Great
Britain

Central & Northern
Highlands & Islands
p892

Argyll, Central &
Northeast Scotland
p836

⭐Edinburgh p771

Glasgow &
Southern
Scotland
p802

The Lake District
& Cumbria
p588

Newcastle &
Northeast England
p624

Manchester, Liverpool
& Northwest England
p553

Yorkshire
p497

Snowdonia &
North Wales
p728

Hay-on-Wye
& Mid-Wales
p704

Birmingham,
the Midlands &
the Marches
p407

Cambridge &
East Anglia
p367

Cardiff, Pembrokeshire
& South Wales
p657

⭐London p62

Bath &
Southwest
England
p229

Canterbury &
Southeast England
p148

Oxford,
Cotswolds &
Around
p184

THIS EDITION WRITTEN AND RESEARCHED BY

Neil Wilson,

Oliver Berry, Fionn Davenport, Marc Di Duca, Belinda Dixon,

Peter Dragicevich, Damian Harper, Anna Kaminski,

Catherine Le Nevez, Andy Symington

PLAN YOUR TRIP

BRITISH MUSEUM, LONDON
P103

ROYAL MILE, EDINBURGH
P773

ON THE ROAD

Contents

ON THE ROAD

Contents

Welcome to Great Britain

Buckingham Palace, Stonehenge, Manchester United, the Beatles – Britain does icons like nowhere else, and travel here is a fascinating mix of famous names and hidden gems.

Variety Packed

From the graceful architecture of Canterbury Cathedral to the soaring ramparts of Edinburgh Castle, via the mountains of Wales and the picture-postcard landscape of the Cotswolds, Britain's astounding variety is a major reason to visit. The cities tempt with top-class shops and restaurants, and some of the world's finest museums, while cutting-edge clubs and world-famous theatres provide endless nights to remember. Next day, you're deep in the countryside, high in the hills or enjoying a classic seaside resort. In Britain, there really is something for everyone, whether you're eight or 80, going solo, or travelling with your friends, your kids or your grandma.

Time Travel

A journey through Britain is a journey through history. But not dull and dusty history – this is history you can immerse yourself in. You can lay hands on the megaliths of a 5000-year-old stone circle, or patrol the battlements of a medieval fortress – just as they were patrolled by chain-mail-clad soldiers many centuries ago. Fast-forward to the future and you're admiring 21st-century architecture in Glasgow or exploring the space-age domes of Cornwall's Eden Project.

English Spoken Here

While Britain has a complex culture and esoteric traditions, it feels familiar to many visitors – on the surface, at least – thanks to a vast catalogue of British film and TV exports. And for most visitors, Britain's national language – English – is equally familiar, and one more reason why travel here is a breeze. Of course Wales and Scotland have their own languages, but everyone speaks English too – and all visitors (even Brits) get a little confused by local accents in places such as Devon, Snowdonia and Aberdeen.

Easy Does It

A final thing to remember while you're planning a trip to Britain: getting from place to place is pretty straightforward. Although the locals may grumble (in fact, it's a national pastime), public transport is pretty good and a train ride through the British landscape can be a memorable experience in itself. Whichever way you get around in this compact country, you're never far from the next town, the next pub, the next national park or the next impressive castle on your hit-list of highlights. The choice is endless, but we've hand-picked the best places for you. Use this book as a guide, but don't let it stop you from making your own discoveries.

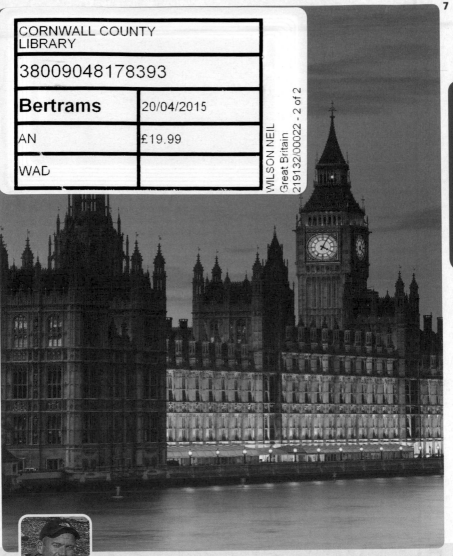

Why I Love Britain

By Neil Wilson, Author

In a word: variety. Few countries pack so much into a small space. Landscapes that range from the sand dunes of South Wales to the snowfields of the Cairngorms, from the lush, quilted farmland of Kent to the naked limestone scarps of the Yorkshire Dales. Three nationalities, two dozen different dialects, more than 60 proudly individual cities, 1000 breweries, 5000 castles – all in a country you could drive across in a day. Plus weather that can offer four seasons in a single afternoon (but remember the old Scandinavian proverb – there's no such thing as bad weather, only the wrong clothes).

For more about our authors, see page 1056

Above: Big Ben & Houses of Parliament (p67), London

Great Britain

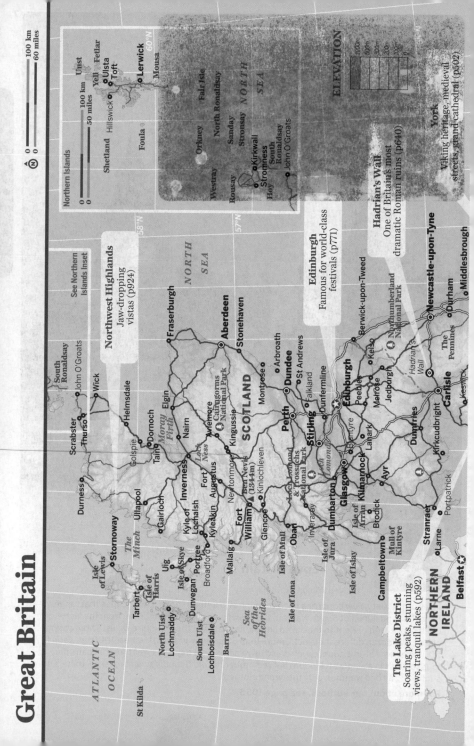

Northern Islands

- Unst
- Fetlar
- Yell
- Ulsta
- Toft
- **Lerwick**
- Mousa
- Fair Isle
- North Ronaldsay
- Orkney
- Sanday
- Stronsay
- Hillswick
- Shetland
- Foula
- Westray
- Rousay
- Kirkwall
- Stromness
- South Ronaldsay
- Hoy
- John O'Groats
- 60°N

N O R T H   S E A

ELEVATION

1000m
500m
300m
200m
100m
0

York
Viking heritage, medieval streets, grand cathedral (p502)

Hadrian's Wall
One of Britain's most dramatic Roman ruins (p640)

Edinburgh
Famous for world-class festivals (p771)

Northwest Highlands
Jaw-dropping vistas (p924)

See Northern Islands Inset

58°N

N O R T H   S E A

57°N

SCOTLAND

- South Ronaldsay
- John O'Groats
- Scrabster
- Thurso
- Wick
- Durness
- Helmsdale
- Golspie
- Dornoch
- Tain
- Elgin
- Fraserburgh
- **Aberdeen**
- Stonehaven
- Nairn
- *Moray Firth*
- Ullapool
- Gairloch
- Inverness
- *Loch Ness*
- Fort Augustus
- Aviemore
- **Cairngorms National Park**
- Kingussie
- Newtonmore
- Kyle of Lochalsh
- Kyleakin
- **Ben Nevis (1344m)**
- **Fort William**
- Glencoe
- Kinlochleven
- Perth
- Montrose
- Arbroath
- **Dundee**
- St Andrews
- Falkland
- Dunfermline
- **Stirling**
- **Edinburgh**
- Berwick-upon-Tweed
- Peebles
- Kelso
- Melrose
- Jedburgh
- **Northumberland National Park**
- *Hadrian's Wall*
- **Newcastle-upon-Tyne**
- Durham
- **Middlesbrough**
- Carlisle
- Dumfries
- Kirkcudbright
- Keswick
- The Pennines
- Lanark
- **Glasgow**
- Dumbarton
- Kilmarnock
- Ayr
- **Loch Lomond & The Trossachs National Park**
- Kintyre
- Inveraray
- Oban
- Isle of Mull
- Isle of Iona
- Isle of Jura
- Isle of Islay
- *Sea of the Hebrides*
- Mallaig
- Broadford
- Portree
- **Isle of Skye**
- Uig
- Dunvegan
- Tarbert
- **Isle of Harris**
- **Isle of Lewis**
- **Stornoway**
- *The Minch*
- North Uist
- Lochmaddy
- South Uist
- Lochboisdale
- Barra
- St Kilda
- Campbeltown
- Mull of Kintyre
- **Stranraer**
- Larne
- Portpatrick
- Brodick
- Isle of Arran
- **Belfast**

NORTHERN IRELAND

The Lake District
Soaring peaks, stunning views, tranquil lakes (p592)

ATLANTIC OCEAN

100 km
60 miles

Northern Islands
100 km
50 miles

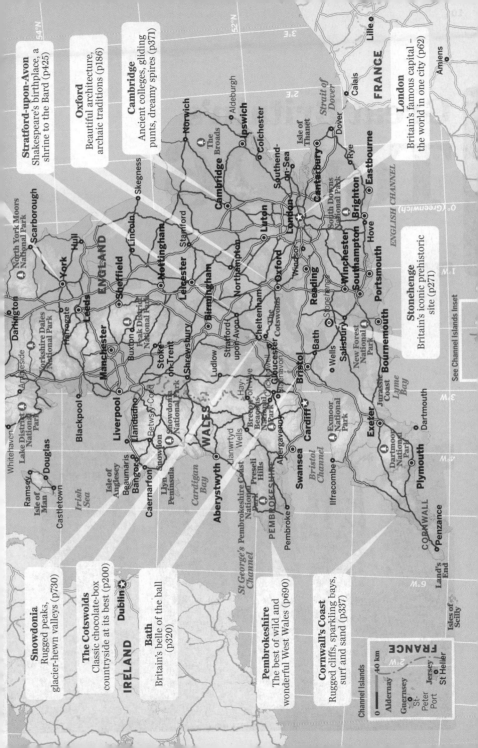

Stratford-upon-Avon
Shakespeare's birthplace, a
shrine to the Bard (p425)

Oxford
Beautiful architecture,
archaic traditions (p186)

Cambridge
Ancient colleges, gliding
punts, dreamy spires (p371)

London
Britain's famous capital –
the world in one city (p62)

Stonehenge
Britain's iconic prehistoric
site (p271)

Snowdonia
Rugged peaks,
glacier-hewn valleys (p730)

The Cotswolds
Classic chocolate-box
countryside at its best (p200)

Bath
Britain's belle of the ball
(p320)

Pembrokeshire
The best of wild and
wonderful West Wales (p690)

Cornwall's Coast
Rugged cliffs, sparkling bays,
surf and sand (p337)

See Channel Islands Inset

Channel Islands

0   40 km

Alderney

Guernsey
St-
Peter
Port   Jersey
         St Helier

Great Britain's
Top 26

1

Stonehenge

1 Mysterious and compelling, Stonehenge (p271) is Britain's most iconic ancient site. People have been drawn to this myth-rich ring of bluestones for the last 5000 years, and we're still not sure why it was built. Most visitors get to gaze at the 50-tonne megaliths from behind the perimeter fence, but with enough planning you can book an early-morning or evening tour and walk around the inner ring. In the slanting sunlight, away from the crowds, it's an ethereal place – an experience that certainly stays with you.

Edinburgh

2 Edinburgh (p771) is a city of many moods – famous for its festivals and especially lively in the summer. It's also worth visiting in the low season for sights such as the castle silhouetted against a blue spring sky with a yellow haze of daffodils misting the slopes below the esplanade. Or on a chilly December morning with the fog snagging the spires of the Old Town, the ancient streets and alleyways more mysterious than ever, rain on the cobblestones and a warm glow beckoning from the window of a pub. Below: Edinburgh Castle (p773)

EURASIA PRESS / GETTY IMAGES ©

MEDIOIMAGES/PHOTODISC / GETTY IMAGES ©

PETER PHIPP / GETTY IMAGES ©

DAVID LYONS / GETTY IMAGES ©

BOISVIEUX CHRISTOPHE / HEMIS.FR / GETTY IMAGES ©

Bath

3 Britain boasts many great cities, but Bath (p320) stands out as the belle of the ball. Thanks to the natural hot water that bubbles to the surface, the Romans built a health resort here. The waters were rediscovered in the 18th century, and Bath became the place to see and be seen by British high society. Today, the stunning Georgian architecture of grand town houses and sweeping crescents (not to mention Roman remains, a beautiful cathedral and a cutting-edge 21st-century spa) means Bath demands your undivided attention.
Above: Roman Baths (p321)

Snowdonia

4 The rugged northwestern corner of Wales has rocky mountain peaks, glacier-hewn valleys, sinuous ridges, sparkling lakes and rivers, and charm-infused villages. The busiest part is around Snowdon (p739) itself, where many people hike to the summit, and many more take the jolly rack-and-pinion railway (p740). To the south and west are rarely trod areas perfect for off-the-beaten-track exploration. And just nearby sit the lovely Llŷn Peninsula and Isle of Anglesey, where the sun often shines, even if it's raining on the mountains.
Top right: Snowdonia National Park (p730)

Isle of Skye

5 Of all Scotland's many islands, Skye (p933) is one of the most famous and best loved by visitors, thanks to a mix of history (the island's link to Bonnie Prince Charlie is forever remembered by 'The Skye Boat Song'), accessibility (the ferry from the mainland has been replaced by a bridge) and sheer beauty. With jagged mountains, velvet moors and towering sea cliffs, Skye's scenery never fails to impress. And for those days when the mist comes in, there are plenty of castles and local museums to explore, and cosy pubs to enjoy. Bottom right: Portree (p936)

London's Museums

6 Institutions bright and beautiful, great and small, wise and wonderful – London (p62) has them all. The range of museums is vast, from generalist exhibitions (British Museum, V&A) to specific themes (Imperial War Museum, London Transport Museum). From intriguing private collections (Sir John Soane's Museum, Wallace Collection) to those celebrating people associated with the city (Handel, Dickens, Freud), you could spend weeks without even scratching the surface. And most of it's free! Top: Great Court, British Museum (p103)

The Cotswolds

7 The most wonderful thing about travel in the Cotswold Hills (p200) is that no matter where you go or how lost you get, you'll still end up in an impossibly picturesque village complete with rose-clad cottages, an ancient church of honey-coloured stone, a pub with sloping floors and fine ales, and a view of the lush green hills. It's easy to leave the crowds behind and find your very own slice of medieval England – and some of the best boutique hotels in the country. Bottom: Arlington Row, Bibury (p203)

PAWEL LIBERA / GETTY IMAGES ©

JOSÃO FUSTE RAGA / GETTY IMAGES ©

Football

8 In some parts of the world it's called 'soccer', but here in Britain it's definitely 'football' (p1014). Despite what the fans may say in Spain or Brazil, the English Premier League has some of the world's finest teams. Globally renowned names include Arsenal, Liverpool and Chelsea, plus *the* most famous club on the planet: Manchester United. North of the border, the Glasgow duo of Rangers and Celtic hold sway, while in Wales the national sport is most definitely rugby. Top: Cardiff City FC Stadium

Oxford

9 For centuries, the brilliant minds and august institutions of Oxford University have made Oxford (p186) famous across the globe. You'll get a glimpse of this revered world as you stroll hushed college quads and cobbled lanes roamed by cycling students and dusty academics. The beautiful buildings and archaic traditions have changed little over the years, leaving Oxford much as it would have been found by alumni such as JRR Tolkien, Lewis Carroll or Oscar Wilde. Bottom: Radcliffe Camera (p191)

Hadrian's Wall

10 Hadrian's Wall (p640) is one of Britain's most revealing and dramatic Roman ruins, its sturdy line of battlements, forts, garrisons, towers and castles disclosing much about the everyday life of the international batallions posted along its length almost 2000 years ago. But this great wall was always about more than mere fortification. Hadrian's edge-of-empire barrier symbolised the boundary of civilised order. To the south was the orderly Roman world of tax-paying, bathhouses and underfloor heating, while to the north was the unruly land of the marauding Celts.

Britain's Pubs

11 The traditional public house (p992) has been the centre of British social life for centuries, and wherever you go there's a range of 'locals' to discover – the ornate Victorian boozers of London, Edinburgh and Leeds; the food-focused gastropubs of Yorkshire, Mid-Wales and Devon; and countless rustic country pubs hunkering under thatched roofs and timber beams. For the true British experience, sup a pint of real ale from one of hundreds of regional breweries or sip on a gin and tonic, and look out for a live music session or a pub quiz night. Top right: West End pub (p133), London

The Lake District

12 William Wordsworth and his Romantic chums were the first to champion the charms of the Lake District (p592), and it's not hard to see what stirred them. With soaring mountains, whaleback fells, razor-edge valleys and – of course – glistening lakes (as well as England's highest peak), this craggy corner of northwest England has some of the country's finest vistas. Come for the comfortable lakeside hotels or the hardy hiking – whatever you choose, inspiration is sure to follow. Bottom right: Lake Windermere (p596)

Cambridge

13 Abounding with exquisite architecture and steeped in tradition, Cambridge (p371) is a university town extraordinaire. The tightly packed core of ancient colleges, the picturesque riverside 'Backs' (college gardens) and the surrounding green meadows give Cambridge a more tranquil appeal than its historic rival Oxford. Highlights include the intricate vaulting of King's College Chapel, while no visit is complete without an attempt to steer a punt (flat-bottomed boat) along the river and under the quirky Mathematical Bridge.

Castles & Stately Homes

14 Britain's turbulent history is nowhere more apparent than in the mighty castles that dot the landscape, from romantic clifftop ruins such as Corfe (p254) or sturdy fortresses such as Caernarfon (p746), to formidable Stirling (p840) and still-inhabited Windsor (p224). And when the aristocracy no longer needed castles, they built vast mansions known as 'stately homes'. Classics of the genre include Blenheim Palace (p199) and Chatsworth House (p495) in England, Powis Castle (p726) in Wales and Scone Palace (p877) in Scotland.

Bottom: Caernarfon Castle (p746)

PHILIP GAME / GETTY IMAGES ©

SLOW IMAGES / GETTY IMAGES ©

Canterbury Cathedral

15 Few other English cathedrals come close to Canterbury (p152), the top temple of the Anglican Church and a place of worship for more than 15 centuries. Its intricate tower dominates the Canterbury skyline, its grandeur unsurpassed by later structures. At its heart lies a 12th-century crime scene, the very spot where Archbishop Thomas Becket was put to the sword – an epoch-making event that launched a million pilgrimages and still pulls in the crowds today. A lone candle mourns the gruesome deed.

Cardiff

16 The exuberant capital of Wales, compact Cardiff (p659) has recently emerged as one of Britain's leading urban centres. After a mid-20th-century decline, the city has entered the new millennium with vigour and confidence, flexing architectural muscles and revelling in a sense of style. From the historic castle to the ultra-modern waterfront, from lively street cafes to infectious nightlife, from Victorian shopping arcades to the gigantic rugby stadium that is the pulsating heart of the city on match days, Cardiff undoubtedly has buzz.

Stratford-upon-Avon

17 The pretty English Midlands town of Stratford-upon-Avon (p425) is famed around the world as the birthplace of the nation's best-known dramatist, William Shakespeare. Today, the town's tight knot of Tudor streets form a living map of Shakespeare's life and times, and crowds of fans and would-be thespians come to enjoy a play at the theatre or visit the five historic houses owned by Shakespeare and his relatives, with a respectful detour to the old stone church where the Bard was laid to rest.

Bottom right: Hall's Croft (p425)

FRANK FELL / GETTY IMAGES ©

VISITBRITAIN/BRITAIN ON VIEW / GETTY IMAGES ©

York

18 With its Roman remains and Viking heritage, ancient city walls and maze of medieval streets, York (p502) is a living showcase for the highlights of English history. For a great introduction, join one of the city's many walking tours through the snickelways (narrow alleys), each the focus of a ghost story or historical character, then admire the intricacies of York Minster, the biggest medieval cathedral in all of Northern Europe, or explore history of another kind at the National Railway Museum, the world's largest collection of historic locomotives. Above left: York Minster (p502)

Scotland's Northwest Highlands

19 In the Highlands of Scotland you're never far from a breathtaking view, but the far northwest (p924) is awe-inspiring, even by these high standards, with the rugged mountainscapes of Assynt, the desolate beauty of Torridon, the piercing incisions of sea lochs and the remote cliffs of Cape Wrath. Add to this the chance to go to sea for Britain's finest whale-watching, polished off with some warm Highland hospitality and you've got an unforgettable corner of the country. Above right: Glen Torridon (p931)

Liverpool

20 For many visitors, Liverpool (p572) will forever be associated with the Beatles, but a visit here proves the city has much more to offer. After a major redevelopment, the waterfront is once again the heart of Liverpool, with Albert Dock declared a World Heritage Site of iconic and protected buildings, a batch of top museums ensuring all sides of the city's history are not forgotten, and the Tate Liverpool gallery and Beatles Story museum, celebrating popular culture and those (still) most famous musical sons. Opposite top: Pier Head (p576)

PICTURES FROM PHIL ORR PHOTOGRAPHY / GETTY IMAGES ©

Pembrokeshire

21 Perched at the tip of wild and wonderful West Wales, the county of Pembrokeshire (p691) boasts one of Britain's most beautiful and dramatic stretches of coast, with sheer cliffs, natural arches, blowholes, sea stacks, and a wonderful hinterland of tranquil villages and secret waterways. It's a landscape of Norman castles, Iron Age hill forts, holy wells and Celtic saints – including the nation's patron, St David – and the remnants of prehistoric inhabitants that left behind intriguing stone circles. Right: Tenby (p692)

DAVID CLAPP / GETTY IMAGES ©

RACHEL DEWIS / GETTY IMAGES ©

HANS-PETER MERTEN / GETTY IMAGES ©

© IAN LEWIS / GETTY IMAGES ©

British Food

22 Britain offers a groaning table full of traditional eating experiences (p45). Tuck into national favourites such as fish and chips, Cornish pasties or toad in the hole, followed of course by rhubarb and custard or spotted dick, or indulge yourself in a quintessentially English afternoon tea. And don't miss the chance to sample regional specialities such as jellied eels (London), Scottish haggis, Cumberland sausage, Stilton cheese, Northumberland kippers, Lancashire hotpot, Melton Mowbray pork pies, Welsh lamb, Yorkshire pudding... the list goes on.

Glen Coe

23 Scotland's most famous glen (p913) combines those two essential qualities of the Highland landscape: dramatic scenery and deep history. The peacefulness and beauty of this valley today belie the fact that it was the scene of a ruthless 17th-century massacre, when the local MacDonalds were murdered by soldiers of the Campbell clan. Some of the glen's finest walks – to the Lost Valley, for example – follow the routes used by the clanspeople trying to flee their attackers, and where many perished in the snow.

Cornwall

24 At Britain's far southwestern extremity, the former kingdom of Cornwall (p337) boasts endless miles of unbroken coastline, with rugged cliffs, sparkling bays, scenic fishing ports and white sandy beaches favoured by everyone from bucket-and-spade families to sun-bronzed surfers. Above the cliffs, the towers of former tin mines now stand like dramatic castles, while inland from the coast is a tranquil landscape of lush farmland and picturesque villages, crowned by the gigantic domes of the Eden Project (p359) – a stunning symbol of Cornwall's renaissance. Bottom right: Port Isaac (p341)

Whisky

25 After tea, Britain's best-known drink is whisky (p991). And while this spirit is also made in England and Wales, it is always most associated with Scotland. With more than 2000 whisky brands available, there are distilleries dotted across Scotland, many open to visitors, with Speyside one of the main concentrations and a favourite spot for connoisseurs. Before enjoying your tipple, heed these warnings: never spell whisky with an 'e' (that's the Irish variety); and when ordering at the bar, never ask for 'Scotch'.

Golf

26 It may be a 'good walk spoilt', but golf (p1015) is one of Britain's most popular sports, for participants of all levels and (at major tournaments) for thousands of spectators too. With courses across the three countries, including some in the most scenic locations, visitors to Britain with a penchant for the little white ball will surely want to try their skill. A highlight for aficionados is a round on the Old Course at St Andrews, the venerable home of golf.

Bottom: Royal & Ancient Golf Club, St Andrews (p871)

KARL BLACKWELL / GETTY IMAGES ©

ANDREA PISTOLESI / GETTY IMAGES ©

Need to Know

For more information, see Survival Guide (p1019)

Currency
Pound; also called
'pound sterling' (£)

Language
English; also Scottish
Gaelic and Welsh

Money
Change bureaux and
ATMs widely available,
especially in cities and
major towns.

Visas
Not required for most
citizens of Europe,
Australia, New Zealand,
USA and Canada.

Mobile Phones
The UK uses the GSM
900/1800 network,
which covers the rest of
Europe, Australia and
New Zealand, but isn't
compatible with the
North American GSM
1900.

Driving
Traffic drives on the left;
steering wheels are on
the right side of the car.
Most rental cars have
manual gears (stick
shift).

When to Go

Aberdeen
GO May–Sep

Fort William
GO May or Sep

Edinburgh
GO Any time

Norwich
GO May–Sep

Brecon
GO May–Sep

London
GO Any time

Exeter
GO Apr–Oct

High Season (Jun–Aug)

➡ Weather at its
best.

➡ Accommodation
rates at their peak –
especially for August
school holidays.

➡ Roads are busy,
especially in seaside
areas, national parks
and popular cities
such as Oxford, Bath,
Edinburgh and York.

Shoulder (Mar–
May & Sep & Oct)

➡ Crowds reduce.
Prices drop.

➡ March to May
is a mix of sunny
spells and sudden
showers; September
to October can
feature balmy
Indian summers. For
outdoor activities in
much of Scotland, the
best times to go are
May and September.

Low Season (Nov–Feb)

➡ Wet and cold.
Snow falls in
mountain areas,
especially up north.

➡ Opening hours
reduced October
to Easter; some
places shut for
winter. Big-city
sights (particularly
London's) operate
all year.

Useful Websites

BBC (www.bbc.co.uk) News and entertainment from the national broadcaster.

Visit Britain (www.visitbritain.com) Comprehensive official tourism website.

Lonely Planet (www.lonelyplanet.com/great-britain) Destination info, hotel bookings, traveller forum and more.

Traveline (www.traveline.org.uk) Great portal site for public transport in all parts of Britain.

British Arts Festivals (www.artsfestivals.co.uk) Listing hundreds of festivals – art, literature, dance, folk and more.

Important Numbers

Area codes vary in length (eg ✆020 for London, ✆01225 for Bath). Omit the code if you're inside that area. Drop the initial ✆0 if you're calling from abroad.

Britain (& UK) country code	✆+44
International access code	✆00
Emergency (police, fire, ambulance, mountain rescue or coastguard)	✆999

Exchange Rates

Australia	A$1	63p
Canada	C$1	62p
Europe	€1	80p
Japan	¥100	77p
New Zealand	NZ$1	49p
USA	US$1	62p

For current exchange rates, see www.xe.com.

Daily Costs

Budget: less than £55

➡ Dorm beds: £15–25

➡ Cheap meals in cafes and pubs: £7–11

➡ Long-distance coach: £15–40 (200 miles)

Midrange: £55–120

➡ Midrange hotel or B&B: £60–130 (London £100–200) per double room

➡ Main course in midrange restaurant: £10–20

➡ Long-distance train: £20–80 (200 miles)

Top end: more than £120

➡ Four-star hotel room: from £130 (London from £200)

➡ Three-course meal in a good restaurant: around £40 per person

➡ Car rental: from £35 per day

Arriving in Britain

Heathrow airport Train to central London (London Paddington station) every 15 minutes (from £18).

Gatwick airport Train to central London (London Victoria station) every 15 minutes (from £16).

Eurostar trains from Paris or Brussels Arrive at London St Pancras International station in central London.

Buses from Europe Arrive at London Victoria Coach Station in central London.

Taxis from airports Trips to central London from Heathrow £40 to £50; from Gatwick £70 to £90 (more at peak hours).

Great Britain on a Shoestring

If you're on a tight budget, there's no getting away from it – Britain isn't cheap. Public transport, admission fees, restaurants and hotel rooms all tend to be expensive compared with their equivalents in many other European countries. But with some careful planning, a trip here doesn't have to break the bank. You can save money by staying in B&Bs instead of hotels, or hostels instead of B&Bs. Motels along motorways and outside large towns are soulless, but who cares? Most of the time you'll be asleep. You can also save by prebooking long-distance coach or train travel – and by avoiding times when everyone else is on the move (like Friday afternoon). Many attractions are free (or offer discounts on quiet days, such as Monday). And don't forget that you won't have to stump up a penny to enjoy Britain's best assets: the wonderful countryside and coastline.

First Time Great Britain

For more information, see Survival Guide (p1019)

Checklist

➡ Check the validity of your passport

➡ Check any visa or entry requirements

➡ Make any necessary bookings (sights, accommodation, travel)

➡ Check airline baggage restrictions

➡ Put all restricted items (eg hair gel, pocket knife) in hold baggage

➡ Inform your credit/debit card company of your trip

➡ Organise travel insurance

➡ Check mobile (cell) phone compatibility

➡ Check rental car requirements

What to Pack

➡ Passport

➡ Credit card

➡ Driving licence

➡ Electrical plug adaptor (UK-specific)

➡ Waterproof jacket

➡ Umbrella

➡ Comfortable shoes

➡ Taste for warm beer

Top Tips for Your Trip

➡ At major London airports, tickets for express trains into central London are usually available in the baggage arrivals hall; this saves queuing or dealing with machines on the station platform.

➡ The best way to get local currency is usually from an ATM, but this term is rarely used in England; the colloquial term 'cash machine' is more common.

➡ If staying more than a few days in London, get an OysterCard, the travel card the locals use.

➡ Pickpockets and hustlers lurk in the more crowded tourist areas, especially in London. No need to be paranoid, but do be on your guard.

➡ Britain's electrical plugs are unlike those in the rest of Europe, so bring (or buy) a UK-specific plug adaptor.

What to Wear

A rain jacket is essential, as is a small backpack to carry it in when the sun comes out. In summer you'll need sunscreen and an umbrella; you're bound to use both.

For sightseeing, comfortable shoes can make or break a trip. If you plan to enjoy Britain's great outdoors, suitable hiking gear is required in higher/wilder areas, but not for casual strolls in the countryside.

Some bars and restaurants have dress codes banning jeans, T-shirts and trainers (sneakers or runners).

Sleeping

Booking your accommodation in advance is recommended, especially in summer, at weekends, and on islands (where options are often limited). Book at least two months ahead for July and August. See p1020 for more accommodation info.

➡ **B&Bs** These small, family-run houses generally provide good value. More luxurious versions are more like a boutique hotel.

➡ **Hotels** British hotels range from half-a-dozen rooms above the pub to restored country houses and castles.

➡ **Hostels** There's a good choice of both institutional and independent hostels, many housed in rustic and/or historic buildings.

Money

ATMs (usually called 'cash machines') are common in cities and towns, but watch out for tampering; a common ruse is to attach a card-reader to the slot. Visa and MasterCard are widely accepted in Britain, except at some smaller B&Bs which take cash or cheque only. Other credit cards, including Amex, are not so widely accepted. Cities and larger towns have banks and exchange bureaux for changing money into pounds, but some bureaux offer poor rates. You can change money at some post offices, which is very handy in country areas; exchange rates are fair.

For more information, see p1025.

Bargaining

A bit of mild haggling is acceptable at flea markets and antique shops, but everywhere else you're expected to pay the advertised price.

Tipping

➡ **Restaurants** Around 10% in restaurants and teashops with table service. Nearer 15% at smarter restaurants. Tips may be added to your bill as a 'service charge'. Paying a tip or a service charge is not obligatory.

➡ **Pubs & Bars** If you order drinks (or food) and pay at the bar, tips are not expected. If you order at the table, your meal is brought to you, and you pay afterwards, then 10% is usual.

➡ **Taxis** Around 10%, or rounded up to the nearest pound, especially in London.

Underground station, London

MATTHEW E. MADDOCK / GETTY IMAGES ©

Etiquette

➡ **Manners** The British have a reputation for being polite, and good manners are considered important in most situations. When asking directions, 'Excuse me, can you tell me the way to...' is a better tactic than 'Hey, where's...'

➡ **Queues** In Britain, queueing ('standing in line' to Americans), whether to board a bus, buy tickets or enter the gates of an attraction, is sacrosanct. Any attempt to 'jump the queue' will result in an outburst of tutting and hard stares.

➡ **Escalators** If you take an escalator or a moving walkway (especially at tube stations in London), be sure to stand on the right, so folks in a hurry can pass on the left.

Eating

It's wise to book ahead for midrange restaurants, especially at weekends. Top-end restaurants should be booked at least a couple of weeks in advance. See Eat & Drink Like a Local (p45) for more information.

➡ **Restaurants** Britain's restaurants range from cheap-and-cheerful to Michelin-starred, and cover every cuisine you can imagine.

➡ **Cafes** Open during daytime (rarely after 6pm), cafes are good for a casual breakfast or lunch, or simply a cup of coffee.

➡ **Pubs** Most of Britain's pubs serve reasonably priced meals, and many can compete with restaurants on quality.

What's New

Stonehenge
A £27 million revamp of Britain's most famous prehistoric site has seen the area around the stones returned to grassland, and the opening of an impressive new visitor centre. (p271)

Shangri-La at the Shard
The first opening in the UK for the luxury Asian hotel chain, this is Europe's first elevated hotel, occupying levels 34 to 52 of London's Shard skyscraper. (p119)

The Making of Harry Potter
Prospective Hogwarts pupils can waggle thier wands and practise their spells during this spectacular new tour at Warner Bros Studios, just outside London. (p223)

Eden Project
Cornwall's iconic eco-centre has an added attraction in the form of a new treetop walkway through the rainforest biome. (p359)

King Richard III: Dynasty, Death & Discovery
The amazing story of the discovery of the skeletal remains of King Richard III beneath a Leicester car park in 2012 is celebrated in this new, high-tech visitor centre. (p475)

Bleak House
Snooze in the very bedroom occupied for 12 productive summers by one Charles Dickens at this new hotel overlooking Broadstairs' tight curve of beach. (p160)

Liverpool International Music Festival
Liverpool's old Mathew St Festival has been expanded into a showcase of local and international talent spread over two weeks in late August. (p578)

Black Sail Youth Hostel
One of England's most remote youth hostels, perched high in the Lake District fells above Ennerdale, now sports double glazing and solar-panel-powered lighting following a major upgrade. (p609)

Northumberland National Park
England's least-populous national park was awarded dark-sky status by the International Dark Skies Association in late 2013 (the largest such designation in Europe), adding to the stargazing appeal of Kielder Observatory. (p647)

Penarth Pavilion
One of Wales' most famous seaside landmarks, the art deco Penarth Pavilion, has been renovated, complete with a brand-new art gallery, cinema and cafe. (p673)

The Hydro
Glasgow's waterfront gained a new 13,000-seat live-performance arena, the Hydro, which hosted the 2014 Commonwealth Games gymnastics and netball events. (p819)

Bannockburn Heritage Centre
To mark the 700th anniversary of the Battle of Bannockburn in 2014, the National Trust for Scotland unveiled a revamped, high-tech heritage centre on the site of the battlefield. (p845)

For more recommendations and reviews, see lonelyplanet.com/great-britain

If You Like...

Castles & Stately Homes

Tower of London Landmark of the capital, patrolled by famous beefeaters and protected by mythical ravens. (p80)

Blenheim Palace A monumental baroque fantasy and one of Britain's greatest stately homes. (p199)

Castle Howard Another stunning baroque edifice, best known as the setting for *Brideshead Revisited*. (p513)

Warwick Castle Preserved enough to be impressive, ruined enough to be romantic. (p422)

Stirling Castle Classic fortress atop volcanic crag, with stunning views from the battlements. (p840)

Beaumaris Castle Wales is the land of castles; imposing Beaumaris, along with nearby Conwy, Caernarfon and Harlech, is a jointly listed World Heritage Site. (p754)

Chatsworth House The quintessential stately home, a treasure trove of heirlooms and works of art. (p495)

Carreg Cennen The most dramatically positioned fortress in Wales, standing guard over a lonely stretch of Brecon Beacons National Park. (p712)

Royal Britain

Buckingham Palace The Queen's official London residence, best known for its royal-waving balcony and the Changing of the Guard. (p69)

Windsor Castle The largest and oldest occupied fortress in the world, a majestic vision of battlements and towers, and the Queen's weekend retreat. (p224)

Westminster Abbey Where British monarchs are crowned and married – most recently William and Kate. (p66)

Royal Yacht Britannia The royal family's floating home during foreign travels, now retired and moored near Edinburgh. (p785)

Balmoral Castle Built for Queen Victoria in 1855 and still a royal Highland hideaway. (p908)

Royal Pavilion Opulent palace built for playboy prince, later King George IV. (p173)

Althorp House Ancestral home and burial place of Diana, Princess of Wales. (p472)

Cathedrals & Ruined Abbeys

St Paul's Cathedral A symbol of the city for centuries, and still an essential part of the London skyline. (p82)

York Minster One of the largest medieval cathedrals in all of Europe, especially renowned for its windows. (p502)

Fountains Abbey Extensive ruins set in more recently landscaped water gardens – one of the most beautiful sites in Britain. (p520)

Canterbury Cathedral The mother ship of the Anglican Church, still attracting pilgrims and visitors in their thousands. (p152)

Melrose Abbey The finest of all the great Border abbeys; the heart of Robert the Bruce is buried here. (p823)

Whitby Abbey Stunning clifftop ruin with an eerie atmosphere that inspired the author of *Dracula*. (p525)

St Davids Cathedral An ancient place of worship in Britain's smallest city. (p696)

Glastonbury Abbey The legendary burial place of King Arthur and Queen Guinevere. (p334)

Glasgow Cathedral A shining example of Gothic architecture, and the only mainland Scottish cathedral to have survived the Reformation. (p809)

Tintern Abbey Riverside ruins that inspired generations of poets and artists. (p678)

Village Idylls

Lavenham A wonderful collection of exquisitely preserved medieval buildings virtually untouched since the 15th century. (p391)

Lacock Well-preserved medieval village, essentially free of modern development and – unsurprisingly – a frequent set for movies and TV period dramas. (p274)

Goathland One of Yorkshire's most attractive villages, complete with village green and traditional steam railway station. (p529)

Mousehole Southwest England overflows with picturesque pint-sized ports, but this is one of the best. (p352)

Beddgelert A conservation village of rough grey stone buildings in the heart of Snowdonia National Park. (p737)

Cromarty At the northeastern tip of the Black Isle, with a fine collection of 18th-century sandstone houses. (p900)

Great Outdoors

Lake District A feast of mountains, valleys, views and – of course – lakes; the landscape that inspired William Wordsworth and entices hikers today. (p592)

Northumberland National Park The dramatically empty landscape of England's far north is remote and off the beaten track. (p647)

Snowdonia The best-known slice of nature in Wales, with the grand but surprisingly accessible peak of Snowdon at its heart. (p730)

Yorkshire Dales A compact collection of moors, hills, valleys, rivers, cliffs and waterfalls, perfect for easy strolls or hardy treks. (p530)

Top: Mousehole (p352), Cornwall
Bottom: Swaledale, Yorkshire Dales National Park (p530)

Ben Nevis Every year thousands of people aim for the summit of Scotland's most famous (and Britain's highest) mountain. (p917)

Industrial Heritage

Ironbridge The place where it all started, the crucible of the Industrial Revolution, where 10 museums for the price of one give fascinating insights. (p447)

Blaenavon A World Heritage Site of well-preserved ironworks and the fascinating Big Pit coal mine. (p679)

New Lanark Once the largest cotton-spinning complex in Britain and a testament to enlightened capitalism. (p821)

National Railway Museum A cathedral to Britain's great days of steam; for railway fans of all ages it's the perfect place to go loco. (p503)

Roman Remains

Roman Baths The city of Bath takes its name from these famous Roman remains – a complex of bathhouses around natural thermal waters, with additions from the 18th century, when restorative waters again became fashionable. (p321)

Hadrian's Wall Snaking coast-to-coast across lonely hills, this 2000-year-old fortified line once marked the northern limit of imperial Roman jurisdiction. (p640)

Caerleon One of three legionary forts in Britain, with impressive remains of barracks, baths and an amphitheatre. (p676)

Corinium Museum The sleepy Cotswold town of Cirencester was once Corinium, the second-largest Roman city in Britain; this excellent museum recalls those days, including beautiful mosaics. (p201)

Shopping

Portobello Road, London Britain's biggest city has shopping galore, with Portobello Rd one of the best-known street markets, surrounded by quirky boutiques and gift stores. (p142)

Victoria Quarter, Leeds Lovely arcades of wrought ironwork and stained glass, home to several top fashion boutiques. (p542)

North Laine, Brighton Narrow streets lined with shops selling books, antiques, collectables, vintage clothing and more. (p179)

Cardiff Arcades Half-a-dozen ornate arcades branch off the city-centre main streets, all with speciality shops and cafes. (p671)

Isle of Skye It seems as if every second cottage on Skye is home to a workshop or an artist's studio, making the island a great place to find quality handmade arts and crafts. (p933)

Hay-on-Wye The self-proclaimed secondhand-book capital of the world boasts over 30 bookshops and millions of volumes, attracting browsers, collectors and academics from around the world. (p719)

Art Galleries

Tate Britain One of the best-known galleries in London, full to the brim with the finest local works. (p95)

Tate Modern London's other Tate focuses on modern art in all its wonderful permutations. (p88)

BALTIC Newcastle's very own 'Tate of the North' with work by some of contemporary art's biggest show-stoppers. (p631)

National Museum Cardiff An excellent collection of Welsh artists, plus works by Monet, Renoir, Matisse, Van Gogh, Francis Bacon and David Hockney. (p660)

Kelvingrove Art Gallery & Museum A national landmark in Glasgow – great collection, and a cracking spot to learn about Scottish art. (p811)

Yorkshire Sculpture Park England's biggest outdoor sculpture collection, dominated by the works of Henry Moore and Barbara Hepworth. (p544)

Barber Institute of Fine Art With works by Rubens, Turner and Picasso, this Birmingham gallery is no lightweight. (p415)

Arts & Music Festivals

Edinburgh International Festival The world's biggest festival of art and culture. 'Nuff said. (p792)

Glastonbury Britain's biggest and best-loved music festival. (p333)

Hay Festival A world-class celebration of all things literary at Britain's bookshop capital. (p720)

Notting Hill Carnival London's Caribbean community shows the city how to party. (p117)

Pride Gay and lesbian street parade through London culminating in a concert in Trafalgar Sq. (p117)

Grassington Festival A village in the scenic Yorkshire Dales hosts this amazing two-week cultural extravaganza. (p532)

ROD EDWARDS / GETTY IMAGES ©

Beach huts, Southwold (p396)

Latitude Festival An eclectic mix of music, literature, dance, drama and comedy, in a stunning location and of manageable size. (p396)

Coastal Attractions

Scarborough The original British beach resort, where 'sea-bathing' first began, way back in the 17th century. (p516)

Pembrokeshire Towering cliffs, rock arches, clean waters and perfect sandy beaches at the tip of West Wales. (p690)

Southwold Genteel old-style seaside town with lovely beach, charming pier and famous rows of colourful beach huts. (p396)

Tongue Sea lochs penetrate the rocky coast in this wild stretch of Scotland's north. (p925)

Holkham Bay A pristine expanse of sand with giant skies stretching overhead. (p404)

Llandudno Beachside Punch-and-Judy shows, a step-back-in-time pier and a classic esplanade. (p758)

Gower Peninsula Family-friendly beaches and surfer hang-outs, backed by sand dunes and tranquil farmland. (p685)

Beachy Head & Seven Sisters Where the South Downs plunge into the sea, these mammoth chalk cliffs provide a dramatic finale. (p172)

Month by Month

January

January is mid-winter in Britain. Festivals and events to brighten the mood are thin on the ground, but luckily some include fire – lots of it.

✸ London Parade

A ray of light in the gloom, the New Year's Day Parade in London (to use its official title; www.london-parade.co.uk) is one of the biggest events of its kind in the world, featuring marching bands, street performers, classic cars, floats and displays winding their way through the streets, watched by over half a million people.

✸ Up Helly Aa

Half of Shetland dresses up with horned helmets and battleaxes in this spectacular re-enactment of a Viking fire festival, with a torchlit procession leading the burning of a full-size Viking longship. (p963)

☆ Celtic Connections

Glasgow plays host to a celebration of Celtic music, dance and culture (www.celticconnections.com), with participants from all over the globe.

February

Britain can be scenic under snow and sunshine, or more likely grey and gloomy under dark skies. Hang in there...

✸ Jorvik Viking Festival

The ancient Viking capital of York becomes home once again to invaders and horned helmets galore, with the intriguing addition of longship races. (p508)

✸ Fort William Mountain Festival

Britain's capital of the outdoors celebrates the peak of the winter season with ski workshops, mountaineering films and talks by famous climbers (www.mountainfestival.co.uk).

March

Spring finally arrives. There's a hint of better weather, and some classic sporting fixtures grace the calendar. Many locals stay hunkered down at home, though, so hotels offer special rates.

☆ Six Nations Rugby Championship

Highlight of the rugby calendar (www.rbs6nations.com), with the home nations playing at London's Twickenham, Edinburgh's Murrayfield and Cardiff's Millennium Stadiums.

☆ University Boat Race

Annual race down the River Thames in London between the rowing teams from Cambridge and Oxford Universities, an institution since 1856 that still enthrals the country. (p117)

April

The weather slowly improves, with warmer and drier days bringing out spring blossoms. Attractions that close for the low season open around the middle of the month or at Easter.

☆ Grand National

Half the country has a flutter on the highlight of the three-day horse race meeting at Aintree on the first Saturday of the month – a steeplechase with a testing course and notoriously high jumps. (p578)

🏃 London Marathon

Super-fit athletes cover 26.22 miles in just over two hours, while others dress up in daft costumes and take considerably longer. (p117)

🎆 Beltane

Thousands of revellers climb Edinburgh's Calton Hill for this modern revival of a pagan fire festival (www.beltane.org) marking the end of winter.

🎆 Spirit of Speyside

Based in Dufftown, a Scottish festival of whisky, food and music, with five days of art, cooking, distillery tours and outdoor activities. (p888)

May

The weather is usually good, with more events to enjoy. There are two public holidays this month (first and last Mondays) so traffic is very busy over the corresponding long weekends.

☆ FA Cup Final

Grand finale of the football (soccer) season for over a century. Teams from across England battle it out over the winter months, culminating in this heady spectacle at Wembley Stadium – the home of English football.

☉ Chelsea Flower Show

The Royal Horticultural Society flower show at Chelsea is the highlight of the gardener's year. (p117)

🎆 Hay Festival

The ever-expanding 'Woodstock of the mind' brings an intellectual influx to booktown Hay-on-Wye. (p720)

☆ Glyndebourne

Famous festival (www.glyndebourne.com) of world-class opera in the pastoral surroundings of East Sussex, running until the end of summer.

June

Now it's almost summer. You can tell because this month sees the music-festival season kick off properly, while sporting events, from rowing to racing, fill the calendar.

☆ Derby Week

Horse-racing, people-watching and clothes-spotting are on the agenda at this week-long meeting in Epsom, Surrey (www.epsomderby.co.uk).

☆ Cotswold Olimpicks

Welly-wanging, pole-climbing and shin-kicking are the key disciplines at this traditional Gloucestershire sports day, held every year since 1612. (p211)

🎆 Trooping the Colour

Military bands and bearskinned grenadiers march down London's Whitehall in this martial pageant to mark the monarch's birthday. (p117)

☆ Royal Ascot

It's hard to tell which matters more, the fashion or the fillies, at this highlight of the horse-racing year in Berkshire. (p226)

☆ Wimbledon Tennis

The world's best-known tennis tournament, attracting all the big names, while crowds cheer and eat tons of strawberries and cream. (p117)

☆ Glastonbury

One of Britain's favourite pop and rock gatherings is invariably muddy, and still a rite of passage for every self-respecting British music fan. (p333)

☆ Royal Regatta

Boats of every description take to the water for Henley's upper-crust river jamboree. (p228)

🎆 Pride

Highlight of the gay and lesbian calendar, this technicolour street parade heads through London's West End. (p117)

🎆 Glasgow's West End Festival

Scotland's second city hosts a major celebration of music and arts. (p812)

July

Proper summer. Festivals every week. School summer breaks begin, so there's a holiday tingle in the air, dulled only by busy roads on Fridays, because everyone's going somewhere for the weekend.

◉ Great Yorkshire Show

Harrogate plays host to one of Britain's largest county shows. This is the place for Yorkshire grit, Yorkshire tykes, Yorkshire puddings, Yorkshire beef... (p515)

🎵 T in the Park

World-class acts since 1994 ensure this major music festival (www.tinthepark.com) is Scotland's answer to Glastonbury.

🎵 Latitude

Relaxed festival in the seaside town of Southwold, with theatre, cabaret, art and literature, plus top names from the alternative music scene. (p396)

☆ International Musical Eisteddfod

Festival of international folk music at Llangollen, with eclectic fringe and big-name evening concerts. (p765)

◉ Royal Welsh Show

Prize bullocks and local produce at this national farm and livestock event in Builth Wells.

☆ Cowes Week

Britain's biggest yachting spectacular on the choppy seas around the Isle of Wight. (p246)

🎵 Womad

Roots and world music take centre stage at this festival (www.womad.org) in a country park in the southern Cotswolds.

🎵 Port Eliot Festival

Beginning life as a literary festival, now branched out into live music, theatre and outdoor art. (p362)

August

Schools and colleges are closed, parliament is in recess, the sun is shining (hopefully), most people go away for a week or two, and the nation is in holiday mood.

🎵 Edinburgh Festivals

Edinburgh's most famous August happenings are the International Festival and Fringe, but this month the city also has an event for anything you care to name – books, art, theatre, music, comedy, marching bands... (www.edinburgh-festivals.co.uk)

🎵 Notting Hill Carnival

London's famous multicultural Caribbean-style street carnival in the district of Notting Hill. Steel drums, dancers, outrageous costumes. (p117)

☆ National Eisteddfod of Wales

The largest celebration of native Welsh culture, steeped in history, pageantry and pomp; held at various venues around the country. (p766)

🎵 Brecon Jazz Festival

Smoky sounds at one of Europe's leading jazz festivals, in the charming Mid-Wales town of Brecon. (p713)

🏃 World Bog Snorkelling Championships

Only in Britain – competitors, many in fancy dress, don snorkel and flippers for a swimming race along a muddy ditch in the middle of a peat bog.

September

The first week of September is still holiday time, but then schools reopen, traffic returns to normal, and the summer party's over for another year. Ironically, the weather's often better than in August, now everyone's back at work.

🏃 Great North Run

Tyneside plays host to one of the biggest half marathons in the world (www.greatrun.org), with the greatest number of runners in any race at this distance.

🍴 Abergavenny Food Festival

The mother of all epicurean festivals and the champion of Wales' burgeoning food scene. (p718)

🍴 Ludlow Food & Drink Festival

Great foodie town and a great foodie festival. (p455)

☆ Braemar Gathering

The biggest and most famous Highland Games

in the Scottish calendar, traditionally attended by members of the royal family. Highland dancing, caber-tossing and bagpipe-playing.

October

October means autumn. The leaves on the trees are changing colour, attractions start to shut down for the low season, and accommodation rates drop as hoteliers try to entice a final few guests before winter.

☆☆ Dylan Thomas Festival

A celebration of the Welsh laureate's work with readings, events and talks in Swansea. (p681)

✖ Falmouth Oyster Festival

The West Country port of Falmouth marks the start of the traditional oyster-catching season (www.falmouthoysterfestival.

co.uk) with a celebration of local food from the sea and fields of Cornwall.

November

Winter's here, and November is a dull month. The weather is often cold and damp, summer is a distant memory and Christmas is still too far away.

☆☆ Guy Fawkes Night

Also called Bonfire Night (www.bonfirenight.net); on 5 November fireworks fill Britain's skies in commemoration of a failed attempt to blow up parliament, way back in 1605.

◉ Remembrance Day

Red poppies are worn and wreaths are laid in towns and cities around the country on 11 November in commemoration of fallen military personnel (www.poppy.org.uk).

December

Schools break up earlier, but shops and businesses keep going until Christmas Eve; the last weekend before Christmas Day is busy on the roads as people visit friends and family, or head for the airport.

☆☆ Stonehaven Fireball Festival

The Scottish fishing town of Stonehaven celebrates Hogmanay with a spectacular procession of fireball-swinging locals (www.stonehavenfireballs.co.uk).

☆☆ New Year Celebrations

The last night of December sees fireworks and street parties in town squares across the country. London's Trafalgar Sq is where the city's largest crowds gather to herald the New Year.

Itineraries

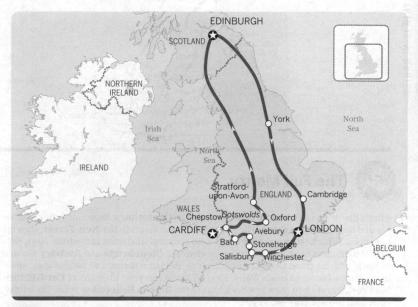

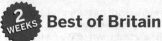

2 WEEKS Best of Britain

Start with a full day in Britain's greatest city, **London**, simply walking the streets to admire the world-famous sights: Buckingham Palace, Tower Bridge, Trafalgar Sq and more. Then head southwest to the grand cathedral cities of **Winchester** and **Salisbury**, across to the iconic menhirs of **Stonehenge** and its less well-known counterpart **Avebury Stone Circle**, then onwards to the beautiful historic city of **Bath**.

Loop over to **Chepstow** for its impressive castle, and then continue to **Cardiff**, the Welsh capital. Retrace slightly, then cruise across the classic English countryside of the **Cotswolds** to reach the university city of **Oxford**. Not far away is **Stratford-upon-Avon**, for everything Shakespeare.

Strike out north to Scotland's capital, **Edinburgh**, for another great castle, before re-crossing the border to **York** for its glorious cathedral and historic city walls. Keep going south to reach **Cambridge**, another landmark university city. Then enjoy the last few days back in **London**, immersed in galleries, museums, luxury shops, street markets, West End shows, East End cafes – or whatever takes your fancy.

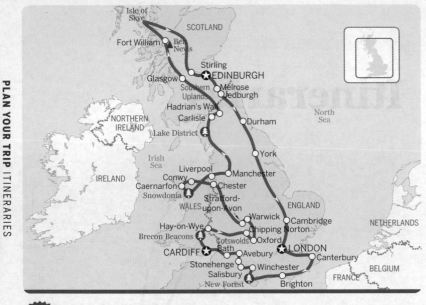

5 WEEKS The Full Monty

After a day or two in **London**, head southeast to **Canterbury**, then along the coast to hip and happening **Brighton**. For a change of pace, divert to the **New Forest**, then up to historic **Winchester** and **Salisbury** with their awe-inspiring cathedrals. Next, religion of a different kind: the ancient stone circles at **Stonehenge** and **Avebury**. Go west to **Bath**, with its grand Georgian architecture, Roman remains and famous spas, and then over the border to reach Wales. Stop off at the energetic little city of **Cardiff**, then head north through to the whaleback hills of the **Brecon Beacons** to reach the quirky book-mad town of **Hay-on-Wye**.

Then it's back to England, and east into the Cotswolds, with its rolling hills, quintessential rural scenery and chocolate-box towns like **Chipping Norton**. Not far away is the famous university town of **Oxford**, as well as the ancient town of **Warwick**, with its spectacular castle, and Shakespeare's birthplace **Stratford-upon-Avon**.

Continue north to **Chester**, for its famous city walls, diverting into North Wales for the grand castles at **Conwy** and **Caernarfon**, and the stunning mountains of **Snowdonia**. If time allows and the weather's good, you can take a train to the top of the highest peak. Then ferry across the Mersey to **Liverpool**, with its famous musical heritage and revitalised waterfront, or to **Manchester** for a taste of big-city life, followed by a total change of scenery in the tranquil mountains of the **Lake District**. To the north is the sturdy border town of **Carlisle**, and one of Britain's most impressive Roman remains, **Hadrian's Wall**.

Hop across the border to Scotland, via the tranquil Southern Uplands, to reach goodtime **Glasgow**. Then trek to **Fort William** (and maybe up Ben Nevis, Britain's highest mountain), from where it's easy to reach the beautiful **Isle of Skye**. Then it's time to head south again, via **Stirling Castle** to **Edinburgh**, and on through the historic abbey towns of **Melrose** and **Jedburgh**.

Back in England, you can marvel at the castle and cathedral of **Durham** and the ancient Viking capital of **York**, before taking in the old university city of **Cambridge** and enjoying the last few days of your trip in **London**.

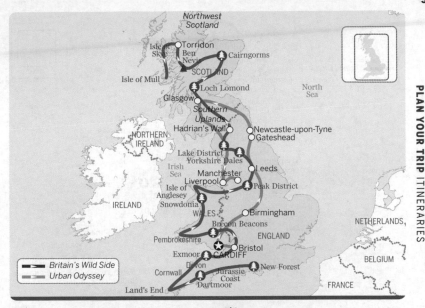

— — — Britain's Wild Side
— — — Urban Odyssey

4 WEEKS Britain's Wild Side

Start in the **New Forest**, then go west via Dorset's fossil-ridden **Jurassic Coast** to reach granite-topped **Dartmoor**. Stop off at **Land's End**, then traverse the stunning **Cornwall** coast and rich farmland of **Devon** to reach the gorse-clad hills of **Exmoor**.

Cross into Wales to hike the **Brecon Beacons** or stroll the beaches of **Pembrokeshire**, then head north to explore **Snowdonia** and the nearby **Isle of Anglesey**. Then it's back to England, through the hills and moors of the **Peak District** and **Yorkshire Dales** to reach the peaks and grand scenery of the **Lake District**.

Head north again, across (or along) the Roman remains of **Hadrian's Wall**, and over the border into Scotland. Saunter through the delightful Southern Uplands, then continue via **Loch Lomond** to the mountain wilderness of the **Cairngorms**.

The top of Britain is crowned by the famous highlands and islands of northwest Scotland, where jewels include peaks like **Ben Nevis** and remote mountain ranges such as **Torridon**, while out to sea the lovely isles of **Skye** and **Mull** bask in the afternoon sun.

3 WEEKS Urban Odyssey

Kick off in **Bristol**, a city with fierce pride and a rich historic legacy, then cross over to **Cardiff**, once a provincial backwater but now the lively Welsh capital.

Next stop is **Birmingham**, oozing transformation, with a renovated waterside, energised museums and a space-age shopping centre. Onwards to **Leeds**, where rundown factories and warehouses have been turned into loft apartments, ritzy boutiques and stylish department stores. Shopping not your thing? No problem. Head for **Newcastle-upon-Tyne** and twin-city **Gateshead**; both have given up on heavy industries in favour of art and architecture – and are famous for to-the-hilt partying.

Still want more? It's got to be **Glasgow**, Scotland's other great city, boasting fabulous galleries and welcoming pubs. Then it's south to **Liverpool**, which has reinvented itself as a cultural hot spot, with a famous musical heritage and very lively current music scene. Finish your tour in **Manchester**, a long-time stage for artistic endeavour, with dramatic new architecture and a rather well-known football club.

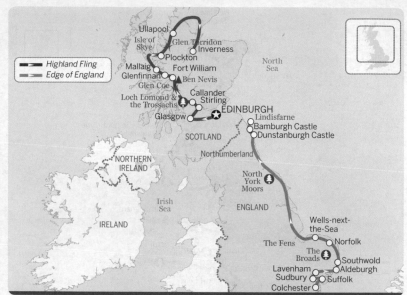

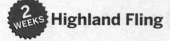 Highland Fling
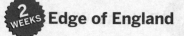 Edge of England

2 WEEKS Highland Fling

Start in **Edinburgh**, where highlights include the renowned castle, as well as the Royal Mile, the new parliament and the haunts of the Old Town. For a change of pace, hop over to **Glasgow** for a day or two as well. Then head northeast to see Scotland's other great castle at **Stirling**. Next stop is **Callander**, a good base for exploring the hills and lochs of the **Trossachs**, part of Loch Lomond and the Trossachs National Park, for a first taste of Highland scenery.

Continue north and the landscape becomes ever more impressive, culminating in the grandeur of **Glen Coe**. Keen hillwalkers will pause for a day at **Fort William** to trek to the top of **Ben Nevis** (plus another day to recover!) before taking the 'Road to the Isles' past glorious **Glenfinnan** to the fishing harbour of **Mallaig**.

Take the ferry to the **Isle of Skye**, then head back to the mainland via the Skye Bridge to reach pretty **Plockton** and magnificent **Glen Torridon**. Onwards, via the outpost of **Ullapool**, takes you into the British mainland's furthest reaches, the remote mountain landscape of Scotland's far northwest, before looping south to finish your tour at **Inverness**.

2 WEEKS Edge of England

Start in **Colchester**, then head out into the sleepy county of Suffolk, where quaint villages and market towns such as **Sudbury** and **Lavenham** dot the landscape, while along the coast are wildlife reserves, shingly beaches, fishing ports such as **Aldeburgh**, and the delightfully retro seaside resort of **Southwold**.

Things get even quieter in Norfolk, especially around the misty lakes and windmill-lined rivers of the **Broads**. For beach strolls or historic country pubs, head for the coastal villages near **Wells-next-the-Sea**.

Across the border in Lincolnshire lies the eerie, pan-flat landscape of the **Fens**, now a haven for otters and bird life.

Continue into the heather-clad **North York Moors** where humpbacked hills roll all the way to the coast to drop dramatically into the choppy waters of the North Sea.

Enjoy a blustery stroll on the wild coast of Northumberland near the landmark castles of **Bamburgh** and **Dunstanburgh**, then end your tour at the historic island of **Lindisfarne**.

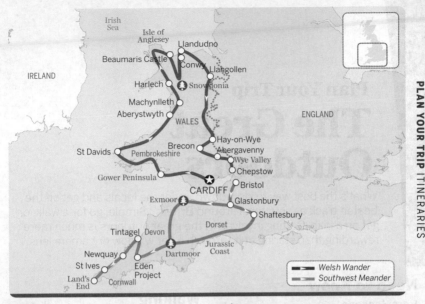

Legend:
- Welsh Wander
- Southwest Meander

Welsh Wander
1 WEEK

Start in **Cardiff**, with its fantastical castle, gigantic rugby stadium, revitalised waterfront and stunning Millennium Centre. Head west via the beautiful **Gower Peninsula** to reach the clear waters and sandy beaches of **Pembrokeshire**. Don't miss the ancient cathedral at **St Davids** – Britain's smallest city. Continue up the coast to **Aberystwyth**, then through 'alternative' **Machynlleth** to reach **Harlech** and its ancient castle. Divert to the tranquil **Isle of Anglesey** and historic **Beaumaris Castle**, then strike through the mountains of **Snowdonia** to reach **Conwy** (another stunning castle) and the seaside resort of **Llandudno**.

Southwards takes you through **Llangollen**, with its jolly steam trains and vertiginous aqueduct, then along the England–Wales borderlands to book-mad **Hay-on-Wye**. Loop inland to peaceful **Brecon** and foodie **Abergavenny**, then saunter down the **Wye Valley** to finish at the frontier town of **Chepstow** – and yet another amazing castle.

Southwest Meander
2 WEEKS

Start in **Bristol**, the capital of the Westcountry, then saunter south to reach **Glastonbury** – famous for its annual music festival and the best place to stock up on candles or crystals at any time of year.

West leads to heathery **Exmoor**. South leads to **Dorset**, where highlights include picturesque **Shaftesbury** and the fossil-strewn Jurassic Coast.

Onwards into **Devon**, and there's a choice of coasts, as well as **Dartmoor**, the highest and wildest hills in southern Britain.

Cross into **Cornwall** to explore the space-age biodomes of the **Eden Project**. Nearby, but in another era entirely, is **Tintagel Castle**, the legendary birthplace of King Arthur. Depending on your tastes, you can hang-ten in surf-flavoured partytown **Newquay**, or browse the galleries at **St Ives**.

The natural finish to this wild-west tour is **Land's End**, where the British mainland comes to a final full stop. Sink a drink in the First and Last Inn in Sennen, and promise yourself a return trip some day...

Plan Your Trip

The Great Outdoors

What's the best way to slow down, meet the locals and get off the beaten track as you travel around Britain? Simple: go for a walk, or get on a bike. Getting involved in the great outdoors is much more rewarding than staring at it through a car window or camera lens.

Need to Know

Best Seasons

Summer (Jun–Aug) Weather usually warm and dry; long evenings with plenty of daylight, too.

Late spring (May) and early autumn (Sep) Fewer crowds; days often mild and sunny. In Scotland, drier weather and fewer midges than high summer.

Best Maps

Ordnance Survey UK's national mapping agency; Explorer series 1:25,000 scale.

Harvey Maps Specially designed for walkers; Superwalker series 1:25,000 scale.

Best Websites

www.walkhighlands.co.uk Superb database of walks of all lengths in Scotland.

www.walkingenglishman.com Short walks in England and Wales.

www.nationaltrail.co.uk Great for specifics on long-distance trails in England and Wales.

www.scotlandsgreattrails.org.uk Long-distance trails in Scotland.

Walking

Walking is the most popular outdoor activity in Britain – for locals and visitors alike. Firstly, because it opens up some beautiful corners of the country, and secondly, because it can be done virtually on a whim. In fact, compared with hiking and trekking in some other parts of the world, it doesn't take much planning at all.

Getting Started

An established infrastructure for walkers already exists in Britain, so everything is easy for visitors or first-timers. Most villages and country towns in areas where walking is popular have shops selling maps and local guidebooks, while the local tourist office can provide leaflets and other information. In the national parks, suggested routes or guided walks are often available. This all means you can arrive in a place for the first time, pick up some info, and within an hour you'll be walking through some of Britain's finest landscape. No fees. No permits. No worries. It really is almost effortless.

Britain's Footpath Network

Britain is covered in a vast network of footpaths, many of which are centuries old, dating from the time when walking was the only way to get from farm to village, from village to town, from town to coast, or from valley to valley. Any walk you do today will follow these historic paths. Even Britain's longest walks simply link up many shorter paths. You'll also sometimes walk along 'bridleways' originally used for horse transport, and old unsurfaced roads called 'byways'.

Rights of Way

The absolute pleasure of walking in Britain is mostly thanks to the 'right of way' network – public paths and tracks across private property, especially in England and Wales. In Britain, nearly all land (including in national parks) is privately owned, but if there's a right of way you can follow it through fields, pastures, woods, even farmhouse yards, as long as you keep to the route and do no damage. In some mountain and moorland areas, walkers can move freely beyond the rights of way and explore at will. Known as 'freedom to roam', where permitted it's clearly advertised with markers on gates and signposts. For more information see the Access pages on www.naturalengland.org.uk.

Scotland has a different legal system, where the **Scottish Outdoor Access Code** (www.outdooraccess-scotland.com) allows walkers to cross most private land providing they act responsibly. There are restrictions during lambing time, bird-nesting periods and the grouse- and deer-hunting seasons.

Britain's Best Walking Areas

Although you can walk just about anywhere in Britain, some areas are better than others. Here's a rundown of favourite places, suitable for short walks of a couple of hours, or longer all-day outings.

Southern England

The chalky hills of the South Downs stride across the counties of West Sussex and East Sussex, while the New Forest in Hampshire is great for easy strolls and the nearby Isle of Wight has excellent walking options. The highest and wildest area in southern England is Dartmoor, dotted with Bronze Age remains and granite outcrops called 'tors' – looking for all the world like abstract sculptures. Exmoor has heather-covered hills cut by deep valleys and a lovely stretch of coastline, while the entire coast of the southwest peninsula from Dorset to Somerset offers dramatic walking conditions – especially along the beautiful cliff-lined shore of Cornwall.

Central England

The gem of central England is the Cotswold Hills, classic English countryside with gentle paths through neat fields, mature woodland and pretty villages of honey-coloured stone. The Marches, where England borders Wales, are similarly bucolic with more good walking options. For something higher, aim for the Peak District, divided into two distinct areas: the White Peak, characterised by limestone, farmland and verdant dales, ideal for gentle strolls; and the Dark Peak, with high peaty moorlands, heather and gritstone outcrops, for more serious hikes.

Northern England

The Lake District is the heart and soul of walking in England, a wonderful area of soaring peaks, endless views, deep valleys and, of course, beautiful lakes. On the other side of the country, the rolling hills of the Yorkshire Dales is another very popular walking area. Further north, keen

WEATHER WATCH

While enjoying the outdoors, it's always worth remembering the fickle nature of the British weather. The countryside can appear gentle and welcoming, and often is, but sometimes conditions can turn nasty – especially on the higher ground. At any time of year, if you're walking on the hills or open moors, it's vital to be well equipped. You should carry warm and waterproof clothing (even in summer); a map and compass (that you know how to use); and drink and food, including high-energy stuff such as chocolate. If you're really going off the beaten track, leave details of your route with someone.

walkers love the starkly beautiful hills of Northumberland National Park, while the nearby coast is less daunting but just as dramatic – perfect for wild seaside strolls.

South & Mid-Wales

The Brecon Beacons is a large range of gigantic rolling whaleback hills with broad ridges and table-top summits, while out in the west is Pembrokeshire, a wonderful array of beaches, cliffs, islands, coves and harbours, with a hinterland of tranquil farmland and secret waterways, and a relatively mild climate year-round.

North Wales

For walkers, North Wales *is* Snowdonia, where the remains of ancient volcanoes bequeath a striking landscape of jagged peaks, sharp ridges and steep cliffs. There are challenging walks on Snowdon itself – at 1085m, the highest peak in Wales – and many more on the nearby Glyder and Carneddau ranges, or further south around Cader Idris.

Southern & Central Scotland

This extensive region embraces several areas just perfect for keen walkers, including Ben Lomond, the best-known peak in the area, and the nearby Trossachs hills, lying within the Loch Lomond and the Trossachs National Park. Also here is the splendid Isle of Arran, with a great choice of coastal rambles and high-mountain hikes.

Northern & Western Scotland

For serious walkers, heaven is the northern and western parts of Scotland, where the forces of nature have created a mountainous landscape of utter grandeur, including two of Scotland's most famous place names, Glen Coe and Ben Nevis (Britain's highest mountain at 1344m). Off the west coast lie the dramatic mountains of the Isle of Skye. Keep going north and west, and things just keep getting better: a remote and beautiful area, sparsely populated, with scenic glens and lochs, and some of the largest, wildest and finest mountains in Britain.

Cycling & Mountain Biking

A bike is the perfect mode of transport for exploring back-road Britain. Once you escape the busy main highways, a vast network of quiet country lanes winds through fields and peaceful villages, ideal for cycletouring. You can cruise through gently rolling landscapes, taking it easy and stopping for cream teas, or you can thrash all day through hilly areas, revelling in steep ascents and swooping downhill sections. You can cycle from place to place, camping or staying in B&Bs (many of which are cyclist-friendly), or you can base yourself in one area for a few days and go out on rides in different directions. All you need is a map and a sense of adventure.

Mountain-bikers can go further into the wilds on the tracks and bridleways that criss-cross Britain's hills and high moors, or head for the many dedicated mountain-bike trail centres where specially built single-track winds through the forests. Options at these centres vary from delightful dirt roads ideal for families to gnarly rock gardens and precipitous dropoffs for hardcore riders, all classified from green to black in ski-resort style.

LONG-DISTANCE TRAILS

Some long-distance walking routes – such as the Pennine Way, the West Highland Way and the Pembrokeshire Coast Path – are well known and well maintained, with signposts and route-markers along the way, as well as being highlighted on Ordnance Survey maps. The most high-profile of these are the national trails, usually very clearly marked on the ground and on the map – ideal for beginners or visitors from overseas (although they're easy to follow, it doesn't mean they're necessarily easy underfoot). A downside of these famous routes is that they can be crowded in holiday times, making accommodation harder to find. An upside is the great feeling of camaraderie with other walkers on the trail.

www.sustrans.org.uk Details of Britain's national network of cycling trails.

www.forestry.gov.uk/england-cycling Guide to forest cycling trails in England.

www.dmbins.com Guide to mountain-biking trails in Scotland.

Fishing in the sea is generally free (except for salmon and sea trout), and neither permit nor rod licence is needed.

www.fishpal.com Information and booking portal for fishing (mostly salmon and trout) all over Britain.

fishing.visitwales.com Guide to fishing in Wales.

Horse Riding & Pony Trekking

If you want to explore the hills and moors but walking or cycling is too much of a sweat, seeing the wilder parts of Britain from horseback is highly recommended. In rural areas and national parks like Dartmoor and Northumberland, riding centres cater to all levels of proficiency, with ponies for kids and beginners and horses for the more experienced.

British Horse Society (www.bhs.org.uk) Lists approved riding centres offering day rides or longer holidays on horseback.

Fishing

After walking, fishing is Britain's most popular outdoor activity. As well as sea angling, there is excellent fishing for brown trout, grayling, pike, perch, carp and other coarse fish all over England, while Scotland offers some of the world's best salmon fishing.

Fishing rights to most inland waters are privately owned and you must obtain a permit to fish in them – these are usually readily available from the local fishing-tackle shop or hotel, which are also great sources of advice and local knowledge. Permits cost from around £5 to £20 per day but salmon fishing on some rivers – notably the Tyne in northeast England, and Scotland's Tweed, Tay and Spey – can be much more expensive (up to £150 a day).

In England and Wales, as well as a permit you will need a rod licence, which can be purchased online (www.postoffice.co.uk/rod-fishing-licence) or from post offices all over the country. This costs £3.75/8/27 for one day/eight days/one year for all freshwater fish except salmon and sea trout, which cost £8/23/72. Rod licences are not required in Scotland.

Canoeing, Kayaking & Rafting

Britain's west coast, with its sheltered inlets, indented shoreline and countless islands, is ideal for sea kayaking, while its inland lakes and canals are great for Canadian canoeing. In addition, the turbulent spate rivers of Scotland and Wales offers some of Britain's best whitewater kayaking and rafting.

Equipment rental and instruction are readily available in major centres such as Cornwall, Anglesey, the Lake District, Loch Lomond and the Isle of Skye.

www.gocanoeing.org.uk Lists approved canoeing centres in England.

www.canoescotland.org Canoe trails in Scotland.

www.ukrafting.co.uk Whitewater rafting in Wales.

Surfing & Windsurfing

Britain may not seem an obvious destination for surfing, but conditions are surprisingly good and the large tidal range often means a completely different set of breaks at low and high tides. If you've come from the other side of the world, you'll be delighted to learn that summer water temperatures in southern England are roughly equivalent to winter temperatures in southern Australia (ie you'll still need a wetsuit). At the main spots, it's easy enough to hire boards and wetsuits.

Top of the list are the Atlantic-facing coasts of Cornwall and Devon (Newquay is surf-central, with all the trappings from Kombi vans to bleached hair), and there are smaller surf scenes elsewhere, notably Pembrokeshire and the Gower in Wales, and Norfolk and Yorkshire in eastern England. Hardier souls can head for northern Scotland and the Outer Hebrides, which have some of the best surf in Europe.

surfinggb.com l istings of approved surf schools, courses, competitions and so on.

Windsurfing is hugely popular all around the coast. Top areas include Norfolk, Suffolk, Devon and Cornwall, the Isle of Wight, and the islands of Tiree, Orkney and the Outer Hebrides.

ukwindsurfing.com A good source of info.

Coasteering

If sometimes a simple clifftop walk doesn't cut the mustard, then coasteering might appeal. It's like mountaineering, but instead of going up a mountain, you go sideways along a coast – a steep and rocky coast – with waves breaking around your feet. And if the rock gets too steep, no problem – you jump in and start swimming. Coasteering centres provide wetsuits, helmets and buoyancy aids; you provide an old pair of training shoes and a sense of adventure. The sport is available all around Britain, but the mix of sheer cliffs, sandy beaches and warm water make Cornwall and Devon prime spots.

www.coasteering.org Info on coasteering in Devon and Cornwall.

Rock Climbing

Britain has a long history of rock climbing and mountaineering, with many of the classic routes having been pioneered in the 19th century. The main rock-climbing areas include the Scottish Highlands, the Lake District, the Peak District and North Wales, plus the sea cliffs of South Wales, Devon and Cornwall, but there are also hundreds of smaller crags situated all over the country.

Comprehensive climbing guidebooks are published by the **Scottish Mountaineering Club** (www.smc.org.uk), the **Fell & Rock Climbing Club** (www.frcc.co.uk) and the **Climbers Club** (www.climbers-club.co.uk), while **UKClimbing** (www.ukclimbing.com) is full of useful information.

Sailing & Boating

Scotland's west coast, with its myriad islands, superb scenery and challenging winds and tides, is widely acknowledged to be one of the finest yachting areas in the world, while the canals of England and Wales offer a classic narrow-boating experience.

Beginners can take a **Royal Yachting Association** (www.rya.org) training course in yachting or dinghy sailing at many sailing schools around the coast. Narrowboaters only need a quick introductory lesson at the start of their trip – for more info see www.canalholidays.com.

Skiing & Snowboarding

Britain's ski centres are all in the Scottish Highlands:

Cairngorm Mountain (www.cairngormmountain. com) 1097m; has almost 30 runs spread over an extensive area.

Glencoe (www.glencoemountain.com) 1108m; has five tows and two chairlifts.

Glenshee (www.ski-glenshee.co.uk) 920m; situated on the A93 road between Perth and Braemar; offers the largest network of lifts and the widest range of runs in Britain.

Lecht (www.lecht.co.uk) 793m; the smallest and most remote centre, on the A939 between Ballater and Grantown-on-Spey.

Nevis Range (www.nevisrange.co.uk) 1221m; near Fort William; offers the highest ski runs, the grandest setting and some of the best off-piste potential.

The high season is from January to April but it's sometimes possible to ski from as early as November to as late as May. It's easy to turn up at the slopes, hire some kit, buy a day pass and off you go.

Weather and snow reports can be obtained from the following:

Ski Scotland (www.ski-scotland.com)

WinterHighland (www.winterhighland.info)

Plan Your Trip
Eat & Drink Like a Local

Britain once had a reputation for bad food, but the nation has enjoyed something of a culinary revolution over the past decade. London is recognised as having one of the best restaurant scenes in the world, while all over the country stylish eateries and gourmet gastropubs are making the most of a newfound passion for quality local produce.

Food Experiences

Meals of a Lifetime

Waterside Inn (p228) Exquisite French food at Michel Roux' classic restaurant, in a romantic setting on the banks of the Thames.

Dinner by Heston Blumenthal (p128) Famous exponent of 'molecular gastronomy' leads you through a tour of Britain's culinary history.

Restaurant Nathan Outlaw (p343) Superb local seafood is the trademark of Cornwall's only Michelin-starred chef.

Three Chimneys (p938) A windswept crofting cottage in a far-flung corner of the Isle of Skye is home to unexpected gastronomic delights.

Hardwick (p718) Set in the heart of Mid-Wales gastropub territory, this rustic inn was one of the first on the scene, and still delivers a meal to remember.

St John (p131) A pioneer of 'nose-to-tail' dining (ie eating every part of the animal), St John offers a memorably 'offal' dining experience.

Cheap Treats

Fish and chips The nation's favourite takeaway meal, served in hundreds of chip shops all over the country.

The Year in Food

Best in Spring (Mar–May)

Spring brings fresh asparagus, new potatoes (notably Jersey Royals), pink rhubarb and tender lamb.

Best in Summer (Jun–Aug)

Strawberries, raspberries and other soft fruits are in season along with salad vegetables such as lettuce and radishes, and seafood such as scallops, langoustines, mackerel and cod.

Best in Autumn (Sep–Nov)

Apples and blackberries (often cooked together in a crumble), game including venison and wood pigeon, and shellfish – oysters, mussels and cockles. Also the main season for food festivals.

Best in Winter (Dec–Feb)

Sweet chestnuts (roasted on an open fire), and that classic Christmas combination of goose, root vegetables and Brussels sprouts.

ANDREW DERNIE / GETTY IMAGES ©

Scotch eggs and pickle

Bacon sandwich The breakfast of champions. Debate rages over the choice of sauce – red (tomato ketchup) or brown (spicy pickled fruit sauce).

Beans on toast A comforting childhood classic of tinned baked beans poured over buttered toast, served in many cafes as a breakfast or lunch dish.

Cockles A classic seaside snack that has been enjoyed by generations of British holidaymakers, sprinkled with vinegar and eaten from a cardboard tub with a wooden fork.

Scotch egg This masterpiece of culinary engineering consists of a hardboiled egg wrapped in sausage meat, coated in breadcrumbs and deep-fried.

Dare to Try

Haggis Scotland's national dish is made from the chopped heart, liver and lungs of a sheep, mixed with oatmeal and onion. Widely available in Scottish restaurants.

Tripe Cow's stomach lining, traditionally poached in milk with onions. A wartime staple, but hard to find in restaurants today – though it's making a comeback.

Stinking Bishop Britain's most pungent cheese, made in Gloucestershire and redolent of old socks. Available from Harrods in London, and many specialist cheese shops.

Jellied eels Traditional London side dish that can still be found in the capital's pie and mash shops.

Local Specialities

Scotland

Scotland may be most famous for haggis, but seafood is where it excels. Fresh lobster, langoustine, salmon and scallops are the favourites of restaurant menus, but look out for traditional dishes such as Arbroath smokies (hot-smoked haddock) and Cullen skink (soup made with smoked haddock, onion, butter and milk). Oats have been a mainstay of the Scottish diet for centuries, appearing in the form of porridge and oatcakes, but also as a coating for fried trout or herring, and in the classic Scottish dessert known as cranachan (whipped cream flavoured with whisky and mixed with raspberries and toasted oatmeal).

Wales

Tender and tasty Welsh lamb is sought after by restaurateurs all over Britain, but it also appears in the rustic local dish known as cawl (pronounced 'cowl') – a one-pot stew of lamb, bacon, cabbage, potato and swede. Better known is laverbread, which is not bread but seaweed, cooked with oatmeal and often served for breakfast with toast and bacon. Sweet-toothed visitors should look out for Welsh cakes (fruity griddle scones) and *bara brith* (a dense and spicy fruit cake flavoured with tea and marmalade).

The Midlands

The Leicestershire town of Melton Mowbray is famed for its pork pies, always eaten cold, ideally with pickle. Only pies handmade in the eponymous town can carry the Melton Mowbray moniker – in the same way that only fizzy wine from the Champagne region of France can carry that name.

Bakewell pudding (pudding, mark you, not 'Bakewell tart' as it's sometimes called) features regularly on local dessert menus and is certainly worth sampling. It is named after the Derbyshire town where it originated in 1860, and consists of a pastry base topped with jam egg custard and almond paste.

North of England

The northeast of England is known for its kippers (smoked herring), traditionally grilled with butter and served for breakfast with toast and marmalade on the side, and for pease pudding (a thick stew of yellow split peas cooked in ham stock). The northwest lays claim to Lancashire hotpot (slow-cooked stew of lamb and onion topped with sliced potatoes), Eccles cakes (rounds of flaky pastry filled with currants), and Cumberland sausage (a spiral shaped pork sausage flavoured with herbs). But the most famous of northern specialities is Yorkshire pudding, a light and puffy batter pudding usually served as a side dish with roast beef, that has now been adopted all over Britain.

Southwest England

Cows reared on the rich pastures of Devon and Cornwall create some of Britain's finest

BRITISH DINERS, INTERNATIONAL TASTES

For most Britons, traditional British food is only one part of a hugely varied diet that takes in everything from Indian and Pakistani curries to Chinese noodles to Italian pasta dishes. Fast food outlets are a favourite lunchtime and postpub destination, with Turkish kebabs, pizza shops and American fried chicken outlets at the top of the popularity stakes.

dairy produce, notably the famous clotted cream (a very thick cream made by heating full-cream milk) that forms an essential component of Cornish cream teas. Less refined but equally tasty are Cornish pasties (crimped pastry parcels containing minced beef, onion and potato), once the lunchtime staple of miners and farm workers.

London & Southeast England

Ask a Londoner about local food specialities, and you're bound to get the answer – pie and mash, and jellied eels. The staple menu of working-class Londoners since the 19th century, the former consists of a small pie filled with minced beef served with mashed potato and 'liquor' – a parsley-rich gravy made from the stock in which eels have been cooked. The eels are cooled and set in the jellied stock, and served as a side dish with malt vinegar – try them out at M Manze (p127) or Poppies (p132).

Oysters today have an expensive reputation, but in the 19th century they were a cheap and plentiful foodstuff, eaten by all. Whitstable oysters, from Kent – the native British species, unlike the more common, farmed Pacific oysters – have been harvested since Roman times, and still grace the tables of London restaurants and oyster bars.

How to Eat & Drink

When to Eat

Breakfast Served in most hotels and B&Bs between 7am and 9am, or perhaps 8am to 10am on weekends. In cafes, the breakfast menu might extend to 11am through the week.

SIX CLASSIC BRITISH CHEESES

Cheddar Sharp and savoury, Britain's most popular cheese originates in Somerset but is now made all over the country (and, indeed, the world).

Stilton A pungent blue cheese, traditionally eaten after dinner with a glass of port.

Wensleydale Crumbly white cheese from Yorkshire, with a mild, honeyed flavour.

Caerphilly From the Welsh town of the same name, this hard, salty cheese has an annual festival dedicated to it.

Cornish Yarg A rich, creamy cheese characterised by its wrapping of nettle leaves.

Caboc A Highland Scottish cream cheese rolled in oatmeal, whose recipe is more than 500 years old.

Lunch Generally taken between noon and 2pm, and can range from a sandwich and a bag of crisps to a three-course meal with wine. Many restaurants offer a set menu two-course lunch at competitive prices on weekdays, while cafes often have a daily lunch special, or offer soup and a sandwich.

Afternoon tea A tradition inherited from the British aristocracy and eagerly adopted by the middle classes, a between-meals snack now enjoying a revival in country hotels and upmarket tearooms. It consists of dainty sandwiches, cakes and pastries plus, of course, a cup of tea, poured from a silver teapot and sipped politely from fine china cups.

Dinner The main meal of the day, usually served in restaurants between 6pm and 9pm, and consisting of two or three courses – starter, main and dessert. Upmarket restaurant might serve a five-course dinner, with an amuse-bouche to begin, and a fish course between starter and main.

Sunday lunch is another great British tradition. It is the main meal of the day, normally served between noon and 4pm. Many pubs and restaurants offer Sunday lunch, where the main course usually consists of roast beef, lamb or pork, accompanied by roast or mashed potatoes, gravy, and boiled vegetables such as carrots and peas.

(In parts of Britain, notably northern England and Scotland, many people use the word 'dinner' for their main midday meal, and 'tea' for a light evening meal. However, this terminology is rarely, if ever, used in restaurants.)

Where to Eat

Cafes Traditional cafes are simple eateries serving simple food – sandwiches, pies, sausage and chips. Quality varies enormously: some cafes definitely earn their 'greasy spoon' handle, while others are neat and clean.

Tearooms The tearoom is a British institution, serving cakes, scones and sandwiches accompanied by pots of tea (though coffee is usually available too). Upmarket tearooms may also serve afternoon tea.

Coffee shops In most cities and towns you'll also find coffee shops – both independents and international chains – serving decent lattes, cappuccinos and espressos, and continental-style snacks such as bagels, panini or ciabattas.

Restaurants London has scores of excellent restaurants that could hold their own in major cities worldwide, while eating places in other British cities can give the capital a run for its money (often for rather less money).

Pubs Many British pubs serve a wide range of food, and it's often a good-value option whether you want a toasted sandwich between museum visits in London, or a three-course meal in the evening after touring the castles of Wales.

Gastropubs The quality of food in some pubs is now so high that they have created a whole new genre of eatery – the gastropub. The finest are almost restaurants (a few have been awarded Michelin stars) but others go for a more relaxed atmosphere.

Plan Your Trip
Travel with Children

Britain is ideal for travelling with children because of its compact size, packing a lot of attractions into a small area. So when the kids in the back of the car say 'are we there yet?' your answer can often be 'yes, we are'.

Britain for Kids

Many places of interest cater for kids as much as adults. At historic castles, for example, mum and dad can admire the medieval architecture, while the kids will have great fun striding around the battlements. In the same way, many national parks and holiday resorts organise specific activities for children. It goes without saying that everything ramps up in the school holidays.

Bargain Hunting

Most visitor attractions offer family tickets – usually two adults plus two children – for less than the sum of the individual entrance charges. Most offer cheaper rates for solo parents and kids, too. Be sure to ask, as these are not always clearly displayed.

On the Road

If you're going by public transport, trains are great for families: intercity services have plenty of room for luggage and extra stuff like buggies (strollers), and the kids can move about a bit when bored. In contrast, they need to stay in their seats on long-distance coaches.

If you're hiring a car, most (but not all) rental firms can provide child seats – but you'll need to check this in advance. Most

Best Regions for Kids

London
The capital has children's attractions galore.

Devon, Cornwall & Wessex
Lovely beaches and reliable weather, though crowded in summer.

The Midlands
Caverns and 'show caves', plus former railways are now traffic-free cycle routes.

Oxford & the Cotswolds
Oxford has Harry Potter connections; the Cotswolds is ideal for little-leg strolls.

Lake District & Cumbria
Zip wires and kayaks for teenagers; boat rides and Beatrix Potter for youngsters.

Wales
Long coast of beaches and pony-trekking in the hill country. And loads of castles...

Southern Scotland
Edinburgh and Glasgow have kid-friendly museums; the Southern Uplands offer mountain biking.

Scottish Highlands & Islands
Hardy teenagers plunge into outdoor activities; dolphin-spotting boat trips are fun for all the family.

will not actually fit the child seats; you need to do that yourself, for insurance reasons.

Dining, not Whining

When it comes to refuelling, most cafes and teashops are child-friendly. Restaurants are mixed: some offer high chairs and kiddy portions; others firmly say 'no children after 6pm'.

Children under 18 are usually not allowed in pubs serving just alcohol. Pubs also serving meals generally allow children of any age (with their parents) in England and Wales, but in Scotland they must be over 14 and must leave by 8pm. If in doubt, simply ask the bar staff.

And finally, a word on another kind of refuelling: Britain is still slightly buttoned up about breastfeeding. Older folks may tut-tut a bit if you give junior a top-up in public, but if done modestly it's usually considered OK.

Children's Highlights

Best Fresh-Air Fun

If the kids tire of castles and museums, you're never far from a place for outdoor activities to blow away the cobwebs.

Wildlife Cruises, Scotland's west coast (p865) What child could resist a boat trip to see seals, porpoises and dolphins, maybe even a whale?

Puzzlewood, Forest of Dean (p220) Wonderful woodland playground with mazy paths, weird rock formations and eerie passageways.

BABY-CHANGING FACILITIES

Most museums and other attractions in Britain usually have good baby-changing facilities (cue old joke: I swapped mine for a nice souvenir). Elsewhere, some city-centre public toilets have baby-changing areas, although these can be a bit grimy; your best bet for clean facilities is an upmarket department store. On the road, baby-changing facilities are generally bearable at motorway service stations and OK at out-of-town supermarkets.

Whinlatter Forest Park, Cumbria (p610) Highlights include a Go Ape adventure park and excellent mountain-bike trails, plus live video feeds from red squirrel cams.

Bewilderwood, Norfolk (p400) Zip wires, jungle bridges, tree houses, marsh walks, boat trips, mazes and all sorts of old-fashioned outdoor adventure.

Lyme Regis, Dorset (p263) Guided tours to find your very own prehistoric fossil.

Cotswold Farm Park (p209) Child-friendly introduction to the world of farm animals.

Tissington Trail, Derbyshire (p487) Cycling this former railway is fun and almost effortless. You can hire kids' bikes, tandems and trailers. Don't forget to hoot in the tunnels!

7stanes MTB Centres, southern Scotland (p833) A network of mountain-biking centres offering everything from easy, family-friendly trails with picnic tables and viewpoints, to more challenging routes for teenagers.

Best Hands-On Action

Please do not touch? No chance. Here are some places where grubby fingers and enquiring minds are positively welcomed.

Science Museum, London (p95) Seven floors of educational exhibits, at the mother of all science museums.

Enginuity, Ironbridge (p449) Endless hands-on displays at the birthplace of the Industrial Revolution.

National Waterfront Museum, Swansea (p681) Great interactive family fun.

Glasgow Science Centre (p811) Bringing science and technology alive through hundreds of engaging exhibits.

Discovery Museum, Newcastle (p628) Tyneside's rich history on display; highlights include a buzzers-and-bells science maze.

Best Rainy-Day Distractions

For those inevitable gloomy days, head for the indoor attractions; don't forget the nation's great collection of museums. Alternatively, try outdoor stuff like coasteering in Pembrokeshire or canyoning in the Lake District. It's always fun – wet or dry.

Cadbury World, Birmingham (p415) Dentists may cry, but kids love the story of chocolate. And yes, there are free samples.

Underground Edinburgh (p778) Take a guided tour of the haunted vaults beneath the medieval Old Town

Eden Project, Cornwall (p359) It may be raining outside, but inside these giant domes it's forever tropical forest or Mediterranean climate.

Cheddar Gorge Caves, Wessex (p331) Finally nail the difference between stalactites and stalagmites in the Westcountry's deep caverns.

Underground Passages, Exeter (p284) Explore medieval catacombs – the only system of its kind open to the public in England.

Best Stealth Learning

Across the country are many excellent museums, where young minds can be exercised while the kids think they are 'just' having fun.

At-Bristol, Bristol (p313) One of Britain's best interactive science museums, covering space, technology and the human brain.

Riverside Museum, Glasgow (p811) Top-class interactive museum with a focus on transport.

Jorvik Viking Centre, York (p505) Excellent smells-and-all Viking settlement reconstruction.

Natural History Museum, London (p95) Highlights include the life-size blue whale and animatronic dinosaurs.

Thinktank, Birmingham (p413) Every display comes with a button or a lever at this 'edutaining' science museum.

National Space Centre, Leicester (p475) Spacesuits, zero-gravity toilets and miniastronaut training – guaranteed to boost little brains.

Centre for Alternative Technology, Machynlleth (p726) Educational, fun and truly green – great for curious kids.

Planning
When to Go

The best time for families to visit Britain is pretty much the best time for everyone else: from April/May to the end of September. It's worth avoiding August – the heart of school summer holidays – when prices go up and roads are busy, especially near the coast. Other school holidays are two weeks around Easter Sunday, and mid-December to early January, plus three week-long 'half-term' breaks – usually late February (or early March), late May and late October.

Places to Stay

Some hotels welcome kids (with their parents) and provide cots, toys and babysitting services, while others maintain an adult atmosphere. Many B&Bs offer 'family suites' of two adjoining bedrooms with one bathroom, and an increasing number of hostels (YHA, SYHA and independent) have family rooms with four or six beds – some even with private bathroom attached. If you want to stay in one place for a while, renting a holiday cottage is ideal. Camping is very popular with British families, and there are lots of fantastic campsites, but you'll usually need all your own gear.

Handy Websites

Baby Goes 2 (www.babygoes2.com) Advice, tips and encouragement (and a stack of advertising) for families on holiday.

MumsNet (www.mumsnet.com) No-nonsense advice on travel and more from a vast network of UK mothers.

Regions at a Glance

From the multicultural melting pot of London to the remote islands of the Outer Hebrides, Britain's regions offer a kaleidoscope of classic experiences. Southern England is where you'll find the archetypal English countryside of lush meadows, thatched cottages and games of cricket on the village green. The southwestern counties of Devon and Cornwall are wilder in nature, known for their surf beaches and seafood restaurants. Lovers of mountain scenery will be spoilt for choice in the Scottish Highlands, the Lake District and North Wales, while those who prefer gritty industrial heritage and lively nightlife will enjoy the northern English cities of Manchester, Liverpool and Newcastle. And bang in the middle is Yorkshire, with everything from the gorgeous city of York to the rolling moors of the Yorkshire Dales.

London

History
Entertainment
Museums

Historic Streets

London's ancient streets contain many of Britain's most famous and history-steeped landmarks. The echoes of the footfalls of monarchs, poets, whores and saints can still be detected in places like the Tower of London, Westminster Abbey and St Paul's Cathedral.

Entertainment

From West End theatres to East End clubs, from Camden's rock venues to Covent Garden's opera house, from tennis at Wimbledon to cricket at Lord's or football at Wembley, London's venues and arenas offer a perpetual clamour of entertainment.

Museums & Galleries

While the British Museum is the big crowd-puller, the capital has museums and galleries of every shape and size and many of the very best are free.

p62

Canterbury & Southeast England

Cathedral
History
Food & Drink

Canterbury Cathedral

A major reason to visit southeast England, Canterbury Cathedral is one of the finest cathedrals in Europe, and one of the most holy places in Christendom.

Invasion Heritage

The southeast has always been a gateway for Continental arrivals, some more welcome than others. Castles and fortresses, the 1066 battlefield and Dover's secret wartime tunnels tell the region's story of invasion and defence.

Hops & Grapes

Kent is known as the Garden of England, long celebrated for its hops, which are still used to flavour traditional English beers. Sussex isn't far behind, with England's finest sparkling wine.

p148

Oxford, Cotswolds & Around

Architecture
Stately Homes
Villages

Oxford Colleges

Oxford's architecture will never leave you indifferent, whether you gaze across the 'dreaming spires' from the top of Carfax Tower, or explore the medieval streets on foot, or admire the fantastic gargoyles on the college facades.

Blenheim Palace

Favoured by the rich and powerful for centuries, this region is scattered with some of the finest country houses in Britain. Top of the pile is the baroque masterpiece of Blenheim Palace.

Cotswold Villages

Littered with picturesque scenes of honey-coloured stone cottages, thatched roofs, neat greens and cobbled lanes, Cotswolds villages provide a charming snapshot of rural England.

p184

Bath & Southwest England

Coastline
History
Activities

Cornish Beaches

Britain's southwest peninsula juts determinedly into the Atlantic, fringed by an almost endless chain of sandy beaches, from the picturesque scenery of Kynance Cove to the rolling surf of Newquay.

Roman Remains

The handsome Georgian city of Bath (the whole town is a Unesco World Heritage Site) is home to one of the best-preserved Roman bath complexes in the world.

Hiking & Surfing

If you like to take it nice and easy, come to walk the moors or tootle along cycle trails. If you prefer life fast and furious, come to surf the best waves in England or learn to dive or kitesurf.

p229

Cambridge & East Anglia

Architecture
Coastline
Waterways

Historic Churches

From the magnificent cathedrals of Ely, Norwich and Peterborough to Cambridge's King's College Chapel, Trinity's Great Court and the New Court at St John's, East Anglia's architectural splendour is second to none.

Seaside Resorts

With wide beaches, great seafood, delightful old pubs, bird reserves, historic villages still proud of their nautical heritage and classic seaside resorts such as Southwold and Cromer, the coastline of East Anglia is rich and varied.

The Broads

The Norfolk and Suffolk Broads is a tranquil area of lakes and rivers, and an ideal spot for boating, birding, canoeing, cycling or walking, or just getting back to nature.

p367

Birmingham, the Midlands & the Marches

Activities
Stately Homes
Food & Drink

Hiking & Biking

The Peak District National Park, plus Cannock Chase, the Shropshire Hills, the Roaches, the Malvern Hills, Offa's Dyke Path, the Tissington Trail and the Pennine Cycleway, make this region great for hiking and biking.

Chatsworth

Grand houses like Haddon Hall, Burghley House and especially Chatsworth promise sprawling deer-filled grounds and grand interiors full of priceless heirlooms and walls dripping with oil paintings.

Curry Capital

Birmingham is the curry capital of the country (and, increasingly, a magnet for Michelin-starred chefs), while the tiny town of Ludlow is an epicentre of gastronomic exploration.

p407

Yorkshire

Activities
Food & Drink
History

Hiking & Biking

With rolling hills, scenic valleys and high moors and a cliff-lined coast all protected by national parks, Yorkshire is a natural adventure playground for hiking, biking, surfing and rock climbing.

Real Ale

Lush pasture means Yorkshire beef and lamb is sought after, while the famous breweries of Masham turn out excellent real ales, always best sampled in one of Yorkshire's equally excellent traditional pubs.

Ancient Abbeys

From York's Viking heritage and the ancient abbeys of Rievaulx, Fountains and Whitby, to the industrial archaeology of Leeds, Bradford and Sheffield, you can follow several of Britain's most important historical narratives in Yorkshire.

p497

Manchester, Liverpool & Northwest England

History
Sport
Seaside Resorts

Historical Museums

The northwest's collection of heritage sites, from the wonderful People's History Museum in Manchester to the International Slavery Museum in Liverpool, is testament to the region's rich history.

Football

Liverpool and Manchester give the world four famous clubs, including the two most successful in English history. The National Football Museum in Manchester is another reason for fans to visit this region.

Blackpool

The epitome of the classic English seaside resort just keeps on going, thanks to the rides of the Pleasure Beach amusement park, where adrenalin junkies can always find a fix.

p553

The Lake District & Cumbria

Scenery
Activities
Literature

Lakes & Mountains

The Lake District National Park is the most mountainous part of England, home to Scafell and countless scenic lakes. Some are big and famous while others are small, hidden and little known.

Walking

The Lake District is the heart and soul of walking in England. Casual strollers find gentle routes through foothills and valleys, while serious hikers tackle high peaks and fells.

William Wordsworth

The beauty of the Lake District famously moved William Wordsworth, and Wordsworth landmarks such as Dove Cottage and Hawkshead Grammar School are among the region's big draws.

p588

Newcastle & Northeast England

History
Landscape
Castles

Hadrian's Wall

One of the world's premier Roman sites, this potent symbol of imperial power strides for over 70 miles across the neck of England, from Tyneside to the Solway Firth. You can travel its length, stopping off at forts along the way.

Northumberland National Park

If it's widescreen vistas you're after, the broad moors, stone villages and expansive views of England's most northerly national park never fail to please.

Alnwick Castle

Northumberland is dotted with some of Britain's finest castles, including the coastal fortresses of Bamburgh and Dunstanburgh, but Alnwick – setting for the Harry Potter movies – is the most famous.

p624

Cardiff, Pembrokeshire & South Wales

Architecture
Coastline
Castles

Victorian Revival

From the whimsical, fairy-tale structures of Cardiff Castle and Castell Coch to the elegant shopping arcades of the city centre, the Welsh capital has plenty to keep fans of Victorian architecture interested.

Pembrokeshire & The Gower

South Wales boasts two of Britain's most beautiful stretches of coast – the Gower Peninsula and Pembrokeshire – between them offering clifftop walks, beaches, surfing hot spots, sea-kayaking and coasteering.

Carreg Cennen

South Wales has some of the country's best castles, including Chepstow and Pembroke, but remote Carreg Cennen is the most spectacularly positioned of them all.

p657

Hay-on-Wye & Mid-Wales

Birdwatching
Local Culture
Food & Drink

Red Kites

In the mountains and moors of the Brecon Beacons and many other parts of the region you can spot birds of prey – most famously the once-rare red kites, most easily spotted at feeding stations such as Gigrin Farm in Rhyader.

Market Towns

From book-obsessed Hay-on-Wye to quirky Llanwrtyd Wells and quaint Llandrindod Wells, the market towns of Mid-Wales are full of charm.

Abergavenny

Restaurants, inns and gastropubs throughout the region are at the forefront of a new Welsh gastronomy, all focused on the nation's foodie capital at Abergavenny.

p704

Snowdonia & North Wales

Mountains
Industrial Heritage
Coastline

Snowdon

Home to some of Britain's finest mountain scenery outside of the Scottish Highlands – and for most visitors much more accessible – the imposing peaks of Snowdon and its neighbours provide a scenic backdrop for innumerable outdoor pursuits.

Welsh Slate

Welsh slate once roofed much of the world and the region's quarries and caverns bear witness to the lives of generations of workers, while rejuvenated railways now shunt tourists through spectacular terrain.

Seaside Resorts

From the North Coast's popular resort towns to the surf spots and quiet bays of Anglesey and the Llŷn Peninsula, North Wales has plenty of beach to go round.

p728

Edinburgh

Culture
History
Food

Festival City

Dubbed the Athens of the North, the Scottish capital is a city of art and literature, home to the world's biggest arts festival. Outside festival time, there's plenty to enjoy in the city's many theatres and world-class art galleries and museums.

Edinburgh Castle

Perched on a brooding black crag overlooking the city centre, Edinburgh Castle has played a pivotal role in Scottish history, the focus of the nation's capital city since medieval times.

Eating Out

Edinburgh has more restaurants per head of population than any city in the UK, while Scottish cuisine has been given a makeover by inventive chefs using top-quality local produce.

p771

Glasgow & Southern Scotland

Museums
Historic Buildings
Stately Homes

Kelvingrove Art Gallery & Museum

Glasgow's mercantile and industrial history has left the city with a wonderful legacy of museums and galleries, dominated by the grand Victorian cathedral of culture that is Kelvingrove.

The Great Abbeys

Rolling countryside and ruined abbeys are the big draws along the country's southern border, where you'll find the Gothic ruins of Melrose, Jedburgh and Dryburgh abbeys.

Dumfries House

This region is rich in Adam-designed mansions such as Culzean Castle and Floors Castle, but the almost perfectly preserved Chippendale time-capsule Dumfries House takes top place.

p802

Argyll, Central & Northeast Scotland

Castles
Islands
Whisky

Stirling Castle

Central and Northeast Scotland are home to the greatest concentration of castles in the country, from the turreted exuberance of Craigievar to the more restrained elegance of Balmoral, and topped by the regal splendour of Stirling.

Island-Hopping

Island-hopping is a great way to explore Scotland's western seaboard, and the islands of this region – wild Jura, scenic Mull and the jewel of Iona – provide a brilliant introduction.

Speyside Distilleries

No trip to Scotland is complete without a visit to a whisky distillery – the Speyside region and the isle of Islay are epicentres of the industry.

p836

Central & Northern Highlands & Islands

Activities
Scenery
History

Hill Walking

Between them, the Cairngorm resort of Aviemore, gateway to snow sports in winter and wild hill-walking in summer, and Fort William, self-styled Outdoor Capital of the UK, offer plenty of adventure.

Mountain Landscapes

Landscape photographers are spoilt for choice, with classic views ranging from the mountain beauty of Glen Coe and the snow-patched summits of the Cairngorms to the rock pinnacles of the Cuillin Hills.

Prehistoric Sites

The region is rich in prehistoric remains, including the standing stones of Callanish, the neolithic tomb of Maes Howe, and Skara Brae – Europe's best-preserved prehistoric village.

p892

On the Road

England

England Highlights

1 Spending more time than you'd planned in England's (and Britain's) endlessly entertaining capital, **London** (p62)

2 Being a Jane Austen character for a day in elegant **Bath** (p320)

3 Wandering lonely as a cloud in the idyllic **Lake District** (p592)

4 Exploring medieval walls, Viking sights and the soaring Gothic minster in historic **York** (p502)

5 Falling in love with the impossibly quaint villages of the **Cotswolds** (p200)

6 Getting some higher education among the dreaming spires of **Oxford** (p186)

7 Punting along the river in **Cambridge** (p371)

8 Seeing wild scenery and ancient engineering at **Hadrian's Wall** (p640)

9 Catching a Shakespeare play or visiting the Bard's grave in **Stratford-upon-Avon** (p425)

10 Marvelling at one of Europe's greatest cathedrals in **Canterbury** (p149)

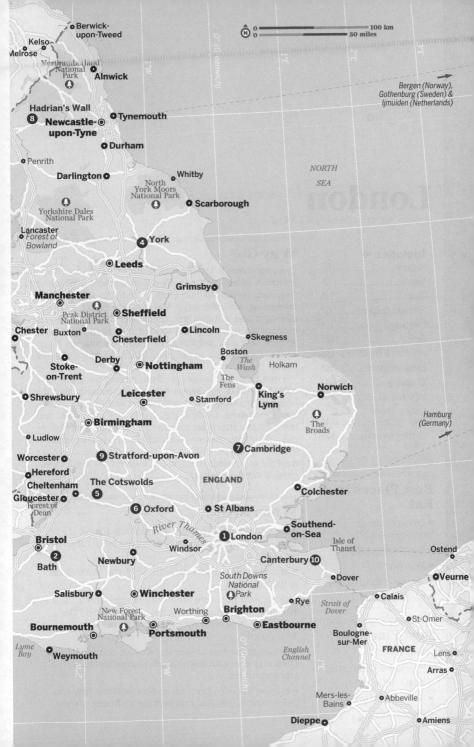

London

📖 020 / POP 8.3 MILLION / AREA 609 SQ MILES

Best Places to Eat

➡ Dinner by Heston Blumenthal (p128)

➡ Five Fields (p128)

➡ Koya (p123)

➡ Brasserie Zédel (p126)

➡ Ledbury (p129)

Best Places to Stay

➡ Haymarket Hotel (p118)

➡ Zetter Hotel (p123)

➡ Hoxton Hotel (p123)

➡ Citizen M (p119)

Why Go?

Everyone comes to London with preconceptions shaped by a multitude of books, movies, TV shows and songs. Whatever yours are, prepare to have them exploded by this endlessly fascinating, amorphous city. You could spend a lifetime exploring it and still find that the slippery thing's gone and changed on you. One thing though is constant: that great serpent of a river enfolding the city in its sinuous loops, linking London both to the green heart of England and the world.

From Roman times people from around the globe have come to London, put down roots and complained about the weather. This is one of the world's most multicultural cities – any given street yields a rich harvest of languages, and those narrow streets are also steeped in fascinating history, magnificent art, imposing architecture and popular culture. When you add an endless reserve of cool to this mix, it's hard not to conclude that London is one of the world's great cities, if not the greatest.

When to Go

➡ London is a place that you can visit any time of the year. That said, different months and seasons boast different charms.

➡ Spring in the city sees daffodils in bloom and blossom in the trees.

➡ In June the parks are filled with people, there's Trooping the Colour, summer arts festivals, Field Day in Victoria Park, other music events, gay pride and Wimbledon.

➡ Although the days are getting shorter, autumn in London is alive with festivals celebrating literature, the arts and culture.

➡ London in December is all about Christmas lights on Oxford and Regent Sts, and perhaps a whisper of snow.

History

London first came into being as a Celtic village near a ford across the River Thames, but the city only really took off after the Roman conquest in AD 43. The invaders enclosed their 'Londinium' in walls that still find refrain in the shape of the City (with a capital 'C') of London today.

By the end of the 3rd century AD, Londinium was home to some 30,000 people. Internal strife and relentless barbarian attacks wore the Romans down, however, and they abandoned Britain in the 5th century, reducing the settlement to a sparsely populated backwater.

The Saxons moved in next, their 'Lundenwic' prospering and becoming a large, well-organised town. As the city grew in importance, it caught the eye of Danish Vikings, who launched numerous invasions. In 1016 the Saxons, finally beaten down, were forced to accept the Danish leader Knut (Canute) as King of England, after which London replaced Winchester as capital. In 1042, the throne reverted to the Saxon Edward the Confessor, who built Westminster Abbey.

The Norman Conquest of 1066 saw William the Conqueror march into London, where he was crowned king. He built the White Tower (the core of the Tower of London), negotiated taxes with the merchants, and affirmed the city's right to self-government. From then until the late 15th century, London politics were largely taken up by a three-way power struggle between the monarchy, the church and city guilds. An uneasy political compromise was reached between the factions, and the city expanded rapidly in the 16th century under the House of Tudor.

In a rerun of the disease that wiped out half of London's population between 1348 and 1350, the Great Plague struck in 1665, and by the time the winter cold arrested the epidemic, 100,000 Londoners had perished. The cataclysm was followed by further devastation when the Great Fire of 1666 sent the city skywards. One upshot of the conflagration was a blank canvas for master architect Sir Christopher Wren to build his magnificent churches.

Despite these setbacks, London continued to grow, and by 1700 it was Europe's largest city, with 600,000 people. An influx of foreign workers brought expansion to the east and south, while those who could afford it headed to the more salubrious environs of the north and west. Georgian London saw a surge in artistic creativity, with the likes of Dr Johnson, Handel, Gainsborough and Reynolds enriching the city's culture, while architects fashioned an elegant new metropolis.

In 1837, 18-year-old Victoria began her epic reign, as London became the fulcrum of the British Empire. The Industrial Revolution saw the building of new docks and railways (including the first underground line in 1863), while the Great Exhibition of 1851 showcased London to the world. During the Victorian era, the city's population mushroomed from just over two million to 6.6 million.

Although London suffered a relatively minor bruising during WWI, it was devastated by the Luftwaffe in WWII, when huge swaths of the centre and East End were flattened and 32,000 people were killed. Ugly housing and low-cost developments followed, and pollutants – both residential and industrial – rose steadily into the air. On 6 December 1952, the Great Smog (a lethal combination of fog, smoke and pollution) descended, killing some 4000 people.

Prosperity gradually returned to the city, and creative energy bottled up in the postwar years was suddenly unleashed. In the 'Swinging Sixties', London became the capital of cool in fashion and music – a party followed morosely by the austere 1970s. Since then the city has surfed up and down the waves of global fortunes, hanging on to its position as the world's leading financial centre.

In 2000, the modern metropolis won its first mayor of London, an elected role covering the City and all 32 urban boroughs. Bicycle-riding Boris Johnson, a Tory (Conservative) with a shock of blond hair and an affable persona, was elected in 2008, and retained his post in the 2012 mayoral election.

Triggered by the shooting of a man by police in Tottenham in August 2011, numerous London boroughs were rocked by riots characterised by looting and arson. Analysts still debate the causes of the disorder, ascribing any number of factors from single-parent families to gang culture, unemployment and criminal opportunism.

Both the Olympics and the Queen's Diamond Jubilee concocted a splendid display of pageantry for London in 2012. New overground train lines opened, a cable car was flung across the Thames and a once rundown and polluted area of East London was regenerated for the Olympic Park. The games themselves were a universally applauded success, kicked off by a stupendous Opening Ceremony orchestrated by Danny Boyle.

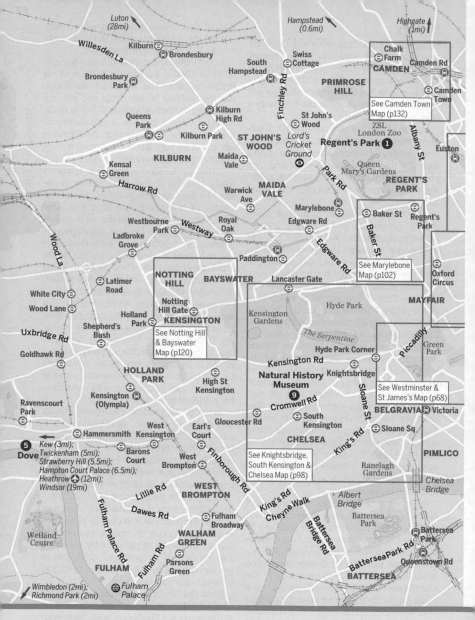

London Highlights

❶ Watching the world pass by on a sunny day in **Regent's Park** (p102) or any of London's other green oases

❷ Sifting through the booty of an empire at the **British Museum** (p103)

❸ Losing your head in history at the **Tower of London** (p80)

❹ Sizing up the awe-inspiring architecture of **Westminster Abbey** (p66)

❺ Raising a glass while overlooking the Thames from the **Dove** (p129) or another riverside London pub

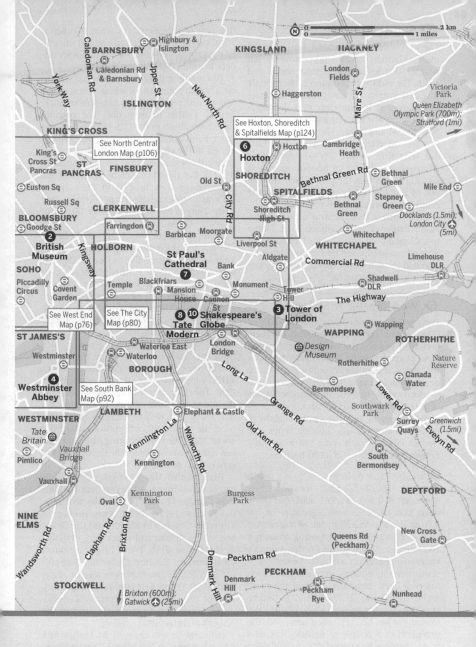

6 Seeing the locals through beer goggles on a Hoxton **bar hop** (p137)

7 Reaching for the heavens at the top of the dome of **St Paul's Cathedral** (p82)

8 Embarking on an eye-opening tour of modern and contemporary art at the **Tate Modern** (p88)

9 Revelling in the astounding stonework and displays at the **Natural History Museum** (p95)

10 Getting your drama fix at **Shakespeare's Globe** (p88) or any of London's outstanding theatres

◉ Sights

The city's main geographical feature is the murky Thames, which snakes around, but roughly divides the city into north and south. The old City of London is the capital's financial district, covering roughly a square mile bordered by the river and the many gates of the ancient (long-gone) city walls: Newgate, Moorgate etc. The areas east of the City are collectively known as the East End. The West End, on the City's other flank, is effectively the centre of London gravity. It actually falls within the City of Westminster, one of London's 32 boroughs and long the centre of government and royalty.

Surrounding these central areas are dozens of former villages (Camden Town, Islington, Clapham etc), each with its own High St, long ago swallowed by London's sprawl.

When the sun shines make like a Londoner and head to the parks.

◉ Westminster & St James's

Purposefully positioned outside the old City (London's fiercely independent burghers preferred to keep the monarch and parliament at arm's length), Westminster has been the centre of the nation's political power for nearly a millennium. The area's many landmarks combine to form an awesome display of authority, pomp and gravitas.

St James's is an aristocratic enclave of palaces, famous hotels, historic shops and elegant edifices, with some 150 historically noteworthy buildings in its 36 hectares.

★ **Westminster Abbey**   CHURCH
(Map p68; ☑ 020-7222 5152; www.westminster -abbey.org; 20 Dean's Yard, SW1; adult/child £18/8, verger tours £3; ⊙ 9.30am-4.30pm Mon, Tue, Thu & Fri, to 7pm Wed, to 2.30pm Sat; ⊜ Westminster) One of London's most imposing treasures, Westminster Abbey serves up the country's venerable history on cold slabs of stone. For centuries, the nation's greatest have been interred here, including most of the monarchs from Henry III (died 1272) to George II (1760). Every sovereign since William the Conqueror has been crowned here, with the exception of a couple of unlucky Eds who were murdered (Edward V) or abdicated (Edward VIII) before the magic moment.

The abbey is not only a sublime place of worship, it's etched with enough history and architectural detail to fill several days' exploration. It has never been a cathedral

(the seat of a bishop). It's what is called a 'royal peculiar' and is administered directly by the Crown. Look out for the curiously underwhelming **Coronation Chair**.

The building itself is an arresting spectacle. Though a mixture of architectural styles, it is considered the finest example of Early English Gothic in existence. The original church was built in the 11th century by King (later Saint) Edward the Confessor, who is buried in the chapel behind the main altar. Henry III began work on the new building in 1245 but didn't complete it; the French Gothic **nave** was finished in 1388. Henry VII's astonishing Late Perpendicular–style **Lady Chapel** was consecrated in 1519 after 16 years of construction.

Apart from the royal graves, keep an eye out for the many famous commoners interred here, especially in **Poets' Corner**, where you'll find the resting places of Chaucer, Dickens, Hardy, Tennyson, Dr Johnson and Kipling, as well as memorials to other literary titans (Shakespeare, Austen, Brontë etc). Elsewhere you'll find the graves of Handel and Sir Isaac Newton.

The octagonal **Chapter House** dates from the 1250s and was where the monks would meet for daily prayer before Henry VIII's suppression of the monasteries in 1536. The door on your right as you enter is the oldest in Britain, dating to around 1050 AD. Used as a treasury and 'Royal Wardrobe', the cryptlike **Pyx Chamber** dates from about 1070. The neighbouring **Abbey Museum** has as its centrepiece the death masks of generations of royalty.

Parts of the Abbey complex are free to visitors. This includes the 900-year-old **College Garden** (10am-6pm Tuesday to Thursday April to September, to 4pm Tuesday to Thursday October to March) and the **Cloister**, where drinks and snacks are available at the Coffee Club. For a proper sit-down meal head for the new **Cellarium** (Map p68; ☑ 020-7222 0516; www.cellariumcafe.com; mains £9.50-14.50; ⊙ 9am-6pm Mon-Fri, to 4.30pm Sat), part of the original 14th-century Benedictine monastery with stunning views of the Abbey's architectural detailing.

Adjacent to the abbey is **St Margaret's Church** (Map p68; ⊙ 9.30am-3.30pm Mon-Fri, to 1.30pm Sat, 2-4.30pm Sun), the House of Commons' place of worship since 1614. There are windows commemorating churchgoers Caxton and Milton, and Sir Walter Raleigh is buried by the altar.

Verger-led tours are held several times a day (except Sunday); call ahead to secure a place. Of course, admission to the Abbey is free if you wish to attend a service. On weekdays, Matins is at 7.30am, Holy Communion at 8am and 12.30pm, and Choral Evensong at 5pm. There are services throughout the day on Sunday. You can sit and savour the atmosphere, even if you're not religious.

★Houses of Parliament   HISTORIC BUILDING
(Map p68; www.parliament.uk; Parliament Sq, SW1; ⊖Westminster) FREE Coming face to face with one of the world's most recognisable landmarks can be a surreal moment, but in the case of the Houses of Parliament, it's a revelation. Photos just don't do justice to the ornate stonework and golden filigree of Charles Barry and Augustus Pugin's neo-Gothic masterpiece (1840). Its most famous feature is its clock tower, aka Big Ben (Map p68) (actually the 13-ton bell, named after Benjamin Hall, commissioner of works when the tower was completed in 1858).

Officially called the Palace of Westminster, the oldest part is Westminster Hall (1097), one of only a few sections that survived a catastrophic fire in 1834. Its roof, added between 1394 and 1401, is the earliest known example of a hammerbeam roof and has been described as the greatest surviving achievement of medieval English carpentry.

At the business end, parliament is split into two houses. The green-hued House of Commons is the lower house, where the 650 elected Members of Parliament sit. Traditionally the home of hereditary bluebloods, the scarlet-decorated House of Lords now has peers appointed through various means. Both houses debate and vote on legislation, which is then presented to the Queen for her Royal Assent (in practice, this is a formality; the last time Royal Assent was denied was 1708). At the annual State Opening of Parliament (usually in November), the Queen takes her throne in the House of Lords, having arrived in the gold-trimmed Irish State Coach from Buckingham Palace. It's well worth lining the route for a gawk at the crown jewels sparkling in the sun.

When parliament is in session, visitors are admitted to the House of Commons Visitors' Gallery. The best time to watch a debate is during Prime Minister's Question Time at noon on Wednesday, but it's also the busiest. Enter via St Stephen's Entrance (Map p68). The House of Lords Visitors' Gallery can also be accessed.

On Saturdays year-round and when Parliament is in summer recess (from mid-July to early September), visitors can join a 75-minute guided tour (☑0844 847 1672; www.ticketmaster.co.uk/housesofparliament; 75min tour adult/child £16.50/7) of both chambers, Westminster Hall and other historic buildings conducted by qualified Blue Badge Tourist Guides in six languages. Tour schedules change with every recess, so check (and book) ahead.

LONDON IN...

Two Days
Only two days? Start in **Trafalgar Sq** and see at least the outside of all the big-ticket sights – **London Eye**, **Houses of Parliament**, **Westminster Abbey**, **St James's Park and Palace**, **Buckingham Palace**, **Green Park**, **Hyde Park** and **Kensington Gardens and Palace**– and then motor around the **Tate Modern** until you get booted out. In the evening, explore **Soho**. On day two, race around the **British Museum**, then head to the **City**. Start with our **walking tour** and finish in the **Tower of London**. In the evening, head to **Clerkenwell** for international eats, then **Hoxton** and **Shoreditch** for hip bars.

Four Days
Take the two-day itinerary but stretch it to a comfortable pace, spending extra time in the Tate Modern, British Museum and Tower of London. Stop at the **National Gallery** while you're in Trafalgar Sq and explore inside Westminster Abbey and **St Paul's Cathedral**. On your extra evenings, check out **Camden** and **Islington** or enjoy a no-expenses-spared dinner in **Kensington** or **Knightsbridge**.

One Week
As above, but slap on a day each for **Greenwich**, **Kew Gardens** and **Hampton Court Palace**.

Westminster & St James's

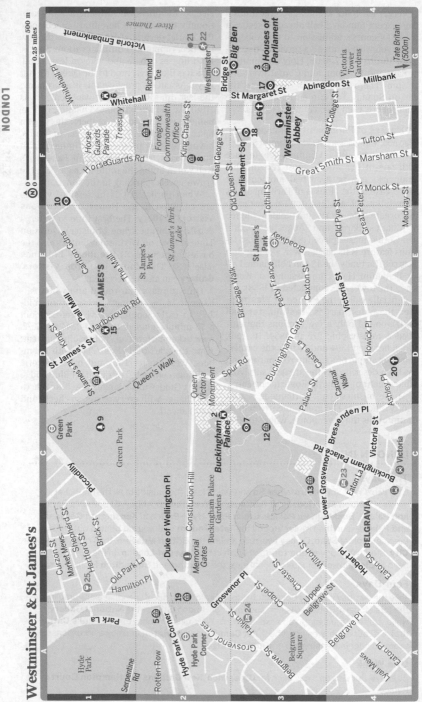

★ **Buckingham Palace** PALACE
(Map p68; ☑ 020-7766 7300; www.royalcollection.
org.uk; Buckingham Palace Rd, SW1; adult/child
£19.75/11.25; ☉ 9.30am-7.30pm late Jul-Aug, to
6.30pm Sep; ☻ St James's Park, Victoria, Green
Park) Built in 1703 for the Duke of Buckingham, Buckingham Palace replaced St
James's Palace as the monarch's official
London residence in 1837. When she's not
giving her famous wave to far-flung parts
of the Commonwealth, Queen Elizabeth
II divides her time between here, Windsor
and Balmoral. To check if she's at home, see
whether the yellow, red and blue standard
is flying. Nineteen lavishly furnished **State
Rooms** are open to visitors when HRH (Her
Royal Highness) takes her holidays.

The two-hour tour includes the **Throne
Room**, with his-and-hers pink chairs ini-
tialed 'ER' and 'P'. Access is by timed tickets
with admission every 15 minutes (audioguide included). Needless to say, the gardens
are an absolute picture.

Your ticket to Buckingham Palace is good
for a return trip if bought direct from the
palace ticket office (ask to have it stamped).
A 'Royal Day Out' is a combined ticket including the State Rooms, Queen's Gallery
and Royal Mews (adult/child £34.50/19.50).

➡ **Changing of the Guard**
At 11.30am daily from April to July, and
on alternate days (weather permitting)
from August to March, the old guard (Foot
Guards of the Household Regiment) comes
off duty to be replaced by the new guard on
the forecourt of Buckingham Palace. Highly
popular, the show lasts about forty minutes
(brace for crowds). If you're here in November, the procession leaving the palace for the
State Opening of Parliament is much more
impressive.

➡ **Queen's Gallery**
(www.royalcollection.org.uk; Southern wing, Buckingham Palace; adult/child £9.50/4.80, with Royal
Mews £16.25/9.10; ☉10am-5.30pm) Originally
designed by John Nash as a conservatory,
the Queen's Gallery showcases some of the
palace's treasures on a rotating basis, through
temporary exhibitions. Entrance to the gallery
is through Buckingham Gate.

➡ **Royal Mews**
(www.royalcollection.org.uk; adult/child £8/5, with
Queen's Gallery £16.25/9.10; ☉10am-5pm Apr-
Oct, to 4pm Mon-Sat Nov & Dec;) Indulge your
Cinderella fantasies while inspecting the
exquisite state coaches in the Royal Mews,
a working stable looking after the immaculately groomed horses and opulent vehicles
the royals use for getting from A to B. Highlights include the magnificent gold coach of
1762 and the 1910 Glass Coach (Prince William and Catherine Middleton actually used
the 1902 State Landau for their wedding in
2011).

Supreme Court LANDMARK
(Map p68; www.supremecourt.gov.uk; Parliament
Sq, SW1; ☉9.30am-4.30pm Mon-Fri; ☻ Westminster) FREE The Supreme Court, the highest court in the UK, is now housed in the
neo-Gothic Middlesex Guildhall (1913) on
Parliament Square. Members of the public
can observe cases when the court is sitting
four days a week (Monday to Thursday). On

Westminster & St James's

LONDON SIGHTS

the lower ground floor is a permanent exhibition on the UK's highest court as well as the history of the building.

St James's Park & Palace
PARK

(⊚ St James's Park, Green Park) With its manicured flower beds and ornamental lake, St James's Park is delightful for strolling and taking in the surrounding palaces. The striking Tudor gatehouse of **St James's Palace** (Map p68; www.royal.gov.uk; Cleveland Row, SW1; ⊜ Green Park), initiated by the palace-mad Henry VIII in 1530, is best approached from St James's St, to the north of the park. This was the residence of Prince Charles and his sons before they shifted next door to **Clarence House** (1828), following the death of its previous occupant, the Queen Mother.

Green Park
PARK

(Map p68; www.royalparks.gov.uk; ⊘ 24hr; ⊜ Green Park) Green Park's 47-acre expanse of meadows and mature trees links St James's Park to Hyde Park and Kensington Gardens, forming a green corridor from Westminster all the way to Kensington. Once a duelling ground, the park became a vegetable garden during WWII. Although it doesn't have lakes, fountains or formal gardens, it's blanketed with daffodils in spring and semi-naked bodies whenever the sun shines.

Westminster Cathedral
CHURCH

(Map p68; www.westminstercathedral.org.uk; Victoria St, SW1; tower adult/child £5/2.50; ⊘ 9.30am-5pm Mon-Fri, to 6pm Sat & Sun; ⊜ Victoria) Begun in 1895, this neo-Byzantine cathedral remains a work in progress, with new areas completed as funds allow. Look out for Eric Gill's highly regarded stone **Stations of the Cross** (1918). The **Treasures of the Cathedral** exhibition is rewarding, there's a cafe near the Baptistry and topping it all, the distinctive 83m red-brick and white-stone **tower** offers tantalising views of London and, unlike St Paul's dome, you can take the lift.

The **Chapel of the Blessed Sacrament** and other parts of the interior are ablaze with Eastern Roman mosaics and ornamented with 100 types of marble; other areas are just bare brick.

Banqueting House
PALACE

(Map p68; www.hrp.org.uk/banquetinghouse; Whitehall, SW1; adult/child £6.60/free; ⊘ 10am-5pm; ⊜ Westminster) Beautiful Banqueting House was conceived by Inigo Jones for James I in 1622. It's the only surviving part of Whitehall Palace after the Tudor bit went

🏃 City Walk
Royal London Tour

START: HOUSES OF PARLIAMENT
END: HOUSES OF PARLIAMENT
LENGTH: 4 MILES; THREE TO FOUR HOURS

From Westminster underground station, cross Bridge St to the Palace of Westminster, aka the ❶ **Houses of Parliament** (p67). Originally built in 1097, Westminster Hall is the oldest surviving part of the original palace, much of which burned down in October 1834. Following the length of the Houses of Parliament along Abingdon St (which becomes Old Palace Yard) brings you to the ❷ **Jewel Tower**, the only other still-extant chunk of the old palace, built in the 14th century for storing Edward III's royal treasures.

Exit the Jewel Tower to breathtaking ❸ **Westminster Abbey** (p66), London's West Minster (as distinct from the minster in the east – St Paul's Cathedral) and traditional venue of coronation for the English monarchy. Walking around Parliament Sq, note the ❹ **Supreme Court** (p69), within the ornate Middlesex Guildhall, dating from 1913.

Round the corner and walk west along Great George St. Turn left down Storey's Gate and then right into Old Queen St, before trotting down ❺ **Cockpit Steps**, said to be haunted by a headless woman dressed in red! The steps lead down to lovely Birdcage Walk, named after the royal Aviary, which was once situated here. Cross over the road and walk into ❻ **St James's Park** (p70) to walk alongside the lake. Near the southwestern end of the park is the ❼ **Guards Museum** on the far side of Birdcage Walk.

Walk up Buckingham Gate to the ❽ **Queen's Gallery** (p69) and the ❾ **Royal Mews** (p69) before walking back to ❿ **Buckingham Palace** (p69) and the ⓫ **Queen Victoria Memorial**, dating from 1911, with its grumpy-looking monarch staring down the Mall. Follow the ceremonial route of the Mall (rhymes with 'shall') and cross into ⓬ **Green Park** (p70) to head up Queen's Walk to grand ⓭ **Spencer House** (p74) before retracing your steps back to the Mall and on to

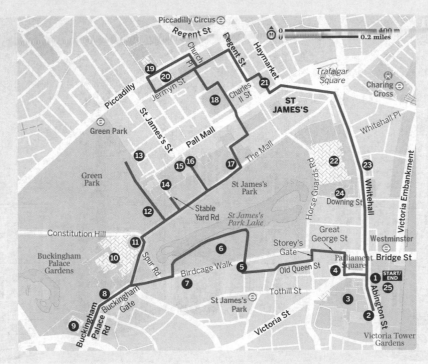

14 Clarence House, residence of Prince Charles and former home of Queen Elizabeth the Queen Mother.

Continue east along the Mall then walk north up Marlborough Road to **15 St James's Palace** (p70) and the **16 Queen's Chapel** opposite. Open during services only, the church interior has exquisite 17th-century fittings. Return to the Mall briefly, then take the steps up alongside a **17 bronze statue** of Queen Elizabeth the Queen Mother with King George VI behind her.

Head up Carlton Gardens and take the first left (also Carlton Gardens) and cross over the pedestrian crossing in Pall Mall to reach **18 St James's Sq**, surrounded by handsome Georgian architecture. With a statue of King William III at its centre, the private gardens are open from 10am to 4.30pm on weekdays.

Head up Duke of York St towards the side-on form of St James's Piccadilly, designed by Christopher Wren, turn left along Jermyn St to cross Duke St St James's and walk up colonnaded Piccadilly Arcade to exit into Piccadilly. On the far side of the road is the impressive entrance of the **19 Royal Academy of Arts**

(p75), founded by George III in 1768, and located within Burlington House. Head back across the road to mint-green **20 Fortnum & Mason** (p141), London's oldest grocery store and holder of many royal warrants.

Walk east along Piccadilly and turn right down Church Pl, then left onto Jermyn St. Take a right at Regent St, then left onto King Charles II St and walk down **21 Royal Opera Arcade**, London's oldest shopping arcade (designed by John Nash). From Pall Mall, walk along Cockspur St to pass Trafalgar Sq and head down Whitehall. Walking past the old Admiralty Building, you will reach **22 Horse Guards Parade**, where the mounted troopers of the Household Cavalry change guard daily at 11am (10am Sunday) and a lite-pomp version takes place at 4pm when the dismounted guards are changed. Open daily, the Household Cavalry Museum is here as well. On the far side of Whitehall stands **23 Banqueting House** (p70), with its bust of Charles I on the corner above the door, while continuing south along Whitehall takes you past **24 No 10 Downing Street** (p74) and returns you to the **25 Houses of Parliament**.

1. Hampton Court Palace 2. Balmoral Castle
3. Tower of London 4. Buckingham Palace

Right Royal Britain

Royalty has long been a British institution, with dynasties of Scottish kings, Welsh princes and, of course, the English monarchs that dominated the scene for centuries. Queen Elizabeth II celebrated 60 years of rule in 2012, and the public displays of loyalty and affection show the institution is still going strong.

Hampton Court Palace

Hampton Court Palace (p112) was used by King Henry VIII – he of the famous six wives – as a retreat from the affairs of state (but not the affairs of the heart). Today, it's Britain's grandest Tudor structure, and you can still relax in the extensive gardens, but don't get lost in the 300-year-old maze.

Buckingham Palace

Buckingham Palace (p69) has been the monarch's residence in London since 1837. If the Queen is at home, the 'royal standard' flag flies on the roof. If she's away, you can take a tour inside. Either way, don't miss the parade of bearskins at the famous Changing of the Guard.

Balmoral Castle

Deep in the Highlands of Scotland, Balmoral Castle (p908) is the Queen's holiday home. Built for Queen Victoria in 1855 as a private residence for the royal family, it popularised the style of architecture known as Scottish Baronial – slender towers, conical-topped turrets, stepped gables, narrow windows, fake battlements and heraldic symbols – that characterises so many of Scotland's 19th-century country houses

Tower of London

The Tower of London (p80) is a world-famous monument with a 1000-year-old history. Over the centuries it's been a royal residence, treasury, mint, prison and arsenal. Today it's home to the spectacular Crown Jewels, as well as red-coated Beefeaters and ravens with mythical power.

heavenwards in a 1698 conflagration. The chief attraction is the ceiling, painted by Rubens in 1635 at the behest of Charles I. The king didn't get to savour it for long, in 1649 he was frogmarched out of the 1st-floor balcony to lose his head for treason.

No 10 Downing Street   HISTORIC BUILDING
(Map p68; www.number10.gov.uk; 10 Downing St, SW1; ⊖Westminster) It's fittingly British that the official seat of the prime minister is a nondescript Georgian town house in White-hall. The street was cordoned off with a rath-er large iron gate during Margaret Thatcher's tenure, so you can't get up close.

Churchill War Rooms   MUSEUM
(Map p68; www.iwm.org.uk; Clive Steps, King Charles St, SW1; adult/child £17.50/free; ⊙9.30am-6pm, last entry 5pm; ⊖Westminster) Winston Churchill coordinated the Allied resistance against Nazi Germany on a Bakelite tele-phone from this underground military HQ during WWII. The Cabinet War Rooms re-main much as they were when the lights were flicked off in 1945, capturing the dra-ma and dogged spirit of the time, while the museum affords intriguing insights into the resolute, cigar-smoking wartime leader.

Institute of Contemporary Arts   ARTS CENTRE
(ICA; Map p68; ☑020-7930 9493; www.ica.org.uk; Nash House, The Mall, SW1; ⊙11am-11pm Tue-Sun, exhibition times vary; ⊖Charing Cross) **FREE** A one-stop contemporary-art bonanza, the excitingly cerebral program at the ICA em-braces film, photography, theatre, installa-tions, talks, performance art, DJs, digital art and book readings. Stroll around the galler-ies, watch a film, browse the left-field book-shop, then hit the bar for a beer.

Spencer House   HISTORIC BUILDING
(Map p68; ☑020-7514 1958; www.spencerhouse.co.uk; 27 St James's Pl, SW1; adult/child £12/10; ⊙10.30am-5.45pm Sun Feb-Jul & Sep-Dec; ⊖Green Park) The ancestral home of Princess Diana's family, Spencer House was built in the Palladian style between 1756 and 1766. It was converted into offices after the Spencers moved out in 1927, but 60 years later an £18 million restoration returned it to its former glory. Visits are by guided tour.

Apsley House   HISTORIC BUILDING
(Map p68; www.english-heritage.org.uk; 149 Picca-dilly, Hyde Park Cnr, W1; adult/child £6.90/4.10, with Wellington Arch £8.90/5.30; ⊙11am-5pm Wed-Sun Apr-Oct, to 4pm Wed-Sun Nov-Mar; ⊖Hyde Park Corner) This stunning house, containing ex-hibits devoted to the Duke of Wellington, was designed by Robert Adam for Baron Apsley in the late 18th century. It was later sold to the first Duke of Wellington, who cut Napoleon down to size in the Battle of Water-loo and lived there for 35 years until his death in 1852. With 10 of its rooms open to visitors, the house has a stairwell dominated by Anto-nio Canova's staggering 3.4m-high statue of a fig-leafed Napoleon with titanic shoulders.

Don't miss the elaborate Portuguese silver service or the impressive Egyptian service, a divorce present from Napoleon to Josephine (she declined it).

Wellington Arch   MUSEUM
(Map p68; www.english-heritage.org.uk; Hyde Park Corner, W1; adult/child £4.20/2.50, with Apsley House £8.90/5.30; ⊙10am-5pm Wed-Sun Apr-Oct, to 4pm Wed-Sun Nov-Mar; ⊖Hyde Park Corner) Throttled by the Hyde Park Corner rounda-bout, this is London's answer to the Arc de Triomphe (except this one commemorates France's *defeat* at the hands of the Duke of Wellington). Erected in 1826, the monument is topped with Europe's largest bronze sculp-ture: *Peace Descending on the Quadriga of War* (1912). Until the 1960s, it housed the capital's smallest police station (complete with pet moggy). The open-air balconies af-ford unforgettable views of Hyde Park, Buck-ingham Palace and the Houses of Parliament.

On the inside is an exhibition on the history of the arch and the newly opened **Quadriga Gallery**.

◉ West End

A strident mix of culture and consumerism, but more a concept than a fixed geographi-cal area, the West End is synonymous with roof-raising musicals, bright lights, outstand-ing restaurants and bag-laden shoppers. It casts its net around Piccadilly Circus and Tra-falgar Sq to the south, Regent St to the west, Oxford St to the north, Covent Garden to the east and the Strand to the southeast.

Named after the elaborate collars (pic-adils) that were the sartorial staple of a local 17th-century tailor, Piccadilly became the fashionable haunt of the well-heeled (and collared), and still boasts establishment icons such as the Ritz hotel and the Fortnum & Mason department store. It meets Regent St, Shaftesbury Ave and Haymarket at the ne-on-lit swirl of Piccadilly Circus, home to the ever-popular and ever-misnamed Eros statue.

Mayfair, west of Piccadilly Circus, hogs all of the most expensive streets from the Monopoly board, including Park Lane and Bond St, which should give you an idea of what to expect: lots of pricey shops, Michelin-starred restaurants, society hotels and gentlemen's clubs. The elegant bow of Regent St and frantic Oxford St are the city's main shopping strips. At the heart of the West End lies Soho, a boho grid of narrow streets and squares hiding gay bars, strip clubs, cafes and advertising agencies. Carnaby St was the epicentre of the swinging London of the 1960s, but is now largely given over to chain fashion stores. Lisle St and, in particular, Gerrard St (north of Leicester Sq) form the heart of Chinatown, a convergence of reasonably priced Asian restaurants, decorative Chinese arches and aromatic Cantonese supermarkets. Heaving with tourists and dominated by huge cinemas (with occasional star-studded premieres), neighbouring Leicester Sq (*les*-ter) has undergone a facelift. Described by Benjamin Disraeli in the 19th century as Europe's finest street, the Strand still boasts a few classy hotels, including the Savoy, but its lustre has dimmed.

Piccadilly Circus   SQUARE
(Map p76; ⊖ Piccadilly Circus) Designed in the 1820s and named after the street Piccadilly (heading west to Hyde Park Corner from the square) as it greets the grand sweep of Regent St and Shaftesbury Avenue, Piccadilly Circus is today a tumult of stop-start traffic, blinking neon advertisement panels and camera-toting out-of-towners. At the heart of the action stands the famous aluminium statue of **Anteros** (Map p76), twin brother of Eros, dedicated to the philanthropist and child-labour abolitionist Lord Shaftesbury.

The statue has long been mistaken for Eros, the God of Love, and the misnomer has stuck (it's even marked on the London A-Z, and signs for 'Eros' lead from the underground).

★**Trafalgar Square**   SQUARE
(Map p76; ⊖ Charing Cross) Trafalgar Sq is the public heart of London, hosting rallies, marches and feverish New Year's festivities. Londoners congregate here to celebrate anything from football victories to the ousting of political leaders. The square is one of the world's grandest public places, with a sandstone Admiral Nelson surveying his fleet from the 43.5m-high **Nelson's Column** at its heart, erected in 1843 to commemorate his 1805 victory over Napoleon off Spain's Cape Trafalgar.

The square is flanked by splendid buildings: Canada House to the west, the **National Gallery** and **National Portrait Gallery** to the north, South Africa House and the church of St Martin-in-the-Fields to the east. Further south stands **Admiralty Arch**, built in honour of Queen Victoria in 1910 (and with a mysterious stone nose around seven foot up from the ground on one of the northernmost arches), and beyond that, the **Mall** (rhymes with 'shall', not 'shawl') is the ceremonial route leading to Buckingham Palace (p69).

★**National Gallery**   GALLERY
(Map p76; www.nationalgallery.org.uk; Trafalgar Sq, WC2; ⊙ 10am-6pm Sat-Thu, to 9pm Fri; ⊖ Charing Cross) **FREE** Gazing grandly over Trafalgar Sq through its Corinthian columns, the National Gallery is the nation's most important repository of largely pre-modern art. Four million visitors flock annually to admire its 2300-plus Western European paintings, ranging from the 13th to the early 20th centuries. Highlights include Turner's *The Fighting Temeraire*, Botticelli's *Venus and Mars* and van Gogh's *Sunflowers*. The medieval religious paintings in the **Sainsbury Wing** are delightful. The comprehensive audioguides (£3.50) are recommended, as are the free introductory tours.

For sustenance, nothing beats the National Dining Rooms (p126) in the Sainsbury Wing.

★**National Portrait Gallery**   GALLERY
(Map p76; www.npg.org.uk; St Martin's Pl, WC2; ⊙ 10am-6pm Sat-Wed, to 9pm Thu & Fri; ⊖ Charing Cross, Leicester Sq) **FREE** The National Portrait Gallery is like stepping into a picture book of English history. Founded in 1856, the permanent collection (around 11,000 works) kicks off with the Tudors on the 2nd floor and descends to contemporary figures (from pop stars to scientists), including Marc Quinn's *Self*, a frozen self-portrait of the artist's head cast in blood and recreated every five years. An audiovisual guide (£3) is available.

The **Portrait** (☎ 020-7312 2490; www.npg.org.uk/visit/shop-eat-drink.php; 3rd fl; mains £18.50; ⊙ 11.45am-2.45pm daily & 5.30-8.15pm Thu-Sat; ⊖ Charing Cross) restaurant pairs superb views towards Westminster with tantalising food.

Royal Academy of Arts   GALLERY
(Map p76; www.royalacademy.org.uk; Burlington House, Piccadilly, W1; adult/child £10/6; prices vary for exhibitions; ⊙ 10am-6pm Sat-Thu, to 10pm Fri;

LONDON SIGHTS

West End

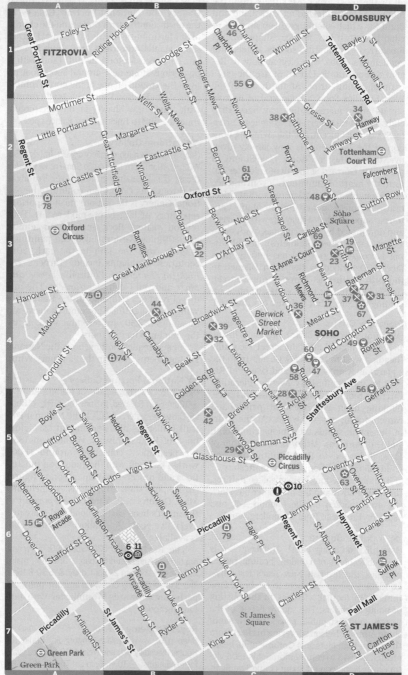

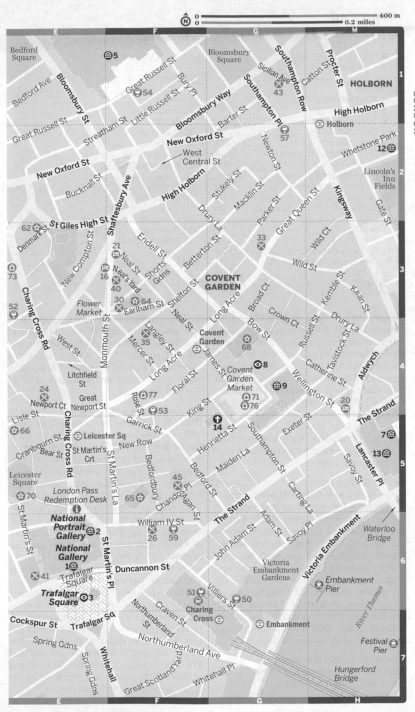

West End

◎ Green Park) Hosting high-profile exhibitions and a small display from its permanent collection, the crafty academy made it a condition of joining its exclusive club of 80 artists for new members to donate one of their artworks. The collection embraces works from such masters as Constable, Turner and Sir Norman Foster, while the Summer Exhibition showcases contemporary art. Free tours of the John Madesjki Fine Rooms are held, and the academy has grown its exhibition space by expanding magnificently into 6 Burlington Gardens.

Covent Garden Piazza SQUARE
(Map p76; ◎ Covent Garden) Hallowed turf – or cobbles – for opera fans descending on the esteemed Royal Opera House, Covent Garden is one of London's biggest tourist hot spots. London's first planned square, Covent Garden Piazza now hosts bands of tourists shopping in quaint old arcades and ringing street entertainers and buskers. On its western flank rises **St Paul's Church** (Map p76; www.actorschurch.org; Bedford St, WC2; ⊙ 8.30am-5pm Mon-Fri, varies Sat, 9am-1pm Sun; ◎ Covent Garden), with a lovely courtyard at the back, ideal for a picnic in the sun.

London Transport Museum MUSEUM
(Map p76; www.ltmuseum.co.uk; Covent Garden Piazza, WC2; adult/child £15/free; ⊙ 10am-6pm Sat-Thu, 11am-6pm Fri; ◎ Covent Garden) Kids and adults alike can tick off all manner of vehicles here, from sedan chairs to train carriages, trams and taxis, along with original advertising posters, photos and a fab shop for tube-map boxer shorts or a pair of 'Mind the Gap' socks.

Sir John Soane's Museum MUSEUM
(Map p76; www.soane.org; 13 Lincoln's Inn Fields, WC2; ⊙ 10am-5pm Tue-Sat & 6-9pm 1st Tue of month; ◎ Holborn) FREE One of the most atmospheric and intriguing of London's museums, this was the remarkable home of architect and collector extraordinaire Sir John Soane (1753–1837). The house has been left largely as it was when Sir John was taken out in a box. Among his eclectic acquisitions are an Egyptian sarcophagus, dozens of Greek and Roman antiquities and the original *Rake's Progress,* William Hogarth's set of caricatures telling the story of a late 18th-century London cad.

The 2nd floor of No 13, including Soane's private apartment and model room, was being restored at the time of writing and will be open to the public for the first time in history. Tours (£10) depart at 11.30am Tuesday and Friday and at 3.30pm Wednesday and Thursday. Audioguides are free. The evening of the first Tuesday of each month, when the house is candle-lit, sees long queues.

Somerset House HISTORIC BUILDING
(Map p76; www.somersethouse.org.uk; The Strand, WC2; ☺galleries 10am-6pm, Safra Courtyard 7.30am-11pm; ⊜Charing Cross, Embankment, Temple) The first Somerset House was built for the Duke of Somerset, brother of Jane Seymour, in 1551. For two centuries it played host to royals (Elizabeth I once lived here), foreign diplomats, wild masked balls, peace treaties, the Parliamentary army (during the Civil War) and Oliver Cromwell's wake. Having fallen into disrepair, it was pulled down in 1775 and rebuilt in 1801 to designs by William Chambers.

Among other weighty organisations, it went on to house the Royal Academy of the Arts, the Society of Antiquaries, the Navy Board and, that most popular of institutions, the Inland Revenue.

The tax collectors are still here, but that doesn't dissuade Londoners from attending open-air events in the grand Safra courtyard, such as films (Film4 Summer Screen) over 12 days in summer and ice skating in winter. Behind the house, there's a sunny terrace and cafe overlooking the embankment.

Near the Strand entrance, the **Courtauld Gallery** (Map p76; www.courtauld.ac.uk; Somerset House, The Strand, WC2; adult/child Tue-Sun £6/free, Mon £3/free; ☺10am-6pm; ⊜Charing Cross, Embankment or Temple) displays a wealth of 14th- to 20th-century art, including a room of Rubens and works by van Gogh, Renoir and Cézanne. Downstairs, the **Embankment Galleries** are devoted to temporary exhibitions; prices and hours vary.

Burlington Arcade SHOPPING ARCADE
(Map p76; www.burlington-arcade.co.uk; 51 Piccadilly, W1; ☺10am-9pm Mon-Fri, 9am-6.30pm Sat, 11am-5pm Sun; ⊜Green Park) The illustrious Burlington Arcade, built in 1819, is famously patrolled by the Burlington Beadles, uniformed guards who constitute one of the world's smallest private police forces.

Broadcasting House TV LOCATION
(☑0370 901 1227; www.bbc.co.uk/showsandtours; Portland Pl, W1; adult/child £13.75/9.25; ☺tour days & times vary; ⊜Oxford Circus) The BBC began radio broadcasting in 1932 from this splendid building north of Oxford Street, and the BBC World Service, other radio broadcasting and TV broadcasting in London recently moved in. Join frequent 1½-hour behind-the-scenes tours, peeking at studios and the state-of-the-art newsroom; check the website for details. No children under nine; pre-booking (at least the day before) essential.

☉ The City

With beguiling churches, hidden gardens and atmospheric lanes stuffed between iconic corporate towers and office blocks, you could spend weeks exploring the City of London, which, for most of its history, *was* London. Its boundaries have changed little since the Romans first founded their gated community here two millennia ago.

It's only in the last 250 years that the City has gone from being the very essence of London and its main population centre to just its central business district. But what a business district it is – the 'square mile' remains at the very heart of world capitalism.

Currently fewer than 10,000 people actually live here, although some 300,000 descend on it each weekday, to generate almost three-quarters of Britain's GDP before squeezing back onto the tube. On Sundays the City (capital 'C') becomes a virtual ghost town; it's nice and quiet, but come with a full stomach – most shops, eateries and pubs are closed.

★ **Tower of London**   CASTLE
(Map p80; ☏ 0844 482 7777; www.hrp.org.uk/toweroflondon; Tower Hill, EC3; adult/child £22/11, audioguide £4/3; ☉ 9am-5.30pm Tue-Sat, 10am-

The City

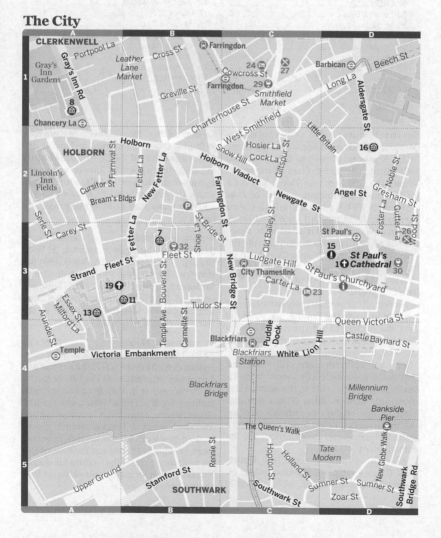

5.30pm Sun & Mon, to 4.30pm Nov-Feb; ⊖ Tower Hill) A World Heritage Site, the Tower possesses a gruesome and compelling history. In the 1070s, William the Conqueror started work on the White Tower to replace the earlier castle. By 1285, two walls with towers and a moat encompassed it and the defences have barely been altered since. A former royal residence, treasury, mint and arsenal, it became most famous as a prison when Henry VIII moved to Whitehall Palace in 1529 and started meting out his preferred brand of punishment.

The most striking building is indeed the central **White Tower**, with its solid Romanesque architecture and four turrets. Today it houses a collection from the **Royal Armouries**, including Henry VIII's commodious suit of armour. On the 2nd floor is **St John's Chapel**, dating from 1080 and therefore the oldest church in London. To the north stands **Waterloo Barracks**, which now contains the spectacular Crown Jewels, including the platinum crown of the late Queen Mother, set with the 105-carat Koh-i-Noor (Mountain of Light) diamond, and the Imperial State Crown. On the far side of the White Tower rises the **Bloody Tower**, where the 12-year-old Edward V and his little brother were held 'for their own safety' and later murdered, probably by their uncle, the future Richard

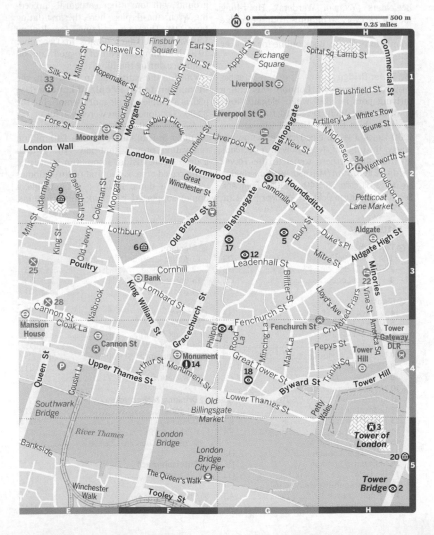

III. Sir Walter Raleigh did a 13-year stretch here, when he wrote his *History of the World*.

On the small green in front of the **Chapel Royal of St Peter ad Vincula** stood Henry VIII's scaffold, where seven people, including Anne Boleyn and her cousin Catherine Howard (Henry's second and fifth wives) were beheaded.

Look out for the latest in the Tower's long line of famous ravens, which legend says could cause the White Tower to collapse should they leave (their wings are clipped in case they get any ideas).

To get your bearings, take the hugely entertaining free guided tour with any of the Beefeaters (Yeoman Warders). Hour-long tours leave every 30 minutes from the bridge near the main entrance; the last tour is an hour before closing. Book online for cheaper rates.

★**Tower Bridge**   BRIDGE
(Map p80; ⊖Tower Hill) London was still a thriving port in 1894 when elegant Tower Bridge was built. Designed to be raised to allow ships to pass (it still lifts around 1000 times a year), electricity has now replaced the original steam power. A lift leads up from the northern tower to the **Tower Bridge Exhibition** (Map p80; www.towerbridge. org.uk; adult/child £8/3.40; ⊙10am-6pm Apr-Sep, 9.30am-5.30pm Oct-Mar; ⊖Tower Hill) 42m

above the water, from where you can walk along the east and west-facing walkways.

The exhibition ticket also gets you into the engine rooms below the southern tower, for the mechanical lowdown.

★**St Paul's Cathedral**   CHURCH
(Map p80; www.stpauls.co.uk; St Paul's Churchyard, EC4; adult/child £16.50/7.50; ⊙8.30am-4.30pm Mon-Sat; ⊖St Paul's) Dominating the City with one of the world's largest church domes (around 65,000 tons worth), St Paul's Cathedral was designed by Christopher Wren after the Great Fire and built between 1675 and 1710. The site is ancient hallowed ground with four other cathedrals preceding Wren's masterpiece here, the first dating from 604. The dome is famed for eludling Luftwaffe incendiary bombs in December 1940, becoming an icon of dogged London resilience during the Blitz.

Outside the cathedral, to the north, the **Monument to the People of London** (Map p80) is a simple and elegant memorial to the 32,000 Londoners who weren't so lucky.

As part of the 300th anniversary celebrations, St Paul's underwent a £40 million renovation project that gave the church a deep clean. Inside, some 30m above the main paved area, is the first of three domes (actually a dome inside a cone inside a dome) supported by eight huge columns.

The City

LOCAL KNOWLEDGE

ALAN KINGSHOTT: CHIEF YEOMAN WARDER AT THE TOWER

Make the Most of Your Visit To understand the Tower's full history, I suggest visitors take a guided tour (in English) by a Yeoman Warder. With such a vast amount of history within the walls, you should allow at least three hours to fully enjoy your experience.

The Crown Jewels The new presentation of the Crown Jewels is a must-see with a new layout, which will help visitors easily explore our sometimes complex history and ceremonies. Just ask a member of the Jewel House staff about any item: you will be amazed at their wealth of knowledge and it will enhance your visit.

The Ravens of the Tower We must have six ravens at the Tower at any one time by a Royal Decree put in place by Charles II. According to an old legend, should the birds leave, the Monarchy and the White Tower will crumble and fall. We tend not to provoke legends so generally we have eight birds.

Recommended Ceremonies There are many ceremonies at the Tower of London, most of which can be viewed by visitors. However, many happen around royal events such as the Queen's Birthday and the State Opening of Parliament. Alternatively there is the Ceremony of the Keys (the locking up of the Tower of London), which takes place, as it has done for 700 years, at 9.30pm every night. (Note: attendance is free but requires that you apply by post at least two months in advance and supply a return-address envelope.)

The walkway around its base, 257 steps up a staircase on the western side of the southern transept, is called the **Whispering Gallery** because if you talk close to the wall, your words will carry to the opposite side 32m away. A further 119 steps brings you to the **Stone Gallery**, 152 iron steps above which is the **Golden Gallery** at the very top, which rewards you with unforgettable views of London.

The **Crypt** has memorials to up to 300 military demigods, including Wellington, Kitchener and Nelson, whose body lies below the dome. But the most poignant memorial is to Wren himself. On a simple slab bearing his name, a Latin inscription translates as: 'If you seek his memorial, look about you'. Also in the crypt is a cafe and the excellent **Restaurant at St Paul's** (☑ 020-7248 2469; www.restaurantatstpauls.co.uk; 2-/3-course lunch £21.50/25.95; ⊙ lunch noon-3pm, tea 2.30-4.30pm Mon-Sat; 🕾 ; ⊜ St Paul's).

The **Oculus** in the former treasury projects four short films onto its walls (you'll need the iPad audiotour to hear the sound). If you're not up to climbing the dome, experience it here (audiovisually). Free audio tours lasting 1½ hours are available. Free 1½-hour guided tours leave the tour desk half-a-dozen times a day (10.30am, 10.45am, 11.15am, 1pm, 1.30pm and 2pm); head to the desk just past the entrance to check times and book a place. Choral evensong is held most days at 5pm.

Museum of London MUSEUM
(Map p80; www.museumoflondon.org.uk; 150 London Wall, EC2; ⊙10am-6pm; ⊜ Barbican) FREE
This riveting museum peels back the layers of historical London for valuable perspectives on this great city. The first gallery, **London before London**, illustrates the settlements predating the Roman era. The Roman section explores the ancient roots of the modern city as we know it, while Saxon, medieval, Tudor and Stuart London are intriguingly brought to life. The museum's new £20 million **Galleries of Modern London** encompasses everything from 1666 (the devastating Great Fire of London) to the present day. While the Lord Mayor's ceremonial coach is the centrepiece, an effort has been made to create an immersive experience: you can enter reconstructions of an 18th-century debtors' prison, a Georgian pleasure garden and a Victorian street.

Guildhall HISTORIC BUILDING
(Map p80; ☑ 020-7606 3030; www.guildhall.city oflondon.gov.uk; Gresham St, EC2; ⊜ Bank) FREE
The Guildhall has been the seat of the City's local government for eight centuries and the present building dates from the early 15th century. Visitors can see the **Great Hall**, where the city's mayor is sworn in – it's an impressive space decorated with the shields and banners of London's 12 principal livery companies, carved galleries and a beautiful oak-panelled roof. Beneath it is London's largest **medieval crypt** (visit by free guided tour only, bookings essential).

Tower of London

TACKLING THE TOWER

Although it's usually less busy in the late afternoon, don't leave your assault on the Tower until too late in the day. You could easily spend hours here and not see it all. Start by getting your bearings on one of the Yeoman Warder (Beefeater) tours; they are included in the cost of admission, entertaining and the easiest way to access the **Chapel Royal of St Peter ad Vincula** ❶, which is where they finish up.

When you leave the chapel, the **Tower Green Scaffold Site** ❷ is directly in front. The building immediately to your left is Waterloo Barracks, where the **Crown Jewels** ❸ are housed. These are the absolute highlight of a Tower visit, so keep an eye on the entrance and pick a time to visit when it looks relatively quiet. Once inside, take things at your own pace. Slow-moving travelators shunt you past the dozen or so crowns that are the treasury's centrepiece, but feel free to double-back for a second or even third pass – particularly if you ended up on the rear travelator the first time around. Allow plenty of time for the **White Tower** ❹, the core of the whole complex, starting with the exhibition of royal armour. As you continue onto the 1st floor, keep an eye out for **St John's Chapel** ❺. The famous **ravens** ❻ can be seen in the courtyard south of the White Tower. Head next through the towers that formed the **Medieval Palace** ❼, then take the **East Wall Walk** ❽ to get a feel for the castle's mighty battlements. Spend the rest of your time poking around the many other fascinating nooks and crannies of the Tower complex.

Chapel Royal of St Peter ad Vincula

This chapel serves as the resting place for the royals and other members of the aristocracy who were executed on the small green out front. Several other historical figures are buried here too, including Thomas More.

MIKE BOOTH/ALAMY ©

Tower Green Scaffold Site

Seven people, including three queens (Anne Boleyn, Catherine Howard and Jane Grey), lost their heads here during Tudor times, saving the monarch the embarrassment of public executions on Tower Hill. The site now features a sculpture by Brian Catling.

Dry Moat

Beauchamp Tower

Main Entrance

Middle Tower

Byward Tower

Bell Tower

White Tower

Much of the White Tower is taken up with an exhibition on 500 years of royal armour. Look for the virtually cuboid suit made to match Henry VIII's bloated body, complete with an oversized armoured codpiece to protect, ahem, the crown jewels.

RYAN MCGINNIS/GETTY IMAGES ©

BEAT THE QUEUES

» **Buy** your fast-track ticket in advance online or at the City of London Information Centre in St Paul's Churchyard.

» **Become a member** An annual Historic Royal Palaces membership allows you to jump the queues and visit the Tower (and four other London palaces) as often as you like.

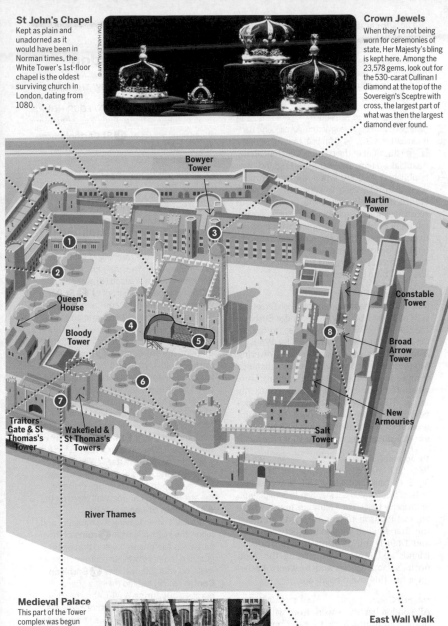

St John's Chapel
Kept as plain and unadorned as it would have been in Norman times, the White Tower's 1st-floor chapel is the oldest surviving church in London, dating from 1080.

Crown Jewels
When they're not being worn for ceremonies of state, Her Majesty's bling is kept here. Among the 23,578 gems, look out for the 530-carat Cullinan I diamond at the top of the Sovereign's Sceptre with cross, the largest part of what was then the largest diamond ever found.

Bowyer Tower

Martin Tower

Constable Tower

Broad Arrow Tower

Queen's House

Bloody Tower

New Armouries

Traitors' Gate & St Thomas's Tower

Wakefield & St Thomas's Towers

Salt Tower

River Thames

Medieval Palace
This part of the Tower complex was begun around 1220 and was home to England's medieval monarchs. Look for the recreations of the bedchamber of Edward I (1272–1307) in St Thomas's Tower and the throne room of his father, Henry III (1216–72) in the Wakefield Tower.

Ravens
This stretch of green is where the Tower's half-dozen ravens are kept, fed on raw meat and blood-soaked bird biscuits. According to legend, if the birds were to leave the Tower, the kingdom would fall.

East Wall Walk
Follow the inner ramparts, starting from the 13th-century Salt Tower, passing through the Broad Arrow and Constable Towers, and ending at the Martin Tower, where the Crown Jewels were stored till the mid-19th century.

The **Clockmakers' Museum** charts 500 years of horology with an intriguing collection of more than 700 clocks; the **Guildhall Art Gallery** displays around 250 artworks. Included in the art gallery admission is entry to the remains of an ancient **Roman amphitheatre**.

Bank of England Museum   MUSEUM

(Map p80; www.bankofengland.co.uk/museum; Bartholomew Lane, EC2; ⊙10am-5pm Mon-Fri; ⊖Bank) **FREE** Guardian of the country's current shaky financial system, the Bank of England was established in 1694 when the government needed to raise cash to support a war with France. The centrepiece of this museum is a reconstruction of architect John Soane's original Bank Stock Office, complete with original mahogany counters. A series of rooms leading off the office are packed with exhibits ranging from silverware and coins to a 13kg gold bar you can lift up (and leave behind).

Monument   TOWER

(Map p80; www.themonument.info; Fish Street Hill, EC3; adult/child £4/2, incl Tower Bridge Exhibition £10.50/4.70; ⊙9.30am-6pm Apr-Sep, to 5.30pm Oct-Mar; ⊖Monument) Designed by Wren to commemorate the Great Fire, the towering Monument is 60.6m high, the exact distance from its base to the bakery on Pudding Lane where the blaze began. Corkscrew your way up the 311 tight spiral steps (claustrophobes beware) for some of London's best wraparound views and twist down again to collect a certificate commemorating your climb.

Dr Johnson's House   MUSEUM

(Map p80; www.drjohnsonshouse.org; 17 Gough Sq, EC4; adult/child £4.50/1.50, audioguide £2; ⊙11am-5.30pm Mon-Sat May-Sep, to 5pm Oct-Apr; ⊖Chancery Lane) The Georgian house where Samuel Johnson and his assistants compiled the first English dictionary (between 1748 and 1759) is full of prints and portraits of friends and intimates, including the good doctor's Jamaican servant to whom he bequeathed this grand residence.

Inns of Court   HISTORIC BUILDINGS

All London barristers work from within one of the four atmospheric Inns of Court, positioned between the walls of the old City and Westminster. It would take a lifetime working here to grasp all the intricacies of their arcane protocols, originating in the 13th-century. It's best just to soak up the dreamy ambience of the alleys and open spaces and consider the roll call of former members that

---

🏃 City Walk
City of London

START: ST BARTHOLOMEW-THE-GREAT
END: HERON TOWER
LENGTH: 2 MILES; TWO TO FOUR HOURS

It's fitting to start at ❶ **St Bartholomew-the-Great** (a five-minute walk southwest from Barbican tube station), as this history-steeped 12th-century church was once a pilgrimage stop for travellers to London.

Head out through the Tudor gatehouse and to your right you'll see the Victorian arches of Smithfield's meat market, on this site just north of the old city walls for 800 years. Executions were held here, most famously the torching of Protestants under Mary I and the grisly killing of Scottish hero William Wallace (Braveheart) in 1305; a plaque on the front of ❷ **St Bartholomew's Hospital** commemorates him.

Head back towards the gate and turn right into Little Britain. Follow it as it curves to the right and look out for the large tree marking the entrance to ❸ **Postman's Park**. This lovely space includes a touching legacy of Victorian socialism: a tiled wall celebrating everyday heroes.

Coming out of the park, turn right onto Aldersgate, then left and left again into Noble St. You're now inside what was once the old City's ❹ **walls**, remnants of which you'll pass on your left. This section was only uncovered after WWII bombs destroyed the buildings covering it. Take the stairs up to the footbridge crossing the street called London Wall towards the ❺ **Museum of London** (p83).

Turn left when leaving the museum and follow the Highwalk past ❻ **ruins** of the barbicans (defensive towers) that once guarded the northwestern corner of the walls, on your left, with the ❼ **Barbican Centre** (p139) behind (filling a space bombed out during WWII). At its heart is an arts centre consisting of concert halls, cinemas, galleries, eateries, a library and a school.

Follow the painted lines on the Highwalk for a closer look, or turn right at Pizza Express, take the escalator down to Wood St and head towards the remaining tower of ❽ **St Alban's**, a Wren-designed church destroyed in WWII. Turn left and you'll find

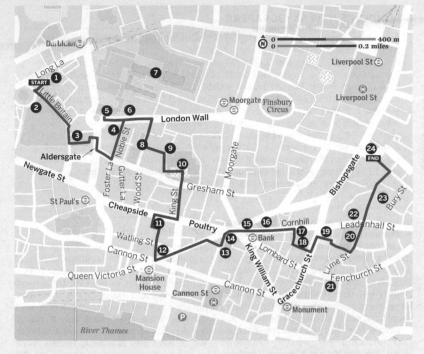

a sweet garden on the site of **9 St Mary Aldermanbury**, with a bust of Shakespeare.

Turn right on to Aldermanbury and head to the **10 Guildhall** (p83). Take King St down to Cheapside, cross the road and head right to elegant **11 St Mary-le-Bow**. The church was rebuilt by Wren after the Great Fire, and then rebuilt again after WWII. The term 'Cockney' traditionally refers to someone born within the sound of this church's bell.

Walk down the west flank of the church and turn left into Bow Churchyard to reach Bow Lane; follow this narrow path south to **12 St Mary Aldermary**, rebuilt in the Perpendicular Gothic style in 1682 following the Great Fire. Turn left on to Queen Victoria St and then right into Bucklersbury, to spot **13 St Stephen's Walbrook** directly in front of you. Rebuilt after the Great Fire, the current St Stephen's is one of Wren's greatest masterpieces, with elegant Corinthian columns supporting a beautifully proportioned dome.

Leaving the church, you'll pass **14 Mansion House**, built in 1752 as the official residence of the Lord Mayor. As you approach the busy Bank intersection, lined with neoclassical temples to commerce, you might think you've stumbled into the ancient Roman forum (the

actual forum was a couple of blocks east). Head for the **15 equestrian statue of the Iron Duke**, behind which a metal pyramid details the many significant buildings here. Directly beyond the statue is the **16 Royal Exchange**; walk through it and exit through the door on the right, then turn left onto Cornhill.

If you're still not churched out, cross the road to **17 St Michael's**, a 1672 Wren design that still has its box pews. Hidden in the warren of tiny passages behind the church is its **18 churchyard**. Head through to Gracechurch St, turn left and cross the road to wonderful **19 Leadenhall Market**. As you wander out the far end, the famous **20 Lloyd's of London** displays its metallic innards for all to see. To the south rises the bulbous, top-heavy form of **21 20 Fenchurch St** (aka the 'Walkie-Talkie') – most impressive from a distance.

Turn left onto Lime St and you'll soon reach the uncompromising wedge of the **22 Leadenhall Building** (aka the 'Cheese Grater'). Ahead of you rises Norman Foster's 180m **23 30 St Mary Axe** (the 'Gherkin'). A short walk beyond, the **24 Heron Tower** is currently the tallest building in the City, from where it's a short walk north to Liverpool Street tube station.

LONDON'S NEW SKYSCRAPERS

A recent scramble for high-altitude, futuristic towers – given further lift by the Olympics – has shaken up the otherwise rather staid, low-lying London skyline. Most famous is the Shard (p93), rising over London Bridge like a vast glass splinter and home to the high-altitude five-star Shangri-La hotel. The City of London's tallest building, the straight-edged **Heron Tower** (Map p80; 110 Bishopsgate, EC2; ⊜ Aldgate or Bank) was completed just up the road from **30 St Mary Axe** (Gherkin; Map p80; www.30stmaryaxe.co.uk; 30 St Mary Axe, EC3; ⊜ Aldgate) in 2011. The top-heavy and bulging **20 Fenchurch St** (Walkie Talkie; Map p80) will be topped with a vast sky garden boasting magnificent views over town, while the wedge-shaped 48-storey, 225m-high **Leadenhall Building** (Cheese Grater; Map p80; 122 Leadenhall St, EC3) cuts into the sky just north of the Lloyd's building. Construction on the concrete stub of the radically-designed **Pinnacle** (Helter Skelter; Map p80; 22-24 Bishopsgate, EC2; ⊜ Aldgate or Bank) – which has earned its nickname due to its cork-screwing top – was on hold at the the time of writing.

includes Oliver Cromwell, Charles Dickens, Mahatma Gandhi and Margaret Thatcher.

Lincoln's Inn (www.lincolnsinn.org.uk; Lincoln's Inn Fields, Newmans Row, WC2; ⊗ grounds 7am-7pm Mon-Fri, chapel noon-2.30pm Mon-Fri; ⊜ Holborn) still has some original 15th-century buildings. It's the oldest and most attractive of the bunch, with a 17th-century chapel and pretty landscaped gardens.

Gray's Inn (Map p80; www.graysinn.org.uk; Gray's Inn Rd, WC1; ⊗ grounds 10am-4pm Mon-Fri, chapel 10am-6pm Mon-Fri; ⊜ Chancery Lane) was largely rebuilt after the Luftwaffe levelled it.

Middle Temple (Map p80; www.middletemple.org.uk; Middle Temple Lane, EC4; ⊗ grounds 10-11.30am & 3-4pm Mon-Fri; ⊜ Temple) and **Inner Temple** (Map p80; www.innertemple.org.uk; King's Bench Walk, EC4; ⊗ grounds 10am-4pm Mon-Fri, gardens 12.30-3pm Mon-Fri; ⊜ Temple) sit between Fleet St and Victoria Embankment. The former is the best preserved, while the latter is home to the 12th-century **Temple Church** (Map p80; ☑ 020-7353 8559; www.templechurch.com; adult/concession £4/2; ⊗ 11am-1pm & 2-4pm Mon-Fri, hours vary), built by the Knights Templar and featuring nine stone effigies of knights in its round chapel. Check the church's website or call ahead for opening hours.

St Katharine Docks HARBOUR
(⊜ Tower Hill) A centre of commerce for 1000 years, St Katharine Docks is today a buzzing waterside area of pleasure boats, shops and eateries. It was badly damaged during WWII, but survivors include the popular **Dickens Inn**, with its original 18th-century timber framework, and **Ivory House** (built 1854), which used to store ivory, perfume and other precious goods. It's the perfect starting point for exploring Wapping and Limehouse.

⦿ South Bank

Londoners once crossed the river to the area controlled by the licentious Bishops of Southwark for all manner of bawdy frolicking frowned upon in the City. It's a much more seemly and temperate area these days, but the frisson of theatre and entertainment survives. While South Bank only technically refers to the area of river bank between Westminster and Blackfriars Bridges (parts of which are actually on the east bank due to the way the river bends), we've used it as a convenient catch-all for those parts of Southwark and Lambeth that sit closest to the river.

★ **Tate Modern** MUSEUM
(Map p92; www.tate.org.uk; Queen's Walk, SE1; ⊗ 10am-6pm Sun-Thu, to 10pm Fri & Sat; ⊜ Southwark, St Paul's) **FREE** One of London's biggest attractions, this outstanding modern and contemporary art gallery is housed in the creatively revamped **Bankside Power Station** south of the Millennium Bridge. A riveting synthesis of funky modern art and capacious industrial brick design, the result is an art-going tour de force. Tate Modern has also been extraordinarily successful in bringing challenging work to the masses, while a stunning extension is under construction, aiming for a 2016 completion date.

The multimedia guides (£3.50) are worthwhile and there are free 45-minute guided tours of the collection's highlights (Level 3 at 11am and midday; Level 5 at 2pm and 3pm).

★ **Shakespeare's Globe** HISTORIC BUILDING
(Map p92; www.shakespearesglobe.com; 21 New Globe Walk, SE1; adult/child £13.50/8; ⊗ 9am-5.30pm; ⊜ London Bridge) Today's Londoners

may flock to Amsterdam to misbehave, but back in the bard's day they'd swarm across London Bridge to Southwark. Free from the city's constraints, men could settle down to a diet of whoring, bear-baiting and heckling of actors. The most famous theatre was the Globe, where a genius playwright was penning box-office hits such as *Macbeth* and *Hamlet*. Admission includes the exhibition hall and a guided tour of the theatre (departing every 15 to 30 minutes).

The original Globe – known as the 'Wooden O' after its circular shape and roofless centre – was erected in 1599. Rival to the Rose Theatre, all was well but did not end well when the Globe burned down within two hours during a performance in 1613 (a stage cannon ignited the thatched roof). A tiled replacement fell foul of the party-pooping Puritans in 1642, who saw the theatre as the devil's workshop, and it was dismantled two years later. Its present-day incarnation – faithfully reconstructed from oak beams, handmade bricks, lime plaster and thatch – is the vision of American actor and director Sam Wanamaker, who sadly died before the opening night in 1997.

From April to October plays are performed, and while Shakespeare and his contemporaries dominate, modern plays are also staged (see the website for upcoming performances). As in Elizabethan times, seatless 'groundlings' (up to 700 of them) can watch in all-weather conditions (£5; seats are £15 to £39) for the best views. There's no protection from the elements (or over-flying jetliners) and you'll have to stand, but it's an unforgettable experience.

The Globe has recently added a new **Sam Wanamaker Playhouse**, an indoor Jacobean theatre, to its repertoire.

Tours of the theatre shift to the nearby **Rose Theatre** instead when matinees are being staged in season.

★ **London Eye**   VIEWPOINT
(Map p92; ☑ 0871 781 3000; www.londoneye.com; adult/child £21/15; ☺10am-8pm; ☻Waterloo) This 135m-tall, slow-moving and refurbed Ferris-wheel-like attraction is the world's tallest 'cantilevered observation wheel'. You

TATE MODERN HIGHLIGHTS

Over 50 million eager art-goers poured through Tate Modern in its first decade since opening, making it one of the most-visited of London's sights. The ambitiously run exhibition space is growing with the conversion of two underground oil tanks, while a funky 11-storey extension is slated for a 2016 opening date.

Note that special exhibitions are held on levels 2 and 3. Free guided highlights tours depart at 11am, noon, 2pm and 3pm daily – no booking is required. Handy multimedia guides are also available. Don't forget that Tate Modern is open till 10pm on Friday and Saturday.

The collection is in perpetual rotation so while the essential themes of the various galleries remain constant, the paintings and art works that represent each concept may vary.

A major highlight of Tate Modern is the architecture. The 4.2 million bricks of the Sir Gilbert Scott–designed Bankside Power Station – generating its last watt in 1981 when rising oil prices finally switched off its turbines – were ambitiously transformed into this modern and contemporary art gallery in 2000.

You can't exactly miss the cavernous 3300-sq-metre **Turbine Hall**, but try to join everyone else streaming down the ramp from Holland St to maximise its impact. Originally housing the power station's colossal turbines, the hall is the imposing venue for large-scale, temporary exhibitions from October to April.

The permanent collection is grouped thematically on levels 2, 3 and 4. For the surrealist dreamscapes of Paul Delvaux, Yves Tanguy, Max Ernst and other artists, immerse yourself in **Poetry & Dream** on Level 2. On Level 3, **Transformed Visions** explores works of expressive abstraction forged in the aftermath of WWII.

Focusing on the evolution of abstraction and radical art on Level 4, **Structure & Clarity** celebrates the abstract work of the interwar years, pieces that tilt towards utopian and universal themes. Also on Level 4, **Energy & Process** takes Art Povera, the revolutionary art of the 1960s, as its focus.

After you have had your fill of modern art, cap your visit with a trip to the restaurant and bar on Level 7 for sublime views of St Paul's and the River Thames. A popular cafe can also be found on Level 2.

The River Thames

A FLOATING TOUR

London's history has always been determined by the Thames. The city was founded as a Roman port nearly 2000 years ago and over the centuries since then many of the capital's landmarks have lined the river's banks. A boat trip is a great way to experience the attractions.

There are piers dotted along both banks at regular intervals where you can hop on and hop off the regular services to visit places of interest. The best place to board is Westminster Pier, from where boats head downstream, taking you from the City of Westminster, the seat of government, to the original City of London, now the financial district and dominated by a growing band of skyscrapers. Across the river, the once shabby and neglected South Bank now bristles with as many top attractions as its northern counterpart, including the slender Shard.

In our illustration we've concentrated on the top highlights you'll enjoy from a waterborne vessel.

MARK DAFFEY / GETTY IMAGES ©

St Paul's Cathedral
Though there's been a church here since AD 604, the current building rose from the ashes of the 1666 Great Fire and is architect Christopher Wren's masterpiece. Famous for surviving the Blitz intact and for the wedding of Charles and Diana, it's looking as good as new after a major clean-up for its 300th anniversary.

Blackfriars

Somerset House
This grand neoclassical palace was once one of many aristocratic houses lining the Thames. The huge arches at river level gave direct access to the Thames until the Embankment was built in the 1860s.

❸ ⊖ Temple

Blackfriars Pier

Blackfriars Bridge

Charing Cross ⊖

Savoy Pier

Waterloo Bridge

Victoria Embankment Gardens

⊖ **Embankment**

National Theatre

Queen Elizabeth Hall
Southbank Centre

OXO Tower

London Eye
Built in 2000 and originally temporary, the Eye instantly became a much-loved landmark. The 30-minute spin takes you 135m above the city from where the views are unsurprisingly amazing.

❷

Westminster Pier

Waterloo Millennium Pier

⊖ **Westminster**

Westminster Bridge

❶

Houses of Parliament
Rebuilt in neo-Gothic style after the old palace burned down in 1834, the most famous part of the British parliament is the clocktower. Generally known as Big Ben, it's named after Benjamin Hall who oversaw its construction.

RICHARD I'ANSON / GETTY IMAGES ©

These are, from west to east the **Houses of Parliament** ❶, the **London Eye** ❷, **Somerset House** ❸, **St Paul's Cathedral** ❹, **Tate Modern** ❺, **Shakespeare's Globe** ❻, the **Tower of London** ❼ and **Tower Bridge** ❽.

Apart from covering this central section of the river, boats can also be taken upstream as far as Kew Gardens and Hampton Court Palace, and downstream to Greenwich and the Thames Barrier.

BOAT HOPPING

Thames Clippers hop-on/hop-off services are aimed at commuters but are equally useful for visitors, operating every 15 minutes on a loop from piers at Embankment, Waterloo, Blackfriars, Bankside, London Bridge and the Tower. Other services also go from Westminster. Oyster cardholders get a discount off the boat ticket price.

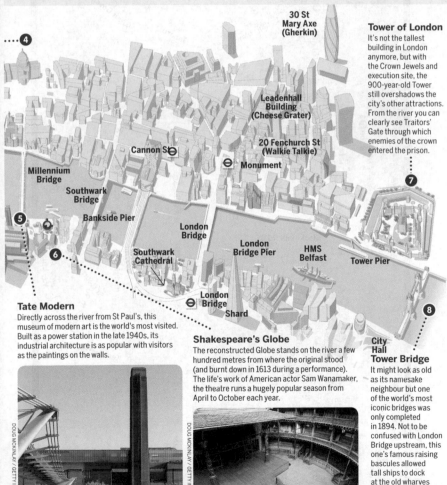

30 St Mary Axe (Gherkin)

Leadenhall Building (Cheese Grater)

Cannon St

20 Fenchurch St (Walkie Talkie)

Monument

Millennium Bridge

Southwark Bridge

Bankside Pier

London Bridge

London Bridge Pier

HMS Belfast

Tower Pier

Southwark Cathedral

London Bridge

Shard

Tower of London
It's not the tallest building in London anymore, but with the Crown Jewels and execution site, the 900-year-old Tower still overshadows the city's other attractions. From the river you can clearly see Traitors' Gate through which enemies of the crown entered the prison.

Tate Modern
Directly across the river from St Paul's, this museum of modern art is the world's most visited. Built as a power station in the late 1940s, its industrial architecture is as popular with visitors as the paintings on the walls.

Shakespeare's Globe
The reconstructed Globe stands on the river a few hundred metres from where the original stood (and burnt down in 1613 during a performance). The life's work of American actor Sam Wanamaker, the theatre runs a hugely popular season from April to October each year.

City Hall

Tower Bridge
It might look as old as its namesake neighbour but one of the world's most iconic bridges was only completed in 1894. Not to be confused with London Bridge upstream, this one's famous raising bascules allowed tall ships to dock at the old wharves to the west and are still lifted up to 1000 times a year.

DOUG MCKINLAY / GETTY IMAGES ©

DOUG MCKINLAY / GETTY IMAGES ©

South Bank

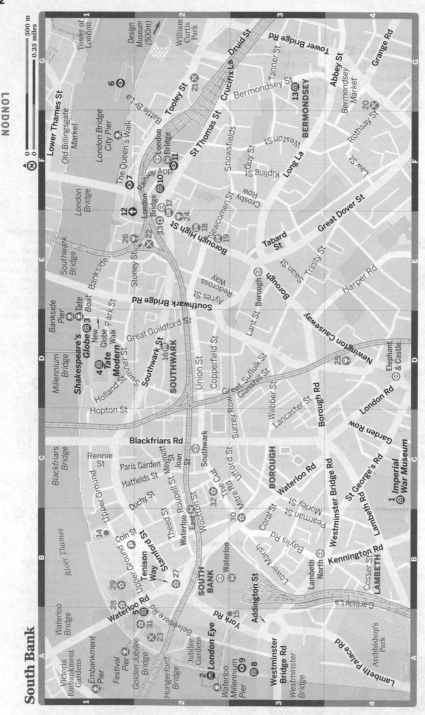

ride in enclosed egg-shaped pods; the wheel takes 30 minutes to rotate completely, offering 25-mile views on clear days. Drawing 0.5 million visitors annually, at peak times (July, August and school holidays), it can seem like they are all in the queue with you. Save money and shorten queues by buying tickets online, or cough up an extra £10 to showcase your fast-track swagger.

Alternatively, visit before 11am or after 3pm to avoid peak density.

★Imperial War Museum   MUSEUM
(Map p92; www.iwm.org.uk; Lambeth Rd, SE1; ⊙10am-6pm; ⊜Lambeth North) FREE Reopened in July 2014 after a massive refurbishment and fronted by a pair of intimidating 15in naval guns that could lob a 1938lb shell over 16 miles, this riveting museum is housed in what was once Bethlehem Royal Hospital, known notoriously as Bedlam.

As well as terrific new World War I galleries and a stunning new Foster+Partners atrium, exhibits include Lawrence of Arabia's 1000cc motorbike, a German V-2 rocket, a doodlebug, a lifelike replica of Little Boy (the atomic bomb dropped on Hiroshima), a Spitfire, Harrier Jet and other classic fighter planes dangling from the ceiling, plus a WWII bomb shelter and a Holocaust exhibition.

Shard   NOTABLE BUILDING
(Map p92; www.the-shard.com; 32 London Bridge St, SE1; adult/child £29.95/23.95; ⊙9am-10pm; ⊜London Bridge) Puncturing the skies above London, the crystalline splinter-like form of the Shard – the tallest building in Western Europe – has rapidly become a dramatic icon of town. The tower boasts the brand new, five-star Shangri-La Hotel at the Shard (p119), restaurants and viewing platforms on floors 68, 69 and 72 – book online to save £5.

Old Operating Theatre
Museum & Herb Garret   MUSEUM
(Map p92; www.thegarret.org.uk; 9a St Thomas St, SE1; adult/child £6.50/3.50; ⊙10.30am-5pm; ⊜London Bridge) The highlight of this unique museum, 32 steps up the spiral stairway of the tower of St Thomas Church (1703), focuses on the nastiness of 19th-century hospital treatment. A fiendish array of amputation knives presages the operating theatre, where doctors operated in rough-and-ready (pre-ether, pre-chloroform, pre-antiseptic) conditions. A demonstration on Victorian speed surgery kicks off at 2pm on Saturdays and one on how drugs were made at 2pm on Sundays. Also browse the natural remedies in the herb garret, including snail water for venereal disease and bladderwrack for goitre and tuberculosis.

South Bank

◎ Top Sights
1 Imperial War Museum	C4
2 London Eye	A2
3 Shakespeare's Globe	D1
4 Tate Modern	D1

◎ Sights
5 Hayward Gallery	A2
6 HMS Belfast	G1
7 London Bridge Experience & London Tombs	F1
8 London Dungeon	A3
9 London Sea Life Aquarium	A3
10 Old Operating Theatre Museum & Herb Garret	F2
11 Shard	F2
12 Southwark Cathedral	E1
13 White Cube Bermondsey	G3

◎ Activities, Courses & Tours
14 London Bicycle Tour	B1
15 London Duck Tours	A3

◎ Sleeping
16 Citizen M	D2
17 Oasis	E2

Shangri-La Hotel at the Shard	(see 11)
18 St Christopher's Inn	E2
19 St Christopher's Village	E2

◎ Eating
20 M Manze	G4
21 Magdalen	G2
22 Monmouth Coffee Company	E2
23 Skylon	A2

◎ Drinking & Nightlife
24 George Inn	E2
25 Ministry of Sound	D4
26 Rake	E1

◎ Entertainment
27 BFI IMAX Cinema	B2
28 BFI Southbank	B1
29 National Theatre	B1
30 Old Vic	B3
31 Southbank Centre	A2
32 Young Vic	C2

◎ Shopping
33 Borough Market	E2

Southwark Cathedral
CHURCH

(Map p92; ☎020-7367 6700; http://cathedral. southwark.anglican.org; Montague Close, SE1; donations welcome; ⊗8am-6pm Mon-Fri, 9am-6pm Sat & Sun; ⊜London Bridge) The earliest surviving chunks of this relatively small cathedral are the retrochoir at the eastern end, some ancient arcading by the southwest door, 12th-century wall cores in the north transept and an arch that dates to the original Norman church, although most of the cathedral is Victorian. In the south aisle of the nave, hunt down the green alabaster monument to William Shakespeare, next to which is a plaque to Sam Wanamaker (1919–93).

Not far away hangs a splendid icon of Jesus Christ illuminated by devotional candles, and don't overlook the exceedingly fine Elizabethan sideboard in the north transept.

Design Museum
MUSEUM

(www.designmuseum.org; 28 Shad Thames, SE1; adult/child £12.40/6.20; ⊗10am-5.45pm; ♠; ⊜Tower Hill) Housed in a 1930s-era warehouse, the rectangular galleries here stage a revolving program of special exhibitions devoted to contemporary design, host the annual *Brit Insurance Design Awards* competition for design innovations, and display a permanent collection of modern British design. The museum is moving to a new site in the former Commonwealth Institute south of Kensington's Holland Park in November 2015.

HMS Belfast
SHIP

(Map p92; www.iwm.org.uk/visits/hms-belfast; Queen's Walk, SE1; adult/child £15.50/free; ⊗10am-5pm; ♠; ⊜London Bridge) White ensign flapping on the Thames breeze, HMS *Belfast* is a magnet for naval-gazing kids. This large, light cruiser served in WWII, helping sink the German battleship *Scharnhorst* and shelling the Normandy coast on D-Day. Explore the nine decks and see the engine room, gun decks, galley, chapel, punishment cells, canteen and dental surgery. The excellent audioguide takes you on a 1½-hour tour of the ship, only available until 3.30pm.

London Dungeon
HISTORIC BUILDING

(Map p92; www.thedungeons.com/london; County Hall, Westminster Bridge Rd, SE1; adult/child £25.20/19.80; ⊗10am-5pm, extended hours holidays; ♠; ⊜Westminster, Waterloo) Older kids will enjoy the London Dungeon: it's all macabre free-fall hangman's drops, spooky boat rides, fake blood and actors hamming it up as gory criminals (including Jack the Ripper and Sweeney Todd), torturers and judges, plus ghastly interactive mayhem, with doses of salacious humour to boot. It recently moved from its old haunt to County Hall, by the London Eye.

London Bridge Experience & London Tombs
HISTORIC ATTRACTION

(Map p92; www.thelondonbridgeexperience.com; 2-4 Tooley St, SE1; adult/child £23/17; ⊗10am-5pm Mon-Fri, to 6pm Sat & Sun; ♠; ⊜London Bridge) Kicking off with the relatively tame London Bridge Experience, where actors bring to life the bridge's history with the assistance of severed heads, the London Tombs turns up the terror once the education bit is out of the way. Adding to the creepiness is the knowledge that these were once plague pits and therefore actual tombs. The experience takes about 45 minutes, with the tombs an optional additional 25 minutes.

Save up to 50% by buying online.

London Sea Life Aquarium
AQUARIUM

(Map p92; www.visitsealife.com; Westminster Bridge Rd, SE1; adult/child £22.20/16.50; ⊗10am-7pm; ⊜Westminster, Waterloo) This is one of the largest aquariums in Europe, with a beautiful and educational array of aquatic (many endangered) creatures from the briny deep grouped into different zones (coral cave, rainforest, River Thames), kicking off with a shark walkway. Check the website for shark-feeding times and book online for a 10% discount.

White Cube Bermondsey
GALLERY

(Map p92; www.whitecube.com; 144-152 Bermondsey St, SE1; ⊗10am-6pm Tue-Sat, noon-6pm Sun; ⊜London Bridge) **FREE** The new White Cube Bermondsey has ample exhibition space, designed to showcase large and ambitious installation pieces.

Hayward Gallery
GALLERY

(Map p92; www.southbankcentre.co.uk; Belvedere Rd, SE1; ⊗10am-6pm Sat-Wed, to 8pm Thu & Fri; ♠; ⊜Waterloo) The 1968 Brutalist architecture is as opinion-dividing as you can get, but the popular international contemporary art shows held here constitute a further rich seam of culture in the Southbank Centre.

◉ Pimlico

The origins of its name highly obscure, Pimlico is a grand part of London, bordered by the Thames but lacking a strong sense of neighbourhood, becoming prettier the further you stray from Victoria station.

★ **Tate Britain** GALLERY
(www.tate.org.uk; Millbank, SW1; ◷ 10am-6pm, to 10pm 1st Fri of month; ❹ Pimlico) FREE Splen didly refurbished with a stunning new staircase and a rehung collection, the more elderly and venerable of the two Tate siblings – in a riverside Portland stone edifice – celebrates paintings from 1500 to the present, with works from Blake, Hogarth, Gainsborough, Barbara Hepworth, Whistler, Constable and Turner – in particular – whose light-infused visions dominate the **Clore Gallery**. It doesn't stop there and vibrant modern and contemporary art finds expression in pieces from Lucian Freud, Francis Bacon and Tracey Emin.

The controversial **Turner Prize** (inviting annual protests outside the gallery) is held here every year between October and January, while a fantastic cafe with an excellent terrace facing the river provides sustenance and views. Free one-hour thematic **tours** are held daily at 11am, noon, 2pm and 3pm, and don't overlook the Late at Tate night (first Friday of the month), when doors are open to 10pm.

◉ Chelsea & Kensington

Known as the royal borough, Chelsea and Kensington lays claim to the highest income earners in the UK. Kensington High St has a lively mix of chains and boutiques, while even the charity shops along King's Rd resemble fashion outlets. Some of London's most beautiful and fascinating museums, clustered together in South Kensington, are must-sees come rain or shine.

★ **Victoria & Albert Museum** MUSEUM
(V&A; Map p98; www.vam.ac.uk; Cromwell Rd, SW7; ◷ 10am-5.45pm Sat-Thu, to 10pm Fri; ❹ South Kensington) FREE This outstanding museum boasts an unparalleled collection of decorative art and design with some 4.5 million objects from Britain and around the globe. The museum setting and gorgeous architecture is as inspiring as the sheer diversity and rarity of its exhibits. Part of Prince Albert's legacy to Londoners in the wake of the Great Exhibition of 1851, the museum is a bit like the nation's attic, spread generously through nearly 150 galleries.

The museum is epic, but it's open late on Friday evenings, for smaller crowds. For food and drink, make for the **V&A Café** in the magnificent Refreshment Rooms, dating from the 1860s, or the **Garden Café** in the John Madejski Garden in summer.

LONDON SIGHTS

TATE-A-TATE

Whisking art lovers between London's Tate galleries, the colourful **Tate Boat** (Map p92; www.tate.org.uk/visit/tate-boat; one-way adult/child £6.50/3.25) stops en route at the London Eye. Services from Bankside Pier run from 9.57am to 4.44pm daily at 40-minute intervals (10.20am to 4.27pm from Millbank Pier). Discounts are available for Travelcard holders.

Free one-hour guided tours leave the main reception area four times daily.

★ **Natural History Museum** MUSEUM
(Map p98; www.nhm.ac.uk; Cromwell Rd, SW7; ◷ 10am-5.50pm; ❹ South Kensington) FREE This ornate building is one of London's finest and a masterpiece: pale blue and honey-coloured stone, broken by Venetian arches decorated with all manner of carved critters. A sure-fire hit with kids of all ages, this awesome museum is crammed with fascinating discoveries, starting with the giant Diplodocus skeleton that greets you in the main hall. In the **dinosaur gallery**, the roaring 4m-high animatronic Tyrannosaurus Rex is a heart-thumping highlight .

Other galleries are equally impressive. An escalator slithers up into a hollowed-out globe where **Volcanoes and Earthquakes** explores the forces that shape our planet; highlights include a plate tectonics room and the mock-up of the Kobe earthquake, a bone-rattling lesson in fault lines.

The **Darwin Centre** houses a team of biologists and a staggering 20-million-plus repertoire of animal and plant specimens. Take a lift to the top of the **Cocoon**, a seven-storey egg-shaped structure encased within a glass pavilion, and make your way down through the floors of interactive displays. Glass windows allow you to watch the scientists at work.

Finally, don't overlook **Sensational Butterflies** by the East Lawn and the charming **Wildlife Garden**, a slice of English countryside in SW7.

★ **Science Museum** MUSEUM
(Map p98; www.sciencemuseum.org.uk; Exhibition Rd, SW7; ◷ 10am-6pm; ❹ South Kensington) FREE With seven floors of interactive and educational exhibits, this scientifically

Victoria & Albert Museum

HALF-DAY HIGHLIGHTS TOUR

The art- and design-packed V&A is vast: we have devised an easy-to-follow tour of the museum highlights to help cover some signature pieces while also allowing you to appreciate some of the grandeur of the museum architecture.

Enter the V&A by the Grand Entrance off Cromwell Rd and immediately turn left to explore the Islamic Middle East Gallery and to discover the sumptuous silk-and-wool **Ardabil Carpet ①**. Among the pieces from South Asia in the adjacent gallery is the terrifying automated **Tipu's Tiger ②**. Continue to the outstanding **Fashion Room ③** with its displays of clothing styles through the ages. The magnificent gallery opposite, which houses the Raphael Cartoons, offers a shortcut via stairs on its far side to Level 2 and the Britain 1500–1760 Gallery; turn left in the gallery to

Fashion Gallery
With clothing from the 18th century to the present day, this circular and chronologically arranged gallery showcases evening wear, undergarments and iconic fashion milestones, such as 1960s dresses designed by Mary Quant.

The Great Bed of Ware
Created during the reign of Queen Elizabeth I, its headboard and bedposts etched with ancient graffiti, the 16th-century oak Great Bed of Ware is famously name-dropped in Shakespeare's *Twelfth Night*.

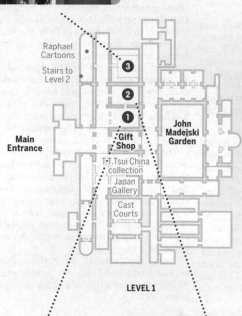

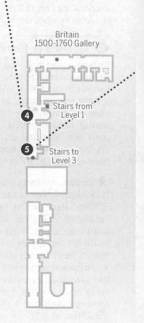

Britain 1500-1760 Gallery

Stairs from Level 1

Raphael Cartoons

Stairs to Level 2

③

②

①

④

⑤

Stairs to Level 3

Main Entrance

Gift Shop

John Madejski Garden

T.T.Tsui China collection

Japan Gallery

Cast Courts

LEVEL 1

LEVEL 2

The Ardabil Carpet
One of the world's most beautiful carpets, the Ardabil was completed in 1540, one of a pair commissioned by Shah Tahmasp, ruler of Iran. The piece is most astonishing for the artistry of the detailing and the subtlety of design.

Tipu's Tiger
This disquieting 18th-century wood-and-metal mechanical automaton depicts a European being savaged by a tiger. When a handle is turned, an organ hidden within the feline mimics the cries of the dying man, whose arm also rises.

INDIAN SCHOOL / GETTY IMAGES ©

DAMIAN HARPER ©

find the **Great Bed of Ware** ➍, beyond which rests the exquisitely crafted artistry of **Henry VIII's writing box** ➎. Head up the stairs into the Metalware Gallery on Level 3 for the **Hereford Screen** ➏. Continue through the Ironwork and Sculpture Galleries and through the Leighton Corridor to the glittering **Jewellery Gallery** ➐, from where a succession of galleries bordering the John Madejski Garden lead you to the **Design Since 1946** ➑ gallery, opposite the 20th Century Gallery (at the end of which are stairs and a lift to the rest of the museum).

Henry VIII's Writing Box
This exquisitely ornate walnut and oak 16th-century writing box has been added to over the centuries, but the original decorative motifs are superb, including Henry's coat of arms, flanked by Venus (holding Cupid) and Mars.

Design Since 1946
Weigh up some innovative classics that defined much of the late 20th century, when mobile phones were seriously chunky and portable audio cassette players were the latest must-have gadget.

Stairs to other Levels

20th Century Gallery

Stairs from level 2

➏

➑

National Art Library

Ironwork Gallery

➐

Sculpture Gallery

Leighton Corridor

Photographers Gallery

LEVEL 3

LEVEL 4

Jewellery Gallery
The beautifully illuminated Jewellery Gallery has a stunning collection of items from ancient Greece to the modern day, including a dazzling gold Celtic breastplate, art-nouveau jewellery and animals fashioned by Fabergé.

The Hereford Screen
Designed by Sir George Gilbert Scott, this awe-inspiring choir screen is a labour of love, originally fashioned for Hereford Cathedral. An almighty conception of wood, iron, copper, brass and hardstone, there were few parts of the V&A that could support its great mass.

Knightsbridge, South Kensington & Chelsea

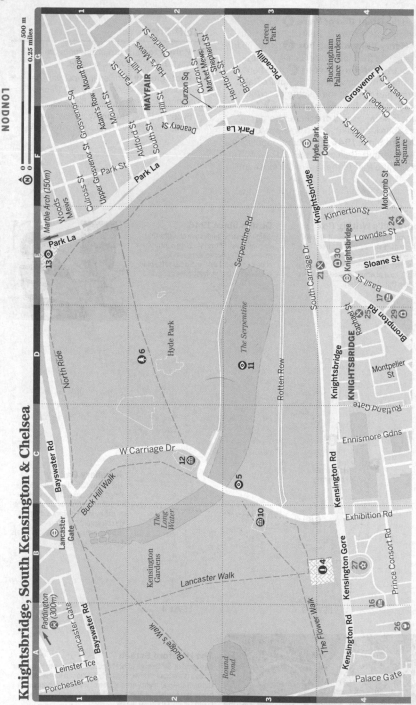

N 0 0
500 m
0.25 miles

Marble Arch (150m)

Paddington (300m)

MAYFAIR

Green Park

Buckingham Palace Gardens

Grosvenor Pl

Chester St

Halkin St

Belgrave Square

Motcomb St

Piccadilly

Park La

Deanery St

Curzon Sq
Curzon St
Market Mews
Shepherd St
Hertford St
Brick St

Hay's Mews
Charles St

Hill St
Farm St

South St
Aldford St

Upper Grosvenor St
Park St

Adam's Row
Grosvenor Sq
Mount Row

Culross St
Mount St

Woods Mews

13 Park La

Park La

North Ride

Hyde Park

6

The Serpentine

Serpentine Rd

11

Rotten Row

South Carriage Dr

21

30

Knightsbridge

Hyde Park Corner

Kinnerton St

Lowndes St

Sloane St

24

KNIGHTSBRIDGE

Knightsbridge

Basil St

Raphael St

Brompton Rd

17

29

25

Montpelier St

Rutland Gate

Ennismore Gdns

W Carriage Dr

Buck Hill Walk

Lancaster Gate

Bayswater Rd

The Long Water

Kensington Gardens

Lancaster Walk

12

5

10

Kensington Rd

Kensington Rd

Kensington Gore

Exhibition Rd

Prince Consort Rd

27

4

The Flower Walk

Budge's Walk

Round Pond

Leinster Tce

Porchester Tce

Lancaster Gate

Bayswater Rd

16

26

Kensington Rd

Palace Gate

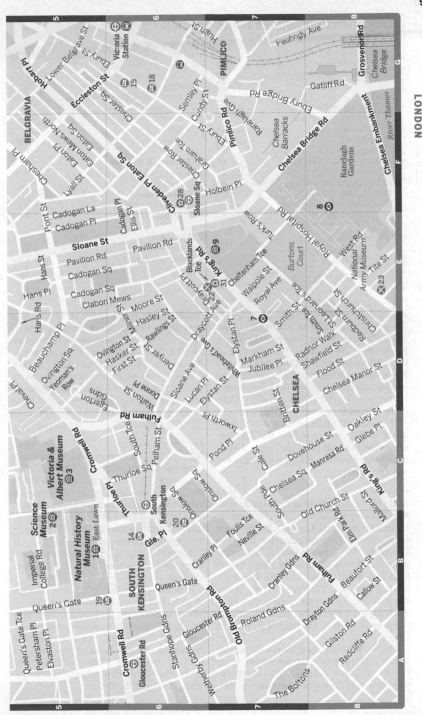

Knightsbridge, South Kensington & Chelsea

spellbinding museum will mesmerise even the most precocious of young Einsteins. Highlights include the **Energy Hall** on the ground floor, the riveting **Flight Gallery** on the 3rd floor and the flight simulator. There's also a 450-seat **Imax cinema**. Some children head straight for voice warpers, lava lamps, boomerangs, bouncy globes and alien babies in the ground-floor shop, and stay put.

If you've kids under the age of five, scoot down to the basement for the **Garden**, where there's a fun-filled play zone, including a water-play area, besieged by tots in red waterproof smocks.

Hyde Park
PARK

(Map p98; ☉5.30am-midnight; ⊖Marble Arch, Hyde Park Corner, Queensway) At 145 hectares, Hyde Park is central London's largest open space. Henry VIII expropriated it from the Church in 1536, when it became a hunting ground and later a venue for duels, executions and horse racing. The 1851 Great Exhibition was held here, and during WWII the park became an enormous potato field. These days, it serves as an occasional concert venue and a full-time green space for fun and frolics.

There's boating on the **Serpentine** (Map p98; ⊖Knightsbridge or South Kensington), while **Speakers' Corner** (Map p98; Park Lane; ⊖Marble Arch) sees oratorical acrobats on Sundays,

maintaining a tradition begun in 1872 as a response to rioting. A wee bit north is **Marble Arch** (Map p102; ⊖Marble Arch), designed by John Nash in 1828 as the entrance to Buckingham Palace and moved here in 1851; it once served as a police lookout. The infamous Tyburn Tree, a three-legged gallows, once stood nearby. It is estimated that up to 50,000 people were executed here between 1196 and 1783.

Kensington Palace
PALACE

(Map p120; www.hrp.org.uk/kensingtonpalace; Kensington Gardens, W8; adult/child £16.50/free; ☉10am-6pm Mar-Oct, to 5pm Nov-Feb; ⊖High St Kensington) Kensington Palace (1605) became the favourite royal residence under the joint reign of William and Mary and remained so until the death of George II (in 1762, George III bought Buckingham Palace for his wife, Charlotte). It still has private apartments where various members of the royal extended family live.

In popular imagination it's most associated with three intriguing princesses: Victoria (who was born here in 1819 and lived here with her domineering mother until her accession to the throne), Margaret (sister of the current queen, who lived here until her death in 2002) and, of course, Diana. The palace recently underwent huge restoration work totalling £12 million.

Kensington Gardens   GARDENS
(Map p120; ☻dawn-dusk; ☻High St Kensington)
Blending in with Hyde Park, these royal
gardens are part of Kensington Palace and
hence popularly associated with Princess
Diana. Diana devotees can visit the **Diana,
Princess of Wales Memorial Fountain**
(Map p98; ☻Knightsbridge), a soothing structure fashioned from 545 pieces of Cornish
granite, channeling a circular stream drawn
from chalk aquifers more than 100m underground that cascades gently and flows
together in a pool at the bottom; paddling
is encouraged.

The astonishing **Albert Memorial** (Map
p98; tours adult/concession £6/5; ☻tours 2pm &
3pm 1st Sun of month Mar-Dec; ☻Knightsbridge,
Gloucester Rd) **FREE** is a unique chunk of Victorian bombast, a lavish marble, mosaic and
gold affair opposite the Royal Albert Hall,
built to honour Queen Victoria's husband,
Albert (1819–61).

The gardens also house the **Serpentine Gallery** (Map p98; www.serpentinegallery.
org; ☻10am-6pm Tue-Sun; ☻Lancaster Gate or
Knightsbridge) **FREE**, one of London's edgiest contemporary art spaces; the recently
opened **Serpentine Sackler Gallery** (Map
p98; www.serpentinegallery.org; West Carriage
Drive; ☻10am-6pm Tue-Sun; ☻Lancaster Gate) is
on the far side of the Serpentine Bridge, in
the former Magazine. The **Sunken Garden**,
near the palace, is at its prettiest in summer,
while tea in the **Orangery** (Map p120; ✐020-
3166 6112; www.hrp.org.uk; Kensington Palace,
Kensington Gardens, W8; afternoon tea £24, with
champagne £34; ☻10am-6pm Mar-Oct, to 5pm
Nov-Feb; ☻Queensway, Notting Hill Gate, High St
Kensington) ✐is a treat any time of the year.

King's Road   STREET
(Map p98; ☻Sloane Sq) Named after King
Charles II who would return to Hampton
Court Palace along a farmer's track here after amorous interludes with Nell Gwyn, this
street was almost synonymous with London
fashion during the '60s and '70s. Its days
at the counter-cultural forefront of London fashion long gone, King's Road today
is more a stamping ground for the leisure-
class shopping set.

Saatchi Gallery   GALLERY
(Map p98; www.saatchi-gallery.co.uk; Duke of
York's HQ, King's Rd, SW1; ☻10am-6pm; ☻Sloane
Sq) **FREE** This enticing gallery hosts temporary exhibitions of experimental and
thought-provoking work across a variety of
media. The white, sanded bare-floorboard
galleries are sharply presented, but save
some wonder for Gallery 15, where Richard Wilson's *20:50* is on permanent display.
Mesmerising, impassive and ineffable, it's a
riveting tour de force. A cool bookshop chips
in down in the basement.

Royal Hospital Chelsea   HISTORIC BUILDINGS
(Map p98; www.chelsea-pensioners.co.uk; Royal
Hospital Rd, SW3; ☻grounds 10am-noon & 2-4pm
Mon-Sat, museum 10am-noon & 2-4pm Mon-Fri;
☻Sloane Sq) **FREE** Designed by Wren, the
Royal Hospital Chelsea was built in 1692
to provide shelter for ex-servicemen. Today
it houses hundreds of war veterans known
as Chelsea Pensioners, charming old chaps
generally regarded as national treasures.
The Chelsea Flower Show takes place in the
hospital grounds in May.

Chelsea Physic Garden   GARDENS
(www.chelseaphysicgarden.co.uk; 66 Royal Hospital
Rd, SW3; adult/child £9.90/6.60; ☻11am-6pm Tue-
Fri & Sun Apr-Oct, to 10pm Wed Jul & Aug; ☻Sloane
Sq) This gorgeous botanical enclave was
established by the Apothecaries' Society
in 1676 for students working on medicinal
plants and healing. One of Europe's oldest
of its kind, the small grounds are a compen-
dium of botany from carnivorous pitcher
plants to rich yellow flag irises, a cork oak
from Portugal, delightful ferns and a treasure trove of rare trees and shrubs. Free tours
are held three times daily.

Fulham Palace   HISTORIC BUILDING
(www.fulhampalace.org; Bishop's Ave; ☻palace &
museum 12.30-4.30pm Mon-Thu, noon-5pm Sun,
gardens dawn-dusk daily; ☻Putney Bridge) **FREE**
Summer home of the bishops of London
from 704 to 1975, this genteel palace near
the Thames has an adorable courtyard that
draws watercolourists on sunny days, a
splendid cafe in the drawing room at the rear
(looking out onto a magnificent lawn), a pretty walled garden and a Tudor Revival chapel.

Guided tours usually take in the Great
Hall, the Victorian chapel, Bishop Sherlock's
Room and the museum and last about 1¼
hours. There are also garden tours (£5);
check the website for details on evening
walks (for a nightfall perspective). Hiking
around the extensive and partially excavated
palace moat (once the longest in England) is
enjoyable. Films are screened on the lawn in
summer, when art fairs and musical festivals
are also held.

LONDON SIGHTS

◉ Marylebone

Not as exclusive as its southern neighbour Mayfair, hip Marylebone has one of London's most pleasant high streets and the famous, if rather disappointing, Baker St, immortalised in the hit song by Gerry Rafferty and strongly associated with Victoria-era sleuth Sherlock Holmes (there's a museum and gift shop at his fictional address, 221b).

Regent's Park   PARK
(www.royalparks.org.uk; ⊙ 5am-dusk; ⊕ Regent's Park, Baker St) A former royal hunting ground, Regent's Park was designed by John Nash

early in the 19th century, although what was actually laid out is only a fraction of the celebrated architect's grand plan. Nevertheless, it's one of London's most lovely open spaces – at once serene and lively, cosmopolitan and local – with football pitches, tennis courts, a boating lake, ZSL London Zoo, and Regent's canal along its northern side.

Queen Mary's Gardens, towards the south of the park, are particularly pretty, with spectacular roses in summer. **Open Air Theatre** (☑ 0844 826 4242; www.openairtheatre.org) hosts performances of Shakespeare and other classics here on summer evenings, along with comedy and concerts.

Marylebone

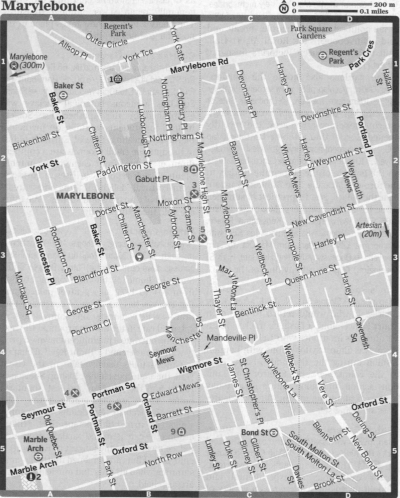

ZSL London Zoo   ZOO
(www.londonzoo.co.uk; Outer Circle, Regent's Park, NW1; adult/child £26/18.50; ⏰10am 6.30pm Mar-Oct, to 4pm Nov-Feb; 🚇Camden Town) These famous zoological gardens have come a long way since being established in 1828, with massive investment making conservation, education and breeding the name of the game. Highlights include Tiger Territory, Penguin Beach, Gorilla Kingdom, Rainforest Life, Nightlife and Butterfly Paradise. Feeding sessions or talks take place during the day. Save 20% off the admission price by booking online.

Regent's Canal   CANAL
To flee the crowded streets and enjoy a picturesque, waterside angle on North London, take to the canals that once played such a vital role in the transport of goods across the capital. The towpath of Regent's Canal also makes an excellent shortcut across North London, either on foot or by bike.

In full, the ribbon of water runs 9 miles from Limehouse to Little Venice (where it meets the Grand Union Canal), but you can make do with walking from Little Venice to Camden in under an hour, passing Regent's Park and London Zoo, as well as beautiful villas designed by architect John Nash and redevelopments of old industrial buildings. Allow 15 to 20 minutes between Camden and Regent's Park, and 25 to 30 minutes between Regent's Park and Little Venice. The London Waterbus Company (p146) and Jason's Trip (p146) run canal boats between Camden Lock and Little Venice.

Madame Tussauds   MUSEUM
(Map p102; ☎0870 400 3000; www.madame-tussauds.com/london; Marylebone Rd, NW1; adult/

Marylebone

◎ Sights
1 Madame Tussauds B1
2 Marble Arch A5

✕ Eating
3 La Fromagerie B2
4 Locanda Locatelli A4
5 Providores & Tapa Room C3
6 Roti Chai B5

◎ Drinking & Nightlife
7 Purl B3

◎ Shopping
8 Daunt Books B2
9 Selfridges B5

---

child £30/26; ⏰9.30am-5.30pm; 🚇Baker St) Tickets may cost a (wax) arm and a (wax) leg and the crowds can be as awesome as the exhibits, but the opportunity to pose beside Posh and Becks has clear-cut kudos. Most of the life-size wax figures – such as Leonardo Di Caprio – are fantastically lifelike and as close to the real thing as most of us will get, but queues for the Queen (and Barack Obama) can get leg-numbing.

Honing her craft making effigies of victims of the French revolution, Tussaud brought her wares to England in 1802. Her Chamber of Horrors still survives (complete with the actual blade that took Marie Antoinette's head), but it's joined by Scream!, where actors lunge at terrified visitors in the dark. The Spirit of London ride in a black cab is tremendous fun and the 4-D Marvel film is top-drawer entertainment, the audience sprayed with air jets and mist and jabbed in the back during a spectacular action film centred on London. Try to arrive early in the morning to avoid long queues.

Tickets are cheaper when ordered online; combined tickets with the London Eye, London Dungeon and London Sealife Aquarium are also available.

◉ Bloomsbury & St Pancras

With the University of London and British Museum within its genteel environs, it's little wonder that Bloomsbury has attracted a lot of very clever, bookish people over the years. Between the world wars, these pleasant streets were colonised by a group of artists and intellectuals known collectively as the Bloomsbury Group, which included novelists Virginia Woolf and EM Forster and the economist John Maynard Keynes. Russell Sq, its very heart, was laid out in 1800 and is one of London's largest and loveliest.

The conversion of spectacular St Pancras station into the Eurostar terminal and a ritzy apartment complex is reviving the area's fortunes.

★ British Museum   MUSEUM
(Map p76; ☎020-7323 8000; www.britishmuseum.org; Great Russell St, WC1; ⏰10am-5.30pm Sat-Thu, to 8.30pm Fri; 🚇Russell Sq, Tottenham Court Rd) FREE The country's largest museum and one of the oldest and finest in the world, this monumental accumulation of treasures boasts vast Egyptian, Etruscan, Greek, Roman, European and Middle Eastern galleries, among many others. Begun in 1753 with a 'cabinet of

The British Museum

A HALF-DAY TOUR

The British Museum, with almost eight million items in its permanent collection, is so vast and comprehensive that it can be daunting for the first-time visitor. To avoid a frustrating trip – and getting lost on the way to the Egyptian mummies – set out on this half-day exploration, which takes in some of the museum's most important sights. If you want to see and learn more, join a tour or hire a multimedia iPad.

A good starting point is the **Rosetta Stone ❶**, the key that cracked the code to ancient Egypt's writing system. Nearby treasures from Assyria – an ancient civilisation centred in Mesopotamia between the Tigris and Euphrates Rivers – including the colossal **Khorsabad Winged Bulls ❷**, give way to the **Parthenon Sculptures ❸**, highpoints of classical Greek art that continue to influence

Winged Bulls from Khorsabad

This awesome pair of alabaster winged bulls with human heads once guarded the entrance to the palace of Assyrian King Sargon II at Khorsabad in Mesopotamia, a cradle of civilisation in present-day Iraq.

Parthenon Sculptures

The Parthenon, a white marble temple dedicated to Athena, was part of a fortified citadel on the Acropolis in Athens. There are dozens of sculptures and friezes with models and interactive displays explaining how they all once fitted together.

Ancient Greece & Rome **❸**

Lion Hunt Reliefs from Nineveh •

❷

West Stairs

South Stairs

❶ ❹

Main Entrance

Great Court

Reading Room

Great Court Shop

China, India & Southeast Asia

North America

Paul Hamlyn Library

Ticket Desk (Temporary Exhibtions)

GROUND FLOOR

Rosetta Stone

Written in hieroglyphic, demotic (cursive ancient Egyptian script used for everyday use) and Greek, the 762kg stone contains a decree exempting priests from tax on the first anniversary of young Ptolemy V's coronation.

Bust of Ramesses the Great

The most impressive sculpture in the Egyptian galleries, this 7.5-tonne bust portrays Ramesses II, scourge of the Israelites in the Book of Exodus, as great benefactor.

us today. Be sure to see both the sculptures and the monumental frieze celebrating the birth of Athena. En route to the West Stairs is a huge bust of **Pharaoh Ramesses II** ❹, just a hint of the large collection of **Egyptian mummies** ❺ upstairs. (The earliest, affectionately called Ginger because of wispy reddish hair, was preserved simply by hot sand.) The Romans introduce visitors to the early Britain galleries via the rich **Mildenhall Treasure** ❻. The Anglo-Saxon **Sutton Hoo Ship Burial** ❼ and the medieval **Lewis Chessmen** ❽ follow.

EATING OPTIONS

» **Court Cafes** At the northern end of the Great Court; takeaway counters with salads and sandwiches; communal tables

» **Gallery Cafe** Slightly out of the way near Room 12; quieter; offers hot dishes

» **Court Restaurant** Upstairs overlooking the former Reading Room; sit-down meals

Lewis Chessmen
The much-loved 78 chess pieces portray faceless pawns, worried-looking queens, bishops with their mitres turned sideways and rooks as 'warders', gnawing away at their shields.

FEARGUS COONEY / GETTY IMAGES ©

Egyptian Mummies
Among the rich collection of mummies and funerary objects is 'Ginger', who was buried at the site of Gebelein, in Upper Egypt, more than 5000 years ago, and Katebet, a one-time chantress (ritual performer) at the Amun temple in Karnak.

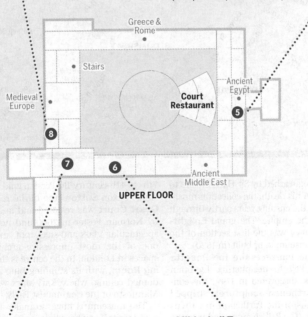

UPPER FLOOR

Sutton Hoo Ship Burial
This unique grave of an important (but unidentified) Anglo-Saxon royal has yielded drinking horns, gold buckles and a stunning helmet with face mask.

Mildenhall Treasure
Roman gods such as Neptune and Bacchus share space with early Christian symbols like the *chi-rho* (short for 'Christ') on the find's three dozen silver bowls, plates and spoons.

North Central London

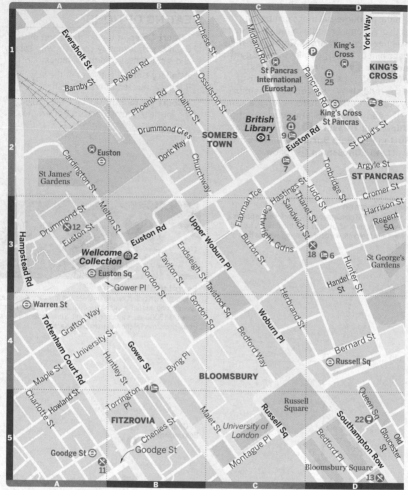

curiosities' bequeathed by Sir Hans Sloane to the nation on his death, the collection mushroomed over the ensuing years partly through plundering the empire. The grand **Enlightenment Gallery** was the first section of the redesigned museum to be built (in 1820).

Among the must-sees are the **Rosetta Stone**, the key to deciphering Egyptian hieroglyphics, discovered in 1799; the controversial **Parthenon Sculptures**, stripped from the walls of the Parthenon in Athens by Lord Elgin (the British ambassador to the Ottoman Empire), and which Greece wants returned; the stunning **Oxus Treasure** of 7th- to 4th-century-BC Persian gold; and the Anglo-Saxon **Sutton Hoo** burial relics. The **Great Court** was restored and augmented by Norman Foster in 2000 and now has a spectacular glass-and-steel roof, making it one of the most impressive architectural spaces in London. In the centre is the **Reading Room**, with its stunning blue-and-gold domed ceiling, where Karl Marx wrote the Manifesto of the Communist Party.

The museum is huge, so make a few focused visits if you have time, and consider the 15 free 30- to 40-minute eyeOpener tours of individual galleries per day. The museum also

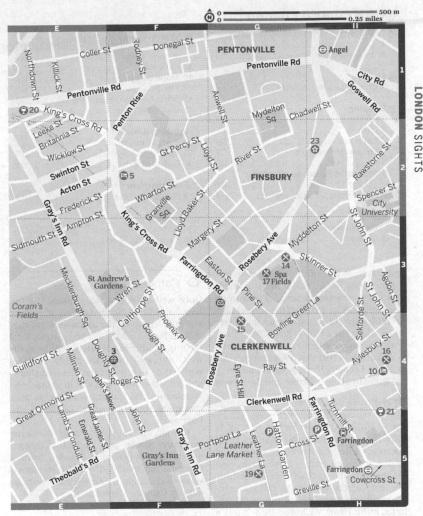

has excellent multimedia iPad tours (adult/child £5/3.50), offering six themed one-hour tours, and eight 35-minute children's trails. Highlights tours (adult/child £12/free) depart at 11.30am and 2pm Saturday and Sunday.

The British Museum's long-awaited new extension, the **World Conservation and Exhibitions Centre** in its northwestern corner, opened in 2014, with an exhibition on the Vikings.

When museum fever strikes you down, pop across the way to the lovely **Museum Tavern** (Map p76; 49 Great Russell St, WC1; ⊙ 11am-11.30pm Mon-Sat, 10am-10pm Sun; ⊖ Holborn, Tottenham Court Rd) where Karl Marx used to polish off a drink or two after a hard day's graft in the Reading Room of the British Library.

★ **British Library**   LIBRARY
(Map p106; www.bl.uk; 96 Euston Rd, NW1; Ritblat Gallery free, special exhibition cost varies; ⊙ 9.30am-6pm Mon & Wed-Fri, to 8pm Tue, to 5pm Sat, 11am-5pm Sun; ⊖ King's Cross St Pancras) For visitors, the real highlight of the British Library is a visit to the **Sir John Ritblat Gallery**, where the most precious manuscripts, spanning almost three millennia, are held. Here you'll find the *Codex Sinaiticus* (the

North Central London

first complete text of the New Testament), a Gutenberg Bible (1455), the stunningly illustrated Jain sacred texts, Leonardo da Vinci's notebooks, a copy of the *Magna Carta* (1215), explorer Captain Scott's final diary and Shakespeare's First Folio (1623).

Further choice selections include the lyrics to 'A Hard Day's Night' (scribbled on the back of Julian Lennon's birthday card) plus original scores by Handel, Mozart and Beethoven.

★ **Wellcome Collection**   MUSEUM
(Map p106; www.wellcomecollection.org; 183 Euston Rd, NW1; ⊙10am-6pm Tue, Wed, Fri & Sat, to 10pm Thu, 11am-6pm Sun; ⊖Euston Sq) FREE
Focusing on the interface of art, science and medicine, this museum – 'a free destination for the incurably curious' – is fascinating. The core of the permanent collection includes objects from around the world collected by Sir Henry Wellcome (1853–1936), a pharmacist, entrepreneur and collector who amassed more than a million objects from different civilisations.

Charles Dickens Museum   MUSEUM
(Map p106; www.dickensmuseum.com; 48 Doughty St, WC1; adult/child £8/4; ⊙10am-5pm, last admission 4pm; ⊖Chancery Lane, Russell Sq) Recently refurbished, Dickens' sole surviving London residence is where his work really flourished – *The Pickwick Papers*, *Nicholas Nickleby* and *Oliver Twist* were all written here. The handsome four-storey house narrowly dodged demolition and opened as a museum in 1925.

⊙ Camden Town

Once well outside the city limits, the former hamlets of North London were long ago gobbled up by the metropolis, yet they still harbour a village feel and distinct local identity. Neither as resolutely wealthy as the west (although there are highly desirable pockets) or as gritty as the east (but there's attitude), the 'Norf' is a mix of genteel terrace houses and featureless council estates, containing some of London's hippest neighbourhoods.

Technicolor hairstyles, facial furniture, elaborate tattoos and alternative threads are the look of bohemian Camden Town, a vibrant neighbourhood of pubs, live-music venues, appealing boutiques and, most famously, Camden Market (p142).

⊙ Hoxton, Shoreditch & Spitalfields

These revitalised and hip areas northeast of the City have enough sightseeing allure to keep daytime travellers occupied, but things really get going in the evening, when the late-night pubs, clubs and restaurants come into their own. Vibrant Hoxton and Shoreditch form the centre of gravity for nightlife, while Sunday is optimum for strolling leisurely through Spitalfields after a Saturday night out. Over the centuries, waves of immigrants have left their mark here, and it's a great place to come for diverse cuisine and vibrant nightlife.

Dennis Severs' House MUSEUM

(Map p124; 020-7247 4013; www.dennissevers house.co.uk; 18 Folgate St, E1; Liverpool St) This Georgian House is set up as if its occupants (a family of Huguenot silk weavers) had just walked out the door, with half-drunk cups of tea, lit candles and, with perhaps more detail than necessary, a full chamber pot by the bed. More than a museum, it's an opportunity to meditate on the minutiae of everyday Georgian life through silent exploration.

Bookings are required for the Monday- and Wednesday-evening candlelit sessions (£14; 6pm to 9pm), but you can just show up on Sundays (£10; noon to 4pm) or selected Mondays (£7; noon to 2pm).

Geffrye Museum MUSEUM

(Map p124; www.geffrye-museum.org.uk; 136 Kingsland Rd, E2; 10am-5pm Tue-Sun; Hoxton, Old St) FREE If you like nosing around other people's homes, you'll love this museum. Devoted to middle-class domestic interiors, these former almshouses (1714) have been converted into a series of living rooms dating from 1630 to the current Ikea generation. On top of the interiors, the back garden has been transformed into period garden 'rooms' and a lovely walled herb garden (April to October only).

⊙ The East End & Docklands

A huge area, the East End and Docklands are not rich in sights, but a dramatic new focus has emerged in the Olympic Park, while recently opened Overground lines make transport a breeze.

The Docklands' Canary Wharf and Isle of Dogs are an island of tower blocks, rivalling those of the City itself. London's port was once the world's greatest, the hub of the enormous global trade of the British Empire. Since being pummelled by the unpleasant Luftwaffe in WWII, its fortunes have been topsy-turvy, but massive development of Canary Wharf replaced its crusty seadogs with battalions of dark-suited office workers.

Museum of London Docklands MUSEUM

(www.museumoflondon.org.uk/docklands; Hertsmere Rd, West India Quay, E17; 10am-6pm; DLR West India Quay) FREE Housed in a heritage-listed warehouse, this museum combines artefacts and multimedia to chart the history of the city through its river and docks. There's a lot to see here, including an informative section on the slave trade. The museum faces West India Quay; head west (towards the City) from the DLR station.

Queen Elizabeth Olympic Park PARK

(www.queenelizabetholympicpark.co.uk; Stratford) From 2008, a vast swath of industrial East London was ambitiously regenerated, becoming London's Olympic Park for the 2012 Games. The 560-acre parkland was renamed the Queen Elizabeth Olympic Park and fully opened to public use in 2014. Complementing its iconic sporting architecture (much of which has been opened to public use) the park was thoughtfully designed with a diverse mix of wetland, woodland, meadow and other wildlife habitats as an environmentally fertile legacy for the future.

LONDON FOR CHILDREN

London is terrific for kids. Many of the city's museums – among the best in the world – are free and will fascinate all ages, with bundles of activities on offer, from storytelling at the National Gallery (p75) to arts and crafts workshops at the Victoria & Albert Museum (p95) and fun sleepovers at the British Museum (p103), Natural History Museum (p95), Science Museum (p95) and others. Theatre, dance and music performances are perfect for older kids and teens. Playgrounds and parks are ideal for relaxation or wearing the young tykes out. On top of that, city farms (see www.london-footprints.co.uk/visitfarms.htm) and the big galleries have activities for children. Ice rinks glisten across London in winter months, at Somerset House (p79), the Natural History Museum (p95), the Tower of London (p80), and Hampton Court Palace (p112). For the Hogwarts fan club, the Making of Harry Potter (Warner Bros studio tour; p223) is a short train trip away from Euston station.

All top-range hotels offer in-house babysitting services. Prices vary enormously from hotel to hotel, so ask the concierge about hourly rates. Get a babysitter or nanny at Greatcare(www.greatcare.co.uk), a site that provides all manner of childcare options.

Under-16s travel free on buses, under-11s travel free on the tube and under-5s go free on the trains.

ℹ EMIRATES AIR LINE CABLE CAR

Capable of ferrying 2400 people per hour across the Thames in either direction, the **Emirates Air Line** (www.emiratesairline.co.uk; adult/child single £4.40/2.30, return £8.80/4.60, with Oyster or Travelcard single £3.20/1.60, return £6.40/3.20; ⊘7am-9pm Mon-Fri, 8am-9pm Sat, 9am-9pm Sun Apr-Sep, closes 1hr earlier Oct-Mar; ▣ DLR Royal Victoria, ⊜North Greenwich) cable car staples together the Greenwich Peninsula and the Royal Docks in a five- to 10-minute journey.

Designed to help regenerate both sides of the river around each embarkation point, the UK's first urban cable car system has cabins every half minute; Oyster card and Travelcard holders nab discounts for journeys, which are bike-friendly, too.

Arriving at Royal Docks, you can hop on the DLR at Royal Victoria DLR station, while in Greenwich, the underground interchange is with North Greenwich station. Open return tickets (£10) can be used any time on the same day and include entry to the Emirates Aviation Experience.

The signature buildings are the sustainably-built **Olympic Stadium**, the uplifting **Aquatics Centre** (now open to swimmers of all abilities), the cutting-edge **Lee Valley VeloPark** (☑0845 6770 603; ⊘9am-10pm), with cycling sessions now bookable, and the **Copper Box Arena**, an indoor venue for sports and concerts. The twisted, abstract tangle of metal overlooking everything is the **ArcelorMittal Orbit** (www.arcelormittalorbit.com; Queen Elizabeth Olympic Park, E20; adult/child £15/7; ⊘10am-6pm Apr-Sep, to 4pm Oct-Mar; ⊜Stratford), a 115m-high observation tower that opened during the games. Panoramic views of the park can also be had from the **View Tube** (www.theviewtube.co.uk; The Greenway; ⊘9am-5pm; ▣DLR Pudding Mill Lane) on the Greenway. Right alongside the park, Westfield Stratford City (p144) is Europe's largest urban shopping mall.

House Mill   HISTORIC BUILDING
(www.housemill.org.uk; Three Mill Lane, E3; adult/child £3/free; ⊘11am-4pm Sun May-Oct, 1st Sun only Mar, Apr & Dec; ⊜Bromley-by-Bow) One of two remaining mills from a trio that once stood on this small island in the River Lea, House Mill (1776) operated as a sluice tidal mill, grinding grain for a nearby distillery until 1941. Tours, which run according to demand and last about 45 minutes, take visitors to all four floors of the mill.

Crystal   MUSEUM
(One Siemens Brothers Way, Royal Victoria Docks, E16; adult/child £8/free; ⊘10am-5pm Tue-Fri, to 7pm Sat & Sun; ▣DLR Royal Victoria, cable car Emirates Royal Docks) Housed in a dramatically modern structure, this creative, highly interactive and thoroughly engaging Siemens-sponsored exhibition focuses on urban sustainability and the pressures facing the modern city, from water to energy consumption, transport needs and beyond. Engaging for both adults and youngsters, you can tie it in with the Emirates Air Line cable car journey across the river from North Greenwich. The ticket includes a complimentary return within two weeks.

⊙ Greenwich

Greenwich (*gren*-itch) straddles the hemispheres and the ages, retaining its own sense of identity based on historic associations with the sea and science and an extraordinary cluster of buildings that have earned 'Maritime Greenwich' a Unesco World Heritage listing.

Greenwich is easily reached on the DLR or via train from London Bridge. **Thames River Services** (www.thamesriverservices.co.uk; adult/child single £12.25/6.10, return £16/8) has boats departing from Westminster Pier (one hour, every 40 minutes), or alternatively take the cheaper **Thames Clippers** (www.thamesclippers.com; adult/child £6.50/3.25) ferry.

★**Old Royal Naval College**   HISTORIC BUILDING
(www.oldroyalnavalcollege.org; 2 Cutty Sark Gardens, SE10; ⊘10am-5pm, grounds 8am-6pm; ▣DLR Cutty Sark) **FREE** Designed by Wren, the Old Royal Naval College is a magnificent example of monumental classical architecture. Parts are now used by the University of Greenwich and Trinity College of Music, but you can visit the **chapel** and the extraordinary **Painted Hall**, which took artist Sir James Thornhill 19 years to complete. The complex was built on the site of the 15th-century Palace of Placentia, the birthplace of Henry VIII and Elizabeth I.

The Tudor connection, along with Greenwich's industrial and maritime history, is explored in the **Discover Greenwich** (www.ornc. urg, Pepys Building, King William Walk; ⊙10am-5pm) **FREE** centre. The tourist office is based here, along with a cafe/restaurant and microbrewery. Yeomen-led tours of the complex leave at 2pm daily, taking in areas not otherwise open to the public (£6, 90 minutes).

★ **National Maritime Museum**   MUSEUM
(www.rmg.co.uk/national-maritime-museum; Romney Rd, SE10; ⊙10am-5pm, Sammy Ofer Wing & ground fl galleries to 8pm Thu; ℝDLR Cutty Sark) **FREE** With its recently opened **Sammy Ofer Wing**, the National Maritime Museum houses a splendid collection of nautical paraphernalia recounting Britain's brine-soaked seafaring history. Exhibits range from **Miss Britain III** (the first boat to top 100mph on open water) from 1933, the 19m-long **golden state barge** built in 1732 for Frederick, Prince of Wales, humdingers such as **Cook's journals** and **Nelson's uniform**, complete with bullet hole, and interactive educational displays. Tours depart from the ship's propeller at noon, 1pm and 3pm.

★ **Royal Observatory**   HISTORIC BUILDING
(www.rmg.co.uk; Greenwich Park, SE10; adult/child £7.70/3.60; ⊙10am-5pm; ℝDLR Cutty Sark, ℝDLR Greenwich, ℝGreenwich) Affording sublime views of London from a hilltop position within idyllic Greenwich Park, the Royal Observatory was commisioned in 1675 by Charles II to help solve the riddle of longitude. Success was confirmed in 1884 when Greenwich was designated as the prime meridian of the world, and Greenwich Mean Time (GMT) became the universal measurement of standard time.

In the north of the observatory is lovely **Flamsteed House** and the **Meridian Courtyard** (where you can stand with your feet straddling the western and eastern hemispheres); admission is by ticket. The southern half contains the highly informative (and free) **Astronomy Centre** and the **Peter Harrison Planetarium** (adult/child £6.50/4.50).

Queen's House   HISTORIC BUILDING
(☑020-8858 4422; www.rmg.co.uk/queens-house; Romney Rd, SE10; ⊙10am-5pm; ℝGreenwich or DLR Cutty Sark) **FREE** The elegant Queen's House is a Palladian peach, designed by Inigo Jones in 1616 for the wife of Charles I. Don't miss the ceremonial **Great Hall** or the delightful helix-shaped **Tulip Staircase**.

Cutty Sark   SHIP
(www.rmg.co.uk/cuttysark; King William Walk SE10; adult/child £13.50/7; ⊙10am-5pm; ℝDLR Cutty Sark) The last of the great clipper ships to sail between China and England in the 19th century has reopened after a serious fire almost scuttled her forever. The vessel has been raised to allow visitors to view the ship from below.

O2   NOTABLE BUILDING
(www.theo2.co.uk; Peninsula Sq, SE10; ⊖North Greenwich) The 380m-wide circular O2 cost £750 million to build. Once *the* definitive white elephant, it finally found a winning direction as a multipurpose venue hosting big-ticket concerts, sporting events (it was the gymnastics and basketball venue for the London Olympics) and blockbuster exhibitions. There are dozens of bars and restaurants inside. The O2 is located on the Greenwich Peninsula, just 10 minutes by bus from Greenwich itself.

⊙ Hampstead & Highgate

These quaint and well-heeled villages, perched on hills north of London, are home to a litany of A- and B-list celebrities.

Hampstead Heath   PARK
(ℝ Gospel Oak, Hampstead Heath, ⊖Hampstead) With its 320 hectares of rolling meadows and wild woodlands, Hampstead Heath is a million miles away – approximately four, actually – from central London. A walk up **Parliament Hill** affords one of the most spectacular views of the city, and on summer days it's picnic heaven. Also bewilderingly popular are the murky brown waters of the single-sex and mixed bathing ponds.

WORTH A TRIP

ESTORICK COLLECTION OF MODERN ITALIAN ART

The outstanding concentration of art in the **Estorick Collection of Modern Italian Art** (www.estorickcollection. com; 39a Canonbury Sq, N1; adult/child £5/free; ⊙11am-6pm Wed-Sat, noon-5pm Sun; ⊖Highbury & Islington) in Islington boasts one of the world's leading collections of futurist painting, from such dazzling talents as Umberto Boccioni, Giacomo Balla and Gino Severini.

LONDON SIGHTS

LONDON SIGHTS

ABBEY ROAD
....

Beatles aficionados can't possibly visit London without making a pilgrimage to **Abbey Road Studios** (www.abbeyroad.com; 3 Abbey Rd, NW8) in St John's Wood. The fence outside is covered with decades of fans' graffiti. Stop-start local traffic is long accustomed to groups of tourists lining up on the zebra crossing to reenact the cover of the fab four's 1969 masterpiece and penultimate swan song *Abbey Road*. In 2010, the crossing was rewarded with Grade II listed status.

For an entertaining live view of the crossing and highlights of the day's action, check out the fun webcam at www.abbeyroad.com/crossing. To get here, take the tube to St John's Wood, cross the road, follow Grove End Rd to its end and turn right.

Kenwood House HISTORIC BUILDING
(www.english-heritage.org.uk; Hampstead Lane, NW3; ⊘10am-5pm; ⊠Gospel Oak, Hampstead Heath) **FREE** Kenwood House is a magnificent neoclassical mansion (1764) on the northern side of Hampstead Heath that houses a collection of paintings by English and European masters including Rembrandt, Vermeer, Turner and Gainsborough.

Highgate Cemetery CEMETERY
(www.highgatecemetery.org; Swain's Lane, N6; East Cemetery adult/child £4/free; ⊘10am-4pm Mon-Fri, 11am-4pm Sat & Sun; ⊖Archway) A Gothic wonderland of shrouded urns, obelisks, broken columns, sleeping angels, classical tomb porticoes and overgrown graves, this boneyard is a sublime Victorian Valhalla. On the eastern side you can pay your respects to the graves of Karl Marx and George Eliot (Mary Ann Evans), but the highlight is the overgrown **West Cemetery**, where a maze of winding paths leads to the Circle of Lebanon, rings of tombs flanking a circular path and topped with a majestic cedar of Lebanon tree.

Admission to the West Cemetery is by tour only (adult/child £12/6); bookings are essential for weekday tours. Tours of the **East Cemetery** take place on Saturdays at 2pm (adult/child £8/4). From Archway station, walk up Highgate Hill until you reach Waterlow Park on the left. Go through the park; the cemetery gates are opposite the exit.

⊙ Outside Central London

★**Kew Gardens** GARDENS
(www.kew.org; Kew Rd; adult/child £15/free; ⊘9.30am-6.30pm Apr-Aug, earlier closing Sep-Mar; ⊠Kew Pier, ⊠Kew Bridge, ⊖Kew Gardens) In 1759 botanists began rummaging around the world for specimens they could plant in the 3-hectare plot known as the Royal Botanic Gardens. They never stopped collecting, and the gardens, which have bloomed to 120 hectares, provide the most comprehensive botanical collection on earth. The beautiful gardens are now recognised as a Unesco World Heritage Site.

No worries if you don't know your golden slipper orchid from your fengoky or your quiver tree from your alang-alang, a visit to Kew is a journey of discovery for everyone. You can easily spend a whole day wandering around, but if you're pressed for time, the Kew Explorer (adult/child £2/1) is a hop-on/hop-off road train that rolls from Victoria Gate, visiting the gardens' main sights.

Highlights include the enormous early Victorian **Palm House**, a hothouse of metal and curved sheets of glass; the impressive **Princess of Wales Conservatory**; the red-brick, 1631 **Kew Palace** (www.hrp.org.uk/kewpalace; ⊘9.30am-5.30pm Apr-Sep), formerly King George III's country retreat; the celebrated **Great Pagoda** designed by William Chambers in 1762; the **Temperate House**, the world's largest ornamental glasshouse; and the fun **Rhizotron and Xstrata Treetop Walkway**, 18m up in the air.

Several fabulous vistas (**Cedar Vista**, **Syon Vista** and **Pagoda Vista**) are channelled by trees from vantage points within Kew Gardens. The idyllic, thatched **Queen Charlotte's Cottage** (⊘11am-4pm Sat & Sun Apr-Sep) in the southwest of the gardens was popular with 'mad' George III and his wife; the nearby carpets of bluebells are a drawcard in spring. The **Orangery** near Kew Palace contains a restaurant, cafe and shop.

The gardens are easily reached by tube, but you might prefer to cruise by riverboat from the **Westminster Passenger Services Association** (Map p68; ☑020-7930 2062; www.wpsa.co.uk; return adult/child to Kew Gardens £18/9), which runs several daily boats from April to October from Westminster Pier (90 minutes).

★**Hampton Court Palace** PALACE
(www.hrp.org.uk/HamptonCourtPalace; adult/child £18.20/9.10; ⊘10am-6pm Apr-Oct, to 4.30pm Nov-Mar; ⊠Hampton Court Palace, ⊠Hampton Court) Built by Cardinal Thomas Wolsey in 1514

but coaxed from him by Henry VIII just before Wolsey (as chancellor) fell from favour, Hampton Court Palace is England's largest and grandest Tudor structure. It was already one of the most sophisticated palaces in Europe when, in the 17th century, Wren was commissioned to build an extension. The result is a beautiful blend of Tudor and 'restrained baroque' architecture.

Take a themed tour led by costumed historians or, if you're in a rush, visit the highlights: **Henry VIII's State Apartments**, including the **Great Hall** with its spectacular hammer-beamed roof; the **Tudor Kitchens**, staffed by 'servants'; and the **Wolsey Rooms**. You could easily spend a day exploring the palace and its 24 hectares of riverside gardens, especially if you get lost in the 300-year-old maze.

Hampton Court is 13 miles southwest of central London and is easily reached by train from Waterloo. Alternatively, the riverboats that head from Westminster to Kew continue here (return adult/child £22.50/11.25, three hours).

Richmond Park PARK
(⊗ 7am-dusk; ⊜Richmond) London's wildest park – and the largest urban parkland in Europe – spans more than 1000 hectares and is home to all sorts of wildlife, most notably herds of red and fallow deer.

To get there from Richmond tube station, turn left along George St then left at the fork that leads up Richmond Hill.

Strawberry Hill HISTORIC BUILDING
(www.strawberryhillhouse.org.uk; 268 Waldegrave Rd, TW1; adult/child £10.80/free; ⊗ house 2-6pm Mon-Wed, noon-6pm Sat & Sun Mar-Oct, garden 10am-6pm daily; ⊜Richmond, then bus R68) With its snow-white walls and Gothic turrets, this fantastical and totally restored 18th-century creation in Twickenham is the whimsical work of art historian, author and politician Horace Walpole. Studded with elaborate stained glass, the building reaches its astonishing apogee in the gallery, with its magnificent papier-mâché ceiling. For the full magic, join a twilight tour (£20).

LONDON SIGHTS

LOCAL KNOWLEDGE

IAN FRANKLIN: HAMPTON COURT PALACE STATE APARTMENT WARDER

An enthusiastic communicator, Ian Franklin has been a State Apartment Warder at Hampton Court Palace for 17 years.

Costumed Guides & State Apartment Warders Trained historians, our interpreters wear extremely accurate representations of period clothes, bringing historic scenarios to life. Warders, such as myself, are found in most of the rooms and can answer questions face to face in a very personal way.

Fascinating Palace Facts The Palace is home to the largest indigenous spider in England. *Tegenaria parietina*, nick-named the Cardinal Spider after Cardinal Wolsey, can measure up to 20cm from leg-tip to leg-tip. You probably won't encounter one, but their webs are often seen in places like the Tudor Kitchens and King's Stairs. If you don't like spiders – watch out!

And another snippet – Jane Seymour, Henry VIII's third wife, died at Hampton Court Palace. It is said that as there was no burial place ready, her body was laid out in the Chapel Royal. To prevent Jane's body decomposing too quickly, her internal organs were removed, and her heart placed in a casket and buried beneath the Chapel altar. There's no evidence the casket was ever dug up, so the heart could still be buried at the palace.

Favourite Part of the Palace I love the Chapel Royal. As it's still used as a place of worship, and visitors are welcome to attend Sunday services, it gives a sense of life and community to the palace.

Recommended Palace Events Check out the special cooking days in the Tudor Kitchens on the first full weekend in any month, and at Easter and Christmas. Where else in the UK can you regularly see cooks creating Tudor dishes, or meals from period recipes, in the greatest surviving Tudor Kitchens in the country?

Spooky Treats Our famous ghost tours, which run from Halloween to March, allow visitors to enter the palace after dark, and take in the most 'haunted' areas. You can visit the infamous 'Haunted Galley' in almost total darkness!

Hampton Court Palace

A DAY AT THE PALACE

With so much to explore and seemingly infinite gardens, it can be tricky knowing where to begin. It helps to understand how the palace has grown over the centuries and how successive royal occupants embellished Hampton Court to suit their purposes and to reflect the style of the time.

As soon as he had his royal hands upon the palace from Cardinal Thomas Wolsey, Henry VIII began expanding the **Tudor architecture** ❶, adding the **Great Hall** ❷, the exquisite **Chapel Royal** ❸, the opulent Great Watching Chamber and the gigantic **kitchens** ❹. By 1540 it had become one of the grandest and most sophisticated palaces in Europe. James I kept things ticking over, while Charles I added a new tennis court and did some serious art-collecting – including acquiring **Mantegna's Triumphs of Caesar** ❺.

❼ The Maze
Around 150m north of the main bulding
Created from hornbeam and yew and planted in around 1700, the maze covers a third of an acre within the famous palace gardens. A must-see conclusion to Hampton Court, the maze takes the average visitor about 20 minutes to reach the centre.

Tudor Architecture
Dating to 1515, the heart of the palace serves as one of the finest examples of Tudor architecture in the nation. Cardinal Thomas Wolsey was responsible for transforming what was originally a grand medieval manor house into a stunning Tudor palace.

Tudor Kitchens
These vast kitchens were the engine room of the palace. With a staff of 200 people, there were six spit-rack-equipped fireplaces, with roast meat always on the menu (to the tune of 8200 sheep and 1240 oxen per year).

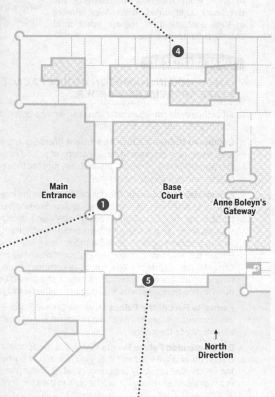

Main Entrance

Base Court

Anne Boleyn's Gateway

↑ **North Direction**

The Triumphs of Caesar
Acquired by Charles I in 1629, Italian artist Andrea Mantegna's nine-painting series *The Triumphs of Caesar* portray Julius Caesar returning to Rome in a triumphant procession, accompanied by the spoils of war.

After the Civil War, puritanical Oliver Cromwell warmed to his own regal proclivities, spending weekends in the comfort of the former Queen's bedroom and selling off Charles I's art collection. In the late 17th century, William and Mary employed Sir Christopher Wren for baroque extensions, chiefly the William III Apartments, reached by the **King's Staircase** ❻. William III also commissioned the world-famous **maze** ❼.

TOP TIPS

» Ask one of the red-tunic-garbed warders for anecdotes and information.

» Tag along with a themed tour led by costumed historians or join a Salacious Gossip Tour for scandalous royal stories.

» Grab one of the audio tours from the Information Centre.

The Great Hall
This grand dining hall is the defining room of the palace, displaying what is considered England's finest hammer-beam roof, 16th-century Flemish tapestries telling the story of Abraham, and some exquisite stained-glass windows.

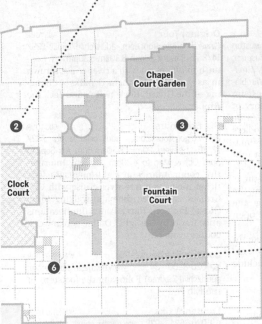

Chapel Court Garden

Clock Court

Fountain Court

Chapel Royal
The blue-and-gold vaulted ceiling was originally intended for Christ Church, Oxford, but was installed here instead; the 18th-century oak reredos was carved by Grinling Gibbons. Books on display include a 1611 1st edition of the King James Bible, printed by Robert Barker.

The King's Staircase
One of five rooms at the palace painted by Antonio Verrio and a suitably bombastic prelude to the King's Apartments, the overblown King's Staircase adulates William III by elevating him above a cohort of Roman emperors.

OPEN FOR INSPECTION
The palace was opened to the public by Queen Victoria in 1838.

POUND SAVERS

As many of London's very best sights are free, you can easily spend a busy week without paying much on admission charges. However, if you're hanging around for longer and have particular attractions that you're keen to see, there are options for saving a few pounds.

London Pass (www.londonpass.com; 1/2/3/6 days £49/68/81/108) The London Pass is a smart card that gains you fast-track entry to over 60 different attractions, including pricier ones such as the Tower of London and St Paul's Cathedral. You'd have to be racing around frantically to get real value from a one-day pass, but you could conceivably save quite a bit with the two- or three-day version.

Passes can be booked online and either shipped or collected from the **London Pass Redemption Desk** (Map p76; 11a Charing Cross Rd, WC2; ⊘10am-4.30pm; ⊜ Leicester Square) opposite the Garrick Theatre. It also sells a version with a preloaded Transport For London (TFL) travel pass, but it's cheaper to buy this separately.

Historic Royal Palaces (www.hrp.org.uk; individual/joint membership £43/65) If you're a royalty buff, taking out an annual membership to the Historic Royal Palaces allows you to jump the queues and visit the Tower of London, Kensington Palace, Banqueting House, Kew Palace and Hampton Court Palace as often as you like.

If you were intending to visit all five anyway, membership will save you £32 (£87 for a couple). There can be a lengthy wait for membership cards, but temporary cards are issued immediately.

Wimbledon Lawn Tennis Museum   MUSEUM
(⏾ 020-89466131; www.wimbledon.com/museum; Gate 4, Church Rd, SW19; adult/child £12/7, museum & tour £22/13; ⊘10am-5pm; ⊠Wimbledon, then bus 93, ⊜Wimbledon) This museum in leafy Wimbledon details the history of tennis – from its French precursor *Jeu de paume* to the supersonic serves of today's champions. It's a state-of-the-art presentation, with plenty of video clips and a projection of John McEnroe in the dressing room at Wimbledon, but the highlight is the chance to see Centre Court from the **360-degree viewing box**. During the championships, the museum is only open to ticket holders.

Regular tours of Wimbledon take in Centre Court, the No 1 Court and other areas of the All England Club, and include access to the museum.

⌲ Tours

One of the best ways to orient yourself when you first arrive in London is with a 24-hour hop-on/hop-off pass for the double-decker bus tours. The buses loop around interconnecting routes throughout the day, providing commentaries as they go, and the price includes a river cruise and three walking tours. Save a few pounds by booking online.

Original Tour   BUS TOUR
(www.theoriginaltour.com; adult/child/family £29/14/86; ⊘every 20min 8.30am-5.30pm) A hop-on/hop-off option with a river cruise thrown in as well as three themed walks – Changing of the Guard, Rock 'n' Roll and Jack the Ripper.

Big Bus Tours   BUS TOUR
(www.bigbustours.com; adult/child/family £32/12/76; ⊘every 20min 8.30am-6pm Apr-Sep, to 5pm Oct & Mar, to 4.30pm Nov-Feb) Informative commentaries in eight languages. The ticket includes a free river cruise with City Cruises and three thematic walking tours (Royal London, Harry Potter film locations and Ghosts by Gaslight). Online booking discounts available.

London Beatles Walks   WALKING TOUR
(⏾020-8200 3438; www.beatlesinlondon.com; adult/child £9/free) Following the footsteps of the Fab Four.

London Walks   WALKING TOUR
(⏾020-7624 3978; www.walks.com; adult/child £9/free) Harry Potter tours, ghost walks and the ever-popular Jack the Ripper tours.

London Mystery Walks   WALKING TOUR
(⏾07957 388280; www.tourguides.org.uk; adult/child/family £10/9/25) Tour Jack the Ripper's old haunts at 7pm on Monday, Wednesday and Friday. You must book in advance.

Greenwich Guided Walks WALKING TOUR
(☑07575 772298; www.greenwichtours.co.uk;
adult/child £8/free, ☻12.15pm & 2.15pm) Guided
tours of Greenwich's sights, leaving twice daily from the tourist office (no need to book).

City Cruises BOAT TOUR
(Map p68; ☑020-7740 0400; www.citycruises.
com; single/return from £9.75/13, day pass £18)
Ferry service between Westminster, Waterloo, Tower and Greenwich piers.

Capital Taxi Tours TAXI TOUR
(☑020-8590 3621; www.capitaltaxitours.co.uk; 2hr
daytime tour per taxi £165, 2½hr evening tour per
taxi £235) Takes up to six people on a variety of tours with Blue Badge, City of London and City of Westminster registered guides/drivers, cheeky Cockney Cabbie option and foreign language availability.

London Bicycle Tour CYCLING TOUR
(Map p92; ☑020-7928 6838; www.londonbicycle.
com; 1a Gabriel's Wharf, 56 Upper Ground, SE1; tour
incl bike from £23.95; ☻Waterloo) Themed 2½-
to 3½-hour tours of the 'West End', 'East', 'Central' or 'Night Tour'.

London Duck Tours ADVENTURE TOUR
(Map p92; ☑020-7928 3132; www.londonduck-
tours.co.uk; County Hall, SE1; adult/child £24/16;
☻Waterloo) Cruise the streets in the same sort of amphibious landing craft used on D-Day before making a dramatic plunge into the Thames.

✴✴ Festivals & Events

Chinese New Year CULTURE
Late January or early February sees Chinatown snap, crackle and pop with fireworks, a colourful street parade, lion dances and dim sum aplenty.

University Boat Race ROWING
(www.theboatrace.org) A grudge match on the Thames held annually since 1829 between the rowing crews of Oxford and Cambridge Universities. Late March.

Virgin Money London Marathon MARATHON
(www.virginmoneylondonmarathon.com) Up to half a million spectators applaud whippet-thin champions and outlandishly clad greenhorns charging down London's streets in late April.

Chelsea Flower Show HORTICULTURE
(www.rhs.org.uk/chelsea; Royal Hospital Chelsea; admission from £23) Held in May, arguably the world's most renowned horticultural show attracts green fingers from all corners.

Trooping the Colour PAGEANT
Celebrating the Queen's official birthday (in June), this ceremonial procession of troops, marching along the Mall for their monarch's inspection, is a pageantry overload.

Field Day MUSIC
(www.fielddayfestivals.com; Victoria Park; tickets £29.50-59.50; ☻Mile End) Fabulously popular indie and alternative music festival, held over a June weekend in Victoria Park.

Royal Academy Summer Exhibition ART
(www.royalacademy.org.uk; adult/child £9.50/5)
Running from mid-June to mid-August, this is an annual showcase of works submitted by artists from all over Britain.

Meltdown Festival MUSIC
(www.southbankcentre.co.uk) The Southbank Centre hands over the curatorial reigns to a legend of contemporary music (such as Nick Cave, Morrissey or Patti Smith) to pull together a program of concerts, talks and films in late June.

**Wimbledon Lawn
Tennis Championships** TENNIS
(www.wimbledon.com) Held at the end of June, the world's most prestigious tennis event is as much about strawberries, cream and tradition as supersonic aces.

Wireless MUSIC
(www.wirelessfestival.co.uk; Queen Elizabeth Olympic Park, E20) One of London's flagship music festivals, with an emphasis on R&B, Wireless moved from Hyde Park to its new home at the Queen Elizabeth Olympic Park in 2013. Usually held in July. Book in advance.

Pride GAY & LESBIAN
(www.prideinlondon.org) The big event on the LGBT calendar; usually held in June or July.

Lovebox MUSIC
(www.loveboxfestival.com; Victoria Park, E9) A popular contribution to the summer music festival circuit, held in Victoria Park in mid-July.

Notting Hill Carnival CARNIVAL
(www.thenottinghillcarnival.com) Held over two days in August, Europe's largest (and London's most vibrant outdoor carnival) sees the Caribbean community showing the city how to party.

🛏 Sleeping

When it comes to finding a place for a good night's kip, London is one of the most expensive places in the world. 'Budget' is pretty much anything below £100 per night for a double; at the top end, how does an £18,000-per-night suite on Hyde Park Corner sound? Double rooms ranging between £90 and £180 per night are considered midrange; more expensive options fall into the top-end category.

London, however, has a delightful selection of characterful hotels, whether brimming with history, zany modern decor or all-stops-out charm. Most of the ritzier places offer substantial discounts on the weekends, for advance bookings and at quieter times.

Public transport is good, so you don't need to be sleeping at Buckingham Palace to be at the heart of things.

Budget accommodation is scattered about, with good options in Bloomsbury and St Pancras, Earl's Court and the South Bank. For something a little nicer, check out Bayswater, Notting Hill Gate or Belgravia. To splash some cash, consider the West End, Kensington and Knightsbridge. Most budget and midrange places offer free wi-fi (top-end properties may charge).

Prices listed here include 20% VAT, when it applies.

🛏 West End

Like in Monopoly, land on a Mayfair hotel and you may have to sell your house, or at least remortgage. This is the heart of the action, and a couple of hostels cater for would-be Soho hipsters of more modest means.

YHA London Oxford Street   HOSTEL £
(Map p76; ☑ 020-7734 1618; www.yha.org.uk; 14 Noel St, W1; dm/tw from £18/46; @ 🛜; ⊖ Oxford Circus) The most central of the YHA London fold, this hostel is a tip-top choice for its location, bright and colourful shared facilities, cleanliness and manageable 104-bed size. There are doubles, twins and three/four-bed dorms, with a charge for wi-fi.

Dean Street Townhouse   BOUTIQUE HOTEL ££
(Map p76; ☑ 020-7434 1775; www.deanstreettownhouse.com; 69-71 Dean St, W1; r £140-310; ❋ 🛜; ⊖ Tottenham Court Rd) This Soho gem of a 39-bedroom boutique hotel enjoys a delightful boudoir atmosphere with choice rooms – everything faultlessly in its place – from 'tiny' options upwards.

Seven Dials Hotel   HOTEL ££
(Map p76; ☑ 020-7240 0823; www.sevendialshotellondon.com; 7 Monmouth St, WC2; s/d/tr/q £95/105/130/150; 🛜; ⊖ Covent Garden, Tottenham Court Rd) The clean, comfortable and affordable Seven Dials offers a highly central location and rooms at the front looking out over delightful Monmouth St and quieter rooms at the back, with less of a view.

★ Haymarket Hotel   HOTEL £££
(Map p76; ☑ 020-7470 4000; www.haymarkethotel.com; 1 Suffolk Pl, off Haymarket, SW1; r £325-425, ste from £505; ❋ 🛜 ✖; ⊖ Piccadilly Circus) An exquisite place to hang your well-trimmed hat, the Tim and Kit Kemp–designed Haymarket is a super-stylish and eye-catching treat, with a knockout swimming pool bathed in serene mood lighting.

Hazlitt's   HISTORIC HOTEL £££
(Map p76; ☑ 020-7434 1771; www.hazlittshotel.com; 6 Frith St, W1; s £216, d/ste from £288/660; ❋ 🛜; ⊖ Tottenham Court Rd) Envelop yourself in Georgian finery at this lovely 1718 house and journey back to the days of four-poster beds, claw-foot baths and panelled walls. Each of the 30 individually decorated rooms overflows with Georgian antiques and days-gone-by charm (plus up-to-the-minute mod cons).

One Aldwych   HOTEL £££
(Map p76; ☑ 020-7300 1000; www.onealdwych.co.uk; 1 Aldwych, WC2; d £255-470, ste £465-1005; ❋ 🛜 ✖; ⊖ Covent Garden) Check in for a tremendous presentation of granite bathrooms, modern art, a majestic bar and restaurant, and a long, chlorine-free swimming pool (with underwater music). The circular suites serve up fabulous views of the Strand and Waterloo Bridge.

Brown's Hotel   HOTEL £££
(Map p76; ☑ 020-7493 6020; www.brownshotel.com; 30 Albemarle St, W1; r/ste from £460/2000; ❋ 🛜; ⊖ Green Park) A stunning five-star choice, this 117-room hotel dates to 1837 when 11 houses were joined together; lovely old-world traditional features (Edwardian oak panelling, working fireplaces) complement individually decorated rooms.

Covent Garden Hotel   BOUTIQUE HOTEL £££
(Map p76; ☑ 020-7806 1000; www.coventgardenhotel.co.uk; 10 Monmouth St, WC2; d/ste from £310/490; ❋ 🛜; ⊖ Covent Garden) Housed in an old French hospital, this well-positioned 58-room Firmdale hotel concocts a classy display of antiques, bright and vibrant

fabrics, quirky bric-a-brac and a winning bar-restaurant.

🛏 The City

It bristles with bankers during the week, but you can often net considerable bargains in the City come weekends.

London St Paul's YHA   HOSTEL £
(Map p80; ☑ 020-7236 4965; www.yha.org.uk; 36 Carter Lane, EC4; dm £17-25, d £40-50; @ 🛜; 🚇 St Paul's) Perfectly placed for hoovering up the sights of the City and the South Bank, this 213-bed hostel in a heritage-listed building is just down the road from St Paul's (the bells, the bells!). There's a licensed cafeteria, but no self-catering, no lift and a seven-night maximum stay.

Hotel Indigo Tower Hill   BOUTIQUE HOTEL ££
(Map p80; ☑ 0843 208 7007; www.hotelindigo.com/lontowerhill; 142 Minories, EC3; r weekend/weekday from £100/200; ❄ 🛜; 🚇 Aldgate) The 46 differently styled rooms at this crisp and affordable hotel north of the Tower of London feature four-poster beds and iPod docking stations.

Andaz Liverpool Street   HOTEL ££
(Map p80; ☑ 020-7961 1234; www.london.liverpool-street.andaz.com; 40 Liverpool St, EC2; r weekend/weekday from £145/290; ❄ 🛜; 🚇 Liverpool St) The former Great Eastern Hotel is now the London flagship for Hyatt's youth-focused Andaz chain. There's no reception here, just black-clad staff who check you in on mini laptops. Rooms are a little generic, but have free juice, snacks and wi-fi.

🛏 South Bank

Immediately on the south side of the Thames is a fab perch for reaching the central sights, while gauging the personality of South London.

St Christopher's Village   HOSTEL £
(Map p92; ☑ 020-7939 9710; www.st-christophers.co.uk; 163 Borough High St, SE1; dm/r from £14/62; @ 🛜; 🚇 London Bridge) The Village – a huge, up-for-it party hostel, with a hopping bar, roof terrace (plus bar), cinema and tons of beds – is the main hub of three locations on the same street. Dorms have four to 14 beds. The other locations are much smaller, quieter and, frankly, more pleasant. **St Christopher's Inn** (Map p92; 121 Borough High St, SE1) is above a very nice pub, while **Oasis** (Map p92; 59 Borough High St) is women-only.

★ Citizen M   BOUTIQUE HOTEL ££
(Map p92; ☑ 020-3519 1680; www.citizenm.com/london-bankside; 20 Lavington St, SE1; r £109-189; ❄ @ 🛜; 🚇 Southwark) Aimed squarely at young, trendy and Tate-going artsy travellers, this Dutch boutique hotel pulls out all the design stops (and rummages around to pull out a few more). Rooms are titchy, but have swish Samsung tablet–controlled mod-cons and free movies on tap. Space comes from the funky lounge area, conceived to hang around in.

New openings in Tower Hill and St Pauls are on the cards for 2014.

Shangri-La Hotel at the Shard   HOTEL £££
(Map p92; ☑ 020-7234 8000; www.shangri-la.com/london/shangrila; 31 St Thomas St, SE1; d/ste £575/3000; ❄ @ 🛜 ☀; 🚇 London Bridge, 🚇 London Bridge) The Shangri-La's first UK opening gives London its first five-star hotel south of the Thames and breathtaking views from the highest hotel in Western Europe, occupying levels 34 to 52 of the Shard. From the 35th floor sky lobby to the rooms, the Shangri-La concocts a stylish blend of Chinese aesthetics, Asian hospitality and sharp modernity.

The Shard's tapering shape puts the suites on lower floors, while each guestroom is slightly different in design. For drop-dead views, zip up to Gŏng on the 52nd floor, but book way ahead.

🛏 Pimlico & Belgravia

Lime Tree Hotel   B&B ££
(Map p98; ☑ 020-7730 8191; www.limetreehotel.co.uk; 135-137 Ebury St, SW1; s/tr/f £110/205/225, d £165-205; @ 🛜; 🚇 Victoria) Family-run for over 40 years, this smartly renovated Georgian town-house hotel has a pleasant back garden to catch the late afternoon rays, while contemporary renovations and polite staff make it an appealing choice. No lift.

B+B Belgravia   B&B ££
(Map p98; ☑ 020-7259 8570; www.bb-belgravia.com; 64-66 Ebury St, SW1; s £89-120, d £100-140, apt £225; @ 🛜; 🚇 Victoria) This lovely place marries contemporary chic with Georgian elegance (and a pleasant courtyard garden out back). Rooms are neat and, although not very spacious, fine studio rooms with compact kitchens are along the road at No 82. No lift.

★ Goring   HOTEL £££
(Map p68; ☑ 020-7396 9000; www.thegoring.com; Beeston Place; r £575-4350; ❄ @ 🛜; 🚇 Victoria) Kate Middleton spent her last night as a

commoner in the Royal Suite here before joining the ranks of the Royal Family, propelling the Goring into an international media glare. Glistening with chandeliers and overseen by magnificent staff, this family-owned hotel is a supremely grand, albeit highly relaxed slice of England and Englishness.

🛏 Knightsbridge

Named after a bridge over the River Westbourne, Knightsbridge is where you'll find some of London's best-known department stores and some top hotels.

Levin Hotel　　　　HOTEL £££

(Map p98; ☑ 020-7589 6286; www.thelevinhotel.co.uk; 28 Basil St, SW3; r from £379; ✴☎; ☻Knightsbridge) As close as you can get to sleeping in Harrods, the 12-room Levin knows its market. Elegance and sophistication permeate this tiny hotel from top to toe, fashioning a highly personable choice in the heart of Knightsbridge.

🛏 Chelsea & Kensington

Well-turned out Chelsea and Kensington offer easy access to the museums, natty

Notting Hill & Bayswater

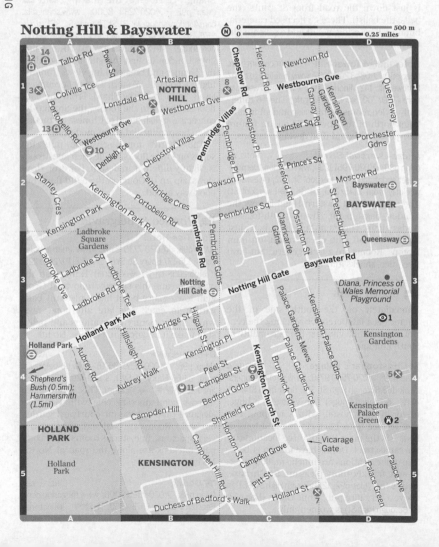

shopping choices and some of London's best-looking streets.

Meininger
HOSTEL £

(Map p98; 020-3318 1407; www.meininger-hostels.com; Baden Powell House, 65-67 Queen's Gate, SW7; dm £16-22, s/tw from £75/90; ✳@🛜; Gloucester Rd, South Kensington) In late-1950s Baden Powell House, opposite the Natural History Museum, this 48-room German-run 'city hostel and hotel' has spic-and-span rooms, most of which are dorms of between four and 12 beds, with pod-like showers, plus 11 private rooms all with bathroom. There's a bar in-house plus a great roof terrace.

Ampersand Hotel
BOUTIQUE HOTEL £££

(Map p98; 020-7589 5895; www.ampersandhotel.com; 10 Harrington Road; s & d £372; ✳@🛜; South Kensington) Housed in the old Norfolk Hotel building, the Ampersand boasts a light, fresh and bubbly feel: its (narrow) corridors and (stylish but smallish) rooms decorated with wallpaper designs celebrating the nearby arts and sciences of South Kensington's museums, a short stroll away. Apero, the cellar Mediterranean restaurant, is excellent.

Halkin by Como
HOTEL £££

(Map p68; 020-7333 1000; www.comohotels.com/thehalkin; Halkin St, SW1; r/ste from £390/540; ✳@🛜; Hyde Park Corner) With muted Asian influences, the chichi Halkin is for business travellers of a minimalist bent. Bedroom

---

Notting Hill & Bayswater

---

doors are hidden within curved wooden hallways, and the 41 swish rooms are filled with natural light, boasting cream walls, burlwood panelling and large all-marble bathrooms.

Number Sixteen
HOTEL £££

(Map p98; 020-7589 5232; www.firmdalehotels.com/hotels/london/number-sixteen; 16 Sumner Pl, SW7; s from £174, d £228-360; ✳@🛜; South Kensington) This is four properties in one delightful whole and a stunning place to stay, with 42 individually designed rooms, a cosy drawing room, a fully stocked library and a simply idyllic back garden.

Gore
HOTEL £££

(Map p98; 020-7584 6601; www.gorehotel.com; 190 Queen's Gate, SW7; r from £204; ✳@🛜; Gloucester Rd) With obliging staff in tails, twinkling chandeliers, walls crowded with portraits and prints, this superb 50-room hotel wallows in old England charm. Rolling Stones fans can celebrate the 1968 *Beggars Banquet* album launch in the bar; Judy Garland aficionados can sleep on her bed.

🛏 Earl's Court & Fulham

West London's Earl's Court is lively, cosmopolitan and so popular with travelling Antipodeans it's nicknamed Kangaroo Valley. There are no real sights, but it has inexpensive digs, an infectious holiday atmosphere and it's a short hop to the action. Further west and abutting the Thames, Fulham is the home of its famous riverside palace.

★ Barclay House
B&B ££

(020-7384 3390; www.barclayhouselondon.com; 21 Barclay Rd, SW6; r £110-125; @🛜; Fulham Broadway) The two dapper, thoroughly modern and comfy bedrooms in this charmingly shipshape Victorian house are a dream, from the Philippe Starck shower rooms, walnut furniture, new double-glazed sash windows and underfloor heating to the small, thoughtful details (fumble-free coat hangers, drawers packed with sewing kits and maps). A four-night minimum stay usually applies.

Rockwell
BOUTIQUE HOTEL ££

(020-7244 2000; www.therockwell.com; 181-183 Cromwell Rd, SW5; s/ste from £90/160, d £100-150; ✳@🛜; Earl's Court) With an understated-cool design ethos, things are muted, dapper and a tad minimalist at 'budget boutique' 40-room Rockwell. All rooms have a shower, the mezzanine suite is an absolute peach, and the three rooms (LG1, 2 and 3) onto the garden are fine. Rooms on Cromwell Rd are triple-glazed to stifle the roar.

Notting Hill, Bayswater & Paddington

Don't be fooled by Julia Roberts' and Hugh Grant's shenanigans, Notting Hill and the areas immediately north of Hyde Park are as shabby as they are chic, but they're still cool. There are some gorgeous gated squares surrounded by Georgian town houses, but the area is better exemplified by the Portobello Road Market and the Notting Hill Carnival.

Scruffy Paddington has lots of cheap hotels, with a major strip of unremarkable ones along Sussex Gardens that may be worth checking if you're short on options.

Tune Hotel HOTEL £

(☑020-7258 3140; www.tunehotels.com; 41 Praed St, W2; r £35-80; ❄@🛜; ⊖Paddington) This 137-room Malaysian-owned budget hotel offers super-duper rates for early birds who book way in advance. You get the bare bones – a twin or double room, the cheapest without window – and pay for add-ons (towel, wi-fi, TV) as you see fit, giving you the chance to simply put a roof over your head. You don't even get a wardrobe, just hangers.

★ La Suite West BOUTIQUE HOTEL £££

(☑020-7313 8484; www.lasuitewest.com; 41-51 Inverness Tce, W2; r £179-489; ❄@🛜; ⊖Bayswater) The black-and-white foyer of the Anouska Hempel–designed La Suite West – bare walls, a minimalist slit of a fireplace, an iPad for guests' use on a bare white marble reception desk – presages the OCD neatness of rooms hidden away down dark corridors. Think impeccable bathrooms, comfortable beds and warm service. Downstairs suites have gardens and individual gated entrances.

Bloomsbury & St Pancras

One step from the West End and crammed with Georgian town-house conversions, these are more affordable neighbourhoods. A stretch of lower-priced hotels runs along Gower St and on the pretty Cartwright Gardens crescent. While hardly a salubrious location, St Pancras is handy with some excellent budget options.

Clink78 HOSTEL £

(Map p106; ☑020-7183 9400; www.clinkhostels. com; 78 King's Cross Rd, WC1; dm/r from £10/25; @🛜; ⊖King's Cross St Pancras) If anyone can

think of a more right-on London place to stay than the courthouse where The Clash went on trial, please let us know. You can watch TV from the witness box or sleep in the converted cells, but the majority of the rooms are custom-built, quite comfortable and all were undergoing a repaint in 2014.

Generator HOSTEL £

(Map p106; ☑020-7388 7666; www.generatorhostels.com/london; 37 Tavistock Pl, WC1; dm/r from £12/50; @🛜; ⊖Russell Sq) Lashings of primary colours and shiny industrial metal are the hallmarks of this huge hostel. This former police barracks has over 850 beds, a bar that stays open until 2am and hosts themed parties, and a large eating area (but no kitchen). Dorm rooms have between four and 12 beds.

London St Pancras YHA HOSTEL £

(Map p106; ☑020-7388 9998; www.yha.org.uk; 79 Euston Rd, NW1; dm/r from £20/61; @🛜; ⊖King's Cross St Pancras) Renovations have converted this 185-bed hostel into a dependable central London choice – despite the busy road. Rooms range from private doubles to six-bed dorms; most have bathrooms. There's a good bar and cafe, but no kitchen.

Arosfa Hotel B&B ££

(Map p106; ☑020-7636 2115; www.arosfalondon. com; 83 Gower St, WC1; s/tr/f £78/145/175, d £130-145; 🛜; ⊖Goodge St) While the immaculately presented rooms are understated, Arosfa's guest lounge is blinged up with chandeliers and clear plastic chairs. Recent refurbishments have added en suites to all bedrooms, but they're tiny. There are a couple of family rooms; room 4 looks onto a small garden.

St Pancras Renaissance London Hotel LUXURY HOTEL £££

(Map p106; ☑020-7841 3540; www.marriott.co.uk; Euston Rd, NW1; d from £230; ❄🛜❄; ⊖King's Cross St Pancras) This iconic George Gilbert Scott–designed Gothic masterpiece is a red-brick Victorian fantasy, its lobby a magnificent conversion of the former train station taxi rank boasting a splendid double-staircase. Disappointingly, only 38 of the 245 rooms are in the original building; the rest are in an extension at the back and rather bland. You can toast the former booking office architecture from the 29m-long bar.

Rough Luxe BOUTIQUE HOTEL £££

(Map p106; ☑020-7837 5338; www.roughluxe.co. uk; 1 Birkenhead St, WC1; r £229-289; ❄🛜; ⊖King's Cross St Pancras) Half rough, half luxury goes the blurb, and the shabby/chic blend at this Grade-II listed property is compelling. Rooms treat you to the finest quality bed linen, eclectic art works cling to walls, you may get a free-standing copper bath and service is top-notch, but the wallpaper is fetchingly distressed and the 1970s TV doesn't quite work. A lovely patio chips in at the rear.

🛏 Clerkenwell & Farringdon

These now-fashionable districts just north of centre contain few echoes of the notorious 'rookeries' of the 19th century, where families were crammed into damp, foetid basements, living in possibly the worst conditions in the city's history (the London documented so vividly by Dickens).

The availability of accommodation hasn't kept pace with Clerkenwell's revival, but it's still a great area to hang your hat. The best pickings aren't exactly cheap.

★ Zetter Hotel & Townhouse   BOUTIQUE HOTEL £££

(Map p106; ☎ 020-7324 4444; www.thezetter.com; 86-88 Clerkenwell Rd, EC1; d from £235, studio £300-450; ❄ 🛜; ☯ Farringdon) ⏸ Guided by a sustainable ethos (water is supplied by its own bore hole), the 59-room Zetter is lovely, from the fine furnishings to the cutting-edge facilities. The rooftop studios with private patios and long views are the icing on this cake. **Bistrot Bruno Loubet** (Map p106; ☎ 020-7324 4455; www.bistrotbrunoloubet. com; mains £12-17; ⏲ 7.30-10.30am, noon-2.30pm & 6-10pm; 🛜) takes care of the fine food end.

Rookery   LUXURY HOTEL £££

(Map p80; ☎ 020-7336 0931; www.rookeryhotel. com; 12 Peter's Lane, Cowcross St, EC1; s £222, d £288-660, ste £474; ❄ 🛜; ☯ Farringdon) Named after London's notorious slums (Fagin's house in *Oliver Twist* was nearby), this antique-strewn charmer fashions an 18th-century ambience with none of the attendant grime or crime. For a bird's-eye view of St Paul's, book the two-storey Rook's Nest, but be warned: Fagin never had a lift.

🛏 Hoxton, Shoreditch & Spitalfields

Its rough-edged reputation well-smoothed by gentrification and the attentions of cash-loaded twenty-somethings, this is a knockout area to roost for some of London's best bars and nightlife.

★ Hoxton Hotel   HOTEL £

(Map p124; ☎ 020-7550 1000; www.hoxtonhotel. com; 81 Great Eastern St, EC2; r from £59; ❄ @ 🛜; ☯ Old St) A revolutionary pricing structure means that while all the rooms are identical, the hip Hoxton aims at constantly full occupancy. Book three months ahead (sign up on the website) and you can, if fortunate, nab a room for £1; you'll also need to book early for £49 to £69 deals.

The reasonably sized rooms have comfy beds, quality linen, a desk and fridge with complimentary bottled water and milk.

🛏 East End & Docklands

40 Winks   BOUTIQUE HOTEL ££

(☎ 020-7790 0259; www.40winks.org; 109 Mile End Rd, E1; s/d £110/185; 🛜; ☯ Stepney Green) This fun Queen Anne town house spills over with charm, eclectic style and whimsy, so much so that the two bedrooms (one single) are devoid of TVs. Fashionistas make this their first port of call, so book way ahead. Breakfast included.

🍴 Eating

Dining out in London has become so fashionable that you can hardly open a menu without banging into some celebrity chef or other. The range and quality of eating options has increased exponentially over the last few decades. Waves of immigrant flavours have deeply infused London cuisine and the expectations of modern-day Londoners are demanding.

In this section we have sieved out choice restaurants and cafes noted for their location, value for money, unique character, ambience and, of course, good food. Vegetarians needn't fret: London has a host of dedicated meat-free joints, while most others have veggie offerings.

🍴 West End

Mayfair, Soho and Covent Garden are the gastronomic heart of London, with a blinding choice of restaurants and cuisines at budgets to suit booze hounds, theatregoers or determined grazers.

★ Koya   NOODLES £

(Map p76; www.koya.co.uk; 49 Frith St, W1; mains £7-15; ⏲ noon-3pm & 5.30-10.30pm; ☯ Tottenham Court Rd, Leicester Sq) Koya's speciality is udon noodles (a type of thick wheat flour noodle) – devoured either with a cold sauce or

Hoxton, Shoreditch & Spitalfields

plunged into a variety of hot broths (from plain to duck or smoked mackerel). The noodles are divine and the simple wooden-table decor wholesome; arrive early or late to avoid queues.

Ceviche　　　　　　　　SOUTH AMERICAN £
(Map p76; www.cevicheuk.com; 17 Frith St, W1; mains £5-11; ☉noon-11.30pm Mon-Sat, to 10.30pm Sun; ☏; ☻Leicester Sq) A big hit with Soho gastronomes, this colourful, vibrant and fabuloso bodega is a must for lovers of Pe-

Hoxton, Shoreditch & Spitalfields

ruvian food, or those keen to kick-start an instant passion for *anticuchos* (grilled skewers), ceviche (citrus-marinated raw fish) and heart-warming shots of pisco.

Orchard   VEGETARIAN £
(Map p76; www.orchard-kitchen.co.uk; 11 Sicilian Ave, WC1; mains £6.50-7; ⊙8am-4pm Mon-Fri; ⚑; ⊜Holborn) Delightfully ensconced amid the charming buildings of Sicilian Ave, this homely eatery is a must for roving vegetarians. The traditional menu is a wholesome delight, from dandelion leaves, baby spinach and poached garlic milk to crushed turnips with pink peppercorns.

Roti Chai   INDIAN £
(Map p102; www.rotichai.com; 3 Portman Mews South, W1; mains from £5-12; ⊙noon-11pm Mon-Sat, 1-9pm Sun; ☎; ⊜Marble Arch) With a refreshing street kitchen menu from India, colourful Roti Chai cooks up a roaring trade in *bel puris*, spiced lamb *chapli kebabs*, *papri chaat* and railway lamb curries for upstairs snackers, with a more expansive dining room menu down below.

Wahaca   MEXICAN £
(Map p76; www.wahaca.com; 66 Chandos Pl, WC2; mains £7-10; ⊙noon-11pm; ☎; ⊜Covent Garden) ⚑ A branch of a chain peppering central London, this delightful cantina is a superb pitstop for Mexican street snacks (tacos, *tostadas, quesadillas*), more traditional mains such as marinated, grilled chicken or fish tacos, and a strong list of tequila and mezqal. Award-winning sustainable credentials to boot.

Nordic Bakery   SCANDINAVIAN £
(Map p76; www.nordicbakery.com; 14a Golden Sq, W1; snacks £4-5; ⊙8am-8pm Mon-Fri, 9am-7pm Sat, 10am-7pm Sun; ⊜Piccadilly Circus) As unfussy and stylish as you'd expect from the Scandinavians, this small cafe has bare wooden walls and uncomplicated Nordic snacks, such as sticky Finnish cinnamon buns, Scandinavian smoked-fish sandwiches, goat's cheese and beetroot salad, and oatmeal cookies.

Monmouth Coffee Company   CAFE £
(Map p76; www.monmouthcoffee.co.uk; 27 Monmouth St, WC2; pastry & cakes from £2.50; ⊙8am-6.30pm Mon-Sat; ⊜Tottenham Court Rd, Leicester Sq) There's an array of treats on the counter, but it's the coffee that's the star, nay god, here. Chat to a caffeinated stranger on one of the tight tables at the back, or grab a takeaway and slink off to a nearby lane for your fix. There's a second outlet in **Borough** (Map p92; 2 Park St, SE1; ⊙7.30am-6pm; underground rail London Bridge).

Hummus Bros   CAFE £
(Map p76; www.hbros.co.uk; 88 Wardour St, W1; mains £3.50-6.50; ⊙noon-10pm Mon-Sat, to 9pm Sun; ☎⚑; ⊜Piccadilly Circus) ⚑ Don't come here if you're chickpea-challenged, because this informal place is hummus heaven. It comes in small or regular bowls with a choice of meat or veggie toppings and a side of pita bread. Other branches can be found in **Holborn** (Map p106; 37-63 Southampton Row, W1; ⊙11am-9pm Mon-Fri, noon-5pm Sat; ☎⚑; ⊜Holborn) ⚑, **Cheapside** (Map p80; 128 Cheapside, EC2; ⊙7.30am-9pm Mon-Thu, to 4pm

Fri; 🔊🖊; 🚇 St Paul's) 🖊 or **Exmouth Market** (Map p106; 62 Exmouth Market; ⏰ 8am-9pm Mon-Sat; 🔊🖊) 🖊.

Fernandez & Wells CAFE £
(Map p76; www.fernandezandwells.com; 73 Beak St, W1; dishes £4.50-6; ⏰ 7.30am-6pm Mon-Fri, 9am-6pm Sat & Sun; 🚇 Piccadilly Circus) One of four central London branches of Fernandez & Wells, each occupying small, friendly and elegant spaces. Both the cafe and the espresso bar do sandwiches and first-rate coffee.

Mildreds VEGETARIAN £
(Map p76; www.mildreds.co.uk; 45 Lexington St, W1; mains £8-10.50; ⏰ noon-11pm Mon-Sat; 🔊🖊; 🚇 Oxford Circus, Piccadilly Circus) Ceaselessly busy, long-standing Mildred's seduces all manner of vegetarians, omnivores and detoxers, so don't be shy about sharing a table in the sky-lit dining room. Vegan and gluten-free options available.

Baozi Inn CHINESE £
(Map p76; 25 Newport Ct, WC2; mains £5-7.50; ⏰ noon-10.30pm; 🚇 Leicester Sq) Decorated vintage-style with kitsch communist pop, Baozi Inn serves authentic Beijing- and Chengdu-style street food, such as piquant *dan dan* noodles (a Sichuan staple) and *baozi* (steamed buns with stuffing), handmade daily.

⭐ **Brasserie Zédel** FRENCH ££
(Map p76; 🖊 020-7734 4888; www.brasseriezedel. com; 20 Sherwood St, W1; mains £8.75-30; ⏰ 11.30am-midnight Mon-Sat, to 11pm Sun; 🔊; 🚇 Piccadilly Circus) This triumphant basement brasserie in the grandly renovated art-deco ballroom of a former Piccadilly hotel offers excellent value set menus (£8.95/11.75 for two/three courses) and *plats du jour* (£12.95), all in a terrific setting.

Great Queen Street BRITISH ££
(Map p76; 🖊 020-7242 0622; 32 Great Queen St, WC2; mains £12-16; ⏰ noon-2.30pm & 6-10.30pm Mon-Sat, noon-3pm Sun; 🚇 Holborn) The menu at what is one of Covent Garden's best places to eat is seasonal (and changes daily), with an emphasis on quality, hearty dishes and good ingredients – with perennial delicious stews, roasts and simple fish dishes. The atmosphere is lively, with a small bar tucked below. Booking is essential.

National Dining Rooms BRITISH ££
(Map p76; 🖊 020-7747 2525; www.peytonandbyrne. co.uk; 1st fl, Sainsbury Wing, National Gallery, Trafalgar Sq, WC2; mains £15.50-20.50; ⏰ 10am-5.30pm Sat-Thu, to 8.30pm Fri; 🚇 Charing Cross) It's fitting that this acclaimed restaurant should celebrate British food, being in the National Gallery and overlooking Trafalgar Sq. For a much cheaper option with the same views, ambience, quality produce and excellent service, try a salad, pie or tart at the adjoining bakery.

Bocca di Lupo ITALIAN ££
(Map p76; 🖊 020-7734 2223; www.boccadilupo. com; 12 Archer St, W1; mains £8-27.50; ⏰ 12.30-3.45pm & 5.30-11pm Mon-Sat, to 9pm Sun; 🚇 Piccadilly Circus) Hidden on a dark Soho backstreet, Bocca radiates elegant sophistication, setting taste buds a quiver with a mouth-watering menu spanning Italy's culinary regions.

Barrafina SPANISH ££
(Map p76; 🖊 020-7813 8016; www.barrafina. co.uk; 54 Frith St, W1; tapas £5-18.50; ⏰ noon-3pm & 5-11pm Mon-Sat, 1-3.30pm & 5.30-10pm Sun; 🚇 Tottenham Court Road) The tapas here (bar seating) may not be as good value as in Spain, but they're standout. No reservations, so prepare to queue. There is a second branch newly opened in **Covent Garden** (Map p76; 10 Adelaide St, WC2).

Canela PORTUGUESE ££
(Map p76; www.canelacafe.com; 33 Earlham St, WC2; mains £9-13; ⏰ 11am-11pm Mon-Sat, to 9pm Sun; 🔊; 🚇 Covent Garden) This sweet Covent Garden cafe flings together a tempting range of Portuguese and Brazilian dishes, including *feijoada* (bean stew with smoked meat) and *pão de queijo* (bread and cheese roll). Great for satiating pre-theatre munchies.

Bar Shu CHINESE ££
(Map p76; 🖊 020-7287 6688; www.barshurestaurant.co.uk; 28 Frith St, W1; mains £10-31; ⏰ noon-11pm; 🚇 Piccadilly Circus, Leicester Sq) Authentic Sichuan food long eluded the sweet-toothed Cantonese chefs of Chinatown, but Bar Shu hits all the right *mala* (numb-spicy) notes with dishes steeped in smoked chillies and the crucial aromatic peppercorn (*hua jiao*).

Pitt Cue Co BARBECUE ££
(Map p76; www.pittcue.co.uk; 1 Newburgh St, W1; mains £11.50-16.50; ⏰ noon-3pm & 5.30-11pm Mon-Sat, noon-4pm Sun; 🚇 Oxford Circus) With only 30 seats jammed into this titchy upstairs-bar, downstairs-dining room affair, prepare to line up (no reservations) for a table and tin trays loaded with slow-cooked meats (pulled pork, beef ribs), classic American BBQ–style. Tuck your elbows in and enjoy.

Hawksmoor Seven Dials   STEAKHOUSE **£££**
(Map p76; ☑020-7420 9390; www.thehawksmoor. co.uk; 11 Langley St, WC2; steak £20-34, 2-/3-course express menu £23/26; ⊗noon-3pm & 5-10.30pm Mon-Sat, noon-9.30pm Sun; 🕾; ⊜Covent Garden) 🏄 Legendary among London carnivores for its mouth-watering and flavour-rich steaks from British cattle, Hawksmoor's sumptuous Sunday roasts, burgers and well-executed cocktails are also show-stoppers. Book ahead.

Arbutus   MODERN EUROPEAN **£££**
(Map p76; ☑020-7734 4545; www.arbutusrestaurant.co.uk; 63-64 Frith St, W1; mains £18-20; ⊗noon-2.30pm & 5-11pm Mon-Sat, noon-3pm & 5.30-10.30pm Sun; 🕾; ⊜Tottenham Court Rd) With seasonal produce and inventive dishes, Anthony Demetre's Michelin-starred brainchild is a winner. The well-priced 'working lunch' menu at £17.95 for two courses and £19.95 for three is a bargain. Bookings crucial.

✖ The City

You'll be sorely dismayed if you've got an empty belly on a Sunday morning in the City. Even during the busy weekdays, the chain eateries are often your best option.

Café Below   CAFE **£**
(Map p80; ☑020-7329 0789; www.cafebelow. co.uk; St Mary-le-Bow Church, Cheapside, EC2; mains £8.75-10.50; ⊗7.30am-2.30pm Mon-Fri; 🖋; ⊜Mansion House) This atmospheric cafe-restaurant, in the crypt of one of London's most famous churches, is breakfast and lunch only these days, but offers excellent value, with many vegetarian choices. In summer there are tables in the shady courtyard.

Duck & Waffle   BRASSERIE **££**
(Map p80; ☑020-3640 7310; www.duckandwaffle. com; 40th fl, Heron Tower, 110 Bishopsgate, EC2; mains £7-32; ⊗24hr; ⊜Liverpool St) The highest restaurant in the UK matches a thoroughly smart (no sportswear, beachwear or flip-flops) and modern perch on the 40th floor of the Heron Tower and a confident British menu (small plates to encourage sharing) – plus waffles – with wrap-around views and round-the-clock hours.

Sweeting's   SEAFOOD **£££**
(Map p80; ☑020-7248 3062; www.sweetingsrestaurant.com; 39 Queen Victoria St, EC4; mains £15-45; ⊗11.30am-3pm Mon-Fri; ⊜Mansion House) 🏄 Hauling in diners since 1889, Sweetings is a massively popular fixture, serving delicious and sustainably sourced fish (grilled, fried or poached), fried whitebait, dover sole and the outstanding chef's fish pie (£15).

✖ South Bank

Popular restaurants feast on iconic riverside views, but cast your net wider and gems crop up everywhere. For a feed with a local feel, head to Borough Market (p142) or Bermondsey St.

M Manze   BRITISH **£**
(Map p92; www.manze.co.uk; 87 Tower Bridge Rd, SE1; mains £2.40-6.25; ⊗11am-2pm Mon-Thu, 10am-2.30pm Fri & Sat; ⊜Borough) Dating to 1902, classic M Manze (Italian roots) began as an ice-cream seller before moving into pie territory. There's lovely tile work and a traditional London working-man's menu: pie and mash, pie and liquor (parsley sauce); take your eels jellied or stewed.

★**Skylon**   MODERN EUROPEAN **££**
(Map p92; ☑020-7654 7800; www.skylon-restaurant.co.uk; 3rd fl, Royal Festival Hall, Southbank Centre, Belvedere Rd, SE1; grill mains £12.50-30, restaurant 2-/3-course £42/48; ⊗grill noon-11pm, restaurant noon-2.30pm & 5.30-10.30pm Mon-Sat, noon-4pm Sun; 🕾; ⊜Waterloo) This looker atop the Royal Festival Hall divides into grill and fine-dining sections. Design is cutting-edge 1950s, with floor-to-ceiling windows rewarding diners with Thames and the City views. Weekday two-/three-course lunches are a tempting £18/21 in the grill. Booking is advised, especially for the restaurant. Dress smart casual (no sportswear).

Magdalen   MODERN BRITISH **££**
(Map p92; ☑020-7403 1342; www.magdalenrestaurant.co.uk; 152 Tooley St, SE1; mains £14.50-21, 2-/3-course lunch £15.50/18.50; ⊗noon-2.30pm Mon-Fri & 6.30-10pm Mon-Sat; 🕾; ⊜London Bridge) A diamond in the Tooley St rough, Magdalen hits the spot for anyone eager to corner some of London's best Modern British fare. With a focus on charcuterie, lovingly cooked and presented, it's not the place to bring a vegetarian or a weight-conscious waif on a date.

✖ Belgravia

★**Pimlico Fresh**   CAFE **£**
(86 Wilton Road, SW1; mains from £6; ⊗7.30am-7.30pm Mon-Fri, 9am-6pm Sat & Sun; ⊜Victoria) A wholesome choice for a healthy breakfast or lunch, this friendly two-room cafe cooks up fine homemade dishes from pies, soups,

baked beans on toast and lasagne to warming bowls of porridge laced with honey, maple syrup, banana, yoghurt or sultanas, while making regular forays into creative cuisine.

✗ Knightsbridge

★ Dinner by Heston Blumenthal
MODERN BRITISH £££

(Map p98; ☑ 020-7201 3833; www.dinnerbyheston. com; Mandarin Oriental Hyde Park, 66 Knightsbridge, SW1; 3-course set lunch £38, mains £28-42; ☉ noon-2.30pm & 6.30-10.30pm; ☎; ◉ Knightsbridge) Double Michelin-star Dinner is a gastronomic tour de force, taking diners on a journey through British culinary history (with inventive modern inflections). Dishes carry dates to convey historical context – the cod in cider (c 1940) is a joy – but unless you order the set lunch (Monday to Friday), your bill may rapidly spiral out of control. Book ahead.

Zuma
JAPANESE £££

(Map p98; ☑ 020-7584 1010; www.zumarestaurant. com; 5 Raphael St, SW7; mains £15-75; ☉ noon-2.30pm Mon-Fri, 12.30-3.30pm Sat & Sun, 6-11pm daily; ☎; ◉ Knightsbridge) A modern-day take on the traditional Japanese *izakaya,* where drinking and eating harmonise, Zuma oozes style, but it's the excellent sushi, sashimi and *robata* (char-grilled) dishes that steal the show. Sake fiends will find more than 40 different types of their favourite tipple at the bar.

✗ Chelsea & Kensington

These highbrow neighbourhoods harbour some of London's very best (and priciest) restaurants.

Wasabi
JAPANESE £

(www.wasabi.uk.com; Kensington Arcade, Kensington High St, W8; mains £5-8; ☉ 10am-10pm Mon-Sat, 11am-9pm Sun; ◉ High St Kensington) Large, bright sit-down and take-out branch of this superb Japanese sushi and bento chain, with delicious rice sets, noodles, rolls and salads, all good value and perfect for a fast lunch. Branches dot central London.

★ Five Fields
MODERN BRITISH £££

(Map p98; ☑ 020-7838 1082; www.fivefieldsrestaurant.com; 8-9 Blacklands Terrace, SW3; 3-course set meal £50; ☉ 6.30-10pm Tue-Sat; ☎; ◉ Sloane Square) The inventive British cuisine, consummate service and enticingly light and inviting decor at this triumphant Chelsea restaurant has won an immediate fan base, but plan early to get a seat.

★ Medlar
MODERN EUROPEAN £££

(☑ 020-7349 1900; www.medlarrestaurant.co.uk, 438 King's Rd, SW10; 3-course lunch £27-30, dinner £35-45; ☉ noon-3pm & 6.30-10.30pm; ☎; ◉ South Kensington, Fulham Broadway, Sloane Sq) With its uncontrived yet crisply modern green-on-grey design, immaculate, Michelin star–rated Medlar has quickly become a King's Rd sensation. With no à la carte menu and scant pretentiousness, the prix fixe modern European cuisine is delightfully assured, with kitchen magic cooked up by chef Joe Mercer Nairne (from Chez Bruce).

Gordon Ramsay
FRENCH £££

(Map p98; ☑ 020-7352 4441; www.gordonramsay. com; 68 Royal Hospital Rd, SW3; 3-course lunch/dinner £55/95; ☉ noon-2.30pm & 6.30-11pm Mon-Fri; ◉ Sloane Sq) One of Britain's finest restaurants and London's longest-running with three coveted Michelin stars, you'll need to book ahead and hop into your best togs: jeans and T-shirts don't get past the door. And if you've seen the chef in action, you'll know not to argue.

✗ Notting Hill, Shepherd's Bush & Hammersmith

Notting Hill teems with good places to eat, from cheap takeaways to atmospheric pubs and restaurants worthy of the fine-dining tag. Shepherd's Bush and Hammersmith to the west pitch in with some fine contenders.

Taquería
MEXICAN £

(Map p120; www.taqueria.co.uk; 139-143 Westbourne Grove; tacos £5-7.50; ☉ noon-11pm Mon-Fri, 10am-11.30pm Sat, noon-10.30pm Sun; ☎; ◉ Notting Hill Gate) ✔ Its sustainable credentials as exacting and appealing as its authentic soft-corn, freshly made tortillas, this place instantly elbows other Mexican restaurants into the Tex-Mex shade. Fish is all sustainably sourced and the pork, chicken and eggs come free range. Great mezcal and tequila menu, too.

Electric Diner
AMERICAN ££

(Map p120; www.electricdiner.com; 191 Portobello Rd, W11; mains from £8-19; ☉ 8am-midnight Mon-Thu, to 1am Fri-Sun; ☎; ◉ Ladbroke Grove) A kitchen fire saw last orders for the Electric Brasserie, prompting redesign as a slender American-style diner with long counter, red-leather booths and a satisying French-American menu of breakfasts, burgers, steak frites and hot dogs.

★ **Ledbury** FRENCH £££
(Map p120; ☑ 020-7792 9090; www.theledbury.com, 127 Ledbury Rd, W11; 4-course set lunch £45, 4-course dinner £90; ⊙ noon-2pm Wed-Sun & 6.30-9.45pm daily; 🐾; ⊜ Westbourne Park, Notting Hill Gate) Two Michelin stars and swooningly elegant, Brett Graham's artful French restaurant attracts well-heeled diners in jeans with designer jackets. Dishes – such as roast sea bass with broccoli stem, crab and black quinoa, or saddle of roe deer with beetroot, pinot lees and bone crisp potato – are triumphant. London gastronomes have Ledbury on speed-dial, so reservations are crucial.

✗ Marylebone

You won't go too far wrong planting yourself on a table anywhere along Marylebone's charming High St.

La Fromagerie CAFE ££
(Map p102; www.lafromagerie.co.uk; 2-6 Moxon St, W1; mains £7-16.50; ⊙ 8am-7.30pm Mon-Fri, 9am-7pm Sat, 10am-6pm Sun; ⊜ Baker St) This delicafe has bowls of delectable salads, antipasto, peppers and beans scattered about the long communal table. Huge slabs of bread invite you to tuck in, and all the while the heavenly waft from the cheese room beckons.

Locanda Locatelli ITALIAN ££
(Map p102; ☑ 020-7935 9088; www.locandalocatelli.com; 8 Seymour St, W1; mains from £13.50; ⊙ noon-3pm daily, 6.45-11pm Mon-Sat, to 10.15pm Sun; 🐾; ⊜ Marble Arch) Known for its sublime but pricey pasta dishes, this dark but quietly glamorous restaurant in an otherwise unremarkable hotel is one of London's hottest tables.

Providores & Tapa Room FUSION £££
(Map p102; ☑ 020-7935 6175; www.theprovidores.co.uk; 109 Marylebone High St, W1; 2-/3-/4-/5-course dinner £33/47/57/63; ⊙ 9am-10.30pm Mon-Fri, 10am-10pm Sat & Sun; 🐾; ⊜ Baker St) New Zealand's most distinctive culinary export since kiwi fruit, chef Peter Gordon works his fusion magic here, matching his creations with NZ wines. Downstairs, in a cute play on words, the Tapa Room (as in the Polynesian barkcloth) serves sophisticated tapas, along with excellent breakfasts.

✗ Bloomsbury & St Pancras

Diwana Bhel Poori House INDIAN £
(Map p106; 121-123 Drummond St, NW1; mains £7-9; ⊙ noon-11.30pm Mon-Sat, to 10.30pm Sun; 🗹; ⊜ Euston, Euston Sq) This ace Indian vegetarian eatery specialises in *bhel poori* (sweet-and-sour, soft and crunchy 'party mix' snacks), dosas (filled rice-flour pancakes),

---

WORTH A TRIP

HAMMERSMITH & SHEPHERD'S BUSH

Well within reach of Notting Hill, Hammersmith and Shepherd's Bush are well worth a detour for their eclectic restaurants and pubs.

Potli (www.potli.co.uk; 319-321 King St, W6; weekday 1-/2-course set lunch £6.95/9.95, mains £6.50-13.50; ⊙ noon-2.45pm & 6-10.30pm Mon-Sat, noon-10.30pm Sun; ⊜ Stamford Brook, Ravenscourt Park) With its Bollywood posters, scattered pieces from Mumbai's Thieves Market, Indian market kitchen/bazaar cuisine, homemade pickles and spice mixes, and accent on genuine flavour, Potli deftly captures the aromas of its culinary home. Downstairs there's an open kitchen and service is very friendly, but it's the alluring menu that's the real crowd-pleaser.

Kerbisher & Malt (www.kerbisher.co.uk; 164 Shepherd's Bush Rd, W6; mains £5.80-6.90; ⊙ noon-2.30pm & 4.30-10pm Tue-Thu, noon-10pm Fri & Sat, to 9pm Sun; ⊜ Hammersmith) The sustainably sourced, delectable, battered-or-grilled coley, haddock, pollock, cod and plaice at popular, blue-fronted Kerbisher & Malt has won over shoals of approving fish fans. The chip butties, crispy servings of whitebait and tasty double-fried chips merit equal applause.

Dove (☑ 020-8748 9474; www.dovehammersmith.co.uk; 19 Upper Mall, W6; ⊙ 11am-11pm Mon-Sat, noon-10.30pm Sun; ⊜ Hammersmith, Ravenscourt Park) Severely inundated by the epic floodwaters of 1928, this gem of a 17th-century Fuller's pub revels in historic charm and superb Thames views. Scottish poet James Thompson was reputedly inspired to write the lyrics to 'Rule Britannia' here in the 18th century, it was Graham Greene's local, and Hemingway and Dylan Thomas drank here, too, while William Morris lived nearby.

thali and the all-you-can-eat, lunchtime buffet (£6.95) is a legendary blowout.

Caravan
MEDITERRANEAN ££

(📞020-7101 7661; www.caravankingscross.co.uk; Granary Bldg, 1 Granary Sq, N1C; mains £7-15; ⊙8am-10.30pm Mon-Thu, to midnight Fri, 10am-midnight Sat, 10am-4pm Sun; 🛜🍴; ⦿King's Cross St Pancras) In the freshly renovated Granary Building by the eye-catching piazza of Granary Sq alongside Regent's Canal, Caravan is a vast, tasty and trendy (industrial chic) stop for fusion Mediterranean cuisine. Book ahead.

North Sea Fish Restaurant
FISH & CHIPS ££

(Map p106; www.northseafishrestaurant.co.uk; 7-8 Leigh St, WC1; mains £10-20; ⊙noon-2.30pm & 5.30-11pm Mon-Sat, 1-6pm Sun; ⦿Russell Sq) Every day is fryday at the North Sea, a classic chippie for eat-in or takeaway with jumbo-sized plaice or halibut steaks, deep-fried or grilled, and lashings of chips.

✖ Fitzrovia

Tucked away behind busy Tottenham Court Rd, Fitzrovia's Charlotte and Goodge Sts form one of central London's most vibrant eating precincts.

Dabbous
MODERN EUROPEAN ££

(Map p106; 📞020-7323 1544; www.dabbous.co.uk; 39 Whitfield St, W1; mains £12-16; ⊙noon-3pm & 5.30-11.30pm Tue-Sat; ⦿Goodge St) You'll need to book ahead for dinner or come for lunch (four courses £28) at this creation from Ollie Dabbous. The rather stark and pared down ambience may not suit all tastes, but it's offset by an inventive menu stuffed with surprises and ideas; the basement cocktail bar is just the place for a pre-meal libation.

★Lima
SOUTH AMERICAN £££

(Map p76; 📞020-3002 2640; www.limalondon. com; 31 Rathbone Place, W1; mains £10-29; ⊙noon-2.30pm & 5.30-10.30pm Mon-Sat; 🛜; ⦿Tottenham Court Rd) Sublimely zestful Peruvian flavours percolate at the heart of this neat and unassuming Fitzrovia restaurant. The stunningly presented cuisine has pulled a Michelin star and helpful staff take pride in their work.

Hakkasan Hanway Place
CHINESE £££

(Map p76; 📞020-7927 7000; www.hakkasan.com; 8 Hanway Place, W1; mains £11-100; ⊙noon-3pm Mon-Fri, to 4pm Sat & Sun, 5.30-11pm Sun-Wed, to 12.15am Thu-Sat; 🛜; ⦿Tottenham Court Rd) Michelin-starred Hakkasan elegantly pairs fine Chinese dining with stunning design

and some persuasive cocktail chemistry. The low-lighting hits all the right romantic notes and the expansive menu runs from *Szechuan mabo tofu* to grilled Shanghai dumplings, Peking duck and beyond.

✖ Camden Town

Camden is great for cheap eats, while neighbouring Chalk Farm and Primrose Hill are salted with gastropubs and upmarket restaurants.

Dirty Burger
BURGERS £

(www.eatdirtyburger.com; 79 Highgate Rd, NW5; burgers £5.50; ⊙5pm-midnight Mon-Fri, noon-midnight Sat, to 10pm Sun; 🚉Gospel Oak, ⦿Kentish Town) More chic shack than restaurant, Dirty Burger is all about burgers (beyond sausages and bacon till 11am) and crinkle-cut fries. And what burgers: thick, juicy and messy, with mustard, gherkin and cheese. The shakes are good, too.

Mango Room
CARIBBEAN ££

(Map p132; 📞020-7482 5065; www.mangoroom. co.uk; 10-12 Kentish Town Rd, NW1; mains £8-15; ⊙noon-11pm; ⦿Camden Town) Mango Room is an upmarket Caribbean experience serving a mix of modern and traditional dishes – Creole snapper, goat curry, jerk chicken – set to ska and reggae beats.

✖ Islington

Allow at least an evening to explore Islington's Upper St, along with the lanes leading off it.

Trullo
ITALIAN ££

(📞020-7226 2733; www.trullorestaurant.com; 300-302 St Paul's Rd, N1; mains £8.50-16, 2-/3-course lunch £15/19; ⊙12.30-3pm daily, 6-10.30pm Mon-Sat; ⦿Highbury & Islington) Alongside fine service, the big plus here is an enjoyable variety beyond pasta or pizza. There are some exquisite pasta dishes, for sure, but the star attraction is the charcoal grill, which churns out succulent T-bone steaks or tasty pork chops with baked borlotti beans or polenta. Bookings essential.

Le Mercury
FRENCH ££

(📞020-7354 4088; www.lemercury.co.uk; 140a Upper St, N1; mains £9.95; ⊙noon-1am Mon-Sat, to 11pm Sun; ⦿Highbury & Islington, Angel) A cosy Gallic haunt ideal for cash-strapped Casanovas, given that it appears much more expensive than it is. Sunday lunch by the open fire upstairs is a treat, though you'll have to book. There's another branch up the road at **Le Mercury Deuxieme** (www.lemercury.co.uk; 154-155 Upper St, N1; mains £9.95; ⊗5pm-midnight Mon-Thu, noon-midnight Fri & Sat, to 11pm Sun; ⊜Highbury & Islington).

Ottolenghi BAKERY, MEDITERRANEAN ££
(☑020-7288 1454; www.ottolenghi.co.uk; 287 Upper St, N1; mains £9-12; ⊗8am-11pm Mon-Sat, 9am-7pm Sun; ⊿; ⊜Highbury & Islington, Angel) Mountains of meringues tempt you through the door, where a sumptuous array of bakery treats and salads greets you. Meals are as light and tasty as the lovely white interior design. Vegetarians are well catered for. There are further branches in **Belgravia** (Map p98; 13 Motcomb St, SW1; ⊗8am-8pm Mon-Fri, to 7pm Sat, 9am-6pm Sun; ⊜Knightsbridge), **Kensington** (Map p120; 1 Holland St, W8; ⊗8am-8pm Mon-Fri, to 7pm Sat, 9am-6pm Sun; ⊜High St Kensington) and **Notting Hill** (Map p120; 63 Ledbury Rd, W11; ⊗8am-8pm Mon-Fri, to 7pm Sat, 8.30am-6pm Sun; ⊜Notting Hill Gate).

✗ Clerkenwell & Farringdon

Clerkenwell's hidden gems are well worth digging for. Pedestrianised Exmouth Market is a good place to start.

Little Bay EUROPEAN £
(Map p106; ☑020-7278 1234; www.little-bay.co.uk; 171 Farringdon Rd, EC1; mains before/after 7pm £6.45/8.45; ⊜Farringdon) The crushed-velvet ceiling, handmade twisted lamps that im-

prove around the room (as the artist got better) and elaborately painted bar and tables showing frolicking nympho are weird but fun. The hearty food is very good value.

Prufrock Coffee CAFE £
(Map p106; www.prufrockcoffee.com; 23-25 Leather Lane, EC1; mains £5.50-9.50; ⊗8am-6pm Mon-Fri, 10am-5pm Sat & Sun; ☎; ⊜Chancery Lane, Farringdon) Coffee-holics and caffeine geeks must trek to Clerkenwell for some of the finest brews in town, served by a talented line-up of staff in an inviting and light-filled space, with practice sessions and classes for baristas-to-be.

Morito TAPAS ££
(Map p106; ☑020-7278 7007; www.morito.co.uk; 32 Exmouth Market, EC1; tapas £4.50-9.50; ⊗noon-4pm daily, 5-11pm Mon-Sat; ☎; ⊜Farringdon, Angel) This titchy venue is an authentic take on a Spanish tapas bar. Seats are at the bar, along the window, or on one of the small tables inside or out. It's relaxed, convivial and often completely crammed. The food is excellent; you can book at lunch, but not in the evening.

St John BRITISH £££
(Map p80; ☑020-7251 0848; www.stjohnrestaurant.com; 26 St John St, EC1; mains £17-23; ⊗noon-3pm & 6-11pm Mon-Sat, 1-3pm Sun; ⊜Farringdon) Bright whitewashed brick walls, high ceilings and simple wooden furniture keep diners free to concentrate on the world-famous nose-to-tail offerings. Expect chitterlings and ox tongue.

CHAIN-CHAIN-CHAIN, CHAIN OF FOODS

Among the endless Caffe Neros and Pret a Mangers are some fab fallback options. Here are some of the best:

Konditor & Cook (www.konditorandcook.com) London's best bakery chain, serving excellent cakes, pastries, bread and coffee.

Jamie's Italian (www.jamieoliver.com) Good Italian food in a modern setting.

Masala Zone (www.masalazone.com) Fantastic Indian chain specialising in thalis (a meal made of several small dishes).

Nando's (www.nandos.co.uk) Loved by Londoners for fantastic value, mouth-watering spicy chicken *a la portuguesa* – with some blindingly hot peri-peri sauces.

Pizza Express (www.pizzaexpress.com) Excellent pizza, neat ambience and standout locations across London.

Wagamama (www.wagamama.com) Japanese noodles taking over the world from their London base.

Wahaca (www.wahaca.com) Working the Mexican street-food angle in fresh, colourful settings.

Wasabi (www.wasabi.uk.com) Cooking up a Japanese storm down the high street.

Zizzi (www.zizzi.co.uk) Wood-fired pizza.

LONDON EATING

Modern Pantry FUSION £££
(Map p106; ☎020-7553 9210; www.themodern-pantry.co.uk; 47-48 St John's Sq, EC1; mains £14-21.50; ⏰noon-3pm Tue-Fri, 11am-4pm Sat & Sun, 6-10.30pm Tue-Sat; 🛜; ⊜Farringdon) One of London's most talked-about eateries, this three-floor Georgian town house in the heart of Clerkenwell has a cracking innovative, all-day menu.

✖ Hoxton, Shoreditch & Spitalfields

From the hit-and-miss Bangladeshi restaurants of Brick Lane to the Vietnamese strip on Kingsland Rd, and the Jewish, Spanish, French, Italian and Greek eateries in between, the East End's cuisine is as multicultural as its residents.

Sông Quê Café VIETNAMESE £
(Map p124; www.songque.co.uk; 134 Kingsland Rd, E2; mains £6-9; ⏰noon-3pm & 5.30-11pm Mon-Fri, noon-11pm Sat & Sun; ⊜Hoxton) Arrive after 7.30pm and you can expect to queue: this humble eatery is one of the best Vietnamese restaurants in London and you'll be shunted out shortly after your last bite.

Brick Lane Beigel Bake BAGELS £
(Map p124; 159 Brick Lane, E2; bagels £1-4; ⏰24hr; ⊜Shoreditch High St, Liverpool St) Always busy, this relic of London's Jewish East End is more takeaway than cafe and sells dirt-cheap bagels, a top late-night snack on a bellyful of booze.

Poppies FISH & CHIPS ££
(Map p124; www.poppiesfishandchips.co.uk; 6-8 Hanbury St, E1; mains £7-16; ⏰11am-11pm Mon-Thu, to 11.30pm Fri & Sat, to 10.30pm Sun; 🛜; ⊜Shoreditch High St, Liverpool St) Frying since 1945, this fantastic Spitalfields chippie is a retro delight, a throwback to the 1950s with iconic jukebox, wall-to-wall memorabilia, waitresses in pinnies and hairnets and classic fish and chips (plus jellied eels).

Camden Town

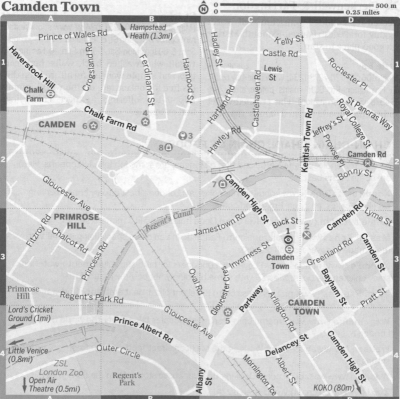

Albion BRITISH ££

(Map p124; 020-7729 1051; www.albioncaff. co.uk; 2-4 Boundary St, E2; mains £9-13; 8am-11pm; ; Old St) For those wanting to be taken back to Dear Old Blighty's cuisine, but with rather less grease and stodge, this self-consciously retro 'caff' serves up top-quality bangers and mash, along with steak-and-kidney pies, devilled kidneys and, of course, fish and chips.

The East End

Formans BRITISH ££

(020-8525 2365; www.formans.co.uk; Stour Rd, Fish Island, E3; mains £11.50-19.50; 7-11pm Thu & Fri, 10am-2pm & 7-11pm Sat, noon-5pm Sun; ; Hackney) Curing fish since 1905, riverside Formans boasts prime views over the Olympic stadium alongside a delectable choice of smoked salmon (including the signature London cure) and seafood, plus a choice of other mouth-watering British dishes. A viewing gallery into the smokery and a lounge bar rounds out an attractive picture.

Drinking & Nightlife

As long as there's been a city, Londoners have loved to drink – and, as history shows, often immoderately. The pub is the hub of social life and, despite depleting numbers, there's always one near at hand. When the sun shines, drinkers spill out into the streets, parks and squares.

Soho is undoubtedly the heart of bar culture, with enough variety to cater to all tastes. Still great for grungy boozers and rock kids, Camden has lost ground on the bohemian-cool front to Hoxton and Shoreditch.

Camden Town

Neighbourhoods such as Clerkenwell, Islington, Southwark, Notting Hill and Earl's Court are bursting at their beer-addled seams with pub-crawl potential.

Mirroring its worker-base, the City is a Monday to Friday spot and several of its historic pubs shut up shop at weekends or on Sundays. South London has some fine historic haunts near the river. The price of beer in pubs is enough to drive you to drink – expect to pay upwards of £3.25 per pint of lager.

The volume and variety of nightclubs in London is staggering. Megaclubs are scattered throughout town wherever there's a venue big enough, cheap enough or quirky enough. The big nights are Friday and Saturday, although some of the most cutting-edge sessions are midweek. Admission prices vary widely; it's often cheaper to arrive early or prebook tickets.

West End

★**Gordon's Wine Bar** BAR

(Map p76; www.gordonswinebar.com; 47 Villiers St, WC2; 11am-11pm Mon-Sat, noon-10pm Sun; Embankment) What's not to love about this cavernous, candlelit wine cellar that's been practically unchanged for the last 120 years? Get here before the office crowd (generally around 6pm) or forget about getting a table.

Opium COCKTAIL BAR

(Map p76; 020-7734 7276; www.opiumchinatown.com; 15-16 Gerrard St, W1; 5pm-midnight Mon-Wed, to 2am Thu-Sat, noon-midnight Sun) Towering above Chinatown's main drag, this self-proclaimed 'cocktail and dim sum parlour' could easily pass as an opium den-cum-brothel, with a jade-coloured door leading to a scarlet-drenched interior and byzantine cocktails.

Spuntino BAR

(Map p76; www.spuntino.co.uk; 61 Rupert St, W1; mains £6-10; noon-midnight Mon-Wed, to 1am Thu-Sat, to 11pm Sun; Piccadilly Circus) Speakeasy decor meets creative fusion American–Italian food at Rupert St cool customer Spuntino. Grab a seat at the bar or one of the counters at the back, but put aside time to queue (no reservations and no phone).

French House BAR

(Map p76; www.frenchhousesoho.com; 49 Dean St, W1; noon-11pm; Leicester Sq) French House is Soho's legendary boho boozer with a history to match: the meeting place of the Free French Forces during WWII, De

Gaulle is said to have knocked back shots here, while Dylan Thomas, Peter O'Toole, Brendan Behan and Francis Bacon all conspired to drink the place dry. The no-phones, no-music and no-TV ruling only amplifies the mystique.

Princess Louise
PUB

(Map p76; 208 High Holborn, WC1; ⊗ 11.30am-11pm; ⊖ Holborn) This late 19th-century Victorian boozer is arguably London's most beautiful pub. Spectacularly decorated with fine tiles, etched mirrors, plasterwork and a gorgeous central horseshoe bar, it gets packed with the after-work crowd.

Terroirs
WINE BAR

(Map p76; www.terroirswinebar.com; 5 William IV St, WC2; ⊗ noon-11pm Mon-Sat; ⊖ Charing Cross

Road) Fab two-floor spot for a pre- or post-theatre glass or some expertly created char-cuterie, with informative staff, affordable £10 lunch specials, a convivial atmosphere and a breathtaking list of organic wines.

Lamb & Flag
PUB

(Map p76; www.lambandflagcoventgarden.co.uk; 33 Rose St, WC2; ⊗ 11am-11pm Mon-Sat, noon-10.30pm Sun; ⊖ Covent Garden) Everyone's Covent Garden 'find', this historic pub is often as jammed with punters as it is packed with history. Built in 1623 and formerly called the 'Bucket of Blood', inside it's all brass fittings and creaky wooden floors.

Galvin at Windows
BAR

(Map p68; www.galvinatwindows.com; London Hilton on Park Lane, 28th fl, 22 Park Lane, W1; ⊗ 11am-1am

GAY & LESBIAN LONDON

The West End, particularly Soho, is the visible centre of gay and lesbian London, with venues clustered around Old Compton St and its surrounds. However, Soho doesn't hold a monopoly on gay life. Vauxhall is a hub for the hirsute, hefty and generally harder-edged sections of the community. The railway arches are filled with dance clubs, leather bars and a sauna. Clapham (South London), Earl's Court (West London), Islington (North London) and Limehouse (East End) have their own miniscenes.

Generally, London is a safe place for lesbians and gays. It's rare to encounter any problem with sharing rooms or holding hands in the inner city, although it would pay to keep your wits about you at night and be conscious of your surroundings.

Some venues to get you started include the following:

George & Dragon (Map p124; 2 Hackney Rd, E2; ⊗ 6-11pm; ⊖ Old St) Appealing corner pub where the crowd is often as eclectically furnished as the venue.

She Soho (☑ 0207 437 4303; www.she-soho.com; 23a Old Compton St, W1D; ⊗ 4-11.30pm Mon-Thu, to 12.30am Fri & Sat, to 10.30pm Sun; ⊖ Leicester Square) Soho Lesbian bar with DJs at weekends, comedy and live music.

Duke of Wellington (Map p76; 77 Wardour St, W1; ⊗ noon-11pm Sun-Wed, to midnight Thu-Sat; ⊖ Leicester Sq) Friendly hang-out for the 30-somethings (and above) gay set.

Edge (Map p76; www.edgesoho.co.uk; 11 Soho Sq, W1; ⊗ 3pm-1am Mon-Thu, to 3am Fri & Sat, to 11.30pm Sun; ⊖ Tottenham Court Rd) London's largest gay bar, hopping nightly across four floors.

Heaven (Map p76; www.heavennightclub-london.com; Villiers St, WC2; ⊗ 11pm-5am Mon, Thu & Fri, 10pm-5am Sat; ⊖ Embankment, Charing Cross) Perennially popular gay club under the arches beneath Charing Cross station with fab club nights.

RVT (www.rvt.org.uk; 372 Kennington Lane, SE11; ⊗ 7pm-midnight Mon, Wed & Thu, 6pm-midnight Tue, 9pm-2am Fri & Sat, 2pm-midnight Sun; ⊖ Vauxhall) Much-loved pub with crazy cabaret and drag acts. Head under the arches from Vauxhall tube station onto Kennington Lane, where you'll see the tavern immediately to your left.

Two Brewers (www.the2brewers.com; 114 Clapham High St, SW4; admission after 10pm £3-6; ⊗ 4pm-2am Sun-Thu, to 4am Fri & Sat; ⊖ Clapham Common) Popular bar with regular acts and a nightclub out the back. From the tube station, head north along Clapham High St (away from the common).

Village (Map p76; www.village-soho.co.uk; 81 Wardour St, W1; ⊗ 4pm-1am Mon-Sat, to 11.30pm Sun; ⊖ Piccadilly Circus) Glitzy gay bar with excellent, lengthy happy hours.

Mon-Wed, to 3am Thu-Sat, to 11pm Sun; ⊜ Hyde Park Corner) Be stunned by both the views and the cocktail prices at this 28th floor eyrie at the Hilton, overlooking Hyde Park.

LAB
COCKTAIL BAR

(Map p76; ☑ 020-7437 7820; www.labbaruk.com; 12 Old Compton St, W1; ⊙ 4pm-midnight Mon-Sat, to 10.30pm Sun; ⊜ Leicester Sq, Tottenham Court Rd) The decor of the London Academy of Bartending has been left behind, but a frisson of creativity runs through the cocktail menu and LAB's mixologists can have your tastebuds singing.

The City

★ Vertigo 42
BAR

(Map p80; ☑ 020-7877 7842; www.vertigo42.co.uk; Tower 42, 25 Old Broad St, EC2; ⊙ noon-3.45pm Mon-Fri & 5-11pm Mon-Sat; ⊜ Liverpool St) Book a two-hour slot in this 42nd-floor champagne bar (no shorts, caps or flip-flops) with vertiginous views across London from the former National Westminster Tower. Reservations only.

Madison
COCKTAIL BAR

(Map p80; www.madisonlondon.net; Roof Terrace, One New Change, EC4; ⊙ 10am-midnight Mon-Sat, to 8pm Sun; ⊜ St Paul's) Perched atop One New Change with a full-frontal view of St Paul's and beyond, Madison offers one of the largest public open-air roof terraces you'll ever encounter. There's a full restaurant on one side and a cocktail bar with outdoor seating on the other.

Ye Olde Cheshire Cheese
PUB

(Map p80; Wine Office Court, 145 Fleet St, EC4; ⊙ 11am-11pm Mon-Fri, noon-11pm Sat; ⊜ Chancery Lane) Rebuilt six years after the Great Fire, this hoary pub was popular with Dr Johnson, Thackeray, Dickens and the visiting Mark Twain. Touristy but always atmospheric and enjoyable for a pub meal.

South Bank

★ Rake
PUB

(Map p92; www.uttobeer.co.uk; 14 Winchester Walk, SE1; ⊙ noon-11pm Mon-Sat, to 8pm Sun; ⊜ London Bridge) The resourceful Rake crams a range of over 100 beers, bitters and real ales into pea-sized premises. There's valuable elbow space on the bamboo-decorated decking outside.

George Inn
PUB

(Map p92; www.nationaltrust.org.uk/george-inn; 77 Borough High St, SE1; ⊙ 11am-11pm; ⊜ London

Bridge) This glorious old boozer is London's last surviving galleried coaching inn, dating from 1676 and now a National Trust property. Getting a mention in Dickens' *Little Dorrit*, it also stands on the site of the Tabard Inn, where the pilgrims in Chaucer's *Canterbury Tales* gathered before hitting the road.

Ministry of Sound
CLUB

(Map p92; www.ministryofsound.com; 103 Gaunt St, SE1; admission £16-25; ⊙ 11pm-6.30am Fri & Sat; ⊜ Elephant & Castle) Where the global brand started, it's London's most famous club and still packs in a diverse crew with big local and international names.

Chelsea & Kensington

★ Queen's Arms
PUB

(Map p98; www.thequeensarmskensington.co.uk; 30 Queen's Gate Mews, SW7; ⊙ noon-11pm; ⊜ Gloucester Rd) Just around the corner from the Royal Albert Hall, this godsend of a blue-grey painted pub in an adorable cobbled mews setting off bustling Queen's Gate beckons with a cosy interior and a right royal selection of ales and ciders on tap.

Bloomsbury & St Pancras

★ Queen's Larder
PUB

(Map p106; www.queenslarder.co.uk; 1 Queen Sq, WC1; ⊙ 11.30am-11pm Mon-Sat, noon-10.30pm Sun; ⊜ Russell Sq) This small and supremely cosy pub in a gorgeous square gets its name from Queen Charlotte, wife of 'Mad' King George III, who rented part of the pub's cellar to store special foods for him while he was undergoing treatment nearby. Poets Sylvia Plath and Ted Hughes married in the church opposite.

Newman Arms
PUB

(Map p76; www.newmanarms.co.uk; 23 Rathbone St, W1; ⊙ noon-11.30pm Mon-Fri; ⊜ Goodge St) One of the few family-run pubs in central London, this tiny one-room affair with upstairs pie room packs a big history; George Orwell and Dylan Thomas drank here and a scene from Michael Powell's *Peeping Tom* was filmed in the passageway alongside the pub in 1960.

69 Colebrooke Row
COCKTAIL BAR

(69 Colebrooke Row, N1; ⊙ 5pm-midnight Sun-Wed, to 1am Thu, to 2am Fri & Sat; ⊜ Angel) London cocktail lovers gravitate to this popular bar run by mixer-maestro Tony Conigliaro, but reserve ahead as seats go faster than a down-in-one. The seasonal drinks menu is steeped in ambitious flavours and blends,

with classic drinks for less adventurous palates. Classes are also offered in cocktail mixing (£40).

Big Chill House
DJ BAR

(Map p106; www.wearebigchill.com; 257-259 Pentonville Rd, N1; ◈ 9am-midnight Mon-Thu, to 3am Fri & Sat, 11am-midnight Sun; 🛜; ◉ King's Cross St Pancras) Come the weekend, the only remotely chilled-out space in this busy bar, split over two levels, is its first-rate and generously proportioned rooftop terrace.

Draft House
BAR

(Map p76; www.drafthouse.co.uk; 43 Goodge St, W1; ◑ noon-11pm Mon-Sat; ◉ Goodge Street) You can line your tummy with ace food, but Draft House is all about the beer choice it crams into its pint-sized premises. This is a public house for ale aficionados, where you can corner a Flying Dog Gonzo Imperial Porter or a head-spinning Samichlaus 14%.

🍸 Notting Hill, Bayswater & Paddington

★ Churchill Arms
PUB

(Map p120; www.churchillarmskensington.co.uk; 119 Kensington Church St, W8; ◑ 11am-11pm Mon-Wed, to midnight Thu-Sat, noon-10.30pm Sun; 🛜; ◉ Notting Hill Gate) Adorned with a gob-smacking array of flower baskets and Union Jacks, this magnificent old boozer is a London classic, famed for its atmosphere, Winston memorabilia, knick-knacks and attached conservatory serving fine Thai food (mains from £7.50).

Windsor Castle
PUB

(Map p120; www.thewindsorcastlekensington. co.uk; 114 Campden Hill Rd, W11; ◑ noon-11pm; 🛜; ◉ Notting Hill Gate) A fine pub with oak partitions separating the original bars at the crest of Campden Hill Rd. One of the loveliest walled gardens of any pub in London is tucked away through the side entrance. The bones of Thomas Paine (*Rights of Man* author) are rumoured to be in the cellar.

Earl of Lonsdale
PUB

(Map p120; 277-281 Portobello Rd, W11; ◑ noon-11pm; ◉ Notting Hill Gate, Ladbroke Grove) Named after the bon vivant founder of the AA (Automobile Association), the Earl is peaceful during the day, with a mixture of old biddies and young hipsters inhabiting the reintroduced snugs. There's a fab backroom with sofas, banquettes and open fires, and a fine beer garden.

🍸 Marylebone

Purl
COCKTAIL BAR

(Map p102; ☑ 020-7935 0835; www.purl-london .com; 50-54 Blandford St, W1; ◈ 5-11.30pm; ◉ Baker St, Bond St) Coined after an old English early morning drink of warm beer, gin, wormwood and spices, Purl is all low lighting, subterranean mellowness and some magnificently presented and unusual cocktails. If you're with a group, book an alcove table. On the musical menu is swing and jazz. Reserve ahead.

Artesian
BAR

(☑ 020-7636 1000; www.artesian-bar.co.uk; Langham Hotel, 1c Portland Pl, W1; ◑ 11am-2am Mon-Sat, to midnight Sun; ◉ Oxford Circus) For doses of colonial glamour with a touch of China, the sumptuous bar at the Langham hits the mark. Rum is the speciality here – award-winning cocktails (from £14) are concocted from the 60 varieties on offer.

🍸 Camden Town

Lock Tavern
PUB

(Map p132; www.lock-tavern.com; 35 Chalk Farm Rd, NW1; ◑ noon-midnight Mon-Thu, to 1am Fri & Sat, to 11pm Sun; ◉ Chalk Farm) The archetypal Camden pub, the Lock has both a rooftop terrace and a beer garden and attracts an interesting crowd with its mix of ready conviviality and regular live music.

🍸 Clerkenwell & Farringdon

★ Jerusalem Tavern
PUB

(Map p106; www.stpetersbrewery.co.uk; 55 Britton St, EC1; ◑ 11am-11pm Mon-Fri; 🛜; ◉ Farringdon) Pick a wood-panelled cubbyhole to park yourself in at this tiny 1720 coffee shop-turned-inn (named after the Priory of St John of Jerusalem) and select from St Peter's fantastic beers and ales, brewed in North Suffolk.

Fabric
CLUB

(Map p80; www.fabriclondon.com; 77a Charterhouse St, EC1; admission £8-18; ◑ 10pm-6am Fri, 11pm-8am Sat, 11pm-6am Sun; ◉ Farringdon) Consistently rated by DJs as one of the world's greatest, Fabric's three dance floors occupy a converted meat cold-store opposite the Smithfield meat market. Friday's FabricLive offers drum and bass, breakbeat and hip hop, Saturdays see house, techno and electronica, while hedonistic Sundays are delivered by the Wetyourself crew.

🍴 Hoxton, Shoreditch & Spitalfields

★ BrewDog
BAR

(Map p124; ☑ 020-7729 8476; www.brewdog.com; 51-55 Bethnal Green Rd, EC1; ☺ noon-midnight Sun-Thu, to 1am Fri & Sat; ☎; ☻ Shoreditch High St) Ale aficionados can migrate to this bar, which overflows with a seasoned and expertly selected choice of cask and bottled beers. There's a strong showing of microbrewery beers, including the Camden Town Brewery and the Redchurch Brewery.

Book Club
BAR

(Map p124; ☑ 020-7684 8618; www.wearetbc.com; 100 Leonard St, EC2A; ☺ 8am-midnight Mon-Wed, to 2am Thu & Fri, 10am-2am Sat & Sun; ☎; ☻ Old St) A cerebral/creative vibe animates this fantastic one-time Victorian warehouse in Shoreditch that hosts cultural events (life drawing, workshops, dance lessons) and DJ nights to complement the drinking, enthusiastic ping-pong-playing and pool-playing shenanigans. Early birds can catch breakfast from 8am weekdays and food continues through the day.

Ten Bells
PUB

(Map p124; cnr Commercial & Fournier Sts, E1; ☺ 11am-11pm Mon-Sat, noon-10.30pm Sun; ☻ Liverpool St) The most famous Jack the Ripper pub, Ten Bells was patronised by his last victim before her grisly end, and possibly by the slayer himself.

Plastic People
CLUB

(Map p124; www.plasticpeople.co.uk; 147-149 Curtain Rd, EC2; admission £5-10; ☺ 10pm-2am Thu, to 4am Fri & Sat; ☻ Old St) Taking the directive 'underground club' literally, Plastic People provides a low-ceilinged subterranean den of dubsteppy, wonky, funky, no-frills fun times.

XOYO
CLUB

(Map p124; www.xoyo.co.uk; 32-37 Cowper St, EC2; ☺ hours vary; ☻ Old St) This excellent Shoreditch warehouse club throws together a pulsingly popular mix of gigs, club nights and art events.

Cargo
CLUB

(Map p124; www.cargo-london.com; 83 Rivington St, EC2; admission free-£16; ☺ noon-1am Mon-Thu, to 3am Fri & Sat, to midnight Sun; ☻ Old St) A popular club with a courtyard where you can simultaneously enjoy big sounds and the great outdoors. Also hosts live bands.

Happiness Forgets
COCKTAIL BAR

(Map p124; ☑ 020-7613 0325; www.happinessforgets.com; 8-9 Hoxton Sq, N1; ☺ 5.30-11pm; ☒ Hoxton, ☻ Old St) Take the stairs down to this trendy basement nook where bar staff know their cocktails, and the seductive, subdued ambience hits all the right moody notes (short hours though).

Worship St Whistling Shop
COCKTAIL BAR

(Map p124; ☑ 020-7247 0015; www.whistlingshop.com; 63 Worship St, EC2; ☺ 5pm-midnight Tue, to 1am Wed & Thu, to 2am Fri & Sat; ☻ Old St) This drinking den's busy master mixologists are content to visit the more unexplored outer regions of cocktail chemistry and aromatic science, concocted within the on-site lab and its rotary evaporators. Many ingredients are made in-house.

Sager & Wilde
WINE BAR

(Map p124; www.sagerandwilde.com; 193 Hackney Rd, E2; ☺ 5-11pm Mon-Fri, 2-11pm Sat & Sun; ☎; ☻ Hoxton) Slightly beyond the Hoxton action along Hackney Rd, this fresh wine bar is a neat, unpretentious and good-looking addition to London drinking culture, with a modish bar bites menu, eye-catching iron-and glass-bricks bar counter and excellent wines by the glass and bottle.

🍴 Greenwich

Greenwich Union
PUB

(www.greenwichunion.com; 56 Royal Hill, SE10; ☺ noon-11pm Mon-Fri, 11am-11pm Sat & Sun; ☒ DLR Cutty Sark) The award-winning and handsome Greenwich Union peddles six or seven local microbrewery beers, including raspberry and wheat varieties, and a strong list of ales and bottled international brews. Sink into a distressed leather armchair or find space in the conservatory and beer garden at the rear.

Cutty Sark Tavern
PUB

(www.cuttysarktavern.co.uk; 4-6 Ballast Quay, SE10; ☺ 11am-11pm Mon-Sat, noon-10.30pm Sun; ☒ DLR Cutty Sark) Housed in a delightful bow-windowed, wood-beamed Georgian building facing the Thames, this historic gem has half a dozen cask-conditioned ales on tap, and riverside seating outside.

🍴 Hampstead & Highgate

Holly Bush
PUB

(www.hollybushhampstead.co.uk; 22 Holly Mount, NW3; ☺ noon-11pm; ☻ Hampstead) Dating from the early 19th century, this beautiful pub has a secluded hilltop location, open fires in winter and a knack for making you stay a bit longer than you had intended. It's above Heath St, reached via the Holly Bush Steps.

Outside Central London

White Cross
PUB

(www.thewhitecrossrichmond.com; Water Lane, TW9; ⊙10am-11pm; ⊜Richmond) The riverside location and fine food and ales make this bay-windowed pub on the site of a former friary a winner. There are entrances for low and high tides, but when the river is at its highest, Cholmondeley Walk running along the Thames floods and the pub is out of bounds to those not willing to wade. Wellies are provided.

Quirky detail: there's a tiny working fireplace *under* the window on your right as you enter.

☆ Entertainment

From West End luvvies to East End geezers, Londoners have always loved a spectacle. With bear-baiting and public executions long on the no-no list, they've fallen back on what London does well: some of the world's best theatre and live-music choices.

For a comprehensive list of what to do on any given night, check out free weekly listings mag *Time Out* and listings in the *Evening Standard* and *Metro*.

Theatre

London is a world capital for theatre across the spectrum from mammoth musicals to thoughtful drama for the highbrow crowd. Blockbuster musicals run and run, with mindboggling longevity. *Les Misérables* and *Phantom of the Opera* lead the pack, but the theatrical biscuit goes to Agatha Christie's *The Mousetrap*, keeping audiences guessing since 1952.

On performance days, you can buy half-price tickets for West End productions (cash only) from the official agency TKTS (Map p76; www.tkts.co.uk; Leicester Sq, WC2; ⊙10am-7pm Mon-Sat, noon-4pm Sun; ⊜Leicester Sq) on the southern side of Leicester Sq. The booth is the one with the clocktower; beware of touts selling dodgy tickets.

The term 'West End' – as with Broadway – generally refers to the big-money productions such as musicals, but also includes other heavyweights. Off West End – including venues such as Almeida and Young Vic – is where you'll generally find the most original works.

National Theatre
THEATRE

(Map p92; ☑020-7452 3000; www.nationaltheatre. org.uk; South Bank, SE1; ⊜Waterloo) Flagship South Bank venue with three theatres and excellent-value tickets for classic and contemporary productions.

Royal Court Theatre
THEATRE

(Map p98; ☑020-7565 5000; www.royalcourttheatre.com; Sloane Sq, SW1; ⊜Sloane Sq) Progressive theatre and champion of new talent.

Old Vic
THEATRE

(Map p92; ☑0844 871 7628; www.oldvictheatre. com; The Cut, SE1; ⊜Waterloo) Kevin Spacey continues his run as artistic director (and occasional performer) at this venue, which features classic, highbrow drama.

Donmar Warehouse
THEATRE

(Map p76; ☑0844 871 7624; www.donmarwarehouse.com; 41 Earlham St, WC2; ⊜Covent Garden) A 251-seat theatre that has forged itself a West End reputation.

Almeida
THEATRE

(☑020-7359 4404; www.almeida.co.uk; Almeida St, N1; ⊜Highbury & Islington) A plush Islington venue that can be relied on for an essential program of imaginative theatre.

Young Vic
THEATRE

(Map p92; ☑020-7922 2922; www.youngvic.org; 66 The Cut, SE1; ⊜Waterloo) One of the capital's most respected theatre troupes, the Young Vic stages winning performances.

Live Music

It goes without saying that London is a crucible of musical talent, with young bands gigging around venues citywide.

★ Vortex Jazz Club
JAZZ

(www.vortexjazz.co.uk; 11 Gillet St, N16; ⊜ 73, ⊞Dalston Kingsland, Dalston Junction) Vortex has an outstanding program of musicians from the UK, US, Europe, Africa and beyond, and hosts jazz musicians, singers and songwriters. It's a small venue, so make sure you book if there is an act you particularly fancy.

★ O2 Academy Brixton
LIVE MUSIC

(www.o2academybrixton.co.uk; 211 Stockwell Rd, SW9; ⊜Brixton) This Grade II–listed art-deco venue is always winning awards for 'best live venue' (something to do with the artfully sloped floor, perhaps) and hosts big-name acts in a relatively intimate setting (5000 capacity).

KOKO LIVE MUSIC

(www.koko.uk.com; 1a Camden High St, NW1; ⊖7-11pm Sun-Thu, to 4am Fri & Sat; ⊖Mornington Cres) Occupying the grand Camden Palace theatre, Koko hosts live bands most nights and the regular Club NME (New Musical Express; £5) on Friday.

12 Bar Club LIVE MUSIC

(Map p76; www.12barclub.com; Denmark St, WC2; admission £6-10; ⊖7pm-3am Mon-Sat, to 12.30am Sun; ⊖Tottenham Court Rd) Small and intimate with a rough-and-ready feel, the 12 Bar is a favourite live-music venue, with anything from solo acts to bands performing nightly. The emphasis is on songwriting and the music is very much indie rock, with anything from folk and jazzy influences to full-on punk and metal sounds.

Dublin Castle LIVE MUSIC

(Map p132; ☑020-7485 1773; www.thedublincastle. com; 94 Parkway, NW1; ⊖Camden Town) There's live punk or alternative music most nights in this pub's back room (cover usually £6).

Barfly LIVE MUSIC

(Map p132; www.mamacolive.com/thebarfly; 49 Chalk Farm Rd, NW1; gigs from £8, club nights £3-5; ⊖7pm-3am Mon-Sat, to midnight Sun; ⊖Chalk Farm) This grungy, indie-rock Camden venue hosts small-time artists looking for their big break. The Killers, Kasabian and Franz Ferdinand have all been on the billing. The lean is clearly towards rock from the US and UK, with alternative-music radio station Xfm hosting regular nights.

Ronnie Scott's JAZZ

(Map p76; ☑020-7439 0747; www.ronniescotts. co.uk; 47 Frith St, W1; ⊖6.30pm-3am Mon-Sat, to midnight Sun; ⊖Leicester Sq, Tottenham Court Rd) London's legendary jazz club has been pulling in jazz titans since 1959.

100 Club LIVE MUSIC

(Map p76; ☑020-7636 0933; www.the100club. co.uk; 100 Oxford St, W1; admission £8-20; ⊖check website for gig times; ⊖Oxford Circus, Tottenham Court Rd) Hosting live music for 70 years, this legendary London venue once showcased the Stones and was at the centre of the punk revolution. It now divides its time between jazz, rock and even a little classical and swing.

606 Club BLUES, JAZZ

(☑020-7352 5953; www.606club.co.uk; 90 Lots Rd, SW10; music fee Sun-Thu £10, Fri & Sat £12; ⊖7-11.15pm Sun-Thu, 8pm-12.30am Fri & Sat; ⊖Im-perial Wharf) Named after its old address on the King's Road, this fantastic tucked-away basement jazz club and restaurant gives centre stage to contemporary British-based jazz musicians nightly. To consume alcohol you'll need to dine to meet some rather antique licensing requirements. There's no entry charge, but a music fee will go on your food/drink bill. Booking advised.

The club is also open most Sundays from 12.30pm to 4.30pm.

Roundhouse LIVE MUSIC

(Map p132; www.roundhouse.org.uk; Chalk Farm Rd, NW1; ⊖Chalk Farm) Built in 1847 as a railway shed, Camden's Roundhouse has been an iconic concert venue since the 1960s (capacity 3300), hosting the likes of the Rolling Stones, Led Zeppelin and The Clash. Theatre and comedy are also staged.

Classical Music

With four world-class symphony orchestras, two opera companies, various smaller ensembles, brilliant venues, reasonable prices and high standards of performance, London is a classical capital. Keep an eye out for the free (or nearly so) lunchtime concerts held in many of the city's churches.

Royal Albert Hall CONCERT VENUE

(Map p98; ☑020-7589 8212, 0845 401 5045; www.royalalberthall.com; Kensington Gore, SW7; ⊖South Kensington) This landmark elliptical Victorian arena – classically based on a Roman ampitheatre – hosts classical concerts and contemporary artists, but is best known as the venue for the annual classical music festival, the Proms.

Barbican PERFORMING ARTS

(Map p80; ☑020-7638 8891, 0845 121 6823; www. barbican.org.uk; Silk St, EC2; ⊖Barbican) Home to the excellent **London Symphony Orchestra** (www.lso.co.uk), this famously hulking complex has a rich program of film, music, theatre, art and dance, including concerts.

Southbank Centre CONCERT VENUE

(Map p92; ☑020-7960 4200; www.southbankcentre.co.uk; Belvedere Rd, SE1; ⊖Waterloo) Home to the **London Philharmonic Orchestra** (www. lpo.co.uk), **Sinfonietta** (www.londonsinfonietta. org.uk) and the **Philharmonia Orchestra** (www.philharmonia.co.uk), among others, this centre hosts classical, opera, jazz and choral music in three premier venues: the **Royal Festival Hall**, the smaller **Queen Elizabeth Hall** and the **Purcell Room**.

Opera & Dance

Royal Opera House OPERA
(Map p76; ☑020-7304 4000; www.roh.org.uk; Bow St, WC2; tickets £4-250; ⊜Covent Garden) Covent Garden is synonymous with opera thanks to this world-famous venue, home of the **Royal Ballet**, Britain's premier classical ballet company. Backstage tours take place three times a day on weekdays and five times on Saturdays (£8.50 to £12, book ahead).

Sadler's Wells DANCE
(Map p106; ☑0844 412 4300; www.sadlerswells. com; Rosebery Ave, EC1; tickets £10-49; ⊜Angel) A glittering modern venue that was, in fact, first established in the 17th century, Sadler's Wells has been given much credit for bringing modern dance to the mainstream.

London Coliseum OPERA
(Map p76; ☑020-7845 9300; www.eno.org; St Martin's Lane, WC2; ⊜Leicester Sq) Home of the progressive English National Opera; the English National Ballet also performs here.

Comedy

When London's comics aren't being outrageously funny on TV, you might find them doing stand-up somewhere in your neighbourhood.

Comedy Store COMEDY
(Map p76; ☑0844 871 7699; www.thecomedy store.co.uk; 1a Oxendon St, SW1; admission £16.50-26; ⊜Piccadilly Circus) One of London's first comedy clubs, featuring the capital's most famous improvisers, the Comedy Store Players, on Wednesdays (8pm) and Sundays (7.30pm).

Comedy Cafe COMEDY
(Map p124; ☑020-7739 5706; www.comedycafe. co.uk; 68 Rivington St, EC2; admission free-£12; ⊙Wed-Sat; ⊜Old St) Have dinner and watch comedy; the free New Act Night on Wednesday is good for toe-curling entertainment.

Soho Theatre COMEDY
(Map p76; ☑020-7478 0100; www.sohotheatre. com; 21 Dean St, W1; £15-20; ⊜Tottenham Court Rd) This is where grown-up comedians graduate to once crowds start paying attention.

Cinemas

Glitzy premieres usually take place in one of the mega multiplexes in Leicester Sq.

Electric Cinema CINEMA
(Map p120; ☑020-7908 9696; www.electriccinema.co.uk; 191 Portobello Rd, W11; tickets £8-22.50; ⊜Ladbroke Grove) Getting Londoners buzzing since 1911, the Electric can help you grab a glass of wine from the bar, head to your leather sofa and snuggle down for a flick.

BFI Southbank CINEMA
(Map p92; ☑020-7928 3232; www.bfi.org.uk; Belvedere Rd, SE1; tickets £8-12; ⊙11am-11pm; ⊜Waterloo) A film-lover's fantasy, screening some 2000 flicks a year, from classics to foreign art-house. There's also the Mediatheque viewing stations, for exploring the British Film Institute's extensive archive of movies and watching whatever you like for free.

BFI IMAX Cinema CINEMA
(Map p92; www.bfi.org.uk/bfi-imax; 1 Charlie Chaplin Walk, SE1; adult/child from £9/5.75; ⊜Waterloo) Watch 3D movies and cinema releases on the UK's biggest screen: 20m high (nearly five double-decker buses) and 26m wide.

Prince Charles CINEMA
(Map p76; www.princecharlescinema.com; 7 Leicester Pl, WC2; tickets £7.50-16; ⊜Leicester Sq) Given the eye-watering prices of West End cinema ticket prices, wait till the first-runs have finished and come here, central London's cheapest picturehouse. Completing the score are mini-festivals, old classics and sing-along screenings.

Football (Soccer)

As the capital of a football-mad nation, expect half of London to be watching the beautiful game during the cooler months.

The home ground for England's national football team, and the venue for the FA Cup final, is **Wembley Stadium** (☑0844 980 8001; www.wembleystadium.com; tours adult/child £16/9).

Tickets for Premier League football matches are like gold dust, but you could try your luck.

London's leading football clubs include the following:

Arsenal STADIUM
(www.arsenal.com/tours; 75 Drayton Park, N5; self-guided tour adult/child £17.50/9; ⊙10am-6pm Mon-Sat, to 4pm Sun; ⊜Arsenal, Finsbury Park, Highbury & Islington) Arsenal Emirates Stadium is the third largest in England. Daily tours available.

Chelsea STADIUM
(☑0871 984 1955; www.chelseafc.com; Stamford Bridge, Fulham Rd, SW6; stadium tours & museum adult/child £20/13; ⊙museum 9.30am-5pm; ⊜Fulham Broadway)

Fulham STADIUM
(www.fulhamfc.com; Craven Cottage, Stevenage Rd, SW6; tours adult/child £12/9; ⊘9am-5pm Mon-Fri; ⊖Putney Bridge)

Tottenham Hotspur STADIUM
(www.tottenhamhotspur.com; White Hart Lane, 748 High Rd, N17; tour adult/child £20/9; ⊠White Hart Lane)

West Ham STADIUM
(www.whufc.com; Boleyn Ground, Green Street, Upton Park, E13; ⊖Upton Park) In 2016, the Olympic Stadium will become the new home of West Ham United FC.

Rugby
Twickenham (www.rfu.com; Rugby Rd, TW1; ⊠Twickenham) is the home of English rugby union, but as with football, tickets for international matches are difficult to get unless you have contacts. The ground also has the **World Rugby Museum** (⊠020-8892 8877; www.rfu.com; adult/child £8/6; ⊘10am-5pm Tue-Sat, 11am-5pm Sun), which can be combined with a tour of the stadium (adult/child £16/10, bookings recommended).

Cricket & Tennis
Cricket is as popular as ever in the home land. Test matches take place at two venerable grounds: Lord's Cricket Ground (which also hosts tours) and the **Brit Oval** (⊠0871 246 1100; www.kiaoval.com; Surrey County Cricket Club, Kennington Oval, SE11; ⊖Oval). Tickets cost from £20 to £80, but if you're a fan it's worth it.

The Wimbledon Lawn Tennis Championships (p117) is one of the biggest events on the city's summer calendar.

Lord's Cricket Ground CRICKET GROUND
(www.lords.org; St John's Wood Rd, NW8; tours adult/child £18/12; ⊖St John's Wood) The next best thing to watching a test at Lord's is the absorbingly anecdotal 100-minute tour of the ground and facilities, held when there's no play. It takes in the famous (members only) Long Room and the **MCC Museum**, featuring evocative memorabilia, including the tiny Ashes trophy.

🔒 Shopping
From world-famous department stores to quirky backstreet retail revelations, London is a mecca for shoppers with an eye for style and a card to exercise.

London's famous department stores are a tourist attraction in themselves, and if there's a label worth having, you'll find it in central London. The capital's most famous designers (Paul Smith, Vivienne Westwood, Stella McCartney, the late Alexander McQueen) have their own stores scattered about and are stocked in major department stores. Look out for dress agencies that sell second-hand designer clothes, bags and shoes – there are particularly rich pickings in the wealthier parts of town.

Nick Hornby's book *High Fidelity* may have done for London music-store workers what *Sweeney Todd* did for barbers, but those obsessive types still lurk in wonderful independent stores all over the city.

🔒 West End
Oxford St is the place for high-street fashion, while Regent St cranks it up a notch. Bond St has designers galore, Savile Row is all about bespoke tailoring and Jermyn St is the place for smart clobber (particularly shirts).

Selfridges DEPARTMENT STORE
(Map p102; www.selfridges.com; 400 Oxford St, W1; ⊘9.30am-9pm Mon-Sat, 11.30am-6.15pm Sun; ⊖Bond St) Famed for its innovative window displays – especially at yuletide – the funkiest of London's one-stop shops bursts with fashion labels and tempts with an unparalleled food hall and the world's largest shoe department.

Fortnum & Mason DEPARTMENT STORE
(Map p76; www.fortnumandmason.com; 181 Piccadilly, W1; ⊘10am-9pm Mon-Sat, noon-6pm Sun; ⊖Piccadilly Circus) It's the byword for quality and service from a bygone era, steeped in 300 years of tradition. The old-world basement food hall is where Britain's elite come for their pantry provisions and epicurean morsels. A new branch opened in 2013 at **St Pancras International** (Map p106; www.fortnumandmason.com; Unit 1a, St Pancras International Station, Pancras Rd, N1; ⊘7am-9pm Mon-Sat, 8am-9pm Sun; ⊖King's Cross St Pancras).

Liberty DEPARTMENT STORE
(Map p76; www.liberty.co.uk; Great Marlborough St, W1; ⊘10am-8pm Mon-Sat, noon-6pm Sun; ⊖Oxford Circus) An irresistible blend of contemporary styles and indulgent pampering in a mock-Tudor fantasyland of carved wood.

Topshop CLOTHING
(Map p76; www.topshop.co.uk; 36-38 Great Castle St, W1; ⊘9am-9pm Mon-Sat, 11.30am-6pm Sun; ⊖Oxford Circus) Billed as the 'world's largest fashion store', the Topshop branch on Oxford Circus is

ROLL OUT THE BARROW

London has over 350 markets selling everything from antiques and curios to flowers and fish. Some, such as Camden and Portobello Rd, are tourist-packed, while others are just for locals.

Columbia Road Flower Market (Map p124; Columbia Rd, E2; ⊙8am-3pm Sun; ⊕Old St) The best place for East End barrow boy banter ('We got flowers cheap enough for ya muvver-in-law's grave'). Unmissable.

Borough Market (Map p92; www.boroughmarket.org.uk; 8 Southwark St, SE1; ⊙11am-5pm Thu, noon-6pm Fri, 8am-5pm Sat; ⊕London Bridge) A farmers market sometimes called London's Larder, it has been here in some form since the 13th century. It's wonderfully atmospheric and you'll find everything from organic falafel to boars' heads.

Maltby Street Market (www.maltby.st; Maltby St, SE1; ⊙10am-4pm Sat; ⊕London Bridge) Hailed as the new Borough Market, Maltby Street is small, delicious and a joy to spend a Saturday afternoon in.

Camden Market (Map p132; Camden High St, NW1; ⊙10am-6pm; ⊕Camden Town, Chalk Farm) London's most famous market is actually a series of markets spread along Camden High St and Chalk Farm Rd. Despite a major fire in 2008, the Camden Lock Market (Map p132; www.camdenlockmarket.com; 54-56 Camden Lock Pl, NW1; ⊙10am-6pm; ⊕Camden Town, Chalk Farm) and Camden Stables Market (Map p132; Chalk Farm Rd, NW1; ⊙10am-6pm; ⊕Chalk Farm) are still the places for punk fashion, cheap food, hippy chic and a whole lotta craziness.

Portobello Road Market (Map p120; www.portobellomarket.org; Portobello Rd, W10; ⊙8am-6.30pm Mon-Wed, Fri & Sat, to 1pm Thu; ⊕Notting Hill Gate, Ladbroke Grove) One of London's most famous street markets, in Notting Hill. New and vintage clothes are its main attraction, with antiques at its south end and food at the north.

Old Spitalfields Market (Map p124; www.oldspitalfieldsmarket.com; Commercial St, btwn Brushfield & Lamb Sts, E1; ⊙10am-4pm Sun-Fri; ⊕Liverpool St) It's housed in a Victorian warehouse, but the market's been here since 1638. Thursdays are devoted to antiques and vintage clothes and Fridays to fashion and art. Sunday's the big day, with a bit of everything.

Broadway Market (www.broadwaymarket.co.uk; London Fields, E8; ⊙9am-5pm Sat; ⊕Bethnal Green) Graze from the organic food stalls, choose a cooked meal and then sample one of the 200 beers on offer at the neighbouring Dove Freehouse. It's a bit of a schlep from the tube.

Brixton Village (www.brixtonmarket.net; Atlantic Rd; ⊙10.30am-6pm Mon-Wed, to 10pm Thu-Sat, 10.30am-5pm Sun; ⊕Brixton) Revitalised and hip transformation of Granville Arcade near Brixton Market, with a host of inventively inclined shops and fantastic restaurants and cafes.

Sunday UpMarket (Map p124; www.sundayupmarket.co.uk; Old Truman Brewery, Brick Lane, E1; ⊙10am-5pm Sun; ⊕Liverpool St) Handmade handbags, jewellery, new and vintage clothes and shoes, plus food if you need refuelling.

Brick Lane Market (Map p124; www.visitbricklane.org; Brick Lane, E1; ⊙8am-2pm Sun; ⊕Liverpool St) An East End pearler, this is a sprawling bazaar featuring everything from fruit and veggies to paintings and bric-a-brac.

Camden Passage Market (www.camdenpassageislington.co.uk; Camden Passage, N1; ⊙8am-2pm Wed, to 5pm Sat; ⊕Angel) Get your fill of antiques and trinkets galore. Not in Camden (despite the name).

Greenwich Market (www.greenwichmarketlondon.com; College Approach, SE10; ⊙10am-5.30pm; ⊠DLR Cutty Sark) Rummage through antiques, vintage clothing and collectables (Thursday and Friday), arts and crafts (Wednesday and weekends), or just chow down in the food section.

Petticoat Lane Market (Map p80; Wentworth St & Middlesex St, E1; ⊙9am-2pm Sun-Fri; ⊕Aldgate) A cherished East End institution overflowing with cheap consumer durables and jumble-sale ware.

a frenzy of shoppers searching for the latest look at reasonable prices. It's home to a range by London's favourite local supermodel rock chick, Kate Moss. Topman is upstairs.

Foyles
BOOKS
(Map p76; www.foyles.co.uk; 107 Charing Cross Rd, WC2; ⊙ 9.30am-9pm Mon-Sat, 11.30am-6pm Sun; ⊜ Tottenham Court Rd) Flogging books since 1906, Foyles is a bookselling institution and retail landmark.

Stanford's
BOOKS, MAPS
(Map p76; www.stanfords.co.uk; 12-14 Long Acre, WC2; ⊙ 9am-8pm Mon-Fri, 10am-8pm Sat, noon-6pm Sun; ⊜ Leicester Sq, Covent Garden) A wonderland of travel titles and maps, with 160 years of experience.

Hamleys
TOYS
(Map p76; www.hamleys.com; 188-196 Regent St, W1; ⊙ 10am-8pm Mon-Sat, noon-6pm Sun; ⊜ Oxford Circus) Reputedly the oldest and largest toy store in the world, Hamleys is five floors of games and toys topped off with Lego world and a cafe.

Waterstones
BOOKS
(Map p76; www.waterstones.com; 203-206 Piccadilly, W1; ⊙ 9am-10pm Mon-Sat, noon-6pm Sun; ⊜ Piccadilly Circus) The chain's mega Piccadilly store is the largest bookstore in Europe, boasting knowledgeable staff and regular author readings and signings. Check out the roof-top **5th View** (Map p76; ✍ 020-7851 2433; www.5thview.co.uk; mains £9-15; ⊙ 9am-10pm Mon-Sat, noon-5pm Sun) bar-restaurant.

Benjamin Pollock's Toy Shop
TOYS
(Map p76; www.pollocks-coventgarden.co.uk; 1st fl, 44 Market Bldg, Covent Garden, WC2; ⊙ 10.30am-6pm Mon-Sat, 11am-4pm Sun; ⊜ Covent Garden) All manner of treasures await at this gem of a traditional toy shop selling Victorian paper toy theatres, children's masks, spinning tops, finger puppets, antique teddy bears, dolls and more.

Moomin Shop
CHILDREN
(Map p76; www.themoominshop.com; 43 Market Bldg, Covent Garden, WC2; ⊙ 10am-8pm Mon-Sat, 11am-7pm Sun; ⊜ Covent Garden) A tiny shrine to Tove Jansson's adorable Moomintrolls: mugs, hot-water bottle sleeves, tea towels, T-shirts, fridge magnets. The whole moomin shebang.

🛍 Knightsbridge, Kensington & Chelsea

Knightsbridge draws the hordes with quintessentially English department stores.

Harrods
DEPARTMENT STORE
(Map p98; www.harrods.com; 87 Brompton Rd, SW1; ⊙ 10am-8pm Mon-Sat, 11.30am-6pm Sun; ⊜ Knightsbridge) Simultaneously stylish and garish, Harrods is an obligatory stop for visitors, both cash-strapped and big spenders alike. The spectacular food hall is a sight in itself.

John Sandoe Books
BOOKS
(Map p98; www.johnsandoe.com; 10 Blacklands Tce, SW3; ⊙ 9.30am-6.30pm Mon-Sat, 11am-5pm Sun; ⊜ Sloane Sq) This atmospheric little bookshop is a treasure trove of literary gems and hidden surprises. In business for decades, loyal customers swear by it and the knowledgeable booksellers spill forth with well-read pointers.

Harvey Nichols
DEPARTMENT STORE
(Map p98; www.harveynichols.com; 109-125 Knightsbridge, SW1; ⊙ 10am-8pm Mon-Sat, 11.30am-6pm Sun; ⊜ Knightsbridge) London's temple of high fashion, jewellery and perfume.

🛍 Bloomsbury & St Pancras

Harry Potter Shop
CHILDREN
(Map p106; www.harrypotterplatform934.com; departure concourse, King's Cross station, N1; ⊙ 10am-6pm; ⊜ King's Cross St Pancras) For all things Potter and Hogwartish.

🛍 Notting Hill, Bayswater & Paddington

Portobello Rd and the lanes surrounding it are the main focus, both for the famous market and the quirky boutiques and gift stores.

Ceramica Blue
HOMEWARES
(Map p120; www.ceramicablue.co.uk; 10 Blenheim Cres, W11; ⊙ 10am-6.30pm Mon-Sat, noon-5pm Sun; ⊜ Ladbroke Grove) For original and eye-catching crockery and coloured glass imported from more than a dozen countries, with Japanese eggshell-glaze teacups, serving plates with traditional South African designs, and more.

🅐 Marylebone

Daunt Books
BOOKS

(Map p102; www.dauntbooks.co.uk; 83 Marylebone High St, W1; ⊙ 9am-7.30pm Mon-Sat, 11am-6pm Sun; ⊖ Baker St) An exquisitely beautiful store, Daunt is one of London's loveliest travel bookshops (and stocks general fiction and nonfiction titles as well).

🅐 Hoxton, Shoreditch & Spitalfields

Rough Trade East
MUSIC

(Map p124; www.roughtrade.com; Dray Walk, Old Truman Brewery, 91 Brick Lane, E1; ⊙ 8am-8pm Mon-Fri, 11am-7pm Sat & Sun; ⊖ Liverpool St) At the forefront of the punk explosion of the 1970s, Rough Trade East – or West (Map p120; ☑ 020-7229 8541; www.roughtrade.com; 130 Talbot Rd, W11; ⊙ 10am-6.30pm Mon-Sat, 11am-5pm Sun; ⊖ Ladbroke Grove) – is the best place to come for anything of an indie or alternative music bent.

Start
CLOTHING

(Map p124; www.start-london.com; 42-44 Rivington St, EC2; ⊙ 10.30am-6.30pm Mon-Wed & Fri, 11am-6pm Sat, noon-5pm Sun; ⊖ Old St) Spilling over three stores on the same lane (womenswear, menswear and men's formal), your quest for designer jeans starts here.

🅐 The East End & Docklands

Westfield Stratford City
MALL

(http://uk.westfield.com; 2 Stratford Place, Montifichet Road, Queen Elizabeth Olympic Park, E20; ⊙ 10am-9pm Mon-Fri, 9am-9pm Sun; ⊖ Stratford) Right by the Queen Elizabeth Olympic Park, this is Europe's largest mall, a shopping behemoth with over 250 shops, dozens of restaurants, a 17-screen cinema, and a casino.

ℹ️ Information

DANGERS & ANNOYANCES

Considering its size and wealth disparities, London is generally safe. That said, keep your wits about you and don't flash your cash unnecessarily. Instances of youth-on-youth knife crime is cause for concern, so walk away if you sense trouble brewing and take care at night. When travelling by tube, choose a carriage with other people in it and avoid deserted suburban stations. Following reports of robberies and sexual attacks, shun unlicensed or unbooked minicabs.

Nearly every Londoner has a story about a wallet/phone/bag being nicked from under their noses – or arses, in the case of bags on floors in bars. Watch out for pickpockets on crowded tube trains, night buses and streets.

When using ATMs, guard your PIN details carefully. Don't use an ATM that looks like it's been tampered with as there have been incidents of card cloning.

EMERGENCY

Police/Fire/Ambulance (☑ 999)

Rape & Sexual Abuse Support Centre (☑ 0808 802 9999; www.rasasc.org.uk; ⊙ noon-2.30pm & 7-9.30pm)

Samaritans (☑ 08457 90 90 90; www.samaritans.org)

INTERNET ACCESS

You'll find free wireless (wi-fi) access at many bars, cafes and hotels (although a few, particularly top-end hotels, continue to charge for the service).

INTERNET RESOURCES

BBC London (www.bbc.co.uk/london)

Evening Standard (www.standard.co.uk)

Londonist (www.londonist.com) London-centric blog.

Lonely Planet (www.lonelyplanet.com/london)

Time Out (www.timeout.com/london)

View London (www.viewlondon.co.uk)

Walk It (www.walkit.com) Enter your destination and get a walking map, time estimate and information on calories burnt and carbon dioxide saved.

MEDIA

Two free newspapers bookend the working day – *Metro* in the morning and the *London Evening Standard* in the evening – both available from tube stations. Also free, *Time Out* is the local listing guide par excellence.

MEDICAL SERVICES

To find a local doctor, pharmacy or hospital, consult the local telephone directory or call ☑ 0845 46 47.

Hospitals with 24-hour accident and emergency units include the following:

St Thomas' Hospital (☑ 020-7188 7188; Lambeth Palace Rd, SE1; ⊖ Waterloo)

University College London Hospital (☑ 0845 155 5000, 020-3456 7890; www.uclh.org; 235 Euston Rd, NW1; ⊖ Euston Sq, Warren St)

TOILETS

If you're caught short around London, public toilets can be elusive. Only a handful of tube stations have them, but the bigger National Rail stations usually do (often coin operated). If you can face five floors on an escalator, department stores are a good bet.

TOURIST INFORMATION

There are tourist information desks at Heathrow Airport, King's Cross St Pancras station, Liverpool Street station, Piccadilly Circus underground station and Victoria Station. **Visit London** (☏ 0870 156 6366; www.visitlondon.com) can fill you in on everything from attractions and events to tours and accommodation.

City of London Information Centre (Map p80; www.visitthecity.co.uk; St Paul's Churchyard, EC4; ⏰ 9.30am-5.30pm Mon-Sat, 10am-4pm Sun; ⊖ St Paul's) Tourist information, fast-track tickets to City attractions and guided walks (adult/child under 12 £7/free).

Greenwich Tourist Office (www.visitgreenwich. org.uk/tourist-information-centre; Pepys House, 2 Cutty Sark Gardens, SE10; ⏰ 10am-5pm; ⊠ DLR Cutty Sark) Information plus guided tours.

ⓘ Getting There & Away

London is the major gateway to England.

AIR

There are a number of London airports. 'For more information, see p1029.

BUS

Most long-distance coaches leave London from **Victoria Coach Station** (Map p98; 164 Buckingham Palace Rd, SW1; ⊖ Victoria).

CAR

Check reservation numbers of the main car-hire firms, all of which have airport and various city locations.

TRAIN

London's main-line terminals are linked by the tube and each serves different destinations. Most stations have left-luggage facilities (around £4) and lockers, toilets (20p) with showers (around £3), newsstands and bookshops, and a range of eating and drinking outlets. St Pancras, Victoria and Liverpool St stations have shopping centres.

If you can't find your destination in the list of main-line terminals, consult the journey planner at www.nationalrail.co.uk.

Charing Cross Canterbury.

Euston Manchester, Liverpool, Carlisle, Glasgow.

King's Cross Cambridge, Hull, York, Newcastle, Scotland.

Liverpool Street Stansted Airport, Cambridge.

London Bridge Gatwick Airport, Brighton.

Marylebone Birmingham.

Paddington Heathrow Airport, Oxford, Bath, Bristol, Exeter, Plymouth, Cardiff.

St Pancras Gatwick and Luton airports, Brighton, Nottingham, Sheffield, Leicester, Leeds, Paris.

Victoria Gatwick Airport, Brighton, Canterbury.

Waterloo Windsor, Winchester, Exeter, Plymouth.

ⓘ Getting Around

TO/FROM THE AIRPORTS
Gatwick

There are **National Rail** (☏ 0845 748 4950; www.nationalrail.co.uk) services between Gatwick's South Terminal and Victoria station (from £15, 37 minutes), running every 15 minutes during the day and hourly through the night. Other trains head to London St Pancras International (from £10, 56 minutes) and London Bridge (£10, 30 minutes, every 15 minutes). Fares are cheaper the earlier you book. If you're racing to make a flight, the **Gatwick Express** (www.gatwickexpress.com; one way/return £19.90/34.90) departs Victoria every 15 minutes from 5am to 11.45pm (30 minutes, first/last train 3.30am/12.32am).

Prices start from £2, depending on when you book, for the **EasyBus** (www.easybus.co.uk) minibus service between Gatwick and Earls Court (allow 1¼ hours, every 30 minutes from 4.20am to 1am). You'll be charged extra if you have more than one carry-on and one check-in bag. Book online for the cheapest deals.

Heathrow

Transport connections to Heathrow are excellent, and the journey to and from the city is usually painless. The cheapest option is the Underground. The Piccadilly line is accessible from every terminal (£5.70, one hour to central London, every five minutes from around 5am to 11.30pm). If there are vast queues at the ticket office, use the automatic machines instead; some accept credit cards as well as cash.

You might save some time on the considerably more expensive **Heathrow Express** (www.heathrowexpress.com; one way/return £21/34), an ultramodern train to Paddington station (15 minutes, every 15 minutes 5.12am to 11.48pm). You can purchase tickets on board (£5 extra), from self-service machines (cash and credit cards accepted) at both stations, or online.

There are taxi ranks for black cabs outside every terminal; a fare to the centre of London will cost between £45 and £85.

London City

The Docklands Light Railway (DLR) connects London City Airport to the tube network, taking 22 minutes to reach Bank station (£4.70). A black taxi costs around £30 to/from central London.

Luton

There are regular **National Rail** (www.nationalrail. co.uk) services from St Pancras (£13.90, 29 to 39 minutes) to Luton Airport Parkway station, where a shuttle bus (£1.60) will get you to the airport within 10 minutes. EasyBus minibuses head from Victoria, Earl's Court and Baker St to Luton (one-way £10, allow 1½ hours, every 30 minutes). A taxi to central London costs around £100 to £110.

Stansted

The **Stansted Express** (☑ 0845 8500150; www. stanstedexpress.com) connects with Liverpool St station (one way/return £23.40/33.20, 46 minutes, every 15 to 30 minutes 6am to 12.30am).

EasyBus (www.easybus.co.uk; one way £10, return from £12) services run between Stansted and Baker St (1¼ hours, every 20 minutes). The **Airbus A6** (☑ 0870 580 8080; www.nationalex-press.com) links with Victoria Coach station (£11, allow 1¾ hours, at least every 30 minutes). **National Express** (www.nationalexpress.com) also runs buses to Stansted from Liverpool St station (£9 one way, 80 mins, every 30 mins).

Terravision (www.terravision.eu) coaches link Stansted to both Liverpool St train station (bus A51, one way/return from £9/15, 55 minutes) and Victoria coach station (bus A50, one way/return from £8/14, 75 minutes) every 20 to 40 minutes between 6am and 1am.

A taxi cab to/from central London costs about £125.

BICYCLE

The central city is flat and relatively compact and traffic moves slowly – all good news for cyclists. Operating 24 hours a day, the excellent **Barclays Cycle Hire Scheme** (☑ 0845 026 3630; www.tfl. gov.uk.) allows you to hire a bike from one of 400 docking stations around London. The access fee is £2 for 24 hours or £10 per week; after that, the first 30 minutes is free (making the bikes perfect for short hops), or £1/4/6/15 for one hour/90 minutes/two hours/three hours. Cycle as often as you like, but leave five minutes between each trip. Visitors to London can pay either online or using a credit or debit card at a docking station. The minimum age for buying access is 18, the minimum age for riding a Barclays Bike is 14.

CAR

The M25 ring road encompasses the 609 sq miles that is broadly regarded as Greater London. For motorists it's the first circle of hell; London's streets can be congested beyond belief. Traffic is heavy, roadwork continuous, parking is either impossible or expensive, and wheel-clampers are diligent. If you drive into central London from 7am to 6pm on a weekday, you'll need to pay a £10 per day congestion charge (visit www.tfl.gov.uk for payment options) or face a hefty fine. If you're hiring a car to continue your trip from London, take the tube to Heathrow and pick it up from there.

PUBLIC TRANSPORT

Although complaining about it is a local sport, London's public transport is excellent, with tubes, trains, buses and boats getting you wherever you need to go. **TFL** (www.tfl.gov.uk), the city's public transport provider, is the glue that binds the network together. Its website has a handy journey planner and information on all services, including cabs. Get yourself an Oyster card and make the most of it.

Boat

Boats plying the Thames are a great way to travel, avoiding traffic jams while affording great views. Passengers with daily, weekly or monthly travelcards (including on Oyster) get a third off all fares.

Thames Clippers (www.thamesclippers. com) runs regular commuter services between Embankment, Waterloo, Blackfriars, Bankside, London Bridge, Tower, Canary Wharf, Greenwich, North Greenwich and Woolwich piers (adult/child £6.80/3.40) from 6am and between 10pm and midnight depending on the day of the week (from 9.30am weekends). Leisure services include the Tate-to-Tate boat (p95) and Westminster–Greenwich services. There are also boats to Kew Gardens and Hampton Court Palace.

London Waterbus Company (☑ 020-7482 2660; www.londonwaterbus.com; single/return £8.20/11.50) and **Jason's Trip** (www.jasons. co.uk; opposite 42 Blomfield Rd, W9; single/return £9/14) both run canal boat journeys between Camden Lock and Little Venice; see websites for times. London has some 40 miles of inner-city canals, mostly built in the 19th century.

Bus

Travelling around London by double-decker bus is great for seeing the city, but it's usually slower than the tube. Heritage 'Routemaster' buses with conductors operate on route 9 (from Aldwych to Royal Albert Hall) and 15 (between Trafalgar Sq and Tower Hill); these are the only buses without wheelchair access. A new fleet of freshly designed hybrid diesel/electric hop-on/hop-off (and wheelchair-accessible) Routemasters is now running on some routes, and will number 600 buses by 2016.

Buses run regularly during the day, while less frequent night buses (prefixed with the letter 'N') wheel into action when the tube stops. Single-journey bus tickets (valid for two hours) cost £2.40 (£1.45 on Oyster, capped at £4.40 per day); a weekly pass is £20.20. Children ride for free. At stops with yellow signs, you must buy your ticket from the automatic machine (or use an Oyster) before boarding. Buses stop on request, so clearly signal the driver with an outstretched arm.

LONDON'S OYSTER DIET

To get the most out of London, you need to be able to jump on and off public transport like a local, not scramble to buy a ticket at hefty rates each time. The best and cheapest way to do this is with an Oyster card, a reusable smartcard on which you can load prepaid credit or Travelcards, valid for periods from a day to a year. The card itself is £5, which is fully refundable when you leave.

London is divided into concentric transport zones, although most visitor destinations are in Zones 1 and 2. Travelcard tickets will give you unlimited transport on the tube, buses and rail services within these zones. All you need to do is touch your card to the yellow sensors on the station turnstiles or at the front of the bus.

For pay-as-you-go, the fare will be deducted from the credit on your card at a much lower rate than if you were buying a one-off paper ticket. An oyster bus trip costs £1.45 as opposed to £2.40 for an individual fare, while a Zone 1 tube journey is £2.20 as opposed to £4.70. Even better, in any single day your fares will be capped at the equivalent of the Oyster day-pass rate for the zones you've travelled in (Zones 1 and 2 peak/off-peak £8.40/7).

Assuming you avoid peak hours (6.30am to 9.30am and 4pm to 7pm), this ready reckoner gives the cheapest options for your length of stay:

One to four days Prepay

Five to 24 days Weeklies topped up with prepay for any remaining days

Twenty-five to 31 days Monthly

London Underground, DLR & Overground

'The tube', as it's universally known, burrows throughout London and into the surrounding counties, with services running every few minutes from roughly 5.30am to 12.30am (from 7am to 11.30pm Sunday).

It's easy to use. Tickets (or Oyster card top-ups) can be purchased from counters or machines at the entrance to each station using either cash or credit card. They're then inserted into the slot on the turnstiles (or you touch your Oyster card on the yellow reader), and the barrier opens.

Also included within the network are the driverless Docklands Light Railway (DLR), and the train lines shown on tube maps as 'Overground'. The DLR links the City to Docklands, Greenwich and London City Airport.

The tube map itself is an acclaimed graphic design work, using coloured lines to show how the 14 different routes intersect. However, it's not remotely to scale. The distances between stations become greater the further from central London you travel, while Leicester Sq and Covent Garden stations are only 250m apart.

Train

Particularly south of the river, where tube lines are in shorter supply, the various rail companies are an important part of the public transport picture. Most stations are now fitted with Oyster readers and accept Travelcards. If you travel outside your zone you'll need to have enough prepay credit on your Oyster card to cover the additional charge. As not all stations have turnstiles, it's important to remember to tap-in and tap-out at the Oyster reader at the station or your card will register an unfinished journey and you're likely to be charged extra. You can still buy a paper ticket from machines or counters at train stations.

TAXI

London's famous black cabs are available for hire when the yellow light above the windscreen is lit. To get an all-London licence, cabbies must do 'The Knowledge', which tests them on up to 25,000 streets within a 6-mile radius of Charing Cross and all points of interest from hotels to churches. Fares are metered, with flag fall of £2.40 and the additional rate dependent on time of day, distance travelled and taxi speed. A one-mile trip will cost between £5.60 and £8.80. To order a black cab by phone, try **Computer Cabs** (cash 020-7908 0207, credit card 020-7432 1432; www.comcablondon.com); it charges a £2 booking fee. Find the nearest black cab by downloading the **Hailo** (www.hailocab.com) app to your mobile.

Licensed minicabs operate via agencies (most busy areas have a walk-in office with drivers waiting). They're a cheaper alternative to black cabs and quote trip fares in advance. To find a local minicab firm, visit www.tfl.gov.uk.

There have been many reports of sexual assault and theft by unlicensed minicab drivers. Only use drivers from proper agencies; licensed minicabs aren't allowed to tout for business or pick you up off the street without a booking, so avoid the shady characters who hang around outside nightclubs or bars.

Canterbury & Southeast England

Best Places to Eat

➜ Deeson's (p156)

➜ Allotment (p165)

➜ Iydea (p177)

➜ Terre à Terre (p177)

➜ Town House (p180)

Best Places to Stay

➜ Bleak House (p160)

➜ Jeake's House (p168)

➜ Wallett's Court (p165)

➜ Reading Rooms (p159)

➜ Hotel Una (p176)

Why Go?

Rolling chalk hills, venerable Victorian resorts, fields of hops and grapes sweetening in the sun: welcome to England's southeast, four soothing counties' worth of country houses, fairy-tale castles and the country's finest food and drink. That fruit-ripening sun shines brightest and longest on the coast, warming a string of seaside towns wedged between formidable chalk cliffs. There's something for everyone here, from the medieval quaintness of Sandwich to the bohemian spirit of hedonistic Brighton and the more genteel air of Eastbourne.

The southeast is also pock-marked with reminders of darker days. The region's position as the front line against Continental invaders has left a wealth of turbulent history, including the 1066 battlefield, Dover Castle's secret war tunnels and scattered Roman ruins.

England's spiritual heart is Canterbury; its cathedral and ancient Unesco-listed attractions are essential viewing for any 21st-century pilgrim.

When to Go

➜ May is a good time to get creative in Brighton at Great Britain's second-largest arts festival.

➜ During June, don your top hat and breeches to revel in frilly Victoriana at the Dickens Festival in Broadstairs.

➜ Any time between May and October is ideal for a hike along the South Downs Way, which runs the length of England's newest national park.

➜ In summer head to Thanet's glorious beaches for some proper seaside fun.

⚡ Activities

The southeast of England may be Britain's most densely populated corner, but there are still plenty of off-the-beaten-track walking and cycling routes to enjoy.

Cycling

Finding quiet roads for cycle touring takes a little extra perseverance in the southeast of England, but the effort is richly rewarded. Long-distance routes that form part of the National Cycle Network (NCN; www.sustrans. org.uk) include the following:

Downs & Weald Cycle Route (110 miles; NCN Routes 2, 20 & 21) London to Brighton and on to Hastings.

Garden of England Cycle Route (165 miles; NCN Routes 1 & 2) London to Dover and then Hastings.

You'll also find less demanding routes on the NCN website. Meanwhile, there are plenty of uppers and downers to challenge mountain bikers on walking trails, such as the South Downs Way National Trail, which takes between two and four days to complete.

Walking

Two long-distance trails meander steadily westward through the region, and there are plenty of shorter ambles to match your schedule, stamina and scenery wishlist.

South Downs Way National Trail (www. nationaltrail.co.uk/southdowns) This 100-mile National Trail through England's newest national park is a beautiful roller-coaster walk along prehistoric drove roads between Winchester and Eastbourne.

North Downs Way National Trail (www. nationaltrail.co.uk/northdowns) This 153-mile walk begins near Farnham in Surrey, but one of its most beautiful sections runs from near Ashford to Dover; a loop takes in Canterbury near its end.

1066 Country Walk Heads from Pevensey Castle to Rye (32 miles) and serves as a continuation of the South Downs Way.

ℹ Information

Kent Attractions (www.kentattractions.co.uk)
Tourism South East (www.visitsoutheastengland.com) The official website for south and southeast England.
Visit Kent (www.visitkent.co.uk)
Visit Surrey (www.visitsurrey.com)
Visit Sussex (www.visitsussex.org)

ℹ Getting There & Around

The southeast is easily explored by train or bus, and many attractions can be visited in a day trip from London. Contact the National Traveline (www.travelinesoutheast.org.uk) for comprehensive information about public transport.

BUS

Explorer Tickets (adult/child £6.20/3.10) provide unlimited day-long travel on most buses throughout the region. Buy them on the first bus you board.

TRAIN

Secure 33% discounts on most rail fares in the southeast by purchasing a **Network Railcard** (www.network-railcard.co.uk; per year £30). Three adults can travel with you for the same discounted fare, and you save 60% on fares for children under 15.

KENT

Kent isn't described as the garden of England for nothing. Within its sea-lined borders you'll find a fragrant landscape of gentle hills, fertile farmland, cultivated country estates and fruit-laden orchards. It could also be described as the beer garden of England as it produces the world-renowned Kent hops and some of the country's finest ales and wines from its numerous vineyards. At its heart is spellbinding Canterbury, crowned by its enthralling cathedral.

You'll also find beautiful coastal stretches dotted with beach towns and villages, from old-school Broadstairs to gentrified Whitstable and the aesthetically challenged port town of Dover.

Canterbury

POP 151,200

Canterbury tops the charts for English cathedral cities and is one of southern England's top attractions. Many consider the World Heritage–listed cathedral that dominates its centre to be one of Europe's finest, and the town's narrow medieval alleyways, riverside gardens and ancient city walls are a joy to explore. But Canterbury isn't just a showpiece for the past – it's a spirited place with an energetic student population and a wide choice of contemporary bars, restaurants and arts venues. Book ahead for the best hotels and eateries: pilgrims may no longer flock here in their thousands, but tourists certainly do.

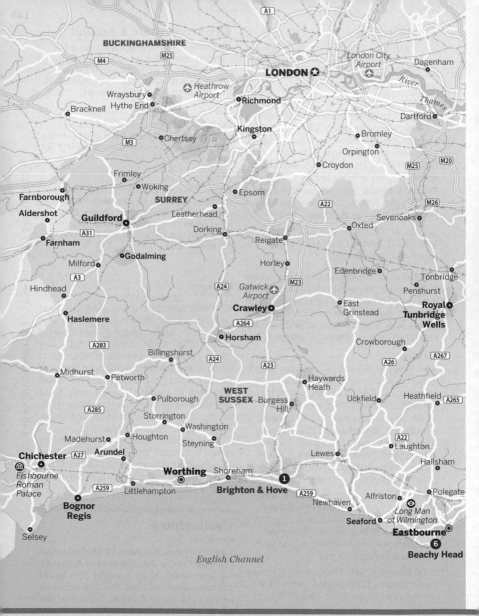

Canterbury & Southeast England Highlights

❶ Shopping, tanning and partying in **Brighton & Hove** (p173), hedonist capital of the southeast

❷ Making a pilgrimage to **Canterbury** (p149), one of England's most important religious sites

❸ Exploring the atmospheric WWII tunnels beneath sprawling **Dover Castle** (p163)

❹ Wandering the cobbled lanes of **Rye** (p168), one of England's prettiest towns

❺ Kicking back at the moated marvel that is **Leeds Castle** (p158)

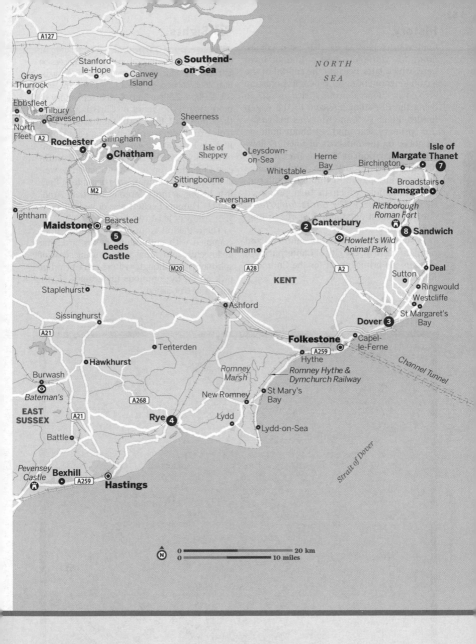

6 Scrambling up **Beachy Head** (p172), a spectacular headland in snow-white chalk

7 Shaking out your beach towel for some seaside fun on the **Isle of Thanet** (p159)

8 Getting hopelessly lost in the crooked medieval streets of **Sandwich** (p161)

History

Canterbury's past is as rich as it comes. From AD 200 there was a Roman town here, which later became the capital of the Saxon kingdom of Kent. When St Augustine arrived in England from Africa in 597 to bring the Christian message to the pagan hordes, he chose Canterbury as his *cathedra* (primary seat) and set about building an abbey on the outskirts of town. Following the martyrdom of Thomas Becket, Archbishop of Canterbury, the town became northern Europe's most important pilgrimage destination, which in turn prompted Geoffrey Chaucer's *The Canterbury Tales*, one of the most outstanding works in English literature.

Despite its blasphemous murders and rampant tourism, the city of Canterbury still remains the primary seat for the Church of England.

◉ Sights

★ Canterbury Cathedral   CATHEDRAL

(www.canterbury-cathedral.org; adult/concession £10.50/9.50, tour adult/concession £5/4, audio tour adult/concession £4/3; ⊙9am-5pm Mon-Sat, 12.30pm-2.30pm Sun) A rich repository of more than 1400 years of Christian history, the Church of England's mother ship is a truly extraordinary place with an absorbing history. This Gothic cathedral, the highlight of the city's World Heritage Sites, is southeast England's top tourist attraction as well as a place of worship. It's also the site of English history's most famous murder: Archbishop Thomas Beckett was done in here in 1170. Allow at least two hours.

The cathedral is an overwhelming edifice crammed with enthralling stories, arresting architecture and a real and enduring sense of spirituality – although visitors can't help but pick up on the ominous undertones of violence and bloodshed.

Canterbury

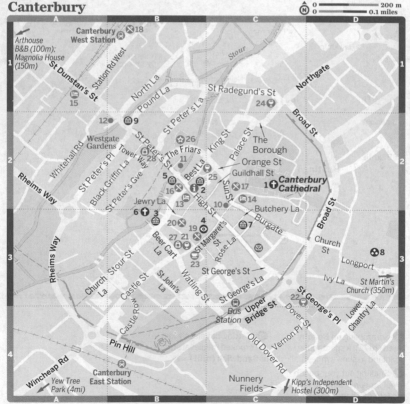

This ancient structure is packed with monuments commemorating the nation's battles. Also here are the grave and heraldic tunic of one of the nation's most famous warmongers, Edward the Black Prince (1330–76). The spot in the northwest transept where Becket met his grisly end has drawn pilgrims for more than 800 years and is marked by a flickering candle and a striking modern altar.

Beside the altar is the doorway to the crypt. This cavernous space is the cathedral's highlight, the only survivor from the last fire in 1174, which destroyed the rest of the building. Look for the amazingly well-preserved carvings among the forest of pillars.

The wealth of detail in the cathedral is immense and unrelenting, so it's well worth joining a one-hour tour (three daily, from Monday to Saturday) or taking a 40-minute self-guided audio tour.

Canterbury Heritage Museum   MUSEUM
(www.canterbury-museums.co.uk; Stour St; adult/child £8/free; ⊙11am-5pm daily) This fine 14th-century building, once the Poor Priests' Hospital, now houses the city's captivating museum. It contains a jumble of exhibits ranging from pre-Roman times to the assassination of Thomas Becket, and from the likes of Joseph Conrad to locally born celebs. The kids' room is excellent, with a memorable glimpse of real medieval poo among other fun activities. Train fans can admire the *Invicta* locomotive, which ran on the world's third passenger railway, the 'Crab & Winkle' Canterbury–Whitstable line.

The building also houses the Rupert Bear Museum (Rupert's creator, Mary Tourtel, was born in Canterbury) and a gallery celebrating another old-time children's favourite TV show, *Bagpuss*.

St Augustine's Abbey   RUIN
(EH; Longport; adult/child £5/3; ⊙10am-6pm Jul & Aug, to 5pm Wed-Sun Apr-Jun & Sep-Oct, to 4pm Sat & Sun Nov-Mar) An integral but often overlooked part of the Canterbury World Heritage Site, St Augustine's Abbey was founded in AD 597, marking the rebirth of Christianity in southern England. Later requisitioned as a royal palace, it fell into disrepair and now only stumpy foundations remain. A small museum and a worthwhile free audio tour do their best to underline the site's importance and put flesh back onto its now-humble bones.

St Martin's Church   CHURCH
(www.martinpaul.org; North Holmes Rd; ⊙11am-4pm Tue, Thu & Sat Apr-Sep, to 3pm Oct-Mar) This stumpy little building just off the road from Canterbury to Sandwich is thought to be England's oldest parish church in continuous use. It's also where Queen Bertha (wife of the Saxon King Ethelbert) welcomed St Augustine when he arrived in England in the 6th century. The original Saxon church has been swallowed up by a medieval refurbishment, but is still worth the walk out of town to see.

CANTERBURY & SOUTHEAST ENGLAND CANTERBURY

Canterbury

Eastbridge Hospital HISTORIC BUILDING

(www.eastbridgehospital.org.uk; 25 High St; adult/child £2/1; ⊘10am-5pm Mon-Sat) A 'place of hospitality' for pilgrims, soldiers and the elderly since 1180, Eastbridge Hospital of St Thomas the Martyr is the last of many such buildings in Canterbury still open to the public. It's worth a visit for the Romanesque undercroft and historic chapel. The 16th-century almshouses, still in use, sit astride Britain's oldest road bridge, dating back more than 800 years.

Roman Museum MUSEUM

(Butchery Lane; adult/child £6/free; ⊘10am-5pm) Given a facelift in 2013 after a reprieve from council cuts, this fascinating subterranean archaeological site gives an insight into Canterbury's everyday life almost two millennia ago. Visitors can stroll a reconstructed Roman marketplace and rooms, including a kitchen, as well as view Roman mosaic floors. Everything you see here was only discovered after WWII bombs did a bit of impromptu excavation.

West Gate Towers MUSEUM

(St Peter's St) The city's only remaining medieval gateway has become Canterbury's most-discussed sight in recent years. Under threat from council cuts in 2011, it was taken over by a local businessman who spent lavishly turning it into a family attraction. His sudden death in early 2012 left the towers closed (again) and it's still uncertain what will become of them. Until they reopen, entertain yourself watching buses, their wing mirrors folded back, as they squeeze through the medieval archway.

Greyfriars Chapel CHURCH

(⊘2-4pm Mon-Sat Easter-Sep) You'll find Greyfriars Chapel in serene riverside gardens behind Eastbridge Hospital. The first monastery built in England by Franciscan monks in 1267, its grounds are a tranquil spot to unfurl the picnic blanket.

Canterbury Tales EXHIBITION

(www.canterburytales.org.uk; St Margaret's St; adult/child £8.50/6.25; ⊘10am-5pm Mar-Oct) This ambitious three-dimensional interpretation of Chaucer's classic tales using jerky animatronics and audioguides is certainly entertaining, but could never do full justice to the original work. It does, however, provide a lighthearted introduction for the young or uninitiated.

Beaney House of Art & Knowledge MUSEUM

(18 High St; ⊘9am-5pm Mon-Wed, Fri & Sat, to 7pm Thu, 10am-5pm Sun) FREE This mock-Tudor edifice is the grandest on the main shopping thoroughfare, if not the most authentic. Formerly called the Royal Museum & Art Gallery, it has housed Canterbury's main library, a museum and an art gallery since 1899 – it's current name is in honour of the 19th-century benefactor who funded the original building. In addition to the city's main library and the tourist office, the mixed bag of museum exhibitions is worth half an hour between the main sights.

There's also a good cafe and interesting temporary exhibitions (admission sometimes charged).

🠪 Tours

Canterbury Historic River Tours BOAT TOUR

(☑07790-534744; www.canterburyrivertours.co.uk; Kings Bridge; adult/child £8.50/5; ⊘10am-5pm Mar-Oct) Knowledgeable guides double up as energetic oars on these fascinating River Stour mini cruises, which depart from behind the Old Weaver's House.

THE MARTYRDOM OF THOMAS BECKET

Not one to shy away from cronyism, in 1162 King Henry II appointed his mate Thomas Becket to the highest clerical office in the land, figuring it would be easier to force the increasingly vocal religious lobby to fall into line if he was pals with the archbishop. Unfortunately for Henry, he underestimated how seriously Thomas would take the job, and the archbishop soon began to disagree with almost everything the king said or did. By 1170 Henry had become exasperated with his former favourite and suggested to four of his knights that Thomas was too much to bear. Becket was murdered on 29 December. Becket's martyrdom – and canonisation in double-quick time (1173) – catapulted Canterbury Cathedral to the top of the league of northern European pilgrimage sites. Mindful of the growing criticism of his role in Becket's murder, Henry arrived in Canterbury in 1174 for a dramatic *mea culpa* and, after allowing himself to be whipped and scolded, was granted absolution.

Canterbury River Navigation Company
BOAT TOUR

(☏ 07816-760869; www.crnc.co.uk; Westgate Gardens; adult/child from £9/4; ⊙ Apr-Oct) Weather permitting, this company offers relaxing punt trips on the River Stour.

Canterbury Guided Tours
WALKING TOUR

(☏ 01227-459779;www.canterburyguidedtours.com; adult/child/concession £7/5/6.50; ⊙ 11am Feb-Oct, 11am & 2pm Jul-Sep) Guided walking tours leave from opposite the Canturbury Cathedral entrance. Tickets can be purchased from the tourist office.

✴✦ Festivals & Events

Canterbury Festival
PERFORMING ARTS

(☏ 01227-787787; www.canterburyfestival.co.uk; ⊙ Oct) Myriad musicians, comedians, theatre groups and other artists from around the world come to party during this festival, which runs for the last two weeks in October.

🛏 Sleeping

Kipp's Independent Hostel
HOSTEL £

(☏ 01227-786121; www.kipps-hostel.com; 40 Nunnery Fields; dm/s/d £19.50/28.50/57; @ 🛜) Occupying a red-brick town house in a quietish residential area less than a mile from the city centre, these superb backpacker digs enjoy a homely atmosphere, clean (though cramped) dorms and rave reviews.

Yew Tree Park
CAMPSITE £

(☏ 01227-700306; www.yewtreepark.com; Stone St; sites per tent & 2 adults £14.20-24.50; ⊙ Apr-Sep; P@🛜🏊) Family-run campsite set in gentle rolling countryside 5 miles southeast of the city. Phone ahead for directions and transport information.

House of Agnes
HOTEL ££

(☏ 01227-472185; www.houseofagnes.co.uk; 71 St Dunstan's St; r from £85-130; @🛜) This rather wonky 13th-century beamed inn, mentioned in Dickens' *David Copperfield,* has eight themed rooms bearing names such as 'Marrakesh' (Moorish), 'Venice' (carnival masks), 'Boston' (light and airy) and 'Canterbury' (antiques and heavy fabrics). If you prefer your room to have straight lines and right angles, there are eight less exciting, but no less comfortable, rooms in an annexe in the walled garden.

Arthouse B&B
B&B ££

(☏ 07976-725457; www.arthousebandb.com; 24 London Rd; r £75; P🛜) A night at Canterbury's most laid-back digs, which are

housed in a 19th-century fire station, is a bit like sleeping over at a really cool art student's pad. The theme is funky and eclectic, with furniture by local designers and artwork by the instantly likeable artist owners, who have a house-studio out back.

The organic continental breakfast is laid out in the guest kitchen, with a hostel-like vibe. Only one of the three rooms is en suite.

Cathedral Gate Hotel
HOTEL ££

(☏ 01227-464381; www.cathgate.co.uk; 36 Burgate; s/d £50/112, without bathroom £50/81.50; 🛜) Predating the spectacular cathedral gate it adjoins, this quaint 15th-century hotel is a medieval warren of steep staircases and narrow passageways leading to 27 pleasingly old-fashioned rooms with angled floors, low doors and cockeyed walls. Some have cathedral views, while others overlook pretty Buttermarket. There's no lift.

Magnolia House
B&B ££

(☏ 01227-765121;www.magnoliahousecanterbury.co.uk; 36 St Dunstan's Tce; s/d from £50/95; P @ 🛜) An alluringly cosy Georgian guesthouse, Magnolia House comes complete with beautifully appointed if slightly over-filled rooms, lovely gardens and big cooked breakfasts. Head up St Dunstan's St from the West Gate for about 400m until you reach a roundabout; turn left and St Dunstan's Terrace is the second on the left.

★ Abode Canterbury
HOTEL £££

(☏ 01227-766266; www.abodehotels.co.uk; 30-33 High St; r from £143; 🛜) The 72 rooms at this supercentral hotel, the only boutique hotel in town, are graded from 'comfortable' to 'fabulous', and for the most part live up to their names. They come with features such as handmade beds, cashmere throws, velour bathrobes, beautiful modern bathrooms and little tuckboxes of locally produced snacks. There's a splendid champagne bar, restaurant and tavern, too.

THE CANTERBURY TALES

If English literature has a father figure, then it is Geoffrey Chaucer (1342–1400). Chaucer was the first English writer to introduce characters – rather than 'types' – into fiction, and he did so to greatest effect in his best-known work, *The Canterbury Tales*.

Written between 1387 and his death, in the hard-to-decipher Middle English of the day, Chaucer's *Tales* is an unfinished series of 24 vivid stories told by a party of pilgrims journeying between London and Canterbury. Chaucer successfully created the illusion that the pilgrims, not Chaucer (though he appears in the tales as himself), are telling the stories, which gave him unprecedented freedom as an author. *The Canterbury Tales* remains one of the pillars of the literary canon. But more than that, it's a collection of rollicking good yarns of adultery, debauchery, crime and edgy romance, and is filled with Chaucer's witty observations about human nature.

✗ Eating

Boho
INTERNATIONAL £

(43 St Peter's St; snacks £4-14; ⊘9am-6pm Mon-Sat, 10am-5pm Sun) This hip eatery in a prime spot on the main drag is extraordinarily popular and you'll be lucky to get a table on busy shopping days. Cool tunes lilt through the chic retro dining space while chilled diners chow down on humungous burgers, full-monty breakfasts and imaginative, owner-cooked international mains. Boho doesn't do bookings, so be prepared to queue.

Veg Box Cafe
VEGETARIAN £

(www.thevegboxcafe.co.uk; 1 Jewry Lane; mains £7; ⊘10am-6pm Mon-Sat; 🖉) Perched above Canterbury's top veggie food store, this laid-back and welcoming spot uses only the freshest, locally sourced organic ingredients in its dishes.

Tiny Tim's Tearoom
CAFE £

(34 St Margaret's St; mains £7-9; ⊘9.30am-5pm Tue-Sat, 10.30am-4pm Sun) Swish 1930s English tearoom offering hungry shoppers big breakfasts bursting with Kentish ingredients, and tiers of cakes, crumpets, cucumber sandwiches and scones plastered in clotted cream.

★ Deeson's
BRITISH ££

(🖉01227-767854; 25-27 Sun St; mains £6-16; ⊘noon-3pm & 5-10pm Mon-Sat, noon-10pm Sun) Put the words 'local', 'seasonal' and 'tasty' together and you have this superb British eatery. Local fruit and veg; award-winning wines, beers and ciders; fish from Kent's coastal waters; and the odd ingredient from the proprietor's own allotment are all served in a straightforward, contemporary setting just a Kentish apple's throw from the Canterbury Cathedral gates.

Goods Shed
MARKET, RESTAURANT ££

(www.thegoodsshed.co.uk; Station Rd West; mains £12-20; ⊘market 9am-7pm Tue-Sat, 10am-4pm Sun, restaurant 8am-9.30pm Tue-Sat, 9am-3pm Sun) Farmers market, food hall and fabulous restaurant rolled into one, this converted warehouse by the Canterbury West train station is a hit with everyone from self-caterers to sit-down gourmets. The chunky wooden tables sit slightly above the market hubbub but in full view of its appetite-whetting stalls, and daily specials exploit fresh farm goodies.

🍺 Drinking & Nightlife

Parrot
PUB

(1-9 Church Lane; ⊘noon-11pm) Built in 1370 on Roman foundations, Canterbury's oldest boozer has a snug, beam-rich pub downstairs and a much-lauded dining room upstairs under yet more ageing oak. Needless to say, many a local microbrewed ale is pulled in both venues.

Thomas Becket
PUB

(21 Best Lane; ⊘noon-3pm & 5-9pm Mon-Thu, to 9.30pm Fri, to 9.30pm Sat, to 9pm Sun) A classic English pub with a garden's worth of hops hanging from its timber frame, Thomas Becket has several quality ales to sample. Traditional decor includes copper pots, comfy seating and a fireplace to cosy up to on winter nights. It also serves decent pub grub.

Micro Roastery
CAFE

(www.microroastery.co.uk; 4 St Margaret's St; ⊘8am-6pm Mon-Fri, from 9am Sat, 10am-5pm Sun; 🛜) Owned by an Anglo-Peruvian couple, this new cafe imports, roasts, grinds and sells its unsurpassed beans and blends. There's local art on the walls; the furniture is upholstered in coffee-bean sacks; and a La Marzocco espresso machine pumps out strong brews.

Alberry's Wine Bar CLUB
(www.alberrys.co.uk; 38 St Margaret's St; ⊙11am-3am) An after-hours music bar that puts on everything from smooth live jazz to DJ-led drum and bass to commercial pop. Relax over a French Kiss cocktail upstairs before heading down to the basement bar.

Chill Nightclub CLUB
(www.chill-nightclub.com; 41 St George's Pl) Small, cheesy nightclub with Alphabeats theme nights on Wednesdays and a big Sound of Saturday that runs well into Sunday morning.

☆ Entertainment

New Marlowe Theatre THEATRE
(☑ 01227-787787; www.newmarlowetheatre.org.uk; The Friars) Canterbury's main theatre attracts top acts and fast-selling productions. Check out the bizarre auditorium, with its dark faux veneers contrasting sharply with the lifejacket-orange seating.

🔒 Shopping

Canterbury has Kent's best shopping. For mainstream stores head for the east end of the main street (High St, St George's St) but for quirkier independents try the west end of High St, St Peter's St and the so-called 'King's Mile' (Palace St, Borough and Northgate).

Revivals CLOTHING
(42 St Peter's St; ⊙10am-5pm Mon-Sat, to 4pm Sun) One of the southeast's best vintage-clothing emporia.

Chaucer Bookshop BOOKS
(6-7 Beer Cart Lane; ⊙10am-5pm Mon-Sat, 11am-4pm Sun) Antiquarian and used books.

ℹ️ Information

Post Office (19 St George's St; ⊙9am-5.30pm Mon-Sat) On the 1st floor of WH Smiths.

Tourist Office (☑ 01227-378100; www.canter bury.co.uk; 18 High St; ⊙9am-5pm Mon-Wed, Fri & Sat, to 7pm Thu, 10am-5pm Sun) In the Beaney House of Art & Knowledge. Staff can help book accommodation, excursions and theatre tickets.

ℹ️ Getting There & Away

The city's **bus station** (St George's Lane) is just within the city walls on St George's Lane. There are two train stations, Canterbury East for London Victoria and Canterbury West for London's Charing Cross/St Pancras stations.

BUS
Canterbury connections:
Dover National Express; £4.90, 40 minutes, hourly
London Victoria National Express; £14.40, two hours, hourly
Margate £5.10, 50 minutes, three per hour
Ramsgate £5.10 45 minutes, hourly
Sandwich £3.50, 40 minutes, three hourly
Whitstable £4.50, 30 minutes, every 10 minutes

TRAIN
Canterbury connections:
Dover Priory £8, 25 minutes, every 30 minutes

A SWIG OF KENT & SUSSEX

With booze cruises over to Calais almost a thing of the past, many Kent and Sussex drinkers are rediscovering their counties' superb home-grown beverages. Both counties produce some of the most delicious ales in the country and the southeast's wines are even outgunning some traditional Continental vintners.

Kent's **Shepherd Neame Brewery** (☑ 01795-542016; www.shepherdneame.co.uk; 10 Court St, Faversham; tours £12.50; ⊙call ahead or see website for tour times) is Britain's oldest and produces aromatic ales brewed from Kent-grown premium hops. Sussex's reply is **Harveys Brewery** (☑ 01273-480217; www.harveys.org.uk; Bridge Wharf, Lewes; per person £2.50; ⊙evenings three times a week Jun-Jul & Sep-Nov), which perfumes Lewes town centre with a hop-laden scent. Book in advance for tours of either brewery.

Mention 'English wine' not too long ago and you'd likely hear a snort of derision. Not any more. Thanks to warmer temperatures and determined winemakers, English wine, particularly of the sparkling variety, is developing a fan base all of its own.

Award-winning vineyards can be found in both Sussex and Kent, whose chalky soils are likened to France's Champagne region. Many vineyards now offer tours and wine tastings. Some of the most popular are **Biddenden Vineyards** (☑ 01580-291726; www.biddenden vineyards.com; admission free ; ⊙tours 10am Wed & Sat), 1.2 miles from Wealden, and **Chapel Down Vinery** (☑ 01580-766111; www.englishwinesgroup.com; Tenterden; admission £10; ⊙tours daily Jun-Sep, weekends May & Oct), located 2.5 miles south of Tenterden on the B2082.

WORTH A TRIP

WHITSTABLE

Perhaps it's the oysters, harvested since Roman times... Maybe it's the weatherboard houses and shingle beach... Perhaps it's the pleasingly old-fashioned main street with petite galleries, been-there-forever outfitters and emporia of vintage clothing... Most likely it's for all of these reasons that Whitstable has become a bit of a weekend mecca for metropolitan types looking for refuge from the city hassle.

If it's the oysters you fancy, **Wheeler's Oyster Bar** (☎ 01227-273311; 8 High St; mains £18.50-22.50; ⊙ 10.30am-9pm Mon & Tue, from 10.15am Thu, 10.15am-9.30pm Fri, 10am-10pm Sat, 11.30am-9pm Sun) is the place to head, but you'll have to book ahead and bring your own wine. Sittings are at 1pm, 3pm, 5pm & 7.30pm. While you're here, take a stroll along the beach or a spin around the **Whitstable Museum & Gallery** (www.whitstable-museum.co.uk; 5 Oxford St; adult/concession £3/2; ⊙ 11am-4.30pm), which has a corner dedicated to actor Peter Cushing, star of several Hammer Horror films and the town's most famous resident, who died in 1994

Whitstable has no tourist office, but you can pick up maps and other information at the **library** (31-33 Oxford St; ⊙ 9am-6pm Mon-Fri, to 5pm Sat, 10am-4pm Sun). Bus 4 departs for Canterbury (30 minutes) every 10 minutes.

London St Pancras High-speed service; £33.70, one hour, hourly

London Victoria/Charing Cross £28.40, 1¾ hours, two hourly

⊙ Getting Around

Canterbury's centre is mostly set up for pedestrians. Car parks are dotted along and just inside the walls, but to avoid heavy traffic day-trippers may prefer to use one of three Park & Ride sites, which cost £3 per day and connect to the centre by bus every eight minutes (7am to 7.30pm Monday to Saturday).

Leeds Castle

This immense moated pile just east of Maidstone is for many the world's most romantic **castle** (www.leeds-castle.com; adult/child £21/13.50; ⊙ 10am-6pm Apr-Sep, to 5pm Oct-Mar), and it's certainly one of the most visited in Britain. The formidable, hefty structure balancing on two islands is known as something of a 'ladies castle'. This stems from the fact that in its more than 1000 years of history, it has been home to a who's who of medieval queens, most famously Henry VIII's first wife, Catherine of Aragon.

The castle was transformed from fortress to lavish palace over the centuries, and its last owner, the high-society hostess Lady Baillie, used it as a princely family home and party pad to entertain the likes of Errol Flynn, Douglas Fairbanks and John F Kennedy.

The castle's vast estate offers enough attractions of its own to justify a day trip: peaceful walks, a duckery, aviary and falconry demonstrations. You'll also find possibly the world's sole dog-collar museum, plenty of kids' attractions and a hedge maze, overseen by a grassy bank from where fellow travellers can shout encouragement or misdirections.

Since Lady Baillie's death in 1974, a private trust has managed the property. This means that some parts of the castle are periodically closed for private events.

Trains run from London Victoria to Bearsted, where you catch a special shuttle coach to the castle.

Margate

POP 40,400

A popular resort for more than two centuries, Margate's late 20th-century slump was long and bleak as British holidaymakers ditched Victorian frump for the carefree *costas* of Spain. But this grand old seaside, with fine-sand beaches and artistic associations, has bounced off the bottom. Major cultural regeneration projects – including the spectacular Turner Contemporary art gallery – are slowly reversing the town's fortunes, and on busy days even the odd non-English speaker can be overheard in the newly minted cafes and rejuvenated old town.

⊙ Sights

★ **Turner Contemporary** GALLERY (www.turnercontemporary.org; Rendezvous (Seafront); ⊙ 10am-6pm Tue-Sun) FREE This blockbuster contemporary art gallery, bolted together on the site of the seafront guesthouse where master painter JMW Turner used to stay, is one of East Kent's top attractions. Within the strikingly featureless shell, the only thing distracting the eye, apart from the artwork on display, is the sea view from the floor-to-ceiling windows. These allow you to appreciate the very thing Turner loved so much about Margate – the sea, sky and refracted light of the north Kent coast.

The gallery is attracting top-notch contemporary installations by high-calibre artists such as Tracey Emin (who grew up in Margate) and Alex Katz, so catch a free gallery tour (Fridays and weekends at 11.30am).

Shell Grotto   GROTTO, CAVE
(www.shellgrotto.co.uk; Grotto Hill; adult/child £3.50/1.50; ⊙10am-5pm Apr-Oct, 11am-4pm Sat & Sun Nov-Mar) Margate's unique attraction is a mysterious subterranean grotto, discovered in 1835. It's a claustrophobic collection of rooms and passageways embedded with 4.6 million shells arranged in symbol-rich mosaics. It has inspired feverish speculation over the years; some think it a 2000-year-old pagan temple, others an elaborate 19th-century hoax. Either way, it's an exquisite place worth seeing.

🛏 Sleeping & Eating

★**Reading Rooms**   B&B £££
(☑01843-225166; www.thereadingroomsmargate.co.uk; 31 Hawley Sq; r £180; ⊛) Occupying an unmarked 18th-century Georgian town house on a tranquil square just five minutes' walk from the sea, this luxury boutique B&B is as stylish as they come. Generously cut rooms with waxed wooden floors and beautiful French antique reproduction furniture contrast with the 21st-century bathrooms fragrant with Ren cosmetics. Breakfast is served in your room. Booking essential.

Sands Hotel   BOUTIQUE HOTEL £££
(☑01843-228228; www.sandshotelmargate.co.uk; 16 Marine Dr; r £120-190; ❋⊛) This beautifully styled boutique hotel sits right on the Margate seafront. It features an understated sand-hued theme throughout; the southeast's best bathrooms; and a restaurant with spectacular bay views, which around half of the rooms also share. The entrance is hidden under the arches on the seafront next to the hotel's very own summertime ice cream parlour.

Mad Hatter   CAFE £
(9 Lombard St; snacks & light meals £3.50-11; ⊙11am-5.30pm Sat) This unmissable cuckoo eatery run by a top-hatted proprietor packs two rooms of a 1690s house with regalia and knick-knackery from down the ages. Christmas decorations stay up all year and the toilets are original Victorian porcelain. The yummy cakes and snacks are all homemade.

Great British Pizza Company   PIZZA £
(14a Marine Dr; pizzas £6-9; ⊙noon-9pm Tue-Sat, to 3pm Sun) A world away from your normal 'British pizza', the delicious cheese-topped wheels at this new hang-out are made using the best local and Italian ingredients. Right on the seafront, this popular feeding spot has a funkily eclectic but simple dining space, heart-pumping coffees and gelato containing nothing that it shouldn't.

❶ Information

Tourist Office (☑01843-577577; www.visit thanet.co.uk; Droit House, Stone Pier; ⊙10am-5pm daily Easter-Oct, to 5pm Tue-Sat Nov-Easter) Next to the Turner Contemporary art gallery, the tourist office serves all of the Isle of Thanet. It hands out *The Isle*, a glossy magazine crammed with Thanet listings.

❶ Getting There & Away

Departure and arrival points for local buses are Queen St and adjacent Cecil St. The train station is just a few steps from the beach.

BUS
Broadstairs Thanet Loop Bus; £1.80, up to every ten minutes
Canterbury £5.10, 50 minutes, three hourly
London Victoria National Express; £16, 2½ hours, four daily
Ramsgate Thanet Loop Bus; £2.20, up to every ten minutes

ISLE OF THANET

You won't need a wetsuit or a ferry to reach the Isle of Thanet and its towns of Margate, Ramsgate and Broadstairs: the 2-mile-wide Wantsum Channel, which divides the island from the mainland, silted up in the 16th century, transforming the East Kent landscape forever. In its island days, Thanet was the springboard for several epoch-making episodes in English history. It was here that the Romans kicked off their invasion in the 1st century AD and where St Augustine landed in AD 597 to launch his conversion of the pagans.

TRAIN

London St Pancras High-speed service, £38.10, 1½ hours, hourly
London Victoria £22.30, one hour and 50 minutes, two hourly

Broadstairs

POP 24,370

While its bigger, brasher neighbours seek to revive and regenerate themselves, quaint little Broadstairs quietly gets on with what it's done best for the past 150 years – wowing visitors with its tight sickle of reddish sand (Viking Bay) and sun-warmed lapping sea. Charles Dickens certainly thought it a pretty spot, spending most summers here between 1837 and 1859. The resort now plays the Victorian nostalgia card at every opportunity and names every second business after the works of its most famous holidaymaker.

◉ Sights

Dickens House Museum   MUSEUM
(www.dickensfellowship.org; 2 Victoria Pde; adult/child £3.60/2; ⊙2-5pm Easter-May, 10am-5pm Jun-Sep) Given a fresh lick of paint for Charles Dickens' 200th birthday in 2012, this quaint museum is Broadstairs' top attraction and the former home of Mary Pearson Strong – Dickens' inspiration for the character of Betsey Trotwood in *David Copperfield*. Diverse Dickensiana on display includes letters from the author.

✴ Festivals & Events

Dickens Festival   ARTS
(www.broadstairsdickensfestival.co.uk) Broadstairs' biggest bash, this annual, nine-day festival held in mid-June culminates in a banquet and ball in Victorian fancy dress.

⊨ Sleeping & Eating

Copperfields Guest House   B&B **££**
(☑ 01843-601247; www.copperfieldsbb.co.uk; 11 Queen's Rd; s/d £50/75; ☜) ✐ This vegetarian B&B offers three homely rooms with en suite, and a warm welcome from the owners and pet Yorkie. It also caters for vegans, and all products in the bathrooms are cruelty-free.

★ **Bleak House**   HISTORIC HOTEL **£££**
(☑ 01843-865338; www.bleakhousebroadstairs.co.uk; Fort Rd; r £155-250, apt £300; ☜) Recently reopened, this former Napoleonic-era fortress overlooking the beach was converted

into an opulent Victorian residence just in time for one Charles Dickens to rent it for 12 summers (1837–1859). From the lounge bar to the Copperfield suite with its Viking Bay views and five-star bathroom, the whole caboodle oozes unique period character. Building tours run from 10am to 6pm.

It was here that Dickens penned *David Copperfield* and the outline of *Bleak House*, declaring the building his favourite place to stay – when you see the views it's not hard to see why. But the highlight must be Dickens' very own bedroom and semicircular seaview study where he would write looking out across the Channel. It's worth every penny of the £250 a night rate and what a place to update your travel journal! There's a labyrinthine smuggling museum in the basement, a fancy restaurant, and a tearoom.

Oscar's Festival Cafe   CAFE **£**
(15 Oscar Rd; snacks £4-6.50; ⊙10.30am-5.30pm Thu-Sun) Just back from the bandstand at the southern end of Viking Bay, this hidden gem successfully recreates the buttered-toast-and-railways brand of sunny 1950s austerity that the British find so comforting.

Wyatt & Jones   BRITISH **££**
(www.wyattandjones.co.uk; 23-27 Harbour St; mains £6-17; ⊙9-11am, noon-3pm & 6-11pm Mon-Sat, 12.30-5pm Sun) Broadstairs was clamouring for a contemporary British restaurant and now, just a few steps off the beach, it has one. Savour unashamedly local dishes such as partridge in crab-apple glaze, or try local bream, mussels and chips or breakfast in the uncluttered interior of gun-metal blue and scratched timber floors. Then admire your expanding waistline in the retro mirror wall.

❶ Getting There & Away

BUS

Canterbury £5.10, 1½ hours, up to three times an hour
London Victoria National Express, £13.90, three hours, seven daily
Margate Thanet Loop Bus; £1.80, up to every ten minutes
Ramsgate Thanet Loop Bus; £1.80, up to every ten minutes

TRAIN

London St Pancras High-speed service, £38.10, one hour 20 minutes, hourly
London Victoria £22.30, two hours, twice hourly

Ramsgate

POP 40,000

The most varied of Thanet's towns, Ramsgate has a friendlier feel than rival Margate and is more vibrant than its quaint little neighbour Broadstairs. A forest of masts whistles serenely in the breeze below the handsomely curved walls of Britain's only royal harbour, and the seafront is surrounded by bars and cosmopolitan street cafes. Just one celebrity chef away from being described as 'up and coming', Ramsgate retains a shabbily undiscovered charm, its sweeping, environmentally sanctioned Blue Flag beaches and some spectacular Victorian architecture making it well worth the visit.

⊙ Sights & Activities

Spitfire Memorial Museum MUSEUM
(www.spitfiremuseum.org.uk; Manston Rd; ☺10am-5pm Apr-Oct, to 4pm Nov-Mar) FREE Around 4 miles northwest of Ramsgate's town centre at Manston Airport, this purpose-built museum stores two WWII planes: one a Spitfire, the other a Hurricane. Both look factory-fresh but are surprisingly delicate and so, sadly, there's no clambering on board. Take bus 38 (hourly) from King St and alight at the airport, then walk about 10 minutes along Manston Rd.

Gathered around the planes are myriad flight-associated exhibits, many relating to Manston's role as an airfield during the Battle of Britain.

Ramsgate Maritime Museum MUSEUM
(www.ramsgatemaritimemuseum.org; The Clock House, Royal Harbour; adult/child £2/1; ☺10am-5pm Tue-Sun Easter-Sep) Interesting but erratically opening museum displaying loot from the more than 600 ships that have been wrecked on the notorious Goodwin Sands off this stretch of coast.

🛌 Sleeping & Eating

Ramsgate has two restaurant rows: Harbour St and Westcliff Arcade.

Glendevon Guesthouse B&B ££
(☑01843-570909; www.glendevonguesthouse.co.uk; 8 Truro Rd; s/d from £52.50/70; ᴾ🛋) ∮ Run by energetic young hosts, this comfy guesthouse takes the whole ecofriendly thing very seriously, with guest recycling facilities, eco-showers and even energy-saving hairdryers. The hallways of this grand Victorian house, a block back from the Ramsgate seafront, are decorated with work by local artists. All rooms have kitchenettes, and breakfast is a convivial affair taken around a communal table.

Bon Appetit FRENCH ££
(4 Westcliff Arcade; mains £7-21; ☺noon-2.30pm & 7pm-late) The best eatery on Westcliff, this first-rate bistro serves up French-inspired dishes in a simple dining room or with alfresco harbour views. Ingredients on the menu are of the seasonal and locally sourced ilk, with finely crafted mains including delights such as pan-fried Kentish pheasant, line-caught sea bass, and lamb rump with rosemary and red-currant preserve.

ℹ Information

Tourist Office (☑01843-598750; Customs House, Harbour Pde; ☺10am-4pm Mon-Sun) A small, staffed visitor centre with out-of-hours brochure stands.

ℹ Getting There & Away

BOAT
Euroferries (☑0844 414 5355; www.euroferries.co.uk) High-speed ferries to Boulogne (from £49 per car, 1¼ hours, four times daily)

BUS
Broadstairs Thanet Loop Bus; £1.80, up to every ten minutes
London Victoria National Express, £13.90, three hours, seven daily
Margate Thanet Loop Bus; £2.20, up to every ten minutes
Sandwich £2.90, 25 minutes, hourly

TRAIN
London Charing Cross £22.30, two hours, two hourly
London St Pancras High-speed service, £38.50, 1¼ hours, hourly

Sandwich

POP 5000

As close as you'll get to a living museum, Sandwich was once England's fourth city (after London, Norwich and Ipswich). It's a fact hard to grasp as you ponder its drowsy medieval lanes, ancient churches, Dutch gables, crooked peg-tiled roofs and overhanging timber-framed houses. Once a port to rival London, Sandwich began its decline when the entrance to the harbour silted up in the 16th century, and this once-vital gateway to and from the Continent spent the next 400 years retreating into quaint rural obscurity. Preservation is big here, with huge local interest in period authenticity. The tiny 100-seat cinema is preserved as an art deco museum piece and the 1920s garage deals more in classic cars than modern vehicles. Within the town's historical core, unlisted buildings are the exception.

Of course, Sandwich indirectly gave the world its favourite snack when the Fourth Earl of Sandwich called for his meat to be served between two slices of bread, thus freeing him to gamble all night without leaving the table or smudging his cards. From then on, it became *de rigueur* to ask for meat 'like Sandwich' and the rest is fast-food history, although the town makes precious little of it.

◉ Sights & Activities

Sandwich's web of medieval and Elizabethan streets is perfect for ambling through and getting pleasantly lost (as many do). **Strand Street** in particular has one of the country's highest concentrations of half-timbered buildings. Ornate brickwork on some houses betrays the strong influence of 350 Protestant Flemish refugees (referred to as 'the Strangers'), who settled in the town in the 16th century at the invitation of Elizabeth I.

Richborough Roman Fort   RUIN
(EH; Richborough Rd; adult/child £5.20/3.10; ⊘10am-6pm Apr-Sep, to 5pm Wed-Sun Oct, to 4pm Sat & Sun Nov-Mar) Roman Britain began here amid the windswept ruins of Richborough's Roman Fort, just 2 miles north of Sandwich. This is where the successful AD 43 invasion of Britain was launched. To celebrate their victory, the Romans planted a colossal triumphal arch here, the base of which remains.

The fort's clearest features today – high walls and scores of deep defensive ditches – came later when the Romans were forced to stave off increasingly vicious seaborne attacks.

To arrive as the Romans did, by boat, you can take the Sandwich River Bus from the Quay.

Sandwich Quay   WATERFRONT
Several attractions line the River Stour. First up is a cute little flint-chequered Barbican tollgate built by Henry VIII, which controls traffic flow over the river's only road bridge. Nearby rises Fishergate, built in 1384 and once the main entrance to the town, through which goods from the Continent and beyond once passed. On fair-weather days, hop aboard the **Sandwich River Bus** (☎07958 376183; www.sandwichriverbus.co.uk; adult/child 30min trip £7/5, 1hr £12/8; ⊘every 30-60min 11am-6pm Thu-Sun Apr-Sep) beside the toll bridge for seal-spotting trips along the River Stour and in Pegwell Bay, or for an interesting way to reach Richborough.

Guildhall Museum   MUSEUM
(adult/child £1/50p; ⊘10.30am-12.30pm & 2-4pm Tue, Wed, Fri & Sat, 2-4pm Thu & Sun Apr-Nov) Sandwich's small but thorough museum is a good place to start exploring the town. Exhibitions examine the town's rich past as a Cinque Port, its role in various wars, and the gruesome punishments meted out to felons, fornicators and phoney fishers.

Salutation Gardens   GARDENS
(www.the-secretgardens.co.uk; The Salutation, Knightrider St; adult/child £6.50/3; ⊘10am-5pm) Just along from Fishergate, this set of exquisite gardens was laid out behind a 1912

CINQUE PORTS

Due to their proximity to Europe, southeast England's coastal towns were the frontline against raids and invasion during Anglo-Saxon times. In the absence of a professional army and navy, these ports were frequently called upon to defend themselves, and the kingdom, on land and at sea.

In 1278 King Edward I formalised this ancient arrangement by legally defining the Confederation of Cinque Ports (pronounced 'sink ports'). The five original ports – Sandwich, Dover, Hythe, Romney and Hastings – were awarded numerous perks and privileges in exchange for providing the king with ships and men. At their peak, the ports were considered England's most powerful institution after Crown and Church.

The ports' importance eventually evaporated when the shifting coastlines silted up several Cinque Port harbours and a professional navy was based at Portsmouth. But still the pomp and ceremony remain. The Lord Warden of the Cinque Ports is a prestigious post now bestowed on faithful servants of the Crown. The Queen Mother was warden until she passed away, succeeded by Admiral Lord Boyce. Previous incumbents include the Duke of Wellington and Sir Winston Churchill.

mansion by leading early 20th-century garden designers Jekyll and Lutyens. There's a superb tearoom in the grounds.

St Peter's
CHURCH

(King St; ⊙10am-5pm) The oldest church in Sandwich is now no longer used for worship. It's a real mixture of styles and years: its tower collapsed in dramatic fashion in 1661 and it was rebuilt with a bulbous cupola by the Flemish 'Strangers'.

St Mary's
CHURCH

(www.stmarysartscentre.org.uk; cnr Church St & Strand St; ⊙10am-5pm) This former church is now a multipurpose venue hosting some surprisingly big acts, and is open during the day for perusal.

🛏 Sleeping & Eating

★ Bell Hotel
HOTEL ££

(⊘01304-613388; www.bellhotelsandwich.co.uk; The Quay; s/tw/d from £95/120/165; 🅟) Today the haunt of celebrity golfers, the Bell Hotel has been sitting on the town's quay since Tudor times, though much of the remaining building is from the 19th century. A splendid sweeping staircase leads to luxurious rooms, some with pretty quay views. The Old Dining Room restaurant is one of East Kent's poshest nosh spots.

King's Arms
INN ££

(⊘01304-617330; www.kingsarms-sandwich.co.uk; cnr Church St St Mary's & Strand St; light meals £3-9, mains £10-17; 🅟) This cosy 15th-century inn opposite St Mary's church serves quality English food and very popular Sunday lunches in a beamed dining room heated by large fireplaces. There are six B&B rooms upstairs.

No Name Shop
DELI, BISTRO ££

(www.nonameshop.co.uk; No Name St; snacks £1.60-6.75, meals £6.50-14.50; ⊙8am-5pm Mon-Sat, 9am-4pm Sun) This far-from-anonymous French-owned deli (downstairs) and bistro (upstairs) near the bus stop is a pleasantly aromatic spot for a quick sandwich in Sandwich or an 'oozylicious' croque-monsieur, as well as more sophisticated dishes, followed by a relaxing glass of something Gallic. Very popular among locals, some of whom seem to regularly prefer it over their own kitchens.

ℹ Information

Tourist Office (⊘01304-613565; www. open-sandwich.co.uk; Guildhall, Cattle Market; ⊙10am-4pm Mon-Sat Apr-Oct) Located in the historic Guildhall.

ℹ Getting There & Away

Trains run from Dover Priory train station (22 minutes, hourly), Ramsgate (12 minutes, hourly) and London Charing Cross (£33.20, 2½ hours, hourly).

Buses also go to Ramsgate (£2.90, 22 minutes, hourly), Dover (£5.50, 45 minutes, hourly) and Canterbury (£3.50, 40 minutes, three hourly).

Dover
POP 37,090

Down-in-the-dumps Dover has certainly seen better days. Its derelict postwar architecture and shabby town centre of vacant shops is a sad introduction to England for travellers arriving on cross-Channel ferries and cruise ships, most of whom pass through quickly. Lucky, then, that the town has a couple of stellar attractions to redeem it. The port's vital strategic position so close to mainland Europe gave rise to a sprawling hilltop castle, which has some 2000 years of history to its credit. The spectacular white cliffs, as much a symbol of English wartime resilience as Winston Churchill or the Battle of Britain, rear in chalky magnificence to the east and west.

⊙ Sights & Activities

★ Dover Castle
CASTLE

(EH; www.english-heritage.org.uk; adult/child £17/10.20; ⊙10am-6pm Apr-Jul & Sep, 9.30am-6pm Aug, to 5pm Oct, 10am-4pm Sat & Sun Nov-Mar; 🅟) Occupying top spot, literally and figuratively, in Dover's townscape, this most impressive of castles was built to bolster the country's weakest point at the shortest sea crossing to mainland Europe. The highlights here are the unmissable secret wartime tunnels and the Great Tower, but the huge area it sprawls across has a lot of other bits, so allow at least three hours for your visit, more if you stand to admire the views across the Channel to France.

The site has been in use for as many as 2000 years. On the vast grounds are the remains of a Roman lighthouse, which dates from AD 50 and may be the oldest standing building in Britain. Beside it lies the restored Saxon Church of St Mary in Castro.

The robust 12th-century Great Tower, with walls up to 7m thick, is a medieval warren filled with interactive exhibits and light-and-sound shows that take visitors back to the times of Henry II.

The biggest draw of all is the network of secret wartime tunnels. The claustrophobic

Dover

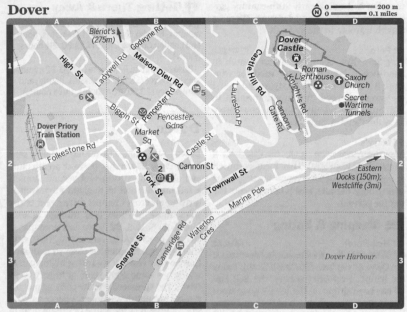

Dover

chalk-hewn passageways were first excavated during the Napoleonic Wars and then expanded to house a command post and hospital in WWII. The highly enjoyable 50-minute guided tour (every 20 minutes) tells the story of one of Britain's most famous wartime operations, code-named Dynamo, which was directed from here in 1940 and saw hundreds of thousands of men evacuated from the beaches at Dunkirk. The story is told in a very effective way, with video projected sharply onto the tunnel walls and sounds rumbling through the rock. At one point the entire passageway is consumed in flames and at others visitors are plunged into complete darkness.

Dover Museum   MUSEUM
(www.dovermuseum.co.uk; Market Sq; adult/child £3.50/2.25; ⊙9.30am-5pm Mon-Sat year-round, 10am-3pm Sun Apr-Sep) By far the most enthralling exhibit in the town's three-storey museum is an astonishing 3600-year-old Bronze Age boat, discovered here in 1992. Vaunted as the world's oldest-known seagoing vessel, it measures a thumping 9.5m by 2.4m and is kept in a huge, low-lit, climate-controlled glass case.

Roman Painted House   RUIN
(New St; adult/child £3/2; ⊙10am-5pm Tue-Sun Jun-Sep) A crumbling 1960s bunker is the unlikely setting for some of the most extensive, if stunted, Roman wall paintings north of the Alps. Several scenes depict Bacchus (Roman god of wine and revelry), which makes perfect sense as this large villa was built around AD 200 as a *mansio* (hotel) for travellers needing a little lubrication to unwind.

🛏 Sleeping

B&Bs are clustered along Castle St, Maison Dieu Rd and Folkestone Rd.

Blériot's
GUESTHOUSE £

(☑01304-211394; www.bleriotsguesthouse.co.uk; 47 Park Ave; s/d £35/52; P☎) Spacious eight-room guesthouse in a quiet residential location but within walking distance of all the sights. Some of the light-filled rooms have original Victorian fireplaces; there's a cosy lounge; and the hosts are the friendliest you'll meet in the southeast. Breakfast is £6 extra.

Dover Marina Hotel
HOTEL ££

(☑01304-203633; www.dovermarinahotel.co.uk; Waterloo Cres; r £89-130; ☎) Just a few steps from Dover's beach, this seafront hotel crams 81 rooms of varying dimensions into a gently curving 1870s edifice. The undulating corridors show the building's age, but there's nothing wonky about the rooms with their trendy ethnic fabrics, big-print wallpaper and contemporary artwork. Half the rooms have unrivalled sea views and 10 boast much-sought-after balconies.

East Lee Guest House
B&B ££

(☑01304-210176; www.eastlee.co.uk; 108 Maison Dieu Rd; d £65-75; P☎) This lovely terracotta-shingled town house impresses with its grand, elegantly decorated communal areas, scrupulously maintained rooms, energetic hosts and excellent, varied breakfasts.

★Wallett's Court
HOTEL £££

(☑01304-852424; www.wallettscourt.com; Westcliffe, St Margaret's-at-Cliffe; d £120-330; P☎⊛) With its soothing spa, first-rate restaurant and perky service, this is one relaxing country retreat. Digs at this country house set in rolling farmland range from spacious Jacobean guestrooms to beamed converted barns to a canvas wigwam (for a night of 'glamping'). Heading towards Deal, turn right off the A258 after almost 2 miles for Westcliffe.

✗ Eating

La Salle Verte
CAFE £

(14-15 Cannon St; snacks £2-6; ⊙9am-4.30pm Mon-Sat) A much-loved coffee or lunch halt with fascinating black-and-white images of old Dover lining the walls, an intimate cellar and friendly staff. Fills up at lunch, even on winter Wednesdays.

★Allotment
BRITISH ££

(www.theallotmentdover.com; 9 High St; mains £7.50-16; ⊙8.30am-10pm Tue-Sat) Dover's best dining spot plates up local fish and regional meat, seasoned with herbs from the tranquil garden out back, for breakfast, lunch and dinner. Cleanse your palette with a Kentish wine in a relaxed setting as you admire the view of the Maison Dieu (13th-century pilgrims' hospital) directly opposite through the exquisite stained-glass frontage.

ℹ Information

Post Office (68-72 Pencester Rd; ⊙7am-10pm Mon-Sat, 8am-8pm Sun)

Tourist Office (☑01304-201066; www.white cliffscountry.org.uk; Market Sq; ⊙9.30am-5pm Mon-Sat year-round, 10am-3pm Sun Apr-Sep) Located in the Dover Museum.

ℹ Getting There & Away

BOAT
Ferries depart for France from the Eastern Docks below the castle. Fares vary according to season and advance purchase. These days services seem to be in a constant state of flux.

DFDS (☑0871 5747235; www.dfdsseaways. co.uk) Services to Dunkirk (two hours, every two hours).

MyFerryLink (☑0844 2482 100; www.my ferrylink.com) Services to Calais (1½ hours, five times daily).

P&O Ferries (☑0871 6642020; www.po ferries.com) Runs to Calais (1½ hours, every 40 to 60 minutes).

BUS
Dover connections:

Canterbury £4.90, 40 minutes, four hourly

London Victoria Coach 007; £14.80, 2½ to 3½ hours, 12 daily

Sandwich £5.50, 40 minutes, hourly

TRAIN
Dover connections:

London Charing Cross £22.30, two hours, twice hourly

London St Pancras High-speed service, £38.50, one hour, hourly

Ramsgate (via Sandwich) £9.30, 35 minutes, hourly

ℹ Getting Around

Between 7am and 9pm, a **port shuttle bus** (£2, five minutes, every 20 minutes) runs between the Eastern Docks and the train station, a long walk apart.

Around Dover

The White Cliffs

Immortalised in song, film and literature, these iconic cliffs are embedded in the national consciousness, and are a big 'Welcome Home' sign to generations of travellers and soldiers. The cliffs rise to 100m high and extend on either side of Dover, but the best bit is the 6-mile stretch that starts about 2 miles east of town, properly known as the Langdon Cliffs.

The Langdon Cliffs are managed by the National Trust, which has a tourist office (☎ 01304-202756; ⊙ 10am-5pm Mar-Oct, 11am-4pm Nov-Feb) and car park (nonmembers £3 per park per day) 2 miles east of Dover along Castle Hill Rd and the A258 road to Deal, or off the A2 past the Eastern Docks. From the tourist office, follow the stony path east along the clifftops for a bracing 2-mile walk to the stout Victorian South Foreland Lighthouse (NT; adult/child £5/2.50; ⊙ guided tours 11am-5.30pm Fri-Mon mid-Mar-Oct). This was the first lighthouse to be powered by electricity and is the site of the first international radio transmissions, in 1898.

A mile further on the same trail brings you to delightful St Margaret's Bay, a gap in the chalk with a sun-trapping shingle beach and the welcoming Coastguard Pub (www.thecoastguard.co.uk; mains £10-16; ⊙ 10.30am-11pm). This is the closest point to France and many a cross-Channel swimmer has stepped into the briny here. From the top of the hill, bus 15 shuttles back to Dover or onward to Deal every hour.

To see the cliffs in all their full-frontal glory, Dover White Cliffs Tours (☎ 01303-271388; www.doverwhiteclifftours.com; adult/child £10/5; ⊙ daily Jul & Aug, Sat & Sun Apr-Jun & Sep-Oct) runs 40-minute sightseeing trips at least three times daily from the Western Docks. Dover Sea Safari (☎ 01304-212880; www.doverseasafari.co.uk; Dover Sea Sports Centre, Esplanade; adult/child £25/13; ⊙ year round) offers exciting, fast-moving rigid inflatable tours of the Cliffs and beyond.

EAST SUSSEX

Home to rolling countryside, medieval villages and gorgeous coastline, this inspiring corner of England is besieged by weekending Londoners whenever the sun pops out. And it's not hard to see why as you explore the cobbled medieval streets of Rye; wander around historic Battle, where William the Conqueror first engaged the Saxons in 1066; and peer over the edge of the breathtaking

🏃 Driving Tour
Dover to Rye

START DOVER EASTERN DOCKS
END RYE
LENGTH 35.5 MILES; AT LEAST FOUR HOURS (WITHOUT DUNGENESS PENINSULA DETOUR)

If you've just rolled off a cross-Channel ferry or have a day away from a cruise ship docked in Dover, instead of heading north to London, why not take this fascinating route along the white cliffs and across the flat marshes of the Kent–Sussex border to discover some of the southeast's hidden corners. Buses 100, 101 and 102 follow this route between Dover, Lydd and Hastings.

Starting at the exit to Dover's frantic ❶ **Eastern Docks**, where all cross-Channel ferries tie up, take the A20 along the seafront. After a few minutes this dual-carriageway begins to climb onto the famous white cliffs west of Dover. Your first stop is just outside town – take the turning for ❷ **Samphire Hoe** nature park, a ledge of parkland created between the white cliffs and the sea using 5 million cu metres of chalk excavated during the construction of the Channel tunnel. It's a fine spot for a picnic as you watch the 30 local species of butterfly flutter by.

Back on the A20, it's a mere 1.75 miles to the exit for the village of Capel-Le-Ferne (on the B2011). Well signposted at the end of the village is the ❸ **Battle of Britain Memorial**, a striking monument to the airmen who took part in the decisive struggle with the Luftwaffe in the skies above Kent and Sussex. An airman seated at the centre of a huge Spitfire propeller looks out serenely across the Channel. At the time of writing a new visitor centre was under construction nearby. Returning to the B2011, a few gear changes will have you on the outskirts of ❹ **Folkestone**. Take a left at the first roundabout then the sixth right onto Dover Rd. This will take you into the centre of this formerly grand old resort, once a favourite stomping ground of royal bon viveur King Edward VII and a forgotten piece of England's seaside past. Take a stroll through the seafront Leas Coastal Park with its subtropical flora, then halt for fish and chips at the old fish market before

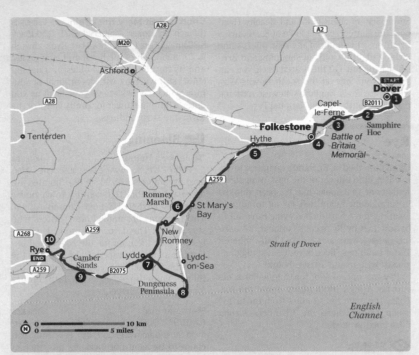

ambling up through the Creative Quarter, Folkestone's old town now occupied by artists studios and craft shops.

Heading out of Folkestone to the west on the A259 Sandgate Rd, you pass through Sandgate with its antique shops and shingle beach. From there it's another 2.5 miles to fascinating little **5 Hythe**. You could spend a full day in this original Cinque Port. Not only is it the eastern terminus of the fascinating narrow-gauge Romney, Hythe and Dymchurch Railway (RH&D Railway), but the Royal Military Canal also flows through the town and there's a quaint high street and beach to explore.

Heading ever west, a series of not-so-attractive shingle resorts such as Dymchurch and St Mary's are strung along the A259, cowering below their huge dykes, which keep the high tides from turning this stretch of the coast into sea bottom.

You've now left the white cliffs behind and are entering the **6 Romney Marsh**, a flat, sparsely populated landscape of reed beds and sheep-dotted fields. There's a visitor centre (www.kentwildlifetrust.org.uk) between St Mary's Bay and New Romney (on the A259) for those with time.

Having negotiated New Romney, another of the original five Cinque Ports, just outside the town take the turning to the left onto the B2075, which leads to **7 Lydd**, a quaint former corporate member of the Cinque Ports. From here detour along the lonely Dungeness Rd, which heads across the flats of the eerie **8 Dungeness Peninsula**, a low shingle spit dominated by a brooding nuclear power station. As well as boasting the southeast's largest seabird colony, it's also the western terminus of the RH&D Railway.

Back in Lydd stick with the B2075 heading west for 6 miles until you reach Camber. Thought the entire south coast had just shingle beaches? Well, the main attraction here is **9 Camber Sands**, a wide expanse of golden grains and dunes, ideal for picnicking and strolling.

The B2075 winds through shingly, scrubby wetlands until it rejoins the A259 at the hamlet of East Guldeford, where you should turn left towards Rye. Along the roads around here you will see the main source of revenue from the Romney Marsh – thousands of sheep grazing on the verdant flats. The A259 barrels across the marshes, eventually depositing you in **10 Rye**, one of the southeast's quaintest towns.

Seven Sisters chalk cliffs and Beachy Head near the genteel seaside town of Eastbourne. Brighton, a highlight of any visit, offers some kicking nightlife, offbeat shopping and British seaside fun. Off the beaten track, you can stretch your legs on the South Downs Way, which traverses England's newest national park, the South Downs National Park.

Rye

POP 4500

Often described as England's quaintest town, Rye is a little nugget of the past, a medieval settlement that looks like it's been dunked in formaldehyde and left for all to admire. Even the most hard-boiled cynic can't fail to be softened by Rye's cobbled lanes, mysterious passageways and crooked half-timbered Tudor buildings. Tales of resident smugglers, ghosts, writers and artists abound.

Rye was once one of the Cinque Ports, occupying a high promontory above the sea. Today the town rises 2 miles from the briny; sheep graze where the Channel's strong tides once swelled.

◉ Sights

Most start their exploration of Rye in famous **Mermaid St**, a short walk from the Rye Heritage Centre. It bristles with 15th-century timber-framed houses with quirky house names such as 'The House with Two Front Doors' and 'The House Opposite'.

Ypres Tower   MUSEUM
(www.ryemuseum.co.uk; adult/child £3/free; ⊙10.30am-5pm Apr-Oct, to 3.30pm Nov-Mar) Just off Church Sq stands the sandcastle-esque Ypres Tower (pronounced 'wipers'). You can scramble through the 13th-century building to learn about its long history as a fort, prison, mortuary and museum (the last two at overlapping times), but it's the views of Rye Bay, Dungeness nuclear power station and even France on very clear days, that will hold your attention longest.

Lamb House   HOUSE, MUSEUM
(NT; West St; adult/child £5/2.60; ⊙2-6pm Tue & Sat late Mar-Oct) This Georgian town house is a favourite stomping ground for local apparitions, but its most famous resident was American writer Henry James, who lived here from 1898 to 1916, during which time he wrote *The Wings of the Dove*.

Church of St Mary the Virgin   CHURCH
(Church Sq; tower adult/child £3/1; ⊙9.15am-5.30pm Apr-Sep, to 4.30 Nov-Mar) Rye's church is a hotchpotch of medieval and later styles, and its turret clock is the oldest in England (1561) still working with its original pendulum, which swings above your head as you enter. Climb the tower for pretty views of the town and surroundings.

🛏 Sleeping

★ Jeake's House   HOTEL ££
(☑01797-222828; www.jeakeshouse.com; Mermaid St; s/d from £70/90; 🅿🐾) Situated on Mermaid St, this 17th-century town house once belonged to US poet Conrad Aitken. The 11 rooms are named after writers who stayed here. The decor was probably slightly less bold then, minus the beeswaxed antiques and lavish drapery. Take a pew in the snug book-lined bar and, continuing the theme, enjoy breakfast in an 18th-century former Quaker chapel.

Mermaid Inn   HOTEL £££
(☑01797-223065; www.mermaidinn.com; Mermaid St; s/d from £90/150; 🅿) Few inns can claim to be as atmospheric as this ancient hostelry, dating from 1420. Each of the 31 rooms is different, but all are thick with dark beams and lit by leaded windows, and some are graced by secret passageways that now act as fire escapes. It also has one of Rye's best restaurants.

George in Rye   HOTEL £££
(☑01797-222114; www.thegeorgeinrye.com; 98 High St; d from £135; @🐾) This old coaching inn has managed to reinvent itself as a contemporary boutique hotel while staying true to its roots. Downstairs, an old-fashioned wood-panelled lounge is warmed by roaring log fires, while the guestrooms in the main building, created by the set designer from the film *Pride & Prejudice*, are chic and understated.

✕ Eating

Haydens   CAFE £
(www.haydensinrye.co.uk; 108 High St; snacks/ meals from £4-9; ⊙10am-5pm) Staunch believer in organic and fair-trade produce, Haydens dishes up delicious omelettes, ploughman's lunches, salads and bagels in a light, breezy cafe. There's a wonderful elevated terrace at the back with great views over town and country. Also runs an excellent seven-room ecofriendly guesthouse upstairs.

Landgate Bistro BRITISH ££
(www.landgatebistro.co.uk; 5-6 Landgate; mains £13-20; ⊘noon-3pm Sat & Sun, 7-9pm Wed-Sat) Escape the medieval excesses of Rye's central eateries to this fresh-feeling bistro slightly off the tourist trail near the impressive 14th-century Landgate. The focus here is on competently crafted dishes using local lamb and fish; locals who eat here love it.

ℹ Information

Post Office (Unit 2, Station Approach; ⊘8.30am-5.30pm Mon-Fri, to 1pm Sat)

Rye Heritage Centre (☑01797-226696; www.ryeheritage.co.uk; Strand Quay; ⊘10am-5pm Apr-Oct, reduced hours Nov-Mar) See a town-model audiovisual history for £3.50 and, upstairs, a freaky collection of penny-in-the-slot novelty machines.

Tourist Office (☑01797-229049; www.visit 1066country.com; 4-5 Lion St; ⊘10am-5pm Apr-Sep, to 4pm Oct-Mar) Accommodation bookings, and train and bus tickets.

ℹ Getting There & Away

BUS
Dover Bus 100, two hours, hourly
Hastings Bus 344 or 100, 40 minutes, two per hour

TRAIN
London Charing Cross £22.30, two hours, hourly (change in Ashford)

Battle

POP 6170

'If there'd been no battle, there'd be no Battle,' goes the saying in this unassuming village, which grew up around the hillside where invading French duke William of Normandy, aka William the Conqueror, scored a decisive victory over local king Harold in 1066. The epicentre of 1066 country, visitors flock here to see the spot where Harold got it in the eye, with the biggest crowd turning up mid-October to witness the annual re-enactment on the original battlefield.

◉ Sights

Battle Abbey HISTORIC SITE
(EH; adult/child £7.80/4.70; ⊘10am-6pm Apr-Sep, to 4pm Sat & Sun Oct-Mar) On this spot raged the pivotal battle in the last successful invasion of England in 1066: an event that had an unparalleled impact on the country's subsequent social structure, language and, well,

pretty much everything. Four years after, the Normans began constructing an abbey on the battlefield, a penance ordered by the pope for the loss of life incurred here. Only the foundations of the original church remain, the altar's position supposedly took the spot King Harold famously took an arrow in his eye.

Other impressive monastic buildings survive and make for atmospheric explorations. The battlefield's innocently rolling lush hillsides do little to evoke the ferocity of the event, but high-tech interactive presentations and a film at the visitors centre, as well as blow-by-blow audio tours, do their utmost to bring the battle to life.

Yesterday's World MUSEUM
(www.yesterdaysworld.co.uk; 89-90 High St; adult/child £7.95/5.75; ⊘10am-5.30pm Apr-Sep, 11am-4pm Oct-Mar) Overshadowed literally and figuratively by the Battle Abbey, this excellent museum constitutes an incredible repository of England's retail past. The first building houses entire streets of quaint old shops where costumed dummies proffer long-discontinued brands, every space in between stuffed with yesteryear products, enamel advertising signs, battered toys, wartime memorabilia and general nostalgia-inducing knick-knackery. The second building houses the Royalty Room where a cardboard cut-out illustrates just how tiny Queen Victoria was (1.40m).

ℹ Information

The town's tourist information point is housed in Yesterday's World (p169) museum.

ℹ Getting There & Away

Bus 304/305 goes to Hastings (26 minutes, hourly).

Trains travel to Hastings (£4.10, 15 minutes, twice hourly) and to London Charing Cross (£22.10, one hour and 20 minutes, twice hourly).

Hastings

POP 90,300

Forever associated with the Norman invasion of 1066 (even though the crucial events took place 6 miles away), Hastings thrived as one of the Cinque Ports and, in its Victorian heyday, was one of the country's most fashionable resorts. After a period of steady decline, the town is enjoying a mini-renaissance, and these days is an intriguing mix of tacky resort, fishing port and arty New Age hang-out.

⊙ Sights

Stade
NEIGHBOURHOOD

(Rock-A-Nore Rd) The seafront area known as the Stade (below East Hill) is home to distinctive black clapboard structures known as Net Shops. These were built to store fishing gear back in the 17th century, but some now house fishmongers who sell off the catch of Europe's largest beach-launched fishing fleet, usually hauled up on the shingle behind. All these fishy goings-on keep the Stade very much a working place, with the combined pong of diesel and guts scenting the air.

Hastings Museum & Art Gallery
MUSEUM

(www.hmag.org.uk; Johns Place, Bohemia Rd; ⊙10am-5pm Tue-Sat, noon-5pm Sun Apr-Sep, shorter hours Oct-Mar) FREE A short walk west of the train station, this marvellous little museum is housed in a red-brick mansion. Highlights inside include the intricately Moorish Durbar Hall and a section on John Logie Baird, who invented television while recuperating from an illness in Hastings between February 1923 and November 1924.

Jerwood Gallery
GALLERY

(www.jerwoodgallery.org; Rock-A-Nore Rd; adult/child £8/3.50; ⊙11am-4pm Tue-Fri, to 6pm Sat & Sun) Large, purpose-built exhibition venue at the end of the Stade used for temporary shows of contemporary British art as well as themed installations from the Jerwood collection. The building has a great cafe with Channel views.

Fishermen's Museum
MUSEUM

(Rock-A-Nore Rd; ⊙10am-5pm Apr-Oct, 11am-4pm Nov-Mar) FREE Shoals of barnacled exhibits swim around the huge *Enterprise* fishing boat at this Stade museum, housed in a former fishers' church.

Hastings Castle
RUIN

(www.discoverhastings.co.uk; Castle Hill Rd; adult/child £4.35/3.60; ⊙10am-4pm Easter-Sep) This

---

A PIER INTO THE FUTURE

Hastings last hit the national news in October 2010 when its Victorian pier burnt down. The ballroom at the end of the structure, where the likes of the Clash, Sex Pistols, Rolling Stones, The Who, Jimi Hendrix and Pink Floyd once performed, was completely destroyed. Work is now under way to rebuild the pier as an open performance space, however, with some of the funding coming from local people.

---

fortress was built by William the Conquerer, and an exhibition in the grounds tells the story of the castle and the Battle of Hastings.

Smugglers Adventure
CAVE

(www.smugglersadventure.co.uk; St Clement Caves; adult/child £7.50/5.50; ⊙10am-5pm Easter-Sep) On West Hill, a short walk east of the Hastings Castle, is the Smugglers Adventure, where you can explore underground caverns and hear smuggling yarns from the Sussex coast.

Shipwreck Museum
MUSEUM

(www.shipwreckmuseum.co.uk; Rock-a-Nore Rd; ⊙10am-5pm Apr-Oct, 11am-4pm Sat & Sun Nov-Mar) FREE An old-school repository of junk salvaged from various vessels that have sunk in the Channel, plus sections on fossils and diving.

🛏 Sleeping & Eating

Swan House
B&B ££

(☑01424-430014; www.swanhousehastings.co.uk; 1 Hill St; s/d from £80/120; @🖙) Inside its 15th-century timbered shell, this place blends contemporary and vintage chic to perfection. The four rooms feature organic toiletries, fresh flowers, hand-painted walls and huge beds. The guest lounge, where pale sofas, painted floorboards and striking modern sculpture rub shoulders with beams and a huge stone fireplace, is a stunner.

Dragon Bar
RESTAURANT ££

(71 George St; mains £10-18, weekday lunch menu £7; ⊙noon-11pm Mon-Sat, to 10.30pm Sun; 🖙) The younger end of the alternative old-town crowd is attracted to this atmospheric bar-restaurant hang-out. It's full of dark walls, mismatched furniture and beaten leather sofas, and the eclectic menu features everything from Thai curry to Winchelsea lamb and pizzas.

🍷 Drinking & Nightlife

Hanushka Coffee House
CAFE

(28 George St; ⊙9.30am-6pm) Hastings' best caffeine stop resembles a well-stocked second-hand bookshop with every inch of wall space packed with titles. The low-lit and tightly packed space in between provokes inter-table interaction, or you can seek sanctuary on the sofas and perches in the window. No wi-fi.

ⓘ Information

Tourist Office (☑01424-451111; www.visit 1066country.com; Aquila House, Breeds Pl; ⊙9am-5.30pm Mon-Fri, to 5pm Sat, 10.30am-4pm Sun Apr-Sep, shorter hours Oct-Mar)

THE LAST INVASION OF ENGLAND

If there's one date that seared itself into every English schoolchild's brain, it's 1066, the year of the most famous battle in the country's history. The punch-up in question was the Battle of Hastings, which began when King Harold's army arrived in a field near what is now the village of Battle on 14 October and created a three-ringed defence consisting of archers, cavalry and massed infantry at the rear. Invading French duke William of Normandy, aka William the Conqueror, marched north from Hastings and took up a position about 400m south of the English. He tried repeatedly to break the cordon, but Harold's men held fast. William's knights then feigned retreat, drawing some of Harold's troops after them. It was a fatal mistake. Seeing the gap in the English wall, William ordered his remaining troops to charge through, and the battle was as good as won. Among the English casualties was King Harold who, as tradition has it, was hit in the eye by an arrow and struck down by Norman knights as he tried to pull it out. At news of his death, the last English resistance collapsed.

In their irreverent parody of a British history textbook, *1066 and All That* (1930), Sellar and Yeatman suggest that 'the Norman conquest was a Good Thing, as from this time onward England stopped being conquered and thus was able to become top nation...'

❶ Getting There & Away

BUS

Eastbourne Bus 99, 80 minutes, four per hour

London Victoria National Express, £14.40, three hours, daily

Rye Buses 100 & 344, 40 minutes, twice hourly

TRAIN

Brighton Via Eastbourne, £12.90, one hour to 80 minutes, twice hourly

London Victoria £17.30, two hours, hourly

❶ Getting Around

Hastings has two delightful Victorian funiculars.

East Hill Cliff Railway (Rock-A-Nore Rd; adult/child £2.50/1.50; ⊙10am-5.30pm Apr-Sep, 11am-4pm Sat & Sun Oct-Mar) The East Hill Cliff Railway funicular ascends from the Stade to Hastings Country Park.

West Hill Cliff Railway (George St; adult/child £2.50/1.50; ⊙10am-5.30pm Mar-Sep, 11am-4pm Oct-Feb) The West Hill Cliff Railway funicular saves visitors' legs when climbing up to Hastings Castle.

Eastbourne

POP 99,000

Despite its official title as 'Britain's sunniest town', Eastbourne has been slow to throw off its unattractive image as death's waiting-room by the chilly Channel, all snoozing octogenarians in deckchairs and fusty guest-houses populated by vitamin D–deprived bank-holidaying Scots. But while much of this is still to be found here, in the last decade an influx of students and the arrival of the southeast's largest Polish community have given the town a sprightlier feel.

Eastbourne's 3.5-mile sweeping, palm-tree-lined seafront is one of the UK's grandest. Add to this a fresh modern art gallery and the recently created South Downs National Park that nudges its western suburbs and Eastbourne certainly makes an enjoyable day trip from London or Brighton. It's also the start and end point for a hike along the 100-mile South Downs Way.

◉ Sights & Activities

Towner Art Gallery ART GALLERY
(☑01323-434670; www.townereastbourne.org. uk; Devonshire Park, College Rd; ⊙10am-5pm Tue-Sun, tours 11.30am & 2pm) **FREE** One of the southeast's most exciting exhibition spaces, this purpose-built structure has temporary shows of contemporary work on the ground and 2nd floors, while the first floor is given over to rotating themed shows created from the gallery's 5000-piece collection. Building tours include a peek inside the climate-controlled art store.

Pier LANDMARK
(☑01323-410466; www.eastbournepier.com; ⊙24hr) Until the summer of 2014, Eastbourne's ramshackle pier was a lovable piece of rusty Victoriana jutting into the Channel. But on 30 July 2014 a fire broke out in the amusement arcade at the land end of the structure, destroying a third of the pier as thousands of tanning holidaymakers looked on. Some clever firefighting saved the other two-thirds, however, and Eastbourne's finest landmark is set to reopen in 2015.

Museum of Shops
MUSEUM

(20 Cornfield Tce; adult/child £5/4; ☺10am-5pm, closed Jan) This small museum is swamped by an obsessive collection of how-we-used-to-live memorabilia.

☞ Tours

Sussex Voyages
BOAT TOUR

(☏01293-888780; www.sussexvoyages.co.uk; Lower Quayside, The Waterfront, Sovereign Harbour Marina; adult/child £25/14) Hour-long Beachy Head and Seven Sisters boat tours leaving from Sovereign Harbour (take hourly bus 51) on rigid-hulled inflatables. Reservations essential.

✯ Festivals & Events

Airbourne
AIR SHOW

(www.airshows.org.uk; ☺mid-Aug) Arguably the UK's best airshow – as it's free! Takes place over the Channel.

⊨ Sleeping

Big Sleep
HOTEL ££

(☏01323-722676; www.thebigsleephotel.com; King Edward's Pde; s/d from £45/60; ☏) Hip, fresh and friendly, this seafront hotel has 50 gob-smacking rooms with big-print wallpaper, retro furnishings, and curtains that resemble sheep that might have been grazing on Beachy Head just a few hours prior. A trendy bar, big basement games room and Channel views make this Eastbourne's coolest kip.

Albert & Victoria
B&B ££

(☏01323-730948; www.albertandvictoria.com; 19 St Aubyns Rd; s/d from £35/70; ☏) Book ahead to stay at this delightful Victorian terraced house, whose fragrant rooms, canopied beds, crystal chandeliers and secluded walled garden for summer breakfasts are mere paces from the seafront promenade. The four rooms are named after four of Queen Victoria's offspring.

✗ Eating

Lamb Inn
PUB ££

(www.thelamb.eu; 36 High St; mains £8.50-11; ☺11am-11.30pm) This Eastbourne institution located less than a mile northwest of the train station in the undervisited Old Town has been plonking Sussex ales on the bar for eight centuries, and now also serves gourmet British pub grub. A holidaying Charles Dickens also left a few beer rings and smudged napkins here when he stayed across the road. Buses 1, 1A and 12 stop nearby.

Belgian Cafe
BELGIAN ££

(www.thebelgiancafe.co.uk; 11-23 Grand Pde; mains £11-22.50) If you didn't know that Belgian beer can taste of fruit; the national dish is mussels and chips; and Tintin hails from its capital, Brussels, you will once you've experienced this popular cafe near the pier. Fifty types of mussel dishes and the same number of Belgian ales are available.

✩ Entertainment

Eastbourne International Tennis Tournament
TENNIS

(www.devonshireparkltc.co.uk; Devonshire Park; ☺mid-Jun) One of the UK's top tennis tournaments played in the week before Wimbledon. Attracts some of the biggest names.

⌂ Shopping

Camilla's Bookshop
BOOKS

(www.camillasbookshop.com; 57 Grove Rd; ☺10am-5pm Mon-Sat) Literally packed to the rafters with half a million musty volumes, this incredible secondhand-book repository, an interesting amble from the train station, fills three floors of a crumbling Victorian town house.

❶ Information

Tourist Office (☏0871 6630031; www.visiteastbourne.com; Cornfield Rd; ☺9.15am-5.30pm Mon-Fri, to 5pm Sat, 10am-1pm Sun Apr-Oct, closed Sun & shorter hours Nov-Mar)

❶ Getting There & Away

BUS

Brighton Bus 12, 75 minutes, up to four hourly

Hastings Bus 98/99, 70 minutes, three per hour

TRAIN

Brighton £10.30, 30 to 40 minutes, twice hourly

London Victoria £17.30, 1½ hours, twice hourly

Around Eastbourne

The **South Downs National Park**, more than 600 sq miles of rolling chalk downs, stretches west from Eastbourne for about 100 miles. The South Downs Way extends its entire length.

Beachy Head

The famous cliffs of Beachy Head are the highest point of the chalky rock faces that slice across the rugged coastline at the southern end of the South Downs. It's off the B2103, from the A259 between Eastbourne and Newhaven. From here the stunning **Seven Sisters Cliffs** undulate their way west. A clifftop path (a branch of the South Downs Way) rides the waves of chalk as far as picturesque Cuckmere Haven.

Eastbourne's **City Sightseeing** (www. city-sightseeing.co.uk; Eastbourne Pier; adult/child £9/5; ⊙ every 30min 10am-5pm mid-Mar–Oct) tour bus stops at the clifftop.

Beachy Head is a spot of thrilling beauty. Unfortunately it is also known as one of Europe's suicide spots.

Along the clifftop path, you'll stumble upon the tiny seaside hamlet of Birling Gap, where you can stop for a drink, snack or ice cream at the **Birling Gap Hotel** (Seven Sisters Cliffs). The secluded beach is a sun-trap popular with locals and walkers taking a breather.

Pevensey Castle

The **ruins** (EH; Castle Rd, Pevensey; adult/child £5/3; ⊙ 10am-6pm Apr-Sep) of William the Conqueror's first stronghold sit 5 miles east of Eastbourne, just off the A259. Regular train services between London Victoria and Hastings via Eastbourne stop at Westham, half a mile from Pevensey. Picturesquely dissolving into its own moat, the castle marks the point where William the Conqueror landed in 1066, just two weeks before the Battle of Hastings.

He wasted no time after his landing by building upon sturdy Roman walls to create this castle, which was used time and again through the centuries, right up to WWII.

Brighton & Hove

POP 273,400

Raves on the beach, Graham Greene novels, mods and rockers in bank-holiday fisticuffs, naughty weekends for Mr and Mrs Smith, classic car runs from London, the UK's biggest gay scene and the Channel's best clubbing – this city by the sea evokes many images for the British. One thing is certain: with its bohemian, cosmopolitan and hedonistic vibe, Brighton is where England's seaside experience goes from cold to cool.

Brighton is without doubt Britain's most colourful and outrageous city, and one with many faces. Here, burlesque meets contemporary design; Spanish students leave Star-

bucks to rub shoulders with stars in Spanish bars; the southeast's grottiest hostels share thin walls with kinky boutique hotels; microbrew ales costing £4 a pint occupy bar space with £1 buckets of 'sex on the beach'; and stags watch drag. This is the city that returned the UK's first Green Party MP, where Valentine's Day is celebrated with more gusto than Christmas, and is the place, according to the 2001 census, with the highest UK population of Jedi.

Brighton rocks all year round, but really comes to life during the summer months when tourists, language students and revellers from London pour into the city, keen to explore the city's legendary nightlife, summer festivals and quirky shops. The highlight for the sightseeing visitor is, without doubt, the weird and wonderful Royal Pavilion, a 19th-century party palace built by the Prince Regent, who kicked off Brighton's enduring love of the outlandish.

◉ Sights

★ Royal Pavilion   PALACE
(www.royalpavilion.org.uk; Royal Pavilion Gardens; adult/child £11/6; ⊙ 9.30am-5.45pm Apr-Sep, 10am-5.15pm Oct-Mar) The city's must-see attraction is the Royal Pavilion, the glittering party pad and palace of Prince George, later Prince Regent and then King George IV. It's one of the most opulent buildings in England, certainly the finest example of early 19th-century chinoiserie anywhere in Europe and an apt symbol of Brighton's reputation for decadence. An unimpressed Queen Victoria called the Royal Pavilion 'a strange, odd Chinese place', but for visitors to Brighton it's an unmissable chunk of Sussex history.

The entire palace is an eye-popping spectacle, but some interiors stand out even amid the riot of decoration. The dragon-themed banqueting hall must be the most incredible in all England; more dragons and snakes writhe in the music room, with its ceiling of 26,000 gold scales; and the then state-of-the-art kitchen must have wowed Georgians with its automatic spits and hot tables. Prince Albert carted away all of the furniture, some of which has been loaned back by the present queen.

Brighton Museum
& Art Gallery   MUSEUM, GALLERY
(www.brighton-hove-museums.org.uk; Royal Pavilion Gardens; ⊙ 10am-5pm Tue-Sun) FREE Set in the Royal Pavilion's renovated stable block, this museum and art gallery has a glittering

Brighton & Hove

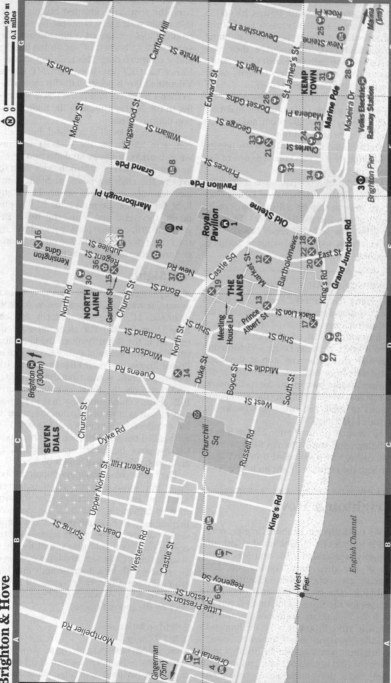

Brighton & Hove

collection of 20th-century art and design, including a crimson Salvador Dalí sofa modelled on Mae West's lips. There's also an enthralling gallery of world art, an impressive collection of Egyptian artefacts, and an 'images of Brighton' multimedia exhibit containing a series of oral histories and a model of the defunct West Pier.

Brighton Pier   LANDMARK
(www.brightonpier.co.uk; Madeira Dr) This grand century-old pier is the place to experience Brighton's tackier side. There are plenty of stomach-churning fairground rides and dingy amusement arcades to keep you amused, and candy floss and Brighton rock to chomp on while you're doing so.

Look west and you'll see the sad remains of the **West Pier**, a skeletal iron hulk that attracts flocks of starlings at sunset. It's a sad end for this Victorian marvel, where the likes of Charlie Chaplin and Stan Laurel once performed.

So far there's no sign of the i360 observation tower ('Hurray!' some may cry), a spectacularly space-age piece of architecture from the creators of the London Eye that may one day loom 175m above the seafront (the completion date of 2015 is unlikely). The venue would include a West Pier Heritage Centre – a pavilion with audiovisual exhibits relating the pier's history.

🎉 Festivals & Events

Brighton Festival   FESTIVAL
(☑ 01273-709709; www.brightonfestival.org; ☺ May) After Edinburgh, this is the UK's biggest arts festival. It draws star performers from around the globe for three weeks by the sea.

Brighton Pride   GAY, LESBIAN
(www.brighton-pride.org; ☺ early Aug) One of the UK's biggest gay bashes with a rainbow-hued parade and concerts in Preston Park.

🛏 Sleeping

Brighton has lots of places to sleep to suit every budget and taste, but beds can be scarce on summer weekends and during events such as the Brighton Festival, when booking ahead is recommended.

Baggies Backpackers   HOSTEL £
(☑ 01273-733740; www.baggiesbackpackers.com; 33 Oriental Pl; dm/d £15/40; ☎) This place may have recently changed hands, but the new proprietors are determined to maintain the warm, familial atmosphere, worn-in charm, attentive service and clean, snug dorms that have made this long-established hostel an institution. The cosy basement music and chill-out room, and a TV lounge piled high with video cassettes have also survived the changeover, as well as the digital revolution.

Kipps Brighton
HOSTEL £

(☑ 01273-604182; www.kipps-brighton.com; 76 Grand Pde; dm/s/d from £15/25/25; @ 🕾) The owners of Canterbury's award-winning hostel have created equally commendable budget digs here in Brighton. There's a real cafe vibe around reception, and facilities include a communal kitchen. Free movie, pizza and pub nights successfully separate guests from their wi-fi-enabled devices.

Hotel Pelirocco
HOTEL ££

(☑ 01273-327055; www.hotelpelirocco.co.uk; 10 Regency Sq; s £59-75, d £109-155; 🕾) One of Brighton's sexiest and nuttiest places to stay, the Pelirocco has become the ultimate venue for a flirty rock-and-roll weekend. Flamboyant rooms, some designed by artists, include the Soviet-chic room with vodka bottles frozen into the walls, the Pin-up Parlour dedicated to Diana Dors, and the Pretty Vacant double, a shrine to the Sex Pistols.

There's also a Play Room suite with 3m circular bed, mirrored ceiling and a pole-dancing area.

Neo Hotel
BOUTIQUE HOTEL ££

(☑ 01273-711104; www.neohotel.com; 19 Oriental Pl; s incl breakfast £55-65, d incl breakfast £100-150; 🕾) You won't be surprised to learn the owner of this gorgeous hotel is an interior stylist. The nine rooms could have dropped straight from the pages of a design magazine, each finished in rich colours and tactile fabrics, with bold floral and Asian motifs, and black-tiled bathrooms. Wonderful breakfasts include homemade smoothies and pancakes.

Snooze
HOTEL ££

(☑ 01273-605797; www.snoozebrighton.com; 25 St George's Tce; s/d from £55/65; 🕾) The retro styling at this eccentric Kemptown pad features everything from vintage posters and bright '60s and '70s wallpaper to Bollywood film posters, floral sinks and mad clashes of colour. It's more than just a gimmick – the rooms are comfortable and spotless, and there are great meat-free breakfasts. You'll find it just off St James' St, about 500m east of New Steine.

Motel Schmotel
B&B ££

(☑ 07557-947449; www.motelschmotel.co.uk; 37 Russell Sq; d £63-120; 🕾) If you can overlook the petite rooms and miniscule bathrooms, this 11-room B&B in a Regency town house, a short stroll from virtually anywhere, is a sound and central place to hit the sack. Rooms are accented with colourful oversized prints and an uncluttered design, and guests heap praise on the breakfast cooked by the always-there-to-help couple who run things.

Paskins Town House
B&B ££

(☑ 01273-601203; www.paskins.co.uk; 18-19 Charlotte St; s £50-75, d £100-150; @ 🕾) 🖈 Around a kilometre east of Brighton Pier along the seafront, this environmentally friendly B&B is spread between two elegant town houses. Paskins prides itself on using ecofriendly products such as recycled toilet paper, low-energy lightbulbs and biodegradable cleaning materials. The individually designed rooms are beautifully maintained, and excellent organic and vegetarian breakfasts are served in the art deco–inspired breakfast room.

myhotel
HOTEL ££

(☑ 01273-900300; www.myhotels.com; 17 Jubilee St; r £70-320; 🕾) There's nothing square about this place: trendsetting rooms look like space-age pods with curved white walls, floor-to-ceiling observation windows and suspended flatscreen TVs, enlivened by the odd splash of neon orange or pink. Hook up your iPod and play music through speakers in the ceiling. There's also a cocoon-like cocktail bar downstairs and, if you've currency to ignite, a suite with a steamroom and harpooned vintage carousel horse.

★ Hotel Una
BOUTIQUE HOTEL £££

(☑ 01723-820464; www.hotel-una.co.uk; 55-56 Regency Sq; s incl breakfast £55-75, d incl breakfast £115-200; ✿ 🕾) All of the 19 generous rooms here wow guests with their bold-patterned fabrics, supersized leather sofas, in-room free-standing baths and vegan/veggie/carnivorous breakfast in bed. Some, such as the two-level suite with its own mini-cinema, and the underpavement chambers with their own spa and jacuzzi, are truly show-stopping and not as expensive as you might expect.

All this plus a cool cocktail bar and lots of timewarp period features make the Una our numero uno.

Drakes
BOUTIQUE HOTEL £££

(☑ 01273-696934; www.drakesofbrighton.com; 43-44 Marine Pde; r £115-345; P ✿ @ 🕾) This minimalist boutique hotel oozes understated class. So understated is the entrance, in fact, you could easily miss it. All rooms have similar decor in bold fabrics and funky European elm panelling, but it's the feature rooms everyone wants – their giant freestanding tubs are set in front of full-length bay windows with widescreen Channel views. The basement restaurant is superb.

✗ Eating

Brighton easily has the best choice of eateries on the south coast, with cafes, diners and restaurants to fulfil every dining whim. It's also one of Britain's best destinations for vegetarians, and its innovative meat-free menus are terrific value for anyone on a budget. For food from the former British Empire and beyond, head for Preston St, which has an incredible concentration of ethnic eateries.

★ Iydea   VEGETARIAN £
(www.iydea.co.uk; 17 Kensington Gardens; mains £6-7.50; ☺9.30am-5.30pm Mon-Sat, from 10am Sun; 🛜📷) Even by Brighton's lofty standards, the food at this award-winning vegetarian cafe is a treat. The daily changing choices of curries, lasagnes, falafel, enchiladas and quiches are full of flavour and can be washed down with a selection of vegan wines, organic ales and homemade lemonades. If you're on the hop, you can get any dish to takeaway in environmentally friendly packaging.

Infinity Foods Cafe   VEGETARIAN £
(www.infinityfoodscafe.co.uk; 50 Gardner St; mains £3.50-8; ☺10.30am-5pm Mon-Fri, from 10am Sat, noon-4pm Sun; 🛜📷) The sister establishment of Infinity Foods wholefoods shop (health-food cooperative and Brighton institution) serves a wide variety of vegetarian and organic food, with many vegan and wheat- or gluten-free options including tofu burgers, mezze platters and veggie sausage sandwiches.

Foodilic   BUFFET £
(www.foodilic.com; 60 North St; buffet £6.45, takeaway per 100g £1.20; ☺9am-9.30pm Mon-Sat, to 6pm Sun) It's as good for breakfast (£2) as for a late dinner, but it's the eat-till-you-burst buffet of scrumptious healthy fare that packs out this funky place all day long.

Tea Cosy   CAFE £
(www.theteacosy.co.uk; 3 George St; teas £3.50-12; ☺noon-5pm Wed-Fri & Sun, to 5.30pm Sat) Tearoom offering cakes and sandwiches, though you can hardly get in the door due to the royal family memorabilia, including ample Kate and Wills paraphernalia.

Mock Turtle   CAFE £
(4 Pool Valley; mains £4-7; ☺9am-6pm Mon-Sat, to 6.30pm Sun) Little has changed at this wonderfully quaintly English tearoom since the mid-20th century. Those who've sipped and munched here that long claim the myriad homemade cakes, Sussex cream teas and light meals are as tasty now as they were back then.

Scoop & Crumb   ICE CREAM £
(5-6 East St; snacks £3-6, sundaes £2.50-6; ☺10am-6pm Sun-Fri, to 7pm Sat) This ice-cream parlour belongs to the city's artisan ice-cream producer, and the sundaes (more than 50 types) are second to none. Freshly cut sandwiches and monster toasties are also available.

★ Terre à Terre   VEGETARIAN ££
(📞01273-729051; www.terreaterre.co.uk; 71 East St; mains £15; ☺noon-10.30pm Mon-Fri, 11am-11pm Sat, to 10pm Sun; 📷) Even staunch meat-eaters will rave about this legendary vegetarian restaurant. A sublime dining experience, from the vibrant modern space to the entertaining menus and inventive dishes stuffed with excitingly zingy ingredients. There's also plenty for vegans. Desserts are on the steep side.

Riddle & Finns   SEAFOOD ££
(www.riddleandfinns.co.uk; 12 Meeting House Lane; mains £13-18; ☺noon-last customer) Regarded as the town's most refined seafood spot, R&F is light on gimmicky interiors (think white butcher's shop tiles, marble tables and candles) but heavy on taste. With the kitchen open to the street outside, chefs put on a public cooking class with every dish as they prepare your smoked haddock in champagne sauce or wild sea bass.

There's an elite wine list to choose from as you wait.

JB's American Diner   FAST FOOD ££
(http://jbsdiner.co.uk; 31 King's Rd; burgers £8-10, mains £6.50-12; ☺10am-10pm Mon-Sat, from 9am Sun) The waft of hotdogs as you push open the door, the shiny red-leather booths, the stars and stripes draped across the wall, the 1950s soundtrack twanging in the background and the colossal portions of burgers, fries and milkshakes – in short, this is a hefty slab of authentic Americana teleported to the Brighton seafront.

Food for Friends   VEGETARIAN ££
(www.foodforfriends.com; 17-18 Prince Albert St; mains £11-13; 📷) An ever-inventive choice of vegetarian and vegan food keeps bringing locals back for seconds and thirds at this place to see and be seen – literally, by every passerby through the huge streetside windows. Be prepared to wait for a table on busy shopping days.

English's Oyster Bar
SEAFOOD ££

(www.englishs.co.uk; 29-31 East St; mains £9-30; ⊙noon-10.15pm Mon-Sat, 12.30-4pm Sun) An almost 70-year-old institution and celebrity haunt, this Brightonian seafood dishes up everything from Essex oysters to locally caught lobster and Dover sole. It's converted from fishers' cottages, with shades of the elegant Edwardian era inside and alfresco dining on the pedestrian square outside.

Gingerman
MODERN EUROPEAN £££

(☑01273-326688; 21a Norfolk Sq; 2-/3-course menu £15/18; ⊙12.30-2pm & 7-10pm Tue-Sun) Hastings seafood, Sussex beef, Romney Marsh lamb, local sparkling wines and countless other seasonal, local and British treats go into the adroitly flash-fried and slow-cooked dishes served at this snug 32-cover eatery. Reservations are advised. Norfolk Sq is a short walk west along Western Rd from the Churchill Square shopping centre.

🍸 Drinking & Nightlife

With the exception of London, Brighton's nightlife is the best in the south, with its unique mix of seafront clubs and bars, and visits by top DJs. On West St, drunken stag and hens' parties and charmless, tacky nightclubs rule. For more ideas, visit www.drinkinbrighton.co.uk or search out publications such as *The List, Source* and *What's On*.

Brighton Rocks
BAR

(www.brightonrocksbar.co.uk; 6 Rock Pl; ⊙4-11pm Mon-Thu, to 1am Sat, from noon Sun; 🛜) Incongruously located in an alley of garages and used-car lots, this cocktail bar is firmly established on the Kemptown gay scene, but welcomes all-comers with 'Shocktails', a 'grazing' menu and theme parties.

Dorset
PUB

(www.thedorset.co.uk; 28 North Rd; ⊙9am-late; 🛜) In fine weather this laid-back Brighton institution throws open its doors and windows, and tables spill out onto the pavement. You'll be just as welcome for a morning coffee as for an evening pint here, and should you not leave between the two, there's a decent gastropub menu.

Black Dove
PUB

(www.blackdovebrighton.com; 74 St James's St; ⊙4pm-late) Eclectic hang-out with shabby-chic furnishings, huge antique ceiling fans, a bar stocked with unusual tipples and a quirky basement snug. Live acoustic music and local DJs provide the soundtrack for evening quaffing that spills out onto the pavements when the mercury is high.

Coalition
BAR

(171-181 Kings Rd Arches; ⊙10am-late) On a summer's day, there's nowhere finer to sit and watch the world go by than at this popular

---

GAY & LESBIAN BRIGHTON

Brighton has the most vibrant gay community in the country outside London and Kemptown (aka Camptown). On and off St James's St is where it's all at. The old Brunswick Town area of Hove is a quieter alternative to the traditionally cruisy (and sometimes seedy) scene in Kemptown. For up-to-date information on the gay scene in Brighton, check out www.gay.brighton.co.uk and www.realbrighton.com, or pick up the free monthly magazine *Gscene* (www.gscene.com) from gay venues.

For Drinking

Poison Ivy (129 St James's St) In-your-face pub featuring drag acts and camp karaoke.

A Bar (www.amsterdam.uk.com; 11-12 Marine Pde; ⊙noon-2am) Extremely hip bar and sauna in the Amsterdam hotel; its sun terrace is a particular hit.

Bulldog (www.bulldogbrighton.com; 31 St James's St) Longest-running gay bar in Brighton, mostly frequented only by men.

Queen's Arms (www.queensarmsbrighton.com; 7 George St; ⊙3pm-late) And they ain't talking Victoria or Elizabeth! Plenty of camp cabaret and karaoke at this pub.

For Dancing

Revenge (www.revenge.co.uk; 32-34 Old Steine) Nightly disco with occasional cabaret.

Legends Club (31-34 Marine Pde) Located beneath the Legends Hotel, arguably the best gay hotel in town and 2009 winner of the Golden Handbag award.

beach bar, diner and club. All sorts of events happen here, from comedy to live music and club nights.

Concorde 2 — CLUB
(www.concorde2.co.uk; Madeira Dr) Brighton's best-known and best-loved club is a disarmingly unpretentious den, where DJ Fatboy Slim pioneered the Big Beat Boutique and still occasionally graces the decks. Each month there's a huge variety of club nights, live bands and concerts by international names.

Audio — CLUB
(www.audiobrighton.com; 10 Marine Pde) Some of the city's top club nights are held at this ear-numbing venue. The music's top priority here, attracting a young, up-for-it crowd.

Digital — CLUB
(www.yourfutureisdigital.com/brighton; 187-193 Kings Rd Arches) Seafront club hosting indie, house and student nights.

☆ Entertainment

Brighton Dome — THEATRE
(☏ 01273-709709; www.brightondome.org; Church St) Once the stables for King George IV's horses, this art deco complex houses three theatre venues within the Royal Pavilion estate. ABBA famously won the 1974 Eurovision Song Contest here.

Theatre Royal — THEATRE
(☏ 08448 717 650; New Rd) Built by decree of the Prince of Wales in 1806, this grand venue hosts musicals, plays and operas.

Komedia Theatre — COMEDY
(☏ 0845 293 8480; www.komedia.co.uk; 44-47 Gardner St) A stylish comedy, theatre and cabaret venue attracting top stand-up acts.

🔒 Shopping

In the market for a pair of vegetarian shoes, a gauche portrait of a Lego man or a letter opener in the shape of something naughty? Whatever item you yearn for, old or new, you'll probably find it in Brighton. The tightly packed Lanes is the most popular shopping district, its every twist and turn jam-packed with jewellers and gift shops, coffee shops and boutiques selling everything from antique firearms to hard-to-find vinyls. There's another, less-claustrophobic shopping district in North Laine, a series of partially pedestrian thoroughfares north of the Lanes, including Bond, Gardner, Kensington and Sydney Sts, lined with retro-cool boutiques

and bohemian cafes. Mainstream chains gather within the Churchill Square shopping centre and along Western Rd.

ⓘ Information

Incredibly, Brighton closed its busy tourist office in 2013.

Brighton City Guide (www.brighton.co.uk)
City Council (www.brighton-hove.gov.uk) A rich seam of city information.
Jubilee Library (Jubilee St; ◷10am-7pm Mon, Tue & Thu, to 5pm Wed, Fri & Sat, 11am-5pm Sun) Bring ID to sign up for free internet sessions.
Post Office (2-3 Churchill Sq; ◷9am-5.30pm Mon-Sat) Located within WH Smiths.
Visit Brighton (☏ 01273-290337; www.visit-brighton.com) There's no tourist office but you can still call or log on for information.

ⓘ Getting There & Away

Transport between London and Brighton is fast and frequent. If arriving by car, parking is plentiful but pricey, and the city-centre traffic, bus-clogged lanes and road layouts can be confusing.

BUS
Standard connections:
Arundel Bus 700, two hours, twice hourly
Chichester Bus 700, 2¾ hours, twice hourly
Eastbourne Bus 12, 70 minutes, up to every 10 minutes
London Victoria National Express, from £8, 2¼ hours, hourly

TRAIN
London-bound services pass through Gatwick Airport (£9.80, 25 to 40 minutes, up to five hourly).
Chichester £12.60, 50 minutes, half-hourly
Eastbourne £10.30, 30 to 40 minutes, half-hourly
Hastings £13, 80 minutes, half-hourly
London St Pancras £22.40, 1¼ hours, half-hourly
London Victoria £24, one hour, three-hourly
Portsmouth £15, 1½ hours, hourly

ⓘ Getting Around

Day bus tickets (£4.60) are available from the drivers of all Brighton and Hove buses. Alternatively a £2 PlusBus ticket on top of your rail fare gives unlimited bus travel for the day.

The city operates a pricey pay-and-display parking scheme. In the town centre, it's usually £3.50 per hour for a maximum stay of two hours. Alternatively, there's a Park & Ride 2.5 miles northwest of the centre at Withdean, from where bus 27 zips into town.

Cab companies include **Brighton Stream-line Taxis** (☑ 01273-202020) and **City Cabs** (☑ 01273-205205), and there's a taxi rank at the junction of East St and Market St.

WEST SUSSEX

West Sussex offers a welcome respite from fast-paced adventures. The serene hills and valleys of the South Downs ripple across the county, fringed by sheltered coastline. Beautiful Arundel and cultured Chichester make good bases from which to explore the county's winding country lanes and remarkable Roman ruins.

Arundel
POP 3410

Arguably the prettiest town in the county, Arundel is clustered around a vast fairy-tale castle, and its hillside streets overflow with antique emporiums, teashops and a host of eateries. While much of the town appears medieval – the whimsical castle has been home to the Dukes of Norfolk for centuries – most of it dates back to Victorian times.

◉ Sights

Arundel Castle CASTLE
(www.arundelcastle.org; adult/child £18/9; ◷ 10am-5pm Tue-Sun Apr-Oct) Arundel Castle was first built in the 11th century but all that's left of the early structure are the modest remains of the keep. It was ransacked during the English Civil War, and most of what you see today is the result of reconstruction by the eigth, 11th and 15th dukes of Norfolk between 1718 and 1900. The current duke still lives in part of the castle, whose highlights include the atmospheric keep, the massive Great Hall and the library.

The castle does a good impression of Windsor Castle and St James's Palace in the popular 2009 film *The Young Victoria,* and occasionally is closed for other film shoots.

Arundel Cathedral CATHEDRAL
(www.arundelcathedral.org; London Rd; ◷ 9am-6pm Apr-Oct, to dusk Nov-Mar) Arundel's ostentatious 19th-century Catholic cathedral is the other dominating feature of the town's impressive skyline. Commissioned by the 15th duke of Norfolk in 1868, this impressive structure was designed by Joseph Aloysius Hansom (inventor of the Hansom cab) in the French Gothic style, but shows much

Victorian economy and restraint. Although small for a cathedral – it holds just 500 worshippers – Hansom's clever layout makes the building seem a lot bigger.

A 1970s shrine in the north transept holds the remains of St Philip Howard, a canonised Catholic martyr who was banged up in the Tower of London by Elizabeth I until his death in 1595 for reverting to Catholicism. The building attracts only a trickle of tourists, rare indeed for a cathedral in southern England.

Arundel Museum MUSEUM
(www.arundelmuseum.org; Mill Rd; adult/child £3/2.50; ◷ 10am-4pm) Located opposite the Arundel Castle gates, this small, brand-new museum has sections on the castle, the South Downs National Park and the River Arun's role in 19th-century trade, as well as various other bits of Arundelia.

🛏 Sleeping & Eating

Arundel House B&B ££
(☑ 01903-882136; www.arundelhouseonline.com; 11 High St; d/ste from £85/120; 🛜) The contemporary chambers at this lovely 'restaurant with rooms' may be slightly low-ceilinged, but they're clean-cut and very comfortable, with showers big enough for two. The restaurant downstairs serves some of the best food in Arundel, which, happily, extends to breakfast.

Arden Guest House B&B ££
(☑ 01903-882544; www.ardenguesthouse.net; 4 Queens Lane; s/d £58/78, without bathroom £48/68; 🅿 🛜) For the classic British B&B experience, head to this eight-room guesthouse just over the river from the historical centre. Rooms are kept fresh and tick all the boxes; the hosts are amiable; and the breakfasts are cooked. No pets or children under 14.

★ Town House BRITISH £££
(☑ 01903-883847; 65 High St; set lunch/dinner from £17.50/25.50; ◷ noon-2.30pm & 7-9.30pm Tue-Sat) The only thing that rivals the 16th-century Florentine gilded-walnut ceiling in this compact and very elegant eatery is the sparkling atmosphere and acclaimed British cuisine with a European twist. Book ahead. Town House also has well-appointed rooms to let.

🛍 Shopping

Arundel is antiques central as far as West Sussex is concerned. If you've come to splurge on old stuff, **Tarrant Street** must have the highest concentration of collectibles shops anywhere in the southeast.

ⓘ Getting There & Away

Trains run to London Victoria (£17.30, 1½ hours, twice hourly) and to Chichester (£4.50, 20 minutes, twice hourly); change at Ford or Barnham. There are also links to Brighton (£10.10, 1¼ hours, twice hourly); again, change at Ford or Barnham.

Bus 700 runs to Brighton (two hours, twice hourly).

Chichester

POP 23,700

A lively Georgian market town still almost encircled by its medieval town walls, the administrative capital of West Sussex keeps watch over the plains between the South Downs and the sea. Visitors flock to Chichester's splendid cathedral, streets of handsome 18th-century town houses and its famous theatre, and of course to its pedestrianised shopping streets. A Roman port garrison in its early days, the town is also a launch pad to other fascinating Roman remains, as well as to Arundel and the coast.

⊙ Sights

Chichester Cathedral CATHEDRAL
(www.chichestercathedral.org.uk; West St; ⊙ 7.15am-7pm, tours 11.15am & 2.30pm Mon-Sat) This understated cathedral was begun in 1075 and largely rebuilt in the 13th century. The free-standing church tower went up in the 15th century; the spire dates from the 19th century, when its predecessor famously toppled over. Inside, three storeys of beautiful arches sweep upwards and Romanesque carvings are dotted around. Interesting features to track down include a smudgy stained-glass window added by artist Marc Chagall in 1978 and a glassed-over section of Roman mosaic flooring. Free guided tours last 45 minutes.

The excellent cathedral choir is guaranteed to give you goosebumps during the daily evensong (5.30pm).

Pallant House Gallery GALLERY
(www.pallant.org.uk; 9 North Pallant; adult/child £9/3.50; ⊙ 10am-5pm Tue, Wed, Fri & Sat, to 8pm Thu, from 11am Sun) A Queen Anne mansion built by a local wine merchant, handsome Pallant House and a 21st-century wing host this superb gallery. The focus is on, mostly British, 20th-century art. Show-stoppers Patrick Caulfield, Lucian Freud, Graham Sutherland, Frank Auerbach and Henry Moore are interspersed with internation-

al names such as Emil Filla, Le Corbusier and RB Kitaj. Most of these older works are in the mansion, while the newer wing is packed with pop art and temporary shows of modern and contemporary work.

Novium Museum MUSEUM
(www.thenovium.org; Tower St; adult/child £7/2.50; ⊙ 10am-5pm Mon-Sat, to 4pm Sun Apr-Oct, to 5pm Tue-Sat Nov-Mar) Chichester's purpose-built museum provides a home for the eclectic collections of the now-defunct District Museum, as well as many artefacts from Fishbourne Palace and a huge mosaic from Chilgrove Roman villa. The highlight is the set of Roman baths discovered in the 1970s, around which the six-million-pound museum was designed.

⌂ Sleeping

Accommodation is very thin on the ground in the city centre. Beds fill when there are goings-on at Goodwood racecourse, just to the north of Chichester.

Ship Hotel BOUTIQUE HOTEL ££
(☎ 01243-778000; www.theshiphotel.net; North St; r from £124; 🛜) The grand central staircase in this former Georgian town house climbs to 36 fairly spacious rooms of commanding period chic. It's the most enticing option in the city centre and it also boasts a brand-new and very snazzily styled restaurant. Book well ahead.

Jubilee House B&B ££
(☎ 01243-536558; www.jubileehousechichester.co.uk; 13 New Park Rd; s £60-80 d £70-90; 🛜) Two-room B&B on the edge of the historical centre with crisp, well-maintained quarters, a communal breakfast table and all of Chichester's sights a short amble away. Book ahead.

✗ Eating

St Martin's Tearooms CAFE £
(3 St Martins St; mains £4-10; ⊙ 10am-6pm Mon-Sat) A little cocoon of nooks and crannies tucked away in a part-18th-century, part-medieval town house, this organic cafe serves freshly ground coffee with wholesome, mostly vegetarian, food and a sinful selection of desserts. There's also a guest piano with which to shatter the tranquil scene, if you so wish. St Martin's St is off East St.

Wests Bar BRITISH £
(14 West St; mains £5-9; ⊙ 11am-11pm Mon-Sat, to 10.30pm Sun; 🛜) In a large deconsecrated church opposite Chichester Cathedral, this

temple of food and ale allows you to refuel and kick back in an incongruously ecclesiastical setting. The sinful menu of British pub favourites, including some typically spicy fare, is sure to bust your belt and invoke a holy thirst.

☆ Entertainment

Chichester Festival Theatre THEATRE
(☑01243-781312; www.cft.org.uk; Oakland's Park) Built in 1962, this somewhat Soviet-looking playhouse has a long and distinguished history. Sir Laurence Olivier was the theatre's first director, and Ingrid Bergman, Sir John Gielgud and Sir Anthony Hopkins have all played here.

ⓘ Information

Post Office (10 West St; ⊘9am-5.30pm Mon & Wed-Fri, from 9.30am Tue, 9am-3pm Sat)
Tourist Office (☑01243-775888; www. visitchichester.org; Tower St; ⊘10am-5pm Mon-Sat, to 4pm Sun) Located in the Novium Museum.

ⓘ Getting There & Away

BUS

Brighton Bus 700, 2½ hours, twice hourly
London Victoria National Express, change at Gatwick Airport; £15.60, three hours 40 minutes, every two hours
Portsmouth Bus 700, 70 minutes, twice hourly

TRAIN

Chichester has train connections to the following destinations:
Arundel Change at Ford or Barnham; £4.50, 20 minutes, twice hourly
Brighton £12.60, 50 minutes, twice hourly
London Victoria £17.30, 1½ hours, half-hourly
Portsmouth £7.50, 30 to 40 minutes, twice hourly

Around Chichester

Fishbourne Palace & Museum

Fishbourne Palace (www.sussexpast.co.uk; Roman Way; adult/child £8.70/4.30; ⊘10am-5pm Mar-Oct, reduced hours & days rest of the year) is the largest-known Roman residence in Britain. The palace lies 1.5 miles west of Chichester, just off the A259 (take bus 700 from outside Chichester Cathedral). Happened upon by labourers in the 1960s, it's thought that this once-luxurious mansion was built around AD 75 for a romanised local king. Housed in a modern pavilion are its foundations, hypocaust and painstakingly re-laid mosaics.

The centrepiece is a spectacular floor depicting Cupid riding a dolphin, flanked by sea horses and panthers. There's also a fascinating little museum and replanted Roman gardens.

SURREY

Surrey is popular with affluent London commuters who've had kids, moved out of the city and bought a country pad. For the most part, though, it's made up of uninspiring towns and dull, sprawling suburbs. Further away from the roaring motorways and packed rush-hour trains, the county reveals some inspiring landscapes made famous by authors Sir Arthur Conan Doyle, Sir Walter Scott and Jane Austen.

Farnham

POP 39,500
Nudging the border with Hampshire and joined at the hip with the garrison settlement of Aldershot, affluent Farnham is Surrey's prettiest town and its best destination. Blessed with lively shopping streets of Georgian symmetry, a 12th-century castle and some soothing river walks, this easygoing market town makes for an undemanding day trip from London, just an hour away.

⊙ Sights

Farnham Castle CASTLE
(EH; ☑01252-721194; www.farnhamcastle.com; Castle St; palace adult/child £3.50/2.50, keep admission free; ⊘palace 2-4pm Wed, keep 9am-5pm Mon-Fri, 10am-4pm Sat & Sun, closed Jan) Farnham Castle was constructed in 1138 by Henry de Blois, the grandson of William the Conqueror. There's not much left of the castle keep today except the beautiful old ramparts. Even if the keep is closed, it's worth walking around the outside for the picturesque views.

Open only one afternoon a week, the residential palace was built in the 13th century as a stopover for the bishops of Winchester on London journeys. From 1926 to the 1950s, it was used by the bishops of Guildford.

The palace is now a private function venue, hence the limited opening hours.

Museum of Farnham
MUSEUM

(38 West St; ⊙ 10am-5pm Tue-Sat) FREE This engaging little museum is located in the splendid Willmer House, a Georgian mansion built in 1718 for the wealthy hop merchant and maltster John Thorne.

Themed rooms trace Farnham's history from flint-tool days to Bakelite nostalgia. A corner is dedicated to William Cobbett, the town's most famous son, a 19th-century reformer, radical member of parliament, writer and journalist who established Hansard (the official record of what is said in Parliament).

Cobbett's bust takes pride of place in the peaceful garden out the back, where you'll also find a timber gallery housing temporary exhibitions.

🛏 Sleeping & Eating

Bush Hotel
HOTEL ££

(☎ 01252-234800; www.mercure-uk.com; The Borough; r from £109; 🅿❋🛜) This 17th-century inn is right in the heart of the action. Rolling renovations keep things fresh, and there's a snug beamed bar and recommended restaurant that spills into the pretty courtyard.

Vintage Cake House
CAFE £

(www.thevintagecakehouse.co.uk; 5 Downing St; light lunch & tea £5-10; ⊙ 9.30am-5pm) Classic English tearoom with wedges of homemade cake, tinkling tea china, staff in vintage attire and lashings of clotted cream.

Brasserie Blanc
FRENCH ££

(www.brasserieblanc.com; 5 Castle St; mains £10-18; ⊙ 9-11am, noon-3pm, 6-10pm Mon-Thu, to 10.30pm Fri, noon-10.30pm Sat, to 9pm Sun) For a bit of Gallic class, head to this understated eatery near Farnham Castle. The simply laid tables, low-Watt art deco lighting and art-packed walls create a modestly stylish atmosphere, and there's a walled garden out the back. The menu is a mostly seasonal list of finely crafted dishes cooked using choice ingredients shipped in from France.

ℹ Information

Farnham has no tourist office, but maps and leaflets are available from the town hall on South St.

ℹ Getting There & Away

BUS

London Victoria National Express; £9.70, two hours, daily

TRAIN

London Waterloo £15.30, one hour, twice hourly

Winchester Change at Woking; £19.40, 60 to 80 minutes, twice hourly

Hindhead

The tiny hamlet of Hindhead, 8 miles south of Farnham off the A287, lies in the middle of the largest area of open heath in Surrey. During the 19th century a number of prominent Victorians bought up property in the area, including Sherlock Holmes' mastermind Sir Arthur Conan Doyle (1859–1930). One of three founders of the National Trust, Sir Robert Hunter lived in nearby Haslemere, and today much of the area is administered by the foundation.

The most beautiful part of the area is to the northeast, where you'll find a natural depression known as the **Devil's Punchbowl**. There are a number of excellent trails and bridleways here. To get the best view, head for **Gibbet Hill** (280m), which was once an execution ground. The **Hindhead YHA Hostel** (☎ 0845 371 9022; www.yha.org. uk; Devil's Punchbowl, Thursley, Godalming; dm from £16) is a completely secluded cottage run by the National Trust on the northern edge of the Punchbowl – perfect digs for walkers.

Buses 18 and 19 run every 30 minutes between Hindhead and Farnham.

Oxford, Cotswolds & Around

Best Places to Eat

➡ Paris House (p222)

➡ Waterside Inn (p228)

➡ Rickety Press (p196)

➡ Horse & Groom (p210)

➡ Edamame (p195)

Best Places to Stay

➡ Bradley (p217)

➡ Glove House (p199)

➡ Star Cottage (p206)

➡ Hope House (p199)

Why Go?

Dotted with gorgeous little villages, this part of the country is as close to the old-world English idyll as you'll get. It's a haven of lush rolling hills, rose-clad cottages, graceful stone churches and thatched roofs. Add to this mix the legendary university city of Oxford, with its gracious architecture and lively student vibe, and it's easy to see why the region is a magnet for visitors.

Although the roads and the most popular villages are busy in summer, it's easy to get off the tourist trail. The Cotswolds are at their best when you find a romantic refuge of your own, and discover the fire-lit inns and grandiose manors that persuade A-list celebrities and the moneyed to buy property here.

Most of the area is an easy day trip from London, but Oxford and the Cotswolds deserve at least a couple of leisurely days.

When to Go

➡ On 1 May you can welcome the dawn with Oxford's Magdalen College Choir, which sings hymns from the college tower.

➡ In July you can sip champagne and watch the rowing at Henley's Royal Regatta and Festival.

➡ September is the best time to sample England's finest ales at the four-day St Albans Beer Festival.

➡ Rambling in the Cotswolds is ideal in spring, early summer and September, when the weather is in your favour, without the July and August crowds.

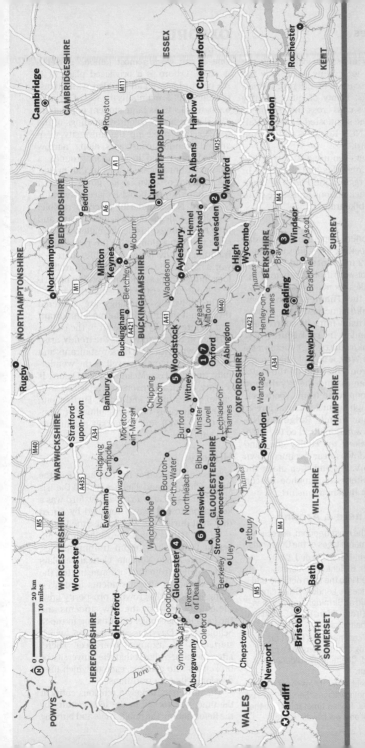

Oxford, Cotswolds & Around Highlights

1 Following in the footsteps of JRR Tolkien, CS Lewis, Evelyn Waugh and Oscar Wilde as you tour the **Oxford colleges** (p187)

2 Having a wizard of a time at the **Making of Harry Potter studio tour** (p223) in Leavesden

3 Getting a glimpse of the regal life at the Queen's weekend hideaway, **Windsor Castle** (p224)

4 Touring the elegant cloisters at the magnificent **Gloucester Cathedral** (p217)

5 Lording it up in **Blenheim Palace** (p199), one of the country's greatest stately homes

6 Meandering around **Painswick** (p214), one of the most beautiful and unspoilt towns in the Cotswolds

7 Exploring the anthropological treasure trove that is the **Pitt Rivers Museum** (p187) in Oxford

🏃 Activities

Cycling

Gentle gradients and scenic vistas make the Cotswolds ideal for cycling, with only the steep western escarpment offering a challenge to the legs. Plenty of quiet country lanes and byways criss-cross the region, or you can follow the signposted **Thames Valley Cycle Way** (NCN Routes 4 and 5) from Windsor to Oxford.

Mountain bikers can use a variety of bridleways in the Cotswolds and Chilterns. In the west of the region, the Forest of Dean has many dirt-track options and some dedicated mountain-bike trails.

Walking

The Cotswolds offers opportunities for day hikes. If you're looking for something more ambitious, the 102-mile **Cotswold Way** (www. nationaltrail.co.uk/cotswold) from Bath to Chipping Campden takes about a week to walk.

Alternatively, the **Thames Path** (www. nationaltrail.co.uk/thamespath) follows the river downstream from its source near Cirencester to London. In Oxfordshire (www. oxfordshire.gov.uk/countryside) there's also the **Oxfordshire Way**, a 65-mile signposted trail running from Bourton-on-the-Water to Henley-on-Thames, and the **Wychwood Way**, a 37-mile loop route from Woodstock, which runs through an ancient royal forest.

The picturesque 87-mile **Ridgeway National Trail** (www.nationaltrail.co.uk/ridgeway) meanders along the chalky grassland of the Wiltshire downs near Avebury, down into the Thames Valley and then along the spine of the Chilterns to Ivinghoe Beacon near Aylesbury in Buckinghamshire.

ℹ️ Getting There & Around

A car will give you the most freedom, especially for exploring the small villages of the Cotswolds.

Oxford, Moreton-in-Marsh, Stroud, Cheltenham, Gloucester, Bletchley, St Albans and Windsor are plugged into the train network and all have direct services to London. Other direct trains go as far afield as Birmingham, Manchester and Newcastle (from Oxford), and Cardiff and Edinburgh (from Cheltenham).

National Express coaches head from London and further-flung destinations to Oxford, Cirencester, Stroud, Cheltenham, Gloucester, Newent and Windsor.

Local buses connect larger towns to each other and to their surrounding villages. Services are run by various operators. To view timetables, use the journey planner tool on www.traveline.info.

OXFORD

POP 171,000

One of the world's most famous university cities, Oxford is a privileged place. It is steeped in history and studded with august buildings, yet it maintains the feel of a young town, thanks to its large student population. The elegant honey-coloured buildings of the colleges that make up the university wrap around tranquil courtyards along narrow cobbled lanes, and inside their grounds, a studious calm reigns. Just as in Cambridge, the existence of 'town' beside 'gown' makes it more than simply a bookish place of learning.

Oxford is a wonderful place to ramble: the oldest colleges date back 750 years, and little has changed inside the hallowed walls since then. But along with the rich history, tradition and lively academic life, there is a world beyond the college walls. Oxford has a long industrial past and the working majority still outnumber the academic elite.

The university buildings are scattered throughout the city, with the most important and architecturally significant in the centre. Jericho, in the northwest, is the trendy, artsy end of town, with slick bars, restaurants and an art-house cinema, as well as the wonderfully tranquil Port Meadow. East Oxford is a gritty, ethnically diverse area packed with cheap places to eat and drink. Further out, in the salubrious northern suburb of Summertown, you'll find upmarket restaurants and bars.

History

Strategically placed at the confluence of the Rivers Cherwell and Thames (called the Isis here, from the Latin *Tamesis*), Oxford was a key Saxon town, heavily fortified by Alfred the Great during the war against the Danes.

By the 11th century, the Augustinian abbey in Oxford had begun training clerics, and when Anglo-Norman clerical scholars were expelled from the Sorbonne in 1167, the abbey began to attract students in droves. Alongside Oxford's growing prosperity grew the enmity between the new students and the local townspeople, culminating in the St Scholastica's Day Massacre in 1355, which started as an argument over beer. Thereafter, the king ordered that the university be broken up into colleges, each of which then developed its own traditions.

The university, largely a religious entity at the time, was rocked in the 16th century by the Reformation; the public trials and burning at the stake of Protestant heretics under Mary I; and by the subsequent hanging, drawing and quartering of Catholics under her successor Elizabeth I. As the Royalist headquarters, Oxford backed the losing side during the Civil War, but flourished after the restoration of the monarchy, with some of its most notable buildings constructed at that time.

The arrival of the canal system in 1790 had a profound effect on the rest of Oxford. By creating a link with the Midlands' industrial centres, work and trade suddenly expanded beyond the academic core. This development was further strengthened by the construction of the railways.

The city's real industrial boom came, however, when William Morris began producing cars here in 1913. With the success of his Bullnose Morris and Morris Minor, his Cowley factory went on to become one of the largest motor plants in the world. Although the works have been scaled down since their heyday, Minis still run off BMW's Cowley production line today.

⦿ Sights

University of Oxford

Much of the centre of Oxford is taken up by graceful university buildings and elegant colleges, each one individual in its appearance and academic specialities. The first colleges (Balliol, Merton and University) were built in the 13th century, with at least three more being added in each of the following three centuries. Newer colleges, such as Keble, were added in the 19th and 20th centuries to cater for an ever-expanding student population. Tradition dies hard at Oxford, however, and it wasn't until 1877 that lecturers were allowed to marry, and another year before female students were admitted. It took another 42 years before women were granted degrees.

Today, there are 38 colleges catering to more than 21,000 students. Not all are open to the public. For those that are, visiting hours change with the term and exam schedule; check www.ox.ac.uk for full details of visiting hours.

Oxford University Museum of Natural History   MUSEUM

(www.oum.ox.ac.uk; Parks Rd; ⊙10am-5pm; ⊞) FREE Housed in a glorious Victorian Gothic building with slender, cast-iron columns, ornate capitals and a soaring glass roof, this museum is worth visiting for its architecture alone. The real draw, however, is the collection of more than five million exhibits. These range from exotic insects and fossils to a towering T Rex skeleton and the remains of the first dinosaur ever to be mentioned in a written text (in 1677).

★ Pitt Rivers Museum   MUSEUM

(www.prm.ox.ac.uk; Parks Rd; ⊙noon-4.30pm Mon, 10am-4.30pm Tue-Sun; ⊞) FREE Hidden away through a door at the back of the main exhibition hall of the Oxford University Museum of Natural History, this wonderfully creepy anthropological museum houses a treasure trove of objects from around the world – more than enough to satisfy any armchair adventurer. One of the reasons this museum is so brilliant is because there are no computers here or shiny modern gimmicks. The dim light lends an air of mystery to the glass cases stuffed with the prized booty of Victorian explorers.

Objects are divided into themes, rather than culture, with subjects such as 'Smoking' or 'Treatment of Dead Enemies' (a particularly disturbing ensemble). Among the feathered cloaks, necklaces of teeth, blowpipes, magic charms, Noh masks, totem poles, fur parkas, musical instruments and shrunken heads, you may spot ceremonial headgear from Uganda worn during circumcision ceremonies, ancient dental implements and a porcupine fish helmet from Kiribati.

Trinity College   COLLEGE

(www.trinity.ox.ac.uk; Broad St; adult/child £2/1; ⊙10am-noon Mon-Fri, 2-4pm daily) Founded in 1555, this small college is worth a visit to see the lovely garden quad, designed by Christopher Wren. Its exquisitely carved chapel is one of the most beautiful in the city and a masterpiece of English baroque. Famous students have included William Pitt the Elder and Cardinal Newman.

LOCAL KNOWLEDGE

ACADEMIC ATTIRE

Don't be surprised to see students wandering around Oxford in black gowns, black 'mortarboard' caps, white bowties and (for graduates) colourful hoods. Oxford students are required to wear their academic dress to take their exams, and some colleges require it every night when dining in the hall.

Oxford

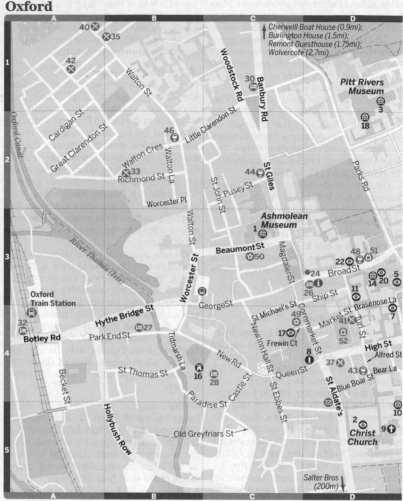

Cherwell Boat House (0.9mi);
Burlington House (1.5mi);
Remont Guesthouse (1.75mi);
Wolvercote (2.7mi)

Salter Bros
(200m)

Exeter College
COLLEGE

(www.exeter.ox.ac.uk; Turl St; ⊙2-5pm) **FREE** Exeter is known for its elaborate 17th-century dining hall and its ornate Victorian Gothic chapel housing *The Adoration of the Magi*, a William Morris tapestry, and a psychedelic bombast of gold mosaic and stained glass.

Museum of the History of Science
MUSEUM

(www.mhs.ox.ac.uk; Broad St; ⊙noon-5pm Tue-Fri, 10am-5pm Sat, 2-5pm Sun) **FREE** Science, art, celebrity and nostalgia come together at this fascinating museum, where the exhibits include everything from a blackboard used by Einstein to the world's finest collection of historical scientific instruments. It's all housed in a beautiful 17th-century building.

Sheldonian Theatre
THEATRE

(www.sheldon.ox.ac.uk; Broad St; adult/child £3.50/2.50; ⊙10am-4.30pm daily Jul & Aug, closed Sun Sep-Jun, closed Sat Dec & Jan) Built in 1663, this monumental building was the first major work of Christopher Wren, at that time a professor of astronomy. Inspired by the classical Theatre of Marcellus in Rome, it has a rectangular front end and a semicircular back, while the ceiling of the main hall is blanketed by a fine 17th-century painting of the triumph

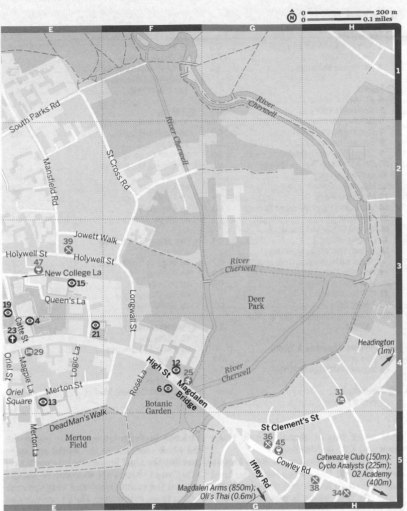

of truth over ignorance. What's remarkable about the ceiling is its length, made possible by ingenious braces made of shorter timbers, for want of trees large enough.

The Sheldonian is now used for college ceremonies and public concerts, but you can climb to the cupola for good views of the surrounding buildings.

New College COLLEGE
(www.new.ox.ac.uk; Holywell St; adult/child £3/2 Mar-Sep, free Oct-Feb; ⏰ 11am-5pm Mar-Sep, 2-4pm Oct-Feb) This 14th-century college was the first in Oxford for undergraduates and is

a fine example of the glorious Perpendicular Gothic style. The chapel here is full of treasures, including superb stained glass, much of it original, and Sir Jacob Epstein's disturbing statue of Lazarus. During term time, visitors can attend the beautiful Evensong, a choral church service held nightly at 6pm.

William Spooner was once a college warden here, and his habit of transposing the first consonants of words gave rise to the term 'spoonerism'. Local lore suggests that he once reprimanded a student by saying, 'You have deliberately tasted two worms and can leave Oxford by the town drain'. Spooner

Oxford

aside, other famous alumni include Hugh Grant and Kate Beckinsale.

New College is also famous for a bizarre medieval ritual. Every three years, the Lord Major of Oxford has to walk along the ruins of the city wall, which is part of New College, to fulfill a medieval obligation that the wall would be repaired if need be (the walk is merely symbolic).

Access for visitors is through the New College Lane gate from Easter to early October, and through the Holywell St entrance the rest of the year. As you walk along New College Lane, look up at the steeped **Bridge of Sighs** linking the two halves of Hertford College to New College. It's sometimes erroneously referred to as a copy of the famous bridge in Venice, but it bears a much closer resemblance to that city's Rialto Bridge.

Bodleian Library   LIBRARY
(☏ 01865-287400; www.bodley.ox.ac.uk; Catte St; tours £5-13; ⊙ 9am-5pm Mon-Sat, 11am-5pm Sun)

Oxford's Bodleian Library is one of the oldest public libraries in the world and quite possibly the most impressive one you'll ever see. Casual visitors are welcome to wander around the central quad and visit the exhibition space in the foyer. For £1 you can also access the Divinity School, but the rest of the complex can only be visited on guided tours (check online or at the information desk for times; it pays to book ahead).

The Bodleian Library has its roots in a 15th-century collection of books and its present state is largely due to the efforts of Sir Thomas Bodley, a 16th-century fellow of Merton College. He came to the agreement with the Stationers' Company of London that the library would receive a copy of every single book published in the UK – an agreement that still stands today. It currently holds more than 11 million items, contains 117 miles of shelving and has seating space for up to 2500 readers. A staggering 4000 books and articles arrive every week, all of which need to be catalogued and stored.

The oldest part of the library surrounds the Jacobean Gothic **Old Schools Quadrangle**, which dates from the early 17th century and sports some of Oxford's odder architectural gems. On the eastern side of the quad is the **Tower of Five Orders**, an ornate building depicting the five classical orders of architecture. On the west side is the **Divinity School**, the university's first teaching room. It is renowned as a masterpiece of 15th-century English Gothic architecture and has a superb fan-vaulted ceiling; it featured as the Hogwarts hospital wing in the *Harry Potter* films.

Half-hour mini tours (£5) include the Divinity School and the medieval **Duke Humfrey's library**, where no fewer than five kings, 40 Nobel Prize winners, 25 British prime ministers, and writers such as Oscar Wilde, CS Lewis and JRR Tolkien studied amid rows filled with grand ancient tomes chained to the shelves. Those wishing to read here (the books may not be borrowed) still have to swear Bodley's Oath, which involves vowing 'not to bring into the Library or kindle therein any fire or flame'.

Hour-long standard tours (£7) also visit the 17th-century **Convocation House**, where parliament was held during the Civil War, and the **Chancellor's Court**. Extended tours (£13) run for 90 minutes and include the Radcliffe Camera and either the Upper Reading Room or underground Gladstone Link.

Radcliffe Camera   LIBRARY
(Radcliffe Sq) The Radcliffe Camera is the quintessential Oxford landmark and one of the city's most photographed buildings. The spectacular circular library/reading room, filled with natural light, was built between 1737 and 1749 in grand Palladian style, and has Britain's third-largest dome. The only way to see the interior is to join one of the extended tours (£13; 90 minutes) of the Bodleian Library (p190).

Brasenose College   COLLEGE
(www.bnc.ox.ac.uk; Radcliffe Sq; admission £2; ⊙ 10-11.30am & 2-4.30pm) Founded in 1509, this small, select and elegant place is named after a 'brass nose', or a brazen door-knocker, to be precise. It's believed that wayward students took the knocker all the way to Stamford, Lincolnshire, in 1533. In 1890 the college purchased a house in Stamford, convinced that the knocker on its front door was the original. The door-knocker in question now takes pride of place above the high table in the dining hall.

Also of interest is the chapel, with its fine painted, vaulted ceiling. Famous alumni include *Lord of the Flies* author William Golding, Monty Python's Michael Palin and British prime minister David Cameron. If the sign outside says that it's shut during supposed open hours, check with the porters as they sometimes hang it to deter tour groups.

University Church of
St Mary the Virgin   CHURCH
(www.university-church.ox.ac.uk; High St; ⊙ 9am-5pm Mon-Sat, 11.30am-5pm Sun) With a tower dating from 1280 and a perpendicular Gothic nave, this relatively unadorned church is most famous as the site of the 1556 trial of three Anglican bishops (including Thomas Cranmer, the first Protestant archibishop of Canterbury) during the reign of Mary I. All three were later burnt at the stake for heresy on Broad St. Inside, there's a memorial to the victims of the Reformation – both Protestant and Catholic.

Mahatma Gandhi spoke here in the 1930s, and his image is inscribed on a ceiling boss above the loft at the rear of the church. A trek to the top of the tower (adult/child £4/3) offers excellent views of the Radcliffe Camera.

All Souls College   COLLEGE
(www.all-souls.ox.ac.uk; High St; ⊙ 2-4pm Mon-Fri) **FREE** One of the wealthiest Oxford colleges, All Souls was founded in 1438 as a centre of prayer and learning. It's one of several graduate colleges, though it doesn't accept just any old Oxford graduate. Each year, the university's top finalists sit a fellowship exam, with an average of only two making the grade. Today fellowship of the college is one of the highest academic honours in the country.

Much of the college facade dates from the 1440s and, unlike other older colleges, the front quad is largely unchanged in five centuries. It also contains a beautiful 17th-century sundial designed by Christopher Wren. Most obvious, though, are the twin mock-Gothic towers on the north quad. Designed by Nicholas Hawksmoor in 1710, they were lambasted for ruining the Oxford skyline when first erected.

St Edmund Hall
COLLEGE

(www.seh.ox.ac.uk; Queen's Lane; ☺10am-4pm)
FREE St Edmund Hall ('Teddy Hall' to its residents) is the sole survivor of the original medieval halls, the teaching institutions that preceded colleges in Oxford. The Mohawk chief Oronhyatekha studied here in 1862 (and eloped with the principal's daughter). The college is best known for its small chapel decorated by William Morris and Edward Burne-Jones.

Magdalen College
COLLEGE

(www.magd.ox.ac.uk; High St; adult/child £5/4; ☺1-6pm) Set amid 40 hectares of lawns, woodlands, river walks and deer park, Magdalen (*mawd*-lin), founded in 1458, is one of the wealthiest and most beautiful of Oxford's colleges. It has a reputation as an artistic college, and some of its famous students have included writers Julian Barnes, Alan Hollinghurst, CS Lewis, John Betjeman, Seamus Heaney and Oscar Wilde, not to mention Edward VIII, TE Lawrence 'of Arabia' and Dudley Moore.

An elegant Victorian gateway leads into a medieval chapel (with its glorious 15th-century tower) and on to the remarkable cloisters (with strange animals perching on the buttresses), some of the finest in Oxford. The fantastic gargoyles and grotesques along the frontage here are said to have inspired CS Lewis' stone statues in *The Chronicles of Narnia*. Behind the cloisters, the lovely Addison's Walk leads through the grounds and along the banks of the River Cherwell for just under a mile. Were you here in the mid-1870s, you would have encountered Oscar Wilde taking his pet lobster for a walk.

The college also has a fine choir that sings Hymnus Eucharisticus at 6am on May Day (1 May) from the top of the 42m bell tower. The event now marks the culmination of a solid night of drinking for most students as they gather in their glad rags on Magdalen Bridge to listen to the dawn chorus.

Botanic Garden
GARDENS

(www.botanic-garden.ox.ac.uk; High St; adult/child £4.50/free; ☺9am-5pm) Sweeping along the banks of the River Cherwell, this peaceful garden was founded in 1621 for the study of medicinal plants, and it's still a department of the university. The bench where Lyra and her extra-universal lover Will intend to haunt in Phillip Pullman's *His Dark Materials* is usually well-attended by mooning students.

Merton College
COLLEGE

(www.merton.ox.ac.uk; Merton St; admission £3; ☺2-5pm Mon-Fri, 10am-5pm Sat & Sun) Founded in 1264, Merton is the oldest of the three original colleges and the first to adopt collegiate planning, bringing scholars and tutors together into a formal community and providing a planned residence for them. Its distinguishing architectural features include large gargoyles whose expressions suggest that they're about to throw up, and the charming 14th-century **Mob Quad** – the first of the college quads.

Just off the quad is a 13th-century **chapel** and the **Old Library** (admission on guided tour only), the oldest medieval library in use (look for the chained books). It is said that Tolkien spent many hours here writing *The Lord of the Rings* and that the trees in the Fellows' Garden inspired the ents of Middle Earth. Other literary giants associated with the college include TS Eliot and Louis MacNeice.

During the summer holidays it may be possible to join a guided tour of the college grounds (£4). Also in summer, look out for posters advertising candlelit concerts in the chapel.

Behind Merton College is the ominously named **Dead Man's Walk**, so called because the medieval Jewish community, who were not allowed to bury their dead within the city, would take bodies along this route to the Jewish cemetery (now the Botanic Garden).

★ Christ Church
COLLEGE

(www.chch.ox.ac.uk; St Aldate's; adult/child £8/6.50; ☺10am-4.30pm Mon-Sat, 2-4.30pm Sun) The largest of all of Oxford's colleges and the one with the grandest quad, Christ Church is also its most popular. Its magnificent buildings, illustrious history and latter-day fame as a location for the *Harry Potter* films have tourists coming in droves. The college was founded in 1524 by Cardinal Thomas Wolsey, who suppressed the monastery existing on the site to acquire the funds for his lavish building project.

Over the years numerous luminaries have been educated here, including philosopher John Locke, poet WH Auden, Charles Dodgson (Lewis Carroll), and no less than 13 British prime ministers. The main entrance is below the imposing **Tom Tower**, the upper part of which was designed by former student Sir Christopher Wren. Great Tom, the 7-tonne tower bell, still chimes 101 times each evening at 9.05pm (Oxford is five minutes west of Greenwich) to sound the curfew imposed on the original 100 students – plus the one added in 1663.

Visitors must go further down St Aldate's to the side entrance. Immediately on entering is the 15th-century cloister, a relic of the ancient Priory of St Frideswide, whose shrine was once a focus of pilgrimage. From here, you go up to the **Great Hall**, the college's magnificent dining room, with its hammerbeam roof and imposing portraits of past scholars; it was replicated in the film studios as the dining hall at Hogwarts for the *Harry Potter* films.

Coming down the grand staircase (where Professor McGonagall welcomed Harry in the first film), you'll enter **Tom Quad**, Oxford's largest and arguably most impressive quadrangle, and from here, 12th-century **Christ Church Cathedral**. It was originally the abbey church and then the college chapel, but it was declared a cathedral by Henry VIII when he broke from the Catholic Church, suppressed more monasteries and convents, and gave the college its current name. It was formerly known as Cardinal's College.

Inside, brawny Norman columns are topped by elegant vaulting, and beautiful stained-glass windows illuminate the walls. Look out for the depiction of the murder of Thomas Becket, dating from 1320, above the side altar on the right. As this is a working Anglican cathedral, there's no charge to visit it for private prayer or to attend a service – talk to the porters at the main gate. Evensong is held at 6pm most days.

To the south of the college is **Christ Church Meadow**, a leafy expanse bordered by the Rivers Cherwell and Isis, ideal for leisurely walking.

The hall often closes between noon and 2pm and the cathedral in late afternoon.

Christ Church Picture Gallery GALLERY
(www.chch.ox.ac.uk/gallery; Oriel Sq; adult/child £3/free; ☉10.30am-4.30pm Mon-Sat, 2-4.30pm Sun, closed Tue Oct-Jun) Christ Church's stash of precious masterpieces dates from 1300 to 1750, and has a particular focus on the Italian Renaissance. Paintings by the likes of Tintoretto, Veronese and Anthony van Dyck take pride of place, and there's an exalted collection of drawings by the likes of Michelangelo, Leonardo da Vinci and Raphael. Admission is half price with a valid Christ Church ticket.

Other Sights

⭐**Ashmolean Museum** MUSEUM
(www.ashmolean.org; Beaumont St; ☉10am-5pm Tue-Sun; ♿) FREE Britain's oldest public museum, second in repute only to London's British Museum, was established in 1683 when Elias Ashmole presented the university with the collection of curiosities amassed by the well-travelled John Tradescant, gardener to Charles I. A 2009 makeover has left the museum with new interactive features, a giant atrium, glass walls revealing galleries on different levels and a beautiful rooftop restaurant.

Its collections, displayed in bright, spacious galleries within one of Britain's best examples of neoclassical architecture, span the world and include Egyptian mummies, Islamic art, ancient documents, rare porcelain, tapestries, silverware, priceless musical instruments and extensive displays of European art.

Oxford Union LIBRARY
(www.oxford-union.org; Frewin Ct; admission £1.50; ☉9.30am-5pm Mon-Fri, longer during university term) Oxford's legendary members' society is famous for its feisty debates, heavyweight international speakers and Pre-Raphaelite murals. Although most of the building is off-limits to nonmembers, you can visit the library to see the murals, which were painted between 1857 and 1859 by Dante Gabriel Rossetti, William Morris and Edward Burne-Jones. They depict scenes from the Arthurian legends but are difficult to see on bright days, as they surround the windows.

Carfax Tower TOWER
(Queen St; adult/child £2.50/1.30; ☉10am-5.30pm) This central landmark, towering over what has been a crossroads for 1000 years, is the sole reminder of medieval St Martin's Church and offers good views over the city centre.

LOCAL KNOWLEDGE

TOLKIEN'S RESTING PLACE

Lord of the Rings author JRR Tolkien is buried with his wife Edith at Wolvercote Cemetery, 2 miles north of the city along Banbury Rd. The names Beren and Luthien are carved on their gravestone, a reference to the love between a mortal man and an elf maiden who gave up her immortality to be with him.

OXFORD, COTSWOLDS & AROUND OXFORD

Oxford Castle Unlocked   CASTLE
(www.oxfordcastleunlocked.co.uk; 44-46 Oxford Castle; adult/child £10/7; ☺tours 10am-4.20pm) It's not England's most imposing fortress, but Oxford Castle dates back more than 1000 years. Access is by tours, departing every 20 minutes, led by costumed guides.

Tours include St George's Tower, offering excellent views of the city; the 11th-century crypt of St George's Chapel (possibly the first formal teaching venue in Oxford); the Victorian prison cells; and the 18th-century Debtors' Tower, where you learn about the inmates' grisly lives, daring escapes and cruel punishments. You can also clamber up the original medieval motte.

🏃 Activities

A quintessential Oxford experience, **punting** is all about sitting back and quaffing Pimms (the typical English summer drink) as you watch the city's glorious architecture float by. Which, of course, requires someone else to do the hard work – punting is far more difficult than it appears. If you decide to go it alone, a deposit for the punt is usually charged. Most punts hold five people including the punter.

Magdalen Bridge Boathouse   BOATING
(☎01865-202643; www.oxfordpunting.co.uk; High St; chauffered per 30min £25, self-punt per hour £20; ☺9.30am-dusk Feb-Nov) The most central location to hire a punt, chauffered or otherwise. From here, you can head downstream around the Botanic Garden and Christ Church Meadow or upstream around Magdalen Deer Park. You can also hire row boats and pedaloes.

Cherwell Boat House   BOATING
(☎01865-515978; www.cherwellboathouse.co.uk; 50 Bardwell Rd; per hour £15-18; ☺10am-dusk mid-Mar–mid-Oct) Head a mile north of the centre for a countryside punt on the River Cherwell, where the most popular destination is the busy pub, the Victoria Arms. Row boats and Canadian canoes are also available. To get here, head north on Banbury Rd and then turn right into Bardwell Rd.

Salter Bros   BOATING, CRUISE
(☎01865-243421; www.salterssteamers.co.uk; Folly Bridge; punt/row boat/motor boat per hr £20/20/35; ☺May-late Sep) Rents punts, row boats and motor boats, and offers a range of cruises along the River Isis from Oxford. The most popular is the scenic journey to the historic market town of Abingdon (adult/

child £13/6.80). The trip takes two hours and passes the college boathouses and several popular riverside pubs en route.

☞ Tours

Bill Spectre's Ghost Trails   WALKING TOUR
(☎07941 041811; www.ghosttrail.org; adult/child £8/6; ☺6.30pm Fri & Sat) For a highly entertaining and informative look at Oxford's dark underbelly, join Victorian undertaker Bill Spectre on a 1¾-hour tour of the city's most haunted sites. It departs from Oxford Castle Unlocked (p194); audience participation likely.

Footprints Tours   WALKING TOUR
(☎020-7558 8706; www.footprints-tours.com) There's no need to book for the 'free' two-hour walking tours (payment is by way of tips), just turn up at the departure point on Broad St at 11am or 2pm. Bookings are required though for the themed pub, bike, *Harry Potter* and Blenheim Palace tours – check times and prices online.

Oxford City Walk   WALKING TOUR
(☎07530 951320; www.oxfordcitywalk.co.uk; 2hr tour for up to 5 people £50) Bespoke tours tweaked to your party's interests, whether that be architecture, literature, history, science, music, university life or detective series *Inspector Morse*.

Oxford Official Guided Walking Tours   WALKING TOUR
(☎01865-252200; www.visitoxfordandoxfordshire.com; 15-16 Broad St; adult/child from £9/8) Book at the tourist office for tours of Oxford city and colleges (10.45am and 1pm year-round, plus 11am and 2pm at busy times) or a bewildering array of themed tours, including *Inspector Morse, Alice in Wonderland* and *Harry Potter*, and family walking tours in the school holidays. Check the website for details.

Oxon Carts   TOUR
(☎07747 024600; www.oxoncarts.com; tours £25) Flexible hour-long tours conducted by a fleet of pedicabs. Passengers receive a copy of a 1904 map of the city and a personal guide to its buildings and history.

🛏 Sleeping

Book ahead between May and September and on weekends. If you're stuck, you'll find a string of B&Bs along Iffley, Abingdon, Banbury and Headington Rds.

Central Backpackers   HOSTEL £

(☑ 01865-242288; www.centralbackpackers.co.uk; 13 Park End St; dm £22-28; @🛜) A friendly budget option located above a bar and right in the centre of town, this small hostel has basic, bright and simple rooms that sleep four to 12 people, a rooftop terrace and a small lounge with satellite TV.

Oxford YHA   HOSTEL £

(☑ 0845 371 9131; www.yha.org.uk; 2a Botley Rd; dm/r from £17/56; @🛜) Particularly convenient for budget travellers arriving by train, this hostel has simple but comfortable four- and six-bed en suite dorms, private rooms and loads of facilities, including a restaurant, library, garden, laundry and a choice of lounges.

★ Oxford Coach & Horses   B&B ££

(☑ 01865-200017; www.oxfordcoachandhorses. co.uk; 62 St Clements St; s/d from £115/130; P 🛜) Once a coaching inn, this 18th-century building has been painted powder blue and given a fresh, modern makeover. Rooms are spacious and light-filled, and the ground floor has been converted into a large, attractive breakfast room.

Burlington House   B&B ££

(☑ 01865-513513; www.burlington-house.co.uk; 374 Banbury Rd, Summertown; s/d from £70/97; P 🛜) Twelve big, bright and elegant rooms with patterned wallpaper and splashes of colour are available at this Victorian merchant's house. The fittings are luxurious and the bathrooms immaculate; the service is attentive; and breakfast comes complete with organic eggs and granola. It has good public transport links to town.

Remont Guesthouse   B&B ££

(☑ 01865-311020; www.remont-oxford.co.uk; 367 Banbury Rd, Summertown; r £112-142; P @🛜) All modern style, subtle lighting and plush furnishings, this 25-room guesthouse has rooms decked out in cool neutrals with silky bedspreads, abstract art and huge plasma-screen TVs. There's also a sunny garden.

Buttery Hotel   HOTEL ££

(☑ 01865-811950; www.thebutteryhotel.co.uk; 11-12 Broad St; s/d from £75/125; 🛜) Right in the heart of the city, the Buttery is wonderfully central and offers views over college grounds from the front rooms. The rooms are spacious but rather modest, so it's the location that you're paying for. Rooms at the rear are smaller but quieter.

University Rooms

Oxford   UNIVERSITY ACCOMMODATION ££

(www.universityrooms.com; s/d from £45/60; 🛜) You can sleep inside hallowed colleges and breakfast in a grand hall by staying in student rooms. Most rooms are functional singles with basic furnishings and shared bathrooms, though there are some en suite, twin and small flats available. Some have views over college quads. They're only available during university holidays (Christmas, Easter and summer).

Old Bank Hotel   HOTEL £££

(☑ 01865-799599; www.oldbank-hotel.co.uk; 92 High St; r from £250; P 🛜) Slap bang in the centre of Oxford, this grand hotel's front rooms look over St Mary's Church and into the very heart of Oxford University. The elegant, pale-hued bedrooms are sleek and spacious, and the whole place is strewn with interesting contemporary art. Downstairs there's a buzzing restaurant.

Malmaison   HOTEL £££

(☑ 01865-268400; www.malmaison-oxford.com; 3 New Rd; d/ste from £180/315; P 🛜) This former Victorian prison is one place you'd wish to be locked up in. Attached to Oxford Castle, it has been converted into a sleek hotel with plush interiors, sultry lighting and giant beds. Each room is made from three cells.

Old Parsonage Hotel   HOTEL £££

(☑ 01865-310210; www.oldparsonage-hotel.co.uk; 1 Banbury Rd; r from £250; P 🛜) Wonderfully quirky, this small boutique hotel inhabits a 17th-century stone building covered with wisteria, and has just the right blend of period charm and modern luxury. Inside, there's a contemporary art collection, artfully mismatched furniture, and chic bedrooms with handmade beds and marble bathrooms. Oscar Wilde once made it his home.

✕ Eating

✕ City Centre

★ Edamame   JAPANESE £

(www.edamame.co.uk; 15 Holywell St; mains £6-8; ⊙ 11.30am-2.30pm Wed-Sun, 5-8.30pm Thu-Sat) The queue out the door speaks volumes about the quality of food here. This tiny joint, all light wood and friendly bustle, is the best place in town for authentic Japanese cuisine. Arrive early and be prepared to wait.

WORTH A TRIP

LE MANOIR AUX QUAT'SAISONS

As Oxford has no Michelin-starred restaurants of its own, local foodies make the pilgrimage 10km east to the famous **Le Manoir aux Quat'Saisons** (☑01844-278881; www.manoir.com; Church Rd, Great Milton; mains £48-54, five-course lunch/dinner £79/134; ⊙7.30-10am, 11.45am-2.15pm & 6.45-9.30pm; ☑) for special occasions. Chef Raymond Blanc has been working his magic at this impressive stone manor house for more than 30 years, presenting imaginative, complex and exquisitely presented dishes to his adoring fans. If you're one of them, consider staying overnight in one of the luxurious rooms. Book well ahead and dress up.

Missing Bean　　　　　　CAFE £
(www.themissingbean.co.uk; 14 Turl St; mains £3-4; ⊙8am-6.30pm Mon-Sat, 10am-5.30pm Sun) Oxford's best coffee can be found here, as well as loose-leaf teas and smoothies for those less caffeine inclined. The fresh muffins, cakes and ciabatta sandwiches make this a great lunchtime stop.

Chiang Mai Kitchen　　　　THAI ££
(☑01865-202233; www.chiangmaikitchen.co.uk; 130a High St; mains £7-16; ⊙noon-10.30pm; ☑) Authentic Thai cuisine in the heart of Oxford, complete with tear-jerkingly spicy *som tum* (spicy papaya salad), a range of curries (including, unusually, venison), noodle dishes and standout classics such as chicken with cashew nuts. There's an extensive separate menu for vegetarians.

✖ Jericho

Al-Shami　　　　　　LEBANESE £
(☑01865-310066; www.al-shami.co.uk; 25 Walton Cres; mains £7-12; ⊙noon-midnight; ☑) The service can be patchy but the food's tasty and authentic at this long-standing Lebanese eatery. Start with a selection of hot and cold mezze before tucking into charcoal-grilled lamb and chicken. There's a great vegetarian selection, too.

Manos　　　　　　　GREEK £
(☑01865-311782; www.manosfoodbar.com; 105 Walton St; mains £7-9; ⊙10.30am-9pm; ☑) For delicious home-cooked tastes of the Mediterranean, head for this Greek deli and restaurant, where you'll find the likes of spinach and feta tart, chicken souvlaki and a great selection of mezze. The ground floor cafe and deli serves inexpensive wraps and salads, while downstairs offers more style and comfort.

★**Rickety Press**　　　MODERN BRITISH ££
(☑01865-424581; www.thericketypress.com; 67 Cranham St; mains £13-17; ⊙noon-2.30pm & 6-9.30pm) Hidden in the back streets of Jericho, this old corner pub serves up beautifully presented, tasty food in casual surrounds. Call in for lunch or before 7pm for a great-value express menu (two/three courses £13/15).

Branca　　　　　　ITALIAN ££
(☑01865-556111; www.branca.co.uk; 110-111 Walton St; mains £10-18; ⊙10am-11pm; ☑) Big, bustling and bright, this glitzy Italian eatery serves delicious cocktails and all the requisite pizza, pasta, and meat and seafood grills that you'd expect. It also runs the deli next door.

✖ East Oxford

Oli's Thai　　　　　　THAI £
(☑01865-790223; www.olisthai.com; 38 Magdalen Rd; mains £7-10; ⊙4-10pm Tue, 11am-10pm Wed-Sat) With a sunny front terrace and a small, brightly coloured interior, this little hot spot is off the tourist track but well worth seeking out. A Thai chef lends authenticity to the short but zingy menu. From Magdalen Bridge, head along Iffley St and turn left at the Magdalen Arms pub; book ahead.

Atomic Burger　　　　AMERICAN £
(www.atomicburger.co.uk; 96 Cowley Rd; mains £7-11; ⊙11.30am-10.30pm) Atomic comes with the Fallout Challenge, which involves consuming a triple burger stack complete with fear-inducing ghost-chilli hot sauce. Not keen on killing your taste buds? Try the Chuck Norris, Dead Elvis, barbeque ribs, nachos or curly fries, all washed down with mega shakes.

Magdalen Arms　　　　BRITISH ££
(☑01865-243159; www.magdalenarms.com; 243 Iffley Rd; mains £12-19; ⊙5-11pm Mon, 11am-11pm Tue-Sun) Claret-coloured walls and mismatched furniture set the scene for a cosy pub, popular with students and foodies alike. It's well worth the 20-minute walk from Magdalen Bridge for hearty fare such as steak-and-ale pie, venison and duck.

Café Coco   MEDITERRANEAN **££**
(📞 01865-200232; www.cafecoco.co.uk; 23 Cowley
Rd; breakfast £4-10, lunch £7-12; ⊙10am-midnight
Thu-Sat, to 5pm Sun) This Cowley Rd institution
is a popular brunching destination for the
hip and hungry, and is decorated with classic
posters on the walls and a bald plaster-cast
clown in an ice bath. The menu ranges from
cooked breakfasts and waffles to pizza, salads,
Mediterranean mains and pecan pie.

Door 74   MODERN BRITISH **££**
(📞 01865-203374; www.door74.co.uk; 74 Cowley Rd;
mains £10-14; ⊙noon-3pm & 5-11pm Tue-Fri, 10am-
11pm Sat, 11am-4pm Sun) This cosy little place
woos its fans with a rich mix of British and
Mediterranean flavours and friendly service.
The menu is limited and the tables tightly
packed, but the food is consistently good and
weekend brunches (full English breakfast,
pancakes etc) supremely filling. Book ahead.

🍷 Drinking & Nightlife

Oxford is blessed with some wonderful traditional pubs (see www.oxfordpubguide.
co.uk), as well as a good selection of funky
bars. Despite a large student population,
Oxford's club scene is fairly limited, with
several large, run-of-the-mill clubs on the
train-station side of the town centre. Paradise St has a couple of gay bars.

Bear Inn   PUB
(www.bearoxford.co.uk; 6 Alfred St; ⊙11am-11pm;
📶) Arguably Oxford's oldest pub (there's
been a pub on this site since 1242), this atmospherically creaky place requires all but
the most vertically challenged to duck their
heads when passing through doorways.
There's a curious tie collection on the walls
and ceiling (though you can no longer exchange yours for a pint), and there are usually a couple of worthy guest ales.

Eagle & Child   PUB
(www.nicholsonspubs.co.uk/theeagleandchildox-
ford; 49 St Giles; ⊙11am-11pm; 📶) Affectionately
known as the 'Bird & Baby', this atmospheric
place, dating from 1650, was once the favourite haunt of author JRR Tolkien and CS Lewis. Its wood-panelled rooms and selection of
real ales still attract a mellow crowd.

Turf Tavern   PUB
(www.theturftavern.co.uk; 4 Bath Pl; ⊙11am-11pm)
Hidden down a narrow alleyway, this tiny
medieval pub (dating from at least 1381) is
one of the town's best loved; it's where US
president Bill Clinton famously 'did not in-

hale'. Home to 11 real ales, it's always packed
with a mix of students, professionals and
lucky tourists who manage to find it. Plenty
of outdoor seating.

White Horse   PUB
(www.whitehorseoxford.co.uk; 52 Broad St; ⊙11am-
11pm) This tiny 16th-century pub was a favourite retreat for TV detective Inspector Morse,
and it can get pretty crowded in the evenings.
It's a great place for a quiet afternoon pint of
whatever the guest ale happens to be.

Raoul's   COCKTAIL BAR
(www.raoulsbar.com; 32 Walton St; ⊙4pm-midnight)
Perfectly mixed cocktails and funky music at
Jericho's finest retro-look bar.

Kazbar   BAR
(www.kazbar.co.uk; 25-27 Cowley Rd; ⊙5pm-
midnight Mon-Fri, noon-12.30am Sat, noon-11pm
Sun) This funky Moroccan-themed bar has
giant windows, low lighting, warm colours
and a cool vibe. It's buzzing most nights with
hip young things sipping cocktails and filling up on Spanish and North African tapas.

Trout   PUB
(www.thetroutoxford.co.uk; 195 Godstow Rd, Wolvercote; ⊙11am-11pm) A 2.5-mile walk northwest
along the Thames from the centre of Oxford
will bring you to this charming old-world
pub, a favourite hang-out since the 17th century. Immortalised by British TV detective series *Inspector Morse*, it's generally crammed
with people enjoying the riverside garden.

☆ Entertainment

If you're a fan of classical music you'll be
spoilt for choice in Oxford, which has a host
of excellent venues and regular concerts
throughout the year. See www.dailyinfo.
co.uk or www.musicatoxford.com for listings.

★ Creation Theatre   THEATRE
(📞 01865-766266; www.creationtheatre.co.uk) Performing in a variety of nontraditional venues,
including city parks, the BMW plant and Oxford Castle, this theatre company produces
highly original, mostly Shakespearean, shows
featuring plenty of magic and special effects.

Oxford Playhouse   THEATRE
(📞 01865-305305; www.oxfordplayhouse.com;
Beaumont St) The city's main stage for quality drama also hosts an impressive selection
of touring music, dance and theatre performances. The Burton Taylor Studio often features quirky student productions.

Catweazle Club LIVE MUSIC
(www.catweazleclub.com; East Oxford Social Club, 44 Princes St; admission £6; ⊗ 8pm Thu) Legendary open-mic night, featuring musos, poets and all sorts of bohemian performers.

O2 Academy LIVE MUSIC
(www.o2academyoxford.co.uk; 190 Cowley Rd) Oxford's best club and live-music venue hosts everything from big-name DJs and international touring artists to indie bands, hard rock and funk nights across three performance spaces.

Cellar LIVE MUSIC
(www.cellaroxford.co.uk; Frewin Crt; ☎) There's live music or DJs most nights at this independent venue, covering a wide spread of genres including indie rock, reggae, folk, hip hop, and drum and bass.

Shopping

★ **Blackwell's** BOOKS
(www.blackwell.co.uk; 48-51 Broad St; ⊗ 9am-6.30pm Mon-Sat, 11am-5pm Sun) The most famous bookshop in the most studenty of cities, Blackwell's doesn't disappoint with its vast range of literature, academic treatises and guilty pleasures. Separate branches on the same street focus on sheet music and art posters. In summer Blackwell's runs literary-themed walking tours.

Make sure you visit the Norrington Room in the basement – an immense inverted step pyramid lined with shelves.

Oxford Covered Market MARKET
(www.oxford-coveredmarket.co.uk; Market St; ⊗ 9am-5.30pm Mon-Sat, 10am-4pm Sun) A haven of traditional butchers, fishmongers, cobblers, barbers, eateries and independent shops, this is the place to go for Sicilian sausage, funky T-shirts and wacky hats for weddings and/or the Ascot horse races. At Christmas the market is a must for its displays of freshly hung deer, wild boar, ostrich and turkey. Be sure to join the queue at Ben's Cookies

ⓘ Information

John Radcliffe Hospital (☎ 01865-741166; www.ouh.nhs.uk; Headley Way, Headington) Located 3 miles east of Oxford city centre.
Post Office (102 St Aldate's; ⊗ 9am-5.30pm Mon-Sat)
Tourist Office (☎ 01865-252200; www. visitoxfordandoxfordshire.com; 15-16 Broad St; ⊗ 9.30am-5pm Mon-Sat, 10am-3.30pm Sun)

ⓘ Getting There & Away

BUS
Oxford's main bus/coach station is at Gloucester Green, near the corner of Worcester and George Sts.

Destinations include the following:
Cambridge (X5) £12.50, 3¾ hours
Chipping Norton (S3) £4.30, 56 minutes
Cheltenham (853) £7.50, 1½ hours
London Victoria (Oxford Tube/X90) £14, 1¾ hours
Woodstock (S3) £3.50, 25 minutes
Oxford Bus Company (☎ 01865-785400; www.oxfordbus.co.uk) Runs 'The Airline' service to/from Heathrow (£23, 1½ minutes) and Gatwick (£28, two hours).
National Express (☎ 08717 818178; www. nationalexpress.com) Coach destinations include London Victoria (£15, two hours), Bath (£6.50, two hours), Bristol (£7.50, 2¾ hours) and Birmingham (£8.50, two hours).

CAR
Driving and parking in central Oxford is a nightmare. There are five Park & Ride car parks on major routes leading into town. Parking costs from £2 to £4 per day; buses leave roughly every 15 minutes into town and cost about £2.70 (journey time from 12 to 25 minutes) .

TRAIN
Oxford's train station is conveniently placed to the west of the city centre. Destinations include the following:
Birmingham £27, 1¼ hours
London Paddington £25, 1¼ hours
Manchester £60, three hours
Newcastle £106, 4¾ hours
Winchester £17, 1¼ hours

ⓘ Getting Around

BICYCLE
Cyclo Analysts (☎ 01865-424444; www. cycloanalysts.com; 150 Cowley Rd; per day/week from £10/36; ⊗ 9am-6pm Mon-Sat) Sells, repairs and rents out bikes, including hybrids.

BUS
Oxford Bus Company and Stagecoach service an extensive local network with regular buses on the major routes. A short journey costs £1.70 (return £2.80); consider a day pass (£4). Tickets can be purchased on the bus.

TAXI
There are taxi ranks at the train station and bus station, as well as on St Giles and at Carfax.

AROUND OXFORD

Rustic charm is in abundant supply in the villages and towns surrounding Oxford. They make excellent day-trip options or stop-off destinations if you're heading on to the Cotswolds.

Woodstock

POP 2520

Don't come expecting tie-dyed clothing, rock music or illicit scents in the English Woodstock; the attractions here are considerably more genteel. Old pubs and antique stores dominate the stone buildings of the well-heeled town centre, but what really draws the crowds is Blenheim Palace, the extravagant baroque pile that was the birthplace of Sir Winston Churchill.

◉ Sights

★ **Blenheim Palace**   PALACE
(www.blenheimpalace.com; adult/child £22/12, park & gardens only £13/6.50; ⊙10.30am-5.30pm daily, closed Mon & Tue Nov–mid-Feb) One of the country's greatest stately homes, Blenheim Palace is a monumental baroque fantasy designed by Sir John Vanbrugh and Nicholas Hawksmoor, and was built between 1705 and 1722. The land and funds to build the house were granted to John Churchill, Duke of Marlborough, by a grateful Queen Anne after his decisive victory at the 1704 Battle of Blenheim. Now a Unesco World Heritage Site, Blenheim (pronounced *blen*-num) is home to the 11th duke and duchess.

Inside, the house is stuffed with statues, tapestries, ostentatious furniture, priceless china and giant oil paintings in elaborate gilt frames. Visits start in the Great Hall, a vast space topped by 20m-high ceilings adorned with images of the first duke. Next up is the Churchill Exhibition, which is dedicated to the life, work and writings of Sir Winston Churchill, who was born at Blenheim in 1874. The British prime minister was a descendant of the Dukes of Marlborough, as was Princess Diana.

From here you can choose to wander through the various grand state rooms at your own pace or wait to join one of the free guided tours, which depart regularly throughout the day (except Sundays). Highlights include the famous Blenheim Tapestries, a set of 10 large wall hangings commemorating the first

duke's achievements; the State Dining Room, with its painted walls and ceilings; and the magnificent Long Library.

Afterwards, head upstairs to the 'Untold Story', where a ghostly chamber maid leads you through a series of tableaux recreating important scenes from the palace's history.

If the crowds in the house become too oppressive, retire to the lavish gardens and vast parklands, parts of which were landscaped by Lancelot 'Capability' Brown. A minitrain takes visitors to the Pleasure Gardens, which feature a yew maze, adventure playground and butterfly house. For quieter and longer strolls, there are glorious walks leading to an arboretum, cascade and temple.

🛏 Sleeping & Eating

★ **Glove House**   B&B £££
(☎01993-813475; www.theglovehouse.co.uk; 24 Oxford St; r/ste from £155/165; ⓢ) Luxuriously renovated but proudly displaying evidence of its venerable age, this elegant 400-year-old town house offers the added bonus of a glorious rear garden. The largest suite has a wonderful free-standing copper bathtub, while another has a rolltop bath.

★ **Hope House**   BOUTIQUE HOTEL £££
(☎01993-815990; www.hopehousewoodstock.co.uk; 14 Oxford St; s/d from £250/350; Ⓟ✳ⓢ) Wallow in pure indulgence in this sumptuous 1708 town house, which has been meticulously restored and furnished with effortless style. Original features blend seamlessly with high-tech gadgetry in the three enormous suites.

WORTH A TRIP

KELMSCOTT MANOR

Tucked away in the countryside 20 miles west of Oxford (near Faringdon), **Kelmscott Manor** (☎01367-252486; www.kelmscottmanor.org.uk; Kelmscott; adult/child £9/4.50; ⊙11am-5pm Wed & Sat Apr-Oct) is a gorgeous Tudor pile that was once the summer home of William Morris, a poet, artist and founder of the Arts and Crafts Movement. The interior is true to his philosophy that one should not own anything that is neither beautiful nor useful, and the house contains many of Morris' personal effects, as well as fabrics and furniture designed by him and his associates.

La Galleria ITALIAN ££
(☑ 01993-813381; www.lagalleriawoodstock.com; 2 Market Pl; mains £11-24; ⊙ noon-2pm & 7-10pm Tue-Sun) Big windows bathe the simple interior of this much-loved restaurant in light. It's an old-fashioned kind of place, with heavy swag curtains, pink tablecloths and flowers on every table, but the food is excellent. Primarily Sardinian, the menu ranges from silky pastas to perfectly cooked veal and fish.

❶ Getting There & Away

Stagecoach (☑ 01865-772250; www.stagecoachbus.com) Buses head to/from Oxford (route S3; £3.50, 25 minutes), Chipping Norton (S3; £3.80, 25 minutes) and Witney (242; £3.40, 28 minutes).

Witney

POP 29,100

The sleepy town of Witney is firmly on Oxford's commuter belt. Make your way through the traffic and new housing developments to the centre of town, however, and you'll find a charming village green flanked by pretty stone houses. At one end is a glorious 13th-century church and 18th-century almshouses, and at the other a 17th-century covered market.

Witney built its wealth through blanket production, which incredibly was its main trade from the Iron Age until 2002. Its mills, wealthy merchants' homes and blanket factories can still be seen today. The baroque 18th-century Blanket Hall dominates genteel High St, while at Wood Green you'll find a second village green and a cluster of old stone cottages.

🛏 Sleeping & Eating

Fleece PUB ££
(☑ 01993-892270; www.fleecewitney.co.uk; 11 Church Green; mains £12-26, s/d from £69/89; Ⓟ🛜) Facing the main village green, this roomy pub has an ambitious seasonal menu, with some wonderful smoked fish, steaks, deli platters and Sunday roasts. Upstairs, the rooms are sleek and spacious.

❶ Information

Tourist Office (☑ 01993-861000; www.westoxon.gov.uk; 3 Welch Way; ⊙ 9am-5pm Mon-Sat) Stocks brochures outlining local walks.

❶ Getting There & Away

Witney Shuttle (☑ 01993-705993; www.witneyshuttle.com) minibuses head to/from Heathrow (£48, 1½ hours) and Gatwick (£68, 2½ hours) airports every two hours. Other destinations:
Burford (route 233) £3, 19 minutes
Chipping Norton (233/X9) £3.40, 45 minutes
Minster Lovell (233/853) £2.50, six minutes
Oxford (11/S1/S2/853) £4.50, 30 minutes
Woodstock (242) £3.40, 28 minutes

Vale of the White Horse

Lying southwest of Oxford, this verdant valley is notable for the historic market town of Wantage, the birthplace of Alfred the Great (in AD 849). But it's most interesting attractions are far older.

Sitting just below the crest of the highest point in Oxfordshire, the Uffington White Horse is the oldest chalk figure in Britain, dating from the Bronze Age. Around 3000 years ago this highly stylised image of a horse was created by cutting trenches out of the hill and filling them with blocks of chalk; local people have maintained the figure for centuries. Perhaps it was designed with the gods in mind, as it's designed to be seen at its best if you're floating in the air above it.

Just below the figure is Dragon Hill, so called because it was believed by locals to be the site where St George slew the dragon, although it's possibly an Iron Age ritual site. Above the figure is Uffington Castle, a hill fort dating from around 700 BC. One mile east from the White Horse along the Ridgeway (an ancient road which may have existed for more than 5000 years) is Waylands Smithy, a neolithic long barrow and chamber tomb named after the Saxon god of smiths.

THE COTSWOLDS

Glorious villages riddled with beautiful old mansions of honey-coloured stone; thatched cottages; atmospheric churches; and rickety almshouses draw crowds of visitors to the Cotswolds. If you've ever coveted exposed beams or lusted after a cream tea in the mid-afternoon, there's no finer place to fulfil your fantasies

The booming medieval wool trade brought the area its wealth and left it with a proliferation of beautiful buildings. In 1966 it was declared an Area of Outstanding Natural Beauty (AONB), and at 790 sq miles, it's the second-largest protected area in England after the Lake District. Spreading from north of Chipping Campden to south of Bath, the Cotswolds cuts across six different counties, although the bulk of it is in Gloucestershire. More than 86% is farmland but, even so, around 158,000 people live within the AONB itself, not counting those in the large towns and small cities on its fringes, such as Cirencester, Cheltenham and Gloucester.

While there are bus routes between the major towns and villages, for flexibility and the option of getting off the beaten track, you can't beat having your own car. The gentle hills are also perfect for walking, cycling and horse riding, as a network of long-distance tracks pass through, most notably the 102-mile **Cotswold Way** (www.nationaltrail.co.uk/cotswold).

Cirencester

POP 17,200

Refreshingly unpretentious, charming Cirencester (siren-sester) is nonetheless an affluent, elegant town. The lovely market square – the heart of the town – is surrounded by Victorian architecture, and the nearby streets showcase a harmonious medley of buildings from various eras.

It's difficult to believe that under the Romans (who called the town Corinium), Cirencester was second only to London in terms of size and importance and, although little of this period remains, you can still see the grassed-over ruins of one of the largest amphitheatres in the country. The medieval wool trade was also good to the town, with wealthy merchants funding the building of a superb church.

Today, Cirencester is the most significant town in the southern Cotswolds, and the lively Monday and Friday markets are as important as the expensive boutiques and trendy delis that line its narrow streets.

⊙ Sights & Activities

Corinium Museum   MUSEUM
(www.coriniummuseum.org; Park St; adult/child £5/2.50; ⊙10am-4pm Mon-Sat, 2-4pm Sun; 🖝) The largest part of this well-presented modern museum is, understandably, dedicated to Cirencester's Roman past. Highlights include an incredible set of floor mosaics and the 'Jupiter column', a carved capital depict-

❶ COTSWOLDS DISCOVERER

If you're planning on seeing much of the Cotswolds in a short space of time and don't have your own wheels, your best bet is the **Cotswolds Discoverer** (www.escapetothecotswolds.org.uk/discoverer; 1-/3-day bus pass £10/25, train pass £8.30/20), which gives you unlimited travel on participating bus or train routes.

ing Bacchus and his drunken mates. Reconstructed rooms and interactive displays bring the era to life, and the kids can dress up as Roman citizens and medieval monks.

St John the Baptist's Church   CHURCH
(www.cirenparish.co.uk; Market Sq; suggested donation £3; ⊙9.30am-4pm) Commenced in 1100, the cathedral-like St John's is one of England's largest parish churches. It boasts an outstanding Perpendicular Gothic tower with flying buttresses (circa 1400) and a majestic three-storey south porch, which was built as an office by late-15th-century abbots but subsequently became the medieval town hall.

Soaring arches, magnificent fan vaulting and a Tudor nave adorn the light-filled interior, where you'll also find a 15th-century painted stone pulpit and some columns recycled from ancient Roman buildings. The east window contains fine 15th- and 16th-century stained glass, and a wall safe displays the Boleyn Cup, made for Anne Boleyn in 1535.

New Brewery Arts   ARTS CENTRE
(www.newbreweryarts.org.uk; Brewery Ct; ⊙9am-5pm Mon-Sat, 10am-4pm Sun) FREE Home to a theatre and more than a dozen resident artisans, this converted Victorian brewery hosts regular exhibitions, workshops and classes.

Cirencester Park   PARK
(www.cirencesterpark.co.uk; Cecily Hill; ⊙8am-5pm) Unusually for a stately home, the Earl of Bathurst's mansion sits right on the edge of town, hidden behind a giant yew hedge. The extensive landscaped grounds are open to the public daily, free of charge.

🛌 Sleeping

Old Brewhouse   B&B ££
(☎01285-656099; www.theoldbrewhouse.com; 7 London Rd; s/d from £68/79; 🅿🛜) Set in a charming 17th-century town house, this

The Cotswolds

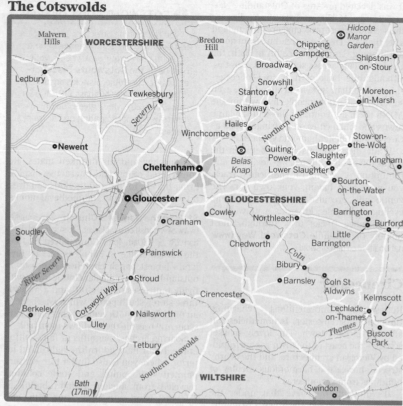

lovely B&B has pretty rooms with cast-iron beds and country-style floral or patchwork quilts. The courtyard rooms are newer and larger.

Greensleeves
B&B ££

(☏ 01285-642516; www.greensleeves4u.co.uk; Baunton Lane, Stratton; s/d £50/65; P ☎) Farmland fringes this modern house on the outskirts of town (off Gloucester Rd). The three comfortable guest rooms share their own wing with a communal kitchenette. Breakfasts include homemade bread.

No 12
B&B ££

(☏ 01285-640232; www.no12cirencester.co.uk; 12 Park St; d/ste £120/140) This Georgian town house right in the centre of Cirencester has four gloriously unfussy rooms kitted out with a tasteful mix of antiques and modern furnishings. Think piles of feather pillows, extra-long beds and slick modern bathrooms.

✖ Eating

Lick the Spoon
CAFE £

(www.lickthespoon.co.uk; 3 Black Jack St; cakes £1-2.50; ⏰9.30am-5pm Mon-Sat) One word: chocolate. It comes both in award-winning solid form, all boxed up for you to take away, and in glorious liquid form. Coffee is roasted on the premises for those desiring a caffeine kick alongside the sugar rush.

Made by Bob
MODERN BRITISH ££

(www.foodmadebybob.com; Corn Hall, 26 Market Pl; breakfast £5-10, lunch £10-19; ⏰7.30am-6.30pm Mon-Sat; ✐) Part deli, part hip brasserie, Bob's has a casual atmosphere and features inventive, sophisticated fare on the daily changing menu. The breakfast selection's the best in town, and light lunch options include soup, salads and charcuterie plates.

Jesse's Bistro
MODERN BRITISH £££

(☏ 01285-641497; www.jessesbistro.co.uk; 14 Black Jack St; mains £18-19; ⏰noon-2.15pm Mon-Sat,

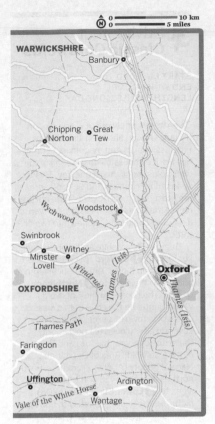

WARWICKSHIRE
Banbury
Chipping Norton
Great Tew
Wychwood
Woodstock
Swinbrook
Witney
Minster Lovell
Windrush (Isis)
Oxford
OXFORDSHIRE
Thames (Isis)
Thames (Isis)
Thames Path
Faringdon
Uffington
Ardington
Vale of the White Horse
Wantage
0 — 10 km
0 — 5 miles

Stroud (54) £3.50, 36 minutes
Tetbury (881) £3.50, 37 minutes

National Express coach destinations:
Birmingham £15, 2½ hours
Leeds £52, 6¾ hours
London £17, 2½ hours
Newcastle-upon-Tyne £68, 10 hours
Nottingham £27, 5¼ hours

Bibury

POP 625

Once described by William Morris as 'the most beautiful village in England', Bibury is the Cotswolds at its most picturesque, with a cluster of riverside cottages and a tangle of narrow streets flanked by wayward stone buildings. **Arlington Row**, a perfectly rustic sweep of cottages, has served as a backdrop for many films (most notably *Stardust*) and is thought to be a contender for the title of the most photographed street in Britain. Also worth a look is the 17th-century **Arlington Mill**, just a short stroll away across **Rack Isle**, a wildlife refuge once used as a cloth-drying area.

◉ Sights

Church of St Mary the Virgin   CHURCH
(Church Rd) The village's Saxon-built church has been much altered since its original construction, but there are many 8th-century features still visible among the 12th- and 13th-century additions.

Bibury Trout Farm   FARM
(www.biburytroutfarm.co.uk; adult/child £4/3, catch per lb £4; ⊘9am-5pm) You can fish for your supper at this trout farm, located at the edge of the village, where the B4425 crosses the River Coln. Otherwise, take the easy option and buy some smoked fish at the little shop.

⌷ Sleeping

The best options are in the nearby villages of Coln St Aldwyns (2 miles east) and Barnsley (3 miles southwest).

New Inn   PUB ££
(☑01285-750651; www.new-inn.co.uk; Coln St Aldwyns; r £100-150; [P] 🛜) The jasmine-clad New Inn offers quirky luxury in 16th-century surroundings, both in the main building and a neighbouring cottage. The 15 bedrooms are spacious and atmospheric, with bold colours and smart furnishings.

6.45-9.15pm Tue-Sat) Hidden away in a cobbled stable yard, Jesse's is a great little place, with flagstone floors, wrought-iron chairs and mosaic tables. The dishes feature local, seasonal produce, such as Cornish crab and Cotswold beef.

❶ Information

Tourist Office (☑01285-654180; www.cotswolds.com; Corinium Museum, Park St; ⊘10am-4pm Mon-Sat, 2-4pm Sun) Stocks a leaflet detailing a self-guided walk around the town (£1.20).

❶ Getting There & Away

Most buses stop outside the Corn Hall on Market Pl. They run to the following from Monday to Saturday:
Cheltenham (route 51) £3.60, 40 minutes
Gloucester (852) £2.60, one hour
Northleach (855) £2.20, 30 minutes

Barnsley House HOTEL £££
(📞01285-740000; www.barnsleyhouse.com; B4425,
Barnsley; r from £290; 🅿️🛜🏊) For pure indulgence and romance, this 1697 house and its
famous garden takes some beating. All of
the 18 rooms are different and while some
have disco balls and jacuzzis, most are demure in their decor. Facilities include a spa
centre, private cinema and restaurant.

ℹ️ Getting There & Away

Pulhams Coaches (www.pulhamscoaches.com)
bus 855 heads to/from Cirencester (£2.20, 15
minutes) and Northleach (£1.70, 19 minutes); no
Sunday service.

Burford

POP 1190

Slithering down a steep hill to a medieval crossing point on the River Windrush,
the remarkable village of Burford is little
changed since its glory days at the height
of the wool trade. It's a particularly picturesque place with higgledy-piggledy stone
cottages, fine Cotswold town houses and
the odd Elizabethan or Georgian treasure.
Antique shops, tearooms and specialist
boutiques peddle nostalgia to the hordes of
visitors who make it here in summer, but despite the crowds it's easy to get off the main
drag and wander along quiet side streets
seemingly lost in time.

👁️ Sights

St John the Baptist's Church CHURCH
(www.burfordchurch.org; Church Lane) Commenced in 1175 and added to over the years,
Burford's sturdy stone church has managed
to survive reformers and Roundheads (supporters of parliament against the king in the
English Civil War) with its fine fan-vaulted
ceiling and several grand tombs intact. The
best of these is the macabre 1626 Tanfield
tomb, which has effigies of a noble couple in
all their finery on top and as skeletons below.

During the Civil War, 340 Levellers were
imprisoned here – Roundhead soldiers who
mutinied due to their leaders' failure to up-
hold the notion of equality of all men before
the law. One of them carved his name in
the lead lining of the font. A plaque outside
the church entrance commemorates the
three ringleaders who were executed in the
churchyard.

Just outside the churchyard, you'll find
the town's 15th-century almshouses

🏃 Driving Tour
Classic Cotswolds

START BURFORD
END WINCHCOMBE
LENGTH 50 MILES; ONE DAY

Given its large network of winding country lanes linking ancient market towns,
timeless villages and magnificent stately
homes, it's impossible to cover all of the
Cotswolds' highlights in one day. This tour
spans three counties and ticks off some of
the most picturesque parts of the northern
half of the range. It can easily be driven in
a day, but could be stretched into two or
three.

Begin in Oxfordshire at the pretty market town of ❶ **Burford** (p204) and then
head west on the A40 into Gloucestershire
and follow the signs to ❷ **Northleach**
(p207). The Escape to the Cotswolds
visitor centre on the edge of this classic
Cotswolds town has excellent displays
covering all you need to know about
the history, geography, flora and fauna
of the Cotswolds Area of Outstanding
Natural Beauty (AONB). From here, head
northeast on the A429 and follow the
signs to ❸ **Lower Slaughter** (p208), a
picture-perfect village lined with houses
made of the golden stone so typical of the
area. If you've got time, take the 1 mile
walk to ❹ **Upper Slaughter** (p208), less
often visited than its sibling but no less
attractive due to its idyllic setting between
a small ford and the hills. If you've had the
wherewithal to book ahead, stop for lunch
at Michelin-starred Lords of the Manor,
housed in a Jacobean mansion.

Continue on to ❺ **Stow-on-the-Wold**
(p208), the highest of the Cotswold villages at 244m and a market town since the
12th century. After perusing the market
square, take the A429 north following the
route of the ancient Roman road, the Fosse
Way. After 4 miles you'll reach ❻ **Moreton-in-Marsh** (p209), a town known for
its weekly market and excellent local food
shops.

From Moreton, take the A44 west
through tiny ❼ **Bourton-on-the-Hill**,
lined with attractive 17th- and 18th-century
cottages and famous for two things: the
gibbeting cage in which the bodies of dead

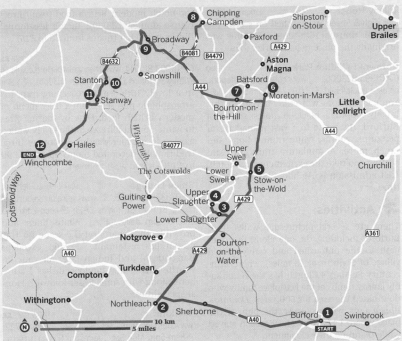

highwaymen were hung in the 19th century, and horse training – there are several stud farms in the vicinity of the village. This is a good alternative spot to pause for lunch.

Continuing on, turn right onto the B4081 and head to **8 Chipping Campden** (p210), one of the Cotswold's prettiest towns. After admiring the buildings on the main street (and if you're not tempted to stay the night), backtrack to the A44, cross into the Worcestershire corner of the Cotswolds and head down the hill to **9 Broadway** (p212). After cruising along the broad main street, take the B4632 south in the direction of Cheltenham.

After three miles, take the left turn-off to **10 Stanton**. A little stunner of a village, its houses are crafted out of that golden Cotswolds stone, with not a shop or quaint tearoom in sight. The buildings most likely to catch your eye are the Jacobean Stanton Court and the fine Perpendicular tower of St Michael & All Angels' Church, which has an absolutely beguiling medieval interior. Stanton Court once belonged to civil architect Sir Philip Stott (1858–1937), who was responsible for the restoration of many other houses in the village.

You'll undoubtedly see walkers passing through the village, heading south along the Cotswold Way to the village of **11 Stanway**, just a mile south; follow the narrow road that runs parallel to the trail. There is little more to Stanway than a few thatched-roofed cottages, a church and Stanway House, a magnificent Jacobean mansion hidden behind a triple-gabled gatehouse. Its baroque water gardens feature Britain's tallest fountain, which erupts, geyser-like, to a height of 300ft. The manor has been the private home of the Earls of Wemyss for 500 years and has a delightful, lived-in charm with much of its original furniture and character intact. It's only open to the public on Tuesday and Thursday afternoons from June to August (adult/child £7/2).

After passing through Stanway, turn right onto the B4077 and then left back onto the B4632. The next stop is **12 Winchcombe** (p212), an ancient Saxon town with some great eating and sleeping options. You'll probably want to stop here for the night so that you can explore wonderful Sudeley Castle in the morning. Otherwise, continue on to the relatively bright lights of Cheltenham.

Tolsey House NOTABLE BUILDING
(cnr High & Sheep Sts) Perched on sturdy pillars, this unusual 16th-century building was originally the place to pay market tolls.

Cotswold Wildlife Park ZOO
(☑ 01993-823006; www.cotswoldwildlifepark.co.uk; adult/child £15/10; ⊙ 10am-5pm; ♠) Younger visitors will enjoy a visit to this hugely popular place, 3 miles south of Burford. It's home to a vast menagerie of penguins, zebras, white rhinos, lions and much more. A miniature train (£1) and petting zoo take the excitement up a notch. Last admission is 1½ hours before closing time.

🏃 Activities

There are several picturesque walks from Burford, including the one along the river path to the untouched and rarely visited village of **Swinbrook** (3 miles), where 12th-century St Mary's Church has the remarkably jaunty tombs of the Fettiplace family who dominated the area for 500 years. *Downton Abbey* fans will recognise the pub as the place where Lady Sybil and Branson stayed while planning their elopement.

🛏 Sleeping & Eating

⭐ **Star Cottage** B&B ££
(☑ 01993-822032; www.burfordbedandbreakfast.co.uk; Meadow Lane, Fulbrook; s/d from £70/80; ♠) In the village of Fulbrook, a 15-minute walk from Burford, this wonderful old Cotswold cottage has two comfortable and character-filled en suite rooms, the smaller of which has a grand canopied bed. The cooked breakfasts are excellent.

Bull HOTEL ££
(☑ 01993-822220; www.bullatburford.co.uk; 105 High St; s/d from £65/80; ℙ♠) You'll be following in the footsteps of guests as illustrious as Charles II and Horatio Nelson if you stay at this 15th-century hotel. The plusher rooms feature four-poster beds and antique furniture, and the restaurant is pure gourmet, with beautifully executed dishes making the most of local ingredients.

Lamb Inn PUB £££
(☑ 01993-823155; www.cotswold-inns-hotels.co.uk/lamb; Sheep St; s/d from £150/160; ♠) At this atmospheric 15th-century inn, expect flagstone floors, exposed beams, creaking stairs, a laidback vibe and luxurious period-style rooms with antique furniture. The restaurant serves top-notch modern British food (two-/three-course dinner £33/39); there's less-formal dining in the bar (mains from £8 to £15).

Angel PUB ££
(☑ 01993-822714; www.theangelatburford.co.uk; 14 Witney St; mains £14-17; ⊙ noon-11.30pm; ♠) Set in a lovely 16th-century coaching inn, this atmospheric pub serves up a tasty menu of modern British food. Dine by roaring fires in winter, or eat alfresco in the lovely walled garden in warmer weather. There are three traditionally decorated rooms upstairs (£90 to £120) if you wish to linger.

Spice Lounge INDIAN, BANGLADESHI ££
(☑ 07833 292255; www.spiceloungeburford.co.uk; 81 High St; mains £7-13; ⊙ noon-2pm Sat-Thu, 6-11pm daily; ♠☑) White linen and brown-leather chairs set the scene for this upmarket restaurant serving excellent Bangladeshi and Indian fare. All your favourite curries and tandoori dishes feature here, along with some lesser-known regional specialities.

Huffkins BAKERY, CAFE ££
(www.huffkins.com; 98 High St; mains £7-12; ⊙ 8am-5pm Mon-Sat, 10am-5pm Sun) Huffkins has been baking and serving delicious scones, cakes and pies since 1890. More substantial fare includes cooked breakfasts, macaroni cheese, Welsh rarebit and burgers.

❶ Information

Tourist Office (☑ 01993-823558; www.oxfordshirecotswolds.org; 33a High St; ⊙ 9.30am-5pm)

❶ Getting There & Away

Most buses stop on the High St or Sheep St. Bus destinations to/from Burford:
Cheltenham (route 853) £3.80, 45 minutes
Gloucester (853) £5, 1¼ hours
Oxford (853) £4.20, 45 minutes
Minster Lovell (233/853) £1.60, nine minutes
Witney (233/853) £3.10, 19 minutes

Minster Lovell
POP 1340

Set on a gentle slope leading down to the meandering River Windrush, Minster Lovell is a gorgeous village with a cluster of stone cottages nestled beside an ancient pub and riverside mill. One of William Morris' favourite spots, the village has changed little since medieval times. It's divided into two halves: Old Minster, recorded in the Domesday Book (1086) and the rather newer Minster Lovell, across the river and up the hill.

◉ Sights

Minster Lovell Hall　　　　HISTORIC BUILDING
The main sight in Old Minster is Minster Lovell Hall, the 15th-century manor house that was home to Viscount Francis Lovell. The manor is now in ruins; you can peek past the blackened walls into the roofless great hall and the interior courtyard, while the wind whistles eerily through the gaping windows.

Lovell fought with Richard III at the Battle of Bosworth in 1485 and joined Lambert Simnel's failed rebellion after the king's defeat and death. Lovell's mysterious disappearance was never explained, and when a skeleton was discovered inside a secret vault in the house in 1708, it was assumed he had died while in hiding.

🍴 Sleeping & Eating

Old Swan & Minster Mill　　HOTEL, PUB £££
(☑ 01993-774441; www.oldswanandminstermill.com; Old Minster; d/ste from £165/285, mains £14-22; ⊘ Old Swan noon-3pm & 6-9pm; P 🛜 ♿ 🐾) This luxurious complex has charming period-style rooms in a 600-year-old pub and sleek, contemporary design in the converted 19th-century mill. Spa treatments are available at the mill, while the Old Swan serves excellent gastropub food, with doorstep sandwiches for lunch, and handmade sausages, daily fish and game for dinner.

❶ Getting There & Away

Buses service the following destinations:
Burford (route 233/853) £1.60, nine minutes
Cheltenham (853) £4.60, 52 minutes
Gloucester (853) £5.60, 1½ hours
Oxford (S2/853) £3.90, 46 minutes
Witney (233/S2/853) £2.60, six minutes

Northleach

POP 1860
Little visited and underappreciated, Northleach has been a little market town since 1227 and comprises late-medieval cottages, imposing merchants' stores and half-timbered Tudor houses. A wonderful mix of architectural styles clusters around the market square and the narrow laneways leading off it.

◉ Sights

Escape to the Cotswolds　　INTERPRETATION CENTRE
(www.cotswoldsaonb.co.uk; A429; ⊘ 9.30am-4.30pm; 🛜) FREE Housed in the Old Prison (an attraction in itself), this is the official visitor centre for the Cotswolds Area of Outstanding Natural Beauty (AONB), and has displays outlining the area's history, ecology and attractions. There's also a cafe and a collection of agricultural wagons in the rear courtyard.

Church of St Peter & St Paul　　CHURCH
(www.northleach.org; Church Walk; ⊘ 10am-dusk) The grandeur and complexity of this masterpiece of the Cotswold Perpendicular style is testimony to its wool-era wealth. Although the chancel dates to around 1350, the building was extensively reworked during the 15th century wool boom. A modern highlight is the large 1964 stained-glass window behind the altar depicting Christ in Glory.

Keith Harding's World of Mechanical Music　　MUSEUM
(www.mechanicalmusic.co.uk; High St; adult/child £8/3.50; ⊘ 10am-5pm) Near Northleach's market square is Oak House, a 17th-century wool house containing this fascinating museum of lovingly restored self-playing musical instruments. Entry is by way of hour-long guided tours.

Chedworth Roman Villa　　ARCHAEOLOGICAL SITE
(NT; www.nationaltrust.org.uk; Yanworth; adult/child £9/4.50; ⊘ 10am-4pm Feb-Nov) Rediscovered in 1864 by a gamekeeper out ferreting, these extensive ruins represent one of the largest and most luxurious Roman villas in England. The earliest section dates to around AD 175, but it's thought to have been at its most magnificent in around AD 362, with two sets of bathhouses, a formal dining room with underfloor heating and a water shrine. It's 4.5 miles southwest of town, signposted from the A429.

🍴 Sleeping & Eating

★ Wheatsheaf　　PUB £££
(☑ 01451-860244; www.cotswoldswheatsheaf.com; West End; d £140-180, mains £11-20; ⊘ 8-10am, noon-3pm & 6-9.30pm; P 🛜 ♿ 🐾) The 14 rooms at this former coaching inn blend nice period touches, such as free-standing baths, with modern comforts, such as power showers. The restaurant is excellent, serving a menu of hearty British dishes including diabolically good devilled kidneys.

ℹ Getting There & Away

Buses head to/from the following:

Cheltenham (route 801/853) £1.80, 30 minutes

Cirencester (855) £2.20, 30 minutes

Gloucester (853) £3, one hour

Moreton-in-Marsh (801) £2.20, 40 minutes

Oxford (853) £6, one hour

The Slaughters

POP 400

The picture-postcard villages of Upper and Lower Slaughter manage to maintain their unhurried medieval charm in spite of receiving a multitude of visitors. The village names have nothing to do with abattoirs; they are derived from the Old English 'sloughtre', meaning slough or muddy place. Today the River Eye is contained within limestone banks and meanders peacefully through the village past the 17th-century Lower Slaughter Manor to the **Old Mill** (www.oldmill-lower-slaughter.com; adult/child £2.50/1; ⊙ 10am-6pm), which houses a small museum, cafe and ice cream parlour.

🛏 Sleeping & Eating

Lords of the Manor   HOTEL £££
(☎ 01451-820243; www.lordsofthemanor.com; Upper Slaughter; d £199-495, 3-course meal £69; ⊙ restaurant noon-3pm Sun, 6-9pm daily; 🅿 🛜) 'Countryside splendour' is what comes to mind when you clap your eyes on this 17th-century mansion. Its rooms are spacious and supremely tasteful, and the Michelin-starred restaurant is one of the best in the Cotswolds, concocting imaginative, beautifully presented dishes.

ℹ Getting There & Away

Pulhams (www.pulhamscoaches.com) bus 801 heads between Lower Slaughter and Northleach (£1.80, 20 minutes), Stow-on-the-Wold (£1.70, seven minutes), Moreton-in-Marsh (£1.70, 17 minutes) and Cheltenham (£3, 33 minutes); no Sunday service.

Stow-on-the-Wold

POP 2050

The highest town in the Cotswolds (244m), Stow is anchored by a large market square surrounded by handsome buildings and steep-walled alleyways, originally used to funnel the sheep into the fair. It's still an important market town and has long held a strategic place in Cotswold history, standing as it does on the Roman Fosse Way and at the junction of six roads. Today, it's famous for its twice-yearly Stow Horse Fair (May and October), where Romany people and other travellers have gathered for more than 500 years.

🛏 Sleeping

Stow-on-the-Wold YHA   HOSTEL £
(☎ 0845 3719540; www.yha.org.uk; Market Sq; dm £19; @ 🛜 🚻) You can't get more central than this location on the market square. The Cotswolds' only YHA is located in a wonderful 16th-century town house, with compact dorms, a children's play area and its own on-site cafe, which serves inexpensive hot meals.

Number 9   B&B ££
(☎ 01451-870333; www.number-nine.info; 9 Park St; s/d from £45/65; 🛜) Centrally located and wonderfully atmospheric, this friendly B&B is all sloping floors, low ceilings and exposed beams. The three rooms are cosy but spacious and each has its own bathroom.

Number Four at Stow   HOTEL £££
(☎ 01451-830297; www.hotelnumberfour.co.uk; Fosse Way; s/d from £115/130; 🅿 🛜) While not exactly 'at Stow' (it's a steep mile's walk from town on the main road to Burford), Number Four has a popular restaurant and 18 modern rooms with bathrooms. Standard rooms are a little cramped (especially for the prices charged), but nicely furnished.

🍴 Eating

Bell at Stow   PUB ££
(☎ 01451-870916; www.thebellatstow.com; Park St; mains £13-16; ⊙ 11am-11pm) Stow has plenty of cool old pubs but the Bell is the best. Lurking on the eastern edge of town, it serves a lively and varied menu stretching from Wiener schnitzel to jerk chicken to jambalaya. A selection of fresh fish dishes is chalked up on the blackboard daily.

Vine Leaf   CAFE ££
(☎ 01451-832010; www.thevineleaf.co.uk; 10 Talbot Ct; mains £9-16, 2-/3-course menu £12/15; ⊙ 11.30am-9pm Tue-Sat Apr-Sep, Wed-Sat Oct-Mar) A wonderful little catch-all cafe, serving chunky lunchtime sandwiches with locally baked bread, burgers, Mediterranean-style mezze and more substantial bistro-style mains crafted from locally sourced produce.

❶ Getting There & Away

➡ Pulhams bus 801 heads to/from Moreton-in-Marsh (£1.70, 15 minutes), Lower Slaughter (£1.70, seven minutes), Northleach (£2.10, 26 minutes) and Cheltenham (£3, one hour), Monday to Saturday.

➡ The Witney Shuttle (www.witneyshuttle.com) has scheduled runs to/from Heathrow (£88, two hours) and Gatwick (£108, three hours) airports.

Chipping Norton

POP 5720

The hilly town of Chipping Norton ('Chippy', to locals) has plenty of quiet side streets to wander and none of the Cotswold crowds. Handsome Georgian buildings and old coaching inns cluster around the market square, while on Church St you'll find a row of beautiful honey-coloured **almshouses** built in the 17th century.

◉ Sights

St Mary's Church   CHURCH
(www.stmaryscnorton.com) This secluded church is a classic example of the Cotswold wool churches, with a magnificent Perpendicular nave and clerestory. While most of the church was built in 1448, two of the arches in the chancel date to around 1200. In the hexagonal porch, take time to gaze up at the carved ceiling bosses that include the possibly pagan but common visitor to British churches, the Green Man.

Bliss Mill   LANDMARK
Chipping Norton's most enduring landmark is the arresting Bliss Mill on the western outskirts of town. This monument to the industrial architecture of the 19th century is more like a stately home than a factory, topped by a domed tower and chimney stack of the Tuscan order. It's been converted into luxury flats, so content yourself with admiring it as you drive along the A44.

✖ Eating

Wild Thyme   MODERN BRITISH £££
(✆ 01608-645060; www.wildthymerestaurant.co.uk; 10 New St; mains £18-19, 2-/3-course lunch £18/23; ◷ noon-2pm Wed-Sun, 7-9pm Tue-Sat) This little 'restaurant with rooms' thrills the palate with top-notch dishes such as goat's-cheese soufflé with red-onion marmalade. The desserts are nothing short of sublime, and the three upstairs rooms (single/double from

WORTH A TRIP

COTSWOLD FARM PARK

Owned by TV presenter Adam Henson, **Cotswold Farm Park** (www.cotswoldfarmpark.co.uk; Guiting Power; adult/child £9/8; ◷ 10.30am-4.30pm Mar-Nov; ⊞) is designed to introduce little ones to the world of farm animals while also preserving rare breeds. There are milking and shearing demonstrations, an adventure playground and pedal tractors to ride on. It's located in Guiting Power, halfway between Stow-on-the-Wold and Winchcombe, signposted from the B4077.

£65/75) have feather duvets and Egyptian cotton bedding.

🛍 Shopping

★ **Jaffé & Neale Bookshop Cafe**   BOOKS
(www.jaffeandneale.co.uk; 1 Middle Row; ◷ 9.30am-5.30pm Mon-Sat, 11am-5pm Sun) This great little independent bookshop serves delicious cakes to tables squeezed between the bookshelves. Upstairs there's a good second-hand selection.

❶ Getting There & Away

Buses head to/from the following:
Oxford (route S3) £4.30, 56 minutes
Stratford-upon-Avon (50) £5.40, 45 minutes
Witney (233/X9) £3.40, 45 minutes
Woodstock (S3) £3.80, 25 minutes

On Sundays buses head to Burford (233; £3.80, 30 minutes).

Moreton-in-Marsh

POP 3500

Home to some beautiful buildings but plagued by heavy traffic that clogs up its broad High St (built on top of the Roman Fosse Way), Moreton-in-Marsh is a major transport hub known for its excellent food shops stocking Cotswold produce. On Tuesdays, the town bursts into life for its weekly market, and if you're here in September, don't miss the one-day **Moreton Show** (www.moretonshow.co.uk), the ultimate agricultural extravaganza, attracting up to 20,000 people with the best of local food and gussied-up livestock competitions.

◉ Sights & Activities

Chastleton House HOUSE
(NT; www.nationaltrust.org.uk; adult/child £8.50/4;
☺12.30-3pm Wed-Sun Mar-Oct) Five miles east
of Moreton (off the A44), Chastleton is one
of England's finest and most complete Jacobean houses. Full of rare tapestries, family portraits and antique furniture, its Long
Gallery is particularly resplendent. Outside,
there's a wonderful topiary garden.

Batsford Arboretum PARK
(www.batsarb.co.uk; Batsford Park; adult/child
£7/3; ☺10am-5pm; ⊛) Created by Bertie
Mitford (Lord Redesdale) in 1880, these
exotic woodlands feature more than 3300
labelled trees, bamboos and shrubs from
Nepal, China, Japan and North America.
Highlights include vast American redwoods,
flowering Japanese cherries (at their best in
spring) and the strangely churchlike 'cathedral' lime.

★Cotswold Falconry Centre AVIARY
(www.cotswold-falconry.co.uk; Batsford Park; adult/
child £10/5; ☺10.30am-5pm mid-Feb–mid-Oct)
Home to numerous species of owl, vulture,
eagle and, of course, falcon, this interesting
place offers displays of the ancient practice
of falconry at 11.30am, 1.30pm and 3pm daily (plus 4.30pm in summer). The birds fly at
their best on windy days. Various hands-on
experiences are also offered (from £40).

⊨ Sleeping & Eating

White Hart Royal Hotel HOTEL ££
(☑01608-650731; www.whitehartroyal.co.uk; High
St; s/d from £72/86) The 'Royal' in the name
relates to the fact that Charles I once stayed
here during the Civil War, and while he
probably didn't make use of the iPod docks,
flatscreen TVs and en suite bathrooms, he
certainly would have walked down the atmospheric half-timbered corridors. The
downstairs restaurant has plenty of charm,
as well.

★Horse & Groom PUB ££
(☑01386-700413; www.horseandgroom.info;
mains £14-20; ☺noon-2pm daily, 7-9pm Mon-Sat;
ℙ�}) In the village of Bourton-on-the-Hill,
2 miles from Moreton-in-Marsh, this relaxed
pub excels at upmarket country cooking
showcasing local lamb and beef, alongside
flavour-filled fish dishes. It's a firm favourite
with the well-heeled horsey types who live
hereabouts. It also has rooms upstairs (sin-
gle/double £80/120).

ℹ Getting There & Away

BUS
From Monday to Saturday buses head to/from
the following:
Broadway (route 21/973) £3, 25 minutes
Cheltenham (801/813) £3.30, 1¼ hours
Chipping Campden (21/22/816) £3, 40
minutes
Stow-on-the-Wold (801/817) £1.70, 15 minutes
Stratford-upon-Avon (21/22/23) £5, one hour

TRAIN
Trains head to/from the following:
Hereford £18, two hours
Ledbury £17, 1½ hours
London Paddington £33, 1¾ hours
Oxford £9.60, 35 minutes
Worcester £12, 45 minutes

Chipping Campden
POP 2290

An absolute gem in an area full of pretty
towns, Chipping Campden is a glorious reminder of life in the Cotswolds in medieval times. The graceful curving main street
is flanked by a picturesque array of stone
cottages, fine terraced houses, ancient inns
and historic homes, many made of that
honey-coloured stone that the Cotswolds is
so famous for. Despite its obvious allure, the
town remains relatively unspoiled by visiting crowds, though it is very popular with
walkers rambling along the Cotswold Way.

While the village's name derives from
the Old English 'ceapen', meaning 'market',
'Chippy's' visible prosperity derives from its
past as a successful wool town.

◉ Sights & Activities

St James' Church CHURCH
(www.stjameschurchcampden.co.uk; Church St;
☺10am-5pm Mon-Sat, 2-5.45pm Sun Apr-Oct,
11am-3pm Mon-Sat, 2-4pm Sun Nov-Mar) Built
in the 15th century in Perpendicular Gothic
style, imposing St James' has a magnificent
tower and some graceful 17th-century monuments. Nearby on Church St is a remarkable row of **almshouses** dating from 1612.

Court Barn Museum MUSEUM
(☑01386-841951; www.courtbarn.org.uk; Church
St; adult/child £4/free; ☺10am-4pm Tue-Sun)
Chipping Campden has been linked with the
Arts and Crafts Movement since architect
and designer Charles Robert Ashbee moved
his Guild of Handicrafts from East London

to here in 1902. This small but interesting design museum features work from luminaries of the movement, which celebrated the work of the traditional artisan in an age of industrialisation.

The barn once belonged to **Campden House**, a grand 17th-century merchant's pad that was burned down by Royalist soldiers during the Civil War. Some of its lodges have since been restored and are available for holiday lets through the Landmark Trust (www.landmarktrust.org.uk); it's closed to nonresidents but you can peer through the gates.

Grevel House
HISTORIC BUILDING

(High St) One of the grandest residences on the High St, 14th-century Grevel House was home to the highly successful wool merchant William Grevel. It's not open to the public, but you can admire the splendid Perpendicular Gothic–style gabled window from the street.

Market Hall
HISTORIC BUILDING

(High St) In the middle of the High St stands the highly photogenic 17th-century Market Hall, an open-sided building where share farmers used to sell their produce. It looks like a cross between a barn and a chapel, with its simple arches, uneven stone floors, multiple gables and elaborate timber roof.

Guild Craft Workshops
ARTS CENTRE

(www.thegalleryattheguild.co.uk; Sheep St; ⊘10am-4.30pm) FREE This former silk mill (circa 1790) was the home of Charles Ashbee's Guild of Handicrafts from 1902 until it went bust in 1908. Many of the artisans stayed on, however, including Hart Gold & Silversmiths, who are still here to this day. Downstairs there's a cafe and a gallery showcasing the work of a cooperative of local artists and craftspeople.

Hidcote
GARDENS

(NT; www.nationaltrust.org.uk; Hidcote Bartrim; adult/child £10/5; ⊘10am-6pm) About 4 miles northeast of Chipping Campden, this is one of the finest examples of Arts and Crafts landscaping in Britain, with outdoor 'rooms' filled with flowers and rare plants for the arboreally inclined.

Cotswold Country Cycles
CYCLING

(⌨01386-438706; www.cotswoldcountrycycles.com; Longlands Farm Cottage; tours from £265) Arranges maps, luggage transfers and B&B accommodation for a range of self-guided cycling itineraries through the Cotswolds countryside.

🛏 Sleeping & Eating

Volunteer Inn
B&B £

(⌨01386-840688; www.thevolunteerinn.net; Lower High St; s/d £35/50, with bathroom £45/60, mains £8-20; 🛜) Attached to a busy locals' pub, this clutch of simple rooms is a favourite haunt of walkers and cyclists travelling along the Cotswold Way. **Maharaja**, the pub's popular Indian restaurant, covers all the classics as well as more unusual dishes such as venison *tikka masala*. The Inn also rent bikes.

Eight Bells Inn
PUB £££

(⌨01386-840371; www.eightbellsinn.co.uk; Church St; s/d from £80/115, mains £13-19) This 14th-century inn is an atmospheric place to stay, featuring bright, modern rooms with iron bedsteads, soothing neutral decor and warm accents. The pub downstairs wins points for its flagstone floors and good modern British country cooking.

Cotswold House & Spa
HOTEL £££

(⌨01386-840330; www.cotswoldhouse.com; The Square; r from £162; ⊘restaurant 6.30-9.30pm Tue-Sat, noon-2.30pm Sun; 🅿🛜🐾) This chic Regency town-house-turned-boutique hotel has ultracomfortable king-sized beds, lush furnishings and, in the top rooms, private gardens and hot tubs. Indulge in a spa treatment and then dine in style in the Dining Room (three-course set dinner £45).

ℹ Information

Tourist Office (⌨01386-841206; www.campdenonline.org; High St; ⊘9.30am-5pm daily Apr-Oct, to 1pm Mon-Thu, to 4pm Fri-Sun Nov-Mar) Pick up a town guide (£1.50) for a self-guided walk around the most significant buildings. Enquire about the guided tours run

---

LOCAL KNOWLEDGE

THE COTSWOLDS OLIMPICKS

The medieval sport of shin-kicking lives on in Chipping Campden, where each year the townspeople gather annually to compete at the **Cotswold Olimpicks** (www.olimpickgames.co.uk; ⊘late May or early Jun), a traditional country sports day first celebrated in 1612. It is one of the most entertaining and bizarre sporting competitions in England, and many of the original events, such as tug o' war, the sack race and climbing a slippery pole, are still held.

by the Cotswold Voluntary Wardens (from May to September; suggested donation £3).

❶ Getting There & Around

Johnsons Excelbus (www.johnsonscoaches.co.uk) services head to/from Moreton-in-Marsh (route 21/22/816; £3, 40 minutes), Broadway (21/608; £3, 17 minutes) and Stratford-upon-Avon (21/22; £4, 35 minutes), from Monday to Saturday.

Broadway

POP 2540

A quintessentially English place with a smattering of antique shops, tearooms and art galleries, Broadway has inspired writers, artists and composers in times past with its graceful, golden-hued cottages set at the foot of a steep escarpment. Take the time to wander down to the lovely 12th-century St Eadburgha's Church, a signposted 1-mile walk from town.

If the neighbouring village of Snowshill looks familiar, that's because it featured in the film *Bridget Jones's Diary;* a local house was used as Bridget's parents' home.

◉ Sights

Broadway Tower   TOWER
(www.broadwaytower.co.uk; Middle Hill; adult/child £4.80/3; ⊙10am-5pm) Near St Eadburgha's Church, a mile from Broadway, a path leads uphill for 2 miles to Broadway Tower, a crenulated 18th-century Gothic folly on the crest of the escarpment, where you'll find all-encompassing views from the top.

Snowshill Manor   HOUSE
(NT; www.nationaltrust.org.uk; adult/child £9.80/4.90; ⊙noon-5pm Wed-Sun Apr-Jun, Sep & Oct, 11.30am-4.30pm Wed-Mon Jul & Aug) About 3 miles south of Broadway lies Snowshill Manor, a wonderful Cotswold mansion that was once home to the marvellously eccentric poet and architect Charles Paget Wade (1883–1956). The house contains Wade's extraordinary collection of crafts and design, with everything from musical instruments to Victorian perambulators and Japanese samurai armour. The impressive gardens were designed as an extension of the house, with pools, terraces and wonderful views.

⫴ Sleeping & Eating

Crown & Trumpet   PUB £ £
(☑01386-853202; www.cotswoldholidays.co.uk; 14 Church St; r £60; ⓟ⑅) For modern comfort within a 300-year-old exterior, this friendly pub offers five en suite rooms complete with sloped floors, exposed beams and low ceilings. Downstairs is a good bet for real ales and a proper roast dinner.

Russell's   HOTEL £ £
(☑01386-853555; www.russellsofbroadway.co.uk; 20 High St; r from £115, 2-/3-course menu £14/17; ⊙restaurant noon-2.30pm daily, 6-9.30pm Mon-Sat; ⓟ⑅) Sleek and stylish Russell's has seven spacious, individually designed rooms, some with exposed beams and four-poster beds, and all with modern luxuries such as contemporary bathrooms and iPod docks. It's known for its beautifully executed modern British fare.

Lygon Arms   HOTEL £ £ £
(☑01386-852255; www.pumahotels.co.uk; High St, Broadway; r from £126; ⓟ⑅⧳) Choose medieval splendour or modern chic at this 16th-century inn in the heart of Broadway. It's a grand old place, with a golden stone exterior and half-timbered walls inside. There's also a good restaurant.

❶ Information

Tourist Office (☑01386-852937; www.beautifulbroadway.com; Russell Sq; ⊙10am-5pm Mon-Sat, 11am-3pm Sun Apr-Oct, 10am-4pm Mon-Sat Nov-Mar)

❶ Getting There & Away

Buses head to/from the following:
Cheltenham (route 606/608) 47 minutes
Chipping Campden (21/22/608) £3, 17 minutes
Moreton-in-Marsh (21/22/973) £3, 25 minutes
Stratford-upon-Avon (21) £4, 52 minutes
Winchcombe (606) 30 minutes

Winchcombe

POP 4540

Winchcombe is very much a working, living town, with butchers, bakers and small independent shops lining the main streets. It was capital of the Saxon kingdom of Mercia and one of the most important towns in the Cotswolds until the Middle Ages. Today, the remnants of its illustrious past can still be seen in its stone and half-timbered buildings. Keep an eye out for the picturesque cottages on Vineyard St and Dents Tce, and the grotesque gargoyles that adorn St Peter's Church.

Winchcombe is ideally situated for walkers, with a spider's web of long-distance trails branching out in every direction including the Cotswold Way, the Gloucestershire Way and the Worcestershire-bound St Kenelm's Way.

◉ Sights & Activities

Sudeley Castle   CASTLE
(www.sudeleycastle.co.uk; adult/child £14/5; ☺10am-5pm mid-Mar–Oct) Winchcombe's main attraction, this magnificent castle has welcomed many a monarch over its thousand year history, including Richard III, Henry VIII and Charles I. It is most famous as the home of Catherine Parr (Henry VIII's widow) and her second husband, Thomas Seymour. Princess Elizabeth (before she became Elizabeth I) was part of the household for a time until Seymour's inappropriate displays of affection towards her prompted Catherine to banish her from the premises.

Lady Jane Grey – the ill-fated 'Nine Days Queen' – was also sent here to live with the Seymours, and she was the chief mourner at Catherine's funeral. You'll find Catherine's tomb in the chapel, making this the only private house in England where a queen is buried.

The house is still used as a family home and some of the interior is off-limits to visitors, but you can get a good sense of its grand proportions while visiting the exhibitions of costumes, memorabilia and paintings, and the surrounding grounds. The gardens include spectacular avenues of sculpted yews, an intricate knot garden and aviaries containing magnificently coloured pheasants.

Enquire at the visitor centre about the 5-mile loop walk from here that leads to a well-preserved Roman mosaic floor hidden within the surrounding woods. Allow 2½ hours for the walk.

Belas Knap Long Barrow ARCHAEOLOGICAL SITE
Dating from more than 5500 years ago, Belas Knap is one of the best-preserved neolithic burial chambers in the country, and the views down to Sudeley Castle and across the surrounding countryside are breathtaking. The remains of 38 people were found when its four chambers were excavated. The barrow can be accessed from Winchcombe by a 2½-mile hike along the Cotswold Way. Otherwise you can park on Corndean Lane and take a steep but shortish walk up across the fields.

Hailes Abbey   RUIN
(EH; www.english-heritage.org.uk; Hailes; adult/child £4.50/2.70; ☺10am-5pm Apr-Nov) Two miles northeast of Winchcombe are the meagre ruins of this Cistercian abbey, once one of the country's main pilgrimage centres, due to a long-running medieval scam. The abbey was said to possess a vial of Christ's blood, which turned out to be merely coloured water. Before the deception came to light, thousands of pilgrims contributed to the abbey's wealth.

🛏 Sleeping & Eating

Wesley House   B&B ££
(☎01242-602366; www.wesleyhouse.co.uk; High St; s/d from £65/90, mains £17-20; ☺restaurant noon-2pm Tue-Sun, 7-9pm Tue-Sat; ☺) Methodist founder John Wesley once stayed in this wonderful 15th-century half-timbered house. The rooms are pleasantly indulgent, especially 'Almsbury', which has its own balcony overlooking the countryside. Downstairs is split between a relaxed bar and grill, and a more formal restaurant serving fabulous Modern British cuisine.

White Hart Inn   HOTEL ££
(☎01242-602359; www.whitehartwinchcombe. co.uk; High St; s/d from £60/70, without bathroom £40/50; ☺) Appealingly old-fashioned, this central inn caters well to walkers. Choose one of the three cheaper 'rambler' rooms, with shared bathrooms and iron bedsteads, or go for greater luxury in a superior room.

★5 North St   MODERN EUROPEAN £££
(☎01242-604566; www.5northstreetrestaurant. co.uk; 5 North St; 2-/3-course lunch £24/28, 3-7-course dinner £44-70; ☺7-9.30pm Tue-Sat) This Michelin-starred restaurant is a treat from start to finish, from its splendid 400-year-old timbered exterior to what you eventually find on your plate. Marcus Ashenford's cooking is rooted in traditional ingredients, but the odd playful experiment (such as Guinness ice cream) adds that extra magic.

ⓘ Information

Tourist Office (☎01242-602925; www. winchcombe.co.uk; High St; ☺10am-4pm daily Apr-Oct, Sat & Sun Nov-Mar)

ⓘ Getting There & Away

Castleways (www.castleways.co.uk) bus 606 travels to/from Broadway (30 minutes) and Cheltenham (20 minutes); no Sunday services.

Painswick

POP 1770

One of the most beautiful and unspoilt towns in the Cotswolds, hilltop Painswick sees only a trickle of visitors, so you can wander the narrow winding streets and admire the picture-perfect cottages, handsome stone town houses and medieval inns in your own good time. Look out for Bisley St, the original main drag, which was superseded by the now ancient-looking New St in medieval times.

⊙ Sights & Activities

St Mary's Church   CHURCH
(www.stmaryspainswick.org.uk; New St; ⊙9.30am-6pm Apr-Sep, to 4pm Oct-Mar) The village centres on this fine 14th-century, Perpendicular Gothic wool church, surrounded by tabletop tombs and clipped yew trees that resemble giant lollipops. Legend had it that only 99 trees could ever grow here, as the devil would appear and shrivel the 100th tree were it ever planted. They planted it anyway, to celebrate the millennium and – lo and behold! – one of the trees toppled several years later. We're assured it's now making a good recovery.

Just behind the churchyard, a rare set of iron stocks stand in the street.

Painswick Rococo Garden   GARDENS
(www.rococogarden.org.uk; adult/child £6.50/3; ⊙11am-5pm mid-Jan–Oct) A mile north of town, this is the only garden of its type in England, designed by Benjamin Hyett in the 1740s and now restored to its former glory. Winding paths soften the otherwise strict geometrical precision, bringing visitors around the central vegetable garden to the many Gothic follies dotted in the grounds. There's also a children's nature trail and maze.

CHEESE-ROLLING AT COOPER'S HILL
....
Cooper's Hill in Cranham, near Painswick, is the location of the Cotswolds' most dangerous sport: the annual **Cheese-Rolling** (www.cheese-rolling. co.uk; ⊙last bank holiday in May). This 200-year-old tradition sees locals running, tumbling and sliding down a steep hill in pursuit of a 7lb round of Double Gloucester cheese; it's only a 90m run, but people get hurt every year. The prize? The cheese itself, and the glory of catching it.

🛏 Sleeping & Eating

Troy House   B&B ££
(☎01452-812339; www.troy-house.co.uk; Gloucester St; s/d £50/75; ⊛) At this great little B&B the two spacious guest rooms occupy their own separate rear cottage accessed from a pretty courtyard. They're nicely decked out with quality toiletries, magazines and *Tintin* books.

Cardynham House   HOTEL ££
(☎01452-814006; www.cardynham.co.uk; Tibbiwell St; s/d from £70/90, lunch £12-14, dinner £14-17; ⊙bistro noon-3pm Tue-Sun, 6.30-9.30pm Tue-Sat; ⊛⊠) Each of the differently themed rooms at 15th-century Cardynham House has four-poster beds and heavy patterned fabrics. For a private pool and garden, book the Pool Room. Downstairs, the bistro (mains from £10 to £20) serves hearty British fare.

Cotswolds88   HOTEL £££
(☎01452-813688; www.cotswolds88.com; Kemps Lane; r/ste from £110/250, 2-/3-course lunch £15/20, dinner £43/50; ⊙restaurant noon-2.30pm &7-9.30pm Wed-Sun; P⊛) This is a happy marriage of 18th-century architecture and over-the-top decor – from the wallpaper to the psychedelic lighting. Spacious, individually decorated rooms come with every creature comfort, and the suites have four-poster beds and spa baths. The restaurant is also excellent, featuring sophisticated yet playful fare.

ℹ Getting There & Away

Stagecoach (www.stagecoachbus.com) bus 46 heads to/from Cheltenham (£3.40, 42 minutes) and Stroud (£2, 10 minutes).

Stroud

POP 32,700

Stroud once hummed with the sound of more than 150 cloth mills operating around the town, but when the bottom fell out of the market, the town went into decline. Although a handful of the handsome old mills are still operating, the hilly town has become a bohemian enclave known for its fair-trade shops, delis and independent stores.

This is still one of the most important market towns in the Cotswolds, with dozens of stallholders converging every Saturday for the **farmers market**. Another great place for organic food, books, craft and more is the **Shambles Market** (www.shamblesmarket-stroud.co.uk), which takes place in the historic Shambles on Fridays and Saturdays.

◉ Sights

Museum in the Park   MUSEUM
(www.museuminthepark.org.uk; Stratford Pk; ⊙11am-4pm Tue-Sun; ♿) **FREE** Set in an 18th-century mansion surrounded by parkland, this museum tells the history of the town and its cloth-making, and there are interactive displays of everything from dinosaurs to Victorian toys. A separate gallery hosts eclectic contemporary art exhibitions.

✖ Eating

Star Anise   CAFE **£**
(www.staraniseartscafe.com; Gloucester St; mains £6-8; ⊙8am-5pm Mon-Sat; ♪) Local produce features heavily in the inventive dishes at this mostly vegetarian cafe (there are some fish dishes). It often hosts live music and other community events.

No 23   TAPAS **££**
(☑01453-298525; www.facebook.com/no23barand bistrostroud; 23 Nelson St; tapas £5-10; ⊙10am-10pm; ♠♪) Tuck into proper Spanish tapas, wine, sherry and brandy at this chilled-out little place. Head upstairs to the balcony for great views of the countryside.

❶ Information

Tourist Office (☑01453-760960; www.visitthecotswolds.org.uk; George St; ⊙10am-5pm Mon-Sat)

❶ Getting There & Away

➧ Buses head to/from Cirencester (route 54; £3.50, 36 minutes), Uley (21/35; £4, 30 minutes), Painswick (46; £2, nine minutes), Cheltenham (46; £3.60, 46 minutes) and Gloucester (14/93; £3.70, 1¼ hours).

➧ National Express coaches head to/from London Victoria (£25, 2¾ hours), Bristol (£8, 45 minutes), Birmingham (£15, 2½ hours), Hereford (£8, 1½ hours) and Scarborough (£56, 10 hours).

➧ Trains head to/from London Paddington (£22, 1½ hours), Gloucester (£4.50, 20 minutes) and Cheltenham (£5.90, 40 minutes).

Tetbury

POP 5480

Once a prosperous wool-trading centre, Tetbury's busy streets are lined with medieval cottages, sturdy old town houses and Georgian gems. The Georgian Gothic Church of **Sts Mary the Virgin & Mary Magadelene** has a towering spire and wonderful interior,

COTSWOLDS FOOD & FARMERS MARKETS

When the locally sourced, seasonal food movement took off, the Cotswolds were already there. Organic, ethically produced produce has long been a staple in its villages. In the delis and independent food shops all over the region, visiting foodies will make tempting discoveries. Edible goodies to look out for include cheese from **Simon Weaver Organic** (www.simonweaver.net), from a farm near Upper Slaughter; organic beef from **LoveMyCow** (www.lovemycow. com) in Bourton-on-the-Water; smoked fish and meats from **Upton Smokery** (www.uptonsmokery.co.uk) in Burford; and fantastic ice cream from Chedworth's **Cotswold Ice Cream Company** (www.cotswold-icecream.co.uk).

Farmers markets take place monthly or fortnightly in many of the villages and towns, with a multitude of local producers selling their seasonal delights to the general public. The best is held every Saturday morning in Stroud.

including its original box pews. From here, it's a short stroll to Market Sq, where the 17th-century Market House stands as if on stilts.

Tetbury is also a great place for antiques fans, with a shop of old curios on almost every corner. A good time to visit is the last Monday in May for the **Woolsack Races** (www.tetburywoolsack.co.uk) – a nod to the town's past – or in August for the **Festival of British Eventing** (www.gatcombe-horse. co.uk) at Princess Anne's Gatcombe Park estate. Her big brother, Charles, also lives near here, at Highgrove.

Buses head to/from Stroud (route 29/129; £3.50, 36 minutes) and Cirencester (881; £3.50, 37 minutes); no Sunday services.

Uley

POP 1000

This lovely little hamlet, with its quaint village green and jumble of pretty houses, sits below the overgrown remains of **Uley Bury**, the largest Iron Age hill fort in England. Dating from about 300 BC, the fort and its perimeter walk provide spectacular views over the Severn Vale; follow the steep path that runs from the village church. If you're driving, access to the car park is off the B4066, north of the village.

Virtually untouched since the mid-1870s, **Woodchester Mansion** (www.woodchester-mansion.org.uk; adult/child £6.50/free; ☺11am-5pm Sat & Sun Apr-Oct) was abandoned before it was finished, yet it's still amazingly grand and graceful. Doors open to nowhere, fireplaces are stuck halfway up walls, and corridors end at ledges with views of the ground below. The house also features an impressive set of gruesome gargoyles and is home to one of England's most important colonies of horseshoe bats and several resident ghosts. It's a mile north of Uley on the B4066.

Buses 21 and 35 head to/from Stroud (£4, 30 minutes) on weekdays.

WESTERN GLOUCESTERSHIRE

West of the Cotswolds, Gloucestershire's greatest asset is the elegant Regency town of Cheltenham. It's home to tree-lined terraces, upmarket boutiques and a tempting collection of dining options. The county capital, Gloucester, is well worth a visit for its magnificent Gothic cathedral, while to the west, the picturesque Forest of Dean is a leafy backwater perfect for cycling and walking.

Berkeley
POP 2040

Tucked away in the thin strip of land between the Cotswolds and the River Severn, Berkeley is a bucolic little place that's none-the-less featured prominently in history.

◉ Sights

Berkeley Castle   CASTLE
(www.berkeley-castle.com; adult/child £10/5.50; ☺11am-5pm Sun-Wed Apr-Oct) Little changed since it was built as a sturdy fortress in Norman times, this fine fortress has been the home of the Berkeleys for nearly 900 years. Edward II was imprisoned and then murdered here in 1327 (allegedly with a hot poker up his rectum) on the order of his wife and her lover. Visits include the King's Gallery (with its cell and dungeon), the medieval Great Hall and the kitchen.

Dr Jenner's House   MUSEUM
(www.jennermuseum.com; Church Lane; adult/child £6.95/5.95; ☺noon-5pm Sun-Wed Apr-Sep)

This beautiful Queen Anne house honours the life and work of Edward Jenner (1749-1823), the country doctor who discovered the principle of vaccination, fundamentally changing the lives of us all. It was here that the doctor performed the first smallpox vaccination in 1796.

❶ Getting There & Away

Berkeley is best visited with your own wheels, as public transport is extremely limited. It's 16 miles south of Gloucester; take the A38 and follow the signs.

Cheltenham
POP 117,000

Cheltenham retains an air of gracious refinement left over from its heyday as a spa resort in the 18th century. At the time, it rivalled Bath as the place for sick rich people to go, and today it still has many Regency buildings and manicured squares. These days, however, it's best known for its racecourse (www.cheltenham.co.uk), which in mid-March attracts up to 40,000 people for one of England's premier steeplechase events.

Cheltenham's excellent accommodation and restaurants make it a more appealing base to the region than the county town of Gloucester, but this mid-tier city is unlikely to be the highlight of your trip.

◉ Sights

Wilson   MUSEUM, GALLERY
(www.thewilson.org.uk; Clarence St; ☺9.30am-5.15pm) FREE Cheltenham's excellent museum depicts local life through the ages and has wonderful displays on William Morris and the Arts and Crafts Movement, as well as British ceramics and fine art. A section on Scott's ill-fated expedition to Antarctica highlights the role of local lad Edward Wilson.

Holst Birthplace Museum   MUSEUM
(www.holstmuseum.org.uk; 4 Clarence Rd; adult/child £5/4.50; ☺10am-5pm Tue-Sat, 1.30-5pm Sun Jun-Sep, 10am-4pm Tue-Sat Feb-May & Oct-mid-Dec) Gustav Holst was born in Cheltenham in 1874, and the rooms of his childhood home are laid out in typical period fashion. They feature many of his personal possessions, including the piano on which most of his orchestral suite *The Planets* was composed, as well as photos of the notoriously camera-shy composer.

GLOUCESTER

Gloucester (*glos*-ter) is the county town of Gloucestershire and a major transport hub, with plenty of train, bus and coach connections. It was originally a settlement for retired Roman soldiers but it came into its own in medieval times, when the pious public flocked to see the grave of Edward II and financed the building of what remains one of England's most beautiful cathedrals.

Gloucester Cathedral (www.gloucestercathedral.org.uk; 12 College Green; tower tours adult/child £4/1; ⊙ 7.40am-5.30pm Mon-Sat, to 3pm Sun) Gloucester Cathedral is among the first and finest examples of the Perpendicular Gothic style. Originally the site of a Saxon abbey, a Norman church was built here by a group of Benedictine monks in the 12th century. When Edward II was murdered in 1327, the church was chosen as his burial place.

Inside, the best of Norman Romanesque and Gothic design are skillfully combined with sturdy columns, creating a sense of gracious solidity. From the elaborate 14th-century wooden choir stalls, you'll get a good view of the imposing Great East Window, one of the largest in England. Beneath the window in the northern ambulatory is Edward II's magnificent tomb, and nearby is the late 15th-century Lady Chapel, a glorious patchwork of carved stone and stained glass.

One of the cathedral's treasures is the exquisite Great Cloister (used in the first two *Harry Potter* films). Completed in 1367, it is the first example of fan vaulting in England and only matched in beauty by Henry VII's chapel at Westminster Abbey.

Gloucester Quays (www.gloucesterquays.co.uk; St Ann Way; ⊙ 10am-8pm Mon-Sat, to 5pm Sun) This set of old brick warehouses is filled with bargain outlet stores for many of the big fashion brands. It's also home to the excellent three-story Gloucester Antiques Centre.

Pittville Pump Room NOTABLE BUILDING
(www.pittvillepumproom.org.uk; Pittville Park; ⊙ 10am-4pm Wed-Sun) **FREE** Built in 1830 as a centrepiece to a large housing subdivision, the Pittville Pump Room is Cheltenham's finest Regency building, based on an ancient Athenian temple. Wander into the main auditorium and sample the pungent spa waters from the fountain, or just explore the surrounding park with its lake, lawns, playground and aviary.

🛏 Sleeping

Accommodation books up well in advance for Cheltenham's horse-racing festival in March, not just in Cheltenham but throughout the surrounding villages as well.

★ **Bradley** B&B ££
(☑ 01242-519077; www.thebradleyhotel.co.uk; 19 Royal Parade, Bayshill Rd; s/d from £80/88; P 🛜) It was the present owner's eccentric great-aunt Madge who brought this lovely Regency house into the family more than 100 years ago. It's lost none of its character in its transition into a fabulous B&B. Each of the six rooms has its own individual style.

Battledown B&B ££
(☑ 01242-233881; www.thebattledown.co.uk; 125 Hales Rd; s/d £60/80; P 🛜) If you don't mind

a 20-minute walk to the city centre, this family-run French colonial–style villa is an especially warm and friendly option. Hales Rd branches off London Rd, just southeast of central Cheltenham.

Wyastone Townhouse B&B ££
(☑ 01242-245549; www.wyastonehotel.co.uk; Parabola Rd; s/d from £80/112; P 🛜) A young couple has taken over this big white Victorian house in the centre of Cheltenham and freshened up the decor. Rooms in the main house are grander than those in the annexe facing the pretty rear courtyard, but all are very comfortable.

Ellenborough Park HOTEL £££
(☑ 01242-545454; www.ellenboroughpark.com; Southam Rd; r from £207; P 🛜🏊) Oozing tradition, this majestic 500-year-old country house has 62 individually designed rooms, mixing original fittings with modern features such as comfy beds and iPod docks. It's 3 miles northeast of the city centre; take Prestbury Rd and follow the signs.

Cowley Manor HOTEL £££
(☑ 01242-870900; www.cowleymanor.com; Cowley; r from £195; P 🛜🏊) In the village of Cowley, 5 miles south of Cheltenham (off the A435), this superb Italianate sandstone mansion

Cheltenham

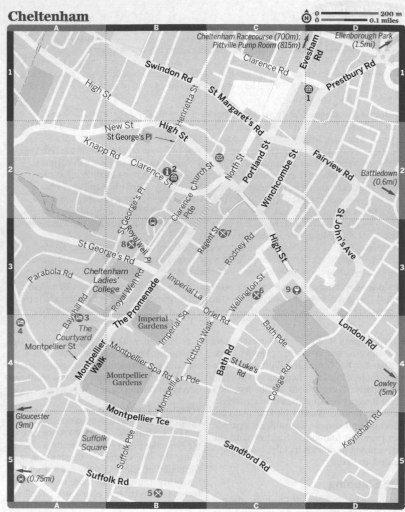

sets both the comfort and the kookiness levels to extreme. Handmade furniture and fabrics by young British designers adorn the bright but elegant rooms; downstairs, oddball art juts out from the walls.

✕ Eating

The Tavern PUB **££**
(☎01242-221212; www.thetaverncheltenham.com; 5 Royal Well Pl; mains £10-20; ⊙9am-10pm; ✸) Delivering 'dude food' at its best, this hiply dishevelled bar (exposed bricks, bare wooden tables) serves fancy burgers, hot dogs, steaks, macaroni cheese, devilled Scotch eggs, calves livers and, for that extra dude pep, Thai-style oysters. There's free popcorn and sparkling water, and the sliders alone justify repeat visits.

Prithvi INDIAN **££**
(☎01242-226229; www.prithvirestaurant.com; 37 Bath Rd; mains £11-16; ⊙noon-1.30pm Wed-Sun, 6-9.45pm Tue-Sun) Prithvi's top-notch service and white-linen ambience matches its immaculate dishes. Each mouth-watering offering is presented with great attention to detail. Various set menus are available, including a good-value lunch option (two/three courses £15/19).

Cheltenham

⊙ Sights
1 Holst Birthplace Museum D1
2 Wilson B2

⊜ Sleeping
3 Bradley A4
4 Wyastone Townhouse A4

⊗ Eating
5 Le Champignon Sauvage B5
6 Prithvi C3
7 Red Pepper C3
8 The Tavern B3

⊙ Drinking & Nightlife
9 Sandford Park Ale House C3

Red Pepper CAFE **££**
(☑ 01242-253900; www.redpeppercheltenham.
co.uk; 13 Regent St; brunch £5-9, dinner £11-17;
⊙ 9.30am-4pm Sun & Mon, to 9.30pm Tue-Sat)
Despite the main dining area being in the
basement, this central cafe still manages
to be surprisingly bright and peppy. In the
evening the lighter meals give way to bistro
fare, with 'steak night' on Wednesdays and
'sausages and wine night' on Thursdays.

★ Le Champignon Sauvage FRENCH **£££**
(☑ 01242-573449; www.lechampignonsauvage.
co.uk; 24-28 Suffolk Rd; 3-course menu £32-59;
⊙ 12.30-3pm & 7.30-10pm Tue-Sat) For nearly 30
years this Cheltenham institution has been
delighting visitors and locals alike with chef
David Everitt-Matthias' finely executed dishes and imaginative flavour combinations.
We're not alone in thinking it Gloucestershire's best restaurant.

Sandford Park Ale House PUB
(www.spalehouse.co.uk; 20 High St; ⊙ noon-midnight) With 10 hand-pulled ales and ciders,
more than 80 bottled beers and 16 taps of Belgian and German brews, this is Cheltenham's
premier beer den. The large back garden is
more appealing than the starkly lit interior.

⊙ Information

Tourist Office (☑ 01242-237431; www.visit
cheltenham.com; The Wilson, Clarence St;
⊙ 9.30am-5.15pm)

⊙ Getting There & Away

BUS
Bus destinations:
Oxford (route 853) £7.50, 1½ hours

Cirencester (51) £3.60, 40 minutes
Gloucester (4/10/94/97-99/377) £3.20, 45
minutes
Stroud (23/46) £3.60, 1¾ hours
Winchcombe (606) 20 minutes

National Express coach destinations:
Birmingham £12, 1½ hours
Leeds £42, 5½ hours
London Victoria £17, three hours
Newcastle-upon-Tyne £55, 8¾ hours
Nottingham £24, four hours

TRAIN
Trains run to/from the following:
Bristol £8.70, 40 minutes
Cardiff £18, 1½ hours
Edinburgh £84, six hours
Exeter £22, 1¾ hours
London Paddington £29, 2¼ hours

Forest of Dean

The Forest of Dean is the oldest oak forest
in England and a wonderfully scenic place to
walk, cycle or paddle. The 42-sq-mile woodland, designated England's first National
Forest Park in 1938, was formerly a royal
hunting ground and a centre of iron and coal
mining. Its mysterious depths supposedly
inspired the forests of JRR Tolkien's Middle
Earth books, and key scenes in *Harry Potter
& the Deathly Hallows* were set here.

The Forest of Dean also gives its name
to one of Gloucestershire's districts, which
includes the small towns of Newent and
Coleford, north and south (respectively) of
the forest itself. A good place to begin your
explorations of the forest proper is the Dean
Forest Centre, near the village of Soudley,
within its eastern fringe. To the west, the forest spills over the Herefordshire border near
the village of Goodrich. The River Wye skirts
its edge, offering glorious views to canoeists
who paddle out from the pretty village of
Symonds Yat.

⊙ Sights

Three Choirs Vineyard WINERY
(☑ 01531-890223; www.threechoirs.com; B4215,
Newent; mains £16-19; ⊙ shop 9am-5pm, restaurant noon-2pm & 7-9pm Tue-Sun) While the
phrase 'quality English wine' might sound
like an oxymoron, a handful of English producers are making just that. Three Choirs is
England's third biggest winery, producing
250,000 bottles annually from varietals such

as pinot noir, bacchus and siegerrebe. Call in for a tasting (five wines, beers or ciders for £6) or take a guided tour of the winery (£12.50, 2.30pm daily). The attached restaurant serves classic brasserie dishes, using locally sourced produce wherever possible.

★ International Centre for Birds of Prey
AVIARY

(⏺ 01531-820286; www.icbp.org; adult/child £11/7; ⏰ 10.30am-4.30pm Feb-Nov) Watch raptors swoop and dive at this large complex in the countryside 2 miles from Newent (follow the signs). There are at least three flyings per day, along with aviaries housing an extensive collection of owls, falcons, kestrels, eagles, buzzards and hawks from all over the world.

Dean Heritage Centre
MUSEUM

(www.deanheritagecentre.com; Camp Mill, Soudley; adult/child £7.20/5.40; ⏰ 10am-4pm; ⏺) This entertaining museum looks at everything from the Forest of Dean's geology to the Roman occupation, medieval hunting laws, cottage crafts and coal mining. There are plenty of sights for kids, too, from a mini-zoo with pigs, rabbits and weasels to the current pride and joy – the Gruffalo Trail, featuring life-sized wooden carvings from Julia Donaldson's classic picture book.

Puzzlewood
FOREST, FARM

(www.puzzlewood.net; Perrygrove Rd, Coleford; adult/child £6.50/5; ⏰ 10am-5pm Apr-Oct, to 3.30pm Sat & Sun Mar, Nov & Dec; ⏺) A pre-Roman open-cast ore mine, overgrown with eerie moss-covered trees, Puzzlewood has a web of paths, weird rock formations, tangled vines and dark passageways seemingly designed to leave you disorientated and uneasy. If it seems familiar, that's because episodes of *Dr Who* and *Merlin* were shot here. Kids will love interacting with the farm animals, and there's also an indoor and outdoor maze. Puzzle Wood is 1 mile south of Coleford on the B4228.

Clearwell Caves
CAVE

(www.clearwellcaves.com; adult/child £6.50/4.50, Christmas display £8.50; ⏰ 10am-5pm mid-Feb–Dec; ⏺) Descend into the damp subterranean world of a 4500-year-old iron mine, comprising a warren of dimly lit passageways, caverns and pools, and home to several species of bats. From November the caves are transformed into a hugely popular Christmas grotto. Clearwell is signposted off the B4228, a mile south of Coleford.

Symonds Yat
VILLAGE

Right on the edge of the Forest of Dean, squeezed between the River Wye and the towering limestone outcrop known as Symonds Yat Rock (504m), Symonds Yat is an endearing tangle of pubs, guesthouses and campsites, with great walks and a canoeing centre. It's split into two halves by the river, connected by an ancient hand-hauled ferry (adult/child/bicycle £1.20/60p/60p). Strong currents make the river dangerous for swimming.

The scenic Peregrine Path follows the River Wye River from Symonds Yat East to Monmouth. Another popular walk from the eastern side picks its way up the side of Symonds Yat Rock, with fabulous views of river and valley. In July and August, you may be lucky enough to spot peregrine falcons soaring by the drop-off. A kiosk atop the rock sells drinks and snacks, and peaceful walking trails continue through the forest.

Experienced rock climbers follow a series of mainly trad routes directly up the face of the cliff, but routes in the easier grades tend to be very polished, and rock falls are common – bring a varied rack and wear your helmet.

Goodrich Castle
CASTLE

(EH; ⏺ 01600-890538; www.english-heritage.org.uk; Castle Lane, Goodrich; adult/child £6/3.60; ⏰ 10am-5pm daily Apr-Oct, to 4pm Sat & Sun Nov-Mar) Seemingly part of its craggy red bedrock, Goodrich is a partly ruined castle topped by a 12th-century keep that affords spectacular views. An audioguide tells the story of the castle from its origins to its demise in the Civil War.

🏃 Activities

Wyedean Canoe & Adventure Centre
ADVENTURE SPORTS

(⏺ 01600-890238; www.wyedean.co.uk; Symonds Yat East; half-day hire from £24) Hires out canoes and kayaks, and organises white-water trips, archery, high ropes, abseiling, caving and rock climbing.

Way2Go Adventures
ADVENTURES SPORTS

(⏺ 01594-800908; www.way2goadventures.co.uk; per person £55) Offers canoeing, kayaking, raft-building and Nordic walking expeditions.

Kingfisher Cruises
CRUISE

(⏺ 01432 267862; Symonds Yat East; adult/child £8/3.50) Fair-weather water-babies can enjoy the Wye without the hard work on a sedate 40-minute gorge cruise leaving Symonds Yat East from beside the ferry crossing.

Pedalabikeaway CYCLING
(📞 01594-860065; www.pedalabikeaway.co.uk; Cannop Valley; hire per day from £18; ☺ 9am-6pm Apr-Oct) Hires both leisure bikes and full suspension mountain bikes, and offers advice on routes. In Cannop Valley, near Coleford.

🛏 Sleeping & Eating

Wye Valley YHA HOSTEL £
(📞 0845 371 9666; www.yha.org.uk; dm/r from £16/46; ☺ Apr-Oct; P) This austere former Victorian rectory surveys the countryside from its lovely riverside grounds. It's on the Wye Valley Walk, 1.5 miles from Goodrich. Drivers should be prepared for a steep and difficult access road; follow the signed road near Goodrich Castle and take the right fork where the road splits.

Garth Cottage B&B ££
(📞 01600-890364; www.garthcottage-symondsyat.com; Symonds Yat East; s/d £43/85; ☺ mid-Mar-Oct; P 🛜) This exceedingly friendly, family-run B&B sits by the river near the ferry crossing, and has spotlessly maintained, chintzy rooms with river views. There are discounted rates for longer stays.

Old Court Hotel HOTEL ££
(📞 01600-890367; www.oldcourthotel.co.uk; s/d/ste from £63/85/155; P 🛜 🐾) Set in gardens on the outskirts of Symonds Yat West, on the main road into the village from the A40, this 16th-century manor house still has its original dining room. The spic-and-span rooms in the newer block are fine but the 'feature rooms' and barn suites (timbered charmers with four-posters) have all the atmosphere.

Ye Olde Ferrie Inn PUB ££
(📞 01600-890232; www.yeoldferrieinn.com; Ferrie Lane; mains £9-11; ☺ noon-11pm; P 🛜) Since 1473 this diamond-in-the-rough has been filling bellies on the western shores of Symonds Yat. Options include ploughman's boards, juicy burgers and all the usual pub-grub suspects (steaks, sausages etc). The upstairs rooms all have bathrooms and river views.

❶ Getting There & Away

➡ Buses head from Gloucester to Coleford (route 23/30/31; £3.40, 1¼ hours) and to Newent (32/132; £2.40, 30 minutes); and from Monmouth to Coleford (35; £2.40, 22 minutes) and Goodrich (34; £2.20, 19 minutes).

➡ National Express coaches head to Newent from London Victoria (£25, 3¾ hours), Cirencester (£6, 1¼ hours), Gloucester (£3, 25 minutes) and Hereford (£5, 45 minutes).

BUCKINGHAMSHIRE, BEDFORDSHIRE & HERTFORDSHIRE

Now on the edge of London's commuter belt, these counties once served as rural boltholes for the city's rich and titled, especially when the stench and grime of the industrial age was at its peak. The sweeping valleys and forested hills are still scattered with majestic stately homes and grand gardens, many of which are open to the public.

Stowe

Located 3 miles northwest of the market town of Buckingham, Stowe has had a manor since before the Norman conquest. While the current incarnation of the house is suitably grand, the real attraction here is the extraordinary Georgian garden. The most spectacular approach is by way of the 1.5-mile-long tree-lined Stowe Ave.

⦿ Sights

Stowe Gardens GARDENS
(NT; www.nationaltrust.org.uk; adult/child £9/5; ☺ 10am-6pm Mar-Oct, to 4pm Nov-Feb) Covering 400 hectares, these glorious gardens were shaped in the 18th century by Britain's greatest landscape gardeners, including Lancelot 'Capability' Brown. They are best known for their 32 temples and other follies, commissioned by the superwealthy Richard Temple (1st Viscount Cobham), whose family motto was *Templa Quam Delecta* (How Delightful are Your Temples).

Stowe House HOUSE
(📞 01280-818166; www.stowe.co.uk/house; adult/child £5.70/free, incl Stowe Gardens £14) Neoclassical Stowe House now houses a private school so exclusive that its driveway is half a mile long. Mere mortals are permitted to visit the eight state rooms by way of guided tours; call or check the website for times. Although the rooms are left bare (the house's contents were sold off to rescue the original owners from financial disaster), the sheer scale and ornamentation of the building is highly impressive.

Bletchley

Once England's best-kept secret, **Bletchley Park** (www.bletchleypark.org.uk; adult/child £15/9; ☺ 9.30am-4pm) was the scene of a huge code-breaking operation during WWII, dramatised in the 2001 film *Enigma*. Almost 8500 people worked here in total secrecy – intercepting, decrypting, translating and interpreting enemy correspondence. Bletchley is just south of Milton Keynes off the B4034. Regular trains head here from London Euston (£19, 40 minutes).

Entry includes an optional hour-long guided tour of the grounds and a multimedia guide. It gives you a real insight into the complex code-breaking process and the hard work, frustration and successes that shaped this secret war effort. Inside Station X you can also see the Enigma machine itself – crucial to the breaking of the code.

Woburn

POP 935

Blissfully set within the Bedfordshire countryside, this peaceful village has existed since the 10th century. Despite having a couple of big attractions and a Michelin-starred restaurant, it's still charmingly sleepy.

Sights

Woburn Abbey HOUSE
(www.woburn.co.uk; Park St; adult/child £15/7.25; ⊙house 11am-5pm Easter-Oct) Originally a Cistercian abbey but dissolved by Henry VIII and awarded to the Earl of Bedford (the current Duke of Bedford still calls it home), Woburn Abbey is a wonderful country pile set within a 1200-hectare deer park. The opulent house displays paintings by Gainsborough, van Dyck and Canaletto. Highlights include Queen Victoria's bedroom, the beautiful wall hangings and cabinets of the Chinese Room, plus the mysterious story of the Flying Duchess.

Woburn Safari Park ZOO
(www.woburnsafari.co.uk; adult/child £21/16; ⊙10am-5pm) This is the country's largest drive-through animal reserve. Rhinos, tigers, lions, zebras, bison, monkeys, elephants and giraffes roam the grounds, while in the 'foot safari' area, you can see sea lions, penguins and lemurs.

Eating

 Paris House MODERN BRITISH £££
(☑01525-290692; www.parishouse.co.uk; London Rd; lunch £39, dinner £71-98; ⊙noon-2pm & 7-10pm Wed-Sat, noon-8pm Sun) On the Woburn Estate, Paris House is a pretty black-and-white structure that a previous duke of Bed-

ford took a shine to on a visit to the French capital and had shipped back here. During WWII the Queen often stayed here. Now it's Bedfordshire's best restaurant, serving exquisite set tasting menus of beautifully presented contemporary cuisine.

ⓘ Information

The Woburn Passport ticket (adult/child £27/20) can be used on two separate days within any 12-month period and gives access to both Woburn Abbey and Safari Park.

Waddesdon

POP 1800

A remarkable French Rensaissance chateau-style fairy-tale palace, **Waddesdon Manor** (NT; www.waddesdon.org.uk; adult/child £18/9, garden only £8/4; ⊙10am-5pm Wed-Sun Apr-Dec) was completed in 1889 for the Baron Ferdinand de Rothschild so that he could showcase his collection of French decorative arts and throw glamorous parties. Taking in the ostentatious magnificence of the house, it's not difficult to imagine the great and good of Victorian society living it up in the palatial rooms.

Very little space is left unadorned – only the Bachelor's Wing stands out as being noticeably more restrained. On display is the outstanding collection of Dutch Old Masters and English portraits, Sèvres porcelain, ornate furniture and the extensive wine cellar. The beautiful gardens boast formal parterres, contemporary sculptures and a rococo-revival aviary filled with exotic birds.

On the edge of the grounds, in Waddeson village, **Five Arrows Hotel** (☑01296-651727; www.thefivearrows.co.uk; s/d from £75/105; P 🛜) is an elaborate half-timbered inn that was originally built to house the artisans working on the manor. Inside, the 16 rooms are nicely renovated, and the downstairs restaurant serves a great cooked breakfast. Guests are entitled to free access to the manor gardens.

Waddesdon is on the A41, 5 miles northwest of Aylesbury.

St Albans

POP 57,800

Under the name Verulamium, this was the third biggest city in Roman Britain. Its current name derives from Alban, a Christian Roman soldier who was martyred here in about AD 250, becoming the first English martyr. These days it's a bustling and prosperous market town with a host of crooked Tudor buildings and elegant Georgian town houses.

Things look a little more crooked and less elegant in late September during the very popular beer and cider festival (http://st albansbeerfestival.org.uk).

⊙ Sights

★ **St Alban's Cathedral** CATHEDRAL
(www.stalbanscathedral.org; off High St & Holywell Hill; ⊙8.30am-5.45pm, free tours 11.30am & 2.30pm Mon-Sat, 2.30pm Sun) Built by King Offa of Mercia in 793 around the tomb of St Alban, this massive cathedral is a magnificent melange of Norman Romanesque and Gothic architecture. The longest medieval nave in the country gives way to ornate ceilings, semi-lost wall paintings, an elaborate nave screen and, of course, the shrine of St Alban, hiding behind a stone reredos.

Verulamium Museum MUSEUM
(www.stalbansmuseums.org.uk; St Michael's St; adult/child £5/2.50; ⊙10am-5.30pm Mon-Sat, 2-5.30pm Sun) This fantastic exposé of everyday life under the Romans includes household objects, legionnaires' armour, statuary, jewellery, glassware and grave goods. The highlight, however, is the Mosaic Room, where five superb mosaic floors, uncovered between 1930 and 1955, are laid out.

Adjacent Verulamium Park has the remains of a basilica, bathhouse and parts of the city wall, and across the busy A4147 are the grassy foundations of a Roman theatre, which once seated 2000 spectators.

✕ Eating

Lussmanns Fish & Grill MODERN BRITISH ££
(✆01727-851941; www.lussmans.com; Waxhouse Gate, off High St; mains £12-20; ⊙noon-9.30pm) This bright, modern restaurant just off the main street serves a changing menu of creative British dishes with Mediterranean touches. Ingredients are ethically and mostly locally sourced.

❶ Information

Tourist Office (✆01727-864511; www.enjoyst albans.com; Market Pl; ⊙10am-4.30pm Mon-Sat)

❶ Getting There & Away

Regular trains run between London St Pancras and St Albans (£12, 30 minutes), with less frequent services from London Blackfriars.

DON'T MISS

WARNER BROS STUDIO TOUR: THE MAKING OF HARRY POTTER

Whether you're a fairweather fan or a full-on Pothead, the **Warner Bros Studio Tour: the Making of Harry Potter** (✆0845 084 0900; www.wbstudiotour.co.uk; Studio Tour Drive, Leavesden; adult/child £31/24; ⊙9am-9.30pm) is well worth the admittedly hefty admission price. You'll need to prebook your visit for an allocated timeslot and then allow two- to three-hours to do the complex justice. It starts with a short film before you're ushered through giant doors into the actual set of Hogwarts' Great Hall – the first of many 'wow' moments.

From here, you're left to explore the rest of the complex on your own, including a large hangar featuring all of the most familiar interior sets (Dumbledore's office, the Gryffindor common room, Hagrid's hut) and an outdoor section with the exterior of Privet Drive, the purple triple-decker Knight Bus and a shop selling butterbeer (super sweet, but worth trying). Along the way, video screens burst into life to discuss elements of the production. The attention to detail is fascinating: there's even a section devoted to the graphic design of elements such as the cereal boxes in the Weasley kitchen!

Other highlights include the animatronic workshop (say 'hi' to the Hippogriff) and a stroll along Diagon Alley. But the most magical treat is kept to last – a giant, gasp-inducing scale-model of Hogwarts, which was used for the exterior shots. Then comes the biggest challenge for true fans and parents, a quite extraordinary gift shop stocked with all your wizardry accessories, including uniforms for each of the Hogwarts houses and replicas of the individually designed wands used by pretty much any character you can think of.

If you're driving, there's a large free car park and extensive directions on the website. Otherwise, train to Watford Junction from London Euston (£9.50, 20 minutes), Bletchley (£15, 34 minutes), Northampton (£22, 40 minutes), Coventry (£20, 45 minutes) or Birmingham (£20, 1½ hours) and then catch the shuttle bus (return £2).

THE THAMES VALLEY

This rather posh and prosperous part of the world acts as a country getaway for some of England's most influential figures. Within easy reach of London and yet entirely different in character, the pastoral landscape features handsome villages and historic houses, as well as some of the top attractions in the country.

Windsor & Eton

POP 33,400

Dominated by the massive bulk of Windsor Castle, these twin towns have a rather surreal atmosphere, with the morning pomp and ceremony of the changing of the guards in Windsor, and the sight of school boys dressed in formal tailcoats wandering the streets of tiny Eton.

Windsor town centre is full of expensive boutiques, grand cafes and trendy restaurants. Eton, by comparison, is far quieter, its one-street centre lined with antique shops and art galleries. Both are easily doable as a day trip from London.

⊙ Sights

★Windsor Castle   CASTLE, PALACE
(www.royalcollection.org.uk; Castle Hill; adult/child £19/11; ⊙9.45am-5.15pm) The largest and oldest occupied fortress in the world, Windsor Castle is a majestic vision of battlements and towers. It's used for state occasions and is one of the Queen's principal residences; if she's at home, you'll see the Royal Standard flying from the Round Tower. Join a free guided tour (every half-hour) or take a multilingual audio tour of the lavish state rooms and beautiful chapels. Note, some sections may be off-limits on any given day if they're in use.

William the Conqueror first established a royal residence in Windsor in 1070; since then successive monarchs have rebuilt,

Windsor & Eton

remodelled and refurbished the castle complex to create the massive and sumptuous palace that stands here today. Henry II replaced the wooden stockade in 1165 with a stone round tower and built the outer walls to the north, east and south; Charles II gave the state apartments a baroque makeover; George IV swept in with his preference for Gothic style; and Queen Victoria refurbished a beautiful chapel in memory of her beloved Albert.

➡ **Queen Mary's Dolls' House**

Your first stop is likely to be the incredible dolls' house designed by Sir Edwin Lutyens for Queen Mary in 1924. The attention to detail is spellbinding – there's running water, electricity and lighting, tiny Crown Jewels and vintage wine in the cellar!

➡ **State Apartments**

The **Grand Staircase** sets the tone for a set of absolutely spectacular rooms, dripping in gilt and screaming 'royal' from every painted surface and sparkling chandelier. Highlights include **St George's Hall**, used for state banquets of up to 160 people. For more intimate gatherings (just 60 people), the Queen entertains in the **Waterloo Chamber**, its paintings commemorating the victory over Napoleon.

➡ **St George's Chapel**

This elegant chapel, commissioned for the Order of the Garter by Edward IV in 1475, is one of Britain's finest examples of Perpendicular Gothic architecture. The nave and fan-vaulted roof were completed under Henry VII, but the final nail was struck under Henry VIII in 1528.

Along with Westminster Abbey, it serves as a royal mausoleum, housing the remains of numerous royals, including Henry VIII, Charles I and the present queen's father (King George VI), mother (Queen Elizabeth) and sister (Princess Margaret).

St George's Chapel closes on Sunday, but time your visit well and you can attend a morning service or Evensong at 5.15pm daily.

➡ **Albert Memorial Chapel**

Built in 1240 and dedicated to St Edward the Confessor, this small chapel was the place of worship for the Order of the Garter until St George's Chapel snatched that honour. After the death of Prince Albert at Windsor Castle in 1861, Queen Victoria ordered its elaborate redecoration as a tribute to her husband. A major feature of the restoration is the magnificent vaulted roof, whose gold mosaic pieces were crafted in Venice. There's a monument to the prince, although he's actually buried with Queen Victoria in the Frogmore Royal Mausoleum in the castle grounds.

➡ **Changing of the Guard**

A fabulous spectacle, with triumphant tunes from a military band and plenty of foot stamping, the changing of the guard draws crowds to the castle gates each day to watch the smartly attired lads in red uniforms and bear-fur hats do their thing. The spectacle takes place at 11am Monday to Saturday from April to July, and on alternate days from August to March. Stay to the right of the crowd for better views.

Eton College　　　　　NOTABLE BUILDING

(www.etoncollege.com) Eton is the largest and most famous public (meaning very private) school in England, and arguably the most enduring and illustrious symbol of England's class system. At the time of writing, it wasn't possible to visit the school due to building work, but check the visitors tab on their website to see whether tours have resumed.

Eton was founded by Henry VI in 1440 with a view towards educating 70 highly qualified boys awarded a scholarship from a fund endowed by the king. Every year since then, 70 King's Scholars (aged 12 to 14) have been chosen based on the results of a highly competitive exam; these pupils are housed in separate quarters from the rest of the 1300 or so other students. All the boys are boarders and must wear

ROYAL ASCOT

Get out your Sunday best and join the glitterati for the biggest **racing meet** (www.ascot.co.uk; Silver Ring per day £25, Grandstand per day £65; ⊘ mid-June) of the year. The royal family, A-list celebrities and the rich and famous gather here to show off their Jimmy Choos and place the odd bet. It's essential to book tickets for this five-day festival well in advance.

You can soak up the atmosphere from the Silver Ring for a mere £25 or head for the Grandstand, where you can rub shoulders with the posh ladies in fancy hats for £65 a day.

formal tailcoats, waistcoats and white collars to lessons (though the top hats went out in 1948).

Those who have studied here include 19 prime ministers, countless princes, kings and maharajahs, famous explorers, authors and economists – among them Princes William and Harry, George Orwell, Ian Fleming, Aldous Huxley, John Maynard Keynes and Bear Grylls.

★ **Windsor Great Park**   PARK
Stretching behind Windsor Castle almost all the way to Ascot, Windsor Great Park covers about 8 sq miles and features a lake, walking tracks, a bridleway and gardens. The Long Walk is a 3-mile jaunt along a tree-lined path from King George IV Gate to the Copper Horse statue (of George III) on Snow Hill, the highest point of the park.

Savill Garden   GARDENS
(www.theroyallandscape.co.uk; Wick Lane, Englefield Green; adult/child £9.50/4.25; ⊘ 10am-6pm Mar-Oct, to 4.30pm Nov-Feb) Created in the 1930s in the southern reaches of the Windsor Great Park, this pretty 14-hectare garden includes ornamental beds and woodlands. Head southeast on the A308 and follow the brown signs. It's 4.5 miles from Windsor Castle.

Runnymede   HISTORIC SITE
(NT; www.nationaltrust.org.uk; Windsor Rd, Old Windsor; parking per hr £1.50; ⊘ car park 8.30am-7pm Apr-Sep, to 5pm Oct-Mar) **FREE** In June 1215, King John met his barons in a field 3 miles southeast of Windsor, and over the next few

days they hammered out an agreement on a basic charter of rights guaranteeing the liberties of the king's subjects and restricting the monarch's absolute power. The document they signed was the Magna Carta, the world's first constitution. Today, the field remains pretty much as it was, except that it now features two lodges (1930) designed by Edward Lutyens.

The Magna Carta formed the basis for statutes and charters throughout the world's democracies. Both the national and state constitutions of the USA, drawn up more than 500 years later, paraphrase it. To recognise its importance, the American Bar Association erected a memorial here in 1957 in the form of a Greek temple. Nearby, an acre of land was gifted to the US in 1963 as a memorial to President John F Kennedy.

After stomping through the muddy field to the two memorials (wear sensible shoes), it's possible to continue up the hill on a two-hour loop track to the moving **Commonwealth Airforces Memorial**, where the names of 20,000 WWII airmen without graves from the UK, Canada, New Zealand, Australia, India and South Africa are inscribed.

Runnymede is on the A308, 3 miles southeast of Windsor.

☞ Tours

French Brothers   BOAT TOUR
(☑ 01753-851900; www.frenchbrothers.co.uk; Windsor Promenade, Barry Ave; ⊘ 11am-5pm Easter-Oct) Offers a variety of boat trips to Runnymede (adult/child £13/8.65) and around Windsor (adult/child from £6.70/4.50).

Royal Windsor Town Walks   WALKING TOUR
(☑ 01753-743900; www.windsor.gov.uk; adult/child £7/6; ⊘ 11.30am Sat & 2.30pm Sun Apr-Sep) Book at the tourist office or online.

🛏 Sleeping

Windsor is an easy day trip from London but overnighting allows you to see the town return to its normally sleepy state after the hordes of visitors have gone home.

76 Duke Street   B&B **££**
(☑ 01753-620636; www.76dukestreet.co.uk; 76 Duke St; s/d £85/100; 🐾) Presided over by a welcoming hostess, this centrally located B&B offers two immaculate double rooms. The second bedroom is only available if booked along with the first, so it's ideal for a family or two couples.

Rutlands   B&B **££**
(✆01753-859533; www.therutlandsbedandbreak-
fast.co.uk; 102 St Leonards Rd; s/d from £55/85, s
without bathroom £40; P✉) Close to the town
centre and with two extremely handy car spaces, this six-room B&B is a comfortable choice.
The rooms are smartly renovated; some have
chandeliers and moulded fireplaces.

Macdonald Windsor Hotel   HOTEL **£££**
(✆0844 879 9101; www.macdonaldhotels.co.uk/
Windsor; 23 High St; r from £149; P✉) Looking
small and quaint from the road but magically hiding 120 spacious rooms within, the
Windsor is the slickest choice in town. Dark
browns and creams add a rich earthy feel to
the resolutely modern decor.

✖ Eating

✖ Windsor

Meimo   MOROCCAN, MEDITERRANEAN **££**
(✆01753-862222; www.meimo.co.uk; 69-70 Peas-
cod St; mains £9-17; ⊙11am-10pm) Bright colours, glass lanterns and draped fabrics bring
North African sunshine into this bastion of
Englishness. The tagines are excellent, delivered bubbling to the table. Pasta, steaks and
fish dishes round out the menu.

Green Olive   GREEK **££**
(✆01753-866655; www.green-olive.co.uk; 10 High
St; mains £13-20; ⊙noon-3pm & 6-10pm; ✎)
A great spot for a light lunch, Green Olive
dishes up generous portions of traditional
Greek mezze and some interesting dessert
choices in bright, simple surroundings.

✖ Eton

Zero 3   SANDWICHES, CAFE **£**
(www.facebook.com/zero3eton; 45 High St; mains
£4-9; ⊙8.30am-4pm) A posh take on a diner,
with lots of shiny chrome and Hollywood
headshots, Zero 3 delivers a lengthy menu of
cooked breakfasts, grills, pasta, salads, burgers and jacket potatoes. Alternatively, grab a
sandwich to eat by the river.

Gilbey's   MODERN BRITISH **£££**
(✆01753-854921; www.gilbeygroup.com; 82-83
High St; 2-/3-course menu £20/26; ⊙noon-3pm
Tue-Sun, 6-10pm daily) Small but perfectly
formed, this restaurant is one of the area's
best. Terracotta tiling, and a sunny courtyard garden and conservatory give Gilbey's
a Continental cafe feel, complemented by a
superb modern British menu.

🍷 Drinking & Nightlife

Two Brewers   PUB
(www.twobrewerswindsor.co.uk; 34 Park St;
⊙11.30am-11pm) Posh folk with dogs congregate in this atmospheric 17th-century inn
perched on the edge of Windsor Great Park.
Think low beamed ceilings, dim lighting,
hearty pub meals and a roaring fire in winter.

Windsor & Eton Brewery   BREWERY
(www.webrew.co.uk; Duke St; ⊙9am-6pm Mon-Fri,
to 3pm Sat) Call into this boutique brewery to
sample and stock up on hoppy delights such
as the award-winning Knight of the Garter
pale ale, Guardsman Best Bitter or the royal-
wedding special, the Windsor Knot.

ℹ Information

Royal Windsor Information Centre (www.
windsor.gov.uk; Old Booking Hall, Windsor
Royal Shopping Arcade; ⊙9.30am-5pm) Pick
up a heritage walk brochure (50p).

ℹ Getting There & Away

➜ Buses head to/from Bray (route 6/16;
£4, 36 minutes) and Heathrow terminal 5
(60/61/71/77; £4.70, 52 minutes).

➜ Green Line (www.greenline.co.uk) coaches
head to London (£5, 1½ hours).

➜ Trains from Windsor Riverside station go
directly to London Waterloo (£9.80, one hour),
although trains from Windsor Central, changing
at Slough for London Paddington, are considerably quicker (between 26 and 44 minutes).

Bray

It's strange to think that this tiny village of
flint, brick and half-timbered cottages strung
along the Thames could be the gastronomic
capital of Britain. Yet Bray is home to two of
only four restaurants in the UK to be rated

READING FESTIVAL

Each August Bank Holiday weekend, up
to 87,000 revellers descend on the industrial town of Reading for one of the
country's biggest rock-music events.
The **Reading Festival** (www.reading-
festival.com; tickets £100-213; ⊙Aug) is
a three-day extravaganza featuring
a top line-up of rock, indie, punk and
alternative artists. Tickets will set you
back about £100 per day or £213 for a
three-day pass.

---

three-star (the highest possible honour) by foodie bible, the Michelin guide. On top of that, two of the local pubs also sport a star.

Arguably the most famous restaurant in the country, The Fat Duck – whizz-bang chef Heston Blumenthal's signature eatery – is exceedingly difficult to get into at the best of times (even at £195 per head), but with the news that he's going to be shifting the entire operation to Melbourne, Australia, for six months in 2015, you might want to leave it on your bucket list a little longer.

✕ Eating

★ **Waterside Inn**   FRENCH £££
(☑ 01628-620691; www.waterside-inn.co.uk; Ferry Rd; mains £50-59, 2-/3-course lunch £46/60; ⊙ noon-2pm & 7-10pm Wed-Sun, closed end Dec–end Jan) From the moment the uniformed valet opens your car door, until the last tray of *petits fours* is served, you know you're somewhere special. For more than 40 years chef Alain Roux has been working his magic here, constructing exceptional dishes for the small army of staff to serve, in a room looking straight out to the Thames. It also has rooms.

★ **Hind's Head**   GASTROPUB £££
(☑ 01628-626151; www.hindsheadbray.com; High St; mains £16-33; ⊙ 11.30am-11pm Mon-Sat, noon-4pm Sun) Oozing atmosphere, this 15th-century pub offers a chance to experience some of Heston Blumenthal's creative cuisine in a relatively affordable and informal setting. The food's less zany than at his sig-nature restaurant, The Fat Duck, but there are still plenty of whimsical touches – try the fish pie topped with 'surf' (crispy kale) and 'sand' (anchovy crumb).

❶ Getting There & Away

Courtney (www.courtneybuses.com) has buses to/from Windsor (route 6/16; £4; 36 minutes).

Henley-on-Thames

POP 11,500

The attractive commuter town of Henley is synonymous with the **Henley Royal Regatta** (www.hrr.co.uk; tickets £18-24 ; ⊙ Jul), a world-famous rowing tournament that sees the town bursting into action in July. The five-day regatta has grown into a major fixture in the social calendar of the upwardly mobile, and although rowers of the highest calibre take part, the main event is rather overshadowed by the champagne-fuelled antics of the wealthy who come here to see and be seen. Still, picnicking in the public enclosure and watching the rowers' straining muscles as the boats whizz by makes for a good day out in sunny weather.

Taking place each July in the week following the famous Henley Royal Regatta, the **Henley Festival** (www.henley-festival.co.uk; ⊙ Jul) is a vibrant dressed-up affair that features everything from opera to rock, jazz, comedy and swing. The main events take place on a floating stage on the Thames.

Bath & Southwest England

Why Go?

England's southwest is simply spectacular. Here the past is ever present – prepare for close encounters with iconic stone circles, Iron Age hill forts and Roman baths. Blockbuster stately homes border romantic castles; serene cathedrals frame sumptuous Georgian cityscapes. The landscape immerses you in the myths of Kings Arthur and Alfred the Great, and the writings of Thomas Hardy, Jane Austen and Daphne du Maurier.

But the southwest also has an eye to the future. Here you can tour alternative eco-towns, pioneering restaurants and cool surfer hang-outs, and sleep in campsites peppered with chic yurts and retro campervans. Then there are three wildlife-rich national parks, fossil-studded shores, England's best surf spots and a coastline flecked with exquisite bays, towering rock formations and tranquil sweeps of sandy beach. It all gives you a bit of a dilemma – with the Westcountry you won't know what to do first.

Best Places to Eat

➡ Restaurant Nathan Outlaw (p343)

➡ Riverford Field Kitchen (p295)

➡ Circus (p328)

➡ The Pig (p243)

Best Places to Stay

➡ Vintage Vacations (p247)

➡ Scarlet (p344)

➡ Lulworth Cove (p256)

➡ Tide House (p349)

When to Go

➡ Cliffs, hillsides and formal gardens burst into fragrance and blooms in April and May, when seasonal attractions also reopen and boat trips start.

➡ Music festival fever takes hold in June at ultra-cool Glastonbury (p333), on the funky Isle of Wight (p247).

➡ The peak holiday season and the best weather (in theory) is in July and August.

➡ The end of school summer holidays in September brings cheaper sleep spots, quieter beaches and warmer seas. The Isle of Wight goes all groovy at bohemian Bestival (p247).

➡ Bigger waves draw surfers to Cornwall and north Devon in October; meanwhile Exmoor's deer rut sees huge stags battle for supremacy and the winter storm watching season begins.

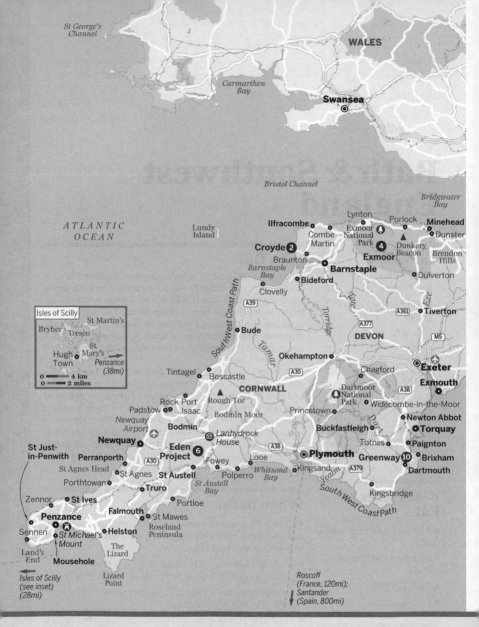

Bath & Southwest England Highlights

1 Securing a space on a magical dawn walk inside the massive sarsen ring at **Stonehenge** (p271)

2 Soaking up beach life on the white sands of Porthcurno

or at a quaint surf spot, such as **Croyde** (p308)

3 Strolling England's most glorious Georgian street, Bath's **Royal Crescent** (p323)

4 Striding the high hills of **Exmoor** (p278), Dartmoor and Bodmin Moor

5 Staring at Henry VIII's warship the Mary Rose, in **Portsmouth** (p238)

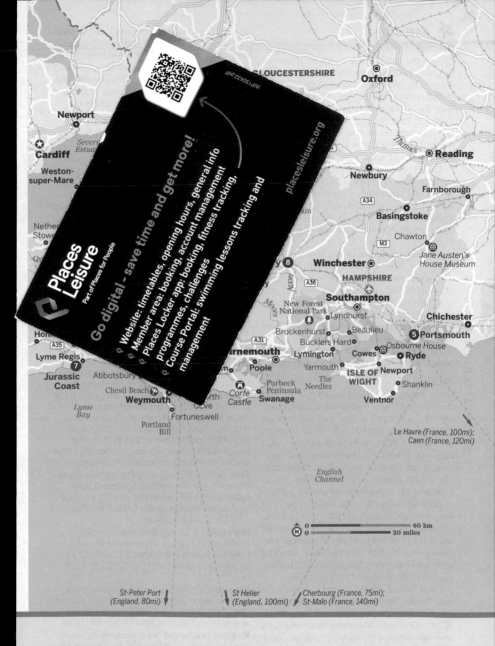

GLOUCESTERSHIRE

Oxford

Newport

Cardiff

Weston-super-Mare

Severn Estuary

Reading

Newbury

Farnborough

A34

Basingstoke

Nether Stowey

Chawton

M3

Jane Austen's House Museum

Winchester

HAMPSHIRE

Southampton

Axe

A36

New Forest National Park

Lyndhurst

Chichester

Home

A35

Brockenhurst

Bucklers Hard

Beaulieu

Portsmouth

5

Osbourne House

Lyme Regis

7

Jurassic Coast

Abbotsbury

rnemouth

Lymington

Cowes

Ryde

Poole

Yarmouth

ISLE OF WIGHT

Newport

Chesil Beach

Weymouth

Corfe Castle

Purbeck Peninsula

The Needles

Shanklin

A31

Bucklers Hard

Fortuneswell

Swanage

Ventnor

Lyme Bay

Portland Bill

Le Havre (France, 100mi); Caen (France, 120mi)

English Channel

0 — 40 km
0 — 20 miles

St-Peter Port (England, 80mi)

St Helier (England, 100mi)

Cherbourg (France, 75mi); St-Malo (France, 140mi)

Places Leisure
Part of Places for People

Go digital – save time and get more!

Website: timetables, opening hours, general info
Member area: booking, account management
Places Locker app: booking, fitness tracking,
programmes, challenges
Course Portal: swimming lessons tracking and
management

placesleisure.org

INP150A32.pdf

6 Marvelling at the space-age biomes of the **Eden Project** (p359)

7 Foraging for 200-million-year-old fossils on Dorset's **Jurassic Coast** (p263)

8 Savouring the serene cathedrals at **Salisbury** (p267), Exeter, Winchester and Wells

9 Stepping on the deck of Brunel's groundbreaking

steamship, the **SS Great Britain** (p310) in Bristol

10 Discovering the locations behind the murder plots at Agatha Christie's enchanting home, **Greenway** (p292)

🏃 Activities

Cycling

Cycling the southwest is a superb, if strenuous, way to experience England's great outdoors. The region's National Cycle Network (NCN) routes include the **West Country Way** (NCN Route 3), a 240-mile jaunt from Bristol to Padstow via Glastonbury, Taunton and Barnstaple, and the 103-mile **Devon Coast to Coast Cycle Route** (NCN Route 27) between Ilfracombe and Plymouth.

The 160-mile, circular **Wiltshire Cycleway** skirts the county's borders. In Hampshire, the New Forest's hundreds of miles of cycle paths snake through a wildlife-rich environment, while the Isle of Wight boasts 62 miles of bike-friendly routes and its very own cycling festival.

Off-road mountain-biking highlights include the North Wessex Downs, Exmoor National Park and Dartmoor National Park. Many cycle trails trace the routes of old railway lines, including Devon's 11-mile **Granite Way** between Okehampton and Lydford, and Cornwall's popular 18-mile **Camel Trail** linking Padstow with Bodmin Moor.

For more information contact **Sustrans** (www.sustrans.org.uk) and local tourist offices.

Walking

Often called the 630-mile adventure, the **South West Coast Path** (www.southwestcoastpath.com) is Britain's longest national walking trail, stretching from Minehead on Exmoor, via Land's End to Poole in Dorset. You can pick it up along the coast for short and spectacular day hikes or tackle longer stretches. The **South West Coast Path Association** (www.swcp.org.uk) publishes an annual guide.

For wilderness hikes, the national parks of Dartmoor and Exmoor are hard to beat. Dartmoor is bigger and more remote; Exmoor's ace in the pack is a cracking 34 miles of precipitous coast. The region's third national park, the New Forest, is a gentler affair, offering hundreds of miles of heritage trails.

Other hiking highlights are Exmoor's 51-mile **Coleridge Way** (www.coleridgeway.co.uk), the Isle of Wight and Bodmin Moor, while Wiltshire's 87-mile **Ridgeway National Trail** (www.nationaltrail.co.uk/ridgeway) starts near Avebury and winds through chalk downland and the wooded Chiltern hills.

Surfing & Boating

North Cornwall, and to a lesser extent north Devon, serve up the best surf in England. Party-town Newquay is the epicentre; other top spots are Bude in Cornwall and Croyde in Devon. Region-wide surf conditions can be found at www.magicseaweed.com.

Sailing highlights includes Britain's 2012 Olympic sailing venues at Weymouth and Portland and the yachting havens of the Isle of Wight, Falmouth, Dartmouth and Poole.

Other Activities

The southwest is also prime territory for kitesurfing, windsurfing, diving, sea kayaking, white-water kayaking and wakeboarding. The sport of stand-up paddleboarding (SUP) continues to grow in popularity, especially in calm water spots.

Plenty of firms also offer caving, coasteering, mountain boarding, climbing and kite-buggying. Check out www.visitsouthwest.co.uk for operators.

ℹ Getting Around

It is possible to travel the southwest using public transport, but services to remote areas are limited; using your own wheels gives you more flexibility. **Traveline South West** (✆0871 200 2233; www.travelinesw.com) provides region-wide bus and train timetable info.

BUS

The region's bus network is fairly comprehensive, but becomes patchy away from main towns. **National Express** (www.nationalexpress.com) often provides the quickest bus link between cities and larger towns. **PlusBus** (www.plusbus.info) adds local bus travel to your train ticket (from £2 per day). Participating cities include Bath, Bournemouth, Bristol, Exeter, Plymouth, Salisbury, Truro and Weymouth. Buy tickets at train stations.

First (www.firstgroup.com) The region's largest bus company. The FirstDay Southwest ticket (adult/child £7/6) is valid for one day on many First buses. Weekly passes (adult/child from £37/23) are also available.

More (Wilts & Dorset; www.wdbus.co.uk) Useful service across Wiltshire and Dorset. Does day tickets (adult/child £8.50/5.50) and seven-day network tickets (£25/20) for south coast routes.

Stagecoach (www.stagecoachbus.com) A key provider in Hampshire and Devon. Offers a range of one-day tickets (adult/child from £4/3) and weekly Megarider fares from £8 (no child fare).

Western Greyhound (www.westerngreyhound.com) Key operator in Cornwall. Its day explorer tickets cost adult/child £8.50/5.50.

CAR

The main car-hire firms have offices at the region's airports and main-line train stations; rates reflect those elsewhere in the UK.

TRAIN

Bristol is a main train hub with links including those to London Paddington, Scotland and Birmingham, plus services to Bath, Swindon, Chippenham, Weymouth, Southampton and Portsmouth. Trains from London Waterloo travel to Bournemouth, Salisbury, Southampton, Portsmouth and Weymouth.

Stops on the London Paddington–Penzance service include Exeter, Plymouth, Liskeard, St Austell and Truro. Spur lines run to Barnstaple, Paignton, Gunnislake, Looe, Falmouth, St Ives and Newquay.

The Freedom of the South West Rover pass (adult/child £110/55) allows eight days' unlimited travel over 15 days in an area west of, and including, Salisbury, Bath, Bristol and Weymouth.

HAMPSHIRE

Hampshire's history is regal and rich. Kings Alfred the Great, Knut and William the Conqueror all based their reigns in its ancient cathedral city of Winchester, whose jumble of historic buildings sits in the centre of undulating chalk downs. The county's coast is awash with heritage too – in rejuvenated Portsmouth you can clamber aboard the pride of Nelson's navy, HMS *Victory*, and wonder at the *Mary Rose* (Henry VIII's flagship), before wandering wharfs buzzing with restaurants, shops and bars. Hampshire's southwestern corner claims the open heath and woods of the New Forest and, just offshore, the hip holiday hot spot that is the Isle of Wight.

Winchester

POP 116,600

Calm, collegiate Winchester is a mellow must-see. The past still echoes strongly around the flint-flecked walls of this ancient cathedral city. It was the capital of Saxon kings and a power base of bishops, and its statues and sights evoke two of England's mightiest myth-makers: Alfred the Great and King Arthur (he of the round table). Winchester's architecture is exquisite, from the handsome Elizabethan and Regency buildings in the narrow streets to the wondrous cathedral at its core, while its river valley location means there are charming waterside trails to explore.

History

The Romans built a defended settlement at Winchester in AD 70, but the city really took off when the powerful West Saxon bishops moved their episcopal see here in AD 670. Thereafter, Winchester was the most important town in the powerful kingdom of Wessex. King Alfred the Great (r 871–99) made it his capital, and it remained so under Knut (r 1016–35) and the Danish kings. After the Norman invasion of 1066, William the Conqueror commissioned local monks to write the ground-breaking Domesday Book (1086), an administrative survey of the entire country and the most significant clerical accomplishment of the Middle Ages. Winchester thrived until the 12th century, when a fire gutted most of the city – after this, London took its crown. In the 18th century the city was revived as a trading centre.

◉ Sights

★ **Winchester Cathedral**　　　CATHEDRAL
(☏ 01962-857225; www.winchester-cathedral.org. uk; The Close; adult/child incl cathedral body & crypt tours £7.50/free; ☉ 9.30am-5pm Sat, 12.30-3pm Sun) One of southern England's most awe-inspiring buildings, 11th-century Winchester Cathedral boasts a fine Gothic facade, one of the longest medieval naves in Europe (164m), and a fascinating jumble of features from all eras. Other highlights include the intricately carved medieval choir stalls, which sport everything from mythical beasts to a mischievous green man, and one of the UK's finest illuminated manuscripts. The cathedral's three separate, excellent tours (p236) of the ground floor, crypt and tower can get busy – book ahead.

Today's cathedral sits beside foundations that mark Winchester's original 7th-century minster church. The cathedral was begun in 1070 and completed in 1093, and was subsequently entrusted with the bones of its patron saint, St Swithin (Bishop of Winchester from 852 to 862). He is best known for the proverb stating if it rains on St Swithin's Day (15 July), it will rain for a further 40 days and 40 nights.

Soggy ground and poor workmanship spelled disaster for the early church. The original tower collapsed in 1107 and major restructuring continued until the mid-15th century. Look out for the monument at the far end of the building to diver William Walker; he saved the cathedral from collapse by delving repeatedly into its waterlogged underbelly from 1906 to 1912 to bolster rotting wooden foundations with vast quantities of concrete and brick.

Choral evensong (5.30pm Monday to Saturday and 3.30pm Sunday) is intensely

Winchester

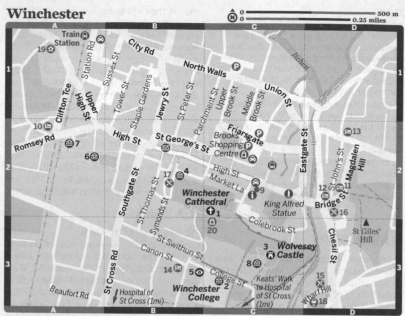

Winchester

atmospheric; Sunday services take place at 7.40am, 8am and 10am.

➡ **Winchester Bible & Triforium Gallery** (🕙10.30am-4pm Tue-Sat, 2-4pm Mon) As the biggest, brightest and best-surviving 12th-century English bible, the dazzling Winchester Bible has vivid illuminated pages. It was commissioned in 1160, possibly by the grandson of William the Conqueror. The treasures in the Triforium Gallery include rare late-Saxon glass and a 15th-century Madonna and child, part of the medieval Great Screen. Admission is included with Winchester Cathedral.

➡ **Jane Austen's Grave**

Jane Austen, one of England's best-loved authors, is buried near the entrance in the cathedral's northern aisle. Austen died a stone's throw away in 1817 at Jane Austen's House, where she spent her last six weeks. It's now a private residence and is marked by a slate **plaque** (8 College St). Another of her former homes, now a museum (p236), is 18 miles away.

➡ **Cathedral Grounds**

The cathedral's tree-fringed lawns make for tranquil spots to take time out, especially on the quieter south side beyond the cloisters; the permanent secondhand book stall in the **Deanery Porch** provides great bargain hunting.

★**Wolvesey Castle**   CASTLE

(EH; ☏02392-378291; www.english-heritage.org.uk; College St; ☉10am-5pm Apr-Oct) **FREE** The fantastical, crumbling remains of early-12th-century Wolvesey Castle huddle in the protective embrace of the city's walls. Completed by Henry de Blois, it served as the Bishop of Winchester's residence throughout the medieval era, with Queen Mary I and Philip II of Spain celebrating their wedding feast here in 1554. According to legend, its name comes from a Saxon king's demand for an annual payment of 300 wolves' heads. Today the bishop lives in the (private) **Wolvesey Palace** next door.

★**Winchester College**   HISTORIC BUILDING

(☏01962-621100;   www.winchestercollege.org; College St; adult/child £6/5; ☉10.45am & noon Mon-Sat, plus 2.15pm & 3.30pm Mon, Wed, Fri-Sun) Winchester College delivers a rare chance to nose around a prestigious English private school. It was set up by William Wykeham, Bishop of Winchester in 1393, 14 years after he founded Oxford's New College. Hour-long guided tours take in the 14th-century Gothic chapel, complete with wooden vaulted roof, the dining room (called College Hall), and a vast 17th-century open classroom (called School), where exams are still held. A revealing insight into how the other half learns.

City Museum   MUSEUM

(www.winchester.gov.uk/heritage-conservation/museums/city-museum; The Square; ☉10am-4pm Mon-Sat, noon-4pm Sun) **FREE** A canter through Winchester's past with jewellery, mosaics, sculpture, coins and tobacco tins charting a narrative from the Iron Age, via the Romans and Anglo Saxons to the present.

Round Table & Great Hall   HISTORIC BUILDING

(☏01962-846476;   www.hants.gov.uk/greathall; Castle Ave; suggested donation £2; ☉10am-5pm) **FREE** Winchester's cavernous Great Hall is the only part of 11th-century Winchester Castle that Oliver Cromwell spared from destruction. Crowning the wall like a giant-sized dartboard of green and cream spokes is what centuries of mythology has dubbed King Arthur's Round Table. It's actually a 700-year-old copy, but is fascinating nonetheless. It's thought to have been constructed in the late 13th century and then painted in the reign of Henry VIII (King Arthur's image is unsurprisingly reminiscent of Henry's youthful face).

This hall was also the stage for several gripping English courtroom dramas, including the trial of adventurer Sir Walter Raleigh in 1603, who was sentenced to death but received a reprieve at the last minute.

Royal Green Jackets Museum   MUSEUM

(The Rifles; ☏01962-828549; www.winchestermilitarymuseums.co.uk; Peninsula Barracks, Romsey Rd; adult/child £4/1.50; ☉10am-5pm Tue-Sat, plus Sun Jul-Sep) The pick of Winchester's cluster of army museums, with a mini rifle-shooting range, a room of 6000 medals and an impressive blow-by-blow diorama of Napoleon's downfall, the Battle of Waterloo.

Hospital of St Cross   HISTORIC BUILDING

(☏01962-853525; www.stcrosshospital.co.uk; St Cross Rd; adult/child £4/2; ☉9.30am-5pm Mon-Sat, 1-5pm Sun Apr-Oct, 10.30am-3.30pm Mon-Sat Nov-Mar) Welcome to the oldest charitable institution in the country, founded in 1132 by the grandson of William the Conqueror, Henry de Blois. As well as healing the sick and housing the needy, the hospital was built to care for pilgrims and crusaders en route to the Holy Land. Today, it's roamed by elderly black- and red-gowned brothers, who hand out the Wayfarer's Dole; a crust of bread and horn of ale (now a small swig of beer) from the Porter's Gate.

Make sure you visit the stumpy church, the brethren hall, the kitchen and the peaceful gardens. The best way to arrive is via the 1-mile Keats' Walk through the water meadows; pick up the trail near Wolvesey Castle.

🏃 **Activities**

Winchester's tempting walks include the 1-mile **Keats' Walk** through the water meadows to the Hospital of St Cross. Its beauty is said to have prompted the poet to pen the ode *To Autumn;* pick up the trail near

JANE AUSTEN'S HOUSE MUSEUM

There's more than a touch of the period dramas she inspired about the former home of Jane Austen (1775–1817). The appealing red-brick house, where the celebrated English novelist lived with her mother and sister from 1809 to 1817, is now a **museum** (☑01420-83262; www.jane-austens-house-museum.org.uk; Chawton; adult/child £7.50/2.50; ☺10.30am-4.30pm mid-Feb–Dec). While here, she wrote *Mansfield Park*, *Emma* and *Persuasion*, and revised *Sense and Sensibility*, *Pride and Prejudice* and *Northanger Abbey*.

The interior showcases a typical well-to-do Georgian family home, complete with elegant furniture and copper pans in the kitchen, plus the occasional table Austen used as a desk, first editions of her novels and the delicate handkerchief she embroidered for her sister.

The museum is 18 miles east of Winchester in Chawton village; take bus 64 from Winchester to Alton Butts (£8, 45 minutes, hourly) then walk 800m to Chawton village.

Wolvesey Castle. Alternatively, head down Wharf Hill, through the water meadows to St Catherine's Hill (1 mile), or take the tranquil **Riverside Walk** from Wolvesey Castle along the River Itchen's banks to High St.

☞ Tours

Cathedral Tours　　　WALKING TOUR
The highly informative, one-hour **Cathedral Body Tours** (Monday to Saturday, 10am to 3pm) and atmospheric **Crypt Tours** (10.30am, 12.30pm and 2.30pm, Monday to Saturday) are included in the admission price for Winchester Cathedral (p233). **Tower and Roof Tours** (2.15pm Monday to Saturday, plus 11.30am Saturday, May to September) cost £6 and take you onto the roof for views as far as the Isle of Wight. These tours are popular – book well in advance.

On the Crypt Tour look out for *Sound II*, an enigmatic life-sized depiction of a contemplative man by Anthony Gormley. The Tower and Roof Tour will see you clambering 213 steps up narrow stairwells, navigating an interior gallery high above the nave and visiting the bell chamber.

Guided Walks　　　WALKING TOUR
(adult/child £6/free; ☺Mon-Sat Apr-Oct, weekly Nov-Mar) These 90-minute walks include City Highlights and Roman and Saxon Winchester. Up to four leave daily from the tourist office in peak season.

🛏 Sleeping

★St John's Croft　　　B&B ££
(☑01962-859976; www.st-johns-croft.co.uk; St John's St; s/d £45/85; P 🕸) You may well fall in love with this oh-so-casually stylish, rambling Queen Anne town house, where rattan carpets are teamed with bulging bookcases, and Indian art with shabby-chic antiques.

The rooms are vast, the garden is tranquil and breakfast is served beside the Aga in the country-house kitchen.

5 Clifton Terrace　　　B&B ££
(☑01962-890053; cliftonterrace@hotmail.co.uk; 5 Clifton Tce; s £65-70, d £75-90, f £110-125; 🕸) There's a captivating air of easygoing elegance about this tall Georgian town house. Family heirlooms sit beside candy-striped rugs and peppermint-green, claw-footed baths – it's great value too.

No 5　　　B&B ££
(☑01962-863838; www.no5bridgestreet.co.uk; 5 Bridge St; d £99-130; 🕸) Subtle tweedy-meets-tartan motifs are used to good effect here, with soft, checked throws book-ending beds draped in gentle grey. Spacious bathrooms, feature fireplaces, while a downstairs bistro adds to the appeal.

Magdalen House　　　B&B ££
(☑01962-869634; www.magdalen-house.co.uk; 5 Magdalen Hill; s/d/f £50/65/75; P 🕸) Smart bedrooms are arranged over three floors in this peaceful, modern hillside house. The family room opens out directly onto a sunny terrace – the doubles trump that though, with views over rooftops to Winchester Cathedral.

★Wykeham Arms　　　INN £££
(☑01962-853834; www.wykehamarmswinchester.co.uk; 75 Kingsgate St; s/d/ste £65/150/180; P 🕸) At 250-odd years old, the Wykeham bursts with history – it used to be a brothel and also put Nelson up for a night (some say the events coincided). Creaking stairs lead to plush bedrooms that manage to be both deeply established but also on-trend; brass bedsteads meet jazzy throws, oak dressers sport stylish lights. Simply smashing.

X Eating

Chesil Rectory
BRITISH ££
(✆ 01962-851555; www.chesilrectory.co.uk; 1 Chesil St; mains £14-20; ⊗noon-2.20pm & 6-9.30pm) It's almost as if they created a checklist for a great date: hushed tones, flickering candles, dark beams. They get the food right too, from lighter offerings such as white onion risotto, to flavourful braised ox cheek, or roasted guinea fowl with red wine.

Wykeham Arms
PUB ££
(✆ 01962-853834; www.wykehamarmswinchester.co.uk; 75 Kingsgate St; mains £14-23; ⊗noon-3pm & 6-9pm; ☎🍴) The menu range here is remarkable, from juicy burgers and fish and chips, to satisfying creations adorned with cheffy flourishes: ham-hock terrine, roasted venison and seared scallops come complete with purees, creams, gels, 'snow' and 'sand'.

Old Vine
PUB ££
(✆ 01962-854616; www.oldvinewinchester.com; 8 Great Minster St; mains £10-20; ⊗noon-2.30pm & 6.30-9pm) Ask for a table with a view of Winchester's captivating Cathedral Green, soak up the mellow, old-inn atmosphere, then choose between comfort food (pork pies and baked eggs) or fancier fare: flaky grilled salmon and hefty rib-eye steaks.

★ Black Rat
FINE DINING £££
(✆ 01962-844465; www.theblackrat.co.uk; 88 Chesil St; mains £23, 2-/3-course lunch £23/26; ⊗7-9pm daily, noon-2.15pm Sat & Sun) The aromas are irresistible, the food frankly fabulous, the cooking highly technical and the ingredients dare to surprise – expect cuttlefish, rabbit saddle, black garlic, seaweed salt, loveage and blowtorched back fat. That'll be why the Black Rat deserves its Michelin star.

♉ Drinking & Entertainment

★ Wykeham Arms
PUB
(www.wykehamarmswinchester.co.uk; 75 Kingsgate St; ⊗11am-11pm; ☎) Winchester's mustn't-miss inn envelops you in an eccentric embrace. Tankards and school canes hang from the ceiling, and worn school desks lend pint-supping an illicit air. The sizzling sausages (75p each) served nightly at 6pm help make it hard to imagine drinking anywhere else. Ever.

Black Boy
PUB
(www.theblackboypub.com; 1 Wharf Hill; ⊗noon-11pm Mon-Thu, to midnight Fri & Sat, to 10.30pm Sun) This adorable old boozer is worth visiting just for the bizarre collections of pocket watches, wax facial features, bear traps and sawn-in-half paperbacks. Then there's the beer: the pumps here produce five well-kept, locally produced real ales.

Railway Inn
LIVE MUSIC
(www.railwaylive.co.uk; 3 St Paul's Hill; ⊗5pm-midnight Sun-Thu, to 2am Fri, to 1am Sat) One of the region's best live-music and DJ spaces, the two-venue Railway puts on everything from indie to country, plus poetry, comedy and even retro gaming (yep).

ℹ Information

Discovery Centre (www3.hants.gov.uk/wdc; Jewry St; ⊗9am-7pm Mon-Fri, to 5pm Sat, 11am-3pm Sun; ☎) Free internet access.

Tourist Office (✆ 01962-840500; www.visitwinchester.co.uk; High St; ⊗10am-5pm Mon-Sat, plus 11am-4pm Sun May-Sep)

ℹ Getting There & Away

Winchester is 65 miles west of London. Direct National Express buses shuttle to London Victoria every two hours (£14, 1¾ hours). Trains leave half-hourly to hourly for London Waterloo (£33, 1¼ hours) and hourly for Portsmouth (£11, 1¼ hours). There are also fast links to the Midlands.

ℹ Getting Around

Bikes can be hired from the Tourist Office, per half/full day £7/10. Park & Ride car parks (per day £3) are signed off junctions 10 and 11 of the M3.

There are taxi ranks on the High St, and outside the train station and tourist office.

Wintax (✆ 01962-878727; www.wintaxcars.com) Operates 24 hours.

Portsmouth
POP 209,100

The world-class collection of maritime heritage at Portsmouth demands a day trip. Here you can roam around three stunning historic ships, a submarine and an impressive cluster of museums. Nauticalia done, the city's Point district tempts with cobbled streets and ancient pubs, the Spinnaker Tower delivers jaw-dropping views, and the port makes a prime jumping-off point for the Isle of Wight.

◉ Sights

★ Portsmouth Historic Dockyard
HISTORIC SHIPS
(✆ 02392-728060; www.historicdockyard.co.uk; Victory Gate; All Attractions ticket adult/child/family £28/21/78; ⊗10am-6pm Apr-Oct, to 5.30pm

Portsmouth

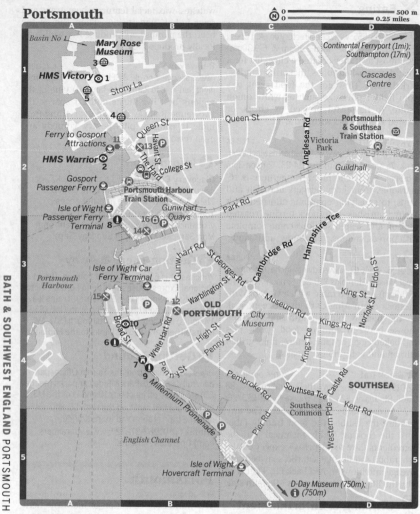

0 — 500 m
0 — 0.25 miles

Basin No 1

Mary Rose Museum 3

HMS Victory 1
5

Stony La

Continental Ferryport (1mi); Southampton (17mi)

Cascades Centre

4

Queen St   Queen St

Ferry to Gosport Attractions 11
13

Queen St

Havant St

The Hard

College St

HMS Warrior 2

Gosport Passenger Ferry

Portsmouth Harbour Train Station

Anglesea Rd

Portsmouth & Southsea Train Station

Victoria Park

Isle of Wight Passenger Ferry Terminal 8

Gunwharf Quays

16   14

Park Rd

Guildhall

Hampshire Tce

Eldon St

Isle of Wight Car Ferry Terminal

Portsmouth Harbour

15

Gunwharf Rd

St Georges Rd

Cambridge Rd

Warblington St

12

OLD PORTSMOUTH

City Museum

Museum Rd

King St

Norfolk St

Kings Rd

Kings Tce

10

6

Broad St

White Hart Rd

High St

Penny St

7   9

Penny St

Millennium Promenade

Pembroke Rd

Southsea Tce

Castle Rd

SOUTHSEA

English Channel

Isle of Wight Hovercraft Terminal

Pier Rd

Southsea Common

Western Pde

Kent Rd

D-Day Museum (750m); (750m)

Nov-Mar) Portsmouth's blockbuster draw sees you gazing at the evocative hulk of Henry VIII's flagship, the *Mary Rose,* and jumping aboard HMS *Victory* – the warship Nelson captained at the Battle of Trafalgar. Then there's the Victorian HMS *Warrior,* the WWII-era submarine HMS *Alliance* and a wealth of imaginative, maritime-themed museums, along with water-borne harbour tours. Visiting more than one exhibit makes the All Attraction ticket (rather than single attraction versions) the best value. Last admission is 1½ hours before closing. Harbour Tours (p240) are also included in the All Attractions ticket.

➡ ★Mary Rose Museum
(www.maryrose.org; adult/child £18/13) The raising of the 16th-century warship the *Mary Rose* in 1982 was an extraordinary feat of marine archaeology. Now the new £35 million, boat-shaped Mary Rose Museum has been built around her. It showcases the massive hull which can be seen from tiered galleries reconstructing life on each deck, using some of the 19,000 artefacts that were raised with her.

This 700-tonne floating fortress was Henry VIII's favourite vessel, but she sank suddenly off Portsmouth while fighting the French in

Portsmouth

1545. Of a crew of 400, it's thought 360 died. Items on display range from the military, including scores of cannons and hundreds of longbows, to the touchingly prosaic: water jugs, hair combs, leather shoes and even the skeleton of Hatch, the ship's dog.

➡ ★**HMS Victory**
(www.hms-victory.com; adult/child £18/13) As resplendent as she is venerable, HMS *Victory* was Lord Nelson's flagship at the Battle of Trafalgar (1805) and the site of his famous dying words 'Kiss me, Hardy', after victory over the French had been secured. This remarkable ship is topped by a forest of ropes and masts, and weighted by a swollen belly filled with cannon and paraphernalia for an 850-strong crew. Clambering through the low-beamed decks and crew's quarters is an evocative experience.

➡ ★**HMS Warrior**
(www.hmswarrior.org; adult/child £18/13) Anywhere else, the magnificent warship HMS *Warrior* would grab centre stage. This stately dame was at the cutting edge of technology when she was built in 1860, riding the transition from wood to iron and sail to steam. The gleaming upper deck, vast gun deck and dimly lit cable lockers conjure up vivid pictures of life in the Victorian navy.

➡ **National Museum of the Royal Navy**
(www.royalnavalmuseum.org; adult/child £13/8) Cannon fire, recoiling guns and injured sailors appear in this museum's multimedia re-creation of the Battle of Trafalgar; Nelson and Napoleon even pop up to give a tactical briefing. The site also features William Wyllie's 42ft painting *The Panorama of the Battle of Trafalgar*, Nelson's 1800 Life Mask and an Enigma machine, used by British WWII code-breakers to crack German signals.

➡ **Action Stations!**
(adult/child £12/9) Stroll into Action Stations!, a warehouse full of child-friendly interactive gadgets, to command a warship, gaze at an astronauts' view of earth, and up a periscope. The whole set-up is a thinly disguised recruitment drive for the modern navy, but it's fun nonetheless.

➡ **Explosion!**
(www.explosion.org.uk; Priddy's Hard, Gosport; adult/child £10/6) This 1771 powder magazine is packed full of ordnance tracing the story of naval munitions from gunpowder to Exocet missiles. Explosion! is in Gosport, on the west side of Portsmouth Harbour – a free waterbus (15 minutes) links it with the main historic dockyard site.

➡ **HMS Alliance at the Submarine Museum**
(www.submarine-museum.co.uk; Haslar Jetty Rd, Gosport; adult/child £14/10) Taking a trip deep into the bowels of the the WWII-era sub HMS *Alliance* is compelling, thanks to the lights, sounds and even smells used to create a sense of dropping by just as the crew has gone ashore. HMS *Alliance* is in Gosport, across the harbour from Portsmouth; free water buses (30 minutes) shuttle to the site from Portsmouth Historic Dockyard.

Your tour leads through the submarine's service years, from the 1940s to the 1970s, and sees you navigating cramped quarters and peering up through periscopes onto the harbour outside.

The Point   HISTORIC SITE
The Point's characteristic cobbled streets are dotted with higgledy-piggledy houses and

---

ℹ **HMS VICTORY**

In the summer, tours of Nelson's flagship are self-guided. But between autumn and spring, hugely popular 40-minute **guided tours** are held. Arrive early to bag a place – you can't book in advance.

salty sea-dog pubs – their terraces prime places to watch streams of ferries and navy ships. Here you can also climb Henry V's **Round Tower** and stroll along the fort's walls to the 15th-century **Square Tower**. Underneath, cavernous vaults frame **Sally Ports**; openings in the defences that used to give captains access to the sea, and now lead sun worshippers onto a tiny shingle beach.

Spinnaker Tower
TOWER

(⌨ 02392-857520; www.spinnakertower.co.uk; Gunwharf Quays; adult/child £9/7; ⏰ 10am-6pm) The Spinnaker Tower soars 170m above Gunwharf Quays, its two sweeping white arcs resembling a billowing sail from some angles, and a skeletal ribcage from others. The 23-mile views take in Portsmouth, the Isle of Wight and the South Downs. Observation Deck 1 has a hair-raising view through the glass floor, while the roofless Crow's Nest on Deck 3 allows you to feel the wind on your face. Tickets are 15% cheaper when booked online.

D-Day Museum
MUSEUM

(⌨ 02392-826722; www.ddaymuseum.co.uk; Clarence Esplanade, Southsea; adult/child £7/5; ⏰ 10am-5pm) The exhibits here recount the assault mounted by Allied D-Day forces in 1944 and Portsmouth's key role in the operation.

☞ Tours

Harbour Tours
BOAT TOUR

(⌨ 01983-864602; Portsmouth Historic Dockyard; adult/child £7/5; ⏰ 10.30am-4pm Apr-Oct, 11am-3pm Nov-Mar) These 45-minute voyages (weather permitting) provide salt-sprayed views of HMS *Warrior* and HMS *Victory*, and you'll go past modern warships too. The tours are included in the All Attractions ticket (p237). The free waterbus to HMS *Alliance*, the Submarine Museum and Explosion! leaves from the same pontoon.

Walking Tours
HERITAGE TOUR

(adult/child £3/free; ⏰ 2.30pm Sun) Themes include Nelson, the Point and Old Fortifications; there are Sunday evening Ghost Walks too. The tourist office has full details.

✖ Eating & Drinking

Still & West
PUB £

(www.stillandwest.co.uk; 2 Bath Sq; mains £8; ⏰ 9am-9pm Mon-Thu, to 10pm Fri & Sat, to 8pm Sun) Genius: two great British institutions in one – a fish and chip shop inside a pub (open 11am to 11pm). Your fried delights come wrapped in traditional chippy paper, so buy a pint, bag

a window table and tuck in while watching the close-up panorama of passing boats.

Lady Hamilton
PUB £

(⌨ 02392-870505; 21 The Hard; mains £7.50; ⏰ kitchen 11am-3pm & 6-9pm Mon-Sat, noon-9pm Sun) Cutlasses and paintings of valiant sea battles plaster the walls of a proper old boozer (open 11am to 11pm) that's named after naval hero Horatio Nelson's mistress. The daily roasts are legendary, the vibe is un-gimmicky and the decor is definitely not smart – and it's all the better for it.

A Bar
BISTRO ££

(⌨ 02392-811585; www.abarbistro.co.uk; 58 White Hart Rd; mains £10-19; ⏰ 11am-11pm; 🐾) A laid-back spot to sample local produce and soak up local life – the menu is strong on fish that's been landed just yards away, while cider-drinking fishermen prop up the bar. The wine list is seriously good; the same people run a specialist retailer from upstairs.

Old Customs House
PUB ££

(www.theoldcustomshouse.com; Gunwharf Quays; mains £10-16; ⏰ 9am-9pm Sun-Thu, to 10pm Fri & Sat; 🐾) The best of Gunwharf Quays' numerous eateries, this smart pub occupies an 18th-century former Royal Marine hospital. Now better-than-average bar food (think mussels steamed in cider, steak and ale pie and Welsh rarebit) is served up alongside its raspberry-red walls and gilt-framed mirrors.

ℹ Information

Net Cafe (www.netcafeportsmouth.com; 4 Market Way; per hr £3; ⏰ 10am-5.30pm Mon-Fri, to 5pm Sat) Some 1.5 miles east of the Historic Dockyard.

Tourist Office (⌨ 02392-826722; www. visitportsmouth.co.uk; Clarence Esplanade; ⏰ 10am-5pm Apr-Sep, to 4.30pm Nov-Mar) In the D-Day Museum in Southsea.

ℹ Getting There & Away

Portsmouth is 100 miles southwest of London.

BOAT

Ferries link Portsmouth to the Isle of Wight (p245).

Several routes run from Portsmouth to France. Prices vary wildly depending on times and dates of travel – an example fare is £120 one way for a car and two adults on the Portsmouth–Cherbourg route. Book in advance, be prepared to travel off-peak and look out for special deals.

Brittany Ferries (www.brittanyferries.co.uk) Services run regularly from Portsmouth to St Malo (10¾ hours), Caen (four hours), Cherbourg (three hours) and Le Havre (3¾ hours) in France, and twice-weekly to Santander (13 hours) and Bilbao in Spain.

Condor Ferries (www.condorferries.co.uk) Runs a weekly car-and-passenger service from Portsmouth to Cherbourg (6½ hours) between June and September.

LD Lines (www.ldlines.co.uk) Shuttles daily to Le Havre (five to eight hours) in France.

BUS

There are hourly, direct National Express buses from London Victoria (£14, 1¾ hours). Bus 700 runs to Chichester (£4.40, one hour) and Brighton (£4.70, four hours) at least hourly.

TRAIN

Direct trains run hourly from London Victoria (£35, two hours) and half-hourly from London Waterloo (£35, two hours). For the Historic Dockyard get off at the final stop, Portsmouth Harbour.

Other departures include:

Brighton (£16, 1½ hours, hourly)

Chichester (£8, 40 minutes, two per hour)

Southampton (£10, one hour, three per hour)

Winchester (£15, 1¼ hours, half-hourly)

❶ Getting Around

Bus 1 runs every 20 minutes between Portsmouth Harbour bus station and South Parade Pier in Southsea, via Old Portsmouth. An all-day ticket is £4.

Ranks for taxis are near the Portsmouth Harbour bus and train stations. Or call **Aquacars** (☎ 02392-811111; www.aquacars.co.uk).

NEW FOREST

With typical, accidental, English irony the New Forest is anything but new – it was first proclaimed a royal hunting preserve in 1079. It's also not much of a forest, being mostly heathland ('forest' is from the Old French for 'hunting ground'). Designated a national park in 2005, the forest's combined charms make it a joy to explore. Wild ponies mooch around pretty scrubland, deer flicker in the distance and rare birds flit among the foliage. Genteel villages dot the landscape, connected by a web of walking and cycling trails.

🏃 Activities

The forest is prime hiking territory. Ordnance Survey (OS) produces a detailed, 1:25,000 Explorer map (*New Forest;* No 22, £8); Pathfinder's *New Forest Short Walks* (£8) features 20 day hikes.

New Forest Activities   ADVENTURE SPORTS
(☎ 01590-612377; www.newforestactivities.co.uk; High St, Beaulieu) Runs sessions in canoeing (adult/child per two hours £32/25), kayaking (per two hours £32) and archery (adult/child per 1½ hours £22/17).

Cycling

The New Forest makes for superb cycling country, with 100 miles of routes linking the main villages and the key railway station at Brockenhurst.

Cycling in the New Forest (£3.25) shows approved off-road and quieter 'on-road' routes. The *New Forest Cycle Experience Route Pack* (£4) features seven trips, ranging from 4 to 24 miles. The *Forest Leisure Cycling Route Pack* (£4) has nine circular trails for all abilities – all start from the village of Burley.

Maps and guides can be bought from Lyndhurst tourist office (p242) or via its website. To rent bikes you'll need to pay a deposit (usually £20) and provide identification.

AA Bike Hire   BICYCLE RENTAL
(☎ 02380-283349; www.aabikehirenewforest.co.uk; Fern Glen, Gosport Lane, Lyndhurst; adult/child per day £10/5)

Country Lanes   BICYCLE RENTAL
(☎ 01590-622627; www.countrylanes.co.uk; train station, Brockenhurst; adult/child/family per day £16/9/43)

New Forest Cycle Hire   BICYCLE RENTAL
(Cyclexperience; ☎ 01590-624204; www.newforestcyclehire.co.uk; 2-4 Brookley Rd, Brockenhurst; adult/child per day £16/6)

Forest Leisure Cycling   BICYCLE RENTAL
(☎ 01425-403584; www.forestleisurecycling.co.uk; The Cross, Burley; adult/child per day £16/6)

Horse Riding

A number of stables welcome beginners.

---

❶ CAMPING IN THE NEW FOREST

The New Forest is a haven for campers. The **Forestry Commission** (www.campingintheforest.co.uk) runs 10 relatively rural sites. Lyndhurst's tourist office (p242) has a free brochure detailing other designated areas; see also www.thenewforest.co.uk.

Arniss Equestrian Centre HORSE RIDING
(☎01425-654114; www.arnissequestrian.co.uk; Godshill, Fordingbridge; per hr £27)

Burley Manor HORSE RIDING
(☎01425-403489; www.burleymanorridingstables.com; Ringwood Rd, Burley; per 1/2hr £33/60)

Burley Villa HORSE RIDING
(☎01425-610278; www.burleyvilla.co.uk; near New Milton; per hr £42)

Tours

Ranger Walks WALKING TOUR
(☎03000 680400; www.forestry.gov.uk; from £5) Day walks including those themed around ecology, flowers and ponies, plus memorable early evening deer-watching strolls.

Information

Tourist Office (☎02380-282269; www.thenewforest.co.uk; main car park, Lyndhurst; ⏲10am-5pm) The national park's main tourist office, set in the New Forest Centre, has a wealth of information, including walking and cycling maps, and camping guides

Getting There & Around

BUS

Regular services run to Bournemouth (£8.50) and Southampton (£7.20).

New Forest Tour (www.thenewforesttour.info; adult per 1/2/5 days £14/19/28, child £7/9/14; ⏲hourly 10am-6pm mid-Jun–mid-Sep) Three connecting routes of hop-on/hop-off buses, passing through Lyndhurst's main car park, Brockenhurst station, Lymington, Beaulieu and Exbury.

TRAIN

Two trains an hour run to Brockenhurst from London Waterloo (£15, two hours) via Winchester (£12, 30 minutes) and on to Bournemouth (£8, 25 minutes). Local trains also shuttle twice an hour between Brockenhurst and Lymington (£4, 10 minutes).

Lyndhurst, Brockenhurst & Around

POP 6579

The quaint country villages of Lyndhurst and Brockenhurst are separated by just 4 miles. Their picturesque sleeping spots and superb eateries ensure they're atmospheric bases from which to explore the New Forest.

Lyndhurst also has the New Forest Centre, which contains the tourist office, and a **library** (main car park; ⏲9.30am-1pm Mon, Wed & Sat, 2-5.30pm Tue & Fri) with free internet access.

Sights

New Forest Museum MUSEUM
(www.newforestcentre.org.uk; main car park, Lyndhurst; adult/child £4/free; ⏲10am-5pm) Features a local labourer's cottage (complete with socks drying beside the fire), potato dibbers and a cider press. The mini-film makes for an accessible introduction to the park – listen too for recordings of the autumn pony sales, which take place after the annual drifts (roundups).

Beaulieu HISTORIC BUILDING
(www.beaulieu.co.uk; adult/child £10/10; ⏲10am-6pm Jun-Sep, to 5pm Oct-May) Petrolheads, historians and ghost-hunters gravitate to Beaulieu (pronounced *bew*-lee), a vintage car museum, stately home and tourist complex based on the site of a key 13th-century Cistercian monastery. Motor-maniacs will be in raptures at Lord Montague's National Motor Museum. Beaulieu is on the Lymington/Brockenhurst route of the New Forest Tour (p242).

Following Henry VIII's monastic land grab of 1536, the abbey fell to the ancestors of current proprietors, the Montague family. Today the **motor museum** presents a splendid collection that spans early classics, F1 cars and jet-powered land-speed record-breakers including *Bluebird,* which broke the 403mph (649km/h) limit in 1964. Celebrity wheels include those driven by James Bond and Mr Bean.

Beaulieu's grand but homely **palace** began life as a 14th-century Gothic abbey gatehouse, but received a 19th-century Scottish baronial makeover from Baron Montague in the 1860s. Listen out for eerie Gregorian chanting – the abbey is supposedly one of England's most haunted buildings.

Sleeping

Lyndhurst House B&B ££
(☎02380-282230; www.lyndhursthousebb.co.uk; 35 Romsey Rd, Lyndhurst; s £55, d £70-76; P 📶) Pine furniture fills floral-themed rooms; steeply slanting eaves add character to those on the top floor. But a real surprise sits in an outhouse: a mini hot tub and sauna combo, for soothing limbs tested by New Forest cycling, hiking or riding.

Daisybank Cottage   BOUTIQUE B&B **££**
(☑ 01590-622086; www.bedandbreakfast-newforest.
co.uk; Sway Rd, Brockenhurst; s £75, d £90-135;
P �🛜) The five gorgeous themed suites here
are mini pamper palaces. Expect aromatic
smellies in gleaming bathrooms, stylish, luxurious furnishings and lots of little extras:
breakfasts laden with New Forest goodies,
handmade chocolates and range-baked cakes
on arrival.

★ **The Pig**   BOUTIQUE HOTEL **£££**
(☑ 01590-622354; www.thepighotel.co.uk; Beaulieu Rd, Brockenhurst; r £139-169; P �🛜) One of
the New Forest's classiest hotels remains an
utter delight: log baskets, croquet mallets
and ranks of guest gumboots give things a
country-house air; espresso machines and
mini-larders lend bedrooms a luxury touch.
In fact, all this effortless elegance makes it
feel like you've just dropped by a friend's
(very stylish) rural retreat.

✕ Eating

Oak Inn   PUB **££**
(☑ 02380-282350; www.oakinnlyndhurst.co.uk;
Pinkney Lane, Bank; mains £8-16; ⊙ noon-2.30pm
& 6-9.30pm Mon-Fri, noon-9pm Sat & Sun) Beams,
panelling, horse brasses, and dried hops
hanging over the bar – this flower-framed
New Forest inn is as English as they come.
The grub though is pure gastropub: monkfish and squid salad; goat-cheese mousse.
It's a mile southwest of Lyndhurst in the
hamlet of Bank.

★ **The Pig**   MODERN BRITISH **££**
(☑ 01590-622354; www.thepighotel.co.uk; Beaulieu Rd, Brockenhurst; mains £10-17; ⊙ noon-
2.30pm & 6.30-9.30pm; ⓢ) Add this to your
must-eat-in list. The '25 mile menu' at this
über-cool hotel is all sourced locally – most
is home-grown, own-reared or foraged. That
means imaginative combos featuring earthy
chard from the kitchen garden, punchy,
own-smoked ham and a creamy risotto of
just-picked mushrooms. You can even join
them for a foraging trip.

❶ Getting There & Away

Bus 6 shuttles between Lyndhurst, Brockenhurst and Lymington (£3.60, hourly Monday
to Saturday, five on Sunday); so does the New
Forest Tour (p242).

Trains run twice an hour between Brockenhurst and Lymington (£4, 10 minutes).

SOUTHAMPTON

Southampton is a useful transport hub.
**Southampton International Air-
port** (www.southamptonairport.com) sits
between Winchester, Portsmouth and
Bournemouth and connects with more
than 30 UK and European destinations,
including Amsterdam, Glasgow, Paris
and Dublin.

Trains run direct from the airport to
Bournemouth (£13, 30 minutes, three
per hour) via Brockenhurst in the New
Forest (£9, 25 minutes). Five trains an
hour link the airport to Southampton's
main train station (seven minutes).
From there, three trains an hour run to
Portsmouth (£10, one hour) and Winchester (£7, 25 minutes).

Ferries (www.redfunnel.co.uk) shuttle
from Southampton to the Isle of Wight.

Buckler's Hard

For such a tiny place, this picturesque huddle of 18th-century cottages, near the mouth
of the River Beaulieu, has a big history. It
started in 1722, when a duke of Montague
built a port to finance a Caribbean expedition. His dream faltered, but when war
with France came, this embryonic village
and sheltered gravel waterfront became a
secret boatyard where several of Nelson's triumphant Battle of Trafalgar warships were
built. In the 20th century it played its part
in the preparations for the D-Day landings.

Buckler's Hard is 2 miles downstream
from Beaulieu; a riverside walking trail links
the two.

⊙ Sights

Buckler's Hard Story   MUSEUM
(☑ 01590-616203; www.bucklershard.co.uk; adult/
child £6.20/4.40; ⊙ 10am-5.30pm Apr-Sep, to
4.30pm Oct-Mar) The hamlet's fascinating
Maritime Museum and heritage centre chart
the inlet's shipbuilding history and WWII
role and feature immaculately preserved
18th-century labourers' cottages.

🛏 Sleeping

Master Builder's House Hotel   HOTEL **££**
(☑ 01590-616253; www.themasterbuilders.co.uk;
Buckler's Hard; d £93-158; P) The luxurious

Master Builder's House Hotel is part of the Buckler's Hard Story complex. This beautifully restored 18th-century hotel has 25 stately but stylish rooms, featuring soft lighting, burnished trunks and plush fabrics. The atmospheric **restaurant** (lunch two/three courses £16/19, dinner mains £16) overlooks the river, while the wood-panelled **Yachtsman's Bar** serves quality pub grub from £7.

Lymington

POP 15,425

A yachting haven, New Forest base and jumping-off point to the Isle of Wight, the appealing Georgian harbour town of Lymington has several strings to its tourism bow. This former smuggler's port offers nautical shops, prime eating and sleep spots and, in Quay St, an utterly quaint cobbled lane.

◉ Sights

St Barbe Museum MUSEUM
(✆01590-676969; www.stbarbe-museum.org.uk; New St; adult/child £4/2; ⊙10am-4pm Mon-Sat) This place explores tales of boat-builders, sailors, smugglers, salt-makers and farmers through a mix of models, hands-on displays and artefacts.

⌖ Tours

Puffin Cruises BOAT TOUR
(✆07850-947618; www.puffincruiseslymington. com; Town Quay) The best trip is an exhilarating, three-hour surge across the Solent to the Isle of Wight (adult/child £19/8, 6pm Wednesday and Friday, May to October), where the Needles lighthouse and towering chalk stacks loom from the water. There is also a 1½-hour evening cruise and a one-hour picnic voyage.

⨶ Sleeping

Auplands B&B ££
(✆01590-675944; www.auplands.com; 22 Southampton Rd; s £45, d £60-70; P☂) Your genial hosts have been running this B&B for more than 30 years, and it shows in their supremely efficient systems and easy charm. Snug rooms feature pine and big plants, while the eateries of Lymington are only a short stroll away.

★ Mill at Gordleton BOUTIQUE HOTEL £££
(✆01590-682219; www.themillatgordleton.co.uk; Silver St, Hordle; d/ste £150/195; P☂) Step inside here and you know, instantly, you're going to be looked after, beautifully. Wicker, velvet and gingham dot exquisite rooms (each one comes with a sweet soft toy duck), while the garden is a magical mix of rushing water, fairy lights and modern sculpture. The acclaimed restaurant (two-course lunch/dinner £16/23, open noon to 2pm daily and 7pm to 9pm Monday to Saturday) focuses firmly on the homemade and the home-grown. The Mill is 4 miles west of Lymington.

Stanwell House BOUTIQUE HOTEL £££
(✆0844 7046820; www.stanwellhouse.com; 14 High St; d £140-180, ste £220; @☂) There are boutique tweaks everywhere at Stanwell. Swish Georgian rooms manage to be both period and modern, the Four Poster ones feature dark woods and zingy colours, while the high-tech suites are simply irresistible – two even have their own roof terrace for sunny days and moonlit nights.

✗ Eating

Fish & Chips FISH & CHIPS £
(130 High St; mains £7.50; ⊙11.30am-2.30pm & 4.30-8.30pm Mon-Thu, 11.30am-9pm Fri & Sat, to 7pm Sun) They're often queuing out the door at this classic British chippy, which boasts great fish, formica tables and pickled eggs. Eat in or take away.

Ship Inn PUB ££
(www.theshiplymington.co.uk; The Quay; mains £9-17; ⊙kitchen noon-9pm; ☑) A pub for all seasons: knock back summertime drinks on the waterside terrace; in winter a toasty log burner gets you warm. Hearty food ranges from prosciutto and poached egg to a sticky marinated chicken; drinks totter from tangy real ales to vintage champagne.

Elderflower MODERN BRITISH £££
(✆01590-676908; www.elderflowerrestaurant.co. uk; 5 Quay St; mains £15-23; ⊙noon-2.30pm & 6.30-9.30pm Wed-Sat, noon-3.30pm Sun) The man running things here used to be head chef at one of the New Forest's finest hotels, and this venture is as ambitious and innovative as you'd expect: prepare for assured rarities like hay-smoked goats' cheese, Dorset snails and cigar-smoked chocolate. The three-course lunch (£25) is a snip.

❶ Information

Library (North Close; ⊙9am-5pm Mon, Wed, Thu & Sat, to 7pm Tue & Fri; ☂) Free internet access.

ⓘ Getting There & Away

Lymington has two train stations: Lymington Town and Lymington Pier. Isle of Wight ferries connect with Lymington Pier. Trains run to Southampton (£11, 40 minutes), via Brockenhurst, every hour.

Wightlink Ferries (☑ 0871 376 1000; www. wightlink.co.uk) Car and passenger ferries run hourly to Yarmouth on the Isle of Wight (30 minutes). An adult/child foot passenger day return costs £14/7. Car fares start at around £60 for a short-break return.

ISLE OF WIGHT

On the Isle of Wight these days there's something groovy in the air. For decades this slab of rock anchored off Portsmouth has been a magnet for family holidays, and it still has seaside kitsch by the bucket and spade. But now the proms and amusement arcades are framed by pockets of pure funkiness. A brace of music festivals draws party-goers, just-caught seafood is served in kooky fishermen's cafes, and cool camping rules – here sites are dotted with ecoyurts and vintage campervans. Yet still the isle's principal appeal remains: a mild climate, myriad outdoorsy activities and a 25-mile shore lined with beaches, dramatic white cliffs and tranquil sand dunes.

🏃 Activities

Water sports are serious business on the Isle of Wight. Cowes is the sailing centre, surfers and wind- and kite-surfers flock to the southwest, especially around Compton Bay, while power boats run trips out to the Needles rocks. See the island's visitor website (www.visitisleofwight.co.uk) for more.

Isle of Wight Adventure ADVENTURE SPORTS
(☑ 01983-755838; www.isleofwightadventureacti ties.co.uk; Freshwater) Runs activities ranging from surfing, stand-up paddleboarding and kayaking (per two hours adult/child £40/25), to archery (£12) and fossil hunting (adult/child £4/3).

Isle of Wight Steam Railway HERITAGE RAILWAY
(☑ 01983-882204; www.iwsteamrailway.co.uk; ☺ mid-Apr–Sep) Chugs regularly from Smallbrook Junction to Wootton Common (return adult/child £12/6, 1st class £17/12, one hour).

Cycling

With 200 miles of cycle routes, the Isle of Wight makes pedal-pushers smile. The island's official visitor website lists suggested trips (complete with maps), ranging from family-friendly tootles along former railway routes to the 50-mile, cliff-climbing **Chalk Ridge Extreme**. A **Cycling Festival** (☑ 01983-821000; www.sunseaandcycling.com) is held every September.

Bike rentals start at around £13/45 per day/week. Many firms deliver and collect on orders over £30.

Tavcycles BICYCLE RENTAL
(☑ 01983- 812989; www.tavcycles.co.uk; 140 High St, Ryde)

Top Gear BICYCLE RENTAL
(☑ 01983-299056; www.top-gearhire.com; 1 Terminus Rd, Cowes)

Wight Cycle Hire BICYCLE RENTAL
(☑ 01983-761800; www.wightcyclehire.co.uk; Station Rd, Yarmouth)

Walking

This is one of the best spots in southern England for rambling, with 500 miles of well-marked walking paths, including 67 miles of coastal routes. The island's two-week **Walking Festival** (www.isleofwightwalkingfestival. co.uk) each May is billed as the UK's largest.

ⓘ Information

At time of writing, the Isle of Wight doesn't have a tourist office. Small-scale info points include one at the Yarmouth Harbour Office.

Visit Isle of Wight (www.visitisleofwight.co.uk) The isle's official tourism website.

ⓘ Getting There & Away

Hovertravel (☑ 08434 87 88 87; www.hov-ertravel.co.uk; day return adult/child £18/9) Shuttles foot passengers between Southsea (a Portsmouth suburb) and Ryde half hourly to hourly.

Red Funnel (☑ 0844 844 9988; www.redfun-nel.co.uk) Operates car-and-passenger ferries between Southampton and East Cowes (day return adult/child £16/8, from £40 with car,

---

ⓘ CAR FERRY COSTS

The cost of car ferries to the Isle of Wight can vary enormously. Make savings by booking ahead, asking about special offers and travelling off-peak (midweek and later in the day). Long stays are cheaper and some deals include admission to island attractions. Booking online can mean paying £20 less.

Isle of Wight

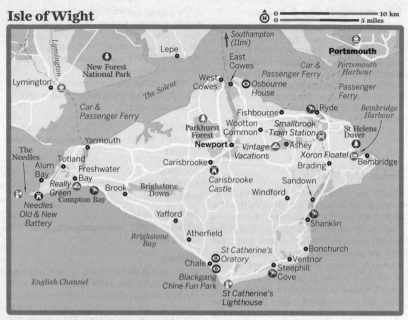

60 minutes, hourly) and high-speed passenger ferries between Southampton and West Cowes (day return adult/child £23/11, 25 minutes, one to two per hour).

Wightlink Ferries (📞 0871 376 1000; www. wightlink.co.uk) Operates passenger ferries every half hour from Portsmouth to Ryde (day-return adult/child £17/9, 22 minutes). It also runs hourly car-and-passenger ferries from Portsmouth to Fishbourne (40 minutes) and from Lymington to Yarmouth (30 minutes). For both, an adult/child foot passenger day return costs £14/7. Car fares start at around £60 for a short-break return.

ℹ Getting Around

BUS
Southern Vectis (www.islandbuses.info) Runs buses between the eastern towns roughly every 30 minutes. Regular services to the remoter southwest, especially between Blackgang Chine and Brook, are less frequent, but between April and September the Island Coaster makes four return circuits a day along the southern shore from Ryde around to Yarmouth, in the west. Rover Tickets are available for one day (adult/child £10/5), two days (adult/child £15/7.30) and a week (adult/child £24/12).

CAR
1st Call (📞 01983-400055; www.1stcallcar-sales.com; 15 College Close, Sandown; per

day/week from £22/160) Collects and delivers island wide.

TRAIN
Island Line (www.southwesttrains.co.uk/island-line) Trains run twice-hourly from Ryde to Shanklin (day return £5.40, 25 minutes), via Smallbrook Junction, Brading and Sandown.

Cowes & Around
POP 10,437

Pack your yachting cap – the hilly Georgian harbour town of Cowes is famous for **Cowes Week** (www.aamcowesweek.co.uk) in late July; first held in 1826, it's one of the biggest and longest-running sailing regattas in the world. Fibreglass playthings and vintage sailboats line Cowes' waterfronts, which are lopped into East and West Cowes by the River Medina; a chain ferry shuttles regularly between the two (foot passengers free, cars £2).

The island's capital, Newport, is 5 miles south.

◎ Sights

★**Osborne House**　　　HISTORIC BUILDING
(EH; 📞 01983-200022; www.english-heritage.org.uk; York Ave, East Cowes; adult/child £14/8; ⊙10am-5pm Apr-Oct; P) Lemon-frosted and

Italianate, Osborne House is pure Victorian pomp. Built in the 1840s at the behest of Queen Victoria, the monarch grieved here for many years after her husband's death. Extravagant rooms include the opulent Royal Apartments and Durbar Room; other highlights are horse and carriage rides, the Swiss Cottage – where the royal ankle-biters would play – and the stroll down Rhododendron Walk to Her Majesty's private beach.

Carisbrooke Castle CASTLE
(EH; ☑ 01983-522107; www.english-heritage.org. uk; Castle Hill, Newport; adult/child £8/5; ☉ 10am-5pm Apr-Oct; ℗) Charles I was imprisoned here before his execution in 1649. Today you can clamber the sturdy ramparts and play bowls on the very green the doomed monarch used.

🛏 Sleeping

onefiftycowes B&B ££
(☑ 07795-296399; www.onefiftycowes.co.uk; 150 Park Rd, West Cowes; s £60-70, d £85-95; ℗ 🛜) Modern art dots the walls, sea-smoothed pebbles are scattered around – this is a crisp, contemporary B&B with beautifully turned-out rooms. Two overlook the water; the pick is top-floor Solent, which comes with mini-binoculars to help you drink in the sea views.

Fountain HOTEL ££
(☑ 01983-292397; www.fountaininn-cowes.co.uk; High St, West Cowes; s £40-100, d £50-110; 🛜) Georgian-repro style rules at this appealing harbourside inn, where mock-flock wallpaper and old, wooden furniture define comfy rooms; number 15 has prime views of the bustling quay. The snug bar and sunny terrace are top places to sample pints and pub-grub classics (mains £9; open noon to 10pm).

Ryde to Shanklin

The nippiest foot-passenger ferries between Wight and Portsmouth alight in **Ryde**, a workaday Victorian town rich in the trappings of the British seaside. Next come the cutesy village of **Brading**, with its fine Roman villa; photogenic **Bembridge Harbour**, fringed by sandy beaches; and the twin resort towns of **Sandown** and **Shanklin**, boasting promenades and hordes of families wielding buckets and spades. The area also features unique places to sleep – including a decommissioned warship and vintage Airstream trailers.

◉ Sights

Brading Roman Villa RUIN
(☑ 01983-406223; www.bradingromanvilla.org.uk; Morton Old Rd, Brading; adult/child £6.50/3.75; ☉ 9.30am-5pm) The exquisitely preserved mosaics here (including a famous cockerel-headed man) make this one of the finest Romano-British sites in the UK. Wooden walkways lead over rubble walls and brightly painted tiles, allowing you to gaze right down onto the ruins below.

St Helens Duver NATURE RESERVE
(NT; www.nationaltrust.org.uk; ☉ 24hr; ℗) At this idyllic sand-and-shingle spit bordering the mouth of the River Yar, trails snake past swaths of sea pink, marram grass and rare clovers. It's signed from the village of St Helens, near Bembridge Harbour.

🛏 Sleeping

★ Vintage Vacations CAMPSITE £
(☑ 07802-758113; www.vintagevacations.co.uk; Ashey, near Ryde; 4-person caravans per week £460-680; ☉ Apr-Oct; ℗) The bevy of 1960s Airstream trailers on this farm are vintage chic personified. The gleaming aluminium shells shelter lovingly selected furnishings ranging from cheerful patchwork blankets to vivid tea cosies. Alternatively, opt for a beach-shack retreat, a 1930s Scout Hut or the Mission: a late-Victorian tin chapel.

Xoron Floatel B&B ££
(☑ 01983-874596; www.xoronfloatel.co.uk; Bembridge Harbour; d £70; ℗) A truly unique spot to drop off – this former WWII gunboat is

---

ISLE OF WIGHT MUSIC FESTIVALS

The isle's festival tradition kicked off in the early 1970s, when 600,000 hippies came to see the Doors, the Who, Joni Mitchell and rock icon Jimi Hendrix's last performance. A generation on, its gatherings are still some of England's top musical events. Mid-June's **Isle of Wight Festival** (www.isleofwightfestival. org) has been headlined by Muse, the Red Hot Chili Peppers, the Kings of Leon and the Rolling Stones, while **Bestival** (www.bestival.net), in early September, delights in an eclectic, alternative feel, drawing the Super Furry Animals, Scissor Sisters, Candi Staton and more.

now a cheery, bunting-draped houseboat. Comfy cabins come complete with tiny bathrooms, while the harbour views from the flower-framed sun deck are simply superb.

Townhouse
B&B **££**

(☑ 07703-171365; www.thetownhouseryde.co.uk; 1 Monkton St, Ryde; d £70-90; 🛜) Swish and quirky sums up the Townhouse; expect smoothly stylish furnishings, brass bedsteads, and a fireside roll-top bath in the poshest room. Breakfast is available until 1.30pm (gasp!), and is either in a nearby, seafront cafe, or is a bacon sandwich delivered to your room.

Eating

Pilot Boat
PUB **££**

(☑ 01983-872077; www.thepilotboatinn.com; Station Rd, Bembridge; mains £9; ⊙ noon-2pm & 6-8pm; P 🛜) It's a good sign when customers can just sit down and play the pub's piano and guitars – a convivial atmosphere added to by a log-burner, ships' flags and quality homemade grub (think local crab salad and big bowls of chilli). Meanwhile, the spic-and-span bedrooms (doubles £90) are attractively nautically themed.

Black Sheep
BISTRO **££**

(www.theblacksheepbar.co.uk; 53 Union St, Ryde; tapas £5-7; ⊙ 10am-11pm Sun-Thu, to 2am Fri & Sat) Fancy sitting on a sunny terrace, sipping an Isle of Wight-brewed beer and eating tapas-style treats – perhaps chargrilled chorizo or buffalo mozzarella with honey and thyme? Then join the cool crowd at this elegant lounge club, with its art-deco vibe.

Ventnor & Around

POP 6300

The Victorian town of Ventnor slaloms so steeply down the island's southern coast that it feels like the south of France. The winding streets are home to a scattering of boutiques, while local hotels, eateries and the atmospheric Steephill Cove are well worth a detour.

To the west, the island's southernmost point is marked by the stocky 19th-century **St Catherine's Lighthouse** and its 14th-century counterpart **St Catherine's Oratory**. Nearby, kid-friendly **Blackgang Chine Fun Park** (☑ 01983-730330; www.blackgangchine.com; admission £17; ⊙ 10am-5pm Apr-Jul, to 6pm Aug, to 4pm Sep-Mar) features water gardens, animated shows and a hedge maze.

🛏 Sleeping

★ Lighthouse
APARTMENT **£**

(☑ 07801-899747; www.theboathouse-steephillcove.co.uk; Steephill Cove; 6 people per week £1400-1850) This is the sea-view sleep spot of your dreams. A white, two-storey, clapperboard lighthouse where the style is pure New England beach chic and the setting is right on the shore. Lie in bed watching the waves, take a few steps to the beach to swim in the sea, stroll out to dine on your private deck. Heavenly. The same people run a house (sleeping six, £700 to £1400 per week) and the romantic, two-person Crow's Nest (£350 to £550) nearby.

St Augustine Villa
B&B **££**

(Harbour View; ☑ 01983-852285; www.harbourviewhotel.co.uk; Esplanade, Ventnor; s £94, d £88-103; P 🛜) Country house collectibles dot this Italianate Victorian villa, wing-backed chairs sit in stately bedrooms and rich red fabrics frame sea views. And what views: watch the sun set from your sofa or the waves roll from your four-poster bed. The window-seated Tower Room sees light pour in from three sides.

Hambrough
BOUTIQUE HOTEL **£££**

(☑ 01983-856333; www.thehambrough.com; Hambrough Rd, Ventnor; d £190-280; P 🛜) It's hard to say which is better: the 180-degree vistas out to sea, or the super-sleek rooms where espresso machines and heated floors keep luxury levels set sky-high.

Eating

Crab Shed
CAFE **£**

(Steephill Cove; snacks £5; ⊙ noon-3pm Apr-Sep) Lobster pots and fishing boats line the slipway outside a shack that's a riot of sea-smoothed spas, cork floats and faded buoys. Irresistible treats include meaty crab salads, mackerel ciabatta and crumbly crab pasties.

★ Boathouse
SEAFOOD **££**

(☑ 01983-852747; www.theboathouse-steephillcove.co.uk; Steephill Cove; mains £18-35; ⊙ noon-3pm Thu-Tue late May-early Sep) Arrive early enough, and you'll see Steephill Cove's fishermen (Jimmy and Mark) landing your lunch – the sanded-wooden tables here are just steps from the sea. It makes a spellbinding spot to sip chilled wine, sample succulent lobster and revel in Wight's new-found driftwood chic. Book.

Pond Cafe
MODERN BRITISH **££**

(☑ 01983-855666; www.thehambrough.com; Bonchurch; mains £15; ⊙ 10.30am-3pm & 6-9.30pm Thu-Mon) Chef Joanne Bennetts loves giving Italian

STEEPHILL COVE

Steephill Cove's tiny, sandy beach is fringed by buildings that range from stone cottages to rickety-looking shacks. Beach finds festoon porches dotted with driftwood furniture and draped with fishing nets; a tiny clapper-board **lighthouse** presides over the scene. That lighthouse is let out as a fabulous self-catering apartment (p248) sleeping six. Two atmospheric places to eat, the Boathouse (p248) and the Crab Shed (p248), add to the appeal.

Steephill Cove is 1 mile west of Ventnor and is off limits to cars. Walk from the nearby Botanical Gardens, or hike from the hillside car park 200m west of Ventnor Esplanade, then follow the (sometimes steep) coast path until you arrive.

twists to prime island ingredients; perhaps roast local pigeon with pancetta, parmesan-flecked island beef carpaccio, or the day's catch with cannellini bean mash. Canny locals book a terrace table for a set lunch or early evening meal (two/three courses £18/22).

Ale & Oyster BISTRO ££
(www.thealeandoyster.co.uk; The Esplanade, Ventnor; £8-22; ⊗ noon-2.30pm & 6-9pm Tue-Sun) Modern takes on pub and bistro standards include monkfish scampi and chips, ham-hock terrine with poached egg, and Isle of Wight cheeses.

West Wight

Rural and remote, Wight's westerly corner is where the island really comes into its own. Sheer white cliffs rear from a surging sea as the stunning coastline peels west to Alum Bay and the most famous chunks of chalk in the region: the **Needles**. These jagged rocks rise, shard-like out of the sea, looking like the backbone of a prehistoric sea monster. West Wight is also home to arguably the isle's best beach: sandy, windswept **Compton Bay**.

⊙ Sights

★**Needles Old & New Battery** FORT
(NT; ☑ 01983-754772; www.nationaltrust.org.uk; The Needles; adult/child £5.30/2.65; ⊗ 11am-4pm mid-Mar–Oct) The Victorian fort complex at the Isle of Wight's western tip houses two gun emplacements where engrossing displays convey how the site was established in 1862, served in two world wars and then became a secret Cold War rocket-testing base. Walk to the battery along the cliffs from Alum Bay (1 mile) or hop on the **tourist bus** (www.islandbuses.info; per 24hr adult/child £10/5; ⊗ 10am-5pm mid-Mar–Sep) that runs twice-hourly between battery and bay.

The whiff of gunpowder seems to linger still at **Old Battery**: shells and powder kegs

lie around, uniforms hang on pegs. You get to pinpoint ships' positions with the rangefinders, then scramble down an ornate spiral staircase, along an echoey 60m tunnel to a searchlight post with close-up views of the eroded cliffs.

In the 1950s the batteries staged top-secret trials of Black Knight rockets, built at East Cowes, that were later used to launch Cold War surveillance satellites into space from Australia. In the tiny underground bunker at **New Battery**, exhibits evoke how this remote location and the existing fortifications proved ideal for keeping clandestine activities away from prying eyes.

⌖ Tours

Needles Pleasure Cruises BOAT TOUR
(☑ 01983-761587; www.needlespleasurecruises.co. uk; Alum Bay; adult/child £5.50/3.50; ⊗ 10.30am-4.30pm Apr-Oct) Twenty-minute voyages run half hourly from Alum Bay beach to the towering Needles chalk stacks, providing close-up views of those soaring white cliffs.

⌷ Sleeping

★**Really Green** CAMPSITE £
(☑ 07802-678591; www.thereallygreenholidaycompany.com; Blackbridge Rd, Freshwater Bay; yurt per week £375-700; ⊗ Apr-Oct; ℗) ✦ Roughing it has never been so smooth. The two- to five-person, fully furnished yurts on this tree-shaded site feature four-poster beds, futons, wood-burning stoves and time-worn antiques. It's set amid secluded fields with river views, and a local farm shop-cum-deli is just a few minutes' walk away.

Totland Bay YHA HOSTEL £
(☑ 01983-752165; www.yha.org.uk; Hirst Hill, Totland Bay; dm/d £17/22; ℗) Creaking, cheerfully run Victorian house with a maximum of eight beds per room and staff happy to share local info.

DORSET

Holiday hot spot Dorset offers a checklist of charms. Its shoreline is one of Britain's best, boasting the Jurassic Coast – a World Heritage Site flecked with sea-carved bays, crumbly cliffs and beaches loaded with fossilised souvenirs. No wonder the swimming, kayaking and hiking here are truly memorable. Inland Thomas Hardy's lyrical landscape serves up vast Iron Age hill forts, rude chalk figures, fairy-tale castles and must-see stately homes. Then there are resorts packed with party animals, golden beaches much loved by multi-millionaires, and Olympic-class sailing waters. Dorset is worth adding to your list.

ⓘ Information

Visit Dorset (www.visit-dorset.com) The county's official tourism website.

ⓘ Getting Around

One main train line runs from Bristol and Bath through Dorchester West to Weymouth. The other connects London with Weymouth, via Southampton, Bournemouth, Poole and Dorchester South.

First (www.firstgroup.com) Runs key bus routes linking the main towns.

More (Wilts & Dorset; www.morebus.co.uk) Key bus operator in Bournemouth, Poole and surrounding rural areas.

Bournemouth

POP 186,700

If one thing has shaped Bournemouth it's the beach. This glorious, 7-mile strip of soft sand first drew holiday-makers in the Victorian days. Today the resort attracts both grey-haired coach parties and boozed-up stag parties – on Saturday nights fancy-dress is everywhere; angels in L-plates meet men in mankinis. But Bournemouth is more than just a full-on party town. It also boasts some hip hideaways, great restaurants, tempting water sports, and in Boscombe, 2 miles east of the centre, a suburb with a cool urban-surfer vibe.

◉ Sights & Activities

Bournemouth Beach   BEACH
Bournemouth's sandy shoreline regularly clocks up seaside awards. It stretches from Southborne in the far east to Alum Chine in the west – an immense promenade backed by 3000 deckchairs, ornamental gardens, kids' playgrounds and cafes. The resort also has two piers. Around **Bournemouth Pier** you can hire brightly painted **beach huts** (🗹 0845 055 0968; www.bournemouthbeachhuts.co.uk; per day/week £36/145), deckchairs (per day £2.50), windbreaks (£3) and parasols (£4.50). Boscombe Pier is a focus for water sports.

East Cliff Lift Railway   HERITAGE RAILWAY
(🗹 01202-451781; Undercliff Dr; adult/child £1.25/85p; ☺ Easter-Oct) These box-like passenger cars on rails whiz up bracken-covered slopes. First built in 1908, the system cuts out the short, steep hike up the zigzag paths from the seafront promenade to the road above.

Alum Chine   GARDENS
(Mountbatten Rd; ☺ 24hr) Bournemouth's 1920s heyday is beautifully evoked at a subtropical enclave containing plants from the Canary Islands, New Zealand, Mexico and the Himalayas; their bright-red bracts, silver thistles and purple flowers are set against a glittering sea. Its 1.5 miles west of Bournemouth Pier.

Russell-Cotes   MUSEUM
(🗹 01202-451858; www.russell-cotes.bournemouth .gov.uk; Russell-Cotes Rd; adult/child £5/4; ☺ 10am-5pm Tue-Sun) Ostentation oozes from almost every inch of this arresting structure: a mash up of Italianate villa and Scottish Baronial pile. It was built at the end of the 1800s for Merton and Annie Russell-Cotes as somewhere to showcase the remarkable range of souvenirs gathered on their world travels. Look out for a plaster version of the Parthenon frieze, Maori woodcarvings and Persian tiles. Paintings include those by Rossetti, Edwin Landseer and William Frith.

Sorted Watersports   WATER SPORTS
(🗹 01202-300668; www.sortedsurfschool.co.uk; Overstrand Bldg, Undercliff Dr) From its base beside Boscombe Pier, Sorted runs lessons in surfing (per two hours adult/child £30/25) and stand-up paddleboarding (per two hours £30). It also hires out wetsuits (two/eight hours £10/30), surfboards (two/eight hours £10/30), stand-up paddleboards (one/two hours £15/20) and kayaks (one/four hours £15/45).

Coastal Activity Park   OUTDOORS
(www.coastalactivitypark.co.uk; Boscombe Promenade) Still in development at time of writing, this 1-mile-long cluster of activities is set to bring bouldering, slacklining, snorkelling, beach volleyball, beach football, table tennis and gym machines to the Boscombe shore.

Sleeping

Bournemouth Backpackers
HOSTEL £

(📞 01202-299491; www.bournemouthbackpackers. co.uk; 3 Frances Rd; dm/d £18/33; P 🖥) Three-to six-bed dorms in a suburban house dotted with travellers' totems – one wall is lined with chocolate bar wrappers from around the world. It's for non-UK citizens only; reservations by email, or by phone: 5pm to 7pm Sunday.

★ B&B By The Beach
B&B ££

(📞 01202-433632; www.bedandbreakfastbythebeach .co.uk; 7 Burtley Rd; d £88-92; P 🖥) Gorgeous rooms, fruit-packed breakfasts and charming, quick-to-laugh owners make this light-filled B&B one of the best in town. Bright, fresh bedrooms sport white shutters and subtle seaside themes, while the sunny patio is perfect for breakfast waffles or a slice of homemade cake.

Mory House
B&B ££

(📞 01202-433553; www.moryhouse.co.uk; 31 Grand Ave; s £50-65, d £72-93, f from £108; P 🖥) There's a delightful air of calm at Mory, where stained glass and an elegant stairwell hint at the house's Edwardian age. The pick of the contemporary bedrooms is no 3, where a pint-sized balcony is an ideal spot to nibble one of the cookies and sweets you'll find scattered around.

Amarillo
B&B ££

(📞 01202-553884; www.amarillohotel.co.uk; 52 Frances Rd; s £30-35, d £60-70; P 🖥) Amarillo's smart, stylish rooms remain ridiculously good value; expect jazzy wallpaper, snazzy throws and subtle lighting.

★ Urban Beach
BOUTIQUE HOTEL ££

(📞 01202-301509; www.urbanbeach.co.uk; 23 Argyll Rd; s £72, d £100-145; P @ 🖥) Still the slumber-spot of choice for Bournemouth's hip visitors, Urban Beach revels in a 'no worries' air that sees free loans of wellingtons, umbrellas and DVDs. Bold black, dark grey and deep brown colour schemes define bedrooms, while the decked terrace is full of dudes tucking into fare from the upscale bistro (open 8am to 10pm).

✗ Eating

★ Urban Reef
BISTRO ££

(📞 01202-443960; www.urbanreef.com; Undercliff Dr, Boscombe; mains £7-35; ⊙ 8am-11pm Mon-Sat, to 6pm Sun; 🖥) On sunny weekends a cool crowd is queuing out the door at funky Urban Reef. No wonder: a waterfront deck and balcony, punchy coffee, top-notch snacks and quality, sustainable restaurant fare. On stormy days snuggle down beside the log burner and listen to the sound of the sea.

West Beach
SEAFOOD ££

(📞 01202-587785; www.west-beach.co.uk; Pier Approach; mains £13-40; ⊙ noon-2.30pm & 6-9pm) The seafood and setting are hard to beat – bag a chair on the decked terrace jutting out over the sand, watch the waves lap Bournemouth Pier and tuck into perfectly cooked, perfectly fresh fish; perhaps plaice braised in cider or a shellfish platter piled high with oysters, langoustines, cockles and clams.

Reef Encounter
BISTRO ££

(www.reef-encounter.com; 42 Sea Rd, Boscombe; mains £7-15; ⊙ 11am-10pm, from 9am Sat & Sun; 🖥) Big squishy sofas, rough wood walls, a mellow soundtrack and a sea-view terrace give this chilled-out eatery a surf-bar vibe. Graze your way through a meat, fish or veggie platter, or just sit alfresco, sipping a tall, cool beer, watching the waves.

🍸 Drinking & Nightlife

Most of the main entertainment venues are clustered around Firvale Rd, St Peter's Rd and Old Christchurch Rd. The gay scene kicks off around the Triangle.

Sixty Million Postcards
PUB

(www.sixtymillionpostcards.com; 19 Exeter Rd; ⊙ noon-midnight Sun-Thu, to 2am Fri & Sat) An oasis of pure funkiness amid drinks-promotion Bournemouth, Sixty Million draws a decidedly beatnik crowd. Worn wooden floors and fringed lampshades frame events encompassing DJ sets, live music (think indie-pop and punk grunge) and musical bingo.

Old Firestation
CLUB

(www.oldfirestation.co.uk; 36 Holdernhurst Rd; ⊙ 10pm-3am Thu-Sat) Mixes gigs, club nights and student parties; music takes in D&B, dubstep, electro and old skool.

ℹ Information

Rio Internet Cafe (📞 01202-312021; 130 Commercial Rd; per hr £1.80; ⊙ 9am-7pm)

Tourist Office (📞 08450-511700; www. bournemouth.co.uk; Westover Rd; ⊙ 10am-5pm Mon-Sat, to 4pm Sun, closed Sun Nov-Feb)

ⓘ Getting There & Away

BUS

Morebus Zone A Dayrider (adult/child £4.10/3.60) Gives a day's unlimited travel in much of Poole, Bournemouth and neighbouring Christchurch.

Direct National Express routes include:

Bristol (£20, four hours, one service Monday to Saturday)

London (£23, 2½ hours, half-hourly)

Oxford (£22, three hours, three daily)

Southampton (£7, 50 minutes, hourly)

Local buses:

Poole (£2, 25 minutes, every 15 minutes) Bus M1/M2.

Salisbury (£6.30, 1¼ hours, at least hourly) Bus X3.

TRAIN

Destinations include Dorchester South (£12, 45 minutes, hourly), London Waterloo (£20, 2¾ hours, half-hourly), Poole (£4, 12 minutes, half-hourly) and Weymouth (£15, one hour, hourly).

Poole

POP 148,600

In the quaint old port of Poole there's a whiff of money in the air: the town borders Sandbanks, a gorgeous beach backed by some of the world's most expensive chunks of real estate. Big bucks aside, Poole also boasts excellent eateries and is the springboard for water sports and some irresistible boat trips.

◎ Sights

Brownsea Island   ISLAND
(NT; ☑ 01202-707744; www.nationaltrust.org.uk; adult/child £6/3; ◷ 10am-5pm late Mar-Oct)

On this small, wooded island in the middle of Poole Harbour trails weave through heath and woods, past peacocks, red squirrels, red deer and a wealth of bird life: the water-framed views onto the Isle of Purbeck are stunning. Free guided walks (at 11.30am and 2pm) focus on the wartime island, smugglers and pirates. Boats, run by **Brownsea Island Ferries** (☑ 01929-62383; www.brownseaislandferries.com; ◷ 10am-5pm late Mar-Oct), leave from Poole Quay (adult/child return £10/6) and Sandbanks (adult/child return £6/4.50) half-hourly.

Brownsea also played a key role in a global movement famous for three-fingered salutes, shorts and toggles – Lord Baden-Powell staged the first ever scout camp here in 1907.

Poole Old Town   HISTORIC AREA
Poole Quay's attractive historic buildings include the Tudor **King Charles pub** on Thames St; the cream **Old Harbour Office** (1820s) next door; and the impressive red-brick **Custom House** (1813) opposite, complete with Union Jack and gilded coat of arms. The tourist office sells the *Poole Cockle Trail* guide to the old town (30p).

Waterfront Museum   MUSEUM
(☑ 01202-262600; www.boroughofpoole.com/museums; 4 High St; ◷ 10am-5pm Mon-Sat, noon-5pm Sun) **FREE** The building alone is worth seeing: a beautifully restored 15th-century warehouse. The star exhibit though is a 2300-year-old **Iron Age logboat** dredged up from Poole Harbour. At 10m long and 14 tonnes, it's the largest to be found in southern Britain and probably carried 18 people. It was hand-chiselled from a single tree; millennia later you can still see the blade marks in the wood.

WATER SPORTS – POOLE HARBOUR

Poole Harbour's sheltered coasts may inspire you to get on the water. Operators cluster near the start of the Sandbanks peninsula.

Pool Harbour Watersports (☑ 01202-700503; www.pooleharbour.co.uk; 284 Sandbanks Rd) This operator does lessons in stand-up paddleboarding (SUP; per two hours £40), windsurfing (per three hours £45) and kitesurfing (per day £99), plus memorable kayak and SUP tours (per three hours £40).

FC Watersports (☑ 01202-707757; www.fcwatersports.co.uk; 19 Banks Rd, Sandbanks) Provides kitesurfing lessons (per day £99).

Watersports Academy (☑ 01202-708283; www.thewatersportsacademy.com; Banks Rd) Offers kitesurfing lessons, and also runs windsurfer taster sessions (per hour £25), plus sailing courses (per two hours/days £55/165) and wakeboarding and water-skiing (per 15 minutes £20).

Sandbanks   BEACH

A 2-mile, wafer-thin peninsula of land that curls around the expanse of Poole Harbour, Sandbanks is studded with some of the most expensive houses in the world. But the white-sand beaches that border them are free, and have some of the best water quality standards in the country. They're also home to a host of water-sports operators. Brownsea Island Ferries (p252) shuttle between Poole Quay and Sandbanks (adult/child return £10/6).

🛏 Sleeping

Corkers   B&B ££

(☑01202-681393; www.corkers.co.uk; 1 High St; s £61-77, d £83-94; 🕾) The decor may be unremarkable, but this neat 'n' tidy B&B punches way above its weight, thanks to a setting right on bustling Poole Quay and the tiny harbour-view roof terrace attached to the Brownsea and Purbeck rooms.

Quayside   B&B ££

(☑01202-683733; www.poolequayside.co.uk; 9 High St; s £35-50, d £60-80, f £80; 🕾) Snug rooms in pine and bright, blocky prints in the heart of the old harbour.

Merchant House   BOUTIQUE B&B £££

(☑01202-661474; www.themerchanthouse.org.uk; 10 Strand St; s £100, d £140-180) Tucked just one street back from the water's edge, tall, red-brick Merchant House is boutiquery at its best. Hefty wood sculptures, wicker rocking chairs and crisp linen ensure it's stylish; the odd teddy bear keeps it cheery too.

🍴 Eating

Storm   SEAFOOD ££

(☑01202-674970; www.stormfish.co.uk; 16 High St; mains £16-20; ☺6-10pm Mon-Sat) Ah, Storm. They've been cooking up one here since 1991 and it's still just as good. Dishes depend on what fisherman-owner, Pete, has caught; it might be intense Goan fish curry, buttery local plaice or fragrant local clams steamed in white wine. They also open some summer lunchtimes; call to check.

Poole Arms   PUB ££

(www.localbiztoday.com/poole-arms; The Quay; mains £9-16; ☺noon-2.30pm & 6-8.30pm) The grub at this ancient pub is strong on locally landed seafood – try the homemade fish pie, local crab or pan-fried herring roe. Order some New Forest beer, then settle down in the snug wood-lined bar with the locals, or on the terrace overlooking the quay.

★ Guildhall Tavern   FRENCH £££

(☑01202-671717; www.guildhalltavern.co.uk; 15 Market St; mains £20, 2-course lunch/dinner £15/22; ☺noon-3pm & 5.30-10pm Tue-Sat; 🅿) Poole's top table delights as it works local ingredients with French flair. Try chargrilled sea bass flambéed with Pernod or the superb-value set menus, where double-baked cheese soufflé and beef bourguignon are followed by crepe au chocolat and ripe cheese.

ℹ Information

Tourist Office (☑0845 234 5560; www.pooletourism.com; Poole Quay; ☺10am-5pm, to 6pm Jul & Aug, closed Sun Nov-Apr)

ℹ Getting There & Around

BOAT

Brittany Ferries (☑0871 244 0744; www.brittany-ferries.com) Sails between Poole and Cherbourg in France (4½ hours, one daily). Summer return prices range from around £80 for foot passengers to £320 for a car and two adults.

Sandbanks Ferry (☑01929-450203; www.sandbanksferry.co.uk; per pedestrian/car £1/3.50; ☺7am-11pm) Makes the four-minute trip from Sandbanks to Studland every 20 minutes. It's a short cut from Poole to Swanage, Wareham and the Isle of Purbeck, but the summer queues can be a pain.

BUS

Bournemouth (£2, 25 minutes, every 15 minutes) Bus M1/M2.

London Victoria (£20, 2¾ hours, every two hours) National Express.

Sandbanks (£3.40, 30 minutes, hourly Monday to Saturday) Bus 52.

TAXI

Dial-a-Cab (☑01202-666822; www.pooletaxis.co.uk)

TRAIN

Bournemouth (£4, 12 minutes, half-hourly)
Dorchester South (£10, 30 minutes, hourly)
London Waterloo (£25, 2¾ hours, half-hourly)
Weymouth (£14, 45 minutes, hourly)

Southeast Dorset

With its string of glittering bays and towering rock formations, the southeast of Dorset can claim the county's most beautiful shores. Also known as the 'Isle' of Purbeck (although it's a peninsula), it's also the start of the Jurassic Coast and the scenery and geology, especially around Lulworth Cove, make swimming here irresistible and hiking memorable. The hinterland harbours the huge, fairy-tale ruins of Corfe Castle, while Wareham sheds light on the mysterious figure of Lawrence of Arabia.

Wareham & Around

POP 5492

Saxons established the sturdy settlement of Wareham beside the River Frome in the 10th century, and their legacy lingers in the remaining defensive walls and one of Dorset's last remaining Saxon churches. Wareham is also famous for its links to the enigmatic TE Lawrence, the British soldier immortalised in the 1962 David Lean epic *Lawrence of Arabia*.

◉ Sights

★ Clouds Hill HOUSE
(NT; ☑ 01929-405616; www.nationaltrust.org.uk; near Bovington; adult/child £5.50/2.50; ⊙ 11am-5pm Wed-Sun mid-Mar–Oct; 🅿) The tiny cottage that was home to TE Lawrence (1888–1935) provides a compelling insight into a complex man. The British soldier became legendary after working with Arab tribes against Turkish forces in WWI. Look out for Lawrence's evocative desert campaign photos, his French crusader castle sketches and the desk where he abridged *Seven Pillars of Wisdom*. The four idiosyncratic rooms include a surprisingly comfortable cork-lined bathroom, an aluminium foil–lined bunk room and a heavily beamed music room.

The house is much as Lawrence left it – he died at the age of 46 after a motorbike accident on a nearby road.

St Martin's on the Walls CHURCH
(North St, Wareham; ⊙ 9am-5pm) This 11th-century church features a 12th-century fresco on the northern wall, and a marble effigy of TE Lawrence. If it's locked during normal shop hours, get the key from Joy's Outfitters in North St.

Monkey World ZOO
(☑ 01929-462537; www.monkeyworld.co.uk; Longthorns; adult/child £12/8.50; ⊙ 10am-5pm, to 6pm Jul & Aug; 🅿) An appealing sanctuary for rescued chimpanzees, orang-utans, gibbons, marmosets and some utterly adorable ring-tailed lemurs.

🛏 Sleeping & Eating

Red Lion INN ££
(☑ 01929-550099; www.redlionwareham.co.uk; 1 North St, Wareham; d £90-115; 🅿) Gorgeous,

elegant and full of fancy touches, the supremely stylish makeover of this old inn sees vast rooms sport brass bedsteads, sweet armchairs and wind-up alarm clocks. The menu (mains £6 to £16, kitchen open noon to 8pm) spans Dorset pâté to Sunday roast.

Anglebury INN ££
(☑ 01929-408094; www.angleburyhouse.co.uk; 15 North St; s/d/f £50/75/95) In an inn that's more than 450 years old you expect a bit of atmosphere, and that's just what you get. A creaking, twisting staircase leading to sedate, traditionally styled bedrooms, and dark wood and beams galore in the bar.

ℹ Information

Purbeck Tourist Office (☑ 01929-552740; www.visitswanageandpurbeck.com; South St, Wareham; ⊙ 9.30am-4pm Mon-Sat)

ℹ Getting There & Away

Rail links include London Waterloo (£25, 2½ hours, half-hourly) and Weymouth (£10, 30 minutes, half-hourly).

Bus 40 runs hourly north to Poole (£4.90, 35 minutes) and south to Swanage (£4.90, 30 minutes) via Corfe Castle (£4, 15 minutes). Bus 104 goes to Lulworth (£4.90, 35 minutes, two daily, Monday to Saturday).

Corfe Castle

The massive, shattered ruins of Corfe Castle loom so dramatically from the landscape it's like blundering into a film set. The defensive fragments tower over an equally photogenic village, which bears the castle's name and makes for a romantic spot for a meal or an overnight stay.

◉ Sights

★ Corfe Castle CASTLE
(NT; ☑ 01929-481294; www.nationaltrust.org.uk; The Square; adult/child £8/4; ⊙ 10am-6pm Apr-Sep, to 4pm Oct-Mar) The startling, fractured battlements of one of Dorset's most iconic landmarks were once home to Sir John Bankes, Charles I's right-hand man. The Civil War saw the castle besieged by Cromwellian forces; in 1646 the plucky Lady Bankes directed a six-week defence and the castle fell only after being betrayed from within. The Roundheads then gunpowdered Corfe Castle apart; today turrets and soaring walls still sheer off at precarious angles, while the splayed-out gatehouse looks like it's just been blown up.

JURASSIC COAST

The kind of massive, hands-on geology lesson you wish you had at school, the Jurassic Coast is England's first natural World Heritage Site, putting it on a par with the Great Barrier Reef and the Grand Canyon. This striking shoreline stretches from Exmouth in East Devon to Swanage in Dorset, encompassing 185 million years of the earth's history in just 95 miles. It means you can walk, in just a few hours, many millions of years in geological time.

It began when layers of rocks formed, their varying compositions determined by different climates: desert-like conditions gave way to higher then lower sea levels. Massive earth movements then tilted all the rock layers, forcing most of the oldest formations to the west, and the youngest to the east. Next, erosion exposed the different strata.

The differences are very tangible. Devon's rusty-red Triassic rocks are 200–250 million years old. Lyme Regis' fossil-rich, dark-clay Jurassic cliffs are 190 million years old. Pockets of much younger, creamy-coloured Cretaceous rocks (a mere 140–65 million years old) pop up, notably around Lulworth Cove, where erosion has sculpted a stunning display of bays, stacks and rock arches.

The coast's **website** (www.jurassiccoast.com) is a great information source; also look out locally for the highly readable *Official Guide to the Jurassic Coast* (£4.95), or buy it at www.jurassiccoasttrust.org.

Swanage Steam Railway HERITAGE RAILWAY
(☑01929-425800; www.swanagerailway.co.uk; adult /child return £11.50/7; ☉daily Apr-Oct, Sat & Sun Nov-Mar) Vintage steam trains run (roughly hourly) between Swanage and Norden (25 minutes), stopping at Corfe Castle.

🛏 Sleeping & Eating

Ammonite B&B £
(☑01929-480188; www.ammonite-corfecastle.co.uk; 88 West St; s £55, d £65-75; ᴘ 🛜) The pleasing bedrooms at this tranquil edge-of-village B&B feature pastels and pine, while the Aga-cooked breakfast includes local eggs, homemade jams and crusty bread from Corfe Castle's bakery.

Olivers B&B ££
(☑01929-477111; www.oliverscorfecastle.com; 5 West St; s £75-85, d £85-95) Tucked away in the heart of the old village in a charismatic street, Olivers combines honey-coloured beams with 21st-century chic: brown leather armchairs, tree silhouette wallpaper and chunky wood furniture – stylish, restful, great-value rooms.

Castle Inn PUB ££
(www.castleinncorfe.com; 63 East St; mains £10-17; ☉noon-3pm & 6-9pm Mon-Sat, noon-9pm Sun; 🐾) The locals' choice. Prepare to dine beside flagstone floors and ancient beams festooned with fairy lights on tasty pub classics, plus some surprises: try the sea bass given a kick by smoked paprika, or the chickpea stew.

ℹ Getting There & Away

Bus 40 shuttles hourly between Poole, Wareham, Corfe Castle and Swanage. The 15-minute trip to Wareham costs £4.

Lulworth Cove & Around

POP 740

South of Corfe Castle the coast steals the show. For millions of years the elements have been creating an intricate shoreline of curved bays, caves, stacks and weirdly wonderful rock formations – most notably the massive natural arch at Durdle Door.

At charismatic Lulworth Cove, a pleasing jumble of thatched cottages and fishing gear leads down to a perfect crescent of white cliffs.

◉ Sights & Activities

★**Durdle Door** LANDMARK
The poster-boy of Dorset's Jurassic Coast, this immense, sea-fringed, 150-million-year-old Portland stone arch was created by a combination of massive earth movements and erosion. Today it's framed by shimmering bays; bring your swimsuit and head down the hundreds of steps for an unforgettable dip.

You can park at the top of the cliffs, but it's best to hike the coast path from Lulworth Cove (1 mile), passing the delightfully named **Lulworth Crumple**, where layers of rock form dramatically zigzagging folds.

Lulworth Castle
CASTLE

(EH; ☎01929-400352; www.lulworth.com; East Lulworth; adult/child £5/3; ⏰10.30am-5pm Sun-Fri, to 4pm Nov-Mar) A confection in creamy, dreamy white, this baronial pile looks more like a French chateau than a traditional English castle. Built in 1608 as a hunting lodge, it's survived extravagant owners, extensive remodelling and a disastrous fire in 1929. It has been extensively restored – check out the reconstructed kitchen and cellars, then climb the tower for sweeping coastal views. It costs £3 to park.

Lulworth Cove Heritage Centre
INTERPRETATION CENTRE

(☎01929-400587; www.lulworth.com; main car park, Lulworth Cove; ⏰10am-5pm) Excellent displays outline how geology and erosion have combined to shape the area's remarkable shoreline. Staff can advise about walks as well.

★ Jurassic Coast Activities
KAYAKING

(☎01305-835301; www.jurassiccoastactivities.co. uk; Lulworth Cove; per person £50; ⏰up to 3 tours daily) This unmissable, three-hour paddle offers jaw-dropping views of Dorset's heavily eroded coast. Starting at Lulworth Cove, you glide through Stair Hole's caves and stacks, across Man O'War Bay then under the stone arch at Durdle Door, stopping for swims and picnics along the way.

🛏 Sleeping & Eating

Lulworth YHA
HOSTEL £

(☎0845 371 9331; www.yha.org.uk; School Lane, West Lulworth; dm £18-23; P) Hills stretch up behind and sheep bleat outside at this cosy, chalet-style, edge-of-village hostel.

Durdle Door Holiday Park
CAMPSITE £

(☎01929-400200; www.lulworth.com; sites £25-35; ⏰Mar-Oct; P) Spacious site, just minutes from the creamy cliffs and 1.5 miles west of Lulworth Cove.

★ Lulworth Cove
INN ££

(☎01929-400333; www.lulworth-coveinn.co.uk; Main Rd, Lulworth Cove; d £110-120; P🐾) Prepare for a vision of driftwood chic – whitewashed floorboards, aquamarine panels, painted wicker chairs and roll-topped baths. It's on the lane leading down to the cove, so add cracking sea views, a mini roof terrace and top-quality gastropub grub (mains £8 to £14, kitchen open noon to 9pm) and you have an irresistible inn.

Cove House
B&B ££

(☎01929-400137; www.covehouse.net; Main Rd, West Lulworth; s £80-95, d £80-100; P) Fragrant, calm, pristine rooms set amid West Lulworth's soaring hills.

Cove Fish
SEAFOOD £

(☎01929-400807; Lulworth Cove; ⏰10am-4pm Tue-Sun Easter-Oct, Sat & Sun Nov-Easter) The seafood piled high in this shed by the path to the beach has been caught by 9th-generation fisherman Joe. Bag a fish kebab for the BBQ, or settle at the wobbly table and tuck into Lulworth Cove crab – a meal that's travelled food yards not miles.

🍸 Drinking & Nightlife

★ Castle
PUB

(www.thecastleinn-lulworthcove.co.uk; West Lulworth; ⏰noon-10pm; 🐾) A head-spinning array of 40-plus ciders make this thatched pub a magnet for fans of the golden elixir. From quaffable Bumble Berry (4%) to epic Old Rosie (7.3%), this 'permanent cider festival' thoughtfully offers sampler trays (three different thirds of a pint) to help you get through a few.

ℹ Getting There & Away

Bus 104 links Lulworth with Wareham (£4.90, 35 minutes, two daily, Monday to Saturday).

Dorchester & Around

POP 19,143

With Dorchester, you get two towns in one: a real-life, bustling county town and Thomas Hardy's fictional Casterbridge. The Victorian writer was born nearby and his literary locations can still be found among Dorchester's white- and red-brick Georgian terraces. Here you can also visit Hardy's former homes and see his original manuscripts. Add cracking archaeological sites and attractive places to eat and sleep and you have an appealing base for a night or two.

⊙ Sights

Thomas Hardy fans will want to hunt down the *Mayor of Casterbridge* locations hidden among modern Dorchester. They include Lucetta's House, a grand Georgian affair with ornate door posts in Trinity St, while in parallel South St, a red-brick, mid-18th-century building (now a bank) is named as the inspiration for the house of the mayor himself. The tourist office sells book location guides.

★**Dorset County Museum**   MUSEUM
(📞 01305-262735; www.dorsetcountymuseum.org; High West St; adult/child £6.35/3.60; ⊙10am-5pm Mon-Sat, to 4pm Nov-Mar) The Thomas Hardy collection here is the world's largest, offering extraordinary insights into his creative process. Reading Hardy's cramped handwriting, you can see where he's crossed out one word and substituted another. There's also an atmospheric reconstruction of his study at Max Gate and a letter in which Siegfried Sassoon requests permission to dedicate his first book of poems to Hardy. In other collections, Jurassic Coast fossil exhibits feature a huge ichthyosaur and 6ft plesiosaur fore paddle.

Bronze and Iron Age finds from Maiden Castle include a treasure trove of coins and neck rings, while Roman artefacts include 70 gold coins, nail cleaners and (toe-curling) ear picks.

Max Gate   HISTORIC BUILDING
(NT; 📞 01305-262538; www.nationaltrust.org.uk; Alington Ave; adult/child £5.50/2.50; ⊙11am-5pm Wed-Sun mid-Mar–Oct; 🅿) Novelist Thomas Hardy was a trained architect and designed this attractive house, where he lived from 1885 until his death in 1928. *Tess of the D'Urbervilles* and *Jude the Obscure* were both written here, and the house contains several pieces of original furniture. It's a mile east of Dorchester, on the A352.

Hardy's Cottage   HISTORIC BUILDING
(NT; 📞 01305-262366; www.nationaltrust.org.uk; adult/child £5.50/2.50; ⊙11am-5pm Wed-Sun mid-Mar–Oct; 🅿) This picturesque cob-and-thatch house is the birthplace of Thomas Hardy and features evocative, sparsely furnished rooms and a lush garden. It's in Higher Bockhampton, 3 miles northeast of Dorchester.

Roman Town House   HISTORIC BUILDING
(www.romantownhouse.co.uk; Northern Hay; ⊙24hr) **FREE** The knee-high flint walls and beautifully preserved mosaics here powerfully conjure up the Roman occupation of Dorchester (then Durnovaria). Peek into the summer dining room to see the underfloor heating system (hypocaust), where charcoal-warmed air circulated around pillars to produce a toasty 18°C (64°F).

🛏 Sleeping

★**Beggars Knap**   BOUTIQUE B&B ££
(📞 01305-268191; www.beggarsknap.co.uk; 2 Weymouth Ave; s £60-70, d £80-90, f £85-130; 🅿) Despite the name, this altogether fabulous, vaguely decadent guesthouse is far from impoverished. Opulent rooms drip with chandeliers and gold brocades; beds draped in fine cottons range from French sleigh to four-poster. You could pay much, much more and get something half as nice.

Yalbury Cottage   HOTEL ££
(📞 01305-262382; www.yalburycottage.com; Lower Bockhampton; s £85, d £120) With its flower-framed patios and quaint village setting, serene Yalbury draws you deftly into rural Westcountry life. Fresh, simple cottage-style rooms overlook fields, the intimate restaurant is acclaimed (two/three courses cost £33/38, booking required) and the superb English tapas (£8, available noon to 4pm Tuesday to Saturday May to September) are packed with prime Dorset goodies.

Westwood   B&B ££
(📞 01305-268018; www.westwoodhouse.co.uk; 29 High West St; s/d/f £75/95/130; 🖥) For a delightful dollop of 18th-century elegance, head to Westwood. Plush bedrooms are decked out in olive, dove grey or duck-egg blue; and mi-

BATH & SOUTHWEST ENGLAND DORCHESTER & AROUND

WORTH A TRIP

MAIDEN CASTLE

Occupying a massive slab of horizon on the southern fringes of Dorchester, Maiden Castle (EH; www.english-heritage.org.uk; ⊙dawn-dusk; 🅿) **FREE** is the largest and most complex Iron Age hill fort in Britain. The huge, steep-sided chalk ramparts flow along a hill's contour lines and surround 48 hectares – the equivalent of 50 football pitches. The first hill fort was built on the site around 500 BC and in its heyday was densely populated with clusters of roundhouses and a network of roads. The Romans besieged and captured it in AD 43 – an ancient Briton skeleton with a Roman crossbow bolt in the spine was found at the site. Up close, the sheer scale of the ramparts is awe-inspiring and the winding complexity of the west entrance reveals just how hard it would be to storm. Finds from the site are displayed at Dorset County Museum (p257). Maiden Castle is 1.5 miles southwest of Dorchester.

ni-armchairs and shaded reading lights are dotted around. Breakfast is a veritable feast.

✗ Eating

No 6 FRENCH ££
(✆01305-267679; www.no6-restaurant.co.uk; 6 North Sq; mains £17; ⊙noon-2pm & 6.30-9pm Tue-Fri, 6-10pm Sat) The locally sourced produce appearing here is dished up with more than a soupçon of French finesse. Expect rich red wine–laced game crock, plump Lyme Bay king scallops and simply cooked but stunning fish. Canny foodies book Tuesday through to Thursday evenings, when a main and a pud is a mere £16.

Trinity SEAFOOD ££
(✆01305-757428; www.trinitybistro.co.uk; Trinity St; mains from £9; ⊙11.30am-3pm Tue-Sat, 6-9.30pm Thu-Sat) Mouth-watering aromas waft around you, and the open-plan kitchen is only yards away. The chalked-up menu might include lemon-fragranced sea bass, Scillian mussel or clams – it's no frills but fun and the fish is super fresh.

Sienna MODERN BRITISH £££
(✆01305-250022; www.siennarestaurant.co.uk; 36 High West St; 2-course lunch/dinner £26/39; ⊙12.30-2pm Wed-Sat, 7-9pm Tue-Sat) At tiny, Michelin-starred Sienna innovation, exquisite presentation and seasonal produce cast a fine culinary spell. Look out for duck egg and asparagus, brill with caviar, and cheeseboards bearing the very best of the west. Reservations required.

❶ Information

Tourist Office (✆01305-267992; www.visit-dorset.com; Antelope Walk; ⊙9am-5pm Mon-Sat Apr-Oct, to 4pm Nov-Mar)

❶ Getting There & Around

BICYCLE
Dorchester Cycles (✆01305-268787; www.dorchestercycles.co.uk; 31 Great Western Rd; per day £12; ⊙9am-5.30pm Mon-Sat)

BUS
London (£20, four hours, one daily) National Express.
Lyme Regis (£4.50, 1¾ hours, hourly) Bus 31.
Poole (£4.30, 1¼ hours, one daily Tuesday and Friday) Bus 186.
Sherborne (£4.10, one hour, four to six daily Monday to Saturday) Bus 216; via Cerne Abbas.
Weymouth (£3, 20 minutes, half-hourly) Bus 10.

TRAIN
There are services, every two hours, from Dorchester West to Bath (£30, two hours) and Bristol (£20, 2½ hours).
Hourly trains from Dorchester South:
Bournemouth (£12, 45 minutes)
London Waterloo (£25, 2¾ hours)
Southampton (£25, 1½ hours)
Weymouth (£5, 10 minutes)

Cerne Abbas & the Cerne Giant

If you had to describe an archetypal sleepy Dorset village, you'd come up with something a lot like Cerne Abbas: houses run the gamut of English architectural styles, roses climb countless doorways and half-timbered houses frame a honey-coloured, 12th-century church. But this village also packs one heck of a surprise: the Cerne Giant, a vast chalk figure of a naked man.

◎ Sights

Cerne Giant LANDMARK
(⊙24hr; ℗) FREE Rarely do you find such a nudge-nudge, wink-wink tourist attraction. Nude, full frontal and notoriously well endowed, this hill-side chalk figure is revealed in all his glory. And he's in a stage of excitement that wouldn't be allowed in most magazines. The giant is around 60m high and 51m wide and his age remains a mystery; some claim he's Roman but the first historical reference comes in 1694, when three shillings were set aside for his repair.

The Victorians found it all deeply embarrassing and allowed grass to grow over his most outstanding feature. Today the hill is grazed by sheep and cattle, though only the sheep are allowed to do their nibbling over the giant – the cows would do too much damage to his lines.

◉ Sleeping

Abbots B&B ££
(✆01300-341349; www.abbotsbedandbreakfast.co.uk; 7 Long St; s/d/f £60/85/130; ☎) The top-floor rooms here are big on atmosphere and small on head space, with duck-or-regret-it lintels for those over 6ft. It's charming throughout though, with rooms decked out in light grey, lemon and blue. The cakes in the cafe (open 10am to 5pm) are real diet busters.

★ **New Inn** INN ££
(☑ 01300-341274; www.thenewinncerneabbas.
co.uk; 14 Long St; d £95-140, ste £170; P 🛜)
What do you get when a retired Michelin
inspector runs a 16th-century English inn?
Sleekly styled boltholes in outhouses, and
luxurious main-building rooms rich in dark
beams. The bar has the easy atmosphere of
a country estate (think mounted antlers and
honey-brown tartan) and rustles up prime
gastropub (mains £9 to £18) delights from
noon to 2pm and 7pm to 9pm.

❶ Getting There & Away

Dorchester is 8 miles south. Bus 216 (four to six
daily Monday to Saturday) goes to Dorchester
(£2.40, 30 minutes) and Sherborne (£2.80, 30
minutes).

Weymouth

POP 65,000

An immense harbour ensured this strip of
Dorset coast was the 2012 Olympic sailing
venue – a state-of-the-art water-sports centre and a soaring viewing tower are among
the legacies. Otherwise, the area's core
character remains: fishing boats pack Weymouth's bustling harbour and candy-striped
beach kiosks line its 3-mile beach.

Weymouth has been a popular seaside spot
since King George III took an impromptu
dip here in 1789. More than 225 years later,
the town is still popular with holidaymakers,
drawn by a curling, golden beach, a revitalised
historic harbour and oodles of seaside kitsch.

◉ Sights & Activities

Weymouth Beach BEACH
The nostalgia-inducing offerings along
Weymouth's fine sandy shore could see you

marvelling at highly skilled sand sculptors,
renting a deckchair or pedalo (per hour £7),
watching Punch and Judy shows, and taking
a donkey ride. Alternatively, go all Califor-
nian and join a volleyball game.

Nothe Fort FORT
(☑ 01305-766626; www.nothefort.org.uk; Barrack
Rd; adult/child £7/1; ⊙ 10.30am-5.30pm Apr-Oct)
Weymouth's 19th-century defences are studded with cannons, searchlights and 12in
coastal guns. Exhibits detail Dorset's Roman
invasion, a Victorian soldier's drill and Weymouth in WWII. Commanding an armoured
car and clambering around the magazine
prove popular with regiments of children.

Sea Life AQUARIUM
(☑ 0871 423 2110; www.sealifeweymouth.com; Lod-
moor Country Park; admission £23; ⊙ 10am-5pm;
P) Aquarium highlights include sharks,
penguins and seahorses. Admission includes
a trip up the 53m **Sea Life Tower** on Weymouth seafront, which rotates to reveal expansive views. Tickets are 25% cheaper online.

Coastline Cruises BOAT CRUISE
(☑ 01305-785000; www.coastlinecruises.com; Brewers
Quay; adult/child return £9/6; ⊙ 2 boats daily
Apr-Oct) This wind-blown 40-minute jaunt
crosses Portland Harbour's vast 2012 Olym-
pic sailing waters, before dropping you off at
Portland Castle. Boats leave from Weymouth
Harbour.

🛏 Sleeping

★ **B+B** B&B ££
(☑ 01305-761190; www.bb-weymouth.com; 68 The
Esplanade; s £60-70, d £80-95; P 🛜) This hip hotel remains remarkable value with its sleek,
minimalist rooms (some have sea views) and
host of freebies; the mineral water, biscuits

WORTH A TRIP

ABBOTSBURY SWANNERY

Every May some 600 free-flying swans choose to nest at the **Abbotsbury Swannery**
(☑ 01305-871858; www.abbotsbury-tourism.co.uk; New Barn Rd, Abbotsbury; adult/child £11/8;
⊙ 10am-5pm late Mar-Oct), which shelters in the Fleet lagoon, protected by the ridge of Chesil
Beach. The swannery was founded by local monks about 600 years ago, and feathers from
the Abbotsbury swans are still used in the helmets of the Gentlemen at Arms (the Queen's
official bodyguard). Wandering the network of trails that wind between the swans' nests is
an awe-inspiring experience that is punctuated by occasional territorial displays (think snuf-
fling, coughing and stand-up flapping), ensuring that even the liveliest children are stilled.

The swannery is at the picturesque village of Abbotsbury, 10 miles from Weymouth off
the B3157.

THE CHANNEL ISLANDS

Clustering just off the coast of France, the islands of Jersey, Guernsey, Sark, Herm and Alderney overflow with exquisite coastlines, beautiful harbours, shaded lanes and old-world charm. The warm Gulf of St Malo ensures subtropical plants, superb local seafood and an incredible array of bird life.

The larger islands of Guernsey and Jersey are the main entry points, with a plethora of flights and ferries from both England and France. Air links between Guernsey, Jersey and Alderney are good, while fleets of ferries also connect them and the other islands. Accommodation and eating options abound; for details and transport information, see the islands' websites.

During WWII, the Channel Islands were the only British soil to be occupied by the Nazis, and poignant museums – some housed in old war tunnels and bunkers – provide an insight into the islanders' fortitude.

The islands are proudly independent, self-governing British Crown dependencies and sport a wealth of quirky anachronisms. English is the main language and although place names may look French, local pronunciation is very different. The islands print their own version of the British pound – it isn't legal tender on the mainland, but you can use British money on the islands. The Channel Islands aren't covered by NHS or EHIC cards, so make sure your travel insurance includes medical treatment. Tourist entry requirements are the same as for the UK.

Jersey

At 9 miles by 5 miles, **Jersey** (www.jersey.com) is the biggest of the Channel Islands. An offshore finance centre with a rugged north coast, key sights are the **Durrell Wildlife Park** (www.durrell.org) and the thought-provoking **Jersey War Tunnels** (www.jerseywartunnels.com), a former WWII underground military hospital.

Guernsey

The second-largest island, **Guernsey** (www.visitguernsey.com) features a captivating capital, St Peter Port and stunning sea cliffs and sandy bays. Victor Hugo's former home, **Hauteville House** (www.victorhugo.gg), and **Castle Cornet** (www.museums.gov.gg) are the big draws.

Alderney

Remote **Alderney** (www.visitalderney.com) is the third-largest island. Its village capital St Anne is picture-perfect; its wealth of bird and wildlife includes blonde hedgehogs and 7000 squawking seabirds.

Sark

On steep-sided, car-free **Sark** (www.sark.co.uk) transport is by bike, tractor or horse and cart – the island (measuring 3 miles by 1.5 miles) has a magical, castaway feel.

Herm

Tiny, traffic-free **Herm** (www.herm.com) is just 1.5 miles long and half a mile wide. Flower-strewn hills are framed by white sandy shores – Shell Beach is a superb spot for a swim.

and espresso machine coffee are best enjoyed in the funky 1st-floor lounge overlooking the bay. They'll loan you a bike as well.

Roundhouse   B&B ££
(☏ 01305-761010;www.roundhouse-hotel-weymouth.com; 1 The Esplanade; d £105-145; ☏) Soak up Weymouth's seaside charms from your bedroom – almost all here have superb views of the beach out front and the harbour behind. Inside, vivid decor combines sky blue, pur-

ple and shocking pink, while fluffy cushions sit beside snazzy modern art.

Old Harbour View   B&B ££
(☏01305- 774633; www.oldharbourviewweymouth.co.uk; 12 Trinity Rd; s/d £78/98; P ☏) In this pristine Georgian terrace you get boating themes in the fresh, white bedrooms and boats right outside the front door. One room overlooks the busy quay, the other faces the back.

Eating

Marlboro FISH & CHIPS £
(www.marlbororestaurant.co.uk; 46 St Thomas St;
mains £7.50; ⊙noon-9.45pm) There's a sustainable slant to this traditional chippy, just
metres from Weymouth's quay, with mackerel featuring among the long list of super-fresh
fish. Take it away or get munching in the
bay-windowed, licensed cafe (open till 8pm).

Dining Room MODERN BRITISH ££
(☑01305-783008; www.thediningroomweymouth.
co.uk; 67 St Mary St; mains £11-24; ⊙noon-2pm daily, 7-9.30pm Mon-Sat) Stand by to see fresh flavours transform local foods – the open-plan
design means you watch the chefs beavering
away. They might make you lime-cured, Wey-
mouth-landed fish, or red wine–laced Westcountry chorizo – the chocolate cheesecake
with Dorset wasabi is a feisty meal's end.

Dorset Burger Co BURGERS ££
(DBC; www.thedorsetburgercompany.co.uk; 97 St
Mary St; burgers £9; ⊙noon-3pm Wed-Sun, 6-9pm
Wed-Sat) These hand-patted, juicy, char-
grilled burgers are made mostly from Dorset
produce.

ⓘ Information

Tourist Office (☑01305-783225; www.
visit-dorset.com; The Esplanade; ⊙10am-6pm)
Inside the Weymouth Pavilion theatre.

ⓘ Getting There & Away

BUS
Axminster (£6, 2¼ hours, hourly) Bus 31.
Dorchester (£3, 20 minutes, half-hourly) Bus 10.
Fortuneswell (£2.50, Isle of Portland; 30
minutes, four per hour) Bus 1.
Jurassic Coast Bus X53 (£7.20, four daily
to hourly, no service winter Sundays) Travels
from Weymouth to Wareham (50 minutes),
Poole (1½ hours), Abbotsbury (35 minutes),
Lyme Regis (1¾ hours) and Exeter (three
hours).
London (£17, 4¼ hours, one direct daily)
National Express.
Lyme Regis (£6, two hours, hourly) Bus 31.
Portland Bill (£2.50, Isle of Portland; 45
minutes, from four daily May to September
only) Bus 501.

BOAT
Condor Ferries (☑0845 609 1024; www.con-
dorferries.co.uk) Sails to the Channel Islands of
Guernsey and Jersey. Prices range from around
£50 return for a foot passenger, to £300 return
for a car and two passengers.

TRAIN
Hourly services:
Bournemouth (£15, one hour)
Dorchester South (£5, 10 minutes)
London Waterloo (£30, three hours)

Services every two hours:
Bath (£17, two hours)
Bristol (£18, 2¾ hours)

Isle of Portland

The 'Isle' of Portland is really a hard, high
comma of rock fused to the rest of Dorset by the ridge of Chesil Beach. Its strip of
once-waste waterfront now features a sailing
centre, business units and new homes. But
inland, on the 500ft central plateau, a quarrying past still holds sway, evidenced by huge
craters and large slabs of limestone. Portland
also offers jaw-dropping views down onto
18-mile Chesil Beach, which is backed by the
Fleet, Britain's biggest tidal lagoon – home to
600 nesting swans. Proud, bleak and rough
around the edges, Portland is decidedly different from the rest of Dorset, and is all the
more compelling because of it. Its industrial
heritage, water-sports, rich bird life and starkly beautiful cliffs make it worth at least a day
trip. The population clusters of Fortuneswell
and Chiswell are towards the north of the isle;
Portland Bill is 4 miles south at the tip.

⊙ Sights

★ Tout Quarry OUTDOORS
(near Fortuneswell; ⊙24hr; Ⓟ) **FREE** Portland's
white limestone has been quarried for centuries, and has been used in some of the world's
finest buildings, such as the British Museum
and St Paul's Cathedral. Tout Quarry's disused
workings now house 53 sculptures that have
been carved into the rock in situ, resulting in
a fascinating combination of the raw material, the detritus of the quarrying process and
the beauty of chiselled works. Labyrinthine
paths snake through hacked-out gullies and
around jumbled piles of rock, revealing the
half-formed bears, bison and lizards that
emerge out of stone cliffs. Highlights include
Still Falling by Antony Gormley, *Woman on
Rock* by Dhruva Mistry and the well-hidden
Green Man. Tout Quarry is signed off the
main road, just south of Fortuneswell.

Portland Lighthouse LIGHTHOUSE
(☑01255-245156; www.trinityhouse.co.uk; Portland Bill; adult/child £4/3; ⊙11am-5pm Sun-Thu

WATER SPORTS – PORTLAND HARBOUR

At 890-hectare Portland Harbour, just south of Weymouth, you can glide in 2012 Olympic sailing waters. The **Weymouth & Portland National Sailing Academy** (☎01305-866000; www.wpnsa.org.uk; Portland Harbour) is home to the **Andrew Simpson Sailing Centre** (☎0753 201 6281; www.andrewsimpsonsailing.org), which runs lessons (adult/child per two days £180/210) and hires lasers (per two hours/day £32/75). Also on-site, **OTC** (☎07817-717904; www.uk.otc-windsurf.com) does lessons in stand-up paddleboarding (SUP; one/two hours £25/40) and windsurfing (per two hours/one day/two days £45/90/165). It also rents out SUP boards (per hour £10) and windsurf boards and sails (per hour £15).

Local waters offer superb diving, with a huge variety of depths, seascapes and wrecks. Operators include **Underwater Explorers** (☎01305-824555; www.underwaterexplorers.co.uk; Mereside, Portland) and **Old Harbour Dive Centre** (☎01305-760888; www.oldharbourdivecentre.co.uk; 11 Nothe Pde, Weymouth). Lessons range from around £50 a day to £475 for a five-day PADI openwater dive course.

late Apr-Aug; **P**) For a real sense of Portland's remote nature, head to its southern tip, Portland Bill. Then climb the 41m-high, candy-striped lighthouse for breathtaking views of rugged cliffs and the Race, a surging vortex of conflicting tides.

Portland Castle   CASTLE
(EH; ☎01305-820539; www.english-heritage.org.uk; Liberty Rd, Chiswell; adult/child £5/3; ☺10am-6pm Apr-Sep, to 5pm Oct) A particularly fine product of Henry VIII's castle-building spree, with expansive views over Portland harbour.

🛏 Sleeping & Eating

Portland YHA   HOSTEL £
(☎0845 371 9339; www.yha.org.uk; Castle Rd; dm/d £18/32) Comfy, rambling Edwardian house with sea views from most dorms.

Queen Anne House   B&B ££
(☎01305-820028; www.queenannehouse.co.uk; 2 Fortuneswell; s £45-55, d £75-90; 🐱) It's impossible to know which room to pick: White, with skylight, beams and a hobbit-esque door; Lotus, with its grand furniture; Oyster with its half tester bed, or the suite with French bath and mini-conservatory. It doesn't matter though – they're all great value and gorgeous.

⭐ **Crab House Cafe**   SEAFOOD ££
(☎01305-788867; www.crabhousecafe.co.uk; Portland Rd, Wyke Regis; mains £16-21; ☺noon-2.30pm & 6-9pm Wed-Sat, noon-3.30pm Sun) This is the place for fresh-as-it-gets seafood and beach-shack-chic. The funky cabin has views onto the cafe's own Fleet Lagoon oyster beds, while the waterside terrace is a prime place to sample clam and cockle spaghetti or cracked whole crab, best washed down with lip-smacking Somerset cider.

Cove House   PUB ££
(www.thecovehouseinn.co.uk; Chiswell Seafront; mains £10-18; ☺noon-2.30pm & 6-9pm Mon-Fri, noon-9pm Sat & Sun) Extraordinary Chesil Beach views, memorable sunsets and great grub (try the crunchy whitebait) in a history-rich fishermen's inn.

ℹ Getting There & Away

Bus 1 runs from Weymouth to Fortuneswell (£2.50, 30 minutes, four per hour). Between May and September bus 501 goes from Weymouth to Portland Bill (£2.50, from four daily).

Coastline Cruises (p259) runs ferries to Portland Castle from Weymouth.

Chesil Beach

One of the most breathtaking beaches in Britain, Chesil is 18 miles long, 15m high and moving inland at the rate of 5m a century. This mind-boggling, 100-million-tonne pebble ridge is the baby of the Jurassic Coast. A mere 6000 years old, its stones range from pea-sized in the west to hand-sized in the east.

◎ Sights & Activities

Chesil Beach Visitors Centre   INTERPRETATION CENTRE
(☎01305-206191; www.chesilbeach.org; Ferrybridge; ☺10am-4pm) **FREE** Just over the bridge to Portland, this centre is a great gateway to the beach. The pebble ridge is at its highest here – 15m compared to 7m at Abbotsbury. From the car park an energy-sapping hike up sliding pebbles leads to the constant surge and rattle of waves on stones and dazzling views of the sea, with the thin pebble line and the expanse of the Fleet Lagoon behind.

The centre details an ecosystem that includes ringed plover, redshank and oyster-catchers, as well as drifts of thrift and sea campion. There's also the Taste cafe here, open 10am to 4pm.

Fleet Observer BOATING
(☑ 01305-759692; www.thefleetobserver.co.uk; adult/child £7/4; ☺ daily Easter-Sep) Offers glass-bottom boat trips on the Fleet Lagoon.

Lyme Regis

POP 3662

Fantastically fossiliferous Lyme Regis packs a heavyweight historical punch. Rock-hard relics of the past pop out repeatedly from the surrounding cliffs – exposed by the landslides of a retreating shoreline. Now a pivot point of the Unesco-listed Jurassic Coast, fossil fever is definitely in the air and everyone, from proper palaeontologists to those out for a bit of fun, can engage in a spot of coastal rummaging. Add sandy beaches and some delightful places to sleep and eat, and you have a charming base for explorations.

○ Sights

Lyme Regis Museum MUSEUM
(☑ 01297-443370; www.lymeregismuseum.co.uk; Bridge St; adult/child £10/5; ☺ 10am-5pm Easter-Oct, 11am-4pm Wed-Sun Nov-Easter) In 1814 local teenager Mary Anning found the first full ichthyosaurus skeleton near Lyme Regis, propelling the town onto the world stage. An incredibly famous fossilist in her day, Miss Anning did much to pioneer the science of modern-day palaeontology. The museum, on the site of her former home, tells her story and exhibits spectacular fossils and other prehistoric finds.

Dinosaurland MUSEUM
(☑ 01297-443541; www.dinosaurland.co.uk; Coombe St; adult/child £5/4; ☺ 10am-5pm mid-Feb–Nov) This joyful, mini, indoor Jurassic Park overflows with fossilised remains; look out for belemnites, plesiosaurus and an impressive locally found ichthyosaur. Lifelike dinosaur models will thrill youngsters – the rock-hard tyrannosaurus eggs and 73kg dinosaur dung will have them in raptures.

Cobb LANDMARK
(☺ 24hr) First built in the 13th century, Lyme's iconic, curling sea defences have been strengthened and extended over the years, so don't present the elegant line they once did, but it's still hard to resist wandering their length to the tip.

Town Mill HISTORIC BUILDING
(www.townmill.org.uk; Mill Lane; ☺ 11am-2pm Mon-Fri, to 4pm Sat & Sun Apr-Oct) FREE An atmospheric, creaking, grinding, 14th-century working watermill. Cafes, art galleries, a cheese deli and microbrewery sit alongside.

🛏 Sleeping

Sanctuary B&B £
(☑ 01297-445815; www.lyme-regis.demon.co.uk; 65 Broad St; s/d £45/56) A B&B for bibliophiles: the charming, chintzy, volume-filled bedrooms here are part of a four-floor, 18-room bookshop. Ancient tomes that just beg to be perused are everywhere – they can delay you en route to (the excellent) breakfast, but handily there's a wonderfully relaxed vibe.

Coombe House B&B ££
(☑ 01297-443849; www.coombe-house.co.uk; 41 Coombe St; s £35, d £62-70, 5-person flat per week £370-650; ℗) The airy, easygoing, stylish

---

FOSSIL HUNTING

Fossil fever is catching. Lyme Regis sits in one of the most unstable sections of Britain's coast, and regular landslips mean nuggets of prehistory keep tumbling from the cliffs.

Joining a guided walk aids explorations. Three miles east of Lyme, the **Charmouth Heritage Coast Centre** (☑ 01297-560772; www.charmouth.org) runs one to seven trips a week (adult/child £7.50/3). Or, in Lyme itself, Lyme Regis Museum holds three to seven walks a week (adult/child £11/6); local expert **Brandon Lennon** (☑ 07944-664757; www.lymeregisfossilwalks.com; adult/child £8/6; ☺ Sat-Mon) also leads expeditions. All are popular; book early.

For the best chances of a find, visit within two hours of low water. If you do hunt by yourself, official advice is to check tide times and collect on a falling tide, observe warning signs, keep away from cliffs, only pick up from the beach and always leave some behind for others. Oh, and tell the experts if you find a stunner.

FORDE ABBEY

This **abbey** ([☎]01460-220231; www.
fordeabbey.co.uk; Chard; house adult/child
£11/free, gardens £9/free; ⊘ house noon-
4pm Tue-Fri & Sun Apr-Oct, gardens 10am-
4.30pm) was built in the 12th century as
a Cistercian monastery, but has been a
private home since 1649. The building
boasts magnificent plasterwork ceilings
and fine tapestries but it's the gardens
that are the main attraction: 12 hectares
of lawns, ponds, shrubberies and flower
beds with hundreds of rare and beautiful species.

It's 10 miles north of Lyme Regis;
public transport is a nonstarter.

bedrooms in this fabulous-value guesthouse
are full of bay windows, wicker and white
wood. Breakfast is delivered to your room on
a trolley, complete with homemade bread and
a toaster – perfect for a lazy lie-in in Lyme.

★ **Hix Townhouse**　　　BOUTIQUE B&B £££
([☎]01297-442499; www.hixtownhouse.co.uk; 1
Pound St; d £130-150, ste £165; 🐾) With its witty designer decor, luxury flourishes and in-
town location, this 18th-century terrace is
hard to resist. Each room echoes a leisure
theme (think gardening, fishing etc); the
pick is Sailing with its mock portholes, artfully arranged ropes, mini roof terrace and
gorgeous sea views.

✕ Eating

★ **Alexandra**　　　　　CAFE £
([☎]01297-442010; www.hotelalexandra.co.uk; Pound
St; afternoon tea £6.50-28; ⊘3-5.30pm; [P]) It's
like the setting for an Agatha Christie, minus
the murder. Wicker chairs dot manicured
lawns, a glittering Lyme Bay sweeps out
behind. The perfect spot for a proper English afternoon tea, complete with scones,
jam and dainty sandwiches. The hotel's
best bedrooms (singles £90, doubles £177 to
£235) boast bay windows and sea views; the
back-facing ones are charming too.

Mill Cafe　　　　　BISTRO ££
([☎]01297-445757; www.townmillcafe.co.uk; The
Town Mill, Mill Lane; lunch mains £8, 2-course dinner £20; ⊘10am-4pm Thu-Sun, 7-9pm Fri & Sat)
The Italian home cooking here is so authentic it feels more like Lombardy than Lyme.
Expect flavour-packed sweet pepper stews,

Sicilian-style cod and irresistible home-
baked bread, best devoured on the tucked-
away terrace out back.

Harbour Inn　　　　　PUB ££
(www.harbourinnlymeregis.co.uk; Marine Pde;
mains £10-19; ⊘noon-2.30pm & 6-9pm) A flower-
framed, beach-side verandah, smart but
snug interior and some of the best bistro-
pub grub in town – the bouillabaisse is suitably intense.

★ **Hix Oyster & Fish House**　　SEAFOOD £££
([☎]01297-446910; www.hixoysterandfishhouse.co.
uk; Cobb Rd; mains £14-25; ⊘10am-10pm) Expect
sweeping views of the Cobb and dazzling
food at this super-stylish, open-plan cabin.
Local asparagus comes with cuttlefish ink
dressing; succulent Portland Race sea bass
comes with kelp broth. Perhaps start by
slurping oysters: Brownsea Island or Portland molluscs come at £2.25 a pop.

ℹ **Information**

Tourist Office ([☎]01297-442138; www.vis-
it-dorset.com; Church St; ⊘10am-5pm Mon-
Sat, to 4pm Sun, to 3pm Mon-Sat Nov-Mar)

ℹ **Getting There & Away**

Bus 31 runs to Dorchester (1¾ hours) and Weymouth (two hours) hourly. Bus X53 goes west
to Exeter (£7, six daily, 1¾ hours) and east to
Weymouth (£7.20, hourly, 1¾ hours); it doesn't
run on winter Sundays.

Sherborne

POP 9495

Sherborne gleams with mellow, orangey-
yellow stone; it's been used to build a
cluster of 15th-century buildings and the
impressive abbey church at their core. This
serene town exudes wealth; the five local fee-
paying schools include the famous Sherborne School, and its pupils are a frequent
sight. Evidence of splashing the cash 16th-
and 18th-century style lies on the edge of
town with two castles: one a crumbling ruin,
the other a marvellous manor house, complete with a Lancelot 'Capability' Brown lake.

◉ Sights

Sherborne Abbey　　　　CHURCH
([☎]01935-812452; www.sherborneabbey.com; suggested donation £3.50; ⊘8am-6pm) [FREE] At the
height of its influence, the magnificent Abbey Church of St Mary the Virgin was the

central cathedral of 26 succeeding Saxon bishops. Established early in the 8th century, it became a Benedictine abbey in 998 and functioned as a cathedral until 1075. The church has mesmerising fan vaulting that's the oldest in the country, a central tower supported by Saxon-Norman piers and an 1180 Norman porch.

The abbey's **tombs** include the elaborate marble effigy belonging to John Lord Digby, Earl of Bristol, and those of the elder brothers of Alfred the Great, Ethelred and Ethelbert.

Sherborne Old Castle
CASTLE

(EH; ☑ 01935-812730; www.english-heritage.org. uk; adult/child £3.70/2.20; ☺ 10am-5pm Apr-Oct; ℗) These days the epitome of a picturesque ruin, Sherborne's Old Castle was built by Roger, Bishop of Salisbury, in 1120 – Elizabeth I gave it to her one-time favourite Sir Walter Raleigh in the late 16th century. It became a Royalist stronghold during the English Civil War, but Cromwell reduced it to rubble after a 16-day siege in 1645, leaving just the fractured southwest gatehouse, great tower and north range.

Sherborne New Castle
CASTLE

(☑ 01935-812072; www.sherbornecastle.com; New Rd; house & gardens adult/child £11/free, gardens only £6/free; ☺ 11am-4.30pm Tue-Thu, Sat & Sun Apr-Oct; ℗) Sir Walter Raleigh began building the impressive Sherborne New Castle in 1594, but only got as far as the central block before being imprisoned by James I. James promptly sold the castle to Sir John Digby who added the splendid wings you see today. In 1753 the grounds received a megamakeover at the hands of landscape-gardener extraordinaire Capability Brown who added a massive lake and 12-hectare waterside gardens.

☞ Tours

Walking Tours
HERITAGE TOUR

(tours £5; ☺ 11am Fri Jul-Sep) Ninety-minute trips exploring the photogenic old town, leaving from the tourist office.

🛏 Sleeping

Cumberland House
B&B ££

(☑ 01935-817554; www.bandbdorset.co.uk; Green Hill; s £55-60, d £70-85; ℗🐾) Artistry oozes from these history-rich rooms – bright scatter rugs sit on flagstone floors; lemon and oatmeal walls undulate between wonderfully wonky beams. Gourmet breakfasts include freshly squeezed orange juice; arrive around 4pm and expect an offer of tea, taken in the garden or beside the fire.

Stoneleigh Barn
B&B ££

(☑ 01935-389288; www.stoneleighbarn.co.uk; North Wootton; s/d £60/80; ℗🐾) Outside, this glorious 18th-century barn delights the senses – it's smothered in bright, fragrant flowers. Inside, exposed trusses frame spacious rooms delicately decorated in lilac and turquoise. Stoneleigh is 3 miles southeast of Sherborne.

✗ Eating

Green
MODERN BRITISH ££

(☑ 01935-813821; www.greenrestaurant.co.uk; 3 The Green; mains £13-25; ☺ noon-2.30pm & 6.30-9.30pm Tue-Sat) In this affable, elegant eatery gently distressed furniture is more chic than shabby, while the food is pure Westcountry élan – local goodies might include a trio of Lyme Bay crab, sole escabeche or wild venison carpaccio. Or plump for the cracking-value *menu du jour* (three courses £20).

George
PUB ££

(www.thegeorgesherborne.co.uk; 4 Higher Cheap St; mains £7-10; ☺ noon-2.30pm & 6-9pm; 🐾) It's five centuries since Sherborne's oldest, cosiest inn pulled its first pint; today it signals its age with wooden settles polished smooth by countless behinds. The food is enduring pub grub fare: robust steaks, ham and eggs, homemade pud and both Sunday and Saturday roasts.

❶ Information

Tourist Office (☑ 01935-815341; www. visit-dorset.com; Digby Rd; ☺ 9.30am-4pm Mon-Sat, to 3pm Dec-Mar) Stocks a self-guided walking tour leaflet (50p).

❶ Getting There & Away

BUS

Dorchester (£4.10, one hour, four to six daily Monday to Saturday) Bus 216; via Cerne Abbas (30 minutes).

Shaftesbury (£6, 30 minutes, daily) National Express.

Yeovil (£4.10, 15 minutes, every two hours Monday to Saturday) Bus 58.

TRAIN

Hourly services to Exeter (£20, 1¼ hours), London Waterloo (£30, 2½ hours) and Salisbury (£13, 40 minutes).

Shaftesbury & Around

POP 7707

Crowning a ridge of hogbacked hills and overlooking pastoral meadows, the agreeable market town of Shaftesbury circles around its medieval abbey ruins. A charismatic castle and a postcard-pretty, ancient street add to the town's appeal.

⊙ Sights

Shaftesbury Abbey   RUIN
(☑ 01747-852910;   www.shaftesburyabbey.org.uk; Park Walk; adult/child £3/free; ⊙10am-5pm Apr-Oct) These hilltop ruins mark the site of what was England's largest and richest nunnery. Founded in 888 by King Alfred the Great, Alfred's daughter, Aethelgifu, was its first abbess. St Edward is thought to have been buried here while King Knut died at the abbey in 1035. Most of the buildings were dismantled by Henry VIII, but you can wander its foundations and search out statuary and illuminated manuscripts in the museum.

Old Wardour Castle   CASTLE
(EH;   ☑ 01747-870487;   www.english-heritage.org. uk; adult/child £4.20/2.50; ⊙10am-5pm Apr-Oct, to 4pm Sat & Sun Nov-Mar; P) Six-sided Old Wardour Castle was built around 1393 and suffered severe damage during the English Civil War, leaving these imposing remains. The views from the upper levels are fabulous while its grassy lawns make a fine spot for a picnic. It's open until 6pm in July and August and is 4 miles west of Shaftesbury.

Gold Hill   STREET
This often-photographed, painfully steep, quaint cobbled slope, lined by chocolate-box cottages, starred in a famous TV advert for Hovis bread.

⊨ Sleeping & Eating

Old Chapel   B&B ££
(☑ 01747-852404;   www.theoldchapelbb.co.uk; 9 Breach Lane; s/d £60/90; P🐾) Sleep spots don't come much more characterful than this: a converted Victorian chapel with slender, two-storey windows, light-filled atriums and massive support beams. Smoothly comfy bedrooms feature fresh flowers and cookie jars; from the guest lounge you can see all the way to Salisbury Plain.

Updown   COTTAGE ££
(☑ 07710-307202;   www.updowncottage.co.uk; 12 Gold Hill; per week £700-1300; P🐾) A supreme-ly picturesque whitewashed, six-person cottage clinging to charming Gold Hill with snug, beam-lined rooms, open fires and a hillside garden.

Fleur de Lys   HOTEL £££
(☑ 01747-853717;   www.lafleurdelys.co.uk; Bleke St; s £95-110, d £130-170; P@🐾) A place to be pampered, whether in the deeply luxurious bedrooms or the acclaimed restaurant (open 7am to 10pm Monday to Saturday; two/three courses cost £27/34).

Mitre   PUB ££
(www.youngs.co.uk/pubs/mitre; 23 High St; mains £9; ⊙noon-3pm Mon-Fri, to 9pm Sat & Sun) It's the decked terrace that'll draw you into this old inn – its cracking views out over Blackmore Vale make for a memorable spot to tuck into homemade pizzas, fish and chips and beefy burgers.

ⓘ Information

Tourist Office (☑ 01747-853514; www.shaftesburydorset.com; 8 Bell St; ⊙10am-4pm Mon-Sat)

ⓘ Getting There & Away

Buses include:

London Victoria (£22, four hours, one daily) National Express; goes via Heathrow.

Salisbury (£4.20, 1¼ hours, five daily Monday to Saturday) Bus 29.

Sherborne (£6, 30 minutes, one daily) National Express.

WILTSHIRE

Wiltshire is rich in the reminders of ritual and packed with not-to-be-missed sights. Its verdant landscape is littered with more mysterious stone circles, processional avenues and ancient barrows than anywhere else in Britain. It's a place that teases and tantalises the imagination – here you'll experience the prehistoric majesty of Stonehenge and the atmospheric stone ring at Avebury. Add the serene 800-year-old cathedral at Salisbury, the supremely stately homes at Stourhead and Longleat and the impossibly pretty village of Lacock, and you have a county crammed full of English charm waiting to be explored.

ⓘ Information

There's a tourist office in Salisbury (p271).

Visit Wiltshire (www.visitwiltshire.co.uk)

ℹ Getting Around

BUS

Wiltshire's bus coverage can be patchy, especially in the northwest.

First (www.firstgroup.com) Serves west Wiltshire.

Salisbury Reds (www.salisburyreds.co.uk) Covers Salisbury and many rural areas. Offers one-day Explorer Tickets (£8.50) and seven-day passes (Salisbury area £15, network-wide £27).

TRAIN

Rail lines run from London Waterloo to Salisbury and beyond to Exeter and Plymouth, branching off north to Bradford-on-Avon, Bath and Bristol.

Salisbury & Around

POP 40,300

Centred on a majestic cathedral that's topped by the tallest spire in England, Salisbury makes an appealing Wiltshire base. It's been an important provincial city for more than a thousand years, and its streets form an architectural timeline ranging from medieval walls and half-timbered Tudor town houses to Georgian mansions and Victorian villas. Salisbury is also a lively, modern town, boasting plenty of bars and restaurants, plus a concentrated cluster of excellent museums.

◉ Sights

★**Salisbury Cathedral**   CATHEDRAL
(☑01722-555120; www.salisburycathedral.org.uk; Cathedral Close; requested donation adult/child £6.50/3; ⊙9am-5pm Mon-Sat, noon-4pm Sun) England is endowed with countless stunning churches, but few can hold a candle to the grandeur and sheer spectacle of 13th-century Salisbury Cathedral. This early English Gothic–style structure has an elaborate exterior decorated with pointed arches and flying buttresses, and a sombre, austere interior designed to keep its congregation suitably pious. Its statuary and tombs are outstanding; don't miss the daily tower tours and the cathedral's original, 13th-century copy of the Magna Carta. It's best experienced on a Tower Tour (p269).

The cathedral was built between 1220 and 1258. Beyond its highly decorative **West Front**, a small passageway leads into the 70m-long **nave**, lined with handsome pillars of Purbeck stone. In the north aisle look out for a fascinating **medieval clock** dating from 1386, probably the oldest working timepiece in the world. At the eastern end of the ambulatory the glorious **Prisoners of Conscience** stained-glass window (1980) hovers above the ornate **tomb** of Edward Seymour (1539–1621) and Lady Catherine Grey. Other monuments and tombs line the sides of the nave, including that of William Longespée, son of Henry II and half-brother of King John. When the tomb was excavated a well-preserved rat was found inside Longespée's skull.

Salisbury's 123m crowning glory, its **spire**, was added in the mid-14th century, and is the tallest in Britain. It represented an enormous technical challenge for its medieval builders; it weighs around 6500 tons and required an elaborate system of cross-bracing, scissor arches and supporting buttresses to keep it upright. Look closely and you'll see the additional weight has buckled the four central piers of the nave.

Sir Christopher Wren surveyed the cathedral in 1668 and calculated that the spire was leaning by 75cm. A brass plate in the floor of the nave is used to measure any shift, but no further lean was recorded in 1951 or 1970. Despite this, reinforcement of the notoriously 'wonky spire' continues to this day.

The cathedral really comes into its own during **evensong**, which takes place at 5.30pm Monday to Saturday and 3pm on Sunday, during term time only.

➡ Magna Carta

(⊙10am-4.30pm Mon-Sat, 12.45-4.30pm Sun) Tucked into Salisbury Cathedral's Chapter House is one of only four surviving original copies of the Magna Carta, the historic agreement made between King John and his barons in 1215 that acknowledged the fundamental principle that the monarch was not above the law. It's a still-powerful document; beautifully written and remarkably well preserved.

WORTH A TRIP

CANAL TRIPS

The 87-mile-long Kennet & Avon (www.katrust.org) runs all the way from Bristol to Reading. **Sally Boats** (☑01225-864923; www.sallyboats.ltd.uk) hires out narrowboats. Weekly rates for a four-berth boat range from around £750 in winter to £995 in high summer.

Salisbury

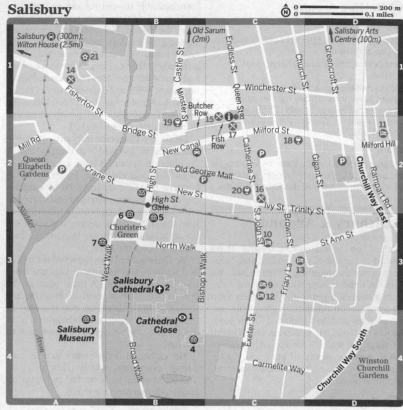

★**Cathedral Close**　　HISTORIC AREA

Salisbury's medieval cathedral close, a hushed enclave surrounded by beautiful houses, has an other-worldly feel. Many of the buildings date from the 13th century, although the area was heavily restored during an 18th-century clean-up by James Wyatt. The close is encircled by a sturdy outer wall, constructed in 1333; the stout gates leading into the complex are still locked every night.

Just inside the narrow High St Gate is the **College of Matrons**, founded in 1682 for widows and unmarried daughters of clergymen. South of the cathedral is the **Bishop's Palace**, now the private Cathedral School, parts of which date from 1220.

★**Salisbury Museum**　　MUSEUM

(☎01722-332151; www.salisburymuseum.org.uk; 65 Cathedral Close; adult/child £5/2; ⊙10am-5pm Mon-Sat, plus noon-5pm Sun Jun-Sep) The hugely important archaeological finds here include the Stonehenge Archer; the bones of a man found in the ditch surrounding the stone circle – one of the arrows found alongside probably killed him. With gold coins dating from 100 BC and a Bronze Age gold necklace, it's a powerful introduction to Wiltshire's prehistory.

Mompesson House　　HISTORIC BUILDING

(NT; ☎01722-335659; www.nationaltrust.org.uk; Cathedral Close; adult/child £6/3; ⊙11am-5pm Sat-Wed mid-Mar–Oct) Magnificent plasterwork ceilings, exceptional period furnishings and a sweeping carved staircase grace this fine Queen Anne (1701) building. All that made it the perfect location for the 1995 film *Sense and Sensibility.*

Rifles　　MUSEUM

(The Wardrobe; ☎01722-419419; www.thewardrobe.org.uk; 58 Cathedral Close; adult/child £5/2; ⊙10am-5pm Mon-Sat, closed Dec & Jan) Collections include a cannonball from the

Salisbury

American War of Independence, Victorian redcoat uniforms and displays on 19th- and 21st-century conflicts in Afghanistan.

Old Sarum
ARCHAEOLOGICAL SITE

(EH; ☑ 01722-335398; www.english-heritage.org.uk; Castle Rd; adult/child £4/2.40; ☉ 10am-5pm Sep-Jun, 9am-6pm Jul & Aug; P) The huge ramparts of Old Sarum sit on a grass-covered hill 2 miles north of Salisbury. You can wander the grassy ramparts, see the original cathedral's stone foundations, and look across the Wiltshire countryside to the spire of Salisbury's new cathedral. Medieval tournaments, open-air plays and mock battles are held on selected days. Bus X5/8 runs twice an hour from Salisbury to Old Sarum (£2.20, hourly on Sundays). It's also a stop on the Stonehenge Tour bus (p273).

It began life as a hill fort during the Iron Age, and was later occupied by both the Romans and the Saxons. By the mid-11th century it was a town – one of the most important in the west of England. William the Conqueror convened one of his earliest councils here and the first cathedral was built in 1092, snatching the bishopric from nearby Sherborne Abbey. But Old Sarum had problems: it was short on water and exposed to the elements, and in 1219 the bishop was given permission to move the cathedral, so founding the modern-day city of Salisbury. By 1331 Old Sarum's cathedral had been demolished for building materials and the settlement was practically abandoned.

Wilton House
HISTORIC BUILDING

(☑ 01722-746700; www.wiltonhouse.com; Wilton; house & grounds adult/child £15/8; ☉ 11.30am-5pm Sun-Thu mid-Apr–Aug; P) Stately Wilton House provides an insight into the rarefied world of the British aristocracy. One of England's finest stately homes, the earls of Pembroke have lived here since 1542, and it's been expanded, improved and embellished by successive generations. Highlights are the Single and Double Cube Rooms, designed by the pioneering 17th-century architect Inigo Jones.

Wilton House is 2.5 miles west of Salisbury; bus R3 runs from Salisbury (£2.60, 10 minutes, one to three hourly).

The result of centuries of embellishments is quite staggering: magnificent period furniture, frescoed ceilings and elaborate plasterwork frame paintings by Van Dyck, Rembrandt and Joshua Reynolds. All the architectural eye candy makes the house a favoured film location: *The Madness of King George, Sense and Sensibility* and *Pride and Prejudice* were all shot here. But Wilton was serving as an artistic haven long before the movies – famous guests include Ben Jonson, Edmund Spenser, Christopher Marlowe and John Donne. Shakespeare's *As You Like It* was performed here in 1603, shortly after the bard had written it. The fine landscaped grounds (adult/child £6/4.50; ☉ 11am-5.30pm early Apr–Sep) were largely laid out by Capability Brown.

👣 Tours

Tower Tour
WALKING TOUR

(adult/child £10/8; ☉ 1-5 daily) The best way to experience Salisbury Cathedral is on a 90-minute tower tour which sees you climbing 332 vertigo-inducing steps to the base of the spire for jaw-dropping views across the city and the surrounding countryside. Booking required.

BATH & SOUTHWEST ENGLAND SALISBURY & AROUND

Salisbury Guides HERITAGE TOUR
(☑ 07873-212941; www.salisburycityguides.co.uk;
adult/child £5/free; ☺ 11am daily Apr-Oct, 11am Sat
& Sun Nov-Mar) These 90-minute trips leave
from the tourist office.

✱✱ Festivals & Events

Salisbury Festival ARTS FESTIVAL
(☑ 01722-33224; www.salisburyfestival.co.uk) A
prestigious, eclectic event running from late
May to early June, encompassing classical,
world and pop music, plus theatre, literature
and art.

🛏 Sleeping

Salisbury YHA HOSTEL £
(☑ 0845 371 9537; www.yha.org.uk; Milford Hill;
dm/d £18/28; ℗ @ ☎) A real gem: neat rooms
in a rambling Victorian house, with a cafe-
bar, laundry and dappled gardens too.

★ St Ann's House BOUTIQUE B&B ££
(☑ 01722-335657; www.stannshouse.co.uk; 32
St Ann St; s £59-64, d £89-110; ☎) The aromas
wafting from breakfast may well spur you
from your room: great coffee; baked peach-
es with raspberry, honey and almonds;
poached eggs and Parma ham. Utter elegance reigns upstairs, where well-chosen
antiques, warm colours and Turkish linen
ensure a supremely comfortable stay.

Spire House B&B ££
(☑ 01722-339213; www.salisbury-bedandbreakfast.
com; 84 Exeter St; s/d/f £60/75/90; ℗ ☎) In
this B&B of beautifully kept, sweet rooms
the easygoing vibe extends to breakfast (add
£5): chalk up your choice on a blackboard
the night before. Options include slow-
cooked, blueberry-studded porridge, croissants and pastries, or local bacon and eggs.

Lazy Cow INN ££
(☑ 01722-412 028; www.thelazycowsalisbury.co.uk;
9 St Johns St; d £75-95, tr £120; ☎) Bordering
on bonkers but beautifully done, a bovine
theme is everywhere here. Highland cattle
peer from walls topped by snaking beams,
cowhide-framed mirrors sit on oak-panelled
walls. Your room key is attached to a tethering ring, and the mainstay of the restaurant?
Steaks galore.

Cathedral View B&B ££
(☑ 01722-502254; www.cathedral-viewbandb.co.uk;
83 Exeter St; s £70-80, d £75-99; ℗ ☎) Admirable attention to detail defines this Georgian
town house. Miniature flower displays and

home-baked cookies sit in quietly elegant
rooms. Breakfasts include prime Wiltshire
sausages and homemade bread and jam.
And the owner's daily what's-on list features
self-guided town trails.

✗ Eating

Fish Row DELI, CAFE £
(www.fishrowdelicafe.co.uk; 3 Fish Row; snacks from
£5; ☺ 8.30am-5.30pm Mon-Sat, 9.30am-4.30pm
Sun) Local produce is piled high at this heavily beamed deli-cafe – the New Forest Blue,
Old Sarum and Nanny Williams cheeses
come from just a few miles away. Grab some
potato salad and a wedge of quiche to go,
or duck upstairs to eat alongside weathered
wood, stained glass and old church pews.

Anokaa INDIAN ££
(☑ 01722-414142; www.anokaa.com; 60 Fisherton
St; mains £11-32; ☺ noon-2pm & 5.30-11pm; ✗)
The pink neon and multicoloured bubble
displays signal what's in store here: a supremely modern version of Indian cuisine.
The spice and flavour combos make the ingredients sing; the meat-free menu range
makes vegetarians beam.

Cloisters PUB ££
(www.cloisterspubsalisbury.co.uk; 83 Catherine St;
mains £9-13; ☺ 11am-9pm Sat & Sun, 11am-3pm &
6-9pm Mon-Fri) The building dates from 1350,
it's been a pub since the 1600s and today improbably warped beams reinforce an age-old
vibe. It's a convivial spot for tasty beef-and-
ale pie, sausage and mash or fancier foods
such as an impressive lamb shank slow-
braised in red wine.

Charter 1227 BRITISH £££
(☑ 01722-333118; www.charter1227.co.uk; 6 Ox
Row, Market Pl; mains £15-26; ☺ noon-2.30pm &
6-9.30pm Tue-Sat, noon-2.30pm Sun) Ingredients
that speak of ancient England have a firm
foothold here – feast on suckling pig, Wiltshire ham hock or roast John Dory. Canny
locals eat between 6pm and 8pm Tuesday to
Thursday (two/three courses for £20/25) or
at lunchtime, when dishes are £5.50 each.

⬤ Drinking & Nightlife

Haunch of Venison PUB
(1 Minster St; ☺ 11am-11pm Mon-Sat, to 6pm Sun)
Featuring wood-panelled snugs, spiral staircases and wonky ceilings, this 14th-century
drinking den is packed with atmosphere –
and ghosts. One is a cheating whist player

whose hand was severed in a game – look out for his mummified bones on display inside.

Chapel
BAR, CLUB
(www.chapelnightclub.com; 34 Milford St; ⊙5pm-3am Wed-Sat) Buzzing bar with adjoining club where the DJ sets range from funk to '90s hip-hop and chart 'n' cheese.

MusicBox
CLUB
(www.themusicboxsalisbury.co.uk; 46 Catherine St; ⊙9pm-3am Thu-Sun) Three-floor venue filled by gigs, open-mic events and DJ sets featuring '80s pop, reggae and dub.

☆ Entertainment

Salisbury Arts Centre
ARTS CENTRE
(☑01722-321744; www.salisburyartscentre.co.uk; Bedwin St) An innovative arts centre showcasing cutting-edge theatre, indie films, dance and live gigs.

Salisbury Playhouse
THEATRE
(☑01722-320333; www.salisburyplayhouse.com; Malthouse Lane) A producing theatre that also hosts top touring shows and musicals.

❶ Information

Library (Market Pl; internet per hr £1; ⊙10am-7pm Mon-Tue & Fri, 9am-5pm Wed-Thu & Sat; ☎)
Tourist Office (☑01722-342860; www.visit-wiltshire.co.uk; Fish Row; ⊙9am-5pm Mon-Fri, 10am-4pm Sat, 10am-2pm Sun)

❶ Getting There & Away

BUS
Direct National Express services include those to Bath (£11, 1¼ hours, one daily), Bristol (£11, 2¼ hours, one daily) and London (£17, three hours, three daily) via Heathrow.

Local services include bus 29 to Shaftesbury (£4.20, 1¼ hours, five daily Monday to Saturday) and bus 2 to Devizes (£5, one hour, hourly Monday to Saturday).

Tour buses leave Salisbury for Stonehenge regularly (p273).

TRAIN
Half-hourly connections include:
Bath (£10, one hour)
Bradford-on-Avon (£13, 40 minutes)
Bristol (£11, 1¼ hours)
London Waterloo (£38, 1¾ hours)
Southampton (£10, 30 minutes)

Hourly connections include:
Exeter (£25, two hours)
Portsmouth (£20, 1¾ hours)

Stonehenge

Welcome to Britain's most iconic archaeological site. This compelling ring of monolithic stones has been attracting a steady stream of pilgrims, poets and philosophers for the last 5000 years and is still a mystical, ethereal place – a haunting echo from Britain's forgotten past, and a reminder of those who once walked the ceremonial avenues across Salisbury Plain.

◉ Sights

★ Stonehenge
ARCHAEOLOGICAL SITE
(EH; ☑0870 333 1181; www.english-heritage.org.uk; adult/child incl visitor centre £14/8.30; ⊙9am-8pm Jun-Aug, 9.30am-7pm Apr, May & Sep, 9.30am-5pm Oct-Mar; ℗) Ancient Stonehenge has had an ultramodern, £27 million makeover. It's brought an impressive new visitor centre and the closure of an intrusive nearby road – now restored to grassland. The result: a far stronger sense of historical context; dignity and mystery returned to an archaeological gem.

A pathway frames the ring of massive stones, and although you can't walk in the circle, unless on a recommended Stone Circle Access Visit (p273), you can get close-up views. Admission is only through prebooked tickets, so secure a place well in advance.

Stonehenge is one of Britain's great archaeological mysteries: despite countless theories about the site's purpose, ranging from a sacrificial centre to a celestial timepiece, in truth no one knows for sure what drove prehistoric Britons to expend so much time and effort on its construction.

The first phase of building started around 3000 BC, when the outer circular bank and ditch were erected. A thousand years later, an inner circle of granite stones, known as bluestones, was added. It's thought that these mammoth 4-tonne blocks were hauled from the Preseli Mountains in South Wales, some 250 miles away – an almost inexplicable feat for Stone Age builders equipped with only the simplest of tools. Although no one is entirely sure how the builders transported the stones so far, it's thought they probably used a system of ropes, sledges and rollers fashioned from tree trunks – Salisbury Plain was still covered by forest during Stonehenge's construction.

Around 1500 BC, Stonehenge's main stones were dragged to the site, erected in a circle and crowned by massive lintels to make

BATH & SOUTHWEST ENGLAND STONEHENGE

Stonehenge

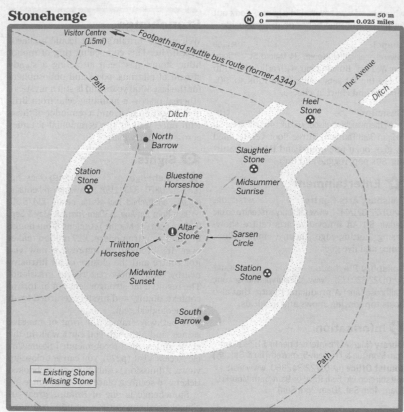

0
0
50 m
0.025 miles

Visitor Centre (1.5mi)

Footpath and shuttle bus route (former A344)

Path

The Avenue

Ditch

Heel Stone

Ditch

North Barrow

Slaughter Stone

Station Stone

Bluestone Horseshoe

Midsummer Sunrise

Altar Stone

Sarsen Circle

Trilithon Horseshoe

Midwinter Sunset

Station Stone

South Barrow

Path

Existing Stone
Missing Stone

the trilithons (two vertical stones topped by a horizontal one). The sarsen (sandstone) stones were cut from an extremely hard rock found on the Marlborough Downs, 20 miles from the site. It's estimated dragging one of these 50-tonne stones across the countryside would require about 600 people.

Also around this time, the bluestones from 500 years earlier were rearranged as an inner **bluestone horseshoe** with an **altar stone** at the centre. Outside this the **trilithon horseshoe** of five massive sets of stones was erected. Three of these are intact; the other two have just a single upright. Then came the major **sarsen circle** of 30 massive vertical stones, of which 17 uprights and six lintels remain.

Much further out, another circle was delineated by the 58 Aubrey Holes, named after John Aubrey, who discovered them in the 1600s. Just inside this circle are the **South** and **North Barrows**, each originally topped

by a stone. Like many stone circles in Britain (including Avebury, 22 miles away) the inner horseshoes are aligned to coincide with sunrise at the midsummer solstice, which some claim supports the theory that the site was some kind of astronomical calendar.

Prehistoric pilgrims would have entered the site via the **Avenue**, whose entrance to the circle is marked by the **Slaughter Stone** and the **Heel Stone**, located slightly further out on one side.

Admission includes an audioguide and is free for EH and NT members.

Visitor Centre INTERPRETATION CENTRE
(EH; ☑0870 333 1181; www.english-heritage.org. uk; 9am-8pm Jun-Aug, 9.30am-7pm Apr, May & Sep, 9.30am-5pm Oct-Mar) Stonehenge's swish new visitor centre sees you standing in the middle of an atmospheric 360-degree projection of the stone circle through the ages and seasons – complete with midsummer sunrise and swirling starscape.

The visitor centre is 1.5 miles from the stones. A fleet of trolley buses makes the 10-minute trip – it's more atmospheric to walk.

Engaging audiovisual displays detail the transportation of the stones and the building stages, while 300 finds from the wider site include flint chippings, bone pins and arrowheads, there's also a striking recreation of the face of a neolithic man whose body was found nearby.

☞ Tours

★**Stone Circle Access Visits**   WALKING TOUR
(☑0870 333 0605; www.english-heritage.org.uk; adult/child £21/12.60) Circle-access visits are an unforgettable experience. Visitors normally have to stay outside the stone circle itself, but on these self-guided walks, you can wander around the core of the site, getting up-close views of the iconic bluestones and trilithons. They take place in the evening or early morning so the quieter atmosphere and the slanting sunlight add to the effect. Each visit takes only 26 people; to secure a place book at least two months in advance.

Salisbury Guided Tours   GUIDED TOUR
(☑07775-674816; www.salisburyguidedtours.com; per person from £80) Runs a wide range of expert-led trips to Stonehenge, the wider ritual landscape and Salisbury.

❶ Getting There & Around

BUS
No regular buses go to the site.
Stonehenge Tour (☑0845 0727 093; www.thestonehengetour.info; adult/child £26/16) Leaves Salisbury's railway station half-hourly from June to August, and hourly between September and May. The ticket includes admission to Stonehenge and the Iron Age hill fort at Old Sarum (p269); it stops there on the return leg.

Around Stonehenge

Stonehenge actually forms part of a huge complex of ancient monuments.

◉ Sights & Activities

North of Stonehenge and running roughly east–west is the **Cursus**, an elongated embanked oval; the smaller **Lesser Cursus** is nearby. Theories abound as to what these sites were used for, ranging from ancient sporting arenas to processional avenues for the dead. Two clusters of burial mounds,

the **Old** and **New Kings Barrows**, sit beside the ceremonial pathway the **Avenue**, which originally linked Stonehenge with the River Avon, 2 miles away.

The **National Trust** (www.nationaltrust.org.uk) website has a downloadable 3.5-mile circular walk (A King's View) that traces tracks across the chalk downland from Stonehenge, past the Cursus and Kings Barrows and along a section of the Avenue itself. The Stonehenge visitor centre also has leaflets detailing walking routes.

Woodhenge   ARCHAEOLOGICAL SITE
(EH; ☑0870 3331181; www.english-heritage.org.uk; ☉dawn-dusk) **FREE** Some 1.5 miles east of Stonehenge, near Amesbury, is Woodhenge, a series of concentric rings that would once have been marked by wooden posts. It's thought there might be some correlation between the use of wood and stone in both henges. Excavations in the 1970s at Woodhenge revealed the skeleton of a child with a cloven skull, buried near the centre.

Stourhead

Overflowing with vistas, temples and follies, **Stourhead** (NT; ☑01747-841152; www.nationaltrust.org.uk; Mere; house or garden adult/child £8/4, house & garden £13/7; ☉house 11am-4.30pm mid-Mar–Oct, 11am-3pm Sat & Sun Nov–mid-Mar; P) is landscape gardening at its finest. The Palladian house has some fine Chippendale furniture and paintings by Claude and Gaspard Poussin, but it's a sideshow to the magnificent 18th-century gardens (open 9am to 5pm, to 7pm April to September), which spread out across the valley. Stourhead is off the B3092, 8 miles south of Frome (in Somerset).

A picturesque 2-mile circuit takes you past the most ornate follies, around the lake and to the Temple of Apollo; a 3.5-mile side trip can be made from near the Pantheon to **King Alfred's Tower** (adult/child £3/2; ⊙noon-4pm Sat & Sun Mar-Oct), a 50m-high folly with wonderful views.

Longleat

Half ancestral mansion, half safari park, **Longleat** (✆01985-844400; www.longleat. co.uk; all-inclusive ticket adult/child £34/22, house & grounds £15.50/10.50; ⊙10am-7pm Jul & Aug, to 5pm Apr-Jun, to 4pm Mar, Sep & Oct; P) was transformed into Britain's first safari park in 1966, turning Capability Brown's landscaped grounds into an amazing drive-through zoo, populated by a menagerie of animals more at home in the African wilderness than the fields of Wiltshire. Longleat also has a throng of attractions, including a narrow-gauge railway, Dr Who exhibit, Postman Pat village, pets' corner and butterfly garden.

Longleat House is just off the A362, 3 miles from both Frome and Warminster.

It was the first English stately home to open its doors to the public, prompted by finance: heavy taxes and mounting post-WWII bills meant the house had to earn its keep.

The house itself contains fine tapestries, furniture and decorated ceilings, as well as seven libraries containing around 40,000 tomes. The highlight, though, is an extraordinary series of paintings and psychedelic murals by the present-day marquess, who was an art student in the '60s and upholds the long-standing tradition of eccentricity among the English aristocracy – check out his website (www.lordbath.co.uk).

Malmesbury

The mellow hilltop town of Malmesbury is peppered with ancient buildings constructed out of honey-coloured Cotswold stone. It's the oldest borough in England, having been awarded that status in AD 880, and boasts one of the county's finest **market crosses** – a 15th-century crown-like structure built to shelter the poor from the rain.

Bus 31 runs to Swindon (£3, one hour, hourly Monday to Saturday); bus 92 heads to Chippenham (£2.70, 45 minutes, hourly Monday to Saturday).

⊙ Sights

Malmesbury Abbey   ABBEY
(✆01666-826666; www.malmesburyabbey.info; suggested donation £3; ⊙9am-4pm) Malmesbury's big draw is Malmesbury Abbey, a blend of ruin and living church, with a somewhat turbulent history. Notable features include the Norman doorway decorated with biblical figures, the Romanesque Apostle carvings and a four-volume illuminated bible dating from 1407. A window at the western end of the church depicts Elmer the Flying Monk, who in 1010 strapped on wings and jumped from the tower. Although he broke both legs during this leap of faith, he survived and became a local hero.

The abbey began life as a 7th-century monastery, which was later replaced by a Norman church. By the mid-15th century the building had been embellished with a spire and twin towers, but in 1479 a storm toppled one tower and spire, destroying the eastern end of the church. The west tower followed suit in 1662, destroying much of the nave. The present-day church is about a third of its original size, and is flanked by ruins at either end.

Just below the abbey are the **Abbey House Gardens** (✆01666-827650; www.abbeyhousegardens.co.uk; adult/child £8/3; ⊙11am-5.30pm mid-Mar–Oct), which include a herb garden, river, waterfall and 2 hectares of colourful blooms.

Lacock

POP 1000

With its geranium-covered cottages and higgledy-piggledy rooftops, pockets of the medieval village of Lacock seem to have been preserved in mid-19th-century aspic. The village has been in the hands of the National Trust since 1944, and in many places is remarkably free of modern development: there are no telephone poles or electric street lights and the main car park on the outskirts keeps it largely traffic-free. Unsurprisingly, it's a popular location for costume dramas and feature films – the village and its abbey pop up in the Harry Potter films, *The Other Boleyn Girl* and BBC adaptations of *Moll Flanders* and *Pride and Prejudice*.

⊙ Sights

Lacock Abbey   ABBEY
(NT; ✆01249-730459; www.nationaltrust.org.uk; adult/child £11.20/5.60; ⊙10.30am-5.30pm Mar-Oct, 11am-4pm Nov-Feb) Lacock Abbey is a window into a medieval world. Founded as an Augustinian nunnery in the 13th century, its deeply atmospheric rooms and stunning Gothic entrance hall are lined with bizarre terracotta figures; spot the scapegoat with a

lump of sugar on its nose. Some of the original structure is evident in the cloisters and there are traces of medieval wall paintings too. On Tuesdays year-round and winter weekdays, access is limited to the cloisters.

Ela, Countess of Salisbury established the abbey in 1232. After the Dissolution it was sold to Sir William Sharington in 1539, who converted the nunnery into a home, demolished the church, built a tower and added a brewery.

The ticket into the abbey also includes admission to the **Fox Talbot Museum**, which profiles the man who pioneered the photographic negative: William Henry Fox Talbot (1800–77). A prolific inventor, he began developing the system in 1834 while working at the abbey. The museum details his ground-breaking work and displays a superb collection of his images.

A cheaper ticket (adult/child £8.50/4.50) gets you into the grounds, museum and abbey cloisters, but not the abbey building itself.

🛏 Sleeping & Eating

★**Red Lion**   INN **££**
(☎01249-730456; www.redlionlacock.co.uk; 1 High St; d £120; 🅿🛜) In atmospheric Lacock where better to sleep than a Georgian coaching inn that oozes ambience. Step on flagstone floors past open fires, up a grand staircase to sweet rooms where padded cushions line mullioned windows with picture-postcard views of ancient streets. The food's notable too (mains £11, served 9am to 8.30pm).

King John's Hunting Lodge   B&B **££**
(☎01249-730313; www.kingjohnslodge.2day.ws; 21 Church St; d/f £95/110; 🅿) An air of peace pervades Lacock's oldest building. The decor matches the beam-lined, irregular-shaped rooms; expect tapestries, dainty chairs and china figurines in meticulous rooms. Afternoon tea in the **cafe** is a must (served 10.30am to 4pm Wednesday to Sunday).

Lacock Pottery   B&B **££**
(☎01249-730266; www.lacockbedandbreakfast. com; Church St; s £56-66, d £89-110; 🅿🛜) A serene, airy former workhouse featuring peat fires, organic breakfasts and, appropriately, fine ceramics.

George Inn   PUB **£**
(www.georgeinnlacock.co.uk; 4 West St; mains £11-19; ⊗noon-2.30pm & 6-9pm) Sample good grub and local ales at this 14th-century, horse brass–hung pub.

ℹ Getting There & Away

Bus 234 runs hourly, Monday to Saturday, from Chippenham (£2.40, 15 minutes).

Avebury

POP 235

While the tour buses head straight for Stonehenge, prehistoric purists make for the massive stone circle at Avebury. Though it lacks the dramatic trilithons of its sister site across Salisbury Plain, Avebury is just as rewarding to visit. It's bigger and older, and a large section of the village is actually inside the stones – footpaths wind around them, allowing you to really soak up the extraordinary atmosphere. Avebury also boasts an encircling landscape that's rich in prehistoric sites and a manor house where restored rooms span five completely different eras.

◉ Sights

★**Avebury Stone Circle**   ARCHAEOLOGICAL SITE
(NT; ☎01672-539250; www.nationaltrust.org.uk; ⊗24hr; 🅿) **FREE** With a diameter of 348m, Avebury is the largest stone circle in the world. It's also one of the oldest, dating from 2500 to 2200 BC. Today, more than 30 stones are in place; pillars show where missing stones would have been. Wandering between them reveals the sheer scale of the site, evidenced also by the massive bank and ditch that lines the circle; the quieter northwest

> ### RITUAL LANDSCAPE
>
> Avebury is surrounded by a network of ancient monuments, including Silbury Hill (p277) and West Kennet Long Barrow (p277). To the south of the village, the West Kennet Avenue stretched out for 1.5 miles, lined by 100 pairs of stones. It linked the Avebury circle with a site called the **Sanctuary**. Post holes indicate that a wooden building surrounded by a stone circle once stood at the Sanctuary, although no one knows quite what the site was for.
>
> The **Ridgeway national trail** (www. nationaltrail.co.uk/ridgeway) starts near Avebury and runs eastwards across Fyfield Down, where many of the sarsen stones at Avebury (and Stonehenge) were collected.

Avebury

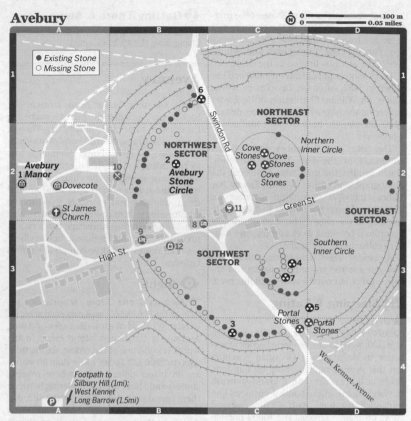

Avebury

◉ Top Sights

◉ Sights

🛏 Sleeping

✗ Eating

🍷 Drinking & Nightlife

🛍 Shopping

quadrant is particularly atmospheric. The National Trust holds guided tours daily.

Avebury Henge originally consisted of an outer circle of 98 standing stones of up to 6m in length, many weighing 20 tonnes. The stones were surrounded by another circle delineated by a 5m-high earth bank and ditch up to 9m deep. Inside were smaller stone circles to the north (27 stones) and south (29 stones).

In the Middle Ages, when Britain's pagan past was an embarrassment to the church, many of the stones were buried, removed or broken up. In 1934, wealthy businessman and archaeologist Alexander Keiller supervised the re-erection of the stones. He later bought the site for posterity using funds from his family's marmalade fortune.

Modern roads into Avebury neatly dissect the circle into four sectors. Starting at High St, near the **Henge Shop**, and walking round the circle in an anticlockwise direction, you'll encounter 11 standing stones in the **southwest sector**. They include the **Barber Surgeon Stone**, named after the skeleton of a man found under it – the equipment buried with him suggests he was a barber-cum-surgeon.

The **southeast sector** starts with the huge **portal stones** marking the entry to the circle from **West Kennet Avenue**. The **southern inner circle** stood in this sector and within this ring was the **obelisk** and a group of stones known as the **Z Feature**. Just outside this smaller circle, only the base of the **Ring Stone** survives.

In the **northern inner circle** in the **northeast sector**, three sarsens remain of what would have been a rectangular **cove**. The **northwest sector** has the most complete collection of standing stones, including the massive 65-tonne **Swindon Stone**, one of the few never to have been toppled.

★**Avebury Manor**   HISTORIC BUILDING
(NT; ☑ 01672-539250; www.nationaltrust.org.uk; adult/child £9/4.50; ⊙ 11am-5pm Thu-Tue Apr-Oct) The mother of all makeovers took place at this 16th-century manor house as part of the BBC TV series *The Manor Reborn*. It used original techniques and materials to recreate interiors spanning five periods, so now you can sit on beds, play billiards and listen to the gramophone in rooms that range from Tudor, through Georgian to the 1930s.

In the garden, the topiary and box hedges create a series of rooms that inspired Vita Sackville-West, creator of **Sissinghurst gardens** (☑ 01580-710700; www.nationaltrust.org.uk/sissinghurst; adult/concession/family £8.80/4.40/22; ⊙ 11am-6.30pm, last entry 5.30pm Mon, Tue & Fri, 10am-6.30pm, last entry 5.30pm Sat & Sun mid-Mar–Nov) in Kent. Visits are by timed tickets only; arrive early to bag a slot.

Silbury Hill   ARCHAEOLOGICAL SITE
(www.english-heritage.org.uk; P) FREE Rising abruptly from the fields just south of Avebury, 40m high Silbury Hill is the largest artificial earthwork in Europe. It was built in stages from around 2500 BC, but the reason for its construction remains unclear. Direct access to the hill isn't allowed, but you can view it from a lay-by on the A4. For more atmospheric views, from Avebury head through the main car park, cross the road, then pick up the footpath south across the fields (3 miles return) to the hill's north side.

West Kennet
Long Barrow   ARCHAEOLOGICAL SITE
(EH; ☑ 01672-539250; www.english-heritage.org.uk; ⊙ dawn-dusk) FREE England's finest burial mound dates from around 3500 BC. Its entrance is guarded by huge sarsens and its roof is made out of gigantic overlapping capstones. About 50 skeletons were found when it was excavated; finds are on display at the Wiltshire Heritage Museum in Devizes. A footpath leads from Avebury to West Kennet (2 miles), passing Silbury Hill en route.

⊨ Sleeping

★**Manor Farm**   B&B ££
(☑ 01672-539294; www.manorfarmavebury.com; High St; s £70-80, d £90-100; P 🛜) Offering a rare chance to sleep in style inside a stone circle, this red-brick farmhouse snuggles just inside Avebury henge. The elegant, comfy rooms blend old woods with bright furnishings, while the windows provide spine-tingling views of those 4000-year-old standing stones.

Avebury Lodge   B&B £££
(☑ 01672-539023; www.aveburylodge.co.uk; High St; d £175; P 🛜) It's as if gentlemanly archaeologists are still in situ: antiquarian prints of stone circles smother the walls, pelmets and chandeliers are dotted around. And whenever you glance from a window, a bit of Avebury henge appears.

✗ Eating & Drinking

Circle   CAFE £
(www.nationaltrust.org.uk; mains from £7; ⊙ 10am-6pm Apr-Oct, to 4pm Nov-Mar; 🍴) A veggie and wholefood cafe beside the Great Barn serving homemade quiches and cakes, chunky sandwiches and afternoon teas.

Red Lion   PUB
(www.oldenglishinns.co.uk; High St; ⊙ 11am-11pm) Having a pint here means downing a drink at the only pub in the world inside a stone circle. The food (served noon to 9pm, mains £7 to £13) is firmly traditional – think pork belly and sausage and mash.

ⓘ Getting There & Away

Bus 49 runs hourly to Swindon (£4.40, 30 minutes) and Devizes (£4, 20 minutes).

BATH & SOUTHWEST ENGLAND AVEBURY

EXMOOR NATIONAL PARK

Exmoor is more than a little addictive. Even when you get home, your mind could well return to its broad, russet views. In the middle sits the higher moor, an empty, expansive, other-worldly landscape of tawny grasses and huge skies. Here picturesque Exford makes an ideal village base. In the north, sheer, rock-strewn river valleys cut into the plateau and coal-black cliffs lurch towards the sea. Amid these towering headlands, charismatic Porlock, and the twin villages of Lynton and Lynmouth, are atmospheric places to stay. Relaxed Dulverton delivers a country-town vibe, while appealing Dunster boasts cobbled streets and a russet-red castle. And everywhere on Exmoor life is attuned to the rhythm of the seasons; it's a glimpse into another world. Visit – but you're likely to be planning to return before you leave.

🏃 Activities

Exmoor Adventures   OUTDOORS
(☑ 01643-863536; www.exmooradventures.co.uk) Runs kayaking, canoeing, mountain biking, coasteering and rock-climbing sessions.

Cycling
Despite the formidable hills, cycling is hugely popular on Exmoor. Several sections of the National Cycle Network (NCN; www.sustrans. org.uk) cross the park, including the Westcountry Way (NCN route 3) from Bristol to Land's End, and the Devon Coast to Coast (NCN route 27), between Illfracombe and Plymouth, via Dartmoor and Exmoor.

Exmoor is also one of the county's most exhilarating off-road cycling destinations, with a wealth of bridleways and permitted tracks. The Exmoor National Park Authority (p279) has produced a colour-coded, off-road cycle map (£10); buy it at tourist offices or from the ENPA website.

Exmoor Adventures (p278) runs a five-hour mountain-biking skills course (£50) and also hires bikes (adult per day £25).

Exmoor Cycle Hire   BICYCLE RENTAL
(☑ 01598-753967; www.exmoorcyclehire.co.uk; adult per day/week £14/50, child £8/28)

Pompys   BICYCLE RENTAL
(☑ 01643-704077; www.pompyscycles.co.uk; Mart Rd, Minehead; per day £15; ⊙ 9am-5pm Mon-Sat)

Pony Trekking & Horse Riding
Exmoor is prime riding country, with stables offering pony and horse treks from around £40 to £45 for a two-hour ride.

Brendan Manor Stables   HORSE RIDING
(☑ 01598-741246; www.ridingonexmoor.co.uk; Brendon Manor, near Lynton)

Burrowhayes Farm   HORSE RIDING
(☑ 01643-862463; www.burrowhayes.co.uk; West Luccombe, near Porlock)

Outovercott Stables   HORSE RIDING
(☑ 01598-753341; www.outovercott.co.uk; near Lynton)

Walking
The open moors and profusion of marked bridleways make Exmoor an excellent area for hiking. The best-known routes are the Somerset & North Devon Coast Path,

Exmoor National Park

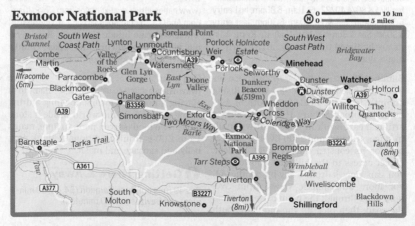

WILDLIFE WATCHING

Exmoor supports one of England's largest wild red deer populations, best experienced in autumn when the annual 'rutting' season sees stags bellowing, charging and clashing horns in an attempt to impress prospective mates. Despite their numbers, these skittish creatures are notoriously difficult to spot without some local knowledge.

The Exmoor National Park Authority (see below) runs regular wildlife-themed guided walks (£3 to £5), or head out on an organised jeep safari to combine scenic sightseeing with a couple of hours of off-road wildlife-spotting.

Barle Valley Safaris (☑01643-841326; www.exmoorwildlifesafaris.co.uk; adult/child £30/25) Runs from Dulverton and Dunster, with pick-ups from Wheddon Cross.

Discovery Safaris (☑01643-863444; www.discoverysafaris.com; per person £25) Twice-daily trips from Porlock.

Exmoor Safari (☑01643-831229; www.exmoorsafari.co.uk; adult/child £35/16) This long-running operator also does special photography-themed trips.

Red Stag Safari (☑01643-841831; www.redstagsafari.co.uk; safari £25-38) Departs from a wide range of Exmoor towns.

which is part of the **South West Coast Path** (www.southwestcoastpath.com), and the Exmoor section of the **Two Moors Way**, which starts in Lynmouth and travels south to Dartmoor and beyond.

Other superb routes include the **Coleridge Way** (www.coleridgeway.co.uk) which winds for 51 miles through Exmoor, the Brendon Hills and the Quantocks. Part of the 180-mile **Tarka Trail** cuts through the park; join it at Combe Martin, hike along the cliffs to Lynton/Lynmouth, then head across the moor towards Barnstaple.

Organised walks run by the ENPA (p279) are held throughout the year and include deer safaris, nightjar walks and dark sky strolls.

ℹ Information

INTERNET RESOURCES

Active Exmoor (www.activeexmoor.com) Info on outdoor activities.

Visit Exmoor (www.visit-exmoor.co.uk) Official visitor website with useful advice on activities, events and accommodation.

TOURIST INFORMATION

There are three **Exmoor National Park Authority** (ENPA; www.exmoor-nationalpark.gov.uk) tourist offices.

Dulverton Tourist Office (☑01398-323841; www.exmoor-nationalpark.gov.uk; 7-9 Fore St, Dulverton; ☺10am-5pm)

Dunster Tourist Office (☑01643-821835; www.exmoor-nationalpark.gov.uk; Dunster Steep, Dunster; ☺10am-5pm)

Lynmouth Tourist Office (☑01598-752509; www.exmoor-nationalpark.gov.uk; The Esplanade, Lynmouth; ☺10am-5pm)

ℹ Getting Around

The **MoorRover** (☑01643-709701) is an on-demand minibus that can take you anywhere on Exmoor. Prices range from £10 to £30, depending on distances involved. It'll also carry bikes and provide a luggage transfer service. Book at least a day ahead.

Exmoor's bus routes are listed at the **ExploreMoor** (www.exploremoor.co.uk) website. Be aware: some services are seasonal, and the more remote ones are particularly prone to change.

300 (one to three daily Monday to Saturday, no Sunday service October to May) Heads along the coast from the resort of Minehead to Lynmouth, via Porlock. One to two services go onto Ilfracombe on Saturday and Sunday.

309/310 (nine daily, Monday to Saturday) Year round; runs from Barnstaple, via Parracombe to Lynmouth.

398 (six daily Monday to Saturday) Year round; cuts through the moor from Minehead to Tiverton via Dunster, Wheddon Cross and Dulverton. One bus a day stops at Exford.

Dulverton

POP 1500

The southern gateway to Exmoor National Park, Dulverton sits at the base of the Barle Valley near the confluence of two key rivers: the Exe and Barle. A traditional country town, it's home to a collection of gun-sellers,

STARGAZING ON EXMOOR

All over Exmoor people are chuffed to bits that it's been named Europe's first International Dark Sky Reserve. The ENPA runs free night-time stargazing strolls; eerie hilltop hikes where the inky blackness is punctuated by mesmerising constellations. The authority's (free) Dark Sky Discovery leaflets feature star-charts and maps. For optimum views, central, higher Exmoor is best; try the hills around Dunkery Beacon.

fishing-tackle stores and gift shops, and makes an attractive edge-of moor base.

◉ Sights

Tarr Steps LANDMARK

(◷24hr) FREE Exmoor's most famous landmark is an ancient stone clapper bridge shaded by gnarled old trees. Its huge slabs are propped up on stone columns embedded in the River Barle. Local folklore aside (which declares it was used by the devil for sunbathing), it first pops into the historical record in the 1600s and has had to be rebuilt after 21st-century floods. The steps are signed off the B3223 Dulverton to Simonsbath road 5 miles northwest of Dulverton.

Or hike there from Dulverton along the banks of the River Barle (12 miles return).

⊨ Sleeping

★ Streamcombe Farm B&B ££

(✍ 01398-323775; www.streamcombefarm.co.uk; Streamcombe Lane, near Dulverton; s £60-65, d £75-100; P) In this enchanting, 18th-century farmhouse stylish, rustic-chic bedrooms feature chimney breasts and reclaimed joists, and the only sounds are the sheep, deer and pheasants outside. There's woodland camping (per person £10) and a two-person shepherd's hut (£75) too.

Town Mills B&B ££

(✍ 01398-323124; www.townmillsdulverton.co.uk; High St; s/d £85/95; P ⊛) The top choice if you want to stay in town is a thoroughly contemporary riverside mill with creamy carpets, magnolia walls and bursts of floral art.

Tarr Farm HOTEL £££

(✍01643-851507; www.tarrfarm.co.uk; Tarr Steps; s/d £85/150; P) This is the place to really lose yourself: a farmhouse nested among the woods near Tarr Steps, 7 miles from Dulverton. The nine rooms are spacious and luxurious, with spoil-yourself extras like organic bath goodies and homemade biscuits.

✗ Eating

Exclusive Cake Co BAKERY £

(www.exclusivecakecompany.co.uk; 19 High St; items from £3; ◷9am-5pm Mon-Fri, to 2pm Sat) Real rarities stack the shelves here: Exmoor ale, cheese and wholegrain mustard bread; Somerset cider cake; venison and port pie (note the typically Exmoor warning: 'Game pies may contain lead shot').

Mortimers CAFE £

(✍ 01398-323850; 13 High St; mains from £6; ◷9.30am-5.15pm Thu-Tue) Top-class teas (including many rare estate varieties) are the order of the day at this charmingly frilly and floral tearoom, but it's worth leaving room for the Welsh rarebits and crumbly cakes.

★ Woods BISTRO £££

(✍ 01398-324007; www.woodsdulverton.co.uk; 4 Bank Sq; mains £19; ◷noon-2pm & 6-9.30pm) Woods has country-but-classy down to a fine art, both in decor and dishes. Deer antlers hang on rough stone walls, and trestle tables sit beside wood-panelled booths. Exmoor beef, lamb, pigeon and cheeses fill the menu; truffle purée, pickled mushrooms and caramelised walnuts add élan.

Lynton & Lynmouth

Tucked in amid precipitous cliffs and steep, tree-lined slopes, these twin coastal towns are a landscape painter's dream. Bustling Lynmouth sits beside the shore, a busy harbour lined with pubs and souvenir shops. On the cliff top, Lynton feels much more genteel and well-to-do. A cliffside railway links the two; it's powered by the rushing West Lyn river, which feeds numerous cascades and waterfalls nearby.

◉ Sights

Cliff Railway HERITAGE RAILWAY

(✍ 01598-753486; www.cliffrailwaylynton.co.uk; adult single/return £2.50/3.50, child £1.50/2; ◷10am-5pm Feb-Oct, to 7pm Jun-Aug) This extraordinary piece of Victorian engineering sees two cars linked by a steel cable descend or ascend the sloping cliff face according to the weight of water in the cars' tanks. All burnished wood and polished brass, it's been running since 1890 and makes for an unmissable ride.

Flood Memorial Hall INTERPRETATION CENTRE
(The Esplanade, Lynmouth; ⊘9am-5pm Easter-Oct) FREE On 16 August 1952 a huge wave of water swept through Lynmouth after torrential rain. The devastation was immense – 34 people lost their lives; four bridges and countless houses were washed away. This exhibition features a scale model of the pre-flood village, photos of the destroyed buildings and personal testimonies of those involved.

🏃 Activities

Popular hiking trails among Lynton and Lynmouth's spectacular scenery include ones to the lighthouse at **Foreland Point**, to **Watersmeet**, 2 miles east of Lynmouth (reached via the gorgeous East Lyn River glade), and along the scenic **Glen Lyn Gorge**.

Valley of the Rocks WALKING
The dramatic geology in this valley was described by poet Robert Southey as 'rock reeling upon rock, stone piled upon stone, a huge terrifying reeling mass'. Look out for the formations dubbed the Devil's Cheesewring and Ragged Jack – and also the feral goats that wander the tracks. It's a mile's walk west of Lynton along a cracking coast path.

🛏 Sleeping

★ Rock House B&B ££
(☑01598-753508; www.rock-house.co.uk; Manor Green, Lynmouth; s £45, d £100-120) The setting is simply superb: set right on Lynmouth's pocket-sized harbour, steep hills slope up on three sides. Contemporary rooms sport leather headboards, lilac scatter-cushions and mini-armchairs. All have extraordinary views; the best is number four, where the window is next to the beach.

North Walk House B&B ££
(☑01598-753372;www.northwalkhouse.co.uk;North Walk, Lynton; d £60-80; P 🛜) Stripped wooden floors, stripy bedspreads and colourful rugs give North Walk House a gently funky feel. The views over the sea and rugged cliffs are fantastic, while the all-organic breakfasts feature Exmoor bacon and sausages, and Aga-baked eggs.

Castle Hill B&B ££
(☑01598-752291; www.castlehill.biz; Castle Hill, Lynton; d £70-95, f £140; 🛜) Despite a stately

Victorian exterior, the rooms in this central Lynton guesthouse are decidedly modern; oatmeal colours combine with chunky wood furniture and the odd cherry-red settee. The mini-suites have tiny balconies with fine hill and town views.

★ Millers at the Tors BOUTIQUE HOTEL £££
(☑01598-753236; www.millerslynmouth.co.uk; Countisbury Hill, Lynmouth; d £180-300; P) With lashings of sculpture, paintings and exotic artefacts, eccentric doesn't even begin to describe this objet d'art–packed enclave. It was set up by the late Martin Miller, of the *Miller's Antiques* books, which explains the delightfully over-the-top furnishings. It's set partway up precipitous Countisbury Hill, which explains the wraparound views.

🍴 Eating

Charlie Friday's CAFE £
(www.charliefridays.co.uk; Church Hill, Lynton; items from £3; ⊘10am-5pm Feb-Nov) A funky, friendly hang-out serving melting pastries, thick sarnies and fair-trade, two-shot espresso that really packs a punch.

Rising Sun FUSION ££
(☑01598-753223; www.risingsunlynmouth.co.uk; mains £12-19; ⊘noon-2.30pm & 6-9pm) Head chef Ben Meill delights in pairing Westcountry produce with European flavours, so tuck into soft, seared scallops with crisp pancetta, or crab with coriander and lime. The building itself has plenty of smugglers' character too, with higgledy-piggledy floors and hefty beams.

ℹ Information

Lynmouth has an ENPA tourist office (p279).

ℹ HOSTELS & CAMPING BARNS

The only YHA hostel inside Exmoor National Park is at **Exford** (☑0845 3719 634; www.yha.org.uk; Exe Mead; dm £18; P). For more basic accommodation, there are camping barns at **Mullacott Farm** (YHA; ☑0800 0191 700; www.yha. org.uk; Mullacott Cross, near Ilfracombe; per person £10) near Ilfracombe and **Northcombe Farm** (YHA; ☑0800 0191 700; www.yha.org.uk; Hollam, near Dulverton; per person £9) near Dulverton; you'll need all the usual camping supplies.

Lynton Tourist Office (☎01598-752225; www.lynton-lynmouth-tourism.co.uk; Lynton Town Hall, Lee Rd; ⏲10am-5pm Mon-Sat, to 2pm Sun)

Porlock & Around

POP 2300

The coastal village of Porlock is one of the prettiest on the north Exmoor coast; the huddle of thatched cottages lining its main street is framed on one side by the sea, and on the other by houses clinging to the steeply sloping hills behind. Winding lanes lead to the charismatic breakwater of **Porlock Weir**, 2 miles to the west, with its arching pebble beach and striking coastal views.

Sights

Holnicote Estate HISTORIC BUILDINGS
(NT; ☎01823-451587; www.nationaltrust.org.uk; near Porlock; ⏲24hr; P) FREE The 5060-hectare Holnicote Estate sweeps southeast out of Porlock, taking in a string of impossibly pretty villages. Picturesque **Bossington** leads to charming **Allerford**, with its 15th-century packhorse bridge. The biggest, **Selworthy**, offers eye-catching Exmoor views, a cafe, shop, and cob-and-thatch cottages clustering around the village green.

Sleeping & Eating

★**Millers at the Anchor** BOUTIQUE HOTEL ££
(☎01643-862753; www.millersuk.com/anchor; Porlock Weir; s £65-95, d £90-155; P 📶) Stuffed with antiques, overflowing with piled-up books, and scattered with exotic rugs, Millers delivers an enjoyably overwhelming dose of English eccentricity. Gilt-framed mirrors jostle with marble busts, vast beds and captivating views of Porlock Weir. But the chess set in the lounge and the quirky home cinema may tempt you from your room.

DRIVING TO PORLOCK

If you're driving, you can choose from two picturesque routes into Porlock village. The New Road Toll Road sweeps through pine forests and round U-bends, while Porlock Hill (A39) is a brake-burning 1:4 descent. Another toll road, the Porlock Scenic (Worthy) Toll Road, provides an alternative, bouncing, route up out of Porlock Weir.

Culbone BRITISH ££
(☎01643-862259; www.theculbone.com; near Porlock; mains £13-25; ⏲noon-10pm Tue-Sat, to 4pm Sun; P) The menu at this smart restaurant (with rooms) is stuffed with local produce – plump for the 28-day aged Devon-red steaks and choose from three different cuts or a huge chateaubriand for two. The contemporary-chic setting, with slate floors and black leather chairs, runs into the upstairs rooms (£85 to £100).

Ship Inn PUB £
(www.shipinnporlock.co.uk; High St, Porlock; mains £8-16; ⏲noon-2.30pm & 6-9pm; P) Coleridge and pal Robert Southey both downed pints in this thatched Porlock inn – you can even sit in 'Southey's Corner'. Substantial pub food – mainly steaks, roasts and stews – is served in the bar, and there are 10 light bedrooms (doubles £70) in pine and cream.

Information

Porlock Tourist Office (☎01643-863150; www.porlock.co.uk; High St, Porlock; ⏲10am-5pm Mon-Sat, to 1pm Sun)

Dunster

POP 850

Centred on a scarlet-walled castle and a medieval yarn market, Dunster is one of Exmoor's oldest villages, a tempting tangle of cobbled streets, bubbling brooks and packhorse bridges.

Sights

Dunster Castle CASTLE
(NT; ☎01643-821314; www.nationaltrust.org.uk; adult/child £9.30/4.60; ⏲11am-5pm Mar-Oct; P) Rosy-hued Dunster Castle crowns a densely wooded hill. Built by the Luttrell family, who once owned much of northern Exmoor, the oldest sections are 13th century, although the turrets and exterior walls are 19th-century additions. Look out for Tudor furnishings, 17th-century plasterwork and a ridiculously grand staircase. Leave time to explore the colourful terraced gardens, with their riverside walks and views across Exmoor's shores.

St George's Church CHURCH
Dunster's beautiful church dates mostly from the 15th century and boasts an intricately carved fan-vaulted rood screen. Just behind the church is a 16th-century dovecote, used for breeding edible squabs (young pigeons) for the dinner table at Dunster Castle.

Watermill
MILL

(☑ 01643-821759; Mill Lane; adult/child £3.75/2.75; ⊕ 11am-4.45pm Apr-Oct) Most of the original cogs, wheels and grinding stones still rotate away in this working 18th-century mill. There's a picturesque riverside tearoom alongside.

🛌 Sleeping & Eating

Mill Stream Cottage
B&B ££

(☑ 01643-821966; www.millstreamcottagedunster. co.uk; 2 Mill Lane; s £55, d £74-84) In the 1600s this was Dunster's workhouse, but now it's a sweet-as-pie guesthouse with country-cottage-style rooms. There are homemade cakes on arrival and home-baked biscuits on the tea tray, plus an oh-so-comfy guest lounge, where you can snooze in front of the wood-burner.

Dunster Castle Hotel
HOTEL ££

(☑ 01643-823030; www.thedunstercastlehotel.co. uk; 5 High St; d £70-160; ⊕ noon-2.30pm & 6-9pm; 🐾) Everything feels rich in this former coaching inn, from the dark purple furnishings and gleaming wooden furniture, to the plush, heraldic-style throws. The bar is comfy, while the buzzy restaurant (mains £14 to £22) specialises in intense flavours; expect beef with chorizo, and scallops with air-dried ham.

Spears Cross
B&B ££

(☑ 01643-821439; www.spearscross.co.uk; 1 West St; d £97-107; 🅿🐾) One for the connoisseur – of cuisine and beams. Age-old elm supports are everywhere, along with panels, floral furnishings and raspberry-red walls. Breakfast features bucks fizz with freshly squeezed orange juice, home-cured bacon, locally smoked trout and spelt and honey artesanal bread.

Reeve's
BRITISH ££

(☑ 01643-821414; www.reevesrestaurantdunster. co.uk; 20 High St; mains £12-25; ⊕ noon-1.30pm Sat & Sun, 7-9pm Tue-Sat) Seriously stylish Reeve's dishes up Dunster's best food. Complex, satisfying creations include piled-up confit of duck and chicken, saffron-fragranced turbot, and a still-warm, zesty lemon meringue.

Cobblestones
CAFE ££

(☑ 01643-821595; www.cobblestonesofdunster.co. uk; 24 High St; mains £5-10; ⊕ 10am-3.30pm daily, 6.30-8.30pm Wed-Sat) Plump for a ham or cheese platter or potted prawns on toast at this village cafe, or drop in for a superior cream tea.

❶ Getting There & Away

Bus 28 stops at Dunster on its way between Taunton and Minehead (£4, half-hourly Monday to Saturday, hourly on Sunday).

The **West Somerset Railway** (☑ 01643-704996; www.west-somerset-railway.co.uk; 24hr rover ticket adult/child £17/8.50) stops at Dunster during the summer, with four to seven trains daily from May to October.

DEVON

Devon offers freedom. Its rippling, beach-fringed landscape is studded with historic homes, vibrant cities and wild, wild moors. So here you can ditch schedules and to-do lists and hike a rugged coast path, take a scenic boat trip, or get lost in hedge-lined lanes that aren't even on your map. Discover collegiate Exeter, touristy Torquay, yachting haven Dartmouth and alternative Totnes. Or escape to wilderness Dartmoor and the remote, surf-dashed north coast. Sample wine made from the vines beside you and food that's fresh from field, furrow or sea. Go surfing, cycling, kayaking, horse riding, sea xswimming and barefoot beachcombing. Heading to Devon? Then prepare for freedom and sandy feet.

❶ Information

Visit Devon (www.visitdevon.co.uk)

❶ Getting Around

Traveline South West (www.travelinesw.com) Searchable database of bus and train times.

BUS

The Devon interactive **bus map** (www.journeydevon.info) helps in route-planning. Central Dartmoor is covered by a fleet of smaller operators.

First (www.firstgroup.com) A key operator in Plymouth and south Devon.

Stagecoach Devon (www.stagecoachbus.com) Runs services around Exeter, north Devon, south Dartmoor and Torquay.

Bus Passes

First Seven Day (adult/child/family £37/23/58) Weeklong pass for most First buses in Devon.

Firstday Southwest (adult/child £7.40/5.30) A day's unlimited bus travel on First buses in Devon and Cornwall.

MegaRiderGold (1/4 weeks £26/94) Unlimited travel on all southwest Stagecoach buses.

Stagecoach Explorer (adult/child/family £7.50/5/15) One day's travel on Stagecoach's southwest network.

TRAIN

Devon's main line skirts southern Dartmoor, running from Exeter to Plymouth and on to Cornwall. Branch lines include the 39-mile Exeter–Barnstaple Tarka Line, the 15-mile Plymouth–Gunnislake Tamar Valley Line and the scenic Exeter–Torquay Paignton line.

Freedom of Devon & Cornwall Rover Allows unlimited train travel in Devon and Cornwall for three days out of seven (adult/child £45/23), or eight days out of 15 (£65/39).

Exeter & Around

POP 117,800

Well heeled and comfortable, Exeter exudes evidence of its centuries-old role as the spiritual and administrative heart of Devon. The city's Gothic cathedral presides over pockets of cobbled streets; medieval and Georgian buildings, and fragments of the Roman city stretch out all around. A snazzy new shopping centre brings bursts of the modern, thousands of university students ensure a buzzing nightlife, and the vibrant quayside acts as a launch pad for cycling or kayaking trips. Throw in some stylish places to stay and eat and you have a relaxed but lively base for explorations.

History

Exeter's past can be read in its buildings. The Romans marched in around AD 55 – their 17-hectare fortress included a 2-mile defensive wall, crumbling sections of which remain, especially in Rougemont and Northernhay Gardens. Saxon and Norman times saw growth: a castle went up in 1068, the cathedral 40 years later. The Tudor wool boom brought Exeter an export trade, riches and half-timbered houses; prosperity continued into the Georgian era when hundreds of merchants built genteel homes. The Blitz of WWII brought devastation. In 1942, in just one night 156 people died and 12 hectares of the city were flattened. In the 21st century the £220 million Princesshay Shopping Centre has added shimmering glass and steel lines to the architectural mix.

⊙ Sights

★**Exeter Cathedral**   CATHEDRAL
(Cathedral Church of St Peter; ☏ 01392-285983; www.exeter-cathedral.org.uk; The Close; adult/child £6/free; ⊙ 9.30am-4.45pm Mon-Sat, 11.30am-3.30pm Sun) Magnificent in warm, honey-coloured stone, Exeter's cathedral is one of Devon's most prestigious sights. Dating largely from the 12th and 13th centuries, one end of the exterior is framed by extraordinary medieval statuary, while inside the ceiling is mesmerising – the longest unbroken Gothic vaulting in the world, it sweeps up to meet ornate ceiling bosses in gilt and vibrant colours. Other highlights include elegant wood carvings and striking sculptures.

The site has been a religious one since at least the 5th century but the Normans started the current building in 1114; the towers of today's cathedral date from that period. In 1270 a 90-year remodelling process began, introducing a mix of Early English and Decorated Gothic styles.

Above the **Great West Front** scores of weather-worn figures line a once brightly painted screen that now forms England's largest collection of 14th-century sculpture. Inside, the exquisitely symmetrical ceiling soars up and along, towards the north transept and the 15th-century **Exeter Clock**: in keeping with medieval astronomy it shows the earth as a golden ball at the centre of the universe with the sun, a fleur-de-lys, travelling round. Still ticking and whirring, it chimes on the hour.

The huge oak canopy over the **Bishop's Throne** was carved in 1312, while the 1350 **minstrels' gallery** is decorated with 12 angels playing musical instruments. Cathedral staff will point out the famous sculpture of the lady with two left feet and the tiny **St James Chapel**, built to repair the one destroyed in the Blitz. Look out for its unusual carvings: a cat, a mouse and, oddly, a rugby player.

The Roof Tours (p285) are superb; as are the 45-minute **ground-floor guided tours** (incl in admission; ⊙ 11am, 12.30pm & 2.30pm Mon-Sat). Evocative choral **evensong** services are held at 5.30pm Monday to Friday, and 4pm Saturday and Sunday.

In the adjoining **Refectory** (Serlo's; mains £6; ⊙ 10am-4.45pm Mon-Sat) you can tuck into cakes, quiches and soups at trestle tables surrounded by vaulted ceilings, stained glass and busts of the great, the good and the dead.

★**Underground Passages**   UNDERGROUND
(☏ 01392-665887; www.exeter.gov.uk/passages; Paris St; adult/child £6/4; ⊙ 9.30am-5.30pm Mon-Sat, 10am-4pm Sun Jun-Sep, 11.30am-4pm Tue-Sun Oct-May) Prepare to crouch down, don a hard

hat and possibly get spooked in what is the only publicly accessible system of its kind in England. These medieval vaulted passages were built to house pipes bringing fresh water to the city. Guides lead you on a scramble through the network telling tales of ghosts, escape routes and cholera. The last tour is an hour before closing; they're popular – book ahead.

★ **RAMM**   MUSEUM
(Royal Albert Memorial Museum & Art Gallery; 01392-265858; www.rammuseum.org.uk; Queen St; 10am-5pm Tue-Sun) **FREE** The imposing, red-brick exterior looks every inch the Victorian museum, but a £24 million revamp has brought the exhibits bang up to date. Interactive displays focus on Exeter's heritage from prehistory to the present, as well as global exploration and the concept of collecting. Look out for Exeter's Roman-era artefacts, local Tudor carvings and the striking ethnographic displays which include African masks, samurai armour and the mummy of Shep en-Mut.

Bill Douglas Centre   MUSEUM
(01392-724321; www.billdouglas.org; Old Library, Prince of Wales Rd; 10am-5pm; P) **FREE** A delightful homage to film and fun, the Bill Douglas Centre is a compact collection of all things celluloid, from magic lanterns to Mickey Mouse. Inside discover just what the butler did see and why the flicks are called the flicks. Among the mass of movie memorabilia are Charlie Chaplin bottle stoppers, Ginger Rogers playing cards, James Bond board games and *Star Wars* toys. It's set on the Exeter University campus, a mile northwest of the city centre.

St Nicholas Priory   HISTORIC BUILDING
(01392-265858; www.exeter.gov.uk/priory; The Mint; adult/child £4.20/1.60; 10am-5pm Sat, plus Mon-Fri school holidays) For a vivid glimpse of life inside a late-Elizabethan town house, head to this 900-year-old former Benedictine monastery. Its beautiful russet stone walls shelter interiors alive with brightly coloured furnishings, elaborate plaster ceilings and intricate oak panelling.

Powderham Castle   HISTORIC BUILDING
(01626-890243; www.powderham.co.uk; adult/ child £11/10; 11am-4.30pm Sun-Fri Apr-Oct; P) The historic, and current, home of the Earl of Devon, Powderham is a stately but still friendly place that was built in 1391 and remodelled in the Victorian era. A visit takes

CATHEDRAL ROOF TOURS

For a sensational view of Exeter Cathedral (p284) book one of these high-rise guided walks (01392-285983; www. exeter-cathedral.org.uk; adult/child £10/5; 2pm Tue-Thu, 11am Sat Apr-Sep). Climb 251 steps up spiral staircases, head out onto the sweeping roof, then gaze down on the city from the edge of the North Tower. They're popular so book two weeks ahead.

in a fine wood-panelled Great Hall, parkland with 650 deer and glimpses of life 'below stairs' in the kitchen. Powderham is on the River Exe near Kenton, 8 miles south of Exeter. Bus 2 runs from Exeter (£3.80, 30 minutes, every 20 minutes Monday to Saturday).

A La Ronde   HISTORIC BUILDING
(NT; 01395-265514; www.nationaltrust.org.uk; Summer Lane; adult/child £8/4; 11am-5pm early Feb-Oct, noon-4pm Sat & Sun Nov-Jan; P) This quirky 16-sided cottage was built in 1796 so two spinster cousins could display a mass of curiosities acquired on their 10-year European grand tour. Its glass alcoves, low lintels and tiny doorways mean it's like clambering through a doll's house – highlights are a delicate feather frieze in the drawing room and a gallery smothered with a thousand seashells. The house is 10 miles south of Exeter, near Exmouth; bus 57 (£4.30, 30 minutes, every 15 minutes) runs close by.

🏃 Activities

The River Exe and the Exeter Canal are framed by foot and cycle paths which wind south from the Quay, past pubs, beside an ever-broadening estuary towards the sea, 10 miles away.

Saddles & Paddles   OUTDOORS
(01392-424241; www.sadpad.com; Exeter Quay; 9azzm-6pm) Rents out bikes (adult per hour/day £6/15), kayaks (£10/35) and Canadian canoes (£15/50); the tourist office stocks maps.

👉 Tours

★ **Redcoat Tours**   WALKING TOUR
(01392-265203; www.exeter.gov.uk/visiting; 3-6pm daily Apr-Oct, 2 daily Nov-Mar) **FREE** For an informed and entertaining introduction to Exeter's history, tag along on one of these

Exeter

Exeter

◎ Top Sights
1 Exeter Cathedral	C3
2 RAMM	C2
3 Underground Passages	D2

◎ Sights
4 St Nicholas Priory	B3

◉ Activities, Courses & Tours
Exeter Cathedral Guided Tours	(see 1)
Exeter Cathedral Roof Tours	(see 1)
5 Redcoat Tours	C3
6 Saddles & Paddles	C4

🛌 Sleeping
7 ABode Exeter	C3
8 Globe Backpackers	C4
9 Magdalen Chapter	D4
10 Raffles	D1

11 Townhouse	A1
12 White Hart	C4

✴ Eating
13 @Angela's	B4
14 Herbies	B3
15 Michael Caines Refectory	C3 (see 1)
16 Ruby	C2
17 Rusty Bike	C1

🍷 Drinking & Nightlife
18 Mamma Stone's	B3
19 Old Firehouse	D2
20 Timepiece	C2

🎭 Entertainment
21 Bike Shed	B3
22 Exeter Picturehouse	B4
23 Phoenix	C2

1½-hour tours. Themes range from murder and trade to the Tudors and religion – there are even torchlit prowls through the catacombs and evening ghost walks. Tours leave from Cathedral Yard or the Quay; there's no need to book.

🛏 Sleeping

⭐**Wood Life**   CAMPSITE **£**
(🗷01392-832509; www.thewoodlife.org; The Linhay; 5/7 nights from £550/800; ☺Apr-Oct; ℗) The trappings that come with this luxurious, six-person safari-style tent don't just include brass bedsteads draped with Egyptian cotton and thick rugs on decked floors. There's also a firepit (plus campfire kettle), tub of fresh herbs and vintage games chest. Add firewood-warmed showers and your very own 3.5-hectare wood, and you have comfy camping heaven. It's on the outskirts of Kenn village, 7 miles south of Exeter.

Globe Backpackers   HOSTEL **£**
(🗷01392-215521; www.exeterbackpackers.co.uk; 71 Holloway St; dm/d £17.50/45; ℗🛜) Rightly a firm favourite among budget travellers, this spotlessly clean, relaxed, rambling house boasts three doubles, roomy dorms and wet room showers that are positively luxurious.

ABode Exeter   HOTEL **££**
(🗷01392-319955; www.abodehotels.co.uk/exeter; Cathedral Yard; r £90-300; 🛜) At ABode, Georgian grandeur meets minimalist chic. Wonky floors and stained glass combine with recessed lighting, pared-down furniture and neutral tones. The rooms range from 'comfortable' and 'enviable' to 'fabulous', where slanted ceilings frame grandstand cathedral views. Prices depend on availability; book ahead to bag bargains.

Raffles   B&B **££**
(🗷01392-270200; www.raffles-exeter.co.uk; 11 Blackall Rd; s/d/f £55/78/88; ℗🛜) The antique dealer owner has peppered each room of this late-Victorian town house with heritage features – look out for Bakelite radios, wooden plant stands and polished trunks. Largely organic breakfasts and a walled garden add to the appeal.

White Hart   INN **££**
(🗷01392-279897; www.whitehartpubexeter.co.uk; 66 South St; s/d £74/84; ℗🛜) They've been putting people up here since the Plantagenets were on the throne in the 1300s. The courtyard is a wisteria-fringed bobble of cobbles and the bar is book-lined and

BLACKDOWN YURTS

Organic bedding, fresh spring water, thick rugs and blazing log burners make this hipster **sleep-spot** (🗷01884-266699; www.blackdownyurts.co.uk; near Exeter; 6-person yurt per 5 days £200; ℗) utterly irresistible. There's a field kitchen, fire pit and an endless supply of logs too. The four, cosy, ecofriendly yurts are tucked away on a sleepy smallholding around 15 miles east of Exeter.

beamed. Rooms are tasteful modern affairs with suede chairs, honey and gold hues and glinting bathrooms.

Townhouse   B&B **££**
(🗷01392-494994; www.townhouseexeter.co.uk; 54 St David's Hill; s/d/f £40/80/90; ℗🛜) Expect simple but delightful rooms with stripped wooden floors and clean, pared-down lines, spiced up by dashes of intense colour. The Victorian exterior drips with ivy and all the rooms are named after literary characters – will you opt for Moneypenny, Lorna Doone or Darcy?

⭐**Magdalen Chapter**   BOUTIQUE HOTEL **£££**
(🗷01392-281000; www.themagdalenchapter.com; Magdalen St; d £160-250; @🛜🏊) Undoubtedly Exeter's coolest hotel (staff wear Converse trainers and low-slung slacks) the Magdalen is replete with funky flourishes. Lush purple corridors lead to dove-grey bedrooms, each with iPad, coffee machine, complimentary mini bar and mood lighting. There's even a tiny, heated outdoor pool that leads into an indoor enclave made toasty by a log burner.

🍴 Eating

⭐**Rusty Bike**   MODERN BRITISH **££**
(🗷01392-214440; www.rustybike-exeter.co.uk; 67 Howell Rd; mains £15-19; ☺6-10pm daily, noon-3pm Sat & Sun) A vintage football table and bashed-about chairs set the scene for some seriously stylish rustic cuisine. Menus change daily depending on deliveries from local suppliers. So expect rarities like confit goose and pistachio; beef chuck and carrots; or truffle-laced pheasant breast – delivered, of course, by the local gamekeeper.

Ruby   BURGERS **££**
(www.rubyburgers.com; 74 Queen St; mains £5.50-10; ☺10am-10pm) The vibe might be retro-hip,

RIVER COTTAGE CANTEEN

TV chef Hugh Fearnley-Whittingstall campaigns on sustainable food, so it's fitting his east Devon canteen (☑ 01297-631715; www.rivercottage.net; Trinity Sq, Axminster; mains £8-16; ☺ 9am-5pm daily, 6.30-9pm Tue-Sat; ☑), 30 miles east of Exeter, champions local, seasonal and organic ingredients. Hearty flavours feature cured wild boar, venison scotch eggs, and sharing platters of local meats, fish and cheese. Drinks include Stinger Beer; brewed from (carefully) hand-picked Dorset nettles. Alternatively, book a four-course gastronomic delight at the nearby **River Cottage HQ** (☑ 01297-630300; www.rivercottage.net; 2-course lunch £55, 4-course dinner £70-90; ☺ noon-3pm Sun, 7.30-11pm Fri & Sat); booking required. There's another River Cottage Canteen in Plymouth (p299).

There's another River Cottage Canteen in Plymouth (p299).

but the focus on prime local ingredients is pure zeitgeist: succulent beef patties from Devon herds, outdoor-reared pork, free-range chicken. Add Devon Blue cheese and edge-of-Exeter veg and you have modern-diner dining that's a cut above the rest.

Herbies
VEGETARIAN ££

(15 North St; mains £7-11; ☺ 11am-2.30pm Mon-Sat, 6.30-9.30pm Tue-Sat; ☑) Cosy and gently groovy, Herbies has been cheerfully feeding Exeter's veggies for more than 20 years. Tuck into delicious Tuscan mushrooms, Moroccan tagine or butter bean, thyme and squash risotto. They take good culinary care of vegans too.

★ Michael Caines
FINE DINING £££

(☑ 01392-319955; www.michaelcaines.com; Cathedral Yard; mains £24; ☺ noon-2.30pm & 6-9pm Mon-Sat) Run by the eponymous, double Michelin-starred chef, the food here is a complex blend of prime Westcountry ingredients and full-bodied French flavours. Gastronomes linger over the seven-course tasting menu (£65), but the set lunches (two/three courses £13/18) are some of the best deals in town.

@Angela's
MODERN BRITISH £££

(☑ 01392-499038; www.angelasrestaurant.co.uk; 38 New Bridge St; mains £20; ☺ 6-9.30pm Mon-Sat) Dedication to sourcing local ingredients sometimes sees the chef here rising before dawn to bag the best fish at Brixham Market. The garlic-infused roasted monkfish is worth the trip alone, while the Devon duck is made memorable by a rich caramelised orange sauce. Also open for reservations only at lunch Friday and Saturday.

🍷 Drinking & Nightlife

★ Old Firehouse
PUB

(www.oldfirehouseexeter.co.uk; 50 New North Rd; ☺ noon-2am Mon-Wed, to 3am Thu-Sat, to 1am Sun)

Step into the snug, candlelit interior of this Exeter institution and feel instantly at home. Here, dried hops hang from rafters above flagstone floors and walls of exposed stone. The range of draught ciders and cask ales is truly impressive while the pizzas, served after 9pm, have kept countless students fed.

Timepiece
CLUB

(www.timepiecenightclub.co.uk; Little Castle St; ☺ 9.30pm-1.30am Mon-Wed, 10pm-2am Fri & Sat) DJ sets range from salsa (Tuesday) and indie electro (Friday), to multi-genre club classics on Saturday nights.

☆ Entertainment

Mamma Stone's
LIVE MUSIC

(www.mamastones.com; 1 Mary Arches St; ☺ 6pm-midnight) A cool venue showcasing everything from acoustic sets to pop, folk and jam nights; many of the acts have been schooled at the artist-development program which operates alongside. Mama Stone's daughter, Joss (yes, *the* Joss Stone) plays sometimes too. It's open 9pm to 3am when bands play.

Phoenix
PERFORMING ARTS

(www.exeterphoenix.org.uk; Gandy St; ☺ 10am-11pm Mon-Sat; ☎) Exeter's art and soul; the Phoenix is a buzzing blend of indy cinema, performance space, galleries and a cool cafe-bar (snacks to 9pm).

Exeter Picturehouse
CINEMA

(☑ 0871 902 5730; www.picturehouses.co.uk; 51 Bartholomew St West) An intimate, independent cinema, screening mainstream and art-house movies.

Bike Shed
THEATRE

(☑ 01392-434169; www.bikeshedtheatre.co.uk; 162 Fore St; ☺ noon-midnight Mon-Thu, to 2am Fri & Sat, 5-11pm Sun) Emerging writers are profiled in the Bike Shed's rough 'n' ready subterranean, brick-lined performance space. Its vintage cocktail bar makes a hip setting for live music and DJ sets on Friday and Saturday nights.

ℹ Information

Exeter Library (Castle St; per 30min £3; ⊙9am-6pm Mon, Tue, Thu & Fri, 10am-5pm Wed, 9am-4pm Sat; 🛜) Internet access and free wi-fi.

Main Tourist Office (🗷 01392-665700; www.heartofdevon.com; Dix's Field; ⊙9.30am-4.30pm)

Police Station (🗷 08452-777444; Heavitree Rd; ⊙24hr)

Royal Devon & Exeter Hospital (Barrack Rd) Accident and emergency.

Tourist Office at the Quay (🗷 01392-271611; www.heartofdevon.com; The Quay; ⊙10am-5pm Apr-Oct, 11am-4pm Sat & Sun Nov-Mar)

ℹ Getting There & Away

AIR

Exeter International (www.exeter-airport.co.uk) Flights connect with Europe and the UK, including Amsterdam, Glasgow, the Isles of Scilly, Manchester, Newcastle and Paris, plus the Channel Islands.

BUS

Services include:

Bude (£6.50, two hours, five daily Monday to Saturday) Bus X9; runs via Okehampton.

Jurassic Coast Bus/Bus X53 Four to six daily to Lyme Regis (£7), Weymouth (£7.20) and Poole (£7.20); no service on winter Sundays.

Moretonhampstead (£3.50, one hour, six daily Monday to Saturday) Bus 359.

Plymouth (£6.50, 1¼ hours, two-hourly Monday to Saturday, three on Sunday) Bus X38.

Totnes (£5.80, 50 minutes, seven daily Monday to Saturday, two on Sunday) Bus X64.

Transmoor Link/Bus 82 Runs on summer Saturdays and Sundays only (mid-May to mid-September), making one trip each way from Exeter to Tavistock (£5.80) via Moretonhampstead, Postbridge, Princetown and Yelverton.

TRAIN

Main-line trains stopping at Exeter St David's include.

Barnstaple (£10, 1¼ hours, one to two hourly)

Bristol (£15, 1¼ hours, half-hourly)

Exmouth (£4, hourly, 40 minutes)

London Paddington (£46, 2½ hours, half-hourly)

Paignton (£7, 50 minutes, half-hourly)

Penzance (£15, three hours, half-hourly to hourly)

Plymouth (£9, one hour, half-hourly)

Torquay (£6, 45 minutes, half-hourly to hourly)

Totnes (£7, 35 minutes, half-hourly)

Some branch-line services also go through Exeter Central.

ℹ Getting Around

TO/FROM THE AIRPORT

Bus 56 runs from the bus station and Exeter St David's train station to Exeter Airport (£2.80, 30 minutes, hourly 7am to 6pm).

BICYCLE

Saddles & Paddles (p285) rents out bikes, kayaks and canoes.

BUS

Bus H (two to four per hour) links St David's train station with Central Station and the High St, passing near the bus station.

CAR

Hire options include **Europcar** (www.europcar.co.uk).

Park & Ride buses (adult/child £2.40/1.60) operate every 20 minutes, running from Sowton (near M5, junction 30) and Matford (near M5, junction 31) Monday to Saturday, and from Honiton Rd (near M5, junction 29) daily.

TAXI

There are ranks at St David's train station and on High St and Sidwell St.

Capital Taxis (🗷 01392-434343; ⊙24hr)

Club Cars (🗷 01392-213030; ⊙24hr)

Gemini (🗷 01392-666666; ⊙24hr)

Torquay & Around

POP 114, 266

It may face the English Channel, rather than the Med, but the coast around Torquay has long been dubbed the English Riviera; famous for palm trees, piers and russet-red cliffs. At first glance, Torquay itself is the quintessential English seaside resort in flux, beloved by both the coach-tour crowd and stag- and hen-party animals. But a mild microclimate and an azure circle of bay have also drawn a smarter set and Torquay now competes with foodie-hub Dartmouth for fine eateries. The area also boasts unique attractions that range from an immense aviary to a surreal model village. Add an Agatha Christie connection, fishing boats and steam trains, and it all adds up to some grand days out beside the sea.

Torquay's neighbouring resort, Paignton, sits 3 miles south; the fishing port of Brixham is 5 miles further south again.

◉ Sights & Activities

Torquay boasts no fewer than 20 beaches and an impressive 22 miles of coast. Holidaymakers flock to the central (but tidal) **Torre Abbey Sands**; locals head for the sand-and-shingle beaches beside the 240ft red-clay cliffs around **Babbacombe**.

Living Coasts   ZOO
(📞0844 474 3366; www.livingcoasts.org.uk; Beacon Quay; adult/child £12/9; ⊙10am-5pm) An enormous open-plan aviary bringing you up close to free-roaming penguins, punk-rocker style tufted puffins and disarmingly cute bank cormorants.

Babbacombe Model Village   EXHIBITION
(📞01803-315315; www.model-village.co.uk; Hampton Ave; adult/child £11/7; ⊙10am-4pm) Prepare for a fabulously eccentric, 1.6-hectare world in miniature, complete with small-scale Stonehenge, football stadium, beach, castle (under attack from a fire-breathing dragon) and thatched village where firefighters are tackling a blaze. Visit in the evening for illuminations; think pocket-sized Piccadilly Circus, complete with flashing banner ads. It's open until 9pm on some summer evenings.

Paignton Zoo   ZOO
(📞0844 474 2222; www.paigntonzoo.org.uk; Totnes Rd, Paignton; adult/child £16/12; ⊙10am-5pm; 🅿) A conservation charity runs this innovative, 80-acre zoo, where spacious enclosures re-create habitats as varied as savannah, wetland, tropical forest and desert. High spots include the orang-utan island, vast glass-walled lion enclosure and a lemur

wood, where you walk over a plank suspension bridge as the primates leap around in the surrounding trees. Then there's the steamy crocodile swamp with pathways winding over and beside Nile, Cuban and saltwater crocs, some up to 6m long.

Babbacombe Cliff Railway   HERITAGE RAILWAY
(📞01803-328750; www.babbacombecliffrailway.co.uk; adult/child return £2/1.40; ⊙9.30am-4.55pm Feb-Oct) At Babbacombe a glorious 1920s funicular railway sees you climbing into a tiny wooden carriage and rattling up and down rails set into the cliff.

Ferry to Brixham   FERRY TRIP
(📞01803-882811; www.greenwayferry.co.uk; Princess Pier; adult/child return £6/4; ⊙12 sailings daily Apr-Oct) This blast across Tor Bay offers spray-dashed views of beaches, crumbling cliffs and grand Victorian hotels. Competition can cause prices to dip wildly; check out the stands lining Torquay's harbour.

🛏 Sleeping

Torquay Backpackers   HOSTEL £
(📞01803-299924; www.torquaybackpackers.co.uk; 119 Abbey Rd; dm/d £17/34; @🛜) Photos of grinning past guests plaster noticeboards; flags of all nations drape the walls at this budget stalwart. There are luxuries too: a DVD den and a decked, alfresco pool table terrace.

Orestone   HOTEL ££
(📞01803-328098; www.orestonemanor.com; Rock House Lane; s £90-275, d £105-190, ste £185-285; 🅿🛜) At this Georgian country house winter brings blazing log fires; summer brings breakfast on a sea-backed terrace. In the bay-view bedrooms, period elegance meets modern comforts: muted blues and greens surround snazzy bathrooms. It's all tucked

---

AGATHA CHRISTIE

Torquay is the birthplace of the 'Queen of Crime', Agatha Christie (1890–1976), author of 75 novels and 33 plays, and creator of Hercule Poirot, the moustachioed, immodest Belgian detective, and Miss Marple, the surprisingly perceptive busybody spinster. Born Agatha Miller, she grew up, courted and honeymooned in Torquay and also worked as a hospital dispenser here during WWI, thus acquiring her famous knowledge of poisons.

The tourist office stocks the free Agatha Christie Mile leaflet, which guides you round significant local sites, while **Torquay Museum** (📞01803-293975; www.torquaymuseum.org; 529 Babbacombe Rd; adult/child £6/3; ⊙10am-4pm Mon-Thu & Sat) has a collection of photos, handwritten notes and displays devoted to her famous detectives. The highlight, though, is Greenway (p292), her summer home near Dartmouth. The Greenway Ferry (p293) sails there from Torquay's Princess Pier – it's best to book. Boats also go from Dartmouth and Totnes; a steam train runs from Paignton.

away in a wooded valley 3 miles north of Torquay. There's also a restaurant open noon to 2pm and 7pm to 9pm.

Seabreeze
B&B ££

(☑ 01803-322429; www.seabreezebabbacombe.co.uk; 39 Babbacombe Downs Rd; s £60-80, d £70-90; P 🛜) The smart rooms here are done out in cheery colours – choose from sea-themed aquamarine or bright 'n' breezy red, white and blue. Swish bathrooms and mini bay-view balconies seal the deal.

Headland View
B&B ££

(☑ 01803-312612; www.headlandview.com; 37 Babbacombe Downs Rd; d £72-75; P 🛜) Set high on the cliffs at Babbacombe, this delightful terrace is peppered with subtle nautical flourishes, from jaunty model lighthouses to boat motifs on the curtains. The wicker chairs on the tiny balconies have grandstand views of a cracking stretch of sea.

★ Cary Arms
BOUTIQUE HOTEL £££

(☑ 01803-327110; www.caryarms.co.uk; Babbacombe Beach; d £195-275, ste £375) The great British seaside has just gone seriously stylish. At this boutique bolthole New England tones are jazzed up by candy-striped cushions; balconies directly overlook the beach and children are given a fishing net and bait on arrival. Prices fall by up to £80 in low season.

✕ Eating & Drinking

At time of writing, sustainable seafood restaurateur Mitch Tonks was about to open one of his aclaimed **Rockfish** (www.therockfish.co.uk) eateries on Torquay Harbour.

Number 7
SEAFOOD ££

(☑ 01803-295055; www.no7-fish.com; 7 Beacon Tce; mains £14-20; ⊙ noon-1.45pm Wed-Sat year-round, 7-9pm daily Jul-Sep, Tue-Sat Oct-Jun) Fabulous smells fill the air at this bustling harbourside bistro, where the chalked-up menus are crowded with crab, lobster and fish fresh from the boats. Accompaniments range from garlic and brandy to Moroccan spices.

Orange Tree
MODERN BRITISH ££

(☑ 01803-213936; www.orangetreerestaurant.co.uk; 14 Park Hill Rd; mains £15-25; ⊙ 7-9pm Tue-Sat) English-meets-European cuisine here in dishes majoring in local fish, meat and game; prepare to enjoy rich Brixham crab bisque with scallops, cod with nutty Serrano ham or south Devon steaks with a Madeira and mushroom sauce.

★ The Room at the Elephant
FINE DINING £££

(☑ 01803-200044; www.elephantrestaurant.co.uk; 3 Beacon Tce; 7 courses £72; ⊙ 6.30-8.30pm Tue-Sat) A restaurant to remember. Torbay's Michelin-starred eatery is defined by a tasting menu showcasing intricate presentation and imaginative flavour fusions: Brixham crab with lovage; roe deer with onion ash; beetroot with smoked blueberries. The window frames bright marina views; a ground-floor brasserie (open noon to 2pm and 6.30pm to 9pm, Tuesday to Saturday) serves simpler fare (mains £16 to £23).

Hole in the Wall
PUB

(www.holeinthewalltorquay.co.uk; 6 Park Lane; ⊙ 11am-11pm) A heavily beamed, Tardis-like boozer with a tiny terrace; an atmospheric spot for a pint.

ℹ Information

Tourist Office (☑ 0844 474 2233; www.theenglishriviera.co.uk; Vaughan Pde, the Harbour; ⊙ 9.30am-5pm Mon-Sat)

ℹ Getting There & Away

BUS

Brixham (£4.10, 50 minutes, half-hourly) Bus 12, via Paignton.

Dartmouth (£4.50, 1¼ hours, hourly Monday to Saturday) Stagecoach Gold.

Totnes (£3.50, 45 minutes, half-hourly Monday to Saturday, seven on Sunday) Stagecoach Gold.

FERRY

Regular ferries (p290) shuttle between Torquay and Brixham.

TRAIN

Trains run from Exeter via Torquay (£6, 45 minutes, half-hourly to hourly) to Paignton (£6, 52 minutes).

Dartmouth Steam Railway (www.dartmouthrailriver.co.uk; Paignton Station; adult/child return £14/8; ⊙ 3-9 trains daily Apr-Oct) These steam trains puff from Paignton via Greenway Halt to Kingswear, which is linked by ferry (p294) to Dartmouth.

Brixham

POP 17,457

An appealing, pastel-painted tumbling of fishermen's cottages leads down to Brixham's horseshoe harbour where arcades and gift shops coexist with winding streets, brightly coloured boats and one of England's busiest fishing ports. Although picturesque, Brixham is far from a neatly packaged resort, and its brand of gritty charm offers an insight into work-a-day life along Devon's coast.

⊙ Sights

Golden Hind
SAILING SHIP

(☎ 01803-856223; www.goldenhind.co.uk; The Quay; adult/child £4/3; ⊙ 10am-4pm Mar-Oct) Devon explorer Sir Francis Drake carried out a treasure-seeking circumnavigation of the globe aboard the *Golden Hind*, in the late 1500s. This full-sized replica sees you crossing the gangplank, clambering below decks, peering into the captain's cabin and prowling around the poop deck.

Brixham Heritage Museum
MUSEUM

(☎ 01803-856267; www.torbaymuseums.com; Bolton Cross; adult/child £2/free; ⊙ 10am-4pm Tue-Sat Apr-Oct, to 1pm Nov-Mar) An eclectic collection of exhibits explores the town's salty history, foscusing on sailboats, smuggling, shipbuilding and sea rescues.

ⓒ Tours

★ Fish Market
MARKET TOUR

(☎ 0741 0617931; www.brixhamtourismpartnership. co.uk; The Quay; tours incl breakfast £10; ⊙ twice monthly late Jun-Sep) Book early for one of these memorable, early-morning tours around a normally off-limits world. You'll see ice-lined fish trays, white-coated buyers and a bustling auction, then have breakfast at the Fishermen's Mission. If you miss a space on the tours, head to the fish market's viewing platform around 6am to watch the fleet's manoeuvrings.

✕ Eating & Drinking

David Walker
SEAFOOD £

(www.davidwalkerandson.com; unit B, Fish Market; ⊙ 9am-3pm Mon-Fri, 8am-3pm Sat) *The* place to connect with Brixham's fishing industry and stock up for your BBQ – the counters are piled high with the day's catch. Picnic goodies include huge, cooked shell-on prawns and dressed crab.

Beamers
SEAFOOD ££

(☎ 01803-854777; www.beamersrestaurant.co.uk; 19 The Quay; mains £16-20; ⊙ 6-9pm Wed-Mon; ✐) Each morning Head Chef Simone strolls to Brixham Fish Market to select the best of the day's catch. The result? Fresh, superbly cooked fish. Samphire, saffron and Pernod spring some menu surprises; bagging a window table secures an absorbing harbour view.

Maritime
PUB

(www.themaritime.co.uk; 79 King St; ⊙ 7-11pm) Eccentric old boozer smothered in thousands of key rings, stone jugs and chamber pots, presided over by a chatty parrot called Mr Tibbs.

ⓘ Getting There & Away

Regular ferries (p290) shuttle between Brixham and Torquay.

Bus 22 to Kingswear (£3.20, 15 minutes, half-hourly to hourly) Ferry (p294) connections continue to Dartmouth.

Bus 12 to Torquay (£4.10, 50 minutes, half-hourly) Via Paignton.

Dartmouth & Around
POP 10,716

A bewitching blend of primary-coloured boats and delicately shaded houses, Dartmouth is irresistible. Buildings cascade down steep, wooded slopes towards the River Dart; 17th-century shops with splendidly carved and gilded fronts line narrow lanes. Its charms have drawn a yachting crowd and a string of top-notch eateries, but fleets of fishing vessels, ferries and pleasure boats ensure it's still a busy working port with an authentic tang of the sea. Hiking trails lead up the river or onto the cliffs, while a unique art-deco house and Agatha Christie's Greenway estate wait in the wings.

Dartmouth is on the west side of the Dart estuary. It's linked to the village of Kingswear on the east bank by fleets of car and foot ferries, providing a key transport link to Torquay.

⊙ Sights & Activities

★ Greenway
HISTORIC BUILDING

(NT; ☎ 01803-842382; www.nationaltrust.org.uk; Greenway Rd, Galmpton; adult/child £9.40/5.20; ⊙ 10.30am-5pm Wed-Sun Mar-Oct, plus Tue late Jul-late Aug) High on Devon's must-see list, the captivating summer home of crime writer Agatha Christie sits beside the placid River Dart. Part-guided tours allow you to wander between rooms where the furnishings and knick-knacks are much as she left them. The bewitching waterside gardens include features that pop up in her mysteries, so you get to spot locations made notorious by fictional murders. Car parking places have to be prebooked; the best way to arrive is by ferry or on foot.

Christie owned Greenway between 1938 and 1959, and the house feels frozen in time: check out the piles of hats in the lobby, the books in her library, the clothes in her wardrobe, and listen to her speak (via a replica radio) in the drawing room. In the gardens, woods speckled with splashes of magnolias, daffodils and hydrangeas frame the water, while the planting creates intimate, secret spaces – the boathouse and views over the river are sublime. In Christie's book *Dead Man's Folly*, Greenway doubles as Nasse House, with the boathouse making an appearance as a murder scene.

The **Greenway Ferry** (✆01803-882811; www.greenwayferry.co.uk) runs to the house from Dartmouth (adult/child return £8/6, eight daily), Totnes (return fare £8, two to seven per week) and Torquay (one daily adult/child return £15/10). It only operates when the house is open – booking is advised. Alternatively, take the Dartmouth Steam Railway (p294) from Paignton to Greenway Halt (adult/child £8.50/5) then walk half a mile through the woods, or hike along the picturesque **Dart Valley Trail** from Kingswear (4 miles).

Coleton Fishacre　　HISTORIC BUILDING
(NT; ✆01803-842382; www.nationaltrust.org.uk; Brownstone Rd, near Kingswear; adult/child £9.40/5.20; ⏱10.30am-5pm Sat-Thu mid-Feb–Oct; ℗) For an evocative glimpse of Jazz Age glamour, drop by the former home of the D'Oyly Carte family of theatre impresarios.

Built in the 1920s, its faultless art-deco embellishments include original Lalique tulip uplighters, comic bathroom tiles and a stunning saloon – complete with tinkling piano. The croquet terrace leads to deeply shelved subtropical gardens and suddenly revealed vistas of the sea. Hike the 4 miles along the cliffs from Kingswear, or drive.

Dartmouth Castle　　CASTLE
(EH; ✆01803-833588; www.english-heritage.org.uk; adult/child £5.50/3.30; ⏱10am-6pm Apr-Sep, to 5pm Oct, to 4pm Sat & Sun Nov-Mar) Encounter mazy passages, atmospheric guardrooms and great views from the battlements. Get there via the tiny, open-top **Castle Ferry** (www.dartmouthcastleferry.co.uk; adult/child return £4/2; ⏱10am-4.45pm Apr-Oct).

Blackpool Sands　　BEACH
Sun-loving locals head 3 miles south of Dartmouth to this curl of coarse sand, lured by beautiful views, kayaking (per hour/day £15/40) and a licensed cafe stacked with organic, local produce. Take bus 93 from Dartmouth (20 minutes, hourly Monday to Saturday).

Dartmouth Steam Railway & River Boat Co　　BOAT CRUISE
(✆01803-555872; www.dartmouthrailriver.co.uk) Cruises along the River Dart to Totnes (adult/child return £14/8.50, 1¼ hours, two to four daily April to September).

LOCAL KNOWLEDGE

EATING & DRINKING LIKE A LOCAL

The southwest is a veritable foodie hot spot. Here are some locals' favourites:

Cornish Pasties Now awarded EU protected status, sample the savoury at bakeries county-wide.

Seafood Net-fresh fish abounds. Prime specialist restaurants include the Seahorse (p294) in Dartmouth, the Wheelhouse (p357) in Falmouth, and the Crab House Cafe (p262) on the Isle of Portland.

Cream Teas Homemade jam, just-baked scones and utterly gooey clotted cream; get stuck in at Alexandra (p264), Brimpts Farm (p303) and the Dwelling House (p360) in Fowey.

Organic & Slow Food Around a quarter of UK-registered organic producers are southwest-based. Try sustainable fare at Riverford (p295) and **River Cottage** (✆01297-630300; www.rivercottage.net; near Axminster; 4-course lunch/dinner £50/80; ⏱noon-4pm Fri-Sun, 7.30-11pm Fri & Sat; ✒).

Drinks Top spots to try regional tipples include the Castle inn (p256) for cider, Camel Valley (p339) and Sharpham (p294) for wine, Grain Barge (p318) in Bristol and the Salamander (p329) in Bath for beer, and Plymouth (p297) for gin.

🛏 Sleeping

★ Bayard's Cove   B&B ££
(📞 01803-839278; www.bayardscoveinn.co.uk; 27 Lower St; d £115-125, ste £135-180, f from £155; 🛜) Crammed with character and bursting with beams, Bayard's Cove sees you sleeping amid whitewashed stone walls and huge church candles. The lavish family suites feature grand double beds and kids' cabins, complete with bunk beds and tiny TVs; there are even estuary glimpses from the rooms.

Just B   GUESTHOUSE ££
(📞 01803-834311; www.justbdartmouth.com; reception 17 Fosse St; r £70-94) The nine chichi options here range from bedrooms with bathrooms to mini-apartments, all featuring snazzy furnishings, crisp cottons and comfy beds. They're scattered over three central properties, and the 'just B' policy (no '&B' means no breakfast) keeps prices down.

Hill View House   B&B ££
(📞 01803-839372; www.hillviewdartmouth.co.uk; 76 Victoria Rd; s/d £47/70; 🅿🛜) 🧺 At this price, you'll be asking, 'what's the catch?' There isn't one. Lloyd loom-style furniture and angle-poise lamps sit in relaxed, beautifully styled rooms above a retro guest lounge. It's a 10-minute walk into Dartmouth.

🍴 Eating

★ Alf Resco   CAFE £
(📞 01803-835880; www.cafealfresco.co.uk; Lower St; mains from £6; ⊘ 7am-2pm; 🛜) An eclectic crowd hangs out at Alf's – you'll be eating among hipsters, families, tourists and riverboat crews. The same menu spans breakfast through to lunch; expect piled-high fry-ups, irresistible pastries and eye-opening espressos. The gorgeous B&B rooms (£75) are pure shabby-chic.

Rockfish   FISH & CHIPS ££
(📞 01803-832800; www.rockfishdevon.co.uk; 8 South Embankment; mains £10-14; ⊘ noon-9.30pm) With its weathered boarding and chilled soundtrack, this place feels more like a beatnik boathouse than your average chippy. The menu is a cut above too; along with sustainable cod there's also monkfish, scallops, oysters and good wine. Eat in (enjoy the atmosphere) or take away (fight the seagulls).

★ Seahorse   SEAFOOD £££
(📞 01803-835147; www.seahorserestaurant.co.uk; 5 South Embankment; mains £23-32; ⊘ noon-3pm Tue-Sun, 6-10pm Tue-Sat) The seafood served at Mitch Tonks' eatery is so fresh, the menu changes daily. So depending on what's been landed at Brixham (7 miles away) or Dartmouth (a few yards) you might get cuttlefish in Chianti, garlicky roast scallops, or *fritto misto di mare*. Their speciality is sublime, charcoal-roasted fish; their two-course lunch menu (£20, Wednesday to Sunday) is a snip.

❶ Information

Tourist Office (📞 01803-834224; www.discoverdartmouth.com; Mayor's Ave; ⊘ 10am-4pm Mon-Sat, to 2pm Sun Apr-Oct, closed Wed & Sun Nov-Mar)

❶ Getting There & Away

BUS
Plymouth (£6.25, 2½ hours, hourly Monday to Saturday) Bus 93; runs via Kingsbridge (one hour).
Torquay (£4.50, 1¼ hours, hourly Monday to Saturday) Stagecoach Gold.
Totnes (£3.50, 50 minutes, hourly Monday to Saturday) Stagecoach Gold.

FERRY
Dartmouth–Kingswear Ferries (www.dartmouthhigherferry.com; car/pedestrian one way £4.70/1.50; ⊘ 7am-10.20pm) Dartmouth's Higher and Lower Ferries both take cars and foot passengers, shuttling across the river to Kingswear every six minutes.

TRAIN
Regular **steam trains** (📞 01803-555872; www.dartmouthrailriver.co.uk) link Kingswear with Paignton (adult/child return £14/8).

Totnes & Around
POP 8041

Totnes has such a reputation for being alternative that local jokers wrote 'twinned with Narnia' under the town sign. For decades famous as Devon's hippie haven, eco-conscious Totnes also became Britain's first 'transition town' in 2005, when it began trying to wean itself off a dependence on oil. Sustainability aside, Totnes boasts a tempting vineyard, a gracious Norman castle and a mass of fine Tudor buildings, and is the springboard for a range of adrenaline sports.

⊙ Sights & Activities

★ Sharpham Wine & Cheese   WINERY
(📞 01803-732203; www.sharpham.com; ⊘ 10am-5pm Mar-Sep; booking required for some tours; 🅿) The vine-lined hills here are more reminis-

cent of Chablis than south Devon. Opt for self-guided rambles (£2.50), wine and cheese tastings (£9) or an expert-led walk, tutored tasting, lunch and bottle of Dart Valley Reserve (£65). The gourmet meals dished up in the award-winning cafe (p295) are a true treat. The vineyard is 3 miles south of Totnes, off the A381. A more atmospheric option is to hike from town along the Dart Valley Trail. Booking is required for some tours.

Totnes Castle   CASTLE
(EH; ☑ 01803-864406; www.english-heritage.org. uk; Castle St; adult/child £3.70/2.20; ⊙ 10am-6pm Apr-Sep, to 5pm Oct, to 4pm Sat & Sun Nov-Mar) The outer keep of Totnes' Norman motte-and-bailey fortress crowns a hill at the top of town, providing engrossing views over higgledy-piggledy rooftops and the river valley. Hunt out the medieval loo, too.

★ **Dynamic Adventures**   ADVENTURE SPORTS
(☑ 01803-862725; www.dynamicadventurescic.co. uk; The Shops at Dartington, Dartington) The superb activities on offer here include canoeing and kayaking (per half/full day £30/60) and sea kayaking (from £75), as well as rock climbing and archery (both per hour £12). Plus, in the winter, exhilarating white-water kayaking on the River Dart (from £30). They're based 2 miles northwest of Totnes.

Totnes Kayaks   KAYAKING
(☑ 07799-403788; www.totneskayaks.co.uk; The Quay, Stoke Gabriel; per 1/6hr £15/40) On these self-guided paddles beside unspoilt hills, it's best to go with the tide (owner Tom will advise); so either upriver past Sharpham Vineyard, or downriver to the charming village of Dittisham, 5 miles southeast of Totnes.

🛏 Sleeping

★ **Dartington Hall**   B&B **££**
(☑ 01803-847147; www.dartington.org; Dartington, near Totnes; d £59-115; P 🖘) The wings of this idyllic, ancient manor house have been carefully converted into rooms that range from heritage-themed to deluxe-modern. Ask for one overlooking the grassy, cobble-fringed courtyard and settle back for a truly tranquil night's sleep.

Sea Trout   INN **££**
(☑ 01803-762274; www.theseatroutinn.co.uk; Staverton, near Totnes; d £95-150; P 🖘) Most of the rooms here are the epitome of carefully judged, contemporary good taste. The feature room though is a deliberately over-the-

top rococo delight, all ornate black-wood, mock chandeliers and a slipper bath. The great-value restaurant (mains £13, open noon to 2pm and 6pm to 9pm) regularly notches up awards.

Steam Packet   INN **££**
(☑ 01803-863880; www.steampacketinn.co.uk; St Peters Quay; s/d £85/105; P) It's almost as if the minimalist bedrooms of this wharf-side former warehouse have been plucked from the pages of a design magazine; expect painted wood panels, willow arrangements and neutral tones. Opt for a river-view room, then watch the world float by.

🍴 Eating

★ **Riverford Field Kitchen**   MODERN BRITISH **££**
(☑ 01803-762074; www.riverford.co.uk; Wash Barn; 2/3 courses £23/27; ⊙ noon-2.30pm daily, 6-10pm most evenings; 🚗) 🌿 Eco-friendly Riverford's bistro is set in a farm, meaning minimal food miles: vegetables are picked to order from the fields outside; meats are organic and locally sourced. Big trestle tables fill a futuristic hangar-like canteen, with diners passing around platters laden with richly flavoured food. Imaginative treatments might include marinated, grilled Moroccan lamb and British veg transformed by cumin or saffron. Bookings required.

Sharpham Vineyard Café   BISTRO **££**
(☑ 01803-732178; www.vineyardcafe.co.uk; Sharpham Estate; mains £10-15, snacks £4-7; ⊙ noon-2pm May-Sep; 🚗) Rustic, organic fare fills the tables of this decked cafe, anchored just yards from Sharpham's vines. Treats include smoked-fish or charcuterie boards, local crab salads and hearty fare such as belly pork and bean cassoulet. And, of course, the

---

DARTINGTON HALL

Henry VIII gave this beguiling 320-hectare **estate** (☑ 01803-847000; www. dartington.org) to two of his wives (Catherines Howard and Parr); now it's home to B&B accommodation (p295), the Barn art-house cinema, a mellow pub (p296), landscaped grounds and a medieval great hall that hosts events ranging from classical music to the **Ways With Words Literature Festival** (☑ 01803-867373; www.wayswithwords.co.uk). The estate is 2 miles northwest of Totnes.

vineyard's own, simply superb cheese and wine. It's 3 miles south of Totnes.

White Hart
PUB ££

(☑ 01803-847111; www.dartingtonhall.com; Dartington Estate, near Totnes; tapas £6, mains £12-17; ☉noon-9pm; ☑) To its already-acclaimed gastropub dishes, the White Hart has added a British tapas menu, so now grazing options include ham hock, lamb cutlets, scallops or wild-mushroom risotto. Winter brings a blazing fire; on fine evenings the lawnside tables are the place to be.

Rumour
PUB ££

(☑ 01803-864682; www.rumourtotnes.com; 30 High St, Totnes; mains £9-18; ☉noon-3pm Mon-Sat, 6-9pm daily) ☑ Rumour is a local institution – a narrow, cosy pub-restaurant with low lighting, funky local art and free newspapers. Famous for its crispy pizzas (£9), it also rustles up stylish cuisine, such as pollock roasted with avocado butter, and irresistible 28-day matured 8oz steaks.

❶ Information

Tourist Office (☑ 01803-863168; www.totnesinformation.co.uk; Coronation Rd; ☉9am-5pm Mon-Fri, 10am-4pm Sat Apr-Oct, 10am-4pm Mon-Fri, to 1pm Sat Nov-Mar)

❶ Getting There & Away

BOAT

Boats (p293) shuttle downriver to Dartmouth.

BUS

Dartmouth (£3.50, 50 minutes, hourly Monday to Saturday) Stagecoach Gold.

Torquay (£3.50, 45 minutes, every half hour Monday to Saturday, seven on Sunday) Stagecoach Gold.

TRAIN

Trains go at least hourly to Exeter (£8, 35 minutes) and Plymouth (£8, 30 minutes). The privately run **South Devon Steam Railway** (www.southdevonrailway.org; adult/child return £12/7; ☉4-9 trains daily Apr-Oct) chuffs to Buckfastleigh, on the edge of Dartmoor.

Plymouth & Around

POP 258,000

For decades, some have dismissed Plymouth as sprawling and ugly, pointing to architectural eyesores and sometimes palpable poverty. But the arrival of high-profile chefs Hugh Fearnley-Whittingstall and Mitch Tonks, and ongoing waterfront regeneration begs a rethink. Yes the city, an important Royal Naval port, suffered WWII bomb damage, and today it is still sometimes more gritty than pretty, but Plymouth is also packed with possibilities: swim in an art-deco lido; tour a gin distillery; learn to kayak; roam an aquarium; take a boat trip across the bay; then see a top-class theatre show and party till dawn. And the ace in the pack? Plymouth Hoe – a cafe-dotted, wide grassy headland offering captivating views of a boat-studded bay.

History

Plymouth's history is dominated by the sea. The first recorded cargo left in 1211 and by the late 16th century it was the port of choice for explorers and adventurers. It's waved off Sir Francis Drake, Sir Walter Raleigh, the fleet that defeated the Spanish Armada, the pilgrims who founded America, Charles Darwin, Captain Cook and countless boats carrying emigrants to Australia and New Zealand.

During WWII Plymouth suffered horrendously at the hands of the Luftwaffe – more than 1000 civilians died in the Blitz, which reduced the city centre to rubble. The 21st century has brought regeneration to waterfront areas, a £200 million Drake Circus shopping centre and a growing university, bringing a burst of new buildings and 30,000 students to the heart of town.

◎ Sights

★**Plymouth Hoe**
HEADLAND

Francis Drake supposedly spied the Spanish fleet from this grassy headland overlooking Plymouth Sound (the city's wide bay); the bowling green on which he finished his game was probably where his **statue** now stands. The wide villa-backed promenade features scores of war memorials, including the immense **Plymouth Naval Memorial**, which commemorates Commonwealth WWI and WWII sailors who have no grave but the sea.

Smeaton's Tower
LIGHTHOUSE

(☑ 01752-304774; www.plymouth.gov.uk/museumsmeatonstower; The Hoe; adult/child £2.60/1.30; ☉10am-4.30pm Apr-Sep, to 3pm Tue-Sat Oct, Nov, Feb & Mar) The red-and-white stripes of Smeaton's Tower rise from the middle of Plymouth Hoe headland. The whole 70ft structure used to stand on the Eddystone Reef, 14 miles offshore, and was transferred here, brick by brick, in the 1880s. For an insight into past lighthouse keepers' lives, head up 93 stone steps and through the circular rooms to emerge onto an open-air platform with stunning views of the city, Dartmoor and the sea.

★ **Barbican** NEIGHBOURHOOD
(www.plymouthbarbican.com) In the historic Barbican district, part-cobbled streets are lined with Tudor and Jacobean buildings, galleries, restaurants and funky bars. The Pilgrim Fathers' *Mayflower* set sail to found America from here in 1620. The **Mayflower Steps** (⊘24hr) FREE mark the approximate embarcation point; track down the passenger list on the side of **Island House** nearby. Other famous departures are also commemorated at the steps, including Captain James Cook's 1768 voyage of discovery, and the first emigrant ships to Australia and New Zealand.

★ **Plymouth Gin Distillery** DISTILLERY
(☑01752-665292; www.plymouthdistillery.com; 60 Southside St; tours £7; ⊘6 tours daily) They've been concocting gin at this heavily beamed distillery since 1793, making it the oldest producer of the spirit in the world. The Royal Navy ferried it round the world in countless officers' messes and the brand was specified in the first recorded recipe for a dry martini in the 1930s. Tours thread past the stills and take in a tutored tasting before retiring to the medieval bar for a complimentary G&T. Book.

National Marine Aquarium AQUARIUM
(☑0844 893 7938; www.national-aquarium.co.uk; Rope Walk; adult/child £14/10; ⊘10am-5pm, to 6pm Apr-Sep) The sharks here swim in coral seas that teem with moray eels and vividly coloured fish – there's even a loggerhead turtle called Snorkel who was rescued from a Cornish beach. Walk-through glass arches ensure huge rays glide over your head, while the gigantic Atlantic reef tank reveals just what's lurking a few miles offshore.

Buckland Abbey HISTORIC BUILDING
(NT; ☑01822-853607; www.nationaltrust.org.uk; near Yelverton; adult/child £9/4.50; ⊘10.30am-5.30pm Mar-Oct, 11.30am-4.30pm Dec & Feb; P) Founded as a Cistercian monastery and abbey church in the 13th century, Buckland Abbey was one of Henry VIII's 'acquisitions' during the Dissolution. Sir Richard Grenville bought it from the land-hungry king, before selling it to his cousin and nautical rival Sir Francis Drake. Highlights include Drake's Drum, said to beat by itself when Britain is in danger of being invaded, exquisite modelled ceilings, a Great Barn, fine Elizabethan gardens and woodland walks. Buckland Abbey is 11 miles north of Plymouth.

🏃 Activities

★ **Tinside Lido** SWIMMING
(☑01752-261915; www.everyoneactive.com; Hoe Rd; adult/child £3.90/2.80; ⊘10am-6pm Jun-Sep) Taking a dip in this Jazz Age, open-air swimspot is an unforgettable experience. Its 1935, art-deco design sees cream curves and light- and dark-blue tiles sweep gracefully out from the foot of the Hoe. Plunge into the chilly saltwater to join the regulars doing laps and the youngsters larking around beside the fountains.

Mount Batten Centre WATER SPORTS
(☑01752-404567; www.mount-batten-centre.com; 70 Lawrence Rd) Two-hour taster sessions include those for sail dinghies, stand-up paddleboarding and canoeing (each £20). Two-day courses include kayaking (£90), sailing (£170) and windsurfing (£145). It's on the Mount Batten peninsula. Ferries run from the Barbican Pontoon.

Mount Batten Ferry FERRY TRIPS
(www.mountbattenferry.com; adult/child return £3/2) A little yellow ferry shuttling from the Barbican Pontoon across to the Mount Batten Peninsula (10 minutes, half-hourly).

🧭 Tours

Plymouth Boat Trips BOAT TOUR
(☑01752-253153; www.plymouthboattrips.co.uk; Barbican Pontoon; ⊘4 daily Apr–mid-Oct) The pick of this firm's trips is the 30-minute blast-across-the-bay to quaint, pub-packed

---

ROYAL WILLIAM YARD

This cluster of 1830s waterfront warehouses once supplied stores for countless Royal Navy vessels. Today it's home to sleek apartments, a couple of art galleries, a relaxed pub, chic wine bar and a string of eateries; the best being River Cottage Canteen (p299) and the Royal William Bakery (p299).

The yard is 2 miles west of the city centre; bus 34 (£1.20, eight minutes, half-hourly) runs there; better still catch the ferry (☑07979-152008; www.royal-williamyardharbour.co.uk; adult/child single £3/1.50; ⊘10am-5pm May-Sep, to 6pm Jul & Aug) from the Barbican Pontoon.

Plymouth

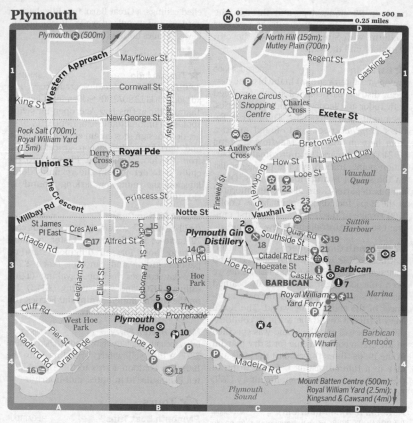

Cornish fishing villages of Kingsand and Cawsand (adult/child return £8/4). They also run one-hour harbour cruises (adult/child £7.50/4) to the warships at Plymouth's naval base.

Sleeping

★ St Elizabeth's House   BOUTIQUE HOTEL ££
(☑ 01752-344840; www.stelizabeths.co.uk; Long-brook St, Plympton St Maurice; d £99-119, ste £150; P ବ) Prepare to be pampered. In this 17th-century manor house turned boutique bolthole, free-standing slipper baths, oak furniture and Egyptian cotton grace the rooms; the suites feature palatial bathrooms and private terraces. It's set in the suburb-cum-village of Plympton St Maurice, 5 miles east of Plymouth.

Imperial   HOTEL ££
(☑ 01752-227311; www.imperialplymouth.co.uk; Lockyer St; s £60, d £62-86, f £92-100; P ବ) In the

1840s an admiral used to slumber in this elegant town house. Now you get to sleep amid heritage features, swish modern furnishings and all the mod-cons, before breakfasting on top-notch local produce (the homemade kedgeree is quite a treat). It's all very high quality for the price.

Sea Breezes   B&B ££
(☑ 01752-667205; www.plymouth-bedandbreakfast.co.uk; 28 Grand Pde; s/d/f £45/72/97; P) The fresh decor at this deeply comfortable guesthouse ranges from subtle gingham to groovy swirls. The bathrooms gleam, the towels are fluffy and the breakfasts feature melon, strawberries and hand-cut toast. Bag a front-facing bedroom (go for the one with the window seat) for smashing sea views.

Acorns & Lawns   B&B ££
(☑ 01752-229474; www.acornsandlawnsguesthouse.com; 171 Citadel Rd; d £60-75; ବ) Simplicity and serenity seem to seep from the walls here.

Plymouth

The guest lounge and breakfast room are all light colours and varnished floors; a bright-white stairwell leads to light-filled rooms. Ask for a front-facing bedroom to look out over the lower slopes of grassy Plymouth Hoe.

Squires　　　　B&B ££
(☎01752-261459; www.squiresguesthouse.com; 7 St James Pl East; s/d £32/65; ☜) Unfussy, squeaky-clean rooms, a quiet but central location and a friendly welcome.

✗ Eating

Royal William Bakery　　CAFE, BAKERY £
(www.royalwilliambakery.com; Royal William Yard; mains £5; ⊙8.30am-4pm; ☞) Piles of huge, just-cooked loaves, tureens full of soup, crumbly pastries and irresistible cakes – this is a bakery like few others. The serve-yourself style is so laid-back you don't get a bill – just tell them what you've eaten and they'll tot it up at the end. The Royal William Yard is 2 miles west of the city centre, on bus route 34.

Cap'n Jaspers　　CAFE £
(www.capn-jaspers.co.uk; Whitehouse Pier, Quay Rd; snacks £3-5; ⊙7.30am-midnight) Beloved by bikers, fishermen, families and tourists, this cabin-kiosk is a local institution thanks to its late hours, motorised gadgets and resolutely burger-van fare – trying to finish the 'half a yard of hot dog' is a Plymouth rite of passage; the Barbican crab rolls are an easier eat.

★Rock Salt　　MODERN BRITISH ££
(☎01752-225522; www.rocksaltcafe.co.uk; 31 Stonehouse St; mains £7-20; ⊙10am-9.30pm, from 8am Wed-Sat; ☞) First-class ingredients and creative flavours – no wonder Rock Salt keeps bagging awards. Their range is remarkable: from stylish all-day breakfasts and afternoon cupcakes to confit Dartmoor lamb. And all in a friendly setting that feels like a funky neighbourhood brasserie.

River Cottage Canteen　　MODERN BRITISH ££
(☎01752-252702; www.rivercottage.net; Royal William Yard; mains £10-17; ⊙11am-10.30pm Mon-Sat, to 4pm Sun; ☞) Hugh Fearnley-Whittingstall's gaff focuses firmly on local, sustainable, seasonal, organic goodies. Expect meats to be roasted beside an open fire, fish to be simply grilled and familiar veg to be given a revelatory makeover. It's in the Royal William Yard, 2 miles west of the city centre; catch bus 34.

Barbican Kitchen　　MODERN BRITISH ££
(☎01752-604448; www.barbicankitchen.com; 60 Southside St; mains £10-20; ⊙noon-2.30pm & 5-9.30pm) The assured menus at this stylish eatery take in everything from chilli dogs and wild-garlic risotto to chateaubriand for two. The express menu (two/three courses £13/16), served at lunch and Monday to Thursday evenings, is a superb deal.

Rockfish　　SEAFOOD ££
(☎01752-255974; www.therockfish.co.uk; 3 Rope Walk; mains £12; ⊙noon-9.30pm) In Mitch Tonks' cheery bistro (handily set right beside the fish market) perfectly cooked cod comes with as many chips as you can eat; roasted scallops, steamed prawns and sweet Devon crab feature on the imaginative menu too.

🍺 Drinking & Nightlife

Like any Royal Navy city, Plymouth has a more-than-lively nightlife. Union St is clubland; Mutley Plain and North Hill have a studenty vibe, while the Barbican has more restaurants amid the bars. All three areas can get rowdy, especially at weekends.

★ Dolpin   PUB
(14 The Barbican; ⊙ 10am-11pm) This gloriously unreconstructed Barbican boozer is all scuffed tables, padded bench seats and an authentic, no-nonsense atmosphere. Feeling peckish? Get a fish-and-chip takeaway from next-door-but-one, then settle down with your pint.

Minerva   PUB
(www.minervainn.co.uk; 31 Looe St; ⊙ 11.30am-11pm Sun-Wed, to midnight Thu-Sat; 🛜) Stone walls, wooden benches, chunks of sailing ships, real ales, live music and Thursday night jam sessions make this 16th-century drinking den a locals' favourite.

Vignoble   WINE BAR
(www.levignoble.co.uk; Royal William Yard; ⊙ noon-11.30pm) A bijou hang-out where you can sample taster-sized glasses of your chosen vintages. It's at the Royal William Yard, 2 miles west of the centre.

☆ Entertainment

★ Annabel's   CABARET, CLUB
(www.annabelscabaret.co.uk; 88 Vauxhall St; ⊙ 9pm-2am Thu, 8.30pm-3am Fri & Sat) The stage spots in this fabulously quirky venue are filled by an eclectic collection of acts (expect anything from comedy or bellydancing to burlesque). Crowd-pleasing tunes fill the dance floor while classy cocktails fill your glass.

Plymouth Arts Centre   CINEMA
(☎ 01752-206114; www.plymouthartscentre.org; 38 Looe St; ⊙ 10am-8.30pm Tue-Sat, from 4pm Sun) Combines a cracking independent cinema, modern-art exhibitions, and a licensed, vegetarian-friendly bistro (closed Sunday).

Theatre Royal   THEATRE
(TRP; ☎ 01752-267222; www.theatreroyal.com; Royal Pde) Plymouth's main theatre stages large-scale touring and home-grown productions; its studio space, the Drum, is renowned for featuring new writing.

ℹ️ Information

Plymouth Library (Drake Circus; per 30min £2; ⊙ 9am-6pm Mon-Fri, to 5pm Sat; 🛜) Internet access and free wi-fi.

Police Station (Charles Cross; ⊙ 24hr)

Tourist Office (☎ 01752-306330; www.visit-plymouth.co.uk; 3 The Barbican; ⊙ 9am-5pm Mon-Sat, 10am-4pm Sun Apr-Oct, 10am-4pm Mon-Sat Nov-Mar)

ℹ️ Getting There & Away

BUS
National Express services include:
Birmingham (£30, five hours, five daily)
Bristol (£20, three hours, four daily)
London (£25, five to six hours, six daily)
Penzance (£10, 3¼ hours, four daily)

Other services:
Exeter (£6.50, 1¼ hours, two-hourly Monday to Saturday, three on Sunday) Bus X38.
Tavistock (£6.20, one hour, one to three hourly) Bus 83/84/86; runs via Yelverton.

TRAIN
Services include:
Bristol (£20, two hours, two or three per hour)
Exeter (£9, one hour, half-hourly)
London Paddington (£40, 3¼ hours, half-hourly)
Penzance (£10, two hours, half-hourly)
Totnes (£8, 30 minutes, half-hourly to hourly)

Dartmoor National Park

Dartmoor is an ancient, compelling landscape, so different from the rest of Devon that a visit feels like falling straight into Tolkien's *Return of the King.* Exposed granite hills (called tors) crest on the horizon, linked by swaths of honey-tinged moors. Streams tumble over moss-smothered boulders in woods of twisted trees. The centre of this 368-sq-mile national park is the higher moor; a vast, treeless expanse.

On sunny, summer days Dartmoor is idyllic; ponies wander at will and sheep graze beside the road; a cinematic location that features in Steven Spielberg's WWI epic *War Horse.* But Dartmoor is also the setting for Sir Arthur Conan Doyle's *The Hound of the Baskervilles,* and in sleeting rain and swirling mists you suddenly see why; the moor morphs into a bleak wilderness where tales of a phantom hound can seem very real indeed.

Dartmoor's settlements range from brooding Princetown and picturesque Widecombe-in-the-Moor to tiny Postbridge and genteel Chagford. In between, lies a natural breakout zone offering superb hiking, cycling, riding, climbing and white-water kayaking; rustic pubs and fancy restaurants; wild camping nooks and country-house hotels – perfect boltholes when the fog rolls in.

Dartmoor is administered by the **Dartmoor National Park Authority** (DNPA; www.dartmoor.gov.uk).

🏃 Activities

Walking

Some 730 miles of public footpaths snake across Dartmoor's open heaths and rocky tors. The Pathfinder *Dartmoor Walks* (£12) guide has 28 hikes of up to 9 miles, while its *Dartmoor Short Walks* (£8) focuses on family-friendly treks.

For multiday hikes, see p302.

★ Moorland Guides   WALKING
(www.moorlandguides.co.uk; adult/child £5-10/free) Wide range of walks, from one-hour rambles to strenuous all-day hikes, on themes spanning heritage, geology, wildlife, myths and navigation.

DNPA Guided Walks   WALKING
(www.dartmoor.gov.uk/visiting; adult/child £5/free) One- to six-hour, ranger-led outings.

Cycling

Routes include the 11-mile **Granite Way**, which runs, now entirely off-road, along a former railway line between Okehampton and Lydford. The 13-mile **Princetown & Burrator Mountain Bike Route** is a challenging moorland circuit along tracks and bridleways taking in Princetown, Sheepstor village and Burrator Reservoir. Tourist offices also sell the *Dartmoor Cycling Map* (£13).

Devon Cycle Hire   BICYCLE RENTAL
(☏ 01837-861141; www.devoncyclehire.co.uk; Sourton Down, near Okehampton; per day adult/child £14/10; ⊙9am-5pm Thu-Tue Apr-Sep) On the Granite Way.

Princetown Cycle Hire   BICYCLE RENTAL
(Fox Tor Cafe; ☏ 01822-890238; www.princetowncyclehire.co.uk; Two Bridges Rd, Princetown; per day

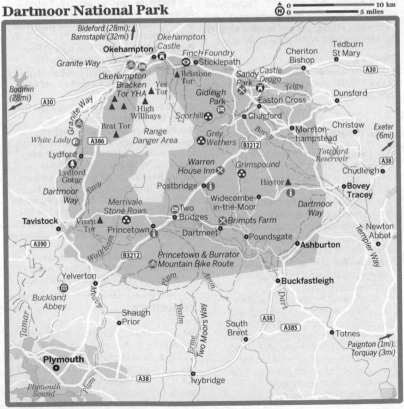

Dartmoor National Park

adult/child £18.50/10; ⊘ 9am-5pm) Handy for the Princetown & Burrator Mountain Bike Route.

Horse Riding

A number of local stables cater to all abilities.

Eastlake   HORSE RIDING
(✆ 01837-52513; www.eastlakeridingstables.co.uk; Eastlake, near Okehampton; per 2hr £35)

Shilstone Rocks   HORSE RIDING
(✆ 01364-621281; www.dartmoorstables.com; Widecombe-in-the-Moor; per 1/2hr £40/55)

Tor Royal   HORSE RIDING
(✆ 01822-890189; www.dartmoorhorseriding.co.uk; Princetown; per 1/2hr £25/40)

White-Water Sports

The raging River Dart makes Dartmoor a top spot for thrill seekers. Experienced kayakers can get permits from the DNPA (p301). For white-water kayaking, go for Dynamic Adventures (p295), near Totnes. Rivers are only open from October to mid-March.

CRS Adventures   WATER SPORTS
(✆ 01364-653444; www.crsadventures.co.uk) For white-water rafting (per two people £100), try this operator near Widecombe-in-the-Moor.

Climbing

Adventure Okehampton   OUTDOORS
(✆ 01837-53916; www.adventureokehampton.com; Klondyke Rd, Okehampton; per day from £60;

DARTMOOR HIKES

The 18-mile **Templer Way** is a two- to three-day leg stretch from Haytor to Teignmouth, while the **West Devon Way** forms a 36-mile trek linking Okehampton and Plymouth. The 95-mile **Dartmoor Way** circles from Buckfastleigh in the south, through Moretonhampstead, northwest to Okehampton and south through Lydford to Tavistock. The 117-mile **Two Moors Way** runs from Wembury on the south Devon coast, across Dartmoor and Exmoor to Lynmouth, on the north coast.

Be prepared for Dartmoor's notoriously fickle weather and carry a map and compass – many trails are not waymarked. The Ordnance Survey (OS) Explorer 1:25,000 map No 28, *Dartmoor* (£8), is the most comprehensive and shows park boundaries and Ministry of Defence firing-range areas.

For shorter hikes, see p301.

---

school holidays only) Runs wall- and rock-climbing sessions, plus activities including archery, abseiling and wild camping.

ⓘ Information

DNPA Haytor (✆ 01364-661520; ⊘ 10am-5pm Apr-Sep, to 4pm Mar & Oct, 10.30am-3.30pm Thu-Sun Nov-Feb)

DNPA Postbridge (✆ 01822-880272; ⊘ 10am-5pm Apr-Sep, to 4pm Mar & Oct, 10.30am-3.30pm Thu-Sun Nov-Feb)

Higher Moorland Tourist Office (DNPA; ✆ 01822-890414; www.dartmoor.gov.uk; Princetown; ⊘ 10am-5pm Apr-Sep, to 4pm Mar & Oct, 10.30am-3.30pm Thu-Sun Nov-Feb) Dartmoor's main tourist office also stocks walking guides, maps and clothes.

ⓘ Getting There & Around

Public transport is an option, but planning is needed and some services are seasonal. Tourist offices stock bus timetables. See www.journeydevon.info.

BUS

The **Dartmoor Sunday Rover** (adult/child/family £8/6/17) offers unlimited Sunday travel on most moorland bus routes; buy from drivers or at Plymouth train station.

Bus 83/84/86 (one to three hourly) From Plymouth to Tavistock, via Yelverton.

Bus 118 (two to six daily) From Barnstaple to Tavistock (2¼ hours), via Lydford and Okehampton.

Bus 359 (six daily Monday to Saturday) From Exeter to Moretonhampstead.

Bus 98 (three daily Monday to Saturday) A year-round service, which runs from Tavistock to Princetown, via Merrivale; one bus a day goes onto Two Bridges and Postbridge.

Haytor Hoppa Runs on Saturdays between April and October only, providing four buses between Newton Abbot, Bovey Tracey, Haytor and Widecombe-in-the-Moor (daily fare £5).

Transmoor Link/Bus 82 Runs on Saturdays and Sundays between mid-May and mid-September only, making one trip each way from Exeter to Tavistock (£5.80) via Moretonhampstead, Postbridge, Princetown and Yelverton. It leaves Exeter in the morning and Tavistock in the afternoon.

Princetown

POP 1767

Set in the heart of the remote, higher moor, Princetown is dominated by the grey, foreboding bulk of Dartmoor Prison and on bad weather days the town can have a bleak feel. But it's also a useful insight into the harsh realities of moorland life and makes an atmospheric base for some excellent walks.

⊙ Sights

Dartmoor Prison Museum　MUSEUM
(☎01822-322130;　www.dartmoor-prison.co.uk;
Princetown; adult/child £3.50/2.50; ⊙9.30am-
12.30pm & 1.30-4pm; ℗) In the early 1800s
Princetown's jail was home to French and
American Prisoners of war, becoming a
convict jail in 1850. Just up from the looming gates, this museum provides a chilling
glimpse of life inside. Look out for straitjack-
ets, manacles, escape stories and the makeshift knives made by modern prisoners. You
can also book a guided walk (adult/child
£6.50/5.50) which skirts the prison perimeter and heads into otherwise out-of-bounds
French and American cemeteries.

Higher Moorland
Tourist Office　INTERPRETATION CENTRE
(DNPA; ☎01822-890414; ⊙10am-5pm Apr-Sep,
to 4pm Mar & Oct, 10.30am-3.30pm Thu-Sun Nov-
Feb) Heritage displays include those on tin
workings, gunpowder factories, legends and
a stunning time-lapse video. The office used
to be the Duchy Hotel; one former guest was
Sir Arthur Conan Doyle, who went on to
write *The Hound of the Baskervilles*. Dartmoor lore recounts local man Henry Bask-
erville took the novelist on a carriage tour,
and the brooding landscape he encountered,
coupled with legends of huge phantom dogs,
inspired the thriller.

🛏 Sleeping & Eating

★Prince of Wales　HOSTEL £
(☎01822-890219; www.theprinceofwalesprince-
town.co.uk; Tavistock Rd; dm/s/d £14/40/60; ℗)
The pick of Dartmoor's bunkhouses, with
central heating, double glazing (on the
moor, this matters) and – joy of joys – a
drying room. The rustic pub (mains £5 to
£16, served 11am to 2.30pm and 5.30pm to
8pm) next door is famous for its three open
fires, mixed-grill platters the size of tea
trays and pints of own-brewed, full-bodied,
Jail Ale.

★Tor Royal Farm　B&B ££
(☎01822-890189; www.torroyal.co.uk; Tor Royal
Lane, near Princetown; s £55, d £85-100; ℗ 🛜)
This is just what a middle-of-the-moor retreat should be – an easygoing, country
cottage–styled farmhouse packed with lived-
in charm. Their own-reared pork appears
on the breakfast menu, and you can book
horse-riding lessons at their stables right
next door.

Two Bridges　HOTEL £££
(☎01822-892300; www.twobridges.co.uk; Two
Bridges; s £95-120, d £140-190; ℗🛜) Perhaps
the definitive historic moorland hotel:
polished wood panels, huge inglenook fireplaces and a guest list that includes Wallis
Simpson, Winston Churchill and Vivien
Leigh. It's 1.5 miles northeast of Princetown.

❶ Getting There & Away
Bus 98 runs from Tavistock to Princetown (£2.30,
three daily, Monday to Saturday). One service a
day goes on to Two Bridges and Postbridge.

Postbridge
POP 170
The quaint hamlet of Postbridge owes its
popularity, and its name, to its medieval
stone slab or clapper bridge; a 13th-century
structure with four, 10ft-long slabs propped
up on sturdy columns of stacked stones.
Walking over takes you across the rushing
East Dart river; a picturesque spot to whip
off your boots and plunge your feet into water that's quite possibly never felt so cold.

🛏 Sleeping & Eating

★Brimpts Farm　B&B £
(☎0845 0345968; www.brimptsfarm.co.uk; site
per person £3, s/d/f £33/55/83; ℗) The brightly
painted, rustic bedrooms above this farmhouse have views over *War Horse* location
Combestone Tor; the back-to-nature camping
fields are idyllic and the cream teas are some

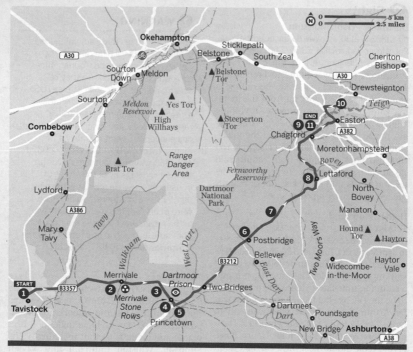

🏃 Driving Tour
A Dartmoor Road Trip

START TAVISTOCK
END CHAGFORD
LENGTH 20 MILES; ONE DAY

Driving on Dartmoor is like being inside a feature film: compelling 360-degree views are screened all around. This scenic, west-to-east transmoor traverse sweeps up and through this wilderness, taking in a bleak prison, prehistoric remains, a rustic pub and a unique castle.

Start by strolling among the fine 19th-century architecture of **1 Tavistock**, perhaps dropping by its Pannier Market to rummage for antiques. Next take the B3357 towards Princetown. It climbs steeply (expect ears to pop), crosses a cattle grid (a sign you're on the moor 'proper') and crests a hill to reveal swaths of honey-coloured tors. Soon you're at **2 Merrivale** (p306). Park up on the right, just after the Dartmoor Inn, and stroll over the rise (due south) to discover a snaking stone row; a tiny stone circle and a standing stone are just 100m further on.

Back in the car, after a short climb, turn right towards Princetown, glimpsing the brooding bulk of Dartmoor Prison (you can't stop here; there's a better vantage point later). Call in at the **3 Dartmoor Prison Museum** (p303) to explore the jail's grim story. Cut through rugged **4 Princetown** (p302), before picking up the B3212 towards Two Bridges; the **5 lay-by** immediately after you leave Princetown provides prime Dartmoor Prison views. As you follow signs for Moretonhampstead, an expansive landscape unfurls. At **6 Postbridge** (p303), park and stroll over the 700-year-old bridge, then dangle hot feet in the cold River Dart. A few miles further on, the **7 Warren House Inn** (p305) makes an atmospheric spot for lunch. Around **8 Lettaford** take one of the signed, plunging lanes to **9 Chagford** (p305) to visit its quaint, thatch-dotted square. Scour some of its wonderfully old-fashioned shops, then head to **10 Castle Drogo** (p305) to explore a unique 1920s stately home. Finish the day back at Chagford at **11 22 Mill Street** (p306); a truly classy spot to eat and sleep.

of the moor's best: freshly baked scones, home-made jams and utterly gooey clotted cream (£5) served 11.30am to 5.30pm on weekends and school holidays. Brimpts is signed off the B3357, Two Bridges–Dartmeet road.

Runnage YHA HUT£
(☐ 0800 0191 700; www.yha.org.uk; dm £10; P) A converted hayloft on a working farm where you bed down to a soundtrack of bleating sheep. It's 1.5 miles east of Postbridge: take the 'Widecombe' turning off the B3212 Moretonhampstead road.

Dartmoor YHA HOSTEL£
(Bellever; ☐ 0845 371 9622; www.yha.org.uk; dm/d £15/48; P) A characterful former farm on the edge of a conifer plantation, with a huge kitchen, lots of rustic stone walls and cosy dorms. It's a mile south of Postbridge.

★ **Warren House Inn** PUB£
(www.warrenhouseinn.co.uk; mains £6-14; ☺ kitchen noon-8.30pm, shorter hours winter) Marooned amid miles of moorland, this Dartmoor institution exudes a hospitality only found in pubs in the middle of nowhere. A fire that's been burning (apparently) since 1845 warms stone floors, trestle tables and hikers munching robust food; the Warreners' Pie (local rabbit) is legendary. It's on the B3212, some 2 miles northeast of Postbridge. The bar's open 11am to 11pm.

ⓘ Getting There & Away
Bus 98 runs to Princetown (£1.25, one per day Monday to Saturday). Postbridge is also served by the Transmoor Link (p302).

Widecombe-in-the-Moor
POP 566
This is archetypal Dartmoor, down to the ponies grazing on a village green encircled by 15th-century buildings of honey-grey stone. The village features in the traditional English folksong, 'Widecombe Fair,' an event that takes place on the second Tuesday of September.

ⓞ Sights

St Pancras Church CHURCH
St Pancras' immense 40m tower has seen it dubbed the Cathedral of the Moor. Inside search out the boards telling the fire-and-brimstone tale of the violent storm of 1638 – it knocked a pinnacle from the roof, killing several parishioners. As ever on Dartmoor, the devil was blamed, said to be in search of souls.

ⓘ DRIVING ON DARTMOOR

Dartmoor's roads are exciting to drive, but large stretches have unfenced grazing so you'll come across Dartmoor ponies, sheep and even cows in the middle of the road. Many sections have a 40mph speed limit. Car parks on the moor can be little more than lay-bys; their surface can be rough to very rough.

🛏 Sleeping & Eating

Manor Cottage B&B£
(☐ 01364-621218; www.manorcottagedartmoor.co.uk; d £50-60; P 🐾) Roses climb around the doorway of this quaint, ancient, village-centre cottage. The best billet is a bedroom-bathroom suite at the top of its own spiral staircase. Breakfasts feature berry compote, local sausages and eggs freshly laid by the hens clucking around outside.

Rugglestone Inn PUB££
(www.rugglestoneinn.co.uk; mains £11; ☺ kitchen noon-2pm & 6.30-9pm) You'll find plenty of locals in front of this intimate old pub's wood-burning stove. Its stone floor and low beams set the scene for hearty dishes; pies are a speciality, including fishermen's, beef in ale, and a rich steak and Stilton.

ⓘ Getting There & Away
Bus 672 stops once a week (Wednesday) en route to Buckfastleigh (£1.60, 40 minutes) and Newton Abbot (£2.60, one hour). On summer Saturdays Widecombe is served by the Haytor Hoppa (p302).

Chagford & Around
POP 1446
With its wonky thatches and cream-and white-fronted buildings, Chagford clusters on the edge of Dartmoor around a picturesque square. But this apparently timeless moorland scene is also now home to some supremely stylish places to eat and sleep.

The bustling market town of Moretonhampstead sits 5 miles east.

ⓞ Sights

★ **Castle Drogo** HISTORIC BUILDING
(NT; ☐ 01647-433306; www.nationaltrust.org.uk; near Drewsteignton; adult/child £8.70/4.30; ☺ 11am-5pm mid-Mar–Oct; P) Magical, unique Castle Drogo really shouldn't be missed.

Designed by Sir Edwin Lutyens for self-made food-millionaire Julius Drewe, it was built between 1911 and 1931. The brief was to combine the medieval grandeur of a castle and the comforts of a 20th-century country house, so today you see Tudor, Georgian and Edwardian styling along with both crenellated battlements and cosy carpeted interiors. The woodland trails have extraordinary alpine-esque views over the plunging Teign Gorge. It's 3 miles northeast of Chagford.

🛏 Sleeping & Eating

Sparrowhawk HOSTEL £
(📞01647-440318; www.sparrowhawkbackpackers.co.uk; 45 Ford St, Moretonhampstead; dm/d/f £17/38/46) 🚲 At this long-standing backpackers' favourite, primary colours meet beams and exposed stone in light dorms overlooking a central courtyard that's ringed by rickety outbuildings.

★ Gidleigh Park HOTEL £££
(📞01647-432367; www.gidleigh.com; Gidleigh; d £315-515, ste £1100-1220; P♿🛜) At Devon's most luxurious hotel crests, crenellations and roaring fires meet shimmering blue-marble bathrooms, complete with waterproof TVs. Culinary alchemy occurs in the double Michelin-starred restaurant where the eight-course tasting menu costs £140 – thrifty cognoscenti opt for the £44 two-course lunch. It's 2 miles west of Chagford.

22 Mill Street B&B £££
(📞01647-432244; www.22millst.com; 22 Mill St, Chagford; d £130-170; 🛜) The elegant rooms of this sleek retreat feature wooden floorboards, satin cushions and bursts of modern art. Its intimate restaurant (two-course lunch/dinner £19/36, served noon

to 2.30pm and 7pm to 9pm Wednesday to Saturday) delivers creative twists on local, seasonal fare: expect scallops with black pudding, and garlic-laced Dartmoor lamb.

★ Horse GASTROPUB ££
(📞01647-440242; www.thehorsedartmoor.co.uk; 7 George St; mains £5-19; ⏱12.30-2.30pm Tue-Sat, 6.30-9pm daily) With a style somewhere between boho-chic and casual country house, this funky gastropub makes for a chilled-out hang-out. Mediterranean-themed goodies crowd a menu which ranges from pizzas and Dartmoor beef bresaola, to worth-forking-out-for à la carte.

Sandy Park BISTRO ££
(📞01647-433267; www.sandyparkinn.co.uk; Sandy Park; mains £8-12; ⏱noon-2.30pm & 6-9pm Mon-Fri, noon-9pm Sat & Sun) A 17th-century thatch with exposed-beam bar, quality restaurant and brightly furnished rooms (£60 to £80).

ℹ Getting There & Away

Bus 173 Goes from Chagford to Exeter (£3.60, one hour, five daily Monday to Saturday), with two services also stopping at Moretonhampstead.

Bus 178 (one daily Monday to Saturday) Runs from Moretonhampstead to Okehampton (£2.40, one hour), via Chagford (45 minutes).

Bus 359 (£3.50, six daily Monday to Saturday) Links Moretonhampstead with Exeter. Moretonhampstead is also served by the Transmoor Link (p302).

Okehampton & Lydford

POP 7831

Okehampton huddles on the edge of an uninhabited tract of bracken-covered slopes and granite tors – the mind-expanding land-

---

PREHISTORIC DARTMOOR

With an estimated 11,000 monuments Dartmoor is ripe for archaeological explorations. It has the largest concentration of Bronze Age (c 2300–700 BC) remains in the country, 75 stone rows (half the national total), 18 stone circles and 5000 huts.

The **Merrivale Stone Rows**, near Princetown, are a handy one-stop shop for most monument types. The site has a parallel stone row, a stone circle, a menhir, burial chambers and dozens of hut circles. To the northeast, near Chagford, the **Grey Wethers** stone circles stand side by side on a stretch of open moor; another stone circle is 400m away near Fernworthy. Also nearby, at Gidleigh, **Scorhill** stone circle is sometimes called the Stonehenge of Dartmoor, although only half of the original stones remain. The biggest site is the Bronze Age village of **Grimspound**, just off the B3212, where you can wander inside the circular stone wall that once surrounded an entire village, and the ruins of several granite roundhouses.

You can buy guides to some sites (£4) from tourist offices.

scape known as the higher moor. The town has a staging-post feel, and its traditional shops and pubs are good places to prepare for a foray into the wilderness.

Some 9 miles southwest, the village of Lydford has an archetypal inn, a string of weathered granite cottages and a stunning gorge.

◎ Sights & Activities

★ Lydford Gorge   WATERFALL
(NT; ☎ 01822-820320; www.nationaltrust.org.uk; Lydford; adult/child £7/3.50; ⊙ 10am-5pm mid-Mar–Oct) The 1.5-mile rugged riverside hikes here snake past a series of bubbling whirlpools (including the fearsome Devil's Cauldron) to the thundering, 30m-high White Lady waterfall.

Okehampton Castle   CASTLE
(EH; ☎ 01837-52844; www.english-heritage.org.uk; Castle Lodge, Okehampton; adult/child £4/2.40; ⊙ 10am-5pm Apr-Oct, to 6pm Jul & Aug) The towering ruined Norman motte and keep of what was once Devon's largest castle cling to a wooded spur, setting the scene for some picturesque rampart clambering.

Finch Foundry   HISTORIC SITE
(NT; ☎ 01837-840046; www.nationaltrust.uk; Sticklepath; adult/child £5/3; ⊙ 11am-5pm mid-Mar–Oct; P) The last working water-powered forge in England sits at the end of a 4-mile (3½-hour) walk east along the Tarka Trail from Okehampton.

🛏 Sleeping & Eating

Okehampton Bracken Tor YHA   HOSTEL £
(☎ 0844 293 0555; www.yha.org.uk; Saxongate; dm £20; P @ 🛜) Budget-conscious outdoors types love this one: a 100-year-old country house, set in 1.6-hectare grounds on the fringe of the higher moor – it also offers climbing, canoeing and bike hire. It's a mile south of Okehampton; be aware, there's another YHA hostel in Okehampton itself.

★ Dartmoor Inn   INN ££
(☎ 01822-820221; www.dartmoorinn.com; Moorside, Lydford; d £100; P) They've pulled off the ancient-meets-modern trick superbly here. Distressed furniture, lavish fabrics and Roberts radios fill chic bedrooms; flagstone floors, roaring open fires and horse brass–hung beams frame diners tucking into elegant gastropub meals (mains £13 to £22, served noon to 2.30pm and 6.45pm to 9pm Tuesday to Saturday, plus noon to 2.30pm Sunday). Irresistible.

ⓘ ENJOY DARTMOOR MAGAZINE

....

The DNPA's *Enjoy Dartmoor* magazine is packed with details of activities, attractions, campsites and guided walks. Pick it up at tourist offices and venues across the moor.

Castle   INN ££
(☎ 01822-820241; www.castleinndartmoor.co.uk; Lydford; d £60-95; P 🛜) The bedrooms in this Elizabethan inn range from smallish 'n' simple to spacious and luxurious – bag room 1 for a private deck and views of tiny, ruined Lydford Castle. The bar is the ultimate snug: lamplight bathes bow ceilings and high-backed benches, while the food, served noon to 3pm and 5pm to 9pm, is tried and tested Dartmoor pub fare (mains £9 to £22).

ⓘ Information

Tourist Office (☎ 01837-53020; www.okehamptondevon.co.uk; Museum Courtyard, 3 West St, Okehampton; ⊙ 10am-5pm Mon-Sat Apr-Oct, to 4pm Mon, Fri & Sat Nov-Mar)

ⓘ Getting There & Away

Bus 118 (two to six daily) Stops at Okehampton and Lydford, en route from Barnstaple to Tavistock (£6.15, 2¼ hours).

Bus 178 (one daily Monday to Saturday) Runs to Okehampton from Moretonhampstead (£2.40, one hour), via Chagford (45 minutes).

Bus X9 (five daily Monday to Saturday) Links Okehampton with Exeter (£3.40, 50 minutes) and Bude (£4.40, one hour).

Croyde & Braunton
POP 8131

The cheerful, chilled village of Croyde is Devon's surf central. Here olde worlde meets new wave: thatched roofs peep out over racks of wetsuits; crowds of cool types in board shorts sip beer outside 17th-century inns.

The businesslike town of Braunton is 4 miles inland.

◎ Sights & Activities

The water's hard to resist in Croyde. **Ralph's** (☎ 01271-890147; Hobbs Hill, Croyde; surfboard & wetsuit per 4/24hr £12/18, bodyboard & wetsuit £10/15; ⊙ 9am-dusk mid-Mar–Dec) is among those hiring equipment. Lessons are provided by **Surf South West** (☎ 01271-890400;

www.surfsouthwest.com; Croyde Burrows, Croyde; per half/full day £32/62; ⊙Mar-Nov) and **Surfing Croyde Bay** (☑01271-891200; www.surfingcroydebay.co.uk; 8 Hobbs Hill, Croyde; per half day adult/child £40/35).

★**Museum of British Surfing**   MUSEUM
(☑01271-815155; www.museumofbritishsurfing.org.uk; Caen St, Braunton; adult/child £3.60/free; ⊙10am-4pm Wed-Mon Easter-Dec) Few museums are this cool. Vibrant surfboards and vintage wetsuits line the walls, sepia images catch your eye. The stories are compelling: 18th-century British sailors riding Hawaiian waves; England's 1920s home-grown surf pioneers – here heritage meets hanging ten.

🛏 Sleeping & Eating

Croyde gets very busy in the summer – book ahead, even for campsites.

★**Baggy**   HOSTEL, B&B £
(www.baggys.co.uk; Baggy Point; dm/d £30/110; 🛜) It doesn't get much sleeker than this surf lodge-cum-cafe set right on the coast path beside Croyde Bay. The dorms here are super-smart, the sea-view doubles positively boutiquey, and breakfast (served till 11am) can be eaten on decking watching the waves.

Bay View Farm   CAMPSITE £
(☑01271-890501; www.bayviewfarm.co.uk; Croyde; site per 2 adults £24; ⊙Apr-Oct; P🛜) One of the area's best campsites, with laundry, showers and surf-view pitches. Often requires a week's minimum booking in summer.

Ocean Pitch   CAMPSITE £
(☑07581-024348; www.oceanpitch.co.uk; Moor Lane, Croyde; site per 2 adults £29-33; ⊙mid-Jun–Aug; P🛜) Set at the northern end of Croyde Bay, a well-equipped site that's two minutes' walk to the beach and has cracking sea views.

Thatch   INN ££
(☑01271-890349; www.thethatchcroyde.com; 14 Hobbs Hill, Croyde; d £50-110, f £130) A legendary venue among surfers, this cavernous, thatched pub's trendy bedrooms feature subtle creams, stripes and checks; the owners offer similar billets above another pub and in the cottage opposite. The pick though are at their nearby (quieter) Priory, where elegant beams frame exposed stone.

ℹ Information

Tourist Office (☑01271-816688; www.visit-braunton.co.uk; Caen St, Braunton; ⊙10am-3pm Mon-Fri, to 1pm Sat) Inside Braunton's museum.

ℹ Getting There & Away

Bus 21/21A (half-hourly Monday to Saturday, hourly Sunday) Runs between Ilfracombe and Barnstaple (£2.30, 40 minutes), via Braunton.

Bus 308 (hourly Monday to Saturday, five on Sunday) Goes from Barnstaple to Braunton, Saunton Sands and Croyde (£2.40, 50 minutes).

Ilfracombe & Around

POP 11,509

Ilfracombe's geology is startling. Precipitous headlands plummet down to pint-sized beaches; waterfront walkways cling to the sides of sheer cliffs. The town seems at first a classic, well-worn Victorian watering hole. Streets slope to a historic harbour lined by touristy shops; crazy golf greens and ropes of twinkling lights line the promenade. But the resort also has a snazzier side, as evidenced by an immense Damien Hirst statue, a string of smart eateries and places to sleep, and some enchanting Victorian bathing pools.

⊙ Sights & Activities

★**Verity**   LANDMARK
(The Pier) FREE Pregnant, naked and holding aloft a huge spear, Damien Hirst's 20m statue, *Verity*, towers above Ilfracombe's harbour mouth. On the seaward side her skin is peeled back, revealing sinew, fat and foetus. Critics say she detracts from the scenery, the artist says she's an allegory for truth and justice. Either way, she's drawing the crowds.

Ilfracombe Aquarium   AQUARIUM
(☑01271-864533; www.ilfracombeaquarium.co.uk; The Pier; adult/child £4.25/3.25; ⊙10am-4.30pm, to 5.45pm late Jul & Aug) Recreates aquatic environments from Exmoor to the Atlantic, via estuary, rock pool and harbour.

★**Tunnelsbeaches**   SWIMMING
(☑01271-879882; www.tunnelsbeaches.co.uk; Granville Rd; adult/child £2.50/2; ⊙10am-5pm Apr-Oct, to 7pm Jul & Aug) It was a remarkable feat – in 1823 hundreds of Welsh miners hacked, by hand, the four tunnels here out of solid rock. They lead to a strip of beach where you can still plunge into the sea from Victorian tidal bathing pools. Extensive exhibits include sepia photos depicting the site in the 19th century, conveying a world of woollen bathing suits, segregated swimming and boating etiquette ('Gentlemen who cannot swim should never take ladies upon the water').

📖 Sleeping & Eating

Ocean Backpackers HOSTEL **£**
(☑ 01271-867835; www.oceanbackpackers.co.uk;
29 St James Pl; dm £15-19, d £45; P @ 🛜) Brightly painted en suite dorms, a convivial kitch-
en and free coffee lend this long-established
indie hostel a laid-back vibe; the giant world
map in the lounge has kick-started countless
travellers' tales.

★Norbury House B&B **££**
(☑ 01271-863888; www.norburyhouse.co.uk; Torrs
Park; d £85-110, f £120-145; P🛜) Each of the
rooms in this gorgeous guesthouse is done
up in a different style: choose from pop art,
art deco or contemporary chic. Fabulous
soft furnishings, a light-filled sitting room
(complete with baby grand piano), charming hosts and cracking sea-and-town views
seal the deal.

Olive Branch & Room B&B **££**
(☑ 01271-879005; www.olivebranchguesthouse.co.
uk; 56 Fore St; s £42-95, d £75-105; 🛜) Georgian
trimmings (bay windows and ceiling roses)
meet modern furnishings (oval armchairs
and beautifully carved wood) in swish
rooms that, mostly, have grandstand views
over the bay and steeply sloping Capstone
Hill. The buzzing bistro downstairs (mains
£12, open 6.30pm to 9pm Wednesday to
Monday) rustles up tasty treats.

11 The Quay EUROPEAN **££**
(☑ 01271-868090; www.11thequay.co.uk; 11 The
Quay; mains £8-25; ⊙10am-10pm) Ilfracombe's
hippest harbourside hang-out by far is
owned by Damien Hirst. His creations line
the walls, so you get to tuck into lobster
macaroni or Exmoor Angus steaks while
studying models of his statue *Verity* and,
with delicious irony, fish in formaldehyde.

ℹ️ Information

Tourist Office (☑ 01271-863001; www.visit-
ilfracombe.co.uk; The Seafront; ⊙9.30am-
4.30pm Mon-Fri, from 10.30am Sat & Sun)
Inside the Landmark Theatre.

ℹ️ Getting There & Away

Bus 21/21A (half-hourly Monday to Saturday,
hourly Sunday) Runs to Barnstaple (£2.30, 40
minutes), via Braunton.

Bus 300 Heads to Lynton and Lynmouth
(£3.70, 45 minutes) twice on Saturday and
once on Sunday; on Sunday the service goes
onto Minehead (£5.40, 1¾ hours).

Clovelly & Around

POP 440

Clovelly is the quintessential, picture-postcard Devon village. Its cottages cascade
down cliffs to meet a curving crab claw of
a harbour which is lined with lobster pots
and set against a deep-blue sea. A clutch of
impossibly picturesque inns and B&Bs make
it even harder to leave.

⊙ Sights

Clovelly Historic Village HISTORIC SITE
(☑ 01237-431644; www.clovelly.co.uk; adult/child
£7/4; ⊙9am-6.30pm Jun-Sep, 9.30am-5pm Apr-
May & Oct, 10am-4pm Nov-Mar; P) Clovelly is
privately owned, and admission is charged
at the hilltop visitor centre. The village's cobbled streets are so steep that cars can't cope,
so supplies are still brought in by sledge;
you'll see these big bread baskets on runners
leaning outside homes. Charles Kingsley, author of the children's classic *The Water Babies*, spent much of his early life in Clovelly –
don't miss his former **house**, or the highly
atmospheric **fisherman's cottage** and the
village's twin **chapels**.

Hartland Abbey HISTORIC BUILDING
(☑ 01237-441496; www.hartlandabbey.com; adult/
child £11/5; ⊙house 2-5pm, grounds 11.30am-5pm
Sun-Thu Apr-Sep; P) History seems to flow
from the walls of this enchanting, warm-
grey manor house. Built in the 12th century,
it was a monastery until Henry VIII grabbed
it in the Dissolution; he then gave it to the
sergeant of his wine cellar. Today its sumptuous interiors house vivid murals, an ornate
Alhambra Passage and a Regency library designed in the Strawberry Hill Gothic style.

It's 5 miles west of Clovelly, off the A39
between Hartland and Hartland Quay.

📖 Sleeping & Eating

Donkey Shoe Cottage B&B **£**
(☑ 01237-431601; www.donkeyshoecottage.co.uk;
21 High St; s/d £30/60) A country-style B&B
plumb on Clovelly's crazily steep hill, with
wooden floors, raspberry-red walls and sea
views – the best is from number 3, under the
eaves.

★Berridon Farm CAMPSITE **££**
(☑ 01409-241552; www.berridonfarm.co.uk; near
Bradworthy; 3 nights £400-515, 7 nights £575-975;
⊙Easter–mid-Oct; P) At Berridon camping
goes seriously comfy. Here five- or six-person,
insulated safari-style tents sport a leather

sofa and wood burner/oven, plus proper beds and a flushing loo. If it's wet, head for the shabby-chic sitting-eating-play space in a converted barn. It's all tucked away 11 miles south of Clovelly.

Red Lion   INN **£££**
(📞 01237-431237; www.clovelly.co.uk; d £150-180) Set right beside the water, the Red Lion has plush bedrooms with either harbour or sea views, a quality restaurant (two/three courses £25/30, booking required), and a welcoming bar (mains £8, served noon to 2.30pm and 6pm to 8.30pm).

❶ Getting There & Away

Bus 319 (five daily Monday to Saturday) runs between Clovelly, Hartland Village, Bideford (£2.10, 40 minutes) and Barnstaple (£2.70, one hour).

BRISTOL

POP 393,300

If ever there was a British city on the rise, it's Bristol. Once a centre for heavy industry, over the last few decades the southwest's largest city has reinvented itself as a hub of culture and creativity. From Clifton's iconic suspension bridge to Brunel's groundbreaking steamship, the SS *Great Britain*, it's a city that's awash with historical interest. But Bristol is also known for its offbeat, alternative character, and you'll find a wealth of art collectives, community-run cafes and music venues dotted around the city's streets – not to mention murals left behind by the city's most notorious son, the mischievous street artist Banksy.

Throw in the revamped harbourside, the landmark new M-Shed history museum and a fast-growing foodie reputation, and it's little wonder that Bristol was recently named Britain's most liveable city. Gert lush, as they might say round these parts.

History

The city began as a Saxon village and developed into the medieval river-port of Brigstow, an important trading centre for cloth and wine.

In 1497, 'local hero' John Cabot (actually a Genoese sailor called Giovanni Caboto) sailed from Bristol to discover Newfoundland in 1497. The city subsequently become one of Britain's major ports, growing rich on the 'Triangular Trade' (in which African slaves were shipped across the Atlantic to New World colonies, where they were bartered for luxury goods such as sugar, rum, tobacco and cotton that fetched a healthy profit back home). Much of Bristol's 18th-century splendour – including Clifton's terraces and the Old Vic theatre – were part-financed on profits from the trade.

After being usurped by rival ports in London and Liverpool, Bristol repositioned itself as an industrial and shipbuilding centre, and in 1840 became the western terminus for the newly built Great Western Railway line from London.

In the early 20th century, local engineers pioneered the development of a groundbreaking aeroplane design, known as the Bristol Boxkite, and the city became a hub for aeronautics; many parts for Concorde were made in nearby Filton. Unfortunately, Bristol's industrial importance made it a target for German bombing during WWII, and much of the city centre and harbourside was reduced to rubble.

In 2006, the city celebrated the bicentenary of the birth of Isambard Kingdom Brunel, the pioneering Victorian engineer responsible (among many other things) for the Great Western Railway, the Clifton Suspension Bridge and SS *Great Britain*.

◉ Sights

★ SS Great Britain   HISTORIC SHIP
(📞 0117-926 0680; www.ssgreatbritain.org; Great Western Dock, Gas Ferry Rd; adult/child/family £13.75/7/36.50; ⏱ 10am-5.30pm Apr-Oct, to 4.30pm Nov-Mar) Bristol's pride and joy is the mighty steamship SS *Great Britain*, designed by the genius engineer Isambard Kingdom Brunel in 1843. Driven by a revolutionary screw propeller, this massive vessel was one of the largest and most technologically advanced steamships ever built, measuring 322ft (98m) from stern to tip. Originally built as a luxury transatlantic liner, she later fell into disrepair but has since been painstakingly restored to her full glory.

The ship has had a chequered history. Between 1843 and 1886, the SS *Great Britain* served her intended duty as a passenger liner, completing the transatlantic crossing between Bristol and New York in just 14 days. Unfortunately, enormous running costs and mounting debts led her towards an ignominious end: she was eventually sold off and subsequently served as a troop vessel, quarantine ship, emigration transport and coal-hulk, before finally being scuttled near Port Stanley in the Falklands in 1937.

Happily, that wasn't the end. The ship was towed back to Bristol in 1970, and has since undergone a 30-year restoration program. The ship's interior has been impeccably refurbished, including the galley, surgeon's quarters, dining saloon and a working model of the original steam engine (weighing 340 tons and measuring three storeys high). The highlight is the 'glass sea' on which the ship sits, enclosing an airtight dry dock that preserves the hull and allows visitors to view the screw propeller.

Tickets remain valid for a year, and also include admission to the nearby **Brunel Institute** (📞0117-926 0680; Great Western Dockyard; ⏱10.30am-4.30pm Tue-Fri & first 2 Sats per month) `FREE`, which houses a wealth of research materials relating to Bristol's maritime past.

Matthew   HISTORIC SHIP
(📞0117-927 6868; www.matthew.co.uk; Princes Wharf; ⏱10am-4pm Tue-Sun) `FREE` For much of the year, a replica of John Cabot's ship, the *Matthew,* is moored in Bristol's Floating Harbour. It's a reconstruction of the vessel in which the explorer made his landmark voyage from Bristol to Newfoundland in 1497. The *Matthew* allows visits Tuesday to Sunday, and also runs trips around the city's harbour (adult/child £10/8) and along the Avon Gorge; see the website for dates.

M Shed   MUSEUM
(📞0117-352 6600; www.mshed.org; Princes Wharf; ⏱10am-5pm Tue-Fri, to 6pm Sat & Sun; ♿) `FREE`
Opened in 2011 alongside the iconic cranes of Bristol's dockside, this impressive museum is a treasure trove of memorabilia rummaging through the city's past. The exhibits are divided into three sections (People, Place and Life), and provide a panoramic overview of Bristol's history – from slaves' possessions and vintage buses to Wallace and Gromit figurines and a set of decks once used by Massive Attack. It's all highly interactive, child-friendly – and, best of all, free.

In summer, look out for special weekend activities including the chance to ride on the dock cranes, watch the old Pyronaut fireboat in action or catch a lift aboard the little steam locomotives of the Bristol Harbour

BANksY

If there's one Bristolian nearly everyone has heard of, it's **Banksy** (www.banksy.co.uk) – the guerrilla street artist whose distinctive stencilled style and provocative artworks have earned him worldwide notoriety.

Though his true identity is a secret, it's believed Banksy was born in 1974 in Yate, 12 miles from Bristol, and honed his artistic skills in a local graffiti outfit. His works take a wry view of 21st-century culture – especially capitalism, consumerism and the cult of celebrity. Among his best-known pieces are the production of spoof banknotes (featuring Princess Diana's head instead of the Queen's), a series of murals on Israel's West Bank barrier (depicting people digging holes and climbing ladders over the wall) and a painting of a caveman pushing a shopping trolley at the British Museum (which the museum promptly claimed for its permanent collection). His documentary *Exit Through The Gift Shop,* about an LA street artist, was nominated for an Oscar in 2011.

Long despised by the authorities, Banksy has become an unlikely tourist magnet. Though many of his works are short-lived, a few still survive around the city. Look out for the **Well Hung Lover (Frogmore St)** on Frogmore St, featuring an angry husband, a two-timing wife, and a naked man dangling from a window; a stencil of the **Grim Reaper** on the side of the Thekla (p319); the **Paint-Pot Angel** outside the Bristol Museum & Art Gallery (p314), a reminder of the artist's hugely popular 2009 exhibition there; and **Mild Mild West** (featuring a Molotov cocktail–wielding teddy bear) on Cheltenham Rd.

Banksy hit the headlines again in 2014 when one of his murals unexpectedly appeared on a wooden panel outside the Broad Plain Boys' Club in April 2014. Known as *Mobile Lovers*, the mural depicted a young couple who appear to be embracing but are actually staring into their phones. Predictably enough, a furore over ownership ensued, but the artist made it clear that he had painted the mural as a gift to the boys' club, which he is thought to have attended as a young man. After a few months on display at the Bristol City Museum, the work was sold for £400,000 to a private collector in August 2014, with all the proceeds going to fund the boys' club's ongoing projects. Good on ya, Banksy.

Bristol

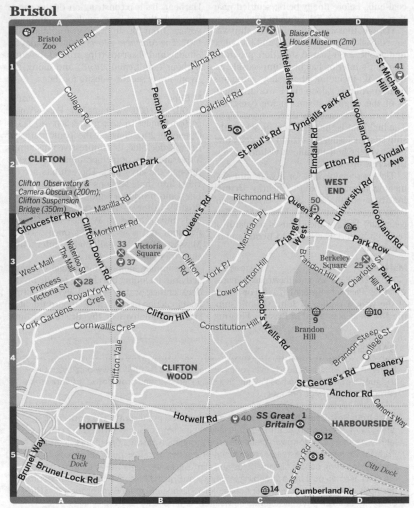

Railway (consult the website for timetables). The museum also runs guided tours exploring the harbour's history.

Spike Island
GALLERY
(☏0117-929 2266; www.spikeisland.org.uk; 133 Cumberland Rd; ☺gallery noon-5pm Tue-Sun, cafe 8.30am-5pm Mon-Fri, noon-5pm Sat & Sun) Culture vultures should make time to visit Spike Island, a lively centre for visual arts that's home to a collective of artists' studios, a contemporary art gallery and a cracking little cafe. It's a short walk south from the SS *Great Britain*.

Arnolfini
GALLERY
(☏0117-917 2300; www.arnolfini.org.uk; 16 Narrow Quay; ☺10am-6pm Tue-Sun) The city's avant-garde art gallery occupies a hulking red-brick warehouse by the river, and remains the top venue in town for modern art, as well as occasional exhibitions of dance, film and photography.

Bristol Aquarium
AQUARIUM
(☏0117-929 8929; www.bristolaquarium.co.uk; Harbourside; adult/child/family £13.50/9.25/43.50; ☺10am-5pm Mon-Fri, to 6pm Sat & Sun) Bristol's harbourside aquarium has underwater habitats including a Bay of Rays, a Coral Sea, a

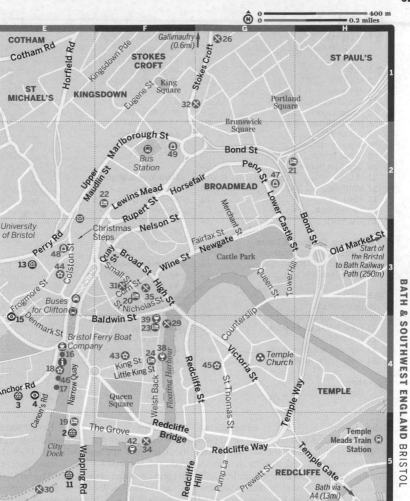

Shark Tank, and an Amazon River Zone, as well as a resident giant Pacific octopus and an underwater viewing tunnel. There's a £2 discount per ticket for buying online.

At-Bristol MUSEUM
(☎ 0845 345 1235; www.at-bristol.org.uk; Anchor Rd; adult/child/family £12.05/7.70/34.15; ⊙ 10am-5pm Mon-Fri, to 6pm Sat & Sun; ♿) Bristol's interactive science museum has several zones spanning space, technology and the human brain. In the Curiosity Zone you get to walk through a tornado, spin on a human gyroscope and strum the strings of a virtual harp. There's also a great planetarium. It's fun and interactive, and should keep kids entertained for hours.

Georgian House HISTORIC BUILDING
(7 Great George St; ⊙ 10am-4pm Tue-Sun Apr-Aug) FREE Once the home of the wealthy West India merchant John Pinney, this 18th-century house provides an evocative insight into aristocratic life in Bristol during the Georgian era. It's decorated in period style, typified by the huge kitchen (complete with cast-iron roasting spit), the book-lined library and the grand drawing rooms, as well as Pinney's cold-water plunge-pool in the basement.

Bristol

Cabot Tower   HISTORIC BUILDING
(⊙8am-dusk) FREE Located in the small park of Brandon Hill, this red-brick tower was built between 1896 and 1898 to commemorate John Cabot's pioneering voyage in search of Canada. It was closed in 2007 when suspicious cracks appeared, but was reopened in 2011 and offers an unparalleled bird's-eye panorama over the whole of Bristol.

Bristol Museum & Art Gallery   MUSEUM
(☑0117-922 3571; Queen's Rd; ⊙10am-5pm Mon-Fri, to 6pm Sat & Sun) FREE A classic old Edwardian museum that's full of mix-and-match exhibits, taking in everything from dinosaurs and Asian antiques to Assyrian reliefs. The French and Eastern Art sections are particularly strong: look out for paintings by Pissarro and Renoir, and a new 'Red Gate' sculpture by the Chinese artist Guan Donghai. As you enter, look up to see the famous Bristol Boxkite, an early design of propeller-powered biplane, dangling from the ceiling.

Red Lodge   HISTORIC BUILDING
(Park Row; ⊙10am-4pm Tue-Sun Apr-Aug) FREE Built in 1590 but remodelled in 1730, this red-brick house is a mix of Elizabethan, Stuart and Georgian architecture. The highlight is the Great Oak Room, which still features its original Elizabethan oak panelling, plasterwork ceiling and carved chimney piece.

Clifton   NEIGHBOURHOOD
During the 18th and 19th centuries, wealthy Bristol merchants transformed the former spa resort of Clifton into an elegant hilltop suburb packed with impressive Georgian mansions. Some of the finest examples can be seen along **Cornwallis Crescent** and **Royal York Crescent**. These days, Clifton is still the poshest postcode in Bristol, with fancy shops and a villagey atmosphere that's far removed from the rest of the city.

Clifton Suspension Bridge   BRIDGE
(www.cliftonbridge.org.uk) Clifton's most famous (and photographed) landmark is a

Brunel masterpiece, the 76m-high Clifton Suspension Bridge, which spans the Avon Gorge. Construction began in 1836, but Brunel died before its completion in 1864. Designed to carry light horse-drawn traffic and foot passengers, these days the bridge carries around 12,000 cars every day – testament to the vision of Brunel's design. It's free to walk or cycle across; car drivers pay a £1 toll.

There's an information point near the tower on the Leigh Woods side. Free tours take place at 3pm on Saturdays and Sundays from Easter to October.

The Downs   PARK

(🚇🚌) Near the Clifton Suspension Bridge, the grassy parks of Clifton Down and Durdham Down (often referred to as just the Downs) make a fine spot for a picnic. Nearby, the small **Clifton Observatory** (🗹0117-974 1242; Clifton Down; adult/child £2/1; ⊙11.30am-5.30pm Mon-Fri, from 10.30am Sat & Sun) houses a **camera obscura** (🗹0117-974 1242; adult/child £2/1; ⊙10.30am-5.30pm) and a tunnel leading down to the **Giant's Cave** (adult/child £1.50/50p), a natural cavern that emerges halfway down the cliff with dizzying views across the Avon Gorge. At the time of writing, the observatory was up for sale for a cool £2 million – so things may have changed by the time you visit. Ring ahead to check.

Bristol Zoo   ZOO

(🗹0117-974 7399; www.bristolzoo.org.uk; adult/child £14.50/8.86; ⊙9am-5.30pm; 🅿🚌) The city's zoo is on the north side of Clifton. Highlights include a brand-new £1 million house for the zoo's family of seven gorillas, as well as reptile and bug zones, a butterfly forest, a lion enclosure, a monkey jungle and the **Zooropia** (adult/child £8/7) treetop adventure park. There's a 10% discount for online tickets. To get there from the city centre, catch bus 15A or 8/9.

Blaise Castle House Museum   MUSEUM

(Henbury Rd; ⊙10am-5pm Wed-Sat) **FREE** In the northern suburb of Henbury is this late-18th-century house and social-history museum. Displays include vintage toys, costumes and other Victorian ephemera. Bus 42/42A (45 minutes, every 15 minutes) passes the castle from Colston Ave; bus 1 (20 minutes, every 10 minutes) runs from the station and St Augustine's Pde.

👉 Tours

Bristol Highlights Walk   WALKING TOUR

(www.bristolwalks.co.uk; adult/under 12yr £5/free; ⊙11am Sat Apr-Sep) Tours of the old town, city centre and Harbourside. It's run every Saturday at 11am; just turn up outside the tourist office (p319). Themed tours exploring Clifton, medieval Bristol and the history of Bristol's slave and wine trades run on request.

LOCAL KNOWLEDGE

BRISTOL'S HOT SPRINGS

Bath isn't the only southwest city with its own outdoor hot tub. It's a little-known fact that Bristol sits on its own system of hot springs, which bubble up through the rocks beneath the Avon Gorge. During the 19th century, these geothermally heated waters turned the area around Hotwells into a popular spa resort, where Georgian bathers flocked to try the curative waters (which were believed to alleviate a variety of conditions including consumption, asthma, dropsy and venereal diseases). The area even had its own funicular railway between Hotwells and Clifton, which served as a bomb shelter during WWII.

Though Bristol's days as a spa town may be over, you can still experience a flavour of its hot-water heyday, thanks to the wonderful **Bristol Lido** (🗹0117-933 9530; www.lido-bristol.com; Oakfield Pl; nonmembers £20; ⊙nonmembers 1-4pm Mon-Fri). Originally opened as the Clifton Lido in 1849, the baths fell into disrepair and were closed in 1990, but have been carefully restored over the last few years. They're now a real local's secret, with a beautiful 24m outdoor swimming pool that's kept at a constant temperature of around 24°C. Spa treatments and massage sessions are also available, and there's even an excellent bistro.

The only drawback for nonlocals is that priority is given to members. On weekends and busy days the lido is closed for day visitors, so phone ahead to make sure there's space.

MP3 Tours
WALKING TOUR

(www.visitbristol.co.uk/about-bristol/video-and-audio/audio-tours) **FREE** Free downloadable MP3 guides covering Bristol's quayside, the slave trade, heritage architecture, historic churches and the city's literary connections.

Bristol Packet Boat Trips
BOAT TOUR

(0117-926 8157; www.bristolpacket.co.uk; Wapping Wharf, Gas Ferry Rd; ☉ 11am-4.15pm Sat & Sun) This boat company cruises around the harbour area (adult/child £5.75/3.75, departures every 45 minutes on weekends, daily during school holidays). There are also weekly cruises along the Avon from May to October (adult/child £16/12) and a Sunday afternoon trip to Beese's Tea Gardens (£11/7). Cruises to Bath (£26.50/20) run once a month from May to September.

Cycle The City
CYCLING

(07873-387167; www.cyclethecity.org; 1 Canon's Rd; bike hire per day £16; ☉ 10am-5.30pm Mon-Sat) Bike rental and cycling tours from Bristol's waterfront. It's based at No 1 Harbourside.

⚡ Festivals & Events

Bristol Shakespeare Festival THEATRE FESTIVAL (www.bristolshakespeare.org.uk) Britain's biggest outdoor festival devoted to the Bard, held between May and September.

Bristol Harbour Festival COMMUNITY FESTIVAL (www.bristolharbourfestival.co.uk) Bands, events and historic ships take over the city's docks in early August.

International Balloon Fiesta HOT-AIR BALLOONS (www.bristolballoonfiesta.co.uk) Hot-air balloons fill the skies at Ashton Court in August.

Encounters FILM FESTIVAL (www.encounters-festival.org.uk) Bristol's largest film fest is in November.

🛏 Sleeping

Bristol's hotels are geared towards the business crowd, but there are some great-value chains and B&Bs dotted around the city centre.

Bristol YHA
HOSTEL £

(0845 371 9726; bristol@yha.org.uk; 14 Narrow Quay; dm £13-22, d from £70; @) Few hostels can boast a position as good as this one, beside the river in a red-brick warehouse. Facilities include kitchens, cycle store, games room and the Grainshed **coffee lounge** – but the dorms are functional, and the doubles are expensive.

Brooks Guest House
B&B ££

(0117-930 0066; www.brooksguesthousebristol.com; Exchange Ave; d £85-120; ☎) If you want to be in the heart of things, this brilliantly central B&B is a fine bet. It's in a modern building opposite St Nick's Market. Rooms are boxy, but pleasantly finished with flock wallpaper, John Lewis bed linen and Hansgröhe power showers. Discounted parking is available for £14 a day at the nearby Queen Charlotte St car park.

Future Inn Cabot Circus
HOTEL ££

(0845 094 5588; www.futureinns.co.uk/bristol-hotels; Bond St South; d £59-99; P ☎) This hotel mini-chain has outlets in Plymouth, Cardiff and Bristol. It's modern and businessy, but the rooms are the best value in town, simply decorated in beige, white and MDF. Prices include parking at the Cabot Circus car park.

Mercure Brigstow Hotel
HOTEL ££

(0117-929 1030; H6548@accor.com; Welsh Back; d £63-125; ☎) A harbourside location and attractive modern design make the Mercure a good, central option. All rooms boast 'floating' beds, curved panel walls and tiny TVs set into bathroom tiles (gimmicky, yes, but fun). Upper rooms have great city views.

Premier Inn, King Street
HOTEL ££

(0871 527 8158; www.premiertravelinn.com; King St; r £59-89; ❋ ☎) Yes, we realise this is a Premier Inn, but stop being snobby and just appreciate the cheap rates and riverside location. Rooms have big beds, desk and wi-fi, and some even have glimpses of the harbour. Worth considering – although the Llandoger Trow pub next door gets rowdy at weekends. Discounted parking is available at the NCP on Queen Charlotte St.

Greenhouse
B&B ££

(0117-902 9166; www.thegreenhousebristol.co.uk; 61 Greenbank Rd, Southville; s/d £70/105; P ☎) 🚭 No bells and whistles here – just a lovely, friendly, quiet B&B in Southville, a few minutes' stride to the river and the centre. Cream rooms, white sheets and an excellent organic breakfast make it worth considering. Free parking's an extra bonus.

★ Number 38
B&B £££

(0117-946 6905; www.number38clifton.com; 38 Upper Belgrave Rd, Clifton; d £135-210; P ☎) Perched on the edge of the Downs, this upmarket B&B is one for the style-conscious. The rooms are huge and contemporary –

sombre greys and smooth blues dictate the palette, luxury is provided by waffle bathrobes and REN bath goodies, and city views unfold from the roof terrace. The two suites have old-fashioned tin baths.

Hotel du Vin
HOTEL **£££**

(☑ 0117-925 5577; www.hotelduvin.com; Narrow Lewins Mead; r £139-254; P 🛜) This luxury British hotel brand is a fave with well-heeled city-breakers. Their Bristol outpost occupies an old sugar warehouse, and mixes industrial chic and sleek minimalism: exposed brick and iron pillars meet futon beds and clawfoot baths. The rooms are named after vintage champagnes; the best are the split-level mezzanine suites. The **bistro** is great, too.

✖ Eating

Bristol's lively food scene takes in everything from ethnic restaurants to wholefood cafes. For a quick lunch, local tips include **Boston Tea Party** (www.bostonteaparty.co.uk; Park St; sandwiches & salads £4-6) and **Bagel Boy** (☑ 0117-922 0417; 39-41 St Nicholas St; bagels £3-5; ☉ 9.30am-5.30pm).

Canteen
CAFE **£**

(☑ 0117-923 2017; www.canteenbristol.co.uk; 80 Stokes Croft; mains £4-10; ☉ 10am-10pm) 🍃 Occupying the ground floor of an old office block in gritty Stokes Croft, this community-run cafe sums up Bristol's alternative character: it's all about slow food, local suppliers and fair prices, whether you pop in for a bacon butty, veggie chilli or sit-down supper. There's regular live music, and artists' studios to explore.

St Nicholas Market
MARKET **£**

(Corn St; ☉ 9.30am-5pm Mon-Sat) The city's lively street market has a bevy of food stalls selling everything from mezze platters to pulled-pork rolls from BBQ specialists **Grillstock**. Lines can be long at lunchtime, but it's worth the wait. Look out for **farmers markets** on Wednesdays and a **slow-food market** on the first Sunday of each month.

Thali Café
INDIAN **£**

(☑ 0117-974 3793; www.thethalicafe.co.uk; 1 Regent St; meals £5.95-10.95; ☉ noon-10pm) This long-standing Indian canteen now has four outlets, including this one in Clifton. It specialises in thalis (multicourse Indian meals), showcasing different curry styles from across India. You can even get takeaway in a reusable tiffin tin.

Gallimaufry
BRITISH **£**

(☑ 0117-942 7319; www.thegallimaufry.co.uk; 26-28 The Promenade; lunch mains £5.50-7, dinner £11.50-13.50; ☉ 11am-midnight) The definition of a locals' cafe, favoured by Gloucester Rd's cool crowd. All the elements are there – upcycled furniture, quirky artworks, scruffy decor – along with a dedication to Bristolian suppliers. The food covers all bases, from quick 'Gallimouthfuls' to plates of pork belly and champ mash.

Pieminister
BRITISH **£**

(24 Stokes Croft; pies around £4.50; ☉ 10am-7pm Sat, 11am-4pm Sun) A Bristol institution: gourmet pies with quirky names (Chicken of Aragon, Deerstalker, Moo and Blue), all drowned in lashings of gravy (meat-free if you wish). The main shop is on Stokes Croft, but there's an outlet in St Nick's market.

Olive Shed
BISTRO **£**

(☑ 0117-929 1960; www.theoliveshed.com; Princes Wharf; mains £4-8; ☉ 6.30-10pm Wed, noon-10pm Thu-Sat, noon-4pm Sun) A good spot for a harbourside lunch, especially after a visit to the SS *Great Britain* or the M Shed. It serves tapas and Med food, with tables on the quayside.

★ Riverstation
BRITISH **££**

(☑ 0117-914 4434; www.riverstation.co.uk; The Grove; 2-/3-course lunch £12.75/15.50, dinner mains £15.50-19.50; ☉ noon-2.30pm & 6-10pm) One of Bristol's original dining-out destinations, and still leading the pack. The riverside location is hard to beat, with a view over the Floating Harbour, but it's the food that keeps the punters coming back: classic in style with a strong European flavour, from French fish soup to steak *à la béarnaise*. The **bar+kitchen** downstairs is open all day for coffee and cakes.

Ox
BRITISH **££**

(☑ 0117-922 1001; www.theoxbristol.com; 43 Corn St; dinner mains £12.50-16; ☉ 12.30-2.30pm Thu & Fri, 5-10.30pm Tue-Sat, noon-4pm Sun) This new addition to Corn St offers a refined dining experience. Located in a basement bank vault, it now resembles a posh Pullman dining car, with wood panelling, a mahogany bar and Pre-Raphaelite murals. As its name suggests, it's for the carnivores – charcuterie platters, gourmet burgers and five choices of steak cut.

Fishers
SEAFOOD **££**

(☑ 0117-974 7044; www.fishers-restaurant.com; 35 Princess Victoria St; mains £11.95-15.50; ☉ noon-2.30pm & 6.30-10pm) Top choice for a fish

TYNTESFIELD

Formerly the aristocratic home of the Gibbs family, **Tyntesfield** (NT; ☑ 01275-461900; www.nationaltrust.org.uk/tyntesfield; adult/child £13.90/7, gardens only £8.55/4.30; ☺ house 11am-5pm Fri-Wed, grounds 10am-6pm) is one of the National Trust's most important acquisitions of recent years. A fairy-tale mansion bristling with pinnacles and turrets, brimful of sweeping staircases and cavernous, antique-filled rooms, the house gives an insight into the lavish lives once enjoyed by England's aristocratic families. Entry is via timed ticket and includes a guided tour. The house is 7 miles southwest of Bristol, off the B3128.

Built in grand Gothic Revival style by the architect John Norton, it was in danger of collapse when the Trust acquired it in 2001, but has since undergone extensive (and very expensive) renovations. Outside, work continues on the orangery and walled gardens.

supper, from baked bream to megrim sole; the hot shellfish platter (£43 for two people) is made for sharing. The simple setting, with its whitewashed walls, ships' lanterns and nautical knick-knacks, contributes to the maritime vibe.

Cowshed BRITISH ££
(☑ 0117-973 3550; www.thecowshedbristol.com; 46 Whiteladies Rd; 3-course lunch £10, dinner mains £12.95-21.50; ☺ noon-3pm & 6-10pm) Country food with a modern twist is served at the Cowshed. The focus is on quality, locally sourced meat – aged beef, wild rabbit, pork belly, plus the *pièce de la résistance* 'steak on stone', served sizzling on a hot lava rock. The three-course lunch and sharing boards (£15.30 to £18.50 for four people) are great value.

Primrose Café BISTRO ££
(☑ 0117-946 6577; www.primrosecafe.co.uk; 1-2 Boyce's Ave; lunch mains £6-12, dinner £13.50-18.50; ☺ 9am-5pm & 6-10pm Tue-Sat, 9.30am-3pm Sun, 9am-5pm Mon) A Clifton classic, as perfect for morning coffee as for a proper sit-down dinner. With its pavement tables and wooden interior, it feels like a Bristolian version of a Parisian street cafe. It's particularly choice for breakfast: the *croque-monsieurs* and Belgian waffles are legendary.

Glassboat FRENCH ££
(☑ 0117-929 0704; www.glassboat.co.uk; Welsh Back; 2-/3-course lunch menu £10/12, dinner mains £15-22; ☺ 8-11am, noon-5pm & 5.30-10pm Mon-Sat, to 4pm Sun) This converted river barge is great for a romantic dinner, with candlelit tables and harbour views through a glass extension. The food revolves around French and Italian flavours.

Soukitchen MIDDLE EASTERN ££
(☑ 0117-966 6880; www.soukkitchen.co.uk; 277 North St; mains £9.50-12.50; ☺ noon-3pm & 6-10pm) Middle Eastern market food is

the stock in trade at this friendly diner in Southville, with characteristic dishes such as *bourek* (filo pies stuffed with meat or vegetables), mix-and-match mezze platters and flame-grilled kebabs. Honest food with heart.

Maitreya Social VEGETARIAN ££
(☑ 0117-951 0100; www.cafemaitreya.co.uk; 89 St Marks Rd; mains £8.95-10.95; ☺ 10am-11.30pm Tue-Sat, to 4pm Sun; ☑) This Easton eatery has won awards for its innovative veggie food, and it's recently branched out with a funky new arts-space-cum-music-venue.

🍷 Drinking & Nightlife

Grain Barge PUB
(www.grainbarge.com; Mardyke Wharf, Hotwell Rd; ☺ noon-11pm Sun-Thu, to 11.30pm Fri & Sat) Built in 1936, this barge opposite the SS *Great Britain* is owned by the Bristol Beer Factory. Descend the decks to down a pint of No. 7 Bitter or dark Exhibition ale.

Highbury Vaults PUB
(164 St Michaels Hill; ☺ noon-midnight Mon-Sat, to 11pm Sun) This endearingly scruffy boozer has a warren of wood-panelled rooms and hallways, and at least eight real ales on tap.

Albion PUB
(www.thealbionclifton.co.uk; Boyce's Ave; ☺ 9am-midnight Mon-Sat, to 11pm Sun) A lovely old-fashioned pub that's popular with evening drinkers from Clifton's well-heeled streets.

BrewDog Bristol PUB
(www.brewdog.com/bars/bristol; 58 Baldwin St; ☺ noon-midnight) Britain's punk brewery has a new Bristol outlet, serving craft beers such as Libertine Black Ale, Dead Pony Club and Hardcore IPA.

Apple BAR
(www.applecider.co.uk; Welsh Back; ☺ noon-midnight Mon-Sat, to 10.30pm Sun summer,

5pm-midnight Mon-Sat winter) Forty varieties of cider are served on this converted barge, including raspberry, strawberry and six perries (pear ciders).

Thekla CLUB
(www.thekla.co.uk; The Grove) Bristol's club-boat has nights for all moods: electro-punk, indie, disco and new wave, plus regular live gigs.

☆ Entertainment

Watershed CINEMA
(www.watershed.co.uk; 1 Canon's Rd) Bristol's digital media centre hosts regular art-house programs and film-related events, including the **Encounters Festival** in November.

Bristol Old Vic THEATRE
(www.bristololdvic.org.uk; 103 The Cut) Bristol's stately theatre (one of England's oldest) hosts big touring productions in its ornate auditorium, plus more experimental work in its smaller studio.

Colston Hall LIVE MUSIC
(www.colstonhall.org; Colston St) Bristol's historic concert hall tends to attract the best bands and big-name comedy acts.

Fleece LIVE MUSIC
(www.fleecegigs.co.uk; St Thomas St) A gig-pub favoured by indie artists.

🛍 Shopping

Bristol is good for shopping, but you'll need to get out of the centre if you want to avoid the high street chains, which cluster around **Cabot Circus** (www.cabotcircus.com) and **Broadmead**.

Stokes Croft and Gloucester Rd are the best areas for independent shops, especially vintage clothing, crafts and secondhand music. Clifton is more upmarket, with high-end designers, homewares and antiques shops.

Rise Music MUSIC
(☑0117-929 7511; bristol@rise-music.co.uk; 70 Queens Rd; ☺10am-7pm Mon-Sat, noon-6pm Sun) Bristol's top independent record shop, with racks of CDs and vinyl, and a coffee bar downstairs.

Dig Haüshizzle VINTAGE
(☑07789-145 175; www.dig-haushizzle.co.uk; 51 Colston St; ☺11am-6pm Mon-Fri, 10am-6pm Sat, noon-4pm Sun) Vintage furniture and retro design pieces, from pine chests to apothecary jars.

Loot CLOTHING
(☑0117-922 0633; facebook.com/LOOTvintagewarehouse; 6-9 Haymarket Walk; ☺10am-5.30pm Mon-Sat, noon-5pm Sun) The city's largest vintage clothing shop.

ℹ Information

Bristol Tourist Information Centre (☑0906 711 2191; www.visitbristol.co.uk; E-Shed, 1 Canon's Rd; ☺10am-4pm Mon-Sat, 11am-4pm Sun) Calling the phone number costs the premium rate of 50p per minute.

ℹ Getting There & Away

The **Travel Bristol** (www.travelbristol.org) website lists comprehensive information on public transport in and around Bristol city.

AIR

Bristol International Airport (☑0871 3344344; www.bristolairport.co.uk) Bristol's airport is 8 miles southwest of the city. Destinations include UK airports such as Newcastle, Edinburgh, Glasgow and Aberdeen (mainly handled by Ryanair and EasyJet) as well as direct flights to cities in Ireland and mainland Europe.

LOCAL KNOWLEDGE

BRISTOL & BATH RAILWAY PATH

This **bike trail** (www.bristolbathrailwaypath.org.uk) between Bristol and Bath is a delightful way to explore the countryside between the two cities. It runs for 13 miles along an old railway track that was decommissioned during Beeching's cuts in the 1950s, and passes several interesting sights, including disused mills and a delightful old station at Bitton (now part of the restored Avon Valley Railway). It also links up with other bike trails including the **Dramway Path** (www.southglos.gov.uk/Documents/The%20Dramway.pdf) and the **River Avon Trail** (www.riveravontrail.org.uk).

The official starts of the path are at St Phillips Lane in Bristol and Brassmill Lane in Bath, but you can access it at various points along the route.

For bike hire, see p320 and p330.

On-the-day parking at the airport is expensive; booking online in advance gets much cheaper rates.

BUS

National Express coaches go to Birmingham (£21.30, two hours, six to eight daily), London (£18.90, 2½ hours, hourly), Cardiff (£6, 1¼ hours, every two hours) and Exeter (£15, two hours, five daily).

Useful local buses:

Bath (£5.50, 50 minutes, several per hour) Express bus X39/339.

Wells (£5.50, one hour, half-hourly Monday to Saturday, hourly on Sunday) Bus 376, with onward connections to Glastonbury (£5.50, 1¼ hours).

TRAIN

Bristol is an important rail hub, with regular services to London Paddington provided by **First Great Western** (www.firstgreatwestern.co.uk) and services to northern England and Scotland mainly covered by **CrossCountry** (www.cross countrytrains.co.uk). Book in advance for cheaper tickets than those listed here.

Birmingham (£51.50, 1½ hours, hourly)
Edinburgh (£163.10, 6½ hours, hourly)
Exeter (£26.90, one hour, hourly)
Glasgow (£148, 6½ hours, hourly)
London (£42, 1¾ hours, hourly)
Penzance (£45, 5½ hours, hourly)
Truro (£45, five hours, hourly)

ⓘ Getting Around

TO/FROM THE AIRPORT

Bristol International Flyer (http://flyer.bristol airport.co.uk) Runs shuttle buses (one way/return £11/7, 30 minutes, every 10 minutes at peak times) from the bus station and Temple Meads.

Checker Cars (🗷 01275-475000; www. checkercars.com) Bristol Airport's official taxi service. Fares start from around £25 to £30 from the city centre.

ⓘ DRIVING IN BRISTOL

Heavy traffic and pricey parking make driving in Bristol a headache. If you do drive, make sure your hotel has parking, or use the **Park & Ride buses** (🗷 01179-222910; return before 10am Mon-Fri £3.50, after 10am Mon-Fri £2.50, Sat £2.50; ⊘ every 10min Mon-Sat) from Portway, Bath Rd and Long Ashton. Note that overnight parking is not permitted at the Park & Ride car parks.

BICYCLE

Bristol Bike Project (🗷 07983-417231; www. thebristolbikeproject.org; City Rd; bike hire per day Mon-Fri £12, Sat & Sun £25; ⊘ 9am-5.30pm Mon-Fri) A community-run bike shop and rental outlet in Stokes Croft.

Roll for the Soul (🗷 07596-917963; www. rollforthesoul.org; 2 Quay St; ⊘ 9am-5.30pm Mon-Fri, 10am-5.30pm Sat) Not-for-profit bike cafe and bike workshop – great for meeting like-minded cycling buddies.

BOAT

Bristol Ferry Boat Company (🗷 0117-927 3416; www.bristolferry.com; adult/child return £4.80/3.80, day pass £6/5) Regular ferry service around the harbour. There are two hourly routes: the red route runs west towards Hotwells, with stops including Millennium Sq and the SS *Great Britain;* the blue route runs east to Temple Meads, with stops including Castle Park (for Cabot Circus), Welsh Back, Millennium Sq and the SS *Great Britain.* Boats leave from the dock near the tourist office.

BUS

Bus journeys in Bristol's city centre cost £1 for up to three stops, otherwise they cost £1.50.

Bus 8/9 to Clifton (10 minutes), Whiteladies Rd and Bristol Zoo Gardens every 15 minutes from St Augustine's Pde. Add 10 minutes from Temple Meads.

Bus 73 Runs from Parkway Station to the centre (30 minutes).

TAXI

You can usually find a cab at the taxi rank on St Augustine's Pde, but there are plenty of dial-a-fares: try **Streamline Taxis** (🗷 0117-926 4001) or **1st Call Taxi** (🗷 0117-955 8880; www.1stcall-taxis.net). If you're taking a non-metered cab, agree on the fare in advance.

BATH

POP 90,144

Britain's littered with beautiful cities, but precious few compare to Bath. Home to some of the nation's grandest Georgian architecture – not to mention one of the world's best-preserved Roman bathhouses – this slinky, sophisticated, snooty city has been a tourist draw for nigh-on 2000 years.

Founded on top of natural hot springs, Bath's heyday really began during the 18th century, when local entrepreneur Ralph Allen and his team of father-and-son architects, John Wood the Elder and Younger, turned this sleepy backwater into the toast of Georgian society, and constructed fabulous landmarks such as the Circus and Royal Crescent.

History

Legend has it King Bladud, a Trojan refugee and father of King Lear, founded Bath some 2800 years ago when his pigs were cured of leprosy by a dip in the muddy swamps. The Romans established the town of Aquae Sulis in AD 44 and built the extensive baths complex and a temple to the goddess Sulis-Minerva.

Long after the Romans left, the Anglo-Saxons arrived, and in 944 a monastery was founded on the site of the present abbey. Throughout the Middle Ages, Bath was an ecclesiastical centre and a wool-trading town, but it wasn't until the early 18th century that Ralph Allen and the celebrated dandy Richard 'Beau' Nash made Bath the centre of fashionable society. Allen developed the quarries at Coombe Down, constructed Prior Park and employed the two John Woods (father and son) to create Bath's signature buildings.

During WWII, Bath was hit by the Luftwaffe during the so-called Baedeker raids, which targeted historic cities in an effort to sap British morale. Several houses on the Royal Crescent and the Circus were badly damaged, and the city's Assembly Rooms were gutted by fire, although all have since been restored.

In 1987, Bath became the only city in Britain to be declared a Unesco World Heritage Site in its entirety, leading to many subsequent wrangles over construction and development, most recently concerning the design of the redeveloped Thermae Bath Spa and SouthGate shopping centre.

◉ Sights

★ **Roman Baths**   MUSEUM
(☑ 01225-477785; www.romanbaths.co.uk; Abbey Churchyard; adult/child/family £13.50/8.80/38; ☺ 9am-6pm, to 9pm Jul & Aug) In typically ostentatious style, the Romans constructed a complex of bathhouses above Bath's three natural hot springs, which emerge at a steady 46°C (115°F). Situated alongside a temple dedicated to the healing goddess Sulis Minerva, the baths now form one of the best-preserved ancient Roman spas in the world, encircled by 18th- and 19th-century buildings. As Bath's premier attraction, the Roman Baths can get very, very busy. Avoid the worst crowds by buying tickets online,

visiting early on a midweek morning, and avoiding July and August.

The heart of the complex is the **Great Bath**, a lead-lined pool filled with steaming, geothermally heated water from the so-called 'Sacred Spring' to a depth of 1.6m. Though now open-air, the bath would originally have been covered by a 45m-high, barrel-vaulted roof.

More bathing pools and changing rooms are situated to the east and west, with excavated sections revealing the **hypocaust system** that heated the bathing rooms. After luxuriating in the baths, Romans would have reinvigorated themselves with a dip in the circular **cold-water pool**, which now has life-size films of bathers projected onto the walls.

The **King's Bath** was added sometime during the 12th century around the site of the original sacred spring. Every day, 1.5 million litres of hot water still pour into the pool. Beneath the Pump Room are the remains of the **Temple of Sulis-Minerva**.

There is also a fascinating **museum** displaying artefacts discovered on the site. Look out for the famous gilded bronze head of Minerva and a striking carved Gorgon's Head, as well as some of the 12,000-odd Roman coins thrown into the spring as votive offerings to the Goddess.

The complex of buildings around the baths were built in stages during the 18th and 19th centuries. The two John Woods designed the buildings around the Sacred Spring, while the famous **Pump Room** (Stall St) was built by their contemporaries, Thomas Baldwin and John Palmer, in neoclassical style, complete with soaring Ionic and Corinthian columns. The building now houses a restaurant which serves a magnificent afternoon tea (£21, or £27.50 with champagne). Should you wish, you can also sample the spring waters, which were believed in Victorian times to have curative properties. If you're lucky, you might even have music provided by the Pump Room's string trio.

Admission includes an audioguide, featuring a commentary in eight languages. The one in English is read by bestselling author Bill Bryson. Free hourly guided tours start at the Great Bath.

★ **Bath Abbey**   CHURCH
(☑ 01225-422462; www.bathabbey.org; requested donation £2.50; ☺ 9am-6pm Mon-Sat, 1-2.30pm & 4.30-5.30pm Sun) Looming above the city centre, Bath's huge abbey church was built

Bath

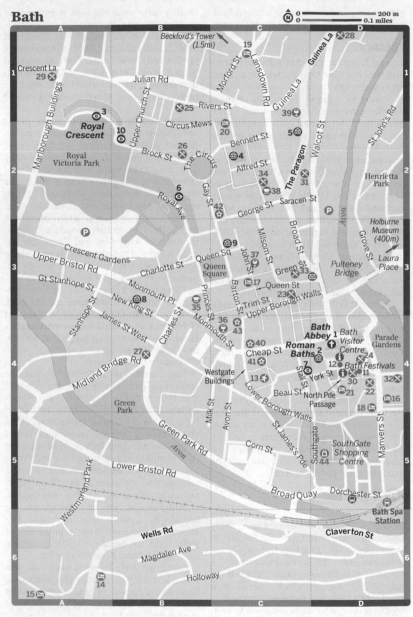

between 1499 and 1616, making it the last great medieval church raised in England. Its most striking feature is the west facade, where angels climb up and down stone ladders, commemorating a dream of the founder, Bishop Oliver King.

Tower tours (towertours@bathabbey.org; adult/child £6/3; ⏱11am-5pm Apr-Aug, to 4pm Sep-Oct, to 3pm Dec-Mar) leave on the hour from Monday to Friday, or every half-hour on Saturdays, but don't run on Sundays. Unfortunately, there's no way out of the 212

Bath

BATH & SOUTHWEST ENGLAND BATH

steps to the top, but the view's worth the slog. If you're feeling really romantic, you can also book a private tour for two.

On the abbey's southern side, the small **Vaults Heritage Museum** explores the abbey's history. Among those buried here are Sir Isaac Pitman (who devised Pitman shorthand) and the celebrated bon viveur Beau Nash.

Jane Austen Centre   MUSEUM
(☑ 01225-443000; www.janeausten.co.uk; 40 Gay St; adult/child £8/4.50; ☺ 9.45am-5.30pm) Bath is known to many as a location in Jane Austen's novels, including *Persuasion* and *Northanger Abbey*. Though Austen only lived in Bath for five years from 1801 to 1806, she remained a regular visitor, and a keen student of the city's social scene. This museum houses memorabilia relating to the writer's life in Bath, and there's a Regency tearoom which serves crumpets and cream teas in suitably frilly surroundings.

Herschel Museum of Astronomy   MUSEUM
(☑ 01225-446865; www.herschelmuseum.org.uk; 19 New King St; adult/child £6/3; ☺ 1-5pm Mon-Fri, 11am-5pm Sat & Sun) In 1781 astronomer William Herschel discovered Uranus from the garden of his home, now converted into a museum. The house is little changed since the 18th century; an astrolabe in the garden marks the position of Herschel's telescope.

★**Royal Crescent**   HISTORIC AREA
Bath is justifiably celebrated for its glorious Georgian architecture, and it doesn't get any grander than on Royal Crescent, a semicircular terrace of majestic town houses overlooking the green sweep of Royal Victoria Park. Designed by John Wood the Younger (1728–82) and built between 1767 and 1775, the houses appear perfectly symmetrical from the outside, but the owners were allowed to tweak the interiors to their own specifications; consequently no two houses on the Crescent are quite the same.

A walk east along Brock St from the Royal Crescent leads to the **Circus**, a ring of 33 houses divided into three semi-circular terraces. Plaques on the houses commemorate famous residents such as Thomas Gainsborough, Clive of India and David Livingstone.

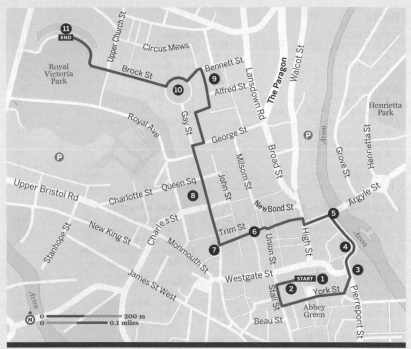

🏃 City Walk
Bath's Architecture

START BATH ABBEY
END ROYAL CRESCENT
LENGTH 1.5 MILES, TWO HOURS

Start this architectural amble at ❶ **Bath Abbey** (p321), the city's iconic ecclesiastical edifice, built on the site of an 8th-century chapel. From the abbey square, head south along Stall St for a view of the 19th-century ❷ **Pump Room** (p321). Turn left onto York St, and follow it west to ❸ **Parade Gardens**, a landscaped Victorian park framed by the River Avon.

From here, the Grand Parade leads north; look out for the building on the corner, ❹ **The Empire**, built as a luxurious hotel in 1901. At the northern end of the Grand Parade is ❺ **Pulteney Bridge**, designed by Robert Adams in 1773, and one of only a handful in the world to be lined with shops (the most famous example is Florence's Ponte Vecchio). West of the bridge, ❻ **Upper Borough Walls** marks the northern extent of medieval Bath; if you look closely, you might spot some sections of the medieval wall that remain.

At Saw Close, you'll see the elaborate facade of Bath's ❼ **Theatre Royal** (p329), which has been staging productions since 1805. From here, follow Barton St onto ❽ **Queen Square**, the oldest of Bath's Georgian squares, built as a showpiece development between 1728 and 1736 to demonstrate the talents of its architect, John Wood the Elder.

Turn north onto Gay St, and right onto George St. Next to the Porter pub, an alley leads north, emerging next to the ❾ **Assembly Rooms** (p325), the heart of Georgian Bath's social life. Continue to Bennett St and turn left until you reach the ❿ **Circus**, designed to echo the Colosseum in Rome. The three-tiered pillars exhibit the key styles of classical architecture (Doric, Ionic and Corinthian).

From here, Brock St leads west to Bath's Georgian glory, the ⓫ **Royal Crescent** (p323). Constructed by John Wood the Younger in 1774, the terrace is now Grade-I listed, making it as architecturally significant as Buckingham Palace. The elegant Royal Crescent Hotel is at number 16.

The terrace was designed by John Wood the Elder, but he died in 1754, and the terrace was completed by his son in 1768.

To the south along Gravel Walk is the Georgian Garden, restored to resemble a typical 18th-century town-house garden.

No 1 Royal Crescent HISTORIC HOUSE
(☑ 01225-428126; www.bath-preservation-trust.org.uk; 1 Royal Cres; adult/child/family £8.50/3.50/17; ☉ 10.30am-5pm Tue-Sun late Feb–mid-Dec) For a glimpse into the splendour and razzle-dazzle of Georgian life, head for the beautifully restored house at No 1 Royal Crescent, given to the city by the shipping magnate Major Bernard Cayzer, and since restored using only 18th-century materials. Among the rooms on display are the drawing room, several bedrooms and the huge kitchen, complete with massive hearth, roasting spit and mousetraps. Costumed guides provide historical background.

Bath Assembly Rooms HISTORIC BUILDING
(www.nationaltrust.org.uk/main/w-bathassembly rooms; 19 Bennett St; adult/child £2.50/free; ☉ 10.30am-6pm) Opened in 1771, the city's glorious Assembly Rooms were where fashionable Bath socialites once gathered to waltz, play cards and listen to the latest chamber music. Rooms open to the public include the card room, tearoom and ballroom, all lit by their original 18th-century chandeliers.

It's free to enter if you already have a ticket to the Fashion Museum.

Fashion Museum MUSEUM
(☑ 01225-477282; www.fashionmuseum.co.uk; Assembly Rooms, Bennett St; adult/child £8/6; ☉ 10.30am-5pm) In the basement of the Assembly Rooms, this museum contains costumes worn from the 16th to late-20th centuries. Exhibitions are changed annually, so check the website for the latest.

Building of Bath Museum MUSEUM
(☑ 01225-333895; www.bath-preservation-trust.org.uk; The Vineyards, The Paragon; adult/child £5/2.50; ☉ 2-5pm Tue-Fri, 10.30am-5pm Sat & Sun mid-Feb–Nov) This museum explores the story of Bath's architecture, with antique tools, displays on Georgian construction methods and a 1:500 scale model of Bath.

Holburne Museum GALLERY
(☑ 01225-388569; www.holburne.org; Great Pulteney St; ☉ 10am-5pm) **FREE** Sir William Holburne, the 18th-century aristocrat and art fanatic, amassed a huge collection that

now forms the core of the Holburne Museum, in a lavish mansion at the end of Great Pulteney St. Fresh from a three-year refit, the museum houses a roll-call of works by artists including Turner, Stubbs, William Hoare and Thomas Gainsborough, as well as 18th-century majollica and porcelain. Temporary exhibitions incur a fee.

Beckford's Tower HISTORIC BUILDING
(www.beckfordstower.org.uk; adult/child £4/1.50; ☉ 10.30am-5pm Sat & Sun Mar-Oct) Built as a study and library for the aristocrat William Beckford in 1827, this 39m neoclassical tower is worth visiting for its eye-popping panoramic view over Bath. A spiral staircase leads to the top-floor Belvedere, while a small collection of paintings and artefacts explores Beckford's eccentric life.

The tower is about 2 miles north of the Royal Crescent along Lansdown Rd.

American Museum in Britain MUSEUM
(☑ 01225-460503; www.americanmuseum.org; Claverton Manor; adult/child £9/5; ☉ noon-5pm) Britain's largest collection of American folk art, including First Nations textiles, patchwork quilts and historic maps, is housed in a fine mansion a couple of miles from the city centre. Several rooms have been decorated to resemble a 17th-century Puritan house, an 18th-century tavern and a New Orleans boudoir c 1860. Catch bus 18/418/U18 from the bus station.

🕴 Activities

Various cruise operators offer boat trips up and down the River Avon from Pulteney

WORTH A TRIP

PRIOR PARK
....

Partly designed by the landscape architect Capability Brown, the grounds of this **18th-century estate** (NT; ☎01225-833422; www.nationaltrust.org. uk/priorpark; Ralph Allen Dr; adult/child £6/3.30; ☺10am-5.30pm Feb-Nov) on Bath's southern fringe feature cascading lakes and a graceful **Palladian bridge**, one of only four such structures in the world (look out for the period graffiti, some of which dates back to the 1800s).

It was built by the entrepreneur Ralph Allen, who founded Britain's first postal service, and owned many of the local quarries from which the city's amber-coloured Bath stone was mined. The house itself is now occupied by a private school, but there are several lovely pathways around the estate, including the **Bath Skyline**, a 6-mile circular trail offering truly inspirational views.

The park is a mile south of Bath's centre. Bus 2 (every 10 minutes) stops nearby, as does the Bath City Sightseeing's 'City Skyline' tour (p326).

Bridge, including **Pulteney Cruisers** (☎01225-312900; www.bathboating.com; adult/child £8/4), the **Pulteney Princess** (☎07791-910650; www.pulteneyprincess.co.uk; adult/child £8/4) and **Bath City Boat Trips** (☎07974-560197; www.bathcityboattrips.com; adult/child £8/4). There's not much difference between the tours; most last around an hour. Depending on the season, there's at least one boat an hour, or more during peak holiday times.

★**Thermae Bath Spa**　　　　SPA
(☎0844 888 0844; www.thermaebathspa.com; Bath St; ☺9am-10pm, last entry 7.30pm) Taking a dip in the Roman Baths might be off limits, but you can still sample the city's curative waters at this fantastic modern spa complex, housed in a shell of local stone and plate glass. Tickets include steam rooms, waterfall showers and a choice of two swimming pools. The showpiece attraction is the open-air rooftop pool, where you can bathe with a backdrop of Bath's cityscape – a mustn't-miss experience, best appreciated at dusk.

Bathwick Boating Station　　BOATING
(☎01225-312900; www.bathboating.co.uk; Forrester Rd; 1st hr adult/child £7/3.50, additional hr £4/2;

☺10am-6pm Easter-Oct) You can pilot your own vessel down the Avon from this Victorian-era boathouse, which rents out traditional skiffs, rowboats and Canadian canoes. It's in the suburb of Bathwick, a 20-minute walk northeast from the city centre.

⚲ Tours

Mayor's Guide Tours　　　WALKING TOUR
(☎01225-477411; www.bathguides.org.uk; ☺10.30am & 2pm Sun-Fri, 10.30am Sat) **FREE** Excellent historical tours provided free by the Mayor's Corp of Honorary guides, leaving from outside the Pump Room. There are extra tours at 7pm on Tuesdays and Thursdays May to September. They cover about 2 miles and are wheelchair accessible.

Jane Austen's Bath　　　WALKING TOUR
(☎01225-443000; www.janeausten.co.uk/jane-austen-centre-walking-tours; adult/child £12/10; ☺11am Sat & Sun) A guided tour of the Georgian city, organised by the Jane Austen Centre. The 1½-hour tours leave from the Abbey churchyard.

Bizarre Bath Comedy Walk　　WALKING TOUR
(☎01225-335124; www.bizarrebath.co.uk; adult/student £8/5; ☺8pm Mar-Oct) Daft city tour mixing street theatre and live performance. Leaves from outside the Huntsman Inn on North Parade Passage. Most of the walk is wheelchair accessible.

Bath City Sightseeing　　　BUS TOUR
(☎01225-330444; www.city-sightseeing.com; adult/child £14/8; ☺9.30am-6.30pm Mar-Nov) Hop-on/hop-off city tour on an open-topped bus, with commentary in seven languages.

✲✲ Festivals & Events

Bath has lots of festivals. All bookings are handled by **Bath Festivals** (☎01225-463362; www.bathfestivals.org.uk; 2 Church St; ☺9.30am-5.30pm Mon-Sat).

Bath Literature Festival　　BOOK FESTIVAL
(www.bathlitfest.org.uk) Major book festival in late February or early March.

Bath International Music Festival　　MUSIC FESTIVAL
(www.bathmusicfest.org.uk) Mainly classical and opera, plus smaller gigs of jazz, folk and world. Mid-May to early June.

Bath Fringe Festival　　THEATRE FESTIVAL
(www.bathfringe.co.uk) Major theatre festival around mid-May to early June.

🛏 Sleeping

Bath gets very busy in the height of summer, when prices are at a premium. Few hotels have on-site parking, although some offer discounted rates at municipal car parks.

Bath YHA   HOSTEL £

(🖉 0845 371 9303; www.yha.org.uk; Bathwick Hill; dm £13-20, d from £29; ☺ reception 7am-11pm; 🅿 @ 🛜) Split across an Italianate mansion and a modern annexe, this impressive hostel is a steep climb (or a short hop on bus 18) from the city centre. The listed building means the rooms are huge, and some have period features such as cornicing and bay windows.

Grays Boutique B&B   B&B ££

(🖉 01225-403020; www.graysbath.co.uk; Upper Oldfield Park; d £120-195; 🛜) An elegant B&B straight out of an interiors magazine. All the rooms are individual: some with feminine flowers or polka-dot prints, others with maritime stripes, but all simple and stylish (we particularly liked Room Two, with its French bed and bay window). Breakfast is served in the conservatory, with eggs, milk and bacon from local farms.

The owners run a smaller but equally smart B&B on the east side of town, **Brindleys** (🖉 01225-310444; www.brindleysbath.co.uk; 14 Pulteney Gardens; d £110-185).

139 Bath   B&B ££

(🖉 01225-314769; www.139bath.co.uk; 139 Wells Rd; r £125-195; 🅿 🛜) It's a bit out of the centre, but this swish B&B has been thoughtfully designed, with swirly fabrics and supremely comfy beds, plus spoils such as cafetière coffee and spa baths in some rooms. Posh, but perhaps pricey for what you get.

Hill House Bath   B&B ££

(🖉 01225-920520; www.hillhousebath.co.uk; 25 Belvedere; s £85, d £110-140) This six-room B&B feels like staying with friends. Renovated in 2011, its decor showcases the quirky tastes of its owners – dog-print cushions, retro pictures and objets d'art abound. Breakfast is served buffet style by owner Douglas – ask him to show you the house's wine cellars. On-street parking permits available.

Henry   B&B ££

(🖉 01225-424052; www.thehenry.com; 6 Henry St; d £95-125, f £155-165; 🛜) This tall town house has one of the best positions in Bath, literally steps from the centre. Seven rooms and a self-catering apartment are finished in crisp whites and smooth beiges, and offer decent value considering the location, but there's no parking, and the house's architecture means some rooms feel cramped. Two-night minimum stay at weekends.

Three Abbey Green   B&B ££

(🖉 01225-428558; www.threeabbeygreen.com; 3 Abbey Green; d £100-160; 🛜) You literally can't get more central – step out of the front door and you're on the abbey's doorstep. It's on a leafy square, and the house has an old-fashioned, country house feel, with original fireplaces and armchairs; three rooms are named after Jane Austen characters. The suites have adjoining singles, ideal for families.

★ Queensberry Hotel   HOTEL £££

(🖉 01225-447928; www.thequeensberry.co.uk; 4 Russell St; d £115-225; 🅿 🛜) The quirky Queensberry is Bath's best boutique spoil. Four Georgian town houses have been combined into one seamlessly stylish whole. Some rooms are cosy in gingham checks and country creams, others feature bright upholstery, original fireplaces and free-standing tubs. The Olive Tree Restaurant is excellent, too. Rates exclude breakfast.

★ Halcyon   HOTEL £££

(🖉 01225-444100; www.thehalcyon.com; 2/3 South Pde; d £125-145; 🛜) Just what Bath needed: a smart city-centre hotel that doesn't break the bank. Situated on a terrace of town houses off Manvers St, the Halcyon offers style on a budget: uncluttered rooms, contemporary bed linen and Philippe Starck bath fittings.

Rooms vary in size and are spread out over three floors – inconvenient as there's no lift. Self-catering apartments (£150 to £300 per night) are also available in a separate building at 15a George St.

Haringtons Hotel   HOTEL £££

(🖉 01225-461278; www.haringtonshotel.co.uk; Queen St; d £148-200) Bath's classical trappings aren't to everyone's taste, so things are kept strictly modern at this city-centre crash pad, with searingly bright colour schemes and clashing wallpapers giving it a fun, young vibe. The location is fantastic, but there's no lift and some rooms are shoebox-sized. Off-site parking costs £11.

🍴 Eating

Many bakeries and cafes serve the city's famous 'Bath Bun', somewhere between a brioche and a bread, and not to be confused with the London Bath Bun, which is small and sweet.

There's a Saturday morning food market at **Green Park Station** (Green Park; ⊘8am-1pm), where you can pick up local cheeses, meats and ciders, plus bread from the **Thoughtful Bread Company** (www.thethoughtfulbreadcompany.com; Green Park Railway Station; ⊘9am-6pm Tue-Sat).

Sam's Kitchen Deli   CAFE £
(☑01225-481159; www.samskitchendeli.co.uk; 61 Walcot St; lunch £8-10; ⊘8am-5pm Mon-Sat, to 10pm every 2nd Fri) Situated on Bath's hippest street, Sam's is a perfect lunch spot, with set dishes (including a daily roast) served from pans on the counter. With its dilapidated piano and reclaimed furniture, it's the epitome of a shabby-chic cafe, and very popular. There are live gigs every other Friday.

Bertinet Bakery   BAKERY, CAFE £
(www.bertinet.com/bertinetbakery; 6 New Bond St Pl; ⊘8am-6pm Mon-Sat, 10.30am-4pm Sun) Renowned baker Richard Bertinet now has his own cafe in Bath, where you can try his feather-light cakes and French-inspired pastries. He also runs a bakery school off George St.

Café Retro   CAFE £
(☑01225-339347; 18 York St; mains £5-11; ⊘9am-5pm Mon-Sat, 10am-5pm Sun) A poke in the eye for the corporate coffee chains. The paint job's scruffy, the crockery's ancient and none of the furniture matches, but that's all part of the charm: this is a cafe from the old school, and there's nowhere better for burgers, butties or cake. Takeaways (in biodegradable containers) are available from Retro-to-Go next door.

Sally Lunn's   TEAROOM £
(4 North Pde Passage; mains £5-15; ⊘10am-9pm) Eating a bun at Sally Lunn's is just one of those things you have to do in Bath. It's all about proper English tea here, brewed in bone-china teapots, with finger sandwiches and dainty cakes served by waitresses in frilly aprons.

The trademark Sally Lunn's Bun is the house speciality – but there are heartier plates too, such as Welsh rarebit and 'Trencher' dishes (with the 'bun' acting as plate).

★ Circus   MODERN BRITISH ££
(☑01225-466020; www.thecircuscafeandrestaurant.co.uk; 34 Brock St; mains lunch £8.30-13.50, dinner £16.50-18.50; ⊘10am-10pm Mon-Sat) Chef Ali Golden has turned this bistro into one of Bath's destination addresses. Her taste is for British dishes with a continental twist, à la Elizabeth David: rabbit, guinea-fowl, roast chicken, spring lamb, infused with herby flavours and rich sauces. It occupies the ground floor and basement of a town house near the Circus. Reservations recommended.

Tasting Room   TAPAS ££
(☑01225-483070; www.tastingroom.co.uk; 6 Green St; 3-course tapas £10; ⊘10am-4.30pm Sun & Mon, 9.30am-11pm Tue-Sat) Plates of tapas and high-class vintages are the *modus operandi* of this slinky cafe-bar, located above Bath's premier wine merchant.

Marlborough Tavern   GASTROPUB ££
(☑01225-423731; www.marlborough-tavern.com; 35 Marlborough Bldgs; lunch £9-13, dinner mains £13.50-21.50; ⊘noon-11pm) The queen of Bath's gastropubs, with food that's closer to a fine-dining restaurant – think duo of venison and pork tenderloin rather than bog-standard meat-and-two-veg. Chunky wooden tables and racks of wine behind the bar give it an exclusive, classy feel.

Sotto Sotto   ITALIAN ££
(☑01225-330236; www.sottosotto.co.uk; 10a North Pde; pasta £9, mains £13-17; ⊘noon-2.30pm & 5-10.30pm) Bath's best Italian, hidden away in a vaulted cellar. Ingredients are shipped in from Italy and everything's just like mamma made, from the classic house lasagne to more unusual options such as veal, grilled swordfish and sea bass in Parma ham.

Chequers   GASTROPUB ££
(☑01225-360017; www.thechequersbar.com; 50 Rivers St; lunch mains £6.95-13.50, dinner £14.50-21.95; ⊘noon-11pm) A local's favourite, this pub has been in business since 1776, but the menu is bang up-to-date thanks to young chef Leigh Evans. Forget bangers and mash – here it's Bath chorizo and spring onion champ. You'll need to book for Sunday lunch.

Yen Sushi   JAPANESE ££
(11-12 Bartlett St; sushi £4-6; ⊘noon-3pm & 5.30-10.30pm) Bath's own *kaiten* (conveyor-belt) restaurant, with colour-coded dishes of nigiri, sushi and sashimi.

Hudson Steakhouse   STEAKHOUSE £££
(☑01225-332323; www.hudsonbars.com; 14 London St; steaks £22-34; ⊘5-10.30pm) Steak, steak and more steak is this place's raison d'être. Tuck into top-quality cuts from porterhouse to prime fillet, all sourced from a Staffordshire farmers' co-op.

Allium
MODERN BRITISH £££

(☑01225-805870; www.alliumbrasserie.co.uk; North Pde; 2-/3-course lunch £17.50/23, dinner mains £16.50-21; ☺noon-3pm & 5.30-9pm) It's not often you find Michelin-level dining inside a Best Western – but that's what you get at the Abbey Hotel, where renowned chef Chris Staines is in charge. This is serious fine dining, awash with emulsions and purées and foams, blending Asian and European flavours.

Menu Gordon Jones
MODERN BRITISH £££

(☑01225-480871; www.menugordonjones.co.uk; 2 Wellsway; 5-course lunch £40, 6-course dinner £50; ☺12.30-2pm & 7-9pm Tue-Sat) If you enjoy dining with an element of surprise, then Gordon Jones' restaurant will be right up your culinary boulevard. Menus are dreamt up daily by the chef, and showcase his taste for experimental ingredients (candied citrus, cod tongues, biodynamic wines) and madcap presentation (test tubes, edible cups, slate plates). It's superb value given the skill on show. Reservations essential.

🍷 Drinking & Nightlife

⭐Colonna & Smalls
CAFE

(www.colonnaandsmalls.co.uk; 6 Chapel Row; ☺8am-5.30pm Mon-Sat, 10am-4pm Sun) This is a connoisseur's coffee house. The espressos and cappuccinos are, quite simply, second to none – so if you care about your caffeine, you won't want to miss it. Proper coffee nuts can even take a barista training course.

⭐Star Inn
PUB

(www.star-inn-bath.co.uk; 23 The Vineyards, off The Paragon; ☺noon-11pm) Not many pubs are registered relics, but the Star is – it still has many of its 19th-century bar fittings. It's the brewery tap for Bath-based Abbey Ales; some ales are served in traditional jugs, and you can even ask for a pinch of snuff in the 'smaller bar'.

Same Same But Different
CAFE, BAR

(7a Prince's Bldgs, Bartlett St; ☺8am-6pm Mon-Wed, to 11pm Thu-Sat, 10am-5pm Sun) Boho hang-out for the town's trendies, tucked down an alley off George St. Savour wine by the glass, snack on tapas or sip a cappuccino with the Sunday papers.

Door 34
COCKTAIL BAR

(www.door34.co.uk; 34 Monmouth St; cocktails from £8; ☺from 7pm) This cocktail bar touts itself as a 'liquid alchemist's lounge', and it certainly mixes a mean martini.

Salamander
PUB

(☑01225-428889; www.bathales.com/pubs/salamander.html; 3 John St; mains £10-14; ☺10am-midnight Mon-Thu, to 1am Fri & Sat, to 11pm Sun) Owned by Bath Ales, the Sally serves in-house beers such as amber Gem and Golden Hare and the stronger, darker Rare Hare. There's an upstairs supper club.

☆ Entertainment

Moles
LIVE MUSIC

(www.moles.co.uk; 14 George St) Bath's main music venue suffered a serious fire in March 2014; it was closed at the time of writing, and won't reopen until 2015 at the earliest.

Theatre Royal
THEATRE

(www.theatreroyal.org.uk; Sawclose) Bath's historic theatre dates back 200 years. Major touring productions go in the main auditorium, while smaller shows appear in the Ustinov Studio.

Komedia
CABARET, COMEDY

(www.komedia.co.uk; 22-23 Westgate St) Live comedy and cabaret at this Bath offshoot of the Brighton-based original.

Little Theatre Cinema
CINEMA

(St Michael's Pl) Bath's excellent art-house cinema screens fringe films as well as foreign-language flicks.

🔒 Shopping

Bath's main shopping centre is Southgate (www.southgatebath.com), where you'll find all the major chain stores.

Smaller shops tend to be situated north from the centre. Milsom St is good for up-market fashion, while Walcot St is lined by quirky independent food shops, design stores and vintage clothing retailers.

ℹ Information

Bath Visitor Centre (☑0906 711 2000, accommodation bookings 0844 847 5256; www.visitbath.co.uk; Abbey Churchyard; ☺9.30am-5pm Mon-Sat, 10am-4pm Sun) Sells the Bath Visitor Card (p325). The general enquiries line is charged at the premium rate of 50p per minute.

Main Post Office (27 Northgate St)

Police Station (Manvers St; ☺7am-midnight)

ℹ Getting There & Away

BUS

Bath's **bus and coach station** (Dorchester St; ☺9am-5pm Mon-Sat) is near the train station.

National Express coaches run direct to London (£17, 3½ hours, eight to 10 daily) via Heathrow. Services to most other destinations change at Bristol or Heathrow.

Local buses:

Bristol (£5.50, 50 minutes, four per hour Monday to Saturday, half-hourly on Sunday) Bus X39/339.

Wells (£5.50, one hour 10 minutes, hourly Monday to Saturday, five on Sunday) Bus 173.

TRAIN

Bath Spa station is at the end of Manvers St. Many services connect through Bristol, especially to the north of England.

Direct services include:

Bristol (£7.10, 15 minutes, several per hour)

Cardiff Central (£19.40, one hour, hourly)

Exeter (£32, 1¼ hours, hourly)

London Paddington (£42, 1½ hours, half-hourly)

Salisbury (£16.90, one hour, hourly)

ⓘ Getting Around

BICYCLE

Bath's hills make getting around by bike challenging, but the canal paths along the Kennet and Avon Canal and the 13-mile Bristol & Bath Railway Path (p319) are great to explore by bike.

Bath Bike Hire (☑ 01225-447276; www.bath-narrowboats.co.uk/bathbikehirecom; Sydney Wharf; half/full day £13/19; ☺9am-11pm) Ten minutes' walk from the centre. Handy for the canal and railway paths.

Bath by Cycle (☑ 01225-807881; www.bathbycycle.com; 3 George's Pl; bike rental from £5; ☺9am-6pm) Rents standard and electric bikes.

BUS

Bus 18 runs from the bus station, High St and Great Pulteney St up Bathwick Hill past the YHA to the university every 10 minutes. Bus 4 runs every 20 minutes to Bathampton.

CAR & MOTORCYCLE

Bath has serious traffic problems, especially at rush hour. **Park & Ride services** (☑ 01225-464446; return Mon-Fri £3, Sat £2.50; ☺6.15am-7.30pm Mon-Sat) operate from Lansdown to the north, Newbridge to the west and Odd Down to the south. It takes about 10 minutes to the centre; buses leave every 10 to 15 minutes.

The best-value car park is underneath the SouthGate shopping centre (two/eight hours £3.30/10, after 6pm £2).

SOMERSET

With its pastoral landscape of hedgerows, fields and hummocked hills, sleepy Somerset is the very picture of the rural English countryside, and makes the perfect escape from the bustle of Bath and the hustle of Bristol. Things certainly move at a drowsier pace around these parts – it's a place to wander, ponder and drink in the sights at your leisure. The cathedral city of Wells is a handy base for exploring the limestone caves and gorges around Cheddar, while the hippie haven of Glastonbury is handy for venturing onto the wetlands of the Somerset Levels and the high hills of the Quantocks.

ⓘ Information

Somerset Visitor Centre (☑ 01934-750833; www.visitsomerset.co.uk; Sedgemoor Services M5 South; ☺9.15am-5pm daily Easter-Oct, Mon-Fri Nov-Easter)

Visit South Somerset (www.visitsouthsomerset.co.uk)

ⓘ Getting Around

Most buses in Somerset are operated by **First** (☑ 08456 064446; www.firstgroup.com). For timetables and general information contact **Traveline South West** (www.travelinesw.com).

Key train services link Bath, Bristol, Bridgwater, Taunton and Weston-super-Mare. The M5 heads south past Bristol, to Bridgwater and Taunton, with the A39 leading west across the Quantocks to Exmoor.

Wells & Around

POP 10,406

In Wells, small is beautiful. This is England's smallest city, and only qualifies for the title thanks to a magnificent medieval cathedral, which sits beside the grand Bishop's Palace – the official residence of the Bishop of Bath and Wells since the 12th century. Medieval buildings and cobbled streets radiate out from the cathedral green to a marketplace that has been the bustling heart of Wells for some nine centuries (Wednesday and Saturday are market days). Film buffs might also recognise it from the hit British comedy, *Hot Fuzz* – the film's final shootout was filmed here.

◉ Sights

Wells Cathedral   CATHEDRAL
(Cathedral Church of St Andrew; www.wellscathedral.org.uk; Cathedral Green; requested donation

adult/child £6/3; ⊙7am-7pm) Wells' gargantuan Gothic cathedral sits plum in the centre of the city, surrounded by one of the largest cathedral closes anywhere in England. It was built in stages between 1180 and 1508, and consequently showcases several Gothic styles. Among its notable features are the **West Front**, decorated with more than 300 carved figures, and the famous **scissor arches** – an ingenious architectural solution to counter the subsidence of the central tower.

In the north transept is a **mechanical clock** dating from 1392 – the second oldest in England after the one at Salisbury Cathedral – which shows the position of the planets and the phases of the moon.

Other highlights include the elegant **Lady Chapel** (1326), the fan-vaulted **Chapter House** (1306) and the celebrated **chained library**, which contains books and manuscripts dating back to 1472. Outside, the covered cloister known as the **Chain Bridge** enabled clerics to reach the cathedral without getting their robes wet.

Free guided tours run every hour from Monday to Saturday, but you'll need a photography permit (£3) to take pictures.

Cathedral Close HISTORIC SITE
Wells Cathedral forms the centrepiece of a cluster of ecclesiastical buildings dating back to the Middle Ages. Facing the west front, on the left are the 15th-century **Old Deanery** and the **Wells & Mendip Museum** (www.wellsmuseum.org.uk; 8 Cathedral Green; adult/child £3/1; ⊙10am-5.30pm Easter-Oct, 11am-4pm Wed-Mon Nov-Easter), with exhibits on local life, cathedral architecture and the infamous Witch of Wookey Hole.

Further along, **Vicars' Close** is a stunning 14th-century cobbled street, with a chapel at the end; members of the cathedral choir still live here. It is thought to be the oldest complete medieval street in Europe.

Penniless Porch, a corner gate leading onto Market Sq, is so-called because beggars asked for alms here.

Bishop's Palace HISTORIC BUILDING
(www.bishopspalacewells.co.uk; adult/child £7/3; ⊙10am-6pm Apr-Oct, to 4pm Nov-Mar) Built for the bishop in the 13th century, this moat-ringed palace is purportedly the oldest inhabited building in England. Inside, the palace's state rooms and ruined great hall are worth a look, but it's the gardens that are the real draw. The natural springs after which Wells is named bubble up in the palace's grounds.

Famously, the palace's population of mute swans have been trained to ring a bell when they want to be fed.

Guided tours are included in the admission price and run at 11.30am and 2.30pm during summer.

Wookey Hole CAVE
(www.wookey.co.uk; adult/child £18/12; ⊙10am-5pm Apr-Oct, 10.30am-4pm Nov-Mar) On the edge of the Mendip Hills, the River Axe has gouged out deep limestone caverns collectively known as Wookey Hole. They're famous for their stalagmites and stalactites, one of which is the legendary Witch of Wookey Hole, who was turned to stone by a local priest. Admission to the caves is by guided tour, while up on top you'll find tacky tourist attractions ranging from a penny arcade to a mirror maze. Wookey Hole is 3 miles northwest of Wells; look out for brown signs on the A371.

At weekends, you might even be greeted by the witch herself. Tickets remain valid for the whole day, and there's a 15% discount for booking online.

Cheddar Gorge CAVE
(www.cheddargorge.co.uk; Explorer Ticket adult/child £18.50/12; ⊙10am-5.30pm) Carved out by glacial meltwater during the last Ice Age, the limestone cliffs of Cheddar Gorge form England's deepest natural canyon, in places towering 138m above the twisting B3135. Beneath the cliffs, the gorge is riddled with miles of subterranean caves. **Cox's Cave** and **Gough's Cave** are the easiest to reach, decorated with impressive displays of stalactites and stalagmites, but you'll need to sign up for a caving trip (p332) if you want to venture deeper underground. The gorge begins about 20 miles northwest of Wells on the A371.

The Cheddar caves have been inhabited since the last Ice Age; a 9000-year-old skeleton (imaginatively named Cheddar Man) was discovered here in 1903, although carbon dating has suggested Gough's Cave was inhabited several thousand years earlier. Rumours of prehistoric cannibalism also seem to have been confirmed by recent discoveries of polished human skulls that are believed to have been used as drinking vessels.

Cheddar is very popular, so expect traffic during summer and school holidays. You can escape the crowds by climbing the 274-step staircase known as **Jacob's Ladder**, which leads to a spectacular viewpoint over the gorge and a 3-mile clifftop trail. There's a 15% discount for online booking.

Cheddar Gorge
Cheese Company
CHEESEMAKER

(☑ 01934-742810; www.cheddargorgecheeseco.co.uk; adult/child £2.25/free; ⊙ 10am-5pm Easter-Oct) Along with its caves, Cheddar is also famous as the home of the nation's favourite cheese, produced here since the 12th century (Henry II considered it 'the best cheese in Britain', and the king's accounts from 1170 record that he purchased 10,240lb of the stuff). Take a guided tour at this cheesemaker and purchase top-quality cheddars at the shop.

🏃 Activities

X-Treme
ADVENTURE SPORTS

(☑ 01934-742343; www.cheddargorge.co.uk/x-treme; 1½-hr trip adult/child £21/19) The Cheddar Gorge's main outdoors company offers guided caving trips lasting around 1½ hours. Inevitably you'll get wet and dirty, and it might not be a great idea if you're averse to small spaces. Rock-climbing trips are also available.

🛏 Sleeping

Beryl
B&B ££

(☑ 01749-678738; www.beryl-wells.co.uk; Hawkers Lane; d £100-150; P 🐾) This grand gabled mansion offers a taste of English eccentricity. Every inch of the house is crammed with antique atmosphere, and the rooms boast grandfather clocks, chaises longues and four-posters galore. It's about a mile from Wells.

Swan Hotel
HOTEL ££

(☑ 01749-836300; www.swanhotelwells.co.uk; Sadler St; d £100-149) A former coaching inn that's a distinct cut above your average Best Western. The building's part-15th-century architecture is packed with period detail, and many rooms have views across the cathedral green – although square footage can be variable, so it might be worth viewing a few before you settle.

Ancient Gate House Hotel
HOTEL ££

(☑ 01749-672029; www.ancientgatehouse.co.uk; Browne's Gate; s £90-100, d £110-130; 🛜) This old hostelry is partly built right into the cathedral's west gate. Rooms are decorated in regal reds and duck-egg blues; the best have four-poster beds and knockout cathedral views through latticed windows. They're £15 extra, but worth it.

Stoberry House
B&B ££

(☑ 01749-672906; www.stoberryhouse.co.uk; Stoberry Park; d £85-145; P 🛜) Just outside the city outskirts, this modern house offers a swanky B&B experience: plush cushions and swags above the beds in the rooms, plus a guest lounge with books to browse and Nespresso coffee on tap.

🍴 Eating

Good Earth
VEGETARIAN £

(☑ 01749-678600; www.thegoodearthwells.co.uk; 4-6 Priory Rd; lunch £8-12; ⊙ 9am-4.30pm) A wholefood store that's branched out into homewares and a fantastic veggie cafe, which offers two daily dishes in a sunny dining room or a secret patio garden.

Strangers with Coffee
CAFE £

(31 St Cuthbert St; cakes £2-5; ⊙ 10am-5.30pm Mon-Sat) This little cafe does the best flat white in town, and has a tempting selection of cakes to match.

Old Spot
BRITISH ££

(☑ 01749-689099; www.theoldspot.co.uk; 12 Sadler St; lunch £18.50, dinner mains £14-21.50; ⊙ 12.30-2.30pm Wed-Sun, 7-9.30pm Tue-Sat) Run by husband-and-wife team Ian and Clare Bates, this restaurant focuses on British classics with a streak of Italian spice – rump of lamb with polenta and peperonata, or guinea-fowl with risotto.

Goodfellows
BISTRO, CAFE £££

(☑ 01749-673866; www.goodfellows.co.uk; 5 Sadler St) There's a choice of settings at Goodfellows: a continental-style cafe (lunch £10-17, dinner £20-25; ⊙ 8.30am-4pm Mon & Tue, 8.30am-5pm & 6-10pm Wed-Sat) for quick lunches, cakes and pastries, or a full-blown seafood bistro (3-/6-course menu £42/55; ⊙ noon-2pm Tue-Sat, 6.30-9.30pm Wed-Sat) for sit-down dining. The quality at both is excellent.

ℹ Information

Tourist office (☑ 01749-672552; www.wellstourism.com; Market Pl; ⊙ 9.30am-5.30pm Apr-Oct, 10am-4pm Nov-Mar) Stocks the *Wells City Trail* leaflet (30p) and sells discount tickets to Wookey Hole and Cheddar Gorge.

ℹ Getting There & Away

The bus station is south of Cuthbert St, on Princes Rd. Useful services:

Bath (£5.50, 1¼ hours, hourly Monday to Saturday, five on Sunday) Bus 173.

Bristol (£5.50, one hour, half-hourly Monday to Saturday, hourly on Sunday) Bus 376.

Cheddar (£4.50, 25 minutes, hourly Monday to Saturday, four on Sunday) Bus 126; continues to Weston-super-Mare (£5.50, 1½ hours).

Glastonbury (£3.50, 15 minutes, several per hour) Bus 377.

Taunton (day rover £10, 1¼ hours, hourly Monday to Saturday) Bus 29 stops in Glastonbury.

Glastonbury

POP 8429

Ley lines converge, white witches convene and every shop is filled with the aroma of smouldering joss-sticks in good old Glastonbury, the southwest's undisputed capital of alternative culture. Now famous for its annual musical mudfest held on Michael Eavis' farm in nearby Pilton, Glastonbury has a much more ancient past: the town's iconic tor was an important pagan site, and is rumoured by some to be the mythical Isle of Avalon, King Arthur's last resting place. It's also allegedly one of the world's great spiritual nodes, marking the meeting point of many mystical lines of power – so if you feel the need to get your chakras realigned, this is definitely the place. Whatever the truth of the various legends swirling round Glastonbury, one thing's for certain – watching the sunrise from the top of the tor is an experience you won't forget in a hurry.

⊙ Sights

★ **Glastonbury Tor** LANDMARK

(NT; www.nationaltrust.org.uk/glastonbury-tor) Topped by the ruined medieval **Chapel of St Michael**, the iconic hump of Glastonbury Tor is visible for miles around, and provides Somerset with one of its most unmistakable landmarks. It takes half an hour to walk up from the start of the trail on Well House Lane; the steepest sections are stepped. You can walk to the trailhead from the town centre in about 20 minutes, or catch the regular Tor Bus, which shuttles from Dunstan's car park near the Abbey to the trailhead on Well House Lane.

The tor is the focal point for a wealth of local legends. According to Celtic legend, the tor is the home of Arawn or Gwyn ap Nudd, king of the Underworld and lord of the faeries. A more famous legend identifies the tor as the mythic Isle of Avalon, where King Arthur was taken after being mortally wounded in battle, and where Britain's 'once and future king' sleeps until his country calls again. Others believe that the Tor marks an ancient mystical node where invisible lines of energy known as ley lines converge.

It's easy to see why the tor has inspired so many myths. It's a strange presence in an

BATH & SOUTHWEST ENGLAND GLASTONBURY

GLASTONBURY FESTIVAL

To many people, Glastonbury is synonymous with the **Glastonbury Festival of Contemporary Performing Arts** (www.glastonburyfestivals.co.uk), a majestic (and frequently mud-soaked) extravaganza of music, theatre, dance, cabaret, carnival, spirituality and general all-round weirdness that's been held on and off on farmland in Pilton, just outside Glastonbury, for the last 40-something years (bar the occasional off-year to let the farm recover).

The first event was held in 1970, when young dairy farmer Michael Eavis decided to stage his own British version of Woodstock on his land at Worthy Farm. Eavis borrowed £15,000 and invited some bands to play on a couple of makeshift stages in a field. Entry was £1, which included a pint of milk from Eavis' dairy herd; among the acts who performed was Marc Bolan of T-Rex, who arrived in typically flamboyant style in his own velvet-covered Buick.

Forty years later, the festival has become the world's longest-running pop-music festival, attracting crowds of more than 120,000. It's even had a feature-length film made about it, directed by Julien Temple. Eavis' daughter Emily has since taken over the day-to-day-running of the festival, and her decision to give headline slots to artists such as Jay-Z and U2 has led many people to grumble that Glastonbury's gone mainstream – but with acts such as the Rolling Stones and the Arctic Monkeys still lining up to play, Glastonbury's status as the UK's premier outdoor party looks safe for years to come.

More importantly, even the local councillors seem to have come around; after years of wrangling, in 2014 the festival was granted an unprecedented 10-year licence, a sign that the powers-that-be have recognised the festival's status as a national treasure. Tickets (which cost £210 in 2014) usually go on sale in the autumn, but always sell out within a matter of minutes, so you need to get in lightning-quick if you want to go.

Glastonbury

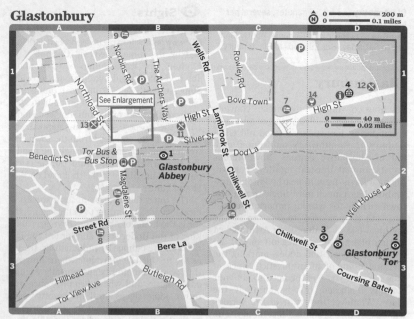

Glastonbury

◎ Top Sights
1 Glastonbury Abbey	B2
2 Glastonbury Tor	D3

◎ Sights
3 Chalice Well & Gardens	D3
4 Lake Village Museum	D1
5 White Spring	D3

⊜ Sleeping
6 Covenstead	B2
7 Crown Glastonbury Backpackers	C1
8 Glastonbury Townhouse	A3
9 Glastonbury White House	B1
10 Parsnips	C2

⊗ Eating
11 Hundred Monkeys Cafe	B2
12 Rainbow's End	D1
13 Who'd a Thought It Inn	A2

⊜ Drinking & Nightlife
14 George & Pilgrim	D1

otherwise pan-flat landscape, and in ancient times (when the area around Glastonbury was covered by water for much of the year), the Tor would indeed have appeared as an island, wreathed in mists and cut off by rivers, marshes and bogs.

Chalice Well & Gardens   GARDENS
(☎01458-831154; www.chalicewell.org.uk; adult/child £4/2; ☺10am-6pm Apr-Oct, to 4.30pm Nov-Mar) Shaded by yew trees and criss-crossed by quiet paths, the Chalice Well and Gardens have been sites of pilgrimage since the days of the Celts. The iron-red waters from the 800-year-old well are rumoured to have healing properties, good for everything from eczema to smelly feet; some legends also identify the well as the hiding place of the Holy Grail. In fact, the reddish waters are caused by iron deposits in the soil. You can drink the water from a lion's-head spout, or rest your feet in basins surrounded by flowers.

The Chalice Well is also known as the 'Red Spring' or 'Blood Spring'; its sister, **White Spring**, surfaces across Well House Lane.

★Glastonbury Abbey   RUIN
(☎01458-832267; www.glastonburyabbey.com; Magdalene St; adult/child £6/4; ☺9am-8pm) The scattered ruins of Glastonbury Abbey give little hint that this was once one of England's great seats of ecclesiastical power. It was torn down following Henry VIII's dissolution of the monasteries in 1539, and the last abbot, Richard Whiting, was hung, drawn and quartered on the tor. Precious little now remains save for a few nave walls, the ruined

St Mary's chapel, and the crossing arches, which may have been scissor-shaped like those in Wells Cathedral.

The grounds also contain a **museum**, **cider orchard** and **herb garden**. According to legend, the abbey's famous holy thorn tree sprang from the staff of Joseph of Arimathea, Jesus' great-uncle, who supposedly visited the abbey following Christ's death. It blooms at Christmas and Easter.

The abbey even has an Arthurian connection. In the 12th century, monks purportedly uncovered a tomb in the abbey grounds inscribed *Hic iacet sepultus inclitus rex arturius in insula avalonia*, or 'Here lies buried the renowned King Arthur in the Isle of Avalon'. Inside the tomb were two entwined skeletons, supposedly those of Arthur and his wife Guinevere. The bones were reburied beneath the altar in 1278, but were lost following the abbey's destruction.

Lake Village Museum MUSEUM
(The Tribunal, 9 High St; adult/child £3/1.50; ⊙10am-3pm) Upstairs from Glastonbury's tourist office, the Lake Village Museum displays finds from a prehistoric bog village discovered in nearby Godney. The houses were clustered in about six groups and built from reeds, hazel and willow. It's thought they were occupied by summer traders who lived the rest of the year around Glastonbury Tor.

🛏 Sleeping

Crown Glastonbury Backpackers HOSTEL £
(☑01458-833353; www.glastonburybackpackers.com; 4 Market Pl; dm £16.50, d £35-60; [P] [@]) Basic but friendly hostel above the old Crown pub, with small, clean rooms as well as a kitchen and laundry.

Covenstead B&B ££
(☑07970-615251; www.covenstead.co.uk; Magdalene St; s £60, d £70-90) Well, what else would you expect in mystical Glastonbury but a witchcraft-themed B&B? There are four rooms, all with their own pagan theme, and the house is a mix of suburban semi and spooky knick-knacks – oil paintings, horned bedside lamps, candelabra and velvet chairs. Thankfully no eye of newt or toe of frog for breakfast, though.

Glastonbury White House B&B ££
(☑01458-830886; www.theglastonburywhitehouse.com; 21 Manor House Rd; s £60-65, d £75-95; [P]) There are only two rooms here, but owner Carey has made them super-cosy, with extra touches such as fridges, fresh milk and bottles of White Spring water. Breakfast is extra (£5 continental, £7.50 cooked). It's about five minutes' walk from High St.

Glastonbury Townhouse B&B ££
(☑01458-831040; www.glastonburytownhouse.co.uk; Street Rd; d £90-120) Nothing too outlandish about this place – just a solid, red-brick, Edwardian town house, with three quiet rooms, lots of antique furniture and a friendly owner, Greg, who has all the local tips.

Parsnips B&B ££
(☑01458-835599; www.parsnips-glastonburyco.uk; 99 Bere Lane; s £55, d £70-75; [P] [@]) This modern B&B is a solid bet, with bright rooms in gingham and cream, complimentary coffee on arrival, and a range of holistic treatments by arrangement. Breakfast is in an attractive conservatory.

✕ Eating & Drinking

Rainbow's End VEGETARIAN £
(☑01458-833896; www.rainbowsendcafe.com; 17a High St; mains £4-8; ⊙10am-5.30pm Mon-Sat, to 4pm Sun; ☑) ⋒ This psychedelic cafe sums up the Glastonbury spirit, with its all-veggie food, potted plants and mix-and-match furniture. Tuck into homity pie or a hot quiche, followed by scrumptious homemade cake. There's a small patio out back.

Bocabar BRITISH ££
(☑01458-440558; http://glastonbury.bocabar.co.uk; Morland Rd; lunch £5-10, dinner £13.50-19.95; ⊙9.30am-midnight Tue-Sat, to 5pm Sun & Mon) In an old factory once occupied by Morlands the sheepskin makers, this has turned into Glastonbury's hippest hang-out. There are live bands and events several times a week, and a pan-global menu that takes in Thai chillies, classic steaks, gourmet burgers and adventurous crêpes. The industrial-chic vibe adds appeal. It's about 1.5 miles southwest of the town centre along Morland Rd.

Hundred Monkeys Cafe BISTRO ££
(www.hundredmonkeyscafe.com; 52 High St; mains £8-15; ⊙8am-8.30pm Mon-Fri, to 9pm Fri & Sat, 9am-4pm Sun; ☑) A cosy bistro with a laid-back, fair-trade, seasonal ethos, decorated in homely fashion with pine furniture and handwritten blackboards. Mezze platters, pasta dishes, curries and risottos are the order of the day – with plenty of gluten-free and vegan options (this is Glastonbury, after all). The tea selection is enormous and the wines are all biodynamic.

Who'd a Thought It Inn
GASTROPUB ££

(17 Northload St; mains £10.95-13.95; ⊙noon-2pm & 6-9pm) A pleasantly peculiar local's pub, covered in paraphernalia including antique bottles and old signs, an old red telephone box and an upside-down bike on the ceiling. The food is solid pub fare – think sausages, pies and steaks – but there are usually specials chalked above the bar.

George & Pilgrim
PUB

(1 High St; mains £7-15; ⊙11am-11pm) Partly 15th-century inn with one of the town's most authentically historic interiors – timbers, flagstones and all.

❶ Information

Glastonbury Tourist Office (☑01458-832954; www.glastonburytic.co.uk; The Tribunal, 9 High St; ⊙10am-5pm)

❶ Getting There & Away

There is no train station in Glastonbury. Bus 377 (several times per hour) travels north to Wells (£3.50, 15 minutes). Bus 29 travels to Taunton (£5.50, 50 minutes, hourly Monday to Saturday).

Taunton & Around

Taunton is in the heart of Somerset in more ways than one; it's bang in the middle of the county geographically, and is also the area's county town and commercial centre.

It's worth a look for its part-12th-century castle, which now houses the Museum of Somerset and the Somerset Military Mu-

seum (☑01823-255088; Castle Green, Taunton; ⊙10am-5pm Tue-Sat) FREE.

It's also a useful gateway to the Quantocks and handy for exploring several local sights.

⊙ Sights

Fleet Air Arm Museum
MUSEUM

(☑01963-840565; www.fleetairarm.com; adult/child £14/10; ⊙10am-5.30pm daily Apr-Oct, 10am-4.30pm Wed-Sun Nov-Mar) This excellent aviation museum houses hundreds of naval aircraft from Sopwiths to Phantom fighters. You can walk onto the flight deck of the first British-built Concorde and take a simulated flight onto the aircraft carrier HMS *Ark Royal*. The museum is 4 miles north of Somerset, near Yeovilton.

West Somerset Railway
HERITAGE RAILWAY

(☑01643-704996; www.west-somerset-railway.co.uk; 24hr rover ticket adult/child £17/8.50) The chuffing steam trains of this vintage railway are a fine way to see the Somerset countryside. The 20-mile route runs from Bishops Lydeard to Minehead, stopping at Dunster, Watchet, Williton, Crowcombe Heathfield and several other stations en route. There are four to eight trains daily from March to October, with a more limited service for the rest of the year. Bikes can be carried on board for £2.

There are discounts if you book online.

Montacute House
HISTORIC BUILDING

(NT; ☑01935-823289; montacute@nationaltrust.org.uk; adult/child £11.20/5.60; ⊙11am-4pm Wed-Mon summer, gardens 10am-5pm year-round) This manor was built in the 1590s for Sir Edward

OFF THE BEATEN TRACK

THE SOMERSET LEVELS

Flat as a pancake, sub-sea-level and criss-crossed with canals (known locally as rhynes), the Somerset Levels are one of England's largest native wetlands. Covering over 64,000 hectares between the Quantock and Mendip Hills, they're brilliant for birdspotters, particularly in October and November, when huge flocks of starlings (properly known as 'murmurations') descend on the area. Nature reserves have been established at Ham Wall, Shapwick Heath, Sedgemoor and Westhay.

More recently, the Levels made the headlines thanks to the serious floods that struck in 2014, submerging the area under several metres of water for much of the winter. In truth, the land here has always been flood-prone, but it's been claimed that the recent floods have been exacerbated by climate change and the cessation of river-dredging.

Along with agriculture, many traditional industries survive on the Levels, including peat digging, reed harvesting and willowcraft, which you can see in action at the Willows & Wetlands Visitor Centre (☑01823-490249; www.englishwillowbaskets.co.uk; ⊙9.30am-5pm Mon-Sat) near Stoke St Gregory.

The flat landscape of the Levels also makes it ideal for cycling. Several trails pass through the village of Langport, including the long-distance River Parrett Trail.

OFF THE BEATEN TRACK

THE QUANTOCKS

The range of red sandstone hills known as the Quantocks traces a 12-mile curve across Somerset's northern edge. A mix of moors, valleys and ancient woods of coppiced oak, these little-visited hills offer stirring views across the Bristol Channel: when the weather's fine, you can see across to the Gower coastline in south Wales.

Designated as an Area of Outstanding Natural Beauty (AONB), the Quantocks receive far fewer visitors than Exmoor and Dartmoor, making them perfect for hikers and bikers in search of quiet trails. The **Quantocks AONB** (www.quantockhills.com; Fyne Ct; ⌚9am-5pm Mon-Fri) runs walks.

Literary buffs might also like to make a stop at the village of **Nether Stowey**, best known for its association with the poet Samuel Taylor Coleridge, who moved to the village with his wife Sara and son Hartley in 1796. **Coleridge Cottage** (NT; ☎01278-732662; 35 Lime St, Nether Stowey; adult £5.80/2.90; ⌚11am-5pm Thu-Mon) is now owned by the National Trust; the poet is thought to have composed some of his greatest works during his three-year stay here, including *The Rime of the Ancient Mariner, Kubla Khan* and *This Lime Tree Bower My Prison*.

Phelips, a Speaker of the House of Commons, and contains some of the finest 16th- and 17th-century interiors in the country. The house is particularly renowned for its plasterwork, chimney pieces and tapestries, but the highlight is the **Long Gallery**, the longest such hall in England. It's decorated with Elizabethan portraits on loan from the National Portrait Gallery in London. It's 24 miles southeast of Taunton on the A358 and A303, or 5 miles west of Yeovil on the A3088.

The house is only open on selected days in winter, so phone ahead.

Ham Hill VIEWPOINT

(www.southsomerset.gov.uk/hamhill; near Stoke-sub-Hamdon) FREE Looming above the village of Stoke-sub-Hamdon, this is the highest point in Somerset. It's served a variety of purposes – Iron Age hill fort, medieval village, stone quarry – but it's now a delightful park covering 156 hectares. Recent archaeological excavations have revealed a huge Iron Age bone-pit that – at least for now – remains a mystery.

Stoke-sub-Hamdon is 7 miles west of Yeovil off the A303; follow the brown signs.

Sleeping & Eating

Queen's Arms INN ££

(☎01963-220317; www.thequeensarms.com; Corton Denham; d £85-130, mains £15-25; ⌚restaurant noon-3pm & 6-9pm; P 📶) Somerset's not short on lovely pubs, but this one in Corton Denham is worth the trip. Rugs, reclaimed pews and flagstones nod to its 18th-century heritage, but the gastropub menu and rustic-chic rooms are altogether modern. It's scooped numerous awards, including CAMRA's Somerset Cider Pub of the Year. It's 8 miles northeast of Yeovil.

Frog St Farmhouse B&B ££

(☎01823-481883; www.frogstreet.co.uk; Hatch Beauchamp; d £90-120; P 📶) The name of this amber-stoned longhouse in nearby Hatch Beauchamp derives from the Anglo-Saxon for 'meeting place'. It's a beauty, with four rooms mixing rusticity (beams, stone, wonky doors) with luxurious furnishings (roll-top baths, cotton linen, wood floors).

★ **Lord Poulett Arms** GASTROPUB ££

(☎01460-73149; www.lordpoulettarms.com; Hinton St George; mains £14-16, r £85-95; ⌚noon-2.30pm & 6-9pm; P) Hinton St George's deliciously olde-worlde village pub has been named Somerset Dining Pub of the Year three times, most recently in 2014. The hearty food is fantastic, and the building oozes country atmosphere, with beams, roaring fires and stacks of ale barrels behind the bar. It even has quirky rooms upstairs. Hard to fault.

It's roughly 15 miles from Yeovil and Taunton.

CORNWALL

You can't get further west than the ancient Celtic kingdom of Cornwall (or Kernow, as it's known to Cornish-speakers). Blessed with the southwest's wildest coastline and most breathtakingly beautiful beaches, this proudly independent peninsula has always marched to its own tune.

While the staple industries of old – mining, fishing and farming – have all but disappeared, Cornwall has since reinvented itself as one of the nation's creative corners. Whether it's exploring the space-age domes of the Eden Project, sampling the culinary creations of a celebrity chef or basking on a deserted beach, you're guaranteed to feel the itch of inspiration. Time to let a little Kernow into your soul.

Since 2006, Cornwall's historic mining areas have formed part of the UK's newest Unesco World Heritage Site, the **Cornwall & West Devon Mining Landscape** (www.cornish-mining.org.uk).

❶ Getting Around

Bus, train and ferry timetables can be found on the **Traveline South West** (☑ 0871 200 2233; www.travelinesw.com) website.

The useful **Great Scenic Railways** (www.greatscenicrailways.com) website features online booking and timetables for Cornwall's regional railways.

BUS

Cornwall has two main bus operators. First Cornwall operates the routes between main towns, and the majority of services in the west of the county, while Western Greyhound operates services between coastal villages and most services in the east of the county.

First Cornwall (☑ customer service 0845 600 1420, timetables 0871 200 2233; www.firstgroup.com/ukbus/devon_cornwall)

Western Greyhound (☑ 01637-871871; www.westerngreyhound.com)

TRAIN

Cornwall's main railway line follows the coast as far as Penzance, with branch lines to Gunnislake, Looe, Falmouth, St Ives and Newquay.

CrossCountry (☑ 0844 811 0124; www.crosscountrytrains.co.uk) Operates services to the north of England, the Midlands and Scotland.

First Great Western (☑ 08457 000125; www.firstgreatwestern.co.uk) Operates the main line from London Paddington via Exeter, Plymouth, St Austell, Truro and Penzance, as well as the regional branch lines.

TRANSPORT PASSES

Several passes cover public transport in Cornwall. Ride Cornwall is the best all-round value covering bus and train. There are also Day Ranger tickets for all of Cornwall's branch railway lines, as well as 'Two Together' and 'Groupsave' tickets for two and four adults travelling together.

FirstDay Southwest (adult/child/family £7.60/6.20/18.70) One-day pass offering unlimited bus travel on First buses in Devon and Cornwall.

Freedom of Devon & Cornwall Rover (3-day adult/child £45, 8-day adult/child £69) Three days' train travel in seven, or eight days' travel in 14. Valid after 9am and anytime weekends.

Ride Cornwall (adult/child/family £10/7.50/20) The best-value all-round travel pass, covering one day's rail and bus travel between Cornwall and Plymouth. Valid after 9am Monday to Friday and weekends.

Western Greyhound Day Explorer (adult/child/family £8.50/5.50/17) Covers one day's travel on any of Western Greyhound's bus routes in Cornwall.

Day Ranger Rail Tickets

Atlantic Coast Line (1-day ranger adult/child £4.60/2.30) Branch line from Newquay to Par.

Looe Valley Line (1-day ranger adult/child £5/3.15) Scenic line from Liskeard to Looe.

Maritime Line (1-day ranger adult/child £4.10/2.05) Truro to Falmouth Docks, with stops at Penryn and Falmouth Town.

Tamar Valley Line (1-day ranger adult/child £5.40/2.70) Plymouth to Gunnislake, with stops including Devonport Dockyard, St Budeaux, Bere Alston and Calstock.

St Ives Bay Line (1-day ranger adult/child/family £4/2/10) Lovely line that runs between St Erth, Carbis Bay and St Ives.

Bude

POP 9242

Just a scant few miles across the Devon border, Bude is a breezy seaside town with a bevy of impressive beaches, as well as a lovely seawater lido built in the 1930s. The town itself isn't much to look at, but the stunning coastline on its doorstep makes it worthy of a stop.

◉ Sights

Bude's beaches are definitely its main asset. Closest is **Summerleaze**, a bucket-and-spade affair with lots of space at low tide, and the beautiful **Bude Sea Pool** (www.budeseapool.net). North across Summerleaze Down is **Crooklets**, offering golden sand and rock pools at low tide.

To reach Bude's other beaches requires either a car or a hike along the coast path. Three miles south of town is **Widemouth Bay** (pronounced 'widmouth'), a broad, sandy beach good for both families and surfers. Two miles further is the shingly beach of **Millook**, followed by the dramatic cliffs around **Crackington Haven**.

Three miles north of town are the National Trust–owned **Northcott Mouth** and **Sandymouth**.

A mile further on is pebbly **Duckpool**, often quiet even in summer.

Bude Castle   MUSEUM
(www.thecastlebude.org.uk; The Castle; ⊙10am-5pm Easter-Oct, 10am-4pm Nov-Easter) **FREE** Housed in a peculiar folly behind Summerleaze Beach, Bude Castle was built by local inventor Sir Goldsworthy Gurney, whose creations included theatrical limelight and steam carriages. The building now houses a small **heritage centre** which roves through Bude's maritime, geological and social history. There's also a cafe on the top floor.

⌊═⌋ Sleeping

Dylan's Guesthouse   B&B £
(☑01288-354705; www.dylansguesthouseinbude.co.uk; Downs View; s £40-50, d £60-75; P �🛜) This snazzy B&B has rooms decked out in white linen, chocolate throws, pine furniture and quirky curios. Most look across the town's golf course and downlands.

Elements Hotel   HOTEL ££
(☑01288-275066; www.elements-life.co.uk; Marine Dr; d £99-120; P 🛜) Smart clifftop hotel with 11 rooms in whites and creams, big views from the outdoor deck, a gym and Finholme sauna, and surf packages courtesy of nearby Raven Surf School.

Beach at Bude   HOTEL £££
(☑01288-389800; www.thebeachatbude.co.uk; Summerleaze Cres; r £95-185; P 🛜) The main sell at this swish hotel are the fine views over Summerleaze beach, but the rooms are attractive too: spacious and smart, with slate-lined bathrooms featuring his-and-hers sinks and Lloyd Loom chairs. They're styled to resemble a New England beach cabin.

✖ Eating

Scrummies   CAFE £
(Lansdown Rd; mains £6-8; ⊙8am-10pm) The best place for fish and chips in town (the skate and monkfish are caught by the owner). For something fancier, try their scallops and lobster (half/whole £12/24).

Life's a Beach   CAFE ££
(☑01288-355222; www.lifesabeach.info; Summerleaze; lunch mains £6-10, dinner £16.50-19; ⊙10.30am-3.30pm & 7-10pm Mon-Sat, 10.30am-3.30pm Sun) This bistro overlooking Summerleaze has a split personality: by day a beach caff serving coffees, panini and ice cream; by night a smart seafood restaurant.

ℹ Information

Bude Tourist Office (☑01288-354240; www.visitbude.info; The Crescent; ⊙10am-5pm Mon-Sat, plus 10am-4pm Sun summer) Beside the main car park near the Castle.

ℹ Getting There & Away

Bus 594/595 (six daily Monday to Saturday, four on Sunday in summer) travels to Boscastle (£4.50 single) via Widemouth and Crackington Haven (£3 or £4).

Boscastle

POP 641

Nestled in the crook of a steep coombe (valley) at the confluence of three rivers, Boscastle's sea-going heritage stretches back to Elizabethan times. With its quaint cottages, flower-clad cliffs, tinkling streams and sturdy quay, it's almost impossibly photogenic.

But the peaceful setting belies some turbulent history: in 2004 Boscastle was devastated by one of Britain's largest-ever flash floods, which carried away cars, bridges and buildings. The village has since been rebuilt, but look closely and you'll still spot reminders of the floods dotted around.

WORTH A TRIP

VINTAGE CORNWALL

Cornwall might not seem like an obvious place for winemaking, but local entrepreneur Bob Lindo has been producing award-winning vintages at his **Camel Valley Vineyard** (☑01208-77959; www.camelvalley.com; ⊙10am-5pm Mon-Sat) since 1989. The range includes award-winning whites and rosés, and a bubbly that's champagne in all but name. Aficionados say the wines have a fresh, light quality that comes from the mild climate and pure sea air. Vineyard tours run regularly, and you can taste and buy the goods in the on-site shop.

◎ Sights

Museum of Witchcraft MUSEUM
(☑01840-250111; www.museumofwitchcraft.com; The Harbour; adult/child £5/4; ☺10.30am-6pm Mon-Sat, 11.30am-6pm Sun Mar-Nov) This odd-ball museum claims to house the world's largest collection of witchy memorabilia, from haunted skulls to hags' bridles and voodoo dolls. It's half-tacky, half-spooky, and some of the more 'controversial' exhibits might perturb kids of a sensitive disposition (or adults, for that matter).

⊨ Sleeping

Boscastle YHA HOSTEL £
(☑01840-250928, 0845 371 9006; boscastle@yha. org.uk; Palace Stables, The Harbour; dm £20-22.50; ☺Apr-Nov) Boscastle's shoebox-sized hostel was all but washed away by the floods, but it's been completely renovated. It's in one of the village's oldest buildings beside the harbour, but be prepared for small dorms, especially considering the price.

Boscastle House B&B ££
(☑01840-250654; www.boscastlehouse.co.uk; Tintagel Rd; s/d from £50/102; P 🛜) The fanciest of Boscastle's B&Bs, in a Victorian house overlooking the valley, with five classy rooms with a bright, contemporary feel, mixing neutral colours with bold print wallpapers. Charlotte has bay window views, Nine Windows has his-and-hers sinks and a free-standing bath, and Trelawney has ample space and a sofa.

Orchard Lodge B&B ££
(☑01840-250418; www.orchardlodgeboscastle.co. uk; Gunpool Lane; d £89-99, 2-night minimum in summer; P 🛜) Uphill from the harbour, Geoff and Shirley Barratt have turned their white-washed house into a charming B&B bolthole, with each room boasting its own mix-and-match furnishings and fabrics, and hallways plastered with Thomas Hardy quotes. There's a two-night minimum in summer, and rates get cheaper the longer you stay.

✗ Eating

For good pub grub, try the cosy Cobweb (☑01840-250278; www.cobwebinn.co.uk; The Bridge; mains £8-14) and the old-time Napoleon (☑01840-250204; High St; mains £6-12).

Boscastle Farm Shop CAFE £
(☑01840-250827; www.boscastlefarmshop.co.uk; cakes & teas £3-5; ☺10am-5pm; P) Half-a-mile from the harbour on the B3263, this excellent farm shop sells its own produce, including ruby-red beef and possibly the best sausages on the north coast. In the cafe, tall windows look onto fields and coast – the perfect setting for a cream tea.

Waterloo Restaurant BRITISH £££
(☑01840-250202; www.wellingtonhotelboscastle. com; The Harbour; 2-/3-course menu £30/37.50) This turreted coaching inn dates back to the 16th century (previous guests include King Edward VII and Guy Gibson of Dambusters fame). It's an old-fashioned place – flock carpets, burnished furniture, upholstered chairs – and the restaurant continues the trad theme. It's now run by Kit Davis, who previously ran his own restaurant in Bude.

❶ Information

Boscastle Tourist Office (☑01840-250010; www.visitboscastleandtintagel.com; The Harbour; ☺10am-5pm Mar-Oct, 10.30am-4pm Nov-Feb)

Tintagel
POP 1822

The spectre of King Arthur looms large over Tintagel and its spectacular clifftop castle. Though the present-day ruins mostly date from the 13th century, archaeological digs have revealed the foundations of a much earlier fortress, fuelling speculation that Arthur may indeed have been born at the castle as locals like to claim.

The village itself isn't terribly exciting, but if you're looking for a cheesy king Arthur souvenir, you'll find them in ample supply.

◎ Sights

★Tintagel Castle CASTLE
(EH; ☑01840-770328; adult/child £6.10/3.70; ☺10am-6pm Apr-Sep, to 5pm Oct, to 4pm Nov-Mar) Famous as the supposed birthplace of King Arthur, Tintagel's stunning clifftop castle has been occupied since Roman times and once served as a residence for Cornwall's Celtic kings. The present castle is largely the work of Richard, Earl of Cornwall, who established the fortress to cash in on its Arthurian connections and curry favour with the local populace.

Though the Arthurian links may be tenuous, there's no doubt that Tintagel's builders chose a fine spot for a fortress. Clinging to the black granite cliffs, surrounded by booming surf and wheeling gulls, it's most people's idea of a fairy-tale castle.

Though much of the structure has crumbled away, it's still possible to make out several walls and much of the original layout. Part of the castle stands on a rocky outcrop cut off from the mainland, and is accessed via a wooden bridge and a very steep staircase (vertigo sufferers beware). Trails lead along the headland to the atmospheric medieval chapel of St Glebe's.

It's a steep walk down to the castle from the village car parks; however, in summer Land Rover taxis shuttle up and down throughout the day.

Old Post Office HISTORIC BUILDING
(NT; ☑01840-770024; Fore St; adult/child £3.70/1.80; ◷10.30am-5.30pm mid-Mar–Sep, 11am-4pm Oct) One of the National Trust's oldest properties, this is also one of the best-preserved examples of a traditional 16th-century Cornish longhouse, and is topped by pepper-pot chimneys and riddled with tiny rooms. As its name suggests, it was used as a post office during the 19th century.

ℹ Getting There & Away

Tintagel is on the route for the 594/595 bus (£4 to £5.50, six daily Monday to Saturday), with connections to Bude, Boscastle and Newquay.

Port Isaac

A few miles southwest of Tintagel is the classic Cornish fishing harbour of Port Isaac, a cluster of cobbled alleyways, slender opes (lanes) and cobwalled cottages collected around a medieval harbour and slipway.

Though still a working harbour, Port Isaac is best known as a filming location: the Brit film *Saving Grace* and the TV series *Doc Martin* have both used the village as a ready-made backdrop (a sign near the quayside directs tourists straight to Doc Martin's cottage). A short walk west leads to the neighbouring harbour of Port Gaverne, while a couple of miles west is Port Quin, now owned by the National Trust.

Cornwall's *chef du jour*, Nathan Outlaw, has opened his latest restaurant right beside the quay. Outlaw's Fish Kitchen (☑01208-881183; www.outlaws.co.uk/fishkitchen; 1 Middle St; mains £6-10; ◷noon-3pm & 6-9pm daily Jun-Dec, Tue-Sat Feb-Jun) serves up seafood tasting plates, with the menu dictated by whatever's brought in on the day by Port Isaac's fishermen. The restaurant is tiny, but bookings are only taken for dinner.

Padstow & Rock
POP 3162

If anywhere symbolises Cornwall's changing character, it's Padstow. This once-sleepy fishing port has been transformed into one of the county's most cosmopolitan corners thanks to celebrity chef Rick Stein, whose property portfolio encompasses several restaurants, shops and hotels, as well as a seafood school and fish-and-chip bar.

The 'Stein Effect' has certainly changed the place: Padstow feels more Kensington-chic than Cornish-quaint these days, with a rash of fancy restaurants and chichi boutiques sitting alongside the old pubs and pasty shops. Whether the town's managed to hold on to its soul in the process is debatable, but it's still hard not to be charmed by the setting.

Across the Camel Estuary from Padstow is Rock, a once-quiet village that's been reinvented as an über-exclusive holiday destination. It's worth a trip for the chance to dine at the Michelin-starred restaurants of Nathan Outlaw, the county's top seafood chef.

Between the two resorts is the silvery sweep of the Doom Bar, a treacherous sandbank that's claimed many ships down the centuries.

◉ Sights & Activities

Padstow is surrounded by fine beaches, including the so-called Seven Bays: Trevone, Harlyn, Mother Ivey's, Booby's, Constantine, Treyarnon and Porthcothan. Bus 556 runs close to most of them.

Between Easter and October, cruise boats including the Jubilee Queen (☑07836-798457; www.padstowboattrips.co.uk; adult/child £11/6) and Padstow Sealife Safaris (☑01841-521613; www.padstowsealifesafaris.co.uk; 2hr cruise adult/child £39/25) run trips to local seal and seabird colonies.

National Lobster Hatchery NATURE DISPLAY
(☑01841-533877; www.nationallobsterhatchery.co.uk; adult/child £3.75/1.50; ◷10am-7.30pm Jul & Aug, to 4pm or 5pm Sep-Jun) ✦ In an effort to combat falling lobster stocks, this harbourside hatchery rears baby lobsters in tanks before returning them to the wild. Displays detail the crustaceans' life cycle, and there are viewing tanks where you can watch the residents in action.

Prideaux Place HISTORIC BUILDING
(☑01841-532411; www.prideauxplace.co.uk; house & grounds adult £8.50, grounds only £3; ◷house

DON'T MISS

BEDRUTHAN STEPS
....

Roughly halfway between Newquay and Padstow loom the stately rock stacks of **Bedruthan** (Carnewas; NT; www.nationaltrust.org.uk/carnewas-and-bedruthan-steps). These mighty granite pillars have been carved out by the relentless action of thousands of years of wind and waves, and now provide a stirring spot for a sunset stroll. The area is owned by the National Trust, who also run the car park and cafe. The beach itself is accessed via a steep staircase and is submerged at high tide. Towards the north end is a rocky shelf known as **Diggory's Island**, which separates the main beach from another little-known cove.

1.30-4pm Sun-Thu, grounds & tearoom 12.30-5.30pm Apr-Oct) Much favoured by directors of costume dramas, the stately manor was built by the Prideaux-Brune family, purportedly descendants of William the Conqueror. Guided tours last around an hour and take in state rooms, staircases and Prideaux-Brune heirlooms.

Camel Trail CYCLING

The old Padstow–Bodmin railway was closed in the 1950s, and has now been turned into Cornwall's most popular bike trail. The main section starts in Padstow and runs east through Wadebridge (5.75 miles), but the trail runs on all the way to Poley Bridge on Bodmin Moor (18.3 miles).

Bikes can be hired from **Padstow Cycle Hire** (☎01841-533533; www.padstowcyclehire.com; South Quay; adult/child per day £14/6; ☺9am-5pm, to 9pm summer) or **Trail Bike Hire** (☎01841-532594; www.trailbikehire.co.uk; Unit 6, South Quay; adult £12, child £5-8; ☺9am-6pm) at the Padstow end, or from **Bridge Bike Hire** (☎01208-813050; www.bridgebikehire.co.uk; adult £12-15, child £6-9; ☺10am-5pm) at the Wadebridge end. Pumps and helmets are usually included, but tandems and kids' trailers cost extra.

🛏 Sleeping

Treyarnon Bay YHA HOSTEL £

(☎0845 371 9664; treyarnon@yha.org.uk; Treyarnon Bay; dm £17-23; 🅿 @) A super 1930s-built beach hostel on the bluffs above Treyarnon Bay. Rooms are big and there's a good cafe, plus barbecues in summer. It's 4.5 miles east of Padstow. Bus 556 stops nearby at Constantine.

Althea Library B&B ££

(☎01841-532579; www.altheahouse-padstow.co.uk; 64 Church St, Padstow; d £98-124; 🅿🐾) If you want to be in the heart of Padstow, this charming ivy-clad house is hard to better. The rooms are both suites, and quite rightly, with sofas, Nespresso coffee machines, in-room fridges and roll-top baths. Rafters is

accessed via a private staircase, while Driftwood has a pine four-poster bed, and there's a cottage for longer stays.

Treann House B&B ££

(☎01841-553855; www.treannhousepadstow.co.uk; 24 Dennis Rd, Padstow; d £100-130; 🐾) This stylish number makes a fancy place to stay. The three rooms are finished with stripped floors, crisp sheets and antique beds, and the Estuary Room has its own dinky balcony with a panorama over Padstow's rooftops.

Treverbyn House B&B ££

(☎01841-532855; www.treverbynhouse.com; Station Rd, Padstow; d £120-125; 🅿🐾) This town house offers four colour-themed rooms (pink, green, lilac or yellow) plus an extra-romantic turret hideaway. The style is classic (oriental rugs, brass bedsteads, traditional tea trays), the rooms are huge, and breakfast includes homemade jams and smoked kippers.

✗ Eating

Chough Bakery BAKERY £

(☎01841-533361; www.thechoughbakery.co.uk; 1-3 The Strand, Padstow; pasties £2-4) This family-run bakery makes Padstow's best pasties, bar none.

Stein's Fish & Chips CAFE £

(South Quay, Padstow; takeaway £6.65-10.95; ☺9-11.30am, noon-3pm & 5-8pm) Stein's fish-and-chips bar uses beef dripping batter for a crisp finish, and often has unusual fish options such as monkfish, John Dory and lemon sole.

Margot's Bistro BRITISH ££

(☎01840-533441; www.margotsbistro.co.uk; 11 Duke St, Padstow; mains £14.50-17.50; ☺noon-2pm Wed-Sat, 7-10pm Tue-Sat) While the food snobs head for Stein's, Margot's is where you'll be sent by the locals. Run by madcap chef Adrian Oliver, known for his chaotic style and seasonal food, it's a fantastically convivial place, but the tables are packed in sardine-tight.

Rojano's in the Square ITALIAN ££
(☏ 01841-532796; www.rojanos.co.uk; 9 Mill Sq, Padstow; pizzas & pastas £12-15) Now run by Paul Ainsworth, this excellent little Italian bistro turns out fantastic wood-fired pizzas, spicy pastas and antipasti.

Rick Stein's Cafe EUROPEAN ££
(☏ 01841-532700; Middle St, Padstow; mains £10-18; ⊙ 8am-9.30pm) Stein's backstreet bistro takes its inspiration from the chef's globetrotting travels, with dishes ranging all the way from the Far East to the Mediterranean: classic mussels with saffron, or Thai-spiced seafood broth. It's a lot more relaxed than its sister restaurant, but you'd still be wise to book.

Basement CAFE ££
(☏ 01841-532846; 11 Broad St, Padstow; lunch mains £5-10, dinner £10-14; ⊙ 8am-10pm) Harbourside cafe that's good for a quick morning coffee, or a bowl of mussels for lunch.

★Paul Ainsworth at No 6 BRITISH £££
(☏ 01840-532093; www.number6inpadstow.co.uk; 6 Middle St, Padstow; 2-/3-course lunch £19/25, dinner mains £26-30; ⊙ noon-2.30pm & 6.30-9pm) Paul Ainsworth is Padstow's hottest chef, and thanks to a shiny Michelin star, his restaurant has become the town's most desirable table. Known for his modern take on surf-and-turf, Ainsworth's cooking combines local seafood, meat and game into fresh, surprising concoctions. His signature dessert, 'A Trip to the Fairground', was created for BBC2's *Great British Menu* in 2011.

★Restaurant Nathan Outlaw SEAFOOD £££
(☏ 01208-862737; www.nathan-outlaw.com; Rock Rd, Rock; tasting menu £99; ⊙ 7-9pm Tue-Sat) A former Rick Stein trainee, Nathan Outlaw has now established his own stellar seafood reputation with two Michelin stars – the only chef in Cornwall to do so. There's a choice of Outlaw venues, both in Rock. Foodies plump for the flagship restaurant, which serves a superb £99 tasting menu. Expensive, but very much a never-to-be-forgotten experience.

Nathan's style is surprisingly classic, and relies on the quality of the seafood rather than cheffy tricks to provide the fireworks. The more relaxed **Outlaw's** (mains £16-25; ⊙ noon-2.30pm & 6-9.30pm) serves similar quality seafood at more affordable prices, while Nathan has also recently opened a new place, Outlaw's Fish Kitchen (p341), in Port Isaac.

Seafood Restaurant SEAFOOD £££
(☏ 01841-532700; www.rickstein.com; Riverside, Padstow; mains £25-65; ⊙ noon-2pm & 6.30-10pm) Rick Stein's flagship seafooderie needs no introduction: it's one of Britain's foremost fish addresses, with an expensive menu offering treats such as fresh Padstow lobster and sumptuous *fruits de mer*. You'll generally need to book months in advance – although last-minute lunch tables sometimes crop up.

ℹ Information

Padstow Tourist Office (☏ 01841-533449; www.padstowlive.com; North Quay, Padstow; ⊙ 10am-5pm Mon-Sat)

ℹ Getting There & Away

There are a couple of car parks beside the harbour in Padstow, but they fill up quickly, so it's usually a better idea to park at one of the large car parks at the top of town and walk down.

Useful bus routes include:

Bude Bus 594/595 (£8, six daily Monday to Saturday) via Wadebridge (£7.50), Boscastle and Tintagel.

Newquay Bus 556 (£6.50, hourly Monday to Saturday, five on Sunday) runs via Padstow's main beaches along the coast to Newquay.

Newquay

POP 19,423

If Padstow is Cornwall's Cannes, then Newquay is its Costa del Sol. Perched on the cliffs above a cluster of white-sand beaches, and packed with enough pubs, bars and dodgy clubs to give Ibiza a run for its money, it's become the summer venue of choice for beer boys, beach bums and surf addicts alike, all of whom descend on the town in their droves in summer. It's also the capital of Cornish surfing, and if you're looking to learn how to brave the waves, this is the place to do it.

◎ Sights

Newquay has a truly stunning location among some of North Cornwall's finest beaches. The best known is **Fistral**, England's most famous surfing beach. It's nestled on the west side of Towan Head, a 10-minute walk from the town centre.

To the east of Towan Head are Newquay's other main beaches. Just below town are **Towan**, **Great Western** and **Tolcarne**, followed by nearby **Lusty Glaze**. All offer good swimming and lifeguard supervision throughout the summer.

You'll need transport to reach Newquay's other beaches. North of Lusty Glaze is Porth, a long, narrow beach that's popular with families, followed a couple of miles later by the massive curve of Watergate Bay, home to Jamie Oliver's much-vaunted restaurant, Fifteen Cornwall. Two miles north brings you to Mawgan Porth, a horseshoe-shaped bay which often stays quieter than its neighbours.

You'll find even more beaches to the southwest of Newquay, including the large, sandy, family-friendly beaches of Crantock (about 3 miles from town) and Holywell Bay (6 miles from town).

Blue Reef Aquarium
AQUARIUM

(🖉 01637-878134; www.bluereefaquarium.co.uk/newquay; Towan Promenade; adult/child/family £10/7.75/33.50; ⊙ 10am-5pm; 🖐) Small aquarium on Towan Beach, with touch-pools and various deep-sea denizens including reef sharks, loggerhead turtles and a giant Pacific octopus. There's a £1 discount for online bookings.

Newquay Zoo
ZOO

(🖉 01637-873342; www.newquayzoo.org.uk; Trenance Gardens; adult/child/family £11.75/9.05/35; ⊙ 9.30am-5pm Apr-Sep, 10am-5pm Oct-Mar; 🖐) Newquay's miniature zoo isn't a world-beater, but its population of penguins, lemurs, parrots and snakes will keep the kids happy. The Tropical House and Toad Hall are particularly good fun.

Trerice
HISTORIC BUILDING

(NT; 🖉 01637-875404; www.nationaltrust.org.uk/trerice; adult/child £7.65/3.80; ⊙ house 11am-5pm, gardens 10.30am-5pm) This Elizabethan manor (1751) is most famous for the elaborate barrel-roofed ceiling of its Great Chamber. It's 3.3 miles southeast of Newquay.

🏃 Activities

Newquay's brimming with surf schools, but the quality is variable. Choose one that offers small-group sessions, and ideally has a no-stag-party policy. Ask about teachers' accreditation and experience, and whether they travel to beaches other than Fistral – good schools follow the best waves.

English Surf School
SURFING

(🖉 01637-879571; www.englishsurfschool.com) This is one of the most experienced and efficient large schools, linked with Rip Curl and staffed by fully English Surfing Federation–approved instructors (including the British team coach).

Extreme Academy
ADVENTURE SPORTS

(🖉 01637-860840; www.extremeacademy.co.uk; Watergate Bay) A well-organised surf school and water-sports centre with a large base at Watergate Bay.

Errant Surf School
SURFING

(🖉 07581-397038; www.errantsurfschool.co.uk; Trebarwith Cres) A small, independent surf school that offers small class sizes, friendly tutors and optional one-to-one lessons. Based at the Trebarwith Hotel.

Kingsurf Surf School
SURFING

(🖉 01637-860091; www.kingsurf.co.uk) A good option if you prefer to avoid the Fistral hustle, this school at Mawgan Porth has five young instructors and gets a tick for personal attention and small class sizes.

EboAdventure
OUTDOORS

(🖉 0800 781 6861; www.eboadventure.co.uk) Surfing's not the only sport in Newquay – you could also try kitebuggying, kayaking, paddle surfing and coasteering (a mix of rock climbing, scrambling and wild swimming). This multi-activity centre is based at the Penhale Training Camp, at the northern end of Holywell Bay.

🛌 Sleeping

Newquay Townhouse
B&B £

(🖉 01637-620009; www.newquaytownhouse.co.uk; 6 Tower Rd; d £50-70; 🅿🛜) A great B&B near Newquay's town centre, with bright rooms livened up with stripy cushions and wicker furniture.

★ Scarlet
HOTEL £££

(🖉 01637-861600; www.scarlethotel.co.uk; r winter/summer from £155/285; 🅿🛜🏊) For out-and-out luxury, Cornwall's fabulously chic, adults-only eco-hotel takes the crown. In a regal location above Mawgan Porth, 5 miles from Newquay, it screams designer style, from the huge sea-view rooms with their funky furniture and minimalist decor to the luxurious spa, complete with meditation lounge, outdoor hot tubs and wild swimming pool. The restaurant's a beauty, too.

★ Bedruthan Hotel
HOTEL £££

(🖉 01637-860555; www.bedruthan.com; Mawgan Porth; d from £130; 🅿🛜🏊) Run by the same team as the Scarlet, the Bedruthan is a family-friendly version but with the same attention to style and detail. It offers contemporary rooms in bright primary colours, artworks and bold pattern prints, plus villas and apartments for longer stays. Activities aplenty will keep the small ones occupied.

✗ Eating

Café Irie   CAFE £
(☑01637-859200; www.cafeirie.co.uk; 38 Fore St; lunch £3-8; ◷9am-5.30pm Mon-Sat) A surfer's favourite in the centre of Newquay, perfect for hot chocolate, sticky cakes and jacket spuds after hitting the waves.

Beach Hut   BISTRO ££
(☑01637-860877; Watergate Bay; mains £10-18; ◷9am-9pm) Lodged beneath Jamie Oliver's Fifteen Cornwall, this beachside bistro is a great bet for simple surf 'n' turf: sticky pork ribs, 'extreme' burgers and a different fish every day.

Lewinnick Lodge   GASTROPUB ££
(☑01637-878117; www.lewinnick-lodge.info; Pentire Head, Newquay; mains £10-16; ◷9am-11pm) Perched on the dramatic outcrop of Pentire Head, the Lewinnick is a super lunch spot. The wraparound views over the clifftops are the main selling point here, but there's a decent choice of gourmet burgers, mussels and Thai-style salads on the menu.

Fifteen Cornwall   ITALIAN £££
(☑01637-861000; www.fifteencornwall.com; Watergate Bay; lunch/dinner menu £28/60; ◷8.30-10am, noon-2.30pm & 6.15-9.15pm) Owned by celeb chef and self-marketing mogul Jamie Oliver, this restaurant on Watergate Bay serves Jamie's trademark Italian food while simultaneously training young apprentices. The vibe is relaxed and the beach view is stunning, but the prices are on the high side.

🍸 Drinking & Nightlife

Newquay's town centre gets rowdy on Friday and Saturday nights.

Chy   BAR
(www.thekoola.com/the-chy-bar; 12 Beach Rd; ◷9am-11pm) Chrome, wood and leather dominate this cafe-bar overlooking Towan Beach. The action continues till late at the Koola nightclub downstairs.

Central   PUB
(11 Central Sq; ◷11am-midnight Sun-Thu, to 1am Fri & Sat) As its name suggests, this pre-club pub is in the heart of town, and is usually packed at weekends.

ℹ Information

Newquay Tourist Office (☑01637-854020; www.visitnewquay.com; Marcus Hill; ◷9.30am-5.30pm Mon-Sat, to 12.30pm Sun)

ℹ Getting There & Away

The 585/586 is the fastest bus service to Truro (50 minutes, twice hourly Monday to Saturday), while the hourly 587 (£3.40 to any stop on the route) follows the coast via Crantock (14 minutes), Holywell Bay (25 minutes) and Perranporth (50 minutes).

There are trains every couple of hours on the branch line between Newquay and Par (£4.50, 45 minutes) on the main London–Penzance line.

Newquay Airport (☑01637-860600; www.newquaycornwallairport.com) Five miles from town, Newquay's airport currently offers direct flights to Belfast, Edinburgh, Glasgow, Manchester, Newcastle and London Gatwick. Bus 556 (22 minutes, hourly Monday to Saturday, five on Sunday) runs from the bus station. A taxi will cost from £15 to £25.

Perranporth to Porthtowan

Southwest of Newquay, Cornwall's craggy northern coastline dips and curves through a stunning panorama of wild, sea-smacked cliffs and golden bays, including the family-friendly beach of Perranporth, the old mining town of St Agnes and the surfy hang-out of Porthtowan.

◉ Sights

Perranporth Beach   BEACH
(🏖) Perranporth's huge, flat, sandy beach is popular with bucket-and-spading families and surfers alike. It's over a mile long, backed by dunes and rocky cliffs, and usually has space even on the busiest days. It's also home to the Watering Hole (p346).

★ Chapel Porth   COVE
Two miles from St Agnes is one of Cornwall's most beautiful coves, Chapel Porth, a wild, rocky beach framed by steep, gorse-covered cliffs, owned by the National Trust. Above the cove is the ruined engine stack of Wheal Coates, which still boasts its chimney and winding house, from where the coast path winds all the way to the blustery outcrop of St Agnes Head.

Trevaunance Cove   COVE
St Agnes' main beach is great for paddling and rock-pooling, and has old-fashioned

beach huts to change in. Koru Kayaking (p355) runs trips from the cove.

Blue Hills Tin Streams
EXHIBITION

(☑ 01872-553341; www.bluehillstin.com; adult/child £6.50/3; ☺ 10am-4pm Tue-Sat mid-Apr–mid-Oct) A mile east of St Agnes (signed to Wheal Kitty) is the rocky valley of Trevellas, home to one of Cornwall's last tin manufacturers where you can watch the whole tinning process, from mining and smelting through to casting and finishing. Handmade jewellery is sold in the shop.

✖ Eating & Drinking

Chapel Porth Cafe
CAFE £

(Chapel Porth; sandwiches & cakes £2-4; ☺ 10am-5pm) The Chapel Porth Cafe is a local institution, serving hot chocolate, cheesy baguettes and the house speciality, hedgehog ice-cream (vanilla ice-cream topped with clotted cream and hazelnuts).

★ No 4 Peterville
BISTRO ££

(☑ 01872-554245; Peterville Sq, St Agnes; mains £12-16.95; ☺ 7-10.30pm Wed-Sat, 10am-1pm Sat & Sun) An impressive address at the bottom of St Agnes that's earned a loyal following with its continental-style bistro food: whole plaice with curried mussel butter, or rib-eye steak with rosemary-salted fries. Pine tables and kilner-jar candles continue the dining-with-friends atmosphere.

Driftwood Spars
PUB ££

(☑ 01872-552428; www.driftwoodspars.com; Trevaunance Cove, St Agnes; mains £8-16; ☺ 11am-11pm; ℗) This classic old inn by Trevaunance Cove has something to suit all-comers: home-brewed beers, good pub food, and nautically themed upstairs rooms.

Bolingey Inn
PUB ££

(☑ 01872-571626; Penwartha Rd, Bolingey; mains £10-16; ☺ noon-11pm) The ivy-covered Bolingey Inn is the best pub around Perranporth for food, and has a valley location about 2 miles' drive inland.

Blue Bar
BISTRO ££

(☑ 01209-890329; www.blue-bar.co.uk; Porthtowan; mains £8-16; ☺ 10am-11pm) For a seaside sundowner or a lunchtime snack by the sand, this Porthtowan cafe is tough to beat (unfortunately everyone knows about it, so arrive early).

Watering Hole
BAR

(www.the-wateringhole.co.uk; Perranporth Beach) One of Cornwall's oldest beach bars, the Watering Hole, which was nearly washed away during heavy storms in 2014.

❶ Getting There & Away

First bus 85 travels at least hourly between Truro and St Agnes (£2.50). Western Greyhound's bus 587 runs twice an hour from Truro to St Agnes (£1.70), and then continues from St Agnes to Perranporth (£2.20) and Newquay (£3.40).

St Ives

POP 9870

Even if you've seen St Ives many times before, it's still hard not to be dazzled as you gaze across its improbably pretty jumble of slate roofs, church towers and turquoise bays. Once a busy pilchard harbour, St Ives later became the centre of Cornwall's arts scene in the 1920s and '30s, and the town is still an artistic centre, with numerous galleries and craft shops lining its winding cobbled streets, as well as the southwestern outpost of the renowned Tate Museum.

DON'T MISS

GWITHIAN & GODREVY TOWANS

Four miles' drive east of St Ives across the Hayle Estuary, the dune-backed flats of Gwithian and Godrevy unfurl in a glimmering golden curve that joins together at low tide to form Hayle's '3 miles of golden sand'. This is one of Cornwall's most glorious beach panoramas, fringed by hectares of rockpools and grassy dunes (known in Cornish as *towans*) and, at the northern end, the lighthouse that inspired Virginia Woolf's stream-of-consciousness classic, *To The Lighthouse*. Don't miss it.

There are several good cafes nearby, including the timber-framed Godrevy Cafe (☑ 01736-757999; www.godrevycafe.com; lunch £6-10; ☺ 10am-5pm), as well as an excellent farm shop, Trevaskis Farm (☑ 01209-713931; www.trevaskisfarm.co.uk; 12 Gwinear Rd, Hayle; ☺ 9am-6pm Jun-Aug, to 5pm Sep-May).

West Cornwall

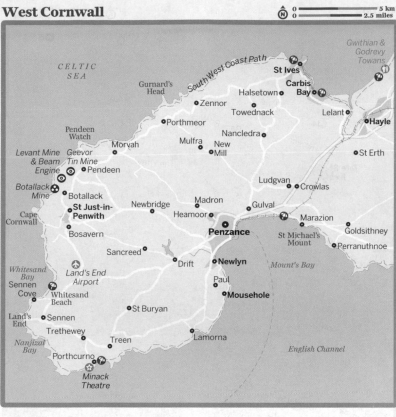

◉ Sights & Activities

The largest town beaches are **Porthmeor** and **Porthminster**, both of which have sand and space aplenty. Between them juts the grassy promontory known as the **Island**, topped by the tiny pre-14th-century **Chapel of St Nicholas**. On the peninsula's east side is the little cove of **Porthgwidden**, often a good place to escape the crowds.

★ Tate St Ives   GALLERY

(☑ 01736-796226; www.tate.org.uk/stives; Porthmeor Beach; adult/child £7/4.50, with Barbara Hepworth Museum £10/6; ☺ 10am-5pm Mar-Oct, to 4pm Nov-Feb) Hovering like a concrete curl above Porthmeor Beach, St Ives' celebrated art museum focuses on the key artists of the 'St Ives School', including luminary names such as Terry Frost, Patrick Heron, Naum Gabo, Ben Nicholson and Barbara Hepworth, displayed alongside more contemporary artists. Of particular local interest are the naive works of fisherman-turned-artist Alfred Wallis, who didn't start painting until the ripe old age of 67.

The top-floor cafe has super views over Porthmeor Beach.

Barbara Hepworth Museum   MUSEUM

(☑ 01736-796226; Barnoon Hill; adult/child £6/4, with Tate St Ives £10/6; ☺ 10am-5pm Mar-Oct, to 4pm Nov-Feb) Barbara Hepworth (1903–75) was one of the leading abstract sculptors of the 20th century and a key figure in the St Ives art scene. Her studio on Barnoon Hill has remained almost untouched since her death and the adjoining garden contains several of her most notable sculptures. Hepworth's work is scattered throughout St Ives; look for works outside the Guildhall and inside the 15th-century parish church of St Ia.

St Ives Boats   BOATING

(☑ 0777 300 8000; www.stivesboats.co.uk; adult/child £10/8) From the harbourfront, several

St Ives

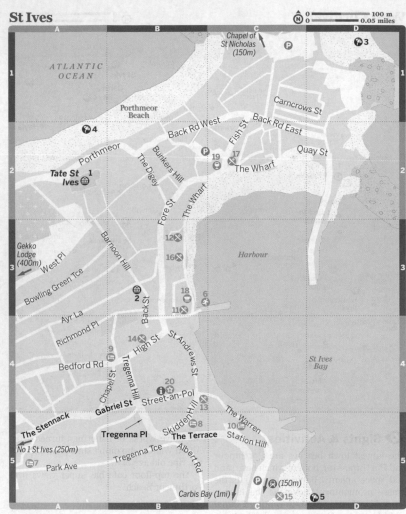

operators including St Ives Boats offer fishing trips and scenic cruises, including to the grey seal colony on Seal Island. If you're really lucky, you might even spot a porpoise or a basking shark in summer.

🛏 Sleeping

No 1 St Ives
B&B ££

(☎01736-799047; www.no1stives.co.uk; 1 Fern Glen; d £95-139; 🅿🖥) Despite its pretentious 'bouchique' tag, this 19th-century granite cottage is still one of the nicest B&Bs in St Ives. Rooms vary in size, but all sport the same palette of cool greys and off-whites,

and have extra spoils such as filtered water, goose-down duvets, iPod docks and White Company bath-stuffs. It's five minutes' walk from town, but there's only space for four cars.

Little Leaf Guest House
B&B ££

(☎01736-795427; www.littleleafguesthouse.co.uk; Park Ave; r £65-120; 🖥) A friendly and cosy five-roomer, on a terrace overlooking the town's rooftops. Rooms are sweet and simple, finished in creamy colours and pine furniture. Ask for rooms 2 or 5 if you're after a sea view.

St Ives

Gekko Lodge   B&B **££**
(✆01736-796591; www.gekkolodge.co.uk; 7 Carthew Tce; d £70-90) A bit of a find, this one: a pebble-dash Victorian house with just two rooms, both of which are enormous and have sea views through bay windows. The style is contemporary, with futon-style beds and funky circular sinks.

Treliska   B&B **££**
(✆01736-797678; www.treliska.com; 3 Bedford Rd; d £60-80; 🛜) This B&B is a bargain in pricey St Ives, especially given the location, just steps from the town centre. The trade-off is the room size: most are on the small side (ask for No 5 if it's space you're after).

★**Tide House**   HOTEL **£££**
(✆01736-791803; www.thetidehouse.co.uk; Skidden Hill; d £140-240) Even in increasingly chi-chi St Ives, this beautiful hotel feels unusually special. It has everything going for it: 16th-century building, harbourside location, gorgeous design and seriously luxurious rooms (all named after Cornish light-

houses), ranging from a romantic penthouse to a split-level mezzanine. Definitely the place to push the boat out.

Trevose Harbour House   B&B **£££**
(✆01736-793267; www.trevosehouse.co.uk; 22 The Warren; d £140-195; 🛜) A stylish six-room town house on the winding Warren, restored with a sea-themed combo of fresh whites and stripy blues. It's been beautifully finished – Neal's Yard bathstuffs, iPod docks and retro design pieces in the rooms, plus a book-lined lounge and minimalist courtyard patio – but the rooms are quite small given the price.

Boskerris   HOTEL **£££**
(✆01736-795295; www.boskerrishotel.co.uk; Boskerris Rd, Carbis Bay; d £130-265; 🅿🛜) In nearby Carbis Bay, this upmarket mini-hotel feels uncluttered, contrasting cool monotones with snazzy design features: pattern-print bedsteads, scatter cushions, minimalist ceramic sinks. The decked patio is an absolute beauty, with grandstand views over the bay.

✖ Eating

Blas Burgerworks   CAFE **£**
(✆01736-797272; The Warren; burgers £5-10; ⏰noon-9.30pm) 🥢 A fantastic boutique burger joint, with an eco-friendly manifesto and an imaginative menu. Go for a 6oz Classic Blasburger, or branch out with a guacamole and corn salsa–topped Rancheros, or a Smokey with beetroot, aged cheddar and homemade piccalilli (plenty of veggie options, too). The owners also run the excellent **Halsetown Inn** (✆01736-795583; www.halsetowninn.co.uk), just outside St Ives.

Pengenna Pasties   BAKERY **£**
(www.pengennapasties.co.uk; 9 High St; pasties £3-4; ⏰10am-5pm Mon-Sat) Generously-stuffed pasties, with a controversial top crimp and flakier texture.

★**Porthminster Beach Café**   BISTRO **££**
(✆01736-795352; www.porthminstercafe.co.uk; Porthminster Beach; mains £10.50-16.50, dinner £10-22; ⏰9am-10pm) This is no ordinary beach cafe: it's a full-blown bistro with a gorgeous suntrap terrace and a superb Mediterranean-influenced menu, specialising in seafood. Tuck into rich bouillabaisse, seafood curry or Provençal fish soup, and settle back to enjoy the breezy beach vistas.

Rum & Crab Shack   SEAFOOD **££**
(✆01736-796353; Wharf Rd; mains £9.95-12.95; ⏰9am-9pm; 👶) If the thought of cracking

your own spider crab and eating it from the shell appeals, then this place will be happy to oblige (aprons and tools are provided). Alternatively, you could just tackle the claws, or tuck into a plate of seafood gumbo or scrowlers on toast (aka sardines). Great fun, and great food to match.

Alba MODERN BRITISH ££
(☑01736-797222; www.thealbarestaurant.com; Old Lifeboat House; 2-/3-course dinner menu £16.95/ 19.95; ☺noon-2pm & 6-10pm) In a converted boathouse near the lifeboat station, this long-standing restaurant has been consistently turning out some of the town's top food for many years. With its banquette seats and sharp decor, it feels classy, especially if you get one of the prime tables next to the panoramic window. The menu is a mix of British and European flavours.

Alfresco BISTRO ££
(☑01736-793737; info@alfrescocafebar.co.uk; The Wharf; 2-/3-course dinner menu £16.95; ☺7-9pm daily, noon-3pm Thu & Fri) Sliding doors onto the quayside allow this tiny restaurant to make the most of its harbourside position, and when the sun's shining it feels positively continental. The Alfresco fish stew is particularly recommended.

Seagrass MODERN BRITISH ££
(☑01736-793763; www.seagrass-stives.com; Fish St; 2-/3-course menu £16.95/19.95; ☺6-9pm) A popular, small bistro just off the wharf, focusing mainly on local seafood – there's a special Oyster and Shells menu, featuring langoustines, whole crab, lobster and oysters.

🍸 Drinking & Entertainment

Hub CAFE, BAR
(www.hub-stives.co.uk; The Wharf; ☺9am-11pm) The open-plan Hub is the heart of St Ives' (limited) nightlife: coffee and burgers by day, cocktails after-dark.

Sloop Inn PUB
(☑01736-796584; www.sloop-inn.co.uk; The Wharf; ☺11am-11pm) This beam-ceilinged boozer is as comfy as an old pair of slippers, with a few tables on the harbour and lots of local ales.

Guildhall CONCERT VENUE
(1 Street-an-Pol) St Ives' concert hall hosts music and theatre, especially during the annual **St Ives September Festival** (www.stivesseptemberfestival.co.uk).

ℹ Information

St Ives Tourist Office (☑01736-796297; www.stivestic.co.uk; Street-an-Pol; ☺9am-5.30pm Mon-Fri, 9am-5pm Sat, 10am-4pm Sun) Inside the Guildhall.

ℹ Getting There & Away

The branch train line from St Ives is worth taking just for the coastal views: trains terminate at St Erth (£3, 14 minutes, half-hourly), where you can catch connections along the Penzance–London Paddington main line.

Bus 17/17A (£4, 30 minutes, half-hourly Monday to Saturday, hourly on Sunday) The quickest route to Penzance.

Bus 16/16A (£5, hourly Monday to Saturday) Round the coast road to Penzance; only the 16A travels via Zennor.

Zennor & St Just

The twisting B3306 from St Ives is a rollercoaster of a road, winding through a stark landscape of ancient drystone walls, barren moorland, tiny villages and rocky bluffs. The landscape here feels wild and ancient, a world away from some of Cornwall's more gentrified corners.

◉ Sights

Church of St Senara CHURCH
(Zennor) This little church in the hamlet of Zennor dates from at least 1150. Inside, a famous carved chair depicts the legendary Mermaid of Zennor, who is said to have fallen in love with the singing voice of local lad Matthew Trewhella. Locals say you can still sometimes hear them singing down at nearby Pendour Cove – and even if you don't, the views along the coast path are reward enough.

★ Geevor Tin Mine MINE
(☑01736-788662; www.geevor.com; adult/child £11/6.50; ☺9am-5pm Sun-Fri Mar-Oct, to 4pm Nov-Feb) Just north of St Just near Pendeen, this historic mine closed in 1990 and now provides a powerful insight into the dark, dingy and dangerous conditions in which Cornwall's miners worked. Above ground, you can view the dressing floors and the original machinery used to sort the minerals and ores, before taking a guided tour into some of the underground shafts. Claustrophobes need not apply.

Botallack Mine
RUIN, MINE

Clinging to the cliffs near Levant, this dramatic engine house has abandoned mine shafts extending right out beneath the raging Atlantic waves. It's a treacherous climb down, so it's best viewed from a distance from nearby **Botallack Head**.

Levant Mine & Beam Engine
HISTORIC SITE

(www.nationaltrust.org.uk/main/w-levantmineandbeamengine; adult/child £6.60/3.30; ☺11am-5pm Sun-Fri) At this clifftop site, one of the world's only working beam engines is still in thunderous action. Built in 1840, these great engines were the powerhouses behind the Cornish mining boom, powering mineral trains and pumping water from the shafts. Lovingly restored by a team of enthusiasts, it's a sight to behold when it's in full steam.

Cape Cornwall
LANDMARK

Jutting out from the cliffs near St Just is Cornwall's only 'official' cape, a craggy finger of land topped by an abandoned minestack. Below the cape is the rocky beach of **Priest's Cove**, while nearby are the ruins of **St Helen's Oratory**, supposedly one of the first Christian chapels built in West Cornwall.

🛏 Sleeping & Eating

Tinner's Arms
INN ££

(☑01736-792697; www.tinnersarms.com; Zennor; s/d £60/100, mains £10-16; P) An old Cornish inn, complete with slate roof, roaring fireplaces, gleaming bar taps and a refreshing lack of commercial clutter (no TV, no jukebox, no mobile signal). Next door, the 'White House' provides fresh, spotless rooms. DH Lawrence drank here while he was writing *Women in Love*.

★ Gurnard's Head
BRITISH ££

(☑01736-796928; www.gurnardshead.co.uk; mains £10-18.50, r £105-170; P 🛜 🐾) On the road between Zennor and St Just, you can't miss the Gurnard's – it's name is written on the roof. Run by the Inkin brothers (who also own Mousehole's Old Coastguard Hotel) this is a perfect country pub, with old-fashioned rooms, book-lined shelves and sepia prints conjuring a cosy, lived-in feel. It's renowned for its delicious, classic British food.

ℹ Getting There & Away

St Just is 6 miles north of Land's End.

Bus 16A (£4, three or four daily Monday to Saturday) Travels from St Ives via Zennor to Penzance.

Bus 10/10A (£5, hourly Monday to Saturday, six on Sunday) Circular route from Penzance via Madron, St Just and Botallack.

Sennen & Land's End

Beyond St Ives, the coastline gets ever wilder and emptier as you near Cornwall's tip at **Land's End**, the westernmost point of mainland England, where the coal-black cliffs plunge into the pounding surf, and the views stretch all the way to the Isles of Scilly on a clear day.

DON'T MISS

MINACK THEATRE & PORTHCURNO

In terms of theatrical settings, the **Minack** (☑01736-810181; www.minack.com) takes top billing. Carved into the crags overlooking Porthcurno Bay and the azure-blue Atlantic, this amazing clifftop amphitheatre was the lifelong passion of local lady Rowena Cade, who dreamt up the idea in the 1930s and oversaw the theatre until her death in 1983. It's now a hugely popular place for alfresco theatre, with a 17-week season running from mid-May to mid-September. Experienced theatre-goers bring wine, picnic supplies, wet-weather gear and – most importantly, considering the seats are carved out of granite – a comfy cushion. Above the theatre, the **visitor centre** (adult/child £3.50/1.40; ☺9.30am-5.30pm Apr-Sep, 10am-4pm Oct-Mar) recounts the theatre's history. It's closed when there's a matinee.

Below the theatre, the sandy wedge of **Porthcurno** is great for swimming and sunbathing, and the lesser-known beach of **Pednvounder** nearby is good if you like to sunbathe au naturel – it's one of Cornwall's few naturist beaches. Inland, the newly redeveloped **Porthcurno Telegraph Museum** (☑01736-810966; www.porthcurno.org.uk; adult/child £8.50/5; ☺10am-5pm) recounts the area's role as Britain's first hub for transatlantic telecommunications.

The Minack is 3 miles from Land's End and 9 miles from Penzance. Bus 1/1A from Penzance stops several times daily.

Unfortunately, the decision to build the **Legendary Land's End** (www.landsendlandmark.co.uk; adult/child £10/7; ⊙10am-5pm Mar-Oct; 🐾) theme park on the headland in the 1980s hasn't done much to enhance the view. Take our advice: just pay for the car park, skip the tacky multimedia shows and opt for an exhilarating clifftop stroll instead. Look out for the slender profile of the historic **Longships Lighthouse**, perched on a rocky reef 1.25 miles out to sea.

From Land's End, you can follow the coast path west to the secluded cove of **Nanjizal Bay**, or east to the old harbour of **Sennen**, which overlooks the glorious – and appropriately named – beach of **Whitesand Bay** (actually pronounced Whitsand), the area's most impressive stretch of sand.

Land's End is 9 miles from Penzance. Bus 1/1A travels from Penzance (£5, one hour, six daily Monday to Saturday) to Land's End; 1 goes via Sennen, while the 1A travels via Treen and Porthcurno.

Mousehole

POP 697

With a tight tangle of cottages and alleyways gathered behind the granite breakwater, Mousehole (pronounced 'mowzle') looks like something from a children's storybook (a fact not unnoticed by the author Antonia Barber, who set her much-loved fairy-tale *The Mousehole Cat* here). In centuries past this was Cornwall's busiest pilchard port, but the fish dried up at the turn of the century, and the village now survives mostly on tourist traffic.

Packed in summer and deserted in winter, it's ripe for a wander, with a maze of slips, net-lofts and courtyards. It's also well-known for its Christmas lights, and as the home of 'stargazey pie', a pilchard pie in which the fish heads are left poking through the pie's crust. It's traditionally eaten on Tom Bawcock's Eve (23 December), named after a local lad who reputedly rescued the town from a famine by braving stormy seas to land a bumper haul of pilchards.

The **Old Coastguard Hotel** (✆01736-731222; www.oldcoastguardhotel.co.uk; d £120-245, mains £11-15; P 🖥 🐾) is the pick of the places to stay, a swanky seaside hotel with to-die-for sea views on the edge of Mousehole.

Bus 6 makes the 20-minute journey (£3) to Penzance half-hourly.

Penzance

POP 21,168

Overlooking the sweep of Mount's Bay, the old harbour of Penzance has a salty, sea-blown charm that feels altogether more authentic than many of Cornwall's polished-up ports. Its streets and shopping arcades still feel real and a touch ramshackle, and there's nowhere better for a windy-day walk than the town's seafront Victorian promenade. The nearby harbour of **Newlyn** is still home to Cornwall's largest fishing fleet.

◎ Sights & Activities

Penlee House Gallery & Museum GALLERY
(www.penleehouse.org.uk; Morrab Rd; adult/child £4.50/3; ⊙10am-5pm Mon-Sat Easter-Sep, 10.30am-4.30pm Oct-Easter) Penzance's historic art gallery displays paintings by artists of the Newlyn School (including Stanhope Forbes) and hosts regular exhibitions. Admission is free on Saturday.

Exchange GALLERY
(www.theexchangegallery.co.uk; Princes St; ⊙10am-5pm Mon-Sat Easter-Sep, Wed-Sat Oct-Easter) FREE Housed in Penzance's former telecoms building, this gallery hosts regular exhibitions of contemporary art. It's the sister gallery to the **Newlyn Art Gallery** (www.newlynartgallery.co.uk; ⊙10am-5pm Mon-Sat Easter-Sep, Wed-Sat Oct-Easter), a mile west along Penzance's prom.

Trengwainton GARDENS
(NT; ✆01736-363148; trengwainton@nationaltrust.org.uk; Madron; adult/child £6.80/3.40; ⊙10am-5pm Sun-Thu mid-Feb–Nov) Two miles north of Penzance near Madron is the walled garden of Trengwainton, which has a subtropical collection of ferns, shrubs, magnolias and rhododendrons.

Jubilee Pool SWIMMING
(www.jubileepool.co.uk) At the eastern end of town is Penzance's 1930s seawater lido. It's usually open in summer, but at the time of writing it was closed due to storm damage – check the website for news.

🛏 Sleeping

Penzance has lots of low-price B&Bs, especially along Alexandra Rd and Morrab Rd.

Penzance YHA HOSTEL £
(✆0845 371 9653; penzance@yha.org.uk; Castle Horneck, Alverton; dm £15-20; P @) Penzance's

Penzance

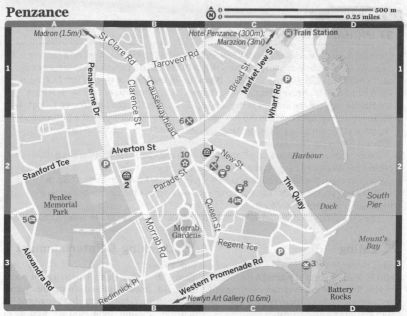

YHA is inside an 18th-century house on the edge of town. It's a rambling place, with a cafe, laundry and four- to 10-bed dorms. It's a 15-minute walk from the front; buses 5 and 6 stop nearby.

★ **Venton Vean**　　　　B&B **££**
(☑ 01736-351294; www.ventonvean.co.uk; Trewithen Rd; r £80-95; ☏) The picture of a modern B&B, finished in greys, blues and pistachios, with stripped wood floors and a keen eye for design. Rooms 1 and 2 are the most spacious; the former overlooks Penlee Memorial Park. The sumptuous breakfast choice includes smoked pollack and Spanish tortillas.

Artist Residence Penzance　　B&B **££**
(☑ 01736-365664; www.arthotelcornwall.co.uk; Chapel St; d £105-145; ☏) This quirky B&B on Chapel St is like sleeping inside an art gallery. All the rooms have their own design courtesy of a local artist: street-art murals by Jo Peel, seascapes by Pinky Vision, butterfly wallpapers by Dolly Divine. They're furnished with retro furniture and most peep across Penzance's rooftops. Great fun.

Hotel Penzance　　　　HOTEL **£££**
(☑ 01736-363117; www.hotelpenzance.com; Briton's Hill; d £140-205; ☏) Perched on a hill

Penzance

◎ Sights
1 Exchange C2
2 Penlee House Gallery & Museum B2

◑ Activities, Courses & Tours
3 Jubilee Pool D3

⊜ Sleeping
4 Artist Residence Penzance C2
5 Venton Vean A3

⊗ Eating
6 Archie Brown's B2
7 Bakehouse C2

◎ Drinking & Nightlife
8 Turk's Head C2
9 Zero Lounge C2

◎ Entertainment
10 Acorn Arts Centre B2

with views across Mount's Bay, this townhouse hotel makes a pleasant Penzance base. Bedrooms are staid in style, with cream-and-magnolia colours, varnished desks and vintage lamps: the best have bay windows looking out to sea. The hotel's restaurant, the Bay, serves quality food.

DON'T MISS

ST MICHAEL'S MOUNT

Looming from the waters of Mount's Bay and connected to the mainland via a cobbled causeway, this **abbey-crowned island** (NT; ☑ 01736-710507; www.stmichaelsmount.co.uk; adult/child £8.75/4.25; ⊙ house 10.30am-5.30pm Sun-Fri late Mar-Oct, gardens Mon-Fri Apr-Jun, Thu & Fri Jul-Sep) is an unforgettable sight. There's been a monastery here since at least the 5th century, but the present abbey was mostly built by Benedictine monks during the 12th century. Highlights include the rococo drawing room, the armoury, the 14th-century church and the amazing clifftop gardens. Though owned by the St Aubyn family, the abbey is run by the National Trust.

Recent excavations including a Bronze Age axe head, dagger and metal clasp have proved the island has been inhabited since ancient times.

You can catch the ferry (adult/child £2/1) from nearby Marazion at high tide, but it's worth timing your arrival for low tide so you can walk across the causeway, just as the monks and pilgrims did centuries ago.

The 13/13A bus shuttles between Marazion and Penzance (£2) three times a day.

✗ Eating

Archie Brown's   CAFE £
(☑ 01736-362828; Bread St; mains £4-10; ⊙ 9am-5pm Mon-Sat) A wholefood cafe and health shop, serving quiches, homity pies and salads to Penzance's arty crowd.

★ Tolcarne Inn   PUB ££
(☑ 01736-363074; www.tolcarneinn.co.uk; Tolcarne Pl, Newlyn; mains £12-18; ⊙ noon-2.15pm & 7-9pm Tue-Sat, noon-2.15pm Sun) This old Newlyn inn is run by talented local chef Ben Tunnicliffe, who's fast turned it into the area's primo gastropub. The ethos is refreshingly honest – top-quality fish, seafood and locally sourced meat, served with minimal fuss. Bookings advisable, especially for Sunday lunch.

Ben's Cornish Kitchen   BRITISH ££
(☑ 01736-719200; www.benscornishkitchen.com; Marazion; mains £14-23; ⊙ noon-2pm & 7-8.30pm Tue-Sat; ☑) You could easily miss Ben Prior's restaurant as you zip along Marazion's main street, but you'd be sorry. Diners travel from far and wide to taste his classical cooking, which focuses on meaty Cornish flavours with a French influence. It's so popular he's recently expanded upstairs.

Bakehouse   MEDITERRANEAN ££
(☑ 01736-331331; www.bakehouserestaurant.co.uk; Chapel St; mains £8.95-19.50; ⊙ 6.15-10pm Mon-Sat) Down an alley off Chapel St, this no-nonsense bistro serves unpretentious food such as fish served with Med-style marinades, and steaks with spicy rubs.

🍷 Drinking & Entertainment

Turk's Head   PUB
(Chapel St; ⊙ 11am-11pm) This salty old boozer could have tumbled from the pages of *Treasure Island*. The bar's covered in maritime memorabilia, and it's said a secret smugglers' tunnel links the pub to the harbour.

Zero Lounge   BAR
(Chapel St; ⊙ 11am-11pm) More urban chic than olde worlde, this open-plan bar also has the town's best beer garden.

Acorn Arts Centre   THEATRE
(www.acornartscentre.co.uk; Parade St) A small theatre hosting film, theatre, comedy and live-music gigs.

❶ Getting There & Away

BUS
Local destinations include:

Helston and Falmouth Bus 2/2A (£5, hourly Monday to Saturday, six on Sunday) via Marazion.

St Ives Buses 17/17A/17B (£4, 30 minutes, half-hourly Monday to Saturday, hourly on Sunday).

TRAIN
Penzance is the last stop on the line from London Paddington.

Exeter (£19.80, three hours)

London Paddington (£60.50, 5½ hours)

Truro (£6.40, 30 minutes)

The Lizard

Once notorious as a smugglers' haven and an ill-famed graveyard for ships, the rugged Lizard Peninsula offers Cornwall's wildest coastal panoramas. Wind-lashed in winter, in summer its heaths and cliffs blaze with wildflowers, and its numerous beaches and coves are perfect for a bracing swim.

The main town is Helston, which is famous for its annual street party, Flora Day, held on 8 May. Pretty villages are dotted all round the peninsula's coastline: the old harbour of Coverack, the beaches of Mullion and the idyllic thatched-cottage cove of Cadgwith are all well worth a visit.

Along the peninsula's northern edge runs the Helford River, lined by creeks and inlets which famously inspired Daphne du Maurier's smuggling yarn, *Frenchman's Creek*. Several local companies offer kayaking tours.

◎ Sights & Activities

Lizard Lighthouse Heritage Centre MUSEUM
(☑ 01326-290202; www.lizardlighthouse.co.uk; adult/child £2.75/1.75; ☺ 11am-5pm Sun-Thu Mar-Oct) Housed in a 1751 lighthouse above Lizard Point, this museum contains exhibits on seafaring and shipwrecks, and you can take guided tours (adult/child £7/4) into the tower to see the lamp room and foghorn.

★ Kynance Cove BEACH
A mile north of Lizard Point, this National Trust–owned inlet is a showstopper, studded with offshore islands rising out of searingly blue seas. The cliffs around the cove are rich in serpentine, a red-green rock popular with Victorian trinket-makers. Drinks and snacks are available at the eco-friendly cafe (www.kynancecovecafe.co.uk; mains £8-14).

National Seal Sanctuary WILDLIFE RESERVE
(☑ 0871 423 2110; www.sealsanctuary.co.uk; adult/child £14.40/12; ☺ 10am-5pm May-Sep, 9am-4pm Oct-Apr) Towards the northwest of the Lizard Peninsula, this sanctuary cares for sick and orphaned seals washed up along the Cornish coastline before returning them to the wild.

Koru Kayaking KAYAKING
(☑ 07794-321827; www.korukayaking.co.uk; 2hr trip £35) Kayaking trips to Frenchman's Creek from the north bank of the Helford River, as well as from Trevaunance Cove near St Agnes.

Aberfal Outdoor Pursuits KAYAKING
(☑ 07968-770756; www.aberfaloutdoorpursuits.co.uk; half/full day £35/50) Half- and full-day guided kayaking trips along the Helford on sit-on-top kayaks.

⊨ Sleeping & Eating

Lizard YHA HOSTEL £
(☑ 0845 371 9550; www.yha.org.uk; dm £17-22; ☺ Apr-Oct) The old lighthouse-keeper's cottage at the heritage centre has now been turned into the UK's most southerly hostel, the Lizard Point YHA.

Ann's Pasties BRITISH £
(☑ 01326-290889; www.annspasties.co.uk; pasties £2.85; ☺ 9am-3pm Mon-Sat) Approved by Rick Stein, no less, Ann Muller serves huge, traditional pasties from her tiny shop near Lizard Point.

Roskilly's ICE CREAM £
(The Harbour; ice cream £2-3; ☺ 9am-5pm) Harbourside outlet for the Lizard's renowned ice-cream maker.

★ Kota INTERNATIONAL ££
(☑ 01326-562407; www.kotarestaurant.co.uk; 2-course menu £17.50, mains £12-20; ☺ 12.30-2.30pm & 6-9pm) New Zealander Jude Kereama takes his culinary inspiration from his globetrotting travels, and his menu is spiced with exotic flavours, from Szechuan to Thai and Malaysian. His main restaurant is in a converted mill in Porthleven, 3 miles south of Helston. He also has a new cafe-bistro, Kota Kai (☑ 01326-574411; www.kotakai.co.uk; mains £11.50-14.95; ☺ noon-2pm & 5.30-9.30pm; ☎), along the quay.

Halzephron Inn PUB ££
(☑ 01326-240406; www.halzephron-inn.co.uk; mains £9.95-21.95; ☺ 11am-11pm) On the cliffs above the cove of Gunwalloe, 5 miles south of Helston, this is a proper Cornish local, whitewashed and slate-topped, with brassy trinkets above the bar, beams on the ceiling and a menu of beer-battered fish and surf-and-turf steak.

❶ Getting There & Away

Services include:

Bus 2 Penzance to Falmouth, with stops at Porthleven and Helston (£5, hourly Monday to Saturday, six on Sunday).

Bus 36 Helston to Gunwalloe, Gweek, Coverack and St Keverne (£3, three or four daily Monday to Saturday).

Bus 37 Helston to Mullion (£3) and the Lizard (£5, every two hours Monday to Saturday, four on Sunday).

Bus 82 (£5, one hour, hourly, five on Sunday) Helston to Truro.

Falmouth & Around

POP 20,775

The world's third-deepest natural harbour, Falmouth made its fortune during the 18th and 19th centuries, when clippers, trading vessels and mail packets stopped off here to unload their cargoes. The town is still an important centre for ship repairs, although these days it's also a lively student town thanks to the ever-expanding campus of University College Falmouth in nearby Penryn.

It's an ideal base for exploring Cornwall's south coast, with a wealth of bars and bistros, a trio of beaches and the nation's foremost maritime museum on its doorstep.

◎ Sights

Falmouth has three beaches. Nearest to town is busy **Gyllyngvase**, a short walk from the town centre, where there's lots of sand and the lively Gylly Beach Café. Around the headland is little **Swanpool**, while **Maenporth** is another mile further west. The 500 bus stops at all three in summer.

National Maritime Museum   MUSEUM
(☑ 01326-313388; www.nmmc.co.uk; Discovery Quay; adult/child £11.50/8; ⊙10am-5pm) This is the sister outpost to the National Maritime Museum in Greenwich, London. It focuses on Falmouth's history as a seafaring port, supplemented by regular nautically themed exhibitions. At the heart of the complex is the impressive **Flotilla Gallery**, where an array of small boats is suspended from the

ceiling on steel wires. From the top floor of the **Lookout tower**, there's a 360-degree panorama across Falmouth Bay.

Pendennis Castle   CASTLE
(EH; ☑ 01326-316594; adult/child £7/4.20; ⊙10am-6pm Jul & Aug, to 5pm Apr-Jun & Sep, to 4pm Oct-Mar) Designed to work in tandem with its sister castle in St Mawes, out across the estuary, this Tudor castle sits proudly on Pendennis Point, and was designed as part of Henry VIII's massive castle-building program to reinforce England's coastline. You can wander around several of the castle floors and the Tudor gun deck, as well as the Governor's bedroom, a WWI guard ouse and the WWII-era Half-Moon Battery. Listen out for the Noonday Gun blasting out at midday.

🛏 Sleeping

Falmouth Lodge Backpackers   HOSTEL **£**
(☑ 01326-319996; www.falmouthbackpackers.co. uk; 9 Gyllyngvase Tce; dm/s £19/26, d £28-35) In a mock-Tudor house at the top of town, this friendly hostel makes a fun budget stay. Rooms are small but clean and cosy, there's an Aga in the kitchen and a DVD lounge, and owner Judi often holds impromptu BBQs for guests.

Highcliffe Contemporary B&B   B&B **££**
(☑ 01326-314466; www.highcliffefalmouth.com; 22 Melvill Rd; s £45-55, d £75-130; ☎) Vintage furniture and upcycled design pieces give each of the rooms here its own individual feel. The pick of the bunch is the light-filled Attic Penthouse, with skylight windows overlooking Falmouth Bay. Room service breakfasts are served in picnic baskets, or you can tuck into pancakes and Hog's pudding in the dining room.

WORTH A TRIP

TREBAH & GLENDURGAN GARDENS

Two of Cornwall's great subtropical gardens sit side by side along the northern bank of the River Helford. First planted in 1840, **Trebah** (☑ 01326-252200; www.trebahgarden.co.uk; adult/child £9/3; ⊙10.30am-4.30pm) is dramatically situated in a steep ravine filled with giant rhododendrons, huge Brazilian rhubarb plants and jungle ferns.

Next-door **Glendurgan** (NT; ☑ 01326-250906; www.nationaltrust.org.uk/glendurgan-garden; adult/child £7.20/3.60; ⊙10.30am-5.30pm Tue-Sun) was established around the same time by the wealthy Fox family, and is now owned by the National Trust. It has amazing views of the River Helford, as well as an original yew-tree maze and a secluded beach near Durgan village.

They're about 4 miles from Falmouth: head for Mawnan Smith and follow the signs.

Bosanneth
B&B ££

(☑01326-314649; www.bosanneth.co.uk; Gyllyngvase Hill; d from £90; 🐾) There's a mix-and-match decorative vibe running through this eight-room B&B. Some of the rooms feel vintage, with old mirrors, reclaimed furniture and classic colours, while others go for a more up-to-date look. The 'oasis' garden is a particular delight.

Greenbank
HOTEL £££

(☑01326-312440; www.greenbank-hotel.co.uk; Harbourside; r £99-245; P 🐾) The queen of Falmouth's old hotels, with a knockout position overlooking the boat-filled estuary towards Flushing. It feels rather like the setting for an Agatha Christie novel – nautical knick-knacks and ships in cabinets dot the public areas, and tall windows look out onto the water. The rooms are more modern, decorated in inoffensive beiges and creams. Sea views command premium prices.

✖ Eating

★ Oliver's
BISTRO ££

(☑01326-218138; www.oliversfalmouth.com; 33 High St; mains £12.50-20.50; ⊙noon-2pm & 7-9pm Tue-Sat) Run by chef Ken Oliver, this little bistro is the place everyone wants to dine in Falmouth, but the tiny dining room means you'll have to book well ahead. White walls and pine tables provide a stripped-back match for Ken's no-fuss, Mediterranean-inspired food. Local foragers provide many ingredients.

Wheelhouse
SEAFOOD ££

(☑01326-318050; Upton Slip; mains £8-15; ⊙6-10pm Wed-Sat) Hidden down a narrow alley, this backstreet shellfish bar is another Falmouth favourite. The dining here is DIY: crab, scallops, mussels and lobsters are served shell-on, complete with cracking tools. There are two sittings, but both are always packed out – book well ahead.

Courtyard Deli
DELI, CAFE ££

(☑01326-319526; http:courtyarddeli.wordpress. com; 2 Bells Ct; mains £8-12; ⊙8.30am-5.30pm Mon-Wed, to 9.30pm Thu-Sat, 10.30am-4pm Sun) Small is beautiful, as this fabulous deli-diner ably demonstrates. Charcuterie, tarts, salads and quiches fill the counter cabinets, and there are evening tapas sessions several times a week. It's up an easy-to-miss alley, next to Beerwolf Books.

Gylly Beach Café
CAFE ££

(☑01326-312884; www.gyllybeach.com; Gyllyngvase Beach; mains £10.95-15.95; ⊙9am-11pm)

When the sun shines, everyone heads to the Gylly Beach for morning coffee or lunch with a sea view. Sliding doors open onto the glass-fronted patio, perched right above Gyllyngvase's sands. Burgers, kebabs, mussels and salads dominate the menu, and the breakfasts are great.

Rick Stein's Fish
FISH & CHIPS ££

(☑01841-532700; Discovery Quay; takeaway £4.95-6.50, mains £10.50-14.50; ⊙noon-2.30pm & 5-9pm) Rick Stein's posh fish-and-chips shop now has a Falmouth branch.

🍸 Drinking & Nightlife

Dolly's
TEAROOM

(☑01326-218400; www.dollysbar.co.uk; 21 Church St; ⊙10am-10pm or 11pm Tue-Sat) Frilly and friendly, Dolly's captures the delights of the English tearoom – complete with charity-shop lamps, bone china teapots and cake stands. It kicks into a different gear after dark, with cocktails and jazz.

Espressini
CAFE

(39 Killigrew St; ⊙8am-6pm Mon-Sat, 10am-4pm Sun; 🐾) Cornwall's best coffee house, bar none. The choice of blends, roasts and coffees are enough to fill a 3m-long blackboard. Literally.

Beerwolf Books
PUB

(☑01326-618474; www.beerwolfbooks.co.uk; 3 Bells Ct; ⊙noon-midnight) Quite possibly the greatest idea ever, anytime, anywhere: a pub and bookshop rolled into one, meaning you can browse for reading material before settling down for a pint of real ale.

Front
PUB

(☑01326-212168; Custom House Quay; ⊙11am-11.30pm) Spit-and-sawdust pub favoured by beer buffs, with scuffed wood floors and real ales served straight from wooden casks.

Chain Locker
PUB

(Quay St; ⊙11am-11pm) A proper old sea-dog's pub, with outside seating on the harbour.

❶ Getting There & Away

Falmouth is at the end of the branch train line from Truro (£4, 20 minutes), which also stops at Penryn.

Bus 2 (£5, hourly Monday to Saturday) To Penzance via Helston.

Bus 35 (£5, twice daily Monday to Saturday) Stops at Glendurgan and Gweek en route to Helston.

Bus 88 (£5, hourly) Fastest bus to Truro.

Truro

POP 17,431

Centred on its three-spired 19th-century cathedral, Truro is Cornwall's capital city. Once a busy river port and one of Cornwall's five Stannary towns (where tin was assayed and stamped for export), these days it's a busy commercial city, with a lively centre dominated by the usual coffee shops and chain stores.

Remnants of the city's elegant Georgian past can be seen on Lemon St and Walsingham Pl.

◉ Sights

Royal Cornwall Museum
MUSEUM

(✆01872-272205; www.royalcornwallmuseum.org.uk; River St; ◷10am-5pm Mon-Sat) FREE Collections at the county's main museum encompass everything from geological specimens to Celtic torques and a ceremonial carriage. Upstairs there's an Egyptian section and a little gallery with some surprising finds: a Turner here, a van Dyck there, and several works by Stanhope Forbes.

Truro Cathedral
CATHEDRAL

(www.trurocathedral.org.uk; High Cross; suggested donation £4; ◷7.30am-6pm Mon-Sat, 9am-7pm Sun) Built on the site of a 16th-century parish church in soaring Gothic Revival style, Truro Cathedral was completed in 1910, making it the first cathedral built in England since St Paul's. Inside, the vast nave contains some fine Victorian stained glass and the impressive Father Willis Organ.

Trelissick Gardens
GARDENS

(NT; www.nationaltrust.org.uk/trelissick-garden; adult/child £8.60/4.30; ◷10.30am-5.30pm) At the head of the Fal estuary, 4 miles south of Truro, Trelissick is one of Cornwall's most beautiful estates, with a formal garden filled with magnolias and hydrangeas, and a huge expanse of fields and parkland criss-crossed by walking trails.

Lemon St Market
MARKET

(www.lemonstreetmarket.co.uk; Lemon St; ◷10.30am-5.30pm Mon-Sat) A covered market housing craft shops, cafes, delis and an upstairs gallery. The willow-and-paper lanterns hanging from the ceiling were built for Truro's Christmas street parade, the City of Lights, held in early December.

🛌 Sleeping

Mannings Hotel
HOTEL ££

(✆01872-270345; www.manningshotels.co.uk; Lemon St; r £79-109; P🕸) The best place to stay in the city centre. The part-Georgian building has been tastefully modernised, with zingy colours and minimalist furniture. There are 'aparthotels' for longer stays (£129).

Merchant House Hotel
HOTEL ££

(✆01872-272450; www.merchant-house.co.uk; 49 Falmouth Rd; s £55, d £70-90, f £95; P) This smart Victorian house is handy for town, and refurbishment has brightened up the rooms. Some rooms have skylights, others overlook the garden. It's popular with business travellers and organised tours, so it's worth reserving well ahead.

WORTH A TRIP

THE ROSELAND

On the opposite side of the Fal Estuary from Truro and Falmouth, the Roseland peninsula gets its name not from flowers, but from the Cornish word *ros*, meaning promontory. Greener and gentler than the harsh granite cliffs of the north coast, it's a pastoral place, criss-crossed by hedgerows and spotted with quiet villages and sandy bays – including the large beaches of Carne and Pendower, which join together at low tide. It's also well worth visiting the chichi town of St Mawes, which has a beautifully preserved Tudor castle (EH; ✆01326-270526; adult/child £4.60/2.80; ◷10am-6pm Apr-Sep, to 5pm Oct-Mar), shaped like a clover leaf.

The quickest route to the Roseland is via the King Harry Ferry (✆01872-862312; www.falriver.co.uk/getting-about/ferries/king-harry-ferry; per car one way/return £5/8, bicycles & pedestrians free), which carries cars and pedestrians over the Fal River from near Trelissick Gardens to the opposite side at Philleigh. Otherwise it's a drive of around 14 miles from Truro.

DON'T MISS

CORNWALL'S GLOBETROTTING GARDENS

Lodged at the bottom of a disused clay-pit, the giant biomes of the **Eden Project** (☎ 01726-811911; www.edenproject.com; adult/child/family £23.50/13.50/68; ☉ 10am-6pm Apr-Oct, to 4.30pm Nov-Mar) – the largest greenhouses in the world – have become Cornwall's most celebrated landmark and a definite must-see. Looking like a Bond villain's lair, Eden's bubble-shaped biomes maintain miniature ecosystems that enable all kinds of weird and wonderful plants to flourish – from stinking rafflesia flowers and banana trees in the rainforest biome to cacti and soaring palms in the Mediterranean biome.

Exhibits around the complex explore ecological and conservation themes, covering everything from global warming to rubber production and chocolate-making. Landscaped gardens wind their way between the biomes, but the highlight is the gravity-defying treetop walkway that winds its way through the canopy of the Rainforest Biome.

In summer, the biomes provide a backdrop for live concerts during the Eden Sessions, and in winter host a full-size ice rink.

The Eden site is at Bodelva, about 5 miles' drive from St Austell. There are discounts for buying tickets online and arriving by public transport. Bus 101 runs regularly from St Austell train station; bus 527 travels from Newquay.

Not far away is Cornwall's real-life secret garden, the **Lost Gardens of Heligan** (☎ 01726-845100; www.heligan.com; adult/child £12/6; ☉ 10am-6pm Mar-Oct, to 5pm Nov-Feb). Formerly the family estate of the Tremaynes, Heligan's magnificent 19th-century gardens fell into disrepair following WWI, and have since been restored to their former splendour by the brains behind the Eden Project, Tim Smit, and a huge army of gardeners, horticulturalists and volunteers.

It's a horticultural wonderland: wandering round the grounds you'll discover formal lawns, working kitchen gardens, fruit-filled greenhouses, a secret grotto and an 25m-high rhododendron (claimed to be the world's largest). For many people, though, it's the jungle valley which really steals the show – a Lost World landscape of gigantic ferns, towering palms and tropical blooms.

Heligan is 7 miles from St Austell. Bus 526 links Heligan with Mevagissey and St Austell train station (£5).

🍴 Eating

Bustopher's   BISTRO ££
(☎ 01872-279029; www.bustophersbarbistro.com; 62 Lemon St; mains £10-14; ☉ noon-10pm Wed-Sat, to 4pm Sun) Modern urban dining comes to Truro at Bustopher's, a classy bistro decked out with shiny wood, candles on the tables and lots of nooks and crannies. The menu is divided into 'Smalls' and 'Bigs', and runs the gamut from clam and fish stew to confit duck. It's really rather good.

Sam's in the City   BISTRO ££
(www.samscornwall.co.uk; 1-2 New Bridge St; mains £11.95-21.95; ☉ 9am-10pm) This long-standing restaurant has a snazzy new city address, in a former jeweller's on one of Truro's oldest streets. The menu is split between seafood classics, steaks, city salads and sharing platters – plus bouillabaisse and seafood feasts for the very hungry.

🍷 Drinking & Entertainment

Old Ale House   PUB
(Quay St; ☉ noon-11pm) A proper ale-drinker's pub, with sawdust on the floor, beer mats on the ceiling and a menu of guest ales.

Old Grammar School   PUB
(19 St Mary St; ☉ 10am-late) Open-plan drinking den with big tables and sofas to sink into. Lunch is served from noon to 3pm; later it's cocktails, candles and Belgian and Japanese beers.

Hall for Cornwall   THEATRE
(☎ 01872-262466; www.hallforcornwall.co.uk; Lemon Quay) The county's main venue for touring theatre and music.

ℹ Information

Tourist Office (☎ 01872-274555; tic@truro.gov.uk; Boscawen St; ☉ 9am-5.30pm Mon-Fri, to 5pm Sat)

❶ Getting There & Away

BUS

Truro's bus station is beside Lemon Quay.

Bus 88 (£5, hourly) Express to Falmouth.

Bus X18 (£5, hourly Monday to Saturday, six on Sunday) To Penzance.

Bus 14/14A (£5, 1½ hours, hourly Monday to Saturday) To St Ives.

TRAIN

Truro is on the main London Paddington–Penzance line and the branch line to Falmouth.

Bristol (£45, 3½ hours)

Exeter (£17.90, 2¼ hours)

Falmouth (£4, 30 minutes)

London Paddington (£60.50, 4½ hours)

Penzance (£6.40, 30 minutes)

Fowey

POP 2273

In many ways, Fowey feels like Padstow's south-coast sister; a workaday port turned well-heeled holiday town, with a tumble of pastel-coloured houses, portside pubs and tiered terraces overlooking the wooded banks of the Fowey River. The town's wealth was founded on the export of china clay from the St Austell pits, but it's been an important port since Elizabethan times, and later became the adopted home of the thriller writer Daphne du Maurier, who used the nearby house at Menabilly Barton as the inspiration for *Rebecca*.

These days, it's an attractive and increasingly upmarket town, handy for exploring Cornwall's southeastern corner.

◎ Sights

Readymoney Cove   BEACH

From the town centre, the Esplanade leads down to this little cove and the remains of the small Tudor fort of **St Catherine's Castle**.

Polkerris Beach   BEACH

(www.polkerrisbeach.com) A couple of miles west of Fowey, this is the area's largest and busiest beach. Sailing lessons, windsurfing and paddle-boarding are all available.

⚡ Activities

Hall Walk   WALKING TRAIL

(www.nationaltrust.org.uk/item379352) This 3.5-mile circular walk starts across the river from Fowey in Bodinnick, winding along the wooded shores of Pont Pill Creek before following the coastline to the harbour of Polruan, from where you can catch a ferry back to Fowey. You can download a route guide from the National Trust website.

Encounter Cornwall   KAYAKING

(☏07976-466123; www.encountercornwall.com; Golant; adult/child £25/12.50) Three-hour trips from Golant, just north of Fowey, with a choice of exploring creek or coastline.

🛏 Sleeping

★ Coriander Cottages   B&B ££

(☏01726-834998; www.foweyaccommodation.co.uk; Penventinue Lane; r £100-130; P🐾🛜) 🐾 A delightfully rural cottage complex on the outskirts of Fowey, with ecofriendly accommodation in a choice of open-plan, self-catering barns, all with quiet country views. The stone barns have been beautifully modernised, and use a combination of solar panels, ground-source heating and rainwater harvesting to reduce environmental impact. A lovely retreat.

Cormorant Hotel   HOTEL ££

(☏01726-833426; www.cormoranthotel.co.uk; Golant; d £115-170) Up the creek in Golant, this small hotel has a superb riverside location, and many of its rooms have water-view balconies. They're split into three comfort levels: go for a Superior with view for the premium price/comfort ratio.

Old Quay House   HOTEL £££

(☏01726-833302; www.theoldquayhouse.com; 28 Fore St; d £145-395; 🛜) The epitome of Fowey's upmarket trend, this exclusive quayside hotel is all natural fabrics, rattan chairs and tasteful tones, and the rooms are a mix of estuary-view suites and attic penthouses. Very Kensington, not very Cornish.

🍴 Eating & Drinking

Lifebuoy Cafe   CAFE £

(☏07715-075869; www.thelifebuoycafe.co.uk; 8 Lostwithiel St; mains £5-10; ⏰8am-5pm) Everyone's favourite brekkie stop in Fowey, this friendly cafe is a riot of character, from the brightly coloured furniture and polka-dot bunting to the vintage Action Men on the shelves. Wolf down a Fat Buoy brekkie or a classic fish-finger butty, washed down with a mug of good old English tea.

Dwelling House   CAFE £

(☏01726-833662; 6 Fore St; tea £3-6; ⏰10am-6.30pm May-Sep, to 5.30pm Wed-Sun Oct-Apr)

Top spot for tea (20-plus varieties) and dainty cakes (decorated with sprinkles and icing swirls, and served on a proper cake stand).

Bistro FRENCH ££
(☑ 01726-832322; www.thebistrofowey.co.uk; 24 Fore St; 2-/3-course menu £15.95/18.95) Solid bistro dining on Fowey's main street, offering a Cornish spin on French classics, with an especially strong focus on seafood. It's stylish inside, with mosaic floors and monochrome photos.

Sam's BISTRO ££
(www.samsfowey.co.uk; 20 Fore St; mains £6.50-13.95; ☻ noon-9pm) Sam's has been a stalwart in Fowey for years. Booth seats, day-glo menus and classic movie posters keep the feel laid-back, and the menu of burgers, fishy specials, salads and 'old favourites' all come in a choice of starter or main sizes. There's a beachside outpost beside Polkerris Beach. No bookings.

King of Prussia PUB
(www.kingofprussia.co.uk; Town Quay; ☻ 11am-11pm) Fowey has lots of pubs, but you might as well go for the one with the best harbour view, named after notorious 'free trader' John Carter.

❶ Getting There & Away

Buses to Fowey all stop at Par Station, where you can catch trains to the Penzance–London Paddington main line. Bus 524/525 (half-hourly) stops in Fowey, St Austell (£4) and Mevagissey (£5); the 525 continues to Heligan (£5).
Bodinnick Ferry (car & 2 passengers/pedestrian/bicycle £4.60/1.70/free; ☻ last ferry 8.45pm Apr-Oct, 7pm Nov-Mar) Car ferry crossing the river to Bodinnick.
Polruan Ferry (adult/child/bicycle £1.80/80p/£1; ☻ last ferry 9pm Sun-Thu, 11pm Fri & Sat) Passenger ferry to Polruan. In winter and on summer evenings, it runs from Town Quay; during the day, it runs from Whitehouse Slipway on the Esplanade.

Polperro
POP 1206
Even in a county where picturesque fishing harbours are 10-a-penny, it's hard not to fall for Polperro – a warren of cottages, boat stores and alleyways, all set around a stout granite harbour. Unsurprisingly, this was once a smugglers' hideout, and it's still a place

with a salty, sea-dog atmosphere, despite the inevitable summer crowds. The coast path between Polperro and Looe is particularly scenic, especially around **Talland Bay**.

The main car park is 750m uphill from the village, from where it's a 15-minute stroll down to the quayside. Apart from simply wandering and soaking up the scenery, it's worth popping into the ramshackle **Polperro Heritage Museum** (☑ 01503-272423; The Warren; adult/child £1.75/50p; ☻ 10am-6pm Mar-Oct), which explores the town's seafaring and smuggling heritage.

The 573 bus (£2.80, hourly) runs between Liskeard, Looe and Polperro, while the 572 (£6.50, hourly Monday to Saturday, three on Sunday) continues to Plymouth.

Looe
POP 5280
Tucked into the long curve of coast between the Fowey River and Plymouth Sound, Looe is half historic fishing port, half bucket-and-spade resort. Split into East and West Looe and linked by a historic arched bridge, it's a pleasant base for exploring Cornwall's southeastern reaches, and has some lovely beaches nearby.

◉ Sights & Activities

Half a mile offshore is tiny **Looe Island**, a 9-hectare nature reserve run by the Cornwall Wildlife Trust. The boat **Islander** (☑ 07814-139223; adult/child return £7/5, plus landing fee £3/1) crosses to the island in summer. Guided nature walks leave from the quay.

Wild Futures Monkey Sanctuary WILDLIFE RESERVE
(☑ 01503-262532; www.monkeysanctuary.org; St Martins; adult/child £8/5; ☻ 11am-4.30pm Sun-Thu Easter-Sep; ⓘ) Half a mile west of town, this wildlife centre is guaranteed to raise some 'aaahhhhs' over its woolly and capuchin monkeys, many of which were rescued from captivity.

Porfell Wildlife Park ZOO
(☑ 01503-220211; www.porfell.co.uk; Lanreath; adult/child £9.50/7.50; ☻ 10am-6pm; ⓘ) A lively animal park a couple of miles outside Looe, with wild denizens including macaws, parakeets, owls, lemurs, meerkats and zebras, as well as a venerable capybara called Bert.

🛏 Sleeping

Penvith Barns B&B £
(☑ 01503-240772; www.penvithbarns.co.uk; St-Martin-by-Looe; s £63-72, d £65-80; 🅿 🛜 🐾) Escape the Looe crowds at this rural barn conversion in nearby of St-Martin-by-Looe. Rooms range from small to spacious: the Piggery is tiny and tucked under the eaves, while the Dairy has enough space for a spare bed and sofa.

Barclay House B&B £££
(☑ 01503-262929; www.barclayhouse.co.uk; St Martins Rd; d £95-130; 🅿 🛜 🐾) This detached Victorian villa sits on 2.4-hectare gardens and has the best bedrooms in East Looe, with wraparound river views and graceful shades of peach, pistachio and aquamarine. It has self-catering cottages available.

ℹ Information

Looe Tourist Office (☑ 01503-262072; www.visit-southeastcornwall.co.uk; Guildhall, Fore St; ⊙ 10am-5pm Easter-Oct)

ℹ Getting There & Away

Bus 572 travels to Plymouth (1¼ hours, seven daily Monday to Saturday). Trains on the Looe Valley Line (every two hours Monday to Saturday, eight on Sunday, day ranger adult/child £5/3.15) trundle along a gorgeous stretch of track to Liskeard.

Southeast Cornwall & the Rame Peninsula

Often called 'Cornwall's forgotten corner', the Rame Peninsula remains one of Cornwall's most unspoilt pockets, and it's a fine place to head when you want to give the crowds the slip. This area was once parcelled up between some of Cornwall's old aristocratic families, and several grand country estates are open to the public. If you have time, it's also worth stopping at the little harbour villages of **Kingsand** and **Cawsand**, and the impressive 3-mile expanse of **Whitsand Bay** (not to be confused with Whitsand Bay, near Sennen). Further inland, Cornwall's southeast is also home to some impressive historic homes.

⊙ Sights

Lanhydrock HISTORIC BUILDING
(NT; ☑ 01208-265950; www.nationaltrust.org.uk/lanhydrock; adult/child £11.30/5.60, grounds only £7/3.50; ⊙ house 11am-5.30pm Tue-Sat, grounds 10am-6pm daily) This huge house provides a fascinating insight into the 'upstairs, downstairs' lives of the Cornish gentry, namely the Robartes family. Extensively rebuilt after a fire in 1881, it's the quintessential Victorian manor, complete with gentlemen's smoking room, toy-strewn nursery and antique-filled dining room – as well as an enormous kitchen which has its original roasting spit. The house is 2.5 miles southeast of Bodmin.

Antony House HISTORIC BUILDING
(NT; ☑ 01752-812191; www.nationaltrust.org.uk/antony; adult/child £8.10/5.10, grounds only £4.10/2.10; ⊙ house 1-5pm, gardens noon-5pm Tue-Thu & Sun) Owned by the National Trust and occupied by the Carew-Pole family, this house's main claim to fame are its decorative gardens, designed by the 18th-century landscape architect Humphry Repton and filled with outlandish topiary, some of which featured in Tim Burton's *Alice in Wonderland*. It's 9 miles east of Looe or 6 miles west from Plymouth.

Port Eliot HISTORIC BUILDING
(☑ 01503-230211; www.porteliot.co.uk; house & grounds adult/child £8/4, grounds only £5/2; ⊙ 2-6pm Sat-Thu Mar-Jun) This glorious 2400-hectare estate is the family seat of the Earl of St Germans. The house is open for three months of the year, and the estate has lots and lots of fabulous walks. The annual **Port Eliot Festival** (www.porteliotfestival.com) of music and literature is held in July.

ℹ Getting There & Away

On the Rame Peninsula's east side, the **Torpoint Ferry** (www.tamarcrossings.org.uk/index.aspx?articleid=36386; cars £2.50, pedestrians & cyclists free; ⊙ 24hr) chugs across the River Tamar to Plymouth.

Bodmin Moor

It can't quite boast the wild majesty of Dartmoor, but Bodmin Moor has a bleak beauty all of its own. Pock-marked with heaths and granite hills, including **Rough Tor** (pronounced 'row-tor'; 400m) and Cornwall's highest point, **Brown Willy** (419m), it's a desolate place that works on the imagination; for years there have been reported sightings of the Beast of Bodmin, a large, black cat-like creature, although no one's ever managed to snap a decent picture.

Apart from the hills, the moor's main landmark is **Jamaica Inn** (☑ 01566-86250;

www.jamaicainn.co.uk; s £65, d £80-110; P), made famous by Daphne du Maurier's novel of the same name – although it's disappointingly been modernised since the author's day.

Bus services are very limited on the moor, so you'll need a car to explore.

Sights & Activities

Golitha Falls WATERFALL
Around 1.25 miles west of St Cleer, these crashing waterfalls are one of the most renowned beauty spots on the moor. Around the falls are the remains of the ancient oak woodland which once covered much of the moor. There is a car park half a mile's walk from the reserve near Draynes Bridge.

Carnglaze Caverns CAVE
(01579-320251; www.carnglaze.com; adult/child £6/4; 10am-5pm) Slate was once extensively mined on the moor, leaving behind a network of deep caverns such as these ones outside St Neot. Several of the caves are open to the public and can be visited on an underground tour.

Bodmin & Wenford Railway HERITAGE RAILWAY
(01208-73555; www.bodminandwenfordrailway.co.uk; rover pass adult/child £12/6; Mar-Oct) Run by enthusiasts, this steam railway chuffs and clatters for 6.5 miles between Bodmin and Boscarne Junction. Many trains are still decked out in their original 1950s livery. At the Boscarne end, the line links up with the Camel Trail (p342); bikes can be taken on the trains if there's space. Look out for special trips in summer, including Pullman-style dining trains that include a silver-service supper.

Cardinham Woods HIKING, BIKING
(01208-72577; www.forestry.gov.uk/cardinham) Just outside Bodmin, this large public forest is a great spot for a woody wander, and also has a network of mountain-bike trails if you're feeling more energetic. The Bodmin and Wenford Railway stops at nearby Coleslogget Halt, from where a 1.5-mile trail leads to Cardinham.

ISLES OF SCILLY

They might only be 28 miles west of the mainland, but in many ways the Isles of Scilly feel like a different world. Life on this archipelago of around 140 tiny islands seems hardly to have changed in decades: there are no traffic jams, no supermarkets, no multinational hotels, and the only noise pollution comes from the sound of breaking waves and cawing gulls. That's not to say that Scilly is behind the times – you'll find a mobile signal and broadband on the main islands – but the people seem perfectly content for life to tick along at their own island pace. Renowned for their glorious beaches, there are few places better to escape the outside world.

Only five islands are inhabited: St Mary's is the largest, followed by Tresco, while only a few hardy souls remain on Bryher, St Martin's and St Agnes. Regular ferry boats run between all five islands.

Unsurprisingly, summer is by far the busiest time. Many businesses shut down completely in winter. Hotels are expensive and the B&B supply is limited, so many people hire a cottage instead – the two main companies are **Island Properties** (01720-422082; www.scillyhols.com) and **Sibley's Island Homes** (01720-422431; www.sibleysonscilly.co.uk).

All the inhabited islands (except Tresco) have a campsite, but you'll need to reserve well ahead for July and August.

Information

Isles of Scilly Tourist Board (01720-422536; tic@scilly.gov.uk; St Mary's; 8.30am-6pm Mon-Fri, 9am-5pm Sat, 9am-2pm Sun May-Sep, shorter hours Oct-Apr) The islands' only tourist office.
Simply Scilly (www.simplyscilly.co.uk) The official tourist site.

Getting There & Away

Bookings for flights and ferries are handled by the **Isles of Scilly Travel Centre** (0845 710 5555; www.islesofscilly-travel.co.uk; Quay St; 8am-6.30pm Mon-Sat) in Penzance.
Isles of Scilly Skybus Since the closure of the helicopter service in 2013, planes provide the only air link to the islands. There are several flights daily from Land's End Airport, near Zennor, and Newquay Airport. Adult fares start at £70 to £80 one way. Summer flights also run from Exeter, Bristol and Southampton.
Scillonian III (Apr-Oct) Scilly's ferry plies the notoriously choppy waters between Penzance and St Mary's (adult fare from £47 each way). There's at least one daily crossing in summer, but there are no ferries in winter.

Getting Around

St Mary's Boatmen Association (01720-423999; www.scillyboating.co.uk) Provides regular ferry services from St Mary's to Scilly's other islands. Returns to/from one island cost adult/child £8.50/4.25, or you can take a 'circular' return via another island for £13/6.50.

St Mary's

POP 2200

St Mary's is the largest and busiest island in Scilly, and the main point of arrival for flights and ferries. About a mile west of the airport is the main settlement of Hugh Town, home to most of the island's hotels, shops and guesthouses, as well as the main harbour.

Most people never get much further than Porthcressa, Hugh Town's narrow sandy beach, but there are plenty of other coves that can be reached on foot or by bike, including Porth Hellick, Watermill Cove and the remote Pelistry Bay.

◉ Sights

Isles of Scilly Museum MUSEUM
(Church St, Hugh Town; adult/child £3.50/1; ⊙10am-4.30pm Mon-Fri, to noon Sat Easter-Sep, 10am-noon Mon-Sat Oct-Easter) The small Isles of Scilly Museum explores the islands' history, with an eclectic mix of archaeological finds and shipwreck artefacts.

☞ Tours

Scilly Walks WALKING TOUR
(☑01720-423326; www.scillywalks.co.uk; adult/child £6/3) Three-hour archaeological and historical tours, plus guided walking trips to other islands.

Island Wildlife Tours WALKING TOUR
(☑01720-422212; www.islandwildlifetours.co.uk; half/full day £6/12) Regular birdwatching and wildlife walks with resident twitcher Will Wagstaff.

Island Sea Safaris BOAT TOUR
(☑01720-422732; www.islandseasafaris.co.uk) Trips to see local seabird and seal colonies (adult/child £33/25). Also rents wetsuits and snorkelling gear.

⎰ Sleeping

Garrison Campsite CAMPSITE £
(☑01720-422670; tedmoulson@aol.com; Tower Cottage, Garrison; sites £8.80-11; ☎) Several hectares of sea-view camping above Hugh Town, with electrical hook-ups, wi-fi and a laundry-cum-shower block. They'll even pre-pitch a tent for you.

Isles of Scilly Country Guesthouse B&B ££
(☑01720-422440; www.scillyguesthouse.co.uk; High Lanes; d £100-124; ☎) Run by Bavarian expat Sabine Schraudolph, this guesthouse is one of the comfiest on St Mary's. The large rooms are chintz-free and look out across St Mary's fields. Sabine serves Bavarian goodies such as *apfelstrudel* in her conservatory-cum-coffee house.

Wingletang B&B ££
(☑01720-422381; www.wingletangguesthouse.co.uk; The Parade; d £72-90) Simple and cosy rooms in a 200-year-old granite cottage in the heart of Hugh Town.

Star Castle Hotel HOTEL £££
(☑01720-422317; www.star-castle.co.uk; The Garrison; r incl dinner £98-398; ☎☀) Shaped like an eight-pointed star, this former fort on Garrison Point is one of Scilly's star hotels, with heritage-style castle rooms and more modern garden suites. It's stuffy and expensive, but prices include dinner.

✕ Eating

Dibble & Grub CAFE ££
(☑01720-423719; www.dibbleandgrub.com; lunch £6-12, dinner £10-16; ⊙10am-10pm Apr-Sep) Sleek new beach cafe beside Porthcressa in the island's old fire station. The menu dabbles in tapas and Mediterranean-style classics.

Juliet's Garden Restaurant BISTRO ££
(☑01720-422228; www.julietsgardenrestaurant.co.uk; mains £8-16; ⊙noon-2pm & 6-9pm) St Mary's long-standing bistro, in business for three decades, and still the best place to eat. It's in a converted barn 15 minutes' walk from town: expect gourmet salads and sandwiches by day, plus classier plates of curried monkfish and spring lamb after dark, served by candlelight.

ⓘ Getting Around

For taxis on St Mary's, try **Island Taxis** (☑01720-422126), **Scilly Cabs** (☑01720-422901) or **Toots Taxis** (☑01720-422142).

All flights are met by **Paulgers Transport** (☑01720-423701), who for a flat-rate fare of £4 will run you to wherever you're staying, or straight to the quayside if you're travelling to other islands.

Island Rover (☑01720-422131; www.islandrover.co.uk; tickets £8) St Mary's only bus service. Runs circular tours from Holgate's Green in Hugh Town at 10.15am and 3.30pm, plus extra tours in high summer.

Tresco

POP 175

Owned by the Duchy of Cornwall, the main attraction of Scilly's second-largest island is the magical **Tresco Abbey Garden** (🖉 01720-424105; www.tresco.co.uk/stay/abbey-garden; adult/child £12/free; ⊙ 10am-4pm), which boasts more than 5000 subtropical plants and a peculiar microclimate, nurtured by the Gulf Stream. Keep an eye out for the Valhalla collection, made up of figureheads and nameplates salvaged from the many ships that have foundered off Tresco's shores.

Most people visit Tresco on a day trip, as accommodation is ludicrously expensive in season, but you should be able to stretch to lunch at the island's lively pub, the **New Inn** (🖉 01720-422849; contactus@tresco.co.uk; mains £10-18).

Bryher

POP 70

Only around 70 people live on Bryher, Scilly's smallest and wildest inhabited island. Covered by rough bracken and heather, this chunk of rock takes the full force of Atlantic storms; Hell Bay in a winter gale is a truly powerful sight. Cloaked in sea-grass and heather, it's a lovely island to explore on foot. **Watch Hill** provides cracking views over the islands, and **Rushy Bay** is one of the finest beaches on Scilly. Several smaller beaches can be reached via the coast path.

🛏 Sleeping & Eating

Bryher Campsite　　　　　CAMPSITE £
(🖉 01720-422886; www.bryhercampsite.co.uk; sites £10.25; 🐾) Bare-bones camping near the quay. Hot showers and tractor transport are included in the rates.

Samson Hill　　　　　　　B&B ££
(🖉 01720-423951; www.samsonhill.co.uk; d £60-75; 🐾) Run by born-and-bred islander Issy Tibbs, this lovely two-room cottage offers a fabulous view towards Tresco. Issy's a keen cook, and breakfast choices range from Canadian pancakes to homemade granola; she also makes her own fudge. Husband Gareth cooks wood-fired pizza in the garden several nights a week.

Hell Bay Hotel　　　　　HOTEL £££
(🖉 01720-422947; www.hellbay.co.uk; d £190-320) Pretty much the poshest place to stay in Scilly – a true island getaway blending New England-style furnishings with sunny golds, sea blues and pale wood beams.

Fraggle Rock　　　　　　CAFE ££
(🖉 01720-422222; www.bryher.co; mains £8-14; ⊙ 9am-9pm; 🐾) This relaxed cafe also doubles as Bryher's pub. The menu's mainly quiches, salads and burgers, but owners Chris and Kim use island suppliers wherever possible. There are a few timber-clad cabins if you feel like staying.

St Martin's

POP 136

The northernmost of the main islands, little St Martin's is rightly renowned for its beaches. Worth hunting out are **Lawrence's Bay** on the south coast, which becomes a broad sweep of sand at low tide; **Great Bay** on the north, arguably Scilly's finest beach; and the secluded cove of **Perpitch** in the southeast.

👁 Sights & Activities

St Martin's Vineyard　　　WINERY
(🖉 01720-423418; www.stmartinsvineyard.co.uk; ⊙ tours 10.45am-4pm Tue-Thu) The UK's smallest and most southwesterly vineyard produces its own range of white wines. Tours are conducted by owners Val and Graham.

Scilly Diving　　　　　　DIVING
(🖉 01720-422848; www.scillydiving.com) Situated in Higher Town, this dive outfit offers diving courses and single dives.

🛏 Sleeping

Accommodation is limited apart from one super-expensive hotel, **St Martin's on the Isle** (🖉 01720-422090; www.stmartinshotel.co.uk; d £300-560), and a handful of B&Bs.

St Martin's Campsite　　　CAMPSITE £
(🖉 01720-422888; www.stmartinscampsite.co.uk; sites £9-11; ⊙ Mar-Oct) The second-largest campsite in Scilly at the western end of Lawrence's Bay, with 50 pitches spread across three fields. Coin-operated laundry and showers are available, and eggs and veg are available for your morning fry-up.

Polreath　　　　　　　　B&B ££
(🖉 01720-422046; www.polreath.com; Higher Town; d £100-110) This friendly granite cottage has small rooms and a sunny conservatory serving cream teas, homemade lemonade and evening meals. Weekly stays only May to September.

✕ Eating

Adam's Fish & Chips
SEAFOOD **£**

(☏ 01720-422457; ⊘ 6-8.30pm Tue-Thu, noon-2.30pm Sat Jul & Aug, 6-8.30pm Tue & Thu Sep-Jun) The fish here is as fresh as it gets – whatever's caught on the day is what ends up in your batter. It's run by Adam and Emma, who live and work on Little Arthur Farm nearby.

Little Arthur Farm
CAFE **£**

(☏ 01720-422457; www.littlearthur.co.uk; ⊘ 10.30am-4pm daily, 6.30-8.30pm Mon-Fri) Home-grown produce, handmade shoes, farm-fresh milk: this organic farm and wholefood cafe does it all.

St Martin's Bakery
BAKERY **£**

(☏ 01720-423444; www.stmartinsbakery.co.uk; ⊘ 9am-6pm Mon-Sat, to 2pm Sun) This home-spun bakery turns out fresh bread, pizzas and, of course, homemade pasties.

St Agnes
POP 170

Scilly's southernmost island feels really remote, with a string of empty coves and a scattering of prehistoric sites. Visitors disembark at Porth Conger, near the decommissioned **Old Lighthouse** – one of the oldest lighthouses in the country.

Other points of interest include the 200-year-old stone **Troy Town Maze** and the island of **Gugh**, where you'll find intriguing standing stones and Bronze Age remains.

🛏 Sleeping & Eating

Troytown Farm
CAMPSITE **£**

(☏ 01720-422360; www.troytown.co.uk; adult £8.75, tents £2-8) Once a flower farm, St Martin's miniscule campsite offers meadow camping with superb sea views, and also rents three self-catering cottages (from £550 to £950 per week).

Covean Cottage
COTTAGE **££**

(☏ 01720-422620; http://st-agnes-scilly.org/cove an.htm; d £60-80) This is a little stone-walled cottage, with three pretty sea-view rooms. There's also a small cafe which serves brekkies and light meals cooked up by the owner.

Turk's Head
PUB **££**

(☏ 01720-422434; mains £8-14; ⊘ 11am-11pm Mon-Sat, noon-10.30pm Sun) Britain's most southerly alehouse is a beauty. Model ships and seafaring photos line the walls, and you can down your pint of homebrewed Turk's Head beside the slipway. You might even be treated to a sea shanty if the lads are in the mood.

Cambridge & East Anglia

Best Places to Eat

➡ Midsummer House (p381)

➡ Roger Hickman's (p402)

➡ Company Shed (p386)

➡ Great House (p392)

Best Places to Stay

➡ Varsity (p380)

➡ Sutherland House (p396)

➡ Angel (p391)

➡ Peacocks (p385)

Why Go?

Unfurling gently eastwards to the sea, the vast flatlands of East Anglia are a rich web of lush farmland, melancholy Fens and sparkling rivers. The area is justly famous for its sweeping sandy beaches, big skies and the bucolic landscape that once inspired Constable and Gainsborough.

It's not all rural idyll though: rising out of the Fens is the world-famous university town of Cambridge, with its stunning classical architecture and earnest attitude, and to the east is the cosmopolitan city of Norwich. Around them magnificent cathedral cities, pretty market towns and implausibly picturesque villages are testament to the enormous wealth amassed here during medieval times, when the wool and weaving industries flourished.

Meanwhile, the meandering coastline is peppered with pretty fishing villages and traditional bucket-and-spade resorts, while inland is the languid, hypnotic charm of the Norfolk Broads, an ideal location for serious relaxation.

When to Go

➡ If the Cambridge colleges are high on your list, avoid Spring (early April to mid-June), when they close to visitors as students prepare for exams.

➡ The (hopefully) better weather between June and August means you'll see the Norfolk and Suffolk beaches and the Norfolk Broads at their best. But school holidays (late-July to August) bring plenty more people, and also push accommodation prices up.

➡ World-class classical music comes to Suffolk in the Aldeburgh Festival (p395) in June. In July, cool-culture fans chill at Southwold's eclectic Latitude Festival (p396).

➡ Come November, the Ways With Words (p396) literature festival draws big-name authors to Southwold.

➡ Exquisite, seasonal music fills Cambridge's King's College Chapel (p371) in December, culminating in the Festival of Nine Lessons and Carols on Christmas Eve.

Cambridge & East Anglia Highlights

❶ Punting past historic colleges in Cambridge and enjoying the heavenly sounds of evensong at **King's College Chapel** (p371)

❷ Soaking up the medieval atmosphere in topsy-turvy **Lavenham** (p391)

❸ Marvelling at the exquisite rib vaulting at **Norwich Cathedral** (p397)

❹ Walking the prom, dining on sublime food and just chilling out in understated **Aldeburgh** (p395)

❺ Noseying around the drawing room of the Queen's country estate at **Sandringham** (p405)

❻ Canoeing your way through the tranquil waterways of the **Norfolk Broads** (p400)

❼ Pondering the history of British and American air forces at the **Imperial War Museum** (p384) in Duxford

❽ Wandering barefoot along the immense, golden sands of **Holkham beach** (p404)

❾ Delighting in one of Britain's grandest stately homes at **Audley End** (p388) in Saffron Walden

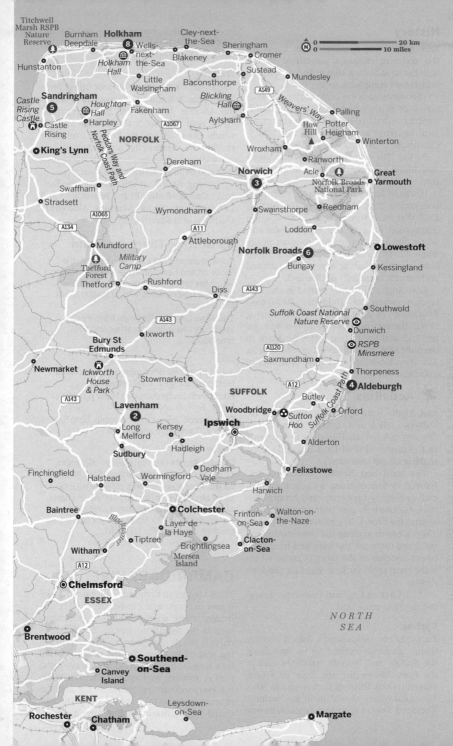

Titchwell
Marsh RSPB
Nature
Reserve
Burnham
Deepdale
Holkham
8
Wells-
next-
the-Sea
Cley-next-
the-Sea
Blakeney
Sheringham
Cromer
Hunstanton
*Holkham
Hall*
Little
Walsingham
Baconsthorpe
Sustead
Mundesley

*Castle
Rising
Castle*
Sandringham
5
*Houghton
Hall*
Fakenham
Aylsham
*Blickling
Hall*
A149
Weavers' Way
Palling

Castle
Rising
Harpley
A1067
How
Hill
Potter
Heigham
Winterton

King's Lynn
NORFOLK
Dereham
Wroxham
Ranworth
Acle
Great
Yarmouth

Swaffham
Norwich
3
Norfolk Broads
National Park

Stradsett
Wymondham
Swainsthorpe
Reedham

A1065
A11
Attleborough
Loddon

A134
Mundford
*Military
Camp*
Diss
A143
Norfolk Broads
6
Lowestoft

*Thetford
Forest*
Thetford
Rushford
Bungay
Kessingland

Bury St
Edmunds
Ixworth
A143
*Suffolk Coast National
Nature Reserve*
Southwold
Dunwich

Newmarket
*Ickworth
House
& Park*
Stowmarket
A1120
Saxmundham
*RSPB
Minsmere*
Thorpeness

A143
Lavenham
2
Kersey
SUFFOLK
A12
Butley
4 **Aldeburgh**

Long
Melford
Woodbridge
*Sutton
Hoo*
Orford

Sudbury
Hadleigh
Ipswich
Alderton

Finchingfield
*Dedham
Vale*

Halstead
Wormingford
Harwich
Felixstowe

Baintree
Colchester
Frinton-
on-Sea
Walton-on-
the-Naze

Witham
Layer de
la Haye
Tiptree
Brightlingsea
**Clacton-
on-Sea**

A12
*Mersea
Island*

◉ **Chelmsford**
ESSEX

*NORTH
SEA*

Brentwood

**Southend-
on-Sea**
Canvey
Island

KENT
Leysdown-
on-Sea

Rochester
Chatham
Margate

0 ── 20 km
0 ── 10 miles

History

East Anglia was a major Saxon kingdom; the dazzling treasures unearthed in the ship burial at Sutton Hoo in Suffolk have revealed how complex a society it was.

The region's heyday came during the wool boom of the Middle Ages when Flemish weavers settled in the area; many of the grand local churches also date from this time – Cambridge University was founded too.

By the 17th century much of the region's marshland and bog had been drained and converted into arable land.

It was in East Anglia's emergent, Puritan bourgeoisie that the seeds of the English Civil War were sown. Oliver Cromwell, the uncrowned king of the Parliamentarians, was a small-time merchant residing in Ely when he answered God's call to take up arms against what he saw as the fattened and corrupt monarchy of Charles I.

East Anglia's fortunes waned in the 18th century, when the Industrial Revolution flourished in northern England. During WWII the region became an ideal base for the RAF and the United States Air Force in the fight against Nazi Germany, thanks to its flat, open landscape and close proximity to mainland Europe.

☆ Activities

East Anglia is an appealing destination for walkers, cyclists and kayakers. Here you can discover miles of coastline, take time touring vast expanses of level land and glide along snaking inland waterways.

The coast and Norfolk Broads are also beloved by sailors, those without their own craft can easily hire boats and arrange lessons. Alternatively putt-putt your way gently around the Broads in a motorboat or paddle a kayak or canoe along the slow-moving rivers. Then there are the wide and frequently empty beaches of the Norfolk coast, which make great spots for land yachting and kitesurfing.

Visit East of England (www.visiteastofengland.com) has more info.

Cycling

Famously one of England's flattest regions, there's gorgeous cycling to be had along the Suffolk and Norfolk coastlines and in the Fens. Meanwhile, the Tour de France snaked its way through East Anglia in 2014. Mountain bikers should head for Norfolk's **Thetford Forest** (www.forestry.gov.uk/thetford

forestpark), while much of the popular on- and off-road Peddars Way (p370) walking route is also open to cyclists.

Walking

The **Peddars Way and Norfolk Coast Path** (www.nationaltrail.co.uk/peddarsway) is a seven-day, 93-mile national trail from Knettishall Heath near Thetford to Cromer. The first half winds along an ancient Roman road, then finishes by meandering along the beaches, sea walls, salt marshes (great for birdwatching) and fishing villages of the coast.

Curving further south, the 50-mile **Suffolk Coast Path** links Felixstowe and Lowestoft, via Snape Maltings, Aldeburgh, Dunwich and Southwold.

ⓘ Getting There & Around

Public transport links between London, the Midlands and East Anglia are excellent. Services within the region are generally good; as ever there are fewer connections to smaller towns and villages.

Traveline East Anglia (www.travelineeast anglia.org.uk) Details local bus and train timetables.

BUS

A host of smaller firms, plus two main companies, run the region's bus networks.

First (www.firstgroup.com) Major provider in Essex, Norfolk and Suffolk.

Stagecoach (www.stagecoachbus.com) Services in Cambridge and around.

TRAIN

Greater Anglia (Abellio; www.greateranglia.co.uk) Runs rail services across East Anglia.

Anglia Plus Pass Secures off-peak train (and some bus) travel in Norfolk, Suffolk and parts of Cambridgeshire. One/three days out of seven costs £18/35. Up to four accompanying children can travel for £2 each.

CAMBRIDGESHIRE

Many visitors to Cambridgeshire never make it past the captivating university city of Cambridge, where august old buildings, student cyclists in academic gowns and glorious chapels await. But beyond this breathtaking seat of learning, the flat reclaimed Fen, lush farmland and myriad waterways make perfect walking and cycling territory, while the extraordinary cathedral at Ely and the rip-roaring Imperial War Museum at Duxford would be headline attractions anywhere else.

ℹ Getting Around

Public transport radiates from Cambridge, a mere 55-minute train ride from London. This line continues north through Ely to King's Lynn in Norfolk. Branch lines run east to Norwich and into Suffolk.

Cambridge

POP 123,900

Abounding with exquisite architecture, oozing history and tradition and renowned for its quirky rituals, Cambridge is a university town extraordinaire. The tightly packed core of ancient colleges, the picturesque 'Backs' (college gardens) leading on to the river and the leafy green meadows that surround the city give it a far more tranquil appeal than its historic rival Oxford.

Like 'the Other Place', as Oxford is known locally, the buildings here seem unchanged for centuries, and it's possible to wander the college buildings and experience them as countless prime ministers, poets, writers and scientists have done. The sheer academic achievement seems to permeate the very walls, with cyclists loaded down with books negotiating narrow cobbled passageways, students relaxing on manicured lawns and great minds debating life-changing research in historic pubs. Meanwhile, first-time punters zigzag erratically across the river, shoppers stroll unhurriedly through the Grand Arcade, and those long past their student days wonder what it would have been like to study in such splendid surroundings.

History

Despite roots stretching back to the Iron Age, Cambridge was little more than a rural backwater until the 11th century, when an Augustinian order of monks set up shop here – the first of the religious institutions that eventually became the colleges. When the university town of Oxford exploded in a riot between town and gown in 1209, a group of scholars, fed up with the constant brawling between locals and students, upped and joined what was to become the University of Cambridge. Cambridge wasn't spared by the riots, and brawls between town and gown took place with disturbing regularity here as well.

The first Cambridge college, Peterhouse (never Peterhouse *College*), was founded in 1284, and in 1318 Pope John XXII's papal bull declared Cambridge to be an official university.

By the 14th century, royalty, nobility, churches, trade guilds and anyone rich enough could court prestige by founding their own colleges, though the system was shaken up during the Reformation with the dissolution of the monasteries. It was 500 years before female students were allowed into the hallowed grounds, though, and even then they were only allowed into the women-only colleges Girton and Newnham, founded in 1869 and 1871 respectively. By 1948 Cambridge minds had broadened sufficiently to allow women to actually graduate.

The honour roll of famous Cambridge students reads like an international who's who of high achievers: 87 Nobel Prize winners (more than any other institution in the world), 13 British prime ministers, nine archbishops of Canterbury, an immense number of scientists, and a healthy host of poets and authors. This is the town where Newton refined his theory of gravity, Whipple invented the jet engine, and Crick and Watson discovered DNA. William Wordsworth, Lord Byron, Vladimir Nabokov, Stephen Hawking and Stephen Fry all studied here too.

Today the university remains one of the best for research worldwide. Thanks to some of the earth-shaking discoveries made here, Cambridge is inextricably linked to the history of learning.

◉ Sights

Cambridge University

Cambridge University comprises 31 colleges, though not all are open to the public.

★ **King's College Chapel**   CHAPEL
(📞 01223-331212; www.kings.cam.ac.uk/chapel; King's Pde; adult/child £7.50/free; ⊙ non-term 9.45am-4.30pm, term 9.45am-3.15pm Mon-Sat, 1.15-2.30pm Sun) In a city crammed with show-stopping buildings, this is the scene-stealer. Grandiose, 16th-century King's College Chapel is one of England's most extraordinary examples of Gothic architecture. Its inspirational, intricate 80m-long, fan-vaulted ceiling is the world's largest and soars upwards before exploding into a series of stone fireworks. This hugely atmospheric space is a fitting stage for the chapel's world-famous choir; hear it in full voice during the magnificent, free, evensong (in term time only – 5.30pm Monday to Saturday, 10.30am and 3.30pm Sunday).

King's **steeples** have long been a magnet for student night climbers and today images

Cambridge

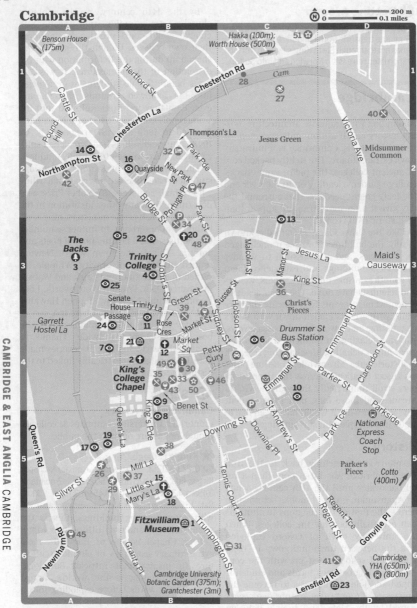

of the chapel adorn thousands of postcards, tea towels and choral CDs. But it was begun in 1446 as an act of piety by Henry VI and was only finished by Henry VIII around 1516.

The lofty **stained-glass windows** that flank the chapel's sides ensure it is remark-

ably light. The glass is original, rare survivors of the excesses of the Civil War in this region. It's said that these windows were ordered to be spared by Cromwell himself, who knew of their beauty from his own studies in Cambridge.

Cambridge

The antechapel and the choir are divided by a superbly carved **wooden screen**, were designed and executed by Peter Stockton for Henry VIII. The screen bears his master's initials entwined with those of Anne Boleyn. Look closely and you may find an angry human face (possibly Stockton's) amid the elaborate jungle of mythical beasts and symbolic flowers. Above is the magnificent batwing **organ**, originally constructed in 1686, though much altered since.

Beyond the thickly-carved, dark-wood choir stalls light suffuses the high **altar**, which is framed by Rubens' masterpiece *Adoration of the Magi* (1634) and the magnificent east window. To the left of the altar in the side chapels, an **exhibition** charts the construction stages and methods.

Note the chapel itself (but not the grounds) *are* open during the exam period (April to June). Each Christmas Eve, King's College Chapel stages the **Festival of Nine Lessons and Carols**. It's broadcast globally by the BBC, and to around 300 American radio stations. You can also queue – if you start early enough (before 9am), you could well get in.

Senate House   HISTORIC BUILDING
(Senate House Passage) This beautiful classical structure (not open to the public), tucked in beside King's College, was designed in 1730 by James Gibbs. Graduations are held here in summer, when gowned and mortar-boarded students parade the streets. Look out for the degree class-lists that are posted outside at the end of the academic year.

Gonville & Caius College   COLLEGE
(www.cai.cam.ac.uk; Trinity St; ⊙9am-2pm, closed early Apr–mid-Jun) **FREE** Known locally as Caius (pronounced 'keys'), Gonville and Caius boasts three fascinating **gates**: Virtue, Humility and Honour. They symbolise the progress of the good student, since the third gate (the Porta Honoris, a fabulous domed and sundial-sided confection) leads to the Senate House and thus graduation. Ex-students

ℹ VISITING THE COLLEGES

Colleges close to visitors over the Christmas break, and while students are preparing for and sitting exams – shutting between early April and mid-June. Be aware too, opening hours can vary from day to day, so if you have your heart set on visiting a particular college, contact it in advance to avoid disappointment.

include Francis Crick (of DNA-discoverers Crick and Watson) and Edward Wilson, of Scott's tragic Antarctic expedition. The megastar of astrophysics, Stephen Hawking, is currently a fellow here.

The college was actually founded twice, first by a priest called Gonville, in 1348, and then again in 1557 by Dr Caius (his given name was Keys – it was common for academics to use the Latin form of their names), a brilliant physician who supposedly spoiled his legacy by insisting in the statutes that the college admit no 'deaf, dumb, deformed, lame, chronic invalids, or Welshmen'.

Trinity Hall College COLLEGE
(www.trinhall.cam.ac.uk; Trinity Lane; admission by donation; ⊙ 9.15am–noon & 2-4pm, closed early Apr–mid-Jun) Wedged cosily among the great and the famous, but unconnected to better-known Trinity, diminutive Trinity Hall was founded in 1350 as a refuge for lawyers and clerics escaping the ravages of the Black Death. The college's 16th-century library has original Jacobean reading desks and chained books on the shelves (to visit, book two weeks in advance), while the chapel is one of the most beautiful of all the colleges – drop by for evensong at 6.30pm Thursday and 6pm Sunday during term time. Writer JB Priestley, astrophysicist Stephen Hawking and actor Rachel Weisz are among Trinity Hall's graduates.

★ Trinity College COLLEGE
(www.trin.cam.ac.uk; Trinity St; adult/child £2/1; ⊙ 10am-4.30pm, closed early Apr–mid-Jun) The largest of Cambridge's colleges, Trinity offers an extraordinary Tudor gateway, an air of supreme elegance and a sweeping Great Court – the largest of its kind in the world. It also boasts the renowned and suitably musty Wren Library (⊙ noon-2pm Mon-Fri), containing 55,000 books dated before 1820 and more than 2500 manuscripts. Works include those by Shakespeare, St Jerome, Newton and Swift – and AA Milne's original

Winnie the Pooh; both Milne and his son, Christopher Robin, were graduates.

As you enter Trinity through the part-gilded gate, look at the statue of the college's founder, Henry VIII, that adorns it. His left hand holds a golden orb, while his right grips not the original sceptre but a table leg, put there by student pranksters and never replaced. It's a wonderful introduction to one of Cambridge's most venerable colleges, and a reminder of who really rules the roost.

In the Great Court beyond, scholastic humour gives way to wonderment, thanks to its imposing architecture and sheer size. To the right of the entrance is a small tree, planted in the 1950s and reputed to be a descendant of the apple tree made famous by Trinity alumnus Sir Isaac Newton. Other alumni include Francis Bacon, Lord Byron, Tennyson, HRH Prince Charles (legend has it his bodyguard scored higher in exams than he did), at least nine prime ministers (British and international) and some 32 Nobel Prize winners.

The college's vast hall has a dramatic hammerbeam roof and lantern, beyond lie the dignified cloisters of Nevile's Court. Henry VIII would have been proud to note, too, that his college would eventually come to throw the best party in town, the lavish May Ball in June, though you will need a fat purse, and a friend on the inside, to get an invitation.

St John's College COLLEGE
(www.joh.cam.ac.uk; St John's St; adult/child £5/3.50; ⊙ 10am-5pm mid-Jun–Oct, to 3.30pm Nov-early Apr) Alma mater of six prime ministers, three saints and Douglas Adams (*The Hitchhiker's Guide to the Galaxy* author), St John's is superbly photogenic. It's also the second-biggest college after Trinity. Founded in 1511 by Henry VII's mother, Margaret Beaufort, it sprawls along both river banks, joined by the Bridge of Sighs (p377), a masterpiece of stone tracery and focus for student pranks. Going into St John's, or a punting tour, are the only ways to get a clear view of the structure.

Over the bridge, is the 19th-century New Court, an extravagant neo-Gothic creation, and out to the left are impressive views of the Backs. Parts of the college are much older and the chapel, though smaller than King's, is one of Cambridge's hidden gems.

Magdalene College COLLEGE
(www.magd.cam.ac.uk; Magdalene St; ⊙ 8am-6pm, closed early Apr–mid-Jun) FREE Riverside

Magdalene often catches people out – the college name is properly pronounced 'Maudlyn'. This former Benedictine hostel's greatest asset is the **Pepys Library** (⊙ 2-4pm Mon-Fri, 11.30am-12.30pm & 1.30-2.30pm Sat May-Aug, 2-3pm Mon-Sat Oct-Apr) housing 3000 books bequeathed by the mid-17th-century diarist to his old college. This idiosyncratic collection of beautifully bound tomes is ordered by height, treasures include vivid medieval manuscripts and the *Anthony Roll,* a 1540s depiction of the Royal Navy's ships.

Magdalene has the dubious honour of being the last college to let women study there; when they were finally admitted in 1988, some male students wore black armbands and flew the college flag at half mast.

Jesus College   COLLEGE
(www.jesus.cam.ac.uk; Jesus Lane; ⊙ 9am-5pm, closed early Apr–mid-Jun) **FREE** This tranquil 15th-century college was once a nunnery of St Radegund before the Bishop of Ely, John Alcock, expelled the nuns for 'improvidence, extravagance and incontinence'. Highlights include a Norman arched **gallery**, a 13th-century **chancel** and art-nouveau features by Pugin, Ford Madox Brown, William Morris (ceilings) and Burne-Jones (stained glass). Illustrious alumni include Thomas Cranmer, burnt for his faith in Oxford during the Reformation, and long-running BBC and PBS radio journalist and presenter Alistair Cooke.

Christ's College   COLLEGE
(www.christs.cam.ac.uk; St Andrew's St; ⊙ 9.30am-4pm, closed early Apr–mid-Jun) **FREE** A great institution at more than 500 years old, Christ's gleaming **Great Gate** is emblazoned with heraldic carving of Tudor roses, portcullis and spotted Beaufort yale (antelope-like creatures). Its founder, Lady Margaret Beaufort, hovers above like a guiding spirit. A stout oak door leads into **First Court**, one of Cambridge's more picturesque front courts and the only circular one. Hunt out the **gardens** dedicated to alumnus Charles Darwin, they feature species brought back from his famous Galapagos voyage.

The Second Court has a gate to the **Fellows' Garden**, which contains a mulberry tree under which 17th-century poet John Milton reputedly wrote 'Lycidas'. Other notable alumni include Sacha Baron Cohen (aka Ali G and Borat) and historian Simon Schama.

Emmanuel College   COLLEGE
(www.emma.cam.ac.uk; St Andrew's St; ⊙ 9am-6pm, closed early Apr–mid-Jun) **FREE** The 16th-century Emmanuel College ('Emma' to students) is famous for its exquisite **chapel** designed by Sir Christopher Wren. The college has a prodigious collection of ducks, they roam the area freely and in early spring produce armies of bright-yellow ducklings. Here, too, is a plaque commemorating John Harvard (BA 1632), a scholar here who later settled in New England and left his money to a certain Cambridge College in Massachusetts – now Harvard University.

Corpus Christi College   COLLEGE
(www.corpus.cam.ac.uk; King's Pde; admission £2.50; ⊙ 10.30am-4.30pm mid-Jun–Sep, 2-4pm Oct-early Apr) One of Cambridge's ancient colleges, Corpus Christi was founded in 1352, a heritage reflected in its exquisite buildings – a monastic atmosphere still radiates from the medieval **Old Court**. Look out for the fascinating sundial and plaque to playwright and past student Christopher Marlowe (1564–93), author of *Doctor Faustus* and *Tamburlaine*. New Court (a mere 200 years old) leads to the **Parker Library**, which holds the world's finest collection of Anglo-Saxon manuscripts (open Thursday afternoons to tourist office–run tours).

Back outside, on the junction of Benet St and King's Pde, look out for the college's new **Corpus Clock**. Made from 24-carat gold, it displays the time through a series of concentric LED lights. A hideous-looking insect 'time-eater' crawls across the top. The clock is only accurate once every five minutes. At other times it slows or stops and then speeds up, which according to its creator, JC Taylor, reflects life's irregularity.

Queens' College   COLLEGE
(www.queens.cam.ac.uk; Silver St; admission £2.50; ⊙ 10am-4pm, closed early Apr–mid-Jun) Gorgeous 15th-century Queens' College sits elegantly

---

CHARIOTS OF FIRE

Trinity College's immense Great Court is the scene of the run made famous by the film *Chariots of Fire* – a 350m-sprint around the courtyard in 43 seconds (the time it takes the clock to strike 12). Although many students attempt it, Harold Abrahams (the hero of the film) never did, and the run in the movie was filmed at Eton. If you fancy your chances, remember that you'll need Olympian speed to even come close.

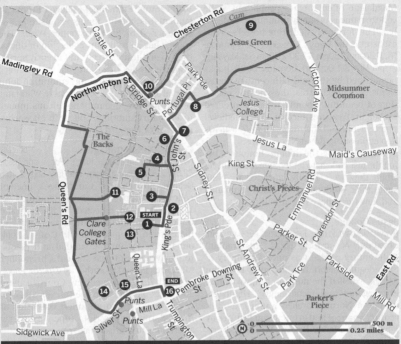

🏃 City Walk
The Colleges & the Backs

START KING'S COLLEGE CHAPEL
END FITZBILLIES
LENGTH 3 MILES; FOUR HOURS

From divine ❶ **King's** (p371), stroll north, diverting into ❷ **Great St Mary's** (p378) and climbing the tower for fine Cambridge views. Next, dodge the bicyclists and touting tour guides before ducking into atmospheric ❸ **Gonville & Caius** (p373) to marvel at its ornate gates. ❹ **Trinity's** (p374) elaborate entranceway towers up on the left; head through it into the college's (genuinely) Great Court; marvel in the architecture, then make for the absorbing ❺ **Wren Library** (p374), with its extraordinary historic books. Next, pause to admire the front of gorgeous ❻ **St John's** (p374), before dropping into the captivating, 12th-century ❼ **Round Church** (p378). Cut right between the sweet terraces of narrow Portugal Place – at the end, the ❽ **Maypole** (p382) pub is a friendly place to eat or drink. Next it's diagonally across Jesus Green, past lounging picnickers and tennis players, to consider a dip in the bijou open-air

❾ **pool** (p379). Then stroll south west beside the river, passing locks and houseboats before a waterside boardwalk leads to a punt launching pad. Cross at the bridge beside ❿ **Magda-lene College** (p374), where the unique Peyps Library is well worth a detour. Northampton St reminds you the 21st century does exist, then it's onto the path through the Backs, where the stately sweep of St John's College shelters amid the trees, Trinity sits next door. Next play zigzag with college paths and the river: nip up ⓫ **Garret Hostel Lane** for a closer view of punts, bridges and college facades. Then it's back to the path, before another detour left leads to the often-open gates of ⓬ **Clare College** (p377), where the Fellow's Garden is a real must-see. Back on the Backs, next comes the impressive west end of Kings College Chapel; the Palladian ⓭ **Fellows' Building** is just to the right. After curving beside ⓮ **Queens'** (p375), cut left. On Silver St's bridge spy the chunky ⓯ **Mathematical Bridge** (p377) on the left, and the fleets of punts on the right. Time to rest. Where better than ⓰ **Fitzbillies** (p381) for a Chelsea bun and a steaming cup of tea.

astride the river, connected by the unscientific-looking Mathematical Bridge (p377). Highlights include two enchanting medieval courtyards: **Old Court** and **Cloister Court**, the beautiful half-timbered **President's Lodge** and the tower in which Dutch scholar and reformer Desiderius Erasmus lodged from 1510 to 1514. His verdict on Cambridge? That the wine tasted like vinegar, the beer was slop and the place was too expensive – he also noted the local women were good kissers.

Peterhouse COLLEGE

(www.pet.cam.ac.uk; Trumpington St; ⊘9am-5pm, closed early Apr–mid-Jun) **FREE** The oldest and smallest college, charming Peterhouse was founded in 1284. Much of the college was rebuilt or added to over the years, including the exceptional little chapel built in 1632, but the beautifully restored **main hall** is bona fide 13th century. Just to the north is **Little St Mary's Church**, which has a memorial to Peterhouse student Godfrey Washington, great-uncle of George. His family coat of arms was the stars and stripes – the inspiration for the US flag.

Rumours abound among students (vigorously denied by college authorities) of hauntings and spectral happenings on the site. Three Nobel Prize winners count themselves among Peterhouse's alumni.

★ The Backs PARK

Behind the Cambridge colleges' grandiose facades and stately courts, a series of gardens and parks line up beside the river. Collectively known as the Backs, the tranquil green spaces and shimmering waters offer unparalleled views of the colleges and are often the most enduring image of Cambridge for visitors. The picture-postcard snapshots of college life and graceful bridges can be seen from the riverside pathways and pedestrian bridges – or the comfort of a chauffeur-driven punt.

The fanciful **Bridge of Sighs**, built in 1831 at St John's (p374), is best observed from the stylish bridge designed by Wren just to the south, also on St John's grounds. The oldest river crossing is at **Clare College**, built in 1639 and ornamented with decorative balls. Its architect was paid a grand total of 15p for his design and, feeling aggrieved at such a measly fee, it's said he cut a chunk out of one of the balls adorning the balustrade so the bridge would never be complete.

Most curious of all is the flimsy-looking wooden construction joining the two halves of Queen's College known as the **Mathematical Bridge**, first built in 1749. Despite what unscrupulous guides may tell you, it wasn't the handiwork of Sir Isaac Newton (he died in 1727), originally built without nails, or taken apart by academics who then couldn't figure how to put it back together.

Other Sights

★ Fitzwilliam Museum MUSEUM

(www.fitzmuseum.cam.ac.uk; Trumpington St; donation requested; ⊘10am-5pm Tue-Sat, noon-5pm Sun) Fondly dubbed 'the Fitz' by locals, this colossal neoclassical pile was one of the first public art museums in Britain, built to house the fabulous treasures that the seventh Viscount Fitzwilliam bequeathed to his old university. Expect Roman and Egyptian grave goods, artworks by many of the great masters and some more quirky collections: banknotes, literary autographs, watches and armour.

PRANKSTERS, NIGHT CLIMBERS AND CUBES

In a city with so much concentrated mental prowess, it is perhaps inevitable that the student community would excel at all kinds of mischief. The most impressive prank ever to take place in Cambridge – lifting an Austin Seven van onto the roof of the landmark Senate House (p373) in 1958 – involved a great deal of planning from four Mechanical Sciences students and spawned a number of copycat pranks, including suspending another Austin Seven from the ornate Bridge of Sighs (p377).

King's College has long been a target of night climbers – students who get their thrills by scaling the lofty heights of out-of-bounds buildings at night. The sport is taken very seriously – to the point where a Trinity College student, Geoffrey Winthrop Young, wrote the *Roof Climber's Guide to Trinity* in 1900. If you're in Cambridge after a particularly spectacular climber excursion, you may find some out-of-place objects atop the pinnacles of King's College Chapel – anything from a traffic cone to a Santa hat.

Finally, there's the Cubes (Cambridge University Breaking and Entering Society); its objective is to access places members shouldn't be and leave distinctive calling cards – the most famous being the wooden mallard in the rafters of Trinity's Great Hall.

The building's unabashedly over-the-top appearance sets out to mirror its contents; this ostentatious jumble of styles mixes mosaic with marble, and Greek with Egyptian. The **lower galleries** are filled with priceless treasures spanning the ancient world; look out for a Roman funerary couch, an inscribed copper votive plaque from Yemen (c AD 100–200), a figurine of Egyptian cat goddess Bastet, splendid Egyptian sarcophagi and mummified animals, plus dazzling illuminated manuscripts. The **upper galleries** showcase works by Leonardo da Vinci, Titian, Rubens, the Impressionists, Gainsborough and Constable, right through to Rembrandt and Picasso; standout works include the tender *Pietà* by Giovanni del Ponte and Salvator Rosa's dark and intensely personal *L'Umana Fragilita*.

The Fitz has a tragic footnote: although begun by George Basevi in 1837, he didn't live to see its completion: while working on Ely Cathedral he stepped back to admire his handiwork, slipped and fell to his death.

One-hour guided tours (£6) of the museum are held at 2.30pm Saturday.

The Polar Museum
MUSEUM
(www.spri.cam.ac.uk/museum; Lensfield Rd; ⊙10am-4pm Tue-Sat) FREE Tales of hostile environments, dogged determination and, sometimes, life-claiming mistakes are evoked powerfully at this compelling museum. Its focus on polar exploration charts the feats of the likes of Roald Amundsen, Fridtjof Nansen and Captain Robert Falcon Scott. The affecting collections include paintings, photographs, clothing, equipment, maps, journals and last messages left for loved ones by Scott's polar crew.

Other engaging exhibits include models of ships that ventured into the frigid Arctic and Antarctic waters, innovative equipment such as the 'Nansen cooker' and interactive displays on ice and climate change. The section devoted to the people of the Arctic includes Inuit carvings and scrimshaw (etched bones), a Sámi knife with a carved reindeer-horn sheath, a walrus tusk with walrus hunt scenes etched on it, and particularly fine examples of *tupilaat* (carved caribou horn figures with ancestor souls captured inside) from Greenland. The museum is run by the Scott Polar Institute, founded with part of the relief fund set up in the wake of the explorer's ill-fated South Pole expedition – these days it takes a lead role in climate-change research.

Great St Mary's Church
CHURCH
(www.gsm.cam.ac.uk; Senate House Hill; ⊙10am-4pm Mon-Sat, 1-4pm Sun) FREE The foundations of Cambridge's sublime university church date from 1010. It was burnt to the ground in the 1290s and rebuilt in 1351. The major expansion of 1478–1519 resulted in the late-Gothic Perpendicular style you see today. Striking features include the mid-Victorian stained-glass windows, seating galleries and two organs – unusual in a church. The tower (adult/child £3.50/2) was added in 1690; climb it for superb vistas of Cambridge's dreamy spires.

Round Church
CHURCH
(www.christianheritageuk.org.uk; Bridge St; adult/child £2/free; ⊙10am-5pm) Cambridge's intensely atmospheric Round Church is one of only four such structures in England. It was built by the mysterious Knights Templar in 1130 and shelters an unusual circular nave ringed by chunky Norman pillars – the carved stone faces that crown them bring the 12th century vividly to life. The church's position on Bridge St reminds you of its original role; that of a chapel for pilgrims crossing the river.

Kettle's Yard
HOUSE
(www.kettlesyard.co.uk; Castle St; ⊙2-5pm Tue-Sun) FREE If you like snooping around other people's houses (and who doesn't?), you'll love this very personal glimpse into the incredible home of HS 'Jim' Ede, a former curator at the Tate Gallery in London. In his deceptively roomy cottage all the furniture, ceramics and art – such as the collection of 20th-century works by Miró, Henry Moore and others – is arranged just so, allowing you a real sense of the man's intriguing personality.

Cambridge University Botanic Garden
GARDENS
(www.botanic.cam.ac.uk; Bateman St; adult/child £4.50/free; ⊙10am-6pm Apr-Sep, to 4pm Oct-Mar) Founded by Charles Darwin's mentor, Professor John Henslow, the beautiful Botanic Garden is home to 8000 plant species, a wonderful arboretum, glasshouses (containing both fierce carnivorous pitcher plants and the delicate slipper orchid), a winter garden and flamboyant herbaceous borders. Hour-long guided tours (£7) are held at 11am on the first Saturday of the month and some Wednesdays. The gardens are 1200m south of the city centre via Trumpington St.

🏃 Activities

Jesus Green Pool
SWIMMING

(www.better.org.uk; Jesus Green; £4.20; ⊙ 8am-6pm May-Sep) A long, thin, 1920s open-air swimspot, popular with pool-side sunbathers too.

Punting

Gliding a self-propelled punt along the Backs is a blissful experience – once you've got the hang of it; it can also be a manic challenge to begin. If you wimp out you can always opt for a relaxing chauffeured punt.

Punt hire costs around £19 per hour, one-hour chauffeured trips of the Backs cost about £15, and a return trip to Grantchester (2½ hours) will set you back around £27.

Cambridge Chauffer Punts
PUNTING

(www.punting-in-cambridge.co.uk; Silver St Bridge) One of the biggest punting companies in Cambridge, with regular chauffeured punting tours.

Granta Canoe & Punt Hire Company
PUNTING

(www.puntingincambridge.com; Newnham Rd) Handily sited punt-rental company if you're heading towards Grantchester. Runs reduced services in the winter.

Scudamore's Punting Cambridge
PUNTING

(www.scudamores.com; Granta Pl) Hires punts, rowboats, kayaks and canoes. Offers up to £5 discount if you buy online.

☞ Tours

As well as running escorted tours, the tourist office (p382) also has information about self-guided walks.

Walking Tours
WALKING TOUR

(☑ 01223-457574; www.visitcambridge.org; Peas Hill) The tourist office runs guided two-hour tours (adult/child £17.50/15.50) of central Cambridge, which take in two of the most memorable colleges; depending on opening hours they might include King's College Chapel, Queens', Pembroke or St John's. The price includes admission to the colleges. Year-round, tours run at 11am Monday to Friday, at 11am, noon and 2pm Saturday, and at 1pm Sunday. In July and August there are extra daily tours at noon and 2pm. They're popular: book.

Colourful, one-hour Ghost Tours (£6) take place on Fridays at 6pm, and – from May to August – on Saturdays at 8pm.

Riverboat Georgina
BOAT TOUR

(☑ 01223-929124; www.georgina.co.uk; Jesus Lock; ⊙ Apr-Sep) One-/two-hour cruises are £7/13, optional extras include lunch, fish and chips, wine or a cream tea.

City Sightseeing
BUS TOUR

(www.city-sightseeing.com; adult/child £14/7; ⊙ every 20min 10am-4.40pm) Hop-on/hop-off bus tours; tickets secure 24 hours' unlimited travel.

✹ Festivals & Events

Cambridge has a jam-packed cultural schedule. For one-off events, check out the notices tied to railings all over the city centre, especially around St Mary's Church.

Bumps
BOAT RACE

(www.cucbc.org/bumps; ⊙ Feb & Jun) Traditional rowing races along the Cam (or the Granta as the Cambridge stretch is called), in

LOCAL KNOWLEDGE

HOW TO PUNT

Punting looks pretty straightforward but, believe us, really – it's not. So here are some tips to stop you zigzagging wildly across the river, losing your pole and falling in.

➡ Standing at the back end of the punt, lift the pole out of the water at the side of the punt.

➡ Let the pole slide through your hands to touch the bottom of the river.

➡ Tilt the pole forward (that is, in the direction of travel of the punt) and push down to propel the punt forward.

➡ Twist the pole to free the end from the mud at the bottom of the river, and let it float up and trail behind the punt. You can then use it as a rudder to steer.

➡ If you haven't fallen in yet, raise the pole out of the water and into the vertical position to begin the cycle again.

➡ Hold on to the pole, particularly when passing under Clare Bridge, as students sometimes snatch them for a giggle.

which college boat clubs compete to 'bump' the crew in front.

Beer Festival
BEER

(www.cambridgebeerfestival.com; ⊘ May) Hugely popular five-day beer and cider extravaganza on Jesus Green, featuring brews from all over the country as well as a great range of British cheeses.

Folk Festival
MUSIC

(www.cambridgefolkfestival.co.uk; ⊘ late Jul-early Aug) Acclaimed four-day music fest in neighbouring Cherry Hinton Hall, which has hosted the likes of Van Morrison, Ladysmith Black Mambazo, Sinéad O'Connor, Paul Simon and kd lang.

May Balls
FORMAL BALLS

(⊘ early Jun) The biggest student events of the year, the name of these formal balls don't match the month they're held in (June) because college authorities decided that May's traditional booze-fuelled revelry – just before the exams – wasn't such a great idea. Now they take place after the exams, but in a typically Cambridge quirk they keep the old name.

Cambridge Shakespeare Festival
THEATRE

(www.cambridgeshakespeare.com; ⊘ Jul & Aug) The bard's best-loved works performed in outdoor settings.

🛏 Sleeping

Cambridge YHA
HOSTEL £

(☎ 0845 371 9728; www.yha.org.uk; 97 Tenison Rd; dm/d £21/30; @ 🛜) Busy, recently renovated, popular hostel with compact dorms and good facilities near the railway station.

Cambridge Rooms
B&B ££

(www.universityrooms.com/en/city/cambridge/home; s/d from £45/75) For an authentic taste of university life check into a student room in one of a range of colleges. Accommodation varies from functional singles (with shared bathroom) overlooking college courts to more modern, en suite rooms in nearby annexes. Breakfast is often in hall (the students' dining room).

Worth House
B&B ££

(☎ 01223-316074; www.worth-house.co.uk; 152 Chesterton Rd; s £65-75, d £65-100; P 🛜) The welcome is wonderfully warm; the great-value rooms utterly delightful. Soft grey and cream meets candy-stripe reds, fancy bathrooms boast claw-footed baths, and tea trays

are full of treats. There's also a three-person, self-catering apartment (per week £550) two doors down.

Benson House
B&B ££

(☎ 01223-311594; www.bensonhouse.co.uk; 24 Huntingdon Rd; s £70, d £90-115; P 🛜) Lots of little things lift Benson a cut above, meaning you can sleep among feather pillows and cotton linen, before breakfasting off Royal Doulton bone china, tucking into kippers, croissants and fresh fruit.

Tudor Cottage
B&B ££

(☎ 01223-565212; www.tudorcottageguesthouse. co.uk; 292 Histon Rd; s/d £45/75; P 🛜) Sweet features help make this neat-as-a-pin guesthouse feel like a home from home, from bedrooms boasting gleaming bathrooms, to the ranks of speciality teas, cereals, cakes and muffins at the breakfast table. It's 2 miles north of the City centre; bus 8 stops just outside.

Rosa's
B&B ££

(☎ 01223-512596; www.rosasbedandbreakfast. co.uk; 53 Roseford Rd; s £45-60; P 🛜) One for solo travellers: a friendly, family-run B&B with four cosy singles that are studies in cream and pale wood. The hosts are engaging without being intrusive, it's 2 miles north of the city centre and bus 8 runs nearby.

★ Varsity
BOUTIQUE HOTEL £££

(☎ 01223-306030; www.thevarsityhotel.co.uk; Thompson's Lane; d £180-345; 🛜) In the 48 individually styled rooms of riverside Varsity, wondrous furnishings and witty features (union-jack footstools, giant postage stamps) sit beside floor-to-ceiling glass windows, monsoon showers and iPod docks. The views from the roof terrace are frankly gorgeous.

★ Hotel du Vin
HOTEL £££

(☎ 01223-227330; www.hotelduvin.com; Trumpington St; d £200-230, ste £250-340; @ 🛜) Arguably the country's swishest, coolest chain delivers again here. Achingly beautiful rooms sport roll-top baths and Egyptian cotton sheets, the cosy cellar bar is vaulted, the bistro (mains £18) is chic and the modern mural in reception depicts a suitably wine-soaked May Ball.

Felix
BOUTIQUE HOTEL £££

(☎ 01223-277977; www.hotelfelix.co.uk; Whitehouse Lane, Huntingdon Rd; s £175, d £210-260, ste £305-325; P @ 🛜) It's the bold modern art and imaginative design (fuchsia-pink chairs amid stately polished wood) that nudges Felix into the boutique sleep spots. That and the silk curtains, luxurious linens and stone-and-slate bathrooms. The Penthouse, up in the eaves, is an utterly romantic retreat. Felix is 1.5 miles northwest of the city.

✖ Eating

Aromi   ITALIAN **£**
(www.aromi.co.uk; 1 Benet St; mains £4.50; ⊘ 9am-8pm Fri-Sun, to 5pm Mon-Thu; ☑) Sometimes you should yield to temptation. So be drawn in by a window full of stunning Sicilian pizza and feast on light, crisp bases piled high with fresh spinach and Parma ham. Then succumb to the indecently thick hot chocolate; may as well make it a large.

Fitzbillies   BAKERY, CAFE **£**
(www.fitzbillies.com; 52 Trumpington St; cafe mains £6-16; ⊘ 9am-9.30pm Thu-Sat, 8am-5pm Mon-Wed, 10am-5pm Sun) Cambridge's oldest bakery has a soft, doughy place in the hearts of generations of students, thanks to its ultra-sticky Chelsea buns and other sweet treats. Pick up a bag-full to take away or munch in comfort in the quaint cafe next door.

Byron   BURGERS **£**
(www.byronhamburgers.com; 12 Bridge St; mains £8; ⊘ 11am-11pm) A bustling, better-than-average burger bar where students, families and business types perch on reclaimed banquettes tucking into prime patties and more.

Dojo   ASIAN **£**
(www.dojonoodlebar.co.uk; Mill Lane; mains £8; ☑) Favoured by students from nearby Queens' and noodle lovers in general, this smart, aroma-filled eatery rustles up the kind of spicy street food you'll find in Thailand, Malaysia, Singapore, Japan and Vietnam.

Gardenia   GREEK **£**
(www.gardis.org.uk; 2 Rose Cres; mains £5; ⊘ noon-4am; ☑) 'Gardi's' is responsible for the late-night nutrition for large numbers of students, and its walls are plastered with photos of happy customers munching on the lamb souvlaki and doner kebabs.

Clowns   CAFE **£**
(54 King St; mains £6; ⊘ 8am-11pm; 🕸) A friendly Italian family has created this Cambridge institution; a top spot for cooked breakfast, homemade lasagne, or lingering over a first-class coffee.

Kingston Arms   PUB **££**
(www.kingston-arms.co.uk; 33 Kingston St; mains £5-16; ⊘ noon-2pm & 6-10pm Mon-Fri, to 10pm Sat & Sun; 🕸) Great gastropub grub – from roasts to white-onion soup and recession-busting mains (held at £4.99), keeps stomachs satisfied at the award-winning Kingston. Meanwhile 12 real ales, stacked board games and a students-meet-locals clientele deliver a contemporary Cambridge vibe. It's 1 mile southeast of the centre, along Parkside then down student-central Mill Rd.

Oak   BISTRO **££**
(☑ 01223-323361; www.theoakbistro.co.uk; 6 Lensfield Rd; mains £12-20; set lunch 2/3 courses £13/16; ⊘ noon-2.30pm & 6-9.30pm Mon-Sat) Truffles (white and black), olive pesto and rosemary jus are the kind of flavour intensifiers you'll find at this friendly but classy neighbourhood eatery where locally sourced duck, fish and beef come cooked just so. The set lunch is a bargain.

Chop House   BRITISH **££**
(www.cambscuisine.com/cambridge-chop-house; 1 Kings Pde; mains £14-20; ⊘ noon-10.30pm Mon-Sat, to 9.30pm Sun) The window seats here deliver some of the best views in town – onto King's College's hallowed walls. The food is pure English establishment too: hearty steaks and chops and chips, plus a scattering of fish dishes and suet puds. Sister restaurant **St John's Chop House** (21-24 Northampton St) sits near the rear entrance to St John's College.

Hakka   CHINESE **££**
(www.hak-ka.co.uk; 24 Milton Rd; mains £10; ⊘ 6.30-9.30pm; ☑) Chef Daniel's mother taught him the secrets of Hakka cooking and once you've tasted his signature salt-and-chilli chicken, you'll be inclined to give her a hug. The menu is extensive but the sizzling dishes stand out.

★ Midsummer House   FINE DINING **£££**
(☑ 01223-369299; www.midsummerhouse.co.uk; Midsummer Common; 5/7/10 courses £45/75/95; ⊘ noon-1.30pm Wed-Sat, 7-9pm Tue-Sat) At the region's top tables Chef Daniel Clifford's double Michelin-starred creations are distinguished by depth of flavour and immense technical skill. Sample braised oxtail, coal-baked celeriac and scallops with truffle before dollops of dark chocolate, blood orange and marmalade ice cream. Wine flights start at £55.

Cotto   INTERNATIONAL **£££**
(☑ 01223-302010; www.cottocambridge.co.uk; 183 East Rd; 3 courses £50; ⊘ 6.30-9pm Wed-Sat; ☑) 🖋 An irresistible blend of artistry and precision ensure chef Hans Schweitzer's creations

look gorgeous and taste fabulous. Delights might include saffron-infused Cromer crab and crayfish tian or herb-encrusted, salt marsh lamb, followed perhaps by a Caribbean palm sugar and vanilla bean brûlée.

🍷 Drinking & Nightlife

Eagle PUB
(www.gkpubs.co.uk; Benet St; ⊙9am-11pm Mon-Sat, to 10.30pm Sun) Cambridge's most famous pub has loosened the tongues and pickled the grey cells of many an illustrious academic; among them Nobel Prize–winning scientists Crick and Watson, who discussed their research into DNA here (note the blue plaque by the door). Dating from the 15th-century, wood-panelled and rambling, its cosy rooms include one with WWII airmens' signatures on the ceiling. The food, served all day, is good too.

Granta PUB
(www.gkpubs.co.uk; Newnham Rd; ⊙11am-11pm, to 10.30pm Sun) If the exterior of this picturesque waterside pub, overhanging a pretty mill pond, looks strangely familiar, it could be because it is the darling of many a TV director. No wonder, with its snug deck, riverside terrace and punts (p379) moored up alongside, it's a highly atmospheric spot to sup and watch the world drift by.

Maypole PUB
(www.maypolefreehouse.co.uk; 20a Portugal Pl; ⊙11.30am-midnight Sun-Thu, to 2am Fri & Sat) A dozen pumps dispensing real ale, a roomy beer garden and a friendly, unreconstructed vibe make this red-brick pub popular with the locals. That and hearty, homemade Italian food and an annual festival championing regional and microbrewery beers.

Fez CLUB
(www.cambridgefez.com; 15 Market Passage; ⊙10pm-3am) Hip-hop, dance, R&B, techno, funk, indie, top-name DJs and club nights – you'll find it all at Cambridge's most popular club, the Moroccan-themed Fez, strewn with Turkish rugs and cushions.

Lola Lo CLUB
(www.lolalocambridge.com; 1 Corn Exchange St; ⊙10pm-3am Wed-Mon) Bringing a South Pacific vibe to the centre of Cambridge, Lola Lo specialises in cocktails and themed nights, featuring commercial dance, drum 'n' bass and club anthems. Grass skirts are de rigueur for ladies (though we might be lying).

☆ Entertainment

Portland Arms LIVE MUSIC
(www.theportlandarms.co.uk; 129 Chesterton Rd; ⊙11am-11.30pm, to 12.30am Fri & Sat) A popular student haunt, the Portland is the best spot in town to catch a gig and see the pick of up-and-coming bands. It has a wood-panelled interior, a spacious terrace and a monthly comedy night too.

ADC THEATRE
(www.adctheatre.com; Park St) This famous student-run theatre is home to the university's Footlights comedy troupe whose past members include Emma Thompson, Hugh Laurie and Stephen Fry.

Junction PERFORMING ARTS
(🖉01223-578000; www.junction.co.uk; Clifton Way) Theatre, dance, comedy, live bands and club nights at a contemporary performance venue near the railway station. It's 1.5 miles southeast of the city centre, down Regent St (later Hills Rd).

Cambridge Arts Theatre THEATRE
(🖉01223-503333; www.cambridgeartstheatre.com; 6 St Edward's Passage) Cambridge's biggest bona fide theatre puts on everything from highbrow drama and dance, to panto and shows fresh from London's West End.

Corn Exchange PERFORMING ARTS
(🖉01223-357851; www.cornex.co.uk; Wheeler St) Venue attracting the top names, from pop and rock to comedy.

ℹ Information

Addenbrooke's (www.cuh.org.uk; Hills Rd) Hospital 4 miles southeast of the centre.

CB1 (www.cb1.com; 32 Mill Rd; per hr £1.80; ⊙9.30am-8pm; 🖥) Internet cafe half a mile southeast of the centre.

Police Station (www.cambs.police.uk; Parkside; ⊙8am-10pm) On the north east corner of Parker's Piece.

Post Office (St Andrew's St; ⊙9.30am-5.30pm Mon-Sat)

Tourist Office (🖉0871 226 8006; www.visitcambridge.org; Peas Hill; ⊙10am-5pm Mon-Sat, plus 11am-3pm Sun Apr-Oct)

ℹ Getting There & Away

BUS

Buses run by **National Express** (www.nationalexpress.com) leave from Parkside. Destinations include the following:

Gatwick £20, 4½ hours, hourly

OLIVER CROMWELL – THE SCOURGE OF KINGS
....

While some believe the enigmatic Cromwell was a regicidal dictator, others hail him as a hero of liberty – although the truth is probably more complex than either.

East Anglia's most notorious son was born in Huntingdon in 1599. His first 40 years or so on a smallholding were spent in obscurity, but after he underwent a religious conversion and became a militant Puritan there was no stopping him, driven as he was by ambition and clarity of purpose before God. After a spell as a Member of Parliament for Huntingdon and then Cambridge, 'Old Ironsides' excelled as a military commander during the English Civil War, fighting on the side of the victorious 'Roundheads' (ie those siding with parliament against the king). Despite the fact that he was only one of several signatories of the death warrant of Charles I, he is the one largely held responsible.

Though modern interpretation suggests Cromwell allowed Jews (expelled in 1290) back into Britain to 'stimulate the economy', the fact that he used the full weight of his office as lord protector to force through this unpopular decision shows how firmly he believed that the conversion of the Jews to Christianity was an essential precondition to the establishment of Christ's rule on earth: 'Was it not our duty in particular to encourage them to settle here, where alone they could be taught the truth?'

His other major actions were the conquests of Ireland and Scotland, acts that – together with the death of Charles I – won him widespread posthumous animosity, to the point where his body was exhumed from Westminster Abbey after the Restoration (of the monarchy) and then treated as if he had been a live rebel: hanged at Tyburn and decapitated. The body was almost certainly thrown into the common pit at Tyburn (the present-day site of Marble Arch), while the head was stuck on Westminster Hall and remained there for several decades, blowing down in a storm in the early 18th century. Picked up, it passed into private ownership and was occasionally exhibited as a curiosity. A descendant of its last owner deeded it to Sidney Sussex College in 1960 – Cromwell's alma mater – and it was buried in the chapel. There is a plaque on the wall but the exact location is kept secret, lest self-proclaimed Royalists dig it up and defile it.

Heathrow £17, four hours, hourly

Oxford £15, 3½ hours, every 30 minutes

Stansted £10, 50 minutes, hourly

CAR

Cambridge's centre is largely pedestrianised. The city's multistorey car parks charge between £2.50 and £4.80 for two hours.

Five free Park & Ride car parks circle the city on the major routes, with buses (return tickets £2.90) shuttling into the city centre every 10 to 15 minutes between around 7am and 8pm.

TRAIN

The **train station** is 1.5 miles southeast of the centre. Destinations include the following:

Birmingham New Street £32, four hours, hourly

Bury St Edmunds £10, 50 minutes, hourly

Ely £4, 15 minutes, three per hour

King's Lynn £10, 45 minutes, hourly

London Kings Cross £18, one hour, two to four per hour

Stansted £15, 30 minutes to 1¼ hours, two per hour

ⓘ Getting Around

BICYCLE

Cambridge is incredibly bike-friendly, with two wheels providing an ideal, and atmospheric, way to get around town.

Station Cycles (www.stationcycles.co.uk; Corn Exchange St; per half-day/day/week £7/10/25; ⊘8am-6pm Mon-Fri, 9am-5pm Sat, 10am-4pm Sun) In the heart of town, underneath the Grand Arcade shopping centre. There's another branch on Station Rd at the train station.

City Cycle Hire (www.citycyclehire.com; 61 Newnham Rd; per half-day/day/week £7/10/25; ⊘9am-5.30pm Mon-Fri, plus 9am-5pm Sat Apr-Oct) A mile southwest of the city centre

BUS

Bus routes run around town from the **main bus station** (Drummer St). Many operate until around 11.30pm. C1, C3 and C7 stop at the train station. A Dayrider ticket (£3.90) provides 24 hours, unlimited, citywide bus travel.

Grantchester

POP 560

Old thatched cottages with gardens covered in flowers, breezy meadows and classic cream teas aren't the only reason to make the pilgrimage along the Cam to the picture-postcard village of Grantchester. You'll also be following in the footsteps of some of the world's greatest minds on a 3-mile walk, cycle or punt that has changed little since Edwardian times. After the idyllic journey, flop into a deck chair under a leafy apple tree and wolf down calorific cakes or light lunches at the quintessentially English **Orchard Tea Garden** (www.orchard-grantchester.com; Mill Way; lunch mains £4-9, cakes £3; ⊘ 9.30am-5pm Mar-Oct, 10am-4pm Nov-Feb). This was the favourite haunt of the Bloomsbury Group who came to camp, picnic, swim and discuss their work.

Imperial War Museum

The romance of the winged war machine is alive and well at Europe's biggest ★ **aviation museum** (www.iwm.org.uk; Duxford; adult/child £17.50/free; ⊘ 10am-6pm Easter-Oct, to 4pm Nov-Easter; Ⓟ 🚗), where almost 200 lovingly preserved vintage aircraft are housed in several enormous hangars. The vast airfield showcases everything from dive bombers to biplanes, Spitfire and Concorde.

The last admission is an hour before closing. Duxford is 9 miles south of Cambridge at Junction 10 of the M11. Bus C7 runs from Emmanuel St in Cambridge to Duxford (£3.50, 50 minutes, two-to-three per hour).

Make this a day trip, especially if you're bringing kids – the interactive rocket launchers and flight simulators prove irresistible.

The awe-inspiring **American Air Museum** hangar, designed by Norman Foster, pays homage to the daring of US WWII servicemen and hosts the largest collection of American civil and military aircraft outside the USA, while the slick **AirSpace** hangar houses an exhibition on British and Commonwealth aviation. The planes aren't here to just look pretty – a number, such as the legendary *Flying Fortress*, take to the skies during the ultra-popular June/July **Winged Legends air show** – an exhilarating spectacle not least because there's considerable risk involved for pilots. Modern battles are also covered, including the latest desert warfare in Afghanistan and Iraq, complete with an assortment of tanks and artillery from WWII onwards.

Ely

POP 20,200

A small but charming city dominated by a jaw-dropping cathedral, Ely makes an excellent day trip from Cambridge. It takes its name (pronounced *ee*-lee) from the eels that once inhabited the undrained Fens surrounding the town. From the Middle Ages onwards, Ely was one of the biggest opium-producing centres in Britain, with high-class ladies holding 'poppy parties' and mothers in the Fens sedating their children with 'poppy tea'. Today, beyond the dizzying heights of the cathedral towers, Ely is a cluster of medieval streets lined with traditional tearooms and pretty Georgian houses; a quaint quayside adds extra appeal.

⊙ Sights

Ely Cathedral   CATHEDRAL
(www.elycathedral.org; The Gallery; adult/child £8/free, entry & tower tour £14.50/free; ⊘ 7am-6.30pm, evensong 5.30pm Mon-Sat, 4pm Sun, choral service 10.30am Sun) Ely Cathedral's stunning silhouette dominates the whole area – it's dubbed the 'Ship of the Fens' because it's so visible across the vast, flat sweeps of land. The early-12th-century **nave** dazzles with clean, uncluttered lines and a lofty sense of space. Look out too for the entrancing ceiling, the masterly 14th-century **Octagon**, and **towers** that soar upwards in shimmering colours. Standard admission includes a ground-floor guided tour. The tower tours (three to five daily) deliver behind-the-scenes glimpses, 165 steps and remarkable views.

Ely has been a place of worship and pilgrimage since at least 673, when Etheldreda, daughter of the king of East Anglia, founded a nunnery here (shrugging off the fact that she had been twice married in her determination to become a nun). She was canonised shortly after her death. The nunnery was sacked by the Danes, rebuilt as a monastery, demolished and then resurrected as a church after the Norman Conquest. In 1109 Ely became a cathedral. Gothic arches were added later to support the weight of the mighty walls.

The vast 14th-century **Lady Chapel** is filled with eerily empty niches that once held statues of saints and martyrs. They were hacked out unceremoniously by iconoclasts during the English Civil War. But the delicate tracery remains, overseen by a rather controversial statue of *Holy Mary* by David Wynne, unveiled in 2000 to mixed reviews. The cathedral's beauty has made it a popular film location: you may recognise some of its fine details from scenes in *Elizabeth: The Golden Age* and *The Other Boleyn Girl*. For optimum atmosphere, visit during evensong or a choral service.

Oliver Cromwell's House　　　MUSEUM
(www.olivercromwellshouse.co.uk; 29 St Mary's St; adult/child £4.60/3.10; ☺10am-5pm Apr-Oct, 11am-4pm Nov-Mar) England's premier Puritan lived in this attractive, half-timbered house with his family from 1636 to 1647, when he was the local tithe collector. The interior has been restored to reflect the fixtures and fittings that would have been part of their daily lives – expect flickering candles, floppy hats and writing quills. It's engaging and entertaining, and also challenges you to answer one question: was this complex character a hero or a villain?

Ely Museum　　　MUSEUM
(www.elymuseum.org.uk; Market St; adult/child £3.50/1; ☺10.30am-5pm Wed-Sat & Mon, 1-5pm Sun Apr-Oct, to 4pm Nov-Mar) Housed in the Old Gaol House, this quirky little museum appropriately features gruesome prison tableaux inside prisoners' cells, plus displays on Romans, Anglo-Saxons, the Long Barrow burial ground at nearby Haddlington, and the formation of the Fens. You are also initiated into the mysteries of old Ely trades such as leatherwork and eel-catching.

🛏 Sleeping & Eating

★**Peacocks**　　　B&B ££
(☑01353-661100; www.peacockstearoom.co.uk; 65 Waterside; d £125-150) Walk into the roomy suites here and feel instantly at home. In Cottage, floral Laura Ashley wallpaper graces a sweet sitting area and bedroom; in Brewery, the vintage books, gilt mirrors and burnished antiques are reminiscent of a grand gentlemen's club. Downstairs, the award-winning cafe (open 10.30am to 5pm Wednesday to Sunday) serves a vast selection of teas and cream teas (from £7), luscious homemade soups, salads, cakes and scones.

Riverside Inn　　　B&B ££
(☑01353-661677; www.riversideinn-ely.co.uk; 8 Annesdale; s/d £65/90; ℗) In this Georgian guesthouse on Ely's quay, rooms team with brocade bedspreads and dark furniture with sparkling new bathrooms. Just the place to gaze at the houseboats and rowers bobbing about on the River Great Ouse.

Old Fire Engine House　　　BRITISH ££
(☑01353-662582; www.theoldfireenginehouse. co.uk; 25 St Mary's St; lunch 2/3 courses £15/20, mains £16; ☺noon-2pm & 7-9pm Mon-Sat, to 2pm Sun) 🌱 Eating here is like sampling the dishes cooked up in a (decidedly classy) classic East Anglian farmhouse kitchen. Seasonal and local produce rules, so treats might include Suffolk venison or quince and Stilton tart with Fen celery or Norfolk samphire, rounded off with some custard-smothered, steamed treacle pud.

ℹ Information

Tourist Office (☑01353-662062; www.visitely. org.uk; 29 St Mary's St; ☺10am-4pm) Stocks leaflets (50p) on the picturesque 'Eel Trail' and Fen Rivers Way circular walks (£2).

ℹ Getting There & Away

You can walk to Ely from Cambridge, along the 17-mile, riverside Fen Rivers Way. Rail connections include:

Cambridge £4, 15 minutes, three per hour
King's Lynn £7, 30 minutes, hourly
Norwich £16, one hour, every 30 minutes

ESSEX

The county's inhabitants have been the butt of snobbery and some of England's cruellest jokes for years, thanks to pop-culture stereotypes. But beyond the fake Burberry bags and slots 'n' bumper car resorts, the county's still-idyllic medieval villages and rolling countryside provided inspiration for Constable, one of England's best-loved painters. Here, too, is the historic town of Colchester, while even Southend-on-Sea, the area's most popular resort, has a softer side in the traditional cockle-sellers and cobbled lanes of the sleepy suburb Leigh.

Colchester
POP 173,074

Dominated by its sturdy castle and extensive Roman walls, Colchester is Britain's oldest recorded city, dating from the 5th century BC. In AD 43, the Romans came, saw, conquered and constructed their northern capital Camulodunum. It was razed by Boudica just 17 years later. In the 11th century the invading Normans built a mighty castle; today it's set amid a maze of narrow streets that are home to a striking new arts space and some half-timbered gems.

◉ Sights

★ Colchester Castle　　CASTLE
(www.cimuseums.org.uk; adult/child £7.50/4.75; ☉ 10am-5pm Mon-Sat, 11am-5pm Sun) Built in 1076 on the foundations of the Roman Temple of Claudius, England's largest surviving Norman keep is bigger than that of the Tower of London. Over the centuries it's been a royal residence, a prison and home to a Witchfinder General. Now a £4-million restoration has brought 21st-century technology to its 11th-century walls. Look out for mobile phone apps and tablet hire, and a cracking *son et lumière* re-creating lost internal structures and bringing the building's history to life.

firstsite　　ARTS CENTRE
(www.firstsite.uk.net; Lewis Gdns; ☉ 10am-5pm Tue-Sun; ⊕) FREE Colchester's shiny curved, glass-and-copper arts centre brings the town bang up to date. It's as striking inside as out: installations flow seamlessly into one another amid a wealth of space and light. Temporary visual art display are cunningly juxtaposed with historical works; the one permanent exhibition is the magnificent Berryfield Mosaic – a Roman artefact found on firstsite's location in 1923, and now under glass in the centre of the gallery space.

Hollytrees Museum　　MUSEUM
(www.cimuseums.org.uk; Castle Park; ☉ 10am-5pm Tue-Sat, 11am-5pm Sun) FREE It's like walking into a period drama: a Georgian town house dating from 1718, filled with toys and costumes, watches and clocks. Reminders of the domestic life of the wealthy owners and their servants are everywhere, with quirky exhibits that include a shipwright's baby carriage in the shape of a boat, a make-your-own Victorian silhouette feature and an intricate, envy-inducing dolls' house.

Dutch Quarter　　HISTORIC NEIGHBOURHOOD
The best of the city's half-timbered houses and rickety roof lines are clustered together in this Tudor enclave just a short stroll north of High St. The area remains as a testament to the 16th-century Protestant weavers who fled here from Holland.

🛏 Sleeping & Eating

North Hill　　HOTEL ££
(Green Room; ☑ 01206-574001; www.north-hillhotel.com; 50 North Hill; s £65-80, d/f/ste £90/120/110; ☎) Ask for a room in the more characterful, back building of this sleek sleep spot and you'll be rewarded with wonky beams, exposed red brick and plush modern furnishings. The restaurant (open noon to 2.30pm daily and 6pm to 9.30pm Monday to Saturday) delights in giving local, seasonal comfort food classics a contemporary twist. Dinner mains are around £15 and their working lunch (mains £7) is a snip.

Four Sevens　　B&B ££
(☑ 01206-546093; www.foursevens.co.uk; 28 Inglis Rd; s £55-60, d £65-75; ℗ ☎) The far-from-frilly furnishings here feature stand-alone bowl sinks, industrial-esque clothes rails and platform beds. Impressive breakfasts include eight cereal options, and guests are often welcomed with sponge cake or even tiramisu. It's a mile southwest of the centre, off the B1022 to Maldon.

★ Company Shed　　SEAFOOD ££
(☑ 01206-382700; www.the-company-shed.co.uk; 129 Coast Rd, West Mersea; mains £4-12; ☉ 9am-5pm Tue-Sat, 10am-5pm Sun) Bring your own bread and wine to this seaside shack to tuck into mussels, Colchester oysters, prawns, lobster, jellied eels and smoked fish, courtesy of the Howard family – eighth-generation oyster-men. It's set on Mersea Island, 9 miles south of Colchester; check the tides – it's cut off for an hour either side of particularly high water.

❶ Information

Tourist Office (☑ 01206-282920; www.visitcolchester.com; Castle Park; ☉ 9.30am-5pm Mon-Sat) Now set inside the Hollytrees Museum.

❶ Getting There & Away

National Express buses run to London Victoria every two hours (£15, 2½ hours).

Trains run to London Liverpool Street (£18, one hour, every 15 minutes).

Dedham Vale

John Constable's romantic visions of country lanes, springtime fields and babbling creeks were inspired by and painted in this serene vale. The artist was born and bred in East Bergholt in 1776 and, although you may not see the rickety old cart pictured in his renowned painting *The Hay Wain*, the picturesque cottages, rolling countryside and languid charm remains.

Now known as Constable Country, **Dedham Vale** (www.dedhamvalestourvalley.org) centres on the villages of Dedham, East Bergholt and Flatford. With leafy lanes, arresting pastoral views and graceful old churches, it's a glorious area to explore on foot or by bike.

◎ Sights

Bridge Cottage   HISTORIC BUILDING
(NT; ☑01206-298260; www.nationaltrust.org.uk; Flatford, nr East Bergholt; parking £3; ⊙10.30am-5pm Apr-Oct, to 3.30pm Sat & Sun Nov-Mar; P) **FREE** Set right beside Flatford Mill – a feature of several Constable paintings – thatched Bridge Cottage has an exhibition that provides a fine introduction to the artist's life and works. Call ahead about the daily guided tours (£6.50) which take in Flatford Mill, Willy Lott's Cottage (which features in *The Hay Wain*) and other sites that pop up in Constable's paintings. There are also self-guided routes.

Flatford Mill   HISTORIC BUILDING
(Flatford, nr East Bergholt; P) Constable fans will recognise red-brick Flatford Mill immediately, as it appears in many of his canvases and remains as idyllic a setting today. It was once owned by the artist's family and is now used as an education centre, so although you can take in picture-perfect views from front and back, you can't go in.

⇄ Courses

Painting Courses   ART
(☑01206-323027; www.dedhamhall.co.uk; Brook St, Dedham; nonresidents per 3/7 days £295/325) For those inspired by Dedham Vale's bucolic landscapes, atmospheric Dedham Hall runs acclaimed painting courses in a converted, 14th-century barn. You can just visit each day for lessons, but it's more fun to stay, when the fee (per three/seven nights from £495/650) includes dinner, bed and breakfast.

🛏 Sleeping & Eating

Sun   INN ££
(☑01206-323351; www.thesuninndedham.com; High St, Dedham; d £110-150; P🐕) Choices, choices, choices. The Rocco-themed, duck-egg-blue room, or the one with a four-poster, beamed bathroom and its own ghost? The lamb kofka and mojitos or the Stilton ploughmans and real ale? Either way the 15th-century Sun delivers wonky walls, creaking floors and

bags of charm. The restaurant (mains £13 to £19) is open noon to 2.30pm and 6.30pm to 9.30pm.

Milsoms   HOTEL ££
(☑01206-322795; www.milsomhotels.com; Stratford Rd, Dedham; d £120-200; P🐕) Sure-footed design gives the rooms here a real sense of fun: red-leather armchairs, Anglepoise lamps and retro phones meet vast leaning mirrors and jazzy modern art. But the peppery pistachio-crusted salmon or lemon posset in the funky brasserie (open noon to 9.30pm, mains £8 to £27) might tempt you from your room.

Dedham Hall   B&B ££
(☑01206-323027; www.dedhamhall.co.uk; Brook St, Dedham; s/d £65/110, 3 courses £35; P) From the beamed bar and cosy lounge to the plump furnishings and shelves of vintage books, it's all atmosphere at this rambling, 15th-century house. Chairs and tables dot landscaped lawns, while the Fountain House restaurant (three courses £35, booking required) dishes up elegant, imaginative fare.

Maison Talbooth   BOUTIQUE HOTEL £££
(☑01206-322367; www.milsomhotels.com; Stratford Rd, Dedham; ste £210-345; P🐕🏊) In secluded grounds overlooking Constable's Dedham Vale, this fabulous retreat sees guests luxuriating in swish suites with goose-feather duvets and don't-want-to-get-up beds, and de-stressing in its heated pool, hot tub, tennis courts and spa.

❶ Getting There & Around

Buses 247 and 102 run from Colchester to Dedham (£2.20, 30 minutes, two to eight daily). Bus 93 links Colchester with East Bergholt (£2.60, 45 minutes, every two hours Monday to Saturday). If coming by train, Flatford Mill is a lovely 2-mile walk from Manningtree station.

Saffron Walden

POP 14,572

The 12th-century market town of Saffron Walden is a delightful knot of half-timbered houses, narrow lanes, crooked roofs and ancient buildings. It gets its name from the purple saffron crocus (source of the world's most expensive spice), which was cultivated in the surrounding fields between the 15th and 18th centuries. It makes an atmospheric day trip from Cambridge.

⊙ Sights

Old Sun Inn   HISTORIC BUILDING
(Church St) Saffron Walden's most famous
landmark sits at a crossroads surrounded by timber-framed buildings. An ornate,
14th-century structure, it was once used as
Cromwell's HQ and its exterior walls still
bear intricate 17th-century pargeting (decorative plaster work).

St Mary the Virgin   CHURCH
(www.stmaryssaffronwalden.org; Church St;
⊙8am-5pm) FREE St Mary's oldest parts
date back to 1250. A symbol of the town's
saffron-inspired golden age, it is one of the
largest churches in the county and features
some impressive Gothic arches, and local
landowner Lord Audley's tomb.

Saffron Walden Museum   MUSEUM
(www.saffronwaldenmuseum.org; Museum St;
adult/child £1.50/free; ⊙10am-4.30pm Tue-Sat,
to 2pm Sun) Eclectic collections here range
from local history, 18th-century costumes
and Victorian toys to geology, ancient Egyptian artefacts and Inuit bone harpoons. The
bramble-covered ruins of **Walden Castle
Keep**, built about 1125, lie in the grounds.

Bridge End Gardens   GARDENS
(⊙gardens 24hr, maze & kitchen garden 9am-3pm
Mon-Thu, to 1pm Fri, 10am-4pm Sat & Sun) FREE
Careful restoration of these seven inter-
linked gardens has brought them back to
their former Victorian glory. Make sure you
visit when the maze and produce-packed
kitchen garden are open too.

✗ Eating

Eight Bells   PUB ££
(www.8bells-pub.co.uk; 18 Bridge St; mains £12-20;
⊙noon-3pm & 6-10pm Mon-Sat, noon-6pm Sun; ⊿)

A warm mix of medieval character and
contemporary style, this 16th-century
gastropub serves up the likes of pork tenderloin with sage-infused apple and home-
cured gravlax. Scrubbed wooden floors,
half-timbered walls, abstract art, deep leather sofas and roaring fires make it an attractive place to sip on a pint too.

Cafe Coucou   CAFE ££
(www.cafecoucou.co.uk; 17 George St; mains £7-10;
⊙9am-5pm Mon-Sat) Delicious homemade
quiches, huge scones, chunky doorstop
sandwiches and salads sell like hotcakes at
this cheerful family-run cafe.

ⓘ Information

Tourist Office (⊿01799-524002; www.vis-
itsaffronwalden.gov.uk; 1 Market Pl; ⊙9.30am-
5pm Mon-Sat) Stocks a good town trail leaflet
on the historic buildings.

ⓘ Getting There & Around

Bus 7 runs between Saffron Walden and Cambridge (£4, one hour, hourly).

The nearest train station is 2 miles west of Saffron Walden at Audley End. Bus 301 links Audley
End train station with Saffron Walden (£1.70, 15
minutes, hourly Monday to Friday). Train services from there include:

Cambridge £7, 20 minutes, every 20 minutes

London Liverpool Street £11, one hour, twice
hourly Monday to Saturday, hourly Sunday

Southend-on-Sea

POP 173,600

Full of flashing lights and fairground rides,
Southend is London's weekend playground,
replete with gaudy amusements and packed
nightclubs. But as well as all that, there's a
glorious stretch of sandy beach, an absurdly

DON'T MISS

AUDLEY END HOUSE PARK

Positively palatial in its scale, style and the all-too-apparent ambition of its creator, the
first earl of Suffolk, the fabulous early-Jacobean **Audley End House Park** (⊙10am-6pm
Wed-Sun) eventually did become a royal palace when it was bought by Charles II in 1668.

Audley End House is 1 mile west of Saffron Walden off the B1383. Audley End train
station is 1.25 miles from the house. Taxis from the town marketplace cost around £5.

Today, the enormous building is one-third of its original size, but it's still magnificent.
Lavishly decorated rooms glitter with silverware, priceless furniture and paintings, making
it one of England's grandest country homes. The interior was remodelled in Gothic style by
the third Baron Braybrooke in the 19th century, and much of his creation remains today.

The house is surrounded by a landscaped park (open 10am to 6pm Wednesday to Sunday) designed by Lancelot 'Capability' Brown and is host to summer concerts.

long pier and, in the suburb of Old Leigh, a traditional fishing village.

◉ Sights

Southend Pier
LANDMARK

(www.southend.gov.uk/pier; ☺ 8am-6pm Mon-Fri, to 8pm Sat & Sun Apr-Sep, 9am-5pm Wed-Sun Oct-Mar) 𝗙𝗥𝗘𝗘 Welcome to the world's longest pier – a staggering 1.34 miles long, to be precise – built in 1830 and a magnet for boat crashes, storms and fires, the last of which ravaged its tip in 2005. Today, a peaceful if windy stroll to the restored pier head reveals a cafe, artists' studios and the 185-seater Royal Pavilion. Hopping on the Pier Railway (single adult/child £3.50/2) saves the long slog back.

Pier Museum
MUSEUM

(www.southendpiermuseum.co.uk; Marine Pde; adult/child £1.50/50p; ☺ 11am-5pm Sat, Sun, Tue & Wed Mar-Oct) Southend's seaside heyday springs to life in this charming museum, where a Victorian toast-rack tram from the pier sits beside a functioning signal box, sepia photos and period costumes. The best bits though are the still-working antique penny-slot machines.

Old Leigh
NEIGHBOURHOOD

Cobbled streets, cockle sheds, art galleries and craft shops define atmospheric Old Leigh. It's a long stroll west along Southend's seafront, or a short hop on the local train.

🛌 Sleeping & Eating

Roslin Beach
HOTEL ££

(☑ 01702-586375; www.roslinhotel.com; Thorpe Esplanade; s/d/ste £87/120/185, mains £14-22; 𝗣🛜🐾) Seafront Roslin is all New England beach-house chic: sculptural driftwood features, seashell-framed mirrors and sand drifting up the steps. De-knot in the sauna, soak in the spa then sample locally-caught whitebait on the water-view terrace, framed by swaying palms. Food is served noon to 3pm and 6pm to 9pm.

Beaches
B&B ££

(☑ 01702-586124; www.beachesguesthouse.co.uk; 192 Eastern Esplanade; s/d from £40/90; 𝗣🛜) A welcome respite from violent florals and heavy swag curtains, rooms at Beaches are bright, simple and tasteful, with white Egyptian-cotton bed linen, feather duvets and subtle colour schemes.

Osborne Bros
SEAFOOD £

(www.osbornebros.co.uk; High St, Leigh-on-Sea; snacks £2.50, mains £6; ☺ 8am-5pm) Part fish stall, part bare-bones cafe, Osbourne's is set right on Old Leigh's waterfront and serves up expansive Thames Estuary views. As it's run by a seafood merchant there are also cockles, mussels, prawns and jellied eels to go with your salad or jacket spud.

ℹ Information

Tourist Office (☑ 01702-618747; www.visit southend.co.uk; Western Esplanade; ☺ 8am-6pm Arp-Oct, 9am-5pm Wed-Sun Nov-Mar) At the entrance to the pier.

ℹ Getting There & Around

Southend has two train stations: Central (10 minutes' walk from the sea) and Victoria (15 minutes from the shore).

London Liverpool Street £15, one hour, four per hour, from Southend Victoria.

London Fenchurch St £11, 55 minutes, four per hour, from Southend Central.

Leigh-on-Sea £3, seven minutes, every 15 minutes, from Southend Central.

SUFFOLK

Suffolk is dotted with picturesque villages seemingly lost in time. The county made its money on the back of the medieval wool trade and magnificent churches and lavish Tudor homes attest to the area's wealthy past. To the west are the picture-postcard villages of Lavenham and Long Melford. Further north Bury St Edmunds ushers in historic buildings and a market-town vibe. While the appealing seaside resorts of Aldeburgh and Southwold overflow with genteel charm.

ℹ Getting Around

Ipswich is the county's main transport hub. Search online for bus routes via **Suffolk County Tourism** (www.suffolkonboard.com) and Traveline (p370).

Trains connections from Ipswich include the following:

Bury St Edmunds £9, 30 minutes, two per hour

London Liverpool Street £30, 1¼ hours, every 20 minutes

Norwich £15, 40 minutes, two per hour

Long Melford

POP 2898

Two Elizabethan manors and some fine eateries make Long Melford deserving of a detour. Its expansive village green, antiques shops and string of independent stores provide other excellent reasons to meander on through.

◉ Sights

Kentwell Hall
HISTORIC BUILDING

(☑01787-310207; www.kentwell.co.uk; adult/child £11.50/8; P) Gorgeous, turreted, haunted Kentwell Hall may date from the 1500s and be full of Tudor grandeur, but the manor house is still used as a private home, resulting in a wonderfully lived-in feel. It's framed by a rectangular moat, glorious gardens and an irresistible rare-breeds farm. Keep an eye out for the Tudor re-enactment events, when the whole estate bristles with bodices, codpieces and hose, and Scaresville – a costumed Halloween extravaganza. Opening hours are erratic, call to check, though it's open noon to 4pm most days in summer, plus other weekends.

Melford Hall
HISTORIC BUILDING

(NT; www.nationaltrust.org.uk; Hall St; adult/child £7/3.40; ⊙1-5pm Wed-Sun Apr-Oct; P) From outside, the romantic Elizabethan mansion of Melford Hall seems little changed since it entertained Queen Elizabeth I in 1578. Inside, there's a panelled banqueting hall, masses of Regency and Victorian finery, and a display on Beatrix Potter, who was a cousin of the Parkers, who owned the house from 1786 to 1960.

Holy Trinity
CHURCH

(www.longmelfordchurch.com; Church Walk; ⊙10am-5pm) Magnificent Holy Trinity is more cathedral-sized than church-sized, a spectacular example of a 15th-century wool church. The stained-glass windows and flint and stone flushwork are outstanding.

🛏 Sleeping & Eating

Black Lion
HOTEL ££

(☑01787-312356; www.blacklionhotel.net; The Green; s/d/ste £100/125/175, mains £16; P🛜) There's more than a hint of the Scottish Highlands at the smashing Black Lion, thanks to tartan carpets, open fires and ancient-looking oil paintings. Flamboyant bedrooms, all swag curtains and feature beds, are named after classy wines – Yquem is, fittingly, floor-to-ceiling rich red. The food, served noon to 2pm and 7pm to 9pm, is a combo of contemporary style and traditional elegance too.

Bull
INN ££

(☑01787-378494; www.oldenglishinns.co.uk; Hall St; s/d £60/80, mains £8-12; P🛜) They've been serving travellers at this rambling village pub since 1580, and its bars are pleasantly businesslike despite ornate carved ceilings and heraldic crests. For maximum atmosphere check into a front-facing bedroom; it'll be rich in aged beams and dark wood. Food is served noon to 9.30pm.

DON'T MISS

SUTTON HOO

Somehow missed by plundering grave robbers and left undisturbed for 1300 years, the hull of an enormous Anglo-Saxon ship was discovered at **Sutton Hoo** (NT; ☑01394-389700; www.nationaltrust.org.uk; Sutton Hoo, nr Woodbridge; adult/child £7.50/3.70; ⊙10.30am-5pm Easter-Oct, 11am-4pm Sat & Sun Nov-Easter; P♿) in 1939, buried under a mound of earth. The vessel was the final resting place of Raedwald, King of East Anglia until AD 625, and was stuffed with Saxon riches, reflecting a sophisticated culture that's conveyed beautifully in on-site displays.

The massive effort that went into Raedwald's burial gives some idea of just how important a man he was, while the elaborate nature of the treasures transformed perceptions of the era.

Many of the original finds and a full-scale reconstruction of his ship and burial chamber can be seen in the visitor centre. The finest treasures, including the king's exquisitely crafted helmet, shields, gold ornaments and Byzantine silver, are displayed in London's British Museum, but replicas are on show here, along with an original prince's sword.

Paths encircle the 18 burial mounds (which look like bumps in the ground) that make up the 'royal cemetery'. You can only walk onto them as part of a one-hour **guided tour** (adult/child £2.50/1.25), which provides a fascinating insight into the site. Call to check for tour times.

Sutton Hoo is 2 miles east of Woodbridge and 6 miles northeast of Ipswich off the B1083.

Scutcher's Bistro BRITISH £££

(☑ 01787-310200; www.scutchers.com; Westgate St; mains £20-30; ☺ noon-2pm & 7-9.30pm Thu-Sat) Beautiful reinventions of traditional ingredients ensure this unpretentious place is renowned throughout the Stour Valley. Local Gressingham duck might be given an Asian twist; wild seabass could be paired with Milanese risotto. It's modern, classy and assured.

❶ Getting There & Away

Bus links include the following:

Bury St Edmunds £3.95, 50 minutes, hourly Monday to Saturday.

Sudbury £1, 10 minutes, hourly Monday to Saturday.

Sudbury

POP 13,000

Besides giving us the celebrated portrait and landscape painter Thomas Gainsborough (1727–88) and being the model for Charles Dickens' fictional town Eatanswill in *The Pickwick Papers* (1837), Sudbury is a bustling market town that prospered during the wool trade, with small-scale silk weaving surviving to this day.

Most visitors to Sudbury come to see **Gainsborough's House** (www.gainsborough. org; 46 Gainsborough St; adult/child £6.50/2; ☺ 10am-5pm Mon-Sat), the artist's birthplace and home to the world's largest collection of his work. The 16th-century house and gardens feature a Georgian facade built by the artist's father. Inside, look for his earliest surviving portrait, *A Boy and a Girl in a Landscape,* the exquisite *Portrait of Harriett, Viscountess Tracy,* celebrated for its delicate portrayal of drapery, and the landscapes that were his passion.

Sudbury's train station has hourly connections to London Liverpool Street (£26, 1¼ hours). Regular buses run to Ipswich (one hour), Long Melford (13 minutes), Lavenham (30 minutes), Bury St Edmunds (one hour) and Colchester (one hour).

Lavenham

POP 1413

One of East Anglia's most beautiful and rewarding towns, the former wool-trade centre of Lavenham is home to a collection of exquisitely preserved medieval buildings that lean and lurch to dramatic effect. Lavenham's 300 half-timbered, pargeted and thatched houses have been left virtually untouched since the 15th century; many are now superb places to eat and stay.

◉ Sights

Guildhall of Corpus Christi HISTORIC BUILDING
(NT; www.nationaltrust.org.uk; Market Pl; adult/child £5.35/2.65; ☺ 11am-5pm Apr-Oct, to 4pm Sat & Sun Mar & Nov) Lavenham's most enchanting buildings are clustered along High St, Water St and around the unusually triangular Market Pl. They're dominated by this early-16th-century whitewashed guildhall – a superb example of a close-studded, timber-framed building. It is now a local-history museum with displays on the wool trade and medieval guilds; in its tranquil garden you can see dye plants that produced the typical medieval colours.

Little Hall HISTORIC BUILDING
(www.littlehall.org.uk; Market Pl; adult/child £3.50/ free; ☺ 2-4.30pm Tue-Thu, Sat & Sun, 10am-1pm Mon Apr-Oct) Caramel-coloured, 14th-century Little Hall was once home to a successful wool merchant. Inside, the rooms of this gem had been restored to period splendour through the efforts of the Gayer-Anderson twins who made it their home in the 1920s and 1930s.

St Peter & St Paul CHURCH
(www.lavenhamchurch.wordpress.com; Church St; ☺ 8.30am-5.30pm) This late-Perpendicular structure seems to lift into the sky, with its beautifully proportioned windows, soaring flint tower and gargoyle waterspouts. Built between 1485 and 1530, it was one of Suffolk's last great wool churches, completed on the eve of the Reformation, and is now a lofty testament to Lavenham's past prosperity.

☞ Tours

Guided Walks WALKING TOUR
(adult/child £4/free; ☺ 2.30pm Sat, 11am Sun Easter-Oct) Delve deep into the stories behind Lavenham's beautiful buildings on these guided strolls. They leave from the tourist office; there's no need to book.

🛏 Sleeping & Eating

★ **Angel** HOTEL ££
(☑ 01787-247388; www.wheelersangel.com; Market Pl; s £85, d £75-125, mains £12-19; ℗ 🐾) For what you get, this is ridiculously good value. In Lavenham's oldest building, dark-green corridors lead to gorgeously renovated large, bright, beam-scored rooms. It also happens to be run by renowned chef Marco Pierre

White; the food (served noon to 2.30pm and 6pm to 9pm) is a seriously good version of bistro-meets-pub-grub.

Lavenham Priory
B&B ££

(☑ 01787-247404; www.lavenhampriory.co.uk; Water St; s/d from £87/120; P 🖗) A rare treat – a sumptuously restored, 13th-century B&B that steals your heart as soon as you walk in. The history-rich bedrooms (here called 'bedchambers', naturally) feature cavernous fireplaces, leaded windows, oak floors, original wall paintings and canopied four-poster beds. Book well in advance.

Guinea House
B&B ££

(☑ 01787-249046; www.guineahouse.co.uk; 16 Bolton St; d £75-85) Get ready to duck – some of the doors in this superbly snug, 15th-century cottage are only 5ft tall. Sloping roofs meet sloping walls, slanting floors support wildly wonky beams. And the Aga-cooked breakfast is served in front of a vast fireplace. Perfect.

★ Swan
HOTEL £££

(☑ 01787-247477; www.theswanatlavenham.co.uk; High St; s £105, d £195-290, ste £350; P 🖗) Marvellously medieval and utterly indulgent, the Swan might just spoil you in terms of other places to stay. Tasteful furnishings team oatmeal with olive and gentle reds, lattice works of ancient wood climb all around. The service is smooth, while the suites are simply stunning; expect soaring arched ceilings criss-crossed with beams.

★ Great House
FRENCH ££

(☑ 01787-247431; www.greathouse.co.uk; Market Pl; 3-course lunch/dinner £24/33; ☉ noon-2.30pm Wed-Sun, 7-9.30pm Tue-Sat; 🖗) Contrasting cultures combine so well here: traditional meets modern, East Anglian ingredients meet French cuisine. Which could see you eating confit of Lavenham lamb or caramelised Suffolk pork, then dispatching melting chocolate moelleux or tangy morsels of French and Suffolk cheese.

❶ Information

Tourist Office (☑ 01787-248207; www.discoverlavenham.co.uk; Lady St; ☉ 10am-4.45pm mid-Mar–Oct, 11am-3pm Sat & Sun Nov–mid-Mar) Tucked in beside central Market Pl.

❶ Getting There & Away

Bus 753/754 runs to Bury St Edmunds (£3.65, 30 minutes) and Sudbury (£3.55, 30 minutes) hourly, Monday to Saturday.

Bury St Edmunds

POP 41,113

In Bury the past is ever present. A centre of pilgrimage for centuries, its history-rich features include an atmospheric ruined abbey, handsome Georgian architecture and tranquil gardens. The chance to visit two breweries proves pretty tempting too.

The event that put Bury on the map was the burial, in 903, of St Edmund, the last Saxon king of East Anglia, He'd become a martyr after been decapitated by the Danes in 869 – his grave became a site of pilgrimage and part of one of Europe's most powerful medieval monasteries. In 1214 the English barons came to the abbey to draw up the petition that formed the basis of the Magna Carta, setting the country on the road to a constitutional government.

◉ Sights

Abbey Gardens
RUIN

(Mustow St; ☉ dawn-dusk) **FREE** Now a picturesque ruin in parkland behind the cathedral, Bury's once-mighty abbey still impresses despite the townspeople having made off with much of the stone after the Dissolution. The walls are striking (especially on the west side), having crumbled and eroded into a series of fantastical shapes. Other highlights are the decorative Great Gate, the diminutive dovecote and the flower-filled gardens.

You enter the Abbey Gardens via one of two well-preserved old gates: opposite the tourist office, the staunch mid-14th-century **Great Gate** is intricately decorated and ominously defensive, with battlements, portcullis and arrow slits. The other entrance sits further up Angel Hill, where a gargoyle-studded early-12th-century **Norman Tower** looms.

Just beyond the Great Gate is a peaceful garden where the **Great Court** was once a hive of activity; further on a **dovecote** marks the only remains of the Abbot's Palace. Most impressive, however, are the remains of the western front, where the original abbey walls were burrowed into in the 18th century to make way for homes. The houses are still in use and look as if they've been carved out of the stone-like caves. Nearby is **Samson Tower** and in front of it a beautiful statue of St Edmund by Dame Elisabeth Frink (1976). The rest of the abbey spreads eastward like a ragged skeleton, with various lumps and pillars hinting at its immense size.

St Edmundsbury Cathedral CATHEDRAL

(www.stedscathedral.co.uk; Angel Hill; requested donation adult/child £3/50p; ⊘8.30am-6pm) The 45m-high tower of this cathedral was only completed in 2005 and is a vision in Lincolnshire limestone – its traditional Gothic-style construction conveys how many English cathedrals must have looked fresh from the stonemason's chisel. Most of the building is early 16th century, though the eastern end is post-1945. The overall effect is light and lofty, with a gorgeous hammerbeam roof and a striking sculpture of the crucified Christ by Dame Elisabeth Frink in the north transept.

The impressive entrance porch has a tangible Spanish influence, a tribute to Abbot Anselm (1121–48), who opted against pilgrimage to Santiago de Compostela in favour of building a church dedicated to St James (Santiago in Spanish) right here.

Stop by the **Treasury** (Angel Hill; ⊘10am-4pm Mon-Sat, 12.30-3pm Sun) in the crypt for a glimpse of church silver and ornate medieval Bibles. Free, 30-minute guided **tours** (Angel Hill; ⊘11.30am Mon-Sat late-Apr–Sep) provide an in-depth insight into the cathedral's heritage.

St Mary's Church CHURCH

(www.stmarystpeter.net/stmaryschurch; Honey Hill; donation requested; ⊘10am-4pm) St Mary's is one of the largest parish church in England and also contains the tomb of Mary Tudor – Henry VIII's sister and a one-time queen of France. Built around 1430, it's famous for its hammer-beam roof, which features a host of vampire-like angels swooping from the ceiling. A bell is still rung to mark curfew, as it was in the Middle Ages.

Greene King Brewery BREWERY

(⊘01284-714297; www.greeneking.co.uk; Crown St; visitor centre free; tours £10; ⊘10am-4.30pm Mon-Sat) They've been crafting some of England's favourite booze in this working brewery since 1799. These days it's a place to explore the town's 900-year-old brewing heritage in the visitor centre, then take a tour (2pm weekdays, plus 11am Wednesday to Sunday, plus 12.30pm and 3.30pm Saturday) that winds past the vats and pipes of the historic brewhouse, takes in sweeping town views from the roof, and heads to the Brewery Tap for tipples from the casks. The tours are popular – book.

Moyse's Hall MUSEUM

(www.stedmundsbury.gov.uk/moyseshall; Cornhill; adult/child £4/2; ⊘10.30am-4.30pm Mon-Sat) Set in an impressive 12th-century undercroft,

DRINK LIKE A LOCAL

Pints produce by Greene King and Adnams have been the top tipples of generations of East Anglians, and two brewery tours provide insights into just how they're made: at the Georgian Greene King brewery in Bury St Edmond's and the Adnams (p396) base in Victorian Southwold. Both are intriguing glimpses into the region's heritage brews – and see you sampling the produce too.

rarities here include a locket containing some of Mary Tudor's hair and finds from Bury's ruined abbey. Displays chart the key episodes in the town's past, including the chilling Bury witch trials. There are also displays about one of England's most notorious murders – that of Maria Marten in the Red Barn at nearby Polstead in 1827. A huge crowd gathered in Bury to see her murderer hang.

Theatre Royal HISTORIC BUILDING

(NT; www.theatreroyal.org; Westgate St; ⊘11.30am-3.30pm Wed-Sun early Aug, 11am-5pm Sat & Sun late-May to Jun) A real treat, Britain's only working Regency playhouse features ornate gilding, sweeps of boxes and a *trompe l'oeuil* ceiling, all revealed on self-led and guided front- and back-stage tours.

🛏 Sleeping

⭐Fox INN ££

(⊘01284-705562; www.oldenglishinns.co.uk; 1 Eastgate St; d £90-150; P🖥) Slumber in these converted animal barns and be surrounded by carefully kept original features: whitewashed beams, weathered brick walls and even the livestock tethering rings. Painted wicker chairs and the odd chandelier add another layer of class.

The Glen B&B ££

(⊘01284-755490; rallov@aol.com; 84 Eastgate St; s £40, d £60-75; P🖥) A wood-burning stove and hanging tapestries lend the lounge of this late-Georgian B&B a cosy air. Upstairs it's all bright elegance, with bedrooms in cream and gentle gold.

Angel HOTEL £££

(⊘01284-714000; www.theangel.co.uk; 3 Angel Hill; d £115-180, ste £350; P🖥) The more expensive rooms at this ivy-clad Georgian coaching inn are pretty special; expect luxury bathrooms, quirky mock-1700s furnishings (the odd bright-pink plastic chair) and suites with stand-alone copper baths. The cheaper rooms have much less pizzaz.

✖ Eating & Drinking

★**Pea Porridge**   INTERNATIONAL **££**
(☑01284-700200; www.peaporridge.co.uk; 28-29 Cannon St; mains £13-18; ☉noon-2pm & 6.30-9.30pm Wed-Sat, 6.30-9.30pm Tue) Warmth, happy chatter and great aromas greet you at this intimate neighbourhood eatery. Imaginative dishes borrow from the cuisines of Turkey, Italy and France – choose from tagines, gnocchi, Normandy black sausage or pigs cheeks and polenta – you're onto a winner any which way.

★**Maison Bleue**   FRENCH **£££**
(☑01284-760 623; www.maisonbleue.co.uk; 31 Churchgate St; mains £18-27; ☉noon-2pm & 7-9.30pm Tue-Sat) Settle onto an elegant chair here for modern French cuisine that's supremely stylish and bursting with flavour. Creations might include roasted Gressingham duck with chicken liver velouté, or a gingery tartar of gilt head bream. The set menus (three-course lunch/dinner £24/33) are great-value deals.

★**Old Cannon**   PUB
(☑01284-768769; www.oldcannonbrewery.co.uk; 86 Cannon St) ✍ How's this for a three-in-one? A microbrewery with its own pub and accommodation (singles/doubles £90/120) alongside. Gleaming mash tuns sit in the funky bar; try the Rusty Gun (ABV 4%) or more feisty Gunner's Daughter (5.5%). Then tuck into modish bistro-meets-pub-grub (mains £12-17, served 8.30am to 9pm Monday to Saturday, to 3pm on Sunday) before droping off in the converted brewery flanked by gentle checks and terracotta walls.

Nutshell   PUB
(www.thenutshellpub.co.uk; The Traverse; ☉11am-11pm Mon-Fri, to midnight Sat, to 10.30pm Fri) See how many of your friends you can squeeze into this thimble-sized, memorabilia-packed, timber-framed pub, recognised by the *Guinness Book of Records* as Britain's smallest.

ⓘ Information

Tourist Office (☑01284-764667; www.visit-burystedmunds.co.uk; 6 Angel Hill; ☉9.30am-5pm Mon-Sat, 10am-3pm Sun Easter-Oct, to 4pm Mon-Fri Nov-Easter)

ⓘ Getting There & Around

BUS
The main bus station is on St Andrew's St North.
Cambridge (£4.80, one hour, hourly Monday to Saturday) Stagecoach bus 11
London (£15, 2½ hours, five daily) National Express

TRAIN
The train station is 900m northwest of the tourist office, with frequent buses to the centre.
Cambridge £10, 45 minutes, hourly
Ely £10, 30 minutes, every two hours

Orford
POP 720

Secluded and seductive, the gorgeous village of Orford, 6 miles south of Snape Maltings, is well worth a detour. It's a laid-back place littered with pretty houses and dominated by a real rarity: curiously polygonal Orford Castle.

⊙ Sights

Orford Castle   CASTLE
(EH; www.english-heritage.org.uk; adult/child £6/3.60; ☉10am-6pm daily Apr-Oct, Sat & Sun Nov-Mar; ℗) This 12th-century structure has an innovative, 18-sided drum design with three square turrets. From the roof there are glorious views of Orford Ness.

Orford Ness   NATURE RESERVE
(NT; www.nationaltrust.org.uk; adult/child incl ferry crossing £4/2; ☉10am-5pm Tue-Sat Jul-Sep, plus Sat Oct & late-Apr–Jun) The largest vegetated shingle spit in Europe was once used as a secret military testing ground; now it's a nature reserve and is home to rare wading birds, animals and plants. Ferries run from Orford Quay: the last leaves Orford at 2pm and returns from the reserve at 5pm. Spaces can be limited – arrive early to reserve a seat.

✖ Eating

Butley Orford Oysterage   FISH **££**
(☑01394-450277; www.pinneysoforford.co.uk; Market Hill; mains £8-17; ☉noon-2pm daily, plus 6.30-9pm Jun–mid-Sep) Make sure you've booked a table at this place, lauded locally for the fish and seafood they catch and smoke themselves (it's open some evenings in low season as well); alternatively get some goodies to go from **Pinney's** (www.pinneysoforford.co.uk; The Quay; ☉10am-4pm), their shop by the harbour.

Aldeburgh

POP 3225

The time-warped coastal town of Alde-burgh (pronounced 'orld-bruh') is one of the region's most charming. Its picturesque streets and sweeping shingle beach are lined with pastel-coloured houses, independent shops, art galleries and ramshackle fresh-fish kiosks. Connections with composer Benjamin Britten and two festivals might also draw you to town.

◎ Sights

Scallop   LANDMARK

(Thorpe Rd car park) Maggi Hambling's sculpture commemorates Aldeburgh's links with 20th-century composer Benjamin Britten, who spent much of his life in the town. With 4m of inscribed, scallop shell–shaped steel, its beachside setting has proved controversial locally. It's a short stroll north of town along the seafront.

Moot Hall   MUSEUM

(www.aldeburghmuseum.org.uk; Market Cross Pl; adult/child £2/free; ◎ noon-5pm Jun-Aug, from 2.30pm Apr, May, Sep & Oct) Displays on fishing, shipbuilding, coastal defences and Regency-era tourism set in an intricately carved, timber-framed, 16th-century house.

☆☆ Festivals

Aldeburgh Festival   MUSIC

(www.aldeburgh.co.uk; ◎ Jun) Founded by local composer Benjamin Britten in 1948, this exploration of classical music is one of East Anglia's biggest, taking in new, re-interpreted and rediscovered pieces, and visual arts.

Aldeburgh Food & Drink Festival   FOOD

(www.aldeburghfoodanddrink.co.uk; ◎ late-Sep) A two-day celebration of Suffolk produce and top-class cooking.

🛏 Sleeping & Eating

★ **Ocean House**   B&B, APARTMENT ££

(✆ 01728-452094;   www.oceanhousealdeburgh.co.uk; 25 Crag Path; d £100, apt per week £1300) Just a pebble's throw from Aldeburg's beach, many of the rustic-chic bedrooms here directly overlook the surging sea. The five-person self-catering flat comes with homely kitchen and pint-sized balcony, while the top floor double is a true delight: water views on three sides and a sitting room with a baby grand.

Dunan House   B&B ££

(✆ 01728-452486; www.dunanhouse.co.uk; 41 Park Rd; d £80-95, f from £117; P ☎) Evidence of the artist owners' efforts are everywhere: bright abstracts, self-portraits and pottery galore. Vivid walls alternate between red, orange and lemon; vintage books and battered travelling chests lie around, while the top-floor family suite even has binoculars for zoomed-in estuary views.

Fish & Chip Shop   FISH & CHIPS £

(www.aldeburghfishandchips.co.uk; 226 High St; mains £5-6; ◎ noon-2pm Tue-Sat, 5-8pm Thu-Sat) Aldeburgh has a reputation for the finest fish and chips in the area; this is the best place to find out why.

★ **Lighthouse**   MODERN BRITISH ££

(✆ 01728-453377; www.lighthouserestaurant.co.uk; 77 High St; mains £11-16; ◎ noon-2pm & 6.30-10pm; 🐾) The bright lighthouse has plenty to keep fish fans happy, and plenty of choices for carnivores too. Flavourful dishes range from

---

WORTH A TRIP

DUNWICH & RSPB MINSMERE

Strung along the coastline north of Aldeburgh is a poignant trail of serene and little-visited coastal heritage towns that are gradually succumbing to the sea. Most dramatically, the once-thriving port town of **Dunwich** is now an eerie village, its 12 medieval churches lost under the waves.

The coast near Dunwich draws ranks of birdwatchers, thanks to **Royal Society for the Protection of Birds Minsmere** (RSPB; www.rspb.org.uk; nr Westleton; adult/child £7.50/3; ◎ reserve dawn-dusk, visitor centre 9am-5pm; P) . The reserve is home to one of England's rarest birds, the bittern, with hundreds of migrant birds dropping by in the autumn. Year-round, binoculars are available for rent from the visitor centre, while the hides along the reserve's trails are prime bird-spotting sites.

With public transport lacking you'll need to drive, cycle or walk.

calves liver and mash, via beer-battered cod and chips, to prime duck confit.

Regatta Restaurant
SEAFOOD ££

(☑ 01728-452011; www.regattaaldeburgh.com; 171 High St; mains £14-20; ⊙ noon-2pm & 6-10pm) Other restaurants must be so envious – your own smokery in the back garden. Oak-smoked treats include meaty salmon and memorable prawns, while the perfectly cooked catch of the day could come with anything from risotto or garlic butter to basil sauce.

ℹ Information

Tourist Office (☑ 01728 453637; www.thesuffolkcoast.co.uk; 48 High St; ⊙ 10am-3pm Mon-Sat)

ℹ Getting There & Away

Bus 165 runs hourly, Monday to Saturday to Ipswich (£4.10, 1½ hours), where you can make connections to the rest of the region.

Southwold

POP 974

Southwold's reputation as a well-heeled holiday getaway has earned it the nickname 'Kensington-on-Sea' after the upmarket London borough, and its lovely sandy beach, pebble-walled cottages, cannon-dotted clifftop and rows of beachfront bathing huts are undeniably picturesque. It's all attracted many artists, including JMW Turner, Charles Rennie Mackintosh, Lucian Freud and Damien Hirst.

◉ Sights

Seafront & Pier
NEIGHBOURHOOD

(www.southwoldpier.co.uk; ⊙ pier 10am-5pm, to 7pm Fri & Sat) **FREE** Southwold's shorefront is its main attraction. Amble along the promenade, admire the squat 19th-century **lighthouse** then drop by the 623ft pier, first built in 1899 but recently reconstructed. Its Under the Pier Show (open same hours as the pier) sports a cooky collection of handmade amusement machines which combine daft fun with political satire.

Adnams
BREWERY

(☑ 01502-727225; www.adnams.co.uk; Adnams Pl; tours £12; ⊙ 2-4 tours daily Mar-Sep) Spend an hour touring the high-tech kit inside this Victorian brewery, indulge in a 30-minute tutored tasting, then select a free bottle of beer to take home. Book.

St Edmund's
CHURCH

(Church St; ⊙ 9am-6pm) Worth a peek for its fabulous medieval screen and 15th-century, bloodshot-eyed 'Southwold Jack' effigy (believed to be part of a clock), grumpily overlooking the church's rear.

☞ Tours

Coastal Voyager
BOAT TOUR

(☑ 07887 525082.; www.coastalvoyager.co.uk; Southwold Harbour) Trips on offer include a 30-minute high-speed blast around the bay (adult/child £24/12), a leisurely 3½-hour cruise up the Blyth Estuary (£28/14) and a three-hour voyage to Scroby Sands (£35/18) to see a seal colony and wind farm.

✸ Festivals

Latitude Festival
ARTS

(www.latitudefestival.co.uk; Henham Park; ⊙ Jul) An eclectic mix of music, literature, dance, drama and comedy set in a country estate.

Ways With Words
LITERATURE

(www.wayswithwords.co.uk; ⊙ Nov) Talks and readings by big-name authors in venues around town.

🛏 Sleeping & Eating

Home@21
B&B ££

(☑ 01502-722573; www.homeat21.co.uk; 21 North Pde; d £80-100; ☜) The rooms in this neat Victorian terrace may be super-compact and relatively simple, but the location is all: plumb on the seafront, with a prime view of Southwold's iconic pier and the surging waves.

★ Sutherland House
HOTEL £££

(☑ 01502-724544; www.sutherlandhouse.co.uk; 56 High St; d £140-220, mains £19; Ⓟ☜) Past guests at this former mayor's house include a future James II and the Earl of Sandwich. They'd probably approve of the present appearance: pargeted ceilings, exposed beams and free-standing baths. Supper time (noon to 2pm and 7pm to 9pm, closed Monday) sees prime local ingredients transformed by bouillabaiss sauce, plantain crisps and clam ragù.

Swan
INN £££

(☑ 01502-722186; www.adnams.co.uk/hotels/theswan; Market Sq; s/d from £115/185; ☜) There's a timeless elegance to the 17th-century Swan, where large fireplaces, grandfather clocks and old-fashioned lamps induce a soporific calm. Bedroom styles range from stately Georgian to contemporary coastal, the atmospheric restaurant (noon to 2pm and

7pm to 9pm) majors on local fish, while barstaff are itching to serve you a Southwold-brewed Adnams beer.

Coasters MODERN BRITISH **££**
(☑ 01502-724734; www.coastersofsouthwold.co.uk; 12 Queen St; mains £10-20; ⊙ 9am-3pm & 6-9pm) Punchy flavours and rich ingredients are the mainstay of this bistro, where a wide-ranging menu skips nimbly from whole baked crab and Stilton-glazed beef, to Dingley Dell Suffolk pork sausages with mustard mash.

❶ Information

Tourist Office (☑ 01502-724729; www.visit-sunrisecoast.co.uk; Child's Yard; ⊙ 10am-5pm Mon-Sat, 11am-4pm Sun) Just off the High St, has extensive accommodation listings.

❶ Getting There & Away

Services are limited: catch bus 61 to Lowestoft (£3.90, 50 minutes, hourly) or bus 88 to Halesworth train station (£2.70, 20 minutes, hourly Monday to Saturday) and continue from there.

NORFOLK

Big skies, sweeping beaches, windswept marshes, meandering inland waterways and pretty flint houses combine to great effect in Norfolk. They say the locals have 'one foot on the land, and one in the sea' and you're never far from water here, whether it's beside the windmill-framed rivers of the tranquil Norfolk Broads or the wide, birdlife-rich sands of the shore. Inland, the bustling city of Norwich offers a fine castle and cathedral, a lively market and some truly excellent places to sleep and eat.

Norwich

POP 132,500

The affluent and easygoing city of Norwich (pronounced 'norr-ich') is a rich tapestry of meandering alleys liberally sprinkled with architectural jewels – spoils of the city's medieval wool boom. A magnificent cathedral and impressive Norman castle bookend the city centre; in between, crooked half-timbered buildings line quiet lanes. Thriving markets and a large student population enhance the city's easygoing vibe. Add easy access to the Broads and Norfolk's beaches, and you have an excellent base from which to explore.

◉ Sights

★ **Norwich Cathedral** CATHEDRAL
(www.cathedral.org.uk; The Close; donations welcome; ⊙ 7.30am-6pm) Norwich's most stunning landmark is the magnificent Anglican cathedral, its barbed spire soaring higher than any in England except Salisbury, while the size of its cloisters is second to none. Highlights include the mesmerising ceiling and striking modern features of the **Hostry**, where high-tech displays explore the cathedral's past. The one-hour **guided tours** (donation requested, hourly Monday to Saturday) are an engaging way to find out more.

Work started on the cathedral in 1096 and it remains one of the finest Anglo-Norman abbey churches in the country. The sheer size of its nave is striking, but its most renowned feature is the superb Gothic rib vaulting added in 1463. Among the spidery stonework are 1200 sculpted roof bosses depicting Bible stories. Together they represent one of the finest achievements of English medieval masonry.

HAUNTED BLICKLING HALL

Largely remodelled in the 17th century for Sir Henry Hobart, James I's chief justice, **Blickling Hall** (NT; www.nationaltrust.org.uk; Blickling; adult/child £12/7; ⊙ noon-5pm Wed-Sun Easter-Oct, 11am-5pm Sat & Sun Nov-Mar; ℙ) began life in the 11th century as a manor house and bishop's palace. Today this grand Jacobean mansion is set in vast parklands and is famous for ghostly sightings and a spectacular Long Gallery.

Blickling Hall is 15 miles north of Norwich off the A140. Buses run twice hourly from Castle Meadow and Tombland in Norwich. Aylsham is the nearest train station, 1.5 miles away.

In 1437 the isolated house was claimed by the Boleyn family and passed through the generations to Thomas, father of Anne Boleyn. Anne was executed by her husband Henry VIII in 1533, who opted to have her beheaded. It's said on the anniversary of her death a coach drives up to the house, drawn by headless horses, driven by headless coachmen and containing the queen with her head on her lap. Ghostly apparitions aside, Blickling's grand state rooms are stuffed with fine Georgian furniture, pictures and tapestries, while the Jacobean plaster ceiling in the Long Gallery is a feast for the eyes.

Norwich

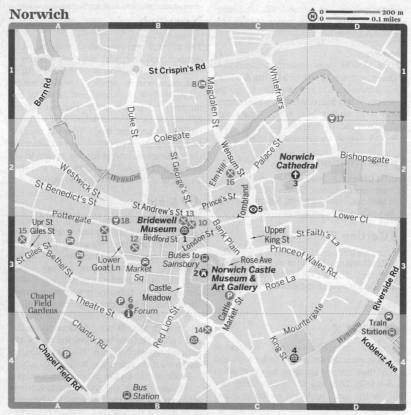

Norwich

◎ Top Sights
1 Bridewell Museum	B3
2 Norwich Castle Museum & Art Gallery	B3
3 Norwich Cathedral	C2

◎ Sights
4 Dragon Hall	C4
5 Tombland & Elm Hill	C2

◆ Activities, Courses & Tours
Ghost Walks	(see 17)
6 Guided Walks	B3

🛏 Sleeping
7 38 St Giles	A3

8 Gothic House	B1
9 St Giles House	A3

✕ Eating
10 Bishops	B3
11 Grosvenor Fish Bar	A3
12 Library	B3
13 Mustard	B3
14 No 12	C4
15 Roger Hickman's	A3
16 Tea House	C2

🍷 Drinking & Nightlife
17 Adam & Eve	D1
18 Birdcage	B3

Similar bosses can be seen in closer detail in the cathedral's two-storey **cloisters**. Built between 1297 and 1430, they are unique in England and were originally built to house a community of about 100 monks.

Above the bronze font (which came from a nearby chocolate factory), look out for

Censing Angel (2012) – a suspended celestial figure woven out of willow branches by sculptor Joy Whiddett, trailing the words 'peace', 'hope' and 'love'.

Outside the cathedral's eastern end is the grave of the WWI heroine Edith Cavell, a Norfolk-born nurse who was executed for helping hundreds of Allied soldiers escape from German-occupied Belgium. The handsome cathedral close also contains the old chapel of King Edward VI School (where naval hero Admiral Nelson was educated). Today's students make up the choir, which performs in services daily.

Tombland & Elm Hill NEIGHBOURHOOD
Leafy Tombland, near Norwich Cathedral, is where the market was originally located ('tomb' is an old Norse word for empty, hence space for a market). From there, follow Princes St to reach Elm Hill, Norwich's prettiest street, with its medieval cobblestones, crooked timber beams and doors, intriguing shops and tucked-away cafes.

★**Bridewell Museum** MUSEUM
(www.museums.norfolk.gov.uk; Bridewell Alley; adult/child £5/3; ⊘10am-4.30pm Tue-Sat) Best be on your best behaviour: 14th-century Bridewell is a former house of correction, a 'prison for women, beggars and tramps'. Displays here explore Norwich's prominence as England's second city in the Middle Ages and its 19th-century industrial heritage. You can also play games in a 1950s parlour, listen to shoe workers' memories, and watch films in a pocket-sized cinema. Look out too for the eccentric, snake-proof boot.

★**Norwich Castle**
Museum & Art Gallery CASTLE
(www.museums.norfolk.gov.uk; Castle Hill; adult/child £7/5; ⊘10am-4.30pm Mon-Sat, from 1pm Sun) Crowning a hilltop overlooking central Norwich, this massive, 12th-century castle is one of England's best-preserved examples of Anglo-Norman military architecture. Its superb interactive museum crams in lively exhibits on Boudica, the Iceni, Anglo-Saxons and Vikings. Perhaps the best bit though is the atmospheric keep itself with its graphic displays on grisly punishments meted out in its days as a medieval prison. Twice-daily, guided tours (£2) run around the battlements and creepy dungeons. The castle's art gallery houses works of the acclaimed 19th-century Norwich School of landscape painting founded by John Crome, and (drumroll) the world's largest collection of novelty teapots.

Dragon Hall HISTORIC BUILDING
(www.dragonhall.org; 123 King St; adult/child £5/3; ⊘10am-4pm Tue-Thu, noon-4pm Sun Apr-Oct) A carved incarnation of the eponymous creature sits amid this medieval trading hall's crown-post roof – a stunning affair of carved and arching beams. The building dates from 1430 and is the only one of its kind to have belonged to one man, Robert Toppes, rather than a guild, suggesting that he was a successful entrepreneur. Engaging displays introduce you to the merchant himself, medieval trade, and 15th-century Norwich life.

Sainsbury Centre for Visual Arts GALLERY
(www.scva.org.uk; University of East Anglia; ⊘10am-5pm Tue-Sun) FREE The region's most important centre for the arts is housed in the first major public building by renowned architect Norman Foster. Its eclectic collections include works by Picasso, Moore, Degas and Bacon, and are displayed beside curios from Africa, the Pacific and the Americas. The gallery is in the University of East Anglia's grounds, 2 miles west of the city centre. To get there take bus 25, 25A or X25 from Castle Meadow (20 minutes).

☞ **Tours**

Guided Walks WALKING TOUR
(✆01603-213999; www.visitnorwich.co.uk; adult/child £4/1.50; ⊘11.30am or 2pm, 2-4 per week Easter-Oct) Art-nouveau Norwich, Georgian dandies and 1000 years of history are among the themes for these 1½-hour guided strolls. Run by the tourist office (p402), many leave from the Forum centre, where the office is based.

Ghost Walks WALKING TOUR
(✆07831-189985; www.ghostwalksnorwich.co.uk; adult/child £7/5; ⊘2-3 walks per week mid-Apr–Dec) A lively immersion in Norwich's haunted history; the tours depart from the Adam & Eve pub (p402) on Bishopsgate at 7.30pm.

🛏 **Sleeping**

★**38 St Giles** B&B ££
(✆01603-662944; www.38stgiles.co.uk; 38 St Giles St; s/d/ste £90/130/160; ⊛) Deep-red rugs sit on varnished floors; silk curtains hang in light rooms dotted with quirky art – this handsome B&B is boutique yet still relaxed. The breakfast table groans with local and organic meats and eggs, as well as home-baked bread.

Gothic House B&B ££
(✆01603-631879; www.gothic-house-norwich.com; King's Head Yard, Magdalen St; s/d £65/95; P⊛)

Step through the door here and be whisked back to the Regency era. Original panelling, columns and cornices border the swirling stairs; fresh fruit and mini-decanters of sherry sit in elegant bedrooms that are studies in olive green, lemon yellow and duck-egg blue.

No 15 B&B **££**
(📞 01603-250283; www.number15bedandbreakfast.co.uk; 15 Grange Rd; s/d £55/75; 🛜) 🍴 The breakfasts at this vegetarian B&B are packed with treats: organic eggs, veggie sausages, artisan-baked walnut bread and grilled haloumi cheese. The furnishings are low allergy, but high on style – expect sanded wooden furniture, soft lights and bright throws. It's a mile west of the centre, bus 25 runs nearby.

Arrandale Lodge B&B **££**
(📞 01603-250150; www.norwichbedandbreakfast.co.uk; 431 Earlham Rd; s/d £50/70; P🛜) Few British B&Bs feature zebra prints and Irish food, but the South African/Southern Irish owners here like to celebrate their twin heritages. Tasteful, contemporary rooms feature springbok and giraffe motifs, while breakfast time brings both white and black pudding. It's 1.5 miles west of the centre.

St Giles House HOTEL **£££**
(📞 01603-275180; www.stgileshousehotel.com; 41 St Giles St; d/ste £130/200; P🛜) There's more than a whiff of art nouveau about luxurious St Giles House; built in 1919. Period flourishes echo on into bedrooms that are full of bold patterns and fluid curves, while the spa, bistro and cocktail terrace are rather splendid too.

🍴 Eating

Grosvenor Fish Bar FISH & CHIPS **£**
(www.fshshop.com; 28 Lower Goat Lane; mains £5; ⊙11am-7pm Mon-Sat) At this groovy chippy-with-a-difference, chips come with fresh cod goujons, sea-bass wraps come with spicy mango salsa and a 'Big Mack' is crispy mackerel fillet tucked into a bread roll. Take away or chow down on the benches inside.

EXPLORING THE NORFOLK BROADS

Why Should I Wish To Visit a Swamp?

These vast wetlands were formed when the Rivers Wensum, Bure, Waveney and Yare flooded the big gaping holes inland which had been dug by 12th-century crofters looking for peat. They comprise fragile ecosystems, and protected as a national park, are home to some of the UK's rarest plants and birds. Apart from that, if you've ever envisioned yourself captaining your own boat and living afloat, there are 125 miles of lock-free waterways to explore. Or if paddling a canoe and losing yourself in the hypnotic lapping of water away from the rest of humanity appeals, there's plenty of scope for that, too.

What Is there to See & Do that Doesn't Involve Water?

Museum of the Broads (www.museumofthebroads.org.uk; The Staithe, Stalham; adult/child £5/2.50; ⊙10.30am-5pm Easter-Oct; 🖭) Five miles north of Potter Heigham off the A149, this museum features fine boats and colourful displays on the local marshmen, their traditional lifestyles, peat extraction and modern conservation.

Toad Hole Cottage (How Hill; ⊙10.30am-5pm Apr-Oct) FREE This tiny cottage delves deeper into the life of Fen-dwellers, showing how the eel-catcher's family lived and the tools they used to work surrounding marshes.

Bewilderwood (www.bewilderwood.co.uk; Hornig Rd, Hoveton; adult/child £14/12; ⊙10am-5.30pm Mar-Oct) A forest playground for children and adults alike, with zip wires, jungle bridges, tree houses and old-fashioned outdoor adventure involving plenty of mud, mazes and marsh walks.

St Helen's Church (Ranworth; ⊙8am-7pm) The Broads' most impressive ecclesiastical attraction is this 14th-century church, known locally as the 'Cathedral of the Broads', which dominates the pretty village of Ranworth and features a magnificent painted medieval rood screen and a 15th-century antiphoner – a rare illustrated book of prayers.

Bure Valley Steam Railway (www.bvrw.co.uk; Aylsham; adult/child return £12/6; ⊙2-6 trains daily Apr-Oct; P) Siderodromophiles will love this train which puffs along 9 miles of narrow-gauge tracks between Aylsham and Wroxham.

Mustard   CAFE **£**
(www.mustardcoffeebar.com; 3 Bridewell Alley;
snacks/mains £2/6; ⊘7.30am-5.30pm Mon-Sat
10am-4pm Sun) Set on the site of the original Colman's Mustard shop, you'll find a
suitably bright yellow colour scheme at this
funky cafe. Quality dishes include rarities
(Mexican style huevos rancheros with salsa), and delight in being home-made; expect
own-baked Scotch eggs and sausage rolls
and their own hand-roasted coffee beans.

Tea House   CAFE **£**
(Elm Hill; snacks from £2; ⊘8.30am-5.30pm Mon-
Sat; 🕾) Tuck into doorstep sarnies, steaming
jacket potatoes, and top tea and scones.

Bishops   MODERN BRITISH **££**
(☑01603-767321; www.bishopsrestaurant.co.uk;
8 St Andrew's Hill; 2-course lunch/dinner £15/27;
⊘noon-2pm & 6-9.30pm) The unusual, the
unexpected and Norfolk ingredients are
the mainstays of menus at Bishops. Sample
smoked eel with pork confit, a ballotine of
Norfolk chicken, or a cockle, mussel and bacon chowder. Then tingle your tongue with
roasted pineapple spiked with chilli.

Library   BRASSERIE **££**
(☑01603-616606; www.thelibraryrestaurant.co.uk;
1 Guildhall Hill; mains £12; ⊘noon-2pm & 6-10pm
Mon-Sat, to 3pm Sun) Victorian bookcases still
line the walls at this cosy former library,
lending dining a club-like feel. The imaginative menu is strong on locally sourced produce, including Lowestoft fish, Havensfield
eggs, East Anglian game and prime Norfolk
cheese.

No 12   BISTRO **££**
(www.number12norwich.org; 12 Farmers Ave; mains
£12; ⊘noon-2.30pm & 5-9pm Mon-Sat, to 3pm
Sun) Lounge music plays, heather-hued
tartan covers the walls, beams sit above
white-leather bar stools; it sounds weird
but it works. Food ranges from homemade
burgers, chilli and fish pie to tasty, breaded
schnitzel.

How Do I Get There?

Driving around the Broads is missing the point and pretty useless. The main centres in the
Broads – Wroxham, on the A1151 from Norwich, and Potter Heigham, on the A1062 from
Wroxham – are reachable by bus from Norwich and Great Yarmouth, respectively, and from
there you can either take to the water or to the trails.

Exploring by Boat

Launches range from large cabin cruisers to little craft with outboards; they can be hired
for anything from a couple of hours' gentle messing about on the water to week-long trips.
Tuition is given. Depending on boat size, facilities and season, a four-person boat costs from
around £15 per hour, from £75 for four hours and from £100 for one day. Week-long rental
ranges from around £650 to £1300, including fuel and insurance. **Boats for the Broads**
(www.dayboathire.com) and **Barnes Brinkcraft** (www.barnesbrinkcraft.co.uk) do short- and
long-term rental, **Broads Tours** (www.broads.co.uk) lets out boats by the week – all are
Wroxham-based. **Blakes** (www.blakes.co.uk) arranges all manner of boating holidays.

Exploring by Canoe

Paddlers can find canoes for hire for around £33 per day; **Rowan Craft** (www.rowancraft.
com; Geldeston) and **Waveney River Centre** (www.waveneyrivercentre.co.uk; Burgh St Peter)
are recommended. **Mark the Canoe Man** (www.thecanoeman.com; half-day trip £25-45)
knows the secrets of the Broads and arranges day and overnight guided trips to areas the
cruisers can't reach, as well as canoe and kayak hire, weekend camping canoe trails (two
nights £65) and bushcraft courses (two days adult/child £95/70).

Exploring by Foot/Bike

Walking trails stretch across the region, including the 61-mile **Weavers' Way** from Cromer to
Great Yarmouth, taking in some choice parts of the landscape along the way. The Broads' high-
est point, How Hill, is just 12m above sea level, so superhero levels of fitness are not required.
Parts of the trail are open to bicycles. **Broadland Cycle Hire** (www.norfolkbroadscycling.co.uk;
Bewilderwood, Hoveton) and **Martha's Cottage** (www.marthascottagecyclehire.co.uk; Barnby) are
among rental firms. Prices start at £16 per day, with child seats and tandems also available.

★ **Roger Hickman's**　　　FINE DINING **£££**
(☑ 01603-633522; www.rogerhickmansrestaurant.
com; 79 Upper St Giles St; dinner 2/3/7 courses
£34/42/55; ⊘ noon-2.30pm & 7-10pm Tue-Sat) Understated elegance is everywhere: pale floorboards, white linen and unobtrusive service.
Dishes might include venison and cherries,
salt-baked turnip, or blow-torched mackerel –
flair, imagination and a simple dedication to
quality run right through. The lunches (two/
three courses £18/22) are a cracking deal.

Drinking & Nightlife

★ **Birdcage**　　　PUB
(www.thebirdcagenorwich.co.uk; 23 Pottergate;
⊘ 11am-midnight; 🎤) Formica tables, chilled
tunes, cupcakes and cocktails make this
beatnik drinking den a one-of-a-kind delight. Drop by for a Bums Life Drawing session (yes, really) and classy nibbles; or ferry
in fish 'n' chips from the shop over the lane.

Adam & Eve　　　PUB
(Bishopsgate; ⊘ 11am-11pm Mon-Sat, noon-
10.30pm Sun) Norwich's oldest-surviving pub
has been slaking thirst since 1249, when the
cathedral builders used to drop by. Tiny,
with a sunken floor and part-panelled walls,
it attracts a mixed band of regulars, choris-
ters and ghost hunters, drawn by the fine
malt whiskies and real ales.

ℹ Information

Tourist Office (☑ 01603-213999; www.
visitnorwich.co.uk; Millenium Plain; ⊘ 9.30am-
5.30pm Mon-Sat, plus 10.30am-3.30pm Sun
mid-Jul–mid-Sep) Inside the Forum centre.

ℹ Getting There & Around

Norwich has free parking at six Park & Ride locations. Buses (£2.40) run to the city centre up to
every 15 minutes from around 6.30am to 7pm,
some routes don't operate at weekends.

AIR
Norwich International Airport (www.nor-
wichinternational.com), 4 miles north of town;
has connections to Amsterdam, Aberdeen,
Edinburgh and Manchester year round, plus
summer flights to the Channel Islands.

BUS
The **bus station** (Queen's Rd) is 400m south
of the castle. Follow Red Lion St into Stephen's
St and then turn left onto Surrey St. **National
Express** (www.nationalexpress.com) and **First**
(www.firstgroup.com) run the following services:
Cromer £3.30, one hour, hourly

King's Lynn £8.60, 1½ hours, hourly
London £15, three hours, hourly

TRAIN
The train station is off Thorpe Rd, 600m east of
the castle.
Cambridge £18, 1¼ hours, hourly
Ely £16, one hour, twice hourly
London Liverpool Street £45, two hours, two
per hour

North Coast Norfolk

Norfolk's north coast has something of a split
personality, with busy seaside towns brim-full
of brash attractions in the east, and a string of
villages dotted with gastropubs and boutique
hotels in the west. In between sit vast sandy
beaches and marshes that attract unusually
rich concentrations of birds, including oys-
tercatchers, plovers, curlews and brent geese.

ℹ Getting There & Away

Coasthopper Bus (www.coasthopper.co.uk;
one-way fares from £2.70, passes per one/
three/seven days £9/18/32.) Runs from
Cromer to Kings Lynn. Stops include Cley,
Blakeney, Wells, Holkham, Burnham Deepdale
and Brancaster. Services range from every 30
minutes to five daily.

Cromer
POP 7294

The once-fashionable Victorian resort of
Cromer is slowly becoming gentrified again,
after years of amusement arcade and souvenir stand rule. Its main attractions remain
sweet-tasting Cromer crab, the atmospheric
pier and an appealing stretch of sandy shore.

⊙ Sights

Henry Blogg Museum　　　MUSEUM
(Lifeboat Museum; www.rnlicromer.org.uk; The
Gangway; ⊘ 10am-4pm Tue-Sun Feb-Nov) **FREE**
Cromer's WWII lifeboat and hands-on giz-
mos help convey tales of remarkably brave
sea rescues in a museum named after one
of the Royal National Lifeboat Institution's
most decorated coxswains.

Felbrigg Hall　　　HISTORIC BUILDING
(NT; www.nationaltrust.org.uk; Felbrigg; adult/child
£10/5; ⊘ 11am-5pm Sat-Wed Mar-Oct; P) This elegant Jacobean mansion boasts a fine Georgian interior and splendid facade, as well as
gorgeous walled gardens and an orangery. It's
2 miles southwest of Cromer, off the B1436.

🛏 Sleeping & Eating

★ Red Lion INN ££

(📞01263-514964; www.redlioncromer.co.uk; Brook St; s £65, d £110, ste £125-180; 🅿🛜) If only all seafront inns were this chic. Cool contemporary rooms feature wood- or brass-framed beds; colours vary from soft grey to purple and red. The enormous Billiard Room suite is superb value (£125), with its chandelier, free-standing bath and chaise longue.

Rocket House CAFE £

(www.rockethousecafe.co.uk; The Gangway; mains £4-10; ⊙10am-5pm) Set right on the seafront inside the Henry Blogg Museum, Rocket House delivers an airy interior, water-view terrace, soups, sandwiches and heaped Cromer crab platters.

Davies SEAFOOD £

(7 Garden St; ⊙8am-4.30pm daily May-Sep, Tue-Sat Oct-Apr) The super-fresh catches here include cooked (and cracked) crab and lobster, cockles, mussel and homemade fish pâté.

❶ Getting There & Away

Trains run to Norwich (£7, 45 minutes) hourly Monday to Saturday, and every two hours on Sunday. The Coasthopper bus (p402) shuttles west along the coast to King's Lynn roughly every half-hour in summer.

Cley-next-the-Sea & Around

POP 420

As the name suggest, the sleepy village of Cley (pronounced 'cly') huddles beside the shore. Here a cluster of pretty cottages surrounds a photogenic windmill and bird-rich marshes fan out all around.

◉ Sights

Cley Marshes NATURE RESERVE

(www.norfolkwildlifetrust.org.uk; nr Cley-next-the-Sea; adult/child £5/free; ⊙10am-5pm Nov-Mar, to 4pm Apr-Oct; 🅿) 🖋 One of England's premier birdwatching sites, Cley Marshes has more than 300 resident bird species, plentiful migrants and a network of walking and bird hides amid its golden reeds. Even if you're not into birding, don't miss the (free) cafe-cum-visitor centre (www.norfolk wildlifetrust.org.uk; ⊙10am-5pm Nov-Mar, to 4pm Apr-Oct) FREE where seats and telescopes line up beside vast picture windows with panoramic reserve views – this is birding for softies; sip a latte enjoying zoomed-in images of marsh harriers.

🛏 Sleeping & Eating

Cookes B&B ££

(📞01263-740776; www.cookes-of-cley.co.uk; High St; d/tr £70/80; 🅿🛜) Satin curtains and restrained checks bring a touch of the 21st century to this 18th-century coaching inn. Fluffy hot water bottles raise a smile, while breakfast is served in the beamed tea shop next door.

★ Cley Windmill B&B £££

(📞01263-740209; www.cleymill.co.uk; High St; d £160-200, apt per week £570.; 🅿) With the kind of wonky walls you'd expect from a circular, 18th-century agricultural building, Cley Windmill is packed with character. Rooms are named after their former functions (the crazy-shaped Barley Bin is gorgeous), and many look out directly over reed-filled salt mashes. A sweet, four-person self-catering cottage sits just next door.

Cley Smokehouse DELI £

(www.cleysmokehouse.com; High St; ⊙9.30am-4.30pm) Flavour-packed, home-smoked fish, shellfish and cured meats.

Picnic Fayre DELI £

(www.picnic-fayre.co.uk; High St; ⊙9am-5pm Mon-Sat, 10am-4pm Sun) Head here for great breads, cheeses, homemade pork pies and cakes, Norfolk ice cream, jams and chutneys.

Blakeney Point

POP 700

Blakeney was once a busy fishing and trading port before its harbour silted up. These days it offers an inviting seafront walk lined with yachts and boat trips out to a colony of common and grey seals that live, bask and breed on nearby Blakeney Point. Several companies, including Bishop's Boats (www.norfolksealtrips. co.uk; Blakeney Quay), and Beans Boat Trips (www.beansboattrips.co.uk; Morston, nr Cley-next-the-Sea) run hour-long trips (adult/child £10/5, one to four boats daily, April to October). The best time to come is between June and August when the common seals pup.

🛏 Sleeping & Eating

Kings Arms INN ££

(📞01263-740341; www.blakeneykingsarms.co.uk; Westgate St; d £80; mains £6-15; 🅿) Sweet simple rooms (expect bright colours and pine) in a pub that is so welcoming you might not want to leave. Order some substantial pub grub (served noon to 9pm) then, for some great theatre gossip, ask landlady Marjorie about her career on the stage.

Moorings   MODERN BRITISH **££**
(☑01263-40054; www.blakeney-moorings.co.uk;
High St; mains £7-17; ⊘10.30am-9pm Fri & Sat,
10am-5.30pm Sun & Tue-Thu) Perfectly pitched
fish dishes have won this bistro a loyal following – try the sea salt–crusted bass or seafood
platter; the classic meat and veg dishes are
tempting too. Mustn't-miss puddings include
pear-and-ginger strudel, and treacle sponge.

Wells-next-the-Sea

POP 2165

Charming Wells excels at both land and sea.
Rows of attractive Georgian houses and flint
cottages snake down to a boat-lined quay; to
the north sits a vast golden beach, backed by
pine-covered dunes.

◉ Sights

Wells Beach   BEACH
Fringed by dense pine forests and undulating dunes, Wells' sandy shore stretches for
miles to the west, with brightly coloured
beach huts clustering beside the water and
wooden steps leading up into the woods.
It's all tucked away at the end of a mile-long
road; you can walk, drive, or hop on a miniature train. Parking is available.

**Wells & Walsingham
Railway**   HERITAGE RAILWAY
(www.wellswalsinghamrailway.co.uk; Stiffkey Rd;
adult/child return £9/7; ⊘3-6 trains daily Apr-Oct;
P) The longest 10.25in narrow-gauge railway
in the world puffs for five picturesque miles
from Wells to the village of Little Walsingham, the site of religious shrines and the ruined but still impressive Walsingham Abbey.

🛏 Sleeping & Eating

Wells YHA   HOSTEL **£**
(☑0845 371 9544; www.yha.org.uk; Church Plains;
dm/d£15/32; P) In the heart of town in an ornately gabled early-20th-century church hall.

Crugmeer   B&B **££**
(☑01328-710622; www.crugmeer-wells.co.uk;
Croft Yard; d £85; P⊚) Walk 20 paces from
Well's atmospheric quay and arrive at the
perfect holiday bolthole. A lattice of beams
criss-crosses the walls (and the walk-in cup-
board), the bed is a study in burgundy and
crisp white, and the standalone bath sits on
a whitewashed floor.

Wells Beach Cafe   CAFE **£**
(Wells Beach; mains £4; ⊘10am-5pm Easter-Oct,
to 4pm Nov-Easter; ⊚) This locals' favourite

rustles up bacon baps, homemade chilli and
an irresistible 'hot chocolate of the week'.
Outside, sits a corral of picnic tables; inside
there's a sofa-surrounded wood-burning
stove for when the wind whips in.

Crown   RESTAURANT **££**
(www.thecrownhotelwells.co.uk; The Buttlands;
mains £12-22; ⊘noon-2.30pm & 6-9pm) Renowned for robust dishes made from locally
sourced ingredients.

ℹ Information

Tourist Office (☑01328-710885; www.vis-
itnorthnorfolk.com; Staithe St; ⊘10am-5pm
Mon-Sat, to 1pm Sun Apr-Oct)

Holkham

The pretty village of Holkham is dominated
by **Holkham Hall and Estate** (www.holkham.
co.uk; Holkham; adult/child £13/5, parking £2.50;
⊘noon-4pm Sun, Mon & Thu Apr-Oct; P), a severe Palladian mansion, largely unadorned
on the outside, set in a vast deer park designed by William Kent.

For many, Holkham's true delight is the
other part of the estate – the **Holkham National Nature Reserve**, where the expansive, pristine **beach** bordering Holkham
Bay is perfumed by the pine forest growing alongside. Ribboning pathways lead
to bird and wildlife hides and onto nearby
villages.

The estate is the ancestral seat of the
original Earl of Leicester and still belongs
to his descendants. The interior is sumptuous, with a red velvet–lined saloon, copies
of Greek and Roman statues, and fluted
columns in the Marble Hall and luxurious
Green State Bedroom. Admission to the
hall includes entry to the **Bygones Museum** (www.holkham.co.uk; Holkham; museum only
adult/child £7/3.50; ⊘10am-5pm Apr-Oct) in
the stable block. Its 4000 exhibits feature
everything from mechanical toys to vintage
cars and steam engines.

Burnham Deepdale & Around

POP 800

Walkers flock to this lovely coastal spot,
with its tiny twin villages of Burnham
Deepdale and Brancaster Staithe strung
along a rural road. Edged by the beautiful
Norfolk Coastal Path, surrounded by beaches and reedy marshes, alive with bird life
and criss-crossed by cycling routes, Burn-

ham Deepdale is also a base for a whole host of water sports.

🛏 Sleeping & Eating

Deepdale Farm   HOSTEL £
(✍ 01485-210256; www.deepdalefarm.co.uk; Burnham Deepdale; dm £13-18, d £30-60, camping £9-20, tipis from £60.; P @ 🛜) For backpackers it really doesn't get much better than Deepdale Farm: spic-and-span en suite dorms and doubles in a converted stables, a homely well-equipped kitchen, BBQ area, and cosy lounge warmed by a wood burning stove. Campers get to go glam – in a tipi or yurt – or casual, in a good old tent.

The hostel also operates a **tourist office** (✍ 01485-210256; ⊙ 10am-4pm), the best place to go to organise kitesurfing or windsurfing on nearby beaches. **Bike hire** (✍ 014852-10258; per half/full day £10/16) is also available.

White Horse   HOTEL £££
(✍ 01485-210262; www.whitehorsebrancaster.co.uk; Main Rd, Brancaster Staithe; mains £10-14; ⊙ 11am-9pm; P 🛜) The award-winning White Horse is a gastropub with a menu strong on seafood; the tapas-style dishes, featuring brown potted shrimp, seared tuna and tempura mackerel, more than set it apart from its competitors. The bedrooms (doubles £140 to £230) embody the seaside with their subtle colour schemes.

Titchwell & Around

Tiny Titchwell, just west of Burnham Deepdale, has a big asset: the **Titchwell Marsh Nature Reserve** (RSPB; www.rspb.org.uk;

Titchwell; parking £5; ⊙ dawn-dusk; P), where marshland, sandbars and lagoons attract vast numbers of birds. Summer brings marsh harriers, avocets, terns and nesting bearded tits; in winter you'll see more than 20 species of wading birds and countless ducks and geese.

Nearby, dreamy **Titchwell Manor** (✍ 01485-210221; www.titchwellmanor.com; Titchwell; d £125-215, mains £12-19; P @) is a swish, oh-so-contemporary hotel set in a grand Victorian house – one of its restaurants focuses on informal eating, the other fine dining. They're open noon to 2pm and 6pm to 9pm.

King's Lynn & Around

POP 12,200

Once one of England's most important ports, King's Lynn was long known as 'the Warehouse on the Wash'. It was said you could cross from one side of the River Great Ouse to the other by simply stepping from boat to boat in its heyday. Something of the salty port-town tang can still be felt in old King's Lynn, with its cobbled lanes, vibrant weekly markets, and narrow streets flanked by old merchants' houses.

◉ Sights

St Margaret's Church   CHURCH
(www.stmargaretskingslynn.org.uk; Margaret Plain; ⊙ 8am-6pm) The patchwork of styles here includes Flemish brasses and a remarkable 17th-century moon dial, which tells the tide. You'll find historic flood-level markings by the west door. Opposite, the 1421 **Trinity Guildhall** has an attractive stone facade.

DON'T MISS

SANDRINGHAM HOUSE

Both monarchists and those bemused by the English system will have plenty to mull over at this, the **Queen's country estate** (www.sandringhamestate.co.uk; Sandringham; adult/child £13/6.50; ⊙ 11am-4.30pm Easter-Oct; P). It's set in 25 hectares of beautifully landscaped gardens, and is open to the public when the royal family is not in residence. Sandringham is 6 miles northeast of King's Lynn off the B1440. Take Hunstanton-bound bus 11 from King's Lynn bus station (30 minutes, hourly Monday to Saturday, four on Sunday).

Queen Victoria bought Sandringham in 1862 for her son, the Prince of Wales (later Edward VII), and the features and furnishings remain much as they were in Edwardian days. Wandering around sumptuous reception rooms regularly used by the royals reveals a wealth of objets d'art and glinting gifts from European and Russian royal families. The stables house a flag-waving **museum** filled with diverse royal memorabilia, while the superb **vintage-car collection** includes the very first royal motor from 1900 and the buggy in which the Queen Mother would bounce around race tracks.

There are **guided tours** (£3.50, 11am and 2pm Wednesday and Saturday) of the gardens. The shop stocks organic goodies produced on the sprawling estate.

Old Gaol House
MUSEUM

(www.kingslynntownhall.com; Sat Market Pl; adult/child £3.30/2.20, Regalia Room free; ⊙ 10am-4pm Wed-Sat Apr-Oct) Explore the old cells and hear grisly tales of smugglers, witches and highwaymen in the former jail. The Regalia Room houses the civic treasures, including the 650-year-old King John Cup, exquisitely decorated with scenes of hunting and hawking.

Lynn Museum
MUSEUM

(www.museums.norfolk.gov.uk; Market St; adult/child £3.70/2.10; ⊙ 10am-5pm Tue-Sat) High points here include a large hoard of Iceni gold coins and the Seahenge Gallery, which tells the story behind the construction and preservation of the early–Bronze Age timber circle which survived for 4000 years, despite being submerged on the Norfolk shoreline – it was only discovered in 1998.

True's Yard
MUSEUM

(www.truesyard.co.uk; North St; adult/child £3/1.50; ⊙ 10am-4pm Tue-Sat) Housed in two restored fishermen's cottages – the only remainder of the district's bustling, fiercely independent fishing community – this museum explores the lives and traditions of the fisherfolk, who were packed into cottages such as these like sardines.

Castle Rising
CASTLE

(www.castlerising.co.uk; Castle Rising; adult/child £4/2.50; ⊙ 10am-5pm Apr-Oct, to 4pm Wed-Sun Nov-Mar; P) There's something bordering on ecclesiastical about the beautifully embellished keep of this castle, built in 1138 and set in the middle of a massive earthwork upon which pheasants scurry about like guards. It's well worth the trip 4 miles northeast of King's Lynn off the A149. Bus 10/11 runs here (20 minutes, hourly Monday to Saturday, four on Sunday) from the King's Lynn bus station.

So extravagant is the stonework that it's no surprise to learn that it shares stonemasons with some of East Anglia's finest cathedrals. It was once the home of Queen Isabella, who (allegedly) arranged the gruesome murder of her husband, Edward II.

Houghton Hall
HISTORIC BUILDING

(www.houghtonhall.com; nr King's Lynn; adult/child £13/5; ⊙ 11am-4pm Wed, Thu & Sun May–mid-Oct; P) Built for Britain's first de-facto prime minister, Sir Robert Walpole, in 1730, the grand Palladian-style Houghton Hall is worth seeing for the ornate staterooms alone, where stunning interiors overflow with gilt, tapestries, velvets and period furniture. Even when the house is closed, the surrounding grounds, home to 600 deer, make for pleasant rambling. Houghton Hall is just off the A148, 13 miles east of Kings Lynn.

Intriguingly, there could have been a whole other dimension to your visit, were it not for the fact that Sir Robert Walpole's grandson sold the estate's splendid art collection to Catherine the Great of Russia to stave off debts – those paintings formed the foundation of the world-renowned collection at the State Hermitage in St Petersburg.

✳ Festivals & Events

King's Lynn Festival
CULTURAL

(www.kingslynnfestival.org.uk; ⊙ Jul) East Anglia's most important cultural gathering, with a diverse mix of music, from medieval ballads to opera, as well as literary talks.

🛏 Sleeping & Eating

Bank House
B&B ££

(☎ 01553-660492; www.thebankhouse.co.uk; King's Staithe Sq; s/d from £90/110; P 🐾) 🍴 A quayside setting, gently funky decor and luxury bathrooms make this stylish Georgian town house pretty hard to turn down. Especially as the hip brasserie (mains £8 to £17) serves seriously good Modern British food.

Market Bistro
MODERN BRITISH ££

(☎ 01553-77148301553-771483; www.marketbistro.co.uk; 11 Sat Market Pl; mains £10-18; ⊙ noon-2pm & 6-8.30pm Tue-Sat) 🍴 A commitment to Norfolk ingredients has won this family-run eatery heaps of fans. Seasonal specials might include succulent Cromer crab, locally smoked fish and tangy samphire from the marshes, not to mention home-made ice cream.

❶ Information

Tourist Office (☎ 01553-763044; www.visitwestnorfolk.com; Purfleet Quay; ⊙ 10am-4pm Mon-Sat, noon-4pm Sun) Arranges guided heritage walks (adult/child £4/1) at 2pm Tuesdays, Fridays and Saturdays between May and October.

❶ Getting There & Away

There are hourly trains from Cambridge (£9, 50 minutes) via Ely and London Kings Cross (£31, 1¾ hours). The **Coasthopper 1** (www.coasthopper.co.uk) bus runs to Hunstanton (35 minutes, hourly) and connects with the Coasthopper 2 service, which runs along the north Norfolk coast. Services are frequent from April to September, less so the rest of the year.

Birmingham, the Midlands & the Marches

Best Places to Eat

➡ Hammer & Pincers (p477)
➡ Old Rectifying House (p436)
➡ Samuel Fox (p492)
➡ Trooper (p434)

Best Places to Drink

➡ Ye Olde Trip to Jerusalem (p461)
➡ Jekyll & Hyde (p418)
➡ Ludlow Brewing Company (p456)
➡ Old Bell Hotel (p480)

Why Go?

Few other places come so close to the dream of England as here, the country's heart. If you're searching for green valleys and chocolate-box villages of wonky timbered houses, the legend surrounding Nottingham's Robin Hood, or stately homes that look like the last lord of the manor just clip-clopped out of the stables, you'll find them here.

You'll also find the relics of centuries of industrial history, best exemplified by the World Heritage–listed mills of Ironbridge and the Derwent Valley. Then there are dynamic cities, including Britain's second-largest, Birmingham: a canal-woven industrial crucible reinvented as a cultural melting pot, with striking architecture and red-hot restaurants, bars and nightlife. And then there are tumbling hills where the air is so clean you can taste it. Walkers and cyclists flock to these areas, particularly the Peak District National Park and the Shropshire Hills, to vanish into the vastness of the landscape.

When to Go

➡ February and March see the wonderful chaos of Shrovetide football in Ashbourne.

➡ Literary buffs take note: Shakespeare takes a back seat to contemporary wordsmiths at Stratford's Literary Festival in April/May.

➡ If you're up for a belt-loosening, belly-stretching good time, head to Ludlow's famous Food and Drink Festival in September.

➡ On weekends from April to September, Shropshire Hills Shuttles provides access to wonderful walking trails on the Long Mynd and the Shropshire Hills, while June to September is the peak season for walking and cycling in the Peak District.

Birmingham, the Midlands & the Marches Highlights

❶ Surveying the buzzing city of Birmingham from the rooftop 'secret garden' of its stunning new **library** (p411)

❷ Hiking, cycling or driving through the rugged **Peak District National Park** (p484)

❸ Contemplating the apple tree that inspired Isaac Newton's theories on gravity at **Woolsthorpe Manor** (p470)

❹ Museum-hopping in **Ironbridge Gorge** (p447), birthplace of the Industrial Revolution

❺ Learning about King Richard III's life, death and the extraordinary discovery of his remains in **Leicester** (p475)

❻ Taking in a Shakespearean performance in the Bard's Tudor hometown **Stratford-upon-Avon** (p431)

❼ Touring Great Malvern's **Morgan Motor Company** (p438) and taking a car for a spin through the surrounding hills

❽ Wandering the opulent halls and grand gardens of Stamford's **Burghley House** (p469)

North Sea

Humber

Scunthorpe
Grimsby
Doncaster
Rotherham
Sheffield
Gainsborough
Market Rasen
Louth
Eyam
Chatsworth House
Worksop
Tuxford
Lincoln
Horncastle
Skegness
Chesterfield
Bakewell
Hardwick Hall
Sherwood Forest National Nature Reserve
Matlock Bath
Cromford
Newstead Abbey
Newark-on-Trent
Withern
Ashbourne
Belper
Southwell
Sleaford
Boston
The Wash
Derby
Nottingham
Grantham
Spalding
East Midlands Airport
Loughborough
Melton Mowbray
3 Woolsthorpe Manor
Burton-upon-Trent
National Forest
Packington
Oakham
Stamford
The Fens
Tamworth
Leicester 5
Rutland Water
Burghley House 8
Peterborough
Drayton Manor
Bosworth Battlefield
Lyddington
Birmingham Airport
Market Harborough
Cambridge
Coventry
Kettering
Kenilworth
Rugby
Althorp House
Stoneleigh Abbey
Warwick
Charlecote Park
Northampton
6 Stratford-upon-Avon
Sulgrave Manor
Stoke Bruerne
Towcester
Banbury
Milton Keynes
Luton

🏃 Activities

The Peak District is the Midlands' number-one spot to get in touch with nature. Famous walking trails such as the Pennine Way and Limestone Way struggle across the hills, while cyclists pit determination and muscle against challenging routes such as the Pennine Cycleway (NCN Route 68) from Derby to Buxton. Other activities include caving and rock climbing.

Tracing the border between England and Wales, the lush green hills of the Marches are scattered with ruined castles. Top walking and cycling areas include the Long Mynd and Stiperstones in Shropshire and the Malvern Hills in Worcestershire.

Sailors, windsurfers and water babies of all ages and levels of experience flock to Rutland Water near Leicester, while canoeing and kayaking are popular diversions in Hereford.

ℹ️ Getting There & Around

Birmingham Airport (☑ 0871 222 0072; www.birminghamairport.co.uk) and **East Midlands Airport** (☑ 0871 919 9000; www.eastmidlands airport.com) near Derby are the main air hubs.

There are excellent rail connections to towns across the Midlands. **National Express** (☑ 08717 818178; www.nationalexpress.com), at Birmingham Coach Station, and local bus companies connect larger towns and villages, though services are reduced in the low season. For general route information, consult **Traveline** (☑ 0871 200 2233; www.travelinemidlands. co.uk) or visit www.networkwestmidlands.com. Ask locally about discounted all-day tickets.

BIRMINGHAM

POP 1,085,800

Britain's second-largest city is also one of its most happening. A state-of-the-art £189 million library, a gleaming shopping centre atop the revitalised New St Station, beautifully restored Victorian buildings and a new 1.4km Midland Metro tram line extension through the city's heart are just some of the initiatives of its Big City Plan. There are also new parks, public spaces, and glitzy residential and commercial buildings. These come hot on the heels of the striking Mailbox and Bullring shopping malls and the 'bubblewrapped' facade of the iconic Selfridges building.

Alongside outstanding museums and galleries you'll find an increasing number of gastronomic restaurants, cool and/or secret cocktail bars, and picturesque canals with waterside bars, restaurants, attractions and cruises. Thriving legacies of Birmingham's industrial heritage include its Jewellery Quarter, Cadbury manufacturing plant and a former custard factory that's been transformed into a cutting-edge creative hub.

With construction on the High Speed Rail (HS2) line – connecting London with Birmingham in just 40 minutes by 2026 – set to boost employment and the economy, 'Brum', as it's dubbed by locals, is buzzing.

History

Birmingham was first mentioned in the Domesday Book of 1086, where it was described

---

EAT & DRINK LIKE A LOCAL

Look out for the following specialities in Birmingham, the Midlands and the Marches:

Balti This fiery one-pot curry, believed to derive from the Urdu word *balty* ('bucket'), is prepared in a cast-iron wok and traditionally served with a giant *karack* naan bread. It was first cooked up in the curry-houses of Sparkbrook in southern Birmingham by Pakistani workers who moved here in the 1970s; the area is now known as the Balti Triangle (p417).

Chocolate Iconic confectionery company Cadbury originated in Birmingham in 1824 when John Cadbury opened a grocer's shop at 93 Bull Street, selling his own preparations of cocoa and drinking chocolate. Learn about chocolate's evolution, watch it being made and taste it too at Cadbury World (p415).

Bakewell Pudding The Peak District's most famous dessert is more rustic than the glazed versions from commercial bakeries. This pastry shell, spread with jam and topped with frangipane, a mixture of egg and ground almonds, was invented following an accidental misreading of a recipe around 1820. Both the Old Original Bakewell Pudding Shop (p495) and Bloomers Original Bakewell Puddings (p495) in Bakewell claim to be the pudding's progenitor.

Cider Crisp, dry ciders have been produced in Herefordshire since medieval times – discover them on the Herefordshire Cider Route (p439).

BIRMINGHAM IN...

Two Days

Start off in the centre, dropping into the eclectic **Birmingham Museum & Art Gallery** (p412). Walk west through Centenary Sq, stopping to check out the **Library of Birmingham** (p411) before reaching the Birmingham Canals. From here you can take a **canal cruise** (p416) or while away an afternoon at the **National Sea Life Centre** (p414) or **Ikon Gallery** (p414). Dine that night at one of Birmingham's cutting-edge restaurants such as **adam's** (p417). On day two, indulge your inner shopaholic at the gleaming shopping malls of the **Bullring** (p419) and **Mailbox** (p419), which both have good options for lunch. In the afternoon, catch up on some social history at the museum **Birmingham Back to Backs** (p412). After dark, kick off a pub crawl at the **Lost & Found** (p418).

Four Days

On day three, head north from the centre to **Aston Hall** (p415) and **Soho House** (p415), or south to the famous **Barber Institute** (p415). End the day with a show at the **Repertory Theatre** (p419) or a concert at **Symphony Hall** (p419). Use day four to explore the fascinating **Jewellery Quarter** (p414) and spend the afternoon reliving *Charlie and the Chocolate Factory* fantasies at **Cadbury World** (p415).

as a small village, home to a handful of villagers and two ploughs, with a total value of £1. From these humble beginnings, Brum exploded into an industrial and mercantile hub, building its fortunes first on the wool trade and then on metal-working from the 16th century.

The Lunar Society brought together the leading geologists, chemists, scientists, engineers and theorists of the mid-18th century and Birmingham became the world's first industrialised town, attracting a tide of workers from across the nation.

In the mid-1800s enlightened mayors such as Joseph Chamberlain (1836–1914) cleaned out the slums and filled the centre with grand civic buildings. Later, WWII bombers and overzealous town planners took their toll, and swaths of the centre were demolished in a bid to transform Birmingham into 'Britain's Motor City'.

Recent years have seen an explosion of regeneration projects, with 21st-century landmarks appearing all over the city.

◉ Sights & Activities

◉ City Centre

Birmingham's grandest civic buildings are clustered around pedestrianised Victoria Square, at the western end of New St, dominated by the stately facade of Council House, built between 1874 and 1879. The square was given a facelift in 1993, with modernist sphinxes and a fountain topped

by a naked female figure, nicknamed 'the floozy in the jacuzzi' by locals, overlooked by a disapproving statue of Queen Victoria.

To the west, Centenary Sq is book-ended by the art deco Hall of Memory War Memorial, the International Convention Centre (ICC) and Symphony Hall. There's a gleaming golden statue of Birmingham's Industrial Revolution leading lights Matthew Boulton, James Watt and William Murdoch. Centenary Sq's showpiece is the spiffing new Library of Birmingham.

⭐ **Library of Birmingham**   LIBRARY
(www.libraryofbirmingham.com; Centenary Sq; ⊙8am-8pm Mon-Fri, 9am-5pm Sat, 11am-4pm Sun) Resembling a glittering stack of gift-wrapped presents, the Francine Houben–designed Library of Birmingham is an architectural triumph. Opened in 2013, the library features a subterranean amphitheatre, a spiralling interior, viewing decks and a glass elevator to the 7th-floor 'secret garden', which provides panoramic views over the city. In addition to its archives, photography and rare-book collections, including Britain's most important Shakespeare collection, are gallery spaces, 160-plus computers and a cafe. The British Film Institute Mediatheque provides free access to the National Film Archive.

The former Central Library is to be demolished to make way for the Paradise Circus redevelopment between Centenary and Chamberlain Sqs, incorporating a new four-star hotel, shops and public squares, due for completion in 2017.

Birmingham Museum & Art Gallery
MUSEUM

(☑ 0121-303 2834; www.bmag.org.uk; Chamberlain Sq; ⏰ 10am-5pm Sat-Thu, 10.30am-5pm Fri; 🚻) **FREE** Major Pre-Raphaelite works by Rossetti, Edward Burne-Jones and others are among the highlights of the delightful Birmingham Museum & Art Gallery's impressive collection of ancient treasures and Victorian art.

Birmingham Back to Backs
HISTORIC BUILDING

(NT; ☑ 0121-666 7671; www.nationaltrust.org.uk; 55-63 Hurst St; tours adult/child £7.25/3.90; ⏰ 1-5pm Tue-Thu, 10am-5pm Fri-Sun, longer hours during school holidays) Quirky tours of this cluster of restored back-to-back terraced houses take you through four working-class homes, telling the stories of those who lived here between the 1840s and the 1970s. Book by phone for the compulsory guided tour.

For an even more vivid impression of what life was like here, you can book to stay in basic three-storey period cottages at 52 and 54 Inge St (doubles from £100). Guests receive a free Back to Backs tour.

Town Hall
HISTORIC BUILDING

(☑ 0121-345 0600; www.thsh.co.uk; Victoria Sq) Constructed in 1834 and styled after the

Birmingham

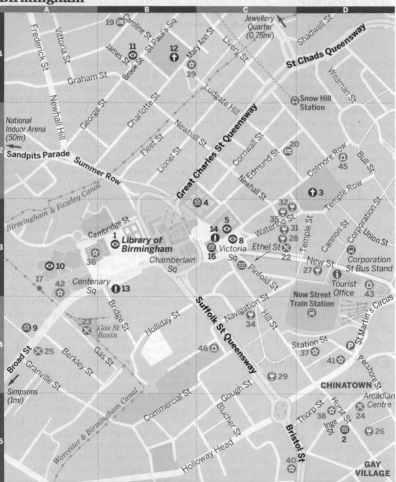

Temple of Castor and Pollux in Rome, Birmingham's neoclassical Town Hall is now used as a venue for classical concerts and stage performances.

Birmingham Cathedral
CATHEDRAL

(☎0121-262 1840; www.birminghamcathedral.com; Colmore Row; entry by donation; ⊙7.30am-6.30pm Mon-Fri, 8.30am-5pm Sat & Sun) Dedicated to St Philip, this small but perfectly formed cathedral was constructed in a neoclassical style between 1709 and 1715. Pre-Raphaelite artist Edward Burne-Jones was responsible for the magnificent stained-glass windows.

Thinktank
MUSEUM

(☎0121-202 2222; www.thinktank.ac; Millennium Point, Curzon St; adult/child £12.25/8.40; ⊙10am-5pm) A 10-minute walk northeast of the centre, surrounded by the footprints of vanished factories, the Millennium Point development contains this entertaining and ambitious attempt to make science accessible to children. Highlights include galleries on the past (Birmingham's industrial breakthroughs), present (how stuff works) and future, as well as an outdoor science garden and digital planetarium (included in the admission price). There's also a **giant screen cinema**

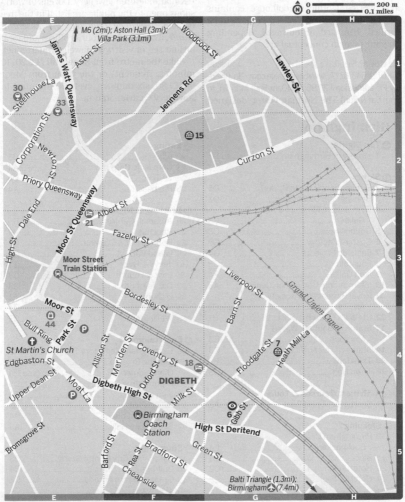

(📞0121-202 3333; www.giantscreencinema.co.uk; adult/child from £8.50/6).

⊙ Birmingham Canals

During the industrial age, Birmingham was a major hub on the English canal network and today the city has more miles of canals than Venice. Narrow boats still float through the heart of the city, passing a string of swanky wharfside developments.

Ikon Gallery   GALLERY
(📞0121-248 0708; www.ikon-gallery.co.uk; 1 Oozells Sq; ⊙11am-6pm Tue-Sun) **FREE** Within the glitzy Brindley Pl development of banking offices and designer restaurants, a converted Gothic schoolhouse contains the cutting-edge Ikon Gallery. Prepare to be thrilled, bemused or outraged, depending on your take on conceptual art.

National Sea Life Centre   AQUARIUM
(📞0121-643 6777; www.visitsealife.com; 3a Brindley Pl; admission £20.95; ⊙10am-5pm Mon-Fri, to 6pm Sat & Sun) The Norman Foster–designed National Sea Life Centre is England's largest inland aquarium. Its tanks teem with exotic marine life including razor-jawed hammerhead sharks, turtles and otters. Tickets for two or more people cost £15 per person. Pre-purchase tickets online for fast-track entry and get discounts of up to 40% off on-the-spot rates.

⊙ Jewellery Quarter

Birmingham has been a major jewellery player since Charles II acquired a taste for it in 17th-century France. The gentrifying Jewellery Quarter, three-quarters of a mile northwest of the centre, still produces 40% of UK-manufactured jewellery. Dozens of workshops open to the public are listed in the free booklet *Jewellery Quarter: the Essential Guide,* available from tourist offices and local businesses, or visit www.jewelleryquarter.net.

Take the metro from Snow Hill (£2.20, 10 minutes, frequent) or the train from Moor St (£1.80, six minutes, every 10 minutes) to Jewellery Quarter station.

Birmingham

Museum of the Jewellery Quarter   MUSEUM
(📞0121-554 3598; www.bmag.org.uk; 75 Vyse St; adult/child £5/free; ⏱10.30am-5pm Tue-Sat) The Smith & Pepper jewellery factory is preserved as it was on its closing day in 1981 after 80 years of operation. Guided tours lasting around one hour explain the long history of the trade in Birmingham and let you watch master jewellers at work. Entry to the temporary exhibition space and shop is free.

St Paul's Church   CHURCH
(www.saintpaulbrum.org; St Paul's Sq; ⏱10am-4pm Tue-Sat) St Paul's Sq is dominated by this beautiful 18th-century Georgian church, where 'Birmingham Brains' Matthew Boulton and James Watt came to pray.

Royal Birmingham Society of Artists   ARTS CENTRE
(📞0121-236 4353; www.rbsa.org.uk; 4 Brook St; ⏱10.30am-5.30pm Mon-Fri, to 5pm Sat, 1-5pm Sun) FREE Local artists and artisans have exhibited their work at the Royal Birmingham Society of Artists since 1814.

Jewellery-Silversmithing Design Academy   COURSE
(📞07780-671 870; www.jsdauk.com; Studio 214b, 120 Vyse St; ⏱1-day courses from £69) Learn how to create your own jewellery during master classes, short courses and workshops in the heart of the Jewellery Quarter.

⊙ Outlying Areas

Soho House   MUSEUM
(📞0121-554 9122; www.bmag.org.uk; Soho Ave, Handsworth; adult/child £4/free; ⏱11.30am-4pm Tue-Sun mid-Apr–Oct) About 1.5 miles northwest of Birmingham's Jewellery Quarter, Soho House is where industrialist Matthew Boulton lived from 1766 to 1809. Among the restored 18th-century chambers is the dining room where Boulton and members of the esteemed Lunar Society met to discuss their world-changing ideas during the greatest technological leap forward since the invention of the wheel. From Priory Queensway, take bus 74 or 75 (£1.70, 25 minutes, every 10 minutes) to the Lozells stop, from where it's a five-minute walk.

Barber Institute of Fine Arts   GALLERY
(📞0121-414 7333; www.barber.org.uk; ⏱10am-5pm Mon-Fri, 11am-5pm Sat & Sun) FREE At the University of Birmingham, 3 miles south of the centre, the Barber Institute of Fine Arts has an astonishing collection of Renaissance masterpieces; European masters such as Rubens and Van Dyck; British greats including Gainsborough, Reynolds and Turner; and classics from modern titans Picasso, Magritte and others. Trains run from New St to University station (£2.10, seven minutes, every five minutes), from where it's a 10-minute walk.

Cadbury World   MUSEUM
(📞0844 880 7667; www.cadburyworld.co.uk; Linden Rd, Bournville; adult/child £15.95/11.70; ⏱10am-4.30pm) The next best thing to Willy Wonka's chocolate factory is Cadbury World, 4 miles south of Birmingham. It aims to educate visitors about the history of cocoa and the Cadbury family, but sweetens the deal with free samples, displays of chocolate-making machines, and chocolate-themed rides. Opening hours vary; bookings are essential at peak times. Last entry is 90 minutes before closing. Frequent trains run from Birmingham New St Station to Bournville (£2.40, 12 minutes, every 10 minutes), from where it's a sign-posted 10-minute walk.

Surrounding the aromatic chocolate works, pretty Bournville Village was built by the philanthropic Cadbury family to accommodate early 20th-century factory workers.

Aston Hall   HISTORIC BUILDING
(📞0121-675 4722; www.bmag.org.uk; Trinity Rd, Aston; house adult/child £4/free, grounds free; ⏱noon-4pm Tue-Sun mid-Apr–Oct) About 3 miles north of the centre, set in lush grounds, this well-preserved hall was built

DIGBETH'S CREATIVE QUARTER
Just over a mile southeast of the centre, Digbeth's creative quarter centres on the Custard Factory (📞0121-224 7777; www.custardfactory.co.uk; Gibb St), a hip art and design enclave set in the converted buildings of the factory that once churned out British favourite Bird's Custard. The open-plan space is now full of small galleries, quirky design boutiques, vintage clothes outlets, skateboard shops and affordable, off-beat cafes. There's also a mini skate ramp and free ping-pong tables.

Check out the artist-run experimental gallery Eastside Projects (www.eastsideprojects.org; 86 Heath Mill Lane; ⏱noon-5pm Wed-Sat) nearby.

in extravagant Jacobean style between 1618 and 1635. The sumptuous interiors are full of friezes, moulded ceilings and tapestries. Trains run from New St to Aston station (£2, eight minutes, every 10 minutes), from where it's a 10-minute walk.

Tours

Big Brum Buz BUS TOUR
(www.birmingham-tours.co.uk; day ticket adult/child £12/5; Sat & Sun May-Sep) Hop-on/hop-off bus tour. On the first Sunday of the month from May to October, it operates as the Museum Heritage Bus (adult/child £5/free) with a different schedule and stops.

Sherborne Wharf Boat Trips BOAT CRUISE
(0121-455 6163; www.sherbornewharf.co.uk; Sherborne St; adult/child £8/6; 11.30am, 1pm, 2.30pm & 4pm daily mid-Apr–Oct, Sat & Sun Nov–mid-Apr) Nostalgic narrow-boat cruises from the quayside by the International Convention Centre.

Festivals & Events

Crufts Dog Show ANIMAL SHOW
(www.crufts.org.uk; Mar) The world's greatest collection of pooches on parade, held annually at the National Exhibition Centre.

Birmingham Pride GAY
(www.birminghampride.com; May) One of the biggest and most colourful celebrations of gay and lesbian culture in the country.

Frankfurt Christmas Market & Craft Fair CHRISTMAS MARKET
(www.birmingham.gov.uk/frankfurtmarket; mid-Nov–mid-Dec) Some 200 food, drink and craft stalls from Birmingham's twin city in Germany and from local purveyors fill the centre during the UK's largest Christmas market.

Sleeping

Most Birmingham hotels are aimed at business travellers, ensuring high prices during the week. Look out for cheap deals at weekends or for longer stays. B&Bs are concentrated outside the centre in Acocks Green (to the southeast) or Edgbaston and Selly Oak (to the southwest).

Birmingham Central Backpackers HOSTEL £
(0121-643 0033; www.birminghambackpackers.com; 58 Coventry St; dm/d from £14/36;) Despite the railway-bridge-right-next-door setting, Birmingham's purple and turquoise backpacker hostel is recommendable for its convenience to the bus station and choice of clean, multicoloured dorms or Japanese-style pods. Excellent facilities include a lounge with DVDs, Wii, an Xbox and PlayStation, a bar and a self-catering kitchen. You mightn't need the latter – breakfast and an evening snack buffet are free.

★ **Hotel La Tour** HOTEL ££
(0121-718 8000; http://hotel-latour.co.uk; Albert St; d from £100;) Sunlight streams through floor-to-ceiling windows into the public areas and spacious rooms of this state-of-the-art independent hotel, purpose-built in 2012. Tech-savvy room features include digitally controlled 'do not disturb' signs and media hubs. There's a 24-hour gym and a swish Modern British restaurant, Aalto.

Hotel du Vin BOUTIQUE HOTEL ££
(0121-200 0600; www.hotelduvin.com; Church St; d from £115;) Housed in the handsome Victorian precincts of the former Birmingham Eye Hospital, this red-brick beauty has real class, with wrought-iron balustrades, classical murals and seasoned charms. Art deco–inspired rooms have spectacular bathrooms; there's a pampering spa and a gym; a bistro with shabby-chic worn floorboards and a stellar wine list; plus a pub and lounge bar with comfy, duffed-up leather furniture.

Bloc HOTEL ££
(0121-212 1223; www.blochotels.com; St Paul's, Caroline St; d from £90;) In the Jewellery Quarter, Bloc excels in sharp, contemporary pod design. Rooms are tiny but space is cleverly stretched – flatscreen TVs are built into walls; storage is under-bed; and bathrooms are compact but with luxe shower-heads. Rooms come with window or without. Good online specials.

Westbourne Lodge B&B ££
(0121-429 1003; www.westbournelodge.co.uk; Fountain Rd; s/d/f from £49.50/69.50/79.50; P) This popular B&B is conveniently located about 2 miles west out in the peaceful suburb of Edgbaston (follow the A456). Rooms are a little chintzy but spacious, and there's a pleasant terrace to enjoy in summer.

Eating

Dining options span cool cafes and cosy pubs to gastronomic extravaganzas. For cheap curries, try the **Balti Triangle**. Spice is also on the menu at inexpensive restaurants throughout Chinatown, on the south-western side of the Bullring shopping mall.

Canalside Cafe
CAFE £

(✆0121-643 3170; 35 Worcester Bar, Gas St; dishes £3.95-4.95; ☻9am-11pm) Narrow boats glide past the terrace of this 18th-century lock-keeper's cottage, where the low-ceilinged interior is strung with nautical paraphernalia and warmed by an open fire. Home-cooked meals such as cottage pie, lasagne and stroganoff are chalked on the blackboard alongside vegetarian (and vegan) specials. Drop by for a cuppa and cake, or a real ale or cider.

Le Truc
FRENCH ££

(✆0121-622 7050; http://letruc.co.uk; 21 Ladywell Way; mains £11.50-23; ☻5-10pm Mon-Fri, 10am-10pm Sat & Sun) Bulldog murals, chandeliers, Scrabble tiles and a cassette-covered DJ console at this funky independent bistro form the backdrop for authentic French regional dishes, served with a contemporary and/or British twist. Regular events include Sunday brunch with 'lashings of Bloody Marys'.

Pushkar
INDIAN ££

(✆0121-643 7978; www.pushkardining.com; 245 Broad St; 2-/3-course lunch menus £10/13, mains £7.25-17; ☻noon-2.30pm & 5-11.30pm Mon-Fri, 5-11.30pm Sat & Sun) Classy North Indian and Punjabi cuisine is served up in this glass-fronted, white tableclothed, gold-trimmed dining room. The elegant presentation extends to boxed menus and serviette-wrapped naan bread as well as stunning cocktails. Lunch menus are an excellent deal.

adam's
MODERN BRITISH £££

(✆0121-643 3745; www.adamsrestaurant.co.uk; 21a Bennett's Hill; 3-course lunch menu £32, 5-/9-course menu £50/80; ☻noon-2pm & 7-9.30pm Tue-Sat) In a small but snazzy dining room with suspended lighting and a space-defying, trompe-l'œil-effect photo of a Victorian columned hallway, Birmingham's newest Michelin-starred restaurant wows with intricately prepared and presented flavour combinations. Five- and nine-course tasting menus are available at lunch and dinner (nine-course only Friday and Saturday). Book well ahead.

★Simpsons
MODERN BRITISH £££

(✆0121-454 3434; www.simpsonsrestaurant.co.uk; 20 Highfield Rd; 3-course lunch menu £40, mains £21-27; ☻noon-2pm & 7-9.30pm Mon-Sat, to 2.30pm Sun) It's worth making the journey 2.5 miles southwest of the centre to this gorgeous Georgian mansion in leafy Edgbaston for Michelin-starred chef Andreas Antona's sensational creations. You can also stay the night in one of four luxurious bedrooms upstairs (£160 to £225; Tuesday to Saturday only), or take an all-day cookery class (£135 including three-course lunch, Saturdays). Reservations recommended.

🍷 Drinking & Nightlife

Nightlife hubs in Birmingham include Broad St (aka the 'golden mile' – some say for the prevalence of fake tan here), which has mainstream pubs and clubs as well as theatres and cinemas.

South of New St station, defunct pubs and warehouses have found new life as bars and clubs; Chinatown's **Arcadian Centre** (www.thearcadian.co.uk; Hurst St) is the gateway to this hedonistic quarter, with numerous party bars and dancing spots.

Post-industrial Digbeth has alternative clubs and club events in and around the Custard Factory (p415).

BALTI TRIANGLE

Birmingham's famous Balti Triangle (www.balti-birmingham.co.uk), 2.5 miles southeast of the centre, is formed by Ladypool Rd, Stoney Lane and Stratford Rd. Dozens of restaurants here serve balti, a Pakistani-inspired one-pot curry, as well as soft drinks, fruit juices and lassis (yoghurt shakes), and diners can bring their own beer or wine.

The Balti Triangle is liveliest at night, especially on Fridays. Take bus 3, 5, 6, 31 or 37 from Selfridges stop PA3 (£1.90, 30 minutes, every five minutes).

Saleem's Restaurant & Sweet House (✆0121-449 1861; www.saleemsrestaurant.com; 256-258 Ladypool Rd; mains £6-8; ☻noon-midnight Mon-Sat, 9am-midnight Sun) This long-established Balti Triangle restaurant is understandably popular for its generous portions of balti and tasty milk-based Indian sweets.

Al Faisal's (✆0121-449 5695; www.alfaisal.co.uk; 136-140 Stoney Lane; mains £7-8; ☻noon-midnight) This Balti Triangle favourite serves delicious dishes from the mountains of Kashmir, as well as for classic Birmingham baltis.

★ **Jekyll & Hyde** PUB
(☑ 0121-236 0345; www.thejekyllandhyde.co.uk; 28 Steelhouse Lane; ◷ noon-11pm Mon-Thu, to 2am Fri & Sat) Potent cocktails (or rather 'elixirs, concoctions and potions') at this trippy spot are served in sweets jars, watering cans, teapots and miniature bathtubs – even a wash bag (with a rum-mint toothpaste and Kaffir lime). Downstairs, Mr Hyde's emporium has a cosy drawing room and *Alice in Wonderland–*themed courtyard; upstairs is Dr Jekyll's Gin Parlour.

If Jekyll & Hyde is your kind of place, check out some of independent Birmingham company Bitters 'n' Twisted's other unique properties, especially the South American–themed **Bodega Bar & Cantina** (www.bodegabirmingham.co.uk; 12 Bennett's Hill; ◷ noon-11pm Mon-Thu, to 2am Fri & Sat, to 8pm Sun); the 19th-century splendour of **Victoria** (www.thevictoriabirmingham.co.uk; 48 John Bright St; ◷ noon-midnight Sun-Wed, to 1am Thu, to 2am Fri & Sat), with awesome DJs; and rum specialist **Island Bar** (☑ 0121-632 5296; www.bar-island.co.uk; 14-16 Suffolk St Queensway; ◷ 5pm-midnight Mon-Wed, to 2am Fri & Sat, 8pm-2am Sun), with giant blow-ups of Hawaiian beaches. All serve top-notch food too.

Lost & Found BAR
(www.the-lostandfound.co.uk; 8 Bennett's Hill; ◷ 11am-11pm Mon-Thu, to midnight Fri, 10am-midnight Sat, 11am-9pm Sun) Fictitious Victorian-era explorer/professor Hettie G Watson is the inspiration for the botanical library theme of this bar in an 1869-built former bank. Inside the domed entrance, elevated seating is surrounded by plants, birdcages, books and maps, while a bookcase conceals the entrance to Hettie's 'secret emporium' bar (try your luck around 7.30pm on a Friday or Saturday).

Wellington PUB
(www.thewellingtonrealale.co.uk; 37 Bennett's Hill; ◷ 10am-midnight) The pastel wallpaper,

timber bar and polished brass give the impression the Welly is frozen in time, but this specialist real ale pub has just been spruced up and has gained a new roof terrace. Its 16 hand-pulled beers (and three ciders) include favourites from Black Country and Wye Valley as well as rare brews.

Bacchus BAR
(☑ 0121-632 5445; www.nicholsonspubs.co.uk; Burlington Arcade, New St; ◷ 11am-11pm Sun-Thu, to 1am Fri & Sat) Beneath the Burlington arcade, down a faux marble-encased staircase, crumbling pillars and giant Grecian murals give way to soaring medieval-style stone arches, swords, suits of armour and candelabras. All of this gives the darkened drinking den the ambience of a decadent underworld.

Old Joint Stock PUB
(☑ 0121-200 1892; www.oldjointstocktheatre.co.uk; 4 Temple Row West; ◷ 11am-11pm Mon-Sat, noon-5pm Sun; ☎) A vast high-ceilinged temple of a pub, housed in a former bank and beloved by a high-spirited after-work crowd. Upstairs, an 80-seat theatre puts on plays and comedy shows.

Q Club CLUB
(www.qclub.co.uk; 212 Corporation St; ◷ hours vary) The old brick Central Hall that houses this legendary club is on its last legs, but the 'Q' is still going strong. DJs pump out boisterous electro, house, jungle and old-school club classics.

☆ **Entertainment**

Tickets for most Birmingham events can be purchased through entertainment megacorp **TicketWeb** (☑ 0870 060 0100; www.ticketweb.co.uk).

Free publications listing gigs and events include the excellent *Brum Notes* (www.brumnotes.com).

Live Music

The **National Indoor Arena** (☑ 0121-780 4141; www.thenia.co.uk; King Edwards Rd), north of Brindley Pl, and the **National Exhibition Centre Arena** (☑ 0121-780 4141; www.thenec.co.uk; off the M42), near Birmingham Airport, host stadium-fillers from the world of rock and pop.

Sunflower Lounge LIVE MUSIC
(☑ 0121-632 6756; www.thesunflowerlounge.com; 76 Smallbrook Queensway; ◷ hours vary) This quirky little indie bar matches a magnificent alternative soundtrack with a regular program of live gigs and DJ nights.

Jam House   LIVE MUSIC
(www.thejamhouse.com; 3-5 St Paul's Sq; ⊙6pm-midnight Tue & Wed, to 1am Thu, to 2am Fri & Sat) Pianist Jools Holland was the brains behind this moody, smart-casual music venue (dress accordingly). Acts range from jazz big bands to famous soul crooners. Over 21s only.

Symphony Hall   CLASSICAL MUSIC
(⏲0121-345 0600; www.symphonyhall.co.uk; Broad St) The City of Birmingham Symphony Orchestra's official home is the ultramodern Symphony Hall. Shows also take place in the handsome auditorium at the Town Hall.

O2 Academy   LIVE MUSIC
(www.o2academybirmingham.co.uk; 16-18 Horsefair, Bristol St; ⊙box office 12-4pm Mon-Sat) Birmingham's leading venue for big-name rockers and tribute bands as well as up-and-coming talent.

Theatre & Cinema

Birmingham Repertory Theatre   THEATRE
(⏲0121-236 4455; www.birmingham-rep.co.uk; Centenary Sq) Founded over a century ago, 'the Rep' now has three performance spaces – the Main House; the more experimental Door; and a new 300-seat studio theatre presenting edgy drama and musicals, with an emphasis on contemporary work.

Electric Cinema   CINEMA
(www.theelectric.co.uk; 47-49 Station St; standard/deluxe seats £7.80/13.50) Topped by its art deco sign, this is the UK's oldest working cinema, operating since 1909. It screens mainly art-house films. Be waited upon in plush two-seater sofas or have a drink in the small bar (complete with an absinthe fountain).

Hippodrome   THEATRE
(⏲0844 338 5000; www.birminghamhippodrome. com; Hurst St) Hosts the Birmingham Royal Ballet.

Sport

Birmingham has three football (soccer) clubs within striking distance: Birmingham City Football Club, West Bromwich Albion ('West Brom') and, most famously, Aston Villa Football Club.

Villa Park   FOOTBALL
(⏲0800 612 0970; www.avfc.co.uk; Trinity Rd, Witton; tours adult/child from £12.95/7.95) Aston Villa Football Club's 19th-century Villa Park is one of the country's largest stadiums. Behind-the-scenes tours (three times weekly by reservation) include the dressing rooms, tunnel

and pitch. The ground is 2 miles north of Birmingham. Trains run from New St to Witton (£2, nine minutes, half-hourly), a five-minute walk away; and every 10 minutes to Aston, a 15-minute walk. Tickets and merchandise are available from the **Aston Villa City Centre Store** (⏲0121-326 1559; www.avfc.co.uk; New St; ⊙9.30am-6pm Mon-Sat, 11am-3pm Sun).

🛍 Shopping

Bustling markets sell fresh food and cheap imported clothes in the pedestrian precincts surrounding the Bullring.

Atop the revitalised New St train station, the gleaming Grand Central Birmingham shopping mall (www.grandcentralbirmingham.com), opening 2015, is anchored by a massive John Lewis department store.

Great Western Arcade   SHOPPING ARCADE
(www.greatwesternarcade.co.uk; btwn Colmore Row & Temple Row; ⊙arcade 9am-11pm Mon-Sat, 11am-8pm Sun, shop hours vary) This glass-roofed, tiled-floored Victorian-era arcade is a jewel filled with mostly independent shops.

Bullring   MALL
(www.bullring.co.uk; St Martin's Circus; ⊙10am-8pm Mon-Fri, 9am-8pm Sat, 11am-5pm Sun) Split into two vast retail spaces – the East Mall and West Mall – the Bullring has all the international brands and chain cafes you could ask for, plus the standout architectural wonder of Selfridges, which looks out over the city like the compound eye of a giant robot insect.

Mailbox   MALL
(www.mailboxlife.com; Wharfside St; ⊙10am-6pm Mon-Wed, to 7pm Thu-Sat, 11am-5pm Sun) Birmingham's stylish waterside shopping experience, the redevelopment of the former Royal Mail sorting office, comes complete with designer hotels, a fleet of upmarket restaurants, the luxury department store Harvey Nichols and designer boutiques. Its snazzy metallic extension, The Cube, houses Marco Pierre White's Steakhouse Bar and Grill on the 25th floor.

ℹ Information

As in most large cities, it's wise to avoid walking alone late at night in unlit areas. In particular, the centre – especially south of the Bullring – can be rowdy with revellers on weekend nights.

Digbeth bus station and its surrounds can be quite rough after dark.

Birmingham Children's Hospital (⏲0121-333 9999; www.bch.nhs.uk; Steelhouse Lane) Has an Accident & Emergency department.

Heart of England Tourist Board (📞 01905-887690; www.visitheartofengland.com)

Heartlands Hospital (📞 0121-424 2000; www.heartofengland.nhs.uk; Bordesley Green East) Located 4 miles east of the centre; has an Accident & Emergency department.

Police Station (📞 101; Steelhouse Lane)

Tourist Office (📞 0844 888 3883; www.visit-birmingham.com; cnr Corporation & New Sts; ⊙ 9am-5pm Mon-Sat, 10am-4pm Sun) Kiosk with racks of info on activities, transport and sights. There's a branch at the Library of Birmingham (p411).

🛈 Getting There & Away

AIR

Birmingham Airport is about 8 miles east of the centre, with direct flights to destinations around the UK and Europe as well as direct long-haul routes to Dubai, India, the USA and Canada.

BUS

Most intercity buses run from **Birmingham Coach Station** (Digbeth High St), but the X20 to Stratford-upon-Avon (£5, 1¼ hours, hourly) leaves from a stop on Moor St, just north of the Pavilions mall.

National Express runs coaches between Birmingham and major cities across the country, including the following destinations:

London Victoria £12.60, 2¾ hours, every 30 minutes

Manchester £14.40, 3 hours, 14 daily

Oxford £15.20, 1½ to four hours, eight daily

TRAIN

Most long-distance trains leave from New St station, but Chiltern Railways runs to London Marylebone (£49, 2½ hours, half-hourly) from Birmingham Snow Hill, and London Midland runs to Stratford-upon-Avon (£7.30, one hour, half-hourly) from Snow Hill and Moor St stations.

Services from New St include the following:

Derby £15.90, 45 minutes, four per hour

Leicester £12.90, one hour, two per hour

London Euston £27.50, 1½ hours, every 15 minutes

Manchester £34.40, 1¾ hours, every half hour

Nottingham £17.40, 1¼ hours, three per hour

Shrewsbury £13.60, one hour, two per hour

🛈 Getting Around

TO/FROM THE AIRPORT

Fast and convenient trains run regularly between New St and Birmingham International station (£3.50, 20 minutes, every 10 minutes), or take bus 97 or 900 (£5, 30 minutes, every 30 minutes) from Moor St Queensway, which runs 24 hours.

A taxi from the airport to the centre costs about £30.

CAR

All the big car-hire companies have town offices.

Avis (📞 0844 544 6038; www.avis.co.uk; 17 Horse Fair)

Enterprise Rent-a-Car (📞 0121-643 7743; www.enterprise.co.uk; 9-10 Suffolk St Queensway)

PUBLIC TRANSPORT

Local buses run from a convenient hub on Corporation St, just north of the New St junction. For routes, pick up a free copy of the *Network Birmingham Map & Guide* from the tourist office. Single-trip tickets start from £1.70.

Commuter trains to destinations in the north of Birmingham (including Aston) operate from Moor St train station, close to Selfridges.

The 2015-opening extension of Birmingham's single tram line, the **Metro** (www.travelmetro.co.uk), links New St Station with Wolverhampton via the Jewellery Quarter, West Bromwich and Dudley. Tickets start from £2.20. A further extension from New St to Birmingham Town Hall and Centenary Sq is due to open in 2017.

Various saver tickets covering buses and trains are available from **Network West Midlands** (📞 0121-2147 7550; www.networkwest-midlands.com; ⊙ 8.30am-5.30pm Mon-Sat) at New St Station.

TOA Taxis (📞 0121-427 8888; www.toataxis.co.uk) is a reliable black-cab taxi firm.

WARWICKSHIRE

Warwickshire could have been just another picturesque English county of rolling hills and market towns were it not for the birth of a rather well-known wordsmith. William Shakespeare was born and died in Stratford-upon-Avon, and the sights linked to his life are a magnet for tourists from around the globe. Famous Warwick Castle attracts similar crowds. Elsewhere visitor numbers dwindle, but Kenilworth has atmospheric castle ruins and Coventry claims two extraordinary cathedrals and an unmissable motoring museum.

🛈 Information

Shakespeare Country (www.shakespeare-country.co.uk)

🛈 Getting There & Around

Coventry is the main transport hub, with frequent rail connections to London Euston and Birmingham New St.

Coventry

POP 325,950

Dominated today by its twin spires and identikit tower blocks, Coventry was once a bustling hub for the production of cloth, clocks, bicycles, automobiles and munitions. It was this last industry that drew the German Luftwaffe in WWII: on the night of 14 November 1940, the city was so badly blitzed that the Nazis coined a new verb, *coventrieren*, meaning 'to flatten'. Postwar planners filled in the gaps with dull concrete developments, and the city faced a further setback with the collapse of the British motor industry in the 1980s. A handful of medieval streets that escaped the bombers offer a glimpse of old Coventry.

◎ Sights

★**Coventry Transport Museum**   MUSEUM
(✐024-7623 4270; www.transport-museum.com; Hales St; ☉10am-5pm) FREE This stupendous museum has hundreds of 'cars' spanning the ages, from horseless carriages to jet-powered, land-speed record breakers. There's a brushed stainless steel DeLorean DMC-12 (of *Back to the Future* fame) with gull-wing doors, alongside a gorgeous Jaguar E-type, a Daimler armoured car and, for 1970s British design oddity enthusiasts, a Triumph TR7 and an Austin Allegro 'Special'. View the Thrust SCC, the current holder of the World Land Speed Record and the Thrust 2, the previous record holder.

Kids will be engrossed by the atmospheric 'Coventry Blitz Experience' and the Thrust speed simulator (£1.50).

Coventry Cathedral   CATHEDRAL
(✐024-7652 1200; www.coventrycathedral.org. uk; Priory Row; adult/child £8/5.75; ☉10am-4pm) The evocative ruins of St Michael's Cathedral, built around 1300 but destroyed by Nazi incendiary bombs in the Blitz, stand as a permanent memorial to Coventry's darkest hour and as a symbol of peace and reconciliation. Climb the Gothic spire's 180 steps for panoramic views (adult/child £2.75/1.50).

Symbolically adjoining St Michael's Cathedral's sandstone walls is the Sir Basil Spence–designed modernist architectural masterpiece, Coventry Cathedral, with a futuristic organ, stained glass and Jacob Epstein statue of the devil and St Michael.

Herbert Art Gallery & Museum   GALLERY
(✐024-7623 7521; www.theherbert.org; Jordan Well; ☉10am-4pm Mon-Sat, noon-4pm Sun) FREE Behind Coventry's twin cathedrals, the Herbert has an eclectic collection of paintings and sculptures (including work by TS Lowry and Stanley Spencer), a delightful cafe and lots of activities aimed at kids. The history gallery and thought-provoking gallery on peace and reconciliation are worth a look-in.

St Mary's Guildhall   HISTORIC BUILDING
(✐024-7683 3328; www.stmarysguildhall.co.uk; Bayley Lane; ☉10am-4pm Sun-Thu mid-Mar–Sep) FREE This hall is where the town's trades came together in the Middle Ages to discuss town affairs. As one of England's finest guildhalls, it was chosen to be a jail for Mary Queen of Scots. Stained-glass windows glorify the kings of England; further down the hall stands WC Marshall's statue of Lady

---

WORTH A TRIP

RUGBY

Warwickshire's second-largest hub, Rugby (population 100,500) is an attractive market town whose history dates back to the Iron Age. But it's most famous for the sport that takes its name, and is a place of pilgrimage for fans.

The game was invented at Rugby School in 1823 when William Webb Ellis is said to have caught the ball during a football match and broke the rules by running with it. The school itself is closed to the public, but you can peek at the hallowed ground through the gates just across from the Webb Ellis Rugby Football Museum (✐01788-533217; www.rugbyfootballmuseum.org.uk; 5-6 Matthews St; ☉9.30am-5pm Mon-Sat) FREE. Intriguing exhibits at the little museum include the evolution of the ball and historic team photos from the Webb Ellis Cup (aka the Rugby World Cup). The museum is attached to the first rugby football workshop, established in 1842, which still manufactures footballs today.

Rugby is 13 miles east of Coventry, served by regular trains (£5.50, 10 minutes, up to four hourly). Trains also serve Birmingham (£9.20, 40 minutes, two to four per hour) and Leicester (£13.60, one hour, hourly).

Godiva. Look out for the medieval tapestry depicting Henry VI.

🛏 Sleeping & Eating

Coventry makes an easy day trip from Birmingham but if you want to stay, the tourist office can help find accommodation.

Spon St, better known as 'Medieval Spon St', has a smattering of restaurants, pubs and cafes as well as boutiques in its half-timbered buildings.

Playwrights   CAFE ££
(📞 024-7623 1441; www.playwrightsrestaurant.co.uk; 4-6 Hay Lane; mains £8-19.50; ⊙ 9am to late) On the lovely cobbled lane leading from Earl St to the cathedral, this bright, inviting cafe, bar and bistro is as good for breakfast as it is for lunch or an intimate dinner. Tables are flung out on the cobbles in warmer weather.

ℹ Information

Tourist Office (📞 024-7622 5616; www.visitcoventry.co.uk; ⊙ 9.30am-4.30pm Mon-Fri, 10am-4.30pm Sat, 10am-noon & 1-4.30pm Sun) Housed in the restored tower of St Michael's Cathedral.

ℹ Getting There & Away

From the main bus station, National Express buses serve most parts of the country. Buses X17 and X19 (every 15 minutes) go to Kenilworth (£1.90, 25 minutes), Leamington Spa (£3.35, 50 minutes) and Warwick (£5, 1¼ hours).

Trains go south to London Euston (£45.90, 1¼ hours, every 10 to 20 minutes) and you will rarely have to wait for a train to Birmingham (£3.40, 30 minutes, every 10 minutes).

Warwick

POP 31,350

Regularly name-checked by Shakespeare, Warwick was the ancestral seat of the Earls of Warwick, who played a pivotal role in the Wars of the Roses. Despite a devastating fire in 1694, Warwick remains a treasure-house of medieval architecture with rich veins of history and charming streets, dominated by the soaring turrets of Warwick Castle.

◉ Sights

★ Warwick Castle   CASTLE
(📞 0871 265 2000; www.warwick-castle.com; castle adult/child £22.80/16.80, castle & dungeon £28.80/24, Kingdom Ticket incl castle, dungeon & exhibition £30.60/27; ⊙ 10am-6pm Apr-Sep, to 5pm

Oct-Mar; 🅿) Founded in 1068 by William the Conqueror, stunningly preserved Warwick Castle is the biggest show in town. The ancestral home of the Earls of Warwick remains impressively intact, and the Tussauds Group has filled the interior with attractions that bring the castle's rich history to life in a flamboyant but undeniably family-friendly way. As well as waxworks populating the private apartments there are jousting tournaments, daily trebuchet-firings, themed evenings and a dungeon. Discounted online tickets provide fast-track entry. Parking costs £6.

Collegiate Church of St Mary   CHURCH
(📞 01926-492909; www.stmaryswarwick.org.uk; Old Sq; church entry by £2 donation, tower adult/child £2.50/1; ⊙ 10am-6pm Apr-Sep, to 4.30pm Oct-Mar) This 1123-founded Norman church was badly damaged in the Great Fire of Warwick in 1694 but is packed with 16th- and 17th-century tombs. Highlights include the Norman crypt with a 14th-century extension; the impressive Beauchamp Chapel, built between 1442 and 1464 to enshrine the mortal remains of the Earls of Warwick; and, up 134 steps, the tower, which provides supreme views over town (kids must be aged over eight).

Lord Leycester Hospital   HISTORIC BUILDING
(📞 01926-491422; www.lordleycester.com; High St; adult/child £4.90/3.90, garden only £2; ⊙ 10am-5pm Tue-Sun Apr-Sep, to 4.30pm Oct-Mar) A survivor of the 1694 fire, the wonderfully wonky Lord Leycester Hospital has been used as a retirement home for soldiers (but not as a hospital) since 1571. Visitors can wander around the chapel, guildhall, regimental museum and restored walled garden, which includes a knot garden and a Norman arch.

Warwickshire Museum   MUSEUM
(📞 01926-412501; Market Pl; ⊙ 10am-5pm Tue-Sat year-round, 11.30am-5pm Sun Apr-Sep) **FREE** Housed in Warwick's striking 17th-century market hall, Warwickshire Museum has some entertaining displays on local history and the Warwick sea dragons (Jurassic-era sea creatures).

🛏 Sleeping & Eating

Reasonably priced B&Bs line Emscote Rd, which runs northeast towards Leamington Spa (2 miles east of Warwick), a genteel spa town that's almost a suburb of Warwick.

Tilted Wig   PUB ££
(📞 01926-400110; www.tiltedwigwarwick.co.uk; 11 Market Pl; d £65-90, mains £8.50-14; 🅿 📶) Bang

Warwick

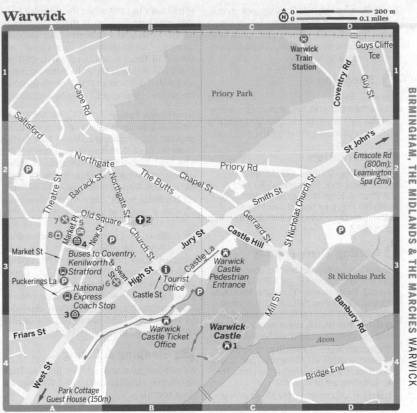

on the epicentral Market Pl, this brilliantly named 17th-century Georgian inn has four freshly refurbished, snug but comfortable rooms and some of the better pub grub in town, such as roast duck breast in port wine reduction. Guests get a three-course meal for just £10 per person.

Park Cottage Guest House   B&B **££**
(☑ 01926-410319; www.parkcottagewarwick.co.uk; 113 West St; s £55-70, d £75-90; P 🛜) Southwest of the centre, this stand-alone 16th-century wattle-and-daub building once served as the dairy for Warwick Castle. There are seven pretty rooms, each with a teddy bear, original floors and a courtyard garden.

Merchants   BRASSERIE **££**
(☑ 01926-403833; www.merchantswarwick.co.uk; Swan St; mains £10.50-19.90; ⊗ noon-9pm Mon-Thu, to 9.30pm Fri & Sat) With stylish leather furniture and chalkboard menus, this restaurant and wine bar specialises in steaks.

Warwick

◎ Top Sights
1 Warwick Castle C4

◎ Sights
2 Collegiate Church of St Mary B3
3 Lord Leycester Hospital A4
4 Warwickshire Museum A3

🛏 Sleeping
5 Tilted Wig A3

✴ Eating
6 Merchants B3
7 Tailors A3

🛍 Shopping
8 Warwick Books A3

Tailors   MODERN BRITISH **£££**
(☑ 01926-410590; www.tailorsrestaurant.co.uk; 22 Market Pl; 2-/3-course lunch menu £15/19, 2-/3-course dinner menu £28/32.50; ⊗ noon-1.45pm

& 6.30-9pm Tue-Sat) Set in a former gentlemen's tailor shop, this elegant eatery serves prime ingredients – guinea fowl, pork belly and lamb from named farms – delicately presented in neat little towers.

🛍 Shopping

Warwick Books BOOKS
(www.warwickbooks.net; 24 Market Pl; ☺9am-5pm Mon-Sat) Small but helpful and friendly bookshop offering great recommendations.

ℹ Information

Tourist Office (✆01926-492212; www.visitwarwick.co.uk; Court House, Jury St; ☺9.30am-4.30pm Mon-Fri, 10am-4pm Sat) Within the flagstone-floored Court House (1725). Sells the informative *Warwick Town Trail* leaflet (50p).

ℹ Getting There & Away

National Express coaches operate from Puckerings Lane. Stagecoach X17 and X19 run to Coventry (£3, 1¼ hours, every 15 minutes Monday to Saturday), via Kenilworth (£2.80, 30 minutes). On Sunday, take bus G1 or 18A for Leamington Sap (£3.35, half-hourly), where you can pick up the U17 for Coventry (£3.10) and Kenilworth (£2).

Stagecoach buses 16 and X18 go to Stratford-upon-Avon (£5.40, 40 minutes, half-hourly) in one direction, and Coventry in the other. The main bus stops are on Market St.

Trains run to Birmingham (£7.50, 40 minutes, half-hourly), Stratford-upon-Avon (£5.40, 30 minutes, hourly) and London (£28.80, 1½ hours, every 20 minutes), from the station, northeast of the centre.

Kenilworth

POP 22,410

A refreshing counterpoint to the commercialism of nearby Warwick's royal ruin, the atmospheric ruin of Kenilworth Castle was the inspiration for Walter Scott's *Kenilworth,* and it still feels pretty inspiring today. It's an easy deviation off the A46 between Warwick and Coventry.

⊙ Sights

Kenilworth Castle CASTLE
(EH; ✆01926-852078; www.english-heritage.org.uk; adult/child £9.30/5.60; ☺10am-5pm Apr-Oct, reduced hours Nov-Mar; P) This spine-tingling ruin sprawls among fields and hedges on Kenilworth's outskirts. Built in the 1120s, the castle survived the longest siege in Eng-

lish history in 1266, when the forces of Lord Edward (later Edward I) threw themselves at the moat and battlements for six solid months. The fortress was dramatically extended in Tudor times, but it fell in the English Civil War and its walls were breached and water defences drained. Don't miss the magnificent restored Elizabethan gardens.

Stoneleigh Abbey HISTORIC BUILDING
(✆01926-858535; www.stoneleighabbey.org; adult/child £8/3.50, garden only £3.50; ☺tours Tue-Sun Easter-Oct, garden 11am-5pm Tue-Sun Easter-Oct; P) The kind of stately home that makes movie directors go weak at the knees, this 850-year-old country house 2 miles east of Kenilworth, off the B4115 by the River Avon, name-drops Charles I and Jane Austen among its roll-call of visitors. Completed in 1726 and only viewable on tours (included in admission), the abbey's splendid Palladian west wing contains richly detailed plasterwork ceilings and wood-panelled rooms. The landscaped grounds are fine picnic territory. The original abbey was founded by Cistercian monks in 1154, but the house was massively expanded by the wealthy Leigh family (distant cousins of the Austens) in the 16th century.

🛏 Sleeping & Eating

Numerous pubs and eateries line the High St (just north of the castle) and Warwick Rd (just south).

The Old Bakery B&B ££
(✆01926-864111; www.theoldbakery.eu; 12 High St; s/d from £75/95; P✆) Located down High St east of the castle, this B&B has attractively attired modern rooms and a cosy, welcoming bar serving real ales on the ground floor.

Harringtons on the Hill MODERN BRITISH ££
(✆01926-852074; www.harringtonsonthehill.com; 42 Castle Hill; mains £10-19; ☺noon-3pm & 6-11pm Mon-Sat, noon-4pm Sun) In an adorable bow-fronted cottage festooned with flower boxes opposite Kenilworth Castle, chef Ryan New recreates his success at some of London's top tables. Dishes include hot smoked salmon with bubble and squeak and soft poached egg, and char-grilled swordfish with chorizo – at impressively reasonable prices.

ℹ Information

Browse the tourist brochures at the town **library** (✆01908-276 2451; www.kenilworthlibrary.org; 11 Smalley Pl; ☺9am-5.30pm Mon, Tue, Thu & Fri, 10.30am-5.30pm Wed, 9am-1pm Sat).

❶ Getting There & Away

From Monday to Saturday, buses X17 and X19 run every 15 minutes from Coventry to Kenilworth (£3.10, 25 minutes) and on to Leamington Spa (£3.10, 15 minutes) and Warwick (£3.35, 20 minutes). On Sundays, take bus U17 for Coventry (£3.10) and Leamington Spa (£2). At Leamington Spa you can change to bus G1 or 18A for Warwick (£3.35, half-hourly).

Stratford-upon-Avon

POP 27,830

The author of some of the most quoted lines ever written in the English language, William Shakespeare was born in Stratford in 1564 and died here in 1616. The five houses linked to his life form the centrepiece of a tourist attraction that verges on a cult of personality.

Experiences in this unmistakably Tudor town range from the touristy (medieval re-creations and Bard-themed tearooms) to the humbling (Shakespeare's modest grave in Holy Trinity Church) and the sublime (taking in a play by the world-famous Royal Shakespeare Company).

❂ Sights & Activities

★ **Shakespeare's Birthplace**   HISTORIC BUILDING
(☑ 01789-204016; www.shakespeare.org.uk; Henley St; incl Nash's House & New Place and Halls Croft £15.90/9.50; ☺ 9am-5.30pm Jul-Sep, to 5pm Oct-Jun) Start your Shakespeare quest at the house where the world's most popular playwright supposedly spent his childhood days. In fact, the jury is still out on whether this really was Shakespeare's birthplace, but devotees of the Bard have been dropping in since at least the 19th century, leaving their signatures scratched onto the windows. Set behind a modern facade, the house has restored Tudor rooms, live presentations from famous Shakespearean characters, and an engaging exhibition on Stratford's favourite son.

Nash's House & New Place   HISTORIC SITE
(☑ 01789-204016; www.shakespeare.org.uk; cnr Chapel St & Chapel Lane; incl Shakespeare's Birthplace & Halls Croft £15.90/9.50; ☺ 10am-5pm mid-Mar–Oct) When Shakespeare retired, he swapped the bright lights of London for a comfortable town house at New Pl, where he died of unknown causes in April 1616. The house was demolished in 1759, but an attractive Elizabethan knot garden occupies part of the grounds. Archaeologists recently dug beneath the plot in search of Shakespearean treasures; their finds are displayed in the adjacent Nash's House, where Shakespeare's granddaughter Elizabeth lived. Displays describe the town's history and there's a collection of 17th-century furniture and tapestries.

Hall's Croft   HISTORIC BUILDING
(☑ 01789-204016; Old Town; incl Shakespeare's Birthplace and Nash's House & New Place £15.90/9.50; ☺ 10am-5pm mid-Mar–Oct) The handsome Jacobean town house belonging to Shakespeare's daughter Susanna and her husband, respected doctor John Hall, stands south of the centre. The exhibition offers fascinating insights into medicine in the 16th and 17th centuries, and the lovely walled garden sprouts with aromatic herbs employed in medicinal preparations.

Holy Trinity Church   CHURCH
(☑ 01789-266316; www.stratford-upon-avon.org; Old Town; Shakespeare's grave adult/child £2/1; ☺ 8.30am-6pm Mon-Sat, 12.30-5pm Sun Apr-Sep, reduced hours Oct-Mar) The final resting place of the Bard is said to be the most visited parish church in all of England. Inside are handsome 16th- and 17th-century tombs (particularly in the Clopton Chapel), some fabulous carvings on the choir stalls and, of course, the grave of William Shakespeare, with its ominous epitaph: 'cvrst be he yt moves my bones'.

Anne Hathaway's Cottage   HISTORIC BUILDING
(☑ 01789-204016; www.shakespeare.org.uk; Cottage Lane, Shottery; adult/child £9.50/5.50; ☺ 9am-5pm mid-Mar–Oct) Before tying the knot with Shakespeare, Anne Hathaway lived in Shottery, a mile west of the centre

---

❶ SHAKESPEARE HISTORIC HOMES

Five of the most important buildings associated with Shakespeare contain museums that form the core of the visitor experience at Stratford. All are run by the Shakespeare Birthplace Trust (www.shakespeare.org.uk).

Tickets for the three houses in town – Shakespeare's Birthplace, Nash's House & New Place and Halls Croft – cost adult/child £15.90/9.50. If you also visit Anne Hathaway's Cottage and Mary Arden's Farm, buy a combination ticket covering all five properties (£23.90/14).

1. Shakespeare's Birthplace (p425), Stratford-upon-Avon
2. West Gate Towers (p154), Canterbury **3.** Laugharne (p689)
4. Wasdale (p608), Lake District

STEPHEN DOREY / GETTY IMAGES ©

ANDREW WILCOX / GETTY IMAGES ©

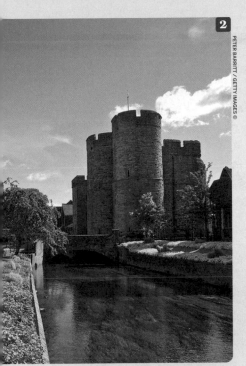

PETER BARRITT / GETTY IMAGES ©

FELLWALKER WITH CAMERA / GETTY IMAGES ©

Literary Britain

Britain's literary heritage is astoundingly rich and globally renowned. As the English language spread around the world in the colonial era, so too did its literature, with novelists such as Charles Dickens and George Eliot and poets including Samuel Taylor Coleridge being read far from home in the late 18th and 19th centuries.

Contemporary Literature

Contemporary British authors whose works are celebrated worldwide range from heavyweights Julian Barnes, Ian McEwan and double Man Booker Prize-winner Hilary Mantel to EL James, author of the smash-hit *50 Shades of Grey* trilogy.

Children's Literature

Beloved characters such as AA Milne's Winnie-the-Pooh, Michael Bond's Paddington Bear, Beatrix Potter's Peter Rabbit, Roald Dahl's Willy Wonka and JK Rowling's Harry Potter are perennially popular. Newcastle's Seven Stories – The Centre for Children's Books (p630) is a wonderful place to get acquainted, or reacquainted, with old and new favourites.

British Playwrights

British playwrights' words come to life on stage in London's West End and right across Britain: cities and even small towns have thriving theatres staging classic and cutting-edge productions.

LITERARY LOCATIONS

➡ **Bath** Grandeur that never tired Jane Austen's heroines.

➡ **Canterbury** Synonymous with Chaucer's *Canterbury Tales*.

➡ **Haworth** Home of the Brontë sisters, surrounded by wuthering moors.

➡ **Lake District** Source of inspiration for William Wordsworth.

➡ **Laugharne (Talacharne)** Dylan Thomas' home, with a 'heron-priested shore' and a 'castle as brown as owls'.

➡ **Edinburgh** Unesco's first City of Literature.

➡ **Stratford-upon-Avon** Birthplace of William Shakespeare.

Stratford-upon-Avon

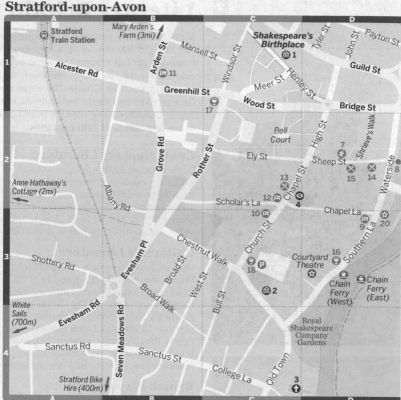

of Stratford, in this delightful thatched farmhouse. As well as period furniture, it has gorgeous gardens and an orchard and arboretum, with examples of all the trees mentioned in Shakespeare's plays. A footpath (no bikes allowed) leads to Shottery from Evesham Pl.

Mary Arden's Farm   HISTORIC SITE, FARM
(☑ 01789-204016; www.shakespeare.org.uk; Station Rd, Wilmcote; adult/child £12.50/8; ☉ 10am-5pm mid-Mar–Oct) Shakespeare genealogists can trace the family tree to the childhood home of the Bard's mother at Wilmcote, 3 miles west of Stratford. Aimed squarely at families, the working farm traces country life over the centuries, with nature trails, falconry displays and a collection of rare-breed farm animals. You can get here on the City Sightseeing bus, or cycle via Anne Hathaway's Cottage, following the Stratford-upon-Avon Canal towpath.

Falstaff's Experience   GHOST EXPERIENCE
(☑ 01789-298070; www.falstaffsexperience.co.uk; 40 Sheep St; adult/child £5.50/3; ☉ 10.30am-5.30pm) Set in an old timbered building, Falstaff's Experience offers a ghostly take on Shakespeare's tales, with oldey-worldey walk-throughs, mannequins of Tudor celebs and live actors hamming it up like Olivier. Night-time adults-only ghost tours are led by famous mediums.

☞ Tours

Guided Town Walks   WALKING TOUR
(☑ 07855-760377; www.stratfordtownwalk.co.uk; adult/child £5/2; ☉ 11am Mon-Thu, 2pm Fri, 11am & 2pm Sat & Sun) Popular and informative two-hour guided town walks departing from Waterside, opposite Sheep St.

Stratford Town Ghost Walk   WALKING TOUR
(☑ 07855-760377; www.stratfordtownwalk.co.uk; adult/child £6/4; ☉ 7.30pm Mon & Thu-Sat)

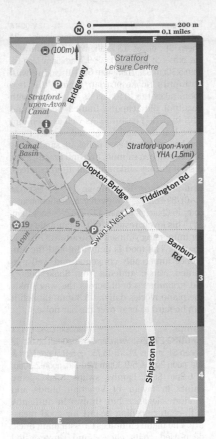

Stratford-upon-Avon

Chill-seekers can take the Stratford Town Ghost Walk departing from Waterside, opposite Sheep St.

City Sightseeing   BUS TOUR
(☑01789-412680; www.city-sightseeing.com; adult/child £12.50/6.50; ☺every 30min Apr-Sep, less frequently Oct-Mar) Open-top, hop-on/hop-off bus tours leave from the tourist office on Bridge Foot, rolling to each of the Shakespeare properties. Tickets are valid for 24 hours (there are also 48-hour tickets costing £19/9.50) and can be bought from the driver. On-board commentary comes in seven languages.

Avon Boating   BOAT TOUR
(☑01789-267073; www.avon-boating.co.uk; The Boathouse, Swan's Nest Lane; river cruises adult/child £5.50/3/50; ☺9am-dusk Apr-Oct) Runs 40-minute river cruises that depart every 20 minutes from either side of the main bridge.

⭐ Festivals & Events

Stratford Literary Festival   LITERATURE
(☑01789-207100; www.stratfordliteraryfestival.co.uk; ☺Apr/May) The top event on Stratford's cultural calendar is the Stratford Literary Festival, which attracts literary big-hitters of the calibre of John Simpson and Jonathan Miller.

🛏 Sleeping

B&Bs are plentiful, particularly along Grove Rd and Evesham Pl, but vacancies can be hard to find during the high season – the tourist office can help with bookings for a £5 fee.

Stratford-upon-Avon YHA   HOSTEL£
(☑0845 371 9661; www.yha.org.uk; Hemmingford House, Alveston; dm/d from £19/40; P@🖥🛜) Set in a large 200-year-old mansion, 1.5 miles east of the town centre along Tiddington Rd, this superior hostel attracts travellers of all ages. Of its 32 rooms and dorms, 16 are en suite. There's a canteen, bar and kitchen.

Buses 18 and 18A run here from Bridge St. Wi-fi is available in common areas.

Legacy Falcon
HOTEL **££**

(☑08444 119 005; www.legacy-hotels.co.uk; Chapel St; d/f from £83/113; P⊛) Definitely request a room in the original 15th-century building, not the souless modern annexe or dingy 17th-century garden house of this epicentral hotel. This way you'll get the full Tudor experience – creaky floorboards, wonky timbered walls and all. Open fires blaze in the wi-fi'd public areas; rooms have wired broadband but the best asset is the unheard-of-for-Stratford free car park.

White Sails
GUESTHOUSE **££**

(☑01789-550469; www.white-sails.co.uk; 85 Evesham Rd; d from £100; ✱) Plush fabrics, framed prints, brass bedsteads and shabby-chic tables and lamps set the scene at this gorgeous and intimate guesthouse on the edge of the countryside. The four individually furnished rooms come with flatscreen TVs, climate control and glamorous bathrooms.

Emsley Guesthouse
B&B **££**

(☑01789-299557; www.theemsley.co.uk; 4 Arden St; d from £64; P⊛) This lovely five-bedroom Victorian property has a personable owner, very clean and attractive accommodation, and a large, pretty family room at the top with an exposed beam ceiling. Weekends require a two-night minimum stay.

Church Street Townhouse
BOUTIQUE HOTEL **£££**

(☑01789-262222; www.churchstreettownhouse.com; 16 Church St; d £110-200; ⊛) Some of the rooms at this exquisite hotel have free-standing baths, and all have iPod docks, flatscreen TVs and luxurious furnishings. Light sleepers should avoid room 1, nearest the bar. The building itself is a centrally located 400-year-old gem with a first-rate restaurant and bar. Minimum two-night stay on weekends.

Arden Hotel
HOTEL **£££**

(☑01789-298682; www.theardenhotelstratford.com; Waterside; d incl breakfast from £129; P⊛@) Facing the Swan Theatre, this elegant property has a sleek brasserie and champagne bar. Rooms feature designer fabrics and bathrooms are full of polished stone.

✖ Eating

Sheep St is clustered with upmarket eating options, mostly aimed at theatre-goers (look out for good-value pre-theatre menus).

Fourteas
TEAROOM **£**

(☑01789-293908; www.thefourteas.co.uk; 24 Sheep St; dishes £3-7, afternoon tea with/without prosecco £17/12.50; ⊙9.30am-5pm Mon-Fri, 9am-5.30pm Sat, 11am-4pm Sun) Breaking with Stratford's Shakespearian theme, this tearoom takes the 1940s as its inspiration with beautiful old teapots, framed posters and staff in period costume. As well as premium loose-leaf teas and homemade cakes, there are hearty breakfasts, delicious sandwiches (fresh poached salmon, brie and grape), a hot dish of the day and indulgent afternoon teas.

Church Street Townhouse
BISTRO **££**

(☑01789-262222; www.churchstreettownhouse.com; 16 Church St; mains £12.25-17; ⊙8am-11pm; ⊛) This lovely restaurant is a fantastic place for immersing yourself in Stratford's historic charms. The food is delightful and the ambience impeccably congenial and well presented. Music students from Shakespeare's old grammar school across the way tinkle the piano ivories daily at 5.30pm, though it can be hard to hear over the bar noise.

Lambs
MODERN EUROPEAN **££**

(☑01789-292554; www.lambsrestaurant.co.uk; 12 Sheep St; mains £11.75-18.75; ⊙5-9.30pm Mon & Tue, noon-2pm & 5-9.30pm Wed-Sat, noon-2.30pm & 6-9pm Sun) Lambs swaps Shakespeare chintz in favour of Venetian blinds and modern elegance but throws in authentic 16th-century ceiling beams for good measure. The menu embraces Gressingham duck, deep-fried goats cheese and slow-roasted lamb shank, backed up by a strong wine list.

Edward Moon's
MODERN BRITISH **££**

(☑01789-267069; www.edwardmoon.com; 9 Chapel St; mains £10-18; ⊙12.30-3pm & 5-10pm Mon-Fri, noon-10pm Sat & Sun) Named after a famous travelling chef who cooked up the flavours of home for the British colonial service, this snug eatery serves delicious, hearty English dishes, many livened up with herbs and spices from the East.

◯ Drinking & Nightlife

★ Old Thatch Tavern
PUB

(http://oldthatchtavernstratford.co.uk; Greenhill St; ⊙11.30am-11pm Mon-Sat, noon-6pm Sun; ⊛) To truly appreciate Stratford's olde-worlde atmosphere, join the locals for a pint at the town's oldest pub. Built in 1470, this thatched-roofed, low-ceilinged treasure has great real ales and a gorgeous summertime courtyard.

Dirty Duck PUB
(Black Swan; Waterside; ⊙ 11am-11pm Mon-Sat, to 10.30pm Sun) Also called the 'Black Swan', this enchanting riverside alehouse is the only pub in England to be licensed under two names. It's a favourite thespian watering hole, with a roll-call of former regulars (Olivier, Attenborough et al) that reads like a who's who of actors.

Windmill Inn PUB
(Church St; ⊙ 11.30am-11pm Mon-Sat, 11am-11pm Sun) Ale was flowing here at the same time as rhyming couplets gushed from Shakespeare's quill – which means this pub with low ceilings has been around a while.

☆ Entertainment

★ **Royal Shakespeare Company** THEATRE
(RSC; ☑ 0844 800 1110; www.rsc.org.uk; Waterside; tickets £10-62.50) Coming to Stratford without seeing a Shakespeare production would be like visiting Beijing and bypassing the Great Wall. The three theatre spaces run by the world-renowned Royal Shakespeare Company have witnessed performances by such legends as Lawrence Olivier, Richard Burton, Judi Dench, Helen Mirren, Ian McKellan and Patrick Stewart.

Stratford has two grand stages – the Royal Shakespeare Theatre and the Swan Theatre on Waterside – as well as the smaller Courtyard Theatre (☑ 0844 800 1110; www.rsc.org.uk; Southern Lane). Contact the RSC for the latest news on performance times. There are often special deals for under 25-year-olds, students and seniors, and a few tickets are held back for sale on the day of the performance, but get snapped up fast. Book well ahead.

ℹ Information

Tourist Office (☑ 01789-264293; www.shakespeare-country.co.uk; Bridge Foot; ⊙ 9am-5.30pm Mon-Sat, 10am-4pm Sun) Just west of Clopton Bridge on the corner with Bridgeway.

ℹ Getting There & Away

CAR
If you're driving, be warned that town car parks charge high fees, 24 hours a day.

BUS
National Express coaches and other bus companies run from Stratford's Riverside bus station (behind the Stratford Leisure Centre on Bridgeway). Services include the following destinations:

Birmingham National Express; £8.40, one hour, twice daily
London Victoria National Express; £7, three hours, three daily
Oxford National Express; £10.70, one hour, twice daily
Warwick Bus 16; £3, 40 minutes, hourly.

TRAIN
From Stratford train station, London Midland runs to Birmingham (£7.30, 50 minutes, half-hourly); Chiltern Railways runs to London Marylebone (£9, 2 hours, up to two per hour).

The nostalgic **Shakespeare Express** (☑ 0121-708 4960; www.shakespeareexpress.com; adult/child £15/10) steam train chugs twice every Sunday in July and August between Stratford and Birmingham Snow Hill; journey time is one hour.

ℹ Getting Around

From April to October, a 1937-built, hand-wound **chain ferry** yo-yos across the Avon (one way 50p).

A bicycle is handy for getting out to the outlying Shakespeare properties. **Stratford Bike Hire** (☑ 07711-776340; www.stratfordbikehire.com; 7 Seven Meadows Rd; per half-day/day from £10/15) will deliver to your accommodation.

Punts, canoes and rowing boats are available for hire from Avon Boating (p429) near Clopton Bridge. Prices for canoes/rowboats per 30 minutes start from £3/5; punts are £20.

Around Stratford-upon-Avon

Charlecote Park

A youthful Shakespeare allegedly poached deer in the grounds of this lavish Elizabethan pile (NT; ☑ 01789-470277; www.nationaltrust.org.uk; adult/child £9.35/7.40, garden only £5/2.50; ⊙ noon-3.30pm Thu-Tue mid-Feb–mid-Mar, 11am-4.30pm Thu-Tue mid-Mar–Oct, noon-3.30pm Sat & Sun Nov & Dec, garden 10.30am-5.30pm Mar-Oct, to 4.30pm Nov-Feb) on the River Avon, 5 miles east of Stratford-upon-Avon. Fallow deer still roam the grounds today. The interiors were restored from Georgian chintz to Tudor splendour in 1823. Highlights include Victorian kitchens, filled with culinary-moulds, and an original 1551 Tudor gatehouse.

Bus 18 (18A on Sunday) runs to Charlecote hourly from Stratford (£2.30, 30 minutes), continuing to Leamington Spa (£2.30, 30 minutes).

STAFFORDSHIRE

Despite being wedged between the ever-expanding conurbations of Birmingham and Manchester, Staffordshire is surprisingly green, with the northern half of the county rising to meet the rugged hills of the Peak District.

❶ Information

Staffordshire Tourism (www.enjoystaffordshire.com)

❶ Getting There & Around

Regular trains and National Express buses serve Stafford and other major towns. The main local bus operator is **First Group** (☑ 08456 020 121; www.firstgroup.com). For details of services, browse the public transport pages at www.staffordshire.gov.uk.

Stafford

POP 68,470

The capital of Staffordshire is a quiet little place that seems somewhat overshadowed by other towns around the county, such as Lichfield. The main shopping street has some handsome Georgian and medieval buildings, but little evidence remains that this was once the capital of the Anglo-Saxon kingdom of Mercia.

◉ Sights

Ancient High House   MUSEUM
(☑ 01785-619131; www.staffordbc.gov.uk; Greengate St; ⊙ 10am-4pm Tue-Sat) FREE Surrounded by high-street shops, the Ancient High House is the largest timber-framed town house in the country, artistically assembled in 1595. Creaking stairways lead to carefully restored rooms, and to displays on the history of the town and medieval construction techniques.

Stafford Castle   RUIN
(☑ 01785-257698; www.staffordbc.gov.uk; Newport Rd; ⊙ visitor centre 11am-4pm Wed-Sun Apr-Oct, 11am-4pm Sat & Sun Nov-Mar) FREE The hilltop remains of Stafford Castle, a classic Norman moat and bailey, sit romantically in a forest glade about 1 mile southwest of town, just off the A518.

⨻ Sleeping & Eating

Swan   PUB ££
(☑ 01785-258142; www.theswanstafford.co.uk; 46-46a Greengate St; s/d from £85/105 mains £9.50-

23; ⊙ kitchen noon-10pm Mon-Sat, noon-4.30pm & 6-8.30pm Sun; P 🕿 🐾) Stafford's best place to sleep, eat and drink is a one-stop-shop. In the centre of town, this former coaching inn has 31 beautiful rooms (some with original stone fireplaces and wooden beams), an excellent brasserie-style restaurant, two bars (cocktail and traditional courtyard) and a cafe/tearoom. Parking's limited but free for overnight guests. The staff is a pleasure to deal with.

❶ Information

Tourist Office (☑ 01785-619619; www.visit-stafford.org; Eastgate St; ⊙ 9.30am-5pm Mon-Sat) For local info, drop into the tourist office at the Stafford Gatehouse Theatre.

❶ Getting There & Away

Bus 101 (£3.50, 1¼ hours, every 20 minutes, hourly on Sunday) runs between Stafford and Hanley (Stoke-on-Trent). Trains run to Birmingham (£10.20, 40 minutes, every 20 minutes).

Lichfield

POP 32,880

Even without its magnificent Gothic cathedral, one of the most spectacular in the country, this quaintly cobbled market town would be worth a visit to tread in the footsteps of lexicographer and wit Samuel Johnson, and natural philosopher Erasmus Darwin, grandfather of Charles. Johnson once described Lichfield folk as 'the most sober, decent people in England', which was rather generous considering that this was the last place in the country to stop burning people at the stake.

◉ Sights

Lichfield Cathedral   CATHEDRAL
(☑ 01543-306100; www.lichfield-cathedral.org; admission by donation; ⊙ 7.30am-6.15pm Sun-Fri, 8am-6.15pm Sat) Crowned by three dramatic towers, Lichfield Cathedral is a Gothic fantasy, constructed in stages from 1200 to 1350. The enormous vaulted nave is set slightly off line from the choir, creating a bizarre perspective when viewed from the west door, and carvings inside the cathedral still bear signs of damage caused by Civil War soldiers sharpening their swords.

In the octagonal Chapter House, you can view the illuminated *Chad Gospels*, created around AD 730; an ornate Anglo-Saxon bas-relief known as the *Lichfield Angel;* and a faded but glorious medieval wall painting above the door.

The grand west facade positively bows under the weight of 113 statues of bishops, saints and kings of England. Be sure to stroll the delightful, once-fortified Cathedral Close, ringed with imposing 17th- and 18th-century houses.

Erasmus Darwin House   HISTORIC BUILDING

(☑ 01543-306260; www.erasmusdarwin.org; Beacon St; adult/child £3/1; ⊙ 11am-5pm Tue-Sun Apr-Oct, noon-4.30pm Thu-Sun Nov-Mar) After turning down the job of royal physician to King George III – perhaps a lucky escape, considering the monarch's descent into madness – Erasmus Darwin became a leading light in the Lunar Society, debating the origins of life with such luminaries as Wedgwood, Boulton and Watt decades before his grandson Charles came up with the theory of evolution. The former house of the 'Grandfather of Evolution' contains some intriguing personal effects. At the back is a fragrant herb garden leading to Cathedral Close.

Samuel Johnson Birthplace Museum   MUSEUM, HISTORIC BUILDING

(☑ 01543-264972; www.samueljohnsonbirthplace.org.uk; Breadmarket St; ⊙ 10.30am-4.30pm Apr-Sep, 11am-3.30pm Oct-Mar) **FREE** This absorbing museum charts the life of the pioneering lexicographer, wit, poet and critic Samuel Johnson, who moved to London from his native Lichfield and devoted nine years to producing the first major dictionary of the English language. Ten years in the making, Johnson's first dictionary helped define the word 'dull' with this example: 'to make dictionaries is dull work'. On the 1st floor, a short dramatised film narrates Johnson's life story. It's a lovely property to explore.

Lichfield Heritage Centre   HERITAGE CENTRE

(☑ 01543-256611; www.stmaryslichfield.co.uk; Market Sq; adult/child £2.50/1, tower adult/child £2.75/1.25; ⊙ 9.30am-4pm Mon-Fri, to 5pm Sat, 10am-4pm Sun) Exhibits cover 1300 years of Lichfield history inside the old St Mary's

---

THEME PARK SHENANIGANS

Staffordshire is famous for its theme parks, which resound with the screams of adrenalin junkies lured here by fast and furious thrills. Buckle up: it's going to be a bumpy ride...

Alton Towers

Phenomenally popular **Alton Towers** (☑ 0871 222 3330; www.altontowers.com; adult/child £48/40.80, water park £16.50/11.75; ⊙ 10am-5pm, water park 10am-6pm, longer hours school holidays, weekends & high season, closed Nov-Mar), east of Cheadle off the B5032, offers maximum G-force for your buck. Roller-coaster fans are well catered for: as well as the vertical drop-ride Th13teen, you can ride lying down, sitting down or suspended from the rails on the Nemesis, Oblivion, Air and Rita; or brave 14 loops on the Smiler. Gentler thrills include log flumes, carousels, stage shows, a pirate-themed aquarium and a splashtastic water park. Book online for discounted entry fees and fast-track entry.

Most large towns in the area offer package coach tours (enquire at tourist offices), or you can ride bus 32A from Stoke-on-Trent (£7, 50 minutes, every two hours), or X52 Nottingham (£10, 40 minutes, hourly) and Derby (£8, 20 minutes, hourly).

Set in pleasant walking country, the miniature **Dimmingsdale YHA** (☑ 0845 371 9513; www.yha.org.uk; Oakamoor; dm from £16) is 2 miles northwest of Alton Towers.

Drayton Manor

Drayton Manor (☑ 0844 472 1960; www.draytonmanor.co.uk; adult/child £36/27; ⊙ 10.30am-5pm Easter-Oct, longer hours May-Sep) has been serving up screams since 1949. Crowd-pleasers include the Apocalypse free-fall tower, voted Britain's scariest ride, and Shockwave, Europe's only stand-up roller coaster. Younger kids will be just as thrilled by Thomas Land, dedicated to the animated steam-train character.

The theme park is on the A4091, between junctions 9 and 10 of the M42. Package coach tours run from Birmingham, or you can take bus 110 from Birmingham Corporation St to Fazeley (£10, one hour, every 20 minutes hourly on Sunday) and walk the last 15 minutes.

The park currently has no on-site accommodation, but Tamworth is just 2 miles away and has plenty of B&Bs and hotels. Contact **Tamworth Tourist Information** (☑ 01827-709581; www.visittamworth.co.uk; Corporation St; ⊙ 9am-7pm Mon-Fri, to 5pm Sat) for recommendations.

Church. Climb the tower's 120 steps for sweeping city views.

🛌 Sleeping

Bogey Hole
B&B **£**

(☎ 01543-264303; www.thebogeyhole.co.uk; 23 Dam St; s/d £40/60) A sweet little place near Lichfield Cathedral with bright and rather feminine en suite rooms, a lounge with TV, and a kitchen at the top and laundry room below. There's no signage; look for the quaint cream-coloured facade.

George Hotel
HOTEL **££**

(☎ 01543-414822; www.thegeorgelichfield.co.uk; 12-14 Bird St; s £80, d £90-103; P @ 🛜) Part of the Best Western chain, this old Georgian pub has been upgraded into a comfortable midrange hotel, scoring points for location rather than atmosphere.

🍴 Eating & Drinking

Chapters Cathedral Coffee Shop
CAFE **£**

(☎ 01543-306125; 19 The Close; dishes £3.50-7.75; ⊙ 8.30am-4pm Mon-Sat, 10am-4pm Sun) A fine 18th-century house overlooking its 13th-century walled garden on one side and the cathedral on the other, serving morning and afternoon tea and Sunday lunches.

Damn Fine Cafe
CAFE **£**

(16 Bird St; dishes £4-8; ⊙ 9am-4pm Tue, Thu & Fri, to 3.30pm Wed, to 5pm Sat, 10am-4pm Sun; 🚼) Teeming with locals, this cafe is a handy spot for sandwiches, soup, filling bacon-and-sausage breakfasts or vegetarian toad-in-the-hole. Order and pay at the counter.

⭐ Trooper
GASTROPUB **££**

(☎ 01543-480413; www.thetrooperwall.co.uk; Watling St, Wall; mains £9.50-23; ⊙ kitchen noon-9.15pm Mon-Wed, to 9.45pm Thu-Sat, to 8pm Sun) Situated 3 miles southwest of Lichfield in the tiny village of Wall, this idyllic gastropub prides itself on ingredients such as aged steak (served with hand-cut, beef-dripping-fried chips and sweet tomato chutney) and pork belly (with apple and quince jus) as well as vegetarian options using herbs from the pub's gardens. Fabulous real ales too.

Wine House
MODERN BRITISH **££**

(☎ 01543-419999; www.thewinehouselichfield. co.uk; 27 Bird St; mains £13-24; ⊙ noon-10pm Mon-Sat, to 6pm Sun) Astutely selected whites, reds, champagnes and rosés, including many by-the-glass options, complement the seriously good cooking at these smart, red-brick premises. Choices range from pancetta-wrapped, fig-stuffed pork fillet to steamed

---

WORTH A TRIP

THE POTTERIES

Situated at the heart of the Potteries – the famous pottery-producing region of Staffordshire – Stoke-on-Trent (population 248,720) is famed for its ceramics.

Don't expect cute little artisanal producers. This was where pottery shifted to mass production during the Industrial Revolution, and Stoke is a sprawl of industrial townships tied together by flyovers and bypasses. You really need your own wheels to get around.

There are dozens of active potteries; the **tourist office** (☎ 01782-236000; www.visit-stoke.co.uk; Victoria Hall, Bagnall St, Hanley; ⊙ 10am-4pm Tue-Sat), in Stoke-on-Trent's 'city centre' Hanley, has leaflets on all the potteries open to the public.

Potteries Museum & Art Gallery (☎ 01782-232323; www.stoke.gov.uk/museum; Bethesda St, Hanley; admission by donation; ⊙ 10am-5pm Mon-Sat & 2-5pm Sun) For a good overview of the history of the Potteries area, this Hanley museum houses an extensive ceramics display, from Toby jugs and jasperware to outrageous ornamental pieces such as the Minton Peacock. You can also see treasures from the outstanding Staffordshire Hoard; displays on the WWII Spitfire, created by the Stoke-born aviator Reginald Mitchell; and artworks by TS Lowry and Sir Henry Moore.

Wedgwood Visitor Centre (☎ 01782-282986; www.wedgwoodvisitorcentre.com; Wedgwood Dr, Barlaston; adult/child £10/8; ⊙ 10am-5pm Mon-Fri, to 4pm Sat & Sun) Set in attractive parkland 8 miles south of Hanley, the modern production centre for Josiah Wedgwood's porcelain empire displays an extensive collection of historic pieces, including plenty of Wedgwood's delicate, neoclassical blue-and-white jasperware. The fascinating industrial process is revealed, and there's an interesting film on Josiah's life and work, including his involvement in canal-building and opposition to slavery.

Scottish mussels with tail-on tiger prawns and squid-ink risotto.

Chandlers' Grande
Brasserie
MODERN EUROPEAN ££

(📞 01543-416688; www.chandlersrestaurant.co.uk; Conduit St; mains £9-24; ⊙ 11am-2pm & 6-11pm Mon-Sat; 🐾) Set in the old Corn Exchange and decked out with natural wood and polished brass. This is where locals go for a big night out, as much for the ambience as for the Mediterranean-inspired cuisine.

ℹ Information

Tourist Office (📞 01543-256611; www.stmaryslichfield.co.uk; Market Sq; ⊙ 9.30am-3.30pm Mon-Sat) In the Lichfield Heritage Centre.

ℹ Getting There & Away

The bus station is opposite the main train station on Birmingham Rd. Bus 825 serves Stafford (£3.40, 1½ hours, half-hourly, hourly on Sunday).

Lichfield has two train stations. Trains to Birmingham (£5.80, 40 minutes, every 20 minutes) leave from Lichfield City station in the centre. Trains to London Euston (£34, 1¾ hours, two per hour) run from Lichfield Trent Valley station.

WORCESTERSHIRE

Famed for its eponymous condiment, invented by two Worcester chemists in 1837, Worcestershire marks the transition from the industrial heart of the Midlands to the peaceful countryside of the Welsh Marches. The southern and western fringes of the county burst with lush countryside and sleepy market towns, while the capital is a classic English county town, whose magnificent cathedral inspired the composer Elgar to write some of his greatest works.

🏃 Activities

The longest riverside walk in the UK, the 210-mile Severn Way winds its way through Worcestershire en route from Plynlimon in Wales to the sea at Bristol. A shorter challenge is the 100-mile Three Choirs Way, linking Worcester to Hereford and Gloucester. The Malvern Hills are also prime country for walking and cycling – information is available at www.malvernhillsaonb.org.uk.

ℹ Information

Visit Worcestershire (www.visitworcestershire.org)

ℹ Getting Around

Worcester is a convenient rail hub. Kidderminster is the southern railhead of the quaint **Severn Valley Railway** (📞 01299-403816; www.svr.co.uk; ⊙ daily May-Sep, Sat & Sun Oct-Apr).

Buses connect larger towns, but services to rural areas can be frustratingly infrequent – search the transport pages at www.worcestershire.gov.uk for bus companies and timetables.

Worcester
POP 100,150

Worcester (pronounced *woos*-ter) has enough historic treasures to forgive the architectural eyesores from the postwar love affair with all things concrete. The home of the famous Worcestershire sauce (an unlikely combination of fermented tamarinds and anchovies), this ancient cathedral city was the site of the last battle of the Civil War, the Battle of Worcester, which took place on 3 September 1651. The defeated Charles II only narrowly escaped the pursuing Roundheads by hiding in an oak tree, an event still celebrated in Worcester every 29 May, when government buildings are decked out with oak sprigs.

◎ Sights

Worcester Cathedral CATHEDRAL
(📞 01905-732900; www.worcestercathedral.co.uk; admission by £5 donation, tower adult/child £4/2, tours £4/free; ⊙ 7.30am-6pm, tower 11am-5pm Sat Apr-Oct, tours 11am & 2.30pm Mon-Sat Mar-Nov, 11am & 2.30pm Sat Dec-Feb; 🐾) Rising above the River Severn, Worcester's majestic cathedral is best known as the final resting place of Magna Carta signatory King John. The strong-legged can tackle the 249 steps to the top of the **tower**, from where Charles II surveyed his troops during the disastrous Battle of Worcester. Hour-long **cathedral tours** run from the gift shop. Several works by local composer Edward Elgar had their first public outings at the cathedral – to appreciate the acoustics, come for **evensong** (5.30pm Monday to Saturday, 4pm Sunday).

Commandery MUSEUM
(📞 01905-361821; www.worcestercitymuseums.org.uk; College St; adult/child £5.50/2.50; ⊙ 10am-5pm Mon-Sat, 1.30-5pm Sun) The town's history museum is housed in a splendid Tudor building that served as King Charles II's headquarters during the Battle of Worcester. Engaging audioguides and interactive exhibits tell the story of Worcester during

WORTH A TRIP

ELGAR BIRTHPLACE MUSEUM

England's most popular classical composer is celebrated with appropriate pomp and circumstance at Elgar Birthplace Museum (☎01905-333224; www.elgarmuseum.org; Crown East Lane, Lower Broadheath; adult/child £7.50/3.50; ⊙11am-5pm Feb-late Dec) , housed in the humble cottage where Edward Elgar was born in 1857. Admission includes an audioguide with musical interludes so that you can appreciate what all the fuss is about.

Bus 308 goes from Worcester to Broadheath Common (£3.10, 15 minutes, three daily Monday to Saturday), from where it's a short walk to the museum.

key periods in its history. A highlight is the 'painted chamber', covered with intriguing 15th-century religious frescos.

Royal Worcester Porcelain Works MUSEUM
(☎01905-21247; www.museumofroyalworcester.org; Severn St; adult/child £6/free; ⊙10am-5pm Mon-Sat Mar-Oct, to 4pm Mon-Sat Nov-Feb) Up there with Crown Derby and Wedgwood, the Royal Worcester porcelain factory gained an edge over its rivals by picking up the contract to provide fine crockery to the English monarchy. An entertaining audio tour reveals some quirkier sides to the Royal Worcester story, including its brief foray into porcelain dentures and 'portable fonts' designed for cholera outbreaks. The shop has some splendid pieces, from monk-shaped candle-snuffers to decorated thimbles and pill boxes.

Tours

Worcester Walks WALKING TOUR
(☎01905-726311; www.worcesterwalks.co.uk; adult £5; ⊙11am Mon-Fri Apr-Sep) Popular half-hour walking tours.

Worcester River Cruises BOAT TOUR
(☎01905-611060; www.worcesterrivercruises.co.uk; adult/child £6/4; ⊙hourly noon-4pm Apr-Sep) Offers a different perspective of Worcester on 45-minute cruises on the River Severn aboard the 1926-built *Earl*. Departure times and days can vary.

Sleeping

Lenchford Inn INN ££
(☎01905-620229; www.thelenchfordinn.co.uk; Shrawley; d from £75; P⊞) An easy 8-mile drive

north of Worcester, this sprawling inn on the banks of the Severn is a tranquil haven. Its nine en suite rooms are old fashioned but spacious and clean, and all open onto a communal balcony or terrace with river views. There's a cavernous restaurant and sociable bar.

Barrington House B&B ££
(☎01905-422965; www.barringtonhouse.eu; 204 Henwick Rd; r £80-90; P@⊞) This lovely Georgian house by the river comes with wonderful views, a pretty walled garden and three plush bedrooms full of brocade, trim and super-king-sized beds. Hearty breakfasts include eggs from the owners' hens.

Ye Olde Talbot Hotel HOTEL ££
(☎01905-235730; www.oldenglishinns.co.uk; Friar St; s/d from £55/70; ⊞) Attached to a popular bar and bistro right in the centre, this tasteful inn dates back to the 13th century, but many of the rooms are housed in a modern extension. Ask for discounted parking in the nearby multistorey car park.

Diglis House Hotel HOTEL ££
(☎01905-353518; www.diglishousehotel.co.uk; Severn St; s/d from £70/105; P⊞) Next to the boathouse in a waterside setting, this rambling yet cosy 28-room Georgian house is a short stroll from the cathedral. The best rooms have four-poster beds and luxe bathrooms. Guests can work out at the nearby gym for free.

Eating

Mac & Jac's DELI, CAFE £
(www.macandjacs.co.uk; 44 Friar St; mains £5-12; ⊙9am-5pm Mon-Sat) This Friar St outfit has a lovely deli downstairs for quality titbits and a relaxing cafe upstairs for caffeine, sandwiches with fillings such as brie and grape, and a wholesome menu of hot dishes such as crispy pork belly with toasted almonds and coriander. There's a second location in Great Malvern (p438).

Little Ginger Pig CAFE, BISTRO £
(☎01905-338913; www.littlegingerpig.co.uk; 9-11 Copenhagen St; dishes £4.50-8; ⊙10am-3.30pm Tue-Fri, 8.30am-4.30pm Sat, 10am-3pm Sun; ⊞) The focus is on locally sourced, free-range produce and independent labels at this pleasant and frequently busy cafe, bistro and bar.

★Old Rectifying House MODERN BRITISH ££
(☎01905-619622; www.theoldrec.co.uk; North Parade; light menu £6-14, mains £12-23.50; ⊙kitchen noon-3pm & 6-9pm Tue-Thu, to 9.30pm Fri & Sat, to 4pm Sun) Worcester's hippest dining

space has a candlelit, painted-brick interior and umbrella-shaded courtyard tables. A switched-on menu of light bites includes burgers (haloumi, wild boar or Wagyu) and mains range from fish pie with curly kale to rare-breed longhorn ribeye steak. DJs often hit the decks in the lounge bar, which mixes mighty cocktails including a sparkling wine-topped 'millionaire's martini'.

🍷 Drinking & Nightlife

Hand in Glove   COCKTAIL BAR
(25 College St; ⊘ 4pm-midnight Mon-Thu, 3pm-1am Fri & Sat, 12.30pm-midnight Sun; 🠲) The muted charcoal-coloured facade doesn't give much away but inside this low-key, independent bar does whizz-bang cocktails.

Cardinal's Hat   PUB
(www.the-cardinals-hat.co.uk; 31 Friar St; ⊘ noon-11pm Mon-Sat, to 10.30pm Sun; 🠲) Despite looking as English as Tudor ruffs and claiming a resident ghost, this atmospheric Worcester institution with log-burning stoves sells Austrian beers in traditional steins and serves authentic Austrian delicacies at lunchtime.

☆ Entertainment

Marr's Bar   LIVE MUSIC
(📋 01905-613336; www.marrsbar.co.uk; 12 Pierpoint St; ⊘8pm-late) The best live-music venue for miles around, Marr's still has its original sprung dance floors from its days as a dance studio. There's a lively schedule of gigs, acts, comedy shows, acoustic and jamming evenings most nights.

🛍 Shopping

Chocolate Deli   FOOD
(📋 01905-611324; www.chocolatedeli.biz; 53 New St; ⊘10am-5pm Mon-Sat) At this cherry-red deli you can buy handcrafted chocolates (such as strawberry and pepper, Jack Daniels truffles or milk-chocolate pencils that actually write); taste them over a cuppa; or sign up for a one-day chocolate-making course (£60 to £99).

❶ Information

Tourist Office (📋 01905-726311; www.visit-worcester.com; Guildhall, High St; ⊘9.30am-5pm Mon-Sat)

❶ Getting There & Away

BUS
The bus station is inside the Crowngate Centre on Friary Walk.

Birmingham Bus 144; £3.50, 1¾ hours, every 20 minutes (hourly Sunday)
Great Malvern Bus 44; £3.50, 30 minutes, every 10 minutes Monday to Saturday (hourly on Sunday)
London Victoria National Express; £22.60, 3½ hours, three daily

TRAIN
Worcester Foregate is the main rail hub, but services also run from Worcester Shrub Hill. Regular trains include the following:
Birmingham £8.40, one hour, every 20 minutes
Hereford £8.90, 50 minutes, hourly
Ledbury £6.50, 25 minutes, half-hourly
London Paddington £30.50, 2½ hours, twice hourly

Great Malvern

POP 36,770

Tumbling down the side of a forested ridge about 7 miles southwest of Worcester, the picturesque spa town of Great Malvern is the gateway to the Malverns, a soaring 9-mile-long range of volcanic hills that rise from the surrounding meadows. In Victorian times, the medicinal waters were prescribed as a panacea for everything from gout to 'sore eyes' – you can test the theory by sampling Malvern water straight from the ground at public wells dotted around the town.

◉ Sights

Great Malvern Priory   MONASTERY
(📋 01684-561020; www.greatmalvernpriory.org.uk; Church St; ⊘9am-5pm) **FREE** The 11th-century Great Malvern Priory is packed with remarkable features, from original Norman pillars to surreal modernist stained glass. The choir is enclosed by a screen of 15th-century tiles and the monks' stalls are decorated with delightfully irreverent 14th-century misericords, depicting everything from three rats hanging a cat to the mythological reptile, the basilisk. Charles Darwin's daughter Annie is buried here.

Malvern Museum of Local History   MUSEUM
(📋 01684-567811;   www.malvernmuseum.co.uk; Priory Gatehouse, Abbey Rd; adult/child £2/50p; ⊘10.30am-5pm Mar-Oct) Straddling Abbey Rd in the grand Priory Gatehouse (c 1470), the town museum offers a thorough exploration of Great Malvern's claims to fame, including spring waters, medieval monasteries, the Malvern Hills and Morgan Motors.

★ **Morgan Motor Company** MUSEUM
(☎ 01684-584580; www.morgan-motor.co.uk; Pickersleigh Rd; tours adult/child £12.50/7.50; ☺ 8.30am-5pm Mon-Thu, to 2.30pm Fri) FREE Morgan has been handcrafting elegant sports cars since 1909, and you can still see the mechanics at work on guided tours of the unassuming shed-like buildings comprising the factory (prebooking essential), and view a fleet of vintage classics. Bus 44 from Church St runs past the factory. If buying one of these beautiful machines is beyond your budget, you can rent one from £190 per day, including insurance, for a spin through the Malvern Hills.

☞ Tours

Great Malvern Walking Tours WALKING TOUR
(adult/child £3/50p; ☺ tours 10.30am Sat & Sun Apr-Sep) Walking tours departing from the tourist office explore the town's medieval and Victorian history.

⌷ Sleeping

Bredon House HOTEL ££
(☎ 01684-566990; www.bredonhouse.co.uk; 34 Worcester Rd; s/d from £45/70; P @) A short saunter from the centre, this genteel family- and pet-friendly Victorian hotel backs onto a stunning vista. Rooms are decorated in a quirky but tasteful mix of new and old, and the books, magazines and family photo-

> ## WALKING IN THE MALVERN HILLS
>
> The jack-in-the-box Malvern Hills, which dramatically pop up out of the Severn plains on the boundary between Worcestershire and Herefordshire, rise to the lofty peak of the Worcester Beacon (419m), reached by a steep 3-mile climb above Great Malvern. More than 100 miles of trails traipse over the various summits, which are mostly capped by exposed grassland, offering the kind of views that inspire orchestral movements.
>
> The Great Malvern tourist office has racks of pamphlets covering popular hikes, including a map of the mineral-water springs, wells and fountains of the town and surrounding hills. The enthusiast-run website www.malvern-trail.co.uk is also a goldmine of useful walking information.
>
> A single £3 parking ticket per day is valid at locations throughout the hills.

graphs dotted around the place mean it feels like staying with relatives.

Abbey Hotel HOTEL £££
(☎ 01684-892332; www.sarova-abbeyhotel.com; Abbey Rd; d £180-220; P @) Tangled in vines like a Brothers Grimm fairy-tale castle, this stately property has 103 elegant rooms in a prime location by the museum and priory.

✗ Eating

Mac & Jac's CAFE £
(www.macandjacs.co.uk; 23 Abbey Rd; dishes £4.50-11; ☺ 9am-7pm Tue-Sat, 10am-4pm Sun) Creative salads, flatbreads, sharing plates, spelt risotto and a savoury tart of the day are served up at this fresh addition to the town's dining scene. It's the sister branch of the Worcester (p436) cafe, set in a chic white-painted shopfront near the Great Malvern Priory. Look out for supper evenings (two-/three-course menus £25/29; dates vary).

St Ann's Well Cafe CAFE £
(☎ 01684-560285; www.stannswell.co.uk; dishes £1.50-4; ☺ 11.30am-3.30pm Tue-Fri, 10am-4pm Sat & Sun Easter-Sep) A s-t-e-e-p climb above St Ann's Rd (so best to check opening times beforehand with the tourist office), this quaint cafe is set in an early 19th-century villa, with mountain-fresh spring water bubbling into a carved basin by the door.

Fig Tree MODERN BRITISH ££
(☎ 01684-569909; www.thefigtreemalvern.co.uk; 99b Church St; mains £13-18; ☺ 10am-10pm Tue-Sat) Tucked down an alleyway off Church St, this 19th-century former stable serves Mediterranean-inspired fare such as marinated pork chops with caramelised apple, red onion and rosemary potatoes, and char-grilled chicken with minted yoghurt and saffron rice.

☆ Entertainment

Malvern Theatres THEATRE
(☎ 01684-892277; www.malvern-theatres.co.uk; Grange Rd) One of the country's best provincial theatres, this long-established cultural hub packs in a lively program of classical music, dance, comedy, drama and cinema.

Theatre of Small Convenience THEATRE
(☎ 01684-568933; www.wctheatre.co.uk; Edith Walk; shows adult/child £2.50/1.50) Set in a converted Victorian public lavatory decked out with theatrical Italianate flourishes, this quirky place has just 12 seats and a program running from puppet shows to poetry and opera. Shows usually last five to 10 minutes.

ℹ Information

Tourist Office (☏ 01684-892289; www.visit-themalverns.org; 21 Church St; ☻10am-5pm Apr-Oct, to 4pm Nov-Mar) The tourist office is a mine of walking and cycling information.

ℹ Getting There & Around

National Express runs one bus daily to London Victoria (£21.70, five hours). For Worcester, take bus 44 (£3.50, 30 minutes, every 10 minutes Monday to Saturday, hourly on Sunday).

The train station is east of the centre, off Ave Rd. Services include the following:

Hereford £7.50, 35 minutes, hourly

Ledbury £4.80, 13 minutes, hourly

Worcester £5, 15 to 20 minutes, two or three hourly

HEREFORDSHIRE

Slumbering in the English countryside, Herefordshire is a patchwork of fields, hills and cute little black-and-white villages, many dating back to the Tudor era and beyond. Getting around is complicated by infrequent bus services and meandering country lanes, but taking the scenic route is part of the appeal of this laid-back rural idyll.

🏃 Activities

As well as the famous **Offa's Dyke Path**, walkers can follow the **Herefordshire Trail** (www.herefordshiretrail.com) on a 150-mile circular loop through Leominster, Ledbury, Ross-on-Wye and Kington. Only slightly less ambitious is the 136-mile **Wye Valley Walk** (www.wyevalleywalk.org), which runs from Chepstow in Wales through Herefordshire and back out again to Plynlimon. Then there's the **Three Choirs Way**, a 100-mile route connecting the cathedrals of Hereford, Worcester and Gloucester.

Cyclists can trace the **Six Castles Cycleway** (NCN Route 44) from Hereford to Leominster and Shrewsbury, or NCN Route 68 to Great Malvern and Worcester.

ℹ Information

Visit Herefordshire (www.visitherefordshire.co.uk)

ℹ Getting Around

For bus timetables, contact Traveline (p410). Alternatively, pick up the chunky *Bus and Train Timetable* from any tourist office (50p). Trains run frequently to Hereford, Leominster and Ledbury, with irregular bus connections on to the rest of the county.

Hereford

POP 60,410

Dozing in the midst of apple orchards and rolling pastures at the heart of the Marches, straddling the River Wye, Hereford is best known for prime steaks, cider and the Pretenders – three of the original band members (guitarist James Honeyman-Scott, bassist Pete Farndon and drummer Martin Chambers) were local boys.

SIPPING (AND SUPPING) YOUR WAY AROUND CIDER COUNTRY

Herefordshire Cider Route (www.ciderroute.co.uk) The Herefordshire Cider Route drops in on numerous local cider producers, where you can try before you buy, and then totter off to the next cidery. Mindful of road safety, tourist offices have maps and guide booklets to help you explore by bus or bicycle.

Westons Cider Mills (☏ 01531-660108; www.westons-cider.co.uk; The Bounds; tours adult/child £7.50/4; ☻9am-5pm Mon-Fri, 10am-4.30pm Sat & Sun) If you only have time to visit one cider-maker, make it Westons Cider Mills, just under a mile west of the tiny village of Much Marcle, whose house brew is even served in the Houses of Parliament. Informative tours (1¼ hours) start at 11am, 12.30pm and 2.30pm, with free cider and perry tastings for the grown-ups. There's also a fascinating bottle museum.

Walwyn Arms (☏ 01531-660601; www.walwynarms.co.uk; Much Marcle; mains £9.50-17; ☻kitchen noon-2.30pm & 6-9.30pm Mon-Sat, noon-4pm & 6-9pm Sun) Westons ciders are served at this welcoming country pub, just across from Westons Cider Mills. Cider is also used in many dishes, such as the scrumptious twice-baked, mature cheddar and Old Rosie scrumpy soufflé, and cider-battered haddock fillet, with chips and mushy peas. Great lunchtime sandwiches (eg prawn and Bloody Mary mayonnaise) on hand-cut bread, too.

⊙ Sights

Hereford Cathedral　　　　　CATHEDRAL
(☑01432-374200; www.herefordcathedral.org; 5 College Cloisters; cathedral entry by £5 donation, Mappa Mundi £6; ⊙9.15am to evensong, Mappa Mundi 10am-5pm Mon-Sat May-Sep, to 4pm Mon-Sat Oct-Apr, evensong 5.30pm Mon-Sat, 3.30pm Sun) After Welsh marauders torched the original Saxon cathedral, the Norman rulers of Hereford erected a larger, grander cathedral on the same site, which was subsequently remodelled in a succession of medieval architectural styles.

The signature highlight is the magnificent **Mappa Mundi**, a single piece of calfskin vellum intricately painted with some rather fantastical assumptions about the layout of the globe in around 1290. The same wing contains the world's largest surviving chained library of rare manuscripts manacled to the shelves.

Heated by four impressive Gurney stoves, the magnificent cathedral comes alive with **evensong**, and every three years in August it holds the famous Three Choirs Festival (www.3choirs.org), shared with Gloucester and Worcester Cathedrals.

In the cloisters you'll find an atmospheric cafe.

Old House　　　　　MUSEUM
(☑01432-260694; ⊙10am-5pm Tue-Sat year-round, to 4pm Sun Apr-Sep) **FREE** This gloriously creaky black-and-white, three-storey wooden house was built in 1621. Climb upstairs for beautifully kept medieval rooms with period furniture (including 17th-century cradles), carved wood panelling and antique cast-iron firebacks.

Hereford Museum & Art Gallery　　　MUSEUM
(☑01432-260692; www.herefordshire.gov.uk/museums; Broad St; ⊙10am-5pm Tue-Sat year-round, to 4pm Sun Apr-Sep) **FREE** The eclectic town museum has displays on just about everything from 19th-century witches' curses to Roman antiquities.

Cider Museum &
King Offa Distillery　　　　　BREWERY
(☑01432-354207; www.cidermuseum.co.uk; 21 Ryeland St; adult/child £5.50/3; ⊙10am-5pm Mon-Sat Apr-Oct, 11am-3pm Mon-Sat Nov-Mar) Displays at this brewery and museum cover cider-making history and you can sample the delicious modern brews. Look for the fine *costrels* (minibarrels) used by agricultural workers to carry their wages, which were partially paid in cider. It's about half-a-mile west of the centre; follow Eign St and turn south along Ryelands St.

⌓ Tours

Guided walks　　　　　WALKING TOUR
(adult/child £3.50/free; ⊙11am Mon-Sat, 3pm Sun May-Sep) Guided walks start from the tourist office, exploring less well known historic sights in the centre.

Ultimate Left Bank　　　　　CANOEING
(☑01432-264807; www.leftbankcanoehire.com; Bridge St; canoe hire half-day/day £20/25) Rents open canoes to paddle along the River Wye.

⌂ Sleeping

Kidwells Guest House　　　　　B&B £
(☑01432-264625; www.kidwellshouse.com; 9 Newtown Rd; s/d with en suite £50/60, without bathroom £35/50; P🖥) This warm and welcoming B&B in the north of town has comfortable rooms in varying categories, some with big balconies. A sunlit conservatory opens onto a large garden. Guests can use a gym, located 3 miles from the guesthouse and run by the same owners, for free.

Charades　　　　　B&B ££
(☑01432-269444; www.charadeshereford.co.uk; 32 Southbank Rd; s/d from £50/65; P@🖥) Handy for the bus station, this imposing Victorian house has five inviting rooms with high ceilings, big and bright windows, and

some with soothing countryside views. The house itself has character in spades – look for old service bells in the hall and the plentiful Titanic memorabilia.

★ **Castle House** BOUTIQUE HOTEL £££
(☑01432-356321; www.castlehse.co.uk; Castle St; s/d/ste from £130/150/195; P@☎) Set in a regal Georgian town house that was once the luxurious digs of the Bishop of Hereford, this tranquil hotel has a sophisticated restaurant, sun-kissed garden spilling down to the river, and magnificent rooms and suites. Eight newer rooms are a short walk away at 25 Castle St. Wheelchair accessible.

✕ Eating & Drinking

Hereford Deli DELI £
(http://thehereforddeli.com; 4 The Mews, St Owen St; sandwiches £2-3; ☺8am-6pm Mon-Fri, 9am-5pm Sat) Great for lunch on the run or eaten at the clutch of tables, sandwiches at this gourmet emporium are a steal. Combinations include curried free-range chicken with mango chutney, Scottish smoked salmon with lemon-and-dill butter, or local roast beef with Cropwell Bishop Stilton and rosehip jelly. It's hidden down a narrow laneway near a large public car park.

Cafe@All Saints CAFE £
(☑01432-370415; www.cafeatallsaints.co.uk; High St; mains £6-10; ☺8am-5pm Mon-Sat; ☎♿) Inside the renovated nave of All Saint's Church, this inviting licensed cafe has wholesome daily specials, kicking off from 8am with bacon butties, eggy bread and breakfasts. There's outside seating for warmer days.

La Madeleine FRENCH ££
(☑01432-265 233; www.la-madeleine.co.uk; 17 Church St; mains £11-16; ☺10am-4pm Mon, Tue & Thu, to 4pm & 6-9pm Wed, to 4pm & 6-10pm Fri, 9am-5pm Sat) ✐ A pretty, bare-boards interior, outdoor tables in the vine-draped garden and a stylish French menu – breakfast croissants, lunchtime tarts and dinner dishes such as fillet steak with horseradish crème fraîche, fries and green-bean salad – are enough to make any Parisian homesick.

Lichfield Vaults PUB
(www.lichfieldvaultshereford.co.uk; 11 Church St; ☺11am-midnight Sun-Thu, to 2am Fri & Sat) On a cobbled lane near the cathedral, sociable 18th-century pub 'The Lich' opens to a decked beer garden out back. Regular live-music events include a monthly jazz Sunday lunch. Jovial Greek Cypriot host Andy serves up superior Greek food including meatballs, mezze plates and more.

Black Lion PUB
(www.theblacklionhereford.co.uk; 31 Bridge St; ☺10am-11pm) The more real ales and local ciders you knock back in this traditional pub, the more you may believe the tales of resident ghosts from the site's history as a monastery, an orphanage, a brothel and even a Chinese restaurant. There's regular live music.

Jailhouse CLUB
(http://thejailhouse.wordpress.com; Gaol St; ☺10pm-3am Wed-Sat) Edgy, underground DJs and alternative sounds are constantly on the billing at Hereford's leading club. Look out for secret sets by big-name spinners.

❶ Information

Tourist Office (☑01432-268430; www.visit herefordshire.co.uk; 1 King St; ☺9.30am-5pm Mon-Sat) Opposite the cathedral.

❶ Getting There & Around

The bus station is on Commercial Rd, northeast of the town centre. National Express goes to London Victoria (£20.20, 4½ hours, five daily) and Gloucester (£5.50, one hour, four daily). Local services include the following:

Ross-on-Wye Bus 44; £3.50, 50 minutes, five daily Monday to Friday, four Saturday

Worcester Bus 420; £8.90, 1¼ hours, five daily Monday to Saturday, four Sunday

The train station is northeast of the centre, with hourly trains to Birmingham (£15.20, 1½ hours), Ledbury (£6.50, 20 minutes), London Paddington (£38.50, three hours) – either direct or with a change in Newport, South Wales. Half-hourly services head to Ludlow (£9.50, 30 minutes).

Ross-on-Wye

POP 10,580

Set on a red sandstone bluff over a kink in the River Wye, hilly Ross-on-Wye was propelled to fame in the 18th century by Alexander Pope and Samuel Taylor Coleridge, who penned tributes to philanthropist John Kyrle, Man of Ross, who dedicated his life and fortune to the poor of the parish.

◉ Sights

Market House HERITAGE CENTRE
(☑01989-260675; ☺10am-5pm Mon-Sat, 10.30am-4pm Sun Apr-Oct, to 4pm Mon-Sat Nov-Mar) FREE The 17th-century Market House sits atop weathered sandstone columns in Market Pl;

inside the salmon-pink building the heritage centre has local history displays.

St Mary's Church
CHURCH

(Church St; ⊙ 9am-5pm) Crowning the hilltop, pin-straight St Mary's Church is a 13th-century building with a fine east window and grand alabaster memorials, including the grave of John Kyrle and the outrageously ostentatious tombs of the noble Rudhall family. Behind the church, Royal Pde runs to the edge of the bluff, lined with realistic-looking but ersatz castle ruins, constructed in 1833.

🛏 Sleeping & Eating

White House Guest House
B&B ££

(☑ 01989-763572; www.whitehouseross.com; 13 Wye St; s/d/tr/f £50/70/90/100; P@🕿) This 18th-century stone house has a great location across the road from the River Wye. Vivid window boxes give it a splash of colour, and the quiet and comfortable rooms are decorated in shades of burgundy and crisp white.

Truffles Delicatessen
DELI £

(www.trufflesdeli.co.uk; 46 High St; dishes £2.50-3.50; ⊙ 8am-5pm Mon-Sat, 11am-5pm Sun) Packed to the rafters with local artisan products (cheeses, breads, chutneys et al), Truffles also has stellar sandwiches, soups and salad boxes to take away for a riverside picnic.

Pots & Pieces
CAFE £

(www.potsandpieces.com; 40 High St; mains £5-6; ⊙ 9am-5pm Mon-Fri, 10am-5pm Sat, 11am-4pm Sun) The best of the tearooms around the market place, with ceramics and crafts to browse.

BLACK-AND-WHITE VILLAGES

A triangle of Tudor England survives almost untouched in northwest Herefordshire, where higgledy-piggledy black-and-white houses cluster around idyllic village greens, seemingly oblivious to the modern world. A delightful 40-mile circular drive follows the Black and White Village Trail (www.blackandwhitetrail.org), meandering past the most handsome timber-framed buildings. It starts at Leominster and loops round through Eardisland and Kington, the southern terminus of the Mortimer Trail from Ludlow.

Pick up guides to exploring the villages by car, bus or bicycle at tourist offices.

King's Head
INN ££

(☑ 01989-763174; www.kingshead.co.uk; 8 High St; d £85-110, mains £11-21; ⊙ kitchen noon-2.15pm & 6.30-9.00pm; 🕿) On the atmospheric High St, this unassuming 14th-century inn is a charmer. Dining highlights – in the low-lit front restaurant or glass conservatory – include seafood in champagne bisque, steaks and pies. Some of its chocolate-toned rooms have four-poster beds; there's limited guest parking. Two caveats: vegetarian options are limited and there's no access for travellers with disabilities.

ℹ Information

Tourist Office (☑ 01989-562768; www.herefordshire.gov.uk; Market House, Market Pl; ⊙ 10.30am-4.30pm Wed-Mon Apr-Sep, to 4pm Sun Oct-Mar) Has information on sights and walks – ask for the *Ross-on-Wye Heritage Trail* booklet (50p). Note that it closes every second Sunday throughout the year.

ℹ Getting There & Around

The bus stand is on Cantilupe Rd. Bus 44 runs hourly to Hereford (£3.50, 45 minutes, five daily Monday to Friday, four on Saturdays).

Ledbury

POP 8860

Creaking with history and dotted with antique shops, Ledbury's crooked black-and-white streets zero in on a delightfully leggy medieval Market House. The timber-framed structure is precariously balanced atop a series of wooden posts supposedly taken from the wrecked ships of the Spanish Armada.

Almost impossibly cute Church Lane runs its cobbled way from the High St to the town church, crowded with tilting timber-framed buildings.

At the top of the lane lies the 12th-century church of St Michael and All Angels (www.ledburyparishchurch.org.uk; ⊙ 9am-5.30pm), with a splendid 18th-century spire and tower divided from its medieval nave.

🛏 Sleeping & Eating

The town pubs offer reasonably priced meals, but budget travellers will struggle to find cheap accommodation.

Feathers Hotel
HOTEL £££

(☑ 01531-635266; www.feathers-ledbury.co.uk; High St; s/d from £97.50/145, mains £13.50-25; P🕿🛏) This charming black-and-white Tudor hotel looms over the main road in Ledbury. Rooms in the oldest part of the building come with sloping floorboards, painted beams and much more character than the modern rooms. There's an atmospheric wood-panelled restaurant and an indoor heated swimming pool.

Chez Pascal FRENCH **££**
(☑ 01531-634443; Church Lane; mains £14-15; ⊙ 9.30am-5.30pm Mon-Thu, to 11pm Fri & Sat) Set in a delightful courtyard with garden tables, this place is the go-to address of locals for fine dining. French owner/chef/patissier Pascal's mains include classics such as pan-fried pheasant in red wine, seafood ragout and fish gratin, but it's desserts such as ginger and lemon torte and raspberry tarts that are the stars of the show.

🛍 Shopping

Three Counties Cider Shop DRINK
(www.threecountiescider.co.uk; 5a The Homend; ⊙ 10am-5.30pm Tue-Thu, to 6pm Fri & Sat) The aroma of apples pervades this charming little shop filled with artisan cider, perry and juices from producers in three counties (Herefordshire, Worcestershire and Gloucestershire). A dozen ciders and perries are on tap to try; you can also buy locally produced gourmet goods including cider chocolates, chutneys and jams.

❶ Getting There & Away

Buses are limited but regular train services include the following:
Great Malvern £4.80, 10 minutes, hourly
Hereford £6.50, 15 minutes, hourly
Worcester £6.50, 30 minutes, hourly

SHROPSHIRE

Sleepy Shropshire is a glorious scattering of hills, castles and timber-framed villages tucked against the Welsh border. Highlights include food-obsessed Ludlow, industrial Ironbridge and the beautiful Shropshire Hills, which offer the best walking and cycling in the Marches.

🏃 Activities

Walking
The towering Shropshire Hills call out to walkers like a siren. Between Shrewsbury and Ludlow, the landscape rucks up into dramatic folds, with spectacular trails

climbing the flanks of **Wenlock Edge** and the **Long Mynd** near Church Stretton. The county is also crossed by long-distance trails, including the famous **Offa's Dyke Path** and the popular **Shropshire Way**, which meanders around Ludlow and Church Stretton. For general information on walking in the county, visit www.shropshire walking.co.uk.

Cycling
Mountain bikers head for the muddy tracks that scramble over the **Long Mynd** near Church Stretton, while road riders aim for the **Six Castles Cycleway** (NCN 44), which runs for 58 miles from Shrewsbury to Leominster.

Tourist offices sell copies of *Cycling for Pleasure in the Marches,* a pack of five maps and guides covering the entire county. You can also download free cycling pamphlets from www.travelshropshire.co.uk.

❶ Information

Secret Shropshire (www.secretshropshire. org.uk)
Shropshire Tourism (www.shropshiretourism. co.uk)

❶ Getting Around

Shrewsbury is the local transport hub, and handy rail services go to Church Stretton and Ludlow. The invaluable *Shropshire Bus & Train Map,* available free from tourist offices, shows useful routes. **Shropshire Hills Shuttles** (www. shropshirehillsshuttles.co.uk) runs useful bus services along popular hiking routes on weekends and bank holidays.

Shrewsbury

POP 71,710
A delightful jumble of winding medieval streets and timbered Tudor houses leaning at precarious angles, Shrewsbury (*shroosbree*) was a crucial front in the conflict between English and Welsh in medieval days. Even today, the road bridge running east towards London is known as the English Bridge to mark it out from the Welsh Bridge leading northwest towards Holyhead. Shrewsbury is also the birthplace of Charles Darwin (1809–82).

◉ Sights

The most handsome buildings can be found on the narrow lanes surrounding **St Alkmond's Church** (AD 912), particularly along **Fish St** and amorously named **Grope Lane**.

Shrewsbury

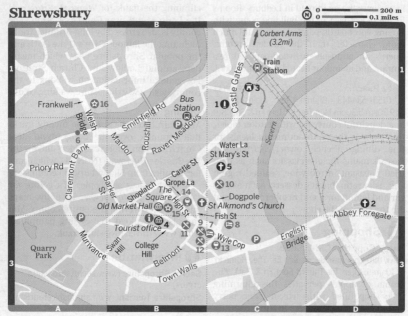

Shrewsbury

◎ Sights
1 Charles Darwin Statue C1
2 Shrewsbury Abbey D2
3 Shrewsbury Castle C1
4 Shrewsbury Museum & Art
   Gallery B3
5 St Mary's Church C2

◆ Activities, Courses & Tours
6 Sabrina A2

🛏 Sleeping
7 Lion Hotel...C3
8 Old House Suites C3

✕ Eating
9 Appleyards Delicatessen......................B3
10 Drapers Hall C2
11 Golden Cross B3
12 Good Life Wholefood
   Restaurant..B3

🍷 Drinking & Nightlife
13 Henry Tudor House.............................C3
14 Three Fishes.......................................B2

✪ Entertainment
15 Old Market Hall Film & Digital
   Media B2
16 Theatre Severn A1

In a cute cobbled square, Shrewsbury's 16th-century **Old Market Hall** contains the town's pocket-sized cinema.

St Mary's Church   CHURCH
(www.visitchurches.org.uk; St Mary's St; ◎10am-5pm Mon-Sat May-early Dec, to 4pm Mon-Sat early Dec-Apr) The fabulous interior of this tall-spired medieval church contains an impressive collection of stained glass, including a 1340 window depicting the Tree of Jesse (a biblical representation of the lineage of Jesus) and a magnificent oak ceiling in the nave, which largely collapsed in a huge gale in 1894 when the top of the spire blew off. Much of the glass in the church is sourced from Europe, including some outstanding Dutch glass from 1500.

Shrewsbury Abbey   CHURCH
(☎01743-232723; www.shrewsburyabbey.com; Abbey Foregate; admission by donation; ◎10am-4pm Apr-Oct, 10.30am-3pm Nov-Mar) All that remains of a vast, cruciform Benedictine monastery founded in 1083 is the lovely red-sandstone Shrewsbury Abbey. Twice the setting for meetings of the English Parliament, the Abbey church lost its spire and

two wings when the monastery was dissolved in 1540. It sustained further damage in 1826 when engineer Thomas Telford ran the London–Holyhead road right through the grounds. Nevertheless, you can still see some impressive Norman, Early English and Victorian features, including an exceptional 14th-century west window.

It's famous as the setting for Ellis Peters' *Chronicles of Brother Cadfael*.

Shrewsbury Museum & Art Gallery MUSEUM
(☎01743-258885; www.shrewsburymuseums.com; The Square; adult/child £4/2; ⏰10am-5pm) Newly housed in the Music Hall along with the tourist office, the town museum has diverse exhibits covering everything from Roman treasures to Shropshire gold, including the Bronze Age Perry bracelet. Its Prehistory and Roman Gallery is free of charge.

Shrewsbury Castle CASTLE
(☎01743-358516; www.shrewsburymuseum.org.uk; adult/child £2.50/1.50; ⏰10.30am-5pm Mon-Wed, Fri & Sat, to 4pm Sun late May–mid-Sep, 10.30am-4pm Mon-Wed, Fri & Sat mid-Sep–late May) Hewn from flaking red Shropshire sandstone, the town castle contains the **Shropshire Regimental Museum**, plus fine views from **Laura's Tower** and the battlements. The lower level of the **Great Hall** dates from 1150.

Charles Darwin Statue MONUMENT
The town's most famous son, naturalist Charles Darwin, was born in the Mount in Shrewsbury's Frankwell area in 1809. He's commemorated by a statue outside the town library, formerly the Shrewsbury School, where he was educated.

Tours

Shrewsbury Walking Tours WALKING TOUR
(☎01743-258888; adult/child £4/2.50; ⏰2.30pm Mon-Sat, 11am Sun May-Sep) Guided walking tours leave from the tourist office.

Sabrina BOAT TOUR
(☎01743-369741; www.sabrinaboat.co.uk; adult/child £7.50/3.50; ⏰hourly 11am-4pm Mar-Oct) Enjoy Shrewsbury from the water on board the Sabrina, which cruises the River Severn. Trips leave from Victoria Quay near the Welsh Bridge. Ghost cruises run from 7.30pm to 10.30pm on Monday evenings ($7.50/3.50). There are music nights from 7.30pm to 10.30pm on Tuesdays (£5).

Sleeping

Pretty Abbey Foregate is lined with B&Bs.

Corbet Arms PUB ££
(☎01743-709232; www.thecorbetarms.com; Church Rd, Uffington; d £65-95; P 📶) Situated 4 miles east of Shrewsbury in the pint-sized village of Uffington, this peaceful, family-friendly pub has nine beautifully appointed en suite rooms reached by a staircase. Try for top-floor room 10, which has exposed beams, a spacious sitting area and panoramic views of the surrounding countryside. Also serves high-quality food including outstanding Sunday roasts.

Old House Suites HISTORIC HOTEL ££
(☎07813-610904; www.theoldhousesuites.com; The Old House, 20 Dogpole; ste £85-125; P @) Shrewsbury's most historic place to hang your tricorn, the Old House has three lavish suites, all with views of the garden from a gloriously crooked timbered Tudor town house that was once owned by one of Catherine of Aragon's courtiers. The owner conducts hour-long history tours of the property for guests. There's no sign, but it's up the steps from the Dogpole bus stop.

Lion Hotel HOTEL ££
(☎01743-353107; www.thelionhotelshrewsbury.com; Wyle Cop; s/d/ste incl breakfast from £80/108/140; P) A gilded wooden lion crowns the doorway of this famous 16th-century coaching inn, decked out inside with portraits of lords and ladies in powdered wigs. Charles Dickens was a former guest, and the lounge is warmed by a grand stone fireplace. Rooms are lovely, right down to the period-pattern fabrics and ceramic water jugs.

Eating

Good Life Wholefood Restaurant VEGETARIAN £
(☎01743-350455; Barracks Passage; mains £3.50-7; ⏰9am-4pm Mon-Sat; 🖉) 🌿 Wholesome, freshly prepared vegetarian food is dished up at this healthy refuge off Wyle Cop. Favourites include quiches, nut loaf, salads, soups, veggie lasagne and a lovely spinach moussaka.

Appleyards Delicatessen DELI £
(☎01743-240180; 85 Wyle Cop; ⏰9am-5pm Tue-Sat) Fantastic traditional shop stuffed with a cornucopia of cheeses and beers.

Golden Cross
MODERN BRITISH ££

(☑ 01743-362507; www.goldencrosshotel.co.uk; 14 Princess St; lunch mains £10.50-14, dinner mains £11.50-19.50; ⊙ kitchen noon-2.30pm & 6-10pm) Overwhelmingly romantic, this candlelit inn dating from 1428 has an inventive, impeccably executed menu, with dishes such as semolina-crusted ricotta-and-nutmeg dumplings, BBQ-glazed ribs with pineapple salsa and smoked garlic, and duck with plum sauce. Upstairs, five exquisite guest rooms (doubles £75 to £150) have luxurious touches including free-standing bathtubs and chaises longues.

Drapers Hall
FRENCH £££

(☑ 01743-344679; www.drapershallrestaurant.co. uk; 10 St Mary's Pl; mains £12-25; ⊙ kitchen noon-2.30pm & 6.30-9pm; ℙ 🛜) The sense of history is palpable in this beautifully preserved 16th-century hall, fronted by an elegant Elizabethan facade. Award-winning Anglo-French haute cuisine is served in rooms adorned with wood panelling and artwork, and upstairs there are spectacular heirloom-filled bedrooms (doubles £105 to £155).

⬛ Drinking & Nightlife

Henry Tudor House
PUB

(www.henrytudorhouse.com; Barracks Passage; ⊙ 11am-11pm Mon-Thu, to 1am Fri & Sat, noon-11pm Sun) Tucked off Wyle Cop, this seriously overhanging black-and-white beauty was built in the early 15th century and is where Henry VII stayed before the Battle of Bosworth. Today it melds old and new with a zinc bar, light-filled conservatory and birdcage-encased chandeliers. Live gigs regularly take to the stage. Good menu, too.

Three Fishes
PUB

(www.realaleshrewsbury.co.uk; 4 Fish St; ⊙ 11.30am-3pm & 5-11pm Mon-Thu, to 11pm Fri & Sat, noon-10.30pm Sun) The quintessential creaky Tudor alehouse, with a jolly publican, mellow regulars and hops hanging from the 15th-century beamed ceiling.

☆ Entertainment

Old Market Hall Film & Digital Media
CINEMA

(☑ 01743-281281; www.oldmarkethall.co.uk; The Square; ⊙ 10am-9pm Mon-Sat, noon-6pm Sun; 🛜) View mainstream and art-house movies in a charming Elizabethan setting.

Theatre Severn
THEATRE

(☑ 01743-281281; www.theatresevern.co.uk; Frankwell Quay) This much-acclaimed and expansive new riverside theatre and music venue hosts everything from pop gigs and comedy nights to plays and classical concerts.

ⓘ Information

Tourist office (☑ 01743-258888; www.visit-shrewsbury.com; The Square; ⊙ 10am-5pm daily Apr-Oct, to 5pm Tue-Sun Nov-Mar) In the Music Hall along with the Shrewsbury Museum & Art Gallery (p445).

ⓘ Getting There & Away

BUS
The **bus station** (Smithfield Rd) is beside the river. Bus 435 runs to Ludlow (£3.50, 1½ hours, hourly Monday to Friday, every two hours Saturday), via Church Stretton (£2.70, 45 minutes). Other useful services include the following:

Birmingham National Express; £7, 1½ hours, twice daily

Ironbridge Bus 96; £3, 50 minutes, every two hours Monday to Saturday

London Victoria National Express; £22.10, 4½ hours, twice daily

TRAIN
From the train station at the bottom of Castle Foregate, trains run to Birmingham (£13.60, one hour, half-hourly), Ludlow (£14.20, 30 minutes, half-hourly) and London Euston (£68, 2¾ hours, every 20 minutes).

If you're bound for Wales, **Arriva Trains Wales** (☑ 0845 606 1660; www.arrivatrainswales. co.uk) runs to Swansea (£44.20, 3¾ hours, hourly) and Holyhead (£57.20, three hours, hourly).

ⓘ Getting Around

Dave Mellor Cycles (☑ 01743-366662; www. davemellorcycles.com; 9a New St, Frankwell; per half-day/day £7.50/15; ⊙ 9am-6pm Mon-Sat) Rents bikes for adults (no kids' bikes available).

Attingham Park

Straight from a bodice-ripping period drama, **Attingham Park** (NT; ☑ 01743-708123; www.nationaltrust.org.uk; house & grounds adult/child £9.45/5.25, grounds only £4.55/2.35; ⊙ house 10.30am-5.30pm mid-Mar–early Nov, grounds 8am-7pm May-Sep, 9am-6pm Mar-Apr & Oct, to 5pm Nov-Mar) was built in imposing neoclassical style in 1785. It has a grand columned facade, manicured lawns, and a stagecoach turning-circle in the courtyard. Home to some 300 fallow deer, the landscaped grounds swirl around an ornamental lake. The restored walled garden is a picture.

Attingham Park is 4 miles southeast of Shrewsbury at Atcham – take bus 81 or 96 (£2.10, 20 minutes, six per day Monday to Saturday).

Ironbridge Gorge

Strolling or cycling through the woods, hills and villages of this peaceful river gorge, it's hard to believe such a sleepy enclave could really have been the birthplace of the Industrial Revolution. Nevertheless, it was here that Abraham Darby perfected the art of smelting iron ore with coke in 1709, making it possible to mass-produce cast iron for the first time.

Abraham Darby's son, Abraham Darby II, invented a new forging process for producing single beams of iron, allowing Abraham Darby III to astound the world with the first-ever iron bridge, constructed in 1779. The bridge remains the focal point of this World Heritage Site, and 10 very different museums tell the story of the Industrial Revolution in the buildings where it took place.

◉ Sights & Activities

★ **Museum of the Gorge**   MUSEUM
(☏ 01952-433424; www.ironbridge.org.uk; The Wharfage; adult/child £4.15/3.25; ⊙10am-5pm Mar-early Nov, to 4pm early Nov-Feb) Kick off your visit at the Museum of the Gorge, which offers an overview of the World Heritage Site using film, photos and 3-D models. Housed in a Gothic warehouse by the river, it's filled with entertaining, hands-on exhibits.

★ **Iron Bridge**   BRIDGE
(www.ironbridge.org.uk; ⊙toll house 10am-5pm Sat & Sun Mar-early Nov, to 4pm Sat & Sun early Nov-Feb, daily during school holidays) FREE The flamboyant, arching and gravel-strewn Iron Bridge, which gives the area its name, was built to flaunt the new technology invented by the pioneering Darby family. At the time of its construction in 1779, nobody could believe that anything so large – it weighs 384 tonnes – could be built from cast iron without collapsing under its own weight. There's a small exhibition on the bridge's history at the former toll house.

Blists Hill Victorian Town   MUSEUM
(☏ 01952-433424; www.ironbridge.org.uk; Legges Way; adult/child £16.50/11; ⊙10am-5pm Mar-early Nov, to 4pm early Nov-Feb) Set at the top of the Hay Inclined Plane (a cable lift that once transported coal barges uphill from the Shropshire Canal), Blists Hill is a lovingly restored Victorian village repopulated with townsfolk in period costume, busy with day-to-day chores. There's even a bank, where you can exchange your modern pounds for shillings to use at the village shops. In summer, a Victorian fair is an added attraction for young ones.

Museum of Iron   MUSEUM
(www.ironbridge.org.uk; Wellington Rd; adult/child, £8.50/5.75, incl Darby Houses £9.25/6.75; ⊙10am-5pm Mar-early Nov, to 4pm early Nov-Feb) Set in the brooding buildings of Abraham Darby's original iron foundry, the Museum of Iron contains some excellent interactive exhibits. As well as producing the girders for the Ironbridge, the factory became famous for heavy machinery and extravagant ornamental castings, including the gates for London's Hyde Park.

Darby Houses   MUSEUM
(☏ 01952-433522; www.ironbridge.org.uk; adult/child £5.25/3.75, incl Museum of Iron £9.25/6.75; ⊙10am-5pm late Mar-early Nov) These beautifully restored 18th-century homes housed generations of the Darby family in gracious but modest Quaker comfort. They're just uphill from the Museum of Iron.

**Coalport China Museum
& Tar Tunnel**   MUSEUM
(www.ironbridge.org.uk; museum adult/child £8.50/5.75, Tar Tunnel £3.25/2.50; ⊙10.30am-4pm Mar-early Nov) As ironmaking fell into decline, Ironbridge diversified into manufacturing china pots, using the fine clay mined around Blists Hill. Dominated by a pair of towering bottle kilns, the atmospheric old china works now contains an absorbing museum tracing the history of the industry, with demonstrations of traditional pottery techniques.

---

❶ IRONBRIDGE GORGE MUSEUM PASSPORT

The 10 Ironbridge museums are administered by the Ironbridge Gorge Museum Trust (☏ 01952-433424; www.ironbridge.org.uk). You'll save considerably by buying a passport ticket (adult/child £27.50/16.50) at any of the museums or the tourist office. Valid for 12 months, it allows unlimited entry to all of Ironbridge Gorge's sites.

Ironbridge Gorge

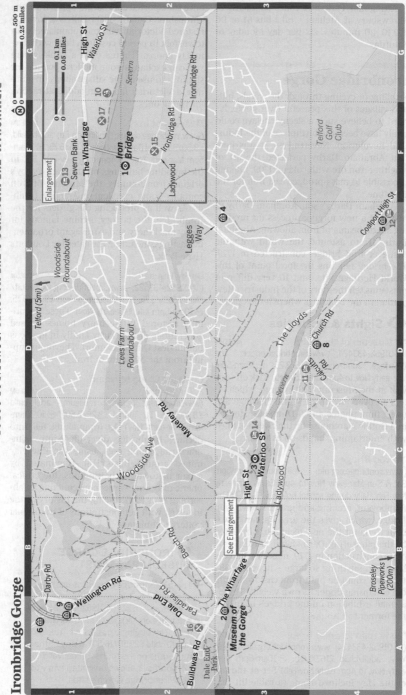

Ironbridge Gorge

A short stroll along the canal brings you to the 200-year-old **Tar Tunnel**, an artificial watercourse that was abandoned when natural bitumen started trickling from its walls.

Jackfield Tile Museum
MUSEUM

(📞 01952-433424; www.ironbridge.org.uk; adult/child £8.50/5.75; ⊙10am-5pm late Mar-early Nov, to 4pm early Nov-late Mar) Once the largest tile factory in the world, Jackfield was famous for its encaustic tiles, with ornate designs produced using layers of different coloured clay. Tiles are still produced here today for period restorations. Gas-lit galleries re-create ornately tiled rooms from past centuries including Victorian public conveniences. The museum is on the south bank of the Severn – cross the footbridge at the bottom of the Hay Inclined Plane. Tile decorating workshops take place on Tuesdays (from 10am; £5).

Enginuity
MUSEUM

(www.ironbridge.org.uk; Wellington Rd; adult/child £8.75/7.25; ⊙10am-5pm late Mar-early Nov, to 4pm early Nov-late Mar) If the kids are starting to look glazed, recharge their batteries at this levers-and-pulleys science centre beside the Museum of Iron, where you can control robots, move a steam locomotive with your bare hands (and a little engineering know-how) and power up a vacuum cleaner with self-generated electricity.

Broseley Pipeworks
MUSEUM

(www.ironbridge.org.uk; adult/child £5.25/3.75; ⊙1-5pm mid-May–mid-Sep) This was once the biggest clay tobacco pipe-maker in the country, but the industry nose-dived after the introduction of prerolled cigarettes in the 1880s, and the factory was preserved much as it was when the lights were turned off in 1957. The pipeworks is a 1-mile walk south of the river (cross the Ironbridge and follow the signs) on a winding lane that passes the old workers' cottages. Ask the tourist office for the *Jitties* leaflet, which has a walking tour of laneways around the pipeworks.

Bedlam Furnaces
NOTABLE BUILDING

By the River Severn, you can see the remains of the 1750s-built coke-fired blast furnaces, which remained in use into the 19th century.

Ironbridge Leisure
CANOEING, KAYAKING

(📞 01952-433518; www.ironbridgeleisure.co.uk; 31 High St; kayak/canoe rental from £20/25; ⊙9am-5pm Tue-Sat) In summer, when the river is at a safe level, you can rent canoes and kayaks to explore the gorge and surrounding areas on 5-mile excursions (around three hours) or multiday camping trips.

🛏 Sleeping

Rooms are everywhere in Ironbridge and nearby Telford has modern hotels. Ironbridge has two YHA hostels but the Coalbrookdale hostel is reserved for groups.

Ye Olde Robin Hood
PUB £

(📞 01952-433071; www.yeolderobinhoodinn.co.uk; 33 Waterloo St; d from £55; 🅿🛜) New managers are revitalising this quaint, white-washed, traditional inn on the banks of the River Severn. Its three spotless rooms come with king-size mattresses; the bar does well-priced, dependable food and you're treated like a regular from the moment you walk in the door.

Coalport YHA
HOSTEL £

(📞 0845 371 9325; www.yha.org.uk; High St; dm/d from £13/50; 🅿🛜) In a converted china factory in the quietest, prettiest corner of Ironbridge. Rooms are modern and functional

WORTH A TRIP

COSFORD ROYAL AIR FORCE MUSEUM

This famous aerospace **museum** (☑ 01902-376200; www.rafmuseum.org. uk; Shifnal; ⊘ 10am-6pm Mar-Oct, to 5pm Nov-Feb) 13 miles east of Ironbridge is run by the Royal Air Force, whose pilots steered many of these winged wonders across the skies. Among the 70 aircraft on display are the Vulcan bomber (which carried Britain's nuclear deterrent) and the tiny helicopter-like FA330 Bachstelze glider that was towed behind German U-boats to warn them of enemy ships. You can also try out a Black Hawk simulator. It's a half-mile walk from Cosford train station, on the Birmingham–Shrewsbury line.

The Red Arrows stunt team paint the sky with coloured smoke during the **Cosford Air Show** (www.cosfordair-show.co.uk) in June .

but the biggest drawcards are the facilities, which include a laundry, kitchen and licensed cafe, with wi-fi in common areas.

★ **Library House**   B&B ££
(☑ 01952-432299; www.libraryhouse.com; 11 Severn Bank; s/d from £75/90; P @ 🖥) Up an alley off the main street, this lovingly restored Georgian library building is hugged by vines, backed by a beautiful garden and decked out with stacks of vintage books, curios, prints and lithographs. There are three charmingly well-preserved, individually decorated rooms, named Milton, Chaucer and Eliot. The affable dog whipping around is Millie.

Calcutts House   B&B ££
(☑ 01952-882631; www.calcuttshouse.co.uk; Calcutts Rd; s/tw/d from £55/70/90; P 🖥) This former ironmaster's pad dates from the 18th century. It's tucked away on the south bank around the corner from the Jackfield Tile Museum, about a mile east of the bridge. Its traditionally decorated rooms have heaps of character, and one is furnished with an outsized two-hundred-year-old four-poster bed.

✕ Eating & Drinking

Most places to eat line the High St, but old-fashioned pubs dot both banks of the River Severn.

Deli-Dale   DELI £
(Dale End, Coalbrookdale; dishes £3-5.50; ⊘ 8.30am-5.30pm Mon-Fri, 10am-4pm Sat, noon-4pm Sun; 🖥 🖼) This wonderful deli is far and away the best place in the area for a light meal. Steaming-hot soups, salads, cakes and sandwiches are all freshly made; take them away or else dine in the cosy shop or at umbrella-shaded picnic tables in the courtyard. Very family-friendly.

D'arcys at the Station   MEDITERRANEAN ££
(☑ 01952-884499; www.darcysironbridge.co.uk; Ladywood; mains £12-14; ⊘ 6-9.30pm Tue-Sat) Just over the bridge by the river, the handsome old station building is the backdrop for flavoursome Mediterranean dishes, from Moroccan chicken to Cypriot kebabs and Tuscan bean casserole.

Restaurant Severn   BRITISH, FRENCH £££
(☑ 01952-432233; www.restaurantsevern.co.uk; 33 High St; 2-/3-course lunch menu £18.95/20.95, 2-/3-course dinner menu from £25.95/27.95; ⊘ 6.30pm-8.30pm Wed-Sat, noon-1.30pm Sun; P) The highly praised fare at this small, unadorned riverside restaurant is a winning English–French hybrid. The locally sourced menu changes weekly but incorporates creations such as Shropshire venison medallions with cognac and sundried cranberry sauce. Menu prices rise slightly on Fridays and Saturdays.

❶ Information

Tourist Office (☑ 01952-433424; www. ironbridge.co.uk; The Wharfage; ⊘ 10am-5pm) Located at the Museum of the Gorge.

❶ Getting There & Away

The nearest train station is 6 miles away at Telford, from where you can travel to Ironbridge on bus 96 (£2.10, 15 minutes, six per day Monday to Saturday). The same bus continues from Ironbridge's tourist office to Shrewsbury (£5.10, 35 minutes). Bus 99 runs from Bridgnorth (£3.20, 45 minutes, nine per day Monday to Saturday) and bus 88 runs to Much Wenlock (£3.50, 30 minutes, every two hours Monday to Saturday).

❶ Getting Around

At weekends and on bank holidays from Easter to October, the Gorge Connect bus (£1.65; Museum Passport holders £1) runs from Telford bus station to all of the museums on the north bank of the Severn. A Day Rover pass costs £2.20/1.55 per adult/child.

Much Wenlock

POP 2210

With one of those quirky names that abound in the English countryside, Much Wenlock is as charming as it sounds. Surrounding the time-worn ruins of Wenlock Priory, the streets are studded with Tudor, Jacobean and Georgian houses, and locals say hello to everyone. This storybook English village also claims to have jump-started the modern Olympics.

◉ Sights

Guildhall   HISTORIC BUILDING
(☑01952-727509; admission £1; ◷10.30am-1pm & 2-4.30pm Mon-Sat & 2-4.30pm Sun Apr-Oct) Built in classic Tudor style in 1540, the wonky Guildhall features some splendidly ornate woodcarving. One of the pillars supporting it was used for public floggings in medieval times.

Holy Trinity Church   CHURCH
(www.muchwenlockchurch.co.uk; ◷9am-5pm) The ancient, eroded Holy Trinity Church was built in 1150 over Saxon foundations. Note the Norman arch as you enter with the (as yet) undeciphered initials 'AB' and 'RI' on either side. Also look out for the old police station nearby, dating from 1864.

Wenlock Priory   RUIN
(EH; ☑01952-727466; www.english-heritage.org.uk; adult/child incl audioguide £4.20/2.50; ◷10am-6pm Apr-Sep, to 5pm Oct, to 4pm Sat & Sun Nov-Mar; ℗) The maudlin Cluniac ruins of Wenlock Priory rise up from vivid green lawns, sprinkled with animal-shaped topiary. Raised by Norman monks over the ruins of a Saxon monastery from AD 680, the hallowed remains include a finely decorated chapterhouse and an unusual carved lavabo, where monks came to ceremonially wash before eating.

⌇ Sleeping & Eating

Raven Hotel   HOTEL **££**
(☑01952-727251; www.ravenhotel.com; Barrow St; d £85-95, ste £105, lunch mains £11-13, dinner 2-/3-course menu £28/36; ℗⍐) Much Wenlock's finest digs, this 17th-century coaching inn and converted stables has oodles of historical charm and rich country-chic styling. Overlooking a flower-filled courtyard, the excellent restaurant serves classic Mediterranean and British fare.

Fox   PUB **££**
(☑01952-727292; www.the-fox-inn.co.uk; 46 High St; s/d from £65/85, mains £13.50-16.50; ◷noon-2pm & 6-9.30pm Tue-Sat, to 2pm Sun; ℗@⍐) Warm yourself by the massive fireplace, then settle down in the dining room to savour locally sourced venison, pheasant and beef, swished down with a pint of Shropshire ale. Candlelit dinners here are lovely. It also has five contemporary rooms.

ℹ Information

Tourist Office (☑01952-727679; www.muchwenlockguide.info; The Square; ◷10.30am-1pm & 1.30-5pm Apr-Oct, 10.30am-1pm & 1.30-4pm Fri-Sun Nov-Mar) Has a modest museum (admission free) of local history.

ℹ Getting There & Away

Bus 436 runs from Shrewsbury to Much Wenlock (£3.30, 35 minutes, hourly Monday to Saturday) and on to Bridgnorth (£3.30, 20 minutes). Bus 88 runs to Ironbridge (£2.60, 30 minutes, every two hours Monday to Saturday).

GRANDADDY OF THE MODERN OLYMPICS

All eyes were on London for the Olympic Games in 2012, but tiny Much Wenlock held its own Olympic Games in July the same year, as it has annually since 1850. The idea of holding a sporting tournament based on the games of ancient Greece was the brainchild of local doctor William Penny Brookes, who was looking for a healthy diversion for bored local youths. Accordingly, he created a tournament for 'every kind of man', with running races, high and long jumps, tilting, hammer throwing and wheelbarrow races – plus glee singing, knitting and sewing for every kind of woman.

The games soon piqued the interest of Baron Pierre Coubertin, who visited in 1890 and consulted Brookes extensively before launching the modern Olympic Games in Athens in 1896. Unfortunately, Brookes was effectively airbrushed out of the Olympic story until 1994, when then-International Olympic Committee President Juan Antonio Samaranch visited Much Wenlock to pay his respects to 'the founder of the Modern Olympic Games'.

The Much Wenlock Olympics are still held every July, with events that range from the triathlon to volleyball; for details visit www.wenlock-olympian-society.org.uk.

Around Much Wenlock

The spectacular limestone escarpment of Wenlock Edge swells up like an immense petrified wave, breaking over the Shropshire countryside. Formed from limestone that once lined the bottom of Silurian seas, the ridge sprawls for 15 miles from Much Wenlock to Craven Arms along the route of the B4371, providing a fantastic hiking backroute from Ludlow and Ironbridge Gorge.

Wilderhope Manor YHA (0845 371 9149; www.yha.org.uk; Longville-in-the-Dale; dm/d/f from £16/48/75; Fri, Sat & school holidays; P) is a gloriously atmospheric gabled greystone Elizabethan manor, with spiral staircases, wood-panelled walls, an impressive stone-floored dining hall and spacious, oak-beamed rooms – this is hostelling for royalty. Bus 155 from Ludlow (£3.70, 50 minutes) runs once daily Monday to Friday to Shipton, a half-mile walk from Wilderhope – call the hostel for timetables.

Bridgnorth & Around

POP 12,315

Cleaved into two by a dramatic sandstone bluff that tumbles down to the River Severn, Bridgnorth is one of Shropshire's finest-looking historic towns, with a wealth of architectural charm despite much of the High Town succumbing to fire in 1646 during the Civil War.

Around its namesake church, the High Town's adorable St Leonard's Close contains some of the most attractive buildings and almshouses in town, including a splendid six-gabled house, once part of the grammar school.

A 19th-century cliff railway and several narrow lanes drop down from the High Town to the Low Town, including the very steep pedestrian Cartway, at the bottom of which is Bishop Percy's House, dating from 1580.

○ Sights & Activities

Northgate   MUSEUM
(www.bridgnorthmuseum.org.uk; Northgate; 1.30-4pm Sat, 11am-4pm Sun Easter-Oct, 11am-4pm Sun-Fri, 1.30-4pm Sat during school holidays) FREE Northgate is the last surviving gate of five that originally guarded the town, and contains a small museum on local history run by volunteers from the Historical Society.

Daniels Mill   MILL
(01746-762753; www.danielsmill.co.uk; adult/child £5/4; 11am-4pm Easter-Oct) One mile south of the centre, Daniels Mill is the largest working water-powered mill in the country, and still produces flour for local bakers. Visitors get a personal tour of the working machinery from the resident miller.

Bridgnorth Cliff Railway   HISTORIC RAILWAY
(01746-762052; www.bridgnorthcliffrailway.co.uk; return £1.20; 8am-8pm Mon-Sat & noon-8pm Sun May-Sep, to 6.30pm Oct-Apr) Britain's steepest inland railway has trundled up the cliff since 1892. At the top of the route, a pedestrian walkway (affording astonishing nighttime panoramas) curves around the bluff to a pretty park dotted with scattered masonry, some leaning at an incredible angle (all that remains of Bridgnorth Castle), and passes the grand and imposing Thomas Telford–designed and cupola-topped St Mary's Church.

Severn Valley Railway   HISTORIC RAILWAY
(01299-403816; www.svr.co.uk; adult one-way/return £12.50/18, child £8/11.50; daily May-Sep, Sat & Sun Oct-Apr) Bridgnorth is the northern terminus of the Severn Valley Railway, whose historic steam or diesel locomotives chug down the valley to Kidderminster (one hour), starting from the station on Hollybush Rd. Check the calendar for additional event dates.

Cyclists can follow a beautiful 20-mile section of the Mercian Way (NCN Route 45) beside the railway line towards the Wyre Forest.

🛏 Sleeping & Eating

Severn Arms Hotel   HOTEL ££
(01746-764616; www.thesevernarms.co.uk; 3 Underhill St; s with/without en suite £32/46, d £64, f £75;) At the bottom of the bluff right next to the cliff railway, this comfortable riverside Georgian property has gorgeous views over the bridge. The helpful owners can direct you to parking a few minute's walk away over the bridge.

Cinnamon Cafe   CAFE £
(01746-762944; Waterloo House, Cartway; mains £5-8; 9am-6pm Mon-Wed & Fri, 10am-4pm Sat & Sun;) Sweeping views extend from the dining room and terrace of this licensed cafe near the top of the Cartway. It serves up savoury bakes (many vegetarian and vegan), plus quiches, homemade muesli and cakes.

Bridgnorth Delicatessen DELI £
(www.delicatessen.tv; 45 High St; ⊙ 9am-5pm Mon-Sat, 11am-4pm Sun) Pick up picnic ingredients from the well-stocked Bridgnorth Delicatessen, a lovely old shop full of gleaming jars.

ⓘ Information

Tourist Office (✆ 01746-763257; www.visit-bridgnorth.co.uk; ⊙ 9.30am-5pm Mon-Wed, Fri & Sat year-round, 10am-1pm & 2-5pm Thu Apr-Oct) Based at the town library.

ⓘ Getting There & Away

Bus 436 runs from Shrewsbury to Bridgnorth (£3.30, one hour, hourly Monday to Saturday), via Much Wenlock (£3.30, 25 minutes). Bus 99 runs to Ironbridge (£3.30, 30 minutes, every two hours Monday to Saturday).

Church Stretton & Around

POP 3700

Set in a deep valley formed by the Long Mynd and the Caradoc Hills, Church Stretton is an ideal base for walks or cycle tours through the Shropshire Hills. Although black-and-white timbers are heavily in evidence, most of the buildings in town are 19th-century fakes, built by the Victorians who flocked here to take the country air. The Norman-era St Laurence's Church features an exhibitionist sheila-na-gig over its north door.

🏃 Activities

Walking

Church Stretton clings to the steeply sloping sides of the Long Mynd, Shropshire's most famous hill, which rises to 517m. Dubbed 'Little Switzerland' by the Victorians, this desolate but dramatic bluff is girdled by walking trails that offer soaring views over the surrounding countryside. Most people start walking from the National Trust car park (per day £2.50) at the end of the Carding Mill Valley (www.cardingmillvalley.org.uk), half a mile west of Shrewsbury Rd. A small tearoom (dishes £3.50-5; ⊙ 10am-5pm Apr-Oct, to 4pm Nov-Mar) here provides refreshments.

A maze of single-track roads climbs over the Long Mynd to the adjacent ridge of Stiperstones, crowned by a line of spooky-looking crags. You can continue right over the ridge, passing the Bog (✆ 01743-792484; www.bogcentre.co.uk; ⊙ 10am-5pm Wed-Sun Easter-Oct) tourist office and cafe in a Victorian-era school by the ruins of an abandoned mining village, heading to the village

of Snailbeach (✆ 01743-790613; www.shropshiremines.org.uk; tours £7.50/3; ⊙ tours 11am-4pm Sun Jun-Sep), with its intriguing mining relics.

Other Activities

The tourist office has maps of local mountain-biking circuits and details of horse-riding stables (visit www.shropshireriding.co.uk for info).

Plush Hill Cycles CYCLING
(✆ 01694-720133; www.plushhillcycles.co.uk; 8 The Square; per half-day/day from £17/22; ⊙ 8.30am-6pm Mon, Tue, Thu & Fri, to 5pm Sat, 10am-4pm Sun) Handy range of mountain bikes and electric bikes. Rates include helmets, maps and child seats.

🛏 Sleeping

Bridges Long Mynd YHA HOSTEL £
(✆ 01588-650656; www.yha.org.uk; Bridges; dm from £16; P) On the far side of the Long Mynd, this wonderfully isolated hiker favourite is housed in a former school in the tiny hamlet of Bridges, 1.1 miles from Ratlinghope. Meals and liquid refreshment are available at the nearby Horseshoe Inn pub. No wi-fi, no phone reception, no credit cards. Cross the Mynd to Ratlinghope, or take the Long Mynd & Stiperstones Shuttle (p454) bus.

Mynd Guest House B&B ££
(✆ 01694-722212; www.myndhouse.co.uk; Ludlow Rd; s/d from £50/80; P @ 🖅) Just under 2 miles south of Church Stretton in Little Stretton, this inviting, family-friendly guesthouse has splendid views across the valley and backs directly onto the Mynd. The lovely rooms are named after local hills; there's a small bar and lounge stocked with local books; and a room for drying your boots.

🍴 Eating & Drinking

Several cosy pubs line Church Stretton's High St.

Berry's Coffee House CAFE £
(✆ 01694-724452; www.berryscoffeehouse.co.uk; 17 High St; mains £6-9.50; ⊙ 9am-5pm Sun-Thu, later Fri & Sat; 🖈) 🍴 A cosy cafe with loads of rooms in an 18th-century house, Berry's offers an organic, free-range, fair-trade, home-cooked menu, including Shropshire breakfasts and wicked desserts. No credit cards.

Bridges PUB ££
(✆ 01588-650260; www.thebridgespub.co.uk; Ratlinghope; lunch mains £9-14, dinner mains £10.50-17.50; ⊙ kitchen noon-3pm & 6.30-9pm) Some 5

miles northeast of Church Stretton, at the base of Long Mynd (tucked away just 160m from Bridges Long Mynd YHA by the river), this is one of those secret country pubs revered for its live music, riverside terrace, relaxed accommodation (dorm/double from £15/50) and impressive food (pork belly in cider; mushroom and goats cheese strudel...). Hard to find but absolutely worth it.

ℹ️ Information

Tourist Office (☎ 01694-723133; www.churchstretton.co.uk; Church St; ⏰ 9.30am-3pm Mon, Tue & Thu-Sat) Adjoining the library. Has abundant walking information and free internet terminals.

ℹ️ Getting There & Around

Trains between Ludlow (£6.80) and Shrewsbury (£5.90) stop in Church Stretton hourly, taking 15 minutes from either end. Alternatively, take bus 435 from Shrewsbury or Ludlow (£2.70, 40 minutes, hourly Monday to Saturday).

Bus 553 runs from Shrewsbury to Bishop's Castle via Stiperstones and Snailbeach (£3.30, 40 minutes, four daily Monday to Saturday).

From Easter to September, the hail-and-ride **Long Mynd & Stiperstones Shuttle** (www.shropshirehillsaonb.co.uk; Day Rover ticket £7; ⏰ 7 daily Sat & Sun Apr-Sep) runs from the Carding Mill Valley near Church Stretton to the villages atop the Long Mynd, passing the YHA at Bridges, and Stiperstones near the Snailbeach mine.

Bishop's Castle

POP 1895

Set amid peaceful Shropshire countryside, Bishop's Castle is a tangle of timbered town houses and Old Mother Hubbard cottages. The High St climbs from the town church to the refurbished Georgian **town hall** (1765) abutting the crooked 16th-century **House on Crutches** (☎ 01588-630556; www.hocmuseum.org.uk; ⏰ 2-5pm Sat & Sun Apr-Sep) FREE, which also houses the town **museum**.

🏃 Activities

Walkers can hike from Bishop's Castle along the **Shropshire Way**, which joins up with the long-distance **Offa's Dyke Path** and **Kerry Ridgeway** to the west. The northern sections of the Shropshire Way climb to the high country of the Stiperstones and the Long Mynd near Church Stretton. Bishop's Castle also lies on the popular **Six Castles Cycleway** (NCN Route 44) between Shrewsbury and Leominster.

🛌 Sleeping & Eating

Castle Hotel HOTEL ££
(☎ 01588-638403; www.thecastlehotelbishopscastle.co.uk; The Square; s/d/f incl breakfast from £100/105/150, mains £11-20; P 🌐) This solid-looking 18th-century coaching inn was built with stones from the now-vanished Bishop's Castle, which also contributed the gorgeous wood panelling in the dining room. All eight en suite rooms are lovely, with modern fabrics meeting old antique furniture. The pub bar in the hotel is decidedly cosy and the garden delightful. Rates increase at the weekends.

Yarborough House CAFE £
(www.yarboroughhouse.com; The Square; dishes £3.50-5; ⏰ 10am-5pm Tue & Thu-Sun) Coffee and cakes in a cosy secondhand bookshop with a simply vast collection of secondhand classical-music recordings.

🍷 Drinking & Nightlife

Three Tuns PUB
(www.thethreetunsinn.co.uk; Salop St; ⏰ noon-11pm Mon-Sat, to 8.30pm Sun) Bishop's Castle's finest watering hole is attached to the tiny **Three Tuns Brewery** (www.threetunsbrewery.co.uk), which has been rolling barrels of nut-brown ale across the courtyard since 1642. It's a lively local, and the ales are delicious.

ℹ️ Information

Tourist Office (☎ 01588-630023; http://bishopscastletownhall.co.uk; ⏰ 10am-4pm Mon-Sat) In the restored Town Hall.

ℹ️ Getting There & Away

Bus 553 runs to and from Shrewsbury (£3.10, one hour, half-hourly Monday to Saturday). On Saturdays, Sundays and bank holidays from mid-April to September, you can jump on the Castle Connect Shuttle from Ludlow (Day Rover ticket/single £7/1.30, 1¼ hours, three per day).

Ludlow

POP 10,515

Exactly why this genteel market town fanning out from the rambling ruins of a fine Norman castle became a national gastronomic phenomenon is not entirely clear, but today Ludlow's delightful muddle of narrow streets are crammed with independent butchers, bakers, grocers, cheesemongers and exceptional restaurants.

◉ Sights & Activities

Ludlow is ringed by wonderful landscapes. Starting just outside Ludlow Castle entrance, the waymarked Mortimer Trail runs for 30 miles through idyllic English countryside to Kington in Herefordshire. The tourist office has various leaflets describing the route, or visit www.exploremortimercountry.com.

Ludlow Castle   CASTLE
(☑01584-873355; www.ludlowcastle.com; Castle Sq; adult/child £5/2.50; ☉10am-6pm daily Aug, to 5pm Apr-Jul & Sep, to 4pm Oct, Nov, Feb & Mar, to 4pm Sat & Sun Dec & Jan) Perched in an ideal defensive location atop a cliff that's above a crook in the river, the town castle was built to ward off the marauding Welsh – or to enforce the English expansion into Wales, perspective depending. Founded after the Norman conquest, the castle was dramatically expanded in the 14th century.

The Norman chapel in the inner bailey is one of the few surviving round chapels in England, and the sturdy keep (built around 1090) offers wonderful views over the hills.

Church of St Laurence   CHURCH
(www.stlaurences.org.uk; King St; admission by £3 donation; ☉10am-5.30pm Apr-Sep, 11am-4pm Oct-Mar) One of Britain's largest parish churches, the church of St Laurence contains grand Elizabethan alabaster tombs and delightfully cheeky medieval misericords carved into its medieval choir stalls, including a beer-swilling chap raiding his barrel. The Lady Chapel contains a marvellous Jesse Window originally dating from 1330 (although the glass is mostly Victorian). Four windows in St John's Chapel date from the mid-15th century, including the honey-coloured Golden Window. Climb 200 steps up the tower (included in donation) for stunning views.

⌲ Tours

Town Tours   WALKING TOUR
(☑01584-874205; www.ludlowhistory.co.uk; adult/child £3/free; ☉2.30pm Sat & Sun Apr-Oct) Popular town tours leave from the Cannon in Castle Sq.

Ghost Walk   WALKING TOUR
(www.shropshireghostwalks.co.uk; adult/child £4/3; ☉8pm Fri) Search for spooks on the ghost walk from outside the Church Inn on the Buttercross.

✲✦ Festivals & Events

Ludlow Festival   ARTS
(www.ludlowartsfestival.co.uk; ☉Jun) The town's cultural calendar peaks with this fortnight of theatre and music that uses the castle as its dramatic backdrop.

Ludlow Food & Drink Festival   FOOD
(www.foodfestival.co.uk; ☉Sep) One of Britain's best foodie celebrations, spanning a long weekend in September.

⌸ Sleeping

Feathers Hotel   HISTORIC HOTEL ££
(☑01584-875261; www.feathersatludlow.co.uk; 21 Bull Ring; s/d from £95/130; Ⓟ) Stepping through the impossibly ornate timbered Jacobean facade, you'll find this hotel is all tapestries, creaky wood furniture, timber beams and stained glass: you can almost hear the cavaliers toasting the health of King Charles. The best rooms are in the old building; rooms in the newer wing lack the character and romance. The restaurant is highly recommended (2-/3-course menus £32.50/39.95).

Charlton Arms   INN ££
(☑01584-872813; www.charltonarms.co.uk; Ludford Bridge; d £90-120; Ⓟ⛢) The pick of the rooms at this landmark inn overlook the River Teme, and the pick of those rooms have terraces (one with an outdoor hot tub as well as a four-poster bed). Its restaurant, also opening to a terrace, serves Ludlow-quality Modern British cuisine, and there's a large free car park and superb service.

Dinham Hall Hotel   HOTEL £££
(☑01584-876464; www.dinhamhall.com; d £145-195, ste £245; Ⓟ⛢) This resplendent 18th-century country manor has views of the castle and the river from gorgeous rooms full of heirloom furniture. There's a superb fine-dining restaurant, Elliots, and afternoon teas.

✕ Eating

Almost every pub and restaurant in town has caught the local-produce-and-deli-ingredients bug. Foodies shouldn't miss the Ludlow Food Centre (p456).

Fish House   SEAFOOD £
(☑01584-879790; www.thefishhouseludlow.co.uk; 50 Bull Ring; taster plates £4-9, shellfish platter £65; ☉9am-5pm Wed-Fri, to 4pm Sat) Except on Saturdays, when it's first-come, first-served,

bookings are recommended for the barrel tables at this stylish fish and oyster bar. It sources Britain's best seafood: Whitby dressed crab, Arbroath smokies and Bigbury Bay oysters included. The house shellfish platter, available Fridays and Saturdays only, is best washed down with champagne.

Green Cafe
CAFE £

(☑ 01584-879872; www.thegreencafe.co.uk; Mill on the Green, Linney; dishes £5-11; ⊙ 10.30am-4.30pm Tue-Sun) Overlooking the weir, the Green Cafe takes full advantage of its riverside position beneath Ludlow Castle with its 25 outdoor seats (plus another 30 inside). Outstanding food spans warm salt beef baps (soft bread rolls) to tagliatelle with pheasant sauce and parmesan shavings. Wines, beers and ciders are from small-scale producers. Its popularity means you should book ahead.

La Bécasse
MODERN FRENCH £££

(☑ 01584-872325; www.labecasse.co.uk; 17 Corve St; 2-/3-course lunch menu £28/32.50, 2-/3-course dinner menu £45/55; ⊙ noon-2pm & 7-9pm Tue-Fri, noon-2pm & 7-9.30pm Sat) Artistically presented and bursting with inventive flavours, meals are served in an oak-panelled, exposed-brick dining room in the 17th-century coach house. Head chef Chris O'Halloran creates remarkable dishes and also runs masterclasses on the second Monday of each month (£99 including lunch).

Mr Underhill's
MODERN BRITISH £££

(☑ 01584-874431; www.mr-underhills.co.uk; Dinham Weir; 8-course menu £67.50-75; ⊙ 7-9.30pm Wed-Sun) ⌀ This dignified Michelin-starred restaurant is set in a converted corn mill that dips its toes in the river. The Modern British food is exquisitely prepared, using market-fresh ingredients in a menu that changes daily. If you're too content to move, one of the four particularly elegant suites (£220 to £365) can oblige.

⬛ Drinking & Entertainment

Real ales are the order of the day in flavour-obsessed Ludlow.

★ Ludlow Brewing Company
BREWERY, PUB

(☑ 01584-873291; www.theludlowbrewingcompany. co.uk; The Railway Shed, Station Dr; ⊙ 10am-5pm Mon-Thu, to 6pm Fri, to 4pm Sat) Up an inconspicuous laneway, the Ludlow Brewing Company produces award-winning brews and sells directly from the brewery and its airy, post-industrial-style bar. Hour-long

tours run at 3pm Monday to Friday and 2pm Saturday (£6 including three half-pints).

Church Inn
PUB

(http://www.thechurchinnludlow.com; Buttercross; ⊙ 10am-midnight Mon-Thu, to 1am Fri & Sat, to 11pm Sun) The hop-strewn Church Inn is a cosy little escape with a pulpit at the bar. It's tucked away on the narrow lane beside the old butter market.

Wheatsheaf Inn
PUB

(www.the-wheatsheaf-inn.co.uk; Lower Broad St; ⊙ noon-11pm) Under the medieval Broadgate, the quiet little Wheatsheaf Inn has a good choice of local ales.

Ludlow Assembly Rooms
CINEMA

(☑ 01584-878141; www.ludlowassemblyrooms. co.uk; adult standard/balcony £6.50/7, child £4/5) Overlooking the market square, Ludlow Assembly Rooms double as the town cinema.

🛍 Shopping

Delis, independent butchers and artisan bakers cluster around the market square and the surrounding lanes.

Ludlow Market
MARKET

(www.ludlowmarket.co.uk; ⊙ Mon, Wed, Fri & Sat) Ludlow Market takes place on the market square on the site of the old Victorian town hall, demolished overnight in 1986.

Ludlow Food Centre
FOOD & DRINK

(☑ 01584-856000; www.ludlowfoodcentre.co.uk; off Bromfield Rd, Bromfield; ⊙ 9am-5.30pm Mon-Wed & Sat, to 6.30pm Thu & Fri, to 4.30pm Sun) ⌀ More than 80% of the cheeses, meats, breads, fruit and vegetables are sourced from the surrounding region and tantalisingly displayed at this enormous farm shop stocking some 4000 products in all. Watch through viewing windows to see traditional preserves, pies, ice cream and more being made. It's signposted 4 miles northwest of Ludlow off Bromfield Rd (the A49).

Produce is utilised by the adjoining cafe/restaurant, the **Ludlow Kitchen** (www.ludlow kitchen.co.uk; breakfast £3.50-10, lunch mains £7-10, dinner mains £7-15; ⊙ 9am-5pm Mon & Tue, to 5pm & 6.30-10pm Wed-Sat, 10am-4pm Sun).

ℹ Information

Tourist Office (☑ 01584-875053; www.ludlow. org.uk; Castle Sq; ⊙ 10am-5pm daily Apr-Sep, to 4pm Mon-Sat Oct-Mar) Contains a small local-history museum (adult/child £1/free).

ⓘ Getting There & Around

Bus 435 runs to Shrewsbury (£4.50, 1½ hours, hourly Monday to Saturday) via Church Stretton (£2.70, 40 minutes). From mid-April to September, the Castle Connect Shuttle links Ludlow with Bishop's Castle (Day Rover ticket/single £7/1.30, 1¼, three daily).

Trains run frequently from the station on the north edge of town to Hereford (£9.50, 25 minutes, half-hourly) and Shrewsbury (£14.20, 30 minutes, half-hourly) via Church Stretton (£6.80, 20 minutes).

Hire bikes from **Wheely Wonderful** (🖉 01568-770755; www.wheelywonderfulcycling.co.uk; Petchfield Farm; adult/child bikes per day from £20/10; ⊙9am-5pm Mon-Sat, by reservation Sun Apr-Oct), 5 miles west of Ludlow.

NOTTINGHAMSHIRE

Say Nottinghamshire and people think of one thing – Robin Hood. Whether the hero woodsman existed is debated, but the county plays up its connections to the outlaw. Storytelling seems to be in Nottinghamshire's blood – local wordsmiths include provocative writer DH Lawrence, of *Lady Chatterley's Lover* fame, and hedonist poet Lord Byron. The city of Nottingham is the bustling hub, but venture into the surrounding countryside and you'll discover historic towns and stately homes surrounding the Sherwood Forest.

ⓘ Information

Experience Nottinghamshire (www.experience nottinghamshire.com)

ⓘ Getting There & Around

National Express and **Trent Barton** (🖉 01773-712265; www.trentbarton.co.uk) buses provide the majority of bus services. See **Traveline** (🖉 0871 200 2233; www.travelineeastmidlands. co.uk) for timetables. Trains run frequently to most large towns, and many smaller villages in the Peak District.

Nottingham

POP 289,300

Forever associated with men in tights and a sheriff with anger-management issues – aka the Robin Hood legend – Nottingham is a dynamic county capital with big-city aspirations, atmospheric historical sights, and a buzzing music and club scene thanks to its spirited student population.

⊙ Sights & Activities

★ Nottingham Castle & Art Gallery
CASTLE, GALLERY

(🖉 0115-876 1400; www.nottinghamcity.gov.uk/ nottinghamcastle; adult/child £5.50/4, Mortimer's Hole tours £3/free; ⊙10am-5pm daily mid-Feb–Oct, to 4pm Wed-Sun Nov–mid-Feb, Mortimer's Hole tours 11am, 1pm, 2pm & 3pm) Nottingham's namesake castle crowns a sandstone outcrop worm-holed with caves and tunnels. The original castle was founded by William the Conqueror and held by a succession of English kings before falling in the English Civil War. Its 17th-century manor-house-like replacement contains a local-history museum and an art gallery.

Burrowing through the bedrock, the underground passageway **Mortimer's Hole** emerges at Brewhouse Yard, where you can visit five atmospheric 17th-century cottages housing the **Museum of Nottingham Life at Brewhouse Yard** (🖉 0115-876 1400; www. nottinghamcity.gov.uk; Castle Blvd; adult/child £2.50/free; ⊙noon-4pm Sat & Sun year-round).

In 1330 supporters of Edward III used Mortimer's Hole to breach the castle security and capture Roger Mortimer, the machiavellian earl of March, who briefly appointed himself ruler of England after deposing Edward II.

City of Caves
CAVE

(🖉 0115-988 1955; www.cityofcaves.com; adult/ child £7.50/5.50, incl Galleries of Justice £12.75/9.75; ⊙10.30am-5pm) Over the centuries, the sandstone underneath Nottingham has been carved into a honeycomb of caverns and passageways. Audio tours (Monday to Friday) and performance tours (weekends and school holidays) lead you from the top level of the Broadmarsh shopping centre through a WWII air-raid shelter, a medieval underground tannery, several pub cellars and a mock-up of a Victorian slum dwelling. Book ahead.

Galleries of Justice
MUSEUM

(🖉 0115-952 0555; www.galleriesofjustice.org.uk; High Pavement; adult/child £9.50/7.50, incl City of Caves £12.75/9.75; ⊙9am-5.30pm Mon-Fri, 10am-5pm Sat & Sun, tours 10am-4pm Mon-Fri, 10.30am-4.30pm Sat & Sun) In the grand Georgian Shire Hall, the Galleries of Justice offers a ghoulish stroll through centuries of British justice, including medieval trials by fire and water. Audio tours run on Mondays and Tuesdays; live-action tours with 'gaolers' run from Wednesday to Sunday (daily during school holidays).

Nottingham

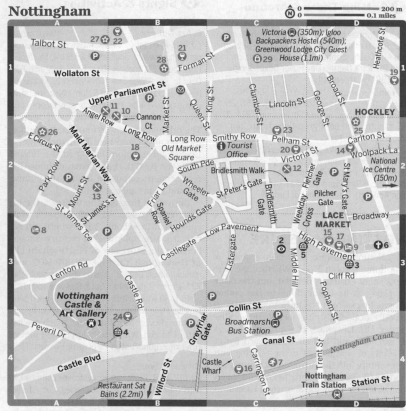

Nottingham Contemporary GALLERY
(☑ 0115-948 9755; www.nottinghamcontemporary.
org; Weekday Cross; ☺ 10am-7pm Tue-Fri, to 6pm Sat,
11am-5pm Sun) FREE Behind its lace-patterned
concrete facade, Nottingham Contemporary
holds edgy, design-driven exhibitions of paintings, prints, photography and sculpture.

St Mary's Church CHURCH
(www.nottinghamchurches.org; High Pavement;
☺ 10am-3pm Mon-Sat) The most atmospheric
time to visit this historic church dating from
Saxon times is during evensong at 6.15pm.

National Ice Centre SKATING
(☑ 0843 373 3000; www.national-ice-centre.com;
Bolero Sq; skating £6, skate hire £2) On Bolero
Sq (named for Nottingham skaters Jayne
Torvill and Christopher Dean's iconic 1984
gold-medal-winning routine) lies the UK's
first ice centre with twin Olympic-sized (60m
x 30m) rinks. The complex incorporates the
East Midland's premier entertainment venue,

the **Capital FM Arena**, which hosts sporting
fixtures, competitions and performances.
Daily skating session times are posted online.

☞ Tours

★**Ezekial Bone Tours** WALKING TOUR
(☑ 07941 210986; www.bonecorporation.co.uk; Robin Hood Town Tours adult/child £12/7, Guts & Gore
tours £7; ☺ Sat May-Sep) Entertaining history
tours are led by Nottingham's 'modern day
Robin Hood' Ezekial Bone, aka Ade Andrews.
In addition to the 2½-hour Robin Hood town
tours, Bone/Andrews runs regular 80-minute
Guts & Gore ghost tours, plus Robin Hood
Sherwood Forest tours and various other
walks year-round by request. Over 10s only.

Nottingham Princess CRUISE
(☑ 0115-910 0400; www.princessrivercruises.co.uk;
2/3hr cruises from £14.85/16.35) Lunch, afternoon tea and dinner (and dance) cruises
along the River Trent.

Nottingham

✴ Festivals & Events

Nottingham hosts an intriguing selection of festivals – search events online at www.experiencenottinghamshire.com.

Splendour   MUSIC
(www.splendourfestival.com; ☺ mid-Jul) The city's biggest live-music festival.

Goose Fair   CULTURAL
(www.nottinghamcity.gov.uk; ☺ Oct) Early October's medieval Goose Fair has evolved from a travelling market to a modern funfair.

Robin Hood Beer & Cider Festival   FOOD & DRINK
(www.beerfestival.nottinghamcamra.org; ☺ Oct) In the castle grounds, this tasting festival in early October features more than 1000 beers and 200 ciders.

Robin Hood Pageant   CULTURAL
(www.experiencenottinghamshire.com; ☺ Oct) A family-friendly pageant in late October.

🛏 Sleeping

Igloo Backpackers Hostel   HOSTEL £
(☑ 0115-947 5250; www.igloohostel.co.uk; 110 Mansfield Rd; dm/d from £16/44; ☎) A favourite with international backpackers, this independent hostel is opposite the Golden Fleece pub and a 24-hour supermarket (handy for the self-catering kitchen). As well as its private-room Annexe, a spiffing new Pods building has private rooms with retro-vintage furniture, grafitti murals, memory foam mattresses and flatscreen TVs.

★ **Lace Market Hotel**   BOUTIQUE HOTEL ££
(☑ 0115-852 3232; www.lacemarkethotel.co.uk; 29-31 High Pavement; s/d incl breakfast from £65/85; ☑ ✳ ☎) Within an elegant Georgian town house in the heart of the trendy Lace Market, sleek rooms have state-of-the-art furnishings and amenities; some have air-conditioning. Its fine-dining restaurant, Merchants (p460), and adjoining genteel pub, the **Cock & Hoop** (☑ 0115-852 3231; 25 High Pavement; ☺ noon-11pm Mon-Thu, to midnight Fri, to 1am Sat, to 10.30pm Sun), are both superb.

Greenwood Lodge City Guest House   B&B ££
(☑ 0115-962 1206; www.greenwoodlodgecityguesthouse.co.uk; Third Ave, Sherwood Rise; s/d from £51.50/86.50; ☑ ☎) A B&B set in a large Victorian house north of the centre. The location is quiet; the house and frilly rooms are full of period character; and there's a pretty courtyard garden. Children under 10 aren't permitted.

Hart's   BOUTIQUE HOTEL £££
(☑ 0115-988 1900; www.hartsnottingham.co.uk; Standard Hill, Park Row; d from £125; ☑ @ ☎)

DON'T MISS

WOLLATON HALL

Built in 1588 for land owner and coal mogul Sir Francis Willoughby by avant-garde architect Robert Smythson, fabulous **Wollaton Hall** (www.nottinghamcity.gov.uk; Wollaton Park, Derby Rd; parking per 3hr/day £2/4, tours adult/child £5/3; ⊙10am-5pm daily mid-Feb–Oct, 11am-4pm Thu-Mon Nov–mid-Feb, tours 11am, 2pm & 3pm) sits within 200 hectares of grounds roamed by fallow and red deer. Along with extravagant rooms from the Tudor, Regency and Victorian periods, there's a natural history museum and industrial museum.

Wollaton Hall is 2.5 miles west of Nottingham city centre; take bus 30 or 2 from Victoria bus station (£2, 15 minutes, every 15 minutes Monday to Saturday, half-hourly Sunday).

The hall starred as Wayne Manor in 2012's Batman film *The Dark Knight Rises*.

Within the former Nottingham General Hospital compound, the city's swishest hotel has ultracontemporary rooms in a striking modernist building, and its renowned **restaurant** (⊡0115-988 1900; www.hartsnottingham.co.uk; Standard Hill, Park Row; mains £15-29.50; ⊙noon-2.30pm & 6-10pm; ⊠) is housed in a historic red-brick wing. Work out in the small gym or unwind in the private garden.

✕ Eating

Nottingham reputedly has more restaurants, pubs and bars per square mile than anywhere else in Europe.

★ Delilah Fine Foods   DELI, CAFE £
(www.delilahfinefoods.co.uk; 12 Victoria St; dishes £6-11; ⊙8am-7pm Mon-Fri, 9am-7pm Sat, 11am-5pm Sun) ❂ Impeccably selected cheeses (more than 150 varieties), pâtés, meats and more from artisan producers are available to take away or eat on-site at this gourmand's dream, housed in a grand former bank with mezzanine seating.

Aubrey's Traditional Crêperie   CREPERIE £
(www.aubreystraditionalcreperie.com; 14-16 West End Arcade; dishes £2.75-7.50; ⊙10am-6pm Mon-Sat) Traditional down to its savoury galettes made with buckwheat flour, its sweet crêpes including salted caramel and its Breton ciders, this little hole-in-the-wall is a charming spot for an inexpensive lunch. Alongside the classics, there are galettes you'll never see in Brittany, such as smoked tofu (with balsamic and plum chutney, beetroot, walnuts, baby spinach and orange zest) too.

Alley Cafe Bar   VEGETARIAN £
(⊡0115-955 1013; www.alleycafe.co.uk; 1a Cannon Ct; mains £5.50-8; ⊙11am-9pm Mon & Tue, to 1am Wed-Sat, noon-5pm Sun; ⊠) ❂ Down a narrow alleyway, this beat-spinning hippie haven serves dishes such as tofu, tempeh and hemp-seed burgers alongside organic beers,

wines and ciders. It hosts events such as open-mic nights and exhibits local art.

Memsaab   INDIAN ££
(⊡0115-957 0009; www.mem-saab.co.uk; 12-14 Maid Marian Way; mains £8.50-19; ⊙5.30-10.30pm Mon-Thu, to 11pm Fri & Sat, 5-10pm Sun) The best of the glamorous modern Indian eateries on Maid Marian Way, Memsaab serves fabulous regional specialities in dinner-date friendly surroundings.

Merchants   GASTRONOMIC £££
(⊡0115-852 3232; www.thefinessecollection.com; 29-31 High Pavement; mains £19-30; ⊙noon-2pm & 7-9.30pm Tue-Thu, noon-2pm & 6-10pm Fri, noon-4pm & 6-10pm Sat) A stunning, coffered-ceilinged dining room sets the stage for some of Nottingham's finest dining. Knockout combinations include smoked eels and pork-belly risotto with lime gel, crackling lollypop, wasabi caviar, and flower and citrus salad. Follow up with desserts such as butternut-squash bavarois with candied purée, basil ice cream and a black-pepper cookie.

Restaurant Sat Bains   GASTRONOMIC £££
(⊡0115-986 6566; www.restaurantsatbains.com; Lenton Lane; tasting menu £75-99; ⊙noon-2pm & 7-9pm Tue-Thu, noon-2pm & 6.30-9.30pm Fri, noon-2pm & 6-10pm Sat; ⊠) Two miles southwest of the centre off the A52, chef Sat Bains has been awarded two Michelin stars for his wildly inventive Modern European cooking. Book well in advance and beware of hefty cancellation charges. It also has eight chic guest rooms (double from £129).

⬤ Drinking & Nightlife

Weekends in Nottingham are boisterous affairs, when the streets throng with lads on stag nights, girls on hens' parties, student revellers and intoxicated grown-ups who really should know better, but there are plenty of low-key alternatives.

★ **Ye Olde Trip to Jerusalem** PUB
(☑0115-947 3171; www.triptojerusalem.com; Brew house Yard, Castle Rd; ⊘11am-11pm Sun-Thu, to midnight Fri & Sat) Carved into the cliff below the castle, this atmospheric alehouse claims to be England's oldest pub. Founded in 1189, it supposedly slaked the thirst of departing crusaders, and its rooms and cobbled court-yards are still the most ambient place in Nottingham for a pint. Book informal tours (£2.50) of its cellars and caves at least two weeks ahead.

Boilermaker COCKTAIL BAR
(http://boilermakerbar.co.uk; 36b Carlton St, Hock-ley; ⊘5pm-1am Mon-Sat, 7pm-1am Sun) Entering what appears to be an industrial boilermak-er's shop and navigating your way through two secret doors brings you into this cav-ernous speakeasy spinning chilled lounge music. The obligatory table service can be slow, and the lighting's so low it's hard to read the inventive cocktails listed (eg Cereal Killer, with rum-soaked cornflakes), but it's a unique-and-then-some experience.

Dragon PUB
(www.the-dragon.co.uk; 67 Long Row; ⊘noon-11pm Mon-Thu, to 1am Fri & Sat, 11am-10pm Sun) The Dragon has a fabulous atmosphere at any time, thanks to homemade food, a good beer garden and funky music on weekends. But it peaks from 8pm on Tuesdays when it hosts the Racing Room (race entry £5) – an awe-some Scalextric slot-car race around a scale model of Nottingham along 180 feet of track.

Tilt COCKTAIL BAR
(www.tiltbar.co.uk; 9 Pelham St; ⊘5pm-midnight Tue-Thu, to 1.30am Fri & Sat) This tiny 1st-floor cocktail bar serves up a brilliant array of live blues offerings as well as cocktails that are giving their competition (in Nottingham, that's a lot of bars) a run for their money. House specialities include a Blues Blazer (cognac and Drambuie flamed with vanilla sugar and orange peel).

Pit & Pendulum PUB
(www.eerie-pubs.co.uk/pit-pendulum; 17 Victoria St; ⊘noon-11pm Sun & Mon, to midnight Tue-Thu, to 1am Fri & Sat; 🛜) Local goths flock to this dimly lit pub for the vampire vibe and the-atrical decor (push the floor-to-ceiling base-ment 'bookcase' to reach the toilets), as well as 'seven deadly sins' cocktails and occasion-al live music.

Brass Monkey BAR
(www.brassmonkeybar.co.uk; High Pavement; ⊘5pm-3am Mon-Sat, 8pm-3am Sun) Notting-ham's original cocktail bar rocks the Lace Market with DJ sets and quirky takes on favourites such as elderflower mojitos. The roof terrace gets packed on summer evenings.

Rocket@Saltwater BAR
(☑0115-924 2664; www.rocketrestaurants.co.uk; The Cornerhouse, Forman St; ⊘noon-midnight Mon-Thu, to 2am Fri & Sat, to 11pm Sun) Slick hip-ster rooftop bar and restaurant with a great open-air terrace.

LOCAL KNOWLEDGE

EZEKIAL BONE AKA ADE ANDREWS

Ade Andrews is a writer, actor, producer and tour guide.

Your background? I did a history degree and worked as a Heritage Ranger at Sherwood Forest, then set up Ezekial Bone Tours to deconstruct the Robin Hood myths and focus on the historic building blocks.

Did Robin Hood actually exist? He's a composite hero: many real outlaws in the me-dieval period were woven together over time by minstrels and storytellers. St Mary's Church (p458) is mentioned in the 1450 *Ballad of Robin Hood and the Monk*, and Old Market Sq in *Robin Hood and the Potter* circa 1500. It was only at the end of the 16th century that playwright Antony Munday elevated Robin Hood from a yeoman to a dis-placed Saxon earl as a symbol of the gentry's dissatisfaction with the Crown.

Robin Hood's relevance in the 21st century? Robin Hood was an original ecowarrior in harmony with the land. I want to put him on the pedestal he deserves – as a figurehead of culture and the environment.

Best places to experience Nottingham's history? The Lace Market area, the City of Caves (p457), Nottingham Castle (p457) and Ye Olde Trip to Jerusalem.

Canal House　　　　　　　　PUB
(☎0115-955 5060; http://thecanalhouse.co.uk; 48-52 Canal St; ⊙11am-11pm Mon-Wed, to midnight Thu, to 1am Fri & Sat, to 10.30pm Sun) The best of the canal-front pubs, run by the independent Castle Rock Brewery, and split in two by a watery inlet.

Malt Cross　　　　　　　　PUB
(www.maltcross.com; 16 St James's St; ⊙11am-11pm Mon-Thu, to 1am Fri & Sat, noon-6pm Sun) A fine place for a pint in a stately old Victorian music hall, where past performers included Charlie Chaplin. It's now a community space run by the Christian Charity Trust hosting art exhibitions and live music.

NG1　　　　　　　　GAY, CLUB
(☎0115-958 8440; www.ng1club.co.uk; 76-80 Lower Parliament St; ⊙11pm-4am Wed, to 6am Fri, to 6.30am Sat, to 4am Sun) Gay-friendly mixed club NG1 is unpretentious, hedonistic fun, with two dance floors belting out house, electro, pop and more.

Stealth　　　　　　　　CLUB
(☎0845 413 4444; www.stealthattack.co.uk; Masonic Pl, Goldsmith St; ⊙10pm-5am Fri & Sat) An underground club for those who like their bass heavy and their beats supercharged. The attached Rescue Rooms has a varied line-up of live bands and DJs.

☆ Entertainment

Theatre Royal &
Royal Concert Hall　　THEATRE, LIVE MUSIC
(☎0115-989 5555; www.trch.co.uk; Theatre Sq; ⊙booking office 9.30am-8.30pm Mon-Sat, 1hr before performance Sun) Sharing the same building and booking office, the Theatre Royal and Royal Concert Hall host musicals, touring theatre shows and veteran music acts. Backstage tours can be arranged (£6, 90 minutes).

Rock City　　　　　　　　LIVE MUSIC
(☎0845 413 4444; www.rock-city.co.uk; 8 Talbot St) This monster venue hosts everything from Goth rock and Midlands metal to Northern Soul.

Rescue Rooms　　　　　　LIVE MUSIC
(☎0115-828 3173; www.rescuerooms.com; ⊙4pm-3am) Attached to Stealth nightclub; has a varied line-up of live bands and DJs.

Nottingham Playhouse　　THEATRE
(☎0115-941 9419; www.nottinghamplayhouse.co.uk; Wellington Circus) Beside Anish Kapoor's enormous *Sky Mirror* dish, the Playhouse puts on serious theatre, from stage classics to the avant-garde. Nottingham's artistic community congregates at its attached restaurant and bar.

Broadway Cinema　　CINEMA, GALLERY
(www.broadway.org.uk; 14-18 Broad St) Artistic hub with an independent cinema, media arts gallery and a cafe-bar where you can actually hear yourself talk.

❶ Information

Tourist Office (☎0844 477 5678; www.experiencenottinghamshire.com; The Exchange, 1-4 Smithy Row; ⊙9.30am-5.30pm Mon-Sat year-round, 11am-5pm Sun late Jul-Aug & mid-late Dec) Friendly office with racks of info and Robin Hood merchandise.

❶ Getting There & Away

AIR
East Midlands Airport (p410) is about 18 miles south of Nottingham; Skylink buses pass the airport (one-way/return £5/8, one hour, at least hourly, 24 hours).

BUS
Local services run from the Victoria bus station, behind the **Victoria Shopping Centre** (Lower Parliament St) on Milton St. Bus 100 runs to Southwell (£4.15, 50 minutes, every 20 minutes Monday to Saturday, hourly Sunday) and bus 90 to Newark (£4.90, 55 minutes, hourly, every two hours Sunday).

Long-distance buses operate from the dingy **Broadmarsh bus station** (Collin St).

National Express services include the following:
Birmingham £10.60, 2¼ hours, five daily
Derby £6.80, 40 minutes, seven daily
Leicester £4.80, 45 minutes, every 20 minutes
London Victoria £13, 3½ hours, 11 daily

TRAIN
The train station is just south of the town centre. Useful services include the following:
Derby £6.60, 25 minutes, four hourly
Lincoln £10.60, one hour, hourly
London King's Cross/St Pancras £23.50, two hours, half-hourly
Manchester £21.50, two hours, two per hour

❶ Getting Around

For information on buses within Nottingham, call **Nottingham City Transport** (☎0115-950 6070; www.nctx.co.uk). A Kangaroo ticket gives you unlimited travel on buses and trams within the city for £4.20.

The single tram line operated by **Nottingham Express Transit** (www.thetram.net; single/day from £2/3.50) runs from Nottingham train station to Hucknall, passing near Broadmarsh bus station, the tourist office and Theatre Royal.

Bunneys Bikes (☑ 0115-947 2713; www. bunneysbikes.com; 97 Carrington St; per day £12.99; ☺ 9am-5.30pm Mon, Thu & Fri, 8am-5.30pm Tue, 9am-7pm Wed, 10am-5pm Sat) is near the train station. Hire bicycles are also available from Nottingham's tourist office and Broadmarsh bus station for £4 per day through a Nottingham City Council bike-share scheme. Bonus: hire includes unlimited use of Nottingham city buses, trams and trains.

Around Nottingham

Newstead Abbey

The evocative lakeside ruins of Newstead Abbey (☑ 01623-455900; www.newsteadabbey. org.uk; adult/child £5/1, garden only £1; ☺ house noon-4pm Sat & Sun, garden 9am-dusk) are inextricably associated with the original tortured romantic, Lord Byron (1788–1824), who owned the house until 1817. Founded as an Augustinian priory in around 1170, it was converted into a residence in 1539.

Newstead Abbey is 12 miles north of Nottingham, off the A60. Pronto buses from Victoria bus station stop at Newstead Abbey gates (£3.10, 25 minutes, every 10 minutes Monday to Saturday, half-hourly Sunday), a mile from the house and gardens.

Byron's old living quarters are full of suitably eccentric memorabilia, and the landscaped grounds include a monument to his yappy dog, Boatswain.

Sherwood Forest National Nature Reserve

If Robin Hood wanted to hide out in Sherwood Forest today, he'd have to disguise himself and the Merry Men as day-trippers on mountain bikes. Now covering just 182 hectares of old-growth forest, it's a major destination for Nottingham city dwellers.

Until a proposed new visitor centre opens, the Sherwood Forest visitor centre (www.nottinghamshire.gov.uk; Swinecote Rd, Edwinstowe; parking £3; ☺ 10am-5pm Easter-Oct, to 4.30pm Nov-Mar), on the B6034, is an uninspiring collection of faded late 20th-century buildings housing cafes, gift shops et al. It's the departure point for walking trails passing Sherwood Forest landmarks such as the Major Oak (1 mile return), a broad-boughed

oak tree (propped up by supporting rods) alleged to have sheltered Robin of Locksley.

🏃 Activities

For informative guided walks try Ezekial Bone Tours (p458).

Sherwood Pines Cycles CYCLING (☑ 01623-822855; www.sherwoodpinescycles. co.uk; Sherwood Pines Forest Park, Clipstone; bike hire adult/child per hr £8/7, per day £24/18; ☺ 9am-5pm Thu-Tue, to 7pm Wed) In the Sherwood Pines Forest Park woodlands area, 2 miles south of Sherwood Forest on the B6030, Sherwood Pines Cycles rents mountain bikes for exploring the area's trails.

🎉 Festivals & Events

Robin Hood Festival CULTURAL (www.nottinghamshire.gov.uk; ☺ Aug) The week-long Robin Hood Festival is a massive medieval re-enactment that takes place every August.

🛏 Sleeping

Sherwood Forest YHA HOSTEL £ (☑ 0845 371 9139; www.yha.org.uk; Forest Corner; dm/d £13/39; 🅿) An arrow's flight from the visitor centre, Sherwood Forest YHA is a modern hostel with comfortable dorms, a bar, a self-catering kitchen and meals.

ℹ Getting There & Away

From Nottingham, take the Sherwood Arrow bus (£3.50, 50 minutes, hourly Monday to Saturday, five on Sunday).

Southwell

POP 6760

A graceful scattering of grand, wisteria-draped country houses, Southwell is straight out of the pages of a novel from the English Romantic period.

◉ Sights

Southwell Minster CHURCH (www.southwellminster.org; suggested donation £5; ☺ 8am-7pm) Rising from the village centre, the awe-inspiring Southwell Minster, built over Saxon and Roman foundations, blends 12th- and 13th-century features including zigzag doorframes and curved arches. Its chapterhouse features some unusual stained glass and detailed carvings of faces, animals and leaves of forest trees.

Southwell Workhouse   MUSEUM

(NT; www.nationaltrust.org.uk; Upton Rd; adult/child £7.70/3.85; ⊙noon-4pm Wed-Sun Mar-Oct) On the road to Newark, Southwell Workhouse is a sobering reminder of the tough life faced by paupers in the 19th century. You can explore the factory floors and workers' chambers accompanied by an audioguide narrated by 'inmates' and 'officials'.

🛏 Sleeping & Eating

Enticing gourmet delis and tearooms line the village streets.

Saracen's Head Hotel   HISTORIC HOTEL ££

(☑01636-812701; www.saracensheadhotel.com; Market Pl; s/d incl breakfast from £75/95, 2-/3-course menus £15.95/19.95; P🐾) This rambling, timbered coaching inn has 27 beautifully refurbished rooms and an oak-panelled restaurant.

Mosedales Bakery   BAKERY £

(7 King St; dishes £3-6.50; ⊙9am-4pm Mon-Fri, 8.30am-4pm Sat, 9.30am-3pm Sun) Queues at this superb bakery regularly extend out the door.

❶ Getting There & Away

Bus 100 runs from Nottingham (£4.15, 50 minutes, every 20 minutes, hourly on Sunday). For Newark-on-Trent, take bus 28 or 29 (£2.50, 20 minutes, half-hourly).

Newark-on-Trent

POP 37,080

Newark-on-Trent paid the price for backing the wrong side in the English Civil War. After surviving four sieges by Oliver Cromwell's men, the town was ransacked by Roundheads when Charles I surrendered in 1646. Today, the riverside town is a peaceful place worth a stop to wander its castle ruins.

◉ Sights

Newark Castle   CASTLE

(www.newark-sherwooddc.gov.uk/newarkcastle; Castlegate; grounds admission free, tours adult/child £3/1.50; ⊙9am-6pm, tours 11am, 1pm & 3pm Wed & Fri-Sun) Set in a pretty park overlooking the River Trent, the ruins include an impressive Norman gate and a series of underground passages and chambers. The real King John, portrayed as a villain in the Robin Hood legend, died here in 1216. Contact the tourist office about tours.

Newark Air Museum   MUSEUM

(☑01636-707170; www.newarkairmuseum.org; adult/child £7.50/4; ⊙10am-5pm Mar-Oct, to 4pm Nov-Feb) About 2 miles east of Newark by the Winthorpe Showground, this air museum has an impressive collection of aircraft, including a fearsome Vulcan bomber.

✕ Eating & Drinking

Old Bakery Tea Rooms   TEAROOM £

(☑01636-611501; www.oldbakerytearooms.co.uk; 4 Queens Head Ct; mains £6-12; ⊙9.30am-5pm Mon-Sat; ☑) Everything, including to-die-for scones, is baked fresh on the premises at the Old Bakery Tea Rooms, housed in an enchanting *Hansel and Gretel*–like 15th-century Tudor building. Lunch specials include soups, frittata, bruschetta and smoked-salmon brioche.

Castle Barge   BAR

(www.castlebarge.co.uk; The Wharf; ⊙11am-11pm) Moored on the River Trent overlooking Newark Castle, this barge is an idyllic spot for a local ale. It serves decent food, and there's picnic seating on the riverbanks.

❶ Information

Tourist Office (☑01636-655765; www.newark-sherwooddc.gov.uk/newarkcastle; Gilstrap Centre, Castlegate; ⊙10am-4pm) In the castle grounds; can help find accommodation.

❶ Getting There & Away

Newark has two train stations. Trains on the East Coast Main Line between London King's Cross (£25, two hours, one to two hourly) and the north stop at Newark North Gate, while East Midlands trains between Leicester (£12.40, two hours, hourly), Nottingham (£6.10, one hour, hourly) and Lincoln (£4.90, 50 minutes, hourly) stop at Newark Castle station.

Bus 90 runs hourly to Nottingham (£4.90, 55 minutes, every two hours Sunday).

LINCOLNSHIRE

One of the most sparsely populated corners of England, Lincolnshire's farmland unfolds over low hills and the pancake-flat Fens. It is dotted with windmills and, more recently, wind turbines. Surrounding the charming county town of Lincoln you'll find seaside resorts, scenic waterways, serene nature reserves and stone-built towns tailor-made for English period dramas.

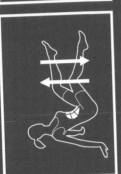

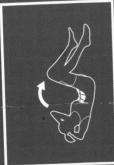
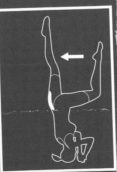

ses, ancient pubs and quirky independ-
stores.

anking the River Witham at the base of
ill, the new town is less absorbing, but
evitalised Brayford Waterfront develop-
by the university is an idyllic spot to
the boats go by.

Sights

ourist office sells the three-day **Visit**
In Pass (adult/family £12/35), giving
to several heritage sites including the
cathedral and Bishops' Palace.

coln Cathedral   CATHEDRAL
22-561600;   http://lincolncathedral.com;
Yard; adult/child £8/1 Mon-Sat, by do-
Sun; ⊙7.15am-8pm Mon-Fri, to 6pm Sat
evensong 5.30pm Mon-Sat, 3.45pm Sun)
ng over Lincoln like a medieval sky-
, Lincoln's magnificent cathedral is a
aking representation of divine power
h. The great tower rising above the
is the third-highest in England at
t in medieval times, a lead-encased
spire added a further 79m, topping
great pyramids of Giza.

our **guided tours** take place at
ice daily; there are less-frequent
the roof and the tower. All are in-
admission; booking is essential.

st interior of the church is too large
ern congregations – services take
tead in **St Hugh's Choir**, a church
church running east from the cross-
choir stalls are accessed through a

1918 and two years later its col-
and's 'Bomber County' was home
(49) than any other in the coun-
d B-29 bombers were based here.
ation legacy.

(☐01522-552222; www.lincolnshire.
ild £6.50/4.50; ⊙10am-5pm Mon-
f Lincoln at the Battle of Britain
urs. Interconnect bus 5 (£3.95, 50
ncoln.

53207; www.lincsaviation.co.uk;
Mon-Sat Easter-Oct, 10am-4pm Mon-
hand airfield complete with its
f Lincoln via the A153; there's no

⊙ Jul) The RAF's Waddington Air
eekend in July. Book well ahead.

Lincoln

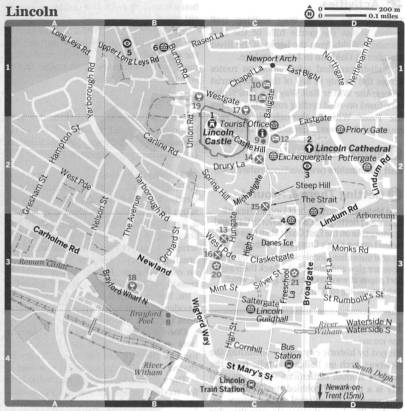

magnificent carved stone screen; look north to see the stunning rose window known as the Dean's Eye (c 1192), mirrored to the south by the floral flourishes of the Bishop's Eye (1330). There's more stained glass in the three Services Chapels in the North Transept.

Beyond St Hugh's Choir, the **Angel Choir** is supported by 28 columns topped by carvings of angels and foliate scrollwork. Other interesting details include the 10-sided **chapterhouse** – where Edward I held his parliament and where the climax of the *Da Vinci Code* was filmed in 2005.

The best time to hear the organ resounding through the cathedral is during **evensong**.

★ **Lincoln Castle**   CASTLE
(www.lincolnshire.gov.uk/lincolncastle; adult/child £2/1.20; ☺10am-6pm May-Aug, to 5pm Apr & Sep, to 4pm Oct-Mar) One of the first castles erected by the victorious William the Conqueror to keep his new kingdom in line, Lincoln Castle offers awesome views over the city and miles of surrounding countryside. Highlights include the chance to view one of the four surviving copies of the **Magna Carta** (dated 1215) and the grim **Victorian prison chapel**, from when this was the county jailhouse and execution ground.

Free 75-minute **guided tours** run once or twice daily (on weekends only in December and January).

Bishops' Palace   HISTORIC SITE
(EH; ☑01522-527468; www.english-heritage.org.uk; adult/child £4.70/2.80; ☺10am-6pm Wed-Sun Apr-Sep, to 5pm Wed-Sun Oct, to 4pm Sat & Sun Nov-Mar) Beside Lincoln Cathedral lie the time-ravaged but still imposing ruins of the 12th-century Bishops' Palace, gutted by parliamentary forces during the Civil War. From here, the local bishops once controlled a diocese stretching from the Humber to the Thames. Entertaining audioguides are included in admission.

Lincoln

Collection MUSEUM
(www.thecollectionmuseum.com; Danes Tce; ⊙10am-4pm, from 10.45am 1st Mon of month) FREE Archaeology bursts into life with loads of hands-on displays. Kids can handle artefacts and dress up in period costume. Check out the crushed skull of a 4000-year-old 'yellowbelly' (the local term for the locals), pulled from a Neolithic burial site near Sleaford.

Usher Gallery GALLERY
(www.thecollectionmuseum.com; Danes Tce; ⊙10am-4pm, from 10.45am 1st Mon of month) FREE A handsome Edwardian building decorated with carvings of cow skulls houses an impressive collection of works by greats such as Turner, Lowry and English watercolourist Peter de Wint (1784–1849).

Museum of Lincolnshire Life MUSEUM
(Old Barracks, Burton Rd; ⊙10am-4pm daily Apr-Sep, closed Sun Oct-Mar) FREE Displays at this charming community museum housed in an old Victorian barracks span everything from Victorian farm implements to the tin-can tank built in Lincoln for WWI. Around the corner from the museum is the cute little Ellis Mill (www.lincolnshire.gov.uk; Mill Rd; ⊙2-5pm Sat & Sun Apr-Sep, 2pm-dusk Sun Oct-Mar) FREE, which ground the town's flour in the 18th century and is still in use today.

☞ Tours

Walking Tours WALKING TOUR
(✐01522-521256; www.lincolnguidedtours.co.uk; adult/child £4/free; ⊙tours 11am daily Jul & Aug,

Sat & Sun Jun, Sep & Oct) History-focused 90-minute guided walking tours run from outside the tourist office.

Ghost Walks WALKING TOUR
(✐01522-874056; adult/child £4/2; ⊙7pm Wed-Sat year-round) Genuinely spooky 75-minute ghost walks depart adjacent to the tourist office in Castle Sq.

Brayford Belle BOAT TOUR
(✐01522-881200; www.lincolnboattrips.co.uk; adult/child £6.50/4) Boat trips along the River Witham and Fossdyke Navigation, a canal system dating back to Roman times, start from Brayford Waterfront. The *Brayford Belle* runs five times daily from Easter to September, and weekends only in October. No credit cards.

⊟ Sleeping

★Castle Hotel BOUTIQUE HOTEL ££
(✐01522-538801; www.castlehotel.net; Westgate; s £90, d £110-140, incl breakfast; P⊛) Each of the 18 rooms at this boutique hotel have been exquisitely refurbished in olive, truffle and oyster tones. Built on the site of Lincoln's Roman forum in 1852, the red-brick building's incarnations variously include a school and WWII lookout station. Take advantage of the great-value dinner, bed and breakfast deals linked to its award-winning restaurant Reform (p468).

Bail House B&B ££
(✐01522-541000; http://bailhouse.jpchotelsand leisure.co.uk; 34 Bailgate; d from £79; P@⊛⊠)

Walking between Lincoln's old and new towns can feel like an Everest expedition, but fortunately there are alternatives.

Walk & Ride (single ticket adult/child £1.50/70p, all-day pass £3/1.60; ⊙9.10am-5.22pm Mon-Sat) Lincoln's 'Little Green Bus' runs every 20 minutes from the Stonebow at the corner of High St and Saltergate to the cathedral and Newport Arch, then back via Brayford Waterfront and the train station.

Tour Lincoln (adult/child £10/4; ⊙10am-3pm Jul & Aug, to 3pm Sat & Sun Mar-May & Jun-Oct) To tour the city in comfort, hop aboard the open-topped Tour Lincoln bus. Tickets are sold at the tourist office and on board. Tours last one hour; tickets are valid all day.

Stone walls, worn flagstones, secluded gardens and one room with an extraordinary timber-vaulted ceiling are just some of the charms of this lovingly restored Georgian town house in central Lincoln. There's limited on-site parking, a garden and children's playground, and even a seasonal heated outdoor swimming pool.

White Hart Hotel　　　　HOTEL **££**
(☑01522-526222; www.whitehart-lincoln.co.uk; Bailgate; s/d from £70/90; P@🤫) You can't get more venerable than this grand dame of Lincoln hotels, sandwiched between castle and cathedral, with a history dating back 600 years through flowing countrified rooms.

✖ Eating

Tearooms are dotted along Steep Hill. Restaurant reservations are generally recommended in the evenings.

La Bottega Delitalia　　　　CAFE, DELI **£**
(9 West Pde; dishes £2.15-7.45; ⊙9am-4pm Mon-Wed, to 9pm Thu & Fri, 8.30am-3pm Sat) Authentic Italian fare such as lobster ravioli in creamy tomato and basil sauce is made from scratch at this inexpensive cafe-deli. Cash only.

Reform　　　　MODERN BRITISH **££**
(☑01522-538801; www.castlehotel.net; The Castle Hotel, Westgate; mains £13.50-23.95; ⊙noon-2.30pm & 7-9pm Mon-Sat, noon-3pm & 7-9pm Sun) Inspired by local, seasonal produce, the Castle Hotel's sophisticated restaurant serves starters such as feta beignets with pomegranate and mint-and-coriander Israeli cous-cous, followed by mains such as pork confit with artichoke risotto and sage onion rings. The real showstoppers, however, are desserts such as warm plum-and-raspberry crumble tart with white-chocolate ice cream and quince purée.

Bronze Pig　　　　MODERN BRITISH **££**
(☑01522-524817; http://thebronzepig.co.uk; 6 West Pde; mains £15-24; ⊙dinner by reservation Wed-Sat) BBC Masterchef 2012 finalist, Irishman Eamonn Hunt, and Sicilian chef Pompeo Siracusa have taken Lincoln's dining scene by storm since opening the Bronze Pig. Their exceptional Modern British cooking has an Italian accent and food is locally sourced. Reserve well ahead and prepare to be wowed.

Brown's Pie Shop　　　　BRITISH **££**
(☑01522-527330; www.brownspieshop.co.uk; 33 Steep Hill; takeaway pies £1.50-3.50, lunch mains £9-12, dinner mains £10-25; ⊙noon-2.30pm & 5-11pm Mon-Sat, noon-8pm Sun) One of Lincoln's top tables, this long-established pie shop encompasses a smart upstairs dining room and cosy brick-lined basement. Hearty pies are stuffed with locally sourced beef, rabbit and game.

Jew's House　　　　MODERN EUROPEAN **££**
(☑01522-524851; www.jewshouserestaurant. co.uk; 15 The Strait (Steep Hill); 2-/3-course lunch menu £16.50/19.95, mains £15.50-21.50; ⊙7-9.30pm Tue, noon-2pm & 7-9.30pm Wed-Sat) This local favourite serves up gourmet fare in atmospheric surrounds in one of England's oldest houses; the Romanesque Jew's House was constructed around 1160. For the ultimate indulgence, go for the six-course tasting menu (by reservation, £59.50).

Wig & Mitre　　　　PUB **££**
(www.wigandmitre.com; 30 Steep Hill; mains £10.50-14.50; ⊙8.30am-10.30pm Mon-Sat, to 10pm Sun; 🖘) Civilised pub-restaurant the Wig & Mitre has an excellent menu yet retains the ambience of a friendly local. Food is served throughout the day, from morning fry-ups to lunchtime sandwiches and filling evening roasts. Bookings not necessary.

🍸 Drinking & Nightlife

Strugglers Inn   PUB
(83 Westgate; ⊘noon-midnight Tue & Wed, to
1am Thu-Sat, to 11pm Sun & Mon) A sunny
walled-courtyard beer garden out back, a
cosy interior and a superb selection of real
ales on tap make this the pick of Lincoln's
independent pubs.

Cloud Bar   BAR
(1 St Pauls Lane; ⊘10.30am-11pm Sun-Thu, to 1am
Fri & Sat; 🎵) The roof terrace at this new bar
near Lincoln Cathedral is a winner on sunny
days. Good tapas menu, too.

Electric Bar & Restaurant   BAR
(🎵01522-565182; www.electricbarandrestaurant.
co.uk; 5th fl, DoubleTree by Hilton Lincoln, Brayford
Wharf North; ⊘11am-11pm Sun-Thu, to midnight Fri
& Sat; 🎵) On the top floor of Lincoln's snazzy four-star DoubleTree Hilton Hotel, this
swish spot with glittering river views has a
great cocktail list, regular live jazz and a restaurant serving sophisticated British dishes
with a retro twist (such as ham-hock terrine
and coconut-ice parfait).

☆ Entertainment

Check www.lovelincoln.co.uk or www.visit
lincolnshire.com for events listings.

Lincoln Drill Hall   ARTS CENTRE
(www.lincolndrillhall.com; Freeschool Lane) Downhill from the station, this stern-looking
building hosts bands, orchestras, stage
shows, comedy and daytime festivals.

Home Nightclub   LIVE MUSIC
(http://homelincoln.co.uk; Park St; ⊘11.30am-11pm
Mon & Wed, to 3am Tue & Thu-Sat, noon-3am Sun)
Spread over six rooms with live music, dance
tunes and a total of eight bars, this cavernous
venue is home to Lincoln's students.

ℹ️ Information

Tourist Office (🎵01522-545458; www.
visitlincoln.com; 9 Castle Hill; ⊘10am-5pm
Mon-Sat, 10.30am-4pm Sun) Friendly office in
a handsome 16th-century building.

ℹ️ Getting There & Away

BUS
National Express runs direct bus services from
Lincoln to London Victoria (£19.60, 5¼ hours,
two daily) and Birmingham (£16.80, three hours,
daily).

Local Stagecoach buses include bus 1 to
Grantham (£4.40, 1¼ hours, hourly Monday to
Saturday, five on Sunday).

TRAIN
Boston £15.10, two hours, hourly, change at
Sleaford
Newark-on-Trent (Newark Castle) £4.90, 25
minutes, every 15 minutes Monday to Saturday,
10 on Sunday
Nottingham £10.60, one hour, hourly
Sheffield £14.10, 80 minutes, hourly
York £36.30, two hours, two per hour

Stamford

POP 19,700
One of England's prettiest towns, Stamford
seems frozen in time, with elegant streets
lined with honey-coloured limestone buildings and hidden alleyways dotted with
alehouses, interesting eateries and small
independent boutiques. A forest of historic
church spires rises overhead and the gently
gurgling River Welland meanders through
the town centre. It's a favourite with film-
makers seeking the postcard vision of England, and appears in everything from *Pride
and Prejudice* to the *Da Vinci Code*.

◉ Sights

Simply strolling Stamford's streets is a delight.

★**Burghley House**   HISTORIC BUILDING
(www.burghley.co.uk; adult/child incl sculpture
garden £13/6.50, garden only £7.50/6.50; ⊘11am-
5pm Sat-Thu mid-Mar–late Oct) Lying just a mile
south of Stamford, opulent Burghley House
('bur-lee') was built by Queen Elizabeth's
chief adviser William Cecil, whose descendants still live here.

Set in more than 810 hectares of grounds,
landscaped by the famous Lancelot 'Capability' Brown, the house bristles with cupolas,
pavilions, belvederes and chimneys. A particular highlight is the lavish staterooms.

The renowned Burghley Horse Trials take
place here in early September.

Follow the marked path for 15 minutes
through the park by Stamford train station.

St Mary's Church   CHURCH
(http://stamfordstmary.weebly.com; St Mary's St;
⊘hours vary) A charmingly wonky broach
spire tops St Mary's Church.

WORTH A TRIP

GRANTHAM & AROUND

Grantham would be just another country town were it not for two famous 'yellowbellies' (as Lincolnshire locals call themselves) – Sir Isaac Newton and the late former prime minister Margaret Thatcher, the daughter of a humble Grantham greengrocer, who plied his trade at 2 North Pde. The town itself has just a few sights, but there are some fascinating properties in the surrounding countryside.

Woolsthorpe Manor (NT; www.nationaltrust.org.uk; Water Lane; adult/child £6.65/3.35; ⊙ 11am-5pm Wed-Mon Mar-Oct, 11am-5pm Fri-Sun Nov-Feb) Newton fans may feel the gravitational pull of the great man's birthplace, about 8 miles south of Grantham. The 17th-century house contains reconstructions of Newton's rooms; the apple that inspired the theory of gravity allegedly fell from the tree in the garden. There's a nifty kids' science room and a cafe. Take Centrebus 28 from Grantham (£2.50, 25 minutes, four per day Monday to Saturday).

Belvoir Castle (☎ 01476-871001; www.belvoircastle.com; adult/child £15/8, gardens only £8/5; ⊙ castle tours 11.15am, 1.15pm & 3.15pm Sun & Mon May-Aug, gardens 11am-5pm Sun & Mon May-Aug) The Duke and Duchess of Rutland's ancestral home, Belvoir (pronounced 'beaver') is a 19th-century baroque and Gothic fantasy built over the ruins of three previous castles. Still inhabited by the Manners family, it overflows with tapestries, priceless furniture and ancient oil paintings. Belvoir Castle is technically in Leicestershire, but Grantham, 6 miles east, is the nearest town. Bus 9 (£1.60, 20 minutes, four per day Monday to Friday) stops at the Chequers Inn, from where it's a 20-minute walk.

Chequers Inn (☎ 01476-870701; www.chequersinn.net; Main St, Woolsthorpe by Belvoir; mains £11-20; ⊙ kitchen noon-2.30pm & 6-9.30pm Mon-Sat, noon-4pm & 6-8.30pm Sun) Dine on some of the finest food in the Midlands in the rambling garden bordering a sheep-filled paddock or inside by the open fire of this charming inn, about 7 miles southwest of Grantham. There's a fabulous range of ciders and real ales on tap and, across the lane, the former stables house four simple but stylish guest rooms (single/double £50/70). The inn's sunny front patio overlooks Belvoir Castle.

William Browne Hospital   MUSEUM
(Broad St; adult/child £2.50/1; ⊙ 11am-4pm Sat, 2-4.30pm Sun May-Sep) Explore the 15th-century chapel and chambers of the medieval almshouse, William Browne Hospital.

🛏 Sleeping

Stamford Lodge   B&B ££
(☎ 01780-482932; www.stamfordlodge.co.uk; 66 Scotgate; s/d £65/85; 🛜) Centrally situated, this 18th-century former bakehouse has five fresh, modern rooms and excellent breakfasts.

★ **George Hotel**   HISTORIC HOTEL £££
(☎ 01780-750750; www.georgehotelofstamford.com; 71 St Martin's; s/d from £95/165, 4-poster d £250; P@🛜) Stamford's luxurious landmark inn opened its doors in 1597. Today its 47 rooms impeccably blend period charm and modern elegance, while its restaurant serves superior Modern British cuisine.

William Cecil at Stamford   HISTORIC HOTEL £££
(☎ 01780-750070; www.thewilliamcecil.co.uk; High St, St Martins; s/d midweek £101/111, weekends £120/130; P🛜) Within the Burghley Estate, rooms at this stunningly renovated hotel are inspired by Burghley House, with period furnishings and luxuries such as claw-foot baths. The smart restaurant opens to a wicker-chair-furnished patio.

🍴 Eating

The finest dining in town is at the George and William Cecil hotels.

Tobie Norris   PUB ££
(www.tobienorris.com; 12 St Pauls St; mains £8-20; ⊙ kitchen noon-2.30pm & 6-9.30pm Mon-Sat, to 4pm & 6-8.30pm Sun) A wonderful stone-walled, flagstone-floored pub with a warren of rooms and a sunny courtyard. It serves international dishes such as wasabi chicken with crushed plum-chutney potatoes and wholesome local ales.

Jim's Yard   MODERN BRITISH ££
(☎ 01780-756080; www.jimsyard.biz; 3 Ironmonger St; mains £12.50-21; ⊙ noon-2.30pm & 6-9.30pm Tue-Sat) Tucked away in a courtyard off a narrow laneway, Jim's Yard serves upmarket fare sourced from local producers.

ⓘ Information

Tourist Office (☑ 01780-755611; www.stamford artscentre.com; 27 St Mary's St; ☺ 9.30am-5pm Mon-Sat; 🐾) In the Stamford Arts Centre.

ⓘ Getting There & Away

Centrebus 4 runs to Grantham (£4, one hour, three per day Monday to Friday, two Saturday) and National Express to London Victoria (£13.50, four hours, one daily).

Trains run to Birmingham (£21.90, 1½ hours, hourly), Leicester (£12.90, 40 minutes, hourly) and Stansted Airport (£31.40, 1¾ hours, hourly) via Cambridge (£24, 1¼ hours) and Peterborough (£7.70, 15 minutes).

Boston

POP 41,340

It's hard to believe that sleepy Boston was the inspiration for its larger and more famous American cousin. Although no Boston citizens sailed on the *Mayflower,* the town became a conduit for persecuted Puritans fleeing Nottinghamshire for religious freedom in the Netherlands and America. In the 1630s, the fiery sermons of Boston vicar John Cotton inspired many locals to follow their lead, among them the ancestors of John Quincy-Adams, the sixth American president. These pioneers founded a namesake town in the new colony of Massachusetts and the rest, as they say, is history.

⊙ Sights

St Botolph's Church   CHURCH
(www.parish-of-boston.org.uk; tower adult/child £3/1; ☺ church 8.30am-4.30pm daily, tower 10am-3.30pm Mon-Sat, last climb 3pm) Built in the early 14th century, St Botolph's Church (the name Boston is a corruption of 'St Botolph's Stone') is known locally as the Stump, in reference to the truncated appearance of its 88m-high tower. Walk up the 365 steps on a clear day and you'll see out to Lincoln, 32 miles away.

Guildhall   MUSEUM
(☑ 01205-365954; www.bostonguildhall.co.uk; South St; ☺ 10.30am-3.30pm Wed-Sat) Before escaping to the New World, the Pilgrim Fathers were briefly imprisoned in the 14th-century Guildhall. It's one of Lincolnshire's oldest brick buildings, dating from the 1390s and situated close to the River Witham. Inside are fun, interactive exhibits, as well as a restored 16th-century courtroom and a re-created Georgian kitchen.

Maud Foster Windmill   MILL
(☑ 01205-352188; www.maudfoster.co.uk; adult/child £4/2; ☺ 10am-5pm Wed & Sat) About 800m northeast of Market Pl, England's tallest working windmill has seven floors that creak and tremble with every turn of the sails; it sells bags of flour milled on-site. Self-caterers can stay in the granary next door (double from £195 for two nights including a windmill tour; children not permitted).

🛏 Sleeping & Eating

White Hart   PUB £€
(☑ 01205-311900; www.whitehartboston.com; 1-5 High St; s/d £49.50/67.50; 🅿 @) Right in the middle of town, this handsome pub-hotel is part of the Best Western chain. Rooms are tastefully modernised and there's a decent Modern British menu (mains £9 to £18).

ⓘ Information

Tourist Office (☑ 01205-365954; www. bostonguildhall.co.uk; South St; ☺ 10.30am-3.30pm Wed-Sat) Inside the Guildhall.

ⓘ Getting There & Away

Trains connect Boston with Leicester (£22.10, 2½ hours, hourly) and Lincoln (£15.10, two hours, hourly) via a change at Sleaford.

NORTHAMPTONSHIRE

Dotted with villages full of pincushion cottages with thatched rooves and Tudor timbers, Northamptonshire also has a string of stately manors, including the ancestral homes of George Washington and Diana, Princess of Wales.

Motoring fans won't want to miss the Formula One British Grand Prix (www.silverstone.co.uk), which roars around Silverstone Circuit, near Towcester, for three days in early July.

ⓘ Information

Visit Northamptonshire (www.visitnorthamptonshire.co.uk; 🐾)

ⓘ Getting Around

Northampton is the county's hub for bus services; see the 'Transport & Streets' pages at www. northamptonshire.gov.uk for routes and timetables. Trains run by London Midland are useful for getting to/from Northampton.

Northampton

POP 215,170

Rebuilt after a devastating fire in 1675, Northamptonshire's county town was one of the prettiest in the Midlands before WWII bombers and postwar town planners wreaked havoc. Still, the city's heart retains some grand architecture. Northampton played a significant role in the Wars of the Roses and the English Civil War, before shifting its attention to manufacturing shoes.

◎ Sights

All Saints' Church   CHURCH
(www.allsaintsnorthampton.com; George Row; ⊙9am-6pm) Constructed after the 1675 fire, All Saints' Church owes an obvious debt to the churches built by Sir Christopher Wren after the Great Fire of London, with an ornate barrel-vaulted ceiling and dark-wood organ and reredos.

Guildhall   HISTORIC BUILDING
(St Giles St) Built between 1861 and 1864, Northampton's landmark Guildhall is adorned with carvings and 14 statues of monarchs, local luminaries and patron saints, including St Michael, patron saint of corporations. Now housing the council offices, it's closed to the public except during heritage events.

**Northampton Museum
& Art Gallery**   MUSEUM, GALLERY
(www.northampton.gov.uk/museums; Guildhall Rd; ⊙10am-5pm Tue-Sat, 2-5pm Sun) FREE Even those without a shoe fetish will get a kick out of the impressive displays, where you can learn about the history of shoemaking and footwear fashions.

St Peter's Church   CHURCH
(⊙10am-4pm Wed-Sat Mar-Oct, 11am-3pm Wed-Sat Nov-Feb) West of the central Market Sq, St Peter's Church is a marvellous Norman edifice built in 1150 and adorned with ancient carvings. The sign on the door tells you where you can collect the key to peek inside.

Church of the Holy Sepulchre   CHURCH
(www.stseps.org; ⊙2-4pm Wed, 11am-3pm Sat May-Sep) North of the centre, beyond the eyesore bus station, Church of the Holy Sepulchre is one of the few surviving round churches in the country. It was founded when the first earl of Northampton returned from the Crusades in 1100.

⎸ Sleeping & Eating

The tourist office can advise on B&Bs in the area.

Church Bar & Restaurant   MODERN EUROPEAN ££
(☑01604-603800; www.thechurchrestaurant.com; 67-83 Bridge St; mains £15; ⊙noon-2.30pm & 6-9.30pm Mon-Sat) At this superbly converted old church, you can feast on modern European cooking (bookings recommended), or sip a cocktail under the stained-glass windows in the bar.

ⓘ Information

Tourist Office (☑01604-838800; www.visitnorthamptonshire.co.uk; George Row; ⊙8am-5.30pm Mon-Fri year-round, 10am-2pm Sat Apr-Sep) Housed in the historic Sessions House, built in 1675.

ⓘ Getting There & Away

Greyfriars bus station is on Lady's Lane, just north of the Grosvenor shopping centre. National Express coach services include the following:
Birmingham £7.40, 2¾ hours, eight daily
London Victoria £13, 2¼ hours, 12 daily
Nottingham £13.20, 2½ hours, two daily

Northampton has good rail links with Birmingham (£14, one hour, every 20 minutes) and London Euston (£26.20, one hour, three hourly). The train station is about half a mile west of town along Gold St.

Around Northampton

Northamptonshire has a cache of ancient churches, some dating back to Saxon times. Many open only from May to September; Northampton's tourist office has information including bus schedules.

Althorp

The ancestral home of the Spencer family, **Althorp House** (☑01604-770107; www.spencerofalthorp.com; adult/child £18.50/11; ⊙1-5pm Sun May–mid-Jul & Sep, 1-5pm daily mid-Jul–Aug) – pronounced 'altrup' – is the final resting place of Diana, Princess of Wales, commemorated by a memorial. The outstanding art collection features works by Rubens, Gainsborough and Van Dyck. Tickets are limited and must be booked by phone or online.

Althorp is off the A428, 5.5 miles northwest of Northampton. Stagecoach bus 96

(Northampton–Rugby, £4.60, hourly, Monday to Saturday) passes the estate gates, from where it's a 20-minute walk.

Profits go to charities supported by the Princess Diana Memorial Fund.

Stoke Bruerne

POP 375

About 8 miles south of Northampton, brightly painted barges frequent this charming little village nestled against the Grand Union Canal, the main drag of England's canal network. From here, you can follow the waterways all the way to Leicester, Birmingham or London.

◉ Sights & Activities

Several boat owners offer summertime cruises.

Canal Museum MUSEUM
(http://canalrivertrust.org.uk/the-canal-museum/stoke-bruerne; adult/child £4.75/2.75; ⊙10am-5pm Apr-Oct, 11am-3pm Wed-Fri, to 4pm Sat & Sun Nov-Mar) Set in a converted corn mill, the entertaining Canal Museum charts the history of the canal network and its bargemen, lock keepers and pit workers. Scale models abound; outside you can see the historic narrowboat *Sculptor*, listed on the National Historic Boat Register.

Indian Chief CRUISE
(✐01604-862428; www.boatinn.co.uk; adult/child from £3/2.50; ⊙11.30am-3pm Sun & bank holiday weekends) Year-round you can take trips lasting 25 minutes aboard the Boat Inn's narrowboat, the *Indian Chief.*

🛏 Sleeping & Eating

Waterways Cottage B&B ££
(✐01604-863865; www.waterwayscottage.co.uk; Bridge Rd; d £75) For overnight stays, try Waterways Cottage, an adorable thatched cottage right off the front of a biscuit box.

Boat Inn PUB ££
(✐01604-862428; www.boatinn.co.uk; mains £7.75-24; ⊙9.30am-3pm & 6-9pm Mon-Fri, to 9pm Sat, to 8.30pm Sun) Meals and brews are served up at the canalside Boat Inn.

ℹ Getting There & Away

Buses 86 and 87 run between Stoke Bruerne and Northampton (£4.40, 30 minutes, four per day Monday to Saturday, four Sunday).

Sulgrave Manor

This impressively preserved Tudor mansion (www.sulgravemanor.org.uk; adult/child £7.90/3.60, garden only £3.60/free; ⊙11am-4pm Sat & Sun Apr-Jul, Sep & Oct, to 4pm Tue-Sun Aug) was built by Lawrence Washington in 1539. The Washington family lived here for almost 120 years before Colonel John Washington, the great-grandfather of America's first president George Washington, sailed to Virginia in 1656.

Sulgrave Manor is about 20 miles southwest of Northampton, just off the B4525 near Banbury; you'll need your own wheels to get here.

LEICESTERSHIRE

Leicestershire was a vital creative hub during the Industrial Revolution, but its factories were a major target for German air-raids in WWII and most towns in the county still bear the scars of war-time bombing. Nevertheless, there are some impressive remains, from Elizabethan castles to Roman ruins. The busy, multicultural capital Leicester is enjoying new-found fame due to the recent discovery of King Richard III's remains.

ℹ Information

Leicestershire Tourism (www.goleicestershire.com)

ℹ Getting There & Around

Leicester is well served by buses and trains. For bus routes and timetables, visit the 'Roads & Transport' pages at www.leics.gov.uk. Regular buses connect Rutland to Leicester, Stamford and other surrounding towns.

Leicester

POP 329,840

Built over the buried ruins of two millennia of history, Leicester (*les*-ter) suffered at the hands of the Luftwaffe and postwar planners. A massive influx of textile workers from India and Pakistan since the 1960s, however, has transformed the city into a bustling global melting pot, with dozens of mosques and temples in and around the centre.

Leicester

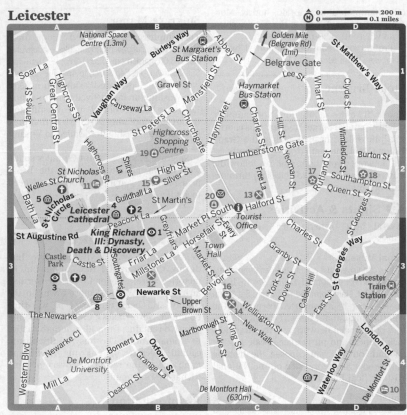

Leicester

◎ Top Sights

◎ Sights

🛏 Sleeping

✕ Eating

🍸 Drinking & Nightlife

🎭 Entertainment

🛍 Shopping

Historical treasures include one of England's finest medieval guildhalls. The 2012 discovery and 2013 identification of the remains of King Richard III in a Leicester car park has sparked a flurry of developments, including a spiffing new visitor centre on the site.

◉ Sights

★ King Richard III: Dynasty, Death & Discovery
HERITAGE CENTRE

(http://kriii.com; St Martin's Pl; adult/child £7.95/4.75; ⊙10am-4pm Mon-Fri, to 5pm Sat & Sun) Leicester's brand-new, high-tech King Richard III visitor centre is split into three sections. Dynasty explores his rise to become the final Plantagenet king. Death delves into the Battle of Bosworth, when Richard became the last English king to be killed in battle. Discovery details the University of Leicester's archaeological dig and identification, allowing you to visit the site of the grave in which he was found.

Guildhall
HISTORIC BUILDING

(www.leicester.gov.uk/museums; Guildhall Lane; ⊙11am-4.30pm Mon-Wed & Sat, 1-4.30pm Sun Feb-Nov) FREE Leicester's perfectly preserved 14th-century guildhall is reputed to be the most haunted building in Leicester. You can search for spooks in the magnificent Great Hall, the wood-panelled 'Mayor's Parlour' and the old police cells, which contain a reconstruction of a 19th-century gibbet.

New Walk Museum & Art Gallery
MUSEUM, GALLERY

(www.leicester.gov.uk/museums; New Walk; ⊙10am-5pm Mon-Sat, from 11am Sun) FREE Highlights of this grand Victorian museum include the dinosaur galleries, the painting collection (with works by Turner and Degas) and the Egyptian gallery, where real mummies rub shoulders with displays about Boris Karloff's *The Mummy* film. Littlies under five can let loose in the interactive Den.

National Space Centre
MUSEUM

(www.spacecentre.co.uk; adult/child £13/11; ⊙10am-4pm Tue-Fri, to 5pm Sat & Sun) Leicester's space museum is a fascinating introduction to the mysteries of the spheres. Although British space missions usually launch from French Guiana or Kazakhstan, the ill-fated *Beagle 2* mission to Mars was controlled from here. Fun, kid-friendly displays cover everything from astronomy to the status of current space missions. The centre is off the A6 about 1.5 miles north of the city centre. Take bus 54 (£1.80, 15 minutes, every 20 minutes) from Charles St.

Newarke Houses Museum
MUSEUM

(www.leicester.gov.uk/museums; The Newarke; ⊙10am-5pm Mon-Sat, from 11am Sun) Sprawling over two 16th-century mansions, exhibits at this entertaining museum detail the lifestyle of locals through the centuries. Don't miss the walk-through re-creation of a WWI trench, and the trophies of the Royal Leicestershire Regiment, including an outrageous snuff box made from a tiger's head.

Leicester Castle
CASTLE

Scattered around the Newarke Houses Museum are the ruins of Leicester's medieval castle, where Richard III spent his final

---

KING RICHARD III

It's an amazing story. Philippa Langley, a member of the Richard III Society, spent four-and-a-half years researching the whereabouts of King Richard's remains after his demise at Bosworth (p478). The society, founded in 1924, aims to research the king's life and to achieve a more balanced characterisation of him than that of a cruel and calculating figure, as portrayed by Shakespeare and various authors and historians. Langley narrowed it down to a Leicester car park, built over the site of the long-since-demolished Greyfriars church. But it took her another three years to persuade the city council to excavate.

Archaeologists from the University of Leicester carried out the dig in August 2012, unearthing a skeleton just three weeks later. In February 2013, the bones were confirmed by DNA analysis as those of the late king.

The university was also able to undertake a facial reconstruction using the king's skull, giving the modern world its first true image of Richard III. The reconstruction is on permanent display at Leicester's new King Richard III: Dynasty, Death & Discovery (p475) visitor centre.

A free Richard III Audio Tour app covers key Richard sites in the city and county.

Leicester Cathedral's arrangements to bury the king were derailed by the Plantagenet Alliance, a group of distant relatives, some of whom wanted Richard to be buried in York, while others sought a public consultation. A High Court ruling in 2014 ordered that the Leicester Cathedral burial go ahead – it's slated for spring 2015, preceded by a procession from Bosworth.

days before the Battle of Bosworth. The most impressive chunk of masonry is the monumental gateway known as the **Magazine** (Newarke St), once a storehouse for cannonballs and gunpowder. Clad in Georgian brickwork, the 12th-century **Great Hall** (Castle Yard) stands behind a 15th-century gate near the church of **St Mary de Castro** (Castle St), where Geoffrey Chaucer was married in 1336.

Jewry Wall Museum   MUSEUM
(www.leicester.gov.uk/museums; St Nicholas Circle; ☺11am-4.30pm Feb-Oct) FREE You can see fine Roman mosaics and frescos in this museum exploring the history of Leicester from Roman times to the modern day. In front of the museum is the **Jewry Wall**, part of Leicester's Roman baths. Tiles and masonry from the baths were incorporated in the walls of neighbouring **St Nicholas Church**.

★ **Leicester Cathedral**   CATHEDRAL
(http://leicestercathedral.org; ☺8am-6pm Mon-Sat, 7am-4.30pm Sun) FREE Look for the striking carvings on the roof supports of this substantial medieval cathedral. Free hour-long tours take place at 2pm from Monday to Saturday.

✦ Festivals & Events

Leicester Comedy Festival   COMEDY
(☑0116-242 3595; www.comedy-festival.co.uk; ☺Feb) England's longest-running comedy festival draws big names as well as fresh talent.

Leicester Caribbean Carnival   CULTURAL
(http://leicestercarnival.com; ☺Aug) The biggest Caribbean celebration in the country (after London's Notting Hill Carnival), with colourful costumes galore on the first Saturday in August.

🛏 Sleeping

★ **Hotel Maiyango**   HOTEL ££
(☑0116-251 8898; www.maiyango.com; 13-21 St Nicholas Pl; d from £89; ✳@☞) At the end of the pedestrian High St, this sophisticated pad has spacious rooms, decorated with handmade Asian furniture, contemporary art and massive plasma TVs. In addition to its candlelit Maiyango Restaurant & Bar, it also has a fabulous Kitchen Deli gourmet cafe and store.

Belmont Hotel   HOTEL ££
(☑0116-254 4773; www.belmonthotel.co.uk; De Montfort St; s/d from £59/79; P✳@☞) Owned and run by the same family for four generations, the 19th-century Belmont has stylish contemporary, individually designed rooms and a fantastic location overlooking leafy New Walk. Its restaurant is highly regarded; the two bars, Jamie's and Will's, open to a terrace and a conservatory respectively.

🍴 Eating

A visit to Leicester isn't complete without singeing your tastebuds on a curry along the **Golden Mile**. Self-caterers should head to the Leicester Market (p477). The glitzy **Highcross Leicester** (www.highcrossleicester.com; Shires Lane; ☺9.30am-8pm Mon-Fri, 9am-7pm Sat, 11am-5pm Sun; ☞) shopping mall has upmarket chain restaurants.

Good Earth   VEGETARIAN £
(☑0116-262 6260; 19 Free Lane; mains £3.50-6.50; ☺10am-3pm Mon-Fri, to 4pm Sat; ✍) ✎ Justifiably popular for its daily changing wholesome veggie bakes; huge, fresh salads; and homemade cakes.

Boot Room   BISTRO ££
(☑0116-262 2555; www.thebootroomeaterie.co.uk; 29 Millstone Lane; mains £13-19.50; ☺noon-2.30pm & 5.30-9.30pm Tue-Fri, noon-10pm Sat) A

DON'T MISS

THE GOLDEN MILE

Lined with sari stores, jewellery emporiums and curry houses, Belgrave Rd – aka the Golden Mile – is an essential stop for authentic Indian vegetarian food.

There are more top-notch eateries than you can shake a chapatti at. Top pick is **Bobby's** (☑0116-266 0106; www.eatatbobbys.com; 154-156 Belgrave Rd; dishes £3.75-6; ☺11am-9pm Mon, to 10pm Wed-Fri, 10am-10pm Sat & Sun; ✍), famed for its *namkeen* – lentil-flour snacks that come in myriad shapes and sizes. Shops along the strip sell *mithai* (Indian sweets), which involve sugary combinations of nuts, fruit and milk curds.

Belgrave Rd is about 1 mile northeast of the centre – follow Belgrave Gate and cross Burleys Flyover, or take bus 5A, 25, 54, or 126 (£1.80, seven minutes, every five minutes) from St Margaret's bus station.

former shoe factory now houses this contemporary independent bistro. Premium ingredients are used in dishes from roast Cornish cod with smoked tomato risotto to duck leg with Clonakilty black pudding. Save room for the soufflé of the day for dessert.

White Peacock
MODERN BRITISH £££

(📞0116-254 7663; www.the-white-peacock.co.uk; 14-16 King St; lunch 2-/3-course menu £16/19, dinner 2-/3-course menu £26.50/28.50; ⊗noon-3pm & 6-9.30pm Tue-Sat, to 3pm Sun) Leicester lacked an independent fine-dining restaurant until it arrived in this beautiful Grade II–listed building overlooking the New Walk pedestrian path. Chef Phillip Sharpe's ambitious dishes span starters such as goats cheese mousse with fig, beetroot and walnut to mains such as chicken with crayfish, mango and tamarind jus, and sublime desserts.

Drinking & Nightlife

The Moroccan-style bar of the Hotel Maiyango mixes Leicester's best cocktails.

Globe
PUB

(www.everards.co.uk; 43 Silver St; ⊗11am-11pm Sun-Thu, to 1am Fri & Sat) In the atmospheric Lanes – a tangle of alleys south of the High St – this old-fashioned pub has fine draught ales and a crowd that rates its drinks by quality rather than quantity.

XY Club
CLUB

(www.superfly-city.com; 2 King St; ⊗10pm-3am Wed & Thu, to 6am Fri & Sat) Behind a towering mock-Tudor facade, XY serves up diverse beats, with resident and visiting DJs.

☆ Entertainment

Curve Theatre
THEATRE

(📞0116-242 3595; www.curveonline.co.uk; Rutland St; backstage tours adult/child £3/2) A sleek artistic space with big-name shows and some innovative modern theatre. Call the ticket office to book backstage tours. The bar is a sophisticated place for a sundowner.

Phoenix Square
CINEMA

(📞0116-242 2800; http://phoenix.org.uk; 4 Midland St) Leicester's premier venue for arthouse films and digital media.

De Montfort Hall
LIVE MUSIC

(📞0116-233 3111; www.demontforthall.co.uk; Granville Rd) Big orchestras, ballets, musicals and other big song-and-dance performances are on the bill at this huge venue.

🛍 Shopping

Leicester Market
MARKET

(www.leicestermarket.co.uk; Market Pl; ⊗outdoor market 7am-6pm Mon-Sat, indoor market 8am-5pm Tue-Sat) More than 300 stalls at Leicester's indoor and outdoor markets sell everything from organic vegetables to aromatic spices, fish and shellfish, new and secondhand clothes, and homewares, electronic goods, cosmetics, jewellery, flowers and fabrics.

🛈 Information

Tourist Office
(📞0116-299 4444; www.goleicestershire.com; 51 Gallowtree Gate; ⊗9.30am-5.30pm Mon-Sat, 11am-5pm Sun) Helpful office with reams of city and county info. Sells the *Richard III Walking Trail* map (50p), which is also downloadable. Ask about guided walking tours (£5).

🛈 Getting There & Away

BUS
Inter-city buses operate from **St Margaret's bus station** (Gravel St), located north of the centre. The useful Skylink bus runs to East Midlands airport (£7, 50 minutes, at least hourly, 24 hours). Bus 440 runs to Derby (£7.70, one hour, at least hourly).

National Express services include the following:

Coventry £6.60, 45 minutes, four daily

London Victoria £10, 2¾ hours, hourly

Nottingham £4.60, 45 minutes, one to two hourly

Rugby £3.60, one hour, hourly

WORTH A TRIP

WYMESWOLD
....

The cute village of Wymeswold, 16 miles north of Leicester via the A46, warrants a visit for a mind-blowing meal. Set in bucolic gardens at the edge of the village, everything at this idyllic **Hammer & Pincers** (📞01509-880735; www.hammerandpincers.co.uk; 5 East Rd; mains £15-24, 8-course menu £45, with wine £65; ⊗noon-2pm & 6-9.30pm Tue-Sat, to 4pm Sun; 🚗) gastropub is homemade, down to the breads and condiments. Steaks are a speciality; value for money is exceptional. Best reached by car; buses from Leicester require changing at Loughborough or Ashfordby.

TRAIN

East Midlands services include the following:
Birmingham £12.90, 50 minutes, hourly
London St Pancras £57, 1¼ hours, two to four hourly

ⓘ Getting Around

The centre is cut off from the suburbs by a tangle of underpasses and flyovers, but downtown Leicester is easy to get around on foot. For unlimited transport on local buses, buy a Flexi Day Ticket (£5).

Around Leicester

Bosworth Battlefield

Given a few hundred years, every battlefield ends up simply a field, but the site of the Battle of Bosworth – where Richard III met his maker in 1485 – is enlivened by an entertaining **heritage centre** (☑01455-290429; www.bosworthbattlefield.com; adult/child £7.95/4.75; ☺10am-5pm Apr-Oct, to 4pm Nov-Mar)

SPLASHING ABOUT ON RUTLAND WATER

Tiny Rutland was merged with Leicestershire in 1974, but in 1997 regained its 'independence' as England's smallest county.

Rutland centres on **Rutland Water**, a vast artificial reservoir created by the damming of the Gwash Valley in 1976. Covering 1255 hectares, the reservoir attracts some 20,000 birds, including ospreys.

Oakham, the main hub, is 20 miles east of Leicester, linked by train (£11.80, 30 minutes, hourly or better). The hail-and-ride Rutland Shore Link bus service (single/day ticket £2.50/4, round trip 1½ hours) runs from Oakham around the lake.

Rutland Water Visitor Centre (☑01780-686800; www.anglianwater.co.uk; ☺10am-4pm Mar-Oct, hours vary Nov-Feb) At Skyes Lane near Empingham, the Rutland Water Visitor Centre has a snack kiosk, walking and cycling trails, and information on the area.

Rutland Water Nature Reserve (www.rutlandwater.org.uk; adult/child incl parking £5.65/3.30; ☺9am-5pm Mar-Oct, to 4pm Nov-Feb) Near Oakham, Rutland Water Nature Reserve has hides where you can view the abundant bird life.

Normanton Church (☑01780-686800; www.anglianwater.co.uk; adult/child £3/2; ☺12.30-3pm Sun-Wed Apr-Aug) This quaint church is saved from inundation by a limestone barrier wall. Inside are displays on the history of the Rutland reservoir.

Rockblok (☑01780-460060; www.rockblok.com; Whitwell Leisure Park, Bull Brigg Lane, Whitwell; climbing/high ropes £4/10, bike hire adult/child £17/10; ☺10am-4.30pm) Tackle a vertigo-inducing high-ropes course, an outdoor climbing wall or rent bikes for a gentle pedal around the Rutland lakeshore. See also www.rutlandcycling.com.

Rutland Watersports (☑01780-460154; www.anglianwater.co.uk/leisure; Whitwell Leisure Park, Bull Brigg Lane, Whitwell; sailboat/windsurf/kayak rental per hr from £17.50/20/7; ☺9am-7pm Fri-Tue, to 8pm Wed & Thu Apr-Oct, reduced hours Nov-Mar) Aquatic activities at Rutland include sailing and windsurfing. You can rent gear, take lessons or do certified courses.

Rutland Belle (☑01572-787630; www.rutlandwatercruises.com; adult/child £8.50/5.50; ☺hourly 1-3pm Mon-Sat, 11am-3pm Sun May-Sep, hourly 1-3pm Sat, noon-3pm Sun Apr & Oct) Cruise from Whitwell to Normanton on the southern shore of the Rutland reservoir, where a stone causeway leads out across the water to Normanton Church.

Giant-Bike (☑01780-720888; www.giant-rutland.co.uk; adult/child per day £17/10; ☺9am-5.30pm) Close to the Normanton boat jetty, Giant-Bike rents bicycles.

Rutland Sailing School (☑01780-721999; www.rutlandsc.co.uk; Gibbet Lane, Edith Weston; sail boat hire per hr from £20, half-day sailing courses from £125; ☺7.30am-dusk) Rents boats and runs sailing courses.

Hambleton Hall (☑01572-756991; www.hambletonhall.com; s/d incl breakfast from £220/285, 2-/3-course lunch menu £25.50/31.50, 3-course dinner menu £65; P 🔊) One of England's finest country hotels, Hambleton Hall sits on a peninsula jutting out into Rutland Water, 3 miles east of Oakham. Its luxuriant floral rooms and Michelin-starred restaurant are surrounded by gorgeous gardens.

full of skeletons and musket balls. Enthusiasts in period costume re-enact the battle each August.

The battlefield is 16 miles southwest of Leicester at Sutton Cheny, off the A447. A taxi from Leicester costs around £25.

Although it lasted just a few hours, the Battle of Bosworth marked the end of the Plantagenet dynasty and the start of the Tudor era. This was where the mortally wounded Richard III famously proclaimed: 'A horse, a horse, my kingdom for a horse'. Well, actually, he didn't: the quote was invented by that great Tudor propagandist William Shakespeare.

Conkers & the National Forest

The National Forest (www.forestry.gov.uk/nationalforest) is an ambitious project to generate new areas of sustainable woodland by planting 30 million trees in Leicestershire, Derbyshire and Staffordshire. More than eight million saplings have already taken root, and all sorts of visitor attractions are springing up in the forest.

⊙ Sights & Activities

Conkers   NATURE CENTRE
(☎01283-216633; www.visitconkers.com; Rawdon Rd; adult/child £8.95/7.25; ⊙10am-6pm Easter–mid-Oct, to 5pm mid-Oct–Easter) A family-oriented nature centre, it has interactive displays, indoor and outdoor playgrounds, and lots of hands-on activities. It's 20 miles northwest of Leicester off the A444; take bus 29 (£3.30, 35 minutes, half-hourly).

Hicks Lodge   CYCLING
(☎01751-460011; www.purplemountain.co.uk; Willesley Wood Side; bike rental per day adult/child £30/15; ⊙trails 8am-dusk, bike hire 10am-4pm Mon-Fri, 9am-5pm Sat & Sun) Bike trails run through the National Forest, including a flat 2km path around the lake, from this cycle centre. Hicks Lodge rents wheels; has a cafe; and also organises guided tours and night rides.

⌂ Sleeping

National Forest YHA   HOSTEL £
(☎0845 371 9672; www.yha.org.uk; dm/d from £13/52; P❋@◈) ✿ Situated 300m west of Conkers visitor centre along Bath Lane, this hostel has impressive ecofriendly features (such as greywater and solar biomass boiler usage), en suite rooms, and a restaurant serving local produce and organic wines.

STEAMING AROUND LEICESTER

Steam locomotives chug from Leicester North station on Redhill Circle to Loughborough Central, following the 8-mile route of the Great Central Railway (☎01509-632323; www.gcrailway.co.uk; return adult/child £15/9) along which Thomas Cook ran the original package tour in 1841. The locos operate several days a week from June to August, and at weekends for the rest of the year – check timetables online.

To reach Leicester North station, take bus 125 (£2.30, 20 minutes, every five minutes) from Leicester's Haymarket bus station on Charles St (take bus 126 to return).

DERBYSHIRE

The Derbyshire countryside is painted in two distinct tones – the lush green of rolling valleys, criss-crossed by dry stone walls, and the barren mottled brown hilltops of the high moorlands. The biggest draw here is the Peak District National Park, which preserves some of England's most evocative scenery, attracting legions of hikers, climbers, cyclists and cave enthusiasts.

❶ Getting There & Around

East Midlands Airport (p410) is the nearest air hub, and Derby is well served by trains, but connecting services to smaller towns are few. In the Peak District, the Derwent Valley Line runs from Derby to Matlock. Edale and Hope lie on the Hope Valley Line from Sheffield to Manchester. For a comprehensive list of Derbyshire bus routes, visit the 'Transport' pages at www.derbyshire.gov.uk.

Derby

POP 255,390

Derby was one of the crucibles of the Industrial Revolution. Almost overnight, a sleepy market town was transformed into a major manufacturing centre, producing everything from silk to bone china, and later locomotives and Rolls-Royce aircraft engines. The city suffered the ravages of industrial decline in the 1980s, but has bounced back with impressive cultural developments and a rejuvenated riverfront.

⊙ Sights

Derby Cathedral CATHEDRAL
(www.derbycathedral.org; 18 Irongate; ⊙9.30am-
4.30pm Mon-Sat & services Sun) Founded in AD
943 and reconstructed in the 18th century,
Derby Cathedral's vaulted ceiling towers
above a fine collection of medieval tombs, including the opulent grave of the oft-married
Bess of Hardwick, who at various times held
court at Hardwick Hall, Chatsworth House
and Bolsover Castle. Peregrine falcons nest
in the tower – follow their progress at www.
derbyperegrines.blogspot.com.

Derby Museum & Art Gallery MUSEUM
(www.derbymuseums.org; The Strand; ⊙10am-5pm
Tue-Sun) FREE Local history and industry displays include fine ceramics produced by Royal Crown Derby and an archaeology gallery.

Quad GALLERY, CINEMA
(☑01332-290606; www.derbyquad.co.uk; Market
Pl; gallery & mediatheque free, cinema £7-15; ⊙gal-
lery 11am-6pm, from noon Sun, BFI Mediatheque
11am-8pm, from noon Sun) A striking modernist
cube on Market Pl, Quad contains a cinema,
futuristic art gallery and mediatheque – an
archive of films and TV covering decades of
broadcasting, run by the British Film Institute (BFI).

Royal Crown Derby Factory CERAMICS
(☑01332-712800; www.royalcrownderby.co.uk;
Osmaston Rd; tour & museum adult/child £5/2.50;
⊙10am-5pm Mon-Sat, tours 11am & 1.30pm Tue-
Thu, 11am Fri by reservation) Derby's historic
potteries still turn out some of the finest
bone china in England, from edgy Asian-
inspired designs to the kind of stuff your
grandma collects.

🛏 Sleeping

Cathedral Quarter Hotel HOTEL ££
(☑01332-546080; www.cathedralquarterhotel.
com; 16 St Mary's Gate; s/d incl breakfast from
£59/69; @�) A bell's peal from the cathedral, this grand Georgian edifice houses
Derby's finest digs. The service is as polished
as the grand marble staircase and there's an
on-site spa and fine-dining restaurant.

Chuckles B&B ££
(☑01332-367193; www.chucklesguesthouse.co.uk;
48 Crompton St; s/d £38/64; �) A friendly and
cosy B&B just south of the centre, Chuckles
is run by an arty couple and is renowned for
its bountiful breakfasts. Take Green Lanes
and turn onto Crompton St by the church.

✗ Eating

★ Jack Rabbits CAFE, DELI £
(☑01332-349966; www.jackrabbitskitchen.co.uk;
50-55 Queen St; mains £6-11; ⊙8.30am-6pm Mon-
Sat, 10am-2pm Sun; ☑) Jack Rabbits serves
gourmet sandwiches, quiches, deli goods
(including homemade jams and chutneys)
and ready-to-eat meals that are perfect for
a riverside picnic. It's proved so popular
that it opened an adjoining sunlit cafe for
lazy grazing on platters, cheese-boards and
scrumptious cakes and slices.

Wonky Table BISTRO ££
(☑01332-295000; www.wonkytable.co.uk; 32
Sadler Gate; lunch mains £5.50-7.25, lunch 2-course
menu £11, dinner 2-/3-course menu £15/19; ⊙5pm-
midnight Mon, 11.30am-3pm & 5pm-midnight Tue-
Sat) Inside a retro-vintage dining room with
exposed brick walls, Wonky Table features a
slimmed-down daytime menu plus sandwiches such as warm goats cheese with caramelised onion and walnuts. But it comes into its
own at dinner with dishes including honey
and balsamic goose breast, rosemary-crusted
lamb rump, and beetroot and goats-cheese risotto balls with watercress cream.

Darleys MODERN BRITISH £££
(☑01332-364987; www.darleys.com; Waterfront,
Darley Abbey; mains £19.75-22.50; ⊙noon-2pm
& 7-9.30pm Mon-Sat, to 2.30pm Sun) Two miles
north of the centre, this upmarket restaurant has a gorgeous setting in a bright, converted mill overlooking the river. Classy fare
includes warm fig tart, goats-cheese mousse
and toasted hazelnuts.

🍷 Drinking & Entertainment

Derby has a wonderful selection of historic
real-ale pubs, many of which have live music.

Catch art-house films at Quad, or check
what's showing at the two theatre spaces
run by **Derby Live** (☑01332-255800; www.
derbylive.co.uk; Market Pl).

★ Old Bell Hotel PUB, TEAROOM
(51 Sadler Gate; ⊙8.30am-5pm Mon, to 11pm Tue-
Thu, to 12.30am Fri & Sat, 10am-10pm Sun) Dating
from 1680 and hosting Bonnie Prince Charlie's soldiers in 1745, this history-steeped
black-and-white inn languished from late
last century until its recent restoration
by valiant local entrepreneur Paul Hurst.
There's a crackling open fire and a central
courtyard (and, allegedly, more than a few
ghosts); boutique accommodation and a microbrewery are planned.

Ye Olde Dolphin PUB
(☑ 01332-267711; www.yeoldedolphin.co.uk; 5a
Queen St; ☺ 10.30am-11pm Mon-Wed, to midnight
Thu-Sat, noon-11pm Sun) Dating from 1530,
Derby's oldest pub has a hearty menu, live
music in the beer garden on weekends, and
it also organises ghost tours.

Brewery Tap PUB
(www.brewerytap-dbc.co.uk; 1 Derwent St; ☺ noon-
11pm Mon-Wed, to midnight Thu, to 1am Fri, 11am-
1am Sat, 1-11pm Sun) This pub serves its own
brews and guest ales in elegant Victorian
surrounds.

Silk Mill PUB
(www.silkmillderby.co.uk; 19 Full St; ☺ noon-11pm
Mon-Thu, 11am-midnight Fri & Sat, noon-10.30pm
Sun; ☎) Live music several times a week including Sunday afternoon jazz.

🛍 Shopping

Bennetts DEPARTMENT STORE
(www.bennettsirongate.co.uk; 8 Irongate; ☺ 9am-
5pm Mon-Sat) Founded as an ironmongers in
1734 and still retaining an ironmongery, Derby's historic department store has evolved
over the centuries to sell beautiful clothes,
homewares, gifts and more. There's a tearoom and cafe, and, on the 1st-floor interi-
or balcony, the excellent **Michael Frith at
Bennetts Brasserie** (☑ 01332-344621; www.
michaelfrithcuisine.co.uk; 8 Irongate; mains £8.50-
11.50, 3-course champagne breakfast £23; ☺ 9am-
3pm Mon-Sat), specialising in three-course
champagne breakfasts (served until 2pm).

ℹ Information

Tourist Office (☑ 01332-643411; www.vis-
itderby.co.uk; Market Pl; ☺ 9.30am-4.30pm
Mon-Sat) Under the Assembly Rooms in the
main square.

ℹ Getting There & Away

AIR
East Midlands Airport, 8 miles northwest of
Derby, is served by regular Skylink buses (£4.20,
30 minutes, at least hourly, 24 hours).

BUS
Local and long-distance buses run from Derby's
bus station, immediately east of the Westfield
shopping mall. From Monday to Saturday,
Transpeak has hourly buses between Derby and
Buxton (£5.70, 1¾ hours), via Matlock (£4.20,
35 minutes) and Bakewell (£4.70, 1¼ hours). Five
buses continue to Manchester (£7.70, 2¼ hours).

Other services include the following:
Leicester National Express; £7.70, one to two
per hour
Nottingham Red Arrow; £7.20, 30 minutes,
nine daily

TRAIN
The train station is about half a mile southeast
of the centre on Railway Tce. Services include
the following:
Birmingham £15.90, 45 minutes, four hourly
Leeds £37.30, 1½ hours, every 30 minutes
London St Pancras £65, 1¾ hours, half-hourly

Around Derby

Ashbourne
POP 8375
Perched at the southern edge of the Peak
District National Park, Ashbourne is a pret-
ty spread of steeply slanting stone streets,
lined with cafes, pubs and antique shops.

The main attraction, however, is the
chance to walk or cycle along the **Tissington Trail**, part of NCN Route 68, which runs
north for 13 miles to Parsley Hay, connecting
with the **Pennine Cycleway** (NCN Route
68) and the **High Peak Trail** towards Buxton
or Matlock. The track climbs gently along
the tunnels, viaducts and cuttings of the disused railway line that once transported local
milk to London.

🛏 Sleeping & Eating

Compton House B&B ££
(☑ 01335-343100; www.comptonhouse.co.uk;
27-31 Compton St; s/d/f from £45/65/85; ☎ 🅿)
Fresh, clean, frilly rooms, a warm welcome
and a central location make this the pick of
Ashbourne's B&Bs.

Bramhalls DELI, CAFE £
(☑ 01335-342631; www.bramhallsdeli.co.uk; 22
Market Pl; dishes £3.25-8; ☺ 8am-5pm Mon-Sat,
9am-5pm Sun) A great little deli and cafe with
posh light meals and sandwiches, and excellent homemade pastries, breads, cold meats
and 60 varieties of cheese.

Flower Cafe CAFE £
(www.theflowercafe.co.uk; 5 Market Pl; mains £6-7;
☺ 8.30am-5pm Sun-Fri, to 8pm Sat) Soups such
as parsnip, chorizo and chestnut, broccoli
and stilton, and spicy bean and lentil are a
speciality at this cute-as-a-button cafe where
everything is homemade.

ROYAL SHROVETIDE FOOTBALL

Some people celebrate Mardi Gras aka Shrove Tuesday (the last day before Lent) by eating pancakes or dressing up in carnival finery. But Ashbourne marks the occasion with a riotous game of football, where the ball is wrestled as much as kicked from one end of town to the other by crowds of revellers.

Following 12th-century rules, villagers are split into two teams – those from north of the river and those from south – and the 'goals' are two millstones, set 3 miles apart. Participants are free to kick, carry or throw the ball, though it's usually squeezed through the crowds like a rugby scrum. Sooner or later, players and the ball end up in the river. Local shops board up their windows and the whole town comes out to watch or play.

Fearless visitors are welcome to participate in the melee but, under a quirk of the rules, only locals are allowed to score goals.

🍷 Drinking & Nightlife

Smith's Tavern   PUB
(36 St John's St; ⏲ noon-11pm Mon-Thu & Sun, to midnight Fri & Sat) A tiny pub on the main shopping street, with a big selection of real ales and an old piano at the back.

❶ Getting There & Away

Bus services include the following:
Buxton Highpeak 441 and 442; £4.20, 80 minutes, every two hours Monday to Saturday, four Sunday
Derby Trent Barton Swift; £4, 30 minutes, hourly Monday to Saturday, five Sunday

❶ Getting Around

Cycle Hire Centre (☑ 01335-343156; www. peakdistrict.gov.uk/visiting/cycle; Mapleton Lane; half-day/day from £13/16; ⏲ 9.30am-5.30pm Mar-Oct, reduced hours Nov-Feb) About a mile above town, the Cycle Hire Centre is right on the Tissington Trail, at the end of a huge and atmospheric old railway tunnel leading under Ashbourne. You can also rent children's bikes, bikes with baby seats, trailers for buggies and tandems.

Matlock Bath

POP 640
Unashamedly tacky, Matlock Bath (not to be confused with the larger, work-a-day town of Matlock 2 miles north) looks like a seaside resort that somehow lost its way and ended up at the foot of the Peak District National Park. Following the River Derwent through a sheer-walled gorge, the main promenade is lined with amusement arcades, tearooms, fish-and-chip shops, pubs and shops catering to the bikers who congregate here on summer weekends. Outside summer, the town is considerably quieter and many lodgings and eateries shut.

◉ Sights & Activities

Steep paths climb the eastern side of the gorge, reached by pedestrian bridges from the A6. The tourist office has details of longer, more challenging walks in the hills.

Beware: many of the lanes up the side of the valley are too narrow for cars, with no space for turning.

Peak District Mining
Museum & Temple Mine   MUSEUM
(www.peakmines.co.uk; The Grand Pavilion, South Pde; museum adult/child £3.50/2.50, mine £3.50/2.50, combined ticket £6/4; ⏲ 10am-5pm Apr-Oct, 11am-3pm Wed-Fri, to 4pm Sat & Sun Nov-Mar) An educational introduction to the mining history of Matlock is provided by this enthusiast-run museum. Set in an old Victorian dancehall, the museum has a maze of tunnels and shafts that kids can wriggle through while adults browse historical displays. At noon and 2pm daily (at weekends only from November to March) you can go into the workings of the Temple Mine and pan for 'gold' (well, shiny minerals).

Gulliver's Kingdom   AMUSEMENT PARK
(☑ 01925-444888; www.gulliversfun.co.uk; admission £16; ⏲ hours vary) This old-fashioned amusement park offers plenty of splashing, churning, looping attractions for anyone as tall as the signs at the start of the rides. Call for opening days and times or check seasonal schedules online.

Heights of Abraham   AMUSEMENT PARK
(☑ 01629-582365; www.heightsofabraham.com; adult/child £14/9.50; ⏲ 10am-4.30pm daily early Feb–mid-Feb & mid-Mar–Nov, 10am-4.30pm Sat & Sun mid-Feb–mid-Mar) A spectacular cable-car

ride (via admission ticket only) from the base of the gorge brings you to this hilltop leisure park, whose cave and mine tours and fossil exhibitions are a winner with kids.

Peak Rail HISTORIC RAILWAY
(☑01629-580381; www.peakrail.co.uk; adult/child £8/4.30) From a tiny platform by Sainsbury's supermarket on the outskirts of Matlock (not Matlock Bath), nostalgic steam trains trundle along a 4-mile length of track to the nearby village of Rowsley, home to Caudwell's Mill, which includes a craft centre. Tickets include unlimited travel on the day of purchase. Services run five times a day Saturday and Sunday (and some weekdays) from May to October, and some weekends at other times of the year – check timetables online.

Would-be engineers can also do a one-hour train-driving course (9.45am March to November, 9.15am January and February; £115); you must be aged between 18 and 70. From March to November, there are also two-hour courses (8.45am; £200)

🛏 Sleeping & Eating

Despite its inland location, Matlock Bath's signature dish is fish and chips, which is served at cafes, tearooms and pubs along the strip.

Hodgkinson's Hotel & Restaurant HOTEL ££
(☑01629-582170; www.hodgkinsons-hotel.co.uk; 150 South Pde; s/d incl breakfast from £77/95,

2-/3-course meal £29.50/34; ⊙restaurant noon-2.30pm & 6.30-10.30pm; P 🛜) Rooms at this central Grade II–listed Victorian beauty conjure up Matlock's golden age with antique furnishings, flowery wallpaper and cast-iron fireplaces. The restaurant has just 16 seats so bookings are advised. Service is superb.

Ashdale Guest House B&B ££
(☑01629-57826; www.ashdaleguesthouse.co.uk; 92 North Pde; s/d from £45/65; P) 🌱 A tall stone house just beyond the bling of the amusement-arcade-lined main promenade, with tasteful rooms and organic breakfasts.

🛍 Shopping

For arts, crafts and discounted clothing brands, check out the Derwent Valley mills.

Scarthin Books BOOKS
(www.scarthinbooks.com; The Promenade, Cromford; ⊙9am-6pm Mon-Sat, noon-6pm Sun) More than 100,000 new and secondhand books cram 12 rooms in this biblioparadise, which hosts regular literary events and has a vegetarian cafe serving organic pizza, wraps, pies and burritos.

ℹ Information

Tourist Office (☑01335-343666; www.visitpeakdistrict.com; The Grand Pavilion, South Pde; ⊙10am-5pm daily Apr-Oct, 11am-3pm Wed-Fri, to 4pm Sat & Sun Nov-Mar) Visitor information point at the Peak District Mining Museum.

DERWENT VALLEY MILLS

Unlikely as it may sound, the industrial mills that line the Derwent Valley are ranked up there with the Taj Mahal on the Unesco World Heritage list.

Cromford Mill (☑01629-823256; www.cromfordmills.org.uk; Mill Lane, Cromford; tour adult/child £3.50/2.50; ⊙9am-5pm, tours 11am, 1pm & 2.30pm Sat-Thu, 11am Fri by reservation) Three miles south of Matlock Bath, the Cromford Mill was founded in the 1770s by Richard Arkwright. It was the first modern factory, producing cotton on automated machines, powered by a series of waterwheels along the River Derwent. This prototype inspired a succession of mills, ushering in the industrial age. The Arkwright Society runs atmospheric tours. It's one train stop from Matlock Bath (60p, three minutes, hourly).

Masson Mills (☑01629-581001; www.massonmills.co.uk; Derby Rd; adult/child £3/2; ⊙10am-4pm Mon-Sat, 11am-4pm Sun, closed Dec) A museum tells the story of the valley's textile mills at this large complex 1 mile south of Matlock Bath. The attached shopping village is full of outlet stores for big clothing brands.

Caudwell's Mill (☑01629-734374; www.caudwellsmillcraftcentre.co.uk; Rowsley; mill tours adult/child £4.50/2; ⊙9.30am-4.30pm) A chugging, grinding, water-powered mill that still produces flour the old-fashioned way, and has various craft workshops and a tearoom. You can get to Rowsley direct from Matlock Bath by Highpeak bus (£2.70, 15 minutes, hourly Monday to Saturday, two services Sunday) on the route to Bakewell, or take the Peak Rail steam train and follow the riverside path from the station.

❶ Getting There & Away

Matlock is a hub for buses around the Peak District.

Bakewell Highpeak; £3.20, 30 minutes, hourly Monday to Saturday

Derby Transpeak; £4.20, 45 minutes, hourly Monday to Saturday, two services Sunday

Trains run hourly between Matlock Bath and Derby (£5, 70 minutes, hourly).

Chesterfield

POP 88,480

The eastern gateway to the Peaks, Chesterfield is worth a stop to see the astonishing crooked spire rising atop **St Mary & All Saints Church** (🖉 01246-206506; www.chesterfieldparishchurch.org.uk; spire tours adult/child £3.50/1.50; ☉ spire tours 11.30am & 2pm Tue & Thu, 11.30am & 2.30pm Mon, Wed, Fri & Sat). Dating from 1360, the 68m-high spire is twisted in a right-handed corkscrew and leans several metres southwest. It's the result of the lead casing on the south-facing side having buckled in the sun. Learn more at the engaging **Chesterfield Museum & Art Gallery** (🖉 01246-345727; www.chesterfieldmuseum.co.uk; St Mary's Gate; ☉ 10am-4pm Mon & Thu-Sat) **FREE**.

The **tourist office** (🖉 012246-345777; www.visitchesterfield.info; Rykneld Sq; ☉ 9am-5.30pm Mon-Sat Easter-early Nov, to 5pm Mon-Sat early Nov-Easter) is directly opposite the crooked spire.

Chesterfield lies on the main rail line between Nottingham/Derby (£8, 30 minutes, up to two per hour) and Sheffield (£4.90, 15 minutes, up to two per hour). The station is just east of the centre. From Chesterfield coach station on Beetwell St, bus 170 serves Bakewell (£3.10, 45 minutes, hourly).

Hardwick Hall

One of the most complete Elizabethan mansions in the country, **Hardwick Hall** (NT; www.nationaltrust.org.uk; house & garden adult/child £12/6, garden only £6/3; ☉ house noon-4.30pm Wed-Sun, garden 9am-6pm daily) was designed by eminent architect Robert Smythson. The hall featured all the latest mod-cons of the time, including fully glazed windows. The atmospheric interiors are decked out with magnificent tapestries and oil paintings of forgotten dignitaries.

Hardwick Hall is 10 miles southeast of Chesterfield, just off the M1; it's best reached by your own wheels.

The hall was home to the 16th-century's second-most powerful woman, Elizabeth, Countess of Shrewsbury – known to all as Bess of Hardwick – who amassed a staggering fortune by marrying wealthy noblemen with one foot in the grave. Hardwick Hall was constructed using her inheritance from hubby number four, who shuffled off this mortal coil in 1590.

Set aside time to explore the formal gardens or the longer walking trails of Hardwick Park.

Next door to the manor is Bess' first house, **Hardwick Old Hall** (EH; www.english-heritage.org.uk; adult/child £5/3, incl Hardwick Hall £14/7; ☉ 10am-5pm Wed-Sun Apr-early Nov, to 5pm Sat & Sun early Nov-Mar), now a romantic ruin administered by English Heritage.

PEAK DISTRICT

Rolling across the southernmost hills of the Pennines is the glorious Peak District. Ancient stone villages are folded into creases in the landscape, and the hillsides are littered with stately homes and rocky outcrops that attract hordes of walkers, climbers and cavers. No one knows how the Peak District got its name – certainly not from the landscape, which has hills and valleys, gorges and lakes, wild moorland and gritstone escarpments, but no peaks. The most popular theory is that the region was named for the Pecsaetan, the Anglo-Saxon tribe who once populated this part of England.

Founded in 1951, the Peak District National Park was England's first national park and is Europe's busiest. But escaping the crowds is easy if you avoid summer weekends. Even at peak times, there are 555 sq miles of open English countryside in which to soak up the scenery.

Locals divide the Peak District into the Dark Peak – dominated by exposed moorland and gritstone 'edges' – and the White Peak, made up of the limestone dales to the south.

Although there are several YHA hostels (www.yha.org.uk) in the Peak District, they're often booked out in advance by groups, so contact them before turning up.

🏃 Activities

Caving & Climbing

The limestone sections of the Peak District are riddled with caves and caverns, includ-

Peak District National Park

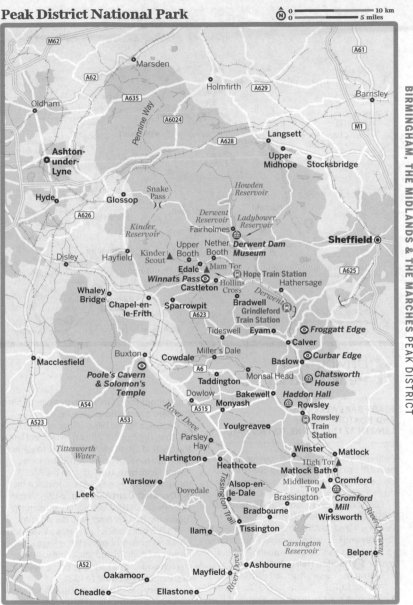

ing a series of 'showcaves' in Castleton, Buxton and Matlock Bath. For serious caving (or potholing) trips, the first port of call should be the website www.peakdistrictcaving.info, run by the caving store **Hitch n Hike** (www.hitchnhike.co.uk; Mytham Bridge, Bamford), near Castleton, which has gear and advice for climbing.

England's top mountaineers train in this area, which offers rigorous technical climbing on a series of limestone gorges, exposed tors (crags) and gritstone 'edges' that extend

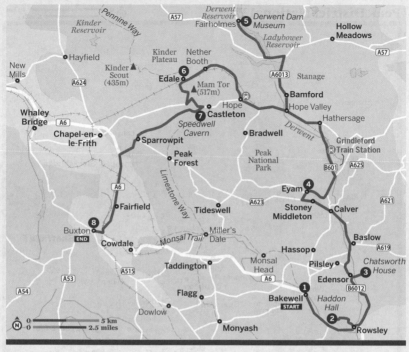

Driving Tour
Peak District

START BAKEWELL
END BUXTON
LENGTH 52 MILES; ONE TO TWO DAYS

Although you can drive this route in just a few hours, there's a lot to see and even more to do, so pack your hiking boots and consider breaking your journey overnight.

Fuel your car and yourself at ❶ **Bakewell** (p494), famed for its distinctive Bakewell Pudding. Head south on the A6 for 3.5 miles to Rowsley and turn left on winding Church Lane for 2 miles to visit the atmospheric medieval manor ❷ **Haddon Hall** (p494).

Return to Rowsley, turn left on the A6 and left on the B6012 – follow it for 2.9 miles before turning right to reach the 'Palace of the Peak', ❸ **Chatsworth House** (p495).

Back on the B6012, turn right to join the A619. At Baslow, home to the country hotel and Michelin-starred restaurant Fischer's Baslow Hall, turn left at the roundabout and travel along the A623 for 3.4 miles to the turn-off for ❹ **Eyam** (p493). Drive up the hill to reach its quaint museum, where you can

learn about the town's poignant plague history. There's fantastic walking here.

Continue up the hill and turn right on Edge Rd, then right on Sir William Hill Rd and left on the B601 at Grindleford. Continue to Hathersage and turn left on the A6187 to Hope Valley. From here, turn right on the A6013, passing Ladybower Reservoir, to reach the ❺ **Derwent Dam Museum** (p492). Pop in to learn about the Dambusters squadron's 'bouncing bombs' tests here during WWII.

It's 5.8 miles back to the Hope Valley turn-off. Then turn right onto Hathersage Rd, right again on Edale Rd and follow the valley to stretch your legs at another prime walking destination, ❻ **Edale** (p492).

Scenery peaks when you travel southwest towards Castleton, climbing the steep hill near 517m-high Mam Tor, to Winnats Rd, then following the former coral reef canyon Winnats Pass to explore ❼ **Speedwell Cavern** (p491), half-a-mile west of charming Castleton.

From Speedwell Cavern, head west along Arthurs Way on to Winnats Rd. Turning right on the A623 brings you to the riot of Victoriana in the former spa town of ❽ **Buxton** (p488).

south into the Staffordshire Moorlands. Gritstone climbing in the Peak District is predominantly on old-school trad routes, requiring a decent rack of friends, nuts and hexes. Bolted sport routes are found on several limestone crags in the Peak District, but many use ancient pieces of gear and most require additional protection. The crags are best reached with your own transport; check seasonal bus services with tourist offices in Trent Barton or Buxton.

Cycling

Plunging dales and soaring scarps provide a perfect testing ground for cyclists, and local tourist offices are piled high with cycling maps and pamphlets. For easy traffic-free riding, head for the 17.5-mile **High Peak Trail**, which follows the old railway line from Cromford, near Matlock Bath, to Dowlow near Buxton. The trail winds through beautiful hills and farmland to Parsley Hay, where the **Tissington Trail**, part of NCN Route 68, heads south for 13 miles to Ashbourne. Trails are off-road on dedicated cycle paths, suitable for road bikes.

Mirroring the Pennine Way, the **Pennine Bridleway** is another top spot to put your calves through their paces. Around 120 miles of trails have been created between Middleton Top and the South Pennines, and the route is suitable for horse riders, cyclists and walkers. You could also follow the **Pennine Cycleway** (NCN Route 68) from Derby to Buxton and beyond. Other popular routes include the **Limestone Way**, running south from Castleton to Staffordshire, and the **Monsal Trail & Tunnels** between Bakewall and Wyedale, near Buxton.

Peak Tours (www.peak-tours.com; mountain bike per day £20) delivers rental bikes anywhere in the Peak District, and offers guided cycling tours. From March to October, the **Peak District National Park Authority** (☎01629-816200; www.peakdistrict.gov.uk; bicycle hire per half-day/day adult £13/16, child £9/11) operates several cycle-hire centres.

Walking

The Peak District is one of England's most popular walking areas, with awe-inspiring vistas of hills, dales and sky that attract legions of hikers in summer. The White Peak is perfect for leisurely strolls, which can start from pretty much anywhere. Be sure to close gates behind you as you go. When exploring the rugged territory of the Dark Peak, make sure your boots are waterproof and beware of slipping into rivulets and marshes.

The Peak's most famous walking trail is the **Pennine Way**, which runs north from Edale for more than 250 miles, finishing in the Scottish Borders. If you don't have three weeks to spare, you can reach the pretty town of Hebden Bridge in Yorkshire comfortably in three days.

The 46-mile **Limestone Way** winds through the Derbyshire countryside from Castleton to Rocester in Staffordshire, following footpaths, tracks and quiet lanes. Many people walk the 26-mile section between Castleton and Matlock in one long, tiring day, but two days is better. Tourist offices have a detailed leaflet.

Other popular routes include the **High Peak Trail**, **Tissington Trail**, and **Monsal Trail & Tunnels**. Numerous short walks are available.

ℹ️ Information

Tourist offices or national park visitor centres include Buxton, Bakewell, Castleton and Edale. The Peak District National Park Authority website (www.peakdistrict.gov.uk) has reams of information on transport, activities and local events.

ℹ️ Getting There & Away

Buses run from regional centres such as Sheffield and Derby to destinations across the Peak District. Be aware that buses are much more frequent at weekends, and many services close down completely in winter. Bakewell and Matlock (not Matlock Bath) are the two main hubs – from here you can get anywhere in the Peak District. Timetables are available from all the tourist offices, or online at www.derbyshire.gov.uk/transport. Trains run to Matlock Bath, Buxton, Edale and several other towns and villages.

ℹ️ PEAK DISTRICT TRANSPORT PASSES

Handy bus passes covering travel in the Peak District include the **Peaks Plus** (adult/child £6/4), offering all-day travel on Trent Barton buses and the Transpeak between Derby and Buxton. The **Derbyshire Wayfarer** (adult/child £11.60/5.80) covers buses and trains throughout the county and as far afield as Manchester and Sheffield.

Buxton

POP 22,110

The 'capital' of the Peak District National Park, albeit just outside the park boundary, Buxton is a confection of Georgian terraces, Victorian amusements and parks in the rolling hills of the Derbyshire dales. The town built its fortunes on its natural warm-water springs, which attracted health tourists in Buxton's turn-of-the-century heyday.

Today, visitors are drawn here by the flamboyant Regency architecture and the natural wonders of the surrounding countryside. Tuesdays and Saturdays are market days, bringing colour to the grey limestone market place.

◉ Sights

Buxton's historic centre overflows with Victorian pavilions, concert halls and glasshouse domes. Its most famous building is the turreted Opera House (p490).

★ Pavilion Gardens   GARDENS
(www.paviliongardens.co.uk; ⊙9.30am-5pm)
FREE Adjoining Buxton's opulent Opera House is the equally flamboyant Pavilion Gardens, dotted with domed pavilions. The main building contains a tropical greenhouse, a nostalgic cafe and the tourist office.

Devonshire Dome   HISTORIC BUILDING
A glorious piece of Victoriana, the Devonshire Dome forms part of the campus of the University of Derby. It is also home to **Devonshire Spa** (☑01298-338408; www.devonshiredome.co.uk; 1 Devonshire Rd; 2hr body spa £20, ocean or frangipani wrap £50, day package from £95), which offers a full range of pampering treatments.

Buxton Baths   HISTORIC BUILDING
In Victorian times, spa activities centred on the extravagant Buxton Baths complex, built in grand Regency style in 1854. The various bath buildings are fronted by a grand, curving facade, known as the **Crescent**, inspired by the Royal Crescent in Bath. It's expected to re-open in 2016 as a five-star hotel and spa.

Slopes   PARK
Opposite the Crescent, a small park called the Slopes rises steeply in a series of grassy terraces. Climbing them provides the definitive view over Buxton's Victorian rooftops.

Pump Room   HISTORIC BUILDING
At the base of the Slopes is the Pump Room, which dispensed Buxton's spring water for nearly a century. Modern-day health-tourists queue up to fill plastic bottles from a small spout known as **St Ann's Well**.

**Buxton Museum
& Art Gallery**   MUSEUM, GALLERY
(www.derbyshire.gov.uk/buxtonmuseum; Terrace Rd; ⊙9.30am-5.30pm Tue-Fri, to 5pm Sat year-round, 10.30am-5pm Sun Easter-Sep) FREE In a handsome Victorian building, the town museum displays local historical bric-a-brac and curiosities from Castleton's Victorian-era 'House of Wonders', including Harry Houdini's handcuffs.

🏃 Activities

★ Buxton Tram   BUS TOUR
(☑01298-79648; http://discoverbuxton.co.uk; adult/child £6/4; ⊙hourly 10am-4pm) From the Pavilion Gardens, this vintage milk float takes you on a 12mph, hour-or-so circuit of the centre on its entertaining Wonder of the Peak tour. There are only eight seats, so booking ahead is recommended.

Poole's Cavern   CAVE
(☑01298-26978; www.poolescavern.co.uk; adult/child £9/5; ⊙9.30am-5pm Mar-Oct, 10am-4pm Sat & Sun Nov-Feb) A pleasant mile stroll southwest from the centre brings you to Poole's Cavern. This magnificent natural limestone cavern is reached by descending 28 steps; the temperature is a cool 7°C. Tours lasting 50 minutes run every 20 minutes from March to October and at 10.30am, 12.30pm and 2.30pm from November to February.

From the cavern's car park, a 20-minute walk leads up through Grin Low Wood to **Solomon's Temple**, a ruined tower with fine views over the town.

Parsley Hay Cycle Hire   CYCLING
(☑01298-84493; www.peakdistrict.gov.uk; bike hire per half-/full day adult £13/16, child £9/11; ⊙9.30am-5pm Mar-Oct) Rent bikes from the Peak District National Park Authority's Parsley Hay Cycle Hire, about 8 miles south of Buxton at the junction of the High Peak and Tissington Trails.

🛏 Sleeping

Buckingham Hotel   HOTEL £
(☑01298-70481; www.buckinghamhotel.co.uk; 1 Burlington Rd; d £55-65, f £67.50-80; P⊙) The eccentric decor isn't for everyone – framed

Buxton

N 0 ——— 100 m
0 ——— 0.05 miles

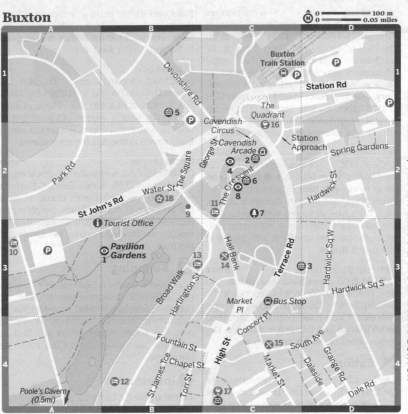

Buxton

⦿ Top Sights
1 Pavilion Gardens B3

⦿ Sights
2 Buxton Baths C2
3 Buxton Museum & Art Gallery D3
4 Crescent C2
5 Devonshire Dome B1
6 Pump Room C2
7 Slopes C2
8 St Ann's Well C2

⦿ Activities, Courses & Tours
9 Buxton Tram B2
Devonshire Spa .... (see 5)

⦿ Sleeping
10 Buckingham Hotel A3
11 Old Hall Hotel C2
12 Roseleigh Hotel B4
13 Victorian Guest House B3

⦿ Eating
14 Columbine Restaurant C3
15 Number 13 .... C4

⦿ Drinking & Nightlife
16 Barbarella's C2
17 Old Sun Inn C4

⦿ Entertainment
18 Opera House B2

photos of Hollywood stars such as Pierce Brosnan or Bruce Willis adorn each of the 57 old-fashioned rooms, and there are more lining the hallways – but there's still a lot to

recommend this oddball town-centre hotel. Rooms are clean and spacious, parking's free, and there's a lively downstairs bar and restaurant.

Old Hall Hotel
HISTORIC HOTEL ££

(☑01298-22841; www.oldhallhotelbuxton.co.uk; The Square; s/d incl breakfast from £69/79; @ 🤖) There's a tale to go with every creak of the floorboards at this history-soaked establishment, supposedly the oldest hotel in England. Among other esteemed residents, Mary, Queen of Scots, stayed here from 1576 to 1578, albeit against her will. The rooms are still the grandest in town, and there are several bars, lounges and dining options.

Roseleigh Hotel
B&B ££

(☑01298-24904; www.roseleighhotel.co.uk; 19 Broad Walk; s/d from £41/80; P @ 🤖) This gorgeous family-run B&B in a roomy old Victorian house has lovingly decorated rooms, many with fine views out over the Pavilion Gardens. The owners are a welcoming couple, both seasoned travellers, with plenty of interesting stories.

Victorian Guest House
B&B ££

(☑01298-78759; www.buxtonvictorian.co.uk; 3a Broad Walk; d from £95; P 🤖) Overlooking the Pavilion Gardens, this elegant house has eight individually decorated bedrooms furnished with Victorian and Edwardian antiques. The home-cooked breakfasts are renowned.

✗ Eating

Number 13
MODERN BRITISH ££

(☑01298-25397; www.number13.co.uk; cnr Market St & South Ave; mains £11-16; ⊙ noon-10.30pm Mon-Thu, to midnight Fri & Sat, to 7pm Sun) 🍴 Don't be fooled by the low prices – this is serious cooking that just happens to be affordable too. Dishes such as coq au vin in garlic and red wine or sausage and root mash with smoked onion marmalade are expertly prepared and exquisitely presented. Live jazz swings in the bar on Sunday afternoons.

Columbine Restaurant
MODERN BRITISH ££

(☑01298-78752; www.columbinerestaurant.co.uk; 7 Hall Bank; mains £13.50-17.50; ⊙ 7-10pm Mon-Sat May-Oct & Dec, 7-10pm Wed-Sat Jan-Apr & Nov) 🍴 On the lane leading down beside the Town Hall, this understated restaurant is the top choice among in-the-know Buxtonites. The chef conjures up imaginative dishes primarily made from local produce. Bookings recommended.

🍷 Drinking & Entertainment

Barbarella's
WINE BAR

(www.barbarellaswinebar.co.uk; 7 The Quadrant; ⊙ noon-11pm Sun-Thu, to midnight Fri & Sat; 🤖) Black-and-white paisley wallpaper, chandeliers and glossy timber tables make this sleek retro wine bar the hottest drinking den in Buxton. Stellar food too.

Old Sun Inn
PUB

(www.theoldsuninnbuxton.com; 33 High St; ⊙ noon-11pm Mon & Wed, to 11.30pm Tue, Thu & Sun, to midnight Fri & Sat) The cosiest of Buxton's pubs, with a warren of rooms full of original features, a dozen ales on tap, and a lively crowd that spans the generations.

Opera House
OPERA

(☑0845 127 2190; www.buxtonoperahouse.org.uk; Water St; tours £2.50; ⊙ tours 11am Sat) Buxton's gorgeously restored Opera House hosts a full program of drama, dance, concerts and comedy. It's the focal point for festivities including the Buxton Festival (www.buxtonfestival.co.uk; ⊙ Jul).

🛍 Shopping

Scrivener's Books & Bookbinding
BOOKS

(☑01298-73100; www.scrivenersbooks.co.uk; 42 High St; ⊙ 9am-5pm Mon-Sat, noon-4pm Sun) A delightfully chaotic bookshop, sprawling over five floors, where books are filed in piles and the Dewey system has yet to be discovered.

ℹ Information

Tourist Office (☑01298-25106; www.visitpeakdistrict.com; Pavilion Gardens; ⊙ 9.30am-5pm; 🤖) Helpful, well-organised office with useful leaflets on walks in the area. Hour-long Roman Buxton town walks, by donation, depart at 11am and 2pm Saturdays.

ℹ Getting There & Away

Buses stop on both sides of the road at Market Pl. The hourly Highpeak runs to Derby (£5.70, 1½ hours), via Bakewell (£3.70, 30 minutes) and Matlock Bath (£3.20, one hour). Five Highpeak services run to Manchester (£5.20, 1¼ hours).

To reach Sheffield take bus 65 (£5.70, 1¼ hours, every two hours Monday to Saturday, three services Sunday).

Northern Rail has trains to/from Manchester (£9.80, one hour, hourly).

Castleton & Around

POP 735

Guarding the entrance to the forbidding Winnats Pass gorge, charming Castleton is a magnet on summer weekends for Midlands visitors – come mid-week if you want to enjoy the sights in relative peace and quiet. The village's streets are lined with leaning stone houses, and walking trails criss-crossing the surrounding hills. An atmospheric castle crowns the ridge above, and the bedrock below is riddled with fascinating caves.

Sights

Peveril Castle   CASTLE
(EH; www.english-heritage.org.uk; adult/child £4.70/2.80; ⊘10am-6pm Apr-Sep, to 5pm Oct, to 4pm Sat & Sun Nov-Mar) Topping the ridge to the south of Castleton, this evocative castle has been so ravaged by the centuries that it almost looks like a crag itself. Constructed by William Peveril, son of William the Conqueror, the castle was used as a hunting lodge by Henry II, King John and Henry III, and the crumbling ruins offer swooping views over the Hope Valley.

Castleton Museum   MUSEUM
(✆01629-816572; Buxton Rd; ⊘10am-5.30pm Apr–mid-Sep, to 5pm mid-Sep–Oct, reduced hours Nov-Mar) FREE Attached to the tourist office, the cute town museum has displays on everything from mining and geology to rock climbing, hang-gliding and the curious Garland Festival.

Peak Cavern   CAVE
(✆01433-620285; http://devilsarse.com; adult/child £9.25/7.25, incl Speedwell Cavern £15.50/11.75; ⊘10am-5pm Apr-Oct, to 5pm Sat & Sun Nov-Mar) Castleton's most convenient cave is easily reached by a pretty streamside walk from the village centre. It has the largest natural cave entrance in England, known (not so prettily) as the Devil's Arse. Dramatic limestone formations are lit with fibre-optic cables.

Speedwell Cavern   CAVE
(✆01433-620512; www.speedwellcavern.co.uk; adult/child £10/8, incl Peak Cavern £15.50/11.75; ⊘9.30am-4pm) About half a mile west of Castleton at the mouth of Winnats Pass, this claustrophobe's nightmare is reached via an eerie boat ride through flooded tunnels, emerging by a huge subterranean lake called the Bottomless Pit. New chambers are discovered here all the time by potholing expeditions.

Treak Cliff Cavern   CAVE
(✆01433-620571; www.bluejohnstone.com; adult/child £8.95/9.95; ⊘10am-5pm Mar-Oct, to 4pm Nov-Feb) Captivating Treak Cliff has a forest of stalactites and exposed seams of colour-ful Blue John Stone, which is still mined to supply the jewellery trade. Tours focus on the history of mining; kids can polish their own Blue John Stone during school holidays.

Blue John Cavern   CAVE
(✆01433-620638; www.bluejohn-cavern.co.uk; adult/child £10/5; ⊘9.30am-5.30pm Apr-Oct, 9.30am-dusk Nov-Mar) Up the side of Mam Tor, Blue John is a maze of natural caverns with rich seams of Blue John Stone that are still mined every winter. You can get here on foot up the closed section of the Mam Tor road.

Activities

At the base of 517m-high Mam Tor, Castleton is the northern terminus of the **Limestone Way**, which follows narrow, rocky Cave Dale, far below the east wall of the castle. The tourist office has maps and leaflets, including details of numerous easier walks.

Festivals & Events

Garland Festival   CULTURAL
(www.visitpeakdistrict.co.uk; ⊘May) Castleton celebrates Oak Apple Day on 29 May (28 May if the 29th is a Sunday) as it has for centuries, with the Garland King (buried under an enormous floral headdress) and Queen parading through the village on horseback.

Sleeping

Prices are often higher at weekends, when booking ahead is advised.

Ye Olde Nag's Head Hotel   PUB £
(✆01433-620248; www.yeoldenagshead.co.uk; Cross St; d from £50; 🐾) The cosiest of the 'residential' pubs along the main road, offering 10 comfortable, well-appointed rooms (some with four-poster beds and spas), ale-tasting trays and a popular restaurant, plus regular live music.

Rowter Farm   CAMPSITE £
(✆01433-620271; 2-person sites £10; ⊘Easter-Oct; 🅿) A simple campsite about 1 mile west of Castleton in a stunning location up in the hills. Drivers should approach via Winnats Pass; on foot, follow the Cave Dale path.

Causeway House   B&B ££
(✆01433-623921; www.causewayhouse.co.uk; Back St; s/d from £35/70) The floors within this ancient character-soaked stone cottage are worn and warped with age, but the quaint bedrooms are bright and welcoming.

Doubles have en suites but the two single rooms (one of which can be used as a twin) share a bathroom.

✖ Eating & Drinking

Tearooms abound in Castleton. The village shop has limited stocks of provisions for walkers and is open seven days.

Three Roofs Cafe
CAFE £

(www.threeroofscafe.co.uk; The Island; dishes £6-9.50; ☺ 9.30am-5pm Mon-Fri, to 5.30pm Sat & Sun; 🗣 🏠) The most popular purveyor of cream teas, opposite the turn-off to the tourist office.

1530
ITALIAN ££

(☑ 01433-621870; www.1530therestaurant.co.uk; Cross St; mains £9.50-17; ☺ noon-2pm & 6-8.30pm Wed & Thu, to 2pm & 6-9.30pm Fri & Sat, to 2pm & 6-8pm Sun & Mon; 🍴) Crispy thin-crust pizzas and fresh pastas such as king prawn, crab, crayfish and calamari linguine are the speciality of Castleton's swish Italian flag-bearer.

★ Samuel Fox
MODERN BRITISH £££

(☑ 01433-621562; www.samuelfox.co.uk; Stretfield Rd, Bradwell; lunch mains £6-18.50, dinner mains £13.50-22.50; ☺ kitchen 6-9pm Tue, noon-2pm & 6-9pm Tue-Sat, to 3.30pm Sun) In the Hope Valley village of Bradwell, 2.5 miles southeast of Castleton, this enchanting inn owned by pedigreed chef James Duckett serves exceptional food such as rare roasted venison with pickled red cabbage, and roast pheasant with braised sprouts, bacon and parsnips. Rates for the gorgeous pastel-shaded guestrooms upstairs (single/double £95/130) include a sumptuous breakfast as well as sherry, grapes and chocolates.

Look out for dinner, bed and breakfast deals.

ℹ Information

Tourist Office (☑ 01433-620679; www.peakdistrict.gov.uk; Buxton Rd; ☺ 10am-5.30pm Apr–mid-Sep, to 5pm mid-Sep–Oct, reduced hours Nov-Mar) In the Castleton Museum.

ℹ Getting There & Away

Bus services include the following:

Bakewell Bus 173; £3, 50 minutes, four daily via Hope (10 minutes) and Tideswell (25 minutes)

Buxton Buses 68 and 173; £3.80, one hour (departs Castleton in the morning and returns in the afternoon from Monday to Saturday)

The nearest train station is at Hope, about 2 miles east of Castleton on the line between Sheffield (£6.60, 30 minutes, half-hourly) and Manchester (£10.80, 50 minutes, half-hourly). On summer Saturdays, a bus runs between Hope station and Castleton to meet the trains, but otherwise it's an easy walk.

Derwent Reservoirs

North of the Hope Valley, the upper reaches of the Derwent Valley were flooded between 1916 and 1935 to create three huge reservoirs to supply Sheffield, Leicester, Nottingham and Derby with water. These constructed lakes soon proved their worth – the **Dambusters** squadron carried out practice runs over Derwent Reservoir before unleashing their 'bouncing bombs' on the Ruhr Valley in Germany in WWII. Their exploits are detailed in the **Derwent Dam Museum** (www.peakdistrict.gov.uk; Fairholmes; ☺ 10am-4pm Sun) **FREE** in a tower atop the dam.

These days, the Ladybower, Derwent and Howden Reservoirs are popular destinations for walkers, cyclists and mountain bikers – and lots of ducks, so drive slowly! **Fairholmes** has a **tourist office** (☑ 01433-650953; www.peakdistrict.gov.uk; Fairholmes; ☺ 10am-5pm Apr-Oct, to 3.30pm Nov-Mar), which dispenses walking and cycling advice, a car park, a snack bar and a good **cycle hire centre** (☑ 01433-651261; per half-/full day adult £13/16, child £9/11; ☺ 9.30am-5.30pm).

Fairholmes is 2 miles north of the A57, the main road between Sheffield and Manchester. Buses are limited at best, so you really need your own wheels.

Edale

POP 290

Surrounded by majestic Peak District countryside, this cluster of stone houses set around a pretty parish church is an enchanting place to pass the time. Edale lies between the White and Dark Peak areas, and is the southern terminus of the Pennine Way. Despite the remote location, the Manchester–Sheffield line passes through the village, bringing throngs of weekend visitors.

🏃 Activities

Walking is the number one drawcard, with plenty of diverting strolls for less committed hill walkers.

As well as trips to Hollins Cross and Mam Tor, on the ridge dividing Edale from Castleton, you can walk north onto the **Kinder Plateau**, dark and brooding in the mist, gloriously high and open when the sun's out. This was the setting for a famous act of civil disobedience by ramblers in 1932 that paved the way for the legal 'right to roam' and the creation of England's national parks.

Weather permitting, a fine circular walk starts by following the **Pennine Way** through fields to **Upper Booth**, then up a path called Jacobs Ladder and along the southern edge of Kinder, before dropping down to Edale via the steep rocky valley of Grindsbrook Clough, or the ridge of Ringing Roger.

About 1.5 miles east of Edale, **Ladybooth Equestrian Centre** (✆ 01433-670205; www. ladybooth.co.uk; Nether Booth; horse riding per hour/day from £25/100) offers horseback trips around the Peak District, lasting anything from one hour to a full day, plus pony farm rides for kids.

🛏️ Sleeping

Fieldhead Campsite
CAMPSITE **£**

(✆ 01433-670386; www.fieldhead-campsite.co.uk; sites per person/car from £5/2.50; **P**) Right next to the Moorland Tourist Office, this pretty and well-equipped campsite spreads over six fields, with some pitches right by the river.

Edale YHA
HOSTEL **£**

(✆ 0845 371 9514; www.yha.org.uk; dm/d from £5/58; **P**@🛜) Spectacular views across to Back Tor unfold from this country-house hostel 1.5 miles east of Edale. The attached **activity centre** is very popular with student groups. It's signposted from the Hope road.

Stonecroft
B&B **££**

(✆ 01433-670262; www.stonecroftguesthouse.co. uk; Grindsbrook; d from £80; **P**🛜) ✓ This handsomely fitted-out stone house, built in the 1900s, has two comfortable bedrooms. Vegetarians and vegans are well catered for – host Julia is an award-winning chef and the organic breakfast is excellent. Picnic baskets (£12) are availble by request when booking.

🍴 Eating

Cooper's Cafe
CAFE **£**

(✆ 01433-670401; Cooper's Camp; dishes £2.20-4.80; ⊗8am-4pm daily Apr-Sep, 9.30am-3pm Thu-Sun Nov-Mar; 🛜) Load up on carbs at this cheerful cafe close to the village school.

Rambler Inn
PUB **££**

(✆ 01433-670268; www.theramblerinn.com; Grindsbrook; mains £9.25-12; 🛜💺) Cosy stone pub with real ales, hearty steaks, pies and casseroles; also B&B rooms and occasional live music.

ℹ️ Information

Moorland Tourist Office (✆ 01433-670207; www.edale-valley.co.uk; Grindsbrook; ⊗9.30am-5pm Mon-Fri, to 5.30pm Sat & Sun Apr-Sep, 10.30am-3.30pm Sat & Sun Oct-Mar) Visitor centre with maps, displays on the moors, a kiosk and a campsite.

ℹ️ Getting There & Away

Trains run from Edale to Manchester (£10.80, every hour, 45 minutes) and Sheffield (£6.90, every two hours, 40 minutes) via Hope.

Eyam
POP 970

Quaint little Eyam (ee-em), a former lead-mining village, has a poignant history. In 1665, the town was infected by the dreaded Black Death plague, carried here by fleas on a consignment of cloth from London, and the village rector, William Mompesson, convinced villagers to quarantine themselves. Some 270 of the village's 800 inhabitants succumbed, while surrounding villages remained relatively unscathed. Today, Eyam's sloping streets of old cottages backed by rows of green hills are delightful to wander.

👁️ Sights

Eyam Parish Church
CHURCH

(www.eyam-church.org; ⊗9am-6pm) Many victims of the village's 1665 Black Death plague outbreak were buried at Eyam's church. You can view stained-glass panels and moving displays telling the story of the outbreak. The churchyard contains a Celtic cross carved in the 8th century.

Eyam Hall
HISTORIC BUILDING

(NT; www.nationaltrust.org.uk; craft centre admission free, house & garden adult/child £7.15/3.70; ⊗craft centre 10am-4.30pm daily year-round, house & garden noon-4pm Wed, Thu & Sun Easter-early May & late Jul-Aug) This solid-looking 17th-century manor house with stone windows and door-frames, home to a craft centre and several eateries, is surrounded by a traditional English walled garden.

Eyam Museum

MUSEUM

(www.eyammuseum.demon.co.uk; Hawkhill Rd; adult/child £2.50/2; ☉10am-4.30pm Tue-Sun late Mar-early Nov) Vivid displays on the Eyam plague are the centrepiece of the engaging town museum, alongside exhibits on the village's history of lead-mining and silk-weaving.

🏃 Activities

Eyam makes a great base for walking and cycling in the White Peak area. For an interesting short walk, follow Water Lane out of the village from the main square, then turn right and climb the hill to reach **Mompesson's Well**, where supplies were left during the Black Death plague time for Eyam folk by friends from other villages. The goods were paid for using coins sterilised in vinegar. To return to Eyam, retrace your steps down the lane, then take a path that leads directly to the church. This 2-mile circuit takes about 1½ hours.

🛏 Sleeping & Eating

Miner's Arms

PUB **££**

(☎01433-630853; Water Lane; s/d £45/70; 🖥) Although its age isn't immediately obvious, this traditional village inn was built shortly before the Black Death hit Eyam in 1665. Inside you'll find beamed ceilings, affable staff, a cosy stone fireplace, comfy en suite rooms and good-value pub food.

Crown Cottage

B&B **££**

(☎01433-630858; www.crown-cottage.co.uk; Main Rd; s/d from £50/70; 🅿) Opposite the post office, this walker- and cyclist-friendly stone house full of pottery ornaments is crammed to the rafters most weekends, when there's a minimum two-night stay.

Village Green

CAFE **£**

(http://cafevillagegreen.com; The Square; dishes £2-6; ☉10am-4pm; 🖥) On the village square, with tables on the cobblestones outside, this sweet cafe has a mouth-watering array of slices and decent coffee.

❶ Getting There & Away

Services include the following:
Bakewell Buses 275 and 350; £3.50, 20 minutes, four per day Monday to Saturday
Buxton Buses 65 and 66; £3.50, 40 minutes, five per day Monday to Saturday, three Sunday
Sheffield Bus 65; £5.60, 40 minutes, five per day Monday to Saturday, three Sunday

Bakewell & Around

POP 3950

The second-largest town in the Peak District, pretty Bakewell is a great base for exploring the White Peak. The town is ringed by famous walking trails and stately homes, but it's probably best known for its famous pudding, a pastry shell filled with jam and frangipane invented in 1820. Like other Peak towns, Bakewell is mobbed during the summer months – expect traffic jams and cut-throat competition for accommodation at weekends. The centre of town is Rutland Sq, the meeting point of the roads from Matlock, Buxton and Chesterfield.

◉ Sights

All Saints Church

CHURCH

(www.bakewellchurch.co.uk; ☉9am-4pm Mon-Sat, to 6pm Sun Apr-Oct, 10am-3.45pm daily Nov-Mar) Up on the hill above Rutland Sq, All Saints Church is packed with ancient features, including a 14th-century font, a pair of Norman arches, some fine heraldic tombs, and a collection of crude stone gravestones and crosses dating from the 12th century.

Old House Museum

MUSEUM

(www.oldhousemuseum.org.uk; Cunningham Pl; adult/child £3.50/2, incl Spirit of the 1940s £5/2; ☉11am-4pm Apr-early Nov) Set in a time-worn stone house near All Saints Church, the Old House Museum explores local history. Check out the Tudor loo and the displays on wattle and daub, a traditional technique for building walls using woven twigs and cow dung.

Spirit of the 1940s

MUSEUM

(www.oldhousemuseum.org.uk; Tanners Yard; adult/child £2/50p, incl Old House Museum £5/2; ☉10.30am-4pm Fri-Mon Apr-early Nov) The Spirit of the 1940s museum incorporates an evocative 1940s street scene, letters and photographs, and wartime memorabilia.

Haddon Hall

HISTORIC SITE

(www.haddonhall.co.uk; adult/child £10/5.50; ☉noon-5pm daily May-Sep, noon-5pm Sat-Mon Mar-Apr & Oct) With stone turrets, time-worn timbers and walled gardens, Haddon Hall, 2 miles south of Bakewell on the A6, looks exactly like a medieval manor house should. Founded in the 12th century, it was expanded and remodelled throughout medieval times. The 'modernisation' stopped when the house was abandoned in the 18th century. Take the Highpeak bus from Bakewell

(£2.10, 10 minutes, hourly) or walk along the footpath through the fields, mostly on the east side of the river.

Spared from the more florid excesses of the Victorian period, Haddon Hall has been used as the location for numerous period blockbusters (such as *Elizabeth*).

Chatsworth House   HISTORIC BUILDING
(☑01246-565300; www.chatsworth.org; house & gardens adult/child £18/10, gardens only £12/7, playground £6, park admission free; ☺11am-4.30pm mid-Mar–late Dec, garden 11am-6pm mid-Mar–late Dec) Known as the 'Palace of the Peak', this vast edifice 3 miles northeast of Bakewell has been occupied by the earls and dukes of Devonshire for centuries. Inside, the lavish apartments and mural-painted staterooms are packed with priceless paintings and period furniture. The house sits in 25 sq miles of grounds and ornamental gardens, some landscaped by Lancelot 'Capability' Brown. Kids will love the farmyard adventure playground.

From Bakewell, take bus 215 (£2.10, 20 minutes, hourly).

The manor was founded in 1552 by the formidable Bess of Hardwick and her second husband, William Cavendish, who earned grace and favour by helping Henry VIII dissolve the English monasteries. Mary, Queen of Scots was imprisoned at Chatsworth on the orders of Elizabeth I in 1569.

Look out for the portraits of the current generation of Devonshires by Lucian Freud.

Walkers can take the footpaths through Chatsworth park via the mock-Venetian village of Edensor (en-sor), while cyclists can pedal via Pilsley.

🏃 Activities

Walking and cycling are, of course, the main activities in the area. The scenic **Monsal Trail** follows the path of a disused railway line from Combs Viaduct on the outskirts of Bakewell to Topley Pike in Wye Dale, about 3 miles east of Buxton, including a number of reopened old railway tunnels, covering 8½ miles in all.

For a rewarding shorter walk, follow the Monsal Trail for 3 miles to the dramatic viewpoint at **Monsal Head**, where you can pause for refreshment at the **Monsal Head Hotel** (☑01629-640250; www.monsalhead.com; s/d incl breakfast from £85/100, mains £11.50-16; ☺kitchen 8am-10am & noon-9.30pm; ℗), which serves real ales and excellent Modern British cuisine. With more time to kill, continue to Miller's Dale, where viaducts give a spectacular vista across the steep-sided valley. The tourist offices at Bakewell and Buxton have full details.

Other walking routes go to the stately homes Haddon Hall and Chatsworth House.

🛏 Sleeping

Melbourne House & Easthorpe   B&B ££
(☑01629-815357; www.bakewell-accommodation. co.uk; Buxton Rd; d from £70; ℗) In a picturesque, creeper-covered building dating back more than three centuries and a new annexe, this inviting B&B is handily situated on the main road leading to Buxton.

Rutland Arms Hotel   HOTEL ££
(☑01629-812812; www.rutlandarmsbakewell.co.uk; The Square; s £82-95, d £139-195; ℗📶) Jane Austen is said to have stayed in room 2 of this aristocratic, recently refurbished stone coaching inn while working on *Pride and Prejudice*. The more expensive of its 33 rooms have lots of Victorian flourishes.

🍴 Eating & Drinking

Bakewell's streets are lined with sweet tearooms and bakeries selling the famous Bakewell Pudding.

Old Original Bakewell Pudding Shop   BAKERY, TEAROOM £
(www.bakewellpuddingshop.co.uk; The Square; dishes £6.50-17; ☺8.30am-6pm) One of the claimants of the Bakewell Pudding, this place has a lovely 1st-floor tearoom with exposed beams that serves light meals and afternoon teas on tiered trays.

Bloomers Original Bakewell Puddings   BAKERY £
(☑01629-814844; Water St; dishes 80p-£4.50; ☺9am-5pm Mon-Sat, 10.30am-5pm Sun) Claims to be the progenitor of the famous Bakewell Pudding. No sit-down dining; head to the pretty riverbanks.

Piedaniel's   FRENCH ££
(☑01629-812687; www.piedaniels-restaurant.com; Bath St; mains £17, 2-/3-course lunch £16/18 Tue-Fri; ☺noon-2pm & 7-9pm Tue-Sat) Chefs Eric and Christiana Piedaniel's Modern French cuisine is the toast of in-town restaurants. A whitewashed dining room is the exquisite setting for the likes of lobster bisque with *quenelles* (feather-light flour, egg and cream dumplings) followed by monkfish in salmon mousse. Weekday lunch menus are exceptional value.

Fischer's Baslow Hall GASTRONOMIC £££
(☑ 01246-583259; www.fischers-baslowhall.co.uk;
259 Calver Rd, Baslow; lunch 2-/3-course menu
from £20/27, dinner 1-/2-/3-course menu from
£34/55/72; ⊙ kitchen noon-1.30pm & from 7pm
daily by reservation) Just over 4 miles northeast of Bakewell, this stately 1907-built stone
manor house has a magnificent Michelin-starred dining room showcasing a roll-
call of British produce (Derbyshire lamb,
Yorkshire game, Cornish crab...) along with
vegetables from its kitchen garden.

Six sumptuous floral bedrooms are in the
main house, with another five larger but less
atmospheric rooms in the adjacent garden
house (doubles from £155 to £250).

Castle Inn PUB
(☑ 01629-812103; www.oldenglishinns.co.uk; Bridge
St; 🕾🚗) The ivy-draped Castle Inn is one
of the better pubs in Bakewell, with four
centuries of practice in rejuvenating ham-
strung hikers. Gourmet burgers are a menu
highlight (mains from £8 to £17).

ℹ Information

Tourist Office (☑ 01629-813227; www.visit-
peakdistrict.com; Bridge St; ⊙ 9.30am-5pm
Apr-Oct, 10.30am-4.30pm Nov-Mar) In the old
Market Hall; the helpful staff can book accommodation.

ℹ Getting There & Away

Bakewell lies on the Highpeak bus route. Buses
run hourly to Derby (£4.70, 1¼ hours), Matlock
Bath (£3.20, 30 minutes) and Buxton (£3.20, 30
minutes). Five services a day continue to Manchester (£5.90, 1¾ hours).

Other services include the following:

Castleton Bus 173; £3, 25 minutes, three per
day

Chesterfield Bus 170; £3.10, 45 minutes,
hourly

Yorkshire

Best Places to Eat

➡ Pipe and Glass Inn (p551)

➡ Van Zeller (p516)

➡ Star Inn (p523)

➡ Crafthouse (p540)

➡ Mannion's (p510)

Best Places to Stay

➡ Millgate House (p536)

➡ Devonshire Fell (p532)

➡ Helaina (p519)

➡ Quebecs (p540)

Why Go?

With a population as big as Scotland's and an area half the size of Belgium, Yorkshire is almost a country in itself. It has its own flag, its own dialect and its own celebration, Yorkshire Day (1 August). While local folk are proud to be English, they're even prouder to be natives of 'God's Own County'.

What makes Yorkshire so special? First, there's the landscape – with its brooding moors and green dales rolling down to a dramatic coastline, Yorkshire has some of Britain's finest scenery. Second, there's the sheer breadth of history – every facet of the British experience is represented here, from Roman times to the 20th century.

But Yorkshire's greatest appeal lies in its people. Industrious and opinionated, they have a wry wit and shrewd friendliness. Stay here for a while and you'll come away believing, like the locals, that God is indeed a Yorkshirewoman.

When to Go

➡ The week-long Jorvik Festival in February sees York taken over by a Viking invasion.

➡ Spring brings drifts of yellow daffodils to brighten the roadsides in the Dales and North York Moors; the Three Peaks Race takes place in Horton-in-Ribblesdale.

➡ Agriculture is celebrated at the Great Yorkshire Show in Harrogate in July. At the same time of year Yorkshire's coastal sea cliffs become a frenzy of nesting seabirds.

➡ September is the ideal time for hiking in the Yorkshire Dales; the Walking Festival in Richmond also takes place in this month. York goes all gourmet with its annual 10-day food festival, while Harrogate gets green-fingered during its Autumn Flower Show.

Yorkshire Highlights

1 Exploring the medieval streets of **York** (p502) and its awe-inspiring cathedral

2 Getting off the beaten track and exploring the lesser-known corners of the **Yorkshire Dales** (p530)

3 Wandering among the atmospheric medieval ruins of **Fountains Abbey** (p520)

4 Being beside the seaside at **Scarborough** (p516) with its traditional bucket-and-spade atmosphere

5 Riding on the **North Yorkshire Moors Railway** (p524), one of England's most scenic train lines

6 Sitting on the pier at **Whitby** (p525) and tucking into the world's best fish and chips

7 Reliving the story of *Brideshead Revisited* amid the aristocratic splendour of **Castle Howard** (p513)

8 Pulling on your hiking boots and tackling the steep paths around scenic **Malham Cove** (p532)

9 Discovering mining's dark side at the **National Coal Mining Museum for England** (p543)

10 Enjoying the high-tech, hands-on exhibits at Bradford's **National Media Museum** (p543)

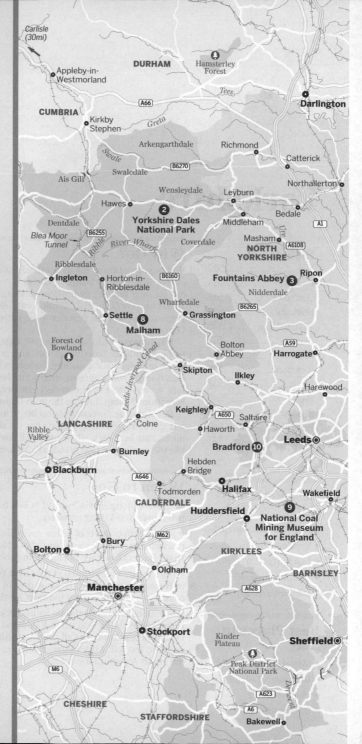

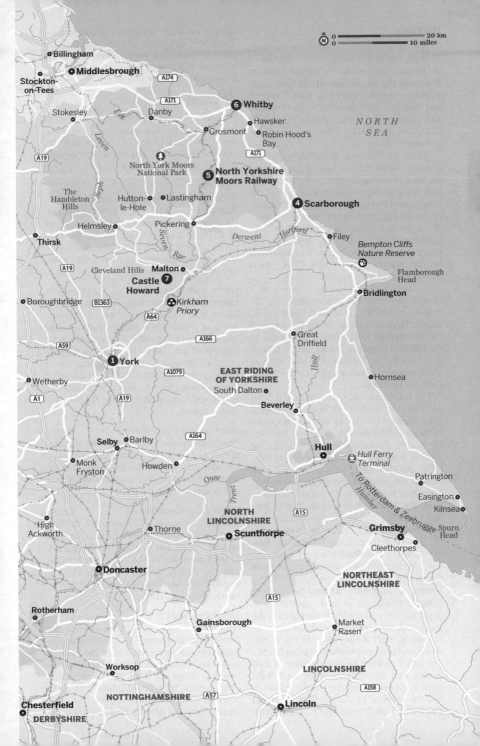

History

As you drive through Yorkshire on the main A1 road, you're following in the footsteps of the Roman legions who conquered northern Britain in the 1st century AD. In fact, many Yorkshire towns – including York, Catterick and Malton – were founded by the Romans, and many modern roads (including the A1, A59, A166 and A1079) follow the alignment of Roman roads.

When the Romans departed in the 5th century, native Britons battled for supremacy with invading Teutonic tribe the Angles and, for a while, Yorkshire was part of the Kingdom of Northumbria. In the 9th century the Vikings arrived and conquered most of northern Britain, an area that became known as the Danelaw. They divided the territory that is now Yorkshire into *thridings* (thirds), which met at Jorvik (York), their thriving commercial capital.

In 1066 Yorkshire was the scene of a pivotal showdown in the struggle for the English crown, when the Anglo-Saxon king, Harold II, rode north to defeat the forces of the Norwegian king, Harold Hardrada, in the Battle of Stamford Bridge, before returning south for his appointment with William the Conqueror – and a fatal arrow – in the Battle of Hastings.

The inhabitants of northern England did not take the subsequent Norman invasion lying down. In order to subdue them, the Norman nobles built a chain of formidable castles throughout Yorkshire, including those at York, Richmond, Scarborough, Pickering and Helmsley. The Norman land grab formed the basis of the great estates that supported England's medieval aristocrats.

By the 15th century, the duchies of York and Lancaster had become so wealthy and powerful that they ended up battling for the English throne in the Wars of the Roses (1455–87). The dissolution of the monasteries by Henry VIII from 1536 to 1540 saw the wealth of the great abbeys of Rievaulx, Fountains and Whitby fall into the hands of noble families, and Yorkshire quietly prospered for 200 years, with fertile farms in the north and the Sheffield cutlery business in the south, until the big bang of the Industrial Revolution transformed the landscape.

South Yorkshire became a centre of coal mining and steel-making while west Yorkshire nurtured a massive textile industry, and the cities of Leeds, Bradford, Sheffield and Rotherham flourished. By the late 20th century another revolution was taking place. The heavy industries had died out, and the cities of Yorkshire were reinventing themselves as shiny, high-tech centres of finance, higher education and tourism.

🏃 Activities

Yorkshire's varied landscape of wild hills, tranquil valleys, high moors and spectacular coastline offers plenty of opportunities for outdoor activities. See www.outdooryorkshire.com for more details.

Cycling

Yorkshire's hosting of the start of the 2014 Tour de France saw a huge upsurge in interest in cycling. The county has a vast network of country lanes that are perfect for road cyclists, although the national parks also attract lots of motorists so even minor roads can be busy at weekends.

North York Moors MOUNTAIN BIKING (www.mtb-routes.co.uk/northyorkmoors) Off-road bikers can avail themselves of the network of bridleways, former railways and disused mining tracks now converted for two-wheel use. Dalby Forest (www.forestry.gov.uk/dalbyforest), near Pickering, sports purpose-built mountain-biking trails of all grades from green to black, and there are newly waymarked trails at the Sutton Bank visitor centre.

Moor to Sea Cycle Route CYCLING (www.moortoseacycle.net) A network of routes between Pickering, Danby and the coast includes a 20-mile traffic-free route that follows a disused railway line between Whitby and Scarborough.

White Rose Cycle Route CYCLING (www.sustrans.org.uk; NCN Route 65) A 131-mile road cruise from Middlesbrough to York and on to Hull and Hornsea, via the dramatic western scarp of the North York Moors and the rolling Yorkshire Wolds. There is a traffic-free section on the old railway between Selby and York.

Yorkshire Dales Cycleway CYCLING, MOUNTAIN BIKING (www.cyclethedales.org.uk) An exhilarating 130-mile loop, taking in the best of the national park; the website also details the route followed by Stage 1 of the 2014 Tour de France. There's scope for off-road riding, with about 500 miles of bridleways and trails – for inspiration, check out www.mtbthedales.org.uk.

Walking

For shorter walks and rambles, the best area is the **Yorkshire Dales**, with a great selection of walks through scenic valleys or over wild hilltops, with a few higher summits thrown in for good measure. The East Riding's **Yorkshire Wolds** hold hidden delights, while the quiet valleys and dramatic coast of the **North York Moors** also offer many opportunities.

Cleveland Way WALKING
(www.nationaltrail.co.uk/clevelandway) A venerable moor-and-coast classic that circles the North York Moors National Park on its 109-mile, nine-day route from Helmsley to Filey.

Coast to Coast Walk WALKING
(www.wainwright.org.uk/coasttocoast.html) One of England's most popular walks: 190 miles across northern England from the Lake District through the Yorkshire Dales and North York Moors National Parks. The Yorkshire section takes a week to 10 days and offers some of the finest walking of its kind in England.

Dales Way WALKING
(www.dalesway.org.uk) A charming and not-too-strenuous amble from the Yorkshire Dales to the Lake District, following the River Wharfe through the heart of the Dales and finishing at Bowness-on-Windermere.

Pennine Way WALKING
(www.nationaltrail.co.uk/pennineway) The Yorkshire section of England's most famous walk runs for more than 100 miles via Hebden Bridge, Malham, Horton-in-Ribblesdale and Hawes, passing near Haworth and Skipton.

White Rose Way WALKING
(www.whiteroseway.co.uk) A long-distance trail covering the 104 miles from Leeds city centre to Scarborough, taking in remote and picturesque Yorkshire villages along the way.

Wolds Way WALKING
(www.nationaltrail.co.uk/yorkshirewoldsway) This beautiful but oft-overlooked walk winds through the most scenic part of Yorkshire's East Riding district.

ℹ Information

Yorkshire Tourist Board (www.yorkshire.com) Plenty of general leaflets and brochures are available, for postal and email enquiries only. For more detailed information, contact local tourist offices.

ℹ Getting There & Around

The major north–south road transport routes – the M1 and A1 motorways – run through the middle of Yorkshire, serving the key cities of Sheffield, Leeds and York. If you're arriving by sea from northern Europe, Hull in the East Riding district is the region's main port.

Traveline Yorkshire (✆ 0871 200 22 33; www. yorkshiretravel.net) provides public transport information for all of Yorkshire.

BUS

Long-distance coaches operated by **National Express** (✆ 08717 81 81 81; www.nationalexpress.com) serve most cities and large towns in Yorkshire from London, the south of England, the Midlands and Scotland.

Bus transport around Yorkshire is frequent and efficient, especially between major towns. Services are more sporadic in the national parks, but are still adequate for reaching most places, particularly in summer months (June to September).

TRAIN

The main rail line between London and Edinburgh runs through Yorkshire, with at least 10 trains calling each day at York and Doncaster, where you can change trains for other Yorkshire destinations. There are also direct services between the major towns and cities of Yorkshire and other northern cities such as Manchester and Newcastle. For timetables, contact **National Rail Enquiries** (✆ 08457 48 49 50; www.nationalrail.co.uk).

NORTH YORKSHIRE

This, the largest of Yorkshire's four counties – and the largest county in England – is also the most beautiful. Unlike the rest of northern England, it survived almost unscathed by the Industrial Revolution. Since the Middle Ages, North Yorkshire has been almost exclusively about sheep and the woolly wealth they produce.

Rather than closed-down factories, mills and mines, the artificial monuments dotting the landscape in these parts are of the stately variety – the great houses and wealthy abbeys that sit, ruined or restored, as a reminder that there was plenty of money to be made off the sheep's back.

All the same, North Yorkshire's biggest attraction is an urban one. While the genteel spa town of Harrogate and the bright and breezy seaside resorts of Scarborough and Whitby have many fans, nothing compares to the unparalleled splendour of York, England's most-visited city outside London.

York

POP 198,000

Nowhere in northern England says 'medieval' quite like York, a city of extraordinary cultural and historical wealth that has lost little of its pre-industrial lustre. A magnificent circuit of 13th-century walls encloses a medieval spider's web of narrow streets. At its heart lies the immense, awe-inspiring York Minster, one of the most beautiful Gothic cathedrals in the world. York's long history and rich heritage are woven into virtually every brick and beam, and the modern, tourist-oriented city – with its myriad museums, restaurants, cafes and traditional pubs – is a carefully maintained heir to that heritage.

Try to avoid the inevitable confusion by remembering that around these parts, *gate* means street and *bar* means gate.

History

In AD 71 the Romans built a garrison called Eboracum, which in time became a large fort with a civilian settlement around it. Hadrian used it as the base for his northern campaign, while Constantine the Great was proclaimed emperor here in AD 306. When the Roman Empire collapsed, the town was taken by the Anglo-Saxons, who renamed it Eoforwic and made it the capital of the independent kingdom of Northumbria.

In 625 a Roman priest, Paulinus, arrived and converted King Edwin and his nobles to Christianity; two years later they built the first wooden church here. For most of the next century, the city was a major centre of learning, attracting students from all over Europe. In 866 the next wave of invaders arrived, this time the Vikings, who gave the town a more tongue-friendly name, Jorvik. It was their capital for the next 100 years, and during that time they turned the city into an important trading port.

King Eadred of Wessex drove out the last Viking ruler in 954 and reunited Danelaw with the south, but trouble quickly followed. In 1066 King Harold II fended off a Norwegian invasion at Stamford Bridge, east of York, but was defeated by William the Conqueror a few months later in the Battle of Hastings.

After William's two wooden castles were captured by an Anglo-Scandinavian army, he torched the entire city (and Durham) and the surrounding countryside. The Normans then set about rebuilding it, adding a grand new minster. Over the next 300 years York (a contraction of the Viking name Jorvik) prospered through royal patronage, textiles, trade and the Church.

Throughout the 18th century the city was a fashionable social centre dominated by the aristocracy, who were drawn by its culture and new racecourse. When the railway arrived in 1839, thousands of people were employed in new industries that sprang up around it, such as confectionery (the Terry's and Rowntree's brands were founded here). These industries went into decline in the latter half of the 20th century, but by then a new invader was asking for directions at the city gates, armed only with a guidebook.

◎ Sights

★ York Minster   CATHEDRAL

(www.yorkminster.org; Deangate; adult/child £10/ free, combined ticket incl tower £15/5; ⊙9am-5.30pm Mon-Sat, 12.45-5.30pm Sun, last admission 5pm) The remarkable York Minster is the largest medieval cathedral in all of Northern Europe, and one of the world's most beautiful Gothic buildings. Seat of the archbishop of York, primate of England, it is second in importance only to Canterbury, seat of the primate of *all* England – the separate titles were created to settle a debate over the true centre of the English church. If this is the only cathedral you visit in England, you'll still walk away satisfied.

The first church on this site was a wooden chapel built for the baptism of King Edwin of Northumbria on Easter Day 627, whose location is marked in the crypt. It was replaced with a stone church built on the site of a Roman basilica, parts of which can be seen in the foundations. The first Norman minster was built in the 11th century and, again, you can see surviving fragments in the foundations and crypt.

The present minster, built mainly between 1220 and 1480, manages to encompass all the major stages of Gothic architectural development. The transepts (1220–55) were built in Early English style; the octagonal chapter house (1260–90) and nave (1291–1340) in the Decorated style; and the west towers, west front and central (or lantern) tower (1470–72) in Perpendicular style.

➜ Choir, Chapter House & Nave

Entrance to the minster is via the south transept, which was badly damaged by fire in 1984, but has now been fully restored. The stained-glass windows, choir screen and chapter house within are superb examples of English Gothic architecture.

As you enter the transept, facing you is the magnificent **Five Sisters Window**, with five lancets over 15m high. This is the minster's oldest complete window; most of its tangle of coloured glass dates from around 1250. Just beyond it to the right is the 13th-century chapter house, a fine example of the Decorated style. Sinuous and intricately carved stonework – there are more than 200 expressive carved heads and figures – surrounds an airy, uninterrupted space.

Back in the main church, take note of the unusually tall and wide nave, the aisles of which (to the sides) are roofed in stone in contrast to the central roof, which is wood painted to look like stone. On both sides of the nave are painted stone shields of the nobles who met with Edward II at a parliament in York. Also note the **dragon's head** projecting from the gallery – it's a crane believed to have been used to lift a font cover. There are several fine windows dating from the early 14th century, but the most impressive is the **Great West Window** (1338), with its beautiful heart-shaped stone tracery.

Beyond the screen and the choir is the **lady chapel** and, behind it, the huge **high altar**, which is dominated by the huge **Great East Window** (1405). At 23.7m by 9.4m – roughly the size of a tennis court – it is the world's largest medieval stained-glass window and the cathedral's single most important treasure. Needless to say, its epic size matches the epic theme depicted within: the beginning and end of the world as described in Genesis and the Book of Revelations.

➡ Undercroft, Treasury & Crypt

A set of stairs in the south transept of York Minster leads down to the architecturally outstanding undercroft, treasury and crypt. The treasury houses 11th-century artefacts including relics from the graves of medieval archbishops. The crypt contains fragments from the Norman cathedral, including the font showing King Edwin's baptism, which also marks the site of the original wooden chapel. Look out for the **Doomstone**, a 12th-century carving showing a scene from the Last Judgment with demons casting doomed souls into Hell.

In 1967 the minster foundations were shored up when the central tower threatened to collapse; while engineers worked frantically to save the building, archaeologists uncovered Roman and Norman remains that attest to the site's ancient history – one of the most extraordinary finds is a **Roman culvert**, still carrying water to the Ouse.

A new interactive exhibit in the Undercroft, **Revealing York Minster**, leads visitors through 2000 years of history on the site of the cathedral.

➡ Tower

At the heart of York's cathedral is the massive tower, which is well worth climbing for the unparalleled views of York. You'll have to tackle a fairly claustrophobic climb of 275 steps and, most probably, a queue of people with cameras in hand.

Access to the tower is near the entrance in the south transept, dominated by the exquisite **Rose Window**, commemorating the union of the royal houses of Lancaster and York through the marriage of Henry VII and Elizabeth of York, which ended the Wars of the Roses and began the Tudor dynasty.

★ **National Railway Museum**   MUSEUM
(www.nrm.org.uk; Leeman Rd; ⏰10am-6pm; P ♿)
FREE While many railway museums are the sole preserve of lone men in anoraks comparing dog-eared notebooks and getting high on the smell of machine oil, coal smoke and nostalgia, this place is different. York's National Railway Museum – the biggest in the world, with more than 100 locomotives – is so well presented and crammed with fascinating stuff that it's interesting even to folk whose eyes don't mist over at the thought of a 4-6-2 A1 Pacific class thundering into a tunnel.

Highlights for the trainspotters among us include a replica of George Stephenson's **Rocket** (1829), the world's first 'modern' steam locomotive; the sleek and streamlined **Mallard**, which set the world speed record for a steam locomotive in 1938 (126mph); a 1960s Japanese **Shinkansen bullet train**; and the world-famous **Flying Scotsman**, the first steam engine to break the 100mph barrier (scheduled to return to the tracks in

ℹ **THE YORK PASS**

If you plan on visiting a number of sights, you can save yourself some money by using a **York Pass** (www.yorkpass.com; 1/2/3 days adult £36/48/58, child £20/24/28). It gives you free access to more than 30 pay-to-visit sights in and around York, including York Minster, Jorvik and Castle Howard. You can buy it at York Tourist Office or online.

York

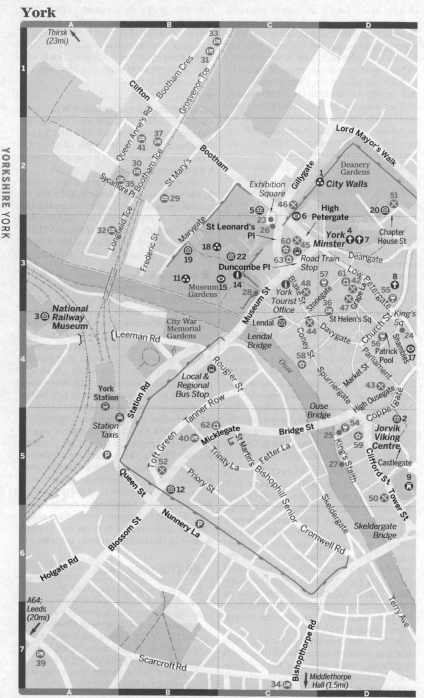

Thirsk
(23mi)

Clifton

Bootham Cres

Grosvenor Tce

Queen Anne's Rd

Bootham Tce

Sycamore Pl

Longfield Tce

Frederic St

St Mary's

Bootham

Marygate

Exhibition
Square

Lord Mayor's Walk

Gillygate

Deanery
Gardens

City Walls

**High
Petergate**

**York
Minster**

Chapter
House St

Deangate

St Leonard's
Pl

Duncombe Pl

Road Train
Stop

Museum
Gardens

Museum St

Low Petergate

Stonegate

Blake St

**York
Tourist
Office**

Lendal

St Helen's Sq

Davygate

Grape La

Church St

Parliament St

King's
Sq

Shambles

Castlegate

**National
Railway
Museum**

Leeman Rd

City War
Memorial
Gardens

Lendal
Bridge

Coney St

Ouse

Spurriergate

Market St

Patrick
Pool

High Ousegate

Coppergate

**Jorvik
Viking
Centre**

Station Rd

Rougier St

Tanner Row

Local &
Regional
Bus Stop

**York
Station**

Station
Taxis

Toft Green

Micklegate

Trinity La

Priory St

Queen St

St Martin's La

Fetter La

Bishophill Senior

Cromwell Rd

Bridge St

Ouse
Bridge

King's Staith

Skeldergate

Clifford St

Tower St

Castlegate

Terry Ave

Skeldergate
Bridge

Blossom St

Nunnery La

Holgate Rd

A64;
Leeds
(20mi)

Scarcroft Rd

Bishopthorpe Rd

Middlethorpe
Hall (1.5mi)

summer 2015, but still undergoing restoration at the time of writing). There's also a massive 4-6-2 loco from 1949 that's been cut in half so you can see how it works.

Even if you're not a rail nerd, you'll enjoy looking through the gleaming, silk-lined carriages of the royal trains used by Queen Victoria and Edward VII, or having a *Brief Encounter* moment over tea and scones at the museum's station platform cafe called, erm, Brief Encounter. Allow at least two hours to do the museum justice.

The museum is about 400m west of the train station and if you don't fancy walking you can ride the **road train** (adult/child £2/1, April to October) that runs between the minster and museum every 30 minutes from 11am to 4pm.

★**Jorvik Viking Centre**   MUSEUM
(www.jorvik-viking-centre.co.uk; Coppergate; adult/child £9.95/6.95; ⊙10am-5pm Apr-Oct, to 4pm Nov-Mar) Interactive multimedia exhibits aimed at bringing history to life often achieve exactly the opposite, but the much-hyped Jorvik manages to pull it off with aplomb. It's a smells-and-all reconstruction of the Viking settlement unearthed here during excavations in the late 1970s, brought to you courtesy of a 'time-car' monorail that transports you through 9th-century Jorvik. You can reduce time waiting in the queue by booking your tickets online and choosing the time you want to visit (£1 extra).

While some of the 'you will now travel back in time' malarkey is a bit naff, it's all done with a sense of humour tied to historical authenticity that will give you a pretty good idea of what life must have been like in Viking-era York. In the exhibition at the end of the monorail, look out for the **Lloyds Bank coprolite**, a fossilised human stool that measures an eye-watering nine inches long and half a pound in weight, and must be the only turd in the world to have its own Wikipedia entry.

★**City Walls**   ARCHAEOLOGICAL SITE
(⊙8am-dusk) **FREE** If the weather's good, don't miss the chance to walk the City Walls, which follow the line of the original Roman walls and give a whole new perspective on the city. Allow 1½ to two hours for the full circuit of 4.5 miles or, if you're pushed for time, the short stretch from **Bootham Bar** to **Monk Bar** is worth doing for the views of the minster.

Start and finish in the Museum Gardens or at Bootham Bar (on the site of a Roman gate), where a multimedia exhibit provides

York

some historical context, and travel clockwise. Highlights include Monk Bar, which is the best-preserved medieval gate and still has a working portcullis, and Walmgate Bar, England's only city gate with an intact barbican.

At Monk Bar you'll find the Richard III Museum (www.richardiiimuseum.co.uk; adult/child £2.50/free; ⊙9am-5pm Mar-Oct, 9.30am-4pm Nov-Feb), which sets out the case of the murdered 'Princes in the Tower' and invites visitors to judge whether their uncle, Richard III, killed them. Micklegate Bar Museum (www.micklegatebar.com; Micklegate; adult/child £3.50/free; ⊙10am-4.30pm May-Sep, 11am-3.30pm Feb-Apr, Oct & Nov) charts the history of

the city walls and the Battle of Towton, chief conflict in the Wars of the Roses.

Yorkshire Museum   MUSEUM
(www.yorkshiremuseum.org.uk; Museum St; adult/child £7.50/free; ⊙10am-5pm) Most of York's Roman archaeology is hidden beneath the medieval city, so the recently revamped displays in the Yorkshire Museum are invaluable if you want to get an idea of what Eboracum was like. There are maps and models of Roman York, funerary monuments, mosaic floors and wall paintings, and a 4th-century bust of Emperor Constantine.

There are excellent exhibits on Viking and medieval York as well, including priceless artefacts such as the beautifully decorated 9th-century York helmet and the exquisite 15th-century Middleham Jewel, an engraved gold pendant adorned with a giant sapphire. Kids will enjoy the dinosaur exhibit, centred around giant ichthyosaur fossils from Yorkshire's Jurassic Coast.

Museum Gardens
GARDENS

(entrances on Museum St & Marygate; ☉ dawn-dusk) In the grounds of the peaceful Museum Gardens, you can see the **Multangular Tower**, a part of the City Walls that was once the western tower of the Roman garrison's defensive ramparts. The Roman stonework at the base has been built over with 13th-century additions. On the other side of the gardens are the ruins of **St Mary's Abbey** dating from 1270 to 1294. The ruined **Gatehall** was its main entrance, providing access from the abbey to the river.

The adjacent **Hospitium** dates from the 14th century, although the timber-framed upper storey is a much-restored survivor from the 15th century, used as the abbey guesthouse. **St Mary's Lodge** was built in about 1470 to provide VIP accommodation.

Shambles
STREET

The Shambles takes its name from the Saxon word *shamel,* meaning 'slaughterhouse' – in 1862 there were 26 butcher shops on this street. Today the butchers are long gone, but this narrow cobbled lane, lined with 15th-century Tudor buildings that overhang so much they seem to meet above your head, is the most picturesque in Britain, and one of the most visited in Europe, often crammed with visitors intent on buying a tacky souvenir before rushing back to the tour bus.

York Castle Museum
MUSEUM

(www.yorkcastlemuseum.org.uk; Tower St; adult/child £8.50/free; ☉ 9.30am-5pm) This excellent museum has displays of everyday life through the centuries, with reconstructed domestic interiors, a Victorian street and a prison cell where you can try out a condemned man's bed – in this case, that of highwayman Dick Turpin (imprisoned here before being hanged in 1739). There's a bewildering array of evocative objects from the past 400 years, gathered together by a certain Dr Kirk from the 1920s onwards for fear the items would become obsolete and disappear completely.

Treasurer's House
HISTORIC BUILDING

(NT; www.nationaltrust.org.uk; Chapter House St; adult/child £7/3.50; ☉ 11am-4.30pm Sat-Thu Apr-Oct, to 3pm Nov) Once home to York Minster's medieval treasurers, this historic house – substantially rebuilt in the 17th and 18th centuries – contains a fine collection of furniture and offers a fascinating insight into 18th-century life. It is also the setting for one of York's most enduring ghost stories: during the 1950s a plumber working in the basement swore he saw a band of Roman soldiers marching *through* the walls.

Dig
MUSEUM

(www.digyork.com; St Saviour's Church, St Saviourgate; adult/child £6/5.50, Dig & Jorvik combined £14.45/11; ☉ 10am-5pm, last admission 4pm; ⊞) Under the same management as Jorvik, Dig cashes in on the popularity of archaeology programs on TV by giving you the chance to be an 'archaeological detective', unearthing the secrets of York's distant past as well as learning something of the archaeologist's world – what they do, how they do it, and so on. Aimed mainly at kids, it's much more hands-on than Jorvik and a lot of its merit depends on how good – and entertaining – your guide is.

Clifford's Tower
CASTLE

(EH; www.english-heritage.org.uk; Tower St; adult/child £4.30/2.60; ☉ 10am-6pm Apr-Sep, to 5pm Oct, to 4pm Nov-Mar) There's precious little left of York Castle except for this evocative stone tower, a highly unusual figure-of-eight design built into the castle's keep after the original one was destroyed in 1190 during anti-Jewish riots. An angry mob forced 150 Jews to be locked inside the tower and the hapless victims took their own lives rather than be killed. There's not much to see inside, but the views over the city are excellent.

Church of the Holy Trinity
CHURCH

(Goodramgate; ☉ 10am-5pm Tue-Sat May-Sep, to 4pm Oct-Apr) FREE Tucked away behind an inconspicuous gate and seemingly cut off from the rest of the town, the Church of the Holy Trinity is a fantastically atmospheric old building, having survived almost unchanged for the past 200 years (it has no electricity or running water). Inside are rare 17th- to 18th-century box pews, 15th-century stained glass and wonky walls that seem to have been built without plumb line or spirit level.

York City Art Gallery · GALLERY

(www.yorkartgallery.org.uk; Exhibition Sq; ⊙10am-5pm) **FREE** Artists represented here include Joshua Reynolds, Paul Nash, Eugène Boudin, LS Lowry and the controversial York artist William Etty, who, back in the 1820s, was the first major British artist to specialise in painting nudes. Closed for redevelopment at the time of writing, the gallery is due to reopen sometime in 2015.

☞ Tours

There's a bewildering range of tours in York, from historic walking tours to ever more competitive night-time ghost tours (York is considered England's most haunted city).

Ghost Hunt of York · WALKING TOUR

(www.ghosthunt.co.uk; adult/child £5/3; ⊙tours 7.30pm) The kids will just love this award-winning and highly entertaining 75-minute tour laced with authentic ghost stories. It begins at the Shambles, whatever the weather (it's never cancelled) and there's no need to book, just turn up and wait till you hear the handbell ringing...

Yorkwalk · WALKING TOUR

(www.yorkwalk.co.uk; adult/child £6/5; ⊙tours 10.30am & 2.15pm Feb-Nov) Offers a series of two-hour walks on a range of themes, from the classics – Roman York, the snickelways (narrow alleys) and City Walls – to walks focused on chocolates and sweets, women in York, and the inevitable graveyard, coffin and plague tour. Walks depart from Museum Gardens Gate on Museum St; there's no need to book.

YorkBoat · BOAT TOUR

(www.yorkboat.co.uk; King's Staith; adult/child from £7.50/3.50; ⊙tours 10.30am, noon, 1.30pm & 3pm Feb-Nov) Hour-long cruises on the River Ouse, departing from King's Staith and, 10 minutes later, Lendal Bridge. Special lunch, dinner and evening cruises are also offered.

Original Ghost Walk of York · WALKING TOUR

(www.theoriginalghostwalkofyork.co.uk; adult/child £5/3; ⊙tours 8pm) An evening of ghouls, ghosts, mystery and history, courtesy of a well-established group departing from the King's Arms pub by Ouse Bridge.

York Citysightseeing · BUS TOUR

(www.city-sightseeing.com; day ticket adult/child £12/5; ⊙9am-5pm mid-Feb–Nov) Hop-on/hop-off route with 16 stops, calling at all the main sights. Buses leave every 20 to 30 minutes from Exhibition Sq near York Minster.

Association of Voluntary Guides · WALKING TOUR

(www.avgyork.co.uk; ⊙tours 10.15am & 2.15pm Apr-Oct, also 6.45pm Jun-Aug, 10.15am Nov-Mar) **FREE** Two-hour walking tours of the city, setting out from Exhibition Sq in front of York City Art Gallery.

⚝ Festivals & Events

Check out the city's full calendar of events at www.yorkfestivals.com.

Jorvik Viking Festival · HISTORY

(www.jorvik-viking-centre.co.uk/festivals) For a week in mid-February, York is invaded by Vikings once again as part of this festival, which

---

LOCAL KNOWLEDGE

ANDY DEXTROUS: GHOST TOUR GUIDE

I love York's outstanding architecture, the maze of 'snickleways' (narrow alleys), the array of small independent shops, the street entertainment and festivals, and the central, green spaces like Museum Gardens. All year round, the streets are full of appreciative visitors from all over the world enjoying the city, relaxing and adding to the atmosphere.

York's Spookiest Spots Haunted pubs like the Old White Swan (p512), plus the Antiques Centre (p512) on Stonegate, which is also haunted. In the streets around the Minster you're always within a breath of a ghost tale.

Best of York For beer and atmosphere, the Blue Bell (p511). For veggie and vegan food and a place that welcomes children, El Piano (p510). And for sheer ambience, Grays Court (p511).

Best of Yorkshire Take the North Yorkshire Moors Railway to Goathland, then walk to Mallyan Spout waterfall. Include a drink at the Birch Hall Inn (p529) at Beck Hole. For a special meal, there's the Star Inn (p523) at Harome or the Stone Trough Inn (p513) at Kirkham; stroll down to the abbey ruins before or after your meal.

features battle re-enactments, themed walks, markets and other bits of Viking-related fun.

York Food Festival   FOOD & DRINK
(www.yorkfoodfestival.com) For 10 days in September, discover all that's good to eat and drink in Yorkshire, with food stalls, tastings, a beer tent, cookery demonstrations and more.

York Christmas   CHRISTMAS
(www.visityork.org/christmas) Kicking off with St Nicholas Fayre market in late November, the run-up to Christmas is an extravaganza of street decorations, market stalls, carol singers and mulled wine.

🛏 Sleeping

Beds are hard to find in midsummer, even with inflated high season rates. The tourist office's accommodation booking service charges £4, which might be the best four quid you spend if you arrive without a reservation.

Needless to say, prices get higher the closer you are to the city centre. However, there are plenty of decent B&Bs on the streets north and south of Bootham. Southwest of the city centre, B&Bs are clustered around Scarcroft Rd, Southlands Rd and Bishopthorpe Rd.

It's also worth looking at serviced apartments if you're planning to stay two or three nights. In York Holidays (☎01904-632660; www.inyorkholidays.co.uk) offers a good selection of places from about £110 a night for a two-person apartment.

★ Fort   HOSTEL £
(☎01904-620222; www.thefortyork.co.uk; 1 Little Stonegate; dm from £22, d from £68; ☎) This new boutique hostel showcases the work of young British designers, creating affordable accommodation with a dash of character and flair. There are six- and eight-bed dorms, along with half a dozen doubles, but don't expect a peaceful retreat – the central location is in the middle of York's nightlife, and there's a lively club downstairs (earplugs are provided!).

York YHA   HOSTEL £
(☎0845 371 9051; www.yha.org.uk; 42 Water End, Clifton; dm/q from £21/99; P@☎) Originally the Rowntree (Quaker confectioners) mansion, this handsome Victorian house makes a spacious and child-friendly youth hostel, with most of its rooms four-bed dorms. Often busy, so book early. It's about a mile northwest of the city centre; there's a riverside footpath from Lendal Bridge (poorly lit, so avoid after dark). Alternatively, take bus 2 from the train station or Museum St.

Safestay York   HOSTEL £
(☎01904-627720; www.safestayyork.co.uk; 88-90 Micklegate; dm £16-34, tw £60-72; @☎) Housed in a Grade I Georgian building that was once home to the High Sheriff of Yorkshire, and recently taken over by London hostel group Safestay, this is a large and well-equipped boutique hostel popular with school groups and stag and hen parties – don't come here looking for peace and quiet!

Abbeyfields   B&B ££
(☎01904-636471; www.abbeyfields.co.uk; 19 Bootham Tce; s/d from £55/84; ☎) ✔ Expect a warm welcome and thoughtfully arranged bedrooms here, with chairs and bedside lamps for comfortable reading. Breakfasts are among the best in town, with sausage and bacon from the local butcher, freshly laid eggs from a nearby farm and the aroma of newly baked bread.

Elliotts B&B   B&B ££
(☎01904-623333; www.elliottshotel.co.uk; 2 Sycamore Pl; s/d from £55/75; P@☎) A beautifully converted 'gentleman's residence', Elliotts leans towards the boutique end of the guesthouse market, with stylish and elegant rooms and some designer touches such as contemporary art and colourful textiles. An excellent location, both quiet and central.

Hedley House Hotel   HOTEL ££
(☎01904-637404; www.hedleyhouse.com; 3 Bootham Tce; r from £113; P☎) ✔ This red-brick terrace-house hotel sports a variety of smart, family-friendly accommodation, including rooms that sleep up to five, and some self-catering apartments – plus it has a spa bath on the outdoor terrace at the back, and is barely five minutes' walk from the city centre through the Museum Gardens.

Dairy Guesthouse   B&B ££
(☎01904-639367; www.dairyguesthouse.co.uk; 3 Scarcroft Rd; d/f from £80/110; ☎) A lovely Victorian home that has retained many of its original features, including pine doors, stained glass and cast-iron fireplaces. But the real heart here is the flower- and plant-filled courtyard leading to the cottage-style rooms. Minimum two-night stay at weekends.

Arnot House   B&B ££
(☎01904-641966; www.arnothouseyork.co.uk; 17 Grosvenor Tce; r £80-88; ☎) ✔ With three beautifully decorated rooms (provided you're a fan of Victorian frills and floral patterns), including two with impressive four-poster

beds, Arnot House has an authentically old-fashioned atmosphere that appeals to a more mature clientele. No children allowed.

Brontë House
B&B ££

(☑ 01904-621066; www.bronte-guesthouse.com; 22 Grosvenor Tce; s/d/f from £45/80/100; ☜) The Brontë has five homely en suite rooms, each individually decorated. Our favourite is the double with a carved 19th-century canopied bed, William Morris wallpaper and assorted bits and pieces from another era.

23 St Mary's
B&B ££

(☑ 01904-622738; www.23stmarys.co.uk; 23 St Mary's; s/d from £52/85; ☜) A smart and stately town house with nine chintzy, country-house-style rooms. Some have hand-painted furniture for that rustic look, others are decorated with antiques, lace and polished mahogany.

Briar Lea Guest House
B&B ££

(☑ 01904-635061; www.briarlea.co.uk; 8 Longfield Tce; s/d from £40/66; ☜) Clean, basic rooms and a friendly welcome in a central location.

St Raphael
B&B ££

(☑ 01904-645028; www.straphaelguesthouse.co.uk; 44 Queen Anne's Rd; s/d from £75/82; ☜) Historic house with that distinctive half-timbered look, a great central location and home-baked bread for breakfast.

Monkgate Guesthouse
B&B ££

(☑ 01904-655947; www.monkgateguesthouse.com; 65 Monkgate; s/d/f from £45/78/117; P ☜) Attractive guesthouse with a special family suite that has a separate bedroom for two children.

★ Middlethorpe Hall
HOTEL £££

(☑ 01904-641241; www.middlethorpe.com; Bishopthorpe Rd; s/d from £139/199; P ☜) This breathtaking 17th-century country house is set in 8 hectares of parkland, once the home of diarist Lady Mary Wortley Montagu. The rooms are divided between the main house, restored courtyard buildings and three cottage suites. All the rooms are beautifully decorated with original antiques and oil paintings that have been carefully selected to reflect the period.

Mount Royale
HOTEL £££

(☑ 01904-628856; www.mountroyale.co.uk; The Mount; s/d/ste from £95/125/225; P ☜ ☒) A grand, early-19th-century heritage-listed building converted into a superb luxury hotel, complete with a solarium, beauty spa

and outdoor heated tub and swimming pool. The rooms in the main house are gorgeous, but best of all are the open-plan garden suites, reached via an arcade of tropical fruit trees and bougainvillea.

✖ Eating

★ Mannion's
CAFE, BISTRO £

(☑ 01904-631030; www.mannionandco.co.uk; 1 Blake St; mains £5-9; ☺ 9am-5.30pm Mon-Sat, 10am-5pm Sun) Expect to queue for a table at this busy bistro (no reservations), with its maze of cosy, wood-panelled rooms and selection of daily specials. Regulars on the menu include eggs Benedict for breakfast, a chunky Yorkshire rarebit made with home-baked bread, and lunch platters of cheese and charcuterie from the attached deli. Oh, and pavlova for pudding.

Your Bike Shed
CAFE £

(☑ 01904-633777; www.yourbikeshed.co.uk; 148-150 Micklegate; mains £3-7; ☺ 9am-5pm Mon-Sat, 10am-5pm Sun; ☜ ☒ ☗) ☞ Reinvigorated by the 2014 Tour de France, York's cycling scene has latched onto this cool new cafe and bike workshop. Fitted out with recycled furniture and colourful artwork, it serves reviving portions of halloumi burger, pie and peas or carrot cake to hungry cyclists, washed down with excellent coffee.

Cafe No 8
CAFE, BISTRO ££

(☑ 01904-653074; www.cafeno8.co.uk; 8 Gillygate; 2-/3-course meal £18/22, Fri & Sat £22/27; ☺ 10am-10pm; ☜ ☗) ☞ A cool little place with modern artwork mimicking the Edwardian stained glass at the front, No 8 offers a day-long menu of classic bistro dishes using fresh local produce, including duck breast with blood orange and juniper, and Yorkshire pork belly with star anise, fennel and garlic. It also does breakfast daily (mains £5) and Sunday lunch (three courses £25). Booking recommended.

El Piano
VEGAN ££

(☑ 01904-610676; www.el-piano.com; 15 Grape Lane; mains £10; ☺ 11am-11pm Mon-Sat, noon-9pm Sun; ☜ ☒ ☗) ☞ With a menu that's 100% vegan, nut-free and gluten-free, this colourful, Hispanic-style spot is a vegetarian haven. Downstairs there's a lovely cafe and upstairs, three themed rooms. The menu offers dishes such as falafel, onion bhaji, corn fritters and mushroom-and-basil salad, either in tapas-size portions or as mixed platters. There's also a takeaway counter.

Parlour at Grays Court   CAFE ££
(www.grayscourtyork.com; Chapter House St; mains
£8-14; ⊙10am-5pm; 🗢) An unexpected find
in the heart of York, this 16th-century house
(now a hotel) has more of a country atmosphere. Enjoy gourmet coffee and cake in the
sunny garden, or indulge in a light lunch in
the historic setting of the oak-panelled Jacobean gallery. The menu runs from Yorkshire
rarebit to confit duck, and includes traditional afternoon tea (£18.50).

Ate O'Clock   BISTRO ££
(☑01904-644080; www.ateoclock.co.uk; 13a High
Ousegate; mains £9-20; ⊙5.30-9pm Mon, noon-
2pm & 6-9.30pm Tue-Sat; 🗢) 🍴 A tempting
menu of classic bistro dishes (sirloin steak,
slow-roasted pork belly, pan-fried duck
breast) made with fresh Yorkshire produce
has made this place hugely popular with
locals – best to book a table to avoid disappointment. A three-course dinner costs £19
from 6pm to 7.55pm, Tuesday to Thursday.

Bettys   TEAHOUSE ££
(www.bettys.co.uk; St Helen's Sq; mains £6-14, afternoon tea £18.50; ⊙9am-9pm; 🖗) Old-school
afternoon tea, with white-aproned waiters,
linen tablecloths and a teapot collection
ranged along the walls. The house speciality
is the Yorkshire Fat Rascal, a huge fruit scone
smothered in melted butter, but the smoked
haddock with poached egg and hollandaise
sauce (seasonal) is our favourite lunch dish.
No bookings – queue for a table at busy times.

Olive Tree   MEDITERRANEAN ££
(☑01904-624433; www.theolivetreeyork.co.uk; 10
Tower St; mains £10-21; ⊙noon-2pm & 5.30-
10pm) Local produce gets a Mediterranean
makeover at this bright and breezy bistro.
Classic pizza and pasta dishes are complemented by more ambitious recipes such as
crayfish and chorizo risotto, and Moroccan
lamb stew. The set menu (lunch and dinner,
pre-6.30pm Friday and Saturday) offers two
courses for £15.

1331   STEAK ££
(☑01904-661130; www.1331-york.co.uk; 13 Grape
Lane; mains £9-17; ⊙6-10pm Mon-Thu, 11am-1am
Fri & Sat, 11am-10pm Sun; 🗢🎘🖗) This courtyard complex houses a bar, cocktail lounge
and even a private cinema, along with this
appealing 1st-floor restaurant serving a
menu of crowd-pleasing classics ranging
from sausage and mash with onion gravy
or slow-braised lamb shank, to good old
steak and chips. Vegetarians are catered for,

too, with a good selection of dishes such as
chickpea and coriander burgers.

Café Concerto   CAFE, MEDITERRANEAN ££
(☑01904-610478; www.cafeconcerto.biz; 21 High
Petergate; mains lunch £5-9, dinner £13-18;
⊙8.30am-10pm) Walls papered with sheet
music, chilled jazz on the stereo, and battered, mismatched tables and chairs set the
bohemian tone in this comforting coffee
shop–cum–bistro. Expect breakfasts, bagels
and cappuccinos big enough to float a boat
in during the daytime, and a sophisticated
Mediterranean-style menu in the evening.

Melton's Too   CAFE, BISTRO ££
(www.meltonstoo.co.uk; 25 Walmgate; tapas £3-
6, mains £11-18; ⊙10.30am-midnight Mon-Sat,
to 11pm Sun; 🗢) A comfortable, chilled-out
cafe, bar and bistro, Melton's Too serves
everything from cake and cappuccino to
tapas-style snacks and three-course dinners
(an early-bird special, served before 7pm, offers three courses for £14).

🍷 Drinking & Nightlife

With only a couple of exceptions, the best
drinking holes in town are the older, traditional pubs. There are some nice cocktail
bars with outdoor seating on Swinegate
Court (off Grape Lane), but the area around
Ousegate and Micklegate can get a bit rowdy, especially at weekends.

★**Blue Bell**   PUB
(53 Fossgate; ⊙11am-11pm Mon-Sat, noon-10.30pm
Sun) This is what a real English pub looks
like: a tiny, 200-year-old wood-panelled
room with a smouldering fireplace, decor
untouched since 1903, a pile of ancient
board games in the corner, friendly and
efficient bar staff, and Timothy Taylor and
Black Sheep ales on tap. Bliss, with froth on
top – if you can get in (it's often full).

Ye Olde Starre   PUB
(www.taylor-walker.co.uk; 40 Stonegate; ⊙11am-
11pm Sun-Wed, to midnight Thu-Sat) Licensed
since 1644, this is York's oldest pub – a warren of small rooms and a small beer garden,
with a half-dozen real ales on tap. It was used
as a morgue by the Roundheads (supporters
of parliament) during the Civil War, but the
atmosphere has improved a lot since then.

Pivni   PUB
(pivni.co.uk; 6 Patrick Pool; ⊙noon-11.30pm Sun-Thu,
11am-11.30pm Fri & Sat; 🗢) A slick, modern pub
set in an ancient half-timbered house, Pivni

provides an atmospheric setting for sampling its range of more than 80 draught and bottled craft beers from all over the world.

Old White Swan   PUB
(www.nicholsonspubs.co.uk; 80 Goodramgate; ⊙10am-midnight Sun-Thu, to 1am Fri & Sat) Popular and atmospheric old pub with a small beer garden and a good range of guest real ales.

King's Arms   PUB
(King's Staith; ⊙11am-11pm Sun-Thu, to 1am Fri & Sat) York's best-known pub enjoys a fabulous riverside location, with tables spilling out onto the quayside. It's the perfect spot on a summer evening, but be prepared to share it with a few hundred other people.

☆ Entertainment

There are a couple of good theatres in York and an interesting art-house cinema.

York Theatre Royal   THEATRE
(☑01904-623568; www.yorktheatreroyal.co.uk; St Leonard's Pl) Well-regarded productions of theatre, opera and dance are staged here.

Grand Opera House   LIVE MUSIC, COMEDY
(☑0844 871 3024; www.grandoperahouseyork. org.uk; Clifford St) Despite the name, there's no opera here; instead, there's a wide range of entertainment from live bands and popular musicals to stand-up comics and pantomime.

City Screen Picturehouse   CINEMA
(☑0871 902 5726; www.picturehouses.co.uk; 13-17 Coney St) An appealing modern building in a converted printing works, screening both mainstream and art-house films. There's also a nice cafe-bar on the terrace overlooking the river.

🛍 Shopping

Coney St, Davygate and the adjoining streets are the hub of York's central-city shopping scene, but the real treat are the antique, bric-a-brac and secondhand bookshops, concentrated in Colliergate, Fossgate and Micklegate.

Ken Spelman Booksellers   BOOKS
(www.kenspelman.com; 70 Micklegate; ⊙9am-5.30pm Mon-Sat) This fascinating shop has been selling rare, antiquarian and secondhand books since 1910. With an open fire crackling in the grate in winter, it's a browser's paradise.

Antiques Centre   ANTIQUES
(www.theantiquescentreyork.co.uk; 41 Stonegate; ⊙9am-5.30pm Mon-Sat, to 4pm Sun) A Georgian town house with a veritable maze of rooms and corridors, showcasing the wares of about 120 dealers selling everything from lapel pins and snuff boxes to oil paintings and longcase clocks. And the house is haunted as well...

Red House   ANTIQUES
(www.redhouseyork.co.uk; Duncombe Pl; ⊙9.30am-5.30pm Mon-Sat, 10.30am-5pm Sun) The goods of about 60 antiques dealers are displayed in 10 showrooms spread over two floors, with items ranging from jewellery and porcelain to clocks and furniture.

ℹ Information

Post Office (22 Lendal; ⊙8.30am-5.30pm Mon-Sat)

York Hospital (☑01904-631313; www.york-hospitals.nhs.uk; Wiggington Rd) Located a mile north of the centre.

York Tourist Office (☑01904-550099; www.visityork.org; 1 Museum St; ⊙9am-6pm Mon-Sat, 10am-5pm Sun Apr-Sep, shorter hours Oct-Mar) Visitor and transport info for all of Yorkshire, plus accommodation bookings, ticket sales and internet access.

ℹ Getting There & Away

BUS

For timetable information, call **Traveline York-shire** (☑0871 200 2233; www.yorkshiretravel. net) or check the computerised 24-hour information points at the train station and Rougier St. All local and regional buses stop on Rougier St, about 200m northeast of the train station.

York connections:

Birmingham £29, 3½ hours, one daily

London £31, 5½ hours, three daily

Newcastle £15.20, 2¾ hours, two daily

CAR

A car is more hindrance than help in the city centre, so use one of the Park & Ride car parks at the edge of the city. If you want to explore the surrounding area, rental options include **Europcar** (☑0844 846 4003; www.europcar. co.uk; Train Station, Station Rd; ⊙8am-8.30pm Mon-Sat, 9am-8.30pm Sun), located in the long-stay car park at the train station; Europcar also stores luggage for £4 per bag.

TRAIN

York is a major railway hub, with frequent direct services to British cities. York connections:

Birmingham £45, 2¼ hours, every 30 minutes

Cambridge (change at Peterborough) £65, three hours, hourly

Edinburgh £80, 2½ hours, every 30 minutes

Leeds £13.50, 25 minutes, every 15 minutes

London Kings Cross £80, two hours, every 30 minutes

Manchester £17, 1½ hours, every 15 minutes

Newcastle £16, one hour, every 30 minutes

Scarborough £8, 50 minutes, hourly

🛈 Getting Around

Central York is easy to get around on foot – you're never more than 20 minutes' walk from any of the major sights.

BICYCLE

The tourist office has a useful free map showing York's cycle routes, or visit **iTravel-York** (www. itravelyork.info/cycling). Castle Howard (15 miles northeast of York via Haxby and Strensall) is an interesting destination, and there's also a section of the **Trans-Pennine Trail cycle path** (www. transpenninetrail.org.uk) from Bishopthorpe in York to Selby (15 miles) along the old railway line.

You can rent bikes from **Cycle Heaven** (🕿 01904-622701; www.cycle-heaven.co.uk; York Railway Station, Station Rd; ⊘8.30am-5.30pm Mon-Fri, 9am-6pm Sat & Sun, closed Sun Sep-Apr) at the train station for £20 per day.

BUS

Local bus services are operated by **First York** (www.firstgroup.com/ukbus/york). Single fares range from £1 to £3, and a day pass valid for all local buses is £3.70 (available at Park & Ride car parks).

TAXI

Station Taxis (🕿 01904-623332; www.yorkstationtaxis.co.uk; Train Station, Station Rd) has a kiosk outside the train station.

Castle Howard

Stately homes may be two-a-penny in England, but you'll have to try pretty damn hard to find one as breathtakingly stately as **Castle Howard** (www.castlehoward.co.uk; adult/child house & grounds £14/7.50, grounds only £9.50/6; ⊘house 11am-4.30pm Apr-Oct, grounds 10am-5pm Mar-Oct & Dec, to 4pm Nov, Jan & Feb; 🅿), a work of theatrical grandeur and audacity set in the rolling Howardian Hills. This is one of the world's most beautiful buildings, instantly recognisable from its starring role in the 1980s TV series *Brideshead Revisited* and in the 2008 film of the same name (both based on Evelyn Waugh's 1945 novel of nostalgia for the English aristocracy).

When the Earl of Carlisle hired his pal Sir John Vanbrugh to design his new home in 1699, he was hiring a bloke who had no formal training and was best known as a playwright. Luckily, Vanbrugh hired Nicholas Hawksmoor who had worked as Christopher Wren's clerk of works – not only would Hawksmoor have a big part to play in the house's design, but he and Vanbrugh would later work wonders with Blenheim Palace. Today the house is still home to the Hon Simon Howard and his family and he can often be seen around the place.

If you can, try to visit on a weekday when it's easier to find the space to appreciate this hedonistic marriage of art, architecture, landscaping and natural beauty. As you wander about the peacock-haunted grounds, views open up over the hills, Vanbrugh's playful Temple of the Four Winds and Hawksmoor's stately mausoleum, but the great baroque house with its magnificent central cupola is an irresistible visual magnet. Inside, the house is full of treasures – the breathtaking Great Hall with its soaring Corinthian pilasters, Pre-Raphaelite stained glass in the chapel, and corridors lined with classical antiquities.

WORTH A TRIP

KIRKHAM PRIORY & STONE TROUGH INN

While crowds queue up to get into Castle Howard, you could turn off on the other side of the A64 along the minor road to the hamlet of Kirkham. Here, the picturesque ruins of **Kirkham Priory** (EH; www.english-heritage.org.uk; adult/child £3.60/2.20; ⊘10am-6pm Wed-Sun Apr-Sep, daily Aug; 🅿) rise gracefully above the banks of the River Derwent, sporting an impressive 13th-century gatehouse encrusted with heraldic symbols.

After a stroll by the river, head up the hill on the far side to the **Stone Trough Inn** (🕿 01653-618713; www.stonetroughinn.co.uk; Kirkham; mains £12-18; ⊘noon-2.30pm & 5.30-9pm Mon-Fri, noon-9pm Sat, to 8pm Sun; 🅿🛜♿🐕) for a spot of lunch. This traditional country inn serves gourmet-style pub grub (try the roast belly pork with black pudding and tarragon cream sauce) and its outdoor terrace has a great view over the valley.

The entrance courtyard has a good cafe, a gift shop and a farm shop filled with foodie delights from local producers.

Castle Howard is 15 miles northeast of York, off the A64. There are several organised tours from York – check with the tourist office for up-to-date schedules. **Stephenson's of Easingwold** (www.stephensonsofeasingwold.co.uk) operates a bus service (£7.50 return, 40 minutes, three times daily Monday to Saturday) linking York with Castle Howard.

Harrogate

POP 73,580

The quintessential Victorian spa town, prim and pretty Harrogate has long been associated with a certain kind of old-fashioned Englishness – the kind that seems the preserve of retired army majors and formidable dowagers who take the *Daily Telegraph* and vote Tory. They come to Harrogate to enjoy the flower shows and gardens that fill the town with magnificent displays of colour, especially in spring and autumn. It is fitting that the town's most famous visitor was Agatha Christie, who fled here incognito in 1926 to escape her broken marriage.

And yet, this picture of Victoriana redux is not quite complete. While it's undoubtedly true that Harrogate remains a firm favourite of visitors in their golden years, the town has plenty of smart hotels and trendy eateries catering to the boom in Harrogate's newest trade – conferences. All those dynamic young sales-and-marketing guns have to eat and sleep somewhere.

◉ Sights & Activities

Royal Pump Room Museum   MUSEUM
(www.harrogate.gov.uk; Crown Pl; adult/child £3.95/2.30; ◷10.30am-5pm Mon-Sat, 2-5pm Sun Apr-Oct, to 4pm Jan-Mar) You can learn all about Harrogate's history as a spa town in the ornate Royal Pump Room, built in 1842 over the most famous of the town's sulphurous springs. It gives an insight into how the phenomenon of visiting spas to 'take the waters' shaped the town and records the illustrious visitors it attracted. At the end, you get the chance to sample the spa water, if you dare.

The ritual of visiting spa towns as a health cure became fashionable in the 19th century and peaked during the Edwardian era in the years before WWI. Charles Dickens visited Harrogate in 1858 and described it as 'the queerest place, with the strangest people in it, leading the oddest lives of dancing, newspaper-reading and dining' – sounds quite pleasant, really.

Montpellier Quarter   NEIGHBOURHOOD
(www.montpellierharrogate.com) The most attractive part of town is the Montpellier Quarter, overlooking Prospect Gardens between Crescent Rd and Montpellier Hill. It's an area of pedestrianised streets lined

---

EAT & DRINK LIKE A LOCAL

Yorkshire pudding *The* classic local dish, these puffy batter puddings are traditionally served with roast beef, but Yorkshire tearooms often serve them as a dish in themselves, with gravy. Try them at Ye Olde Naked Man (p533) in Settle.

Theakston's ale Theakston's was turning out best bitter long before the term 'craft beer' had ever been thought of. Try it at pubs all over Britain, or at Theakston's Brewery (p519) in Masham.

Wensleydale cheese Famous as the favourite snack of animated characters Wallace and Gromit, this crumbly white cheese is made in the heart of the Yorkshire Dales. Try it at the source, at Wensleydale Creamery (p534) in Hawes.

Yorkshire rhubarb Traditionally grown in the 'rhubarb triangle' near Wakefield, Yorkshire forced rhubarb (early season rhubarb grown in darkness) has achieved Protected Designation of Origin status. Try the Michelin-starred rhubarb trifle at the Pipe and Glass (p551) near Beverley.

Curd tart A very old Yorkshire dish, a bit like cheesecake, traditionally baked for the Whitsun holiday. Try it at Bettys (p516) in Harrogate.

Parkin A rich and sticky cake made with oatmeal and flavoured with ginger and treacle. Try it at Thomas of Helmsley (p523).

with restored 19th-century buildings that are now home to art galleries, antique shops, fashion boutiques, cafes and restaurants – an upmarket annexe to the main shopping area around Oxford and Cambridge Sts.

Turkish Baths
SPA

(☑01423-556746; www.turkishbathsharrogate.co.uk; Parliament St; admission £17-29.50, guided tours per person £3.75; ⊘check website, guided tours 9-10am Wed) Plunge into Harrogate's past at the town's fabulously tiled Turkish Baths. This mock-Moorish facility is gloriously Victorian and offers a range of watery delights – hot rooms, steam rooms, plunge pools and so on. A visit is likely to last about 1½ hours. There's a complicated schedule of opening hours that are by turns ladies-only and mixed, so call or check online for details. If you prefer to stay dry, there are also guided tours of the building.

🎉 Festivals & Events

All three of Harrogate's major events are held at the Great Yorkshire Showground, just off the A661 on the southeastern edge of town.

Spring Flower Show
HORTICULTURE

(www.flowershow.org.uk; admission £14.50-16) The year's main event, held in late April. A colourful three-day extravaganza of blooms and blossoms, flower competitions, gardening demonstrations, market stalls, crafts and gardening shops.

Great Yorkshire Show
AGRICULTURE

(www.greatyorkshireshow.co.uk; adult/child £25/11) Staged over three days in mid-July by the Yorkshire Agricultural Society. Expect all manner of primped and prettified farm animals competing for prizes, and entertainment ranging from show jumping and falconry to cookery demonstrations and hot-air-balloon rides.

Autumn Flower Show
HORTICULTURE

(www.flowershow.org.uk; admission £14.50-16) Held in late September, this show has vegetable- and fruit-growing championships, cookery demonstrations, a heaviest-onion competition and children's events.

🛏 Sleeping

There are lots of excellent B&Bs and guesthouses just north of Harrogate town centre, on and around Franklin and Ripon Rds.

Bijou
B&B ££

(☑01423-567974; www.thebijou.co.uk; 17 Ripon Rd; s/d from £74/104; P @ 🛜) Bijou by name and bijou by nature, this Victorian villa sits firmly at the boutique end of the B&B spectrum – you can tell that a lot of thought and care has gone into its design. The husband-and-wife team who own the place make fantastic hosts, warm and helpful but unobtrusive.

Acorn Lodge
B&B ££

(☑01423-525630; www.acornlodgeharrogate.co.uk; 1 Studley Rd; s/d from £49/89; P 🛜) Attention to detail makes the difference between an average and an excellent B&B, and the details at Acorn Lodge are spot on – stylish decor, crisp cotton sheets, powerful showers and perfect poached eggs for breakfast. The location is good too, just 10 minutes' walk from the town centre.

Harrogate Brasserie Hotel
BOUTIQUE HOTEL ££

(☑01423-505041; www.harrogatebrasserie.co.uk; 26-30 Cheltenham Pde; s/d/f from £85/110/120; P 🛜) Stripped pine, leather armchairs and subtle colour combinations make this one of Harrogate's most appealing places to stay. The cheerful and cosy accommodation is complemented by an excellent restaurant and bar, with live jazz every evening except Saturday.

Arden House Hotel
B&B ££

(☑01423-509224; www.ardenhousehotel.co.uk; 69-71 Franklin Rd; s/d from £50/80; P 🛜) This grand old Edwardian house has been given a modern makeover with stylish contemporary furniture, Egyptian-cotton bed linen and posh toiletries, but still retains some lovely period details, including tiled cast-iron fireplaces. Attentive service, good breakfasts and a central location are the icing on the cake.

Hotel du Vin
BOUTIQUE HOTEL £££

(☑01423-856800; www.hotelduvin.com; Prospect Pl; r/ste from £155/315; P @ 🛜) An extremely stylish boutique hotel that has made the other lodgings in town sit up and take notice. The loft suites with exposed oak beams, hardwood floors and designer bathrooms are among the nicest rooms in town, but even the standard bedrooms are spacious and very comfortable (though they can be noisy), each with a huge bed draped in soft Egyptian cotton.

🍴 Eating

Le Jardin
BISTRO £

(☑01423-507323; www.lejardin-harrogate.com; 7 Montpellier Pde; lunch mains £5-9, 2-/3-course dinner £10/13; ⊘11.30am-2.30pm Tue-Fri, 6-8.30pm

Tue-Sat, noon-3pm Sun; 🖈) This cool little bistro has a snug atmosphere, especially in the evening when candlelight adds a romantic glow. During the day, locals throng to the tables to enjoy great salads, sandwiches and homemade ice cream.

Bettys TEAROOM ££
(www.bettys.co.uk; 1 Parliament St; mains £6-14, afternoon tea £18.50; ⊙9am-9pm) A classic tearoom in a classic location with views across the park, Betty's is a local institution. It was established in 1919 by a Swiss immigrant confectioner who took the wrong train, ended up in Yorkshire and decided to stay. There are exquisite home-baked breads, scones and cakes, quality tea and coffee, and a gallery hung with art-nouveau marquetry.

Le D2 BISTRO, FRENCH ££
(www.led2.co.uk; 7 Bower Rd; 2-/3-course dinner £21/25; ⊙noon-2pm & 6-11.30pm Tue-Sat) 🍽 This bright and airy bistro is always busy, with diners drawn back again and again by its relaxed atmosphere, warm and friendly service, and hearty menu that takes fresh local produce and adds a twist of French sophistication. A one-course lunch costs £8.95 including a drink.

Tannin Level MODERN BRITISH ££
(☑01423-560595; www.tanninlevel.co.uk; 5 Raglan St; mains £15-25; ⊙noon-9pm Mon-Thu, to 9.30pm Fri & Sat, to 8pm Sun) 🍽 Old terracotta floor tiles, polished mahogany tables and gilt-framed mirrors and paintings create a relaxed yet elegant atmosphere at this popular neighbourhood bistro. A competitively priced menu based on seasonal British produce – think beef braised in Yorkshire ale, or hazelnut-crusted sea bream – means you'd best book a table or face being turned away.

Sasso ITALIAN ££
(☑01423-508838; www.sassorestaurant.co.uk; 8-10 Princes Sq; mains £10-22; ⊙noon-3pm & 6pm-midnight Mon-Sat) A top-class basement trattoria where homemade pasta is served in a variety of traditional and authentic ways, along with a host of other Italian specialities.

⭐**Van Zeller** MODERN BRITISH £££
(☑01423-508762; www.vanzellerrestaurants.co.uk; 8 Montpellier St; 3-course lunch/dinner £35/50; ⊙noon-2pm & 6-10pm Tue-Sat) 🍽 Michelin-trained Yorkshire chef Tom van Zeller (who began his career in Bettys) offers exquisite and unusual interpretations of classic British dishes in a refreshingly relaxed atmosphere – 'fine food without the fuss' is his motto. Imaginative starters include smoked hen's egg with morels and a wild garlic and pine nut pesto. The 10-course chef's tasting menu is £85.

⭐ Entertainment

Harrogate Theatre THEATRE
(☑01423-502116; www.harrogatetheatre.co.uk; Oxford St) A historic Victorian building that dates from 1900, staging variety, comedy, musicals and dancing.

Royal Hall MUSIC
(☑01423-500500; www.royalhall.co.uk; Ripon Rd) A gorgeous Edwardian theatre that is now part of the conference and events venue Harrogate International Centre. The musical program covers orchestral and choral performances, piano recitals, jazz and more.

ℹ Information

Harrogate Tourist Office (☑01423-537300; www.visitharrogate.co.uk; Crescent Rd; ⊙9am-5.30pm Mon-Sat, 10am-1pm Sun Apr-Oct, 9.30am-5pm Mon-Sat Nov-Mar)
Post Office (11 Cambridge Rd; ⊙9.30am-5.30pm Mon-Sat)

ℹ Getting There & Away

Bus National Express coaches run from Leeds (£3.90, 40 minutes, four daily). Bus 36 comes from Ripon (£6, 30 minutes, every 15 minutes) and continues to Leeds.
Train Trains run to Harrogate from Leeds (£7.90, 40 minutes, every 30 minutes) and York (£8.10, 45 minutes, hourly).

Scarborough
POP 61,750

Scarborough is where the tradition of English seaside holidays began – and it began earlier than you might think. It was in the 1660s that a book promoting the medicinal properties of a local spring (now the site of Scarborough Spa) pulled in the first flood of visitors. A belief in the health-giving effects of sea bathing saw wheeled bathing carriages appear on the beach in the 1730s, and with the arrival of the railway in 1845 Scarborough's fate was sealed. By the time the 20th century rolled in, it was all donkey rides, fish and chips, and boat trips round the bay, with saucy postcards, beauty contests and slot-machine arcades only a decade or two away.

Scarborough

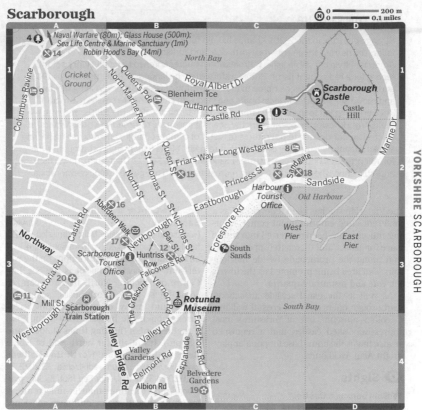

0 ___ 200 m
0 ___ 0.1 miles

Scarborough

◉ Top Sights
1 Rotunda Museum B3
2 Scarborough Castle D1

◉ Sights
3 Grave of Anne Brontë C1
4 Peasholm Park A1
5 St Mary's Church C1

⊕ Activities, Courses & Tours
6 Secretspot Surf Shop B3

🛏 Sleeping
7 Helaina B1
8 Interludes C2
9 North Bay Guest House A1

10 Regency Central Hotel B3
11 Windmill A3

✕ Eating
12 Bonnet's B3
13 Golden Grid C2
14 Jeremy's A1
15 Lanterna B2
16 Naylor's B2
17 Roasters B3
18 Tunny Club C2

✪ Entertainment
19 Scarborough Spa B4
20 Stephen Joseph Theatre A3

Like all British seaside towns, Scarborough suffered a downturn in recent decades as people jetted off to the Costa Blanca on newly affordable foreign holidays, but things are looking up again. The town retains all the trappings of the classic seaside resort, but is in the process of reinventing itself as a centre for the creative arts and digital industries.

THE TUNNY CLUB

Strange but true: in the 1930s Atlantic bluefin tuna (also known as tunny) started to follow the herring shoals into the North Sea, and Yorkshire became the hub of an American-style big-game fishery. Professional hunter Lorenzo Mitchell-Henry set the record for a rod-caught fish in British waters when he landed a 386kg monster in 1933, and Scarborough was soon home to the Tunny Club of Great Britain. Visiting millionaires and movie stars chartered local boats and vied with each other to smash the record.

Overfishing led to the disappearance of the herring shoals in the 1950s, and with them the tunny. However, in recent years the ocean giants have returned to British waters, attracted by warmer sea temperatures (a result of climate change) and recovering herring stocks. Meanwhile, the only evidence that remains of the fishery in Scarborough is the former premises of the **Tunny Club** (1 Sandgate; mains £4-7; ◷ 11am-11pm), now a fish-and-chip shop whose upstairs dining room is filled with big-game fishing memorabilia.

The Victorian spa has been redeveloped as a conference and entertainment centre, a former museum has been converted into studio space for artists, and there's free, open-access wi-fi along the promenade beside the harbour – an area being promoted as the town's bar, cafe and restaurant quarter.

As well as the usual seaside attractions, Scarborough offers excellent coastal walking, a geology museum, one of Yorkshire's most impressively sited castles, and a renowned theatre that is the home base for popular playwright Alan Ayckbourn.

◉ Sights

★**Scarborough Castle** CASTLE
(EH; www.english-heritage.org.uk; adult/child £5/3; ◷ 10am-6pm Apr-Sep, to 5pm Oct, to 4pm Sat & Sun only Nov-Mar) The massive medieval keep of Scarborough Castle occupies a commanding position atop its headland. Legend has it that Richard I loved the views from here so much that his ghost just keeps coming back. Take a walk out to the edge of the cliffs, where you can see the 2000-year-old remains of a **Roman signal station**; clearly the Romans appreciated this viewpoint, too.

★**Rotunda Museum** MUSEUM
(www.rotundamuseum.co.uk; Vernon Rd; adult/child £3/free; ◷ 10am-5pm Tue-Sun; ⊞) The Rotunda Museum is dedicated to the coastal geology of northeast Yorkshire, which has yielded many of Britain's most important dinosaur fossils. The strata in the local cliffs were also important in deciphering England's geological history. Founded by William Smith, 'the father of English geology', who lived in Scarborough in the 1820s, the museum has original Victorian exhibits as well as a hands-on gallery for kids.

Sea Life Centre & Marine Sanctuary AQUARIUM
(www.sealife.co.uk; Scalby Mills; admission £16.20, family per person £13.20; ◷ 10am-5pm; ℗ ⊞) Of all the family-oriented attractions on the waterfront, the best of the lot is the Sea Life Centre overlooking North Bay. You can see coral reefs, turtles, octopuses, seahorses, otters and many other fascinating creatures, though the biggest draw is the **Seal Rescue Centre** (feeding times 11.30am and 2.30pm). It's at the far north end of North Beach – the miniature **North Bay Railway** (www.nbr.org.uk; return adult/child £3.30/2.70; ◷ 10.30am-3pm daily Apr-Sep, Sat & Sun year-round) runs the three-quarter-mile route. A lot of the attractions are outdoors, so it's not an ideal rainy-day refuge.

Peasholm Park PARK
(www.peasholmpark.com; Columbus Ravine; ◷ 24hr) Set back from North Bay, Scarborough's beautiful Edwardian pleasure gardens are famous for their summer sessions of **Naval Warfare** (adult/child £3.90/2.10; ◷ 3pm selected dates Jun-Aug), when large model ships re-enact famous naval battles on the boating lake (check the website for dates).

St Mary's Church CHURCH
(Castle Rd; ◷ 10am-4pm Mon-Fri, 1-4pm Sun May-Sep) This church dates from the 12th to the 15th centuries (boards inside explain its history), but it is most notable for the little cemetery across the lane that contains the **grave of Anne Brontë**.

🏃 Activities

There are some decent waves on England's northeast coast, supporting a growing surf scene. A top spot is **Cayton Bay**, 4 miles south of town, where you'll find **Scarborough Surf School** ([☎]01723-585585; www.scarboroughsurfschool.co.uk; Cayton Bay; parking £2) offering full-day lessons for £45 per person and surfboard hire for £18 per day.

Back in town, you can get information and advice from the **Secretspot Surf Shop** (www.secretspot.co.uk; 4 Pavilion Tce) near the train station.

[🛏] Sleeping

In Scarborough, if a house has four walls and a roof it will offer B&B. Competition is intense, and in such a tough market multi-night-stay special offers are a dime a dozen, which means single-night rates are the highest of all.

Scarborough YHA HOSTEL **£**
([☎]01723-361176; www.yha.org.uk; Burniston Rd; dm/q from £18/60; [P]) An idyllic hostel set in a converted 17th-century water mill, 2 miles north of town along the A166 to Whitby. Take bus 3 or 3A from York Pl.

[★] **Helaina** B&B **££**
([☎]01723-375191; www.hotelhelaina.co.uk; 14 Blenheim Tce; s/d from £79/89; [◷]daily Apr-Nov, Fri & Sat only Feb & Mar; [☎]) Location, location, location – you'd be hard pushed to find a place with a better sea view than this elegant guesthouse perched on the clifftop overlooking North Beach. And the view inside is pretty good, too, with sharply styled contemporary furniture and cool colours. It's well worth paying extra for the deluxe sea-view room with bay window (£119).

Waves B&B **££**
([☎]01723-373658; www.scarboroughwaves.co.uk; 39 Esplanade Rd, South Cliff; s/d from £39/68; [P][☎]) [✎] Crisp cotton sheets and powerful showers make for comfortable accommodation at this B&B, but it's the second B that's the real star – the breakfasts range from vegan-friendly fruit salads and smoothies to fry-ups, kippers and kedgeree. A unique selling point is the jukebox in the lounge, loaded with 1960s and '70s hits.

The property is 0.75 miles south of the centre, off the A165 (Ramshill Rd).

North Bay Guest House B&B **££**
([☎]01723-374406; www.northbay-scarborough.co.uk; 137 Columbus Ravine; s/d from £28/60; [☎][☎]) Cosy and colourful bedrooms, big breakfasts and wonderfully welcoming owners come together to create exceptional value at this excellent B&B, within easy walking distance of Peasholm Park, North Bay Railway and the beach at North Bay.

Windmill B&B **££**
([☎]01723-372735; www.windmill-hotel.co.uk; Mill St; d from £85; [P][☎]) Quirky doesn't begin to

---

WORTH A TRIP

BLACK SHEEP OF THE BREWING FAMILY

The village of Masham (pronounced 'Massam') is a place of pilgrimage for connoisseurs of real ale – it's the frothing fountainhead of Theakston's beers, brewed here since 1827. The company's most famous brew, Old Peculier, takes its name from the Peculier of Masham, a parish court established in medieval times to deal with religious offences, including drunkenness, brawling and 'taking a skull from the churchyard and placing it under a person's head to charm them to sleep'. The court seal is used as the emblem for Theakston Ales.

To the horror of real-ale fans, and after much falling-out among Theakston family members, the Theakston Brewery was taken over by megabrewer Scottish & Newcastle in 1987. Five years later, Paul Theakston, who refused to work for S&N and was determined to keep small-scale artisan brewing alive, bought an old maltings building in Masham and set up his own brewery, which he named Black Sheep. He managed to salvage all kinds of traditional brewing equipment, including six Yorkshire 'stone square' brewing vessels, and was soon running a successful enterprise.

History came full circle in 2004 when Paul's four brothers took the Theakston brewery back into family ownership. Both **Black Sheep Brewery** ([☎]01765-680101; www.blacksheepbrewery.com; tours £6.95; [◷]10am-5pm Sun-Wed, to 11pm Thu-Sat) and **Theakston's Brewery** ([☎]01765-680000; www.theakstons.co.uk; tours £6.95; [◷]10.30am-5.30pm Jul & Aug, to 4.30pm Sep-Jun) have visitor centres and offer guided tours (best booked in advance).

Masham is 9 miles northwest of Ripon on the A6108 to Leyburn. Bus 159 from Richmond to Ripon stops at Masham (£4, 30 minutes, two or three daily).

describe this place, a beautifully converted 18th-century windmill in the middle of town. There are two self-catering cottages and three four-poster doubles around a cobbled courtyard, but try to secure the balcony suite (from £110 a night) in the upper floors of the windmill itself, with great views from the wraparound balcony.

Interludes B&B **££**
(☑01723-360513; www.interludeshotel.co.uk; 32 Princess St; s/d £45/70; ☎) Owners Ian and Bob have a flair for the theatrical and have enacted it with visible success on this lovely, gay-friendly Georgian home plastered with old theatre posters, prints and other thespian mementos. The individually decorated rooms are guaranteed to put a smile on your face. No children.

Regency Central Hotel HOTEL **£££**
(☑01723-365766; www.regencycentralhotel.com; 1-3 The Crescent; s/d from £100/149; ℗☎) Set in an elegant Georgian terrace in the middle of town, on a quiet street overlooking gardens, this recently refurbished hotel combines old-fashioned style – think swagged drapes and sink-up-to-your-waist sofas – and spacious rooms with attentive but friendly and informal service.

✖ Eating

Glass House CAFE **£**
(☑01723-368791; www.glasshousebistro.co.uk; Burniston Rd; mains £4-8; ⊙10am-4.30pm; ☎♨) Homemade lasagne, steak-and-ale pie and filled baked potatoes pull in the lunchtime crowds at this appealing (and always busy) cafe beside the start of the North Bay Rail-

---

FOUNTAINS ABBEY & STUDLEY ROYAL

Nestled in the secluded valley of the River Skell are two of Yorkshire's most beautiful attractions, an absolute must on any northern itinerary.

The alluring and strangely obsessive water gardens of the Studley Royal estate were built in the 18th century to enhance the picturesque ruins of 12th-century **Fountains Abbey** (NT; www.fountainsabbey.org.uk; adult/child £10.50/5.25; ⊙10am-6pm Apr-Sep, to 5pm Sat-Thu Oct-Mar). Together, they present a breathtaking picture of pastoral elegance and tranquillity that have made them a Unesco World Heritage Site and the most visited of all the National Trust's pay-to-enter properties.

After falling out with the Benedictines of York in 1132, a band of rebel monks came here to establish their own monastery. Struggling to make it alone, they were formally adopted by the Cistercians in 1135. By the middle of the 13th century, the new abbey had become the most successful Cistercian venture in the country. After the Dissolution, when Henry VIII confiscated church property, the abbey's estate was sold into private hands, and between 1598 and 1611 **Fountains Hall** was built using stone from the abbey ruins. The hall and ruins were united with the Studley Royal estate in 1768.

Studley Royal was owned by John Aislabie, once Chancellor of the Exchequer, who dedicated his life to creating the park after a financial scandal saw him expelled from parliament. The main house of Studley Royal burnt down in 1946, but the superb landscaping, with its serene artificial lakes, survives almost unchanged from the 18th century.

A choice of scenic walking trails leads for a mile to the famous water gardens, designed to enhance the romantic views of the ruined abbey. Don't miss **St Mary's Church** (Studley Royal; ⊙noon-4pm Apr-Sep) **FREE** above the gardens, a neo-Gothic jewel designed by William Burgess, and ask the attendant to point out the trademark mouse carved into the stone of the mausoleum.

The remains of the abbey are impressively grandiose, gathered around the sunny Romanesque **cloister**, with a huge vaulted **cellarium** leading off the west end of the church. Here, the abbey's 200 lay brothers lived, and food and wool from the abbey's farms were stored. At the east end is the soaring **Chapel of Nine Altars** and on the outside of its northeast window is a Green Man carving (a pre-Christian fertility symbol).

Fountains Abbey is 4 miles west of Ripon off the B6265. Bus 139 travels from Ripon to Fountains Abbey visitor centre year-round (£2.60 return, 15 minutes, four times daily Monday to Saturday, seven on Sundays in summer).

way. Fried breakfasts, sandwiches, cakes and scones fill the menu for the rest of the day.

Roasters   CAFE £
(www.roasterscoffee.co.uk; 8 Aberdeen Walk; mains £4-6; ☺9am-5pm) A funky coffee shop with chunky pine tables, bentwood chairs and an excellent range of freshly ground coffees. There's a juice and smoothie bar, too, and the lunch menu includes ciabatta sandwiches, salads and jacket potatoes.

Bonnet's   TEAROOM £
(38-40 Huntriss Row; mains £5-9; ☺9am-5pm Mon-Sat, 11am-4pm Sun) One of the oldest cafes in town (established in 1880), Bonnet's serves delicious cakes and light meals in a quiet courtyard.

Naylor's   FISH & CHIPS £
(45 Aberdeen Walk; mains £4-5; ☺11.30am-6pm Mon-Thu, to 7pm Fri & Sat) Currently riding high in the local charts for best fish and chips in Scarborough.

★ Jeremy's   BRITISH, FRENCH ££
(☑01723-363871; www.jeremys.co; 33 Victoria Park Ave; mains £16-24, 3-course Sun lunch £25; ☺6-9.30pm Wed-Sat, noon-3pm Sun; ⏰) ✔ A fantastic neighbourhood bistro run by a chef who won his Michelin credential with Marco Pierre White, this off-the-beaten-track gem sports an art-deco ambience and a menu that blends the best of Yorkshire and British produce with French inventiveness and flair. Best to book at weekends.

Golden Grid   FISH & CHIPS ££
(www.goldengrid.co.uk; 4 Sandside; mains £8-18; ☺11.30am-11pm; ⏰) Whoever said fish and chips can't be eaten with dignity hasn't tried the Golden Grid, a sit-down fish restaurant that has been serving the best cod in Scarborough since 1883. Its starched white tablecloths and starched white aprons are staunchly traditional, as is the menu – as well as seafood there's sausage and mash, liver and bacon, and steak and chips.

★ Lanterna   ITALIAN £££
(☑01723-363616; www.lanterna-ristorante.co.uk; 33 Queen St; mains £15-24; ☺7-10pm Mon-Sat) ✔ A snug, old-fashioned Italian trattoria that specialises in fresh local seafood (including lobster from £32) and classic dishes from the old country such as *stufato de ceci* (chickpea stew with oxtail) and white-truffle dishes in season (October to December; £30 to £45). As well as sourcing Yorkshire produce, the chef imports delicacies direct from Italy.

☆ Entertainment

Stephen Joseph Theatre   THEATRE
(☑01723-370541; www.sjt.uk.com; Westborough) A good range of drama is staged here, including the premieres of plays by the renowned chronicler of middle-class mores, Alan Ayckbourn.

Scarborough Spa   VARIETY
(☑01723-821888; www.scarboroughspa.co.uk; Foreshore Rd) The revitalised spa complex stages a varied program of entertainment, especially in the summer months – orchestral performances, variety shows, popular musicals and old-fashioned afternoon-tea dances.

ℹ Information

FreeBay Wifi (📶) Free wi-fi internet access along the harbourfront from West Pier to East Pier.

Harbour Tourist Office (Sandside; ☺10am-5.30pm Easter-Oct, to 9pm Jul & Aug)

Post Office (11-15 Aberdeen Walk; ☺9am-5.30pm Mon-Fri, to 12.30pm Sat)

Scarborough Tourist Office (☑01723-383637; www.discoveryorkshirecoast.com; Brunswick Shopping Centre, Westborough; ☺9.30am-5.30pm Apr-Oct, 10am-4.30pm Mon-Sat Nov-Mar; 📶)

ℹ Getting There & Away

Bus Bus 128 travels along the A170 from Helmsley to Scarborough (£7.60, 1½ hours, hourly Monday to Saturday, six on Sunday) via Pickering, while buses 93 and X93 come from Whitby (£5.60, one hour, every 30 minutes) via Robin Hood's Bay (hourly). Bus 843 goes to Scarborough from Leeds (£12, 2¾ hours, hourly) via York (£11, 1¾ hours, hourly).

Train There are regular trains from Hull (£15.10, 1½ hours, hourly), Leeds (£18, 1¼ hours, hourly) and York (£15, 50 minutes, hourly).

ℹ Getting Around

Tiny Victorian-era **funicular railways** (per person 80p; ☺9.30am-5.30pm Feb-Oct) rattle up and down Scarborough's steep cliffs between town and beach. Local buses leave from the western end of Westborough and outside the train station.

For a taxi, call **Station Taxis** (☑01723-366366; www.taxisinscarborough.co.uk); £5 should get you to most places in town.

NORTH YORK MOORS NATIONAL PARK

Inland from the north Yorkshire coast, the wild and windswept North York Moors rise in desolate splendour. Three-quarters of all the world's heather moorland is to be found in Britain, and this is the largest expanse in England. Ridge-top roads climb up from lush green valleys to the bleak open moors, where weather-beaten stone crosses mark the lines of ancient roadways. In summer, heather blooms in billowing drifts of purple haze.

This is classic walking country. The moors are criss-crossed with footpaths old and new, and dotted with pretty, flower-bedecked villages. The national park is also home to one of England's most picturesque steam railways.

The park produces the useful *Out & About* visitor guide, available from tourist offices and hotels, with information on things to see and do. See also www.northyorkmoors.org.uk.

ℹ Information

There are two national park visitor centres, providing information on walking, cycling, wildlife and public transport:

Moors National Park Centre (☑ 01439-772737; www.northyorkmoors.org.uk; Lodge Lane, Danby; ⊙10am-5pm Apr-Oct, 10.30am-4pm Nov-Mar, Sat & Sun only Jan-Feb)

Sutton Bank National Park Centre (☑ 01845-597426; www.northyorkmoors.org.uk; Sutton Bank, by Thirsk; ⊙10am-5pm Apr-Oct, 10.30am-4pm Nov-Mar, Sat & Sun only Jan-Feb; 🛜)

ℹ Getting Around

On Sundays and bank holiday Mondays from late May to September, the **Moors Explorer** (☑ 01482-592929; www.eyms.co.uk) bus service runs from Hull to the Moors National Park Centre in Danby, via Beverley, Pickering, Hutton-le-Hole and the Lion Inn at Blakey, with a shuttle between Danby and Pickering. An all-day hop-on/hop-off ticket costs £12.50.

If you're planning to drive on the minor roads over the moors, beware of wandering sheep and lambs – hundreds are killed by careless drivers every year.

Helmsley

POP 1515

Helmsley is a classic North Yorkshire market town, a handsome huddle of old stone houses, historic coaching inns and – inevitably – a cobbled market square (market day is Friday), all basking under the watchful gaze of a sturdy Norman castle. Nearby are the romantic ruins of Rievaulx Abbey and a fistful of country walks.

North York Moors National Park

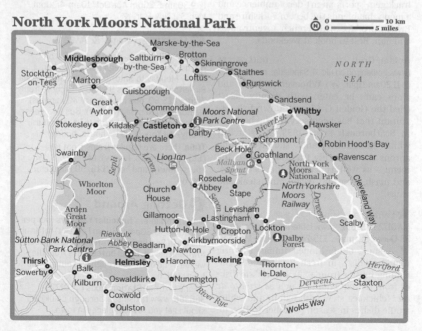

⊙ Sights & Activities

Helmsley Castle
CASTLE

(EH; www.english-heritage.org.uk; adult/child £5.20/ 3.10; ⊙10am-6pm Apr-Sep, to 5pm Oct, to 4pm Sat & Sun Nov-Mar) The impressive ruins of 12th-century Helmsley Castle are defended by a striking series of deep ditches and banks, to which later rulers added the thick stone walls and defensive towers. Only one tooth-shaped tower survives today, following the dismantling of the fortress by Sir Thomas Fairfax after the Civil War. The castle's tumultuous history is well explained in the visitor centre.

Helmsley Walled Garden
GARDENS

(www.helmsleywalledgarden.org.uk; adult/child £6/ free; ⊙10am-5pm Apr-Oct) Helmsley Walled Garden would be just another plant and produce centre were it not for its dramatic position next to Helmsley Castle and fabulous selection of flowers, fruits and vegetables (some of them rare), not to mention the herbs, which include 40 varieties of mint. If you're into horticulture with a historical twist, this is Eden.

Duncombe Park Gardens
GARDENS

(www.duncombepark.com; adult/child £5/3; ⊙10.30am-5pm Sun-Fri May-Aug) South of Helmsley lies the superb landscape of Duncombe Park estate, with the stately home of Duncombe Park House at its heart. From the house (not open to the public) and formal gardens, grassy walkways and terraces lead through woodland to mock-classical temples, while longer walking trails are set out in the landscaped parkland, now protected as a nature reserve. You could easily spend a day here, especially if you take in one of the many walks. Cream of the crop is the 3.5-mile route to Rievaulx Abbey, and the tourist office can provide route leaflets and advise on buses if you don't want to walk both ways. This route is also the opening section of the Cleveland Way.

⌂ Sleeping

Helmsley YHA
HOSTEL £

(☎0845 371 9638; www.yha.org.uk; Carlton Lane; dm/q £21/91; ℗) This hostel's location, just 400m east of the market square at the start of the Cleveland Way, means it's often busy, so book in advance.

Wrens of Ryedale
CAMPSITE £

(☎01439-771260; www.wrensofryedale.co.uk; Gale Lane; site & 1 person £12, with car & 2 people £20; ⊙Apr-Oct; ☎) A sheltered campsite with more than a hectare of pristine parkland 3 miles east of Helmsley, just south of Beadlam.

Feathers Hotel
INN ££

(☎01439-770275; www.feathershotelhelmsley.co. uk; Market Pl; s/d from £70/80) One of a number of old coaching inns on the market square that offer B&B, decent grub and a pint of hand-pumped real ale. There are four-poster beds in some rooms and historical trimmings throughout.

Feversham Arms
HOTEL £££

(☎01439-770766; www.fevershamarms.com; High St; r from £130; ℗⊙⊛⊛) A rustic hotel given a designer makeover, the Feversham Arms has a snug and sophisticated atmosphere where country charm meets boutique chic. Individually decorated bedrooms are complemented by an excellent restaurant, spa treatments and a heated outdoor pool in the central courtyard.

✕ Eating

Helmsley is a bit of a foodie town, sporting a couple of quality delicatessens on the main square. There's **Thomas of Helmsley** (18 Market Pl; ⊙7.30am-5.30pm Mon-Sat, 10am-4pm Sun), a butcher and deli specialising in local produce, and **Hunters of Helmsley** (www. huntersofhelmsley.com; 13 Market Pl; ⊙8am-5.30pm), offering a cornucopia of locally made chutneys, jams, beers, cheeses, bacon, humbug sweets and ice cream – a great place to stock up for a gourmet picnic.

★ Star Inn
GASTROPUB £££

(☎01439-770397; www.thestaratharome.co.uk; Harome; mains £19-29; ⊙11.30am-2pm Tue-Sat, 6.15-9.30pm Mon-Sat, noon-6pm Sun; ℗⊛) ∂ This thatch-roofed country pub is home to one of Yorkshire's best restaurants, with a menu specialising in top-quality produce from the surrounding countryside: Whitby turbot with smoked eel and beetroot or roast English quail with wild mushrooms and truffle. There's also a set three-course menu for £25 (Monday to Saturday). Harome is about 2 miles southeast of Helmsley off the A170.

The Star is the sort of place you won't want to leave, and the good news is you don't have to – the adjacent lodge has eight magnificent bedrooms (£170 to £260), each decorated in classic but luxurious country style.

ℹ Information

The **tourist office** (☎01439-770173; Castlegate; ⊙9.30am-5.30pm Mar-Oct, 10am-4pm Fri-Sun Nov-Feb) at the castle entrance sells maps and books, and can help with accommodation.

ⓘ Getting There & Away

All buses stop in the main square. Bus 31X runs from York to Helmsley (£7.60, 1¼ hours, four daily Monday to Saturday). From Scarborough, take bus 128 (£7.60, 1½ hours, hourly Monday to Saturday, four times on Sunday) via Pickering.

Rievaulx

In the secluded valley of the River Rye, amid fields and woods loud with birdsong, stand the magnificent ruins of Rievaulx Abbey (www.english-heritage.org.uk; adult/child £6.20/3.70; ☺10am-6pm Apr-Sep, to 5pm Oct, to 4pm Sat & Sun only Nov-Mar; P), pronounced 'ree-voh'. The extensive remains give a wonderful sense of the size and complexity of the community that once lived here, and their story is fleshed out in a series of fascinating exhibits in the neighbouring visitor centre.

This idyllic spot was chosen by Cistercian monks in 1132 as a base for their missionary activity in northern Britain. St Aelred, the third abbot, famously described the abbey's setting as 'everywhere peace, everywhere serenity, and a marvellous freedom from the tumult of the world'. But the monks of Rievaulx were far from unworldly and soon created a network of commercial interests ranging from sheep farms to lead mines.

In the 1750s, landscape-gardening fashion favoured a Gothic look and many aristocrats had mock ruins built in their parks. The Duncombe family were able to go one better, as their lands contained a real medieval ruin, Rievaulx Abbey. They built Rievaulx Terrace and Temples (www.nationaltrust.org.uk; adult/child £5.95/3; ☺11am-5pm Mar-Oct; P) so that lords and ladies could stroll effortlessly in 'the wilderness' and admire the abbey in the valley below. Visitors today can do the same, with views over Ryedale and the Hambleton Hills forming a perfect backdrop.

Rievaulx is located about 3 miles west of Helmsley. Note that there's no direct access between the abbey and the terrace. Their entrance gates are about a mile apart, though easily reached along a lane (steeply uphill if you're heading from the abbey to the terrace).

Pickering

POP 6590

Pickering is a lively market town with an imposing Norman castle that advertises itself as the 'gateway to the North York Moors'. That gateway is the terminus of the wonderful North Yorkshire Moors Railway, a picturesque survivor from the great days of steam. The tourist office (☎01751-473791; The Ropery; ☺9.30am-5.30pm Mon-Sat, to 4pm Sun Mar-Oct, 10am-4pm Mon-Sat Nov-Feb) has the usual details, as well as plenty of railway-related info.

◉ Sights

North Yorkshire Moors Railway
HERITAGE RAILWAY

(NYMR; www.nymr.co.uk; Pickering-Whitby Day Rover ticket adult/child £25/12.50; ☺May-Oct) The privately owned North Yorkshire Moors Railway runs for 18 miles through beautiful countryside from Pickering to Grosmont. Lovingly restored steam locos pull period carriages resplendent with polished brass and bright paintwork, and the railway appeals to train buffs and day trippers alike. For visitors without wheels, it's excellent for reaching out-of-the-way spots. Grosmont is on the main railway line between Middlesbrough and Whitby, which opens up yet more possibilities for walking or sightseeing day trips.

Pickering Castle
CASTLE

(EH; www.english-heritage.org.uk; adult/child £4.20/2.50; ☺10am-6pm Apr-Sep, to 5pm Oct) Pickering Castle is a lot like the castles we drew as kids: thick stone outer walls circle the keep, and the whole lot is perched atop a high motte (mound) with great views of the surrounding countryside. Founded by William the Conqueror, it was added to and altered by later kings.

🛏 Sleeping & Eating

There's a strip of B&Bs on tree-lined Eastgate (on the A170 to Scarborough) and a few more on Westgate (heading towards Helmsley). Decent options include Eleven Westgate (☎01751-475111; www.elevenwestgate.co.uk; 11 Westgate; s/d from £49/75; ☎), a pretty house with patio and garden, and the elegant Georgian town house at 17 Burgate (☎01751-473463; www.17burgate.co.uk; 17 Burgate; s/d from £85/99; @☎).

There are several cafes and teashops on Market Pl, but don't overlook the tearoom (mains £4-6; ☺8.30am-4pm) at Pickering station, which serves excellent home-baked goodies and tasty lunch specials such as Yorkshire pudding with roast beef and gravy.

★ White Swan Hotel
HOTEL £££

(☎01751-472288; www.white-swan.co.uk; Market Pl; r from £149; P☎) ✔ The top spot in town successfully combines a smart pub, a superb restaurant serving local produce cooked with a continental twist (mains £14 to £25), and a luxurious boutique hotel. Nine modern rooms in the converted coach house up the ante, with flatscreen TVs and other stylish paraphernalia adding to the luxury found throughout the hotel.

❶ Getting There & Away

In addition to the NYMR trains, bus 128 between Helmsley (£4.50, 40 minutes) and Scarborough (£5.50, 50 minutes) runs hourly via Pickering. Bus 840 between Leeds and Whitby links Pickering with York (£8.80, 70 minutes, hourly).

Whitby

POP 13,215

Whitby is a town of two halves, split down the middle by the mouth of the River Esk. It's also a town with two personalities – on the one hand, a busy commercial and fishing port with a bustling quayside fish market; on the other, a traditional seaside resort, complete with sandy beach, amusement arcades and promenading holidaymakers slurping ice-cream cones in the sun.

It's the combination of these two facets that makes Whitby more interesting than your average resort. The town has managed to retain much of its 18th-century character, recalling the time when James Cook – Whitby's most famous adopted son – was making his first forays out to sea on his way to becoming one of the best-known explorers in history. The narrow streets and alleys of the old town hug the riverside, now lined with restaurants, pubs and cute little shops, all with views across the handsome harbour where colourful fishing boats land their catch. Keeping a watchful eye over the whole scene is the atmospheric ruined abbey atop the East Cliff.

But Whitby also has a darker side. Most famously, it was the inspiration and setting for part of Bram Stoker's Gothic horror story *Dracula*. Less well known is the fact that Whitby is famous for the jet (fossilised wood) that has been mined from its sea cliffs for centuries. This smooth black substance was popularised in the 19th century when Queen Victoria took to wearing mourning jewellery made from Whitby jet. In recent years these morbid associations have seen the rise of a series of hugely popular goth festivals.

◉ Sights

★ **Whitby Abbey** RUIN
(EH; www.english-heritage.org.uk; adult/child £6.60/4; ⏰ 10am-6pm Apr-Sep, to 5pm Oct, to 4pm Sat & Sun only Nov-Mar; Ⓟ) There are ruined abbeys; and there are picturesque ruined abbeys; and then there's Whitby Abbey, dominating the skyline above the East Cliff like a great Gothic tombstone silhouetted against the sky. Looking as though it was built as an atmospheric film set rather than a monastic establishment, it is hardly surprising that this medieval hulk inspired the Victorian novelist Bram Stoker (who holidayed in Whitby) to make it the setting for Count Dracula's dramatic landfall.

From the end of Church St, which has many shops selling jet jewellery, the 199 steps of Church Stairs will lead you steeply up to Whitby Abbey, passing the equally atmospheric St Mary's Church (⏰ 10am-5pm Apr-Oct, to 4pm Nov-Mar) and its spooky graveyard, a favourite haunt of courting goth couples.

★ **Captain Cook Memorial Museum** MUSEUM
(www.cookmuseumwhitby.co.uk; Grape Lane; adult/child £4.80/3.30; ⏰ 9.45am-5pm Apr-Oct, 11am-3pm Mar) This fascinating museum occupies the house of the ship owner with whom Cook began his seafaring career. Highlights include the attic where Cook lodged as a young apprentice, Cook's own maps and letters,

> ### CAPTAIN COOK – WHITBY'S ADOPTED SON
>
> Although he was born in Marton (now a suburb of Middlesbrough), the renowned explorer Captain James Cook has been adopted by Whitby. Ever since the first tourists got off the train in Victorian times, local entrepreneurs have mercilessly cashed in on Cook's memory, as endless Endeavour Cafes and Captain Cook Chip Shops testify.
>
> Still, Whitby played a key role in Cook's eventual success as a world-famous explorer. It was here that he first went to sea, serving his apprenticeship with local ship owners, and the designs of the ships used for his voyages of discovery – including the *Endeavour* – were based on the design of Whitby 'cats', flat-bottomed ships that carried coal from Newcastle to London.

Whitby

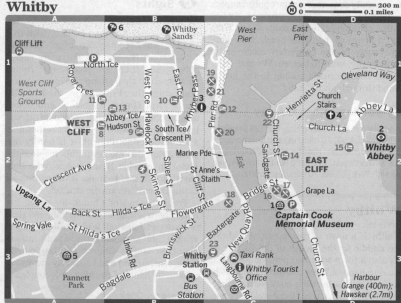

Whitby

etchings from the South Seas, and a wonderful model of the *Endeavour,* with the crew and stores all laid out for inspection.

Whitby Sands BEACH
Whitby Sands, stretching west from the harbour mouth, offers donkey rides, ice-cream vendors and bucket-and-spade escapades. The beach can be reached from West Cliff via the **cliff lift** (per person 60p; ☺10am-5.30pm May-Sep), an elevator that has been in service

since 1931. Atop the cliff at the beach's east end, the **Captain Cook Monument** shows the great man looking out to sea, often with a seagull perched on his head. Nearby is the **Whalebone Arch**, which recalls Whitby's days as a whaling port.

Whitby Museum MUSEUM
(www.whitbymuseum.org.uk; Pannett Park; adult/child £5/free; ☺9.30am-4.30pm Tue-Sun) Set in a park to the west of the town centre is the

wonderfully eclectic Whitby Museum, with displays of fossil plesiosaurs and dinosaur footprints, Captain Cook memorabilia, ships in bottles, jet jewellery and even the 'Hand of Glory', a preserved human hand reputedly cut from the corpse of an executed criminal.

🏃 Activities

For a cracking day out, take a bus to Robin Hood's Bay, explore the village, have lunch, and then hike the 6-mile **clifftop footpath** back to Whitby (allow three hours).

First choice for a bike ride is the excellent 20-mile Whitby to Scarborough **Coastal Cycle Trail**, which starts a mile south of the town centre and follows the route of an old railway line via Robin Hood's Bay. Bikes can be hired for £15 to £25 a day from **Dr Crank's Bike Shack** (✆ 01947-606661; 20 Skinner St; ⏱ 10am-4.30pm Mon, Tue & Thu-Sat) in Whitby, or **Trailways** (✆ 01947-820207; www.trailways.info; Old Railway Station, Hawsker; ⏱ 9.30am-6pm) at Hawsker.

🎊 Festivals & Events

Whitby Goth Weekends   COUNTER CULTURE (www.whitbygothweekend.co.uk; tickets £55) Goth heaven, with gigs, events and the Bizarre Bazaar – dozens of traders selling goth gear, jewellery, art and music. Held twice yearly on the last weekends of April and October.

Whitby Spring Session   MUSIC, ART (www.moorandcoast.co.uk; tickets from £40) Beards, sandals and real ale abound at this traditional festival of folk music, dance and dubious Celtic art on the May Bank Holiday weekend.

🛏 Sleeping

B&Bs are concentrated in West Cliff in the streets to the south and east of Royal Cres. If a house here ain't offering B&B, the chances are it's derelict. Accommodation can be hard to find at festival times when it's wise to book ahead.

Whitby YHA   HOSTEL £ (✆ 0845 371 9049; www.yha.org.uk; Church Lane; dm/q £25/109; P @ 🕾) With an unbeatable position next to the abbey, this hostel is incredibly popular – you'll have to book well in advance to get your body into one of the bunks here. Hike up the 199 steps from the town, or take bus 97 from the train station to Whitby Abbey (twice hourly Monday to Saturday).

Harbour Grange   HOSTEL £ (✆ 01947-600817; www.whitbybackpackers.co.uk; Spital Bridge; dm from £18) Overlooking the harbour and less than 10 minutes' walk from the train station, this clean and basic hostel is conveniently located and has great views, but has an 11.30pm curfew – just the ticket for a night when you don't want to paint the town red.

★**La Rosa Hotel**   HOTEL ££ (✆ 01947-606981; www.larosa.co.uk/hotel; 5 East Tce; d £86-135; 🕾) 🍴 Weird, but wonderful. Lewis Carroll, author of *Alice in Wonderland*, once stayed in this house while holidaying in Whitby. And entering today is like stepping through the looking-glass into an antique world of love-it-or-hate-it Victorian bric-a-brac and kitsch. Eight quirky and atmospheric bedrooms (one with a wooden bath!), great sea views, no TVs, and breakfast served in a basket in your room.

Langley Hotel   B&B ££ (✆ 01947-604250; www.langleyhotel.com; 16 Royal Cres; s/d from £70/105; 🕾) With its cream-and-crimson colour scheme, and a gilt four-poster bed in one room, this grand old guesthouse exudes a whiff of Victorian splendour. Go for room 1 or 2, if possible, to make the most of the panoramic views – the same as those enjoyed in 1897 by Bram Stoker, who holidayed a few doors along at No 6.

Shepherd's Purse   GUESTHOUSE ££ (✆ 01947-820228; www.theshepherdspurse.com; 95 Church St; r £60-75) This place combines

---

DRACULA IN WHITBY

The famous story of *Dracula*, inspiration for a thousand lurid horror movies, was written by Bram Stoker while holidaying in Whitby in 1897 (a blue plaque at 6 Royal Cres marks the house where he stayed). Although most Hollywood versions of the tale concentrate on deepest, darkest Transylvania, a large part of the original book was set in Whitby, and many of the sites can still be seen today.

The tourist office sells a *Dracula Trail* leaflet (£1), which will direct you to the **Bram Stoker memorial seat** on Khyber Pass. From here, you can see all the Whitby-based settings used in the novel.

a beads-and-baubles boutique and wholefood shop with guest accommodation in the courtyard at the back. The cheaper rooms share a bathroom and are perfectly adequate, but we recommend the rustic en suite bedrooms; while the four-poster beds feel a bit as though they've been shoehorned in, the atmosphere is cute rather than cramped. Breakfast is not provided.

Trailways   SELF-CATERING ££
(☑ 01947-820207; www.trailways.info; Hawsker; per week high season £699; P) If travelling on the North Yorkshire Moors Railway has given you a taste for trains, how about sleeping in one? Trailways has a beautifully converted InterCity 125 coach parked at the old Hawsker train station on the Whitby–Scarborough cycle route, offering luxurious self-catering accommodation with all mod cons for two to six people.

Rosslyn House   B&B ££
(☑ 01947-604086; www.rosslynhousewhitby.co.uk; 11 Abbey Tce; s/d from £65/75; ☎) Bright and cheerful with a friendly welcome.

Bramblewick   B&B ££
(☑ 01947-604504; www.bramblewickwhitby.com; 3 Havelock Pl; s/d £35/78; P ☎) Friendly owners, hearty breakfasts and abbey views from the top-floor room.

Argyle House   B&B ££
(☑ 01947-602733; www.argyle-house.co.uk; 18 Hudson St; per person £37-43; ☎) ✐ It's as comfortable as old slippers, and serves kippers for breakfast.

★ Marine Hotel   INN £££
(☑ 01947-605022; www.the-marine-hotel.co.uk; 13 Marine Pde; r £135-150; ☎) Feeling more like mini-suites than ordinary hotel accommodation, the four bedrooms at the Marine are quirky, stylish and comfortable; it's the sort of place that makes you want to stay in rather than go out. Ask for one of the two rooms with a balcony – they have great views across the harbour.

✗ Eating & Drinking

Humble Pie 'n' Mash   BRITISH £
(www.humblepienmash.com; 163 Church St; mains £6; ⊙ noon-8pm Mon-Sat, to 4pm Sun) Superb homemade pies with fillings ranging from lamb, leek and rosemary to roast veg and goats cheese, served in a cosy timber-framed cottage.

Java Cafe-Bar   CAFE £
(2 Flowergate; mains £5-8; ⊙ 8am-6pm; ☎) A cool little diner with stainless-steel counters and retro decor, music videos on the flatscreen and a menu of healthy salads, sandwiches and wraps washed down with excellent coffee.

★ Green's   SEAFOOD ££
(☑ 01947-600284; www.greensofwhitby.com; 13 Bridge St; mains £10-20; ⊙ noon-2pm & 6-9pm Mon-Fri, noon-10pm Sat & Sun) ✐ The classiest eatery in town is ideally situated to take its pick of the fish and shellfish freshly landed at the harbour. Grab a hearty lunch in the ground-floor bistro (mussels and chips, sausage and mash, fish and chips), or head to the upstairs restaurant for a sophisticated dinner date. Two-course lunch for £10 Monday to Friday.

Moon & Sixpence   BRASSERIE ££
(☑ 01947-604416; www.moon-and-sixpence.co.uk; 5 Marine Pde; mains £10-20; ⊙ 9am-midnight; ☎) ✐ This brasserie and cocktail bar has a prime position, with views across the harbour to the abbey ruins. The seafood-dominated menu concentrates on hearty, straightforward dishes such as chunky vegetable soup, seafood chowder, fish pie, homemade burgers, and mussels and chips. Good breakfasts, too, including local kippers with brown bread and butter.

Magpie Cafe   SEAFOOD ££
(www.magpiecafe.co.uk; 14 Pier Rd; mains £7-23; ⊙ 11.30am-9pm; ☗) ✐ The Magpie flaunts its reputation for serving the 'World's Best Fish and Chips'. Damn fine they are, too, but the world and his dog knows about it and summertime queues can stretch along the street. Takeaway fish and chips cost £4.95; the sit-down restaurant is more expensive, but offers a wide range of seafood dishes, from grilled sea bass to paella.

Quayside   FISH & CHIPS ££
(www.quaysidewhitby.co.uk; 7 Pier Rd; mains £10-14; ⊙ 11am-7pm Sun-Thu, to 8pm Fri & Sat; ☗) Top-notch fish and chips minus the 'world's best' tag line – this place is your best bet if you want to avoid queues. Takeaway fish and chips are £4.40.

Station Inn   PUB
(www.stationinnwhitby.co.uk; New Quay Rd; ⊙ 10am-midnight Mon-Sat, to 11.30pm Sun; ☎) The best place in town for atmosphere

and real ale, with its impressive range of cask-conditioned beers including Timothy Taylor's Golden Best and Ossett Silver King. Live music Wednesday, Friday, Saturday and Sunday.

Duke of York PUB
(www.dukeofyork.co.uk; Church St; ⊙11am-11pm Sun-Thu, to midnight Fri, to 1am Sat; 🛜) A popular watering hole at the bottom of the Church Stairs, serving Timothy Taylor ales and great views over the harbour.

❶ Information

Post Office (Langbourne Rd; ⊙8.30am-5.30pm Mon-Sat) Located inside the Co-op supermarket.
Whitby Tourist Office (✆01947-602674; www.visitwhitby.com; Langbourne Rd; ⊙9.30am-6pm Apr-Oct, to 4.30pm Nov-Mar)

❶ Getting There & Away

Bus Buses 93 and X93 run south to Scarborough (£5.60, one hour, every 30 minutes), with every second bus going via Robin Hood's Bay (£3.90, 15 minutes, hourly); and north to Middlesbrough (£5.60, one hour, hourly), with fewer services on Sunday. The Coastliner service 840 runs from Leeds to Whitby (£13, 3¼ hours, six times daily Monday to Saturday) via York and Pickering.

Train Coming from the north, you can get to Whitby by train along the Esk Valley Railway from Middlesbrough (£6, 1½ hours, four per day), with connections from Durham and Newcastle. From the south, it's easier to get a train from York to Scarborough, and then a bus from Scarborough to Whitby.

Robin Hood's Bay

Picturesque **Robin Hood's Bay** (www.robin-hoods-bay.co.uk) is the end point of the Coast to Coast Walk (p501). It has nothing to do with the hero of Sherwood Forest – the origin of its name is a mystery, and the locals call it Bay Town or just Bay. But there's no denying that this fishing village is one of the prettiest spots on the Yorkshire coast.

Leave your car at the parking area in the upper village (£3.50 for four hours), where 19th-century ships' captains built comfortable Victorian villas, and walk downhill to Old Bay, the oldest part of the village (don't even think about driving down). This maze of narrow lanes and passages is dotted with

---

WORTH A TRIP

GOATHLAND

This picture-postcard halt on the North Yorkshire Moors Railway (p524) stars as Hogsmeade train station in the Harry Potter films, and the village appears as Aidensfield in the British TV series *Heartbeat*. It's also the starting point for lots of easy and enjoyable walks, often with the chuff-chuff-chuff of passing steam engines in the background.

One of the most popular hikes is to head northwest from the station (via a gate on the platform on the far side from the village) to the hamlet of Beck Hole, where you can stop for a pork pie and a pint of Black Sheep at the wonderfully atmospheric **Birch Hall Inn** (www.beckhole.info; ⊙11am-11pm mid-Apr–mid Sep, shorter hours & closed Tue mid-Sep–mid-Apr), where it's like stepping into the past. Return to Goathland via the waterfall at **Mallyan Spout** (total 4 miles).

An alternative to the hike is to walk or cycle from Goathland along Beck Hole Rd (just over 1 mile); it's best not to drive, as the road is narrow and twisty and there's nowhere to park.

---

tearooms, pubs, craft shops and artists' studios (there's even a tiny cinema) and at low tide you can go down onto the beach and fossick around in the rock pools. The NT-listed **Old Coastguard Station** (www.nationaltrust.org.uk; The Dock; ⊙10am-5pm Apr-Oct, to 4pm Sat & Sun Nov-Mar) FREE houses an exhibition about local geology and natural history.

There are several pubs and cafes. The best pub for ambience and real ale is **Ye Dolphin** (King St; ⊙11.30am-11pm), while the **Swell Cafe** (www.swell.org.uk; Chapel St; mains £3-8; ⊙10am-4pm Mon-Fri, to 4.30pm Sat & Sun; 🛜👶) does great coffee and has a terrace with a view over the beach.

Robin Hood's Bay is 6 miles southeast of Whitby. You can walk here along the coastal path in two or three hours, or bike to it along the cycle trail in 40 minutes. Bus 93 runs hourly between Whitby and Scarborough via Robin Hood's Bay – the bus stop is at the top of the hill, in the new part of town.

YORKSHIRE DALES NATIONAL PARK

The Yorkshire Dales – named from the old Norse word *dalr,* meaning 'valleys' – is the central jewel in the necklace of three national parks strung across the neck of northern England, with the dramatic fells of the Lake District to the west and the brooding heaths of the North York Moors to the east.

From well-known names such as Wensleydale and Ribblesdale to the obscure and evocative Langstrothdale and Arkengarthdale, the park's glacial valleys are characterised by a distinctive landscape of high heather moorland, stepped skylines and flat-topped hills. Down in the green valleys, patchworked with drystone dykes and little barns, are picture-postcard villages where sheep and cattle still graze on village greens. And in the limestone country of the southern Dales you'll find England's best examples of karst scenery (a landscape created by rainwater dissolving the underlying limestone bedrock).

The Dales have been protected as a national park since the 1950s, assuring their status as a walker's and cyclist's paradise. But there's plenty for nonwalkers as well, from exploring the legacy of literary vet James Herriot of *All Creatures Great and Small* fame to sampling the favourite teatime snack of the British TV characters Wallace and Gromit at the Wensleydale Creamery.

The *Visitor* newspaper, available from tourist offices, lists local events and walks guided by park rangers, as well as many places to stay and eat. The official park website (www.yorkshiredales.org.uk) is also useful.

ⓘ Getting There & Around

About 90% of visitors to the park arrive by car, and the narrow roads can become extremely crowded in summer. Parking can also be a serious problem. If you can, try to use public transport as much as possible.

Yorkshire Dales National Park

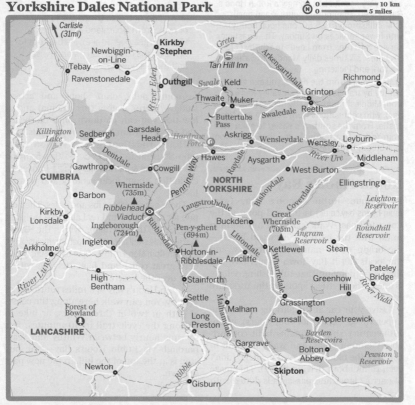

Pick up a DalesBus Timetable from tourist offices, or consult the **DalesBus** (www.dalesbus.org) website.

By train, the best and most interesting access to the Dales is via the famous Settle–Carlisle Line (p535). Trains run between Leeds and Carlisle, stopping at Skipton, Settle and numerous small villages, offering unrivalled access to the hills straight from the station platform.

Skipton

POP 14,625

This busy market town on the southern edge of the Dales takes its name from the Anglo-Saxon *sceape ton* (sheep town). There are no prizes for guessing how it made its money. Monday, Wednesday, Friday and Saturday are market days, bringing crowds from all over and giving the town something of a festive atmosphere. The **tourist office** (☑ 01756-792809; www.welcometoskipton.com; Town Hall, High St; ⊙ 9.30am-4pm Mon-Sat, 10am-4pm 1st Sun of month) is in the town hall.

◉ Sights & Activities

High Street   STREET
Skipton's pride and joy is the broad and bustling High St, one of the most attractive shopping streets in Yorkshire. There's a general market on High St four days a week, and on the first Sunday of the month the nearby canal basin hosts the **Northern Dales Farmers Market** (www.northerndalesfarmersmarkets.com; ⊙ 8.30am-2.30pm 1st Sun of month).

Skipton Castle   CASTLE
(www.skiptoncastle.co.uk; High St; adult/child £7.30/4.50; ⊙ 10am-6pm Mon-Sat, noon-6pm Sun Mar-Sep, to 4pm Oct-Feb) A gate to the side of the church at the north end of High St leads to Skipton Castle, one of the best-preserved medieval castles in England and a fascinating contrast to the ruins you'll see elsewhere.

Pennine Cruisers   BOAT CRUISE
(www.penninecruisers.com; The Wharf, Coach St; per person £4; ⊙ 10.30am-dusk Mar-Oct) No trip to Skipton is complete without a cruise along the Leeds–Liverpool Canal, which runs through the middle of town. Pennine Cruisers runs half-hour trips to Skipton Castle and back.

⌊▅ Sleeping

There's a strip of B&Bs just outside the centre on Keighley Rd.

OFF THE BEATEN TRACK

DELVE INTO THE DALES

Whether on two wheels or four, one of the joys of the Yorkshire Dales is exploring the hidden corners of the lesser known valleys. From Swaledale, climb up to the moors above Arkengarthdale in search of the **Tan Hill Inn** (☑ 01833-628246; www.tanhillinn.com; Tan Hill; ⊙ 8am-11.30pm Jul & Aug, noon-9.30pm Sep-Jun; 🕙🐾), Britain's highest pub, or seek out the picture-postcard village green at **West Burton**, at the entrance to Bishopdale. From Grassington, make your way north along lovely Littondale and stop for a pint at the **Falcon Inn** (www.thefalconinn.com; Arncliffe), where beer is still served from a jug on the counter.

Park Hill   B&B ££
(☑ 01756-792772; www.parkhillskipton.co.uk; 17 Grassington Rd; d £80; 🅿@🕙) 🐾 From the complimentary glass of sherry on arrival to the hearty breakfasts based on local produce, farm-fresh eggs and homegrown tomatoes, this B&B provides a real Yorkshire welcome. It enjoys an attractive rural location half a mile north of the town centre, on the B6265 road towards Grassington.

Carlton House   B&B ££
(☑ 01756-700921; www.carltonhouseskipton.co.uk; 46 Keighley Rd; s/d from £30/60) A handsome house with five pretty and comfortable rooms – there are no frills, but lots of floral prints. This B&B is deservedly popular on account of its friendly welcome.

✗ Eating & Drinking

Cafe 76   BRITISH £
(☑ 01756-795460; www.cafe76.co.uk; 76 High St; mains £4-8; ⊙ 8.15am-4.30pm Mon, Wed, Fri & Sat, 9am-4.30pm Thu & Sun; 🕙🔧) Squeezed into a tall and narrow building (best seats are upstairs), this popular local lunch spot serves hearty homemade food including roast chicken, cheese burgers, roast beef sandwiches, and daily specials such as minted lamb and vegetable pasty with onion gravy. Full English breakfast served all day.

Bizzie Lizzies   FISH & CHIPS £
(www.bizzielizzies.co.uk; 36 Swadford St; mains £4-8; ⊙ 11am-9pm; 🔧🐾) An award-winning sit-down fish-and-chip restaurant overlooking

the canal. There's also a takeaway counter offering fish and chips for £5; it's open until 11.30pm.

Bean Loved
CAFE £
(www.beanloved.co.uk; 17 Otley St; mains £5-9; ⏰7.30am-5pm Mon-Sat, 9am-5pm Sun; 🛜) This place just off High St serves the best coffee in town, along with good cakes and freshly prepared sandwiches.

Le Caveau
FRENCH ££
(🖉01756-794274; www.lecaveau.co.uk; 86 High St; mains £13-20; ⏰noon-2pm & 7-9.30pm Tue-Fri, 5-10pm Sat) 🍴 Set in a stylishly decorated 16th-century cellar with barrel-vaulted ceilings, this friendly bistro offers a seasonal menu built lovingly around fresh local produce. Daily specials include dishes such as a light and flavourful quiche made with black pudding, bacon and mushrooms, and a succulent smoked haddock and leek pie. On weekdays you can get a two-course lunch for £11.

Narrow Boat
PUB
(www.markettowntaverns.co.uk; 38 Victoria St; ⏰noon-11pm) A traditionally styled pub with a great selection of local ales and foreign beers, friendly service and bar meals.

❶ Getting There & Away

Skipton is the last stop on the Metro rail network from Leeds and Bradford (£9.10, 45 minutes, half-hourly, hourly on Sunday). Three buses a day (weekdays only) link Skipton with Settle (£6, 40 minutes).

Grassington

The perfect base for jaunts around the south Dales, Grassington's handsome Georgian centre teems with walkers and visitors throughout the summer months, soaking up an atmosphere that – despite the odd touch of faux rusticity – is as attractive and traditional as you'll find in these parts.

Highlight of the year is the Grassington Festival (www.grassington-festival.org.uk), a two-week arts extravaganza held in June that attracts many big names in music, theatre and comedy, and also includes offbeat events like drystone-walling workshops.

The tourist office (🖉01756-751690; Hebden Rd; ⏰10am-5pm Apr-Oct, Fri-Sun only Nov-Mar) is beside the big car park on the edge of town.

🛏 Sleeping & Eating

Ashfield House
B&B ££
(🖉01756-752584; www.ashfieldhouse.co.uk; Summers Fold; r from £100; 🅿@🛜) A secluded 17th-century country house behind a walled garden, with exposed stone walls, open fireplaces and an all-round cosy feel. It's just off the main square.

★Devonshire Fell
HOTEL £££
(🖉01756-718111; www.devonshirefell.co.uk; Burnsall; r from £140; 🅿@🛜) A sister property to Bolton Abbey's Devonshire Arms Country House Hotel, this former gentleman's club for mill owners has a much more contemporary feel, with beautiful modern furnishings crafted by local experts. The conservatory (used as a lounge and breakfast room) has a stunning view over the valley. It's 3 miles southeast of Grassington on the B6160.

Whimsical Cottage
CAFE £
(🖉01756-752414; 1 Garr's Lane; mains £4-9; ⏰10am-4pm; 🚼) This cute little white cottage, just uphill from the village square, serves good coffee and unusual homemade cakes (parsnip and apple sponge is unexpectedly delicious), as well as hot pies for lunch - chicken, ham and leek, or steak and Guinness. Breakfast served till 11.30am.

Malham
POP 120

Stretching west from Grassington to Ingleton is the largest area of limestone country in England, a distinctive landscape pockmarked with potholes, dry valleys, limestone pavements and gorges. Two of the most spectacular features – Malham Cove and Gordale Scar – lie near the pretty village of Malham.

The national park centre (🖉01969-652380; www.yorkshiredales.org.uk; ⏰10am-5pm Apr-Oct, to 4pm Sat & Sun only Nov-Mar) at the southern edge of the village has the usual wealth of information. See also www.malhamdale.com.

◉ Sights & Activities

A 0.75-mile walk north from Malham village leads to Malham Cove, a huge rock amphitheatre lined with 80m-high vertical cliffs. Peregrine falcons nest here in spring, when the Royal Society for the Protection of Birds (RSPB) sets up a birdwatching lookout. You can hike up the steep steps on the left-hand side of the cove (on the Pennine

Way footpath) to see the extensive limestone pavement above the cliffs. Another 1.5 miles further north is Malham Tarn, a glacial lake and nature reserve.

A mile east of Malham along a narrow road (with very limited parking) is spectacular Gordale Scar, a deep limestone canyon with scenic cascades and the remains of an Iron Age settlement. The national park centre has a leaflet describing the Malham Landscape Trail, a 5-mile circular walk that takes in Malham Cove, Gordale Scar and the Janet's Foss waterfall.

The Pennine Way (p501) passes through Malham, with Horton-in-Ribblesdale a day's hike away to the northwest.

🛏 Sleeping

Malham YHA   HOSTEL £
(☎0845 371 9529; www.yha.org.uk; dm/tw £22/49; Ⓟ) You will find this recently refurbished, purpose-built hostel in the village centre. The facilities are top-notch, including a restaurant, and young children are well catered for.

Beck Hall   HOTEL ££
(☎01729-830332; www.beckhallmalham.com; s/d from £45/65; Ⓟ 🞄) This rambling 17th-century country house on the edge of the village, a gurgling stream flowing through the garden, has 18 individually decorated rooms; we recommend the Green Room, with its old-style furnishings and antique four-poster bed.

❶ Getting There & Away

There are between two and five buses a day (except Tuesday and Thursday) from Skipton to Malham (45 minutes), and the Malham Tarn Shuttle bus links Settle and Malham (25 minutes) four times daily on Sundays only, Easter to October. Check the DalesBus website or ask at Skipton tourist office for details.

Note that Malham is reached via narrow roads that can get very congested in summer, so leave your car at the national park centre and walk into the village.

Ribblesdale & the Three Peaks

Scenic Ribblesdale cuts through the southwestern corner of the Yorkshire Dales National Park, where the skyline is dominated by a trio of distinctive hills known as the Three Peaks – Whernside (735m), Ingleborough (724m) and Pen-y-ghent (694m).

Easily accessible via the Settle–Carlisle railway line, this is one of England's most popular areas for outdoor activities, attracting thousands of hikers, cyclists and cavers each weekend.

Settle

POP 3660

The busy market town of Settle, dominated by its grand neo-Gothic town hall, is the gateway to Ribblesdale and marks the beginning of the scenic part of the famous Settle–Carlisle railway line. Narrow cobbled streets lined with shops and pubs lead out from the central market square (Tuesday is market day), and the town offers plenty of accommodation options.

The tourist office (☎01729-825192; Town Hall, Cheapside; ⊙9.30am-4pm Mon, Tue & Thu-Sat, to 1pm Wed) has maps and guidebooks.

Around the main square are several good cafes, including Ye Olde Naked Man (Market Pl; mains £4-8; ⊙9am-5pm Thu-Tue, to 4pm Wed; 🞄), formerly an undertaker's (look for the 'naked man' on the outside wall, dated 1663), which serves superb Yorkshire pudding with a choice of fillings.

Trains from Leeds heading to Carlisle stop at Settle station near the town centre (£12, one hour, eight daily). Those heading for Morecambe (on the west coast) stop at Giggleswick, about 1.5 miles outside town.

Horton-in-Ribblesdale

POP 560

A favourite with outdoor enthusiasts, the little village of Horton and its railway station is 5 miles north of Settle. Everything centres on the Pen-y-Ghent Cafe, which acts as the village tourist office, wet-weather retreat and hikers' information centre.

Horton is the starting point for climbing Pen-y-ghent and doing the Three Peaks Walk; it's also a stop on the Pennine Way. At the head of the valley, 5 miles north of Horton, is the spectacular 30m-high Ribblehead Viaduct, built in 1874 and, at 400m, the longest on the Settle–Carlisle Line (p535). You can hike there along the Pennine Way and travel back by train from Ribblehead station.

🍴 Sleeping & Eating

Horton is popular, so it's advisable to book accommodation in advance.

THREE PEAKS CHALLENGES

Since 1968 more than 200,000 hikers have taken up the challenge of climbing York-shire's Three Peaks in less than 12 hours. The circular 25-mile route begins and ends at the Pen-y-Ghent Cafe in Horton-in-Ribblesdale (where you clock-in and clock-out to verify your time) and takes in the summits of Pen-y-ghent, Whernside and Ingleborough. Succeed and you become a member of the cafe's Three Peaks of Yorkshire Club. You can find details of the route at www.merseyventure.com/yorks and download a guide (£4) at www.walkingworld.com (walk ID 4228 and 4229).

Fancy a more gruelling test of your endurance? Then join the fell-runners in the an-nual **Three Peaks Race** (www.threepeaksrace.org.uk) on the last Saturday in April, and run the route instead of walking it. First held in 1954 when six people competed, it now attracts about 900 entrants. The course record is two hours, 43 minutes and three seconds.

In the last week of September, cyclists get their chance in the **Three Peaks Cyclo-Cross** (www.3peakscyclocross.org.uk), which covers 38 miles of rough country and climbs 1524m.

Golden Lion   INN £
(☑ 01729-860206; www.goldenlionhotel.co.uk; s/d from £45/70, bunkhouse per person £12) The Golden Lion is a lively pub that offers com-fortable B&B rooms, a 15-bed bunkhouse, and three public bars where you can tuck into a bit of grub washed down with a pint of hand-pulled ale.

Holme Farm Campsite   CAMPSITE £
(☑ 01729-860281; Horton-in-Ribblesdale; tent sites per person £5, shower £1) A basic, no-frills campsite next door to the Golden Lion pub, much used by Pennine Way hikers.

Pen-y-Ghent Cafe   CAFE £
(mains £3-6; ⊙ 9am-5.30pm Mon & Wed-Fri, 8.30am-5pm Sat & Sun; ☑ 🐾) A traditional cafe run by the same family since 1965, the Pen-y-Ghent fills walkers' fuel tanks with fried eggs and chips, homemade scones and pint-sized mugs of tea. It also sells maps, guide-books and walking gear.

Hawes

POP 885

Hawes is the beating heart of Wensleydale, a thriving and picturesque market town (market day is Tuesday) that has the added attraction of its own waterfall in the village centre. On busy summer weekends, howev-er, Hawes' narrow arteries can get serious-ly clogged with traffic. Leave the car in the parking area beside the national park cen-tre (☑ 01969-666210; Station Yard; ⊙ 10am-5pm Apr-Oct, limited hours Nov-Mar, closed Jan) at the eastern entrance to the village.

⊙ Sights

Dales Countryside Museum   MUSEUM
(☑ 01969-666210; Station Yard; adult/child £4/ free; ⊙ 10am-5pm, closed Jan; Ⓟ) Sharing a building with the national park centre is the Dales Countryside Museum, a beauti-fully presented social history of the area that explains the forces shaping the land-scape, from geology to lead mining to land enclosure.

Wensleydale Creamery   MUSEUM
(www.wensleydale.co.uk; adult/child £2.50/1.50; ⊙ 10am-4pm; 🐾) This museum is devoted to the production of the animated TV charac-ters Wallace and Gromit's favourite crumbly white cheese. You can visit the cheese muse-um, see cheesemakers in action in the view-ing gallery, and then try-before-you-buy in the shop, which is free to enter.

Hardraw Force   WATERFALL
About 1.5 miles north of Hawes is 30m-high Hardraw Force. It's the highest unbroken waterfall in England, but by internation-al standards not really all that impressive (except after heavy rain). Access is through the Green Dragon Inn, which levies a £2 admission fee.

Sheepdog Demonstrations   FARM
(www.sheepdogdemo.co.uk; adult/child £4/1; ⊙ 6.30pm Thu May-Aug, 2.30pm Thu Sep; Ⓟ) On Thursdays from May to September, a local farmer gives demonstrations of working sheepdogs, held in a field 800m north of Hawes on the minor road towards Hardraw.

🛏 Sleeping & Eating

Bainbridge Ings Caravan & Camp Site   CAMPSITE **£**
(☑ 01969-667354; www.bainbridge-ings.co.uk; hikers & cyclists per person £6, site, car & 2 adults £15; 🐕🍽) An attractive site set around a spacious farmhouse in stone-walled fields about half a mile east of Hawes. Fresh-laid eggs are sold on-site.

Hawes YHA   HOSTEL **£**
(☑ 0845 371 9120; www.yha.org.uk; Lancaster Tce; dm/tw £19.50/47) A modern place on the western edge of town, at the junction of the main A684 (Aysgarth Rd) and B6255, this is a family-friendly hostel with great views of Wensleydale.

Herriot's Guest House   B&B **££**
(☑ 01969-667536; www.herriotsinhawes.co.uk; Main St; d from £75; 🐕) A delightful guesthouse set in an old stone building close to the bridge by the waterfall, Herriot's has seven comfy en suite bedrooms set above an art gallery and coffee shop.

Green Dragon Inn   INN **££**
(☑ 01969-667392; www.greendragonhardraw.co.uk; Hardraw; B&B per person £35-50; 🐕) A fine old pub with flagstone floors, low timber beams, ancient oak furniture and Theak-ston's on draught. The Dragon serves up a tasty steak-and-ale pie and offers bunkhouse accommodation (per person £15), camping (per person £8) or B&B in plain but adequate rooms, as well as a pair of larger, more comfortable suites. One mile northwest of Hawes.

Cart House   TEAROOM **£**
(☑ 01969-667691; Hardraw; mains £4-7; ⏰ 10am-5pm mid-Mar–Oct) This craft shop and tearoom offers a healthier diet of homemade soup, organic bread and a 'Fellman's Lunch' of Wensleydale cheese, pickle and salad. There's a basic campsite at the back (per person £7, including tent and car). One mile northwest of Hawes.

❶ Getting There & Away

Buses 156 and 157 run from Hawes to Leyburn (50 minutes, four daily Monday to Saturday), where you can connect with buses to or from Richmond.

From Garsdale station on the Settle–Carlisle Line, bus 113 runs to Hawes (20 minutes, three daily Monday to Friday). On Sundays and bank holidays from April to October, bus 831 goes to Hawes from Ribblehead station (25 minutes, one daily). Check bus times with Traveline Yorkshire or a tourist office before using these routes.

THE SETTLE–CARLISLE LINE

The 72-mile **Settle–Carlisle Line** (SCL; www.settle-carlisle.co.uk), built between 1869 and 1875, offers one of England's most scenic railway journeys. The line's construction was one of the great engineering achievements of the Victorian era: 5000 labourers armed with picks and shovels built 325 bridges and 21 viaducts and blasted 14 tunnels in horrific conditions – nearly 200 of them died in the process. Trains run between Leeds and Carlisle via Settle about eight times per day.

The first section of the journey from Leeds is along the Aire Valley, stopping at Keighley, where the Keighley & Worth Valley Railway (p547) branches off to Haworth, Skipton (gateway to the southern Dales) and Settle. The train then labours up the valley beside the River Ribble, through Horton-in-Ribblesdale, across the spectacular **Ribblehead Viaduct** and then through Blea Moor Tunnel to reach remote **Dent station**, at 350m the highest main-line station in the country.

The line reaches its highest point (356m) at Ais Gill, where it leaves the Dales behind before easing down to Kirkby Stephen. The last halts are Appleby and Langwathby, just northeast of Penrith (a jumping-off point for the Lake District), before the train finally pulls into Carlisle.

The entire journey from Leeds to Carlisle takes two hours and 40 minutes and costs £28/34 for a single/day return. Various hop-on/hop-off passes are also available for one or three days. You can pick up a free SCL timetable – which includes a colour map of the line and brief details about places of interest – from most Yorkshire stations. For more information, contact **National Rail Enquiries** (www.nationalrail.co.uk) or see www.settle-carlisle.co.uk.

Richmond

POP 8415

The handsome market town of Richmond is one of England's best-kept secrets, perched on a rocky outcrop overlooking the River Swale and guarded by the ruins of a massive castle. A maze of cobbled streets radiates from the broad, sloping market square (market day is Saturday), lined with elegant Georgian buildings and photogenic stone cottages, with glimpses of the surrounding hills and dales peeking through the gaps.

In September/October the town hosts the Richmond Walking & Book Festival (www. booksandboots.org), 10 days of guided walks, talks, films and other events.

◉ Sights

Richmond Castle   CASTLE
(www.english-heritage.org.uk; Market Pl; adult/child £4.90/2.90; ⊙10am-6pm Apr-Sep, to 5pm Oct, to 4pm Sat & Sun only Nov-Mar) The impressive heap that is Richmond Castle, founded in 1070, was one of the first castles in England since Roman times to be built of stone. It's had many uses through the years, including a stint as a prison for conscientious objectors during WWI (there's a small and sobering exhibition about their part in the castle's history). The best part of a visit is the view from the top of the remarkably well-preserved 30m-high keep, which towers over the town.

Green Howards Museum   MUSEUM
(www.greenhowards.org.uk; Trinity Church Sq; adult/child £4/2; ⊙10am-4.30pm Mon-Sat Feb-Dec, also 12.30-4.30pm Sun Apr-Oct) Military buffs will enjoy the three floors of this museum (recently reopened after a major revamp), which pays tribute to the famous Yorkshire regiment.

Richmondshire Museum   MUSEUM
(www.richmondshiremuseum.org.uk; Ryder's Wynd; adult/child £3/free; ⊙10.30am-4pm Apr-Oct) The Richmondshire Museum is a delight, with local history exhibits including an early Yorkshire cave-dweller and displays about lead mining, which forever altered the Swaledale landscape a century ago. You can also see the original set that served as James Herriot's surgery in the TV series *All Creatures Great and Small*.

Georgian Theatre Royal   HISTORIC BUILDING
(www.georgiantheatreroyal.co.uk; Victoria Rd; tour per person £3.50; ⊙tours hourly 10am-4pm Mon-Sat mid-Feb–mid-Nov) The Georgian Theatre

Royal, built in 1788, is the most complete Georgian playhouse in Britain. Tours include a look at the country's oldest surviving stage scenery, painted between 1818 and 1836.

⩓ Activities

Walkers can follow paths along the River Swale both upstream and downstream from the town. A longer option is to follow part of the famous long-distance Coast to Coast Walk (p501) all the way to Reeth (11 miles) and take the bus back (see www.dalesbus. info/richmond).

Cyclists can also follow Swaledale – as far as Reeth may be enough, while a trip along Arkengarthdale and then over the high wild moors to Kirkby Stephen via the Tan Hill Inn is a more serious (but very rewarding) 40-mile undertaking.

⌷ Sleeping

There's a batch of pleasant places to stay along Frenchgate, and a couple more on Pottergate (the road into town from the east).

Frenchgate Hotel   HOTEL ££
(☏01748-822087; www.thefrenchgate.co.uk; 59-61 Frenchgate; s/d from £88/118; P) Nine elegant bedrooms occupy the upper floors of this converted Georgian town house, now a boutique hotel decorated with local art. The rooms have cool designer fittings that set off a period fireplace here, a Victorian roll-top bath there. Downstairs there's an excellent restaurant (three-course dinner £39) and a hospitable lounge with oak beams and an open fire.

Willance House   B&B ££
(☏01748-824467; www.willancehouse.com; 24 Frenchgate; s/d £55/75; ☎) This oak-beamed house, built in 1600, has three immaculate rooms (one with a four-poster bed) that combine old-fashioned charm and all mod cons.

66 Frenchgate   B&B ££
(☏01748-823421; www.66frenchgate.co.uk; 66 Frenchgate; s/d/f £70/84/120; ☎) Three of the six stylish bedrooms have superb river views.

★ Millgate House   B&B £££
(☏01748-823571; www.millgatehouse.com; Market Pl; r £110-145; P @ ☎) ✿ Behind an unassuming grey door lies the unexpected pleasure of one of the most attractive guesthouses in England. While the house itself is a Georgian gem crammed with period details, it is overshadowed by the multi-award-winning garden at the back, which offers superb views

over the River Swale and the Cleveland Hills. If possible, book the Garden Suite.

✗ Eating & Drinking

Cross View Tearooms TEAROOM £
(www.crossviewtearooms.co.uk; 38 Market Pl; mains £5-8; ☺9am-5.30pm; 🚼) 🍴 So popular with locals that you might have to queue for a table at lunchtime, the Cross View is the place to go for a hearty breakfast, homemade cakes, a hot lunch, or just a nice cup of tea.

Barkers FISH & CHIPS £
(Trinity Church Sq; mains £6-10; ☺11am-9.30pm) The best fish and chips in town, sit-down or takeaway.

Rustique FRENCH ££
(📞01748-821565; www.rustiqueyork.co.uk; Chantry Wynd, Finkle St; mains £10-21; ☺noon-9pm) Tucked away in an arcade, this cosy bistro has consistently impressed with its mastery of French country cooking, from *confit de canard* (duck slow roasted in its own fat) to *paupiette de poulet* (chicken breast stuffed with brie and sun-dried tomatoes). Booking is recommended.

Black Lion Hotel PUB
(www.blacklionhotelrichmond.co.uk; Finkle St; ☺11am-11pm) Cosy bars, low beams and good beer and food.

Unicorn Inn PUB
(2 Newbiggin; ☺10.30am-11pm Mon-Thu, to midnight Fri & Sat, to 10.30pm Sun) A determinedly old-fashioned free house, serving Theakston's and Old Speckled Hen.

ℹ Information

The **tourist office** (📞01748-850549; www.richmond.org; 2 Queens Rd; ☺10am-4pm Mon-Sat), in Calverts shop on the central traffic roundabout, has the usual maps and guides, plus several leaflets showing walks in town and the surrounding countryside.

ℹ Getting There & Away

From Darlington (on the railway between London and Edinburgh), it's easy to reach Richmond on bus X26 or X27 (£4.50, 30 minutes, every half hour, hourly on Sunday). All buses stop in Market Pl.

On Sundays and bank holiday Mondays only, from May to October, the Northern Dalesman bus 830 runs from Richmond to Hawes (£6.25, 1½ hours, one daily) via Reeth, and continues on to Ribblehead and Ingleton (£8.90, two hours, one daily).

WEST YORKSHIRE

It was the tough and unforgiving textile industry that drove West Yorkshire's economy from the 18th century onward. The woollen mills, factories and canals built to transport raw materials and finished products defined much of the county's landscape. But that's all in the past, and recent years have seen the transformation of this once hard-bitten area into quite the picture postcard.

Leeds and Bradford, two adjoining cities so big they've virtually become one, are the perfect case in point. Though both were founded amid the dark satanic mills of the Industrial Revolution, both are undergoing radical redevelopment and reinvention, prettifying their town centres and trying to tempt the more adventurous tourist with a host of new museums, galleries, restaurants and bars.

Beyond the cities, West Yorkshire is a landscape of bleak moorland dissected by deep valleys dotted with old mill towns and villages. The relics of the wool and cloth industries are still visible in the rows of weavers' cottages and workers' houses built along ridges overlooking the towering chimneys of the mills in the valleys – landscapes that were so vividly described by the Brontë sisters, West Yorkshire's most renowned literary export and biggest tourist draw.

ℹ Getting Around

The Metro is West Yorkshire's highly efficient train and bus network, centred on Leeds and Bradford – which are also the main gateways to the county. For transport information, contact **West Yorkshire Metro** (📞0113-245 7676; www.wymetro.com).

Day Rover tickets (£7.70) are good for one day's unlimited travel on Metro buses and trains after 9.30am on weekdays and all day at weekends. A range of additional Rover tickets covering buses and/or trains, plus heaps of useful Metro maps and timetables, are available from bus and train stations and most tourist offices in West Yorkshire.

Leeds

POP 751,500

One of the fastest-growing cities in the UK, Leeds is the glitzy embodiment of rediscovered northern self-confidence. More than a decade of redevelopment has seen the city centre transform from near-derelict mill town into a vision of 21st-century urban chic, with towering office blocks, glass-and-steel

Leeds

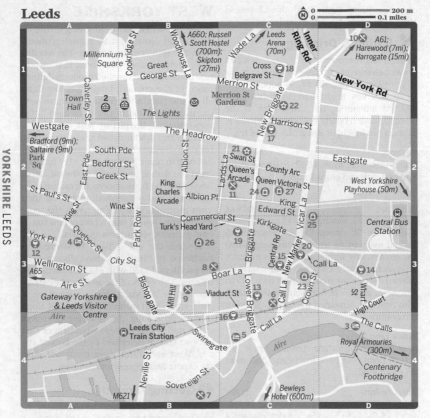

⊙ Sights

Royal Armouries
MUSEUM

(www.royalarmouries.org; Armouries Dr; ⊙10am-5pm; P ⊞) FREE Leeds' most interesting museum was originally built in 1996 to house armour and weapons from the Tower of London, but subsequently expanded to cover 3000 years' worth of combat and self-defence. It all sounds a bit macho, but the exhibits are as varied as they are fascinating, covering subjects as diverse as jousting and Indian elephant armour. To get here, walk east along the river from Centenary Footbridge (10 minutes), or take bus 28 from Albion St.

Leeds Industrial Museum
MUSEUM

(www.leeds.gov.uk/armleymills; Canal Rd; adult/child £3.60/1.80; ⊙10am-5pm Tue-Sat, 1-5pm Sun; P ⊞) One of the world's largest textile mills has been transformed into a museum telling the story of Leeds' industrial past, both glorious and ignominious. The city grew rich

waterfront apartment complexes and renovated Victorian shopping arcades. The financial crisis of 2008–10 saw many flagship development projects grind to a halt, but tower cranes are beginning to sprout on the skyline again and a massive new entertainment venue, the Leeds Arena (www.firstdirectarena.com; Clay Pit Lane), opened in 2013.

Known as the 'Knightsbridge of the North', Leeds has made itself a shopping mecca, its streets lined with bustling malls sporting the top names in fashion. And when you've shopped till you've dropped, there's a plethora of pubs, clubs and excellent restaurants to relax in. From cutting-edge couture to contemporary cuisine, Leeds will serve it to you on a plate (or more likely in a stylishly designed bag). Amid all this fashion-conscious finery, it seems fitting that the network of city bus routes includes peach, mauve and magenta lines as well as the more humdrum red, orange and blue.

Leeds

YORKSHIRE LEEDS

from the textile industry, but at some cost in human terms – working conditions were Dickensian. As well as a selection of mill machinery, there's a particularly informative display about how cloth is made. The museum is 2 miles west of the city centre; take bus 5 from the train station.

Leeds Art Gallery   GALLERY
(www.leeds.gov.uk/artgallery; The Headrow; ⊙10am-5pm Mon, Tue & Thu-Sat, noon-5pm Wed, 1-5pm Sun) **FREE** The municipal gallery is packed with 19th- and 20th-century British heavyweights – Turner, Constable, Stanley Spencer, Wyndham Lewis et al – along with contemporary pieces by more recent arrivals such as Antony Gormley, sculptor of the *Angel of the North*.

Henry Moore Institute   GALLERY
(www.henry-moore.org; The Headrow; ⊙11am-5.30pm Tue & Thu-Sun, to 8pm Wed) **FREE** Housed in a converted Victorian warehouse in the city centre, this gallery showcases the work of 20th-century sculptors, but not, despite the name, anything by Henry Moore (1898–1986), who graduated from the Leeds School of Art. To see works by Moore, head to the Yorkshire Sculpture Park (p544).

🎪 Festivals & Events

Leeds Festival   MUSIC
(www.leedsfestival.com) The August Bank Holiday (the weekend preceding the last Monday in August) sees 50,000-plus music fans converge on Bramham Park, 10 miles outside the city centre, for the Leeds Festival. Spread across four stages, it's one of Englands's biggest rock-music extravaganzas.

🛏 Sleeping

There are no budget options in the city centre, and the midrange choices here are either chain hotels or places we wouldn't recommend. If you want somewhere cheapish you'll be forced to head for the suburbs, where there are plenty of decent B&Bs and smallish hotels.

Russell Scott Hostel   HOSTEL £
(☑0113-245 9046; www.rshostels.co.uk; 47a Well Close Rise, Woodhouse; dm £15; 🛜) There's a reason there are no photos of this new hostel on its website – it's just an anonymous red-brick suburban semi on a council estate. But it's the only hostel in Leeds, and if you can find it, the facilities are fine and the location is quiet. It's 1.5 miles (a half-hour walk) north of the train station.

Roomzzz Leeds City   APARTMENT ££
(☑0844 499 4888; www.roomzzz.co.uk; 10 Swinegate; 2-person apt from £82; @🛜) This outfit offers bright and modern luxury apartments complete with fitted kitchen, with the added advantage of 24-hour hotel reception, and a great city centre location; a second branch, Roomzzz Leeds City West, is half a mile west on Burley Rd.

Headingley Lodge   HOTEL ££
(☑0844 858 2858; www.headingleylodge.co.uk; Headingley Stadium, St Michael's Lane; d/f from £60/75; 🅿🛜) Smart, comfortable rooms

with views of Headingley cricket ground; part of the stadium complex.

Bewleys Hotel
HOTEL ££

(☑0113-234 2340; www.bewleyshotels.com/leeds; City Walk, Sweet St; r from £68; P@🐾) Bewleys is super-convenient for motorists, just off Junction 3 on the M621, but also just 10 minutes' walk from the city centre and with secure basement parking. Rooms are stylish and well appointed, with soundproofed walls and windows. The flat rate accommodates up to two adults plus two children under 12.

★ Quebecs
BOUTIQUE HOTEL £££

(☑0113-244 8989; www.quebecshotel.co.uk; 9 Quebec St; d/ste from £110/300; @🐾) Victorian grace at its opulent best is the theme of our favourite hotel in town, a conversion of the former Leeds & County Liberal Club. The elaborate wood panelling and heraldic stained-glass windows in the public areas are matched by the contemporary design of the bedrooms. Booking online can get you a suite for as little as half the rack rate.

42 The Calls
BOUTIQUE HOTEL £££

(☑0113-244 0099; www.42thecalls.co.uk; 42 The Calls; r/ste from £150/280; @🐾) A snazzy boutique hotel in what was once a 19th-century grain mill overlooking the river, this place is a big hit with the trendy business crowd, who love its sharp, polished lines and designer aesthetic. The smaller 'study' rooms are pretty compact and breakfast is not included – it'll cost you an extra £15 for the full English.

✖ Eating

The Leeds restaurant scene is constantly evolving, with new places springing up in the wake of new shopping and residential developments.

Pickles & Potter
DELI, CAFE £

(www.picklesandpotter.co.uk; 18-20 Queens Arcade; mains £4-7; ⊙9am-5pm Mon-Fri, to 6pm Sat, 10.30am-5pm Sun; 🐾) 🌱 This rustic cafe is famous for its superb sandwiches, especially the sumptuous roast-beef version complete with mustard, onion marmalade and fresh salad. There's also homemade soup, delicious cakes and a meat or vegetarian main course of the day.

Hansa's Gujarati
INDIAN, VEGETARIAN £

(www.hansasrestaurant.com; 72-74 North St; mains £6-8; ⊙5-10pm Mon-Fri, 6-11pm Sat, noon-2pm Sun; 🌱🐾) A Leeds institution, Hansa's has been dishing up wholesome Gujarati vegetarian cuisine for almost 20 years. The restaurant is plain and unassuming (save for a Hindu shrine), but the food is exquisite – specialities of the house include *samosa chaat*, a mix of spiced potato and chickpea samosas with a yoghurt and tamarind sauce.

Dish
MODERN BRITISH ££

(☑0113-318 2274; www.dishdining.co.uk; 19 Boar Lane; mains £11-22; ⊙5-10pm Tue-Sat, noon-2.30pm Fri & Sat; 🐾) 🌱 One of Yorkshire's best up-and-coming restaurants, Dish offers fine dining in an informal setting, while the menu takes an imaginative approach to the best of British and especially Yorkshire produce – the Yorkshire beef Wellington (£55 for two) is not to be missed. Unusually, vegetarians are not forgotten, with several gourmet options to choose from. Two-/three-course set menu £16.50/19.50.

Brasserie Blanc
FRENCH ££

(☑0113-220 6060; www.brasserieblanc.com; Victoria Mill, Sovereign St; mains £10-20; ⊙noon-2.45pm & 5.30-10pm Mon-Fri, noon-10.30pm Sat, to 9pm Sun; 🐾) Raymond Blanc manages to create a surprisingly intimate and romantic space amid the cast-iron pillars and red brick of an old Victorian warehouse, with a scattering of outdoor tables for sunny lunchtimes beside the river. The menu is unerringly French, from *escargots* (edible snails) to Toulouse sausage. The lunch and pre-7pm menu (except Sunday) offers three courses for £14.

Art's Cafe Bar & Restaurant
INTERNATIONAL ££

(www.artscafebar.co.uk; 42 Call Lane; mains £11-17; ⊙noon-11pm; 🐾) Local art on the walls and a bohemian vibe throughout make this a popular place for quiet reflection, a chat and a really good cup of coffee. The dinner menu offers a half-dozen classic dishes, while the early bird menu (pre-7pm, except Saturday) offers three courses for £15.

★ Crafthouse
MODERN BRITISH £££

(☑0113-897 0444; www.crafthouse-restaurant.com; Level 5, Trinity Leeds, 70 Boar Lane; mains £14-21; ⊙noon-3pm & 5-11pm Mon-Sat, noon-10pm Sun; 🐾) 🌱 This new rooftop restaurant makes a big impression, with cool grey and black decor and huge picture windows overlooking the neighbouring church tower. The food is similarly striking, with bold flavour combinations such as ham hock and dandelion salad or sea bream with fennel salad and sautéed beetroot. The three-course set menu (£22.50) is available lunchtimes and from 5pm to 6.30pm.

🍷 Drinking & Nightlife

Leeds is renowned for its selection of pubs and bars. Glammed-up hordes of party animals crawl the cluster of venues around Boar and Call Lanes, where bars are opening (and closing) all the time. Most bars open till 2am and many turn into clubs after 11pm or midnight.

The tremendous club scene attracts people from miles around. In true northern tradition, people brave the cold wearing next to nothing, even in winter, which is a spectacle in itself. Clubs charge a variety of admission prices, ranging from as little as £1 on a slow weeknight to £10 or more on Saturday. In order to make sense of the ever-evolving scene, check out **Leeds Guide** (www.leeds-guide.co.uk). The tourist office provides a free *Gay Leeds* map and guide.

North Bar   BAR
(www.northbar.com; 24 New Briggate; ⊙11am-1am Mon & Tue, to 2am Wed-Sat, noon-midnight Sun; ☎) There's a Continental feel to this long and narrow, minimalist bar, enhanced by the unfamiliar beer labels, from Dortmunder and Duvel to Schneider and Snake Dog. In fact, North is dedicated to the best of world beers, with more than a dozen ales on tap and scores more in bottles. Good selection of malt whisky, too.

Duck & Drake   PUB
(www.duckndrake.co.uk; 43 Kirkgate; ⊙10am-midnight Mon-Thu, to 1am Fri & Sat, 11am-midnight Sun; ☎) A down-to-earth, traditional boozer with a well-worn atmosphere, a cast of regular characters, a pub piano, pork pie and mushy peas on the menu, and no fewer than 15 hand-pulled real ales to choose from. It also provides a stage for local rock and blues bands from Wednesday to Sunday nights.

Whitelocks   PUB
(www.whitelocksleeds.com; 6-8 Turk's Head Yard; ⊙11am-midnight Mon-Thu, to 1am Fri & Sat, to 11.30pm Sun; ☎ 🅿 🐾) There's lots of polished wood, gleaming brass and colourful stained glass in this popular traditional pub, which dates from 1715. Theakston's, Deuchars IPA and several other real ales are on tap, there's a log fire in winter, and in summer the crowds spill out into the courtyard.

Baby Jupiter   BAR
(www.babyjupiter.co.uk; 11 York Pl; ⊙noon-midnight Mon-Wed, to 2am Thu & Fri, 5pm-2am Sat) A retro gem with lots of purple velvet, hanging fishbowls and images from old sci-fi films, this basement bar sports a cool soundtrack that ranges from indie, funk and soul to punk, new wave and electro.

Sandinista   COCKTAIL BAR
(www.sandinistaleeds.co.uk; 5/5a Cross Belgrave St; ⊙11am-3am Sun-Fri, 10am-4am Sat; ☎) This laid-back bar has a Latin look, but a unifying theme, attracting an eclectic clientele with its mixed bag of music and unpretentious atmosphere. If you enjoy a well-mixed cocktail, but aren't too fussed about looking glam, this is the spot for you.

Bar Fibre   GAY
(www.barfibre.com; 168 Lower Briggate; ⊙noon-1am Sun-Wed, to 3am Thu & Fri, to 4am Sat) Leeds' most popular gay bar, which spills out onto the cheekily named Queen's Court, is where the beautiful people congregate. There's another cluster of gay bars downhill at the junction of Lower Briggate and The Calls.

HiFi Club   CLUB
(www.thehificlub.co.uk; 2 Central Rd; ⊙11pm-3am Wed & Fri-Sun) This intimate club is a good break from the hardcore sound of electronic dance: if it's Tamla Motown or the percussive beats of dance-floor jazz that shake your booty, this is the spot for you.

Mission   CLUB
(www.clubmission.com; Viaduct St; ⊙11pm-4am Mon & Fri, to 6am Sat, 10pm-3.30am Thu) Fresh from a huge refit, this massive club redefines the term 'up for it'. Thursday sees the Full Moon Thai Beach Party student night, while Saturdays offer a range of house, dance and classic-anthem club nights, plus the Queer-Do gay club (11pm to 6am).

Wire   CLUB
(www.wireclub.co.uk; 2-8 Call Lane; ⊙10pm-3am) This small, atmospheric basement club, set in a forest of Victorian cast-iron pillars, throbs to a different beat every night, from rock and roll to drum and bass. Popular with local students.

☆ Entertainment

City Varieties   VARIETY
(www.cityvarieties.co.uk; Swan St) Founded in 1865, City Varieties is the world's longest running music hall, where the likes of Harry Houdini, Charlie Chaplin and Lily Langtry once trod the boards. Reopened after a major revamp, the program now features stand-up comedy, live music, pantomime and old-fashioned variety shows.

Grand Theatre & Opera House THEATRE, OPERA
(www.leedsgrandtheatre.com; 46 New Briggate)
Hosts musicals, plays and opera, including performances by the acclaimed Opera North (www.operanorth.co.uk).

West Yorkshire Playhouse THEATRE
(www.wyp.org.uk; Quarry Hill Mount) The Playhouse has a reputation for excellent live drama, from the classics to cutting-edge new writing. It's on the eastern edge of the city centre.

🛍 Shopping

Leeds' city centre has so many shopping arcades they all seem to blend into one giant mall. The latest development, Trinity Leeds (www.trinityleeds.com; ⊘ 9am-8pm Mon-Sat, 11am-5pm Sun), opened in 2013, is the city's biggest, while the historic Corn Exchange (www.leedscornexchange.co.uk; ⊘ 10am-6pm Mon-Sat, 10.30am-4.30pm Sun; 🖹), with its dramatic wrought-iron dome, is reinventing itself as a home for designer boutiques and fashion markets.

Victoria Quarter MALL
(www.v-q.co.uk) The mosaic-paved, stained-glass-roofed Victorian arcades of Victoria Quarter, between Briggate and Vicar Lane, are well worth visiting for aesthetic reasons alone. Dedicated shoppers can join the footballers' wives browsing boutiques by Louis Vuitton, Vivienne Westwood and Swarovski. The flagship store here, of course, is Harvey Nichols (www.harveynichols.com; 107-111 Briggate; ⊘ 10am-6pm Mon-Wed, to 8pm Thu, to 7pm Fri, 9am-7pm Sat, 10.30am-5pm Sun).

Leeds City Market MARKET
(www.leedsmarket.com; Kirkgate; ⊘ 9am-5pm Mon, Tue & Thu-Sat, to 1pm Wed, open-air market Thu-Tue) Sitting at the opposite end of the retail spectrum to its flashy Victoria Quarter neighbour, this is Britain's largest covered market, selling fresh meat, fish and fruit and vegetables, as well as household goods. It was once the home of Michael Marks, who later joined forces with Spencer to become the retailing giant.

ℹ Information

Gateway Yorkshire & Leeds Visitor Centre
(📋 0113-242 5242; www.visitleeds.co.uk; The Arcade, Leeds City Train Station; ⊘ 10am-5.30pm Mon, 9am-5.30pm Tue-Sat, 10am-4pm Sun)
Post Office (St John's Centre, 116 Albion St; ⊘ 9am-5.30pm Mon-Sat)

ℹ Getting There & Away

Air Eleven miles northwest of the city via the A65, **Leeds Bradford International Airport** (www.leedsbradfordairport.co.uk) has flights to a range of domestic and international destinations. The Metroconnect 757 bus (£3.50, 40 minutes, every 30 minutes, hourly on Sunday) runs between Leeds bus station and the airport. A taxi costs about £20.

Bus National Express (www.nationalexpress.com) serves most major cities, including services from London (from £12, 4½ hours, hourly) and Manchester (from £5, 1¼ hours, every 30 minutes). **Yorkshire Coastliner** (www.coastliner.co.uk) buses run from Leeds to York (£6.20, 1¼ hours), Whitby (£13, 3¾ hours) and Scarborough (£12, three hours). A Freedom Ticket (£15) gives unlimited bus travel on all of these services for a day.

Train Leeds City Train Station has hourly services from London King's Cross (£90, 2½ hours), Sheffield (£14, one hour), Manchester (£16, one hour) and York (£13.50, 25 minutes, every 15 minutes). Leeds is also the starting point for trains on the famous Settle–Carlisle railway line (p535).

ℹ Getting Around

Leeds City Bus (www.wymetro.com; flat fare 50p) runs every few minutes from 6.30am to 7.30pm Monday to Saturday, linking the bus and train stations with all the main shopping areas in the city centre.

The various WY Metro DayRover passes covering trains and/or buses are good for reaching Bradford, Haworth and Hebden Bridge.

Bradford

Their suburbs may have merged into one sprawling urban conurbation, but Bradford remains far removed from its much more glamorous neighbour, Leeds. Thanks to its role as a major player in the wool trade, Bradford attracted large numbers of immigrants from Bangladesh and Pakistan during the 20th century. Despite occasional racial tensions, these new arrivals have helped reinvigorate the city and give it new energy (plus a reputation for superb curry restaurants). A high point of the year is the colourful Bradford Mela, now incorporated into the mid-June Bradford Festival (www.bradfordfestival.org.uk), a celebration of Asian music, dance, arts, crafts and food.

Bradford is on the Metro train line from Leeds (£3.60, 20 minutes, three or four per hour).

⊙ Sights

★ **National Media Museum**　　　MUSEUM
(www.nationalmediamuseum.org.uk; off Little Horton Lane; ⊘10am-6pm) FREE Bradford's top attraction is the National Media Museum, an impressive glass-fronted building that chronicles the story of photography, film, TV, radio and the web from 19th-century cameras and early animation to digital technology and the psychology of advertising. There's lots of hands-on stuff, too. You can film yourself in a bedroom scene, pretend to be a TV newsreader, or play 1970s and '80s video games. The IMAX cinema (adult/child £11.50/9) here shows the usual combination of in-your-face nature films, space documentaries and 3D animations.

The museum looks out over City Park, Bradford's new central square, which is home to the Mirror Pool, the country's largest urban water feature.

✗ Eating

Bradford is famous for its curries – it was voted the UK's Curry Capital for three years running from 2011 to 2013 – so don't miss out on trying one of the city's hundred or so restaurants. A great help is the Bradford Curry Guide (www.visitbradford.com/explore/Bradford_Curry_Guide.aspx).

Kashmir　　　INDIAN £
(27 Morley St; mains £4-6; ⊘11am-3am; ✍) Bradford's oldest curry house has top tucker, served with no frills and no booze (although it is BYO). Whatever you do, go for a table upstairs, as the soul-destroying, windowless basement has all the character of a 1950s factory canteen. It's just around the corner from the National Media Museum.

Zouk Tea Bar　　　INDIAN ££
(www.zoukteabar.co.uk; 1312 Leeds Rd; mains £7-13; ⊘11am-midnight; 🛜✍📶) This modern and stylish cafe-restaurant staffed by chefs from Lahore serves everything from *chana puri* (curried chickpeas) for breakfast to legendary lamb Nihari (slow-cooked lamb with a thick and spicy sauce) for dinner.

Saltaire

A Victorian-era landmark, Saltaire was a model industrial village built in 1851 by philanthropic wool baron and teetotaller Titus Salt. The rows of neat, honey-coloured cottages – now a Unesco World Heritage Site – overlook what was once the largest factory in the world.

The factory is now Salts Mill (www.saltsmill.org.uk; ⊘10am-5.30pm Mon-Fri, to 6pm Sat & Sun; 🅿) FREE, a splendidly bright and airy building where the main attraction is a permanent exhibition of 1970s and '80s artworks by local boy David Hockney (1937–). In a fitting metaphor for the shift in the British economy from making things to selling them, this former engine of industry is now a shrine to retail therapy, with shops selling books, crafts and outdoor equipment, and a cafe and restaurant.

Saltaire's tourist office (☏01274-437942; www.saltairevillage.info; Salts Mill, Victoria Rd; ⊘10am-5pm Apr-Sep, to 4pm Oct-Mar) has maps of the village and provides information on local walks.

Saltaire is 9 miles west of Leeds city centre and 3 miles north of Bradford centre, and is easily reached by Metro rail from either.

National Coal Mining Museum for England

For close to three centuries, West and South Yorkshire were synonymous with coal production. The collieries shaped and scarred the landscape and entire villages grew up around the pits. The industry came to a shuddering halt in the 1980s, but the imprint of coal is still very much in evidence, even if there's only a handful of collieries left. One of these, the former Caphouse Colliery, is now this fascinating museum (www.ncm.org.uk; Overton, near Wakefield; ⊘10am-5pm, last tour 3.15pm; 🅿♿) FREE, a superb testament to the inner workings of a coal mine.

The highlight of a visit is the underground tour (departing every 10 minutes): equipped with helmet and head-torch, you descend almost 140m in the 'cage', then follow subterranean passages to the coal seam where massive drilling machines now stand idle. Former miners work as guides and explain the detail – sometimes with a suitably authentic and almost impenetrable mix of local dialect (known in Yorkshire as 'Tyke') and technical terminology.

At ground level there are audiovisual displays, some fascinating memorabilia (including sketches by Henry Moore), and exhibits about trade unions, strikes and the wider mining communities – only a bit over-romanticised in parts. You can also stroll round the pit-pony stables (their equine inhabitants also now retired) or the slightly eerie bathhouse, unchanged since the miners scrubbed off the coal dust for the last time and emptied their lockers.

The museum is 10 miles south of Leeds on the A642 between Wakefield and Huddersfield, reached via Junction 40 on the M1. By public transport, take a train from Leeds to Wakefield (£3.30, 15 minutes, at least hourly), and then bus 232 towards Huddersfield (£3, 25 minutes, hourly).

Yorkshire Sculpture Park

One of England's most impressive collections (www.ysp.co.uk; Bretton Park, near Wakefield; admission free, 4hr parking £4; ☉10am-6pm Apr-Oct, to 5pm Nov-Mar; P) of sculpture is scattered across the formidable 18th-century estate of Bretton Park, 200-odd hectares of lawns, fields and trees. A bit like the art world's equivalent of a safari park, the Yorkshire Sculpture Park showcases the work of dozens of sculptors both national and international. But the main focus of this outdoor gallery is the work of local kids Barbara Hepworth (1903–75), who was born in nearby Wakefield, and Henry Moore (1898–1986).

The rural setting is especially fitting for Moore's work, as the artist was hugely influenced by the outdoors and preferred his art to be sited in the landscape rather than indoors. Other highlights include pieces by Andy Goldsworthy and Eduardo Paolozzi, and Richard Hiorns' famous work *Seizure 2008/2013,* an apartment coated in blue copper sulphate crystals (open weekends only). There's also a program of temporary exhibitions and installations by visiting artists, plus a bookshop and cafe.

The park is 12 miles south of Leeds and 18 miles north of Sheffield, just off Junction 38 on the M1 motorway. If you're on public transport, take a train from Leeds to Wakefield (£3.30, 15 minutes, at least hourly), or from Sheffield to Barnsley (£3.80, 20 minutes, at least hourly), and then take bus 9, which runs between Wakefield and Barnsley via Bretton Park (£3, 30 minutes, hourly Monday to Saturday).

Hepworth Wakefield

West Yorkshire's standing in the international arts scene got a boost in 2011 when the Yorkshire Sculpture Park was joined by this award-winning gallery (☑01924-

247360; www.hepworthwakefield.org; Gallery Walk, Wakefield; admission free, parking £4.50; ☉10am-5pm Tue-Sun; P) of modern art, housed in a stunningly angular building on the banks of the River Calder. The gallery has been built around the works of Wakefield-born sculptor Barbara Hepworth, perhaps best known for her work *Single Form,* which graces the United Nations Headquarters in New York.

The gallery showcases more than a dozen Hepworth originals, as well as works by other 20th-century British artists including Ivon Hitchens, Paul Nash, Victor Pasmore, John Piper and Henry Moore. The Gott Collection of 19th-century art includes a 1793 painting of Wakefield Bridge and Chantry Chapel, which you can compare with the real thing by looking out the neighbouring window.

The gallery is near the centre of Wakefield, a 10-minute walk south of Wakefield Kirkgate train station, easily reached from Leeds (£3.30, minutes, at least hourly).

Hebden Bridge

POP 4235

Tucked tightly into a fold of a steep-sided valley, Yorkshire's funkiest little village is a former mill town that refused to go gently with the dying of industry's light. Instead, it raged a bit and then morphed into an attractive little tourist trap with a distinctly bohemian atmosphere. The town is home to university academics, artists, die-hard hippies and a substantial gay community. All of this explains the abundance of craft shops, organic cafes and secondhand bookstores.

⊙ Sights

Alternative Technology Centre   INTERPRETATION CENTRE
(www.alternativetechnology.org.uk; Hebble End Mill; ☉10am-5pm Mon-Fri, noon-5pm Sat, noon-4pm Sun) FREE From the town centre, a short stroll along the attractive waterfront of the Rochdale Canal leads to the Alternative Technology Centre, which promotes renewable energy, recycling and sustainable lifestyles through a series of intriguing exhibits and workshops.

Heptonstall   VILLAGE
Above Hebden Bridge is the much older village of Heptonstall, its narrow cobbled street lined with 500-year-old cottages and the ruins of a beautiful 13th-century church. But it's the churchyard of the new-

er **St Thomas' Church** that draws literary pilgrims, for here is buried the poet Sylvia Plath (1932–63), wife of another famous poet, Ted Hughes (1930–98), who was born in nearby Mytholmroyd.

Gibson Mill HISTORIC BUILDING
(www.nationaltrust.org.uk; adult/child £3.60/1.80; ⊙11am-4pm Tue-Thu, Sat & Sun Mar-Oct, to 3pm Sat & Sun Nov-Feb; P) / This renovated 19th-century cotton mill houses a visitor centre with exhibitions covering the industrial and social history of the mill and its former workers.

🛏 Sleeping & Eating

Hebden Bridge Hostel HOSTEL £
(☏01422-843183; www.hebdenbridgehostel.co.uk; Birchcliffe Centre, Birchcliffe Rd; dm/tw £20/55; ⊙Easter-early Nov; P🐾) / Just 10 minutes' walk uphill from the town centre, this hostel is set in a peaceful stone building, complete with sunny patio, tucked behind a former Baptist chapel (look for the green hostel signs). There's a cosy library, comfy and clean en suite rooms, and a vegetarian-food-only kitchen. The hostel is closed from 10.30am to 5pm daily.

Thorncliffe B&B B&B ££
(☏01422-842163; Alexandra Rd; s/d £50/70; 🐾) This delightful Victorian house is perched on the hill above town, and the guest accommodation is perched at the top of the house – a spacious attic double with en suite and lovely views across the valley (there's a second double room, but without views and en suite). A continental, vegetarian breakfast is served in your room.

Mooch CAFE £
(www.moochcafebar.co.uk; 24 Market St; mains £4-9; ⊙9am-8pm Mon-Thu, to 11pm Fri, 10am-11pm Sat, to 8pm Sun; 🐾) This chilled-out little cafe-bar exemplifies Hebden's alternative atmosphere, with a menu that includes a full-vegan breakfast, brie-and-grape ciabatta, and Mediterranean lunch platters of olives, hummus, stuffed vine leaves, tabouli and more. There's also Krombacher beer on draught, and excellent espresso.

Organic House CAFE £
(www.organic-house.co.uk; 2 Market St; mains £6-13; ⊙9am-5pm Mon-Sat, 10am-5pm Sun; 🐾) / Practically everything on the menu at this busy local cafe is organic, locally produced or fair-trade, from the veggie breakfast to the *pâté du jour* (served with toast

and chutney). There are outdoor tables in the garden, and a shiatsu and reflexology studio upstairs.

★ **Green's Vegetarian Café** VEGETARIAN ££
(☏01422-843587; www.greensvegetariancafe.co.uk; Old Oxford House, Albert St; mains £11; ⊙11am-3pm Wed-Sun, 6.30-9pm Fri & Sat; 🐾) / One of Yorkshire's best vegetarian restaurants, Green's adopts a gourmet attitude towards veggie and vegan cuisine, serving dishes such as Sicilian *caponata* (aubergines, red pepper, celery, olives and capers) with spaghetti, and Thai green curry with chickpeas, squash and tofu. Best book a table to avoid disappointment, especially for dinner.

ⓘ Information

Hebden Bridge Visitor & Canal Centre
(☏01422-843831; www.hebdenbridge.co.uk; Butlers Wharf, New Rd; ⊙10am-5pm mid-Mar–mid-Oct, shorter hours rest of year) Has a good stock of maps and leaflets on local walks, including a saunter to Hardcastle Crags, the local beauty spot, and the nearby NT-listed Gibson Mill.

ⓘ Getting There & Away

Hebden Bridge is on the train line from Leeds (£5.30, 50 minutes, every 20 minutes Monday to Saturday, hourly on Sunday) to Manchester.

Haworth
POP 6380

It seems that only Shakespeare himself is held in higher esteem than the beloved Brontë sisters – Emily, Anne and Charlotte – judging by the 8 million visitors a year who trudge up the hill from the train station to pay their respects at the handsome parsonage where the literary classics *Jane Eyre* and *Wuthering Heights* were penned.

Not surprisingly, the whole village is given over to Brontë-linked tourism, but even without the literary associations Haworth is still worth a visit, though you'll be hard pushed not to be overwhelmed by the cottage industry that has grown up around the Brontës and their wonderful creations.

◉ Sights

Haworth Parish Church CHURCH
(Church St; ⊙9am-5.30pm) Your first stop in Haworth should be the parish church, a lovely old place of worship built in the late 19th century on the site of the older

church that the Brontë sisters knew, which was demolished in 1879. In the surrounding churchyard, gravestones are covered in moss or pushed to one side by gnarled tree roots, giving the place a tremendous feeling of age.

Brontë Parsonage Museum   MUSEUM
(www.bronte.info; Church St; adult/child £7.50/3.75; ⊙ 10am-5.30pm) Set in a pretty garden overlooking the church and graveyard, the house where the Brontë family lived from 1820 to 1861 is now a museum. The rooms are meticulously furnished and decorated exactly as they were in the Brontë era, including Charlotte's bedroom, her clothes and her writing paraphernalia. There's also an informative exhibition, which includes the fascinating miniature books the Brontës wrote as children.

🏃 Activities

Above Haworth stretch the bleak moors of the South Pennines – immediately familiar to Brontë fans – and the tourist office has leaflets on local walks to endless Brontë-related places. A 6.5-mile favourite leads to Top Withins, a ruined farm thought to have inspired *Wuthering Heights,* even though a plaque clearly states that the farmhouse bore no resemblance to the one Emily wrote about.

Other walks can be taken around the **Brontë Way**, a longer route linking Bradford and Colne via Haworth. Alternatively, you can walk or cycle the 8 miles south to Hebden Bridge via the scenic valley of Hardcastle Crags.

🛏 Sleeping & Eating

Virtually every second house on Main St offers B&B; they're mostly indistinguishable from each other, but some are just that little bit cuter. There are a couple of good restaurants in town, and many of the B&Bs have small cafes that are good for a spot of lunch.

Apothecary Guest House   B&B £
(☑ 01535-643642; www.theapothecaryguesthouse. co.uk; 86 Main St; s/d £35/55; 🐾) Oak beams and narrow, slanted passageways lead to smallish rooms with cheerful decor.

Haworth YHA   HOSTEL £
(☑ 0845 371 9520; www.yha.org.uk; Longlands Dr; dm/tw £18.50/47; P @) A big old house with a games room, lounge, cycle store and laundry. It's on the northeastern edge of town, off Lees Lane.

BAD-LUCK BRONTËS

The Reverend Patrick Brontë, his wife Maria and six children moved to Haworth Parsonage in 1820. Within four years Maria and the two eldest daughters had died from cancer and tuberculosis. This triple tragedy led the good reverend to keep his remaining family close to him, and for the next few years the children were home-schooled in a highly creative environment.

The children conjured up mythical heroes and fantasy lands, and produced miniature homemade books. It was an auspicious start, at least for the three girls, Charlotte, Emily and Anne. The lone boy, Branwell, was more of a painter, but lacked his sisters' drive and discipline. After a short stint as a professional artist, he ended up spending most of his days in the Black Bull pub, drunk and stoned on laudanum obtained across the street at Rose & Co Apothecary.

While the three sisters were setting the London literary world alight with the publication of three superb novels – *Jane Eyre, Wuthering Heights* and *Agnes Grey* – in one extraordinary year (1847), Branwell was fading quickly and died of tuberculosis in September 1848. The family was devastated, but things quickly got worse. Emily fell ill with tuberculosis soon after her brother's funeral; she never left the house again, and died on 19 December. Anne, who had also been sick, was next; Charlotte took her to Scarborough to seek a sea cure, but she died on 28 May 1849.

The remaining family never recovered. Despite her growing fame, Charlotte struggled with depression and never quite adapted to her high position in literary society. Despite her misgivings, she eventually married, but died in the early stages of pregnancy on 31 March 1855. All things considered, it's hardly surprising that poor old Patrick Brontë spent the remainder of his life going steadily insane.

Old Registry   B&B ££
(☑01535-646503; www.theoldregistryhaworth.co
.uk; 2-4 Main St; r £75-120; ⬤) This place is a bit
special. It's an elegantly rustic guesthouse
where each of the carefully themed rooms
has a four-poster bed, whirlpool bath or valley view. The Blue Heaven room is just that –
at least for fans of Laura Ashley's delphin-
ium blue.

Ye Sleeping House   B&B ££
(☑01535-546992; www.yesleepinghouse.co.uk; 8
Main St; s/d from £29/58; P⬤) This welcoming B&B has a cosy, country-cottage atmosphere, with just three small rooms and two
friendly resident cats.

Try to get the one en suite room, which
can sleep a family of four and has great
views over the valley.

Old White Lion Hotel   INN ££
(☑01535-642313; www.oldwhitelionhotel.com;
West Lane; s/d from £70/98; P⬤) Pub-style
accommodation, comfortable if not spectacular – though some rooms have good views –
above an oak-panelled pub and highly rated
restaurant.

Cookhouse   CAFE, BISTRO £
(☑01535-958904; www.thecookhousehaworth.co.
uk; Main St; mains £4-9; ⬤10am-5.30pm; ⬤⬤) A
bright and breezy cafe that serves a bracing
breakfast menu (till 11.45am) that includes
eggs Benedict and bacon, cheese and onion
hash, and mouth-watering lunch dishes
such as bangers and mash with onion gravy, pulled pork sandwiches with barbecue
sauce or toasted crumpets with Wensleydale
cheese and chutney.

Cobbles & Clay   CAFE £
(www.cobblesandclay.co.uk; 60 Main St; mains
£5-8; ⬤9am-5pm; ⬤⬤) This attractive,
child-friendly cafe not only offers fair-trade
coffee and healthy salads and snacks – Tuscan bean stew, or hummus with pita bread
and raw veggie sticks – but also provides the
opportunity to indulge in a bit of pottery
painting.

Haworth Old Hall   PUB ££
(☑01535-642709; www.hawortholdhall.co.uk; Sun
St; mains £10-15) A 16th-century pub serving
real ale and decent food, with a glorious
beer garden for alfresco drinking and dining. If you want to linger longer, two comfortable doubles cost from £60 each.

STEAM ENGINES & RAILWAY CHILDREN

The **Keighley & Worth Valley Railway** (www.kwvr.co.uk; adult/child return
£11/5.50, Day Rover £15/7.50) runs steam
and classic diesel engines between
Keighley and Oxenhope via Haworth,
of Brontë fame. It was here, in 1969,
that the classic 1970 movie *The Railway Children* was shot: Mr Perks was
station master at Oakworth, where the
Edwardian look has been meticulously
maintained. Trains operate about hourly
at weekends all year, and in holiday
periods they run hourly every day.

❶ Information

Haworth Tourist Office (☑01535-642329;
www.haworth-village.org.uk; 2-4 West Lane;
⬤9am-5.30pm) The tourist office has an excellent supply of information on the village, the
surrounding area and, of course, the Brontës.

❶ Getting There & Away

From Leeds, the easiest approach is via Keighley,
which is on the Metro rail network. Bus 500 runs
from Keighley bus station to Haworth (£2.10, 15
minutes, hourly) and continues to Todmorden
and Hebden Bridge. However, the most interesting way to get from Keighley to Haworth is via
the Keighley & Worth Valley Railway (see above).

SOUTH YORKSHIRE

What wool was to West Yorkshire, so steel
was to South Yorkshire. A confluence of natural resources – coal, iron ore and ample water – made the region a crucible of the British iron and steel industries. From the 18th
to the 20th centuries, the region was the
industrial powerhouse of northern England.

Sheffield's and Rotherham's blast furnaces and the coal pits of Barnsley and
Doncaster may have closed long ago, but
the hulking reminders of that irrepressible
Victorian dynamism remain, not only in the
old steelworks and pit heads (some of which
have been converted into museums and exhibition spaces), but also in the grand civic
buildings that grace Sheffield's city centre,
fitting testaments to the untrammelled ambitions of their 19th-century patrons.

Sheffield

POP 551,800

Steel is everywhere in Sheffield. Today, however, it's not the steel of the foundries, mills and forges that made the city's fortune, nor the canteens of cutlery that made 'Sheffield Steel' a household name, but the steel of scaffolding and cranes, of modern sculptures and supertrams, and of new steel-framed buildings rising against the skyline.

The steel industry that made the city famous is long since gone, but after many years of decline Sheffield is on the up again – like many of northern England's cities, it has grabbed the opportunities presented by urban renewal with both hands and is working hard to reinvent itself. The new economy is based on services, shopping and the 'knowledge industry' that flows from the city's universities.

◉ Sights

Since 2000 the city centre has been in the throes of a massive redevelopment that will continue into 2020 and beyond, so expect building sites and roadworks for several years to come.

Winter Gardens   GARDENS
(Surrey St; ⊘8am-6pm) Pride of place in Sheffield's city centre goes to this wonderfully ambitious public space with a soaring glass roof supported by graceful arches of laminated timber. The 21st-century architecture contrasts sharply with the Victorian **town hall** nearby, and is further enhanced by the **Peace Gardens** – complete with fountains, sculptures, and lawns full of lunching office workers whenever there's a bit of sun.

Millennium Gallery   GALLERY, MUSEUM
(www.museums-sheffield.org.uk; Arundel Gate; ⊘10am-5pm Mon-Sat, 11am-4pm Sun) FREE
Sheffield's cultural revival is spearheaded by the Millennium Gallery, a collection of four galleries under one roof. Inside, the **Ruskin Gallery** houses an eclectic collection of paintings, drawings and manuscripts established and inspired by Victorian artist, writer, critic and philosopher John Ruskin, while the **Metalwork Gallery** charts the transformation of Sheffield's steel industry into craft and design – the 'Sheffield steel' stamp on locally made cutlery and tableware now has the cachet of designer chic.

Graves Gallery   GALLERY
(www.museums-sheffield.org.uk; Surrey St; ⊘10am-5pm Mon-Sat) This gallery has a neat and accessible display of British and European modern art. The big names represented include Cézanne, Gaugin, Miró, Klee and Picasso.

Abbeydale Industrial Hamlet   MUSEUM
(www.simt.co.uk; Abbeydale Rd S; adult/child £4/free; ⊘10am-4pm Mon-Thu, 11am-4.45pm Sun; P ⛟) In the days before steel mills, metalworking was a cottage industry (just like wool and cotton). For a glimpse of that earlier, more innocent era, explore the restored 18th-century forges, workshops and machines at the Abbeydale Industrial Hamlet, 4 miles southwest of the centre on the A621 (towards the Peak District).

🛏 Sleeping & Eating

Tourism has not quite taken off in Sheffield, and most of the city-centre hotels cater primarily to business travellers. New restaurants are springing up, but the main restaurant areas are outside the centre.

There's a mile-long strip of bars, restaurants, cafes and takeaways on Ecclesall Rd, a mile to the southwest of the city centre, while London Rd, a mile south of the central city, has a concentration of good-value ethnic restaurants ranging from Turkish to Thai. To find student bars and eateries, head along Division St and Devonshire St just west of the city centre.

Leopold Hotel   BOUTIQUE HOTEL ££
(☏0845 078 0067; www.leopoldhotel.co.uk; 2 Leopold St; r from £65; ☎) Housed in a former grammar school building, Sheffield's first boutique hotel brings some much-needed style and sophistication to the city's accommodation scene (but without a London-sized price tag). Rooms can suffer late-night noise from the bars on Leopold Sq – ask for a quiet room at the back.

Houseboat Hotels   HOUSEBOAT ££
(☏01909-569393; www.houseboathotels.com; Victoria Quays, Wharfe St; s/d/q from £79/99/159; P) Here's something a bit different: kick off your shoes and relax on board your very own permanently moored houseboat, complete with self-catering kitchen and patio area. Guests are entitled to use the gym and pool facilities at the Hilton across the road.

Marmaduke's　　　　　　　　　　CAFE £

(www.marmadukescafedeli.co.uk; 22a Norfolk Row; mains £6-9; ⊘9am-5pm Mon-Sat, 10am-4pm Sun; 🐾�ⓐ🖊) 🖊 This appealingly cramped and chaotic cafe, crammed with recycled furniture and run by a young and enthusiastic crew, serves an imaginative breakfast menu (until 11.30am) that includes corn fritters with avocado salsa, and lunch dishes that range from deli sandwiches and quiche to vegetarian specials. Cash only.

Blue Moon Cafe　　　　　　　VEGETARIAN £

(2 St James St; mains £6-7; ⊘8am-8pm Mon-Sat; 🖊) A Sheffield institution offering tasty veggie and vegan creations, soups and other healthy dishes, all served with the ubiquitous salad, in a very pleasant atmosphere – perfect for a spot of Saturday afternoon lounging.

★ **Vero Gusto**　　　　　　　　ITALIAN ££

(🖊0114-276 0004; www.gustosheffield.com; 12 Norfolk Row; mains £9-25; ⊘4-10pm Tue-Sat; 🕿) Gusto is a *real* Italian restaurant, from the Italian owners serving homemade Italian food to the genuine Italian coffee enjoyed by Italian customers reading Italian newspapers...you get the idea. Coffee and home-baked Italian cakes and pastries are served in the late afternoon, plus a dinner menu of exquisite Italian cuisine. It's best to book for dinner.

ℹ Information

Post Office (Norfolk St; ⊘8.30am-5.30pm Mon-Fri, to 3pm Sat)

Sheffield Tourist Office (🖊0114-221 1900; www.welcometosheffield.co.uk; Winter Gardens, Surrey St; ⊘9.30am-5pm Mon-Fri, to 4pm Sat, closed 1-1.30pm)

ℹ Getting There & Away

For all travel-related info for Sheffield and South Yorkshire, contact **Travel South Yorkshire** (🖊01709-515151; www.travelsouthyorkshire.com).

Bus The bus station, called the Interchange, is just east of the centre, about 250m north of the train station. National Express services link Sheffield with most major centres in the north. There are frequent buses to Leeds (£4.50, one hour, hourly), Manchester (£8.60, 1½ hours, four daily) and London (£14, four hours, four daily).

Train Sheffield is served by trains from all directions: Leeds (£12, one hour, twice hourly); London St Pancras (£65, 2½ hours, hourly) via Derby or Nottingham; Manchester (£14, one hour, twice hourly); and York (£15, 1¼ hours, twice hourly).

EAST RIDING OF YORKSHIRE

The rolling farmland of the East Riding of Yorkshire meets the sea at Hull itself, a no-nonsense port that looks to the North Sea and the broad horizons of the Humber estuary for its livelihood. Just to its north, and in complete contrast to Hull's salt and grit, is Beverley, the East Riding's most attractive town, with lots of Georgian character and one of England's finest churches.

Hull

POP 284,320

Properly known as Kingston-upon-Hull – the ancient harbour on the River Hull was granted a royal charter in 1299 and became King's Town – Hull has long been the principal port of England's east coast, with an economy that grew up around carrying wool out and bringing wine in. It was also a major whaling and fishing port until the trawling industry died out.

Though it's not going to win any prizes for prettiness, the city has a gritty appeal for those who appreciate Britain's industrial past and enjoy getting away from the beaten tourist path. Famous as the home of poet Philip Larkin, Hull harbours a clutch of fascinating museums and one of Britain's best aquariums. Named as UK City of Culture 2017, the town has set about the regeneration of its waterfront.

A minor cultural renaissance has taken place in the Fruitmarket district around Humber St, where derelict buildings have been reclaimed as artists' studios and performance spaces, but progress is slow.

◉ Sights & Activities

Deep　　　　　　　　　　AQUARIUM

(www.thedeep.co.uk; Tower St; adult/child £11.50/9.50; ⊘10am-6pm, last entry 5pm; 🅿♿) Hull's biggest tourist attraction is the Deep, a vast aquarium housed in a colossal angular building that appears to lunge above the muddy waters of the Humber like a giant shark's head. Inside, it's just as dramatic, with echoing commentaries and computer-generated interactive displays that guide you through the formation of the oceans and the evolution of sea life.

The largest aquarium is 10m deep, filled with sharks, stingrays and colourful coral fishes, with moray eels draped over rocks like scarves of iridescent slime. A glass elevator plies up and down inside the tank, though you'll get a better view by taking the stairs. Don't miss the cafe on the top floor, which has a great view of the Humber estuary.

Streetlife Museum
MUSEUM

(www.hullcc.gov.uk/museums; High St; ⊙10am-5pm Mon-Sat, 1.30-4.30pm Sun) FREE This fascinating museum contains re-created street scenes from Georgian and Victorian times and from the 1930s, with all sorts of historic vehicles to explore, from stagecoaches to bicycles, buses and trams.

Hull & East Riding Museum
MUSEUM

(www.hullcc.gov.uk/museums; ⊙10am-5pm Mon-Sat, 1.30-4.30pm Sun) FREE This museum traces local history and archaeology from Roman times to the present, with new Anglo-Saxon, medieval and geology galleries.

Arctic Corsair
HISTORIC SHIP

(www.hullcc.gov.uk/museums; ⊙10am-4.30pm Wed & Sat, 1.30-4.30pm Sun Apr-Oct) FREE Behind the Streetlife Museum, marooned in the mud of the River Hull, is the Arctic Corsair. Tours of this Atlantic trawler, a veteran of the 1970s so-called 'Cod Wars', when the UK and Iceland clashed over fishing rights, demonstrate the hardships of fishing north of the Arctic Circle.

Spurn Lightship
MUSEUM

(Castle St; ⊙1.30-4pm Sun late Jun-mid Sep) FREE Built in 1927, Hull's lighthouse-ship once served as a navigation mark for ships entering the notorious Humber estuary. Now safely retired in the marina, it houses an engaging exhibition about its own history, and offers an interesting contrast between the former living quarters of captain and crew.

Old Town
NEIGHBOURHOOD

Hull's Old Town, whose grand public buildings retain a sense of the prosperity the town once knew, occupies the thumb of land between the River Hull to the east and Princes Quay to the west. The most impressive legacy is the Guildhall (Low Gate; ⊙8.30am-4.30pm Mon-Thu, to 3.30pm Fri) FREE, a huge neoclassical building that dates from 1916 and houses vast areas of polished marble, and oak and walnut panelling, plus the Hull Tapestry, which records the city's history (on view near reception).

Wilberforce House
MUSEUM

(www.hullcc.gov.uk/museums; High St; ⊙10am-5pm Mon-Sat, 1.30-4.30pm Sun) FREE Wilberforce House (1639) was the birthplace in 1759 of politician and antislavery crusader William Wilberforce. It is now a museum chronicling the slave trade and its abolition.

Larkin Trail
WALKING TOUR

(www.thelarkintrail.co.uk) Hull's most famous son, the poet Philip Larkin, is commemorated in this self-guided walking tour, which begins beside a bronze statue of the man himself in the railway station. It leads past places mentioned in his poetry, and on to some of his favourite pubs. Pick up a free leaflet at the tourist office.

🛏 Sleeping & Eating

Good accommodation in the city centre is pretty thin on the ground and is mostly business-oriented chain hotels and a few mediocre guesthouses. The tourist office will help book accommodation for free.

The best concentration of eating places is found around Dock St in the city centre, and along Princes Ave, from Welbeck St to Blenheim St, a mile northwest of the centre.

Kingston Theatre Hotel
HOTEL ££

(☑01482-225828; www.kingstontheatrehotel.com; 1-2 Kingston Sq; s/d/ste from £60/80/110; 🛜) Overlooking leafy Kingston Sq, close to the New Theatre, this hotel is one of the best options in the city centre, with elegant bedrooms, friendly service and an excellent breakfast.

Fudge
CAFE, BRASSERIE ££

(☑01482-441019; www.fudgefood.com; 93 Princes Ave; mains £7-21; ⊙10.30am-2.30pm Tue-Thu & Sun, 9am-3pm Fri & Sat, 6-9pm Tue-Sun) This funky cafe decked out in pink and peppermint colours serves hearty breakfasts, cakes and coffee all day, but also offers a tempting brasserie menu at lunch and dinner, with dishes that include juicy burgers (beef or veggie), herby crab cakes and Portuguese fish stew.

Hitchcock's Vegetarian Restaurant
VEGETARIAN ££

(☑01482-320233; www.hitchcocksrestaurant.co.uk; 1 Bishop Lane, High St; buffet £18; ⊙8-10.30pm Tue-Sat; 🖉) The word 'quirky' could have been invented to describe this place. It's an atmospheric maze of small rooms, with an all-you-can-eat vegetarian buffet whose theme – Thai, Indian, Spanish, whatever – is chosen by the first person to book that evening. But, hey, the food is excellent and the welcome is warm. Bookings required.

1884 Dock Street Kitchen
MODERN BRITISH £££

(☑01482-222260; www.1884dockstreetkitchen.co.uk; Humber Dock St; mains £17-32; ⊙noon-2pm & 6-9.30pm Tue-Sat, noon-3pm Sun; ☎) ∅ Poster boy for the city's redeveloping waterfront, this big and bold enterprise tries to blend British cuisine with a sepia-tinted, late-19th-century New York steakhouse look, and just about pulls it off. As well as the steaks, the menu is strong on Scottish seafood, Yorkshire pork and Lancashire lamb, and dishes dotted with wild garlic and duck egg. Three-course set menu £22.

▼ Drinking & Entertainment

Come nightfall – especially at weekends – Hull can be raucous and often rowdy, especially in the streets around Trinity Sq in the Old Town and on the strip of pubs along Beverley Rd to the north of the city centre.

Minerva
PUB

(Nelson St; ⊙11am-11pm Mon-Sat, noon-10.30pm Sun) If you're more into pubbing than clubbing, try a pint of Black Sheep at this lovely 200-year-old pub down by the waterfront. On a sunny day you can sit outdoors and watch the ships go by.

Fruitspace
LIVE MUSIC, COMEDY

(☑01482-221113; www.fruitspace.co.uk; 62-63 Humber St) A focus for the cultural revival of Hull's Fruitmarket district, this former industrial space is now a multipurpose venue incorporating a bar, cinema and stage. There are regular live gigs by local bands (and occasional big names), a monthly comedy club and, on the third Sunday of the month, the Humber Street Market.

Hull Truck Theatre
THEATRE, JAZZ

(www.hulltruck.co.uk; Spring St) Home to acclaimed playwright John Godber, who made his name with the gritty comedies *Bouncers* and *Up 'n' Under* (Godber is one of the most-performed playwrights in the English-speaking world), Hull Truck presents a lively program of drama, comedy and Sunday jazz. It's just northwest of the Old Town.

ℹ Information

Hull Tourist Office (☑0844-811 2070; www.visithullandeastyorkshire.com; 1 Paragon St; ⊙10am-5pm Mon-Sat, 11am-3pm Sun)

Post Office (63 Market Pl; ⊙9am-5.30pm Mon-Sat)

ℹ Getting There & Away

Boat The ferry port is 3 miles east of the centre at King George Dock. A bus connects the train station with the ferries. There are ferry services to Zeebrugge and Rotterdam.

Bus There are buses direct from London (£26, 6½ hours, one daily), Leeds (£9, 1¾ hours, hourly) and York (£6.90, 1¾ hours, six daily).

Train Hull has rail links north and south to Newcastle (£40, 2½ hours, hourly, change at York or Doncaster) and London Kings Cross (£75, 2¾ hours, every two hours), and west to York (£25, 1¼ hours, hourly) and Leeds (£15, one hour, hourly).

Beverley

POP 30,590

Handsome, unspoilt Beverley is one of the most attractive towns in Yorkshire, largely on account of its magnificent minster – a rival to any cathedral in England – and the tangle of streets that lie beneath it, each brimming with exquisite Georgian and Victorian buildings.

All the sights are a short walk from either train or bus station. There's a large market in the main square on Saturday, and a smaller one on Wednesday on the square called... Wednesday Market.

◎ Sights

★**Beverley Minster**
CHURCH

(www.beverleyminster.org; ⊙9am-4.45pm Mon-Sat, noon-5.30pm Sun) One of the great glories of English religious architecture, Beverley Minster is the most impressive church in the country that is not a cathedral. The soaring lines of the exterior are imposing, but it is inside that the charm and beauty lie. The

---

WORTH A TRIP

PIPE & GLASS INN

Set in a picturesque hamlet 4 miles northwest of Beverley, this charming **country pub** (☑01430-810246; www.pipeandglass.co.uk; West End, South Dalton; mains £11-27; ⊙noon-2pm & 6.30-9.30pm Tue-Fri, noon-11pm Sat, noon-4pm Sun; P☎∅☲) has held a Michelin star since 2010. The setting may be delightfully informal, with weathered timber tables, stone hearths and leather sofas, but a great deal of care is lavished on the food – even seemingly simple dishes such as fish pie are unforgettable.

14th-century north aisle is lined with original stone carvings, mostly of musicians. Much of our knowledge of early musical instruments comes from these images. You'll also see goblins, devils and grotesque figures. Look out for the bagpipe player.

Construction began in 1220 – the third church to be built on this site, with the first dating from the 7th century – and continued for two centuries, spanning the Early English, Decorated and Perpendicular periods of the Gothic style.

Close to the altar, the elaborate and intricate Percy Canopy (1340), a decorative frill above the tomb of local aristocrat Lady Eleanor Percy, is a testament to the skill of the sculptor and the finest example of Gothic stone carving in England. In complete contrast, in the nearby chancel is the 10th-century Saxon frith stool, a plain and polished stone chair that once gave sanctuary to anyone escaping the law.

In the roof of the tower is a restored treadwheel crane, where workers ground around like hapless hamsters to lift the huge loads necessary to build a medieval church. Access to the roof is by guided tour only (per person £5).

St Mary's Church CHURCH
(☉9.30am-4.30pm Mon-Fri, 10am-4pm Sat, 2-4pm Sun Apr-Sep, shorter hours Oct-Mar) Doomed to play second fiddle to Beverley Minster, St Mary's Church at the other end of town was built between 1120 and 1530. The west front (early 15th century) is considered one of the finest of any parish church in England. In the north choir aisle there is a carving (c 1330) of a rabbit dressed as a pilgrim, said to have inspired Lewis Carroll's White Rabbit.

⊫ Sleeping & Eating

Friary YHA HOSTEL £
(☑0845 371 9004; www.yha.org.uk; Friar's Lane; dm/d £18.50/69; ℗) In Beverley, the cheapest accommodation also has the best setting and location. This hostel is housed in a beautifully restored 14th-century Dominican friary mentioned in Chaucer's *The Canterbury Tales*, and is only 100m from the minster and a short walk from the train station.

Kings Head INN ££
(☑01482-868103; www.kingsheadpubbeverley.co. uk; 38 Saturday Market; s/d £70/80; @♠) A Georgian coaching inn given a modern makeover, the Kings Head is a lively pub with 12 bright and cheerful rooms above the bar. The pub opens late on weekend nights, but earplugs are supplied for those who don't want to join the revelry!

Vanessa Delicafe CAFE ££
(☑01482-868190; www.vanessadelicafe.co.uk; 21-22 Saturday Market; mains £7-15; ☉9am-4.30pm Mon, Tue, Fri & Sat, to 9pm Wed & Thu, 10am-3.30pm Sun; ♠⚑) This popular cafe sits above a delicatessen, with sofas and bookshelves scattered among the tables, and window seats overlooking the market square. Settle down for cappuccino and cake with the Sunday papers, or tuck into hearty lunch and dinner specials such as homemade lasagne or venison burger.

Grant's Bistro 22 MODERN BRITISH £££
(☑01482-887624; 22 North Bar Within; mains £16-25; ☉noon-2pm Fri & Sat, 6-9.30pm Mon-Sat) ⚑ A great place for a romantic dinner *à deux*, with dark-wood tables, fresh flowers and candlelight. The menu makes the most of fresh local beef, game and especially seafood, with dishes such as pan-fried scallops with black pudding. A two-/three-course lunch is £15/20.

❶ Information

Beverley Tourist Office (☑01482-391672; www.beverley.gov.uk; 34 Butcher Row; ☉9.30am-5.30pm Mon-Fri, to 4.30pm Sat year-round, also 10am-3.30pm Sun Apr-Sep)
Post Office (Register Sq; ☉9am-5.30pm Mon-Fri, to 12.30pm Sat)

❶ Getting There & Away

Bus There are frequent bus services from Hull, including numbers 121, 122, 246 and X46/X47 (£4.05, 30 minutes, every 20 minutes). Bus X46/X47 links Beverley with York (£6.45, 1¼ hours, hourly).
Train Trains run regularly to Scarborough (£13.70, 1¼ hours, every two hours) and Hull (£6.60, 15 minutes, twice hourly).

Manchester, Liverpool & Northwest England

Best Places to Eat

➡ Australasia (p563)
➡ Monro (p579)
➡ Lime Tree (p563)
➡ Upstairs at the Grill (p571)
➡ Tanroagan (p586)

Best Places to Stay

➡ Stone Villa (p570)
➡ Great John Street Hotel (p563)
➡ Hope Street Hotel (p578)
➡ Malmaison (p563)
➡ Richmond Hotel (p578)

Why Go?

If you're looking for clues as to what once made Britain great, you'll find plenty of them in the Northwest. Dominating the region is Manchester, a paradigm of reinvention that has transformed itself from 20th-century industrial hulk into a modern city with accompanying distractions – from football to fine food. Nearby Liverpool has plenty of its own diversions including a fine collection of galleries and museums, terrific shopping and a sporting pedigree every bit as impressive as that of its neighbour across the Pennines. Within easy reach of both is Chester, a historic postcard to its Tudor past and beyond, to when it was the Roman Castra Devana. And, for a bit of respite from humankind's concrete pawprint, some of Britain's most beautiful – and walkable – countryside can be found in northern Lancashire and on the Isle of Man.

When to Go

➡ The world's most famous steeplechase – the Aintree Grand National – is run just outside Liverpool over the first weekend in April.

➡ May and June are Tourist Trophy (TT) Festival season on the Isle of Man – beloved of motor enthusiasts the world over.

➡ In the arts, the highlight is the Manchester International Festival, a biennial showstopper held in July.

➡ Music buffs should visit Liverpool in the last week of August for madness at Creamfields dance-fest and for the Mathew St Festival, an ode to all things Beatles.

➡ The football (soccer) season runs from late August until May.

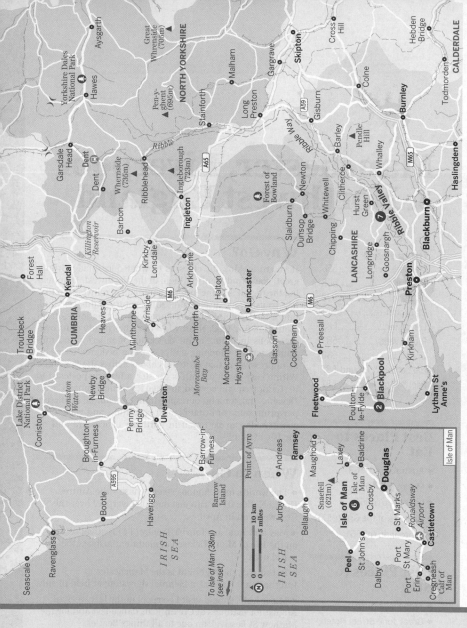

Manchester, Liverpool & Northwest England Highlights

1 Learning a valuable history lesson at Liverpool's **International Slavery Museum** (p576)

2 Having your insides churned at Blackpool's **Pleasure Beach** (p581)

3 Learning exactly what kind of hell war is in the **Imperial War Museum North** (p561) in Manchester

4 Tramping Chester's **City Walls** (p569) like the Romans did 2000 years ago

5 Sampling Manchester's culinary delights at one (or more!) of its superb **restaurants** (p563)

6 Getting to grips

Isle of Man

To Isle of Man (38m) (see inset)

0 ——— 10 km
0 ——— 5 miles

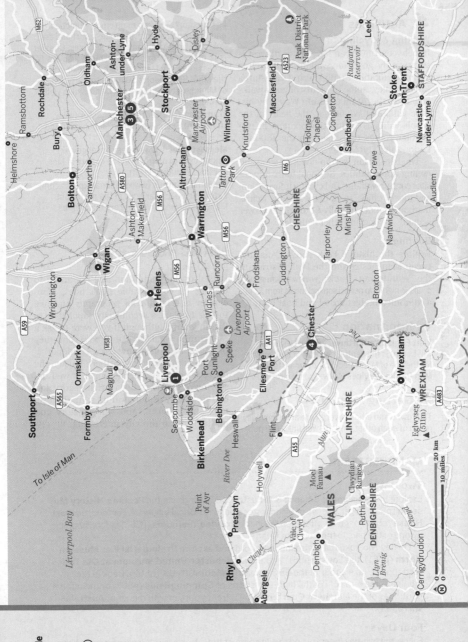

with wild, exciting **Isle of Man** (p585)

7 Going for a rural constitutional in the **Ribble Valley** (p583)

🏃 Activities

Walking & Cycling

In between the urban bits, the northwest is surprisingly good for walking and cycling options, notably in northern Lancashire's Ribble Valley, home to plenty of good walks including the 70-mile Ribble Way. The historic village of Whalley, in the heart of the Ribble Valley, is the meeting point of the two circular routes that make up the 260-mile Lancashire Cycle Way.

The Isle of Man has top-notch walking and cycling opportunities. Regional tourism websites contain walking and cycling information, and tourist offices stock free leaflets as well as maps and guides (usually £1 to £5) that cover walking, cycling and other activities.

Boating

Explore the historic Peak Forest Canal between Manchester and the Peak District on the Wandering Duck (www.wanderingduck. co.uk; 2-night trip per person incl meals from £145), a combined budget hostel and boat tour.

ℹ Information

Visit England's Northwest (www.visitnorthwest.com) is the centralised tourist authority; for the Isle of Man, check out the main Isle of Man Public Services (www.gov.im) site.

ℹ Getting Around

The towns and cities covered are all within easy reach of each other, and are well linked by public transport. The two main cities, Manchester and Liverpool, are only 34 miles apart and are linked by hourly bus and train services. Chester is 18 miles south of Liverpool, but is also easily accessible from Manchester by train or via the M56. Blackpool is 50 miles to the north of Manchester and Liverpool, and is also well connected.

Transport for Greater Manchester (www. tfgm.com) Extensive info on Manchester and its environs.

Merseytravel (www.merseytravel.gov.uk) Taking care of all travel in the county of Merseyside, including Liverpool.

National Express (www.nationalexpress.com) Extensive coach services in the northwest; Manchester and Liverpool are major hubs.

MANCHESTER

POP 503,100

Raised on lofty ambition and not afraid to declare its considerable bona fides, Manchester is – by dint of geography and history – England's second city (apologies to Birmingham), although if you were to ask a Mancunian what it's like to be second they might reply, 'Don't know, ask a Londoner'.

Even accounting for northern bluster, the uncrowned capital of the north is well deserving of the title. It has a rich history and culture, easily explored in its myriad museums and galleries. And while history and heritage make the city interesting, its dis-

---

MANCHESTER IN...

Two Days

Explore the **Museum of Science & Industry** (p557) and visit the **People's History Museum** (p557) to get a sense of Manchester's huge historical influence. For food, try **Oast House** (p564) or go for afternoon tea in the **Rosylee Tearooms** (p563) before stopping by one of the bars in the Northern Quarter.

On day two, take the Metrolink to Salford and explore the **Imperial War Museum North** (p561), the **Lowry** (p561) and the **Manchester United Museum at Old Trafford** (p561). Take a tour of the BBC spread at **MediaCityUK** (p562). Back in the city, indulge some retail *chi* at the high-end shops of **Spinningfields** (p567) or the offbeat boutiques of the **Northern Quarter** (p564). Treat yourself with dinner at **Australasia** (p563).

Four Days

Follow the two-day itinerary and tackle some of the city's lesser-known museums like the **John Rylands Library** (p560) and examine the riches of the **Manchester Art Gallery** (p560). End the day with a gig at one of the city's excellent **live music venues** (p566). The next day, take a walking tour – the tourist office has details of a whole host of themed ones – and if you're serious about clubbing, make the pilgrimage to Ancoats for the absolutely fabulous **Sankey's** (p565).

tractions of pure pleasure make Manchester fun: you can dine, drink and dance yourself into happy oblivion in the swirl of hedonism that is one of Manchester's most cherished characteristics.

History

Canals and steam-powered cotton mills were what transformed Manchester from a small disease-infested provincial town into a big disease-infested industrial city. It all happened in the 1760s, with the opening of the Bridgewater Canal between Manchester and the coal mines at Worsley in 1763, and with Richard Arkwright patenting his super cotton mill in 1769. Thereafter Manchester and the world would never be the same again. When the canal was extended to Liverpool and the open sea in 1776, Manchester – dubbed 'Cottonopolis' – kicked into high gear and took off on the coal-fuelled, steam-powered gravy train.

There was plenty of gravy to go around, but the good burghers of 19th-century Manchester made sure that the vast majority of the city's swollen citizenry (with a population of 90,000 in 1801, and two million 100 years later) who produced most of it never got their hands on any of it. Their reward was life in a new kind of urban settlement: the industrial slum. Working conditions were dire, with impossibly long hours, child labour, work-related accidents and fatalities commonplace. Mark Twain commented that he would like to live here because the 'transition between Manchester and Death would be unnoticeable'. So much for Victorian values.

The wheels started to come off towards the end of the 19th century. The USA had begun to flex its own industrial muscles and was taking over a sizeable chunk of the textile trade; production in Manchester's mills began to slow, and then it stopped altogether. By WWII there was hardly enough cotton produced in the city to make a tablecloth. The postwar years weren't much better: 150,000 manufacturing jobs were lost between 1961 and 1983, and the port – still the UK's third largest in 1963 – finally closed in 1982 due to declining traffic. The nadir came on 15 June 1996, when an IRA bomb wrecked a chunk of the city centre, but the subsequent reconstruction proved to be the beginning of the glass-and-chrome revolution so much in evidence today.

◉ Sights & Activities

◉ City Centre

★**Museum of Science & Industry** MUSEUM
(MOSI; ☑0161-832 2244; www.msim.org.uk; Liverpool Rd; charges vary for special exhibitions; ⊙10am-5pm) **FREE** If there's anything you want to know about the Industrial (and post-Industrial) Revolution and Manchester's key role in it, you'll find the answers here among this collection of steam engines and locomotives, factory machinery from the mills, and the excellent exhibition telling the story of Manchester from the sewers up.

It's an all-ages kind of museum, but the emphasis is on making sure the young 'uns don't get bored – they could easily spend a whole day poking about this 'urban heritage park', testing an early electric-shock machine here and trying out a printing press there. A unifying theme is that Manchester and Mancunians had a key role to play: this is the place to discover that Manchester was home to the world's first stored-program computer (a giant contraption nicknamed 'baby') in 1948 and that the world's first submarine was built to the designs of local curate Reverend George Garrett in 1880.

★**People's History Museum** MUSEUM
(☑0161-838 9190; www.phm.org.uk; Left Bank, Bridge St; ⊙10am-5pm) **FREE** The story of Britain's 200-year march to democracy is told in all its pain and pathos at this superb museum, housed in a refurbished Edwardian pumping station. You clock in on the 1st floor (literally: punch your card in an old mill clock, which managers would infamously fiddle with so as to make employees work longer) and plunge into the heart of Britain's struggle for basic democratic rights, labour reform and fair pay.

Amid displays like the (tiny) desk at which Thomas Paine (1737–1809) wrote *Rights of Man* (1791), and an array of beautifully made and colourful union banners, are compelling interactive displays, including a screen where you can trace the effects of all the events covered in the museum on five generations of the same family. The 2nd floor takes up the struggle for equal rights from WWII to the current day, touching on gay rights, antiracism initiatives and the defining British sociopolitical landmarks of the last 50 years, including the founding of the National Health Service (NHS), the Miners' Strike and the widespread protests against the Poll Tax.

Manchester

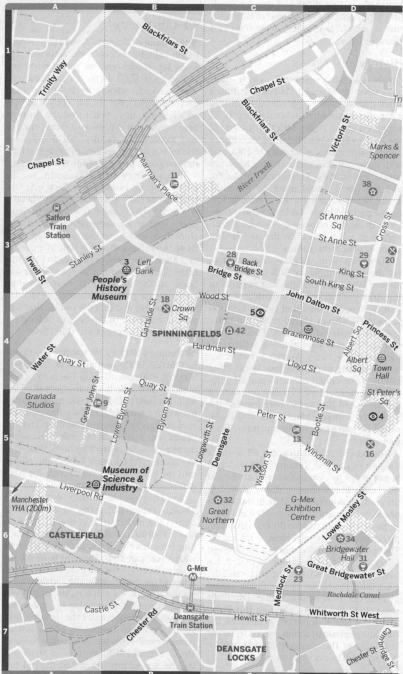

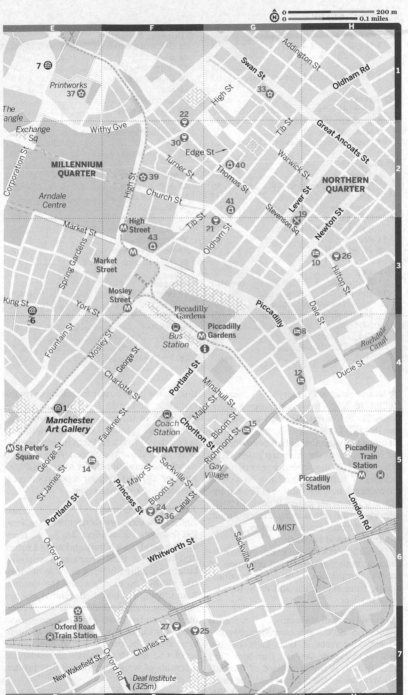

Manchester

★ **Manchester Art Gallery**   GALLERY
(☎0161-235 8888; www.manchestergalleries.org; Mosley St; ⊙10am-5pm Mon-Wed & Fri-Sun, to 9pm Thu) FREE A superb collection of British art and a hefty number of European masters are on display at the city's top gallery. The older wing has an impressive selection that includes 37 Turner watercolours, as well as the country's best assemblage of Pre-Rapha-elite art. The newer gallery is home to 20th-century British art starring Lucien Freud, Francis Bacon, Stanley Spencer, Henry Moore and David Hockney.

The Gallery of Craft & Design, in the Athenaeum, houses a permanent collection of pre-17th-century art, with works predominantly from the Dutch and early Renaissance masters.

National Football Museum   MUSEUM
(☎0161-605 8200; www.nationalfootballmuseum.com; Corporation St, Urbis, Cathedral Gardens; ⊙10am-5pm Mon-Sat, 11am-5pm Sun) FREE Britain is the birthplace of football and Manchester the home of both the most popular and richest clubs in the world. Fit-tingly, this blockbuster museum charts the evolution of British football from its earliest days to the multi-billion pound phenomenon it is today. One of the highlights is **Football Plus**, a series of interactive stations that allow you to test your skills in simulated conditions; buy a credit (£2.50, four for £9) and try your luck – it's recommended for kids over seven.

John Rylands Library   LIBRARY
(☎0161-306 0555; www.library.manchester.ac.uk; 150 Deansgate; ⊙noon-5pm Mon & Sun, 10am-5pm Tue-Sat) Less a library and more a cathedral to books, Basil Champneys' stunning building is a breathtaking example of Victorian Gothic, no more so than the Reading Room, complete with high-vaulted ceilings and stained-glass windows. The collection of early printed books and rare manuscripts is equally impressive, and includes a Gutenberg Bible, the earliest extant New Testament text and the country's second-largest assembly of works by Britain's first printer, William Caxton.

◉ Salford Quays

Just west of the city centre lies Salford Quays, home to some of Manchester's big-ticket attractions and the new hub of the BBC's northern HQ. It is easily reached via Metrolink (£2). Check out www.thequays.co.uk for more info.

Imperial War Museum North
MUSEUM

(☑0161-836 4000; www.iwm.org.uk/north; Trafford Wharf Rd; ⊙10am-5pm; ⊟Harbour City, MediaCityUK) FREE War museums generally appeal to those with a fascination for military hardware and battle strategy (toy soldiers optional), but Daniel Libeskind's visually stunning Imperial War Museum North takes a radically different approach. War is hell, it tells us, but it's a hell we revisit with tragic regularity.

The exhibits cover the main conflicts of the 20th century through a broad selection of displays, including regular screenings of the Big Picture Show, which include three permanent 15-minute films (*Children and War, The War at Home* or *Weapons of War*) and other topical ones, including (in 2014) *Al-Mutanabbi Street: A Reaction*, about a 2007 street bombing in Baghdad.

Although the audiovisuals and displays are quite compelling, the extraordinary aluminium-clad building itself is a huge part of the attraction, and the exhibition spaces are genuinely breathtaking.

Old Trafford (Manchester United Museum & Tour)
STADIUM

(☑0161-868 8000; www.manutd.com; Sir Matt Busby Way; tours adult/child £18/12; ⊙museum 9.30am-5pm, tours every 10min except match days 9.40am-4.30pm; ⊟Old Trafford) You don't have to be a fan of the world's most famous football club to enjoy a visit to their impressive 75,000-plus capacity stadium, but it helps. The museum tour includes a walk down the tunnel onto the edge of the playing surface of the 'Theatre of Dreams', where Manchester United's superstar footballers exercised their Premier League supremacy for 20 years, guided by the peerless Sir Alex Ferguson.

Fergie retired in 2013 and the team's fortunes dipped accordingly; the success of their cross-town rivals Manchester City (league winners in 2012 and 2014) puts added pressure on United to reclaim the top spot, and the appointment of Dutchman Louis Van Gaal as manager in 2014 (replacing the hapless David Moyes, Fergie's successor) is a measure of their intent.

Other highlights of the excellent tour include a seat in the stands, a stop in the changing rooms and a peek at the players' lounge (from which the manager is banned unless invited by the players) – all ecstatic experiences for a Man United devotee. The museum has a comprehensive history of the club and a state-of-the-art call-up system that means you can view your favourite goals.

Lowry
ARTS CENTRE

(☑0161-876 2020; www.thelowry.com; Pier 8, Salford Quays; ⊙11am-6pm Sun-Fri, 10am-8pm Sat; ⊟Harbour City, MediaCity UK) Looking more like a shiny steel ship than an arts centre, the Lowry is the quays' most notable success. With multiple performance spaces, bars, restaurants and shops, it attracts more than a million visitors a year to its myriad functions, which include everthing from big-name theatrical productions to comedy, kids' theatre and even weddings. The centre is also home to 300 beautifully humanistic

---

MORE NOTABLE BUILDINGS

Demonstrating a vibrant medley of architectural styles, Manchester has no shortage of eye-catching buildings dating from the 19th century (when the city was flush with industrial wealth). Keep an eye out for these showstoppers on your travels.

Town Hall (☑0161-234 5000; www.manchester.gov.uk; Albert Sq) The Victorian town hall is Manchester's most impressive building. It is crowned by an 85m-high tower and features an especially ornate interior.

Central Library (☑0161-234 1900; www.manchester.gov.uk; St Peter's Sq) Built in 1934 to resemble the Roman Pantheon, this is Britain's largest municipal library. It reopened in late 2014 after a two-year restoration.

Midland Bank (100 King St) The year 1935 saw the opening of Edwin Lutyens' stunning art-deco Midland Bank, now home to a branch of Jamie's Italian (p564) – even if you don't eat there it's well worth having a look inside; be sure to go downstairs and peek in at the deposit vaults.

depictions of urban landscapes by LS Lowry (1887–1976), who was born in nearby Stretford, and after whom the complex is named.

MediaCityUK
MEDIA CENTRE

(☑0161-886 5300; www.mediacityuk.co.uk; Salford Quays; adult/child £10/6.50; ☺ tours 10.30am, 12.30pm & 3pm Mon-Wed, Sat & Sun; 🖥 MediaCity UK) The BBC's northern home is but one significant element of this vast, 81-hectare site. Besides hosting six departments of the national broadcaster (BBC Breakfast, Children's, Sport, Radio 5 Live, Learning, and Future Media & Technology), it is also home to the set of the world's longest-running soap opera, the perennially popular *Coronation Street* (which broadcasts on ITV).

There are no plans as yet to offer tours of the Corrie set, but you can visit the BBC's impressive set-up and see the sets of some of TV's most iconic programs on a guided 90-minute tour that also includes a chance for kids to 'make' a program in an interactive studio; see www.bbc.co.uk/shows andtours. For refuelling, there are plenty of cafes and restaurants in the area.

☞ Tours

The tourist office (p567) sells tickets for guided walks on all aspects of the city, from architecture to radical history, which operate almost daily year-round and cost £7/6 per adult/child.

✸ Festivals & Events

Screenfields
FILM

(www.spinningfieldsonline.com; Spinningfields; admission £3; ☺ 8pm Thu May-Jul) Summer season of outdoor films, complete with deckchairs and picnics beginning in May.

Manchester Day
ARTS, PARADE

(www.themanchesterdayparade.co.uk) A day to celebrate all things Manchester: art, music and performances, including a parade through the city centre.

Manchester International Festival
ARTS

(☑0161-238 7300; www.mif.co.uk) A three-week-long biennial arts festival of new work across visual arts, performance and popular culture. The next festival is scheduled for July 2015.

Manchester Pride
GAY & LESBIAN

(☑0161-831 7700; www.manchesterpride.com) One of England's biggest celebrations of gay, lesbian, bisexual and transgender life, held over 10 days in late August.

Manchester Food & Drink Festival
FOOD

(www.foodanddrinkfestival.com) Manchester's superb foodie scene shows off its wares over 10 days in mid-October. Farmers markets, pop-up restaurants and gourmet events are just part of the UK's biggest urban food fest.

🛏 Sleeping

Manchester's hotels cater primarily for business travellers and sports fans but, keeping up the capital-of-chic reputation, there are a handful of designer digs and cool hotels around town. Beds can be tough to get during home matches during the football season (August to May). The tourist office has a free accommodation service.

Manchester YHA
HOSTEL £

(☑0845 371 9647; www.yha.org.uk; Potato Wharf; dm/d from £11/58; 🅿 @ 🛜) This canalside hostel in the Castlefield area is one of the best in the country. It's a top-class option with four- and six-bed dorms, all with bathroom, as well as three doubles and a host of good facilities. Potato Wharf is just left off Liverpool Rd.

Hatters
HOSTEL £

(☑0161-236 9500; www.hattersgroup.com; 50 Newton St; dm/s/d/tr from £16/30/55/70; 🅿 @ 🛜) The old-style lift and porcelain sinks are the only leftovers of this former milliner's factory, now one of the best hostels in town, with location to boot – smack in the heart of the Northern Quarter, you won't have to go far to get the best of alternative Manchester.

ABode
HOTEL ££

(☑0161-247 7744; www.abodehotels.co.uk; 107 Piccadilly St; r from £100; @ 🛜) The original fittings at this converted textile factory have been combined successfully with 61 bedrooms divided into four categories of ever-increasing luxury: Comfortable, Desirable, Enviable and Fabulous, the latter being five seriously swanky top-floor suites. Vispring beds, monsoon showers, LCD-screen TVs and stacks of Aquae Sulis toiletries are standard. In the basement, star chef Michael Caines has a champagne-and-cocktail bar adjacent to his very own restaurant.

Roomzzz
APARTMENT ££

(☑0161-236 2121; www.roomzzz.co.uk; 36 Princess St; r £65-180; @ 🛜) The inelegant name belies the designer digs inside this beautifully restored Grade II building, which features serviced apartments equipped with a kitchen and the latest connectivity gadgetry, including sleek iMac computers and free wi-fi throughout. There's a small pantry with food for sale downstairs. Highly recommended if you're planning a longer stay.

Radisson Blu Edwardian
HOTEL **££**

(☑0161-835 9929; www.radissonblu-edwardian.com/manchester; Peter St; r from £100; P@☎) Gladstone, Dickens and Fitzgerald...just some of the names associated with the historic Free Trade Hall, now a business hotel with high-end decor. It has done its best to preserve the memories of the building's most famous visitors: suites are named after Bob Dylan and Shirley Bassey, while meeting rooms carry the names of Disraeli, Thackeray and Pankhurst.

★ Great John Street Hotel
HOTEL **£££**

(☑0161-831 3211; www.greatjohnstreet.co.uk; Great John St; r £160-320; @☎) Elegant designer luxury? Present. Fabulous rooms with all the usual delights (Egyptian cotton sheets, fabulous toiletries, free-standing baths and lots of high-tech electronics)? Present. This former schoolhouse (ah, now you get it) is small but sumptuous – beyond the art-deco lobby are the fabulous bedrooms, each an example of style and luxury. If only school left such comfortable memories.

Malmaison
HOTEL **£££**

(☑0161-278 1000; www.malmaison.com; Piccadilly St; r from £119; ☐Piccadilly) Drop-dead trendy and full of crushed-red velvet, deep purples, art-deco ironwork and signature black-and-white tiles, Malmaison Manchester follows the chain's quirky design style and passion for cool, although rarely at the expense of comfort: the rooms are terrific. The **Smoak Grill** (☑0161-278 1000; www.smoak-grill.com; mains £13-25) downstairs is hugely popular.

Velvet Hotel
BOUTIQUE HOTEL **£££**

(☑0161-236 9003; www.velvetmanchester.com; 2 Canal St; r from £119; ☎) Nineteen beautiful bespoke rooms each oozing style: there's the sleigh bed in room 24, the double bath of room 34, the saucy framed photographs of a stripped-down David Beckham (this is Gay Village, after all!). Despite the tantalising decor and location, this is not an exclusive hotel and is as popular with straight visitors as it is with the same-sex crowd.

Lowry
HOTEL **£££**

(☑0161-827 4000; www.roccofortecollection.com; 50 Dearman's Pl; r £120-950; P@☎) Visiting rock stars and luxury hunters tend to favour this modern, five-star hotel (not to be confused with the arts centre in Salford

Quays), where the fabulous bedrooms have enormous beds and ergonomically designed furniture...for maximum comfort, of course. There's an excellent restaurant on the premises, and a health spa where you can soothe yourself with a skin-brightening treatment or an aromatherapy head-massage.

✖ Eating

With a choice of restaurants unrivalled outside of London, there's something for every palate and budget. You can eat well throughout the city. Spinningfields, just off Deansgate, has a handful of trendy contemporary restaurants; the Northern Quarter is the spot to go for organic eats; while the outlying suburb of Didsbury (5 miles south of the city centre, and easily reached by Metrolink) is where in-the-know Mancunians like to dine.

Rosylee Tearooms
CAFE **£**

(www.rosyleetearooms.com; 11 Stevenson Sq; lunch £6.95, 2-/3-course menu £15.95/17.95; ⊙noon-10pm Tue-Thu, 10am-10pm Fri-Sun) One of the nicest of the Northern Quarter's cafes opened in 2014, combining Edwardian and Georgian decor with a touch of Parisian bistro. The room is bright, the cakes are fabulous and the afternoon tea (£18.95), with its selection of freshly made sandwiches, is one of the nicer experiences to be had in Manchester.

★ Australasia
MODERN AUSTRALIAN **££**

(☑0161-831 0288; www.australasia.uk.com; 1 The Avenue, Spinningfields; mains £13-26; ⊙noon-midnight; ☑) One of Manchester's most successful building conversions has been that of the basement archive of the *Manchester Evening News* into this suprisingly bright and beautiful restaurant, which serves contemporary Australian cuisine with flavours of Southeast Asia – the lunchtime selection of fresh sushi

WORTH A TRIP

FINE DINING IN DIDSBURY

The ambience at **Lime Tree** (☑0161-445 1217; www.thelimetreerestaurant.co.uk; 8 Lapwing Lane; mains £16-26; ⊙noon-2.30pm Tue-Fri, 5.30-10pm Mon-Sat, noon-8pm Sun; ☐West Didsbury) is refined without being stuffy, the service is relaxed but spot on, and the food is divine – Mancunians book in advance and travel from far afield just to enjoy the superb menu. The 21-day dry-aged fillet steak in peppercorn sauce (£21) is to die for.

is particularly good, as are the specials. A late licence sees it turn into a very cool bar.

Sam's Chop House
BRITISH ££

(☑0161-834 3210; www.samschophouse.co.uk; Back Pool Fold, Chapel Walks, off Cross St; mains £12.50-20; ⊙noon-3pm & 5-9.30pm Mon-Fri, 12.30-10pm Sat, noon-8pm Sun) Arguably the city's top gastropub, Sam's is a Victorian classic that serves dishes straight out of a Dickens novel. The highlight is the crispy corned beef hash cake starter, which is salt-cured for 10 days on the premises. The gravy-loving Mrs Todgers from *Martin Chuzzlewit* would certainly approve.

James Martin Manchester
MODERN BRITISH ££

(☑0161-828 0345; www.jamesmartinmanchester.co.uk; Manchester235, Great Northern, Watson St; mains £16-18; ⊙5-11pm) Inside the opulent Manchester235 casino, itself a converted linen warehouse, this elegant restaurant is all wooden floors, exposed brick walls and wonderfully comfortable seating. The perfect ambience to enjoy celebrity chef James Martin's terrific menu, a tasty exploration of modern British dishes like slow roast belly of Redhill pork or West Coast plaice, served with herb dumplings.

Oast House
INTERNATIONAL ££

(☑0161-829 3830; www.theoasthouse.uk.com; Crown Sq, Spinningfields; mains £9-15; ⊙noon-midnight) An oast house is a 16th-century kiln used to dry out hops as part of the beer-making process. In Manchester, the Oast House is Tim Bacon's exciting BBQ restaurant, a slice of medieval charm in the heart of (slightly) po-faced Spinningfields' contemporary designer chic.

The kitchen is an outdoor covered grill, so staff have to shuttle the barbecued delights (nothing fancy: burgers, kebabs, steaks and rotisserie chickens) to diners inside, but it works brilliantly. The deli boards (lots of cheeses and cured meats) are equally delicious.

Jamie's Italian
ITALIAN ££

(☑0161-241 3901; www.jamieoliver.com; 100 King St; mains £11-18; ⊙noon-11.30pm) The magnificent banking hall of Edwin Lutyens' castle-like art-deco Midland Bank (1935) is now home to a branch of Jamie Oliver's fast-expanding gourmet empire. And while the food is perfectly adequate – it's an appealing blend of British staples given the Italian treatment – the real treat is the building itself. In the basement, the old deposit vaults have been converted into private dining rooms.

French
MODERN BRITISH £££

(☑0161-236 3333; www.the-french.co.uk; Midland Hotel, Peter St; 6-/10-course menu £59/84; ⊙noon-1.30pm Wed-Sat, 6.30-9.30pm Tue-Sat) 🍴 The revamped restaurant of the Midland Hotel (where Rolls met Royce to make motoring history) is now home to Simon Rogan's exquisite Modern British cuisine, which uses exclusively local produce grown on his farm in Cartmel, Cumbria, home to his Michelin-starred L'Enclume restaurant. The 10-course tasting menu is a feast you won't soon forget.

🍷 Drinking & Nightlife

There are all kinds of bars in town – from old-fashioned watering holes where nostalgia is on tap to trendy cocktail lounges where the beautiful people take selfies and update their social media profiles. Like most other British cities, club nights generally take place in bars with late licences and dance floors. Check the *Manchester Evening News* for details of what's on.

Bluu
BAR

(☑0161-839 7740; www.bluu.co.uk; Smithfield Market Bldgs, Thomas St; ⊙10am-midnight; 🐾) Our favourite of the Northern Quarter's collection of great bars. Bluu is cool, comfortable and comes with a great terrace on which to enjoy a pint and listen to music selected by folks with really good taste.

Black Dog Ballroom
BAR

(www.blackdogballroom.co.uk; 52 Church St; ⊙10am-midnight; 🐾) A basement bar with a speakeasy vibe, but there's nothing illicit about drinking here: the cocktails are terrific, the atmosphere is always buzzing and the music always good and loud.

Britons Protection
PUB

(☑0161-236 5895; www.britons-protection.com; 50 Great Bridgewater St; ⊙noon-11pm) Whisky (over 300 different kinds) is the beverage of choice at this liver-threatening, proper English pub that also does home-style meals. An old-fashioned boozer with open fires in the back rooms and a cosy atmosphere...perfect on a cold evening.

Lass O'Gowrie
PUB

(☑0161-273 6932; 36 Charles St; ⊙noon-11pm) A Victorian classic off Princess St that brews its own beer in the basement. It's a favourite with students, old-timers and anyone looking for an authentic pub experience. It also does good-value bar meals.

Liar's Club   BAR
(www.theliarsclub.co.uk; 19a Back Bridge St; ☺5pm-
4am; 🔊) A basement bar designed in the style
of a speakeasy/tiki lounge, the Liar's Club
serves strong cocktails to an assorted clientele
of revellers, students and off-duty barstaff. A
great atmosphere any night of the week.

Odd   BAR
(✉0161-833 0070; www.oddbar.co.uk; 30-32
Thomas St; ☺11am-midnight Sun-Wed, to 1am Thu,
to 2am Fri & Sat) This eclectic little bar – with
its oddball furnishings, wacky tunes and
anti-establishment crew of customers – is
the perfect antidote to the increasingly similar look of so many modern bars. A slice of
Mancuniana to be treasured.

Mr Thomas' Chop House   PUB
(www.tomschophouse.com; 52 Cross St; ☺11am-
11pm Mon-Thu, to midnight Fri & Sat, noon-10.30pm
Sun) An old-style boozer that is very popular
for a pint as well as a meal (mains £13).

Peveril of the Peak   PUB
(✉0161-236 6364; 127 Great Bridgewater St;
☺11am-11pm) An unpretentious pub with
wonderful Victorian glazed tilework outside.

Sankey's   CLUB
(✉0161-950 4201; www.sankeys.info; Radium St,
Ancoats; admission free-£12; ☺10pm-3am Thu &
Fri, to 4am Sat) If you're a fan of techno, electro or any kind of nonmainstream house
music, then a pilgrimage to Manchester's
best nightclub should on no account be
missed. Its commitment to top-class music

is unwavering, with world-renowned DJs
mixing it up with residents.

Sankey's has earned itself legendary status for being at the vanguard of dance music (The Chemical Brothers, Daft Punk and
others got their start here); these days, you'll
hear the likes of Timo Maas, Séb Léger and
Thomas Schumacher mix it up to an ever-
adoring crowd. Choon! The best way to get
here is to board the free Disco Bus that picks
up at locations throughout the city from
Thursday to Saturday night; see the website
for details.

Fac251   CLUB
(✉0161-272 7251; www.factorymanchester.com;
112-118 Princess St; admission £1-6; ☺11pm-3am
Mon-Sat) Located in Tony Wilson's former
Factory Records HQ, Fac251 is one of the
most popular venues in town. There are
three rooms, all with a broad musical appeal, from drum and bass to Motown and
indie rock. Something for everybody.

☆ Entertainment

Cinemas

Cornerhouse   CINEMA
(www.cornerhouse.org; 70 Oxford St; ☺11am-
8.30pm Mon-Thu, to 11pm Fri-Sun) Your only destination for good art-house releases; also has
a gallery, bookshop and cafe.

Odeon Cinema   CINEMA
(www.odeon.co.uk; The Printworks, Exchange Sq;
☺noon-11pm) A 20-screen complex in the
middle of the Printworks centre.

MANCHESTER, LIVERPOOL & NORTHWEST ENGLAND MANCHESTER

GAY & LESBIAN MANCHESTER

The city's gay scene is unrivalled outside London and caters to every taste. Its healthy
heart beats loudest in the Gay Village, centred on handsome Canal St. Here you'll find
bars, clubs, restaurants and – crucially – karaoke joints that cater almost exclusively to
the pink pound.

Manchester Pride (p562) is a 10-day festival that runs from the middle of August each
year and attracts more than 500,000 people.

There are bars to suit every taste, but you won't go far wrong in **Lammar's** (www.
lammarsbar.com; 57 Hilton St; ☺noon-late Wed-Sat, to 6pm Sun), which was voted best bar in
the city two years running in the Pride of Manchester awards.

For your clubbing needs, look no further than **Club Alter Ego** (105-107 Princess St;
☺11pm-5am Thu-Sat).

And then there's karaoke, the ultimate choice for midweek fun. The best of the lot is at
the **New Union Hotel & Showbar** (✉0161-228 1492; 111 Princess St; r from £40; ☺noon-
10pm Mon, to 2am Tue-Thu & Sun, to 3.30am Fri, to 4am Sat), where you can find your inner
Madonna and Cyndi Lauper every Tuesday and Thursday – for a top prize of £50.

For more information, check with the **Lesbian & Gay Foundation** (✉0161-235 8035;
www.lgf.org.uk; 105-107 Princess St; ☺4-10pm). Up-to-date information is also available at
www.visitmanchester.com under LGBT.

AMC Cinemas
CINEMA

(www.amccinemas.co.uk; The Great Northern, 235 Deansgate; ⊙noon-11pm) A 16-screen multiplex in a retail centre that was formerly a goods warehouse for the Northern Railway Company.

Theatre

Royal Exchange
THEATRE

(☑0161-833 9833; www.royalexchange.co.uk; St Anne's Sq) Interesting contemporary plays are standard at this magnificent, modern theatre-in-the-round.

Live Music

Band on the Wall
LIVE MUSIC

(☑0161-834 1786; www.bandonthewall.org; 25 Swan St) A top-notch venue that hosts everything from rock to world music, with splashes of jazz, blues and folk thrown in.

Deaf Institute
LIVE MUSIC

(www.thedeafinstitute.co.uk; 135 Grosvenor St; ⊙10am-midnight) Excellent midsized venue in a former institute for the deaf; also includes a smaller venue in the basement and a cafe on the ground floor.

MEN Arena
CONCERT VENUE

(www.men-arena.com; Great Ducie St) A giant arena north of the centre that hosts rock concerts (as well as being the home of the city's ice-hockey and basketball teams). It's about 300m north of Victoria Station.

Ruby Lounge
LIVE MUSIC

(☑0161-834 1392; www.therubylounge.com; 28-34 High St; ⊙noon-midnight) Terrific live-music venue in the Northern Quarter that features mostly rock bands. It gets very loud.

Classical Music

Bridgewater Hall
CONCERT VENUE

(☑0161-907 9000; www.bridgewater-hall.co.uk; Lower Mosley St) The world-renowned Hallé Orchestra has its home at this enormous and impressive concert hall, which hosts up to 250 concerts and events a year. It has a widespread program that includes opera, folk music, children's shows, comedy and contemporary music.

THE MADCHESTER SOUND

It's often claimed that Manchester was the engine room of British pop and that its chief engineer was TV presenter and music impresario Tony Wilson (1950–2007), founder of Factory Records, owner of the Hacienda and the man responsible for Joy Division and New Order. In 1983, Wilson released New Order's ground-breaking 'Blue Monday', whose successful fusion of punk and a pulsating dance beat laid the foundations for the trippy, soul-infused dance music that became known as the Manchester Sound.

The Hacienda was open from 1982 to 1997, and even though it struggled financially for much of its existence (the club was supported by New Order's record sales) it was the HQ of acid house and then rave, as the club embraced the house music coming out of Chicago and Detroit. By the late 1980s, ecstasy hit the scene and it seemed every kid in town was 'mad for it'.

Meanwhile, the city's homegrown guitar bands took notice and began shaping their sound to suit the clubbers' needs. Happy Mondays and the Stone Roses were particularly good at it, as were the Charlatans and other local producers like A Guy Called Gerald ('Voodoo Ray') and 808 State ('Pacific'). Taking no part in the revolution, but admired by everybody in it, were The Smiths, who brought a sardonic and literate tone to the grey-grim state of play that was 1980s Britain before disappearing just as the party known as Madchester was taking off.

Overdanced and overdrugged, the city awoke with a terrible hangover in 1992. Within a year or so the party was over and the fertile crossover scene, which had seen clubbers go mad at rock gigs, and rock bands play the kind of dance sounds that kept the floor thumping until the early hours, virtually disappeared and the two genres withdrew into a more familiar isolation. Taking its place was a new generation of bands, led by Oasis, the self-styled biggest band in the world, and then followed on by a host of other names like The Verve, The Chemical Brothers, Badly Drawn Boy and Elbow.

If you missed the party, you can get a terrific sense of what it was like by watching Michael Winterbottom's *24-Hour Party People* (2002), which captures the hedonism, extravagance and genius of Madchester's cast of characters, and the superb *Control* (2007) by Anton Corbijn, which tells the story of Ian Curtis, Joy Division's tragic lead singer.

Lowry   CONCERT VENUE
(☑0161-876 2020; www.thelowry.com; Pier 8, Salford Quays) Two separate venues in one: the Lyric Theatre, with the country's largest stage outside the West End, hosts all kinds of performances including Opera North. The smaller Quays hosts more intimate gigs.

Sport

For most people, Manchester plus sport equals football, and football means Manchester United (p561). But the last few years has seen the arrival on the main stage of their cross-town rivals Manchester City, whose ambition is to match United's global footprint.

Manchester City   FOOTBALL
Perennial underdogs turned 2014 league champions, Manchester City is now one the world's wealthiest clubs, and fans from all over the world come for the Etihad Stadium Tour (☑0161-444 1894; www.mcfc.co.uk; tours adult/child £14/10; ☉tours 11am, 1.30pm & 3.30pm Mon-Sat, 11.45am, 1.45pm & 3.30pm Sun except match days), a circuit of the ground, dressing rooms and museum before the inevitable steer into the kit shop. Tours must be booked in advance.

The club owes its new-found success to Sheikh Mansour of Abu Dhabi, who bought the club in 2008 and transformed them into big-time contenders. A lineup of mediocre talent was replaced at great expense with some of the brightest stars of the game, and success followed soon after: two league championships and an FA Cup win in three years.

Take bus 53, 54, 185, 186, 216, 217, 230–37, X36 or X37 from Piccadilly Gardens.

Lancashire County Cricket Club   CRICKET
(☑0161-282 4000; www.lccc.co.uk; Warwick Rd; matches £11-17; 🏏Old Trafford) The genteel game of cricket is a big deal here and the biggest game of Lancashire's season is the Roses match against Yorkshire. They play their matches at Old Trafford (same name, different but adjacent ground to the football stadium) where international test matches are also played occasionally.

Lancashire – founded in 1816 as the Aurora before changing their name in 1864 – are one of the most beloved of England's county teams, despite the fact that they haven't won the county championship since 1934. Still, a match at the ground remains a great day out.

🛍 Shopping

From the boho indie boutiques of the Northern Quarter to the swanky stores of Spinningfields (www.spinningfieldsonline.com), including Emporio Armani (☑0161-220 2980; Unit G1 & 2, The Avenue; ☉10am-6pm Mon-Sat, 11am-6pm Sun), Brooks Brothers (☑0161-834 6649; Unit G19, The Avenue; ☉10am-6pm Mon-Sat, 11am-6pm Sun) and DKNY (☑0161-833 3277; Unit G18, The Avenue; ☉10am-6pm Mon-Sat, 11am-6pm Sun), Manchester's retail credentials are assured. New Cathedral St, part of the Millennium Quarter, and King St also have fancy shops, while the Arndale Centre is the city's equivalent of the English high street.

Oi Polloi   CLOTHING
(www.oipolloi.com; 63 Thomas St) Besides the impressive range of casual footwear, this hip boutique also stocks a range of designers including APC, Lyle & Scott, Nudie Jeans and Fjällräven.

Tib Street Market   MARKET
(☑0161-234 7357; Tib St; ☉10am-5pm Sat) Up-and-coming local designers get a chance to display their wares at this weekly market where you can pick up everything from purses to lingerie and hats to jewellery.

Oxfam Originals   VINTAGE
(Unit 8, Smithfield Bldg, Oldham St; ☉10am-6pm Mon-Sat, 11am-6pm Sun) If you're into retro, this terrific store has high-quality gear from the 1960s and '70s. Shop in the knowledge that it's for a good cause.

ℹ Information

EMERGENCY
Ambulance (☑0161-436 3999)
Police Station (☑0161-872 5050; Bootle St)

MEDICAL SERVICES
Cameolord Chemist (St Peter's Sq; ☉10am-10pm) A pharmacy conveniently located in the city centre.
Manchester Royal Infirmary (Oxford Rd; ☉24hr) The most centrally located of the city's hospitals.

POST
Post Office (Brazennose St; ☉9am-5.30pm Mon-Fri)

TOURIST INFORMATION
Tourist Office (www.visitmanchester.com; Piccadilly Plaza, Portland St; guided tours daily £7/6 per adult/child; ☉10am-5.15pm Mon-Sat, to 4.30pm Sun) This is mostly a self-service

tourist office, with brochures and interactive maps to help guide visitors.

WEBSITES

Manchester City Council (www.manchester. gov.uk) The council's official website, which includes a visitors section.

Manchester Evening News (www.menmedia. co.uk) The city's evening paper in electronic form.

Real Manchester (www.realmanchester.com) Online guide to nightlife.

Restaurants of Manchester (www.restaurantsofmanchester.com) Thorough, reliable and up-to-date reviews of restaurants in the city and suburbs.

Visit Manchester (www.visitmanchester.com) The official website for Greater Manchester.

ℹ Getting There & Away

AIR

Manchester Airport (☎ 0161-489 3000; www. manchesterairport.co.uk) is the largest airport outside London and is served by 13 locations throughout Britain as well as more than 50 international destinations.

BUS

National Express (☎ 08717 81 81 81; www. nationalexpress.com) serves most major cities almost hourly between the coach station (Chorlton St) in the city centre. Destinations include Leeds (£9.70, one hour, hourly), Liverpool (£7.10, 1¼ hours, hourly) and London (£26.20, 3¾ hours, hourly).

TRAIN

Manchester Piccadilly (east of the Gay Village) is the main station for trains to and from the rest of the country, although Victoria station (north of the National Football Museum) serves Halifax and Bradford. The two stations are linked by Metrolink. Off-peak fares are considerably cheaper. Destinations include Blackpool (£16.30, 1¼ hours, half-hourly), Liverpool Lime St (£11.90, 45 minutes, half-hourly), London Euston (£78.70, three hours, seven daily) and Newcastle (£62.70, three hours, six daily).

ℹ Getting Around

TO/FROM THE AIRPORT

The airport is 12 miles south of the city. A train to or from Victoria station costs peak/off-peak £4.10/3.50, and a coach is £3.50. A taxi is nearly four times as much in light traffic.

PUBLIC TRANSPORT

The excellent public transport system can be used with a variety of Day Saver tickets. For enquiries about local transport, including night buses, contact **Travelshop** (☎ 0161-228 7811; www.tfgm.com; 9 Portland St, Piccadilly Gardens; ☉ 8am-8pm).

Bus

Centreline bus 4 provides a free service around the heart of Manchester every 10 minutes. Pick up a route map from the tourist office. Most local buses start from Piccadilly Gardens.

Metrolink

The **Metrolink** (www.metrolink.co.uk) is the best way to get between Victoria and Piccadilly train stations (and the G-Mex for Castlefield), as well as further afield to Salford Quays and other suburbs. Buy your tickets from the platform machine.

Train

Castlefield is served by Deansgate station with rail links to Piccadilly, Oxford Rd and Salford stations.

CHESHIRE

Cheshire is genteel, southern hinterland to both Liverpool and Manchester, the postal code of choice for many of its better-off citizens (including the cities' football millionaires) who opt for the amenity-laden bucolic charm of the county's contemporary version of ye olde Englande – complete with fields of Friesian cows, half-timbered Tudor houses and high-speed internet and transport links. For everybody else, Cheshire is really about Chester.

Chester

POP 90,525

Chester is one of English history's greatest gifts to the contemporary visitor. Its red-sandstone wall, which today gift-wraps a tidy collection of Tudor and Victorian buildings, was built during Roman times. The town was then called Castra Devana, and was the largest Roman fortress in Britain.

Beyond the cruciform-shaped historic centre, Chester is an ordinary, residential town; it's hard to believe today, but throughout the Middle Ages Chester made its money as the most important port in the northwest. However, the River Dee silted up over time and Chester fell behind Liverpool in importance.

◉ Sights & Activities

★ City Walls   LANDMARK

A good way to get a sense of Chester's unique character is to walk the 2-mile circuit along the walls that surround the historic centre. Originally built by the Romans around AD 70, the walls were altered substantially over the following centuries but have retained their current position since around 1200. The tourist office's *Walk Around Chester Walls* leaflet is an excellent guide.

Of the many features along the walls, the most eye-catching is the prominent **Eastgate**, where you can see the most famous clock in England after London's Big Ben, built for Queen Victoria's Diamond Jubilee in 1897.

At the southeastern corner of the walls are the **wishing steps**, added in 1785. Local legend claims that if you can run up and down these uneven steps while holding your breath your wish will come true.

Just inside Southgate, known here as **Bridgegate** (as it's located at the northern end of the Old Dee Bridge), is the **Bear & Billet** (www.bearandbillet.com; Southgate; ⊙noon-11pm) pub, Chester's oldest timber-framed building, built in 1664, and once a toll gate into the city.

★ Rows   ARCHITECTURE

Besides the city walls, Chester's other great draw is the Rows, a series of two-level galleried arcades along the four streets that fan out in each direction from the **Central Cross**. The architecture is a handsome mix of Victorian and Tudor (original and mock) buildings that house a fantastic collection of individually owned shops.

The origin of the Rows is a little unclear, but it is believed that as the Roman walls slowly crumbled, medieval traders built their shops against the resulting rubble banks, while later arrivals built theirs on top.

Chester Cathedral   CATHEDRAL

(☑01244-324756; www.chestercathedral.com; 12 Abbey Sq; admission £3; ⊙9am-5pm Mon-Sat, 1-4pm Sun) Originally a Benedictine abbey built on the remains of an earlier Saxon church dedicated to St Werburgh (the city's patron saint), it was shut down in 1540 as part of Henry VIII's dissolution frenzy, but reconsecrated as a cathedral the following year. Although the cathedral itself was given a substantial Victorian facelift, the 12th-century cloister and its surrounding buildings are essentially unaltered and retain much of the structure from the early monastic years.

Grosvenor Museum   MUSEUM

(☑01244-972197; www.grosvenormuseum.co.uk; 27 Grosvenor St; ⊙10.30am-5pm Mon-Sat, 2-5pm Sun) **FREE** Excellent museum with the country's most comprehensive collection of Roman tombstones. At the back of the museum is a preserved Georgian house, complete with kitchen, drawing room, bedroom and bathroom.

Dewa Roman Experience   MUSEUM

(☑01244-343407; www.dewaromanexperience.co.uk; Pierpoint Lane; adult/child £5.50/3.75; ⊙9am-5pm Mon-Sat, 10am-5pm Sun) Walk through a reconstructed Roman street to reveal what Roman life was like.

Roman Amphitheatre   ARCHAEOLOGICAL SITE

(Little St John St) **FREE** Just outside the city walls is what was once an arena that seated 7000 spectators (making it the country's largest); some historians have suggested that it may have also been the site of King Arthur's Camelot and that his knights' 'round table' was really just this circular construction. Excavations continue; during summer months there are occasional shows held here.

St John the Baptist Church   CHURCH

(Vicar's Lane; ⊙9.15am-6pm) Built on the site of an older Saxon church in 1075, it's been a peaceful ruin since 1581. It includes the remains of a Norman choir and medieval chapels.

Boat Hire   BOATING

(The Groves; per hr £6-8; ⊙9am-6pm Apr-Sep) Steps at the back of St John the Baptist Church (Vicar's Lane) lead down to the riverside promenade known as the Groves. Here you can hire different kinds of boats with pedals, oars or small engines.

☞ Tours

Chester Visitor Information Centre offers a broad range of walking tours departing from the town hall, including food, historical and ghost tours. Each lasts between 1½ and two hours. Recommended are the cruises up and down the Dee run by **Chester Boat** (☑01244-325394; www.chesterboat.co.uk; Boating Station, Souters Lane, The Groves; tours £6.50-15), which include a foray into the gorgeous Eaton Estate, home of the duke and duchess of Westminster.

Chester

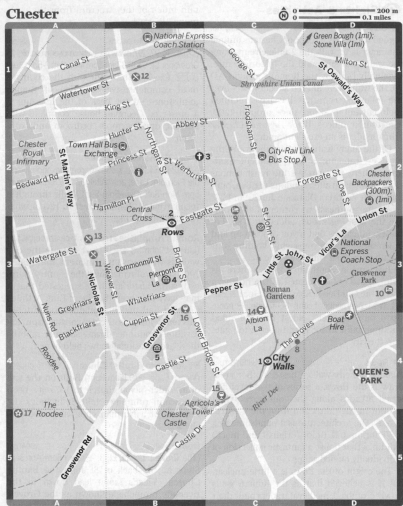

MANCHESTER, LIVERPOOL & NORTHWEST ENGLAND CHESTER

Sleeping

If you're visiting between Easter and September, you'd better book early if you want to avoid going over budget or settling for far less than you hoped for. Except for a handful of options, most of the accommodation is outside the city walls, but within easy walking distance of the centre.

Chester Backpackers　　　HOSTEL **£**
(☎01244-400185; www.chesterbackpackers.co.uk; 67 Boughton; dm/s/d from £16/22/34; ☎) Comfortable dorm rooms with nice pine beds in a typically Tudor white-and-black building.

It's just a short walk from the city walls and there's also a pleasant garden.

★**Stone Villa**　　　B&B **££**
(☎01244-345014; www.stonevillachester.co.uk; 3 Stone Pl, Hoole Rd; s/d from £45/75; P☎; ☐9) Twice winner of Chester's B&B of the Year in the last 10 years, this beautiful villa has everything you need for a memorable stay. Elegant bedrooms, a fabulous breakfast and welcoming, friendly owners all add up to one of the best lodgings in town. The property is about a mile from the city centre.

Chester

Grove Villa   B&B **££**
(☑ 01244-349713; www.grovevillachester.com; 18 The Groves; r from £75; ℗) A wonderfully positioned Victorian home overlooking the Dee. The rooms have antique beds and great river views.

Chester Grosvenor Hotel & Spa   HOTEL **£££**
(☑ 01244-324024; www.chestergrosvenor.com; 58 Eastgate St; r from £175; ℗ @ 🛜) Perfectly located, the Chester Grosvenor has huge rooms with exquisite period furnishings and all mod cons. The spa, which is also open to nonguests, offers a range of body treatments, including reiki, LaStone therapy, Indian head massage and four-handed massage. There's also a Michelin-starred restaurant downstairs.

✕ Eating

Chester has great food – it's just not in any of the tourist-oriented restaurants that line the Rows. Besides the better restaurants, you'll find the best grub in some of the pubs.

Joseph Benjamin   MODERN BRITISH **££**
(☑ 01244-344295; www.josephbenjamin.co.uk; 134-140 Northgate St; mains £13-17; ☺ 9am-5pm Tue

& Wed, 9am-midnight Thu-Sat, 10am-5pm Sun) A bright star in Chester's culinary firmament is this combo restaurant, bar and deli that delivers carefully prepared local produce to take out or eat in. Excellent sandwiches and gorgeous salads are the mainstay of the takeout menu, while the more formal dinner menu features fine examples of modern British cuisine.

Bar Lounge   MODERN BRITISH **££**
(www.barlounge.co.uk; 75 Watergate St; mains £11-18) One of the most popular spots in town is this bistro-style bar that serves up good burgers, pies and a particularly tasty beer-battered haddock and chips. There's a heated outdoor terrace for alfresco drinks.

Upstairs at the Grill   STEAKHOUSE **£££**
(☑ 01244-344883; www.upstairsatthegrill.co.uk; 70 Watergate St; mains £17-29; ☺ 5-11pm Mon-Thu, noon-11pm Fri-Sun) This two-storey Manhattan-style steakhouse is the place to devour every cut of meat from American-style porterhouse to a sauce-sodden chateaubriand. All of the cuts are locally sourced and dry aged for five weeks to guarantee succulence; most cuts are available in 225g or 340g except for the bone-in rib eye, which comes in a daunting racket-sized 680g hunk of meat.

⬛ Drinking & Nightlife

Albion   PUB
(4 Albion St; ☺ noon-11pm) No children, no music and no machines or big screens (but plenty of Union Jacks). This 'family hostile' Edwardian classic pub is a throwback to a time when ale-drinking still had its own rituals. Still, this is one of the finest pubs in northwest England precisely because it doggedly refuses to modernise.

Falcon   PUB
(Lower Bridge St; ☺ noon-11pm) An old-fashioned boozer with a lovely atmosphere, the Falcon is great for a pint, especially the selection of Samuel Smyth ales, wheat beers and ciders – they also serve organic fruit beers.

☆ Entertainment

Roodee   HORSE RACING
(www.chester-races.co.uk; The Racecourse; ☺ May-Sep) Chester's ancient and very beautiful racetrack, on the western side of the walls, has been hosting races since the 16th century. Highlights of the summer flat season include the two-day July Festival and the August equivalent.

ℹ Information

Cheshire Constabulary (☎ 01244-350000; Town Hall, Northgate St)

Countess of Chester Hospital (☎ 01244-365000; Health Park, Liverpool Rd)

Post Office (2 St John St; ⊙ 9am-5.30pm Mon-Sat)

Tourist Office (☎ 01244-402111; www.visitchester.com; Town Hall, Northgate St; ⊙ 9am-5.30pm Mon-Sat, 10am-4pm Sun May-Oct, 10am-5pm Mon-Sat Nov-Apr)

ℹ Getting There & Away

BUS

National Express (☎ 08717 81 81 81; www.nationalexpress.com) coaches stop on Vicar's Lane, just opposite the tourist office by the Roman amphitheatre. Destinations include Birmingham (£14.30, two hours, four daily), Liverpool (£8.20, one hour, four daily), London (£23, 5½ hours, three daily) and Manchester (£7.70, 1¼ hours, three daily).

For information on local bus services, ring the **Cheshire Bus Line** (☎ 01244-602666). Local buses leave from the **Town Hall Bus Exchange** (Princess St).

TRAIN

The train station is about a mile from the city centre via Foregate St and City Rd, or Brook St. City-Rail Link buses are free for people with rail tickets, and operate between the station and **Bus Stop A** (Frodsham St). Destinations include Liverpool (£6.65, 45 minutes, hourly), London Euston (£78.70, 2½ hours, hourly) and Manchester (£16.10, one hour, hourly).

ℹ Getting Around

Much of the city centre is closed to traffic from 10.30am to 4.30pm, so a car is likely to be a hindrance. The city is easy to walk around anyway, and most places of interest are close to the wall.

Around Chester

The largest of its kind in the country, **Chester Zoo** (www.chesterzoo.org; Upton-by-Chester; adult/child £20/16, monorail £2/1.50, waterbus £2/1.50; ⊙ 10am-dusk, last admission 4pm Mon-Fri, to 5pm Sat & Sun) is about as pleasant a place as caged animals in artificial renditions of their natural habitats could ever expect to live. It's so big that there's even a monorail and a waterbus for getting around. The zoo is on the A41, 3 miles north of Chester's city centre. Bus 1 (return £8, 15 minutes, every 15 minutes Monday to Saturday, every 30 minutes Sunday) runs between Chester's Town Hall Bus Exchange and the zoo.

LIVERPOOL

POP 466,400

Few English cities are as shackled by reputation as Liverpool, and none has worked so hard to outgrow the clichés that for so long have been used to define it.

A hardscrabble town with a reputation for wit and an obsessive love of football, Liverpool also has an impressive cultural heritage: it has more listed museums than any other city outside London, its galleries are among the best in the country, and it has recently undergone an impressive program of urban regeneration. And then there's the Beatles. Liverpool cherishes them not because it's stuck in the past and hasn't gotten over the fact that they're long gone – it's because their worldwide popularity would make it crazy *not* to do so.

The main attractions are Albert Dock (west of the city centre), and the trendy Ropewalks area (south of Hanover St and west of the two cathedrals). Lime St station, the bus station and the Cavern Quarter – a mecca for Beatles fans – lie just to the north.

History

Liverpool grew wealthy on the back of the triangular trading of slaves, raw materials and finished goods. From 1700 ships carried cotton goods and hardware from Liverpool to West Africa, where they were exchanged for slaves, who in turn were carried to the West Indies and Virginia, where they were exchanged for sugar, rum, tobacco and raw cotton.

As a great port, the city drew thousands of Irish and Scottish immigrants, and its Celtic influences are still apparent. Between 1830 and 1930, however, nine million emigrants – mainly English, Scots and Irish, but also Swedes, Norwegians and Russian Jews – sailed from here to the New World.

The start of WWII led to a resurgence of Liverpool's importance. More than one million American GIs disembarked here before D-Day and the port was, once again, hugely important as the western gateway for transatlantic supplies. The GIs brought with them the latest American records, and Liverpool was thus the first European port of call for the new rhythm and blues that would eventually become rock and roll. Within 20 years, the Mersey Beat was *the* sound of British pop, and four mop-topped Scousers had formed a skiffle band...

◉ Sights

The wonderful Albert Dock is the city's biggest tourist attraction and the key to understanding the city's history, but the city centre is where you'll find most of Liverpool's real day-to-day life.

◉ City Centre

★ World Museum   MUSEUM
(☎0151-478 4399; www.liverpoolmuseums.org.uk/wml; William Brown St; ⊙10am-5pm) FREE Natural history, science and technology are the themes of the oldest museum in town, which opened in 1853 and whose exhibits range from live bugs to human anthropology. This vastly entertaining and educational museum is spread across five themed floors, from the live fish aquarium on the 1st floor to the planetarium on the 5th, where you'll also find exhibits dedicated to space (moon rocks, telescopes etc) and time (clocks and timepieces from the 1500s to 1960). Highly recommended.

★ Liverpool Cathedral   CATHEDRAL
(☎0151-709 6271; www.liverpoolcathedral.org.uk; Upper Duke St; visitor centre & tower admission £5; ⊙8am-6pm) Liverpool's Anglican cathedral is a building of superlatives. Not only is it Britain's largest church, it's also the world's largest Anglican cathedral. It is the work of Sir Gilbert Scott, who also gave us the red telephone box and the Southwark Power Station in London, now the Tate Modern. The central bell is the world's third largest (with the world's highest and heaviest peal), while the organ, with its 9765 pipes, is likely the world's largest operational model.

The visitor centre features *Great Space*; this 10-minute, panoramic high-definition movie about the history of the cathedral is followed by your own audiovisual tour, courtesy of a headset. Your ticket also gives you access to the cathedral's 101m tower, from which there are terrific views of the city and beyond – on a clear day you can see Blackpool Tower.

★ Walker Art Gallery   GALLERY
(☎0151-478 4199; www.liverpoolmuseums.org.uk/walker; William Brown St; ⊙10am-5pm) FREE The city's foremost art gallery is the national gallery for northern England, housing an outstanding collection of art from the 14th to the 21st centuries. Its strong suits are pre-Raphaelite art, modern British art and sculpture – not to mention the rotating exhibits of contemporary expression. It's a family-friendly place, too: the ground-floor Big Art for Little People gallery is designed for under-eights and features interactive exhibits and games that will (hopefully) result in a lifelong love affair with art.

St George's Hall   CULTURAL CENTRE
(☎0151-707 2391; www.stgeorgesliverpool.co.uk; William Brown St; ⊙10am-5pm Tue-Sat, 1-5pm Sun) FREE Arguably Liverpool's most impressive building is the Grade I–listed St George's Hall, a magnificent example of neoclassical architecture that is as imposing today as it was when it was completed in 1854.

MANCHESTER, LIVERPOOL & NORTHWEST ENGLAND LIVERPOOL

LIVERPOOL IN...

Two Days

Start at the waterfront's collection of superb museums. Visit the **Museum of Liverpool** (p577) and, just south, the **International Slavery Museum** (p576) in Albert Dock.

Pay the Fab Four their due at the **Beatles Story** (p576) before heading into town to the Cavern Quarter around Mathew St. The **Monro** (p579) is worth a visit for lunch and the **London Carriage Works** (p579) for dinner. Round off the day with a pint at the marvellous **Philharmonic** (p579), and wrap yourself in the crisp sheets of the **Malmaison** (p579). Night hawks can tear it up in the bars and clubs of the hip **Ropewalks** area. The next day, explore the city's two **cathedrals** and check out the twin delights of the **World Museum** (p573) and the **Walker Art Gallery** (p573).

Four Days

Follow the two-day itinerary and make a pilgrimage to **Mendips** and **20 Forthlin Road** (p577), the childhood homes of John Lennon and Paul McCartney respectively. For dinner, try **HoSt** (p579). The next day, walk on holy ground at Anfield, home of **Liverpool Football Club** (p580). Race junkies can head to the visitor centre at Aintree racecourse, which hosts England's beloved race, the **Grand National** (p578).

Liverpool

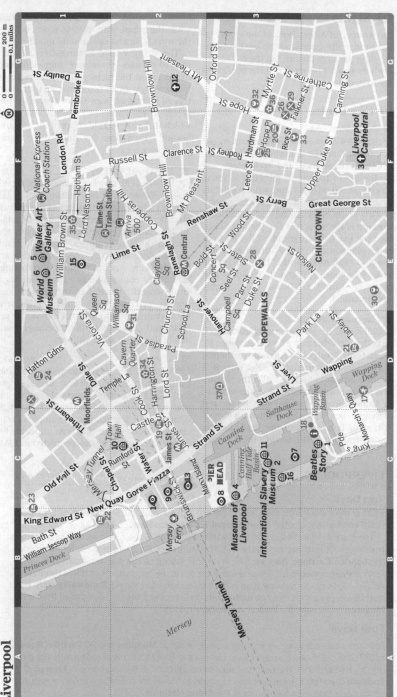

Liverpool

Curiously, it was built as law courts and a concert hall – presumably a judge could pass sentence and then relax to a string quartet.

Inside, you can visit the recently refurbished courtroom and robing room, stop by the cells below, and get a nice vantage point on the Great Hall, home to Britain's second-largest organ (its 7000 pipes are pipped by the organ in London's Albert Hall). The building also hosts concerts, corporate gigs and a host of other civic get-togethers; it is also the focal point of any city-wide celebration.

**Metropolitan Cathedral
of Christ the King**   CATHEDRAL
(☑0151-709 9222; www.liverpoolmetrocathedral.
org.uk; Brownlow Hill; ◷7.30am-6pm) Known colloquially as Paddy's Wigwam, Liverpool's Catholic cathedral is a mightily impressive modern building that looks like a soaring concrete tepee, hence its nickname. It was completed in 1967 according to the design of Sir Frederick Gibberd after the original plans by Sir Edwin Lutyens, whose crypt is inside. The central tower frames the world's largest stained-glass window, created by John Piper and Patrick Reyntiens.

Liverpool War Museum   MUSEUM
(www.liverpoolwarmuseum.co.uk; 1 Rumford St; adult/child £6/4; ◷10.30am-4.30pm Mon-Thu & Sat Mar-Oct) The secret command centre for the Battle of the Atlantic, the Western Approaches, was abandoned at the end of the war with virtually everything left intact. You can get a good glimpse of the labyrinthine nerve centre of Allied operations, including the all-important map room, where you can imagine playing a real-life, full-scale version of Risk.

◉ **Albert Dock**

Liverpool's biggest tourist attraction is Albert Dock (☑0151-708 8854; www.albertdock. com) **FREE**, 2.75 hectares of water ringed by enormous cast-iron columns and impressive five-storey warehouses that make up the country's largest collection of protected buildings and are a World Heritage Site. A fabulous development program has really brought the dock to life – here you'll find several outstanding museums and an extension of London's Tate Gallery, as well as a couple of top-class restaurants and bars.

MANCHESTER, LIVERPOOL & NORTHWEST ENGLAND LIVERPOOL

LIVERPOOL FOR CHILDREN

The waterfront museums are extremely popular with kids, especially the Museum of Liverpool (p577) and the Merseyside Maritime Museum (p576), which has a couple of boats for kids to mess about on. A visit to Anfield Rd (p580) is a must if your kids have any kind of interest in football. The Big Art for Little People gallery at the Walker Art Gallery (p573) is perfect for kids who want to find out that art is more than just something adults stare at.

★ **International Slavery Museum**　MUSEUM
(☑ 0151-478 4499; www.liverpoolmuseums.org. uk/ism; Albert Dock; ☉ 10am-5pm) **FREE** Museums are, by their very nature, like a still of the past, but the extraordinary International Slavery Museum resonates very much in the present. It reveals slavery's unimaginable horrors – including Liverpool's own role in the triangular slave trade – in a clear and uncompromising manner. It does this through a remarkable series of multi-media and other displays, and it doesn't baulk at confronting racism, slavery's shadowy ideological justification for this inhumane practice.

The history of slavery is made real through a series of personal experiences, including a carefully kept ship's log and captain's diary. These tell the story of one slaver's experience on a typical trip, departing Liverpool for West Africa. The ship then purchased or captured as many slaves as it could carry before embarking on the gruesome 'middle passage' across the Atlantic to the West Indies. The slaves that survived the torturous journey were sold for sugar, rum, tobacco and raw cotton, which were then brought back to England for profit. Exhibits include original shackles, chains and instruments used to punish rebellious slaves – each piece of metal is more horrendous than the next.

It's heady, disturbing stuff, but as well as providing an insightful history lesson, we are reminded of our own obligations to humanity and justice throughout the museum, not least in the Legacies of Slavery exhibit, which explores the continuing fight for freedom and equality.

★ **Beatles Story**　MUSEUM
(☑ 0151-709 1963; www.beatlesstory.com; Albert Dock; adult/child £12.95/7, incl Elvis & Us £15.95/7;

☉ 9am-7pm, last admission 5pm) Liverpool's most popular museum won't illuminate any dark corners in the turbulent history of the world's most famous foursome – there's ne'er a mention of internal discord, drugs or Yoko Ono – but there's plenty of genuine memorabilia to keep a Beatles fan happy. You can also get a combo ticket for the Elvis & Us (p577) exhibit at the Beatles Story extension on Pier Head.

Particularly impressive is the full-size replica Cavern Club (which was actually tiny) and the Abbey Rd studio where the lads recorded their first singles, while George Harrison's crappy first guitar (now worth half a million quid) should inspire budding, penniless musicians to keep the faith.

Merseyside Maritime Museum　MUSEUM
(☑ 0151-478 4499; www.liverpoolmuseums.org.uk/ maritime; Albert Dock; ☉ 10am-5pm) **FREE** The story of one of the world's great ports is the theme of this excellent museum and, believe us, it's a graphic and compelling page-turner. One of the many great exhibits is Emigration to a New World, which tells the story of nine million emigrants and their efforts to get to North America and Australia; the walk-through model of a typical ship shows just how tough conditions on board really were.

Tate Liverpool　GALLERY
(☑ 0151-702 7400; www.tate.org.uk/liverpool; Albert Dock; special exhibitions adult/child from £5/4; ☉ 10am-5.50pm Jun-Aug, closed Mon Sep-May) **FREE** Touted as the home of modern art in the north, this gallery features a substantial checklist of 20th-century artists across its four floors, as well as touring exhibitions from the mother ship on London's Bankside. But it's all a little sparse, with none of the energy we'd expect from the world-famous Tate.

◉ North of Albert Dock

The area to the north of Albert Dock is known as Pier Head, after a stone pier built in the 1760s. This is still the departure point for ferries across the River Mersey, and was for millions of migrants their final contact with European soil.

The Museum of Liverpool is an impressive architectural interloper, but pride of place in this part of the dock still goes to the trio of Edwardian buildings known as the 'Three Graces', dating from the days when Liverpool's star was still ascending. The southernmost, with the dome mimicking St Paul's Cathedral, is the Port of Liverpool

Building, completed in 1907. Next to it is the Cunard Building, in the style of an Italian palazzo, once HQ to the Cunard Steamship Line. Finally, the Royal Liver Building (pronounced *lie*-ver) was opened in 1911 as the head office of the Royal Liver Friendly Society. It's crowned by Liverpool's symbol, the famous 5.5m copper Liver Bird.

★ **Museum of Liverpool**   MUSEUM
(☑0151-478 4545; www.liverpoolmuseums.org.uk/mol; Pier Head; ☺10am-5pm) FREE Liverpool's storied past is explored through an interactive exploration of the city's cultural and historical milestones – the railroad, poverty, wealth, *Brookside* (a popular '80s TV soap opera set in the city), the Beatles and football (the film on the meaning of the game to the city is worth the 15 minutes). The desire to tell all of the city's rich story means there isn't a huge amount of depth, but the kids will love it.

Beatles Story: Elvis & Us   EXHIBITION
(☑0151-709 1963; www.elvisandus.com; Mersey Ferries Terminal, Pier Head; admission £6; ☺9am-7pm Apr-Sep, 10am-6pm Oct-Mar) The meeting of pop music's most iconic figures on 27 August 1965 forms the basis of this exhibit atop the Pier Head ferry terminal. Want to gawk at the white Fender bass Paul played at the meeting? Stare lovingly at the shirt Elvis wore in *Jailhouse Rock*? Look at rare footage and examine a ticket to the '68 comeback special? Then this is the place to do it.

☞ Tours

Beatles Fab Four Taxi Tour   TAXI TOUR
(☑0151-601 2111; www.thebeatlesfabfourtaxitour.co.uk; 2/3hr tour £45/55) Themed tours of the city's mop-top landmarks – there's the three-hour original Lennon tour or the two-hour Epstein express tour. Pick-ups arranged when booking. Up to five people per tour.

Liverpool Beatles Tour   GUIDED TOUR
(☑0151-281 7738; www.beatlestours.co.uk; tours from £65) Your own personalised tour of every bit of Beatles minutiae, from cradle to grave. Tours range from the three-hour Helter Skelter excursion to the Fantastic All-Day Tour, by the end of which, presumably, you'll be convinced you were actually in the band. Pick-ups are arranged upon booking.

Magical Mystery Tour   GUIDED TOUR
(☑0151-709 3285; www.cavernclub.org; per person £16.95; ☺tours 10.30am, 11.30am, 1pm & 2pm) This two-hour tour takes in all Beatles-related landmarks – their birthplaces, childhood homes, schools and places such as Penny Lane and Strawberry Field – before finishing up in the Cavern Club (which isn't the original). Departs from opposite the tourist office on Albert Dock.

MANCHESTER, LIVERPOOL & NORTHWEST ENGLAND LIVERPOOL

(NEVER) LET IT BE

They broke up more than 40 years ago and two of their members are dead, but the Beatles are bigger business than ever in Liverpool.

Most of it centres around tiny Mathew St, site of the original Cavern Club, which is now the main thoroughfare of the 'Cavern Quarter'. Here you can shuck oysters in the Rubber Soul Oyster Bar, buy a George pillowcase in the From Me to You shop and put it on the pillows of the Hard Day's Night Hotel. Ringo may have disparaged the city in 2008 by declaring that he missed nothing about it, but the city's tourist authorities continue to exploit Liverpool's ties to the world's most famous group and have done so with enormous success – the original, Beatles-oriented Mathew St Festival was enormously popular, attracting over 350,000 fans (it's now the Liverpool International Music Festival (p578) and explores music beyond the Fab Four).

Wandering around Mathew St is plenty of fun – and the Beatles Shop is best for memorabilia – but if you really want a bit of Beatles lore, you'll have to visit the National Trust–owned Mendips, the home where John lived with his Aunt Mimi from 1945 to 1963 (which is also the time period covered by Sam Taylor-Wood's superb 2009 biopic of the young Lennon, *Nowhere Boy*) and 20 Forthlin Road, the plain terraced home where Paul grew up; you can only do so by prebooked tour (☑0151-427 7231; www.nationaltrust.org.uk; Jury's Inn, 31 Keel Wharf, Wapping Dock; adult/child £22/7; ☺10am, 11am & 2.15pm Wed-Sun Mar-Nov). Tours also leave from Speke Hall (☑0151-427 7231; www.nationaltrust.org.uk; The Walk, Speke; ☺3.15pm Wed-Sun Mar-Oct).

If you'd rather do it yourself, the tourist offices stock the *Discover Lennon's Liverpool* guide and map, and Ron Jones' *The Beatles' Liverpool*.

✿ Festivals & Events

Creamfields   MUSIC, DANCE
(www.cream.co.uk) An alfresco dance-fest that brings together some of the world's best DJs and dance acts during the last weekend in August. It takes place at the Daresbury Estate near Halton, Cheshire.

International Beatleweek   MUSIC
(www.cavernclub.org) Tribute bands keep the crowds entertained across a week in late August of Beatles-inspired music and talks organised by the Cavern Club.

**Liverpool International
Music Festival**   MUSIC
(☑0151-239 9091; www.limfestival.org) A festival showcasing local bands and international acts across five different venues spread throughout the city during the last two weeks of August.

🛏 Sleeping

Liverpool's choice of accommodation ranges from sexy boutique to strictly functional. Rooms are at a premium when Liverpool FC are playing at home and during the mobbed-out music festivals of late August. If you fancy self-catering options, the tourist office has all the information you need.

📍 City Centre

★ **Richmond Hotel**   HOTEL ££
(www.richmondliverpool.com; 24 Hatton Garden; d from £80, 2-bedroom apt from £199) Centrally located and fully renovated, the Richmond offers a convenient choice of accommodation, from classic doubles and suites to fully equipped, self-catering one-, two- and three-bedroom apartments. All of the rooms have high-spec decor, including 50in

THE GRAND NATIONAL
The world's most famous **steeple-chase** (☑0151-522 2929; www.aintree.co.uk) – and one of England's most cherished events – takes place on the first Saturday in April across 4.5 miles and over the most difficult fences in world racing. Its protagonists are 40-odd veteran stalwarts of the jumps, ageing bruisers full of the oh-so-English qualities of grit and derring-do. If you want to attend the race, you'd better book tickets far in advance.

flatscreen TVs and fancy toiletries. Guests also have access to the hotel spa.

Radisson Blu   HOTEL ££
(☑0151-966 1500; www.radissonblu.co.uk; 107 Old Hall St; r from £95; @ 🐾) The rooms at this funky Scandinavian design hotel are divided into 'Ocean', with regal blues and views of the docks and the Mersey, and 'Urban', with luscious reds and purples and city views. Each comes with all the designer gadgetry you'd expect: flatscreen TVs, free highspeed wi-fi and super-hip bathrooms. They're not especially huge, but they're very cool, baby.

62 Castle St   BOUTIQUE HOTEL ££
(☑0151-702 7898; www.62castlest.com; 62 Castle St; r from £80; P @ 🐾) This elegant property successfully blends the traditional Victorian features of the neoclassical building with a sleek, contemporary style. The 20 fabulously different suites come with high-definition plasma-screen TVs, drench showers and luxe toiletries as standard.

Roscoe House   BOUTIQUE HOTEL ££
(☑0151-709 0286; www.roscoehouse.com; 27 Rodney St; r from £70; 🐾) A handsome Georgian home once owned by Liverpool-born writer and historian William Roscoe (1753–1831) has been given the once-over and is now a chic boutique hotel. The elegant rooms combine period touches (original coving, fireplaces and furnishings) with contemporary comforts such as flatscreen TVs and fancy Egyptian cotton sheets.

★ **Hope Street Hotel**   BOUTIQUE HOTEL £££
(☑0151-709 3000; www.hopestreethotel.co.uk; 40 Hope St; r/ste from £130/190; @ 🐾) Luxurious Liverpool's pre-eminent flag-waver is this stunning boutique hotel on the city's most elegant street. King-sized beds draped in Egyptian cotton, oak floors with underfloor heating, LCD TVs and sleek modern bathrooms (with REN bath and beauty products) are but the most obvious touches of class at this supremely cool address. Breakfast, taken in the marvellous London Carriage Works, is not included.

🛏 Around Albert Dock

Liverpool YHA   HOSTEL £
(☑0845 371 9527; www.yha.org.uk; 25 Tabley St; dm from £18; P 🐾) It may have the look of an Eastern European apartment complex, but this award-winning hostel, adorned with plenty of Beatles memorabilia, is one of the

most comfortable you'll find anywhere in the country. The dorms with en suite bathrooms even have heated towel rails.

★ **Malmaison**   HOTEL **££**
(☑0151-229 5000; www.malmaison.com; 7 William Jessop Way, Princes Dock; r from £89; P @ 🛜) Malmaison's preferred colour scheme of plum and black is everywhere in this purpose-built hotel, which gives it an air of contemporary sophistication. Everything about the Liverpool Mal is plush, from the huge beds and the deep baths to the heavy velvet curtains and the excellent buffet breakfast.

✖ Eating

Top-grade international cuisine, the best of British and the greasy spoon...you'll find plenty of choices to satisfy every taste. Best spots include Ropewalks, along Hardman St and Hope St.

Monro   GASTROPUB **££**
(☑0151-707 9933; www.themonro.com; 92 Duke St; 2-course lunch £11.95, dinner mains £14-20; ☉11am-11pm) 🍴 The Monro has fast become one of the city's favourite spots for lunch, dinner and, especially, weekend brunch. The constantly changing menu of classic British dishes made with ingredients sourced as locally as possible has transformed this handsome old pub into a superb dining experience. It's tough to find pub grub this good elsewhere, unless you go to its sister pub, the James Monro (☑0151-236 9700; www.thejamesmonro.com; 69 Tithebarn St; ☉11am-11pm).

HoSt   ASIAN, FUSION **££**
(www.ho-st.co.uk; 31 Hope St; mains £9.50-13; ☉11am-11pm; 🚲🦽) A bright, airy room with the look of a chic, contemporary New York brasserie serves up excellent pan-Asian dishes like Indonesian braised lamb with fried rice and red duck coconut curry with lychees. The starter nibbles are pretty delicious, too.

Quarter   BISTRO **££**
(☑0151-707 1965; www.thequarteruk.com; 7-11 Falkner St; mains £9-15; ☉8am-11pm Mon-Fri, 9am-11pm Sat & Sun) A gorgeous little wine bar and bistro with outdoor seating for that elusive summer's day.

London Carriage Works   MODERN BRITISH **£££**
(☑0151-705 2222; www.thelondoncarriageworks.co.uk; 40 Hope St; 2-/3-course meal £17.50/22.50, mains £16-30; ☉7-10am & noon-10pm Mon-Fri, 8-11am & noon-10pm Sat, to 9pm Sun) Liverpool's dining revolution is being led by Paul Askew's award-winning restaurant, which successfully blends ethnic influences from around the globe with staunch British favourites and serves up the result in a beautiful dining room – actually more of a bright glass box divided only by a series of sculpted glass shards. Reservations are recommended.

🍷 Drinking & Nightlife

Unless specified, all the bars included here open from 11am until 2am Monday to Saturday, and most have a nominal entry charge after 11pm. Most of the city's clubs are concentrated in Ropewalks, where they compete for customers with a tonne of late-night bars; considering the number of punters in the area on a Friday or Saturday night, we're guessing there's plenty of business for everyone.

Everyman Bistro   BAR
(www.everymanplayhouse.com; Williamson Sq; ☉10am-10pm) This Liverpool institution reopened in 2014 in a new location and is better than ever. The downstairs bar and bistro are packed most evenings, making this one of the best places in town for a drink and a bite. The wi-fi is stronger than in most other bars.

Philharmonic   PUB
(36 Hope St; ☉10am-11.30pm) This extraordinary bar, designed by the shipwrights who built the *Lusitania*, is one of the most beautiful bars in all of England. The interior is resplendent with etched and stained glass, wrought iron, mosaics and ceramic tiling – and if you think that's good, just wait until you see inside the marble men's toilets, the only heritage-listed lav in the country.

Ye Cracke   PUB
(13 Rice St; ☉11am-11pm) A traditional pub with a beer garden; the fact that John and Cynthia Lennon liked coming here when they were students is completely incidental to its charms.

DON'T MISS

BEST PUBS FOR A PINT IN THE NORTHWEST

➡ Philharmonic (p579), Liverpool

➡ Britons Protection (p564), Manchester

➡ Albion (p571), Chester

➡ Peveril of the Peak (p565), Manchester

24 Kitchen Street
CLUB

(www.facebook.com/24kitchenstreet; 24 Kitchen St; tickets £8-12; ☺9pm-4am Fri & Sat) A multipurpose venue that splits its focus between the arts and electronic music. The converted Victorian building is one of the best places in town to dance in.

☆ Entertainment

Philharmonic Hall
CLASSICAL MUSIC

(☑0151-709 3789; www.liverpoolphil.com; Hope St) One of Liverpool's most beautiful buildings, the art-deco Phil is home to the city's main classical orchestra, but it also stages the work of avant-garde musicians such as John Cage and Nick Cave.

O2 Academy
LIVE MUSIC

(☑0151-794 6868; www.o2academyliverpool.co.uk; Liverpool University, 11-13 Hotham St) Good spot to see midsize bands on tour.

Cavern Club
LIVE MUSIC

(☑0151-236 1965; www.cavernclub.org; 8-10 Mathew St; admission before/after 2pm free/£4; ☺10am-midnight Mon-Wed & Sun, to 1.30am Thu, to 2am Fri & Sat) It's a reconstruction, and not even on the same spot, but the 'world's most famous club' is still a great spot to see local bands.

Liverpool FC
FOOTBALL

(☑0151-263 9199, ticket office 0151-220 2345; www.liverpoolfc.com; Anfield Rd) Doff o' the cap to Evertonians and Beatle-maniacs, but no single institution represents the Mersey spirit and strong sense of identity more powerfully than Liverpool FC, who dominated British football in the '70s and '80s, but have had to watch as their bitter rivals Manchester United did the same in the decades since.

New manager Brendan Rodgers was appointed in 2012 and has re-established the club as viable contenders for the league title: in 2014 they were pipped to the prize by Manchester City, but the club's millions of fans worldwide have a renewed sense of hope for the future.

After years of discussion, plans to enlarge the utterly marvellous Anfield Road were approved in 2014 and the 60,000-capacity ground should be ready by 2017. In the meantime, the experience of a live match remains a sporting highlight of a visit to England, especially the sound of 40,000 fans singing the club's anthem, 'You'll Never Walk Alone'. The **Anfield Stadium Tour** (www.liverpoolfc.com; Anfield Stadium; stadium tour adult/child £16.50/10)

brings fans to the home dressing room and down the tunnel past the famous 'This is Anfield' sign into the pitchside dugout. Take bus 26 or 27 from Paradise St Interchange or bus 17 or 217 from the Queen St Bus Station.

Everton Football Club
FOOTBALL

(☑0151-330 2400, ticket office 0151-330 2300; www.evertonfc.com; Goodison Park) Founded in 1878, Liverpool's blue half, Everton FC, consoles itself for existing in the shadow of its more successful neighbour with the historical truth of 'we were there first'. **Goodison Park Tours** (☑0151-530 5212; www.evertonfc.com; adult/child £10/5; ☺11am & 1pm Mon, Wed, Fri & Sun) run throughout the year, except on the Friday before home matches. Take bus 19, 20 or 21 from Paradise St Interchange or Queen St Bus Station.

🔒 Shopping

Sandwiched between Albert Dock, the Cavern Quarter and Ropewalks is the simply enormous **Liverpool ONE** (www.liverpool-one.com; ☺9.30am-8pm Mon-Fri, 9am-7pm Sat, 11am-5pm Sun) shopping district ('centre' just feels too small) – 17 hectares of retail and restaurant pleasure.

ℹ Information

There is a small **tourist office** (☑0151-707 0729; www.visitliverpool.com; Anchor Courtyard; ☺10am-6pm) in Albert Dock, and a separate **accommodation hotline** (☑0845 601 1125; ☺9am-5.30pm Mon-Fri, 10am-4pm Sat).

Liverpool Magazine (www.liverpool.com) Insiders' guide to the city run by the *Liverpool Echo*, including lots of great recommendations for food and nights out.

Mars Pharmacy (68 London Rd) Open until 10pm every night.

Mersey Guide (www.merseyguide.co.uk) Guide to the Greater Mersey area.

Merseyside Police Headquarters (☑0151-709 6010; Canning Pl) Opposite Albert Dock.

Post Office (Ranelagh St; ☺9am-5.30pm Mon-Sat)

Royal Liverpool University Hospital (☑0151-706 2000; Prescot St)

ℹ Getting There & Away

AIR

Liverpool John Lennon Airport (☑0870 750 8484; www.liverpoolairport.com; Speke Hall Ave) serves a variety of international destinations as well as destinations in the UK (Belfast, London and the Isle of Man).

BUS

The **National Express Coach Station** (www.nationalexpress.com; Norton St) is 300m north of Lime St station. There are services to/from most major towns including Birmingham (£13.80, 2¾ hours, five daily), London (£28, five to six hours, six daily), Manchester (£7.10, 1¼ hours, hourly) and Newcastle (£25.70, 6½ hours, three daily).

TRAIN

Liverpool's main station is Lime St. It has hourly services to almost everywhere, including Chester (£6.65, 45 minutes), London Euston (£78.70, 3¼ hours) and Manchester (£11.90, 45 minutes).

❶ Getting Around

TO/FROM THE AIRPORT

The airport is 8 miles south of the centre. **Arriva Airlink** (www.arriva.co.uk; adult £2; ⊙6am-11pm) buses 80A and 180 depart from Paradise St Interchange, and **Arriva 500** (www.arriva.co.uk; £2.50; ⊙5.15am-12.15am) buses leave from outside Lime St station. Buses from both stations take half an hour and run every 20 minutes. A taxi to the city centre should cost no more than £18.

BOAT

The famous **Mersey ferry** (www.merseyferries.co.uk; one way/return £2.30/2.80) crossing for Woodside and Seacombe departs from Pier Head Ferry Terminal, next to the Royal Liver Building (to the north of Albert Dock).

CAR & MOTORCYCLE

You won't have much use for a car in Liverpool, and it'll no doubt end up costing you in parking fees. If you have to drive, there are parking meters around the city and a number of open and sheltered car parks. Car break-ins are a significant problem, so leave nothing of value in the car.

PUBLIC TRANSPORT

Local public transport is coordinated by **Merseytravel** (www.merseytravel.gov.uk). Highly recommended is the Saveaway ticket (adult/child £5/2.50), which allows for one day's off-peak (after 9.30am) travel on all bus, train and ferry services throughout Merseyside. Tickets are available at shops and post offices throughout the city. Paradise St Interchange is in the city centre.

Merseyrail (www.merseyrail.org) is an extensive suburban rail service linking Liverpool with the Greater Merseyside area. There are four stops in the city centre: Lime St, Central (handy for Ropewalks), James St (close to Albert Dock) and Moorfields (for the Liverpool War Museum).

TAXI

Mersey Cabs (☏0151-298 2222) operates tourist taxi services and also has some wheelchair-accessible cabs.

LANCASHIRE

As you travel north, past the concrete blanket that covers much of the southern half of the county, Lancashire's undulating landscape begins to reveal itself in all its bucolic glory. Beyond Blackpool – the faded queen of beachside holidays – the Ribble Valley is a gentle and beautiful warm-up for the Lake District that lies beyond the county's northern border. North of the Ribble Valley is the county's handsome Georgian capital, Lancaster.

Blackpool

POP 148,185

Blackpool is the queen of England's faded fun-by-the-seaside resorts, a defiant tribute to a traditional past before the advent of low-cost airlines and sun holidays in Spain. It's tacky, trashy and a little tawdry, but Blackpool doesn't care because 15 million-plus annual visitors don't either.

The town is famous for its tower, its three piers, its Pleasure Beach and its Illuminations, the latter being a successful ploy to extend the brief summer holiday season. From early September to early November, 5 miles of the Promenade are illuminated with thousands of electric and neon lights.

◉ Sights

Blackpool Pleasure Beach AMUSEMENT PARK (www.blackpoolpleasurebeach.com; Central Promenade; Pleasure Beach Pass £6, Unlimited Ride wristband 1-day adult/child £30/27, Speedy Pass/ VIP Speedy Pass per person £12/42; ⊙hours vary) The main reason for Blackpool's immense popularity is the Blackpool Pleasure Beach, a 16-hectare collection of more than 145 rides that attracts some seven million visitors annually. As amusement parks go, it's easily the best in Britain.

Rides are divided into categories, and once you've gained entry to the park with your Freedom Ticket you can buy tickets for individual categories or for a mixture of them all. Alternatively, an Unlimited Ride wristband includes the £5 entrance fee; there are great discounts if you book your tickets online in advance. The Speedy Pass saves you the hassle of queuing for rides by allocating you a specific ride time; rent it and add as many people to it as you want; they've just added a VIP Speedy Pass that allows you get in ahead of regular Speedy Pass users.

There are no set times for closing; it depends how busy it is.

Blackpool Tower   ENTERTAINMENT COMPLEX

(☑0844 856 1000; www.theblackpooltower.com; Tower Ticket adult/child £52/40; ⊙hours vary) Built in 1894, this 154m-high tower is Blackpool's most recognisable landmark. Watch a 4D film on the town's history in the **Blackpool Tower Eye** (a 2011 addition), before taking the elevator 154m up to the observation deck, which has splendid views and only a (thick) glass floor between you and the ant-sized people below.

Back at ground level, the **dungeon** exhibit sits alongside the old Moorish circus and the magnificent rococo ballroom, with its extraordinary sculptured and gilded plasterwork, murals, chandeliers and couples gliding across the beautifully polished wooden floor to the melodramatic tones of a huge Wurlitzer organ. There's also **Jungle Jim's** adventure playground for kids.

Visitors are strongly urged to buy their tickets online as buying them at the door can be up to 50% more expensive.

Sandcastle Waterpark   AMUSEMENT PARK

(www.sandcastle-waterpark.co.uk; adult/child £14.50/11.50, Hyperzone £5/2.50; ⊙hours vary) Across from Pleasure Beach is this indoor water complex with 15 different slides and rides, including the Hyperzone, which has the complex's most popular slides: Aztec Falls, Montezooma, the Sidewinder and Master Blaster, the world's largest indoor water slide.

North Pier   LANDMARK

(Promenade) **FREE** Built in 1862 and opening a year later, the most famous of the three Victorian piers once charged a penny for admission; its plethora of unexciting rides are now free.

🛏 Sleeping

If you want to stay close to the waterfront, prepare for a noisy, boisterous night; accommodation along Albert and Hornby Rds, 300m back from the sea, is that little bit quieter. The tourist office will assist you in finding a bed.

Number One   BOUTIQUE HOTEL ££

(☑01253-343901; www.numberoneblackpool.com; 1 St Lukes Rd; s/d from £70/100; P🐾) Far fancier than anything else around, this stunning boutique guesthouse is all luxury and contemporary style. Everything exudes a kind of discreet elegance, from the dark-wood furniture and high-end mod cons to the top-notch breakfast. It's on a quiet road just set back from the South Promenade near the Pleasure Beach amusement park.

Big Blue Hotel   HOTEL ££

(☑01253-400045; www.bigbluehotel.com; Blackpool Pleasure Beach; r from £80; P@🐾) A handsome family hotel with smartly kitted-out rooms. Kids are looked after with DVD players and computer games, while its location at the southern entrance to Blackpool Pleasure Beach should ensure that everyone has something to do.

🍴 Eating

Forget gourmet meals – the Blackpool experience is all about stuffing your face with burgers, doughnuts, and fish and chips. Most people eat at their hotels, where roast and three vegetables often costs just £5 per head.

There are a few restaurants around Talbot Sq (near the tourist office) on Queen St, Talbot Rd and Clifton St.

ℹ️ Information

Tourist Office (☑01253-478222; www.visitblackpool.com; 1 Clifton St; ⊙9am-5pm Mon-Sat)

ℹ️ Getting There & Away

BUS

The central coach station is on Talbot Rd, near the town centre. Services include London (£34.20, seven hours, four daily) and Manchester (£8.90, 1¾ hours, four daily).

TRAIN

The main train station is Blackpool North, about five blocks east of the North Pier on Talbot Rd. There is a direct service from Manchester (£16.30, 1¼ hours, half-hourly) and Liverpool (£17.60, 1½ hours, seven daily), but most other arrivals change in Preston (£7.60, 30 minutes, half-hourly).

ℹ️ Getting Around

A host of travel-card options for trams and buses ranging from one day to a week are available at the tourist office and most newsagents. With more than 14,000 car-parking spaces in Blackpool, you'll have no problem parking. The (recently upgraded) **tramway** (one stop £1, up to 16 stops £2; ⊙from 10.30am Apr-Oct) shuttles funsters for 11 miles, including along the pier as far as the Fylde Coast (also serving the central corridor car parks), every eight minutes or so throughout the day. Otherwise, the town's **bike hire scheme** (www.hourbike.com; per hr £1) has bikes available for hire from stations along the Promenade and in Stanley Park.

Lancaster

POP 44,500

Lancashire's county seat is genteel, austere and much, much quieter than it was in its 18th-century heyday, when it served as an important trading port for all manner of goods, including people. The city's handsome Georgian architecture was one of the slave trade's ancillary benefits.

◉ Sights

Lancaster Castle & Priory   CASTLE
(☑01524-64998; www.lancastercastle.com; Castle Park; adult/child £8/6.50; ⊘10am-5pm, guided tours every 30min 10am-4pm) Lancaster's imposing castle was originally built in 1150. Later additions include the Well Tower, more commonly known as the Witches' Tower because it was used to incarcerate the accused of the famous Pendle Witches Trial of 1612, and the impressive twin-towered gatehouse, both from the 14th century. Visits are by guided tour only as the castle is used as a Crown Court.

The castle was heavily restored in the 18th and 19th centuries to suit a new function as a prison, and it continued to house Category C prisoners until 2011.

Immediately next to the castle is the equally fine priory church (Priory Cl; ⊘9.30am-5pm), founded in 1094 but extensively remodelled in the Middle Ages.

Judges' Lodgings   MUSEUM
(Church St; adult/child £3/2; ⊘10am-4pm Jun & Jul, 1-4pm Easter-May & Aug-Oct) Once the home of witch-hunter Thomas Covell (who 'caught' the poor Pendle women), Lancaster's oldest town house, a Grade I–listed Georgian building, is now home to a Museum of Furnishings by master builders Gillows of Lancaster, whose work graces the Houses of Parliament. It also houses a Museum of Childhood with memorabilia from the turn of the 20th century.

Williamson Park &
Tropical Butterfly House   GARDENS
(Tropical Butterfly House adult/child £3.70/2.70; ⊘10am-5pm Apr-Sep, to 4pm Oct-Mar) Lancaster's highest point is the 22-hectare spread of this elegant park, whose highlights are (besides the views) the Tropical Butterfly House, full of exotic and stunning species, and the Ashton Memorial, a 67m-high baroque folly built by Lord Ashton (the son of the park's founder, James Williamson) for his wife. Take bus 25 or 25A from the station, or else it's a steep, short walk up Moor Lane.

🛌 Sleeping & Eating

Sun Hotel & Bar   HOTEL ££
(☑01524-66006; www.thesunhotelandbar.co.uk; 63 Church St; r from £90; P🐕) An excellent hotel in a 300-year-old building with a rustic, old-world look that stops at the bedroom doors – beyond them are 16 stylish and contemporary rooms. The pub downstairs is one of the best in town and a top spot for a bit of grub; the two-course roast of the day (£8) is excellent.

Whale Tail Cafe   VEGETARIAN £
(www.whaletailcafe.co.uk; 78a Penny St; mains £8-11; ⊘10am-4pm Mon-Fri, to 5pm Sat, to 3pm Sun; 🍽) 🍴 This gorgeous 1st-floor veggie restaurant has an elegant dining room and a more informal plant-filled courtyard for lunch on a sunny day. The spicy bean burger is particularly good. Food here is locally produced and, where possible, organic.

❶ Information

Tourist Office (☑01524-582394; www.citycoastcountryside.co.uk; Storey Creative Industries Centre, Meeting House Lane; ⊘9am-5pm Mon-Sat)

❶ Getting There & Away

Lancaster is on the main west coast railway line and on the Cumbrian coast line. Destinations include Carlisle (£19.50, one hour, hourly), Manchester (£8.60, one hour, hourly) and Morecambe (£2.30, 15 minutes, half-hourly).

Ribble Valley

Known locally as 'Little Switzerland', Lancashire's most attractive landscapes lie east of the brash tackiness of Blackpool and north of the sprawling urban areas of Preston and Blackburn.

The northern half of the valley is dominated by the sparsely populated moorland of the Forest of Bowland, which is a fantastic place for walks, while the southern half features rolling hills, attractive market towns and ruins, with the River Ribble flowing between them.

🏃 Activities

Ribble Way   WALKING
(www.visitlancashire.com) The Ribble Way, a 70-mile footpath that follows the River Ribble from its source at Ribblehead (in the Yorkshire Dales) to the estuary at Preston, is one of the more popular walks in the area and passes through Clitheroe.

THE PENDLE WITCHES

A lovely walk brings you to the top of Pendle Hill (558m) from which there are marvellous views of the surrounding countryside.

In 1612, however, the surrounding villages in the shadow of Pendle Hill were the scene of dramatic witch trials. Ten people, two of them older women who were known locally as 'healers', were accused of practising witchcraft, including murder, and were convicted to hang based on the sole testimony of a nine-year-old child (a legal reference point that would later influence the Salem Witch Trials of the New World). Every Halloween a pseudomystical ceremony is performed here to commemorate their 'activities'. If that's not enough, in 1652 George Fox, the founder of the Quakers, felt compelled to climb Pendle Hill and experienced visions there – an event that was to add momentum to the growth of the Quaker religion.

Lancashire Cycle Way
CYCLING

The Ribble Valley is well covered by the northern loop of the Lancashire Cycle Way; for more information about routes, safety and so on, contact Blazing Saddles (☑01442-844435; www.blazingsaddles.co.uk; 35 West End, Hebden Bridge, West Yorkshire), a Yorkshire-based bike shop.

Clitheroe

POP 14,700

Located northeast of Preston, the Ribble Valley's largest market town is best known for its impressive Norman keep (⊙dawn-dusk) FREE, built in the 12th century and now, sadly, standing empty; from it there are great views of the river valley below. The extensive grounds are home to the newly refurbished Castle Museum (Castle Hill; adult/child £4/3; ⊙11am-4pm Mar-Oct, noon-4pm Mon, Tue & Fri-Sun Nov-Feb), which explores 350 million years of local history.

🛏 Sleeping & Eating

Old Post House Hotel
HOTEL ££

(☑01200-422025; www.posthousehotel.co.uk; 44-48 King St; s/d from £50/70; P🖒) A former post office is now Clitheroe's most handsome hotel, with 11 superbly decorated rooms.

Halpenny's of Clitheroe
TEAROOM £

(Old Toll House, 1-5 Parson Lane; mains £7-9) A traditional teashop that serves sandwiches, and dishes such as Lancashire hotpot.

ℹ Information

Tourist Office (☑01200-425566; www.visitribblevalley.co.uk; Church Walk; ⊙9am-5pm Mon-Sat) Info on the town and surrounding area.

Forest of Bowland

This vast grouse-ridden moorland is somewhat of a misnomer. The use of 'forest' is a throwback to an earlier definition, when it served as a royal hunting ground. Today it is an Area of Outstanding Natural Beauty (AONB), which makes for good walking and cycling. The Pendle Witch Way, a 45-mile walk from Pendle Hill to northeast of Lancaster, cuts right through the area, and the Lancashire Cycle Way runs along the eastern border. The forest's main town is Slaidburn, about 9 miles north of Clitheroe on the B6478.

Other villages worth exploring are Newton, Whitewell and Dunsop Bridge.

🛏 Sleeping & Eating

Slaidburn YHA
HOSTEL £

(☑0845 371 9343; www.yha.org.uk; King's House; dm £18; ⊙Apr-Oct) A converted 17th-century village inn that is especially popular with walkers and cyclists.

Inn at Whitewell
INN ££

(☑01200-448222; www.innatwhitewell.com; s/d from £90/119) Once the home of Bowland's forest keeper, this is now a superb guesthouse with antique furniture, peat fires and Victorian claw-foot baths. The restaurant specialises in traditional English game dishes (mains £11 to £19).

Hark to Bounty Inn
INN ££

(☑01200-446246; www.harktobounty.co.uk; Slaidburn; s/d from £45/90) This marvellous 13th-century inn has atmospheric rooms with exposed oak beams. An excellent restaurant downstairs specialises in homemade herb breads (mains £9 to £17).

ℹ Getting There & Away

Clitheroe is served by regular buses from Preston and Blackburn and hourly trains from Manchester (£9.30, 75 minutes) and Preston (£6.70, 50 minutes). Once here, you're better off having your own transport: there is only a Sunday bus service between Clitheroe and the rest of the valley villages.

ISLE OF MAN

Deliberately different and not-so-ferociously independent, the Isle of Man (Ellan Vannin in Manx, the local lingo) has doggedly held onto its semi-autonomous status (it is home to the world's oldest continuous parliament, the Tynwald) so as to continue doing its own thing, which really means operating as a popular tax haven.

The islanders' rejection of England's warm embrace has led to an oft-quoted prejudice that there's something odd about them, but the only thing that's odd here is the local tailless cat.

Crass commercialism and mass tourism have no place here, except of course for the world-famous summer season of Tourist Trophy (TT) motorbike racing, which attracts around 50,000 punters and bike freaks every May and June, bringing noise and mayhem to the otherwise lush valleys, barren hills and rugged coastlines of this beautiful island. Needless to say, if you want a slice of silence, be sure to avoid the high-rev bike fest.

🏃 Activities

With plenty of great marked trails, the Isle of Man is a firm favourite with walkers and is regularly voted one of the best walking destinations in Britain. Ordnance Survey (OS) Landranger Map 95 (£6.99) covers the whole island, while the free *Walks on the Isle of Man* is available from the tourist office in Douglas. The Millennium Way is a walking path that runs the length of the island amid some spectacular scenery. The most demanding of all the island's walks is the 95-mile Raad ny Foillan (Road of the Gull), a well-marked path that makes a complete circuit of the island and normally takes about five days to complete. The Isle of Man Walking Festival (www.iomevents.com; ☺mid-May) takes place over five days in May.

The island has six designated off-road mountain-biking trails, each with varying ranges of difficulty. See www.visitisleofman.com for details.

ℹ Information

Most of the island's historic sites are operated by Manx Heritage, which offers free admission for National Trust or English Heritage members. Unless otherwise indicated, **Manx Heritage** (www.manxnationalheritage.im) sites are open 10am to 5pm daily, from Easter to October. The Manx Heritage **Holiday Pass** (www.manxheritageshop.com; adult/child £20/10) grants you entry to all nine of the island's heritage attractions; pick it up at any of the tourist offices or online.

You can also check out www.iomevents.com for listings of what's on in the Isle of Man, along with accommodation and other tourist information.

ℹ Getting There & Away

AIR
Ronaldsway Airport (www.iom-airport.com) is 10 miles south of Douglas near Castletown. Airlines that service the region:

Aer Lingus Regional (www.aerlingus.com; from £75) From Dublin.

Citywing (www.citywing.com; from £50) From Belfast, Blackpool, Leeds-Bradford, Gloucester M5, Newcastle and East Midlands.

EasyJet (www.easyjet.com; from £59) From Liverpool and London Gatwick.

Flybe (www.flybe.com; from £21) From Birmingham, Bristol, Jersey, London Gatwick, Luton, Liverpool, Manchester, Glasgow and Edinburgh.

BOAT
Isle of Man Steam Packet (www.steampacket.com; foot passenger single/return £22/40, car & 2 passengers return from £115) Isle of Man Steam Packet is a car ferry and high-speed catamaran service from Liverpool and Heysham to Douglas. There is also a summer service (mid-April to mid-September) to Dublin (three hours) and Belfast (three hours). It's usually cheaper to buy a return ticket than to pay the single fare.

ℹ Getting Around

Buses link the airport with Douglas every 30 minutes between 7am and 11pm; a taxi should cost you no more than £18.

The island has a comprehensive **bus service** (www.gov.im); the tourist office in Douglas has timetables and sells tickets. It also sells the **Island Explorer** (1-day adult/child £16/8, 3-day £32/16), which gives you unlimited public transport use, including the tram to Snaefell and Douglas' horse-trams.

Bikes can be hired from **Eurocycles** (www.eurocycles.co.im; 8 Victoria Rd; per day £14-20; ☺9am-5.30pm Mon-Sat).

Petrolheads will love the scenic, sweeping bends that make for some exciting driving – and the fact that outside of Douglas town there's no speed limit. Naturally, the most popular drive is along the TT route. Car-hire operators have desks at the airport, and charge from around £38 per day.

The 19th-century electric and steam **rail services** (☎01624-663366; www.iombusandrail.info; ☺Mar-Oct) are a thoroughly satisfying way of getting from A to B:

Douglas–Castletown–Port Erin Steam Train (return £10.80)

Douglas–Laxey–Ramsey Electric Tramway (return £10.80)

Laxey–Summit Snaefell Mountain Railway (return £10.80)

Douglas

POP 28.940

Much like Blackpool across the water, Douglas' heyday was in the middle of the 19th century, when it was a favourite destination for Victorian mass tourism. It's not nearly as popular – or as pretty – today, but it still has the best of the island's hotels and restaurants – as well as the bulk of the finance houses that are frequented so regularly by tax-allergic Brits.

The **Manx Museum** (www.gov.im/mnh; Kingswood Grove; ⊙10am-5pm Mon-Sat) **FREE** gives an introduction to everything from the island's prehistoric past to the latest TT race winners.

🛏 Sleeping

The seafront promenade is crammed with B&Bs. Unless you booked back at the beginning of the millennium, however, there's little chance of finding accommodation during TT week and the weeks either side of it. The tourist office's camping information sheet lists sites all around the island.

Sefton Hotel   HOTEL **££**
(✆01624-645500; www.seftonhotel.co.im; Harris Promenade; r from £70; P🛜) Douglas' best hotel is an upmarket oasis with its own indoor water garden and rooms that range from plain and comfy to elegant and very luxurious. The rooms overlooking the water garden are superb, even better than the ones with sea views. Save up to 10% by booking online.

Admiral House   B&B **££**
(✆01624-629551; www.admiralhouse.com; Loch Promenade; s/d from £60/75; P🛜) This elegant guesthouse overlooks the harbour near the ferry port. The 23 spotless and modern rooms are a cheerful alternative to the worn look of a lot of other seafront B&Bs.

Palace Hotel   HOTEL **££**
(✆01624-662662; www.palacehotel.co.im; Central Promenade; r from £75; P@🛜) Tidy, modern rooms, a small gym and a casino – a Best Western hotel that takes care of your every need.

✗ Eating & Drinking

There are a few good drinking spots around, including **Bar George** (www.bargeorge.im; St George's Chambers, 3 Hill St), an elegant option for a glass of wine, and **Rover's Return** (11 Church St), which specialises in the local brew, Bushy Ales.

14North   MEDITERRANEAN **££**
(✆01624-664414; www.14north.im; mains £14-21; ⊙noon-2.30pm & 6-9.30pm Mon-Sat) An old timber merchant's house is now home to this smart eatery serving North African–style flatbreads (basically gourmet pizzas with a variety of toppings) and a selection of fish and meat dishes.

Tanroagan   SEAFOOD **£££**
(✆01624-472411; www.tanroagan.co.uk; 9 Ridgeway St; mains £19-31; ⊙noon-2pm & 6.30-9.30pm Mon-Sat) The place for all things from the sea, this elegant eatery is Douglas' smartest. It serves fresh fish straight off the boats, giving them the merest of Continental twists or just a spell on the hot grill. Reservations are recommended.

❶ Information

Tourist Office (✆01624-686766; www.visitisleofman.com; Sea Terminal Bldg; ⊙9.15am-7pm May-Sep, closed Sun Oct-Apr) Makes free accommodation bookings.

Around Douglas

You can follow the TT circuit up and over the mountain or wind around the coast. The mountain route goes close to the summit of **Snaefell** (621m), the island's highest point. It's an easy walk up to the summit, or take the electric tram from Laxey, near the coast.

On the edge of Ramsey, on the north of the island, is the **Grove Museum of Victorian Life** (MH; Andreas Rd; admission £5; ⊙10am-5pm Apr-Oct), where you can see the summer home of a well-to-do family preserved in aspic – and learn what it was like to be a scullery maid! The church in the small village of **Maughold** is on the site of an ancient monastery; a small shelter houses quite a good selection of stone crosses and ancient inscriptions.

It's no exaggeration to describe the **Lady Isabella Laxey Wheel** (MH; Mines Rd, Laxey; admission £5; ⊙10am-5pm Apr-Oct), built in 1854 to pump water from a mine, as a 'great' wheel: it measures 22m across and can draw 1140L of water per minute from a depth of 550m. The largest wheel of its kind in the world, it's named after the wife of the then lieutenant-governor.

The wheel-headed cross at Lonan Old Church, just north of Douglas, is the island's most impressive early Christian cross.

Castletown & Around

At the southern end of the island is Castletown, a quiet harbour town that was originally the capital of the Isle of Man. The town is dominated by the impressive 13th-century Castle Rushen (MH; Castletown Sq; admission £6; ⊙ 10am-5pm Apr-Oct). The flag tower affords fine views of the town and coast. There's also a small Nautical Museum (MH; Bridge St; admission £5; ⊙ 10am-5pm Easter-Oct) displaying, among other things, its pride and joy, *Peggy*, a boat built in 1791 and still housed in its original boathouse. There is a school dating back to 1570 in St Mary's Church (MH; ⊙ 10am-5pm Mar-Nov) FREE, behind the castle.

The Garrison Tapas Bar (www.thegarrison.co.im; 5 Castle St; tapas £7-8; ⊙ 10am-4pm Mon, to 9pm Tue-Sat) brings Iberian flavour to a handsome 17th-century building in the town centre. The paella is fantastic and huge, so is best shared.

Between Castletown and Cregneash, the Iron Age hill fort at Chapel Hill encloses a Viking ship burial site.

On the southern tip of the island, the Cregneash Village Folk Museum (MH; admission £5; ⊙ 10am-5pm Apr-Oct) recalls traditional Manx rural life. The Calf of Man, the small island just off Cregneash, is a bird sanctuary. Calf Island Cruises (☑ 01624-832339; adult/child £14/7; ⊙ 10.15am, 11.30am & 1.30pm Apr-Oct, weather permitting) run between Port Erin and the island.

Port Erin & Port St Mary

Port Erin, another Victorian seaside resort, plays host to the small Railway Museum (Station Rd; adult/child £2/1; ⊙ 10am-5pm Apr-Oct), which reveals the history of steam railway on the island.

Port Erin has a good range of accommodation, as does Port St Mary, across the headland and linked by steam train. The Victorian Falcon's Nest Hotel (☑ 01624-834077; www.falconsnesthotel.co.uk; Station Rd, Port Erin; d from £80; ⊛), once supremely elegant, is now just handsome in a nostalgic sort of way. The rooms aren't noteworthy, but the views over the water are superb. The slightly more splendid Victorian-style Aaron House (☑ 01624-835702; www.aaronhouse.co.uk; The Promenade, Port St Mary; s/d from £38/70) is a B&B that has fussed over every detail, from the gorgeous brass beds and claw-foot baths to the old-fashioned photographs on the walls. The sea views are also sensational.

Peel & Around

The west coast's most appealing town has a fine sandy beach, but its real attraction is the 11th-century Peel Castle (MH; admission £5; ⊙ 10am-5pm Apr-Oct), stunningly positioned atop St Patrick's Island and joined to Peel by a causeway.

The House of Manannan (MH; admission £6; ⊙ 10am-5pm Apr-Oct) museum uses interactive displays to explain Manx history and its seafaring traditions.

Three miles east of Peel is Tynwald Hill at St John's, where the annual parliamentary ceremony takes place on 5 July.

Peel has several B&Bs, including the Fernleigh Hotel (☑ 01624-842435; www.isleofman-bedandbreakfast.com; Marine Pde; d from £72; ⊙ Feb-Nov), which has 12 decent bedrooms. For a better-than-average bite, head for the Creek Inn (☑ 01624-842216; www.thecreekinn.co.uk; East Quay; mains around £8, r from £35; ⊙ 10am-11pm), opposite the House of Manannan, which serves Manx queenies (scallops served with white cheese sauce).

The Lake District & Cumbria

Best Traditional Inns

➜ Drunken Duck (p605)

➜ Wasdale Head Inn (p609)

➜ Pheasant Inn (p612)

➜ Mortal Man (p598)

➜ Kirkstile Inn (p615)

Best Beauty Spots

➜ Wasdale (p608)

➜ Tarn Hows (p604)

➜ Great Langdale (p607)

➜ Buttermere (p615)

➜ Derwentwater (p611)

Why Go?

'No part of the country is more distinguished by its sublimity', mused the grand old bard of the lakes, William Wordsworth, and a couple of centuries on his words still ring true. In terms of natural splendour, nowhere in England can compare to the Lake District. For centuries, poets, painters and perambulators alike have been flocking here in search of inspiration and escape, and it's still the nation's favourite place to revel in the majesty of the English landscape.

The main draw here is undoubtedly the Lake District National Park – England's largest, at 885 sq miles. Every bend in the road reveals more eye-popping views: deep valleys, plunging passes, glittering lakes, whitewashed inns, barren hills. But it's worth exploring beyond the national park's boundaries too: the old towns of Carlisle, Kendal and Penrith are full of historical interest, and Cumbria's coast has a windswept charm all of its own.

When to Go

➜ The Lake District is the UK's most popular national park; visit in early spring and late autumn for the fewest crowds. Its weather is also notoriously fickle – showers can strike at any time of year, so bring wet-weather gear just in case.

➜ Cumbria's largest mountain festival is held in Keswick in mid-May, while the Beer Festival in June welcomes ale aficionados from across the globe.

➜ Ambleside's traditional sports day on the last Saturday in July features events such as hound trailing and Cumbrian wrestling; Grasmere's annual sports day takes place on the August Bank Holiday.

➜ In November, the world's greatest liars congregate on Santon Bridge for their annual fibbing contest.

History

Neolithic settlers arrived in the Lake District around 5000 BC. The region was subsequently occupied by Celts, Angles, Vikings and Romans, and during the Dark Ages marked the centre of the ancient kingdom of Rheged.

During the Middle Ages, Cumbria marked the start of the 'Debatable Lands', the wild frontier between England and Scotland. Bands of raiders known as Border Reivers regularly plundered the area, prompting the construction of defensive *pele* towers and castles at Carlisle, Penrith and Kendal.

The area became a centre for the Romantic movement during the 19th century, largely thanks to the Cumbrian-born poet William Wordsworth, who also championed the need to protect the Lake District's landscape from overdevelopment – a dream that was achieved in 1951, when the Lake District National Park was formed.

The present-day county of Cumbria was formed from the neighbouring districts of Cumberland and Westmorland in 1974.

Activities

Cycling

Cycling is a great way to explore the Lake District and Cumbria, as long as you don't mind the hills. For short mountain-bike rides, the trails of Grizedale Forest (p604) and Whinlatter Forest Park (p610) are very popular.

Long-distance touring routes include the 70-mile Cumbria Way between Ulverston, Keswick and Carlisle; the 140-mile Sea To Sea Cycle Route (C2C; NCN 7; www.c2c-guide.co.uk), which begins in Whitehaven and cuts east across the northern Pennines to Newcastle; and the 173-mile Reivers Route (NCN 10; www.reivers-route.co.uk) from the River Tyne to Whitehaven.

Several local buses (including bus 599 from Bowness to Grasmere, bus X33 from Ambleside to Ravenglass and the Cross Lakes Experience) have space for bikes. There's also the new summer-only bus 800 along Windermere's eastern shore, which can carry 12 bikes. It runs several times a day in July and August, plus on weekends in May and June. You pay the standard bus fare plus £1.50 for each bike. For more information see www.golakes.co.uk/travel/New-Bike-Bus.aspx.

Walking

For many people, hiking is the main reason for a visit to the Lake District. All tourist offic-

es and bookshops sell maps and guidebooks, such as Collins' *Lakeland Fellranger* and Ordnance Survey's *Pathfinder Guides*. Purists prefer Alfred Wainwright's seven-volume *Pictorial Guides to the Lakeland Fells* (1955–66) – part walking guides, part illustrated artworks, part philosophical memoirs, with painstakingly hand-penned maps and text.

Maps are essential: the Ordnance Survey's 1:25,000 *Landranger* maps are used by most official bodies, while some hikers prefer the Harvey *Superwalker* 1:25,000 maps.

Long-distance trails which pass through Cumbria include the 54-mile Allerdale Ramble from Seathwaite to the Solway Firth, the 70-mile Cumbria Way from Ulverston to Carlisle and the 191-mile Coast to Coast from St Bees to Robin Hood's Bay in Yorkshire. Door-to-door baggage services such as Coast to Coast Packhorse (017683-71777; www.c2cpackhorse.co.uk) or Sherpa Van (0871 520-0124; www.sherpavan.com) transport luggage from one destination to the next.

Other Activities

Cumbria is a haven for outdoor activities, including rock climbing, orienteering, horse riding, archery, fell (mountain) running and *ghyll* (waterfall) scrambling. Contact the Holmescales Activity Centre (01539-722147; www.holmescales.com; Old Hutton, Kendal), Rookin House (017684-83561; www.rookinhouse.co.uk; Troutbeck) or Keswick Adventure Centre (017687-75687; www.keswickadventurecentre.co.uk; Newlands).

Getting There & Away

Carlisle is on the main West Coast train line from London Euston to Manchester and Glasgow. To get to the Lake District, you need to change at Oxenholme for Kendal and Windermere. The lines around the Cumbrian coast and between Settle and Carlisle are particularly scenic.

National Express coaches run direct from London Victoria and Glasgow to Windermere, Carlisle and Kendal.

Getting Around

Traveline (0871 200 22 33; www.traveline-northeast.info) provides comprehensive travel information. Bus timetables are available from tourist offices.

There are round-the-lake ferry services on Windermere, Coniston Water, Ullswater and Derwentwater. Windermere also has a ferry service (p597).

Traffic can be heavy during peak season and holiday weekends. Many Cumbrian towns use

The Lake District & Cumbria Highlights

1 Conquering England's highest mountain, **Scafell Pike** (p608)

2 Spotting the inspirations for Beatrix Potter's tales at **Hill Top** (p604)

3 Cruising Coniston Water aboard the **Steam Yacht Gondola** (p606)

4 Cycling the trails of **Grizedale Forest** (p604)

5 Delving into the slate mines of **Honister Pass** (p615)

6 Catching the miniature steam trains of **La'al Ratty** (p620) into Eskdale

7 Visiting Wordsworth's houses, **Dove Cottage** (p602) and **Rydal Mount** (p599)

8 Patrolling the battlements of **Carlisle Castle** (p620)

9 Sampling world-famous gingerbread at **Sarah Nelson's shop** (p603) in Grasmere

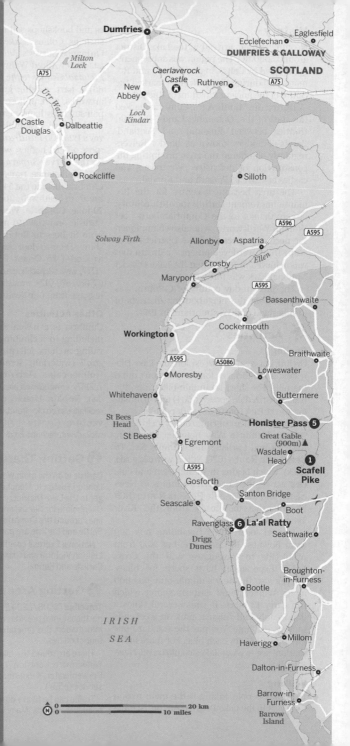

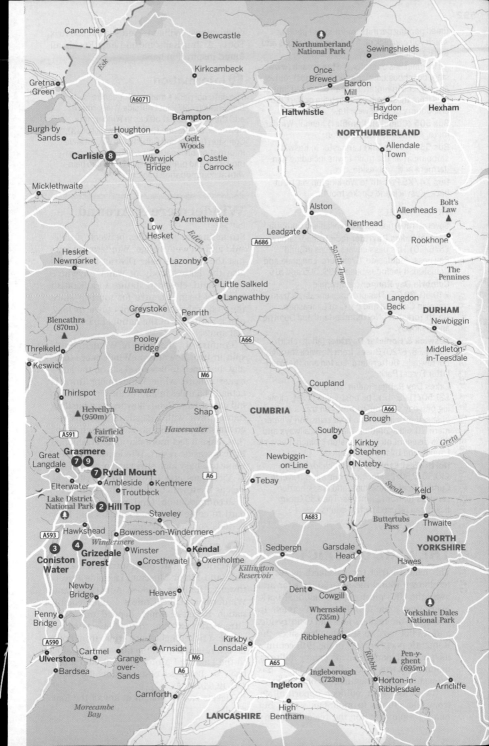

timed parking permits for on-street parking, which you can pick up free from local shops and tourist offices.

The main bus operator is **Stagecoach** (www.stagecoachbus.com). Services on most routes are reduced in winter. You can download timetables from the Stagecoach website or the Cumbria County Council website.

Bus 505 (Coniston Rambler) Kendal, Windermere, Ambleside and Coniston.

Bus 555 (Lakeslink) Lancaster to Keswick, stopping at all the main towns including Windermere and Ambleside.

Bus X4/X5 Penrith to Workington via Troutbeck, Keswick and Cockermouth.

TRAVEL PASSES

Several travel passes are available in Cumbria.

Central Lakes Dayrider (adult/child/family £8/6/20) This pass covers buses around Bowness, Ambleside, Grasmere, Langdale and Coniston; it includes buses 599, 505 and 516.

Cumbria Day Ranger (adult/child £40.50/20.25) This provides one day's train travel in Cumbria and parts of Lancashire, North Yorkshire, Northumberland and Dumfries and Galloway.

Keswick & Honister Dayrider (adult/child/family £8/6/20) Buses from Keswick through Borrowdale, Buttermere, Lorton and the Whinlatter Forest Park.

Lakes Day Ranger (adult/child/family £21.50/11.75/42) The best-value ticket, allowing one day's unlimited travel on trains and buses. It also includes a boat cruise on Windermere, 10% discount on the steam railways and 20% discount on the Coniston Launch, Keswick Launch and Ullswater Steamers.

North West Explorer (adult/child/family £10.50/7.50/25) Includes one day's travel in Cumbria and Lancashire, and cross-border services to/from Dumfries. The £30 Group ticket can be used by five adults.

THE LAKE DISTRICT

The Lake District (or Lakeland, as it's often known round these parts) is by far and away the UK's most popular national park. Every year, some 15 million people pitch up to explore the region's fells and countryside, and it's not hard to see why. Ever since the Romantic poets arrived in the 19th century, its postcard panorama of craggy hilltops, mountain tarns and glittering lakes has been stirring the imaginations of visitors.

It's awash with outdoor opportunities, from lake cruises to mountain walks, but many people visit for the region's literary connections; William Wordsworth, Beatrix Potter, Arthur Ransome and John Ruskin all found inspiration here.

ⓘ Information

The national park's main visitor centre is at Brockhole (p597), just outside Windermere, and there are tourist offices in Windermere, Bowness, Ambleside (p601), Keswick (p613), Coniston (p607) and Carlisle (p622). All have information on local sights, activities, accommodation and public transport, and can help with accommodation bookings.

Windermere & Around

POP 5423

Stretching for 10.5 miles between Ambleside and Newby Bridge, Windermere isn't just the queen of Lake District lakes – it's also the largest body of water anywhere in England, closer in stature to a Scottish loch. It's been a centre for tourism since the first trains chugged into town in 1847, and it's still one of the national park's busiest spots.

Confusingly, the town of Windermere is split in two: Bowness-on-Windermere (usually shortened to Bowness) sits on the lake's eastern shore, while Windermere Town is actually 1.5 miles inland, at the top of a steep hill called Lake Road. Bowness is a bustling tourist town, with a gaggle of teashops, ice-cream stalls, restaurants and souvenir shops that make it feel more like an old-fashioned British seaside resort. Windermere Town is home to a busy high street and orderly ranks of Victorian- and Edwardian-era villas, as well as the town's bus and train stations.

Accommodation (and parking) can be hard to come by during holidays and busy periods, so plan accordingly.

⊙ Sights

Windermere's four main attractions – the Lakeland Motor Museum, Lakeside Haverthwaite Railway, Lakes Aquarium and Windermere Lake Cruises – offer combination tickets. Savings depend on which attractions you want to combine: as an example, a ticket including a cruise from Bowness, a return trip on the railway, admission to the Lakeland Motor Museum and a bus back to Bowness costs adult/child/family £21/12.65/58.35.

Tickets can be bought at any of the four sights.

Lake District

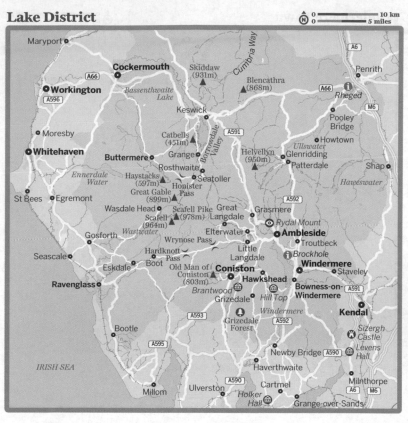

World of Beatrix Potter   MUSEUM
(www.hop-skip-jump.com; Crag Brow, Bowness-on-Windermere; adult/child £6.95/3.65; ⊙10am-5.30pm Apr-Sep, to 4.30pm Oct-Mar) This themed attraction brings to life various scenes from Beatrix Potter's books, including Peter Rabbit's garden, Mr McGregor's greenhouse, Mrs Tiggywinkle's kitchen, Jemima Puddle-Duck's glade (there's even a themed tearoom). It's squarely aimed at kids, but adult Potter fans might enjoy indulging their inner child. Be prepared for queues (and lots of Japanese tourists) during holiday times.

Blackwell House   HISTORIC BUILDING
(www.blackwell.org.uk; adult/child under 16yr £7.25/free; ⊙10.30am-5pm Apr-Oct, to 4pm Feb-Mar, Nov & Dec) Two miles south of Bowness on the B5360, Blackwell House is a glorious example of the 19th-century Arts and Crafts Movement, which championed the importance of handmade goods and craftsman-

ship over the mass-produced mentality of the Industrial Revolution.

Designed by Mackay Hugh Baillie Scott for a wealthy brewer, the house has many hallmarks of Arts and Crafts design: light, airy rooms, detailed decor and bespoke craftwork (including wood panelling, stained glass and Delft tiles).

Of note are the huge wood-panelled Great Hall and the serene White Drawing Room. The cafe has brilliant views over Windermere.

Fell Foot Park   GARDENS
(NT; www.nationaltrust.org.uk/fell-foot-park; ⊙8am-8pm Apr-Sep, 9am-5pm Oct-Mar) **FREE** Located at the southern end of Windermere, 7 miles south of Bowness, this 7-hectare lakeside estate originally belonged to a manor house. It's now owned by the National Trust, and its shoreline paths and grassy lawns are ideal for a sunny-day picnic. The small cafe is open 10am to 5pm, and rowing boats are available for hire.

Windermere Town

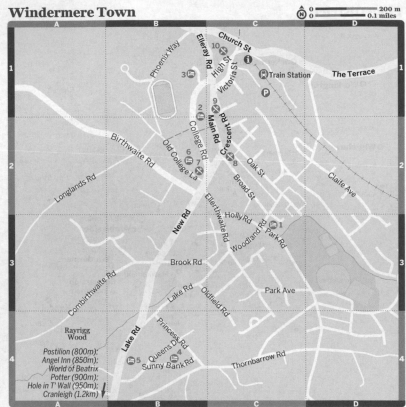

Windermere Town

🛏 Sleeping
1 1 Park Road	C3
2 Archway	B1
3 Lake District Backpackers Lodge	B1
4 Rum Doodle	B4
5 The Boundary	B4
6 Wheatlands Lodge	B2

🍴 Eating
7 Hooked	B2
8 Lazy Daisy's Lakeland Kitchen	C2
9 Lighthouse	C1
10 Mojo's Bistro	C1

Lakes Aquarium   AQUARIUM
(☎ 015395-30153; www.lakesaquarium.co.uk; Lakeside; adult/child £6.95/4.95; ⏰ 9am-6pm Apr-Oct) At the southern end of the lake near Newby Bridge, this aquarium explores a range of underwater habitats from tropical Africa through to Morecambe Bay. Windermere Lake Cruises and the Lakeside & Haverthwaite Railway stop right beside the aquarium, or you could catch bus 618 from Bowness. Discounts for tickets purchased online.

Lakeland Motor Museum   MUSEUM
(www.lakelandmotormuseum.co.uk; Backbarrow; adult/child £8/5; ⏰ 9.30am-5.30pm Apr-Sep, to 4.30pm Oct-Mar) In a purpose-built new home 2 miles south of Newby Bridge, this car museum houses a wonderful collection of antique cars: classic (Minis, Austin Healeys, MGs), sporty (DeLoreans, Audi Quattros, Aston Martins) and plain odd (Scootacars, Amphicars).

The museum is on the A590 from Newby Bridge towards Kendal. Bus X35 (hourly Monday to Saturday, three on Sunday) from Newby Bridge to Ulverston and Kendal stops nearby.

A separate building explores Donald and Malcolm Campbell's record attempts on

Coniston Water, with replicas of the 1935 Bluebird car and 1967 boat, *Bluebird K7*.

Lakeside & Haverthwaite Railway
HERITAGE RAILWAY

(☑ 015395-31594; www.lakesiderailway.co.uk; adult/child/family return £6.50/3.25/18; ☺ mid-Mar–Oct) Originally built to carry ore and timber to the ports at Ulverston and Barrow, these vintage steam trains puff their way between Haverthwaite, near Ulverston, to Newby Bridge and Lakeside. There are five to seven trains a day, timed to correspond with the Windermere cruise boats.

🏃 Activities

Windermere Lake Cruises
BOATING

(☑ 015395-31188; www.windermere-lakecruises.co.uk; tickets from £2.70) Since the launch of the first passenger ferry in 1845, cruising has been an essential part of every Windermere itinerary. Some of the vessels are modern, but there are a couple of period beauties dating back to the 1930s. All cruises allow you to disembark as you please and catch a later ferry back.

There are various colour-coded cruise options available. The **Freedom of the Lake** ticket (adult/child/family £18.50/9.25/50) remains valid all day, and allows unlimited travel on all routes.

The **Blue Cruise** (adult/child/family £7.50/3.80/20) is a 45-minute circular cruise around Windermere's shoreline and islands. The north-lake **Red Cruise** (adult/child/family £10/6/29) goes from Bowness to Ambleside, while the south-lake **Yellow Cruise** (adult/child/family £10.50/6.30/30) heads down to Lakeside and the Lakes Aquarium. Running in summer only, the **Green Cruise** (adult/child/family £7.50/3.80/20) takes in Waterhead/Ambleside via Wray Castle and Brockhole Visitor Centre. For a cross-lake dash, the **Bowness to Ferry House** (adult/child/family £2.70/1.60/7.60) service links up with buses to Hill Top and Hawkshead. Seasonal twilight cruises are also available.

If you're visiting other attractions such as the Lakeland Motor Museum and the Lakes Aquarium, look out for combination tickets; see p597.

🛏 Sleeping

Windermere's popularity means accommodation is pricier than elsewhere.

Archway
B&B £

(☑ 015394-45613; www.the-archway.com; 13 College Rd, Windermere Town; d £50-86) Value is the name of the game here: this place is a no-nonsense, old-fashioned, home-away-from-home. Some of the rooms have fell views, and the breakfast is enormous, but there's no parking.

Lake District Backpackers Lodge
HOSTEL £

(☑ 015394-46374; www.lakedistrictbackpackers.co.uk; High St, Windermere Town; dm £16, r £36; @) Not the fanciest hostel in the Lake District, but these Windermere digs are about the only option in town for backpackers. There are two small four-bed dorms, plus two private rooms with a double bed and a single bed above.

Boundary
B&B ££

(☑ 015394-48978; www.theboundaryonline.co.uk; Lake Rd, Windermere Town; d £100-191; P 🤶) Not the cheapest sleep in Windermere, but definitely one of the swishest. Owners Steve and Helen have given this Victorian house a sleek, boutique makeover: chic decor, monochrome colours, retro furniture and all. Steve's a cricket obsessive, so all the rooms are named after famous batsmen.

Rum Doodle
B&B ££

(☑ 015394-45967; www.rumdoodlewindermere.com; Sunny Bank Rd, Windermere Town; d £85-119; P 🤶) Forget boutique B&B: this little place is all about quirky English style. Each of the nine rooms is named after an explorer with corresponding decorative twist: Jungle has old suitcases and giant map, Wish has a four-poster and faux-bookcase wallpaper, while Summit and Burley hunker under attic eaves. There's a two-night minimum in summer.

Wheatlands Lodge
B&B ££

(☑ 015394-43789; www.wheatlandslodge-windermere.co.uk; Old College Lane; d £80-170; P 🤶)

WORTH A TRIP

WRAY CASTLE & CLAIFE HEIGHTS

Windermere's quieter west side is a good place to escape the crowds. North of the ferry landings at Ferry House, a network of woodland paths winds across **Claife Heights**, while the nearby National Trust–owned estate of **Wray Castle** (NT; www.nationaltrust.org.uk/wray-castle; adult/child £7.20/3.60; ☺ 10am-5pm) encompasses 25 hectares of lakeside grounds and a turreted 19th-century mansion, once used as a holiday home by Beatrix Potter's family.

DON'T MISS

WINDERMERE & THE ISLANDS

Like many places in Cumbria, Windermere gets its name from the old Norse, Vinandr mere, or Vinandr's lake (so Lake Windermere is actually a tautology). Encompassing 5.7 sq miles between Ambleside and Newby Bridge, the lake is a mile wide at its broadest point, with a maximum depth of about 220m.

The lake's shoreline is owned by a combination of private landholders, the National Park Authority and the National Trust, but the lake bed itself (and thus the lake itself) officially belongs to the people of Windermere (local philanthropist Henry Leigh Groves purchased it on their behalf in 1938).

There are 18 islands on Windermere: the largest is Belle Isle, encompassing 16 hectares and an 18th-century Italianate mansion, while the smallest is Maiden Holme, little more than a patch of soil and a solitary tree.

From April to October, rowing boats can be hired for £12. Motorboats cost from £18 to £22 for two adults per hour; children under 16 go free. There's a 10mph speed limit.

Between Bowness and Windermere, this detached house looks Victorian, but the eight rooms are nice and modern. They're split into three categories (Comfortable, Deluxe and Master); extra money buys more space and luxury spa baths. Breakfast is a high point, with homemade muesli, local bacon and sausages, plus smoked salmon from Loch Ewe.

1 Park Road　　　　　　　B&B ££
(www.1parkroad.com; 1 Park Rd, Windermere Town; d £76-104; P 🌐) It's the little treats that keep this cosy guesthouse a cut above: bath goodies from Pure Lakes and The White Company, iPod docks in every room, and home-made baked beans and marmalade for breakfast. Rooms are comfortable, and the rates stay reasonable year-round – a rarity in Windermere.

Cranleigh　　　　　　　HOTEL ££
(☏ 015394-43293; www.thecranleigh.com; Kendal Rd, Bowness-on-Windermere; d £109-189, ste £220-425; P 🌐) This guesthouse has gone all-out on the decor, but strip away the snazziness and it's still just a B&B. It's worth bumping up to the Superior for the spacious bathrooms, or maybe blowing the budget on one of the two over-the-top suites (check out the Sanctuary, complete with Bose stereo, glass bath and picture-fireplace).

Samling　　　　　　　HOTEL £££
(☏ 015394-31922; www.thesamlinghotel.co.uk; Ambleside Rd; r £220-670) If money's no object, this deluxe country house is the choice. The chic rooms and cottages are classically styled, and feature luxury touches such as split-level mezzanines, rain showers and private lounges. Its restaurant has recently scooped a Michelin star, too. Early bookings score a substantial

discount. The hotel is 3 miles northwest of Windermere Town, off the A591.

🍴 Eating

Lazy Daisy's Lakeland Kitchen　　CAFE £
(☏ 015394-43877; 31-33 Crescent Rd, Windermere Town; lunch £4-10, dinner £10-16; ⊙ 10am-9pm Mon-Sat) Filling comfort food is the order of the day at this trad cafe: the cakes and giant Yorkshire puddings are a highlight.

Lighthouse　　　　　　　CAFE £
(Main Rd, Windermere Town; mains £8-15; ⊙ 8.30am-5.30pm) This three-storey cafe downhill from the train station offers a continental-style menu, quality coffee and freshly baked pastries.

Hooked　　　　　　　SEAFOOD ££
(☏ 015394-48443; www.hookedwindermere.co.uk; Ellerthwaite Sq, Windermere Town; mains £16.95-19.95; ⊙ 5.30-10.30pm Tue-Sun) This seafood restaurant in Windermere Town has a loyal following. Fish arrives daily from the Fleetwood docks, and chef Paul White dabbles in everything from fish classics to fusion concoctions: *moules marinières* (mussels in white wine) to start, perhaps, then a whole Thai-spiced sea bass or king scallops with pea purée and black pudding. The only drawback is the limited space: bookings essential.

Brown Horse Inn　　　　　PUB ££
(☏ 015394-43443; www.thebrownhorseinn.co.uk; Winster; mains £11.95-17.95; ⊙ lunch noon-2pm, dinner 6-9pm) Three miles from Windermere in Winster, the Brown Horse is one of Windermere's top dining pubs. Produce is sourced from the Brown Horse Estate, furnishing the chefs with meat and game such as venison, spring lamb and roast pigeon. Beams and

fireplaces conjure rustic atmosphere, and there are two home-brewed ales on tap (Old School and Best Bitter). Worth the drive.

Watermill   PUB ££
(☑ 01539-821309; www.watermillinn.co.uk; Ings; mains £12-20; ☺ 11am-11pm Mon-Sat, to 10.30pm Sun) Two miles from Windermere in Ings, this resolutely traditional inn is exactly what you'd expect from a Cumbrian pub – beamed ceilings, whitewashed walls, log fires, hand-pumps and all. Throw in good food and a choice of 16 ales – including home-brewed Collie Wobbles – and it's no wonder it's scooped lots of local awards.

Mason's Arms   PUB ££
(☑ 015395-68486; www.masonsarmsstrawberry bank.co.uk; Winster; mains £13-20) Three miles east of the lake near Bowlands Bridge, the marvellous Mason's Arms is a local secret. The rafters, flagstones and cast-iron range haven't changed in centuries, and the patio has to-die-for views across fields and fells. In short, a cracker.

Mojo's Bistro   BRITISH ££
(☑ 015394-449540; www.mojosbistro.co.uk; 4 High St, Windermere Town; 2-/3-course menu £13.95/ 17.95; ☺ 6-9pm Mon-Sat) Quality bistro-style food and a handy High St location make Mojo's a winner. The menu is largely old British classics: bangers-and-mash, beef-and-ale cobbler, chargrilled chicken with mushroom sauce.

Angel Inn   GASTROPUB ££
(☑ 015394-44080; www.the-angelinn.com; Helm Rd, Bowness-on-Windermere; mains £10.95-16.50; ☺ 11.30am-4pm & 5-9pm) Bowness' gastropub is on a hummock behind the shoreline. Settle into a sofa and order a sharing platter, or go upmarket with a paupiette of plaice. The front lawn is the spot when the sun shines.

Postilion   BISTRO ££
(☑ 015394-45852; www.postilionrestaurant.co.uk; Ash St, Bowness-on-Windermere; mains £12-16, set menu £18.95; ☺ 6-10pm) Reliable bistro tucked away off Ash St with a French-Mediterranean menu.

☕ Drinking & Nightlife

Hole in T' Wall   PUB
(Falbarrow Rd, Bowness-on-Windermere; ☺ 11am-11pm) Bowness' best-loved boozer is also the town's oldest, dating back to 1612, and offering lashings of rough-beamed, low-ceilinged atmosphere.

Hawkshead Brewery   BREWERY
(☑ 01539-822644; www.hawksheadbrewery.co.uk; Mill Yard, Staveley) This craft brewery has its own brewhall in Staveley, 3 miles east of Windermere. Core beers include Hawkshead Bitter, dark Brodie's Prime and fruity Red. Guided tours can be arranged in advance.

ℹ Information

Bowness Tourist Office (☑ 015394-42895; bownesstic@lake-district.gov.uk; Glebe Rd, Bowness-on-Windermere; ☺ 9.30am-5.30pm Easter-Oct, 10am-4pm Fri-Sun Nov-Easter) Beside the lake jetties.

Brockhole National Park Visitor Centre (☑ 015394-46601; www.lake-district.gov.uk; ☺ 10am-5pm Easter-Oct, to 4pm Nov-Easter) In a 19th-century mansion 3 miles north of Windermere on the A591, this is the Lake District's flagship visitor centre, and also has a teashop, an adventure playground and gardens.

Windermere Tourist Office (☑ 015394-46499; windermeretic@southlakeland.gov.uk; Victoria St, Windermere Town; ☺ 9am-5.30pm Mon-Sat, 9.30am-5.30pm Sun Apr-Oct, shorter hours winter) Opposite Natwest bank.

ℹ Getting There & Away

BOAT
The **Windermere Ferry** (car/bike/pedestrian £4.30/1/50p; ☺ 6.50am-9.50pm Mon-Fri, 9.10am-9.50pm Sat & Sun Mar-Oct, to 8.50pm

---

ℹ THE CROSS LAKES EXPERIENCE

The **Cross Lakes Experience** (http://www.lakedistrict.gov.uk/visiting/plan-yourvisit/travelandtransport/crosslakes; ☺ Apr-Nov) is a boat, bus and minibus service that enables car-free travel from Windermere to Coniston.

Tickets include travel on the Windermere Ferry from Bowness to Ferry House, from where buses run to Hill Top, Hawkshead, Grizedale and Coniston. For info, timetables and tickets, contact **Mountain Goat** (☑ 015394-45161; www.mountain-goat.com; Victoria Rd, Windermere) or local tourist offices. A return from Bowness to Coniston costs adult/child £20.20/11.90. Single fares for adult/child:

➡ Ferry House (£2.70/1.60)

➡ Hill Top (£5.65/3.25)

➡ Hawkshead (£6.70/3.70)

➡ Coniston (£12.05/6.85)

winter) carries vehicles and pedestrians from Ferry Nab, just south of Bowness, across to Ferry House on the lake's west side. There's a ferry roughly every 20 minutes, although queues can be horrendous in summer. You can also take lake cruises (p595).

BUS

There's one daily National Express coach from London (£31.50, eight hours) via Lancaster and Kendal.

Combo tickets include a day's bus travel and one boat journey: the Central Lakes version costs adult/child/family £12/8/32, or there's an Explorer version for £15/11/36.

Bus 505 Coniston Rambler (hourly including Sundays) Travels from Windermere to Coniston (£4, 50 minutes) via Troutbeck, Brockhole, Ambleside, Skelwith Fold, Hawkshead and Hawkshead Hill. Two buses a day serve Kendal.

Bus 555/556 Lakeslink (at least hourly including Sundays) Starts at the train station, stopping at Troutbeck Bridge (five minutes), Brockhole Visitor Centre (seven minutes), Ambleside (£6.30, 15 minutes), Grasmere (£6.80, 30 minutes) and Keswick (£8.55, one hour). In the opposite direction it continues to Kendal (£9.30, 25 minutes) and Lancaster (one hour 40 minutes).

Bus 599 Lakes Rider (£4 to £6, three times hourly including weekends) Open-top bus between Bowness, Troutbeck, Brockhole, Rydal Church (for Rydal Mount), Dove Cottage and Grasmere. Some buses stop at Windermere train station.

TRAIN

Windermere is the only town inside the national park accessible by train. It's on the branch line to Kendal and Oxenholme.

Edinburgh (£59.10, 2½ hours)
Glasgow (£51.50, 2¼ to 2¾ hours)
Kendal (£4.50, 15 minutes)
Lancaster (£13.50, 45 minutes)
London Euston (£99, 3½ hours)
Manchester Piccadilly (£22.70, 1½ hours)

Troutbeck

Nestled among the fells to the north of Windermere, on the road towards Kirkstone Pass, this rural hamlet feels a world away from the Bowness bustle, with wonderful views over Windermere.

◎ Sights

Townend   HISTORIC BUILDING
(NT; ☑01539-432628; www.nationaltrust.org.uk/townend; adult/child £5.25/2.60; ☺1-5pm Wed-Sun Mar-Oct, daily school holidays) The historic farmhouse at Townend contains a collection of vintage farming tools and furniture that belonged to the Browne family, who owned the house until 1943. Public visiting hours are from 1pm to 5pm, but you can join hourly guided tours from 11am to 1pm.

🛏 Sleeping & Eating

Windermere YHA   HOSTEL £
(☑0845 371 9352; www.yha.org.uk/hostel/windermere; Bridge Lane; dm £15, r £29; ☺reception 7.30-11.30am & 1-11pm; [P] [@]) Downhill from Troutbeck village is the Windermere YHA, the closest YHA to Windermere. The rooms are modern, and facilities include a well-stocked shop, canteen and gear-drying room. Buses stop about a mile downhill from the village, at the river crossing of Troutbeck Bridge.

★ **Mortal Man**   PUB ££
(☑015394-33193; www.themortalmaninn.co.uk; mains £8.95-14.95, r £85-130; [P] [🐾]) Troutbeck has a couple of excellent pubs; top of the heap is the 17th-century Mortal Man, which has a lovely beer garden offering panoramic fell and lake views.

❶ Getting There & Away

Bus 508 from Windermere costs £3.20.

Ambleside & Around

POP 2529

Once a busy mill and textile centre at Windermere's northern tip, Ambleside is an attractive little town, built from the same slate and stern grey stone that's so characteristic of the rest of Lakeland. Ringed by fells, it's a favourite base for hikers, with a cluster of outdoors shops and plenty of cosy pubs and cafes providing fuel for their adventures.

◎ Sights & Activities

Bridge House   HISTORIC BUILDING
The town's best-known landmark is Bridge House, a tiny cottage that spans the clattering brook of Stock Ghyll; now occupied by a National Trust shop, it's thought to have originally been built as an apple store.

Armitt Museum   MUSEUM
(www.armitt.com; Rydal Rd; adult £2.50; ☺10am-5pm) Ambleside's excellent little museum hosts some intriguing seasonal exhibitions alongside its core collection, populated with artefacts relating to important Lakeland

FIVE CLASSIC LAKELAND HIKES
....

The Lake District's most famous fell-walker, the accountant-turned-author Alfred Wainwright, recorded 214 official fells in his seven-volume *Pictorial Guides* (as if that weren't enough, he usually outlined at least two possible routes to the top, or in the case of Scafell Pike, five). If you only have limited time, here are five hikes which offer a flavour of what makes fell-walking in the Lake District so special.

Scafell Pike (978m) The daddy of Lakeland hikes, a six- to seven-hour slog to the top of England's highest peak. The classic route is from Wasdale Head.

Helvellyn (950m) Not for the faint-hearted; a vertiginous scramble along the knife-edge ridge of Striding Edge. It takes at least six hours starting from Glenridding or Patterdale.

Blencathra (868m) A mountain on its own, Blencathra offers a panoramic outlook on Keswick and the northern fells. Count on four hours from Threlkeld.

Haystacks (597m) Wainwright's favourite mountain, and the place where his ashes were scattered. It's a steep three-hour return hike from Buttermere village.

Catbells (451m) The fell for everyone, accessible to six-year-olds and septuagenarians. It's on the west side of Derwentwater, and takes a couple of hours to climb.

characters such as Beatrix Potter, National Trust founder Canon Hardwicke Rawnsley and pioneering photographers Herbert Bell and the Abraham Brothers. There are also original canvases by the modernist artist Kurt Schwitters, a German refugee who settled in Ambleside after WWII.

★**Rydal Mount** HISTORIC BUILDING
(www.rydalmount.co.uk; adult/child £7/3; ⊙ 9.30am-5pm Mar-Oct, 11am-4pm Wed-Mon Nov, Dec & Feb) The poet William Wordsworth's most famous residence in the Lake District is Dove Cottage, but he actually spent a great deal more time at Rydal Mount, a much grander house halfway between Ambleside and Grasmere. This was the Wordsworth family's home from 1813 until the poet's death in 1850, and the house contains a treasure trove of Wordsworth memorabilia. The house is 1.5 miles northwest of Ambleside, off the A591. Bus 555 (and bus 599 from April to October) stops at the end of the drive.

Downstairs you can wander around the library, dining room and drawing room (look out in the cabinets for William's pen, inkstand and picnic box, and a famous portrait of the poet by the American painter Henry Inman hanging above the fireplace). Upstairs are the family bedrooms and Wordsworth's attic study, containing his encyclopedia and a sword belonging to his brother John, who was lost in a shipwreck in 1805. Below the house is Dora's Field, which Wordsworth planted with daffodils in memory of his eldest daughter, who died from tuberculosis in 1847.

Stock Ghyll Force WALKING
Ambleside's most popular walk is the half-hour stroll up to the 18m waterfall of Stock Ghyll Force; the trail is signposted behind the old Market Hall at the bottom of Stock Ghyll Lane. If you feel energetic, you can follow the trail beyond the falls up **Wansfell Pike** (482m), a reasonably steep walk of about two hours.

Low Wood Watersports BOATING
(☑ 015394-39441; www.englishlakes.co.uk/watersports; Low Bay Marina) This water-sports centre offers water-skiing, sailing and kayaking, and also has rowboats and motorboats for hire.

🛏 Sleeping

Ambleside YHA HOSTEL £
(☑ 0845 371 9620; ambleside@yha.org.uk; Windermere Rd; dm £20-23; P 🛱) One of the YHA's flagship Lake District hostels, this huge lakeside house is a fave for activity holidays (everything from kayaking to *ghyll* scrambling). Great facilities (kitchen, bike rental, boat jetty and bar) mean it's heavily subscribed, so book well ahead. Families can book out dorms as private rooms. The hostel is halfway between Ambleside and Windermere on Lake Rd (the A591).

Ambleside Backpackers HOSTEL £
(☑ 015394-32340; www.amblesidehostel.co.uk; Old Lake Rd; dm £21-25; P @) Independent cottage hostel a short walk south from Ambleside's centre.

❶ NATIONAL TRUST CAMPSITE BOOKINGS

The National Trust has four fantastic campsites in the Lake District at Low Wray near Ambleside, Hoathwaite near Coniston, Wasdale and Great Langdale.

The centralised National Trust Lake District Campsite Bookings (☎01539-432733; www.nationaltrust.org. uk/holidays/camping/camping-in-the-lake-district; ⊙10am-3pm Mon-Fri) service handles reservations for all NT campsites in the Lake District. Bookings can be made up to 24 hours before arrival. There's a fee of £5 for booking online, or £7.50 by telephone and email, and stays must be for a minimum of two nights.

Low Wray CAMPSITE £
(NT; ☑bookings 015394-63862; www.ntlakescampsites.org.uk; 2 adults & tent £14.50-19, eco-pods £35-55; ⊙campsite arrivals 3-7pm Sat-Thu, to 9pm Fri Mar-Oct) Lakeside camping courtesy of the National Trust. It's 3 miles from town along the B5286, near the Wray Castle estate; bus 505 stops nearby. Yurts and tepees also available.

Regent Hotel HOTEL ££
(☑015394-32254; www.regentlakes.co.uk; Waterhead Bay; d £89-159; P☎) This attractive hotel has a near-the-lake location, but for once doesn't charge sky-high prices. The rooms offer different settings: some have balconies overlooking the garden, others have bunks for the kids or walk-in wet rooms, and a few sneak in views over Windermere. The top-floor Sail Loft has its own private deck terrace.

Lakes Lodge B&B ££
(☑015394-33240; www.lakeslodge.co.uk; Lake Rd; r £99-129; P☎) This modish mini-hotel offers a touch more luxury than Ambleside's other guesthouses. The 16 rooms are all about clean lines, stark walls and zero clutter, and most have a full-size wall mural featuring a local beauty spot. Some are in the main building, while others are in an attached annexe.

Gables B&B ££
(☑015394-33272; www.thegables-ambleside.co.uk; Church Walk; s £45-50, d £90-120; P☎) One of the best value of Ambleside's B&Bs, in a quiet spot overlooking the recreation ground. Spotty cushions and colourful prints keep things cheery, but room sizes are variable (in this instance, bigger is definitely better).

Guests receive discounts at the owner's restaurant, Sheila's Cottage.

Compston House Hotel B&B ££
(☑015392-32305; www.compstonhouse.co.uk; Compston Rd; s from £45, d from £65; ☎) Americans will feel at home here: the owners are expat New Yorkers, and each room is themed after a different state: sunny Hawaii, bright Florida, maritime Maine. Breakfast includes blueberry muffins and maple pancakes. There's a three-night minimum in season.

Waterhead Hotel HOTEL £££
(☑0845 850 4503; www.englishlakes.co.uk; r £135-215; P☎☎) Ambleside's main hotel has a super position beside the lakeshore. The exterior is classic Lakeland, all solid stone and bay windows, but inside it's very much a modern hotel, with spacious rooms stocked with heritage furniture and designer fabrics, and a sophisticated restaurant, the Mountain View.

Cote How B&B £££
(☑015394-32765; www.bedbreakfastlakedistrict. com; Rydal; d £150-180; P☎) ✿ In Rydal, 1.5 miles from Ambleside, this detached house is all about the good life. Food is 100% local and organic, power's sourced from an eco-supplier, and there's a discount for non-drivers. The three rooms are olde Edwardian, with cast-iron beds, roll-top baths and fireplaces (ex-president Woodrow Wilson once visited the Rydal Suite). Two-night minimum at weekends.

🍴 Eating

Zeffirelli's ITALIAN £
(☑015394-33845; www.zeffirellis.com; Compston Rd; pizzas & mains £8-12; ⊙11am-10pm) A beloved local landmark, Zeff's is often packed out for its quality pizza and pasta. The £19.75 Double Feature deal includes two courses and a ticket to the cinema next door.

Lucy 4 TAPAS £
(2 St Mary's Lane; tapas £4-10; ⊙5-10.30pm Mon-Fri, noon-10.30pm Sat & Sun) A cosy wine-bar that also does good tapas.

Apple Pie CAFE £
(Rydal Rd; lunches £4-10; ⊙9am-5.30pm) Sunny cafe popular for its sandwiches, buns and hearty pies.

Atelier BISTRO ££
(☑015394-31156; www.atelier-ambleside.co.uk; Kelsick Rd; mains £11.95-20.95; ⊙6.30-10pm Thu-Sat) Sometimes, simplicity is strength. This

small street-corner bistro specialises in fresh, zesty Mediterranean flavours, served in an intimate modern dining room, characterised by framed prints and Arne Jacobsen–style chairs. Dishes are classic but accomplished: eg Barbary duck with sautéed potatoes, or balsamic-marinated Lakeland lamb.

Fellini's   VEGETARIAN **££**
(☏015394-32487; www.fellinisambleside.com; Church St; mains £11.95; ⊙5.30-10pm; ⏚) Fear not, veggies: even in the land of the Cumberland sausage and the tattie hotpot, you won't go hungry thanks to Fellini's sophisticated 'vegeteranean' food. It's run by Zeffirelli's owners; a small upstairs cinema shows art-house and opera performances.

Glass House   MEDITERRANEAN **££**
(☏015394-32137; www.theglasshouserestaurant.co.uk; Rydal Rd; mains £10.25-14.75; ⊙noon-2pm & 6.30-10pm) Classy dining in a converted fulling mill (with original mill wheels and machinery still in place). It's known for its accomplished French-inspired food, so expect plenty of rich flavours underpinned by Lakeland ingredients.

☕ Drinking & Entertainment

Ambleside has plenty of pubs: locals favour the **Golden Rule** (Smithy Brow) for its ale selection, while the **Royal Oak** (Market Pl) packs in the post-hike punters.

Zeffirelli's Cinema   CINEMA
(☏015394-33100; Compston Rd) Ambleside's two-screen Zeffirelli's Cinema is next to Zeffirelli's, with extra screens in a converted church down the road.

🛍 Shopping

Gaynor Sports   OUTDOOR EQUIPMENT
(☏01524-734938; www.gaynors.co.uk; Market Cross) Compston Rd has enough equipment shops to launch an assault on Everest. The largest is Gaynor Sports, with three floors of outdoor gear.

ⓘ Information

Hub (☏015394-32582; tic@thehubofambleside.com; Central Bldgs, Market Cross; ⊙9am-5pm) The tourist office and the post office are both here.

ⓘ Getting There & Around

BICYCLE
Bikes and gear can be hired from **Biketreks** (☏015394-31505; www.biketreks.net; Rydal Rd; per day £20) and **Ghyllside Cycles** (☏015394-33592; www.ghyllside.co.uk; The Slack; per day £18).

BUS
Bus 505 to Hawkshead and Coniston (£4, hourly including Sundays).

LOCAL KNOWLEDGE

TOP LAKE DISTRICT CAMPSITES

In addition to the four excellent campsites run by the National Trust (near Ambleside, Great Langdale, Wasdale and Coniston), there are more great places to sleep under the stars. Here's our top five:

The Quiet Site (☏07768 727016; www.thequietsite.co.uk; sites £18-30, pods £50; ⊙year-round; 🐾) Eco-camping on the fells above Ullswater, with pre-erected tents and eco-pods available.

Syke Farm (☏01768-770222; adult/child £7/3.50; ⊙Easter-Oct) Back-to-basics camping beside the river in Buttermere. Fresh milk and homemade ice cream are sold at the farm shop.

Bowkerstead Farm (☏01229-860208; www.grizedale-camping.co.uk; Satterthwaite; adult/child £7/3, camping pods £30; ⊙Apr-Sep) Pitch beside the trees of Grizedale Forest, either in your own tent, a luxury yurt or a timber eco-pod.

Seatoller Farm (☏01768-777232; www.seatollerfarm.co.uk; adult/child £6/3; ⊙Easter-Oct) A tucked-away site on a 500-year-old farm near Seatoller in Borrowdale, with a choice of riverside or woodland pitches.

Fisherground Farm (☏019467-23349; www.fishergroundcampsite.co.uk; adult/child £6.50/3.50, car £2.50; ⊙Mar-Oct) Family-friendly camping in idyllic Eskdale, handy for the Ravenglass & Eskdale Railway (see p620).

Bus 516 to Elterwater and Langdale (£3.60, seven daily).
Bus 555 to Grasmere and Windermere (£6.30, at least hourly including Sundays).

Grasmere

POP 1458

Even without its connections to the Romantic poets, gorgeous Grasmere would still be one of the Lakes' biggest draws. It's one of the prettiest of the Lakeland hamlets, huddled at the edge of an island-studded lake surrounded by woods, pastures and slate-coloured hills, but most of the thousands of trippers come in search of its famous former resident, the poet William Wordsworth, who set up home at nearby Dove Cottage in 1799. With such a rich literary heritage, Grasmere unsurprisingly gets busy.

◎ Sights

★ Dove Cottage   HISTORIC BUILDING
(☑ 015394-35544; www.wordsworth.org.uk; adult/child £7.50/4.50; ⊙ 9.30am-5.30pm) On the edge of Grasmere, this tiny, creeper-clad cottage (formerly a pub called the Dove & Olive Bough) was famously inhabited by William Wordsworth between 1799 and 1808. The cottage's cramped rooms are full of artefacts: try to spot the poet's passport, a pair of his spectacles and a portrait of his favourite dog Pepper, given to him by Sir Walter Scott. Entry is by timed ticket to avoid overcrowding, and includes an informative guided tour.

Wordsworth lived here happily with his sister Dorothy, wife Mary and three children John, Dora and Thomas until 1808, when the family moved to another nearby house at Allen Bank, and the cottage was rented by Thomas de Quincey (author of *Confessions of an English Opium Eater*).

Tickets also include admission to the **Wordsworth Museum & Art Gallery** next door, which houses one of the nation's main collections relating to the Romantic movement – including many original manuscripts and some creepy death masks of some famous Romantic figures.

St Oswald's Church   CHURCH
(Church Stile) In the churchyard of this tiny chapel in the centre of Grasmere are the Wordsworths' family graves: look out for tombstones belonging to William, Mary, Dorothy and all three children. Samuel Taylor Coleridge's son Hartley is also buried here.

Grasmere Lake & Rydal Water   LAKE
Quiet paths lead along the shorelines of Grasmere's twin-set lakes. Rowing boats can be hired at the northern end of Grasmere Lake from the **Faeryland Tea Garden** (⊙ 10.30am-4pm), a five-minute walk from the village centre.

🏃 Activities

Popular hikes starting from Grasmere include **Helm Crag** (405m), often known as the 'Lion and the Lamb', thanks to its distinctive shape, Silver Howe (394m), **Loughrigg Fell** (335m) and the multipeak circuit known as the **Easedale Round** (five to six hours, 8.5 to 9 miles).

A less taxing option is to follow the **Old Coffin Trail** between Grasmere and Rydal Mount, which was once used by pallbearers carrying coffins to St Oswald's Church. The trail begins near Dove Cottage.

🛏 Sleeping

Butharlyp How YHA   HOSTEL £
(☑ 0845 371 9319; www.yha.org.uk; Easedale Rd; dm £18-21; ⊙ reception 7am-10pm daily Feb-Nov, Sat & Sun Dec & Jan; 🅿 @) Grasmere's YHA is in a large Victorian house set among grassy grounds. There's a good range of different-sized dorms and a cafe-bar.

Grasmere Hostel   HOSTEL £
(☑ 015394-35055; www.grasmerehostel.co.uk; Broadrayne Farm; dm £20-22; 🅿 @) This independent hostel is in a converted farmhouse on the A591, near the Traveller's Rest pub. There are two kitchens, and each dorm has its own en suite bathroom. There's even a Nordic sauna.

Thorney How   HOSTEL £
(☑ 015394-35597; www.thorneyhow.co.uk; Easedale Rd; dm £21-5) Now independent, this former YHA is in a Grade II–listed farmhouse off Easedale Rd, 15 minutes' walk from Grasmere. Accommodation is in six- to 10-bed dorms, and it all feels pretty cramped – although there are a few double rooms available. Facilities include a kitchen, cafe and bike shelter.

How Foot Lodge   B&B ££
(☑ 015394-35366; www.howfoot.co.uk; Town End; d £75-80; 🅿) Just a stroll from Dove Cottage, this stone house has six rooms finished in fawns and beiges; the nicest are the Deluxe Doubles, one with sun terrace and the other with private sitting room. Rates are an absolute bargain considering the location.

Raise View House　　　　　B&B **££**
(☑ 015394-35215; www.raiseviewhouse.co.uk; White Bridge; s £53-58, d £106-116; P 🔊) Fell views unfurl from nearly every room here: Helm Crag, Easedale and Stone Arthur are particularly impressive. On the edge of Grasmere, the house is smartly appointed: Farrow & Ball paints, Gilchrist & Soames bathstuffs and Wedgwood china on the breakfast table.

Heidi's Grasmere Lodge　　　B&B **££**
(☑ 015394-35248;　　www.heidisgrasmerelodge. co.uk; Red Lion Sq; r £79-110; 🔊) This plush B&B plonked above Heidi's cafe offers six super-feminine rooms full of frilly cushions and Cath Kidston–style patterns. They're quite small but very comfy: room 6 has its own sun patio, reached via a spiral staircase.

⭐**Moss Grove Organic**　　　HOTEL **£££**
(☑ 015394-35251; www.mossgrove.com; r Sun-Thu £114-209, Fri & Sat £129-259; P 🔊) 🥗 This eco-chic hotel champions its green credentials: sheep-wool insulation, organic paints, reclaimed timber beds, but for once, eco also equals elegance. Rooms are enormous, and bathrooms sparkle with sexy showers and underfloor heating. Breakfast is served buffet-style in the kitchen-diner downstairs.

✕ Eating

Heidi's of Grasmere　　　　CAFE **£**
(Red Lion Sq; mains £4-8; ⊕ 9am-5.30pm) This cute pine-clad cafe makes a welcome refuge if the weather turns. Thick-cut sandwiches and hot soups are its mainstay, but the house special, 'cheese smokeys', is the choice if you're hungry.

Baldry's Tea Room　　　　CAFE **£**
(Red Lion Sq; lunch £3-8; ⊕ 10am-5pm) This lacy cafe is the spot for a classic cream tea, served in a bone-china pot and accompanied by buttery scones or Victoria sponges.

⭐**Jumble Room**　　　MODERN BRITISH **££**
(☑ 015394-35188; www.thejumbleroom.co.uk; Langdale Rd; dinner mains £14.50-21; ⊕ 5.30-10pm Wed-Mon) Husband-and-wife team Andy and Crissy Hill have turned this village bistro into a dining landmark. It's really fun and friendly place to dine. Spotty crockery, cow murals and primary colours set the boho tone, matched by a magpie menu taking in everything from Dithose chicken to a 9oz 'flatiron' steak.

Sara's Bistro　　　　　BISTRO **££**
(Broadgate; mains £10-16; ⊕ 6-9pm Tue-Sun) Hearty homespun cooking is Sara's raison d'être – big portions of roast chicken, honey-roasted duck and thyme-infused belly pork. There's nothing fancy about the food or the decor, but warm welcomes are guaranteed.

Miller Howe Cafe　　　　CAFE **££**
(Red Lion Sq; mains £5-14; ⊕ 8.30am-5.30pm) A smart cafe on the main square, serving upmarket lunch fare: smoked-salmon muffins, club toasties and excellent Farrers coffee.

🛍 Shopping

⭐**Sarah Nelson's Gingerbread Shop**　　　FOOD
(www.grasmeregingerbread.co.uk; Church Cottage; ⊕ 9.15am-5.30pm Mon-Sat, 12.30-5pm Sun) In business since 1854, this famous sweetshop next to the village church makes Grasmere's essential souvenir: traditional gingerbread with a half-biscuit, half-cakey texture, cooked according to the same top-secret recipe (12 pieces for £4.95). Friendly service by ladies dressed in frilly pinafores and starched bonnets is an added bonus.

ⓘ Getting There & Away

The regular 555 bus runs from Windermere to Grasmere (15 minutes), via Ambleside, Rydal Church and Dove Cottage.

The open-top 599 (two or three per hour in summer) runs from Grasmere via Ambleside, Troutbeck Bridge, Windermere and Bowness.

Both buses charge the same fares: Grasmere to Ambleside is £6.30, to Windermere it's £6.80.

Hawkshead & Around
POP 1640

Lakeland villages don't come much more perfect than Hawkshead, a jumble of whitewashed cottages, cobbled lanes and old pubs lost among bottle-green countryside between Ambleside and Coniston. The village has literary cachet too – Wordsworth went to school here, and Beatrix Potter's husband, William Heelis, worked here as a solicitor for many years (his old office is now an art gallery).

Cars are banned in the village centre.

◉ Sights

Hawkshead Grammar School　　HISTORIC BUILDING
(www.hawksheadgrammar.org.uk; admission £2; ⊕ 10am-1pm & 2-5pm Mon-Sat, 1-5pm Sun Apr-Sep) In centuries past, promising young gentlemen were sent to Hawkshead's village school for their educational foundation.

DON'T MISS

GRIZEDALE FOREST

Sprawling across the hills between Coniston Water and Esthwaite Water, Grizedale Forest (from the Old Norse for 'wild boar') is one of the Lake District's most beautiful woodlands – not to mention its largest outdoor art project. More than 90 large-scale artworks and sculptures are sprinkled throughout the forest, from an enormous xylophone to a Tolkienesque 'man of the forest'.

Bus X30, the Grizedale Wanderer (four daily March to November), runs from Haverthwaite to Grizedale via Hawkshead and Moor Top.

Grizedale Visitors Centre (☑ 01229-860010; www.forestry.gov.uk/grizedaleforestpark; ☺ 10am-5pm, 11am-4pm winter) The main information point has lots of leaflets and maps covering activities in the forest.

Grizedale Mountain Bikes (☑ 01229-860369; www.grizedalemountainbikes.co.uk; adult/child per day from £25/18; ☺ 9am-5pm) Rents out mountain bikes and supplies trail maps. Last hire at 3pm.

Go Ape (www.goape.co.uk; adult/child £30/24; ☺ 9-5pm daily Mar-Oct, Sat & Sun Nov-Feb) Children (big and little) will love this treetop assault course.

Among the former pupils was a certain William Wordsworth, who attended the school from 1779 to 1787.

The curriculum was punishing: 10 hours' study a day, covering weighty subjects such as Latin, Greek, geometry, science and rhetoric. Hardly surprising young William felt the urge to carve his name into a desk.

Upstairs is a small exhibition exploring the history of the school.

Beatrix Potter Gallery　　　GALLERY
(NT; www.nationaltrust.org.uk/beatrix-potter-gallery; Red Lion Sq; adult/child £5/2.50; ☺ 10.30am-5pm Sat-Thu mid-Mar–Oct) As well as being a children's author, Beatrix Potter was also a talented botanical painter and amateur naturalist. This small gallery (housed in the offices of Potter's husband, solicitor William Heelis) contains a collection of her watercolours depicting local flora and fauna. She was particularly fascinated by mushrooms.

There's discounted admission if you show your ticket from Hill Top.

★ **Tarn Hows**　　　LAKE
(NT; www.nationaltrust.org.uk/coniston-and-tarn-hows) FREE Two miles off the B5285 from Hawkshead, a winding country lane wends its way to this famously photogenic artificial lake, now owned by the National Trust. Trails wind their way around the lakeshore and surrounding woodland – keep your eyes peeled for red squirrels in the treetops.

There's a small National Trust car park, but it fills quickly. Several buses, including the 505 and X30, stop nearby.

Hill Top　　　HISTORIC BUILDING
(NT; ☑ 015394-36269; www.nationaltrust.org.uk/hill-top; adult/child £9/4.50; ☺ 10.30am-4.30pm Sat-Thu mid-Feb–Oct, longer hours Jul & Aug) In the tiny village of Near Sawrey, 2 miles south of Hawkshead, this idyllic farmhouse is a must for Beatrix Potter buffs: it was the first house she lived in after moving to the Lake District, and also where she wrote and illustrated many of her famous tales. Purchased in 1905 (largely on the proceeds of her first bestseller, *The Tale of Peter Rabbit*), Hill Top is crammed with decorative details that fans will recognise from the author's illustrations. Entry is by timed ticket; try visiting later in the day to avoid the worst crowds.

The house features directly in *Samuel Whiskers*, *Tom Kitten* and *Jemima Puddle-Duck*, and you might recognise the cast-iron kitchen range from many of Potter's underground burrows.

Thanks to its fame (helped by the 2006 biopic *Miss Potter*), Hill Top is one of the Lakes' most popular spots, so queues are inevitable in season.

🛏 Sleeping & Eating

Hawkshead YHA　　　HOSTEL £
(☑ 0845 371 9321; hawkshead@yha.org.uk; dm £15-21; P @) This large hostel occupies a Regency house a mile along the Newby Bridge road. The dorms and kitchen are spacious, there's on-site bike rental and buses stop outside the door.

Yewfield   B&B **££**
([✓]015394-36765; www.yewfield.co.uk; Hawkshead Hill; s £49-65, d £98-130; [P][🛜]) [🚭] This detached house occupies a hilltop spot near Tarn Hows, halfway between Coniston and Hawkshead. It's run by the owners of Zeffirelli's, and though the building itself is Victorian, it's run along eco lines: breakfast is veggie and organic, power comes from a wood-mass boiler, and produce comes from the kitchen garden.

Randy Pike   B&B **£££**
([✓]015394-36088; www.randypike.co.uk; r Mon-Fri £200, Sat & Sun £225) Managed by the owners of Grasmere's Jumble Room restaurant, Andy and Chrissy Hill, this former hunting lodge feels more like a stay in the country with friends than a night in a B&B. The three rooms ooze bohemian style: distressed wood floors, quirky furniture and mix-and-match fabrics, plus iPods loaded up with music. There's even a Tardis in the garden.

Love Shack   COTTAGE **£££**
([✓]015394-41242; www.lakedistrictloveshack.com; Cunsey; [⊙]r Sat & Sun £350-650, per week £600-850) [🚭] A cooler cottage you simply will not find. Built on the site of a 1960s love shack (hence the name), this eco-friendly cabin is the brainchild of artists Karen Guthrie and Adam Sutherland. It's a mix of modern and retro – reclaimed timber, organic paints and oak floors meet funky furnishings and shagadelic love seats, all in a secluded woodland location not far from Near Sawrey.

Hawkshead Relish Company   DELI **£**
([✓]015394-36614; www.hawksheadrelish.com; The Square; [⊙]9.30am-5pm winter, 9am-5.30pm summer) This village chutney company sells an enormous choice of relishes and jams.

Queen's Head   PUB **££**
([✓]015394-36271; www.queensheadhawkshead.co.uk; Main St; mains £14-22, s £70, d £100-130; [⊙]noon-3pm & 6-10pm) Hawkshead has several decent pubs, but the old Queen's Head beats them all in age and atmosphere. Head-knockingly low ceilings and the oak-panelled walls give it period character, and the food is packed with local flavour (roast Herdwick lamb, shepherd's pie, sticky toffee pudding). Rooms in the main inn are small and prim, decked out in elegant gingham checks and neutral tones.

★Drunken Duck   PUB **£££**
([✓]015394-36347; www.drunkenduckinn.co.uk; Barngates; mains £13-25; [⊙]noon-2pm & 6-10pm;

[P][🛜]) For top-class dining in the Lakes, nowhere beats the Drunken Duck. It's become one of the region's premier foodie destinations, closer to a fine-dining restaurant than a country pub. The food is full of flair, and ales come from the pub's own Barngates Brewery out back. You'll need to book weeks in advance for dinner, although lunch is first-come, first-served.

If you fancy staying, you'll find the rooms (£95 to £275) are just as fancy as the food. The pub's tricky to find: drive along the B5286 from Hawkshead towards Ambleside, and look out for the brown signs.

❶ Getting There & Away

Hawkshead is linked with Windermere (£6.50), Ambleside (£4) and Coniston (£4) by bus 505 (hourly including Sundays).

Coniston

POP 641

Hunkered beneath the pockmarked peak known as the **Old Man of Coniston** (803m), this lakeside village was originally established to support the local mining industry, and the surrounding hilltops are littered with the remains of old copper workings. These days most people visit with two things in mind: to cruise on the lovely old Coniston Launch, or to tramp to the top of the Old Man, a steep but rewarding return hike of around 7 miles.

Coniston's other claim to fame is as the location for a string of world-record speed attempts made here by Sir Malcolm Campbell and his son, Donald, between the 1930s and 1960s. Tragically, after beating the record several times, Donald was killed during an attempt in 1967, when his futuristic jet-boat *Bluebird* flipped at around 320mph. The boat and its pilot were recovered in 2001, and Campbell was buried in the cemetery of St Andrew's church.

◉ Sights

Brantwood   HISTORIC BUILDING
([✓]015394-41396; www.brantwood.org.uk; adult/child £7.20/free, gardens only £4.95/free; [⊙]10.30am-5pm mid-Mar–mid-Nov, to 4pm Wed-Sun mid-Nov–mid-Mar) John Ruskin (1819–1900), who lived at Brantwood for 28 years, was one of the great thinkers of 19th-century society. A polymath, philosopher, painter and critic, as well as an inveterate shell collector, he expounded views on everything from Venetian architecture to the finer points of lace-making.

In 1871 Ruskin purchased this lakeside house and spent the next 20 years expanding and modifying it, championing his passion for traditional 'Arts and Crafts' over factory-made materials. He even dreamt up the wallpaper designs.

Of particular note are Ruskin's enormous shell collection in the downstairs study, and several works by JMW Turner (Ruskin's favourite artist) in an upstairs bedroom. The formal gardens are also delightful to wander, with unsurprisingly majestic views.

The best way to arrive is by boat from Coniston (you also get a 50p discount on admission). While you wait, you can have lunch at the Jumping Jenny (lunches £4-8) in the house's former stables. If you'd prefer to drive, take the B5285 towards Coniston from Hawkshead and follow the signs.

Ruskin Museum   MUSEUM
(www.ruskinmuseum.com; adult/child £5.25/2.50; ☺10am-5.30pm Easter–mid-Nov, 10.30am-3.30pm Wed-Sun mid-Nov–Easter) Coniston's little museum explores the village's history, touching on copper mining, Arthur Ransome and the Campbell story. There's also a section on John Ruskin, with displays of his writings, watercolours and sketchbooks.

The new Bluebird Wing currently houses the recovered engine from Donald Campbell's *Bluebird* boat, but it's hoped that the whole boat will be displayed here when (and if) it's finally restored.

🏊 Activities

Lake Coniston famously inspired Arthur Ransome's classic children's tale *Swallows and Amazons*. Peel Island, towards the southern end of Coniston Water, doubles in the book as Wild Cat Island, while the *Gondola* steam yacht allegedly gave Ransome the idea for Captain Flint's houseboat.

Steam Yacht Gondola   BOATING
(NT; ☑015394-63850; www.nationaltrust.org.uk/gondola; Coniston Jetty; half-lake return adult/child £11/5.50) ✈ Built in 1859 and restored in the 1980s by the National Trust, this wonderful steam yacht looks like a cross between a Venetian *vaporetto* and an English houseboat, complete with cushioned saloons and polished wood seats. It's a stately way of seeing the lake, especially if you're visiting Brantwood, and it's even ecofriendly: since 2008 it's been powered by waste-wood.

There are several 'Half Lake' trips a day from mid-March to October. Longer 'Full

Lake' cruises run a few times a week, and cover the history of Ransome, the Campbells and Ruskin. Special picnic and Sunday afternoon tea cruises also run in summer. There's a 10% discount for online bookings.

Coniston Launch   BOATING
(☑015394-36216; www.conistonlaunch.co.uk; Coniston Jetty; northern service adult/child return £10.50/5.25, southern £15.50/7.75) ✈ Coniston's two launches have been solar-powered since 2005. The regular 45-minute northern service calls at the Waterhead Hotel, Torver and Brantwood, while the 105-minute southern service sails from Monday to Thursday with a different theme depending on the day; it's Swallows and Amazons on Monday and Wednesday, and the Campbells on Coniston on Tuesday and Thursday.

Coniston Boating Centre   BOATING
(☑015394-41366; www.conistonboatingcentre.co.uk; Coniston Jetty) Hires out rowing boats, Canadian canoes and motorboats.

🛏 Sleeping

Coniston Holly How YHA   HOSTEL £
(☑0845 371 9511; conistonhh@yha.org.uk; Far End; dm £15-21.50; ☺reception 7.30-10am & 5-10pm) A fine period house offering the usual YHA standards: decent dorms, well-equipped kitchens, organised walks and an in-house cafe.

Coppermines YHA   HOSTEL £
(☑0845 371 9630; coppermines@yha.org.uk; dm from £16; ☺reception 7-11am & 5-10pm Easter-Oct) Up a steep rock road 1.5km from the village, this rustic hostel once provided accommodation for local copper miners. It's now a walkers' favourite; dorms are small but there's a kitchen, showers and even a licensed bar.

Hoathwaite Campsite   CAMPSITE £
(NT; ☑bookings 015394-63862; www.ntlakescampsites.org.uk; adult, tent & car from £6; ☺Easter-Nov) This 'back-to-basics' National Trust-owned campsite is on the A5394 between Coniston and Torver. There's a toilet block, water taps and not much else – but the views over Coniston Water are super.

Bank Ground Farm   B&B ££
(☑015394-41264; www.bankground.com; East of the Lake; d from £90, 2-night minimum; ℗) This lakeside farmhouse has literary cachet: Arthur Ransome used it as the model for Holly Howe Farm in *Swallows and Amazons*. Parts of the house date back to the 15th

century, so the rooms are snug. Some have sleigh beds, others exposed beams. The tearoom is a beauty, too, and there are cottages for longer stays. Two-night minimum.

Lakeland House B&B **££**
(🖉 015394-41303; www.lakelandhouse.co.uk; Tilberthwaite Ave; s £30-55, d £60-95) Perched above the village's internet cafe is this no-fuss B&B. Budget doubles border on the utilitarian, so it's worth stretching to Superior for space and comfort. The Lookout Suite has its own sitting room.

✖ Eating & Drinking

Bluebird Cafe CAFE **£**
(Lake Rd; mains £4-8; ⊙ 9.30am-5.30pm) This lakeside cafe does a brisk trade from people waiting for the Coniston launches. The usual salads and sandwiches are on offer, and there are lots of outside tables.

Sun Hotel PUB **££**
(www.thesunconiston.com; mains £12-20; ⊙ 10am-11pm) A Coniston landmark, this 400-year-old gabled inn was famously used as an HQ by Donald Campbell during his final fateful campaign. There's lots of Campbell memorabilia to spot inside, dotted around the inn's beamed interior, and a pleasant garden overlooking the lake. The food is solid (beer-battered fish, oak-smoked roast chicken), washed down with guest ales from local breweries.

Black Bull PUB
(www.conistonbrewery.com/black-bull-coniston.htm; Yewdale Rd; mains £8-16; ⊙ 10am-11pm) Coniston's main meeting spot, the old Black Bull offers a warren of rooms and a popular outside terrace. The pub grub's good, but it's mainly known for its home-brewed ales: Bluebird Bitter and Old Man Ale are always on tap, and there are seasonal ones too.

ℹ Information

Coniston Tourist Office (🖉 015394-41533; www.conistontic.org; Ruskin Ave; ⊙ 9.30am-5.30pm Easter-Oct, to 4pm Nov-Easter) Sells the Coniston Loyalty Card offering local discounts.

ℹ Getting There & Away

Bus 505 runs to Windermere (£4, hourly including Sundays), via Ambleside (£4), with a couple of daily connections to Kendal (£9.30, 1¼ hours).

The Coniston Bus-and-Boat ticket (adult/child £17.90/7.50) includes return bus travel on the 505, plus a trip on the launch and entry to Brantwood.

Elterwater & Great Langdale

Travelling north from Coniston, the road passes into the wild, empty landscape of Great Langdale, one of Lakeland's iconic hiking valleys. As you pass the pretty village of Elterwater, imposing fells stack up like dominoes along the horizon, looming over a pastoral patchwork of tumbledown barns and lime-green fields.

Langdale's best-known hike is the multipeak route up and over the Langdale Pikes: Pike O' Stickle (709m), Loft Crag (682m), Harrison Stickle (736m) and Pavey Ark (700m). Across the valley are the rippled summits of Bowfell (902m) and the Crinkle Crags, which represent a serious challenge even for experienced walkers.

🛏 Sleeping

Great Langdale Campsite CAMPSITE **£**
(NT; 🖉 015394-63862; www.ntlakescampsites.org.uk; tent sites £10.50-13, extra adult £6, pods £35-50; ⊙ arrivals 3-7pm Sat-Thu, 3-9pm Fri; 🅿) Quite possibly the most spectacularly positioned campsite in the Lake District, spread out over grassy meadows overlooked by Langdale's fells. It gets crowded in season, but around three-quarters of the sites can be booked in advance; the remainder are available on a first-come, first-served basis. Camping pods and yurts are also available.

Langdale YHA HOSTEL **£**
(🖉 0845 371 9748; langdale@yha.org.uk; High Close, Loughrigg; dm £15-21; ⊙ reception 7-10am & 5-10.15pm Mar-Oct; 🅿 @) Hostel in a grand Victorian house on the road towards Grasmere. It's a rambling old affair, with big rooms, high ceilings and a huge communal lounge.

Elterwater YHA HOSTEL **£**
(🖉 0845 371 9017; elterwater@yha.org.uk; dm £15-21; ⊙ reception 7.30-10am & 5-10.30pm Easter-Oct; @) A pleasant hostel in a former farmhouse, a stone's throw from Elterwater's village green.

★ **Old Dungeon Ghyll** HOTEL **££**
(🖉 015394-37272; www.odg.co.uk; d from £106, half-board £156; 🅿 🛜 🕸) Affectionately known as the ODG, this historic inn is awash with Lakeland heritage: many famous walkers have stayed here, including Prince Charles and mountaineer Chris Bonington. It's endearingly olde-worlde (well-worn furniture, four-poster beds), and even if you're not staying here, the Hiker's Bar is a must for a

THE STEEPEST ROAD IN ENGLAND?

Zigzagging over fells between the valleys of **Little Langdale** and **Eskdale** is one of the Lake District's most infamous mountain roads. Used since ancient times and later substantially improved by the Romans, this old packhorse route provided a vital trading link between the central valleys of Lakeland and the ports dotted along the Cumbrian coast. En route, it traverses both of England's highest road passes, **Wrynose** and **Hardknott**, and in places the road reaches forbidding gradients of 1 in 3. At the top of Hardknott Pass, there's a ruined Roman fort, where you can still see the remains of the walls, parade ground and commandant's house. The views from here to the coast are stunning.

It's perfectly driveable if you take things slow and steady, but probably best avoided if you're a hesitant reverser or don't like driving next to steep drops (caravans and buses should definitely steer clear). Things to note: it's single-carriage most of the way, and passing places few and far between, so be prepared for vehicles going the opposite way. Also, make sure your brakes are in good order, and top up the water in your radiator – you'll do most of it in first or second gear.

To get to the passes from Ambleside, follow road signs on the A593 to Skelwith Bridge, then turn off to Little Langdale. When you reach the Three Shires Inn, the road becomes really steep. Alternatively, you can approach from the west; drive along the A595 coast road and turn off towards Eskdale, and follow the road past Boot to the passes.

post-hike pint – it's been the hub of Langdale's social life for decades.

★ **Eltermere Inn** HOTEL **£££**

(☑ 015394-37207; www.eltermere.co.uk; r £125-225) Lovingly refurbished by hoteliers Mark and Ruth Jones, this Elterwater inn is one of Lakeland's loveliest backwater bolt-holes. Rooms are simple and classic, tastefully decorated in fawns and taupes, with quirky features such as window seats and free-standing tubs. The food's excellent, too, served in the inn's snug bar, and afternoon tea is served on the lawn on sunny days.

Brimstone Hotel HOTEL **£££**

(☑ 015394-38062; www.brimstonehotel.co.uk; Langdale Estate; r £200-300) This lavish cottage complex on the Langdale Estate takes luxury to another level. The huge suites are more London-chic than Lakeland-cosy; mezzanine floors, sleek tiles, private patios and futuristic log-burners are standard, and then of course there's a reading room, spa, restaurant and private woodland.

✕ Eating

Stickle Barn PUB **£**

(☑ 015394-37356; mains £6-12) A walkers' fave, this lively pub near the ODG serves filling food such as curries, chillies and hotpots.

Chesters by the River CAFE **££**

(☑ 015394-32553; www.chestersbytheriver.co.uk; lunch mains £8-14; ☉ 10am-5pm) A fine riverside cafe handily placed between Amble-

side and Elterwater, serving gastro-gourmet grub and superb cakes. There's a gift shop, too, and you can pick up slate souvenirs from the workshop around the corner.

❶ Getting There & Away

Bus 516 (seven daily) is the only bus, with stops at Ambleside, Skelwith Bridge, Elterwater, and the Old Dungeon Ghyll Hotel in Great Langdale. Fares from Ambleside are £3.60 to all destinations.

Wasdale

Carving its way for 5 miles from the Cumbrian coast, the craggy, wind-lashed valley of Wasdale is where the Lake District scenery takes a turn for the wild. Ground out by a long-extinct glacier, the valley is home to the Lake District's highest and wildest peaks, as well as the steely grey expanse of Wastwater, England's deepest and coldest lake.

Wasdale's fells are an irresistible draw for hikers, especially those looking to conquer England's tallest mountain, **Scafell Pike** (978m). The classic route starts from Wasdale Head and is well within the reach of most walkers, although it's long, steep and hard to navigate in bad weather. You're looking at around six to seven hours out on the mountain, so you'll need proper supplies.

The valley is also home to one of England's tiniest chapels, 16th-century **St Olaf's Church**. Legend claims the roof beams were salvaged from a Viking longboat.

The **Barn Door Shop** (☑019467-26384; www.wasdaleweb.com), next door to the Wasdale Head Inn, sells camping and walking supplies.

🛏 Sleeping

Wasdale Head Campsite CAMPSITE £
(NT; ☑ bookings 015394-63862; www.ntlakescampsites.org.uk; sites £10.50-13, extra adult £6, pods £35-50; ⊙ reception 8-10.30am Mon-Fri, 8-10.30am & 5-6.30pm Sat & Sun) This campsite is in a fantastically wild spot, nestled beneath the Scafell range. Facilities are basic (laundry room, showers), but the views are out of this world.

Wastwater YHA HOSTEL £
(☑0845 371 9350; wasdale@yha.org.uk; Wasdale Hall, Nether Wasdale; dm £18-23; ⊙ reception 8-10am & 5-10.30pm; ☐) This lakeside hostel on the shores of Wastwater has the kind of location you'd normally pay through the nose for. It's in a 19th-century mansion that still boasts most of its period architecture, including original roof trusses and latticed windows. It has the usual self-catering facilities plus a decent restaurant.

★Wasdale Head Inn B&B ££
(☑019467-26229; www.wasdale.com; s £59, d £118-130, tr £177; ☐) Hunkering beneath the brooding bulk of Scafell Pike is this 19th-century hostelry full of hill-walking heritage. It's wonderfully old-fashioned, covered in vintage photos and climbing memorabilia. The rooms are cosy, with roomier suites in a converted stable. The wood-panelled dining room serves fine food, with humbler grub and ales from the Great Gable Brewing Co available in Ritson's Bar.

ℹ Getting There & Away

There are no longer any scheduled bus services to Wasdale Head, but you could order a taxi from **Gosforth Taxis** (☑01946-734800).

Cockermouth

POP 9146

Set along the River Cocker, the Georgian town of Cockermouth is best known as the birthplace of William Wordsworth and the home base of the renowned Jenning's Brewery, but hit the headlines in 2009 when the town suffered serious flooding. Since then, Cockermouth's elegant streets have been restored, and the town makes an interesting detour from the better-known and busier Lakeland towns.

⊙ Sights

★Wordsworth House HISTORIC BUILDING
(NT; ☑01900-824805; Main St; adult/child £6.70/3.35; ⊙ 11am-5pm Sat-Thu Mar-Oct) William Wordsworth was born on 7 April 1770 at this handsome Georgian house at the end of Main St. Built around 1745, the house has been restored based on accounts from the Wordsworth archive. Costumed guides help bring the house to life.

The kitchen garden (mentioned in Wordsworth's autobiographical poem *The Prelude*) was badly damaged during the floods, but has since been carefully replanted.

Jenning's Brewery BREWERY
(☑01900-821011; www.jenningsbrewery.co.uk; adult/child £8/4.50; ⊙ guided tours noon & 2pm Mon-Sat Apr-Oct, fewer in winter) Real ale aficionados will be well familiar with the name of Jenning's, a renowned brewery that's been in business since 1874. It's possible to take a guided tour to see the brewing process, followed by a tasting session in the Old Cooperage Bar. Take your pick from golden Cocker Hoop, classic Bitter and the superbly named Sneck Lifter. Children must be over 12.

OFF THE BEATEN TRACK

ENNERDALE

If you really want to leave the outside world behind, the remote valley of Ennerdale is definitely the place. Just to the north of Wasdale, this valley and its namesake lake was once home to slate mines and large timber plantations, but these are slowly being removed and the valley is being returned to nature as part of the **Wild Ennerdale project** (www.wildennerdale.co.uk).

Needless to say, the valley is paradise if you prefer your trails quiet. Several popular routes head over the fells to Wasdale, while walking towards Buttermere takes you past the **Black Sail YHA** (☑0845 371 9680; www.yha.org.uk/hostel/black-sail; dm £20.50-22.50), a marvellously remote hostel inside a shepherd's bothy. Much-loved by mountaineers and hikers, it's become a YHA landmark. and has recently been kitted out with solar panels, LED lighting and double glazing at a cost of around £260,000. Space is very limited, so make sure you book ahead.

🛏 Sleeping

Six Castlegate   B&B ££

(☑ 01900-826749;   www.sixcastlegate.co.uk;   6 Castlegate; s £45-50, d £70-80; 🖥) A Grade II–listed town house combining Georgian heritage with a modern twist, and feathery pillows, lofty ceilings and shiny showers in all six rooms.

Croft House   B&B ££

(☑ 01900-827533; www.croft-guesthouse.com; 6/8 Challoner St; s £50, d £70-80; 🖥) This swish lemon-yellow B&B offers rooms in a Georgian house, all with exposed stone and reclaimed maple-wood floors.

🍴 Eating & Drinking

Merienda   CAFE £

(7a Station St; mains £4-8; ☺ 9am-5pm Mon-Sat) The town's best bet for lunch, this bright cafe serves fresh soups and open-face sandwiches.

Quince & Medlar   VEGETARIAN ££

(www.quinceandmedlar.co.uk; 13 Castlegate; mains £13.95; ☺ 7-10pm Tue-Sat; 🍴) 🍃 Imaginative veggie food served in the refined surrounds of one of Castlegate's Georgian houses, complete with panelled walls and flickering candles. Even committed carnivores will be tempted by the creative creations. Butternut squash layered with spiced ginger and cumin quinoa, anyone?

Honest Lawyer   BISTRO ££

(☑ 01900-824888; 2 Main St; 2-course meal £18.95; ☺ 5.30-9.30pm) Tucked away by the river, this attractive bistro specialises in French-Italian fusion: grilled sea bass with scallops with sauce vierge, perhaps, or supreme of duck with pommes Anna. There's a range of veggie options too. They can usually squeeze you in even at the busiest of times.

Bitter End   PUB

(☑ 01900-828993; www.bitterend.co.uk; 15 Kirkgate; mains £10-15; ☺ noon-2.30pm & 6-10pm) This well-regarded brewpub produces its own award-winning beers such as Cockermouth Pride, Lakeland Honey Beer and Cuddy Lugs. You can watch the vats at work through a glass partition in the bar.

ℹ Information

Tourist Office (☑ 01900-822634; cockermouthtic@co-net.com; ☺ 10am-4pm Mon-Fri, to 2pm Sat) Inside the town hall.

ℹ Getting There & Away

Bus X4/X5 (half-hourly Monday to Saturday, hourly Sunday) travels from Penrith to Keswick and Cockermouth (£6.40), and Workington (£7.60, 1¼ hours).

Keswick

POP 4821

The most northerly of the Lake District's major towns, Keswick has perhaps the most beautiful location of all: encircled by cloud-capped fells and nestled alongside the idyllic, island-studded lake of Derwentwater, a silvery curve criss-crossed by puttering cruise boats. It's also brilliantly positioned for further adventures into the nearby valleys of Borrowdale and Buttermere.

⊙ Sights

The heart of Keswick is the old Market Place, in the shadow of the town's former prison and meeting rooms at the **Moot Hall** (now occupied by the tourist office). Keswick's oddball museum is still closed for refurbishment; ask at the tourist office for the latest news.

Castlerigg Stone Circle   MONUMENT

FREE Set on a hilltop a mile east of town, this jaw-dropping stone circle consists of 48 stones that are between 3000 and 4000 years old, surrounded by a dramatic ring of mountain peaks.

Pencil Museum   MUSEUM

(www.pencilmuseum.co.uk; Southy Works; adult/child £4.25/3.25; ☺ 9.30am-5pm) Vying for top spot in Cumbria's weirdest museum chart, this pencil-themed museum's exhibits include the world's longest pencil (8m from end to end) and a replica of a Borrowdale slate mine. There is method in the madness, though – when graphite was discovered in the Borrowdale fells during the 17th century, Keswick became one of the world's main pencil producers. You can buy luxury Derwent colouring pencils in the shop.

Whinlatter Forest Park   FOREST

(www.forestry.gov.uk/whinlatter) FREE Encompassing 1200 hectares of pine, larch and spruce, Whinlatter is England's only true mountain forest, rising sharply to 790m about 5 miles from Keswick. The forest is a designated red squirrel reserve; you can check out live video feeds from squirrel cams at the **visitor centre** (☑ 017687-78469; ☺ 10am-4pm).

It's also home to two exciting mountain-bike trails and the **Go Ape** (www.goape.co.uk/days-out/whinlatter; adult/child £30/25; ☺9am-5pm mid-Mar–Oct) tree-top assault course. You can hire bikes from **Cyclewise** (☑017687-78711; www.cyclewise.co.uk; ☺10am-5pm), next to the visitor centre.

Entry to the forest is free, but you have to pay for parking. Bus 77 (four daily) runs from Keswick. If you're driving, head west on the A66 and look for the brown signs near Braithwaite.

🏃 Activities

Keswick has a wealth of fantastic walks on its doorstep. The most popular is the family-friendly fell of **Catbells** (451m), on the lake's west side; the trailhead starts next to the jetty at Hawse End, served by the Keswick Launch. There's also an easy trail along the **old railway path** to Threlkeld.

Hardcore hikers will prefer the more challenging slog up **Skiddaw** (931m), the huge mountain that looms on Keswick's northern skyline. Alternatively, near Threlkeld is the lonely fell of **Blencathra** (868m), which was recently put up for sale by the Earl of Lonsdale with a price tag of £1.75 million.

Keswick Launch   BOATING
(☑017687-72263; www.keswick-launch.co.uk; round-the-lake adult/child £9.25/4.50) Said to have been Beatrix Potter's favourite lake (she's supposed to have got the idea for Squirrel Nutkin while watching red squirrels on the shoreline), **Derwentwater** is certainly a real beauty. As always, the best way to appreciate its charms is by getting out on the water. There are six daily boats from March to November, with a couple of extra afternoon sailings and a twilight cruise in summer, dropping to just a couple of sailings a day in winter.

Apart from the main jetties in Keswick, the lake's other landing stages are at Ashness Gate, Lodore Falls, High Brandlehow, Low Brandlehow, Hawse End and Nichol End. Departures run clockwise and anti-clockwise. Rowboats and motorboats can be hired next to the launch jetties.

🎉 Festivals & Events

Keswick Mountain Festival   OUTDOORS
(www.keswickmountainfestival.co.uk) This May festival celebrates all things mountainous.

Keswick Beer Festival   BEER
(www.keswickbeerfestival.co.uk) Lots of beer is drunk during Keswick's real ale fest in June.

THE BASSENTHWAITE OSPREYS

In 2001 the first wild ospreys to breed in England for 150 years set up home at **Bassenthwaite Lake**, near Keswick. Over the last few years, the birds have usually arrived at Bassenthwaite in April, spending the summer at the lake before heading for Africa in late August or early September.

There are two official viewpoints, both in **Dodd Wood**, about 3 miles north of Keswick on the A591 (follow signs for Dodd Wood and Cattle Inn). The lower hide (open 10am to 5pm) is about 15 minutes' walk from the car park at Mirehouse, and the new upper hide (open 10.30am to 4.30pm) is half an hour further. Find out more at www.ospreywatch.co.uk.

🛏 Sleeping

Keswick is simply crammed with good-value B&Bs, especially around Stanger and Helvellyn Sts.

Keswick YHA   HOSTEL £
(☑0845 371 9746; keswick@yha.org.uk; Station Rd; dm £13-21; ☺) Keswick's YHA is a beauty, lodged inside a converted woollen mill by the clattering River Rothay, and renovated thanks to the benevolence of a generous doctor. Dorms are cosy, there's an excellent cafe, and some rooms even have balconies over Fitz Park.

★**Howe Keld**   B&B ££
(☑017687-72417; www.howekeld.co.uk; 5-7 The Heads; s £58, d £110-130; ⓟ☺) This B&B pulls out all the stops: goose-down duvets, slate-floored bathrooms, chic colours and locally made furniture. The best rooms have views across Crow Park and the golf course, and the breakfast is a pick-and-mix delight. Free parking is available on the Heads if there's space.

Linnett Hill   B&B ££
(☑017687-44518; www.linnetthillkeswick.co.uk; 4 Penrith Rd; s/d £45/80; ☺) Much recommended by travellers, this lovingly run B&B has lots going for it: crisp white rooms, a great location near Fitz Park and keen prices that stay the same year-round. Breakfast is good too: there's a blackboard of specials to choose from, and the dining room has

gingham-check tablecloths and a crackling woodburner.

Oakthwaite House B&B ££

(☑017687-72398; www.oakthwaite-keswick.com; 35 Helvellyn St; d £76-90; 🛜) One of the top choices in the B&B-heavy neighbourhood around Helvellyn St. There are just four rooms (so it's not too crowded), all with power showers, white linen and soothingly neutral tones. Rooms 4 and 5 are up in the eaves, while Room 2 is the most spacious, with views of Walla Crag.

★ Cottage in the Wood HOTEL £££

(☑017687-78409; www.thecottageinthewood. co.uk; Braithwaite; d £110-190; ☺restaurant 6.30-9pm Tue-Sat) For a secluded spoil, this out-of-the-way hotel is a real find. It's on the way to Whinlatter Forest, in a 17th-century coaching inn that's been thoroughly modernised. Elegant rooms survey woods and countryside: the Mountain View rooms overlook the Skiddaw Range, but we liked the super-private Attic Suite and Garden Room, with its wood floors and wet-room. The restaurant's fantastic, too.

🍴 Eating & Drinking

Abraham's Tea Rooms CAFE £

(2 Borrowdale Rd; mains £6-10; ☺10am-5pm Mon-Sat, 10.30am-4.30pm Sun) On the top floor of George Fishers, in the former photography studio of the Abraham brothers, this cosy cafe is great for a country lunch: hot rarebit (toasted-cheese-on-toast), mackerel paté or a classic baked spud.

Lakeland Pedlar Wholefood Cafe CAFE £

(www.lakelandpedlar.co.uk; Hendersons Yard; mains £4-10; ☺9am-5pm) 🚲 Down a narrow side alley off the high street, this veggie-organic wholefood emporium is a hallowed destination for hikers and bikers, renowned for its chunky sandwiches, homemade soups and enormous cakes. There's a bike shop upstairs.

Bryson's CAFE £

(42 Main St; cakes £2-5; ☺8.30am-5.30pm) An old-fashioned bakery known for its fruitcakes, Battenbergs and Florentines.

Pumpkin Cafe CAFE £

(19 Lake Rd; lunches £3-6; ☺8.30am-5pm Mon-Sat) Metropolitan cafe culture comes to Keswick: order a make-your-own salad or a deli sandwich, followed by a fresh-baked croissant and a flat white. There's seating upstairs, or you can order to go.

★ Pheasant Inn PUB ££

(☑017687-72219; www.the-pheasant.co.uk; Bassenthwaite; mains £14-18; ☺restaurant 7-9pm Tue-Sat, noon-2pm Sun, bistro noon-4.30pm & 6-9pm) A short drive along Bassenthwaite Lake is this fine dining pub. Hunting prints and pewter tankards cover the old bar, stocked with vintage whiskies and Lakeland ales, and the brace of restaurants (informal bistro and smart restaurant) both serve superior country food. The afternoon tea's done in the proper English fashion, too, complete with cucumber sandwiches.

★ Chalet BISTRO ££

(☑017687-72757; www.thechaletportinscale.co.uk; lunch £5-8.50, dinner £12.95-17.95; ☺9am-5pm Tue & Wed, 9am-5pm & 6.30-11pm Thu-Mon) This cafe-bistro opened in 2013 in Portinscale and has fast become one of Keswick's gastronomic hot spots. The architecture blends old (wood-burners, log piles) and new (plate glass, Scandinavian minimalism), and the food's a similar blend of styles; comforting crumpets and sharing platters for lunch, sophisticated plates of confit duck and dry-aged steak for supper, all accompanied by a suggested wine. Classy.

Morrel's BRITISH ££

(☑017687-72666; www.morrels.co.uk; Lake Rd; 3-course menu £21.95, mains £12.50-16.50; ☺5.30-9pm Tue-Sun) A reliable bistro that serves Mediterranean-tinged food. The stripped-back interior and spotlights make it feel formal, but it's actually a very relaxed affair.

Cafe-Bar 26 CAFE, BAR

(26 Lake Rd; tapas £4-10; ☺9am-11pm Mon-Sat, 10am-10pm Sun) An attractive corner wine-bar that also serves good tapas.

Dog & Gun PUB

(2 Lake Rd; ☺11am-11pm) Benches, beams, hearths, rugs: the old Dog is the picture of a Lakeland pub. Look out for Thirst Rescue ale, which donates part of its proceeds to the Keswick Mountain rescue team.

🛍 Shopping

George Fisher OUTDOOR EQUIPMENT

(2 Borrowdale Rd; ☺9am-5.30pm Mon-Sat, 10am-4pm Sun) Keswick has plenty of outdoor shops, but the traditionalists' choice is George Fisher, one of the Lake District's oldest outdoors suppliers. There are three floors of boots, tents and gear, and the boot-fitting service is superb.

ℹ Information

Tourist Office (☑ 017687-72645; keswicktic@
lake-district.gov.uk; Moot Hall, Market Pl;
⊙ 9.30am-5.30pm Apr-Oct, to 4.30pm Nov-Mar)
Sells discounted tickets for the Keswick Launch.

ℹ Getting There & Away

The Keswick & Honister Dayrider (adult/child/
family £8/6/22) buys unlimited travel on buses
in the Keswick area.

Useful buses from Keswick:

555/556 Lakeslink Hourly to Ambleside
(£7.95, 40 minutes), Windermere (£8.55, 50
minutes) and Kendal (£9.30, 1½ hours).

77/77A Honister Rambler Circular route (Keswick & Honister Dayrider adult/child £8/6, four
daily) from Keswick via Portinscale, Catbells,
Grange, Seatoller, Honister Pass, Buttermere,
Lorton and Whinlatter.

78 Borrowdale Rambler (Keswick & Honister
Dayrider adult/child £8/6, at least hourly Mon-
day to Friday, half-hourly weekends) The main
Borrowdale bus, with stops at Lodore, Grange,
Rosthwaite and Seatoller.

X4/X5 Penrith to Workington via Keswick
(£6.40, hourly Monday to Friday, six on Sunday).

ℹ Getting Around

Keswick Mountain Bikes (☑ 017687-75202;
www.keswickmountainbikes.co.uk; 133 Main St;
adult bikes per day £15-40; ⊙ 9.30am-5.30pm)
Mountain bikes can be hired from Keswick
Mountain Bikes. The road-specific shop is
above the Lakeland Pedlar Wholefood Cafe.

Borrowdale

With their patchwork of craggy hills, broad
fields, tinkling streams and drystone walls,
the side-by-side valleys of Borrowdale and
Buttermere are many people's idea of the
quintessential Lakeland landscape. Once
a centre for mineral mining (especially for
slate, coal and graphite), this is walkers'
country these days, and apart from the odd
rickety barn or puttering tractor, there's precious little to spoil the view.

South of Keswick, the B5289 tracks Derwentwater into the heart of Borrowdale,
winding past the small farming villages
of Grange-in-Borrowdale, Rosthwaite and
Stonethwaite.

◉ Sights & Activities

Lodore Falls   WATERFALL
At the southern end of Derwentwater, this
famous waterfall featured in a poem by Robert Southey, but it's only worth visiting after a
spell of rain. It's in the grounds of the Lodore
Hotel; there's an honesty box for donations.

Bowder Stone   OUTDOORS
A mile south from Grange, a turn-off leads
up to the geological curiosity known as the
Bowder Stone, a 1696-tonne lump of rock
left behind by a retreating glacier. A small
stepladder leads up to the top of the rock.

Watendlath Tarn   LAKE
This National Trust–owned tarn is reached
via a turn-off on the B5285 south of Keswick.
On the way, the road passes over one of the
Lake District's most photographed packhorse crossings at **Ashness Bridge**. Parking
at the tarn is free for NT members, but the
road is narrow and has few passing places,
so it's more pleasant to walk up in summer.

Platty+   BOATING
(☑ 017687-76572; www.plattyplus.co.uk; kayaks &
canoes per hr £8-15) Based at the Lodore Boat
Landings, this company hires out kayaks, canoes and sailing dinghies, and runs instruction courses.

🛏 Sleeping

Derwentwater Independent Hostel HOSTEL £
(☑ 017687-77246; www.derwentwater.org; Barrow
House; dm £19-21, r from £66; ℗ ◉) Built as a
19th-century mansion for the local notable
George Pocklington, this grand hostel was
previously YHA-owned, but it's now independently run and offers clean, basic dorms
(most have four to eight beds, but one has 22
beds) plus self-catering facilities. The house
still has many of its original architectural
features, and sits in 7-hectare grounds complete with waterfall.

Borrowdale YHA   HOSTEL £
(☑ 0845 371 9624; borrowdale@yha.org.uk; Long-
thwaite; dm £19-23; ⊙ Feb-Dec) Purpose-built
chalet hostel, specialising in walking and
activity trips.

Langstrath Inn   B&B ££
(☑ 017687-77239; www.thelangstrath.com; Stonethwaite; d £100-128, mains from £11.30; ⊙ restaurant
noon-10.30pm Tue-Sun; ℗ 🕸) Borrowdale's
country hotels are expensive, so you'll be better off basing yourself at this out-of-the-way
inn in Stonethwaite. The eight rooms feature
white walls, crimson throws and pleasant en
suites, and the countryside views are to die
for. Hearty food and beers from Hawkshead
Brewery are served in the restaurant.

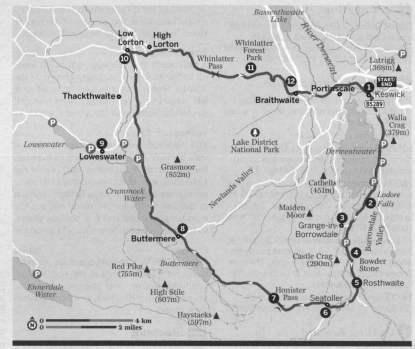

🏃 Driving Tour
Borrowdale & Buttermere

START KESWICK
END KESWICK
LENGTH 28 MILES, THREE TO FOUR HOURS

This is one of the Lakes' most beautiful road trips, taking in the unspoilt scenery of the Borrowdale, Buttermere and Lorton Valleys. Begin with breakfast in ❶ **Keswick**, then head along the B5289 into Borrowdale. First stop is ❷ **Lodore Falls** (p613), a pretty cascade at the southern end of Derwentwater. Next, detour to the little hamlet of ❸ **Grange-in-Borrowdale**, where a trail leads up the slate-strewn sides of Castle Crag, a small fell with great views over Borrowdale.

From Grange, carry on to the huge boulder known as the ❹ **Bowder Stone** (p613), shifted into position by the glacier which carved out the Borrowdale Valley. Pootle on to ❺ **Rosthwaite** for tea and cake at the Flock-In tearoom, or continue to ❻ **Seatoller** for lunch.

In the afternoon, tackle the steep crawl up to ❼ **Honister Pass** (p615), where you can pick up some slate souvenirs or take a mine tour. From here, the road drops down into the beautiful valley of ❽ **Buttermere**. Spot the zigzag peaks of High Stile, Haystacks and Red Pike looming on your left-hand side over the lake, stop off for a drink at the Fish Inn, and remember to pay your respects to Alfred Wainwright inside St James' Church.

Continue along the shore of Crummock Water past ❾ **Loweswater**, where you could make an optional but very worthwhile detour via the excellent Kirkstile Inn. When you reach ❿ **Low Lorton**, a right-hand turn carries you over Whinlatter Pass to ⓫ **Whinlatter Forest Park** (p610). The forest park makes a good spot for a late-afternoon stop; there's a pleasant cafe at the visitor centre, as well as displays on the local wildlife.

There are a couple of great options for dinner on your way back to Keswick such as ⓬ **Cottage in the Wood** (p612) just before Braithwaite.

Seatoller House
B&B ££

(☑ 017687-77218; www.seatollerhouse.co.uk; s £55, d £90-100; ℗) A tiny hideaway in Seatoller that feels like a Beatrix Potter burrow. It's tucked beneath Honister Pass and all the rooms are named after animals: attic Osprey has skylight views, Rabbit is pine-filled and Badger looks over the garden. Rooms including a four-course dinner for two cost £139.

Yew Tree Farm
B&B ££

(☑ 017687-77675; www.borrowdaleherdwick.co.uk; Rosthwaite; d £80; ℗) There are floral patterns galore at this sturdy Cumbrian farmhouse in rural Rosthwaite, with three rooms snuggled among cob walls and tiny windows (no wi-fi or TVs!). It's run by working sheep farmers, and you'll be able to spot Herdwicks in the nearby fields. Breakfast is huge, and the Flock-In tearoom over the road serves delicious cakes and puddings.

❶ Getting There & Away

Buses 77/77A and 78 connect Borrowdale and Buttermere with Keswick. Get the Keswick & Honister Dayrider pass (adult/child £8/6).

Honister Pass

From Borrowdale, a narrow, perilously steep road snakes up the fellside to Honister Pass and Buttermere Valley beyond.

Overlooking the top of the pass is the **Honister Slate Mine** (☑ 017687-77230; www.honister-slate-mine.co.uk; mine tour adult/child £12.50/7.50, all-day pass £34/25; ☺ tours 10.30am, 12.30pm & 3.30pm Mar-Oct), where underground tours venture deep into the bowels of the old 'Edge' and 'Kimberley' mines (a tour into the 'Cathedral' mine runs on Friday by request, but you'll need eight people and it costs £19.75).

Honister is also home to the UK's first **Via Ferrata** (Classic route adult/child £35/25, Xtreme £39.50/29.50), a vertiginous system of clifftop ropes and ladders once used by slate miners. It's exhilarating and great fun, but unsurprisingly you'll need a head for heights. Combination tickets are available for both activities.

A brand-new attraction opened in April 2014 combines the mining-and-climbing experience: a subterranean 'Burma Bridge', which involves clambering along underground passages on fixed ropes. It costs adult/child £19.95/14.95, and you need to be 10 or older.

Buttermere

From the high point of Honister, the road drops sharply into the deep bowl of Buttermere, skirting the lakeshore to Buttermere village, 4 miles from Honister and 9 miles from Keswick. From here, the B5289 cuts past Crummock Water before exiting the valley's northern edge.

Buttermere marks the start of Alfred Wainwright's all-time favourite circuit: up **Red Pike** (755m), and along **High Stile** (807m), **High Crag** and **Haystacks** (597m). In fact, the great man liked it so much, he stayed here for good: after his death in 1991, his ashes were scattered across the top of Haystacks as requested in his will. A small plaque in Buttermere's little chapel, **St James' Church**, commemorares the great man.

🛏 Sleeping & Eating

Buttermere YHA
HOSTEL £

(☑ 0845 371 9508; buttermere@yha.org.uk; dm £17-22; ☺ reception 8.30-10am & 5-10.30pm) A fine YHA, with a lake-view location halfway between Honister and Buttermere village.

★ Kirkstile Inn
PUB ££

(☑ 01900-85219; www.kirkstile.com; mains £12-16, s £63.50-90, d £99-109) A finer country pub you could not hope to find. Hidden away near the little lake of Loweswater, a mile or so north of Buttermere, the Kirkstile is a joy: crackling fires, oak beams, worn carpets, wooden bar and all. It's particularly known for its award-winning ales (try the Loweswater Gold). Rooms are quaint; some have views across Lorton Vale.

Fish Inn
PUB ££

(☑ 017687-70253; www.fishinnbuttermere.co.uk; mains £8-14, d £90-110; ℗) This inn once employed the 18th-century beauty known as the 'Maid of Buttermere', but these days it's just a welcoming local's pub, serving staples such as lasagne and battered haddock, washed down with ales from several local breweries.

❶ Getting There & Away

Bus 77/77A serves Buttermere and Honister Pass from Keswick. Use the Keswick & Honister Dayrider (adult/child £8/6).

Ullswater & Around

After Windermere, the second-largest lake in the Lake District is **Ullswater**, stretching for 7.5 miles between **Pooley Bridge**, and **Glenridding** and **Patterdale** in the south. Carved out by a long-extinct glacier, the deep valley in which the lake sits is flanked by an impressive string of fells, most notably the razor ridge of **Helvellyn**, Cumbria's third-highest mountain at 950m.

It's also famous as the place where William Wordsworth was inspired to write his best-known poem, 'Daffodils'.

◉ Sights & Activities

Gowbarrow Park
& Aira Force   PARK, WATERFALL
FREE This rolling park stretches out across the lakeshore between Pooley Bridge and Glenridding. Well-marked paths lead up to the impressive 20m waterfall of **Aira Force**. Another waterfall, **High Force**, is further up the hillside.

South of Gowbarrow Park is **Glencoyne Bay**, where the springtime daffodils inspired Wordsworth to pen the immortal lines: 'I wandered lonely as a cloud/That floats on high over hills and dales/When all at once I saw a crowd/A host, of golden daffodils...'

February and March are the best months if you want to see the flowers for yourself.

Ullswater 'Steamers'   BOATING
(☑017684-82229; www.ullswater-steamers.co.uk; round-the-lake adult/child £13.20/6.60) Ullswater's historic steamer service has been running since 1855. There are now four boats, all dressed in the company's distinctive livery; the stately *Lady of the Lake* was launched in 1888, making it the oldest passenger boat still working in the world.

The boats run east–west from Pooley Bridge, stopping at the village of Howtown on the southern shore en route to Glenridding. There are up to 11 sailings a day in summer, dropping to four in winter.

🛏 Sleeping

Helvellyn YHA   HOSTEL £
(☑0845 371 9742; helvellyn@yha.org.uk; Greenside; dm £13-18; ☺Easter-Oct) A high-level hostel, in an old miners' cottage 275m above the valley at the end of a rough track. It's a favourite with hikers looking to get a headstart on Helvellyn; dorms are small and facilities are basic, but meals are provided by hostel staff.

Patterdale YHA   HOSTEL £
(☑0845 371 9337; patterdale@yha.org.uk; Patterdale; dm £17-22.50; ☺reception 7.30-10am &

5-10.30pm Easter-Oct) This 1970s hostel lacks the heritage of some of the Lakeland YHAs, but it has a great location by the lake and all the usual YHA trappings (kitchen, cafe, TV lounge) – as long as you don't mind the institutional architecture.

Lowthwaite Farm   B&B ££
(☑017684-82343; www.lowthwaiteullswater.com; Matterdale; d £86-90; ℗) This lovely farmhouse in Matterdale is all about the good life. The owners have filled the place with souvenirs collected on their travels, such as chunky wooden beds made in Tanzania that match the house's hefty wooden beams. It's a couple of miles from the lake, off the A5091 to Dockray; ring ahead for directions, as it's tricky to find. Two-night minimum on weekends.

Old Water View   B&B ££
(☑017684-82175; www.oldwaterview.co.uk; Patterdale; d £72-86) Patterdale has several B&Bs, but this one's the pick. It's a simple place focusing on the essentials: friendly service, comfy rooms and good value. The split-level Bothy room is ideal for families, with attic beds for the kids, while Little Gem overlooks a stream and Place Fell is said to have been a favourite of Alfred Wainwright.

✖ Eating

Traveller's Rest   PUB ££
(Glenridding; mains £5.50-15; ☺10am-11pm) Down a pint with a view of the fells at Traveller's Rest, a Glenridding stalwart. The food might be plain (steaks, pies, prawn cocktails) but the portions are huge.

Fellbites   CAFE ££
(Glenridding; mains £5-15; ☺11am-8.30pm, to 5.30pm Wed) Popular Glenridding cafe that serves a good selection of spuds, sarnies and all-day breakfasts, plus a daily roast and chunky steaks.

ℹ Information

Ullswater Information Centre (☑017684-82414; ullswatertic@lake-district.gov.uk; Glenridding; ☺9am-5.30pm Apr-Oct)

ℹ Getting There & Away

The Ullswater Bus-and-Boat Combo ticket (adult/child/family £15.50/8.50/33) includes a day's travel on bus 108 with a return trip on an Ullswater Steamer; buy the ticket on the bus.

108 Travels from Penrith to Patterdale via Pooley Bridge and Glenridding (£5.50 to £6.50, five daily Monday to Friday, four on weekends).

Kendal

POP 28,586

Technically Kendal isn't in the Lake District, but it's a major gateway town. Often known as the 'Auld Grey Town' thanks to the sombre grey stone used for many of its buildings, Kendal is a bustling shopping centre with some good restaurants, a funky arts centre and intriguing museums. But it'll forever be synonymous in many people's minds with its famous mint cake, a staple item in the nation's hiking packs ever since Edmund Hillary and Tenzing Norgay munched it during their ascent of Everest in 1953.

◉ Sights

Kendal Museum MUSEUM
(www.kendalmuseum.org.uk; Station Rd; ⊗10.30am-5pm Tue-Sat) **FREE** Founded in 1796 by the inveterate Victorian collector William Todhunter, this mixed-bag museum features everything from stuffed beasts and transfixed butterflies to medieval coin hoards. There's also a reconstruction of the office of Alfred Wainwright, who served as honorary curator at the museum from 1945 to 1974: look out for his pipe and knapsack.

Abbot Hall Art Gallery GALLERY
(www.abbothall.org.uk; adult/child £5/free; ⊗10.30am-5pm Mon-Sat Apr-Oct, to 4pm Nov-Mar) Kendal's fine art gallery houses one of the northwest's best collections of 18th- and 19th-century art. It's especially strong on portraiture and Lakeland landscapes: look out for works by Constable, John Ruskin and local boy George Romney, a key figure in the Kendal School.

**Museum of Lakeland
Life & Industry** MUSEUM
(www.lakelandmuseum.org.uk; adult/child £5/free; ⊗10.30am-5pm Mon-Sat Mar-Oct, to 4pm Nov-Feb) Directly opposite Abbot Hall, this museum recreates various scenes from Lakeland life during the 18th and 19th centuries, including a farmhouse parlour, a Lakeland kitchen, an apothecary and the study of Arthur Ransome, author of *Swallows and Amazons*.

☆ Festivals & Events

Kendal Mountain Festival OUTDOORS
(www.mountainfest.co.uk) An annual mountain-themed celebration that encompasses films, books and talks in November.

🛏 Sleeping

Crosthwaite House B&B ££
(☏015395-68264; www.crosthwaitehouse.co.uk; d £80; P🐾) Zingy and zesty, this bright number has lots of imagination: the six rooms are colourfully decorated with swirly wallpapers, funky fabrics and retro furniture, and all named after a type of damson fruit. Tasty breakfast options include blueberry pancakes and huevos rancheros. It's in Crosthwaite, about 6 miles west of Kendal.

Beech House B&B ££
(☏01539-720385; www.beechhouse-kendal.co.uk; 40 Greenside; d £75-100; P🐾) Top Kendal honours go to this extremely elegant B&B at the top of the steep hill of Beast Banks. Rooms are a prim-and-proper treat: some feature sleigh beds and fluffy cushions, others free-standing baths and comfy sofas.

✗ Eating

Baba Ganoush DELI £
(☏01539-738210; Finkle St; mains £5-8; ⊗9.30am-4pm Tue-Sat) Down a side alley, this super cafe-deli serves delicious Mediterranean-tinged food such as falafels, lamb stews, veggie mezze and Moroccan tagines.

Waterside Wholefoods CAFE £
(Kent View; light meals £4-10; ⊗8.30am-4.30pm Mon-Sat) 🐾 Kendal's veggies make a beeline for this riverside cafe, a long-standing staple for sandwiches, pancakes and naughty-but-nice cakes.

1657 Chocolate House CAFE £
(54 Branthwaite Brow; lunches £3-8) A chocoholics' delight: handmade chocolates and Kendal mint cake in the basement, plus umpteen varieties of hot chocolate in the upstairs cafe.

New Moon BISTRO ££
(☏01539-729254; www.newmoonrestaurant.co.uk; 129 Highgate; mains £11.95-16.95; ⊗11.30am-2.15pm & 5.30-9pm Tue-Sat) A good bet for a pre-theatre supper, the New Moon is one of Kendal's longest-standing bistros, strong on filling dishes spiced with Asian and African flavours. The two-course pre-7pm menu is great value at £13.50.

Grain Store BISTRO ££
(Highgate; pizzas £6.50-10, mains £10-16.50; ⊗10am-11pm Mon-Sat) The Brewery Arts Centre's restaurant does a decent line in pub grub and stone-baked pizzas.

★ Punch Bowl Inn   PUB £££
(☑015395-68237; www.the-punchbowl.co.uk; Crosthwaite; mains £14.50-19.95; ☺noon-4pm & 5.30-8.30pm; P) This country inn in Crosthwaite, halfway between Kendal and Bowness, is one of the Lake District's epicurian pubs par excellence. Chef Scott Fairweather favours classic flavours, but his menu is sprinkled with cheffy ingredients such as salsify, pickled carrot, pak choi and cep purées. The elegant rooms are lovely too (£105 to £305), with reclaimed beams and Roberts Revival radios.

☆ Entertainment

Brewery Arts Centre   THEATRE, CINEMA
(☑01539-725133; www.breweryarts.co.uk; Highgate) One of the best arts centres in the northwest, it has a gallery, cafe, theatre and two cinemas, with regular live events to boot.

❶ Getting There & Around

The train line from Windermere runs to Kendal (£4.50, 15 minutes, hourly) en route to Oxenholme.

Bus 106 To Penrith (£4.50, 80 minutes, six to eight daily Monday to Saturday).

Bus 505 To Windermere, Ambleside, Hawkshead and Coniston (£9.30, hourly including Sundays).

Buses 555/556 Regular bus (£8 to £9.30, half-hourly Monday to Saturday, hourly at weekends) to Windermere (30 minutes), Ambleside (40 minutes) and Grasmere (1¼ hours).

Around Kendal

The countryside around Kendal feels gentler than the dramatic fells and valleys of the rest of the Lakes. It's mainly worth visiting for its stately homes and one of the county's top farm shops.

◉ Sights

Sizergh Castle   CASTLE
(NT; ☑015395-60070; www.nationaltrust.org.uk/sizergh-castle; adult/child £9.45/4.73, gardens only £5.85/2.93; ☺house 1-5pm Sun-Thu, gardens 11am-5pm daily) Three-and-a-half miles south of Kendal along the A591, this castle is the feudal seat of the Strickland family. Set around a *pele* tower, its finest asset is the lavish wood panelling on display in the Great Hall. There are private house tours between noon and 1pm.

Levens Hall   HISTORIC BUILDING
(☑015395-60321; www.levenshall.co.uk; adult/child £12.50/free, garden only £8.50/free; ☺house noon-4.30pm, gardens 10am-5pm Sun-Thu Mar-Oct) This Elizabethan manor is built around a mid-13th-century *pele* tower, and fine Jacobean furniture litters the house, although the real draw is the 17th-century topiary garden: a surreal riot of pyramids, swirls, curls, pom-poms and peacocks straight out of *Alice in Wonderland*. It's 2 miles south from Sizergh Castle along the A6. The 555/556 bus runs past the castle gates.

🛍 Shopping

Low Sizergh Barn   FOOD
(☑015395-60426; www.lowsizerghbarn.co.uk; ☺9am-5.30pm) A prodigious selection of Lakeland goodies are available at this beamed farm shop, one of the Lake District's very best. Breads from Grange Bakery, meats from Mansergh Hall, cheeses from Thornby Moor Dairy and beers from the Coniston Brewery Co are just some of the gourmet treats in store. There's also a farm trail and woodland walk to follow if the weather's nice. Look out for the signs just outside Kendal on the A590.

CUMBRIAN COAST

While the central lakes and fells pull in a never-ending stream of visitors, surprisingly few ever make the trek west to explore Cumbria's coastline. And that's a shame: while it might not compare to the wild grandeur of Northumberland or the rugged splendour of Scotland's shores, Cumbria's coast is well worth exploring. Less attractive is the nuclear plant of Sellafield, still stirring up controversy some 50 years after its construction.

◉ Sights

Holker Hall   HISTORIC BUILDING
(☑015395-58328; www.holker.co.uk; adult/child £12/free; ☺house 11am-4pm Sun-Fri, grounds 10.30am-4.30pm Mar-Oct, longer hours Jul & Aug) Holker Hall has been the family seat of the Cavendish family for nigh on 400 years. Though parts of the house date from the 16th century, the house was almost entirely rebuilt following a devastating fire in 1871. It's a typically ostentatious Victorian affair, covered with mullioned windows, gables

and copper-topped turrets outside, and filled inside with a warren of lavishly over-the-top rooms. The estate is about 3 miles east of Cartmel on the B5278.

Of particular note are the library and lavish Long Gallery (renowned for its elaborate plasterwork) and the amazing Wedgwood Dressing Rooms, covered in blue-and-white Wedgwood Jasperware. Also look out for various pieces of priceless Chippendale furniture, especially in the Drawing Room.

Outside, Holker's grounds sprawl for more than 10 hectares, encompassing a rose garden, a woodland, ornamental fountains and a 22m-high lime tree. There's also a food hall stocking produce from the estate, including venison and saltmarsh lamb.

Muncaster Castle   CASTLE
(www.muncaster.co.uk; adult/child £13/7.50; ⊗gardens & owl centre 10.30am-5pm, castle noon-4.30pm Sun-Fri) Like many Cumbrian castles, Muncaster was originally built around a 14th-century *pele* tower, constructed to resist Reiver raids. Home to the Pennington family for seven centuries, the castle's architectural highlights are its great hall and octagonal library, and outside you'll find an ornamental maze and owl centre.

The castle is also known for its numerous ghosts: keep your eyes peeled for the Muncaster Boggle and a malevolent jester known as Tom Fool (hence 'tomfoolery'). The castle is about 1.5 miles east of Ravenglass.

Laurel & Hardy Museum   MUSEUM
(☑01229-582292; www.laurel-and-hardy.co.uk; Brogden St, Ulverston; adult/child £4.50/2.50; ⊗10am-5pm Tue & Thu-Sun) Founded by avid Laurel and Hardy collector Bill Cubin back in 1983, this madcap museum in Ulverston (the birthplace of Stan Laurel) has new premises inside the town's old Roxy cinema. It's crammed floor-to-ceiling with cinematic memorabilia, from original posters to film props, and there's a shoebox-sized cinema showing back-to-back Laurel and Hardy classics.

Furness Abbey   ABBEY
(EH; adult/child £4.20/2.50; ⊗10am-6pm) Eight-and-a-half miles southwest of Ulverston, the rosy ruins of Furness Abbey are all that remains of one of northern England's largest and most powerful monasteries. Founded

CARTMEL

Tiny Cartmel is known for three things: its 12th-century **priory** (⊗9am-5.30pm May-Oct, to 3.30pm Nov-Apr) FREE, its **miniature racecourse** and its world-famous sticky toffee pudding, sold at the **Cartmel Village Shop** (☑015395-36280; www.stickytoffeepudding.co.uk; ⊗9am-5pm Mon-Sat, 10am-4.30pm Sun).

More recently it's become known as the home of chef Simon Rogan (dubbed Cumbria's answer to Heston Blumenthal). His flagship restaurant, **L'Enclume** (☑015395-36362; www.lenclume.co.uk; Cavendish St; set lunch £45, dinner menu £120; ⊗noon-1pm Wed-Sun & 6.30-9pm daily), showcases his boundary-pushing cuisine and madcap presentation, as well as his passion for foraged ingredients.

He also runs a less formal bistro, **Rogan & Company** (☑015395-35917; www.roganandcompany.co.uk; The Square; 3-course menu £40; ⊗noon-2pm Tue-Sat, 6.30-9pm Mon-Sat), across the village. Bookings for both are essential.

in the 12th century, it met an ignominious end in 1537 during the Dissolution. You can make out its footprint; arches, windows and some transept walls are still standing, along with the shell of the bell tower.

A recently unearthed gold crozier and gemstone ring are displayed in the **abbey museum** with other archaeological finds. Several buses, including bus X35, stop nearby.

St Bees Head   WILDLIFE RESERVE
(RSPB; stbees.head@rspb.org.uk) Five-and-a-half miles south of Whitehaven and 1.5 miles north of the tiny town of St Bees, this wind-battered headland is one of Cumbria's most important reserves for nesting seabirds. Depending on the season, species nesting here include fulmars, kittiwakes and razorbills, as well as Britain's only population of resident black guillemots. There are over 2 miles of cliff paths to explore.

ⓘ Getting Around

The Furness and Cumbrian Coast railway lines loop 120 miles from Lancaster to Carlisle,

DON'T MISS

LA'AL RATTY

Officially known as the **Ravenglass & Eskdale Railway** (☎ 01229-717171; www. ravenglass-railway.co.uk; adult/child/family return £13/16.50/33), but universally known hereabouts as La'al Ratty, this pocket-sized railway was originally built to ferry iron ore from the Eskdale mines out to the coast. These days it's one of Cumbria's most beloved family attractions, with miniature steam trains that chug for 7 miles down the Eskdale valley between the coastal town of Ravenglass and the village of Dalegarth.

Even if you're not a train nerd, it's a fabulously odd way to see the Lake District countryside. There are between seven and 14 trains a day depending on the season, and the trains stop at various stations en route.

stopping at the coastal resorts of Grange, Ulverston, Ravenglass, Whitehaven and Workington. The Cumbrian Coast Day Ranger (adult/child £19/9.50) covers a day's unlimited travel on the line, and works out cheaper than a return journey from Carlisle or Lancaster.

NORTHERN & EASTERN CUMBRIA

Many visitors speed through the northern and eastern reaches of Cumbria in a headlong dash for the Lake District, but it's worth taking the time to venture inland from the national park. It might not have the big-name fells and chocolate-box villages, but it's full of interest: traditional towns, crumbling castles, abandoned abbeys and sweeping moors, all set alongside the magnificent Roman engineering project of Hadrian's Wall.

Carlisle

POP 75,306

Carlisle isn't Britain's prettiest city, but it has history and heritage aplenty. Precariously perched on the frontier between England and Scotland, in the area once ominously dubbed the 'Debatable Lands', Cumbria's capital is a city with a notoriously stormy past: sacked by the Vikings, pillaged by the Scots, and plundered by the Border Reivers,

the city has been on the frontline of England's defences for more than 1000 years.

Reminders of the past are evident in its great crimson castle and cathedral, built from the same rosy-red sandstone as most of the city's houses. On English St, you can also see two massive circular **towers** which once flanked the city's gateway.

The nearest section of Hadrian's Wall begins at nearby Brampton; see p645 for details.

◉ Sights

★**Carlisle Castle**   CASTLE
(EH; www.english-heritage.org.uk/daysout/properties/carlisle-castle; Castle Way; adult/child £5.90/3.50; ☺ 9.30am-5pm Apr-Sep, 10am-4pm Oct-Mar) Carlisle's brooding, rust-red castle lurks on the north side of the city. Founded around a Celtic and Roman stronghold, the Norman keep was added in 1092 by William Rufus, and later refortified by Henry II, Edward I and Henry VIII (who added the supposedly cannon-proof towers). From the battlements, the stirring views stretch as far as the Scottish borders.

The castle has witnessed some dramatic events over the centuries: Mary, Queen of Scots was imprisoned here in 1568, and the castle was the site of a notorious eight-month siege during the English Civil War, when the Royalist garrison survived by eating rats, mice and the castle dogs before finally surrendering in 1645. Look out for some medieval graffiti and the 'licking stones' in the dungeon, which Jacobite prisoners supposedly lapped for moisture.

Admission includes entry to the **Kings Own Royal Border Regiment Museum**, which details the history of Cumbria's Infantry Regiment. There are guided tours from April to September.

Carlisle Cathedral   CATHEDRAL
(www.carlislecathedral.org.uk; 7 The Abbey; suggested donation £5, photography £1; ☺ 7.30am-6.15pm Mon-Sat, to 5pm Sun) Built from the same red sandstone as the castle, Carlisle's cathedral began life as a priory church in 1122, and became a cathedral when its first abbot, Athelwold, became the first Bishop of Carlisle. Among its notable features are the 15th-century choir stalls, the barrel-vaulted roof and the 14th-century East Window, one of the largest Gothic windows in England. Surrounding the cathedral are other priory relics, including the 16th-century **Fratry** and the **Prior's Tower**.

Tullie House Museum   MUSEUM
(www.tulliehouse.co.uk; Castle St; adult/child £7/
free; ⏱10am-5pm Mon-Sat, 11am-4pm Sun) Carlisle's main museum covers the city's past,
from Roman foundations to the present day.
There's an awesome view of the castle from
the rooftop Lookout.

The highlight is the Roman Frontier
Gallery, which uses a mix of archaeological
exhibits and interactive displays to tell the
story of the Roman occupation of Carlisle.
Upstairs, the Border Galleries cover the rest
of the city's history, from the Bronze Age
through to the Border Reivers, the Jacobite
Rebellion and the Industrial Revolution.
The Carlisle Life Gallery details the city's
social history through photos, films and archive recordings, and Old Tullie House has
a collection of art, sculpture and porcelain.

🛏 Sleeping

Carlisle's accommodation leaves a lot to be
desired. The B&Bs in the centre are pretty
uninspiring, so you're better off heading further out.

Warwick Lodge   B&B £
(✓01228-523796; www.warwicklodgecarlisle.co.
uk; 112 Warwick Rd; s/d £40/75) Decent budget
B&B, with clean rooms, flouncy furnishings
and a generous breakfast.

Willowbeck Lodge   B&B ££
(✓01228-513607; www.willowbeck-lodge.com; Lamb-
ley Bank, Scotby; d £100-130; P 🐾) Escape the
city hustle at this modern venue, 3 miles
from the centre. Six deluxe rooms are closer
to hotel standard than B&B, offering tasteful
shades of beige and taupe, luxurious bathrooms and a gabled lounge overlooking a
private pond.

Premier Inn Carlisle Central   HOTEL ££
(✓0871 527 8210; www.premierinn.com; Warwick
Rd; d from £60; P 🐾) A Premier Inn it may
be, but this is actually one of Carlisle's best-
value and best-located options. It's about
a mile from the centre along Warwick Rd,
and offers the usual bog-standard facilities:
decent-sized rooms, generic decor, wi-fi and
plenty of parking. It's about a mile east of
the centre on Warwick Rd.

Warwick Hall   B&B £££
(✓01228-561546; www.warwickhall.org; Warwick-on-
Eden; s £95, d £126-180) This fine country house
2 miles from the centre along Warwick Rd is
a real country retreat. With its huge rooms,
high ceilings and antique decor, it feels a bit
like staying on an aristocratic friend's estate.
There are hectares of grounds and it even has
its own stretch of river for fishing.

🍴 Eating

Shabby Scholar   CAFE £
(✓01228-402813; 11-13 Carlyle Ct; mains £7-10;
⏱9.30am-9pm Tue-Sat) As its name suggests, this popular place is stylishly shabby, with scruffy furniture, a bar made out
of old crates and a determinedly chilled
vibe. It's great for tapas and light bites such
as pulled-pork rolls, mackerel salad and
'carnivore' nachos, but it does not take
bookings.

Prior's Kitchen Restaurant   CAFE £
(Carlisle Cathedral; lunches £4-6; ⏱9.45am-4pm
Mon-Sat) Carlisle's best place for traditional afternoon tea is in the cathedral's fratry,
once used as a monk's mess hall.

Foxes Cafe Lounge   CAFE £
(www.foxescafelounge.co.uk; 18 Abbey St; mains
£4-10; ⏱10am-7pm Tue-Thu, to 11pm Fri, to 4.30pm
Sat) This cool cafe-gallery provides a venue
for all kinds of creative happenings, from
open-mic nights and live gigs to photo exhibitions. Count on Continental cafe food and
excellent coffee.

David's   BRITISH ££
(✓01228-523578; www.davidsrestaurant.co.uk; 62
Warwick Rd; 2-course lunch £13.95, 2-course dinner
£18.95; ⏱noon-3.30pm & 6.30-11pm Tue-Sat) For
sit-down dining in Carlisle, David's townhouse restaurant is definitely the place.
Gourmet gastronomy is the order of the day
here – herb-crusted lamb, saffron-infused
cod or roast Goosnargh duck – with a formal
setting to match (think chandeliers, fireplaces, cornicing).

Holme Bistro   BRITISH ££
(✓01228-534343; www.holmebistro.co.uk; 56-58
Denton St; mains £10.95-15.95; ⏱12.30-2pm &
6-9pm Tue-Sat) This slick bistro is run by
brother-and-sister team Rob Don and Kirsty
Robson, and has earned a loyal clientele for
its unpretentious cuisine.

🍷 Drinking & Entertainment

Botchergate's the centre of Carlisle's nightlife, but it gets rowdy at closing time.

Fats   PUB
(✓01228-511774; 48 Abbey St; ⏱11am-11pm) A
less hectic alternative to Botchergate's pubs.
DJs and comedy nights are held regularly.

Hell Below & Co
BAR

(☑ 01228-548481; 14 Devonshire St; ☺ noon-1am) Bare brick and wood floors give this lively bar a hint of hipsterdom; the house specialities are mojitos and craft beer, ideally served with a wood-fired pizza.

Brickyard
CONCERT VENUE

(www.thebrickyardonline.com; 14 Fisher St) Carlisle's grungy gig venue, housed in the former Memorial Hall.

ℹ Information

Tourist Office (☑ 01228-625600; www.historic-carlisle.org.uk; Greenmarket; ☺ 9.30am-5pm Mon-Sat, 10.30am-4pm Sun)

ℹ Getting There & Away

BUS

National Express coaches depart from the bus station on Lonsdale St for destinations including London (£22 to £34.80, 7½ hours, two direct daily), Manchester (£22.90 to £27.40, three to 3½ hours, four daily) and Glasgow (£16.40 to £19.50, two hours, four to six daily).

104 To Penrith (£5.40, 40 minutes, half-hourly Monday to Saturday, nine on Sunday).

554 To Keswick (£7.75, 70 minutes, four daily Monday to Saturday, three on Sunday).

TRAIN

Carlisle is on the west coast line from London to Glasgow. It's also the terminus for the scenic Cumbrian Coast and Tyne Valley Lines, as well as the historic **Settle to Carlisle Railway** (www.settle-carlisle.co.uk; anytime single to Settle £20.30, anytime return £26.20) across the Yorkshire Dales. Main destinations:

Glasgow £27, 1¼ hours

Lancaster £29.70, 45 minutes

London Euston £109.70, 3½ hours

Manchester £53, two hours

Newcastle-upon-Tyne £15.50, 1½ hours

ℹ Getting Around

To book a taxi, call **Radio Taxis** (☑ 01228-527575) or **Cumbria Cabs** (☑ 01228-899599).

Alston
POP 1105

Surrounded by the bleak hilltops of the Pennines, isolated Alston's main claim to fame is its elevation: at 305m above sea level, it's thought to be the highest market town in England (despite no longer having a market). It's also famous among steam enthusiasts thanks to the **South Tynedale Railway** (☑ 01434-381696, timetable 01434-382828; www.south-tynedale-railway.org.uk; adult/child return to Lintley £10/4; ☺ Apr-Oct), which puffs and clatters through the hilly country between Alston and Lintley, along a route that originally operated from 1852 to 1976.

The line was partly reopened by enthusiasts in 1983. It's now run as a registered charity, and a recent £4.2 million lottery grant will fund the long-awaited extension of the line all the way to Slaggyford over the next few years.

The return trip takes about an hour; there are up to five daily trains in midsummer.

Penrith
POP 15,181

Just outside the borders of the national park, red-brick Penrith perhaps has more in common with the stout market towns of the Yorkshire Dales. It's a solid, traditional place, with plenty of cosy pubs and quaint teashops, and a lively market on Tuesdays. It's also the main gateway for exploring the picturesque Eden Valley.

Two miles west of Penrith, the **Rheged visitor centre** (www.rheged.com; ☺ 10am-6pm) houses a large-screen Imax cinema and retail hall. The name commemorates the Celtic kingdom of Rheged, of which the Eden Valley was once the centre.

◉ Sights

Penrith Castle
RUIN

(☺ 7.30am-9pm Easter-Oct, to 4.30pm Nov-Easter) The ruins of Penrith Castle loom on the edge of town, opposite the train station. Built in the 14th century, by William Strickland (later Bishop of Carlisle and Archbishop of Canterbury), it was later expanded by Richard III to resist Scottish raids, one of which razed the town in 1345.

🛏 Sleeping

Brooklands
B&B ££

(☑ 01768-863395; www.brooklandsguesthouse.com; 2 Portland Pl; s £40, d £80-90; 🛜) The town's most elegant B&B is this Victorian red-brick on Portland Pl. Rich furnishings and posh extras (such as White Company toiletries, fridges and chocolates on the tea tray) keep it a cut above the competition.

★ **Augill Castle**
HOTEL £££

(☑ 01768-341967; www.stayinacastle.com; Kirkby Stephen; r £170-240; 🅿🛜) If you've always

HAWESWATER & LOWTHER

The most easterly of the Lake District's waters, **Haweswater** is also one of its most remote; it can only be reached via a narrow, winding road. In fact, it's not actually a lake but an artificial reservoir, created in 1935; sometimes during exceptionally dry spells, the remains of the drowned village of Mardale appear above the water-line. It's a great area to escape the hiking crowds, and is popular with wildlife-spotters too; sometimes golden eagles can be seen soaring over the fells.

Nearby is the sprawling estate of **Lowther** (☑01931-712192; www.lowthercastle.org; admission £8; ☻10am-5pm), which belonged to one of the Lake District's most venerable families and is currently undergoing a huge, multimillion-pound restoration project. The 400-year-old crenellated castle and the estate's grounds are now open to the public for the first time in many years; though the castle itself is to remain a ruin, restoration work is slowly breathing life back into the gardens, which have been largely forgotten since the estate fell into disrepair following WWII. The estate has a new cafe and shop, but the nearby **George & Dragon** (☑01768-865381; www.georgeanddragonclifton.co.uk; mains £12.95-21.95; ☻noon-2.30pm & 6-9pm) in Clifton is the best bet for lunch.

dreamt of staying in a bona-fide British castle, then this stately pile in Kirkby Stephen is definitely the place. All the trappings are here – crenellated turrets, stained-glass windows, cavernous rooms – and inside the design vibe is rather groovy, with a mix of antique furniture and contemporary furnishings. There's even a mini-cinema. It's 25 miles southeast of Penrith.

George Hotel HOTEL **£££**
(☑01768-862696; www.lakedistricthotels.net/georgehotel; Devonshire St; d £134-204; P☏) Penrith's venerable red-brick coaching inn offers classically decorated rooms in prim stripes and country patterns, plus a quaint bar and restaurant.

✖ Eating

No 15 CAFE **£**
(15 Victoria Rd; lunches £6-10; ☻9am-5pm Mon-Sat) Lively cafe-cum-art emporium specialising in gourmet lunch fare such as ciabattas, burgers, salads and veggie quiches. After lunch, browse the latest exhibition in the attached gallery.

★**Four & Twenty** BISTRO **££**
(☑01768-210231; www.fourandtwentypenrith.co.uk; 14 King St; mains £13-16; ☻noon-2.30pm

&6.30-9.30pm) Proper fine dining with a reasonable price tag is the modus operandi at this much-admired new bistro, which blends sleek decor with rustic wood, banquette seats and mix-and-match furniture. Expect sophisticated dishes such as twice-baked Stilton soufflé and braised blade of beef with caramelised onion rosti. If you're going to eat out in Penrith, this is the place to do it.

❶ Information

Tourist Office (☑01768-867466; pen.tic@eden.gov.uk; Middlegate; ☻9.30am-5pm Mon-Sat, 1-4.45pm Sun) Also houses Penrith's tiny museum.

❶ Getting There & Away

There are frequent train connections to Carlisle (£7.30, 15 minutes) and Lancaster (£16.80, one hour).

The bus station is northeast of the centre, off Sandgate.

104 To Carlisle (£5.40, 40 minutes, half-hourly Monday to Saturday, nine on Sunday).

X4/X5 Via Rheged, Keswick and Cockermouth to the Cumbrian coast (£6.40 to £7.60, half-hourly Monday to Saturday, hourly Sunday).

THE LAKE DISTRICT & CUMBRIA PENRITH

Newcastle & Northeast England

Best Places to Eat

➜ Jolly Fisherman (p650)

➜ Mizen Head (p652)

➜ Bouchon Bistrot (p645)

➜ Blackfriars (p632)

➜ Broad Chare (p632)

Best Places to Stay

➜ Otterburn Castle (p648)

➜ Jesmond Dene House (p631)

➜ Ashcroft (p646)

➜ 2 The Crofts (p644)

Why Go?

The irrepressible city of Newcastle-upon-Tyne anchors England's northeast. Set on the mighty River Tyne, this former industrial powerhouse's steep hills are lined with handsome Victorian buildings, and many of its one-time factories and warehouses have been transformed into galleries, museums, bars and entertainment venues. Newcastle's nightlife is legendary and revelling in an evening on the tiles here is a quintessential experience.

Newcastle is also an ideal gateway for escaping into the northeast's utterly wild, starkly beautiful countryside – from the rounded Cheviot Hills to brooding Northumberland National Park and the remote North Pennines. Spectacular Hadrian's Wall cuts a lonely path through the landscape, dotted with dramatic fortress ruins that are haunting reminders of the bloody struggle with the Scots to the north, while the region's unspoilt coastline takes in long, desolate beaches, wind-worn castles and tiny, magical islands offshore.

When to Go

➜ May in the northeast brings the chance to celebrate all things Roman at the week-long Hadrian's Wall Festival.

➜ The best time to discover the region's miles of wide sandy beaches is during the summer season (June to August), although for surfers, Tynemouth's world-class waves are best (if chilliest) in winter and spring.

➜ September through October is great for losing yourself in the autumnal landscapes of the North Pennines.

➜ September is also the month to grab a Newkie Brown ale, or your running shoes, and join the party along the route of Tyneside's Great North Run, one of the world's biggest half marathons.

History

Violent history has shaped this region more than any other in England, primarily because of its frontier position. Although Hadrian's Wall didn't serve as a defensive barrier, it marked the northern limit of Roman Britain and was the empire's most heavily fortified line. Following the Romans' departure, the region became part of the Anglian kingdom of Bernicia, which united with the kingdom of Deira (encompassing much of modern-day Yorkshire) to form Northumbria in 604.

The kingdom changed hands and borders shifted several times over the next 500 years as Anglo-Saxons and Danes struggled to seize it. The land north of the River Tweed was finally ceded to Scotland in 1018, while the nascent kingdom of England kept everything below it.

The arrival of the Normans in 1066 saw William I eager to secure his borders against the Scots. He commissioned most of the castles you see along the coast, and cut deals with the prince bishops of Durham to ensure their loyalty. The new lords of Northumberland became very powerful because, as Marcher Lords (from the use of 'march' as a synonym of 'border'), they kept the Scots at bay.

Northumberland's reputation as a hotbed of rebellion intensified during the Tudor years, when the largely Catholic north, led by the seventh duke of Northumberland, Thomas Percy, rose up against Elizabeth I in the defeated Rising of the North in 1569. The Border Reivers, raiders from both sides of the border in the 16th century, kept the region in a perpetual state of lawlessness that only subsided after the Act of Union between England and Scotland in 1707.

Coal mines were the key to the 19th-century industrialisation of the northeast, powering steelworks, shipyards and armament works that grew up along the Tyne and Tees. In 1825 the mines also spawned the world's first steam railway, the Stockton & Darlington, built by local engineer George Stephenson. Social strife emerged in the 20th century, however, with mines, shipbuilding, steel production and the railway industry all winding down during the Great Depression and postwar years. Reinventing the northeast has been a mammoth task but regeneration continues apace.

🏃 Activities

Walking and cycling opportunities abound in this region, but be prepared for wind and rain at any time of year and for very harsh conditions in winter. Regional tourism websites all contain walking and cycling information, and tourist offices stock free leaflets, plus maps and guides covering walking, cycling and other activities.

Cycling

The northeast has some of England's most inspiring cycle routes. Part of the National Cycle Network (NCN), a longtime favourite is the **Coast & Castles Cycle Route** (www.coast-and-castles.co.uk; NCN Route 1), which runs south–north along the glorious Northumberland coast between Newcastle-upon-Tyne and Berwick-upon-Tweed and Edinburgh, Scotland.

The 140-mile **Sea to Sea Cycle Route** (C2C; www.c2c-guide.co.uk) runs across northern England between the Cumbrian coast (Whitehaven or Workington) and Tynemouth or Sunderland via the northern Lake District and wild North Pennines' hills.

The other coast-to-coast option is the **Hadrian's Cycleway** (www.cycle-routes.org), a 175-mile route between South Shields or Tynemouth and Ravenglass in Cumbria along Hadrian's Wall.

Walking

The North Pennines – along with the Cheviots further north – are considered 'England's last wilderness'. Long routes through the hills include the famous **Pennine Way National Trail**, which keeps mainly to the high ground between the Yorkshire Dales and the Scottish border, but also crosses sections of river valley and some tedious patches of plantation. The whole route is around 270 miles, but the 70-mile section between Bowes and Hadrian's Wall is a fine four-day taster.

Hadrian's Wall has a huge range of easy loop walks taking in forts and other historical highlights.

One of the finest walks along the windswept **Northumberland coast**, between the villages of Craster and Bamburgh via Dunstanburgh, includes two of the region's most spectacular castles.

ℹ️ Getting There & Around

BUS

Bus transport around the region can be difficult, particularly around the more remote reaches of western Northumberland. Contact **Traveline** (☑ 0871 200 2233; www.travelinenortheast. info) for information on connections, timetables and prices.

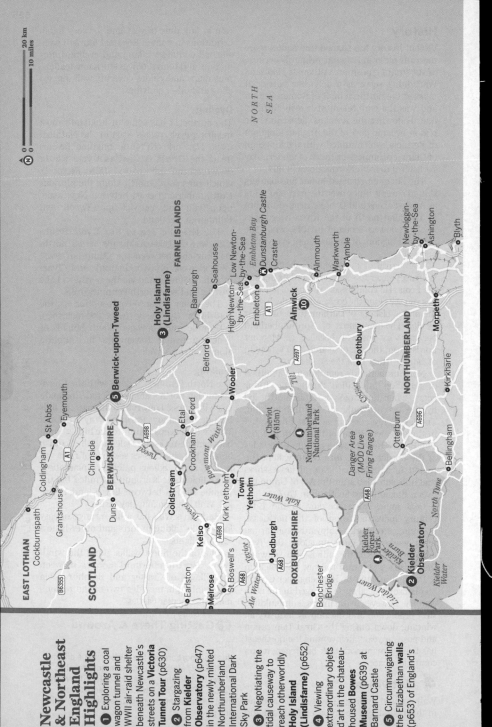

Newcastle & Northeast England Highlights

❶ Exploring a coal wagon tunnel and WWII air-raid shelter beneath Newcastle's streets on a **Victoria Tunnel Tour** (p630)

❷ Stargazing from **Kielder Observatory** (p647) in the newly minted Northumberland International Dark Sky Park

❸ Negotiating the tidal causeway to reach otherworldly **Holy Island (Lindisfarne)** (p652)

❹ Viewing extraordinary objets d'art in the chateau-housed **Bowes Museum** (p639) at Barnard Castle

❺ Circumnavigating the Elizabethan **walls** (p653) of England's

0 20 km
0 10 miles

EAST LOTHIAN

Cockburnspath
Grantshouse
Coldingham
St Abbs
Eyemouth

SCOTLAND

B6355
A1

Chirnside
Duns

BERWICKSHIRE

A698

❺ Berwick-upon-Tweed

Earlston
Melrose
St Boswell's
Kelso
A698
Coldstream
Kirk Yetholm
Town Yetholm

A68
Jedburgh
A68
ROXBURGHSHIRE

Bonchester Bridge

Kielder Forest Park
❷ **Kielder Observatory**

Kielder Water
Kielder Burn
Liddel Water

A68
North Tyne
Bellingham

A696
Kirkharle

Otterburn

Danger Area (MOD Live Firing Range)

❹ Northumberland National Park

▲ Cheviot (815m)

Bowmont Water
Kale Water
Teviot
Ale Water
Tweed

Crookham
Etal
Ford

Wooler

Belford

Bamburgh
Seahouses

FARNE ISLANDS

❸ Holy Island (Lindisfarne)

High Newton-by-the-Sea
Low Newton-by-the-Sea
Embleton Bay
Embleton
A1
❹ Dunstanburgh Castle
Craster

Alnwick ❿
Alnmouth

A697
Rothbury
Coquet
Till

NORTHUMBERLAND

Warkworth
Amble

Newbiggin-by-the-Sea
Ashington
Blyth

Morpeth

NORTH SEA

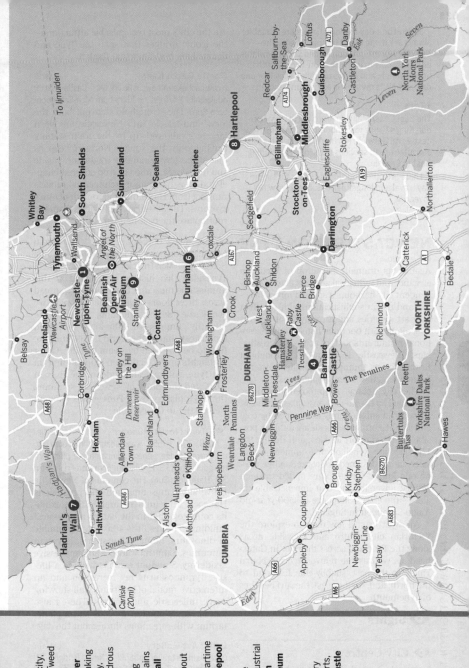

Several one-day Explorer tickets are available; always ask if one might be appropriate. The Explorer North East (adult/child £9/8), available on buses, covers Berwick-upon-Tweed south to Scarborough, and allows unlimited travel for one day, as well as numerous admission discounts.

TRAIN

The East Coast Main Line runs north from London King's Cross to Edinburgh via Durham, Newcastle and Berwick; Northern Rail operates local and inter-urban services in the north, including west to Carlisle.

There are numerous Rover tickets for single-day travel and longer periods; check www.rail rover.org.

NEWCASTLE-UPON-TYNE

POP 279,100

Against its dramatic backdrop of Victorian elegance and industrial grit, this fiercely independent city harbours a spirited mix of heritage and urban sophistication, with excellent new art galleries and a magnificent concert hall, along with boutique hotels, some exceptional restaurants and, of course, interesting bars; Newcastle is renowned throughout Britain for its thumping nightlife, bolstered by an energetic student population.

The city retains deep-rooted traditions, embodied by the no-nonsense, likeable locals. Raised and subsequently abandoned by coal and steel, Geordies (as locals are dubbed, possibly due to support for George II during the 1745 Jacobite Rebellion or to miners' use of safety lamps designed by George Stephenson – no one knows for sure) are united through history, adversity and that impenetrable dialect – the closest language to 1500-year-old Anglo-Saxon left in England.

Allow at least a few days to explore the Victorian city centre and quayside areas along the Tyne and across the river in Gateshead, as well as the rejuvenated Ouseburn Valley to the east, shabby-chic Jesmond to the north, and, on the coast, the surf beaches of Tynemouth.

◉ Sights

◉ City Centre

Newcastle's grand Victorian centre, a compact area bordered roughly by Grainger St to the west and Pilgrim St to the east, is one of the most compelling examples of urban rejuvenation in England. Down by the quays

are the city's most recognisable attractions – the iconic bridges that span the Tyne and the striking buildings that flank it.

Castle Garth Keep   CASTLE

(www.castlekeep-newcastle.org.uk; Castle Garth; adult/child £4/free; ⊙10am-5pm Mon-Sat, noon-5pm Sun) The stronghold that put both the 'new' and 'castle' into Newcastle has been largely swallowed up by the train station, leaving only the square Norman keep as one of the few remaining fragments. Inside you'll discover a fine chevron-covered chapel and an exhibition of architectural models ranging from Hadrian's Wall to 20th-century eyesores. The 360-degree city views from the rooftop are the best in town.

★ Discovery Museum   MUSEUM

(www.discoverymuseum.org.uk; Blandford Sq; ⊙10am-4pm Mon-Fri, 11am-4pm Sat & Sun) FREE Tyneside's rich history is explored at this unmissable museum. Exhibitions are spread across three floors of the former Co-operative Wholesale Society building around the mightily impressive 30m-long *Turbinia*, the fastest ship in the world in 1897 and first to be powered by steam turbine. Other highlights are a section on shipbuilding on the Tyne, with a scale model of the river in 1929, and the 'Story of Newcastle' spanning the city's history from Pons Aelius (Roman Newcastle) to Cheryl Cole.

★ Great North Museum   MUSEUM

(☐0191-208 6765; www.greatnorthmuseum.org. uk; Barras Bridge; general admission free, planetarium adult/child £3/2; ⊙10am-5pm Mon-Fri, to 4pm Sat, 11am-4pm Sun) The contents of Newcastle University's museums and the prestigious Hancock Museum's natural history exhibits come together in the latter's neoclassical building. The result is a fascinating jumble of dinosaurs, Roman altar stones, Egyptian mummies, Samurai warriors and impressive taxidermy. Standout exhibits include a life-size Tyrannosaurus rex recreation and an interactive model of Hadrian's Wall showing every milecastle and fortress. There's also lots of hands-on stuff for kids and a planetarium with screenings throughout the day.

Laing Art Gallery   GALLERY

(www.laingartgallery.org.uk; New Bridge St; ⊙10am-5pm Tue-Sat, 2-5pm Sun) FREE The exceptional collection at the Laing includes works by Gainsborough, Gauguin and Henry Moore, and an important collection of paintings by Northumberland-born artist

Newcastle-upon-Tyne

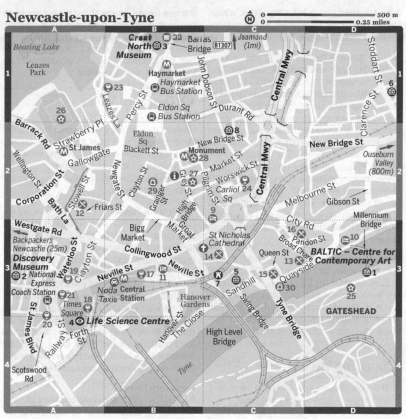

Newcastle-upon-Tyne

John Martin (1789–1854). Check the 'What's On' section of the website for free events including talks and tours.

★ **Life Science Centre**   SCIENCE CENTRE
(☑0191-243 8210; www.life.org.uk; Times Sq; family/adult/concession £29.50/12.00/£9.50, child 2-17yr £7.50, child under 2yr free; ☺10am-6pm Mon-Sat, 10am-8pm Thu, 11am-6pm Sun) Part of a sober-minded institute devoted to the study of genetic science, this centre lets you discover the secrets of life through a fascinating series of hands-on exhibits. The highlight is the Motion Ride, a simulator that lets you 'experience' bungee jumping and the like (the 3D film changes every year). There are lots of thought-provoking arcade-style games, and if the information sometimes gets lost on the way, never mind, kids will love it. Book ahead at busy times.

Bessie Surtees House   HISTORIC BUILDING
(EH; www.english-heritage.org.uk; 41-44 Sandhill; ☺10am-4pm Mon-Fri) `FREE` The Tyne's northern bank was the hub of commercial Newcastle in the 16th century and on Sandhill a row of leaning merchant houses has survived from that era. One of them is Bessie Surtees House, where three rooms are open to the public. The daughter of a wealthy banker, feisty Bessie annoyed Daddy by falling in love with pauper John Scott (1751–1838). It all ended in smiles as John went on to become Lord Chancellor.

◉ Ouseburn Valley

Around a mile east of the city centre, Newcastle's 19th-century industrial heartland, Ouseburn Valley, is now an up-and-coming, semi-regenerated district, with potteries, glass-blowing studios and other creative workspaces, along with pubs, bars and entertainment venues.

★ **Victoria Tunnel**   HISTORIC SITE
(☑0191-261 6596; www.ouseburntrust.org.uk; adult/child £6/3; ☺by reservation) Walking Newcastle's streets, you'd never know this extraordinary tunnel runs for 4km beneath your feet. Built between 1839 and 1842 as a thoroughfare for coal wagons, it was used as an air-raid shelter during WWII. Volunteer-led, two-hour tours take you through an atmospheric 700m-long level section of the tunnel. Book ahead as numbers are limited to 12 participants, and wear good shoes and a washable jacket for the limewashed walls. Tours usually depart from Ouseburn Farm.

Ouseburn Farm   FARM
(☑0191-232 3698; www.bykerbridge.org.uk/farm; Ouseburn Rd, adjacent Lime St; admission by donation; ☺9.30am-4.30pm) Shetland ponies, pigs, sheep, goats, chickens and agricultural crops are the last thing you'd expect to find in Newcastle, but you can see them all at this community farm.

Biscuit Factory   GALLERY
(www.thebiscuitfactory.com; 16 Stoddart St; ☺10am-5pm Mon-Fri, to 6pm Sat, 11am-5pm Sun) No prizes for guessing what this commercial art gallery used to be. These days, it's the UK's biggest contemporary art shop, where you can peruse and/or buy works by artists from near and far in a variety of mediums, including painting, sculpture, glassware and furniture, many with a northeast theme.

Seven Stories – The Centre for Children's Books   MUSEUM
(www.sevenstories.org.uk; 30 Lime St; adult/child £7/6; ☺10am-5pm Mon-Sat, to 4pm Sun) A marvellous conversion of a handsome Victorian mill has resulted in Seven Stories, a very hands-on museum dedicated to the

---

BRIDGING THE TYNE

The most famous view in Newcastle is the cluster of Tyne bridges, the most famous of these being the **Tyne Bridge** (1925–28). Its resemblance to Australia's Sydney Harbour Bridge (1923–32) is no coincidence, as both were built by the same company, Dorman Long of Middlesbrough. The quaint little **Swing Bridge** (1876) pivots in the middle to let ships through. Nearby, the **High Level Bridge** (1849) designed by Robert Stephenson, was the world's first combined road and railway bridge. The most recent addition is the multiple-award-winning **Millennium Bridge** (aka Blinking Bridge; 2002), which opens like an eyelid to let ships pass.

Beneath the Tyne between Howdon in North Tyneside and Jarrow in South Tyneside, east of the centre, are the Grade II–listed, 1951-built **Tyne Pedestrian and Cyclist Tunnels** (www.tynepedestrianandcyclisttunnels.co.uk) as well as two tollway **vehicle tunnels** (TT2; www.tt2.co.uk; one-way £1.60, notes & copper coins not accepted).

wondrous world of children's literature. Across the seven floors you'll find original manuscripts and artwork from the 1930s onwards, and a constantly changing program of kid-oriented exhibitions, activities and events designed to encourage the AA Milnes of the new millennium.

⊙ Gateshead

The area of Newcastle south of the Tyne is the 'town' of Gateshead. Local authorities are now promoting the whole kit-and-caboodle-on-Tyne as 'NewcastleGateshead'.

★ BALTIC – Centre
for Contemporary Art   GALLERY

(www.balticmill.com; Gateshead Quays; ⊙10am-6pm) **FREE** Once a huge mustard-coloured grain store, the BALTIC is now a huge mustard-coloured art gallery rivalling London's Tate Modern. There are no permanent exhibitions; instead, rotating shows feature the work and installations of some of contemporary art's biggest show-stoppers. The complex has artists in residence, a performance space, a cinema, a bar, a spectacular rooftop restaurant (bookings essential) and a ground-floor restaurant with riverside tables. A 4th-floor outdoor platform and 5th-floor viewing box offer fabulous panoramas of the Tyne.

🛏 Sleeping

Although the number of city-centre accommodation options is increasing, they are still generally restricted to the chain variety – either budget or business – catering to party people and execs. Most of the other properties are in the handsome northern suburb of Jesmond, where the forces of gentrification and student power fight it out for territory.

🛏 City Centre

Backpackers Newcastle   HOSTEL £

(☑0191-340 7334; www.backpackersnewcastle. com; 262 Westgate Rd; dm from £18; 🛜) This clean, well-run budget hostel has just 26 beds, lending it a bit more of a backpacker vibe than its competitors in the city. Great facilities include bike storage, a kitchen, a big games room with an X-box, and power-showers.

Grey Street Hotel   BOUTIQUE HOTEL ££

(☑0191-230 6777; www.greystreethotel.com; 2-12 Grey St; d from £80; ✱🛜) On the classiest street in the city centre, this beautiful Grade II–listed building has been adapted for contemporary needs, including triple-glazing on the sash windows. Gorgeous, individually designed rooms boast flatscreen TVs, big beds and handsome modern furnishings.

Royal Station Hotel   HOTEL ££

(☑0191-232 0781; www.royalstationhotel.com; Neville St; s £53-93, d £80-150, f £90-120; P🛜✉) Newcastle's hotels don't come better located than this Grade I– and II–listed Victorian beauty attached to Central Station. Above the chandeliered lobby, the 144 streamlined, unfussy rooms include cheaper 'small doubles' (from £55). Staff couldn't be friendlier or more helpful. Arrive early – the 20 free on-street car spaces are first-come, first-served.

Malmaison   BOUTIQUE HOTEL £££

(☑0191-245 5000; www.malmaison.com; Quayside; d/ste from £99/174; P@🛜) The affectedly stylish Malmaison touch has been applied to this former warehouse with considerable success, even down to the French-speaking lifts. Big beds, sleek lighting and designer furniture embellish the bouncy boudoirs and slick chambers.

🛏 Jesmond

About a mile-and-a-half north of the centre, Jesmond has a host of budget and midrange accommodation. Catch the Metro to Jesmond or West Jesmond.

Newcastle Jesmond Hotel   HOTEL ££

(☑0191-239 9943; www.newcastlejesmondhotel. co.uk; 105 Osborne Rd; s/d from £55/65; P🛜) Rooms aren't huge at this freshly refurbished red-brick property footsteps from the bars and restaurants of Osborne Rd, but they're cosy, comfy and come with the bonus of free parking (though spaces are limited, so get in quick). Wi-fi can be patchy.

★ Jesmond Dene House   HOTEL £££

(☑0191-212 3000; www.jesmonddenehouse.co.uk; Jesmond Dene Rd; s/d/ste from £115/130/180; P@🛜) Large, gorgeous bedrooms at this exquisite property are furnished in a modern interpretation of the Arts and Crafts style and are bedecked with all manner of technological goodies (flatscreen digital TVs, digital radios). Wonderful bathrooms come complete with underfloor heating. The fine-dining restaurant (p632) is sublime.

Eating

The Geordie palate is pretty refined and there are a host of dining options in all price ranges.

City Centre

Quay Ingredient CAFE £

(☎0191-447 2327; www.quayingredient.co.uk; 4 Queen St; dishes £2-7; ⊙8am-5pm Tue-Sun; 📶) Beneath the Tyne Bridge's soaring steel girders, this chic little hole-in-the-wall has a devoted following for its eggs Benedict (and Florentine, and Montreal), but don't discount the rest of the menu – Craster kippers with pickled beetroot, scampi with homemade tartar sauce, pulled beef with bourbon…

★Broad Chare GASTROPUB ££

(☎0191-211 2144; www.thebroadchare.co.uk; 25 Broad Chare; mains £11.50-18.50; ⊙kitchen noon-2.30pm & 5.30-10pm Mon-Sat, noon-5pm Sun) Spiffing English classics – the grilled pork chop with black pudding and cider sauce is divine – and splendid cask ales are served in the dark-wood bar and mezzanine of this perfect gastropub.

Oak Newcastle INTERNATIONAL ££

(☎0191-232 3200; www.oaknewcastle.co.uk; Milburn House, Dean St; mains £8-20; ⊙restaurant 7.30am-11pm Mon-Fri, 10am-11pm Sat & Sun, bar noon-2am daily) This hybrid restaurant/deli/bar is an equally good spot to pick up takeaways like pies, dine on dishes spanning black truffle risotto to Moroccan lamb burgers, or sip a cocktail while listening to DJs or live music. Energetic staff ensure it all comes together.

Silk Room INTERNATIONAL ££

(☎0191-260 3506; www.silkroom.co.uk; Pandon Bankside, Trinity Gardens; mains £13-28; ⊙11am-2pm & 5pm-midnight Mon-Fri, 5pm-midnight Sat & Sun) Glamorous fare like Kobe wagyu burgers and kangaroo with port and caramelised pears is complemented with over 25 brands of bubbly and 16 champagne cocktails at this glitzy Quayside establishment.

★Blackfriars BRITISH £££

(☎0191-261 5945; www.blackfriarsrestaurant.co.uk; Friars St; mains £12-25; ⊙noon-2.30pm & 5.30-11pm Mon-Sat, noon-4pm Sun) 🍃 A 12th-century friary is the atmospheric setting for 'modern medieval' cuisine. Check the table-mat map for the provenance of your cod, woodpigeon or rare-breed pork. Everything else is made from scratch on-site, including breads, pastries, ice creams and sausages. Bookings recommended.

Jesmond

Fat Hippo BURGERS ££

(☎0191-340 8949; www.fat-hippo.co.uk; 35a St Georges Tce, West Jesmond; burgers £7.50-14.50; ⊙11.30am-9.30pm Tue-Fri, 9am-9.30pm Sat, 9am-3.30pm Sun) Humongous burgers arrive on wooden planks with stainless-steel buckets of triple-fried, hand-cut chips at this local success story. The Shenton's three beef patties weigh in at one-and-a-half pounds; veggie options include My Big Fat Bean Burger with halloumi and garlic mayo. Sides (if you can squeeze them in) span deep-fried gherkins to breaded jalapeno poppers with sour cream.

Around the corner, the **Little Hippo** (☎0191-447 2114; www.fat-hippo.co.uk; 7 Acorn Rd, West Jesmond; dishes £4-5.50; ⊙11am-8.30pm) has smaller burgers, street food and specials like pulled pork and mac 'n' cheese.

Pizzeria Francesca PIZZERIA ££

(134 Manor House Rd; pizza & pasta £5-7, other mains £9-17; ⊙noon-2.30pm & 5-9.30pm Mon-Sat) This chaotic, cheerful place is how all Italian restaurants should be. Excitable waiters and huge portions of pizza and pasta keep locals queuing at the door – get in line and wait because you can't book in advance.

Jesmond Dene House MODERN BRITISH £££

(☎0191-212 5555; www.jesmonddenehouse.co.uk; Jesmond Dene Rd; mains £20-35; ⊙7am-9.30pm) 🍃 Head chef Michael Penaluna is the architect of an exquisite regional menu – venison from County Durham, oysters from Lindisfarne and herbs plucked straight from the garden. The result is a gourmet extravaganza.

Drinking & Nightlife

Are you up for it? You'd better be, because Newcastle's nightlife doesn't mess about. While it's no secret that Geordies love a night on the razzle, the nightlife beyond the coloured cocktails of the boisterous Bigg Market (just south of Newgate St) is infinitely less raucous. Jesmond has loads of bars, while Ouseburn Valley attracts a mellower crowd.

City Centre

QB Tea House TEAHOUSE

(☎0191-261 4861; www.quilliambrothers.com; Claremont Bldgs, 1 Eldon Pl; ⊙10am-midnight Mon-Fri, 9am-midnight Sat) Set up by a trio of brothers as 'an alternative to Newcastle's boozy scene', this hip Hungarian-style teahouse with post-industrial decor has over 100 types of tea as well as a tiny cinema screening cult films (dates vary), plus various gigs and art events.

Centurion Bar
BAR

(www.centurion-newcastle.com; Central Station; ⊙noon-11pm Mon-Thu, 11am-midnight Fri, noon-midnight Sat, to 10.30pm Sun) Dating from 1893, with floor-to-ceiling ornate Victorian tiling, Central Station's former first-class waiting room is ideal for a pre-club drink in style.

World Headquarters
CLUB

(www.welovewhq.com; Curtis Mayfield House, Carliol Sq; ⊙from 11pm, days vary) Dedicated to the genius of black music – funk, rare groove, dance-floor jazz, northern soul, genuine R&B, lush disco, proper house, reggae and more – this brilliant club is a world away from commercial blandness.

Trent House
PUB

(1-2 Leazes Lane; ⊙noon-11pm) Old-school boozer Trent House out-cools every other bar because it isn't trying. There's a free jukebox and fabulous atmosphere.

Digital
CLUB

(www.yourfutureisdigital.com; Times Sq; ⊙11pm-3am Mon & Wed-Sat) A two-floored cathedral to dance music, this megaclub was voted one of the top 20 clubs in the world by *DJ Magazine* thanks to one of the best sound systems you're ever likely to hear. Live acts rock the house, too.

🍽 Ouseburn Valley

★Tyne Bar
PUB

(☑0191-265 2550; www.thetyne.com; 1 Maling St; ⊙11am-11pm Sun-Thu, to midnight Fri & Sat; 🐾) An outdoor stage hosting free gigs, a disco ball spinning beneath the Glasshouse Bridge and a sprawling expanse of grass with knock-out river views make this tucked-away waterfront pub a magnet for in-the-know locals.

Ship Inn
PUB

(☑0191-222 1322; www.ship-inn.co.uk; Stepney Bank; ⊙3-11.30pm Mon-Wed, noon-11.30pm Thu, to 12.30am Fri & Sat, to 11pm Sun) Maritime memorabilia and historic photos of the Ouseburn Valley fill this red-brick charmer, which has been pouring pints since the early 1800s. On busy days the elbow-bending spills out onto the small green in front.

Cumberland Arms
PUB

(www.thecumberlandarms.co.uk; off Byker Bank, Ouseburn Valley; ⊙11am-1am Mon-Sat, noon-

12.30am Sun; 🐾) Sitting on a hill at the top of the Ouseburn, this 19th-century bar has a sensational selection of ales and ciders as well as a range of Northumberland meads. There's a terrace, regular live music and if you can't bear to leave, four comfy B&B rooms upstairs (double £80).

☆ Entertainment

Free monthly magazine *The Crack* (www.thecrackmagazine.com), available from clubs, tourist offices and some hotels, contains comprehensive theatre, music, cinema and club listings for the entire northeast.

Sage Gateshead
LIVE MUSIC

(☑0191-443 4666; www.sagegateshead.com; Gateshead Quays) Norman Foster's magnificent chrome-and-glass horizontal bottle is a stunner in itself but as the home of the Northern Sinfonia and Folkworks also presents outstanding live music.

Tyneside Cinema
CINEMA

(www.tynesidecinema.co.uk; Pilgrim St) Opened in 1937 as Newcastle's first newsreel cinema, this art-deco picture house with plush red-velvet seats still screens newsreels (11.15am daily) as well as mainstream and offbeat movies, and archive British Pathé films. Free one-hour guided tours of the building run at 11am on Monday, Tuesday, Friday and Saturday.

Theatre Royal THEATRE
(☑08448 11 21 21; www.theatreroyal.co.uk; 100
Grey St) The winter home of the Royal
Shakespeare Company is full of Victorian
splendour and has an excellent program of
drama, along with major musicals, pantomimes, opera, ballet, comedy and contemporary dance.

Head of Steam @ The Cluny LIVE MUSIC
(☑0191-230 4474; www.headofsteam.co.uk; 36
Lime St; ⊙ noon-11pm Mon-Thu, to midnight Fri &
Sat, to 10.30pm Sun) Based at the artist cooperative 36 Lime St, touring acts and local talent – from experimental prog-rock heads to
up-and-coming pop goddesses – fill the bill
every night of the week.

Newcastle United Football Club FOOTBALL
(NUFC; www.nufc.co.uk) NUFC is more than
just a football team – it's the collective expression of Geordie hope and pride. The
club's hallowed ground, **St James Park**
(Strawberry Pl), is always packed, but you can
get a **stadium tour** (☑0844 372 1892; adult/
child £15/8; ⊙11.30am, 12.30pm & 2.30pm daily,
10.30am match days) that includes the dugout
and changing rooms. Match tickets go on
public sale about two weeks before a game.

🛍 Shopping

Newcastle Quayside Market MARKET
(☑0191-211 5533; under the Tyne Bridge; ⊙ 9am-
4pm Sun) Stalls displaying jewellery, photographic prints, art, clothing, homewares
and more set up along the quays around the
Tyne Bridge every Sunday. Buskers and food
stalls add to the street-party atmosphere.

Grainger Market MARKET
(www.graingermarket.org.uk; btwn Grainger & Clay-
ton Sts; ⊙ 9am-5pm Mon-Sat) Trading since
1835, Newcastle's gorgeous, heritage-listed
covered market has over 100 stalls selling
everything from fish, farm produce, meat
and vegetables to clothes, accessories and
homewares. Between alleys 1 and 2, look out
for the historic Weigh House, where goods
were once weighed.

ℹ Information

Newcastle City Centre Police Station
(☑ emergency 999, nonemergency 101; www.
northumbria.police.uk; Forth Banks; ⊙ 24hr)
Tourist Office Main Branch (☑ 0191-277
8000; www.visitnewcastlegateshead.com;
Central Arcade, Market St; ⊙ 9.30am-5pm
Mon-Sat, 2-5pm Sun Jul & Aug, 10am-5pm
Mon-Sat Sep-Jun)

ℹ Getting There & Away

AIR
Newcastle International Airport (☑ 0871 882
1121; www.newcastleairport.com) Seven miles
north of the city off the A696, the airport has direct services to many UK and European cities as
well as long-haul flights to Dubai. Tour operators
fly charters to the USA, Middle East and Africa.

BUS
Local and regional buses leave from Haymarket
or Eldon Sq bus stations. National Express buses arrive and depart from the coach station (St
James Blvd). For local buses around the northeast, the excellent-value Explorer North East
ticket (£9.30) is valid on most services.

Buses X15 and X18 run north to Berwick-upon-
Tweed (£6.50, two hours, nine daily). National
Express offers services to Edinburgh (£14.90,
three hours, two daily), London (£16, seven hours,
nine daily) and Manchester (£12.50, 4½ hours,
four daily).

TRAIN
Newcastle is on the main rail line between Lon-
don and Edinburgh and is the starting point of
the scenic Tyne Valley Line west to Carlisle.
Alnmouth (for bus connections to Alnwick)
£9.70, 25 minutes, hourly
Berwick-upon-Tweed £23.60, 45 minutes,
hourly
Carlisle £15.50, 1½ hours, hourly
Edinburgh £48, 1½ hours, every 30 minutes
Hartlepool £8.90, 45 minutes, hourly
London King's Cross £121, three hours, every
30 minutes
York £32, one hour, every 20 minutes

ℹ Getting Around

TO/FROM THE AIRPORT
The airport is linked to town by the Metro (£3.30,
20 minutes, every 12 minutes).

PUBLIC TRANSPORT
There's a large bus network, but the best means
of getting around is the excellent Metro, with
fares from £1.80. Several saver passes are also
available. The tourist office can supply you with
route plans for the bus and Metro networks.

The DaySaver (£2.60 to £4.50) gives unlimited
Metro travel for one day for travel after 9am, and
the DayRover (adult/child £6.80/3.70) gives unlimited travel on all modes of transport in Tyne
and Wear for one day for travel any time.

TAXI
On weekend nights taxis can be rare; try **Noda
Taxis** (☑ 0191-222 1888; www.noda-taxis.co.uk),
which has a kiosk outside Central Station.

AROUND NEWCASTLE

Angel of the North

Nicknamed the Gateshead Flasher, this extraordinary 200-tonne, rust-coloured, winged human frame has loomed over the A1 (M) some 6 miles south of Newcastle since 1998. At 20m high and with a wingspan wider than a Boeing 767, Sir Antony Gormley's iconic work (which saw him knighted in 2014) is the UK's largest sculpture and most viewed public artwork. Buses 21 and 22 from Newcastle's Eldon Sq (£2, 20 minutes) stop here. There's a free car park by the base.

Tynemouth

POP 67,520

One of the most popular Geordie days out is to this handsome seaside resort some 9 miles east of Newcastle. The mouth of the Tyne is one of the best surf spots in England, with great all-year breaks off the immense, crescent-shaped Blue Flag beach, which occasionally hosts the National Surfing Championships.

◉ Sights & Activities

Tynemouth Priory   RUIN
(EH; www.english-heritage.org.uk; adult/child £4.80/2.90; ⊙10am-6pm Apr-Sep, to 4pm Oct, 10am-4pm Sat & Sun Nov-Mar) Built by Benedictine monks on a strategic bluff above the mouth of the Tyne in the 11th-century ruins, Tynemouth Priory was ransacked during the Dissolution in 1539. The military took over for four centuries, only leaving in 1960, and today the skeletal remains of the priory church sit alongside old military installations, their guns aimed out to sea at an enemy that never came.

Tynemouth Surf Company   SURFING
(☑0191-258 2496; www.tynemouthsurf.co.uk; Grand Pde; ⊙10am-5.30pm) For all your surfing needs, call into this friendly surf company, which also provides two-hour group lessons for £25 per person.

✕ Eating & Drinking

Opposite the priory, village-like Front St runs inland from the ocean and is lined with bars, restaurants, cafes and arty shops.

Barca Art Cafe   CAFE ££
(☑0191-257 7959; www.barcaart.co.uk; 68 Front St; mains £10.50-19; ⊙kitchen 5-10pm Mon-Sat, noon-4pm Sun, bar noon-1am) This funky hybrid restaurant, bar and art gallery (the works by local artists are all for sale) has an ambitious, contemporary menu, though vegetarian options, aside from starters like mezze boards to share, are few. DJs spin on Saturday nights from 10pm.

Turks Head   PUB
(☑0191-257 6547; www.johnbarras.com; 41 Front St; ⊙11am-11pm Mon-Wed, to 11.30pm Thu-Sat, noon-11.30pm Sun; ☎) Encased in ivory-coloured tiles, this salt-of-the-earth 1850-built traditional pub is great for a pint of real ale while watching a Newcastle United match.

❶ Getting There & Away

From Newcastle, the easiest way to reach Tynemouth is by Metro (£3.20, 25 minutes).

Segedunum

The last strong post of Hadrian's Wall was the fort of **Segedunum** (☑0191-236 9347; www.twmuseums.org.uk; Buddle St, Wallsend; adult/child £5.50/free; ⊙10am-5pm Apr-Aug, to 4pm Sep & Oct, 10am-2.30pm Mon-Fri Nov-Mar), 5 miles east of Newcastle at the 'wall's end', now the Newcastle suburb of Wallsend. Beneath the 35m-high tower, which you can climb for terrific views, is an absorbing site that includes a reconstructed Roman bathhouse (with steaming pools and frescoes) and a museum offering a fascinating insight into life during Roman times.

Segedunum is a three-minute walk from the Wallsend Metro station (from Newcastle £3.95, 20 minutes).

HARTLEPOOL

POP 88,895

Steelworks and shipyards made this North Sea coastal town's fortunes in the 19th century, but also made it a WWI target. On 16 December 1914, it was hit by 1150 shells, killing 117 people including 29-year-old Durham Light Infantry Private Theophilus Jones, the war's first soldier killed on British soil. Hartlepool's defence batteries returned fire, damaging three enemy ships and becoming England's only coastal battery to fire its guns in the conflict.

After WWII, the collapse of both the steel and ship-building industries saw Hartlepool languish until the revitalisation of its marina around the turn of the millennium, and it makes a fascinating stop to explore its wartime and maritime heritage.

◉ Sights

Hartlepool's Maritime Experience INTERPRETATION CENTRE
(☑ 01429-860077; www.hartlepoolsmaritimeexperience.com; Jackson Dock, Maritime Ave; adult/child £8.95/6.85, museum free; ◷ 10am-5pm Apr-Oct, 11am-4pm Nov-Mar) This superb family attraction incorporates both the Museum of Hartlepool, with exhibits from the Bronze Age to today, and the 1817-built HMS *Trincomalee,* the oldest British warship still afloat, as well as recreated businesses – gunsmith, swordsmith and so on – along its historic quayside. Costumed staff and audioguides do a great job of bringing it to life.

Heugh Gun Battery Museum MUSEUM
(☑ 01429-270746; www.heughbattery.com; Moor Tce; adult/child £5/3; ◷ 10am-4pm Thu-Sun) Atop the windswept Hartlepool Headland, about 2 miles west of the centre, you can visit the underground magazines, parade ground, museum and panoramic observation tower at the 19th-century Heugh (pronounced 'yuff') Gun Battery – one of Hartlepool's two defence batteries to return WWI fire.

⊨ Sleeping

Hillcarter Hotel HOTEL ££
(☑ 01429-855800; www.hillcarterhotel.com; 31-32 Church St, enter via Whitby St; s £65, d £75-85, f £95; P ⧂) This central Hartlepool landmark was built in 1887 as the Hill and Carter department store and converted to a hotel a century later. Rooms are spacious and comfortable, service is top notch and there's an enclosed rooftop restaurant, a bar serving meals, and two nightclubs, plus nearby late bars, so beware noisy Friday and Saturday nights (other nights are quiet).

✗ Eating & Drinking

By far the best place to eat and/or drink is Navigation Point, where a slew of bars, cafes and restaurants serving a wide range of cuisines – traditional and contemporary British, Chinese, Indian, Italian – overlook the boats moored at Hartlepool Marina.

Cinnamons BANGLADESHI £
(☑ 01429-269666; 29 Navigation Point, Hartlepool Marina; mains £6-11; ◷ noon-2pm & 5.30-11.30pm Mon-Sat, 5.30-11.30pm Sun) Fresh, fiery Bangladeshi cuisine at this elegant restaurant

spans clay oven tikka and tandoori favourites, Bengal curries, baltis and countless *chingri* (prawn) dishes.

❶ Information

Tourist Office (☑ 01429-869706; www.destinationhartlepool.com; Church Sq; ◷ 10am-5.30pm Tue-Sat, 2-5pm Sun) At the Hartlepool Art Gallery.

❶ Getting There & Away

Trains link Hartlepool with Newcastle (£8.90, 45 minutes, hourly). Bus 22 to/from Durham (£5.70, 1¼ hours, hourly) stops at the train station.

COUNTY DURHAM

Spread across the lonely, rabbit-inhabited North Pennines and Teesdale's ochre hills, County Durham's star attraction is its county town. Its cathedral and adjoining castle were the seat of the once powerful prince bishops, rulers since 1081 of the Palatinate of Durham, a political entity created by William the Conqueror as a bulwark against Saxons and Scots.

The county was at the heart of the region's coal-mining industry, a brutal business that saw the last pit close in 1984 and left the landscape with some fast-dissolving yet evocative scarring.

Durham

POP 47,785

England's most beautiful Romanesque cathedral, a huge castle, and, surrounding them both, a cobweb of hilly, cobbled streets usually full of upper-crust students attending England's third university of choice (after Oxford and Cambridge) make Durham an ideal day trip from Newcastle or overnight stop.

◉ Sights

★**Durham Cathedral** CATHEDRAL
(www.durhamcathedral.co.uk; by donation, tower £5, guided tours adult/child £5/free; ◷ 7.30am-6pm Mon-Sat, to 5.30pm Sun) This monumental cathedral is the definitive structure of the Anglo-Norman Romanesque style, a resplendent monument to the country's ecclesiastical history and, since 1986, a Unesco World Heritage Site. Beyond the main door – and the famous **Sanctuary Knocker**, which medieval felons would strike to gain 37 days

asylum within the cathedral before standing trial or leaving the country – the interior is spectacular. Climbing the tower's 325 steps rewards you with show-stopping vistas.

Durham was the first European cathedral to be roofed with stone-ribbed vaulting, which upheld the heavy stone roof and made it possible to build pointed transverse arches – the first in England, and a great architectural achievement. The central tower dates from 1262, but was damaged in a fire caused by lightning in 1429 and unsatisfactorily patched up until it was entirely rebuilt in 1470. The western towers were added in 1217–26.

The northern side of the beautiful, 1175-built **Galilee Chapel** features rare surviving examples of 12th-century wall painting (thought to feature portraits of Sts Cuthbert and Oswald). Galilee Chapel also contains the **tomb of the Venerable Bede**, the 8th-century Northumbrian monk turned historian: his *Ecclesiastical History of the English People* is still the prime source of information on the development of early Christian Britain. Among other things, Bede introduced the numbering of years from the birth of Jesus. He was first buried at Jarrow, but in 1022 a miscreant monk stole his remains and brought them here.

Other highlights include the 14th-century **Bishop's Throne**; the beautiful stone **Neville Screen** (1372–80), which separates the high altar from **St Cuthbert's tomb**; and the mostly 19th-century **Cloisters** where you'll find the **Monk's Dormitory**, now a library of 30,000 books, with Anglo-Saxon carved stones. There are audiovisual displays on the building of the cathedral and the life of St Cuthbert.

★**Durham Castle**   CASTLE
(☑0191-334 2932; www.dur.ac.uk/durham.castle; admission by guided tour only, adult/child £5/3.50; ☺by reservation) Built as a standard motte-and-bailey fort in 1072, Durham Castle was the prince bishops' home until 1837, when it became the University of Durham's first college. It remains a university hall, and it's possible to stay here (contact the castle for information and availability). Highlights of the 45-minute tour include the groaning 17th-century **Black Staircase** and the beautifully preserved **Norman chapel** (1080).

Each successive prince bishop sought to put his particular imprint on the place, but heavy restoration and reconstruction were necessary in any case as the castle is built of soft stone on soft ground.

WORTH A TRIP

BEAMISH OPEN-AIR MUSEUM
....
County Durham's living, breathing, working **museum** (☑0191-370 4000; www.beamish.org.uk; adult/child £17.50/10; ☺10am-5pm Apr-Oct, 10am-4pm Tue-Thu, Sat & Sun Nov-Mar) offers an unflinching glimpse into industrial life in the northeast during the 19th and 20th centuries. Spread over 121 hectares, it is instructive and fun for all ages. Allow at least three hours here, but check ahead in the winter months as some sections close.

Beamish is about 8 miles northwest of Durham. Take buses 28 and 28A from Newcastle (£4.70, one hour, every 30 minutes) or 128 from Durham (£3.20, 30 minutes, hourly).

Highlights include going underground, exploring mine heads, visiting a working farm, school, dentist and pub, and marvelling at how every cramped pit cottage seemed to find room for a piano. Don't miss a ride behind an 1815 Steam Elephant locomotive or a replica of Stephenson's *Locomotion No 1*.

🏃 **Activities**

Prince Bishop River Cruiser   BOAT CRUISE
(☑0191-386 9525; www.princebishoprc.co.uk; Browns Boathouse, Elvet Bridge; adult/child £7/4; ☺cruises 12.30pm, 2pm & 3pm Jun-Sep, call for times Oct-May) Wonderfully scenic one-hour cruises on the Wear.

Browns Boathouse   BOATING
(☑0191-386 3779; Elvet Bridge; per hr adult/child £5/4; ☺dawn-dusk Apr-Oct) Rent a row boat for a romantic river excursion.

🛌 **Sleeping**

Honest Lawyer   INN **££**
(☑0191-378 3780; www.honestlawyerhotel.com; Croxdale; d £68-88; P⚛) An easy 3-mile drive south of Durham on the A167, this handy spot has mostly motel-style rooms with countrified chequered fabrics and parking outside the door. The main building has a timber bar and restaurant serving good pub grub in generous portions.

Cathedral View   B&B **££**
(☑0191-386 9566; www.cathedralview.com; 212 Gilesgate; s/d from £75/90; P⚛) This discreet Georgian house has no sign, but inside, two of its six large rooms decorated with lots of

Durham

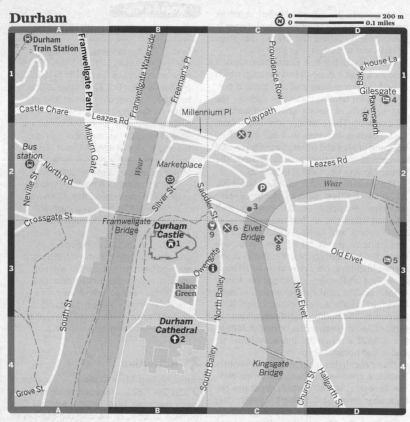

cushions and coordinated bed linen and window dressings indeed have sensational cathedral views. Breakfast, including home-baked bread, is cooked to order and served on the terrace or in the art-lined dining room.

Gadds Townhouse   BOUTIQUE HOTEL **£££**
(☑0191-384 1037; www.gaddstownhouse.com; 34 Old Elvet; d £110-250; ☎) Each of Gadds' 11 opulent rooms has a theme, with Le Jardin featuring a shed and garden furniture, a huge projection screen and popcorn machine in Premiere, and the Edwardian Express recreating a night in a yesteryear sleeper compartment. The most 'normal' room is the Garden Lodge, with outdoor tub and underfloor heating. The restaurant is superb.

✖ Eating

Tealicious   CAFE **£**
(☑0191-340 1393; www.tealicioustearoom.co.uk; Elvet Bridge; dishes £2-5.25; ☺10am-4pm Tue-Sat)

A gingerbread-house replica of this quaint pastel-blue and white building sits in the window, while inside, amid vintage decor, treats include homemade cakes (such as white chocolate cheesecake or ginger and lime), soups, and over a dozen blends of tea served from individual pots on fine bone china. It's tiny so book ahead.

Cellar Door Durham   MODERN BRITISH **££**
(☑0191-383 1856; www.thecellardoordurham.co.uk; 41 Saddler St; mains £14-17.50; ☺11.30am-10.30pm) Accessed from an inconspicuous door on Saddler St, this 12th-century building boasts glorious river views, including from the outdoor terrace. The Mediterranean-meets-Britain menu features starters such as twice-baked goats cheese soufflé, mains such as seared venison with chestnut dressing, and desserts including brioche bread-and-butter pudding. Service is spot on.

Durham

Oldfields　　　　　　　　　BRITISH ££
(⟁ 0191-370 9696; www.oldfieldsrealfood.co.uk;
18 Claypath; 2-/3-course lunch £10/13, dinner
mains £12-17.50; ⊙ noon-10pm; ☏) ⌖ Serving
strictly seasonal menus that use only local
or organic ingredients sourced within a 60-
mile radius of Durham – such as North Sea
fish casserole, pan haggerty and wild boar
pie – this award-winning restaurant, in the
1881 boardroom of the former HQ of the
Durham Gas Company, is passionate about
great British food.

⚑ Drinking & Nightlife

Shakespeare Tavern　　　　　　　PUB
(www.shakespearedurham.com; 63 Saddler St;
⊙ 11am-11.30pm) Built in 1190, this authentic-
as-it-gets locals' boozer is complete with
dartboard, cosy snugs, a terrific selection
of beers and spirits and wise-cracking characters propping up the bar – as well as,
allegedly, a resident ghost. Folk music jam
sessions take place on Wednesday evenings.

ⓘ Information

Tourist Office (World Heritage Site Visitor Centre; ⟁ 0191-334 3805; www.thisisdurham.com; 7
Owengate; ⊙ 9.30am-6pm Jul & Aug, to 5pm late
Mar-Jun & Sep, to 4.30pm Oct-late Mar) Small
but helpful, with all the usual tourist information.

ⓘ Getting There & Away

BUS
Destinations include Hartlepool (bus 22; £5.70,
1¼ hours, hourly), London (National Express;
£32, 6½ hours, four daily) and Newcastle (bus

21, 43, 44, X2, X21, X41; £3.60, one hour to 1¾
hours, several hourly).

TRAIN
The East Coast Main Line provides speedy
connections to many destinations including
Edinburgh (£56.20, two hours, hourly), London
King's Cross (£121, three hours, hourly), Newcastle (£5.10, 15 minutes, four hourly) and York
(£30.50, 50 minutes, four hourly).

ⓘ Getting Around

Pratt's (⟁ 0191-386 0700; www.prattstaxis.
co.uk) Reliable taxi company.

Barnard Castle

POP 7040
The charming market town of Barnard Castle, better known as 'Barney', is a tradition-
alist's dream, full of antiquarian shops and
atmospheric old pubs that serve as a wonderful setting for its twin draws: a daunting
ruined castle at its edge and an extraordinary French chateau. If you can drag yourself away, it's also a terrific base for exploring
Teesdale and the North Pennines.

◎ Sights

Barnard Castle　　　　　　　CASTLE
(EH; www.english-heritage.org.uk; adult/child £4.60/
2.80; ⊙ 10am-6pm Apr-Sep, to 5pm Oct, 10am-4pm
Sat & Sun Nov-Mar) Built on a cliff above the River Tees by Guy de Bailleul and rebuilt around
1150, Barnard Castle was partly dismantled
some four centuries later, but still manages
to cover more than two very impressive hectares with wonderful river views.

★ Bowes Museum　　　　　　MUSEUM
(www.thebowesmuseum.org.uk; adult/child £9/free;
⊙ 10am-5pm) About half a mile east of town
a monumental chateau contains the lavishly furnished Bowes Museum. Funded by
19th-century industrialist John Bowes, and
opened in 1892, this brainchild of his Parisian actress wife, Josephine, was built by
French architect Jules Pellechet to display
a collection the Bowes had travelled the
world to assemble. The star attraction is the
marvellous 18th-century mechanical swan,
which performs every day at 2pm. If you
miss it, a film shows it in action.

Look for works by Canaletto, El Greco and
Goya as well as 55 paintings by Josephine
herself. Among the 15,000 other objets d'art
are incredible dresses from the 17th century
through to the 1970s as part of an exhibit on

WORTH A TRIP

RABY CASTLE
··

About 7 miles northeast of Barnard Castle, sprawling **Raby Castle** (www.rabycastle.com; adult/child £10/4.50; ☺1-4.30pm Sun-Fri Jul & Aug, Sun-Wed May, Jun & Sep) was a stronghold of the Catholic Neville family until it engaged in some ill-judged plotting (the 'Rising of the North') against the oh-so Protestant Queen Elizabeth in 1569. Most of the interior dates from the 18th and 19th centuries, but the exterior remains true to the original design, built around a courtyard and surrounded by a moat. Bus 8 zips between Barnard Castle and Raby (£3, 15 minutes, eight daily).

There are beautiful formal gardens and a deer park.

---

textiles through the ages, and clocks, watches and tableware in gold and silver in the precious-metals section.

🍴 Sleeping & Eating

Old Well Inn   INN **££**
(☎01833-690130; www.theoldwellinn.co.uk; 21 The Bank; s/d/f from £50/70/96; 🛜) Built over a huge well (not visible), this old coaching inn has 10 enormous rooms. No 9 is the most impressive with its own private entrance, flagstone floors and a bath. The pub has a reputation for excellent grub like rabbit and black pudding casserole (mains £7.50 to £9) as well as regional real ales that you can sip in the leafy beer garden in fine weather.

Jersey Farm Country Hotel   HOTEL **££**
(☎01833-638223; www.jerseyfarmhotel.co.uk; Darlington Rd; s/d from £72/99; ☺kitchen noon-2pm & 6-9pm; 🅿🛜) Another genteel farmhouse conversion, right? Wrong. Rooms here sport cool retro colour schemes and gadgets galore. The restaurant is a clean-cut affair (mains £10 to £19). It's a mile east of town just off the A67.

ⓘ Information

Tourist Office (☎01833-631107; www.thewitham.org.uk; 3 Horsemarket; ☺10am-4pm Mon & Wed-Sat) In the Witham building's new arts and community centre.

ⓘ Getting There & Away

From Durham, take bus 75 via Darlington (£3.80, 1½ hours, twice hourly).

North Pennines

The North Pennines stretch from western Durham to just short of Hadrian's Wall in the north. In the south is Teesdale, the gently undulating valley of the River Tees; to the north is the much wilder Weardale, carved by the River Wear. Both dales are marked by ancient quarries and mines – industries that date back to Roman times. The wilds of the North Pennines are also home to the picturesque Derwent and Allen Valleys, north of Weardale.

For information on the area check out www.northpennines.org.uk and www.exploreteesdale.co.uk.

HADRIAN'S WALL

What exactly have the Romans ever done for us? The aqueducts. Law and order. And this enormous wall, built between AD 122 and 128 to separate Romans and Scottish Picts. Named in honour of the emperor who ordered it built, Hadrian's Wall was one of Rome's greatest engineering projects, a spectacular 73-mile testament to ambition and the practical Roman mind. Even today, almost 2000 years after the first stone was laid, the awe-inspiring sections that remain are proof that when the Romans wanted something done, they just knuckled down and did it.

It wasn't easy. When completed, the mammoth structure ran across the narrow neck of the island, from the Solway Firth in the west almost to the mouth of the Tyne in the east. Every Roman mile (0.95 miles) there was a gateway guarded by a small fort (milecastle) and between each milecastle were two observation turrets. Milecastles are numbered right across the country, starting with Milecastle 0 at Wallsend (where you can visit the wall's last stronghold, Segedunum (p635)) and ending with Milecastle 80 at Bowness-on-Solway.

A series of forts were developed as bases some distance south (and may predate the wall), and 16 lie astride it.

Carlisle, in Cumbria, and Newcastle are logical start/end points; Haltwhistle, Hexham and Corbridge make good bases. The B6318 follows the course of the wall from the outskirts of Newcastle to Birdoswald. The main A69 road and the railway line follow 3 or 4 miles to the south.

Every May the Hadrian's Wall Festival features lots of recreations of Roman life along the wall – contact tourist offices for details.

🏃 Activities

Hadrian's Wall Path

WALKING

(www.nationaltrail.co.uk/hadrianswall) This 84-mile National Trail runs the length of the wall from Wallsend in the east to Bowness-on-Solway in the west. The entire route should take about seven days on foot, giving plenty of time to explore the rich archaeological heritage along the way. Local bookshops and tourist offices sell detailed guides.

ℹ Information

Hadrian's Wall Country (www.visithadrianswall.co.uk) The official portal for the whole of Hadrian's Wall Country.

Northumberland National Park Visitor Centre (☏ 01434-344396; www.northumberlandnationalpark.org.uk; Bardon Mill, Once Brewed; ⏰ 9.30am-5.30pm Apr-Oct, 10am-3pm Sat & Sun Nov-Mar) On Military Rd (B6318).

ℹ Getting There & Around

BUS

The AD122 Hadrian's Wall bus (one-day adult/child £12/6, five daily, April to October) is a hail-and-ride service that runs between Hexham and Carlisle, with one bus a day starting and ending at Newcastle's Central Station and not all services covering the entire route. Bikes can be taken aboard AD122 buses, but space is limited. Bus 185 zips from Haltwhistle to Carlisle the rest of the year (Monday to Saturday only).

West of Hexham the wall runs parallel to the A69, which connects Carlisle and Newcastle. Bus 685 runs along the A69 hourly, passing 2 miles to 3 miles south of the main sites throughout the year.

All these services can be used with the **Hadrian's Wall Rover Ticket** (adult/child one-day £9/4.50, three-day £18/9, seven-day £36/18), available from bus drivers and tourist offices, where you can also get timetables.

Hadrian's Wall & Northumberland National Park

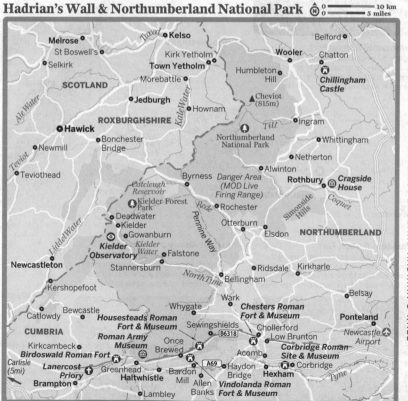

Hadrian's Wall

ROME'S FINAL FRONTIER

Of all Britain's Roman ruins, Emperor Hadrian's 2nd-century wall, cutting across northern England from the Irish Sea to the North Sea, is by far the most spectacular; Unesco awarded it world cultural heritage status in 1987.

We've picked out the highlights, one of which is the prime remaining Roman fort on the wall, Housesteads, which we've reconstructed here.

Housesteads' granaries
Nothing like the clever underground ventilation system, which kept vital supplies of grain dry in Northumberland's damp and drizzly climate, would be seen again in these parts for 1500 years.

Milecastle

North Gate

Interval Tower

Birdoswald Roman Fort
Explore the longest intact stretch of the wall, scramble over the remains of a large fort then head indoors to wonder at a full-scale model of the wall at its zenith. Great fun for the kids.

Housesteads Roman Fort
See Illustration Right

[Map showing: Brampton, Birdoswald Roman Fort, Harrow Scar Milecastle, Irthing, Greenhead, Roman Army Museum, Once Brewed, Haltwhistle, South Tyne, Sewingshields, Housesteads Roman Fort & Museum, B6318, Vindolanda Roman Fort & Museum, Bardon Mill, Haydon Bridge, Acomb, Hadrian's Wall, Chesters Roman Fort & Museum, Chollerford, Low Brunton, A69, Hexham, 10 km / 5 miles]

Chesters Roman Fort
Built to keep watch over a bridge spanning the River North Tyne, Britain's best-preserved Roman cavalry fort has a terrific bathhouse, essential if you have months of nippy northern winter ahead.

Hexham Abbey
This may be the finest non-Roman sight near Hadrian's Wall, but the 7th-century parts of this magnificent church were built with stone quarried by the Romans for use in their forts.

Housesteads' hospital
Operations performed at the hospital would have been surprisingly effective, even without anaesthetics; religious rituals and prayers to Aesculapius, the Roman god of healing, were possibly less helpful for a hernia or appendicitis.

Housesteads' latrines
Communal toilets were the norm in Roman times and Housesteads' are remarkably well preserved – fortunately no traces remain of the vinegar-soaked sponges that were used instead of toilet paper.

ALISON ROSCHE / GETTY ©

QUICK WALL FACTS & FIGURES

» **Latin name** Vallum Aelium
» **Length** 73.5 miles (80 Roman miles)
» **Construction date** AD 122–128
» **Manpower for construction**
Three legions (around 16,000 men)
» **Features** At least 16 forts, 80 milecastles, 160 turrets
» **Did you know** Hadrian's wasn't the only wall in Britain – the Antonine Wall was built across what is now central Scotland in the AD 140s, but it was abandoned soon after

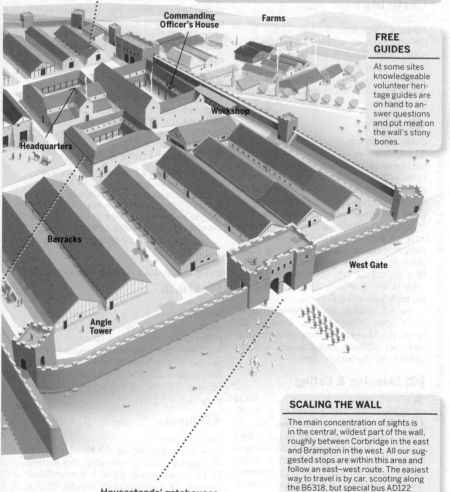

Commanding Officer's House

Farms

Workshop

Headquarters

Barracks

Angle Tower

West Gate

FREE GUIDES

At some sites knowledgeable volunteer heritage guides are on hand to answer questions and put meat on the wall's stony bones.

Housesteads' gatehouses
Unusually at Housesteads neither of the gates faces the enemy, as was the norm at a Roman fort – builders aligned them east-west. Ruts worn by cart wheels are still visible in the stone.

SCALING THE WALL

The main concentration of sights is in the central, wildest part of the wall, roughly between Corbridge in the east and Brampton in the west. All our suggested stops are within this area and follow an east–west route. The easiest way to travel is by car, scooting along the B6318, but special bus AD122 will also get you there. Hiking along the designated Hadrian's Wall Path (84 miles) allows you to appreciate the achievement up close.

CAR & MOTORCYCLE

Your own wheels are the easiest way to get around, with one fort or garrison usually just a short hop from the next. Parking costs £4/15 per day/week; tickets are valid at all sites along the wall.

TRAIN

The railway line between Newcastle and Carlisle (Tyne Valley Line; £12.20, one hour, hourly) has stations at Corbridge, Hexham, Haydon Bridge, Bardon Mill, Haltwhistle and Brampton. Not all services stop at all stations.

Corbridge

POP 2950

Above a green-banked curve in the Tyne, Corbridge's shady, cobbled streets are lined with old-fashioned shops and pubs. Inhabited since Saxon times when there was a substantial monastery, many of its charming buildings feature stones nicked from nearby Corstopitum.

◎ Sights

**Corbridge Roman
Site & Museum**   HISTORIC SITE
(EH; www.english-heritage.org.uk; adult/child £5.60/3.40; ⊙10am-6pm Apr-Sep, to 5pm Oct, 10am-4pm Sat & Sun Nov-Mar) What's left of the Roman garrison town of Corstopitum lies about half a mile west of Market Pl on Dere St, once the main road from York to Scotland. It's the oldest fortified site in the area, predating the wall itself by some 40 years. Most of what you see here though dates from around AD 200, when the fort had developed into a civilian settlement and was the main base along the wall.

You get a sense of the domestic heart of the town from the visible remains. The Corbridge Museum displays Roman sculpture and carvings, including the amazing 3rd-century **Corbridge Lion**.

🛏 Sleeping & Eating

★2 The Crofts   B&B ££
(☑01434-633046; www.2thecrofts.co.uk; B6530; d from £80; 🅿🛜) By far the best place in town to drop your pack, this secluded B&B occupies a beautiful period home around half a mile's walk east of the town centre on Newcastle Rd. The three high-ceilinged, spacious rooms are all en suite and the energetic owners cook a mean breakfast.

Corbridge Larder   DELI, CAFE £
(☑01434-632948; www.corbridgelarder.co.uk; 18 Hill St; dishes £4-7; ⊙9.30am-5pm Mon-Fri, 9am-5.30pm Sat) Gourmet picnic fare at this fabulous deli includes bread, over 100 varieties of cheese, chutneys, cakes, chocolates and wine (you can get hampers made up) as well as made-to-order sandwiches, pies, quiches, tarts, and antipasti and mezze delicacies. Upstairs from the wonderland of provisions there's a small sit-down cafe.

Black Bull   BRITISH ££
(Middle St; mains £8-17; ⊙kitchen noon-9pm; 🛜🍴) A menu of British comfort food, such as beef burgers, fish in beer batter and slow-cooked lamb, and a series of low-ceilinged, atmospheric dining rooms, make this tavern a cosy spot to hole up. Sundays offer a choice of five different roasts.

❶ Information

Tourist Office (☑01434-632815; www.thisiscorbridge.co.uk; Hill St; ⊙10am-4.30pm Mon-Sat Easter-Oct, 11am-4pm Wed, Fri & Sat Nov-Mar) Occupies a corner of the library.

❶ Getting There & Away

Buses 85, 685 and X85 between Newcastle and Carlisle come through Corbridge (£4.70 to either, up to one hour, every 30 minutes), as does the half-hourly bus 10 from Newcastle (£5, one hour) to Hexham (£2.90, 20 minutes), where you can connect with the Hadrian's Wall bus AD122.

Corbridge is also on the Newcastle–Carlisle railway line.

Hexham

POP 11,390

Bustling Hexham is a handsome if somewhat scuffed market town centred on its grand Augustinian abbey. Its cobbled alleyways have more shops and amenities than any other wall town between Carlisle and Newcastle, making it a good place to pick up supplies if you're heading out into the windswept wilds beyond.

◎ Sights

Hexham Abbey   MONASTERY
(www.hexhamabbey.org.uk; ⊙9.30am-5pm, Saxon crypt 11am & 3.30pm) Dominating tiny Market Pl, Hexham's stately abbey is a marvellous example of Early English architecture. It cleverly escaped the Dissolution of 1537 by rebranding as Hexham's parish church, a

role it still has today. The highlight is the 7th-century **Saxon crypt**, the only surviving element of St Wilifrid's Church, built with inscribed stones from Corstopitum in 674.

Old Gaol   HISTORIC BUILDING
(adult/child £4/2; ⊙ 11am-4.30pm Tue-Sat Apr-Sep, Tue & Sat only Oct-Nov & Feb-Mar) Completed in 1333 as England's first purpose-built prison, today this strapping stone structure's four floors tell the history of the jail in all its gruesome glory. The history of the Border Reivers – a group of clans who fought, kidnapped, blackmailed and killed each other in an effort to exercise control over a lawless tract of land along the Anglo-Scottish border throughout the 16th century – is also retold, along with tales of the punishments handed out in the prison.

🍴 Sleeping & Eating

Hallbank Guest House   B&B ££
(☑ 01434-605567; www.hallbankguesthouse.com; Hallgate; s/d from £70/90; 🅿 🛜) Behind the Old Gaol, this fine Edwardian house combines period elegance with stylishly furnished rooms equipped with flatscreen TVs and huge beds. It's very popular so book ahead.

Deli at Number 4   DELI, CAFE £
(☑ 01434-608091; www.deliatnumber4.co.uk; 4 Beaumont St; dishes £2-5; ⊙ 9am-5pm Mon-Sat, 11am-4pm Sun) Opposite Hexham's abbey, colourful window displays of breads, cheeses, olives, jams, homemade cakes and more entice you in, and the aromas from the kitchen tempt you upstairs to dine on soups, sandwiches and various specials.

★**Bouchon Bistrot**   FRENCH ££
(www.bouchonbistrot.co.uk; 4-6 Gilesgate; mains £12-20; ⊙ noon-2pm & 6-9.30pm Mon-Sat) Hexham may be an unlikely setting for some true fine dining, but this Gallic affair has an enviable reputation. Classically inspired dishes range from proper French onion soup with gruyère or garlic snails to pan-fried Coley fillet with watercress velouté. Ingredients are as fresh as nature can provide and the wine list is an elite selection of champagnes, reds and whites.

ℹ️ Information

Tourist Office (☑ 01434-652220; www.visitnorthumberland.com/hexham; Wentworth Car Park; ⊙ 9.30am-5pm Mon-Sat, 10am-4pm Sun Apr-Oct, 10am-4.30pm Mon-Sat Nov-Mar) Northeast of the town centre.

ℹ️ Getting There & Away

Buses 85, 685 and X85 between Newcastle and Carlisle come through Hexham (£4.70, 1¼ hours, every 30 minutes); the AD122 Hadrian's Wall bus connects with other towns along the wall. Bus 10 (£5.40, 1¼ hours, every 30 minutes) links Hexham with Newcastle.

Hexham is on the scenic railway line between Newcastle (£6.60, 30 minutes, hourly) and Carlisle (£5, one hour, hourly).

Chesters Roman Fort & Museum

This Roman **cavalry fort's** (EH; ☑ 01434-681379; www.english-heritage.org.uk; adult/child £5.60/3.40; ⊙ 10am-6pm Apr-Sep, to 5pm Oct, 10am-4pm Sat & Sun Nov-Mar) superbly preserved remains are set among green woods and meadows near the village of Chollerford. Originally constructed to house a unit of troops from Asturias in northern Spain, they include part of a bridge (best appreciated from the eastern bank), four gatehouses, a bathhouse and an underfloor heating system. The museum has a large Roman sculpture collection. It's served by Hadrian's Wall bus AD122.

Haltwhistle & Around
POP 3790

It's one of the more intriguing debates in Britain: where exactly is the centre of the mainland? The residents of Haltwhistle, basically one long street just north of the A69, claim it's here. But then so do the folks in Dunsop Bridge, 71 miles to the south.... No matter, Haltwhistle is a handy spot to get some cash and load up on gear and groceries. Thursday is market day.

◎ Sights

Vindolanda Roman Fort & Museum   HISTORIC SITE
(www.vindolanda.com; adult/child £6.50/4, with Roman Army Museum £10/5.50; ⊙ 10am-6pm Apr-Sep, to 5pm Oct, to 4pm Nov & Dec) The extensive site of Vindolanda offers a fascinating glimpse into the daily life of a Roman garrison town. The time-capsule museum is just one part of this large, extensively excavated site, which includes impressive parts of the fort and town (excavations continue) and reconstructed turrets and temple.

It's 1.5 miles north of Bardon Mill between the A69 and B6318 and a mile from Once Brewed.

Highlights of the Vindolanda museum displays include leather sandals, signature Roman toothbrush-flourish helmet decorations, and numerous writing tablets recently returned from the British Library. These include a student's marked work ('sloppy'), and a parent's note with a present of socks and underpants (things haven't changed – in this climate you can never have too many).

Roman Army Museum MUSEUM

(www.vindolanda.com; adult/child £5.25/3, with Vindolanda £10/5.50; ⏲10am-6pm Apr-Sep, to 5pm Oct, 10am-4pm Sat & Sun Nov & Dec) A mile northeast of Greenhead, near Walltown Crags, this kid-pleasing museum provides lots of colourful background detail to Hadrian's Wall life, such as how the soldiers spent their R&R time in this lonely outpost of the empire.

Housesteads Roman Fort & Museum HISTORIC SITE

(EH; www.english-heritage.org.uk; adult/child £6.40/3.80; ⏲10am-6pm Apr-Sep, to 5pm Oct, to 4pm Nov-Mar) The most dramatic site of Hadrian's Wall – and the best-preserved Roman fort in the whole country – is at Housesteads, 2.5 miles north of Bardon Mill on the B6318, and about 6 miles from Haltwhistle. From here, high on a ridge and covering 2 hectares, you can survey the moors of Northumberland National Park, and the snaking wall, with a sense of awe at the landscape and the aura of the Roman lookouts.

Housesteads' remains include an impressive hospital, granaries with a carefully worked out ventilation system and barrack blocks. Most memorable are the spectacularly situated communal flushable latrines. Information boards show what the individual buildings would have looked like in their heyday. There's a scale model of the entire fort in the small museum at the ticket office.

Birdoswald Roman Fort HISTORIC SITE

(EH; ☎01697-747602; www.english-heritage.org.uk; adult/child £5.60/3.40; ⏲10am-6pm Apr-Sep, to 5pm Oct, 10am-4pm Sat & Sun Nov-Mar) Technically in Cumbria, the remains of this once-formidable fort on an escarpment overlooking the beautiful Irthing Gorge are on a minor road off the B6318, about 3 miles west of Greenhead; a fine stretch of wall extends from here to Harrow's Scar Milecastle.

Lanercost Priory RUIN

(EH; www.english-heritage.org.uk; adult/child £3.60/2.20; ⏲10am-6pm Apr-Sep, to 5pm Oct, 10am-4pm Sat & Sun Nov-Mar) Situated 2.6 miles northeast of Brampton, these peaceful ruins are all that remain of a priory founded in 1166 by Augustinian canons. Post-dissolution it became a private house and a priory church was created from the Early English nave.

Sleeping

Once Brewed YHA HOSTEL £

(☎0845 371 9753; www.yha.org.uk; Military Rd, Bardon Mill; dm/d from £19.50/37.50; ⏲Mar-Nov; P) This modern, well-equipped hostel, with a kitchen, laundry and meals available, is central for visiting the Roman forts of Vindolanda, 1 mile away, and Housesteads, 3 miles away. The Hadrian's Wall bus AD122 drops you at the door.

Greenhead HOSTEL £

(☎01697-747411; www.greenheadhotelandhostel.co.uk; Greenhead; dm from £15) A converted Methodist chapel by a stream and a pleasant garden houses this independent hostel 3 miles west of Haltwhistle near the Roman Army Museum. There's a laundry and kitchen, but if you don't feel like cooking, Greenhead's hotel across the road has a restaurant and bar. It's served by the Hadrian's Wall bus AD122.

★Ashcroft B&B ££

(☎01434-320213; www.ashcroftguesthouse.co.uk; Lanty's Lonnen, Haltwhistle; s/d from £65/89; P 📶) British B&Bs don't get better than this elegant Edwardian vicarage surrounded by nearly a hectare of beautifully manicured, terraced lawns and gardens. Inside, the nine rooms – some with private balconies and terraces – have soaring ceilings and come with every gadget 21st-century beings need. The dining room is grander than some snooty hotels and the welcome certainly more genuine.

Holmhead Guest House B&B ££

(☎01697-747402; www.bandbhadrianswall.com; Greenhead Brampton; dm/s/d from £12.50/56/72, camping per person £7; P 📶) Built using recycled bits of the wall on whose foundations it stands, this superb farmhouse half a mile north of Greenhead offers comfy rooms, a basic bunk barn and unpowered campsites. The Pennine Way and the Hadrian's Wall Path pass through the grounds and Thirwall Castle's jagged ruins loom above. Ask to see the 3rd-century Roman graffiti.

Information

Tourist Office (☎01434-322002; www.northumberland.gov.uk; Mechanics Institute, Westgate; ⏲10am-4.30pm Mon-Sat Apr-Oct)

NORTHUMBERLAND NATIONAL PARK

England's last great wilderness is the 405 sq miles of natural wonderland that make up the country's least populated national park. The finest sections of Hadrian's Wall run along its southern edge and the landscape is dotted with prehistoric remains and fortified houses – the thick-walled *peles* were the only solid buildings built here until the mid-18th century.

Adjacent to the national park itself, the Kielder Water & Forest Park is home to Kielder Water, Europe's largest artificial lake, holding 200,000 million litres. Surrounding its 27-mile-long shoreline is England's largest forest, with 150 million spruce and pine trees.

The lack of population here helped see the area awarded dark-sky status by the International Dark Skies Association in late 2013 (the largest such designation in Europe), with controls to prevent light pollution.

The towns of Wooler (population 1990) and Rothbury (population 2330) make handy bases for exploring the area.

Sights

★ **Kielder Observatory**   OBSERVATORY
(☑ 07805-638469; www.kielderobservatory.org; off Shilling Pot; public observing session adult/child £15/10; ☺ by reservation) For the best views of the Northumberland International Dark Sky Park, attend a stargazing session at this state-of-the-art, 2008-built observatory. In addition to public observing there are a host of events including family astronomy, astrophotography and star camps. Book well ahead for all events, which sell out quickly, and dress as you would for the ski slopes (it's seriously chilly here at night). At the signs towards Kielder Observatory and Skyspace, turn left; it's a 2-mile drive up the track.

Cragside House, Garden & Estate   HISTORIC BUILDING, GARDENS
(NT; ☑ 01669-620333; www.nationaltrust.org.uk; adult/child £15.85/7.90, gardens & estate only £10.20/5.20; ☺ house 1-5pm or 11am-5pm Tue-Sun depending on the month, gardens 10.30am-5pm Tue-Sun mid-Mar–Oct) Situated 1 mile northeast of Rothbury is the astonishing country retreat of the first Lord Armstrong. In the 1880s the house had hot and cold running water, a telephone and alarm system, and was the first in the world to be lit by electricity, generated through hydropower. The sprawling Victorian gardens feature lakes, moors and one of Europe's largest rock gardens. Visit late May to mid-June to see Cragside's famous rhododendrons in bloom. It's just off the B6341.

Chillingham Castle   CASTLE
(☑ 01668-215359; www.chillingham-castle.com; adult/child £9/5; ☺ noon-5pm Sun-Fri Apr-Oct) Steeped in history, warfare, torture and ghosts, Chillingham is said to be one of the country's most haunted places, with spectres from a phantom funeral to Lady Mary Berkeley seeking her errant husband. Owner Sir Humphrey Wakefield has passionately restored the castle's extravagant medieval staterooms, stone-flagged banquet halls and grisly torture chambers. Chillingham is 6 miles southeast of Wooler. Bus 470 (three daily Monday to Saturday) between Alnwick (£3.70, 25 minutes) and Wooler (£3.10, 20 minutes) stops at Chillingham.

It's possible to stay at the medieval fortress in one of eight self-catering apartments where the likes of Henry III and Edward I once snoozed. Doubles start from £100.

Activities

The most spectacular stretch of the **Hadrian's Wall Path** is between Sewingshields and Greenhead in the south of the park.

There are many fine walks through the Cheviots (including a clamber to the top of the 815m-high **Cheviot**, the highest peak in the range), frequently passing by prehistoric remnants; local tourist offices can provide maps, guides and route information.

Though at times strenuous, **cycling** is a pleasure here; roads are good and traffic is light.

Kielder Water is a water-sports playground (and midge magnet; bring insect repellent). There are also walking and cycling trails here as well as great birdwatching. Visit www.visitkielder.com for more information.

Sleeping & Eating

Wooler YHA   HOSTEL £
(☑ 01668-281365; www.yha.org.uk; 30 Cheviot St; dm/d from £15.50/32; ☺ Mar-Nov; ℗ ☺) In a low, red-brick building above Wooler, this handy hostel contains 57 beds in a variety of rooms including four handcrafted 'shepherds' huts', a modern lounge and a small restaurant.

★ Otterburn Castle
Country House Hotel   HISTORIC HOTEL ££
(☑ 01830-520620; www.otterburncastle.com; Main
St, Otterburn; s £59-69, d £99-119, f £129; P 🛜)
Founded by William the Conqueror's cousin Robert Umfraville in 1086 and set in 13
hectares of grounds, this storybook castle's
18 rooms (some with four-poster beds)
are recently refurbished and astonishing
value. Rates include breakfast, served in
the wood-panelled Oak Room restaurant.
Cheaper meals are available in the Stable
Bar & Bistro.

Katerina's Guest House   B&B ££
(☑ 01669-620691; www.katerinasguesthouse.co.uk;
High St, Rothbury; d £78; 🛜) Beamed ceilings,
stone fireplaces and en suite rooms with
fridges and canopied four-poster beds make
Katerina's one of Rothbury's best choices.
Bakeries, cafes and pubs abound along the
street.

ⓘ Information

For information, contact the **National Park**
(☑ 01434-605555; www.northumberlandna-
tionalpark.org.uk). As well as tourist offices
in towns including **Wooler** (☑ 01668-282123;
www.wooler.org.uk; Cheviot Centre, 12 Padge-
pool Pl; ⊙ 10am-4.30pm Apr-Oct, 10am-4.30pm
Mon-Sat Nov-Mar) and **Rothbury** (☑ 01669-
620887; www.theheartofnorthumberland.co.uk;
Church St; ⊙ 10am-4.30pm), there's a national
park office in **Once Brewed** (☑ 01434-344396;
Military Rd; ⊙ 9.30am-5pm Apr-Oct, 10am-3pm
Sat & Sun Nov-Mar). All offices can help find
accommodation.

ⓘ Getting There & Around

Public transport options are limited – to explore
properly you really need your own wheels.

Kielder Bus 880 (£3.50, 50 minutes, two daily,
Tuesday, Friday and Saturday) runs between
Hexham and Kielder.

Otterburn Bus 808 (£3.50, 55 minutes, three
daily, Monday to Saturday) runs between Otterburn and Newcastle. A National Express service
calls at Otterburn (£5.80, 50 minutes, daily)
between Newcastle and Edinburgh.

Rothbury Bus 14 runs hourly between Morpeth
and Rothbury (£5, 1¼ hours, hourly, Monday to
Saturday).

Wooler Buses 470 and 473 link Wooler and
Alnwick (£3.70, 50 minutes, nine daily).
Buses 267 and 464 run between Wooler and
Berwick-upon-Tweed (£3.70, 50 minutes, nine
daily).

NORTHUMBERLAND COAST

Like Northumberland's wild and remote
interior, its coast is also sparsely populated.
You won't find any hurdy-gurdy seaside resorts, but instead charming, castle-crowned
villages strung along miles of wide, sandy
beaches that you might just have to yourself.

Alnwick

POP 8120

Northumberland's historic ducal town, Alnwick (pronounced 'annick') is an elegant
maze of narrow cobbled streets beneath the
watchful gaze of a colossal medieval castle. Alnwick is also home to an enchanting
bookshop and spectacular Alnwick Garden.

⊙ Sights

★ **Alnwick Castle**   CASTLE
(www.alnwickcastle.com; adult/child £14.50/7.50,
with Alnwick Garden £26.25/10.40; ⊙ 10am-
5.30pm Apr-Oct) The outwardly imposing
ancestral home of the Duke of Northumberland, and a favourite set for film-makers (it
was Hogwarts for the first couple of Harry
Potter films), has changed little since the
14th century. The interior is sumptuous and
extravagant; the six rooms open to the public – staterooms, dining room, guard chamber and library – have an incredible display
of Italian paintings, including Titian's *Ecce
Homo* and many Canalettos.

Various free tours include several focusing on Harry Potter and other productions
that have used the castle as a backdrop, including British comedy series *Blackadder*.

The castle is set in parklands designed by
Lancelot 'Capability' Brown. The woodland
walk offers some great aspects of the castle,
or for a view looking up the River Aln, take
the B1340 towards the coast.

Alnwick Garden   GARDENS
(www.alnwickgarden.com; adult/child £13.75/4.40;
⊙ 10am-7pm Jan-Oct, noon-6pm Nov & Dec) This
4.8-hectare walled garden has been transformed from a derelict site into a series of
magnificent green spaces surrounding the
breathtaking Grand Cascade – 120 separate
jets spurting more than 30,000L of water
down 21 weirs for everyone to marvel at and
kids to splash around in.

There are six other gardens, including
the Franco-Italian-influenced Ornamental

🏃 Driving Tour
Northumberland Coast

START NEWBIGGIN-BY-THE-SEA
END BERWICK-UPON-TWEED
LENGTH 78 MILES; ONE DAY

It's possible to shadow the coast to the Scottish border from Tynemouth, but the scenery really picks up at ❶ **Newbiggin-by-the-Sea**. Newbiggin's beach was recently restored, when over 500,000 tonnes of Skegness' sand was relocated here to counteract erosion, and Sean Henry's gigantic bronze sculpture *The Couple* was installed offshore.

Continuing north along the A1068 coast road for 13 miles brings you to the fishing port of ❷ **Amble**, with a boardwalk along the seafront and puffin cruises. Less than 2 miles north, biscuit-coloured ❸ **Warkworth** is a cluster of houses around a loop in the River Coquet, dominated by the craggy ruin of 14th-century Warkworth Castle. The castle features in Shakespeare's *Henry IV* Parts I and II, and the 1998 film *Elizabeth* was shot here. A few hundred yards upriver, the tiny 14th-century Warkworth Hermitage is carved into the rock.

Some 5 miles north of Warkworth is ❹ **Alnmouth**, with brightly painted houses and pretty beaches. It's another 5 miles inland to the bustling town of ❺ **Alnwick** to see its imposing castle – which starred as Harry Potter's Hogwarts – and glorious Alnwick Garden. Turn back towards the coast and follow the B1339 for 4.7 miles before turning east on Windside Hill to ❻ **Craster**, famed for its smoked kippers, which you can buy direct from the smokery. Don't miss a meal at the Jolly Fisherman, which has spectacular views of brooding Dunstanburgh Castle. Around 5 miles north at ❼ **Low Newton-by-the-Sea**, in Embleton Bay, pause for a pint brewed at the Ship Inn.

Past the village of Seahouses (jumping-off point for the Farne Islands), quaint ❽ **Bamburgh** is home to the most dramatic castle yet. Another 17 miles on, via a tidal causeway (check tide times!), the sacred priory ruins of isolated, other-worldly ❾ **Holy Island (Lindisfarne)** still attract spiritual pilgrims. Return to the mainland where, 14 miles north, you can walk almost the entire length of the Elizabethan walls encircling England's northernmost city, beautiful ❿ **Berwick-upon-Tweed**.

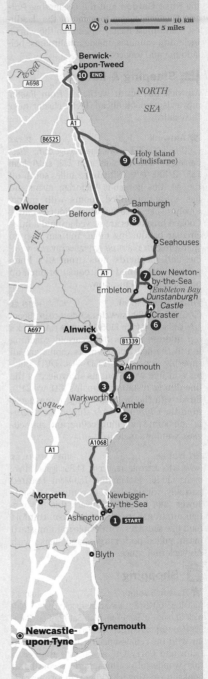

Garden (with more than 15,000 plants), the Rose Garden and the fascinating Poison Garden, home to some of the deadliest – and most illegal – plants in the world, including cannabis, magic mushrooms, belladonna and tobacco.

🛌 Sleeping & Eating

Alnwick fills up at weekends from Easter onwards so book ahead. B&Bs cluster near the castle.

⭐ Alnwick Lodge   B&B ££
(🖃01665-604363; www.alnwicklodge.com; West Cawledge Park, A1; sites from £12, s/d/f from £55/72/100; 🅿🛜) Situated 2 miles south off the A1, this gorgeous Victorian farmstead has 15 antique-filled rooms with quirky touches like free-standing, lidded baths. Cooked breakfasts are served around a huge circular banqueting table. You can also go 'glamping' in restored gypsy caravans, wagons and shepherds' huts (from £45, linen per bed £15; shared bathrooms), or pitch up on the sheltered meadow.

White Swan Hotel   HOTEL ££
(🖃01665-602109; www.classiclodges.co.uk; Bondgate Within; d/f from £105/115; 🅿🛜) Alnwick's top address is this 300-year-old coaching inn in the heart of town. Its rooms are all superbly appointed (LCD TVs, DVD players and free wi-fi), but its showpiece is the fine-dining restaurant (mains £11 to £19), fitted with the original dining room decor from the *Olympic,* sister ship to the *Titanic* – elaborate panelling, ceiling and stained-glass windows included.

Art House   INTERNATIONAL ££
(www.arthouserestaurant.com; 14 Bondgate Within; mains £10-16; ⊙11am-11pm Thu-Mon) Located partially within the 15th-century Hotspur Tower (aka Bondgate Tower), this hip restaurant/art gallery serves upmarket comfort food like sausages with wholegrain mustard mash, pulled pork burgers and steaks with Alnwick rum sauce.

🔒 Shopping

⭐ Barter Books   BOOKS
(🖃01665-604888; www.barterbooks.co.uk; Alnwick Station; ⊙9am-7pm Mon-Sat Apr-Sep, 9am-5pm Mon-Fri, to 7pm Sat Oct-Mar) If you're familiar with the renaissance of the WWII 'Keep Calm and Carry On' slogan, it's thanks to this wonderfully atmospheric secondhand bookshop in Alnwick's Victorian former railway station. While converting the station, the owner came across a set of posters – the framed original is above the till – and turned it into a successful industry.

Coal fires, velvet ottomans, reading rooms and a cafe make this a place you could spend days in, the silence interrupted only by the tiny rumble of the toy train that runs along the track above your head.

ℹ Information

Tourist Office (🖃01670-622152; www.visitalnwick.org.uk; 2 The Shambles; ⊙9am-5pm Mon-Sat, 10am-4pm Sun Easter-Oct, 9.30am-4.30pm Mon-Fri, 10am-4pm Sat Nov-Easter) By the marketplace.

ℹ Getting There & Away

Alnwick's nearest train station is at Alnmouth, connected to Alnwick by bus X18 (£2.65, 10 minutes, hourly). Buses X15 and X18 run to Berwick-upon-Tweed (£5.90, 50 minutes, 10 daily) and Newcastle (£5.90, one hour, 10 daily).

Craster
POP 435

Sandy, salty Craster is a small, sheltered fishing village about 6 miles northeast of Alnwick, and is famous for its kippers. In the early 20th century, 2500 herring were smoked here daily. The kippers they still produce today often grace the Queen's breakfast table, no less.

⊙ Sights

Dunstanburgh Castle   CASTLE
(EH & NT; www.english-heritage.org.uk; adult/child £4.30/2.60; ⊙10am-6pm Apr-Sep, to 4pm Oct, 10am-4pm Sat & Sun Nov-Mar) The dramatic 1.5-mile walk along the coast from Craster (not accessible by car) is the most scenic path to this moody, weather-beaten castle. Its construction began in 1314, it was strengthened during the Wars of the Roses, but left to crumble, becoming ruined by 1550. Parts of the original wall and gatehouse keep are still standing and it's a tribute to its builders that so much remains.

You can also reach the castle on foot from Embleton (1.5 miles).

🍴 Eating

⭐ Jolly Fisherman   PUB ££
(🖃01665-0576461; www.thejollyfishermancraster.co.uk; Haven Hill, Craster; lunch mains £7-10, dinner mains £12-20; ⊙kitchen 11am-3pm & 5-8.30pm

Mon-Sat, noon-7pm Sun;) Crab (in sensational soup, sandwiches, fish platters and more) is the speciality of this superb gastropub, but Paul Bocuse–trained chef John Blackmore's other amazing creations include apricot-stuffed pheasant leg and Northumbrian venison with juniper berry jus. Great wine list, wonderful real ales, a roaring fire in the bar and a stunning beer garden overlooking Dunstanburgh Castle, too.

Shopping

Robson & Sons FOOD
(01665-576223; www.kipper.co.uk; Haven Hill, Craster; kippers per kilo £6) Four generations have operated this traditional fish smokers. It's best known for its kippers, but also smokes salmon and other fish.

Information

Tourist Office (01665-576007; Quarry Car Park; 10am-5pm Easter-Oct)

Getting There & Away

Bus X18 runs to Berwick-upon-Tweed (£5.90, 1½ hours, nine daily) and Newcastle (£5.40, 1½ hours, nine daily). Bus 418 links Craster to Alnwick (£4.90, 30 minutes, hourly).

Embleton Bay

Beautiful Embleton Bay, a pale wide arc of sand, stretches from Dunstanburgh past the endearing, sloping village of Embleton and curves in a broad vanilla-coloured strand around to end at Low Newton-by-the-Sea, a tiny whitewashed, National Trust–preserved village.

Sights & Activities

Behind the bay is a path leading to the **Newton Pool Nature Reserve**, an important spot for breeding and migrating birds such as black-headed gulls and grasshopper warblers. There are a couple of hides where you can peer out at them. You can continue walking along the headland beyond Low Newton, where you'll find **Football Hole**, a delightful hidden beach between headlands.

Dunstanburgh Castle Golf Club GOLF
(01665-576562; www.dunstanburgh.com; green fee per round weekday/weekend £26/30; by reservation) First laid out in 1900, this stunning course was improved upon by golf legend and 'inventor' of the dogleg, James Braid (1870–1950) in 1922.

Sleeping & Eating

Joiners Arms PUB £££
(01665-576112; www.joiners-arms.com; High Newton-by-the-Sea; d £140-155;) Locals love this gastropub and for good reason: ingredients are sourced nearby, the seafood and steaks are excellent (mains £8 to £21) and families are warmly welcomed. But for visitors, it's also a fantastic place to stay – five contemporary guest rooms are individually and exquisitely decorated with details like exposed brick, free-standing baths and four-poster beds.

Ship Inn PUB ££
(01665-576262; www.shipinnnewton.co.uk; Low Newton-by-the-Sea; mains £8.50-18; bar 11am-11pm Mon-Sat, noon-11pm Sun, kitchen noon-2.30pm daily & 7-8pm Wed-Sat) Set around a village green, this wonderful pub brews 20 different beers – blond, wheat, rye, bitter, stout and seasonal – using local Coquet river water. Food is first-rate, too, from local crab to slow-cooked Peelham Farm lamb shanks with lemon and parsley couscous. No credit cards.

Getting There & Away

Bus X18 to Newcastle (£5.40, 1¾ hours, nine daily) and Berwick-upon-Tweed (£5.40, 1¼ hours, nine daily) stops outside the Joiners Arms. Bus 418 (£4.90, 40 minutes, hourly) links the village of Embleton with Alnwick.

Farne Islands

During breeding season (roughly May to July), you can see feeding chicks of 20 species of seabird, including puffin, kittiwake, Arctic tern, eider duck, cormorant and gull, as well as some 6000 grey seals on this rocky **archipelago** (NT; 07901-922143; www.nationaltrust.org.uk; adult/child excl boat transport £6.80/3.50; by reservation, season and conditions permitting) about 3 miles offshore from the fishing village of Seahouses, reached from its dock with operators including **Billy Shiel** (01665-720308; www.farne-islands.com; 2½hr tour adult/child £13/9, 6hr tour £30/18).

Crossings can be rough (impossible in bad weather); wear warm, waterproof clothing and an old hat to guard against the birds!

Inner Farne is the more interesting of the two islands accessible to the public (along with Staple Island); its tiny chapel (1370; restored 1848) commemorates St Cuthbert, who lived here for a spell and died here in 687.

ℹ Information

Tourist Office (☑ 01670-625593; www.
seahouses.org; Seafield car park; ☺10am-5pm
Apr-Oct, 11am-3pm Sat & Sun Nov-Mar)

ℹ Getting There & Away

Seahouses bus connections include bus X18
to Berwick-upon-Tweed (£5.70, nine daily, 45
minutes) and Newcastle (£6.20, nine daily, two
hours). Bus 418 runs to Alnwick (£5.10, 55 minutes, hourly).

Bamburgh

POP 280

Roosting high up on a basalt crag, Bamburgh's mighty castle looms over the
quaint village – a clutch of houses around
a pleasant green – which continues to commemorate the valiant achievements of local heroine, Grace Darling.

◉ Sights

Bamburgh Castle   CASTLE
(www.bamburghcastle.com; adult/child £9.95/4.50;
☺10am-5pm mid-Feb–Oct, 11am-4.30pm Nov-
mid-Feb) Northumberland's most dramatic
castle was built around a powerful 11th-
century Norman keep by Henry II. The castle played a key role in the border wars of the
13th and 14th centuries, and in 1464 was the
first English castle to fall during the Wars of
the Roses. It was restored in the 19th century by the great industrialist Lord Armstrong,
and is still home to the Armstrong family.

Its name is a derivative of Bebbanburgh,
after the wife of Anglo-Saxon ruler Aedel-
frip, whose fortified home occupied this
basalt outcrop 500 years earlier. Antique
furniture, suits of armour, priceless ceramics and artworks cram the castle's rooms
and chambers, but top billing goes to the
neo-Gothic **King's Hall** with wood panelling, leaded windows and hefty beams supporting the roof.

RNLI Grace Darling Museum   MUSEUM
(www.rnli.org; 1 Radcliffe Rd; ☺10am-5pm Easter-
Sep, 10am-4pm Tue-Sun Oct-Easter) 𝗙𝗥𝗘𝗘 Born
in Bamburgh, Grace Darling was the lighthouse keeper's daughter on Outer Farne
who rowed out to the grounded, flailing SS
Forfarshire in 1838 and saved its crew in the
middle of a dreadful storm. This recently refurbished museum even has her actual coble
(row boat) as well as a film on the events of

that stormy night. Grace was born just three
houses down from the museum and is buried in the churchyard opposite.

Her ornate wrought-iron and sandstone
tomb was built tall so as to be visible to
passing ships.

✕ Eating

★**Mizen Head**   MODERN BRITISH £££
(☑01668-214254; www.mizenheadhotel.co.uk; Luc-
ker Rd; mains £10-29; ☺noon-2pm & 6-9pm; ℙ🛜)
Since it opened in 2011, Bamburgh's best
place to eat and/or stay is this stunning restaurant with rooms. Local seafood (lobster
thermidor, and roast turbot with asparagus,
tarragon and lemon butter) is the kitchen's
speciality, along with chargrilled steaks. Its
six rooms with chequered fabrics and black-
and-white coastal prints are light, bright
and spacious (doubles from £100 to £140).
Switched-on staff know their stuff.

There's wi-fi in public areas only.

ℹ Getting There & Away

Take bus X18 north to Berwick-upon-Tweed
(£5.90, 35 minutes, nine daily) or south to Newcastle (£5.90, two hours, nine daily).

Holy Island (Lindisfarne)

POP 160

There's something almost other-worldly
about this tiny, 2-sq-mile island. Connected
to the mainland by a narrow causeway that
only appears at low tide, it's fiercely desolate
and isolated, scarcely different from when St
Aidan arrived to found a monastery in 635.

As you cross the empty flats, it's easy to
imagine the marauding Vikings who repeatedly sacked the settlement between 793 and
875, when the monks finally took the hint
and left. They carried with them the illuminated *Lindisfarne Gospels* (now in the British Library in London) and the miraculously
preserved body of St Cuthbert, who lived
here for a couple of years but preferred the
hermit's life on Inner Farne. A priory was
re-established in the 11th century, but didn't
survive the Dissolution in 1537.

Pay close attention to the crossing-time
information, posted at tourist offices and
on notice boards throughout the area, and
at www.holy-island.info. Every year drivers
are caught midway by the incoming tide and
have to abandon their cars.

◉ Sights

Lindisfarne Priory　　　　　RUIN
(EH; www.english-heritage.org.uk; adult/child £5.40/
3.20; ◷ 10am-6pm Apr-Sep, to 5pm Oct, 10am-
4pm Sat & Sun Nov-Mar) The skeletal, red and
grey ruins of the priory are an eerie sight
and give a glimpse into the isolated life led
by the Lindisfarne monks. The later 13th-
century **St Mary the Virgin Church** is
built on the site of the first church between
the Tees and the Firth of Forth, and the adjacent **museum** displays the remains of
the first monastery and tells the story of
the monastic community before and after
the Dissolution.

Lindisfarne Heritage Centre　　MUSEUM
(www.lindisfarne-centre.com; Marygate; adult/child
£4/2; ◷ 10am-5pm Apr-Oct, reduced hours Nov-
Mar) Twenty pages of the luminescent
Lindisfarne Gospels can be flicked through
on touch-screens here, though there's normally a queue. While you wait your turn
there are fascinating exhibitions on the Vikings and the sacking of Lindisfarne in 793.

Lindisfarne Castle　　　　　CASTLE
(NT; www.nationaltrust.org.uk; adult/child £7.40/
3.70; ◷ 10am-3pm Tue-Sun Mar-Oct) Half a mile
from the village stands this tiny, storybook
castle, moulded onto a hunk of rock in 1550,
and extended and converted by Sir Edwin
Lutyens from 1902 to 1910 for Mr Hudson,
the owner of *Country Life* magazine – you
can imagine some of the decadent Gats-
by-style parties to have graced its alluring
rooms. Opening times can vary due to tide
times.

🛏 Sleeping & Eating

It's possible to stay on the island, but you'll
need to book well in advance.

Crown & Anchor　　　　　INN **££**
(☎ 01289-389215; www.holyislandcrown.co.uk; Market Pl; d £75-100) The only locally run inn on
the island is a relaxed, down-to-earth spot
with brightly coloured guest rooms and solid pub grub (steak-and-ale pie, rib-eye steak
with onion rings; mains £8 to £18), but the
biggest winner is the beer garden with a
postcard panorama of the castle, priory and
harbour.

Lindisfarne Inn　　　　　INN **££**
(☎ 01289-381223; www.lindisfarneinn.co.uk; Beal;
s/d from £60/85; 🛜) Although on the mainland (on the A1 next to the turn-off to the

causeway), this is a handy alternative to
staying and/or dining on the island if you're
cutting it fine with crossing times. Its 21
spotless, modern rooms are set far back
enough that road noise isn't a problem. The
well-above-average bar food includes a catch-
of-the-day fisherman's pie (mains £9 to £15).
There's wi-fi in the bar only.

Open Gate　　　　　GUESTHOUSE **££**
(☎ 01289-389222; www.aidanandhilda.org; Marygate; s £48-58, d £78-85) An Elizabethan farmhouse is the setting for this Christian retreat.
In addition to four en suite rooms, the top
floor has some cheaper single rooms that
share bathrooms (£38).

ℹ Getting There & Around

The sea covers the causeway and cuts the island
off from the mainland for about five hours each
day.

Holy Island can sometimes be reached by bus
477 from Berwick-upon-Tweed (£4.50, 40 minutes, depends on tides); check with Berwick's
tourist offices for updated information.

Drivers need to park in one of the signposted
car parks (£4.60 per day). A shuttle bus (£2
return) runs from the car park to the castle every
20 minutes.

Berwick-upon-Tweed

POP 13,265

England's northernmost city is a picturesque fortress town, cleaved by the River
Tweed, which is spanned by the Grade I–
listed Berwick Bridge (aka Old Bridge), built
from sandstone between 1611 and 1624, and
the Royal Tweed (1925–28).

Berwick is the stubborn holder of two
unique honours: it is the most fought-over
settlement in European history (between
1174 and 1482 it changed hands 14 times
between the Scots and the English); and its
football team, Berwick Rangers, are the only
English team to play in the Scottish League
(albeit in lowly Scottish League Two). Although firmly English since the 15th century, Berwick retains its own identity, with
locals south of the border speaking with a
noticeable Scottish whirr.

◉ Sights & Activities

Berwick Walls　　　　　WALLS
(EH; ◷ daylight hours) **FREE** You can walk almost the entire length of Berwick's hefty
Elizabethan walls, begun in 1558 to reinforce an earlier set built during the reign

of Edward II. The mile-long walk is a must, with wonderful, wide-open views. Only a small fragment remains of the once-mighty **border castle**, most of the building having been replaced by the train station.

Berwick Barracks   MUSEUM, GALLERY
(EH; www.english-heritage.org.uk; The Parade; adult/child £4.20/2.50; ⊙10am-6pm Mon-Fri Apr-Sep, to 4pm Oct) Designed by Nicholas Hawksmoor, Britain's oldest purpose-built barracks (1717) now house an assortment of museums and art galleries, covering a history of the town and British soldiery since the 17th century. The **Gymnasium Gallery** hosts big-name contemporary art exhibitions.

Cell Block Museum   MUSEUM
(Marygate; adult/child £2/50p; ⊙tours 10.30am & 2pm Mon-Fri Easter-Sep) The original jail cells in the upper floor of the town hall (1750–61) have been preserved as a chilling museum devoted to crime and punishment. Tours take in the public rooms, museum, jail and belfry.

☞ Tours

Time to Explore Guided Tours   WALKING TOUR
(✍01289-330218; www.visitberwick.com; 106 Marygate; Town & Walls adult/child £5/free, Hidden Berwick adult/child £6/free; ⊙by reservation Easter-Oct) Passionate local Derek Sharman leads 1¼-hour Town & Walls tours taking in the town's highlights, and 1¾-hour Hidden Berwick tours including entry to an Elizabethan bastion and the 18th-century gunpowder magazine, which aren't normally open to the public. Tours depart from the tourist office.

⌂ Sleeping

Accommodation in Berwick is limited – the tourist office can help find places to stay.

Berwick YHA   HOSTEL £
(✍01629-592700; www.yha.org.uk; Dewars Lane; dm/d from £18/59; @ ⑨) A 240-year-old granary has been converted into a state-of-the-art hostel with contemporary facilities: comfortable dorms, a handful of en suite doubles, a TV room, a laundry and wi-fi in common areas. Staff are terrifically friendly and helpful.

Granary Guesthouse   BOUTIQUE B&B ££
(✍01289-304403; www.granaryguesthouse.co.uk; 11 Bridge St; s/d from £80/96; P⑨) ✿ In a charming town-centre location, Berwick's most romantic B&B has three fresh, elegant and contemporary guest rooms, locally sourced and/or organic breakfasts and an on-site beauty treatment room offering massages.

✗ Eating & Drinking

Audela   MODERN BRITISH ££
(✍01289-308827; www.audela.co.uk; 41-47 Bridge St; breakfast dishes £3-8, lunch mains £5-9.50, dinner mains £8-19; ⊙9am-9pm; ☝) ✿ Named for the last vessel to be built at Berwick Shipyard (in 1979), this brand-new addition to Berwick's dining scene has become the town's top table. Local suppliers provide the ingredients for dishes like twice-baked blue cheese soufflé, halibut with lemon butter sauce and herb-crusted rack of lamb, served in a striking sage-green dining room.

Barrels Alehouse   PUB
(59-61 Bridge St; ⊙noon-midnight; ⑨) Berwick's best watering hole attracts a mixed, laid-back crowd who can be found sipping real ales and micro-distilled gins and whiskies at all hours. There's regular live music in the atmospherically dingy basement bar.

ⓘ Information

Tourist Office (✍01670-622155; www.visitberwick.com; 106 Marygate; ⊙10am-5pm Apr-Oct, 10am-4pm Mon-Sat Nov-Mar)

ⓘ Getting There & Away

BUS
Buses stop on Golden Sq (where Marygate becomes Castlegate). National Express coaches between Edinburgh (£11.60, 1¼ hours, twice daily) and London (£36.50, eight hours, twice daily) stop here. Other options include buses X15 (via Alnwick) and X18 to Newcastle (£6.50, 2½ hours, nine daily) and bus 477 to Holy Island (£4.50, 35 minutes, depends on tides; check with Berwick's tourist offices for updated information).

TRAIN
Berwick is almost exactly halfway between Edinburgh (£19.90, 40 minutes, every 30 minutes) and Newcastle (£23.60, 45 minutes, every 30 minutes) on the East Coast Main Line linking London and Edinburgh.

Wales

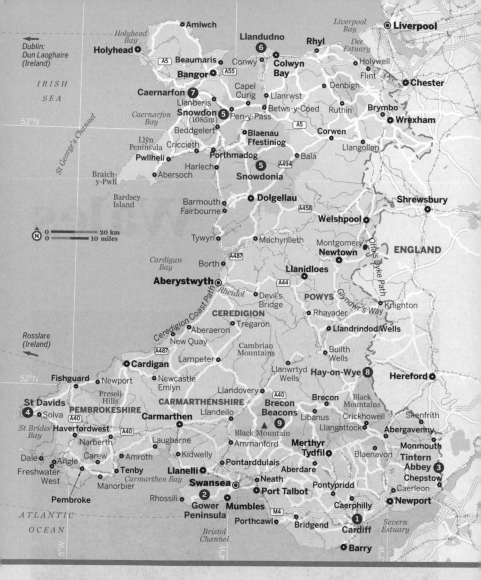

Wales Highlights

1 Exploring **Cardiff** (p659), the Welsh capital, with its castle, shopping arcades and nightlife

2 Catching some breaks or just enjoying the views along the **Gower Peninsula** (p685)

3 Marvelling at the picture-perfect ruins of **Tintern Abbey** (p678) in the beautiful Wye Valley

4 Enjoying tiny **St Davids** (p696), with its beautiful cathedral and idyllic setting

5 Climbing Wales' highest peak, Snowdon, or enjoying more gentle exercise in **Snowdonia** (p730)

6 Buying fish and chips and strolling along the pier in **Llandudno** (p758)

7 Seeing **Caernarfon Castle** (p746), maybe the most impressive of Wales' fortresses

8 Wandering through **Hay-on-Wye** (p719), a book-lover's heaven

9 Walking in the mountains, then eating in the gastropubs of the **Brecon Beacons** (p710)

Cardiff, Pembrokeshire & South Wales

Best Places to Eat

➡ Purple Poppadom (p669)

➡ Halen Môr (p695)

➡ Cors (p690)

➡ Food at Williams (p695)

➡ Coffee Barker (p668)

Best Places to Stay

➡ Grove (p691)

➡ Manor Town House (p702)

➡ Old School Hostel (p700)

➡ Old Rectory (p677)

Why Go?

Stretching from historic border town Chepstow through to the jagged Pembrokeshire Coast in the west, South Wales really packs in the sights.

Hugging the border, the Wye Valley is the birthplace of British tourism. For more than 200 years people have come to explore this tranquil waterway and its winding, wooded vale, where the majestic ruins of Tintern Abbey have inspired generations of poets and artists.

The nation's capital, Cardiff, flies the flag for big-city sophistication in the land of the red dragon. Just out of Swansea, Wales' second city, the Gower Peninsula revels in its coastal beauty. To the north, the fecund heartland of rural Carmarthenshire offers country comfort in abundance.

Beyond Cardiff, the biggest draw in South Wales remains Pembrokeshire, where almost 200 miles of magical shoreline has been declared a national park, delineated by craggy cliffs, golden sands, chocolate-box villages and seaside resorts.

When to Go

➡ Wales' home matches in the Six Nations Rugby Championship warm the spirits of locals and visitors alike during chilly February and March. Early daffodils pop out to celebrate St David's Day on 1 March – spend it in the saint's city, St Davids.

➡ If you're planning some coastal walking, April to July are the driest months.

➡ In July the summer-long Cardiff Festival kicks off, incorporating theatre, comedy, music and a food festival.

➡ In August, the warmest month, knights storm Cardiff Castle, classic cars converge and gay pride hits the streets. Swansea Bay's summer festival continues right through to September.

Cardiff, Pembrokeshire & South Wales Highlights

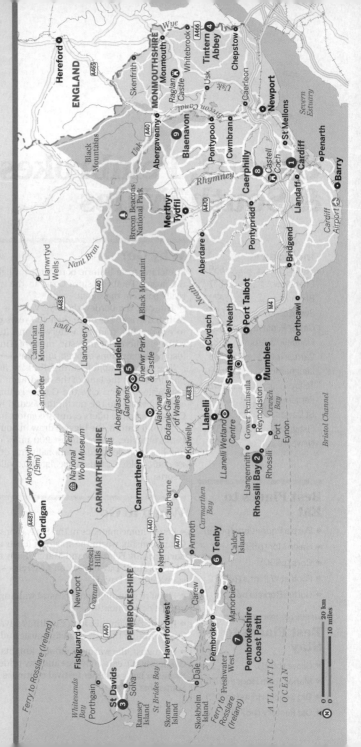

① Diving into the attractions and nightlife of Wales' dynamic capital city, **Cardiff** (p659)

② Watching the surf break at **Rhossili Bay** (p685) on the spectacular Gower Peninsula

③ Unwinding in **St Davids** (p696), Wales' most beguiling little city

④ Strolling among the ruins of **Tintern Abbey** (p678) in the glorious Wye Valley

⑤ Discovering gardens and manors in the countryside around **Llandeilo** (p687)

⑥ Building sandcastles in the shadow of the real thing at **Tenby** (p692)

⑦ Tracing a breathtaking collision of rock and sea along the **Pembrokeshire Coast Path** (p692)

⑧ Crossing the moat at **Caerphilly Castle** (p674) and wandering into a fairy tale

⑨ Feasting on World Heritage industrial sites and world-class cheese at **Blaenavon** (p679)

🏃 Activities

For outdoor activities, the region's main draw is Pembrokeshire. Walkers love the **Pembrokeshire Coast Path**, a 186-mile jaunt through some of Britain's most spectacular scenery. Watersports on offer include excellent sea kayaking, surfing and, most thrilling of all, coasteering. Another area popular with surfers and walkers is the Gower Peninsula.

The **Lôn Geltaidd** (Celtic Trail; NCN Routes 4 and 47) cycle route cuts clear across South Wales from the Severn Bridge to Fishguard via Chepstow, Swansea and Carmarthen. Off-road cycling fans should head for the tracks and byways of the Preseli Hills, south of Newport, or to the dedicated **Cognation** (www.cognation.co.uk) mountain-bike areas between Cardiff and the Brecon Beacons.

ℹ️ Getting There & Around

Frequent train and coach services connect South Wales to England and the rest of Wales. The main railway continues west to the ferry terminals of Fishguard and Pembroke Dock (both ports for Ireland). Trains also trundle through Carmarthenshire on the famously scenic **Heart of Wales line** (www.heart-of-wales.co.uk) between Swansea and Shrewsbury.

For information on routes and timetables, refer to www.traveline-cymru.info.

CARDIFF (CAERDYDD)

POP 447,000

The capital of Wales since only 1955, Cardiff has embraced the role with vigour, emerging in the new millennium as one of Britain's leading urban centres. Caught between an ancient fort and an ultramodern waterfront, compact Cardiff seems to have surprised even itself with how interesting it has become.

The city has entered the 21st century pumped up on steroids, flexing its recently acquired architectural muscles as if it's astonished to have them. This newfound confidence is infectious, and these days it's not just the game of rugby that draws crowds into the city. Come weekends, a buzz reverberates through the streets as swarms of shoppers hit the Hayes, followed by waves of revellers descending on the capital's thriving pubs, bars and live-music venues.

History

In AD 75 the Romans built a fort where Cardiff Castle now stands. The name 'Cardiff' probably derives from the Welsh Caer Tâf (Fort on the River Taff) or Caer Didi (Didius' Fort), referring to the Roman general Aulus Didius. After the Romans left Britain, the site remained unoccupied until the Norman Conquest. In 1093 a Norman knight named Robert Fitzhamon, conqueror of Glamorgan and later earl of Gloucester, built himself a castle here (the remains stand within the grounds of Cardiff Castle) and a small town grew up around it. Both were damaged during a Welsh revolt in 1183, and the town was sacked in 1404 by Owain Glyndŵr during his unsuccessful rebellion against English domination.

The first of the Tudor Acts of Union in 1536 put the English stamp on Cardiff and brought some stability. But despite Cardiff's importance as a port, market town and bishopric, only 1000 people were living here in 1801.

Cardiff owes its present-day stature to iron and coal mining in the valleys to the north. Coal was first exported, on a small scale, as early as 1600. In 1794 the Bute family, which owned much of the land from which Welsh coal was mined, built the Glamorganshire Canal to enable iron to be shipped to Cardiff from Merthyr Tydfil.

In 1840 the canal was superseded by the Taff Vale Railway. A year earlier the second marquess of Bute had completed the first docks at Butetown, just south of Cardiff, getting the jump on other South Wales ports. By the time it dawned on everyone that the valleys held immense reserves of coal, which triggered a kind of black gold rush, the Butes were in a position to insist the coal be shipped from Butetown. Cardiff was off and running.

The docklands expanded rapidly; the Butes grew staggeringly rich; and the town boomed, its population rising to 170,000 by the end of the 19th century and to 227,000 by 1931. A large, multiracial workers' community known as Tiger Bay grew up in the harbourside area of Butetown.

In 1905 Cardiff was officially designated a city, and a year later its elegant Civic Centre was inaugurated. The city's wealth and its hold on the coal trade persuaded Captain Robert Scott to launch his ill-fated expedition to the South Pole from here in 1910. Cardiff became the world's top coal port in

1913, exporting some 13 million tonnes of the stuff.

The slump in the coal trade after WWI and the Great Depression of the 1930s slowed Cardiff's expansion. Bombing in WWII badly damaged the city and claimed more than 350 lives. Shortly afterwards the coal industry was nationalised, prompting the Butes to pack their bags and leave town in 1947.

Wales had no official capital, and the need for one was seen as an important focus for Welsh nationhood. Cardiff had the advantage of being the country's biggest city and boasting the architectural riches of the Civic Centre, which today includes the National Museum Cardiff, City Hall, police headquarters, law courts, crown offices and Cardiff University. A ballot of members of the Welsh authorities gave Cardiff 36 votes against Caernarfon's 11 and Aberystwyth's four, and it was proclaimed the capital of Wales in 1955.

◉ Sights

◉ Central Cardiff

★ **National Museum Cardiff** MUSEUM
(Map p666; www.museumwales.ac.uk; Gorsedd Gardens Rd; ⊙10am-5pm Tue-Sun) **FREE** Devoted mainly to natural history and art, this grand neoclassical building is the centrepiece of the seven institutions dotted around the country that together form the Welsh National Museum. It's one of Britain's best museums; you'll need at least three hours to do it justice, but it could easily consume the best part of a rainy day.

The excellent art collection's treasures include a trio of Monet's *Water Lilies,* alongside his scenes of London, Rouen and Venice; Sisley's *The Cliff at Penarth* (the artist was married in Cardiff); Renoir's shimmering *La Parisienne;* and Van Gogh's anguished *Rain: Auvers.* Welsh artists such as

Cardiff

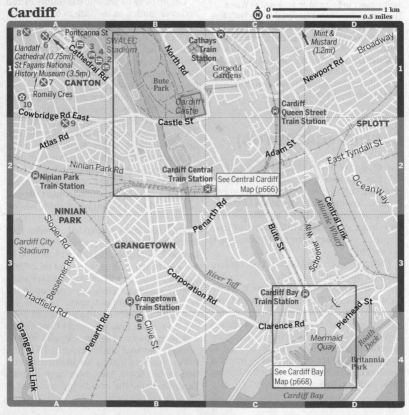

Gwen and Augustus John, Richard Wilson, Thomas Jones, David Jones and Ceri Richards are well represented. A large new space is devoted to contemporary exhibitions.

★ **Cardiff Castle**   CASTLE
(Map p666; www.cardiffcastle.com; Castle St; adult/child £12/9, incl guided tour £15/11; ⊙9am-5pm) The grafting of Victorian mock-Gothic extravagance onto Cardiff's most important historical relics makes Cardiff Castle the city's leading attraction. Far from a traditional Welsh castle, it's more a collection of disparate buildings scattered around a central green and which encompasses practically the entire history of Cardiff. The most conventionally castlelike bits are the 12th-century motte-and-bailey **Norman keep** at its centre and the 13th-century **Black Tower**, which forms the entrance gate.

In the 19th century it was discovered that the Normans had built their fortifications on top of the original 1st-century Roman fort. The high walls that surround the castle are largely a Victorian reproduction of the 3m-thick Roman walls from the 3rd century. Also from the 19th century are the towers and turrets on the west side, dominated by the colourful 40m clock tower. This faux-Gothic extravaganza was dreamed up by the third marquess of Bute and his architect, the eccentric William Burges. Both were obsessed with Gothic architecture, religious symbolism and astrology, influences that were incorporated into the designs.

A 50-minute guided tour takes you through the interiors of this flamboyant fantasy world, from the winter smoking room in the clock tower with decor expounding on the theme of time, to the mahogany-and-mirrors narcissism of Lord Bute's bedroom. The banqueting hall boasts Bute-family heraldic shields and a fantastically over-the-top fireplace. Marble, sandalwood, parrots and acres of gold leaf create an elaborate Moorish look in the Arab room. The neighbouring nursery is decorated with fairy-tale and nursery-rhyme characters, while the Roman-style roof garden seems to underline how much of a fantasy all this really was – designed with southern Italy in mind, rather than Wales. Some but not all of these rooms can be accessed with a regular castle entry, which includes an excellent audioguide (also available in a children's edition and a range of languages).

Below the ticket office is **Firing Line**, a small museum devoted to Welsh soldiers.

★ **Bute Park**   PARK
(Map p666; ⊙7.30am-sunset) Flanked by the castle and the River Taff, Bute Park was donated to the city along with the castle in 1947. With Sophia Gardens, Pontcanna Fields and Llandaff Fields, it forms a green corridor that stretches northwest for 1½ miles to Llandaff. All were once part of the Bute family's vast holdings.

Forming the park's southern edge, the **Animal Wall** (Map p666) is topped with stone figures of lions, seals, bears and other creatures. In the 1930s they were the subject of a newspaper cartoon strip and many Cardiff kids grew up thinking the animals came alive at night.

★ **Millennium Stadium**   STADIUM
(Map p666; ☎029-2082 2228; www.millenniumstadium.com; Westgate St; tours adult/child £9.50/6) This spectacular stadium squats like a stranded spaceship on the River Taff's east bank. Attendance at matches has increased dramatically since this 74,500-seat, £168-million, three-tiered stadium with sliding roof was completed in time to host the 1999 Rugby World Cup. Rugby is the national game and when the crowd begins to sing at Millennium, the whole of Cardiff resonates. If you can't get tickets to a match, it's well worth taking a tour. Book online or at the **WRU Store** (Map p666; 8 Westgate St; ⊙10am-5.30pm Mon-Sat, 11am-4pm Sun).

Cardiff Story   MUSEUM
(Map p666; www.cardiffstory.com; Old Library, The Hayes; ⊙10am-4pm) This excellent little museum uses interactive displays, video footage and everyday objects to tell the story of Cardiff's transformation from a small market

---

Cardiff

🛏 **Sleeping**

🍴 **Eating**

🎭 **Entertainment**

CARDIFF IN...

Two Days

Wander around the central city, stopping to explore **Cardiff Castle** (p661) and the **National Museum Cardiff** (p660). Lunch could be a picnic in **Bute Park** (p661) with treats acquired at **Cardiff Market** (p671) or, if the weather's not cooperating, a meal at any of the reasonably priced central-city eateries. Spend your second day heading back to the future at **Cardiff Bay**, where you can immerse yourself in forward-thinking architecture and have a **Doctor Who Experience** (p662).

Four Days

Spend your third morning steeped in history at **St Fagans National History Museum** (p663), then check out **Barry Island** (p674). On your last day, head north to explore **Llandaff Cathedral** (p664), then continue on to **Castell Coch** (p674) and **Caerphilly Castle** (p674). For your last night in the Welsh capital, blast away the cobwebs in one of the city's live-music venues.

town into the world's biggest coal port and then into the capital city of today. Check out the original entrance to the library, lined with beautiful Victorian tiles, and head upstairs to see temporary art exhibitions.

St John the Baptist Church   CHURCH

(Map p666; Working St; ⊙10am-3pm Mon-Sat) A graceful Gothic tower rises from this 15th-century church, its delicate stonework looking almost like filigree. A church has stood on this site since at least 1180. Inside there are regimental flags, elegant pointed arches and a spectacular Elizabethan-era tomb. Regular lunchtime organ concerts are held here.

◉ Cardiff Bay

Lined with important national institutions, Cardiff Bay is where the modern Welsh nation is put on display in an architect's playground of interesting buildings, large open spaces and public art. The bay's main commercial centre is Mermaid Quay, which is packed with bars, restaurants and shops.

It wasn't always this way. By 1913 more than 13 million tonnes of coal were being shipped from Cardiff docks. Following the post-WWII slump the docklands deteriorated into a wasteland of empty basins, cut off from the city by the railway embankment. The bay outside the docks, which has one of the highest tidal ranges in the world (more than 12m between high and low water), was ringed for up to 14 hours a day by smelly, sewage-contaminated mudflats. The nearby residential area of Butetown became a neglected slum.

Since 1987 the area has been radically redeveloped. The turning point came with the completion of a state-of-the-art tidal barrage in 1999.

Doctor Who Experience   EXHIBITION

(Map p668; ☑0844 801 2279; www.doctorwho-experience.com; Porth Teigr; adult/child £15/11; ⊙10am-5pm (last admission 3.30pm) Wed-Mon, daily school holidays) The huge success of the reinvented classic TV series *Doctor Who*, produced by BBC Wales, has brought Cardiff to the attention of sci-fi fans worldwide. City locations have featured in many episodes; and the first two series of the spin-off *Torchwood* were also set in Cardiff Bay. Capitalising on Timelord tourism, this interactive exhibition is located right next to the BBC studios where the series is filmed – look out for the Tardis hovering outside.

Visitors find themselves sucked through a crack in time and thrown into the role of the Doctor's companion. It's great fun – especially when you come face to face with full-size Daleks in full 'ex-ter-min-ate' mode. But don't blink – there are weeping angels about. The 'experience' only takes about 20 minutes but afterwards you're transported into a large two-level warehouse, where you can wander at your leisure around the displays of sets, costumes and props spanning the show's 50-year run.

★ Wales Millennium Centre   ARTS CENTRE

(Map p668; ☑029-2063 6464; www.wmc.org.uk; Bute Pl; tours £6; ⊙tours 11am & 2.30pm) FREE The centrepiece and symbol of Cardiff Bay's regeneration is the superb Wales Millennium Centre, an architectural masterpiece of stacked Welsh slate in shades of purple, green and grey topped with an overarching bronzed steel shell. Designed by Welsh architect Jonathan Adams, it opened in 2004 as Wales' premier arts complex, housing major cultural organisations such as the Welsh National Opera, National Dance Company, National Orchestra, Literature Wales, HiJinx Theatre and Ty Cerdd (Music Centre of Wales).

The roof above the main entrance is pierced by 2m-high letter-shaped windows, spectacularly backlit at night, which spell out phrases from poet Gwyneth Lewis: 'Creu Gwir fel Gwydr o Ffwrnais Awen' (Creating truth like glass from inspiration's furnace) and 'In these stones horizons sing'.

You can wander through the large public lobby at will. Guided tours lead visitors behind the giant letters, onto the main stage and into the dressing rooms, depending on what shows are on.

Senedd
NOTABLE BUILDING
(National Assembly Building; Map p668; ☑ 0845 010 5500; www.assemblywales.org; ☉ 10.30am-4.30pm) FREE Designed by Lord Richard Rogers (the architect behind London's Lloyd's Building and Millennium Dome and Paris' Pompidou Centre), the Senedd is a striking structure of concrete, slate, glass and steel, with an undulating canopy roof lined with red cedar. It has won awards for its environmentally friendly design, which includes a huge rotating cowl on the roof for power-free ventilation and a gutter system that collects rainwater for flushing the toilets.

When they're not on recess, the National Assembly for Wales meets in a plenary session from 1.30pm on Tuesday and Wednesday. Seats in the public gallery may be prebooked, although there's usually space if you turn up on the day. Free tours take place at 11am, 2pm and 3pm, except for sitting days when only the 11am tour is held.

Pierhead
MUSEUM
(Map p668; www.pierhead.org; ☉ 10.30am-4.30pm) FREE One of the waterfront's few Victorian remnants, Pierhead is a red-brick and glazed-terracotta French Gothic confection, built in 1897 with Bute family money in order to impress the maritime traffic. Its ornate clocktower earned it the nickname 'Wales' Big Ben'. Inside there's an interesting little display on the history of the bay (including a short film and a slideshow), some important historical documents and a gallery.

Butetown History & Arts Centre
GALLERY
(Map p668; www.bhac.org; Bute St; ☉ 10am-5pm Tue-Sun) FREE This centre is devoted to preserving oral histories, documents and images of the multiethnic neighbourhood that was best known as Tiger Bay. Displays range from old photographs to contemporary art.

⊙ St Fagans

St Fagans National History Museum
MUSEUM
(☑ 029-2057 3500; www.museumwales.ac.uk; carpark £3.50; ☉ 10am-5pm) FREE Five miles west

THE BEAUT BUTES

The Butes, an aristocratic Scottish family related to the Stuart monarchy, arrived in Cardiff in 1766 in the shape of John, Lord Mountstuart, who had served briefly as prime minister under King George I. He married a local heiress, Charlotte Jane Windsor, and in the process acquired vast estates and mineral rights in South Wales.

Their grandson, the second marquess of Bute, grew fabulously wealthy from coal mining and then, in 1839, chanced his fortune to create the first docks at Cardiff. The gamble paid off. The coal-export business boomed, and his son, John Patrick Crichton-Stuart, the third marquess of Bute, became one of the richest people on the planet. Not your conventional Victorian aristocrat, John was an intense, scholarly man with a passion for history, architecture, ritual and religion (Catholicism). He neither hunted nor fished, but instead supported the antivivisection movement and campaigned for the rights of women to a university education.

The Butes had interests all over Britain and never spent more than about six weeks at a time in Cardiff. Soon after WWII ended they had sold or given away all of their Cardiff assets, the fifth marquess gifting Cardiff Castle and Bute Park to the city in 1947. The present marquess, the seventh, lives in the family seat at Mount Stuart House on the Isle of Bute in Scotland's Firth of Clyde. Another maverick, he's better known as Johnny Dumfries, the former Formula One racing driver.

WORTH A TRIP

LLANDAFF CATHEDRAL

Set in a hollow on the west bank of the River Taff, **Llandaff Cathedral** (☑029-2056 4554; www.llandaffcathedral.org.uk; Cathedral Green; ⊙7am-6.30pm Sun, 9am-6.30pm Mon-Sat) is built on the site of a 6th-century monastery. Derelict by the 18th century, it was largely rebuilt in the 19th century and extensively restored after being damaged by a German bomb in 1941.

Regular buses run along Cathedral Rd from Cardiff to Llandaff, 2 miles from the city centre.

The present cathedral was begun in 1120, but it crumbled throughout the Middle Ages, and during the Reformation and Civil War it was used as an alehouse and then an animal shelter. The towers at the western end epitomise the cathedral's fragmented history – one was built in the 15th century, the other in the 19th. Inside, a giant arch supports sculptor Sir Jacob Epstein's huge aluminium work *Majestas*, its modern style a bold contrast in this gracious vaulted space.

of central Cardiff, the little village of St Fagans is the semirural setting for the St Fagans National History Museum. More than 40 historic buildings from all over the country have been re-erected here, including thatched farmhouses, barns, a watermill, a school, an 18th-century Unitarian chapel and shops stocked with period-appropriate goods.

Buses 32A, 320 and 322 (£1.80, 23 minutes) head here from Cardiff's Central bus station. By car, it's reached from the continuation of Cathedral Rd.

You'll need half a day to do the whole complex justice and you could easily spend longer, picnicking in the grounds. It's a great place for kids, with special events in summer, tractor-and-trailer rides (£1) and an old-time funfair. Craftspeople work in many of the buildings, showing how blankets, clogs, barrels, tools and cider were once made. In winter, fires are stoked by people in period clothes.

Highlights include a 16th-century farmhouse imbued with the smell of old timber, beeswax and wood smoke, and a row of six miners' cottages from Merthyr Tydfil, each one restored and furnished to represent different periods in the town's history, from the austere minimalism of 1805 to all the mod cons of 1985. It took 20 years to move St Teilo's church here (built 1150 to 1530), stone by stone. It's been restored to its original look, before Protestant whitewash covered the vividly painted interior.

St Fagans Castle is no johnny-come-lately to this site; it was built by the Normans in 1091 as a motte-and-bailey castle before being rebuilt in stone. The manor house at its heart was grafted on in 1580 and is recognised as one of the finest Elizabethan houses in Wales. The property was donated by the earl of Plymouth in 1948, along with its extensive formal gardens, which form the basis of the museum.

The museum is in the midst of a multi-million-pound redevelopment, which isn't due to be completed until 2018. Until that time the reproduction Celtic village and indoor galleries are likely to remain closed.

☞ Tours

Cardiff History & Hauntings   WALKING TOUR
(☑07538 878609; www.cardiffhistory.co.uk) Runs a selection of guided history walks, the most acclaimed of which is the Llandaff Ghost Walk, a two-hour torch-lit stroll through the ruins, lanes and graveyards of old Llandaff (£8.50).

Cardiff On Foot   WALKING TOUR
(☑0790 5923421; www.cardiffwalkingtours.com; from £6) Offers guided strolls around the city centre, Cardiff Bay and Penarth.

Where When Wales   BUS TOUR
(☑07773 786228; www.wherewhenwales.com; adult/child from £45/25) Operates a range of one-day itineraries: South Wales Valleys, Wye Valley, the Gower, Wales Borders, West Wales, Mid-Wales. Overnight tours can be customised.

See Wales   BUS TOUR
(☑029-2022 7227; www.seewales.com; adult/child £45/25) Themed day tours include Mines & Mountains, Romans & Ruins and Golden Gower.

City Sightseeing   BUS TOUR
(☑07808 713928; www.city-sightseeing.com; adult/child £12/7) Open-top double-decker tours, departing every 30 to 60 minutes from outside Cardiff Castle and making a short circuit of the city. Tickets last 24 hours, and you can hop on and off at any of the stops.

Cardiff Cycle Tours CYCLING TOUR
(Map p666; ✏07500 564389; www.cardiffcycletours.
com; NosDa, 53-59 Despenser St; per person £20)
Three-hour guided rides around Cardiff Bay
(Docks & Doctor) or the city (Parks & Canals).

☆☆ Festivals & Events

Cardiff Festival SUMMER FESTIVAL
(www.cardiff-festival.com; ☺Jun-Aug) Acts as an
umbrella for most of Cardiff's regular summertime festivals, including the Welsh Proms
(two weeks of classical concerts at St David's
Hall), Cardiff International Food & Drink Festival, Grand Medieval Melee, Pride Cymru,
Classic Car & Boat Rally, Everyman Summer
Theatre Festival, and lots of crazy one-offs.

Cardiff Winter Wonderland WINTER FESTIVAL
(www.cardiffswinterwonderland.com; ☺late Nov-
early Jan) Festivities include an outdoor
ice-skating rink, Christmas lights, Santa's
grotto and family-friendly activities.

🛏 Sleeping

🛏 Central Cardiff

★**River House Backpackers** HOSTEL £
(Map p666; ✏029-2039 9810; www.riverhouse-
backpackers.com; 59 Fitzhamon Embankment;
dm/r incl breakfast from £18/42; @🛜) Professionally run by a young brother-and-sister
team, the River House has a well-equipped
kitchen, small garden and cosy TV lounge.
The private rooms are basically small dorm
rooms and share the same bathrooms. A free
breakfast of cereal and toast is provided.

Premier Inn Cardiff City Centre HOTEL £
(Map p666; ✏029-2034 9910; www.premierinn.
com; 10 Churchill Way; r from £39; 🛜) The Cardiff branch of Britain's biggest chain has 200
beds in a squat mirror-clad former office
tower, right in the city centre. It's not flash,
but it's comfortable, clean and terrific value – although you'll need to book early and
pay in advance to secure the cheapest rates.
Request a higher floor for a quieter room.

NosDa HOSTEL £
(Map p666; ✏029-2037 8866; www.nosda.co.uk;
53-59 Despenser St; dm from £21, s/d from £42/60,
without bathroom £32/48, incl breakfast; P@🛜)
Directly across the river from the Millennium Stadium, NosDa ('goodnight' in Welsh)
has brightly painted rooms above a grungy
bar. Free basic breakfasts and parking make
this an appealing budget option.

Park Plaza HOTEL ££
(Map p666; ✏029-2011 1111; www.parkplazacardiff.
com; Greyfriars Rd; r from £86; 🛜🎐) Luxurious
without being remotely stuffy, the Plaza has
all the five-star facilities you'd expect from
an upmarket business-oriented hotel. The
snug reception sets the scene, with a gas fire
blazing along one wall and comfy wingback
chairs. The rear rooms have leafy views over
the Civic Centre.

🛏 Cardiff Bay

St David's Hotel & Spa HOTEL ££
(Map p668; ✏029-2045 4045; www.thestdavids-
hotel.com; Havannah St; r from £119; @🛜🎐) A
glittering, glassy tower topped with a sail-
like flourish, St David's is already starting
to look a little dated. The rooms have been
recently renovated and almost all of them
have a small private balcony with a bay
view. Facilities include a restaurant, bar
and day spa.

🛏 Pontcanna

Lincoln House HOTEL ££
(Map p660; ✏029-2039 5558; www.lincolnhotel.
co.uk; 118 Cathedral Rd; r from £90; P🛜) Walking a middle line between a large B&B and
a small hotel, Lincoln House is a generously proportioned Victorian property with a
separate bar, and heraldic emblems in the
stained-glass windows of its sitting room.
For added romance, book a room with a
four-poster bed.

Number 62 GUESTHOUSE ££
(Map p660; ✏07974 571348; www.number62.com;
62 Cathedral Rd; s/d from £49/65; @🛜) The
only thing stopping us calling Number 62
a B&B is that breakfast isn't offered. In all

CARDIFF FOR CHILDREN

Compact and easy to navigate, Cardiff is
welcoming to families. Interactive **Tech-
niquest** (Map p668; www.techniquest.
org; Stuart St; adult/child £7/5; ☺9.30am-
4.30pm Tue-Sun, daily school holidays)
is the main attraction for challenging
junior brains, while the National Museum Cardiff (p660) is full of weird and
wonderful animals and other fascinating
exhibits. For a day trip, try the living
history of St Fagans (p663), Caerphilly
Castle (p674) or Castell Coch (p674).

Central Cardiff

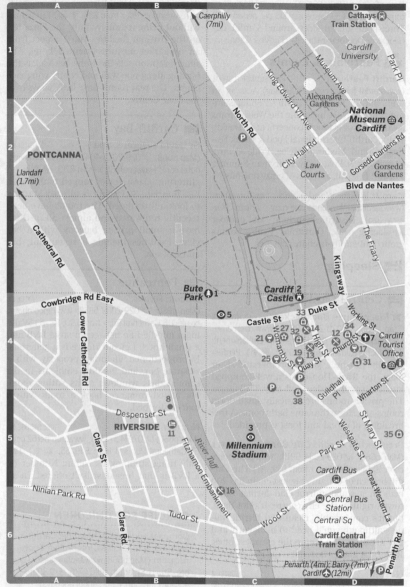

other respects it's very similar to the other converted town houses on this strip, although it does have one of the most lovingly tended front gardens. The cosy rooms are simply decorated in demure colours.

Town House   B&B ££

(Map p660; ☎029-2023 9399; www.thetownhouse-cardiff.co.uk; 70 Cathedral Rd; s/d £53/73; P ⊜) Succinctly named, this elegant Victorian town house on the Cathedral Rd strip has

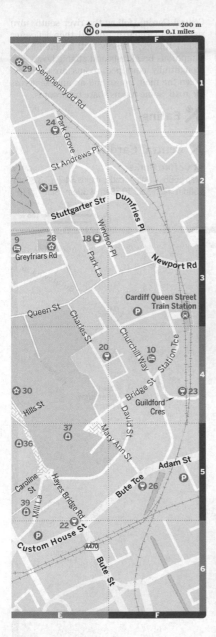

Central Cardiff

◎ Top Sights
1 Bute Park	C3
2 Cardiff Castle	C4
3 Millennium Stadium	C5
4 National Museum Cardiff	D2

◎ Sights
5 Animal Wall	C4
6 Cardiff Story	D4
7 St John the Baptist Church	D4

◎ Activities, Courses & Tours
8 Cardiff Cycle Tours	B5

◎ Sleeping
NosDa	(see 8)
9 Park Plaza	E3
10 Premier Inn Cardiff City Centre	F4
11 River House Backpackers	B5

◎ Eating
12 Cafe Cittá	D4
13 Coffee Barker	D4
14 Goat Major	D4
15 Park House	E2
16 Riverside Market	C6

◎ Drinking & Nightlife
17 10 Feet Tall	D4
18 Buffalo Bar	E3
19 City Arms	C4
20 Eagle	E4
21 Full Moon	C4
22 Golden Cross	E6
23 Gwdihŵ	F4
24 Pen & Wig	E1
25 Pica Pica	C4
26 Porter's	F5

◎ Entertainment
27 Clwb Ifor Bach	C4
28 New Theatre	E3
29 Sherman Cymru	E1
30 St David's Hall	E4

◎ Shopping
31 Cardiff Market	D4
32 Castle Arcade	C4
33 Castle Welsh Crafts	C4
34 High St Arcade	D4
35 Morgan Quarter	D5
36 Spillers Records	E5
37 St David's	E5
38 WRU Store	C5
39 Wyndham Arcade	E5

welcoming owners and a relaxed vibe. It retains lots of period features, including original fireplaces, stained-glass windows and a tiled hallway with busy wallpaper. The rooms are more restrained.

Saco House APARTMENT **£££**
(Map p660; ☎0845 122 0405; www.sacoapartments.co.uk; 74-76 Cathedral Rd; apt from £138; ☎) This large town house has been given

a contemporary makeover and converted into serviced apartments, complete with comfortable lounges and fitted kitchens. They're set up for longer visits but one-day stays are possible midweek. The two-bedroom apartments are good value for families with kids; there's an extra sofa bed in the lounge.

🛏 Grangetown

Tŷ Rosa B&B ££
(Map p660; ☑ 0845 643 9962; www.tyrosa.com; 118 Clive St; s/d from £50/69, without bathroom £40/50; 🛜) Half an hour's walk from either the bay or

Central Cardiff (follow the river south, turn right on to Penarth Rd and then left after 650m), this gay-friendly B&B is noted for its sumptuous breakfasts and affable hosts. The thoughtfully equipped rooms are split between the main house and an annexe across the road. Some rooms share bathrooms.

✕ Eating

✕ Central Cardiff
★**Coffee Barker** CAFE £
(Map p666; Castle Arcade; mains £4-7; ⊗8.30am-5.30pm Mon-Sat, 10.30am-4.30pm Sun; 🛜♿)

Cardiff Bay

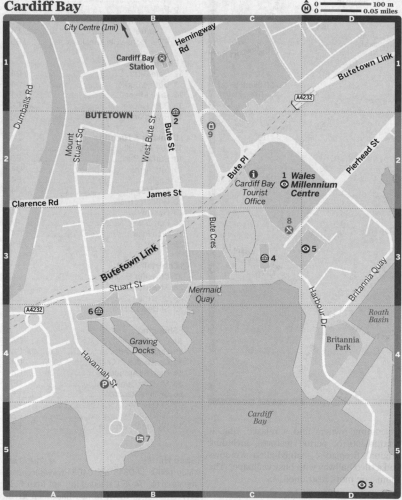

Slink into an armchair, sip on a silky coffee and snack on salmon scrambled eggs or a sandwich in what is Cardiff's coolest cafe. There are plenty of magazines and toys to keep everyone amused.

Riverside Market
MARKET £
(Map p666; www.riversidemarket.org.uk; Fitzhamon Embankment; ⊗10am-2pm Sun; ⌖) What it lacks in size, Riverside Market makes up for in sheer yumminess, its stalls heaving with cooked meals, cakes, cheese, organic meat, charcuterie, bread, apple juice and real ale. There are lots of options for vegetarians, and the Welsh cakes, hot off the griddle, are exceptional.

Goat Major
PUB £
(Map p666; www.sabrain.com/goatmajor; 33 High St; pies £7.50; ⊗kitchen noon-6pm Mon-Sat, to 4pm Sun; ⌖) A solidly traditional wood-lined pub with a fireplace and Brains craft beers, the Goat Major's gastronomic contribution takes the form of a selection of homemade pot pies served with chips. Try the Wye Valley pie, a mixture of chicken, leek, asparagus and Tintern Abbey cheese.

Cafe Cittá
ITALIAN ££
(Map p666; ✆029-2022 4040; 4 Church St; mains £9-12; ⊗noon-9pm Tue-Sat; ⌖) Once you're lured through the door by the delicious scents wafting out of the wood-fired oven, you won't want to escape this little slice of *la dolce vita*. The authentic linguine puttanesca is proof that some traditions shouldn't be messed with. There are only a handful of tables, so book ahead.

Cardiff Bay

◉ Top Sights

◉ Sights

◉ Sleeping

◉ Eating

◉ Shopping

Park House
MODERN BRITISH £££
(Map p666; ✆029-2022 4343; www.parkhouse-restaurant.co.uk; 20 Park Pl; mains £26, 2-/3-course lunch £16/21; ⊗11am-10pm Wed-Sat, to 6pm Sun) The ambience is rather stuffy, but the menu at this private members' club is anything but conservative, adding subtle Indian and Southeast Asian touches to classic European dishes. Dress up and push the buzzer for admittance.

⚔ Cardiff Bay

Ffresh
MODERN WELSH ££
(Map p668; ✆029-2063 6465; www.ffresh.org.uk; Wales Millennium Centre; mains £14-18; ⊗noon-9.30pm Mon-Sat, to 5pm Sun) ⊘ Overlooking the Senedd from the glassed-in end of the Millennium Centre, Ffresh has the Welshiest of settings and a menu to match. Local, seasonal produce features heavily in a creative menu that includes some traditional favourites, such as Welsh lamb and Perl Wen cheese.

⚔ Pontcanna

★ Purple Poppadom
INDIAN ££
(Map p660; ✆029-2022 0026; www.purplepoppadom.com; 185A Cowbridge Rd East; mains £8-18; ⊗5.30-11pm Tue-Fri, noon-2.30pm & 5.30-11pm Sat, 1-9pm Sun; ⌖) Trailblazing a path for 'nouvelle Indian' cuisine, Anand George's kitchen offers its own unique take on regional dishes from all over the subcontinent – from Kashmir to Kerala. Meals are thoughtfully constructed and artfully presented.

Conway
GASTROPUB ££
(Map p660; ✆029-2022 4373; www.knifeandforkfood.co.uk; 58 Conway Rd; mains £10-15; ⊗noon-11pm; ⛽) With a sun-trap front terrace and a pleasantly laid-back vibe, this wonderful corner pub chalks up its delicious 'seasonal, fresh and local' offerings daily. Kids get their own menu, while the grown-ups can ponder the large selection of wines served by the glass.

Brava
CAFE, BISTRO ££
(Map p660; www.bravacardiff.co.uk; 71 Pontcanna St; brunch £6-9, dinner £9-15; ⊗9am-4pm Sun & Mon, 8am-10pm Tue-Sat) With local art on the walls and an informal vibe, this cool cafe is a favourite brunch spot on the strength of its eggs Benedict, silky coffee and attentive service. Tables spill out onto the pavement in summer and in the evening it morphs into a licensed bistro. *Brava,* indeed.

Bully's
FRENCH £££

(Map p660; ☎029-2022 1905; www.bullysrestaurant.co.uk; 5 Romilly Cres; mains £19-23, 1-/2-/3-course lunch £10/14/18; ⊙noon-2pm & 6.30-9pm Mon-Sat, noon-3.30pm Sun) An assortment of odd things (bank notes, receipts from famous restaurants etc) cover the walls of this cosy neighbourhood bistro, giving little indication of the high-quality French-style dishes served here. The set lunch menus are great value, including a free glass of house wine.

✗ Cathays

Mint & Mustard
INDIAN ££

(☎029-2062 0333; www.mintandmustard.com; 134 Whitchurch Rd; mains £8-16, lunch thali £10; ⊙noon-2pm & 6-11pm; ✐) A rewarding short detour to student hub Cathays, north of the city centre, will bring you to this upmarket Indian eatery, specialising in seafood dishes from Kerala. If you're not enticed by the lobster, crab, prawn and fish dishes, there are plenty of vegetarian options and an excellent crusted lamb biryani.

🍷 Drinking & Nightlife

Cardiff is a prodigiously boozy city. Friday and Saturday nights see the city centre invaded by hordes of generally good-humoured, beered-up lads and ladettes tottering from bar to club to kebab shop, whatever the weather (someone fetch that young woman a coat!). It's not as tacky as it sounds: a lively alternative scene, some swish bars and a swath of old-fashioned pubs keep things interesting.

Try the local Brains SA (meaning Special Ale, Same Again or Skull Attack, depending on how many you've had), brewed by the same family concern since 1882.

★ Gwdihŵ
BAR

(Map p666; www.gwdihw.co.uk; 6 Guildford Cres; ⊙3pm-midnight Sun-Wed, noon-2am Thu-Sat) The last word in Cardiff hipsterdom, this cute little bar has an eclectic line-up of entertainment (comedy nights, markets and lots of live music, including microfestivals that spill over into the car park) but it's a completely charming place to stop for a drink at any time.

Buffalo Bar
BAR

(Map p666; www.buffalocardiff.co.uk; 11 Windsor Pl; ⊙noon-3am) A haven for cool kids about town, the laid-back Buffalo features retro furniture, tasty food, life-affirming cocktails and alternative tunes. There's a small beer garden at the rear, while upstairs a roster of cutting-edge indie bands takes to the stage.

Full Moon
BAR

(Map p666; www.thefullmooncardiff.com; 1/3 Womanby St; ⊙5pm-late) There are no pretences at this friendly, grungy rock bar, directly opposite well-known live-music venue Clwb Ifor Bach. Sample from the large selection of rum, whisky and vodka, or try the 'jar of green shit' if you dare. Upstairs, the Moon Club thrums to live bands.

City Arms
PUB

(Map p666; www.thecityarmscardiff.com; 10-12 Quay St; ⊙11am-11pm Mon-Wed, to 2am Thu-Sun; ☎) What's affectionately known in these parts as an 'old man's pub' – despite it attracting just as many young people – the City Arms is an unpretentious, old-fashioned kind of place, its walls lined with rugby memorabilia and beer labels. It gets packed out on rugby weekends, but on weekday afternoons it's a quiet place for a pint.

Pen & Wig
PUB

(Map p666; www.penandwigcardiff.co.uk; 1 Park Grove; ⊙11am-midnight) Latin legal phrases are printed on the walls of this solidly traditional pub, but there's nothing stuffy about the large beer garden or the entertainment roster (open mic Mondays, quiz Tuesdays, 'Gig @ the Wig' Saturdays). *Caveat emptor:* the impressive range of ales may induce *mens rea* (guilty mind) the morning after.

Porter's
BAR

(Map p666; www.porterscardiff.com; Bute Tce; ⊙4pm-12.30am Sun-Thu, to 3am Fri, noon-3am Sat) There's something on most nights at this friendly attitude-free bar, whether it's live music, a quiz or a movie screening (there's a little cinema attached).

10 Feet Tall
BAR

(Map p666; www.10feettallcardiff.com; 12 Church St; ⊙noon-3am) This three-storey venue merges a cafe, a cocktail and tapas bar, and a live-music venue. Handsome bartenders swish together two-for-one cocktails between 5pm and 10pm, and all day Sundays.

Pica Pica
BAR

(Map p666; www.picapicacardiff.com; 15-23 Westgate St; ⊙noon-midnight Wed-Sat; ☎) Housed in a series of low-ceilinged brick vaults, this cool bar serves tapas, mezze and two-for-one cocktails before 7.30pm.

☆ Entertainment

Pick up a copy of *Buzz* (www.buzzmag.co.uk), a free monthly magazine with up-to-date entertainment listings, available from the tourist office and venues.

Most of the large arts companies are based at the Wales Millennium Centre (p662).

St David's Hall
CLASSICAL MUSIC

(Map p666; ☑029-2087 8444; www.stdavidshallcardiff.co.uk; The Hayes) The National Concert Hall of Wales hosts the Welsh Proms in July and a full roster of classical music performances.

★ Clwb Ifor Bach
LIVE MUSIC

(Map p666; ☑029-2023 2199; www.clwb.net; 11 Womanby St) Truly an independent music great, Y Clwb has broken many a Welsh band since the early 1980s. It started as a venue for Welsh-language music in Anglophone Cardiff and has built a reputation as the city's most eclectic and important venue. It's the best place to catch gigs by up-and-coming new acts as well as by more established artists.

Chapter
THEATRE, CINEMA

(Map p660; ☑029-2030 4400; www.chapter.org; Market Rd, Canton) The city's edgiest arts venue, Chapter has a varied rota of contemporary drama, art exhibitions, art-house cinema, workshops, alternative theatre and dance performances.

Sherman Cymru
THEATRE

(Map p666; ☑029-2064 6900; www.shermancymru.co.uk; Senghennydd Rd, Cathays) South Wales' leading theatre company, Sherman stages a wide range of material, from classics and children's theatre to works by new playwrights.

New Theatre
THEATRE

(Map p666; ☑029-2087 8889; www.newtheatrecardiff.co.uk; Park Pl) A restored Edwardian playhouse, New Theatre hosts touring productions, including musicals, ballet and pantomime.

🛍 Shopping

If you thought Cardiff's 21st-century makeover was all about political edifices, arts centres and sports stadia, think again. One of the most dramatic developments in the central city is the transformation of the Hayes shopping strip, with the giant, glitzy extension of the St David's shopping centre now eating up its entire eastern flank. Balancing this modern mall is a historic network of Victorian and Edwardian shopping arcades, which spread their dainty tentacles either side of St Mary St.

★ St David's
MALL

(Map p666; www.stdavidscardiff.com; The Hayes; ⊙9.30am-8pm Mon-Sat, 11am-5pm Sun; ☎) Immense is the best way to describe this shiny shopping centre. All the high-street chains you could name have a home here, along with a smorgasbord of eateries, a cinema multiplex and a large branch of the John Lewis department store dominating its southern end.

Cardiff Market
MARKET

(Map p666; www.cardiff-market.co.uk; btwn St Mary & Trinity Sts; ⊙8am-5.30pm Mon-Sat) For an age-old shopping experience, head to this Victorian covered market, which is packed with stalls selling everything from fresh fish to mobile phone covers. Stock up here for a picnic in Bute Park.

Craft in the Bay
ARTS & CRAFTS

(Map p668; www.makersguildinwales.org.uk; Lloyd George Ave; ⊙10.30am-5.30pm) This retail showcase for the Welsh Makers Guild cooperative sells work by its members, including a wide range of ceramics, textiles, woodwork, jewellery, glassware and ironwork.

Castle Welsh Crafts
SOUVENIRS

(Map p666; www.castlewelshcrafts.co.uk; 1 Castle St; ⊙9am-5.30pm) If you're after stuffed dragons, lovespoons or Cardiff T-shirts, this is the city's biggest souvenir shop, conveniently located across the street from the castle.

Spillers Records
MUSIC

(Map p666; www.spillersrecords.co.uk; Morgan Arcade; ⊙10am-6pm Mon-Sat, 11am-4pm Sun) The world's oldest record shop, founded in 1894 (when it sold wax phonograph cylinders), Spillers stocks a large range of CDs and vinyl; prides itself on catering to the non-mainstream end of the market (it's especially good for punk music); and promotes local talent through in-store gigs.

Morgan Quarter
SHOPPING ARCADE

(Map p666; www.morganquarter.com; btwn St Mary St & The Hayes) Cardiff's oldest arcade (1858), the Royal connects up with the Morgan Arcade via a series of covered lanes, forming this ritzy shopping precinct. Look out for Spillers Records, the excellent Wally's Delicatessen and Liam Gallagher's pricey menswear boutique, Pretty Green.

High St Arcade
SHOPPING ARCADE

(Map p666; www.cardiffhighstreetarcade.co.uk; btwn High & St John Sts) Stop into the NY Deli for a burger or sandwich, then head on to Hobo's for vintage clothing, or to Catapult for dance music.

Castle Arcade
SHOPPING ARCADE

(Map p666; www.cardiffcastlearcade.co.uk; btwn Castle & High Sts) The most decorative of the city's arcades houses Troutmark Books (secondhand and Welsh-language titles), Claire Grove Buttons (beads and buttons of every description), Madame Fromage and Coffee Barker.

Wyndham Arcade
SHOPPING ARCADE

(Map p666; btwn St Mary St & Mill Lane) This historic arcade houses the gloriously old-fashioned Bear Shop, a specialist tobacconist featuring a prominently displayed 200-year-old piece of taxidermy called Bruno.

❶ Information

Cardiff Bay Tourist Office (Map p668; ☑029-2087 7927; www.visitcardiffbay.info; Wales Millennium Centre; ⊙10am-6pm, extended on show nights)
Cardiff Tourist Office (Map p666; ☑029-2087 3573; www.visitcardiff.com; Old Library,

The Hayes; ⊙9.30am-5.30pm Mon-Sat, 10am-4pm Sun; @) Internet access costs £1 per 30 minutes.
University Hospital of Wales (☑029-2074 7747; www.cardiffandvaleuhb.wales.nhs.uk; Heath Park) Cardiff's main accident and emergency department, located 2 miles north of the Civic Centre.

❶ Getting There & Away

AIR

Cardiff Airport (☑01446-711111; www.cardiff-airport.com) is mainly used by budget operators. Aside from summer-only services and charters, a number of airlines fly into Cardiff and serve international and national destinations.
Aer Lingus (www.aerlingus.com) Flies to Dublin.
CityJet (www.cityjet.com) Services to Edinburgh, Glasgow, Jersey and Paris Orly.
Citywing (www.citywing.com) Flights to Anglesey.
Eastern Airways (www.easternairways.com) Sevices to Aberdeen and Newcastle.
Flybe (www.flybe.com) Flights to Belfast and Jersey.
KLM (www.klm.com) Services to Amsterdam.
Thomson (www.thomson.co.uk) Flights to Málaga, Alicante, Gran Canaria, Tenerife, Lanzarote, Paphos and Sharm el-Sheikh.

BUS

➜ Cardiff's **Central bus station** (Map p666; Wood St) is next to the train station.
➜ Bus destinations include Swansea (route 100/701; £3, one hour), Aberystwyth (701; four hours), Abergavenny (X4; £9.10, 2¼ hours), Hereford (X4; 3¼ hours) and Bristol (100; £11, 1½ hours).
➜ **National Express** (www.nationalexpress.com) coach destinations include London (£19, 3½ hours), Bristol (£6, 1¼ hours), Birmingham (£27, 2¾ hours), Manchester (£37, six hours) and Leeds (£51, 6¾ hours).
➜ **Greyhound** (www.greyhounduk.com) coaches head to/from Swansea (£3.30, one hour), Newport (£3.30, 35 minutes) and Bristol Airport (£11, 1¾ hours).

CAR

Cardiff is easily reached from the M4 (which runs from London to northwest of Swansea). All major rental car companies have branches in the capital.

TRAIN

Trains from major British cities arrive at Cardiff Central station, on the southern edge of the city centre. Direct services from Cardiff:
Abergavenny £13, 45 minutes
Birmingham £26, two hours

Bristol £13, 35 minutes
Cheltenham £18, 1½ hours
London Paddington £39, 2¼ hours

ⓘ Getting Around

TO/FROM THE AIRPORT

➡ Cardiff Airport is 12 miles southwest of Cardiff, past Barry.

➡ Cardiff Airport Express bus (£5, 38 minutes, every 20 minutes) heads between the airport and Central bus station.

➡ The 905 shuttle bus (£1, seven minutes) links the airport terminal to nearby Rhoose Cardiff Airport train station. Trains to Cardiff Central station (£4.20, 30 minutes) run hourly from Monday to Saturday and two-hourly on Sundays.

➡ A taxi from the airport to the city centre takes 20 to 30 minutes, depending on traffic, and costs £31.

PUBLIC TRANSPORT

Local buses are operated by **Cardiff Bus** (Map p666; ☑ 029-2066 6444; www.cardiffbus.com; single trip/day pass £1.70/3.40); buy your ticket from the driver (no change given). Free route maps and timetables are available from its Wood St office. Generally buses are more convenient for short trips than trains, although there are a handful of stations scattered around the city.

Two boats run alternating water-bus services along the River Taff from Bute Park to Mermaid Quay, departing every half-hour from 10.30am to 5pm. The journey takes about 25 minutes and costs £3 each way.

TAXI

Reliable companies include **Capital Cabs** (☑ 029-2077 7777; www.capitalcabs.co.uk) and **Dragon Taxis** (☑ 029-2033 3333; www.dragontaxis.com). **Checker Cars** (☑ 01446 711747; www.checkercars.com) operates the cabs leaving from the airport.

AROUND CARDIFF

If you're based in Cardiff, there's a diverting selection of day trips to choose between.

Penarth

POP 27,300

Well-heeled Penarth is slowly transforming from an old-fashioned seaside resort to a virtual suburb of Cardiff, despite it being in the neighbouring county, the Vale of Glamorgan. It's connected to Cardiff Bay by the freshwater lake formed by the construction of the barrage and it now sports a busy marina on the lakefront.

⊙ Sights

Penarth Pavilion   ARTS CENTRE
(www.penarthpavilion.co.uk; Penarth Pier; ⊙10am-5pm Sun-Wed, to 8pm Thu-Sat Apr-Oct, 10am-5pm daily Nov-Mar) Penarth's rock-strewn shoreline may not be particularly attractive but it is the closest beach to Cardiff. In 1894 it was graced with that stereotype of the Victorian seaside, a pier. This elegant art deco pavilion followed in 1927, and has been recently restored, complete with a brand-new gallery, cinema and cafe.

Alexandra Gardens   PARK
This pretty Edwardian-era park slopes from Penarth's bustling town centre down to the esplanade. Its formal gardens are filled with topiary and colourful flowerbeds.

Ffotogallery   GALLERY
(☑ 029-2034 1667; www.ffotogallery.org; Plymouth Rd; ⊙11am-5pm Tue-Sat) **FREE** Also known as the Turner House Gallery, this red-brick building near the train station hosts edgy

---

MUSICAL CYMRU

With such a small population and a culture that's been overshadowed by England for centuries, it's something of a surprise that Wales (Cymru in Welsh) has produced plenty of musical maestros who have hit the big time. Everyone knows perma-tanned warbler Tom Jones, who, together with the likes of Shirley Bassey, has kept Welsh pop on the map since the 1960s.

Along with Lou Reed, valleys-born John Cale was responsible for the experimental edge that made the Velvet Underground one of the most influential bands of all time. He's gone on to become a respected solo performer and producer.

Since then major names have included The Alarm, Manic Street Preachers, Catatonia, Stereophonics, Gorky's Zygotic Mynci, Charlotte Church, Jem, Christopher Rees, Bullet For My Valentine, Kate Le Bon and Duffy. The genre-defying Super Furry Animals produced the biggest-selling Welsh-language album of all time, the dreamy *Mwng*.

The Welsh wave shows no signs of breaking anytime soon, with bands such as Marina & the Diamonds, Kids In Glass Houses and Future of the Left flying the red dragon flag.

photographic, video and multimedia exhibitions. It's at its busiest during the month-long Diffusion international photography festival in May.

❶ Getting There & Away

Buses head to/from Cardiff (route 89/92–95; £1.80, 28 minutes) and Barry (88/93/94; £2.50, 30 minutes) and there are frequent trains (£2.60, 12 minutes).

It's possible to walk or cycle along the barrage from Cardiff Bay to Penarth Marina (allow 40 minutes on foot). From here it's a steep but short walk up to the town centre and down again to the pier.

Barry (Y Barri)

POP 54,700

Nowhere have the recent triumphs of the BBC Wales television department been more keenly felt than in Barry, a seaside town 8 miles southwest of Cardiff. If you watch *Doctor Who* or *Being Human,* you'll no doubt be aware that the town is infested with aliens, zombies, ghosts, werewolves and vampires. Yet it's the massive popularity of the altogether more down-to-earth comedy *Gavin & Stacey* that has given the town a new cache. The staff at Island Leisure (on the Promenade) are used to fans of the show making a pilgrimage to the booth where Nessa (played in the show by co-writer Ruth Jones) worked. Other sites include nearby Marco's Cafe, where Stacey worked, and Trinity St, where Stacey's mum and Uncle Bryn lived.

The real attraction here is **Barry Island**, which is well signposted at the south end of the town. It stopped being a real island in the 1880s when it was joined to the mainland by a causeway. Amusement arcades and fun parks line the waterfront at sandy Whitmore Bay, which is easily the best beach this side of the Gower.

It's also worth stopping at **Porthkerry Country Park**, where an impressive Victorian railway viaduct passes over a lovely wooded valley leading down to a stony beach. There are plenty of trails to explore, a popular playground and the potential to spot buzzards, adders and foxes. It's well signposted from the road to Barry Island.

❶ Getting There & Away

Frequent trains head to the Barry and Barry Island train stations from Cardiff (£3.20, 24 minutes).

Cardiff Bus services head to/from Penarth (route 88/93/94; £2.50, 30 minutes) and Cardiff (93–96/304; £2.50, one hour).

Castell Coch

Cardiff Castle's little brother is perched atop a thickly wooded crag on the northern fringes of the city. Fanciful **Castell Coch** (Cadw; ☏ 029-2081 0101; www.cadw.wales.gov.uk; adult/child £5.50/4.10; ◷ 10am-4pm) was the summer retreat of the third marquess of Bute and, like Cardiff Castle, was designed by William Burges in gaudy Victorian medieval style.

Stagecoach buses 26 and 132 (£2.30, 27 minutes) stop at Tongwynlais, a 10-minute walk from the castle. Bus 26 continues to Caerphilly Castle, and the two can be combined in a day trip.

Raised on the ruins of Gilbert de Clare's 13th-century Castell Coch, the Butes' Disneyesque holiday home is a monument to high camp. Lady Bute's huge, circular bedroom is pure fantasy: her bed, with crystal globes on the bedposts, sits beneath an extravagantly decorated and mirrored cupola, with painted panels around the walls depicting monkeys (fashionable at the time, apparently; just plain weird now). The corbels are carved with images of birds nesting or feeding their young, and the wash basin is framed between two castle towers.

Lord Bute's bedroom is small and plain by comparison, but the octagonal drawing room is another hallucinogenic tour de force. Its walls are painted with scenes from Aesop's *Fables*, while the domed ceiling is a flurry of birds and stars. The tower to the right of the entrance has exhibits explaining the castle's history.

Caerphilly (Caerffili)

POP 32,700

The town of Caerphilly, with its fairy-tale castle, guards the entrance to the Rhymney Valley to the north of Cardiff. Its name is synonymous with a popular variety of mild, slightly crumbly, hard white cheese that originated in the surrounding area.

◉ Sights

★ **Caerphilly Castle**　　　　CASTLE
(Cadw; ☏ 029-2088 3143; www.cadw.wales.gov.uk; adult/child £5.50/4.10; ◷ 9.30am-5pm) You could be forgiven for thinking that Caerphilly Castle – with its profusion of towers and

crenellations reflected in a duck-filled lake – was a film set rather than an ancient monument. While it is often used as a film set, it is also one of Britain's finest examples of a 13th-century fortress with water defences.

Most of the construction was completed between 1268 and 1271 by the powerful English baron Gilbert de Clare (1243–95), Lord Marcher of Glamorgan, in response to the threat of attack by Prince Llywelyn ap Gruffydd, prince of Gwynedd (and the last Welsh Prince of Wales), who had already united most of the country under his control. Edward I's subsequent campaign against the Welsh princes put an end to Llywelyn's ambitions and Caerphilly's short-lived spell on the front line came to an end.

In the 13th century Caerphilly was state-of-the-art, being one of the earliest castles to use lakes, bridges and a series of concentric fortifications for defence. To reach the inner court you had to overcome no fewer than three drawbridges, six portcullises and five sets of double gates. In the early 14th century it was remodelled as a grand residence and the magnificent great hall was adapted for entertaining, but from the mid-14th century onward the castle began to fall into ruin.

Much of what you see today is the result of restoration by the castle-loving Bute family. The third marquess of Bute purchased and demolished houses built up against the walls, and in 1870 the great hall was given a magnificent wooden ceiling. The fourth marquess instituted a major restoration from 1928 to 1939, giving jobs to many Great Depression–affected locals in the process. Work continued after 1950, when the fifth marquess gifted the castle to the state. In 1958 the dams were reflooded, creating its current fairy-tale appearance.

You can enter through the outside gate and into the first tower before reaching the ticket office. Upstairs, there are detailed displays about the castle's history. A cartoonish film projected onto the walls of one of the inner towers tells a truncated version of the same story.

On the south dam platform you can see reconstructions of medieval siege weapons; they are working models and lob stone projectiles into the lake during battle re-enactments.

❶ Information

Caerphilly Tourist Office (☑ 029-2088 0011; www.visitcaerphilly.com; The Twyn; ☺10am-5.30pm) Not only is this friendly office a good

THE BIG CHEESE

Any festival that includes a Cheese Olympics and a Tommy Cooper Tent has got to be worth a look. On the last weekend of July, Caerphilly welcomes more than 70,000 people to the **Big Cheese** (www.caerphilly.gov.uk/bigcheese; admission free), three days of family-oriented fun and games that offer everything from fireworks to falconry, comedy acts to cheese tasting, plus medieval battle re-enactments, food and craft stalls, archery demonstrations, live music and a traditional funfair.

The Cheese Olympics are held on Friday evening, with events including cheese throwing, rolling and stacking. The Tommy Cooper Tent – named after the much-loved British comedian, who was born in Caerphilly and died in 1984 – stages comedy acts, including a Tommy Cooper tribute act. A statue of Cooper, in his trademark fez and with a rabbit at his feet, overlooks the castle near the tourist office.

place to stock up on information, it's also the only place in town selling Caerphilly cheese – along with Penderyn spirits and locally made chocolates. There's a small cafe attached.

❶ Getting There & Away

The easiest way to reach Caerphilly from Cardiff is by train (£4.20, 19 minutes).

Buses head here from Cardiff's Central bus station (route 26/A/B; £3.80, 40 minutes).

SOUTHEAST WALES

You need only contemplate the preponderance of castles to realise that the pleasantly rural county of Monmouthshire was once a wild frontier. The Norman Marcher lords kept stonemasons extremely busy, erecting mighty fortifications to keep the unruly Welsh at bay. The River Wye forms the Wales–England border before emptying into the River Severn below Chepstow. Much of it is designated as an Area of Outstanding Natural Beauty (AONB; www.wyevalleyaonb. org.uk), famous for its limestone gorges and dense broad-leaved woodland.

To the west, the serried South Wales valleys were once the heart of industrial Wales.

Although the coal, iron and steel industries have withered, the valleys still evoke a world of tight-knit working-class communities, male voice choirs and rows of neat terraced houses set amid a scarred, coal-blackened landscape. Today, the region is fighting back against decline by creating a tourist industry based on its industrial heritage.

Newport (Casnewydd)

Sitting at the muddy mouth of the River Usk and flanked by the detritus of heavy industry, Newport is never going to win any awards for beauty. Despite its grim appearance and gritty undercurrents, however, Wales' third-largest city does have some fascinating things to see. It's well worth a day trip, but you're unlikely to be tempted to stay over.

◎ Sights

Tredegar House   HISTORIC BUILDING
(NT; ☑ 01633-815880; www.nationaltrust.org.uk; house adult/child £7.20/3.60, parking £2; ☺ park 9am-dusk year-round, house 11am-5pm Feb-Oct; ℗) The seat of the Morgan family for more than 500 years, Tredegar House is a stone and red-brick 17th-century country house set amid extensive gardens. It is one of the finest examples of a Restoration mansion in Britain, the oldest parts dating to the 1670s. The National Trust took over management of the property in late 2011 and has done a great job bringing the fascinating stories of its owners to life. Tredegar House is 2 miles west of Newport city centre.

The Morgans, once one of the richest families in Wales, were an interesting lot – Sir Henry was a 17th-century pirate (Captain Morgan's Rum is named after him); Lord Godfrey survived the Charge of the Light Brigade; and Viscount Evan was an occultist, a Catholic convert and a twice-married homosexual who kept a boxing kangaroo.

Transporter Bridge   BRIDGE
(www.newport.gov.uk/transporterbridge; Usk Way; vehicle/passenger £1/50p; ☺ 10am-5pm Wed-Sun Easter-Sep) The spidery towers of the 1906 Transporter Bridge rise over the river, about a mile south of the city centre. A remarkable piece of Edwardian engineering, the bridge can carry up to six cars across the river in a gondola suspended beneath the high-level track, while still allowing high-masted ships to pass beneath. It's the largest of eight such bridges remaining in the world. The day

visitor rate (adult/child £2.75/1.75) includes access to the motor house and high-level walkway.

ℹ Information

Tourist Office (☑ 01633-656656; www.newport.gov.uk/tourism; John Frost Sq; ☺ 9am-6pm Mon-Fri, to 4pm Sat)

ℹ Getting There & Away

BUS
➜ Newport's bus station is on Kings Way, across from the river, but it can also be accessed from John Frost Sq.

➜ Buses head to Cardiff (route 30; £2, 40 minutes), Caerleon (27–29; £1.60, 15 minutes), Chepstow (74; £2, one hour) and Blaenavon (X24; £4.50, 51 minutes).

➜ **National Express** (www.nationalexpress.com) coach destinations include Swansea (£9.10, 1½ hours), Cardiff (£3.20, 30 minutes), Birmingham (£23, 2¼ hours), Bristol (£8.10, 40 minutes) and London (£23, three hours).

➜ Greyhound coaches stop at the train station en route to/from Swansea (£6.60, two hours), Cardiff (£3.30, 35 minutes) and Bristol Airport (£11, 1¾ hours).

TRAIN
Newport train station is on Queensway, immediately north of the High St. Direct train destinations:

Abergavenny £8.50, 25 minutes
Bristol £11, 30 minutes
Cardiff £4.80, 20 minutes
London Paddington £39, two hours
Shrewsbury £37, 1¾ hours

Caerleon

POP 8750

Hidden in plain view beneath the small, genteel town of Caerleon is one of the largest and most important Roman settlements in Britain. After the Romans invaded in AD 43, they controlled their new territory through a network of forts and military garrisons. The top tier of military organisation was the legionary fort, of which there were only three in Britain – at Eboracum (York), Deva (Chester) and Isca (Caerleon).

Caerleon (meaning, 'Fort of the Legion') was the headquarters of the elite 2nd Augustan Legion for more than 200 years, from AD 75 until the end of the 3rd century. It wasn't just a military camp but a purpose-built township some 9 miles in circumference, complete with a 6000-seat amphitheatre and a state-of-the-art Roman baths complex.

⊙ Sights

National Roman Legion Museum MUSEUM (www.museumwales.ac.uk/en/roman; High St; ⊙10am-5pm Mon-Sat, 2-5pm Sun) **FREE** Put your Caerleon explorations into context at this excellent museum, which paints a vivid picture of what life was like for soldiers in one of the most remote corners of the Roman Empire. It displays a host of intriguing Roman artefacts uncovered locally, from jewellery to armour, and from teeth to tombstones.

Caerleon Roman Fortress Baths RUIN (Cadw; www.cadw.wales.gov.uk; High St; ⊙9.30am-5pm daily Apr-Oct, 9.30am-5pm Mon-Sat, 11am-4pm Sun Nov-Mar) **FREE** Like any good Roman town, Caerleon had a grand public bath complex. Parts of the outdoor swimming pool, *apodyterium* (changing room) and *frigidarium* (cold room) remain under a protective roof, and give some idea of the scale of the place. Projections of bathers splashing through shimmering water help bring it to life.

Roman Amphitheatre RUIN (Cadw; www.cadw.wales.gov.uk; The Broadway; ⊙9.30am-5pm) **FREE** The turf-covered terraces of the only fully excavated Roman amphitheatre in Britain can be found here; it once lay just outside the old Roman fortress walls. Take the side street opposite the National Roman Legion Museum, which leads to a park on the left. Follow the signs on the other side of the Broadway to see the foundations of the Barracks.

⌂ Sleeping

★Old Rectory B&B **££** (☎01633-430700; www.the-oldrectory.co.uk; Christchurch Rd; r £75; P�) One mile south of Caerleon, in the village of Christchurch, the Old Rectory offers a warm welcome and three luxurious rooms with views over the Severn Estuary to England.

❶ Information

Tourist Office (☎01633-422656; www.newport.gov.uk/tourism; 5 High St; ⊙10am-4pm)

❶ Getting There & Away

Regular buses head to/from Newport (routes 27–29; £1.60, 15 minutes).

Chepstow (Cas-gwent)
POP 16,200

Chepstow is an attractive market town nestled in a great S-bend in the River Wye, with a splendid Norman castle perched dramatically on a cliff above the water. The town was first developed as a base for the Norman conquest of southeast Wales, later prospering as a port for the timber and wine trades. As river-borne commerce gave way to the railways, Chepstow's importance diminished to reflect its name, which means 'marketplace' in Old English.

⊙ Sights

★Chepstow Castle CASTLE (Cadw; www.cadw.wales.gov.uk; Bridge St; adult/child £4.50/3.40; ⊙10am-4pm) Magnificent Chepstow Castle perches atop a sheer limestone cliff overhanging the river, guarding the main river crossing from England into South Wales. It is one of the oldest castles in Britain (building began in 1067) and it's remarkably well preserved.

Chepstow Museum MUSEUM (Bridge St; ⊙11am-5pm Mon-Sat, 2-5pm Sun) **FREE** Housed in an 18th-century town house across the road from the castle, this small, child-friendly museum covers Chepstow's industrial and social history.

✗ Eating

Lime Tree CAFE **£** (www.facebook.com/limetreecafebar; 24 St Mary St; mains £4-11; ⊙8.30am-11pm; �) This appealing eatery handles the transition from cosy daytime cafe into trendy gastro bar seamlessly. The vastly varied menu stretches from breakfast into sandwiches, burgers and all the traditional tapas favourites. Grab a newspaper and settle into one of the nooks.

Riverside Wine Bar TAPAS **££** (☎01291-628300; www.theriversidewinebar.co.uk; 18a The Back; mains €7-11; ⊙10.30am-11pm, reduced hours in winter) Sink into a leather couch and quaff on wine while grazing through antipasto and cheese platters, skewers, burgers, pizza and tapas. Heavy gilt-framed mirrors and feature wallpaper set the tone, while in summer the action spills outside.

Mythos! GREEK **££** (☎01291-627222; www.facebook.com/MythosMezeBar; Welsh St; mains £9-18; ⊙noon-midnight Mon-Thu, to 2am Fri & Sat, 5pm-midnight Sun) Exposed beams, stone walls and dramatic lighting make this lively Greek bar and restaurant memorable, but it's the authentic, delicious food that justifies that exclamation mark in the name: tzatziki, grilled haloumi, moussaka – served as mezze or main-sized portions.

ℹ Information

Tourist Office (☑ 01291-623772; www.chepstowtowncrier.org.uk; Castle car park, Bridge St; ⊙ 9.30am-5pm Apr-Oct, to 3.30pm Nov-Mar) Ask about local walking trails, such as the Tintern & Return path.

ℹ Getting There & Away

➜ Buses head to/from Newport (route 74; £2, one hour), Tintern (69; £2.65, 19 minutes) and Monmouth (65/69; £3, one hour).

➜ **National Express** (www.nationalexpress. com) coach destinations include London (£19, three hours), Cardiff (£5.40, one hour), Swansea (£12, two hours), Carmarthen (£17, 2½ hours) and Tenby (£18, 3¼ hours).

➜ There are direct trains from Cardiff (£9.30, 40 minutes), Gloucester (£9.50, 30 minutes), Cheltenham (£12, 40 minutes) and Birmingham (£26, 1½ hours).

Lower Wye Valley

The A466 road follows the snaking, steep-sided valley of the River Wye from Chepstow to Monmouth, passing through the straggling village of Tintern. It's a beautiful drive, rendered particularly mysterious when a twilight mist rises from the river and shrouds the illuminated ruins of Tintern Abbey.

There are plenty of possibilities for riverside walks around Tintern. One of the best begins at the old railway bridge just upstream from the abbey, and leads to the **Devil's Pulpit**, a limestone crag on the east side of the river with a spectacular view over the abbey (2.5 miles round-trip).

◉ Sights

★ **Tintern Abbey**   HISTORIC BUILDING
(Cadw; www.cadw.wales.gov.uk; adult/child £4.50/3.40; ⊙ 10am-4pm; ℙ) Founded in 1131 by the Cistercian order, this monastic complex and its riverside setting has been immortalised in many famous paintings and poems. The huge abbey church was built between 1269 and 1301, the stone shell of which remains surprisingly intact; the finest feature is tracery that once contained the magnificent west windows.

🛏 Sleeping

Tintern Old Rectory   B&B ££
(☑ 01291-689920; www.tintern-oldrectory.co.uk; A466; s/d from £75/85; ℙ🛜🐾) Dressed in pale pink and blue, the four sweet rooms in this 18th-century house either look over the river or have access to the rear garden. The breakfast menu offers an impressive array of options.

Tŷ Bryn   B&B ££
(☑ 01594-531330; www.wyevalleystay.co.uk; A466; r £70-80; ℙ🛜) Perched on a hillside overlooking a pretty stretch of the River Wye in the village of Llandogo, 3 miles north of Tintern Abbey, this old stone house has three comfortable en suite rooms looked after by friendly young owners.

Crown at Whitebrook   HOTEL ££
(☑ 01600-860254; www.crownatwhitebrook.co.uk; Whitebrook; r £110-140) Hidden away on the narrow country lane that runs along the west bank of the Wye (a mile north of the turn-off where the A466 crosses the river into England, and 5 miles north of Tintern Abbey), this little restaurant-with-rooms is a peaceful and elegant bolt-hole.

ℹ Getting There & Away

Bus 69 follows the A466 along the river between Chepstow (£2.65, 19 minutes) and Monmouth (£3.55, 34 minutes).

Monmouth (Trefynwy)

POP 10,200

The compact market town of Monmouth sits at the confluence of the Rivers Wye and Monnow, and has hopped in and out of Wales over the centuries as the border shifted back and forth. Henry V was born in 1397 in **Monmouth Castle**, the meagre remains of which can be seen on Castle Hill.

Monmouth's main drag, Monnow St, starts at car-free **Monnow Bridge**, the UK's only complete example of a medieval fortified bridge. It was built in 1270, although much of what you see now was restored in 1705. Before you cross into town, it's worth poking your head into **St Thomas the Martyr's Church**; parts of it date from around 1180.

✕ Eating

Bistro Prego   ITALIAN ££
(☑ 01600-712600; www.pregomonmouth.co.uk; 7 Church St; mains £12-19; ⊙ noon-2.30pm & 6.30-

9.30pm) Set down a cobbled lane in the heart of the town, this little Italian eatery dishes up tasty pasta and more substantial mains. Save room for dessert – the semifreddo is delicious. It also has rooms.

❶ Information

Tourist Office (☏01600-775257; www.shirehallmonmouth.org.uk; Shire Hall, Agincourt Sq; ⊙10am-4pm)

❶ Getting There & Away

➡ Buses head to/from Chepstow (route 65/69; £3, one hour), Newport (60; £5.50, one hour), Abergavenny (83; £3, 45 minutes), the Forest of Dean (34/35; £2.20, 20 minutes) and Hereford (36; one hour).

➡ National Express coaches head here from Newport (£8.40, 35 minutes), Cardiff (£11, one hour), Ross-on-Wye (£4.80, 20 minutes) and Birmingham (£20, 1¾ hours).

Skenfrith

A chocolate-box village of stone buildings set around a hefty castle and ancient church, and skirted by the River Monnow, Skenfrith encapsulates the essence of the Monmouthshire countryside. **Skenfrith Castle** was built around 1228 on the site of earlier Norman fortifications. Its keep and walls are partially intact, and there are no barriers to prevent you entering and picnicking on the central lawn. Nearby, a squat tower announces 800-year-old **St Bridget's Church**, accessed by a low wooden door with a foothigh step. The riverside village pub, the **Bell at Skenfrith** (☏01600-750235; www.skenfrith. co.uk; s/d from £75/110; 🅿 🛜 🐾), has a popular restaurant and elegant rooms.

Skenfrith is 5 miles northwest of Monmouth along the B4233; there's no public transport.

Blaenavon (Blaenafon)

POP 5700

Of all the valley settlements that were decimated by the demise of heavy industry, the one-time coal and iron town of Blaenavon shows the greenest shoots of regrowth, helped in large part by the awarding of Unesco World Heritage Site status in 2000 to its conglomeration of industrial sites. Its proximity to Brecon Beacons National Park and Abergavenny doesn't do it any harm either.

◉ Sights

Blaenavon World Heritage Centre INTERPRETATION CENTRE
(☏01495-742333; www.visitblaenavon.co.uk; Church Rd; ⊙9am-4pm Tue-Sun) **FREE** Housed in an artfully converted old school, this centre contains a cafe, tourist office, gallery, gift shop and, more importantly, excellent interactive, audiovisual displays that explore the industrial heritage of the region.

★**Big Pit National Coal Museum** MINE, MUSEUM
(☏029-2057 3650; www.museumwales.ac.uk; car park £3; ⊙9.30am-5pm, guided tours 10am-3.30pm; 🅿) **FREE** The atmospheric Big Pit provides an opportunity to explore a real coal mine and get a taste of what life was like for the miners who worked here up until 1980. Tours descend 90m into the mine and explore the tunnels and coalfaces in the company of an ex-miner guide. Above ground, you can see the pit-head baths, blacksmith's workshop and other colliery buildings, filled with displays on the industry and the reminiscences of ex-miners.

Blaenavon Ironworks HISTORIC SITE
(Cadw; www.cadw.wales.gov.uk; North St; ⊙10am-5pm) **FREE** When it was completed in 1789, this ironworks was one of the most advanced in the world. Today the site is one of the best preserved of all its Industrial Revolution contemporaries – although the

---

WORTH A TRIP

RAGLAN CASTLE
....
Raglan Castle (Cadw; www.cadw.wales. gov.uk; adult/child £4.50/3.40; ⊙10am-4pm; 🅿) was the last great medieval castle to be built in Wales, designed more as a swaggering declaration of wealth and power than a defensive fortress. A magnificent, sprawling complex built of dusky pink and grey sandstone, its centrepiece is the lavish Great Tower, a hexagonal keep ringed by a moat, badly damaged during the Civil War of the 1640s.

Buses from Newport (route 60; £5.50, 39 minutes), Monmouth (60/83; £2.85, 19 minutes) and Abergavenny (83; £3.40, 26 minutes) stop in Raglan, a five-minute walk to the castle.

hulking remains of the kilns and towers are now a home for ravens. Also on display are the tiny terraced workers' cottages.

Pontypool & Blaenavon Railway
HERITAGE RAILWAY

(☎01495-792263; www.pontypool-and-blaenavon. co.uk; adult/child £7/4) Built to haul coal and passengers, this railway has been restored by local volunteers, allowing you to catch a steam train from the town centre to Big Pit or to Whistle Halt, the highest train station in England and Wales (396m). Check online for timetables.

🛏 Sleeping & Eating

Oakfield
B&B ££

(☎01495-792829; www.oakfieldbnb.com; 1 Oakfield Tce, Varteg Rd; s/d £41/68; P 🛜) The clued-up owners of this spick-and-span B&B moonlight at the World Heritage Centre, so they're a fount of local knowledge. There are only three rooms, but twins, doubles and families are all catered for.

Butterflies Restaurant
PUB ££

(☎01495-791044; www.butterflies-restaurant.co.uk; 31-33 Queen St; mains £12-18; ⊙6-9.30pm Tue-Sat, 12.30-2.30pm Sun) This bistro-style place has a good menu of meaty mains – Beef Wellington and Welsh lamb cutlets, for example – as well as a few fish and veggie options.

🛍 Shopping

Blaenavon Cheddar Company
FOOD

(☎01495-793123; www.chunkofcheese.co.uk; 80 Broad St; ⊙10am-5pm Mon-Sat) Showcasing the company's range of handmade cheese, some of which is matured down in the Big Pit mineshaft, this little store also stocks a range of Welsh speciality ales, wines and whisky. It offers bike hire and small-group cycling and walking tours.

❶ Getting There & Away

Bus X24 heads to Blaenavon from Newport (£4.50, 50 minutes).

SWANSEA & THE GOWER

Wales' second-largest city sprawls along the 5-mile sweep of Swansea Bay, ending to the southwest in the smart seaside suburb of Mumbles at the head of the beautiful Gower Peninsula.

Swansea (Abertawe)
POP 301,000

Dylan Thomas called Swansea an 'ugly, lovely town' and that remains a fair description today. It's currently in the grip of a Cardiff-esque bout of regeneration that's slowly transforming the drab, postwar city centre into something worthy of the natural assets of its bay-side setting. Swansea makes up for some visual shortcomings with a visceral charm. A hefty student population takes to the city's bars with enthusiasm, and pockets of hipness have emerged in inner suburbs such as Uplands – which is, conveniently, where all the best B&Bs are located.

Swansea's Welsh name, Abertawe, describes its location at the mouth of the Tawe, where the river empties into Swansea Bay. The Vikings named the area Sveins Ey (Swein's Island), probably referring to the sandbank in the river mouth.

The Normans built a castle here, but Swansea didn't really get into its stride until the Industrial Revolution, when it developed into an important copper-smelting centre. Ore was first shipped in from Cornwall, across the Bristol Channel, but by the 19th century it was arriving from Chile, Cuba and the USA, in return for Welsh coal.

By the 20th century the city's industrial base had declined, although Swansea's oil refinery and smaller factories were still judged a worthy target by the Luftwaffe, which devastated the city centre in 1941.

◎ Sights

Swansea Castle
CASTLE

(Castle Sq) A small pocket of the central city around Wind St and Castle Sq escaped the wartime bombing and retains a remnant of Georgian and Victorian Swansea, and the ruins of 14th-century Swansea Castle (closed to the public). The castle was mostly destroyed by Oliver Cromwell in 1647, but had a brief lease of life as a prison in the 19th century.

Dylan Thomas Centre
MUSEUM

(www.dylanthomas.com; Somerset Pl; ⊙10am-4.30pm) FREE Housed in the former Guildhall, this unassuming museum contains absorbing displays on the Swansea-born poet's life and work. Aside from the collection of memorabilia, what really brings Dylan Thomas' work to life is a series of recordings, including the booming baritone of Richard

Burton performing *Under Milk Wood* and Thomas himself reading *Do Not Go Gentle into That Good Night,* the celebrated paean to his dying father.

Swansea Museum   MUSEUM
(www.swansea.gov.uk/swanseamuseum; Victoria Rd; ⊙10am-5pm Tue-Sun; 🔊) **FREE** Dylan Thomas referred to this august institution as 'the museum which should have *been* in a museum'. Founded in 1834, it remains charmingly low-tech, from the eccentric Cabinet of Curiosities to the glass cases of archaeological finds from Gower caves. Pride of place goes to the Mummy of Hor.

National Waterfront Museum   MUSEUM
(www.museumwales.ac.uk/en/swansea; South Dock Marina, Oystermouth Rd; ⊙10am-5pm) **FREE** Housed in a 1901 dockside warehouse with a striking glass and slate extension, the museum's 15 hands-on galleries explore Wales' industrial history and the impact of industrialisation on its people, making much use of interactive computer screens and audiovisual presentations. The effect can be a bit overwhelming, but there is a lot of interesting stuff here.

Egypt Centre   MUSEUM
(www.egypt.swan.ac.uk; Mumbles Rd, Sketty; ⊙10am-4pm Tue-Sat) **FREE** Swansea University's musem of ancient Egyptian antiquities includes a fascinating collection of everyday artefacts, ranging from a 4000-year-old razor to a mummified crocodile. Kids can try their hand at muppet mummification.

Dylan Thomas Birthplace   HOUSE
(☑01792-472555; www.dylanthomasbirthplace.com; 5 Cwmdonkin Dr, Uplands; adult/child £8/6; ⊙10.30am-4.30pm) The bad boy of Welsh poetry was born in this unassuming Uplands house and it's here that he wrote two-thirds of his poetry. It's now been lovingly restored and furnished in period style. Call ahead to arrange a tour, or if you're really keen, you can stay the night (rooms £150).

🏃 Activities

LC2   SWIMMING
(www.thelcswansea.com; Oystermouth Rd; waterpark adult/child £7/4; ⊙4-8pm Mon-Fri, 9am-8pm Sat & Sun; 🐾) The Marine Quarter's £32-million leisure centre includes a toddler's play area, a gym and a 9m indoor climbing wall. Best of all though is the waterpark, complete with a wave pool, water slides and the world's first indoor surfing ride.

Action Bikes   CYCLING
(☑01792-464640; www.actionbikesswansea.co.uk; 5 St David's Sq; half-/full day £12/18) Rent a bike and hit the cycle trail that hugs the bay from downtown Swansea to Mumbles.

🎊 Festivals & Events

Swansea Bay Festival   SUMMER FESTIVAL
(www.swanseabayfestival.co.uk; ⊙Jul-Sep) From July to September, the waterfront is taken over by shows, fun fairs, carnivals, music and exhibitions.

Dylan Thomas Festival   LITERARY FESTIVAL
(www.dylanthomas.com; ⊙Oct-Nov) Poetry readings, talks, films and performances; held from 27 October (Thomas' date of birth) to 9 November (the date he died).

🛏 Sleeping

Leonardo's   GUESTHOUSE £
(☑01792-470163; www.leonardosguesthouse.co.uk; 380 Oystermouth Rd; s/d from £38/48, without bathroom £30/45; 🔊) With small rooms in bright, sunny colours, Leonardo's is the best choice in the long strip of budget seafront guesthouses on Oystermouth Rd. Five of the nine bedrooms enjoy views over Swansea Bay.

★ Christmas Pie B&B   B&B ££
(☑01792-480266; www.christmaspie.co.uk; 2 Mirador Cres, Uplands; s/d £49/78; 🅿🔊) The name suggests something warm and comforting, and this suburban villa does not disappoint. The three en suite bedrooms are all individually and tastefully decorated. Plus there's fresh fruit and an out-of-the-ordinary, vegetarian-friendly breakfast selection.

Mirador Town House   B&B ££
(☑01792-466976; www.themirador.co.uk; 14 Mirador Cres, Uplands; s/d from £60/80; 🔊) Kooky in the extreme, all the rooms are well kitted out and elaborately themed – Roman, Mediterranean, African, Venetian, Egyptian, Asian, French – with murals on the walls and sometimes the ceilings as well. The exuberant hosts are enthusiastic cheerleaders for the area.

Crescent   B&B ££
(☑01792-465782; www.thecrescentswansea.co.uk; 132 Eaton Cres, Uplands; s/d/ste from £40/70/109; 🔊) Perched on a slope with views across the rooftops to Swansea Bay, the Crescent is a grand old Edwardian gent, daringly dressed in bright blue. The larger bedrooms are quite spacious, although the bathrooms are small.

Swansea

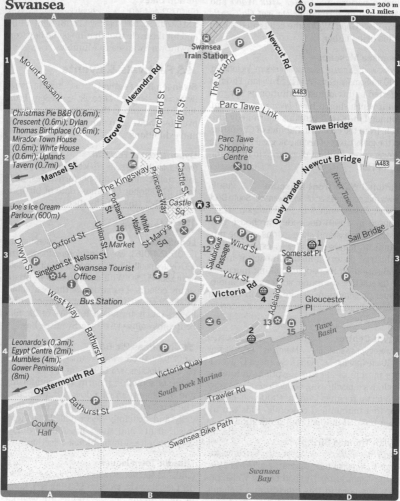

Dragon Hotel
HOTEL ££

(📞 01792-657141; www.dragon-hotel.co.uk; The Kingsway; r from £69; 🅿❄🛜🖼) This 1960s city-centre hotel has been given an expensive upgrade, with dragon-red carpets, orange backlighting and well-turned-out bedrooms. There's also a gym and an 18m indoor pool. The double-glazing helps combat the noise in this extremely busy location, but you're still better off requesting a higher floor.

White House
HOTEL ££

(📞 01792-473856; www.thewhitehousehotel.co.uk; 4 Nyanza Tce, Eaton Cres, Uplands; s/d £49/79)

More modest than its name suggests, this three-storey suburban house has an old-fashioned vibe, with chandeliers downstairs and colourful leadlights. The reasonably priced rooms all have their own bathrooms.

Morgans
HOTEL £££

(📞 01792-484848; www.morganshotel.co.uk; Somerset Pl; r £65-250; 🅿) Set in the gorgeous red-brick and Portland-stone former Ports Authority building, Morgans combines historic elegance with contemporary design and a high pamper factor. An annexe across the road has lower ceilings but similar standards.

Swansea

✕ Eating & Drinking

In a city synonymous with Dylan Thomas you'd expect some hard drinking to take place...and you'd be right. Swansea's main boozing strip is Wind St (pronounced to rhyme with 'blind', as in drunk) and on weekends it can be a bit of a zoo, full of generally good-natured alcopop-fuelled teens teetering around on high heels. *Buzz* magazine (free from the tourist office and bars around town) has its finger on the pulse.

The dining scene is more hit and miss, although Sketty Rd, Uplands, is worth exploring.

Joe's Ice Cream Parlour   ICE CREAM £
(www.joes-icecream.com; 85 St Helen's Rd; cones/ sundaes from £1.30/3.70; ☺noon-7.30pm) For an ice-cream sundae or a cone, locals love Joe's – a Swansea institution founded in 1922 by Joe Cascarini, son of immigrants from Italy's Abruzzi mountains. There are also branches at **Parc Tawe Shopping Centre** (The Strand; ☺10.30am-5.15pm) and **Mumbles** (☑01792-368212; 526 Mumbles Rd; ☺10.30am-7.30pm).

Hanson at the Chelsea Restaurant   SEAFOOD ££
(☑01792-464068; www.hansonatthechelsea.co.uk; 17 St Mary's St; mains £13-20, 2-/3-course lunch £13/17; ☺noon-2.15pm daily, 7-9.30pm Mon-Sat) Perfect for a romantic liaison, this elegant little dining room is discreetly tucked away behind the frenzy of Wind St. Seafood's the speciality, although the menu contains plenty of meaty dishes, and blackboard specials are chalked up daily.

No Sign Bar   BAR
(www.nosignwinebar.com; 56 Wind St; ☺11am-midnight) Once frequented by Dylan Thomas (it appears as the Wine Vaults in his story *The Followers*), the No Sign stands out as the only vaguely traditional bar left on Wind St. On weekends there's live music downstairs in the Vault. The food's very good too (mains from £6 to £11).

Kon-Tiki   COCKTAIL BAR
(10 The Strand; ☺6pm-midnight) Hidden down the hill from Wind St, cool Kon-Tiki offers all the requisite elements for a tropical beach fantasy: faux Polynesian statues, cocktails served in tiki cups, flax matting on the walls and Bob Marley on the stereo.

Uplands Tavern   PUB
(www.facebook.com/TheUplandsTavern; 42 Uplands Cres; ☺11am-11pm) Yet another Thomas hangout, Uplands still serves a quiet daytime pint in the Dylan Thomas snug. Come nightfall, it turns into a different beast altogether as the hub of the city's live-music scene.

☆ Entertainment

Swansea Grand Theatre   THEATRE
(☑01792-475715; www.swanseagrand.co.uk; Singleton St) The city's largest theatre stages a mixed line-up of ballet, opera, musicals, theatre, pantomimes and a regular comedy club.

Taliesin Arts Centre   PERFORMING ARTS
(☑01792-602060; www.taliesinartscentre.co.uk; Swansea University, Mumbles Rd) Part of Swansea University, this vibrant arts centre showcases live music, theatre, dance and film.

Dylan Thomas Theatre   THEATRE
(☑01792-473238; www.dylanthomastheatre.org. uk; Gloucester Pl) Home to Swansea Little Theatre, an amateur dramatic group of which Dylan Thomas was once a member, the company stages a wide repertoire of plays, including regular performances of your man's *Under Milk Wood*.

Shopping

Swansea Market   MARKET
(www.swanseaindoormarket.co.uk; Oxford St;
⊙ 8am-5.30pm Mon-Sat) There's been a covered market in Swansea since 1652 and at this site since 1830. Rebuilt in 1961 after being bombed in WWII, the current version is a buzzing place to stock up on local specialities, such as cockles, laver bread and Welsh cakes fresh from the griddle.

Mission Gallery   ART
(www.missiongallery.co.uk; Gloucester Pl; ⊙ 11am-5pm Tue-Sun) FREE Set in a converted 19th-century seamen's chapel, Mission stages Swansea's most striking exhibitions of contemporary art, as well as selling glassware, ceramics, jewellery and art magazines.

ⓘ Information

Morriston Hospital (✆ 01792-702222; Heol Maes Eglwys, Morriston) Accident and emergency department, 5 miles north of the centre.
Police Station (✆ 101; Grove Pl)
Swansea Tourist Office (✆ 01792-468321; www.visitswanseabay.com; Plymouth St; ⊙ 9.30am-5.30pm Mon-Sat)

ⓘ Getting There & Away

BUS
➤ Buses head to/from Cardiff (route 701; £3, 1¼ hours), Kidwelly (111; £5.20, 1½ hours), Carmarthen (X11/701; £5.20, one hour), Llandeilo (X13; £5.20, 1½ hours) and Aberystwyth (701; 2¾ hours).

➤ National Express destinations include Cardiff (£3.50, one hour), Chepstow (£12, two hours), Bristol (£10, 2½ hours), Birmingham (£35, 4¼ hours) and London Victoria (£24, 5¼ hours).

➤ Greyhound coaches head to/from Cardiff (£3.30, one hour), Newport (£6.60, two hours) and Bristol Airport (£11, three hours).

TRAIN
Direct trains head to/from Cardiff (£8.60, one hour), Llandrindod Wells (£13, 2¼ hours), Bristol (£26, 1½ hours), London Paddington (£45, three hours) and Shrewsbury (£45, three hours).

ⓘ Getting Around

First Cymru (www.firstgroup.com) runs local services. A FirstDay ticket offers all-day bus travel in the Swansea Bay area (including Mumbles and the Gower Peninsula) for £4.70; buy tickets from the driver.

Mumbles (Y Mwmbwls)

Strung out along the shoreline at the southern end of Swansea Bay, Mumbles has been Swansea's seaside retreat since 1807, when the Oystermouth Railway was opened. Built for transporting coal, the horse-drawn carriages were soon converted for paying customers, and the now defunct Mumbles train became the first passenger railway service in the world.

Once again fashionable, with restaurants vying for trade along the promenade, Mumbles received a boost to its reputation when its most famous daughter, Hollywood actress Catherine Zeta-Jones, built a £2-million luxury mansion at Limeslade, on the south side of the peninsula. Singer Bonnie Tyler also has a home here.

The origin of Mumbles' unusual name is uncertain, although one theory is that it's a legacy of French seamen who nicknamed the twin rounded rocks at the tip of the headland Les Mamelles ('the breasts').

⊙ Sights

Clyne Gardens   GARDENS
(www.breatheswansea.com) FREE Spanning 20 hectares, these magnificent gardens are particularly impressive in spring when the azaleas and rhododendrons are at their most spectacular. Plus there are bluebell woods, wildflower meadows and a bog garden to explore. The entrance is behind the Woodman Pub at the Swansea end of the Mumbles Rd strip.

Oystermouth Castle   CASTLE
(www.abertawe.gov.uk/oystermouthcastle; Castle Ave; adult/child £2.50/1.50; ⊙ 11am-5pm Apr-Sep) It wouldn't be Wales without a castle, hence the trendy shops and bars of Newton Rd are guarded by a majestic ruin. Once the stronghold of the Norman lords of Gower, it's now the focus of summer Shakespeare performances. There's a fine view over Swansea Bay from the battlements.

Mumbles Pier   PIER
(✆ 01792-365220; www.mumbles-pier.co.uk; Mumbles Rd) At the end of Mumbles' mile-long strip of pastel-painted houses, pubs and restaurants lies a rocky headland abutted by a Victorian pier with a sandy beach below. Built in 1898, it houses the usual amusement arcade and a once-grand cafe, festooned with chandeliers.

🛏 Sleeping

★Tides Reach Guest House B&B **££**
(📞 01792-404877; www.tidesreachguesthouse.
com; 388 Mumbles Rd; s/d from £60/70; 🅿 @ 🛜)
Delicious eco-conscious breakfasts and
stacks of local information are served with
a smile at this smart waterfront B&B. Some
rooms have sea views; our favourite is suite-
like room 9, where the dormer windows
open out to create a virtual deck.

Patricks with Rooms BOUTIQUE HOTEL **£££**
(📞 01792-360199; www.patrickswithrooms.com;
638 Mumbles Rd; r £115-175; 🛜) Patricks has
16 individually styled designer bedrooms
in bold contemporary colours with art on
the walls, and with fluffy robes. Some are
set back in a separate annexe. Downstairs
there's an upmarket restaurant and bar.

ℹ Information

Mumbles Tourist Office (📞 01792-361302;
www.mumbleshead.info; Methodist Church,
Mumbles Rd; ⊙ 10.30am-4pm Mon-Sat)

ℹ Getting There & Away

Buses 2, 3 and 27 head between Swansea and
Mumbles (£3.70, 20 minutes).

Gower Peninsula (Y Gŵyr)

With its broad butterscotch beaches, pounding surf, precipitous clifftop walks and rugged, untamed uplands, the Gower Peninsula
feels a million miles away from Swansea's
urban bustle – yet it's just on the doorstep.

This 15-mile-long thumb of land stretching
west from Mumbles was in 1956 designated
the UK's first official Area of Outstanding
Natural Beauty (AONB).

⊙ Sights

The main family beaches, patrolled by lifeguards during the summer, are **Langland
Bay**, **Caswell Bay** and **Port Eynon** on the
south coast. The most spectacular, however,
is the 3-mile sweep of **Rhossili Bay** at the
western tip of the peninsula – which has
been recently ranked on Trip Advisor as one
of the top 10 beaches in the world.

From Rhossili village you can follow the
1-mile tidal causeway to rocky, wave-blasted
Worm's Head (from Old English 'wurm',
meaning dragon) but only for a two-hour
period either side of low tide. At the Outer
Head, look out for choughs, peregrine falcons, razorbills, guillemots and oystercatch-
ers, as well as seals bobbing in the swell.

The village of **Llangennith**, at the north
of Rhossili Bay, is the infrastructure hub for
surfers.

At the heart of the peninsula is **Cefn
Bryn**, a ruggedly beautiful expanse of moorland that rises to a height of 186m. On a
suitably desolate ridge above the village of
Reynoldston stands a mysterious neolithic burial chamber capped by the 25-tonne
quartz boulder known as **Arthur's Stone**
(Coeten Arthur).

🏃 Activities

The Gower has the best surfing in Wales outside Pembrokeshire.

LOCAL KNOWLEDGE

WALES COAST PATH

Fancy a stroll? We asked Quentin Grimley, Coastal Access Project Officer for Natural
Resources Wales, to tell us about the **Wales Coast Path** (www.walescoastpath.gov.uk),
the first walking track to encompass a country's entire coastline.

Tell us about the path. The project started in 2007 with the intention to create a continuous coastal path around all of Wales. It opened in 2012, linking up existing coastal paths
like Pembrokeshire, which has been around since 1970, and others such as Ceredigion
and Anglesey. If you then walk the Offa's Dyke Path you can circle the whole of Wales.

How long does it take to walk the whole thing? It's 870 miles long. Walking every day
for an average of 13 miles, it would take two months to complete – plus an additional two
weeks if you finish with Offa's Dyke Path.

**Are there any sections that you'd recommend for travellers with only a day or two
to spare?** Well, places like Pembrokeshire are already well known, so for somewhere a
little less obvious, try the Gower Peninsula by Swansea. It's an Area of Outstanding Natural Beauty, it's easy to get to and it's never had a continuous coastal path before now.

PJ's Surf Shop
SURFING

(☑ 01792-386669; www.pjsurfshop.co.uk; wetsuits/surfboards/bodyboards per day £11/11/6; ☺ 9am-5.30pm) Run by former surf champion Peter Jones in the village of Llangennith, at the north of Rhossili Bay, this is a centre of activity for surfers.

Gower Coast Adventures
CRUISE

(☑ 07866-250440; www.gowercoastadventures.co.uk) Speedboat trips to Worm's Head from Port Eynon (adult/child £38/22) or Mumbles (adult/child £48/28), or from Mumbles to Three Cliffs and Oxwich Bay (adult/child £30/18).

Parc-Le-Breos Pony Trekking
HORSE RIDING

(☑ 01792-371636; www.parc-le-breos.co.uk; Parkmill; half-/full day £35/48) The rural byways and bridleways of the Gower are ideal territory for horseback explorations.

Welsh Surfing Federation Surf School
SURFING

(☑ 01792-386426; www.wsfsurfschool.co.uk; Llangennith) The governing body for surfing in Wales offers initial two-hour surfing lessons for £25.

🛏 Sleeping & Eating

Port Eynon YHA
HOSTEL £

(☑ 0845 371 9135; www.yha.org.uk; Port Eynon; dm/r from £21/84) Worth special mention for its spectacular location, this former lifeboat station is as close as you could come to the sea without sleeping on the beach itself. It's cosier than your average YHA, with sea views from the lounge.

Nicholaston Farm
CAMPSITE £

(☑ 01792-371209; www.nicholastonfarm.co.uk; Penmaen; sites £18-25; ☺ Apr-Sep) Field camping in a working farm overlooking Oxwich Bay. There's a little farm shop/cafe and an excellent ablutions block.

King's Head
PUB ££

(☑ 01792-386212; www.kingsheadgower.co.uk; Llangennith; r from £99; P 🛜) The centre of Llangennith's social life, the King's Head serves real ales and meals. Behind it are two custom-made stone blocks, stylishly fitted out with modern bathrooms, pale tiles and underfloor heating.

Culver House
APARTMENT ££

(☑ 01792-720300; www.culverhousehotel.co.uk; Port Eynon; apt incl breakfast from £79; @ 🛜) This renovated 19th-century house offers eight modern self-contained apartments with all the mod cons, and continental breakfasts delivered daily to your fridge. The upper apartments have balconies, while those on the ground floor open onto cute little gardens.

Parc-le-Breos House
B&B ££

(☑ 01792-371636; www.parc-le-breos.co.uk; Parkmill; r from £90; P 🛜) Set in its own private estate north of the main road, Parc-le-Breos offers en suite B&B accommodation in a Victorian hunting lodge. The majestic lounge and dining room downstairs have grand fireplaces that crackle into action in winter.

King Arthur Hotel
PUB ££

(☑ 01792-390775; www.kingarthurhotel.co.uk; Higher Green, Reynoldston; r £75-105, mains £8-14; P 🛜) As traditional as swords in stone and ladies of the lake, the King Arthur serves real ales in a cosy wood-panelled bar and offers a lengthy menu in the neighbouring bistro. The bedrooms above are less atmospheric but clean and comfortable.

★ Fairyhill
HOTEL £££

(☑ 01792-390139; www.fairyhill.net; s/d from £170/190; P 🛜) Hidden (as any proper fairy place should be) down a narrow lane north of Reynoldston, this Georgian country house has a suitably magical setting. The rooms are excellent and less old-fashioned than the restaurant downstairs, which serves pleasantly Welsh food with few surprises.

ⓘ Information

Rhossili Visitor Centre (☑ 01792-390707; www.nationaltrust.org.uk/gower; Coastguard Cottages, Rhossili; ☺ 10.30am-5pm daily mid-Feb–Dec, 10.30am-4pm Wed-Sun Jan–mid-Feb) The National Trust's centre has information on local walks and wildlife, and an audiovisual display upstairs.

ⓘ Getting There & Around

The Gower is included in the First Cymru (www.firstgroup.com) Swansea Bay zone. Buses zip all around the peninsula, with additional services in summer.

CARMARTHENSHIRE (SIR GAERFYRDDIN)

Castle-dotted Carmarthenshire has gentle valleys, deep-green woods and a small, partly sandy coast. Caught between dramatic neighbours – Pembrokeshire to the west and the Brecon Beacons to the east – it remains much quieter and less explored. Yet the appeal of its tranquil countryside hasn't gone entirely unnoticed, and charming places like Llandeilo are sprouting upmarket galleries and shops. If your interests stretch to gardens, stately homes and all things green, add this quiet county to your itinerary.

Llandeilo & Around

POP 1800

Set on a hill encircled by the greenest of fields, Llandeilo is little more than a handful of narrow streets lined with grand Georgian and Victorian buildings and centred on a picturesque church and graveyard. The surrounding region was once dominated by large country estates and, though they have long gone, the deer, parkland trees and agricultural character of the landscape are their legacy.

Sights

★Dinefwr HISTORIC BUILDING
(NT; www.nationaltrust.org.uk; adult/child £4/2, parking £6; ⏲ house 11am-6pm daily Apr-Oct, 10am-4pm Fri-Sun Nov-Mar; P) At the heart of this large estate, immediately west of Llandeilo, is **Newton House**, a wonderful 17th-century manor with a Victorian facade. It's presented as it was in Edwardian times, focusing particularly on the experience of servants in their downstairs domain. Striking 12th-century **Dinefwr Castle** is set on a hilltop in the southern corner of the estate. In the 17th century it suffered the indignity of being converted into a picturesque garden feature.

Aberglasney Gardens GARDENS
(www.aberglasney.org; Llangathen; adult/child £8/4; ⏲ 10am-6pm Apr-Oct, 10.30am-4pm Nov-Mar) Wandering through these formal walled gardens feels a bit like walking into a Jane Austen novel. They date back to the 17th century and contain a unique cloister built solely as a garden decoration. There's also a pool garden, a 250-year-old yew tunnel and a 'wild' garden in the bluebell woods to the west.

At its heart stands a semirestored Elizabethan manor house, where you can watch a video on the estate's history and view temporary art exhibitions. The derelict kitchens have been converted into a glass-roofed atrium garden full of subtropical plants such as orchids, palms and cycads.

Aberglasney is in the village of Llangathen, just off the A40, 4 miles west of Llandeilo.

National Botanic Garden of Wales GARDENS
(www.gardenofwales.org.uk; Llanarthne; adult/child £8.50/4.50; ⏲ 10am-6pm Apr-Sep, to 4.30pm Oct-Mar) Concealed in the rolling Tywi Valley, this lavish complex opened in 2000 and is still maturing. Formerly an aristocratic estate, the garden has a wide range of plant habitats, from lakes and bogs to woodland and heath, with lots of decorative areas and educational exhibits on plant medicine and organic farming. The centrepiece is the Norman Foster–designed **Great Glasshouse**, an arresting glass dome sunken into the earth. The garden is 8 miles southwest of Llandeilo, signposted from the road to Carmarthen (A40).

Sleeping

Cawdor HOTEL ££
(☎ 01558-823500; www.thecawdor.com; Rhosmaen St; r £65-200; P 📶) Grey-and-pink-striped carpet leads to well-appointed rooms with marble-clad bathrooms in this grand Georgian inn in Llandeilo. The downstairs bar serves tasty meals, or you can opt for a more formal meal in the restaurant.

Plough HOTEL ££
(☎ 01558-823431; www.ploughrhosmaen.com; s/d from £75/95; P 📶 👪 🐾) On the A40, just north of Llandeilo, this baby-blue inn offers hip, contemporary rooms, some with countryside views. The standard rooms are spacious enough but the corner-hogging executives have cat-swinging space and then some.

Getting There & Away

BUS

Buses head to/from Swansea (route X13; £5.20, 1½ hours) and Carmarthen (279–281; £3.30, 40 minutes).

TRAIN

Direct trains head to/from Cardiff (£21, 2½ hours), Swansea (£7, 1¼ hours), Llanwrtyd Wells (£5, 45 minutes), Llandrindod Wells (£15, 1¼ hours) and Shrewsbury (£25, three hours).

Kidwelly (Cydweli)

POP 2790

The unassuming little town of Kidwelly, at the mouth of the River Gwendraeth Fach, is dominated by the impressive pigeon-inhabited remains of Kidwelly Castle.

WORTH A TRIP

LLANELLI WETLAND CENTRE

Covering 97 hectares on the northern shore of the Burry Inlet, across from the Gower Peninsula, **Llanelli Wetland Centre** (☑ 01554-741087; www.wwt. org.uk/llanelli; Llwynhendy; adult/child £8.14/4.50; ⊗ 9.30am-5pm; Ⓟ) is one of Wales' most important habitats for waders and waterfowl. Winter is the most spectacular season, when up to 60,000 birds converge on the salt marsh and mudflats. Flashiest of all are the resident flock of nearly fluorescent pink Caribbean flamingos.

There's plenty on for kids during school holidays. Late spring's Duckling Days are filled with downy cuteness, while in summer there are canoes and bikes to borrow.

⊙ Sights

Kidwelly Castle   CASTLE
(Cadw; www.cadw.wales.gov.uk; Castle Rd; adult/child £4/3; ⊗ 10am-5pm) Rising above a narrow waterway dotted with swans, this forbidding grey eminence was founded by the Normans in 1106, but most of the system of towers and curtain walls was built in the 13th century in reaction to Welsh uprisings. If it looks familiar, that may be because it featured in the opening scene of *Monty Python and the Holy Grail*.

ⓘ Getting There & Away

Trains head to Kidwelly from Swansea (£8.50, 30 minutes), Cardiff (£13, 1½ hours), Abergavenny (£30, 2¼ hours), Shrewsbury (£48, 3½ hours) and Manchester (£75, five hours); buses run from Carmarthen (route X11/198; £2.80, 27 minutes).

Carmarthen (Caerfyrddin)

POP 15,900

Carmarthenshire's county town is a place of legend and ancient provenance, but it's not the kind of place you'll feel inclined to linger in. It's a handy transport and shopping hub but there's not a lot to see. The Romans built a town here, complete with a fort and an amphitheatre. A couple of solid walls, a gatehouse and a few crumbling towers are all that remain of Carmarthen's Norman castle, which was largely destroyed in the Civil War.

Most intriguingly, Carmarthen is reputed to be the birthplace of the most famous wizard of them all (no, not Harry Potter) – Myrddin of the Arthurian legends, better known in English as Merlin. An oak tree planted in 1660 for Charles II's coronation came to be called 'Merlin's Tree' and was linked to a prophecy that its death would mean curtains for the town. The tree died in the 1970s, but the town, while a little down at heel, is still standing.

⊙ Sights

Carmarthen Market   MARKET
(www.carmarthenmarket.co.uk;   Market   Way; ⊗ 9.30am-4.30pm Mon-Sat) **FREE** There's been a market here since Roman times, and in 1180 it was given a royal charter. Now housed in an edgy new building, the market sells a bit of everything, from produce to antiques. On Wednesdays and Saturdays it spills out onto the street.

Oriel Myrddin   GALLERY
(☑ 01267-222775; www.orielmyrddingallery.co.uk; Church Lane; ⊗ 10am-5pm Mon-Sat) **FREE** Stages changing exhibitions of contemporary art.

ⓕ Tours

Creepy Carmarthen   WALKING TOUR
(☑ 01267-231557; www.thespookymagiccompany. co.uk; adult/child £7.50/5; ⊗ 7pm Thu & 5pm Sat Apr-Nov) Stroll around the town's dark corners while being regaled with ghost stories and chilling tales from its history.

✕ Eating

Carmarthen's contribution to Welsh gastronomy is a salt-cured, air-dried ham. Local legend has it that the Romans liked the recipe so much they took it back to Italy with them (as proscuitto). Look for it at Carmarthen market.

Waverley Restaurant   VEGETARIAN £
(23 Lammas St; mains £6; ⊗ 11.30am-2pm; ☑) Hiding at the rear of a wholefoods store, this cheap-and-cheerful eatery serves up simple vegetarian meals such as soups, salads, quiches, lasagne and jacket potatoes.

ⓘ Information

Tourist Office (☑ 01267-231557; www. discovercarmarthenshire.com; Old Castle House; ⊗ 9.30am-4.30pm Mon-Sat)

❶ Getting There & Away

BUS

➡ The main bus stop is on Blue St. Destinations include Aberystwyth (route 701; 1¾ hours), Haverfordwest (322; £5, one hour), Llandeilo (279–281; £3.30, 40 minutes), Swansea (X11/701; £5.20, one hour) and Cardiff (701; 2¼ hours).

➡ National Express coaches head to/from London Victoria (£24, six hours), Birmingham (£38, five hours), Bristol (£18, three hours), Cardiff (£11, two hours) and Swansea (£6.50, 45 minutes).

TRAIN

The train station is 300m south of town, across the river. There are direct trains to Swansea (£9, 45 minutes), Cardiff (£19, 1¾ hours), Abergavenny (£35, 2½ hours), Shrewsbury (£54, four hours) and Manchester (£75, 5¼ hours).

Laugharne (Talacharn)

POP 820

Sleepy little Laugharne (pronounced 'larn') sits above the tide-washed shores of the Taf Estuary, overlooked by a Norman castle. Dylan Thomas spent the last four years of his life here, during which he produced some of his most inspired work, including *Under Milk Wood;* the town is one of the inspirations for the play's fictional village of Llareggub (spell it backwards and you'll get the gist).

On Thomas' first visit he described it as the 'strangest town in Wales', but he returned repeatedly throughout his restless life. Many Thomas fans make a pilgrimage here to see the Boathouse where he lived, the shed where he wrote, Brown's Hotel where he drank (he used to give the pub telephone number as his contact number) and the churchyard where he's buried.

◉ Sights & Activities

Dylan Thomas Boathouse MUSEUM
(www.dylanthomasboathouse.com; Dylan's Walk; adult/child £4.20/3.20; ⊗10am-5.30pm May-Oct, 10.30am-3.30pm Nov-Apr) Dylan Thomas lived here from 1949 to 1953 with his wife Caitlin and their three children. It's a beautiful setting, looking out over the estuary with what his 'Poem in October' called its 'heron-priested shore'. The parlour has been restored to its 1950s appearance, with the desk that once belonged to Thomas' schoolmaster father, and there are recordings of the poet reading his own works. Upstairs are photographs, manuscripts, a short video about his life, and his death mask, which once belonged to Richard Burton.

Along the lane from the Boathouse is the old shed where Thomas did most of his writing. It looks as if he has just popped out, with screwed-up pieces of paper littered around. Thomas and Caitlin are buried in a grave marked by a simple white wooden cross in the grounds of St Martin's Church, on the northern edge of the town.

Laugharne Castle CASTLE
(Cadw; www.cadw.wales.gov.uk; Wogan St; adult/child £3.80/2.85; ⊗10am-5pm Apr-Oct) Built in the 13th century, Laugharne Castle was converted

---

WORTH A TRIP

NORTH CARMARTHENSHIRE

Most travellers continue west from Carmarthen, leaving the lush green hills and valleys of northern Carmarthenshire relatively unexplored. Although the sights are few, it's a pleasant place to potter about.

Positioned in verdant countryside, 14 miles north of Carmarthen (signposted from the A484), is the surprisingly interesting **National Wool Museum** (☑029-2057 3070; www.museumwales.ac.uk; ⊗10am-5pm daily Apr-Sep, Tue-Sat Oct-Mar) FREE. It's based in the former Cambrian Mills factory, which was world famous for its high-quality woollen products until it closed in 1984. Former mill workers are often on hand to get the machines clickety-clacking, but there's also a working commercial mill next door where you can watch the operations from a viewing platform. There's a cafe on-site and a gift shop selling snug woollen blankets.

Continuing on into the Teifi Valley, the town of **Newcastle Emlyn** has a ruined 13th century castle and a wonderful old coaching inn that's been transformed into a slick little hotel. **Gwesty'r Emlyn Hotel** (☑01239-710317; www.gwestyremlynhotel.co.uk; Bridge St; s/d from £90/130; ℗ 🛜) has spacious rooms, a restaurant and a 'fitness suite', with gym equipment, a spa pool and a sauna.

into a mansion in the 16th century for John Perrot, thought to be the illegitimate son of Henry VIII. It was landscaped with its current lawns and gardens in Victorian times.

Marros Riding Centre　　　HORSE RIDING
(☏01994-453777; www.marros-farm.co.uk; Marros) Based 7 miles west of Laugharne, past the broad sands of Pendine, this riding centre offers lessons (half-hour £25) and treks (two hours £43) including beach rides (£60).

🛏 Sleeping & Eating

Boat House　　　B&B **££**
(☏01994-427263; www.theboathousebnb.co.uk; 1 Gosport St; s/d £60/80; 🐾) Friendly, homely and tastefully decorated, this is the smartest B&B in town. The breakfasts are exceptional, with lots of yummy home baking. The building was formerly the Corporation Arms pub, where Dylan Thomas told stories in exchange for free drinks.

Keepers Cottage　　　B&B **££**
(☏01994-427404; www.keepers-cottage.com; A4066; s/d from £60/80; P🐾) Sitting on the top of the hill by the main approach to town, this white-painted brick cottage has four simply decorated but very comfortable rooms. Complimentary bottled water, chocolates and little bottles of wine are a nice touch.

Corran　　　HOTEL **£££**
(☏01994-427417; www.thecorran.com; East Marsh; r from £200; P🐾🐕) Having had a £5-million makeover, you would expect this converted Georgian farm on the salt-marsh flats south of Laugharne to be luxurious. And it is. Rooms have big beds and roll-top baths, and the complex includes a bar, restaurant and day spa.

★**Cors**　　　MODERN BRITISH **£££**
(☏01994-427219; www.thecors.co.uk; Newbridge Rd; mains £19-27, s/d £50/80; ⊙7pm-midnight Thu-Sat; P🐾) Tucked away in a rambling old house behind a wonderful bog garden ('cors' means bog), this colourful and pleasantly eccentric restaurant-with-rooms serves excellent local seasonal food. The upstairs bedrooms are spacious and brimming with character.

❶ Getting There & Away

Bus 222 runs from Carmarthen to Laugharne (£3, 30 minutes) on weekdays.

PEMBROKESHIRE (SIR BENFRO)

The rugged Pembrokeshire Coast is what you would imagine the world would look like if God was a geology teacher. There are knobbly hills of volcanic rock, long thin inlets scoured by glacial meltwater, and stratified limestone pushed up vertically and eroded into natural arches, blowholes and sea stacks. Stretches of towering red and grey cliff give way to perfect sandy beaches, only to resume around the headland painted black.

It's a landscape of Norman castles, Iron Age hill forts, holy wells and Celtic saints – including the nation's patron, Dewi Sant (St David). Predating even the ancient Celts are the remnants of an older people, who left behind them dolmens and stone circles – the same people who transported their sacred bluestones all the way from the Preseli Hills to form the giant edifice at Stonehenge.

MYTHS & LEGENDS
....

Wales is awash with sagas inspired by bloody conflict and untamed landscapes. From generation to generation, elaborate tales of enchantment and wizardry have been bequeathed like rich family legacies. As early as the 9th century tales of mystery and heroism were compiled in the *Historia Britonum*. But the finest impressions come from the *Mabinogion*, a 14th-century tome containing occasionally terrifying tales of Celtic magic.

King Arthur is a recurrent character, especially in the *Mabinogion*. One of British legend's most romanticised heroes, he was believed to have been a 5th- or 6th-century cavalry leader who rallied British fighters against the marauding Saxon invaders. Time transformed Arthur into a king of magic deeds, with wise magician Myrddin (Merlin) by his side and a loyal band of followers in support. Arthur went on to slay Rita Gawr, a giant who butchered kings, in an epic battle on Snowdon. Finally, Myrddin delivered the dying hero to Avalon, which may well have been saintly Bardsey Island off the Llŷn Peninsula.

The world of Welsh myths is richly imaginative. For more see Robin Gwyndaf's detailed bilingual *Chwedlau Gwerin Cymru: Welsh Folk Tales*.

Pembrokeshire

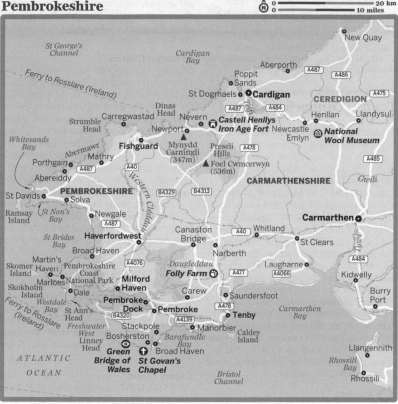

Narberth (Arberth)

POP 2270

An arty little town full of independent shops, Narberth is a gem. Despite being light on specific sights, it's well worth a stop for its lively vibe, passion for food and thriving retail scene. Somehow managing to beat the economic odds, butchers, delis, antique shops and boutiques line the streets. There's a friendly food festival (www.narberthfood-festival.com; ⊙Sep) in September, a ruined Norman castle, a whizz-bang local history museum (www.narberthmuseum.co.uk; Church St; adult/child £3.50/2.50; ⊙10am-5pm) and an interesting town hall with a double stairway.

🛌 Sleeping & Eating

Canaston Oaks   B&B **££**
(☑01437-541254; www.canastonoaks.co.uk; A4075, Canaston Bridge; r/ste from £113/137; 🐾) Set alongside a working farm, 3 miles west of Narberth near the intersection of the A40 and A4075, this luxurious B&B has eight en suite rooms positioned around a Celtic cross–shaped garden. Expect hearty breakfasts and charming Welsh hospitality.

★ Grove   HOTEL **£££**
(☑01834-860915; www.thegrove-narberth.co.uk; Molleston; s/d from £162/171; 3-course lunch/dinner £28/54; ⊙restaurant noon-9.30pm; P🐾✉️) 🍴 A truly magical place to stay, this luxury hotel is hidden in the countryside south of Narberth, surrounded by manicured lawns, mature trees and wildflower meadows. The sumptuous rooms blend period character with contemporary styling, while the renowned restaurant serves a creative menu of Modern Welsh cuisine.

ℹ️ Getting There & Away

➔ Buses head to/from Carmarthen (route 322; £4.80, 38 minutes), Saundersfoot (381; £3.15,

30 minutes), Tenby (381; £3.75, 42 minutes), Haverfordwest (322/381; £3.65, 21 minutes) and Cardigan (430; one hour); no Sunday services.

➡ Direct trains head to/from Cardiff (£25, 2½ hours), Swansea (£15, 1½ hours), Carmarthen (£7.80, 30 minutes), Tenby (£4.70, 19 minutes) and Pembroke (£8.10, 45 minutes).

Tenby (Dinbych-y-Pysgod)

POP 4700

Perched on a headland with sandy beaches on either side, Tenby is a postcard-maker's dream. Houses are painted from the pastel palette of a classic fishing village, interspersed with the white elegance of Georgian mansions. The main part of town is still constrained by its Norman-built walls, funnelling holidaymakers through medieval streets lined with pubs, ice-creameries and gift shops. Without the tackiness of the promenade-and-pier beach towns, it tastefully returns to being a sleepy little place in the off-season. In the summer months it has a boisterous, boozy holiday-resort feel.

Tenby flourished in the 15th century as a centre for the textile trade, exporting cloth in exchange for salt and wine. Clothmaking declined in the 18th century, but the town soon reinvented itself as a fashionable watering place, assisted by the coming of the railway in the 19th century.

◉ Sights

Tudor Merchant's House HISTORIC BUILDING
(NT; www.nationaltrust.org.uk; Quay Hill; adult/child £3.50/1.75; ⊙11am-5pm Wed-Mon Apr-Jul, Sep & Oct, daily Aug, 11am-3pm Sat & Sun Mar, Nov & Dec) Tenby's handsomely restored 15th-century Tudor house is set up like it would have been in its heyday, with colourful wall hangings, period-style beds and kitchen implements. The curators have drawn the line at recreating the scent of the open cesspit next to the kitchen though.

St Mary's Church CHURCH
(High St) The graceful vaulted roof of this 13th-century church is studded with fascinating wooden bosses, mainly dating from the 15th century, carved into flowers, cheeky faces, mythical beasts, fish and even a mermaid holding a comb and mirror. There's a memorial here to Robert Recorde, the 16th-century writer and mathematician who invented the 'equals' sign, along with a confronting cadaver-topped tomb, intended to remind the viewer of their own mortality.

The young Henry Tudor – later to become Henry VII – was hidden here before fleeing to Brittany. It's thought that he left by means of a tunnel into the cellars under Mayor Thomas White's house across the road.

Tenby Museum & Art Gallery MUSEUM
(www.tenbymuseum.org.uk; Castle Hill; adult/child £4/3; ⊙10am-5pm daily Apr-Oct, Tue-Sat Nov-Mar) Housed within the ruins of a Norman castle, this museum covers local history (summarised in an interesting short film) and includes paintings by Augustus and Gwen John.

Caldey Island ISLAND
(☑01834-844453; www.caldey-island.co.uk; adult/child £11/6; ⊙Mon-Sat May-Sep, Mon-Fri Apr & Oct) Boat trips run from Tenby harbour to Caldey Island, home to lots of grey seals and seabirds, and a red-topped, whitewashed monastery that houses a community of Cistercian monks. There are great walks around the island, and good views from the lighthouse.

PEMBROKESHIRE COAST NATIONAL PARK

Established in 1952, **Pembrokeshire Coast National Park** (Parc Cenedlaethol Arfordir Sir Benfro) takes in almost the entire Pembrokeshire Coast and its offshore islands, as well as the Preseli Hills in the north and the inland waters of the River Cleddau near Milford Haven. Pembrokeshire's sea cliffs and islands support huge breeding populations of seabirds, while seals, dolphins, porpoises and whales are frequently spotted in coastal waters.

There are three national park information centres – in Tenby, St Davids and Newport – and the local tourist offices scattered across Pembrokeshire are well stocked with park paraphernalia. The free annual newspaper *Coast to Coast* (online at www.pembrokeshirecoast.org.uk) has lots of information on park attractions, a calendar of events and details of park-organised activities. It's worth picking it up for the tide tables alone – they're an absolute necessity for many legs of the spectacular 186-mile **Pembrokeshire Coast Path**, which traverses the entire coast of the park.

Dragon Reptile Experience   REPTILE HOUSE
(📞 07970 441346; www.dragonreptiles.co.uk; Brewery Tce, Saundersfoot; adult/child £8/5; ⏱ 10am-5pm Apr-Oct, call ahead Nov-Mar) Come face to face with huge snakes, hairy spiders and all sorts of other slippery, creepy and crawly critters during an hour-long hands-on experience. Saundersfoot is 3 miles north of Tenby, about an hour's walk along the coast path. There's also an excellent beach here.

🛌 Sleeping

Myrtle House   HOTEL **££**
(📞 01834-842508; www.myrtlehousehoteltenby. com; St Mary's St; s/d £35/70; 📶) Located just a few metres from the steps down to Castle Beach, this late-Georgian house has eight attractive rooms with en suite bathrooms. The friendly owners serve up good breakfasts (vegetarians are well catered for).

St Lawrence Country Guesthouse   B&B **££**
(📞 01834-849727; www.stlawrencecountryguesthouse.co.uk; Gumfreston; s/d from £50/84; P📶) Set in 7.5 hectares of gardens, pasture and woodland, this tranquil B&B offers spacious rooms, refined elegance and wonderful sea views. The guesthouse is 1.5 miles from Tenby, just off the B4318 west of town.

Penally Abbey   HOTEL **£££**
(📞 01834-843033; www.penally-abbey.com; Penally; r £150-188; P📶♨) Set on a hillside overlooking the sea, this lovely old house offers high ceilings, roaring fires and leather Chesterfields. Rooms in the adjacent Coach House have a more cottagey feel. Penally is 2 miles southwest of Tenby, off the A4139.

St Brides Spa Hotel   HOTEL **£££**
(📞 01834-812304; www.stbridesspahotel.com; St Brides Hill, Saundersfoot; s/d from £130/160; P@📶♨) Pembrokeshire's premier spa hotel offers the chance to relax after a massage in a small hydrotherapy pool overlooking the beach, before dining in **Cliff restaurant** (mains £16-20). The bedrooms are stylish and modern, in colours that evoke the seaside. It's in Saundersfoot, 3 miles north of Tenby.

✘ Eating

D Fecci & Sons   FISH & CHIPS **£**
(Lower Frog St; mains £4-7; ⏱ 11.30am-9pm) Eating fish and chips on the beach is a British tradition, and D Fecci & Sons is a Tenby institution, having been in business since 1935. The same family runs the traditional Fecci's Ice Cream Parlour around the corner on St George's St.

WORTH A TRIP

FOLLY FARM

If your toddler's tolerance for castles and churches is wearing thin, this combination **zoo/petting farm/funfair/amusement park** (www.folly-farm. co.uk; A478, Begelly; adult/child £11/9.25; ⏱ 10am-5pm) could be the antedote. Once they've tired of the pirate ship, dragon playground and ride-on diggers, there's a large menagerie to explore, featuring lemurs, meerkats, monkeys, giraffes, zebras and an excellent penguin enclosure.

Folly Farm is 6 miles north of Tenby.

Blue Ball Restaurant   INTERNATIONAL **££**
(📞 01834-843038; www.theblueballrestaurant. co.uk; Upper Frog St; mains £12-22; ⏱ 6-9pm Wed-Sat, 12.30-2.30pm Sun) Polished wood, old timber beams and exposed brickwork create a cosy, rustic atmosphere in what is Tenby's best restaurant. The menu makes good use of local produce, notably seafood.

Mooring   CAFE, BISTRO **££**
(📞 01834-842502; www.themooringtenby.com; 15 High St; lunch £5-8, dinner £14-17; ⏱ 10.30am-4pm Sun & Mon, to 9pm Tue-Sat) Although it's firmly anchored to the High St, this upmarket but casual eatery drifts breezily from a daytime cafe serving comfort food (sandwiches, cakes, bangers and mash, mac cheese) into a sophisticated bistro after dark.

Plantagenet House   MODERN WELSH **£££**
(📞 01834-842350; www.plantagenettenby.co.uk; Quay Hill; lunch £9-13, dinner £16-27; ⏱ noon-2.30pm Sat & Sun, 6-10pm Fri & Sat, extended hours in summer) Atmosphere-wise, this place instantly impresses – perfect for a romantic, candle-lit dinner. Tucked down an alley in Tenby's oldest house, it's dominated by an immense 12th-century Flemish hearth. The menu ranges from seafood to organic beef.

ℹ Information

National Park Centre (📞 01834-845040; www.pembrokeshirecoast.org.uk; South Pde; ⏱ 9.30am-5pm daily Apr-Sep, 10am-3.30pm Mon-Sat Oct-Mar)

Tourist Office (📞 01834-842402; www.visit-pembrokeshire.com; Upper Park Rd; ⏱ 9am-5pm Mon-Sat Sep-Jun, daily Jul & Aug)

❶ Getting There & Away

BUS

➜ The bus station is next to the tourist office on Upper Park Rd.

➜ Buses head to/from Saundersfoot (route 351/352/361/381; £2.10, 13 minutes), Manorbier (349; £3.10, 20 minutes), Pembroke (349; £3.80, 43 minutes), Haverfordwest (349/381; £5.20, 1½ hours) and Narberth (381; £3.75, 42 minutes).

➜ National Express coach destinations include Carmarthen (£5.80, 45 minutes), Swansea (£8.60, 1½ hours), Cardiff (£18, 3¼ hours), Birmingham (£40, six hours) and London Victoria (£29, seven hours).

TRAIN

There are direct services to/from Cardiff (£25, three hours), Swansea (£15, 1¾ hours), Carmarthen (£9, 50 minutes), Narberth (£4.70, 19 minutes) and Pembroke (£5.30, 20 minutes).

West of Tenby

Craggy, lichen-spotted **Manorbier Castle** (www.manorbiercastle.co.uk; adult/child £5/3; ⊙10am-5pm Apr-Sep) guards a little village of leafy, twisting lanes nestled above a lovely sandy beach, 5.5 miles southwest of Tenby. **Manorbier YHA** (✆0845 371 9031; www.yha. org.uk; site/dm/d £10/16/48; ℗ 🛜) occupies a futuristic ex–Ministry of Defence building, 1.5 miles east of the village centre, on a remote clifftop.

Further west, the National Trust's **Stackpole Estate** (NT; ✆01646-661359; www.nationaltrust.org.uk; ⊙dawn-dusk) **FREE** takes in 8 miles of coast, including two fine beaches (**Barafundle Bay** and **Broad Haven**), a wooded valley and the **Bosherston Lily Ponds**, a system of artificial lakes famous for their spectacular display of water lilies in summer.

From the car park at the end of St Govan's Head road, steps hacked into the rock lead down to tiny **St Govan's Chapel**, wedged into a slot in the cliffs just out of reach of the sea. The chapel dates from the 5th or 6th century, and is named for an itinerant 6th-century Irish preacher. The car park at **Stack Rocks**, 3 miles to the west, gives access to even more spectacular cliff scenery, including the **Green Bridge of Wales**, the biggest natural arch in the country. Unfortunately, this part of the coast lies within an army firing range, so you won't be able to access these sights if the red flags on the access roads are flying.

Wild and windblown **Freshwater West**, a 2-mile strand of golden sand and silver shingle backed by acres of dunes, is Wales' best surf beach, sitting wide open to the Atlantic rollers. But beware – although great for surfing, its big waves, powerful rips *and* quicksand make it dangerous for swimming; several people have drowned here and the beach has year-round red-flag status. Scenes from *Harry Potter and the Deathly Hallows* and Ridley Scott's *Robin Hood* were filmed here.

At the southern head of the Milford Haven waterway, the village of **Angle** feels a long way off the beaten track. The main attraction is the tiny beach at **West Angle Bay**, which has great views across the mouth of Milford Haven to St Ann's Head, and offers good coastal walks with lots of rock pools to explore.

The **Coastal Cruiser bus** (www.pembrokeshiregreenways.co.uk; ⊙daily May-Sep) loops in both directions between Pembroke, Angle, Freshwater West, Bosherston and Stackpole, terminating at Pembroke Dock.

Carew

Looming romantically over the River Carew, its gaping windows reflected in the glassy water, craggy **Carew Castle** (www.carewcastle.com; adult/child £4.75/3.50; ⊙10am-5pm Apr-Oct) is an impressive sight. These rambling limestone ruins range from functional 12th-century fortification to Elizabethan country house. Abandoned in 1690, the castle is now inhabited by a large number of bats. A summer program of events includes re-enactments and open-air theatre.

Buses head here from Pembroke Dock (route 361; £3.15, eight minutes), Tenby (360/361; £3.25, 17 minutes) and Saundersfoot (361; £2.65, 34 minutes).

The castle ticket also gives you admission to Carew Tidal Mill, the only intact tidal mill in Wales.

Near the castle entrance is the 11th-century Carew Cross, one of the grandest of its kind – around 4m tall and covered in psychedelic Celtic squiggles.

Pembroke (Penfro)

POP 7560

Pembroke is not much more than a single street of neat Georgian and Victorian houses sitting beneath a whopping great castle.

⊙ Sights

Pembroke Castle
CASTLE

(🖰01646-684585; www.pembrokecastle.co.uk; Main St; adult/child £5/4, guided tours £1.50 May-Aug; ⊙10am-5pm) Spectacular and forbidding Pembroke Castle is the oldest in West Wales. It was the home of the earls of Pembroke for more than 300 years and the birthplace of Henry VII, the first Tudor king. A fort was established here in 1093, but most of the present buildings date from the 12th and 13th centuries. It's a great place for kids to explore – wall walks and passages run from tower to tower, and there are vivid exhibitions detailing the castle's history.

Falconry displays and costumed re-enactments are held in summer. Phone ahead for guided tour times.

⊨ Sleeping

Tregenna
B&B ££

(🖰01646-621525; www.tregennapembroke.co.uk; 7 Upper Lamphey Rd; s/d £50/65; P🐾🛜) When the treats in the room include a sewing kit, shaving kit, mini toothbrush and toothpaste, bottled water and Welsh cakes, you know you're somewhere special. It's a newly built house, so everything's modern, shiny and crisp.

Lovesgrove
HOTEL ££

(🖰01646-687514; www.lovesgrove.com; A477; s/d from £60/70; P🛜) Is it a small hotel, a large B&B or a particularly upmarket motel? Whatever label you settle on, Lovesgrove is a handsome choice, with large, modern rooms and a rural setting on the main road east of Pembroke Dock.

✕ Eating

★ Food at Williams
CAFE £

(www.foodatwilliams.co.uk; 18 Main St; mains £5-8; ⊙9am-5.30pm Mon-Sat, 10am-3.30pm Sun; 🛜) Pop into this bright, cheerful cafe in the morning for a cooked breakfast, and then again in the afternoon for a glass of wine and Welsh cheese platter on the terrace.

Old King's Arms Hotel
PUB ££

(🖰01646-683611; www.oldkingsarmshotel.co.uk; Main St; mains £14-23) Dark timber beams, ochre walls and polished copperware lend a country kitchen atmosphere to the restaurant here. The locally sourced protein (Welsh lamb, Carmarthen ham) comes accompanied with enough potatoes and vegetables to fill even a Tudor king.

ⓘ Information

Tourist Office (🖰01437-776499; Commons Rd; ⊙10am-5pm Tue, Thu & Fri, to 1pm Wed & Sat; @)

ⓘ Getting There & Away

BOAT

Irish Ferries (🖰08717-300 500; www.irishferries.com) has two sailings a day on the four-hour route between Pembroke Dock and Rosslare in the southeast of Ireland (car and driver from £79, foot passenger from £35).

BUS

➤ Bus 349 heads to Tenby (£3.80, 43 minutes) and Haverfordwest (£4.30, 53 minutes), while the Coastal Cruiser loops around Angle, Freshwater West and Stackpole (£2.90).

➤ National Express destinations include Carmarthen (£5.80, one hour), Swansea (£8.80, two hours), Cardiff (£18, 3½ hours), Birmingham (£40, 6¼ hours) and London Victoria (£26, 7¼ hours).

TRAIN

Direct trains run to/from Swansea (£15, two hours), Carmarthen (£9, 1¼ hours), Narberth (£8.10, 45 minutes), Tenby (£5.30, 20 minutes) and Manorbier (£3.40, 11 minutes).

Marloes Sands & Around

The fishing village of **Dale** sits on a rugged and remote peninsula, forming the northern head of the Milford Haven waterway. As you round beautiful **St Ann's Head**, all vestiges of the harbour's heavy industry and, indeed, human habitation disappear from view. Little **Westdale Bay** follows and then the impressive sweep of **Marloes Sands**, with views over tidal **Gateholm Island** – a major Iron Age Celtic settlement where the

---

HALEN MÔR

The industrial town of Milford Haven needn't trouble your itinerary but if you're passing through, it's well worth stopping in at **Halen Môr** (🖰01646-693017; 2 Agamemnon House, The Quay; lunch £8-12, dinner £12-16; ⊙noon-2.30pm daily, 6-9.30pm Mon-Sat) down by the marina. There's a tapas-style 'bites' menu, ciabatta and wraps for lunch, and interesting mains including daily seafood specials and lots of Greek, Spanish and Moroccan flavours.

remains of 130 hut circles have been found. Housed in a group of National Trust–owned farm buildings near the Pembrokeshire Coast Path, **Marloes Sands YHA** (✆0845 371 9333; www.yha.org.uk; Runwayskiln, Marloes; dm/tw from £21/60; ☻Easter-Oct; Ⓟ🔧) offers a mixture of dorms and private rooms.

Around Wooltack Point is **Martin's Haven**, the tiny harbour that is the jumping-off point for boat trips to the Skomer Island and Skokholm Island nature reserves. An unstaffed **information room** here has displays on the marine environment, including touchscreen displays of wildlife activity around Skomer. Look for a 7th-century **Celtic cross** set into the wall outside.

Further around the headland the cliffs change from red to black and **Musselwick Sands** comes in to view: a large, sandy beach with plenty of craggy inlets to explore.

Solva (Solfach)

POP 710

With its colourfully painted cottages, art galleries and inviting pubs, Solva is a North Pembrokeshire gem. Lower Solva sits at the head of a peculiar L-shaped **harbour**, where the water drains away completely at low tide leaving its flotilla of yachts tilted onto the sand. **Clifftop walks** provide wonderful views over the village and surrounding coastline.

Buses head to Solva from Marloes (route 400; £3.30, 1½ hours), Martin's Haven (400; £4.05, 1¼ hours), St Davids (400/411; £1.70, 10 minutes) and Haverfordwest (411; £3.05, 30 minutes).

St Davids (Tyddewi)

POP 1410

Charismatic St Davids (yes, it has dropped the apostrophe from its name) is Britain's smallest city, its status ensured by the magnificent 12th-century cathedral that marks Wales' holiest site. The birth and burial site of the nation's patron saint, St Davids has been a place of pilgrimage for 1500 years.

The setting itself has a numinous presence. With the sea just beyond the horizon on three sides, you're constantly surprised by glimpses of it at the ends of streets. Then there are those strangely shaped hills in the distance, sprouting from an ancient landscape.

Dewi Sant (St David) founded a monastic community here in the 6th century. In 1124 Pope Calixtus II declared that two pilgrimages to St Davids were the equivalent of one to Rome, and three were equal to one to Jerusalem. The cathedral has seen a constant stream of visitors ever since.

Today St Davids attracts hordes of nonreligious pilgrims too, drawn by the laid-back vibe and the excellent hiking, surfing and wildlife-watching in the surrounding area.

◉ Sights & Activities

★**St Davids Cathedral** CATHEDRAL (www.stdavidscathedral.org.uk; suggested donation £3, tours £4; ☻8.30am-6pm Mon-Sat, 12.45-5.30pm Sun) Hidden in a hollow and behind high walls, St Davids Cathedral is intentionally unassuming. The valley site was chosen in the vain hope that the church would be overlooked by Viking raiders, but it was ransacked at least seven times. Yet once you pass through the gatehouse that separates it from the town and its stone walls come into view, it's as imposing as any of its contemporaries.

Built on the site of a 6th-century chapel, the building dates mainly from the 12th to the 14th centuries. Extensive works were carried out in the 19th century by Sir George Gilbert Scott (architect of London's Albert Memorial and St Pancras) to stabilise the building. The distinctive **west front**, with its four pointed towers of purple stone, dates from this period.

The atmosphere inside is one of great antiquity. As you enter the **nave**, the oldest surviving part of the cathedral, the first things you notice are the sloping floor and the outward lean of the massive, purplish-grey pillars linked by semicircular Norman Romanesque arches, a result of subsidence. Above is a richly carved 16th-century oak ceiling, adorned with pendants and bosses.

At the far end of the nave is a delicately carved 14th-century Gothic **pulpitum** (screen), separating it from the magnificent **choir**. Check out the mischievous carved figures on the 16th-century misericords (under the seats), one of which depicts pilgrims being seasick over the side of a boat. Don't forget to look up at the colourfully painted lantern tower above (those steel tie rods around the walls were installed in the 19th century to hold the structure together).

Between the choir and the high altar is the object of all those religious pilgrimages – a **shrine** containing the bones of St David and St Justinian. Destroyed during the Reformation, it was restored and rededicated in 2012.

St Davids

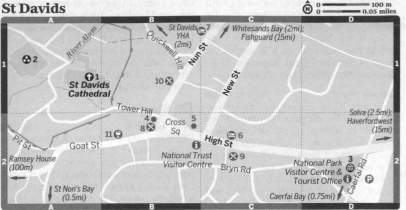

Accessed from the north wall of the nave, the **Treasury** displays vestments and religious paraphernalia crafted from precious metals and stones.

The St Davids Cathedral Festival starts on the bank holiday weekend at the end of May and continues for 10 days, with classical musicians performing within the hallowed walls. Many other concerts are performed at the cathedral throughout the year.

Bishop's Palace
RUIN

(Cadw; www.cadw.wales.gov.uk; adult/child £3.50/2.65; ⏱10am-4pm) This atmospheric ruined palace was begun at the same time as the cathedral just across the river, but its final, imposing form owes most to Henry de Gower, bishop from 1327 to 1347. Its most distinctive feature is the arcaded parapet that runs around the courtyard, decorated with a chequerboard pattern of purple and yellow stone blocks. The corbels that support the arches are richly adorned with a menagerie of carved figures.

The palace courtyard provides a spectacular setting for open-air plays in summer.

Oriel y Parc
GALLERY

(Landscape Gallery; ☎01437-720392; www.oriel-yparc.co.uk; High St; ⏱10am-4.30pm) Occupying a bold, semicircular, environmentally friendly building on the edge of town, this gallery is a winning collaboration between the Pembrokeshire Coast National Park Authority and the National Museum Wales. Not only does it function as a tourist office and national park visitor centre, it houses changing exhibitions from the museum's art collection.

St Davids

◎ Top Sights
1 St Davids Cathedral	A1

◎ Sights
2 Bishop's Palace	A1
3 Oriel y Parc	D2

◐ Activities, Courses & Tours
4 Thousand Islands Expeditions	B2
5 TYF Adventure	B2
Voyages of Discovery	(see 5)

⊜ Sleeping
6 Coach House	C2
7 Y Glennydd	C1

⊗ Eating
8 Bishops	B2
9 Cwtch	C2
10 Sampler	B1

◎ Drinking & Nightlife
11 Farmer's Arms	B2

St Non's Bay
RUIN, CHURCH

Immediately south of St Davids, this is a ruggedly beautiful spot, named after St David's mother and traditionally accepted as his birthplace. A path leads down to the 13th-century **ruins of St Non's Chapel**. Only the base of the walls remains, along with a stone marked with a cross within a circle, believed to date from the 7th century. Standing stones in the surrounding field suggest that the chapel may have been built within an ancient pagan stone circle.

On the approach to the ruins is a pretty little holy well. The spring is said to have emerged at the moment of the saint's birth and the water is believed to have curative powers.

Nearby, the Catholic **Chapel of Our Lady and St Non** was built in 1935 out of the stones of ruined religious buildings. Its dimensions echo those of the original chapel.

Ramsey Island   WILDLIFE RESERVE

Ramsey Island lies off the headland to the west of St Davids, ringed by dramatic sea cliffs and an offshore armada of rocky islets and reefs. The island is a Royal Society for the Protection of Birds reserve, famous for its large breeding population of choughs – members of the crow family with glossy black feathers and distinctive red bills and legs – and for its grey seals.

You can reach the island by boat from the tiny harbour at St Justinian's, 2 miles west of St Davids. Longer boat trips run up to 20 miles offshore, to the edge of the Celtic Deep, to spot whales, porpoises and dolphins. What you'll see depends on the weather and the time of year: July to September are the best months, although seabirds are at their most numerous from April to July. Porpoises are seen on most trips, dolphins on four out of five, and there's a 40% chance of seeing whales. The most common species is the minke, but pilot whales, fin whales and orcas have also been spotted.

Thousand Islands Expeditions (☑ 01437-721721; www.thousandislands.co.uk; Cross Sq) is the only operator permitted to land day trippers on the island (adult/child £17/8.50). It has a range of other boat trips, including 2½-hour whale- and dolphin-spotting cruises (£60/30) and one-hour jet-boat trips (£25/12).

Voyages of Discovery (☑ 01437-721911; www.ramseyisland.co.uk; 1 High St; ⊙ Apr-Oct) offers a similar selection of cruises, without the island landings. For a racier experience, try **Venture Jet** (☑ 01348-8377764; www.venturejet.co.uk; ⊙ Apr-Oct), which bills itself as a 'New Zealand jet, Pembrokeshire-style'. Trips range from the 90-minute Ramsey Island Adventure (adult/child £26/14) to a 3½-hour Offshore Adventure (£64/38).

🛏 Sleeping

St Davids YHA   HOSTEL £

(☑ 0845 371 9141; www.yha.org.uk; Llaethdy; dm/r £22/52; ⊙ Apr-Oct; P �‚ ⊛) If you're an enthusiastic walker or you have your own transport, this former farmhouse tucked beneath Carn Llidi, 2 miles northwest of town, is a wonderful option. The cow sheds now house snug dorms and twins, and an inviting communal kitchen.

Caerfai Bay Caravan & Tent Park CAMPSITE £

(☑ 01437-720274; www.caerfaibay.co.uk; 2-person sites from £15; ⊙ Mar-Nov; P @ 🙚) A 15-minute walk south of St Davids, this large campsite has good facilities and exceptional views across St Brides Bay.

Ramsey House   B&B ££

(☑ 01437-720321; www.ramseyhouse.co.uk; Lower Moor; r £105-115; P 🙚) The young owners have fashioned a boutique-style B&B from their new house on the outskirts of the little city. The six rooms feature bold wallpaper, matching chandeliers and stylish bathrooms.

Coach House   B&B ££

(☑ 01437-720632; www.thecoachhouse.biz; 15 High St; s/d from £55/80; 🙚) The bright, simple rooms are just part of the Coach House's appeal. Friendly and helpful hosts, excellent breakfasts and its central location all conspire to make it one of St Davids' better options.

COASTEERING

If you fancy a spot of rock climbing, gully scrambling, cave exploration, wave riding and cliff jumping, all rolled together, then try coasteering. More or less conceived on the Pembrokeshire Coast, this demanding activity is the mainstay of the local adventure-sports scene. It's also risky, so take guidance from an instructor.

Celtic Quest (☑ 01348-881530; www.celticquest.co.uk; per person from £39) Coasteering specialists, taking to the cliffs near Abereiddy.

Preseli Venture (☑ 01348-837709; www.preseliventure.co.uk) Has its own excellent backpackers lodge near Mathry, between St Davids and Fishguard. Activities include coasteering, sea kayaking, surfing and coastal hiking.

TYF Adventure (☑ 01437-721611; www.tyf.com; 1 High St, St Davids) Organises coasteering, surfing, sea-kayaking and rock-climbing trips.

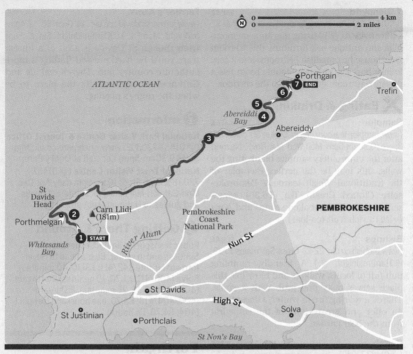

🏃 Walking Tour
Whitesands to Porthgain

START WHITESANDS
END PORTHGAIN
LENGTH 10 MILES; FOUR TO SIX HOURS

Covering a beautiful but remote stretch of coast from popular Whitesands Bay near St Davids to the historic port of Porthgain, this rewarding walk takes you over rugged headlands and past dramatic cliffs, pretty coves and flooded quarries. It's a taxing route with several steep descents and ascents but it's well worth the effort. Bring provisions, as it's a long way between villages.

Start out at the busy surfer hang-out **1 Whitesands Bay** and head northwest onto wild and rocky St Davids Head. The start of the route is fairly easy with a good path, wide open views and craggy volcanic outcrops to admire. The only signs of human habitation here are ancient, with the simple **2 neolithic burial chamber** on the headland predating the surrounding remnants of Celtic forts.

The path soon becomes more rugged with a rock scramble down to and up from the lovely little cove at **3 Aber-pwll**. Continue on past crumbling cliffs to **4 Abereiddi**, looking out for seals in the coves, gannets and possibly porpoises diving for fish out at sea. The beach at Abereiddi is famous for its black sand full of tiny fossils. Ruined quarry buildings and slate workers' cottages flank the path beyond the beach that leads to the **5 Blue Lagoon**, a deep turquoise flooded slate quarry now popular with coasteerers and, in early September, cliff divers from all over the world who compete here, diving 27m into the icy water below.

The half-hour walk from Abereiddi to Porthgain is one of the best stretches along the entire coast path, following a clifftop plateau past the often-deserted beach at **6 Traeth Llyfn**. A long flight of steep metal stairs leads down to the golden sand, but beware of strong undercurrents and the tide, which can cut off parts of the beach from the steps. Continue on for the last descent into the tiny harbour of **7 Porthgain**, where you can reward yourself with some superb food or a drink at the pub.

Y Glennydd B&B ££
(✆ 01437-720576; www.yglennydd.co.uk; 51 Nun St; s/d from £45/70; ✿) Mixing maritime memorabilia and antique oak furniture, this 10-room guesthouse has smallish bedrooms and a cosy lounge bar. The cheapest double room has a private bathroom entered from the corridor.

✗ Eating & Drinking

Sampler CAFE £
(www.sampler-tearoom.co.uk; 17 Nun St; cakes £2-3; ◷ 10.30am-5pm Mon-Wed Mar-Nov) Named after the embroidery samples blanketing the walls, this may be the perfect exemplar of the traditional Welsh tearoom. Pembrokeshire Clotted Cream Tea (£6.30) comes served with freshly baked scones and *bara brith* (a rich fruit tea-loaf).

Bishops PUB ££
(www.thebish.co.uk; 22-23 Cross Sq; mains £7-19; ◷ 11am-midnight; ✿) A friendly, rambling pub full of locals, walkers and blow-ins, this place serves tasty pub grub with a smile. There's a roaring fire in winter, a decent pint on offer and great views of the cathedral from the beer garden.

Cwtch MODERN WELSH £££
(✆ 01437-720491; www.cwtchrestaurant.co.uk; 22 High St; 2-/3-courses £22/26; ◷ 6-9.30pm Wed-Sat, noon-2.30pm Sun, daily high season, closed Jan–mid-Feb) Stone walls and wooden beams mark this out as a sense-of-occasion place, yet there's a snugness that lives up to its name (*cwtch* means a 'cosy place' or a 'cuddle'). There's an emphasis on local produce, so expect plenty of fresh seafood on the menu.

WORTH A TRIP

MELIN TREGWYNT

For more than 100 years the same family has run **this traditional woollen mill** (✆ 01348-891288; www.melintregwynt.co.uk; ◷ 9.30am-5pm Mon-Sat, 11am-4.30pm Sun) that churns out some of Wales' best blankets, cushions and upholstery fabrics. New designs have brought the traditional weaves bang up to date and the full range now includes clothing, bags and lampshades, all of which are on display in the mill shop. You can see the looms and giant water wheel in action on weekdays, and there's a small cafe on-site. It's near Abermawr; follow the signs from the A487.

Farmer's Arms PUB
(www.farmersstdavids.co.uk; 14 Goat St; ◷ 4pm-midnight Mon-Fri, 11.30am-midnight Sat & Sun) Even though St Davids is a bit of a tourist trap, you'd be hard-pressed finding a more authentic country pub. There's real ale and Guinness on tap, and it's the place to be when the rugby's playing.

ⓘ Information

National Park Visitor Centre & Tourist Office (✆ 01437-720392; www.orielyparc.co.uk; High St; ◷ 9.30am-5pm) Located at Oriel y Parc.

National Trust Visitor Centre (✆ 01437-720385; High St; ◷ 10am-5pm daily Apr-Dec, Mon-Sat Jan-Mar) Sells local-interest books and guides to National Trust properties.

ⓘ Getting There & Around

Public transport is limited, especially on Sundays and in winter. Buses head to Haverfordwest (route 342/411; £3.30, 40 minutes), Solva (400/411; £1.70, 10 minutes), Porthgain (404/413; £2.35, 25 minutes), Fishguard (400/404/413; £3.70, one hour) and Newport (404; £4.70, 1½ hours).

Porthgain

POP 30

For centuries the tiny harbour of Porthgain consisted of little more than a few sturdy cottages wedged into a rocky cove. In the mid-19th century it began to prosper as the port for shipping slate quarried just down the coast at Abereiddy, and by the 1870s its own deposits of granite and fine clay had put it on the map as a source of building stone. The post-WWI slump burst the bubble, and the sturdy stone quays and overgrown brick storage 'bins' are all that remain.

Despite having been an industrial harbour, Porthgain is surprisingly picturesque and today it is home to a couple of art galleries and restaurants.

🛏 Sleeping & Eating

★ Old School Hostel HOSTEL £
(✆ 01348-831800; www.theoldschoolhostel.co.uk; Ffordd-yr-Afon, Trefin; dm/s/d from £16/21/36; P✿🌢) ✔ Set in a converted school, this is an exemplar of the new breed of independent, brightly painted, personably run backpackers, with six appealing little rooms. It's in the village of Trefin, 2 miles east of Porthgain.

Shed SEAFOOD ££
(☑01348-831518; www.theshedporthgain.co.uk; mains £10-17; ☺10am-9pm Mon & Wed-Sat, to 5pm Tue & Sun, extended hours in summer) Housed in a converted machine shop right by the little harbour, the Shed describes itself as a 'fish and chip bistro', which nicely understates the quality of the local seafood served.

Sloop Inn PUB ££
(☑01348-831449; www.sloop.co.uk; mains £7-21; ☺11.30am-9.30pm Mon-Fri, 9.30am-9.30pm Sat & Sun; ☜) With wooden tables worn smooth by many a bended elbow, old photos of Porthgain in its industrial heyday and interesting nautical clutter all over the place, the Sloop is a cosy and deservedly popular pub. The hearty home-cooked meals will satisfy even the hungriest Coast Path walker.

❶ Getting There & Away

Buses head to/from St Davids (route 404/413; £2.35, 25 minutes), Abereiddy (404; £1.40, 11 minutes), Trevin (404/413; £1.20, seven minutes), Fishguard (404/413; £3.50, 50 minutes) and Newport (404; £4.20, one hour).

Fishguard (Abergwaun)

POP 3420

Perched on a headland between its modern ferry port and former fishing harbour, Fishguard is often overlooked by travellers, most of whom pass through on the way to or from Ireland. It doesn't have any sights as such, but it's an appealing little town and was the improbable setting for the last foreign invasion of Britain.

Fishguard is split into three distinct areas. The main town is centred on Market Sq, where the buses stop. To the east is the picturesque harbour of the Lower Town (Y Cwm), which was used as a setting for the 1971 film version of *Under Milk Wood*. The train station and ferry terminal lie a mile to the northwest of the town centre in Goodwick.

Much that goes on in Fishguard happens in the Town Hall on Market Sq. The tourist office is here, as is the library (handy for free internet access) and the market hall. It hosts a general market on Thursday mornings and a farmers market on Saturday mornings.

THE LAST INVASION OF BRITAIN
....

While Hastings in 1066 may get all the press, the last invasion of Britain was actually at Carregwastad Point, northwest of Fishguard, on 22 February 1797. The ragtag collection of 1400 French mercenaries and bailed convicts had intended to land at Bristol and march to Liverpool, keeping English troops occupied while France mounted an invasion of Ireland. Bad weather blew them ashore at Carregwastad, where, after scrambling up a steep cliff, they set about looting for food and drink.

The invaders had hoped that the Welsh peasants would rise up to join them in revolutionary fervour but, not surprisingly, their drunken pillaging didn't endear them to the locals. The French were quickly seen off by volunteer 'yeoman' soldiers, with help from the people of Fishguard including, most famously, one Jemima Nicholas who, armed with a pitchfork, single-handedly captured 12 mercenaries.

◉ Sights & Activities

Last Invasion Gallery EXHIBITION
(Library, Market Sq; ☺9.30am-5pm Mon-Sat Apr-Sep, 9.30am-5pm Mon-Fri, to 1pm Sat Oct-Mar) FREE Inspired by the Bayeux Tapestry, which recorded the 1066 Norman invasion at Hastings, the Fishguard Tapestry was commissioned in 1997 to commemorate the bicentenary of the failed Fishguard invasion. It uses a similar cartoonish style as Bayeux' (albeit with less rude bits) and tells the story in the course of 37 frames and 30m of cloth. A film about its making demonstrates what a huge undertaking it was.

Kayak-King KAYAKING
(☑07967 010203; www.kayak-king.com; tour £45) Twice-daily sea-kayaking tours, tailored to either family groups or adults.

Mike Mayberry Kayaking KAYAKING
(☑01348-874699; www.mayberrykayaking.co.uk; ☺May-Sep) Offers sea-kayaking tours for families and active adults.

WORTH A TRIP

CASTELL HENLLYS IRON AGE FORT

If you've ever wondered what a Celtic village looked, felt and smelt like, take a trip back in time to Castell Henllys (www.castellhenllys.com; Felindre Farchog; adult/child £4.75/3.50; ☺10am-5pm Apr-Oct, to 3pm Nov-Mar), 4 miles east of Newport. From about 600 BC and right through the Roman occupation there was a thriving Celtic settlement here, and the whole thing has been reconstructed on its original foundations. Costumed staff bring the site to life, stoking the fires and performing traditional crafts.

🛏 Sleeping

★ Manor Town House B&B ££
(☎01348-873260; www.manortownhouse.com; 11 Main St; s/d from £65/85; 🕿) This graceful Georgian house has a lovely garden terrace where you can sit and gaze over the harbour. The young owners are charm personified and the house has been tastefully renovated.

Pentower B&B ££
(☎01348-874462; www.pentower.co.uk; Tower Hill; s/d from £50/80; P) Built by Sir Evan Jones, the architect who designed the harbour, this rambling home is perched on a hill at the edge of town, overlooking his creation. The house is pretty and unassuming, apart from the grand tiled atrium. Rooms are spacious and romantic.

ℹ Information

Tourist Office (☎01437-776636; www.visitpembrokeshire.com; Market Sq, Town Hall; ☺9am-5pm Mon-Fri; @)

ℹ Getting There & Away

BOAT
Stena Line (☎08447 707070; www.stenaline.co.uk; car & driver from £79; foot passenger £30) Has two regular ferries a day, year-round, between Rosslare in the southeast of Ireland and Fishguard Harbour.

BUS
Buses head to/from St Davids (route 400/404/413; £3.70, one hour), Porthgain (404/413; £3.50, 50 minutes), Newport (404/405/412; £2.45, 15 minutes), Haverfordwest (343/344/412; £3.40, 30 minutes) and Cardigan (405/412; £3.75, 1¼ hours).

TRAIN
Direct trains run to Fishguard Harbour from Cardiff (£25, 2½ hours), Swansea (£15, two hours) and Carmarthen (£9.20, 55 minutes).

Newport (Trefdraeth)
POP 850

In stark contrast to the industrial city of Newport near the English border, the Pembrokeshire Newport is a pretty cluster of flower-bedecked cottages huddled beneath a small, privately owned Norman castle. It sits at the foot of Mynydd Carningli (347m), a large bump on the seaward side of the Preseli Hills.

Newport makes a pleasant base for walks along the coastal path or south into the Preseli Hills, but it does get crowded in summer. At the northwest corner of the town is little Parrog Beach, dwarfed by Newport Sands (Traeth Mawr) across the river.

Right in town there's a little dolmen Carreg Coetan Arthur, which is well signposted from the main road just past the Golden Lion. At first glance it looks like its capstone is securely supported by four standing stones. A closer inspection suggests that some old magic has held it together all these thousands of years, as it's balanced on only two of them.

The back roads around the Preseli Hills and Cwm Gwaun offer some of the best on-road cycling in southwest Wales. Mountainbikers will find plenty of enjoyment on the ridges and bridleways.

🛏 Sleeping & Eating

★ Cnapan B&B ££
(☎01239-820575; www.cnapan.co.uk; East St; s/d £65/95, 2-/3-courses £26/32; ☺restaurant 6.30-9pm Wed-Mon; P🕿) Light-filled rooms and a flower-filled garden are offered at this listed Georgian town house above an accomplished restaurant. If you're game enough for the floral wallpaper, ask for room 4 – it's bigger. The dining room offers candlelight and crisp white linen tablecloths, but the service is friendly and relaxed.

Llys Meddyg B&B ££
(☎01239-820008; www.llysmeddyg.com; East St; s/d from £100/120, mains £17-20; ☺restaurant 6.30-9.30pm Wed-Sun; 🕿🎧🍴) This converted doctor's residence takes contemporary big-city cool and plonks it firmly by the seaside. Bedrooms are large and bright and decked

out in an unassuming but stylish manner. The restaurant is superb, with the seasonal menu reflecting the best of local produce.

Golden Lion   PUB **££**
(📍01239-820321; www.goldenlionpembrokeshire. co.uk; East St; s/d £70/90, mains £11-16; P 🛜 ♿) Sunny decor and pine furniture make for a warm atmosphere in this appealing country pub. In contrast to the modern bedrooms, there's a snug traditional bar with log fire and low ceilings downstairs, serving real ales and good-quality meals.

Lou Lou's   CAFE **£**
(www.loulouscafenewport.com; Market St; mains £8; ⊙10am-5pm Mon-Sat) This friendly little cafe offers a range of organic soups, salads, baguettes, tarts and the obligatory indulgent cakes. It's a wonderfully relaxed place with cheerful service.

ⓘ Information

National Park Information Centre & Tourist Office (📍01239-820912; Long St; ⊙10am-3.30pm Mon, Wed, Fri & Sat, extended hours in summer)

ⓘ Getting There & Away

Buses head to/from St Davids (route 404; £4.70, 1½ hours), Porthgain (404; £4.20, one hour), Fishguard (404/405/412; £2.45, 15 minutes), Cardigan (412; £3.35, 29 minutes) and Haverfordwest (412; £4.05, 50 minutes).

Preseli Hills (Mynydd Preseli)

The only upland area in Pembrokeshire Coast National Park – rising to a height of 536m at Foel Cwmcerwyn – the Preseli Hills are at the centre of a fascinating prehistoric landscape. Scattered with hill forts, standing stones and burial chambers, the area is famous as the source of the mysterious bluestones of Stonehenge.

The largest dolmen in Wales, **Pentre Ifan**, can be found here. This 4500-year-old burial chamber is set on a remote hillside 3 miles southeast of Newport (signposted from the A487). The 5m-long capstone, weighing more than 16 tonnes, is delicately poised on three tall, pointed, upright bluestones.

Hay-on-Wye & Mid-Wales

Best Places to Eat

➡ Checkers (p726)

➡ Hardwick (p718)

➡ Felin Fach Griffin (p715)

➡ St John's Place (p720)

➡ Ultracomida (p709)

Best Hikes

➡ Pen-y-Fan (p716)

➡ Ysgyryd Fawr (p718)

➡ Sugar Loaf (p718)

➡ Crug Hywell (p717)

➡ Fan Brycheiniog (p712)

Why Go?

The big draw here is the magnificent upland scenery of Brecon Beacons National Park, with book-loving Hay-on-Wye within its confines and food-loving Abergavenny on its doorstep. By contrast the Powys countryside is Wales at its most rural – a landscape of lustrous green fields, wooded river valleys and small market towns; it's the part that the Industrial Revolution missed. Isolated, sea-battered Ceredigion is home to some of country's most unspoiled beaches, as well as the exuberant hot spot of Aberystwyth. Thrills can be found outside urban areas along lonely trails in the hills and valleys, and on two wheels down narrow country lanes. Central Wales is thoroughly Welsh, with around 40% of people speaking the mother tongue – and more than 50% in Ceredigion.

When to Go

➡ If you're planning on walking, you'll get the most rain-free days between April and July; July and August are generally the warmest months.

➡ In May and June, the world's intelligentsia heads to Hay for its literary festival and for philosophy and music at HowTheLightGetsIn.

➡ In August, cap off the Green Man and Brecon Jazz music festivals with a spot of bog snorkelling.

➡ As the weather starts to cool, fill up at the Abergavenny Food Festival in September, and earn your laurel wreath in Llanwrtyd Wells' mountain-bike chariot race in January.

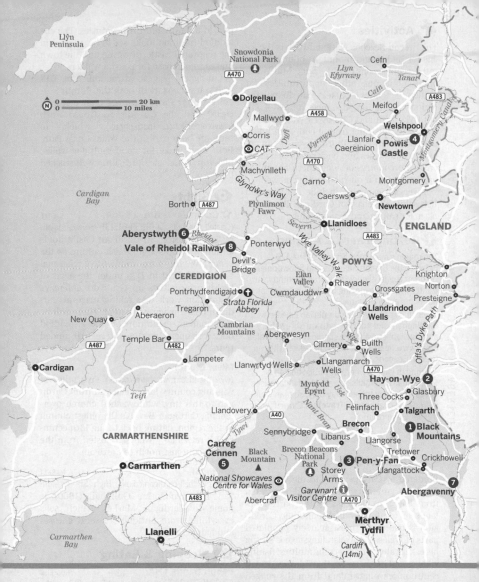

Hay-on-Wye & Mid-Wales Highlights

1 Soaking up the tranquillity of the remote Vale of Ewyas in the **Black Mountains** (p719)

2 Experiencing charming **Hay-on-Wye** (p719), a town surrounded by nature but infatuated with books

3 Conquering blustery **Pen-y-Fan** (p716) peak in the heart of the Brecon Beacons

4 Admiring the treasures of India and the sculptured yew paths of **Powis Castle** (p726)

5 Gazing up at **Carreg Cennen** (p712), Wales' most dramatically positioned fortress

6 Revelling in the high culture and student-inspired high jinks that come together

by the seaside at **Aberystwyth** (p707)

7 Exploring a countryside seasoned with Wales' best restaurants in the fields around **Abergavenny** (p717)

8 Reliving the age of steam with a scenic ride to Devil's Bridge on the **Vale of Rheidol Railway** (p708)

🏃 Activities

The Brecon Beacons National Park is the focus for hiking and mountain biking (www.mtbbreconbeacons.co.uk) but Mid-Wales offers numerous other opportunities for outdoor activities. Walkers can follow the region's main long-distance routes – Offa's Dyke Path and Glyndŵr's Way national trails – for anything from a couple of hours to a couple of weeks. Touring cyclists can enjoy the quiet lanes and back roads that crisscross the countryside, and there are many opportunities for off-road cycling as well.

Rivers for canoeing include the Wye and Usk, while the coast of Cardigan Bay is the place for sailing and sea kayaking.

❶ Getting There & Around

The region's main road artery is the A470 between the Brecon Beacons and Snowdonia. On other roads, expect to be stuck behind farm tractors and slow-moving trucks; just relax, slow down and enjoy the view.

The main railway is the Cambrian Line between Birmingham and Aberystwyth via Shrewsbury and Machynlleth, and the scenic **Heart of Wales Line** (www.heart-of-wales.co.uk) skirts the Brecon Beacons.

Trying to get anywhere by public bus on a Sunday can be a fool's errand. Most local buses operate Monday to Saturday only, so plan your journey in advance with **Traveline Cymru** (www.traveline-cymru.info).

CEREDIGION

Bordered by Cardigan Bay to the west, buffeted by gun-metal waves and separated from Powys to the east by the barren uplands of the Cambrian Mountains, Ceredigion is one of the most sparsely populated parts of Wales. The Welsh language is strong here, kept alive in rural communities, fishing villages and in Aberystwyth, Wales' esteemed centre of learning. Inland from the rugged cliffs and the clean, isolated beaches, waterfalls and abbey ruins beckon travellers willing to get lost in the maze of narrow country lanes.

Cardigan (Aberteifi)

POP 4180

Cardigan's present sedate state belies its past greatness – it was the site of the first ever eisteddfod in 1176 and was a busy seaport in the 18th and 19th centuries. The eisteddfod tradition looks set to be revived in the renovated castle, however, and the town makes a good base for coastal walkers.

Cardigan's biggest attractions are DIY walks; it's the start of both the **Pembrokeshire Coast Path national trail** (nt.pcnpa.org.uk) and the **Ceredigion Coast Path** (www.ceredigioncoastpath.org.uk), which, in turn, are both part of the Wales Coast Path. Both trails make for good multiday walks; pick up maps at Cardigan's well-stocked tourist office.

◎ Sights

★**Cardigan Castle**   CASTLE
(Castell Aberteifi; ☎01239-615131; www.cardigan-castle.com; 2 Green St) Cardigan Castle holds an important place in Welsh culture as the venue for the first competitive National Eisteddfod, held in 1176 under the aegis of Welsh prince Rhys ap Gruffydd. Intensive restoration work was taking place at Cardigan Castle when we visited. There will be a permanent exhibition on the eisteddfod once it re-opens in 2015, and regular guided tours.

Mwnt Church   CHURCH
(www.friendsofmwntchurch.co.uk) Five miles of winding country lanes lead you from Cardigan to this tiny, whitewashed church overlooking Cardigan Bay. It's the oldest church in the region, dating back to the 13th century. It's reasonably well signposted from the roundabout just north of Cardigan.

Guildhall   MARKET
(www.guildhall-cardigan.co.uk; High St; ◎Mon-Sat) The neo-Gothic Guildhall (1860) is home to Cardigan Market, which sells everything from antiques to local cheeses and handicrafts.

🛏 Sleeping & Eating

Poppit Sands YHA   HOSTEL £
(☎0845 371 9037; www.yha.org.uk; dm £19, r with/without bathroom £47/42; ◎daily Jul & Aug, Tue-Sat Sep-Jun; ℗) Reached by the narrowest road imaginable, this hostel is tucked into a hillside overlooking a Blue Flag beach, 4 miles northwest of town. It makes a great base for cycling ventures along the disused railway that follows the river, plus trails near nearby Fishguard and Tregarron, and for water sports in nearby St Davids. There's a well-equipped guest kitchen.

★ **Fforest Camp** CAMPSITE ££
(⌨01239-623751; www.coldatnight.co.uk; Cilgerran; per 3-night stay from £300; ⊛) Perched on the edge of Teifi Marshes Nature Reserve, 2 miles south of Cardigan, just off the A478, Fforest's large nomad tents, threepis, geodesic domes, camp-shacks and crofters' cottages are a study in how to get close to nature without giving up your creature comforts. Cooking facilities are included and active adventures are organised on land and water.

Ty-Parc B&B B&B ££
(⌨01239-615452; www.ty-parc.com; Park Ave; s/d £50/65; 🅿�) Appealing Edwardian house on the western edge of town, featuring five bright en suite rooms decked out in cream shades, with thoughtful touches such as radios in the showers, and fresh flowers.

★ **25 Mile** MODERN WELSH ££
(⌨01239-623625; www.the25mile.com; 1 Pendre; mains £8-16; ⊙10am-9pm Mon-Sat; 🖋⊛) 🖉 All main ingredients at this 'local eating house' come from within a 25-mile radius, and the menu uses its seasonal produce in simple, beautifully crafted dishes that really hit the spot. The 25 Mile is an informal, friendly place where dog-walkers and families mingle, brought together by what is hands-down the best food in town.

ℹ Information

Tourist Office (⌨01239-613230; www.discoverceredigion.co.uk; Bath House Rd; ⊙10am-5pm) In the lobby of the Theatr Mwldan.

ℹ Getting There & Around

Hire bikes from **New Image Bicycles** (⌨01239-621275; www.bikebikebike.co.uk; 29-30 Pendre; per half-/full day £14/20; ⊙10am-5pm Mon-Sat).

Bus routes include X50 to Aberystwyth (£5.35, 1¾ hours); 407 to Poppit Sands (£1.50, 15 minutes); and 412 to Newport (£3.35, 29 minutes), Fishguard (£3.75, 45 minutes) and Haverfordwest (£4.90, 1½ hours).

Aberystwyth

POP 18,090

Hemmed in between two rocky heads – Pen Dinas and Constitution Hill – and skirted by a long stretch of pebbled beach, compact and cosmopolitan Aberystwyth ('Aber' to its friends) is one of Wales' prettiest towns. Its long promenade is lined with pastel-coloured Georgian buildings.

Aberystwyth is distinguished by the presence of its prestigious university and a correspondingly youthful vibe. It also has a strong Welsh heritage and a rebellious spirit: the now-ruined castle on the rocky headland was once occupied by national hero Owain Glyndŵr in defiance of the English. The town's history, coupled with its lively nightlife, dining scene and spectacular natural setting make Aberystwyth an essential stop along the Ceredigion coast.

⊙ Sights

National Library of Wales LIBRARY
(⌨01970-632800; www.llgc.org.uk; A487; ⊙9.30am-6pm Mon-Fri, to 5pm Sat) FREE One of the UK's six copyright libraries, the National Library holds an ever-increasing (by 100-plus crates per week!) collection of written material. The **Hengwrt Room** houses the Welsh literary Holy Grail – the 13th-century *Tintern Abbey Bible* and the Four Ancient Books, one of which is the 12th-century *Black Book of Carmarthen* (the oldest existing Welsh poetry collection). The World of Books exhibition charts the history of the written word in Wales, while the Gregynog Gallery features temporary displays.

Constitution Hill HILL
Constitution Hill rises from the northern end of the seafront Promenade and on a clear day you can see the Llŷn Peninsula from its blustery top. On the hilltop is a Victorian **camera obscura** (£1) – the world's largest – that allows you to spy on the people of Aberystwyth. If your, ahem, constitution is not up to walking up the hill, the 1896 **cliff railway** (Rheilffordd y Graig; ⌨01970-617642; www.aberystwythcliffrailway.co.uk; Cliff Tce; adult/child 1-way £3/2, return £4/2.50; ⊙10am-5pm Apr-Oct, shorter hours Nov-Mar) can carry you up. Albeit very, very slowly.

Ceredigion Museum MUSEUM
(⌨01970-633088; http://museum.ceredigion.gov.uk; Terrace Rd; ⊙10am-5pm Mon-Sat Apr-Sep, noon-4.30pm Mon-Sat Oct-Mar) FREE This Edwardian former music hall houses entertaining displays devoted to Aberystwyth's history. Exhibits include anything from Roman coins, farming equipment and knitted woollen knickers to Victorian fashion and the famous *Salem* painting, in which the face of the Devil is said to be hiding in the old lady's shawl.

🏃 Activities

⭐ Vale of Rheidol Railway   HERITAGE RAILWAY
(Rheilffordd Cwm Rheidol; ☎01970-625819; www.rheidolrailway.co.uk; Park Ave; adult/child return £18/6; ⏱up to 5 daily Feb-Dec) Old steam locomotives (built between 1923 and 1938), formerly laden with lead and timber, have been lovingly restored by volunteers. They chug for almost 12 miles high above the picturesque valley of the River Rheidol to Devil's Bridge in a cloud of coal smoke. The trip lasts an hour each way; check the timetable online.

Ystwyth Trail   CYCLING, WALKING
Suitable for cyclists and walkers, this 20-mile waymarked route starts from the footbridge on Riverside Tce. It follows for the most part an old rail line from Aberystwyth southeast to Tregaron, at the foot of the Cambrian Mountains. For the first 12 miles it shadows the River Ystwyth, and at the end it enters the Teifi Valley.

🛏 Sleeping & Eating

Maes-y-Môr   GUESTHOUSE £
(☎01970-639270; www.maesymor.co.uk; 25 Bath St; s/d £35/55; 🛜) Yes, that is a launderette. But don't be fooled: venture upstairs from the drying machine and you will find clean, bright, inviting rooms and a warm welcome. Breakfast is not included but there's a kitchen for guest use. A lockable shed is available for bicycles.

Gwesty Cymru   HOTEL ££
(☎01970-612252; www.gwestycymru.com; 19 Marine Tce; s/d from £80/100, mains £13-19, 2-course Sunday lunch from £16; 🛜) This gem of a hotel is a character-filled boutique property with eight stylish, homely rooms (though outside noise can be an issue in room 7). Local slate features throughout, and the elegant little restaurant downstairs serves imaginative dishes such as gingerbread-crusted lamb.

Aberystwyth

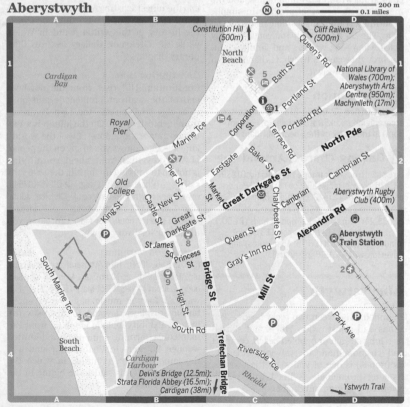

Glyn Garth   B&B ££
(☑01970-615050; www.glyngarth.pages.qpg.com; South Rd; s/d from £33/66; 🛜) A stone's throw from the sea (literally), this friendly B&B is a boon for budget-conscious and solo travellers. Chintzy decor aside, all rooms are cosy and spotless; cheaper rooms share facilities. A full cooked breakfast is thrown in.

★**Ultracomida**   TAPAS, DELI £
(☑01970-630686; www.ultracomida.co.uk; 31 Pier St; tapas £5-6.70; ⊙10am-5pm Mon, to 9pm Tue-Sat, noon-4pm Sun; 🖋) Perch at one of the immense communal tables at this deli-cum-tapas-bar and sample the love children of Cymru and España: authentic *fábada Asturiana* (savoury bean and smoked meat stew), Welsh rarebit, meatballs, *patatas bravas* (fried cubed potatoes and sauce) and deli platters featuring Spanish and Welsh cold cuts and cheeses. Chase down all this bounty with a wide range of Spanish wines, Asturian and Welsh ciders, and real ales.

Baravin   ITALIAN ££
(www.baravin.co.uk; Llys y Brenin, Terrace Rd; mains £8-13; ⊙10am-late Mon-Sat; 🛜) This busy, buzzy bistro serves Italian food with Welsh touches, such as pizza with Penlan pulled belly pork, and vermicelli with locally sourced clams and cockles. Not hungry? Prop up at the horseshoe-shaped bar with a pint of real ale or an imaginative cocktail-of-the-week.

🍺 Drinking & Nightlife

Thanks to its large student population, during term time you may find yourself sharing a bar with a bunch of toga-clad Romans or cross-dressed schoolgirls.

Aberystwyth

Academy   BAR
(Great Darkgate St; ⊙noon-1am Sun-Fri, to 2am Sat) This former chapel has a mezzanine supported by slender cast-iron columns and red lights illuminating a wooden staircase leading to an eagle-fronted pulpit. Most importantly, it serves cask ales and ciders.

Ship & Castle   PUB
(www.shipandcastle.co.uk; 1 High St; ⊙2pm-midnight) Cosy and welcoming 1830 pub, with sports on the big screen and a respectable selection of real ales on tap.

☆ Entertainment

Aberystwyth Arts Centre   THEATRE
(Canolfan Y Celfyddydau; ☑01970-623232; www.aberystwythartscentre.co.uk; Penglais Rd) Stages opera, drama, dance and concerts. There's also a cinema, a contemporary pottery and sculpture gallery, bar and cafe. The centre is on the Penglais university campus.

**Aberystwyth Male
Voice Choir**   TRADITIONAL MUSIC
(www.aberchoir.co.uk; Plascrug Ave) Rehearses at the Aberystwyth Rugby Club from 7pm to 8.30pm most Thursdays.

ℹ Information

Bronglais Hospital (☑01970-623131; Caradoc Rd) Emergency services.
Tourist Office (☑01970-612125; www.tourism.ceredigion.gov.uk; Terrace Rd; ⊙10am-5pm; 🛜) Below the Ceredigion Museum.

ℹ Getting There & Away

BUS
Routes include the T2 to Bangor (£5.40, 3½ hours, two to three daily) via Machynlleth (£4.25, 45 minutes, three to seven daily), Dolgellau (£4.75, 1¼ hours, three to seven daily) and Porthmadog (£5.40, 2¼ hours, two to four daily); and the twice-daily 701 to Carmarthen (£7.80, 1¾ hours), Swansea (£11, 2¾ hours) and Cardiff (£16.50, four hours).

A daily National Express coach heads to/from Welshpool (£12, 1¾ hours), Shrewsbury (£15, 2¼ hours), Birmingham (£30, four hours) and London Victoria (£34, 6¾ hours).

TRAIN
Aberystwyth is the terminus of the Cambrian Line, which crosses Mid-Wales every two hours en route to Birmingham (£28.80, 3½ hours) via Machynlleth (£6.20, 45 minutes), Welshpool (£14.20, 1¾ hours) and Shrewsbury (£19.20, 2¼ hours).

Devil's Bridge

Mysterious Devil's Bridge (www.devilsbridge-falls.co.uk; adult/child £3.50/2) spans the Rheidol Valley on the lush western slopes of Plynlimon Fawr (752m), source of the Rivers Wye and Severn. Here the Rivers Mynach and Rheidol tumble together in a narrow gorge.

The Mynach is spanned by three stone bridges, stacked on top of each other. The lowest and oldest is believed to have been built by the monks of Strata Florida Abbey before 1188. It's one of many bridges associated with an arcane legend that involves the devil building the bridge on the condition that he gets the first thing to cross it. An old lady outwits the devil by throwing some food over, which her dog chases and everybody's happy – except the devil and, presumably, the dog.

Just above the confluence, the Rheidol drops 90m in a series of spectacular waterfalls. Punch Bowl (£1), a steep 10-minute circuit, takes in the bridges and an emerald pool. The Waterfalls & Nature Trail (£2) is a 40-minute loop through striking hilly countryside, with viewpoints overlooking the 90m falls en route and an almost vertical descent of 100 steps (Jacob's Ladder).

The Vale of Rheidol Railway (p708) heads to Devil's Bridge from Aberystwyth, as does the 18-mile Rheidol Cycle Trail.

WORTH A TRIP

STRATA FLORIDA ABBEY

This ruined Cistercian abbey (Cadw; Abaty Ystrad Fflur; www.cadw.wales.gov.uk; B4343; adult/child £3.50/2.65; ⊙10am-5pm Apr-Oct, unattended & free other months) sits in splendid isolation. To get here, head a mile down a rural road from the village of Pontrhydfendigaid, which is on the B4343, 15 miles southeast of Aberystwyth or 9 miles south of Devil's Bridge. Founded in 1164, the abbey's best-preserved remnant is an arched doorway, decorated with mazelike lines of stone. At the rear of the site, two chapels still have some of their 14th-century tiling, and Welsh chieftains are seeing out eternity in graves found in a small enclosure.

This monastery was once a hub of activity: the industrious monks ran a lead mine, a sheep farm and corn mills; grew wheat; produced peat; and bred freshwater fish.

BRECON BEACONS NATIONAL PARK

Rippling dramatically for 45 miles from Llandeilo in the west, all the way to the English border, Brecon Beacons National Park (Parc Cenedlaethol Bannau Brycheiniog) encompasses some of the finest scenery in Mid-Wales. High mountain plateaux of grass and heather, their northern rims scalloped with glacier-scoured hollows, rise above wooded, waterfall-splashed valleys and green, rural landscapes.

There are four distinct regions within the park, neatly bounded by main roads and offering hundreds of walking routes as well as mountain-biking trails: the wild, lonely Black Mountain in the west, with its high moors and glacial lakes; Fforest Fawr, which lies between the A4067 and A470, whose rushing streams and spectacular waterfalls form the headwaters of the Rivers Tawe and Neath; the Brecon Beacons proper, a group of very distinctive, flat-topped hills that includes Pen-y-Fan (p716; 886m), the park's highest peak; and, from the A40 northeast to the English border, the rolling heathland ridges of the Black Mountains (not to be confused with Black Mountain, singular).

Black Mountain (Mynydd Du) & Fforest Fawr

The western half of the Brecon Beacons National Park, centred around Black Mountain, is sparsely inhabited. This lonely land of barren peaks throws down an irresistible gauntlet to hikers.

Fforest Fawr (Great Forest; www.fforestfawr-geopark.org.uk), once a Norman hunting ground, is now a Unesco geopark famous for its varied landscapes, ranging from bleak moorland to flower-flecked limestone pavement and lush, wooded ravines choked with moss and greenery.

◉ Sights & Activities

A series of dramatic waterfalls lies between the villages of Pontneddfechan and Ystradfellte, where the Rivers Mellte, Hepste and Pyrddin pass through steep forested gorges. The Elidir Trail (2½ miles each way; allow four hours) leaves from the Waterfalls Centre and takes in four falls. This can be combined with the

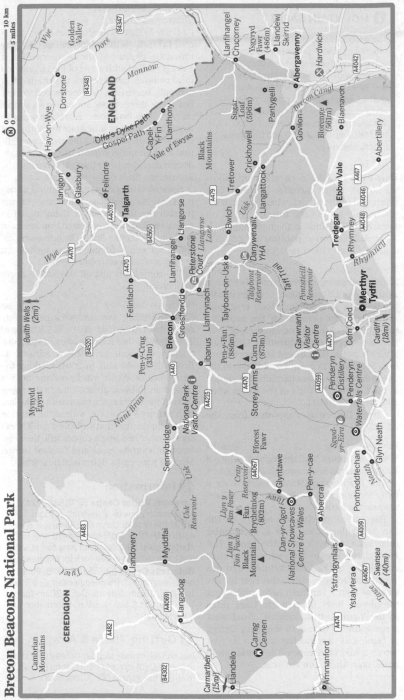

Brecon Beacons National Park

ⓘ MOUNTAIN SAFETY

The Brecon Beacons are serious mountains. The weather is very change-able and descending fog can obscure visibility within minutes even on a fine day. Wear hiking boots and take warm clothes, waterproofs, food and water, and a map and compass or a GPS. Weather forecasts are available from the Met Office (☎ 0870 900 0100; www. metoffice.gov.uk).

Four Falls Trail for a 12-mile loop (allow six hours), which includes Sgwd-yr-Eira (Waterfall of the Snow), where you can ac-tually walk behind the torrent. Walks on the area are outlined in the national park's *Waterfall Country* publication (£3.50), available from visitor centres.

Carreg Cennen   CASTLE
(Cadw; www.carregcennencastle.com; adult/child £4/3.50; ⊙ 9.30am-5.30pm) Dramatically perched atop a steep limestone crag high above the River Cennen are the brooding ruins of the ultimate romantic castle, vis-ible for miles in every direction. Originally a Welsh castle, the current structure dates back to Edward I's conquest of Wales in the late 13th century. It was partially dismantled in 1462 during the Wars of the Roses when taken by the Yorkists.

Carreg Cennen is signposted from the A483.

Fan Brycheiniog   MOUNTAIN
The finest feature (and the highest point) of Black Mountain is the sweeping escarpment of Fan Brycheiniog (802m), reached via a fairly strenuous 11.5-mile loop from Glyn-tawe on the A4067.

The initial precipitous ascent of the Fan Hir ridge eases into a spectacular ridge walk, with views of the Llyn y Fan Fawr glacial lake to the east. A steep path climbs up to Fan Brycheiniog and it's worth detouring to climb Fan Foel for the views of Llyn y Fan Fach before following the almost level Bannau Sir Gaer ridge to the Waun Lefrith summit. Head west across pathless terrain to the rocky Carreg yr Ogof, and descend the trail to its east across a wild landscape of limestone sink-holes, marshland and streams.

Dan-yr-Ogof National Showcaves Centre for Wales   CAVE
(☎ 01639-730284; www.showcaves.co.uk; adult/child £13.75/9; ⊙ 10am-4pm Apr-Oct; 🖈) The limestone plateau of the southern Fforest Fawr is riddled with some of the largest and most complex cave systems in Britain. Most can only be visited by experienced cavers, but these three caves are easily accessible on a self-guided tour. Attractions range from the glistening limestone formations of Dan-yr-Ogof Cave and the two waterfalls that feed an underground lake to the high-domed chamber of Cathedral Cave and the Bronze Age finds of the tiny Bone Cave.

Somewhat at odds with the natural attrac-tions are the plexiglass dinosaurs peeking through the trees, some of them locked in mortal combat, and a recreated Iron Age farm with mushroomlike huts. The admission fee covers other child-friendly draws, including a petting zoo and a shire-horse centre.

The complex is just off the A4067, north of Abercraf.

Penderyn Distillery   DISTILLERY
(☎ 01685-810651; www.welsh-whisky.co.uk; Pen-deryn; tours adult/child £6/4; ⊙ 9.30am-5pm) Though Wales has a long history of spirit dis-tillation, this boutique distillery released its first malt whisky only in 2004, marking the resurgence of Welsh whisky-making after a more than 100-year absence due to the popu-larity of the temperance movement in the late 19th century. Visitors can witness the creation of the liquid fire that's distilled with fresh spring water in a single copper still, then ma-tured in bourbon casks and finished in rich Madeira wine casks. Tours include tastings.

ⓘ Information

Garwnant Visitor Centre (☎ 01685-722481; www.forestry.gov.uk/garwnant; ⊙ 10am-4pm; 🖈) At the head of Llwyn Onn Reservoir, 5 miles north of Merthyr Tydfil on the A470, this is the starting point for a couple of easy forest walks and has a mountain-bike park for children.

Waterfalls Centre (☎ 01639-721795; Pont-neathvaughan Rd, Pontneddfechan; ⊙ 9.30am-1pm & 1.30-5pm daily Apr-Oct, 9.30am-1pm & 1.30-3pm Sat & Sun Nov-Mar) Information on waterfall walks.

ⓘ Getting There & Away

Bus X63 (eight daily Monday to Saturday) stops at Dan-yr-Ogof en route from Brecon (£3.30, 33 minutes) to Swansea (£3.70, one hour).

Brecon (Aberhonddu) & Around

POP 8250

The handsome stone market town of Brecon stands at the meeting of the River Usk and the River Honddu. For centuries the town thrived as a centre of wool production and weaving. Today it's a handy jumping-off point for the Brecon Beacons, and you'll find a high concentration of hikers and soldiers from the nearby military base in its bars, eateries and outdoor-gear shops. The conical hill of **Pen-y-Crug** (331m), capped by an Iron Age hill fort, rises northwest of the town, and makes a good objective for a short hike (2.5 miles round trip).

◎ Sights & Activities

★**Brecon Cathedral**   CHURCH
(Eglwys Gadeiriol Aberhonddu; www.breconcathedral.org.uk; Cathedral Close) Perched on a hill above the River Honddu, Brecon Cathedral was founded as part of a Benedictine monastery in 1093. Only the carved font and parts of the nave remain of the original structure, but this stark stone church features an ornate 1937 reredos and a cross that seems to hover in mid-air at the end of the nave.

In the cathedral grounds is a **Heritage Centre** (◎10am-4.30pm Mon-Sat) **FREE**, cafe and gift shop housed in a restored 15th-century tithe barn.

Monmouthshire & Brecon Canal   CANAL
Brecon is the northern terminus of this canal, built between 1799 and 1812 to move coal, iron, limestone and agricultural goods. The 33 miles from Brecon to Pontypool is back in business, transporting a generally less grimy cargo of holidaymakers and river-dwellers.

The busiest section is around Brecon, with craft departing from the canal basin, 400m south of the town centre. **Dragonfly Cruises** (☑07831-685222; www.dragonfly-cruises.co.uk; adult/child £7.50/4.50; ◎Mar-Oct) runs 2½-hour narrowboat trips and **Backwaters Adventure Equipment Ltd** (☑01873-831825; www.backwatershire.co.uk; kayak/canoe per day £27.50/45) rents kayaks and canoes.

Llangorse Lake   LAKE
(Llyn Syfaddan) Reed-fringed Llangorse Lake, to the east of Brecon, is Wales' second-largest natural lake, but it's barely more than a mile long and half a mile wide. The lake is the Brecon Beacons National Park's main water-sports location, used for sailing, windsurfing, canoeing and water-skiing. **Lakeside Caravan Park** rents rowing boats (per hour/day £12/30), Canadian canoes (per hour/day £12/36) and Wayfarer sailing dinghies (per hour £25). There's a **crannog** (lake dwelling) dating back to AD 900 near the northern shore.

Cantref Adventure Farm & Riding Centre   HORSE RIDING
(☑01874-665223; www.cantref.com; Llanfrynach, Upper Cantref Farm; height more than/less than 93cm £8.75/free; ◎10.30am-5.30pm) In the countryside south of Brecon, Cantref operates a child-focused fun farm, complete with pig races, lamb feeding and indoor play areas. The adjoining riding centre offers equestrian lessons, horse treks (£35) into the Brecon Beacons and 20-minute pony rides. Follow the horseshoe signs down narrow country lanes from the A40, southeast of town.

★✿ Festivals & Events

Brecon Jazz Festival   MUSIC
(www.breconjazz.org; ◎Aug) On the second weekend in August, Brecon hosts one of Europe's leading jazz events, and there's plenty of free alternative-music events in the local pubs as part of the coinciding **Brecon Fringe Festival** (www.breconfringe.co.uk).

Brecon Beast   SPORTS
(www.breconbeast.co.uk; ◎Sep) A gruelling mountain-bike challenge over either 31 or 47 miles, held in mid-September. The fee (£30 prepaid online or £35 on the day) covers camping, refreshments en-route, a 'pasta party' and a brag-worthy T-shirt.

---

❶ THE DEMISE OF THE BEACONS BUSES

The very useful Beacons Buses service that ferried walkers and cyclists all over the Brecon Beacons on Sundays and bank holidays has been curtailed. The only bus route currently operating is the bike-bus service operated by **Cardiff Bus** (www.cardiffbus.com), which runs between Cardiff and Brecon (Sundays and bank holidays, late May to September); it interchanges with bus 39A in Brecon and runs between Brecon and Abergavenny twice a day.

🛏 Sleeping & Eating

🛏 Brecon

Bridge Cafe B&B **£**
(☑ 01874-622024; www.bridgecafe.co.uk; 7 Bridge St; s/d from £45/55; 🛜) With a particular focus on refuelling weary walkers and mountain-bikers, Bridge Cafe offers three comfortable double rooms with down-filled duvets and crisp, cotton sheets upstairs, and hearty dishes downstairs in cosy surrounds (mains £9 to £13; dinner Friday and Saturday, breakfast on Sundays; bookings advised).

Coach House GUESTHOUSE **££**
(☑ 07974 328437; www.coachhousebrecon.com; 12 Orchard St; d incl breakfast £95) This hospitable 19th-century coaching inn is well attuned to the needs of walkers, with a drying room for hiking gear, generous breakfasts (including good vegetarian options) and packed lunches put together by the hosts. The seven stylish, modern rooms, decorated in soothing creams, have ultracomfy beds and good showers.

Roberto's ITALIAN **££**
(☑ 01874-611880; www.robertos.netau.net; St Mary St; mains £9-15; ⊗ 6-11pm Mon-Sat; 🖋) Roberto's pairs mostly authentic Italian recipes, executed using fresh local ingredients, with an Italian-style ambience (plastic vines, wine racks). The quality of the specials can be variable, but the pizza hits the spot and the 'planks' – cured meat/fish/veggie platters – are very popular. Service can be slow.

🛏 Around Brecon

Beacons Backpackers HOSTEL **£**
(☑ 01874-730215; www.beaconsbackpackers.co.uk; The New Inn, Bwlch; dm £22) The one thing better than a good hostel is a good hostel inside a 14th-century pub. This compact, friendly place comes with comfy bunks, reliable hot showers, a chillout room with a crackling

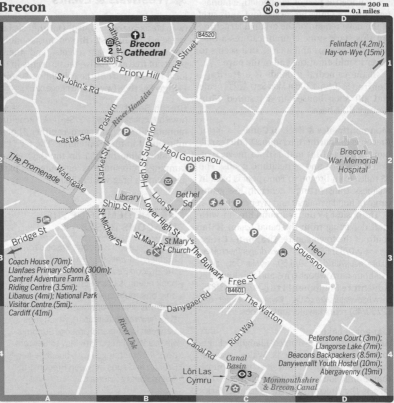

Brecon

🧭 N 0 ─── 200 m
0 ─── 0.1 miles

Felinfach (4.2mi);
Hay-on-Wye (15mi)

① 1
Brecon
Cathedral

B4520

Cathedral Cl

The Struet

St John's Rd

Priory Hill

River Honddu

Pastern

Castle Sq

Market St

High St Superior

Heol Gouesnou

The Promenade

Watergate

Brecon
War Memorial
Hospital

Library

Ship St

Lion St

Lower High St

Bethel
Sq

① 4

St Michael St

St Mary St

St Mary's
Church

The Bulwark

Heol
Gouesnou

5

Bridge St

Coach House (70m);
Llanfaes Primary School (300m);
Cantref Adventure Farm &
Riding Centre (3.5mi);
Libanus (4mi); National Park
Visitor Centre (5mi);
Cardiff (41mi)

6

Free St

B4601

The Watton

Danygaer Rd

River Usk

Canal Rd

Rich Way

Lôn Las
Cymru

Canal
Basin

③ 3

7

Monmouthshire
& Brecon Canal

Peterstone Court (3mi);
Llangorse Lake (7mi);
Beacons Backpackers (8.5mi);
Danywenallt Youth Hostel (10mi);
Abergavenny (19mi)

wood fire, and knowledgeable owners. With good hikes on its doorstep, it's also a great place to mingle with fellow ramblers.

Danywenallt YHA HOSTEL **£**
(☑0800 0195 465; www.yha.org.uk; Talybont-on-Usk; dm/r from £18/54, sites £9; P) Ideally located for hiking and biking around Talybont Reservoir, this secluded, converted farmhouse lacks a guest kitchen but has a cafe. Camping is available in the orchard. Danywenallt is half way between Brecon and Crickhowell.

★Peterstone Court HOTEL **£££**
(☑01874-665387; www.peterstone-court.com; A40, Llanhamlach; r from £145; P🕭🔊) At this elegant Georgian manor house, the decor is classic, and the rooms large and comfortable. Its excellent restaurant (mains from £14-22) uses produce from the manor's own farm. The views across the valley to the Beacons are superb, and the boutique spa pampers guests with organic products. Llanhamlach is 3 miles southeast of Brecon, just off the A40.

★Felin Fach Griffin PUB **£££**
(☑01874-620111; www.felinfachgriffin.co.uk; Felinfach; mains £13-20; ⊙noon-2.30pm & 6-10pm) Heavy wooden beams and the scent of woodsmoke from the open fires create a cosy, rustic ambience at this award-winning inn. The gourmet kitchen makes the most of local fish, meat and game, and the wine list spans the world. Rooms (single/double from £100/130) are TV-free. The Griffin is 5 miles northeast of Brecon on the A470.

Brecon

☆ Entertainment

Brecon & District
Male Choir TRADITIONAL MUSIC
(www.breconchoir.co.uk; Llanfaes Primary School, Orchard St; ⊙7-9pm Fri) For booming harmonies, head to the practice sessions of the local men's choir. Visitors welcome.

Theatr Brycheiniog THEATRE
(☑01874-611622; www.brycheiniog.co.uk; Canal Wharf) The town's main venue for drama, dance, comedy and music. It often hosts big-name touring acts.

❶ Information

Brecon War Memorial Hospital (☑01874-622443; Cerrigcochion Rd) Emergency services.

National Park Visitor Centre (☑01874-623366; www.breconbeacons.org; Libanus; ⊙9.30am-5pm) The Brecon Beacons National Park's main visitor centre has full details of walks, hiking and biking trails, outdoor activities, wildlife and geology. Signposted off the A470 road, 5 miles southwest of Brecon.

Tourist Office (☑01874-622485; Market car park; ⊙9.30am-5pm Mon-Sat, 10am-4pm Sun)

❶ Getting There & Away

BICYCLE
Bikes + Hikes (☑01874-610071; www.bikesandhikes.co.uk; Lion Yard; per half-/full day £18/20) rents bikes and offers guided mountain-bike rides. The Taff Trail heads south from here to Cardiff (67km). This forms part of the Lôn Las Cymru national cycling route, which also heads north to Builth Wells (28km).

BUS
Bus routes include the X43 to Abergavenny (£3.40, 40 minutes, 12 daily) via Crickhowell (£2.60, 25 minutes, 13 daily); X63 to Swansea (£7, 2 hours 20 minutes, six daily,) via Dan-yr-Ogof (£3.30, 33 minutes, nine daily); no Sunday service. The 39 runs to Hay-on-Wye (£3.80, 35 minutes, up to 10 daily).

Crickhowell (Crughywel)

This prosperous, picturesque village sits on the northern shore of the River Usk, straddled by a 17th-century stone bridge famous for having 12 arches on one side and 13 on the other. Crickhowell grew up around a Norman motte-and-bailey castle, which was reduced to its present remains of a gatehouse tower and keep by the marauding forces of Owain Glyndŵr. Crickhowell is named after the distinctive flat-topped Crug Hywel.

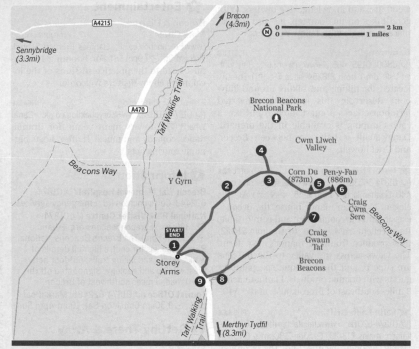

Walking Tour
Climbing Pen-y-Fan

START STOREY ARMS
END STOREY ARMS
LENGTH 5 MILES; THREE HOURS

Of all the possible routes up the Brecon Beacons' highest peak, Pen-y-Fan (886m), this loop is reasonably straightforward to follow and the trailhead is easy to find. The ascent is along one of the quieter paths, which avoids the crowds along the 'motorway' – the main route – and offers particularly impressive views along the approach. Carry maps and a GPS (and know how to use it) as fog can descend suddenly.

Start at the **1** **Storey Arms car park** off the A470. A clear trail crosses the moorland that covers the southern approach to the Y Gyrn summit on your left. Once you reach a broad ridge, cross a stile and follow the trail down to the **2** **River Taf Fawr**. The rocky path then heads up the hillside along the right-hand side of the valley. Once you reach the **3** **steep escarpment edge** overlooking the Cwm Llwch Valley and a small lake, if you

have the energy, do a 275m detour northwest down along the escarpment edge to the **4** **Tommy Jones memorial obelisk**, commemorating a lost local boy who died here of exposure in 1900.

The main path bears right along the escarpment and rises steeply to the crags that guard the approach to Corn Du (873m). It's a short, steep scramble to **5** **the Corn Du summit**, followed by a short dip and a less precipitous final ascent to the exposed, wind-buffeted top of **6** **Pen-y-Fan**, marked with a large cairn. Walk to the southern edge of the plateau for stupendous views of the Craig Gwaun Taf ridge to the south and the almost vertical drop-off along the northern flank of Craig Cwm Sere ridge. When you're ready to descend, take the path that skirts the eastern flank of Corn Du and leads to a **7** **major trail junction**. Descend into the valley along the obvious trail paved with natural stone. After a mile or so, cross a **8** **wooden bridge** and enter a **9** **large car park**. Bear right and follow the path along the A470 back to Storey Arms.

⊙ Sights & Activities

Crug Hywel MOUNTAIN
(Table Mountain) Crug Hywel (Hywel's Rock; 451m), better known as Table Mountain, rises to the north of Crickhowell. A hike to the top (3 miles round trip) starts behind the White Hart Inn, heads up through the woods, follows a stream and then a stone wall. The summit and the allegedly haunted remains of an Iron Age fort are a short scramble from the path. Exit through the fort gate and follow the path downhill through five stiles and a farmyard.

Tretower Court & Castle HISTORIC BUILDING
(Cadw; www.cadw.wales.gov.uk; Tretower; adult/child £4.75/3.60; ⊙10am-5pm Apr-Oct; ℗) Tretower consists of two historic buildings: a 15th-century manor house with a mock-up kitchen, a disembodied calf's head in the pantry, a cheery banquet hall and vast, bare rooms upstairs; and the remains of a Norman motte-and-bailey castle. Access to the 13th-century circular tower is through a vine-and-trellis-bedecked patio and a sheep-filled meadow.
Tretower is 3 miles northwest of Crickhowell on the A479.

✵ Festivals & Events

Green Man Festival MUSIC
(www.greenman.net; Glanusk Park; adult/student/child £159/135/5; ⊙mid-Aug; ♿) Staged over a weekend in mid-August, 2 miles west of Crickhowell via the B4558, Green Man is an alternative, folk and indie music festival, which also features performance art, comedy, drumming workshops and children's events.

Walking Festival SPORTS
(www.crickhowellfestival.com; ⊙Mar) Eight-day walking fest in early March, with guided treks and walks, talks on keeping safe in the wilderness, navigating and more.

🛏 Sleeping & Eating

★ Gwyn Deri B&B ££
(☎01873-812494; www.gwynderibedandbreakfast.co.uk; Mill St; s/d/f £40/65/90; ℗🐾📶) The friendly couple who run this homely B&B keep its three modern rooms immaculately clean, and are happy to share their knowledge of the area. Bonuses include iPod docks, fresh fruit in the rooms and an excellent breakfast selection. Connecting rooms are available for family groups.

Tŷ Gwyn B&B ££
(☎01873-811625; www.tygwyn.com; Brecon Rd; s/d from £40/68; ℗@) Once the home of Regency architect John Nash, Tŷ Gwyn is a lovely old Georgian house with four spacious en suite rooms, each themed around a Welsh literary figure. The hosts are exceptionally helpful. It's five minutes' walk from the town centre.

Number Eighteen CAFE, BRASSERIE ££
(☎01873-810337; 18 High St; breakfast & lunch £6-7, dinner £10-20; ⊙cafe daily 9am-6pm, restaurant 6-11.30pm Wed-Sat, noon-4pm Sun; ♿) By day it's a bright, modern cafe serving good coffee, hearty breakfasts, panini and other light bites, but at night the action shifts to the glassed-in brasserie upstairs. It's a relaxed spot for a burger, steak or pork chop; live music serenades diners on Wednesday evenings.

Nantyffin Cider Mill MODERN WELSH ££
(☎01873-810775; www.cidermill.co.uk; mains £11-17; ⊙12.30-2.30pm & 6-9.30pm Wed-Sun) This 16th-century drovers' inn uses quality local produce to create simple, unfussy dishes, with a focus on meats cooked in the charcoal oven. The dining room is a blend of bare stone, exposed roof beams and designer chairs, set around the original 19th-century cider press. Nantyffin is a mile northwest of Crickhowell on the A40.

ℹ Information

Tourist Office (☎01873-811970; www.visit-crickhowell.co.uk; Beaufort St; ⊙10am-5pm Mon-Sat, to 1pm Sun; 📶) Has leaflets for local walks.

ℹ Getting There & Away

Bus X43 connects Crickhowell with Abergavenny (£1.20, 20 minutes) and Brecon (£2.60, 42 minutes); no service on Sundays.

Abergavenny (Y Fenni)
POP 13,420

In a millennium of existence, Abergavenny has played many roles on history's stage: Norman stronghold, tanning and weaving centre and prison for Hitler's deputy. Its enviable location between three of the Black Mountains – Blorenge (561m) to the southwest; Ysgyryd Fawr (486m) to the northeast; and Sugar Loaf (596m) to the northwest – make it a superb base for walkers, while its annual food festival and its acclaimed restaurants attract lovers of fresh, organic and seasonal Welsh cuisine from all over the country, and beyond.

Sights

Ysgyryd Fawr   MOUNTAIN
(Skirrid) Of the glacially sculpted hills that surround Abergavenny, Skirrid (486m) is the most dramatic looking and was once considered holy.

Take the B4521 to the layby at the base of the hill. It's a steep climb from here through the woods along a muddy track. Once you clear the tree line the walk is less steep, with a final short climb to the summit where you'll be rewarded with extravagant views and the ruins of a clandestine Catholic chapel.

Sugar Loaf   MOUNTAIN
(Mynydd Pen-y-Fâl) The cone-shaped pinnacle of Sugar Loaf (596m) is a 4½-mile round trip from the Mynydd Llanwenarth viewpoint car park. Take the middle track that follows a stone wall, skirts a wood and climbs steeply uphill, turning right to bisect a grassy ridge before a final steep summit scramble. The descent route flanks the head of the valley.

Head west on the A40; at the edge of town turn right for Sugarloaf Vineyards, then go left at the next two junctions.

★ St Mary's Priory Church   CHURCH
(www.stmarys-priory.org; Monk St; ☺9am-5pm Mon-Sat) The austere interior of St Mary's contains a remarkable treasury of aristocratic tombs, including that of Eva de Braose (d 1246), Lady of Abergavenny. The church was founded at the same time as the castle (1087) as part of a Benedictine priory, but the present building dates mainly from the 14th century, with 15th- and 19th-century additions and alterations. In the northern transept is a monumental 15th-century wooden representation of the biblical figure of Jesse.

Next door, the restored 13th-century tithe barn has been converted into an excellent heritage centre and cafe.

Abergavenny Castle & Museum   MUSEUM
(www.abergavennymuseum.co.uk; Castle St; ☺11am-1pm & 2-5pm Mon-Sat, 2-5pm Sun) FREE The banquet hall of the now-ruined Abergavenny Castle witnessed a terrible act of treachery when Lord William de Braose massacred his dining guests – Seisyll ap Dyfnwal and his men – during a feast on Christmas Day, 1175. The castle keep now houses a small museum devoted to the history of the town.

★ Festivals & Events

South Wales Three Peaks Trial   SPORTS
(www.threepeakstrial.co.uk; ☺Mar) Annual walking challenge held in late March.

Abergavenny Festival of Cycling   SPORTS
(www.abergavennyfestivalofcycling.co.uk; ☺Jul) Mid-July lycra-enthusiasts' meet incorporating the Iron Mountain Sportif, a participatory event with 20-mile, 41-mile, 67-mile and 100-mile courses.

Abergavenny Food Festival   FOOD
(www.abergavennyfoodfestival.co.uk; ☺Sep) The most important gastronomic event in Wales, held on the third weekend in September.

Sleeping & Eating

Guest House   B&B ££
(☎01873-854823; www.theguesthouseabergavenny. co.uk; 2 Oxford St; s/d from £45/80; ⓟ⑦❀) This family-friendly B&B features six cheerful, eclectically furnished, en suite rooms with mountain views and a minimenagerie of pigs, rabbits and chickens. The gregarious owners slap up fantastic breakfasts (with good veggie options).

Angel   HOTEL ££
(☎01873-857121; www.angelhotelabergavenny. com; 15 Cross St; r from £111, cottage from £293; ⓟ⑦) Abergavenny's top hotel is a fine Georgian building that was once a famous coaching inn. Choose between sleek, sophisticated rooms and luxury cottages nearby. The menus at the informal Foxhunter bar and the refined Oak Room (mains £13-£28, 3-course meals £25) put an international twist on local produce.

Cwtch Cafe   CAFE £
(58 Cross St; mains from £6; ☺9am-5pm Mon-Sat; ⓩ) This wonderfully friendly cafe entices a crowd of regulars with its homemade cakes, good coffee and lunchtime dishes such as buck rarebit, Canadian pancakes with crispy bacon, quiche and veggie lasagne. Get here early or risk elbowing your neighbour every time you lift your fork.

★ Hardwick   MODERN WELSH £££
(☎01873-854220; www.thehardwick.co.uk; Old Raglan Rd, Abergavenny; mains £17-25, 2-/3-course lunch £21/26; ☺9-11am, noon-3pm & 6.30-10pm) The Hardwick is a traditional inn with an old stone fireplace and low ceiling beams. Ex-Walnut Tree alumnus Stephen Terry has created a gloriously unpretentious menu

that celebrates the very best of country cooking. Attached are eight elegant, modern **rooms** (from £155). The Hardwick is 2 miles south of Abergavenny on the B4598.

Walnut Tree MODERN WELSH **£££**
(☑ 01873-852797; www.thewalnuttreeinn.com; Llanddewi Skirrid; mains £19-27, 2-/3-course lunch £25/30; ☉ noon-2.30pm & 6.30-10pm Tue-Sat) Established in 1963, Michelin-starred Walnut Tree serves the imaginative meat and seafood creations of chef Shaun Hill, made from fresh, local produce. When we visited, the flavours were merely good rather than outstanding, however, and the service was brusque. The Walnut Tree is 3 miles northeast of Abergavenny on the B4521.

❶ Information

Nevill Hall Hospital (☑ 01873-732732; Brecon Rd; ☉ 24hr) Emergency service.

Tourist Office (☑ 01873-853254; www.visit-abergavenny.co.uk; Swan Meadow, Monmouth Rd; ☉ 10am-5pm Apr-Sep, 10am-1pm & 2-4pm Oct-Mar) Has merged with the Brecon Beacons National Park visitor centre.

❶ Getting There & Away

BUS

Bus routes include the T4 to Cardiff (£5.90, 2½ hours, 11 daily) and Hereford (£5.30, one hour, six daily); and X43 to Brecon (£3.40, 45 minutes, 12 daily) via Crickhowell (£1.20, 20 minutes).

Daily National Express coaches head to Worcester (£12, 1¾ hours) and Birmingham (£13, three hours).

TRAIN

Direct trains run from Cardiff (£12.70, 45 minutes, regular); Shrewsbury (£27.20, 1¼ hours, regular) via Hereford (£9.90, 25 minutes); and Holyhead (£74, 4¼ hours, two to six daily) via Bangor (£68.10, 3½ hours).

Black Mountains (Y Mynyddoedd Duon)

The hills that stretch northward from Abergavenny to Hay-on-Wye are bleak, untamed and largely uninhabited, their summits and pathways best explored on foot, hoof or two wheels. The scenic and secluded Vale of Ewyas runs through the heart of the area, from Llanfihangel Crucorney to the exposed Gospel Pass (542m), the single-track road winding its way down to Hay-on-Wye in between enchanted-forest-like hedgerows.

◉ Sights & Activities

Llanthony Priory RUIN
(☉ 10am-4pm) Halfway along the Vale of Ewyas lie these atmospheric 13th-century ruins, set among grasslands and wooded hills by the River Honddu. JMW Turner painted the bleak grandeur of the still-standing arches and the chapel's remains in 1794.

Grange Trekking Centre HORSE RIDING
(☑ 01873-890215; www.grangetrekking.co.uk; Capel-Y-Fin; per hour/half-day/day £17/32/52; ☝) The friendly Griffiths family offers pony trekking in the Black Mountains for all abilities. **B&B accommodation** (per person £38) and **camping** (per person £6) are also available.

⊨ Sleeping & Eating

Llanthony Priory Hotel INN **££**
(☑ 01873-890487; www.llanthonyprioryhotel.co.uk; r from £80; ℗) Seamlessly merging with the priory ruins, and incorporating some of the original medieval buildings, the Abbey Hotel is wonderfully atmospheric, with four-poster beds, stone spiral staircases, and four rooms squeezed into turrets; all share facilities. Hearty pub food, Welsh beers and real ales served.

Skirrid Inn PUB **££**
(☑ 01873-890258; www.skirridmountaininn.co.uk; Llanfihangel Crucorney; d £90; ℗) Those with a taste for the macabre and a fondness for ghost-hunting will adore this place. Wales' oldest inn (pre-1110) once doubled as a court and more than 180 people were hung here. Just so you don't forget, a noose dangles from the well-worn hanging beam, outside the doors to the three old-fashioned bedrooms. Good **pub** (mains £7-13) downstairs.

Hay-on-Wye (Y Gelli Gandryll)

POP 1955

The credit for putting this pretty little town on the literary map goes largely to the charismatic and forthright local maverick Richard Booth, who triggered an explosion in secondhand bookshops by opening his eponymous store in the 1960s and proclaiming himself the King of Hay. A festival of literature and culture followed in 1988, growing in stature every year until it became an international fixture, though old-timers grumble that it has now been hijacked by celebrities and has lost its 'alternative' vibe.

The printed word still rules this town, as evidenced by the number of bookshops and tongue-in-cheek anti-Kindle posters. It's easy for a bibliophile to drift into insolvency here, but Hay is also an excellent base for active pursuits, whether you wish to mount Lord Hereford's Knob (aka Twmpa) or walk Offa's Dyke Path.

🏃 Activities

Drover Cycles   CYCLING
(☑01497-822419; www.drovercycles.co.uk; Forest Rd) Rents mountain and touring bikes (per half-day/day/week £25/35/100).

🎊 Festivals

Hay Festival   LITERARY
(☑01497-822629; www.hayfestival.com; ☺May) The 10-day Hay Festival in late May is Britain's leading festival of literature and the arts. Far more celebrity-driven these days, it consists of readings, workshops, book signings, concerts and club nights, and its internationally famous speakers include the likes of Terry Pratchett, Al Gore, Stephen Fry and Margaret Atwood. Book tickets for headlining acts as early as possible.

HowTheLightGetsIn   MUSIC, PHILOSOPHY
(howthelightgetsin.org; ☺Jun) A low-key and appealing week-long philosophy and music event in late June.

🛏 Sleeping & Eating

★Bear   B&B ££
(☑01497-821302; www.thebearhay.com; 2 Bear St; s £55, d £75-95; ℗🖱) This 1590 coaching inn, run by a friendly young owner, retains its historic ambience and combines it with interesting art, sisal floors and bathtubs in each of the bathrooms – succour for tired hikers. The 'romantic' bedroom features a four-poster bed, and the excellent breakfasts include imaginative vegetarian options. Curl up with a book by the immense fireplace.

★Old Black Lion   PUB ££
(☑01497-820841; www.oldblacklion.co.uk; Lion St; s/d £55/99; ℗) This traditional coaching inn is Hay's most atmospheric sleeping option. Parts of it date from the 13th century – expect low ceilings, heavy wooden beams and uneven floors. The accumulated weight of centuries of hospitality is cheerfully carried by the current staff. The **food** (mains £13-19) is leagues beyond pub grub: think stuffed Guinea fowl, roast halibut and beef Wellington.

Hay Stables   B&B ££
(☑01497-820008; www.haystables.co.uk; Oxford Rd; s/d £40/60; 🖱) Three modern, homely en suite twins and doubles, decked out in neutral tones, welcome you at this friendly guesthouse. There's a common area and a large, fully equipped guest kitchen. Breakfast is a self-serve affair. The owners are very accommodating.

Tomatitos Tapas Bar   SPANISH £
(☑01497-820770; 38 Lion St; tapas £2.25-4.95; ☺11am-11pm; 🖱) Friendly, bustling Tomatitos combines the atmosphere of everyone's favourite pub with a Spanish-centric menu. Staples such as *patatas bravas* and *calamares* aside, the menu's guest stars include mushrooms stuffed with Cabrales cheese and lamb tagine. Wash it down with Spanish, Chilean and Argentine wine by the glass. Book a table or prop up the bar with the locals.

Bookshop Cafe   CAFE £
(www.boothbooks.co.uk; 44 Lion St; mains £4-10; ☺9.30am-4.30pm Tue-Thu, to 7pm Fri & Sat, 11am-4pm Sun; 🖉) Tucked into the rear of Richard Booth's Bookshop, this sun-filled cafe offers adventurous, modern breakfast and lunch menus with plenty of vegetarian options and greens straight out of its kitchen garden.

★St John's Place   MODERN WELSH ££
(☑07855 783799; stjohnsplacehay.tumblr.com; Lion St; mains £12-16; ☺6-10pm Thu-Sat) The menu at this intimate restaurant inside St John's Chapel is limited, but each of the three-to-four unusual starters, mains and desserts is conceived and executed with imagination and flair. Expect the likes of brown shrimp with duck egg, palm sugar and chilli; mackerel with samphire; and date and pecan tart.

🍷 Drinking & Entertainment

Blue Boar   PUB
(Oxford Rd; ☺9am-11pm) This creeper-clad, family-run traditional pub is ideal for whiling away a wet afternoon with a pint of Timothy Taylor's ale, a home-cooked lunch of Glamorgan sausage, and a good book.

Globe at Hay   LIVE MUSIC, PERFORMING ARTS
(☑01497-821762; www.globeathay.org; Newport St; ☺10am-midnight Thu-Sat, to 5pm Sun, 6-11pm Tue; 🖱) This converted Methodist chapel wears many hats: cafe, bar, music venue, theatre and all-round community hub. It hosts DJs, world music, comedy, theatre, film, festivals such as HowTheLightGetsIn and political talks.

🛍 Shopping

Richard Booth's Bookshop   BOOKS
(www.boothbooks.co.uk; 44 Lion St; ☺9.30am-5.30pm Mon-Sat, 11am-5pm Sun) The most famous, and still the best; has a sizeable Anglo-Welsh literature section, and a Wales travel section.

Murder & Mayhem   BOOKS
(☑01497-821613; 5 Lion St; ☺10am-5.30pm Mon-Sat) Body outline on the floor, monsters on the ceiling, and stacks of detective fiction, true crime and horror.

Hay Cinema Bookshop   BOOKS
(☑01497-820071; www.haycinemabookshop.co.uk; Castle St; ☺9am-6pm Mon-Sat, 10am-5.30pm Sun) Converted cinema housing a huge collection of books about filmmaking and cinema.

Mostly Maps   MAPS
(☑01497-820539; www.mostlymaps.com; 2 Castle St) Exquisite antiquarian maps and prints, many hand-coloured. Hours vary; call ahead.

Addyman Books   BOOKS
(☑01497-821136; www.hay-on-wyebooks.com; 39 Lion St; ☺10am-5.30pm) A dedicated sci-fi room and plenty of books on art, photography and architecture within a 19th-century Transylvanian church interior.

ⓘ Information

Tourist Office (☑01497-820144; www.hay-on-wye.co.uk; Oxford Rd; ☺10am-1pm & 2-5pm) The helpful tourist office stocks a free guide and map profiling all of Hay's bookshops (most bookshops stock the map, too).

ⓘ Getting There & Away

Buses 39, 39A and 39B stop in Hay-on-Wye, en route between Brecon (£3.80, 32 minutes, three to seven daily) and Hereford (£8.40, one hour).

POWYS

By far Wales' biggest county, Powys is named after the ancient Welsh kingdom that succeeded Roman rule. Overwhelmingly rural, it is dotted with charming little villages. Along the border, the communities of Knighton and Presteigne play host to hikers tackling the 177-mile Offa's Dyke Path national trail – the symbolic line that separates Wales from England. Sheltered by the Cambrian Mountains to the west, this county isn't just green in a literal sense – successful conservation

efforts have brought the threatened red kite back from brink of extinction, and Machynlleth has long been a focal point for the nation's environmental aspirations.

Llanwrtyd Wells (Llanwrtyd)

POP 630

Llanwrtyd (khlan-*oor*-tid) Wells is one strange little town: mostly deserted, it becomes packed to the rafters with an influx of contestants and their merry-making supporters during its many oddball festivals. At the beginning of July Llanwrtyd is also busy with attendees of the Royal Welsh Show, held in nearby Builth Wells, which involves everything from gussied-up livestock to lumberjack competitions. According to the *Guinness Book of Records*, Llanwrtyd is the UK's smallest town – some local residents even claim that in order to cling onto this status there's a periodic cull.

🛏 Sleeping & Eating

Ardwyn House   B&B ££
(☑01591-610768; www.ardwynhouse.co.uk; Station Rd; s/d £60/80; P⏥) This beautifully restored art nouveau house wins you over with its yesteryear grandeur and the congeniality of its young owners. Some rooms have clawfoot baths and rural views, and there is oak parquet flooring, period wallpaper, and a guest lounge with a pool table and bar.

Plasnewydd B&B   B&B ££
(☑01591-610293; www.plasnewydd90.co.uk; Irfon Tce; s/d £35/60; P⏥) Located in the heart of town, this spick-and-span B&B has numerous fans thanks to its warm, cosy, individually styled rooms, an extensive breakfast spread (which caters well for vegetarians) and the accommodating attitude of its owners. There's a drying room for wet cycling gear, and other nice touches include delicious homemade Welsh cakes.

★Carlton Riverside   WELSH ££
(☑01591-610248; www.carltonriverside.com; Irfon Cres; mains £13-27; ☺12.30-3pm Mon-Sat, 7-10.30pm Tue-Sat; P⏥) This upmarket restaurant-with-rooms has a boutique feel. The restaurant executes classic dishes (slow-cooked pork, roast lamb, fillet steak) with aplomb. The **rooms** (s/d £50/65) are modern, simple and tasteful, and cater to bon vivants, with late breakfasts and check-outs.

LLANWRTYD'S UNCONVENTIONAL EVENTS

While mulling over how to encourage tourism in Llanwrtyd, some citizens started an inspired roll call of unconventionality. There's something on most months (see www. green-events.co.uk) but here are some of the wackiest.

Saturnalia Beer Festival & Mountain-Bike Chariot Racing (☉Dec) Roman-themed festival that includes a 'Best-Dressed Roman' competition, the devouring of stuffed bulls' testicles and a chariot race.

Man vs Horse Marathon (☉mid-Jun) One of Llanwrtyd's many oddball events, this marathon has been held every year since 1980 and has resulted in some tense finishes. Two-legged runners have won only twice, most recently in 2007.

World Bog Snorkelling Championships (☉Aug) Competitors are permitted wetsuits, snorkels and flippers in order to traverse a trench cut out of a peat bog, but may use no recognisable swimming stroke and may surface only to navigate. Spin-off events include Mountain-Bike Bog Snorkelling and the Bog-Snorkelling Triathlon, both held in July.

Real Ale Wobble & Ramble (☉Nov) Held in conjunction with the Mid-Wales Beer Festival, this event sees cyclists and walkers following waymarked routes (10, 15 or 25 miles, or 35 miles for the 'wobblers' on bikes), and supping real ales at the 'pintstops' along the way.

Mari Llwyd (New Year Walk In; ☉Dec) A revival of the ancient practice of parading a horse's skull from house to house while reciting Welsh poetry.

Drovers Rest WELSH ££
(☑01591-610264; www.food-food-food.co.uk; Y Sgwar; mains £15-21; ☉10.30am-3.30pm & 7.30-9.30pm Tue & Thu-Sat, 12.30-2.30pm Sun; 🛜) The menu at the Drovers, a restaurant-with-rooms, showcases some adventurous pairings of ingredients, plucked from the best local produce. The three-course Sunday lunches (£14.95) are particularly good value, and the owners run regular cooking classes, including a Welsh Cooking Day (£185).

🍷 Drinking & Nightlife

Neuadd Arms PUB
(☑01591-610236; www.neuaddarmshotel.co.uk; Y Sgwar) A focal point for the community, Neuadd Arms hosts the farmers' dogs on the couch in front of the fire and brews its own real ales (including seasonal offerings). All this is complemented by an unusually good bar-food menu.

ⓘ Getting There & Away

Bus 48 heads to Builth Wells (£2.20, 23 minutes, six daily Monday to Saturday).

Llanwrtyd is on the **Heart of Wales** (www.heart-of-wales.co.uk) railway line, with direct services to Swansea (£10.60, 1¾ hours, two to four daily) via Llandeilo (£5, 44 minutes); and Shrewsbury (£13.40, two hours, two to four daily) via Llandrindod Wells (£4, 30 minutes) and Knighton (£7, 1¼ hours).

Llandrindod Wells (Llandrindod)

POP 5310

This spa town struck gold in Victorian times by touting its waters to the well-to-do gentry who rolled in for rest and recuperation following the arrival of the railway in 1864. Though its heyday is long past, this languid place is worth a stop to admire the grand architecture of the era, such as the Gwalia on High St, the elaborate iron and woodwork of the original Victorian shopfronts on Middleton St, the 1865 signal box on the train station platform and the Pump Room.

◎ Sights

Rock Park PARK
The sulphur and saline springs of the forested Rock Park were used as far back as Roman times, and the Victorians sought out their therapeutic properties when the spa Pump Room was built in 1867. The allure of pungent-smelling water diminished by the 1970s, but these days you can still wander past the blue-and-cream cast ironwork of the building and drink from the salty-tasting, iron-rich Chalybeate Spring beside Arlais Brook: apparently the water is good for treating gout, rheumatism, anaemia and more.

National Cycle Collection   MUSEUM
(☑ 01597-825531;   www.cyclemuseum.org.uk;
Temple St; adult/child £4/2; ☺ 10am-4pm Tue-Fri
Apr-Oct) The art nouveau Automobile Palace houses more than 250 bikes, tracing
the progression from clunky boneshakers
to slick modern-day examples, such as the
reserve bike of the 1992 Olympic gold med-
allist Chris Boardman. Curios include penny
farthings, bamboo bikes from the 1890s and
the vertiginous 'Eiffel Tower' of 1899.

Llandrindod Lake   LAKE
Just southeast of the centre is a sedately
pretty, tree-encircled lake constructed at the
end of the 19th century to allow Victorians
to engage in sedate rowing.

Radnorshire Museum   MUSEUM
(☑ 01597-824513; www.powys.gov.uk/radnorshire-
museum; Temple St; adult/child £1/free; ☺ 10am-
4pm Tue-Sat) Small but entertaining, this
museum offers a taste of local history. Look
out for the carved sheila-na-gig figure with
a prominent vulva; a 12th-century log boat;
and a special centenary exhibition on WWI.

✲✲ Festivals & Events

Victorian Festival   CULTURAL
(www.victorianfestival.co.uk; ☺ Aug) In the middle of August Llandrindod Wells indulges
in nine days of capering in 19th-century
costume.

🛏 Sleeping

The Cottage   B&B ££
(☑ 01597-825435;   www.thecottagebandb.co.uk;
Spa Rd; s/d £43/65) The original owner of this
large, appealing Edwardian house requested
that no room be made square. The end result? Comfortable, odd-angled twins, doubles
and a single, all with heavy wooden furniture
and without TV, some with funky wallpaper,
and all presided over by the irrepressibly
chatty host, who makes his own delicious
preserves.

Metropole Hotel   HOTEL ££
(☑ 01597-823700; www.metropole.co.uk; Temple
St; s/d from £98/126; P ☎ ☜) The grand dame
of Llandrindod's hotels, turreted Metropole
retains an old-fashioned elegance – particularly in the lobby. The facilities, however,
are modern, and include a spa and sizeable
pool. What some of its staff lack in the congeniality department, the hotel makes up for
with its sheer size, and its brasserie is one of
the better dining options in town.

ⓘ Information

Tourist Office (☑ 01597-822600; www.
llandrindod.co.uk; Temple St; ☺ 10am-5pm
Mon-Sat) In the old town hall.

ⓘ Getting There & Around

Bus routes include the T4 to Cardiff (£11, 2¾
hours, four daily), Brecon (£8.50, one hour, six
daily), Builth Wells (£2, 22 minutes, seven daily)
and Newtown (£4.80, 48 minutes, six daily); and
X47 to Rhayader (£2.60, 25 minutes, six daily).

Llandrindod is on the Heart of Wales railway
line, with direct services to Swansea (£12.20, 2¼
hours, two to four daily) via Llanwrtyd Wells (£4,
30 minutes), and Shrewsbury (£11.20, 1½ hours)
via Knighton (£4.50, 35 minutes).

Rhayader (Rhaeadr Gwy)
POP 1825

This small town, infamous in the mid-19th
century for the Rebecca Riots, in which farmers disguised as women rebelled against un-
fair taxation, is a sleepy place that revolves
around its Wednesday livestock market. Skirted by the River Wye, the town is a gateway
for walkers and cyclists bound for the nearby
Elan Valley and the 136-mile Wye Valley Walk,
which passes through town; and draws visitors to the red-kite feeding at Gigrin farm.

◉ Sights & Activities

Elan Valley   OUTDOORS
(Cwm Elan) ✐ In the early 19th century, dams
were built on the River Elan (pronounced
'ellen'), west of Rhayader, in order to supply a rapidly expanding Birmingham. The
70-sq-mile watershed has been turned into
an important wildlife conservation area,
with red kites and other rare bird species
now flourishing. The **Elan Valley Visitor
Centre** (☑ 01597-810880; www.elanvalley.org.uk;
☺ 10am-4.30pm Mar-Oct) FREE, 3 miles from
Rhayader on the B4518, downstream of the
lowest dam, has leaflets on the estate's 80
miles of nature trails and rents bicycles.

The 8-mile **Elan Valley Trail**, a walking,
horse-riding and cycling path, starts just
west of Rhayader at Cwmdauddwr and
mostly follows the line of the long-gone Birmingham Corporation Railway alongside
the River Elan and its reservoirs. The wall of
water gushing from the Pen-y-Garreg dam is
particularly impressive.

The Elan Valley Visitor Centre arranges
numerous events for visitors, including birdwatching safaris and helicopter tours.

Gigrin Farm Red-Kite Feeding Station
BIRDWATCHING

(☑ 01597-810243; www.gigrin.co.uk; South St, A470; adult/child £5/3; ☉ 2pm Nov-Mar, 3pm Apr-Oct) Once the most common bird of prey throughout Britain, by the 19th century the red kite was flirting with extinction. Now, visitors to Gigrin Farm can watch conservation efforts in action from strategically placed hides. Once the meat scraps (from a local abattoir) are spread on the field, the kites descend, swooping acrobatically – as many as 400 at a time – followed by crows, and later ravens and buzzards.

Clive Powell Mountain Bike Centre
MOUNTAIN BIKING

(☑ 01597-811343; www.clivepowell-mtb.co.uk; West St; ☉ 9am-5.30pm, closed Thu) Mountain/hybrid-bike rental (per day £24/16) and all-inclusive mountain-biking 'Dirty Weekends', which hit trails around the Elan Valley and are run by a former cycling champion.

ⓘ Getting There & Away
Buses include the weekday X47 to Aberystwyth (£3.85, 1¾ hours, one daily) and Llandrindod Wells (£2.60, 22 minutes, six daily); and X75 to Shrewsbury (£9, 2¾ hours, one daily) and Newtown (£4.50, one hour, twice-daily).

Presteigne (Llanandras)
POP 2055

Pressed right up against the English border, Presteigne (www.presteigne.org.uk) is a bohemian little place, lined with attractive old buildings.

☉ Sights

Radnorshire Arms
HISTORIC BUILDING

(High St) One of the most impressive buildings in town is the half-timbered Radnorshire Arms, the former private residence of Sir Christopher Hatton, alleged lover of Queen Elizabeth I.

Judge's Lodging
HISTORIC BUILDING

(☑ 01544-260650; www.judgeslodging.org.uk; Broad St; adult/child £7.50/3.90; ☉ 10am-5pm Tue-Sun Mar-Oct) The Judge's Lodging offers an intimate glimpse into Victorian times through a wander led by audioguide through the town's 19th-century courthouse, lock-up and the apartments where circuit judges used to stay. You'll 'meet' a motley crew of characters along the way.

⌂ Sleeping

★ Old Vicarage
B&B ££

(☑ 01544-260038; www.oldvicarage-nortonrads.co.uk; Norton; s/d from £78/112; ℗) The Old Vicarage is a three-bedroom, gay-friendly, boutique B&B that makes you feel as if you're on the set of a Victorian period drama, and serves up sumptuous three-course dinners. It's in the town of Norton, 1.5 miles north of Presteigne on the B4355.

ⓘ Getting There & Away
Bus 41 heads to Knighton (£1.85, 15 minutes, up to eight Monday to Saturday).

Knighton (Tref-Y-Clawdd)
POP 3010

Hilly Knighton (www.visitknighton.co.uk) sits midway along the Offa's Dyke Path national trail and at one end of the Glyndŵr's Way national trail, a 132-mile walking route to Welshpool.

⌂ Sleeping & Eating

Offa Dyke House
B&B ££

(☑ 01547-528886; www.offadykehouse.com; 4 High St; s/d from £49/75; ℗ 🛜) Centrally located Offa Dyke House provides succour to weary hikers with its three sumptuous rooms, countryside views and delicious home-cooked dinners.

Horse & Jockey Inn
B&B ££

(☑ 01547-520062; www.thehorseandjockeyinn.co.uk; Station Rd; mains bar £5-9, restaurant £9-18) The town's best refuelling option is the Horse & Jockey, a horseshoe-shaped 14th-century coaching inn. You can eat in the bar or on the sunny terrace, or opt for a substantial meal at the restaurant.

ⓘ Information

Tourist Office & Offa's Dyke Centre (☑ 01547-528753; www.offasdyke.demon.co.uk; West St; ☉ 10am-5pm Apr-Oct, to 4pm Mon-Sat Nov-Mar) The two-in-one Tourist Office & Offa's Dyke Centre is full of information for walkers and interactive displays about the dyke, a section of which runs behind the centre.

ⓘ Getting There & Away
Train destinations from Knighton include Swansea (£15.80, 3¼ hours, two to four daily) via Llanwrtyd Wells (£7, 1¼ hours) and Llandrindod Wells (£4.50, 34 minutes), and Shrewsbury (£9.50, 50 minutes, two to four daily). Bus 41

heads to Presteigne (£1.85, 15 minutes, up to eight Monday to Saturday).

Newtown (Y Drenewydd)

POP 11,360

Newtown used to be a major textiles centre but these days it's as somnolent as Heaven on a Sunday. Its big claim to fame is that Robert Owen (1771–1858), the factory reformer, founder of the cooperative movement and 'father of Socialism', was born and died here. His life and legacy are on display at the **Robert Owen Museum** (📞01686-622510; www.robert-owen-museum.org.uk; The Cross) **FREE**, which was under renovation at the time of writing.

A more contemporary attraction, **Davies Gallery** (Oriel Davies; 📞01686-625041; www.orieldavies.org; The Park; ⊙10am-5pm Mon-Sat) **FREE**, often hosts edgy exhibitions. Its glassed-in **Relish Cafe** (mains £5-7) is the best place for light bites and the shop sells funky handmade jewellery by local designers.

Splendid half-timbered 1651 farmhouse **Highgate** (📞01686-623763; www.highgatebandb.co.uk; Bettws Cedewain; s/d from £55/85; P🐾🛜🐕) makes for a bucolic retreat near Newtown. It offers understated decor, heavy oak beams, inglenook fireplaces and hospitable owners.

Bus routes include the X75 to Shrewsbury (£4.50, 1½ hours, six daily) via Welshpool

(£2.20, 35 minutes, seven daily), and the T4 to Cardiff (£14, 3¾ hours, three daily) via Brecon (£4.80, two hours, six Monday to Saturday). Daily National Express coaches run to Aberystwyth (£10, 1¼ hours) and London Victoria (£34, 5½ hours).

Newtown is on the Cambrian train line between Aberystwyth (£12.50, one hour 20 minutes, five to eight daily) and Birmingham (£19, 1¾ hours, five to eight daily).

Montgomery

Genteel Montgomery sits around a market square lined with Georgian houses in stone and brick, near a well-preserved section of Offa's Dyke Path national trail.

⊙ Sights

St Nicholas' Church   CHURCH

(Church Bank; ⊙9am-dusk) The appealing 13th-century St Nicholas' Church has a vaulted ceiling decorated with intricate coloured bosses, a carved altar screen and an elaborate Elizabethan tomb.

Montgomery Castle   RUIN

FREE The ruins of the 13th-century Montgomery Castle rise from the craggy outcrop above the town, and there are picture-perfect views of Montgomery along the short walk from the car park to the castle.

OFFA'S DYKE PATH

They say that good fences make good neighbours, but King Offa may have taken the idea a bit far. The 8th-century Mercian king built Offa's Dyke, Britain's longest archaeological monument, to mark the boundary between his kingdom and that of the Welsh princes. Even today, though only 80 miles of the dyke remains, the modern Wales–England border roughly follows the line it defined.

The Offa's Dyke Path national trail criss-crosses that border around 30 times in its journey from the Severn Estuary near Chepstow, through the beautiful Wye Valley and Shropshire Hills, to the coast at Prestatyn in North Wales. The dyke itself usually takes the form of a bank next to a ditch, although it's overgrown in some places and built over in others. The trail often strays from the dyke, covering an astonishing range of scenery and vegetation, including river valleys, hill country, oak forests, heathland and bracken, conifer forest, green fields, high moors and the mountainous terrain of the Clwydian Ranges in the north.

While it can be walked in either direction, it's best done south to north, with the wind and sun mainly on your back. Most people take 12 days to complete the 177-mile walk, though it's wise to allow at least two rest days, bringing your adventure to an even two weeks.

The best sources of information about the route are Offa's Dyke Centre in Knighton and www.nationaltrail.co.uk/offasdyke.

Becky Ohlsen

✕ Eating

★**Checkers** MODERN BRITISH £££
(☑01686-669822; www.thecheckersmontgomery.
co.uk; Broad St; mains £18-28, r from £145; ⊘lunch
Wed-Sat, dinner Thu-Sat; 🐾) This truly excellent
restaurant-with-rooms is possibly the main
drawcard of Montgomery. Its Modern British menu, put together from fresh, locally
sourced ingredients, and its first-rate service
have earned it a Michelin star. There are five
stylish, contemporary rooms upstairs.

🛈 Getting There & Away

Bus X71 stops in Montgomery five times daily
(Monday to Saturday) en route from Newtown
(£2.20, 19 minutes) to Welshpool (£1.85, 16
minutes).

Machynlleth

POP 2235
It was in little Machynlleth (ma-*hun*-khleth)
that Welsh hero Owain Glyndŵr established
the country's first Parliament in 1404. But
even that legacy is close to being trumped
by the town's reinvention as the green capital of Wales – thanks primarily to the Centre
for Alternative Technology (CAT).

⊙ Sights

★**Centre for Alternative
Technology (CAT)** ECO-CENTRE
(Canolfan y Dechnoleg Amgen; ☑01654-705950;
www.cat.org.uk; Pantperthog; adult/child £8.50/4;
⊘10am-5pm; P🚻) 🌿 Founded in 1974 in a
disused slate quarry, CAT is a pioneer education centre and an ecologically driven labora-
tory that believes that all of Britain's energy
needs can be met through biomass, hydro,
solar and wind power. A water-balanced funicular whisks you up to the primarily outdoor display area that covers 3 hectares and
is devoted to environmentally friendly construction, renewable energy sources, organic
gardening and alternative technologies.

To get to the CAT from Machynlleth, take
bus 32, X32 or 34 (£1.20, six minutes).

Interactive eco-games, pond dipping
and the Mole Hole's gigantic subterranean dwellers keep younger visitors entertained. CAT hosts workshops for children
during the main school holidays and offers
an extensive program of courses for adults
throughout the year at its state-of-the-art
WISE (Wales Institute for Sustainable Education) building. It also works with local
communities at a grassroots level and advis-
es relevant government bodies on how Britain can adapt to environmental challenges
in a sustainable manner. There's also an
increasing focus on on-site demonstrations,
talks and tours.

★**MOMA Wales** GALLERY
(☑01654-703355; www.momawales.org.uk; Pen-
rallt St; ⊘10am-4pm Mon-Sat) **FREE** Housed
partly in a neoclassical chapel (1880), the
Museum of Modern Art exhibits contemporary Welsh art, such as photography, dra-

---

DON'T MISS

POWIS CASTLE & GARDEN

Surrounded by magnificent gardens, just over a mile south of Welshpool, **Powis Castle**
(NT; ☑01938-551944; www.nationaltrust.org.uk; adult/child castle & gardens £11.80/5.90,
garden only £8.70/4.30; ⊘garden 10am-6pm, castle 12.30-5pm) was originally constructed in
the 13th-century by Gruffydd ap Gwenwynwyn, Prince of Powys, and subsequently en-
riched by generations of the Herbert and Clive families. The castle's highlight, the **Clive
Museum**, houses exquisite treasures brought back from India and the Far East by Clive
of India (British conqueror of Bengal at the Battle of Plassey in 1757) and his son Edward,
who married the daughter of the first Earl of Powys.

The extravagant mural-covered, wood-panelled interior, the mahogany beds, tiger
skins and what is one of Wales' finest collection of paintings proclaim the family's wealth,
while the Clive Museum, with its cache of armour, bejewelled weapons, textiles, diaries
and letters is testimony to a life richly lived in colonial India. You may spot a gold tiger's
head encrusted with rubies and diamonds – one of only two to survive from the throne of
Tipu Sultan, as well as delicately carved ivory chess pieces.

The baroque garden is peerless, dotted with ornamental lead statues and an orangery,
formal gardens, wilderness, terraces and orchards.

matic Snowdonia landscapes and sculpture. The annual Machynlleth Festival, which combines music events with masterclasses and talks, takes place here in late August.

Owain Glyndŵr Centre MUSEUM
(Canolfan Owain Glyndŵr; ☑01654-702932; www. canolfanglyndwr.org; Maengwyn St; adult/child £2.50/1; ⊙10am-4pm) Housed in a rare example of a late-medieval Welsh town house, the eponymous Centre charts the life and times of Owain Glyndŵr, a Welsh independence hero. Displays (some of which are interactive) focus on his military campaigns against the English – so successful initially that by 1404 he controlled most of what is now Wales – as well as his subsequent, swift downfall.

🏃 Activities

Dyfi Mountain Biking MOUNTAIN BIKING
(www.dyfimountainbiking.org.uk) Dyfi maintains three waymarked mountain-bike routes from Machynlleth: Mach 1 (10 miles), 2 (15 miles) and 3 (19 miles), each of which is more challenging than the last. The group also maintains the custom-built 15km Climachx loop trail in the Dyfi Forest, near Corris, with an extension planned. Each May the same crew runs the Dyfi Enduro (www. summitcycles.co.uk/enduro), a noncompetitive, long-distance mountain-bike challenge limited to 650 riders.

🛏 Sleeping & Eating

Reditreks Bunkhouse BUNKHOUSE £
(☑07590-282374; www.reditreks.co.uk; Heol Powys; dm/f £17.55/55; ℙ🅿🛜) 🍴 Run by an outdoor enthusiast involved with Enduro cycling events (www.summitcycles.co.uk/enduro), this comfy, ecofriendly bunkhouse is a fantastic base for self-catering cyclists. The owner has cycle trail maps on hand and the three rooms are spacious and warm. Bring your own bedding and towels.

Wynnstay Hotel INN ££
(☑01654-702941; www.wynnstay-hotel.com; Maengwyn St; s/d from £59/90, mains £12-20; ℙ🛜) The rooms at this erstwhile Georgian coaching inn (1780) have old-fashioned decor and uneven floors, but wi-fi works in most rooms. The menu at the rustic bar-eatery revels in local meats, flying in the face of Machynlleth's veg-warrior image. The on-site pizzeria serves some of the UK's best pizza, including a sensational version topped with goats cheese and chargrilled vegetables.

Number Twenty One MODERN WELSH ££
(☑01654-703382; www.numbertwentyone.co.uk; 21 Maengwyn St; mains £10-17; ⊙noon-10pm Wed-Sun; 🍴♿) This bright and friendly little bistro is consistently packed full of happy customers thanks to its mantra (local, sustainable); its roster of fresh, expertly executed dishes (spiced lamb chops, pearl-barley risotto, slow-cooked pork belly); and its professional service. A warm welcome is extended to children, and there are homemade cakes to munch on between meals.

Farmers Market MARKET £
(www.machynllethmarket.co.uk; Maengwyn St; ⊙Wed) This market has been held for more than seven centuries and remains a lively affair, with produce, baked goods and bric-a-brac for sale.

ℹ Getting There & Away

Routes include the T2 to Aberystwyth (£4.25, 40 minutes, three to six daily) and Bangor (£5.40, 2¾ hours, two to five daily) via Dolgellau (£3.45, 35 minutes), Porthmadog (£4.75, 1¾ hours) and Caernarfon (£5.40, 2½ hours).

Machynlleth is on both the Cambrian and Cambrian Coast train lines. Destinations include Aberystwyth (£6.20, 35 minutes, five to eight daily) and Birmingham (£21.80, 2½ hours, five to eight daily) via Newtown (£9.50, 42 minutes). Train services to Pwllheli and Porthmadog have been replaced by bus services until further notice.

Snowdonia & North Wales

Why Go?

Rugged mountain trails, historic train lines, World Heritage castles and rejuvenated seaside towns ensure North Wales holds its own against attractions down south. The region is dominated by Snowdonia National Park, where mighty peaks scrape moody skies. Protected by such a formidable mountain shield, it's little wonder that the less-visited Llŷn Peninsula and the ancient island enclave of Anglesey have retained their traditional language and culture. In fact, the whole region feels properly Welsh: you'll hear the language on the street, see the Celtic legacy in the landscape, and soak up the cultural pride in galleries, museums and attractions, all the way from the beaches of the North Coast to the river-threaded heartland of northeast Wales. In many ways, North Wales distils the very essence of Welshness – just don't mention that to the folks in Cardiff.

Best Castles

➡ Conwy Castle (p761)

➡ Caernarfon Castle (p746)

➡ Beaumaris Castle (p754)

➡ Harlech Castle (p745)

Best Heritage Railways

➡ Ffestiniog Railway (p753)

➡ Welsh Highland Railway (p753)

➡ Snowdon Mountain Railway (p740)

➡ Talyllyn Railway (p744)

When to Go

➡ May is the driest month and Llandudno celebrates the warming weather with its Victorian Extravaganza festival.

➡ May to September arguably gives you the best hiking weather, but the warmest months – July and August – bring crowds.

➡ The Snowdon train runs to the summit between Easter and November.

➡ In July you can shuttle between the beaches and Llangollen's International Musical Eisteddfod and Fringe Festival.

➡ Late autumn and early winter bring the heaviest rains, while late winter and early spring are particularly raw and bracing.

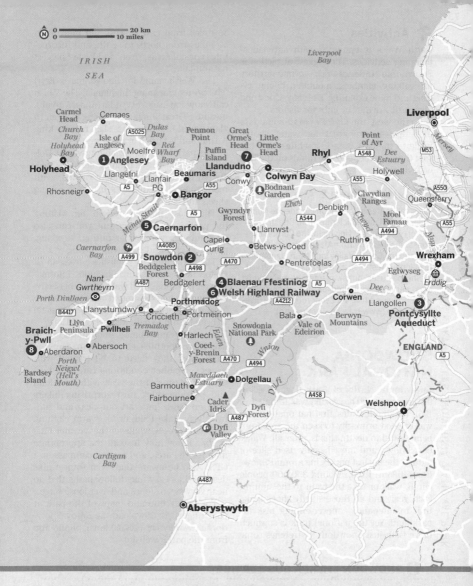

Snowdonia & North Wales Highlights

① Exploring the coves, cliffs and neolithic remains of **Anglesey** (p754)

② Climbing **Snowdon** (p739), Wales' highest peak – or cheating by taking the rack-and-pinion train to the top

③ Sailing across **Pontcysyllte Aqueduct** (p764), Britain's latest World Heritage Site

④ Disappearing underground into the slate caverns at **Blaenau Ffestiniog** (p736)

⑤ Witnessing the fearsome beauty and strength of **Caernarfon Castle** (p746)

⑥ Taking an unforgettable coast-to-coast journey on the narrow-gauge **Welsh Highland Railway** (p753)

⑦ Revelling in all things Victorian – pier, promenade and Mr Punch – at the seaside resort of **Llandudno** (p758)

⑧ Gazing towards the holy island of Bardsey from end-of-the-world headland **Braich-y-Pwll** (p750)

🏃 Activities

North Wales is crammed with adrenaline-pumping activities. The biggest attraction is **Snowdonia National Park** – prime territory for walking, climbing, mountain biking, cycling and mine exploring. **Betws-y-Coed** and **Llanberis** are the key hubs for visitors.

To the west, the **Llŷn Peninsula** and **Isle of Anglesey** are great for water sports, while to the east **Bala** is a white-water hot spot thanks to dependable rapids on the River Tryweryn.

ⓘ Getting There & Around

Major rail routes in the region include the North Wales Coast Line, which runs from Chester to the ferry terminal at Holyhead; the Cambrian Coast Line, heading from Machynlleth to Pwllheli; and the Conwy Valley Line from Llandudno to Blaenau Ffestiniog. Snowdonia is well served by Sherpa buses, but away from the main tourist areas services are limited and getting anywhere on a Sunday is a trial. Plot your route with **Traveline Cymru** (www.traveline-cymru.info).

SNOWDONIA NATIONAL PARK

Snowdonia National Park (Parc Cenedlaethol Eryri; www.eryri-npa.gov.uk) was founded in 1951, making it Wales' first national park. It was created primarily to keep the area from being loved to death: this is, after all, Wales' best known and most heavily used slice of nature, the busiest part being around **Snowdon** (1085m) itself. Around 350,000 people climb, walk or take the train to the summit each year, and all those sturdy shoes make trail maintenance a never-ending task for park staff. Yet the national park is so much more than just Snowdon; it stretches some 35 miles from east to west and more than 50 miles from north to south, and incorporates coastal areas, rivers and Wales' biggest natural lake.

The Welsh name for Snowdonia is Eryri (eh-*ruh*-ree) meaning 'highlands'. The Welsh call Snowdon itself Yr Wyddfa (uhr-*with*-vuh), meaning 'Great Tomb' – according to legend a giant called Rita Gawr was slain here by King Arthur and is buried at the summit.

The park includes sizeable towns at Dolgellau, Bala, Harlech and Betws-y-Coed. Two-thirds of it is privately owned, with more than three-quarters used for raising sheep and cattle.

The most popular reason for visiting the park is for walking, but you can also go climbing, white-water rafting, kayaking, pony trekking and even windsurfing.

The park authority publishes a free annual visitor newspaper, which includes information on park-organised walks and other activities and on getting around. The **Met Office** (www.metoffice.gov.uk/loutdoor/mountainsafety) website has up-to-date weather conditions.

Though Snowdonia's mountains seem like mere foothills compared to, say, the Himalayas, they need to be treated with respect. Weather conditions can turn hostile at any time of the year, with low cloud and porridge-thick mist surprising hikers even on days that start out clear and sunny. Always take food, drink, warm clothing and waterproofs, whatever the weather. Carry *and* know how to read the appropriate map for the area, and carry a compass or a GPS. Also be aware that even some walks described as easy may follow paths that go near very steep slopes and over loose scree.

For handy info and maps of the park at your fingertips, download the **Enjoy Snowdonia** (www.eryri-npa.gov.uk) smartphone app from the park's website.

ⓘ SNOWDON SHERPA BUS SERVICE

The Snowdon Sherpa service, a circuit of buses that scurries around the slopes of Snowdon, linking up the six main trailheads, is a boon for walkers. It means you can access trailheads by public transport from nearby towns; or you can walk up the mountain by one path and come down by another, and then hop on a bus to take you back to your starting point. Check timetables carefully, however; the S6 service, for example, is extremely limited.

Services S1, S2, S3 and S6 link Llanberis, Pen-y-Pass, Betws-y-Coed and Llanrwst. The S4 runs between Caernarfon, Waunfawr and Beddgelert. The S6 joins Bangor, Bethesda and Betws-y-Coed. The S97 runs from Porthmadog to Beddgelert and Pen-y-Pass.

A day ticket costs adult/child £4/2, but may be a false economy: a single trip on services S1, S4 and S6 costs £2/1 and on the S2 and S3 £1.50/75p. For up-to-date timetables, see the **Gwynedd Council website** (www.gwynedd.gov.uk).

Llanberis

POP 1845

Llanberis acts as a gateway to Snowdon for scores of rugged Gore-Tex and fleece wearers who flow steadily through the little town year-round. The Llanberis Path, the most popular route up Wales' most famous mountain, starts from here, as does the Snowdon Mountain Railway (p740), so it's little wonder that Llanberis receives the lion's share of visitors to the national park, although it sits just outside the park border.

Synonymous these days with hiking, biking and climbing, for much of its existence Llanberis was a mining town whose residents coaxed a living out of the steep sides of Elidir Fawr. The last of the mines closed down in 1969, but visitors can delve into Llanberis' industrial heritage via the Dinorwig slate quarry, now part of Europe's largest underground power station, and the attractions that stem from it. The narrow-gauge railway that once used to haul slate to the coast now slowly chugs its way along the shore of Llyn Padarn lake.

You can't get lost in Llanberis; most of its points of interest are along the High St, which runs parallel to the A4086.

◉ Sights & Activities

★ **National Slate Museum** MUSEUM
(www.museumwales.ac.uk/en/slate; ⊙10am-5pm) FREE The immense jagged scar of a quarry gouged into the mountainside, a stone archway and a yard full of heavy machinery usher you into the slate-mining world – the former lifeblood of Llanberis. You can attend slate-cutting demonstrations taken by wise-cracking staff and learn the difference between a Duchess and a Lady; check out Britain's largest water wheel; follow the tramways; and peer into the recreated slate workers' cottages for a glimpse of their lives in 1861, 1901 and 1969.

Electric Mountain INTERPRETATION CENTRE
(☑01286-870636; www.electricmountain.co.uk; tour adult/child £8.50/4.35; ⊙10am-4.30pm Easter-Oct) Dinorwig Power Station is the largest hydroelectricity scheme of its kind in Europe. It harnesses the power of Marchlyn Mawr reservoir, the release of which through its turbines is enough to cover the national grid's evening demand surge. Guided bus tours run into the station's guts under the mountain pretty much hourly, but booking

in advance is advised. Electric Mountain is located by the lakeside on the A4086, near the south end of High St.

Dolbadarn Castle CASTLE
(Castell Dolbadarn; ⊙10am-4pm) FREE Built before 1230 by the Princes of Gwyneth, the castle keep rises like a perfect black chessboard rook from a green hilltop between two lakes. It's reached via a short walk from the main road leading towards the National Slate Museum through gnarly woods, where a giant moss-covered rock by the path looks poised to release the Headless Horseman, à la *Sleepy Hollow*.

🛏 Sleeping

Llanberis YHA HOSTEL £
(☑0845 371 9645; www.yha.org.uk; Capel Goch Rd; dm/r from £15/45; ⊙reception 8-10am & 5-10pm; ℗) This former quarry-manager's house on the slopes above town has twin-bunk rooms and dorms with shared facilities and two en suite doubles. Lock-out between noon and 5pm.

★ **Beech Bank** B&B ££
(☑01286-871085; www.beech-bank.co.uk; 2 High St; s/d £60/80; ℗ 🛜) The effusive, gregarious manner of proprietress Annie has won her repeat guests, as have the five individually styled rooms inside this double-gabled, wrought-iron-trimmed stone house. Room 1 features a roof garden; room 2 has a super-king-size bed. Flasks and packed meals can be arranged and rooms come equipped with wine coolers for posthike R&R.

Plas Coch Guest House HOTEL ££
(☑01286-872122; www.plascochsnowdonia.co.uk; High St; s/d £55/80; ℗ 🛜) This large ivy-draped 1865-built house is operated by a friendly couple with lots of local knowledge to impart. Hikers are well looked after with a boot-washing nook, and packed lunches and flasks. Of the eight unique rooms, one comes with its own balcony and the family room has proper beds for children rather than bunks.

✗ Eating

Pete's Eats CAFE £
(☑01286-870117; www.petes-eats.co.uk; 40 High St; mains £3-7; ⊙8am-8pm; 🛜) Photos of local mountain-related exploits adorn the walls of this busy, bright cafe where hikers and climbers swap tips over monster portions of soup, pasta and sandwiches in a hostel-like

Snowdonia & Llŷn Peninsula

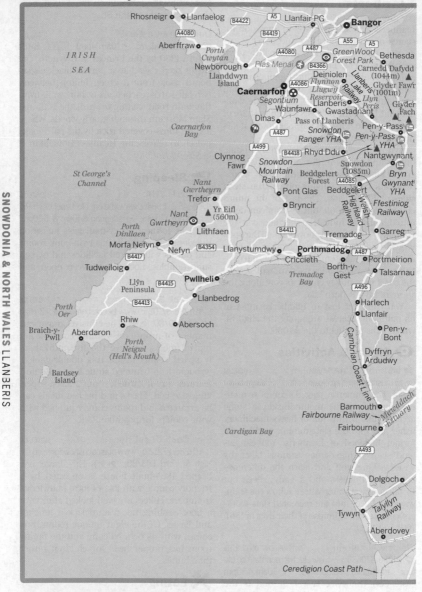

environment. There's a huge noticeboard full of travellers' information, a book exchange, a map and guidebook room, and computers for internet access, and you can crash in the bunkrooms and private digs upstairs.

Llygad yr Haul
(90 High St; mains from £5; ⊙10am-5pm; 🕿🖶🐾) The delicious homemade bread and cakes have won this friendly little cafe a local fan base, while walkers crowd in for the generous helpings of jacket potato with toppings,

CAFE £

noon-2pm Wed-Fri & Sun, 7-10pm Wed-Sat; ✍) Charming owners and imaginative menus underpin this modern, brasserie-style restaurant's popularity and longevity, and the open kitchen allows you to see the masters at work. Fine local ingredients (Welsh lamb, beef, cheeses, seasonal vegetables) form the basis of the internationally inspired dishes. There are tasty veggie options and a good wine list.

ℹ Information

Tourist Office (☎ 01286-870765; www.visit-snowdonia.info; ⏰10am-4pm Fri-Tue Easter-Sep) Located inside Electric Mountain.

ℹ Getting There & Away

Snowdon Sherpa bus S1 heads to Pen-y-Pass (£2, 20 minutes, up to 13 daily) while S2, S3 (both £1.50) and S6 (£2) continue on to Capel Curig (30 minutes, up to 12 daily) and Betws-y-Coed (40 minutes). Buses 85 and 86 head to Bangor (£3.30, 40 minutes, 16 daily Monday to Friday), and buses 88 and 89 head to Caernarfon (£2.20, 20 minutes, one to two per hour Monday to Friday).

Betws-y-Coed

POP 2250

Blessed with an almost Alpine atmosphere, the bustling little stone village of Betws-y-Coed (bet-us-ee-koyd) makes an excellent base for exploring Snowdonia National Park. It sports a postcard-perfect setting above an inky river, engulfed in the verdant leafiness of the Gwydyr Forest, near the junction of three river valleys: the Llugwy, the Conwy and the Lledr. Betws is a walker and cyclist magnet *par excellence*, as evidenced by a disproportionately high number of outdoor-gear shops and bike-hire joints.

The town has been Wales' most popular inland resort since Victorian times, when a group of countryside painters founded an artistic community here. The arrival of the railway in 1868 cemented its popularity, and today Betws-y-Coed is as busy with families and coach parties as it is with walkers.

⊙ Sights & Activities

★ **Gwydyr Forest** FOREST
The 28-sq-mile Gwydyr Forest, planted since the 1920s with oak, beech and larch, encircles Betws-y-Coed and is ideal for a day's walking – though it gets very muddy in wet weather. *Walks Around Betws-y-Coed*, available from the Betws-y-Coed Tourist

chunky sandwiches, and panini-and-soup meal deals.

★ **Peak Restaurant** INTERNATIONAL ££
(Bwyty'r Copa; ☎01286-872777; www.peakrestaurant.co.uk; 86 High St; lunch £4-7, dinner £11-19;

SNOWDONIA & NORTH WALES BETWS-Y-COED

1. Snowdon Mountain Railway (p740) 2. Lake District (p592)
3. Cape Cornwall (p351) 4. Eilean Donan Castle (p932), Scotland

Breathtaking Britain

Britain is best known for the historic capitals of London and Edinburgh, the university towns of Cambridge and Oxford, and the well-preserved Roman remains in Bath. However, beyond the urban sprawl lies another Britain: a landscape of high mountain vistas, dramatic valleys lined with lakes, and – as befitting an island – thousands of miles of spectacular coastline.

Lake District

The Lake District (p592) is home to the highest mountains in England, as well as some of the longest and most beautiful lakes. With summits snow-capped in winter, and spectacular at any time of year, this landscape inspired the poet William Wordsworth, and is a major magnet for hikers today.

Snowdonia

Wales is crowned with Snowdonia (p730) – a range of rocky peaks and glacier-hewn valleys stretching across the north of the country. Snowdon itself is accessible by Swiss-style cog railway, while Tryfan and Glyder Fawr offer equally challenging hikes and spectacular views, as well as more chance of solitude.

Cornwall's Coast

In Britain, you're spoilt for choice when it comes to beautiful coastline, but in the far southwest, the coast of Cornwall (p337) is hard to beat, with its stunning combination of sandy beaches, tranquil coves, picture-postcard fishing ports, adrenaline-pumping surf spots and rugged cliffs carved by Atlantic waves.

Scotland's Northwest Highlands

The long journey to the far northwest corner of the Scottish Highlands (p924) is repaid with some of the finest scenery anywhere in Britain. In this wild and remote region, the sheer mountainsides drop to the sea, while narrow sea lochs cut deep inland, creating a landscape that is almost other-worldly in its beauty.

Office, details several circular forest walks. Mountain-bikers are challenged by two mountain-biking trails (both waymarked), particularly the tough Marin Trail, as well as the Penmachno Loops, 4km south of town near the village of Penmachno.

Swallow Falls   WATERFALL

(Rhaeadr Ewynnol; admission £1.50) Located 2 miles west of Betws-y-Coed alongside the A5, this much-visited spot consists of a series of viewpoints flanking a straightforward descent to a mesmeric emerald pool, fed by the torrent weaving through the rocks.

Go Below Underground
Adventures   ADVENTURE TOUR

(☑ 01690-710108; www.go-below.co.uk; adult/child from £49/39) Explore the depths of an abandoned slate mine, armed with a harness, headlamp and helmet. Five- to six-hour adventures involve abseiling down shafts, zip-lining, (and perilous traverses in the case of Challenge Xtreme). Book in advance. It's based on the A5 south of Betws-y-Coed at the turn-off to Penmachno.

Beics Betws   BICYCLE RENTAL

(☑ 01690-710766; www.bikewales.co.uk; Vicarage Rd; ☺ 9am-5.30pm Mon-Sat Mar-Nov, call ahead at other times) Can advise on cycling trails; and repairs and hires mountain bikes (per day £28 to £32).

🛏 Sleeping

Betws-y-Coed YHA   HOSTEL, CAMPGROUND £

(☑ 01690-710796; www.swallowfallshotel.co.uk; Holyhead Rd, Swallow Falls; dm/tw £18/40, site per adult/child £8/4; P 🛜 🛋) Popular with ram-blers and cyclists, this hostel is part of a bustling traveller hub with a year-round campsite, pub and upmarket inn next door. There's a kitchen for guest use, en suite dorms sleeping four to 10 people, functional twins and doubles, and an indoor games room.

Tŷ Gwyn Hotel   HISTORIC HOTEL ££

(☑ 01690-710383; www.tygwynhotel.co.uk; A5; r £60-140; P 🛜) This ex-coaching inn has been welcoming guests since 1636, its venerable age borne out by misshapen rooms, low ceilings and exposed beams. Four rooms share facilities, while the others are en suite. The **restaurant** (mains £14-20) menu focuses on hearty, meaty mains, but vegetarian choices and lighter bar-style meals are also available. It's just across Waterloo Bridge.

Maes-y-Garth   B&B ££

(☑ 01690-710441; www.maes-y-garth.co.uk; Lon Muriau, off A470; r £76-118; P 🛜) Just across the river and a field from the township, this hillside home has earned itself many fans. Inside you'll find a warm welcome from owners happy to share their knowledge of the area. Five quietly stylish guest rooms have gorgeous views; perhaps the nicest is room 4, where you can watch the sunset over Snowdonia from your own balcony.

Afon Gwyn   B&B £££

(☑ 01690-710442; www.guest-house-betws-y-coed.com; A470, Coed-y-Celyn; r £176-256; P 🛜) Down in the valley, this old stone house has been skilfully converted into a grand boutique guesthouse run by attentive management. The decor is faultlessly tasteful, with white-painted wooden panelling, a bright and sunny conservatory where meals are

BLAENAU FFESTINIOG

Most of the slate used to roof 19th-century Britain came from Wales, and much of that came from the mines of Blaenau (blay-nye) Ffestiniog. Encircled by dark, bare mountains of slate, Blaenau feels oddly like a ski town in the off-season, with few people on the streets and frequently miserable weather, so it's a good thing that its main attraction lies underground.

Don a helmet, grab a seat in the cramped yellow funicular, and you're ready to descend into the subterranean gloom of the **Llechwedd Slate Caverns** (☑ 01766-830306; www.llechwedd-slate-caverns.co.uk; tours adult/child £15/10; ☺ 9.30am-5.30pm): Blaenau's former lifeblood. On the hour-long tour, a guide leads you through the 1846 network of narrow, dripping tunnels and vast caverns – including one occasionally used now as a wedding chapel – describing the harsh lives of Victorian miners who worked 12-hour days here by candlelight.

The final section involves mounting a flight of 70 steps; once back up to the surface, you can potter around the workshops and watch slate being expertly cut into tiles.

served, glittering chandeliers, and bathrooms bedecked in Italian tiles and marble. Wi-fi reception in all rooms but one.

✖ Eating

Cwmni Cacen Gri CAFE £
(www.cwmnicacengri.co.uk; Station approach; Welsh cakes each £0.50; ⊙ 9am-4.30pm Tue-Sun; ✐) At this pint-sized spot, two local ladies serve Welsh cakes straight off the griddle – from traditional to unusually flavoured sweet and savoury. Pies, homemade cake and good coffee also available: ideal picnic fodder.

★ Bistro Betws-y-Coed WELSH ££
(✐ 01690-710328; www.bistrobetws-y-coed.com; Holyhead Rd; lunch £6-9, dinner £13-20; ⊙ noon-3pm & 6.30-9.30pm Jun-Sep, closed Mon & Tue Oct-May) This cottage-style brasserie's statement of intent is 'modern and traditional Welsh' and it gets the pairings of ingredients just right. Treats may include wood pigeon with blueberry pancakes, goats cheese rarebit and spiced honey belly pork, served by ultrafriendly, professional staff. Book days in advance during high season or taste bitter disappointment.

❶ Information

Tourist Office (✐ 01690-710426; www.eryri-npa.gov.uk; Royal Oak Stables; ⊙ 9.30am-5.30pm) Across the road from the train station. Sells books and maps.

❶ Getting There & Away

Snowdon Sherpa buses S2, S3 (£1.50) and S6 (£2) stop outside the train station, with services to Swallow Falls (five minutes, up to 12 daily), Capel Curig (10 minutes), Pen-y-Pass (20 minutes) and Llanberis (30 minutes).

Betws-y-Coed is on the **Conwy Valley Line** (www.conwyvalleyrailway.co.uk), with six daily train services (three on Sundays) to Llandudno (£5.60, 52 minutes) and Blaenau Ffestiniog (£4.50, 27 minutes).

Blaenau is a stop between Caernarfon and Porthmadog on the historic Ffestiniog Railway (p753).

Beddgelert

POP 500

Charming little Beddgelert is a conservation village of rough grey stone buildings overlooking the trickling River Glaslyn with its ivy-covered bridge.

The name, meaning 'Gelert's Grave', is said to refer to a folk tale concerning 13th-century Welsh prince Llywelyn. Believing that his dog Gelert had savaged his baby son, Llywelyn slaughtered the dog, only to discover that Gelert had fought off the wolf that had attacked the baby. More likely, the name Beddgelert is derived from a 5th-century Irish preacher, Celert, who is believed to have founded a church here. Regardless, the 'grave' of Gelert the dog is a popular attraction, reached by a pretty riverside trail. It was probably constructed by a 19th-century hotelier in an attempt to boost business – clearly a successful gambit.

⊙ Sights & Activities

Sygun Copper Mine MINE
(www.syguncoppermine.co.uk; adult/under 15yr £8.95/6.95; ⊙ 9.30am-5pm Mar-Oct, 10am-4pm Nov-Feb) A mile east of Beddgelert, this mine was first worked by Romans, then by 19th-century miners. Disembodied voices guide you throughout the 45-minute self-guided tour through narrow, glistening tunnels, up steep steps and into caverns with dioramas evoking Victorian miner life. There's an absorbing little Museum of Antiquities on-site and you can also try your hand at metal-detecting or panning for gold.

Aberglaslyn Gorge & Moel Hebog WALKING
Two excellent walks start near Beddgelert. The Aberglaslyn Gorge trail runs alongside the pretty River Glaslyn through the gorge until you hit the main road at Pont Aberglaslyn (3 miles return, two hours). The ascent of Moel Hebog hill (783m) is a more strenuous hike (8-mile loop, five hours), made particularly worthwhile by the scenic ridge walk that takes in two more peaks. The tourist office has leaflets on the hikes.

Beddgelert Forest MOUNTAIN BIKING
Within this forestry commission block, 2 miles north of Beddgelert along the A4805, is a popular campsite and two mountain-bike trails: the 9.5km Hir Trail and the easier 4km Byr Trail. Beddgelert Bikes, by the West Highland railway station in the village, rents out mountain bikes, tandems and child seats.

⫞ Sleeping & Eating

★ Bwyty & Wety Hebog B&B ££
(✐ 01766-890400; www.hebog-eatandsleep.co.uk; Fford Caernarfon; s/d £45/75; ☎) A welcome addition to Beddgelert's sleeping and dining scene, Bwyty features three cheerful en suite singles and a compact double with eye-catching wallpaper. The downstairs

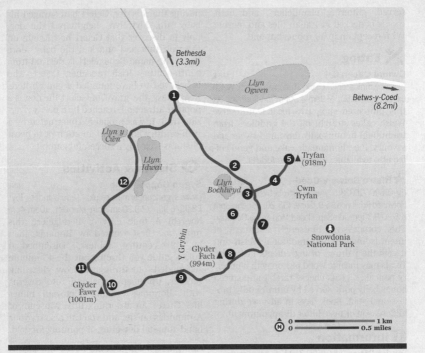

Walking Tour
The Glyder Traverse

START IDWAL COTTAGE
END IDWAL COTTAGE
LENGTH 6.5 MILES; SIX TO EIGHT HOURS

Snowdon often steals the fanfare but in nearby Ogwen Valley other equally challenging peaks clamour for attention. This rugged day hike takes in Glyder Fach and Glyder Fawr, with an optional scramble up 'peak (recommended for fit hikers with a head for heights). Come prepared with wet-weather gear, map and GPS in case fog rolls in.

Cross the footbridge from the car park at Idwal Cottage (off the A5). As the path forks, carry on straight ahead up the **1 Miner's Track** that crosses some bracken-covered, boggy ground before climbing steeply up Cwm Bochlwyd to the sheltered **2 Llyn Bochlwyd** lake. Ignore the track veering off to the right and continue ascending instead towards the gap between Tryfan and Glyder Fach. Once you've reached the **3 ridge** with its stone wall, you can detour up the **4 Tryfan's South Ridge**. It's a 30-minute, straightforward scramble up giant rocks to Tryfan's famous summit (918m) feature – the **5 Adam and Eve rocks**. Tempted to climb up and jump the 5ft gap? Don't do it on a windy day!

Once you've taken in the view of Llyn Ogwen below and the Carnedd mountains opposite, retrace your steps to the stone wall. Use the ladder crossing and then either power up the steep shortcut of **6 Bristly Ridge** or take the moderately inclined **7 footpath** that cuts across the eastern flank of Glyder Fach; make a sharp right up towards the jumble of dark rock slabs that mark the **8 Glyder Fach summit** (994m), with the famous Cantilever – a slab of rock balanced on two shorter rocks – just a few metres away. A straightforward, cairn-marked walk passes the dramatic black-rock spikes of **9 Castell y Gwynt** (Castle of the Winds) en route across the bare, rock-strewn plateau to **10 Glyder Fawr** (1001m). A steep, scree-strewn path zigzags down to the **11 Devil's Kitchen** ridge. Head right along the path that makes its way between giant boulders to the shores of **12 Llyn Idwal**. Skirt the lake from the left for the best views of Cwm Idwal, cross the footbridge, turn left and follow the footpath back to the car park.

cafe morphs into a sleek **bistro** (mains £9-22) by night, serving the likes of brie tart and Welsh lamb with samphire. An on-site chip shop and summer terrace overlooking the babbling Glaslyn seal the deal.

Plas Tan y Graig B&B **££**
(📞01766-890310; www.plas-tanygraig.co.uk; Smith St; s £54-78, d £88-90; ☺mid-Feb–Oct; 🛜) This bright, friendly place is an appealing B&B in the heart of the village. It has seven uncluttered rooms, five with bathrooms, and a lounge full of maps and books. Minimum two-night stay April to October.

Glaslyn Ices & Cafe Glandwr ICE CREAM **£**
(www.glaslynices.co.uk; mains £4-10; ☺10am-5pm Sun-Fri, 9.30am-8.30pm Sat; 🖲) In summer you'll spot this ice-cream parlour by the massive queues out the door. It serves 24 highly lickable homemade flavours and is attached to a family **restaurant** offering paninis, pizza, sandwiches and more.

ℹ️ Information

Tourist Office (📞01766-890615; www.eryri-npa.gov.uk; Canolfan Hebog; ☺9.30am-5.30pm daily Easter-Oct, to 4.30pm Fri-Sun Nov-Easter) Sells leaflets on hikes around Beddgelert.

ℹ️ Getting There & Away

Beddgelert is a stop on the historic Welsh Highland Railway, which runs between Caernarfon (£26.80 return, 1½ hours) and Porthmadog (£19.20 return, 50 minutes).

Snowdon Sherpa bus S4 runs to Caernarfon (£2, 30 minutes, daily), while S97 heads to Porthmadog (£2, 25 minutes, three to four daily) in one direction and Pen-y-Pass (20 minutes) in the other.

Capel Curig

POP 205

Tiny Capel Curig, 5 miles west of Betws-y-Coed and ringed by looming mountains, is one of Snowdonia's oldest hill stations, and has long been a magnet for walkers, climbers and other outdoor junkies. The village spreads out along the A5, but the main hub of activity is at the intersection of the A4086.

Plas y Brenin (📞01690-720214; www.pyb.co.uk; A4086), at the western edge of the village, is a multiactivity centre offering an array of year-round courses on both land and water, ranging from basic rock climbing and summer and winter mountaineering to kayaking, canoeing and abseiling. Taster days for youngsters are available throughout the school holidays.

Plas Curig Hostel (📞01690-720225; www.snowdoniahostel.co.uk; A5; dm/d/f from £23/50/90; 🅿️🛜🖲) pays great attention to the comfort of its guests. Most bunks have privacy curtains, there's a large, well-equipped kitchen and a drying room for soggy hiking gear.

Snowdon Sherpa buses S2 and S6 stop here.

Snowdon

No Snowdonia National Park experience is complete without coming face-to-face with Snowdon (1085m), one of Britain's most awe-inspiring mountains and the highest in Wales. On a clear day the views stretch to Ireland and the Isle of Man over Snowdon's fine jagged ridges, which drop away in great swoops to sheltered *cwms* (valleys) and deep lakes. Even on a gloomy day you could find yourself above the clouds. The Snowdon Mountain Railway and several well-marked trails make the mountain extremely accessible; however, that does mean that you're highly unlikely to have the summit or the approach all to yourself.

⊙ Sights & Activities

Climbing Snowdon

Your prize, the barren peak of Snowdon, awaits. Seven routes lead up to the summit, each with its own difficulties and rewards. Now that you've accepted the challenge, will it be the path of least resistance or the road less taken?

ℹ️ HERITAGE RAILWAY DISCOUNT CARD

Wales is the Holy Grail for lovers of steam engines. Ten narrow-gauge railways used for mining and quarrying during Wales' industrial heyday have been lovingly restored to form a group called **Great Little Trains of Wales** (www.greatlittletrainsofwales.co.uk; £10). A discount card entitles the holder to a 20% discount for a return trip on each of the 10 participating railways, which include Talyllyn Railway, Welsh Highland Railway and Snowdon Mountain Railway.

Llanberis Path (5 miles; three hours) Starts in Llanberis. The longest route but with a gentle incline and popular with families. Runs beside the railway line.

Snowdon Ranger Path (4 miles; three hours) Starts at Snowdon Ranger YHA. Straightforward but with two steep sections. Relatively uncrowded.

Miners' Track (4 miles; 2½ hours) Starts at Pen-y-Pass car park. Broad and flat for much of the way; skirts Llyn Llydaw and climbs steeply to meet Pyg Track. Then there's a final steep zigzag to meet Llanberis Path near the summit.

Pyg Track (3.5 miles; 2½ hours) Starts at the western end of Pen-y-Pass car park. Climbs quite steeply up to Bwlch y Moch and skirts Crib Goch with great views down on Llyn Llydaw before switchbacking up to the summit.

Snowdon Horseshoe (8-mile loop; six to eight hours) Starts with the Pyg Track, but involves a short, steep scramble up to the exposed knife-edge Crib Goch ridge (only attempt if you're very experienced), a traverse to Crib-y-Dddysgl pinnacle and a precipitous descent down the scree-covered east side of Snowdon. Another short scramble takes you up to the twin summits of Y Lliwedd, and then it's a straightforward descent into Cwm Dyli to rejoin the Miners' Track.

Rhyd Ddu Path (4 miles; three hours) Starts off the Caernarfon–Beddgelert road (A4085). Follows grazing land before skirting the rim of Cwm Clogwyn and Yr Wyddfa's south ridge. Beautiful and uncrowded.

Watkin Path (4 miles; three hours). Starts from Bethania Bridge in Nantgwynant. A challenging route that involves an ascent of more than 1000m. A wooded track narrows and ascends Cwm Llan before skirting the base of Craig Ddu. Then it's a scramble across a steep-sided scree-covered slope to Bwlch Ciliau, the saddle between Snowdon's summit and Y Lliwedd, and another steep ascent to Snowdon itself.

Make sure you're well prepared with warm, waterproofed clothing and sturdy footwear, and always take food, drink, a map and a compass or GPS. Conditions can deteriorate quickly; check the weather forecast before setting out.

Snowdon by Rail

★ **Snowdon
Mountain Railway**   HERITAGE RAILWAY
(☑ 0844 493 8120; www.snowdonrailway.co.uk; return diesel adult/child £27/18, steam £35/25; ⊙ 9am-5pm mid-Mar–Oct) Those industrious, railway-obsessed Victorians have gifted today's visitors with an alternative to a three-hour mountain walk: the UK's highest and only public rack-and-pinion railway, opened in 1896. Vintage steam and modern diesel locomotives haul carriages from Llanberis up to Snowdon's summit in an hour. Single tickets can only be booked for the journey up (adult/child £20/15) and return trips involve a scant half-hour at the top before heading back down again. Book in advance due to huge popularity.

Departures are weather-dependent and based on customer demand; from March to May the trains head only as far as Clogwyn Station (adult/child return £21/13) – at an altitude of 779m.

🛏 Sleeping

Accommodation options are scattered around Snowdon's slopes and make ideal hiking bases.

Pen-y-Pass YHA   HOSTEL £
(☑ 0845 371 9534; www.yha.org.uk; A4086; dm/d £20/52.50; ⊙ Mar-Dec) Superbly situated 5.5 miles up the A4086 from Llanberis, right at the start of two trails up Snowdon. Reopened in June 2014 after extensive renovations.

Snowdon Ranger YHA   HOSTEL £
(☑ 0800 0191 700; www.yha.org.uk; dm/tr/q £19/57/73; Ⓟ @) On the A4085, 5 miles north of Beddgelert, at the trailhead for the Snowdon Ranger Path, this former inn is full of character and has its own adjoining lakeside beach.

Bryn Gwynant YHA   HOSTEL £
(☑ 0800 0195 465; www.yha.org.uk; Nantgwynant; dm/tw/f £19/50/73; ⊙ Mar-Oct; Ⓟ) Victorian mansion with splendid lake views, 4 miles east of Beddgelert, well-located for various outdoor sports and near the start of the tricky Watkin Path up Snowdon. Three-course meals are available on request, as are maps of the area.

Pen-y-Gwryd   HOTEL ££
(☑ 01286-870211; www.pyg.co.uk; Nant Gwynant; s/d £43/86; Ⓟ 🛜 🐾) Creeper-clad Pen-y-Gwryd was used as a training base by Ed-

mund Hilary's 1953 Everest team. Their signatures are on the dining-room ceiling and if your child under 12 makes it up and down Snowdon without having to be carried, they get to drink from Hilary's own tankard. Five of the rooms are en suite; full board and sauna are available for dedicated hikers. You'll find the hotel below Pen-y-Pass, at the junction of the A498 and A4086.

ℹ️ Information

Hafod Eryri (☉10am to 20min before last train departure; 🛜) Just below the cairn that marks Snowdon's summit, the Hafod Eryri centre is clad in oak and granite and curved to blend into the mountain. Ambient interpretative elements are built into the structure itself, and inside there are toilets and a decent cafe. The centre (including toilets) closes in the winter or if the weather's terrible.

ℹ️ Getting There & Away

Snowdon Sherpa buses stop at all of the trailheads. Buses S1, S2, S6 cost £1.50 to £2; adult/child day ticket costs £4/2.

Car parks fill up quickly; on a fine day you won't find a parking space at the Pen-y-Pass car park after 8am (even though it costs £10 per day). Park near the junction of A4086 and A498 and walk up, or drive to the free car park at Gwastadnant along the A4086 and catch either a Sherpa bus to Pen-y-Pass or a minivan shuttle (£1).

The Welsh Highland Railway (p753) stops at the trailhead of the Rhyd Ddu path, and there is a request stop (Snowdon Ranger Halt) where you can alight for the Snowdon Ranger path.

Bala (Y Bala)

POP 1975

The quiet Welsh-speaking town of Bala draws scores of kayakers, canoeists, windsurfers and rafters due to its proximity to Wales' largest natural lake, 4-mile-long **Llyn Tegid** (Bala Lake), as well as the River Tryweryn, hallowed in white-water kayaking circles.

⊙ Sights & Activities

National White Water Centre RAFTING (Canolfan Dŵr Gwyn Genedlaethol; ☑01678-521083; www.ukrafting.co.uk; Frongoch; 1-/2hr trip £32/66; ☉9am-4.30pm Mon-Fri) This centre runs year-round rafting, kayaking, inflatable Orca and canoeing trips on a 1.5-mile stretch of the Tryweryn that is almost continuous class-III white water with some class IV sections. Trips can be combined with rock

climbing, mountain biking, pony trekking, bushcraft, canyoning, and quad biking on an Adventure Breaks package (£135 including accommodation). Book at least two days in advance. Located 3.5 miles northwest of Bala on A4212.

Bala Adventure & Watersports Centre WATER SPORTS (☑01678-521059; www.balawatersports.com; Pensarn Rd) This one-stop activity and hire centre, behind the leisure centre by the lakeshore, offers windsurfing, sailing, paddleboarding, canoeing, kayaking, white-water rafting, mountain-biking, rock-climbing and abseiling courses (costing from £38/75 per half-/full day). Rental gear includes paddleboards (£20), kayaks (£12), canoes (£25), windsurfers (£18) and sailing boats (from £28); all prices are per hour.

🛌 Sleeping & Eating

Good accommodation and dining options are rather thin on the ground in Bala proper.

Bala Backpackers HOSTEL £ (☑01678-521700; www.bala-backpackers.co.uk; 32 Tegid St; dm/tw from £21/49; ☉reception 8-10am & 5-10pm) Pros: central location, brightly painted dorms (some windowless) with four single beds maximum, private rooms in a separate building, fully equpped kitchen, and plenty of local info. Cons: the owner may not win prizes for congeniality; you have to bring your own bed linen; there's a midnight curfew; and there's no wi-fi or internet.

DON'T MISS

TYDDYN LLAN

An elegant property set among gardens in the tranquil Vale of Edeirion, **Tyddyn Llan** (☑01490-440264; www.tyddynllan. co.uk; r £195-230, ste £300; 🅿🛜) is a cosy bolthole for a rural retreat. The 12 rooms and a suite each boast their own individual style, some frou-frou romantic, some shabby-chic modern. We are still salivating at the memory of our last visit to the hotel's **restaurant** (2-/3-course dinner £45/55; ☉lunch Fri-Sun, dinner daily; 🅿); some dishes were extraodinary, while others merely good, but the rack of lamb and rib-eye were cooked to juicy perfection. It's 7.5 miles east of Bala on the B4401.

★ **Abercelyn Country House**　　B&B **££**
(☏01678-521109; www.abercelyn.co.uk; Llanycil; s £60, d £80-100; ℙ🛜) Luxurious rooms in classical style, excellent breakfasts and a lovely setting in gardens with a gurgling brook win rave reviews for this former rectory (1729). The owner is a mountain guide and whitewater enthusiast. It's located on the A494, a mile along the lake from the town. Two-night minimum stays apply in high season.

Eagles Inn (Tafarn Yr Eryod)　　PUB **£**
(☏01678-540278; www.yr-eagles.co.uk; Llanuwchllyn; mains £8-16.50; ☺11am-11pm Sun-Wed, to midnight Thu-Sat, closed lunch Mon; 🐾) Your consummate Welsh-speaking village pub but with food that's a step above: most of the vegetables and some of the meat comes from its own garden.

① Information

Bala Information Point (www.visitbala.org; Penllyn Leisure Centre, Pensarn Rd; ☺10am-4pm Fri-Tue Easter-Sep; 🛜) Unstaffed information point located inside the leisure centre by the lake.

① Getting There & Away

Buses stop on the High St. Bus X94 heads to/from Barmouth (£4.60, one hour, eight daily Monday to Saturday) via Dolgellau (£3.80, 35 minutes), and Wrexham (£5, 1½ hours) via Llangollen (£4.80, 53 minutes); and bus X6 heads to Betws-y-Coed (£3.20, 1¼ hours, daily Monday to Friday).

Dolgellau

POP 2690

The seat of Owain Glyndŵr's Welsh Parliament, a safe haven for Quakers, even a gold-rush town: charming little market-town Dolgellau has worn many hats over the centuries. The prosperous wool industry that ruled here in the 18th and early 19th centuries is responsible for the highest concentration of listed buildings in Wales.

Dolgellau's enviable location, its clutch of boutique B&Bs and a surprisingly diverse dining scene for a place of its size make the town an ideal springboard for tackling Snowdonia's varied terrain on two legs or two wheels.

◉ Sights & Activities

Tŷ Siamas　　MUSEUM
(☏01341-421800; www.tysiamas.com; Eldon Sq; ☺10am-4pm Tue-Fri, to 1pm Sat; ♿) As Dolgellau has been an important folk-music hub ever since it held the first Welsh folk festival in 1952, the town's former market hall has been transformed into Tŷ Siamas, the National Centre for Welsh Folk Music. It's named after the creator of the Welsh triple harp, which you can try playing by using the touch screens in the interactive music exhibition.

Cader Idris　　MOUNTAIN
Cader Idris (893m), or the 'Seat of Idris' (a legendary giant), is a hulking, menacing-looking mountain whose peaks are said to attract hounds of the underworld, and strange light effects are often sighted in the area. It's also said that anyone who spends the night on the summit will awake either mad or a poet, but in spite of its reputation (or because of it) its trails attract serious hikers and it's Snowdonia's favourite locale for rock climbers.

When tackling Cader Idris, the main route is the **Pony Path** (6 miles return, five hours), which begins from the Tŷ Nant car park on the A493 southwest of Dolgellau. At the south side of the mountain is the start of the longest but easiest **Tywyn** or **Llanfihangel y Pennant Path** (10 miles, seven hours), northeast from the Talyllyn Railway terminus at Abergynolwyn. The shortest and most picturesque trail is the **Minffordd Path** (6 miles, five hours), which skirts the rim of Cwm Cau and begins from the Dôl Idris car park, 6 miles south of Dolgellau at the junction of the A487 and the B4405. A visitor centre and tearoom by the car park provides information and succour.

Coed-y-Brenin Forest Park　　MOUNTAIN BIKING
(www.forestry.gov.uk/coedybrenin; A470) 🚴 Covering 3600 hectares, this woodland park is mountain-biker central. It's laced with more than 70 miles of purpose-built cycle trails, divided into seven graded routes, ranging from 'easy' (green) to 'severe' (black), along with a family-friendly flat forest trail. Routes are impressively presented by way of old-fashioned waterproof trail cards or downloadable geocaches and MP3 audio files. Bike hire available. The visitor centre is 8 miles north of Dolgellau off the A470.

Precipice Walk　　WALKING
This 3-mile circular walk through the private Nannau estate leads you through woodland, down lakeside paths, into conifer plantations and along the brink of a dramatic sheer-sided precipice, with stunning views of Cader Idris, Snowdon and the Mawddach Estuary along the way. The walk starts from Saith Groesffordd car park, Llanfachreth, around 2½ miles from Dolgellau (well signposted).

🛏 Sleeping

HYB Bunkhouse   HOSTEL £
(☑ 01341-421755; www.medi-gifts.com; 2 Bridge
St; dm/r £21/84; P ?) The only budget accommodation in town, this oak-beamed
hostel has spartan rooms, each sleeping four
people (in bunk beds), with handy kitchenettes. Accommodation is rented by the room
during busy periods – enquire at the Medi
gift shop below.

Bryn Mair House   B&B ££
(☑ 01341-422640; www.brynmairbedandbreak-
fast.co.uk; Love Lane; s £75-85, d £95-105; P ?)
On wistfully monikered Love Lane, this former Georgian rectory has three comfortable
B&B rooms, all kitted out with DVDs, iPod
docks and supremely comfortable beds, and
presided over by effusive hosts. Room 1 has
sublime mountain views, and breakfast is
superb.

Pandy Isaf   B&B ££
(☑ 01341-423949; www.pandyisaf-accommodation.
co.uk; s/d from £55/80; P) This peaceful old
mill houses three spotless, luxurious rooms
with classic decor and supremely comfortable beds. All rooms overlook the river, where
frolicking otters can be spotted. The warm,
welcoming hosts provide the perfect start to
the day by cooking up a fantastic breakfast.
It's 2 miles northeast of Dolgellau off the
A494.

★ Ffynnon   B&B £££
(☑ 01341-421774; www.ffynnontownhouse.com;
Love Lane; s £100, d £150-215; P ?) With a
keen eye for contemporary design and a su-
perfriendly welcome, this first-rate boutique
guesthouse feels both homely and stylish.
French antiques are mixed in with modern
chandeliers, claw-foot tubs and electronic
gadgets, and each of the six individually decorated rooms has a seating area so you can
admire the views in comfort. There's also an
outdoor hot tub.

🍴 Eating

TH Roberts   CAFE £
(Parliament House, Glyndŵr St; mains £4.50-7;
⊙ 9.30am-5.30pm Mon-Sat; ?) This former
ironmonger's shop, complete with tall ceilings, original counter, antique lamp holders
and 'Produce of India' barrels, has morphed
into the town's favourite coffee shop. If the
aroma of freshly ground brew is not enough
to lure you in, perhaps you'll come for the
light meals (soup, Welsh rarebit, sandwiches, cakes), friendly service and a leisurely
newspaper read.

Y Sospan   CAFE, BISTRO ££
(☑ 01341-423174; Queen's Sq; breakfast & lunch
£5-9, dinner £12-17; ⊙ 9am-9.30pm; ?) With its
encroaching wooden-beamed ceilings and
book-lined walls, this 1606 building once
served as a prison (though the food has much
improved since). A cafe by day, serving fry-
up breakfasts, sandwiches, jacket potatoes,
light-cooked meals and great homemade
cakes, Y Sospan turns into a cosy bistro by
night: lamb and steak play the starring roles,
but vegetarians will find options too.

Mawddach Restaurant   MODERN WELSH ££
(Bwyty Mawddach; ☑ 01341-421752; www.mawd-
dach.com; Llanelltyd; mains £14-21; ⊙ noon-
2.30pm & 6-9.30pm Wed-Sat, noon 3.30pm Sun)
Located 2 miles west of Dolgellau on the
A496, Mawddach brings a touch of urban
style to what was once a barn. Slate floors,
leather seats and panoramic views across to
Cader Idris set the scene. The food is equally impressive: meat straight from nearby
farms, fresh local fish specials and imaginative Sunday lunches (two/three courses
£20.95/22.95).

ℹ Information

Tourist Office (☑ 01341-422888; www.eryri-
npa.gov.uk; Eldon Sq; ⊙ 9.30am-5pm) Plenty of
local info; also sells maps, local-history books,
the *Dolgellau Town Trail* (£1) brochure and
trail leaflets for climbing Cader Idris. Upstairs
there's an interesting little exhibition on the
region's Quaker heritage.

WORTH A TRIP

LIVING IN A TREEHOUSE
....
A *Peter Pan* and *The Swiss Family Robinson* fantasy come alive, the five cosy,
rustic-glam **Living Room Treehouses**
(☑ 01654-703700; www.living-room.co; 3
day & 2 night stay £349) are found in an
enchanting forest off the A470. You're
as close to nature as can be (you're up
a tree!), yet the beds are luxurious, the
wood-burning stoves keep you warm
and the seclusion is glorious; it's perfect for a romantic getaway. The Bryn
Meurig treehouse, lower off the ground,
makes for a memorable family weekend away. Arrival days are Sundays,
Wednesdays and Fridays.

ⓘ Getting There & Away

Dolgellau Cycles (☑ 01341-423332; www. dolgellaucycles.co.uk; Smithfield St) rents bikes, performs repairs and offers advice on local cycle routes. Lôn Las Cymru, the Welsh National Cycle Route (NCN Route 8), passes through Dolgellau, heading north to Porthmadog and south to Machynlleth.

All buses stop on Eldon Sq in the heart of town. Routes include T2 to Machynlleth (£2.60, 35 minutes, two to four daily) and Aberystwyth (£5.40, 1¼ hours), and in the other direction to Porthmadog (£3.80, 50 minutes), Caernarfon (£5.40, 1½ hours) and Bangor (£5.40, two hours); bus 35 to Blaenau Ffestiniog (£4.20, 50 minutes, Monday to Saturday); and X94 to Barmouth (£1.80, 20 minutes, four to eight daily), Bala (£2.20, 35 minutes) and Llangollen (£4.80, 1½ hours).

Mawddach Estuary

An important bird habitat, the glorious Mawddach Estuary is a striking sight – flanked by woodlands, wetlands and the romantic mountains of southern Snowdonia.

Mawddach Trail (www.mawddachtrail.co.uk) is a 9½-mile flat walking and cycling path that skirts the estuary's southern edge. It follows an old railway line from the bridge in Dolgellau, through woods and past wetlands, before crossing over the rail viaduct to Barmouth (from where you can grab the bus back).

Mawddach Way (www.mawddachway.co.uk) is a 30-mile, two- to three-day track looping through the hills on either side of the estuary. Although the highest point is 346m, by the end of the undulating path you'll have climbed 2226m. An A5 booklet can be ordered or downloaded online from the website (booklet/download £10/5); GPS route data can be downloaded for free.

Fairbourne

POP POP 720

Fairbourne is a small seaside settlement with a lovely long beach. In the next couple of decades, however, it's likely the village will have to begin retreating inland as holding back the sea is becoming too costly. Until then, visitors can enjoy the steam-hauled **Fairbourne Railway** (☑ 01341-250362; www. fairbournerailway.com; Beach Rd; adult/child return £9/5.25; ◷ Easter-Oct), Wales' only seaside narrow-gauge railway. The line heads north along the coast for 2.5 miles to Penrhyn Point, where there are ferries across the mouth of the Mawddach to Barmouth, timed to meet the trains.

Fairbourne is on the Cambrian Coast train line and bus 28 from Dolgellau (£2.70, 25 minutes, eight daily Monday to Friday) stops here.

Barmouth (Abermaw)

POP 2315

In the summer months, and particularly in late June when it hosts the **Three Peaks Yacht Race** (www.threepeaksyachtrace.com; ◷ Jun), the seaside resort of Barmouth is an assault on the senses. Wall-to-wall chip shops, ice-cream stalls, pubs and dodgem rides cater to the summertime train-loads of tourists. Outside those times, however, you can

---

WORTH A TRIP

TALYLLYN RAILWAY

Talyllyn Railway (Rheilffordd Talyllyn; ☑ 01654-710472; www.talyllyn.co.uk; Wharf Station; adult/under 15yr return £15.95/2.20; ◷ Easter-Oct, select days rest of year), or the locomotive that plies its narrow-gauge rails, was the inspiration behind Rev W Awdry's *Thomas the Tank Engine* stories. This enchanting little railway was saved from closure in 1950 by the world's first railway-preservation society. The locomotive puffs for 7.3 scenic, steam-powered miles up the Fathew Valley from Tywyn to Nant Gwernol. Hop out at one or more of the five stations along the way for a ramble along the waymarked walking trails.

Your ticket entitles you to all-day travel and you can take your canine friend along on a 'dog Rover' ticket. If you've always dreamed of driving a steam locomotive yourself, afternoon, evening and full-day driving experiences (£350/400/700) take place on select days under the watchful eye of a locomotive driver.

The **Narrow Gauge Railway Museum** (www.ngrm.org.uk; ◷ 10.30am-4.30pm Apr-Sep) at Tywyn's Wharf Station is one for the history buffs. It features shiny narrow-gauge steam locomotives, the story of the volunteers who preserved the railway, and regular temporary exhibitions on train- and Tywyn-related subjects.

enjoy the vast, windswept and dune-studded Blue Flag beach at your leisure.

Wales' only surviving wooden rail viaduct spans the estuary and has a handy pedestrian walkway across it.

◉ Sights

Tŷ Crwn Roundhouse HISTORIC BUILDING
(The Quay; ⊙10.30am-5pm) **FREE** Barmouth's attractions include the Tŷ Crwn Roundhouse, a squat, round 17th-century stone prison where drunk sailors and slatterns were once locked up for 'wanton mischief'.

Last Haul MONUMENT
(Church St) This carved slab of marble along Church St hails from the coast's most famous shipwreck.

⊨ Sleeping & Eating

Richmond House B&B **££**
(✆01341-281366; www.barmouthbedandbreakfast.co.uk; High St; s/d £65/80; P ⊠) Bed down for the night at supercentral Richmond House, which features contemporary rooms and an attractive garden for summer lounging.

Harbour Fish Bar FISH & CHIPS
(Church St; mains from £7; ⊙noon-10pm) Queue for your perfectly battered fish and then head for a picnic on the beach.

♀ Drinking & Nightlife

Last Inn PUB
(✆01341-280530; Church St; ⊙noon-11pm) Stop for a drink at this characterful 15th-century building where the mountain behind it forms its rear wall.

❶ Information

Tourist Office (✆01341-280787; www.visit-snowdonia.info; Station Rd; ⊙10am-5pm daily Apr-Oct, 10am-3.30pm Mon-Sat Nov-Mar; ⊠) The helpful tourist office is inside the train station.

❶ Getting There & Away

Bus routes to/from Barmouth include 38 to Harlech (£1.60, 33 minutes, 11 daily Monday to Saturday) and X94 to Llangollen (£5, two hours, eight daily Monday to Saturday) via Dolgellau (£2.20, 24 minutes) and Bala (£3.80, one hour).

Barmouth is on the **Cambrian Coast Line** (www.thecambrianline.co.uk). Services to Machynlleth, Fairbourne, Harlech, Porthmadog and Pwllheli have been replaced by buses until further notice.

Harlech
POP 1760

Dramatically positioned on a rocky outcrop and framed by gleaming Tremadog Bay in the distance, Harlech is best known for the mighty, grey-stone towers of its castle, the southernmost of Edward I's 'iron ring' fortifications, designed to keep the Welsh firmly beneath his boot.

Gentrified Harlech consists of just a handful of streets, dotted with antique shops, and a few good places to slumber and dine. As such, it's a wonderful place to base yourself for your forays to the coast or deeper into Snowdonia National Park.

◉ Sights

★Harlech Castle CASTLE
(Cadw; www.cadw.wales.gov.uk; Castle St; adult/child £4.25/3.20; ⊙9.30am-5pm) The southernmost of Edward I's 'iron ring' of fortresses, this formidable concentric castle (1289) has been called the 'Castle of Lost Causes' because it has been lucklessly defended so many times. Owain Glyndŵr captured it after a long siege in 1404; it fell to the Yorks in the Wars of the Roses; and gave in to Cromwell's forces in 1647. From the crumbling ramparts there are all-encompassing views of the surrounding countryside, best seen from the southern wall privy.

⊨ Sleeping & Eating

Maelgwyn House B&B **££**
(✆01766-780087; www.maelgwynharlech.co.uk; Ffordd Isaf; r £70-95; P ⊠) A model B&B, Maelgwyn offers delicious breakfasts and six elegant rooms stocked with DVD players, with tremendous views across the bay from the largest two. Bridget and Derek really give this place a 'home away from home' ambience, and can arrange birdwatching trips and autumn fungus forays; Derek also shows you his artwork and regales you with life stories.

★Castle Cottage HOTEL **£££**
(✆01766-780479; www.castlecottageharlech.co.uk; Ffordd Pen Llech; s £85-125, d £130-175; P ⊠) Within arrow's reach of the castle, Castle Cottage has spacious bedrooms in a contemporary style – all creams and exposed beams paired with flatscreen TVs. The award-winning fine-dining **restaurant** (2-/3-/5-course dinner £35/40/45) serves

a delicious menu that revels in local produce (Welsh lamb, beef and cod, Ruthin chicken, Menai mussels, wild duck) and traditional dishes, executed in classical French style.

Cemlyn Tea Shop TEAROOM £
(www.cemlynteashop.co.uk; High St; snacks around £5; ◷10am-5pm Wed-Sun; 🐾) The Coles (Jan and Geoff) may be merry old souls, but it's tea that's king here. There are more than 30 varieties on offer, along with a simple range of snacks. Splurge on high tea (from 2.30pm to 4.30pm) served on fine bone china, complete with finger sandwiches, *bara brith* (a dense and spicy fruit cake flavoured with tea and marmalade), scones, Welsh cakes and sponge (reservations essential).

★**Soul Food** CARIBBEAN ££
(☑01766-780416; www.caribbeancrabharlech.com; High St; lunch mains £5-8, dinner mains £15-19; ◷12.30-2.30pm & 6.30-10.30pm Mon-Sat) Having changed its name and location without losing its spicy Trinidadian flavours, Soul Food has added lunchtime Louisiana-style jerk-chicken- or prawn-stuffed po'boys and full British breakfasts to its culinary arsenal. If you can, though, come for dinner to feast on the likes of curry goat, jerk Welsh lamb and blackened salmon. Dinner reservations recommended.

❶ Information

Harlech Tourist Office (☑01766-780658; www.eryri-npa.gov.uk; High St; ◷9.30am-5.30pm) Due to relocate to the new visitor centre being built opposite the castle at the time of writing.

---

❶ STORM DAMAGE AFFECTS TRAFFIC

Following storm surges and subsequent flooding in December 2013, the railway line between Machynlleth and Pwllheli was damaged, and all rail services along that stretch were replaced by buses until September 2014. The railway is once again operational and the new rail bridge that connects the A496 with Porthmadog and Penrhyndeudraeth across the estuary reopened in September 2014. The road/cycle bridge will not be functional until mid-2015.

---

❶ Getting There & Away

Bus 38 heads to Barmouth (£1.60, 30 minutes, 11 daily Monday to Saturday).

Direct train services run up the coast to Pwllheli via Porthmadog and down the coast to Machynlleth.

WEST OF SNOWDONIA

The region between the western fringe of the Snowdonia National Park and the Isle of Anglesey is a staunchly Welsh-speaking area. Indeed, the county of Gwynedd is the traditional heartland of Welsh nationalism; around 70% of people here still use Welsh as their first language.

Caernarfon

POP 9490

Wedged between the gleaming Menai Strait and the stark mountains of Snowdonia, compact Caernarfon consists of a few medieval streets clustered around North Wales' most formidable fortifications, with the modern town fanning out beyond the ancient town walls and the attractive yacht marina. Given the town's reputation as a centre of Welsh culture (it has the highest percentage of Welsh speakers anywhere), it is highly ironic that Caernarfon's dominant feature is the castle. The last link in Edward I's 'Iron Ring', it was built for the express purpose of suppressing the Welsh.

Caernarfon's proximity to the Snowdonia National Park and its proliferation of good eating and slumbering options make it a popular launchpad for Snowdon-bound travellers.

◉ Sights & Activities

★**Caernarfon Castle** CASTLE, MUSEUM
(Cadw; www.cadw.wales.gov.uk; adult/child £6.75/5.10; ◷9.30am-5pm) Mighty Caernarfon Castle was built on Edward I's orders between 1283 and 1330 as a military stronghold, a seat of government and a royal palace. It was used to consolidate the English hold over the Welsh in two ways: its fortifications repelled Owain Glyndŵr's army in 1404 with a garrison of only 28 men; and when Edward I's son was made by him the Prince of Wales in 1301, the legitimacy of the title was apparently granted by his son's birth at Caernarfon.

Inspired by the dream of Macsen Wledig recounted in the *Mabinogion*, Caernarfon echoes the 5th-century walls of Constantinople, with colour-banded masonry and polygonal towers, instead of the traditional round towers and turrets. Despite its fairytale aspect, you can see just how formidable the castle's defences are as you explore the interconnected walls and towers: it successfully resisted three sieges during the Civil War before surrendering to Cromwell's army in 1646.

Segontium Roman Fort
RUIN

(Cadw; www.cadw.wales.gov.uk; Ffordd Cwstenin; ⊘10am-4pm Tue, Wed & Sat Apr-Oct) **FREE** These stony foundations, dating back to AD 77, represent the westernmost Roman legionary fort of the Roman Empire, with a crucial strategic position overlooking the Menai Strait. It served as the base for Maximus, whose march on Rome failed spectacularly after he was proclaimed emperor by his British troops. The on-site museum has been recently refurbished. Segontium is located on a hill, about half a mile along the A4085 (heading towards Beddgelert).

GreenWood Forest Park
ADVENTURE PARK

(www.greenwoodforestpark.co.uk; Y Felinheli; admission £12; ⊘10am-5pm late Mar-Oct) ✔ This 7-hectare adventure park makes a brilliant family day out. It offers a slew of activities for infant and junior-school-aged kids, all of which are underpinned by a strong green ethos. You'll find mazes, a giant web to climb, a sledge run, archery, a tree-top playground, den-building, paddle boats, a forest theatre, and the world's first people-powered roller coaster, the Green Dragon. It's signposted from the A487 near Y Felinheli, 4 miles northeast of Caernarfon.

Plas Menai
WATER SPORTS

(☑01248-670964;www.plasmenai.co.uk;⊘8.30am-7pm) The excellent National Watersports Centre, 3 miles along the A487 towards Bangor, offers year-round water-based courses (sailing, power-boating, kayaking and windsurfing) for all interests and ability levels. Advance reservations are necessary. Bus 5 (Caernarfon to Bangor) stops a five-minute walk away.

Beics Menai
BICYCLE RENTAL

(☑01286-676804; www.beicsmenai.co.uk; 1 Cei Llechi; per 2/4/6/8hr £15/17/19/22; ⊘9.30am-4pm Tue-Sat) Hires bikes (including tandems, children's bikes and child seats) and can advise on local cycle routes. Recreational

ℹ CADW EXPLORER PASS
A boon for culture vultures looking to do plenty of sightseeing, the **Cadw Explorer Pass** (www.cadw.cymru.gov.uk; 3-/7-day pass £17.50/26.00) allows you to visit as many Cadw-run castles and other properties as you like within a set period of time. The three-day pass is valid for seven days, while a seven-day pass can be used within 14 days. See website for a full list of properties.

cycle routes include the 12.5-mile Lôn Eifion (starting near the Welsh Highland Railway station and running south to Bryncir) and the 4-mile Lôn Las Menai (following the Menai Strait to the village of Y Felinheli).

🛏 Sleeping

★ Totters
HOSTEL £

(☑01286-672963; www.totters.co.uk; 2 High St; dm/d/tr/q incl breakfast £17/47/54/68; 🛜) Modern, clean and very welcoming, this ubercentral independent hostel is the only backpacker joint in town. In addition to traveller-friendly facilities – lockers, guest kitchen, book swap – the 14th-century arched basement gives a sense of history to guests' breakfasts. There's also a spillover town house across the street with doubles for couples.

Caer Menai
B&B £

(☑01286-672612; www.caermenai.co.uk; 15 Church St; s/d/f from £45/57/78; @🛜) Inside this elegant former county school building (1894), the hospitable hosts preside over seven individually styled, en suite rooms; number 7 has sunset sea views. A full breakfast is provided and vegetarians are well catered for.

★ Victoria House
B&B ££

(☑01286-678263; www.thevictoriahouse.co.uk; Church St; r £75-80; @🛜) Victoria House is a wonderfully homely four-bedroom guesthouse. Spacious modern rooms come with memory-foam mattresses, and nothing's too much trouble for hostess Jan. Thoughtful touches abound, such as an impressive selection of free toiletries and a DVD on the town's history in each room. Breakfast is a joy.

Black Boy Inn
INN ££

(☑01286-673604; www.black-boy-inn.com; Northgate St; s/d from £57/86; 🅿🛜) ✔ Though its emblem may incur ire, this traditional inn dates back to 1522 and offers the most atmospheric digs in town, with original wooden beams and four-poster beds in some of the rooms. The snug **restaurant-bar** (mains £9-18) serves real ale, as well as monster portions of fish and chips, cassoulet and game pie.

✗ Eating

Y Gegin Fach   CAFE **£**
(www.facebook.com/YGeginFach; 5-9 Pool Hill; mains £5-7; ⊘ 9.30am-3pm) 'The Little Kitchen' is a proper old-fashioned Welsh-speaking *caffi*, right down to the floral drapes. Kick off your day with the Works breakfast or tuck into traditional faves such as rarebit, faggots (meatballs) and Welsh cakes. You'll wish you had a Welsh granny.

★ Blas   MODERN WELSH **££**
(⊘ 01286-677707; www.blascaernarfon.co.uk; 23-25 Hole in the Wall St; mains lunch £7-16, dinner £13-18; ⊘ noon-2.30pm & 6.30-11pm) You'll think the chef must be some kind of mad genius, pairing wood pigeon with rhubarb and smoked salmon with tangy horseradish ice, but the flavours come together seamlessly and each of the dishes on the short menu really makes your tastebuds sing. The setting is intimate, the service efficient and friendly, and the food's the best in town.

Oren   FUSION **££**
(⊘ 01286-669683; www.orencaernarfon.wordpress. com; 12 Church St; 3-course menu £16.50; ⊘ 7pm-late Fri & Sat) The eccentric Dutchman runs his small operation out of Abel's B&B, and if you're lucky enough to be in town on a weekend, you can join him in his 'weekly wonder wanderings through world cuisine.'

☆ Entertainment

Galeri Caernarfon   THEATRE, CINEMA
(⊘ 01286-685222; www.galericaernarfon.com; Victoria Dock; ⊘ 7.30am-11pm Mon-Fri, from 9am Sat & Sun) This excellent multipurpose arts centre hosts exhibitions, theatre, film and events. The stylish in-house **DOC Cafe Bar** serves all-day snacks and pre-event suppers.

🛍 Shopping

Celtica   GIFTS, HANDICRAFTS
(www.celtica-wales.com; Doc Fictoria; ⊘ 8.30am-5pm Mon-Sat, 10am-4pm Sun) Love spoons, Halen Môn salt and jewellery sit alongside deli and food-store goods inside this gleaming venue by the yacht marina. A good selection of books and maps of Wales, too.

ℹ Information

Tourist Office (⊘ 01286-672232; www.visit-snowdonia.info; Castle St; ⊘ 9.30am-4.30pm; 🖥) Helpful centre opposite the castle's main entrance.

ℹ Getting There & Away

BUS

Buses depart from stands along Penllyn, two blocks north of Castle Sq. Routes include the following:

➠ 1/1A to Bangor (£2.20, 25 minutes, one to two per hour Monday to Saturday), Criccieth (£3.40, 40 minutes, six daily Monday to Saturday) and Porthmadog (£3.60, 45 minutes, 11 daily Monday to Saturday)

➠ X5 to Conwy (£3.50, 1¼ hours, one to two per hour) and Llandudno (£3.50, 1½ hours, one to two per hour)

➠ 12 to Pwllheli (£3, 45 minutes, hourly Monday to Saturday)

➠ 87/88/89 to Llanberis (£2.70, 30 minutes, four daily Monday to Friday)

Snowdon Sherpa S4 bus heads to Beddgelert (£2, 30 minutes, two to eight daily) via the Snowdon Ranger (20 minutes) and Rhyd Ddu (24 minutes) trailheads.

A daily National Express service runs to London Victoria (£36, 9½ hours) via Bangor (£6.90, 30 minutes), Llandudno (£8.30, one hour) and Birmingham (£29.60, 6½ hours). From June to August a direct service runs to Manchester (£24.40, five hours) via Liverpool (£18.80, four hours).

CAR

Free parking in Caernarfon is as rare as unicorns, but you might be able to grab a space by the water on the south embankment of Victoria Dock.

TRAIN

The northern terminus of the Welsh Highland Railway (p753) is on St Helen's Rd. Trains run to Porthmadog (£35 return, 2½ hours) via Dinas, Waunfawr, Rhd Ddu and Beddgelert.

Llŷn Peninsula

Jutting out into the Irish Sea from the mountains of Snowdonia, the Llŷn Peninsula (also spelled 'Lleyn') is a green finger of land some 25 miles long and 8 miles wide. It's a mountainous, largely unpeopled region rich with legend (particularly those of King Arthur), a former pirate haven and home to lobster fishers. The bracken-covered slopes of its hills give way to pristine coves. Llŷn is criss-crossed with isolated walking and cycling routes, good beaches with a scattering of small fishing villages, particularly along the south coast, and 70 miles of wildlife-rich coastline. Over the centuries the heaviest footfalls have been those of pilgrims on their way to Bardsey Island.

Welsh is the language of everyday life here. The Llŷn (pronounced *khlee'en*) and the Isle of Anglesey were the last places on the Roman and Norman itineraries, and both have maintained a separate identity, the Llŷn especially. Isolated physically and culturally, it's been an incubator of Welsh activism. It was also the birthplace of David Lloyd George, the first Welsh prime minister of the UK, and of Plaid Cymru (Party of Wales), founded in Pwllheli in 1925 and now the main opposition party in the Welsh Assembly.

Pwllheli (poolth-*heh*-lee; meaning 'saltwater pool') is the Llŷn's largest town and the peninsula's public transport hub.

❶ Getting There & Away

BUS

Bus 1 (Porthmadog–Caernarfon–Bangor) stops in Criccieth. All of the peninsula's other bus services originate or terminate at Pwllheli, including bus 3 to Llanystumdwy (£1, 20 minutes), Criccieth (£1.20, 24 minutes) and Porthmadog (£2, 50 minutes); bus 12 to Caernarfon (£3, 45 minutes, hourly Monday to Saturday); bus 17/17B to Aberdaron (£2.70, 40 minutes, eight daily Monday to Friday); and bus 18 to Abersoch (£1.30, 25 minutes, six daily Monday to Friday).

A National Express coach heads between Pwllheli and London Victoria (£33, 10½ hours) daily, via Criccieth (£5.70, 17 minutes), Caernarfon (£7.40, one hour), Bangor (£7.80, 1½ hours) and Birmingham (£25, seven hours).

TRAIN

Pwllheli is the terminus of the Cambrian Coast Line, with direct services to Criccieth, Porthmadog, Harlech, Barmouth, Fairbourne and Machynlleth.

Pwllheli

Pwllheli, a small market town with a lively marina, is the main transport hub of the Llŷn Peninsula and the launchpad for boat trips to Bardsey Island. Stop in at **Pwllheli Tourist Office** (☑ 01758-613000; www.visitsnowdonia.info; Station Sq; ☺ 9.30am-5pm Apr-Oct) to stock up on information about the area.

In July skateboarders, BMX bikers and wakeboarders and their audiences gravitate to Pwllheli for **Wakestock** (www.wakestock.co.uk; ☺ Jul), a street culture and music fest.

Gourmets should not miss the best food on the Llŷn at **Plas Bodegroes** (☑ 01758-612363; www.bodegroes.co.uk; r £130-170, dinner £45, lunch Sun £22.50; P ⹁), a stately 1780 manor house with immaculately coiffured gardens, a mile inland from Pwllheli along the A497. Its Michelin-starred restaurant thrills with culinary creations made from local ingredients, paired with a long wine list and wonderfully friendly service. The restaurant is open for lunch on Sundays and dinner from Tuesdays to Saturdays.

Nant Gwrtheyrn

The village of Nant Gwrtheyrn was built for workers in the 19th century, but when the granite quarries closed after WWII it was gradually abandoned. In 1978 the place was given a new lease of life when bought and restored as a residential **Welsh Language & Heritage Centre** (☑ 01758-750334; www.nant-gwrtheyrn.org; weekend course £240, 3-day course incl full board £295; ☺ call ahead for times). The centre has a small but compelling exhibition on the history of the Welsh language, but its main focus is offering Welsh language and literature courses to suit all levels of ability. Even if you're not here to immerse yourself in Cymraeg (Welsh language), it's well worth taking a walk along the world's-end cliffs.

Nant Gwrtheyrn is reached from the village of Llithfaen (on the B4417) by following a hair-raisingly precipitous path down a steep valley.

Porth Dinllaen

It's hard to believe that this was once a busy cargo, ship-building and herring port, the only safe haven on the peninsula's north coast. Today, this long sweep of sand, backed with a few cottages, is owned in its entirety by the National Trust.

At the western end of the beach lies an isolated cluster of buildings, which includes the legendary **Tŷ Coch Inn** (www.tycoch.co.uk; ☺ 11am-4pm Sun-Thu, to 10pm Fri & Sat). It's famous for its views and for pints that you can drink while dabbling your toes in the sea.

Parking costs £5 in summer; free to NT members.

Braich-y-Pwll & Mynydd Mawr

While the boats for Bardsey Island now leave from Porth Meudwy outside of Aberdaron, medieval pilgrims once set sail from

Braich-y-Pwll (NT; www.nationaltrust.org.uk), a rugged National Trust property on the very tip of the Llŷn Peninsula. A narrow, hedge-fringed country lane runs from Abersoch to the base of the promontory. A path then leads down past the earthworks that are all that remains of St Mary's Abbey to a neolithic standing stone known as Maen Melyn, bent like a finger towards the island and suggesting this was a holy place long before the Celts or their saints arrived.

A single serpentine track winds its way up the exposed hillside to the wind-blasted summit of Mynydd Mawr. One glimpse of Bardsey rising out of the gunmetal-grey sea far beyond the surf-pounded rocks below will reinforce what a terrifying voyage it would have been.

Aberdaron

Aberdaron is an ends-of-the-earth kind of place with whitewashed, windswept houses contemplating Aberdaron Bay. It was traditionally the last resting spot before pilgrims made the treacherous crossing to Bardsey Island.

◉ Sights & Activities

St Hywyn's Church   CHURCH
(www.st-hywyn.org.uk; ⊙10am-6pm Apr-Oct, to 4pm Nov-Mar) St Hywyn's Church is stoically positioned above the pebbly beach. Its left half dates from 1100 while the right half was added 400 years later, to cope with the volume of pilgrims.

Porth Oer   BEACH
(Whistling Sands; NT; www.nationaltrust.org.uk; car park £1.50) Two miles north of Aberdaron lies Porth Oer; the beach known as 'Whistling Sands' is popular with local hard-nut surfers and known for its eerily squeaky white sands. The turn-off is marked with a blink-and-you'll-miss-it sign; parking is at the designated car park only.

🛏 Sleeping & Eating

Tŷ Newydd   HOTEL **££**
(☑01758-760207; www.gwesty-tynewydd.co.uk; s/d/f from £65/100/120; 🐾) Right on the beach, the friendly Tŷ Newydd has light-drenched, spacious, carpeted rooms, most of them dreamily looking out to sea. The tide comes in right under the terrace off the pub restaurant, which seems designed with afternoon gin and tonics in mind.

Y Gegin Fawr   WELSH **££**
(The Big Kitchen; mains from £7; ⊙9am-6pm) After tending to their spiritual needs, Bardsey-bound penitents could claim a meal at Y Gegin Fawr. Dating from 1300, it now dishes up locally caught crab and lobster, as well as homemade cakes (no longer free for pilgrims).

Bardsey Island (Ynys Enlli)

This mist-shrouded, rugged island, 2 miles long and 2 miles off the tip of the Llŷn Peninsula, is a teardrop off the remotest coast of Wales, isolated further by the churning waters of the strait. In the 6th or 7th century the obscure St Cadfan founded a monastery here, giving shelter to Celts fleeing the Saxon invaders, and medieval pilgrims followed in their wake.

A Celtic cross amid the abbey ruins commemorates the pilgrims who came here to die and gave the island its poetic epithet: the Isle of 20,000 Saints. Due to the sheer number of buried dead, it was difficult to do any farming without hitting an unmarked grave or three, and it's said that in the 1850s human femurs were used as fencing, as there were so many of them. The home of buccaneers in the 16th century, Bardsey is also rumoured to be the mythical Isle of Avalon where King Arthur was taken after being mortally wounded in the Battle of Camlan. It's said that King Arthur lies in a glass castle somewhere on the island, together with the Thirteen Treasures of the British Isles.

Most modern pilgrims to Bardsey are sea-birdwatchers: the island is home to Manx shearwaters, guillemots and fulmars. The Bardsey Island Trust (☑0845811 22 33; www.bardsey.org) can arrange holiday lets in cottages on the island. You can buy snacks from the single farming family resident on the island year-round.

In the summer months Bardsey Boat Trips (☑07971-769895; www.bardseyboattrips.com; adult/child £30/20) sails to Bardsey from Porth Meudwy, a little cove outside Aberdaron; Enlli Charters (☑0845 811 3655; www.enllicharter.co.uk; per person £40) sails from the marina in Pwllheli. Dolphins are occasionally spotted en route.

Abersoch

Abersoch comes alive in summer with a 30,000-person influx of boaties, surfers and beach bums. Edged by gentle blue-green hills, the town's main attraction is its long stretch of beach, one of the most popular on the peninsula. Surfers should head further south around the coast for the Atlantic swell at Porth Neigwl (Hell's Mouth) and Porth Ceiriad.

🏄 Activities

West Coast Surf Shop
SURFING
(📞01758-713067; www.westcoastsurf.co.uk; Lôn Pen Cei; lessons incl equipment from £30; ⊗10am-5pm Mon, Tue & Thu-Sat, noon-5pm Wed & Sun) Hires out boards and wetsuits all year round.

Offaxis
WAKEBOARDING, SURFING
(📞01758-713407; www.offaxis.co.uk; Lôn Engan; lessons incl equipment from £30) An outdoors and surf shop that specialises in wakeboarding, windsurfing and surfing lessons.

Abersoch Sailing School
SAILING
(📞07917-525540; www.abersochsailingschool.co.uk; sailing lessons from £45; ⊗Sat, Sun & school holidays Mar-Oct) Offers sailing lessons, and hires laser fun boats (one/two hours £30/40), catamarans (one/two hours £40/60), sea kayaks (per hour single/double £10/20) and skippered day racers and keel boats (per hour £75; minimum two hours).

🛏 Sleeping & Eating

Camping is available at several farms near Abersoch.

★ Venetia
HOTEL ££
(📞01758-713354; www.venetiawales.com; Lôn Sarn Bach; r £108-148; 🅿🐾) A splurge-worthy lodging with five beautifully styled rooms decked out with designer lighting and modern art. The excellent Italian restaurant (mains £12-24) downstairs specialises in fresh seafood and pasta dishes.

★ Coconut Kitchen
THAI ££
(📞01758-712250; www.thecoconutkitchen.co.uk; Lôn Port Morgan; mains £11-21; ⊗5.30-10pm; 🅿🐾) Coconut Kitchen adds spice to the Abersoch culinary scene with authentic and imaginative Thai cuisine.

Oriel Plas Glyn-y-Weddw

Oriel Plas Glyn-y-Weddw (www.oriel.org.uk; ⊗10am-5pm Wed-Mon, daily school holidays) FREE is an excellent art gallery, but its lively collection of work by contemporary Welsh artists, such as Stephen John Owen, is only part of the attraction. The gallery is worth visiting just to wonder at the flamboyant Victorian Gothic mansion it's housed in, which features heavy exposed beams and stained glass. The bustling conservatory serves paninis, wraps and cakes, and paths run through the wooded grounds to the National Trust–owned Llanbedrog beach.

It's 3 miles from Abersoch and 4 miles west of Pwllheli.

Llanystumdwy

Tiny Llanystumdwy is the boyhood home and final resting place of David Lloyd George, one of Wales' finest political statespersons, and the British prime minister from 1916 to 1922.

The short video, photos, posters and personal effects held at the Lloyd George Museum (📞01766-522071; www.gwynedd.gov.uk/museums; adult/child £5/4; ⊗10.30am-5pm) show him as a fiery orator and ladies' man who was largely responsible for introducing National Insurance in a two-pronged attack on unemployment and poverty. Later on in his career, his loyalty to Wales was

---

THE BARDSEY PILGRIMAGE

At a time when journeys from Britain to Italy were long, perilous and beyond the means of most people, the pope decreed that three pilgrimages to the holy island of Bardsey would have the same spiritual value as one to Rome. Tens of thousands of penitents took advantage of this get-out-of-purgatory-free (or at least quickly) card and many came here to die. In the 16th century, Henry VIII's ban on pilgrimages put paid to the practice – although a steady trickle of modern-day pilgrims still walk the route.

The traditional path ran along the Llŷn coast, stopping at ancient churches and holy wells along the way. It's broken into nine legs on the Edge of Wales Walk (www.edgeofwaleswalk.co.uk) website, which is run by a cooperative of local Llŷn Peninsula residents. They can help to arrange a 47-mile, self-guided walking tour, including five nights' accommodation and baggage transfers (£320 per person). A similar service is also offered for the 95-mile Llŷn Coastal Path, which circumnavigates the peninsula (£682 per person).

SNOWDONIA & NORTH WALES LLŶN PENINSULA

challenged by his ambitions in Westminster and, although a friend of Churchill, Lloyd George became a war apologist by WWII.

Highgate, his uncle's house that he grew up in, lies 50m away from the museum. His mortal remains rest in a boulder-topped grave, about 150m away, by a babbling brook.

The turn-off to the village is 1.5 miles west of Criccieth on the A497.

Criccieth

This genteel and slow-moving seaside town sits above a sweep of sand-and-stone beach about 5 miles west of Porthmadog. Criccieth is an excellent spot to base yourself if exploring the Llŷn.

◎ Sights

Criccieth Castle   CASTLE
(Cadw; www.cadw.wales.gov.uk; Castle St; adult/child £3.50/2.65; ⊘10am-5pm) Criccieth's main claim to fame is ruined Criccieth Castle, perched up on the clifftop and offering views stretching along the southern coast and across Tremadog Bay to Harlech. Constructed by Welsh prince Llywelyn the Great in 1239, it was overrun in 1283 by Edward I's forces and recaptured for the Welsh in 1404 by Owain Glyndŵr, whose forces promptly sacked it.

⌨ Sleeping & Eating

Marine Tce, running parallel to the sea, is lined with lodgings.

Marine Hotel   HOTEL **££**
(☑01766-522946; Marine Tce; s/d £48/77; P �) The pick of accommodation on Marine Tce, this hotel offers an appealing maze of rooms presided over by a congenial local couple.

Castle Fish & Chips   FISH & CHIPS **£**
(5 Castle St; mains from £7; ⊘5.30-9pm) Join the queue of locals at the perpetually popular Castle Fish & Chips.

Tir a Môr   BRASSERIE **££**
(☑01766-523084; www.tiramor-criccieth.co.uk; 1 Mona Tce; mains £14-23; ⊘6-9.30pm Tue-Sat mid-Feb–Nov) Once you've been sandblasted by the winds up at the castle, head for a warming plate of Welsh lamb or fresh monkfish at stylish Tir a Môr – bookings advised.

Porthmadog & Around

POP 2980

Busy little Porthmadog (port-*mad*-uk) was founded by (and named after) reforming landowner William Alexander Madocks, who went to work on a grand scale, laying down the mile-long Cob causeway, draining some 400 hectares of wetland habitat, and creating a brand-new harbour. After his death in 1828, the causeway became the route for the new Ffestiniog Railway: at its peak in 1873 it transported more than 116,000 tonnes of slate from the mines to the harbour.

Today Porthmadog is railway-buff heaven, with no less than two of Wales' finest narrow-gauge train journeys, run by the oldest independent railway company in the world. They depart from Harbour Station in pungent puffs of smoke.

◎ Sights & Activities

Portmeirion Village   ARCHITECTURE
(www.portmeirion-village.com; adult/child £10/6.50; ⊘9.30am-7.30pm; P) The lifetime project of eccentric Welsh architect Sir Clough Williams-Ellis, Portmeirion is an Italian-influenced, whimsical, colourful collection of buildings, columns and statuary, centred around a Mediterranean-looking plaza with a fountain. Starting in 1926, Clough designed and built his seaside utopia from pieces of disintegrating stately mansions he'd collected; 50 years later, Clough deemed the village to be complete. Porthmeirion formed the ideally surreal background for cult TV series *The Prisoner,* filmed here from 1966 to 1967. It's a straightforward 1.5-mile walk east of Porthmadog.

A mishmash of architectural styles, painted turquoise, yellow and ochre, it all somehow comes together, with surprises around every corner: a Buddha statue in a pavilion, a cherub peeking out of a hidden opening. Several buildings contain cafes, art galleries and gift shops, including one selling the famously florid Portmeirion pottery. A network of walking paths thread along the coast and through the private forested peninsula; if you want to enjoy them in solitude, most of the village's kooky cottages and minimansions are available for holiday lets.

Online ticket discounts are available; half-price entry after 3.30pm.

SNOWDONIA & NORTH WALES PORTHMADOG & AROUND

★ **Ffestiniog Railway**   HERITAGE RAILWAY
(Rheilffordd Ffestiniog; ☑01766-516024; www.fes-
trail.co.uk; adult/child return £20.20/18.20) The
Ffestiniog Railway is Wales' most spectacular and beautiful narrow-gauge journey. The
twisting and precipitous line was built between 1832 and 1836 to haul slate down to
Porthmadog from the mines at Blaenau Ffestiniog, 13.5 miles away. Steam locomotives
took over from horses in the 1860s and the
line opened to passengers in the 1920s. Views
are best on the right-hand side as the steam
engines chug their way up through the lush,
green valley to the slate-strewn final terminus.

★ **Welsh Highland Railway**   HERITAGE RAILWAY
(☑01766-516000; www.festrail.co.uk; adult/child
return £35/31.50) The Welsh Highland Railway is an amalgamation of several late-19th-
century slate railways that runs for 25 miles
through lovely Snowdonian landscapes from
Porthmadog to Caernarfon via Beddgelert.
En route it passes through the splendid Aberglaslyn Gorge, flanking the fast-flowing river, and between Beddgelert and Caernarfon
it chugs along Snowdon's south flank, rising
steeply to its highest point of 650ft.
　Walkers can hop off at either Rhyd Ddu
(£23/20.70) station or the Snowdon Ranger
request stop to follow paths up Snowdon.

Purple Moose Brewery   BREWERY
(Bragdy Mŵs Piws; ☑01766-515571; www.purp-
lemoose.co.uk; Madoc St; tours £5; ☉9am-5pm
Mon-Fri) One of more than 50 microbreweries across Wales, Purple Moose has grown
into an award-winning company – it picked
up a Silver Award in 'Best Bitters' at the
2013 CAMRA Champion Beer competition.
Its four regular tipples are Snowdonia Ale,
Madog's Ale, Glaslyn Ale and Dark Side of
the Moose; there's usually a seasonal one as
well. Hour-long brewery tours are available
for ale aficionados from Tuesdays to Thursdays at noon; these include free tastings.

🛏 **Sleeping & Eating**

★ **Yr Hen Fecws**   B&B ££
(☑01766-514625; www.henfecws.com; 16 Lombard
St; s/d from £65/80; P🐾) This stylish stone
cottage has seven compact, individually decorated en suite rooms with exposed-slate
walls and fireplaces. Breakfast is served at
the excellent cafe next door – a lunchtime
gathering point for the local contingent of
yummy mummies who come for the paninis, wraps, salads, waffles and sandwiches
(£4.95 to £7.85).

Golden Fleece Inn   PUB ££
(☑01766-512421; www.goldenfleeceinn.com; Market Sq, Tremadog; s/d from £60/75; mains £8-16;
P🐾) This dark, atmospheric pub is a cross
between a cavern and an enchanted forest –
an illusion created by hop flowers hanging
from the ceiling. After sampling the real ales
and the classic dishes with a twist (mains
£8 to £16), bed down on Egyptian cotton
sheets in one of the three historic buildings
on Tremadog's square. There's live acoustic
music on Tuesday nights.

**Hotel Portmeirion
& Castell Deudraeth**   HOTEL, COTTAGE £££
(☑01766-770000; www.portmeirion-village.com;
Portmeirion; hotel s/d £204/219, castle & village
s/d from £145/179; P🐾) You can stay within
the famous fairy-tale village of Portmeirion
at Hotel Portmeirion (1926), overlooking the
estuary. It has classic, elegant rooms and a
dining room designed by Sir Terence Con-
ran. Up the drive, Castell Deudraeth is, per-
versely, a more modern alternative. There
are also 17 whimsical cottages. Prices drop
considerably in low season.

Eric Jones' Cafe   CAFE £
(☑01766-512199; www.ericjones-tremadog.co.uk;
Bwlch-y-Moch; mains from £4; ☉8am-5pm; P🐾)
A mile east of Tremadog, this friendly little
cafe attracts a lively clientele of climbers and
cyclists with its all-day breakfasts, toasties,
jacket potatoes and more. Eric, a 79-year-old
local legend with the first solo ascent of the
Eiger and the first base jump off the Eiger
under his belt, also runs a campsite (per
person per night £6) and bunk barns (per
person per night £7.50).

ℹ **Information**

Porthmadog Tourist Office (☑01766-512981;
www.visitsnowdonia.info; High St; ☉9.30am-
5pm daily Easter-Oct, 10am-3.30pm Mon-Sat
Nov-Easter; 🐾)

ℹ **Getting There & Away**

BUS
Bus 3 heads to Tremadog (£0.80, four minutes),
Criccieth (£3.50, 13 minutes), Llanystumdwy
(£3.50, 16 minutes) and Pwllheli (£3.50, 40
minutes).
　Bus T2 runs to Dolgellau (£2.60, 50 minutes),
Machynlleth (£3.80, 1½ hours) and Aberystwyth
(£5.40, 2¼ hours), and in the other direction
to Caernarfon (£2.60, 40 minutes) and Bangor
(£3.80, one hour). Snowdon Sherpa bus S97
goes to Beddgelert (£2, 20 minutes, eight daily

Monday to Saturday) and Pen-y-Pass (£2, 40 minutes, three daily Monday to Saturday).

A daily National Express coach heads to London Victoria (£35, 10 hours) via Caernarfon (£7.60, 45 minutes), Llandudno (£8.30, 1¾ hour) and Birmingham (£29.60, 6¾ hours).

TRAIN

Direct services run to Machynlleth via Harlech, Fairbourne and Barmouth, and to Pwllheli.

ISLE OF ANGLESEY

At 276 sq miles, the Isle of Anglesey is the largest island in England and Wales. Holy to the Celts, Anglesey was the last part of Wales to fall to the Romans around AD 60. You can imagine even the disciplined imperial troops blanching when faced with fearsome blue-skinned Druids and their followers bellowing and shaking their weapons from across the Menai Strait.

The ancient name for the island was 'Môn mam Cymru' (Mother of Wales): its outpost status, singular character and the proliferation of the Welsh language gives Anglesey a fair claim to being the Welsh heartland. The industrial age arrived in 1826 when Thomas Telford's iconic 174m Menai Suspension Bridge straddled the Menai Strait, its 30m-high central span allowing the passage of tall ships. It was joined in 1850 by Robert Stephenson's Britannia Bridge to carry the newly laid railway.

Today, Anglesey beckons visitors with its extensive hiking trails, secluded coves and cliffs rich with bird life, the greatest concentration of ancient and prehistoric sites

HALEN MÔN SALT

What started as two ex–Bangor University students selling fish out of a van turned into a prosperous salt-extracting business. Today, Halen Môn Salt is known in most foodie circles and used in Michelin-starred restaurants such as the Fat Duck and Tyddyn Llan. At the **Halen Môn** (www.halenmon.com; ◷10am-4pm Mon-Fri) headquarters, you can purchase the salt both in its 100% undiluted form and in seven delectable flavours. A **visitor centre** was being built at research time so that soon you'll be able to follow the entire process, from piping in the seawater to evaporation and harvesting.

in Wales, a mighty castle and some excellent seafood. Beaumaris makes the most convenient base on the island, but if you're looking for countryside seclusion, there's plenty of that to be found, too.

For more information about the island, see www.visitanglesey.co.uk.

Beaumaris (Biwmares)

POP 1370

Beaumaris was once Wales' largest port, notorious for its smugglers and pirates. It hides its shady past well: today it's a delightfully refined spot, offering a romantic castle and pretty Georgian buildings, an attractive waterfront and a newly refurbished pier. It's also home to a growing number of boutiques, deli-cafes and galleries.

◉ Sights & Activities

★**Beaumaris Castle**   CASTLE
(Cadw; www.cadw.wales.gov.uk; Castle St; adult/child £5.25/3.90; ◷9.30am-5pm) The last and largest of Edward I's great castles of North Wales, Beaumaris is a perfectly symmetrical masterpiece, its concentric 'walls within walls' design making it difficult for enemies to breach – though Owain Glyndŵr managed to do just that in 1403. Though never fully completed, remarkably much of the castle was built within one year, in the late 13th century.

The castle is surrounded by a brackish moat that once allowed supply ships to dock by its wall at high tide. Crossing the drawbridge, you can wander beneath the moss-covered mighty battlements, overlooked by murder holes and arrow slits; stroll the crumbling outer wall; and peer into half-decayed towers.

Beaumaris Gaol   HISTORIC BUILDING
(www.visitanglesey.co.uk; Steeple Lane; adult/child £4.80/3.80, incl Beaumaris Courthouse £7.50/6.20; ◷10.30am-5pm Sat-Thu Apr-Oct) This fortress-like jail, built in the early 19th century, was modern for its time, with toilets in every cell and a treadmill water pump. None of that is enough, however, to dispel the gloom of the windowless punishment cell, the condemned cell where prisoners awaited their demise at the gibbet or hard labour in the stone-breaking yard.

Beaumaris Courthouse   HISTORIC BUILDING
(Llys Biwmares; www.visitanglesey.co.uk; Castle St; adult/child £3.60/2.80, incl Beaumaris Gaol £7.50/6.20; ◷10.30am-5pm Sat-Thu Apr-Oct)

The Beaumaris Court, opposite the castle, was an instrument of justice dispensed by the English between 1614 and 1971. Welsh-speaking defendants here were at a distinct disadvantage as the proceedings were held in English. An excellent audio-guide paints the picture.

Puffin Island Cruises BOAT TOUR
(📞07854-028393; www.beaumarismarine.com; adult/child £9.50/7.50; ☺Apr-Oct) Designated a Special Protection Area, Puffin Island resounds with the squawks and grunts of bird and marine life. The (weather-dependent) boat trips take in spectacular views across the Menai Strait to the Snowdonia range, and promise encounters with 12 species of seabirds in their natural habitat. Book at the entrance to the pier, or by phone.

🛏 Sleeping & Eating

**Ye Olde Bulls Head Inn
& Townhouse** HOTEL ££
(📞01248-810329; www.bullsheadinn.co.uk; Castle St; s/d from £80/100; 📶) The original wooden beams and wrought-iron bedsteads at the stately Ye Olde Bulls Head Inn contrast with the contemporary, high-tech and design-driven rooms at the Townhouse across the street. Head to the Ye Olde Bulls Head for light dishes at its cheery brasserie (mains £13-16) or for a bit of romance at the refined Loft Restaurant (3-course dinner £47.50).

EXPLORING ANGLESEY

Its two main towns aside, Anglesey has plenty to keep you exploring.

Thomas Telford Centre (www.menaibridges.co.uk; Mona Rd; adult/child £3/free; ☺10am-5pm Sun-Thu Jul-Sep) Anglesey is synonymous with the twin iconic bridges that connect the island to the Welsh mainland. The Menai Heritage Experience explains the feat of Victorian engineering and explores the ecology of the Menai Strait.

Llanfair PG Train Station In case you were wondering whether the name Llanfairpwll-gwyngyllgogerychwyrndrobwllllantysiliogogogoch (Llanfair PG for short) is some kind of joke, well, it is: the last five syllables were added by a local tailor in 1880 in a bid to attract visitors to this nondescript town. And since you're here, the ploy clearly worked. Elbow your way past coach parties to take a photo of the sign at the train station.

Anglesey Sea Zoo (www.angleseyseazoo.co.uk; Brynsiencyn; adult/concession £7.50/6.50; ☺10am-5.30pm Feb-Oct; 🅿🚼) With great pains taken to simulate different marine environments, Anglesey Sea Zoo introduces you to the denizens of the local waters: from lobster to tiny brine shrimp and flatfish that look like they're from a Picasso painting. Daily eel and shark feeds keep the children entertained. Head south along the A4080 from Llanfair PG towards Brynsiencyn and follow the signs.

Plas Newydd (NT; www.nationaltrust.org.uk; adult/child £8.90/4.45, garden only £7/3.50; ☺house noon-4.30pm Sat-Wed Mar-Oct, garden 10am-5.30pm Sat-Wed Mar-Oct, 11am-4pm Sat-Wed Nov-Feb; 🅿) If you only visit one National Trust property in North Wales, make it Plas Newydd. It was home to the first marquess of Anglesey, who commanded the cavalry during the 1815 battle of Waterloo, and is famous for its massive Whistler mural in the dining room. The house is 2 miles southwest of Llanfair PG, along the A4080.

Bryn Celli Ddu Burial Chamber The Bryn Celli Ddu Burial Chamber is one of Anglesey's most impressive neolithic remains, with an earthen mound you can enter to pass into a stone-lined burial chamber that was used as a communal grave 5000 years ago. From Llanfair PG follow the signpost off the A4080 down the country lane to the marked car park.

Oriel Ynys Môn (www.orielynysmon.info; ☺10.30am-5pm) Oriel Ynys Môn is the lynchpin of Anglesey's visual arts scene. Its History Gallery explores Anglesey's past, and it features wonderful landscape paintings by local talent, but the main draw is the Oriel Kyffin Williams Gallery, featuring 400-odd works by Wales' most celebrated artist. It's 600m north along the B5111 from Llanfegni.

Funsport (📞01407-810899; www.funsportonline.co.uk; 1 Beach Tce; ☺9am-5pm) Anglesey's top surfing and windsurfing spots include Rhosneigr on the western coast. Funsport rents out wetsuits and equipment here, and can arrange two-hour taster courses (£35) in surfing, windsurfing and kitesurfing.

DON'T MISS

ANGLESEY'S TOP THREE SEASIDE LUNCH SPOTS

Ann's Pantry (☑ 01248-410386; www.annspantry.co.uk; Moelfre; lunch £5-11, dinner £11-21; ⊙ 11am-5pm daily, 6-9pm Thu-Sat) With a delightful garden setting and funky, beach-hut-chic interior, Ann's serves great homemade food and fair-trade drinks in the village of Moelfre.

Oyster Catcher (www.oystercatcher-anglesey.co.uk; Main Rd; mains £10-16; ⊙ noon-11pm; P) This striking glass-fronted structure, backed by windswept sand dunes, serves hearty, well-prepared gastropub dishes and sandwiches. It also serves a second purpose by letting ex-offenders retrain as chefs. Situated near Rhosneigr, along the southwest coast of Anglesey.

Lobster Pot (☑ 01407-730241; www.thelobsterpotrestaurant.co.uk; Church Bay; mains £13-30; ⊙ noon-2pm & 6-10pm Tue-Sat) For a decadent lobster lunch, follow the narrow country roads down to the sea at Church Bay for this north-coast institution, famous for its fresh seafood and scenic location.

Cleifiog   B&B £££
(☑ 01248-811507; www.cleifiogbandb.co.uk; Townsend; s £60-80, d £90-110; 🐾) This artistic town house oozes character and history, and boasts superb views of the Menai Strait. Of the three rooms, all stylishly designed, Tapestry is the largest and features the original 18th-century panelling. The owner displays her artworks around the house.

Red Boat Ice Cream Parlour   ICE CREAM £
(www.redboatgelato.com; 34 Castle St; scoop £2.20; ⊙ 10am-6pm Mon-Thu, 10am-7pm Fri-Sun) Red Boat uses authentic Italian recipes to prepare the tastiest gelato this side of Florence. The sherry-trifle flavour more than passes the taste test; new flavours are added weekly.

★**Cennin**   MODERN WELSH £££
(☑ 01248-811230; www.restaurantcennin.com; 13 Castle St; mains £18-22; ⊙ 6.30-9pm Fri & Sat) 🍴 Having worked with the likes of Heston Blumenthal, local lad Aled Williams now cooks up his own skilfully executed takes on classic dishes. Settle in beneath the centuries-old beams and tuck into the best-quality local black beef, lamb and sea trout.

ℹ️ Information

Tourist Office (www.visitbeaumaris.co.uk; Town Hall, Castle St; ⊙ 10am-2pm Mon-Fri) The frequently unstaffed volunteer-run tourist office is well-stocked with brochures and maps.

ℹ️ Getting There & Away

Buses stop on Church St. Buses 53/56/57/58 run to Bangor (£3.30, 20 to 50 minutes, roughly half-hourly Monday to Saturday, every two hours Sunday) via Menai Bridge for onward connections.

Holyhead (Caergybi)

POP 11,430

Holyhead (pronounced *holly-head*) is a major travel hub for ferries to Ireland, but few visitors linger in this lacklustre town. It is, however, the starting point for the **Lôn Las Cymru** Welsh National Cycle Route (NCN route 8) and a handy base from which to expore the dramatic coastal scenery. Its **St Cybi's Church** (which has beautiful stained-glass windows from William Morris' workshop) marks the official starting point for the Isle of Anglesey Coastal Path.

Holyhead is divided from the west coast of Anglesey by a narrow channel on Holy Island (Ynys Gybi), a 7-mile stretch of land. It's 'Holy' because this was the domain of St Cybi, a well-travelled monk thought to have lived in the 6th century.

◉ Sights & Activities

★**South Stack Cliffs RSPB Reserve**   WILDLIFE RESERVE
(Ynys Lawd; ☑ 01407-762100; www.rspb.org.uk/wales; South Stack Rd; ⊙ visitor centre 10am-5pm; P) **FREE** Two miles west of Holyhead, the sea vents its fury against the cliffs of South Stack, an important RSPB reserve – home to thousands of seabirds. A steep, serpentine flight of steps leads down to the suspension bridge that crosses over to the **South Stack Lighthouse** for tremendous cliff views. Numerous paths lead into the bracken-covered and hilly interior, climbing **Holyhead Mountain** (Mynydd Twr; 200m) and skirting neolithic stone circles. **South Stack Kitchen**, an interpretive-centre-cum-cafe, provides maps and information.

Holyhead Maritime Museum   MUSEUM
(www.holyheadmaritimemuseum.co.uk; Newry Beach; adult/child £4.50/2; ⊙ 10am-4pm Tue-Sun Easter-Oct) The oldest lifeboat house in Wales (c 1858) charts Holyhead's maritime history

from Roman times onwards. There's a focus on local shipwrecks alongside model lifeboats, a permanent display on Holyhead's struggles during WWII and a whale's eardrum that looks like a human head.

Ucheldre Centre ARTS CENTRE

(Canolfan Ucheldre; ☑ 01407-763361; www.ucheldre.org; Millbank; ☉ 10am-5pm Mon-Sat, 2-5pm Sun) A former convent chapel turned artistic hub, Ucheldre holds concerts, poetry readings, comedy nights and art exhibitions. Its cinema screens films on Wednesdays, Fridays and Sundays.

🛏 Sleeping & Eating

Yr Hendre B&B ££

(☑ 01407-762929; www.yr-hendre.net; Porth-y-Felin Rd; r £65-70; ℗ @ ☎) Professionally run Yr Hendre's three luxurious, individually styled rooms have girls' names and are a real treat for walkers and cyclists (safe bicycle storage available). Choose 'Bethany' for sea views.

Sea Breezes B&B B&B ££

(☑ 01407-765682; 95 Newry St; s/d £45/66; ☎) Welcoming B&B just a short stroll from the ferry terminal – ideal for those middle-of-the-night departures to Ireland. Cosy rooms share facilities.

Ucheldre Kitchen CAFE £

(www.ucheldre.org; Millbank; mains £4-6; ☉ 10am-4.30pm Mon-Sat, 2-4.30pm Sun) Attached to Holyhead's excellent arts hub, this friendly cafe serves delicious homemade food (including a vegetarian menu) and better-than-average coffees.

★ **Harbourfront Bistro** INTERNATIONAL ££

(☑ 01407-763433; www.harbourfrontbistro.co.uk; Newry Beach; lunch £6-12, dinner £11-15; ☉ noon-2.30pm & 6-9pm Thu-Sat, noon-2.30pm Sun) With waves lapping right against it, this cosy little bistro adjoining the maritime museum serves rarebit and other light bites at lunchtime, and more substantial fishy offerings.

ℹ Information

Tourist Office (☑ 01407-762004; 63 Market St; ☉ 9am-5pm Mon-Sat) Community-run tourist office, gift shop and fish-pedicure spa on the main shopping street.

ℹ Getting There & Away

BUS

From the ferry terminal, National Express coaches head to/from Bangor (£19.50, 35 minutes), Liverpool (£31, 2¾ hours), Manchester (£36, 4¾ hours), Birmingham (£35, four hours) and London Victoria (£29.50, 7¼ hours).

Local bus stops are on Summer Hill. X4 runs to Bangor (£3.50, 1¼ hours, one to two per hour Monday to Saturday) via Llanfair PG and Menai Bridge.

FERRY

Irish Ferries (☑ 08717 300 200; www.irish-ferries.com; foot passenger/motorcycle/car from £29/52/119) runs two daily slow ferries (3¼ hours) and two fast services (one hour 50 minutes) to Dublin, while **Stena Line** (☑ 08447 70 70 70; www.stenaline.co.uk; foot passenger/bicycle/ car from £35/55/115) has four daily services to Dublin (3¼ hours) and one daily service to Dun Laoghaire (two hours).

WALKING THE ISLE OF ANGLESEY COASTAL PATH

Anglesey is a big draw for walkers thanks to the **Isle of Anglesey Coastal Path** (www.angleseycoastalpath.co.uk), a 125-mile coastal walking path with spectacular views. The full trail takes an average of 12 days and passes through a changing landscape of coastal heath, saltmarsh, beaches and Wales' largest Area of Outstanding Natural Beauty (AONB). Although the path reaches a maximum altitude of just 219m, don't be fooled – its up-and-down nature means your total height gain will be more than 4km.

The official trailhead is at St Cybi's Church in Holyhead, but the 12 stages can easily be tackled as individual day hikes, ranging from 7 to 13 miles per day. Some of the stages, particularly the far-northern legs from Cemaes Bay to Church Bay, make for bracing strolls against a dramatic backdrop of wild, windswept scenery.

A great, introductory day walk from Beaumaris takes in the ancient monastic site of Penmon Priory, Penmon Point, with views across to Puffin Island.

OS Explorer Maps 262 (west coast) and 263 (east coast) are helpful, as is the Isle of Anglesey Coastal Path – Official Guide by Carl Rogers.

Anglesey Walking Holidays (www.angleseywalkingholidays.com; per person from £385) offers self-guided walking packages, including accommodation, breakfast, luggage transfers and transport between trailheads.

TRAIN

Direct trains head to/from Bangor (£8.70, 30 minutes), Conwy (£13.50, one hour) and London Euston (£89, 3¾ hours).

NORTH COAST & BORDERS

The North Wales coast has both perennial charms and cultural black spots in equal measure. Stick with the former and you'll not be disappointed – they include a glorious, Unesco-listed castle at Conwy and the limestone-cliff-backed Victorian beach resort of Llandudno.

Moving southeast towards the English border, Llangollen has a reputation for its surrounding attractions (both natural and constructed), adventure sports and cultural festivals. Most of all, it is known as the home of the annual International Musical Eisteddfod.

More details on this region are available from www.northwalesborderlands.co.uk and www.visitllandudno.org.uk.

Llandudno

POP 15,370

Llandudno is a master of reinvention. Backed against an enormous limestone headland, this formerly upmarket Victorian holiday town retains much of its 19th-century grandeur, yet continues to find new fans with its booming boutique accommodation, Welsh art scene and varied dining options.

While for active travellers there can be no bigger highlight than hiking, biking and birding along the Great Orme, for many visitors there are simpler pleasures to be had at sea level: strolling along the promenade or the pier and catching the entertaining beachside Punch and Judy show.

◉ Sights & Activities

★ Great Orme   HEADLAND
(Y Gogarth) 'Orme' comes from the Old Norse for 'sea serpent', perhaps because to seafaring Vikings the vast limestone plateau that towers above present-day Llandudno appeared as a leviathan raising its great head above the water. Traversed by three waymarked summit trails, the vast, grass-covered and largely flat peak is the town's dominant feature, and it's home to several neolithic sights, ample bird life, a lighthouse-cum-cafe and a **visitor centre** (☑01492-874151; www.greatorme.org.uk/canolfan.html; ◷9.30am-5pm mid-Mar–Oct).

You can reach the summit on your own two feet or by two or four wheels via the scenic **Marine Drive**; a **tram** and **cable car** operate in high season.

Llandudno Promenade & Pier   WATERFRONT
(◷pier 9am-6pm) A trip to Llandudno isn't complete until you've strolled along the majestic sweep of the promenade. Queen Victoria herself watched **Professor Codman's Punch & Judy Show**, performed here by the same family since 1860. Audiences are still enthralled by displays of puppet violence and hijinks involving a crocodile and a policeman. Mr Punch's iconic red-and-white-striped tent sits by the entrance to the 1878-built Victorian pier, the longest in Wales at 670m.

Mostyn Gallery   GALLERY
(www.mostyn.org; 12 Vaughan St; ◷10.30am-5pm Tue-Sun) **FREE** A listed 1901 terracotta exterior hides the striking innards of Wales' leading contemporary art gallery – all sharp white angles and light. Its five galleries – the result of an imaginative three-year expansion program – house anything from bleak urban photography to abstract installations. Explore the art shop or grab a coffee at **Café Lux**.

Great Orme Mines   MINE
(☑01492-870447; www.greatormemines.info; adult/child £6.75/4.75; ◷10am-5pm mid-Mar–Oct) Halfway up the tramline to Great Orme is the oldest Bronze Age copper mine

---

WORTH A TRIP

BODNANT GARDEN

Lying 10km south of Llandudno off the A470, **Bodnant Garden** (NT; www.nationaltrust.org.uk; adult/child £9.50/4.75; ◷10am-5pm; **P**) is one of Wales' most beautiful gardens and a must for green-fingered visitors. Laid out in 1875, its 80 lush acres unfurl around picturesque Bodnant Hall (closed to the public). Formal Italianate terraces and rectangular ponds creep away from the house into orderly disorder, transforming themselves into a picturesque wooded valley and wild garden, complete with rushing stream. Key features are the 55m laburnum tunnel; fragrant rose gardens; great banks of azaleas and rhododendrons; and some of the tallest giant redwoods in Britain.

Llandudno

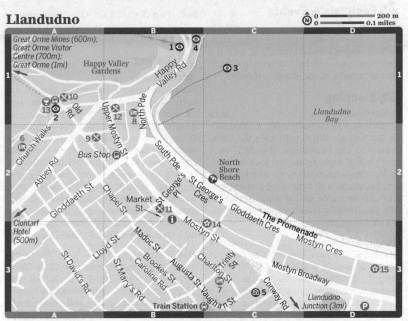

Llandudno

◉ Sights
1 Great Orme Aerial Cable Car	B1
2 Great Orme Tramway	A1
3 Llandudno Promenade & Pier	C1
4 Marine Drive	B1
5 Mostyn Gallery	C3

⬤ Sleeping
6 Escape B&B	A2
7 Llandudno Hostel	C3
8 Osborne House	B1

❋ Eating
9 Characters	A2
10 Fish Tram Chips	A1
11 Ham Bone Food Hall & Brasserie	B2
12 Seahorse	B1

◉ Drinking & Nightlife
13 King's Head	A1

✦ Entertainment
14 St John's Methodist Church	C3
15 Venue Cymru	D3

SNOWDONIA & NORTH WALES LLANDUDNO

in the world that's open to visitors. Copper has been mined here as far back as 4000 years ago, thanks to the rock-softening process that allowed early miners to extract the metal using nothing but bone-and-stone tools.

Marine Drive   SCENIC DRIVE
(drivers & cyclists £2.50; ⊘9am-8pm) Starting by the pier, this one-way, 4-mile narrow road loops anticlockwise around the Great Orme, with immense sea vistas opening up on your right-hand side. There are few places to pull over, but you can take the branch road that heads up to the Great Orme summit a quarter of the way along.

Great Orme Tramway   TRAM
(☎01492-577877; www.greatormetramway.co.uk; Church Walks; adult/child return £6/4.20; ⊘10am-6pm Easter-Oct) This original 1902 tram, one of only three cable-operated trams in the world (the other two are in Lisbon and San Francisco), runs to the top of the Great Orme every 20 minutes, weather permitting.

Great Orme Aerial Cable Car   CABLE CAR
(☎01492-877205; adult/child return £8/6; ⊘10am-6pm Easter-Oct) When it's not too windy, Britain's longest cable car whisks passengers up to the summit of the Great Orme from the Happy Valley Gardens above the pier.

✯ Festivals & Events

Victorian Extravaganza   PERFORMING ARTS
(www.victorian-extravaganza.com; ☺May) Llandudno's biggest annual event, held over the
early-May Bank Holiday weekend and comprising parades, magic shows and music.

🛏 Sleeping

Beach Cove   B&B £
(☑01492-879638; 8 Church Walks; s £35 d £60-
70; 🛜) A stone's throw both from the Great
Orme and the Promenade, this B&B on a
street full of B&Bs represents excellent value for money, particularly for single travellers. The decor is all light wood and creams;
breakfast is ample; and if you're travelling
with your sweetie, consider splurging on the
four-poster room.

Llandudno Hostel   HOSTEL £
(☑01492-877430; www.llandudnohostel.co.uk; 14
Charlton St; dm £21, tw £48-52, f £74-126; P🛜)
Central cheapie with clean, cavernous
rooms, tea- and coffee-making facilities, a
continental breakfast and about as much
atmosphere as the moon.

★Clontarf Hotel   HOTEL ££
(☑01492-877621; www.clontarf.co.uk; 2 Great
Ormes Rd; s £45 d £65-88; P🛜) The nine
individually styled rooms at this small,
friendly hotel come with luxurious touches: there are sophisticated showers in
three of the rooms, and a four-poster bed
and whirlpool bath in the Romantic room.
All rooms look out either to the sea or the
Great Orme, and a small bar contributes to
evening relaxation.

Escape B&B   B&B ££
(☑01492-877776; www.escapebandb.co.uk; 48
Church Walks; r £89-120; P🛜) Llandudno's
first boutique B&B has nine five-star rooms
decorated in designer style and which include a host of energy-saving and luxurious
features. It's hard to choose a favourite, but
the Loft, with its split-level accommodation
and retro vibe, does it for us. All rooms come
with Blu-Ray players and Bose iPod docks,
and there are tasty breakfasts.

Osborne House   HOTEL £££
(☑01492-860330; www.osbornehouse.co.uk; 17
North Pde; ste £145-176; P@) All about marble, antique four-poster beds, fireplaces and
fancy drapes, lavish Osbourne House takes a
classical approach to aesthetics, and the results are impressive. All rooms are suites; the

best is on the 1st floor with Victorian-style
sitting rooms and sea views. Guests have use
of spa facilities at the Empire Hotel.

🍴 Eating

★Characters   CAFE £
(www.charactersllandudno.com; 11 Llewelyn Ave;
lunch £4-6, dinner £14-16; ☺11am-5pm Mon-
Sat, 6-8pm Fri & Sat; 🖉) If you're wondering
whether it's the place that's full of character
or the people running it, well, it's both. Llandudno's hippest tearoom serves wonderful
cream teas (£4) and three-tiered high teas
(£7.95), six types of scones (including choc
chip and Turkish delight flavours), along
with light lunches of sandwiches, lobscows
(beef, beef bone, potato and vegetable stew)
and jacket potatoes. Weekend nights sizzle
with cook-it-yourself hot-stone dinners.

Fish Tram Chips   FISH & CHIPS £
(www.fishtramchipsllandudno.co.uk; 22-24 Old Rd;
mains £7-10; ☺noon-2pm & 5-9pm Tue-Sat, noon-
2.30pm Sun) Come to this firm local favourite
for crispy battered plaice, cod, haddock and
hake, and moreish, fried-to-perfection chips,
or take it all away to munch on the pier.

Ham Bone Food Hall & Brasserie DELI, CAFE £
(www.hambone.co.uk; 3 Lloyd St; mains £6-10;
☺8am-5pm Mon-Sat, 10am-4pm Sun; 🛜) The
best deli-cafe in Llandudno, the Hambone
stocks a range of freshly made wraps, sandwiches and award-winning pork pies, perfect
for a picnic. At night it becomes a brasserie,
with great food made from scratch: paprika-
maple-chicken burgers, huge pizzas, and an
ever-changing range of specials.

Carmel Bistro   MODERN WELSH ££
(☑01492-877643; www.carmelbistro.co.uk; 17 Craig
y Don Pde; 2-course menu £18.50; ☺6.45pm-late
Tue-Sat) With its short-but-sweet menu and
an emphasis on fresh local ingredients, this is
the place for the discerning carnivore. Choose
one of three starters and then have your mature Welsh rump steak cooked one of five different ways, or else sink your teeth into some
slow-grilled lamb chops. Book ahead.

Seahorse   SEAFOOD £££
(☑01492-875315; 7 Church Walks; mains £15-23;
☺4.30pm-late Tue-Sat) Llandudno's only proper seafood restaurant reels you in with delights such as haddock chowder, local wild
seabass, Conwy mussels and – drum roll,
please! – the Codfather. The chef is a keen
fisherman, and the menu reflects his passion for the local catch.

LLANDUDNO JUNCTION'S CULINARY DELIGHTS

A mere blip on the map between Conwy and Llandudno, Llandudno Junction boasts a cafe and a fish-and-chip joint that would do any city proud.

Providero (148 Conwy Rd; coffee £1.85; ⊘ 8am-6pm Mon-Fri, 9.30am-6pm Sat) Providero started out as a North Coast–plying coffee van but has found a more permanent home in this wonderful thimble-sized cafe. You may well find yourself lingering over a cup of locally roasted coffee or one of the 30-plus types of tea, propping up the bar and watching the friendly barista work his latte-art magic.

Enoch's (⊋ 01492-581145; www.enochs.co.uk; 146 Conwy Rd; mains £8-18; ⊘ 11.30am-8.30pm; ⊕) Enoch's, the first chip shop dedicated to Marine Stewartship Council (MSC), attracts customers from many miles. Mains are a perfect blend of tender fish and crispy batter; nonpescatarians are kept happy with award-winning Edwards sausages and deluxe burgers; and one of the specials – cod rarebit – actually made us groan out loud with pleasure.

🍸 Drinking & Entertainment

King's Head   PUB
(www.kingsheadllandudno.co.uk; Old Rd; ⊘ noon-11pm) For a quiet pint and good pub grub, head to this Victorian pub overlooking the tramway station.

Venue Cymru   THEATRE, MUSIC
(⊋ 01472-872000; www.venuecymru.co.uk; Penrhyn Cres; ⊘ box office 10am-7pm Mon-Sat, plus 1hr before performances) The town's leading arts venue for shows and events, from rock gigs to highbrow classical performances.

St John's Methodist Church   LIVE MUSIC
(www.stjohnsllandudno.org; 53 Mostyn St) Choir and soloist performances between May and October.

ℹ️ Information

Llandudno General Hospital (⊋ 01492-860066; Hospital Rd) One mile south of the town centre.

Llandudno Tourist Office (⊋ 01492-577577; www.visitllandudno.org.uk; ⊘ 9.30am-5pm Apr-Oct, closed Sun Nov-Mar) In the library building, with helpful staff, maps and plenty of brochures on local attractions.

ℹ️ Getting There & Away

BUS

Local buses stop on the corner of Upper Mostyn St and Gloddaeth St. Bus 5 runs to Bangor (£3.50, one hour, one to two per hour) and Caernarfon (£3.50, 1½ hours, hourly). Bus 15/19 runs to Conwy (£2.50, 22 minutes, one to two per hour).

National Express runs direct services to London Victoria (£34, 8¼ to 10½ hours, two daily) and Manchester (£15, 3½ hours, one to two daily) via Liverpool (£11.70, 2½ hours).

CAR

Parking on the Promenade is at a premium. The Parc Llandudno complex, just off the A470 close to the railway station, has lots of spaces.

TRAIN

Direct services head to/from Betws-y-Coed (£5.90, 48 minutes), Blaenau Ffestiniog (£8.10, 1¼ hours), Chester (£18, one hour) and Manchester Piccadilly (£30, 2¼ hours); for other destinations you'll need to change at Llandudno Junction (£2.60, eight minutes).

Conwy

POP 3870

Unesco-designated Conwy Castle dominates the cute little walled town: approaching from the east, three bridges span the river and add a further theatrical flourish to the splendid sight of its turrets and towers. The regenerated Conwy Quay at the castle's feet makes for ideal strolling, and – for a place of its size – compact Conwy has a wonderful range of places to eat, drink and be merry.

A highlight of the year is the **Gwledd Conwy Feast** (www.gwleddconwyfeast.co.uk; ⊘ Oct), a food festival with music and arts events, held annually in late October. If you've dragged your feet with booking lodgings, fear not: nearby Llandudno can accommodate the Conwy spillover.

⊙ Sights

★ **Conwy Castle**   CASTLE
(Cadw; ⊋ 01492-592358; www.cadw.wales.gov.uk; Castle Sq; adult/child £5.75/4.35; ⊘ 9.30am-5pm; ℗) Perhaps the most impressive of all Edward I's 'Iron Ring' of fortresses, built between 1277 and 1307 to subdue the rebellious Welsh,

Conwy

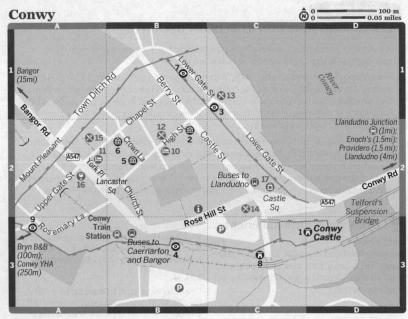

Conwy Castle rises from a rocky outcrop with commanding views across the estuary and Snowdonia National Park. Its moss-covered walls and eight mighty towers enclose a largely intact Great Hall used for feasting; there's a disembodied King's Head in the King's Apartments, and that cloaked man up one of the towers just might be the resident phantom.

Plas Mawr
HISTORIC BUILDING
(Cadw; www.cadw.wales.gov.uk; High St; adult/under 16yr £5.75/4.35; ⊙9am-5pm Apr-Sep) Plas Mawr, one of Britain's finest surviving Elizabethan town houses, was built in 1576 for Robert Wynn. The owner's pride in his noble credentials is evident in the vivid interior, with its colourful friezes, splendid plasterwork ceilings and references to the Wynn dynasty's descent from the princes of Gwynedd. The audioguide-enhanced exhibition on disease in Tudor and Stuart times is an eye-opener; and on summer evenings Blodwen the Maid leads you on a spooky hunt for resident spectres.

Town Wall
FORTIFICATIONS
FREE Encircling the old town and built concurrently with the castle, the 1300m-long wall, punctuated by 21 towers, was erected to protect the English colonists from the Welsh. Ascend the battlements through the Lower Gate on Berry St and follow the wall round to the Upper Gate. Then pick up the other accessible section of the wall at the Mill Gate for the best views of the castle.

Aberconwy House
HISTORIC BUILDING
(NT; www.nationaltrust.org.uk; Castle St; adult/child £3.50/1.75; ⊙11am-5pm) This timber-and-plaster building is the town's oldest medieval house, dating from around 1300. It's worn several hats in its lifetime – from merchant's house and a naval captain's abode to temperance hotel, bakery and antiques shop. The unevenly floored rooms are lined with period furniture, including an 18th-century clock made by local craftsman Moses Evans.

Royal Cambrian Academy
GALLERY
(www.rcaconwy.org; Crown Lane; ⊙11am-5pm Tue-Sat) FREE The twin white-walled galleries host exhibitions by Academy members, such as watercolours depicting Snowdonia by Maurice Greenwood; visiting shows from the National Museum of Wales; and the excellent Annual Summer Exhibition from July to September.

Smallest House in Great Britain
BUILDING
(www.thesmallesthouseingreatbritain.co.uk; Lower Gate St; adult/child £1/50p; ⊙10am-4pm Apr-

Conwy

Oct) Even hobbit-sized visitors to this tiny red construction will wonder how the last resident – a 6ft 3in fisherman – managed to live in the two minute rooms that together measure 9ft by 6ft.

⊨ Sleeping

★**Conwy YHA** HOSTEL **£**
(☑ 0845 371 9732; www.yha.org.uk; Larkhill, Sychnant Pass Rd; dm/r £22/49; ℗ 🛜) Perched on a hill above the town, this former hotel has been converted into a top-notch hostel with a full range of facilities, two- and four-bed dorms and mostly en suite private rooms. It's a 10-minute walk from Upper Gate St onto Sychnant Pass Rd and then up a long drive to the left.

★**Gwynfryn** B&B **££**
(☑ 01492-576733; www.gwynfrynbandb.co.uk; 4 York Pl; r £70-85; 🛜) The helpful owners of this family B&B – set in a refurbished, five-bedroom Victorian property just off the main square – preside over brightly coloured, individually styled rooms; the Rouge Room comes with the best views. Thoughtful touches throughout: fridges; biscuits and chocolates; and books and DVDs to borrow.

Bryn B&B B&B **££**
(☑ 01492-592449; www.bryn.org.uk; Sychnant Pass Rd; s/d £65/80; ℗ 🛜) Appealing Victorian house just beyond the town walls, with five sumptous guest rooms decked out in a soothing cream colour scheme. Breakfast is delightful, with freshly baked bread and organic and fair-trade ingredients. Nothing is too much trouble for the congenial proprietor.

Castle Hotel HOTEL **£££**
(☑ 01492-582800; www.castlewales.co.uk; High St; s/d/ste from £89/166/270; ℗ 🛜) The rooms at Conwy's swishest lodgings feature purple-and-gold decor and Bose sound systems; higher-priced rooms boast castle views, four-poster beds and free-standing baths. The hotel's **Dawson's Restaurant** (light bites £7-13, mains £15-23) serves well-executed brasserie-style meals in elegant surroundings.

✖ Eating

★**Parisella's of Conwy Ice Cream** ICE CREAM **£**
(www.parisellasicecream.co.uk; Conwy Quay; per scoop £1.90) The kiosk on the quay sells some of the finest ice cream in Wales. The picks of the 50-plus flavours include mint choc-chip, salted caramel, death by chocolate, and amaretto and black cherry.

Press Room CAFE **£**
(☑ 01492-592242; 3 Rose Hill St; mains £6-9; ⊗ 10.30am-3.30pm; 🖉🍴) With an outdoor courtyard facing the castle, this arty, friendly cafe-cum-health-food-shop serves up the likes of Welsh rarebit, veggie quiches, black pudding and potato patties, and homemade cakes, along with fair-trade coffees.

★**Watson's Bistro** MODERN WELSH **££**
(☑ 01492-596326; www.watsonsbistroconwy.co.uk; Bishop's Yard, Chapel St; 2-course lunch £11, mains £16-23; ⊗ noon-2pm Wed-Sun, 5.30-8pm daily) For modern Welsh food in an intimate bistro setting, Watson's is the smartest option in town. Everything is homemade, from the chicken-liver pâté to the ice cream. Wraps, burgers and topped ciabatta grace the lunchtime menu; at night, the bistro's trio of lamb shares the spotlight with the likes of hake with samphire.

Amelie's FRENCH **££**
(☑ 01492-583142; 10 High St; lunch £5-7, dinner £13-20; ⊗ 11.30am-2.15pm & 6-9pm Tue-Sat; 🖉) The heroine of the Audrey Tautou film would feel at home in this cheery French-motif

bistro with wood floors and flowers on the tables. Mains – from the lunchtime goats cheese and onion marmalade tart to the evening's melt-in-your-mouth cod with pancetta – are prepared with great attention to both flavour and presentation.

🍸 Drinking & Nightlife

★ Albion Ale House   PUB
(www.albionalehouse.weebly.com; 1-4 Upper Gate St; ⊙noon-11pm) Born out of a collaboration of four Welsh craft breweries (Purple Moose, Conwy, Nant and Great Orme), this heritage-listed 1920s pub is a beer-drinker's nirvana with eight real ales on tap. There's no TV or background music – just the crackle of the fire, the hum of conversation and the click of knitting needles from the local Stich'n'Bitch club.

🛍 Shopping

Knight Shop   GIFTS
(☑01492-541300; www.theknightshop.co.uk; Castle Sq; ⊙9am-5pm Mon-Fri) Always buying boring ol' souvenirs for your loved ones? Then why not go for a Henry VIII–era replica helmet, a war-hammer, some chainmail or perhaps a bottle of locally brewed whisky mead instead?

❶ Information

Tourist Office (☑01492-577566; www.visit-llandudno.org.uk; Rose Hill St; ⊙9am-5pm Mon-Fri, 10am-4pm Sat & Sun) Extremely busy, well-stocked office, with an interesting interactive exhibition on the princes of Gwynedd.

❶ Getting There & Away

Most buses stop by the train station. Bus routes include 5/X5 to Caernarfon (£3.50, 1¼ hours, one to two per hour), Bangor (£3.50, 30 minutes); 15/19 to Llandudno (£2.50, 22 minutes, one to two per hour) and 19 to Betws-y-Coed (£3.50, one hour).

Conwy's train station is inside the town walls, on Rosemary Lane. Direct services head to/from Holyhead (£13.50, one hour), Bangor (£6.30, 17 minutes) and Shrewsbury (£20, 2¼ hours).

Llangollen

POP 3470

Llangollen (lan-goch-len), huddled in the fertile Vale of Llangollen around the banks of the tumbling River Dee, is a scenic, quintessential Welsh town. Both steam-powered and watery attractions lie on its fringes, and it's a popular destination for walkers, bikers

and general fresh-air fiends. In July, Llangollen's streets become packed with attendees of its international arts festival.

◉ Sights & Activities

★ Pontcysyllte Aqueduct
& Canal World Heritage Site   CANAL
(☑01978-292015; www.pontcysyllte-aqueduct.co.uk; guided tours £3; ⊙visitor centre 10am-4pm Mar-Oct) FREE In the 18th century the horse-drawn canal barge was the most efficient way of hauling goods over long distances. These days the Llangollen Canal that was once used to carry drinking water from the River Dee to the Hurleston Reservoir in Cheshire is in use once more, with **Jones the Boats** (☑01978-824166; www.canaltrip.co.uk; Old Wharf, Trevor; adult/child £5/3; ⊙Apr-Oct) carrying passengers on boat rides over the head-spinningly high miracle of engineering that is the Pontcysyllte Aqueduct, designed by the great civil engineer Thomas Telford (1757–1834). The old towpaths also offer peaceful, traffic-free walking.

Castell Dinas Brân   CASTLE
FREE The ragged arches and tumbledown walls of Dinas Brân mark the remnants of a short-lived 13th-century castle that fell to Edward I's campaign against Llywellyn ap Gruffydd. The all-encompassing 360-degree views from the hilltop are well worth the two-hour return walk up the steep track; follow the Offa's Dyke Path arrows from Llangollen Wharf.

Plas Newydd   HISTORIC BUILDING
(www.denbighshire.gov.uk/heritage; Hill St; adult/child £5.50/4.50; ⊙10am-5pm Wed-Mon Apr-Sep) Ornate Plas Newydd was home to Lady Eleanor Butler and Miss Sarah Ponsonby, two society ladies who ran away from Ireland to Wales disguised as men, and settled down here to enjoy 'friendship, celibacy and the knitting of stockings'. Various high-profile figures of the day, attracted by the romantic story, came to call on the Ladies of Llangollen: admirers included the Duke of Wellington and William Wordsworth. There's a good self-guided audio tour of the house, and tranquil gardens to explore.

Valle Crucis Abbey   RUIN
(Abaty Glyn y Groes; Cadw; www.cadw.wales.gov.uk; A542; adult/concession Apr-Oct £3.50/2.65, Nov-Mar free; ⊙10am-5pm) The mournful ruins of this 13th-century Cistercian abbey are a 2-mile walk from Llangollen. The abbey is particularly atmospheric on grey days, when

Llangollen

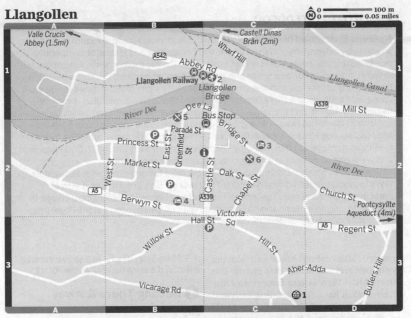

N 0 — 100 m
0 — 0.05 miles

Valle Crucis Abbey (1.5mi)

Castell Dinas Brân (2mi)

A542

Abbey Rd

Llangollen Railway 2

Llangollen Bridge

Llangollen Canal

A539 Mill St

River Dee

Dee La

5

Bus Stop

Bridge St

Parade St

Princess St

East St

Greenfield St

Market St

Castle St

3

6

Oak St

Chapel St

River Dee

Church St

A5

P

Berwyn St 4

A539

Victoria Sq

Pontcysyllte Aqueduct (4mi)

Hall St

A5 Regent St

Willow St

Hill St

Aber-Adda

Butlers Hill

Vicarage Rd

1

---

its intact wall rises out of the mist. The vaulted chapter house is remarkably well preserved; the cloister is not, but a small interpretation centre brings the monks' daily routines to life.

Llangollen Railway HERITAGE RAILWAY
(☑01978-860979; www.llangollen-railway.co.uk; Abbey Rd; adult/under 15yr return £12/6; ⊙daily Apr-Sep) The 7.5-mile jaunt through the Dee Valley via Berwyn (near Horseshoe Falls) and Carrog on the former Ruabon-to-Barmouth line is a superb day out for families and heritage-rail-lovers alike. The 2½ mile extension to Corwen was completed in October 2014.

🎭 Festivals & Events

Llangollen Fringe Festival PERFORMING ARTS
(www.llangollenfringe.co.uk; ⊙Jul) This small-town, volunteer-run arts festival, held in July, manages to attract some big names: 2014's line-up included Gruff Rhys of the Super Furry Animals.

International Musical Eisteddfod MUSIC
(http://international-eisteddfod.co.uk; ⊙Jul) Choral performances, costumed dances and more. Staged at the Royal International Pavilion in early July.

Llangollen

◉ Sights
1 Plas Newydd..C3

⊕ Activities, Courses & Tours
2 Llangollen Railway..................................C1

⌂ Sleeping
3 Cornerstones Guesthouse..................C2
4 Llangollen Hostel...................................B2

⊗ Eating
5 Corn Mill..B1
6 Gales of Llangollen.............................C2

🛏 Sleeping & Eating

Llangollen Hostel HOSTEL £
(☑01978-861773; www.llangollenhostel.co.uk; Berwyn St; dm/d/tr from £18/45/60; ⓟ⑀) An uber-central hostel that doesn't have a Dickensian orphanage vibe is a rare beast in Wales. In this welcoming home-away-from-home cyclists and canoeists haunt the well-equipped kitchen and guest lounge; there's both storage for your bike/boat and laundry facilities for mucky gear. A light breakfast seals the deal.

Cornerstones Guesthouse B&B ££
(☑01978-861569; www.cornerstones-guesthouse. co.uk; 15 Bridge St; r £100-120; ⓟ⑀⑁) This

ESSENTIAL EISTEDDFOD

National Eisteddfod (www.eisteddfod.org.uk; ☺Aug), pronounced *'ey-steth-vot'*, is an eight-day celebration of Welsh culture, and Europe's largest festival of competitive music-making and poetry. Descended from ancient bardic tournaments, it is conducted in Welsh, with prizes for best prose and poetry presented by robed Druids (modern-day bards). Many people come in search of Welsh ancestry, while musical fringe events featuring local bands lend a slight Glastonbury-style atmosphere. Eisteddfod is generally held in early August, and the venue swings annually between North and South Wales.

Urdd Eisteddfod (www.urdd.org; ☺May/Jun) is a separate young people's festival – *urdd* (pronounced *'irth'*) is Welsh for 'youth' – held in late May/early June. The format resembles its bigger brother, National Eisteddfod, and involves around 15,000 children and teenagers competing in singing, dancing and other competitions.

International Musical Eisteddfod (p765) is the most famous of all, established after WWII to promote international harmony. Held over six days in early July, it attracts participants from around 50 countries, transforming Llangollen into a global village. In addition to daily folk-music and dancing competitions, gala concerts at the Royal International Pavilion feature international stars.

converted 16th-century house, all sloping floorboards and oak beams, has charm and history. River View is our favourite of the three rooms; it has a free-standing bath and the gentle lapping of the River Dee sends you off to sleep. Breakfast is a sumptuous affair for carnivores and vegetarians alike.

Gales of Llangollen EUROPEAN ££
(www.galesofllangollen.co.uk; 18 Bridge St; mains £11-19; ☺noon-2pm & 6-9.30pm Mon-Sat; ✍) Turn up early to grab a table at the friendly, wood-panelled Gales wine bar–restaurant, a Llangollen institution. The formidable wine list is 100-strong, and the succinct food menu includes firm favourites (Welsh black rib-eye, pork belly), daily changing specials (dolcelatte and walnut tortelli), and platters of cold cuts and artisan cheeses. When it's busy, continents may drift before you get served.

Corn Mill GASTROPUB ££
(✆01978-869555; www.brunningandprice.co.uk/cornmill; Dee Lane; light meals £7-11, mains £10-18; ☺noon-9.30pm; ☜) The water wheel still turns at the heart of this converted mill, now a well-lit, buzzy, multistorey gastropub. The deck overlooking the River Dee is a great spot for an alfresco lunch, and the well-executed dishes – from crab linguine and steak sandwiches to slow-cooked pork belly – are real crowd pleasers.

❶ Information

Tourist Office (✆01978-860828; www.north-walesborderlands.co.uk; The Chapel, Castle St;

☺9.30am-5pm) Helpful well-stocked tourist office, in the same building as the library.

❶ Getting There & Away

BUS

Bus X94 heads to Wrexham (£3.30, 35 minutes, eight daily Monday to Saturday), Bala (£5, 48 minutes), Dolgellau (£5.40, 1½ hours) and Barmouth (£5.40, 1¾ hours).

National Express coaches head to Wrexham (£2.80, 25 minutes), Shrewsbury (£4.70, 55 minutes) and Birmingham (£11.90, 2½ hours).

CAR

Parking is at a premium in Llangollen. If your accommodation doesn't provide parking, check whether it can provide a pass for the council car parks.

Ruthin

POP 5500

Tucked away in the quiet Clwyd Valley, Ruthin is a town with a particularly appealing historic heart. **St Peter's Square** features some fine half-timbered houses, including the Old Courthouse with a protruding beam that served as a gibbet (now home to Nat-West Bank).

Offa's Dyke Path national trail passes through the nearby Clwydian Range Area of Outstanding Natural Beauty (AONB).

❍ Sights

Nantclwyd y Dre HISTORIC BUILDING
(www.nantclwydydre.co.uk; Castle St; adult/child £4/3; ☺10.30am-5pm Fri-Sun Apr-Sep) The

15th-century Nantclwyd y Dre is the oldest timber-framed building in Wales, with rooms restored to various eras and an attic full of endangered bats.

Ruthin Gaol   HISTORIC BUILDING
(www.ruthingaol.co.uk; 46 Clwyd St; adult/child £4/3; ☺10am-5pm Wed-Sun Apr-Oct) An audio-guided tour around Ruthin Gaol, a sombre Victorian construction, initiates you into the grisly world of 17th-century penal correction.

Ruthin Craft Centre   ARTS CENTRE
(www.ruthincraftcentre.org.uk; Park Rd; ☺10am-5pm; ℗) FREE The town's arts hub, with a decent cafe and information centre.

🛏 Sleeping & Eating

Manorhaus   BOUTIQUE HOTEL ££
(☑01824-704830; www.manorhaus.com; 10 Well St; s/d from £87.50/115; ☎) This boutique restaurant-with-rooms is the place to stay in town. It has eight gorgeously styled bedrooms, each decorated in collaboration with a different local or national artist.

★ On the Hill   MODERN BRITISH ££
(☑01824-707736; www.onthehillrestaurant.co.uk; 1 Upper Clwyd St; mains £13-17, 1-/2-/3-course lunch £10/13/16; ☺6.30-9pm Tue, noon-2pm & 6.30-9pm Wed-Sat) A brief stopover in Ruthin is worth it for the sophisticated cooking at On the Hill alone.

🛈 Getting There & Away

Bus X1/1/2 runs to Chester (£5.50, one hour, two daily Monday to Saturday).

Bangor

POP 17,990

If you've ever descended on the university town of Bangor on a rainy day and were confronted with the sight of a forlorn, mostly emply High St where a homeless man was playing 'Moon River' on his saxophone, you can understand why most travellers dismiss Bangor as unlovely. It's a useful transport hub, however, and may yet undergo a cultural renaissance once the ambitious new performance arts centre is completed in 2015.

🌑 Sights

Penrhyn Castle   CASTLE
(NT; www.nationaltrust.org.uk; off Llandegai Rd; adult/child £10.35/5.18; ☺castle noon-5pm, grounds 11am-5pm Mar-Oct) Bangor's main attraction, Penrhyn Castle is an immense 19th-century neo-Norman fortress flanked by a Victorian walled garden. Funded by the vast profits from the slate mine of the Caribbean sugar plantation owner and anti-abolitionist First Baron Penrhyn, it is both tasteless and formidable, with darkly extravagant rooms in the neo-Gothic hall.

🍴 Eating

Blue Sky   CAFE £
(☑01248-355444; www.blueskybangor.co.uk; 236 High St; mains £4-9; ☺9.30am-5.30pm Mon-Sat) Get to Blue Sky early to beat the crowds who come for the best breakfasts, soups, sandwiches, burgers and salads in town.

Noodle One   ASIAN £
(www.noodleone.com; 166 High St; mains £7.50-9; ☺noon-3pm & 5-10pm Sun-Thu, noon-10pm Fri & Sat) If you're in Bangor on a Sunday, Noodle One is your one good option. It serves ample portions of noodle dishes from all over Asia.

🛈 Getting There & Away

From the bus station, National Express coaches head to Porthmadog (£8.30, one hour), Caernarfon (£6.80, 25 minutes), Holyhead (£19.50, 50 minutes) and Birmingham (£27.90, 5½ hours) daily and to London Victoria (£32.50, nine to 11 hours) twice daily.

Bus routes include the following:

➡ 5/X5 to Caernarfon (£3.50, 30 minutes, one to two per hour), Conwy (£3.50, 35 minutes, one to two per hour) and Llandudno (£3.50, 56 minutes, one to two per hour).

➡ 53–58 to Beaumaris (£3.30, 30 minutes, two hourly Monday to Saturday).

➡ 85/86 to Llanberis (£2.20, 27 minutes, one to two per hour).

➡ T2 to Aberystwyth (£5.40, 3¼ hours, two daily) via Caernarfon (£2.60, 25 minutes), Porthmadog (£5.40, one hour), Dolgellau (£5.40, two hours), Machynlleth (£5.40, 2½ hours) and Aberystwyth (£5.40, 3¼ hours).

➡ X4 to Holyhead (£3.50, 50 minutes, one to two per hour).

➡ Snowdon Sherpa S6 morning service to Capel Curig (£2, 33 minutes) and Betws-y-Coed (£2, 45 minutes).

Bangor's train station is on Holyhead Rd. Direct trains run to/from Holyhead (£8.70, 30 minutes), Conwy (£6.30, 17 minutes) and London Euston (£86, 3¼ hours).

Scotland

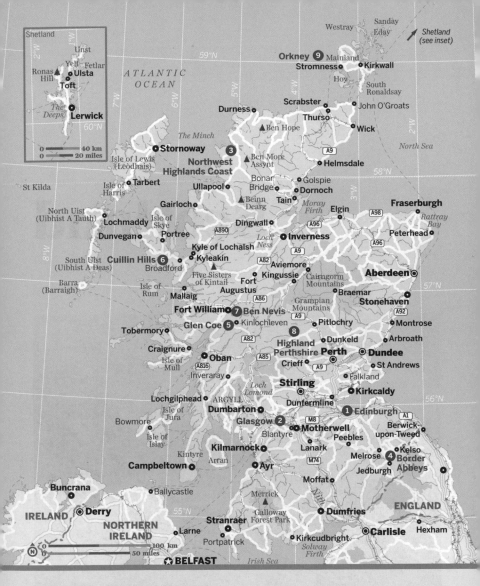

Scotland Highlights

1 Exploring Scotland's capital, **Edinburgh** (p771), one of the world's most fascinating cities

2 Enjoying Victorian architecture, great nightlife and friendly locals in **Glasgow** (p803)

3 Getting permanent jawdrop along the **northwest Highlands coast** (p924)

4 Experiencing the romantic ruins of the **Border Abbeys** (p822)

5 Uncovering scenic beauty and tragic history at **Glen Coe** (p913)

6 Capturing the brooding splendour of Skye's **Cuillin Hills** (p935)

7 Climbing **Ben Nevis** (p917), the highest point in Britain

8 Admiring the magnificent forests and lochs of **Highland Perthshire** (p909)

9 Discovering 5000-year-old neolithic sites on **Orkney** (p946)

Edinburgh

POP 460,400 / AREA 116 SQ KM

Best Places to Eat

➡ The Kitchin (p796)

➡ Gardener's Cottage (p795)

➡ The Dogs (p796)

➡ Ondine (p795)

Best Places to Stay

➡ Witchery by the Castle (p793)

➡ Hotel Missoni (p793)

➡ Sandaig Guest House (p794)

Why Go?

Edinburgh is a city that begs to be explored. From the vaults and wynds (narrow lanes) that riddle the Old Town to the urban villages of Stockbridge and Cramond, it's filled with quirky come-hither nooks that tempt you to walk just a little bit further. And every corner turned reveals sudden views and unexpected vistas – green sunlit hills, a glimpse of rust-red crags, a blue flash of distant sea.

But there's more to Edinburgh than sightseeing – there are top shops, world-class restaurants and a bacchanalia of bars to enjoy. This is a city of pub crawls and impromptu music sessions, mad-for-it clubbing and all-night parties, overindulgence, late nights and wandering home through cobbled streets at dawn.

All these superlatives come together in August at festival time, when it seems as if half the world descends on Edinburgh for one enormous party. If you can possibly manage it, join them.

When to Go

➡ In May there's good weather (usually), flowers and cherry blossom everywhere, and (gasp!) no crowds.

➡ August is festival time – crowded and mad, but unmissable.

➡ In December there are Christmas decorations, cosy pubs with open fires and ice skating in Princes Street Gardens.

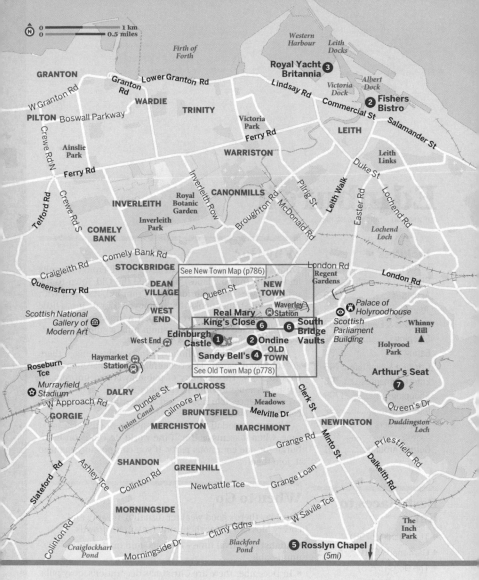

Edinburgh Highlights

❶ Taking in the views from the battlements of **Edinburgh Castle** (p773)

❷ Enjoying the finest of Scottish seafood at **Ondine** (p795) or **Fishers Bistro** (p796)

❸ Nosing around the Queen's private quarters on the former **Royal Yacht Britannia** (p785) at Leith

❹ Listening to live folk music at **Sandy Bell's** (p798)

❺ Trying to decipher the Da Vinci code at mysterious **Rosslyn Chapel** (p788)

❻ Exploring Edinburgh's subterranean history in the haunted vaults of **South Bridge** (p784) and **Real Mary King's Close** (p778)

❼ Climbing to the summit of the city's miniature mountain, **Arthur's Seat** (p780)

History

Back in the 7th century the Castle Rock was called Dun Eiden (meaning 'Fort on the Hill Slope'). When invaders from the kingdom of Northumbria in northeast England captured it in 638, they took the existing Gaelic name 'Eiden' and tacked it onto their own Old English word for fort, *burh*, to create the name Edinburgh.

Originally a purely defensive site, Edinburgh began to expand in the 12th century when King David I held court at the castle and founded the abbey at Holyrood. The city's first effective town wall was constructed around 1450, enclosing the Old Town; this overcrowded area became a medieval Manhattan, forcing its inhabitants to build tenements five and six storeys high.

The capital played an important role in the Reformation (1560–1690), led by the firebrand John Knox. Mary, Queen of Scots held court in the Palace of Holyroodhouse for six brief years, but when her son James VI succeeded to the English throne in 1603, he moved his court to London. The Act of Union in 1707 further reduced Edinburgh's importance.

Nevertheless, cultural and intellectual life flourished during the Scottish Enlightenment (roughly from 1740 to 1830), and Edinburgh became known as 'a hotbed of genius'. In the second half of the 18th century, the New Town was built, and in the 19th century the population quadrupled to 400,000 as suburbs of Victorian tenements spread to the north and south.

In the 1920s, the city's borders expanded again to encompass Leith in the north, Cramond in the west and the Pentland Hills in the south. Following WWII, the city's cultural life blossomed, stimulated by the Edinburgh International Festival and its fellow traveller the Fringe, both held for the first time in 1947 and now recognised as world-class arts festivals.

Edinburgh entered a new era following the 1997 referendum vote in favour of a devolved Scottish parliament, which first convened in July 1999. The parliament is housed in a controversial new building in Holyrood at the foot of the Royal Mile, where the 2007 elections saw the Scottish National Party – whose long-term aim is independence for Scotland – take power for the first time. However, in a 2014 referendum on independence, the Scots voted by 55% to 45% to remain in the UK.

◉ Sights

Edinburgh's main attractions are concentrated in the city centre – on and around the Old Town's Royal Mile between the castle and Holyrood, and in New Town. A major exception is the Royal Yacht Britannia, which is in the redeveloped docklands district of Leith, 2 miles northeast of the centre.

◉ Old Town

Edinburgh's Old Town stretches along a ridge to the east of the castle, and tumbles down Victoria St to the broad expanse of the Grassmarket. It's a jagged and jumbled maze of masonry riddled with closes (alleys) and wynds (narrow lanes), stairs and vaults, and cleft along its spine by the cobbled ravine of the Royal Mile.

This mile-long street earned its regal nickname in the 16th century when it was used by the king to travel between the castle and the Palace of Holyroodhouse. There are five sections – the Castle Esplanade, Castlehill, Lawnmarket, High St and Canongate – whose names reflect their historical origins.

Until the founding of New Town in the 18th century, old Edinburgh was an overcrowded and insanitary hive of humanity squeezed between the boggy ground of the Nor' Loch (North Loch, now drained and occupied by Princes Street Gardens) to the north and the city walls to the south and east. The only way for the town to expand was upwards, and the five- and six-storey tenements that were raised along the Royal Mile in the 16th and 17th centuries were the skyscrapers of their day, remarked upon with wonder by visiting writers such as Daniel Defoe. All classes of society, from beggars to magistrates, lived cheek by jowl in these urban ants' nests, the wealthy occupying the middle floors – high enough to be above the noise and stink of the streets, but not so high that climbing the stairs would be too tiring – while the poor squeezed into attics, basements, cellars and vaults amid the rats, rubbish and raw sewage.

★ **Edinburgh Castle** CASTLE
(Map p778; www.edinburghcastle.gov.uk; adult/child incl audioguide £16/9.60; ⊙9.30am-6pm Apr-Sep, to 5pm Oct-Mar, last admission 45min before closing; ▣23, 27, 41, 42) Edinburgh Castle has played a pivotal role in Scottish history, both as a royal residence – King Malcolm Canmore (r 1058–93) and Queen Margaret first made their home here in the 11th

Royal Mile

A GRAND DAY OUT

Planning your own procession along the Royal Mile involves some tough decisions – it would be impossible to see everything in a single day, so it's wise to decide in advance what you don't want to miss and shape your visit around that. Remember to leave time for lunch, for exploring some of the Mile's countless side alleys and, during festival time, for enjoying the street theatre that is bound to be happening in High St.

The most pleasant way to reach the Castle Esplanade at the start of the Royal Mile is to hike up the zigzag path from the footbridge behind the Ross Bandstand in Princes Street Gardens (in springtime you'll be knee-deep in daffodils). Starting at **Edinburgh Castle** ❶ means that the rest of your walk is downhill. For a superb view up and down the length of the Mile, climb the **Camera Obscura's Outlook Tower** ❷ before visiting **Gladstone's**

ROYAL VISITS TO THE ROYAL MILE

1561: Mary, Queen of Scots arrives from France and holds an audience with John Knox.
1745: Bonnie Prince Charlie fails to capture Edinburgh Castle, and instead sets up court in Holyroodhouse.
2004: Queen Elizabeth II officially opens the Scottish Parliament building.

Edinburgh Castle
If you're pushed for time, visit the Great Hall, the Honours of Scotland and the Prisons of War exhibit. Head for the Half Moon Battery for a photo looking down the length of the Royal Mile.

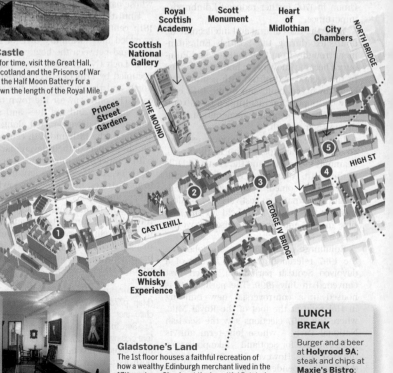

Royal Scottish Academy

Scott Monument

Heart of Midlothian

City Chambers

NORTH BRIDGE

Scottish National Gallery

Princes Street Gardens

THE MOUND

❺

HIGH ST

❹

❸

❷

GEORGE IV BRIDGE

❶

CASTLEHILL

Scotch Whisky Experience

Gladstone's Land
The 1st floor houses a faithful recreation of how a wealthy Edinburgh merchant lived in the 17th century. Check out the beautiful Painted Bedchamber, with its ornately decorated walls and wooden ceilings.

LUNCH BREAK

Burger and a beer at **Holyrood 9A**; steak and chips at **Maxie's Bistro**; slap-up seafood at **Ondine**.

Land ❸ and **St Giles Cathedral** ❹. If history's your thing, you'll want to add **Real Mary King's Close** ❺, **John Knox House** ❻ and the **Museum of Edinburgh** ❼ to your must-see list.

At the foot of the mile, choose between modern and ancient seats of power – the **Scottish Parliament** ❽ or the **Palace of Holyroodhouse** ❾. Round off the day with an evening ascent of Arthur's Seat or, slightly less strenuously, Calton Hill. Both make great sunset viewpoints.

TAKING YOUR TIME

Minimum time needed for each attraction:

» **Edinburgh Castle**: two hours
» **Gladstone's Land**: 45 minutes
» **St Giles Cathedral**: 30 minutes
» **Real Mary King's Close**: one hour (tour)
» **Scottish Parliament**: one hour (tour)
» **Palace of Holyroodhouse**: one hour

Real Mary King's Close
The guided tour is heavy on ghost stories, but a highlight is standing in an original 17th-century room with tufts of horsehair poking from the crumbling plaster, and breathing in the ancient scent of stone, dust and history.

Canongate Kirk

CANONGATE

ST MARY'S ST

SOUTH BRIDGE

Tron Kirk

Our Dynamic Earth

St Giles Cathedral
Look out for the Burne-Jones stained-glass window (1873) at the west end, showing the crossing of the River Jordan, and the bronze memorial to Robert Louis Stevenson in the Moray Aisle.

Scottish Parliament
Don't have time for the guided tour? Pick up a 'Discover the Scottish Parliament Building' leaflet from reception and take a self-guided tour of the exterior, then hike up to Salisbury Crags for a great view of the complex.

Palace of Holyroodhouse
Find the secret staircase joining Mary, Queen of Scots' bedchamber with that of her husband, Lord Darnley, who restrained the queen while his henchmen stabbed to death her secretary (and possible lover), David Rizzio.

DANITA DELIMONT/GETTY IMAGES ©

RICK LEWGETTI IMAGES © ARCHITECT ENRIC MIRALLES

RIEGER BERTRAND/GETTY IMAGES ©

century – and as a military stronghold. The castle last saw military action in 1745; from then until the 1920s it served as the British army's main base in Scotland. Today it is one of Scotland's most atmospheric and most popular tourist attractions.

The brooding, black crags of Castle Rock, rising above the western end of Princes St, are the very reason for Edinburgh's existence. This rocky hill was the most easily defended hilltop on the invasion route between England and central Scotland, a route followed by countless armies from the Roman legions of the 1st and 2nd centuries AD to the Jacobite troops of Bonnie Prince Charlie in 1745.

The Entrance Gateway, flanked by statues of Robert the Bruce and William Wallace, opens to a lane that leads up beneath the 16th-century Portcullis Gate to the cannons ranged along the Argyle and Mills Mount batteries. The battlements here have great views over New Town to the Firth of Forth.

At the far end of Mills Mount Battery is the famous One O'Clock Gun, where crowds gather to watch a gleaming WWII 25-pounder fire an ear-splitting time signal at exactly 1pm (every day except Sunday, Christmas Day and Good Friday).

South of Mills Mount, the road curls up leftwards through Foog's Gate to the highest part of Castle Rock, crowned by the tiny, Romanesque St Margaret's Chapel, the oldest surviving building in Edinburgh. It was probably built by David I or Alexander I in memory of their mother, Queen Margaret, sometime around 1130 (she was canonised in 1250). Beside the chapel stands Mons Meg, a giant 15th-century siege gun built at Mons (in what is now Belgium) in 1449.

The main group of buildings on the summit of Castle Rock is ranged around Crown Sq, dominated by the shrine of the Scottish National War Memorial. Opposite is the Great Hall, built for James IV (r 1488–1513) as a ceremonial hall and used as a meeting place for the Scottish parliament until 1639. Its most remarkable feature is the original, 16th-century hammer-beam roof.

The Castle Vaults beneath the Great Hall (entered from Crown Sq via the Prisons of War exhibit) were used variously as storerooms, bakeries and a prison. The vaults have been renovated to resemble 18th- and early-19th-century prisons, where graffiti carved by French and American prisoners can be seen on the ancient wooden doors.

THE STONE OF DESTINY

On St Andrew's Day 1996 a block of sandstone – 26.5in by 16.5in by 11in in size, with rusted iron hoops at either end – was installed with much pomp and ceremony in Edinburgh Castle. For the previous 700 years it had lain in London, beneath the Coronation Chair in Westminster Abbey. Almost all English, and later British, monarchs from Edward II in 1307 to Elizabeth II in 1953 have parked their backsides firmly over this stone during their coronation ceremony.

The legendary Stone of Destiny – said to have originated in the Holy Land, and on which Scottish kings placed their feet during their coronation (not their bums; the English got that bit wrong) – was stolen from Scone Abbey near Perth by King Edward I of England in 1296. It was taken to London and there it remained for seven centuries – except for a brief removal to Gloucester during WWII air raids, and a three-month sojourn in Scotland after it was stolen by Scottish Nationalist students at Christmas in 1950 – an enduring symbol of Scotland's subjugation by England.

The Stone of Destiny returned to the political limelight in 1996, when the then Scottish Secretary and Conservative Party MP, Michael Forsyth, arranged for the return of the sandstone block to Scotland. An attempt to boost the flagging popularity of the Conservative Party in Scotland prior to a general election, Forsyth's publicity stunt failed. The Scots said thanks very much for the stone and then, in May 1997, voted against every Conservative MP in Scotland.

Many people, however, believe that Edward I was fobbed off with a shoddy imitation in 1296 and that the true Stone of Destiny remains safely hidden somewhere in Scotland. This is not impossible – some descriptions of the original stone state that it was made of black marble and decorated with elaborate carvings. Interested parties should read Scotland's Stone of Destiny, by Nick Aitchinson, which details the history and cultural significance of Scotland's most famous lump of rock.

EDINBURGH IN...

Two Days

A two-day trip to Edinburgh should start at **Edinburgh Castle**, followed by a stroll down the **Royal Mile** to the **Scottish Parliament Building** and the **Palace of Holyroodhouse**. You can work up an appetite by climbing **Arthur's Seat**, then satisfy your hunger with dinner at **Ondine** or **Timberyard**. On day two, spend the morning in the **National Museum of Scotland**, then catch the bus to **Leith** for a visit to the **Royal Yacht Britannia**. In the evening, have dinner at one of Leith's many excellent restaurants, or scare yourself silly on a guided **ghost tour**.

Four Days

Two more days will give you time for a morning stroll around the **Royal Botanic Garden**, followed by a trip to the enigmatic and beautiful **Rosslyn Chapel**, or a relaxing afternoon visit to the seaside village of **Cramond** – bring binoculars (for birdwatching and yacht-spotting) and a book (to read in the sun). Dinner at **Gardener's Cottage** could be before or after your sunset walk to the summit of **Calton Hill**. On day four, head out to the pretty harbour village of **Queensferry**, nestled beneath the **Forth Bridges**.

On the eastern side of the square is the **Royal Palace**, built during the 15th and 16th centuries, where a series of historical tableaux leads to the highlight of the castle – a strongroom housing the **Honours of Scotland** (the Scottish crown jewels), the oldest surviving crown jewels in Europe. Locked away in a chest following the Act of Union in 1707, the crown (made in 1540 from the gold of Robert the Bruce's 14th-century coronet), sword and sceptre lay forgotten until they were unearthed at the instigation of the novelist Sir Walter Scott in 1818. Also on display here is the **Stone of Destiny**.

Among the neighbouring **Royal Apartments** is the bedchamber where Mary, Queen of Scots gave birth to her son James VI, who was to unite the crowns of Scotland and England in 1603.

Scotch Whisky Experience   EXHIBITION

(Map p778; www.scotchwhiskyexperience.co.uk; 354 Castlehill; adult/child incl tour & tasting £13.50/6.75; ⊙10am-6.30pm Jun-Aug, to 6pm Sep-May; ☐2, 23, 27, 41, 42, 45) A former school houses this multimedia centre explaining the making of whisky from barley to bottle in a series of exhibits, demonstrations and tours that combine sight, sound and smell, including the world's largest collection of malt whiskies; look out for Peat the distillery cat! More expensive whisky tours include more extensive whisky tastings and samples of Scottish cuisine. There's also a restaurant (p795) that serves traditional Scottish dishes with, where possible, a dash of whisky thrown in.

Camera Obscura   EXHIBITION

(Map p778; www.camera-obscura.co.uk; Castlehill; adult/child £12.95/9.50; ⊙9.30am-9pm Jul & Aug, to 7pm Apr-Jun & Sep-Oct, 10am-6pm Nov-Mar; ☐2, 23, 27, 42) Edinburgh's camera obscura is a curious 19th-century device – in constant use since 1853 – that uses lenses and mirrors to throw a live image of the city onto a large horizontal screen. The accompanying commentary is entertaining and the whole experience has a quirky charm, complemented by an intriguing exhibition dedicated to illusions of all kinds. Stairs lead up through various displays to the **Outlook Tower**, which offers great views over the city.

Gladstone's Land   HISTORIC BUILDING

(NTS; Map p778; www.nts.org.uk; 477 Lawnmarket; adult/child £6.50/5; ⊙10am-6.30pm Jul & Aug, to 5pm Apr-Jun & Sep-Oct; ☐23, 27, 41, 42) One of Edinburgh's most prominent 17th-century merchants was Thomas Gledstanes, who in 1617 purchased the tenement later known as Gladstone's Land. It contains fine painted ceilings, walls and beams, and some splendid furniture from the 17th and 18th centuries. The volunteer guides provide a wealth of anecdotes and a detailed history.

St Giles Cathedral   CHURCH

(Map p778; www.stgilescathedral.org.uk; High St; suggested donation £3; ⊙9am-7pm Mon-Fri, to 5pm Sat, 1-5pm Sun May-Sep, 9am-5pm Mon-Sat, 1-5pm Sun Oct-Apr; ☐23, 27, 41, 42) The great grey bulk of St Giles Cathedral dominates Edinburgh's High St. Properly called the High Kirk of Edinburgh (it was only a true

Old Town

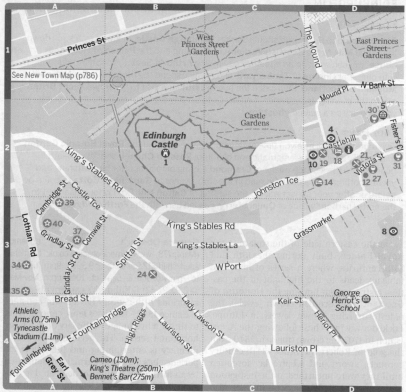

See New Town Map (p786)

cathedral – the seat of a bishop – from 1633 to 1638 and from 1661 to 1689), the church was named after the patron saint of cripples and beggars. The present building dates largely from the 15th century – the beautiful crown spire was completed in 1495 – but much of it was restored in the 19th century.

The interior lacks grandeur but is rich in history: a Norman-style church was built here in 1126 but was destroyed by English invaders in 1385 (the only substantial remains are the central piers that support the tower). St Giles was at the heart of the Scottish Reformation, and John Knox served as minister here from 1559 to 1572. One of the most interesting corners of the kirk is the **Thistle Chapel**, built in 1911 for the Knights of the Most Ancient & Most Noble Order of the Thistle. The elaborately carved Gothic-style stalls have canopies topped with the helms and arms of the 16 knights – look out for the bagpipe-playing angel amid the vaulting.

By the side of the street, outside the western door of St Giles, is the **Heart of Midlothian**, set into the cobblestone paving. This marks the site of the Tolbooth. Built in the 15th century and demolished in the early 19th century, the Tolbooth served variously as a meeting place for parliament, the town council and the General Assembly of the Reformed Kirk, before becoming law courts and, finally, a notorious prison and place of execution. Passers-by traditionally spit on the heart for luck (don't stand downwind!).

At the other end of St Giles is the Mercat Cross (p844), a 19th-century copy of the 1365 original, where merchants and traders met to transact business and royal proclamations were read.

⭐ **Real Mary King's Close**   HISTORIC BUILDING
(Map p778; ☎ 0845 070 6244; www.realmarykings-close.com; 2 Warriston's Close, High St; adult/child £12.95/7.45; ⊙ 10am-9pm daily Apr-Oct, to 11pm

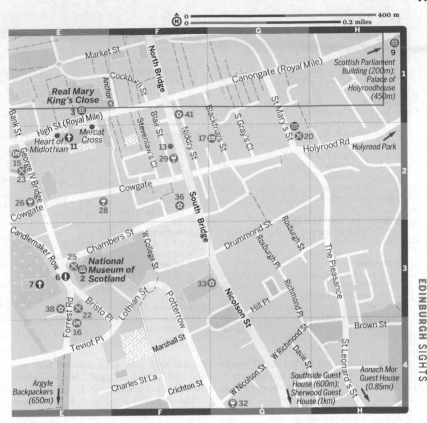

Aug; 10am-5pm Sun-Thu & 10am-9pm Fri & Sat Nov-Mar; 📱 23, 27, 41, 42) Edinburgh's 18th-century City Chambers were built over the sealed-off remains of Mary King's Close, and the lower levels of this medieval Old Town alley have survived almost unchanged amid the foundations for 250 years. Now open to the public, this spooky, subterranean labyrinth gives a fascinating insight into the everyday life of 17th-century Edinburgh. Costumed characters lead tours through a 16th-century town house and the plague-stricken home of a 17th-century gravedigger. Advance booking recommended.

The scripted tour, complete with ghostly tales and gruesome tableaux, can seem a little naff, milking the scary and scatological aspects of the close's history for all they're worth. But there are many things of genuine interest to see; there's something about the crumbling 17th-century **tenement room** that makes the hairs rise on the back of your neck, the tufts of horsehair poking from the collapsing lath-and-plaster walls, the ghost of a pattern on the walls, and the ancient smell of stone and dust thick in your nostrils.

In one of the former bedrooms off the close, a psychic once claimed to have been approached by the ghost of a little girl called Annie. It's hard to tell what's more frightening – the story of the ghostly child, or the bizarre heap of tiny dolls and teddies left in a corner by sympathetic visitors.

Museum of Edinburgh   MUSEUM

(Map p778; www.edinburghmuseums.org.uk; 142 Canongate; ⊙ 10am-5pm Mon-Sat year-round, noon-5pm Sun Aug; 📱 35) **FREE** You can't miss the colourful facade of Huntly House, brightly renovated in red and yellow ochre, opposite the Tolbooth clock on the Royal Mile. Built in 1570, it houses a museum covering Edinburgh from its prehistory to the present. Exhibits of national importance include an original copy of the National

Old Town

Covenant of 1638, but the big crowd-pleaser is the dog collar and feeding bowl that once belonged to Greyfriars Bobby, the city's most famous canine citizen.

Palace of Holyroodhouse　　　PALACE
(www.royalcollection.org.uk; Horse Wynd; adult/child £11.30/6.80; ◎9.30am-6pm Apr-Oct, to 4.30pm Nov-Mar; ☐35, 36) This palace is the royal family's official residence in Scotland, but is more famous as the 16th-century home of the ill-fated Mary, Queen of Scots. The highlight of the tour is **Mary's Bed Chamber**, home to the unfortunate queen from 1561 to 1567. It was here that her jealous first husband, Lord Darnley, restrained the pregnant queen while his henchmen murdered her secretary – and favourite – Rizzio. A plaque in the neighbouring room marks the spot where he bled to death.

The palace developed from a guesthouse, attached to Holyrood Abbey, which was extended by King James IV in 1501. The oldest surviving part of the building, the northwestern tower, was built in 1529 as a royal apartment for James V and his wife, Mary of Guise. Mary, Queen of Scots spent six turbulent years here, during which time she debated with John Knox, married both her first and second husbands, and witnessed the murder of her secretary David Rizzio.

The self-guided audio tour leads you through a series of impressive royal apartments, culminating in the **Great Gallery**. The 89 portraits of Scottish kings were commissioned by Charles II and supposedly record his unbroken lineage from Scota, the Egyptian pharaoh's daughter who discovered the infant Moses in a reed basket on the banks of the Nile. The tour continues to the oldest part of the palace, which contains Mary's Bed Chamber, connected by a secret stairway to her husband's bedroom, and ends with the ruins of Holyrood Abbey.

Holyrood Park　　　PARK
(☐35, 36) In Holyrood Park Edinburgh is blessed with a little bit of wilderness in the heart of the city. The former hunting ground of Scottish monarchs, the park covers 263 hectares of varied landscape, including crags, moorland and loch, and the 251m summit of **Arthur's Seat**. Holyrood Park can be circumnavigated by car or bike along Queen's Dr.

⭐**National Museum of Scotland** MUSEUM
(Map p778; www.nms.ac.uk; Chambers St; fee for special exhibitions; ⏱10am-5pm; 🚇2, 23, 27, 35, 41, 42, 45) FREE Broad, elegant Chambers St is dominated by the long facade of the National Museum of Scotland. Its extensive collections are spread between two buildings, one modern, one Victorian – the golden stone and striking modern architecture of the new building, opened in 1998, is one of the city's most distinctive landmarks. The five floors of the museum trace the history of Scotland from geological beginnings to the 1990s, with many imaginative and stimulating exhibits – audioguides are available in several languages.

The new building connects with the original Victorian museum, dating from 1861, the stolid, grey exterior of which gives way to a beautifully bright and airy, glass-roofed exhibition hall. The old building houses an eclectic collection covering natural history, archaeology, scientific and industrial technology, and the decorative arts of ancient Egypt, Islam, China, Japan, Korea and the West.

Greyfriars Kirk CHURCH
(Map p778; www.greyfriarskirk.com; Candlemaker Row; ⏱10.30am-4.30pm Mon-Fri & 11am-2pm Sat Apr-Oct, closed Nov-Mar; 🚇2, 23, 27, 41, 42, 45) FREE One of Edinburgh's most famous churches, Greyfriars Kirk was built on the site of a Franciscan friary and opened for worship on Christmas Day 1620. Surrounding the church, **Greyfriars Kirkyard** (Map p778) is one of Edinburgh's most evocative cemeteries, a peaceful green oasis dotted with elaborate monuments. Many famous Edinburgh names are buried here, including the poet Allan Ramsay (1686–1758), architect William Adam (1689–1748) and William Smellie (1740–95), the editor of the first edition of the *Encyclopedia Britannica*.

In 1638 the **National Covenant** was signed in the kirk, rejecting Charles I's attempts to impose episcopacy and a new English prayer book on the Scots, and affirming

SCOTTISH PARLIAMENT BUILDING

The **Scottish Parliament Building** (📞0131-348 5200; www.scottish.parliament.uk; Horse Wynd; ⏱9am-6.30pm Tue-Thu, 10am-5.30pm Mon, Fri & Sat in session, 10am-6pm Mon-Sat in recess; 🚇35, 36) FREE, built on the site of a former brewery close to the Palace of Holyroodhouse, was officially opened by HM the Queen in October 2005.

The public areas of the parliament building – the Main Hall, where there is an exhibition, a shop and a cafe, and the **public gallery** in the Debating Chamber – are open to visitors (tickets needed for public gallery; see website for details). You can also take a free, one-hour **guided tour** (advance booking recommended) that includes a visit to the Debating Chamber, a committee room, the Garden Lobby and, when possible, the office of an MSP (Member of the Scottish Parliament). If you want to see the parliament in session, check the website to see when it will be sitting – business days are normally Tuesday to Thursday year-round.

Enric Miralles (1955–2000), the architect who conceived the design of the Scottish Parliament Building, believed that a building could be a work of art. However, the weird concrete confection that has sprouted at the foot of Salisbury Crags has left the good people of Edinburgh staring and scratching their heads in confusion. What does it all mean? The strange forms of the exterior are all symbolic in some way, from the oddly shaped windows on the west wall (inspired by the silhouette of the *Reverend Robert Walker Skating on Duddingston Loch*, one of Scotland's most famous paintings), to the ground plan of the whole complex, which represents a 'flower of democracy rooted in Scottish soil' (best seen looking down from Salisbury Crags).

The **Main Hall**, inside the public entrance, has a low, triple-arched ceiling of polished concrete, like a cave, cellar or castle vault. It is a dimly lit space, the starting point for a metaphorical journey from this relative darkness up to the **Debating Chamber** (sitting directly above the Main Hall), which is, in contrast, a palace of light – the light of democracy. This magnificent chamber is the centrepiece of the parliament, designed not to glorify, but to humble the politicians who sit within it. The windows face Calton Hill, allowing MSPs to look up to its monuments (reminders of the Scottish Enlightenment), while the massive, pointed oak beams of the roof are suspended by steel threads above the MSPs' heads like so many Damoclean swords.

the independence of the Scottish Church. Many who signed were later executed at the Grassmarket and, in 1679, 1200 Covenanters were held prisoner in terrible conditions in the southwestern corner of the kirkyard. There's a small exhibition inside the church.

If you want to experience the graveyard at its scariest – inside a burial vault, in the dark, at night – go on one of the City of the Dead (p788) guided tours.

Greyfriars Bobby Statue   MONUMENT

(Map p778; cnr George IV Bridge & Candlemaker Row; ▣ 2, 23, 27, 35, 41, 42, 45) Probably the most popular photo opportunity in Edinburgh, the life-size statue of Greyfriars Bobby, a Skye terrier who captured the hearts of the British public in the late 19th century, stands outside Greyfriars Kirkyard. From 1858 to 1872, the wee dog maintained a vigil over the grave of his master, an Edinburgh police officer. The story was immortalised in a novel by Eleanor Atkinson in 1912, and in 1963 was made into a movie by – who else? – Walt Disney.

◉ New Town

Edinburgh's New Town lies north of the Old Town, on a ridge running parallel to the Royal Mile and separated from it by the valley of Princes Street Gardens. Its regular grid of elegant, neoclassical terraces is the world's most complete and unspoilt example of Georgian architecture and town planning. Along with the Old Town, it was declared a Unesco World Heritage Site in 1995.

Princes St is one of the world's most spectacular shopping streets. Built up on the north side only, it catches the sun in summer and allows expansive views across Princes Street Gardens to the castle and the crowded skyline of the Old Town.

Princes Street Gardens lie in a valley that was once occupied by the Nor' Loch, a boggy depression that was drained in the early 19th century. The gardens are split in the middle by The Mound, which was created by around two million cart-loads of earth excavated from the foundations of New Town being dumped here to provide a road link across the valley to the Old Town. It was completed in 1830.

Scott Monument   MONUMENT

(Map p786; www.edinburghmuseums.org.uk; East Princes Street Gardens; admission £4; ◷10am-7pm Apr-Sep, 10am-4pm Oct-Mar; ▣all Princes St buses) The eastern half of Princes Street

---

🏃 Walking Tour
Old Town Alleys

START CASTLE ESPLANADE
END COCKBURN ST
LENGTH ONE MILE; ONE TO TWO HOURS

This walk explores the alleys and side streets around the the Royal Mile, and involves a bit of climbing up and down steep stairs.

Begin on the ❶ **Castle Esplanade**, which provides a grandstand view south over the Grassmarket; the prominent quadrangular building with all the turrets is George Heriot's School, which you'll be passing later on. Head towards Castlehill and the start of the Royal Mile.

The 17th-century house on the right is known as ❷ **Cannonball House** because of the iron ball lodged in the wall (look between, and slightly below, the two largest windows on the wall facing the castle). It was not fired in anger, but marks the gravitation height to which water would flow naturally from the city's first piped water supply.

The low, rectangular building across the street (now a touristy tartan-weaving mill) was originally the reservoir that held the Old Town's water supply. On its west wall is the ❸ **Witches Well**, where a bronze fountain commemorates around 4000 people (mostly women) who were executed between 1479 and 1722 on suspicion of witchcraft.

Go past the reservoir and turn left down Ramsay Lane. Take a look at ❹ **Ramsay Garden** – one of Edinburgh's most desirable addresses – where late-19th-century apartments were built around the octagonal Ramsay Lodge, once home to poet Allan Ramsay. The cobbled street continues around to the right below student residences, to the towers of the ❺ **New College**, home to Edinburgh University's Faculty of Divinity. Nip into the courtyard to see the statue of John Knox (a firebrand preacher who led the Protestant Reformation in Scotland, and was instrumental in the creation of the Church of Scotland in 1560).

Just past New College turn right and climb the stairs into Milne's Court, a student residence belonging to Edinburgh University. Exit into Lawnmarket, cross the street (bearing slightly left) and duck into

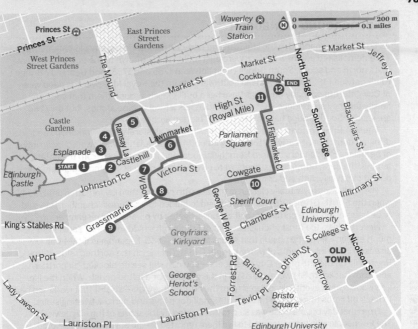

6 Riddell's Court, a typical Old Town close at No 322-8. You'll find yourself in a small courtyard, but the house in front of you (built in 1590) was originally the edge of the street (the building you just walked under was added in 1726 – look for the inscription in the doorway on the right). The arch with the inscription 'Vivendo discimus' (we live and learn) leads into the original 16th-century courtyard.

Go back into the street, turn right and right again down Fisher's Close, which leads to the delightful Victoria Terrace, strung above the cobbled curve of shop-lined Victoria St. Wander right, enjoying the view – **7 Maxie's Bistro**, at the far end of the terrace, is a great place for a drink – then descend the stairs at the foot of Upper Bow and continue downhill to the Grassmarket. At the east end, outside Maggie Dickson's pub, is the **8 Covenanters Monument**, which marks the site of the gallows where more than 100 Covenanters were martyred in the 17th century.

If you're feeling peckish, the Grassmarket has several good places to eat and a couple of good pubs – Robert Burns once stayed at the **9 White Hart Inn**. Head east along the gloomy defile of the Cowgate, passing under

the arch of George IV Bridge – the buildings to your right are the new law courts, while high up to the left you can see the complex of buildings behind Parliament Sq. Past the courts, on the right, is **10 Tailors Hall** (built 1621, extended 1757), now a hotel and bar but formerly the meeting place of the Companie of Tailzeours (Tailors' Guild).

Turn left and climb steeply up Old Fishmarket Close, a typical cobbled Old Town wynd, and emerge once more onto the Royal Mile. Across the street and slightly downhill is **11 Anchor Close**, named for a tavern that once stood there. It hosted the Crochallan Fencibles, an 18th-century drinking club that provided its patrons with an agreeable blend of intellectual debate and intoxicating liquor. The club was founded by William Smellie, editor of the first edition of the Encyclopedia Brittanica; its best-known member was the poet Robert Burns.

Go down Anchor Close, to finish the walk on **12 Cockburn St**, one of the city's coolest shopping streets, lined with record shops and clothing boutiques. The street was cut through Old Town tenements in the 1850s to provide an easy route between Waverley Station and the Royal Mile.

UNDERGROUND EDINBURGH

As Edinburgh expanded in the late 18th and early 19th centuries, many old tenements were demolished and new bridges were built to link the Old Town to the newly built areas to its north and south. South Bridge (built between 1785 and 1788) and George IV Bridge (built between 1829 and 1834) lead southwards from the Royal Mile over the deep valley of Cowgate, but so many buildings have been built closely around them that you can hardly tell they are bridges – George IV Bridge has a total of nine arches, but only two are visible; South Bridge has no less than 18 hidden arches.

These **subterranean vaults** were originally used as storerooms, workshops and drinking dens. But as early-19th-century Edinburgh's population was swelled by an influx of penniless Highlanders cleared from their lands, and Irish refugees from the potato famine, the dark, dripping chambers were given over to slum accommodation and abandoned to poverty, filth and crime.

The vaults were eventually cleared in the late 19th century, then lay forgotten until 1994 when the **South Bridge Vaults** were opened to guided tours. Certain chambers are said to be haunted and one particular vault was investigated by paranormal researchers in 2001.

Nevertheless, the most ghoulish aspect of Edinburgh's hidden history dates from much earlier – from the plague that struck the city in 1645. Legend has it that the disease-ridden inhabitants of **Mary King's Close** (a lane on the northern side of the Royal Mile on the site of the City Chambers – you can still see its blocked-off northern end from Cockburn St) were walled up in their houses and left to perish. When the lifeless bodies were eventually cleared from the houses, they were so stiff that workmen had to hack off limbs to get them through the small doorways and narrow, twisting stairs.

From that day on, the close was said to be haunted by the spirits of the plague victims. The few people who were prepared to live there reported seeing apparitions of severed heads and limbs, and the largely abandoned close fell into ruin. When the Royal Exchange (now the City Chambers) was constructed between 1753 and 1761, it was built over the lower levels of Mary King's Close, which were left intact and sealed off beneath the building.

Interest in the close revived in the 20th century when Edinburgh's city council began to allow occasional guided tours to enter. Visitors have reported many supernatural experiences – the most famous ghost is 'Sarah', a little girl whose sad tale has prompted people to leave gifts of dolls in a corner of one of the rooms. In 2003 the close was opened to the public as the Real Mary King's Close (p778).

Gardens is dominated by the massive Gothic spire of the Scott Monument, built by public subscription in memory of the novelist Sir Walter Scott after his death in 1832. The exterior is decorated with carvings of characters from his novels; inside you can see an exhibition on Scott's life, and climb the 287 steps to the top for a superb view of the city.

Scottish National Gallery　　GALLERY
(Map p786; www.nationalgalleries.org; The Mound; fee for special exhibitions; ⊙10am-5pm Fri-Wed, to 7pm Thu; 🚇all Princes St buses) **FREE** Designed by William Playfair, this imposing classical building with its Ionic porticoes dates from the 1850s. Its octagonal rooms, lit by skylights, have been restored to their original Victorian decor of deep-green carpets and dark-red walls. The gallery houses an important collection of European art from the Renaissance to post-Impressionism, with works by Verrocchio (Leonardo da Vinci's teacher), Tintoretto, Titian, Holbein, Rubens, Van Dyck, Vermeer, El Greco, Poussin, Rembrandt, Gainsborough, Turner, Constable, Monet, Pissarro, Gauguin and Cézanne.

The upstairs galleries house portraits by Sir Joshua Reynolds and Sir Henry Raeburn, and a clutch of **Impressionist paintings**, including Monet's luminous *Haystacks,* Van Gogh's demonic *Olive Trees* and Gauguin's hallucinatory *Vision After the Sermon.* But the painting that really catches your eye is the gorgeous portrait of Lady Agnew of Lochnaw by John Singer Sargent.

The basement galleries dedicated to **Scottish art** include glowing portraits by Allan Ramsay and Sir Henry Raeburn, rural scenes by Sir David Wilkie and Impressionistic landscapes by William MacTaggart. Look out for Raeburn's iconic *Reverend Robert Walker Skating on Duddingston*

Loch, and Sir George Harvey's hugely entertaining *A Schule Skailin* (A School Emptying) – a stern dominie (teacher) looks on as the boys stampede for the classroom door, one reaching for a confiscated spinning top. Kids will love the fantasy paintings of Sir Joseph Noel Paton in room B5; the incredibly detailed canvases are crammed with hundreds of tiny fairies, goblins and elves.

Each January the gallery exhibits its collection of Turner watercolours, bequeathed by Henry Vaughan in 1900. Room X is graced by Antonio Canova's white marble sculpture, The Three Graces; it is owned jointly with London's Victoria & Albert Museum.

Georgian House   HISTORIC BUILDING
(NTS; Map p786; www.nts.org.uk; 7 Charlotte Sq; adult/child £6.50/5; ⊘10am-6pm Jul & Aug, 10am-5pm Apr-Jun & Sep-Oct, 11am-4pm Mar, 11am-3pm Nov; ☐47) The National Trust for Scotland's Georgian House has been beautifully restored and furnished to show how Edinburgh's wealthy elite lived at the end of the 18th century. The walls are decorated with paintings by Allan Ramsay, Sir Henry Raeburn and Sir Joshua Reynolds.

Scottish National Portrait Gallery   GALLERY
(Map p786; www.nationalgalleries.org; 1 Queen St; ⊘10am-5pm Fri-Wed, to 7pm Thu) FREE The Venetian Gothic palace of the Scottish National Portrait Gallery reopened its doors in 2011 after a two-year renovation, emerging as one of the city's top attractions. Its galleries illustrate Scottish history through paintings, photographs and sculptures, putting faces to famous names from Scotland's past and present, from Robert Burns, Mary, Queen of Scots and Bonnie Prince Charlie to Sean Connery, Billy Connolly and poet Jackie Kay.

The gallery's interior is decorated in Arts and Crafts style, and nowhere more splendidly than in the Great Hall. Above the gothic colonnade a processional frieze painted by William Hole in 1898 serves as a 'visual encyclopedia' of famous Scots, shown in chronological order from Calgacus (the chieftain who led the Caledonian tribes into battle against the Romans) to writer and philosopher Thomas Carlyle (1795–1881). The murals on the first-floor balcony depict scenes from Scottish history, while the ceiling is painted with the constellations of the night sky.

The gallery's selection of 'trails' leaflets adds background information while leading you around the various exhibits; the Hidden Histories trail is particularly interesting.

◉ Calton Hill

Calton Hill (100m), rising dramatically above the eastern end of Princes St, is Edinburgh's acropolis, its summit scattered with grandiose memorials mostly dating from the first half of the 19th century. It is also one of the best viewpoints in Edinburgh, with a panorama that takes in the castle, Holyrood, Arthur's Seat, the Firth of Forth, New Town and the full length of Princes St.

Looking a bit like an upturned telescope – the similarity is intentional – and offering even better views, the Nelson Monument (Map p786; www.edinburghmuseums.org. uk; Calton Hill; admission £4; ⊘10am-7pm Mon-Sat & noon-5pm Sun Apr-Sep, 10am-3pm Mon-Sat Oct-Mar; ☐all Leith St buses) was built to commemorate Admiral Lord Nelson's victory at Trafalgar in 1805.

◉ Leith

Two miles northeast of the city centre, Leith has been Edinburgh's seaport since the 14th century and remained an independent burgh with its own town council until it was incorporated by the city in the 1920s. Like many of Britain's dockland areas, it fell into decay in the decades following WWII but has been undergoing a revival since the late 1980s.

★Royal Yacht Britannia   SHIP
(www.royalyachtbritannia.co.uk; Ocean Terminal; adult/child £12.75/7.75; ⊘9.30am-6pm Jul-Sep, to 5.30pm Apr-Jun & Oct, 10am-5pm Nov-Mar, last admission 90min before closing; ☐11, 22, 34, 35, 36) Built on Clydeside, the former Royal Yacht *Britannia* was the British royal family's floating holiday home during their foreign travels from the time of her launch in 1953 until her decommissioning in 1997, and is now moored permanently in front of Ocean Terminal. The tour, which you take at your own pace with an audioguide (included in admission fee and available in 20 languages), lifts the curtain on the everyday lives of the royals, and gives an intriguing insight into the Queen's private tastes.

Britannia is a monument to 1950s decor, and the accommodation reveals Her Majesty's preference for simple, unfussy surroundings. There was nothing simple or unfussy, however, about the running of the ship. When the Queen travelled, with her went 45 members of the royal household, five tons of luggage and a Rolls-Royce that was carefully

New Town

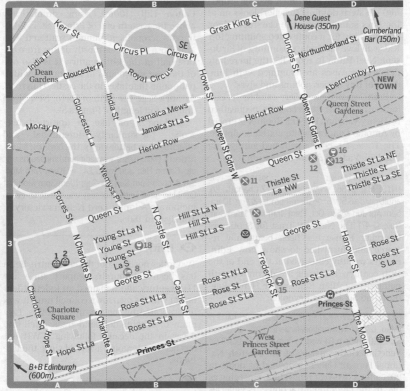

EDINBURGH SIGHTS

New Town

squeezed into a specially built garage on the deck. The ship's company consisted of an admiral, 20 officers and 220 yachtsmen.

The decks (of Burmese teak) were scrubbed daily, but all work near the royal accommodation was carried out in complete

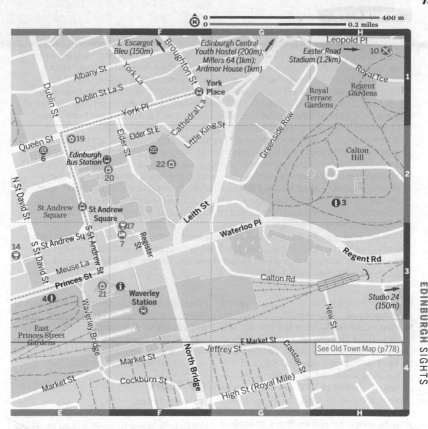

silence and had to be finished by 8am. A thermometer was kept in the Queen's bathroom to make sure the water was the correct temperature, and when in harbour one yachtsman was charged with ensuring that the angle of the gangway never exceeded 12 degrees. Note the mahogany windbreak that was added to the balcony deck in front of the bridge. It was put there to stop wayward breezes from blowing up skirts and inadvertently revealing the royal undies.

Britannia was joined in 2010 by the 1930s racing yacht Bloodhound, which was owned by the Queen in the 1960s. It is moored alongside *Britannia* (except in July and August, when it is away cruising) as part of an exhibition about the Royal family's love of all things nautical.

The Majestic Tour (p789) bus runs from Waverley Bridge to *Britannia* during opening times.

⊙ Greater Edinburgh

Edinburgh Zoo   ZOO
(www.edinburghzoo.org.uk; 134 Corstorphine Rd; adult/child £16.50/12; ☺ 9am-6pm Apr-Sep, to 5pm Oct & Mar, to 4.30pm Nov-Feb) Opened in 1913, Edinburgh Zoo is one of the world's leading conservation zoos. Edinburgh's captive breeding program has helped save many endangered species, including Siberian tigers, pygmy hippos and red pandas. The main attractions are the two giant pandas, Tian Tian and Yang Guang, who arrived in December 2011; the penguin parade (the zoo's penguins go for a walk every day at 2.15pm), and the sea lion training session (daily at 11.15am).

The zoo is 2.5 miles west of the city centre; take Lothian Bus 12, 26 or 31, First Bus 16, 18, 80 or 86, or the Airlink Bus 100 westbound from Princes St.

WORTH A TRIP

ROSSLYN CHAPEL

The success of Dan Brown's novel *The Da Vinci Code* and the subsequent Hollywood film has seen a flood of visitors descend on Scotland's most beautiful and enigmatic church: **Rosslyn Chapel** (Collegiate Church of St Matthew; www.rosslynchapel.org.uk; Chapel Loan, Roslin; adult/child £9/free; ⊘ 9.30am-5pm Mon-Sat, noon-4.45pm Sun). The chapel was built in the mid-15th century for William St Clair, third earl of Orkney, and the ornately carved interior – at odds with the architectural fashion of its time – is a monument to the mason's art and rich in symbolic imagery. As well as flowers, vines, angels and biblical figures, the carved stones include many examples of the pagan 'Green Man'; other figures are associated with Freemasonry and the Knights Templar. Intriguingly, there are also carvings of plants from the Americas that predate Columbus' voyage of discovery. The symbolism of these images has led some researchers to conclude that Rosslyn is some kind of secret Templar repository, and it has been claimed that hidden vaults beneath the chapel could conceal anything from the Holy Grail or the head of John the Baptist to the body of Christ himself. The chapel is owned by the Episcopal Church of Scotland and services are still held here on Sunday mornings.

The chapel is on the eastern edge of the village of Roslin, 7 miles south of Edinburgh's centre. Lothian Bus 15 (not 15A) runs from the west end of Princes St in Edinburgh to Roslin (£1.50, 30 minutes, every 30 minutes) via Penicuik (it may be faster to catch any bus to Penicuik, then the 15 to Roslin).

Royal Botanic Garden GARDENS
(www.rbge.org.uk; Arboretum Pl; ⊘ 10am-6pm Mar-Sep, to 5pm Feb & Oct, to 4pm Nov-Jan; 🚍 8, 23, 27) **FREE** Edinburgh's Royal Botanic Garden is the second oldest institution of its kind in Britain (after Oxford), and one of the most respected in the world. Founded near Holyrood in 1670 and moved to its present location in 1823, its 70 beautifully landscaped acres include splendid Victorian glass houses, colourful swaths of rhododendron and azalea, and a world famous rock garden. The garden's new visitor centre, the John Hope Gateway, is housed in a striking, environmentally friendly building overlooking the main entrance on Arboretum Place.

The centre has exhibitions on biodiversity, climate change and sustainable development, as well as displays of rare plants from the institution's collection and a specially created biodiversity garden. Take Lothian Bus 8, 23 or 27 to the East Gate, or the Majestic Tour (p789) bus to the main entrance.

🏃 Activities

Edinburgh is lucky to have several good walking areas within the city boundary, including Arthur's Seat, Calton Hill, Blackford Hill, Hermitage of Braid, Corstorphine Hill, and the coast and river at Cramond.

You can follow the **Water of Leith Walkway** from the city centre to Balerno (8

miles), and continue across the Pentlands to Silverburn (6.5 miles) or Carlops (8 miles), and return to Edinburgh by bus. Another good walk is along the towpath of the **Union Canal**, which begins in Fountainbridge and runs all the way to Falkirk (31 miles).

👣 Tours

Walking Tours

There are plenty of organised walks around Edinburgh, many of them related to ghosts, murders and witches. For starting times of individual walks, check the tour websites.

City of the Dead Tours WALKING TOUR
(www.cityofthedeadtours.com; adult/concession £10/8) This tour of Greyfriars Kirkyard is probably the scariest of Edinburgh's 'ghost' tours. Many people have reported encounters with the 'McKenzie Poltergeist', the ghost of a 17th-century judge who persecuted the Covenanters, and now haunts their former prison in a corner of the kirkyard. Not suitable for young children.

Cadies & Witchery Tours WALKING TOUR
(Map p778; www.witcherytours.com; adult/child £8.50/6) The becloaked and pasty-faced Adam Lyal (deceased) leads a 'Murder & Mystery' tour of the Old Town's darker corners. These tours are famous for their 'jumper-ooters' – costumed actors who 'jump oot' when you least expect it.

Edinburgh Literary Pub Tour WALKING TOUR
(www.edinburghliterarypubtour.co.uk; adult/student
£14/10) An enlightening two-hour trawl
through Edinburgh's literary history – and its
associated *howffs* (pubs) – in the entertaining
company of Messrs Clart and McBrain. One
of the city's best walking tours.

Mercat Tours WALKING TOUR
(Map p778; www.mercattours.com; adult/child
£10/5) Mercat offers a wide range of fascinating history walks and 'Ghosts & Ghouls'
tours, but its most famous is a visit to the
hidden, haunted, underground vaults beneath South Bridge.

Rebus Tours WALKING TOUR
(www.rebustours.com; adult/student £10/9) A
two-hour guided tour of the 'hidden Edinburgh' frequented by novelist Ian Rankin's
fictional detective, John Rebus. Not recommended for children under 10.

Bus Tours

Open-topped buses leave from Waverley
Bridge outside the main train station and offer hop-on/hop-off tours of the main sights,
taking in New Town, the Grassmarket and
the Royal Mile. They're a good way to get
your bearings, although with a bus map and
a Day Saver bus ticket (£3) you could do
much the same thing but without the commentary. Tours run daily, year-round, except
for 24 and 25 December.

Tickets for the following two tours remain valid for 24 hours.

City Sightseeing BUS TOUR
(www.edinburghtour.com; adult/child £13/6; ☺ daily year-round except 25 Dec) Bright-red, open-
top buses depart every 20 minutes from
Waverley Bridge.

Majestic Tour BUS TOUR
(www.edinburghtour.com; adult/child £13/6; ☺ daily
year-round except 25 Dec) Hop-on/hop-off tour
departing every 15 to 20 minutes from Waverley Bridge to the Royal Yacht Britannia
at Ocean Terminal via the New Town, Royal
Botanic Garden and Newhaven, returning
via Leith Walk, Holyrood and the Royal Mile.

✹ Festivals & Events
April
**Edinburgh International
Science Festival** SCIENCE
(www.sciencefestival.co.uk) First held in 1987,
it hosts a wide range of events, including
talks, lectures, exhibitions, demonstrations,

guided tours and interactive experiments
designed to stimulate, inspire and challenge.
From dinosaurs to ghosts to alien life forms,
there's something to interest everyone. The
festival runs over two weeks in April.

May
Imaginate Festival ARTS
(www.imaginate.org.uk) This is Britain's biggest
festival of performing arts for children, with
events suitable for kids aged from three to 12.
Groups from around the world perform classic tales like *Hansel and Gretel,* as well as new
material written specially for children. The
one-week festival takes place annually in May.

June
Scottish Real Ale Festival FOOD, DRINK
(www.scottishbeerfestival.org.uk) A celebration
of all things fermented and yeasty, Scotland's
biggest beer-fest gives you the opportunity to sample a wide range of traditionally
brewed beers from Scotland and around
the world. Froth-topped bliss. The festival is
held over a weekend in June or July.

Royal Highland Show AGRICULTURAL
(www.royalhighlandshow.org; Royal Highland Centre, Ingliston) Scotland's hugely popular national agricultural show is a four-day feast of
all things rural, with everything from show-
jumping and tractor driving to sheep shearing and falconry. Countless pens are filled
with coiffed show cattle and pedicured prize
ewes. The show is held over a long weekend
(Thursday to Sunday) in late June.

**Edinburgh International
Film Festival** FILM
(www.edfilmfest.org.uk) One of the original Edinburgh Festival trinity, having first been staged
in 1947 along with the International Festival
and the Fringe, the two-week June film festival is a major international event, serving
as a showcase for new British and European
films, and staging the European premieres of
one or two Hollywood blockbusters.

July
**Edinburgh International
Jazz & Blues Festival** MUSIC
(www.edinburghjazzfestival.com) Held annually
since 1978, the Jazz & Blues Festival pulls in
top talent from all over the world. It runs
for nine days, beginning on a Friday, a week
before the Fringe and Tattoo begin. The first
weekend sees a carnival parade on Princes
St and an afternoon of free, open-air music
in Princes Street Gardens.

Rosslyn Chapel

DECIPHERING ROSSLYN

Rosslyn Chapel is a small building, but the density of decoration inside can be overwhelming. It's well worth buying the official guidebook by the Earl of Rosslyn first; find a bench in the gardens and have a skim through before going into the chapel – the background information will make your visit all the more interesting. The book also offers a useful self-guided tour of the chapel, and explains the legend of the Master Mason and the Apprentice.

Entrance is through the **north door** ❶. Take a pew and sit for a while to allow your eyes to adjust to the dim interior; then look up at the ceiling vault, decorated with engraved roses, lilies and stars, (Can you spot the sun and the moon?). Walk left along the north aisle to reach the Lady Chapel, separated from the rest of the church by the **Mason's Pillar** ❷ and the **Apprentice Pillar** ❸.
Here you'll find carvings of **Lucifer** ❹, the Fallen Angel, and the **Green Man** ❺. Nearby are **carvings** ❻ that appear to resemble Indian corn (maize). Finally, go to the western end and look up at the wall – in the left corner is the head of the **Apprentice** ❼; to the right is the (rather worn) head of the **Master Mason** ❽.

ROSSLYN CHAPEL & THE DA VINCI CODE

Dan Brown was referencing Rosslyn Chapel's alleged links to the Knights Templar and the Freemasons – unusual symbols found among the carvings, and the fact that a descendant of its founder, William St Clair, was a Grand Master Mason – when he chose it as the setting for his novel's denouement. Rosslyn is indeed a coded work, written in stone, but its meaning depends on your point of view. See The Rosslyn Hoax? by Robert LD Cooper for an alternative interpretation of the chapel's symbolism.

SANDRO VANNINI/CORBIS ©

EXPLORE SOME MORE

After visiting the chapel, head downhill to see the spectacularly sited ruins of Roslin Castle, then take a walk along leafy Roslin Glen.

Lucifer, the Fallen Angel
At head height, to the left of the second window from the left, is an upside-down angel bound with rope, a symbol often associated with Freemasonry. The arch above is decorated with the Dance of Death.

The Apprentice
High in the corner, beneath an empty statue niche, is the head of the murdered Apprentice, with a deep wound in his forehead above the right eye. Legend says the Apprentice was murdered in a jealous rage by the Master Mason. The worn head on the side wall to the left of the Apprentice is that of his mother.

North Door

The Master Mason ❽

Baptistery

PRACTICAL TIPS

Buy your tickets in advance through the chapel's website (except in August, when no bookings are taken). No photography is allowed inside the chapel.

Green Man

On a boss at the base of the arch between the second and third windows from the left is the finest example of more than a hundred 'green man' carvings in the chapel, pagan symbols of spring, fertility and rebirth.

SANDRO VANNINI/CORBIS ©

Green Man
② **④**
Mason's Pillar **⑤**
Lady Chapel
③
Sacristy
① **North Aisle**
Altar
Choir
⑥
South Aisle
⑦

The Apprentice Pillar

This is perhaps the chapel's most beautiful carving. Four vines spiral up the pillar, issuing from the mouths of eight dragons at its base. At the top is Isaac, son of Abraham, lying bound upon the altar.

CHRISTOPHER FURLONG/GETTY IMAGES ©

Indian Corn

The frieze around the second window on the south wall is said to represent Indian corn (maize), but it predates Columbus' discovery of the New World in 1492. Other carvings seem to resemble aloe vera.

JOHN HESELTINE/ALAMY ©

AUGUST FESTIVALS

August in Edinburgh sees a frenzy of festivals, with four world-class events running at the same time.

Edinburgh Festival Fringe (☎ 0131-226 0026; www.edfringe.com) When the first Edinburgh Festival was held in 1947, there were eight theatre companies who didn't make it onto the main program. Undeterred, they grouped together and held their own mini-festival, on the fringe, and an Edinburgh institution was born. Today the Edinburgh Festival Fringe is the biggest festival of the performing arts anywhere in the world. The Fringe takes place over 3½ weeks in August, the last two weeks overlapping with the first two of the Edinburgh International Festival.

Edinburgh International Festival (☎ 0131-473 2099; www.eif.co.uk) First held in 1947 to mark a return to peace after the ordeal of WWII, the Edinburgh International Festival is festooned with superlatives – the oldest, the biggest, the most famous, the best in the world. The original was a modest affair, but today hundreds of the world's top musicians and performers congregate in Edinburgh for three weeks of diverse and inspirational music, opera, theatre and dance. The festival takes place over three weeks ending on the first Saturday in September; the program is usually available from April. Tickets for popular events – especially music and opera – sell out quickly, so it's best to book as far in advance as possible. You can buy tickets in person at the **Hub** (Map p778; ☎ 01131-473 2015; www.thehub-edinburgh.com; Castlehill; admission free; ☺ ticket centre 10am-5pm Mon-Sat), or by phone or over the internet.

Edinburgh Military Tattoo (☎ 0131-225 1188; www.edintattoo.co.uk) The month kicks off with the Edinburgh Military Tattoo, a spectacular display of military marching bands, massed pipes and drums, acrobats, cheerleaders and motorcycle display teams, all played out in front of the magnificent backdrop of the floodlit castle. The Tattoo takes place over the first three weeks of August (from a Friday to a Saturday); there's one show at 9pm Monday to Friday and two (at 7.30pm and 10.30pm) on Saturday, but no performance on Sunday.

Edinburgh International Book Festival (☎ 0845 373 5888; www.edbookfest.co.uk) Held in a little village of marquees in the middle of Charlotte Sq, the Edinburgh International Book Festival is a fun fortnight of talks, readings, debates, lectures, book signings and meet-the-author events, with a cafe and tented bookshop thrown in. The festival lasts for two weeks in August (usually the first two weeks of the Edinburgh International Festival).

August

Half a dozen world-class events run simultaneously. See the boxed text for details.

December

Edinburgh's Christmas CHRISTMAS
(www.edinburghschristmas.com) The youngest of the Scottish capital's festivals, first held in 2000, the Christmas bash runs from late November to early January and includes a big street parade, a Christmas market, a fairground and Ferris wheel, and an open-air ice rink in Princes Street Gardens.

Edinburgh's Hogmanay CULTURAL
(www.edinburghshogmanay.com) Edinburgh's Hogmanay is the biggest winter festival in Europe. Events run from 27 December to 1 January, and include a torchlight procession, a huge street party and the famous 'Loony Dook', a chilly sea-swimming event on New Year's Day. To get into the main party area in the city centre after 8pm on 31 December you'll need a ticket – book well in advance.

🛏 Sleeping

Edinburgh is not short of accommodation, but you can guarantee the city will be packed to the gills during the festival period (August) and over Hogmanay (New Year). If you want a room during these periods, book as far in advance as possible. In general, it's best to book ahead for accommodation at Easter and from mid-May to mid-September.

🛏 Old Town

★ **Malone's Old Town Hostel** HOSTEL £
(Map p778; ☎ 0131-226 7648; www.maloneshostel.com; 14 Forrest Rd; dm £16-25; @🛜) No fancy

decor or style credentials here, but they've got the basics right: it's clean, comfortable and friendly, and set upstairs from an Irish pub where guests get discounts on food and drink. The cherry on the cake is its superbly central location, an easy walk from the Royal Mile, the castle, the Grassmarket and Princes St.

Smart City Hostel   HOSTEL £
(Map p778; ☑ 0131-524 1989; www.smartcityhostels.com; 50 Blackfriars St; dm £24-28, tr £99; @ �) A big, modern hostel, with a convivial cafe where you can buy breakfast, and mod cons such as keycard access and charging stations for mobile phones, MP3 players and laptops. Lockers in every room, a huge bar and a central location just off the Royal Mile make this a favourite among the young, party-mad crowd – don't expect a quiet night!

Castle Rock Hostel   HOSTEL £
(Map p778; ☑ 0131-225 9666; www.scotlands-top-hostels.com; 15 Johnston Tce; dm £14-24, tr £54-60; @ ☎) With its bright, spacious, single-sex dorms, superb views and friendly staff, the 200-bed Castle Rock has lots to like. It has a great location – the only way to get closer to the castle would be to pitch a tent on the esplanade – a games room, reading lounge and big-screen video nights.

Hotel Missoni   BOUTIQUE HOTEL £££
(Map p778; ☑ 0131-220 6666; www.hotelmissoni.com; 1 George IV Bridge; r £125-290; ☎) The Italian fashion house has established a style icon in the heart of the medieval Old Town with this bold statement of a hotel – modernistic architecture, black-and-white decor with well-judged splashes of colour, impeccably mannered staff and, most importantly, very comfortable bedrooms and bathrooms with lots of nice little touches, from fresh milk in the minibar to plush bathrobes.

★Witchery by the Castle   B&B £££
(Map p778; ☑ 0131-225 5613; www.thewitchery.com; Castlehill, Royal Mile; ste £325-360) Set in a 16th-century Old Town house in the shadow of Edinburgh Castle, the Witchery's nine lavish Gothic suites are extravagantly furnished with antiques, oak panelling, tapestries, open fires, four-poster beds and roll-top baths, and supplied with flowers, chocolates and complimentary champagne. Overwhelmingly popular – you'll have to book several months in advance to be sure of getting a room.

🛏 New Town & Around

Haggis Hostel   HOSTEL £
(Map p786; ☑ 0131-557 0036; www.haggishostels.co.uk; 3 West Register St; dm £18-30; @ ☎) The Haggis is a small, clean and relatively quiet hostel, with pinewood bunks and comfy mattresses in four-, eight- and 10-bed dorms. There's a small kitchen and recreation area, and a laundry. The location is great, off the east end of Princes St and just two minutes' walk from train and bus stations.

B+B Edinburgh   HOTEL ££
(☑ 0131-225 5084; www.bb-edinburgh.com; 3 Rothesay Tce; d/ste from £110/170; ☎) Built in 1883 as a grand home for the proprietor of the *Scotsman* newspaper, this Victorian extravaganza of carved oak, parquet floors, stained glass and elaborate fireplaces was given a designer makeover in 2011 to create a striking contemporary hotel. Rooms on the 2nd floor are the most spacious, but the smaller top-floor rooms enjoy the finest views.

Dene Guest House   B&B ££
(☑ 0131-556 2700; www.deneguesthouse.com; 7 Eyre Pl; per person £25-50; ☎) The Dene is a friendly and informal place, set in a charming Georgian town house, with a welcoming owner and spacious bedrooms. The inexpensive single rooms make it ideal for solo travellers; children under 10 staying in their parents' room pay half price.

Tigerlily   BOUTIQUE HOTEL £££
(Map p786; ☑ 0131-225 5005; www.tigerlilyedinburgh.co.uk; 125 George St; r from £210; ☎) Georgian meets gorgeous at this glamorous, glittering boutique hotel (complete with its own nightclub) decked out in mirror mosaics, beaded curtains, swirling Timorous Beasties textiles and wall coverings, and atmospheric pink uplighting. Book the Georgian Suite (from £410) for a truly special romantic getaway.

🛏 South Edinburgh

Argyle Backpackers   HOSTEL £
(☑ 0131-667 9991; www.argyle-backpackers.co.uk; 14 Argyle Pl; dm £18-22, s/tw £56/58; @ ☎) The Argyle, spread across three adjacent terraced houses, is a quiet and relaxed hostel offering single, double and twin rooms as well as four- to 10-bed dorms (mixed sex). There is a comfortable TV lounge, an attractive little conservatory and a pleasant walled garden at the back where you can sit outside in summer.

★ **Southside Guest House**　　B&B **££**
(☎ 0131-668 4422; www.southsideguesthouse.
co.uk; 8 Newington Rd; s/d £75/95; ☎) Though
set in a typical Victorian terrace, the Southside transcends the traditional guesthouse
category and feels more like a modern
boutique hotel. Its eight stylish rooms ooze
interior design, standing out from other
Newington B&Bs through the clever use of
bold colours and modern furniture. Breakfast is an event, with Buck's Fizz (champagne mixed with orange juice) on offer to
smooth the rough edges off your hangover!

No 45　　B&B **££**
(☎ 0131-667 3536; www.edinburghbedbreakfast.
com; 45 Gilmour Rd; s/d £70/140; ☎) A peaceful
setting, a large garden and friendly owners
contribute to the appeal of this Victorian
terraced house, which overlooks the local bowling green. The decor is a blend of
19th- and 20th-century, with bold Victorian
reds, pine floors and period fireplace in the
lounge, a rocking horse and art-nouveau
lamp in the hallway, and a 1930s vibe in the
three spacious bedrooms.

Aonach Mor Guest House　　B&B **££**
(☎ 0131-667 8694; www.aonachmor.com; 14 Kil-
maurs Tce; r £50-125; @ ☎) This elegant Victorian terraced house is located on a quiet
back street and has seven bedrooms, beautifully decorated, with many original period
features. Our favourite is the four-poster
bedroom with polished mahogany furniture
and period fireplace. Located 1 mile southeast of the city centre.

Sherwood Guest House　　B&B **££**
(☎ 0131-667 1200; www.sherwood-edinburgh.com;
42 Minto St; d £55-100; P ☎) One of the most
attractive guesthouses on Minto St's B&B
strip, the Sherwood is a refurbished Georgian
terraced house decked out with hanging baskets and shrubs. Inside are six en suite rooms
that combine Regency-style striped wallpaper with modern fabrics and pine furniture.

⌕ Northeast Edinburgh

Edinburgh Central Youth Hostel　　HOSTEL **£**
(SYHA; ☎ 0131-524 2090; www.edinburghcen-
tral.org; 9 Haddington Pl, Leith Walk; dm/s/tw
£25/49/74; @ ☎) This modern, purpose-built
hostel, about a half-mile north of Waverley
train station, is a big (300 beds), flashy, five-
star establishment with its own cafe-bistro
as well as self-catering kitchen, smart and
comfortable eight-bed dorms and private

rooms, and mod cons including keycard entry and plasma- screen TVs.

Sandaig Guest House　　B&B **££**
(☎ 0131-554 7357; www.sandaigguesthouse.co.uk; 5
East Hermitage Pl, Leith Links; s/d from £70/90; ☎)
From the welcoming tot of whisky liqueur to
the cheerful goodbye wave, the owners of the
Sandaig know a thing or two about hospitality. Staying here is a pleasure, from the boldly
coloured decor to the crisp cotton sheets, big
fluffy towels and refreshing power showers,
and a breakfast menu that includes porridge
with cream and maple syrup.

Ardmor House　　B&B **££**
(☎ 0131-554 4944; www.ardmorhouse.com; 74 Pilrig St; s £60-85, d £85-170; ☎) The 'gay-owned,
straight-friendly' Ardmor is a stylishly renovated Victorian house with five en suite bedrooms, and all the touches that make a place
special – an open fire, thick towels, crisp white
bed linen and free newspapers at breakfast.

Millers 64　　B&B **££**
(☎ 0131-454 3666; www.millers64.com; 64 Pilrig St;
s from £80, d £90-150; ☎) Luxury textiles, colourful cushions, stylish bathrooms and fresh
flowers added to a warm Edinburgh welcome
make this Victorian town house a highly desirable address. There are just two bedrooms
(and a minimum three-night stay during festival periods), so book well in advance.

✗ Eating

In the last decade there has been a boom in
the number of restaurants in Edinburgh –
the city now has more restaurants per head
of population than any other UK city.

For good-value eats, head for the
student-populated areas south of the city
centre: Bruntsfield, Marchmont and Newington. Fine dining is concentrated in the
New Town, Stockbridge and Leith.

✗ Old Town

★ **Mums**　　CAFE **£**
(Map p778; www.monstermashcafe.co.uk; 4a Forrest
Rd; mains £6-9; ⊙ 9am-10pm Mon-Sat, 10am-10pm
Sun; ☐ 23, 27, 41, 42) ✎ This nostalgia-fuelled
cafe serves up classic British comfort food
that wouldn't look out of place on a 1950s
menu – bacon and eggs, bangers and mash,
shepherd's pie, fish and chips. But there's a
twist – the food is all top-quality nosh freshly prepared from local produce, including
Crombie's gourmet sausages. There's even a

wine list, though we prefer the real ales and Scottish-brewed cider.

★ Timberyard SCOTTISH ££

(Map p778; ☑0131-221 1222; www.timberyard.co; 10 Lady Lawson St; mains £16-21; ☺noon-9.30pm Tue-Sat; ☎; ☐2, 35) ✐ Ancient floorboards, cast-iron pillars, exposed joists and tables made from slabs of old mahogany create a rustic atmosphere in this slow-food restaurant where the accent is on locally sourced produce from artisan growers and foragers. Typical dishes include seared scallop with apple, jerusalem artichoke and sorrel; and juniper-smoked pigeon with wild garlic flowers and beetroot.

David Bann VEGETARIAN ££

(Map p778; ☑0131-556 5888; www.davidbann. com; 56-58 St Mary's St; mains £9-13; ☺noon-10pm Mon-Fri, 11am-10pm Sat & Sun; ☑; ☐35) ✐ If you want to convince a carnivorous friend that cuisine à la veg can be as tasty and inventive as a meat-muncher's menu, take them to David Bann's stylish restaurant – dishes such as parsnip and blue cheese pudding, and spiced aduki bean and cashew pie, are guaranteed to win converts.

Amber SCOTTISH ££

(Map p778; ☑0131-477 8477; www.amber-restaurant.co.uk; 354 Castlehill; mains £12-20; ☺10am-7.30pm Sun-Thu, to 9pm Fri & Sat; ☐23, 27, 41, 42) You've got to love a place where the waiter greets you with the words, 'My name is Craig, and I'll be your whisky adviser for this evening'. Located in the Scotch Whisky Experience (p777), this whisky-themed restaurant manages to avoid the tourist clichés and creates genuinely interesting and flavoursome dishes blending top Scottish produce with whisky-inspired sauces.

★ Ondine SEAFOOD £££

(Map p778; ☑0131-226 1888; www.ondinerestaurant.co.uk; 2 George IV Bridge; mains £14-39, 2-/3-course lunch £22/25; ☺noon-3pm & 5.30-10pm Mon-Sat; ☐23, 27, 41, 42) Ondine is one of Edinburgh's finest seafood restaurants, with a menu based on sustainably sourced fish. Take a seat at the Oyster Bar and tuck into oysters Kilpatrick, lobster thermidor, a roast shellfish platter or just good old haddock and chips (with minted pea purée, just to keep things posh).

Tower SCOTTISH £££

(Map p778; ☑0131-225 3003; www.tower-restaurant.com; National Museum of Scotland, Chambers St; mains £18-39, 2-course lunch & pretheatre menu £19, afternoon tea £19; ☺10am-11pm; ☐23, 27, 41, 42) Chic and sleek, with a great view of the castle, Tower is perched in a turret atop the National Museum of Scotland building. A star-studded guest list of celebrities has enjoyed its menu of quality Scottish food, simply prepared – try half a dozen oysters followed by roast loin of venison. Afternoon tea (£18) is served from 2.30pm to 5.30pm.

✖ New Town

★ Gardener's Cottage SCOTTISH ££

(Map p786; ☑0131-558 1221; www.thegardenerscottage.co; 1 Royal Terrace Gardens, London Rd;

BEST VALUE BISTROS

Many restaurants in Edinburgh offer good-value lunches. Here are a few suggestions from various parts of the city:

L 'Escargot Bleu (☑0131-556 1600; www.lescargotbleu.co.uk; 56 Broughton St; mains £13-18; ☺noon-2.30pm & 5.30-10pm Mon-Thu, noon-3pm & 5.30-10.30pm Fri & Sat; ☐8) This cute little bistro is as Gallic as garlic, but makes fine use of quality Scottish produce – the French-speaking staff will lead you knowledgeably through a menu that includes authentic Savoyard *tartiflette*, quenelle of pike with lobster sauce, and pigs' cheeks braised in red wine with roasted winter vegetables.

Urban Angel (Map p786; ☑0131-225 6215; www.urban-angel.co.uk; 121 Hanover St; mains £5-13; ☺8am-5pm Mon-Fri, 9am-5pm Sat & Sun; ☑☒; ☐23, 27) ✐ A wholesome deli that puts the emphasis on fair-trade, organic and locally sourced produce, Urban Angel also has a delightfully informal cafe-bistro that serves all-day brunch (porridge with honey, French toast, eggs Benedict), tapas, and a wide range of light, snacky meals.

La P'tite Folie (Map p786; ☑0131-225 7983; www.laptitefolie.co.uk; 61 Frederick St; mains £16-25; ☺lunch & dinner) This is a delightful little restaurant with a Breton owner whose menu includes French classics – onion soup, *moules marinières* – alongside steaks, seafood and a range of plats du jour. The two-course lunch is a bargain at £9.95.

lunch mains £16-17, dinner set menu £30; ☺noon-2.30pm & 5-10pm Thu-Mon, 10am-2pm Sat & Sun; 🚍all London Rd buses) 🏃 This country cottage in the heart of the city, bedecked with flowers and fairy lights, offers one of Edinburgh's most interesting dining experiences – two tiny rooms with communal tables made of salvaged timber, and a set menu based on fresh local produce (most of the vegetables and fruit are grown in an organic garden in the city suburbs). Booking is essential.

The Dogs
BRITISH ££
(Map p786; ✍0131-220 1208; www.thedogsonline. co.uk; 110 Hanover St; mains £10-15; ☺noon-4pm & 5-10pm; 🚍23, 27) 🏃 One of the coolest tables in town, this bistro-style place uses cheaper cuts of meat and less-well-known, more-sustainable species of fish to create hearty, no-nonsense dishes such as lamb sweetbreads on toast, baked coley with *skirlie* (fried oatmeal and onion), and devilled liver with bacon and onions.

Café Marlayne
FRENCH ££
(Map p786; ✍0131-226 2230; www.cafemarlayne. com; 76 Thistle St; mains £12-15; ☺noon-10pm; 🚍24, 29, 42) All weathered wood and candlelit tables, Café Marlayne is a cosy nook offering French farmhouse cooking – *brandade de morue* (salt cod) with green salad, slow-roast rack of lamb, *boudin noir* (black pudding) with scallops and sautéed potato – at very reasonable prices. Booking is recommended.

✖ Leith

Chop Chop
CHINESE £
(✍0131-553 1818; www.chop-chop.co.uk; 76 Commercial St; mains £7-11; ☺noon-2pm & 6-10pm Mon & Wed-Fri, noon-2pm & 5-10pm Sat, 12.30-2pm & 5-10pm Sun) A Chinese restaurant with a difference, in that it serves dishes popular in China rather than Britain – as its slogan says, 'Can a billion people be wrong?' No sweet-and-sour pork here, but a range of delicious dumplings filled with pork and coriander, beef and chilli, or lamb and leek, and unusual vegetarian dishes such as aubergine fried with garlic and Chinese spices.

★Fishers Bistro
SEAFOOD ££
(✍0131-554 5666; www.fishersbistros.co.uk; 1 The Shore; mains £11-23; ☺noon-10.30pm Mon-Sat, 12.30-10.30pm Sun; 🚍🏃🚻; 🚍16, 22, 35, 36) This cosy little restaurant, tucked beneath a 17th-century signal tower, is one of the city's best seafood places. The menu ranges widely in price, from cheaper dishes such as classic fishcakes with lemon and chive mayonnaise, to more expensive delights such as North Berwick lobster thermidor.

★The Kitchin
SCOTTISH £££
(✍0131-555 1755; www.thekitchin.com; 78 Commercial Quay; mains £33-38, 3-course lunch £28.50; ☺12.15-2.30pm & 6.30-10pm Tue-Thu, to 10.30pm Fri & Sat; 🏃; 🚍16, 22, 35, 36) Fresh, seasonal, locally sourced Scottish produce is the philosophy that has won a Michelin star for this elegant but unpretentious restaurant. The menu moves with the seasons, of course, so expect fresh salads in summer and game in winter, and shellfish dishes such as seared scallops with endive *tarte tatin* when there's an 'r' in the month.

🍸 Drinking & Nightlife

Edinburgh has more than 700 bars, which are as varied as the population – everything from Victorian palaces to rough-and-ready drinking dens, and from bearded, real-ale *howffs* to trendy cocktail bars.

🍺 Old Town

★Bow Bar
PUB
(Map p778; 80 West Bow; 🚍23, 27, 41, 42) One of the city's best traditional-style pubs (it's not as old as it looks), serving a range of excellent real ales and a vast selection of malt whiskies, the Bow Bar often has standing-room only on Friday and Saturday evenings.

Jolly Judge
PUB
(Map p778; www.jollyjudge.co.uk; 7a James Ct; ☎; 🚍2, 23, 27, 41, 42, 45) A snug little howff tucked away down a close, the Judge exudes a cosy 17th-century atmosphere (low, timber-beamed painted ceilings) and has the added attraction of a cheering open fire in cold weather. No music or gaming machines, just the buzz of conversation.

BrewDog
BAR
(Map p778; www.brewdog.com; 143 Cowgate; ☎; 🚍36) The Edinburgh outpost of Scotland's self-styled 'punk brewery', BrewDog stands out among the grimy, sticky-floored dives that line the Cowgate, with its cool, industrial-chic designer look. As well as its own highly rated beers, there's a choice of four guest real ales.

Pear Tree House
PUB
(Map p778; www.pear-tree-house.co.uk; 38 West Nicolson St; ☎; 🚍2, 41, 42, 47) Set in an 18th-century house with cobbled courtyard, the Pear Tree is a student favourite with an

open fire in winter, comfy sofas and board games inside, plus the city's biggest and most popular beer garden in summer.

Bongo Club
CLUB

(Map p778; www.thebongoclub.co.uk; 66 Cowgate; ⬤; 🚌2) Owned by a local arts charity, the weird and wonderful Bongo Club boasts a long history of hosting everything from wild club nights to local bands to performance art to kids' comedy shows, and is open as a cafe and exhibition space during the day.

★Cabaret Voltaire
CLUB

(Map p778; www.thecabaretvoltaire.com; 36-38 Blair St; 🚌all South Bridge buses) An atmospheric warren of stone-lined vaults houses this self-consciously 'alternative' club, which eschews huge dance floors and egotistical DJ worship in favour of a 'creative crucible' hosting an eclectic mix of DJs, live acts, comedy, theatre, visual arts and the spoken word. Well worth a look.

Liquid Room
ROCK, CLUB

(Map p778; www.liquidroom.com; 9c Victoria St; admission free-£10) Set in a subterranean vault deep beneath Victoria St, the Liquid Room is a superb club venue with a thundering sound system. There are regular club nights Wednesday to Saturday as well as live bands.

Studio 24
CLUB

(www.facebook.com/studio24edinburgh; 24 Calton Rd; 🚌35, 36) Studio 24 is the dark heart of Edinburgh's underground music scene, with a program that covers all bases, from house to nu metal via punk, ska, reggae, crossover, tribal, electro, techno and dance.

❓ New Town

Oxford Bar
PUB

(Map p786; www.oxfordbar.co.uk; 8 Young St; 🚌19, 36,37,41,47) The Oxford is that rarest of things: a real pub for real people, with no 'theme', no music, no frills and no pretensions. 'The Ox' has been immortalised by Ian Rankin, author

---

TOP FIVE TRADITIONAL PUBS

Edinburgh is blessed with a large number of traditional 19th- and early-20th-century pubs, which have preserved much of their original Victorian or Edwardian decoration and serve cask-conditioned real ales and a staggering range of malt whiskies.

Athletic Arms (Diggers; 1-3 Angle Park Tce; 🚌1, 34, 35) Nicknamed after the cemetery across the street – the gravediggers used to nip in and slake their thirst after a hard day's interring – the Diggers dates from the 1890s. It's still staunchly traditional – the decor has barely changed in 100 years – and has recently revived its reputation as a real-ale drinker's mecca by serving locally brewed Diggers' 80-shilling ale. Packed to the gills with football and rugby fans on match days.

Abbotsford (Map p786; www.theabbotsford.com; 3 Rose St) Dating from 1902, and named after Sir Walter Scott's country house, the Abbotsford is one of the few pubs in Rose St that has retained its Edwardian splendour. It has long been a hang-out for writers, actors, journalists and media people, and has many loyal regulars. The pub's centrepiece is a splendid, mahogany island bar with a good selection of Scottish and English real ales.

Bennet's Bar (www.bennetsbar.co.uk; 8 Leven St; 🚌all Tollcross buses) Situated beside the King's Theatre, Bennet's has managed to hang on to almost all of its beautiful Victorian fittings, from the leaded, stained-glass windows and ornate mirrors to the wooden gantry and the brass water taps on the bar (for your whisky – there are over 100 malts to choose from).

Cafe Royal Circle Bar (Map p786; www.caferoyaledinburgh.co.uk; 17 West Register St; 🚌all Princes St buses) Perhaps the classic Edinburgh bar, the Cafe Royal's main claims to fame are its magnificent oval bar and the series of Doulton tile portraits of famous Victorian inventors. Check out the bottles on the gantry – staff line them up to look like there's a mirror there, and many a drink-befuddled customer has been seen squinting and wondering why he can't see his reflection.

Sheep Heid (www.thesheepheidedinburgh.co.uk; 43-45 The Causeway; ⬤; 🚌42) Possibly the oldest inn in Edinburgh – with a licence dating back to 1360 – the Sheep Heid feels more like a country pub than an Edinburgh bar. Set in the semi-rural shadow of Arthur's Seat, it's famous for its 19th-century skittles alley and the lovely little beer garden.

of the Inspector Rebus novels, whose fictional detective is a regular here.

Bramble
COCKTAIL BAR

(Map p786; www.bramblebar.co.uk; 16a Queen St; 🚇 23, 27) One of those places that easily earns the sobriquet 'best-kept secret', Bramble is an unmarked cellar bar where a maze of stone and brick hideaways conceals what is arguably the city's best cocktail venue. No beer taps, no fuss, just expertly mixed drinks.

Cumberland Bar
PUB

(www.cumberlandbar.co.uk; 1-3 Cumberland St; 🕿; 🚇 23, 27) Immortalised as the stereotypical New Town pub in Alexander McCall Smith's serialised novel *44 Scotland Street*, the Cumberland has an authentic, traditional wood-brass-and-mirrors look (despite being relatively new) and serves well-looked-after, cask-conditioned ales and a wide range of malt whiskies. There's also a pleasant little beer garden outside.

Amicus Apple
COCKTAIL BAR

(Map p786; www.amicusapple.com; 15 Frederick St; 🕿; 🚇 all Princes St buses) This laid-back cocktail lounge is the hippest hang-out in the New Town. The drinks menu ranges from retro classics such as bloody Marys and mojitos, to original and unusual concoctions such as the Cuillin martini (Tanqueray No 10 gin, Talisker malt whisky and smoked rosemary).

🍷 Leith

★Roseleaf
CAFE, BAR

(📞 0131-476 5268; www.roseleaf.co.uk; 23-24 Sandport Pl; ⏰ 10am-1am; 🕿 📶; 🚇 16, 22, 35, 36) Cute and quaint and verging on chintzy, the Roseleaf could hardly be further from the average Leith bar. Decked out in flowered wallpaper, old furniture and rose-patterned china (cocktails are served in teapots), the real ales and bottled beers are complemented by a range of speciality teas, coffees and fruit drinks (including rose lemonade) and well-above-average pub grub (served 10am to 10pm).

Port O'Leith
PUB

(www.portoleithpub.com; 58 Constitution St; 🚇 16, 22, 35, 36) This is a good, old-fashioned, friendly local boozer, swathed with flags and cap bands left behind by visiting sailors – Leith docks are just down the road. Pop in for a pint and you'll probably stay until closing time.

☆ Entertainment

The comprehensive source for what's-on info is *The List* (www.list.co.uk), an excellent listings magazine covering both Edinburgh and Glasgow. It's available from most newsagents, and is published fortnightly on a Thursday.

Live Music

★Sandy Bell's
LIVE MUSIC

(Map p778; www.sandybellsedinburgh.co.uk; 25 Forrest Rd) This unassuming pub is a stalwart of the traditional music scene (the founder's wife sang with The Corries). There's music almost every evening at 9pm, and from 3pm Saturday and Sunday, plus lots of impromptu sessions.

Henry's Cellar Bar
LIVE MUSIC, BLUES

(Map p778; www.henryscellarbar.com; 16 Morrison St; admission free-£5) One of Edinburgh's most eclectic live-music venues, Henry's has something going on most nights of the week, from rock and indie to 'Balkan-inspired folk', funk to hip-hop to hardcore, staging both local bands and acts from around the world. Open till 3am at weekends.

Whistle Binkie's
LIVE MUSIC

(Map p778; www.facebook.com/WhistleBinkies-Edinburgh; 4-6 South Bridge; admission free; 🚇 all South Bridge buses) This crowded cellar bar, just off the Royal Mile, has live music every night till 3am, from rock and blues to folk and jazz. Open mic night on Monday and breaking bands on Tuesday are showcases for new talent.

Jazz Bar
JAZZ, BLUES

(Map p778; www.thejazzbar.co.uk; 1a Chambers St; admisson £3-7; 🕿) This atmospheric cellar bar, with its polished parquet floors, bare stone walls, candlelit tables and stylish steel-framed chairs, is owned and operated by jazz musicians. There's live music every night from 9pm to 3am, and on Saturday from 3pm; as well as jazz, expect bands playing blues, funk, soul and fusion too.

Cinemas

Cameo
CINEMA

(www.picturehouses.co.uk; 38 Home St; 🚇 all Tollcross buses) The three-screen, independently owned Cameo is a good, old-fashioned cinema showing an imaginative mix of mainstream and art-house movies. There is a good program of late-night movies and Sunday matinees, and the seats in screen 1 are big enough to get lost in.

Filmhouse CINEMA
(Map p778; www.filmhousecinema.com; 88 Lothian Rd, ☏, ♿ all Lothian Rd buses) The Filmhouse is the main venue for the annual Edinburgh International Film Festival and screens a full program of art-house, classic, foreign and second-run films, with lots of themes, retrospectives and 70mm screenings. It has wheelchair access to all three screens.

Classical Music, Opera & Ballet

Edinburgh Festival Theatre PERFORMING ARTS
(Map p778; www.edtheatres.com/festival; 13-29 Nicolson St; ◎box office 10am-6pm Mon-Sat, to 8pm show nights, 4pm-showtime Sun; ♿all South Bridge buses) A beautifully restored art-deco theatre with a modern frontage, the Festival is the city's main venue for opera, dance and ballet, but also stages musicals, concerts, drama and children's shows.

Usher Hall CLASSICAL MUSIC
(Map p778; www.usherhall.co.uk; Lothian Rd; ◎box office 10.30am-5.30pm, to 8pm show nights) The architecturally impressive Usher Hall hosts concerts by the Royal Scottish National Orchestra (RSNO) and performances of popular music.

Sport
Edinburgh is home to two rival football (soccer) teams playing in the Scottish Premier League. Heart of Midlothian (aka Hearts) has its home ground at Tynecastle Stadium (www.heartsfc.co.uk; Gorgie Rd), while the Hibernian (aka Hibs) home ground is at Easter Road Stadium (www.hibernianfc.co.uk; 12 Albion Pl).

Each year, from January to March, Scotland's national rugby team takes part in the Six Nations Rugby Union Championship. Murrayfield Stadium (www.scottishrugby.org; 112 Roseburn St), about 1.5 miles west of the city centre, is the venue for international matches.

Theatre, Musicals & Comedy

Royal Lyceum Theatre THEATRE, MUSIC
(Map p778; www.lyceum.org.uk; 30b Grindlay St; ◎box office 10am-6pm Mon-Sat, to 8pm show nights; 🎭) A grand Victorian theatre located beside the Usher Hall, the Lyceum stages drama, concerts, musicals and ballet.

Traverse Theatre THEATRE, DANCE
(Map p778; www.traverse.co.uk; 10 Cambridge St; ◎box office 10am-6pm Mon-Sat, to 8pm show nights) The Traverse is the main focus for new Scottish writing and stages an adven-turous program of contemporary drama and dance. The box office is only open on Sunday (from 4pm) when there's a show on.

King's Theatre THEATRE, PERFORMING ARTS
(www.edtheatres.com/kings; 2 Leven St; ◎box office open 1hr before show; ♿all Tollcross buses) King's is a traditional theatre with a program of musicals, drama, comedy and its famous Christmas pantomimes.

The Stand Comedy Club COMEDY
(Map p786; www.thestand.co.uk; 5 York Pl; ◎from 7.30pm Mon-Sat, from 12.30pm Sun; ♿all York Pl buses) The Stand, founded in 1995, is Edinburgh's main independent comedy venue. It's an intimate cabaret bar with performances every night and a free Sunday lunchtime show.

🛍 Shopping

Princes St is Edinburgh's principal shopping street, lined with all the big high-street stores, with many smaller shops along pedestrianised Rose St and more expensive designer boutiques on George St. There are also two big shopping centres in the New Town – Princes Mall (Map p786), at the eastern end of Princes St, and the nearby St James Centre (Map p786) at the top of Leith St – plus Multrees Walk (Map p786), a designer shopping complex with a flagship Harvey Nichols store on the eastern side of St Andrew Sq. The huge Ocean Terminal (☏0131-555 8888; www.oceanterminal.com; Ocean Dr; ◎10am-8pm Mon-Fri, to 7pm Sat, 11am-6pm Sun; ♿11, 22, 34, 35, 36) in Leith is the biggest shopping centre in the city.

For more off-beat shopping – including fashion, music, crafts, gifts and jewellery – head for the cobbled lanes of Cockburn, Victoria and St Mary's Sts, all near the Royal Mile in the Old Town; William St in the western part of New Town; and the Stockbridge district, immediately north of the New Town.

ℹ️ Information

EMERGENCY
Edinburgh Rape Crisis Centre (☏08088 01 03 02; www.rapecrisisscotland.org.uk)

Police Information Centre (☏0131-226 6966; 188 High St; ◎10am-1pm & 2-5.30pm, to 9.30pm during Fringe Festival) Report a crime, ask a question or make lost-property inquiries here.

Police Scotland (☏non-emergency 101; www.scotland.police.uk; 3-5 Torphichen Pl)

INTERNET ACCESS

There are several internet-enabled telephone boxes (10p a minute, 50p minimum) scattered around the city centre, and countless wi-fi hot spots – search on www.jiwire.com. Internet cafes are spread around the city. Some convenient ones include:

Coffee Home (www.coffeehome.co.uk; 28 Crighton Pl, Leith Walk; per 20min 60p; ◔10am-9pm Mon-Fri, 10am-8pm Sat, noon-8pm Sun)

e-corner (www.e-corner.co.uk; 54 Blackfriars St; per 20min £1; ◔10am-7pm Mon-Sat, noon-7pm Sun; 🛜)

G-Tec (www.grassmarket-technologies.com; 67 Grassmarket; per 20min £1; ◔10am-5.30pm Mon-Fri, to 4pm Sat)

MEDICAL SERVICES

For urgent medical advice you can call the **NHS 24 Helpline** (☑08454 24 24 24; www.nhs24. com). Chemists (pharmacists) can advise you on minor ailments. At least one local chemist remains open round the clock – its location will be displayed in the windows of other chemists.

Chalmers Street Dental Clinic (3 Chalmers St; ◔9am-4.45pm Mon-Thu, to 4.15pm Fri; 🚍23, 27, 35, 45, 47). Walk-in clinic for urgent dental treatment.

Lothian Dental Advice Line (☑0131-536 4800; ◔5-10pm Mon-Fri, 9am-10pm Sat & Sun) In the case of a dental emergency in the evenings or at weekends.

Royal Infirmary of Edinburgh (☑0131-536 1000; www.nhslothian.scot.nhs.uk; 51 Little France Cres, Old Dalkeith Rd; ◔24hr) Edinburgh's main general hospital; has 24-hour accident and emergency department.

POST

Main Post Office (Map p786; St James Shopping Centre, Leith St; ◔9am-5.30pm Mon-Sat) Hidden away inside a shopping centre.

TOURIST INFORMATION

Edinburgh Airport Information Centre (☑0131-344 3120; main concourse, Edinburgh Airport; ◔7.30am-9pm)

Edinburgh Information Centre (Map p786; ☑0131-473 3868; www.edinburgh.org; Princes Mall, 3 Princes St; ◔9am-9pm Mon-Sat, 10am-8pm Sun Jul & Aug, 9am-7pm Mon-Sat, 10am-7pm Sun May, Jun & Sep, 9am-5pm Mon-Wed, to 6pm Thu-Sun Oct-Apr) Includes an accommodation booking service, currency exchange, gift and bookshop, internet access and counters selling tickets for Edinburgh city tours and Scottish Citylink bus services.

USEFUL WEBSITES

Edinburgh Architecture (www.edinburgh-architecture.co.uk) Informative site dedicated to the city's modern architecture.

Edinburgh Festival Guide (www.edinburgh-festivals.co.uk) Everything you need to know about Edinburgh's many festivals.

Events Edinburgh (www.eventsedinburgh.org. uk) The city council's official events guide.

The List (www.list.co.uk) Listings of restaurants, pubs, clubs and nightlife.

VisitScotland Edinburgh & Lothians (www. edinburgh.org) Official tourist-board site, with listings of accommodation, sights, activities and events.

❶ Getting There & Away

AIR

Edinburgh Airport (☑0844 448 8833; www. edinburghairport.com) Eight miles west of the city; has numerous flights to other parts of Scotland and the UK, Ireland and mainland Europe.

FlyBe/Loganair (☑0871 700 2000; www. loganair.co.uk) Operates daily flights to Inverness, Wick, Orkney, Shetland and Stornoway.

BUS

Edinburgh bus station (Map p786; left luggage lockers per 24hr £3-10; ◔4.30am-midnight Sun-Thu, 4.30am-12.30am Fri & Sat) At the north-east corner of St Andrew Sq, with pedestrian entrances from the square and from Elder St. For timetable information, call **Traveline** (☑0871 200 22 33; www.travelinescotland.com).

THE FORTH BRIDGES

At Queensferry, west of Edinburgh, the narrowest part of the Firth of Forth is spanned by two spectacular bridges. Ferries have crossed to Fife here from the earliest times – the village takes its name from Queen Margaret (1046–93), who gave pilgrims free passage across the firth on their way to St Andrews. Ferries continued to operate until 1964 when the graceful Forth Road Bridge was opened. Construction has started on a second road bridge, the Queensferry Crossing, scheduled to open in 2016.

Predating the road bridge by 74 years, the magnificent Forth Bridge – only outsiders ever call it the Forth Rail Bridge – is one of the finest engineering achievements of the 19th century. Completed in 1890 after seven years' work, its three huge cantilevers span 1447m and took 59,000 tonnes of steel, eight million rivets and the lives of 58 men to build.

Scottish Citylink (☑ 0871 266 3333; www. citylink.co.uk) buses connect Edinburgh with all of Scotland's cities and major towns. The following are one-way fares departing from Edinburgh:

Aberdeen £30

Dundee £16

Fort William £34

Glasgow £7.30

Inverness £30

Portree £54

Stirling £8

It's also worth checking with **Megabus** (☑ 0900 1600 900; www.megabus.com) for cheap intercity bus fares (from as little as £5) from Edinburgh to Aberdeen, Dundee, Glasgow, Inverness and Perth.

There are various buses to Edinburgh from London and the rest of the UK.

TRAIN

The main terminus in Edinburgh is **Waverley train station**, located in the heart of the city. Trains arriving from, and departing for, the west also stop at Haymarket station, which is more convenient for the West End.

You can buy tickets, make reservations and get travel information at the **Edinburgh Rail Travel Centre** (⊙ 4.45am-12.30am Mon-Sat, 7am-12.30am Sun) in Waverley station. For fare and timetable information, phone the **National Rail Enquiry Service** (☑ 08457 48 49 50; www. nationalrail.co.uk) or use the journey planner on the website.

First ScotRail (☑ 08457 55 00 33; www. scotrail.co.uk) operates a regular shuttle service between Edinburgh and Glasgow (£13.20, 50 minutes, every 15 minutes), and frequent daily services to all Scottish cities, including Aberdeen (£34, 2½ hours), Dundee (£17.30, 1¼ hours) and Inverness (£72, 3½ hours).

ⓘ Getting Around

TO/FROM THE AIRPORT

The Lothian Buses **Airlink** (www.flybybus.com) service 100 runs from Waverley Bridge, outside the train station, to the airport (one way/return £4/7, 30 minutes, every 10 minutes, 4am to midnight) via the West End and Haymarket.

Edinburgh Trams (www.edinburghtrams. com) run from the airport to the city centre (one way/return £4.50/7.50, 33 minutes, every six to eight minutes, 6am to midnight).

An airport taxi to the city centre costs around £20 and takes about 20 to 30 minutes. Trams, buses and taxis all depart from outside the arrivals hall; go out through the main doors and turn left.

CAR & MOTORCYCLE

Though useful for day trips beyond the city, a car in central Edinburgh is more of a liability than

---

EDINBURGH'S TRAMS

After six years of street closures, traffic chaos, ballooning costs and accusations of mismanagement, trams finally returned to Edinburgh's streets on 31 May 2014 after an absence of 58 years. Several hundred million pounds over budget, several years behind schedule, and half the length originally planned, the new tram line runs for 8.7 miles from Edinburgh Airport to York Place in the New Town, passing Murrayfield Stadium, Haymarket and Princes St.

---

a convenience. There is restricted access on Princes St, George St and Charlotte Sq, many streets are one-way, and finding a parking place is like striking gold. Queen's Dr around Holyrood Park is closed to motorised traffic on Sunday.

All the big international car-rental agencies have offices in Edinburgh, but there are many smaller local agencies that offer better rates. **Arnold Clark** (☑ 0141-237 4374; www.arnold-clarkrental.co.uk) near Portobello, charges from £30 a day, or £180 a week for a small car, including VAT and insurance.

PUBLIC TRANSPORT

Edinburgh's public transport system consists of an extensive bus network and a single tram line that runs from the airport via Haymarket and Princes St to York Pl at the east end of the city centre. The main operators are Edinburgh Trams, **Lothian Buses** (www.lothianbuses.com) and **First** (☑ 0131-663 9233; www.firstedin-burgh.co.uk); for timetable information contact Traveline.

Adult fares within the city are £1.50 on both bus and tram; purchase from the bus driver, or from machines at tram stops. Children aged under five travel free and those aged five to 15 pay a flat fare of 70p.

On Lothian Buses you must pay the driver the exact fare, but First buses will give change. Lothian Bus drivers also sell a day ticket (£3.50) that gives unlimited travel (on Lothian buses and trams) for a day. Night-service buses, which run hourly between midnight and 5am, charge a flat fare of £3.

TAXI

Central Taxis (☑ 0131-229 2468; www.taxis-edinburgh.co.uk)

City Cabs (☑ 0131-228 1211; www.citycabs. co.uk)

ComCab (☑ 0131-272 8000; www.comcab-edinburgh.co.uk)

Glasgow & Southern Scotland

Best Places to Eat

➜ The Ubiquitous Chip (p816)

➜ Stravaigin (p815)

➜ Coltman's (p828)

➜ Loon Fung (p815)

Best Places to Stay

➜ Old Bank House (p823)

➜ Malmaison (p813)

➜ Corsewall Lighthouse Hotel (p835)

➜ Knockinaam Lodge (p835)

➜ Hotel du Vin (p814)

Why Go?

For many, southern Scotland is what you drive through on the way further north. Big mistake. But it means there are plenty of peaceful corners here. The south's proximity to England brought strife, but the ruins of Borders castles and the abbeys they protected make wonderfully atmospheric historic sites. The hillier west enjoys extensive forest cover; hills cascade down to sandy coasts blessed with Scotland's sunniest weather.

The region's premier urban attraction is marvellous Glasgow, Scotland's biggest city and a fascinatingly vital place. Glaswegians are proud of their working-class background, black humour and leftist traditions, and their city combines art, architecture, great food and nightlife, style, edgy urbanity and the people's legendary friendliness in a captivating blend that will leave you wanting more.

When to Go?

➜ Take a fortnight to cross the whole region hiking the gorgeous Southern Upland Way in May

➜ The West End Festival and the Jazz Festival make Glasgow music heaven in June, while spectacular gardens bloom at the region's numerous stately homes.

➜ Glasgow is super-friendly at any time, but when the sun is shining in August there's no happier city in Britain.

ℹ Getting There & Around

Train services are limited. There are stations at Berwick-upon-Tweed on the main Edinburgh–London line (on the English side of the border); at Dumfries on the main Glasgow–London line; and at Stranraer and Ayr, linked to Glasgow. Bus transport is the mainstay of the region. Check details with **Traveline Scotland** (☑ 0871 200 22 33; www.travelinescotland.com).

GLASGOW

POP 595,100

Disarmingly blending sophistication and earthiness, Scotland's biggest city has evolved over the last couple of decades to become one of Britain's most intriguing metropolises.

At first glance, the soberly handsome Victorian buildings, legacies of wealth generated from manufacturing and trade, suggest a staid sort of place. Very wrong. They are packed with stylish bars, top-notch restaurants, hedonistic clubs and one of Britain's best live music scenes. The place's sheer vitality is gloriously infectious: the combination of edgy urbanity and the residents' legendary friendliness is captivating.

Glasgow also offers plenty by day. Its shopping - whether you're looking for Italian fashion or pre-loved denim – is famous and there are great museums and galleries. Charles Rennie Mackintosh's sublime designs dot the city, which – always proud of its working-class background – also innovatively displays its industrial heritage. The River Clyde, traditionally associated with Glasgow's earthier side, is now a symbol of the city's renaissance.

History

Glasgow grew around the cathedral founded by St Kertigan, later to become St Mungo, in the 6th century. Unfortunately, with the exception of the cathedral, virtually nothing of the medieval city remains. It was swept away by the energies of a new age – the age of capitalism, the Industrial Revolution and the British Empire.

In the 18th century, much of the tobacco trade between Europe and the USA was routed through Glasgow, providing a great source of wealth. Even after the tobacco trade declined in the 19th century, the city continued to prosper as a centre of textile manufacturing, shipbuilding and the coal and steel industries. The outward appearance of prosperity, however, was tempered by the dire working conditions in the factories.

In the first half of the 20th century Glasgow was the centre of Britain's munitions industry; postwar, however, the port and heavy industries dwindled, and by the early 1970s, the city had become synonymous with unemployment, economic depression and urban violence, centred around highrise housing schemes such as the infamous Gorbals. More recently, urban development and a booming cultural sector have injected style and confidence into the city; though the standard of living remains low for Britain and life continues to be tough for many, ongoing regeneration gives grounds for optimism. The successful hosting of the 2014 Commonwealth Games highlighted this regeneration to a wide global audience.

GLASGOW IN...

Two Days

On your first day, hit the East End for **Glasgow Cathedral**, **St Mungo's Museum** and a wander through the hillside necropolis. Later take in one of the city's top museums: either the **Burrell Collection** or the **Kelvingrove**. As evening falls, head to trendy **Merchant City** for a stroll and dinner – perhaps **Café Gandolfi**. Check out **Artá** for a pre- or post-meal drink. The next day, visit whichever museum you missed yesterday, and then it's Mackintosh time. **Glasgow School of Art** is his finest work: if you like his style, head to the West End for **Mackintosh House**. Hungry? Thirsty? Some of the city's best restaurants and bars are up this end of town, so you could make a night of it. Be sure to check out one of the numerous excellent music venues around the city.

Four Days

A four-day stay gives better scope to get to grips with Glasgow. Spend a day along the Clyde visiting the **Riverside Museum** and the **Science Centre**. Plan your weekend around a night out at **Arches** or the legendary **Sub Club**, a day strolling the stylish city-centre clothing emporia or attending a football game. Try at least one of the city's classic curry houses.

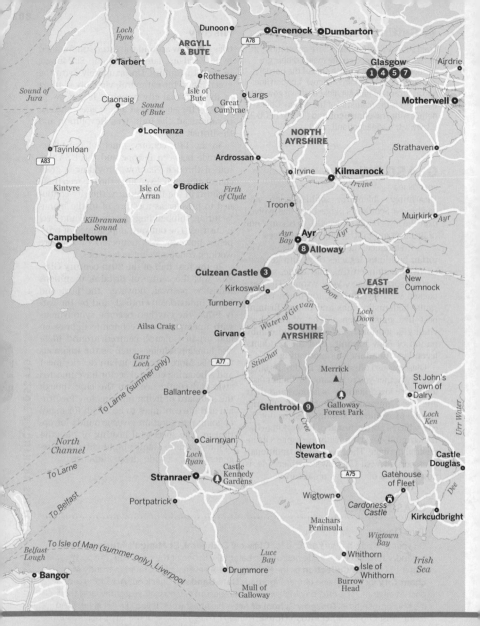

Glasgow & Southern Scotland Highlights

❶ Gazing at Glasgow's fabulous wealth of paintings in the **Burrell Collection** (p812), the **Kelvingrove** (p811) and **Hunterian Art Gallery** (p812)

❷ Hiking or cycling between the ruins of the **Border Abbeys** (p822)

❸ Admiring 18th-century architectural genius at **Culzean Castle** (p830)

❹ Deciding which of Glasgow's excellent **West End restaurants** (p815) you are going to dine at next

❺ Discovering the work of **Charles Rennie Mackintosh**

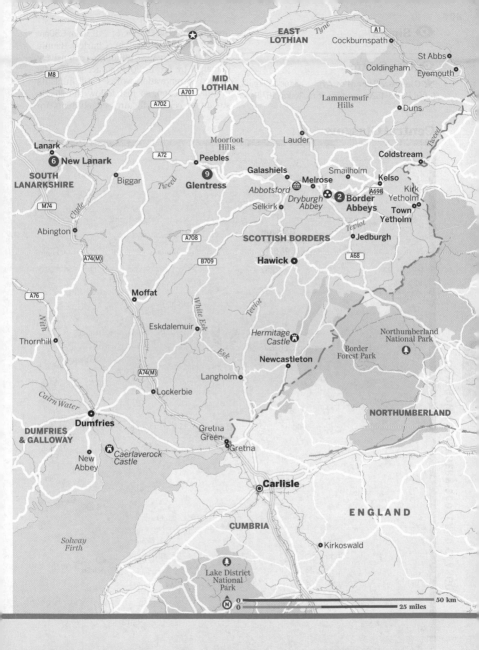

◉ Sights

◉ City Centre

★ **Glasgow School of Art**   HISTORIC BUILDING
(☑ 0141-353 4526; www.gsa.ac.uk/tours; 167 Ren-

frew St; adult/child £9.75/4.75; ⊘ 9.30am-6.30pm Mar-Oct, 10am-5pm Nov-Feb) Charles Rennie Mackintosh's greatest building – extensively damaged by fire in 2014, so access may be limited by renovation works – still fulfils its original function, so just follow the steady stream of eclectically dressed students up

Central Glasgow

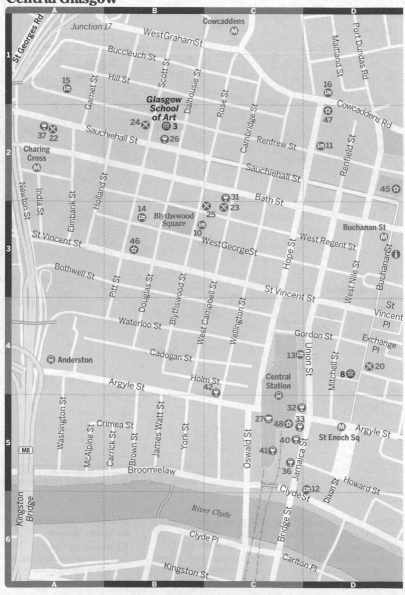

the hill to find it. It's one of Glasgow's architectural showpieces and has now been joined by Steven Holl's spectacular glacial, green School of Design (the Reid Building) right opposite. A risqué combination, but it works.

Visits are by excellent hour-long guided tours (roughly hourly in summer; 11am, 1pm and 3pm in winter; multilingual translations available). These leave from the new building; book online or by phone at busy times.

★**City Chambers** HISTORIC BUILDING
(www.glasgow.gov.uk; George Sq; ⏲9am-5pm Mon-Fri) The grand seat of local government

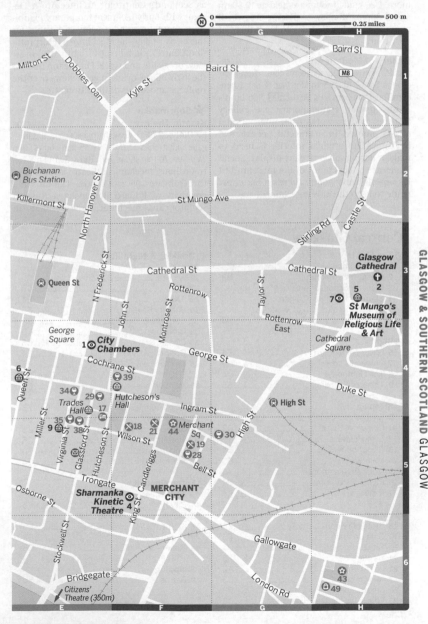

was built in the 1880s at the high point of Glasgow's wealth. The interior is even more extravagant than the exterior, and the chambers have sometimes been used as a movie location to represent the Kremlin or the Vatican. You can have a look at the opulent ground floor during opening hours: to see more, free guided tours are held at 10.30am and 2.30pm Monday to Friday; it's worth popping in earlier that day to book them at busy times.

Gallery of Modern Art   GALLERY
(GoMA; www.glasgowmuseums.com; Royal Exchange Sq; ⊙10am-5pm Mon-Wed & Sat, 10am-8pm Thu, 11am-5pm Fri & Sun) FREE Scotland's most popular contemporary art gallery features modern works from international artists, housed in a graceful neoclassical building. The original interior is used to make a daring, inventive art display. Social issues are a focal point of the museum but it's not all heavy going: there's a big effort made to keep the kids entertained.

The Lighthouse   HISTORIC BUILDING
(☑0141-276 5365; www.thelighthouse.co.uk; 11 Mitchell Lane; ⊙10.30am-5pm Mon-Sat, noon-5pm Sun) FREE Mackintosh's first building, designed in 1893, was a striking new headquarters for the *Glasgow Herald*. Tucked up a narrow lane off Buchanan St, it now serves as Scotland's Centre for Architecture & Design, with fairly technical temporary exhibitions (sometimes admission is payable for these), as well as the Mackintosh Interpretation Centre, a detailed (if slightly dry) overview of his life and work. On the top floor of the 'lighthouse', drink in great views over the rooftops and spires of the city centre.

★ Sharmanka
Kinetic Theatre   EXHIBITION
(☑0141-552 7080; www.sharmanka.com; 103 Trongate; adult/child £5/free; ⊙45-min shows 3pm Wed-Sun, 70-min shows 7pm Thu & Sun) This extraordinary mechanical theatre is located at the Trongate 103 arts centre. The amazing creativity of Eduard Bersudsky, a Russian sculptor and mechanic, now resident in

Central Glasgow

THE GENIUS OF CHARLES RENNIE MACKINTOSH

Great cities have great artists, designers and architects contributing to their urban environment while expressing its soul and individuality. Charles Rennie Mackintosh was all of these and his quirky, linear and geometric designs have had enormous influence on Glasgow. Many of the buildings Mackintosh designed are open to the public, and you'll see his tall, thin, art nouveau typeface repeatedly reproduced.

Born in 1868, Mackintosh studied at the Glasgow School of Art. It was there that he met the also influential artist and designer Margaret Macdonald, whom he married; they collaborated on many projects and were major influences on each other's work. In 1896, aged only 27, he won a competition for his design of the School of Art's new building, Mackintosh's supreme architectural achievement. The first section was opened in 1899 and is considered to be the earliest example of art nouveau in Britain. This building demonstrates his skill in combining function and style.

Although Mackintosh's genius was quickly recognised on the Continent, he did not receive the same encouragement in Scotland. His architectural career here lasted only until 1914, when he moved to England to concentrate on furniture design. He died in 1928, and it is only since the last decades of the 20th century that Mackintosh's genius has been widely recognised. For more about the man and his work, contact the **Charles Rennie Mackintosh Society** (☑ 0141-946 6600; www.crmsociety.com; 870 Garscube Rd, Mackintosh Church). Check its website for special events.

Another of Mackintosh's finest works is **Hill House** (NTS; ☑ 0844 493-2208; www.nts. org.uk; Upper Colquhoun St; adult/child £10.50/7.50; ☺ 1.30-5.30pm Apr-Oct), in Helensburgh. If you're planning to visit some of the farther-flung attractions, the **Mackintosh Trail ticket** (£10), available at the tourist office or any Mackintosh building, gives you a day's admission to Hill House, the Mackintosh Church and House for an Art Lover as well as unlimited bus and subway travel.

Scotland, has created a series of large, wondrous figures sculpted from bits of scrap and elaborate carvings. Set to haunting music, these perform humorous and tragic stories of the human spirit. The gallery is open from 1pm to 3pm Wednesday to Sunday – the sculptures and their stories are fascinating even when not in motion.

It's great for kids and very moving for adults: inspirational one moment and macabre the next, but always colourful, clever and thought-provoking.

◉ East End

The oldest part of the city, given a facelift in the 1990s, is concentrated around Glasgow Cathedral, to the east of the modern city centre. It takes 15 to 20 minutes to walk from George Sq, but numerous buses pass nearby.

★ Glasgow Cathedral   CHURCH

(HS; www.historic-scotland.gov.uk; Cathedral Sq; ☺ 9.30am-5.30pm Mon-Sat, 1-5pm Sun Apr-Sep, closes 4.30pm Oct-Mar) **FREE** Glasgow Cathedral has a rare timelessness. The dark, imposing interior conjures up medieval might and can send a shiver down the spine. It's a shining example of Gothic architecture, and, unlike nearly all Scotland's cathedrals, survived the turmoil of the Reformation mobs almost intact. Most of the current building dates from the 15th century.

★ St Mungo's Museum
of Religious Life & Art   MUSEUM

(www.glasgowmuseums.com; 2 Castle St; ☺ 10am-5pm Tue-Thu & Sat, 11am-5pm Fri & Sun) **FREE** Set in a reconstruction of the bishop's palace that once stood in the cathedral forecourt, this museum audaciously attempts to capture the world's major religions in an artistic nutshell. A startling achievement, it presents the similarities and differences of how various religions approach common themes such as birth, marriage and death. The attraction is twofold: firstly, impressive art that blurs the lines between religion and culture; and secondly, the opportunity to delve into different faiths, as deep or shallow as you wish.

Provand's Lordship   HISTORIC HOUSE

(www.glasgowmuseums.com; 3 Castle St; ☺ 10am-5pm Tue-Thu & Sat, 11am-5pm Fri & Sun) **FREE** Near the cathedral is Provand's Lordship, the oldest house in Glasgow. A rare example

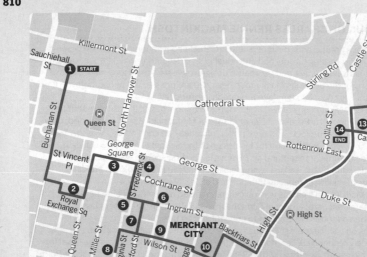

🏃 City Walk
Glasgow

START BUCHANAN ST
END GLASGOW CATHEDRAL
LENGTH 1¾ MILES; 1½ HOURS

This stroll takes you to Glasgow Cathedral through trendy Merchant City.

Start at the junction of two major shopping thoroughfares, Sauchiehall and Buchanan Streets, overseen by a bronze ❶ **statue of Donald Dewar**, Scotland's inaugural First Minister. Stroll down pedestrian Buchanan St, then left through one of the handsome gateways into Merchant City. Here, the strikingly colonnaded ❷ **Gallery of Modern Art** (p808) was once the Royal Exchange and now hosts some of the country's best contemporary art displays. Turn left up Queen St to ❸ **George Square**, surrounded by imposing Victorian architecture, including the grandiose ❹ **City Chambers** (p807).

Walk down South Frederick St. Ahead of you, the former Court House cells now house the ❺ **Corinthian Club** (p816); drop into the bar for a glimpse of the extravagant interior, then continue to ❻ **Hutcheson's Hall**. This was built in 1805 as a hospital and school for the poor. Retrace your steps one block and continue south down Glassford St past ❼ **Trades Hall**, designed by Robert Adam in 1791 to house the trades guild. Turn right into Wilson St and left along Virginia St, lined with the old warehouses of the Tobacco Lords. The ❽ **Tobacco Exchange** is flanked by pretty Virginia Court. Sugar and tobacco were traded here in the 18th and 19th centuries.

Back on Wilson St, the ❾ **Old Sheriff Court** fills a whole block and has been both Glasgow's town hall and main lawcourt. Continue east on Wilson St past Ingram Sq to ❿ **Merchant Square**, a covered courtyard that was once the city's fruit market, but now bustles with cafes and bars.

Head up Albion St, then right into Blackfriars St. Emerging onto High St, turn left and follow it up to the ⓫ **cathedral** (p809). Behind the cathedral wind your way up through the ⓬ **Necropolis**, which offers great city views. Lastly, check out ⓭ **St Mungo's Museum of Religious Life & Art** (p809) and ⓮ **Provand's Lordship** (p809).

of 15th-century domestic Scottish architecture, it was built in 1471 as a manse. The ceilings and doorways are low, and the rooms are sparsely furnished with period artefacts, except for an upstairs room, which has been furnished to reflect the living space of an early-16th-century chaplain. The building's biggest draw is its authentic feel – if you ignore the tacky imitation-stone linoleum covering the ground floor.

◉ The Clyde

Once a thriving shipbuilding area, the Clyde sank into dereliction during the post-war era, but is being rejuvenated.

★ Riverside Museum   MUSEUM

(www.glasgowmuseums.com; 100 Pointhouse Pl; ☺10am-5pm Mon-Thu & Sat, 11am-5pm Fri & Sun; ⦿) **FREE** This visually impressive modern museum at Glasgow Harbour (west of the centre – get bus 100 from the north side of George Sq, or the Clyde Cruises boat service) owes its striking curved forms to British-Iraqi architect Zaha Hadid. A transport museum forms the main part of the collection, featuring a fascinating series of cars made in Scotland, plus assorted railway locos, trams, bikes (including the world's first pedal-powered bicycle from 1847) and model Clyde-built ships.

An atmospheric recreation of a Glasgow shopping street from the early 20th century puts the vintage vehicles into a social context.

The magnificent three-masted *Glenlee*, launched in 1896, is the **Tall Ship** (www.thetallship.com; Riverside Museum; ☺10am-5pm; ⦿) **FREE** that is berthed alongside the museum. On board are family-friendly displays about the ship's history, restoration and shipboard life during its heyday. Upkeep costs are high, so do donate something or have a coffee below decks. The Riverside is west of the centre at Glasgow Harbour; you can reach it on bus 100 from the north side of George Sq, or via the Clyde Cruises boat service. There's also a cafe.

★ Glasgow Science Centre   MUSEUM

(☑0141-420 5000; www.glasgowsciencecentre.org; 50 Pacific Quay; adult/child £10.50/8.50, Imax, tower or planetarium extra £2.50; ☺10am-5pm Wed-Sun Nov-Mar, 10am-5pm daily Apr-Oct; ⦿) This ultramodern science museum will keep the kids entertained for hours (that's middle-aged kids, too!). It brings science and technology alive through hundreds of interactive exhibits on four floors: a bounty of discovery for inquisitive minds. There's also an **Imax theatre** (see www.cineworld.com for current screenings), a rotating 127m-high **observation tower**, a planetarium, and a **Science Theatre**, with live science demonstrations. To get here, take bus 89 or 90 from Union St.

◉ West End

With its expectant buzz, trendy bars and cafes and nonchalant swagger, the bohemian West End is great for people-watching. From the city centre, buses 9, 16 and 23 run towards Kelvingrove, buses 8, 11 and 16 to the university, and buses 20, 44 and 66 to Byres Rd (among others).

★ Kelvingrove Art
Gallery & Museum   GALLERY, MUSEUM

(www.glasgowmuseums.com; Argyle St; ☺10am-5pm Mon-Thu & Sat, 11am-5pm Fri & Sun) **FREE** A magnificent stone building, this grand Victorian cathedral of culture is a fascinating and unusual museum, with a bewildering variety of exhibits. You'll find fine art alongside stuffed animals, and Micronesian shark-tooth swords alongside a Spitfire plane, but it's not mix 'n' match: rooms are carefully and thoughtfully themed, and the collection is a manageable size. There's an excellent room of Scottish art, a room of fine French Impressionist works, and quality Renaissance paintings from Italy and Flanders.

Salvador Dalí's superb *Christ of St John of the Cross* is also here. Best of all, nearly everything, including the paintings, has an easy-reading paragraph of interpretation. You can learn a lot about art here, and it's excellent for children, with plenty to do and displays aimed at a variety of ages. Free hour-long guided tours begin at 11am and 2.30pm. Bus 17, among many others, runs here from Renfield St.

Hunterian Museum   MUSEUM

(www.hunterian.gla.ac.uk; University Ave; ☺10am-5pm Tue-Sat, 11am-4pm Sun) **FREE** Housed in the glorious sandstone university building, which is in itself reason enough to pay a visit, this quirky museum contains the collection of renowned one-time student of the university, William Hunter (1718–83). Hunter was primarily an anatomist and physician but, as one of those gloriously well-rounded Enlightenment figures, he interested himself in everything the world had to offer. Pickled organs in glass jars take their place alongside geological phenomena, potsherds gleaned from ancient brochs, dinosaur skeletons and a creepy case of deformed animals. The main halls of the exhibition, with their high vaulted roofs, are magnificent in themselves. A highlight is the 1674 Chinese *Map of the Whole World* in the World Culture section.

Hunterian Art Gallery
GALLERY

(www.hunterian.gla.ac.uk; 82 Hillhead St; ⊙10am-5pm Tue-Sat, 11am-4pm Sun) FREE Across the road from the Hunterian Museum, and part of the same bequest, the bold tones of the Scottish Colourists (Samuel Peploe, Francis Cadell, JD Fergusson and Leslie Hunter) are well represented in this gallery. There are William MacTaggart's Impressionistic Scottish landscapes and a gem by Thomas Millie Dow. There's also a special collection of James McNeill Whistler's limpid prints, drawings and paintings. Upstairs, in a section devoted to late-19th-century Scottish art, you can see works by several of the Glasgow Boys.

★ Mackintosh House
HISTORIC BUILDING

(www.hunterian.gla.ac.uk; 82 Hillhead St; ⊙10am-5pm Tue-Sat, 11am-4pm Sun) FREE Attached to the Hunterian Art Gallery, this is a reconstruction of the first home that Charles Rennie Mackintosh bought with his wife, noted designer-artist Margaret Macdonald. It's fair to say that interior decoration was one of their strong points; Mackintosh House is startling even today. The quiet elegance of the hall and dining room on the ground floor give way to a stunning drawing room.

⊙ South Side

★ Burrell Collection
GALLERY

(www.glasgowmuseums.com; Pollok Country Park; ⊙10am-5pm Mon-Thu & Sat, 11am-5pm Fri & Sun) FREE One of Glasgow's top attractions was amassed by wealthy industrialist Sir William Burrell then donated to the city, and is housed in an outstanding museum, in a park 3 miles south of the city centre. Burrell collected all manner of art from his teens to his death at 97, and this idiosyncratic collection of treasure includes everything from Chinese porcelain and medieval furniture to paintings by Degas and Cézanne. It's not so big as to be overwhelming, and the stamp of the collector lends an intriguing coherence.

Visitors will find their own favourite part of this museum, but the exquisite tapestry galleries are outstanding. Intricate stories capturing life in Europe are woven into staggering wall-size pieces dating from the 13th to 16th centuries.

Within the spectacular interior, carved-stone Romanesque doorways are incorporated into the structure so you actually walk through them. Floor-to-ceiling windows admit a flood of light. In springtime, it's worth making a full day of your trip here and spending some time wandering in the beautiful park, studded with flowers. If you're not heading further north, here's the place to see shaggy Highland cattle, as well as heavy horses.

Many buses pass the park gates (including buses 45, 47, 48 and 57), and there's a twice-hourly bus service between the gallery and the gates (a pleasant 10-minute walk). Alternatively catch a train to Pollokshaws West from Central station (four per hour; second station on the line for East Kilbride or Kilmarnock).

🏃 Activities

The **Clyde Walkway** extends from Glasgow upriver to the Falls of Clyde near New Lanark, some 40 miles away. The tourist office has a good leaflet pack detailing different sections of this walk. The 10-mile section through Glasgow has interesting parts, though modern buildings have replaced most of the old shipbuilding works.

The well-trodden **West Highland Way** footpath begins in Milngavie, 8 miles north of Glasgow (you can walk to Milngavie from Glasgow along the River Kelvin), and runs for 95 spectacular miles to Fort William.

There are several long-distance pedestrian/cycle routes that begin in Glasgow and follow off-road routes for most of the way. Check www.sustrans.org.uk for more details.

🎉 Festivals & Events

Glasgow Jazz Festival
MUSIC

(www.jazzfest.co.uk) Excellent festival held in June.

Glasgow International Festival of Visual Art
VISUAL ART

(☑0141-276 8384; www.glasgowinternational.org) Held in late April in even years, this festival features a range of innovative installations, performances and exhibitions around town.

West End Festival
PERFORMING ARTS

(☑0141-341 0844; www.westendfestival.co.uk) This music and arts event is Glasgow's biggest festival, running for three weeks in June.

🛌 Sleeping

The city centre gets very rowdy at weekends, and accommodation options fill up fast, mostly with groups who will probably roll home boisterously some time after 3am. If you prefer an earlier appointment with your bed, you'll be better off in a smaller, quieter lodging, or in the West End. Booking ahead is essential at weekends and in July and August.

📍 City Centre

Euro Hostel   HOSTEL £

(📞0141-222 2828; www.euro-hostels.co.uk; 318 Clyde St; dm £14-22, s £22-60, d £44-80; @ 🛜) With hundreds of beds, this mammoth hostel is handily central. While it feels a bit institutional and businesslike, and is often booked out by rowdy groups, it has lots of facilities, including en suite dorms with lockers, internet access, a compact kitchen, breakfast, an on-site public bar, a games room and a laundry. Dorms range in size from four to 14 beds, and price varies on a daily basis. Renovations are ongoing.

McLay's Guesthouse   GUESTHOUSE £

(📞0141-332 4796; www.mclays.com; 264 Renfrew St; s/d £42/56, without bathroom £35/48; 🛜) The string of cheapish guesthouses along the western end of Renfrew St are a mixed bag offering no luxury, but they are in a tempting location right by the Sauchiehall nightlife and College of Art. This is among the best of them: a solid choice with decent warm rooms and fair prices. There's a big variety of rooms and rates. Wi-fi doesn't reach the rooms.

★Citizen M   HOTEL ££

(📞0141-404 9485; www.citizenm.com; 60 Renfrew St; r £75-105; @ 🛜) This modern chain does away with some normal hotel accoutrements in favour of self-check-in terminals and minimalist, plasticky modern rooms with just two features: a big, comfortable king-sized bed and a decent shower with mood lighting. The idea is that guests make liberal use of the public areas, and why wouldn't you, with upbeat and super-comfortable designer furniture, 24-hour cafe, and a table full of iMacs.

★Grasshoppers   HOTEL ££

(📞0141-222 2666; www.grasshoppersglasgow.com; 87 Union St; r £85-115; 🛜) Discreetly hidden atop a timeworn railway administration building right alongside Glasgow Central, this small, well-priced hotel is a modern, upbeat surprise. Rooms are compact – a few larger ones are available – but well-appointed, with unusual views over the station roof's glass sea. Numerous nice touches (friendly staff, interesting art, proper in-room coffee, free cupcakes, and weeknight suppers available) make this one of the centre's homeliest choices.

There's a very good deal available (£6 per day) at a car park a block away.

Rab Ha's   INN ££

(📞0141-572 0400; www.rabhas.com; 83 Hutcheson St; r £69-89; 🛜) This Merchant City favourite is an atmospheric pub-restaurant with four stylish rooms upstairs. They are all quite distinct and colourful. Room 1 is the best and largest, but all are comfortable, and the location is great. The personal touches, like fresh flowers, iPod docks, a big welcome and any-time breakfast, make you feel special.

Pipers Tryst Hotel   HOTEL ££

(📞0141-353 5551; www.thepipingcentre.co.uk; 30-34 McPhater St; s/d £65/80; 🛜) The name is no tartan tourist trap: this intimate, cosy hotel in a noble building is actually run by the adjacent bagpiping centre, and profits go towards maintaining it. Cheery staff, great value and a prime city-centre location make this a wise choice. You won't have far to migrate after a night of Celtic music and fine single malts in the snug bar-restaurant downstairs.

Malmaison   HOTEL £££

(📞0141-572 1000; www.malmaison.com; 278 West George St; r/ste £160/210; 🛜) A longtime favourite for its decadent decor and plush lines, this former church is sexy, slinky and a cornerstone of accommodation faith. Stylish rooms with mood lighting have a dark, brooding tone and opulent furnishings. It's a hedonistic sort of place so can be cheerfully boisterous at weekends. It's best to book online, as it's cheaper, and various suite offers can be mighty tempting.

Blythswood Square   HOTEL £££

(📞0141-248 8888; www.blythswoodsquare.com; 11 Blythswood Sq; r £145-249; @ 🛜 ♨ 🛁) In a gorgeous Georgian terrace, this elegant five-star offers plenty of inner-city luxury, with grey and cerise tweeds providing casual soft-toned style throughout. Grades of rooms go from standard to penthouse with corresponding increases in comfort; it's hard to resist the traditional 'classic' ones with windows onto the delightful square, but at weekends you'll have a quieter sleep in the new wing at the back.

🛏 West End

Glasgow SYHA
HOSTEL £

(📞 0141-332 3004; www.syha.org.uk; 8 Park Tce; dm/tw £22/64; @ 🤝) Perched on a hill overlooking Kelvingrove Park in a charming town house, this place is one of Scotland's best official hostels. Dorms are mostly four to six beds with padlock lockers and all have their own en suite. The common rooms are spacious, plush and good for lounging about. There's no curfew, a good kitchen, and meals are available. The prices listed reflect maximums and are usually cheaper.

Heritage Hotel
HOTEL £

(📞 0141-339 6955; www.theheritagehotel.net; 4 Alfred Tce, Great Western Rd; s/d £40/60; P 🤝 ❄) A stone's throw from all the action of the West End, this friendly hotel has an open, airy feel despite the rather dilapidated raised terrace it's located on. Generally, the rooms on the 1st and 2nd floors are a bit more spacious (No 21 is best of the doubles) and have a better outlook. The location, parking option and very fair prices mark it out.

★ Alamo Guest House
B&B ££

(📞 0141-339 2395; www.alamoguesthouse.com; 46 Gray St; basic/superior d £89/149, s/d without bathroom £49/59; @ 🤝) The Alamo may not sound like a peaceful spot, but that's exactly what this great place is. Opposite Kelvingrove Park, it feels miles from the city's hustle, but several of the best museums and restaurants in town are very close by. The decor is an enchanting mixture of antique furnishings and modern design, with excellent bathrooms, and the owners will make you very welcome.

Amadeus Guest House
B&B ££

(📞 0141-339 8257; www.amadeusguesthouse. co.uk; 411 North Woodside Rd; s £40-60, d £72-88; 🤝) Just off the bustle of Great Western Rd, a minute's walk from the subway, but on a quiet street by the riverside pathway, this B&B has compact bright rooms with cheerful cushions on the comfortable beds. There's a variety of room types, but prices are very good for all of them and come down substantially midweek. Breakfast is continental.

Embassy Apartments
APARTMENT ££

(📞 0141-946 6698; www.glasgowhotelsandapartments.co.uk; 8 Kelvin Dr; 1-/2-/4-person apt £60/80/99; P 🤝) This elegant self-catering place offers both facilities and location. Situated on a quiet, exclusive street right on the edge of the Botanical Gardens, the studio-style apartments sleep one to seven, have fully equipped kitchens and are sparkling clean. They're a particularly good option for couples and families with older kids. Prices are per night, but drop for longer rentals and vary extensively by demand.

Hotel Du Vin
HOTEL £££

(One Devonshire Gardens; 📞 0141-339 2001; www. hotelduvin.com; 1 Devonshire Gardens; r/ste from £180/440; P @ 🤝 ❄) This is traditionally Glasgow's favoured hotel of the rich and famous, and the patriarch of sophistication and comfort. A study in elegance, it's sumptuously decorated and occupies three classical sandstone terrace houses. There's a bewildering array of room types, all different in style and size. The hospitality is old-school courteous, and there's an excellent restaurant on site with a wine selection exceeding 600 varieties. Breakfast is extra.

✖ Eating

Glasgow is the best place to eat in Scotland, with an excellent range of eateries. The West End is the culinary centre of the city, with Merchant City also boasting an incredible concentration of quality restaurants and cafes. Pubs and bars mentioned in the Drinking section are often good lunchtime options.

✖ City Centre

★ Saramago Café Bar
CAFE £

(www.facebook.com/saramagocafebar; 350 Sauchiehall St; light meals £3-9; ☺ food 10am-10pm Mon-Wed, 10am-11.30pm Thu-Sat, noon-11.30pm Sun; 🤝 ✈) In the airy atmosphere of the Centre for Contemporary Arts, this place does a great line in eclectic vegan fusion food, with a range of top flavour combinations from around the globe. The upstairs bar has a great deck on steep Scott St and packs out inside with a friendly hipstery crowd enjoying the eclectic DJ sets and quality tap beers.

Brutti Ma Buoni
MEDITERRANEAN £

(📞 0141-552 0001; www.brunswickhotel.co.uk; 106 Brunswick St; mains £8-12; ☺ 11am-10pm Sun-Thu, to 11pm Fri & Sat; 🤝 🍴) Brutti is the antithesis of some of the pretentious places around the Merchant City. With dishes such as 'ugly but good' pizza and 'angry or peaceful' prawns, Brutti's menu draws a smile for its quirkiness and its prices. Italian and Spanish influences give rise to tapas-like servings or full-blown meals, which are imaginative, fresh and frankly delicious.

Where the Monkey Sleeps   CAFE £
(www.monkeysleeps.com; 182 West Regent St; dishes
£3-7; ⊙7am-4pm Mon-Fri; ⊛) This funky little
number in the middle of the business district
is a perfect escape from the ubiquitous coffee
chains. Laid-back and a little hippy, the bagels
and panini – with names like Witchfynder or
Meathammer – are highlights, as are some
very inventive dishes, such as the 'nuclear'
beans, dripping with cayenne and Tabasco.

Chippy Doon the Lane   FISH & CHIPS £
(www.thechippyglasgow.com; McCormick Lane, 84
Buchanan St; meals £6-10; ⊙noon-9.30pm; ⊛) ◢
Don't be put off by its location in an alleyway
off the shopping precinct: this is a cut above
your average chip shop. Sustainable seafood is
served in a chic space, all old-time brick, metal archways and jazz. Otherwise, chow down
on your takeaway at the wooden tables in the
lane or on Buchanan St itself.

★**Loon Fung**   CHINESE ££
(⌨0141-332 1240; www.loonfungglasgow.co.uk; 417
Sauchiehall St; mains £9-15; ⊙noon-4am; ⊛◢)
Accessed down the side of a travel agent, this
elegant Cantonese oasis is one of Scotland's
most authentic Chinese restaurants; indeed,
it's quite a surprise after a spot of late-night
dining to emerge to boisterous Sauchiehall
rather than Hong Kong. The dim-sum choices are very toothsome, and the seafood – try
the sea bass – really excellent. The ultra-late
opening hours make it a very flexible option.

Café Gandolfi   CAFE, BISTRO ££
(⌨0141-552 6813; 64 Albion St; mains £9-15;
⊙8am-11.30pm Mon-Sat, 9am-11.30pm Sun; ⊛)
In Merchant City, this cafe was once part
of the old cheese market. It's been pulling
in the punters for years and attracts an interesting mix of die-hard Gandolfers, the
upwardly mobile and tourists. It covers all
the bases with excellent breakfasts and coffee, an enticing upstairs bar, and top-notch
bistro food, covering Scottish and Continental bases in an atmospheric medieval-like
setting. There's an expansion, specialising in
fish, next door, with a takeaway outlet.

Red Onion   BISTRO ££
(⌨0141-221 6000; www.red-onion.co.uk; 257 West
Campbell St; mains £11-20; ⊙noon-10pm; ⊛◉)
This comfortable bistro buzzes with contented chatter. French, Mediterranean and Asian
touches add intrigue to the predominantly
British menu, and a good-value fixed-price
deal is available at lunch and dinnertime daily, though only for early diners at weekends.

Dakhin   INDIAN ££
(⌨0141-553 2585; www.dakhin.com; 89 Candleriggs;
mains £10-19; ⊙noon-2pm & 5-11pm Mon-Fri, 1-11pm
Sat & Sun; ⊛◢) This South Indian restaurant
breathes some fresh air into the city's curry
scene. Dishes are from all over the south, and
include dosas (thin rice-based crêpes) and
a yummy variety of fragrant coconut-based
curries. If you're really hungry, try a thali: an
assortment of Indian 'tapas'.

✖ **West End**

There are numerous excellent restaurants
in the West End. They cluster along Byres
Rd and just off it, on Ashton Lane and Ruth-
ven Lane. Gibson St and Great Western Rd
also have plenty to offer, while the Argyle
Rd strip in Finnieston has lots of interesting
new options.

Bay Tree Café   CAFE £
(www.thebaytreewestend.co.uk; 403 Great Western
Rd; mains £7-11; ⊙9am-10.30pm Mon-Sat, 9am-
9.30pm Sun; ⊛◢) There are many good cafes
in the two or three blocks around here, but
the Bay Tree is still a solid choice. With lots
of vegan and vegetarian options, it has smiling staff, filling mains (mostly Middle Eastern
and Greek), generous salads and a good range
of hot drinks. The cafe is famous for its all-day
breakfasts.

★**Stravaigin**   SCOTTISH ££
(⌨0141-334 2665; www.stravaigin.co.uk; 28 Gibson
St; mains £10-18; ⊙9am-11pm; ⊛) Stravaigin is
a foodie's delight, with a menu pushing the
boundaries of originality and offering creative culinary excellence. The contemporary
dining space in the basement has booth
seating, and helpful, laid-back waiting staff
to assist in deciphering the audacious menu.
Entry-level has a buzzing two-level bar; you
can also eat here. There are always plenty of
menu deals and special culinary nights.

★**Mother India**   INDIAN ££
(⌨0141-221 1663; www.motherindia.co.uk; 28 Westminster Tce, Sauchiehall St; mains £9-15; ⊙5.30-
10.30pm Mon-Thu, noon-11pm Fri, 1-11pm Sat, 1-10pm
Sun; ⊛◢⊞) Glasgow curry buffs forever
debate the merits of the city's numerous excellent South Asian restaurants; this features
in every discussion. It may lack the trendiness
of some of the up-and-comers but it's been a
stalwart for years, and the quality and innovation on show are superb. The three separate
dining areas are all attractive and they make
an effort for kids, with a separate menu.

Left Bank BISTRO ££

(🖉 0141-339 5969; www.theleftbank.co.uk; 33 Gibson St; mains £8-15; ⊘ 9am-10pm Mon-Fri, 10am-10pm Sat & Sun; 🗟🖉🗟🗟) 🖋 Huge windows fronting the street greet patrons of this outstanding eatery specialising in gastronomic delights and lazy afternoons. There are lots of little spaces filled with couches and chunky tables, reflecting a sense of intimacy. The large starter-menu can be treated like tapas, making it good for sharing. Lots of delightful creations use seasonal and local produce, with an eclectic variety of influences. Breakfasts and brunches are another highlight.

Finnieston SEAFOOD, PUB ££

(www.thefinniestonbar.com; 1125 Argyle St; mains £13-19; ⊘ noon-10pm Mon-Sat, noon-9pm Sun; 🗟) 🖋 A flagship of this increasingly vibrant strip, this gastropub recalls the area's sailing heritage with a cosily romantic below-decks atmosphere and artfully placed nautical motifs. It's been well thought through, with excellent mixed drinks and cocktails accompanying a short menu of really high-quality upmarket pub fare focusing on sustainable Scottish seafood.

★**Ubiquitous Chip** SCOTTISH £££

(🖉 0141-334 5007; www.ubiquitouschip.co.uk; 12 Ashton Lane; 2-/3-course lunches £16/20, mains £23-27, brasserie mains £9-14; ⊘ noon-2.30pm & 5-11pm; 🗟) 🖋 The original champion of Scottish produce, this is legendary for its unparalleled Scottish cuisine and lengthy wine list. Named to poke fun at Scotland's culinary reputation, it offers a French touch but resolutely Scottish ingredients, carefully selected and following sustainable principles. The elegant courtyard space offers some of Glasgow's highest-quality dining, while above, the cheaper brasserie menu offers exceptional value for money.

🍷 Drinking & Nightlife

Some of Britain's best nightlife is found in the din and sometimes roar of Glasgow's pubs and bars. There are as many different styles of bar as there are punters to guzzle in them. Some pubs and, especially, clubs have begun to enforce a 21-year-old minimum age.

Glasgow has one of Britain's biggest and best clubbing scenes, attracting devotees from afar. Glaswegians usually hit clubs after the pubs have closed, so many clubs offer discounted admission and cheaper drinks if you go early. Entry costs £5 to £10 (up to £25 for big events), although bars often hand out free passes. By law, clubs shut at 3am, so keep your ear to the ground to find out where the after parties are at.

Bars & Pubs

📍 City Centre

★**Artà** BAR, CLUB

(www.arta.co.uk; 62 Albion St; ⊘ 5pm-3am Thu-Sat; 🗟) This extraordinary place is so baroque that when you hear a Mozart concerto over the sound system, it wouldn't surprise you to see the man himself at the other end of the bar. Set in a former cheese market, it really does have to be seen to be believed. Despite the luxury, it's got a relaxed, chilled vibe. The big cocktails are great.

Babbity Bowster PUB

(www.babbitybowster.com; 16-18 Blackfriars St; ⊘ 11am-midnight Mon-Sat, 12.30pm-midnight Sun; 🗟) In a quiet corner of Merchant City, this handsome spot is perfect for a tranquil daytime drink, particularly in the adjoining beer garden. Service is attentive, and the smell of sausages may tempt you to lunch; it also offers accommodation. This is one of the city centre's most charming pubs, in one of its noblest buildings.

Corinthian Club BAR

(www.thecorinthianclub.co.uk; 191 Ingram St; ⊘ 11am-6am Mon-Sat, noon-6am Sun; 🗟) A breathtaking domed ceiling and majestic chandeliers make this casino a special space. Originally a bank and later Glasgow's High Court, this regal building's main bar, Teller's, has to be seen to be believed. Cosy wraparound seating and space to spare are complemented by a snug wine bar and a plush club downstairs in old court cells.

MacSorley's BAR

(www.macsorleys.com; 42 Jamaica St; ⊘ 11am-midnight Mon-Sat, 12.30pm-midnight Sun; 🗟) There's nothing better than a good horseshoe-shaped bar in Glasgow, and here the elegantly moulded windows and ceiling add a touch of class to this happy place, which offers live music every night and some excellent, inventive pub food. There's live music and good DJs at weekends – check the schedule on the website.

Butterfly & The Pig PUB

(www.thebutterflyandthepig.com; 153 Bath St; ⊘ 11am-1am Mon-Thu, 11am-3am Fri & Sat, 12.30pm-midnight Sun; 🗟) A breath of fresh air, the piggery is a little offbeat and makes you feel comfortable as soon as you plunge into its basement depths. The decor is eclectic with a retro feel and this adds to its familiarity. There's regular live jazz or similar, a sizeable menu – if you can decipher it – of pub grub, and a rather wonderful tearoom upstairs, great for breakfast before the pub opens.

Arches CAFE, BAR
(www.thearches.co.uk; 253 Argyle St; ⊙11am-midnight Mon-Sat; 🎅) A one-stop culture-entertainment fix, Arches is a cafe, bar, nightclub and theatre showing contemporary, avant-garde productions. The hotel-like entrance belies the deep interior, which make you feel as though you've discovered Hades' bohemian underworld. The crowd is mixed – hiking boots are as welcome as Versace. It also does a more-than-acceptable line in pub food.

Nice 'n' Sleazy BAR, CLUB
(www.nicensleazy.com; 421 Sauchiehall St; ⊙noon-3am; 🎅) On the rowdy Sauchiehall strip, students from the nearby School of Art make the buzz here reliably friendly. If you're over 35 you'll feel like a professor not a punter, but retro decor, a big selection of tap and bottled beers, 3am closing, and nightly alternative live music downstairs followed by a club at weekends make this a winner. There's also popular, cheap Tex-Mex food (dishes £6 to £9).

🍷 West End

Brewdog PUB
(www.brewdog.com; 1397 Argyle St; ⊙noon-midnight; 🎅) Perfect for a pint after visiting the Kelvingrove Museum, this is a great small spot offering the delicious range of artisanal beers from the brewery of the same name. Punk IPA is refreshingly hoppy and

GAY & LESBIAN GLASGOW

Glasgow has a vibrant scene, with the gay quarter found in and around the Merchant City (particularly Virginia, Wilson and Glassford Sts). The city's gay community has a reputation for being very friendly.

To tap into the scene, check out *The List* (www.list.co.uk), the free *Scots Gay* (www.scotsgay.co.uk) magazine and website. If you're in Glasgow in autumn, check out **Glasgay** (⊘0141-552 7575; www.glasgay.co.uk), a gay performing arts festival, held around October/November each year.

Many straight clubs and bars have gay and lesbian nights. The following are just a selection of gay and lesbian pubs and clubs in the city:

AXM (www.axmgroup.co.uk; 80 Glassford St; ⊙11pm-3am Wed & Thu, 10pm-3am Fri-Sun) This popular Manchester club's Glasgow branch is a cheery spot, not too scene-y, with all welcome.

Delmonica's (⊘0141-552 4803; www.delmonicas.co.uk; 68 Virginia St; ⊙noon-midnight) In the heart of the Pink Triangle, this is a popular bar, packed on weekday evenings but a pleasant spot for a quiet drink during the day. Drop in here before heading to the adjacent Polo Lounge, as they often give out free passes.

FHQ (www.fhqbar.co.uk; 10 John St; ⊙10pm-3am Fri & Sat) Fashionable women-only location in the heart of the Pink Triangle.

Polo Lounge (www.pologlasgow.co.uk; 84 Wilson St; ⊙11pm-3am Sun-Thu, 10pm-3am Fri, 9pm-3am Sat) This doesn't have the friendliest of staff, but it still attracts talent. The downstairs Polo Club and Club X areas pack out on weekends; just the main bars open on other nights.

Underground (www.underground-glasgow.com; 6a John St; ⊙noon-midnight Mon-Sat, 1pm-midnight Sun) Downstairs on cosmopolitan John St, this bar sports a relaxed crowd and, crucially, a free jukebox. You'll be listening to indie rather than Abba here.

Speakeasy (www.speakeasyglasgow.co.uk; 10 John St; ⊙5pm-1am Thu, 5pm-3am Fri & Sat) Relaxed and friendly bar that starts out pub-like and gets louder with gay anthem DJs as the night progresses. Serves food too.

Waterloo Bar (306 Argyle St; ⊙noon-midnight) This traditional pub is Scotland's oldest gay bar. It attracts punters of all ages. It's very friendly and, with a large group of regulars, a good place to meet people away from the scene.

fruity, more so than the formidable WattDickie, which comes in at a whisky-like 35%. Tasting flights mean you can try several, while burgers and dogs are on hand to soak it up.

Hillhead Bookclub   BAR
(www.hillheadbookclub.com; 17 Vinicombe St; ⊙ 11am-midnight Mon-Fri, 10am-midnight Sat & Sun; 🛜) Atmosphere in spades is the call sign of this easygoing West End bar. An ornate wooden ceiling overlooks two levels of well-mixed cocktails, seriously cheap drinks, comfort food and numerous intriguing decorative touches. There's even a ping-pong table in a cage.

Òran Mór   BAR, CLUB
(www.oran-mor.co.uk; 731 Great Western Rd; ⊙ 9am-3am Mon-Sat, 12.30pm-3am Sun; 🛜) Now some may be a little uncomfortable with the thought of drinking in a church. But we say: the Lord giveth. This sizeable converted church is now a bar, restaurant, club and theatre venue. Look out for the 'A Play, a Pie and a Pint' deals. There's an excellent array of whiskies. The only thing missing is holy water on your way in.

Brel   BAR
(www.brelbar.com; 39 Ashton Lane; ⊙ 11am-midnight Mon-Sat, 12.30pm-midnight Sun; 🛜) Perhaps the best bar on Ashton Lane, this can seem tightly packed, but there's a conservatory for eating out the back, so you can pretend you're sitting outside when it's raining, and when the sun does peek through, there's a beer garden. It has a huge range of Belgian beers, and also does mussels and langoustines, among other tasty fare.

Nightclubs

Sub Club   CLUB
(www.subclub.co.uk; 22 Jamaica St; ⊙ 11pm-3am Tue-Sun) Saturdays at the Sub Club are one of Glasgow's legendary nights, offering serious clubbing with a sound system that aficionados usually rate as the city's best.

The Arches   CLUB
(www.thearches.co.uk; 30 Midland St; ⊙ to 3am Thu-Sun, opening time varies) The Godfather of Glaswegian clubs, this has a design based around hundreds of arches slammed together, and has a range of different club nights. A must for funk and hip-hop freaks, it's one of the city's biggest clubs, pulling top DJs, and you'll also hear some of the UK's up-and-coming turntable spinners. The dingy road under the railway adds atmosphere.

Classic Grand   CLUB
(www.classicgrand.com; 18 Jamaica St; ⊙ 11pm-3am Thu-Sat) Rock, industrial, electronic, and powerpop grace the stage and the turntables at this unpretentious central venue. It doesn't take itself too seriously, drinks are cheap and the locals are welcoming.

Cathouse   CLUB
(www.cathouse.co.uk; 15 Union St; ⊙ 10.30pm-3am Thu-Sun) It's mostly rock, alternative and metal with a touch of goth and post-punk at this long-standing indie venue. There are two dance floors: upstairs is pretty intense with lots of metal and hard rock, downstairs is a little more tranquil.

ABC   CLUB
(O2 ABC; www.o2abcglasgow.co.uk; 300 Sauchiehall St) Both nightclub and venue, this star of Sauchiehall has two large concert spaces and several attractive bars. It's a good all-rounder, with a variety of DJs playing every Thursday to Saturday. Punters scrub up fairly well here.

☆ Entertainment

Glasgow is Scotland's entertainment city, from classical music, fine theatres and ballet to cheesy chart tunes and contemporary Scottish bands at the cutting edge of modern music. For concerts, a useful booking centre is **Tickets Scotland** (☑ 0141-204 5151; www.tickets-scotland.com; 237 Argyle St; ⊙ 9am-6pm Mon-Wed, Fri & Sat, 9am-7pm Thu, noon-5pm Sun).

Live Music

Glasgow is the king of Scotland's live-music scene. There are so many venues it's impossible to keep track of them all. Pick up a copy or check the website of the *Gig Guide* (www.gigguide.co.uk), available free in most pubs and venues, for the latest listings.

Several of the bars mentioned under Drinking & Nightlife are great for live music, including Classic Grand, MacSorley's (p816) and Nice 'n' Sleazy (p817). The ABC is also a popular venue.

King Tut's Wah Wah Hut   LIVE MUSIC
(☑ 0141-221 5279; www.kingtuts.co.uk; 272a St Vincent St; ⊙ noon-midnight) This is one of the city's premier live-music pub venues; it hosts bands every night of the week.

Barrowland   LIVE MUSIC
(www.glasgow-barrowland.com; 244 Gallowgate) A down-at-heel but exceptional old dancehall presenting some of the larger acts.

Clyde Auditorium
LIVE MUSIC

(☑0844 395 4000; www.secc.co.uk; Finnieston Quay) Also known as the Armadillo because of its bizarre shape, the Clyde adjoins the SECC auditorium, and caters for big national and international acts.

Hydro
LIVE MUSIC, SPORT

(☑0141-248 3000; www.thessehydro.com; Finnieston Quay) Another spectacular modern building to keep the adjacent Armadillo company, the Hydro amphitheatre is a phenomenally popular venue for big-name concerts and shows, and also hosted gymnastics and netball in the Commonwealth Games.

Theatres & Concert Halls

Theatre Royal
OPERA & BALLET

(☑0844 871 7627; www.atgtickets.com; 282 Hope St) Proudly sporting an eyecatching modern facelift, Glasgow's oldest theatre is the home of Scottish Opera and Scottish Ballet.

City Halls
CLASSICAL MUSIC

(☑0141-353 8000; www.glasgowconcerthalls.com; Candleriggs) In the heart of Merchant City, there are regular performances here by the Scottish Chamber Orchestra and the Scottish Symphony Orchestra. The adjacent Old Fruitmarket venue also has concerts.

Glasgow Royal Concert Hall
MUSIC

(☑0141-353 8000; www.glasgowconcerthalls.com; 2 Sauchiehall St) A feast of classical music is showcased at this concert hall, the modern home of the Royal Scottish National Orchestra.

Citizens' Theatre
THEATRE

(☑0141-429 0022; www.citz.co.uk; 119 Gorbals St) This is one of the top theatres in Scotland and it's well worth trying to catch a performance here.

Football

Two football clubs – Rangers (☑0871 702 1972; www.rangers.co.uk; Ibrox Stadium, 150 Edmiston Dr) and Celtic (☑0871 226 1888; www.celticfc.net; Celtic Park, Parkhead) – dominate the sporting scene in Scotland, having vastly more resources than other clubs and a long history (and rivalry). This runs along partisan lines, with Rangers representing Protestant supporters, and Celtic, Catholic. It's worth going to a game; both play in magnificent arenas with great atmosphere. Rangers have had to work their way back up the divisions after a financial meltdown.

🛍 Shopping

Boasting the UK's largest retail phalanx outside London, Glasgow is a shopaholic's paradise. The 'Style Mile' around Buchanan St, Argyle St and Merchant City (particularly upmarket Ingram Street) is a fashion hub, while the West End has quirkier, more bohemian shopping options: Byres Rd is great for vintage clothing.

Barras
MARKET

(www.glasgow-barrowland.com; btwn Gallowgate & London Rd; ⊙10am-5pm Sat & Sun) At Glasgow's legendary weekend flea market, the Barras on Gallowgate, cheap tat rules the roost these days, but it's still an intriguing stroll, as much for the assortment of local characters as what's on offer. People come here just for a wander, and it has the feel of a nearly vanished Britain of whelk stalls and rag-and-bone merchants. Watch your wallet.

ℹ Information

The List (www.list.co.uk), available from newsagents (£2.50), is an invaluable four-weekly guide to

---

LOCAL KNOWLEDGE

CINDY-LOU RAMSAY: TV CAMERA OPERATOR & PHOTOGRAPHER

Top photography spot? Pollok Park. The park itself is gorgeous and full of lots of good walks for walkers and cyclists to explore. It also takes you to the famous Burrell Collection, which may not look like much from the outside, but it's a really calming, beautiful building on the inside and jam-packed with exhibits from all over the world.

Favourite spots for live music? Barrowland and King Tut's Wah Wah Hut. Barrowland is an old, tired-looking ballroom badly in need of a bit of a wee facelift, but you're guaranteed to get an unforgettable atmosphere; this is the reason that the biggest bands in the world continue to grace its stage. King Tut's is a much smaller venue for getting 'up close and personal' with some great bands.

Pub for a pint and read of the paper? Blackfriars in the Merchant City.

Typical local words? Blethering (chatting)! Glaswegians tend to do a lot of it, especially if you decide to ask them about their city!

films, theatre, cabaret, music, clubs – the works – in Glasgow and Edinburgh. The excellent *Eating & Drinking Guide* (£5.95), published by the *List* every second April, covers both Glasgow and Edinburgh.

INTERNET ACCESS

Gallery of Modern Art (☑ 0141-229 1996; Royal Exchange Sq; ⊘ 10am-5pm Mon-Wed & Sat, 10am-8pm Thu, 11am-5pm Fri & Sun; ☎) Basement library; free internet access. Bookings recommended.

iCafe (www.icafe.uk.com; 250 Woodlands Rd; per hr £2.50; ⊘ 8.30am-10.30pm; ☎) Sip a coffee and munch on a pastry while you check your emails on super-fast connections. Wi-fi too. It's actually a very good cafe in its own right. There are other branches, including one on Sauchiehall St (www.icafe.uk.com; 315 Sauchiehall St; ⊘ 7am-11pm Mon-Sat, 8am-11pm Sun; ☎).

MEDICAL SERVICES

Glasgow Royal Infirmary (☑ 0141-211 4000; www.nhsggc.org.uk; 84 Castle St) Medical emergencies and outpatient facilities.

TOURIST INFORMATION

Airport Tourist Office (☑ 0141-848 4440; Glasgow International Airport; ⊘ 7.30am-5pm Mon-Sat, 8am-3.30pm Sun)

Glasgow Information Centre (☑ 0845 225 5121; www.visitscotland.com; 170 Buchanan St; ⊘ 9am-6pm Mon-Sat, noon-4pm or 10am-5pm Sun; ☎) In the heart of the shopping area.

❶ Getting There & Away

AIR

Ten miles west of the city, **Glasgow International Airport** (GLA; ☑ 0844 481 5555; www.glasgowairport.com) handles international and domestic flights. **Prestwick Airport** (PIK; ☑ 0871 223 0700; www.glasgowprestwick.com), 30 miles southwest of Glasgow, is used by **Ryanair** (www.ryanair.com) and some other budget airlines, with connections to the rest of Britain and Europe.

BUS

All long-distance buses arrive at and depart from **Buchanan bus station** (☑ 0141-333 3708; www.spt.co.uk; Killermont St), which has pricey lockers, ATMs, and a cafe with wi-fi.

Your first port of call if you're looking for the cheapest fare should be **Megabus** (www.megabus.com), which offers very cheap demand-dependent prices on many major bus routes, including to Edinburgh and London.

Scottish Citylink (☑ 0871 266 3333; www.citylink.co.uk) has buses to Edinburgh (£7.30, 1¼ hours, every 15 minutes) and most major towns in Scotland. National Express also runs daily to several English cities.

CAR & MOTORCYLE

There are numerous car-rental companies; both big names and discount operators have airport offices. Companies include the following:

Arnold Clark (☑ 0141-423 9559; www.arnoldclarkrental.com; 43 Allison St)

Avis (☑ 0844 544 6064; www.avis.co.uk; 70 Lancefield St)

Europcar (☑ 0844 384 8471; www.europcar.co.uk; 76 Lancefield Quay)

TRAIN

As a general rule, Glasgow Central station serves southern Scotland, England and Wales, and Queen St station serves the north and east. Buses run between the two stations every 10 minutes. There are direct trains to London's Euston station; they're much quicker (advance purchase single £56, full fare off-peak/peak £130/176, 4½ hours, more than hourly) and more comfortable than the bus.

Scotrail (☑ 08457 55 00 33; www.scotrail.co.uk) runs Scottish trains. Destinations include: Edinburgh (£12.50, 50 minutes, every 15 minutes), Oban (£23.10, three hours, three to six daily), Fort William (£28.20, 3¾ hours, four to five daily), Dundee (£21.30, 1½ hours, hourly), Aberdeen (£38.20, 2½ hours, hourly) and Inverness (£84.70, 3½ hours, 10 daily, four on Sunday).

❶ Getting Around

TO/FROM THE AIRPORT

There are buses every 10 or 15 minutes from Glasgow International Airport to Buchanan bus station via Central and Queen St stations (single/return £6/8.50, 25 minutes). This is a 24-hour service. The 747 bus covers the same route via Finnieston and Kelvingrove, taking longer. A taxi costs £24. There are also buses from Buchanan bus station direct to/from Edinburgh Airport (£11, one hour, half-hourly).

BICYCLE

There are several places to hire a bike; the tourist office has a full list.

Alpine Bikes (www.alpinebikes.com; 6 St Georges Pl; per day £20; ⊘ 9.30am-6pm Mon-Sat, 11am-5pm Sun, 9.30am-7pm Thu) Hardtail and roadbikes available.

PUBLIC TRANSPORT

Bus City bus services, mostly run by **First Glasgow** (☑ 0141-423 6600; www.firstglasgow.com), are frequent. You can buy tickets when you board buses, but on most you must have the exact change. Short journeys in town cost £1.20 or £1.95; a day ticket (£4.10) is good value and valid until 1am, when a night service starts. A weekly ticket is £16.50. The tourist office hands out the highly complicated SPT Bus Map, detailing all routes in and around the city.

Train & Underground There's an extensive suburban network of trains in and around Glasgow; tickets should be bought before travel if the station is staffed, or from the conductor if it isn't. There's also an underground line, the subway, that serves 15 stations in the centre, west and south of the city (single £1.60). The train network connects with the subway at Buchanan St station. The Discovery Ticket (£4) gives unlimited travel on the subway for a day, while the Roundabout ticket gives a day's unlimited train and subway travel for £6.30. The subway annoyingly shuts down at around 6pm on a Sunday.

Combined Ticket The Daytripper ticket gives you a day's unlimited travel on buses, the Subway, rail and some ferries in the Glasgow region. It costs £11.20 for one or £19.80 for two. Two kids per adult are included free.

AROUND GLASGOW

Other appealing destinations within easy reach of Glasgow, such as Loch Lomond, are covered elsewhere.

Lanark & New Lanark

POP 8900

Below the market town of Lanark, in an attractive gorge by the River Clyde, is the World Heritage Site of **New Lanark**, an intriguing collection of restored mill buildings and warehouses.

Once the largest cotton-spinning complex in Britain, it was better known for the pioneering social experiments of Robert Owen, who managed the mill from 1800. New Lanark is really a memorial to this enlightened capitalist. You'll need at least half a day to explore this site, as there's plenty to see, and appealing walks along the riverside.

◉ Sights & Activities

★**New Lanark Visitor Centre**   MUSEUM
(www.newlanark.org; adult/child/family £8.50/6/25; ⊙10am-5pm Apr-Oct, 10am-4pm Nov-Mar) The main attractions of this World Heritage mill town are accessed via a single ticket. These include a huge working spinning mule, producing woollen yarn, and the **Historic Schoolhouse**, which contains an innovative, high-tech journey to New Lanark's past via a 3D hologram of the spirit of Annie McLeod, a 10-year-old mill girl who describes life here in 1820. The kids will love it as it's very realistic, although the 'do good for all mankind' theme is a little overbearing.

**Falls of Clyde
Wildlife Centre**   WILDLIFE RESERVE
(www.scottishwildlifetrust.co.uk; New Lanark; adult/child £3/1; ⊙10am-4pm) The wildlife centre is by the river in New Lanark and features child-friendly displays focused on badgers, bats, peregrine falcons and other prominent species. In season (April to July), there's a live video feed of peregrines nesting nearby. Entry is a pound cheaper if you buy it together with the New Lanark Visitor Centre entrance. The centre also organises various activities in summer, including badger-watching.

From the centre, you can walk through the beautiful nature reserve up to Corra Linn (¾ mile, 30 minutes) and Bonnington Linn (1½ miles, one hour), two of the Falls of Clyde that inspired Turner and Wordsworth. You could return via the muddier path on the opposite bank, pass New Lanark, and cross the river a little further downstream to make a circular walk of it (3 miles, three hours).

🛏 Sleeping

New Lanark makes a very relaxing, attractive place to stay.

New Lanark SYHA   HOSTEL £
(☑01555-666710; www.syha.org.uk; dm/tw £17/45; ⊙mid-Mar–mid-Oct; P@🕿) This hostel has a great location in an old mill building by the River Clyde, in the heart of the New Lanark complex. It has comfortable en suite dormitories and a really good downstairs common area. It does breakfasts and dinners and will also make a packed lunch. Closed between 10am and 4pm.

New Lanark Mill Hotel   HOTEL ££
(☑01555-667200; www.newlanarkmillhotel.co.uk; r £99-119; P@🕿🐾) Cleverly converted from an 18th-century mill, this hotel is full of character and is a stone's throw from the major attractions. It has luxury rooms (only a little extra for a spacious superior room), with contemporary art on the walls and views of the churning Clyde below, as well as self-catering accommodation in charming **cottages** (£89 to £109). There are good facilities for the disabled here. The hotel also serves decent meals (bar meals £5 to £11, restaurant mains £14 to £16).

ℹ Information

Lanark Information Centre (☑01555-661661; lanark@visitscotland.com; Ladyacre Rd; ⊙10am-5pm) Close to the bus and train stations. Closed Sundays October to March.

ⓘ Getting There & Around

Lanark is 25 miles southeast of Glasgow. Express bus 240X runs hourly Monday to Saturday (£6, one hour); trains from Glasgow Central also run (£6.60, 55 minutes, every 30 minutes, hourly on Sunday).

It's a pleasant walk to New Lanark, but there's also a half-hourly bus service from the train station (daily). If you need a taxi, call **Clydewide** (☏ 0800-050 9264; www.clydewidetaxis.co.uk).

BORDERS REGION

The Borders has had a rough history: centuries of war and plunder have left a battle-scarred landscape, encapsulated by the magnificent ruins of the Border abbeys. Their wealth was an irresistible magnet during cross-frontier wars, and they were destroyed and rebuilt numerous times. Today these massive stone shells are the region's finest attraction.

But the Borders is also genteel. Welcoming villages with ancient traditions pepper the countryside and grandiose mansions await exploration. It's fine walking and cycling country too.

Kelso

POP 5600

Kelso, a prosperous market town with a broad, cobbled square flanked by Georgian buildings, has a cheery feel and historic appeal. During the day it's a busy little place,

---

WALKING ROUTES

··

The region's most famous walk is challenging 212-mile **Southern Upland Way** (www.southernuplandway.gov.uk). If you want a sample, one of the best bits is the three- to four-day section from Dalry to Beattock.

Another long-distance walk is 62-mile **St Cuthbert's Way** (www.stcuthbertsway.info), inspired by the travels of St Cuthbert, a 7th-century saint who lived at the first Melrose monastery. It crosses some superb scenery between Melrose and Lindisfarne (in England).

The **Borders Abbeys Way** (www.bordersabbeysway.com) links all the great Border abbeys in a 65-mile circuit. For shorter walks and especially circular loops in the hills, Melrose, Jedburgh and Kelso all make ideal bases.

---

but after 8pm you'll have the streets to yourself. The town has a lovely site at the junction of the Tweed and Teviot, and is one of the most enjoyable places in the Borders.

◉ Sights

Floors Castle   CASTLE
(www.floorscastle.com;   adult/child   £8.50/4.50; ⊙ 10.30am-5pm mid-Apr–mid-Oct) Grandiose Floors Castle is Scotland's largest inhabited mansion, home to the Duke of Roxburghe, and overlooks the Tweed about a mile west of Kelso. Built by William Adam in the 1720s, the original Georgian simplicity was 'improved' in the 1840s with the addition of rather ridiculous battlements and turrets. Inside, view the vivid colours of the 17th-century Brussels tapestries in the drawing room and the intricate oak carvings in the ornate ballroom.

Kelso Abbey   RUIN
(HS;   www.historic-scotland.gov.uk;   Bridge St; ⊙ 9.30am-6.30pm Apr-Sep, 9.30am-4.30pm Sat-Wed Oct-Mar) **FREE** Once one of the richest abbeys in southern Scotland, Kelso Abbey was built by the Tironensians, an order founded in Picardy and brought to the Borders around 1113 by David I. English raids in the 16th century reduced it to ruins, though what little remains today is some of the finest surviving Romanesque architecture in Scotland.

🛏 Sleeping

★ **Old Priory**   B&B **££**
(☏ 01573-223030;   www.theoldpriorykelso.com; 33 Woodmarket St; s/d £55/85; P 🛜) Fantastic rooms here are allied with numerous personal details – they turn down the beds at night and make you feel very welcome. Doubles are top-notch and the family room has to be seen to be believed. The good news extends to the garden – perfect for a coffee in the morning – and a comfortable sitting room and conservatory lounge. The huge windows flood the rooms with natural light.

★ **Edenbank House**   B&B **££**
(☏ 01573-226734; www.edenbank.co.uk; Stichill Rd; s/d £45/80; P 🛜) Half a mile down the road to Stichill, this grand Victorian house sits in spacious grounds where only the bleating of lambs in the green fields and birds in the garden break the silence. It's a fabulous place, with huge opulent rooms, lovely views over the fields, and incredibly warm, generous hospitality. Breakfast features homemade produce, and a laissez-faire attitude makes for an utterly relaxing stay. Call ahead.

Ednam House Hotel   HOTEL **£££**
(☑ 01573-224168; www.ednamhouse.com; Bridge
St; P ♠ ⊛) The genteel, Georgian Ednam
House, touched with a quiet dignity, contains
many of its original features, with fine gardens overlooking the river. We've not included
prices, for at the time of writing a new owner
planned to gradually convert it into a luxury
country-house hotel, keeping it open all the
while. During salmon season, from the end of
August until November, the hotel is very busy.
Some of the rooms have lovely river views.

✗ Eating & Drinking

★ **Cobbles**   PUB FOOD **££**
(☑ 01573-223548; www.thecobblesinn.co.uk; 7
Bowmont St; mains £10-17; ⊙ noon-2.30pm & 5.45-
9pm; ♠) We've included the phone number
for a reason: this inn off the main square
is so popular you will need to book a table
at weekends. It's cheery, very welcoming,
warm, and serves excellent upmarket pub
food in generous portions. Pick and mix
from the bar menu, blackboard specials and
upmarket options. Leave room for cheese
and/or dessert. The bar's own microbrewed
ales are really excellent. A cracking place.

ⓘ Information

Kelso Information Centre (☑ 01573-228055;
www.visitscottishborders.com; The Square;
⊙ 10am-4pm Mon-Sat Apr-Oct, to 5pm plus
10am-2pm Sun Jul & Aug)

ⓘ Getting There & Away

There are frequent services to Edinburgh (£7.20,
two hours), other Borders towns and Berwick-
upon-Tweed.

Melrose

POP 2300

Charming Melrose is a village running on the
well-greased wheels of tourism. Sitting at the
feet of the three heather-covered Eildon Hills,
Melrose has a classic market square and one
of the great abbey ruins. Just outside town
is Abbotsford, the home of Sir Walter Scott,
which makes another superb visit.

◎ Sights

★ **Melrose Abbey**   RUIN
(HS; www.historic-scotland.gov.uk; adult/child
£5.50/3.30; ⊙ 9.30am-5.30pm Apr-Sep, to 4.30pm
Oct-Mar) Perhaps the most interesting of the
Border abbeys, red-sandstone Melrose was re-
peatedly destroyed by the English in the 14th

WORTH A TRIP

SMAILHOLM TOWER

Perched on a rocky knoll above a small
lake, this narrow stone **tower** (HS;
www.historic-scotland.gov.uk; adult/child
£4.50/2.70; ⊙ 9.30am-5.30pm Apr-Sep)
provides one of the most evocative
sights in the Borders and keeps its
bloody history alive. Although displays
inside are sparse, the panoramic view
from the top is worth the climb. The
tower is 6 miles west of Kelso, a mile
south of Smailholm village on the
B6397. First bus 66 between Kelso and
Galashiels stops in Smailholm village.

The nearby privately-owned farm,
Sandyknowe, was owned by Sir Walter
Scott's grandfather. As Scott himself
recognised, his imagination was fired
by the ballads and stories he heard as a
child at Sandyknowe, and by the ruined
tower a stone's throw away.

---

century. The remaining broken shell is pure
Gothic and the ruins are famous for their decorative stonework – look out for the pig gargoyle playing the bagpipes. Though Melrose
had a monastery way back in the 7th century,
this abbey was founded by David I in 1136 for
Cistercian monks, and later rebuilt by Robert
the Bruce, whose heart is buried here.

✲ Festivals & Events

Melrose Rugby Sevens   SPORT
(www.melrose7s.com) In mid-April rugby followers fill the town to see the week-long
competition.

⊨ Sleeping

★ **Old Bank House**   B&B **££**
(☑ 01896-823712; www.oldbankhousemelrose.co.uk;
27 Buccleuch St; s/d £45/70; ♠ ⊛) In the middle
of town, this is a superb B&B in a charming
old building. The owner's artistic touch is
evident throughout, from walls covered with
paintings, some his own, a house full of curios
and Art Nouveau features, and a sumptuous
breakfast room. Rooms are spacious with
comfortable furniture and top modern bathrooms; they are complemented by a generous
can-do attitude. They go the extra mile here
and that makes it a great Borders base.

★ **Townhouse**   HOTEL **£££**
(☑ 01896-822645; www.thetownhousemelrose.
co.uk; Market Sq; s/d £95/130; P ♠) The classy

HERMITAGE CASTLE

The 'guardhouse of the bloodiest valley in Britain', **Hermitage Castle** (HS; www.historic-scotland.gov.uk; adult/child £4.50/2.70; ⊘ 9.30am-5.30pm Apr-Sep) embodies the brutal history of the Scottish Borders. Desolate but proud, with its massive squared stone walls, it looks more like a lair for orc raiding parties than a home for Scottish nobility, and is one of the bleakest and most stirring of Scottish ruins.

Strategically crucial, the castle was the scene of many a dark deed and dirty deal with the English invaders, all of which rebounded heavily on the perfidious Scottish lord in question. Here, in 1338, Sir William Douglas imprisoned his enemy Sir Alexander Ramsay and deliberately starved him to death. Ramsay survived for 17 days by eating grain that trickled into his pit (which can still be seen) from the granary above. In 1566, Mary, Queen of Scots famously visited the wounded tenant of the castle, Lord Bothwell, here. Fortified, he recovered to (probably) murder her husband, marry her himself, then abandon her months later and flee into exile.

The castle is about 12 miles south of Hawick on the B6357.

Townhouse exudes warmth and professionalism, and has some of the best rooms in town, tastefully furnished. There are superior rooms (£147) that are enormous in size with lavish furnishings and excellent en suites, some with Jacuzzi. Standard rooms are a fair bit smaller but recently refurbished and very comfortable. It's well worth the price.

✖ Eating

Townhouse   SCOTTISH ££
(☑ 01896-822645; www.thetownhousemelrose.co.uk; Market Sq; mains £10-16; ⊘ noon-2pm & 6-9pm Mon-Thu, noon-2pm & 6-9.30pm Fri & Sat, noon-2.30pm & 6-9pm Sun; 🐾) The brasserie and restaurant here turn out just about the best gourmet cuisine in town and offer decent value. There's some rich, elaborate, beautifully presented fare here, with plenty of venison and other game choices, but for a lighter feed you can always opt for the range of creative lunchtime sandwiches.

Marmion's Brasserie   SCOTTISH ££
(☑ 01896-822245; www.marmionsbrasserie.co.uk; 5 Buccleuch St; mains £11-17; ⊘ noon-3pm & 6-9pm Mon-Sat; 🐾✏) This atmospheric, oak-panelled niche serves snacks all day, but the lunch and dinner menus include modern Scottish bistro classics: expect duck breast, chicken stuffed with haggis, smoked salmon and the like, but also several more-than-token offerings for vegetarians.

ⓘ Information

Melrose Information Centre (☑ 01896-822283; www.visitscottishborders.com; Abbey St; ⊘ 10am-4pm Mon-Sat, noon-4pm Sun Apr-Oct) Located by the abbey.

ⓘ Getting There & Away

Buses run to/from nearby Galashiels, with connections for Edinburgh (£7.20, two hours, hourly) and other Borders destinations.

Around Melrose

In the vicinity of Melrose are a couple of excellent attractions intimately connected with Sir Walter Scott.

⊙ Sights

★ **Abbotsford**   HISTORIC HOUSE
(www.scottsabbotsford.co.uk; visitor centre free, house adult/child £8.75/4.50; ⊘ 10am-5pm Apr-Sep, 10am-4pm Oct-Mar) Just outside Melrose, this is where to discover the life and works of Sir Walter Scott, to whom we arguably owe both the modern novel and our mind's-eye view of Scotland. This whimsical, fabulous house where he lived – and which ruined him when his publishers went bust – really brings this 19th-century writer to life. The grounds on the banks of the Tweed are lovely, and Scott drew much inspiration from rambles in the surrounding countryside.

★ **Dryburgh Abbey**   RUIN
(HS; www.historic-scotland.gov.uk; adult/child £5/3; ⊘ 9.30am-5.30pm Apr-Sep, 9.30am-4.30pm Oct-Mar) This is the most beautiful and complete of the Border abbeys, partly because the neighbouring town of Dryburgh no longer exists (another victim of the wars) and partly for its lovely site by the Tweed in a sheltered birdsong-filled valley. Dating from about 1150, the abbey belonged to the Premonstratensians, a religious order founded

in France, and conjures 12th-century monastic life more successfully than its nearby counterparts. The pink-hued stone ruins are the burial place of Sir Walter Scott.

The abbey is 5 miles southeast of Melrose on the B6404, which passes the famous Scott's View outlook. Hike there along the southern bank of the River Tweed, or take a bus to the nearby village of Newtown St Boswells.

Jedburgh

POP 4000

Attractive Jedburgh, where many old buildings and wynds (narrow alleys) have been intelligently restored, invites exploration by foot. It's centred on the noble skeleton of its ruined abbey.

⊙ Sights

★ **Jedburgh Abbey**   RUIN
(HS; www.historic-scotland.gov.uk; Abbey Rd; adult/child £5.50/3.30; ⊙ 9.30am-5.30pm Apr-Sep, 9.30am-4.30pm Oct-Mar) Dominating the town skyline, this was the first of the great Border abbeys to be passed into state care, and it shows – audio and visual presentations telling the abbey's story are scattered throughout the carefully preserved ruins (good for the kids). The red-sandstone ruins are roofless but relatively intact, and the ingenuity of the master mason can be seen in some of the rich (if somewhat faded) stone carvings in the nave. The abbey was founded in 1138 by David I as a priory for Augustinian canons.

Mary, Queen of Scots House   HISTORIC HOUSE
(Queen St; ⊙ 9.30am-4.30pm Mon-Sat, 10.30am-4pm Sun early Mar-Nov) FREE Mary stayed at this beautiful 16th-century tower house in 1566 after her famous ride to visit the injured earl of Bothwell, her future husband, at Hermitage Castle. The interesting exhibition evokes the sad saga of Mary's life and death. Various objects associated with her – including a lock of her hair – are on display.

⌂ Sleeping

Maplebank   B&B £
(☎ 01835-862051; maplebank3@btinternet.com; 3 Smiths Wynd; s/d £30/50; P 🐾) It's very pleasing to come across places like this, where it really feels like you're staying in someone's home. In this case, that someone is a bit like your favourite aunt: friendly, chaotic and generous. There's lots of clutter and it's very informal.

The rooms are comfortable and large, and share a good bathroom. Breakfast (particularly if you like fruit, yoghurts, homemade jams and a selection of everything) is much better than you get at most posher places.

Willow Court   B&B £££
(☎ 01835-863702; www.willowcourtjedburgh.co.uk; The Friars; d £80-86; P 🐾) It seems inadequate to call this impressive option a B&B; it's more like a boutique hotel. Three impeccable rooms with elegant wallpaper, showroom bathrooms and great beds are complemented by a courteous professional welcome. Breakfast can include a grapefruit medley or smoked salmon, and you could spend hours in the conservatory lounge admiring the views over the garden and town.

✗ Eating

Clock Tower   BISTRO ££
(☎ 01835-869788; www.clocktowerbistro.co.uk; Abbey Pl; mains £9-15; ⊙ 10am-4pm & 6-9pm Tue-Sat; 🐾) Opposite the skeleton of the abbey, this place has an eclectic menu of upmarket bistro fare, drizzling truffle oil or Rioja jus over ingredients like tuna steaks, duck confit or west coast scallops. Prices are good for this level of food, though some of the flavours could be more adventurous.

ⓘ Information

There's a free wi-fi zone around the town centre.
Jedburgh Information Centre (☎ 01835-863170; jedburgh@visitscotland.com; Murray's

---

THE RIDING OF THE MARCHES

The Riding of the Marches, also known as the Common Riding, takes place in early summer in the major Borders towns. Like many Scottish festivals it has ancient origins, dating back to the Middle Ages, when riders would be sent to the town boundary to check on the common lands. The colourful event normally involves extravagant convoys of horse riders following the town standard as it is paraded along a well-worn route. Festivities vary between towns but usually involve lots of singing, sport, pageants, concerts and plenty of whisky. If you want to zero in on the largest of the Ridings, head to Jedburgh for the **Jethart Callant's Festival** (www.jethartcallantsfestival.com) in late June.

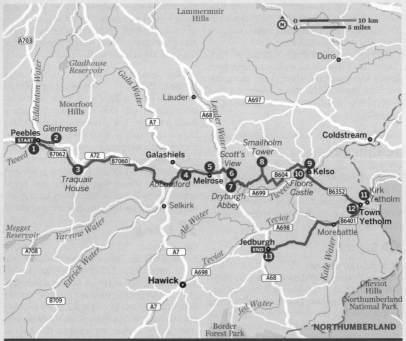

Cycling Tour
Cycling the Borders

START PEEBLES
END JEDBURGH
LENGTH 80 MILES; TWO TO THREE DAYS

With the exception of the main A-roads, traffic is sparse, which, along with the beauty of the countryside, makes the Borders ideal cycling country. This route takes you through classic Borders countryside, visiting abbey ruins and stately homes along the way.

1 Peebles is easily accessed on the bus from Edinburgh and offers bike hire. Check out the downhill routes at nearby **2 Glentress** (p827) before following the south bank of the Tweed eastwards on the B7062. **3 Traquair House** (p827) is a great stop on this route. Continue on the south side, signposted as part of the National Cycle Network, before crossing the river, bearing right onto the A708, then turning left (B7060) before the river recrosses the Tweed at a bridge with traffic lights. Following signposts, this will eventually take you past **4 Abbotsford** (p824), home of Sir Walter Scott, into **5 Melrose**, a good overnighting option.

From Melrose, it's a short but stiff ascent to **6 Scott's View**, where you can get your breath back with the marvellous vista, then a swift descent back to river level and **7 Dryburgh Abbey** (p824). Past the abbey, turn left on the B6404, then detour left for just over a mile to visit **8 Smailholm Tower** (p823) (signposted). From here it's an easy six miles into **9 Kelso**, where you should leave time to see impressive **10 Floors Castle** (p822).

You've seen three of the four great ruined Border Abbeys by now, so it's time to complete the set by heading south to the fourth. There are several possible routes, but a nice quiet, picturesque one (25 miles) heads out of Kelso southeast on the B6352. Have a pint in the twin walkers' villages of **11 Town Yetholm** and **12 Kirk Yetholm**, then head west on the B6401 through the village of Morebattle, then left 1½ miles beyond down a rustic road signposted to Cessford/Crailinghall. Follow this south, then west all the way to **13 Jedburgh**. There are bus connections from here back to Peebles.

All the towns mentioned have good overnighting options. Other routes are also detailed at www.cyclescottishborders.com.

Green; ☉ 9.15am-5pm Mon-Sat, 10am-4pm Sun Apr-Oct, 10am-4pm Mon-Sat Nov-Mar; ☎) Head tourist office for the Borders region. Very helpful.

❶ Getting There & Away

Jedburgh has good bus connections to Hawick, Melrose and Kelso (all around 25 minutes, roughly hourly, two-hourly on Sunday). Buses also run to Edinburgh (£7.20, two hours, hourly Monday to Saturday, five Sunday).

Peebles

POP 8400

With a picturesque main street set on a ridge between the River Tweed and the Eddleston Water, Peebles is one of the most handsome of the Border towns. Though it lacks a major sight, the agreeable atmosphere and good walking options in the rolling, wooded hills thereabouts will entice you to linger for a couple of days. There are some excellent eating choices.

🏃 Activities

Two miles east of town, off the A72 and in **Glentress forest**, the busiest of the **7stanes** (www. 7stanesmountainbiking.com) mountain-biking hubs also has osprey viewing and marked walking trails. The **shop** (☑ 01721-724522; www. alpinebikes.com; ☉ 9am-5pm Mon Fri, 9am 5.30pm Sat & Sun) here hires rigs and will put you on the right trail for your ability. These are some of Britain's best biking routes. **Go Ape** (www. goape.co.uk) also has swing and zipline forest routes here, and there are camping huts available (see www.glentressforestlodges.co.uk). In town, you can hire bikes to explore the region from **Glentress Bikes** (☑ 01721-729756; 20A Northgate; day hire £22).

🛏 Sleeping & Eating

Tontine Hotel HOTEL **££**
(☑ 01721-720892; www.tontinehotel.com; High St; s £55, d £110-120; P 🛜 🐾) Right in the heart of things, this is a bastion of Borders hospitality. Refurbished rooms have high comfort levels, modish colours and top-notch bathrooms, while service couldn't be more helpful. There's a small supplement for rooms with four-poster beds and/or river views. There's a good restaurant and bar here: it's the heart of town.

Rowanbrae B&B **££**
(☑ 01721-721630; www.aboutscotland.co.uk/peebles/rowanbrae.html; 103 Northgate; s/d £42/65;

DON'T MISS

TRAQUAIR HOUSE

One of Scotland's great country houses, **Traquair House** (www.traquair.co.uk; adult/child/family £8.50/4.25/23; ☉ 11am-5pm Easter-Sep, 11am-4pm Oct, 11am-3pm Sat & Sun Nov) has a powerful, ethereal beauty, and exploring it is like time travel. Odd, sloping floors and a musty odour bestow a genuine feel, and parts of the building are believed to have been constructed long before the first official record of its existence in 1107. The massive tower house was gradually expanded over the next 500 years, but has remained virtually unchanged since the 17th century. Traquair is 1.5 miles south of Innerleithen, about 6 miles southeast of Peebles.

Since the 15th century, the house has belonged to various branches of the Stuart family, and the family's unwavering Catholicism and loyalty to the Stuart cause led to famous visitors like Mary, Queen of Scots and Bonnie Prince Charlie, but also to numerous problems after the deposal of James II of England in 1688. The family's estate, wealth and influence were gradually whittled away, as life as a Jacobite became a furtive, clandestine affair.

One of Traquair's most interesting places is the concealed room where priests secretly lived and performed Mass – up until 1829 when the Catholic Emancipation Act was finally passed. Other beautiful, time-worn rooms hold fascinating relics, including the cradle used by Mary for her son, James VI of Scotland (who also became James I of England), and fascinating letters from the Jacobite Earls of Traquair and their families, including a particularly moving one written from death row in the Tower of London.

The main gates to the house were locked by one earl in the 18th century until the day a Stuart king reclaims the throne in London, so meanwhile you'll have to enter by a side gate.

In addition to the house, there's a garden **maze**, a small **brewery** producing the tasty Bear Ale, and a series of **craft workshops**.

Bus 62 runs from Edinburgh via Peebles to Innerleithen and on to Galashiels and Melrose.

🖤) In a quiet cul-de-sac but not far from the main street, this hospitable spot treats its guests like family friends. It's pleasantly and comfortably old-fashioned; there are three upstairs bedrooms, two en suite, and a commodious guest lounge for relaxation.

★ Coltman's
BISTRO, DELI ££

(www.coltmans.co.uk; 71 High St; mains £11-19; ⊙10am-5pm Sun-Wed, 10am-10pm Thu-Sat; 🖤) ✐ This main street deli has numerous temptations, such as excellent cheeses and Italian smallgoods, as well as perhaps Scotland's tastiest sausage roll. Behind the shop, the good-looking dining area serves up confident bistro fare and light snacks with a variety of culinary influences, using top-notch local ingredients.

Sunflower Restaurant
FUSION ££

(☑01721-722420; www.thesunflower.net; 4 Bridgegate; lunch £6-9, dinner mains £12-16; ⊙noon-3pm Mon-Sat, plus 6-9pm Fri & Sat; 🖉) ✐ The Sunflower, with its warmly decorated dining room, is in a quiet spot off the main drag and has a reputation that brings diners from all over southern Scotland. It serves good salads for lunch and has an admirable menu in the evenings, with creative and elegant dishes that always include standout vegetarian fare.

ℹ Information

Peebles Information Centre (☑01721-723159; www.visitscottishborders.com; High St; ⊙9am-5pm Mon-Sat, 11am-4pm Sun) Closed Sundays from January to March. Open until 5.30pm July and August.

ℹ Getting There & Away

The bus stop is beside the post office on Eastgate. Bus 62A/X62 runs half-hourly (hourly on Sundays) to Edinburgh (£5.10, one hour). In the other direction it heads for Galashiels, where you can change for Melrose (£6).

AYRSHIRE

Ayrshire is synonymous with golf and with Robert Burns – and there's plenty on offer here to satisfy both of these pursuits. Troon has six golf courses for starters, and there's enough Burns memorabilia in the region to satisfy even his most fanatic admirers.

The best way to appreciate the Ayrshire coastline is on foot: the **Ayrshire Coastal Path** (www.ayrshirecoastalpath.org) offers 100 miles of spectacular waterside walking.

Ayr

POP 46,800

Ayr's long sandy beach has made it a popular family seaside resort since Victorian times, but it has struggled in the recent economic climate. Parts of the centre have a neglected air, though there are many fine Georgian and Victorian buildings, and it makes a convenient base for exploring this section of coast. The huge drawcard is Alloway, 3 miles south, with its Robert Burns heritage.

⊙ Sights

Most things to see in Ayr are Robert Burns related. The bard was baptised in the **Auld Kirk** (Old Church) off High St. Several of his poems are set here in Ayr; in *Twa Brigs,* Ayr's old and new bridges argue with one another. The **Auld Brig** (Old Bridge) was built in 1491 and spans the river just north of the church. **St John's Tower** (Eglinton Tce) is the only remnant of a church where a parliament was held in 1315, the year after the celebrated victory at Bannockburn.

🛏 Sleeping & Eating

★ 26 The Crescent
B&B ££

(☑01292-287329; www.26crescent.co.uk; 26 Bellevue Cres; s £53, d £75-97; 🖤) When the blossom's out, this is Ayr's prettiest street, with an excellent place to stay on it. The rooms are impeccable – an upgrade to the spacious four-poster room is a sound investment – but it's the warm welcome given by the hosts that makes this special. It's with the numerous little extras, like iPod docks, Arran toiletries, bottled water, and silver cutlery at breakfast, that this B&B is at its best.

Beresford
BISTRO ££

(☑01292-280820; www.theberesfordayr.co.uk; 22 Beresford Tce; mains £10-13; ⊙food 9am-9pm; 🖤) Style and fun go hand in hand at this upbeat establishment serving offbeat martinis and luring churchgoing ladies with artisanal chocolates and delicious desserts. The food is a creative fusion of Mediterranean, particularly Italian influences, and is solidly backed by a wide choice of wines, with lots available by the glass.

ℹ Information

Ayr Information Centre (☑01292-290300; www.ayrshire-arran.com; 22 Sandgate; ⊙9am-5pm Mon-Sat year-round, 10am-5pm Sun Apr-Sep; ♿) In the centre.

ℹ Getting There & Around

AMG Cycles (☑ 01292-287580; www.irvine-cycles.co.uk; 55 Dalblair Rd; per day/weekend/week £15/20/35-50; ⊙ 9.30am-5pm Mon-Sat) hires out bikes.

Ayr is 33 miles from Glasgow and is Ayrshire's major transport hub. There are very frequent express services to Glasgow (£5.90, one hour) via Prestwick Airport, as well as services to Stranraer (£8.20, two hours, four to eight a day), other Ayrshire destinations, and Dumfries (£6.60, 2¼ hours, five to seven a day).

There are at least two trains an hour that run between Ayr and Glasgow Central station (£8, 50 minutes), and some trains continue south from Ayr to Stranraer (£10.50, 1½ hours).

Alloway

The pretty, lush village of Alloway (3 miles south of Ayr) should be on the itinerary of every Robert Burns fan – he was born here on 25 January 1759. Even if you haven't been seduced by Burnsmania, it's still well worth a visit, as the Burns-related exhibitions give a good impression of life in Ayrshire in the late 18th century.

⊙ Sights

Robert Burns Birthplace Museum   MUSEUM
(NTS; www.burnsmuseum.org.uk; adult/child £8.50/6.50; ⊙ 10am-5pm Oct-Mar, to 5.30pm Apr-Sep) This impressive museum has collected a solid range of Burns memorabilia, including manuscripts and possessions of the poet, like the pistols he packed in order to carry out his daily work as a taxman. There's good biographical information, and a series of displays that bring to life individual poems via background snippets, translations, and audiophones with recitations. Appropriately, the museum doesn't take itself too seriously: there's plenty of humour that the man himself surely would have approved of, and entertaining audio and visual performances will keep the kids amused.

The admission ticket also covers the atmospheric **Burns Cottage**, connected via a walkway to the Birthplace Museum. Born in the little box-bed in this cramped thatched dwelling, the poet spent the first seven years of his life here. It's an attractive display that gives you a context for reading plenty of his verse. Much-needed translation of some of

THE SCOTTISH BARD

Best remembered for penning the words of 'Auld Lang Syne', Robert Burns (1759–96) is Scotland's most famous poet and a popular hero; his birthday (25 January) is celebrated as Burns Night by Scots around the world.

Burns was born in 1759 in Alloway to a poor family, who scraped a living gardening and farming. At school he soon showed an aptitude for literature and a fondness for the folk song. He later began writing his own songs and satires. When the problems of his arduous farming life were compounded by the threat of prosecution from the father of Jean Armour, with whom he'd had an affair, he decided to emigrate to Jamaica. He gave up his share of the family farm and published his poems to raise money for the journey.

The poems were so well reviewed in Edinburgh that Burns decided to remain in Scotland and devote himself to writing. He went to Edinburgh in 1787 to publish a 2nd edition, but the financial rewards were not enough to live on and he had to take a job as an excise man in Dumfriesshire. Though he worked well, he wasn't a taxman by nature, and described his job as 'the execrable office of whip-person to the blood-hounds of justice'. He contributed many songs to collections, and a 3rd edition of his poems was published in 1793. A prodigious writer, Burns composed more than 28,000 lines of verse over 22 years. He died (probably of heart disease) in Dumfries in 1796, aged 37, having fathered more than a dozen children to several different women. Generous-spirited Jean bore nine of them and took in another, remarking 'Oor Robbie should hae had twa wives'.

Many of the local landmarks mentioned in the verse-tale 'Tam o' Shanter' can still be visited. Farmer Tam, riding home after a hard night's drinking in a pub in Ayr, sees witches dancing in Alloway churchyard. He calls out to the one pretty witch, but is pursued by them, and has to reach the other side of the River Doon to be safe. He just manages to cross the Brig o' Doon, but his mare loses her tail to the witches.

The Burns connection in southern Scotland is milked for all it's worth and tourist offices have a *Burns Heritage Trail* leaflet leading you to every place that can claim some link with the bard. Burns fans should have a look at www.robertburns.org.

ℹ ARDROSSAN

An otherwise unremarkable coastal town, Ardrossan is the main ferry port for Arran. Trains leave Glasgow Central station (£7.20, 40 to 50 minutes, half-hourly) to connect with ferries. From May to September there are also services to Campbeltown on the Kintyre peninsula.

the more obscure Scots farming terms he loved to use decorate the walls.

Alloway Auld Kirk   CHURCH
(⊙24hr) **FREE** Near the Birthplace Museum are the ruins of the kirk, the setting for part of 'Tam o' Shanter'. Burns' father, William, is buried in the kirkyard; read the poem on the back of the gravestone.

Burns Monument & Gardens   GARDENS
The monument was built in 1823; the gardens afford a view of the 13th-century Brig o' Doon.

ℹ Getting There & Away

Bus 361 runs hourly between Alloway and Ayr (seven minutes). Otherwise, walk or rent a bike and cycle here.

Culzean Castle & Country Park

The Scottish National Trust's flagship property, magnificent **Culzean Castle** (NTS; ☑01655-884400; www.culzeanexperience.org; castle adult/child/family £15.50/11.50/38; ⊙castle 10.30am-5pm Apr-Oct, last entry 4pm, park 9.30am-sunset year-round), pronounced kull-*ane*, is one of the most impressive of Scotland's great stately homes. The entrance is an unusual viaduct, and on approach the castle appears like a mirage, floating into view. Designed by Robert Adam, who was encouraged to exercise his romantic genius, this 18th-century mansion is perched dramatically on the edge of the cliffs. Adam was the most influential architect of his time, renowned for his meticulous attention to detail and the elegant classical embellishments with which he decorated his ceilings and fireplaces.

ℹ Getting There & Away

Culzean is 12 miles south of Ayr; buses (£4.20, 30 minutes, 11 daily Monday to Saturday) pass the park gates, from where it's a 20-minute walk through the grounds to the castle.

DUMFRIES & GALLOWAY

Some of the region's finest attractions lie in the gentle hills and lush valleys of Dumfries and Galloway. Ideal for families, there's plenty on offer for the kids. Galloway Forest is a highlight, with its sublime views, mountain-biking and walking trails, red deer, kites and other wildlife, as are the dreamlike ruins of Caerlaverock Castle. Adding to the appeal of this enticing region is a string of southern Scotland's most idyllic towns, which are charming when the sun shines. And shine it does. Warmed also by the Gulf Stream, this is the mildest region in Scotland, a phenomenon that has allowed the development of some famous gardens.

Dumfries

POP 32,900

Lovely, red-hued sandstone bridges criss-cross pleasant Dumfries, bisected by the wide River Nith, with grassy banks. Historically, Dumfries held a strategic position in the path of vengeful English armies; consequently, although it has existed since Roman times, the oldest standing building dates from the 17th century. Plenty of famous names have passed through: Robert Burns lived here and worked as a tax collector; JM Barrie, creator of Peter Pan, was schooled here; and former racing driver David Coulthard also hails from the town.

◉ Sights

There are more Burns-related sights scattered throughout town; you'll find Robert Burns' **mausoleum** (St Michael's Kirk) in the graveyard at **St Michael's Kirk**; it's in the far left corner as you go in. His wife is also buried here. At the top of High St is a **statue** of the bard.

★ Burns House   MUSEUM
(www.dumgal.gov.uk/museums; Burns St; ⊙10am-5pm Mon-Sat & 2-5pm Sun Apr-Sep, 10am-1pm & 2-5pm Tue-Sat Oct-Mar) **FREE** This is a place of pilgrimage for Burns enthusiasts. It's here that the poet spent the last years of his life, and there are various possessions of his in glass cases, as well as manuscripts and, entertainingly, letters: make sure you have a read.

Robert Burns Centre   MUSEUM
(www.dumgal.gov.uk/museums; Mill Rd; audiovisual presentation £2.25; ⊙10am-5pm Mon-Sat & 2-5pm

Sun Apr-Sep, 10am-1pm & 2-5pm Tue-Sat Oct-Mar) FREE A worthwhile Burns exhibition in an old mill on the banks of the River Nith. It tells the story of the poet and Dumfries in the 1790s. The optional audiovisual presentations give more background on Dumfries, and explain the exhibition's contents.

🛏 Sleeping

Merlin   B&B £
(📞 01387-261002;   www.themerlin.webeden.co.uk; 2 Kenmure Tce; s/d without bathroom £35/56; 🛜) Beautifully located on the riverbank across a pedestrian bridge from the centre, this is a top place to hole up in Dumfries. So much work goes on behind the scenes here that it seems effortless: numerous small details and a friendly welcome make this a very impressive set-up. Rooms share a bathroom, and have super-comfy beds; the breakfast table is also quite a sight.

Ferintosh Guest House   B&B ££
(📞 01387-252262;   www.ferintosh.net;   30 Lovers Walk; s £35, d £60-66; 🛜🐕) A Victorian villa opposite the train station, Ferintosh is a good-humoured place with excellent rooms and a warm welcome. These people have the right attitude towards hospitality, with comfortable plush beds, a free dram on arrival, and plenty of good chat on distilleries and kilts. The showers sound like light aircraft taking off but deliver impressive results. The owner's original artwork complements the decor, and cyclists are welcomed with a shed and bike-washing facilities.

🍴 Eating & Drinking

Cavens Arms   PUB FOOD £
(20 Buccleuch St; mains £8-14; ⏱ 11.30am-9pm Tue-Sat, 12.30-8.30pm Sun; 🛜) Engaging staff, 10 real ales on tap, and a warm contented buzz make this a legendary Dumfries pub. Generous portions of typical pub nosh backed up by a long list of more adventurous daily specials make it one of the town's most enjoyable places to eat too. It gets packed at weekends but they still try and find a table for all.

ℹ Information

Dumfries Information Centre (📞 01387-253862; www.visitdumfriesandgalloway.co.uk; 64 Whitesands; ⏱ 9.30am-4pm Mon-Sat Nov-Mar, to 5pm Apr-Jun & Sep-Oct, to 5.30pm Jul-Aug, plus 11am-4pm Sun Jul-Sep) Offers plenty of information on the region.

ℹ Getting There & Away

BUS
Buses run to towns along the A75 to Stranraer (£7, 2¼ hours, eight daily Monday to Saturday, three on Sunday) as well as to Castle Douglas and Kirkcudbright. Bus 100/101 runs to/from Edinburgh (£8.80, 2¾ hours, four to seven daily), via Moffat and Biggar.

TRAIN
There are trains between Carlisle and Dumfries (£10.40, 35 minutes, every hour or two), and direct trains between Dumfries and Glasgow (£15.60, 1¾ hours, eight daily Monday to Saturday). Services are reduced on Sundays.

South Of Dumfries

Caerlaverock Castle

The ruins of **Caerlaverock Castle** (HS; www. historic-scotland.gov.uk; adult/child £5.50/3.30; ⏱ 9.30am-5.30pm Apr-Sep, 9.30am-4.30pm Oct-Mar), by Glencaple on a beautiful stretch of the Solway coast, are among the loveliest in Britain. Surrounded by a moat, lawns and stands of trees, the unusual pink-stoned triangular castle looks impregnable. In fact, it fell several times, most famously when it was attacked in 1300 by Edward I: the siege became the subject of an epic poem, 'The Siege of Caerlaverock'.

The current castle dates from the late 13th century, but once defensive purposes were no longer a design necessity it was refitted as a luxurious Scottish Renaissance mansion house in 1634. Ironically, the rampaging Covenanter militia sacked it a few years later. With nooks and crannies to explore, passageways and remnants of fireplaces, this castle is great for the whole family.

New Abbey

The small, picturesque village of New Abbey lies 7 miles south of Dumfries and contains the remains of the 13th-century Cistercian **Sweetheart Abbey** (HS; www.historic-scotland. gov.uk; adult/child £4.50/2.70; ⏱ 9.30am-5.30pm Apr-Sep, 9.30am-4.30pm Sat-Wed Oct-Mar). The shattered, red-sandstone remnants of the abbey are impressive and stand in stark contrast to the manicured lawns surrounding them. The abbey, the last of the major monasteries to be established in Scotland, was founded by Devorgilla of Galloway in 1273 in honour of her dead husband John Balliol (with whom she had founded Balliol College, Oxford). On his death, she had his heart embalmed and carried it with her until she died 22 years later. She and the heart were buried by the altar – hence the name.

To get to New Abbey, take Bus 372 from Dumfries (15 minutes).

Kirkcudbright

POP 3400

Kirkcudbright (kirk-*coo*-bree), with its dignified streets of 17th- and 18th-century merchants houses and appealing harbour, is the ideal base from which to explore the south coast. Look out for the nook-and-cranny wynds in the elbow of beautifully restored High St. With its architecture and setting, it's easy to see why Kirkcudbright has been an artists' colony since the late 19th century.

Sights & Activities

Broughton House GALLERY
(NTS; www.nts.org.uk; 12 High St; adult/child £6.50/5; noon-5pm Apr-Oct) The 18th-century Broughton House displays paintings by EA Hornel (he lived and worked here), one of the Glasgow Boys. The library, with its wood panelling and stone carvings, is probably the most impressive room. Behind the house is a lovely Japanese-style garden (also open 11am to 4pm Monday to Friday in February and March).

MacLellan's Castle CASTLE
(HS; www.historic-scotland.gov.uk; Castle St; adult/child £4.50/2.70; 9.30am-1pm & 2-5.30pm Apr-Sep) Near the harbour, this is a large, atmospheric ruin built in 1577 by Thomas MacLellan, then provost of Kirkcudbright, as his town residence. Inside look for the 'lairds' lug', a 16th-century hidey-hole designed for the laird to eavesdrop on his guests.

Tolbooth Art Centre ARTS CENTRE
(www.dumgal.gov.uk; High St; 10am-4pm Mon-Sat, 1-4pm Sun mid-Apr–Sep, 11am-4pm Mon-Sat Oct–mid-Apr) FREE As well as catering for today's local artists, this centre has an exhibition on the history of the town's artistic development. The place is as interesting for the building itself as for the artistic works on display; it's one of the oldest and best-preserved tollbooths in Scotland, and there are interpretive signboards to explain its past.

Sleeping & Eating

Kirkcudbright has a swath of good B&Bs.

★**Selkirk Arms Hotel** HOTEL ££
(01557-330402; www.selkirkarmshotel.co.uk; High St; s/d £84/110, superior d £130; P@) What a haven of good hospitality this is. All the rooms have been recently refurbished, and are looking good with a stylish purply finish and slate-floored bathroms. Superior rooms are excellent – wood furnishings and views over the back garden give them a rustic appeal. Staff are happy to be there, and you will be too.

Baytree House B&B ££
(01557-330824; www.baytreekirkcudbright.co.uk; 110 High St; s/d £65/82; @) This is a very high standard B&B, but its focus is always directed towards the guest's comfort, and it never feels too posh. Rooms are ample size and feature plush, comfortable beds and lots of little extras like a sherry decanter, earplugs (not that you need them) and fresh milk. A great lounge space has DVDs and reading material. There's a self-catering flat out the back too.

Selkirk Arms Hotel BISTRO ££
(www.selkirkarmshotel.co.uk; High St; mains £11-19; noon-2pm & 6-9pm; P) Cheery servers and a wide-ranging menu of well-presented dishes give you plenty of options here, where you can sit in the more formal restaurant area or the more casual bar zone. Local scallops are a highlight, and some fairly elaborate mains can round out the meal, but you can also chow down on 'posh fish 'n' chips'. All positive.

Information

Check out www.kirkcudbright.co.uk and www.artiststown.org.uk for heaps of information on the town.

Kirkcudbright Information Centre (01557-330494; www.visitdumfriesandgalloway.co.uk; Harbour Sq; 10am-5pm Mon-Sat & 11am-3pm Sun Apr-Jun & Sep-Oct, 9.30am-6pm Mon-Sat & 10am-5pm Sun Jul & Aug, 11am-4pm Mon-Sat Nov-Mar) Handy office with useful brochures detailing walks and road tours in the surrounding district.

Getting There & Away

Kirkcudbright is 28 miles southwest of Dumfries. Buses run to Dumfries (one hour) via either Castle Douglas or changing in Dalbeattie. Change at Gatehouse of Fleet for Stranraer.

Galloway Forest Park

South and northwest of the small town of New Galloway is 300-sq-mile Galloway Forest Park, with numerous lochs and great whale-backed, heather- and pine-covered mountains. The highest point is **Merrick** (843m). The park is criss-crossed by off-road bike routes and some superb signposted walking trails, from gentle strolls to long-distance paths, including the **Southern Upland Way**. The park is very family focused; look out for the booklet of annual events in tourist offices.

The park is also great for **stargazing**; it has been declared a Dark Sky Park by the International Dark-Sky Association (www.darksky.org).

The scenic 19-mile A712 (Queen's Way) between New Galloway and Newton Stewart slices through the southern section of the park.

On the shore of **Clatteringshaws Loch**, 6 miles west of New Galloway, is **Clatteringshaws Visitor Centre** (☑ 01671-402420; www.forestry.gov.uk/scotland; ⊙ 10am-4pm, to 5pm Jul & Aug), which is basically a cafe but has the odd display panel; pick up a copy of the *Galloway Kite Trail* leaflet here, which details a circular route through impressive scenery that offers a good chance to spot one of the majestic reintroduced red kites. From the visitor centre you can walk to a replica of a Romano-British homestead, and to **Bruce's Stone**, where Robert the Bruce is said to have rested after defeating the English at the Battle of Rapploch Moss in 1307

About a mile west of Clatteringshaws, **Raiders Rd** is a 10-mile drive through the forest with various picnic spots, child-friendly activities, and short walks marked along the

way. It costs £2 per vehicle; drive slowly as there's plenty of wildlife about.

Further west is the **Galloway Red Deer Range**, where you can observe Britain's largest land-based beast. During rutting season in autumn it's a bit like watching a bullfight as snorting, charging stags compete for the harem. From April to September there are guided **ranger-led visits** (adult/child £5/3) to see these impressive beasts.

Walkers and cyclists should head for **Glentrool** in the park's west, accessed by the forest road east from Bargrennan off the A714, north of Newton Stewart. Located just over a mile from Bargrennan is the **Glentrool Visitor Centre** (⊙ 10am-4pm, to 5pm Jul & Aug), which has a cafe and stocks information on activities, including mountain biking. The road then winds and climbs up to **Loch Trool**, where there are magnificent views.

The Machars

In the south, the Galloway Hills give way to the softly rolling pastures of the triangular peninsula known as the Machars. The south has many early Christian sites and the 25-mile Pilgrims Way walk.

Bus 415 runs every hour or so between Newton Stewart and Isle of Whithorn (one hour) via Wigtown (15 minutes) and Whithorn.

Wigtown

POP 900

Little Wigtown, officially Scotland's National Book Town, has more than a dozen bookshops offering an astonishingly wide selection of volumes, giving book enthusiasts the opportunity to get lost here for days. A

MOUNTAIN-BIKING HEAVEN

A brilliant way to experience southern Scotland's forests is by pedal power. The **7stanes** ('stanes' means stones) are seven mountain-biking centres around the region with trails through some of the finest forest scenery you'll find in the country.

Glentrool is one of these centres and the **Blue Route** here is 5.6 miles in length and a lovely ride climbing up to Green Torr Ridge overlooking Loch Trool. If you've more serious intentions, the **Big Country Route** is 36 miles of challenging ascents and descents that afford magnificent views of the Galloway Forest. It takes a full day and is not for wimps.

Another of the trailheads is at **Kirroughtree Visitor Centre**, 3 miles southeast of Newton Stewart. This offers plenty of singletrack at four different skill levels. You can hire bikes here (www.thebreakpad.com). For more information on routes see www.7stanes-mountainbiking.com.

major **book festival** (www.wigtownbookfestival.com) is held here in late September.

The **Bookshop** (www.the-bookshop.com; 17 North Main St; ⊙ 9am-5pm Mon-Sat) claims to be Scotland's largest secondhand bookshop, and has a great collection of Scottish and regional titles.

A noble stone building in a quiet part of town, **Hillcrest House** (☑ 01988-402018; www.hillcrest-wigtown.co.uk; Station Rd; s £40-45, d £70-78; ℗ 🛜 🐾) features high ceilings and huge windows; spend the extra for one of the superior rooms, which have stupendous views overlooking rolling green hills and the sea beyond. This is all complemented by a ripper breakfast involving fresh local produce. **ReadingLasses Bookshop Café** (www.reading-lasses.com; 17 South Main St; mains £7-8; ⊙ 10am-5pm Mon-Sat, plus 11am-4pm Sun May-Oct; 🛜 🐾) 🐾 is set around a brilliantly welcoming cafe serving decent coffee to prolong your reading time and a toothsome range of home cooking prepared with care and offering several vegetarian/vegan options.

Whithorn

POP 800

Whithorn has a broad, attractive High St which is virtually closed at both ends (it was designed to enclose a medieval market). There are few facilities in town, but it's worth visiting because of its fascinating history.

In 397, while the Romans were still in Britain, St Ninian established the first Christian mission beyond Hadrian's Wall in Whithorn (pre-dating St Columba on Iona by 166 years). After his death, **Whithorn Priory**, the earliest recorded church in Scotland, was built to house his remains, and Whithorn became the focus of an important medieval pilgrimage.

Today the ruined priory is part of the excellent **Whithorn Trust Discovery Centre** (www.whithorn.com; 45 George St; adult/child £4.50/2.25, 20% Historic Scotland discount; ⊙ 10.30am-5pm Apr-Oct), which introduces you to the history of the town through a very informative audiovisual exhibition. Outside, you can see the site of earlier churches. There's also a museum with some fascinating early Christian stone sculptures, including the **Latinus Stone** (c 450), reputedly Scotland's oldest Christian artefact. Learn about the influences their carvers drew on, from around the British Isles and beyond.

Stranraer

POP 10,600

The friendly but somewhat ramshackle port of Stranraer has seen its tourist mainstay, the ferry traffic to Northern Ireland, move up the road to Cairnryan. The town's still wondering what to do with itself, but there's lots to explore in the surrounding area.

⊙ Sights

Castle Kennedy Gardens　　GARDENS, CASTLE
(www.castlekennedygardens.co.uk; adult/child £5/1.50; ⊙ 10am-5pm daily Apr-Oct, Sat & Sun only Feb-Mar) Three miles east of Stranraer, these magnificent gardens are among Scotland's most renowned. They cover 30 hectares and are set on an isthmus between two lochs and two castles. The landscaping was undertaken in 1730 by the Earl of Stair, who used unoccupied soldiers to do the work. Buses heading east from Stranraer stop at the gate on the main road; it's a pleasant 20-minute stroll from here to the entrance to the gardens.

🛏 Sleeping & Eating

Ivy House　　B&B £
(☑ 01776-704176;　www.ivyhouse-ferrylink.co.uk; 3 Ivy Pl; s/d £30/50, s without bathroom £25; 🛜) This is a great guesthouse that does Scottish hospitality proud, with excellent facilities, tidy en suite rooms and a smashing breakfast. Nothing is too much trouble for the genial host, who always has a smile for her guests. The room at the back overlooking the churchyard is particularly light and quiet.

Balyett Farm　　B&B ££
(☑ 01776-703395; www.balyettbb.co.uk; Cairnryan Rd; s £55, d £65-75; ℗ 🛜) A mile north of town on the A77, Balyett has top relaxing rooms in a tranquil setting; they are light, bright, clean as a whistle and boast lovely views over the surrounding country. Ring ahead, as they might be further up the road in Cairnryan by the time you read this.

❶ Information

Stranraer Information Centre (☑ 01776-702595; 28 Harbour St; ⊙ 10am-4pm Mon-Sat Sep-Jun, 9am-5pm daily Jul & Aug, plus 11am-3pm Sun Jul) Efficient and friendly.

❶ Getting There & Away

BOAT

Stranraer is 6 miles south of Cairnryan, which is on the eastern side of Loch Ryan. Bus 358 runs frequently between Stranraer and Ayr, stopping in Cairnryan. For a taxi to Cairnryan (around £8), contact **McLean's Taxis** (☑ 01776-703343; 21 North Strand St; ⊙24hr), just up from the tourist office.

P&O (☑ 08716 64 20 20; www.poferries.com) Runs six to eight fast ferries a day from Cairnryan to Larne (Northern Ireland). The crossing takes two hours.

Stena Line (☑ 08447 70 70 70; www.stenaline. co.uk; passenger £20-29, driver plus car £99-150) Runs five to six ferries from Cairnryan to Belfast (2¾ hours).

BUS

Scottish Citylink buses run to Glasgow (£18.50, 2½ hours, three daily) and Edinburgh (£21.50, four hours, three daily).

There are also several daily local buses to Kirkcudbright and the towns along the A75, such as Newton Stewart (45 minutes, at least hourly) and Dumfries (£7, 2¼ hours, nine daily Monday to Saturday, three on Sunday).

TRAIN

First Scotrail runs to/from Glasgow (£12.40, 2¼ hours, two to seven trains daily); it may be necessary to change at Ayr.

Portpatrick

POP 500

Portpatrick is a charming harbour village on the rugged west coast of the Rhinns of Galloway peninsula; it's the starting or finishing point for the **Southern Upland Way**. You can follow part of the way to Stranraer (9 miles). It's a clifftop walk, with sections of farmland and heather moor.

🛌 Sleeping & Eating

Harbour House Hotel   INN **££**
(☑ 01776-810456;   www.theharbourhousehotel.
co.uk; 53 Main St; s/d £60/100; 🐕🐾) Formerly the customs house, this is now a popular, solid old pub. Some of the tastefully furnished, recently refurbished rooms have brilliant views over the harbour. The hotel is

also a warm nook for a traditional bar meal (mains £8 to £10).

★**Knockinaam Lodge**   HOTEL **£££**
(☑ 01776-810471;   www.knockinaamlodge.com; dinner, bed & breakfast s £200-310, d £320-420; P🐾🐕) For a real dose of luxury, head 3 miles southeast to this former hunting lodge in a dramatic, secluded location with grassy lawns rolling down to a sandy cove. It's where Churchill plotted the endgame of WWII – you can stay in his suite – and it's a very romantic place to get away from it all. The excellent French-influenced cuisine (lunch/dinner £40/65) is backed up by a great range of wines and single malts, and breakfast features homemade jams.

★**Campbell's**   SEAFOOD **££**
(☑ 01776-810314; www.campbellsrestaurant.co.uk; 1 South Crescent; mains £11-18; ⊙noon-2pm & 5.30-9pm Tue-Sun) Fresh local seafood is the stock-in-trade of this unprepossessing local favourite, and they do it very well. Ask for whatever is good that day and enjoy the flavour burst of locally caught fish or shellfish.

❶ Getting There & Away

Bus 367 runs to Stranraer (20 minutes, hourly Monday to Saturday, three times Sunday).

Argyll, Central & Northeast Scotland

Includes ➡

Best Places to Eat

➡ Café Fish (p866)

➡ Breizh (p879)

➡ Cellar Restaurant (p875)

➡ Seafood Temple (p863)

Best Places to Stay

➡ Old Manse Guest House (p862)

➡ Monachyle Mhor (p849)

➡ George Hotel (p852)

➡ Argyll Hotel (p868)

Why Go?

Covering everything from the green pastures of the northeast to the ferry port of Oban, from urban Dundee to the far Mull of Kintyre, this chapter's title is less a geographical region than a catch-all term for everything between the Lowlands and the northern Highlands. Anything you ever dreamed about Scotland can be found here: lochs aplenty, from romantic Lomond to the picturesque Trossachs; castles, ranging from royal Glamis to noble Stirling; whiskies, from the honeyed lotharios of Speyside to the peaty clan chiefs of Islay; and islands, from brooding, deer-studded Jura to emerald Iona, birthplace of Scottish Christianity.

The active are well catered for, with a welter of hills to climb and some of Britain's best long-distance trails to hike. Cyclists and walkers are spoiled for choice, with scenery ranging from the plains of Stirling to the rugged Argyll hills; from the fishing hamlets of Fife to the epic landscapes of Mull.

When to Go

➡ If the weather is kind, May is a magical time for exploring Loch Lomond and the Trossachs before the summer crowds arrive.

➡ August is the best month of the year for whale-watching off the west coast.

➡ In September there's the Spirit of Speyside whisky and music festival in Dufftown.

🏃 Activities

Cycling

Long-distance routes include much of the northern section of the 214-mile **Lochs & Glens Cycle Way** (NCN route 7). Starting in Glasgow, it winds its way through the region's heart via Pitlochry to Inverness, and includes some wonderful traffic-free sections in the Trossachs and Cairngorms. **NCN route 77** crosses picturesque Perthshire heading west from Dundee to Pitlochry (54 miles). **NCN route 78** is a 120-mile ride between Oban and Campbeltown, while part of **NCN route 1** bisects Fife then follows the coast to Dundee, Aberdeen and on to Inverness. Browse www.sustrans.org.uk for details and maps of these routes.

For shorter rides, the Trossachs and the islands of Islay and Mull are ideal for a day or more's exploration by bike; cycle hire is available.

A great two-week tour could start by circling Arran. From here, take a ferry to the Kintyre Peninsula and loop down to Campbeltown. Then cross to Islay and Jura, timing your trip so you can take the Wednesday-only ferry from Islay to Oban and crossing by ferry to Mull. From Mull, you can cross to remote Kilchoan, and head north to Mallaig.

Fife takes cycling very seriously, and produces several maps and leaflets detailing cycle routes in this area (www.fifedirect.org.uk/cycleways). There are only a few steep hills here, and the country roads are fairly quiet.

Check out http://active.visitscotland.com for more details and further routes in the region.

Walking

One of Britain's best-known long-distance walks, the **West Highland Way** (www.west-highland-way.co.uk), starts just outside Glasgow and finishes at Fort William. It covers 96 miles through mountains and glens via Loch Lomond and Rannoch Moor.

The route begins in the Lowlands, but the greater part of the trail is among the mountains, lochs and fast-flowing rivers of the western Highlands. After following the eastern shore of Loch Lomond and passing Crianlarich and Tyndrum, the route crosses the vast wilderness of Rannoch Moor and reaches Fort William via Glen Nevis, in the shadow of Britain's highest peak, Ben Nevis.

The path is easy to follow, making use of old drovers' roads (along which Highland cattle were once driven to Lowland markets), an old military road (built by troops to help subdue the Highlands in the 18th century) and disused railway lines.

Best done from south to north, the walk takes about six or seven days, and is completed by about 30,000 hikers each year.

The 66-mile **Speyside Way** (www.speysideway.org) is a picturesque route running from Buckie on the northeast coast, through lush green whisky country, and finishing at Aviemore in the Cairngorms (or vice versa). Much of the route is along a peaceful disused railway line well away from traffic.

Both of these routes have baggage-carrying services available.

ℹ️ Getting Around

BOAT

Most ferries to the west-coast islands are run by **CalMac** (☎ 0800 066-5000; www.calmac.co.uk) Car space on busier routes should be reserved by phone ahead of your trip.

If you plan to island-hop, you'll save money with an Island Hopscotch ticket, which offers 30 combinations that can save you more than 20% off the normal fares.

Island Rover Passes (passengers 8/15 consecutive days £55/79, vehicles 8/15 consecutive days £259/388) cover the whole system and are good value if you want to see a lot of islands fast. Bicycles travel free on this pass.

BUS

Citylink (☎ 0871 266 33 33; www.citylink.co.uk) is the major intercity bus operator. Most local bus transport is operated by Stagecoach (p899).

TRAIN

Scotrail (☎ 08457 55 00 33; www.scotrail.co.uk) runs three north–south lines, including the spectacular West Highland line, running from Glasgow to Fort William with a branch to Oban. Another line runs from Glasgow and Edinburgh (via Stirling) to Perth, Pitlochry and Inverness; the third line goes from Perth to Dundee and Aberdeen, then northwest via Elgin to Inverness. Fife also has a rail network. See individual towns for transport details.

The **Central Scotland Rover** pass allows unlimited travel (for three days out of seven) between Edinburgh and Glasgow and the Fife and Stirling areas. It costs £36.30 and is available from all train stations. Similarly, the **Highland Rover** pass (£81.50) allows travel on four days out of eight and includes Oban, Aberdeen and buses on Mull.

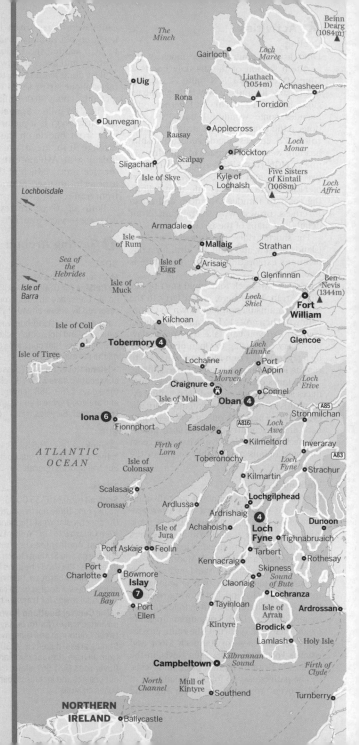

Argyll, Central & Northeast Scotland Highlights

1 Exploring the lovely lochscapes and accessible walking and cycling routes of the **Trossachs** (p846)

2 Pacing through the historic birthplace of golf, **St Andrews** (p869), to play the famous Old Course

3 Admiring the views from magnificent **Stirling Castle** (p840), overlooking ancient independence battlefields

4 Scoffing at critics of British cuisine as you sample the super seafood in **Tobermory** (p865), **Oban** (p861) or **Loch Fyne** (p852)

5 Strolling the verdant **Speyside Way** (p837) and sauntering into distilleries for a sly dram along the way

6 Unwinding totally on delightful tiny **Iona** (p867), holy island and tomb of Scottish kings

7 Experiencing the astonishing hospitality of **Islay** (p857), whisky and bird paradise and Scotland's friendliest island

8 Strutting with peacocks at noble **Scone Palace** (p877), where Scottish kings were once crowned

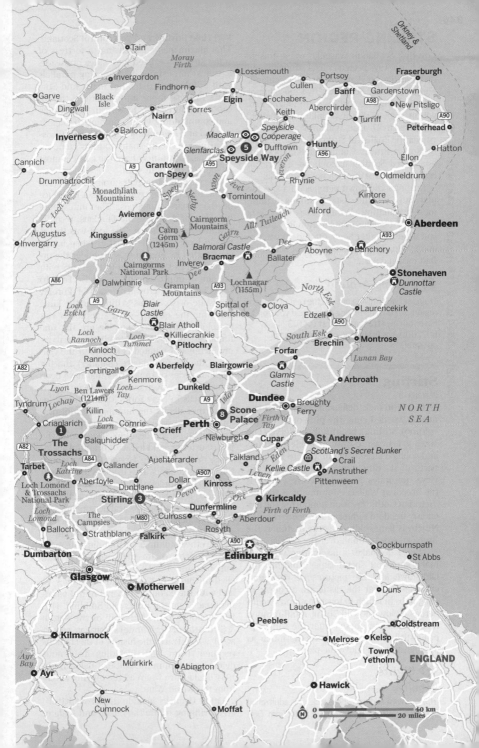

STIRLING REGION

Covering Scotland's wasplike waist, this region has always been a crucial strategic point dividing the Lowlands from the Highlands. For this reason, Scotland's two most important independence battles were fought here, within sight of Stirling's hilltop stronghold. Separated by 17 years, William Wallace's victory over the English at Stirling Bridge, followed by Robert Bruce's triumph at Bannockburn, established Scottish nationhood. The region remains a source of much national pride.

Stirling's Old Town perches on a spectacular crag, and the castle is among Britain's most fascinating. Within easy reach, the dreamy Trossachs, home to Rob Roy and inspiration to Walter Scott, offer great walking and cycling in the eastern half of Scotland's first national park.

❶ Getting Around

Trains service Stirling but not the rest of the region, so you'll be relying on buses if you don't have your own transport. **First** (☑ 01324-602200; www.firstgroup.com) is the main operator.

Stirling

POP 36,150

With a supremely defensible position atop a mighty wooded crag (the plug of an extinct volcano), Stirling's beautifully preserved Old Town is a treasure-trove of noble buildings and cobbled streets winding up to the ramparts of its dominant castle, which offer views for miles around. Clearly visible is the brooding Wallace Monument, a strange Victorian Gothic creation honouring the legendary freedom fighter of *Braveheart* fame. Nearby is Bannockburn, scene of Robert the Bruce's major triumph over the English.

The castle makes a fascinating visit, but make sure you spend time exploring the Old Town and the picturesque path that encircles it. Near the castle are a couple of snug pubs in which to toast Scotland's hoary heroes. Below the Old Town, retail-minded modern Stirling doesn't offer the same appeal; stick to the high ground as much as possible and you'll love the place.

◎ Sights

★**Stirling Castle**   CASTLE
(HS; www.stirlingcastle.gov.uk; adult/child £14/7.50; ⊙9.30am-6pm Apr-Sep, to 5pm Oct-

Mar) Hold Stirling and you control Scotland. This maxim has ensured that a fortress of some kind has existed here since prehistoric times. You cannot help drawing parallels with Edinburgh Castle, but many find Stirling's fortress more atmospheric – the location, architecture, historical significance and commanding views combine to make it a grand and memorable sight. It's best to visit in the afternoon; many tourists come on day trips, so you may have the castle almost to yourself by about 4pm.

The current castle dates from the late 14th to the 16th century, when it was a residence of the Stuart monarchs. The undisputed highlight of a visit is the fabulous, recently restored **Royal Palace**. The idea was that it should look brand new, just as when it was constructed by French masons under the orders of James V in the mid-16th century with the aim of impressing his new (also French) bride and other crowned heads of Europe. The suite of six rooms – three for the king, three for the queen – is a sumptuous riot of colour. Particularly notable are the fine fireplaces, the **Stirling Heads** (modern reproductions of painted oak discs in the ceiling of the king's audience chamber) and the fabulous series of **tapestries** that have been painstakingly woven over many years. Based on originals in New York's Metropolitan Museum, they depict the hunting of a unicorn, an event ripe with Christian metaphor, and are breathtakingly beautiful. Don't miss the palace exterior, studded with beautiful sculptures, or the **Stirling Heads Gallery** above the royal chambers. This displays the original carved oak roundels that decorated the king's audience chamber – a real rogue's gallery of royals, courtiers and classical personalities. In the vaults beneath the palace is a kid-friendly **exhibition** on various aspects of castle life.

The other buildings surrounding the main castle courtyard are the vast **Great Hall**, built by James IV; the **Royal Chapel**, remodelled in the early 17th century by James VI and with the colourful original mural painting intact; and the King's Old Building. This is now home to the **Museum of the Argyll & Sutherland Highlanders** (donations encouraged), which traces the history of this famous regiment from 1794, including its famous defensive action in the Battle of Balaclava in 1854. Make sure you read the moving letters from the World Wars.

Other displays include the **Great Kitchens**, bringing to life the bustle and scale of

Stirling

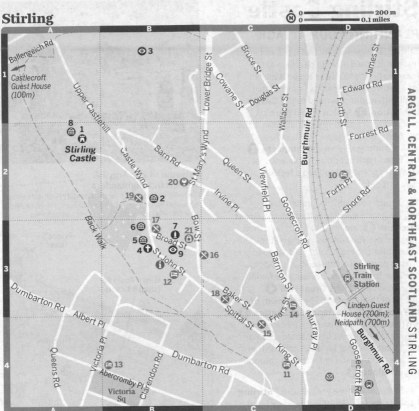

Stirling

◎ Top Sights
1 Stirling Castle	A2

◎ Sights
2 Argyll's Lodging	B2
3 Beheading Stone	B1
4 Church of the Holy Rude	B3
5 Cowane's Hospital	B3
6 Mar's Wark	B3
7 Mercat Cross	B3
8 Museum of the Argyll & Sutherland Highlanders	A2
9 Tolbooth	B3

🛏 Sleeping
10 Forth Guest House	D2
11 Sruighlea	C4

the enterprise of cooking for the king and, near the entrance, the **Castle Exhibition**, which gives good background information on the Stuart kings and updates on current archaeological investigations. The magnificent vistas from the ramparts are stirring.

Stirling Castle

PLANNING YOUR ATTACK

Stirling's a sizeable fortress, but not so huge that you'll have to decide what to leave out – there's time to see it all. Unless you've got a working knowledge of Scottish monarchs, head to the **Castle Exhibition ❶** first: it'll help you sort one James from another. That done, take on the sights at leisure. First, stop and look around you from the **ramparts ❷**; the views high over this flat valley, a key strategic point in Scotland's history, are magnificent.

Track back towards the citadel's heart, stopping for a quick tour through the **Great Kitchens ❸**; looking at all that fake food might make you seriously hungry, though. Then enter the main courtyard. Around you are the principal castle buildings. During summer there are events (such as Renaissance dancing) in the **Great Hall ❹** – get details at the entrance. The **Museum of the Argyll & Sutherland Highlanders ❺** is a treasure trove if you're interested in regimental history, but missable if you're not. Leave the best for last – crowds thin in the afternoon – and enter the sumptuous **Royal Palace ❻**.

Take time to admire the beautiful **Stirling Tapestries ❼**, skillfully woven by hand on-site between 2001-2014.

THE WAY UP & DOWN

If you have time, take the atmospheric Back Walk, a peaceful, shady stroll around the Old Town's fortifications and up to the castle's imposing crag-top position. Afterwards, wander down through the Old Town to admire its facades.

TOP TIPS

» **Admission** Entrance is free for Historic Scotland members. If you'll be visiting several Historic Scotland sites a membership will save you plenty.

» **Vital Statistics** First constructed: before 1110; number of sieges: at least nine; last besieger: Bonnie Prince Charlie (unsuccessful); money spent refurbishing the Royal Palace: £12 million.

Museum of the Argyll & Sutherland Highlanders
The history of one of Scotland's legendary regiments – now subsumed into the Royal Regiment of Scotland – is on display here, featuring memorabilia, weapons and uniforms.

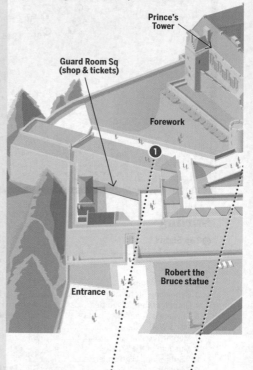

Prince's Tower

Guard Room Sq (shop & tickets)

Forework

❶

Robert the Bruce statue

Entrance

Castle Exhibition
A great overview of the Stewart dynasty here will get your facts straight, and also offers the latest archaeological titbits from the ongoing excavations under the citadel. Analysis of skeletons has revealed surprising amounts of biographical data.

Royal Palace
The impressive new highlight of a visit to the castle is this recreation of the royal lodgings originally built by James V. The finely worked ceiling, ornate furniture and sumptuous unicorn tapestries dazzle.

Great Hall & Chapel Royal

Creations of James IV and VI, respectively, these elegant spaces around the central courtyard have been faithfully restored. The vast Great Hall, with its imposing beamed roof, was the largest medieval hall in Scotland.

King's Old Building

⑤

⑥ ⑦

④

Nether Bailey

③

Grand Battery

②

The Stirling Tapestries

Copies of an exquisite series of 16th-century tapestries hang in the Royal Palace. They were painstakingly reproduced by hand using medieval techniques – each one took four years to make – and depict a unicorn hunt rich with Christian symbolism.

Ramparts

Perched on the walls you can appreciate the utter dominance of the castle's position atop this lofty volcanic crag. The view includes the site of Robert the Bruce's victory at Bannockburn and the monument to William Wallace.

Great Kitchens

Dive into this original display that brings home the massive enterprise of organising, preparing and cooking a feast fit for a Renaissance king. Your stomach may rumble at the lifelike haunches of meat, loaves of bread, fowl and fishes.

Admission includes an audioguide, and free guided tours leave regularly from near the entrance. Tours also run to **Argyll's Lodging**, at the top of Castle Wynd. Complete with turrets, this spectacular lodge is Scotland's most impressive 17th-century town house. It's the former home of William Alexander, Earl of Stirling and noted literary figure. It has been tastefully restored and gives an insight into lavish, 17th-century aristocratic life. There are four or five tours daily (you can't enter by other means).

Old Town
HISTORIC DISTRICT

Sloping steeply down from Stirling Castle, the Old Town has a remarkably different feel to modern Stirling, its cobblestone streets packed with 15th- to 17th-century architectural gems, and surrounded by Scotland's best-surviving town wall. Its growth began when Stirling became a royal burgh (about 1124), and in the 15th and 16th centuries rich merchants built their houses here.

Stirling's **town wall** was built around 1547 when Henry VIII of England began the 'Rough Wooing' – attacking the town in order to force Mary, Queen of Scots to marry his son so the two kingdoms could be united. The wall can be explored on the **Back Walk**, which follows the line of the wall from Dumbarton Rd to the castle. You pass the town cemeteries (check out the **Star Pyramid**, an outsized affirmation of Reformation values dating from 1863), then continue around the back of the castle to Gowan Hill, where you can see the **Beheading Stone**, now encased in iron bars to prevent contemporary use.

Mar's Wark, on Castle Wynd at the head of the Old Town, is the ornate facade of a Renaissance town house commissioned in 1569 by the wealthy Earl of Mar, regent of Scotland during James VI's minority.

The **Church of the Holy Rude** (www.holyrude.org; St John St; suggested donation £2; ⊙11am-4pm Easter & May-Sep) **FREE** has been the town's parish church for 600 years and James VI was crowned here in 1567. The nave and tower date from 1456, and the church has one of the few surviving medieval open-timber roofs. Stunning stained-glass windows and huge stone pillars create a powerful effect.

Behind the church is **Cowane's Hospital** (www.cowanes.org.uk; 49 St John St; ⊙10.30am-4.30pm May-Oct, 10.30am-5pm Tue-Sun Nov-Apr) **FREE**, built as an almshouse in 1637 by the merchant John Cowane. The high vaulted hall was much modified in the 19th century.

The **Mercat Cross**, in Broad St, is topped with a unicorn (known as 'The Puggie') and was once surrounded by a bustling market. Nearby is the **Tolbooth**, built in 1705 as the town's administrative centre and now an arts venue, and **Stirling Bagpipes** (✆01786-448886; www.stirlingbagpipes.com; 8 Broad St; ⊙10am-6pm Mon, Tue & Thu-Sat), a combined shop and workshop that also houses a collection of antique bagpipes and piping paraphernalia. The place is a focus for local pipers, and sells books and CDs of pipe music.

National Wallace Monument
MONUMENT

(www.nationalwallacemonument.com; adult/child £9.50/5.90; ⊙10am-5pm Apr-Jun, Sep & Oct, to 6pm Jul & Aug, 10.30am-4pm Nov-Mar) Perched high on a crag above the floodplain of the River Forth, this Victorian monument is so Gothic it deserves circling bats and croaking ravens. In the shape of a medieval tower, it commemorates William Wallace, the hero of the bid for Scottish independence depicted in the film *Braveheart*. The view from the top over the flat, green gorgeousness of the Forth Valley, including the site of Wallace's 1297 victory over the English at Stirling Bridge, almost justifies the steep entry fee.

The climb up the narrow staircase inside leads through a series of galleries including the Hall of Heroes, a marble pantheon of lugubrious Scottish luminaries. Admire Wallace's 66 inches of broadsword and see the man himself re-created in a 3-D audiovisual display.

Buses 62 and 63 run from Murray Pl in Stirling to the visitor centre; otherwise it's a half-hour walk from central Stirling. From the visitor centre, walk or shuttle-bus up the hill to the building itself. There's a cafe here.

Bannockburn
HISTORIC SITE

Though William Wallace's heroics were significant, it was Robert the Bruce's defeat of the English on 24 June 1314 at Bannockburn that finally established a lasting Scottish nation. Exploiting the marshy ground, Bruce won a great tactical victory against a much larger and better-equipped force (the Scots were outnumbered by two or three to one), and, in the words of the popular song 'The Flower of Scotland', sent Edward II 'homeward, tae think again' (Roy Williamson, The Corries (Music) Ltd, by permission).

The problem with 700-year-old battlefields is that there isn't much left to see today. There has been much debate over exactly where the main battle took place, but it was somewhere on what is now the southern edge of Stirling's urban sprawl – the **Bannockburn Heritage Centre** (NTS; battleofbannockburn.com; Glasgow Rd; adult/child/family £11/8/30; ⊙10am-5.30pm Mar-Oct, to 5pm Nov-Feb) looks for all the world like a 1970s community centre set in suburban parkland. Reopened after a major refurbishment in time for the 700th anniversary of the battle, the centre uses animated films, 3D imagery and interactive technology in an attempt to bring the battle to life – great fun for kids, a little naff for history buffs. The highlight is a digital projection of the battlefield onto a 3D landscape that shows the progress of the battle and the movements of infantry and cavalry.

Outside, the 'battlefield' itself is no more than an expanse of neatly trimmed grass, crowned with a circular monument inscribed with a poem by Kathleen Jamie, and a Victorian statue of the victor astride his horse.

Bannockburn is 2 miles south of Stirling; you can reach it on First bus 24 or 54 from Stirling bus station (£1.80, 10 minutes, three per hour).

🛏 Sleeping

Neidpath
B&B £

(☏01786-469017; www.neidpath-stirling.co.uk; 24 Linden Ave; s/d/f from £40/60/70; P 🛜) Offering excellent value and a genuine welcome, this fine choice is easily accessed by car. A particularly appealing front room is one of three excellent modernised bedrooms with fridges and good bathrooms. The owners also run various self-catering options around town (see the website for details).

Forth Guest House
B&B £

(☏01786-471020; www.forthguesthouse.co.uk; 23 Forth Pl; s/d £55/60; P 🛜) Just a couple of minutes' walk from town, on the other side of the railway, this elegant Georgian terrace offers attractive and stylish accommodation at a fair price. The rooms are very commodious, particularly the cute garret rooms with their coombed ceilings and modern bathrooms. Even cheaper in low season.

Sruighlea
B&B £

(☏01786-471082; www.sruighlea.com; 27 King St; s/d £45/60; 🛜) This place feels like a secret hideaway – there's no sign – but it's conveniently located smack bang in the centre of town. Staying here, you'll feel like a local, and there are eating and drinking places practically on the doorstep. It's a B&B that welcomes guests with the kind of warmth that keeps them returning.

Willy Wallace Backpackers Hostel
HOSTEL £

(☏01786-446773; www.willywallacehostel.com; 77 Murray Pl; dm/tw £18/38; @🛜) This highly convenient central hostel is friendly, roomy and sociable. The colourful, spacious dormitories are clean and light, and it has free tea and coffee, a good kitchen and a laissez-faire atmosphere. Other amenities include bicycle hire, laundry service and free internet and wi-fi.

Stirling SYHA
HOSTEL £

(☏01786-473442; www.syha.org.uk; St John St; dm/tw £21/55; P @🛜) This hostel has an unbeatable location and great facilities. Though its facade is that of a former church, the interior is modern and efficient. The dorms are compact but comfortable, with lockers and en suite bathrooms; other highlights include a pool table, a bike shed and, at busy times, cheap meals on offer. Lack of atmosphere can be the only problem.

Castlecroft Guest House
B&B ££

(☏01786-474933; www.castlecroft-uk.com; Ballengeich Rd; s/d £50/65; P @🛜) Nestling into the hillside under the back of the castle, this great hideaway feels like a rural retreat but is a short, spectacular walk from the heart of Stirling. The lounge and deck area enjoy views over green fields to the nearby hills, the rooms have excellent modern bathrooms and the welcome couldn't be more hospitable. Breakfast features homemade bread, among other delights.

Victoria Square Guesthouse
B&B ££

(☏01786-473920; www.victoriasquareguesthouse. com; 12 Victoria Sq; s/d £70/105; 🛜) Though close to the centre of town, Victoria Sq is a quiet oasis with elegant Victorian buildings surrounding a verdant swath of lawn. This luxury guesthouse's huge rooms, bay windows and period features make it a winner – there's a great four-poster room for romantic getaways, and some bedrooms have views to the castle towering above. No children.

Linden Guest House
B&B ££

(☏01786-448850; www.lindenguesthouse.co.uk; 22 Linden Ave; d £65-80, f £90-150; P @🛜) The warm welcome and easy parking here offer understandable appeal. The rooms, two of which are great for families, have fridges and posh TVs with DVD and iPod dock, and the gleaming bathrooms could feature in ads for cleaning products. Breakfast features fresh fruit and kippers, among other choices.

✕ Eating & Drinking

Darnley Coffee House CAFE £

(☑ 01786-474468; www.facebook.com/Darnley-
CoffeeHouse; 18 Bow St; mains £3-5; ☺ 11am-4pm
Mon-Sat, noon-4pm Sun) Just down the hill
from Stirling Castle, this is a good pit stop
for home-baked goods, soup and speciality coffees during a walk around the Old
Town. The cafe is in the vaulted cellars of
a 16th-century house where Darnley, lover
and later husband of Mary, Queen of Scots,
once stayed while visiting her.

Breá CAFE ££

(www.breastirling.com; 5 Baker St; mains £9-18;
☺ 10am-9.30pm Tue-Sun; 🖽) ⌀ Bringing a bohemian touch to central Stirling, this busy
bistro has pared-back contemporary decor
and a short menu showcasing carefully
sourced Scottish produce, including Brewdog beers. Best in show is perhaps the pork
burger with apple and black pudding – a
huge thing served with homemade bread.

Hermann's AUSTRIAN, SCOTTISH ££

(☑ 01786-450632; www.hermanns.co.uk; 58 Broad
St; 3-course lunch/dinner £13/22, mains £12-
23; ☺ noon-3pm & 6-10pm; 🖉) This elegant
Scottish-Austrian restaurant is reliable and
popular. The solid, conservative decor is oddly offset by magazine-spread skiing photos,
but the food doesn't miss a beat and ranges
from Scottish favourites to gourmet schnitzel
and *spätzle* noodles. Vegetarian options are
good, and quality Austrian wines provide an
out-of-the-ordinary accompaniment.

Mamma Mia ITALIAN ££

(www.mammamiastirling.co.uk; 52 Spittal St; mains
£10-17; ☺ noon-3pm Tue-Sat, 5-10pm Mon-Sat)
This Old Town split-level favourite has a
short menu of southern Italian cuisine augmented by weekly specials, which are definitely worth going for. It shows a sure touch
with sea bass and Scottish steaks alike,
though it's hard not to feel the pasta dishes
are a mite overpriced.

Portcullis PUB FOOD ££

(☑ 01786-472290; www.theportcullishotel.com;
Castle Wynd; bar meals £9-13; ☺ food noon-3.30pm
& 5.30-9pm; 🖀) Built in stone as solid as
the castle that it stands below, this former
school is just the spot for a pint and a pub
lunch after your castle visit. With bar meals
that would have had even William Wallace
loosening his belt a couple of notches, a little
beer garden and a cosy buzz indoors, it's well
worth a visit.

Settle Inn PUB

(☑ 01786-474609; 91 St Mary's Wynd; ☺ 11am-
11pm; 🖀) A warm welcome is guaranteed
at Stirling's oldest pub (1733), a spot redolent with atmosphere, what with its log fire,
vaulted back room and low-slung ceilings.
Guest ales, atmospheric nooks for settling in
for the night and a blend of local characters
make it a classic of its kind.

❶ Information

Stirling Community Hospital (☑ 01786-
434000; www.nhsforthvalley.com; Livilands
Rd) South of the town centre; has a minor
injuries unit. Nearest emergency department is
Forth Valley Royal Hospital in Larbert, 9 miles
southeast of Stirling.

Stirling Tourist Office (☑ 01786-475019;
www.visitstirling.org; Old Town Jail, St John
St; ☺ 10am-5pm) Accommodation booking,
internet access.

❶ Getting There & Away

BUS

The bus station is on Goosecroft Rd. Citylink
(p837) offers a number of services to/from
Stirling:

Dundee £14, 1¾ hours, hourly

Edinburgh £8, one hour, hourly

Glasgow £7.50, 40 minutes, hourly

Perth £9, 50 minutes, at least hourly

Some buses continue to Aberdeen, Inverness
and Fort William; more frequently a change will
be required.

TRAIN

First ScotRail (www.scotrail.co.uk) has services
to/from a number of destinations, including the
following:

Aberdeen £32, 2¼ hours, hourly weekdays,
every two hours Sunday

Dundee £14, one hour, hourly weekdays, every
two hours Sunday

Edinburgh £8.30, one hour, twice hourly
Monday to Saturday, hourly Sunday

Glasgow £8.60, 50 minutes, twice hourly
Monday to Saturday, hourly Sunday

Perth £12.60, 30 minutes, hourly weekdays,
every two hours Sunday

The Trossachs

The Trossachs region has long been a favourite weekend getaway, offering outstanding
natural beauty and excellent walking and cycling routes within easy reach of the southern population centres. With thickly forested

hills, romantic lochs, national-park status and an interesting selection of places to stay and eat, its popularity is sure to continue.

The Trossachs first gained popularity in the early 19th century, when curious visitors came from across Britain, drawn by the romantic language of Walter Scott's poem *Lady of the Lake*, inspired by Loch Katrine, and *Rob Roy*, about the derring-do of the region's most famous son.

In summer the Trossachs can be overburdened with coach tours, but many of these are daytrippers – peaceful, long evenings gazing at the reflections in the nearest loch are still possible. If you can, it's worth timing your visit not to coincide with a weekend.

Aberfoyle & Around

Crawling with visitors on most weekends and dominated by a huge car park, little Aberfoyle is easily overwhelmed by daytrippers. Instead of staying here, we recommend Callander or other Trossachs towns.

Half a mile north of Aberfoyle on the A821 is the **David Marshall Lodge Visitor Centre** (David Marshall Lodge; www.forestry.gov.uk; car park £1-3; ☉10am-4pm Nov-Mar, to 5pm Apr-Jun, Sep & Oct, to 6pm Jul & Aug) **FREE** in the **Queen Elizabeth Forest Park**, which has info about the many walks and cycle routes in and around the park. The Royal Society for the Protection of Birds (RSPB) has a display here on local bird life, the highlight being a live video link to the resident osprey family. The visitor centre is worth visiting solely for the views.

Three miles east is the **Lake of Menteith** (called lake, not loch, due to a mistranslation from Gaelic). A ferry takes visitors to the substantial ruins of **Inchmahome Priory** (HS; www.historic-scotland.gov.uk; adult/child incl ferry £5.50/3.30; ☉10am-5pm Apr-Sep, 10am-4pm Oct, last ferry to island 1hr before closing). Mary, Queen of Scots was kept safe here as a child during Henry VIII's 'Rough Wooing'. Henry attacked Stirling in an attempt to force Mary to marry his son so that the kingdoms could be united.

🏃 Activities

Several picturesque but busy waymarked trails start from the David Marshall Lodge Visitor Centre in the forest park. These range from an easy 20-minute stroll (to a nearby waterfall) to a hilly 4-mile circuit. Also here, **Go Ape!** (☎0845 519 3023; www.goape.co.uk; adult/child £30/24; ☉Sat & Sun Nov & Feb-Easter, Wed-Mon Easter-Oct) will bring out the monkey in you on its exhilarating adventure course of long ziplines, swings and rope bridges through the forest.

An excellent 20-mile circular **cycle route** links with the boat at Loch Katrine. From Aberfoyle, join the Lochs & Glens Cycle Way on the forest trail, or take the A821 over Duke's Pass. Following the southern shore of Loch Achray, you reach the pier on Loch Katrine. The ferry can take you to Stronachlachar (one way with bike £16) on the western shore, from where you can follow the beautiful B829 via Loch Ard back to Aberfoyle.

🛏 Sleeping & Eating

Forth Inn   PUB FOOD **£** (☎01877-382372; www.forthinn.com; Main St, Aberfoyle; mains £8-12; ☉noon-5.30pm & 6-8.30pm; **P 🤖 📶 🐕**) In the middle of the village, locals and visitors alike queue up here for good, honest pub fare: the best bar meal in Aberfoyle. It has a top selection of Scottish craft beers on tap and drinkers spilling outside into the sunny courtyard. Single (£60) and double (£80 to £90) rooms are available, but they can be noisy at weekends.

ⓘ Information

Aberfoyle Information Centre (☎01877-382352; www.visitscottishheartlands.com; Main St, Aberfoyle; ☉10am-5pm Apr-Oct, 10am-4pm Nov-Mar; 🤖) Large office with good selection of walking information.

ⓘ Getting There & Away

First (www.firstgroup.com) has six daily buses (Monday to Saturday) from Stirling (£4.60, 40 minutes).

Callander

POP 3100

Callander, the principal Trossachs town, has been pulling in tourists for over 150 years, and has a laid-back ambience along its main

---

TROSSACHS TRANSPORT

In a bid to cut public transport costs, 'Demand Responsive Transport' (DRT) now covers the Trossachs area. Sounds complex, but basically it means you get a taxi to where you want to go, for the price of a bus. There are various zones. Taxis should preferably be booked 24 hours in advance; call ☎01877-330496. A cab between Callander and Aberfoyle, for example, costs £5.

thoroughfare that quickly lulls visitors into lazy pottering. There's an excellent array of accommodation options here.

The Trossachs is a lovely area to cycle around. The excellent **Wheels Cycling Centre** (☑ 01877-331100; www.wheelscyclingcentre. com; bike per hr/day/week from £8/20/90; ⊙ 10am-6pm Mar-Oct) has a wide range of hire bikes.

🛏 Sleeping

White Shutters
B&B £
(☑ 01877-330442; www.incallander.co.uk/whiteshutters.htm; 6 South Church St; s/d £26/46; 🛜) A cute house just off the main street, White Shutters offers pleasing rooms with shared bathroom and a friendly welcome. The large double is particularly appealing, but it's all clean and comfortable and offers exceptional value.

Callander Hostel
HOSTEL £
(☑ 01877-330141; www.callanderhostel.co.uk; 6 Bridgend; dm/d £23/70; P 🛜) 🅿 This hostel in a mock-Tudor building run by a youth project has well-furnished dorms and a welcoming, if not wholly professional, attitude.

Arden House
B&B ££
(☑ 01877-339405; www.ardenhouse.org.uk; Bracklinn Rd; s from £70, d £85-100; ⊙ Mar-Oct; P 🛜) This elegant home has a fabulous hillside location with verdant garden and lovely vistas; it's close to the centre but far from the crowds. The commodious rooms are impeccable, with lots of natural light. They include large upstairs doubles with great views. Welcoming owners, noble architectural features – super bay windows – and a self-catering studio make this a top option.

Abbotsford Lodge
HOTEL ££
(☑ 01877-330066; www.abbotsfordlodge.com; Stirling Rd; s/d £65/85; ⊙ Mar-Nov; P 🛜) This Victorian house offers something different to the norm, with tartan and florals consigned to the bonfire, replaced by stylish, comfortable contemporary design that enhances the building's original features. There are spacious superiors with modish grey fabrics (from £125) as well as cheaper top-floor rooms – shared bathroom – with lovably offbeat under-roof shapes. Room-only rates are available.

Roslin Cottage
B&B ££
(☑ 01877-339787; www.roslincottage.co.uk; Stirling Rd; s £40, d £55-65; P 🛜) A characterful cottage that's a haven of good hospitality holds three snug en suite rooms that make an enticing Trossachs base. They all have charm: we love the Kirtle room with the original 17th-century wall exposed. Other delights include a lovely big back garden, a log fire in the lounge and sociable chef-cooked breakfasts. It's on the right as you enter Callander from the east, before the petrol station.

★ Roman Camp Hotel
HOTEL £££
(☑ 01877-330003; www.romancamphotel.co.uk; Main St; s/d/superior £110/160/210; P 🛜 🐾) Callander's best hotel is centrally located but feels rural, set by the river in beautiful grounds. Endearing features include a lounge with blazing fire and a library with a tiny secret chapel. It's an old-fashioned warren of a place with four grades of room; standards are certainly luxurious, but superiors are even more appealing, with period furniture, excellent bathrooms, armchairs and fireplace. The upmarket restaurant is open to the public. Reassuringly, the name refers not to toga parties but to a ruin in the adjacent fields.

🍴 Eating & Drinking

★ Callander Meadows
SCOTTISH ££
(☑ 01877-330181; www.callandermeadows.co.uk; 24 Main St; lunches £10, mains £12-16; ⊙ 9am-9pm Thu-Sun Jun-Sep; 🛜) Informal but smart, this restaurant in the town centre occupies the two front rooms of a house on the main street. There's a contemporary flair for presentation and unusual flavour combinations, but a solidly British base underpins the cuisine. There's a great beer/coffee garden out the back, where you can also eat.

Mhor Fish
SEAFOOD ££
(☑ 01877-330213; www.mhor.net; 75 Main St; mains £7-16; ⊙ noon-9pm Tue-Sun) 🅿 This simply decorated spot, with formica tables and a hodge-podge of chairs, sources brilliant sustainable seafood. Browse the fresh catch then eat it pan-seared in the dining area accompanied by a decent wine selection, or fried and wrapped in paper with chips to take away. It's all great – calamari and oysters are wonderfully toothsome starters.

Lade Inn
PUB
(www.theladeinn.com; Kilmahog; ⊙ noon-11pm Mon-Thu, noon-1am Fri & Sat, 12.30-10.30pm Sun; 🛜 ♿) Callander's best pub isn't in Callander – it's a mile west of town. They pull a good pint (with their own real ales) and, next door, they have a shop with a dazzling selection of Scottish beers. There's low-key live music here at weekends. The food (noon to 9pm, from 12.30pm Sunday; mains £9 to £12) at last visit was overpriced and mediocre.

ℹ Information

Callander Visitor Centre (☑ 01877-330342; www.lochlomond-trossachs.org; 52 Main St; ⊙9.30am-5pm Apr-Oct, to 4pm Nov-Mar; 🛜) Very helpful for information on the region and national park.

ℹ Getting There & Away

First (☑ 0871 200 2233; www.firstgroup. com) operates buses from Stirling (£5.20, 45 minutes, hourly Monday to Saturday, every two hours Sunday), while **Kingshouse** (☑ 01877-384768; www.kingshousetravel.com) buses run from Killin (£5.70, 45 minutes, five to six Monday to Saturday). For Aberfoyle, use DRT (p847) or get off a Stirling-bound bus at Blair Drummond safari park and cross the road. There are also **Citylink** (www.citylink.co.uk) buses via Callander from Edinburgh (£16.20, 1¾ hours, two daily mid-May to mid-October) to Oban (£21.30, 2¼ hours) or Fort William (£23.20, 2½ hours).

Loch Katrine

This rugged area, 7 miles north of Aberfoyle and 10 miles west of Callander, is the heart of the Trossachs. From April to October two **boats** (☑ 01877-376315; www.lochkatrine. com; Trossachs Pier; 1hr cruise adult/child £13/8; ⊙Easter-Oct) run seven cruises from Trossachs Pier at the eastern tip of Loch Katrine. One of these is the fabulous centenarian steamship *Sir Walter Scott*; check the website departures, as it's worth coinciding with this veteran if you can. It runs various one-hour afternoon sailings, and at 10.30am (plus additional summer departures) there's a departure to Stronachlachar at the other end of the loch before returning (single/return adult £13/15.50, child £8/9.50, two hours return). From Stronachlachar (also

accessible by car via a 12-mile road from Aberfoyle), you can reach the eastern shore of Loch Lomond at isolated Inversnaid. A tarmac path links Trossachs Pier with Stronachlachar, so you can take the boat out and walk/cycle back (14 miles). At Trossachs Pier **Katrinewheelz** (☑ 01877-376366; www.katrinewheelz.co.uk; hire per half-/full day from £15/20; ⊙9am-5pm Apr-Oct, 11am-3pm Sat & Sun Nov, Dec, Feb & Mar) hires out good bikes and even electric buggies. Bring a picnic; the cafe is mediocre.

Killin

POP 800

A fine base for the Trossachs or Perthshire, this lovely village sits at the western end of Loch Tay and has a spread-out, relaxed sort of feel, particularly around the scenic **Falls of Dochart**, which tumble through the town centre. On a sunny day people sprawl over the rocks by the bridge, with a pint or picnic in hand. Killin offers some fine walking around the town, and mighty mountains and glens close at hand.

🏃 Activities

Five miles northeast of Killin, **Ben Lawers** rises above Loch Tay. Other routes abound; one rewarding **circular walk** heads up into the Acharn forest south of town, emerging above the treeline to great views of Loch Tay and Ben Lawers. Killin Outdoor Centre offers walking advice.

Killin is on the Lochs & Glens cycle route from Glasgow to Inverness. Hire bikes at **Killin Outdoor Centre** (☑ 01567-820652; www. killinoutdoor.co.uk; Main St; bike per 24hr £25, kayak/canoe per 2hr £25/30; ⊙8.45am-5.45pm). It also rents out canoes and kayaks.

WORTH A TRIP

MONACHYLE MHOR

Monachyle Mhor (☑ 01877-384622; www.mhor.net; d £195-265; ⊙Feb-Dec; P🛜🐕) is a luxury hideaway with a fantastically peaceful location overlooking two lochs. It's a great fusion of country Scotland and contemporary attitudes to design and food. The rooms are superb and feature quirkily original decor, particularly the fabulous 'feature rooms'; you might get your own steam room or a wonderful double bathtub. The restaurant serves soup-and-sandwich deals, delicious lunches and five-course dinners (£50), which are high in quality, sustainably sourced and deliciously innovative. Enchantment lies in its successful combination of top-class hospitality with a relaxed rural atmosphere; dogs and kids happily romp on the lawns, and no one looks askance if you come in flushed and muddy after a day's fishing or walking.

📖 Sleeping & Eating

There are numerous good guesthouses strung along the road through town, and a couple of supermarkets for trail supplies.

High Creagan   CAMPSITE £

(📞01567-820449; www.highcreagan.co.uk; Aberfeldy Rd; per person tent/caravan sites £5/8; ☺Apr-Oct; 🅿🐾) This place has a well-kept, sheltered campsite with plenty of grass, set high on the slopes overlooking sparkling Loch Tay, 3 miles east of Killin. Kids under five aren't allowed in the tent area (for insurance reasons) as there's a stream running through it.

Falls of Dochart Inn   PUB FOOD ££

(📞01567-820270; www.falls-of-dochart-inn.co.uk; mains £11-14; ☺noon-3pm & 6-9pm Mon-Thu, to 9.30pm Fri, noon-9.30pm Sat, noon-8.30pm Sun; 🅿🐾) In a prime position overlooking the falls, this is a terrific pub, a snug, atmospheric space with a roaring fire, real ales, personable service and decent pub grub, with some Asian flavours adding a dimension to tasty staples and daily specials. The rooms (singles/doubles from £60/80) are handsome, but a few glitches like poor heating let some of them down. The outside tables are great spots on a sunny day.

❶ Getting There & Away

Two daily **Citylink** (www.citylink.co.uk) buses between Edinburgh (£20.70, 2¼ hours) and Crianlarich/Oban/Fort William stop here; two buses from Dundee to Oban also pass through. Kingshouse (p849) runs five to six buses Monday to Saturday to Callander, where you can change for Stirling. A summer **bus** (www.breadalbane.org; ☺Tue, Wed & Sun Jun–mid-Oct, plus Sat Jul-Aug) does a hop-on hop-off Breadalbane circuit, running to Ben Lawers, Kenmore, Aberfeldy, Crieff and back.

ARGYLL

An ancient and disparate area, Argyll comprises a series of peninsulas and islands along Scotland's ragged southwestern coast, pierced by long sea lochs knifing their way into the hilly, moody landscape. Because of its dramatic geography, places such as the Mull of Kintyre – not so far from Glasgow as the crow flies – can seem impossibly remote.

The islands offer great diversity. Romantic Mull is the gateway to sacred Iona, whereas cheery Islay reverberates with the names of the heavyweights of the whisky world and Jura's wild hillscapes show nature's ultimate mastery and majesty. Meanwhile, the banks of Loch Lomond, the oysters of Loch Fyne and the prehistoric sites of Kilmartin Glen, all within easy striking distance of Glasgow, mean the mainland has nothing to envy.

Loch Lomond & Around

The 'bonnie banks' and 'bonnie braes' of Loch Lomond have long been Glasgow's rural retreat – a scenic region of hills, lochs and healthy fresh air within easy reach of Scotland's largest city. Today the loch's popularity shows no sign of decreasing.

The main tourist focus is along the A82 on the loch's western shore, and at the southern end, around Balloch, which can occasionally be a nightmare of jet skies and motorboats. The eastern shore, which is followed by the West Highland Way long-distance footpath, is a little quieter.

The region's importance was recognised when it became the heart of **Loch Lomond & the Trossachs National Park** (www.lochlomond-trossachs.org), Scotland's first national park, created in 2002.

ROB ROY

Nicknamed Red (*ruadh* in Gaelic, anglicised to 'roy') for his ginger locks, Robert MacGregor (1671–1734) was the wild leader of the wildest of Scotland's clans, outlawed by powerful neighbours, hence their sobriquet, Children of the Mist. Incognito, Rob became a prosperous livestock trader, before a dodgy deal led to a warrant for his arrest.

A legendary swordsman, the fugitive from justice then became notorious for daring raids into the Lowlands to carry off cattle and sheep. Forever hiding from potential captors, he was twice imprisoned, but escaped dramatically on both occasions. He finally turned himself in and received his liberty and a pardon from the king. He lies buried – perhaps – in the churchyard at Balquhidder; his uncompromising later epitaph reads 'MacGregor despite them'. His life has been glorified over the years due to Walter Scott's novel and the 1995 film. Many Scots see his life as a symbol of the struggle of the common folk against the inequitable ownership of vast tracts of the country by landed aristocrats.

⚡ Activities

Walking

The big walk around here is the West Highland Way (p837), which runs along the eastern shore of the loch. There are shorter lochside walks at Firkin Point on the western shore and at several other places around the loch.

Rowardennan is the starting point for an ascent of Ben Lomond (974m), a popular and relatively straightforward (if strenuous) five- to six-hour round trip. The route starts at the car park just past the Rowardennan Hotel.

Boat Trips & Canoeing

The main centre for boat trips is Balloch, where Sweeney's Cruises (☑ 01389-752376; www.sweeneyscruises.com; Balloch Rd, Balloch) offers a range of trips including a one-hour cruise to Inchmurrin and back (adult/child £8.50/5, departs hourly).

Cruise Loch Lomond   BOATING
(☑ 01301-702356; www.cruiselochlomond.co.uk; Tarbet/Luss; ⊘ 8.30am-5.30pm early Apr-late Oct) Based in Tarbet and offers trips to Inversnaid and Rob Roy MacGregor's Cave. You can also be dropped off at Rowardennan and picked up at Inversnaid after a 9-mile hike along the West Highland Way (£15).

Can You Experience   BOATING
(☑ 01389-756251; www.canyouexperience.com; Loch Lomond Shores, Balloch; ⊘ 9am-5.30pm Easter-Oct) Offers a huge range of activities on water and land from various bases around Loch Lomond. Hire mountain bikes (£13/17 per half/full day), canoes and kayaks or take a full-day guided canoe safari (£50).

🛏 Sleeping & Eating

★ Rowardennan SYHA   HOSTEL £
(☑ 01360-870259; www.syha.org.uk; Rowardennan; dm/tw £18/42; ⊘ late Mar-early Oct; ℗ 🛜) Where the road ends on the eastern side of the loch, this is a wonderful retreat in an elegant ex-hunting lodge with lawns stretching right down to the water's edge. Whether you're walking the West Highland Way, climbing Ben Lomond or just putting your feet up, it's a great choice, with atmosphere, genial staff and a huge lounge that has windows overlooking Loch Lomond.

Cashel Campsite   CAMPSITE £
(☑ 01360-870234; www.campingintheforest.co.uk; Rowardennan; sites £15-17, incl car £20-31; ⊘ Mar-Oct; ℗ 🐾) The most attractive campsite in the area is 3 miles north of Balmaha, on the shore.

Oak Tree Inn   INN ££
(☑ 01360-870357; www.oak-tree-inn.co.uk; Balmaha; dm/s/d £30/50/85; ℗ 🛜) An attractive traditional inn built in slate and timber, this place offers bright modern guest bedrooms for pampered hikers, super-spacious superior chambers, self-catering cottages and two four-bed bunkrooms for hardier souls. The rustic restaurant brings locals, tourists and walkers together and dishes up hearty meals that cover lots of bases (mains £9 to £12, food noon to 9pm). There's lots of outdoor seating and they brew their own beers.

★ Drover's Inn   PUB FOOD ££
(☑ 01301-704234; www.thedroversinn.co.uk; Ardlui; bar meals £8-12; ⊘ 11.30am-10pm Mon-Sat, 11.30am-9.30pm Sun; ℗ 🛜) This is one howff (drinking den) you shouldn't miss – a low-ceilinged place just north of Ardlui with smoke-blackened stone, barmen in kilts, and walls festooned with stags' heads and stuffed birds. The bar, where Rob Roy allegedly dropped by for pints, serves hearty hill-walking fuel and hosts live folk at weekends. We recommend this more as an atmospheric place to eat and drink than somewhere to stay.

ℹ Information

Balloch Tourist Office (☑ 01389-753533; Balloch Rd, Balloch; ⊘ 9.30am-6pm Jun-Aug, 10am-5pm Sep-May) Opposite Balloch train station.

Balmaha National Park Centre (☑ 01389-722100; www.lochlomond-trossachs.org; Balmaha; ⊘ 9.30am-4.30pm Apr-Sep, 9.30am-4pm Sat & Sun Oct-Mar) Has maps showing local walking routes.

National Park Gateway Centre (☑ 01389-751035; www.lochlomondshores.com; Loch Lomond Shores, Balloch; ⊘ 10am-6pm Apr-Sep, 10am-5pm Oct-Mar; 🛜) Crowded information desk with shop and cafe.

Tarbet Tourist Office (☑ 01301-702260; Tarbet; ⊘ 10am-4pm Easter & May-Sep) At the junction of the A82 and the A83.

ℹ Getting There & Away

BUS

First Glasgow (p820) bus 1A runs from Argyle St in central Glasgow to Balloch (£4.50, 1½ hours, at least two per hour) and bus C8 to Drymen (£5.20, 1¼ hours, two daily).

Scottish Citylink (☑ 0871 266-3333; www.citylink.co.uk) coaches from Glasgow stop at Luss (£8.50, 55 minutes, nine daily), Tarbet (£8.50, 65 minutes, nine daily) and Ardlui (£14.90, 1¼ hours, four daily).

TRAIN

Glasgow to Balloch £5.10, 45 minutes, every 30 minutes

Glasgow to Arrochar & Tarbet £11.40, 1¼ hours, three or four daily

Glasgow to Ardlui £14.90, 1½ hours, three or four daily, continuing to Oban and Fort William

Inveraray

POP 600

There's no 50 shades of grey around here: this historic planned village is all black and white – even logos of high street shops conform. Spectacularly set on the shores of Loch Fyne, Inveraray was built by the Duke of Argyll in Georgian style when he revamped his nearby castle in the 18th century.

◉ Sights

Inveraray Castle   CASTLE
(☑ 01499-302203; www.inveraray-castle.com; adult/child £10/7, parking £2; ⊙ 10am-5.45pm Apr-Oct) This visually stunning castle has been the seat of the Dukes of Argyll – chiefs of Clan Campbell – since the 15th century. The 18th-century building, with its fairy-tale turrets and fake battlements, houses an impressive armoury hall, its walls patterned with more than 1000 pole-arms, dirks, muskets and Lochaber axes. The castle is 500m north of town, entered from the A819 Dalmally road.

Inveraray Jail   MUSEUM
(☑ 01499-302381; www.inverarayjail.co.uk; Church Sq; adult/child £9.50/5.25; ⊙ 9.30am-6pm Apr-Oct, 10am-5pm Nov-Mar; ⊕) At this entertaining interactive tourist attraction you can sit in on a trial, try out a cell and discover the harsh tortures that were meted out to unfortunate prisoners. The attention to detail – including a life-sized model of an inmate squatting on a 19th-century toilet – more than makes up for the sometimes tedious commentary.

⌸ Sleeping & Eating

Inveraray Hostel   HOSTEL £
(☑ 01499-302454; www.inverarayhostel.co.uk; Dalmally Rd; dm £17-18; ⊙ Apr-Oct; P◉) To get to this hostel, housed in a comfortable, modern bungalow, go through the right-hand-side arched entrance (there are two) on the seafront. Metal bunk beds (rooms sleep only two or four) are comfortable, and there's a wee lounge and kitchen with plenty of stoves.

George Hotel   HOTEL ££
(☑ 01499-302111; www.thegeorgehotel.co.uk; Main St E; d £80-100; P◈◉) The George boasts a magnificent choice of opulent rooms complete with four-poster beds, period furniture, Victorian roll-top baths and private Jacuzzis (superior rooms cost £145 to £170 per double). Some are in an annexe across the way. The cosy wood-panelled bar, with rough stone walls, flagstone floor and peat fires, is a delightful place for all-day bar meals (mains £9 to £16; noon to 9pm) and has a beer garden.

★**Loch Fyne Oyster Bar**   SEAFOOD ££
(☑ 01499-600236; www.lochfyne.com; Clachan, Cairndow; mains £11-22; ⊙ 9am-7pm or 8pm; ◉) ✦ The success of this cooperative is such that it now lends its name to dozens of restaurants throughout the UK. But the original's still the best, with salty oysters straight out of the lake, and fabulous salmon dishes. The atmosphere and decor is simple, friendly and unpretentious; there's also a shop and deli.

⊙ Getting There & Away

Scottish Citylink (www.citylink.co.uk) buses run from Glasgow to Inveraray (£11.90, 1¾ hours, seven daily). Five continue to Campbeltown (£13, 2½ hours); the others go to Oban (£9.90, 1¼ hours, two daily). There are buses to Dunoon (£3.90, 1¼ hours, three daily Monday to Saturday).

Kilmartin Glen

This glen is the focus of one of the biggest concentrations of prehistoric sites in Scotland. Burial cairns, standing stones, stone circles, hill forts and cup-and-ring-marked rocks litter the countryside. Within a 6-mile radius of Kilmartin village there are 25 sites with standing stones and over 100 rock carvings.

In the 6th century, Irish settlers arrived in this part of Argyll and founded the kingdom of Dál Riata (Dalriada), which eventually united with the Picts in 843 to create the first Scottish kingdom. Their capital was the hill fort of Dunadd, on the plain to the south of Kilmartin.

◉ Sights

Your first stop should be **Kilmartin House Museum** (☑ 01546-510278; www.kilmartin.org; Kilmartin; adult/child £5/2; ⊙ 10am-5.30pm Mar-Oct, 11am-4pm Nov-23 Dec), in Kilmartin village, a fascinating interpretative centre that provides a context for the ancient monuments you can go on to explore, alongside displays of artefacts recovered from various sites. There's also an excellent **cafe** (☑ 01546-510278; mains £5-9; ◔ 10am-5pm Mar-Oct, 11am-4pm Nov-Christmas; ☜) and a shop with handcrafts and books on Scotland.

The oldest monuments at Kilmartin date from 5000 years ago and comprise a linear cemetery of **burial cairns** that runs south 1.5 miles from Kilmartin village. There are also two stone circles at **Temple Wood**, 0.75 miles southwest of Kilmartin.

Kilmartin Churchyard contains 10th-century Celtic crosses and medieval grave slabs with carved effigies of knights. Some researchers have surmised that these were the tombs of Knights Templar who fled persecution in France in the 14th century.

The hill fort of **Dunadd**, 3.5 miles south of Kilmartin village, was the seat of power of the first kings of Dál Riata, and may have been where the **Stone of Destiny** was originally located. Faint rock carvings of a boar and two footprints with an Ogham inscription may have been used in some kind of inauguration ceremony. The prominent little hill rises straight out of the boggy plain of **Moine Mhor Nature Reserve**. A slippery path leads to the summit where you can gaze out on much the same view that the kings of Dál Riata enjoyed 1300 years ago.

ⓘ Getting There & Away

Bus 423 between Oban and Ardrishaig (three to five Monday to Friday, two on Saturday) stops at Kilmartin (£5.60, one hour).

You can walk or cycle along the Crinan Canal from Ardrishaig, then turn north at Bellanoch on the minor B8025 road to reach Kilmartin (12 miles one way).

Kintyre

Almost an island, the 40-mile-long Kintyre Peninsula has only a narrow isthmus at Tarbert connecting it to the rest of Scotland. Magnus Barefoot the Viking, who could claim any island he circumnavigated, made his people drag their longship across this strand to validate his claim to Kintyre.

Tarbert

POP 1200

The attractive fishing village and yachting centre of Tarbert is the gateway to Kintyre, and most scenic, with buildings strung around its excellent natural harbour. It's well worth a stopover.

◉ Sights & Activities

The harbour is overlooked by the ivy-covered ruins of **Tarbert Castle**, rebuilt by Robert the Bruce in the 14th century. You can hike up via a signposted footpath beside **Loch Fyne Gallery** (www.lochfynegallery.com; Harbour St; ◔ 10am-5pm Mon-Sat, 10.30am-5pm Sun), which showcases the work of local artists.

Tarbert is the starting point for the 100-mile **Kintyre Way**. The 9-mile first section to Skipness makes a pleasant day-hike, climbing through forestry plantations to a high moorland plateau where you can soak up superb views to the Isle of Arran.

🛏 Sleeping & Eating

Knap Guest House   B&B ££

(☑ 01880-820015;   www.knapguesthouse.co.uk; Campbeltown Rd; s/d from £50/70; @ ☜) A flight of stairs lit by Edwardian stained glass leads to this 1st-floor flat with three spacious en suite bedrooms sporting an attractive blend of Scottish and Far Eastern decor. The welcome is warm, and there are great harbour views from the lounge (leather sofas, log fire and a small library) and breakfast room.

★ Starfish   SEAFOOD ££

(☑ 01880-820733; wwwstarfishtarbert.com; Castle St; mains £11-19; ◔ noon-2pm & 6-9pm Tue-Sun) Simple but stylish describes not only the decor in this friendly restaurant, but the seafood too. A great variety of specials – anything from classic French fish dishes to Thai curries – are prepared with whatever's fresh off the Tarbert boats that day. Best to book a table. Reduced hours off-season.

Campbeltown

POP 4900

Blue-collar Campbeltown, set around a beautiful harbour, still suffers from the decline of its fishing and whisky industries and the closure of the nearby air force base, but is rebounding on the back of golf tourism and a ferry link to Ayrshire. The spruced-up seafront, backed by green hills, lends the town a distinctly optimistic air.

The **Mull of Kintyre Music Festival** (☑ 01586-551053; www.mokfest.com), held in late August, is a popular event featuring traditional Scottish and Irish music.

◉ Sights & Activities

Springbank   DISTILLERY

(☑ 01586-552009;   www.springbankwhisky.com; 85 Longrow; tours from £6.50; ◔ tours 10am & 2pm

Mon-Sat) There were once no fewer than 32 distilleries around Campbeltown, but most closed in the 1920s. Today this is one of only three that are operational. It is also one of the few that distils, matures and bottles all its whisky on the one site, making for an interesting tour. It's a quality malt, one of Scotland's finest.

Davaar Cave   CAVE

A very unusual sight awaits in this cave on the southern side of Davaar island, at the mouth of Campbeltown Loch. On the wall of the cave is an eerie painting of the Crucifixion by local artist Archibald MacKinnon, dating from 1887. You can walk to the island at low tide: check tide times with the tourist office.

Machrihanish Bay   BEACH, GOLF

Five miles northwest of Campbeltown, this has a 3-mile-long sandy beach popular with surfers and windsurfers. There are two great golf courses here, both very competitively priced compared to their more famous rivals: **Machrihanish Golf Club** (✑01586-810213; www.machgolf.com; green fee £65) is a classic links course, designed by Old Tom Morris. Much-newer **Machrihanish Dunes** (✑01586-810000; www.machrihanishdunes.com; Campbeltown; green fee around £70) offers another impressive seaside experience, commendably light on snobbery: the clubhouse is a convivial little hut, kids play free, and there are always website offers.

Mull of Kintyre Seatours   BOAT TOUR

(✑07785-542811; www.mull-of-kintyre.co.uk; ⏱Apr-Sep) Operates high-speed boat trips out of Campbeltown harbour to the spectacular sea cliffs of the Mull of Kintyre, Arran, Ailsa Craig (£30; gannet colony and puffins), or Sanda Island (£25; seals, puffins and other seabirds) as well as whalewatching (£30, best late July to early September). Book in advance by phone or at the tourist office.

🛏 Sleeping & Eating

Campbeltown Backpackers   HOSTEL £

(✑01586-551188; www.campbeltownbackpackers.co.uk; Big Kiln St; dm £20; 🅿🛜) 🌿 This beautiful hostel occupies a central former school building: it's great, with a modern kitchen, disabled access and state-of-the-art wooden bunks. Profits maintain the Heritage Centre running it. Rates are £2 cheaper if you pre-book.

Redknowe   B&B ££

(✑01586-550374; www.redknowe.co.uk; Witchburn Rd; s £35, d £60-70; 🅿🛜🐾) An interesting Victorian home that's a short walk from the centre of town but feels rural with a lovely garden and an outlook over green fields. There's a fine welcome from the friendly couple that run it, a very decent breakfast, and comfortable rooms, a couple of which share an immaculate bathroom.

Royal Hotel   HOTEL £££

(✑01586-810000; www.machrihanishdunes.com; Main St; r £142-152; ⏱food noon-9pm Sun-Thu, noon-10pm Fri & Sat; 🅿🛜) Historically Campbeltown's best address, this hotel opposite the harbour is looking swish again. It caters mostly to yachties and golfers; though rack rates feel overpriced, there are often online specials and rooms are very spacious and attractive. The restaurant (mains £11 to £30) is the town's best, with fresh seafood and tasty grilled steaks the highlight.

ℹ Getting There & Away

BOAT

Kintyre Express (✑01586-555895; www.kintyreexpress.com) operates a small, high-speed passenger ferry from Campbeltown to Ballycastle in Northern Ireland (£35/60 one way/return, 1½ hours, daily May to August, four weekly April and September, two weekly October to March). You must book in advance.

Calmac (✑0800 066-5000; www.calmac.co.uk) run thrice weekly May to September between Ardrossan in Ayrshire and Campbeltown (adult/car £9.80/60, 2¾ hours); the Saturday return service stops at Brodick on Arran.

BUS

Scottish Citylink (www.citylink.co.uk) runs from Campbeltown to Glasgow (£19.80, 4¼ hours, five daily) via Tarbert, Inveraray and Loch Lomond. Change at Inveraray for Oban.

Mull of Kintyre

A narrow winding road, 15 miles long, leads south from Campbeltown to the **Mull of Kintyre**, passing some good sandy beaches near Southend. This remote headland was immortalised in Paul McCartney's famous song – the former Beatle owns a farmhouse in the area. From where the road ends, a 30-minute steep downhill walk leads to a clifftop **lighthouse**, with Northern Ireland, only 12 miles away, visible across the channel. Don't leave the road when the frequent mists roll in as it's easy to become disoriented.

Isle of Arran

Enchanting Arran is a jewel in Scotland's scenic crown. The island is a visual feast, and boasts culinary delights, its own brewery and distillery, and stacks of accommodation options. The variations in Scotland's dramatic landscape can all be experienced on this one island, best explored by pulling on the hiking boots or jumping on a bicycle. Arran offers some challenging walks in the mountainous north while the island's circular coastal road is very popular with cyclists.

ℹ Information

Brodick Information Centre (☑ 01770-303774; www.ayrshire-arran.com; Brodick; ☺9am-5pm Mon-Sat) Efficient. Located by Brodick ferry pier; also open Sundays in summer. Slightly reduced hours in winter.

ℹ Getting There & Away

CalMac (☑ 0800 066-5000; www.calmac.co.uk) runs between Ardrossan and Brodick (passenger/car return £11.35/70, 55 minutes, four to 10 daily), and from April to late October also runs services between Claonaig on the Kintyre peninsula and Lochranza (passenger/car return £10.35/47, 30 minutes, seven to nine daily).

ℹ Getting Around

Four to seven buses daily go from Brodick pier to Lochranza (£2.95, 45 minutes), and many head to Lamlash (£2.05) and Whiting Bay (£2.95, 30 minutes), then on to Kildonan and Blackwaterfoot. Grab a timetable from the tourist office. An Arran Dayrider (a day's travel) costs £5.40 from the driver. Bicycle and car hire are available in Brodick.

Brodick & Around

Most visitors arrive in Brodick, the beating heart of the island, and congregate along the coastal road to admire the town's long curving bay. Main attractions are just out of town, off the Lochranza road.

⊙ Sights & Activities

The 55-mile coastal circuit is popular with cyclists and has few serious hills – more in the south than the north. There are plenty of walking booklets and maps available, and trails are clearly signpost-

Isle of Arran

ed around the island. Several leave from Lochranza, including the spectacular walk to the island's northeast tip, the **Cock of Arran**, finishing in the village of Sannox (8 miles one-way).

Tackling **Goatfell** (the island's tallest peak) takes up to eight hours return, starting in Brodick. If the weather's fine, there are superb views to Ben Lomond and the coast of Northern Ireland.

Brodick Castle   CASTLE
(NTS; www.nts.org.uk; castle & park adult/child £12.50/9, park only £6.50/5.50; ☺castle 11am-4pm May-Sep, 11am-3pm Apr & Oct, park 9.30am-sunset year-round) This elegant castle 2 miles north of Brodick evolved from 13th-century origins into a stately home and hunting lodge for the Dukes of Hamilton and was used until the 1950s. You enter via the hunting gallery, wallpapered with deer heads. The rest of the interior is characterised by fabulous 19th-century wooden furniture and an array of horses 'n' hounds paintings. Helpful guides and laminated sheets – the kids' ones are more entertaining – provide extra info.

The extensive grounds, now a country park with various trails among the rhododendrons, justify the steep entry fee.

🛏 Sleeping

Glenartney   B&B **££**

(📞01770-302220; www.glenartney-arran.co.uk; Mayish Rd; s/d £52/85; ⊙ Easter-Sep; P🕸🛜♨) 🚲 Uplifting bay views and genuine, helpful hosts make this a cracking option. Airy, stylish rooms make the most of the natural light available at the top of the town. Cyclists will appreciate bike wash, repair and storage facilities, while hikers can benefit from drying rooms and expert trail advice. They make big efforts to be sustainable.

★Kilmichael Country House Hotel   HOTEL **£££**

(📞01770-302219; www.kilmichael.com; s £95, d £163-204; ⊙ Apr-Oct; P🛜♨) The island's best hotel is also the oldest building – one bit dates from 1650. Luxurious and tastefully decorated, it's a mile outside Brodick but seems a world away in deep countryside. With just eight spacious, very individual rooms and excellent four-course dinners (£45, open to nonguests), it's an ideal, utterly relaxing hideaway, that feels very classy without being overly formal.

In the grounds there are also five self-catering cottages.

✕ Eating

★Brodick Bar   BRASSERIE **££**

(📞01770-302169; www.brodickbar.co.uk; Alma Rd; mains £9-19; ⊙ noon-2.30pm & 5.30-8.45pm or later Mon-Sat; 🛜) Don't leave Brodick without stopping here. The regularly changing blackboard menu brings modern French flair to this Arran pub, with great presentation, efficient service and delicious flavour combinations. You'll have a hard time choosing, as it's all brilliant. It's very buzzy on weekend evenings.

Lochranza

The village of Lochranza has a stunning location in a small bay at the island's north. On a promontory stands ruined 13th-century **Lochranza Castle** (HS; www.historic-scotland. gov.uk; ⊙ 24hr; **FREE**), basically a draughty shell inside.

Isle of Arran Distillery (📞01770-830264; www.arranwhisky.com; tours adult/child £6/free; ⊙ 10am-5.30pm Apr-Oct, 11am-4pm Mon-Sat Nov-Mar) produces a light, aromatic single malt. The tour is a good one; it's a small set-up, and the whisky-making process is thoroughly explained. More expensive tours (£15) include extra tastings.

🛏 Sleeping

★Lochranza SYHA   HOSTEL **£**

(📞01770-830631; www.syha.org.uk; dm/d £19/50; ⊙ mid-Mar–Oct plus Sat & Sun year-round; P@🛜♨) 🚲 An excellent hostel in a charming place, with lovely views. Rooms sport chunky wooden furniture, keycards, and lockers. Rainwater toilets, energy-saving heating solutions, and an excellent accessible room show thoughtful design, while plush lounging areas, a kitchen you could run a restaurant out of, a laundry, a drying room, red deer in the garden, and welcoming management combine to make this a top option.

Castlekirk   B&B **££**

(📞01770-830202; www.castlekirkarran.co.uk; s £35-40, d £60-75; ⊙ Mar-Oct; P🛜♨) This unusual and warmly welcoming place to stay is a converted church chock-full of excellent artworks; there's a gallery downstairs, and paintings decorate the passageways and rooms. The breakfast area is dignified by a rose window, and there are great views of the castle opposite. Rooms are cosy under the sloping ceiling.

West Coast

On the western side of the island is **Machrie Moor Stone Circle**, a pleasant 20-30 minute stroll from the parking area on the coastal road. There are actually several separate groups of stones of varying sizes, erected around 4000 years ago. You pass a Bronze Age burial cairn along the path.

Blackwaterfoot is the west coast's largest village, with shop and hotel. You can walk to **King's Cave** from here – Arran is one of several islands that claim the cave where Robert the Bruce had his famous arachnid encounter. This walk can easily be extended to the Machrie stones.

South Coast

The landscape in the south is gentler; the road drops into little wooded valleys, and it's particularly lovely around **Lagg**, where a 10-minute walk goes to **Torrylinn Cairn**, a chambered tomb over 4000 years old. **Kildonan** has pleasant sandy beaches, a gorgeous water outlook, hotel, campground and ivy-clad ruined castle.

In genteel **Whiting Bay** you'll find small sandy beaches and local walks.

🛏 Sleeping & Eating

Sealshore Campsite CAMPSITE £
(✆01770-820320; www.campingarran.com; Kildonan; sites per adult/child £6/3, per tent £2-4; ⊙Apr-Oct; P 🛜 🐾) Living up to its name, this excellent small campsite is right by sea (and the Kildonan Hotel) with one of Arran's finest views from its grassy camping area. There's a good washroom area with heaps of showers, kitchen facilities, and the breeze keeps the midges away. Cosy camping pods cost £30 for two people.

Kildonan Hotel HOTEL ££
(✆01770-820207; www.kildonanhotel.com; Kildonan; s/d/ste £75/99/135; P @ 🛜 🐾) Appealing rooms and a grounded attitude – dogs and kids are made very welcome – combine to make this one of Arran's better options. Oh, and it's right by the water, with seals basking on the rocks. The standard rooms could do with a pep-up but are decent; the suites – with private terrace or small balcony – are great.

Nearly all rooms have sea views; other attractions include great staff, a bar and restaurant serving tasty meals (mains £9 to £17; noon to 3pm and 6pm to 9pm), and live folk music.

Lagg Hotel INN ££
(✆01770-870255; www.lagghotel.com; Lagg, Kilmory; s/d £50/90; ⊙Apr-Oct; P 🛜 🐾) This 18th-century coaching inn has a beautiful location and is the perfect place for a romantic weekend away from the cares of modern life. Rooms are smart; grab a superior one (£100) with garden views. There's also a cracking beer garden, a fine bar with log fire and an elegant restaurant (mains £9 to £13; noon to 3pm and 5.30pm to 9pm) with good veggie options.

Lamlash

Lamlash is in a dazzling setting, strung along the beachfront. Just off the coast is **Holy Island**, owned by the Samye Ling Tibetan Centre and used as a retreat, but day visits are allowed. Depending on tides, the **ferry** (✆01770-600998; tomin10@btinternet.com; adult/child return £12/6; ⊙May-Sep, by arrangement Tue & Fri winter) makes around seven daily trips from Lamlash (15 minutes) between May and September. You can stay at the **Holy Island Centre for World Peace & Health** (✆01770-601100; www.holyisle.org; dm/s/d £28/47/72; ⊙Apr-Oct). Prices include full (vegetarian) board.

🛏 Sleeping & Eating

★Glenisle Hotel HOTEL ££
(✆01770-600559; www.glenislehotel.com; Shore Rd; s/d/superior d £83/128/167; 🛜) This stylish hotel offers great service and high comfort levels. Rooms are decorated with contemporary fabrics; the 'cosy' ones under the sloping ceiling upstairs are a little cheaper. All feel fresh and include binoculars for scouring the seashore; upgrade to a superior for the best views over the water. Downstairs is excellent pub food (mains £10 to £13; 8am to 9pm, reduced hours in winter), with Scottish classics and a good wine list.

★Drift Inn PUB FOOD ££
(✆01770-600608; www.driftinnarran.com; Shore Rd; mains £10-18; ⊙food noon-9pm; 🛜) Recently refurbished, this is now the island's best pub, with a plush interior with leather chairs and a fireplace, as well as a fabulous beer garden – enjoy magnificent views from both across to Holy Island. Great bar food is on offer – upmarket fare with thoughtful vegetarian options – as well as Arran ales on tap and soul and blues on the stereo.

Isle of Islay

POP 3200

The home of some of the world's greatest and peatiest whiskies, whose names reverberate on the tongue like a pantheon of Celtic deities, Islay (eye-lah) is a wonderfully friendly place whose welcoming inhabitants offset its lack of the scenic splendour of Mull or Skye. The distilleries are well-geared up for visits; even if you're not a fan of single malt, the bird life, fine seafood, turquoise bays and basking seals are ample reason to visit. Locals are among Britain's most genial: a wave or cheerio to passers-by is mandatory, and you'll soon find yourself unwinding to relaxing island pace. The only drawback is that the waves of well-heeled whisky tourists have induced many sleeping and eating options to raise prices to eye-watering levels.

🎊 Festivals & Events

Fèis Ìle MUSIC, WHISKY
(Islay Festival; www.islayfestival.com) A week-long celebration of traditional Scottish music and whisky at the end of May. Events include *ceilidhs,* pipe-band performances, distillery tours, barbecues and whisky tastings.

Islay, Jura & Colonsay

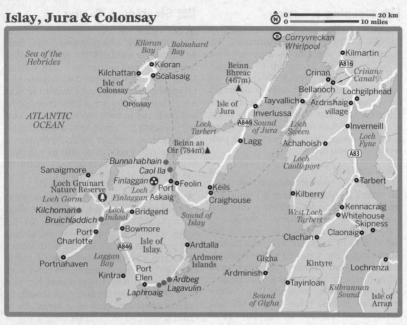

Islay Jazz Festival

MUSIC

(www.islayjazzfestival.co.uk) This three-day festival takes place over the second weekend in September. A varied line-up of international talent plays at venues across the island.

ℹ Information

Islay Tourist Office (☎ 01496-810254; The Square, Bowmore; ☺10am-5pm Mon-Sat, noon-3pm Sun Easter-Oct, 10am-3pm Mon-Fri Nov-Mar)

ℹ Getting There & Away

There are two ferry terminals on the island, both served by ferries from Kennacraig in West Loch Tarbert: Port Askaig on the east coast and Port Ellen in the south. Islay airport lies midway between Port Ellen and Bowmore.

AIR

Loganair/FlyBe (www.loganair.co.uk) flies daily from Glasgow to Islay, while **Hebridean Air Services** (☎ 0845 805-7465; www.hebrideanair.co.uk) operates twice daily Tuesday and Thursday from Oban to Colonsay and Islay.

BOAT

CalMac (www.calmac.co.uk) runs ferries from Kennacraig to Port Ellen or Port Askaig (passenger/car £6.45/32, two to 2¼ hours, three to five daily). On Wednesday and Saturdays in summer

you can continue to Colonsay (£3.95/16.55, 1¼ hours) and Oban (£11.10/54, four hours).

ℹ Getting Around

BICYCLE

There are various places to hire bikes, including **Islay Cycles** (☎ 07760-196592; www.islaycycles.co.uk; Port Ellen; bikes per day/week from £15/60) in Port Ellen.

BUS

A bus links Ardbeg, Port Ellen, Bowmore, Port Charlotte, Portnahaven and Port Askaig (limited service on Sunday). Pick up a copy of the *Islay & Jura Public Transport Guide* from the tourist office.

CAR

D&N MacKenzie (☎ 01496-302300; www.carhireonislay.co.uk; Islay Airport) offers car hire from £32 a day and can meet ferries.

TAXI

There are various drivers; **Carol** (☎ 01496-302155; www.carols-cabs.co.uk) can take bikes in her taxi.

Port Ellen & Around

Port Ellen is the main point of entry for Islay. While there's nothing to see in the town itself, the coast stretching northeast from Port Ellen is one of the loveliest parts of the island.

There are three **whisky distilleries** in close succession (check websites for tour times):

Laphroaig DISTILLERY
(www.laphroaig.com; tours from £6; ⏰ 9.45am-5pm daily Mar-Oct, 9.45am-4.30pm daily Nov & Dec, 9.45am-4.30pm Mon-Fri Jan-Feb)

Lagavulin DISTILLERY
(www.discovering-distilleries.com; tours from £6; ⏰ 9am-7pm Mon-Fri, to 5pm Sat & Sun Jun-Sep, 9am-5pm daily Apr, May & Oct, 10am-4pm Mon-Sat Nov-Feb, 10am-4pm daily Mar)

Ardbeg DISTILLERY
(www.ardbeg.com; tours from £5; ⏰ 9.30am-5pm Mon-Fri, plus Sat Apr-Oct & Sun May-Sep)

A pleasant bike ride leads past the distilleries to the atmospheric, age-haunted **Kildalton Chapel**, 8 miles northeast of Port Ellen. In the kirkyard is the exceptional late-8th-century **Kildalton Cross**, the only remaining Celtic high cross in Scotland (most surviving high crosses are in Ireland). There are carvings of biblical scenes on one side and animals on the other. There are also several extraordinary grave slabs around the chapel, some carved with swords and Celtic interlace patterns.

🛏 Sleeping & Eating

Kintra Farm CAMPSITE, B&B £
(☑ 01496-302051; www.kintrafarm.co.uk; tent sites £6-8, plus adult/child £4/2, s/d £50/80; ⏰ Apr-Sep; 🅿) At the southern end of Laggan Bay, Kintra is a basic but beautiful campsite on buttercup-sprinkled turf amid the dunes, with a sunset view across the beach. There's also a B&B available.

★**Oystercatcher B&B** B&B £££
(☑ 01496-300409; www.islay-bedandbreakfast.com; 63 Frederick Cres; s/d £60/80; 🛜) Two beautifully decorated upstairs rooms with a maritime theme and water views make inviting Islay bases in this excellent B&B. Thoughtful breakfast options and a super-welcoming host add appeal. If you want to dine here, you can organise to order in a seafood platter.

Old Kiln Café CAFE £
(☑ 01496-302244; www.ardbeg.com; Ardbeg; mains £5-11; ⏰ 10am-4.30pm daily May-Sep, Mon-Sat Apr & Oct, Mon-Fri Nov-Mar) Housed in the former malting kiln at Ardbeg distillery, this cafe serves homemade soups, tasty light meals, heartier daily specials and a range of desserts, including traditional clootie dumpling (a steamed pudding filled with currants and raisins).

Bowmore

The attractive Georgian village of Bowmore was built in 1768 to replace the village of Kilarrow, which just had to go – it was spoiling the view from the laird's house. Its centrepiece is the distinctive **Round Church** at the top of Main St, built in circular form to ensure that the devil had no corners to hide in.

Bowmore Distillery (☑ 01496-810441; www.bowmore.com; School St; tours from £6; ⏰ 9am-5pm Mon-Fri & 9am-12.30pm Sat Oct-Mar, 9am-5pm Mon-Sat & noon-4pm Sun Apr-Sep) is the only distillery on the island that still malts its own barley. The tour (check website for times), which begins with an overblown 10-minute marketing video, is redeemed by a look at (and taste of) the germinating grain laid out in golden billows on the floor of the malting shed, and a free dram at the end.

🛏 Sleeping & Eating

Lambeth House B&B ££
(☑ 01496-810597; lambethguesthouse@tiscali.co.uk; Jamieson St; s/d £60/94; 🛜) Cheerily welcoming, and with smart refurbished rooms with top-notch en suite bathrooms, this is a sound option in the centre of town. Breakfasts are reliably good. Rooms vary substantially in size.

Harbour Inn INN £££
(☑ 01496-810330; www.harbour-inn.com; The Sq; s/d from £110/145; 🛜) The plush seven-room Harbour Inn, now owned by Bowmore whisky, is the poshest place in town. The restaurant (mains £19 to £26; open noon to 2pm and 6pm to 9pm) has harbour views and serves fresh local oysters, lobster and scallops, Islay lamb and Jura venison. It's tasty, but feels a little overpriced.

Port Charlotte

Eleven miles from Bowmore, on the opposite shore of Loch Indaal, is the attractive village of Port Charlotte. It has a **general store** (⏰ 9am-12.30pm & 1.30-5.30pm Mon-Sat, 11.30am-1.30pm Sun) and post office.

Islay's long history is lovingly recorded in the **Museum of Islay Life** (☑ 01496-850358; www.islaymuseum.org; Port Charlotte; adult/child £3/1; ⏰ 10.30am-4.30pm Mon-Fri Apr-Sep), housed in the former Free Church. Prize exhibits include an illicit still, 19th-century crofters' furniture, and a set of leather boots once worn by the horse that pulled the lawnmower at Islay House (so it wouldn't leave hoof prints on the lawn!).

The **Bruichladdich Distillery** (☎01496-850190; www.bruichladdich.com; tours £5; ⊙9am-6pm Mon-Fri & 9.30am-4pm Sat, plus 12.30-3.30pm Sun Apr-Aug), at the northern edge of the village, reopened in 2001 with all of its original Victorian equipment restored to working condition. Independently owned and independently minded, Bruichladdich (brook-*lah*-day) produces an intriguing range of distinctive, very peaty whiskies. Call ahead to book a tour.

🛏 Sleeping & Eating

Islay SYHA   HOSTEL £
(☎01496-850385; www.syha.org.uk; dm/q £19/80; ⊙Apr-Oct; @🗢) This modern and comfortable hostel is housed in a former distillery building with views over the loch.

Port Mòr Campsite   CAMPSITE £
(☎01496-850441; www.islandofislay.co.uk; tent sites per adult/child £8/4; @🗢) The sports field in Port Charlotte doubles as a campground – there are toilets, showers, a laundry and a children's play area in the main building. Open all year.

Port Charlotte Hotel   HOTEL £££
(☎01496-850360; www.portcharlottehotel. co.uk; s/d £115/190; P🗢🐾) This lovely old Victorian hotel has stylish, individually decorated bedrooms with sea views, and a candlelit **restaurant** (mains £21-33; ⊙6.30-9pm) serving local seafood, Islay beef, venison and duck. The **bar** (mains £10 to £16; meals noon to 2pm and 5.30pm to 8.30pm) also does great food, is well stocked with Islay malts and real ales, and has a nook at the back with a view over the loch towards the Paps of Jura.

Finlaggan

Lush meadows swathed in buttercups and daisies slope down to reed-fringed Loch Finlaggan, the medieval capital of the Lords of the Isles. This bucolic setting, 3 miles southwest of Port Askaig, was once the most important settlement in the Hebrides, the central seat of power of the Lords of the Isles from the 12th to the 16th centuries. From the little island at the northern end of the loch the descendants of Somerled administered their island territories and entertained visiting chieftains in their great hall. Little remains now except the tumbled ruins of

houses and a chapel, but the setting is beautiful and the history fascinating. A wooden walkway leads over the reeds and water lilies to the island, where information boards describe the remains.

The **Finlaggan Visitor Centre** (www.finlaggan.com; adult/child £3/1; ⊙10.30am-4.30pm Mon-Sat, 1.30-4.30pm Sun Apr-Sep), in a nearby cottage (plus modern extension), explains the site's history and archaeology. The island itself is open at all times.

Buses from Bowmore to Port Askaig stop at the road-end, from where it's a 15-minute walk to the loch.

Isle of Jura
POP 200

Jura lies off the coast of Argyll – long, dark and low like a vast Viking longship, its billowing sail the distinctive triple peaks of the Paps of Jura. A magnificently wild and lonely island, Jura is the perfect place for getting away from it all – as George Orwell did in 1948. Orwell wrote his masterpiece *1984* while living at the remote farmhouse of Barnhill in the north of the island. Jura takes its name from the Old Norse *dyr-a* (deer island) – an apt appellation, as the island supports a population of around 6000 red deer, who outnumber their human cohabitants by about 30 to one.

Apart from the wilderness walking and wildlife watching, there's not a whole lot to do on the island apart from visit the **Isle of Jura Distillery** (☎01496-820385; www.jurawhisky.com; Craighouse; tours from £6; ⊙9.30am-4.30pm Mon-Sat Apr-Oct, 10am-2pm Mon-Fri Nov-Mar) or attend the **Jura Music Festival** (www.juramusicfestival. com) in late September, a convivial weekend of traditional Scottish folk music.

You can hire bikes from **Jura Bike Hire** (☎07768-450000; www.jurabikehire.com; Craighouse; bike hire per day £12.50).

🛏 Sleeping & Eating

Places to stay on the island are very limited, so book ahead. Most of Jura's accommodation is in self-catering cottages that are let by the week (see www.juradevelopment.co.uk). You can camp for free in the field below the Jura Hotel.

Jura Hotel   HOTEL ££
(☎01496-820243; www.jurahotel.co.uk; Craighouse; s £50-60, d £94-120; P🗢) The heart of Jura's community is this hotel, which is warmly

welcoming and efficiently run. Rooms vary in size and shape, but all are renovated and feel inviting. The premier rooms – all of which have sea views – are just lovely, with understated elegance and polished modern bathrooms. You can eat (mains £9 to £14; noon to 2.30pm and 6.30pm to 8.30pm) in the elegant restaurant or the convivial pub.

Antlers CAFE £££
(✆ 01496-820496; www.juradevelopment.co.uk; Craighouse; light meals £4-7; ⊙ 10am-5pm Mar-Oct, plus 6.30-8.30pm Fri) ✎ This community-owned cafe has a craft shop and displays on Jura heritage. It does tasty home baking, sandwiches and the like, and is also open for more elaborate dinners on Fridays. Not licensed (£3 corkage).

ⓘ Getting There & Around

A car ferry shuttles between Port Askaig on Islay and Feolin on Jura (passenger/car/bicycle £1.60/8.55/free, five minutes, hourly Monday to Saturday, every two hours Sunday). There is no direct car-ferry connection to the mainland.

From April to September **Jura Passenger Ferry** (✆ 07768-450000; www.jurapassengerferry. com; one-way £20 ; ⊙ mid-Apr–Sep) runs from Tayvallich on the mainland to Craighouse on Jura (one hour, one or two daily except Wednesday). Booking recommended.

The island's only **bus service** (✆ 01436-810200; www.garelochheadcoaches.co.uk) runs between the ferry slip at Feolin and Craighouse (20 minutes, three or four a day), timed to coincide with ferry arrivals and departures. One or two of the runs continue north as far as Inverlussa.

Oban

POP 8600

Oban, main gateway to many of the Hebridean islands, is a peaceful waterfront town on a bay, with sweeping views to Kerrera and Mull. OK, that first bit about peaceful is true only in winter; in summer the town centre is jammed with traffic and crowded with holidaymakers and travellers headed for the islands. But the setting is still lovely, and Oban's brilliant seafood restaurants are marvellous places to be as the sun sets over the bay.

⊙ Sights

McCaig's Tower HISTORIC BUILDING
(cnr Laurel & Duncraggan Rds; ⊙ 24hr) Crowning the hill above town is this Colosseum-like Victorian folly, commissioned in 1890 by local worthy John Stuart McCaig, with the philanthropic intention of providing work for unemployed stonemasons. To reach it on foot, make the steep climb up Jacob's Ladder (a flight of stairs) from Argyll St; the bay views are worth the effort.

Oban Distillery DISTILLERY
(✆ 01631-572004; www.discovering-distilleries. com; Stafford St; tour £7.50; ⊙ noon-4.30pm Dec-Feb, 9.30am-5pm Mar-Jun, Oct & Nov, 9.30am-7.30pm Mon-Fri & 9.30am-5pm Sat & Sun Jul-Sep) This handsome distillery has been producing since 1794. The standard guided tour leaves regularly (worth booking) and includes a dram and a taste straight from the cask. Specialist tours (£35) run once daily in summer. Even without a tour, it's still worth a look at the small exhibition in the foyer.

Dunollie CASTLE, MUSEUM
(✆ 01631-570550; www.dunollie.org; Dunollie Rd; adult/child £4/2; ⊙ 10am-4pm Mon-Sat & 1-4pm Sun Easter-Oct) A pleasant 1-mile stroll along the coast road leads to Dunollie Castle, built by the MacDougalls of Lorn in the 13th century and unsuccessfully besieged for a year during the 1715 Jacobite rebellion. It's very much a ruin, but the nearby 1745 House – seat of Clan MacDougall – is an intriguing museum of local and clan history. Ongoing improvement works are in progress.

⚞ Activities

A tourist-office leaflet lists local **bike rides**, which include a 7-mile Gallanach circular tour, a 16-mile route to the Isle of Seil and routes to Connel, Glenlonan and Kilmore. You can hire mountain bikes from **Oban Cycles** (✆ 01631-566033; www.obancycleshop.com; 87 George St; per day/week £15/70; ⊙ 10am-5pm Tue-Sat, plus Sun in summer).

Sea Kayak Oban (✆ 01631-565310; www. seakayakoban.com; Argyll St; ⊙ 10am-5pm Mon-Fri, 9am-5pm Sat, 10am-4pm Sun) has a well-stocked shop, and offers **sea-kayaking** courses, including a two-day intro for beginners (£170 per person).

Various operators offer **boat trips** to spot seals and other marine wildlife, departing from the North Pier slipway (adult/child £10/5); ask for details at the tourist office.

⎙ Sleeping

Despite having lots of B&B accommodation, Oban's beds can still fill up quickly in July and August so try to book ahead. If you can't find a bed in Oban, consider staying at Connel, 4 miles to the north.

Oban SYHA
HOSTEL £

(☎01631-562025; www.syha.org.uk; Corran Esplanade; dm/tw £21/48; P@🖥🛜) Set in a grand Victorian villa on the Esplanade, 0.75 miles north of the train station, this is modernised to a high standard with comfy wooden bunks, lockers, good showers and a lounge with great views across Oban Bay. All dorms are en suite; the neighbouring lodge has three- and four-bed rooms. Breakfast available.

Oban Backpackers
HOSTEL £

(☎01631-562107; www.obanbackpackers.com; Breadalbane St; dm £15-18; @🛜) Simple, colourful, relaxed and casual, this has plenty of atmosphere. Dorms are cheap and cheerful – price varies according to the number of bunks – and there's a sociable downstairs lounge with big windows and 'zebrapard' couches. Breakfast available for £2. Don't confuse with the similarly named (also decent) Backpackers Plus across the road.

Jeremy Inglis Hostel
HOSTEL £

(☎01631-565065; www.jeremyinglishostel.co.uk; 21 Airds Cres; dm/s £17/25; 🛜🖥) More eccentric B&B than a hostel – most 'dorms' have only two or three beds, and might come decorated with colourful duvets, original artwork, books, fresh flowers and more. It's grungy, friendly, decent value and there's a good kitchen–eating area. It won't be for everyone, but the spirit of hospitality thrives here. Breakfast is included and features homemade jams. Wi-fi doesn't reach the rooms.

Oban Caravan & Camping Park
CAMPSITE £

(☎01631-562425; www.obancaravanpark.com; Gallanachmore Farm; tent/campervan sites £15/20; ⊙Apr-Oct; 🐾) This campground has a superb location overlooking the Sound of Kerrera, 2.5 miles south of Oban (two buses on schooldays). A one-person tent with no car is £8. No prebooking – it's first come, first served. There are also bungalows and camping pods that sleep up to four (two/four people £40/50).

★ Old Manse Guest House
B&B ££

(☎01631-564886; www.obanguesthouse.co.uk; Dalriach Rd; s/d £65/90; P🛜) Set on the hillside above town, this place commands magnificent views over to Kerrera and Mull. It's run with genuine enthusiasm, and the owners are constantly adding thoughtful new features to the bright, cheerful rooms – think binoculars, DVDs, poetry, corkscrews and tartan hot-water bottles – and breakfast menus, with special diets catered for.

Barriemore
GUESTHOUSE ££

(☎01631-566356; www.barriemore-hotel.co.uk; Corran Esplanade; s from £70, d £99-119; ⊙Mar-Nov; P🛜) With a grand location overlooking the entrance to Oban Bay, this offers top-notch hospitality with tartan carpets on the stairs and plump Loch Fyne kippers on the breakfast menu. Rooms are all spacious, recently refurbished, and full of features. The front ones – pricier but enormous – have fabulous vistas; there's also a great family suite up the back and solicitous service.

Sandvilla Guesthouse
B&B ££

(☎01631-564483; www.holidayoban.co.uk; Breadalbane St; s/d £50/70; P🛜) Upbeat and modern, the rooms in this welcoming spot – all en suite by the time you read this – are lovely, bright and very well kept. Enthusiastic owners guarantee a personal welcome and service with a smile. It's our favourite of several options on this street.

Heatherfield House
B&B ££

(☎01631-562806; www.heatherfieldhouse.co.uk; Albert Rd; s £50, d £80-115; P🛜) Welcoming Heatherfield House occupies a converted 1870s rectory set in extensive grounds and has six spacious rooms. One comes complete with fireplace, sofa and a view over the garden to the harbour.

Kathmore Guest House
B&B ££

(☎01631-562104; www.kathmore.co.uk; Soroba Rd; s £35-50, d £60-75; P🛜) Warmly welcoming, this guesthouse, a 10-minute stroll from the centre, combines traditional Highland hospitality and hearty breakfasts with a touch of boutique flair in its stylish bedspreads and colourful artwork. It's actually two adjacent houses combined; each has a comfortable lounge and shares an outdoor garden deck where you can enjoy a glass of wine on summer evenings.

✖ Eating

Oban Seafood Hut
SEAFOOD £

(www.obanseafoodhut.co.uk; Railway Pier; mains £3-13; ⊙10am-6pm Mar-Oct) If you want to savour Scottish seafood without the expense of an upmarket restaurant, head for Oban's famous seafood stall – the green shack on the quayside near the ferry terminal. Here you can buy fresh and cooked seafood to take away – excellent prawn sandwiches (£2.95), dressed crab (£4.95), and fresh oysters (95p each).

Kitchen Garden
DELI, CAFE £

(☎01631-566332; www.kitchengardenoban.co.uk; 14 George St; light meals £4-8; ⊙9am-5.30pm

Mon-Sat, 10am-4.30pm Sun) A deli packed with delicious picnic food. Also has a great little cafe – good coffee, scones, cakes, homemade soups and sandwiches.

Waterfront Fishouse Restaurant SEAFOOD ££
(☑ 01631-563110; www.waterfrontoban.co.uk; Railway Pier; mains £12-20; ⊗ noon-2.15pm & 5.30-9.30pm Sun-Fri, noon-9.30pm Sat; 🛜🖼) Housed on the top floor of a converted seamen's mission, the Waterfront's stylish, unfussy decor in burgundy and brown, with dark wooden furniture, does little to distract from the superb seafood freshly landed at the quay just a few metres away. The menu ranges from classic haddock and chips to fresh oysters, scallops and langoustines. Best to book for dinner.

Cuan Mór BISTRO ££
(☑ 01631-565078; www.cuanmor.co.uk; 60 George St; mains £9-14; ⊗ 10am-10pm; 🛜🖼) This always-busy bar and bistro brews its own beer and sports a no-nonsense menu of old favourites: from haddock and chips or homemade lasagne to sausage and mash with onion gravy. The menu's spiced with a few more sophisticated plates such as squat lobster carbonara, and a decent range of vegetarian dishes. And the sticky toffee pudding is not to be missed!

★ Seafood Temple SEAFOOD £££
(☑ 01631-566000; www.obanseafood.com; Gallanach Rd; mains £16-25; ⊗ 6.15-8.30pm Apr-Sep, 6.15-8.30pm Wed-Sat Oct-Dec, Feb & Mar) 🥦 Locally sourced seafood is the god that's worshipped at this tiny temple – a former park pavilion with glorious views over the bay. Oban's smallest restaurant serves up whole lobster cooked to order, baked crab, plump langoustines, and a seafood platter (£75 for two), which offers a taste of everything. Dinner is in two sittings (6.15pm and 8.30pm); bookings essential.

Ee-usk SEAFOOD £££
(☑ 01631-565666; www.eeusk.com; North Pier; mains £12-24; ⊗ noon-3pm & 5.45-9.30pm; 🛜) 🥦 Bright and modern Ee'usk (it's how you pronounce *iasg*, Gaelic for fish) occupies a prime pier location. Floor-to-ceiling windows allow diners on two levels to enjoy sweeping views while sampling locally caught seafood ranging from fragrant fish cakes to langoustines and succulent fresh fish. A bevy of serving staff make it swift and efficient, and they make an effort to give you the best view available.

It's a little pricey, perhaps, but both food and location are first class. Closes 9pm in winter.

ℹ Information

Lorn & Islands District General Hospital (☑ 01631-567500; Glengallan Rd) Southern end of town.

Oban Tourist Office (☑ 01631-563122; www.oban.org.uk; 3 North Pier; ⊗ 10am-5pm daily, extended weekday hours Apr-Oct) Helpful; on the waterfront.

ℹ Getting There & Away

The bus, train and ferry terminals are conveniently grouped together next to the harbour on the southern edge of the bay.

BOAT
CalMac (☑ 0800 066 5000; www.calmac.co.uk) ferries link Oban with the islands of Mull, Coll, Tiree, Lismore, Colonsay, Barra and Lochboisdale (South Uist). See the relevant island entries for details. Information and reservations for all CalMac ferry services are available at the **ferry terminal** (☑ 01631-562244; Railway Pier; ⊗ 9am-6pm Mar-Oct) near the train station.

BUS
Scottish Citylink (www.citylink.co.uk) operates most intercity coaches, while **West Coast Motors** (www.westcoastmotors.co.uk) runs local and regional services.

Glasgow (via Inveraray and Arrochar) £23.10, 3¼ hours, three daily

Fort William (via Appin and Ballachulish) £9.40, 1½ hours, two Monday to Saturday

TRAIN
Oban is at the terminus of a scenic route that branches off the West Highland line at Crianlarich. The train isn't much use for travelling north – to reach Fort William requires a long detour (3¾ hours). Take the bus instead.

Glasgow £22, three hours, three daily
Tyndrum/Crianlarich £10.70, one hour, three daily

Isle of Mull
POP 2800

From the rugged ridges of Ben More and the black basalt crags of Burg to the white sand, rose-pink granite and emerald waters that fringe the Ross, Mull can lay claim to some of the finest and most varied scenery in the Inner Hebrides. Noble birds of prey soar over mountain and coast, while the western waters provide good whale-watching. Add a lovely waterfront 'capital', an impressive castle, the sacred island of Iona and easy access from Oban and you can see why it's sometimes impossible to find a spare bed on the island.

Mull, Coll & Tiree

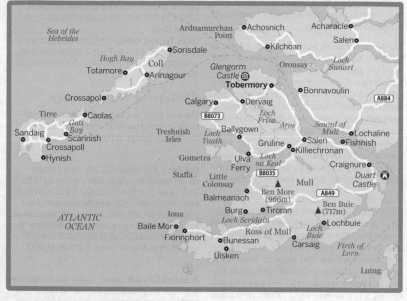

🕝 Tours

West Coast Tours COACH TOUR
(☑ 01631-566809; www.westcoasttours.co.uk; 1 Queens Park Pl; ⊙ Apr-Oct) Offers a Three Isles day trip (adult/child £60/30, 10 hours, daily) from Oban that visits Mull, Iona and Staffa. The crossing to Staffa is weather dependent. Without Staffa, the trip is £40/20 and takes eight hours. Also runs various trips on Mull.

Sea Life Surveys WILDLIFE WATCHING
(☑ 01688-302916; www.sealifesurveys.com; Ledaig) Whale-watching trips head from Tobermory harbour to the waters north and west of Mull. An all-day whale-watch gives up to seven hours at sea (£80), and has a 95% success rate for sightings. The four-hour Wildlife Adventure cruise (adult/child £50/40) is better for young kids. Shorter seal-spotting excursions are also available.

ℹ Information

There's a bank with ATM in Tobermory, otherwise you can get cashback with a purchase from Co-op food stores.
Craignure Tourist Office (☑ 01680-812377; ⊙ 8.30am-5pm Mon-Sat, 10am-5pm Sun, to 7pm Jul & Aug) Opposite the ferry slip.
Explore Mull (☑ 01688-302875; www.exploremull.com; Ledaig, Tobermory; ⊙ 9am-5pm

Easter-Oct, to 7pm Jul-Aug; 🛜) In Tobermory car park. Local information, books all manner of island tours, hires bikes and has internet access.

ℹ Getting There & Away

Three **CalMac** (www.calmac.co.uk) car ferries link Mull with the mainland.
Lochaline to Fishnish (£3.30/14.45, 15 minutes, at least hourly) On the east coast of Mull.
Oban to Craignure (passenger/car £5.55/49.50, 40 minutes, every two hours) The busiest route – booking advised for cars.
Tobermory to Kilchoan (£5.30/27.50, 35 minutes, seven daily Monday to Saturday, plus five Sunday May to August) Links to the Ardnamurchan peninsula.

ℹ Getting Around

BICYCLE
You can hire bikes for around £15 per day from various places around the island, including Explore Mull in Tobermory.

BUS
West Coast Motors (☑ 01631-566809; www.westcoastmotors.co.uk) connects ferry ports and main villages. Its Discovery Day Pass (adult/child £15/7.50) is available from April to October and grants a day's unlimited bus travel.

Craignure to Tobermory (single/return £7/10, one hour, four to seven daily)
Craignure to Fionnphort (£9/14 single/return, 1¼ hours, three to four Monday to Saturday, one Sunday)
Tobermory to Dervaig and Calgary (single/return £3/5.10, two to four Monday to Saturday)

CAR
Almost all of Mull's road network consists of single track roads. There are petrol stations at Craignure, Fionnphort, Salen and Tobermory. **Mull Self Drive** (☑ 01680-300402; www.mullselfdrive.co.uk) rents small cars for £45/237 per day/week.

TAXI
Mull Taxi (☑ 07760-426351; www.mulltaxi.co.uk) is based in Tobermory, and has a vehicle that is wheelchair accessible.

Duart Castle
The **ancestral seat of the Maclean clan** (☑ 01680-812309; www.duartcastle.com; adult/child £5.75/2.85; ⊙ 10.30am-5pm daily May–mid-Oct, 11am-4pm Sun-Thu Apr) enjoys a spectacular position on a rocky outcrop overlooking the Sound of Mull. Originally built in the 13th century, it was abandoned for 160 years before a 1912 restoration. As well as the dungeons, courtyard and battlements with memorable views, there's a lot of clan history – pantomime boos go to Lachlan Cattanach, who took his wife on an outing to an island in the strait, then left her there to drown when the tide came in.

A bus to the castle meets some of the incoming ferries at Craignure, but it's a pretty walk too.

Tobermory
POP 1000
Mull's main town is a picturesque fishing port with brightly painted houses arranged around a sheltered harbour. The children's TV program *Balamory* was set here, and though the series stopped filming in 2004 regular repeats mean that the town still swarms in summer with toddlers (and nostalgic teenagers) towing parents around (you can get a *Balamory* info sheet from tourist offices).

⊙ Sights & Activities

Hebridean Whale and Dolphin Trust   EXHIBITION
(☑ 01688-302620; www.whaledolphintrust.co.uk; 28 Main St; ⊙ 10am-5pm Mon-Fri, 11am-4pm Sun Apr-Oct, 11am-5pm Mon-Fri Nov-Mar) ⫸ **FREE**
This has displays, videos and interactive exhibits on whale and dolphin biology and ecology, and is a great place for kids to learn about sea mammals. It also provides information about volunteering and reporting sightings of whales and dolphins. Opening times are rather variable.

Mull Museum   MUSEUM
(☑ 01688-302603; www.mullmuseum.org.uk; Main St; admission by donation; ⊙ 10am-4pm Mon-Fri plus most Sat Easter-Oct) Places to go on a rainy day include Mull Museum, which records the history of the island. There are interesting exhibits on crofting, and on the *Tobermory Galleon*, a ship from the Spanish Armada that sank in Tobermory Bay in 1588 and has been the object of treasure seekers ever since.

Marine Visitor Centre   MUSEUM
(www.tobermorymarinevisitorcentre.com; Ledaig; admission by donation; ⊙ 9am-5pm Easter-Oct) By the harbour car park, this has good information on the local marine environment, and little touch pools with crabs and the like for the kids.

🛏 Sleeping
Tobermory has dozens of B&Bs, but the place can still be booked solid in July and August, especially on weekends.

Tobermory SYHA   HOSTEL £
(☑ 01688-302481; www.syha.org.uk; Main St; dm/q £19/84; ⊙ Mar-Oct; @🛜) Great location in a Victorian house right on the waterfront, with dorms and good triples and quads for families. Was up for sale at the time of research with an uncertain future; it will hopefully remain a hostel.

Tobermory Campsite   CAMPSITE £
(☑ 01688-302624; www.tobermory-campsite.co.uk; Newdale, Dervaig Rd; tent sites per adult/child £7.50/3; ⊙ Mar-Oct; P🐕) ⫸ A quiet, family-friendly campground 1 mile west of town on the road to Dervaig. It also has a self-catering house and static caravans available. Credit and debit cards not accepted.

Cuidhe Leathain   B&B ££
(☑ 01688-302504; www.cuidhe-leathain.co.uk; Breadalbane St; r £85; 🛜) A handsome 19th-century house in the upper town, Cuidhe Leathain (coo-lane), which means Maclean's Corner, exudes a cosily cluttered Victorian atmosphere. The rooms are

THAR SHE BLOWS!

The North Atlantic Drift, a swirling tendril of the Gulf Stream, carries warm water into the cold, nutrient-rich seas off the Scottish coast, resulting in huge blooms of plankton. Small fish feed on the plankton, and bigger fish feed on the smaller fish... This huge seafood smorgasbord attracts large numbers of marine mammals, from harbour porpoises and dolphins to minke whales and even – though sightings are rare – humpback and sperm whales.

In contrast to Iceland and Norway, Scotland has cashed in on the abundance of minke whales off its coast by embracing whale watching rather than whaling. There are now dozens of operators around the coast offering whale-watching boat trips lasting from a couple of hours to all day; some have whale-sighting success rates of 95% in summer.

While seals, porpoises and dolphins can be seen year-round, minke whales are migratory. The best time to see them is from June to August, with August being the peak month for sightings. The website of the **Hebridean Whale & Dolphin Trust** (www.whaledolphintrust.co.uk) has lots of information on the species you are likely to see, and how to identify them.

A booklet titled *Is It a Whale?* is available from tourist offices and bookshops, and provides tips on identifying the various species of marine mammal that you're likely to see.

beautifully plush, with plunger coffee and decent teas, breakfasts will set you up for the rest of the day, and the owners are a fount of knowledge about Mull and its wildlife. Minimum two-night stay.

Harbour View B&B **££**
(☎ 01688-301111; www.tobermorybandb.com; 1 Argyll Tce; s £65, d £80-90; ☎) This beautifully renovated fisherman's cottage is perched on the edge of Tobermory's 'upper town'. Exposed patches of original stone walls add a touch of character, while a new extension provides the family suite (two adjoining rooms with shared bathroom, sleeps four) with an outdoor terrace that enjoys breathtaking views across the harbour.

Sonas House B&B **££**
(☎ 01688-302304; www.sonashouse.co.uk; The Fairways, Erray Rd; s/d £110/125, apt from £90; P ☎ ☎) Here's a first – a B&B with a heated, indoor 10m swimming pool! Sonas is a large, modern house – follow signs for the golf course – offering luxury B&B in a beautiful setting with superb views over Tobermory Bay; ask for the 'Blue Poppy' bedroom, which has its own balcony. There's also a self-contained studio apartment with double bed.

Eating & Drinking

Fish & Chip Van FISH & CHIPS **£**
(☎ 01688-301109; www.tobermoryfishandchipvan.co.uk; Main St; mains £6-9; ⊙12.30-9pm Mon-Sat Apr-Dec, plus Sun Jun-Sep, 12.30-7pm Mon-Sat Jan-Mar) If it's a takeaway you're after, you can tuck into some of Scotland's best gourmet fish and chips down on the waterfront. And where else will you find a chip van selling freshly cooked scallops?

★**Café Fish** SEAFOOD **££**
(☎ 01688-301253; www.thecafefish.com; The Pier; mains £13-24; ⊙11am-3pm & 5.30-9.30pm mid-Mar–Oct) Seafood doesn't come much fresher than the stuff served at this warm and welcoming little restaurant overlooking Tobermory harbour – as its motto says, 'The only things frozen are our fisherman'! Langoustines and squat lobsters go straight from boat to kitchen to join rich Tuscan-style seafood stew, fat scallops, fish pie and catch-of-the-day on the daily-changing menu, where confident use of Asian ingredients adds an extra dimension.

Mishnish Hotel PUB FOOD **££**
(☎ 01688-302009; www.mishnish.co.uk; Main St; mains £13-18; ⊙food noon-2pm & 6-9pm; ☎) 'The Mish' is a favourite hang-out for visiting yachties and a good place for a pint, or a meal at the restaurant. Wood-panelled and flag-draped, this is a good old traditional pub where you can listen to live folk music, toast your toes by the open fire, or challenge the locals to a game of pool.

North Mull

The road from Tobermory west to Calgary cuts inland, leaving most of the north coast of Mull wild and inaccessible. Just outside Tobermory, a long, single-track road leads north for 4 miles to majestic **Glengorm Castle** (☎ 01688-302321; www.glengormcastle.

co.uk; Glengorm; ⊙10am-5pm May-Aug) **FREE**, with views across the sea to Ardnamurchan, Rum and the Outer Hebrides. The castle outbuildings house an art gallery featuring the work of local artists, a farm shop selling local produce and an excellent coffee shop. The castle itself is not open to the public, but you're free to explore its beautiful grounds.

Mull's best (and busiest) silver-sand beach, flanked by cliffs and with views out to Coll and Tiree, is at Calgary, about 12 miles west of Tobermory. And yes – this is the place from which the more famous Calgary in Alberta, Canada, takes its name.

🛏 Sleeping & Eating

Calgary Bay Campsite   CAMPSITE £
(Calgary) **FREE** You can camp for free in a lovely setting at the southern end of the beach at Calgary Bay. There are no facilities other than the public toilets across the road; water comes from the stream.

Dervaig Hostel   HOSTEL £
(✐01688-400491; www.mull-hostel-dervaig.co.uk; Dervaig; dm/q £18/60; P🐾) Basic but very comfortable bunkhouse accommodation in Dervaig's village hall, with self-catering kitchen and sitting room.

★ Calgary Farmhouse   SELF-CATERING ££
(✐01688-400256; www.calgary.co.uk; Calgary; apt & cottages per week summer £400-1275; P🐾) 🐾 This brilliant complex near Calgary beach offers fantastic apartments, cottages and a farmhouse (sleeps two to nine), beautifully designed and fitted out with timber furniture and wood-burning stoves. The Hayloft is spectacular, with noble oak and local art. We loved romantic Kittiwake (one/three days £100/225), a beautiful wooden camping cabin among the trees, with bay views, a boat for a ceiling and chemical toilet below decks.

Bellachroy   HOTEL ££
(✐01688-400225; www.thebellachroy.co.uk; Dervaig; s/d £70/100; P🐾) The Bellachroy is an atmospheric 17th-century droving inn with six plain but comfortable bedrooms. The bar is a focus for local social life and serves decent, if somewhat overpriced, food.

Glengorm Coffee Shop   CAFE £
(www.glengormcastle.co.uk; Glengorm; light meals £3-8; ⊙10am-5pm May-Aug; 🐾) 🐾 Set in a cottage courtyard in the grounds of Glengorm Castle, this licensed cafe serves superb lunches (from noon to 4.30pm) – the menu changes daily, but includes sandwiches and salads (much of the salad veg is grown on the Glengorm estate), soups and tasty specials.

Am Birlinn   SCOTTISH ££
(✐01688-400619; www.ambirlinn.com; Penmore, Dervaig; mains £13-23; ⊙6-9pm Wed-Sun, plus noon-2pm Wed-Sun May-Oct) 🐾 Occupying a spacious modern wooden building between Dervaig and Calgary, this is an interesting dining option. Locally caught crustaceans and molluscs are the way to go here, though there are burgers, venison and other meat dishes available. Free pick-up and drop-off from Tobermory or other nearby spots is offered.

South Mull

The road from Craignure to Fionnphort climbs through some wild and desolate scenery before reaching the southwestern part of the island, which consists of a long peninsula called the Ross of Mull. The Ross has a spectacular south coast lined with black basalt cliffs that give way further west to white-sand beaches and pink granite crags.

At the western end of the Ross, 38 miles from Craignure, is Fionnphort (*finn*-a-fort) and the ferry to Iona. The coast here is a beautiful blend of pink granite rocks, white sandy beaches and vivid turquoise sea.

Isle of Iona
POP 200

Like an emerald teardrop off Mull's western shore, enchanting, idyllic Iona, holy island and burial ground of kings, is a magical place that lives up to its lofty reputation. From the moment you embark on the ferry towards its sandy shores and green fields, you'll notice something different about it.

St Columba sailed from Ireland and landed on Iona in 563 before setting out to spread Christianity throughout Scotland. He established a monastery on the island and it was here that the *Book of Kells* – the prize attraction of Dublin's Trinity College – is believed to have been transcribed. It was taken to Kells in Ireland when Viking raids drove the monks from Iona.

The monks returned and the monastery prospered until its destruction during the Reformation. The ruins were given to the Church of Scotland in 1899, and by 1910 a group of enthusiasts called the Iona Community had reconstructed the abbey. It's still a flourishing spiritual community that holds regular courses and retreats.

◉ Sights & Activities

Past the abbey, look for a footpath on the left signposted **Dun I** (dun-ee). An easy 15-minute walk leads to Iona's highest point, with fantastic 360-degree views.

Iona Abbey   HISTORIC BUILDING
(HS; ☑01681-700512; adult/child £7.10/4.30; ◎9.30am-5.30pm Apr-Sep, to 4.30pm Oct-Mar) Iona's ancient but heavily reconstructed abbey is the spiritual heart of the island. The spectacular **nave**, dominated by Romanesque and early Gothic vaults and columns is a powerful space; a door on the left leads to the beautiful **cloister**, where medieval grave slabs sit alongside modern religious sculptures. Out the back, the new **museum** displays fabulous carved high crosses and other inscribed stones, along with lots of background information. A replica of the intricately carved St John's Cross stands outside the abbey.

Next to the abbey is an ancient **graveyard** where there's an evocative Romanesque chapel as well as a mound that marks the burial place of 48 of Scotland's early kings, including Macbeth; the ruined **nunnery** nearby was established at the same time as the Benedictine abbey.

Iona Heritage Centre   MUSEUM
(☑01681-700576; adult/child £2.50/1.50; ◎10.30am-5pm Mon-Sat Easter-Oct) Covers the history of Iona, crofting and lighthouses; there's a craft shop and cafe that serves delicious home baking.

ISLE OF STAFFA

Felix Mendelssohn, who visited the uninhabited island of Staffa in 1829, was inspired to compose *The Hebrides* overture after hearing waves echoing in the impressive and cathedral-like **Fingal's Cave**. The cave walls and surrounding cliffs are composed of vertical, hexagonal basalt columns that look like pillars (Staffa is Norse for 'Pillar Island'). You can land on the island and walk into the cave via a causeway. Nearby **Boat Cave** can be seen from the causeway, but you can't reach it on foot. Staffa also has a sizeable puffin colony, north of the landing place.

Unless you have your own boat, the only way to reach Staffa and the Treshnish Isles is on an organised boat trip.

🛏 Sleeping & Eating

★ Iona Hostel   HOSTEL £
(☑01681-700781; www.ionahostel.co.uk; dm adult/child £21/17.50; P 🐶 🛜) ✔ This working ecological croft and environmentally sensitive hostel is one of Scotland's most rewarding and tranquil places to stay. Lovable black Hebridean sheep surround the building, which features pretty, practical and comfy dorms, and an excellent kitchen-lounge. There's a fabulous beach nearby, and a hill to climb for views. It's just over a mile from the ferry, past the abbey.

Iona Campsite   CAMPSITE £
(☑01681-700112; www.ionacampsite.co.uk; tent sites per adult/child £6.50/3; ◎Apr-Oct; 🛁) Basic campsite about 1 mile west of the ferry.

★ Argyll Hotel   HOTEL ££
(☑01681-700334; www.argyllhoteliona.co.uk; s £69, d £82-99; ◎Mar-Oct; @🐶🛜🛁) ✔ This cute, higgledy-piggledy warren of a hotel has great service and appealing snug rooms (a sea view costs more – £150 for a double), including good-value family options. Most of the rooms look out to the rear, where a huge organic garden supplies the country-house **restaurant** (☑01681-700334; www.argyllhoteliona.co.uk; lunch £6-8, dinner mains £12-16; ◎12.15-2pm & 6.30-8pm; 🛜) ✔ with wooden fireplace and antique tables and chairs. The menu includes home-grown salads, local seafood and Scottish beef and lamb.

ℹ Getting There & Away

The passenger ferry from Fionnphort to Iona (£5.10 return, five minutes, hourly) runs daily. There are also various day trips available from Oban to Iona.

FIFE

Protruding like a serpent's head from Scotland's east coast, Fife (www.visitfife.com) is a tongue of land between the Firths of Forth and Tay. An atmosphere distinct from the rest of Scotland and a place in royal history has seen the region style itself as 'The Kingdom of Fife'.

Though overdeveloped southern Fife is commuter-belt territory, the eastern part's rolling green farmland and quaint fishing villages are prime turf for exploration, and the fresh sea air feels like it's doing a power of good. Fife's biggest attraction, St Andrews, has Scotland's most venerable university and a wealth of historic buildings. It's also, of course, the home of golf, and draws professionals and keen amateurs alike to take on the Old Course – the classic links experience.

🏃 Activities

The **Fife Coastal Path** (www.fifecoastalpath. co.uk) runs more than 80 miles following the entire Fife coastline from the Forth Road Bridge to the Tay Bridge and beyond. It's well waymarked, picturesque and not too rigorous, though winds can buffet. It's easily accessed for shorter sections or day walks, and long stretches of it can be tackled on a mountain bike too.

ⓘ Getting Around

The main bus operator here is **Stagecoach Fife** (☏ 0871 200 2233; www.stagecoachbus.com). For £8 you can buy a Fife Dayrider ticket, which gives one day's unlimited travel around Fife on Stagecoach buses.

If you are driving from the Forth Road Bridge to St Andrews, a slower but much more scenic route than the M90/A91 is along the signposted **Fife Coastal Tourist Route**.

St Andrews

POP 16,900

For a small place, St Andrews has made a big name for itself. Firstly as religious centre, then as Scotland's oldest university town (and third-oldest in Britain), but it is its status as the home of golf that has propelled it to even greater fame, and today's pilgrims mostly arrive with a set of clubs. Nevertheless, it's a lovely place to visit even if you've no interest in the game, with impressive medieval ruins, stately university buildings, idyllic white sands and excellent accommodation and eating options.

The Old Course (p872), the world's most famous golf links, has a striking seaside location at the western end of town – it's a thrilling experience to stroll the hallowed turf.

History

St Andrews is said to have been founded by St Regulus (also known as St Rule), who arrived from Greece in the 4th century bringing with him the bones of St Andrew, Scotland's patron saint. The town soon grew into a major pilgrimage centre and St Andrews developed into the ecclesiastical capital of the country. The university, the first in Scotland, was founded in 1410.

Golf has been played at St Andrews for more than 600 years; the game's governing body was founded here in 1754 and the imposing Royal & Ancient clubhouse was built 100 years later.

⊙ Sights

★ St Andrews Cathedral   RUIN

(HS; www.historic-scotland.gov.uk; The Pends; adult/child £4.50/2.70, incl castle £7.20/4.40; ⊙9.30am-5.30pm Apr-Sep, to 4.30pm Oct-Mar) The ruins of this cathedral are all that's left of one of Britain's most magnificent medieval buildings. You can appreciate the scale and majesty of the edifice from the small sections that remain standing. Although founded in 1160, it was not consecrated until 1318. It stood as the focus of this important pilgrimage centre until 1559, when it was pillaged during the Reformation.

St Andrew's bones supposedly lie under the altar; until the cathedral was built, they had been enshrined in the nearby **Church of St Regulus** (or Rule). All that remains of this church is **St Rule's Tower**, worth the climb for the view across St Andrews. There's also a museum with a collection of Celtic crosses and gravestones found on the site. The entrance fee only applies for the tower and museum; you can wander freely around the atmospheric ruins, a fine picnic spot.

★ St Andrews Castle   CASTLE

(HS; www.historic-scotland.gov.uk; The Scores; adult/child £5.50/3.30, incl cathedral £7.20/4.40; ⊙9.30am-5.30pm Apr-Sep, to 4.30pm Oct-Mar) The town's castle is mainly in ruins, but the site itself is evocative and has dramatic coastline views. It was founded around 1200 as a fortified home for the bishop of St Andrews. After the execution of Protestant reformers in 1545, other reformers retaliated by murdering Cardinal Beaton and taking over the castle. They spent almost a year holed up, during which they and their attackers dug a complex of **siege tunnels**; you can walk (or stoop) along their damp mossy lengths.

The visitor centre gives a good audiovisual introduction and has a small collection of Pictish stones.

The Scores   STREET

From the castle, the Scores follows the coast west down to the first tee at the Old Course. Family-friendly **St Andrews Aquarium** (www.standrewsaquarium.co.uk; adult/child £10/7; ⊙10am-5pm Mon-Fri, to 6pm Sat & Sun; 👶) has a

St Andrews

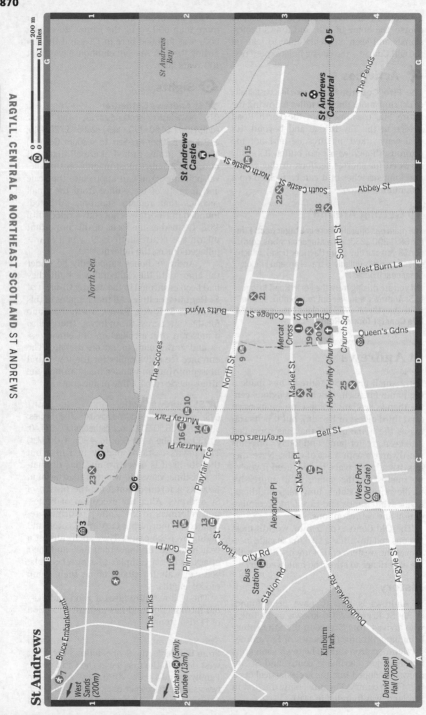

200 m
0.1 miles

St Andrews Bay

St Andrews Castle

North Castle St

St Andrews Cathedral

2

The Pends

1

North Sea

15

22 South Castle St

18

Abbey St

South St

West Burn La

Butts Wynd

College St

Church St

21

Mercat Cross

19 20

Holy Trinity Church

Church Sq

Queen's Gdns

The Scores

North St

9

Market St

24

25

Murray Park

10

14

Murray Pl

16

Greyfriars Gdn

Bell St

4

23

St Mary's Pl

17

6

West Port (Old Gate)

Playfair Tce

Alexandra Pl

3

12

13

Hope St

City Rd

Argyle St

Golf Pl

Pilmour Pl

11

Bus Station

Station Rd

Doubledykes Rd

8

The Links

Kinburn Park

David Russell Hall (700m)

Bruce Embankment

7

West Sands (200m)

Leuchars (5mi); Dundee (13mi)

St Andrews

seal pool, rays and sharks from Scottish waters and exotic tropical favourites. Once introduced to our finny friends, you can snack on them with chips in the cafe.

Nearby, the **British Golf Museum** (www.britishgolfmuseum.co.uk; Bruce Embankment; adult/child £6.50/3; ⊙9.30am-5pm Mon-Sat, 10am-5pm Sun Apr-Oct, 10am-4pm Sun Nov-Mar) has an extraordinarily comprehensive overview of the history and development of the game and the role of St Andrews in it. Favourite fact: bad players were formerly known as 'foozlers'. Interactive panels allow you to relive former British Opens (watch Paul Azinger snapping his putter in frustration), and there's a large collection of memorabilia from Open winners, both male and female.

Opposite the museum is the **Royal & Ancient Golf Club**, which stands proudly at the head of the Old Course (p872). Beside it stretches magnificent **West Sands** beach, made famous by the film *Chariots of Fire*.

🛏 Sleeping

St Andrews accommodation is often heavily booked (especially in summer), so you're well advised to book in advance. Almost every house on Murray Park and Murray Pl is a guesthouse.

St Andrews Tourist Hostel   HOSTEL £
(☑01334-479911; www.cowgatehostel.com/st-andrews; St Marys Pl; dm £11-13; 🛜) Laid-back and central, this hostel is the only backpacker accommodation in town. Occupying a stately old building, it has high corniced ceilings, especially in the huge lounge.

There's a laissez-faire approach, which can verge on chaotic at times, but the staff and location can't be beat. Reception closed between 2pm and 5pm.

Five Pilmour Place   B&B ££
(☑01334-478665; www.5pilmourplace.com; 5 Pilmour Pl; s/d from £75/110; @🛜) Just around the corner from the Old Course, this luxurious and intimate spot offers stylish, compact rooms with an eclectic range of styles as well as modern conveniences such as flatscreen TV and DVD player. The king-size beds are especially comfortable, and the lounge area is a stylish treat.

Aslar House   B&B ££
(☑01334-473460; www.aslar.com; 120 North St; s/d/ste £55/100/110; ⊙Feb–mid-Nov; 🛜) The rooms are so impeccable at this place that it's frightening to imagine how much work goes on behind the scenes. The modern comforts don't detract from the house's historical features (including a whimsical turret room) and certainly add value. The master suite is very spacious and a good small extra investment. No under-16s.

Old Fishergate House   B&B ££
(☑01334-470874; www.oldfishergatehouse.co.uk; North Castle St; s/d £80/110; 🛜) This historic 17th-century town house, furnished with period pieces, is in a great location – the oldest part of town, close to the cathedral and castle. The two twin rooms are very spacious and even have their own sitting room. On a scale of one to 10 for quaintness, we'd rate it about 9½. Cracking breakfast menu features fresh fish and pancakes.

PLAYING THE OLD COURSE

Golf has been played at St Andrews since the 15th century. By 1457 it was so popular that James II placed a ban on it because it interfered with his troops' archery practice. Although it lies beside the exclusive, all-male-membership Royal & Ancient Golf Club, the **Old Course** (www.standrews.org.uk; Golf Pl) is public.

You'll need to book in advance to play via **St Andrews Links Trust** (☏ 01334-466666; www.standrews.org.uk). Reservations open on the first Wednesday in September the year before you wish to play. No bookings are taken for Saturdays or the month of September.

Unless you've booked months in advance, getting a tee-off time is literally a lottery; enter the ballot at the **caddie pavilion** (☏ 01334-466666; West Sands Rd) before 2pm two days before you wish to play (there's no Sunday play). Be warned that applications by ballot are normally heavily oversubscribed, and green fees are £160 in summer. Singles are not accepted in the ballot and should start queuing as early as possible on the day – 5am is good – in the hope of joining a group. You'll need a handicap certificate (24/36 for men/women). If your number doesn't come up, there are six other public courses in the area (book up to seven days in advance on ☏ 01334-466718, no handicap required), including the prestigious Castle Course (£120). Other summer green fees: New £75, Jubilee £75, Eden £45, Strathtyrum £30 and Balgove (nine-holer for beginners and kids) £15. There are multiple-day tickets available. A caddie for your round costs £45 plus tip. If you play on a windy day, expect those scores to balloon.

Guided walks (per person £3; ⊙ 11am & 2pm Tue-Sun Jul & Aug) of the Old Course take in famous landmarks such as the Swilcan Bridge and the Road Hole bunker. They run from outside the shop by the 18th green and last 50 minutes. On Sunday, a three-hour walk (£6) takes you around the whole course. You are free to walk over the course on Sunday, or follow the footpaths around the edge at any time.

Cameron House   B&B ££
(☏ 01334-472306; www.cameronhouse-sta.co.uk; 11 Murray Park; s/d £50/90; ☏) Beautifully decorated rooms and warm, cheerful hosts make this a real home away from home on this guesthouse-filled street. The two single rooms share a bathroom. Prices drop £10 per person outside peak season.

Six Murray Park   B&B ££
(☏ 01334-473319; www.sixmurraypark.co.uk; 6 Murray Park; s/d from £65/100; ☏) Enticing rooms with classy contemporary styling make this a most appealing option on this street bristling with guesthouses.

University of St Andrews   APARTMENT, B&B ££
(☏ 01334-463000; www.discoverstandrews.com; ⊙ Jun-Aug; P @ ☏) ✎ During the university summer vacation, three student residences open up as visitor accommodation. There's the B&B-style **Agnes Blackadder Hall** (North Haugh; s/d £61/88) and self-catering apartments sleeping up to six at **David Russell Hall** (Buchanan Gardens; s/d £77/131); both are on the main campus west of town. There are cheaper rooms in the central **McIntosh Hall** (s/d £41/70). These prices are all good value for the standard of accommodation on offer.

Fairways of St Andrews   B&B £££
(☏ 01334-479513; www.fairwaysofstandrews.co.uk; 8a Golf Pl; d £130-170; ☏) Just a few paces from golf's most famous 18th green, this is more of a boutique hotel than a B&B, despite its small size. There are just three super-stylish rooms; the best on the top floor is huge and has its own balcony with views over the Old Course.

Ogstons on North Street   HOTEL £££
(☏ 01334-473387; www.ogstonsonnorthst.com; 127 North St; r £120-180; ☏) If you want to eat, drink and sleep in the same stylish place, this inn could be for you. Rooms feature elegant contemporary styling and beautiful bathrooms, some with spa. There are also DVD players, iPod docks, crisp white linen and large windows that give the rooms an airy feel.

✖ Eating

Northpoint Cafe   CAFE £
(24 North St; mains £3-7; ⊙ 8.30am-5pm Mon-Fri, 10am-5pm Sat; ☏) The cafe where Prince William famously met his future wife Kate Middleton while they were both students at St Andrews. It serves good coffee and a broad range of breakfast fare, from porridge topped with banana to toasted bagels, pancake stacks and classic fry-ups.

Café in the Square CAFÉ £
(www.cafeinthesquare.co.uk; 4 Church Sq; mains £4-8; ☺ 11am-5pm Mon-Sat, plus Sun in summer) Hidden away down the side of the library, this upbeat wee coffee stop also makes a good venue for a light lunch, with sandwiches, panini and salads and a couple of secluded picnic tables out the back.

The Tailend FISH & CHIPS £
(www.thetailend.co.uk; 130 Market St; takeaway £4-8; ☺ 11.30am-10pm, seven days) ✏ Delicious fresh fish sourced from Arbroath, just up the coast, puts this a class above most chippies. It fries to order and it's worth the wait. The array of exquisite smoked delicacies at the counter will have you planning a picnic or fighting for a table in the licensed cafe out the back.

B Jannetta ICE CREAM £
(☑ 01334-473285; www.jannettas.co.uk; 31 South St; 2-scoop cones £2.25; ☺ 9am-9pm) Jannetta's is a St Andrews institution, offering 52 varieties of ice cream, from the weird (Irn-Bru sorbet) to the decadent (strawberries and champagne).

Doll's House SCOTTISH ££
(☑ 01334-477422; www.dolls-house.co.uk; 3 Church Sq; mains £12-18; ⚐) With its high-backed chairs, bright colours and creaky wooden floor, the Doll's House blends a Victorian child's bedroom with modern stylings. The result is a surprising warmth and no pretensions. The menu makes the most of local fish and other Scottish produce, and the £6.95 two-course lunch is unbeatable value. The early evening two-course deal for £11.95 isn't bad, either.

Glass House ITALIAN, SCOTTISH ££
(www.glasshouse-restaurant.co.uk; 80 North St; mains £8-11; ☺ noon-10.30pm) Casual but comfortable, this restaurant offers plenty of light in its split-level, open-kitchen dining area. The menu is basically Italian, with attractively presented pizzas and pastas popular with students. But a handful of daily specials offer more Scottish meat-and-game choices of notable quality. Two-course lunches cost £7.

★**Vine Leaf** SCOTTISH £££
(☑ 01334-477497; www.vineleafstandrews.co.uk; 131 South St; 2-/3-course dinners £27/30; ☺ 6-10pm Tue-Sat; ☑) Classy, comfortable and well-established, the friendly Vine Leaf offers a changing menu of sumptuous Scottish seafood, game and vegetarian dishes. There's a huge selection within the set-price menu, all well presented, and an interesting, mostly old-world wine list. It's down a close off South St.

Seafood Restaurant SEAFOOD £££
(☑ 01334-479475; www.theseafoodrestaurant.com; The Scores; mains £13-28; ☺ noon-2.30pm Mon-Sat, 12.30-3pm Sun, 6-10pm daily) ✏ The Seafood Restaurant occupies a stylish glass-walled room, built out over the sea, with plush navy carpet, crisp white linen, an open kitchen and panoramic views of St Andrews Bay. It offers top-notch seafood and an excellent wine list; look out for its special winter deals.

❶ Information

J&G Innes (www.jg-innes.co.uk; 107 South St; ☺ 9am-5.15pm Mon-Sat, 12.30-4.30pm Sun) Plenty of local-interest books, such as ones about Fife's history of burning witches.

Library (Church Sq; ☺ 9.30am-5pm Mon, Fri & Sat, to 7pm Tue-Thu) Free internet access – drop-in only; no bookings.

St Andrews Community Hospital (☑ 01334-465656; www.nhsfife.org; Largo Rd) Has a minor injuries unit.

St Andrews Tourist Office (☑ 01334-472021; www.visitstandrews.com; 70 Market St; ☺ 9.15am-6pm Mon-Sat, 10am-5pm Sun Jul & Aug, shorter hours rest of year) Helpful staff with good knowledge of St Andrews and Fife.

❶ Getting There & Away

BUS

All buses leave from the bus station on Station Rd. There are frequent services to the following:
Anstruther £3.20, 25 minutes, hourly
Crail £4, 25 minutes, hourly
Dundee £4.50, 30 minutes, half-hourly
Edinburgh £10.45, two hours, hourly
Glasgow £10.45, 2½ hours, hourly
Stirling £7.80, two hours, every two hours Monday to Saturday

TRAIN

There is no train station in St Andrews itself, but you can take a train from Edinburgh (grab a seat on the right-hand side of the carriage for great firth views) to Leuchars (£13.50, one hour, hourly), 5 miles to the northwest. From here, buses leave regularly for St Andrews (£2.75, 10 minutes).

❶ Getting Around

For a cab, call **Golf City Taxis** (☑ 01334-477788; www.golfcitytaxis.co.uk). A taxi between Leuchars train station and the town centre costs around £12.

Spokes (☑ 01334-477835; www.spokescycles.com; 37 South St; per day/week £15/80; ☺ 9am-5.30pm Mon-Sat) hires out mountain bikes.

East Neuk

This charming stretch of coast runs south from St Andrews to the point at Fife Ness, then west to Leven. Neuk is an old Scots word for corner, and it's certainly an appealing nook of the country to investigate, with picturesque fishing villages, some great restaurants and pretty coastal walks; the Fife Coastal Path's most scenic stretches are in this area. It's easily visited from St Andrews, but also makes a very pleasant place to stay.

Crail

POP 1640

Pretty and peaceful, little Crail has a much-photographed stone-built harbour surrounded by wee cottages with red-tiled roofs. You can buy lobster and crab from a shed (34 Shoregate; mains £4-5; ⊙noon-4pm Sat & Sun) here – the benches in the nearby grassed area are perfectly placed for munching your alfresco crustaceans while admiring the view across to the Isle of May.

The village's history and involvement with the fishing industry is outlined in the Crail Museum (www.crailmuseum.org.uk; 62 Marketgate; ⊙11am-4pm Mon-Sat, 1-4pm Sun Jun-Sep, Sat & Sun only May) FREE, which also offers tourist information.

Eighteenth-century Selcraig House (☑01333-450697; www.selcraighouse.co.uk; 47 Nethergate; s/d £35/70; 🛜🐾) is a characterful, well-run place with a variety of rooms. Across the road from the museum, a lot of work has gone into making Hazelton Guest House (☑01333-450250; www.thehazelton.co.uk; 29 Marketgate North; s £45-50, d £70-85; 🛜) what it is. Attractively remodelled rooms make full use of the abundant natural light in this lovely old building.

Crail is 10 miles southeast of St Andrews. Stagecoach bus 95 between Leven, Anstruther, Crail and St Andrews passes through Crail hourly every day (£4, 25 minutes to St Andrews).

Anstruther

POP 3450

Once among Scotland's busiest ports, cheery Anstruther has ridden the tribulations of the fishing industry better than some, and now has a very pleasant mixture of bobbing boats, historic streets, and visitors ambling around the harbour grazing on fish and chips or contemplating a trip to the Isle of May.

◉ Sights

The displays at the excellent Scottish Fisheries Museum (www.scotfishmuseum.org; adult/child £7/free; ⊙10am-5.30pm Mon-Sat, 11am-5pm Sun Apr-Sep, 10am-4.30pm Mon-Sat, noon-4.30pm Sun Oct-Mar) include the Zulu Gallery, which houses the huge, partly restored hull of a traditional Zulu-class fishing boat, redolent with the scent of tar and timber. Afloat in the harbour outside the museum lies the Reaper, a fully restored Fifie-class fishing boat built in 1902.

The mile-long Isle of May, 6 miles southeast of Anstruther, is a stunning nature reserve. Between April and July the intimidating cliffs are packed with breeding kittiwakes, razorbills, guillemots, shags and around 40,000 puffins.

The five-hour trip to the island on the May Princess (☑01333-311808; www.isleofmayferry.com; adult/child £24/12), including two to three hours ashore, sails almost daily from April to September; check times by phone or via the website. There's also a faster boat, the 12-seater rigid-hull inflatable Osprey (☑07473 631671; www.isleofmayboattrips.co.uk; adult/child £25/12; ⊙Apr-Sep), which makes nonlanding circuits of the island and longer visits.

🛏 Sleeping & Eating

⭐ Spindrift   B&B ££

(☑01333-310573; www.thespindrift.co.uk; Pittenweem Rd; s/d £58/85; 🅿🛜🐾) Arriving from the west, there's no need to go further than Anstruther's first house on the left, a redoubt of Scottish cheer and warm hospitality. The rooms are elegant, classy and extremely comfortable – some have views across to Edinburgh and one is like a ship's cabin, courtesy of the sea captain who once owned the house.

Wee Chippy   FISH & CHIPS £

(4 Shore St; takeaway £4-6; ⊙noon-10pm Apr-Sep, to 9pm Oct-Mar) 🍴 The Anstruther Fish Bar is one of Britain's best chippies, but we – and plenty of locals – reckon this one might be even better. The fish is of a very high quality and there's less of a queue too. Eat your catch by the water.

Dreel Tavern   PUB FOOD ££

(www.dreeltavern.com; 16 High St W; mains £8-12; ⊙food served noon-2.30pm & 6-9pm Mon-Sat, 1-7.30pm Sun; 🚸) This charming old pub on the banks of the Dreel Burn has bucketloads of character and serves reliably tasty bar meals. Chow down in the outdoor beer garden in summer. There are also some top-quality cask ales.

★ Cellar Restaurant
SEAFOOD £££

(☑ 01333-310378; www.thecellaranstruther.co.uk; 24 East Green; menus £42 ; ⊘ lunch Thu-Sun, dinner Wed-Sun) Tucked away in an alley behind the Scottish Fisheries Museum, the elegant and upmarket Cellar has been famous for its superb seafood and fine wines since 1982; recently under new management, it is as good as ever. Try the local crab, lobster or whatever delicacies have been brought in that day. Advance bookings are essential.

ℹ Information

Anstruther Tourist Office (☑ 01333-311073; www.visitfife.com; Harbourhead; ⊘ 10am-5pm Mon-Sat, 11am-4pm Sun Apr-Oct) The best tourist office in the East Neuk.

ℹ Getting There & Away

Stagecoach bus X60 runs hourly from Edinburgh to Anstruther (£10.45, 2¼ hours) and on to St Andrews (£3.20, 25 minutes). Bus 95 runs from Anstruther to Crail (£2.05, 12 minutes, hourly).

Falkland

POP 1100

Below the soft ridges of the Lomond Hills in the centre of Fife lies the charming village of Falkland. Rising majestically out of the town centre is 16th-century **Falkland Palace** (NTS; www.nts.org.uk; adult/child £12.50/9; ⊘ 11am-5pm Mon-Sat, noon-5pm Sun Mar-Oct), a country residence of the Stuart monarchs, where Mary, Queen of Scots, is said to have spent the happiest days of her life 'playing the country girl in the woods and parks'. The palace was built between 1501 and 1541 to replace a castle dating from the 12th century; French and Scottish craftspeople were employed to create a masterpiece of Scottish Gothic architecture. The **king's bedchamber** and the **chapel**, with its beautiful painted ceiling, have both been restored. Don't miss the prodigious 17th-century Flemish hunting **tapestries** in the hall, and the oldest **royal tennis court** in Britain, built in 1539 for James V. It's in the grounds and still in use.

Falkland village is 11 miles north of Kirkcaldy. Stagecoach bus 64 links St Andrews to Falkland direct (£5.30, 1½ hours, hourly Monday to Saturday, five on Sunday). If trav-

elling from Edinburgh (£11.70, hourly Monday to Saturday, five on Sunday), change buses at Glenrothes.

Dunfermline

POP 49,700

Historic, monastic Dunfermline is Fife's largest population centre, sprawling eastwards through once-distinct villages. Its noble history is centred on evocative **Dunfermline Abbey** (HS; www.historic-scotland.gov.uk; St Margaret St; adult/child £4.50/2.70; ⊘ 9.30am-5.30pm daily Apr-Sep, to 4.30pm Oct, 9.30am-4.30pm Sat-Wed Nov-Mar), founded by David I in the 12th century as a Benedictine monastery. Dunfermline was already favoured by religious royals; Malcolm III married the exiled Saxon princess Margaret here in the 11th century, and both chose to be interred here. There were many more royal burials, none more notable than Robert the Bruce, whose remains were discovered here in 1818.

What's left of the abbey are the **ruins** of the impressive three-tiered refectory building, and the atmosphere-laden nave of the church, endowed with geometrically patterned columns and fine Romanesque and Gothic windows. It adjoins the 19th-century **church** (⊘ 10am-4.30pm Mon-Sat, 2-4.30pm Sun Apr-Oct) **FREE** where Robert the Bruce now lies under the ornate pulpit.

Next to the refectory (and included in your abbey admission price) is **Dunfermline Palace**. Once the abbey guesthouse, it was converted for James VI, whose son, the ill-fated Charles I, was born here in 1600. Below stretches the bosky, strollable **Pittencrieff Park**.

There are frequent buses between Dunfermline and Edinburgh (£5.30, 50 minutes), Stirling (£4.70, 1¼ hours) and St Andrews (£10.45, 1¼ hours), and trains to/from Edinburgh (£5.10, 40 minutes).

Culross

POP 400

An enchanting little town, Culross (kooross) is Scotland's best-preserved example of a 17th-century Scottish burgh: the National Trust for Scotland (NTS) owns 20 of the town's buildings, including the palace. Small, red-tiled, whitewashed buildings line the cobbled streets, and the winding Back Causeway to the abbey is embellished with whimsical stone cottages.

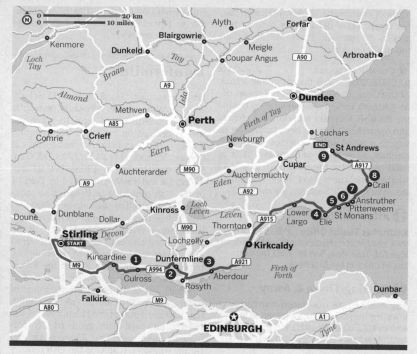

🏃 Driving Tour
The Fife Coast

START STIRLING
END ST ANDREWS
LENGTH 76 MILES; ONE DAY

This tour links two of the most popular tourist towns in Central Scotland via the scenic delights of the Fife coast.

Head south from Stirling on the M9 and at Junction 7 turn east towards Kincardine Bridge. As you approach the bridge, follow signs for Kincardine and Kirkcaldy then, once across the Firth of Forth, follow the Fife Coastal Tourist Route signposts to the historic village of ❶ **Culross**. Spend an hour or so exploring the medieval buildings of Culross before continuing via the A994 to ❷ **Dunfermline**, for a look at its fine abbey and palace ruins.

From Dunfermline take the M90 towards the Forth Road Bridge, but leave at Junction 1 (signposted A921 Dalgety Bay) and continue to the attractive seaside village of ❸ **Aberdour** for lunch at the Aberdour Inn or the Room with a View restaurant. Stay on the A921 as far as Kirkcaldy, then take the faster

A915 (signposted St Andrews) as far as Upper Largo where you follow the A917 towards Elie; from here on, you will be following the brown Fife Coastal Tourist Route signs.

❹ **Elie**, with its sandy beaches and coastal footpaths, is a great place to stretch your legs and take in some bracing sea air before driving just a couple of miles further on to explore the neighbouring fishing villages of ❺ **St Monans** and ❻ **Pittenweem**. Just 1 mile beyond Pittenweem, ❼ **Anstruther** deserves a slightly longer stop for a visit to the Scottish Fisheries Museum, a stroll by the harbour, and an ice cream. If time allows, you may want to detour inland a couple of miles to visit Kellie Castle or Scotland's Secret Bunker.

The final stop before St Andrews is the pretty fishing village of ❽ **Crail**, where the late afternoon or early evening light will provide ideal conditions for capturing one of Scotland's most photographed harbours. A brisk hike along the coastal path towards Fife Ness, keeping an eye out for seals and seabirds, will round off the day before driving the last 10 miles into St Andrews.

As birthplace of St Mungo, Glasgow's patron saint, Culross was an important religious centre from the 6th century. The burgh developed, under laird George Bruce, by mining coal through extraordinary underwater tunnels. When mining was ended by flooding of the tunnels, the town switched to making linen and shoes.

Culross Palace (NTS; www.nts.org.uk; adult/child £10.50/7.50; ☉ noon-5pm Thu-Mon Apr, May & Sep, noon-5pm daily Jun-Aug, noon-4pm Thu-Mon Oct) is more a large house than a palace, and features extraordinary decorative painted woodwork, barrel-vaulted ceilings and an interior largely unchanged since the early 17th century. The **Town House** (tourist office downstairs) and the **Study**, also completed in the early 17th century, are open to the public (via guided tour included in palace admission), but the other NTS properties can only be viewed from the outside.

Ruined **Culross Abbey** (HS; www.historic-scotland.gov.uk; ☉ 9.30am-7pm Mon-Sat, 2-7pm Sun Apr-Sep, 9.30am-4pm Mon-Sat, 2-4pm Sun Oct-Mar) **FREE**, founded by the Cistercians in 1217, is on the hill in a lovely peaceful spot with vistas of the firth. Part of the ruins were converted into the parish church in the 16th century; it's worth a peek inside for the stained glass and the Gothic Argyll tomb.

Culross is 12 miles west of the Forth Road Bridge. Stagecoach bus 78 runs from Dunfermline (£2.75, 25 minutes, hourly) via Culross to Stirling (£4.70, 50 minutes, hourly Monday to Saturday).

LOWLAND PERTHSHIRE

Perth

POP 46,970

Elegantly arranged along the banks of the Tay, this former capital of Scotland is a most liveable place, with large tracts of enticing parkland surrounding an easily managed centre. On its outskirts lies Scone Palace, a country house of staggering luxury built alongside the ancient crowning place of Scotland's kings. The palace is a must-see, and the town itself – known as the Fair City – is endowed with fine galleries and excellent restaurants, and is within easy striking distance of both Edinburgh and Glasgow.

⊙ Sights

★**Scone Palace**   PALACE
(www.scone-palace.co.uk;   adult/child/family £10.50/7.60/33; ☉ palace & grounds 9.30am-5pm Apr-Oct, grounds only 10am-4pm Fri-Sun Nov-Mar) 'So thanks to all at once and to each one, whom we invite to see us crowned at Scone.' This line from *Macbeth* indicates the importance of Scone (pronounced 'skoon') as the coronation place of Scottish monarchs. The original palace of 1580, built on a site intrinsic to Scottish history, was rebuilt in the early 19th century as a Georgian mansion of extreme elegance and luxury. The visit takes you through a succession of sumptuous rooms filled with fine French furniture and noble portraits.

Scone has belonged for centuries to the Murray family, Earls of Mansfield, and many of the objects have fascinating history attached to them (friendly guides are on hand to explain). Each room has comprehensive multilingual information; there are also panels relating histories of some of the Scottish kings crowned at Scone over the centuries. Outside, peacocks – each named after a monarch – strut around the magnificent grounds, which incorporate woods, a butterfly garden and a maze.

Ancient kings were crowned on **Moot Hill**, now topped by a chapel next to the palace. It's said that the hill was created by bootfuls of earth, brought by nobles attending the coronations as an acknowledgement of the king's rights over their lands, although it's more likely the site of an ancient motte-and-bailey castle. Here in 838, Kenneth MacAlpin became the first king of a united Scotland and brought to Scone the **Stone of Destiny**, on which Scottish kings were ceremonially invested. In 1296 Edward I of England carted this talisman off to Westminster Abbey, where it remained for 700 years before being returned to Scotland in 1997.

Scone Palace is 2 miles north of Perth; from the town centre, cross the bridge, turn left, and keep bearing left until you reach the gates of the estate. From here, it's a another half-mile to the palace (about 30 minutes' walk). Various buses from town stop here; the tourist office has a printout of timetables.

★**Fergusson Gallery**   GALLERY
(www.pkc.gov.uk; cnr Marshall Pl & Tay St; ☉ 10am-5pm Mon-Sat, plus noon-4.30pm Sun May-Sep) **FREE** Beautifully set in a circular cast-iron building that was once a waterworks, this

ARGYLL, CENTRAL & NORTHEAST SCOTLAND PERTH

Perth

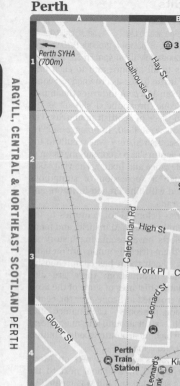

Perth

◎ Top Sights
1 Fergusson Gallery	C4
2 St John's Kirk	C3

◎ Sights
3 Black Watch Museum	B1
4 Perth Museum & Art Gallery	C2

🛏 Sleeping
5 Kinnaird Guest House	C4
6 Parklands	B4
7 Pitcullen Guest House	D1

✕ Eating
8 63 Tay Street	C4
9 Breizh	C3
10 Deans@Let's Eat	C2
11 Pig'Halle	C3

◉ Drinking & Nightlife
12 Twa Tams	B4

gallery exhibits an extensive collection of paintings by the Scottish Colourist JD Fergusson in a most impressive display. Fergusson spent time in Paris, and the influence of artists such as Matisse on his work is evident; his voluptuous female portraits against a tropical-looking Riviera background are memorable, as is the story of his lifelong relationship with noted Scottish dancer Margaret Morris.

★ **St John's Kirk** CHURCH
(www.st-johns-kirk.co.uk; St John's St; ⊙ 10am-4pm Mon-Sat May-Sep) **FREE** Daunting St John's Kirk, surrounded by cobbled streets, was founded in 1126 and is still the centrepiece of the town. In 1559 John Knox preached a powerful sermon here that helped begin the Reformation, inciting a frenzied destruction of Scone abbey and other religious sites. Perth used to be known as St John's Town after this church, and the local football team is still called St Johnstone.

Perth Museum & Art Gallery
MUSEUM

(www.pkc.gov.uk; cnr George & Charlotte Sts; ⊙10am-5pm Mon-Sat, plus 10am-5pm Sun Apr-Oct) **FREE** The city's main museum is worth wandering through for the elegant neoclassical interior alone. There's a varied range of exhibits, from portraits of dour lairds to interesting local social history. A geological room provides more entertainment for the young, while there are often excellent temporary exhibitions.

Black Watch Museum
MUSEUM

(www.theblackwatch.co.uk; Hay St; adult/child £7.50/3.50; ⊙9.30am-5pm Mon-Sat, plus 10am-4pm Sun Apr-Oct) Housed in Balhousie Castle on the edge of North Inch, this museum honours what was once Scotland's foremost regiment. Formed in 1725 to combat rural banditry, the Black Watch fought in numerous campaigns, re-created here with paintings, memorabilia and anecdotes.

Little attempt at perspective is evident: there's justifiable pride in the regiment's role in the gruelling trench warfare of WWI, where it suffered nearly 30,000 casualties, but no sheepishness about less glorious colonial engagements, such as against the 'Fuzzy Wuzzies' of Sudan. In 2006 the Black Watch was subsumed into the new Royal Regiment of Scotland.

🛏 Sleeping

Perth SYHA
HOSTEL £

(☑01738-877800; www.syha.org.uk; Crieff Rd; dm/tw £23/46; ⊙late Jun-late Aug) A 20-minute stroll from the centre, this summer-only hostel is set in a student residence at Perth College. The rooms are all en suite twins, with good share kitchens and common rooms. For some reason, there's a price jump for a week in July. Turn into the Brahan entrance on Crieff Rd, and the hostel is by the large car park. Numerous buses stop outside.

Parklands
HOTEL ££

(☑01738-622451; www.theparklandshotel.com; 2 St Leonard's Bank; s/d from £94/119; P@🅢) Tucked away near Perth train station, this relaxing, renovated hotel sits amid a lush hillside garden overlooking the parklands of South Inch. While the rooms conserve the character of this beautiful building, formerly the residence of the town's mayors, they also offer modern conveniences and plenty of style. There's a great terrace and garden area to lap up the Perthshire sun.

Pitcullen Guest House
B&B ££

(☑01738-626506; www.pitcullen.co.uk; 17 Pitcullen Cres; s/d £50/70; P🅢) This excellent place has a much more contemporary look than other guesthouses on this strip. Great-looking fabrics and modern styling give the rooms an upbeat feel. Lots of thought has gone into making your stay more comfortable, with things like fridges with free drinks in the rooms, plenty of plugs to make recharging easy and handy maps on the walls.

Kinnaird Guest House
B&B ££

(☑01738-628021; www.kinnaird-guesthouse.co.uk; 5 Marshall Pl; s £45-65, d £60-80; P🅢) The best of the handful of guesthouses enjoying a privileged position opposite the lovely South Inch park, this elegant old house has original features and appealing, bright rooms with big beds. It's all impeccable, with nice touches like bathrobes and teddy bears on the beds. The owners are engaging and helpful; breakfast features organic produce and quality bacon. The back rooms receive occasional train noise.

🍴 Eating & Drinking

★63 Tay Street
SCOTTISH ££

(☑01738-441451; www.63taystreet.com; 63 Tay St; lunch mains £13.50, 4-course dinners £42; ⊙noon-2pm Thu-Sat, 5.45-9pm Tue-Fri, 6.30-9pm Sat) Classy and warmly welcoming, this understated restaurant is Perth's best, featuring a lightly decorated dining area, excellent service and quality food. In a culinary Auld Alliance, French influence is applied to the best of Scottish produce to produce memorable game, seafood, beef and vegetarian plates.

Breizh
BISTRO ££

(☑01738-444427; www.cafebreizh.co.uk; 28 High St; mains £7-17; ⊙9am-9pm Sun-Thu, to 9.30pm Fri & Sat) This funkily French bistro – the name is Breton for Brittany – is a treat. Dishes are served with real panache, and the salads, featuring all sorts of delicious ingredients, are a feast of colour, texture and subtle flavours. The blackboard specials offer great value and a real taste of northwest France, including traditional *galettes* (Breton buckwheat pancakes with savoury fillings).

Deans@Let's Eat
SCOTTISH ££

(☑01738-643377; www.letseatperth.co.uk; 77 Kinnoull St; mains £14-20; ⊙noon-3pm & 6-9pm Tue-Sat) A Perth favourite for splashing out on a special meal, this busy corner restaurant has a can-do attitude and an excellent line in fresh

Scottish produce. Juicy scallops, fine Orkney beef, local venison or lamb may feature, but you can't really go wrong. Recession-busting lunch and dinner set menus are a good way to graze here on a budget.

Pig'Halle FRENCH ££
(www.pighalle.co.uk; 38 South St; mains £10-19; ⊘noon-3pm & 5.30-9.30pm Tue-Sun) A spacious bistro that presents the very best of pork products through traditional regional French cuisine. The sample platter of charcuterie is fabulous value, there are succulent mains and there's a decent selection of Gallic wines to accompany them. There are other dishes on the menu if pig ain't your thing, and a cheap early dinner deal.

Twa Tams PUB
(www.twatams-perth.co.uk; 79 Scott St; ⊘11am-11pm Mon-Wed, to 12.30am Thu-Sat, 12.30pm-midnight Sun) Perth's best pub has a strange outdoor space with windows peering out onto the street, an ornate entrance gate and a large, cosy interior. There are regular events, including live music every Friday and Saturday night; it has a sound reputation for attracting talented young bands.

ℹ Information

AK Bell Library (York Pl; ⊘9.30am-5pm Mon, Wed & Fri, to 8pm Tue & Thu, to 4pm Sat) Free internet; lots of terminals.
Perth Tourist Office (☑01738-450600; www.perthshire.co.uk; West Mill St; ⊘9am-5pm daily Apr-Oct, Mon-Sat Nov-Mar) Efficiently run tourist office.
Perth Royal Infirmary (☑01738-623311; www.nhstayside.scot.nhs.uk; Taymount Tce) West of the town centre.

ℹ Getting There & Away

BUS
Citylink (www.citylink.co.uk) operates, from the **bus station** (Leonard St), services to/from these cities:
Dundee £7.50, 40 minutes, hourly
Edinburgh £12, 1¾ hours, hourly
Glasgow £12, 1½ hours, hourly
Inverness £21, three hours, at least five daily
Stirling £9, 55 minutes, hourly

Further buses run from the Broxden Park & Ride on Glasgow Rd; this is connected regularly with the bus station by shuttle bus. These include **Megabus** (www.megabus.com) discount services to Aberdeen, Edinburgh, Glasgow, Dundee and Inverness.

Stagecoach (www.stagecoachbus.com) buses serve Perthshire destinations regularly, with reduced Sunday service. A Tayside Megarider ticket gives you seven days travel in Perth and Kinross, and Dundee and Angus for £26.

TRAIN
Trains run between Perth and various destinations, including the following:
Dundee £7.60, 20 to 30 minutes, twice hourly, fewer on Sunday
Edinburgh £15.60, 1¼ hours, at least hourly Monday to Saturday, every two hours Sunday
Glasgow £15.60, one hour, at least hourly Monday to Saturday, every two hours Sunday
Pitlochry £13.20, 30 minutes, two hourly, fewer on Sunday
Stirling £8, 30 minutes, one or two per hour

DUNDEE & ANGUS

Angus is a region of fertile farmland stretching north from Dundee – Scotland's fourth-largest city – to the Highland border. It's an attractive area of broad straths (valleys) and low, green hills contrasting with the rich, red-brown soil of freshly ploughed fields. Romantic glens finger their way into the foothills of the Grampian Mountains, while the scenic coastline ranges from the red-sandstone cliffs of Arbroath to the long, sandy beaches around Montrose. This was the Pictish heartland of the 7th and 8th centuries, and many interesting Pictish symbol stones survive here.

Apart from the crowds visiting Discovery Point in newly confident Dundee and the coach parties shuffling through Glamis Castle, Angus is a bit of a tourism backwater – a good place to get away from it all.

Dundee

POP 147,300
London's Trafalgar Sq has Nelson on his column, Edinburgh's Princes St has its monument to Sir Walter Scott and Belfast has a statue of Queen Victoria outside City Hall. Dundee's City Sq, on the other hand, is graced – rather endearingly – by the bronze figure of Desperate Dan. Familiar to generations of British school children, Dan is one of the best-loved cartoon characters from the children's comic *The Dandy*, published by Dundee firm DC Thomson since 1937.

Dundee enjoys perhaps the finest location of any Scottish city, spreading along the northern shore of the Firth of Tay, and boasts tourist attractions of national importance in Discovery Point and the Verdant Works museum. Add in the attractive seaside town of Broughty Ferry and the Dundonians themselves – among the friendliest, most welcoming and most entertaining people you'll meet – and Dundee is definitely worth a stopover.

The waterfront around Discovery Point is currently undergoing a massive redevelopment, preparing the ground for a branch of London's **Victoria & Albert Museum** (scheduled to open in 2016). In the meantime, be prepared for construction sites, temporary street layouts and traffic diversions on the approach to the Tay Bridge.

◉ Sights

★**Discovery Point**   MUSEUM
(www.rrsdiscovery.com; Discovery Quay; adult/child/family £8.75/5.25/25; ⊙10am-6pm Mon-Sat, 11am-6pm Sun Apr-Oct, to 5pm Nov-Mar) The three masts of Captain Robert Falcon Scott's famous polar expedition vessel the **RRS Discovery** dominate the riverside to the south of the city centre. Exhibitions and audiovisual displays in the neighbouring visitor centre provide a fascinating history of both the ship and Antarctic exploration, but *Discovery* itself – afloat in a protected dock – is the star attraction. You can visit the bridge, the galley and the mahogany-panelled officers' wardroom, and poke your nose into the cabins used by Scott and his crew.

The ship was built in Dundee in 1900, with a wooden hull at least half a metre thick to survive the pack ice, and sailed for the Antarctic in 1901, where it spent two winters trapped in the ice. From 1931 on it was laid up in London where its condition steadily deteriorated, until it was rescued by the efforts of Peter Scott (Robert's son) and the Maritime Trust, and restored to its 1925 condition. In 1986 the ship was given a berth in its home port of Dundee, where it became a symbol of the city's regeneration.

A joint ticket that gives entry to both Discovery Point and the Verdant Works costs £15/8.50/40 per adult/child/family.

★**Verdant Works**   MUSEUM
(www.verdantworks.com; West Henderson's Wynd; adult/child/familiy £8.75/5.25/25; ⊙10am-6pm Mon-Sat, 11am-6pm Sun Apr-Oct, 10.30am-4.30pm Wed-Sun Nov-Mar) One of the finest industrial museums in Europe, the Verdant Works explores the history of Dundee's jute industry. Housed in a restored jute mill, complete with

original machinery still in working condition, the museum's interactive exhibits and computer displays follow the raw material from its origins in India through to the manufacture of a wide range of finished products, from sacking to rope to wagon covers for the pioneers of the American West.

The museum is 250m west of the city centre and is operating while undergoing a major renovation that will restore more buildings and double the size of the exhibition space.

McManus Galleries   MUSEUM
(www.mcmanus.co.uk; Albert Sq; ⊙10am-5pm Mon-Sat, 12.30-4.30pm Sun) FREE Housed in a solid Victorian Gothic building designed by Gilbert Scott in 1867, the McManus Galleries are a city museum on a human scale – you can see everything there is to see in a single visit, without feeling rushed or overwhelmed. The exhibits cover the history of the city from the Iron Age to the present day, including relics of the Tay Bridge Disaster and the Dundee whaling industry.

Computer geeks will enjoy the Sinclair ZX81 and Spectrum (pioneering personal computers with a whole 16K of memory!) which were made in Dundee in the early 1980s.

Dundee Contemporary Arts   ARTS CENTRE
(www.dca.org.uk; Nethergate; ⊙11am-6pm Tue, Wed & Fri-Sun, 11am-8pm Thu) FREE The focus for the city's Cultural Quarter is Dundee Contemporary Arts, a centre for modern art, design and cinema. The galleries here exhibit work by contemporary UK and international artists, and there are printmakers' studios where you can watch artists at work, or even take part in craft demonstrations and workshops. There's also the Jute Cafe-Bar (p882).

⛏ Sleeping

Dundee Backpackers   HOSTEL £
(☑01382-224646; www.hoppo.com/dundee; 71 High St; dm £16-18.50, s/tw from £25/40; @☎) Set in a beautifully converted historic building, with a clean, modern kitchen, a pool room, and an ideal location right in the city centre. Can get a bit noisy at night, but that's because it's close to pubs and nightlife.

Aabalree   B&B £
(☑01382-223867; www.aabalree.com; 20 Union St; s/d £26/44) This is a pretty basic B&B – there are no en suites – but the owners are

WORTH A TRIP

GLAMIS CASTLE

Looking every inch the archetypal Scottish Baronial castle, with its roofline sprouting a forest of pointed turrets and battlements, **Glamis Castle** (www.glamis-castle.co.uk; adult/child £10.90/8; ⊙10am-6pm Apr–Oct, last entry 4.30pm; P⊠) claims to be the legendary setting for Shakespeare's *Macbeth* (his character is the Thane of Glamis at the start of the play). A royal residence since 1372, it is the family home of the Earls of Strathmore and Kinghorne: the Queen Mother (born Elizabeth Bowes-Lyon; 1900–2002) spent her childhood at Glamis (pronounced 'glams') and Princess Margaret (the Queen's sister; 1930–2002) was born here. The one-hour guided tours depart every 15 minutes (last tour at 4.30pm, or 3.30pm in winter).

Glamis Castle is 12 miles north of Dundee. There are two to four buses a day from Dundee (35 minutes) to Glamis; some continue to Kirriemuir.

welcoming (don't be put off by the dark entrance) and it couldn't be more central, close to both the train and bus stations. This makes it popular, so book ahead.

Balgowan House B&B ££
(☑01382-200262; www.balgowanhouse.co.uk; 510 Perth Rd; s/d from £60/85; P☎) Built in 1900 and perched in a prime location with stunning views over the Firth of Tay, Balgowan is a wealthy merchant's mansion converted into a luxurious guesthouse with three sumptuous en suite bedrooms. It's 2 miles west of the city centre, overlooking the university botanic gardens.

Apex City Quay Hotel HOTEL ££
(☑0845 365 0000; www.apexhotels.co.uk; 1 West Victoria Dock Rd; r from £77; P☎☀) Though it looks plain and boxy from the outside, the Apex sports the sort of stylish, spacious, sofa-equipped rooms that make you want to lounge around all evening munching chocolate in front of the TV. If you can drag yourself away from your room, there are spa treatments, saunas and Japanese hot tubs to enjoy.

Errolbank Guest House B&B ££
(☑01382-462118; www.errolbank-guesthouse.com; 9 Dalgleish Rd; s/d £49/69; P) A mile east of the city centre, just north of the road to Broughty Ferry, Errolbank is a lovely Victorian family home with small but beautifully decorated en suite rooms set on a quiet street.

 Eating

⭐**Parlour Cafe** CAFE £
(☑01382-203588; 58 West Port; mains £5-7; ⊙8am-7pm Mon-Fri, to 5pm Sat, 10am-3pm Sun; ☎☑) ⭐ Tiny but terrific, this friendly neighbourhood cafe is bursting with good things to eat including filled tortillas, savoury tarts, bean burgers, bagels and homemade soup, all freshly prepared using seasonal produce. Great coffee and cakes too, but be prepared to wait for a table or squeeze in among the locals.

Jute Café Bar BISTRO ££
(☑01382-909246; www.jutecafebar.co.uk; 152 Nethergate; lunch mains £9-13, dinner £10-18; ⊙noon-9.30pm; ☎⊠) The industrial-chic cafe-bar in the Dundee Contemporary Arts centre (p881) serves excellent deli sandwiches and burgers, as well as more adventurous Mediterranean-Asian fusion cuisine. The early-bird menu (5pm to 6.30pm weekdays) offers a two-/three-course meal for £14/16. Tables spill out into the sunny courtyard in summer.

⭐**Metro** BRASSERIE ££
(☑0845 365 0002; www.apexhotels.co.uk/eat; Apex City Quay Hotel, 1 West Victoria Dock Rd; mains £11-27; ⊙noon-2.30pm & 6-9.30pm) Sleek, champagne-coloured banquettes, white linen napkins, black-clad staff and a view of Victoria Dock lend an air of sophistication to this stylish hotel brasserie, with a menu that ranges from steaks and burgers to wild mushroom and truffle risotto. There's a three-course pre-theatre menu for £22.50 (before 7pm).

Blue Marlin SEAFOOD £££
(☑01382-221397; www.thebluemarlin.co.uk; City Quay; mains £14-26; ⊙noon-2pm & 5.30-10pm Tue-Sat) The ongoing redevelopment of Dundee's former docks means that the setting for the city's best fish restaurant doesn't look too promising. But once inside, there is sleek and understated nautical-themed decor, and the chance to feast on the best of Scottish seafood. Two-course lunch and pretheatre menu £15.

ℹ️ **Information**

Dundee Tourist Office (☑01382-527527; www.angusanddundee.co.uk; Discovery Point;

⊘10am-5pm Mon-Sat, noon-4pm Sun Jun-Sep, 10am-4pm Mon-Sat Oct-May)
Ninewells Hospital (☏01382-660111; www. nhstayside.scot.nhs.uk; ⊘casualty 24hr) At Menzieshill, west of the city centre.

❶ Getting There & Around

AIR
Dundee Airport (www.hial.co.uk), 2½ miles west of the city centre, has daily scheduled services to London City airport, Birmingham and Belfast. A taxi from the city centre to the airport takes 10 minutes and costs around £4.

BUS
The bus station is northeast of the city centre. Some Aberdeen buses travel via Arbroath, others via Forfar.
Aberdeen £16.80, 1½ hours, hourly
Edinburgh £16.10, 1½ hours, hourly, some change at Perth
Glasgow £16.10, 1¾ hours, hourly
London £40, 11 hours; National Express, daily
Perth £7.50, 35 minutes, hourly
Oban £35.50, 5½ hours, three daily

TRAIN
Trains from Dundee to Aberdeen travel via Arbroath and Stonehaven.
Aberdeen £19.10, 1¼ hours, twice an hour
Edinburgh £17.30, 1¼ hours, at least hourly
Glasgow £21.30, 1½ hours, hourly

Arbroath

POP 23,900

Arbroath is an old-fashioned seaside resort and fishing harbour, home of the famous **Arbroath smokie** (a form of smoked haddock). The humble smokie achieved EU 'Protected Geographical Indication' status in 2004 – the term 'Arbroath smokie' can only be used legally to describe haddock smoked in the traditional manner within an 8km radius of Arbroath. No visit is complete without buying a pair of smokies from one of the many fish shops and eating them with your fingers while sitting beside the harbour. Yum.

◉ Sights

Arbroath Abbey   ABBEY
(HS; Abbey St; adult/child £5.50/3.30; ⊘9.30am-5.30pm Apr-Sep, to 4.30pm Oct-Mar) The magnificent, red-sandstone ruins of Arbroath Abbey, founded in 1178 by King William the Lion, dominate the town of Arbroath. It is thought that Bernard of Linton, the abbot here in the early 14th century, wrote the famous Declaration of Arbroath in 1320, asserting Scotland's right to independence from England. You can climb to the top of one of the towers for a grand view over the town.

St Vigeans Museum   MUSEUM
(HS; ☏01241-878756; St Vigeans Lane; adult/child £4.50/2.70) About a mile north of Arbroath town centre, this cottage museum houses a superb collection of Pictish and medieval sculptured stones. The museum's masterpiece is the **Drosten Stone**, beautifully carved with animal figures and hunting scenes on one side, and an interlaced Celtic cross on the other (look for the devil perched in the top left corner). Phone ahead or ask at Arbroath Abbey to check current opening hours.

🛏 Sleeping & Eating

Harbour Nights Guest House   B&B ££
(☏01241-434343; www.harbournights-scotland. com; 4 The Shore; s/d from £50/70; 🐾) With a superb location overlooking the harbour, four stylishly decorated bedrooms and a gourmet breakfast menu, Harbour Nights is our favourite place to stay in Arbroath. Rooms 2 and 3, with harbour views, are a bit more expensive (doubles £75 to £80), but well worth asking for when booking.

But'n'Ben Restaurant   SCOTTISH ££
(☏01241-877223; www.butnbenauchmithie.co.uk; 1 Auchmithie; lunch mains £8-11, dinner £12-22; ⊘noon-2pm Wed-Mon, 6-9pm Mon & Wed-Sat, 4-7pm Sun; 🖗) 🍃 Above the harbour in Auchmithie, this cosy cottage restaurant with open fireplace, rustic furniture and sea-themed art serves the best of local seafood – the Arbroath smokie pancakes are recommended – plus great homemade cakes and desserts, and high teas on Sunday (£14). Best to book.

❶ Getting There & Away

BUS
Bus 140 runs from Arbroath to Auchmithie (£1.90, 15 minutes, six daily Monday to Friday, three daily on Saturday and Sunday).

TRAIN
Trains from Dundee to Arbroath (£5.40, 20 minutes, two per hour) continue to Aberdeen (£18.70, 55 minutes) via Montrose and Stonehaven.

ABERDEENSHIRE & MORAY

Since medieval times Aberdeenshire and its northwestern neighbour Moray have been the richest and most fertile regions of the Highlands. Aberdeenshire is famed for its Aberdeen Angus beef cattle, its many fine castles and the prosperous 'granite city' of Aberdeen. Moray's main attractions are the Speyside whisky distilleries that line the valley of the River Spey and its tributaries.

Aberdeen

POP 195,000

Aberdeen is the powerhouse of the northeast, fuelled by the North Sea petroleum industry. Oil money has made the city as expensive as London and Edinburgh, and there are hotels, restaurants and clubs with prices to match the depth of oil-wealthy pockets. Fortunately, most of the cultural attractions, such as the excellent Maritime Museum and Aberdeen Art Gallery, are free.

Royal Deeside and the Cairngorms National Park are easily accessible to the west, Dunnottar Castle to the south, sandy beaches to the north and whisky country to the northwest.

◉ Sights & Activities

★ **Aberdeen Maritime Museum**   MUSEUM
(☑ 01224-337700; www.aagm.co.uk; Shiprow; ⊙ 10am-5pm Tue-Sat, noon-3pm Sun) **FREE** Overlooking the nautical bustle of Aberdeen harbour is the Maritime Museum. Centred on a three-storey replica of a North Sea oil production platform, it explains all you ever wanted to know about the petroleum industry. Other galleries, some situated in **Provost Ross's House**, the oldest building in the city and part of the museum, cover the shipbuilding, whaling and fishing industries.

Sleek and speedy Aberdeen clippers were a 19th-century shipyard speciality, used by British merchants for the importation of tea, wool and exotic goods (opium, for instance) to Britain, and, on the return journey, the transportation of emigrants to Australia.

★ **Aberdeen Art Gallery**   GALLERY
(☑ 01224-523700; www.aagm.co.uk; Schoolhill; ⊙ 10am-5pm Tue-Sat, 2-5pm Sun) **FREE** Behind the grand facade of Aberdeen Art Gallery is a cool, marble-lined space exhibiting the work of contemporary Scottish and English painters, such as Gwen Hardie, Stephen Conroy, Trevor Sutton and Tim Ollivier. There are also several landscapes by Joan Eardley, who lived in a cottage on the cliffs near Stonehaven in the 1950s and '60s and painted tempestuous oils of the North Sea and poignant portraits of slum children.

Among the Pre-Raphaelite works upstairs, look out for the paintings by Aberdeen artist William Dyce (1806–64), ranging from religious works to rural scenes.

★ **Marischal College**   HISTORIC BUILDING
(Broad St) Marischal College, founded in 1593 by the 5th Earl Marischal, merged with King's College (founded 1495) in 1860 to cre-

---

WORTH A TRIP

OLD ABERDEEN

Just over a mile north of the city centre is the district called Old Aberdeen. The name is misleading – although Old Aberdeen is certainly old, the area around Castlegate is older still. This part of the city was originally called Aulton, from the Gaelic for 'village by the pool', and this was anglicised in the 17th century to Old Town.

Old Town House (☑ 01224-273650; www.abdn.ac.uk/oldtownhouse; High St; admission free; ⊙ 9am-5pm Mon-Sat) At the north end of High St, the Old Town House now houses a visitor centre with information and exhibits on the history of Old Aberdeen. It also houses **King's Museum**, with changing exhibits of items from the universities 18th-century collection.

St Machar's Cathedral (www.stmachar.com; The Chanonry; ⊙ 10am-4pm) The 15th-century St Machar's Cathedral, with its massive twin towers, is a rare example of a fortified cathedral. According to legend, St Machar was ordered to establish a church where the river takes the shape of a bishop's crook, which it does just here. The cathedral is best known for its impressive **heraldic ceiling**, dating from 1520, which has 48 shields of kings, nobles, archbishops and bishops. Sunday services are held at 11am and 6pm.

ate the modern University of Aberdeen. The college's huge and impressive facade overlooking Broad St, in Perpendicular Gothic style – unusual in having such elaborate masonry hewn from notoriously hard-to-work granite – dates from 1906 and is the world's second-largest granite structure (after L'Escorial near Madrid).

A recent renovation project saw the facade returned to its original silvery grey glory, and the building now houses Aberdeen City Council's new headquarters; the square outside is undergoing redevelopment into a pedestrian plaza, creating controversy over plans for modern architecture juxtaposed with the college's neo-Gothic facade.

Clyde Cruises   BOAT TRIPS
(☑01475-721281; www.clydecruises.com; Aberdeen Harbour; adult/child from £16/8; ☺daily Jul-late Aug, Thu-Sun late Aug-mid-Sep) Operates 45-minute cruises around Aberdeen's bustling commercial harbour, and 1¼-hour trips outside the harbour to look for dolphins and other marine wildlife.

🛏 Sleeping

There are clusters of B&Bs on Bon Accord St and Springbank Tce (both 400m southwest of the train station) and along Great Western Rd (the A93, a 25-minute walk southwest of the city centre. Prices tend to be lower on weekends.

Aberdeen Youth Hostel   HOSTEL £
(SYHA; ☑01224-646988; 8 Queen's Rd; dm/q £22/100; @�) This unexceptional but good-value hostel, set in a granite Victorian villa, is a mile west of the train station. Walk west along Union St and take the right fork along Albyn Pl until you reach a roundabout; Queen's Rd continues on the western side of the roundabout.

★ Globe Inn   B&B ££
(☑01224-624258; www.the-globe-inn.co.uk; 13-15 North Silver St; r £119) This popular pub has seven appealing and comfortable guest bedrooms upstairs, done out in dark wood with burgundy bedspreads. There's live music in the pub on weekends so it's not a place for early-to-bed types, but the price-versus-location factor can't be beaten. No dining room, so breakfast is continental, served on a tray in your room.

Butler's Guest House   B&B ££
(☑01224-212411; www.butlersguesthouse.com; 122 Crown St; s/d from £63/74; @�) Butler's is a

cosy place with a big breakfast menu that includes fresh fruit salad, kippers and kedgeree as alternatives to the traditional fry-up (rates include a continental breakfast – cooked breakfast is £6.50 extra per person). There are cheaper rooms with shared bathrooms.

City Wharf Apartments   APARTMENT ££
(☑0845 094 2424; www.citywharfapartments.co.uk; 19-20 Regent Quay; d from £120; �) You can watch the bustle of Aberdeen's commercial harbour as you eat breakfast in one of these luxury serviced apartments, complete with stylish, fully equipped kitchen, champagne-stocked minibar and daily cleaning service. Available by the night or the week, with discounts for longer stays.

Brentwood Villa   B&B ££
(☑01224-480633; www.brentwoodvillabandb.com; 560 King St; s/d £60/90; �) Comfortable beds, spotless bathrooms and friendly and helpful owners tick all the right boxes in this homely B&B, attractively set opposite a park. The Brentwood is a mile north of the city centre (take bus 20) and close to Old Aberdeen and the university.

Adelphi Guest House   B&B ££
(☑01224-583078; www.adelphiguesthouse.com; 8 Whinhill Rd; s/d from £45/70; �) Basic but comfortable and good value, located 400m south from western end of Union St.

Aberdeen Douglas Hotel   HOTEL £££
(☑01224-582255; www.aberdeendouglas.com; 43-45 Market St; r Mon-Fri from £165, Sat & Sun from £145; �) You can't miss the grand Victorian facade of this historic landmark, which first opened its doors as a hotel in 1853. Now renovated, it offers classy modern rooms with polished woodwork and crisp white bedlinen, and is barely a minute's walk from the train station.

Jurys Inn   HOTEL £££
(☑01224-381200; www.jurysinns.com; Union Sq, Guild St; r from £129; �) Stylish and comfortable hotel right next to the train station.

✕ Eating

Beautiful Mountain   CAFE £
(www.thebeautifulmountain.com; 11-13 Belmont St; mains £7-10; ☺8am-3.30pm & 5.30-11pm Wed-Sat, 10.30am-2.45pm Sun; ☑) This cosy cafe is squeezed into a couple of tiny rooms (seating upstairs), but serves all-day breakfasts and tasty sandwiches (smoked salmon, Thai chicken, pastrami) on sourdough, bagels,

Aberdeen

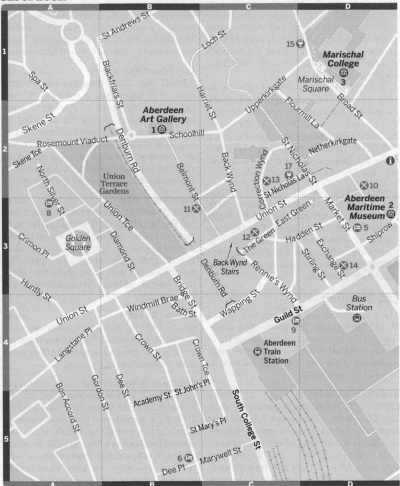

ciabatta and lots of other breads, along with exquisite espresso and consummate cappuccino. It's also open for dinner, when the menu switches to Spanish-style tapas.

★ **Café 52**   BISTRO **££**
(☏01224-590094; www.cafe52.net; 52 The Green; mains £9-13; ☉noon-midnight Mon-Sat, to 6pm Sun; ☏) This little haven of laid-back industrial chic – a high, narrow space lined with bare stonework, rough plaster and exposed ventilation ducts – serves some of the finest and most inventive cuisine in the northeast. Try starters such as crisp black pudding with

wine-poached pear, or mains like pan-fried herring with orange butter sauce.

★ **Adelphi Kitchen**   MODERN SCOTTISH **££**
(☏01224-211414; www.theadelphikitchen.co.uk; 28 Adelphi Ln, Union St; mains £12-28; ☉noon-2.30pm & 5-10pm Tue-Sat; ☏) 🍴 Cool and clever flavour combinations are the hallmark of this unsuspected little gem hidden down an alley off Union St, a small but sophisticated space decorated with weathered timber and muted natural colours. Charcoal grilling is a speciality, with aged Aberdeen Angus beef and pulled pork given the barbecue treat-

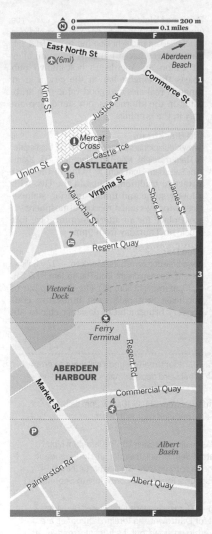

Aberdeen

◎ Top Sights
1 Aberdeen Art Gallery	B2
2 Aberdeen Maritime Museum	D3
3 Marischal College	D1

◉ Activities, Courses & Tours
4 Clyde Cruises	F4

⊜ Sleeping
5 Aberdeen Douglas Hotel	D3
6 Butler's Guest House	B5
7 City Wharf Apartments	E3
8 Globe Inn	A3
9 Jurys Inn	C4

⊗ Eating
10 Adelphi Kitchen	D2
11 Beautiful Mountain	B3
12 Café 52	C3
13 Moonfish Café	C2
14 Musa Art Cafe	D3

◉ Drinking & Nightlife
15 BrewDog	D1
Globe Inn	(see 8)
16 Old Blackfriars	E2
17 Prince of Wales	C2

ment alongside seafood treats such as west coast scallops and Shetland mussels.

Sand Dollar Café　　　　　CAFE **£**
(☑ 01224-572288; www.sanddollarcafe.com; 2 Beach Esplanade; mains £6-12; ☉ 7.30am-6pm Sun-Tue, to 7.30pm Wed, to 4pm Thu-Sat, also 6-9pm Thu-Sat) A cut above your usual seaside cafe – on sunny days you can sit at the wooden tables on the prom and share a bottle of chilled white wine, or choose from a menu that includes pancakes with maple syrup, homemade burgers and chocolate brownie with Orkney ice cream.

Moonfish Café　　　　MEDITERRANEAN **££**
(☑ 01224-644166; www.moonfishcafe.co.uk; 9 Correction Wynd; 2-/3-course dinners £27/32; ☉ noon-2pm & 6-9.30pm Tue-Sat) ✐ The menu of this funky little eatery tucked away on a back street concentrates on good quality Scottish produce that draws its influences from cuisines all around the world, from simple smoked haddock kedgeree to spiced monkfish with pickled carrot, mustard seed, yoghurt and coriander.

Musa Art Cafe　　　　MODERN SCOTTISH **££**
(☑ 01224-571771; www.musaaberdeen.com; 33 Exchange St; lunch mains £10, dinner £13-29; ☉ noon-11pm Tue-Sat; 🛜☑) ✐ The bright paintings on the walls match the vibrant furnishings and smart gastronomic creations at this great cafe-restaurant, set in a former church. As well as a menu that focuses on quality local produce cooked in a quirky way – think haggis-and-black-pudding spring rolls with chilli jam – there are Brewdog beers from Fraserburgh, and interesting music, sometimes live.

Silver Darling　　　　SEAFOOD **£££**
(☑ 01224-576229; www.thesilverdarling.co.uk; Pocra Quay, North Pier; 2-/3-course lunches £20/24, dinner mains £22-30; ☉ noon-1.45pm

Mon-Fri, 6.30-9.30pm Mon-Sat) The Silver Darling (an old Scottish nickname for herring) is the place for a special meal, housed in a former Customs office at the entrance to Aberdeen harbour with picture windows overlooking the sea. Here you can enjoy fresh Scottish seafood prepared by a top French chef while you watch the porpoises playing in the harbour mouth. Bookings are recommended.

🍸 Drinking & Nightlife

Globe Inn   PUB
(www.the-globe-inn.co.uk; 13-15 North Silver St; ⏱11am-midnight, to 1am Fri & Sat) This lovely Edwardian-style pub with wood panelling, marble-topped tables and walls decorated with old musical instruments is a great place for a quiet lunchtime or afternoon drink. It serves good coffee as well as real ales and malt whiskies, and has live music (rock, blues, soul) Friday to Sunday. It's also got probably the poshest pub toilets in the country.

Prince of Wales   PUB
(www.princeofwales-aberdeen.co.uk; 7 St Nicholas Lane; ⏱10am-midnight Mon-Thu, to 1am Fri & Sat, 11am-midnight Sun; 🍴) Tucked down an alley off Union St, Aberdeen's best-known pub boasts the longest bar in the city, a great range of real ales and good-value pub grub. Quiet in the afternoons, but standing-room only in the evenings.

Old Blackfriars   PUB
(www.oldblackfriars-aberdeen.co.uk; 52 Castlegate; ⏱11am-midnight Mon-Thu, 11am-1am Fri, 10am-1am Sat, 10am-11pm Sun; 🛜) One of the most attractive traditional pubs in the city, with a lovely stone and timber interior, stained-glass windows and a relaxed atmosphere – a great place for an afternoon pint. Live folk music on Thursday from 9pm.

BrewDog   BAR
(www.brewdog.com/bars/aberdeen; 17 Gallowgate; ⏱noon-midnight Mon-Thu, to 1am Fri & Sat, 12.30pm-midnight Sun; 🛜) The flagship bar of northeast Scotland's most innovative craft brewery brings a bit of designer chic to Ab-

---

BLAZE YOUR OWN WHISKY TRAIL

Visiting a distillery can be memorable, but only hardcore malt-hounds will want to go to more than one or two. Some are great to visit; others are depressingly corporate. The following are some recommendations.

Aberlour (📞01340-881249; www.aberlour.com; tours from £14; ⏱10am & 2pm daily Apr-Oct, by appointment Mon-Fri Nov-Mar) Has an excellent, detailed tour with a proper tasting session. It's on the main street in Aberlour.

Glenfarclas (📞01807-500257; www.glenfarclas.co.uk; admission £5; ⏱10am-4pm Mon-Fri Oct-Mar, to 5pm Mon-Fri Apr-Sep, plus to 4pm Sat Jul-Sep) Small, friendly and independent, Glenfarclas is 5 miles south of Aberlour on the Grantown road. The last tour leaves 90 minutes before closing. The in-depth Connoisseur's Tour (Friday only July to September) is £20.

Glenfiddich (www.glenfiddich.com; ⏱9.30am-4.30pm daily year-round, closed Christmas & New Year) FREE It's big and busy, but handiest for Dufftown, and foreign languages are available. The standard tour starts with an overblown video, but it's fun, informative and free. An in-depth Connoisseur's Tour (£20) must be prebooked. Glenfiddich kept single malt alive during the dark years.

Macallan (📞01340-872280; www.themacallan.com; tours £15; ⏱9.30am-6pm Mon-Sat Easter-Oct, 9.30am-5pm Mon-Fri Nov-Mar) Excellent sherry-casked malt. Several small-group tours are available (last tour at 3.30pm), including an expert one (£20); all should be prebooked. Lovely location 2 miles northwest of Craigellachie.

Speyside Cooperage (📞01340-871108; www.speysidecooperage.co.uk; adult/child £3.50/2; ⏱9am-4pm Mon-Fri, closed mid Dec-early Jan) Here you can see the fascinating art of barrel-making in action. It's a mile from Craigellachie on the Dufftown road.

Spirit of Speyside (www.spiritofspeyside.com) This biannual whisky festival in Dufftown has a number of great events. It takes place in early May and late September; both accommodation and events should be booked well ahead.

erdeen's pub scene along with a vast range of guest beers from around the world.

ⓘ Information

Aberdeen Royal Infirmary (☑0845 456 6000; www.nhsgrampian.org; Foresterhill) Medical services. About a mile northwest of the western end of Union St.

Aberdeen Tourist Office (☑ 01224-288828; www.aberdeen-grampian.com; 23 Union St; ⊗9am-6.30pm Mon-Sat, 10am-4pm Sun Jul & Aug, 9.30am-5pm Mon-Sat Sep-Jun) Handy for general information; has internet access (£1 per 20 minutes).

ⓘ Getting There & Away

AIR

Aberdeen Airport (ABZ; ☑0844 481 6666; www.aberdeenairport.com) is at Dyce, 6 miles northwest of the city centre. There are regular flights to numerous Scottish and UK destinations, including Orkney and Shetland, and international flights to the Netherlands, Norway, Denmark, Germany and France.

Stagecoach Jet bus 727 runs regularly from Aberdeen bus station to the airport (single £2.70, 35 minutes). A taxi from the airport to the city centre takes 25 minutes and costs £15.

BOAT

Car ferries from Aberdeen to Orkney and Shetland are run by **Northlink Ferries** (www.northlinkferries.co.uk). The ferry terminal is a short walk east of the train and bus stations.

BUS

The **bus station** (Guild St) is next to Jurys Inn, close to the train station.

Braemar £11, 2¼ hours, every two hours; via Ballater and Balmoral

Dundee £16.80, 1½ hours, hourly

Edinburgh £30, three hours, three daily direct, more frequent changing at Perth

Glasgow £30, three hours, at least hourly

Inverness £12.50, four hours, hourly; via Huntly, Keith, Fochabers, Elgin and Nairn

London £47, 12 hours, twice daily; National Express

Perth £23.50, two hours, hourly

TRAIN

The train station is south of the city centre, next to the massive Union Square shopping mall.

Dundee £19.10, 1¼ hours, twice an hour

Edinburgh £34, 2½ hours, hourly

Glasgow £34, 2¾ hours, hourly

Inverness £27, 2¼ hour, eight daily

London King's Cross £110, eight to 11 hours, hourly; some direct, most change at Edinburgh

ⓘ Getting Around

BUS

The main city bus operator is **First Aberdeen** (www.firstaberdeen.com). Local fares cost from £1.20 to £2.50; pay the driver as you board the bus. A FirstDay ticket (adult/child £4.30/2.60) allows unlimited travel from the time of purchase until midnight on all First Aberdeen buses. Information, route maps and tickets are available from the **First Travel Centre** (47 Union St; ⊗8.45am-5.30pm Mon-Sat).

The most useful services for visitors are buses 15 and 19 from Union St to Great Western Rd (for B&Bs); bus 11 from Union St to Aberdeen Youth Hostel and the airport; and bus 20 from Marischal College to Old Aberdeen.

CAR

Car rental companies:

Arnold Clark (☑01224-622714; www.arnoldclarkrental.com; Canal Rd)

Enterprise Car Hire (☑01224-642642; www.enterprise.co.uk; 80 Skene Sq)

TAXI

The main city-centre taxi ranks are at the train station and on Back Wynd, off Union St. To order a taxi, phone **ComCab** (☑01224-353535; www.comcab-aberdeen.co.uk) or **Rainbow City Taxis** (☑01224-878787; www.rainbowcitytaxis.com).

Around Aberdeen

⊙ Sights

Dunnottar Castle   CASTLE
(☑01569-762173;   www.dunnottarcastle.co.uk; adult/child £6/2; ⊗9am-6pm Apr-Sep, 10am-5pm or dusk Oct-Mar) A pleasant, 15-minute walk along the clifftops south of Stonehaven harbour leads to the spectacular ruins of Dunnottar Castle, spread out across a grassy promontory 50m above the sea. As dramatic a film set as any director could wish for, it provided the backdrop for Franco Zeffirelli's *Hamlet* (1990), starring Mel Gibson. The original fortress was built in the 9th century; the keep is the most substantial remnant, but the drawing room (restored in 1926) is more interesting.

Crathes Castle   CASTLE
(NTS;   ☑01330-844525;   adult/child   £12.50/9; ⊗10.30am-5pm Apr-Oct, 11am-4pm Sat & Sun Nov-Mar; ⓟ) The atmospheric, 16th-century Crathes Castle is famous for its Jacobean painted ceilings, magnificently carved canopied beds, and the 'Horn of Leys', presented to the Burnett family by Robert the Bruce in

the 14th century. The beautiful formal gardens include 300-year-old yew hedges and colourful herbaceous borders. The castle is signposted off the A93; Stagecoach buses 201 and 202 from Aberdeen stop at the castle entrance (£4.80, 45 minutes, every 30 minutes).

Moray

The old county of Moray (*murr*-ree), centred on the county town of Elgin, lies at the heart of an ancient Celtic earldom and is famed for its mild climate and rich farmland – the barley fields of the 19th century once provided the raw material for the Speyside whisky distilleries, one of the region's main attractions for present-day visitors.

Elgin

POP 23,130

Elgin has been the provincial capital of Moray for over eight centuries and was an important town in medieval times. Dominated by a hilltop monument to the 5th duke of Gordon, Elgin's main attraction is its impressive ruined cathedral, where the tombs of the duke's ancestors lie.

◉ Sights

Elgin Cathedral   CATHEDRAL
(HS; King St; adult/child £5.50/3.30; ◷9.30am-5.30pm daily Apr-Sep, 9.30am-4.30pm Sat-Wed Oct-Mar) Many people think that the ruins of Elgin Cathedral, known as the 'lantern of the north', are the most beautiful and evocative in Scotland; its octagonal chapter house is the finest in the country. Consecrated in 1224, the cathedral was burned down in 1390 by the infamous Wolf of Badenoch, the illegitimate son of Robert II, following his excommunication by the Bishop of Moray. Guided tours are available on weekdays.

Johnstons of Elgin   FASHION
(☑01343-554009; www.johnstonscashmere.com; Newmill; ◷9am-5.30pm Mon-Sat, 11am-5pm Sun) Founded in 1797, Johnstons is famous for its cashmere woollen clothing, and is the only UK woollen mill that still sees the manufacturing process through from raw fibre to finished garment. There's a retail outlet and coffee shop, and free guided tours of the works.

🛏 Sleeping & Eating

Croft Guesthouse   B&B £££
(☑01343-546004; www.thecroftelgin.co.uk; 10 Institution Rd; s/d from £55/78; P🐾🅿) The Croft offers a taste of Victorian high society, set in a spacious mansion built for a local lawyer back in 1848. The house is filled with period features – check out the cast-iron and tile fireplaces – and the three large bedrooms are equipped with easy chairs and crisp bed linen.

Southbank Guest House   B&B £££
(☑01343-547132; www.southbankguesthouse.co.uk; 36 Academy St; s/d/f from £55/75/120; P) The family-run, 15-room Southbank is set in a large Georgian town house in a quiet street south of Elgin's centre, just five minutes' walk from the cathedral and other sights.

Johnstons Coffee Shop   CAFE £
(Newmill; mains £5-10; ◷10am-5pm Mon-Sat, 11am-4.30pm Sun; P🐾🅿) The coffee shop at Johnstons woollen mill is the best place to eat in town, serving breakfast till 11.45am, hot lunches noon to 3pm (crepes with a range of fillings, inlcuding smoked salmon with cream cheese and dill), and cream teas.

❶ Getting There & Away

BUS
Elgin is a stop on the hourly Stagecoach bus 10 service between Inverness (£10.20, 1½ hours) and Aberdeen (£12.50, 2½ hours). Bus 35 goes from Elgin to Banff and Macduff (£12.50, 1¾ hours, hourly), continuing to Aberdeen via Fyvie. Bus 36 goes to Dufftown (£5.60, 50 minutes, hourly Monday to Saturday).

WORTH A TRIP

DUFF HOUSE

One of Scotland's hidden gems, **Duff House** (☑01261-818181; www.duffhouse.org.uk; adult/child £7.10/4.30; ◷11am-5pm Apr-Oct, 11am-4pm Thu-Sun Nov-Mar) is an art gallery that displays a superb collection of Scottish and European art, including important works by Raeburn and Gainsborough. The house is an impressive baroque mansion on the southern edge of Banff, built between 1735 and 1740 as the seat of the Earls of Fife. It was designed by William Adam and bears similarities to that Adam masterpiece, Hopetoun House near Edinburgh.

TRAIN

There are five trains a day to Aberdeen (£18.20, 1½ hours) and Inverness (£11.90, 40 minutes).

Dufftown & Aberlour

Rome may be built on seven hills, but **Dufftown** is built on seven stills, say the locals. Founded in 1817 by James Duff, 4th Earl of Fife, Dufftown is 17 miles south of Elgin and lies at the heart of the Speyside whisky-distilling region. With seven working distilleries nearby, Dufftown has been dubbed Scotland's malt-whisky capital and is host to the biannual Spirit of Speyside (p888) whisky festival. Ask at the whisky museum about the **Malt Whisky Trail** (www.maltwhiskytrail. com), a self-guided tour around the local distilleries.

Five miles to the northwest, **Aberlour** (www.aboutaberlour.co.uk) – or Charlestown of Aberlour, to give it its full name – is prettier than Dufftown, straggling along the banks of the River Spey. It is famous as the home of Walkers Shortbread, and has Aberlour Distillery right on the main street. Attractions include salmon fishing, and some lovely walks along the Speyside Way.

Buses link Elgin to Aberour (£5.30, 35 minutes) and Dufftown (£5.60, 50 minutes) hourly Monday to Saturday, continuing to Huntly, Aberdeen and Inverness.

On summer weekends, you can take a train from Aberdeen or Inverness to Keith (£16.40, one hour, five daily), and then ride the Keith and Dufftown Railway to Dufftown.

Central & Northern Highlands & Islands

Why Go?

Scotland's vast melancholy soul is here, an epic land whose stark beauty indelibly imprints upon the hearts of those who see it. Mist, peat, whisky, heather...and long, sunblessed summer evenings that repay the many days of horizontal drizzle.

The glorious hills and glens of western Perthshire offer a memorable first taste. The region's capital, Inverness, is backed by the craggy Cairngorms, which draw skiers and walkers to its slopes. Further north, ancient stones are testament left by prehistoric builders in Caithness, and across the water on the magical Orkney and remote Shetland Islands – where wind keeps the vegetation at a minimum – isolation makes it a haven for sea birds and more.

The most epic scenery – you really need an orchestra to do it justice – is in the far northwest, and it continues on to Skye, where the mighty Cuillin Ridge towers jaggedly in the setting sun. Beyond here, the Outer Hebrides offer the nation's best beaches and a glimpse of traditional life.

Best Places to Eat

➡ The Albannach (p928)

➡ Three Chimneys (p938)

➡ Lime Tree (p916)

➡ Côte du Nord (p925)

Best Places to Stay

➡ The Torridon (p931)

➡ Toravaig House Hotel (p935)

➡ Rocpool Reserve (p897)

➡ West Manse (p958)

When to Go

➡ In January hit the Cairngorms for skiing or the Shetland Islands for Up Helly Aa, a fiery Viking festival.

➡ Long June evenings see the Highlands at their most romantic, while Fort William hosts the Mountain Bike World Cup.

➡ September is the ideal time for hiking and hill walking – midges are dying off, but the weather is still reasonably good.

Activities

For outdoor fans, especially hikers and hill-walkers, the Highlands are heaven. Famous spots like Ben Nevis, Glen Coe, Skye and the Cairngorms offer endless opportunities for experienced walkers – and several options for strollers too. Long-distance walking routes include the **Great Glen Way** (www.greatglenway.com), while the **West Highland Way** and **Speyside Way** are nearby (covered in the Argyll, Central & Northeast Scotland chapter).

For touring cyclists, the roads of the Highlands are enjoyable, as car traffic is often fairly light. The islands are also ideal: Skye is ever popular, as is the end-to-end tour of the Outer Hebrides, where south-to-north (Barra to Lewis) gives you the best chance of a following wind. Gateways for mountain-biking include Fort William and Laggan. The Great Glen Way is also suitable for off-road bikes.

Other activities include sea kayaking around the islands, fishing in rivers and the sea, scuba diving (notably at Scapa Flow in the Orkney Islands) and mountaineering on Ben Nevis or the Cairngorms. The main skiing and snowboarding areas include the Cairngorms and the Nevis Range near Fort William.

Getting There & Around

Inverness is the main train hub, with connections south to England and the rest of Scotland, and lines north to Thurso and west to Kyle of Lochalsh – both passing through fabulous scenery. The West Highland line from Glasgow to Fort William and Mallaig is similarly scenic. Inverness is also the main hub for bus travel. Check details with **Traveline Scotland** (☑ 0871 200 2233; www.travelinescotland.com).

Ferries to/from the Western islands are mostly run by **Caledonian MacBrayne** (☑ 0800 066-5000; www.calmac.co.uk) , with mainland ports including Mallaig and Ullapool (plus Uig on Skye), while ferries to Orkney depart mainly from three different crossings in the Thurso–John O'Groats area. The main port for Shetland is Aberdeen.

INVERNESS & THE GREAT GLEN

Inverness, one of the fastest growing towns in Britain, is the capital of the Highlands. It's a transport hub and jumping-off point for the central, western and northern Highlands, the Moray Firth coast and the Great Glen.

The Great Glen is a geological fault running in an arrow-straight line, filled by a series of lochs, across Scotland from Fort William to Inverness. In 1822 the various lochs were linked by the Caledonian Canal to create a cross-country waterway. The modern A82 road along the glen was completed in 1933 – a date that coincides neatly with the first modern sightings of the Loch Ness Monster.

Inverness

POP 61,235

Inverness has a great location astride the River Ness at the northern end of the Great Glen. In summer it overflows with visitors intent on monster hunting at nearby Loch Ness, but it's worth a visit in its own right for a stroll along the picturesque River Ness, a cruise on Loch Ness, and a meal in one of the city's excellent restaurants.

Sights

★ **Ness Islands** PARK

The main attraction in Inverness is a leisurely stroll along the river to the Ness Islands. Planted with mature Scots pine, fir, beech and sycamore, and linked to the river banks and each other by elegant Victorian footbridges, the islands make an appealing picnic spot. They're a 20-minute walk south of the castle – head upstream on either side of the river (the start of the Great Glen Way), and return on the opposite bank.

Tours

Jacobite Cruises BOAT TOUR

(☑ 01463-233999; www.jacobite.co.uk; Glenurquhart Rd; adult/child £31.50/25; ☉ daily Apr-Sep) Boats depart from Tomnahurich Bridge at 2pm for a 1½-hour 'Discovery' cruise along Loch Ness, followed by a visit to Urquhart Castle and a return to Inverness by coach. You can buy tickets at the tourist office and catch a free minibus to the boat. Other cruises and combined cruise–coach tours, from one to 6½ hours, are also available.

Sleeping

Inverness has a good range of backpacker accommodation, and also has some excellent boutique hotels. There are lots of guesthouses and B&Bs along Old Edinburgh Rd and Ardconnel St on the east side of the river, and on Kenneth St and Fairfield Rd on the west bank.

Central & Northern Highlands & Islands Highlights

1 Exploring the hills around gorgeous **Glen Lyon** (p913)

2 Dipping your toes in the water at some of the world's most beautiful beaches on **Harris** (p942) and **Barra** (p945)

3 Shouldering the challenge of the **Cuillin Hills** (p935), whose rugged silhouettes brood over the skyscape of Skye

4 Marvelling at the epic Highland scenery of the **far northwest** (p924)

5 Launching into a sea kayak to explore the otter-rich waters around the **Isle of Skye** (p933)

6 Being astonished at extraordinary **Skara Brae** (p953) and **Maes Howe** (p952), prehistoric perfection that predates the pyramids

7 Exploring the castles, villages, hills and forests of **Royal Deeside** (p908), home to the Queen's Balmoral Castle

8 Capering with puffins, spotting offshore orcas, or dodging dive-bombing skuas in Shetland's **nature reserves** (p961)

9 Soaking up the scenery (when you can see it!) in moody but magnificent **Glen Coe** (p913)

10 Making it to the summit of **Ben Nevis** (p917) – and being able to see the view

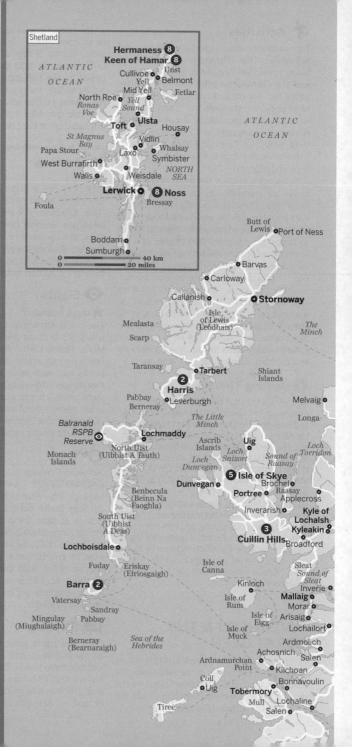

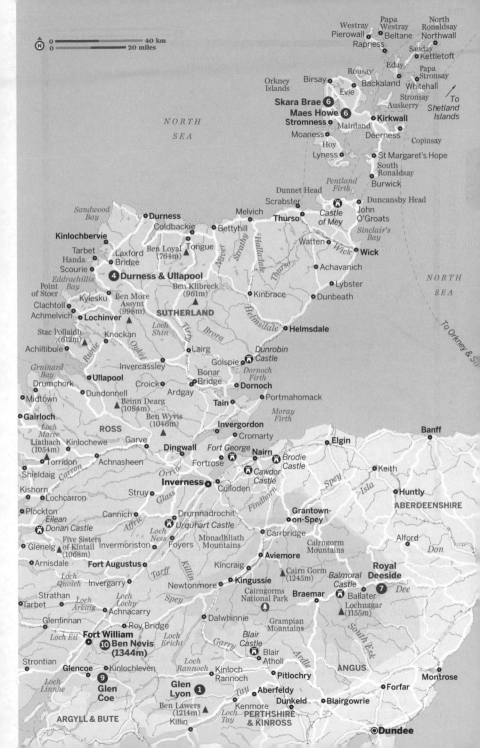

Inverness

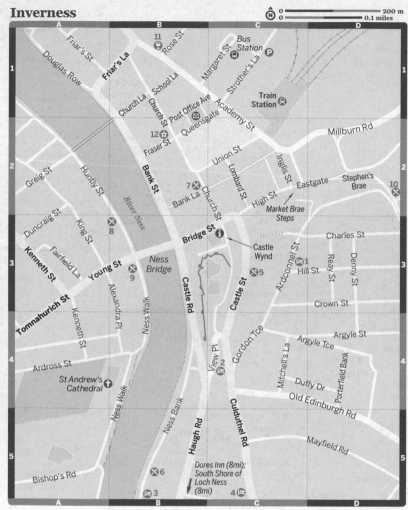

CENTRAL & NORTHERN HIGHLANDS & ISLANDS INVERNESS

Bazpackers Backpackers Hotel HOSTEL £
(☎ 01463-717663; www.bazpackershostel.co.uk;
4 Culduthel Rd; dm/tw £17/44; @ ☎) This may
be Inverness' smallest hostel (34 beds),
but it's hugely popular. It's a friendly, quiet
place – the main building has a convivial
lounge centred on a wood-burning stove,
and a small garden and great views (some
rooms are in a separate building with no
garden). The dorms and kitchen can be a bit
cramped, but the showers are great.

Inverness Millburn SYHA HOSTEL £
(SYHA; ☎ 01463-231771; www.syha.org.uk; Victoria
Dr; dm/tw £19/54; ☉ Apr-Dec; P @ ☎) Inver-

ness' modern 166-bed hostel is 10 minutes'
walk northeast of the city centre. With its
comfy beds and flashy stainless-steel kitch-
en, some reckon it's the best SYHA hostel in
the country. Booking is essential, especially
at Easter and in July and August.

★ **Trafford Bank** B&B ££
(☎ 01463-241414; www.traffordbankguesthouse.
co.uk; 96 Fairfield Rd; d £120-132; P ☎) Lots of
word-of-mouth rave reviews for this elegant
Victorian villa, which was once home to a
bishop, just a mitre-toss from the Caledonian Canal and 10 minutes' walk west from

Inverness

the city centre. The luxurious rooms include fresh flowers and fruit, bathrobes and fluffy towels – ask for the Tartan Room, which has a wrought-iron king-size bed and Victorian roll-top bath.

Ardconnel House B&B ££
(☎01463-240455; www.ardconnel-inverness.co.uk; 21 Ardconnel St; r per person £35-40; ☎) The six-room Ardconnel is one of our favourites – a terraced Victorian house with comfortable en suite rooms, a dining room with crisp white table linen, and a breakfast menu that includes Vegemite for homesick Antipodeans. Kids under 10 not allowed.

Ach Aluinn B&B ££
(☎01463-230127; www.achaluinn.com; 27 Fairfield Rd; r per person £25-35; P) This large, detached Victorian house is bright and homely, and offers all you might want from a B&B – private bathroom, TV, reading lights, comfy beds with two pillows each, and an excellent breakfast. Less than 10 minutes' walk west from the city centre.

MacRae Guest House B&B ££
(☎01463-243658; joycemacrae@hotmail.com; 24 Ness Bank; s/d from £45/64; P☎) This flower-bedecked Victorian house on the eastern bank of the river has smart, tastefully decorated bedrooms (one is wheelchair accessible), and vegetarian breakfasts are available. Minimum two-night bookings in July and August.

★**Rocpool Reserve** BOUTIQUE HOTEL £££
(☎01463-240089; www.rocpool.com; Culduthel Rd; s/d from £185/220; P☎) Boutique chic meets the Highlands in this slick and sophisticated little hotel, where an elegant Georgian exterior conceals an oasis of contemporary cool. A gleaming white entrance hall lined with red carpet and contemporary art leads to designer rooms in shades of chocolate, cream and gold; a restaurant by Albert Roux completes the luxury package.

✖ Eating

Velocity Cafe CAFE £
(☎01463-419956; velocitylove.co.uk; 1 Crown Ave; mains £4-7; ⊙9am-5pm Fri-Mon & Wed, 10am-5pm Tue, 9am-9pm Thu; ☎☎) ✦ This cyclists' cafe serves soups, sandwiches and salads prepared with organic, locally sourced produce, as well as yummy cake and coffee. There's also a workshop where you can repair your bike or book a session with a mechanic.

★**Café 1** BISTRO ££
(☎01463-226200; www.cafe1.net; 75 Castle St; mains £10-24; ⊙noon-2.30pm & 5-9.30pm Mon-Fri, noon-2.30pm & 6-9.30pm Sat) ✦ Café 1 is a friendly and appealing bistro with candlelit tables amid elegant blonde-wood and wrought-iron decor. There is an international menu based on quality Scottish produce, from Aberdeen Angus steaks to crisp pan-fried sea bass and meltingly tender pork belly. The set lunch menu (two courses for £8) is served noon to 2.30pm Monday to Saturday.

Contrast Brasserie BRASSERIE ££
(☎01463-227889; www.glenmoristontownhouse.com; 20 Ness Bank; 2-course lunch £10.95, 2-course early bird £12.95, à la carte £4.95-25) Book early for what we think is one of the the the best-value restaurants in Inverness – a dining room that drips designer style, with smiling professional staff and truly delicious food prepared using fresh Scottish produce. The two-course lunch menu and three-course early-bird menu (£16, 5pm to 6.30pm) are bargains.

Joy of Taste BRITISH ££
(☎01463-241459; www.thejoyoftaste.co.uk; 25 Church St; mains £15-19; ⊙noon-3pm & 5.30-10.30pm Mon-Sat, 5.30-9.30pm Sun) ✦ Here's a novel concept – a restaurant run by a head chef and 25 volunteers who work a shift a week just for 'the love of creating a beautiful restaurant' (plus a share of the profits). And a very good job they have made of it, with a menu of classic British cuisine and a growing fan club of satisfied customers.

Rocpool
MEDITERRANEAN ££

(☑ 01463-717274; www.rocpoolrestaurant.com; 1 Ness Walk; mains £18-25; ⊙ noon-2.30pm & 5.45-10pm Mon-Sat) 🥢 Lots of polished wood, crisp white linen and leather booths and banquettes lend a nautical air to this relaxing bistro, which offers a Mediterranean-influenced menu that makes the most of quality Scottish produce, especially seafood. The two-course lunch is £15.

Kitchen Brasserie
MODERN SCOTTISH ££

(☑ 01463-259119; www.kitchenrestaurant.co.uk; 15 Huntly St; mains £8-19; ⊙ noon-10pm; 🛜 ♿) This spectacular glass-fronted restaurant offers a great menu and a view over the River Ness – try to get a table upstairs. Great value two-course lunch (£7, noon-3pm) and early-bird menu (£12, 5pm to 7pm).

🍷 Drinking & Nightlife

Clachnaharry Inn
PUB

(☑ 01463-239806; www.clachnaharryinn.co.uk; 17-19 High St; ⊙ 11am-11pm, to midnight Fri & Sat) Just over a mile northwest of the city centre, on the bank of the Caledonian Canal just off the A862, this is a delightful old coaching inn (with beer garden out back) serving an excellent range of real ales and good pub grub.

Phoenix
PUB

(☑ 01463-233685; 108 Academy St; ⊙ 11am-11pm) Recently refurbished, this is the most traditional of the pubs in the city centre, with a mahogany horseshoe bar and several real ales on tap, including beers from the Cairngorm, Cromarty and Isle of Skye breweries.

☆ Entertainment

Hootananny
LIVE MUSIC

(☑ 01463-233651; www.hootananny.com; 67 Church St) Hootananny is the city's best live-music venue, with traditional folk- and/or rock-music sessions nightly, including big-name bands from all over Scotland (and, indeed, the world). The bar is well stocked with a range of beers from the local Black Isle Brewery.

❶ Information

Inverness Tourist Office (☑ 01463-252401; www.visithighlands.com; Castle Wynd; internet access per 20min £1; ⊙ 9am-6pm Mon-Sat, 9.30am-5pm Sun Jul & Aug, 9am-5pm Mon-Sat, 10am-4pm Sun Jun, Sep & Oct, 9am-5pm Mon-Sat Apr & May) Bureau de change and accommodation booking service; also sells tickets for tours and cruises. Opening hours limited November to March.

❶ Getting There & Away

AIR
Inverness Airport (INV; ☑ 01667-464000; www.hial.co.uk/inverness-airport) At Dalcross, 10 miles east of the city, off the A96 towards Aberdeen. There are scheduled flights to Amsterdam, London, Manchester, Orkney, Shetland and the Outer Hebrides, as well as other places in the British Isles.

BUS
Services depart from **Inverness bus station** (Margaret St).

Aberdeen £12.50, 3¾ hours, hourly
Aviemore £9.80, 45 minutes, eight daily
Edinburgh £30, 3½ to 4½ hours, hourly
Fort William £11.20, two hours, five daily
Glasgow £30, 3½ to 4½ hours, hourly
London £45, 13 hours, one daily; more frequent services requiring a change at Glasgow.

Operated by **National Express** (☑ 08717 81 81 78; www.gobycoach.com).

Portree £25, 3¼ hours, three daily
Thurso £19, three hours, three to five daily
Ullapool £12.80, 1½ hours, two daily except Sunday

If you book far enough in advance, **Megabus** (☑ 0871 266 3333; www.megabus.com) offers fares from as little as £1 for buses from Inverness to Glasgow and Edinburgh, and £10 to London.

TRAIN
Aberdeen £27, 2¼ hours, eight daily
Edinburgh £41, 3½ hours, eight daily
Glasgow £41, 3½ hours, eight daily
Kyle of Lochalsh £22, 2½ hours, four daily Monday to Saturday, two Sunday; one of Britain's great scenic train journeys
London £100, eight to nine hours, one daily direct; others require a change at Edinburgh
Wick £19, 4½ hours, four daily Monday to Saturday, one or two on Sunday; via Thurso

❶ Getting Around

TO/FROM THE AIRPORT
Stagecoach Jet (www.stagecoachbus.com) Buses run from the airport to Inverness bus station (£3.90, 20 minutes, every 30 minutes).

BICYCLE
Ticket to Ride (☑ 01463-419160; www.ticket-toridehighlands.co.uk; Bellfield Park; per day from £22; ⊙ 9am-6pm Apr-Oct) Hires mountain bikes, hybrids and tandems; can be dropped off in Fort William. Will deliver bikes free to local hotels and B&Bs.

BUS

City services and buses to places around Inverness, including the Culloden battlefield, are operated by **Stagecoach** (www.stagecoachbus.com). An Inverness City Dayrider ticket costs £3.40 and gives unlimited travel for a day on buses throughout the city.

Around Inverness

Culloden Battlefield

The Battle of Culloden in 1746, the last pitched battle ever fought on British soil, saw the defeat of Bonnie Prince Charlie and the end of the Jacobite dream when 1200 Highlanders were slaughtered by government forces in a 68-minute rout. The Duke of Cumberland, son of the reigning King George II and leader of the Hanoverian army, earned the nickname 'Butcher' for his brutal treatment of the defeated Jacobite forces. The battle sounded the death knell for the old clan system, and the horrors of the Clearances soon followed. The sombre moor where the conflict took place has scarcely changed in the ensuing 260 years.

Culloden is 6 miles east of Inverness. Bus 2 runs from Queensgate in Inverness to Culloden battlefield (£2.40, 30 minutes, hourly).

The impressive **Culloden visitor centre** (NTS; www.nts.org.uk/culloden; adult/child £11/8.50; ☉ 9am-6pm Jun-Aug, to 5.30pm Apr, May, Sep & Oct, 10am-4pm Nov-Mar) has everything you need to know about the Battle of Culloden in 1746, including the lead-up and the aftermath, with perspectives from both sides. An innovative film puts you on the battlefield in the middle of the mayhem, and a wealth of other audio presentations must have kept Inverness' entire acting community in business for weeks. The admission fee includes an audioguide for a self-guided tour of the battlefield itself.

Fort George

The headland guarding the narrows in the Moray Firth opposite Fortrose is occupied by the magnificent and virtually unaltered 18th-century artillery fortification of Fort George.

One of the finest artillery fortifications in Europe, **Fort George** (HS; ☑ 01667-462777; adult/child £8.90/5.40; ☉ 9.30am-5.30pm Apr-Sep, to 4.30pm Oct-Mar) was established in 1748 in the aftermath of the Battle of Culloden, as a base for George II's army of occupation in the Highlands. By the time of its completion in 1769 it had cost the equivalent of around £1 billion in today's money. It still functions as a military barracks; public areas have exhibitions on 18th-century soldiery, and the mile-plus walk around the ramparts offers fine views out to sea and back to the Great Glen.

Given its size, you'll need at least two hours to do the place justice. The fort is off the A96 about 11 miles northeast of Inverness; there is no public transport.

Cawdor Castle

This **castle** (☑ 01667-404615; www.cawdorcastle.com; adult/child £10/6.50; ☉ 10am-5.30pm May-Sep) was once the seat of the Thane of Cawdor, one of the titles prophesied by the three witches for the eponymous character of Shakespeare's *Macbeth*. Macbeth couldn't have lived here, though, since the central tower dates from the 14th century (the wings were 17th-century additions) and he died in 1057. The castle is 5 miles southwest of Nairn.

Glen Affric

The broad valley of **Strathglass** extends about 18 miles inland from the town of Beauly, followed by the A831 road to **Cannich**, the only village in the area, where there's a grocery store and a post office.

Glen Affric (www.nnr-scotland.org.uk/glen-affric), one of the most beautiful glens in Scotland, extends deep into the hills beyond Cannich. The upper reaches of the glen, now designated as **Glen Affric National Nature Reserve**, are a scenic wonderland of shimmering lochs, rugged mountains and native Scots pine, and they are home to pine marten, wildcat, otter, red squirrel and golden eagle.

It's possible to walk all the way from Cannich to **Glen Shiel** on the west coast (35 miles) in two days, spending the night at the remote Glen Affric Youth Hostel. The route is now part of the newly waymarked **Affric-Kintail Way** (www.glenaffric.info), a 56-mile walking or mountain-biking trail leading from Drumnadrochit to Kintail via Cannich.

🛏 Sleeping

Glen Affric SYHA   HOSTEL £
(☑ 0845 293 7373; www.syha.org.uk; Allt Beithe; dm £22; ☉ Apr–mid-Sep) This remote and rustic hostel is set amid magnificent scenery at

the halfway point of the cross-country walk from Cannich to Glen Shiel, 8 miles from the nearest road. Facilities are basic and you'll need to take all supplies with you (and all litter away). Book in advance. There is no phone, internet or mobile phone signal at the hostel.

★**Kerrow House**   B&B **££**
(☑ 01456-415243; www.kerrow-house.co.uk; Cannich; per person £40-45; P) ✦ This wonderful Georgian hunting lodge has bags of old-fashioned character – it was once the home of Highland author Neil M Gunn – and has spacious grounds with 3.5 miles of private trout fishing. It's a mile south of Cannich on the minor road along the east side of the River Glass.

❶ Getting There & Away

Stagecoach (www.stagecoachbus.com) buses 17 and 117 run from Inverness to Cannich (£5.40, one hour, three a day Monday to Saturday) via Drumnadrochit.

Black Isle

The Black Isle – a peninsula rather than an island – is linked to Inverness by the Kessock Bridge.

At **Fortrose Cathedral** you'll find the vaulted crypt of a 13th-century chapter house and sacristy, and the ruinous 14th-century south aisle and chapel. In **Rosemarkie**, the **Groam House Museum** (☑ 01381-620961; www.groamhouse.org.uk; High St; ☉ 11am-4.30pm Mon-Fri, 2-4.30pm Sat & Sun Easter-Oct) FREE has a superb collection of Pictish stones engraved with designs similar to those on Celtic Irish stones.

The pretty village of **Cromarty** at the northeastern tip of the Black Isle has lots of 18th-century red-sandstone houses. The 18th-century **Cromarty Courthouse** (☑ 01381-600418; www.cromarty-courthouse.org. uk; Church St; ☉ noon-4pm daily Jul-Aug, Sun-Thu Easter-Jun & Sep) FREE details the town's history using contemporary references. Kids will love the talking mannequins.

From Cromarty harbour, **Ecoventures** (☑ 01381-600323; www.ecoventures.co.uk; Cromarty Harbour; adult/child £26/20) runs 2½-hour boat trips (adult/child £22/16) into the Moray Firth to see bottlenose dolphins and other wildlife.

Stagecoach buses 26 and 26A run from Inverness to Fortrose and Rosemarkie (£3.30, 30 to 40 minutes, twice hourly Monday to Saturday); half of them continue to Cromarty (£4.70, one hour).

Loch Ness

Deep, dark and narrow, Loch Ness stretches for 23 miles between Inverness and Fort Augustus. Its bitterly cold waters have been extensively explored in search of Nessie, the elusive Loch Ness monster, but most visitors see her only in cardboard-cutout form at Drumnadrochit's monster exhibitions. The busy A82 road runs along the northwestern shore, while the more tranquil and picturesque B862 follows the southeastern shore. A complete circuit of the loch is about 70 miles – travel anticlockwise for the best views.

🕱 Activities

The 79-mile **Great Glen Way** (www.greatglenway.com) long-distance footpath stretches from Inverness to Fort William, where walkers can connect with the **West Highland Way**. It can also be ridden (strenuous!) by mountain bike, while the **Great Glen Mountain Bike Trails** at Nevis Range and Abriachan Forest offer challenging cross-country and downhill trails. (You can hire a mountain bike in Fort William and drop it off in Inverness, and vice versa.)

The **South Loch Ness Trail** (www.visitlochness.com/south-loch-ness-trail) links a series of footpaths and minor roads along the less-frequented southern side of the loch. The 28 miles from Loch Tarff near Fort Augustus to Torbreck on the fringes of Inverness can be done on foot, by bike or on horseback.

There's also the option of the **Great Glen Canoe Trail** (www.greatglencanoetrail.info), a series of access points, waymarks and informal campsites that allow you to travel the length of the glen by canoe or kayak.

Drumnadrochit

POP 1100

Seized by monster madness, its gift shops bulging with Nessie cuddly toys, Drumnadrochit is a hotbed of beastie fever, with two monster exhibitions battling it out for the tourist dollar.

◉ Sights & Activities

Urquhart Castle   CASTLE
(HS; ☑ 01456-450551; adult/child £7.90/4.80; ☉ 9.30am-6pm Apr-Sep, to 5pm Oct, to 4.30pm Nov-Mar; P) Commanding a brilliant location 1.5 miles east of Drumnadrochit, with outstanding views (on a clear day), Urquhart Castle is a popular Nessie-watching hot spot.

A huge visitor centre (most of which is beneath ground level) includes a video theatre (with a dramatic 'unveiling' of the castle at the end of the film) and displays of medieval items discovered in the castle.

The castle was repeatedly sacked and rebuilt (and sacked and rebuilt) over the centuries; in 1692 it was blown up to prevent the Jacobites from using it. The five-storey tower house at the northern point is the most impressive remaining fragment and offers wonderful views across the water. The site includes a huge gift shop and a restaurant, and is often very crowded in summer.

Loch Ness Centre

& Exhibition   INTERPRETATION CENTRE

(☑ 01456-450573;   www.lochness.com;   adult/child £7.45/4.95;   ☉ 9.30am-6pm Jul & Aug, to 5pm

Easter-Jun, Sep & Oct, 10am-3.30pm Nov-Easter; Ⓟ) This Nessie-themed attraction adopts a scientific approach that allows you to weigh the evidence for yourself. Exhibits include the original equipment – sonar survey vessels, miniature submarines, cameras and sediment coring tools – used in various monster hunts, as well as original photographs and film footage of sightings. You'll find out about hoaxes and optical illusions, as well as learning a lot about the ecology of Loch Ness – is there enough food in the loch to support even one 'monster', let alone a breeding population?

Nessie Hunter   BOAT TOUR

(☑ 01456-450395;   www.lochness-cruises.com; adult/child £15/10;   ☉ Easter-Oct) One-hour monster-hunting cruises, complete with sonar and underwater cameras. Cruises depart

THE MONSTER OF LOCH NESS

Highland folklore is filled with tales of strange creatures living in lochs and rivers, notably the kelpie (water horse) that lures unwary travellers to their doom. The use of the term 'monster', however, is a relatively recent phenomenon, the origins of which lie in an article published in the *Inverness Courier* on 2 May 1933, entitled 'Strange Spectacle on Loch Ness'.

The article recounted the sighting of a disturbance in the loch: 'There the creature disported itself, rolling and plunging for fully a minute, its body resembling that of a whale, and the water cascading and churning like a simmering cauldron.'

The story was taken up by the London press and sparked off a rash of sightings that year, including a notorious on-land encounter with London tourists Mr and Mrs Spicer on 22 July 1933, again reported in the *Inverness Courier*:

It was horrible, an abomination. About 50 yards ahead, we saw an undulating sort of neck, and quickly followed by a large, ponderous body. I estimated the length to be 25 to 30 feet, its colour was dark elephant grey. It crossed the road in a series of jerks, but because of the slope we could not see its limbs. Although I accelerated quickly towards it, it had disappeared into the loch by the time I reached the spot. There was no sign of it in the water. I am a temperate man, but I am willing to take any oath that we saw this Loch Ness beast. I am certain that this creature was of a prehistoric species.

The London newspapers couldn't resist. In December 1933 the *Daily Mail* sent Marmaduke Wetherall, a film director and big-game hunter, to Loch Ness to track down the beast. Within days he found 'reptilian' footprints in the shoreline mud (soon revealed to have been made with a stuffed hippopotamus foot). Then in April 1934 came the famous 'long-necked monster' photograph taken by the seemingly reputable Harley St surgeon Colonel Kenneth Wilson. The press went mad and the rest, as they say, is history.

In 1994, however, Christian Spurling – Wetherall's stepson, by then 90 years old – revealed that the most famous photo of Nessie ever taken was in fact a hoax, perpetrated by his stepfather with Wilson's help. Today, of course, there are those who claim that Spurling's confession is itself a hoax. And, ironically, the researcher who exposed the surgeon's photo as a fake still believes wholeheartedly in the monster's existence.

There have been regular sightings of the monster through the years (see www.lochness-sightings.com), with a peak in 1996–97 (the Hollywood movie *Loch Ness* was released in 1996), but reports have tailed off in recent years – there were no sightings at all in 2013.

Hoax or not, there's no denying that the bizarre mini-industry that has grown up around Loch Ness and its mysterious monster since that eventful summer three-quarters of a century ago is a spectacle in its own right.

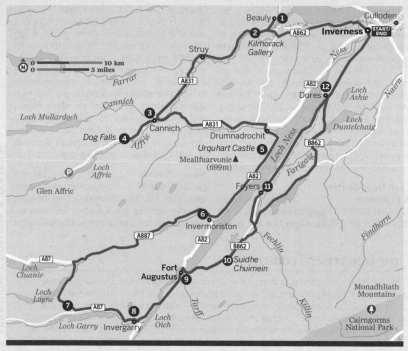

Driving Tour
A Loch Ness Circuit

START INVERNESS
END INVERNESS
LENGTH 130 MILES; FOUR HOURS

Head out of Inverness on the A862 to **1 Beauly**, arriving in time for breakfast. Backtrack a mile and turn right on the A831 to Cannich, passing **2 Kilmorack Gallery**, which exhibits contemporary art in a converted church. The scenery gets wilder as you approach **3 Cannich**; turn right and follow the single-track road to the car park at **4 Dog Falls**. Take a stroll along the rushing river, or hike to the viewpoint (one-hour round trip) for a glimpse of remote Glen Affric.

Return to Cannich and turn right on the A831 to Drumnadrochit, then right on the A82 past picturesque **5 Urquhart Castle** (p900) and along the shores of Loch Ness. At **6 Invermoriston**, pause to look at the old bridge, built by Telford in 1813, then head west on the A897 towards Kyle of Lochalsh;

after 16 miles go left on the A87 towards Invergarry. You are now among some of the finest mountain scenery in the Highlands; as the road turns east above Loch Garry, stop at the famous **7 viewpoint** (the layby on the right; it's not signposted). By a quirk of perspective, the lochs to the west appear to form the map outline of Scotland.

At **8 Invergarry**, turn left on the A82 to reach **9 Fort Augustus** and a late lunch at the Lovat (p903) or Lock Inn (p903). Take the B862 out of town, following the line of General Wade's 18th-century military road, to another viewpoint at **10 Suidhe Chuimein**. A short walk (800m) up the well-worn path to the summit affords an even better panorama.

Ahead, you can choose the low road via the impressive **11 Falls of Foyers**, or stay on the the high road (B862) for more views; both converge on Loch Ness at the **12 Dores Inn**, where you can sip a pint with a view along Loch Ness, and even stay for dinner before returning to Inverness.

from Drumnadrochit hourly (except 1pm) from 9am to 6pm daily.

🛏 Sleeping & Eating

Loch Ness Backpackers Lodge HOSTEL £
(☑ 01456-450807; www.lochness-backpackers.com; Coiltie Farmhouse, East Lewiston; per person from £16; P ⊚) This snug, friendly hostel housed in a cottage and barn has six-bed dorms, one double and a large barbecue area. It's about 0.75 miles from Drumnadrochit, along the A82 towards Fort William; turn left where you see the sign for Loch Ness Inn, just before the bridge.

Loch Ness Inn INN ££
(☑ 01456-450991; www.staylochness.co.uk; Lewiston; d/f £90/120; P ⊚) The Loch Ness Inn ticks all the weary traveller's boxes, with comfortable bedrooms (the family suite sleeps two adults and two children), a cosy bar pouring real ales from the Cairngorm and Isle of Skye breweries, and a rustic restaurant (mains £9 to £19) serving hearty, wholesome fare such as whisky-flambéed haggis, and roast rump of Scottish lamb. It's conveniently located in the quiet hamlet of Lewiston, between Drumnadrochit and Urquhart Castle.

Drumbuie Farm B&B ££
(☑ 01456-450634; www.loch-ness-farm.co.uk; Drumnadrochit; s/d from £44/68; P) Drumbuie is a B&B in a modern house on a working farm – the surrounding fields are full of sheep and highland cattle – with views over Urquhart Castle and Loch Ness. Walkers and cyclists are welcome.

❶ Getting There & Away

Scottish Citylink (☑ 0871 266 3333; www.citylink.co.uk) and Stagecoach (p899) buses from Inverness to Fort William run along the shores of Loch Ness (six to eight daily, five on Sunday); those headed for Skye turn off at Invermoriston. There are bus stops at Drumnadrochit (£3.20, 30 minutes), and Urquhart Castle (£3.50, 35 minutes).

Fort Augustus

POP 620

Fort Augustus, at the junction of four old military roads, was originally a government garrison and the headquarters of General George Wade's road-building operations in the early 18th century. Today it's a neat and picturesque little place, often overrun by coach-tour crowds in summer.

◎ Sights & Activities

Caledonian Canal CANAL
(www.scottishcanals.co.uk) At Fort Augustus, boats using the Caledonian Canal are raised and lowered 13m by a 'ladder' of five consecutive locks. It's fun to watch, and the landscaped canal banks are a great place to soak up the sun or compare accents with fellow tourists. The **Caledonian Canal Visitor Centre** (☑ 01320-366493; Ardchattan House, Canalside; ⊙10am-1.30pm & 2-5.30pm Apr-Oct) FREE, beside the lowest lock, showcases the canal's history.

🛏 Sleeping & Eating

Morag's Lodge HOSTEL £
(☑ 01320-366289; www.moragslodge.com; Bunoich Brae; dm/tw/f from £21/50/69; P @ ⊚) This large and well-run hostel is based in a big Victorian house with great views of Fort Augustus' hilly surrounds, and has a convivial bar with open fire. It's hidden away in the trees up the steep side road just north of the tourist office car park.

★ Lovat HOTEL £££
(☑ 01456-459250; www.thelovat.com; Main Rd; d from £121; P ⊚) 🖉 A boutique-style makeover has transformed this former huntin'-and-shootin' hotel into an eco-conscious retreat set apart from the tourist crush around the canal. The bedrooms are spacious and stylishly furnished, while the lounge is equipped with a log fire, comfy armchairs and grand piano. It has an informal brasserie and a highly acclaimed restaurant (five-course dinner £50), which serves top-quality cuisine.

Lock Inn PUB FOOD ££
(Canal Side; mains £9-14; ⊙meals noon-8pm) A superb little pub right on the canal bank, the Lock Inn has a vast range of malt whiskies and a tempting menu of bar meals, which includes Orkney salmon, Highland venison and daily seafood specials; the house speciality is beer-battered haddock and chips.

❶ Information

Fort Augustus Tourist Office (☑ 01320-366367; ⊙9am-6pm Mon-Sat & 9am-5pm Sun Easter-Oct) In the central car park.

❶ Getting There & Away

Scottish Citylink (www.citylink.co.uk) and **Stagecoach** (www.stagecoachbus.com) buses from Inverness to Fort William stop at Fort Augustus (£6 to £10.20, one hour, five to eight daily Monday to Saturday, five on Sunday).

THE CAIRNGORMS

The **Cairngorms National Park** (www.cairngorms.co.uk) encompasses the highest landmass in Britain – a broad mountain plateau, riven only by the deep valleys of the Lairig Ghru and Loch Avon, with an average altitude of over 1000m and including five of the six highest summits in the UK. This wild mountain landscape of granite and heather has a sub-Arctic climate and supports rare alpine tundra vegetation and high-altitude bird species, such as snow bunting, ptarmigan and dotterel.

The harsh mountain environment gives way lower down to scenic glens softened by beautiful open forests of native Scots pine, home to rare animals and birds such as pine martens, wildcats, red squirrels, ospreys, capercaillies and crossbills.

This is prime hill-walking territory, but even couch potatoes can enjoy a taste of the high life by taking the Cairngorm Mountain Railway up to the edge of the Cairngorm plateau.

Aviemore

POP 3150

The gateway to the Cairngorms, Aviemore is the region's main centre for transport, accommodation, restaurants and shops. It's not the prettiest town in Scotland by a long stretch – the main attractions are in the surrounding area.

The Cairngorm skiing area and funicular railway lie 9 miles southeast of Aviemore along the B970 (Ski Rd) and its continuation, past Coylumbridge and Glenmore.

◉ Sights & Activities

Strathspey Steam Railway   HERITAGE RAILWAY
(☑ 01479-810725;   www.strathspeyrailway.co.uk; Station Sq; return ticket per adult/child £13.95/6.98) Strathspey Steam Railway runs steam trains on a section of restored line between Aviemore and Broomhill, 10 miles to the northeast, via Boat of Garten. There are four or five trains daily from June to August, and a more limited service in April, May, September, October and December, with the option of enjoying afternoon tea, Sunday lunch or a five-course dinner on board.

An extension to Grantown-on-Spey is under construction (see www.railstograntown.org); in the meantime, you can continue from Broomhill to Grantown-on-Spey by bus.

★**Rothiemurchus Estate**   FOREST
(www.rothiemurchus.net) The Rothiemurchus Estate, which extends from the River Spey at Aviemore to the Cairngorm summit plateau, is famous for having Scotland's largest remnant of **Caledonian forest**, the ancient forest of Scots pine that once covered most of the country. The forest is home to a large population of red squirrels, and is one of the last bastions of the Scottish wildcat.

The **Rothiemurchus Estate visitor centre** (☑ 01479-812345; ◷ 9.30am-5.50pm) FREE, a mile southeast of Aviemore along the B970, sells an *Explorer Map* detailing more than 50 miles of **footpaths** and **cycling trails**, including the wheelchair-accessible 4-mile trail around **Loch an Eilein**, with its ruined castle and peaceful pine woods.

🛏 Sleeping

Aviemore Bunkhouse   HOSTEL £
(☑ 01479-811181;   www.aviemore-bunkhouse.com; Dalfaber Rd; dm/d/f from £19/50/65; 🅿 @ 🛜) This independent hostel provides accommodation in bright, modern six- or eight-bed dorms, each with private bathroom, and one twin/family room. It has a drying room, secure bike storage and wheelchair-accessible dorms. From the train station, cross the pedestrian bridge over the tracks, turn right and walk south on Dalfaber Rd.

Aviemore SYHA   HOSTEL £
(☑ 01479-810345; www.syha.org.uk; 25 Grampian Rd; dm £20; 🅿 @ 🛜) Upmarket hostelling in a spacious, well-equipped modern building, five minutes' walk south of the village centre. There are four- and six-bed rooms, and a comfortable lounge with views of the mountains.

Rothiemurchus Camp & Caravan Park   CAMPSITE £
(☑ 01479-812800; www.rothiemurchus.net; Coylumbridge; sites per adult/child £11/2) The nearest camping ground to Aviemore is this year-round park, beautifully sited among Scots pines at Coylumbridge, 1.5 miles along the B970.

Old Minister's House   B&B ££
(☑ 01479-812181;   www.theoldministershouse.co.uk; Rothiemurchus; s/d £70/110; 🅿 🛜) This former manse dates from 1906 and has four rooms with a homely, country-farmhouse feel. It's in a lovely setting amid Scots pines on the banks of the River Druie, just 0.75 miles southeast of Aviemore.

The Cairngorms

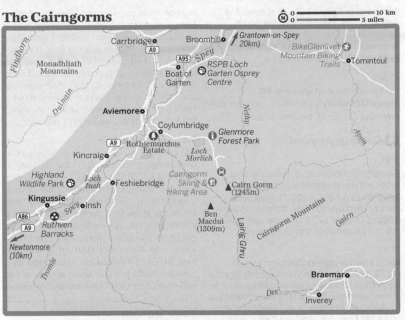

Ardlogie Guest House B&B **££**
(☑ 01479-810747; www.ardlogie.co.uk; Dalfaber Rd; s/d from £40/62, cabins per 3 nights £165; P ⓢ) Handy to the train station, the five-room Ardlogie has great views over the River Spey towards the Cairngorms. There's also self-catering accommodation in the Bothy, a cosy, two-person timber cabin. Facilities include a boules pitch in the garden, and guests can get free use of the local country club's pool, spa and sauna.

Ravenscraig Guest House B&B **££**
(☑ 01479-810278; www.aviemoreonline.com; Grampian Rd; s/d £48/82 ; P ⓢ) Ravenscraig is a large, flower-bedecked Victorian villa with six spacious en suite rooms, plus another six in a modern chalet at the back (one wheelchair accessible). It serves traditional and veggie breakfasts in an attractive conservatory dining room.

Eating & Drinking

★ Mountain Cafe CAFE **£**
(www.mountaincafe-aviemore.co.uk; 111 Grampian Rd; mains £4-10; ⏱ 8.30am-5pm Tue-Thu, to 5.30pm Fri-Mon; P ☑ ♿) The Mountain Cafe offers freshly prepared local produce with a Kiwi twist (the owner is from New Zealand) – healthy breakfasts of muesli, por-

ridge and fresh fruit (till 11.30am), hearty lunches of seafood chowder, burgers and imaginative salads, and homebaked breads, cakes and biscuits. Vegan, coeliac and nut-allergic diets catered for.

Old Bridge Inn PUB
(☑ 01479-811137; www.oldbridgeinn.co.uk; 23 Dalfaber Rd; ⏱ noon-midnight Sun-Thu, to 1am Fri & Sat; ⓢ) The Old Bridge has a snug bar, complete with roaring log fire in winter, and a cheerful, chalet-style **restaurant** (mains £10-24; ⏱ noon-2pm & 6-9pm, to 10pm Fri & Sat) at the back serving quality Scottish cuisine.

ℹ Information

Aviemore Tourist Office (☑ 01479-810930; www.visitaviemore.com; The Mall, Grampian Rd; ⏱ 9am-6pm Mon-Sat, 9.30am-5pm Sun Jul & Aug, 9am-5pm Mon-Sat, 10am-4pm Sun Easter-Jun, Sep & Oct) Hours are limited from October to Easter.

ℹ Getting There & Away

BUS
Buses stop on Grampian Rd opposite the train station; buy tickets at the tourist office. Services include the following:
Edinburgh £26, four hours, five daily
Glasgow £26, 2¾ hours, five daily

Grantown-on-Spey £3.50, 35 minutes, five daily weekdays, two Saturday; bus 33 via Carrbridge (15 minutes)

Inverness £9.80, 45 minutes, eight daily

Perth £19.20, 2¼ hours, five daily

TRAIN

The train station is on Grampian Rd.

Glasgow/Edinburgh £40, three hours, six daily

Inverness £11.70, 40 minutes, 12 daily

ℹ Getting Around

BIKE

Several places in Aviemore, Rothiemurchus Estate and Glenmore hire mountain bikes. **Bothy Bikes** (☑ 01479-810111; www.bothybikes.co.uk; 5 Granish Way, Dalfaber; ⊘ 9am-5.30pm) Charges £20 a day for a quality bike with front suspension and disc brakes.

BUS

Bus 31 links Aviemore to Cairngorm car park (£2.50, 30 minutes, hourly) via Coylumbridge and Glenmore. A Strathspey Dayrider/Megarider ticket (one/seven days £6.50/17) gives unlimited bus travel from Aviemore as far as Cairngorm, Carrbridge and Kingussie (buy from the bus driver).

Around Aviemore

Cairngorm Mountain

⊙ Sights & Activities

Cairngorm Mountain Railway FUNICULAR RAILWAY
(☑ 01479-861261; www.cairngormmountain.org; adult/child return £10.50/6.80; ⊘ every 20min, 10am-4pm May-Nov, 9am-4.30pm Dec-Apr) The region's most popular attraction is a funicular railway that will whisk you to the edge of the Cairngorm plateau (1085m) in just eight minutes. The bottom station is at the Coire Cas car park at the end of Ski Rd; at the top is an exhibition, a shop (of course) and a restaurant. Unfortunately, for environmental and safety reasons, you're not allowed out of the top station in summer unless you book a guided walk or mountain-bike descent.

Cairngorm Mountain Ski Area SNOW SPORTS
(www.cairngormmountain.org; 1-day ski pass per adult/child £33.50/20) Aspen or Val d'Isère it ain't, but with 19 runs and 23 miles of piste, Cairngorm is Scotland's biggest ski area. When the snow is at its best and the sun is shining, you can close your eyes and imagine you're in the Alps; sadly, low cloud, high winds and horizontal sleet are more common. Ski or snowboard hire is around £23/17 per adult/child per day; there are lots of hire outlets at Coire Cas, Glenmore and Aviemore.

Loch Morlich

Six miles east of Aviemore, Loch Morlich is surrounded by some 8 sq miles of pine and spruce forest that make up the **Glenmore Forest Park**. Its attractions include a sandy beach (at the east end).

⊙ Sights & Activities

★**Glenmore Lodge** ADVENTURE SPORTS
(☑ 01479-861256; www.glenmorelodge.org.uk) One of Britain's leading adventure sports training centres, offering courses in hill walking, rock climbing, ice climbing, canoeing, mountain biking and mountaineering.

MOUNTAIN WALKS IN THE CAIRNGORMS

The climb from the car park at the Coire Cas ski area to the summit of **Cairn Gorm** (1245m) takes about two hours (one way). From there, you can continue south across the high-level plateau to Ben Macdui (1309m), Britain's second-highest peak. This takes eight to 10 hours return from the car park and is a serious undertaking; it's for experienced and well-equipped walkers only.

The **Lairig Ghru trail**, which can take eight to 10 hours, is a demanding 24-mile walk from Aviemore through the Lairig Ghru pass (840m) to Braemar. An alternative to doing the full route is to make the six-hour return hike up to the summit of the pass and back to Aviemore. The path starts from Ski Rd, a mile east of Coylumbridge, and involves some very rough going.

Warning – the Cairngorm plateau is a sub-Arctic environment where navigation is difficult and weather conditions can be severe, even in midsummer. Hikers must have proper hill-walking equipment, and know how to use a map and compass. In winter it is a place for experienced mountaineers only. Trip durations are estimates only.

The centre's comfortable **B&B accommodation** (tw £76) is available to all, even if you're not taking a course, as is the indoor-climbing wall, gym and sauna.

Cairngorm Reindeer Centre GUIDED TOUR
(www.cairngormreindeer.co.uk; adult/child £12/6) The warden here will take you on a guided walk to see and feed Britain's only herd of reindeer, who are very tame and will even eat out of your hand. Walks take place at 11am daily year-round (weather-dependent), plus another at 2.30pm from May to September, and 3.30pm Monday to Friday in July and August.

Loch Morlich
Watersports Centre WATER SPORTS
(☑01479-861221; www.lochmorlich.com; ⊙9am-5pm May-Oct) This popular outfit rents out Canadian canoes (£21 an hour), kayaks (£8), sailboards (£17.50), sailing dinghies (£25) and rowing boats (£21), and also offers instruction.

🛏 Sleeping

Cairngorm Lodge SYHA HOSTEL **£**
(☑01479-861238; dm/tw £17/45; ⊙closed Nov & Dec; @☑) Set in a former shooting lodge that enjoys a great location at the east end of Loch Morlich; booking is essential.

Glenmore Campsite CAMPSITE **£**
(☑01479-861271; www.campingintheforest.co.uk; tent & campervan sites £27) Campers can set up base at this attractive lochside site with pitches amid the Scots pines; rates include up to four people per tent/campervan. Open year round.

Boat of Garten

Boat of Garten is known as the Osprey Village because these rare and beautiful birds of prey nest nearby at the **RSPB Loch Garten Osprey Centre** (☑01479-831694; www.rspb.org.uk/lochgarten; Tulloch; osprey hide adult/child £5/2; ⊙osprey hide 10am-6pm Apr-Aug). The ospreys migrate here each spring from Africa and nest in a tall pine tree – you can watch from a hide as the birds feed their young. The centre is signposted about 2 miles east of the village.

Boat of Garten is 6 miles northeast of Aviemore. The most interesting way to get here is on the Strathspey Steam Railway (p904) from Aviemore.

Kingussie & Newtonmore

The gracious old Speyside towns of Kingussie (kin-*yew*-see) and Newtonmore, 2.5 miles apart, sit at the foot of the great heather-clad humps known as the Monadhliath Mountains. Newtonmore is best known as the home of the excellent Highland Folk Museum.

◉ Sights & Activities

Highland Folk Museum MUSEUM
(☑01540-673551; www.highlandfolk.museum; Kingussie Rd, Newtonmore; ⊙10.30am-5.30pm Apr-Aug, 11am-4.30pm Sep & Oct) **FREE** The open-air Highland Folk Museum comprises a collection of historical buildings and artefacts revealing many aspects of Highland culture and lifestyle. Laid out like a farming township, it has a community of traditional thatch-roofed cottages, a sawmill, a schoolhouse, a shepherd's bothy (hut) and a rural post office. Actors in period costume give demonstrations of woodcarving, wool-spinning and peat-fire baking. You'll need at least two to three hours to make the most of a visit here.

Laggan Wolftrax MOUNTAIN BIKING
(scotland.forestry.gov.uk/visit/laggan-wolftrax; Strathmashie Forest; admission free, parking £3; ⊙10am-6pm Mon, 9.30am-5pm Tue, Thu & Fri, 9.30am-6pm Sat & Sun) Ten miles southwest of Newtonmore, on the A86 road towards Spean Bridge, this is one of Scotland's top mountain-biking centres with purpose-built trails ranging from open-country riding to black-diamond downhills with rock slabs and drop-offs. At the time of research, a new centre with cafe and bike shop was scheduled to open in summer 2014.

🛏 Sleeping & Eating

★**Eagleview Guest House** B&B **££**
(☑01540-673675; www.eagleviewguesthouse.co.uk; Perth Rd, Newtonmore; r per person £39-40; ℗☑) Welcoming Eagleview is one of the best places to stay in the area, with beautifully decorated bedrooms, super-king-size beds, spacious bathrooms with power showers (except room 4, which has a Victorian slipper bath!), and nice little touches such as cafetières (coffee plungers) with real coffee – and fresh milk – on your hospitality tray, and Scottish kippers on the breakfast menu.

Hermitage B&B ££
(☑01540-662137; www.thehermitage-scotland. com; Spey St, Kingussie; s/d from £40/70; P 🛜) The five-bedroom Hermitage is a lovely old house with plenty of character, filled with Victorian period features – ask for room 5 (superior king), with double bed, Chesterfield sofa, and a view of the hills. The lounge has deep sofas ranged by a log fire, and there are good views of the Cairngorms from the breakfast room and garden.

★**Cross** SCOTTISH £££
(☑01540-661166; www.thecross.co.uk; Tweed Mill Brae, off Ardbroilach Rd, Kingussie; 2-course lunches £23, 3-course dinners £60; ☺noon-2pm & 7-8.30pm; P 🛜) 🍴 Housed in a converted water mill, the Cross is one of the finest restaurants in the Highlands. The intimate, low-raftered dining room has an open fire and a patio overlooking the stream, and serves a daily-changing menu of fresh Scottish produce accompanied by a superb wine list. If you want to stay the night, there are eight stylish rooms (double or twin £100 to £180) to choose from.

❶ Getting There & Away

BUS
Kingussie and Newtonmore are served by Scottish Citylink (p903) buses:
Aviemore £7.70, 25 minutes, five to seven daily
Inverness £13.40, one hour, six to eight Monday to Saturday, three Sunday
Perth £16.30, 1¾ hours, five daily

TRAIN
Kingussie's train station is at the southern end of town. Kingussie and Newtonmore are served by the following:
Edinburgh £35, 2½ hours, seven a day Monday to Saturday, two Sunday
Inverness £11.70, 50 minutes, eight a day Monday to Saturday, four Sunday

Royal Deeside

The upper valley of the River Dee stretches west from Aboyne to Braemar, closely paralleled by the A93 road. Made famous by its long association with the monarchy – today's royal family still holiday at Balmoral Castle, built for Queen Victoria in 1855 – the region is often called Royal Deeside.

The River Dee, renowned world-over for its **salmon fishing**, has its source in the Cairngorm Mountains west of Braemar, the starting point for long walks into the hills. The

FishDee website (www.fishdee.co.uk) has all you need to know about fishing on the river.

Ballater

POP 1530

The attractive little village of Ballater owes its 18th-century origins to the curative waters of nearby Pannanich Springs (now bottled commercially as Deeside Natural Mineral Water), and its prosperity to nearby Balmoral Castle. The **tourist office** (☑01339-755306; Station Sq; ☺9am-6pm Jul & Aug, 10am-5pm Sep-Jun) is in the Old Royal Station.

When Queen Victoria travelled to Balmoral Castle she would alight from the royal train at Ballater's **Old Royal Station** (☑01339-755306; Station Sq; admission £2; ☺10am-6pm Jul & Aug, 10am-5pm Sep-Jun). The station has been beautifully restored and now houses the tourist office, a cafe and a museum with a replica of Victoria's royal coach (the original is in the National Railway Museum in York).

You can hire bikes from **CycleHighlands** (☑01339-755864; www.cyclehighlands. com; The Pavilion, Victoria Rd; bicycle hire per day £18; ☺9am-6pm) and **Bike Station** (☑01339-754004; www.bikestationballater.co.uk; Station Sq; bicycle hire per 3hr/day £12/18; ☺9am-6pm), which also offer guided bike rides and advice on local trails.

Balmoral Castle

Eight miles west of Ballater lies **Balmoral Castle** (☑01339-742334; www.balmoralcastle. com; adult/child £11/5; ☺10am-5pm Apr-Jul, last entry 4.30pm), the Queen's Highland holiday home, screened from the road by a curtain of trees. Built for Queen Victoria in 1855 as a private residence for the royal family, it kicked off the revival of the Scottish Baronial style of architecture that characterises so many of Scotland's 19th-century country houses.

The admission fee includes an interesting and well thought-out audioguide, but the tour is very much an outdoor one through garden and grounds; as for the castle itself, only the **ballroom**, which displays a collection of Landseer paintings and royal silver, is open to the public. Don't expect to see the Queen's private quarters! The main attraction is learning about Highland estate management, rather than royal revelations.

Balmoral is beside the A93 at Crathie and can be reached on the Aberdeen–Braemar bus.

Braemar

POP 450

Braemar is a pretty little village with a grand location on a broad plain ringed by mountains where the Dee valley and Glen Clunie meet. In winter this is one of the coldest places in the country – temperatures as low as -29°C have been recorded – and during spells of severe cold, hungry deer wander the streets looking for a bite to eat. Braemar is an excellent base for hill walking, and there's also skiing at nearby Glenshee.

The **tourist office** (☑ 01399-741600; The Mews, Mar Rd; ☉ 9am-6pm Aug, 9am-5pm Jun, Jul, Sep & Oct, 10am-5pm Mon-Sat, 2-5pm Sun Nov-May), opposite the Fife Arms Hotel, has lots of useful info on walks in the area.

Just north of the village, turreted **Braemar Castle** (www.braemarcastle.co.uk; adult/child £8/4; ☉ 10am-4pm Sat & Sun Jun-Sep, also Wed Jul–mid-Sep, daily Aug, 11am-3pm Sat & Sun May & Oct) dates from 1628 and served as a government garrison after the 1745 Jacobite rebellion. It was taken over by the local community in 2007, and now offers guided tours of the historic castle apartments.

An easy walk from Braemar is up **Creag Choinnich** (538m), a hill to the east of the village above the A93. The 1-mile route is waymarked and takes about 1½ hours. For a longer walk (4 miles; about three hours) and superb views of the Cairngorms, head for the summit of **Morrone** (859m), southwest of Braemar. Ask at the tourist office for details of these and other walks.

You can hire mountain bikes from **Braemar Mountain Sports** (☑ 01339-741242; www.braemarmountainsports.com; 5 Invercauld Rd; bike hire per day £18; ☉ 9am-6pm). It also rents skiing and mountaineering equipment.

⌂ Sleeping

★**Rucksacks Bunkhouse**　　HOSTEL £
(☑ 01339-741517; 15 Mar Rd; bothy £7, dm £12-15, tw £36; ℗) An appealing cottage with a dorm, and cheaper beds in an alpine-style bothy (shared sleeping platform for 10 people; bring your own sleeping bag). Extras include a drying room (for wet-weather gear), a laundry and even a sauna (£10 an hour). The friendly owner is a font of knowledge about the area.

Braemar SYHA　　HOSTEL £
(☑ 01339-741659; www.syha.org.uk; 21 Glenshee Rd; dm/tw £18.50/44; ☉ Feb-Oct; @) This hostel is housed in a grand former shooting lodge just south of Braemar village centre on the A93 to Perth. It has a comfy lounge with pool table, and a barbecue in the garden.

Craiglea　　B&B ££
(☑ 01339-741641; www.craigleabraemar.com; Hillside Dr; d/f from £74/105; ℗ 🛜) Craiglea is a homely B&B set in a pretty stone cottage with three en suite bedrooms. Vegetarian breakfasts are available and the owners can give advice on local walks.

St Margarets　　B&B ££
(☑ 01339-741697; soky37@hotmail.com; 13 School Rd; s/tw £34/56; 🛜) Grab this place if you can, but there's only one room, a twin with a serious sunflower theme. The genuine warmth of the welcome is delightful. It's tucked behind the church on the south side of the A93 road.

✕ Eating

Taste　　CAFE £
(☑ 01339-741425; www.taste-braemar.co.uk; Airlie House, Mar Rd; mains £4-7; ☉ 10am-5pm Tue-Sat; 🖶) 🖉 Taste is a relaxed little cafe with armchairs in the window, serving homemade soups, sandwiches, coffee and cake.

★**Gathering Place**　　BISTRO ££
(☑ 01339-741234; www.the-gathering-place.co.uk; 9 Invercauld Rd; mains £12-19; ☉ 6-9pm Tue-Sat; 🛜) This bright and breezy bistro is an unexpected corner of culinary excellence, with a welcoming dining room and sunny conservatory, tucked below the main road junction at the entrance to Braemar village.

ℹ Getting There & Away

Bus 201 runs from Aberdeen to Braemar (£11, 2¼ hours, every two hours Monday to Saturday, five on Sunday). The 50-mile drive from Perth to Braemar is beautiful, but there's no public transport on this route.

HIGHLAND PERTHSHIRE

Dunkeld & Birnam

POP 1005

The Tay runs like a storybook river between the twin towns of Dunkeld and Birnam, nestled in the heart of Perthshire's Big Tree Country. As well as Dunkeld's lovely cathedral, there's much walking to be done in this area of magnificent forested hills. These same walks were one of the inspirations for Beatrix Potter to create her children's tales.

◉ Sights

Dunkeld Cathedral CHURCH

(HS; www.dunkeldcathedral.org.uk; High St; ◎ 9.30am-6.30pm Apr-Sep, to 4pm Oct-Mar) **FREE** Situated on the grassy banks of the River Tay, Dunkeld Cathedral is one of the most beautifully sited churches in Scotland; don't miss it on a sunny day, when there are few lovelier places to be. Half the cathedral is still in use as a church; the rest is in ruins. It partly dates from the 14th century, having suffered damage during the Reformation and the battle of Dunkeld (Jacobites versus government) in 1689.

Birnam VILLAGE

Across the bridge from Dunkeld is Birnam, a name made famous by *Macbeth*. There's not much left of Birnam Wood, but there is a small, leafy **Beatrix Potter Park** (the children's author, who wrote the evergreen story of *Peter Rabbit*, spent childhood holidays in the area). Next to the park, in the **Birnam Arts Centre** (www.birnaminstitute.com; Station Rd; admission £1.50; ◎ 10am-5pm mid-Mar–Nov, 10am-4.30pm Mon-Sat & 11am-4.30pm Sun Dec–mid-Mar), is a small exhibition on Potter and her characters.

Loch of the Lowes
Wildlife Centre WILDLIFE RESERVE

(☑ 01350-727337; www.swt.org.uk; adult/child £4/50p; ◎ 10am-5pm Mar-Oct, 10.30am-4pm Fri-Sun Nov-Feb) Loch of the Lowes, 2 miles east of Dunkeld off the A923, has a visitor centre devoted to red squirrels and the majestic osprey. There's a birdwatching hide (with binoculars provided), where you can see the birds nesting during breeding season (late April to August).

🛏 Sleeping & Eating

★ Jessie Mac's HOSTEL, B&B £

(☑ 01350-727324; www.jessiemacs.co.uk; Murthly Tce, Birnam; dm £18, d £70; 🕾) 🛇 Set in a Victorian manse complete with baronial turret, Jessie Mac's is a glorious cross between B&B and luxury hostel, with three gorgeous doubles and five shared rooms with bunks. Guests make good use of the country-style lounge, sunny dining room and well-equipped kitchen, and breakfasts are composed of local produce, from organic eggs to Dunkeld smoked salmon.

★ Taybank PUB FOOD £

(☑ 01350-727340; www.thetaybank.co.uk; Tay Tce; mains £6-9; ◎ 11am-11pm Mon-Thu, to midnight Fri & Sat, 12.30-11pm Sun) Top choice for a sun-kissed pub lunch by the river is the Taybank, a regular meeting place and performance space for musicians of all creeds and a wonderfully welcoming bar serving ales from the local Strathbraan Brewery. There's live music several nights per week, and the menu runs to burgers and stovies (stewed potato and onion with meat or other ingredients).

ℹ Information

Dunkeld Tourist Office (☑ 01350-727688; www.dunkeldandbirnam.org.uk; The Cross; ◎ 9am-5pm Apr-Oct, Fri-Sun Nov-Mar) Has information on local hiking and biking trails.

ℹ Getting There & Away

Dunkeld is 15 miles north of Perth. Citylink buses running between Glasgow/Edinburgh (£16.60, two hours, five daily) and Inverness stop at the Birnam Hotel. **Stagecoach** (www.stagecoachbus.com) runs hourly buses (only five on Sunday) between Perth and Dunkeld (£2.50, 40 minutes), continuing to Aberfeldy.

There are also buses from Dunkeld to Blairgowrie (£2.50, 35 minutes), twice daily on Tuesday, Thursday and Saturday only.

Pitlochry

POP 2780

Pitlochry, with the scent of the Highlands already in the air, is a popular stop on the way north. In summer the main street can be a conga line of tour groups, but linger a while and it can still charm – on a quiet spring evening it's a pretty place with salmon leaping in the Tummel and good things brewing at the Moulin Hotel.

◉ Sights

One of Pitlochry's attractions is its beautiful **riverside**; the River Tummel is dammed here, and if you're lucky you might see salmon swimming up the **fish ladder** to Loch Faskally above (May to November, best month is October).

★ Edradour Distillery DISTILLERY

(☑ 01796-472095; www.edradour.co.uk; tour adult/child £7.50/2.50 ; ◎ 10am-5pm Mon-Sat Apr-Oct; 🅿🚼) This is proudly Scotland's smallest and most picturesque distillery, and it's one of the best to visit: you can see the whole process, easily explained, in one building. It's 2.5 miles east of Pitlochry by car, along the Moulin road, or a pleasant 1-mile walk.

Explorers Garden GARDENS
(✐01796-484600; www.explorersgarden.com; Foss Rd; adult/child £4/1; ⊙10am-5pm Apr-Oct) This garden is based around plants brought to Scotland by 18th- and 19th-century Scottish botanists and explorers such as David Douglas, and it celebrates 300 years of collecting and the 'plant hunters' who tracked down these exotic species.

🛏 Sleeping

Ashleigh B&B £
(✐01796-470316; www.realbandbpitlochry.co.uk; 120 Atholl Rd; s/d £30/57; 🛜) Genuine welcomes don't come much better than Nancy's, and her place on the main street makes a top Pitlochry pit stop. Two comfortable doubles share an excellent bathroom, and there's an open kitchen stocked with goodies where you make your own breakfast in the morning. A home away from home and a standout budget choice. Cash only; no kids.
She also has a good self-catering apartment with great views, available by the night.

Pitlochry Backpackers Hotel HOSTEL £
(✐01796-470044; www.scotlands-top-hostels.com; 134 Atholl Rd; dm/tw/d £18/47/52; ⊙Apr-mid-Nov; P@🛜) Friendly, laid-back and very comfortable, this is a cracking hostel smack bang in the middle of town, with three- to eight-bed dorms that are in mint condition. There are also good-value en suite twins and doubles, with beds, not bunks. Cheap breakfast and a pool table add to the convivial party atmosphere. No extra charge for linen.

Pitlochry SYHA HOSTEL £
(✐01796-472308; www.syha.org.uk; Knockard Rd; dm/tw £17/45; ⊙Mar-Oct; P@🛜) Great location overlooking the town centre. Popular with families and walkers.

★Craigatin House B&B ££
(✐01796-472478; www.craigatinhouse.co.uk; 165 Atholl Rd; s £80, standard/deluxe d £90/100; P@🛜) Several times more tasteful than the average Pitlochry lodging, this elegant house and garden is set back from the main road. Chic contemporary fabrics covering expansive beds offer a standard of comfort above and beyond the reasonable price; the rooms in the converted stable block are particularly inviting. A fabulous breakfast and lounge area gives views over the lush garden.
Breakfast choices include whisky-laced porridge, smoked-fish omelettes and apple pancakes. Kids not allowed.

Tir Aluinn B&B ££
(✐01796-473811; www.tiraluinn.co.uk; 10 Higher Oakfield Rd; r per person £35-37; P🛜) Tucked away above the main street, this is a little gem of a place with bright rooms and easy-on-the-eye furniture, and a warm personal welcome. Breakfasts are a pleasure too.

🍴 Eating & Drinking

★Moulin Hotel PUB FOOD ££
(✐01796-472196; www.moulinhotel.co.uk; Kirkmichael Rd; mains £8-12; P🛜🐕) A mile away from town but a world apart, this atmospheric inn was trading centuries before the tartan tack came to Pitlochry. With its low ceilings, ageing wood and booth seats, the Moulin is a wonderfully romantic spot for a house-brewed ale and a portion of Highland comfort food: try the mince and tatties, or venison stew. It's a pleasant uphill stroll from Pitlochry, and an easy roll down afterwards.

Port-na-Craig Inn BAR, BISTRO ££
(✐01796-472777; www.portnacraig.com; Port Na Craig; mains £13-22, 2-/3-course lunches £13/15; ⊙11am-8.30pm; P🐕) Across the river from the town centre, this cute little cottage sits in what was once a separate hamlet. Top-quality main meals are prepared with confidence and panache; there are also simpler sandwiches, kids' meals and light lunches. Or you could just sit outdoors by the river with a pint and watch the anglers.

☆ Entertainment

★Pitlochry Festival Theatre THEATRE
(✐01796-484626; www.pitlochryfestivaltheatre.com; Port-na-Craig; tickets £26-35) Founded in 1951 (in a tent!), this famous and much-loved theatre is the focus of Highland Perthshire's cultural life. The summer season, from May to mid-October, stages a different play each night of the week except Sunday.

ℹ Information

Pitlochry Tourist Office (✐01796-472215; www.perthshire.co.uk; 22 Atholl Rd; ⊙9am-5pm Mar-Oct, Mon-Sat Nov-Feb) Good information on local walks.

ℹ Getting There & Away

Pitlochry is on the main railway line from Perth (£13.20, 30 minutes, nine daily Monday to Saturday, five on Sunday) to Inverness.
Citylink (www.citylink.co.uk) Buses run every two hours to Inverness (£16.60, 2¼ hours), Perth

(£10.70, 40 minutes), Edinburgh (£16.60, two to 2½ hours) and Glasgow (£16.60, 2¼ hours).
Megabus (🖉 0871 266 3333; www.megabus.com) Offers discounted fares to Inverness, Perth, Edinburgh and Glasgow.
Stagecoach (www.stagecoachbus.com) Buses run to Aberfeldy (£2, 30 minutes, hourly Monday to Saturday, three Sunday), Dunkeld (£2, 30 minutes, hourly Monday to Saturday) and Perth (£3.40, 1¼ hours, hourly Monday to Saturday).

Blair Castle

One of the most popular tourist attractions in Scotland, magnificent **Blair Castle** (🖉 01796-481207; www.blair-castle.co.uk; adult/child/family £9.90/5.95/26.75; ☉ 9.30am-5.30pm Apr-Oct, 10am-4pm Sat & Sun Nov-Mar; P ⚑), and the 108 sq miles it sits on, is the seat of the Duke of Atholl, head of the Murray clan. It's an impressive white building set beneath forested slopes above the River Garry. Thirty rooms are open to the public and they present a wonderful picture of upper-class Highland life from the 16th century on.

The original tower was built in 1269, but the castle has undergone significant remodelling since. The **dining room** is sumptuous – check out the 9-pint wine glasses – and the **ballroom** is a vaulted chamber that's a virtual stag cemetery. The current duke visits the castle every May to review the **Atholl Highlanders**, Britain's only private army.

For a great walk, drive or cycle (it's strenuous!), take the steep, winding road to **Glenfender** and Loch Moraig from Blair Atholl. It's about 3 miles on a long, narrow uphill road to a farmhouse; the view of the peaks Beinn a'Ghlo at the top is spectacular.

Blair Atholl is 6 miles northwest of Pitlochry, and the castle a further mile beyond it. Local buses run between Pitlochry and Blair Atholl (£2, 25 minutes, three to seven daily). Four buses a day (Monday to Saturday) go directly to the castle. There are trains from Perth (£13.20, 40 minutes, nine daily Monday to Saturday, five on Sunday).

Lochs Tummel & Rannoch

The scenic route along Lochs Tummel and Rannoch (www.rannochandtummel.co.uk) is worth doing any way you can – by foot, bicycle or car. Hillsides shrouded with ancient birchwoods and forests of spruce, pine and larch make up the fabulous **Tay Forest Park**. These wooded hills roll into the glittering waters of the lochs; a visit in autumn is recommended, when the birch leaves are at their finest.

The **Queen's View Visitor Centre** (www.forestry.gov.uk; admission free, parking £2; ☉ visitor centre 10am-6pm late Mar-mid-Nov), at the eastern end of Loch Tummel, provides access to a magnificent viewpoint along the loch to the conical peak of **Schiehallion** (1083m). A new cafe and shop was under construction here at the time of research.

Eighteen miles west, the road ends at romantic, isolated **Rannoch Station**, which is on the Glasgow–Fort William railway line. Beyond is desolate, intriguing **Rannoch Moor**. There's a tearoom on the platform, and a welcoming small hotel alongside.

Loch Tay

Loch Tay is the heart of the ancient region known as Breadalbane (from the Gaelic *Bràghad Albainn*, 'the heights of Scotland') – mighty **Ben Lawers** (1214m), looming over the loch, is the highest peak outside the Ben Nevis and Cairngorms regions. Much of the land to the north of Loch Tay falls within the **Ben Lawers National Nature Reserve** (www.nnr-scotland.org.uk/ben-lawers), known for its rare alpine flora. The minor road along the south shore is narrow and twisiting (unsuitable for large vehicles), but offers great views of the hills to the north.

Less than a mile south of Kenmore is the fascinating **Scottish Crannog Centre** (🖉 01887-830583; www.crannog.co.uk; tours adult/child £8/6; ☉ 10am-5.30pm Apr-Oct), perched on stilts above the loch. Crannogs – effectively artificial islands – were a favoured form of defensive dwelling from the 3rd millennium BC onwards. This superb re-creation (based on studies of Oakbank crannog, one of 18 discovered in Loch Tay) offers a guided tour that includes an impressive demonstration of fire making and Iron Age crafts.

The picturesque village of **Kenmore** lies at Loch Tay's eastern end. Dominated by a striking archway leading to Taymouth Castle (not open to the public), it was built by the 3rd Earl of Breadalbane in 1760 to house his estate workers.

The heart of the village, **Kenmore Hotel** (🖉 01887-830205; www.kenmorehotel.com; The Square; r from £89; P @ 🛜 🐾) has a bar with a roaring fire and some scribbled on the chimney piece by Robert Burns in 1787, when the inn was already a couple of centuries old. There's also a riverbank beer garden, great views from the restaurant and a wide range of accommodation. **Culdees Bunkhouse** (✆ 01887-830519; www.culdeesbunkhouse.co.uk; dm/tw/f £18/50/69; P @ 🛜 🐾) is a wonderfully offbeat hostel with majestic vistas: the whole of the loch stretches out below you. It's a fine base for hill walking or for mucking in with the volunteers who help run the sustainable farm here. It's half a mile above the village of Fearnan, 4 miles west of Kenmore.

Glen Lyon

This remote and romantic glen stretches for 34 unforgettable miles of rickety stone bridges, Caledonian pine forest and heather-clad peaks. It becomes wilder and more uninhabited as it snakes its way west, and is proof that hidden treasures still exist. The ancients believed it to be a gateway to Faerieland, and even the most sceptical of visitors will be entranced by the valley's magic.

From the pretty village of Fortingall, a narrow road winds up the glen, while another from Loch Tay crosses the hills to **Bridge of Balgie**, halfway along. The road continues as far as the dam on Loch Lyon, passing a memorial to Robert Campbell (1808–94; a Canadian explorer and fur trader, who was born in the glen). **Cycling** through Glen Lyon is a wonderful way to experience this special place.

There are no villages in the valley – the majestic and lonely scenery is the main reason to be here – just a cluster of houses at Bridge of Balgie, where the **Bridge of Balgie Tearoom** (✆ 01887-866221; Bridge of Balgie; snacks £3-5; ⊙ 10am-5pm Apr-Oct) serves homemade cakes, sandwiches and soups to hungry walkers and cyclists.

Milton Eonan (✆ 01887-866337; www.miltoneonan.com; Bridge of Balgie; per person £43; P 🛜 🐾) is a must for those seeking tranquillity in a glorious natural setting. On a bubbling stream where a watermill once stood, it's a working rare-breed croft with a romantic one-bedroom self-catering cottage (breakfast available) at the bottom of the garden. The lively owners offer packed lunches and evening meals (£20) using local and home-grown produce. It's signposted to the right a short distance beyond Bridge of Balgie, on the road towards Loch Tay. There is no public transport in the glen.

CENTRAL WESTERN HIGHLANDS

This region extends from the bleak blanket-bog of the Moor of Rannoch to the west coast beyond Glen Coe and Fort William, and includes the southern reaches of the Great Glen. The scenery is grand throughout, with high and wild mountains dominating the glens. Expanses of moor alternate with lochs and patches of commercial forest. Fort William, at the inner end of Loch Linnhe, is the only sizeable town in the area.

Since 2007 the region has been promoted as **Lochaber Geopark** (www.lochabergeopark.org.uk), an area of outstanding geology and scenery.

Glen Coe

Scotland's most famous glen is also one of the grandest and, in bad weather, the grimmest. The southern side is dominated by three massive, brooding spurs, known as the **Three Sisters**, while the northern side is enclosed by the continuous steep wall of the knife-edged Aonach Eagach ridge. The main road threads its lonely way through the middle of all this mountain grandeur.

Glencoe village was written into the history books in 1692 when the resident MacDonalds were murdered by Campbell soldiers in what became known as the Glencoe Massacre.

🏃 Activities

There are several short, pleasant walks around **Glencoe Lochan**, near the village. A more strenuous hike, but well worth the effort on a fine day, is the climb to the **Lost Valley**, a magical mountain sanctuary still haunted by the ghosts of the murdered Mac-Donalds (only 2.5 miles round trip, but allow three hours). A rough path from the car park at Allt na Reigh (on the A82, 6 miles east of Glencoe village) climbs up the wooded valley between Beinn Fhada and Gearr Aonach (the first and second of the Three Sisters) before emerging – quite unexpectedly – into a broad, open valley with an 800m-long meadow as flat as a football pitch.

Glencoe Mountain Resort   OUTDOORS
(✆ 01855-851226; www.glencoemountain.com; Kingshouse; ⊙ 9am-8.30pm) A few miles east of Glen Coe proper is the Glencoe Mountain Resort, where commercial skiing in Scotland

first began back in 1956. The **chairlift** (adult/child £10/5; ⊘9am-4.30pm Mon-Fri, 8.30am-4.30pm Sat & Sun) continues to operate in summer – there's a grand view over the Moor of Rannoch from the top – providing access to mountain-biking trails. The **Lodge Café-Bar** has comfy sofas where you can soak up the view through the floor-to-ceiling windows. In winter a lift pass costs £30 a day; equipment hire is £25.

Glencoe Village

POP 360

The little village of Glencoe stands on the south shore of Loch Leven at the western end of the glen, 16 miles south of Fort William.

⊙ Sights

Glencoe Folk Museum　　　　　　MUSEUM
(✆01855-811664; www.glencoemuseum.com; adult/child £3/free; ⊘10am-4.30pm Mon-Sat Easter-Oct) This small, thatched museum houses a varied collection of military memorabilia, farm equipment, and tools of the woodworking, blacksmithing and slate-quarrying trades.

Glencoe Visitor Centre　INTERPRETATION CENTRE
(NTS; ✆01855-811307; www.glencoe-nts.org.uk; adult/child £6.25/5; ⊘9.30am-5.30pm Easter-Oct, 10am-4pm Thu-Sun Nov-Easter; P) ∅ The centre provides comprehensive information on the geological, environmental and cultural history of Glencoe via high-tech interactive and audiovisual displays, charts the history of mountaineering in the glen, and tells the story of the Glencoe Massacre in all its gory detail. It's 1.5 miles east of Glencoe village.

🛏 Sleeping & Eating

Glencoe Independent Hostel　　HOSTEL **£**
(✆01855-811906; www.glencoehostel.co.uk; dm £13-16.50, bunkhouse £12.50-14.50; P@🌐) This handily located hostel, just 1.5 miles southeast of Glencoe village, is set in an old farmhouse with six- and eight-bed dorms, and a bunkhouse with another 16 bed spaces in communal, alpine-style bunks. There's also a cute little wooden cabin that sleeps up to three (£19 to £25 per person).

Clachaig Inn　　　　　　HOTEL **££**
(✆01855-811252; www.clachaig.com; per person from £51; P🌐) The Clachaig has long been a favourite haunt of hill walkers and climbers. As well as comfortable en suite accommodation, there's a smart, wood-panelled lounge bar with lots of sofas and armchairs, moun-

taineering photos, and climbing magazines to leaf through.

Climbers usually head for the lively **Boots Bar** (mains £9-18) on the other side of the hotel – it has log fires, serves real ale and good pub grub (mains £9 to £18), and has live Scottish music on Saturday nights. It's 2 miles southeast of Glencoe village.

❶ Getting There & Away

Scottish Citylink (p903) buses run between Fort William and Glencoe (£7.80, 30 minutes, eight daily) and from Glencoe to Glasgow (£21, 2½ hours, eight daily). Buses stop at Glencoe village, Glencoe Visitor Centre and Glencoe Mountain Resort.

Stagecoach (p899) bus 44 links Glencoe village with Fort William (£3.70, 35 minutes, hourly Monday to Saturday, three on Sunday) and Kinlochleven (£2, 25 minutes).

Kinlochleven

POP 900

Kinlochleven is hemmed in by high mountains at the head of beautiful Loch Leven, about 7 miles east of Glencoe village.

🏃 Activities

The final section of the **West Highland Way** stretches for 14 miles from Kinlochleven to Fort William. The village is also the starting point for easier walks up the glen of the River Leven, through pleasant woods to the Grey Mare's Tail waterfall, and harder mountain hikes into the Mamores.

Ice Factor　　　　ADVENTURE SPORTS
(✆01855-831100; www.ice-factor.co.uk; Leven Rd; ⊘9am-10pm Tue & Thu, to 7pm Mon, Wed & Fri-Sun; 🚼) If you fancy trying your hand at ice-climbing, even in the middle of summer, the world's biggest indoor ice-climbing wall offers a one-hour beginner's 'taster' session for £30. You'll also find a rock-climbing wall, an aerial adventure course, a sauna and steam room, and a cafe and bar-bistro.

🛏 Sleeping & Eating

Blackwater Hostel　HOSTEL, CAMPSITE **£**
(✆01855-831253; www.blackwaterhostel.co.uk; Lab Rd; dm/tw £16.50/40, tent sites per person £7, pods from £35; 🌐) This 40-bed hostel has spotless dorms with en suite bathrooms and TV, and a level, well-sheltered camping ground with the option of wooden 'glamping' pods.

★**Lochleven Seafood Cafe**   SEAFOOD ££
(☑01855-821048;   www.lochlevenseafoodcafe.
co.uk; mains £11-22, whole lobster £40; ☺noon-
3pm & 6-9pm Apr-Oct; ℗) This outstanding
place serves superb shellfish freshly plucked
from live tanks – oysters on the half shell, razor clams, scallops, lobster and crab – plus a
daily fish special and some nonseafood dishes. For warm days, there's an outdoor terrace with a view across the loch to the Pap
of Glencoe, a distinctive conical mountain.

ⓘ Getting There & Away

Stagecoach (p899) bus 44 runs from Fort William to Kinlochleven (£4.70, 50 minutes, hourly
Monday to Saturday, three on Sunday) via Ballachulish and Glencoe village.

Fort William

POP 9900

Basking on the shores of Loch Linnhe amid
magnificent mountain scenery, Fort William
has one of the most enviable settings in Scotland. If it wasn't for the busy dual carriageway
crammed between the town centre and the
loch, and one of the highest rainfall records
in the country, it would be almost idyllic. Even
so, the Fort has carved out a reputation as the
Outdoor Capital of the UK (www.outdoorcapi-
tal.co.uk), and easy access by rail and bus make
it a good place to base yourself for exploring
the surrounding mountains and glens.

Magical **Glen Nevis** begins near the
northern end of the town and wraps itself
around the southern flanks of **Ben Nevis**
(1344m) – Britain's highest mountain and a
magnet for hikers and climbers.

◉ Sights

Jacobite Steam Train   HERITAGE RAILWAY
(☑0844 850 4685; www.westcoastrailways.co.uk;
day return adult/child £34/19; ☺daily Jul & Aug,
Mon-Fri mid-May–Jun, Sep & Oct) The Jacobite
Steam Train, hauled by a former LNER K1 or
LMS Class 5MT locomotive, travels the scenic two-hour run between Fort William and
Mallaig. Classed as one of the great railway
journeys of the world, the route crosses the
historic Glenfinnan Viaduct, made famous in
the Harry Potter films – the Jacobite's owners
supplied the steam locomotive and rolling
stock used in the film.

West Highland Museum   MUSEUM
(☑01397-702169; www.westhighlandmuseum.org.uk;
Cameron Sq; ☺10am-5pm Mon-Sat Apr-Oct, to 4pm

Mar, Nov & Dec, closed Jan & Feb) **FREE** This small
but fascinating museum is packed with all
manner of Highland memorabilia. Look out
for the secret portrait of Bonnie Prince Charlie – after the Jacobite rebellions all things
Highland were banned, including pictures of
the exiled leader, and this tiny painting looks
like nothing more than a smear of paint until
viewed in a cylindrical mirror, which reflects
a credible likeness of the prince.

ⓖ Tours

Crannog Cruises   CRUISE
(☑01397-700714;   www.crannog.net/cruises;
adult/child £14/7; ☺4 daily) Operates 1½-hour
wildlife cruises on Loch Linnhe, visiting a
seal colony and a salmon farm.

⚜ Festivals & Events

**UCI Mountain
Bike World Cup**   MOUNTAIN BIKING
(www.fortwilliamworldcup.co.uk) In June, Fort
William pulls in crowds of more than 18,000
spectators for this World Cup downhill
mountain-biking event. The gruelling downhill course is at nearby Nevis Range ski area.

🛏 Sleeping

It's best to book well ahead in summer, especially for hostels.

Calluna   APARTMENT £
(☑01397-700451;   www.fortwilliamholiday.co.uk;
Heathercroft, Connochie Rd; dm/tw £16/36,
6–8-person apt per week £550; ℗☏) Run by
well-known mountain guide Alan Kimber
and wife Sue, the Calluna offers self-catering
apartments geared to groups of hikers and
climbers, but also takes individual travellers
prepared to share; there's a fully equipped
kitchen and an excellent drying room for
your soggy hiking gear.

Bank Street Lodge   HOSTEL £
(☑01397-700070; www.bankstreetlodge.co.uk; Bank
St; dm/tw from £17/55; ℗) Part of a modern hotel and restaurant complex, the Bank Street
Lodge offers the most central budget beds in
town, only 250m from the train station. It has
kitchen facilities and a drying room.

Fort William Backpackers   HOSTEL £
(☑01397-700711; www.scotlands-top-hostels.com;
Alma Rd; dm/tw £18/47; ℗@☏) A 10-minute
walk from the bus and train stations, this
lively and welcoming hostel is set in a grand
Victorian villa, perched on a hillside with
great views over Loch Linnhe.

CENTRAL & NORTHERN HIGHLANDS & ISLANDS FORT WILLIAM

★**Grange** B&B ££
(☑ 01397-705516; www.grangefortwilliam.com; Grange Rd; r per person £65-70; P🖥) An exceptional 19th-century villa set in its own landscaped grounds, the Grange is crammed with antiques and fitted with log fires, chaise longues and Victorian roll-top baths. The Turret Room, with its window seat in the turret overlooking Loch Linnhe, is our favourite. It's 500m southwest of the town centre. No children.

Lime Tree HOTEL ££
(☑ 01397-701806; www.limetreefortwilliam.co.uk; Achintore Rd; s/d from £100/110; P) Much more interesting than your average guesthouse, this former Victorian manse overlooking Loch Linnhe is an 'art gallery with rooms', decorated throughout with the owner's atmospheric Highland landscapes. Foodies rave about the restaurant, and the gallery space – a triumph of sensitive design – stages everything from serious exhibitions (works by David Hockney and Andy Goldsworthy have appeared) to folk concerts.

St Andrew's Guest House B&B ££
(☑ 01397-703038; www.standrewsguesthouse. co.uk; Fassifern Rd; s/d £55/68; P🖥) Set in a lovely 19th-century building that was once a rectory and choir school, St Andrew's retains period features, such as carved masonry, wood panelling and stained-glass windows. It has six spacious bedrooms; those at the front have stunning views.

Crolinnhe B&B £££
(☑ 01397-703795; www.crolinnhe.co.uk; Grange Rd; r £130-140; Easter-Oct; P) This grand 19th-century villa enjoys a lochside location, beautiful gardens and sumptuous accommodation – a welcome dose of luxury at the end of the West Highland Way. Breakfast porridge comes with cream and a wee jug of whisky!

✗ Eating & Drinking

Sugar and Spice CAFE £
(☑ 01397-705005; 147 High St; mains £8-11; 11am-4pm Mon-Wed, 11am-9pm Thu-Sat; 🖥👶) Enjoy what is probably the best coffee in town at this colourful cafe, just a few paces from the official finishing line of the West Highland Way. In the evening (Thursday to Saturday only) it serves authentic Thai dishes (BYOB).

Crannog Seafood Restaurant SEAFOOD ££
(☑ 01397-705589; www.crannog.net; Town Pier; mains £15-20, 2-course lunches £15; noon-2.30pm & 6-9pm) The Crannog wins the prize for best location in town – perched on the Town Pier, giving window-table diners an uninterrupted view down Loch Linnhe. Informal and unfussy, it specialises in fresh local fish – there are three or four daily fish specials plus the main menu – though there are lamb, venison and vegetarian dishes, too.

★**Lime Tree** SCOTTISH £££
(☑ 01397-701806; www.limetreefortwilliam.co.uk; Achintore Rd; mains £14-23; 6.30-9.30pm; P) Fort William is not over-endowed with great places to eat, but the restaurant at this small hotel and art gallery has put the UK's Outdoor Capital on the gastronomic map. The chef turns out delicious dishes built around fresh Scottish produce, ranging from partan bree (crab soup) to roast cod to venison sausage.

Grog & Gruel PUB
(☑ 01397-705078; www.grogandgruel.co.uk; 66 High St) The Grog & Gruel is a traditional-style, wood-panelled pub with an excellent range of cask ales from regional Scottish and English microbreweries. Bar meals are served from noon to 9pm.

ⓘ Information

Fort William Tourist Office (☑ 01397-703781; www.visithighlands.com; 15 High St; internet per 20min £1; 9am-6pm Mon-Sat, 10am-5pm Sun Apr-Sep, limited hours Oct-Mar) Internet access.

ⓘ Getting There & Away

Both bus and train station are next to the huge Morrisons supermarket, reached from the town centre via an underpass next to the Nevisport shop.

BUS

Scottish Citylink (p903) buses link Fort William with other major towns and cities.

Edinburgh £34, 4½ hours, one daily direct, seven with a change at Glasgow; via Glencoe and Crianlarich
Glasgow £23, three hours, eight daily
Inverness £11.20, two hours, six daily
Oban £9.40, 1½ hours, three daily
Portree £30, three hours, three daily

Shiel Buses (☑ 01397-700700; www.shielbuses.co.uk) service 500 runs to Mallaig (£6.10, 1½ hours, three daily Monday to Friday only) via Glenfinnan (30 minutes) and Arisaig (one hour).

TRAIN

The spectacular West Highland line runs from Glasgow to Mallaig via Fort William. The overnight **Caledonian Sleeper** (www.scotrail.co.uk/sleeper) service connects Fort William and London Euston (from £113 sharing a twin-berth cabin, 13 hours).

There's no direct rail connection between Oban and Fort William – you have to change at Crianlarich, so it's faster to use the bus.

Edinburgh £42, five hours; change at Glasgow's Queen St station

Glasgow £28, 3¾ hours, three daily, two on Sunday

Mallaig £11.80, 1½ hours, four daily, three on Sunday

❶ Getting Around

BIKE

Alpine Bikes (☑ 01397-704008; www.lochaberbikehire.com; 117 High St; ☉ 9am-5.30pm Mon-Sat, 10am-5.30pm Sun) Mountain-bike rental from £20 a day; bikes can be hired here and dropped off in Inverness. Also hires out full-suspension downhill bikes and body armour for use on Nevis Range trails.

BUS

The Fort Dayrider ticket (£3.20) gives unlimited travel for one day on Stagecoach bus services in the Fort William area. Buy from the bus driver.

Around Fort William

Glen Nevis

You can walk the 3 miles from Fort William to scenic Glen Nevis in about an hour or so. The **Glen Nevis Visitor Centre** (☑ 01397-705922; www.bennevisweather.co.uk; ☉ 9am-5pm Apr-Jun, Sep & Oct, 8.30am-6pm Jul & Aug, 9am-3pm Nov-Mar) **FREE** is situated 1.5 miles up the glen, and provides information on walking, weather forecasts, and specific advice on climbing Ben Nevis.

From the car park at the far end of the road along Glen Nevis, there is an excellent 1.5-mile walk through the spectacular Nevis Gorge to **Steall Meadows**, a verdant valley dominated by a 100m-high bridal-veil waterfall. You can reach the foot of the falls by crossing the river on a wobbly, three-cable wire bridge – one cable for your feet and one for each hand – a real test of balance!

🍴 Sleeping & Eating

⭐**Ben Nevis Inn** HOSTEL £
(☑ 01397-701227; www.ben-nevis-inn.co.uk; Achintee; dm £15.50; ☉ noon-11pm daily Apr-Oct, Thu-Sun only Nov-Mar; 🅿) This great barn of a pub serves real ale and tasty bar meals (mains £9 to £15, food served noon to 9pm), and has a

CENTRAL & NORTHERN HIGHLANDS & ISLANDS AROUND FORT WILLIAM

CLIMBING BEN NEVIS

As the highest peak in the British Isles, Ben Nevis (1344m) attracts many would-be ascensionists who would not normally think of climbing a Scottish mountain – a staggering (often literally) 100,000 people reach the summit each year.

Although anyone who is reasonably fit should have no problem hiking to the summit of Ben Nevis on a fine summer's day, an ascent should not be undertaken lightly. Every year people have to be rescued from the mountain. You will need proper walking boots (the path is rough and stony, and there may be soft, wet snowfields on the summit), warm clothing, waterproofs, a map and compass, and plenty of food and water. And don't forget to check the weather forecast (see www.bennevisweather.co.uk).

In thick cloud, visibility at the summit can be 10m or less; and in such conditions the only safe way off the mountain requires careful use of a map and compass to avoid walking over 700m cliffs.

There are three possible starting points for the tourist track (the walkers' route) ascent: Achintee Farm; the footbridge at Glen Nevis Youth Hostel; and the car park at Glen Nevis Visitor Centre. The path climbs gradually to the shoulder at Lochan Meall an t-Suidhe (known as the Halfway Lochan), then zigzags steeply up beside the Red Burn to the summit plateau.

The total distance to the summit and back is 8 miles; allow at least four or five hours to reach the top, and another 2½ to three hours for the descent. Afterwards, as you celebrate in the pub with a pint, consider the fact that the record time for the annual Ben Nevis Hill Race is just under 1½ hours – up *and* down. Then have another pint.

comfy 24-bed bunkhouse downstairs. It's at the start of the path from Achintee up Ben Nevis, and only a mile from the end of the West Highland Way.

Achintee Farm   B&B, HOSTEL £
(☑ 01397-702240; www.achinteefarm.com; Achintee; B&B per person £39-45, hostel £21; P 🛜) This attractive farmhouse offers excellent B&B accommodation and also has a small hostel attached. It's at the start of the path up Ben Nevis.

**Glen Nevis Caravan
& Camping Park**   CAMPSITE £
(☑ 01397-702191; www.glen-nevis.co.uk; tent sites £7.20, incl car £11, campervan £12.10, plus per person £3.50; ☺ mid-Mar–Oct; 🛜) This big, well-equipped site is a popular base camp for Ben Nevis and the surrounding mountains. The site is 2.5 miles from Fort William, along the Glen Nevis road.

❶ Getting There & Away

Bus 41 runs from Fort William bus station to the Glen Nevis SYHA (£2, 15 minutes, two daily year round, five daily Monday to Saturday June to September). Check at the tourist office for the latest timetable, which is subject to alteration.

Nevis Range

🏃 Activities

Nevis Range   OUTDOORS
(☑ 01397-705825; www.nevisrange.co.uk; gondola return trip per adult/child £11.50/6.75; ☺ 10am-5pm summer, 9.30am-dusk winter, closed mid-Nov–mid-Dec) The Nevis Range ski area, 6 miles north of Fort William, spreads across the northern slopes of Aonach Mor (1221m). The gondola that gives access to the bottom of the ski area at 655m operates year-round (15 minutes each way). At the top there's a restaurant and a couple of hiking trails through nearby Leanachan Forest, as well as mountain-biking trails.

**Nevis Range Downhill
& Witch's Trails**   MOUNTAIN BIKING
(☑ 01397-705825; bike.nevisrange.co.uk; multitrip ticket £31, single £13; ☺ 10.15am-3.45pm mid-May–mid-Sep) A world championship downhill mountain-bike trail – for experienced riders only – runs from the Snowgoose restaurant at the Nevis Range ski area to the base station; bikes are carried up on a rack on the gondola cabin. A multitrip ticket gives unlimited up-lift for a day; full-suspension bike hire costs from £40/70 per single run/full day.

Road to the Isles

The 46-mile A830 from Fort William to Mallaig is traditionally known as the Road to the Isles, as it leads to the jumping-off point for ferries to the Small Isles and Skye, itself a stepping stone to the Outer Hebrides.

Glenfinnan

POP 100

Glenfinnan is hallowed ground for fans of Bonnie Prince Charlie; the monument here marks where he raised his Highland army. It is also a place of pilgrimage for steam train enthusiasts and Harry Potter fans – the famous railway viaduct features in the films, and is regularly traversed by the Jacobite Steam Train (p915).

By the monument, the Glenfinnan Visitor Centre recounts the story of the '45, as the Jacobite rebellion of 1745 is known, when the prince's loyal clansmen marched and fought from Glenfinnan south to Derby, then back north to final defeat at Culloden.

A delightful old coaching inn from 1658, the Prince's House is a great place to pamper yourself – ask for the spacious, tartan-clad Stuart Room (£190), complete with four-poster bed, if you want to stay in the oldest part of the hotel. The relaxed but well-regarded restaurant specialises in Scottish produce (four-course dinners £43.50).

Arisaig & Morar

The 5 miles of coast between Arisaig and Morar is a fretwork of rocky islets, inlets and gorgeous silver-sand beaches backed by dunes and machair, with stunning sunset views across the sea to the silhouetted peaks of Eigg and Rum. The Silver Sands of Morar, as they are known, draw crowds of bucket-and-spade holidaymakers in July and August, when the many camping grounds scattered along the coast are filled to overflowing.

Built as a hunting lodge in 1840, Garramore House (☑ 01687-450268; r per person £25-35; P 🐾) served as the headquarters of the Special Operations Executive (SOE, forerunner of MI6) during WWII. Today it's a wonderfully atmospheric, old-fashioned guesthouse set in lovely woodland gardens with resident peacocks and great views to the Small Isles and Skye. Garramore is sign-posted off the coastal road, 4 miles north of Arisaig village.

Mallaig

POP 800

If you're travelling between Fort William and Skye, you may find yourself overnight-ing in the bustling fishing and ferry port of Mallaig (*mahl*-ig). Indeed, it makes a good base for a series of day trips by ferry to the Small Isles and Knoydart.

🛏 Sleeping & Eating

Seaview Guest House B&B ££

(☑ 01687-462059; www.seaviewguesthousemal-laig.com; Main St; r per person £30-38, cottages per week £400-495; ☺ Mar–mid-Nov; ℗) This com-fortable five-bedroom B&B has grand views over the harbour, not only from the upstairs bedrooms but also from the breakfast room. There's also a cute little cottage next door that offers self-catering accommodation (www.selfcateringmallaig.com; one double and one twin room) for a week.

Fish Market Restaurant SEAFOOD ££

(☑ 01687-462299; Station Rd; mains £10-21) 🐟 At least half-a-dozen signs in Mallaig ad-vertise 'seafood restaurant', but this bright, modern, bistro-style place next to the har-bour is our favourite, serving simply pre-pared scallops, smoked salmon, mussels, and fresh Mallaig haddock fried in bread-crumbs, as well as the tastiest Cullen skink on the west coast.

Upstairs is a **coffee shop** (mains £6-7; ☺ 11am-5pm) that serves delicious hot roast-beef rolls with horseradish sauce, and scones with clotted cream and jam.

❶ Getting There & Away

BOAT

Ferries run from Mallaig to Skye and South Uist among other places. See the relevant sections for details.

BUS

Shiel Buses (☑ 01397-700700; www.shielbus-es.co.uk) bus 500 runs from Fort William to Mallaig (£6.10, 1½ hours, three daily Monday to Friday, one on Saturday) via Glenfinnan (30 minutes) and Arisaig (one hour).

TRAIN

The West Highland line runs between Fort Wil-liam and Mallaig (£11.10, 1½ hours) four times a day (three on Sunday).

NORTHEAST COAST

The east coast landscapes of the old coun-ties of Ross and Sutherland unfold real wil-derness and Highland character. While the interior is dominated by mournful moor landscapes, along the coast great heath-er-covered hills heave themselves out of the wild North Sea. Rolling farmland drops suddenly into icy waters, and small, historic towns are moored precariously alongside.

Tain

POP 3700

Scotland's oldest royal burgh, Tain is a proud sandstone town that rose to prominence as pilgrims descended to venerate the relics of St Duthac, who is commemorated by the 12th-century ruins of **St Duthac's Chapel**, and St Duthus Church.

🅞 Sights

Tain Through Time MUSEUM

(☑ 01862-894089; www.tainmuseum.org.uk; Tow-er St; adult/child £3.50/2.50; ☺ 10am-5pm Mon-Fri Apr-Oct, also Sat Jun-Aug) Set in the grounds of **St Duthus Church** is Tain Through Time, an entertaining heritage centre with a col-ourful and educational display on St Duthac, King James IV and key moments in Scottish history. Another building focuses on the town's fine silversmithing tradition. Admis-sion includes an audioguided walk around town.

Glenmorangie DISTILLERY

(www.glenmorangie.com; tours £5; ☺ 10am-5pm Mon-Fri, plus 10am-4pm Sat & noon-4pm Sun Jun-Aug) Located on Tain's northern outskirts, Glenmorangie (emphasis on the second syllable) produces a fine lightish malt, sub-jected to a number of different cask finishes for variation. The tour is less in-depth than some, but finishes with a free dram. A spe-cial tour is £30.

🛏 Sleeping & Eating

Golf View House B&B ££

(☑ 01862-892856; www.bedandbreakfasttain.co.uk; 13 Knockbreck Rd; s/d £60/85; ℗ 🛜) Set in an old manse in a secluded location just off the main drag, this spot offers magnifi-cent views over fields and water. Impecca-ble rooms are very cheerful and bright, and there's an upbeat feel, with delicious break-fasts and welcoming hospitality. It's worth the extra for a room with a view.

ⓘ Getting There & Away

Stagecoach (www.stagecoachbus.com) buses run from Inverness (£9.70, 50 minutes, roughly hourly); some continue north as far as Thurso.

Trains run daily to Inverness (£13.50, 1¼ hours) and Thurso (£16.50, 2¾ hours).

Portmahomack

Portmahomack is a former fishing village in a flawless spot – off the beaten track, gazing across the water at sometimes snowcapped peaks. Intriguing **Tarbat Discovery Centre** (☑01862-871351; www. tarbat-discovery.co.uk; Tarbatness Rd; adult/child £3.50/1; ☺10am-5pm Mon-Sat May-Sep, 2-5pm Mon-Sat Apr & Oct, plus 2-5pm Sun Jun-Oct) has great carved Pictish stones. The foundations of an Iron Age settlement were discovered around the village church; ongoing investigation revealed a Pictish monastery with evidence of manuscript production. The exhibition is excellent and includes the church's spooky crypt.

Seafood aficionados shouldn't miss bright and cheerful **Oystercatcher Restaurant** (☑01862-871560; www.the-oystercatcher.co.uk; Main St; lunch mains £8-14, dinner £15-20; ☺12.15-2.45pm Thu-Sun, plus 6.30-8.30pm Wed-Sat Mar-Oct; ℙ 중 ♿). A lunchtime bistro menu lets you choose your serving size, and a classy brasserie evening menu includes lots of lobster among other temptations. Fourteen-course tasting menus (£60) are a delight, with invention and quality given levity by the whimsical dish names. It also offers three cosy rooms (singles/doubles £52/108). Rates include what has to be Scotland's most amazing breakfast, with numerous gourmet options.

Stagecoach (www.stagecoachbus.com) runs from Tain to Portmahomack (£1.95, 25 minutes, four to five Monday to Friday).

Dornoch

POP 1200

On the north shore of Dornoch Firth, two miles off the A9, this attractive old market town is one of the east coast's most pleasant settlements. Dornoch is best known for its championship **golf course**, but there's a fine cathedral among other noble buildings. Other historical oddities: the last witch to be executed in Scotland was boiled alive in hot tar here in 1722 and Madonna married Guy Ritchie here in 2000.

⊙ Sights & Activities

Have a walk along Dornoch's golden-sand **beach**, which stretches for miles. South of Dornoch, **seals** are often visible on the sandbars of Dornoch Firth.

Dornoch Cathedral   CHURCH
(www.dornoch-cathedral.com; St Gilbert St; ☺9am-7pm or later) **FREE** Consecrated in the 13th century, Dornoch Cathedral is an elegant Gothic edifice with an interior softly illuminated through modern stained-glass windows. The controversial first Duke of Sutherland, whose wife restored the church in the 1830s – lies in a sealed burial vault beneath the chancel.

Royal Dornoch   GOLF
(☑01862-810219; www.royaldornoch.com; Golf Rd, Dornoch; summer green fee £120) One of Scotland's most famous links, described by Tom Watson as 'the most fun I have ever had on a golf course'. It's public, and you can book a slot online. Twilight rates are the most economical. A golf pass (www.dornochfirthgolf. co.uk) lets you play several courses in the area at a good discount.

🛏 Sleeping & Eating

★**Dornoch Castle Hotel**   HOTEL ££
(☑01862-810216; www.dornochcastlehotel.com; Castle St; s/d £73/125, superior/deluxe d £169/250; ℙ 중) This 16th-century former bishop's palace makes a wonderful place to stay, particularly if you upgrade to one of the superior rooms, which have views, space, whisky and chocolates on the welcome trays and (in some) a four-poster bed; the deluxe rooms are unforgettable. Cheaper rooms (singles/ doubles £50/65), simpler, without the historic atmosphere, are also available in adjoining buildings.

ⓘ Information

Tourist Office (☑01862-810594; Castle St; ☺9am-12.30pm & 1.30-4pm Mon-Fri, plus 10am-4pm Sat May-Aug & 10am-4pm Sun Jul & Aug) In the council building alongside Dornoch Castle Hotel.

ⓘ Getting There & Away

There are buses roughly hourly from Inverness (£10.20, 1¼ hours), with some services continuing north to Wick or Thurso.

Dunrobin Castle

Magnificent **Dunrobin Castle** (✆01408-633177; www.dunrobincastle.co.uk; adult/child £10.50/5.75; ◷10.30am-4.30pm Mon-Sat & noon-4.30pm Sun Apr, May & Sep–mid-Oct, 10am-5pm daliy Jun & Aug), a mile past Golspie, is the Highlands' largest house. Although it dates to 1275, most of what you see was built in French style between 1845 and 1850. A home of the dukes of Sutherland, it's richly furnished and offers an intriguing insight into the aristocratic lifestyle. The beautiful castle inspires mixed feelings locally; it was once the seat of the first Duke of Sutherland, notorious for some of the cruellest episodes of the Highland Clearances.

This classic fairy-tale castle is adorned with towers and turrets, but only 22 of its 187 rooms are on display, with hunting trophies much to the fore. Beautiful gardens, where impressive falconry displays take place two or three times a day, extend down to the sea. In the gardens is a museum with an eclectic mix of archaeological finds, natural-history exhibits, more un-PC animal remains and an excellent collection of Pictish stones.

Both trains (£18.20, 2¼ hours, two or three daily) and buses (£11.60, 1½ hours) between Inverness and Wick/Thurso stop in Golspie, a mile south, and at Dunrobin Castle.

Helmsdale

POP 700

Surrounded by breathtaking coastline and gorse-covered hills that explode mad-yellow in spring, this sheltered fishing town, like many on this coast, was a major emigration point during the Clearances and a booming herring port.

Timespan Heritage Centre (www.timespan.org.uk; Dunrobin St; adult/child £4/2; ◷10am-5pm Easter-Oct, 10am-3pm Sat & Sun & 2-4pm Tue Nov-Easter) has an impressive display covering local history (including the 1869 gold rush) and Barbara Cartland, queen of romance novels, who was a Helmsdale regular. There are also local art exhibitions, a geology garden and a cafe.

🛏 Sleeping & Eating

Helmsdale Hostel   HOSTEL £
(✆07971-516287, 01431-821636; www.helmsdale-hostel.co.uk; Stafford St; dm/tw/f £19/45/60;

◷Apr-Sep; 🛜🐕) This caringly run hostel is in very good nick, well-equipped and spotlessly clean; it makes a cheerful, comfortable budget base for exploring Caithness. Dorms have mostly cosy single beds rather than bunks, and en suite rooms are great for families. The lofty central space has a lounge with wood stove and good kitchen.

La Mirage   BISTRO £
(✆01431-821615; www.lamirage.org; 7 Dunrobin St; mains £7-12; ◷11am-8.45pm Mon-Sat, noon-8.45pm Sun; 🛜) Created in homage to Barbara Cartland, this is a '70s throwback with pink walls, kitschy installations and a retro menu. Meals aren't gourmet – think chicken Kiev – but portions are huge. Fish and chips are also available takeaway; eat 'em by the pretty harbour.

ℹ Getting There & Away

Buses from Inverness (£11.60, 1¾ hours) and Thurso stop in Helmsdale, as do trains (from Inverness £18.20, 2½ hours, two to three daily).

CAITHNESS

Once you pass Helmsdale, you are entering Caithness, a place of jagged gorse-and-grass-topped cliffs hiding tiny fishing harbours. Scotland's top corner was once Viking territory, historically more connected to Orkney and Shetland than the rest of the mainland. It's a mystical, ancient land peopled by wise folk with long memories who are fiercely proud of their Norse heritage.

Lybster & Around

Lybster is a purpose-built fishing village dating from 1810, with a stunning harbour area surrounded by grassy cliffs. In its heyday, it was Scotland's third busiest port.

There are several interesting prehistoric sites nearby.

⊙ Sights & Activities

Achavanich Stone Setting   HISTORIC SITE
Six miles to the northwest of Lybster and a mile off the A9, these 30 standing stones date from around 2000 BC. These crumbling monuments of the distant past still capture the imagination with their desolate location. Nearby are the remains of a burial cairn, another millennium older.

Grey Cairns of Camster   HISTORIC SITE

Dating from between 4000 BC and 2500 BC, these burial chambers are hidden in long, low mounds rising from an evocatively lonely moor. The **Long Cairn** measures 60m by 21m. You can enter the main chamber, but must first crawl into the well-preserved **Round Cairn**, which has a corbelled ceiling.

From a turn-off a mile east of Lybster on the A99, the cairns are 4 miles north. You can continue a further 7 miles to approach Wick on the A882.

Hill o'Many Stanes   HISTORIC SITE

Two miles beyond the Camster turn-off on the A99 is a curious, fan-shaped arrangement of 22 rows of small stones, probably from around 2000 BC. Staggeringly, there were 600 in the original pattern. On a sunny day, the views from this hill are stunning.

Wick

POP 7200

More gritty than pretty, Wick has been down on its luck since the collapse of the herring industry. It was once the world's largest fishing port for the 'silver darlings', but when the market dropped off after WWII, job losses were huge and the town hasn't totally recovered. It's worth a visit though, particularly for its excellent museum and attractive, spruced-up harbour area.

◉ Sights & Activities

★ **Wick Heritage Centre**   MUSEUM

(☑ 01955-605393; www.wickheritage.org; 20 Bank Row; adult/child £4/50p; ⊙ 10am-5pm Apr-Oct, last entry 3.45pm) Tracking the rise and fall of the herring industry, this great town museum displays everything from fishing equipment to complete herring boats. It's absolutely huge inside, and is crammed with memorabilia and extensive displays describing Wick's heyday in the mid-19th century.

The Johnston collection is the star exhibit. From 1863 to 1977, three generations photographed everything that happened around Wick; the 70,000 photographs are an amazing record.

⊨ Sleeping & Eating

Mackays Hotel   HOTEL **££**

(☑ 01955-602323; www.mackayshotel.co.uk; Union St; s/d £89/119; ☎) Hospitable Mackays is Wick's best hotel by a long stretch. Attrac-

tive, mostly refurbished rooms vary in layout and size, so ask to see a few; prices are usually lower than these rack rates. On-site **No 1 Bistro** (Union St; mains £11-17; ⊙ noon-2pm & 5-9pm; ☎) is a fine option for lunch or dinner. The world's shortest street, 2.06m-long Ebenezer Place, is one side of the hotel.

Bord de l'Eau   FRENCH **££**

(☑ 01955-604400; 2 Market St; mains £14-19; ⊙ noon-2.30pm & 6-9pm Tue-Sat, 6-9pm Sun) This serene, relaxed French restaurant is Wick's best place to eat. It overlooks the river and serves a changing menu of mostly meat-and-game French classics, backed up by daily fish specials. Starters are great value, and mains include a huge assortment of vegetables, so you won't go hungry. The conservatory dining room with water views is lovely on a sunny evening.

❶ Information

Wick Information Centre (☑ 01955-602547; www.visithighlands.com; 66 High St; ⊙ 9am-5.30pm Mon-Sat) Good selection of information; upstairs in McAllans Clothing Store.

❶ Getting There & Away

Wick is a Caithness transport gateway. **Flybe/Loganair** (☑ 0871 700 2000; www.flybe.com) flies from Edinburgh; **Eastern Airways** (☑ 0870 366 9100; www.easternairways.com) from Aberdeen.

Stagecoach (p920) and **Citylink** (www.citylink.co.uk) operate to/from Inverness (£19, three hours, six daily) and Stagecoach to Thurso (£3.30, 35 minutes, hourly). There's also connecting service to John O'Groats and Gills Bay (£3.30, 40 minutes, two to three daily) for the passenger and car ferries to Orkney.

Trains service Wick from Inverness (£19.30, 4¼ hours, four daily).

John O'Groats

POP 300

Though not the northernmost point of the British mainland (that's Dunnet Head), John O'Groats still serves as the end point of the 874-mile trek from Land's End in Cornwall, a popular if arduous route for cyclists and walkers, many of whom raise money for charitable causes. There's a passenger ferry from here to Orkney. Most of the settlement is taken up by a stylish modern self-catering complex, which has given a dose of new life to the once-tawdry locale.

◎ Sights & Activities

Ninety-minute wildlife cruises to the island of Stroma or Duncansby Head cost £18 (late June to August).

Duncansby Head   LOOKOUT
Two miles east, Duncansby Head has a small lighthouse and 60m-high cliffs sheltering nesting fulmars. A 15-minute walk through a sheep paddock yields spectacular views of the sea-surrounded monoliths known as Duncansby Stacks.

⟁ Sleeping & Eating

Natural Retreats   SELF-CATERING ££
(☑ 0844 384-3166; www.naturalretreats.com; apt £125-250; P ⟐ 🐾) Nearly all of John O'Groats is now taken up by this company, which has erected a series of modern wooden holiday chalets offering spectacular views, and transformed the old hotel – with the addition of some eye-catchingly colourful giant Scandi-modern 'fish warehouses' – into self-catering apartments. All are stylish and well-equipped. Minimum two-night stay.

Storehouse   CAFE £
(www.naturalretreats.com; light meals £5-10; ⊙ 8am-5pm; ⟐) The best of the eating options, this modern cafe does pizzas, panini, sandwiches on tasty thick-cut bread, and deli platters with Arran cheeses and local smoked salmon.

❶ Getting There & Away

Stagecoach (p920) runs between John O'Groats and Wick (£3.30, 40 minutes, two to three daily) or Thurso (£4, 40 minutes, regular Monday to Saturday).

From May to September, a passenger ferry (p946) shuttles across to Burwick in Orkney. Three miles west, a car ferry (p946) runs from Gills Bay to St Margaret's Hope in Orkney.

Mey

The Castle of Mey (www.castleofmey.org.uk; adult/child £11/6.50; ⊙ 10.20am-5pm May-Sep, last admission 4pm), a big crowd-puller for its Queen Mother connections, is 6 miles west of John O'Groats. The exterior is grand, but inside it feels domestic and everything is imbued with the Queen Mum's character. The highlight is the genteel guided tour, with various anecdotes recounted by staff who once worked for her. In the grounds there's a farm zoo, an unusual walled garden that's worth

a stroll, and lovely views over the Pentland Firth. The castle normally closes for a couple of weeks at the end of July for royal visits.

Just off the main road nearby, Mey House (☑ 01847-851852; www.meyhouse.co.uk; East Mey; r £100-120; ⊙ Easter-Oct; P ⟐) is beautifully situated among green fields running down to the water with majestic views of Orkney and Dunnet Head. This modern top-drawer sleep is a welcoming, sumptuous place to stay. They've thought it all through: huge, luxurious rooms have arty designer decor, excellent custom-made beds, Nespresso machines, big flatscreens, sound bar and stunning modern bathrooms with shower and tub. There's fast satellite wi-fi and transfers: free for nearby ferries and inexpensive for Wick or Thurso. No toddlers are allowed, as there's an interior balcony.

Dunnet Head

Eight miles east of Thurso a minor road leads to dramatic Dunnet Head, the **most northerly point on the British mainland**. There are majestic cliffs dropping into the turbulent Pentland Firth, inspiring views of Orkney, basking seals and nesting seabirds below, and a lighthouse built by Robert Louis Stevenson's grandad.

Just west, **Dunnet Bay** offers one of Scotland's finest beaches, backed by high dunes.

Thurso & Scrabster
POP 7900

Britain's most northerly mainland town, Thurso makes a handy overnight stop if you're heading west or across to Orkney. There's a pretty town beach, riverbank strolls and a good museum. Ferries for Orkney leave from Scrabster, 2.5 miles away.

◎ Sights

Caithness Horizons   MUSEUM
(www.caithnesshorizons.co.uk; High St; ⊙ 10am-6pm Mon-Sat, also 11am-4pm Sun Apr-Sep) FREE
This museum brings Caithness history and lore to life through excellent displays. Fine Pictish cross-slabs greet the visitor downstairs; the main exhibition is a wide-ranging look at local history using plenty of audiovisuals – check out the wistful account of the now-abandoned island of Stroma. There's also a gallery space, an exhibition on the Dounreay nuclear reactor, tourist information and a cafe.

🛏 Sleeping

Sandra's Hostel HOSTEL **£**
(☑ 01847-894575; www.sandras-backpackers.co.uk;
24 Princes St; dm/d/f £16/38/60; 🅿 @ 🛜) In the
heart of town above a chip shop, this budget
backpacker option offers en suite dorms,
mostly four-berthers with elderly mattresses, a spacious kitchen and traveller-friendly
facilities such as internet and help-yourself
cereals and toast. It's not luxurious but it's a
reliable cheap sleep.

⭐ **Pennyland House** B&B **££**
(☑ 01847-891194; www.pennylandhouse.co.uk;
s/d/tr £60/80/90; 🅿 🛜 🐾) A super conversion of an historic house, this is a standout
B&B choice. It offers phenomenal value for
this level of accommodation, with huge oak-
furnished rooms named after golf courses.
We especially loved St Andrews: super-
spacious, with a great chessboard-tiled bathroom. Hospitality is enthusiastic and helpful,
and there's an inviting breakfast space, garden and terraced area with views across to
Hoy. Two-night minimum stay in summer.

Marine B&B **££**
(☑ 01847-890676; www.themarinethurso.co.uk; 38
Shore St, Thurso; s £75, d £90-99; 🅿 🛜) Tucked
away in Thurso's most appealing corner
you'll find a top spot right by the pretty town
beach, offering spectacular vistas over it
and across to Orkney. Surfers can study the
breakers from the stunning conservatory-
lounge, and rooms are just fabulous, with a
designer's touch and a subtle maritime feel.
Two rooms in the adjacent house make a
great family option.

🍴 Eating

Holborn Hotel BISTRO **££**
(☑ 01847-892771; www.holbornhotel.co.uk; 16 Princes St; bar meals £8-11, ⊙ noon-2pm & 6-8pm or 9pm;
🛜) A trendy, comfortable place decked out in
light wood, the Holborn contrasts starkly with
more traditional Thurso watering holes. In
the bar, uncomplicated but decent meals are
available, while quality seafood – including
delicious home-smoked salmon – is the mainstay of a short but solid menu fleshed out by
specials at **Red Pepper restaurant** (mains £13-
20), where desserts are excellent too. Service
can be slow when busy.

⭐ **Captain's Galley** SEAFOOD **£££**
(☑ 01847-894999; www.captainsgalley.co.uk; Scrabster; 5-course dinner £49; ⊙ 7-9pm Tue-Sat) 🍃 By
the Scrabster ferry, this is classy but friendly,

offering a short, seafood-based menu featuring local and sustainably-sourced produce
prepared in relatively simple ways, letting
natural flavours shine through. The chef
picks the best fish off the local boats, and
the menu describes exactly which fishing
grounds your morsel came from. Cheaper,
quality fish 'n' chips are also available to take
away from 4.30pm until 6.30pm.

ℹ Information

Thurso Information Centre (☑ 01847-893155;
www.visithighlands.com; High St; ⊙ 10am-6pm
Mon-Sat, plus 11am-4pm Sun Apr-Sep) In the
Caithness Horizons museum.

ℹ Getting There & Around

It's a 2-mile walk from Thurso train station to the
ferry at Scrabster; there are buses from Olrig St.

BUS

From Inverness, Stagecoach/Citylink run to
Thurso/Scrabster (£19, three hours, five
daily). There are buses roughly hourly to Wick,
as well as every couple of hours to John
O'Groats (£4, 40 minutes, Monday to Saturday).
There's one bus on Tuesday and Friday west-
wards to Tongue via Bettyhill; it also runs some
Saturdays.

TRAIN

There are four daily trains from Inverness
(£19.30, 3¾ hours), with connecting bus to
Scrabster.

NORTH & NORTHWEST COAST

Quintessential wilderness such as this,
marked by single-track roads, breathtaking
emptiness and a wild, fragile beauty, is a rarity on the modern, crowded, highly urban-
ised island of Britain. The scenic majesty is
never forgotten.

Thurso to Durness

It's 80 winding, and often spectacular, coastal miles from Thurso to Durness.

Bettyhill

POP 500

Bettyhill is a crofting community of resettled
tenant farmers kicked off their land during
the Clearances; the spectacular panorama
of a sweeping, sandy beach backed by vel-

vety green hills with rocky outcrops makes a sharp contrast to that sad history.

Strathnaver Museum (☏01641-521418; www.strathnavermuseum.org.uk; adult/child £2/1; ⏰10am-5pm Mon-Sat Apr-Oct), housed in an old church, tells the story of the Strathnaver Clearances through posters written by local kids. The museum contains Clan Mackay memorabilia, crofting equipment and a boat-shaped container that was used by St Kildans to send messages to the mainland. Outside the back door is the **Farr Stone**, a fine carved Pictish cross-slab.

A good B&B option is **Farr Cottage** (☏01641-521755; www.bettyhillbedandbreakfast.co.uk; Farr; s/d £40/64; 🅿🐶), a welcoming white bungalow amid the bleating of sheep and beautiful scenery a mile off the main road (follow signs to Farr). Rooms are modern and compact, with sparkling bathrooms. Good dinners (£16 for two courses) as well as packed lunches are available.

An extraordinary place to eat, **Côte du Nord** (☏01641-521773; www.cotedunord.co.uk; The School House, Kirtomy; degustation £39; ⏰7-9pm Wed, Fri & Sat Apr-Oct) 🍃 is in the nearby village of Kintory. Brilliantly innovative cuisine, local ingredients and wonderfully whimsical presentation are the highlights of the excellent degustation menu here. It's an unlikely spot to find such a gourmet experience and the chef is none other than the local GP who forages for wild herbs and flavours in between patients. Top value. It's tiny, so reserve well ahead.

Bettyhill tourist office (☏01641-521244; www.visithighlands.com; ⏰10.45am-4.30pm Mon-Thu, to 4pm Fri, 11am-4pm Sat) has information on the area and the **cafe** (☏01641-521244; mains £5-9; ⏰10.30am-4pm Mon-Thu, 10.30am-4pm & 5-7.30pm Fri, 11am-4pm & 5-7.30pm Sat) here serves home baking and light meals.

Coldbackie & Tongue
POP 500

Coldbackie has outstanding views over sandy beaches, turquoise waters and offshore islands. Two miles further is Tongue, with the evocative 14th-century ruins of **Castle Varrich**, once a Mackay stronghold. To get to the castle, take the trail next to the Royal Bank of Scotland – it's an easy stroll.

CROFTING & THE CLEARANCES

The wild empty spaces up here are among Europe's least populated zones, but this wasn't always so. Ruins of cottages in desolate areas are mute witnesses to one of the most heartless episodes of Scottish history: the Highland Clearances.

Until the 19th century the most common form of farming settlement here was the *baile*, a group of a dozen or so families who farmed the land granted to them by the local chieftain in return for military service and a portion of the harvest. The arable land was divided into strips called *rigs,* which were allocated to different families by annual ballot so that each took turns at getting the poorer soils; this system was known as *runrig.* The families worked the land communally and their cattle shared grazing land.

After Culloden, however, the king banned private armies and new laws made the clan chiefs actual owners of their traditional lands, often vast tracts of territory. With the prospect of unimagined riches allied to a depressing failure of imagination, the lairds decided that sheep were more profitable than agriculture and proceeded to evict tens of thousands of farmers. These desperate folk were forced to head for the cities in the hope of finding work or to emigrate to the Americas or southern hemisphere. Those who stayed were forced to eke a living from narrow plots of marginal agricultural land, often close to the coast. This form of smallholding became known as crofting. The small patch of land barely provided a living and had to be supplemented by other work such as fishing and kelp-gathering. It was always precarious, as rights were granted on a year-by-year basis, so at any moment a crofter could lose not only the farm but also the house they'd built on it.

The late 19th-century economic depression meant many couldn't pay their rent. This time, however, they resisted expulsion, instead forming the Highland Land Reform Association and their own political party. Their resistance led the government to accede to several demands, including security of tenure, fair rents and eventually the supply of land for new crofts. Crofters now have the right to purchase their farmland and 2004 laws finally abolished the feudal system, which created so much misery.

🛏 Sleeping & Eating

Kyle of Tongue

Hostel & Holiday Park   HOSTEL, CAMPSITE £
(📞01847-611789; www.tonguehostelandholiday-
park.co.uk; dm £18, d £42-50; P 🛜) In a wonderful spot right by the causeway across the
Kyle of Tongue, a mile west of town, this
is the top budget option in the area, with
clean, spacious dorms, great family rooms,
views, a decent kitchen and a cosy lounge.
It's bright and helpful, and there's bikeshed
as well as camping (£7 per person).

Tongue Hotel   HOTEL ££
(📞01847-611206; www.tonguehotel.co.uk; s/d
£75/110, superior d £130; P 🛜) A stalwart of the
north coast, this former hunting lodge is offers attractive, roomy chambers, including
plush superiors with top views, and classic
standards, some with recently renovated
bathrooms. It has a restaurant, plus bar meals
in the snug Brass Tap basement bar, a good
spot to chat with locals. Food is served noon
to 2pm and 6pm to 9pm.

Tigh-nan-Ubhal   B&B ££
(📞01847-611281; www.tigh-nan-ubhal.com; Main
St; d £60-70; P 🛜 🐾) In the middle of Tongue
and within stumbling distance of two pubs,
is this charming B&B. There are snug, loft-
style rooms with plenty of natural light, but
the basement double with spa is the pick of
the bunch – it's the biggest en suite we've
seen in northern Scotland. There's also a
caravan in the garden and a cheaper room
(£50) that shares a bathroom.

Craggan Hotel   SCOTTISH ££
(📞01847-601278; www.thecraggan.co.uk; Talmine;
mains £10-21; ⊙11am-9.15pm) On the side road
to Melness, across the causeway from Tongue
village, the Craggan Hotel doesn't look much
from outside, but go in and you'll find smart,
formal service and a menu ranging from
exquisite burgers to classy game and local
scallops, crab and langoustines, presented
beautifully. It also does pizzas and curries to
take away and the wine list's not bad either.

Durness

POP 400

Scattered Durness (www.durness.org) is wonderfully located, strung out along cliffs rising
from a series of pristine beaches. When the
sun shines, the effects of blinding white sand,
the cry of seabirds and the spring-green-
coloured seas combine in a magical way.

There are shops, an ATM, petrol and plenty of accommodation options.

⊙ Sights & Activities

Walking around the sensational sandy coastline is a highlight, as is a visit to Cape Wrath.
Durness' beautiful **beaches** include Ris-
pond to the east, Sango Sands below town
and Balnakeil to the west. At **Balnakeil**, less
than a mile beyond Durness, a craft village
occupies a onetime early-warning radar station. A walk along the beach to the north
leads to **Faraid Head**, where you can see
puffin colonies in early summer. You can
hire bikes from a shed on the square.

Smoo Cave   CAVE
(www.smoocave.org) A mile east of the centre
is a path down to Smoo Cave. From the vast
main chamber, you can head through to a
smaller flooded cavern, where a waterfall
sometimes cascades from the roof. There's
evidence the cave was inhabited about 6000
years ago. You can take a **boat trip** (📞01971-
511704; adult/child £4/2; ⊙11am-4pm Apr, May &
Sep, 10am-5pm Jun-Aug) to explore a little further into the interior.

🛏 Sleeping & Eating

Lazy Crofter Bunkhouse   HOSTEL £
(📞01971-511202; www.durnesshostel.com; dm
£17.50; 🛜) Durness' best budget accommodation is here, opposite the supermarket.
A bothy vibe gives it a very Highland feel.
Inviting dorms have plenty of room and
lockers, and there's also a sociable shared table for meals and board games, and a great
wooden deck with sea views, perfect for
midge-free evenings.

Sango Sands Oasis   CAMPSITE £
(📞01971-511222; www.sangosands.com; sites per
adult/child £7/5; P 🐾) You couldn't imagine a
better location for a campsite: great grassy
areas on the edge of cliffs, descending to two
lovely sandy beaches. Facilities are good and
very clean, and there's a pub next door. Electric hookup is an extra £4. You can camp
free from November to March, but don't
complain about the cold.

★Mackays Rooms   HOTEL ££
(📞01971-511202; www.visitdurness.com; standard/
deluxe d £125/139; ⊙Easter-Oct; P 🛜 🐾) You really feel you're at the furthest corner of Scotland here, where the road turns through 90
degrees. But whether heading south or east,
you'll go far before you find a better place to

stay than this haven of Highland hospitality. With big beds, contemporary colours and soft fabrics, it's a romantic spot with top service and numerous boutique details.

Smoo Cave Hotel PUB FOOD **££**
(www.smoocavehotel.co.uk; mains £9-15; ⊘food 11.30am-9.30pm; ☏) Signposted off the main road at the eastern end of town, this amiable local offers quality bar food in hefty portions. Haddock or daily seafood specials are an obvious and worthwhile choice; there's also a restaurant area with clifftop views.

❶ Information

Durness Information Centre (☑ 01971-511368; www.visithighlands.com; ⊘10am-4.30pm Mon-Sat & 10am-3pm Sun Easter-Jun & Sep, 9.30am-5.30pm Mon-Sat & 10am-4pm Sun Jul & Aug, 10am-4.30pm Mon-Sat Oct) Very helpful. Phone for possible winter opening.

❶ Getting There & Away

From mid-May to mid-September, one **bus** (☑ 01463-222444; www.decoaches.co.uk; ⊘mid-May–mid-Sep) runs Monday to Saturday from Durness to Inverness (£16.70) via Ullapool (£12.50). You can take bikes (£6), but they must be booked ahead (office hours). Another, year-round **bus** (☑ 07782 110007; www.thedurnessbus.com) heads daily Monday to Saturday to Lairg (£7.85), which has a train station. On Saturday a bus heads to either Inverness or Thurso.

Durness to Ullapool

Perhaps Scotland's most spectacular road, the 69 miles connecting Durness to Ullapool is a smorgasbord of dramatic scenery, almost too much to take in. From Durness you pass through a broad heathered valley with the looming grey bulk of Foinaven and Arkle to the southeast. Heather gives way to a rockier landscape of Lewisian gneiss pockmarked with hundreds of small lochans, and gorse-covered hills prefacing the magnificent Torridonian sandstone mountains of Assynt and Coigach, including Suilven's distinctive sugarloaf, ziggurat-like Quinag and pinnacled Stac Pollaidh. The area has been named **Northwest Highlands Geopark** (www.nwhgeopark.com).

Kylesku & Loch Glencoul

Hidden away on the shores of Loch Glencoul, tiny Kylesku offers **cruises** (☑ 01971-502239; www.rachaelclare.com; adult/child £25/18; ⊘mid-May–Sep) out to see local seal colonies and the 213m drop of **Eas a'Chual Aulin**, Britain's highest waterfall.

Run with pride and enthusiasm, the **Kylesku Hotel** (☑ 01971-502231; www.kyleskuhotel.co.uk; s/d from £55/80; ℗) is a great place to stay, or to gorge yourself on delicious sustainable seafood in the convivial bar (food served noon to 9pm, mains £10 to £19). Local langoustines and mussels are a speciality. There's a variety of rooms; the small extra charge for loch views is well worthwhile.

Lochinver & Assynt

With its otherworldly scenery of isolated peaks rising above a sea of crumpled, lochan-spattered gneiss, Assynt epitomises the northwest's wild magnificence. Glaciers have sculpted the hills of Suilven (731m), Canisp (846m), Quinag (808m) and Ben More Assynt (998m) into strange, wonderful silhouettes.

WORTH A TRIP

CAPE WRATH

Though its name actually comes from the Norse word for 'turning point', there is something daunting and primal about Cape Wrath, the remote northwestern point of the British mainland, crowned by a Stevenson lighthouse and close to the seabird colonies of **Clo Mor**, Britain's highest coastal cliffs. Getting to Cape Wrath involves a **boat ride** (☑ 01971-511284; www.capewrathferry.co.uk; single/return £4/6; ⊘Easter-Oct) – passengers and bikes only – across the Kyle of Durness (10 minutes), connecting with a **minibus** (☑ 01971-511284; www.visitcapewrath.com; single/return £7/12; ⊘Easter-Oct) running 11 miles to the cape (40 minutes). This combination is a friendly but eccentric, sometimes shambolic service with limited capacity, so plan on waiting in high season, and ring beforehand to make sure the ferry is running. The ferry leaves from two miles southwest of Durness, and runs twice or more daily from April to September. If you eschew the minibus, it's a spectacular 11-mile ride or hike from boat to cape over bleak scenery occasionally used by the Ministry of Defence as a firing range. A cafe at the lighthouse serves soup and sandwiches.

Lochinver is the main settlement, a busy little fishing port that's a popular port of call with its laid-back atmosphere, good facilities and striking scenery.

Sleeping & Eating

Achmelvich Beach SYHA HOSTEL £
(☑ 01571-844480; www.syha.org.uk; dm/tw £18/46; ☺ Apr-Sep) The Achmelvich Beach SYHA is a whitewashed cottage set beside a great beach at the end of a side road. Dorms are simple, and there's a sociable common kitchen/eating area. They sell heat-up meals; there's a basic summer shop and chip van at the adjacent campsite or it's a 4-mile walk from Lochinver.

Veyatie B&B ££
(☑ 01571-844424; www.veyatie-scotland.co.uk; Lochinver; s/d £70/90; P ☎ ☺) This choice, at the end of the road across the bay, has perhaps the finest views of all, best enjoyed from the grassy garden or conservatory lounge on a sunny day. There are two enormous rooms with lovely plush beds, great en suites, flatscreens and ipod docks. Breakfast is highly recommended.

★ Albannach HOTEL £££
(☑ 01571-844407; www.thealbannach.co.uk; Lochinver; s/d/ste incl dinner £220/300/380; ☺ Tue-Sun Mar-Dec; P ☎) ✔ One of the Highlands' top places to stay and eat, this hotel combines old-fashioned country-house elements – steep creaky stairs, stuffed animals, fireplaces, and noble antique furniture – with strikingly handsome showroom-class rooms that range from a sumptuous four-poster to more modern spaces with features such as underfloor heating and, in one case, a private deck with outdoor spa.

Lochinver Larder & Riverside Bistro CAFE, BISTRO ££
(☑ 01571-844356; www.lochinverlarder.co.uk; 3 Main St, Lochinver; pies £5, mains £11-20; ☺ 10am-7.45pm, to 8.30pm Jun-Sep; ☎) This offers an outstanding menu of inventive food made with local produce. The bistro turns out delicious seafood dishes in the evening, while the takeaway counter (open till 7pm) sells delicious pies with a wide range of gourmet fillings: try the wild boar and apricot. It also does quality meals to take away and heat up: great for hostellers and campers.

Caberfeidh PUB FOOD ££
(☑ 01571-844321; www.caberfeidhlochinver.co.uk; Main St, Lochinver; tapas £6-8; ☺ food noon-

2.30pm & 6-8.45pm; ☎) ✔ This convivial pub (with riverside beer garden) serves a range of real ales and some excellent food. The menu is based around tapas-sized portions of, say, venison meatballs or local langoustines. A sustainable, low-food-mile philosophy is at work and the quality shines through.

ℹ Information

Assynt Visitor Centre (☑ 01571-844194; www. discoverassynt.co.uk; Main St; ☺ 10am-4.30pm Mon-Sat & 11am-3pm Sun Easter-Jun, Sep & Oct, 9.30am-5pm Mon-Sat & 10am-4pm Sun Jul & Aug) Has leaflets on hill walks in the area and a display on the story of Assynt.

Ullapool

POP 1500

This pretty port on the shores of Loch Broom is the largest settlement in Wester Ross and one of the most alluring spots in the Highlands, a wonderful destination in itself as well as a gateway to the Western Isles. Offering a row of whitewashed cottages arrayed along the harbour and special views of the loch and its flanking hills, the town has a very distinctive appeal. The harbour served as an emigration point during the Clearances, with thousands of Scots watching Ullapool recede behind them as the diaspora cast them across the world.

◉ Sights & Activities

Ullapool Museum MUSEUM
(www.ullapoolmuseum.co.uk; 7 West Argyle St; adult/child £3.50/free; ☺ 10am-5pm Mon-Sat Apr-Oct) Housed in a converted Telford church, this museum relates the prehistoric, natural and social history of the town and Lochbroom area, with a particular focus on the emigration to Nova Scotia and other places. There's also a genealogy section if you want to trace your Scottish roots.

Seascape BOAT TOUR
(☑ 01854-633708; www.sea-scape.co.uk; adult/ child £30/20; ☺ Jun-Aug) Enjoyable two-hour tours out to the Summer Isles in an orange rigid inflatable boat (RIB).

Summer Queen BOAT TOUR
(☑ 01854-612472; www.summerqueen.co.uk; ☺ Mon-Sat May-Sep) The stately *Summer Queen* takes you out (weather permitting) around Isle Martin (adult/child £20/10, two hours) or to the Summer Isles (£30/15, four hours), with a stop on Tanera Mor.

🛌 Sleeping

Note that during summer Ullapool is very busy and finding accommodation can be tricky – book ahead.

Ullapool SYHA HOSTEL £
(☑ 01854-612254; www.syha.org.uk; Shore St; dm/tw/q £20/45/88; ☺ Apr-Oct; 🛜) You've got to hand it to the SYHA; it's chosen some very sweet locations for its hostels. This is as close to the water as it is to the town's best pub: about four seconds' walk. The front rooms have harbour views, but the busy dining area and little lounge are also good spots for contemplating the water.

Ceilidh Clubhouse HOSTEL £
(☑ 01854-612103; www.theceilidhplace.com; West Lane; s £23-30, tw/f £58/68; P 🛜) Opposite the Ceilidh Place, which runs it, this annexe offers no-frills accommodation for walkers, journeyers and staff. A big building, it has hostel-style rooms with sturdy bunks and basins. Though shared showers and toilets are a little institutional, rooms are private: if you're woken by snores, at least they'll be familiar ones. Prices drop substantially outside high summer.

Broomfield Holiday Park CAMPSITE £
(☑ 01854-612020; www.broomfieldhp.com; West Lane; tent sites £12-19; ☺ Apr-Sep; P 🛜 🐕) Great grassy headland location, very close to centre. Midge-busting machines in action.

★ West House B&B ££
(☑ 01854-613126; www.ullapoolaccommodation. net; West Argyle St; s £60, d £75-85; P 🛜) 🖍 Slap bang in the centre, this solid white house, once a manse, offers excellent rooms with contemporary style and great bathrooms. Breakfast is continental: rooms come with a fridge stocked with fresh fruit, cheeses, yoghurts, homemade bread, proper coffee and juice, so you can eat at your leisure in your own chamber. Most rooms have great views, as well as iPod docks and other conveniences.

★ Tamarin Lodge B&B ££
(☑ 01854-612667; www.tamarinullapool.com; The Braes; s/d £42/84; P 🛜 🐕) Effortlessly elegant modern architecture in this hilltop house is noteworthy in its own right, but the glorious vistas over the hills opposite and the water far below are unforgettable. All rooms face the view; some have a balcony, and all are very spacious, quiet and utterly relaxing, with unexpected features and gadgets. The great lounge and benevolent hosts are a delight. Follow signs for Braes from the Inverness road.

★ Ceilidh Place HOTEL £££
(☑ 01854-612103; www.theceilidhplace.com; 14 West Argyle St; s £58-92, d £140-164; ☺ Feb-Dec; P 🛜 🐕) This hotel, which includes a bookshop, is a celebration of Scottish culture: we're talking literature and traditional music, not tartan and Nessie dolls. It's one of the Highlands' more unusual and delightful places to stay. Rooms go for character over modernity: instead of a TV they come with a selection of books chosen by Scottish literati, eclectic artwork and cosy touches. The sumptuous lounge has sofas, chaises longues and an honesty bar.

🍴 Eating & Drinking

Arch Inn PUB FOOD ££
(☑ 01854-612454; www.thearchinn.co.uk; West Shore St; mains £10-18; ☺ food noon-2.30pm & 5-9pm Mon-Sat, 12.30-2.30pm & 5-9pm Sun; 🛜) There's pleasing pub food to be had at this shorefront establishment, where the cosy bar and restaurant area dishes up generously proportioned, well-presented mains that range from tender chicken and fish dishes to more advanced blackboard specials with local seafood a highlight. Service is helpful and efficient. The outdoor tables right beside the lapping water are a top spot for a pint.

ℹ️ Information

Ullapool Information Centre (☑ 01854-612486; ullapool@visitscotland.com; Argyle St; ☺ 9.30am-5pm Mon-Sat Easter-Oct, plus 10am-3pm Sun Jun-Aug) Can book ferries and buses.

ℹ️ Getting There & Away

Citylink (www.citylink.co.uk) has one to three daily buses from Inverness to Ullapool (£12.80, 1½ hours), connecting with the Lewis ferry.

Ullapool to Kyle of Lochalsh

Although it's less than 50 miles as the crow flies from Ullapool to Kyle of Lochalsh, it's more like 150 miles along the circuitous coastal road – but don't let that put you off. It's a deliciously remote region and there are fine views of beaches and bays backed by mountains all the way along.

The A832 doubles back to the coast from the A835, 12 miles from Ullapool. Just after the junction, the Falls of Measach spill 45m into the spectacularly deep and narrow Corrieshalloch Gorge. You can cross from side to side on a wobbly suspension bridge; the thundering falls and misty vapours rising from the gorge are very impressive.

If you're hurrying to Skye, head inland on the A835 (towards Inverness) and catch up with the A832 further south, near Garve.

Gairloch

POP 1000

Gairloch is a group of villages (comprising Achtercairn, Strath and Charlestown) around the inner end of a loch of the same name. Gairloch is a good base for whale- and dolphin-watching excursions and the surrounding area has beautiful sandy beaches, good trout fishing and birdwatching.

◉ Sights & Activities

Gairloch Marine Wildlife Centre   NATURE DISPLAY

(☑ 01445-712636; www.porpoise-gairloch.co.uk; Pier Rd; ◷ 10am-4pm Easter-Oct) ✔ FREE This has audiovisual and interactive displays, lots of charts, photos and knowledgeable staff. Cruises (adult/child £20/15) run from the centre up to three times daily (weather permitting); during the two-hour trips you may see basking sharks, porpoises and minke whales. The crew collects data on water temperature and conditions, and monitors cetacean populations, so you are subsidising important research.

Inverewe Garden   GARDENS

(NTS; www.nts.org.uk; adult/concession £10.50/7.50; ◷ 10am-3pm Nov-Mar, to 5pm Apr & Sep, to 5.30pm May, to 6pm Jun-Aug, to 4pm Oct) Six miles north of Gairloch, this splendid garden is a welcome splash of colour on this otherwise bleak coast. The climate here is warmed by the Gulf Stream, which allowed Osgood MacKenzie to create this exotic woodland garden in 1862. There are free guided tours on weekdays at 1.30pm (March to October). The cafe has great cakes.

🛏 Sleeping & Eating

Wayside Guest House   B&B £

(☑ 01445-712008; issmith@msn.com; Strath; s/d £40/60; 🛜) Cosy and compact, Wayside provides comfortable and welcoming accommodation in Strath, the spiritual heart

of Gairloch. The spotless rooms come with either en suite bathroom or a fabulous view; you can decide what's more important. It offers excellent value and hosts full of kind thoughts.

Rua Reidh Lighthouse   LODGE £££

(☑ 01445-771263; www.stayatalighthouse.co.uk; d/f £60/110; ◷ Easter-Oct; P 🛜 🐾) Three miles down a private road beyond Melvaig (11 miles north of Gairloch), this simple, excellent lodge gives a taste of a lighthouse keeper's life. It's a wild, lonely location that's great for walking and birdwatching. Breakfast is included and tasty evening meals are available. It's open Easter to October, but there's a self-catering apartment open almost year-round. Book well ahead.

Badachro Inn   PUB FOOD £££

(☑ 01445-741255; www.badachroinn.com; Badachro; light meals £5-8, mains £11-16; ◷ food noon-3pm & 6-9pm, from 12.30pm Sun; P) ✔ Set in an enchanting location, overlooking a sheltered yacht harbour at Badachro, 5 miles southwest of Gairloch, this old Highland inn serves local real ales and platters of fresh local seafood: crab, scallops and langoustines, some landed right alongside. There are also tasty panini and sandwiches; eating out on the deck on a sunny day here is a real treat.

ℹ Information

Gairloch Information Centre (☑ 01445-712071; ◷ 10am-4pm Mon-Sat Oct-Apr, 10am-5pm Mon-Sat & 10am-4pm Sun May-Sep) In the wooden Gale Centre, on the road through town, this has good walking pamphlets. Opening hours are slightly variable.

Loch Maree & Kinlochewe

Stretching for 12 miles southeast of Gairloch, **Loch Maree** is often regarded as one of the most beautiful lochs in Scotland. At the southern end of the loch, tiny **Kinlochewe** makes a good base for outdoor activities. **Kinlochewe Hotel** (☑ 01445-760253; www.kinlochewehotel.co.uk; Kinlochewe; dm £15.50, s £50, d £90-98; P 🛜 🐾) ✔ is a welcoming place that's very walker-friendly. There are nice features such as a handsome lounge well stocked with books, a great bar with several real ales on tap and a thoughtful menu of locally sourced food. There's also a bunkhouse with one no-frills 12-bed dorm, a decent kitchen and clean bathrooms.

Torridon

Southwest from Kinlochewe, the A896 follows **Glen Torridon**, overlooked by multiple peaks, including Beinn Eighe (1010m) and Liathach (1055m). The drive along Glen Torridon is one of the most breathtaking in Scotland. Mighty, brooding mountains, often partly obscured by clumps of passing clouds, seemingly drawn to their peaks like magnets, loom over the tiny, winding, single-track road.

The road reaches the sea at the spectacularly sited Torridon village, where there is a **Countryside Centre** (NTS; www.nts.org.uk; donation £3; ⊙10am-5pm Sun-Fri Easter-Sep) offering information on flora, fauna and walks in the rugged area. There's a **camping ground** (☑01445-791368; sites free) here.

Modern, squat **Torridon SYHA** (☑01445-791284; www.syha.org.uk; dm £20, tw £45-49; ⊙Mar-Oct, plus weekends Nov-Feb; P@®❅) is in a magnificent location surrounded by spectacular mountains. It's a very popular walking base, so book ahead in summer.

If you prefer the lap of luxury to the sound of rain beating on your tent, head for **The Torridon** (☑01445-791242; www.thetorridon.com; standard/superior/master r £235/290/440; ⊙closed Jan, plus Mon & Tue Nov, Dec, Feb & Mar; P@®❅), a lavish Victorian shooting lodge with a romantic lochside location. Service is excellent, with muddy boots positively welcomed, and dinners are sumptuous affairs, also open to nonresidents (£55). Part of the same set-up, adjacent **Torridon Inn** (☑01445-791242; www.thetorridon.com; s/d/q £100/110/175; ⊙daily May-Oct, Thu-Sun Nov, Dec, Mar & Apr, closed Jan & Feb; P®❅) offers excellent modern rooms that vary substantially in size and layout, and a sociable bar offering all-day food.

Applecross

POP 200

The delightfully remote seaside village of Applecross feels like an island retreat due to its isolation and the magnificent views of Raasay and the hills of Skye that set the pulse racing, particularly at sunset. On a clear day it's an unforgettable place, though the campsite and pub fill to the brim in school holidays.

Twenty-five winding miles of road leads here from Shieldaig, but a more spectacular route (accessed from further south on the A896) is the magnificent **Bealach na Ba** (626m; Pass of the Cattle), the third-highest motor road in the UK, and the longest continuous climb. Originally built in 1822, it climbs steeply and hair-raisingly via hairpin bends perched over sheer drops, with gradients up to 25%, then drops dramatically to the village with views of Skye.

Mountain & Sea Guides (☑01250-744394; www.applecross.uk.com) runs sea-kayaking, hill-walking and mountaineering excursions, as well as more serious expeditions.

🛏 Sleeping & Eating

Applecross Campsite   CAMPSITE £
(☑01520-744268; www.applecross.uk.com; sites per adult/child £9/4.50, 2-person huts £45; ⊙Mar-Oct; P®❅) Offers green grassy plots, cute little wooden cabins and a good greenhouse-like cafe.

★**Applecross Inn**   INN ££
(☑01520-744262; www.applecross.uk.com; Shore St; s/d £85/130, mains £9-18; ⊙food noon-9pm; P®❅) ⬦ The hub of the spread-out community and the perfect shoreside location for a sunset pint, this inn is famous for its food – mostly daily blackboard specials concentrate on local seafood and venison – and sports seven snug bedrooms. All have a view of the Skye hills and the sea.

Plockton

POP 400

There's something distinctly tropical about idyllic little Plockton, a filmset-like village with palm trees, whitewashed houses and a small bay dotted with islets and hemmed in by green-fuzzed mountains. It's a great place to stay and to eat.

Calum's Seal Trips (☑01599-544306; www.calums-sealtrips.com; adult/child £10/6; ⊙Apr-Oct) runs seal-watching cruises. There are swarms of the slippery fellas just outside the harbour and the trip comes with an excellent commentary.

🛏 Sleeping & Eating

Plockton Station Bunkhouse   HOSTEL £
(☑01599-544235; mickcoe@btinternet.com; dm £15; P®) Airily set in the former train station (the new one is opposite), this has cosy four-bed dorms, a garden and kitchen/lounge with plenty of light and good views of the frenetic comings and goings (OK, that last bit's a lie) of the platforms below. It can get a bit cramped when there are lots of folk in. The owners also do good-value B&B (singles/doubles £30/50) next door in the inaccurately named Nessun Dorma.

MADDENING MIDGES

Forget Nessie; the Highlands have a real monster – a voracious bloodsucking female fully 3mm long and named *culicoides impunctatus*, or the Highland midge. The bane of campers and as much a symbol of Scotland as the kilt or dram, they drive sane folk to distraction, descending in biting clouds.

Though normally vegetarian, the female midge needs a dose of blood in order to lay her eggs. And, like it or not, if you're in the Highlands between June and August, you just volunteered as a donor. Midges especially congregate near water, and are most active in the early morning, though squadrons also patrol in the late evening.

Repellents and creams are reasonably effective, though some walkers favour midge veils. Light-coloured clothing also helps. Many pubs and campsites have midge-zappers. Check www.midgeforecast.co.uk for activity levels by area, but don't blame us: we've been eaten alive when the forecast said moderate too.

Plockton Hotel
INN ££

(☑ 01599-544274; www.plocktonhotel.co.uk; 41 Harbour St; s/d £90/130, cottage s/d £55/80; ⃰) *✿* Black-painted Plockton Hotel is one of those classic Highland spots that manages to make everyone happy, whether it's thirst, hunger or fatigue that brings you knocking. Assiduously tended rooms are a delight, with excellent facilities and thoughtful touches. Those without a water view are consoled with more space and a balcony with rock-garden perspectives. The cottage nearby offers simpler comfort.

The cosy bar, or the wonderful beer garden on a sunny day, are memorable places for a pint, and food ranges from sound-value bar meals to seafood platters and local langoustines brought in on the afternoon boat (mains £6 to £12).

★ Plockton Shores
SEAFOOD ££

(☑ 01599-544263; www.plocktonshoresrestaurant.com; 30 Harbour St; mains £11-18; ⃝ noon-2.30pm & 6-8.30pm Mon-Sat, from 11am Sun; ⃰) *✿* This welcoming restaurant attached to a shop sports a tempting menu of local seafood, including good-value platters with langoustines, mussels, crab, squat lobster and more, or succulent hand-dived tempura scallops. There's also a very tasty line in venison, steaks and a small selection of tasty vegetarian dishes that are more than an afterthought. Breakfast, teas and snacks are served from morning until night.

Plockton Inn
SEAFOOD ££

(☑ 01599-544222; www.plocktoninn.co.uk; mains £10-18; ⃝ noon-2.15pm & 6-9pm; ⃰) Offering a wide range of anything from haggis to toothsome local langoustines (Plockton prawns) and daily seafood specials, this covers lots of bases and offers genuinely welcoming service. A range of rooms – some substantially more spacious than others, and some in an annexe, are available at a decent price.

Kyle of Lochalsh

POP 700

Before the bridge was opened in 1995, this was Skye's main ferry port. Visitors now tend to buzz through town, but Kyle has some good boat trips if you're interested in marine life.

Citylink runs two to three daily buses from Inverness (£19.90, two hours) and three from Glasgow (£36.20, five to six hours).

The train route between Inverness and Kyle of Lochalsh (£22, 2½ hours, up to four daily) is marvellously scenic.

Eilean Donan Castle

Photogenically sited at the entrance to Loch Duich, near Dornie village, Eilean Donan Castle (☑ 01599-555202; www.eileandonancastle.com; adult/child/family £6.50/5.50/16; ⃝ 10am-6pm Feb-Dec, from 9am Jul & Aug) is one of Scotland's most evocative castles, and must be represented in millions of photo albums. It's on an offshore islet, magically linked to the mainland by an elegant, stone-arched bridge. It's very much a re-creation inside with an excellent introductory exhibition. Keep an eye out for the photos of castle scenes from the movie *Highlander*. There's also a sword used at the battle of Culloden in 1746. The castle was ruined in 1719 after Spanish Jacobite forces were defeated at the Battle of Glenshiel, and it was rebuilt between 1912 and 1932.

Citylink buses from Fort William and Inverness to Portree will stop at the castle.

ISLE OF SKYE

POP 10,000

The Isle of Skye (an t-Eilean Sgiathanach in Gaelic) takes its name from the old Norse *sky-a,* meaning 'cloud island', a Viking reference to the often-mist-enshrouded Cuillin

Hills. It's the second-largest of Scotland's islands, a 50-mile-long patchwork of velvet moors, jagged mountains, sparkling lochs and towering sea cliffs. The stunning scenery is the main attraction, but when the mist closes in there are plenty of castles, crofting museums and cosy pubs and restaurants;

Skye & Outer Hebrides

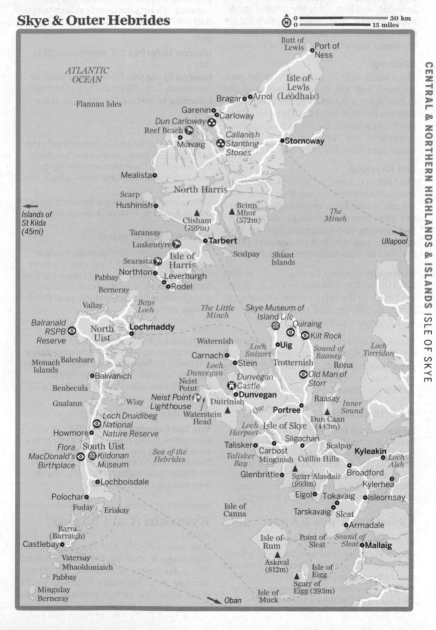

there are also dozens of art galleries and craft studios.

🏃 Activities

Walking

Skye offers some of the finest – and in places, the roughest and most difficult – walking in Scotland. There are many detailed guidebooks available. You'll need Ordnance Survey (OS) 1:50,000 maps 23 and 32. Don't attempt the longer walks in bad weather or in winter.

Climbing

The Cuillin Hills is a playground for rock climbers, and the two-day traverse of the Cuillin Ridge is the finest mountaineering expedition in the British Isles. There are several mountain guides in the area who can provide instruction and safely introduce inexperienced climbers to the more difficult routes.

Sea Kayaking

The sheltered coves and sea lochs around the coast of Skye provide water lovers with magnificent sea-kayaking opportunities. The centres listed here can provide kayaking instruction, guiding and equipment hire for both beginners and experts. It costs around £40 to £50 for a half-day kayak hire with instruction.

Whitewave Outdoor Centre KAYAKING
(☑ 01470-542414; www.white-wave.co.uk; 19 Linicro, Kilmuir; ☉ Mar-Oct) Provides kayaking instruction, guiding and equipment hire for both beginners and experts.

Skyak Adventures KAYAKING
(☑ 01471-820002; www.skyakadventures.com; 29 Lower Breakish, Breakish) Expeditions and courses to take both beginners and experienced paddlers to otherwise inaccessible places.

ℹ Information

Portree Tourist Office (☑ 01478-612137; Bayfield Rd, Portree; internet per 20min £1; ☉ 9am-6pm Mon-Sat & 10am-4pm Sun Jun-Aug, 9am-5pm Mon-Fri & 10am-4pm Sat Apr, May & Sep, shorter hours Oct-Mar) The only tourist office on the island; provides internet access (£1 per 20 minutes) and currency exchange.

ℹ Getting There & Away

BOAT

Despite the bridge, there are still a couple of ferry links between Skye and the mainland. Ferries also operate from Uig on Skye to the Outer Hebrides.

CalMac (www.calmac.co.uk; per person/car £4.65/23.90) The Mallaig to Armadale ferry

(30 minutes, eight daily Monday to Saturday, five to seven on Sunday) is very popular on weekends and in July and August, so book ahead if you're travelling by car.

Skye Ferry (www.skyeferry.co.uk; car with up to four passengers £15; ☉ Easter–mid-Oct) Runs a tiny vessel (six cars only) on the short Kylerhea to Glenelg crossing (five minutes, every 20 minutes). The ferry operates from 10am to 6pm daily (till 7pm June to August).

BUS

Glasgow to Portree £41, seven hours, three daily

Glasgow to Uig £41, 7½ hours, two daily; via Crianlarich, Fort William and Kyle of Lochalsh

Inverness to Portree £24, 3¼ hours, three daily

CAR & MOTORCYCLE

The Isle of Skye became permanently tethered to the Scottish mainland when the Skye Bridge opened in 1995. The controversial bridge tolls were abolished in 2004 and the crossing is now free.

There are petrol stations at Broadford (open 24 hours), Armadale, Portree, Dunvegan and Uig.

ℹ Getting Around

Getting around the island by public transport can be a pain, especially if you want to explore away from the main Kyleakin–Portree–Uig road. Here, as in much of the Highlands, there are fewer buses on Saturday and only a handful of Sunday services.

BUS

Stagecoach (p920) operates the main bus routes on the island, linking all the main villages and towns. Its **Skye Dayrider/Megarider ticket** (per day/week £8/32) gives unlimited bus travel. For timetable info, call **Traveline** (☑ 0871 200 22 33).

TAXI & CAR HIRE

Kyle Taxi Company (☑ 01599-534323; www.skyecarhire.co.uk) You can order a taxi or hire a car from Kyle Taxi Company. Car hire costs from around £40 a day, and you can arrange for the car to be waiting at Kyle of Lochalsh train station.

Kyleakin (Caol Acain)

POP 100

Poor wee Kyleakin had the carpet pulled from under it when the Skye Bridge opened. The village went from being the island's gateway to a backwater bypassed by the main road. It's now a pleasant, peaceful little place, with a harbour used by yachts and fishing boats.

There are two hostels and a couple of B&Bs in the village. The friendly **Skye Backpackers** (☑ 01599-534510; www.skye-backpackers.com; dm/tw £18/47; @☎) is our favourite, with even cheaper beds (£13) in caravans out back.

A shuttle bus runs half-hourly between Kyle of Lochalsh and Kyleakin (£1.20, five minutes), and there are eight to 10 buses daily (except Sunday) to Broadford (£2.40, 15 minutes), and three or four to Portree (£6.20, one hour).

Broadford (An T-Ath Leathann)

POP 750

Broadford is a service centre for the scattered communities of southern Skye. The long, straggling village has a 24-hour petrol station, a large supermarket with ATM, a laundrette and a bank.

There are lots of B&Bs in and around Broadford and the village is well placed for exploring southern Skye by car.

🛏 Sleeping & Eating

★ **Tigh an Dochais**   B&B £££
(☑ 01471-820022; www.skyebedbreakfast.co.uk; 13 Harrapool; d £90; ℗) ✦ A cleverly designed modern building, Tigh an Dochais is one of Skye's best B&Bs – a little footbridge leads to the front door, which is on the 1st floor. Here you'll find the dining room (gorgeous breakfasts) and lounge offering a stunning view of sea and hills; the bedrooms (downstairs) open onto an outdoor deck with that same wonderful view.

Creelers   SEAFOOD £££
(☑ 01471-822281; www.skye-seafood-restaurant.co.uk; Lower Harrapool; lunch mains £10, dinner mains £14-19; ☒ noon-9.30pm Mon-Sat Mar-Nov; 🖶) ✦ Broadford has several places to eat but one really stands out: Creelers is a small, bustling, no-frills restaurant that serves some of the best seafood on Skye. The house speciality is a rich, spicy seafood gumbo. Best to book ahead.

Sleat

If you cross over the sea to Skye on the ferry from Mallaig you arrive in Armadale, at the southern end of the long, low-lying peninsula known as Sleat (pronounced 'slate'). There are six or seven buses a day Monday to Saturday (three on Sunday) from Armadale to Broadford (£3.50, 30 minutes) and Portree (£6.80, 1¼ hours).

◉ Sights & Activities

Museum of the Isles   MUSEUM
(☑ 01471-844305; www.clandonald.com; adult/child £8/6.50; ☒ 9.30am-5.30pm Apr-Oct, occasionally shorter hours Oct; ℗) Just along the road from Armadale pier is the part-ruined **Armadale Castle**, former seat of Lord MacDonald of Sleat. The neighbouring museum will tell you all you ever wanted to know about Clan Donald, as well as providing an easily digestible history of the Lordship of the Isles. Prize exhibits include rare portraits of clan chiefs, and a wine glass that was once used by Bonnie Prince Charlie. The ticket also gives admission to the lovely **castle gardens**.

🛏 Sleeping

★ **Toravaig House Hotel**   HOTEL ££
(☑ 01471-820200; www.skyehotel.co.uk; d £99-130; ℗☎) This hotel, 3 miles south of Isleornsay, is one of those places where the owners know a thing or two about hospitality – as soon as you arrive you'll feel right at home, whether relaxing on the sofas by the log fire in the lounge or admiring the view across the Sound of Sleat from the lawn chairs in the garden.

The spacious bedrooms – ask for room 1 (Eriskay), with its enormous sleigh bed – are luxuriously equipped, from the crisp bed linen to the huge, high-pressure shower heads. The elegant restaurant serves the best of local fish, game and lamb. After dinner you can retire to the lounge with a single malt and flick through the yachting magazines – you can even arrange a day trip aboard the owners' 42ft sailing yacht.

Cuillin Hills

The Cuillin are Britain's most spectacular mountain range. Though small in stature (**Sgurr Alasdair**, the highest summit, is only 993m), the peaks are near-alpine in character, with knife-edge ridges, jagged pinnacles, scree-filled gullies and acres of naked rock. While they are a paradise for experienced mountaineers, the higher reaches of the Cuillin are off limits to the majority of walkers.

The good news is that there are also plenty of good, low-level hikes within the ability of most. One of the best (on a fine day) is the steep climb from Glenbrittle camping ground to **Coire Lagan** (6 miles round trip; allow at least three hours).

There are two main bases for exploring the Cuillin – **Sligachan** to the north, and **Glenbrittle** to the south.

Sleeping & Eating

Sligachan Hotel
HOTEL **£££**

(☑ 01478-650204; www.sligachan.co.uk; Sligachan; r per person £68-78; P@🖸) The Slig, as it has been known to generations of climbers, is a near village in itself, encompassing a comfortable hotel, a microbrewery, self-catering cottages, a small mountaineering museum, a big barn of a pub – **Seamus's Bar** (Sligachan Hotel; mains £8-13; ⊙ food served 11am-9.30pm; 🖸🚻) – and an adventure playground.

❶ Getting There & Away

Bus 53 runs five times a day Monday to Friday (once on Saturday) from Portree to Carbost via Sligachan (50 minutes); for Glenbrittle, you'll have to hitch or walk the remaining 8 miles.

Minginish

Loch Harport, to the north of the Cuillin, divides the Minginish Peninsula from the rest of Skye. On its southern shore lies the village of **Carbost**, home to the smooth, sweet and smoky malt whisky produced at **Talisker Distillery** (☑ 01478-614308; www.discovering-distilleries.com; guided tour £7; ⊙ 9.30am-5pm Mon-Sat Apr-Oct, 11am-5pm Sun Jul & Aug, 10am-4.30pm Mon-Fri Nov-Mar) This is the only distillery on Skye; the guided tour includes a free dram. Magnificent **Talisker Bay**, 5 miles west of Carbost, has a sandy beach, sea stack and waterfall.

There's one bus a day (school days only) from Portree to Carbost (£3.70, 40 minutes) via Sligachan.

Portree (Port Righ)

POP 2300

Portree is Skye's largest and liveliest town. It has a pretty harbour lined with brightly painted houses, and there are great views of the surrounding hills. Its name (from the Gaelic for King's Harbour) commemorates James V, who came here in 1540 to pacify the local clans.

Sleeping

Portree is well supplied with B&Bs, but accommodation fills up fast in July and August so be sure to book ahead.

Bayfield Backpackers
HOSTEL **£**

(☑ 01478-612231; www.skyehostel.co.uk; Bayfield; dm £18; P@🖸) Clean, central and modern, this hostel provides the best backpacker accommodation in town. The owner really makes you feel welcome, and is a fount of advice on what to do and where to go in Skye.

Torvaig Campsite
CAMPSITE **£**

(☑ 01478-612209; www.portreecampsite.co.uk; Torvaig; sites per adult/child £7/3; ⊙ Apr-Oct; 🖸) An attractive, family-run campsite located 1.5 miles north of Portree, on the road to Staffin.

Ben Tianavaig B&B
B&B **££**

(☑ 01478-612152; www.ben-tianavaig.co.uk; 5 Bosville Tce; r £75-88; P🖸) ⏪ A warm welcome awaits from the Irish-Welsh couple who run this appealing B&B bang in the centre of town. All four bedrooms have a view across the harbour to the hill that gives the house its name, and breakfasts include free-range eggs and vegetables grown in the garden. Two-night minimum stay April to October; no credit cards.

Woodlands
B&B **££**

(☑ 01478-612980; www.woodlands-portree.co.uk; Viewfield Rd; r £70; ⊙ Mar-Oct; P🖸) A great location, with views across the bay, and unstinting hospitality make this B&B, a half-mile south of the town centre, a good choice.

Peinmore House
B&B **£££**

(☑ 01478-612574; www.peinmorehouse.co.uk; r £135-145; P🖸) Signposted off the main road about 2 miles south of Portree, this former manse has been cleverly converted into a guesthouse that is more stylish and luxurious than most hotels. The bedrooms and bathrooms are huge (one bathroom has an armchair in it!), as is the choice of breakfast (kippers and smoked haddock on the menu), and there are panoramic views to the Old Man of Storr.

✕ Eating

Café Arriba
CAFE **£**

(☑ 01478-611830; www.cafearriba.co.uk; Quay Brae; mains £5-10; ⊙ 7am-6pm daily May-Sep, 8am-5pm Thu-Sat Oct-Apr; 🖸) ⏪ Arriba is a funky little cafe, brightly decked out in primary colours and offering delicious flatbread melts (bacon, leek and cheese is our favourite) as well as the best choice of vegetarian grub on the island, ranging from a veggie breakfast fry-up to falafel wraps with hummus and chilli sauce. Also serves excellent coffee.

★ Harbour View
Seafood Restaurant
SEAFOOD ££

(☑ 01478-612069; www.harbourviewskye.co.uk; 7 Bosville Tce; mains £14-19; ⊗ noon-3pm & 5.30-11pm Tue-Sun) ✔ The Harbour View is Portree's most congenial place to eat. It has a homely dining room with a log fire in winter, books on the mantelpiece and bric-a-brac on the shelves. And on the table, superb Scottish seafood such as fresh Skye oysters, seafood chowder, king scallops, langoustines and lobster.

Sea Breezes
SEAFOOD ££

(☑ 01478-612016; www.seabreezes-skye.co.uk; 2 Marine Buildings, Quay St; mains £12-20; ⊗ noon-2pm & 5-9.30pm Apr-Oct) ✔ Sea Breezes is an informal, no-frills restaurant specialising in local fish and shellfish fresh from the boat – try the impressive seafood platter, a small mountain of langoustines, crab, oysters and lobster (£48 for two). Book early, as it's often hard to get a table.

❶ Getting There & Around

BUS
The main bus stop is in Somerled Sq. There are six Scottish Citylink buses every day from Kyle of Lochalsh to Portree (£6.50, one hour) continuing to Uig.

Local buses (mostly six to eight Monday to Saturday, three on Sunday) run from Portree to:
Armadale (£6.80, 1¼ hours) connecting with the ferry to Mallaig
Broadford (£5.20, 40 minutes)

Dunvegan Castle (£4.65, 40 minutes, one daily)

There are also three buses a day on a circular route around Trotternish (in both directions), taking in Flodigarry (£4.65, 45 minutes), Kilmuir (£4.65, 45 minutes) and Uig (£3.50, 30 minutes).

BIKE
Island Cycles (☑ 01478-613121; www.island-cycles-skye.co.uk; The Green; ⊗ 9am-5pm Mon-Sat) You can hire bikes here for £8.50/15 per half/full day.

Dunvegan (Dun Bheagain) & Around

Skye's most famous historic building, and one of its most popular tourist attractions, is **Dunvegan Castle** (☑ 01470-521206; www.dunvegancastle.com; adult/child £10/7; ⊗ 10am-5.30pm Apr–mid-Oct; ℗), seat of the chief of Clan MacLeod. It has played host to Samuel Johnson, Sir Walter Scott and, most famously, Flora MacDonald. The oldest parts are the 14th-century keep and dungeon, but most of it dates from the 17th to 19th centuries.

There are some interesting artefacts, most famous being the **Fairy Flag**, a diaphanous silk banner that dates from some time between the 4th and 7th centuries.

🛏 Sleeping & Eating

★ Red Roof Café
CAFE £

(☑ 01470-511766; www.redroofskye.co.uk; Glendale; mains £6-9; ⊗ 11am-5pm Sun-Fri Apr-Oct; ℗ ♿) ✔ Tucked away up a glen, a mile off the main road, this restored 250-year-old

---

FLORA MACDONALD

Flora MacDonald, who became famous for helping Bonnie Prince Charlie escape after his defeat at the Battle of Culloden, was born in 1722 at Milton in South Uist, where a memorial cairn marks the site of one of her early childhood homes.

In 1746, she helped Bonnie Prince Charlie make his way from Benbecula to Skye disguised as her Irish maidservant. With a price on the prince's head, their little boat was fired on, but they managed to land safely and Flora escorted the prince to Portree where he gave her a gold locket containing his portrait before setting sail for Raasay.

Waylaid on the way home, the boatmen admitted everything. Flora was arrested and imprisoned in the Tower of London. She never saw or heard from the prince again.

In 1747, she returned to Skye, marrying Allan MacDonald and having nine children. Dr Samuel Johnson stayed with her in 1773 during his trip to the Western Isles, but later poverty forced her family to emigrate to North Carolina. There her husband was captured by rebels. Flora returned to Kingsburgh on Skye where she died in 1790. She was buried in Kilmuir churchyard, wrapped in the sheet on which both Bonnie Prince Charlie and Dr Johnson had slept.

byre is a wee haven of home-grown grub. As well as great coffee and cake, there are lunch platters (noon to 3pm) of Skye seafood, game or cheese served with salad leaves and edible flowers grown just along the road.

★ **Three Chimneys**   MODERN SCOTTISH **£££**
(☑ 01470-511258; www.threechimneys.co.uk; Colbost; 3-course lunch/dinner £37/60; ⊘ 12.15-1.45pm Mon-Sat mid-Mar–Oct, plus Sun Easter-Sep, 6.15-9pm daily year-round; P) ✔ Halfway between Dunvegan and Waterstein, the Three Chimneys is a superb romantic retreat combining a gourmet restaurant in a candlelit crofter's cottage with sumptuous five-star rooms (doubles £345) in the modern house next door. Book well in advance, and note that children are not welcome in the restaurant in the evenings.

Trotternish

The Trotternish Peninsula to the north of Portree has some of Skye's most beautiful – and bizarre – scenery. On the eastern coast, the 50m-high, pot-bellied pinnacle of crumbling basalt known as the **Old Man of Storr**, is prominent above the road 6 miles north of Portree. North again is spectacular **Kilt Rock**, a stupendous cliff of columnar basalt whose vertical ribbing is fancifully compared to the pleats of a kilt, and the Quiraing, an impressive land-slipped escarpment bristling with crags and pinnacles.

On the western side of the peninsula, the peat-reek of crofting life in the 18th and 19th centuries is preserved in thatched cottages at **Skye Museum of Island Life** (☑ 01470-552206; www.skyemuseum.co.uk; adult/child £2.50/50p; ⊘ 9.30am-5pm Mon-Sat Easter-Oct; P). Behind the museum is Kilmuir Cemetery, where a tall Celtic cross marks the grave of Flora MacDonald.

Whichever way you arrive at **Uig** (oo-ig), the picture-perfect bay, ringed by steep hills, rarely fails to impress. There's a cluster of B&Bs.

🛌 Sleeping & Eating

Dun Flodigarry Hostel   HOSTEL **£**
(☑ 01470-552212; www.hostelflodigarry.co.uk; Flodigarry; dm/tw £18/40, tent sites per person £9; P@�) A bright and welcoming hostel that enjoys a stunning location above the sea, with views across Raasay to the mainland mountains. A nearby hiking trail leads to the Quiraing (2.5 miles away), and there's a hotel bar barely 100m from the door. You can also camp nearby and use all the hostel facilities.

Flodigarry Hotel   HOTEL **£££**
(☑ 01470-552203; www.hotelintheskye.co.uk; Flodigarry; r £130-250; P�) From 1751 to 1759 Flora MacDonald lived in a cottage that is now part of this atmospheric hotel, given a new lease of life by adventurous new owners. You can stay in the cottage itself (there are four bedrooms here), or in the more spacious rooms in the main hotel; nonresidents are welcome at the stylish bar and restaurant, with great views over the sea.

Isle Of Raasay

POP 200

Raasay (www.raasay.com) is the rugged, 10-mile-long island that lies off Skye's east coast. There are several good walks here, including one to the flat-topped conical hill of **Dun Caan** (443m), and another to the extraordinary ruin of **Brochel Castle**, perched on a pinnacle at the northern end of Raasay.

Beautifully renovated **Raasay House** (☑ 01478-660266; www.raasay-house.co.uk; dm £25, s/d £105/125; P�) provides outdoor-activity courses, and accommodation ranging from hostel bunks to luxury B&B. It also has the island's only bar and restaurant (mains £12 to £20), serving quality pub grub and locally brewed beers.

A **CalMac ferry** (www.calmac.co.uk; return passenger/car £6.45/24.80) runs from Sconser, on the road from Portree to Broadford, to Raasay (25 minutes, nine daily Monday to Saturday, twice daily Sunday). There are no petrol stations on the island.

OUTER HEBRIDES

POP 27,700

The Outer Hebrides – also known as the Western Isles, or Na h-Eileanan an Iar in Gaelic – are a 130-mile-long string of islands lying off the northwest coast of Scotland. There are 119 islands in total, of which the five main inhabited islands are: Lewis and Harris (two parts of a single island, although often described as if they are separate islands), North Uist, Benbecula, South Uist and Barra. The middle three (often referred to simply as 'the Uists') are connected by road-bearing causeways.

The ferry crossing from Ullapool or Uig to the Western Isles marks an important cultural divide – more than a third of Scotland's registered crofts are in the Outer Hebrides, and no less than 60% of the population are Gaelic speakers. The rigours of life in the old island blackhouses are still within living memory.

The name Hebrides is likely a corruption of the Roman name for the islands. But the alternative derivation from the Norse *havbredey* ('isles at the edge of the sea') has a much more poetic ring, alluding to the broad vistas of sky and sea that characterise the islands' often bleak and treeless landscapes. But there is beauty here too, in the machair (grassy, wildflower-speckled dunes) and dazzling white-sand beaches, majesty in the rugged hills and sprawling lochs, and mystery in the islands' fascinating past. It's a past signalled by Neolithic standing stones, Viking place names, deserted crofts and folk memories of the Clearances.

❶ Information

Castlebay Tourist Office (☑ 01871-810336; Main St, Castlebay; ⊙ 9am-1pm & 2-5pm Mon-Sat & noon-4pm Sun Apr-Oct)

Lochboisdale Tourist Office (☑ 01878-700286; Pier Rd, Lochboisdale, South Uist; ⊙ 9am-5pm Mon-Sat Apr-Oct)

Stornoway Tourist Office (☑ 01851-703088; www.visithebrides.com; 26 Cromwell St, Stornoway; ⊙ 9am-6pm Mon-Sat year-round)

Tarbert Tourist Office (☑ 01859-502011; Pier Rd, Tarbert; ⊙ 9am-5pm Mon-Sat Apr-Oct)

❶ Getting There & Away

AIR

There are airports at Stornoway (Lewis), Benbecula and Barra. Flights operate to Stornoway from Edinburgh, Inverness, Glasgow and Aberdeen. There are also two flights a day (Tuesday to Thursday only) between Stornoway and Benbecula.

There are daily flights from Glasgow to Barra, from Tuesday to Thursday only to Benbecula. At Barra, the planes land on the hard-sand beach at low tide, so the timetable depends on the tides.

FlyBe/Loganair (☑ 01857-873457; www.loganair.co.uk)

Eastern Airways (☑ 0870 366 9100; www.easternairways.com)

BOAT

Standard one-way fares on **CalMac** (☑ 0800 066 5000; www.calmac.co.uk) ferries:

CROSSING	DURATION (HOURS)	CAR	PER PERSON
Ullapool–Stornoway	2¾	£48	£9.15
Uig–Lochmaddy	1¾	£29	£6
Uig–Tarbert	1½	£29	£6
Oban–Castlebay	4¾	£65	£14.25
Oban–Lochboisdale	6¾	£65	£14.25

There are two or three ferries a day to Stornoway, one or two a day to Tarbert and Lochmaddy, and one a day to Castlebay and Lochboisdale. You can also take the ferry from Lochboisdale to Castlebay (car/passenger £22.90/7.95, 1½

KEEPING THE SABBATH

The Protestants of the Outer Hebrides have succeeded in maintaining a distinctive fundamentalist approach to their religion, with Sunday being devoted largely to religious services, prayer and Bible reading. On Lewis and Harris, the last bastion of Sabbath observance in the UK, almost everything closes down on a Sunday. In fact, Stornoway must be the only place in the UK to suffer a Sunday rush hour as people drive to church around 10.30am; it's then a ghost town for an hour and a half until the services are over. But a few cracks have begun to appear.

There was outrage when British Airways/Loganair introduced Sunday flights to Stornoway in 2002, with members of the Lord's Day Observance Society spluttering that this was the thin end of the wedge. They were probably right – in 2003 a Stornoway petrol station began to open on a Sunday, and now does a roaring trade in Sunday papers and takeaway booze. Then in 2006, CalMac ferries between Leverburgh and Berneray began operating on Sundays, followed in 2009 by the Ullapool to Stornoway crossing, despite strong opposition from the residents (ironically, they were unable to protest at the ferries' arrival, as that would have meant breaking the Sabbath).

hours, one daily Monday, Tuesday and Thursday) and from Castlebay to Lochboisdale (one daily Wednesday, Friday and Sunday).

Advance booking for cars is recommended (essential in July and August); foot and bicycle passengers should have no problems. Bicycles are carried free.

❶ Getting Around

Despite their separate names, Lewis and Harris are actually one island. Berneray, North Uist, Benbecula, South Uist and Eriskay are all linked by road bridges and causeways. There are car ferries between Leverburgh (Harris) and Berneray; Tarbert (Harris) and Lochmaddy (North Uist); Eriskay and Castlebay (Barra); and Lochboisdale (South Uist) and Castlebay (Barra).

The local council publishes timetables of all bus and ferry services within the Outer Hebrides, available at tourist offices.

Timetables can also be found online at www.cne-siar.gov.uk/travel.

BICYCLE
The wind is often strong, so south to north is usually the easier direction. Bikes can be hired for around £15 a day or £60 to £80 a week in Stornoway (Lewis), Leverburgh (Harris), Howmore (South Uist) and Castlebay (Barra).

BUS
The bus network covers almost every village in the islands, with around four to six buses a day on all the main routes; however, there are no buses at all on Sunday.

CAR & MOTORCYCLE
Cars can be hired from around £35 per day. One option:
Lewis Car Rentals (☑ 01851-703760; www.lewis-car-rental.co.uk; 52 Bayhead St, Stornoway; ⊘ 8am-5pm Mon-Sat)

Lewis (Leodhais)
POP 21,000 (INCLUDES HARRIS)

The northern part of Lewis is dominated by the desolate expanse of the Black Moor, a vast, undulating peat bog dimpled with glittering lochans, seen clearly from the Stornoway–Barvas road. But Lewis' finest scenery is on the west coast, from Barvas southwest to Mealista, where the rugged landscape of hill, loch and sandy strand is reminiscent of the northwestern Highlands. The Outer Hebrides' most evocative historic sites – Callanish Standing Stones, Dun Carloway and Arnol Blackhouse Museum – are also to be found here.

Stornoway (Steornabhagh)
POP 5700

Stornoway is the bustling 'capital' of the Outer Hebrides and the only real town in the whole archipelago. It's a surprisingly busy little place, with cars and people swamping the centre on weekdays. Though set on a beautiful natural harbour, the town isn't going to win any prizes for beauty or atmosphere, but it's a pleasant enough introduction to this remote corner of the country.

◉ Sights

Lews Castle CASTLE
The Baronial mansion across the harbour from Stornoway town centre was built in the 1840s for the Matheson family, then owners of Lewis; it was gifted to the community by Lord Leverhulme in 1923. A major redevelopment sees the new **Museum nan Eilean** (Museum of the Isles) opening here from summer 2015, covering the history of the

FOR PEAT'S SAKE

In the Outer Hebrides, where trees are few and far between and coal is absent, peat has been the main source of domestic fuel for many centuries. Although oil-fired central heating is now the norm, many houses have held on to their peat fires for nostalgia's sake.

Peat in its raw state is extremely wet and can take a couple of months to dry out. It is cut from roadside bogs, where the cuttings are at least a metre deep. Rectangular blocks of peat are cut using a long-handled tool called a *tairsgeir* (peat-iron) and carefully assembled into a *cruach-mhonach* (peat stack), each balanced on top of the other in a grid pattern thus creating maximum air space. Once the peat has dried out it is stored in a shed.

Peat burns much more slowly than wood or coal and produces a not unpleasant smell, but in the old blackhouses (which had no chimney) it permeated every corner of the dwelling, not to mention the inhabitants' clothes and hair, hence the expression 'peat-reek' – the ever-present smell of peat smoke that was long associated with island life.

Outer Hebrides and exploring traditional island life. The beautiful **wooded grounds**, criss-crossed with walking trails, are open to the public and host the Hebridean Celtic Festival in July.

An Lanntair Arts Centre ARTS CENTRE
(✆ 01851-703307; www.lanntair.com; Kenneth St; ⊙ 10am-9pm Mon-Wed, to 10pm Thu, to midnight Fri & Sat) FREE The modern, purpose-built An Lanntair (Gaelic for 'lighthouse'), complete with art gallery, theatre, cinema and restaurant, is the centre of the town's cultural life; it hosts changing exhibitions of contemporary art and is a good source of information on cultural events.

★⁂ Festivals

Hebridean Celtic Festival MUSIC
(www.hebceltfest.com) A four-day extravaganza of folk, rock and Celtic music held in the second half of July.

⊨ Sleeping

Heb Hostel HOSTEL £
(✆ 01851-709889; www.hebhostel.co.uk; 25 Kenneth St; dm £18; @ �🛜) The Heb is a friendly, easygoing hostel close to the ferry, with comfy wooden bunks, a convivial living room with peat fire and a welcoming owner who can provide all kinds of advice on what to do and where to go.

Hal o' the Wynd B&B ££
(✆ 01851-706073; www.halothewynd.com; 2 Newton St; s/d from £60/80; 🛜) Touches of tartan and Harris Tweed lend a tradtional air to this welcoming B&B, conveniently located directly opposite the ferry pier. Most rooms have views over the harbour to Lews Castle. There's also a cafe on the premises.

Park Guest House B&B ££
(✆ 01851-702485; www.theparkguesthouse.co.uk; 30 James St; s/d from £58/110; @ 🛜) A charming Victorian villa with a conservatory and eight luxurious rooms (mostly en suite), the Park Guest House is comfortable and central and has the advantage of an excellent **restaurant** specialising in Scottish seafood, beef and game plus one or two vegetarian dishes (three-course dinners £30). Rooms overlooking the main road can be noisy on weekday mornings.

Braighe House B&B £££
(✆ 01851-705287; www.braighehouse.co.uk; 20 Braighe Rd; s/d from £115/130; ℗) This spacious and luxurious guesthouse, 3 miles east of the town centre on the A866, has stylish, modern bedrooms and a great seafront location. Good bathrooms with powerful showers, hearty breakfasts and genuinely hospitable owners round off the perfect package.

✗ Eating

Most restaurants in Stornoway close on Sunday, but a couple of options ensure you won't starve.

Thai Café THAI £
(✆ 01851-701811; www.thai-cafe-stornoway.co.uk; 27 Church St; mains £5-10; ⊙ noon-2.30pm & 5.30-11pm Mon-Sat; 🛜) Here's a surprise – authentic, inexpensive Thai food in the heart of Stornoway. This spick-and-span, no-frills restaurant has a genuine Thai chef and serves some of the most delicious, best-value Asian food in the Hebrides. If you can't get a table, it does takeaway.

★ Digby Chick BISTRO £££
(✆ 01851-700026; www.digbychick.co.uk; 5 Bank St; mains £17-25, 2-course lunches £13.50; ⊙ noon-2pm & 5.30-9pm Mon-Sat; 🖟) ⌁ A modern restaurant that dishes up bistro cuisine such as haddock and chips, slow-roast pork belly or roast vegetable panini at lunchtime, the Digby Chick metamorphoses into a candlelit gourmet restaurant in the evening, serving dishes such as grilled langoustines, seared scallops, venison and steak. The three-course early-bird menu (5.30pm to 6.30pm) costs £19.

🔒 Shopping

Sandwick Rd Petrol Station FOOD, DRINK
(Engebret Ltd; ✆ 01851-702304; Sandwick Rd; ⊙ 6am-11pm Mon-Sat, 10am-4pm Sun) The only shop in town that's open on a Sunday, selling groceries, alcohol, hardware, fishing tackle and outdoor kit; the Sunday papers arrive around 2pm.

❶ Getting There & Around

The bus station is on the waterfront, next to the ferry terminal (left luggage desk, £1.50 per piece). Bus W10 runs from Stornoway to Tarbert (£4.40, one hour, four or five daily Monday to Saturday) and Leverburgh (£6.20, two hours).

The Westside Circular bus W2 runs a circular route from Stornoway through Callanish (£2.50, 30 minutes), Carloway, Garenin and Arnol; the timetable means you can visit one or two of the sites in a day.

Arnol

One of Scotland's most evocative historic buildings, the **Arnol Blackhouse** (HS; ☏ 01851-710395; adult/child £4.50/2.70; ⊙ 9.30am-5.30pm Mon-Sat Apr-Sep, to 4.30pm Oct-Mar; P) is not so much a museum as a perfectly preserved fragment of a lost world. Built in 1885, this traditional blackhouse – a combined byre, barn and home – was inhabited until 1964 and has not been changed since the last inhabitant moved out. The staff faithfully rekindle the central peat fire every morning so you can experience the distinctive peat-reek; there's no chimney, and the smoke finds its own way out through the turf roof, windows and door – spend too long inside and you might feel like you've been kippered! The museum is just off the A858, about 3 miles west of Barvas.

Garenin (Na Gearrannan)

The picturesque and fascinating **Gearrannan Blackhouse Village** is a cluster of nine restored thatch-roofed blackhouses perched above the exposed Atlantic coast. One of the cottages is home to the **Blackhouse Museum** (☏ 01851-643416; www.gearrannan. com; adult/child £3/1; ⊙ 9.30am-5.30pm Mon-Sat Apr-Sep), a traditional 1955 blackhouse with displays on the village's history, while another houses the **Taigh an Chocair Cafe** (mains £3-6; ⊙ 9.30am-5.30pm Mon-Sat).

The other blackhouses in the village are let out as self-catering **holiday cottages** (☏ 01851-643416; www.gearrannan.com; 2-person cottage for 3 nights £226), offering the chance to stay in a unique and luxurious modernised blackhouse with attached kitchen and lounge. There's a minimum five-night stay from June to August.

Carloway (Carlabagh)

Dun Carloway (Dun Charlabhaigh) is a 2000-year-old, dry-stone broch, perched defiantly above a beautiful loch with views to the mountains of North Harris. The site is clearly signposted along a minor road off the A858, a mile southwest of Carloway village. One of the best-preserved brochs in Scotland, its double walls (with internal staircase) still stand to a height of 9m and testify to the engineering skills of its Iron Age architects.

The tiny, turf-roofed **Doune Broch Centre** (☏ 01851-643338; admission free; ⊙ 10am-5pm Mon-Sat Apr-Sep) FREE nearby has interpretative displays and exhibitions about the history of the broch and the life of the people who lived there.

Callanish (Calanais)

The **Callanish Standing Stones**, 15 miles west of Stornoway on the A858 road, form one of the most complete stone circles in Britain. It is one of the most atmospheric prehistoric sites anywhere; its ageless mystery, impressive scale and undeniable beauty leave a lasting impression. Sited on a wild and secluded promontory overlooking Loch Roag, 13 large stones of beautifully banded gneiss are arranged, as if in worship, around a 4.5m-tall central monolith. Some 40 smaller stones radiate from the circle in the shape of a cross, with the remains of a chambered tomb at the centre. Dating from 3800 to 5000 years ago, the stones are roughly contemporary with the pyramids of Egypt.

The nearby **Calanais Visitor Centre** (☏ 01851-621422; www.callanishvisitorcentre.co.uk; admission free, exhibition £2.50; ⊙ 9.30am-8pm Mon-Sat Jun-Aug, 10am-6pm Mon-Sat Apr, May, Sep & Oct, 10am-4pm Tue-Sat Nov-Mar; P) is a tour de force of discreet design. Inside is a small exhibition that speculates on the origins and purpose of the stones, and an excellent **cafe** (mains £4-7).

If you plan to stay the night, you have a choice of **Eschol Guest House** (☏ 01851-621357; www.eschol.com; 21 Breasclet; r per person £43; P) and neighbouring **Loch Roag Guest House** (☏ 01851-621357; www.lochroag. com; 22a Breasclet; r per person £39-55; P 🛜), half a mile north of Callanish. Both are modern bungalows with the same friendly owner, who is very knowledgeable about the local area (evening meals available).

Harris (Na Hearadh)

Harris, to the south of Lewis, is the scenic jewel in the necklace of islands that comprise the Outer Hebrides. It has a spectacular blend of rugged mountains, pristine beaches, flower-speckled machair and barren rocky landscapes. The isthmus at Tarbert splits Harris neatly in two: North Harris is dominated by mountains that rise forbiddingly above the peat moors to the south of Stornoway – Clisham (799m) is the highest point. South Harris is lower-lying, fringed by beautiful white-sand beaches in the west and a convoluted rocky coastline to the east.

Harris is famous for **Harris tweed**, a high-quality woollen cloth still hand-woven in islanders' homes. The industry employs around 400 weavers; staff at Tarbert tourist office can tell you about weavers and workshops you can visit.

Tarbert (An Tairbeart)

POP 480

Tarbert is a harbour village with a spectacular location, tucked into the narrow neck of land that links North and South Harris. It has ferry connections to Uig on Skye. Under construction at the time of research, **Isle of Harris Distillery** will be open to visitors daily (except Sunday) from spring 2015.

Village facilities include two petrol stations, a bank, an ATM and two general stores.

🛏 Sleeping & Eating

Tigh na Mara   B&B £

(☑ 01859-502270; East Tarbert; r per person £25-30; P) Excellent-value B&B (though the single room is a bit cramped) just five minutes from the ferry – go up the hill above the tourist office and turn right. The owner bakes fresh cakes every day, which you can enjoy in the conservatory with a view over the bay.

Harris Hotel   HOTEL ££

(☑ 01859-502154; www.harrishotel.com; s/d from £70/98; P@🛜) Run since 1903 by four generations of the Cameron family, Harris Hotel is a 19th-century sporting hotel, built in 1865 for visiting anglers and deer stalkers, and retains a distinctly old-fashioned atmosphere. It has spacious, comfy rooms and a decent restaurant; look out for JM Barrie's initials scratched on the dining-room window (the author of *Peter Pan* visited in the 1920s).

South Harris

The west coast of South Harris has some of the most beautiful beaches in Scotland. The blinding white sands and turquoise waters of **Luskentyre** and **Scarasta** would be major holiday resorts if they were transported to somewhere with a warm climate; as it is, they're usually deserted.

The **east coast** is a complete contrast – a strange, rocky moonscape of naked gneiss pocked with tiny lochans.

◉ Sights

Clò Mòr   EXHIBITION

(☑ 01859-511189; Old School, Drinishader; ⊘ 9am-5.30pm Mon-Sat; P) **FREE** The Campbell family has been making Harris tweed for 90 years, and this exhibition (behind the family shop) celebrates the history of the fabric known in Gaelic as *clò mòr* (the 'big cloth'); ask about live demonstrations of tweed weaving on the 70-year-old Hattersley loom. Drinishader is 5 miles south of Tarbert on the east coast road.

Seallam! Visitor Centre   EXHIBITION

(www.seallam.com; Northton; adult/child £2.50/2; ⊘ 10am-5pm Mon-Sat; P) The culture and landscape of the Hebrides are celebrated in the fascinating exhibition at Seallam! Visitor Centre (*Seallam* is Gaelic for 'Let me show you'). The centre, which is in Northton, 3 miles north of Leverburgh, also has a genealogical research centre for people who want to trace their Hebridean ancestry.

🛏 Sleeping & Eating

Am Bothan   HOSTEL £

(☑ 01859-520251; www.ambothan.com; Ferry Rd, Leverburgh; dm £20; P🛜) An attractive, chalet-style hostel, Am Bothan has small, neat dorms and a great porch where you can enjoy morning coffee with views over the creek. The hostel offers bike hire and can arrange wildlife-watching boat trips.

Carminish House   B&B ££

(☑ 01859-520400; www.carminish.com; 1a Strond, Leverburgh; s/d £60/80; P🛜) One of the few B&Bs in Harris that is open all year, the welcoming Carminish is a modern house with three comfy bedrooms. There's a view of the ferry from the dining room, and lots of nice little touches such as handmade soaps, a carafe of drinking water in the bedroom and fresh fruit salad at breakfast.

Sorrel Cottage   B&B ££

(☑ 01859-520319; www.sorrelcottage.co.uk; 2 Glen, Leverburgh; s/d from £48/72; 🐾) Sorrel Cottage is a pretty crofter's house, about 1.5 miles west of the ferry at Leverburgh. Vegetarians and vegans are happily catered for. Bike hire available.

ℹ Getting There & Around

A **CalMac** (☑ 0800 066 5000; www.calmac.co.uk) car ferry zigzags through the reefs of the Sound of Harris from Leverburgh to Berneray (pedestrian/car £7.35/33.50, one hour, three or four daily Monday to Saturday, two or three Sunday).

There are two to four buses a day (except Sunday) from Tarbert to Leverburgh.

Berneray (Bearnaraigh)

POP 140

Berneray was linked to North Uist by a causeway in October 1998, but that hasn't altered the peace and beauty of the island. The beaches on its west coast are some of the most beautiful and unspoilt in Britain, and seals and otters can be seen in Bays Loch on the east coast.

The basic but atmospheric Gatliff Hostel (www.gatliff.org.uk; adult/child dm £12/7, camping per person £8), housed in a pair of restored blackhouses right by the sea, is the place to stay. You can camp outside, or on the grass above the gorgeous white-sand beach just to the north.

Bus W19 runs from Berneray (Gatliff Hostel and Harris ferry) to Lochmaddy (£2.10, 20 to 30 minutes, eight daily Monday to Saturday). There are daily ferries to Leverburgh (Harris).

North Uist (Uibhist A Tuath)

POP 1300

North Uist, an island half-drowned by lochs, is famed for its trout fishing but also has some magnificent beaches on its north and west coasts. For birdwatchers this is an earthly paradise, with regular sightings of waders and wildfowl ranging from redshank to red-throated diver to red-necked phalarope. The landscape is less wild and mountainous than Harris, but it has a sleepy, subtle appeal.

Little Lochmaddy is the first village you hit after arriving on the ferry from Skye. There's a tourist office, a couple of stores, a bank with an ATM, a petrol station, a post office and a pub.

⊙ Sights & Activities

Balranald RSPB Reserve   WILDLIFE RESERVE
FREE Birdwatchers flock to this Royal Society for the Protection of Birds (RSPB) nature reserve, 18 miles west of Lochmaddy, in the hope of spotting the rare red-necked phalarope or hearing the distinctive call of the corncrake. There's a visitor centre (admission free; ⊙9am-6pm Apr-Aug) with a resident warden who offers 1½-hour guided walks (£5, depart visitor centre 10am Tuesday, May to September).

🛏 Sleeping & Eating

Rushlee House   B&B **££**
(☑01876-500274;   www.rushleehouse.co.uk; Lochmaddy; s/d £50/75; 🅿) A lovely modern bungalow with three luxuriously appointed bedrooms and great views of the hills to the south. No evening meals, but it's just a short walk to the restaurant at Hamersay House. The B&B is 0.75 miles from the ferry pier; take the first road on the right, then first left.

Langass Lodge Hotel   HOTEL **££**
(☑01876-580285;   www.langasslodge.co.uk; Locheport; s/d from £80/109; 🅿🛜) The delightful Langass Lodge Hotel is a former shooting lodge set in splendid isolation overlooking Loch Langais. Refurbished and extended, it now offers a dozen appealing rooms, many with sea views, and one of the Hebrides' best restaurants (mains £13-23; ⊙noon-2pm & 6-9pm), noted for its fine seafood and game.

Benbecula (Beinn Na Faoghla)

POP 1300

Benbecula is a low-lying island with a flat, lochan-studded landscape that's best appreciated from the summit of Rueval (124m), the island's highest point. There's a path around the south side of the island (signposted from the main road; park beside the landfill site) that is said to be the route taken to the coast by Bonnie Prince Charlie and Flora MacDonald during the prince's escape in 1746.

The main village, Balivanich, is headquarters for a military missile station on South Uist and has a bank with an ATM, a post office, a large Co-op supermarket (⊙8am-8pm Mon-Sat, 11am-6pm Sun) and a petrol station (open on Sunday).

South Uist (Uibhist A Deas)

POP 1800

South Uist is the second-largest island in the Outer Hebrides and saves its choicest corners for those who explore away from the main north–south road. The low-lying west coast is an almost unbroken stretch of white-sand beach and flower-flecked machair – a waymarked hiking trail, the Machair Way, follows the coast – while the multitude of inland lochs provide excellent trout fishing. The east coast, riven by four large sea lochs, is hilly and remote, with spectacular **Beinn Mhor** (620m) the highest point.

Driving south from Benbecula, you cross from the predominantly Protestant northern half of the Outer Hebrides into the mostly Roman Catholic south, a religious transition marked by the granite statue of **Our Lady of the Isles** on the slopes of Rueval (the hill with the military radomes on its summit) and the presence of many roadside shrines.

The ferry port of **Lochboisdale** is the island's largest settlement, with a tourist office, a bank with an ATM, a grocery store and a petrol station.

⊙ Sights & Activities

Loch Druidibeg National Nature Reserve   WILDLIFE RESERVE

FREE The northern part of North Uist is mostly occupied by the watery expanses of Loch Bee and Loch Druidibeg. Loch Druidibeg National Nature Reserve is an important breeding ground for birds such as dunlin, redshank, ringed plover, greylag goose and corncrake; you can take a 5-mile self-guided walk through the reserve. Ask for details at the Scottish Natural Heritage office on the main road beside the loch.

Kildonan Museum   MUSEUM

(☑ 01878-710343; www.kildonanmuseum.co.uk; Kildonan; adult/child £2/free; ☺ 10am-5pm Apr-Oct; P) Six miles north of Lochboisdale, Kildonan Museum explores the lives of local crofters through its collection of artefacts, an absorbing exhibition of black-and-white photography and first-hand accounts of harsh Hebridean conditions. There's also an excellent **tearoom** (mains £3-8; ☺ 11am-4pm) and craft shop.

Amid Milton's ruined blackhouses, half a mile south of the museum, a cairn marks the site of **Flora MacDonald's birthplace**.

🛌 Sleeping & Eating

Tobha Mor Crofters' Hostel   HOSTEL £

(www.gatliff.org.uk; Howmore; adult/child dm £12/7) An atmospheric hostel housed in a restored thatched blackhouse, about 12 miles north of Lochboisdale.

★ Polochar Inn   INN ££

(☑ 01878-700215; www.polocharinn.com; Polochar; s/d from £70/90; P 🛜) An 18th-century inn that has been transformed into a stylish, welcoming hotel with a stunning location looking out across the sea to Barra. The excellent restaurant and bar menu (mains £14

to £18) includes fish chowder, haddock and chips, local salmon and Uist lamb. Polochar is 7 miles southwest of Lochboisdale, on the way to Eriskay.

Eriskay (Eiriosgaigh)

POP 140

In 1745 Bonnie Prince Charlie first set foot in Scotland on the west coast of Eriskay, on the sandy beach (immediately north of the ferry terminal) still known as **Prince's Strand** (Coilleag a'Phrionnsa).

More recently the SS *Politician* sank just off the island in 1941. The islanders salvaged much of its cargo of around 250,000 bottles of whisky and, after a binge of dramatic proportions, the police intervened and a number of the islanders landed in jail. The story was immortalised by Sir Compton Mackenzie in his comic novel *Whisky Galore,* later made into a famous film.

A **car ferry** links Eriskay with Ardmhor at the northern end of Barra.

Barra (Barraigh)

POP 1200

With its beautiful **beaches**, wildflower-clad dunes, rugged little hills and strong sense of community, diminutive Barra – just 14 miles in circumference – is the Outer Hebrides in miniature. For a great view of the island, walk up to the top of **Heaval** (383m), a mile northeast of Castlebay.

Castlebay (Bagh a'Chaisteil), in the south, is the largest village. There's a tourist office (p939), a bank with an ATM, a post office and two grocery stores.

⊙ Sights & Activities

Kisimul Castle   CASTLE

(HS; ☑ 01871-810313; Castlebay; adult/child incl ferry £5.50/3.30; ☺ 9.30am-5.30pm Apr-Sep) Castlebay takes its name from the island fortress of Kisimul Castle, first built by the MacNeil clan in the 11th century. A short boat trip (weather permitting) takes you out to the island, where you can explore the fortifications and soak up the view from the battlements.

The castle was restored in the 20th century by American architect Robert MacNeil, who became the 45th clan chief; he gifted the castle to Historic Scotland in 2000 for an annual rent of £1 and a bottle of whisky (Talisker single malt, if you're interested).

🛏 Sleeping & Eating

Wild camping (on foot or by bike) is allowed almost anywhere.

Dunard Hostel   HOSTEL **£**
(☑ 01871-810443; www.dunardhostel.co.uk; Castlebay; dm/tw from £18/40; P) Dunard is a friendly, family-run hostel just five minutes' walk from the ferry terminal. The owners can organise sea-kayaking tours for £35/65 a half/full day.

Castlebay Hotel   HOTEL **££**
(☑ 01871-810223; www.castlebayhotel.com; Castlebay; s/d from £65/110; P 🛜) The Castlebay Hotel offers spacious bedrooms decorated with a subtle tartan motif – it's worth paying a bit extra for a sea view – and there's a comfy lounge and conservatory with grand views across the harbour to the islands south of Barra.

The hotel bar is the hub of island social life, with regular sessions of traditional music, and the restaurant specialises in local seafood and game (rabbit is often on the menu).

🛈 Getting There & Around

There are two daily flights from Glasgow to Barra airport, whose runway is the beach.

A **CalMac** (☑ 0800 066 5000; www.calmac.co.uk) car ferry (pedestrian/car £8/22.90, 40 minutes, three to five daily) links Eriskay with Ardmhor at the northern end of Barra.

Ferries also run from Castlebay to Oban and Lochboisdale.

A bus service links ferry arrivals and departures at Ardmhor with Castlebay (£1.60, 20 minutes). Bus W32 makes a circuit of the island up to five times daily (not Sunday), and also connects with flights.

Barra Cycle Hire (☑ 01871-810284; Castlebay; per day £12)

ORKNEY

There's a magic to Orkney that you begin to feel as soon as the Scottish mainland slips astern. An archipelago of mostly flat, green-topped islands stripped bare of trees and ringed with red sandstone cliffs, its heritage dates back to the Vikings whose influence is still strong today. Famed for ancient standing stones and prehistoric villages, for sublime sandy beaches and spectacular coastal scenery, it's a region whose ports tell of lives shared with the blessings and rough moods of the sea, and a destination where seekers can find melancholy wrecks of warships and the salty clamour of remote seabird colonies.

🧭 Tours

Wildabout Orkney   GUIDED TOUR
(☑ 01856-877737; www.wildaboutorkney.com) Operates tours covering Orkney's history, ecology, folklore and wildlife. Day trips operate year-round and cost £59, with pick-ups in Stromness and Kirkwall.

John O'Groats Ferries   BUS TOUR
(☑ 01955-611353; www.jogferry.co.uk; ☺ May-Sep) For the hurried; runs a one-day tour of the main sites for £58, including the ferry from John O'Groats. You can do the whole thing as a long day trip from Inverness.

🛈 Getting There & Away

AIR
Flybe (☑ 0871 700 2000; www.flybe.com) flies daily from Kirkwall to Aberdeen, Edinburgh, Glasgow, Inverness and Sumburgh (Shetland). Most summers it also serves Bergen (Norway).

BOAT
During summer, book ahead for car spaces. Peak season fares are quoted here.

From Scrabster, Shetland & Aberdeen
Northlink Ferries (☑ 0845 6000 449; www.northlinkferries.co.uk) operates ferries from Scrabster to Stromness (passenger/car £19.15/58, 1½ hours, two to three daily), from Aberdeen to Kirkwall (passenger/car £31/110, six hours, three or four weekly) and from Kirkwall to Lerwick (passenger/car £24.30/101, six to eight hours, three or four weekly) on Shetland. Fares are up to 30% lower off-season.

From Gills Bay
Pentland Ferries (☑ 01856-831226, 0800 688-8998; www.pentlandferries.co.uk; adult/child/car/bike £15/7/35/free) leave from Gills Bay, 3 miles west of John O'Groats, and head to St Margaret's Hope on South Ronaldsay three to four times daily.

From John O'Groats
From May to September, **John O'Groats Ferries** (☑ 01955-611353; www.jogferry.co.uk; single £15, incl bus to Kirkwall £17; ☺ May-Sep) operates a passenger-only service from John O'Groats to Burwick, on the southern tip of South Ronaldsay. A bus to Kirkwall meets the ferry. There are two to three departures daily.

BUS
John O'Groats Ferries has summer-only 'Orkney bus' service from Inverness to Kirkwall. Tickets (one way/return £40/55, five hours) include

Orkney

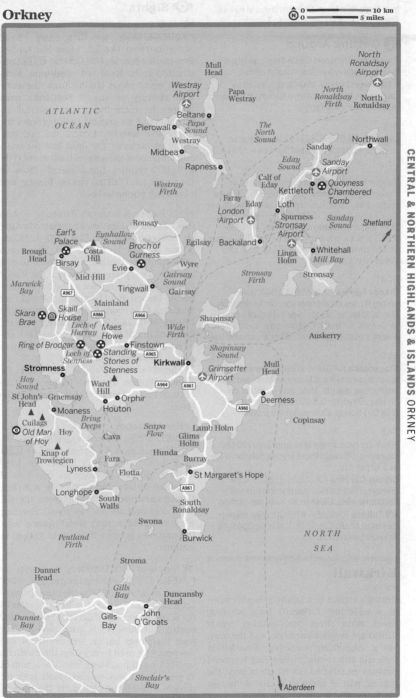

bus–ferry–bus travel from Inverness to Kirkwall. There are two daily from June to August.

ℹ️ Getting Around

The *Orkney Transport Guide* details all island transport and is free from tourist offices.

The largest island, Mainland, is linked by causeways to four southern islands; others are reached by air and ferry.

AIR

Loganair (📞 01856-873457; www.loganair. co.uk) operates interisland flights from Kirkwall.

BICYCLE

Various locations on Mainland hire bikes, including **Cycle Orkney** (📞 01856-875777; www. cycleorkney.com; Tankerness Lane, Kirkwall; per day/3 days/week £15/30/60; ⊙ 9am-5.30pm Mon-Sat) and **Orkney Cycle Hire** (📞 01856-850255; www.orkneycyclehire.co.uk; 54 Dundas St, Stromness; per day £10-12.50). Both offer out-of-hours pick-ups.

BOAT

Orkney Ferries (📞 01856-872044; www. orkneyferries.co.uk) operates car ferries from Mainland to the islands. See individual islands for details. An Island Explorer pass costs £42 for a week's passenger travel. Bikes are carried free.

BUS

Stagecoach (📞 01856-878014; www.stage-coachbus.com) Runs buses on Mainland and connecting islands. Most don't operate on Sunday. Dayrider (£8.30) and 7-Day Megarider (£18.55) tickets allow unlimited travel.

CAR

Small-car rates begin at around £35/190 per day/week, although there are specials for as low as £30 per day.

Orkney Car Hire (📞 01856-872866; www. orkneycarhire.co.uk; Junction Rd, Kirkwall) Recommended. Close to Kirkwall bus station.

WR Tullock (📞 01856-875500; www.orkney-carrental.co.uk; Castle St, Kirkwall) Opposite Kirkwall bus station.

Kirkwall

POP 7000

Orkney's capital is a bustling market town on a wide bay. Kirkwall's long, winding, paved main street and twisting wynds (lanes) are very atmospheric, and the town has a magnificent cathedral. Founded in the early 11th century, when Earl Rognvald Brusson established his kingdom here, the original part of Kirkwall is one of the best examples of an ancient Norse town.

◉ Sights

★ **St Magnus Cathedral**   CATHEDRAL
(📞 01856-874894; www.stmagnus.org; Broad St; ⊙ 9am-6pm Mon-Sat, 1-6pm Sun Apr-Sep, 9am-1pm & 2-5pm Mon-Sat Oct-Mar) **FREE** Constructed from local red sandstone, Kirkwall's centrepiece, dating from the early 12th century, is among Scotland's most interesting cathedrals. The powerful atmosphere of an ancient faith pervades the impressive interior. Lyrical and melodramatic epitaphs of the dead line the walls and emphasise the serious business of 17th- and 18th-century bereavement. Tours of the upper level (£7.25) run on Tuesday and Thursday; phone to book.

Earl's Palace & Bishop's Palace   RUINS
(HS; 📞 01856-871918; www.historic-scotland.gov. uk; Watergate; adult/child £4.50/2.70; ⊙ 9.30am-5.30pm Apr-Sep, to 4.30pm Oct) These two adjacent ruined palaces are worth poking around. The more intriguing, the **Earl's Palace**, was once known as the finest example of French Renaissance architecture in Scotland. One room features an interesting history of its builder, Earl Patrick Stewart, executed in Edinburgh for treason. He started construction in about 1600, but ran out of money and never completed it.

The **Bishop's Palace** was built for Bishop William the Old in the mid-12th century. There's a good cathedral view from the tower.

Orkney Museum   MUSEUM
(📞 01856-873191; www.orkney.gov.uk; Broad St; ⊙ 10.30am-12.30pm & 1.30-5pm Mon-Sat) **FREE** In a former merchant's house, this labyrinthine display includes an overview of Orcadian history and prehistory, including Pictish carvings and a display on the Ba'. Most engaging are the last rooms, covering 19th- and 20th-century social history. Note, the museum is open 10.30am to 5.30pm in summer.

★ **Highland Park Distillery**   DISTILLERY
(📞 01856-874619; www.highlandpark.co.uk; Holm Rd; tour adult/child £7.50/free; ⊙ 10am-5pm Mon-Sat & noon-5pm Sun May-Aug, 10am-5pm Mon-Fri Apr & Sep, 1-5pm Mon-Fri Oct-Mar) South of the centre, this distillery is great to visit. They malt their own barley; you can see it and the peat kiln used to dry it on the excellent, well-informed hour-long tour. The standard 12-year-old is a soft, balanced malt, great for novices and aficionados alike; the 18-year-

Kirkwall

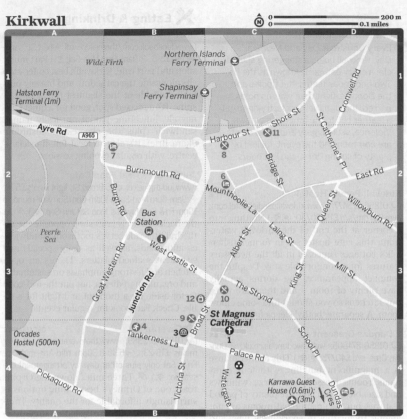

old is among the world's finest drams. This and older whiskies can be tasted on more specialised tours (£20 to £75), which you can prearrange.

✦✦ Festivals & Events

St Magnus Festival ARTS, MUSIC
(☎01856-871445; www.stmagnusfestival.com) A colourful celebration of music and the arts in late June.

🛏 Sleeping

Orcades Hostel HOSTEL £
(☎01856-873745; www.orcadeshostel.com; Muddisdale Rd; dm/s/d £20/40/52; P@🛜) Book ahead to get a bed in this cracking hostel on the western edge of town. It's a guesthouse conversion so there's a very smart kitchen and lounge, and great-value doubles. Comfortable dorms with just four bunks make for sound sleeping; young, enthusiastic owners give the place spark.

Kirkwall

◉ Top Sights
1 St Magnus Cathedral C4

◉ Sights
2 Earl's Palace & Bishop's Palace......... C4
3 Orkney Museum................................B4

◉ Activities, Courses & Tours
4 Cycle Orkney....................................B4

🛏 Sleeping
5 2 Dundas Crescent............................ D4
6 Albert Hotel.....................................C2
7 Kirkwall Peedie Hostel.......................B2

🍴 Eating
8 Helgi's...C2
9 Judith Glue Real Food Cafe B3
10 Reel...C3
11 Shore...C2

🛍 Shopping
12 Longship B3

THE BA'

Every Christmas Day and New Year's Day, Kirkwall holds a staggering spectacle: a crazy ball game known as the Ba'. Two enormous teams, the Uppies and the Doonies, fight their way, no holds barred, through the streets, trying to get a leather ball to the other end of town. Violence, skulduggery and other stunts are common and the event, fuelled by plenty of strong drink, can last hours.

Kirkwall Peedie Hostel HOSTEL £
(☑ 01856-875477; www.kirkwallpeediehostel.com; Ayre Rd; dm/s/d £15/20/30; P 🛜) Nestling into a corner at the end of the Kirkwall waterfront, this cute hostel set in former fisherfolk's cottages squeezes in all the necessary features for a comfortable stay. Despite the compact appearance, the dorms actually have plenty of room – and there are three tiny kitchens so you should find some elbow room. A separate 'bothy' sleeps four.

2 Dundas Crescent B&B ££
(☑ 01856-874805; www.twodundas.co.uk; 2 Dundas Cres; s/d £40/75; P 🛜) This former manse is a magnificent building with four enormous rooms blessed with large windows and sizeable beds. There are plenty of period features, but the en suite bathrooms are not among them: they're sparklingly new, and one has a free-standing bathtub. Both the welcome and the breakfast will leave you most content.

Karrawa Guest House GUESTHOUSE ££
(☑ 01856-871100; www.karrawaguesthouseorkney.co.uk; Inganess Rd; s/d £64/68; P 🛜🛜) In a peaceful location on the southeastern edge of Kirkwall, this enthusiastically run guesthouse offers significant value for its well-kept modern double rooms with comfortable mattresses. Breakfast is generously proportioned.

★ Albert Hotel HOTEL £££
(☑ 01856-876000; www.alberthotel.co.uk; Mounthoolie Lane; s/d £96/135; 🛜) Stylishly refurbished in plum and grey, this central but peaceful hotel is Kirkwall's finest address. Comfortable contemporary rooms in a variety of categories sport superinviting beds and smart bathrooms. A great Orkney base, with the more-than-decent Bothy Bar downstairs. Walk-in prices are often cheaper.

🍴 Eating & Drinking

Reel CAFE £
(www.facebook.com/thereelkirkwall; Albert St; sandwiches £3-6; ☉ 9am-6pm Mon-Sat; 🛜) Part music shop and part cafe, Kirkwall's best coffee-stop sits alongside the cathedral, and bravely puts tables outside at the slightest threat of sunshine. It's a relaxed spot, good for a quiet Orkney ale, lunchtime panini musically named sandwich (plus the cheese-and-mushroom Skara Brie). It's also a local folk-musicians' centre, with regular evening sessions.

Judith Glue Real Food Cafe CAFE £
(www.judithglue.com; 25 Broad St; light meals £5-10; ☉ 9am-Mon-Sat & 10am-6pm Sun year-round, to 10pm Fri & Sat May plus Mon-Sat Jun-Sep; 🛜) ✎ At the back of a lively craft shop opposite the cathedral, this cafe serves toothsome sandwiches and salads, as well as daily specials and succulent seafood platters. There's an open kitchen and a strong emphasis on sustainable and organic ingredients, but put the feel-good factor aside for a moment and fight for a table. Check Facebook for regular events.

★ Foveran ORCADIAN ££
(☑ 01856-872389; www.thefoveran.com; St Ola; mains £15-23; ☉ 6.30-8.30pm mid-Apr–mid-Oct, Fri & Sat only plus other days by arrangement off-season; 🛜) ✎ Three miles down the Orphir road, one of Orkney's best dining options is surprisingly affordable for the quality. Tranquilly located, with a cosy eating area overlooking the sea, it shines through its use of classic Orcadian ingredients – the steak with haggis and whisky sauce is feted throughout, while North Ronaldsay lamb comes in four different, deliciously tender cuts.

Shore GASTROPUB ££
(www.theshore.co.uk; 6 Shore St; bar meals £8-10, restaurant mains £12-18; ☉ food 11am-9.30pm; 🛜) This popular harbourside eatery offers bar meals combined with more adventurous evening fare in the restaurant section. It's run with a customer-comes-first attitude, and the seafood is especially good.

Helgi's PUB FOOD ££
(www.helgis.co.uk; 14 Harbour St; mains £10-12; ☉ food noon-9pm, from 12.30pm Sun; 🛜) There's a traditional cosiness about this place, but the decor has moved beyond the time-honoured beer-soaked carpet to a contemporary slate floor and quotes from the *Orkneyinga Saga* plastering the walls. It's more find-a-table than jostle-at-the-bar and

serves cheerful, well-priced comfort food – light bites only between 2pm and 5pm. Take your pint upstairs for some quiet harbour contemplation.

🛍 Shopping

Kirkwall has some gorgeous jewellery and crafts along Albert St. The **Longship** (✆01856-888790; www.olagoriejewellery.com; 7 Broad St; ⏰10am-5pm Mon-Sat Sep-May, 9am-5.30pm daily Oct-Apr), established in 1859, has Orkney-made crafts, food, gifts and exquisite designer jewellery across adjacent shops.

ℹ Information

Kirkwall Information Centre (✆01856-872856; kirkwall@visitscotland.com; West Castle St; ⏰9am-6pm daily Jun-Sep, 9am-5pm Mon-Fri & 10am-2pm Sat Oct-Apr, 9am-6pm Mon-Sat & 10am-2pm Sun May) Has a good range of Orkney info. Shares building with the bus station.

ℹ Getting There & Away

AIR

Flybe (p946) and Loganair (p948) services use **Kirkwall Airport** (www.hial.co.uk), located a few miles east of town and served by bus 4.

BOAT

Ferries to the Northern Islands depart from the town harbour; however, ferries to Aberdeen and Shetland use the Hatston terminal, 1 mile northwest. Bus X10 shuttles out there regularly.

BUS

All services leave from the **bus station** (West Castle St):
Bus X1 Stromness (£3, 30 minutes, hourly, seven Sunday); St Margaret's Hope (£2.80)
Bus 2 Orphir and Houton (£2.70, 20 minutes, four or five Monday to Saturday)
Bus 5 Evie (£2.70, 30 minutes, three to five daily Monday to Saturday), Tingwall (Rousay ferry) and Birsay

Mainland To South Ronaldsay

After a German U-boat sank battleship HMS *Royal Oak* in 1939, Winston Churchill had causeways of concrete blocks erected across the channels on the eastern side of Scapa Flow, linking Mainland to the islands of Lamb Holm, Glims Holm, Burray and South Ronaldsay. The Churchill Barriers, flanked by rusting wrecks of blockships, now support the main road from Kirkwall to Burwick.

ℹ Getting There & Away

Bus X1 goes to South Ronaldsay's St Margaret's Hope (£2.80, 30 minutes, almost hourly Monday to Saturday).

Lamb Holm

On the tiny island of Lamb Holm, the **Italian Chapel** (✆01865-781268; ⏰9am-dusk) **FREE** is all that remains of a POW camp that housed the Italian soldiers who worked on the Churchill Barriers. They built the chapel in their spare time, using two Nissen huts, scrap metal and their considerable artistic skills. One of the artists returned in 1960 to restore the paintwork. It's quite extraordinary inside.

South Ronaldsay

South Ronaldsay's main village, pristine St Margaret's Hope, was named after the Maid of Norway, who died here in 1290 on her way to marry Edward II of England (strictly a political affair: Margaret was only seven years old). The ferry from Gills Bay on mainland Scotland docks here, while the passenger ferry from John O'Groats lands at Burwick, at the island's southern tip.

⊙ Sights

★**Tomb of the Eagles** ARCHAEOLOGICAL SITE (✆01865-831339; www.tomboftheeagles.co.uk; Liddel; adult/child £7.50/3.50; ⏰9.30am-5.30pm Apr-Sep, 10am-noon Mar, 9.30am-12.30pm Oct) Two significant archaeological sites were found here by a farmer on his land. The first is a Bronze Age stone building with a firepit, indoor well, and plenty of seating: a communal cooking site or the original Orkney pub? Beyond, in a spectacular clifftop position, the Neolithic tomb (wheel yourself in prone on a trolley) is an elaborate stone construction that held the remains of up to 340 people who died some five millennia ago.

An excellent personal explanation is given to you at the **visitor centre**; you meet a few spooky skulls and can handle some of the artefacts found, plus absorb information on the Mesolithic period. It's about a mile's airy walk to the tomb from the centre, which is near Burwick.

Banks Chambered Tomb ARCHAEOLOGICAL SITE (Tomb of the Otters; www.bankschamberedtomb.co.uk; Cleat; adult/child £6/free; ⏰10am-5pm Apr-Oct) Discovered while digging a car park, this 5000-year-old chambered tomb is still being investigated, but has yielded a vast quantity of human bones (well preserved thanks to the saturation of the earth). The tomb is dug into bedrock and makes for an atmospheric if claustrophobic visit. The guided tour from the guy who found it mixes homespun archaeological theories with astute observations.

In the visitor centre, which has a good bistro too, you can handle finds of stones and bones, including the remains of otters, who presumably used this as a den. Follow the signs for the Tomb of the Eagles.

🛏 Sleeping & Eating

St Margaret's Hope Backpackers HOSTEL £
(☎01856-831225; www.orkneybackpackers.com; dm £15; P) Just a stroll from the Gills Bay ferry, this hostel is a lovely stone cottage offering small, simple rooms with up to four berths – great for families. There's a lounge, kitchen, laundry and good, hot showers. Book in at the Trading Post shop next door.

★ Bankburn House B&B ££
(☎01856-831310; www.bankburnhouse.co.uk; A961; s/d £52/68, without bathroom £41/62; P@🛜🅿) 🍽 This large rustic house does everything right, with smashing good-sized rooms and engaging owners who put on quality breakfasts and take pride in constantly innovating to improve guests' comfort levels. The huge lawn overlooks St Margaret's Hope and the bay – perfect for sunbathing on shimmering Orkney summer days. Prices drop substantially for multinight stays.

★ Creel SEAFOOD £££
(☎01856-831311; www.thecreel.co.uk; Front Rd, St Margaret's Hope; 2-/3-course dinners £33/40; ⊗7-9pm Tue-Sat Apr–mid-Oct; 🛜) 🍽 On the waterfront in an unassuming house, on unpretentious wooden tables, some of Scotland's best seafood has been served up for well over 20 years. Upstairs, three most comfortable rooms (singles/doubles £75/110) face the spectacular sunset over the water. Wooden ceilings and plenty of space give them an airy feel. It was up for sale at the time of research, so fingers crossed.

West & North Mainland

This part of the island is sprinkled with outstanding prehistoric monuments: the journey to Orkney is worth it for these alone. It would take the best part of a day to see all of them – if pushed for time, visit Skara Brae then Maes Howe, but book your visit to the latter in advance.

◉ Sights

★ Maes Howe ARCHAEOLOGICAL SITE
(HS; ☎01856-761606; www.historic-scotland.gov.uk; adult/child £5.50/3.30; ⊗tours hourly 10am-4pm) Egypt has pyramids, Scotland has Maes Howe. Constructed about 5000 years ago, it's an extraordinary place, a Stone-Age tomb built from enormous sandstone blocks, some of which weighed many tons and were brought from several miles away. Creeping down the long stone passageway to the central chamber, you feel the indescribable gulf of years that separate us from the architects of this mysterious place. Though nothing is known about who and what was interred here, the scope of the project suggests it was a structure of great significance.

In the 12th century, the tomb was broken into by Vikings searching for treasure. A couple of years later, another group sought shelter in the chamber from a three-day blizzard. Waiting out the storm, they carved runic graffiti on the walls. As well as the some-things-never-change 'Olaf was 'ere' and 'Thorni bedded Helga', there are also more intricate carvings, including a particularly fine dragon and a knotted serpent.

Buy tickets in Tormiston Mill across the road. Entry is by 45-minute guided tours on the hour: reserve your tour-slot ahead by phone. Oversized groups mean guides tend to only show a couple of the Viking inscriptions, but they'll happily show more if asked.

Standing Stones of Stenness ARCHAEOLOGICAL SITE
(HS; www.historic-scotland.gov.uk; ⊗24hr) FREE Within sight of Maes Howe, four mighty stones remain of what was once a circle of 12. Recent research suggests they were perhaps erected as long ago as 3300 BC, and they impose by their sheer size; the tallest measures 5.7m in height. The narrow strip of land they're on, the Ness of Brodgar, separates the Harray and Stenness lochs and was the site of a large settlement, inhabited throughout the Neolithic period (3500–1800 BC).

Barnhouse Neolithic Village RUINS
(HS; www.historic-scotland.gov.uk; ⊗24hr) FREE Alongside the Standing Stones of Stenness are the excavated remains of a village thought to have been inhabited by the builders of Maes Howe. Don't skip this – it brings the area to life. The houses are well

preserved and similar to Skara Brae with their stone furnishings. One of the buildings was entered by crossing a fireplace: possibly of ritual significance.

Ring of Brodgar
ARCHAEOLOGICAL SITE
(HS; www.historic-scotland.gov.uk; ⊘24hr) FREE
A mile north of Stenness is this wide circle of standing stones, some over 5m tall. The last of the three Stenness monuments to be built (2500–2000 BC), it remains a most atmospheric location. Twenty-one of the original 60 stones still stand among the heather. On a grey day with dark clouds thudding low across the sky, the stones are a spine-tingling sight.

★ Skara Brae
ARCHAEOLOGICAL SITE
(HS; www.historic-scotland.gov.uk; joint ticket with Skaill House adult/child £7.10/4.30; ⊘9.30am-5.30pm Apr-Sep, to 4.30pm Oct-Mar) Idyllically situated by a sandy bay 8 miles north of Stromness, and predating Stonehenge and the pyramids of Giza, extraordinary Skara Brae is northern Europe's best-preserved prehistoric village. Even the stone furniture (beds, boxes and dressers) has survived the 5000 years since a community lived and breathed here. It was hidden under dunes until an 1850 storm exposed the houses.

There's an excellent interactive exhibit and short video, arming visitors with facts and theory, which will enhance the impact of the site. You then enter a reconstructed house, giving more meaning to the excavation, which you head on to next.

The joint ticket also gets you into Skaill House (HS; ⊘Apr-Sep), a mansion built for the bishop in 1620. It's a bit anticlimactic catapulting straight from the Neolithic to the 1950s decor, but you can see a smart hidden compartment in the library as well as the bishop's original 17th-century four-poster bed.

Buses run to Skara Brae from Kirkwall and Stromness a few times weekly in summer, but not all are useful to visit the site. It's possible to walk along the coast from Stromness to Skara Brae (9 miles), or it's an easy taxi (£15), hitch or cycle from Stromness. If you ring before 3pm the day before, you can book Octobus (☑01856-871536; www.octocic. co.uk) from Kirkwall (£3.20 each way).

Birsay

The small village of Birsay is 6 miles north of Skara Brae. The ruins of the Earl's Pal-

ace (⊘24hr) FREE, built in the 16th century by the despotic Robert Stewart, earl of Orkney, dominate the village centre. Today it's a mass of half walls and crumbling columns, the latter climbing like dilapidated chimney stacks.

At low tide (check tide times at the shop in Earl's Palace) you can walk out to the Brough of Birsay (HS; www.historic-scotland. gov.uk; adult/child £4.50/2.70; ⊘9.30am-5.30pm mid-Jun–Sep), where you'll find the extensive ruins of a Norse settlement and the 12th-century St Peter's Church.

Evie

On an exposed headland at Aikerness, a 1.5-mile walk northeast from the straggling village of Evie, you'll find the Broch of Gurness (HS; www.historic-scotland. uk; adult/child £5.50/3.30; ⊘9.30am-12.30pm & 1.30-5.30pm Apr-Sep), a fine example of these drystone fortified towers that were both status symbol for powerful farmers and useful protection from raiders some 2200 years ago. The imposing entranceway and sturdy stone walls – originally 10m high – impress; inside you can see the hearth and where a mezzanine floor would have fitted. Around the broch are the remains of the settlement centred on it.

Stromness
POP 1800
This appealing grey-stone port has a narrow, elongated, flagstone-paved main street and tiny alleys leading down to the waterfront between tall stone houses. It lacks Kirkwall's size, but makes up for that with bucketloads

---

A NEOLITHIC VATICAN?

Ongoing excavations on the Ness of Brodgar, between the Stenness standing stones and the Ring of Brodgar, are rapidly revealing that this was a Neolithic site of huge importance. Probably a major power and religious centre and used for over a millennium, the settlement had a mighty wall, a large building (temple or palace?) and as many as 100 other structures, some painted. Each dig season reveals new intriguing finds. During the season, mid-July to late August, free guided tours of the excavation run at 11am, 1pm and 3pm.

of character, having changed little since its heyday in the 18th century. Stromness is ideally located for trips to Orkney's major prehistoric sites.

Sights

★Stromness Museum
MUSEUM
(☑ 01856-850025; www.stromnessmuseum.co.uk; 52 Alfred St; adult/child £4.50/1; ☉ 10am-5pm daily Apr-Sep, 11am-3.30pm Mon-Sat Oct-Mar) A superb museum full of knick-knacks from maritime and natural-history exhibitions covering whaling, the Hudsons Bay Company and the sunk German fleet. You can happily nose around for a couple of hours. Across the street is the house where local poet and novelist George Mackay Brown lived.

Pier Arts Centre
GALLERY
(☑ 01856-850209; www.pierartscentre.com; 30 Victoria St; ☉ 10.30am-5pm Tue-Sat, plus Mon Jun-Aug) **FREE** This gallery has really rejuvenated the Orkney modern-art scene with its sleek lines and upbeat attitude. It's worth a look as much for the architecture as its high-quality collection of 20th-century British art and the changing exhibitions.

★ Festivals & Events

Orkney Folk Festival
MUSIC
(www.orkneyfolkfestival.com) A four-day event in late May, with folk concerts, *ceilidhs* and casual pub sessions. Stromness packs out, and late-night buses from Kirkwall are laid on. Book tickets and accommodation ahead.

🛏 Sleeping

Hamnavoe Hostel
HOSTEL £
(☑ 01856-851202; www.hamnavoehostel.co.uk; 10a North End Rd; dm/s/tw £20/22/44; ☎) This well-equipped hostel is efficiently run and boasts excellent facilities, including a fine kitchen and a lounge room with great perspectives over the water. The dorms are very commodious, with duvets, decent mattresses and reading lamps (bring a pound coin for the heating), and the showers are good. Ring ahead as the owner lives off-site.

Brown's Hostel
HOSTEL £
(☑ 01856-850661; www.brownsorkney.co.uk; 45 Victoria St; s £20, d £36-45; @☎) On the main street, this handy, sociable place has cosy private rooms – no dorms, no bunks – at a good price. There's an inviting common area, where you can browse the free internet or swap pasta recipes in the open kitchen. There are en suite rooms in a house up the street, with self-catering options available.

Point of Ness Caravan & Camping Park
CAMPSITE £
(☑ office hours 01856-873535, site 01856-850532; www.orkney.gov.uk; Ness Rd; tent sites 1/2 people £7.20/11.20; ☉ Apr-Sep; P☎🐕) This breezy, fenced-in campsite has a super location overlooking the bay at the southern end of town and is as neat as a pin. There's free wi-fi.

★Brinkies Guest House
B&B ££
(☑ 01856-851881; www.brinkiesguesthouse.co.uk; s £50, d £75-80; P☎) Just a short walk from

---

DIVING SCAPA FLOW'S WRECKS

One of the world's largest natural harbours, Scapa Flow, the sheltered bay enclosed by the archipelago's main islands, has been in near-constant use by various fleets from the Vikings onwards. After WWI, 74 German ships were interned here; when the terms of the armistice included a severely reduced German navy, Admiral von Reuter, who was in charge of the fleet, decided to take matters into his own hands. A secret signal was passed from ship to ship and the British watched incredulously as every German ship began to sink. Fifty-two of them went to the bottom, with the rest left aground in shallow water.

Most were salvaged, but seven vessels remain to attract divers. There are three battleships – the *König*, the *Kronprinz Wilhelm* and the *Markgraf* – all of which weigh over 25,000 tonnes. The first two were subjected to blasting for scrap metal, but the *Markgraf* is undamaged and considered one of Scotland's best dives.

Numerous other ships rest on the sea bed in Scapa Flow. HMS *Royal Oak*, sunk by a German U-boat in October 1939 with the loss of 833 crew, is an official war grave – diving here is prohibited.

The wreck dives are for experienced divers only. **Scapa Scuba** (☑ 01856-851218; www. scapascuba.co.uk; Lifeboat House, Stromness; beginner's try dive £80, 2 guided dives £125-145; ☉ noon-7pm Mon-Fri & 3-6pm Sat & Sun May-Sep) is an excellent operator.

the centre, but with a lonely, king-of-the-castle position overlooking the town and bay, this exceptional place offers five-star islander hospitality. Compact, modern rooms are handsome, stylish and comfortable, and public areas are done out most attractively in wood, but above all it's the charming owner's flexibility and can-do attitude that makes this so special.

Burnside Farm   B&B ££

(☑ 01856-850723; www.burnside-farm.com; North End Rd; s £50, d £80-95; ℗ ☜) A most pleasing option on a working dairy farm on the edge of Stromness, this offers lovely views over green fields, the town and harbour. Rooms are elegant, and maintain the style from when the house was built in the late '40s, with elegant period furnishings. The top-notch bathrooms, however, are sparklingly contemporary. Breakfast is served with vistas, and the kindly owner couldn't be more welcoming.

✗ Eating & Drinking

Ferry Inn   PUB FOOD £

(☑ 01856-850280; www.ferryinn.com; 10 John St; mains £7-14; ⊘ food noon-2pm & 5-9pm Mon-Fri, noon-9pm Sat & Sun; ☜) Every port has its pub, and in Stromness it's the Ferry. Convivial and central, it warms the cockles with folk music, local beers and characters, and pub food that offers plenty of value in a dining area done out like the deck of a ship. The fish and chips are excellent, and a few blackboard specials fill things out. It's also open for breakfast.

Hamnavoe Restaurant   SEAFOOD ££

(☑ 01856-850606; 35 Graham Pl; mains £15-22; ⊘ 6-9pm Tue-Sun Jun-Aug) Tucked away off the main street, this Stromness favourite specialises in excellent local seafood in an intimate, cordial atmosphere. There's always something good off the boats, and the chef prides himself on his lobster. Booking is a must. It usually opens weekends off-season.

ⓘ Information

Stromness Information Centre (☑ 01856-850716; www.visitorkney.com; Ferry Rd; ⊘ 10am-4pm Mon-Fri & 8.30am-2.30pm Sat Apr-May, 9am-5pm daily Jun-Oct) In the ferry terminal.

ⓘ Getting There & Away

Northlink Ferries (☑ 0845 6000 449; www.northlinkferries.co.uk) runs services from Stromness to Scrabster on the mainland (passenger/car £19.15/58, 1½ hours, two to three daily).

Bus X1 runs regularly to Kirkwall (£3, 30 minutes) and on to St Margaret's Hope.

Hoy

Orkney's second-largest island, Hoy (meaning 'High Island'), got the lion's share of the archipelago's scenic beauty. Shallow turquoise bays lace the east coast and massive seacliffs guard the west, while peat and moorland cover Orkney's highest hills. Much of the north is a reserve for breeding seabirds. Book the car ferry to Hoy ahead.

⊙ Sights

Scapa Flow Visitor Centre   MUSEUM

(☑ 01856-791300; www.orkney.gov.uk; Lyness; admission by donation; ⊘ 9am-4.30pm Mon-Fri Mar-Oct, plus 9am-4.30pm Sat May-Oct, first ferry arrival to 4pm Sun May-Sep) Lyness was an important naval base during both world wars, when the British Grand Fleet was based in Scapa Flow. This fascinating museum and photographic display, located in an old pumphouse that once fed fuel to the ships, is a must-see for anyone interested in Orkney's military history. Take your time to browse the exhibits and have a look at the folders of supplementary information: letters home from a seaman, killed when the *Royal Oak* was torpedoed, are particularly moving.

Old Man of Hoy   HEADLAND

Hoy's best-known sight is this spectacular 137m-high rock stack jutting from the ocean off the tip of an eroded headland. It's a tough ascent for experienced climbers only, but a great walk from Rackwick (6 miles return). You can see it from the Scrabster–Stromness ferry.

▭ Sleeping

Hoy Centre   HOSTEL £

(☑ office hours 01856-873535, warden 01856-791315; www.orkney.gov.uk; dm/tw £18/49; ℗) This clean, bright modern hostel has an enviable location, around 15 minutes' walk from Moaness Pier, at the base of the rugged Cuilags. Rooms are all en suite and include good-value family options; there's also a spacious kitchen and DVD lounge. The same people run a simpler hostel at Rackwick, five miles away.

Wild Heather   B&B ££

(☑ 01856-791098; www.wildheatherbandb.co.uk; Lyness; s/d £43/69; ℗) Turn right from the Lyness ferry to reach this great place right on the bay. The lovely room is frilly and spotless, with soul-soothing water views from your own wee conservatory, where you also tuck into breakfast. Packed lunches and three-course dinners (£16.50) are available, as well as cycle storage and a genuine welcome. The owners' daughter runs a cute craft shop alongside.

ℹ Getting There & Away

Orkney Ferries (p948) runs a passenger and bike ferry (adult £4.25, 30 minutes, two to six daily) between Stromness and Moaness at Hoy's northern end, and a car ferry to Lyness from Houton on Mainland (passenger/car £4.25/13.60, 40 minutes, up to seven daily Monday to Friday, two or three Saturday and Sunday); book cars in advance. Sunday service is May to September only.

A bus meets the ferries and runs to Hoy's main settlements.

Northern Islands

The group of windswept islands north of Mainland is a haven for birds, rich in archaeological sites, and blessed with wonderful white-sand beaches and azure seas. Some give a real sense of what Orkney was like before the modern world infringed upon island life.

The tourist offices in Kirkwall and Stromness on Mainland have the useful Islands of Orkney brochure with maps and details of these islands. Note that the 'ay' at the end of island names (from the Old Norse for 'island') is pronounced 'ee'.

Rousay

Off the north coast of Mainland, Rousay makes a great day trip, but you'll feel like staying longer. This hilly island is famous for its numerous excellent archaeological sites.

◉ Sights & Activities

You can hire a bike at Trumland Farm (£7 per day) and make the hilly 14-mile circuit of the island. You can walk from the ferry pier to Midhowe Broch, taking in all the main historic sites (12 miles return, allow six hours).

★ Midhowe Cairn & Broch   ARCHAEOLOGICAL SITE
(HS; www.historic-scotland.gov.uk; ⊙24hr) FREE Six miles from the ferry, mighty Midhowe Cairn has been dubbed the 'Great Ship of Death'. Built around 3500 BC and enormous, it's divided into compartments, in which the remains of 25 people were found. Covered by a protective stone building, it's nevertheless memorable. Adjacent Midhowe Broch, whose sturdy stone lines echo the rocky shoreline's striations, is a muscular Iron Age fortified compound with a mezzanine floor. The sites are on the water, a 10-minute walk downhill from the main road.

Prehistoric Sites   ARCHAEOLOGICAL SITE
(HS; www.historic-scotland.gov.uk; ⊙24hr) FREE The major archaeological sites are clearly labelled from the road ringing the island. Heading west from the ferry, you soon come to Taversoe Tuick, an intriguing burial cairn constructed on two levels, with separate entrances – perhaps a joint tomb for different families; a semidetached solution in posthumous housing. Not far beyond are two other significant cairns: Blackhammer, then Knowe of Yarso, the latter a fair walk up the hill but with majestic views.

Rousay Tours   GUIDED TOUR
(☎01856-821234; www.rousaytours.co.uk; adult/child £30/10) Friendly Patrick offers taxi service and recommended guided tours of the island, including wildlife-spotting (seals and otters), visits to the prehistoric sites and a tasty packed lunch.

🛏 Sleeping & Eating

Trumland Farm   HOSTEL £
(☎01856-821252; trumland@btopenworld.com; sites £5, dm £12-14; ℗🐾) 🐾 An easy stroll from the ferry (turn left at the main road), this organic farm has a wee hostel with two dorms and a pretty little kitchen and common area. You can pitch tents and use the facilities; there's also well-equipped self-catering in a cottage and various farm buildings.

Taversoe Hotel   HOTEL ££
(☎01856-821325; www.taversoehotel.co.uk; s/d £50/80; ℗) Two miles west from the ferry pier, the island's only hotel is a low-key place, with neat, simple doubles that have water vistas and share a bathroom, and a twin with en suite but no view. The best views are from the dining room, which serves good-value meals (noon to 5pm Monday, noon to 9pm Tuesday to Saturday and noon to 7.30pm Sunday in summer). The friendly owners will collect you from the ferry.

ℹ Getting There & Around

A small **ferry** (☑ 01856-751360; www.orkneyferries.co.uk) connects Tingwall on Mainland with Rousay (passenger/bicycle/car return £8.50/ free/27.20, 30 minutes, up to six daily) and the nearby islands of Egilsay and Wyre. Vehicle bookings are compulsory.

ℹ Getting There & Around

There's a Monday and Wednesday flight from Kirkwall (one way £37, 30 minutes) to London airport – that's London, Eday.

Ferries sail from Kirkwall, sometimes via Stronsay or Sanday (passenger/car £8.35/19.70, two hours, two to three daily).

Stronsay

Stronsay attracts walkers and cyclists for its lack of serious inclines and the beautiful landscapes of its four curving bays. You can spot wildlife here: chubby seals basking on the rocks, puffins and other seabirds.

🛏 Sleeping & Eating

Stronsay Hotel   HOTEL ££
(☑ 01857-616213; www.stronsayhotelorkney.co.uk; s/d £50/79; 🐾🐕) The island's watering hole is near the ferry and has immaculate refurbished rooms. There's also recommended pub grub in the bar.

ℹ Getting There & Away

Loganair (☑ 01857-873457; www.loganair.co.uk) flies from Kirkwall to Stronsay (£37 one way, 20 minutes, one or two daily).

A **ferry** (☑ 01856-872044; www.orkneyferries.co.uk) links Kirkwall with Stronsay (passenger/car £8.35/19.70, 1½ hours, two to three daily) and Eday.

Eday

This slender island was extensively cut for peat to supply the surrounding islands. The interior is hilly and covered in peat bog, while the coast and the north of the island are low-lying and green.

👁 Sights & Activities

Eday Heritage & Visitor Centre   MUSEUM
(☑ 01857-622283; www.visiteday.com; ⏰9am-5.30pm daily May-Sep, 10am-5pm Sun Oct-Apr) FREE Has a range of local history exhibits, as well as an audiovisual about tidal energy initiatives: there's a big test project just offshore.

🛏 Sleeping & Eating

Eday Hostel   HOSTEL £
(☑ 07977-281084; dm £12-15; P@🐾) Four miles north of the ferry pier, this recently renovated, community-run hostel is a simple but comfortable place to stay. You can camp alongside too at no cost and there are bikes available to hire.

Sanday

Aptly named, blissfully quiet flat Sanday is ringed by Orkney's best beaches, with dazzling white sand of the sort you'd expect in the Caribbean. It's a peaceful, green, pastoral landscape with the sea revealed at every turn.

👁 Sights

Quoyness Chambered Tomb   ARCHAEOLOGICAL SITE
(⏰24hr) FREE There are several archaeological sites on Sanday, the most impressive being the Quoyness chambered tomb, similar to Maes Howe and dating from the 3rd millennium BC. It has triple walls, a main chamber and six smaller cells.

Sanday Heritage Centre   MUSEUM
(Lady Village; entry by donation; ⏰9am-5pm Mar-Oct) This new museum in the former temperance hall has intriguing displays on various aspects of island history, including fishing, the wars, archaeology and shipwrecks. In an adjacent field, a typical croft house has been preserved.

🛏 Sleeping

Two adjacent pubs in the main settlement, Kettletoft, offer accommodation and basic bar meals.

Ayre's Rock Hostel & Campsite   HOSTEL, CAMPSITE £
(☑ 01857-600410; www.ayres-rock-hostel-orkney.com; tent sites 1-/2-person £7/9, pods per person £10, dm/s/tw £15/18/30; P🐾🐕) This super-friendly spot six miles north of the ferry by a beach offers a cosy hostel with three rooms sleeping two or four in beds, and a sweet grassy campsite by the water. As well as tent pitches, there are heated two-person pods and a static caravan. There's a craft shop and Saturday chip shop on site, and hosts are extremely helpful.

Backaskaill   B&B ££
(☑ 01857-600305; www.bedandbreakfastsandayorkney.com; s/d £45/75; P🐾) Set on a working cattle farm by the sea, Backaskaill offers

comfortable accommodation in a noble stone farmhouse. The polished interior features an eclectic collection of art and curios and cordial, professional hospitality. Rooms feel light and modern, and there's a fabulous guest lounge. The island's best meals (mains £9 to £16) are here and can be booked by non-guests.

❶ Getting There & Around

There are flights from Kirkwall to Sanday (one way £37, 20 minutes, once or twice daily).

Ferries run from Kirkwall (passenger/car £8.35/19.70, 1½ hours), with a link to Eday. A bus meets the boat.

Westray

If you've time to visit only one of Orkney's Northern Islands, make it **Westray** (www.westraypapawestray.co.uk). The largest of the group, it has rolling farmland, handsome sandy beaches, great coastal walks and several appealing places to stay.

◉ Sights & Activities

Noup Head   NATURE RESERVE

FREE This bird reserve at Westray's north-western tip is a dramatic area of sea cliffs with vast numbers of breeding seabirds from April to July. You can walk here along the clifftops from a car park, passing the impressive chasm of **Ramni Geo**, and return via the lighthouse access road (4 miles).

Westray Heritage Centre   HERITAGE CENTRE

(☑ 01857-677414; www.westrayheritage.co.uk; Pierowall; adult/child £3/50p; ⊙10am-noon Tue-Sat & 2-5pm Sun May-Sep) This has displays on local history, nature dioramas, and archaeological finds, with some famous Neolithic carvings (including the 5000-year-old 'Westray Wife'). These small sandstone figurines are the oldest known depictions of the human form so far found in the British Isles.

★ Noltland Castle   CASTLE

(⊙8am-8pm) **FREE** A half-mile west of Pierowall stands this sturdy ruined tower house, built in the 16th century by Gilbert Balfour, aide to Mary, Queen of Scots. The castle is super-atmospheric and bristles with shot holes, part of the defences of the deceitful Balfour, who plotted to murder Cardinal Beaton and, after being exiled, the king of Sweden. Like a pantomime villain, he met a sticky end.

🛏 Sleeping & Eating

★ West Manse   B&B **£**

(☑ 01857-677482; www.westmanse.co.uk; Westside; r per person £20; P🤶🎱) ✏ No timetables reign at this imposing house with arcing coastal vistas; make your own breakfast when you feel like it. Your welcoming hosts have introduced a raft of green solutions for heating, fuel and more. Kids will love this unconventional place, with its play nooks and hobbit house, while art exhibitions, cooking and blacksmithing classes, venerably comfortable furniture and clean air are drawcards for parents.

Chalmersquoy & The Barn   B&B, HOSTEL **£**

(☑ 01857-677214; http://chalmersquoywestray.co.uk; Pierowall; dm £20, apt £60-100, tent sites £5-8 plus per adult/child £2/1; P🎱) This excellent, intimate, modern hostel is an Orcadian gem. It's heated throughout and has pristine kitchen facilities and an inviting lounge; rooms sleep two or three in comfort. Out the front, the lovely owners have top self-catering apartments with great views, and three spacious en suite B&B rooms. There's also a campground on-site. A recommended all-round choice.

Pierowall Hotel   PUB FOOD **£**

(☑ 01857-677472; www.pierowallhotel.co.uk; Pierowall; mains £8-11; ⊙food noon-1.30pm & 5-8.30pm; 🎱) The heart of this island community, the refurbished local pub is famous throughout Orkney for its popular fish and chips – whatever has turned up in the day's catch by the hotel's boats is displayed on the blackboard. There are also some curries available, but the sea is the way to go here. It also has rooms, hires bikes and offers internet access.

❶ Getting There & Away

There are daily flights from Kirkwall to Westray (one way £37, 20 minutes).

A ferry (p948) links Kirkwall with Rapness (passenger/car £8.35/19.70, 1½ hours, daily). A bus to the main town, Pierowall, meets the ferry.

Papa Westray

Known locally as Papay, this exquisitely peaceful, tiny island (4 miles by 1 mile) is home to possibly Europe's oldest domestic building, the 5500-year-old **Knap of Howar** (⊙24hr) **FREE**, plus its largest arctic tern colony. Plus the two-minute hop from Westray is the world's shortest scheduled air service. The island was the cradle of Christianity in

Orkney – **St Boniface Kirk** (⊙24hr) **FREE** was founded in the 8th century, though most of it dates to the 12th.

🛏 Sleeping

Beltane House GUESTHOUSE, HOSTEL £
(📞01857-644224; www.papawestray.co.uk; dm/s/d £17/25/35; 🅿🤶🛜) Owned by the local community co-op, this comprises a 20-bed hostel and a guesthouse with four simple and immaculate rooms with en suite and self-catering kitchen access. It's just over a mile north of the ferry. You can camp here (adult/child £5/3).

ℹ Getting There & Away

There are daily flights to Papa Westray (£18, 15 minutes) from Kirkwall, and a special £21 return fare if you stay overnight. Some of the Kirkwall flights go via Westray (£17, 2 minutes) or North Ronaldsay (£17, 10 minutes).

A passenger-only ferry runs from Pierowall on Westray to Papa Westray (£4.15, 25 minutes, three to six daily in summer). From October to April the boat sails by arrangement (📞01857-677216).

North Ronaldsay

North Ronaldsay is a real outpost surrounded by rolling seas and big skies. Delicious peace-and-quiet and excellent birdwatching lure visitors. There are enough semiferal sheep to seize power, but as a 13-mile drystone wall running around the island keeps them off the grass; they make do with seaweed, which gives their meat a unique flavour.

⊙ Sights

North Ronaldsay Tour GUIDED TOUR
(📞07703-112224; lighthouse or mill adult/child £6/4, combined £9/7) Offers excellent tours of one of North Ronaldsay's two lighthouses and a wool mill.

🛏 Sleeping & Eating

Observatory Guest House HOSTEL, CAMPSITE ££
(📞01857-633200; www.nrbo.co.uk; sites £4.50, dm/s/d £17.50/40.50/81; 🅿@🤶) 🍃 Powered by wind and solar energy, this offers first-rate accommodation and ornithological activities next to the ferry pier. There's a cafe-bar with lovely coastal views and convivial communal dinners (£14.50) in a sun-kissed (sometimes) conservatory; if you're lucky, local lamb might be on the menu. You can also camp here.

ℹ Getting There & Away

There are two or three daily flights to North Ronaldsay (£18, 20 minutes) from Kirkwall. The £21 return offer (you must stay overnight) is great value.

A ferry runs from Kirkwall on Tuesday and Friday (passenger/car £8.35/19.70, 2½ hours).

SHETLAND

Close enough to Norway geographically and historically to make nationality an ambiguous concept, the Shetland Islands are Britain's most northerly outpost. There's a Scandinavian lilt to the local accent, and streets named King Haakon or St Olaf remind that Shetland was under Norse rule until 1469, when it was gifted to Scotland in lieu of the dowry of a Danish princess.

Though the stirringly bleak setting still feels uniquely Scottish, Shetland is far from a backwater: offshore oil makes it quite a busy, well-heeled place, with hotels frequently block-booked for workers. Nevertheless, nature still rules the seas and islands, and the bird life is spectacular: pack binoculars.

ℹ Getting There & Around

AIR

The main **airport** (LSI; 📞01950-461000; www.hial.co.uk) is at Sumburgh, 25 miles south of Lerwick. **Flybe** (📞0871 700 2000; www.flybe.com)

OFFBEAT ACCOMMODATION

Shetland offers intriguing options for getting off the beaten accommodation track. There's a great network of *böds* – simple rustic cottages or huts with peat fires. They cost £10 per person, or £8 for the ones without electricity, and are available March to October. Contact and book via **Shetland Amenity Trust** (📞01595-694688; www.camping-bods.com; ⊙9am-5pm Mon-Thu, 9am-4pm Fri).

The same organisation runs three **Lighthouse Cottages** (📞01595-694688; www.shetlandlighthouse.com; per 3 days £277-320, per week £600-700), commanding dramatic views of rugged coastline: one, recently renovated and classy, at Sumburgh, one on the island of Bressay near Lerwick, and one at Eshaness. They sleep six to seven, and prices drop substantially off-season.

Shetland

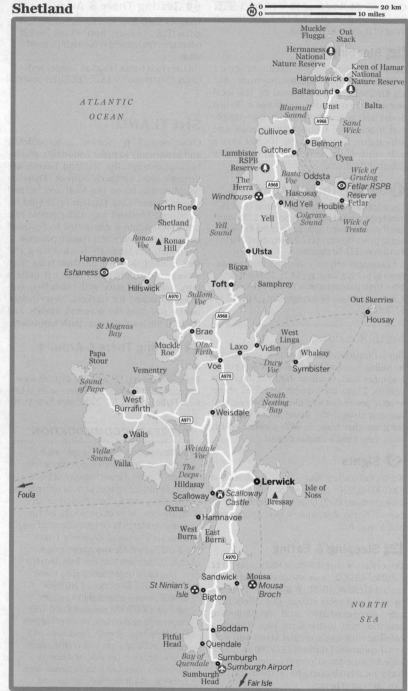

CENTRAL & NORTHERN HIGHLANDS & ISLANDS SHETLAND

runs daily services to Aberdeen, Kirkwall, Inverness, Edinburgh and Glasgow, and summer services to Bergen (Norway).

BICYCLE
You can hire bikes from several places, including Grantfield Garage (£12.50/50 per day/week) in Lerwick.

BOAT
Northlink Ferries (☎0845 600 0449; www.northlinkferries.co.uk; 🗬) runs daily overnight car ferries between Aberdeen and Lerwick (passenger/car high-season one-way £41/144, 12 to 15 hours), some stopping at Kirkwall, Orkney. With a basic ticket you can sleep in recliner chairs or the bar area. It's £36 for a berth in a shared cabin and up to £137 for a comparatively luxurious double cabin. Sleeping pods (£18) are comfortable, reclinable seats. There's a cafe, bar, paid lounge and cinema on-board plus slow wi-fi.

BUS
An extensive bus network, coordinated by **ZetTrans** (www.zettrans.org.uk), radiates from Lerwick to all corners of Mainland, and on (via ferry) to the islands of Yell and Unst. Schedules aren't great for day tripping from Lerwick.

CAR & MOTORCYCLE
Shetland has broad, well-made roads (think 'oil money'). Car hire is fuss-free, and vehicles can be delivered to transport terminals. Prices are usually around £35/180 per day/week.
Bolts Car Hire (☎01595-693636; www.boltscarhire.co.uk; 26 North Rd, Lerwick) Also has an office at Sumburgh airport.
Grantfield Garage (☎01595-692709; www.grantfieldgarage.co.uk; North Rd, Lerwick; ◷9am-5.30pm Mon-Sat) The cheapest. A short walk towards town from the Northlink ferry terminal.
Star Rent-a-Car (☎01595-692075; www.starrentacar.co.uk; 22 Commercial Rd, Lerwick) Opposite the bus station. Has an office at Sumburgh airport.

Lerwick
POP 7000
Built on the herring trade, Lerwick is Shetland's only real town, home to a third of the islands' population. It has a solidly maritime feel, with aquiline oilboats competing for space in the superb natural harbour with the dwindling fishing fleet. Wandering along atmospheric Commercial St is a delight, and the excellent museum provides cultural background.

NATURE-WATCHING IN SHETLAND
For birdwatchers, Shetland is paradise – a stopover for migrating Arctic species and host to vast seabird breeding colonies; June is the height of the season.

Every bird has its own name here: rain geese are red-throated divers, bonxies are great skuas, and alamooties are storm petrels. Clownish puffin antics are a highlight. The **RSPB** (RSPB; www.rspb.org.uk) maintains several reserves plus there are National Nature Reserves at **Hermaness**, **Keen of Hamar** and **Noss**. **Foula** and **Fair Isle** also support large seabird populations.

Keep an eye on the sea: sea otters, orcas and other cetaceans are regularly sighted. Latest sightings are logged at useful www.nature-shetland.co.uk.

Shetland Nature Festival (www.shetlandamenity.org) in early July has guided walks, talks, boat trips, open days and workshops.

◉ Sights
★**Shetland Museum**   MUSEUM
(☎01595-695057; www.shetland-museum.org.uk; Hay's Dock; ◷10am-5pm Mon-Sat, noon-5pm Sun) **FREE** This is an impressive recollection of 5000 years' worth of culture, people and their interaction with this ancient landscape. Comprehensive but never dull, the display covers everything from the archipelago's geology to its fishing industry, via local mythology – find out about scary *nyuggles* (ghostly horses), or detect *trows* (fairies). Pictish carvings and replica jewellery are among the finest pieces; the museum also includes a working lighthouse mechanism, a small gallery, a boat-building workshop and an archive for tracing Shetland ancestry.

Clickimin Broch   ARCHAEOLOGICAL SITE
FREE This fortified site, just under a mile southwest of the town centre, was occupied from the 7th century BC to the 6th century AD. It's impressively large, and its setting on a small loch gives it a feeling of being removed from the present day.

Böd of Gremista   MUSEUM
(Shetland Textile Museum; www.shetlandtextilemuseum.com; Gremista Rd; admission £2; ◷noon-5pm Tue-Sat, to 7pm Thu May–mid-Oct) A mile north

Lerwick

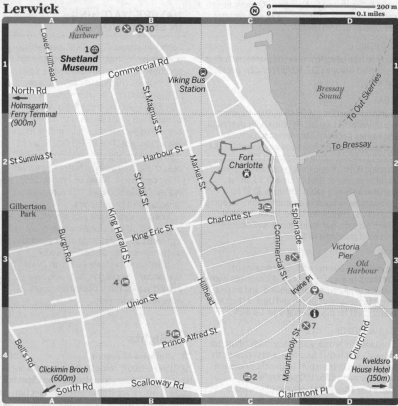

Lerwick

◎ **Top Sights**

🛏 **Sleeping**

✗ **Eating**

🍷 **Drinking & Nightlife**

✪ **Entertainment**

of the centre, this house, birthplace of P&O founder Arthur Anderson, was also once a fish-curing station. It now holds a display on the knitted and woven textiles and patterns that take their name from the islands.

🎉 Festivals & Events

Shetland Folk Festival MUSIC
(www.shetlandfolkfestival.com) Held in late April or early May.

🛏 Sleeping

Lerwick has very average hotels but excellent B&Bs. It fills year-round; book ahead. There's no campsite within 15 miles.

Islesburgh House Hostel HOSTEL £
(☎01595-745100; www.islesburgh.org.uk; King Harald St; dm/tw/q £20/40/60; ☉Apr-Sep; ℗@🛈) This typically grand Lerwick mansion houses an excellent hostel, with com-

fortable dorms, a shop, a laundry, a cafe and an industrial kitchen. Electronic keys offer excellent security and no curfew. It's wise to book ahead, and ask about winter availability as it sometimes opens for groups.

Woosung B&B £
(✆ 01595-693687; conroywoosung@hotmail.com; 43 St Olaf St; s without bathroom £30-35, d without bathroom £50-55; 🛜🖿) A budget gem in the heart of Lerwick B&B-land, this has a wise and welcoming host, and comfortable, clean, good-value rooms that share a bathroom. The solid stone house dates from the 19th century, built by a clipper captain who traded tea out of the Chinese port it's named after.

⭐ **Alder Lodge Guesthouse** B&B ££
(✆ 01595-695705; www.alderlodgeguesthouse.com; 6 Clairmont Pl; s/d £35/75; 🅿🛜) This stone former bank is a delightful place to stay. Imbued with a sense of space and light, the rooms are large and very well furnished, with good en suites, fridges and DVD players. Excellent hosts really make the effort to help you feel at home, and do a great breakfast, with a smoked fish option and special diets catered for. There is also a self-catering house nearby.

⭐ **Fort Charlotte Guesthouse** B&B £££
(✆ 01595-692140; www.fortcharlotte.co.uk; 1 Charlotte St; s/d £35/70; 🛜🖿) Sheltering under the fortress walls, this friendly place offers summery en suite rooms, including great singles. Views down the pedestrian street are on offer in some; sloping ceilings and oriental touches add charm to others. There's a bike shed and local salmon for breakfast. Very popular; book ahead.

Kveldsro House Hotel HOTEL ££
(✆ 01595-692195; www.shetlandhotels.com; Greenfield Pl; s/d £110/135; 🅿🛜) Lerwick's best hotel overlooks the harbour and has a quiet but central setting. It's a dignified small setup that will appeal to older visitors or couples. All doubles cost the same, but some are markedly better than others, with four-poster beds or water views. All boast new stylish bathrooms and iPod docks. The bar area is elegant and has fine perspectives.

 Eating

Peerie Shop Cafe CAFE £
(✆ 01595-692816; www.peerieshopcafe.com; Esplanade; light meals £3-8; ⏰ 9am-6pm Mon-Sat; 🛜) If you've been craving proper espresso since leaving the mainland, head to this gem, with art exhibitions, wire-mounted halogens and industrial-gantry chic. Newspapers, scrumptious cakes and sandwiches, hot chocolate that you deserve after that blasting wind outside, and – more rarely – outdoor seating give everyone a reason to be here.

Mareel Cafe CAFE £
(Mareel; light meals £3-5; ⏰ 10am-11pm Sun-Thu, to 10am-1am Fri & Sat; 🛜) Buzzy, arty and colourful, this cheery venue in Mareel overlooks the water and does sandwiches and baked potatoes by day, and some cute Shetland tapas in the evenings. The coffee is decent, too, and it's a nice place for a cocktail.

⭐ **Hay's Dock** CAFE, RESTAURANT ££
(✆ 01595-741569; www.haysdock.co.uk; Hay's Dock; lunch mains £7-11, dinner £15-22; ⏰ 10.30am-3.30pm Mon-Sat, noon-4.30pm Sun, plus 6.30-9pm Fri & Sat year round and Tue-Thu Jun-Aug; 🛜♿) 🌱 Upstairs in the Shetland Museum, Hay's Dock sports a wall of picture windows and a fairweather balcony overlooking the harbour. Clean lines and pale wood recall Scandinavia, but the menu relies on carefully selected local and Scottish produce. Lunch ranges from delicious fish-and-chips to chowder, while evening menus focus on seafood and steak.

Monty's Bistro BRITISH ££
(✆ 01595-696555; www.montys-shetland.co.uk; 5 Mounthooly St; mains lunch £8-10, dinner £13-17; ⏰ 5-9pm Mon, noon-2pm & 5-9pm Tue-Sat, noon-9.30pm Sun; 🛜) 🌱 Though well hidden away behind the tourist office, Monty's is far from a secret and Shetlanders descend on it with alacrity. The upstairs dining room, with proper floorboards and an upbeat atmosphere, is a cheerful venue for good-quality British bistro fare.

UP HELLY AA!!!

Shetland's long Viking history has rubbed off in more ways than just street names and square-shouldered locals. Most villages have a fire festival, a continuation of Viking midwinter celebrations of the rebirth of the sun. The most spectacular happens in Lerwick.

Up Helly Aa (www.uphellyaa.org) takes place on the last Tuesday in January. Squads of *guizers* dress in Viking costume and march through the streets with blazing torches, dragging a replica longship, which they then surround and burn, bellowing out Viking songs from behind bushy beards.

⚲ Drinking & Entertainment

Check what's on at **Mareel** (☑01595-745555; www.mareel.org), a swish new arts venue near the museum.

Captain Flint's PUB
(2 Commercial St; ☻11am-1am; 🐾) This lively port-side bar – Lerwick's liveliest – throbs with happy conversation and loud music, and has a distinctly nautical, creaky-wooden feel. There's a cross-section of young 'uns, tourists, boat folk and older locals. There's live music some nights and a pool table upstairs.

ℹ Information

Lerwick Tourist Office (☑01595-693434; lerwick@visitscotland.com; cnr Commercial St & Mounthooly St; ☻9am-5pm Mon-Sat & 10am-4pm Sun Apr-Sep, 10am-4pm Mon-Sat Oct-Mar) Helpful, with a good range of books and maps.

ℹ Getting There & Around

From **Viking bus station** (☑01595-694100; Commercial Rd), buses service various corners of the archipelago, including regular services to/from Sumburgh Airport.

Northlink Ferries (☑0845 6000 449; www.northlinkferries.co.uk) dock at Holmsgarth terminal, a 15-minute walk northwest from the town centre.

Bressay & Noss

POP 400
These islands lie across Bressay Sound just east of Lerwick. Bressay (*bress*-ah) has interesting walks, especially along the cliffs and up **Ward Hill** (226m), which has good views of the islands. Much smaller Noss is a nature reserve.

◉ Sights & Activities

★**Isle of Noss** NATURE RESERVE
(☑0800-107-7818; www.nnr-scotland.org.uk/noss; boat adult/child £3/1.50; ☻10am-5pm Tue, Wed & Fri-Sun mid-Apr–Aug) Little Noss, 1.5 miles wide, lies just east of Bressay. High seacliffs harbour over 100,000 pairs of breeding seabirds, while inland heath supports hundreds of pairs of great skua.

Access is by dinghy from Bressay; phone in advance to check that it's running. Walking anticlockwise around Noss is easier, with better cliff viewing. There's a small visitor centre by the dock.

Seabirds & Seals CRUISE
(☑07595-540224; www.seabirds-and-seals.com; adult/child £45/25; ☻10am & 2pm mid-Apr–mid-Sep) Runs three-hour wildlife cruises (10am and 2pm) around Bressay and Noss, departing from Lerwick. Includes underwater viewing. Trips run year-round, weather permitting; book by phone or at Lerwick tourist office.

ℹ Getting There & Away

Ferries (passenger/car return £5.20/12.80, seven minutes, frequent) link Lerwick and Bressay. The Noss crossing is 2.5 miles across the island.

Central & West Mainland

Scalloway

POP 1200
Surrounded by bare, rolling hills, Scalloway (*scall*-o-wah) – Shetland's former capital – is a busy fishing and yachting harbour with a thriving seafood-processing industry. It's 6 miles from Lerwick.

◉ Sights & Activities

Scalloway Museum MUSEUM
(www.scallowaymuseum.org; Castle St; adult/child £3/1; ☻11am-4pm Mon-Sat, 2-4pm Sun May-Sep; 🔄) This enthusiastic modern museum has an excellent display on Scalloway life and history, with prehistoric finds, witch-burnings and local lore all featuring. There's a detailed section on the Shetland Bus, and a fun area for kids.

Scalloway Castle CASTLE
(HS; www.historic-scotland.co.uk; ☻24hr) **FREE**
The town's most prominent landmark is Scalloway Castle, built around 1600 by Earl Patrick Stewart. The turreted and corbelled tower house is fairly well preserved. If it's locked, get keys from Scalloway Museum or Scalloway Hotel.

🛏 Sleeping & Eating

★**Scalloway Hotel** HOTEL **££**
(☑01595-880444; www.scallowayhotel.com; Main St; s/d £80/115; 🅿🐾) One of Shetland's best, this energetically run waterfront place has very stylish rooms featuring sheepskins, local tweeds and other fabrics, and views over the harbour. Some are larger than others; the best is the fabulous superior, with handmade furniture, artworks and a top-of-

the-line mattress on its four-poster bed. The restaurant (mains £11 to £15) is good for quality seafood and Scottish cheeses.

❶ Getting There & Away

Buses run from Lerwick (25 minutes, roughly hourly Monday to Saturday, two Sunday) to Scalloway.

South Mainland

From Lerwick, it's 25 miles down this narrow, hilly tail of land to Sumburgh Head. The lapping waters are an inviting turquoise – if it weren't for the raging Arctic gales, you'd be tempted to have a dip.

Sandwick & Around

Opposite scattered Sandwick is the small isle of Mousa, an RSPB reserve protecting some 7000 breeding pairs of storm petrels. It's also home to rock-basking seals and impressive **Mousa Broch**. Rising to 13m, it's an imposing double-walled structure with a spiral staircase to access a 2nd floor. It features in Viking sagas as a hideout for eloping couples.

◉ Sights & Activities

Mousa Boat   BOAT TOUR
(☑ 07901-872339; www.mousa.co.uk; ☺ Apr–mid-Sep) This operator runs daily boat trips to Mousa (adult/child return £16/7, 15 minutes) from Sandwick, allowing three hours ashore on the island. It also offers night petrel-viewing trips (dates on the website).

Sumburgh

With sea cliffs, and grassy headlands jutting out into sparkling blue waters, Sumburgh is one of the most scenic places on the island, with a far greener landscape than the peaty north.

◉ Sights

Jarlshof   ARCHAEOLOGICAL SITE
(HS; ☑ 01950-460112; www.historic-scotland.gov.uk; adult/child £5.30/3.30; ☺ 9.30am-5.30pm Apr-Sep, 9.30am-4.30pm Oct-Mar) Old and new collide here, with Sumburgh airport right by this picturesque, instructive archaeological site. Periods of occupation from 2500 BC to AD 1500 can be seen; the complete change upon the Vikings' arrival is clear: their rectangular longhouses present a marked contrast to the preceding brochs, roundhouses

and wheelhouses. Atop the site is 16th-century Old House, named 'Jarlshof' in a novel by Sir Walter Scott. There's an informative audio tour included with admission.

★**Sumburgh Head**
Visitor Centre   LIGHTHOUSE, MUSEUM
(☑ 01595-694688;   www.sumburghhead.com; adult/child £6/2; ☺ 10am-4pm May-Aug) High on the cliffs at Sumburgh Head, this excellent new attraction is set across several buildings. Displays explain about the lighthouse, foghorn and radar station that operated here, while there's a good exhibition on the local marine- and bird-life. You can visit the lighthouse itself on a guided tour.

Sumburgh Head   BIRDWATCHING
(www.rspb.org.uk) At Mainland's southern tip, these spectacular cliffs offer a good chance to get up close to puffins, and huge nesting colonies of fulmars, guillemots and razorbills. If you're lucky, you might spot dolphins, minke whales or orcas. Also here is an excellent visitor centre, in the lighthouse buildings.

🛏 Sleeping & Eating

Other options are the atmospheric Sumburgh Lighthouse cottage and a camping **böd** behind Old Scatness.

Sumburgh Hotel   HOTEL ££
(☑ 01950-460201; www.sumburghhotel.com; s/d £85/110; Ⓟ @ 🛜 🐾) A reliable country-style hotel. Rooms have been recently renovated and feature soft duvets, attractive colour schemes and big towels. Larger sea-view rooms looking out to Fair Isle cost a tenner more. This is handy for the airport or Sumburgh Head birdwatching, though food is mediocre.

❶ Getting There & Away

To get to Sumburgh from Lerwick, take the airport bus (45 minutes, four to seven daily).

North Mainland

The north of Mainland is very photogenic. Around Hillswick, there's stunning scenery.

Brae & Around

Just outside Brae and built in 1588, luxurious, genteel **Busta House Hotel** (☑ 01806-522506; www.bustahouse.com; s/d £99/115; Ⓟ @ 🛜 🐾) 🐾 has a long, sad history and the inevitable rumours of a (friendly) ghost.

Built in the late 18th century (though the oldest part dates from 1588), its refurbished rooms – all individually decorated – are compact and retain a classy but homey charm. Sea views and/or four-poster bed cost a bit more. There are excellent dinners with local produce (£35).

Buses from Lerwick to Eshaness and North Roe stop in Brae (35 minutes, four to six daily Monday to Saturday).

Eshaness & Hillswick

Eleven miles northwest of Brae the road ends at the red basalt cliffs of Eshaness, which form some of the most impressive, wild coastal scenery in Shetland. When the wind subsides there is superb walking and panoramic views from the lighthouse on the headland.

◉ Sights

Tangwick Haa Museum　　　MUSEUM
(☑01806-503389; ⊘11am-5pm mid-Apr–Sep) FREE A mile east of Eshaness, a side road leads south to the Tangwick Haa Museum, housed in a restored 17th-century house. The wonderful collection of ancient B&W photos capture the sense of community in this area.

⌂ Sleeping & Eating

Braewick Cafe & Caravan Park　CAMPSITE £
(☑01806-503345; www.eshaness.shetland.co.uk; sites for 1/2 £6/8, wigwams £42; ⊘mid-Mar–mid-Sep; 🅿🛜🐕) 🐾 Decent tent pitches and tasty light meals served in a cafe (dishes £4 to £10; 10am to 5pm Thursday to Monday mid-March to mid-September, daily in July and August) with stunning views over St Magnus Bay's weird and wonderful rock formations, are on offer here. Much food is sourced from the owners' croft next door. It also has 'wigwams' – wooden huts (with fridge and kettle) that sleep four (six at a pinch). It's on the road between Hillswick and Eshaness.

★Almara　　　B&B £££
(☑01806-503261; www.almara.shetland.co.uk; s/d £35/70; 🅿🛜) 🐾 Follow the puffin signpost a mile short of Hillswick to find Shetland's finest welcome. With sweeping views over the bay, this house has a great lounge, unusual features in the excellent rooms and bathrooms (including thoughtful extras such as USB chargers) and a good eye on the environment. You'll feel completely at home and appreciated; this is B&B at its best.

The North Isles

Yell, Unst and Fetlar make up the North Isles, connected to each other by ferry.

Yell
POP 1000

Yell if you like, but nobody will hear; the desolate peat moors here are typical Shetland scenery. The bleak landscape has an undeniable appeal.

◉ Sights & Activities

Lumbister RSPB Reserve　　NATURE RESERVE
(www.rspb.org.uk) At this nature reserve red-throated divers, merlins, skuas and other bird species breed. The area is home to a large otter population, too, best viewed around Whale Firth, where you may also spot common and grey seals.

Old Haa Museum　　　MUSEUM
(☑01957-702431; ⊘10am-4pm Tue-Thu & Sat & 2-5pm Sun Apr-Sep) FREE This museum has a medley of curious objects (pipes, piano, doll-in-cradle, tiny bibles, ships in bottles and a whale jaw) as well as an archive of local history, and a tearoom. It's in Burravoe, 4 miles east of the southern ferry terminal in Ulsta.

⌂ Sleeping & Eating

There are lots of excellent self-catering cottages dotted around the island: check www.visitshetland.com for options.

Pinewood House　　　B&B ££
(☑01957-702092; www.pinewoodhouseshetland.co.uk; Aywick; s/d £35/70; 🅿🛜🐕) Next to Aywick shop, this three-roomer boasts glorious water views from the lounge and bedrooms, and offers a warm welcome and optional, very tasty evening meals (£16).

Windhouse Lodge　　　BÖD £
(☑office 01595-694688, warden 01957-702350; www.camping-bods.co.uk; dm £10) Below the haunted ruins of Windhouse, and on the A968, you'll find this well-kept, clean, snug camping böd with power and a pot-belly stove to warm your toes. It's one of the cosiest, with a modern interior. Mattresses are thin. Book via phone or the website.

❶ Getting There & Away

Yell is connected with Mainland by ferries between Toft and Ulsta (passenger/car return

£5.20/7.60, 20 minutes, frequent). It's wise to book in summer.

Buses run Monday to Saturday from Lerwick to Yell (£4.50) and Unst; connecting services cover other parts of the island.

Unst

POP 600

You're fast running out of Scotland once you cross to rugged Unst (www.unst.org). Britain's most northerly inhabited island is prettier than Yell, with bare, velvety-smooth hills and settlements clinging to waterside locations, fiercely resisting the buffeting winds.

⊙ Sights & Activities

★**Hermaness**
Nature Reserve   NATURE RESERVE
(www.nnr-scotland.org.uk) At marvellous Hermaness headland, a 4.5-mile round walk takes you to cliffs where gannets, fulmars and guillemots nest, and numerous puffins frolic. You can see Scotland's most northerly point, the rocks of **Out Stack**, and **Muckle Flugga**, with its lighthouse built by Robert Louis Stevenson's uncle. Duck into the **visitor centre** (☑01595-711278; ☺9am-5pm May-early Sep) **FREE**, with its poignant story about long-time resident Albert Ross. To visit Muckle Flugga, you can charter a **boat** (☑01806-522447; www.muckleflugga.co.uk; 2hr charter £150; ☺Jun-Aug) in summer.

★**Unst Bus Shelter**   LANDMARK
(www.unstbusshelter.shetland.co.uk; Baltasound) At the turnoff to Littlehamar, just past Baltasound, is Britain's most impressive bus stop. Enterprising locals, tired of waiting in discomfort, decided to do a job on it, and it now boasts posh seating, novels, numerous decorative features and a visitors' book to sign. The theme and colour scheme changes yearly.

Unst Heritage Centre   MUSEUM
(☑01957-755244, 01957-711528; www.unstheritage.com; Haroldswick; adult/child £3/free, combined ticket with Unst Boat Haven £5; ☺11am-4pm May-Sep) This heritage centre houses a modern museum with a history of the Shetland pony and a re-creation of a croft house.

Unst Boat Haven   MUSEUM
(☑01957-755282, 01957-711528; Haroldswick; adult/child £3/free, combined ticket with Unst Her-

itage Centre £5; ☺11am-4pm May-Sep) This large shed is a boaty's delight, packed with a beautifully cared-for collection of Shetland rowing and sailing boats, all with a backstory. Old photos and maritime artefacts speak of the glory days of Unst fishing.

🛏 Sleeping & Eating

★**Gardiesfauld Hostel**   HOSTEL £
(☑01957-755279; www.gardiesfauld.shetland.co.uk; 2 East Rd, Uyeasound; tent sites per adult/child £6/2, dm £15; ☺Apr-Sep; P🐾) This spotless hostel has very spacious dorms with lockers, family rooms, a garden, an elegant lounge and a wee conservatory dining area with great bay views. You can camp here too, with separate areas for tents and vans. The bus stops right outside. Bring 20p for a shower.

Saxa Vord   HOSTEL £
(☑01957-711711; www.saxavord.com; Haroldswick; s/d £21/42; ☺late May-early Sep; P🐾) This former RAF base is not the most atmospheric lodging, but the barracks-style rooms offer great value. The restaurant dishes out reasonable local food, and there's a bar – Britain's northernmost, by our reckoning – and a friendly, helpful atmosphere. Self-catering houses (£450 to £595 per week) are good for families and available year-round.

Baltasound Hotel   HOTEL, PUB ££
(☑01957-711334; www.baltasoundhotel.co.uk; Baltasound; s £45-60, d £90-100; ☺May–mid-Oct; P🐾) Brightly decorated, commodious rooms – some bigger than others – are complemented by wooden chalets arrayed around the lawn. It's worth the tenner upgrade to the 'large doubles', which sport good modern bathrooms. There's a lovely country outlook, and evening bar meals (mains £7 to £12; food served 6pm to 8pm) in a dining room dappled by the setting sun.

ⓘ Getting There & Away

Unst is connected with Yell and Fetlar by a small **ferry** (☑01595-745804; www.shetland.gov.uk/ferries) between Gutcher and Belmont (free if coming from Mainland that day, otherwise passenger/car £5.20/7.60 return, 10 minutes, frequent).

Three buses a day (except Sunday) run from Lerwick to Unst (£4.60, 2½ hours), via the ferries. There are also services around Unst itself (£1.70 to £1.80).

Understand Great Britain

Great Britain Today

For Britain and the British, the first 15 years of the 21st century has been a time of change, controversy and national soul-searching. Despite a boost to the national mood from the successful London Olympics and Glasgow Commonwealth Games, and signs of the economy emerging from recession, there is a nagging uncertainty about the future. Can Britain survive in its present form?

Best on Film

Brief Encounter (1945)
Under Milk Wood (1972)
Trainspotting (1996)
Sense & Sensibility (1996)
The Full Monty (1997)
Elizabeth: The Golden Age (2007)
War Horse (2011)

Best Music

God Save The Queen by The Sex Pistols
Teardrop by Massive Attack
Town Called Malice by The Jam
Sultans of Swing by Dire Straits
Waterloo Sunset by The Kinks
Patience of Angels by Eddi Reader
Ghost Town by The Specials
Bonkers by Dizzee Rascal
Hounds of Love by Kate Bush
A Design for Life by Manic Street Preachers
I Predict a Riot by Kaiser Chiefs
Common People by Pulp
Down By The Water by PJ Harvey
Shipbuilding by Elvis Costello

The End of the UK?

Where once the United Kingdom of Great Britain and Northern Ireland was a single political entity, it's now anything but united. From 1999 onwards, the process of devolution has seen the nations of Scotland, Wales, and Northern Ireland get their own ruling bodies – the Scottish Parliament in Edinburgh, the Welsh Assembly in Cardiff, and the Northern Ireland Assembly in Belfast – with power over domestic affairs such as health and education.

However, when the Scottish National Party won a surprise majority in the Scottish Parliament elections of 2011 they went further, and pledged to hold a referendum on full Scottish independence in 2014. The implications of Scotland breaking away from the UK were hotly debated. Would an independent Scotland need a new currency, or be able to continue using the pound? Would there be border controls with England? Would Scotland be able to remain in the EU? Would the Queen still be head of state?

The referendum took place on 18 September 2014, posing the question: 'Should Scotland be an independent country?' The result was that 55% voted to maintain the status quo (with a turnout of 85%). What this means for the future of Scotland – and Britain – remains unclear. Will there be increased powers for the Scottish Parliament? Will there be increased devolution to the English regions? Will the UK become a federal state?

This questioning of the balance of power across Britain has led to a reassessment – both by politicians and the people themselves – of what it actually means to be British. This has occurred especially in England where for centuries 'British' and 'English' have meant essentially the same thing. While Wales and Scotland, as smaller nations, have always been more aware of the institutions that bind the countries together – and the tensions that threaten to drive them apart – the English are now having to confront the questions of what Britain actually represents.

A Crumbling Coalition

A key milestone in Britain's recent history was the general election of 2010 when the Labour government was ousted after 13 years in power, but no party won an overall majority. An agreement between the Conservative and Liberal-Democrat parties created the first coalition government in Westminster since WWII.

But the relationship between the coalition parties has been turbulent, battered by disagreements over how to tackle the country's problems. Conservative 'rebels' blocked Lib-Dem moves to reform the House of Lords, and the Lib-Dems vetoed Tory plans to cut taxes on the rich, ditch the Human Rights Act and reduce the number of MPs at Westminster.

The constraints of coalition have also forced the Lib-Dems to abandon some of their 2010 election pledges, notably a promise not to raise tuition fees for university students in England and Wales. As a result, their support has plummeted. Nonetheless, opinion polls suggest that, once again, no party will win an overall majority in the 2015 UK general election, raising the prospect of minority government, or yet another uneasy coalition.

The Rise of UKIP

Although British politics since 2010 has been dominated by austerity measures supposed to combat the impact of the global financial crisis, by the start of 2014 the economy had been joined by immigration as the issue of most concern. The same year saw the rise to prominence of UKIP (the United Kingdom Independence Party), a right-wing, libertarian party whose flagship policies include cutting back on immigration and taking Britain out of the European Union.

UKIP took first place in the European elections of May 2014 with 27.5% of the vote (on a turnout of 34%) – the first time any party other than Labour or Conservative had come first in a UK-wide election since 1906. The result threw Britain into a spin. Did this herald a fundamental change in the direction of British politics? Or was it a protest vote from an electorate fed up with Westminster politicians?

Opinion polls suggesting that UKIP might win a couple of Westminster seats in the 2015 election saw both Labour and the Conservatives harden their positions on immigration, while the Tory leader David Cameron pledged that he would offer the country a referendum on whether to stay in the EU if he remained as prime minister after 2015.

POPULATION: **61.4 MILLION**

AREA: **88,500 SQ MILES (230,000 SQ KM)**

GDP PER CAPITA: **£21,800 (USD$37,300)**

GDP GROWTH: **1.8%**

INFLATION: **2%**

UNEMPLOYMENT: **7.2%**

if Britain were 100 people

85 would be Caucasian
4 would be South Asian
2 would be African & Afro Caribbean
9 would be other

belief systems
(% of population)

59 Christian
25 No Religion
4 Other
5 Muslim
7 Not Stated

population per sq km

BRITAIN   USA   FRANCE

≈ 30 people

History

Britain may be a small country on the edge of Europe, but it has never been on the sidelines of history. For thousands of years, invaders and immigrants have arrived, settled and made their mark. The result is Britain's fascinating mix of landscape, culture and language. That rich historic legacy – everything from Stonehenge to Culloden, via Hadrian's Wall, Canterbury Cathedral, Caernarfon Castle and the Tower of London – is one of the country's main attractions for visitors.

First Arrivals

Probably built around 3000 BC, Stonehenge has stood on Salisbury Plain for more than 5000 years and is older than the famous Great Pyramids of Egypt.

Around 4000 BC, as glaciers retreated in the wake of the Ice Age, a group of migrants arrived from Europe, but instead of hunting and moving on, they settled in one place and started farming. Alongside their fields, Britain's Stone Age people used rocks and turf to build massive burial mounds; the remains of many of these can still be seen, including West Kennet Long Barrow in Wiltshire, Pentre Ifan in Pembrokeshire and Maes Howe in Orkney. But the most impressive legacies left by these nascent Britons were the enigmatic stone circles of Callanish, Avebury and Stonehenge.

Iron & Celts

During the Iron Age (from 800 BC to AD 100) the population expanded and began to divide into specific tribes. Forests were cleared as more land was used for farming. This led to a patchwork pattern of fields, woods and small villages that still exists today in many parts of rural Britain. As the population grew, territorial defence became an issue, so the Iron Age people left another legacy; the great 'earthwork' castles of southern England, stone forts in northern England and brochs (defensive towers) in Wales and Scotland.

The Celts, a people who originally migrated from Central Europe, had settled across much of Britain by around 500 BC. A Celtic-British population developed, comprising around 20 tribes including the Cantiaci (in today's county of Kent), the Iceni (Norfolk), the Brigantes (northwest England), the Picts and Caledonii (Scotland), the Ordivices (parts of Wales) and the Scotti (Ireland).

TIMELINE	c 500 BC	AD 43	60
	The Celts, a group originally from Central Europe, arrive in Britain, and by the middle of the 1st millennium BC have settled across much of the island, absorbing the indigenous people.	Emperor Claudius leads the first proper Roman invasion of England. His army wages a ruthless campaign, and the Romans control most of southern England by AD 50.	Warrior-queen Boudica leads an army against the Romans, destroys the Roman town of Colchester and gets as far as Londinium, the Roman port on the present site of London.

You noticed the Latin-sounding names? That's because the tribal tags were first handed out by the next arrivals on Britain's shores...

Enter the Romans

Julius Caesar, the Roman ruler everyone remembers, made forays to the island of Britain in 55 BC. But the real Roman invasion happened a century later, when Emperor Claudius led a ruthless campaign resulting in the Romans controlling pretty much everywhere in southern England by AD 50.

Much of the occupation was straightforward: several Celtic-British tribal kings realised collaboration was more profitable than battle. It wasn't all plain sailing, though, and some locals fought back. The most famous freedom fighter was warrior-queen Boudica, who led an army as far as Londinium, the Roman port on the present site of London.

However, opposition was mostly sporadic and no real threat to the legions' military might. By around AD 80 the new province of Britannia (much of today's England and Wales) was firmly under Roman rule.

Exit the Romans

Settlement by the Romans in Britain lasted almost four centuries. Intermarriage was common between locals and incomers (many from other parts of the empire, including today's Belgium, Spain and Syria), and a Romano-British population evolved, particularly in the towns, while indigenous Celtic-British culture remained in rural areas.

Along with stability and wealth, the Romans introduced a new religion called Christianity, officially recognised by Emperor Constantine in AD 313. Although Romano-British culture was thriving by this time, back in its Mediterranean heartland the empire was already in decline.

It was an untidy finale. Britannia was simply dumped by Rome, and the colony slowly fizzled out of existence. But historians are tidy folk, and the end of Roman power in Britain is generally dated at AD 410.

The Emergence of England

Britain's post-Roman power vacuum didn't go unnoticed and once again invaders arrived from the European mainland. Angles and Saxons

> Christianity was introduced to Britain by the Romans and adopted by the Celts, but the Anglo-Saxons were pagans, and their invasion of Britain forced the Christian religion, along with other aspects of Celtic culture, to the edges of the British Isles – today's Wales, Scotland and Ireland.

LEGACY OF THE LEGIONS

To control the territory they'd occupied, the Romans built castles and garrisons across Britain, especially in Wales and England. Many of these developed into towns, which can be recognised by names ending in 'chester' or 'caster' (from the Latin castrum, meaning military camp) – Lancaster, Winchester, Manchester, Cirencester and Chester, to name but a few.

60	122	c 410	5th century
In Wales the Celts, led by their mystic faith-healers, the druids, fight a last stand on Anglesey against the Roman army; they are beaten but not totally conquered.	Rather than conquer wild north British tribes, Emperor Hadrian settles for building a coast-to-coast barricade. For nearly 300 years, Hadrian's Wall marks the northernmost limit of the Roman Empire.	As the classical world's greatest empire finally declines after more than three centuries of relative peace and prosperity, Roman rule ends in Britain with more of a whimper than a bang.	Teutonic tribes (known today as the Anglo-Saxons) from the area now called Germany migrate to England and quickly spread across much of the country.

(Teutonic tribes from the land we now call Germany) advanced across the former Roman turf.

Historians disagree on exactly what happened next. Either the Anglo-Saxons largely replaced or absorbed the Romano-British and Celtic population, or the indigenous tribes simply adopted Anglo-Saxon language and culture. Either way, by the late 6th century much of the area we now call England was dominated by the Anglo-Saxons and divided into three kingdoms: Wessex (in today's southern England), Mercia (the Midlands) and Northumbria (northern England).

In many areas the original inhabitants lived alongside the Anglo-Saxons and remained unaffected by the incomers (the Celtic language was still being spoken in parts of southern England when the Normans invaded 500 years later), but the overall impact was immense: the core of the modern English language is Anglo-Saxon, many place names have Anglo-Saxon roots, and the very term 'Anglo-Saxon' has become a (much-abused and factually incorrect) byword for 'pure English'.

A History of Britain, by historian and TV star Simon Schama, is a highly accessible set of three books, examining events from 3000 BC to AD 2000.

The Waking of Wales

The Celts on the western fringes of the British Isles (particularly in Ireland) kept alive their own distinct yet Roman-influenced culture. And while the Anglo-Saxons occupied eastern Britain, towards the end of the 5th century the Scotti (from today's Ireland) invaded what is today Wales and western Scotland.

In response to the invasion, people from the kingdom of Gododdin (near today's Edinburgh) moved to northwest Wales to drive out the invaders, then stayed and settled in the area, which became the kingdom of Gwynedd. (The modern county in northern Wales still proudly bears this name.) More settlers came to Wales from Cornwall and western France, and Christian missionaries arrived from Ireland in the 6th and 7th centuries.

The people of Wales were also under pressure to the east, harassed by the Anglo-Saxons. In response, by the 8th century the disparate tribes of Wales had started to band together and sow the seeds of nationhood. They called themselves *cymry* (fellow countrymen), and today Cymru is the Welsh word for Wales.

Myths and Legends of the British Isles by Richard Barber is an ideal read if you want a break from firm historical facts. Learn about King Arthur and the Knights of the Round Table, plus much more from the mists of time.

The Stirring of Scotland

While Wales was becoming established in the west of Britain, similar events were taking place to the north. The Picts were the region's dominant indigenous tribe and named their kingdom Alba, which remains to this day the Gaelic word for Scotland.

Following the end of Roman rule in Britannia, Alba was invaded from two sides: first, towards the end of the 5th century, the Scotti crossed the sea from Ireland and established the kingdom of Dalriada (in what is

Late 5th century	597	7th century	685
The Scotti people (from today's Ireland) invade the land of the Picts (today's Scotland). In today's Argyll they establish the kingdom of Dalriada.	Pope Gregory sends missionary St Augustine to southern England to revive interest in Christianity among the southern Anglo-Saxons. His colleague St Aidan similarly converts many people in northern England.	Anglo-Saxons from the expanding English kingdom of Northumbria attempt to colonise southeast Alba (today's southern Scotland) and are met by the Scotti.	The Pictish king Bridei defeats the Northumbrians at Nechtansmere in Angus, an against-the-odds victory that sets the foundations for Scotland as a separate entity.

now Argyll); then in the 7th century Anglo-Saxons, from the expanding English kingdom of Northumbria, moved in to colonise the southeast. But by this time the Scotti were well dug in alongside the Picts, foreshadowing the time when yet another name – Scotland – would be applied to northern Britain.

The Viking Era

In the 9th century, just as the new territories of England, Wales and Scotland were becoming established, Britain was yet again invaded by a bunch of pesky continentals. This time it was the Vikings – Nordic people from today's Scandinavia.

It's another classic historical image: blonde hair, horned helmets, big swords, square-sailed longboats, rape and pillage. Tradition has it that Vikings turned up, killed everyone, took everything and left. There's *some* truth in that, but in reality many Vikings settled in Britain, and their legacy is especially evident in today's northern England, Orkney and Shetland.

After conquering northern and eastern areas, the Vikings started to expand into central England. Blocking their route were the Anglo-Saxon armies led by Alfred the Great, the king of Wessex and one of English history's best-known characters.

The battles that followed were seminal to the foundation of the nation-state of England, but the fighting didn't all go Alfred's way. For a few months he was on the run, wading through swamps, hiding in peasant hovels and famously burning cakes. It was the stuff of legend, and by 886 Alfred had gathered his strength and pushed the Vikings back to the north.

United England?

Thus England was divided in two: north and east was the Viking 'Danelaw', while south and west was Anglo-Saxon territory. Alfred was hailed as king of the English – the first time the Anglo-Saxons regarded themselves as a truly united people.

Alfred's son and successor was Edward the Elder. After more battles, he gained control of the Danelaw, and thus became the first king to rule the whole of England. His son, Athelstan, took the process a stage further and was specifically crowned King of England in 927. But it was hardly cause for celebration: the Vikings were still around, and later in the 10th century more raids from Scandinavia threatened this fledgling English unity. Over the following decades, control swung from Saxon (King Edgar) to Dane (King Knut) and back to Saxon again (King Edward the Confessor). As England came to the end of the 1st millennium AD, the future was anything but certain.

The Year 1000 by Robert Lacey and Danny Danziger looks long and hard at English life a millennium ago. Apparently it was cold and damp then, too.

8th century	850	872	9th century
King Offa of Mercia orders the construction of a clear border between his kingdom and Wales – a defensive ditch called Offa's Dyke, still visible today.	Vikings come from today's Denmark and conquer east and northeast England. They establish their capital at Jorvik, today's city of York.	The King of Norway creates an earldom in Orkney; Shetland is also governed from here. These island groups become a Viking base for raids and colonisation into Scotland and northern England.	Kenneth MacAilpin, the king of the Scotti, declares himself ruler of both the Scots *and* the Picts, thus uniting Scotland north of the Firth of Forth into a single kingdom.

Highs & Lows in Wales

Meanwhile, as England fought off the Viking threat, Wales was also dealing with the Nordic intruders. Building on the initial cooperation forced upon them by Anglo-Saxon oppression, in the 9th and 10th centuries the small kingdoms of Wales began cooperating, through necessity, to repel the Vikings.

King Rhodri Mawr (who died in 878) defeated a Viking force off the Isle of Anglesey and began the unification process. His grandson Hywel the Good is thought to have been responsible for drawing up a set of laws to bind the disparate Welsh tribes. But just as Wales was becoming a recognisable entity, the fledgling country was faced with more destructive onslaughts than it could handle and in 927 the Welsh kings recognised the Anglo-Saxon King Athelstan as their overlord, in exchange for an anti-Viking alliance.

Scotland Becomes a Kingdom

In the 9th century, the king of the Scotti of Dalriada was one Kenneth MacAlpin. His father was a Scot, but his mother was a Pictish princess, so MacAlpin took advantage of the Pictish custom of matrilineal succession to declare himself ruler of both the Scots *and* the Picts, and therefore king of all Alba.

In a surprisingly short time, the Scots gained cultural and political ascendancy. The Picts were absorbed, and their culture disappeared; Alba became known as Scotia.

In the 11th century, Scottish nation-building was further consolidated by King Malcolm III (whose most famous act was the 1057 murder of Macbeth, immortalised by William Shakespeare). With his English queen, Margaret, he founded the Canmore dynasty that would rule Scotland for the next two centuries.

1066 & All That

Back in England things were unsettled, as the royal pendulum swung between Saxon and Viking monarchs. When King Edward the Confessor died, the crown passed to Harold, his brother-in-law. That should've settled things, but Edward had a cousin in Normandy (the northern part of today's France) called William, who thought that *he* had a right to the throne of England.

The result was the Battle of Hastings in 1066, the most memorable of dates for anyone who's studied English history – or for anyone who hasn't. William sailed from Normandy with an army of Norman soldiers, the Saxons were defeated and Harold was killed (according to tradition, by an arrow in the eye).

927	1018	1040	1066
Athelstan, grandson of Alfred the Great, son of Edward the Elder, is the first monarch to be specifically crowned King of England, building on his ancestors' success in regaining Viking territory.	Scottish King Malcolm II defeats the Northumbrians at the battle of Carham and gains the Lothian region, thus expanding the size of Scotland.	Macbeth takes the Scottish throne after defeating Duncan in battle. This, and the fact that he was later killed by Duncan's son Malcolm, are the only parallels with the Shakespeare play.	Battle of Hastings – a crucial date in English history. Incumbent King Harold is defeated by an invading Norman army, and England has a new monarch: William the Conqueror.

Norman Wisdom

William became king of England, earning the title William the Conqueror. It was no idle nickname – to control the Anglo-Saxons, the Norman invaders wisely built castles across their newly won territory, and by 1085–86 the Domesday Book provided a census of England's current stock and future potential.

In the years after the invasion, the French-speaking Normans and the English-speaking Anglo-Saxons kept pretty much to themselves. A strict hierarchy of class developed, known as the feudal system.

Intermarriage was not completely unknown; William's son, Henry I, married a Saxon princess. Nonetheless, such unifying moves stood for nothing after Henry's death: a bitter struggle for succession followed, finally won by Henry II, who took the throne as the first king of the Plantagenet dynasty.

> At the top of the feudal system came the monarch, followed by nobles (barons, dukes and bishops), then earls, knights, lords and ladies. At the bottom were peasants or 'serfs'. This strict hierarchy became the basis of a class system that still exists in Britain today.

Post-Invasion Wales & Scotland

To secure his new kingdom, and keep the Welsh in theirs, William the Conqueror built castles and appointed feudal barons along the border. The Lords Marcher, as they were known, became massively rich and powerful, and the parts of western England along the Welsh border are still called the Marches today.

In Scotland, King Malcolm III and Queen Margaret were more accommodating to Norman ways. Malcolm's successor, David I (1124–53), adopted the Norman feudal system, as well as granting land to great Norman families. By 1212 a courtier called Walter of Coventry remarked that the Scottish court was 'French in race and manner of life, in speech and in culture'.

But while the French-Norman effect changed England and lowland Scotland over the following centuries, further north the Highland clans remained inaccessible in their glens, and were a law unto themselves for another 600 years.

Royal & Holy Squabbling

When the reign of England's Henry I came to an end, the enduring British habit of competition for the throne introduced an equally enduring tendency for bickering between royalty and the church. Things came to a head in 1170 when Henry II had the 'turbulent priest' Thomas Becket murdered in Canterbury Cathedral, where a memorial to Becket can still be seen today.

Perhaps the next king, Richard I, wanted to make amends for his forebears' unholy sentiments by leading a crusade (a Christian 'holy war') to liberate Jerusalem and the Holy Land from occupation by Muslim 'heathens' under their leader Saladin. The campaign became known as the Third Crusade, and although the Christian armies captured the cities of Acre and Jaffa, they did not take Jerusalem.

1085–86	1124–53	12th century	1215
The new Norman rulers establish the Domesday Book census. Within three years they have a snapshot of England's current stock and future potential.	The rule of David I of Scotland – the Scottish aristocracy adopts the Norman feudal system, and the king grants land to great Norman families.	Oxford University is founded. There's evidence of teaching in the area since 1096, but King Henry II's 1167 ban on students attending the University of Paris solidified Oxford's importance.	King John signs the Magna Carta, limiting the monarch's power for the first time in English history in an early step along the path towards constitutional rule.

Unfortunately, Richard's overseas activities meant he was too busy crusading to bother about governing England and in his absence the country fell into disarray, although his bravery and ruthlessness earned him the sobriquet Richard the Lionheart.

Richard was succeeded by his brother John, but under his harsh rule things got even worse for the general population. According to legend, during this time a nobleman called Robert of Loxley, better known as Robin Hood, hid in Sherwood Forest and engaged in a spot of wealth redistribution.

Expansionist Edward

Edward I of England (1272–1307) was a skilled ruler and ambitious general. During a busy 35-year reign he was unashamedly expansionist in his outlook, leading campaigns into Wales and Scotland.

Some decades earlier, the Welsh king Llywelyn the Great (died 1240) had attempted to set up a state in Wales, and his grandson Llywelyn the Last was recognised by Henry III as the first Prince (but not King) of Wales. But Edward I had no time for such niceties, and descended on Wales in a bloody invasion that lasted much of the 1270s. In the end, Wales became a dependent principality, owing allegiance to England. There were no more Welsh kings, and Edward made his own son Prince of Wales. Ever since, the British sovereign's eldest son has automatically been given the title. (Most recently, Prince Charles was formally proclaimed Prince of Wales at Caernarfon Castle in 1969, much to the displeasure of Welsh nationalists.)

Edward I then looked north. For 200 years, Scotland had been ruled by the Canmores, but the dynasty effectively ended in 1286 with the death of Alexander III. He was succeeded by his four-year-old granddaughter Margaret ('the Maid of Norway'), who was engaged to the son of Edward I, but she died in 1290 before the wedding could take place.

Scotland Wins Independence

There followed a dispute for the Scottish throne between John Balliol and Robert Bruce of Annandale. Arbitration was needed and Edward I chose Balliol. But Edward then sought to formalise his feudal overlordship and travelled through Scotland forcing local leaders to swear allegiance. In a final blow to Scottish pride, Edward removed the Stone of Destiny, on which the kings of Scotland had been crowned for centuries, and sent it to London.

That was too much. In response, Balliol got in touch with Edward's old enemy, France, and arranged a treaty of cooperation, the start of an anti-English partnership 'the Auld Alliance', which was to last for many centuries (and to the present day when it comes to rugby or football).

13th century	1295	1296	1298–1305
Wales is invaded by English King Edward I, bringing to an end the rule of Welsh leader 'Llywelyn the Last'. Edward builds a ring of castles to suppress further Welsh uprisings.	John Balliol of Scotland and Philip IV of France sign a mutual defence treaty that establishes the 'Auld Alliance' – this predominantly anti-English agreement remains in place for several centuries.	King Edward I marches on Scotland with an army of 30,000 men, and in a brutal invasion captures the castles of Berwick, Edinburgh, Roxburgh and Stirling.	William Wallace is proclaimed Guardian of Scotland in 1298. After Edward's army defeats the Scots at the Battle of Falkirk, Wallace goes into hiding but is betrayed and executed in 1305.

Edward wasn't the sort of bloke to brook opposition, though. In 1296 the English army defeated Balliol, forcing the Scottish barons to accept Edward's rule, and his ruthless retaliation earned him the title 'Hammer of the Scots'. But still the Scottish people refused to lie down; in 1297, at the Battle of Stirling Bridge, the English were defeated by a Scots army under the leadership of William Wallace. Over 700 years later, Wallace is still remembered as a Scottish hero.

By this time, Robert the Bruce (grandson of Bruce of Annandale) had crowned himself king of Scotland (1290), been beaten in battle, gone on the run and, while hiding in a cave, been famously inspired to renew his efforts by a spider persistently spinning its web. Bruce's army went on to defeat Edward II's superior English forces at the Battle of Bannockburn in 1314, a famous victory that led to the official recognition of Scotland as an independent nation, with Bruce as its king, in 1328.

Stewarts Enter the Scene

While the Hundred Years' War (1337–1453) rumbled on between England and France, things weren't much better in Scotland. After the death of Robert the Bruce in 1329, the country was ravaged by endless internal conflicts and plague epidemics.

Bruce's son became David II of Scotland, but he was soon caught up in battles against fellow Scots disaffected by his father and aided by England's Edward III. So when David died in 1371, the Scots quickly crowned Robert Stewart (Robert the Bruce's grandson) as king, marking the start of the House of Stewart, which was to crop up again in England later.

Houses of York & Lancaster

In 1399 the ineffectual Richard II of England was ousted by a powerful baron called Henry Bolingbroke, who became Henry IV, the first monarch of the House of Lancaster. Less than a year later, his rule was disrupted by a final cry of resistance from the downtrodden Welsh, led by royal descendant Owain Glyndŵr (Owen Glendower). But the rebellion was crushed, Glyndŵr died an outlaw and the Welsh elite were barred from public life for many years.

Henry IV was followed by Henry V, who stirred up the dormant Hundred Years' War and defeated France at the Battle of Agincourt. The patriotic speech penned for him by Shakespeare in *Henry V* ('Cry "God for Harry, England, and St George!"') has ensured his position among the most famous English kings of all time.

When the Hundred Years' War finally ground to a halt in 1453, you'd have thought things would be calm for a while, but no. The English forces returning from France threw their energies into a civil war dubbed the Wars of the Roses.

The story of William Wallace is told in the Mel Gibson epic *Braveheart*. In devolution debates of the 1990s, the patriotic pride engendered by this movie did more for Scottish nationalism than any politician's speech.

Shakespeare's *Henry V* was filmed as a superb epic starring Kenneth Branagh as the eponymous king. Also worth catching is the earlier movie of the same name starring Laurence Olivier, made in 1944 as a patriotic rallying cry.

HISTORY STEWARTS ENTER THE SCENE

1314	1328	1337–1453	1348
An army under Robert the Bruce wins against the English at the Battle of Bannockburn – a victory that consolidated Scottish independence for the next 400 years.	Continuing raids by the Scots into northern England force the English to sue for peace; the Treaty of Northampton gives Scotland its independence, with Robert I, the Bruce, as king.	England battles France in a long conflict known as the Hundred Years' War. It was actually a series of small conflicts. And it lasted for more than a century, too...	The bubonic plague (called the Black Death) arrives, ultimately killing more than a third of the population. For peasant labourers who survived, an upside was a rise in wages.

Briefly it went like this: Henry VI of the House of Lancaster (emblem, a red rose) was challenged by Richard, Duke of York (emblem, a white rose). Henry was weak and it was almost a walkover for Richard. But Henry's wife, Margaret of Anjou, was made of sterner stuff and her forces defeated the challenger. It didn't rest there. Richard's son Edward entered the scene with an army, turned the tables and finally drove out Henry. He became King Edward IV, first monarch of the House of York.

Dark Deeds in the Tower

Edward IV hardly had time to catch his breath before Richard Neville, Earl of Warwick, and Margaret of Anjou teamed up in 1471 to force him into exile and bring Henry VI back to the throne. But a year later Edward IV came bouncing back: he killed Warwick, captured Margaret and had Henry snuffed out in the Tower of London.

Although Edward IV's position seemed secure, he ruled for only a decade before being succeeded by his 12-year-old son, Edward V. But the boy-king's reign was even shorter than his dad's. In 1483 he was mysteriously murdered, along with his brother, and once again the Tower of London was the scene of the crime.

With the 'little princes' dispatched, this left the throne open for their dear old Uncle Richard. Whether he was the princes' killer is still the subject of debate, but his rule as Richard III was short-lived. Despite being given another famous Shakespearean sound bite ('A horse, a horse! My kingdom for a horse!'), few tears were shed in 1485 when he was tumbled from the top job by a nobleman from Wales called Henry Tudor, who became Henry VII.

Moves Towards Unity

After the Wars of the Roses, Henry VII's Tudor neutrality was important. He mended fences with his northern neighbours by marrying his daughter to James IV of Scotland, linking the Tudor and Stewart lines, though this didn't stop James IV invading England in 1513, only to be killed at the Battle of Flodden. Henry VII married Edward IV's daughter, Elizabeth of York (daughter of Edward IV and niece of Richard III), further cementing his claim to the throne.

Matrimony may have been more useful than warfare for Henry VII, but the multiple marriages of his successor, Henry VIII, were a very different story. Fathering a male heir was his problem, hence the famous six wives, but the pope's disapproval of divorce and remarriage led to a split with the Roman Catholic Church. Parliament made Henry the head of the Protestant Church of England – the beginning of a pivotal division between Catholics and Protestants that still exists in some areas of Britain.

Six Wives: The Queens of Henry VIII, by historian David Starkey, is an accessible modern study of the multi-marrying monarch.

1371	1381	1400	1459–71
The last of the Bruce dynasty dies, succeeded by the Stewards (Stewarts), who rule Scotland and then Britain for the next three centuries.	Richard II is confronted by the Peasants' Revolt. This attempt by commoners to overthrow the feudal system is brutally suppressed, further injuring an already deeply divided country.	Welsh nationalist hero Owain Glyndŵr leads the Welsh in rebellion, declaring a parliament in Machynlleth, but his rebellion is short-lived and victory fleeting.	The Wars of the Roses takes place – an ongoing conflict between two competing dynasties, the Houses of Lancaster and York. The Yorkists are eventually successful, enabling King Edward IV to gain the throne.

In 1536 Henry followed this up by 'dissolving' many monasteries in Britain and Ireland, a blatant takeover of their land and wealth rather than a symptom of the struggle between church and state. Nonetheless, the general populace felt little sympathy for the wealthy (and often corrupt) abbeys, and in 1539–40 another monastic land grab swallowed the larger ones as well.

At the same time, Henry signed the Acts of Union (1536 and 1543), formally uniting England and Wales for the first time. Meanwhile, in Scotland, James IV had been succeeded by James V, who died in 1542. His baby daughter Mary became queen, and Scotland was ruled by regents.

The Elizabethan Age

Henry VIII died in 1547, succeeded by his son Edward VI, then by his daughter Mary I, but their reigns were short. So, unexpectedly, Elizabeth, third in line, came to the throne.

As Elizabeth I, she inherited a nasty mess of religious strife and divided loyalties, but after an uncertain start she gained confidence and turned the country around. Refusing marriage, she borrowed biblical imagery and became known as the Virgin Queen, making her perhaps the first British monarch to create a cult image.

It paid off. Her 45-year reign was a period of boundless optimism, characterised by the naval defeat of the Spanish Armada, the expansion of trade due to the global explorations of seafarers such as Walter Raleigh and Francis Drake, not to mention a cultural flourishing thanks to writers such as William Shakespeare and Christopher Marlowe.

The 1998 film *Elizabeth*, directed by Shekhar Kapur and starring Cate Blanchett, covers the early years of the Virgin Queen's rule, as she graduates from princess to commanding monarch – a time of forbidden love, unwanted suitors, intrigue and death.

MARY, QUEEN OF SCOTS

During Elizabeth I's reign, her cousin Mary (the Catholic daughter of Scottish King James V) had become known as Mary, Queen of Scots. She'd spent her childhood in France and had married the French *dauphin* (crown prince), thereby becoming queen of France as well. Why stop at two? After her husband's death, Mary returned to Scotland, where she claimed the English throne as well, on the grounds that Elizabeth I was illegitimate.

However, Mary's plans failed. She was imprisoned and forced to abdicate in favour of her son (a Protestant, who became James VI of Scotland), but she escaped to England and appealed to Elizabeth for help. This was a bad move; Mary was seen, not surprisingly, as a security risk and imprisoned once again. In an uncharacteristic display of indecision, Elizabeth held Mary under arrest for nearly 19 years before finally ordering her execution. As a prisoner, Mary was frequently moved from house to house, so that today England has many stately homes (and even a few pubs) claiming 'Mary, Queen of Scots slept here'.

1468–69	1485	1509–47	1536 & 1543
Orkney and then Shetland are mortgaged to Scotland as part of a dowry from Danish King Christian I, whose daughter is to marry the future King James III of Scotland.	Henry Tudor defeats Richard III at the Battle of Bosworth to become King Henry VII, establishing the Tudor dynasty and ending York-Lancaster rivalry for the throne.	The reign of King Henry VIII. The Pope's disapproval of Henry's serial marriage and divorce results in the English Reformation – the founding of the Church of England.	English authority is exerted over Wales; the Laws in Wales Acts, also known as the Acts of Union, formally tie the two countries as a single political entity.

United & Disunited Britain

Elizabeth I died in 1603 without an heir, and was succeeded by her closest relative James, the Protestant son of the executed Mary. He became James I of England and James VI of Scotland, the first English monarch of the House of Stuart (Mary's time in France had Gallicised the Stewart name). Most importantly, James united England, Wales and Scotland into one kingdom for the first time in history – another step towards British unity.

James' attempts to smooth religious relations were set back by the anti-Catholic outcry that followed the infamous Guy Fawkes Gunpowder Plot, a terrorist attempt to blow up parliament in 1605. The event is still celebrated every 5 November with fireworks, bonfires and burning effigies of Guy himself.

Alongside the Catholic-Protestant rift, the divide between king and parliament continued to smoulder. The power struggle worsened during the reign of the next king, Charles I, and eventually degenerated into the Civil War of 1642–49. The antiroyalist (or 'parliamentarian') forces were led by Oliver Cromwell, a Puritan who preached against the excesses of the monarchy and established Church. His army (known as the Roundheads) was pitched against the king's forces (the Cavaliers) in a conflict that tore England apart. It ended with victory for the Roundheads, with the king executed, England declared a republic and Cromwell hailed as 'Protector'.

The Civil War extended into Scotland where the main struggle was between royalists and radical 'Covenanters', who sought freedom from state interference in church government.

On the chilly day of his execution, dethroned King Charles I reputedly wore two shirts to avoid shivering and being regarded as a coward.

Return of the King

By 1653 Cromwell was finding parliament too restrictive and he assumed dictatorial powers, much to his supporters' dismay. On his death in 1658, he was followed half-heartedly by his son, but in 1660 parliament decided to re-establish the monarchy, as republican alternatives were proving far worse.

Charles II (the exiled son of Charles I) came to the throne, and his rule, known as 'the Restoration', saw scientific and cultural activity bursting forth. Exploration and expansion were also on the agenda. Backed by the army and navy (modernised, ironically, by Cromwell), British colonies stretched down the American coast, while the East India Company set up headquarters in Bombay (now Mumbai), laying foundations for what was to become the British Empire.

The next king, James II, had a harder time. Attempts to ease restrictive laws on Catholics ended with his defeat at the Battle of the Boyne by William III, the Protestant king of Holland, better known as William of Orange. William was married to James' own daughter Mary, but it didn't stop him having a bash at his father-in-law.

1560	1588	1558–1603	1603
The Scottish Parliament creates a Protestant Church that is independent of Rome and the monarchy, as a result of the Reformation. The Latin Mass is abolished and the pope's authority denied.	The first complete translation of the Bible into Welsh helps the cause of Protestantism and also helps the survival of the neglected Welsh language.	The reign of Queen Elizabeth I, a period of boundless English optimism. Enter stage right playwright William Shakespeare. Exit due west navigators Walter Raleigh and Francis Drake.	James VI of Scotland inherits the English throne in the so-called Union of the Crowns, becoming James I of England and James VI of Scotland.

William and Mary came to the throne as King and Queen, each in their own right (Mary had more of a claim, but William would not agree to be a mere consort), and their joint accession in 1688 was known as the Glorious Revolution.

Act of Union

In 1694 Mary died, leaving William as sole monarch. He died a few years later and was succeeded by his sister-in-law Anne (the second daughter of James II). In 1707, during Anne's reign, the Act of Union was passed, bringing an end to the independent Scottish Parliament and linking the countries of England, Wales and Scotland under one parliament (based in London) for the first time. The nation of Britain was now established as a single state, with a bigger, better and more powerful parliament, and a constitutional monarchy with clear limits on the power of the king or queen.

The new-look parliament didn't wait long to flex its muscles. The Act of Union banned any Catholic, or anyone married to a Catholic, from ascending the throne – a rule still in force today. In 1714 Anne died without leaving an heir, marking the end of the Stuart line. The throne was then passed to distant (but still safely Protestant) German relatives: the House of Hanover.

Walks Through Britain's History (published by the Automobile Association) guides you on foot to castles, battlefields and hundreds of other sites with a link to the past. Take the air. Breathe in history!

The Jacobite Rebellions

Despite, or perhaps because of, the 1707 Act of Union, anti-English feeling in Scotland refused to disappear. The Jacobite rebellions, most notably those of 1715 and 1745, were attempts to overthrow the Hanoverian monarchy and bring back the Stuarts. Although these are iconic events in Scottish history, in reality there was never much support for the Jacobite cause outside the Highlands: the people of the lowlands were mainly Protestant, and feared a return to the Catholicism that the Stuarts represented.

The 1715 rebellion was led by James Edward Stuart (the Old Pretender), the son of the exiled James II of England (James VII of Scotland), but when the attempt failed he fled to France. To impose control on the Highlands, General George Wade was commissioned to build a network of military roads through many previously inaccessible glens.

In 1745 James' son Charles Edward Stuart (Bonnie Prince Charlie, the Young Pretender) landed in Scotland to claim the crown for his father. He was initially successful, moving south into England as far as Derby, but the prince and his Highland army suffered a catastrophic defeat at the Battle of Culloden in 1746; his legendary escape to the western isles is remembered in 'The Skye Boat Song'. General Wade is remembered too, as many of the roads his troops built are still in use today.

1642–49	1688	1707	1745–46
English Civil War between the king's Cavaliers and Oliver Cromwell's Roundheads establishes the Commonwealth of England.	William of Orange and his wife, Mary, daughter of King James II, jointly ascend the throne after William defeats his father-in-law in the Glorious Revolution.	The Act of Union brings England and Scotland under one parliament, one sovereign and one flag.	The culmination of the Jacobite uprisings sees Bonnie Prince Charlie land in Scotland, gather an army and march southwards, to be eventually defeated at the Battle of Culloden.

The Empire Strikes Out

By the mid-18th century, struggles for the British throne seemed a thing of the past, and the Hanoverian kings increasingly relied on parliament to govern the country. As part of the process, from 1721 to 1742 a senior parliamentarian called Sir Robert Walpole effectively became Britain's first prime minister.

Meanwhile, the British Empire continued to grow in America, Canada and India. The first claims were made on Australia after Captain James Cook's epic voyage of exploration in 1768.

The empire's first major reverse came when the American colonies won the War of Independence (1776–83). This setback forced Britain to withdraw from the world stage for a while, a gap not missed by French ruler Napoleon. He threatened to invade Britain and hinder the power of the British overseas, before his ambitions were curtailed by naval hero Admiral Nelson and military hero the Duke of Wellington at the famous battles of Trafalgar (1805) and Waterloo (1815).

Captain Cook's voyage to the southern hemisphere was primarily a scientific expedition. His objectives included monitoring the transit of Venus, an astronomical event that happens only twice every 180 years or so (most recently in 2004 and 2012). 'Discovering' Australia was just a sideline.

The Industrial Age

While the empire expanded abroad, at home Britain became the crucible of the Industrial Revolution. Steam power (patented by James Watt in 1781) and steam trains (launched by George Stephenson in 1830) transformed methods of production and transport, and the towns of the English Midlands became the first industrial cities.

From about 1750, much of the Scottish Highlands was emptied of people, as landowners expelled entire farms and villages to make way for more profitable sheep, a seminal event in Scotland's history known as the Clearances. Although many of the dispossessed left for the New World, others headed to the cotton mills of Lanarkshire and the shipyards of Glasgow.

By the early 19th century, copper, iron and slate were being extracted in the Merthyr Tydfil and Monmouth areas of Wales. The 1860s saw the Rhondda valleys opened up for coal mining, and Wales soon became a major exporter of coal, as well as the world's leading producer of tin plate.

Across Britain, industrialisation meant people were on the move as never before, leaving the farms and villages their families had occupied for generations. The rapid change from rural to urban society caused great dislocation, and although knowledge of science and medicine also improved alongside industrial advances, for many people the adverse side effects of Britain's economic blossoming were poverty and deprivation.

Age of Empire

Despite the social turmoil of the early 19th century, by the time Queen Victoria took the throne in 1837 Britain's factories dominated world trade and British fleets dominated the oceans. The rest of the 19th cen-

1799–1815	1837–1901	1847	1926
In the Napoleonic Wars, Napoleon threatens invasion on a weakened Britain, but his ambitions are curtailed by Nelson and Wellington at the famous battles of Trafalgar (1805) and Waterloo (1815).	The reign of Queen Victoria, during which the British Empire – 'on which the sun never sets' – expands from Canada through Africa and India to Australia and New Zealand.	Publication of a government report, dubbed the 'Treason of the Blue Books', suggests the Welsh language is detrimental to education in Wales, and fuels the Welsh-language struggle.	Increasing mistrust of the government, fuelled by soaring unemployment, leads to the General Strike. Millions of workers – train drivers, miners, shipbuilders – down tools and bring the country to a halt.

tury was seen as Britain's Golden Age, a period of confidence not enjoyed since the days of the last great queen, Elizabeth I.

Victoria ruled a proud nation at home and great swaths of territories abroad, from Canada through much of Africa and India to Australia and New Zealand, trumpeted as 'the empire on which the sun never sets'.

The times were optimistic, but it wasn't all tub-thumping jingoism. Disraeli and his successor William Gladstone also introduced social reforms to address the worst excesses of the Industrial Revolution. Education became universal, trade unions were legalised and the right to vote was extended in a series of reform acts, finally being granted to all men over the age of 21 in 1918, and to all women in 1928.

> At its height, the British Empire covered 20% of the land area of Earth and contained a quarter of the world's population.

World War I

When Queen Victoria died in 1901, it seemed Britain's energy fizzled out too. The new king, Edward VII, ushered in the relaxed Edwardian era – and a long period of decline.

Meanwhile, in continental Europe, other states were more active: four restless military powers (Russia, Austria-Hungary, Turkey and Germany) focused their sabre-rattling on the Balkan states, and the assassination of Archduke Ferdinand at Sarajevo in 1914 finally sparked a clash that became the 'Great War' we now call WWI. Soldiers from Britain and Allied countries were drawn into a conflict of horrendous slaughter, most infamously on the killing fields of Flanders and the beaches of Gallipoli.

By the war's weary end in 1918, over a million Britons had died (plus millions more from many other countries) and there was hardly a street or village untouched by death, as the sobering lists of names on war memorials all over Britain still show.

> One of the finest novels about WWI is *Birdsong* by Sebastian Faulks. Understated, perfectly paced and intensely moving, it tells of passion, fear, waste, incompetent generals and the poor bloody infantry.

Disillusion & Depression

For the soldiers who did return from WWI, the war had created disillusion and a questioning of the social order. Many supported the ideals of a new political force, the Labour Party, to represent the working class.

Meanwhile, the bitter Anglo-Irish War (1919–21) saw most of Ireland achieving full independence from Britain. Six counties in the north remained British, creating a new political entity called the United Kingdom of Great Britain and Northern Ireland. But the decision to partition the island of Ireland was to have long-term repercussions that still dominate political agendas in both the UK and the Republic of Ireland today.

The Labour Party won for the first time in the 1923 election, in coalition with the Liberals. James Ramsay MacDonald was the first Labour prime minister, but by the mid-1920s the Conservatives were back. The world economy was now in decline and in the 1930s the Great Depression meant another decade of misery and political upheaval.

1948	1955 & 1959	1971	1979
Aneurin Bevan, the health minister in the Labour government, launches the National Health Service – the core of Britain as a 'welfare state'.	Cardiff is declared the Welsh capital in 1955, and Wales gets its own official flag (the red dragon on a green and white field) in 1959.	Britain adopts the 'decimal' currency (one pound equals 100 pence) and drops the ancient system of one pound equals 20 shillings or 240 pennies, the centuries-old bane of school maths lessons.	A Conservative government led by Margaret Thatcher wins the national election, a major milestone of Britain's 20th-century history, ushering in a decade of dramatic political and social change.

World War II

In 1933 Adolf Hitler came to power in Germany and in 1939 Germany invaded Poland, drawing Britain once again into war. The German army swept through Europe and pushed back British forces to the beaches of Dunkirk (northern France) in June 1940. An extraordinary flotilla of rescue vessels turned total disaster into a brave defeat, and Dunkirk Day is still remembered with pride and sadness every year in Britain.

By mid-1940 most of Europe was controlled by Germany. In Russia, Stalin had negotiated a peace agreement. The USA was neutral, leaving Britain virtually isolated. Into this arena came a new prime minister, Winston Churchill.

Between September 1940 and May 1941, the German air force launched the Blitz, a series of (mainly night-time) bombing raids on London and other cities. Despite this, morale in Britain remained strong, thanks partly to Churchill's regular radio broadcasts. In late 1941 the USA entered the war, and the tide began to turn.

By 1944 Germany was in retreat. Russia pushed back from the east, and Britain, the USA and other Allies were again on the beaches of France. The Normandy landings (or D-Day, as they are better remembered) marked the start of the liberation of Europe's western side. By 1945 Hitler was dead and the war was finally over.

Normandy Landings Statistics

Largest military armada in history

More than 5000 ships

Approximately 150,000 Allied troops landed

Campaign time: four days

Swinging & Sliding

Despite victory in WWII, there was an unexpected swing on the political front in 1945. An electorate tired of war and hungry for change tumbled Churchill's Conservatives in favour of the Labour Party.

WINSTON CHURCHILL

Born in 1874 to an aristocratic family, Winston Churchill is Britain's most famous prime minister. As a young man he joined the British Army and saw action in India and Africa. He was first elected to parliament as a Conservative MP (Member of Parliament) in 1900, and held various ministerial positions through the 1920s.

In 1939 Britain entered WWII, and by 1940 Churchill was prime minister, taking additional responsibility as minister of defence. Hitler had expected an easy victory, but Churchill's dedication, not to mention his radio speeches (most famously offering 'nothing but blood, toil, tears and sweat' and promising to 'fight on the beaches'), inspired the British people to resist.

Between July and October 1940 the Royal Air Force withstood Germany's aerial raids to win what became known as the Battle of Britain, a major turning point in the war – in Churchilll's words of praise for the RAF, 'never was so much owed by so many to so few'. It was an audacious strategy, but it paid off and Churchill was lauded as a national hero – praise that continued to the end of the war, and well beyond his death in 1965.

1982	1990	1997	1999
Britain is victorious in a war against Argentina over the invasion of the Falkland Islands, leading to a rise in patriotic sentiment.	Mrs Thatcher is ousted as leader and the Conservative Party enters a period of decline, but remains in power thanks to inept Labour opposition.	The general election sees Tony Blair lead 'New' Labour to victory in the polls, with a record-breaking parliamentary majority, ending more than 20 years of Tory rule.	The first National Assembly is elected for Wales, with the members sitting in a new building in Cardiff; Rhodri Morgan becomes First Minister.

In 1952 George VI was succeeded by his daughter Elizabeth II and, following the trend set by earlier queens Elizabeth I and Victoria, she has remained on the throne for over six decades, overseeing a period of massive social and economic change.

By the late 1950s, recovery was strong enough for Prime Minister Harold Macmillan to famously remind the British people they had 'never had it so good'. By the time the 1960s had started, grey old Britain was suddenly more fun and lively than it had been for generations.

Although the 1960s were swinging, the 1970s saw an economic slide thanks to a grim combination of inflation, the oil crisis and international competition. The rest of the decade was marked by strikes, disputes and all-round gloom.

Neither the Conservatives (also known as the Tories), under Edward Heath, nor Labour, under Harold Wilson and Jim Callaghan, proved capable of controlling the strife. The British public had had enough, and in the elections of 1979 the Conservatives won a landslide victory, led by a little-known politician named Margaret Thatcher.

The six decades since the end of WWII are neatly covered in *A History of Modern Britain*, a handy overview focusing on political events, by TV presenter and commentator Andrew Marr.

The Thatcher Years

Soon everyone had heard of Margaret Thatcher. Love her or hate her, no one could argue that her methods weren't dramatic. Looking back from a 21st-century vantage point, most commentators agree that by economic measures the Thatcher government's policies were largely successful, but by social measures they were a failure and created a polarised Britain: on one side were the people who gained from the prosperous wave of opportunities in the 'new' industries, while on the other side were those left unemployed and dispossessed by the decline of the 'old' industries such as coal-mining and steel production.

Despite, or perhaps thanks to, policies that were frequently described as uncompromising, Margaret Thatcher was, by 1988, the longest-serving British prime minister of the 20th century.

For detail on the 1980s, read *No Such Thing as Society*, by Andy McSmith. Drawing on Margaret Thatcher's famous quotation, this book studies the era dominated by the Iron Lady.

New Labour, New Millennium

The political pendulum started to swing again in the early 1990s. The turning point came in 1997, when 'New' Labour swept to power, with leader Tony Blair declared the new Prime Minister.

The Labour Party enjoyed an extended honeymoon period, and the 2001 election was another walkover. The Conservative Party continued to struggle, allowing Labour to win a historic third term in 2005. A year later Tony Blair became the longest-serving Labour prime minister in British history.

In May 2010, a record 13 years of Labour rule came to an end, and a new coalition between the Conservative and Liberal-Democrat Parties became the new government.

1999–2004	2003	2010	2014
Scottish Parliament is convened for the first time on 12 May 1999. Five years later, after plenty of scandal and huge sums of money, a new parliament building is opened at Holyrood in Edinburgh.	Britain joins America and other countries in the invasion of Iraq, initially with some support from parliament and public, despite large antiwar street demonstrations in London and other cities.	Labour is narrowly defeated in the general election as the minority Liberal-Democrats align with the Conservatives to form the first coalition government in Britain's postwar history.	A referendum is held in Scotland, asking the question 'Should Scotland be an independent country?' The result: 55% voted No, 45% voted Yes.

The British Table

The idea of British cuisine was once a bit of a joke. But a culinary landmark came in 2005, when food bible *Gourmet* magazine famously singled out London as having the best collection of restaurants in the world. In the years since then the choice for food lovers – whatever their budget – has continued to improve. London is now regarded as a global gastronomic capital, and it's increasingly easy to find great food all over Britain.

Eating in Britain

Britain's most popular restaurant dish is chicken tikka masala, an 'Indian' curry dish created specifically for the British palate and unheard of in India itself.

The infamous outbreaks of 'mad cow' disease in the 1990s are ancient history now, and British beef is once again exported to the world, but an upside of the bad press at the time was a massive surge in demand for good-quality food. That means wherever you go in Britain today, you'll find a plethora of organic, natural, unadulterated, chemical-free, free-range, hand-reared, locally farmed, nonintensive foods available in shops, markets, cafes and restaurants.

Alongside this greater awareness of quality and provenance, there have been other changes to British food thanks to outside influences. For decades most towns have boasted Italian, Chinese and Indian restaurants, so spaghetti carbonara, chow mein or vindaloo are no longer considered exotic, and in more recent times dishes from Japan, Korea or Thailand and other Asian countries have also become widely available.

The overall effect of these foreign influences has been the introduction to 'traditional' British cuisine of new techniques, new ingredients and new herbs and spices. So now we have 'modern British cuisine', where even humble bangers and mash (sausage with mashed potato) are raised to new heights when handmade pork, apple and thyme-scented sausages are paired with lightly chopped fennel and red wine gravy.

But beware the domination of style over substance: you're often better spending £5 on a top-notch curry in Birmingham or a homemade steak-and-ale pie in a country pub than forking out £30 in a city restaurant for a 'modern European' concoction that tastes like it came from a can.

The Full British

In Yorkshire, the eponymous pudding is traditionally a *starter*, a reminder of days when food was scarce and the pudding was a pre-meal stomach-filler.

Although grazing on a steady supply of snacks is increasingly common-place in Britain, as it is in many other industrialised nations, the British culinary day is still punctuated by the three traditional meals of breakfast, lunch and dinner. And just to keep you on your toes, those later meals are also called dinner and tea or lunch and supper – depending on social class and geographical location.

Breakfast

Many people in Britain make do with toast or a bowl of cereal before dashing to work, but visitors staying in hotels and B&Bs will undoubt-edly encounter a phenomenon called the 'Full English Breakfast' – or one of its regional equivalents. This usually consists of bacon, sausages, eggs, tomatoes, mushrooms, baked beans and fried bread. In Scotland the 'full Scottish breakfast' might include oatcakes instead of fried bread.

In Wales you may be offered laver bread, which is not a bread at all but seaweed – a tasty speciality often served with oatmeal and bacon on toast. In northern England you may get black pudding. And just in case you thought this insufficient, it's still preceded by cereal, and followed by toast and marmalade.

If you don't feel like eating half a farmyard first thing in the morning, most places offer a lighter alternative or local speciality such as kippers (smoked fish) or a 'continental breakfast', which completely omits the cooked stuff and may even add something exotic such as croissants.

Lunch

One of the many great inventions that England gave the world is the sandwich, often eaten as a midday meal. Slapping a slice of cheese or ham between two bits of bread may seem a simple concept, but no one apparently thought of it until the 18th century, when the Earl of Sandwich (his title comes from the Southeast England town of Sandwich that originally got its name from the Viking word for sandy beach) ordered his servants to bring cold meat between bread so he could keep working at his desk, or, as some historians claim, continue playing cards late at night.

Another lunch classic that perhaps epitomises British food more than any other – especially in pubs – is the ploughman's lunch. Basically it's bread and cheese, and although hearty yokels probably did carry such food to the fields (no doubt wrapped in a red-spotted handkerchief) in days of yore, the meal is actually a modern phenomenon. It was invented in the 1960s by the marketing chief of the national cheese-makers' organisation as a way to boost consumption, neatly cashing in on public nostalgia and fondness for tradition.

You can still find a basic ploughman's lunch offered in some pubs – and it undeniably goes well with a pint or two of local ale at lunchtime – but these days the meal has usually been smartened up to include butter, salad, pickle, pickled onion and dressings. At some pubs you get a selection of cheeses. You'll also find other variations, such as a farmer's lunch (bread and chicken), stockman's lunch (bread and ham), Frenchman's lunch (brie and baguette) and fisherman's lunch (you guessed it, with fish).

For cheese and bread in a different combination, try Welsh rarebit – a sophisticated variation of cheese on toast, seasoned and flavoured with butter, milk and sometimes a little beer. For a takeaway lunch in Scotland, look out for stovies (tasty pies of meat, mashed onion and fried potato).

Dinner

For generations, a typical British dinner has been 'meat and two veg'. The meat is pork, beef or lamb, one of the vegetables is potatoes and the other inevitably carrots, cabbage or cauliflower – and just as inevitably cooked

> According to the Soil Association (www.soilassociation.org), the leading organic-food campaign group, more than 85% of people in Britain want pesticide-free food. See www.organicfood.com for more information.

THE BRITISH TABLE THE FULL BRITISH

NAME THAT PASTY

A favourite speciality in southwest England is the Cornish pasty. Originally a mix of cooked vegetables wrapped in pastry, it's often available in meat varieties (much to the scorn of the Cornish people) and now sold everywhere in Britain. The pasty was originally an all-in-one-lunch pack that tin miners carried underground and left on a ledge ready for mealtime. So that pasties weren't mixed up, they were marked with their owner's initials – always at one end, so the miner could eat half and safely leave the rest to snack on later without it mistakenly disappearing into the mouth of a workmate. Before going back to the surface, the miners traditionally left the last few crumbs of the pasty as a gift for the spirits of the mine, known as 'knockers', to ensure a safe shift the next day.

NOSE TO TAIL CUISINE

One of the many trends enjoyed by modern British cuisine is the revival of 'nose to tail' cooking – that is, making use of the entire animal, not just the more obvious cuts. This doesn't mean boiling or grilling a pig or sheep all in one go – it means utilising the parts that may at first seem unappetising or, frankly, inedible. So as well as dishes involving liver, heart, chitterlings (intestines) and other offal, traditional delights such as bone marrow on toast, or tripe (cow's stomach lining) with onions are once again gracing the menus of fashionable restaurants. The movement has been spearheaded by chef Fergus Henderson at his St John restaurant in London, and through his influential book, *Nose to Tail Eating: A Kind of British Cooking* (1999) and its follow-up *Beyond Nose to Tail* (2007).

long and hard. Although tastes and diets are changing, this classic combination still graces the tables of many British families several times a week.

And when the British say beef, they usually mean roast beef – a dish that's become a symbol of the nation, and the reason why the French call the British *les rosbifs*. Perhaps the most famous beef comes from Scotland's Aberdeen Angus cattle, while the best-known meat from Wales is lamb. Venison – usually from red deer – is readily available in Scotland, as well as in parts of Wales and England, most notably in the New Forest.

With beef – especially at Sunday lunches – comes another British classic: Yorkshire pudding. It's simply roast batter, but very tasty when cooked properly. Yet another classic British dish brings together Yorkshire pudding and sausages to create the delightfully named 'toad-in-the-hole'.

Perhaps the best-known British meal is fish and chips, often bought from the 'chippie' wrapped in paper to carry home – it's especially popular with families on Friday evenings. Late at night, epicures may order their fish and chips 'open' to eat immediately while walking back from the pub. It has to be said that quality varies outrageously across the country; sometimes the chips are limp and soggy, and the fish greasy and tasteless, especially once you get away from the sea, but in towns with salt in the air, this classic deep-fried delight is always worth trying.

Puddings & Desserts

In British English, 'pudding' has two meanings: the course that comes after the main course (ie dessert); and a type of food that might be sweet (such as Bakewell pudding) or savoury (such as Yorkshire pudding).

A classic British dessert is rhubarb crumble: the juicy stem of a large-leafed garden plant, stewed and sweetened, then topped with a crunchy mix of flour, butter and more sugar, and served with custard or ice cream.

Scotland's classic pudding is 'clootie dumpling' (a rich fruit pudding that is wrapped in a cotton cloth, or cloot in Scots dialect, while being steamed). Other sweet temptations include bannocks (half-scone, half-pancake), shortbread (a sweet biscuit) and Dundee cake (a rich fruit mix topped with almonds).

Other favourite British puddings include treacle sponge, bread-and-butter pudding and plum pudding, a dome-shaped cake with fruit, nuts and brandy or rum, traditionally eaten at Christmas, when it's called – surprise, surprise – Christmas pudding. This pudding is steamed (rather than baked), cut into slices and served with brandy butter.

While key ingredients of most puddings are self-explanatory, they are perhaps not so obvious for another well-loved favourite: spotted dick. The origin of 'dick' in this context is unclear (it may be a corruption of 'dough' or derived from the German *dicht,* meaning 'thick', or even from 'spotted dog') but the ingredients are easy: it's just a white suet pudding dotted with black currants. Plus sugar, of course. Most British puddings

Sherry trifle was considered the height of sophistication at dinner parties during the 1970s, but then fell out of fashion. A few decades later this combination of custard, fruit, sponge cake, whipped cream, and – of course – sherry is back in style, and enjoying a renaissance in many British restaurants.

have loads of butter or loads of sugar, preferably both. Light, subtle and healthy? No chance!

Drinking in Britain

The drinks most associated with Britain are tea, beer and whisky. The first two are unlike drinks of the same name found elsewhere in the world, and all three are well worth sampling on your travels around the country.

Tea & Coffee

In Britain, if a local asks 'Would you like a drink?', don't automatically expect a gin and tonic. They may well mean a 'cuppa' – a cup of tea – Britain's best-known beverage. It's usually made with dark tea leaves to produce a strong, brown drink, more bitter in taste than tea served in some other Western countries, which is partly why it's usually served with a dash of milk.

Although tea is sometimes billed as the national drink, coffee is equally popular these days; the Brits consume 165 million cups a day and the British coffee market is worth almost £700 million a year – but with the prices some coffee shops charge, maybe that's not surprising.

A final word of warning: when you're ordering a coffee and the server says 'white or black', don't panic. It simply means 'Do you want milk in it?'

Beer, Wine & Whisky

British beer typically ranges from dark brown to amber in colour, and is often served at room temperature. Technically it's called ale and is more commonly called 'bitter' (or 'heavy' in Scotland). This is to distinguish it from lager – the drink that most of the rest of the worlfod calls 'beer', which is generally yellow and served cold.

Bitter that's brewed and served traditionally is called 'real ale' to distinguish it from mass-produced brands, and there are many regional varieties. But be ready! If you're used to the 'amber nectar' or 'king of beers', a traditional British brew may come as a shock – a warm, flat and expensive shock. This is partly to do with Britain's climate, and partly to do with the beer being served by hand pump rather than gas pressure. Most important, though, is the integral flavour: traditional British beer doesn't need to be chilled or fizzed to make it palatable.

The increasing popularity of real ales and a backlash against the bland conformity of globalised multinational brewing conglomerates has seen a huge rise in the number of artisan brewers and microbreweries springing up all over Britain – by 2014 there were more than 1000 in operation, with more than 50 in London alone. They take pride in using only natural ingredients, and many try to revive ancient recipes, such as heather-and-seaweed-flavoured ales.

Another key feature is that real ale must be looked after, which usually means a willingness on the part of the pub manager or landlord to put in extra effort. This often translates into extra effort on food, atmosphere, cleanliness and so on, too. But the extra effort is why many pubs don't serve real ale.

If beer doesn't tickle your palate, try cider – available in sweet and dry varieties. In western parts of England, notably Herefordshire and the southwestern counties of Devon and Somerset, you could try 'scrumpy', a very strong dry cider traditionally made from local apples. Many pubs serve it straight from the barrel.

On hot summer days, you could go for shandy – beer and lemonade mixed in equal quantities. You'll usually need to specify 'lager shandy' or 'bitter shandy'.

Many visitors are surprised to learn that wine is produced in Britain, and has been since the time of the Romans. Today, more than 400

Like meat, but not battery pens? Go to the Royal Society for the Prevention of Cruelty to Animals (www.rspca.org.uk) and follow links to Freedom Food.

THE BRITISH TABLE DRINKING IN BRITAIN

vineyards produce between three and four million bottles a year – many highly regarded and frequently winning major awards. English sparkling wines have been a particular success story, especially those produced in southeast England where the chalky soil and climatic conditions are similar to those of the Champagne region in France.

The spirit most visitors associate with Britain – and especially Scotland – is whisky (note the spelling – it's Irish whiskey that has an 'e'). There's a big difference between single malt whisky, made purely from malted barley in a single distillery, and blended whisky, made from a blend of cheaper grain whisky and malt whiskies from several distilleries. Single malts are like fine wines, and command similarly high prices.

A final word of warning: when ordering a dram in Scotland remember to ask simply for a 'whisky' – only the English and other foreigners say 'Scotch'. After all, what else would you be served in Scotland?

Bars & Pubs

In Britain the difference between a bar and a pub is sometimes vague, but generally bars are smarter, larger and louder than pubs, possibly with a younger crowd. Drinks are more expensive too, unless there's a gallon-of-vodka-and-Red-Bull-for-a-fiver promotion – which there often is.

As well as beer, cider and wine, pubs and bars offer the usual choice of spirits, often served with a 'mixer', producing English favourites such as gin and tonic, rum and coke or vodka and lime. These drinks are served in measures called 'singles' and 'doubles'. A single is 35mL – just over one US fluid ounce. A double is, of course, 70mL – still disappointingly small when compared with measures in other countries. To add further to your disappointment, the vast array of cocktail options, as found in America, is generally restricted to more upmarket city bars in Britain.

And while we're serving up warnings, here are two more: first, if you see a pub calling itself a 'free house', it's simply a place that doesn't belong to a brewery or pub company, and thus is 'free' to sell any brand of beer. Unfortunately, it doesn't mean the booze is free of charge. Second, remember that drinks in British pubs are ordered and paid for at the bar. You can always spot the freshly arrived tourists – they're the ones sitting forlornly at an empty table hoping to spot a waiter.

When it comes to gratuities, it's not usual to tip pub and bar staff. However, if you're ordering a large round, or the service has been good all evening, you can say to the person behind the bar '...and one for yourself'. They may not have a drink, but they'll add the monetary equivalent to the total you pay and keep it as a tip.

Rick Stein is a TV chef, energetic restaurateur and good-food evangelist. His books *Food Heroes* and *Food Heroes: Another Helping* extol small-scale producers and top-notch local food, from organic vegetables to wild boar sausages.

Architecture in Britain

The history of British architecture spans more than three millennia, from the mysterious stone circles of Stonehenge and Callanish to the glittering skyscrapers of modern London. The country's built heritage includes Roman baths and parish churches, mighty castles and magnificent cathedrals, humble cottages and grand stately homes, and exploring it all is one of the great joys of a visit to Britain.

Early Foundations

The oldest surviving structures in Britain are the grass-covered mounds of earth called 'tumuli' or 'barrows', used as burial sites by the country's prehistoric residents. These mounds, measuring anything from a rough hemisphere just 2m high to oval domes around 5m high and 10m long, are dotted across the countryside and are especially common in areas of chalk such as Salisbury Plain and the Wiltshire Downs in southern England.

Perhaps the most famous barrow, and certainly the largest and most mysterious, is Silbury Hill (p277) near Marlborough. Historians are not sure exactly why this huge conical mound was built – there's no evidence of it actually being used for burials. Theories include the possibility it was used at cultural ceremonies or in the worship of deities in the style of South American pyramids. Whatever its original purpose, it's still awe-inspiring today.

Even more impressive than the giant tumuli are the most prominent legacy of the neolithic era – the iconic stone circles of Stonehenge (p271) and Avebury (p275), both in Wiltshire. Again, their original purpose is a mystery, providing fertile ground for hypothesis and speculation. The most recent theories suggest that Stonehenge may have been a place of pilgrimage for the sick, like modern-day Lourdes, though it was also used as a burial ground and a place of ancestor worship.

> The Callanish Standing Stones on Scotland's Isle of Lewis, dating from 3800 to 5000 years ago, are even older than those at Stonehenge and Avebury.

Bronze Age & Iron Age

After the neolithic era's great stone circles, the Bronze Age architecture we can see today is more domestic in scale. Hut circles from this period can still be seen in parts of Britain, most notably on Dartmoor in Devon. The Scottish islands hold many of Europe's best surviving Bronze and Iron Age remains, in places like the stone villages of Skara Brae in Orkney and Jarlshof in Shetland.

During the Iron Age, the early peoples of Britain began organising themselves into clans or tribes. Their legacy includes forts built to defend territory and protect from rival tribes or other invaders. Most forts consisted of a steep mound of earth behind a large circular or oval ditch; a famous example is Maiden Castle (p257) in Dorset.

The Roman Era

Remains of the Roman Empire are found in many towns and cities (mostly in England and Wales, as the Romans didn't colonise Scotland). There are impressive remains in Chester, Exeter and St Albans, as well as in the lavish Roman spa and bathhouse complex in Bath. Britain's largest and most impressive Roman relic is the 73-mile-long sweep of Hadrian's Wall, built in the 2nd century as a defensive line stretching from coast to coast across the country. Originally intended to defend the empire's territories in the south from the marauding tribes further north, it became as much a symbol of Roman power as a fortification.

Medieval Masterpieces

Founded by German immigrant Nikolaus Pevsner after WWII, the Pevsner Architectural Guides are the classic travellers' handbooks of British architecture. Around 80 volumes, published between 1951 and the present day, lovingly document the significant buildings of England, Scotland and Wales.

In the centuries following the Norman Conquest of 1066, the perfection of the mason's art saw an explosion of architecture in stone, inspired by the two most pressing concerns of the day: religion and defence. Early structures of timber and rubble were replaced with churches, abbeys and monasteries built in dressed stone. The round arches, squat towers and chevron decoration of the Norman or Romanesque style (11th to 12th centuries) slowly evolved into the tall pointed arches, ribbed vaults and soaring spires of the Gothic (13th to 16th centuries), a history that can often be seen all in the one church – construction often took a couple of hundred years to complete. Many cathedrals remain modern landmarks, such as Salisbury, Winchester, Canterbury and York.

Stone was also put to good use in the building of elaborate defensive structures. Castles range from the atmospheric ruins of Tintagel (p340) and Dunstanburgh (p650), and the sturdy ramparts of Conwy (p761) and Beaumaris (p754), to the stunning crag-top fortresses of Stirling (p840) and Edinburgh (p773). And then there's the most impressive of them all: the Tower of London (p80), guarding the capital for more than 900 years.

Stately Homes

The medieval period was tumultuous, but by the start of the 17th century life had become more settled and the nobility had less need for fortifications. While they were excellent for keeping out the riff-raff, castles were often too cold and draughty for comfortable aristocratic living.

Many castles underwent the home improvements of the day, with larger windows, wider staircases and better drainage installed. Others were simply abandoned for a brand-new dwelling next door, as at Hardwick Hall (p484) in Derbyshire.

Following the Civil War, the trend away from castles gathered pace, and throughout the 17th century the landed gentry developed a taste for fine 'country houses' designed by famous architects of the day. Many became the stately homes that are a major feature of the British landscape and a major attraction for visitors. Among the most extravagant are Chatsworth House (p495) and Blenheim Palace (p199) in England, Powis Castle (p726) in Wales and Floors Castle (p822) in Scotland.

HOUSE & HOME

In Britain, it's not all about big houses. Alongside the stately homes, ordinary domestic architecture can still be seen in rural areas. Black-and-white 'half-timbered' houses characterise counties such as Worcestershire, brick-and-flint buildings pepper Suffolk and Sussex, and hardy, centuries-old cottages and farm buildings of slate and local stone are a feature of North Wales. In northern Scotland, the blackhouse is a classic basic dwelling, with walls of dry, unmortared stone packed with earth and a roof of straw and turf.

The great stately homes all display the proportion, symmetry and architectural harmony that was in vogue during the 17th and 18th centuries. These styles were later reflected in the fashionable town houses of the Georgian era, most notably in the city of Bath, where the stunning Royal Crescent (p323) is the ultimate example of the genre.

Victoriana

The Victorian era was a time of great building activity. A style called Victorian Gothic developed, imitating the tall, narrow windows and ornamented spires featured in the original Gothic cathedrals. The most famous example is London's Houses of Parliament (p67) and the clock tower that everyone knows as Big Ben (p67), which was officially renamed Elizabeth Tower in 2012 to celebrate the Queen's diamond jubilee. Other Victorian-Gothic highlights in England's capital include the Natural History Museum (p95) and St Pancras train station. The style was copied all around the country, especially for civic buildings, with the finest examples including Manchester Town Hall (p561) and Glasgow City Chambers (p807).

As well as many grand cathedrals, Britain has thousands of parish churches, many with historical or architectural significance, especially in rural areas.

Industrialisation

Through the late 19th and early 20th centuries, as Britain's cities grew in size and stature, the newly moneyed middle classes built smart town houses in streets and squares. Elsewhere, the first town planners oversaw the construction of endless terraces of 'back-to-back' and 'two-up-two-down' houses to accommodate the massive influx of workers required for the country's factories. In South Wales, similar, though often single-storeyed houses were built for the burgeoning numbers of coal miners. The industrial areas of Scotland saw the construction of tenements, usually three or four storeys high, with a central communal staircase and two dwellings on each floor. In many cases the terraced houses and basic tenements are not especially scenic, but they are perhaps the most enduring mark on the British architectural landscape.

Postwar Pains & Pride

During WWII, bombing damaged many of Britain's cities and the rebuilding that followed showed little regard for the overall appearance of the cities or for the lives of people who lived in them. Rows of terraces were swept away in favour of high-rise tower blocks, while the brutalist architecture of the 1950s and '60s embraced the modern and efficient building materials of steel and concrete.

Perhaps this is why the British are largely conservative in their architectural tastes. They often resent ambitious or experimental designs, especially applied to public buildings or when a building's form appears more important than its function. However, a familiar pattern unfolds: after a few years of resentment, the building is given a nickname, then it gains grudging acceptance, and finally it becomes a source of pride and affection. The British just don't like to be rushed, that's all.

Perhaps the best-known example of 1950/60s brutalist architecture is London's Southbank Centre. A building of its time, it was applauded when finished, then reviled for its ugliness, and is now regarded by Londoners with something close to pride and affection.

21st Century

During the first decade of this century, many areas of Britain placed new importance on having progressive, popular architecture as part of a wider regeneration. Top examples include Manchester's Imperial War Museum North (p561), Birmingham's Bullring shopping centre (p419), the Welsh National Assembly building and the Wales Millennium Centre (p662; both on the Cardiff waterfront), the overlapping arches of Glasgow's Scottish Exhibition & Conference Centre (affectionately called 'the Armadillo') and The Sage concert hall in Gateshead in northeast England.

DOMINATING THE LANDSCAPE

If you're travelling through Wales, it won't take you long to notice the country's most striking architectural asset: castles. There are about 600 in all, giving Wales the dubious honour of being Europe's most densely fortified country. Most were built in medieval times, first by William the Conqueror and then by other Anglo-Norman kings, to keep the Welsh in check. In the late 13th century Edward I built spectacular castles at Caernarfon, Harlech, Conwy and Beaumaris, now jointly listed as a Unesco World Heritage Site. Other castles to see include Rhuddlan, Denbigh, Cricceith, Raglan, Pembroke, Kidwelly, Chepstow and Caerphilly. While undeniably great for visitors, the castles are a sore point for patriotic Welsh; the writer Thomas Pennant called them 'the magnificent badge of our subjection'.

Britain's largest and highest-profile architectural project of recent times was the Olympic Park, the centrepiece of the 2012 Olympic Games. Situated in the London suburb of Stratford, it was renamed the Queen Elizabeth Olympic Park after the games. The main Olympic Stadium and other arenas, including the Velodrome and Aquatics Centre, were built using cutting-edge techniques and are all dramatic structures in their own right.

Meanwhile, in the centre of the capital, the London Bridge Tower (p93) – its tall and jagged shape quickly earning it the nickname of 'the Shard' – dominates the South Bank; at 306m, it's one of Europe's tallest buildings. On the other side of the River Thames, two more giant skyscrapers were completed in 2014: 20 Fenchurch St (thanks to its shape, already nicknamed 'the Walkie-Talkie') and the slanting-walled Leadenhall Building (dubbed, inevitably, 'the Cheese Grater').

London continues to grow upwards and British architecture continues to push new boundaries of style and technology. The buildings may look a little different, but they're still iconic and impressive.

The Arts in Britain

Britain's contributions to the worlds of literature, drama, cinema and pop are celebrated around the world, thanks in no small part to the global dominance of the English language. As you travel around Britain today you'll see landscapes made famous as movie sets and literary locations, or mentioned in songs, so for this chapter we've picked some major milestones and focused on works with a connection to real places where you can experience something of your favourite artist.

Literature

The roots of Britain's literary heritage stretch back to Norse sagas and Early English epics such as *Beowulf*, but most scholars agree that modern English-language literature starts in the late 14th century: yes, that counts as 'modern' in history-soaked Britain.

First Stars

The first big name in Britain's literary canon is Geoffrey Chaucer, best known for *The Canterbury Tales*. This mammoth collection of fables, stories and morality tales, using travelling pilgrims (the Knight, the Wife of Bath, the Nun's Priest and so on) as a narrative hook, is considered an essential of the canon.

After Chaucer, two centuries passed before Britain's next major literary figure rose to prominence: enter stage left William Shakespeare. Best known for his plays (discussed in the Theatre section) he was also a prolific and influential poet. 'Shall I compare thee to a summer's day?' is just one of his famous lines still widely quoted today.

A collection of folk tales discovered in medieval Welsh manuscripts of the 14th century, *The Mabinogion* was translated into English in the mid-19th century. Drawing on pre-Christian Celtic myths, several of the stories deal with the legendary feats of King Arthur and the knights of the round table.

The 17th & 18th Centuries

The 17th century saw the publication of John Milton's epic blank verse poem *Paradise Lost,* a literary landmark inspired by the biblical tale of Adam and Eve's expulsion from the Garden of Eden. This was followed a few years later by the equally seminal *Pilgrim's Progress* by John Bunyan, an allegorical tale of the everyday Christian struggle. For mere mortals, reading these books in their entirety can be hard going, but they're worth dipping into for a taste of the rich language.

More familiar to most British people are the words of 'Auld Lang Syne', penned by Scotland's national poet Robert Burns, and traditionally sung at New Year. His more unusual 'Address to a Haggis' is also still recited annually on Burns Night, a Scottish celebration held on 25 January (the poet's birthday).

Another milestone literary work of this period is Daniel Defoe's *Robinson Crusoe*. On one level it's an adventure story about a man shipwrecked on an uninhabited island, but it's also a discussion on civilisation, colonialism

The *Oxford Literary Guide to Great Britain & Ireland*, edited by Daniel Hahn and Nicholas Robins, gives details of towns, villages and the countryside immortalised by writers, from Chaucer's Canterbury and Austen's Bath to Scott's Highlands.

and faith, and is regarded by many scholars as the first English-language novel. It's also been an armchair travellers' favourite since its publication in 1719.

The Romantic Era

As industrialisation began to take hold in Britain during the late 18th and early 19th century, a new generation of writers, including William Blake, John Keats, Percy Bysshe Shelley, Lord Byron and Samuel Taylor Coleridge, drew inspiration from human imagination and the natural world (in some cases aided by a healthy dose of laudanum). The best-known of the 'Romantics' was William Wordsworth; his famous line from the poem commonly known as 'Daffodils', 'I wandered lonely as a cloud', was inspired by a hike in the hills of the Lake District.

The painter, writer, poet and visionary William Blake (1757–1827) mixed fantastical landscapes and mythological scenes with motifs drawn from classical art, religious iconography and legend. For more, see www.blakearchive.org.

Victoriana

During the reign of Queen Victoria (1837–1901), key novels of the time explored social themes. Charles Dickens is the best-known writer of the period: *Oliver Twist* is a tale of child pickpockets surviving in the London slums, while *Hard Times* is a critique of the excesses of capitalism.

At around the same time, but in a rural setting, George Eliot (the pen name of Mary Anne Evans) wrote *The Mill on the Floss*, whose central character, Maggie Tulliver, searches for true love and struggles against society's expectations.

Meanwhile, Thomas Hardy's classic *Tess of the D'Urbervilles* deals with the peasantry's decline, and *The Trumpet Major* paints a picture of idyllic English country life interrupted by war and encroaching modernity. Many of Hardy's works are in the fictionalised county of Wessex, largely based on today's Dorset and surrounding counties, where towns such as Dorchester are popular stops on tourist itineraries today.

Displaying similarly close links to the landscape is *Waverley* by Scotland's greatest historical novelist, Sir Walter Scott. Written in the early 19th century and set in the mountains and glens of Scotland during the time of the Jacobite rebellion, it is usually regarded as the first historical novel in the English language. Scott's bestselling works, which include the narrative poem *The Lady of the Lake* and the novel *Rob Roy,* are often credited with kick-starting the Scottish tourist industry.

The Modern World

Britain – and its literature – changed forever following WWI and the social disruption of the period. This fed into the modernist movement, with DH Lawrence perhaps its finest exponent. *Sons and Lovers* follows

BEST-LOVED LIT: AUSTEN & THE BRONTËS

The beginning of the 19th century saw the emergence of some of English literature's best-loved writers: Jane Austen and the Brontë sisters.

Austen's fame stems from her exquisite observations of love, friendship, intrigues and passions boiling under the buttoned-up reserve of middle-class social convention. These observations have spawned countless films and TV costume dramas based on her works. The location now most associated with Austen is the city of Bath – a beautiful place even without such a literary link. As one of her heroines said, 'Oh! Who can ever be tired of Bath?'.

Of the Brontë sisters' prodigious output, Emily Brontë's *Wuthering Heights*, an epic tale of obsession and revenge, where the dark and moody landscape plays a role as great as any human character, is the best known, while Charlotte Brontë's *Jane Eyre* and Anne Brontë's *The Tenant of Wildfell Hall* are classics of passion and mystery. Visitors still flock to the former Brontë home (p546) in the Yorkshire town of Haworth, perched on the edge of the wild Pennine moors that inspired so many of their books.

the lives and loves of generations in the English Midlands as the country changes from rural idyll to industrial landscape, while his controversial exploration of sexuality in *Lady Chatterley's Lover* was banned until 1960 because of its 'obscenity'.

Other highlights of this period included Daphne du Maurier's romantic suspense novel *Rebecca*, with close connections to Cornwall; Evelyn Waugh's *Brideshead Revisited*, an exploration of moral and social disintegration among the English aristocracy; and Richard Llewellyn's Welsh classic *How Green Was My Valley*. A decade or so later, after WWII, Compton Mackenzie lifted postwar spirits with *Whisky Galore*, a comic novel about a cargo of booze shipwrecked on a Scottish island.

In the 1950s, the poet Dylan Thomas found fame with his *Portrait of The Artist as a Young Dog*, although his most celebrated work is a radio play *Under Milk Wood* (1954), exposing the tensions of small-town Wales.

Then came the swinging '60s. Liverpool poet Roger McGough and friends determined to make art relevant to daily life produced *The Mersey Sound* – landmark pop poetry for the streets. Other new writers included Muriel Spark, who introduced the world to a highly unusual Edinburgh school mistress in *The Prime of Miss Jean Brodie*.

The 1970s saw the arrival of two novelists who went on to become prolific through the rest of the century and beyond. Martin Amis produced a string of novels whose common themes include the absurdity and unappealing nature of modern life, such as *London Fields* (1989). Ian McEwan made his debut with *The Cement Garden* (1978), and earned critical acclaim for finely observed studies of the English character in works such as *Atonement* (2001) and *On Chesil Beach* (2007).

Modern novels in a different vein include *Trainspotting* (1993) by Irvine Welsh, a dark look at Edinburgh's drug culture, and the birth of a new genre coined 'Tartan Noir' – crime fiction set in Scottish cities. Ian Rankin, best known for his Edinburgh-set *Inspector Rebus* novels, is a master of the form.

New Millennium

As the 20th century came to a close, and the new millennium dawned, Britain's multicultural landscape proved a rich inspiration for contemporary novelists. Hanif Kureishi sowed the seeds with his ground-breaking 1990 novel *The Buddha of Suburbia*, examining the hopes and fears of a group of Anglo-Asians in London. This was followed by Zadie Smith's acclaimed debut *White Teeth* (2000) and a string of bestsellers, including her most recent novel, *NW* (2012). Andrea Levy found acclaim with *Small Island* (2004), about a Jamaican couple settled in postwar London, and Monica Ali's *Brick Lane* was shortlisted for the 2003 Man Booker Prize, a high-profile literary award.

Other big-name writers of the current era include Will Self, known for his surreal, satirical novels, including *The Book of Dave* (2006), and Nick Hornby, whose most recent novel is *Juliet, Naked* (2009), although he's perhaps best known for the autobiographical memoir *Fever Pitch*, a study of the insecurities of English blokishness.

Also popular is Julian Barnes, whose book *England, England* is a darkly ironic study of nationalism and tourism, while *The Sense of an Ending* won the 2011 Man Booker Prize. Hilary Mantel, author of many novels on an astoundingly wide range of subjects, won the Man Booker Prize twice, first in 2009 for historical blockbuster *Wolf Hall* (about Henry VIII and his ruthless advisor Thomas Cromwell), and then in 2012 for its sequel *Bring Up the Bodies*; the third and final instalment, *The Mirror and the Light*, is due out in 2015.

Britain's greatest literary phenomenon of the 21st century is JK Rowling's *Harry Potter* series, a set of other-worldly adventures that have

---

Graham Greene's novel *Brighton Rock* (1938) is a classic account of wayward English youth. For an even more shocking take, try *A Clockwork Orange* by Anthony Burgess, later infamously filmed by Stanley Kubrick in 1971.

For a taste of surreal humour, try two of Britain's funniest (and most successful) writers: Douglas Adams (*The Hitchhiker's Guide to the Galaxy* plus sequels) and Terry Pratchett (the *Discworld* series).

Helen Fielding's *Bridget Jones's Diary* is a fond look at the heartache of a modern single girl's blundering search for love and epitomised the late-1990s 'chick lit' genre.

THE ARTS IN BRITAIN LITERATURE

entertained millions of children (and many grown-ups too) since the first book was published in 1996. The magical tales are the latest in a long line of British children's classics enjoyed by adults, stretching back to the works of Lewis Carroll *(Alice's Adventures in Wonderland)*, E Nesbit *(The Railway Children)*, AA Milne *(Winnie-the-Pooh)* and CS Lewis *(The Chronicles of Narnia)*.

Cinema

British cinema has a long history, with many early directors cutting their teeth in the silent-film industry. Perhaps the best-known of these was Alfred Hitchcock, who directed *Blackmail*, one of the first British 'talkies' in 1929, and who went on to direct a string of films during the 1930s, before migrating to Hollywood in the early 1940s.

Patriot Games

During WWII, British films were dominated by patriotic stories designed to raise morale: *Went the Day Well?* (1942), *In Which We Serve* (1942) and *We Dive at Dawn* (1943) are prime examples of the genre. During this period David Lean directed the classic tale of repressed passion, *Brief Encounter* (1945), before graduating to Hollywood epics, including *Lawrence of Arabia* and *Doctor Zhivago*.

Another great film of the 1940s is *How Green Was My Valley,* a tale of everyday life in the coal-mining villages of Wales. Perhaps the best-known movie about Wales, it manages to annoy more Welsh people than any other with its stereotyped characters, absence of Welsh actors, and the fact that it was shot in a Hollywood studio. It's worth seeing, though, for its period flavour.

After the War

The Ladykillers (1955) is a classic Ealing comedy about a band of hapless bank robbers holed up in a London guesthouse, and features Alec Guinness sporting quite possibly the most outrageous set of false teeth ever captured on celluloid.

Following the hardships of the war, British audiences were in the mood for escape and entertainment. During the late 1940s and early '50s, the domestic film industry specialised in eccentric British comedies epitomised by the output of Ealing Studios: notable titles include *Passport to Pimlico* (1949), *Kind Hearts and Coronets* (1949) and *The Titfield Thunderbolt* (1953).

Dramatic box-office hits of the time included *Hamlet* (the first British film to win an Oscar in the Best Picture category), starring Laurence Olivier, and Carol Reed's *The Third Man*. In a post-war Britain still struggling with rationing and food shortages, tales of heroic derring-do such as *The Dam Busters* (1955) and *Reach for the Sky* (1956) helped lighten the national mood.

HAMMER HORROR

The British company Hammer Film Productions produced low-budget horror films in the 1950s and '60s, still revered by fans around the globe. Early flicks included *The Quatermass Experiment* (1955) and *The Curse of Frankenstein* (1957). The stars of the latter, Peter Cushing as Dr Frankenstein and Christopher Lee as the Monster, would feature in many of Hammer's best films over the next 20 years, including a string of nine *Dracula* films (most of which star Lee as Dracula and Cushing as Van Helsing or his descendants) and six *Frankenstein* sequels.

The studio also launched the careers of several other notable actors (including Oliver Reed, who made his debut in *The Curse of the Werewolf*, 1961) and even spawned its very own spoof, *Carry On Screaming* – the ultimate British seal of approval. From 1979 the company went into hibernation, but its fortunes revived in 2012 with the release of *The Woman in Black*, starring *Harry Potter* lead Daniel Radcliffe.

Swinging '60s

In the late 1950s, 'British New Wave' and 'Free Cinema' explored the gritty realities of life in an intimate, semidocumentary style, with Lindsay Anderson and Tony Richardson crystallising the movement with films such as *This Sporting Life* (1961) and *A Taste of Honey* (1961).

At the other end of the spectrum were the *Carry On* films, packed with bawdy gags and double entendres, and starring a troupe of 'national treasures' including Barbara Windsor, Sid James and Kenneth Williams.

The 1960s saw the birth of another classic British icon: super-spy James Bond, adapted from the Ian Fleming novels and first played by Sean Connery in *Dr No* (1962). Since then over 20 Bond movies have been made, with Bond played by a series of actors, from Roger Moore and George Lazenby to Pierce Brosnan and Daniel Craig.

Burning Gold

After the boom of the 1960s, British cinema entered troubled waters for a decade or so, but was revived in the 1980s, thanks partly to David Puttnam's *Chariots of Fire*, the Oscar-winning tale of two British athletes competing at the 1924 Olympics.

The newly established (1982) Channel 4 invested in edgy films such as *My Beautiful Laundrette* (1985), while the British production duo of Ismail Merchant and James Ivory played Hollywood at its own game with period epics such as *Heat and Dust* (1983) and *A Room With A View* (1986), capitalising on the success of Richard Attenborough's big-budget *Gandhi* (1982), which bagged eight Academy Awards.

Brit Flicks

In the 1990s, the massively successful *Four Weddings and a Funeral*, which introduced Hugh Grant in his trademark role as the likeable, self-deprecating Englishman (an archetype he reprised in subsequent hits *Notting Hill* and *Love, Actually*) spearheaded the 'Brit-flick' genre. *The Full Monty* (1997), about a troupe of laid-off steel workers turned male strippers, was Britain's most successful film ever (until overtaken by the Harry Potter franchise in 2001) and *The Englishman Who Went Up a Hill and Came Down a Mountain*, an affectionate story about a hill in North Wales deemed too low.

Grittier films of the 1990s included *Trainspotting*, a visually innovative, hard-hitting film about Edinburgh's drugged-out underworld, which launched the careers of Scottish actors Ewan McGregor and Robert Carlyle, while Mike Leigh's *Secrets and Lies*, a Palme d'Or winner at Cannes, tells the story of an adopted black woman who seeks out her white mother.

Other landmark films of the decade included gangster movie *Lock, Stock and Two Smoking Barrels*, which spawned a host of copycats; *Breaking the Waves*, a perfect study of culture clash in 1970s Scotland; *Human Traffic*, an edgy romp through Cardiff's clubland; and the Oscar-winning Austen adaptation *Sense and Sensibility,* starring English doyennes Emma Thompson and Kate Winslet as the Dashwood sisters, with Hugh Grant as (you guessed it) a likeable and self-deprecating Englishman.

Award-winning Welsh-language films of the time include *Hedd Wynn*, a heartbreaking story of a poet killed in WWI, and *Solomon and Gaenor*, a passionate tale of forbidden love at the turn of the 20th century, staring Ioan Gruffudd and filmed twice: once in the Welsh language and once in English.

The decade ended with films such as *East Is East* (1999), a beautifully understated study of the clash between first- and second-generation immigrant Pakistanis in Britain, and *Billy Elliott* (2000), about a boy's quest to learn ballet and escape the slag-heaps of post-industrial northern England.

Withnail and I (1987) is one of the great British cult comedies. Directed by Bruce Robinson, it stars Paul McGann and Richard E Grant as a pair of hapless out-of-work actors on a disastrous holiday to the Lake District.

The British Film Institute (BFI) is dedicated to promoting film and cinema in Britain, and publishes the monthly academic journal *Sight & Sound.* See www.bfi.org.uk and www.screenonline.org.uk for complete coverage of Britain's film and TV industry.

A GRAND SUCCESS

One of the great success stories of British television and cinema has been Bristol-based animator Nick Park and the production company Aardman Animations, best known for the award-winning series starring the man-and-dog duo Wallace and Gromit. This lovable pair first appeared in Park's graduation film, *A Grand Day Out* (1989), and went on to star in *The Wrong Trousers* (1993), *A Close Shave* (1995) and their full-length feature debut, *The Curse of the Were-Rabbit* (2005).

Known for their intricate plots, movie references and amazingly realistic animation, the Wallace and Gromit films have netted Nick Park four Oscars. Other Aardman films include *Chicken Run* (2000), *Flushed Away* (2006) and *The Pirates! – In an Adventure with Scientists* (2012).

The 21st Century

In the early part of the 21st century, literature continued to provide the richest seam mined by the British film industry. Hits include the blockbuster *Harry Potter* franchise (based on the books of the same name, and the most financially successful film series of all time), starring Daniel Radcliffe, as well as *The Constant Gardener* (2005; based on a John Le Carré novel), *Atonement* (2008; based on Ian McEwan's novel), *War Horse* (2011; directed by Stephen Spielberg and based on Michael Morpurgo's novel), and *Anna Karenina* (2012; directed by Joe Wright and staring Keira Knightley).

The BBC is a public-service broadcaster, financed by the licence fee of £145, paid annually by every house in Britain with a TV set, rather than by advertising. This means shows are not interrupted by commercial breaks.

Biopics are a perennial favourite, especially, it seems, of famous females, with recent highlights including: Queen Elizabeth I (*Elizabeth: The Golden Age;* 2007), Queen Elizabeth II (*The Queen;* 2006) and Margaret Thatcher (*The Iron Lady;* 2011).

Comedy continues to thrive: building on the success of zombie-spoof *Shaun of the Dead* (2004) and cop-movie spoof *Hot Fuzz* (2007), Simon Pegg (who stars as Scotty in the most recent Star Trek movies) and Nick Frost returned in alien-invasion spoof *The World's End* (2013), while Richard Curtis produced another crowd-pleasing romantic comedy with *About Time* (2013).

Meanwhile, the oldest of British film franchises rolls on, with James Bond now a tough, toned and occasionally fallible character played by Daniel Craig in *Casino Royale* (2006), *Quantum of Solace* (2008) and *Skyfall* (2012); the next instalment is scheduled for 2015.

Television

Since the earliest days of TV broadcasting, Britain has produced some of the world's finest shows and programs, from classic comedy to ground-breaking drama. Many of the world's most popular formats have their origins in British broadcasting, including the phenomenon known as reality TV.

Britain's main broadcasters are known for their long-running 'soaps' (soap operas) such as *Eastenders* (BBC), *Emmerdale* and *Coronation Street* (both ITV), which have collectively been running on British screens for well over a century.

The main broadcasters are BBC and ITV, each with several channels. Others include Channels 4 and 5. The BBC is a national institution, especially famous for its news and natural-history programming, epitomised by landmark series such as *Planet Earth* and *The Blue Planet* (reassuringly helmed by Sir David Attenborough, a similarly precious national institution since the 1970s).

The big-budget costume drama is a British staple; BBC viewers have been treated to adaptations of practically every Dickens, Bronte and Thackeray novel, while ITV has entered the same territory, notably with Jane Austen's *Mansfield Park* and *Northanger Abbey*. But top of the tree is ITV's *Downton Abbey*, a saga of Edwardian manners and class conflict that went through five award-winning seasons since 2010, and became the world's most-watched TV drama.

Pop & Rock Music

Britain's been putting the world through its musical paces ever since a mop-haired four-piece from Liverpool tuned up their Rickenbackers and created The Beatles. And while some may claim that Elvis invented rock 'n' roll, it was the Fab Four who transformed it into a global phenomenon, backed by the other bands of the 1960s 'British Invasion' – The Rolling Stones, The Who, Cream, The Kinks and soul man Tom Jones.

Glam to Punk

Glam rock swaggered onto the stage at the start of the 1970s, led by the likes of Marc Bolan and David Bowie in their tight-fitting jumpsuits and chameleon guises, and succeeded by early boy-band Bay City Rollers, art-rockers Roxy Music, outrageously costumed Elton John and anthemic popsters Queen. In the same era, Led Zeppelin, Deep Purple and Black Sabbath laid down the blueprint for heavy metal, while the psychedelia of the previous decade morphed into the spacey noodlings of prog rock, epitomised by Pink Floyd, Genesis and Yes.

By the late '70s, glam and prog bands were looking out of touch in a Britain wracked by rampant unemployment and industrial unrest, and punk rock exploded onto the scene, summing up the air of doom with nihilistic lyrics and three-chord tunes. The Sex Pistols remain the best-known band of the era, while other punk pioneers included The Clash, The Damned, The Buzzcocks and The Stranglers.

Punk begat New Wave, with acts such as The Jam and Elvis Costello blending spiky tunes and sharp lyrics into a more radio-friendly sound. A little later, along came bands like The Specials and baggy-trousered rude boys Madness, mixing punk, reggae and ska sounds. Meanwhile, another punk-and-reggae-influenced band called The Police – fronted by bassist Sting – became one of the biggest names of the decade.

Mode, Metal & Miserabilism

The conspicuous consumption of Britain in the early 1980s was reflected in the decade's pop scene. Big hair and shoulder pads became the uniform of New Romantics such as Spandau Ballet, Duran Duran and Culture Club, while the increased use of synthesisers led to the development

Around Britain, buildings associated with notable people are marked with a (usually blue) plaque. In early 2012, a plaque was placed at 23 Heddon St in London to commemorate fictional pop character Ziggy Stardust.

THE ARTS IN BRITAIN POP & ROCK MUSIC

ROCK 'N' ROLL LOCATIONS

Fans buy the music, then the T-shirt. However, true fans visit the locations featured on album covers. Here are some favourites, many in London, plus a few others around the country:

Abbey Rd, St John's Wood, London – *Abbey Road*, The Beatles

Battersea Power Station, London – *Animals*, Pink Floyd

Berwick St, Soho, London – *(What's the Story) Morning Glory*, Oasis

Big Ben, London – *My Generation* (US version), The Who

Camden Market, London – *The Clash*, The Clash

Heddon St, off Regent St, London – *The Rise and Fall of Ziggy Stardust & the Spiders from Mars*, David Bowie

Black Rock Sands, near Porthmadog – *This is My Truth Tell Me Yours*, Manic Street Preachers

Salford Boys Club, Manchester – *The Queen is Dead*, The Smiths

Thor's Cave, Manifold Valley, near Ashbourne, Peak District National Park – *A Storm In Heaven*, The Verve

Yes Tor, Dartmoor, Devon – *Tomato*, Yes

POP ON FILM

If you want to combine British pop music with British cinema, try some of these films: *Backbeat* (1994), a look at the early days of The Beatles; *Sid and Nancy* (1986), following The Sex Pistols bassist and his American girlfriend; *Velvet Goldmine* (1998), a tawdry glimpse of the glam-rock scene; *24 Hour Party People* (2002), a totally irreverent and suitably chaotic film about the 1990s Manchester music scene; *Control* (2007), a biopic about Joy Division singer Ian Curtis; and *Nowhere Boy* (2009), about John Lennon in his pre-Beatles days.

of a new electronic sound in the music of Depeche Mode and The Human League. More hits and highlights were supplied by Texas, Eurythmics and Wham! – a boyish duo headed by a bright young fellow named George Michael.

Away from the glitz, fans enjoyed the doom-laden lyrics of The Cure, Bauhaus and Siouxsie & the Banshees, while Britain's heavy rock heritage inspired acts such as Iron Maiden. In a different tone entirely, the disaffection of mid-1980s Britain was summed up by the arch-priests of 'miserabilism', The Smiths, fronted by quiffed wordsmith Morrissey.

Raves, Indie & Britpop

The beats and bleeps of 1980s electronica fuelled the burgeoning dance-music scene of the early '90s. An eruption of ecstasy-saturated rave culture, centred on famous clubs like Manchester's Haçienda and London's Ministry of Sound, overflowed into the mainstream through chart-topping artists such as The Prodigy and Fatboy Slim. Manchester was also a focus for the burgeoning British 'indie' scene, driven by guitar-based bands such as The Charlatans, The Stone Roses, James and Happy Mondays.

Indie grew up in the mid- to late-1990s, and the term 'Britpop' was coined, with Oasis at the forefront and covering a wide range of bands including Blur, Elastica, Suede, Supergrass, Ocean Colour Scene, The Verve, Pulp, Travis, Feeder, Super Furry Animals, Stereophonics, Catatonia and the Manic Street Preachers.

Pop Today, Gone Tomorrow

The new millennium saw no let-up in the British music scene's shape-shifting and reinvention. Jazz, soul, R&B and hip-hop have fused into an 'urban' sound epitomised by artists like Dizzee Rascal, Tinie Tempah and Plan B.

In a totally different genre, British folk and roots music, and folk-influenced acoustic music, is enjoying its biggest revival since the 1960s, with major names including Eliza Carthy and Mumford & Sons.

Meanwhile, the singer-songwriter, exemplified by Katie Melua, Ed Sheeran, the late Amy Winehouse and the all-conquering Adele, has made a comeback, and the spirit of British punk and indie stays alive thanks to the likes of Snow Patrol, Florence & the Machine, Coldplay, Muse, Kasabian, Radiohead and The Horrors.

But the biggest commercial success of all has been boy-band One Direction, seeing their first three albums debut at No 1 in the US charts, releasing the biggest-selling British album of 2013, and being named the top global act of 2013.

The Spice Girls were one of the most famous pop creations of the 1990s, and they became the world's best-selling all-female group. Sporty, Scary, Baby, Ginger and Posh famously reunited in 2012 to perform at the London Olympics closing ceremony.

Painting & Sculpture

For many centuries, continental Europe – especially Holland, Spain, France and Italy – set the artistic agenda. The first artist with a truly British style and sensibility was arguably William Hogarth, whose riotous canvases exposed the vice and corruption of 18th-century London. His most celebrated work is *A Rake's Progress*, which kick-started a long tradition of British caricatures that can be traced right through to the work of modern-day cartoonists such as Gerald Scarfe and Steve Bell. It's displayed at Sir John Soane's Museum in London.

Portraits & Landscapes

While Hogarth was busy satirising society, other artists were hard at work showing it in its best light. The leading figures of 18th-century British portraiture were Sir Joshua Reynolds, Thomas Gainsborough and George Romney, while George Stubbs is best known for his intricate studies of animals (particularly horses). Works by these artists are displayed at Tate Britain (p95) or the National Gallery (p75) in London.

In the 19th century, leading painters favoured the landscape. John Constable's best-known works include *Salisbury Cathedral* and *The Haywain*, depicting a mill in Suffolk (and now on show in the National Gallery, London), while JMW Turner was fascinated by the effects of light and colour, with his works becoming almost entirely abstract by the 1840s – vilified at the time, but prefiguring the Impressionist movement that was to follow 50 years later.

Fables & Flowers

In the mid- to late 19th century, the Pre-Raphaelite movement harked back to the figurative style of classical Italian and Flemish art, tying in with the prevailing Victorian taste for fables, myths and fairy tales. Key members of the movement included Sir John Everett Millais and William Holman Hunt. Millais' *Ophelia,* showing the damsel picturesquely drowned in a river, is an excellent example of their style, and can be seen the Tate Britain. However, one of the best collections of Pre-Raphaelite art is in the Birmingham Museum and Art Gallery (p412).

A good friend of the Pre-Raphaelites was William Morris; he saw late-19th-century furniture and interior design as increasingly vulgar, and with Dante Gabriel Rossetti and Edward Burne-Jones founded the Arts and Crafts movement to encourage the revival of a decorative approach to features such as wallpaper, tapestries and windows. Many of his designs are still used today.

North of the border, Charles Rennie Mackintosh, fresh from the Glasgow School of Art, fast became a renowned artist, designer and architect. He is still Scotland's greatest art nouveau exponent, and much of his work remains in Glasgow. He also influenced a group of artists from the 1890s that became known as the Glasgow School (often divided into two groups: the Glasgow Boys and the Glasgow Girls), among them Margaret and Frances MacDonald, James Guthrie and EA Walton. Much of their work can be seen in the Kelvingrove Art Gallery (p811) in Glasgow.

Stone & Sticks

In the tumultuous 20th century, British art became increasingly experimental, with key painters including Francis Bacon, whose work was influenced by Freudian psychoanalysis, and the group known as the Scottish Colourists – Francis Cadell, SJ Peploe, Leslie Hunter and JD Ferguson. Meanwhile, pioneering sculptors such as Henry Moore and Barbara Hepworth experimented with natural forms in stone and new materials.

At around the same time, Welsh artist Gwen John painted introspective portraits of women friends, cats and nuns (and famously became the model and lover of French artist Rodin), while her brother Augustus John became Britain's leading portrait painter, with famous sitters such as Thomas Hardy and George Bernard Shaw. One place to admire the their works is at the Glynn Vivian Art Gallery in Swansea.

After WWII, Howard Hodgkin and Patrick Heron developed a British version of American abstract expressionism. At the same time, but in

The works of Henry Moore and Barbara Hepworth can be seen at the Yorkshire Sculpture Park, between Sheffield and Leeds, in northern England. Hepworth is also forever associated with St Ives in Cornwall, while the Hepworth Wakefield gallery is dedicated to her life and work.

Antony Gormley's *Angel of the North* is one of the most viewed works of art in the world. Standing beside the busy A1 London-to-Edinburgh road, millions of drivers each year can't help but see it.

great contrast, Manchester artist LS Lowry was painting his much-loved 'matchstick men' figures set in an urban landscape of narrow streets and smoky factories. A good place to see his work is in The Lowry (p561), Manchester.

Pop Art

The mid-1950s and early '60s saw an explosion of British artists plundering TV, music, advertising and popular culture for inspiration. Leaders of this new 'pop art' movement included David Hockney, who used bold colours and simple lines to depict his dachshunds and swimming pools, and Peter Blake, who designed the collage cover for the Beatles' landmark *Sgt Pepper's Lonely Hearts Club Band* album.

The '60s also saw the rise of sculptor Anthony Caro, who held his first ground-breaking exhibition at the Whitechapel Art Gallery in 1963. Creating large abstract works in steel and bronze, he remains one of Britain's most influential sculptors.

Britart & Beyond

Thanks partly to the support (and money) of advertising tycoon Charles Saatchi, a new wave of British artists came to the fore in the 1990s. The movement was dubbed, inevitably, 'Britart'; its leading members included Damien Hirst, initially famous (or infamous) for works involving pickled sharks, semi-dissected human figures and, more recently, a diamond-encrusted skull entitled *For the Love of God*.

A contemporary is Tracey Emin. Once considered an enfant terrible, she incurred the wrath of the tabloids for works such as *My Bed*, a messed-up bedroom scene which sold for £2.2 million in 2014, but is now a respected figure and patron of the new Turner Gallery in Margate, named for the famous English artist JMW Turner.

Turner also gives his name to the Turner Prize, a high-profile (and frequently controversial) annual award for British visual artists. As well as Hirst, other winners have included Martin Creed (his work was a room with lights going on and off), Mark Wallinger (a collection of anti-war objects), Simon Starling (a shed converted to a boat and back again), Rachel Whiteread (a plaster cast of a house) and Antony Gormley (best known for his gigantic *Angel of the North*).

Theatre

Theatre in Britain has its roots in medieval morality plays, court jesters and travelling storytellers. Its origins can possibly be traced all the way back to dramas during Roman times in amphitheatres, a few of which still remain at places such as Chester and Cirencester. Most scholars agree that the key milestone in the story is the opening of England's first theatre, called simply The Theatre, in London in 1576. A few years later, two more theatres appeared, the Rose and the Globe, and the stage was set for the entrance of Britain's best-known playwright.

Shakespeare

For most visitors to Britain (and for many locals) drama means just one name: Shakespeare. Born in 1564 in the Midlands town of Stratford-upon-Avon, William Shakespeare made his name in London, where most of his plays were performed at the Globe Theatre.

He started writing plays around 1585, and his early theatrical works are grouped together as 'comedies' and 'histories', many of which have household names today, such as *All's Well that Ends Well, The Taming of the Shrew, A Midsummer Night's Dream, Richard III* and *Henry V*. Later in his career Shakespeare wrote the plays known collectively as the 'tragedies', including *Romeo and Juliet, Macbeth, Julius Caesar, Hamlet* and *King Lear*. His bril-

WHAT A PANTOMIME

If any British tradition is guaranteed to bemuse outsiders, it's the pantomime. This over-the-top Christmas spectacle graces stages across the land in December and January, and traces its roots back to Celtic legends, medieval morality plays and the British music hall. The modern incarnation is usually based on a classic fairy tale and features a mix of saucy dialogue, comedy skits, song-and-dance routines and plenty of custard-pie humour, mixed in with topical gags for the grown-ups. Tradition dictates that the leading 'boy' is played by a woman, and the leading lady, or 'dame', is played by a man. B-list celebrities, struggling actors and soap stars famously make a small fortune hamming it up for Christmas panto, and there are always a few staple routines that everyone knows and joins in with. The hero (or villain) asks 'Where's that dragon/wizard/pirate/lion?' and the audience shouts back 'He's behind you!' It's cheesy, daft and frequently rather surreal, but guaranteed to be great fun for the family. Oh, no it isn't! Oh, yes it is! Oh, no it isn't!

liant plots and spectacular use of language, plus the sheer size of his body of work have turned him into a national – and international – icon.

Today, almost 400 years after he shuffled off his mortal coil, the Bard's plays still pull in big crowds, and can be enjoyed at the rebuilt Globe on London's South Bank or at the Royal Shakespeare Company's own theatre in his original hometown of Stratford-upon-Avon.

British Theatre Today

However you budget your time and money during your visit to Britain, be sure to see some theatre. It easily lives up to its reputation as the finest in the world, especially in London (whatever New Yorkers may say), while other big cities around the country boast their own top-class venues, such as the Birmingham Repertory Theatre, the Bristol Old Vic, the Chichester Festival Theatre, the Playhouse in Nottingham, the New Theatre in Cardiff and the Royal Lyceum in Edinburgh.

Many accomplished British actors, including Judi Dench, Ralph Fiennes, Brenda Blethyn, Toby Stephens and Simon Callow juggle high-paying Hollywood roles with appearances on the British stage, while over the last decade or so several American stars, including Glenn Close, Kevin Spacey, Gwyneth Paltrow, Gillian Anderson, Christian Slater and Danny DeVito, have taken hefty pay cuts to tread the London boards.

Other options in London include the Donmar Warehouse and Royal Court Theatre, best known for new and experimental works. For big names, most people head for the West End, where famous spots include the Shaftsbury, Adelphi and Theatre Royal at Drury Lane. These venues are mostly the preserve of classic plays, including *The Mousetrap*, the legendary whodunnit and world's longest-running play, which has shown continuously since 1952.

In 2012, the massively successful musical *Matilda*, based on the novel by Roald Dahl, broke records by winning seven Olivier Awards, the most prestigious prize in British theatre, going on to take four US Tony Awards in 2013.

West End Musicals

As well as drama, London's West End means big musicals, with a long history of crowd-pullers such as *Cats*, *The Wizard of Oz*, *Les Misérables*, *Sweeney Todd*, *The Phantom of the Opera* and *The Lion King*, with many of today's shows raiding the pop world for material, such as *We Will Rock You*, inspired by the music of Queen, and Abba-based *Mamma Mia!*

For details of other top shows and venues, and how to buy tickets, see the Entertainment section of the London chapter. Details of major theatres in other cities around Britain are also given in the relevant chapters.

The British Landscape

When it comes to landscapes, Britain is not a place of extremes; there are no Alps or Himalaya here, no Amazon or Sahara. But there's plenty to keep you enthralled. The country may be small, but even a relatively short journey takes you through a surprising mix of scenery. Seeing the change – subtle in some areas, dramatic in others – as you travel is one of this country's great attractions.

Location, Location, Location

Geologically at least, Britain is part of Europe. It's on the edge of the Eurasian landmass, separated from the mother continent by the shallow English Channel. (The French are not so proprietorial, and call it La Manche – 'the sleeve'.) About 10,000 years ago, Britain was physically part of Europe, but then sea levels rose and created the island we know today. Only in more recent times has there been a reconnection, in the form of the Channel Tunnel.

Southern England is covered in a mix of cities, towns and gently undulating countryside. Eastern England (especially the area called East Anglia) is almost entirely low and flat, while southwest England has wild moors, granite outcrops and rich pastures (Devon's cream is world famous), plus a rugged coast with sheltered beaches, making it a favourite holiday destination.

In the north of England, farmland is interspersed with towns and cities, but the landscape is noticeably more rugged. A spine of large hills called the Pennines (fondly tagged 'the backbone of England') runs from Derbyshire to the Scottish border, and includes the peaty plateaus of the Peak District, the wild moors around Haworth (immortalised in Brontë novels), the delightful valleys of the Yorkshire Dales and the frequently windswept but starkly beautiful hills of Northumberland.

Perhaps England's best-known landscape is the Lake District, a small but spectacular cluster of mountains and lakes in the northwest, where Scafell Pike (a towering 978m) is England's highest peak.

BRITAIN'S BEST BEACHES

Britain has a great many beaches, each with their own distinct character, from tiny hidden coves in Cornwall and Pembrokeshire to vast neon-lined strands in resorts such as Brighton or Blackpool. Favourite spots line the entire southwest peninsula and much of the south coast. Other great beaches can be found in Suffolk, Norfolk, Lancashire, Yorkshire and Northumberland in England, and pretty much anywhere on the Welsh coast between the Gower Peninsula and Llandudno. Scotland offers even more choice, from the rocky bays of the west coast to the gorgeous white-sand beaches of the Outer Hebrides. Britain's best resort beaches earn the coveted international Blue Flag (www.blueflag. org) award, meaning sand and water are clean and unpolluted. Other parameters include the presence of lifeguards, litter bins and recycling facilities – meaning some wild beaches may not earn the award, but are still stunning nonetheless.

The landscape of Wales is also defined by hills: notably the rounded Black Mountains and Brecon Beacons in the south, and the spiky peaks of Snowdonia in the north, with Snowdon (1085m) the highest summit in Wales. In between lie the wild Cambrian Mountains of central Wales, rolling to the west coast of spectacular cliffs and shimmering river estuaries.

For real mountains, you need to head to Scotland, especially the wild, remote and thinly populated northwest Highlands – separated from the rest of the country by a diagonal gash in the earth's crust called the Great Glen Fault. Ben Nevis (1343m) is Scotland's – and Britain's – highest summit, but there are many more to choose from. The Highlands are further enhanced by the vast cluster of beautiful islands that lie off the loch-indented west coast.

South of the Scottish Highlands is the relatively flat Central Lowlands, home to the bulk of Scotland's population. Further south, down to the border with England, things get hillier again; this is the Southern Uplands, an area of rounded heather-clad hills and fertile farms.

National Parks

Back in 1810, English poet and outdoor fan William Wordsworth suggested that the wild landscape of the Lake District in Cumbria, northwest England, should be 'a sort of national property, in which every man has a right'. More than a century later the Lake District did indeed become a national park, followed by the Brecon Beacons, Cairngorms, Dartmoor, Exmoor, Loch Lomond and the Trossachs, New Forest, Norfolk and Suffolk Broads, Northumberland, North York Moors, Peak District, Pembrokeshire Coast, Snowdonia, South Downs and Yorkshire Dales.

Britain's national parks combined cover over 10% of its area, but the term 'national park' can cause confusion. First, these areas are not state owned: nearly all land in Britain is privately owned, belonging mostly to aristocratic families, private trusts and conservation organisations. Second, they are not areas of wilderness as in many other countries. In Britain's national parks you'll see crop-fields in lower areas and grazing sheep on the uplands, as well as roads, railways and villages. Some national parks even contain towns, quarries and factories. It's a reminder of the balance that needs to be struck in this crowded country between protecting the natural environment and catering for the people who live in it.

But don't be put off. Despite these apparent anomalies, Britain's national parks still contain mountains, hills, downs, moors, woods, river valleys and other areas of quiet countryside, all ideal for long walks, easy rambles, cycle rides, sightseeing or just lounging around. To help you get the best from the parks, they all have information centres, and all provide various recreational facilities (trails, car parks, campsites etc) for visitors.

Finally, it's worth noting that there are many beautiful parts of Britain that are *not* national parks (such as central Wales, the North Pennines in England, and many parts of Scotland). These can be just as good for outdoor activities or simply exploring by car or foot, and are often less crowded than the popular national parks.

Wildlife

For a small country, Britain has a diverse range of plants and animals. Many native species are hidden away, but there are some undoubted gems, from lowland woods carpeted in shimmering bluebells to stately herds of deer on the high moors. Taking the time to have a closer look will enhance your trip enormously, especially if you have the time and inclination to enjoy some walking or cycling through the British landscape.

Britain's most wooded county is Surrey, despite its proximity to London. The soil is too poor for agriculture, and while woodland areas elsewhere in Britain were cleared, Surrey's trees were spared.

Wildlife of Britain by George McGavin et al is subtitled 'the definitive visual guide'. Although too heavy to carry around, this beautiful photographic book is great for pre-trip inspiration or post-trip memories.

Farmland

In farmland areas, rabbits are everywhere, but if you're hiking through the countryside be on the lookout for brown hares, an increasingly rare species. They're related to rabbits but much larger. Males who battle for territory by boxing on their hind legs in early spring are, of course, as 'mad as a March hare'.

Although hare numbers are on the decline, otters are making a comeback. In southern Britain they inhabit the banks of rivers and lakes, and in Scotland they frequently live on the coast. Although their numbers are growing, they are mainly nocturnal, but keep your eyes peeled in daytime and you might be lucky.

You're much more likely to see a red fox. This classic British mammal was once seen only in the countryside, but these wily beasts adapt well to any situation, so these days you're just as likely to see them scavenging in towns and even in city suburbs.

Britain's Best Wildlife by Chris Packham and Mike Dilger is a 'Top 40' countdown of favourites compiled by experts and the public, with details on when and where to see wildlife at its finest.

Elsewhere, another British classic, the badger, is under threat from farmers who believe they transmit bovine tuberculosis to cattle, although conservationists say the case is far from proven.

Common birds of farmland and similar landscapes (and urban gardens) include: the robin, with its instantly recognisable red breast and cheerful whistle; the wren, whose loud trilling song belies its tiny size; and the yellowhammer, with a song that sounds like (if you use your imagination) 'a-little-bit-of-bread-and-no-cheese'. In open fields, the warbling cry of a skylark is another classic, but now threatened, sound of the British outdoors. You're more likely to see a pheasant, a large bird originally introduced from Russia to the nobility's shooting estates, but now considered naturalised.

Between the fields, hedges provide cover for flocks of finches, but these seed-eaters must watch out for sparrowhawks – birds of prey that come from nowhere at tremendous speed. Other predators include barn owls, a wonderful sight as they fly silently along hedgerows listening for the faint rustle of a vole or shrew. In rural Wales or Scotland you may see a buzzard, Britain's most common large raptor.

Woodland

In woodland areas, mammals include the small white-spotted fallow deer and the even smaller roe deer. Woodlands are full of birds too, but you'll hear them more than see them. Listen out for willow warblers (which, as the name suggests, have a warbling song with a descending cadence) and chiffchaffs (once again, the clue is in the name: they make a repetitive 'chiff chaff' noise).

WILDLIFE IN YOUR POCKET

Is it a rabbit or a hare? A gull or a tern? Buttercup or cowslip? If you need to know a bit more about Britain's plant and animal kingdoms the following field guides are ideal for entry-level naturalists:

➡ *Complete Guide to British Wildlife* by Paul Sterry is portable and highly recommended, covering mammals, birds, fish, plants, snakes, insects and even fungi, with brief descriptions and excellent photos.

➡ If feathered friends are enough, the *Complete Guide to British Birds* by Paul Sterry combines clear photos and descriptions, plus when and where each species may be seen.

➡ *Wildlife of the North Atlantic* by world-famous film-maker Tony Soper beautifully covers the animals seen from beach, boat and clifftop in the British Isles and beyond.

➡ Collins Gem series includes handy little books on wildlife topics such as *Birds, Trees, Fish* and *Wild Flowers*.

Sporting Britain

If you want a shortcut into the heart of British culture, then watch the British at play. They're passionate about their sport – as participants or spectators. Every weekend thousands of people turn out to cheer their favourite team, and sporting highlights such as Wimbledon keep the entire nation enthralled.

The British invented many of the world's favourite team sports – or at least codified the modern rules – including cricket, tennis, rugby, golf and football (soccer) although, it has to be said, the national teams in the high-profile sports aren't always that successful internationally. This applies especially to the male teams, whereas the women's national teams have a better record of success, with the England women's national football team reaching the quarter finals in the FIFA Women's World Cup on three occasions, and the England women's cricket team winning the World Cup in 2009.

But whether the British 'home teams' are winning or losing – be they the individual teams of England, Wales and Scotland, or national teams representing Great Britain or the whole of the UK – nothing dulls the enthusiasm of the fans.

Football (Soccer)

Despite what the football fans may say in Madrid or São Paulo, the English Premier League has some of the finest teams in the world, dominated in recent years by the four top teams – Manchester United, Chelsea, Arsenal and Liverpool – joined in 2012 by a fifth big player in the shape of Manchester City.

Down from the Premier League, 72 other teams play in the English divisions called the Championship, League One and League Two.

The Scottish football scene has a similar pattern: the best teams in the Scottish Premier League, the rest in the Scottish Football League. The top flight has long been dominated by Glasgow teams Celtic and Rangers

THE SWEET FA CUP

e Football Association held its first interclub knockout tournament in 1871. Fifteen
took part, playing for a nice piece of silverware called the FA Cup – then worth
20.

days, around 600 clubs compete for this legendary and priceless trophy. It
many other competitions in that every team – from the lowest-ranking
the stars of the Premier League – is in with a chance. The preliminary
August, and the world-famous Cup Final is held in May at the iconic
n in London.

ed are the team with the most cup victories, but public attention, and
focused on the 'giant-killers' – minor clubs that claw their way up
xpectedly beating higher-ranked competitors. The best-known
d in 1992, when Wrexham, then ranked 24th in Division 3, fa-
ons Arsenal.

SPORTING COVERAGE

Perhaps surprisingly, unlike many countries, Britain has no dedicated large-circulation sports newspaper (apart from perhaps *The Sportsman*, which concentrates mainly on the betting angle). But read the excellent coverage in the back pages of the *Daily Telegraph*, the *Times* and the *Guardian* and you'll see there's no need for one. The tabloid newspapers also cover sport, especially if a star has been caught with their pants down. Talking of which, the *Daily Sport* is not a sports newspaper, despite the name, unless photos of glamour models wearing only a pair of Arsenal socks count as 'sport'.

(although in 2012 the latter went into financial administration and was relegated to the third division – they are now in the process of clawing their way back up the league ladder).

In Wales football is less popular (rugby is the national sport) and the main Welsh football teams such as Cardiff and Swansea drift between the two top leagues.

The football season is the same for all divisions (August to May), so seeing a match can easily be tied into most visitors' itineraries. However, tickets for Premier League matches are like gold dust – your chances of bagging one are pretty much zilch unless you're a club member or know someone who is – so you're better off buying tickets for a lower-division game, which are cheaper. You can often buy tickets on the spot at stadiums, or go to club websites or online agencies such as www.ticketmaster.co.uk and www.myticketmarket.com.

The word 'soccer', often used outside Britain, derives from the sport's official name Association Football (as opposed to rugby football), or possibly from 'sock' – a leather foot-cover worn in medieval times, ideal for kicking a pig's bladder around the park on a Saturday afternoon.

Golf

Golf is a very popular sport in Britain, with millions taking to the fairways every week. The main tournament for spectators is the Open Championship, often referred to simply as The Open (or the 'British Open' outside the UK). It's the oldest of professional golf's major championships (dating back to 1860) and the only one held outside the USA, and is watched by many thousands of golf fans. It is usually played over the third weekend in July and the location changes each year, using nine courses around the country – check www.theopen.com for details of past, present and future championships.

Perhaps the UK'S most famous golfing destination is the Old Course at St Andrews (p872), often dubbed the 'home of golf' as it was one of the first places the sport was played, all the way back in the early 1400s. Playing here is almost a spiritual experience for golf enthusiasts, but you'll need to plan well ahead to get a game. If you fancy a round as part of your visit to Britain, there are around 2000 private and public golf courses to choose from, with 500 in Scotland alone. (There are more golf courses per capita in Scotland than in any other country in the world.) Some private clubs admit members or golfers with a handicap certificate, but most welcome visitors. Public golf courses are open to anyone. A round costs around £10 to £30 on public courses, and up to £200 on famous championship courses.

Rugby Football

A wit once said that football was a gentlemen's game played by hooligans, while rugby was a hooligans' game played by gentlemen. That may be true, but rugby union is very popular, especially since England became world champions in 2003 (and nearly did it again in 2007). It's worth catching a game for the display of skill (OK, and brawn), and the fun atmosphere in the grounds. Tickets for games cost around £15 to £50 depending on the club's status and fortunes.

There are two versions of the game in Britain: rugby union (www.rfu. com) is played more in southern England, Wales and Scotland, and is traditionally the game of the middle and upper classes, while rugby league (www.therfl.co.uk) is played predominantly in northern England, traditionally by the working classes, although these days there's a lot of crossover.

Both rugby codes trace their roots back to a football match in 1823 at Rugby School, in Warwickshire. A player called William Webb Ellis, frustrated at the limitations of mere kicking, reputedly picked up the ball and ran with it towards the opponents' goal. True to the British tradition of fair play, rather than Ellis being dismissed from the game, a whole new sport was developed around his tactic, and the Rugby Football Union was formally inaugurated in 1871. Today, the Rugby World Cup trophy is named the Webb Ellis Cup after this enterprising young tearaway.

The highlight of rugby union's international calendar is the annual Six Nations Championship (www.rbs6nations.com), between teams from England, Wales, Scotland, Ireland, France and Italy. A simple points system sees teams compete to win the Grand Slam or Triple Crown, or at least avoid the 'wooden spoon' for coming last.

The Rugby League World Cup is dominated by Australia and New Zealand (the 2017 tournament will be held in Australia), but an even bigger event on the horizon is the Rugby Union World Cup to be hosted by England in 2015, with the final played at Twickenham. For details see www.rugbyworldcup.com.

Cricket

One of the most popular sports in Britain, cricket remains a predominantly English activity at home, although it became an international game during Britain's colonial era, when it was exported to the countries of the Commonwealth. Australia, the Caribbean and the Indian subcontinent took to the game with gusto, and a century on the former colonies delight in giving the old country a good spanking on the cricket pitch.

While many English people follow cricket like a religion, to the uninitiated it's an impenetrable spectacle. Spread over half-day games, one-day games or five-day test matches, progress seems so *slow* (surely, say the unbelievers, this is the game for which TV highlights were invented) and dominated by arcane terminology such as innings, over, googly, out-swinger, leg-

Causing ructions in the cricket world, the fast-paced Twenty20 format emphasises big-batting scores, rather than slow and careful run-building. Traditionalists say it's changing the character of the game, but there's no doubting its popularity – many Twenty20 matches are sell-outs.

THE ASHES

The historic test cricket series between England and Australia known as the Ashes has been played every other year since 1882 (bar a few interruptions during wartime). It is played alternately in England and Australia with each of the five matches in the series held at a different cricket ground, always in the summer in the host location.

The contest's name dates back to the landmark test match of 1882, won (for the very first time) by the Australians. Defeat of the mother country by the colonial upstarts was a source of profound national shock: a mock obituary in the *Sporting Times* lamented the death of English cricket and referred to the game's ashes being taken to Australia.

Later the name was given to a terracotta urn presented the following year to the English captain Ivo Bligh, purportedly containing the cremated ashes of a stump or bail used in this landmark match. Since 1953 this hallowed relic has resided at the Marylebone Cricket Club (MCC) Museum at Lord's Cricket Ground. Despite the vast importance given ɔ winning the series, the urn itself is a diminutive 6in high.

The recent history of the Ashes is not without drama. In the 2010–11 series England ashed Australia, winning on Australian turf for the first time since the 1986–87 series. in 2013 Australia thrashed England 5-0, the third time in Ashes history the Aussies ad a clean sweep. The 2015 Ashes tournament will be held in England.

BRITISH GOLD

The highlight of the nation's entire sporting history was the outstanding achievements by Team GB at the 2012 Olympic and Paralympic Games in London. The team (which represented the whole of the UK – with athletes from Northern Ireland choosing whether to compete for the UK or Irish team) won 65 medals, including 29 golds, and third place overall on the medals table behind China and the USA. The British Paralympic athletes exceeded even this impressive total by winning 120 medals, and notching up another third place in the medals table behind China and Russia.

bye and silly-mid-off. Nonetheless, at least one cricket match should feature in your travels. If you're patient and learn the intricacies, you could find cricket as enriching and absorbing as all the fans who remain glued to their radio or computer all summer, 'just to see how England are getting on'.

International Twenty20, one-day test matches are played at grounds including Lord's in London, Edgbaston in Birmingham and Headingley in Leeds. Tickets cost from £30 to well over £200. The County Championship pits the best teams from around the country against each other; tickets cost £5 to £25, and only the most crucial games tend to sell out. Details are on the website of the **English Cricket Board** (www.ecb.co.uk).

The easiest way to watch cricket – and often the most enjoyable – is stumbling across a local game on a village green as you travel around the country. There's no charge for spectators, and no one will mind if you nip into the pub during a quiet period.

Horse Racing

The tradition of horse racing in Britain stretches back centuries, and there's a 'meeting' somewhere pretty much every day. For all but the major events you should be able to get a ticket on the day, or buy in advance from the British Horse Racing Authority's website (www.lovetheraces. com), which also has lots of information about social events such as music festivals that coincide with the races.

The top event in the calendar is **Royal Ascot** (www.ascot.co.uk) at Ascot Racecourse in mid-June, where the rich and famous come to see and be seen, and the fashion is almost as important as the nags. Even the Queen turns up to put a fiver each way on Lucky Boy in the 3.15.

Other highlights include the Grand National steeplechase at Aintree (p578) in early April; and the Derby at **Epsom** (www.epsomdowns.co.uk) on the first Saturday in June. The latter is especially popular with the masses so, unlike at Ascot, you won't see many morning suits or outrageous hats.

Tennis

Tennis is widely played in Britain, but the best known tournament for spectators is the All England Championships – known to everyone as Wimbledon – when tennis fever sweeps through Britain in the last week of June and first week of July. Although there's something quintessentially English (yes, more English than British) about the combination of grass courts, polite applause and umpires in straw hats, it was a Scotsman, Andy Murray, who in 2013 became the first British men's singles champion since 1936.

Demand for seats at Wimbledon always outstrips supply, but to give everyone an equal chance tickets are sold through a public ballot. You can also take your chance on the spot; about 6000 tickets are sold each day (excluding the final four days), but you'll need to be an early riser: dedicated fans start queuing before dawn. For more information, see www.wimbledon.com.

For the dates and details of major football and cricket matches, horse racing and other sporting fixtures across Britain, a great place to start is the sports pages of www.britevents.com.

Over 27 tonnes of strawberries and 7000L of cream are consumed every year during the two weeks of the Wimbledon Tennis Championships.

Survival Guide

Directory A–Z

Accommodation

Accommodation in Britain is as varied as the sights you visit. From hip hotels to basic barns, the wide choice is all part of the attraction.

B&Bs

The B&B (bed and breakfast) is a great British institution. At smaller places it's pretty much a room in somebody's house; larger places may be called a 'guesthouse' (halfway between a B&B and a full hotel). Prices start from around £25 per person for a simple bedroom and shared bathroom; for around £30 to £35 per person you get a private bathroom – either down the hall or en suite.

In cities, some B&Bs are for long-term residents or people on welfare; they don't take passing tourists. In country areas, most B&Bs cater for walkers and cyclists, but some don't, so let them know if you'll be turning up with dirty boots or wheels.

When booking, check where your B&B actually is. In country areas, postal addresses include the nearest town, which may be 20 miles away – important if you're walking! Some B&B owners will pick you up by car for a small charge.

Prices Usually quoted per person, based on two people sharing a room. Single rooms for solo travellers are harder to find, and attract a 20% to 50% premium. Some B&Bs simply won't take single people (unless you pay the full double-room price), especially in summer.

Booking Advance reservations are preferred at B&Bs and are essential during popular periods. You can book many B&Bs via online agencies but rates may be cheaper if you book direct. If you haven't booked in advance, most towns have a main drag of B&Bs; those with spare rooms hang up a 'Vacancies' sign.

Many B&Bs require a minimum two-night stay at weekends. Some places reduce rates for longer stays (two or three nights) midweek. If a B&B is full, owners may recommend another place nearby (possibly a private house taking occasional guests, not in tourist listings).

Food Most B&Bs serve enormous breakfasts; some offer packed lunches (around £6)

and evening meals (around £15 to £20).

Bunkhouses

A bunkhouse in Britain is a simple place to stay, usually in country areas, with a communal sleeping area and bathroom, plus stoves for self-catering. You provide a sleeping bag and possibly cooking gear. Most charge around £12 per person per night.

Some basic places are called 'camping barns' – usually converted farm buildings. Take everything you'd need to camp except the tent. Charges are from around £6 per person.

Camping

Campsites range from farmers' fields with a tap and basic toilet, costing from £3 per person per night, to smarter affairs with hot showers and many other facilities, charging up to £13. You usually need all your own kit.

A few campsites also offer self-catering accommodation in chalets, caravans, tepees, yurts and stylish wooden camping 'pods', often dubbed 'glamping'.

If you're touring Britain with a tent or campervan (motorhome), consider joining the **Camping & Caravanning Club** (www. campingandcaravanningclub. co.uk), which provides up to 30% discount on its sites for an annual membership fee of £37. The club owns almost 100 campsites and lists thousands more in the invaluable *Big Sites Book* (free to members).

Hostels

There are two types of hostel in Britain: those run by the **Youth Hostels Association** (YHA; www.yha.org.uk) and **Scottish Youth Hostels Association** (SYHA; www.syha.org.uk); and independent hostels, most listed in the **Independent Hostel Guide** (www.independenthostelguide.co.uk).

Hostels can be found in rural areas, towns and cities, and are aimed at all types of traveller, young and old. Some hostels are converted cottages, country houses and even castles – often in wonderful locations. Sleeping is usually in dormitories; some hostels also have twin or four-bed rooms.

YHA & SYHA HOSTELS

The simplest YHA and SYHA hostels cost around £15 per person per night. Larger hostels with more facilities are £18 to £25. London's YHA hostels cost from £30. Advance bookings and payments with credit card are usually possible.

You don't have to be a member of the YHA or SYHA (or another Hostelling International organisation) to stay, but most hostels charge extra if you're not a member (£3 at YHA hostels; £1 at SYHA hostels), so it's usually worth joining. Annual YHA membership costs £20; annual SYHA membership costs £10; younger people and families get discounts.

Most hostel prices vary according to demand and season. Book early for a Tuesday night in May and you'll get the best rate. Book late for a weekend in August and you'll pay top price – if there's space at all. We have generally quoted the cheaper rates (in line with those listed on the YHA's website); you may find yourself paying more.

YHA hostels tend to have complicated opening times and days, especially in remote locations or out of tourist season, so check before turning up.

INDEPENDENT HOSTELS

In rural areas some independent hostels are little more than simple bunkhouses (charging around £12), or almost up to B&B standard (£20 or more). In cities, independent backpacker hostels are usually aimed at young budget travellers. Most are open 24 hours, with a lively atmosphere, a range of rooms (doubles or dorms), bar, cafe, wi-fi and laundry. Prices go from around £20 for a dorm bed to £40 for a bed in a private room.

Hotels

There's a massive choice of hotels in Britain, from small town houses to grand country mansions, from no-frills locations to boutique hideaways. At the bargain end, single/double rooms cost from £40/50. Move up the scale and you'll pay £100/150 or beyond.

If all you want is a place to put your head down, budget chain hotels can be a good option. Most are lacking in ambience, but who cares? You'll only be there for 12 hours, and eight of them you'll be asleep. Prices vary on demand: at quiet times twin-bed rooms start from £30; at the height of the tourist season you'll pay £60 or more. Options include the following:

Ibis Hotels (www.ibis.com)

Premier Inn (www.premierinn.com)

Travelodge (www.travelodge.co.uk)

RATES

There's no such thing as a 'standard' hotel rate in Britain. Many hotels, especially larger places or chains, vary prices according to demand – or have different rates for online, phone or walk-in bookings – just like airlines and train operators. So if you book early for a night when the hotel is likely to be quiet, rates are cheap. If you book late, or aim for a public holiday weekend, you'll pay a lot. But wait until the very last minute, and you *sometimes* get a bargain as rates drop again. The end result: you can pay anything from £25 to £200 for the very same hotel room. With that in mind, the hotel rates we quote are often guide prices only. (In contrast, B&B prices tend to be much more consistent.)

SOMETHING DIFFERENT FOR THE WEEKEND?

For some more unusual accommodation options, the **Landmark Trust** (☎01628-825925; www.landmarktrust.org.uk) rents historic buildings; your options include ancient cottages, medieval castles, Napoleonic forts and 18th-century follies. Or try **Distinctly Different** (www.distinctlydifferent.co.uk), specialising in unusual and bizarre places to stay.

Houseboats

A popular English holiday option is renting a houseboat on one of England's picturesque waterways, combining accommodation and transport for a few days or a week.

UK Boat Hire (www.ukboathire.com)

Hoseasons (www.hoseasons.co.uk)

Wandering Duck (www.wanderingduck.co.uk) 'Floating hostels' for budget travellers.

Pubs & Inns

As well as selling drinks, many pubs and inns offer lodging, particularly in country areas. For bed and breakfast, you'll pay around £25 per person for a basic room, around £40 for something better. An advantage for solo tourists: pubs often have single rooms.

Rental Accommodation

If you want to stay in one place, renting for a week can be ideal. Choose from neat apartments in cities or quaint old houses (always called 'cottages', whatever the size) in country areas. Cottages for four people cost between £250 and £650 in high season. Rates fall at quieter times and you may be able to rent for a long weekend. Handy websites:

Bed & Breakfast Nationwide (www.bedandbreakfastnationwide.com)

Cottages & Castles (www.cottages-and-castles.co.uk)

Cottages4you (www.cottages4you.co.uk)

Hoseasons (www.hoseasons.co.uk)

National Trust (www.nationaltrust.org.uk/holidays)

Stilwell's (www.stilwell.co.uk)

University Accommodation

During vacations, many universities offer accommodation to visitors. You usually get a functional single bedroom, and self-catering flats are also available. Prices range from £25 to £60 per person. A handy portal is www.universityrooms.co.uk.

Customs Regulations

Travellers arriving in the UK from EU countries don't have to pay tax or duty on goods for personal use, and can bring in as much EU duty-paid alcohol and tobacco as they like. However, if you

Climate

London

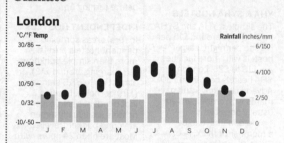

Newquay

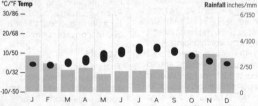

York

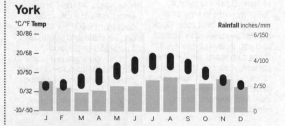

bring in more than the following, you'll probably be asked some questions:

➜ 800 cigarettes

➜ 1kg of tobacco

➜ 10L of spirits

➜ 90L of wine

➜ 110L of beer

Travellers from outside the EU can bring in, duty-free:

➜ 200 cigarettes or 100 cigarillos or 50 cigars or 250g of tobacco

➜ 16L of beer

➜ 4L of nonsparkling wine

➜ 1L of spirits or 2L of fortified wine or sparkling wine

➜ £390 worth of all other goods, including perfume, gifts and souvenirs

Anything over this limit must be declared to customs officers on arrival. Check www.hmrc.gov.uk/customs for further details, and for information on reclaiming VAT on items purchased in the UK by non-EU residents.

Discount Cards

There's no specific discount card for visitors to Britain, although travel cards are discounted for younger and older people.

Electricity

230V/50Hz

Cardiff

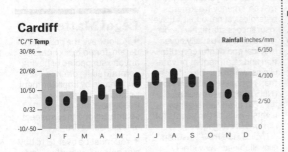

Inverness

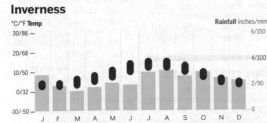

Edinburgh

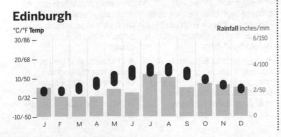

Embassies & Consulates

This is a selection of embassies, consulates and high commissions in London. For a complete list, go to www.fco.gov.uk and search for 'foreign embassies'.

Australia (☑020-7379 4334; www.uk.embassy.gov.au; The Strand, WC2B 4LA)

Canada (☑020-7258 6600; www.canadainternational.gc.ca; 1 Grosvenor Sq, W1X 0AB)

China (☑020-7299 4049; www.chinese-embassy.org.uk; 49-51 Portland Pl, W1B 4JL)

France (☑020-7073 1000; www.ambafrance-uk.org; 58 Knightsbridge, SW1 7JT)

Germany (☑020-7824 1300; www.london.diplo.de; 23 Belgrave Sq, SW1X 8PX)

Ireland (☑020-7235 2171; www.embassyofireland.co.uk; 17 Grosvenor Pl, SW1X 7HR)

Japan (☑020-7465 6500; www.uk.emb-japan.go.jp; 101 Piccadilly, W1J 7JT)

Netherlands (☑020-7590 3200; www.dutchembassyuk.org; 38 Hyde Park Gate, SW7 5DP)

EATING PRICE RANGES

In reviews, the following price ranges refer to a main dish.

£ less than £9.

££ £9 to £18

£££ more than £18

New Zealand (☑020-7930 8422; www.nzembassy.com/uk; 80 Haymarket, SW1Y 4TQ)

Poland (☑020-7291 3520; www.london.mfa.gov.pl; 47 Portland Pl, W1B 1HQ)

USA (☑020-7499 9000; www.usembassy.org.uk; 24 Grosvenor Sq, W1A 1AE)

Gay & Lesbian Travellers

Britain is a generally tolerant place for gays and lesbians. London, Manchester and Brighton have flourishing gay scenes, and in other sizeable cities (even some small towns) you'll find communities not entirely in the closet. That said, you'll still find pockets of homophobic hostility in some areas. Resources include the following:

Diva (www.divamag.co.uk)

Gay Times (www.gaytimes. co.uk)

London Lesbian & Gay Switchboard (www.llgs. org.uk)

Health

➡ If you're an EU citizen, a European Health Insurance Card (EHIC) – available from health centres or, in the UK, post offices – covers you for most medical care. An EHIC will not cover you for non-urgent cases, or emergency repatriation.

➡ Citizens from non-EU countries should find out if there is a reciprocal arrangement for free medical care between their country and the UK.

➡ If you do need health insurance, make sure you get a policy that covers you for the worst possible scenarios, including emergency flights home.

➡ No jabs (vaccinations) are required to travel to Britain. For more information, check with your medical provider in your own country before you travel.

➡ Chemists (pharmacies) can advise on minor ailments such as sore throats and earaches. In large cities, there's always at least one 24-hour chemist.

Insurance

Although everyone receives free emergency treatment, regardless of nationality, travel insurance is still highly recommended. It will usually cover medical and dental consultation and treatment at private clinics, which can be quicker than National Health Service (NHS) places – as well as the cost of any emergency flights – plus all the usual stuff like loss of baggage.

Worldwide travel insurance is available at www.lonely planet.com/travel_services. You can buy, extend and claim online anytime, even if you're already on the road.

Internet Access

➡ 3G and 4G mobile broadband coverage is good in large population centres, but limited or nonexistent in rural areas. However, beware high charges for data roaming – check with your mobile/cellphone provider before travelling.

➡ Most hotels, B&Bs, hostels, stations and coffee shops (even some trains and buses) have wi-fi access, charging anything from nothing to £6 per hour.

➡ Internet cafes are surprisingly rare in Britain, especially away from big cities and tourist spots. Most charge from £1 per hour, but out in the sticks you can pay £5 per hour.

➡ Public libraries often have computers with free internet access, but only for 30-minute slots, and demand is high. All the usual warnings apply about keystroke-capturing software and other security risks.

➡ We've indicated accommodation and eating and drinking options that have wi-fi with the 🛜 symbol in the text. Wi-fi is often free, but some places (usually upmarket hotels) charge.

➡ If you see the @ symbol in our listings, then the place has an internet terminal.

Legal Matters

➡ Police have the power to detain, for up to six hours, anyone suspected of having committed an offence punishable by imprisonment (including drugs offences). Police have the right to search anyone they suspect of possessing drugs.

➡ You must be over 18 to buy alcohol and cigarettes. You usually have to be 18 to enter a pub or bar, although rules are different for under-18s if eating. Some bars and clubs are over-21 only.

➡ Illegal drugs are widely available, especially in clubs. Cannabis possession is a criminal offence; punishment for carrying a small amount may be a warning, a fine or imprisonment. Dealers face stiffer penalties, as do people caught with other drugs.

➡ On buses and trains (including the London Underground), people without a valid ticket are fined on the spot – usually around £20.

Money

The currency of Britain is the pound sterling (£). Paper money ('notes') comes in £5, £10, £20 and £50 denominations. Some shops don't accept £50 notes because fakes circulate.

Other currencies are very rarely accepted, except at some gift shops in London, which may take euros, US dollars, yen and other major currencies.

Exchange rates are given in the Need to Know chapter.

ATMs

ATMs (usually called 'cash machines' in Britain) are common in cities and even small towns. Cash withdrawals from some ATMs may be subject to a small charge, but most are free. If you're not from the UK, your home bank will likely charge you for withdrawing money overseas. Watch out for tampered ATMs; a common ruse is to attach a card-reader or minicamera.

Credit & Debit Cards

Visa and MasterCard credit and debit cards are widely accepted in Britain. Most businesses will assume your card is 'Chip and PIN' enabled (using a PIN instead of signing). If it isn't, you should be able to sign instead, but some places may not accept your card. Some smaller country B&Bs don't take cards, so you'll need to pay with cash.

Moneychangers

Cities and larger towns have banks and exchange bureaux for changing your money into pounds. Check rates first; some bureaux offer poor rates or levy outrageous commissions. You can also change money at some post offices – very handy in country areas, and exchange rates are fair.

Tipping

In Britain you're not obliged to tip if the service or food was unsatisfactory (even if it's been automatically added to your bill as a 'service charge').

Restaurants Around 10%. Also at teashops and smarter cafes with full table service. At smarter restaurants waiters expect tips nearer 12% or 15%.

Taxis Around 10%, or rounded up to the nearest pound, especially in London. It's less usual to tip minicab drivers.

Pubs Around 10% if you order food at the table and your meal is brought to you. If you order and pay at the bar (food or drinks), tips are not expected.

Opening Hours

Banks

➡ 9.30am to 4pm or 5pm Monday to Friday.

➡ main branches 9.30am to 1pm Saturday.

Bars, Pubs & Clubs

➡ Standard hours for pubs: 11am to 11pm Monday to Sunday. Some pubs shut from 3pm to 6pm; some open to midnight or 1am Friday and Saturday.

➡ Standard hours for bars: 11am to midnight, often later, especially at weekends.

➡ Clubs open any time from 8pm to 11pm, until 2am or beyond.

Cafes & Restaurants

Most restaurants and cafes are open for lunch or dinner or both, so precise opening times and days are given in reviews only if they differ markedly from the pattern outlined here.

➡ Standard hours for cafes: 9am to 5pm. Most cafes open daily.

➡ In cities, some cafes open at 7am for breakfast, then shut at 6pm or later.

➡ In country areas, some cafes open until 7pm or later in the summer. In winter months, hours are reduced; some cafes close completely from October to Easter.

➡ Standard hours for restaurants: lunch noon to 3pm, dinner 6pm to 11pm (to midnight or later in cities). Most restaurants open daily; some close Sunday evening or all day Monday.

➡ A few restaurants open for breakfast (usually 9am), but mainly cafes do this.

Museums & Sights

➡ Large museums and sights usually open daily.

➡ Some smaller places open Saturday and Sunday but close Monday and/or Tuesday.

➡ Smaller places open daily in high season but operate weekends only or completely close in low season.

Post Offices

➡ 9am to 5pm (5.30pm or 6pm in cities) Monday to Friday.

➡ 9am to 12.30pm Saturday; main branches to 5pm.

Shops

➡ 9am to 5pm (5.30pm or 6pm in cities) Monday to Friday; 9am to 5pm Saturday.

➡ Larger shops open 10am to 4pm Sunday. London and

SCOTTISH BANKNOTES

Scottish banks issue their own sterling banknotes. They are interchangeable with Bank of England notes, but you'll sometimes run into problems outside Scotland – shops in the south of England may refuse to accept them. They are also harder to exchange once you get outside the UK, though British banks will always exchange them.

other cities have convenience stores open 24/7.

➡ In smaller towns and country areas shops often shut for lunch (normally 1pm to 2pm) and on Wednesday or Thursday afternoon.

Public Holidays

Holidays for the whole of Britain:

New Year's Day 1 January (plus 2 January in Scotland)

Easter March/April (Good Friday to Easter Monday inclusive)

May Day First Monday in May

Spring Bank Holiday Last Monday in May

Summer Bank Holiday Last Monday in August

Christmas Day 25 December

Boxing Day 26 December

If a public holiday falls on a weekend, the nearest Monday is usually taken instead. In England and Wales most businesses and banks close on official public holidays (hence the quaint term 'bank holiday'). In Scotland, bank holidays are just for the banks, and many businesses stay open. Many Scottish towns normally have a spring and autumn holiday, but the dates vary.

On public holidays, some small museums and places

of interest close, but larger attractions have their busiest times. If a place closes on Sunday, it'll probably be shut on bank holidays as well.

Virtually everything – attractions, shops, banks, offices – closes on Christmas Day, although pubs are open at lunchtime. There's usually no public transport on Christmas Day, and a very minimal service on Boxing Day.

Safe Travel

Britain is a remarkably safe country, but crime is not unknown in London and other cities.

➡ Watch out for pickpockets and hustlers in crowded areas popular with tourists such as around Westminster Bridge in London.

➡ When travelling by tube, tram or urban train services at night, choose a carriage containing other people.

➡ Many town centres can be rowdy on Friday and Saturday nights when the pubs and clubs are emptying.

➡ Unlicensed minicabs – someone with a car earning money on the side – operate in large cities, and are worth avoiding unless you know what you're doing.

Telephone
Mobile Phones

The UK uses the GSM 900/1800 network, which covers the rest of Europe, Australia and New Zealand, but isn't compatible with the North American GSM 1900. Most modern mobiles can function on both networks – but check before you leave home just in case.

Though roaming charges within the EU are due to be entirely eliminated in December 2015, other international roaming charges can be prohibitively high, and you'll probably find it cheaper to get a UK number. This is easily done by buying a SIM card (around £10 including calling credit) and sticking it in your phone.

Your phone may be locked to your home network, however, so you'll have to either get it unlocked, or purchase a pay-as-you-go phone along with your SIM card (around £50).

Pay-as-you-go phones can be recharged by buying vouchers from shops.

Phone Codes

Dialling into the UK Dial your country's international access code then ☑44 (the UK country code), then the area code (dropping the first ☑0) followed by the telephone number.

Dialling out of the UK The international access code is ☑00; dial this, then add the code of the country you wish to dial.

Making a reverse-charge (collect) international call Dial ☑155 for the operator. It's an expensive option, but not for the caller.

Area codes in the UK These do not have a standard format or length, eg Edinburgh ☑0131, London ☑020, Ambleside ☑015394.

Directory Assistance A host of agencies compete for your business and charge from 10p

---

SCHOOL HOLIDAYS

Roads get busy and hotel prices go up during school holidays. Exact dates vary from year to year and region to region, but are roughly as follows:

Easter Holiday Week before and week after Easter

Summer Holiday Third week of July to first week of September

Christmas Holiday Mid-December to first week of January

There are also three week-long 'half-term' school holidays – usually late February (or early March), late May and late October. These vary between Scotland, England and Wales.

to 40p; numbers include ☎118 192, ☎118 118, ☎118 500 and ☎118 811.

Mobile phones Codes usually begin with ☎07.

Free calls Numbers starting with ☎0800 are free; calls to ☎0845 numbers are charged at local rates.

National operator ☎100

International operator ☎155

Time

Britain is on GMT/UTC. The clocks go forward for 'summer time' one hour at the end of March, and go back at the end of October. The 24-hour clock is used for transport timetables.

Time Differences

Paris, Berlin, Rome One hour ahead of Britain.

New York Five hours behind.

Sydney Nine hours ahead between April and September, 10 hours October, 11 hours between November and March.

Los Angeles Eight hours behind.

Mumbai 5½ hours ahead, 4½ hours bewteen March and October.

Tokyo Nine hours ahead, eight hours between March and October.

Tourist Information

Most British cities and towns, and some villages, have a tourist information centre or visitor information centre – for ease we've called all these places 'tourist offices'. Such places have helpful staff, books and maps for sale, leaflets to give away, and advice on things to see or do. Some can also assist with booking accommodation. Some are run by national parks and often have small exhibits about the area.

HERITAGE ORGANISATIONS

A highlight of a journey through Britain is visiting the numerous castles and historic sites that pepper the countries. Membership of a heritage organisation gets you free admission (usually a good saving) as well as information handbooks and so on.

The **National Trust** (NT; www.nationaltrust.org.uk) is a charity protecting historic buildings and land with scenic importance across England and Wales. Annual membership £58 (discounts for under-26s and families). A Touring Pass allows free entry to NT properties for one/two weeks (£25/30 per person); families and couples get cheaper rates. The **National Trust for Scotland** (NTS; www.nts.org.uk) is a similar organisation in Scotland; annual membership £52.

English Heritage (EH; www.english-heritage.org.uk) is a state-funded organisation responsible for numerous historic sites. Annual membership is £49 (couples and seniors get discounts). An Overseas Visitors Pass allows free entry to most sites for nine/16 days for £25/30 (cheaper rates for couples and families). In Wales and Scotland the equivalent organisations are **Cadw** (www.cadw.wales.gov.uk) and **Historic Scotland** (HS; www.historic-scotland.gov.uk).

You can join at the first site you visit. If you join an English heritage organisation, it covers you for Wales and Scotland, and vice versa.

Most tourist offices keep regular business hours; in quiet areas they close from October to March, while in popular areas they open daily year-round. In recent years, cost-cutting has seen many smaller tourist offices close down.

Before leaving home, check the comprehensive website of Britain's official tourist board, **Visit Britain** (www.visitbritain.com), covering all the angles of national tourism, with links to numerous other sites.

Travellers with Disabilities

All new buildings have wheelchair access, and even hotels in grand old country houses often have lifts, ramps and other facilities. Hotel and B&Bs in historic buildings

are often harder to adapt, so you'll have less choice here.

Modern city buses and trams have low floors for easy access, but few have conductors who can lend a hand when you're getting on or off. Many taxis take wheelchairs, or just have more room in the back.

For long-distance travel, coaches may present problems but the main operator, **National Express** (www.nationalexpress.com) has wheelchair-friendly coaches on many routes. For details, see the website or ring the dedicated Disabled Passenger Travel Helpline on ☎08717 81 81 79.

On most intercity trains there's more room and better facilities, compared with travel by coach, and usually station staff around; just have a word and they'll be happy to help. A **Disabled**

PRACTICALITIES

Newspapers Tabloids include the *Sun* and *Mirror*, and *Daily Record* (in Scotland); quality 'broadsheets' include (from right to left, politically) the *Telegraph, Times, Independent* and *Guardian*.

TV All TV in the UK is digital. Leading broadcasters include BBC, ITV and Channel 4. Satellite and cable TV providers include Sky and Virgin Media.

Radio Main BBC stations and wavelengths are Radio 1 (98–99.6MHz FM), Radio 2 (88–92MHz FM), Radio 3 (90–92.2 MHz FM), Radio 4 (92–94.4MHz FM) and Radio 5 Live (909 or 693 AM). National commercial stations include Virgin Radio (1215Hz MW) and non-highbrow classical specialist Classic FM (100–102MHz FM). All are available on digital.

DVD PAL format (incompatible with NTSC and Secam).

Weights & Measures Britain uses a mix of metric and imperial measures (eg petrol is sold by the litre but beer by the pint; mountain heights are in metres but road distances in miles).

Person's Railcard (www.disabledpersons-railcard.co.uk) costs £20 and gets you 33% off most train fares.

Useful organisations include the following:

Disability Rights UK (www.disabilityrightsuk.org) Published titles include a Holiday Guide. Other services include a key for 7000 public disabled toilets across the UK.

Good Access Guide (www.goodaccessguide.co.uk)

Tourism for All (www.tourismforall.org.uk)

Visas

➡ If you're a citizen of the EEA (European Economic Area) nations or Switzerland, you don't need a visa to enter or work in Britain – you can enter using your national identity card.

➡ Visa regulations are always subject to change, and immigration restriction is currently big news in Britain, so it's essential to check with your local British embassy, high commission or consulate before leaving home.

➡ Currently, if you're a citizen of Australia, Canada, New Zealand, Japan, Israel, the USA and several other countries, you can stay for up to six months (no visa required), but are not allowed to work.

➡ Nationals of many countries, including South Africa, will need to obtain a visa: for more info, see www.ukvisas.gov.uk.

➡ The Youth Mobility Scheme, for Australian, Canadian, Japanese, Hong Kong, Monegasque, New Zealand, South Korean and Taiwanese citizens aged 18 to 31, allows working visits of up to two years, but must be applied for in advance.

➡ Commonwealth citizens with a UK-born parent may be eligible for a Certificate of Entitlement to the Right of Abode, which entitles them to live and work in the UK.

➡ Commonwealth citizens with a UK-born grandparent could qualify for a UK Ancestry Employment Certificate, allowing them to work full time for up to five years in the UK.

➡ British immigration authorities have always been tough; dress neatly and carry proof that you have sufficient funds with which to support yourself. A credit card and/or an onward ticket will help.

Transport

GETTING THERE & AWAY

Most visitors reach Britain by air. As London is a global transport hub, it's easy to fly to Britain from just about anywhere. In recent years, the massive growth of budget ('no-frills') airlines has increased the number of routes – and reduced the fares – between Britain and other countries in Europe.

The other main option for travel between Britain and mainland Europe is ferry, either port-to-port or combined with a long-distance bus trip, although journeys can be long and financial savings not huge compared with budget airfares.

International trains are much more comfortable and a 'green' option; the Channel Tunnel allows direct rail services between Britain, France and Belgium, with onward connections to many other European destinations.

Flights, cars and rail tickets can be booked online at lonelyplanet.com/bookings.

Air

London Airports

London's main airports are listed here. For details of getting from the airports into the city, see p145.

Heathrow (LHR; www.heathrowairport.com) Britain's main airport for international flights; often chaotic and crowded. About 15 miles west of central London.

Gatwick (LGW; www.gatwickairport.com) Britain's number-two airport, mainly for international flights, 30 miles south of central London.

Stansted (STN; www.stanstedairport.com) About 35 miles northeast of central London, mainly handling charter and budget European flights.

Luton (LTN; www.london-luton.co.uk) Some 35 miles north of central London, well known as a holiday-flight airport.

London City (LCY; www.londoncityairport.com) A few miles east of central London, specialising in flights to/from European and other UK airports.

Regional Airports

Some planes on European and long-haul routes avoid London and use major regional airports including Manchester and Glasgow. Smaller regional airports such as Southampton, Cardiff and Birmingham are served by flights to and from continental Europe and Ireland.

Land

Bus & Coach

You can easily get between Britain and other European countries via long-distance bus or coach. The international network **Eurolines** (Map p68; www.eurolines.com;

CLIMATE CHANGE & TRAVEL

Every form of transport that relies on carbon-based fuel generates CO_2, the main cause of human-induced climate change. Modern travel is dependent on aeroplanes, which might use less fuel per kilometre per person than most cars but travel much greater distances. The altitude at which aircraft emit gases (including CO_2) and particles also contributes to their climate change impact. Many websites offer 'carbon calculators' that allow people to estimate the carbon emissions generated by their journey and, for those who wish to do so, to offset the impact of the greenhouse gases emitted with contributions to portfolios of climate-friendly initiatives throughout the world. Lonely Planet offsets the carbon footprint of all staff and author travel.

SW1) connects a huge number of destinations; you can buy tickets online via one of the national operators.

Services to/from Britain are operated by **National Express** (www.national express.com). Sample journey times to/from London include Amsterdam 12 hours; Barcelona 24 hours; Dublin 12 hours; and Paris eight hours.

If you book early, and can be flexible with timings (ie travel when few other people want to), you can get some very good deals. For example, between London and Paris or Amsterdam from about £20 one-way (although paying £30 to £40 is more usual).

Train
CHANNEL TUNNEL PASSENGER SERVICE

High-speed **Eurostar** (www. eurostar.com) passenger services shuttle at least 10 times daily between London and Paris (2½ hours) or Brussels (two hours). Buy tickets from travel agencies, major train stations or the Eurostar website.

The normal one-way fare between London and Paris/ Brussels costs £140 to £180; advance booking and off-peak travel gets cheaper fares as low as £39 one-way.

CHANNEL TUNNEL CAR SERVICE

Drivers use **Eurotunnel** (www.eurotunnel.com). At Folkestone in England or Calais in France, you drive onto

a train, get carried through the tunnel and drive off at the other end.

Trains run about four times an hour from 6am to 10pm, then hourly through the night. Loading and unloading takes an hour; the journey lasts 35 minutes.

Book in advance online or pay on the spot. The one-way cost for a car and passengers is between £75 and £165 depending on time of day; promotional fares often bring it down to £55.

Sea
Ferry Routes

The main ferry routes between Britain and other European countries include the following:

➡ Dover to Calais (France)

➡ Dover to Boulogne (France)

➡ Newhaven to Dieppe (France)

➡ Harwich to Hook of Holland (Netherlands)

➡ Hull to Zeebrugge (Belgium)

➡ Hull to Rotterdam (Netherlands)

➡ Portsmouth to Santander (Spain)

➡ Portsmouth to Bilbao (Spain)

➡ Holyhead to Dun Laoghaire (Ireland)

➡ Cairnryan to Larne (Ireland)

Ferry Fares

Most ferry operators offer flexible fares, meaning great bargains at quiet times of day or year. For example, short cross-channel routes such as Dover to Calais or Boulogne can be as low as £20 for a car plus up to five passengers, although around £50 to £90 is more likely. If you're a foot passenger, or cycling, there's less need to book ahead; fares on short crossings cost about £10 to £30 each way.

Ferry Bookings

Book direct with one of the operators listed following, or use the very handy www. ferrybooker.com – a single site covering all sea-ferry routes, plus Eurotunnel.

Brittany Ferries (www. brittany-ferries.com)

DFDS Seaways (www. dfdsseaways.co.uk)

Irish Ferries (www.irish ferries.com)

P&O Ferries (www.poferries. com)

Stena Line (www.stenaline. com)

GETTING AROUND

For getting around Britain your first big decision is whether to travel by car or public transport.

Having your own car makes the best use of time, and helps reach remote places, but rental and fuel costs can be expensive for budget travellers (while traffic jams in major cities hit everyone) – public transport is often the better choice. As long as you have time, using a mix of train, bus, taxi, walking and occasionally hiring a bike, you can get almost anywhere in Britain without having to drive.

The main public transport options are train and long-distance bus (called coach in Britain). Services between major towns and cities are generally good,

---

TRAIN & FERRY CONNECTIONS

As well as Eurostar, many 'normal' trains run between Britain and mainland Europe. You buy one ticket, but get off the train at the port, walk onto a ferry, then get another train on the other side. Routes include Amsterdam–London (via Hook of Holland and Harwich). Travelling between Ireland and Britain, the main train-ferry-train route is Dublin to London, via Dun Laoghaire and Holyhead. Ferries also run between Rosslare and Fishguard or Pembroke (Wales), with train connections on either side.

although at peak times you must book in advance to be sure of getting a ticket. If you book ahead early or travel at off-peak periods – ideally both – train and coach tickets can be very cheap.

Air

Britain's domestic airline companies include British Airways, FlyBe/Loganiar, EasyJet and Ryanair. If you're really pushed for time, flights on longer routes across Britain (eg Exeter or Southampton to Newcastle, Edinburgh or Inverness), or to the Scottish islands, are handy, although you miss the glorious scenery in between. On some shorter routes (eg London to Newcastle, or Manchester to Newquay) trains compare favourably with planes on time, once airport downtime is factored in. On costs, you might get a bargain airfare, but trains can be cheaper if you buy tickets in advance.

Bicycle

Britain is a compact country, and hiring a bike – for an hour or two, or a week or longer – is a great way to really see the country if you've got time to spare.

Rental in London

London is famous for its Barclays Cycle Hire Scheme, known as 'Boris bikes' after the mayor that introduced them to the city. Bikes can be hired on the spot from automatic docking stations. For more information visit the **Transport for London** (www.tfl.gov.uk) website. Other rental options in the capital are listed at www.lcc. org.uk.

Rental Elsewhere

The **nextbike** (www.nextbike. co.uk) bike-sharing scheme currently has stations in Glasgow, Stirling and Bath,

while tourist towns such as Oxford and Cambridge have plentiful bike-rental options. Bikes can also be hired in national parks or forestry sites now primarily used for leisure activities, such as Kielder Water in Northumberland, Grizedale Forest in the Lake District and the Elan Valley in Mid-Wales. In some areas, disused railway lines are now bike routes, notably the Peak District in Derbyshire. Rental rates start at about £10 per day, or £20 for something half decent.

Bikes on Trains

Bicycles can be taken free of charge on most local urban trains (although they may not be allowed at peak times when the trains are crowded with commuters) and on shorter trips in rural areas, on a first-come, first-served basis – though there may be space limits.

Bikes can be carried on long-distance train journeys free of charge, but advance booking is required for most conventional bikes. (Folding bikes can be carried on pretty much any train at any time.) In theory, this shouldn't be too much trouble as most long-distance rail trips are best bought in advance anyway, but you have to go a long way down the path of booking your seat before you start booking your bike – only to find space isn't available. A better course of action is to buy in advance at a major rail station, where the booking clerk can help you through the options.

A final warning: when railways are repaired, cancelled trains are replaced by buses, and they won't take bikes.

A very useful leaflet called *National Rail Cycling by Train* is available at major stations or downloadable from www. nationalrail.co.uk (from the homepage follow links to 'Stations & On-train' then 'Cyclists').

Boat

There are around 90 inhabited islands off the western and northern coasts of Scotland, which are linked to the mainland by a network of car and passenger ferries. There are two main ferry operators.

Caledonian MacBrayne (CalMac; ☎0800 066 5000; www.calmac.co.uk) Operates car ferry services to the Inner and Outer Hebrides and the islands in the Firth of Clyde.

Northlink Ferries (☎0845 600 0449; www.northlink -ferries.co.uk) Operates car ferry services to the Orkney and Shetland Islands.

Bus & Coach

If you're on a tight budget, long-distance buses (called coaches in Britain) are nearly always the cheapest way to get around, although they're also the slowest – sometimes by a considerable margin. Many towns have separate stations for local buses and long-distance coaches; make sure you go to the right one!

National Express (www. nationalexpress.com) is the main coach operator, with a wide network and frequent services between main centres. North of the border, services tie in with those of

INFORMATION SERVICE

Traveline (☎0871 200 2233; www.traveline.info) is a very useful information service covering bus, coach, taxi and train services nationwide. The website offers access to online timetables, a journey planner, route maps and limited fares information.

Scottish Citylink (☎0871 266 3333; www.citylink.co.uk), Scotland's leading coach company. Fares vary: they're cheaper if you book in advance and travel at quieter times, and more expensive if you buy your ticket on the spot and it's Friday afternoon. As a guide, a 200-mile trip (eg London to York) will cost £15 to £30 if you book a few days in advance.

Megabus (www.megabus. com) operates a budget coach service between about 30 destinations around the country. Go at a quiet time, book early and your ticket will be very cheap. Book later, for a busy time and... You get the picture.

Passes & Discounts

National Express offers discount passes to full-time students and under-26s, called Young Persons Coachcards. They cost £10 and give you 30% off standard adult fares. Also available are coachcards for people over 60, families and disabled travellers.

For touring the country, National Express offers Brit Xplorer passes, allowing unlimited travel for seven/14/28 days (£79/139/219). You don't need to book journeys in advance: if the coach has a spare seat, you can take it.

Car & Motorcycle

Travelling by car or motorbike around Britain means you can be independent and flexible, and reach remote places. Downsides for drivers include traffic jams, the high price of fuel, and high parking costs in cities.

Car Rental

Compared with many countries (especially the USA), hire rates are expensive in Britain; the smallest cars start from about £120 per week, and it's around £250 per week for a medium car. All rates include insurance and unlimited mileage, and can rise at busy times (or drop at quiet times).

Some main players:

Avis (www.avis.co.uk)

Budget (www.budget.co.uk)

Europcar (www.europcar. co.uk)

Sixt (www.sixt.co.uk)

Thrifty (www.thrifty.co.uk)

Another option is to look online for small local car-hire companies in Britain that can undercut the international franchises. Generally those in cities are cheaper than in rural areas. Using a rental-broker or comparison site such as **UK Car Hire** (www. ukcarhire.net) or **Kayak** (www. kayak.com) can also help find bargains.

Motorhome Rental

Hiring a motorhome or campervan (£500 to £900 a week) is more expensive than hiring a car, but saves on accommodation costs and gives almost unlimited freedom. Sites to check include the following:

Just Go (www.justgo.uk.com)

Wild Horizon (www.wildhori zon.co.uk)

Motoring Organisations

Motoring organisations in Britain include the **Automobile Association** (www.

theaa.com) and the **Royal Automobile Club** (www. rac.co.uk). For both, annual membership starts at around £50, including 24-hour roadside breakdown assistance. A greener alternative is the **Environmental Transport Association** (www.eta.co.uk); it provides breakdown assistance but doesn't campaign for more roads.

Insurance

It's illegal to drive a car or motorbike in Britain without (at least) third-party insurance. This will be included with all rental cars. If you're bringing a car from Europe you'll need to arrange it.

Parking

Many cities have short-stay and long-stay car parks; the latter are cheaper though may be less convenient. 'Park & Ride' systems allow you to park on the edge of the city then ride to the centre on frequent nonstop buses for an all-in-one price.

Yellow lines (single or double) along the edge of the road indicate restrictions. Nearby signs spell out when you can and can't park. In London and other big cities, traffic wardens operate with efficiency; if you park on the yellow lines at the wrong time, your car will be clamped or towed away, and it'll cost you £100 or more to get driving again. In some cities there are also red lines, which mean no stopping at all. Ever.

Roads

Motorways and main A-roads deliver you quickly from one end of the country to another. Lesser A-roads, B-roads and minor roads are much more scenic – ideal for car or motorcycle touring. You can't travel fast, but you won't care.

Speed limits are usually 30mph (48km/h) in built-up areas, 60mph (96km/h) on main roads and 70mph (112km/h) on motorways and most (but not all) dual carriageways.

Road Rules

A foreign driving licence is valid in Britain for up to 12 months.

Drink driving is taken very seriously; you're allowed a maximum blood-alcohol level of 80mg/100mL (0.08%) – campaigners want it reduced to 50mg/100mL (0.05%), in line with most European countries.

Some other important rules:

➡ drive on the left (!)

➡ wear fitted seat belts in cars

➡ wear helmets on motorcycles

➡ give way to your right at junctions and roundabouts

➡ always use the left lane on motorways and dual carriageways unless overtaking (although so many people ignore this rule, you'd think it didn't exist)

➡ don't use a mobile phone while driving unless it's fully hands-free (another rule frequently flouted)

Hitching

Hitching is not as common as it used to be in Britain: maybe because more people have cars and maybe because few drivers give lifts any more. It's perfectly possible, however, if you don't mind long waits, although travellers should understand they're taking a small but potentially serious risk, and we don't recommend it. If you decide to go by thumb, note that it's illegal to hitch on motorways; you must use approach roads or service stations.

However, it's all different in remote rural areas such as Mid-Wales or northwest Scotland, where hitching is a part of getting around – especially if you're a walker heading back to base after a hike on the hills. On some Scottish islands, local drivers may stop and offer a lift without you even asking.

HOW MUCH TO...?

When travelling by long-distance bus, coach or train in Britain, it's important to realise that there's no such thing as a standard fare. Prices vary according to demand and when you buy your ticket. Book long in advance and travel on Tuesday midmorning and it's cheap. Buy your ticket on the spot late Friday afternoon and it'll be a lot more expensive. Ferries use similar systems. We have generally quoted sample fares somewhere in between the very cheapest and most expensive options. The price you pay will almost certainly be different.

Local Transport

British cities usually have good public transport systems – a combination of bus, train and tram – often run by a confusing number of separate companies. Tourist offices can provide maps and information.

Local Bus

There are good local bus networks year-round in cities and towns. Buses also run in some rural areas year-round, although timetables are designed to serve schools and businesses, so there aren't many midday and weekend services (and they may stop running during school holidays), or buses may link local villages to a market town on only one day each week.

In tourist areas (especially national parks), there are frequent services from Easter to September. However, it's worth double-checking at a tourist office before planning your day's activities around a bus that may not actually be running.

In this book, along with the local bus route number, frequency and duration, we have provided indicative fares.

LOCAL BUS PASSES

If you're taking a few local bus rides in one area, day passes (with names like Day Rover, Wayfarer or Explorer) are cheaper than buying several single tickets. Often

they can be bought on your first bus, and may include local rail services. It's always worth asking ticket clerks or bus drivers about your options.

Local Ferry

Local ferries are another option when travelling around Britain; for example, from the mainland to the Isle of Wight, and to or among the Scottish islands.

Taxi

There are two sorts of taxi in Britain: those with meters that can be hailed in the street; and minicabs, which are cheaper but can only be called by phone. Unlicensed minicabs operate in some cities.

In London, most taxis are the famous 'black cabs' (some with advertising livery in other colours) which charge by distance and time. Depending on the time of day, a 1-mile journey takes five to 10 minutes and cost £6 to £9. Longer journeys are proportionally cheaper.

Black cabs also operate in some other large cities around Britain, with rates usually lower than in London.

In London, taxis are best flagged down in the street; a 'for hire' light on the roof indicates availability. In other cities, you can flag down a cab if you see one, but it's usually easier to go to a taxi rank.

In rural areas, taxis need to be called by phone; the best place to find the local taxi's phone number is the local pub. Fares are £2 to £4 per mile.

Train-Taxi (www.traintaxi. co.uk) is a portal site that helps 'bridge the final gap' between the train station and your hotel or other final destination.

Train

For long-distance travel around Britain, trains are generally faster and more comfortable than coaches but can be more expensive, although with discount tickets they're competitive – and often take you through beautiful countryside. The British like to moan about their trains, but around 85% run on time. The other 15% that get delayed or cancelled mostly impact commuter services rather than long-distance journeys.

Information

Your first stop should be **National Rail Enquiries** (☎08457 48 49 50; www. nationalrail.co.uk), the nationwide timetable and fare information service. Its website advertises special offers and has real-time links to station departure boards and downloadable maps of the rail network.

Operators

About 20 different companies operate train services in Britain, while Network Rail operates track and stations. For some passengers this system can be confusing at first, but information and ticket-buying services are mostly centralised. If you have to change trains, or use two or more train operators, you still buy one ticket – valid for the whole journey. The main railcards and passes are also accepted by all train operators.

Where more than one train operator services the same route, eg York to Edinburgh, a ticket purchased from one company may not be valid on trains run by another. So if you miss the train you originally booked, it's worth checking which later services your ticket will be valid for.

Tickets & Reservations

BUYING TICKETS

Once you've found the journey you need on the National Rail Enquiries website, links take you to the relevant train operator to buy the ticket. This can be mailed to you (UK addresses only) or collected at the station on the day of travel from automatic machines. There's usually no booking fee on top of the ticket price.

You can also use a centralised ticketing service to buy your train ticket. These cover all train services in a single site, and make a small booking fee on top of every ticket price. The main players include the following:

QJump (www.qjump.co.uk)

Rail Easy (www.raileasy. co.uk)

Train Line (www.thetrainline. com)

To use operator or centralised ticketing websites, you always have to state a preferred time and day of travel, even if you don't mind when you go, but you can change it as you go through the process, and with a little delving around you can find some real bargains.

You can also buy train tickets on the spot at stations, which is fine for short journeys (under about 50 miles), but discount tickets for longer trips are usually not available and must be bought in advance by phone or online.

COSTS

For longer journeys, on-the-spot fares are always available, but tickets are much cheaper if bought in advance. The earlier you book, the cheaper it gets. You can also save if you travel off-peak. Advance purchase usually gets a reserved seat, too.

Whichever operator you travel with and wherever you buy tickets, these are the three main fare types:

Anytime Buy anytime, travel anytime – usually the most expensive option.

Off-peak Buy ticket any time, travel off-peak (what is off-peak depends on the journey).

Advance Buy ticket in advance, travel only on specific trains – usually the cheapest option.

For an idea of the price difference, an Anytime single ticket from London to York will cost £125 or more, an Off-peak around £95, with an

---

STATION NAMES

London has several mainline train stations, including Victoria, Paddington, King's Cross, Waterloo, Charing Cross and Liverpool St, positioned in a rough circle around the city's central area (and mostly linked by the Circle Underground line). The stations' proper names are London Victoria, London Paddington, London King's Cross and so on, and this is how you'll see them on official timetables, information boards and booking websites – although the British never use the full names in everyday speech.

In this guide, for clarity, we have used the full name for London stations. This is also to help distinguish the London stations from stations in some other British cities that also share names such as Victoria and Charing Cross.

Advance around £30 to £40, and possibly less if you book early enough or don't mind arriving at midnight.

The cheapest fares are nonrefundable, so if you miss your train you'll have to buy a new ticket.

ONWARD TRAVEL

If the train doesn't get you all the way to your destination, you can add a **PlusBus** (www. plusbus.info) supplement when making your reservation to validate your train ticket for onward travel by bus. This is more convenient, and usually cheaper, than buying a separate bus ticket.

Train Classes

There are two classes of rail travel: 1st and standard. First class costs around 50% more than standard fare (up to double at busy periods) and gets you bigger seats, more leg-room, and usually a more peaceful businesslike atmosphere, plus extras such as complimentary drinks and

newspapers. At weekends some train operators offer 'upgrades' to 1st class for an extra £5 to £25 on top of your standard class fare, payable on the spot.

Train Passes

DISCOUNT PASSES

If you're staying in Britain for a while, passes known as **Railcards** (www.railcard.co.uk) are available:

16-25 Railcard For those aged 16 to 25, or a full-time UK student.

Senior Railcard For anyone over 60.

Family & Friends Railcard Covers up to four adults and four children travelling together.

Railcards cost £30 (valid for one year, available from major stations or online) and get 33% discount on most train fares, except those already heavily discounted. With the Family card, adults get 33% and children get 60% discounts, so the fee is easily repaid in a couple of journeys.

LOCAL & REGIONAL PASSES

Local train passes usually cover rail networks around a city (many include bus travel too) and are detailed in the relevant sections throughout this guide.

If you're concentrating your travels on southeast England (eg London to Dover, Weymouth, Cambridge or Oxford), a **Network Railcard** (www.railcard.co.uk/network; per year £30) covers up to four adults and up to four children travelling together outside peak times.

NATIONAL PASSES

For country-wide travel, **BritRail** (www.britrail.net) passes are available for visitors from overseas. They must be bought in your country of origin (not in Britain) from a specialist travel agency. Available in seven different versions (eg England only; Scotland only; all Britain; UK and Ireland) for periods from four to 30 days.

Behind the Scenes

SEND US YOUR FEEDBACK

We love to hear from travellers – your comments keep us on our toes and help make our books better. Our well-travelled team reads every word on what you loved or loathed about this book. Although we cannot reply individually to your submissions, we always guarantee that your feedback goes straight to the appropriate authors, in time for the next edition. Each person who sends us information is thanked in the next edition – the most useful submissions are rewarded with a selection of digital PDF chapters.

Visit **lonelyplanet.com/contact** to submit your updates and suggestions or to ask for help. Our award-winning website also features inspirational travel stories, news and discussions.

Note: We may edit, reproduce and incorporate your comments in Lonely Planet products such as guidebooks, websites and digital products, so let us know if you don't want your comments reproduced or your name acknowledged. For a copy of our privacy policy visit lonelyplanet.com/privacy.

OUR READERS

Many thanks to the travellers who used the last edition and wrote to us with helpful hints, useful advice and interesting anecdotes:

Alice Gossington, Charlotte Dawes, Chris Girdler, Chuck Wiener, Eric Pellissier Tanon, Susanne Lanz, Tohru Yukimura

AUTHOR THANKS

Neil Wilson

Many thanks to all the helpful and enthusiastic staff at tourist information centres throughout the country, and to the many travellers I met on the road who chipped in with advice and recommendations. Thanks also to Carol Downie, and to Steven Fallon and Keith Jeffrey, Steve Hall, Russell Leaper, Brendan Bolland, Jenny Neil, and Tom and Christine Duffin. Finally, many thanks to all my co-authors and to the ever-helpful and patient editors and cartographers at Lonely Planet.

Oliver Berry

Thanks for help and assistance on this book go to Alice Sommerlad, Thom Hunt, Rupert Ellis, Dave Grimstead, Jim Burns, Lucy Granger, Simon Timms and Hetty at Koru Kayaking. Special thanks to Susie & Gracie Berry, to Belinda Dixon for co-authoring skills, to Neil Wilson for steering the ship, and James Smart

and all the folks at Lonely Planet for guidance and sage advice.

Fionn Davenport

Thanks to Andy Parkinson at Visit Manchester and Joe Keggin at Marketing Liverpool for their help; big thanks to Saralinda Turner at Lonely Planet for her patience and perseverance, and also to Neil for being the good steward and James for, well, everything else.

Marc Di Duca

A huge 'ta' goes to all the staff at tourist offices across the Southeast (those that haven't been axed that is) but especially to the helpful guys in Hastings, Canterbury and Rye. Also thanks to Therese at Canterbury Cathedral and my Kyiv parents-in-law Mykola and Vira for looking after sons Taras and Kirill while I was on the road. And last, but certainly not least, heartfelt gratitude must go to my wife Tanya, for all those long days we spend apart.

Belinda Dixon

Huge thanks go to: James Smart for having faith (and the gig!), Lonely Planet's behind the scenes teams, and fellow authors for humour, wisdom and travellers' tales. Everyone encountered on southwest-wide travels for tips, facts and countless kindnesses. And JL for sharing the road trips (especially kayaking, fossil-hunting and afternoon tea drinking) and still making me smile.

Peter Dragicevich

Many thanks to the friends on the road who made this such an enjoyable assignment, especially Kerri Tyler, Tim Benzie, Paul Joseph and Kurt Crommelin. Extra special thanks to Matt, Clare, Charlie and Artie Swaine for the Bristol bonhomie. Much love to Phillippa Steel – an absolute inspiration and a true friend.

Damian Harper

Many thanks to a long list of helpful individuals: John Patrick Egan, Fiona Jenkins, Stephanie Francis, Daisy Harper, Amy Williams, Arlene Fraser, Matthew Scudamore, Daniel Hands and last but certainly not least, Timothy Benjamin and Emma Rosalind. A tip of the hat also to the people of London who make this city such an exciting and fascinating place to call home.

Anna Kaminski

I would like to thank the supportive *Great Britain* team, particularly Neil and James, plus everyone who helped me during my travels. In particular, a huge thank you to Christopher in Hay-on-Wye; Cate and Asher in Conwy; Jo, Manu, James and CAT staff in Machynlleth; Geoff in Brecon; Martin in Harlech; and the good people of AA for towing me to Swansea. I am also grateful to Jan Morris and her partner Elizabeth for the gracious hospitality shown to a complete stranger turning up on their doorstep.

Catherine Le Nevez

Cheers first and foremost to Julian, and to all of the locals, tourism professionals and fellow travellers who provided insights, inspiration and good times. Thanks especially to Ade Andrews for the interview, and to Steven, Jeremy, Jayni and Alan in Birmingham, Nadia in Nottingham, and Raisa and Jonny in Newcastle. Thanks too to Neil Wilson, James Smart, Cliff Wilkinson, Joe Revill and everyone at Lonely Planet. As ever, *merci encore* to my parents, brother, *belle-sœur* and *neveu*.

Andy Symington

Many thanks are due in many places, but firstly to Jenny Neil and Brendan Bolland for a big welcome and cracking cemetery stay and to Juliette and David Paton for guaranteed warm and generous hospitality. Old mate Hugh O'Keefe was grand company on the Highlands' winding roads, while John Campbell brightened an Unst evening. Gratitude goes also to Eleanor Hamilton, Cindy-Lou Ramsay, Riika Åkerlind, the Jackson-Hevia family and numerous helpful folk met along the way. Big thanks to Neil for coordinating and Taybank pints, and cheers to James, Cliff and the Lonely Planet team for a top organising job.

ACKNOWLEDGMENTS

Climate map data adapted from Peel MC, Finlayson BL & McMahon TA (2007) 'Updated World Map of the Köppen-Geiger Climate Classification', *Hydrology and Earth System Sciences*, 11, 1633–44.

Cover photograph: Land's End, Cornwall, Pietro Canali/4Corners.

Illustrations: pp84-5, pp642-3, pp756-7, pp790-1 and pp842-3 by Javier Zarracina; pp90-1 by Javier Zarracina and Michael Weldon

THIS BOOK

This 11th edition of Lonely Planet's *Great Britain* guidebook was researched and written by Neil Wilson, Oliver Berry, Fionn Davenport, Marc Di Duca, Belinda Dixon, Peter Dragicevich, Damian Harper, Anna Kaminski, Catherine Le Nevez and Andy Symington. This guidebook was produced by the following:

Destination Editors James Smart, Clifton Wilkinson

Product Editor Elin Berglund

Senior Cartographer Mark Griffiths

Book Designer Cam Ashley

Assisting Editors Peter Cruttenden, Kate Evans, Carly Hall, Victoria Harrison, Anne Mulvaney, Susan Paterson, Monique Perrin, Ross Taylor, Saralinda Turner, Jeanette Wall

Assisting Cartographers Julie Dodkins, Corey Hutchison, David Kemp

Cover Researcher Naomi Parker

Thanks to Penny Cordner, Bruce Evans, Ryan Evans, Justin Flynn, Larissa Frost, Anna Harris, Jouve India, Andi Jones, Katherine Marsh, Virginia Moreno, Claire Naylor, Karyn Noble, Katie O'Connell, Martine Power, Dianne Schallmeiner, Ellie Simpson, Luna Soo, John Taufa, Samantha Tyson, Lauren Wellicome, Amanda Williamson

Index

Map Legend

Sights
- Beach
- Bird Sanctuary
- Buddhist
- Castle/Palace
- Christian
- Confucian
- Hindu
- Islamic
- Jain
- Jewish
- Monument
- Museum/Gallery/Historic Building
- Ruin
- Shinto
- Sikh
- Taoist
- Winery/Vineyard
- Zoo/Wildlife Sanctuary
- Other Sight

Activities, Courses & Tours
- Bodysurfing
- Diving
- Canoeing/Kayaking
- Course/Tour
- Sento Hot Baths/Onsen
- Skiing
- Snorkelling
- Surfing
- Swimming/Pool
- Walking
- Windsurfing
- Other Activity

Sleeping
- Sleeping
- Camping

Eating
- Eating

Drinking & Nightlife
- Drinking & Nightlife
- Cafe

Entertainment
- Entertainment

Shopping
- Shopping

Information
- Bank
- Embassy/Consulate
- Hospital/Medical
- Internet
- Police
- Post Office
- Telephone
- Toilet
- Tourist Information
- Other Information

Geographic
- Beach
- Hut/Shelter
- Lighthouse
- Lookout
- Mountain/Volcano
- Oasis
- Park
- Pass
- Picnic Area
- Waterfall

Population
- Capital (National)
- Capital (State/Province)
- City/Large Town
- Town/Village

Transport
- Airport
- Border crossing
- Bus
- Cable car/Funicular
- Cycling
- Ferry
- Metro station
- Monorail
- Parking
- Petrol station
- S-Bahn/Subway station
- Taxi
- T-bane/Tunnelbana station
- Train station/Railway
- Tram
- Tube station
- U-Bahn/Underground station
- Other Transport

Note: Not all symbols displayed above appear on the maps in this book

Routes
- Tollway
- Freeway
- Primary
- Secondary
- Tertiary
- Lane
- Unsealed road
- Road under construction
- Plaza/Mall
- Steps
- Tunnel
- Pedestrian overpass
- Walking Tour
- Walking Tour detour
- Path/Walking Trail

Boundaries
- International
- State/Province
- Disputed
- Regional/Suburb
- Marine Park
- Cliff
- Wall

Hydrography
- River, Creek
- Intermittent River
- Canal
- Water
- Dry/Salt/Intermittent Lake
- Reef

Areas
- Airport/Runway
- Beach/Desert
- Cemetery (Christian)
- Cemetery (Other)
- Glacier
- Mudflat
- Park/Forest
- Sight (Building)
- Sportsground
- Swamp/Mangrove

Belinda Dixon

Bath & Southwest England; Cambridge & East Anglia Belinda made a gleeful bolt for the sunny southwest for her post-grad, having been drawn there by the palm trees on campus. Like the best Westcountry limpets, she's proved hard to shift since and now writes and broadcasts in the region. Research highlights for this latest adventure included fossil hunting on the Jurassic Coast, white-water kayaking on Dartmoor, pony spotting on Exmoor, 'researching' cider in Dorset and sampling afternoon tea in Lyme.

Read more about Belinda at:
lonelyplanet.com/members/belindadixon

Peter Dragicevich

Oxford, Cotswolds & Around; Cardiff, Pembrokeshire & South Wales Wales has held a fascination for Peter ever since he was sent to write about Welsh castles for one of his first ever newspaper travel features. Since then he's co-authored dozens of Lonely Planet titles, including the *Wales* guidebook. And while his name may not be very Welsh, it does at least have over half a dragon in it.

Damian Harper

London Born off the Strand within earshot of Bow Bells (favourable wind permitting), Damian grew up in Notting Hill way before it was discovered by Hollywood. A onetime Shakespeare and Company bookseller and radio presenter, Damian has been authoring guidebooks for Lonely Planet since the late 1990s. He lives in South London with his wife and two kids, frequently returning to China (his second home).

Anna Kaminski

Hay-on-Wye & Mid-Wales; Snowdonia & North Wales No stranger to Wales, Anna spent this research trip gleefully rediscovering childhood highlights: castles, narrow-gauge railways, the beaches of North Wales and the many hiking paths of Snowdonia and the Brecon Beacons. In spite of (or perhaps because of) nearly bringing a rockslide down on herself on Mt Snowdon and her car breaking down for the first time ever, it has been Anna's most memorable venture into Cymru's remotest parts. Anna has contributed to over a dozen Lonely Planet titles.

Catherine Le Nevez

Birmingham, the Midlands & the Marches; Newcastle & Northeast England Catherine first roadtripped around Great Britain aged four and she's been roadtripping here at every opportunity since, completing her Doctorate of Creative Arts in Writing, Masters in Professional Writing, and post-grad qualifications in editing and publishing along the way. She's also written dozens of Lonely Planet guidebooks and newspaper, magazine and online articles covering the UK, Europe and beyond. Roaming castle ruins and corridors of stately homes were highlights of researching this book, as was discovering idyllic countryside pubs.

Andy Symington

Glasgow & Southern Scotland; Central & Northern Highlands & Islands Andy's Scottish forebears make their presence felt in a love of malt, a debatable ginger colour to his facial hair and a love of wild places. From childhood treks up the M1 he graduated to making dubious roadtrips around the firths in a disintegrating Mini Metro and thence to peddling whisky in darkest Leith. While living there, he travelled widely around the country in search of the perfect dram, and, now resident in Spain, continues to visit very regularly.

OUR STORY

A beat-up old car, a few dollars in the pocket and a sense of adventure. In 1972 that's all Tony and Maureen Wheeler needed for the trip of a lifetime – across Europe and Asia overland to Australia. It took several months, and at the end – broke but inspired – they sat at their kitchen table writing and stapling together their first travel guide, *Across Asia on the Cheap*. Within a week they'd sold 1500 copies. Lonely Planet was born.

Today, Lonely Planet has offices in Franklin, London, Melbourne, Oakland, Beijing and Delhi, with more than 600 staff and writers. We share Tony's belief that 'a great guidebook should do three things: inform, educate and amuse'.

OUR WRITERS

Neil Wilson

Coordinating Author; Yorkshire; Edinburgh; Argyll, Central & Northeast Scotland Neil was born in Scotland and, save for a few years spent abroad, has lived there most of his life. A lifelong enthusiast for the great outdoors has inspired hiking, biking and sailing expeditions to every corner of Britain. Researching this edition took him from the country's most westerly point at Ardnamurchan Lighthouse to its most easterly at Fraserburgh, and to every corner of Yorkshire. Neil has been a full-time author since 1988 and has written around 65 guidebooks for various publishers, including Lonely Planet's *Scotland* and *Scotland's Highlands & Islands*.

Oliver Berry

Bath & Southwest England; The Lake District & Cumbria A professional writer and photographer based in Cornwall and Bristol, Oliver likes nothing better than exploring his local beaches and clifftops in the name of research. For this book he covered his home county, and also ventured across the Tamar to write the sections on Somerset, Bristol, Bath and Cumbria. Research highlights included kayaking down the Helford River and watching the sunset from the top of Scafell Pike. You can see his latest work at www.oliverberry.com.

Fionn Davenport

Manchester, Liverpool & Northwest England As a Dubliner, Fionn feels an affinity with the Northwest. Maybe it's his lifelong support of Liverpool Football Club, or his longtime love of The Smiths, but a visit to Liverpool or Manchester is always that little bit special. Over the years and various editions of this guide he's had plenty of occasion to visit and get to know the region better, exploring Chester and the Wirral, and tramping through Lancaster and into the north Lancashire hills.

Marc Di Duca

Canterbury & Southeast England Originally from Darlington, County Durham, Marc has been a northerner-gone-south since 2000 and has covered his adopted corner of weald and down for the past three editions of Lonely Planet's *England* and *Great Britain*. A full-time travel author for a decade, Marc has updated and written Lonely Planet guides to Ukraine, Russia, the Trans-Siberian Railway, Poland, Austria and Germany, though he can usually be found in Sandwich, Kent, where he lives with wife Tanya and their two sons.

Read more about Marc at:
lonelyplanet.com/members/madidu

OVER PAGE | MORE WRITERS

Published by Lonely Planet Publications Pty Ltd
ABN 36 005 607 983
11th edition – April 2015
ISBN 978 1 74321 472 5
© Lonely Planet 2015   Photographs © as indicated 2015
10 9 8 7 6 5 4 3 2 1
Printed in China